PRAISE FOR
THE BANTAM NEW COLLEGE
ITALIAN AND ENGLISH DICTIONARY

". . . thorough, accurate, well-organized, clear, and up to date . . . Relevant to the student's contemporary life . . . It is bound to become a mainstay in the field."
—Albert N. Mancini, Professor of Romance Languages, The Ohio State University

"Both the method and the execution seem to me excellent . . . It would be impossible to find elsewhere as good a dictionary of this size."
—Beatrice Corrigan, Professor Emeritus, Editor, University of Toronto Press

"Apart from its accurate philological approach, its most useful grammatical apparatus, and other singular features, this concise dictionary is the first which is based primarily on *American* English usage . . . It contains numerous up-to-date colloquial and technical terms which cannot be found in any other similar dictionary."
—M. Ricciardelli, Professor of Italian and Comparative Literatures, Editor of *Forum Italicum*

Comprehensive, authoritative, and completely modern, **THE BANTAM NEW COLLEGE ITALIAN AND ENGLISH DICTIONARY** is a landmark in foreign language reference works.

THE BANTAM NEW COLLEGE DICTIONARY SERIES

Robert C. Melzi, Author

ROBERT C. MELZI, D. in L., A.M., Ph.D., was trained in Italy, at the University of Padua, and in the United States, at the University of Pennsylvania. He has done extensive linguistic research, traveling frequently to his native country. Now professor of Romance Languages at Widener College, he has contributed articles and reviews to many learned journals, is the author of *Castelvetro's Annotations to the Inferno,* The Hague and Paris, 1966 (Castelvetro was one of Italy's foremost philologists), and is an associate editor of *The Scribner-Bantam English Dictionary* (Scribner's, 1977; Bantam Books, 1979). Professor Melzi is a Cavaliere in the Order of Solidarity of the Republic of Italy.

Edwin B. Williams, General Editor

EDWIN B. WILLIAMS (1891–1975), A.B., A.M., Ph.D., Doct. d'Univ., LL.D., L.H.D., was chairman of the Department of Romance Languages, dean of the Graduate School, and provost of the University of Pennsylvania. He was a member of the American Philosophical Society and the Hispanic Society of America. Among his many lexicographical works are *The Williams Spanish and English Dictionary* (Scribner's, formerly Holt) and *The Bantam New College Spanish and English Dictionary.* He created and coordinated the Bantam series of original dictionaries—English, French, German, Italian, Latin, and Spanish. The University of Pennsylvania named "Williams Hall" in honor of Edwin B. Williams and his wife, Leonore, and is establishing the "Williams Chair in Lexicography," as the first chair in lexicography in an English-speaking country.

THE BANTAM NEW COLLEGE
ITALIAN & ENGLISH
DICTIONARY

ROBERT C. MELZI, Ph.D.
Widener College, Philadelphia

THE BANTAM NEW COLLEGE
ITALIAN & ENGLISH DICTIONARY

A Bantam Book | April 1976

2nd printing	*...... January 1978*	*4th printing*	*............ April 1980*
3rd printing	*.... February 1979*	*5th printing*	*.............. May 1981*

ISBN 0–553–20267–7

Published simultaneously in the United States and Canada

PRINTED IN THE UNITED STATES OF AMERICA

14 13 12 11 10 9 8 7 6 5

CONTENTS

CONTENTS

PREFACE

Inasmuch as the basic function of a bilingual dictionary is to provide semantic equivalences, syntactical constructions are shown in both the source and the target languages on both sides of the Dictionary. In performing this function, a bilingual dictionary must fulfill six purposes. That is, an Italian and English dictionary must provide (1) Italian words which an English-speaking person wishes to use in speaking and writing (by means of the English-Italian part), (2) English meanings of Italian words which an English-speaking person encounters in listening and reading (by means of the Italian-English part), (3) the spelling, pronunciation, and inflection of Italian words and the gender of Italian nouns which an English-speaking person needs in order to use Italian words correctly (by means of the Italian-English part), (4) English words which an Italian-speaking person wishes to use in speaking and writing (by means of the Italian-English part), (5) Italian meanings of English words which an Italian-speaking person encounters in listening and reading (by means of the English-Italian part), and (6) the spelling, pronunciation, and inflection of English words which an Italian-speaking person needs in order to use English words correctly (by means of the English-Italian part).

It may seem logical to provide the pronunciation and inflection of English words and the pronunciation and inflection of Italian words and the gender of Italian nouns where these words appear as target words inasmuch as target words, according to (1) and (4) above, are sought for the purpose of speaking and writing. Thus the user would find not only the words he seeks but all the information he needs about them in one and the same place. But this technique is impractical because target words are not alphabetized and could, therefore, be found only by the roundabout and uncertain way of seeking them through their translations in

PREFAZIONE

Dato che la funzione principale di un dizionario bilingue è quella di fornire all'utente equivalenze semantiche, le costruzioni sintattiche sono indicate in entrambe le lingue, quella di partenza e quella di arrivo, in entrambe le parti del Dizionario. Per compiere questa funzione, un dizionario bilingue deve raggiungere sei scopi differenti. Cioè, un dizionario italiano e inglese deve fornire (1) nella parte inglese-italiano, le parole italiane che la persona anglofona vuole adoperare parlando e scrivendo l'italiano; (2) nella parte italiano-inglese, il significato in inglese delle parole italiane che tale persona oda nella lingua parlata o legga in libri o giornali; (3) nella parte italiano-inglese, l'ortografia, la pronunzia, la flessione delle parole italiane e il genere dei nomi italiani che la persona anglofona deve conoscere per servirsi correttamente della lingua italiana; (4) nella parte italiano-inglese, le parole inglesi che la persona italofona vuole adoperare parlando o scrivendo l'inglese; (5) nella parte inglese-italiano, il significato in italiano delle parole inglesi che tale persona oda nella lingua parlata o legga in libri o giornali; (6) nella parte inglese-italiano, l'ortografia, la pronunzia figurata e la flessione delle parole inglesi che la persona italofona deve conoscere per servirsi correttamente della lingua inglese.

A prima vista potrebbe sembrare logico che la pronunzia e la flessione delle parole inglesi e la pronunzia e la flessione delle parole italiane e il genere dei nomi italiani fossero indicati dove queste parole si trovano nella lingua d'arrivo, dato che le parole della lingua d'arrivo, secondo i punti (1) e (4) enunciati più sopra, sono consultate da coloro che vogliono parlare e scrivere in lingua straniera. In questa maniera l'utente troverebbe non solo le parole che cerca, ma tutte le informazioni che gli sono necessarie, nello stesso luogo. Questa tecnica, peraltro, non è pratica poiché le parole della lingua d'arrivo non si trovano in ordine

the other part of the dictionary. And this would be particularly inconvenient for persons using the dictionary for purposes (2) and (5) above. It is much more convenient to provide immediate alphabetized access to pronunciation and inflection where the words appear as source words.

alfabetico e potrebbero quindi essere trovate solo in maniera complicata nella parte opposta del dizionario. E ciò sarebbe specialmente scomodo per coloro che usano il dizionario per gli scopi (2) e (5) menzionati più sopra. È molto più semplice aggiungere la pronunzia e la flessione nella serie alfabetica in cui le parole si trovano nella loro lingua di partenza.

Since Italian is an almost perfectly phonetic language, IPA transcription of Italian words has been omitted. The only elements of pronunciation not shown by standard spelling are the values of tonic e and o (§1; pp. 3, 4) the stress of words stressed on the third syllable from the end (§3,3; p. 5), the value of intervocalic s when unvoiced, and the values of z and zz when voiced (§1; p. 4); these are shown in the entry words themselves.

Dato che l'italiano è una lingua quasi perfettamente fonetica, non si è data la trascrizione delle parole italiane nell'alfabeto dell'Associazione Fonetica Internazionale. Considerando che l'ortografia comune non mostra il vario timbro della e (§1, p. 3) e della o (§1, p. 4) quando esse sono toniche, l'accento delle parole sdrucciole (§3,3, p. 5), la pronunzia della s sorda (§1, p. 4) e la pronunzia delle z e zz sonore (§1, p. 4), si è data tale informazione nell'esponente stesso.

All words are treated in a fixed order according to the parts of speech and the functions of verbs, as follows: adjective, article, substantive, pronoun, adverb, preposition, conjunction, transitive verb, intransitive verb, reflexive verb, auxiliary verb, impersonal verb, interjection.

Ogni singola voce è trattata secondo uno schema fisso che si riferisce alle parti del discorso o alle funzioni del verbo, nel seguente ordine: aggettivo, articolo, sostantivo, pronome, avverbio, preposizione, congiunzione, verbo transitivo, verbo intransitivo, verbo riflessivo, verbo ausiliare, verbo impersonale e interiezione.

Meanings with labels come after more general meanings. Labels (printed in roman and in parentheses) refer to the preceding entry or phrase (printed in boldface).

I significati accompagnati da sigle si trovano dopo quelli di accezione più generale. Tali sigle (che sono sempre stampate in carattere romano e in parentesi) si riferiscono all'esponente precedente, stampato in grassetto, o alla frase precedente, ugualmente stampata in grassetto.

In view of the fact that the users of this Italian and English bilingual dictionary are for the most part English-speaking people, definitions and discriminations are provided in English. They are printed in italics and in parentheses and refer to the English word which they particularize:

Dato che gli utenti di questo dizionario bilingue italiano e inglese sono per lo più anglofoni, definizioni e locuzioni esplicative sono apportate in inglese. Sono stampate in corsivo e in parentesi e si riferiscono sempre alla parola inglese il cui significato cercano di spiegare:

porter ['portər] *s (doorman)* portiere *m; (man who carries luggage)* facchino; . . .
órdine *m* order; . . . series *(e.g., of years);* college *(e.g., of surgeons);* . . .

English adjectives are always translated by the Italian masculine form

Gli aggettivi inglesi sono sempre tradotti in maschile italiano, anche se il

regardless of whether the translation of the exemplary noun modified would be masculine or feminine:

nome che qualificano sia un femminile italiano:

tough [tʌf] *adj* duro; ...; (*luck*) cattivo; ...

In order to facilitate the finding of the meaning and use sought for, changes within a vocabulary entry in part of speech and function of verb, in irregular inflection, in the use of an initial capital, in the gender of Italian nouns, and in the pronunciation of English words are marked with parallels: ||, instead of the usual semicolons.

Per facilitare l'uso del Dizionario, i raggruppamenti sono stati fatti secondo le parti del discorso, la funzione del verbo, la flessione irregolare, l'uso della maiuscola iniziale, il genere dei nomi italiani e la pronunzia delle parole inglesi e sono separati da sbarrette verticali: ||, invece del punto e virgola che è stato generalmente usato.

Since vocabulary entries are not determined on the basis of etymology, homographs are included in a single entry. When the pronunciation of an English homograph changes, this is shown in the proper place after parallels:

Dato che gli esponenti in questo Dizionario non sono stati selezionati su base etimologica, tutti gli omografi sono inclusi sotto il medesimo esponente. Il cambio di pronunzia di un omografo inglese è indicato al posto adatto dopo sbarrette verticali:

frequent [ˈfrikwənt] *adj* frequente || [friˈkwent] or [ˈfrikwənt] *tr* ...

However, when the pronunciation of an Italian homograph changes, the words are entered separately:

Però, quando la pronunzia di un omografo italiano cambia, si hanno esponenti separati:

retina *f* small net
rètina *f* (anat) retina
tóc·co -ca (-**chi -che**) *adj* ... || *m* touch; ...
tòc·co *m* (-**chi**) chunk, piece; ...

Periods are omitted after labels and grammatical abbreviations and at the end of vocabulary entries.

Il punto è stato omesso dopo sigle, abbreviazioni grammaticali, ed alla fine di ogni articolo.

Proper nouns are listed in their alphabetical position in the main body of the Dictionary. Thus **Svezia** and **svedese** do not have to be looked up in two different sections of the book. And all subentries are listed in strictly alphabetical order.

Tutti i nomi propri sono posti nella loro posizione alfabetica nel corpo del Dizionario: quindi **Svezia** e **svedese** non si trovano in sezioni separate di questo libro. Per la medesima ragione di semplicità d'uso, le parole e frasi contenute sotto ogni esponente sono poste in ordine alfabetico.

The gender of Italian nouns is shown on both sides of the Dictionary, except that the gender of masculine nouns ending in **-o**, feminine nouns ending in **-a** and **-ione**, masculine nouns modified by an adjective ending in **-o**, and feminine nouns modified by an adjective

Il genere dei nomi italiani è indicato in entrambe le parti del Dizionario, eccezion fatta nella parte inglese-italiano, per le parole maschili che terminano in **-o**, per le parole femminili che terminano in **-a** e in **-ione**, per i nomi maschili accompagnati da un

ending in -a is not shown on the English-Italian side.

aggettivo che termina in -o e per i nomi femminili accompagnati da un aggettivo che termina in -a.

The feminine form of an Italian adjective used as a noun (or an Italian feminine noun having identical spelling with the feminine form of an adjective) which falls alphabetically in a separate position from the adjective is treated in that position and is listed again as a cross reference under the adjective:

Quando un nome femminile italiano ha la medesima grafia della forma femminile di un aggettivo o quando tale forma femminile di aggettivo è usata come nome, lo si trova elencato nella sua posizione alfabetica come nome e poi di nuovo come rinvio interno sotto l'aggettivo:

nòta *f* mark, score, . . .
nò·to -ta *adj* . . . ‖ *m* . . . ‖ *f* see **nota**

The centered period is used in vocabulary entries of inflected words to mark off, according to standard orthographic principles in the two languages, the final syllable that has to be detached before the syllable showing the inflection is added:

Qualora l'esponente italiano o inglese sia un vocabolo a flessione, un punto leggermente elevato sopra il rigo è stato usato per separare, secondo le regole ortografiche di ciascuna delle due lingue, la sillaba finale che dev'essere rimossa prima che la nuova desinenza di flessione possa essere attaccata al corpo dell'esponente, per es.:

vèc·chio -chia (-chi -chie) *adj* . . .
put·ty [ˈpʌti] *s* (**-ties**) . . . ‖ *v* (*pret & pp* -tied) . . .
hap·py [ˈhæpi] *adj* (**-pier; -piest**) . . .

If the entry word cannot be divided by a centered period the full form is given in parentheses:

Se l'esponente non può essere scisso a mezzo del suddetto punto, la forma completa è indicata in parentesi:

mouse [maʊs] *s* (**mice** [maɪs]) . . .
mouth [maʊθ] *s* (**mouths** [maʊðz]) . . .
die [daɪ] *s* (**dice** [daɪs]) . . . ‖ *s* (**dies**) . . . ‖ *v* (*pret & pp* **died**; *ger* **dying**) *intr* . . .

Many Italian verbs which take an indirect object have, as their equivalent, English verbs which take a direct object. This is shown on both sides of this Dictionary by the insertion of (with *dat*) after the Italian verb, e.g.,

Molti verbi italiani che reggono un oggetto indiretto hanno come equivalenti inglesi verbi che reggono un oggetto diretto. Questa equivalenza è indicata in entrambe le parti del Dizionario con l'aggiunta di (with *dat*) dopo il verbo italiano, per es.:

ubbidire §176 *intr* . . . ; (with *dat*) to obey
obey [oˈbe] *tr* ubbidire (with *dat*)

On the Italian-English side inflection is shown by: a) numbers that refer to the grammatical tables of articles, pronouns, etc., and to the tables of model verbs: they are placed before the abbreviation indicating the part of speech:

Nella parte italiano-inglese la flessione si indica: a) con numeri che si riferiscono alle tavole grammaticali degli articoli, dei pronomi, ecc., e alle tavole dei verbi modello; questi numeri sono posti innanzi all'abbreviazione indicante la parte del discorso:

mì·o -a §6 *adj & pron poss*
lui §5 *pron pers*
congiùngere §183 *tr & ref*

x

b) the first person singular of the present indicative of verbs in which the stress falls on either an **e** or an **o** not stressed in the infinitive or on the third syllable from the end, whatever the vowel may be:

b) con la prima persona singolare del presente dell'indicativo dei verbi non sdruccioli all'infinito in cui l'accento tonico cade o su una **e** o su una **o**, o su qualsiasi vocale di una parola sdrucciola:

> ritornare (ritórno) *tr* . . .
> visitare (vìsito) *tr* . . .

---

c) the feminine endings of all adjectives which end in **-o**:

c) con la desinenza femminile di tutti gli aggettivi che terminano in **-o** nel maschile:

> laborió•so -sa [s] *adj* . . .

---

d) the plural endings of nouns and adjectives which are formed irregularly:

d) con la desinenza plurale dei nomi e aggettivi che si formano in maniera irregolare:

> bràc•cio *m* (-cia *fpl*) . . . || *m* (-ci) . . .
> cit•tà *f* (-tà) . . .
> dià•rio -ria (-ri -rie) *adj* . . . || *m* . . . || *f* . . .
> fotogram•ma *m* (-mi) . . .
> fràn•gia *f* (-ge) . . .
> laburi•sta (-sti -ste) *adj* . . . || *mf* . . .
> la•go *m* (-ghi) . . .
> òr•co *m* (-chi) . . .
> òtti•co -ca (-ci -che) *adj* . . . || *m* . . . || *f* . . .

---

e) the full plural forms of all nouns that cannot be divided by a center period or whose plural cannot be shown by such division:

e) con la completa forma plurale di quei nomi che non possono essere scissi col suddetto punto o che hanno mutamenti interni:

> re *m* (re) . . .
> caporeparto *m* (capireparto) . . .

I wish to express my gratitude to many persons who helped me in the production of this book and particularly to Dr. Edwin B. Williams who, ever since graduate school, has been a constant inspiration and who has established the principles upon which this book was compiled, to my wife and children, who patiently aided and abetted me through ten years of research and compilation, to Richard J. Nelson, Sebastiano DiBlasi, Walter D. Glanze, and to Giacomo De Voto, Miro Dogliotti, and Michele Ricciardelli.

Labels and abbreviations

Sigle ed abbreviazioni

abbr abbreviation—abbreviazione
(acronym) word formed from the initial letters or syllables of a series of words—parola costituita dalle lettere o sillabe iniziali di una serie di parole
adj adjective—aggettivo
adv adverb—avverbio
(aer) aeronautics—aeronautica
(agr) agriculture—agricoltura
(alg) algebra—algebra
(anat) anatomy—anatomia
(archaic) arcaico
(archeol) archeology—archeologia
(archit) architecture—architettura
(arith) arithmetic—aritmetica
art article—articolo
(astr) astronomy—astronomia
(astrol) astrology—astrologia
(aut) automobile—automobile
aux auxiliary verb—verbo ausiliare
(bact) bacteriology—batteriologia
(baseball) baseball
(basketball) pallacanestro
(bb) bookbinding—legatoria
(Bib) Biblical—biblico
(billiards) biliardo
(biochem) biochemistry—biochimica
(biol) biology—biologia
(bot) botany—botanica
(bowling) bowling
(boxing) pugilato
(bridge) bridge
(Brit) British—britannico
(cards) carte da gioco
(carp) carpentry—falegnameria
(checkers) gioco della dama
(chem) chemistry—chimica
(chess) scacchi
(coll) colloquial—familiare
(com) commercial—commerciale
comb form elemento di parola composta
comp comparative—comparativo
cond conditional—condizionale
conj conjunction—congiunzione
(cricket) cricket
(culin) cooking—cucina
dat dative—dativo
def definite—determinativo, definito
dem demonstrative—dimostrativo
(dentistry) medicina dentaria
(dial) dialectal—dialettale
(dipl) diplomacy—diplomazia

(disparaging) sprezzante
(eccl) ecclesiastical—ecclesiastico
(econ) economics—economia
(educ) education—istruzione
e.g., or *e.g.*, per esempio
(elec) electricity—elettricità
(electron) electronics—elettronica
(ent) entomology—entomologia
(equit) horseback riding—equitazione
f feminine noun—nome femminile
(fa) fine arts—belle arti
fem feminine—femminile
(fencing) scherma
(fig) figurative—figurato
(fin) financial—finanziario
(football) football americano
fpl feminine noun plural—nome femminile plurale
fut future—futuro
(geog) geography—geografia
(geol) geology—geologia
(geom) geometry—geometria
ger gerund—gerundio
(golf) golf
(gram) grammar—grammatica
(herald) heraldry—araldica
(hist) history—storia
(hort) horticulture—orticoltura
(hunt) hunting—caccia
(ichth) ichthyology—ittiologia
i.e., cioè
imperf imperfect—imperfetto
impers impersonal verb—verbo impersonale
impv imperative—imperativo
ind indicative—indicativo
indef indefinite—indefinito, indeterminativo
inf infinitive—infinito
(ins) insurance—assicurazione
interj interjection—interiezione
interr interrogative—interrogativo
intr intransitive verb—verbo intransitivo
invar invariable—invariabile
(Italian cards) carte italiane
(jewelry) gioielleria
(joc) jocular—faceto
(journ) journalism—giornalismo
(law) diritto, legge
(letterword) word in the form of an abbreviation which is pronounced by sounding the names of its letters in

succession and which functions as a part of speech—parola in forma di abbreviazione che si ottiene pronunziando consecutivamente la denominazione di ciascuna lettera e che funziona come parte del discorso

(lexicography) lessicografia
(ling) linguistics—linguistica
(lit) literary—letterario
(log) logic—logica
m masculine noun—nome maschile
(mach) machinery—macchinario
masc masculine—maschile
(math) mathematics—matematica
(mech) mechanics—meccanica
(med) medicine—medicina
(metallurgy) metallurgia
(meteor) meteorology—meteorologia
mf masculine or feminine noun according to sex—nome maschile o nome femminile secondo il sesso
m & f see below between (mythol) and (naut)
(mil) military—militare
(min) mining—lavorazione delle miniere
(mov) moving pictures—cinematografo
mpl masculine noun plural—nome maschile plurale
(mus) music—musica
(mythol) mythology—mitologia
m & f masculine and feminine noun without regard to sex—nome maschile e femminile senza distinzione di sesso
(naut) nautical—nautico
(nav) naval—navale
neut neuter—neutro
num number—numero
(obs) obsolete—in disuso
(obstet) obstetrics—ostetricia
(opt) optics—ottica
(orn) ornithology—ornitologia
(painting) pittura
(pathol) pathology—patologia
(pej) pejorative—peggiorativo
perf perfect—perfetto, passato
pers personal—personale; person—persona
(pharm) pharmacy—farmacia
(philately) filatelia
(philol) philology—filologia
(philos) philosophy—filosofia
(phonet) phonetics—fonetica
(phot) photography—fotografia
(phys) physics—fisica
(physiol) physiology—fisiologia
pl plural—plurale
(poet) poetical—poetico
(poker) poker
(pol) politics—politica
pp past participle—participio passato
poss possessive—possessivo
pref prefix—prefisso
prep preposition—preposizione

prep phrase prepositional phrase—frase preposizionale
pres present—presente
pret preterit—passato remoto
pron pronoun—pronome
(pros) prosody—prosodia
(psychoanal) psychoanalysis—psicanalisi
(psychol) psychology—psicologia
(psychopath) psychopathology—psicopatologia
qlco or qlco qualcosa—something
qlcu or qlcu qualcuno—someone
(racing) corse
(rad) radio—radio
ref reflexive verb—verbo riflessivo o pronominale
rel relative—relativo
(rel) religion—religione
(rhet) rhetoric—retorica
(rok) rocketry—studio dei razzi
(rowing) canottaggio
(rr) railroad—ferrovia
(rugby) rugby
s substantive—sostantivo
(scornful) sprezzante
(Scot) Scottish—scozzese
(sculp) sculpture—scultura
(sew) sewing—cucito
sg singular—singolare
(slang) gergo
s.o. or *s.o.* someone—qualcuno
(soccer) calcio
spl substantive plural—sostantivo plurale
(sports) sport
ssg substantive singular—sostantivo singolare
s.th or *s.th* something—qualcosa
subj subjunctive—congiuntivo
suf suffix—suffisso
super superlative—superlativo
(surg) surgery—chirurgia
(surv) surveying—agrimensura, topografia
(taur) bullfighting—tauromachia
(telg) telegraphy—telegrafia
(telp) telephone—telefonia
(telv) television—televisione
(tennis) tennis
(tex) textile—tessile
(theat) theater—teatro
(theol) theology—teologia
tr transitive verb—verbo transitivo
(trademark) marchio di fabbrica
(typ) printing—tipografia
(U.S.A.) S.U.A.
v verb—verbo
var variant—variante
(vet) veterinary medicine—medicina veterinaria
(vulg) vulgar—volgare, ordinario
(wrestling) lotta
(zool) zoology—zoologia

PART ONE

Italian-English

Italian Spelling and Pronunciation

§1. The Italian Alphabet. 1. The twenty-one letters of the Italian alphabet are listed below with their names and their sounds in terms of approximate equivalent English sounds. Their gender is masculine or feminine.

LETTER	NAME	APPROXIMATE SOUND
a	a	Like *a* in English *father*, e.g., **facile, padre.**
b	bi	Like *b* in English *boat*, e.g., **bello, abate.**
c	ci	When followed by **e** or **i**, like *ch* in English *cherry*, e.g., **cento, cinque**; if the **i** is unstressed and followed by another vowel, its sound is not heard, e.g., **ciarla, cieco.** When followed by **a, o, u,** or a consonant, like *c* in English *cook*, e.g., **casa, come, cura, credere.** The digraph **ch**, which is used before **e** and **i**, has likewise the sound of *c* in English *cook*, e.g., **chiesa, perché.**
d	di	Like *d* in English *dance*, e.g., **dare, madre.**
e	e	Has two sounds. One like *a* in English *make*, shown on stressed syllables in this DICTIONARY by the acute accent, e.g., **séra, trénta**; and one like *e* in English *met*, shown on stressed syllables in this DICTIONARY by the grave accent, e.g., **fèrro, fèsta.**
f	effe	Like *f* in English *fool*, e.g., **farina, efelide.**
g	gi	When followed by **e** or **i**, like *g* in English *general*, e.g., **gelato, ginnasta**; if the **i** is unstressed and followed by another vowel, its sound is not heard, e.g., **giallo, giorno.** When followed by **a, o, u,** or a consonant, like *g* in English *go*, e.g., **gamba, goccia, gusto, grado.** The digraph **gh**, which is used before **e** and **i**, has likewise the sound of *g* in English *go*, e.g., **gherone, ghisa.** When the combination **gli** (a) is a form of the definite article or the personal pronoun, (b) is final in a word, or (c) is intervocalic, it has the sound of Castilian *ll*, which is somewhat like *lli* in English *million*, e.g., (a) **gli uomini, gli ho parlato ieri,** (b) **battagli,** (c) **figlio, migliore.** When it is (a) initial (except in the word **gli**, above), (b) preceded by a consonant, or (c) followed by a consonant, it is pronounced like *gli* in English *negligence*, e.g., (a) **glioma,** (b) **ganglio,** (c) **negligenza.** The combination **gl** followed by **a, e, o,** or **u** is pronounced like *gl* in English *globe*, e.g., **glabro, gleba, globo, gluteo, inglese, poliglotto.** The digraph **gn** has the sound of Castilian *ñ*, which is somewhat like *ni* in English *onion*, e.g., **signore, gnocco.**
h	acca	Always silent, e.g., **ah, hanno.** See **ch** under **c** above and **gh** under **g** above.
i	i	Like *i* in English *machine*, e.g., **piccolo, sigla.** When unstressed and followed by another vowel, like *y* in English *yes*, e.g., **piatto, piede, fiore, fiume.** For **i** in **ci**, see **c** above, in **gi**, see **g** above, and in **sci**, see **s** below.

3

LETTER	NAME	APPROXIMATE SOUND
l	elle	Like *l* in English *lamb*, e.g., **labbro, lacrima.**
m	emme	Like *m* in English *money*, e.g., **mano, come.**
n	enne	Like *n* in English *net*, e.g., **nome, cane.**
o	o	Has two sounds. One like *o* in English *note*, shown on stressed syllables in this DICTIONARY by the acute accent, e.g., **dópo, sóle;** and one like *ou* in English *ought*, shown on stressed syllables in this DICTIONARY by the grave accent, e.g., **còsa, dònna.**
p	pi	Like *p* in English *pot*, e.g., **passo, carpa.**
q	cu	This letter is always followed by the letter u and the combination has the sound of *qu* in English *quart*, e.g., **quanto, questo.**
r	erre	Like *r* in English *rubber*, with a slight trill, e.g., **roba, carta.**
s	esse	Has two sounds. When initial and followed by a vowel, when preceded by a consonant and followed by a vowel, and when followed by c [k] f, p, q, or t, like *s* in English *see*, e.g., **sale, falso, scappare, spazio, stoffa;** and when standing between two vowels and when followed by b, d, g [g], l, m, n, r or v, like *z* in English *zero*, e.g., **paese, sbaglio, svenire.** However, s standing between two vowels in some words and initial s followed by b, d, g [g], l, m, n, r, or v in some foreign borrowings are pronounced like *s* in *see*, e.g., **casa*, tesa, smoking, slam** In this DICTIONARY this is indicated by the insertion of [s] immediately after the entry word. However, when initial s stands between two vowels in a compound, its pronunciation remains that of initial s, e.g., **autoservizio** and this is not indicated. The digraph sc, when followed by e or i has the sound of *sh* in English *shall*, e.g., **scelta, scimmia;** if the i is unstressed and followed by another vowel, its sound is not heard, e.g., **sciame, sciopero.** The trigraph sch has the sound of *sc* in English *scope*, e.g., **scherzo, schiavo.**
t	ti	Like *t* in English *table*, e.g., **terra, pasto.**
u	u	Like *u* in English *rule*, e.g., **luna, mulo.** When followed by a vowel, like *w* in English *was*, e.g., **quanto, guerra, nuovo.**
v	vu	Like *v* in English *vain*, e.g., **vita, uva.**
z	zeta	Has two sounds. One like *ts* in English *nuts*, e.g., **grazia, zucchero;** and one like *dz* in English *adze*, e.g., **zero, mezzo.** In this DICTIONARY the sound of *dz* in *adze* is indicated by the insertion of [dz] immediately after the entry word. If the sound is long, [ddzz] is inserted

* Intervocalic s is generally voiced in the north of Italy.

2. The following five letters are found in borrowings from other languages.

LETTER	NAME	EXAMPLES
j	i lunga	**jazz, jingo**
k	cappa	**kiosco, kodak**
w	doppia vu	**water-polo, whisky**
x	ics	**xenofobo, xilofono**
y	ipsilon	**yacht, yoghurt**

3. Consonants written double are longer than consonants written single, that is, it takes a longer time to pronounce them, e.g., **camino** *chimney* and **cam-**

mino *road*, **capello** *hair* and **cappello** *hat*. Special attention is called to the following double consonants: **cc** followed by **e** or **i** has the sound of *ch ch* in English *beach chair*, that is, a lengthened *ch* (not the sound of *ks*), e.g., **accento; cch** has the sound of *kk* in English *bookkeeper*, e.g., **becchino; cq** has the sound of *kk* in English *bookkeeper*, e.g., **acqua; gg** followed by **e** or **i** has the sound of *ge j* in English *carriage joiner*, e.g., **peggio; ggh** has the sound of *g g* in English *tag game*, e.g., **agghindare.**

§2. Division of Syllables. In the application of the following rules for the syllabic division of words, the digraphs **ch, gh, gl, gn,** and **sc** count as single consonants.

(a) When a single consonant stands between two vowels it belongs to the following syllable, e.g., **ca·sa, fu·mo, ami·che, la·ghi, fi·glio, biso·gno, la·sciare.**

(b) When a consonant group consisting of two consonants of which the second is **l** or **r** stands between two vowels, the group belongs to the following syllable, e.g., **nu·cleo, so·brio, qua·dro.**

(c) When a consonant group consisting of two or more consonants of which the first or the second is **s** stands between two vowels, that part of the group beginning with **s** belongs to the following syllable, e.g., **ta·sca, bo·schi, fine·stra, super·sti·zione, sub·strato.**

(d) When a consonant group consisting of two or three consonants of which the first is **l, m, n,** or **r** stands between two vowels, the **l, m, n,** or **r** belongs to the preceding syllable, the other consonant or consonants to the following syllable, e.g., **al·bero, am·pio, prin·cipe, mor·te, in·flazione, com·pleto.**

(e) When a double consonant stands between two vowels or between a vowel and **l** or **r**, the first belongs to the preceding syllable, the second to the following syllable, e.g., **bab·bo, caval·lo, an·no, car·ro, mez·zo, sup·plica, lab·bro, quat·tro.**

§3. Stress and Accent Marks. 1. Whenever stress is shown as part of regular spelling, it is shown on **a, i,** and **u** by the grave accent mark, e.g., **libertà, giovedì, gioventù,** on close **e** and **o** by the acute accent mark, e.g., **perché,** and on open **e** and **o** by the grave accent mark, e.g., **caffè, parlò.** This occurs (a) in words ending in a stressed vowel, as in the above examples, (b) in stressed monosyllables in which the vocalic element is a diphthong of which the first letter is unstressed **i** or **u**, e.g., **già, più, può,** and (c) on the stressed monosyllable of any pair of monosyllables of which one is stressed and the other unstressed, in order to distinguish one from the other, e.g., **dà** *he gives* and **da** *from,* **è** *is* and **e** *and,* **sé** *himself* and **se** *if,* **sì** *yes* and **si** *himself.*

2. Whenever stress is not shown as part of regular spelling, it is often difficult to determine where it falls.

(a) In words of two syllables, the stress falls on the syllable next to the last, e.g., **ca'sa, mu'ro, ter'ra.** If the syllable next to the last contains a diphthong, that is, a combination of a strong vowel (**a, e,** or **o**) and a weak vowel (**i** or **u**), the strong vowel is stressed, regardless of which vowel comes first, e.g., **da'ino, ero'ico, ne'utro, fia'to, dua'le, sie'pe, fio're, buo'no.**

(b) In words of more than two syllables, the stress may fall on the syllable next to the last, e.g., **anda'ta, canzo'ne, pasto're** or on a preceding syllable, e.g., **fis'sile, gòn'dola, man'doria.** In these positions also the stressed syllable may contain a diphthong, e.g., **inca'uto, idra'ulico, fio'cina.**

(c) If a weak vowel in juxtaposition with a strong vowel is stressed, the two vowels constitute two separate syllables, e.g., **abba·i'no, ero·i'na, pa·u'ra, miri'ade, vi'a.**

(d) Two strong vowels in juxtaposition constitute two separate syllables, e.g., **pa·e'se, aure'ola, ide'a, oce'ano.**

(e) Two weak vowels in juxtaposition generally constitute a diphthong in which the first vowel is stressed in some words, e.g., **flu'ido** and the second vowel in others, e.g., **piu'ma.**

(f) If a word ends in a diphthong, the diphthong is stressed, e.g., **marina'i, parla'i, ero'i.**

3. In this DICTIONARY, stress is understood or shown on all words that do not bear an accent mark as part of regular spelling according to the following principles. In the application of these principles, individual vowels and not diphthongs are counted as units. In some words in which it is not necessary to show stress, an accent mark is used to show the quality of the stressed vowels **e** and **o.**

As in regular Italian spelling, stress is shown on **a, i,** and **u** by the grave accent mark, on close **e** and **o** by the acute accent mark, and on open **e** and **o** by the grave accent mark.

(a) It is understood that in words of more than one syllable in which no accent mark is shown, the stress falls on the vowel next to the last, e.g., **casa,**

5

fiato, duale, abbaino, paura. In such words as **sièpe, fióre, buòno, paése, fluènte, eròe, nói, pòi,** the accent mark is used to show the quality of the vowel.

(b) An accent mark is placed on the stressed vowel if the word is stressed on the third vowel from the end, e.g., **mùsica, sìmbolo, dàino, incàuto, marinàio, contìnuo, infànzia.** If this vowel is **e** or **o,** the acute or grave accent mark must correspond to the quality of the vowel, e.g., **fiòcina, rómpere, nèutro, eròico, assèdio, filatóio.**

(c) Contrary to the above-mentioned principle of counting vowels, an accent mark is placed on the strong vowel of a final diphthong, e.g., **marinài, assài.**

(d) Contrary to the above-mentioned principle of counting vowels, an accent mark is placed on the **i** of final **ia, ie, ii,** and **io,** e.g., **farmacìa, scìa, farmacìe, mormorìi, gorgoglìo, fìo.**

(e) An accent mark is placed on some borrowings ending in a consonant, e.g., **hàrem, revòlver.**

(f) The loss of the last vowel or last syllable of a word does not alter the position of the stress of the word, e.g., **la maggior parte, in alcun modo, fan bene.**

84. The Definite Article and Combinations with Prepositions.

		MASC BEFORE CONSONANT	MASC BEFORE S IMPURE OR Z[1]	MASC BEFORE VOWEL	FEM BEFORE CONSONANT	FEM BEFORE VOWEL
	SG	il	lo	l'	la	l'
	PL	i	gli	gli[2]	le	le[3]
WITH a	SG	al	allo	all'	alla	all'
	PL	ai	agli	agli[2]	alle	alle[3]
WITH di	SG	del	dello	dell'	della	dell'
	PL	dei	degli	degli[2]	delle	delle[3]
WITH con	SG	col	collo	coll'	colla	coll'
	PL	coi	cogli	cogli[2]	colle	colle[3]
WITH da	SG	dal	dallo	dall'	dalla	dall'
	PL	dai	dagli	dagli[2]	dalle	dalle[3]
WITH in	SG	nel	nello	nell'	nella	nell'
	PL	nei	negli	negli[2]	nelle	nelle[3]
WITH su	SG	sul	sullo	sull'	sulla	sull'
	PL	sui	sugli	sugli[2]	sulle	sulle[3]

[1] Other letters and groups of letters, which occur in a few words, are gn, pn, ps, sc, x, and i before a vowel, sometimes spelled j or y.

[2] These forms may drop the l before words beginning with i, e.g., gl'inglesi.

[3] The e of these forms is not elided, e.g. le erbe.

7

§5. Personal and Reflexive Pronouns.

PERSONS	SUBJECT	PERSONAL DIRECT OBJECT	PERSONAL INDIRECT OBJECT	REFLEX. & RECIPROCAL DIRECT & INDIRECT OBJECT	PERSONAL PREPOSITIONAL OBJECT	REFLEX. & RECIPROCAL PREPOSITIONAL OBJECT
SG						
1	io *I*	mi *me*	mi *to me*	mi *myself; to myself*	me *me*	me *myself*
2	tu *you*	ti *you*	ti *to you*	ti *yourself; to yourself*	te *you*	te *yourself*
3 MASC	egli, lui *he*	lo *him or it*	gli *to him*	si *himself; to himself*	lui *him*	sé *himself*
3 FEM	lei, essa *she*	la *her or it*	le *to her*	si *herself; to herself*	lei, essa *her*	sé *herself*
2 FORMAL	Lei *you*	La *you*	Le *to you*	si *yourself; to yourself*	Lei *you*	sé *yourself*
PL						
1	noi *we*	ci *us*	ci *to us*	ci *ourselves; to ourselves; each other; to each other*	noi *us*	noi *ourselves; each other*
2	voi *you*	vi *you*	vi *to you*	vi *yourself; yourselves; to yourself; each other; to each other*	voi *you*	voi *yourself; yourselves; each other*
3 MASC	loro, essi *they*	li *them*	loro *to them*	si *themselves; to themselves; each other; to each other*	loro, essi *them*	sé *themselves; each other*
3 FEM	loro, esse *they*	le *them*	loro *to them*	si *themselves; to themselves; each other; to each other*	loro, esse *them*	sé *themselves; each other*
2 FORMAL	Loro *you*	Li Le } *you*	Loro *to you*	si *yourselves; to yourselves; each other; to each other*	Loro *you*	sé *yourselves; each other*

ci and **vi** both mean also *here, there, to it, in it, to them, in them, about it.*
ne means *of, from,* or *with him, her, it, them; some, any; from here, from there, thence, about it.*

meco *with me,* **teco** *with you,* and **seco** *with him, with himself; with her, with herself; with you, with yourself, with yourselves; with them, with themselves; with each other* may be used instead of **con me, con te, con e,** and **con sé** respectively.

8

COMBINATION OF DIRECT AND INDIRECT OBJECT

PERSONS		
1 SG & 3 SG	me lo / me la }	*him, her, it to me*
1 SG & 3 PL	me li / me le }	*them to me*
2 SG & 3 SG	te lo / te la }	*him, her, it to you*
2 SG & 3 PL	te li / te le }	*them to you*
3 SG & 3 SG	glielo / gliela }	*him, her, it to him; him, her, it to her*
3 SG & 3 PL	glieli / gliele }	*them to him; them to her*
2 SG FORMAL & 3 SG	Glielo / Gliela }	*him, her, it to you*
2 SG FORMAL & 3 PL	Glieli / Gliele }	*them to you*

PERSONS		
1 PL & 3 SG	ce lo / ce la }	*him, her, it to us*
1 PL & 3 PL	ce li / ce le }	*them to us*
2 PL & 3 SG	ve lo / ve la }	*him, her, it to you*
2 PL & 3 PL	ve li / ve le }	*them to you*
3 SG & 3 PL	lo / la } VERB loro	*him, her, it to them*
3 PL & 3 PL	li / le } VERB loro	*them to them*
3 SG FORMAL & 2 PL FORMAL	lo / la } VERB Loro	*him, her, it to you*
3 PL & 2 PL FORMAL	li / le } VERB Loro	*them to you*

The form **si** (third singular and plural reflexive and reciprocal indirect object) changes to **se** before one of the direct objects **lo, la, li,** and **le,** and before **ne,** e.g., **se lo mette** he puts it on; **se n'è andato** he went away.

In combinations, **ne** occupies the same position as **lo, la, li,** and **le,** e.g., **me ne,** and forms one word with **gli,** namely, **gliene, gliene.**

9

§6 Possessive Adjectives and Pronouns

PERSON, NUMBER & SEX OF POSSESSOR	GENDER & NUMBER OF POSSESSIVE ADJECTIVE OR PRONOUN ACCORDING TO THE GENDER & NUMBER OF THE PERSON OR THING POSSESSED				MEANING OF ADJECTIVE	MEANING OF PRONOUN
	MSG	MPL	FSG	FPL		
SG						
1	il mio	i miei	la mia	le mie	*my*	*mine*
2	il tuo	i tuoi	la tua	le tue	*your*	*yours*
3 MASC	il suo	i suoi	la sua	le sue	*his*	*his*
3 FEM	il suo	i suoi	la sua	le sue	*her*	*hers*
3 NEUT	il suo	i suoi	la sua	le sue	*its*	*its*
2 FORMAL	il Suo	i Suoi	la Sua	le Sue	*your*	*yours*
PL						
1	il nostro	i nostri	la nostra	le nostre	*our*	*ours*
2	il vostro	i vostri	la vostra	le vostre	*your*	*yours*
3	il loro	i loro	la loro	le loro	*their*	*theirs*
2 FORMAL	il Loro	i Loro	la Loro	le Loro	*your*	*yours*

The definite article, shown here, is not generally used (a) in direct address, e.g., mio caro amico *my dear friend*, (b) after the verb essere, e.g., la casa è nostra *the house is ours*, and (c) when a singular form modifies the name of a relative, e.g., sua sorella *his sister*.

With forms of the indefinite article, the possessive adjective, whether standing before or after the noun, is translated by *of* plus the possessive pronoun, e.g., un amico mio *a friend of mine*; una sua zia *an aunt of his* (or *of hers*).

The forms of the possessive pronouns also have the force of nouns, e.g., il mio *my property, my belongings*; i suoi *his people, relatives, followers, troops, retinue*, etc.; la mia *my letter*; la sua *his opinion*.

10

§7. The Demonstrative Adjective.

		MASC BEFORE CONSONANT	MASC BEFORE S IMPURE OR Z (see note 1, p. 7)	MASC BEFORE VOWEL	FEM BEFORE CONSONANT	FEM BEFORE VOWEL
SG		quel *that*	quello	quell'	quella	quell'
PL		quei *those*	quegli	quegli	quelle	quelle
SG		questo *this*	questo	questo or quest'	questa	questa or quest'
PL		questi *these*	questi	questi	queste	queste

§8. The Demonstrative Pronoun.

	MASC	FEM	MASC
SG	quello *that one*	quèlla	quegli *that one;* *the former*
PL	quelli *those*	quelle	
SG	questo *this one*	questa	questi *this one;* *the latter*
PL	questi *these*	queste	

The demonstrative pronoun **quello** is often followed by **che, di,** or **da** and the masculine singular form may be shortened to **quel** before these words.

SG	colui *that one*	colei
PL	coloro *those*	coloro
SG	costui *this one*	costei
PL	costoro *these*	costoro

code·sto -sta -sti -ste and **cote·sto -sta -sti -ste** are demonstrative adjectives and demonstrative pronouns and mean *that (of yours)*.

§9. Indefinite Article and Numeral Adjective.

MASC	MASC	MASC	FEM	FEM
BEFORE CONSONANT	BEFORE S IMPURE OR z (see note 1, p. 7)	BEFORE VOWEL	BEFORE CONSONANT	BEFORE VOWEL
un *a, an; one*	uno	un	una	un'

13

§10. Indefinite Pronoun uno.

MASC	FEM
uno *one*	una

§11. Correlative Indefinite Pronoun.

	MASC	FEM
SG	l'uno . . . l'altro *one . . . the other*	l'una . . . l'altra
PL	gli uni . . . gli altri *some . . . the others*	le une . . . le altre

§12. Reciprocal Indefinite Pronoun.

	MASC	FEM
SG	l'un l'altro *each other, one another*	l'una l'altra
PL	gli uni gli altri	le une le altre

Table of Regular Endings of Italian Verbs

The stem to which the endings of the gerund, past participle, present participle, imperative, present indicative, present subjunctive, imperfect indicative, preterit indicative, and imperfect subjunctive are attached is obtained by dropping the ending of the infinitive, viz., **-are**, **-ere**, **-ire**.

The stem to which the endings of the future indicative and present conditional are attached is obtained by dropping the **-e** of the ending of the infinitive of all conjugations and changing the **a** of the ending of the infinitive of the first conjugation to **e**.

The letters before the names of some of the tenses of this table correspond to the designation of the tenses shown on the following page.

Letters printed in italics have a written accent that is not part of the regular spelling.

TENSE	FIRST CONJUGATION	SECOND CONJUGATION	THIRD CONJUGATION
inf	**-are**	**-ére** (or **-ere**)	**-ire**
ger	-ando	-èndo	-èndo
pp	-ato	-uto	-ito
pres part	-ante	-ènte	-ènte
(a) *impv*	-a -ate	-i -éte	-i -ite
(b) *pres ind*	-o -i -a -iamo -ate -ano	-o -i -e -iamo -éte -ono	-o -i -e -iamo -ite -ono
(c) *pres subj*	-i -i -i -iamo -iate -ino	-a -a -a -iamo -iate -ano	-a -a -a -iamo -iate -ano
(d) *imperf ind*	-avo -avi -ava -avamo -avate -àvano	-évo -évi -éva -evamo -evate -évano	-ivo -ivi -iva -ivamo -ivate -ìvano
(e) *pret ind*	-ài -asti -ò -ammo -aste -àrono	-éi -ésti -è -émmo -éste -érono	-ìi -isti -ì -immo -iste -ìrono
imperf subj	-assi -assi -asse -àssimo -aste -àssero	-éssi -éssi -ésse -éssimo -éste -éssero	-issi -issi -isse -ìssimo -iste -ìssero
(f) *fut ind*	-er-ò -er-ài -er-à -er-émo -er-éte -er-anno	-ò -ài -à -émo -éte -anno	-ò -ài -à -émo -éte -anno

TENSE	FIRST CONJUGATION	SECOND CONJUGATION	THIRD CONJUGATION
pres cond	-er-ə̀i -er-ésti -er-ə̀bbe -er-émmo -er-éste -er-ə̀bbero	-ə̀i -ésti -ə̀bbe -émmo -éste -ə̀bbero	-ə̀i -ésti -ə̀bbe -émmo -éste -ə̀bbero

MODEL VERBS
ORDER OF TENSES

(a) imperative
(b) present indicative
(c) present subjunctive

(d) imperfect indicative
(e) preterit indicative
(f) future indicative

In addition to the infinitive, gerund, and past participle, which are shown in line one of these tables, all simple tenses are shown if they contain at least one irregular form, except (1) the present conditional, which is always formed on the stem of the future indicative, (2) the imperfect subjunctive, which is always formed on the stem of the *2nd sg* of the preterit indicative, and (3) the present participle, which is generally formed by changing the final -do of the gerund to -te (exceptions being shown in parentheses after the gerund).

Letters printed in italics have a written accent that is not part of the regular spelling.

§100 **ACCÈDERE**—accedèndo—acceduto
  (e) accedètti *or* accedéi *or* accèssi; accedésti; accedètte *or* accedé *or* accèsse; accedémmo; accedéste; accedèttero *or* accedérono *or* accèssero

§101 **ACCÈNDERE**—accendèndo—accéso
  (e) accési, accendésti, accése, accendémmo, accendéste, accésero

§102 **ADDURRE**—adducèndo—addótto
  (b) adduco, adduci, adduce, adduciamo, adducéte, addùcono
  (c) adduca, adduca, adduca, adduciamo, adduciate, addùcano
  (d) adducévo, adducévi, adducéva, adducevamo, adducevate, adducévano
  (e) addussi, adducésti, addusse, adducémmo, adducéste, addùssero

§103 **AFFÌGGERE**—affiggèndo—affisso
  (e) affissi, affiggésti, affisse, affiggémmo, affiggéste, affìssero

17

§104 **AFFLÌGGERE**—affliggèndo—afflitto
    (e) afflissi, affliggésti, afflisse, affliggémmo, affliggéste, afflìssero

§105 **ALLÙDERE**—alludèndo—alluso
    (e) allusi, alludésti, alluse, alludémmo, alludéste, allùsero

§106 **ANDARE**—andando—andato
    (a) va *or* va' *or* vai, andate
    (b) vò *or* vado, vai, va, andiamo, andate, vanno
    (c) vada, vada, vada, andiamo, andiate, vàdano
    (f) andrò, andràI, andrà, andrémo, andréte, andranno

§107 **ANNÈTTERE**—annettèndo—annèsso *or* **annéttere**, annetténdo, annésso
    (e) annettéi *or* annèssi *or* annéssi; annettésti; annetté *or* annèsse *or* annésse; annettémmo; annettéste; annettérono *or* annèssero *or* annéssero

§108 **APPARIRE**—apparèndo—apparso
    (a) apparisci *or* appari; apparite
    (b) apparisco *or* appàio; apparisci *or* appari; apparisce *or* appare; appariamo; apparite; apparìscono *or* appàiono
    (c) apparisca *or* appàia; apparisca *or* appàia; apparisca *or* appàia; appariamo; appariate; apparìscano *or* appàiano
    (e) apparvi *or* apparìi *or* apparsi; apparisti; apparve *or* apparì *or* apparse; apparimmo; appariste; appàrvero *or* apparìrono *or* appàrsero

§109 **APPÈNDERE**—appendèndo—appéso
    (e) appési, appendésti, appése, appendémmo, appendéste, appésero

§110 **APRIRE**—aprèndo—apèrto
    (e) aprìi *or* apèrsi; apristi; aprì *or* apèrse; aprimmo; apriste; aprìrono *or* apèrsero

§111 **ÀRDERE**—ardèndo—arso
    (e) arsi, ardésti, arse, ardémmo, ardéste, àrsero

§112 **ASPÈRGERE**—aspergèndo—aspèrso
    (e) aspèrsi, aspergésti, aspèrse, aspergémmo, aspergéste, aspèrsero

§113 **ASSÌDERE**—assidèndo—assiso
    (e) assisi, assidésti, assise, assidémmo, assidéste, assìsero

§114 **ASSÌSTERE**—assistèndo—assistito
    (e) assistéi *or* assistètti; assistésti; assisté *or* assistètte; assistémmo; assistéste; assistérono *or* assistèttero

§115 ASSÒLVERE—assolvèndo—assòlto *or* assoluto
(e) assolvéi *or* assolvètti *or* assòlsi; assolvésti; assolvé *or* assolvètte *or* assòlse; assolvémmo; assolvéste; assolvérono *or* assolvèttero *or* assòlsero

§116 ASSÙMERE—assumèndo—assunto
(e) assunsi, assumésti, assunse, assumémmo, assuméste, assùnsero

§117 ASSÙRGERE—assurgèndo—assurto
(e) assursi, assurgésti, assurse, assurgémmo, assurgéste, assùrsero

§118 AVÈRE—avèndo—avuto
(a) abbi, abbiate
(b) ho, hai, ha, abbiamo, avete, hanno
(c) àbbia, àbbia, àbbia, abbiamo, abbiate, àbbiano
(e) èbbi, avésti, èbbe, avémmo, avéste, èbbero
(f) avrò, avràì, avrà, avrémo, avréte, avranno

§119 AVVIARE—avviando—avviato
(b) avvìo, avvìì, avvìa, avviamo, avviate, avvìano
(c) avvìì, avvìì, avvìì, avviamo, avviate, avvìino

§120 BÉRE—bevèndo—bevuto
(a) bévi, bevéte
(b) bévo, bévi, béve, beviamo, bevéte, bévono
(c) béva, béva, béva, beviamo, beviate, bévano
(d) bevévo, bevévi, bevéva, bevevamo, bevevate, bevévano
(e) bévvi *or* bevéi *or* bevètti; bevésti, bévve *or* bevé *or* bevètte; bevémmo; bevéste; bévvero *or* bevérono *or* bevèttero
(f) berrò, berràì, berrà, berrémo, berréte, berranno

§121 CADÉRE—cadèndo—caduto
(e) caddi, cadésti, cadde, cadémmo, cadéste, càddero
(f) cadrò, cadràì, cadrà, cadrémo, cadréte, cadranno

§122 CECARE—cecando—cecato
(a) cièca *or* cèca; cecate
(b) cièco *or* cèco; cièchi *or* cèchi; cièca *or* cèca; cechiamo; cecate; ciècano *or* cècano
(c) cièchi *or* cèchi; cièchi *or* cèchi; cièchi *or* cèchi; cechiamo; cechiate; cièchino *or* cèchino
(f) cecherò, cecheràì, cecherà, cecherémo, cecheréte, cecheranno

§123 CÈDERE—cedèndo—ceduto
(e) cedéi *or* cedètti; cedésti; cedé *or* cedètte; cedémmo; cedéste; cedérono *or* cedèttero

§124 CHIÈDERE—chiedèndo—chièsto
(e) chièsi, chiedésti, chièse, chiedémmo, chiedéste, chièsero

§125 CHIÙDERE—chiudèndo—chiuso
(e) chiusi, chiudésti, chiuse, chiudémmo, chiudéste, chiùsero

§126 CÌNGERE—cingèndo—cinto
(e) cinsi, cingésti, cinse, cingémmo, cingéste, cìnsero

§127 CÒGLIERE—coglièndo—còlto
(a) còlgi, cogliéte
(b) còlgo, còlgi, còglie, cogliamo, cogliéte, còlgono
(c) còlga, còlga, còlga, cogliamo, cogliate, còlgano
(e) còlsi, cogliésti, còlse, cogliémmo, cogliéste, còlsero

§128 COMINCIARE—cominciando—cominciato
(b) comìncio, cominci, comìncia, cominciamo, cominciate, comìnciano
(c) cominci, cominci, cominci, cominciamo, cominciate, comìncino
(f) comincerò, comincerài, comincerà, cominceremo, cominceréte, cominceranno

§129 COMPÈTERE—competèndo—*pp* missing

§130 CÒMPIERE—compièndo—compiuto
(a) cómpi, compite
(b) cómpio, cómpi, cómpie, compiamo, compite, cómpiono
(c) cómpia, cómpia, cómpia, compiamo, compiate, cómpiano
(d) compivo, compivi, compiva, compivamo, compivate, compìvano
(e) compiéi *or* compìi; compiésti *or* compisti; compié *or* compì; compiémmo *or* compimmo; compiéste *or* compiste; compiérono *or* compìrono

§131 COMPRÌMERE—comprimèndo—comprèsso
(e) comprèssi, comprimésti, comprèsse, comprimémmo, compriméste, comprèssero

§132 CONCÈDERE—concedèndo—concèsso
(e) concedéi *or* concèssi *or* concedètti; concedésti; concedé *or* concèsse *or* concedètte; concedémmo; concedéste; concedérono *or* concèssero *or* concedèttero

§133 CONCÈRNERE—concernèndo—*pp* missing
(e) concernéi *or* concernètti; concernésti; concerné *or* concernètte; concernémmo; concernéste; concernérono *or* concernèttero

20

§134 **CONÓSCERE**—conoscèndo—conosciuto
(e) conóbbi, conoscésti, conóbbe, conoscémmo, conoscéste, conóbbero

§135 **CONQUÌDERE**—conquidèndo—conquiso
(e) conquisi, conquidésti, conquise, conquidémmo, conquidéste, conquìsero

§136 **CONSÙMERE**—*ger* missing—consunto
(a) missing
(b) missing
(c) missing
(d) missing
(e) consunsi, consunse, consùnsero
(f) missing

§137 **CONVÈRGERE**—convergèndo—convèrso
(e) convèrsi *or* convergéi; convergésti; convèrse *or* convergé; convergémmo; convergéste; convèrsero *or* convergérono

§138 **CONVERTIRE**—convertèndo—convertito
(e) convertìi *or* convèrsi; convertisti; convertì *or* convèrse; convertimmo; convertiste; convertìrono *or* convèrsero

§139 **CÓRRERE**—corrèndo—córso
(e) córsi, corrésti, córse, corrémmo, corréste, córsero

§140 **COSTRUIRE**—costruèndo—costruito
(a) costruisci, costruite
(b) costruisco, costruisci, costruisce, costruiamo, costruite, costruìscono
(c) costruisca, costruisca, costruisca, costruiamo, costruiate, costruìscano
(e) costruìi *or* costrussi; costruisti; costruì *or* costrusse; costruimmo; costruiste; costruìrono *or* costrùssero

§141 **CRÉDERE**—credèndo—creduto
(e) credéi *or* credètti; credésti; credé *or* credètte; credémmo; credéste; credérono *or* credèttero

§142 **CRÉSCERE**—crescèndo—cresciuto
(e) crébbi, crescésti, crébbe, crescémmo, crescéste, crébbero

§143 **CUCIRE**—cucèndo—cucito
(b) cùcio, cuci, cuce, cuciamo, cucite, cùciono
(c) cùcia, cùcia, cùcia, cuciamo, cuciate, cùciano

§144a **CUÒCERE**—cuocèndo *or* cocèndo (cocènte)—còtto *or* cociuto

(a) cuòci, cocéte
(b) cuòcio, cuòci, cuòce, cociamo, cocéte, cuòciono
(c) cuòcia, cuòcia, cuòcia, cociamo, cociate, cuòciano
(d) cocévo, cocévi, cocéva, cocevamo, cocevate, cocévano
(e) còssi, cocésti, còsse, cocémmo, cocéste, còssero
(f) cocerò, coceràì, cocerà, cocerémo, coceréte, coceranno

§144b **DARE**—dando—dato
(a) dà *or* dàì *or* da'; date
(b) dò *or* dò; dàì; dà; diamo; date; danno
(c) dìa, dìa, dìa, diamo, diate, dìano
(e) dièdi *or* dètti; désti; d*i*ède *or* dètte *or* diè; démmo; déste; dièdero *or* dèttero
(f) darò, daràì, darà, darémo, daréte, daranno

§145 **DECÌDERE**—decidèndo—deciso
(e) decisi, decidésti, decise, decidémmo, decidéste, decìsero

§146 **DELÌNQUERE**—delinquèndo—*pp* missing
(a) missing
(c) missing
(e) missing

§147 **DEVÒLVERE**—devolvèndo—devoluto
(e) devolvéi *or* devolvètti; devolvésti; devolvé *or* devolvètte; devolvémmo; devolvéste; devolvérono *or* devolvèttero

§148 **DIFÈNDERE**—difendèndo—diféso
(e) difési, difendésti, difése, difendémmo, difendéste, difésero

§149 **DILÌGERE**—diligèndo—dilètto
(a) missing
(b) missing
(c) missing
(d) missing
(e) dilèssi, diligésti, dilèsse, diligémmo, diligéste, dilèssero
(f) missing

§150 **DIPÈNDERE**—dipendèndo—dipéso
(e) dipési, dipendésti, dipése, dipendémmo, dipendéste, dipésero

§151 **DIRE**—dicèndo—détto
(a) di' *or* dì; dite
(b) dico, dici, dice, diciamo, dite, dìcono
(c) dica, dica, dica, diciamo, diciate, dìcano
(d) dicévo, dicévi, dicéva, dicevamo, dicevate, dicévano
(e) dissi, dicésti, disse, dicémmo, dicéste, dìssero
(f) dirò, diràì, dirà, dirémo, diréte, diranno

22

§152 **DIRÌGERE**—dirigèndo—dirètto
    (e) dirèssi, dirigésti, dirèsse, dirigémmo, dirigéste, dirèssero

§153 **DISCÈRNERE**—discernèndo—*pp* missing
    (e) discernéi; discernésti; discerné *or* discernètte; discernémmo; discernéste; discernérono *or* discernèttero

§154 **DISCÙTERE**—discutèndo—discusso
    (e) discussi, discutésti, discusse, discutémmo, discutéste, discùssero

§155 **DISSÒLVERE**—dissolvèndo—dissòlto
    (e) dissòlsi *or* dissolvéi *or* dissolvètti; dissolvésti; dissòlse *or* dissolvé *or* dissolvètte; dissolvémmo; dissolvéste; dissòlsero *or* dissolvérono *or* dissolvèttero

§156 **DISTÌNGUERE**—distinguèndo—distinto
    (e) distinsi, distinguésti, distinse, distinguémmo, distinguéste, distìnsero

§157 **DIVÈRGERE**—divergèndo—*pp* missing
    (e) obsolete

§158 **DIVÌDERE**—dividèndo—diviso
    (e) divisi, dividésti, divise, dividémmo, dividéste, divìsero

§159 **DOLÉRE**—dolèndo—doluto
    (a) duòli, doléte
    (b) dòlgo, duòli, duòle, doliamo, doléte, dòlgono
    (c) dòlga, dòlga, dòlga, doliamo, doliate, dòlgano
    (e) dòlsi, dolésti, dòlse, dolémmo, doléste, dòlsero
    (f) dorrò, dorrài, dorrà, dorrémo, dorréte, dorranno

§160 **DOVÉRE**—dovèndo—dovuto
    (b) dèbbo *or* dèvo; dèvi; dève; dobbiamo; dovéte; dèbbono *or* dèvono
    (c) dèva *or* dèbba; dèva *or* dèbba; dèva *or* dèbba; dobbiamo; dobbiate; dèvano *or* dèbbano
    (e) dovéi *or* dovètti; dovésti; dové *or* dovètte; dovémmo; dovéste; dovérono *or* dovèttero

§161 **ELÌDERE**—elidèndo—eliso
    (e) elisi, elidésti, elise, elidémmo, elidéste, elìsero

§162 **EMÈRGERE**—emergèndo—emèrso
    (e) emèrsi, emergésti, emèrse, emergémmo, emergéste, emèrsero

§163 **ÉMPIERE & EMPIRE**—empièndo—empito *or* empiuto
    (a) émpi, empite

(b) émpio, émpi, émpie, empiamo, empite, émpiono

(c) émpia, émpia, émpia, empiamo, empiate, émpiano

(d) empivo, empivi, èmpiva, empivamo, empivate, empìvano

(e) empiéi *or* empìi; empiésti; *or* empisti; empié *or* empì; empiémmo *or* empimmo; empiéste *or* empiste; empiérono *or* empìrono

(f) empirò, empiràì, empirà, empirémo, empiréte, empiranno

§164 ÈRGERE—ergèndo—èrto
(e) èrsi, ergésti, èrse, ergémmo, ergéste, èrsero

§165 ESÌGERE—esigèndo—esatto
(e) esigéi *or* esigètti; esigésti; esigé *or* esigètte; esigémmo; esigéste; esigérono *or* esigèttero

§166 ESÌMERE—esimèndo—*pp* missing
(e) esiméi *or* esimètti; esimésti; esimé *or* esimètte; esimémmo; esiméste; esimérono *or* esimèttero

§167 ESPÀNDERE—espandèndo—espanso
(e) espandéi *or* espandètti *or* espansi; espandésti; espandé *or* espandètte *or* espanse; espandémmo; espandéste; espandérono *or* espandèttero *or* espànsero

§168 ESPÈLLERE—espellèndo—espulso
(e) espulsi, espellésti, espulse, espellémmo, espelléste, espùlsero

§169 ESPLÒDERE—esplodèndo—esplòso
(e) esplòsi, esplodésti, esplòse, esplodémmo, esplodéste, esplòsero

§170 ÈSSERE—essèndo—stato
(a) sii, siate
(b) sóno, sèi, è, siamo, sièto, sóno
(c) sìa, sìa, sìa, siamo, siate, sìano
(d) èro, èri, èra, eravamo, eravate, èrano
(e) fui, fósti, fu, fummo, fóste, fùrono
(f) sarò, saràì, sarà, sarémo, saréte, saranno

§171 ESTÒLLERE—estollèndo—*pp* missing
(e) missing

§172 EVÀDERE—evadèndo—evaso
(e) evasi, evadésti, evase, evadémmo, evadéste, evàsero

§173 FARE—facèndo—fatto
(a) fa *or* fàì *or* fa'; fate

24

(b) fàccio or fò; fài; fa; facciamo; fate; fanno
(c) fàccia, fàccia, fàccia, facciamo, facciate; fàcciano
(d) facévo, facévi, facéva, facevamo, facevate, facévano
(e) féci, facésti, féce, facémmo, facéste, fécero
(f) farò, farài, farà, farémo, faréte, faranno

§174 **FÈNDERE**—fendèndo—fenduto or fésso
(e) fendéi or fendètti; fendésti; fendé or fendètte; fendémmo; fendéste; fendérono or fendèttero

§175 **FÈRVERE**—fervèndo—*pp* missing
(e) fervéi or fervètti; fervésti; fervé or fervètte; fervémmo; fervéste; fervérono or fervèttero

§176 **FINIRE**—finèndo—finito
(a) finisci, finite
(b) finisco, finisci, finisce, finiamo, finite, finìscono
(c) finisca, finisca, finisca, finiamo, finiate, finìscano

§177 **FLÈTTERE**—flettèndo—flèsso
(e) flettéi or flèssi; flettésti; flettè or flèsse; flettémmo; flettéste; flettérono or flèssero

§178 **FÓNDERE**—fondèndo—fuso
(e) fusi, fondésti, fuse, fondémmo, fondéste, fùsero

§179 **FRÀNGERE**—frangèndo—franto
(e) fransi, frangésti, franse, frangémmo, frangéste, frànsero

§180 **FRÌGGERE**—friggèndo—fritto
(e) frissi, friggésti, frisse, friggémmo, friggéste, frìssero

§181 **GIACÉRE**—giacèndo—giaciuto
(b) giàccio; giaci; giace; giacciamo or giaciamo; giacete; giàcciono
(c) giàccia, giàccia, giàccia, giacciamo, giacciate, giàcciano
(e) giàcqui, giacésti, giàcque, giacémmo, giacéste, giàcquero

§182 **GIOCARE**—giocando—giocato
(a) giuòca or giòca; giocate
(b) giuòco or giòco; giuòchi or giòchi; giuòca or giòca; giochiamo; giocate; giuòcano or giòcano
(c) giuòchi or giòchi; giuòchi or giòchi; giuòchi or giòchi; giochiamo; giochiate; giuòchino or giòchino
(f) giocherò, giocherài, giocherà, giocherémo, giocheréte, giocheranno

§183 **GIÙNGERE**—giungèndo—giunto
(e) giunsi, giungésti, giunse, giungémmo, giungéste, giùnsero

25

§184 GODÉRE—godèndo—goduto
    (e) godéi *or* godètti; godésti; godé *or* godètte; godémmo; godéste; godérono *or* godèttero
    (f) godrò, godrài, godrà, godrémo, godréte, godranno

§185 IMBÉVERE—imbevèndo—imbevuto
    (e) imbévvi, imbevésti, imbévve, imbevémmo, imbevéste, imbévvero

§186 INCÓMBERE—incombèndo—*pp* missing
    (e) incombéi *or* incombètti; incombésti; incombé *or* incombètte; incombémmo; incombéste; incombérono *or* incombèttero

§187 INDÙLGERE—indulgèndo—indulto
    (e) indulsi, indulgésti, indulse, indulgémmo, indulgéste, indùlsero

§188a INFERIRE—inferèndo—inferito *or* infèrto
    (a) inferisci, inferite
    (b) inferisco, inferisci, inferisce, inferiamo, inferite, inferìscono
    (c) inferisca, inferisca, inferisca, inferiamo, inferiate, inferìscano
    (e) inferìi *or* infèrsi; inferisti; inferì *or* infèrse; inferimmo; inferiste; inferìrono *or* infèrsero

§188b INSTARE—instando—*pp* missing

§189 INTRÌDERE—intridèndo—intriso
    (e) intrisi, intridésti, intrise, intridémmo, intridéste, intrìsero

§190 INTRÙDERE—intrudèndo—intruso
    (e) intrusi, intrudésti, intruse, intrudémmo, intrudéste, intrùsero

§191 IRE—*ger* missing—ito
    (a) *sg* missing, ite
    (b) missing
    (c) missing
    (d) ivo, ivi, iva, ivamo, ivate, ìvano
    (e) *1st sg* missing, isti, *3rd sg* missing, *1st pl* missing, iste, ìrono

§192 LÈDERE—ledèndo—léso *or* lèso
    (e) lési, ledésti, lése, ledémmo, ledéste, lésero

§193 LÈGGERE—leggèndo—lètto
    (e) lèssi, leggésti, lèsse, leggémmo, leggéste, lèssero

26

§194 LIQUEFARE—liquefacèndo—liquefatto
(a) liquefà, liquefate
(b) liquefò or liquefàccio; liquefài; liquefà liquefacciamo; liquefate; liquefanno
(c) liquefàccia, liquefàccia, liquefàccia, liquefacciamo, liquefacciate, liquefàcciano
(d) liquefacévo, liquefacévi, liquefacéva, liquefacevamo, liquefacevate, liquefacévano
(e) liqueféci, liquefacésti, liqueféce, liquefacémmo, liquefacéste, liquefécero
(f) liquefarò, liquefaràì, liquefarà, liquefarémo, liquefaréte, liquefaranno

§195 MALEDIRE—maledicèndo—maledétto
(a) maledici, maledite
(b) maledico, maledici, maledice, malediciamo, maledite, maledìcono
(c) maledica, maledica, maledica, malediciamo, malediciate, maledìcano
(d) maledicévo or maledivo; maledicévi or maledivi; maledicéva or malediva; maledicevamo or maledivamo; maledicevate or maledivate; maledicévano or maledìvano
(e) maledìi or maledissi; maledisti or maledicésti; maledì or maledisse; maledimmo or maledicémmo; malediste or maledicéste; maledìrono or maledìssero
(f) maledirò, maledirài, maledirà, maledirémo, maledirétе, malediranno

§196 MALVOLÉRE—*ger* missing—malvoluto
(a) missing
(b) missing
(c) missing
(d) missing
(e) missing
(f) missing

§197 MANCARE—mancando—mancato
(b) manco, manchi, manca, manchiamo, mancate, màncano
(c) manchi, manchi, manchi, manchiamo, manchiate, mànchino
(f) mancherò, mancherài, mancherà, mancherémo, mancheréte, mancheranno

§198 MÉTTERE—mettèndo—mésso
(e) misi, mettésti, mise, mettémmo, mettéste, mìsero

§199 MÌNGERE—mingèndo—minto
(e) minsi, mingésti, minse, mingémmo, mingéste, mìnsero

§200 **MÒRDERE**—mordèndo—mòrso
    (e) mòrsi, mordésti, mòrse, mordémmo, mordéste, mòrsero

§201 **MORIRE**—morèndo—mòrto
    (a) muòri, morite
    (b) muòio, muòri, muòre, moriamo, morite, muòiono
    (c) muòia. muòia, muòia, moriamo, moriate, muòiano
    (f) morrò or morirò; morràì or moriràì; morrà or morirà; morrémo or morirémo; morréte or moriréte; morranno or moriranno

§202 **MUÒVERE**—muovèndo or movèndo (movènte)—mòsso
    (a) muòvi, movéte
    (b) muòvo, muòvi, muòve, moviamo, movéte, muòvono
    (c) muòva, muòva, muòva, moviamo, moviate, muòvano
    (d) movévo, movévi, movéva, movevamo, movevate, movévano
    (e) mòssi, movésti, mòsse, movémmo, movéste, mòssero
    (f) moverò, moveràì, moverà, moverémo, moveréte, moveranno

§203 **NÀSCERE**—nascèndo—nato
    (e) nàcqui, nascésti, nàcque, nascémmo, nascéste, nàcquero

§204 **NASCÓNDERE**—nascondèndo—nascósto
    (e) nascósi, nascondésti, nascóse, nascondémmo, nascondéste, nascósero

§205 **NEGLÌGERE**—negligèndo—neglètto
    (a) missing
    (b) missing
    (c) missing
    (e) neglèssi, negligésti, neglèsse, negligémmo, negligéste, neglèssero

§206 **NUÒCERE**—nuocèndo—nociuto
    (a) nuòci, nocéte
    (b) nuòccio or nòccio; nuòci; nuòce; nociamo; nocéte; nuòcciono or nòcciono
    (c) nòccia, nòccia, nòccia, nociamo, nociate, nòcciano
    (d) nocévo, nocévi, nocéva, nocevamo, nocevate, nocévano
    (e) nòcqui, nocésti, nòcque, nocémmo, nocéste, nòcquero
    (f) nocerò, noceràì, nocerà, nocerémo, noceréte, noceranno

§207 **OFFRIRE**—offrèndo (offerènte)—offèrto
    (e) offrìi or offèrsi; offristi; offrì or offèrse; offrimmo; offriste; offrìrono or offèrsero

§208 **OTTÙNDERE**—ottundèndo—ottuso
    (e) ottusi, ottundésti, ottuse, ottundémmo, ottundéste, ottùsero

§209 PAGARE—pagando—pagato
  (b) pago, paghi, paga, paghiamo, pagate, pàgano
  (c) paghi, paghi, paghi, paghiamo, paghiate, pàghino
  (f) pagherò, pagherài, pagherà, pagherémo, pagheréte, pagheranno

§210 PARÉRE—parèndo (parvènte)—parso
  (a) missing
  (b) pàio; pari; pare; pariamo *or* paiamo; paréte; pàiono
  (c) pàia; pàia; pàia; pariamo *or* paiamo; pariate *or* paiate; pàiano
  (e) parvi, parésti, parve, parémmo, paréste, pàrvero
  (f) parrò, parrài, parrà, parrémo, parréte, parranno

§211 PÀSCERE—pascèndo—pasciuto
  (a) pascéi *or* pascètti; pascésti; pascé *or* pascètte; pascémmo; pascéste; pascérono *or* pascèttero

§212 PÈRDERE—perdèndo—pèrso *or* perduto
  (e) perdéi *or* pèrsi *or* perdètti; perdésti; perdé, *or* pèrse *or* perdètte; perdémmo; perdéste; perdérono *or* pèrsero *or* perdèttero

§213 PERSUADÉRE—persuadèndo—persuaso
  (e) persuasi, persuadésti, persuase, persuadémmo, persuadéste, persuàsero

§214 PIACÉRE—piacèndo—piaciuto
  (b) piàccio, piaci, piace, piacciamo, piacéte, piàcciono
  (c) piàccia, piàccia, piàccia, piacciamo, piacciate, piàcciano
  (e) piàcqui, piacésti, piàcque, piacémmo, piacéste, piàcquero

§215 PIÀNGERE—piangèndo—pianto
  (e) piansi, piangésti, pianse, piangémmo, piangéste, piànsero

§216 PIÒVERE—piovèndo—piovuto
  (e) piòvvi, piovésti, piòvve, piovémmo, piovéste, piòvvero

§217 PÒRGERE—porgèndo—pòrto
  (e) pòrsi, porgésti, pòrse, porgémmo, porgéste, pòrsero

§218 PÓRRE—ponèndo—pósto
  (a) póni, ponéte
  (b) póngo, póni, póne, poniamo, ponéte, póngono
  (c) pónga, pónga, pónga, poniamo, poniate, póngano
  (d) ponévo, ponévi, ponéva, ponevamo, ponevate, ponévano
  (e) pósi, ponésti, póse, ponémmo, ponéste, pósero

§219 POTÉRE—potèndo (potènte *or* possènte)—potuto
  (a) missing
  (b) pòsso, puòi, può, possiamo, potéte, pòssono

(c) pòssa, pòssa, pòssa, possiamo, possiate, pòssano
(e) potéi *or* potètti; potésti, poté *or* potètte; potémmo; potéste; potérono *or* potèttero
(f) potrò, potrài, potrà, potrémo, potréte, potranno

§220 **PRÈNDERE**—prendèndo—préso
(e) prési, prendésti, prése, prendémmo, prendéste, présero

§221 **PROVVEDÉRE**—provvedèndo—provveduto *or* provvisto
(e) provvidi, provvedésti, pròvvide, provvedémmo, provvedéste, provvìdero

§222 **PRÙDERE**—prudèndo—*pp* missing
(e) *1st sg* missing; *2nd sg* missing; prudé *or* prudètte; *1st pl* missing; *2nd pl* missing; prudérono *or* prudèttero

§223 **RÀDERE**—radèndo—raso
(e) rasi, radésti, rase, radémmo, radéste, ràsero

§224 **REDÌGERE**—redigèndo—redatto
(e) redassi, redigésti, redasse, redigémmo, redigéste, redàssero

§225 **REDÌMERE**—redimèndo—redènto
(e) redènsi, redimésti, redènse, redimémmo, rediméste, redènsero

§226 **RÈGGERE**—reggèndo—rètto
(e) rèssi, reggésti, rèsse, reggémmo, reggéste, rèssero

§227 **RÈNDERE**—rendèndo—réso
(e) rési *or* rendéi *or* rendètti; rendésti; rése *or* rendé *or* rendètte; rendémmo; rendéste; résero *or* rendérono *or* rendèttero

§228 **RETROCÈDERE**—retrocedèndo—retrocèsso *or* retroceduto
(e) retrocèssi *or* retrocedéi *or* retrocedètti; retrocedésti; retrocèsse *or* retrocedé *or* retrocedètte; retrocedémmo; retrocedéste; retrocèssero *or* retrocedérono *or* retrocedèttero

§229 **RIAVÉRE**—riavèndo—riavuto
(a) riabbi, riabbiate
(b) riò, riài, rià, riabbiamo, riavéte, rianno
(c) riàbbia, riàbbia, riàbbia, riabbiamo, riabbiate, riàbbiano
(e) rièbbi, riavésti, rièbbe, riavémmo, riavéste, rièbbero
(f) riavrò, riavrài, riavrà, riavrémo, riavréte, riavranno

§230 **RIDARE**—ridando—ridato
(a) ridài *or* ridà; ridate
(b) ridò, ridài, ridà, ridiamo, ridate, ridanno
(c) ridìa, ridìa, ridìa, ridiamo, ridiate, ridìano

30

(e) ridièdi *or* ridètti; ridésti; ridiède *or* ridètte; ridémmo; ridéste; ridièdero *or* ridèttero

(f) ridarò, ridaràì, ridarà, ridarémo, ridaréte, ridaranno

§231 RÌDERE—ridèndo—riso

(e) risi, ridésti, rise, ridémmo, ridéste, rìsero

§232 RIFLÈTTERE—riflettèndo—riflèsso *or* riflettuto

§233 RIFÙLGERE—rifulgèndo—rifulso

(e) rifulsi, rifulgésti, rifulse rifulgémmo, rifulgéste, rifùlsero

§234 RILÙCERE—rilucèndo—*pp* missing

§235 RIMANÉRE—rimanèndo—rimasto

(b) rimango, rimani, rimane, rimaniamo, rimanéte, rimàngono

(c) rimanga, rimanga, rimanga, rimaniamo, rimaniate, rimàngano

(e) rimasi, rimanésti, rimase, rimanémmo, rimanéste, rimàsero

(f) rimarrò, rimarràì, rimarrà, rimarrémo, rimarréte, rimarranno

§236 RINCORARE—rincorando—rincorato

(a) rincuòra, rincorate

(b) rincuòro, rincuòri, rincuòra, rincoriamo, rincorate, rincuòrano

(c) rincuòri, rincuòri, rincuòri, rincoriamo, rincoriate, rincuòrino

§237 RISOLARE—risolando—risolato

(a) risuòla, risolate

(b) risuòlo, risuòli, risuòla, risoliamo, risolate, risuòlano

(c) risuòli, risuòli, risuòli, risoliamo, risoliate, risuòlino

§238 RISPÓNDERE—rispondèndo—rispósto

(e) rispósi, rispondésti, rispóse, rispondémmo, rispondéste, rispósero

§239 RÓDERE—rodèndo—róso

(e) rósi, rodésti, róse, rodémmo, rodéste, rósero

§240 RÓMPERE—rompèndo—rótto

(e) ruppi, rompésti, ruppe, rompémmo, rompéste, rùppero

§241 ROTARE—rotando—rotato

(a) ruòta, rotate

(b) ruòto, ruòti, ruòta, rotiamo, rotate, ruòtano

(c) ruòti, ruòti, ruòti, rotiamo, rotiate, ruòtino

§242 **SALIRE**—salèndo—salito
   (b) salgo, sali, sale, saliamo, salite, sàlgono
   (c) salga, salga, salga, saliamo, saliate, sàlgano

§243 **SAPÉRE**—sapèndo (sapiènte)—saputo
   (a) sappi, sappiate
   (b) sò, sai, sa, sappiamo, sapéte, sanno
   (c) sàppia, sàppia, sàppia, sappiamo, sappiate, sàppiano
   (e) sèppi, sapésti, sèppe, sapémmo, sapéste, sèppero
   (f) saprò, sapràì, saprà, saprémo, sapréte, sapranno

§244 **SCÉGLIERE**—sceglièndo—scélto
   (a) scégli, scegliéte
   (b) scélgo, scégli, scéglie, scegliamo, scegliéte, scélgono
   (c) scélga, scélga, scélga, scegliamo, scegliate, scélgano
   (e) scélsi, scegliésti, scélse, scegliémmo, scegliéste, scélsero

§245 **SCÉNDERE**—scendèndo—scéso
   (e) scési, scendésti, scése, scendémmo, scendéste, scésero

§246 **SCÈRNERE**—scernèndo—*pp* missing
   (e) scernéi *or* scernètti; scernésti; scerné *or* scernètte; scer-
   némmo; scernéste; scernérono *or* scernèttero

§247 **SCÌNDERE**—scindèndo—scisso
   (e) scissi, scindésti, scisse, scindémmo, scindéste, scìssero

§248 **SCOIARE**—scoiando—scoiato
   (a) scuòia, scoiate
   (b) scuòio, scuòi, scuòia, scoiamo, scoiate, scuòiano
   (c) scuòi, scuòi, scuòi, scoiamo, scoiate, scuòino

§249 **SCÒRGERE**—scorgèndo—scòrto
   (e) scòrsi, scorgésti, scòrse, scorgémmo, scorgéste, scòrsero

§250 **SCRÌVERE**—scrivèndo—scritto
   (e) scrissi, scrivésti, scrisse, scrivémmo, scrivéste, scrìssero

§251 **SCUÒTERE**—scotèndo—scòsso
   (a) scuòti, scotéte
   (b) scuòto, scuòti, scuòte, scotiamo, scotéte, scuòtono
   (c) scuòta, scuòta, scuòta, scotiamo, scotiate, scuòtano
   (d) scotévo, scotévi, scotéva, scotevamo, scotevate, scoté-
   vano
   (e) scòssi, scotésti, scòsse, scotémmo, scotéste, scòssero

§252 **SEDÉRE**—sedéndo—seduto
   (a) sièdi, sedéte
   (b) sièdo *or* sèggo; sièdi; siède; sediamo; sedéte; sièdono
   or sèggono
   (c) sièda *or* sègga; sièda *or* sègga; sièda *or* sègga; sediamo;
   sediate; sièdano *or* sèggano
   (e) sedéi *or* sedètti; sedésti; sedé *or* sedètte; sedémmo;
   sedéste; sedérono *or* sedèttero

§253 SEPPELLIRE—seppellèndo—sepólto *or* seppellito
(a) seppellisci, seppellite
(b) seppellisco, seppellisci, seppellisce, seppelliamo, seppellite, seppellìscono
(c) seppellisca, seppellisca, seppellisca, seppelliamo, seppelliate, seppellìscano

§254 SODDISFARE—soddisfacèndo—soddisfatto
(a) soddisfa *or* soddisfài *or* soddisfa'
(b) soddisfàccio *or* soddisfò *or* soddisfo; soddisfài *or* soddisfi; soddisfà *or* soddisfa; soddisfacciamo; soddisfate; soddisfanno *or* soddìsfano
(c) soddisfàccia *or* soddisfi; soddisfàccia *or* soddisfi; soddisfàccia *or* soddisfi; soddisfacciamo; soddisfacciate; soddisfàcciano *or* soddìsfino
(d) soddisfacévo, soddisfacévi, soddisfacéva, soddisfacevamo, soddisfacevate, soddisfacévano
(e) soddisféci, soddisfacésti, soddisféce, soddisfacémmo, soddisfacéste, soddisfécero
(f) soddisfarò, soddisfaràì, soddisfarà, soddisfarémo, soddisfaréte, soddisfaranno

§255 SOLÉRE—solèndo—sòlito
(a) missing
(b) sòglio, suòli, suòle, sogliamo, soléte, sògliono
(c) sòglia, sòglia, sòglia, sogliamo, sogliate, sògliano
(e) missing
(f) missing

§256 SÒLVERE—solvèndo—soluto
(e) solvéi *or* solvètti; solvésti; solvé *or* solvètte; solvémmo; solvéste; solvérono *or* solvèttero

§257 SONARE—sonando—sonato
(a) suòna, sonate
(b) suòno, suòni, suòna, soniamo, sonate, suònano
(c) suòni, suòni, suòni, soniamo, soniate, suònino

§258 SÓRGERE—sorgèndo—sórto
(e) sórsi, sorgésti, sórse, sorgémmo, sorgéste, sórsero

§259 SOSPÈNDERE—sospendèndo—sospéso
(e) sospési, sospendésti, sospése, sospendémmo, sospendéste, sospésero

§260 SPÀNDERE—spandèndo—spanto
(e) spandéi *or* spandètti *or* spansi; spandésti; spandé *or* spandètte *or* spanse; spandémmo; spandéste; spandérono *or* spandèttero *or* spànsero

§261 SPÀRGERE—spargèndo—sparso
(e) sparsi, spargésti, sparse, spargémmo, spargéste, spàrsero

33

§262 **SPÈGNERE**—spegnèndo—spènto
    (b) spéngo *or* spèngo; spég i *or* spègni; spégne *or* spègne; spegniamo; spegnéte; spéngono *or* spèngono
    (c) spénga *or* spènga; spénga *or* spènga; spénga *or* spènga; spegniamo; spegniate; spéngano *or* spèngano
    (e) spènsi, spegnésti, spènse, spegnémmo, spegnéste, spènsero

§263 **STARE**—stando—stato
    (a) sta *or* stai *or* sta'; state
    (b) stò, stài, sta, stiamo, state, stanno
    (c) stìa, stìa, stìa, stiamo, stiate, stìano
    (e) stètti, stésti, stètte, stémmo, stéste, stèttero
    (f) starò, starài, starà, starémo, staréte, staranno

§264 **STRÌDERE**—stridèndo—*pp* missing
    (e) stridéi *or* stridètti; stridésti; stridé *or* stridètte; stridémmo; stridéste; stridérono *or* stridèttero

§265 **STRÌNGERE**—stringèndo—strétto
    (e) strinsi, stringésti, strinse, stringémmo, stringéste, strìnsero

§266 **STRÙGGERE**—struggèndo—strutto
    (e) strussi, struggésti, strusse, struggémmo, struggéste, strùssero

§267 **SVÈLLERE**—svellèndo—svèlto
    (b) svèllo *or* svèlgo; svèlli; svèlle; svelliamo; svelléte; svèllono *or* svèlgono
    (c) svèlla *or* svèlga; svèlla *or* svèlga; svèlla *or* svèlga; svelliamo; svelliate; svèllano *or* svèlgano
    (e) svèlsi, svellésti, svèlse, svellémmo, svelléste, svèlsero

§268 **TACÉRE**—tacèndo—taciuto
    (b) tàccio, taci, tace, taciamo, tacéte, tàcciono
    (c) tàccia, tàccia, tàccia, taciamo, taciate, tàcciano
    (e) tàcqui, tacésti, tàcque, tacémmo, tacéste, tàcquero

§269 **TÀNGERE**—tangèndo—pp missing
    (a) missing
    (b) *1st sg* missing; *2nd sg* missing; tange; *1st pl* missing; *2nd pl* missing; tàngono
    (c) *1st sg* missing; *2nd sg* missing; tanga; *1st pl* missing; *2nd pl* missing; tàngano
    (d) *1st sg* missing; *2nd sg* missing; tangéva; *1st pl* missing; *2nd pl* missing; tangévano
    (e) missing
    (f) *1st sg* missing; *2nd sg* missing; tangerà; *1st pl* missing; *2nd pl* missing; tangeranno

34

§270 TÈNDERE—tendèndo—téso
(e) tési, tendésti, tése, tendémmo, tendéste, tésero

§271 TENÉRE—tenèndo—tenuto
(a) tièni, tenéte
(b) tèngo, tièni, tiène, teniamo, tenéte, tèngono
(c) tènga, tènga, tènga, teniamo, teniate, tèngano
(e) ténni, tenésti, ténne, tenémmo, tenéste, ténnero
(f) terrò, terrài, terrà, terrémo, terréte, terranno

§272 TÒRCERE—torcèndo—tòrto
(e) tòrsi, torcésti, tòrse, torcémmo, torcéste, tòrsero

§273 TRARRE—traèndo—tratto
(a) trài, traéte
(b) traggo, trài, trae, traiamo, traéte, tràggono
(c) tragga, tragga, tragga, traiamo, traiate, tràggano
(d) traévo, traévi, traéva, traevamo, traevate, traévano
(e) trassi, traésti, trasse, traémmo, traéste, tràssero

§274 UCCÌDERE—uccidèndo—ucciso
(e) uccisi, uccidésti, uccise, uccidémmo, uccidéste, uccìsero

§275 UDIRE—udèndo *or* udièndo—udito
(a) òdi, udite
(b) òdo, òdi, òde, udiamo, udite, òdono
(c) òda, òda, òda, udiamo, udiate, òdano
(f) udirò *or* udrò; udirài *or* udrài; udirà *or* udrà; udirémo
   or udrémo; udiréte *or* udréte; udiranno *or* udranno

§276 ÙRGERE—urgèndo—*pp* missing
(a) missing
(e) missing

§277 USCIRE—uscèndo—uscito
(a) èsci, uscite
(b) èsco, èsci, èsce, usciamo, uscite, èscono
(c) èsca, èsca, èsca, usciamo, usciate, èscano

§278 VALÉRE—valèndo—valso
(b) valgo, vali, vale, valiamo, valéte, vàlgono
(c) valga, valga, valga, valiamo, valiate, vàlgano
(e) valsi, valésti, valse, valémmo, valéste, vàlsero
(f) varrò, varrài, varrà, varrémo, varréte, varranno

§279 VEDÉRE—vedèndo—veduto *or* visto
(e) vidi, vedésti, vide, vedémmo, vedéste, vìdero
(f) vedrò, vedrài, vedrà, vedrémo, vedréte, vedranno

§280 VEGLIARE—vegliando—vegliato
(b) véglio, végli, véglia, vegliamo, vegliate, végliano
(c) végli, végli, végli, vegliamo, vegliate, véglino

§281 VÉNDERE—vendèndo—venduto
(e) vendéi *or* vendètti; vendésti; vendé *or* vendètte; vendémmo; vendéste; vendérono *or* vendèttero

§282 VENIRE—venèndo (veniènte)—venuto
(a) vièni, venite
(b) vèngo, vièni, vjène, veniamo, venite, vèngono
(c) vènga, vènga, vènga, veniamo, veniate, vèngano
(e) vénni, venisti, vénne, venimmo, veniste, vénnero
(f) verrò, verrài, verrà, verrémo, verréte, verranno

§283 VÈRTERE—vertèndo—*pp* missing

§284 VÌGERE—vigèndo—*pp* missing
(a) missing
(b) *1st sg* missing; *2nd sg* missing; vige; *1st pl* missing; *2d pl* missing; vìgono
(c) *1st sg* missing; *2d sg* missing; viga; *1st pl* missing; *2d pl* missing; vìgano
(d) *1st sg* missing; *2d sg* missing; vigéva; *1st pl* missing; *2d pl* missing; vigévano
(e) missing

§285 VÌNCERE—vincèndo—vinto
(e) vinsi, vincésti, vinse, vincémmo, vincéste, vìnsero

§286 VÌVERE—vivèndo—vissuto
(e) vissi, vivésti, visse, vivémmo, vivéste, vìssero
(f) vivrò, vivrài, vivrà, vivrémo, vivréte, vivranno

§287 VIZIARE—viziando—viziato
(b) vìzió, vizi, vìzia, viziamo, viziate, vìziano
(c) vizi, vizi, vizi, viziamo, viziate, vìzino

§288 VOLÉRE—volèndo—voluto
(a) vògli, vogliate
(b) vòglio, vuòi, vuòle, vogliamo, volète, vògliono
(c) vòglia, vòglia, vòglia, vogliamo, vogliate, vògliano
(e) vòlli, volésti, vòlle, volémmo, voléste, vòllero
(f) vorrò, vorrài, vorrà, vorrémo, vorréte, vorranno

§289 VÒLGERE—volgèndo—vòlto
(e) vòlsi, volgésti, vòlse, volgémmo, volgéste, vòlsero

§290 VOLTEGGIARE—volteggiando—volteggiato
(b) voltéggio, voltéggi, voltéggia, volteggiamo, volteggiate, voltéggiano
(c) voltéggi, voltéggi, voltéggi, volteggiamo, volteggiate, voltéggino
(f) volteggerò, volteggerài, volteggerà, volteggerémo, volteggeréte, volteggeranno

36

A

A, a [α] *m & f* first letter of the Italian alphabet

a *prep* (**ad** in front of a vowel) to, e.g., **diede il libro a Giovanni** he gave the book to John; in, e.g., **a Milano** in Milan; at, e.g., **a casa** at home; within, e.g., **a tre miglia da qui** within three miles from here; on, e.g., **portare una catena al collo** to wear a chain on one's neck; e.g., **al sabato** on Saturdays; for, e.g., **a vita** for life; by, e.g., **fatto a mano** made by hand; with, e.g., **una gonna a pieghe** a skirt with pleats; as, e.g., **eleggere a presidente** to elect as chairman; into, e.g., **fu gettato a mare** he was thrown into the sea; of, e.g., **un quarto alle due** fifteen minutes of two

àba·co *m* (**-chi**) (*archit*) abacus

abate *m* abbot

abbacchiare §287 *tr* to knock down (*e.g., olives*); to sell too cheap ‖ *ref* to lose courage; to be dejected

abbacchia·to -ta *adj* (*coll*) dejected

abbàc·chio *m* (**-chi**) baby lamb (*slaughtered*)

abbacinare (**abbàcino**) *tr* to dazzle; to deceive

abbadéssa *f* var of **badessa**

abbagliante *adj* dazzling ‖ *m* (*aut*) bright light, high beam

abbagliare §280 *tr* to dazzle; to deceive; to blind (*with the lights of a car*)

abbà·glio *m* (**-gli**) error; **prendere abbaglio** to make a mistake

abbaiaménto *m* bark (*of dog*)

abbaiare §287 *intr* to bark; to yelp

abbaino *m* dormer window; skylight; attic

abbambinare *tr* to walk (*a heavy piece of furniture*)

abbandonare (**abbandóno**) *tr* to abandon; to give up; to let go (*e.g., the reins*); to let fall; (*sports*) to withdraw from ‖ *ref* to yield; to lose courage

abbandóno *m* abandon, abandonment; desertion; neglect; relaxation; renunciation (*of a right*); cession (*of property*); withdrawal (*from a fight*)

abbarbicare §197 (**abbàrbico**) *intr & ref* to cling; to hold on

abbassalin·gua *m* (**-gua**) tongue depressor

abbassaménto *m* lowering; reduction; drop, fall

abbassare *tr* to lower; to dim (*lights*); to turn (*the radio*) lower; **abbassare le armi** to surrender; **abbassare la cresta** to yield ‖ *ref* to lower oneself; to drop

abbàs·so *m* (**-so**) angry shout (*of a crowd*) ‖ *adv* down, below; downstairs ‖ *interj* down with!

abbastanza *adj invar* enough ‖ *adv* enough; rather, fairly

abbàttere *tr* to demolish; to fell; to shoot down; to refute (*an argument*); to depress ‖ *ref* to be depressed, be downcast

abbattiménto *m* demolition; felling; shooting down; chill; (*fig*) depression; **abbattimento alla base** (*econ*) basic exemption (*from taxes*)

abbattu·to -ta *adj* dejected, downcast ‖ *f* clearing (*of trees*)

abbazìa *f* abbey; abbacy

abbecedà·rio *m* (**-ri**) speller, primer

abbelliménto *m* embellishment, ornamentation

abbellire §176 *tr* to embellish, adorn; to landscape

abbeverare (**abbévero**) *tr* to water (*animals*) ‖ *ref* to quench one's thirst

abbevera·tóio *m* (**-tói**) watering trough

abbìc·cì *m* (**-cì**) alphabet; speller, primer; ABC's, rudiments

abbiènte *adj* well-to-do ‖ *m*—**gli abbienti** the haves; **gli abbienti e nullatenenti** the haves and the have-nots

abbiettézza or **abiettézza** *f* abjectness, baseness

abbièt·to -ta or **abièt·to -ta** *adj* abject, base, low

abbiezióne or **abiezióne** *f* wretchedness, baseness

abbigliaménto *m* attire, wear

abbigliare §280 *tr & ref* to dress; to dress up

abbinaménto *m* coupling; merger

abbinare *tr* to couple; to join, merge

abbindolare (**abbìndolo**) *tr* to dupe, deceive

abbiosciare §128 *ref* to fall down; to lose heart, be downcast

abbisognare (**abbisógno**) *intr* to be in need

abboccaménto *m* interview, conversation

abboccare §197 (**abbócco**) *tr* to swallow (*the hook*); to fit (*pipes*) ‖ *intr* to bite (*said of fish*); to fall; to fit (*said of pipes*) ‖ *ref* to confer

abbocca·to -ta *adj* palatable; slightly sweet (*wine*)

abbonacciare §128 *ref* to calm down, abate (*said of weather*)

abbonaménto *m* subscription; **abbonamento postale** mailing permit

abbonare (**abbòno**) *tr* to take out a subscription for (*s.o.*) ‖ *ref* to subscribe ‖ §257 *tr* to remit (*a debt*); to forgive

abbona·to -ta *mf* subscriber; commuter

abbondante *adj* abundant, plentiful; heavy (*rain*)

abbondanza *f* abundance, plenty

abbondare (**abbóndo**) *intr* (ESSERE & AVERE) to abound; to exceed; **abbondare di** or **in** to abound in

abbonire §176 *tr* to calm; to placate ‖ *ref* to calm down

abbordàbile *adj* accessible, approachable; negotiable (*curve*)

abbordàg·gio *m* (-gi) boarding (*of an enemy ship*); **andare all'abbordaggio di** to board

abbordare (**abbórdo**) *tr* to board (*an enemy ship*); to negotiate (*a curve*); to face (*a problem*); (fig) to button-hole

abborracciare §128 *tr* to botch, bungle

abborracciatura *f* botch, bungle

abbottonare (**abbottóno**) *tr* to button ‖ *ref* (coll) to keep to oneself

abbottonatura *f* buttoning; row of buttons

abbozzare (**abbòzzo**) *tr* to sketch; to hew (*e.g., a statue*); (naut) to tie up ‖ *intr* (coll) to take it

abbòzzo *m* sketch, draft

abbracciabò·sco *m* (-schi) (bot) woodbine

abbracciare *m* embrace, embracing ‖ §128 *tr* to embrace, hug; to seize (*an opportunity*); to become converted to (*e.g., Christianity*); to enter (*a profession*); to span, encompass ‖ *ref* to cling; to embrace one another

abbràc·cio *m* (-ci) embrace, hug

abbrancare §197 *tr* to grab; to herd ‖ *ref* to cling; to join a herd

abbreviaménto *m* abbreviation, shortening

abbreviare §287 (**abbrèvio**) *tr* to abbreviate, shorten, abridge

abbreviatura *f* shortening, abridgment

abbreviazióne *f* abbreviation

abbrivo *or* **abbrìvio** *m* headway (*of a ship*); **prendere l'abbrivio** to gather momentum

abbronzante [dz] *adj* suntanning ‖ *m* suntan lotion

abbronzare [dz] (**abbrónzo**) *tr* & *ref* to bronze; to tan

abbronza·to -ta [dz] *adj* tanned, suntanned

abbronzatura [dz] *f* tan, suntan

abbruciacchiare §287 *tr* to singe

abbrunare *tr* to brown; to hang crepe on ‖ *ref* to wear mourning

abbrunire §176 *tr* to turn brown; to tan; to burnish

abbrustolire §176 *tr* to toast; to singe ‖ *ref* to tan; to become sunburned

abbrutiménto *m* degradation, brutishness

abbrutire §176 *tr* to degrade; to brutalize ‖ *intr* & *ref* to become brutalized

abbuiare §287 *tr* to darken; to hush up, hide ‖ *ref* to grow dark; to become gloomy ‖ *impers*—**abbuia** it's growing dark

abbuòno *m* allowance, discount; handicap (*in racing*)

abburattaménto *m* sifting

abburattare *tr* to sift, bolt

abdicare §197 (**àbdico**) *tr* & *intr* to abdicate; **abdicare a** to give up, renounce; to abdicate (*e.g., the throne*)

abdicazióne *f* abdication

aberrare (**abèrro**) *intr* to deviate

aberrazióne *f* aberration

abéte *m* fir

abetina *f* forest of fir trees

abiàti·co *m* (-ci) (coll) grandson

abièt·to -ta *adj* abject, base, low

abigeato *m* (law) cattle rustling

àbile *adj* able, clever, capable; (mil) fit

abili·tà *f* (tà) ability, skill

abilitare (**abìlito**) *tr* to certify (*e.g., a teacher*); to qualify, license

abilita·to -ta *adj* certified (*teacher*)

abilitazióne *f* qualification; certification (*of teachers*)

abissale *adj* abysmal

Abissinia, l' *f* Abyssinia

abissi·no -na *adj* & *mf* Abyssinian

abisso *m* abyss; fountain (*of knowledge*); slough (*of degradation*)

abitàbile *adj* inhabitable

abitàcolo *m* (aer) cockpit; (aut) cab, interior; (naut) compass bowl; **abitàcolo eiettabile** (aer) ejection capsule

abitante *mf* inhabitant; resident

abitare (**àbito**) *tr* to inhabit; to occupy ‖ *intr* to dwell, live, reside

abitati·vo -va *adj* living, e.g., **condizioni abitative** living conditions

abita·to -ta *adj* inhabited, populated ‖ *m* built-up area

abita·tóre -trice *mf* dweller

abitazióne *f* dwelling; housing

àbito *m* suit (*for men*); dress (*for women*); garb, attire; habit; **abiti** clothes; **abito da ballo** evening gown; **abito da cerimonia** formal dress; **abito da inverno** winter suit; winter clothes; **levarsi l'abito** to doff the cassock; **prender l'abito** to enter the Church

abituale *adj* habitual

abituare (**abìtuo**) *tr* to accustom ‖ *ref* to grow accustomed

abitudinà·rio -ria *adj* (-ri -rie) set in his ways

abitùdine *f* habit, custom

abituro *m* (poet) shanty, hut

abiura *f* abjuration

abiurare *tr* to abjure

ablati·vo -va *adj* & *m* ablative

ablazióne *f* (med) removal; (geol) erosion

abluzióne *f* ablution

abnegare §209 (**abnégo** & **abnègo**) *tr* to renounce, abnegate

abnegazióne *f* abnegation, self-denial

abnòrme *adj* abnormal

abolire §176 *tr* to abolish

abolizióne *f* abolition

abominàbile *adj* abominable

abominare (**abòmino**) *tr* to abominate, detest

abominazióne *f* abomination

abominévole *adj* abominable

aborige·no -na *adj* aboriginal ‖ *m* aborigine; **aborigeni** aborigines

aborrire §176 & (**abòrro**) *tr* to abhor, loathe ‖ *intr*—**aborrire da** to shun, shrink from

abortire §176 *intr* to abort

abòrto *m* abortion, miscarriage; **aborto di natura** monstrosity

abrasióne *f* abrasion; erosion

abrasi·vo -va *adj* & *m* abrasive

abrogare §209 (**àbrogo**) *tr* to abrogate

abrogazióne *f* abrogation

abruzzése adj of the Abruzzi || mf person of the Abruzzi || m dialect of the Abruzzi

àbside f (archit) apse

abusare intr—**abusare di** to go to excesses in (e.g., smoking); to take advantage of; to impose on

abusì·vo -va adj illegal, abusive; unwarranted

abuso m abuse, excess

acà·cia f (-cie) acacia

acanto m acanthus

àcaro m (ent) acarus, mite, tick; **acaro della scabbia** itch mite

ac·ca m & f (-ca or -che) h (letter); **non valere un'acca** (coll) to not be worth a fig

accadèmia f academy

accadèmi·co -ca (-ci -che) adj academic || mf academician

accadére §121 intr (ESSERE) to happen, occur

accadu·to -ta adj happened, occurred || m fact, event; what has taken place

accagliare §280 tr, intr (ESSERE) & ref to curdle, coagulate

accalappiaca·ni m (-ni) dogcatcher

accalappiare §287 tr to catch (a dog); to snare; (fig) to fool

accalcare §197 tr to crowd || ref to throng

accaldare ref to get hot; to become flushed

accalda·to -ta adj hot; perspired

accalorare (accalóro) tr to excite || ref to get excited

accalora·to -ta adj excited, animated

accampaménto m encampment, camp; camping

accampare tr to encamp; to advance, lay (a claim) || ref to camp, encamp

accaniménto m animosity, bitterness; obstinacy, stubbornness

accanire §176 tr to persist; to work doggedly; **accanirsi contro** to harass

accani·to -ta adj obstinate, persistent; furious; fierce, ruthless, bitter (fight)

accanto adv near, nearby; **accanto a** near

accantonaménto m tabling (e.g., of a discussion); reserve (of money); (mil) billeting; (sports) camping

accantonare (accantóno) tr to set aside (money); (mil) to billet

accaparraménto m cornering (of market)

accaparrare tr to corner (merchandise); to hoard; to put a down payment on (e.g., a house); (coll) to gain (somebody's affection)

accaparra·tóre -trice mf monopolizer; hoarder

accapigliare §280 ref to pull each other's hair; to scuffle; to come to blows

accapo or **a capo** m paragraph

accappa·tóio m (-tói) bathrobe

accapponare (accappóno) tr to castrate (a rooster) || ref to wrinkle; **mi si accappona la pelle** I get gooseflesh

accarezzare (accarézzo) tr to caress, fondle; to pet; to nurture (e.g., a hope); **accarezzare le spalle di** to strike; to club

accartocciare §128 **(accartòccio)** tr to wrap up in a cone || ref to curl up

accartoccia·to -ta adj curled up

accasare [s] tr & ref to marry

accasciaménto m dejection

accasciare §128 tr to weaken, enfeeble; to depress || ref to weaken; to lose heart

accasermare [s] **(accasèrmo)** tr to quarter, billet

accatastare tr to register (real estate); to pile, heap up

accattàbri·ghe mf (-ghe) quarrelsome person, scrapper

accattare tr to beg for; to borrow (e.g., ideas) || intr to beg

accattonàg·gio m (-gi) begging, mendicancy

accattó·ne -na mf mendicant, beggar

accavalcare §197 tr to straddle; to go over

accavalciare §128 tr to bestride

accavallare tr to superimpose; to cross (one's legs) || ref to pour forward, run high (said of waves)

accecaménto m blinding

accecare §122 tr to blind; to countersink || intr (ESSERE) to become blind || ref to blind oneself

acceca·tóio m (-tói) countersink

accèdere §100 intr (ESSERE) to enter, approach; to accede

acceleraménto m acceleration

accelerare (accèlero) tr & intr to accelerate

accelera·to -ta adj accelerated; intensive (course); local (train) || m local train

acceleratóre m accelerator

accelerazióne f acceleration

accèndere §101 tr to kindle; to turn on (e.g., the light); to light (e.g., a match, a cigar) || ref to catch fire; to become lit; **accendersi in viso** to become flushed

accendisìgaro m lighter

accendi·tóio m (-tói) candle lighter

accenditóre m lighter

accennare (accénno) tr to nod; to point at; to sketch || intr to refer; to hint

accénno m nod; sign; allusion

accensióne f lighting, kindling; (aut) ignition; (law) contraction (of a debt); **accensione improvvisa** spontaneous combustion

accentare (accènto) tr to accent

accènto m accent; stress; (poet) accent (word); **accento tonico** stress accent

accentraménto m centralization

accentrare (accèntro) tr to concentrate, centralize

accentuare (accèntuo) tr to accentuate || ref to become aggravated

accentuazióne f accentuation

accerchiaménto m encirclement

accerchiare §287 **(accérchio)** tr to encircle, surround

accertàbile adj verifiable

accertaménto m ascertainment, verification; determination (e.g., of taxes)

accertare (accèrto) *tr* to assure; to ascertain, verify; to determine (*the tax due*) || *ref* to make sure

accé·so -sa [s] *adj* lit; turned on; on (*e.g., radio*); excited, aroused; bright (*color*)

accessìbile *adj* accessible; moderate (*price*)

accessióne *f* accession

accèsso *m* access, approach; admittance, entry; fit (*of anger, of coughing*)

accessò·rio -ria (-ri -rie) *adj* accessory || *m* accessory; (mach) accessory, attachment

accétta *f* hatchet, axe, cleaver; **tagliato con l'accetta** rough-hewn

accettàbile *adj* acceptable

accettare (accètto) *tr* to accept

accettazióne *f* acceptance; receiving room; (econ) acceptance

accèt·to -ta *adj* agreeable; welcome; **male accetto** unwelcome

accezióne *f* meaning, acceptation

acchiappafarfal·le *m* (-le) butterfly net

acchiappamó·sche *m* (-sche) fly catcher

acchiappare *tr* to grab, seize; (coll) to catch in the act

acchito *m* (billiards) break; **di primo acchito** at first

acciaccare §197 *tr* to crush; to trample upon; (coll) to lay low (*e.g., by illness*)

acciac·co *m* (-chi) illness, infirmity, ailment

acciaiare §287 *tr* to convert into steel; to strengthen with steel

acciaierìa *f* steel mill, steelworks

ac·ciàio *m* (-ciài) steel; **acciaio inossidabile** stainless steel

acciaiòlo *m* whetstone

acciambellare (acciambèllo) *tr* to shape in the form of a doughnut || *ref* to curl up

acciarino *m* flintlock; linchpin; (nav) war nose (*of a torpedo*)

accidèmpoli *interj* (slang) darn it!

accidentale *adj* accidental

accidenta·to -ta *adj* paralyzed; uneven, rough (*road*); broken (*ground*)

accidènte *m* accident; crack-up; (coll) paralytic stroke; (coll) hoot, fig; (coll) pest, menace (*child*); (mus) accidental; **accidenti!** (coll) darn!, damn!; **correre come un accidente** to run like the devil; **mandare un accidente a** to wish ill luck to; **per accidente** perchance

accìdia *f* sloth

accidió·so -sa [s] *adj* slothful

accigliare §280 *ref* to frown, knit one's brow

accingere §126 *ref*—**accingersi a** to get ready to

-àccio -àccia *suf adj & mf* (-acci -acce) no good, e.g., **gentaccia** no good people; good-for-nothing, e.g., **ragazzaccio** good-for-nothing boy

acciò or **acciocché** *conj* (poet) so that

acciottolare (acciòttolo) *tr* to pave with cobblestones

acciottola·to -ta *adj* cobblestone || *m* cobblestone pavement

acciottolì·o *m* (-ìi) clatter (*e.g., of dishes*)

accipìcchia *interj* (coll) darn·it!

acciuffare *tr* to seize, grab, pinch (*a thief*)

acciu·ga *f* (-ghe) anchovy

acclamare *tr* to acclaim || *intr* to voice one's approval

acclamazióne *f* acclamation

acclimatare (acclìmato) *tr & ref* to acclimate

acclimatazióne *f* acclimatation

acclive *adj* (poet) steep

acclivi·tà *f* (-tà) acclivity

acclùdere §105 *tr* to enclose

acclu·so -sa *adj* enclosed

accoccare §197 (accòcco & accócco) *tr* (poet) to nock (*the arrow*)

accoccolare (accòccolo) *ref* to squat down

accodare (accódo) *tr* to line up || *ref* to line up, queue

accogliènte *adj* cozy, hospitable, inviting

accogliènza *f* reception, welcome

accògliere §127 *tr* to receive; to welcome; to grant (*a request*) || *ref* (poet) to gather

accoglitrice *f* receptionist

accòlito *m* acolyte, altar boy; follower

accollare (accòllo) *tr* to overload (*a cart*); **accollare qlco a qlcu** to charge s.o. with s.th || *intr* to go up to the neck (*said of a dress*) || *ref* to assume, take upon oneself

accolla·to -ta *adj* high-necked (*dress*); high-cut (*shoes*) || *f* accolade

accollatura *f* neck, neckhole

accòlta *f* (poet) gathering

accoltellare (accoltèllo) *tr* to knife

accomandante *m* limited partner

accomandatà·rio *m* (-ri) (law) general partner

accomàndita *f* (law) limited partnership

accomiatare *tr* to dismiss || *ref* to take leave

accomodaménto *m* arrangement; compromise; settlement

accomodante *adj* accommodating, obliging

accomodare (accòmodo) *tr* to arrange; to fix; to settle || *intr* to be convenient || *ref* to adapt oneself; to agree; to sit down; **si accomodi** have a seat, make yourself comfortable

accomodatura *f* arrangement; repair

accompagnaménto *m* retinue; cortege; (mus) accompaniment; (law) writ of mandamus; (mil) softening-up (*by gunfire*)

accompagnare *tr* to accompany; to escort; to follow; to match || *ref*—**accompagnarsi a** or **con** to join

accompagna·tóre -trice *mf* escort; guide; (mus) accompanist

accomunare *tr* to mingle, mix; to unite, associate; to share

acconciaménto *m* arrangement

acconciare §128 (accóncio) *tr* to prepare for use; to arrange; to set (*e.g., the hair*) || *ref* to adorn oneself; to dress one's hair; to adapt oneself

acconcia·tóre -trice *mf* hairdresser

acconciatura f hairdo; headdress

accòn·cio -cia adj (-ci -ce) proper, fitting

accondiscendènte adj acquiescing, acquiescent

accondiscendènza f acquiescence

accondiscéndere §245 intr to acquiesce, consent; to yield

acconsentire (acconsènto) intr to consent, acquiesce

acconsenziènte adj consenting, acquiescing

accontentare (accontènto) tr to satisfy, please || ref to be satisfied, be pleased

accónto m installment

accoppare (accòppo) tr (coll) to kill; (coll) to beat to death || ref (coll) to get killed

accoppiaménto m pairing; mating; (mach) parallel operation

accoppiare §287 (accòppio) tr to couple, pair, cross (e.g., animals) || ref to mate, copulate

accoppiata f daily double (in races)

accoraménto m sadness, sorrow

accorare (accòro) tr to stab to death; to sadden || ref to sadden, grieve

accora·to -ta adj saddened, grieving

accorciare §128 (accórcio) tr & ref to shorten; to shrink

accorciatura f shortening; shrinking

accordare (accòrdo) tr to harmonize (colors); to reconcile (people); to tune up; to grant; (gram) to make agree || ref to agree; to match

accorda·to -ta adj tuned up || m (econ) credit limit

accorda·tóre -trice mf (mus) tuner

accordatura f tuning

accòrdo m agreement, accordance; (law) mutual consent; (mus) harmony; **d'accordo** O.K., agreed; **d'accordo con** in accord with; **di comune accordo** with one accord; **essere d'accordo** to agree; **mettersi d'accordo** to come to an agreement

accòrgere §249 ref to perceive, notice; **accorgersi di** to become aware of, realize; **senza accorgersi** inadvertently

accorgiménto m smartness; device, trick

accórrere §139 intr (ESSERE) to run up, rush up

accortézza f alertness; shrewdness, perspicacity

accòr·to -ta adj alert; shrewd, perspicacious

accosciare §128 (accòscio) ref to squat

accostàbile adj approachable

accostaménto m approach; combination (e.g., of colors)

accostare (accòsto) tr to approach; to bring near; to leave (a door) ajar || intr to be near; to cling, adhere; (naut) to come alongside; (naut) to maneuver alongside a pier; (naut) to change direction, haul || ref to approach, come near; to cling (e.g., to a faith)

accosta·to -ta adj ajar

accò·sto -sta adj (coll) near || m approach; help || **accosto** adv near; **accosto a** near, close to

accovacciare §128 ref to crouch

accovonare (accovóno) tr to sheave

accozzàglia f hodgepodge; motley crowd

accozzare (accòzzo) tr to jumble up; to collect, gather (people) together || ref to collect, congregate

accòzzo m jumble, medley

accreditàbile adj chargeable (e.g., account); creditable

accreditaménto m crediting

accreditare (accrédito) tr to credit, believe; to accredit (an ambassador); to credit (one's account)

accredita·to -ta adj confirmed (news); accredited

accréscere §142 tr & ref to increase

accresciménto m increase

accucciare §128 ref to curl up (said of dogs)

accudire §176 tr (coll) to attend (a sick person) || intr—**accudire a** to take care of

acculturazióne f acculturation

accumulare (accùmulo) tr, intr & ref to accumulate; to gather

accumulatóre m storage battery

accumulazióne f accumulation

accuratézza f care, carefulness

accura·to -ta adj careful, painstaking

accusa f accusation, charge; **pubblica accusa** (law) public prosecutor

accusare (accùso) tr to accuse, charge; to betray; to acknowledge (receipt); (cards) to declare, bid

accusati·vo -va adj & m accusative

accusa·to -ta adj accused || mf defendant

accusató·re -trice mf accuser; **pubblico accusatore** (law) public prosecutor, district attorney

accusatò·rio -ria adj (-ri -rie) accusatory, accusing

acèfa·lo -la adj headless; without the first page (said of a manuscript)

acèr·bo -ba adj unripe, green, sour

àcero m maple tree, sugar maple

acèrri·mo -ma adj bitter, fierce

acetato m acetate

acèti·co -ca adj (-ci -che) acetic

acetificare §197 (acetífico) tr to acetify

acetilène m acetylene

acéto m vinegar; **aceto aromatico** aromatic spirits; **sotto aceto** pickled

acetóne m acetone

acetósa [s] f (bot) sorrel

acetosèlla [s] f wood sorrel

acetó·so -sa [s] adj vinegarish || f see acetosa

Acherónte m Acheron

Achille m Achilles

acidificare §197 (acidífico) tr to acidify

acidi·tà f (-tà) acidity; **acidità di stomaco** heartburn

àci·do -da adj acid, sour || m acid; **sapere d'acido** to taste sour

acidu·lo -la adj acidulous

àcino m berry (of grapes); bead (of rosary)

acme f acme; crisis

acne f acne

acònito *m* (bot) monkshood

àcqua *f* water; rain; purity (*e.g., of a diamond*); acqua a catinelle pouring rain; acqua alta high water; acqua corrente running water; acqua dolce fresh water; drinking water; acqua in bocca! mum's the word!; acqua morta stagnant water; acqua ossigenata hydrogen peroxide; acqua potabile drinking water; acqua salata salt water; acqua viva spring; all'acqua di rose very mild; avere l'acqua alla gola to be in dire straits; della più bell'acqua of the first water; fare acqua to leak (*said of a boat*); fare un buco nell'acqua to waste one's efforts; portare acqua al mare to carry coals to Newcastle; prendere l'acqua to get wet; sott'acqua (fig) underhand; tirare l'acqua al proprio mulino to be grist to one's mill; versare acqua in un cesto to waste one's efforts

acquafòrte *f* (acquefòrti) etching

acquaforti·sta *mf* (-sti -ste) etcher

ac·quàio -quàia (-quài -quàie) *adj* watering (*trough*) || *m* sink

acquaiò·lo -la *adj* water || *m* water carrier; (sports) water boy

acquamarina *f* (acquemarine) aquamarine

acquaplano *m* aquaplane

acquaràgia *f* turpentine

acquarèllo *m* var of acquerello

acquà·rio *m* (-ri) aquarium || Acquario *m* (astr) Aquarius

acquartierare (acquartièro) *tr* (mil) to quarter || *ref* to be quartered

acquasanta *f* holy water

acquasantièra *f* (eccl) stoup

acquàti·co -ca *adj* (-ci -che) aquatic, water

acquattare *ref* to crouch, squat

acquavite *f* brandy; liquor, rum

acquazzóne *m* downpour, heavy shower

acquedótto *m* aqueduct

àcque·o -a *adj* aqueous, watery

acquerelli·sta *mf* (-sti -ste) watercolorist

acquerèllo *m* watercolor; watered-down wine

acquerùgiola *f* fine drizzle

acquiescènte *adj* acquiescent

acquietare (acquièto) *tr* to pacify, placate || *ref* to quiet down

acquirènte *mf* buyer, purchaser; il miglior acquirente the highest bidder

acquisire §176 *tr* to acquire

acquisi·tóre -trice *mf* salesperson, agent || *m* salesman || *f* saleswoman

acquistare *tr* to purchase, buy; to acquire; to gain (*e.g., ground*) || *intr* to improve

acquisto *m* buy, purchase; acquisition

acquitrino *m* marsh

acquitrinó·so -sa [s] *adj* marshy

acquolina *f*—far venire l'acquolina in bocca a to make one's mouth water

acquó·so -sa [s] *adj* watery

acre *adj* sour; pungent; acrid; bitter (*words*)

acrèdine *f* acrimony, sourness

acrimònia *f* acrimony

acro *m* acre

acròba·ta *mf* (-ti -te) acrobat

acrobàti·co -ca (-ci -che) *adj* acrobatic || *f* acrobatics

acrobatismo *m* acrobatics

acrobazia *f* acrobatics; stunt, feat

acrocòro *m* plateau

acrònimo *m* acronym

acròpo·li *f* (-li) acropolis

acròsti·co *m* (-ci) acrostic

acuire §176 *tr* to sharpen, whet

acuità *f* acuity

acùle·o *m* (-i) quill; prickle, thorn; stinger (*of an insect*)

acume *m* acumen

acuminare (acùmino) *tr* to sharpen, whet

acumina·to -ta *adj* pointed, sharp

acùsti·co -ca (-ci -che) *adj* acoustic(al) || *f* acoustics

acutézza *f* acuteness, sharpness

acutizzare [ddzz] *tr & ref* to sharpen

acu·to -ta *adj* acute, sharp || *m* high note

ad *prep* var of a before words beginning with a vowel

adagiare §290 *tr* to lay down gently; to lower gently || *ref* to lie down; to stretch out

adà·gio *m* (-gi) adage; (mus) adagio || *adv* slowly; gently; (mus) adagio

Adamo *m* Adam

adattàbile *adj* adaptable

adattaménto *m* adaptation; adaptability

adattare *tr* to adapt, fit || *ref* to adapt oneself; to become adapted; adattarsi a to go with; to match; to be becoming to

adat·to -ta *adj* suitable, adequate

addebitaménto *m* debiting

addebitare (addébito) *tr* to debit; addebitare una spesa a qlcu to debit s.o. with an expense

addébito *m* charge; (com) debit; elevare l'addebito di qlco a qlcu (law) to charge s.o. with s.th

addènda *mpl* addenda

addèndo *m* (math) addend

addensare (addènso) *tr* to thicken || *ref* to thicken; to gather, throng

addentare (addènto) *tr* to bite || *ref* (mach) to mesh

addentatura *f* bite; (carp) tongue (*of tongue and groove*)

addentella·to -ta *adj* toothed, notched || *m* chance, occasion; (archit) toothing

addentrare (addéntro) *tr* to penetrate || *ref* to penetrate; to proceed

addéntro *adv* inside; addentro in into; inside of

addestraménto *m* training

addestrare (addèstro) *tr & ref* to train

addestra·tóre -trice *mf* trainer

addét·to -ta *adj* assigned; attached; pertaining || *m* attaché; addetto stampa press secretary

addì *adv* the (+ *a certain date*), e.g., addì 27 gennaio the 27th of January

addiàc·cio *m* (-ci) sheepfold; bivouac

addiètro *m* (naut) stern; per l'addietro in the past || *adv* behind; ago; dare

addietro to back up; **lasciarsi addietro** to delay; **tempo addietro** some time ago; **tirarsi addietro** to back away

addì·o m (-i) farewell; **dare l'addio to** say good-bye; **dare l'estremo addio** to pay one's last respects; **fare gli addii** to say good-bye || *interj* farewell!, good-bye!

addire §151 tr (poet) to consecrate || ref to be suitable, be becoming; **addirsi a** to be becoming to

addirittura adv directly; even, without hesitation; absolutely, positively

addirizzare tr to straighten up; **addirizzare le gambe ai cani** to try the impossible

additare tr to point out

additi·vo -va adj & m additive

addivenire §282 intr (ESSERE)—**addivenire a** to come to, reach (e.g., an agreement)

addizionale adj additional || f supplementary tax

addizionare (addizióno) tr & intr to add

addizionatrice f adding machine

addizióne f addition

addobbaménto m adornment, decoration

addobbare (addòbbo) tr to adorn, bedeck, decorate

addobba·tóre -trice mf decorator

addòbbo m adornment, decoration; hangings (in a church)

addocilire §176 tr to soften up

addolcire §176 tr to sweeten; to calm down || ref to mellow, soften

addolorare (addolóro) tr & ref to grieve; **addolorarsi per** to grieve over, lament

addolora·to -ta adj sorrowful || **l'Addolorata** f (eccl) Our Lady of Sorrows

addòme m abdomen

addomesticàbile adj tamable

addomesticaménto m taming

addomesticare §197 (**addomèstico**) tr to tame; to accustom || ref to become accustomed

addomestica·to -ta adj tame, domesticated

addominale adj abdominal

addormentare (addorménto) tr to put to sleep; to numb || ref to fall asleep; to be asleep (said of a limb)

addormenta·to -ta adj asleep; numbed

addossare (addòsso) tr to put on; **addossare qlco a qlco** to lean s.th against s.th; **addossare qlco a qlcu** to put s.th on s.o.; (fig) to entrust s.o. with s.th || ref to take upon oneself; to crowd together; **addossarsi a** to lean against; to crowd

addossa·to·-ta adj leaning

addòsso adv on; on oneself, on one's back; about oneself; **addosso a** on, upon; against; **avere la sfortuna addosso** to be always unlucky; **dare addosso a qlcu** to assail s.o.; **levarsi d'addosso** to get rid of; **levarsi i panni d'addosso** to take the shirt off one's back

addót·to -ta adj adduced, alleged

addottorare (addottóro) tr to confer the doctor's degree on || ref to receive the doctor's degree

addurre §102 tr to adduce; to allege; (poet) to bring

Ade m Hades

adeguare (adéguo) tr to equalize; to bring in line || ref to conform, adapt oneself

adegua·to -ta adj adequate

adeguazióne f equalization

adémpiere §163 tr to fulfill, accomplish || ref to come true

adempiménto m fulfillment, discharge (of one's duty)

adempire §176 tr to fulfill, accomplish || ref to come true

adenòide adj adenoid || **adenoidi** fpl adenoids

adèpto m follower; initiate

aderènte adj adherent || mf adherent, supporter

aderènza f adherence; (mach) friction; (pathol) adhesion; **aderenze** connections

aderire §176 intr to adhere; to stick; **aderire a** to grant (e.g., a request); to concur with; to subscribe to

adescare §197 (**adésco**) tr to lure, bait, entice; (mach) to prime (a pump)

adesióne f adhesion; support; (phys) adherence

adesi·vo -va adj & m adhesive

adèsso adv now, just now; **da adesso in poi** from now on; **per adesso** for the time being

adiacènte adj adjacent

adiacènza f adjacency; **adiacenze** vicinity

adianto m (bot) maidenhair

adibire §176 tr to assign; to use

àdipe m fat

adipó·so -sa [s] adj adipose

adirare ref to get angry

adira·to -ta adj angry, mad

adire §176 tr to apply to (the court); to enter into possession of (an inheritance)

adocchiare §287 (**adòcchio**) tr to eye; to ogle; to spot

adolescènte adj & mf adolescent

adolescènza f adolescence

adombrare (adómbro) tr to shade; to hide, veil || ref to shy (said of a horse); (fig) to take umbrage

Adóne m Adonis

adontare (adónto) tr (obs) to offend || ref to take offense

adoperare (adòpero & adópero) tr to use, employ || ref to exert oneself; to do one's best

adoràbile adj adorable

adorare (adóro) tr to adore; to worship || intr (archaic) to pray

adora·tóre -trice mf worshiper || m (joc) admirer, suitor

adorazióne f adoration, worship

adornare (adórno) tr to adorn || ref to bedeck oneself

adór·no -na adj adorned, bedecked; (poet) fine, beautiful

adottante mf (law) adopter

adottare (adòtto) *tr* to adopt
adotti·vo -va *adj* adoptive; foster (*child*)
adozióne *f* adoption
Adriàti·co -ca *adj* (-ci -che) Adriatic ‖ **Adriatico** *m* Adriatic
adulare (àdulo) *tr* to flatter; to fawn on
adula·tóre -trice *mf* flatterer
adulatò·rio -ria *adj* (-ri -rie) flattering; fawning
adulazióne *f* adulation; fawning
adulterante *adj* & *m* adulterant
adulteri·no -na *adj* bastard; adulterated
adultè·rio *m* (-ri) adultery
adùlte·ro -ra *adj* adulterous ‖ *m* adulterer ‖ *f* adulteress
adul·to -ta *adj* & *mf* adult
adunanza *f* assembly
adunare *tr* & *ref* to assemble, gather
adunata *f* reunion, meeting; (mil) muster
adun·co -ca *adj* (-chi -che) hooked, crooked
adunghiare §287 *tr* (poet) to claw
adu·sto -sta *adj* skinny; (poet) burnt
aerare (àero) *tr* to air, ventilate
aerazióne *f* aeration; airing
aère·o -a *adj* aerial; air; overhead; high, lofty; airy, fanciful ‖ *m* airplane; (rad & telv) aerial
aerobrigata *f* (mil) wing
aerocistèrna *f* (aer) tanker
aerodinàmi·co -ca -a (-ci -che) *adj* aerodynamic(al); streamlined ‖ *f* aerodynamics
aeròdromo *m* airfield, airdrome
aerofaro *m* airport beacon
aerofotogram·ma *m* (-mi) aerial photograph
aerogiro *m* helicopter
aerògrafo *m* spray gun (*for painting*)
aerolinea *f* airline; **aerolinea principale** trunkline
aeròlito *m* meteorite, meteorite
aeromaritti·mo -ma *adj* air-sea
aeròmetro *m* aerometer
aeromòbile *m* aircraft; **aeromobile senza pilota** drone, pilotless aircraft
aeromodellismo *m* model-airplane building
aeromodelli·sta *mf* (-sti -ste) model-airplane builder
aeromodèllo *m* model airplane
aeromotóre *m* windmill; aircraft motor
aeronàu·ta *m* (-ti) aeronaut
aeronàuti·co -ca -a (-ci -che) *adj* aeronautic(al) ‖ *f* aeronautics
aeronave *f* airship, aircraft
aeroplano *m* airplane
aeropòrto *m* airport, airfield
aeroportuale *adj* airport
aerorazzo [ddzz] *m* rocket spaceship
aeroriméssa *f* hangar
aerosbar·co *m* (-chi) landing of airborne troops
aeroservi·zio [s] *m* (-zi) air service
aerosilurante [s] *f* torpedo plane
aerosiluro [s] *m* aerial torpedo
aerosòl [s] *m* aerosol
aerosostenta·to -ta [s] *adj* airborne
aerospaziale *adj* aerospace
aerospà·zio *m* (-zi) aerospace

aerostàti·co -ca (-ci -che) *adj* aerostatic(al) ‖ *f* aerostatics
aeròstato *m* aerostat
aerostazióne *f* air terminal
aerotas·sì *m* (-sì) taxiplane
aerotrasportare (aerotraspòrto) *tr* to airlift
aerotrasporta·to -ta *adj* airlifted; airborne
aerovia *f* (aer) beam (*course indicated by a radio beam*); (aer) air lane
afa *f* sultriness; **fare afa** (coll) to be a pain in the neck to
afèresi *f* apheresis
affàbile *adj* affable, agreeable
affaccendare (affaccèndo) *tr* to busy ‖ *ref* to busy oneself, bustle
affaccenda·to -ta *adj* busy, bustling; occupied with busywork
affacciare §128 *tr* to show or display at the window; to bring forward (*e.g., an objection*); to raise (*a doubt*) ‖ *ref* to show oneself (*at the door or window*); to present itself (*said of a doubt*)
affaccia·to -ta *adj* facing
affagottare (affagòtto) *tr* to bundle ‖ *ref* to bundle up; to dress sloppily
affamare *tr* to starve
affama·to -ta *adj* starved, ravenous ‖ *mf* starveling; hungry person; wretch
affannare *tr* to worry, to afflict ‖ *intr* to pant; to be out of breath ‖ *ref* to worry; to bustle around
affanna·to -ta *adj* panting; out of breath; worried
affanno *m* shortness of breath; grief, sorrow
affannó·so -sa [s] *adj* panting; wearisome
affardellare (affardèllo) *tr* to bundle together; (mil) to pack
affare *m* affair, matter; business; condition, quality; deal; **affari** business; **affari esteri** foreign affairs; **un buon affare** a good deal; a bargain
affarismo *m* sharp business practice
affari·sta *mf* (-sti -ste) unscrupulous operator
affaristi·co -ca *adj* (-ci -che) sharp
affascinante *adj* fascinating, charming
affascinare (affàscino) *tr* to fascinate, charm; to seduce; to spellbind ‖ (affàscino) *tr* to bundle, to sheave
affascina·tóre -trice *adj* fascinating, charming ‖ *mf* charmer, spellbinder
affastellare (affastèllo) *tr* to fagot (*twigs*): to sheave, bundle (*e.g., hay*); to pile, heap (*wood, crops, etc*); (fig) to jumble up
affaticare §197 *tr* to fatigue, tire, weary ‖ *ref* to get tired; to weary; to toil
affatica·to -ta *adj* weary, tired
affatto *adv* quite, entirely; **niente affatto** not at all; **non . . . affatto** not at all
affatturare *tr* to bewitch; to adulterate (*e.g., food*)
affermare (affèrmo) *tr* to affirm, assert ‖ *intr* to nod assent ‖ *ref* to take hold (*said, e.g., of a new product*)
affermati·vo -va *adj* & *f* affirmative
affermazióne *f* affirmation; assertion,

statement; success (e.g., of a new product); (sports) victory

afferrare (**affèrro**) tr to grab, grasp; to catch, nab || ref to cling

affettare (**affétto**) tr to slice; to cut up || (**affètto**) tr to affect

affetta·to -ta adj affected || m cold cuts

affettatrice f slicing machine

affettazióne f affectation

affetti·vo -va adj emotional

affèt·to -ta adj afflicted, burdened || m affection, love; feeling

affettuosi·tà [s] f (-tà) love, affection

affettuó·so -sa [s] adj affectionate, loving, tender

affezionare (**affezióno**) tr to inspire affection in || ref—affezionarsi a to become fond of

affeziona·to -ta adj affectionate, loving; Suo affezionatissimo best regards; tuo affezionatissimo love, as ever

affezióne f affection

affiancare §197 tr to place next; to favor, help; (mil) to flank

affiatamento m harmony; teamwork

affiatare tr to harmonize

affibbiare §287 tr to buckle, fasten; to deliver (a blow); to play (a trick); to slap (a fine)

affidaménto m consignment, delivery; trust, confidence; dare affidamento to be trustworthy; fare affidamento su to rely upon

affidare tr to entrust; to commit (to memory); affidare qlco a qlcu to entrust s.o with s.th || ref to trust; affidarsi a to trust in

affievoliménto m weakening

affievolire §176 tr to weaken || ref to grow weaker

affiggere §103 tr to post; to fix (one's eyes or glance) || ref to gaze, stare

affigliare §287 tr & ref var of affiliare

affilacoltèl·li m (-li) steel (for sharpening knives)

affilara·sóio m (-sói) strop

affilare tr to sharpen, hone, whet; to make thin || ref to become thin

affila·to -ta adj sharp, sharpened; thin || f sharpening

affila·tóio m (-tói) sharpener

affilatrice f grindstone

affiliare §287 tr to affiliate || ref to become affiliated; affiliarsi a to become a member of

affilia·to -ta adj affiliated || mf affiliate; foster child; member of a secret society

affiliazióne f affiliation

affinare tr to sharpen; to refine, purify; to improve (e.g., one's style) || ref to improve

affinché conj so that, in order that; affinché non lest

affine adj akin, related; similar || mf in-law || m kinsman || f kinswoman || adv—affine di in order to

affini·tà f (-tà) affinity

affiochire §176 tr to make hoarse; to weaken || ref to become hoarse; to grow dim (said of a candle)

affioraménto m surfacing; (min) outcrop

affiorare (**affióro**) intr to surface, emerge; to appear, to show

affissare tr (poet) to fix || ref to concentrate; (poet) to gaze

affissióne f posting, bill posting

affis·so -sa adj fixed; posted || m bill, poster; door or window; (gram) affix

affittacàme·re m (-re) landlord || f landlady

affittanza f rent

affittare tr to rent || ref—si affitta for rent

affitto m rent, rental; dare in affitto to rent (to grant by lease); prendere in affitto to rent (to take by lease)

affittuà·rio -ria mf (-ri -rie) renter; tenant

affliggente adj tormenting, distressing

affliggere §104 tr to afflict, distress || ref to grieve

afflit·to -ta adj afflicted, grieving || mf afflicted person, wretch

afflizióne f affliction, distress

afflosciare §128 (**afflòscio**) tr to cause to sag; to weaken || ref to droop; to sag; to be deflated; to faint

afflosire §176 tr & ref var of afflosciare

affluènte adj & m confluent

affluènza f confluence; abundance; crowd

affluire §176 intr (ESSERE) to flow (said of river); to flock (said of people); to pour in (said of earnings)

afflusso m flow

affogaménto m drowning

affogare §209 (**affógo**) tr to drown; to smother || intr (ESSERE) to drown

affoga·to -ta adj drowned; poached (egg)

affollaménto m crowd, throng

affollare (**affóllo** & **affòllo**) tr to crowd; to overcome || ref to crowd

affolla·to -ta adj crowded

affondaménto m sinking

affondami·ne m (-ne) mine layer

affondare (**affóndo**) tr to sink; to stick || ref to sink

affondata f (aer) nosedive

affóndo m (fencing) lunge || adv deeply

afforestare (**afforèsto**) tr to reforest

affossare (**affòsso**) tr to ditch; (fig) to table (e.g., a proposal); to hollow out || ref to become sunken or hollow (said, e.g., of cheeks)

affossatóre m ditchdigger; gravedigger

affrancare §197 tr to set free; to free; to redeem (a property); to stamp || ref to free oneself; to take heart

affrancatrice f postage meter

affrancatura f stamp, stamping

affràngere §179 tr to weary; (obs) to break down (the spirit)

affran·to -ta adj weary; broken down, broken-hearted

affratellaménto m fraternization

affratellare (**affratèllo**) tr to bind in brotherly love || ref to fraternize

affrescare §197 (**affrésco**) tr to fresco; to paint in fresco affré·sco *m* (-schi) fresco

affrettare (affrétto) *tr* & *ref* to hurry, hasten

affretta· to -ta *adj* hurried

affrontare (affrónto) *tr* to face, confront || *ref* to meet in combat; to come to blows

affronta·to -ta *adj*—affrontati (herald) combattant

affrónto *m* affront, offense

affumicare §197 (affùmico) *tr* to smoke; to blacken; to smoke out; to smoke (*meat or fish*)

affumica·to -ta *adj* smoked; dark (*glasses*)

affusolare [s] (affùsolo) *tr* & *ref* to taper

affusola·to -ta [s] *adj* tapered; slender

affusto *m* gun carriage

afga·no -na *adj* & *mf* Afghan

àfo·no -na *adj* voiceless

afori·sma *m* (-smi) aphorism

afó·so -sa [s] *adj* sultry

Africa, l' *f* Africa

africa·no -na *adj* & *mf* African

afrodisìa·co -ca *adj* & *m* (-ci -che) aphrodisiac

afta *m* mouth ulcer; afta epizootica (vet) foot-and-mouth disease

àgata *f* agate || Agata *f* Agatha

agènda *f* notebook; agenda

agènte *adj* active || *m* agent; broker; merchant; officer; agente delle tasse tax collector; agente di cambio stockbroker; money changer; agente di commercio broker, commission merchant; agente di custodia jailer; agente di polizia police officer, policeman; agente di spionaggio informer; agente provocatore agent provocateur

agenzìa *f* agency; office, branch; agenzia immobiliare real-estate office

agevolare (agévolo) *tr* to facilitate, help

agevolazióne *f* facility; agevolazione di pagamento easy terms

agévole *adj* easy

agevolézza *f* facility

agallare *intr* to come to the surface

agganciaménto *m* docking (*in space*); (rr) coupling

agganciare §128 *tr* to hook; (rr) to couple; (mil) to engage (*the enemy*)

aggàn·cio *m* (-ci) docking (*in space*); (rr) coupling

aggég·gio *m* (-gi) gadget

aggettivale *adj* adjectival

aggettivo *m* adjective

agghiacciaménto *m* freezing

agghiacciante *adj* hair-raising, frightful

agghiacciare §128 *tr* to freeze || *ref* to freeze; to be horrified

agghiaccia·to -ta *adj* frozen, icy

agghindare *tr* & *ref* to preen, primp

àg·gio *m* (-gi) agio; fare aggio to be at a premium

aggiogare §209 (aggiógo) *tr* to yoke

aggiornaménto *m* adjournment (*e.g., of a meeting*); bringing up to date

aggiornare (aggiórno) *tr* to bring up to date; to adjourn || *ref* to keep up with the times

aggiraménto *m* surrounding, outflanking

aggirare *tr* to surround, outflank; to swindle || *ref* to roam, wander; aggirarsi su to approximate; to be almost

aggiudicare §197 (aggiùdico) *tr* to adjudicate, award || *ref* to win

aggiudicazióne *f* adjudication, award

aggiùngere §183 *tr* to add; to join, connect || *ref* to be added; to join

aggiunta *f* addition

aggiuntare *tr* to attach, join

aggiun·to -ta *adj* & *m* associate, assistant, deputy || *f* see aggiunta

aggiustàbile *adj* repairable

aggiustaménto *m* settlement; adjustment; (mil) correction (*of fire*)

aggiustare *tr* to fix, repair; to adjust; (mil) to correct (*cannon fire*); aggiustare per le feste (coll) to fix; (coll) to give a good beating to || *ref* (archaic) to come closer; (coll) to manage; (coll) to come to an agreement

aggiusta·tóre -trice *mf* repairer, fixer || *m* repairman

aggiustatura *f* fixing, repairing, repair

agglomerare (agglòmero) *tr* & *ref* to pile up; to crowd together

agglomerato *m* built-up area; agglomerato urbano urban center

agglutinare (agglùtino) *tr* & *ref* to agglutinate

agglutinazióne *f* agglutination

aggobbire §176 *tr* to bend, bend over || *intr* (ESSERE) & *ref* to hunch over

aggomitolare (aggomitolo) *tr* to coil || *ref* to curl up

aggradare *intr* (with *dat*) (poet) to please; come Le aggrada as you please

aggradire §176 *tr* to appreciate || *intr* (poet) (with *dat*) to please

aggraffare *tr* to hook; to grab; to join (*metal sheets*) with a double seam; to stitch, staple

aggraffatrice *f* folding machine; (mach) can sealer

aggranchire §176 *tr* to benumb; to deaden, stupefy || *intr* to become numb

aggrappare *tr* to grab; to clamp || *ref* to cling

aggravaménto *m* aggravation

aggravante *adj* (law) aggravating (*circumstances*)

aggravare *tr* to aggravate; to overload (*e.g., one's stomach*) || *ref* to get worse

aggrà·vio *m* (-vi) burden (*e.g., of taxes*); fare aggravio a qlcu di qlco to impute s.th to s.o.

aggraziare §287 *tr* to embellish; to render graceful || *ref* to win, gain; to ingratiate oneself

aggrazia·to -ta *adj* graceful; polite

aggredire §176 *tr* to assail, attack, assault

aggregare §209 (aggrègo) *tr* & *ref* to join, unite

aggrega·to -ta *adj* adjunct || *m* aggregation

aggressióne *f* aggression

aggressi·vo -va adj aggressive || m (mil) poison gas

aggressóre m aggressor

aggricciare §128 tr to wrinkle; (slang) to knit (e.g., the brow) || ref (poet) to shiver

aggrinzare tr & ref to wrinkle

aggrinzire §176 tr & ref var of **aggrinzare**

aggrondare (aggróndo) tr to knit (the brow)

aggrottare (aggròtto) tr to knit (the brow)

aggrovigliare §280 tr to tangle, entangle || ref to become entangled

aggrumare tr & ref to clot; to coagulate

aggruppare tr to group

agguagliare §280 tr to level; to equalize; to compare

agguantare tr to grab; to nab; (coll) to hit; **agguantare per il collo** to grab by the neck || ref—**agguantarsi a** to get hold of

agguato m ambush; **cadere in un agguato** to fall into a trap; **stare in agguato** to wait in ambush

agguerrire §176 tr to train for war; to inure to war; to inure

aghétto m shoestring; (mil) lanyard

agiatézza f comfort, wealth; **vivere nell'agiatezza** to live in comfort

agia·to -ta adj well-to-do, comfortable

àgile adj agile, nimble; prompt

agili·tà f (-tà) agility, nimbleness; promptness

à·gio m (-gi) comfort; opportunity; ease; **agi** conveniences, comforts; **a Suo agio** at your convenience; **aver agio** to have time; **stare a proprio agio** to feel at ease; to be comfortable; **vivere negli agi** to live comfortably

agiografia f hagiography

agiògrafo m hagiographer

agire §176 intr to act; to work; (theat) to act, perform

agitare (àgito) tr to agitate, shake; to stir; to stir up; to discuss (e.g., a problem) || ref to toss; to shake; to stir; to get excited

agita·to -ta adj rough, choppy (sea); troubled, upset || mf violently insane person

agita·tóre -trice mf agitator || m shaker

agitazióne f agitation

agli §4

agliàce·o -a adj garlicky

à·glio m (-gli) garlic

agnellino m little lamb, lambkin

agnèllo m lamb

agnizióne f recognition

agnòsti·co -ca adj & mf (-ci -che) agnostic

a·go m (-ghi) needle; pointer (of scales); stem (of valve)

agognare (agógno) tr to covet

agóne m contest; arena

agonia f agony, death struggle; anguish

agonisti·co -ca adj (-ci -che) competitive, aggressive (spirit); athletic (competition) || f athletics

agonizzare [ddzz] intr to agonize, be in agony; (fig) to die out

agopuntura f acupuncture

ago·ràio m (-rài) needle case

agosta·no -na adj August, e.g., **pomeriggio agostano** August afternoon

agostinia·no -na adj & m Augustinian

agósto m August

agrà·rio -ria (-ri -rie) adj & m agrarian || m landlord || f agriculture

agrèste adj country

agrìco·lo -la adj agricultural

agricoltóre m farmer; agriculturist

agricoltura f agriculture

agrifò·glio m (-gli) holly

agrimensóre m surveyor

agrimensura f surveying

a·gro -gra adj sour, bitter || m citrus juice; sourness, bitterness; surrounding country

agrodólce adj sweet and sour; (fig) acidulous (tone)

agronomia f agronomy

agrònomo m agronomist

agrume m citrus (tree and fruit); **agrumi** citrus fruit

aguchiare §287 intr to knit or sew idly

agùglia f spire; top; (ichth) gar; (poet) eagle; (obs) needle

aguzzare tr to sharpen; to whet (the appetite)

aguzzino [ddzz] m slave driver; jailer

aguz·zo -za adj sharp, pointed

ah interj ah!

ahi interj ouch!

ahimè interj alas!

àia f yard, barnyard; threshing floor; governess || **L'Aia** f the Hague

Aiace m Ajax

àio m (ài) tutor

aiòla f lawn; flower bed

àire m push; short run (preparing for a jump); **dare l'aire a** to start off; **prendere l'aire** to take off

airóne m heron

aitante adj robust, stalwart

aiuòla f (poet) var of **aiola**

aiutante adj helping || mf assistant || m (mil) adjutant; **aiutante di campo** aide-de-camp; **aiutante di sanità** orderly

aiutare tr to help || ref to strive; to help oneself; to help one another

aiutato m first assistant (e.g., of a surgeon)

aiuto m aid, help; assistant; first assistant (of a surgeon)

aizzare (aìzzo) tr to incite, to incite to riot; to sic (a dog)

al §4

a·la f (-li & -le) wing; sail, vane (of windmill); blade (e.g., of fan); brim (of hat); (football) end; **ala a freccia** backswept wing; **ala di popolo** throng; **fare ala a** to line up along

alabarda f halberd

alabardière m halberdier

alabastri·no -na adj alabaster; white as alabaster

alabastro m alabaster

àlacre adj eager, lively

alacrità f alacrity

alàg·gio *m* (-gi) hauling, towing
alamaro *m* braid, gimp
alambìc·co *m* (-chi) still
alano *m* Great Dane
alare *adj* wing (*e.g., span*) || *m* andiron || *tr* to haul
Alasca, l' *f* Alaska
ala·to -ta *adj* winged, sublime
alba *f* dawn, daybreak
albagìa *f* haughtiness
albanése [s] *adj & mf* Albanian
Albanìa, l' *f* Albania
àlbatro *m* (orn) albatross
albeggiaménto *m* dawning
albeggiare §290 (albéggio) *intr* (ESSERE) to dawn; (poet) to sparkle (*said, e.g., of ice*) || *impers* (ESSERE)—albeggia the day dawns
alberare (àlbero) *tr* to plant (*trees*); to reforest; to hoist (*a mast*); to mast (*a ship*)
albera·to -ta *adj* tree-lined; (naut) masted
alberèllo *m* small tree; apothecary's jar
albergare §209 (albèrgo) *tr* to lodge; to put up at a hotel; (fig) to harbor || *intr* to lodge; to put up
alberga·tóre -trice *mf* hotelkeeper
alberghiè·ro -ra *adj* hotel
albèr·go *m* (-ghi) hotel; refuge; hospitality; albergo diurno day hostel; albergo per la gioventù youth hostel
àlbero *m* tree; poplar; (mach) shaft; (naut) mast; albero a camme (aut) camshaft; albero a gomito (aut) crankshaft; albero di distribuzione (aut) camshaft; albero di Natale Christmas tree; albero di trasmissione (aut) transmission; albero genealogico family tree
albicòc·ca *f* (-che) apricot
albicòc·co *m* (-chi) apricot tree
al·bo -ba *adj* (poet) white || *m* album; bulletin board; (law) roll; comic book; albo d'onore honor roll || *f* see alba
albóre *m* (poet) whiteness; (poet) dawn
album *m* (album) album, scrapbook
albume *m* albumen
albumina *f* albumin
àlca·li *m* (-li) alkali
alcali·no -na *adj* alkaline
alce *m* moose; elk
alchimìa *f* alchemy
alchimi·sta *m* (-sti) alchemist
alcióne *m* halcyon
alciò·nio -nia *adj* (-ni -nie) halcyon
àlco·le *m* alcohol
alcolici·tà *f* (-tà) alcoholic content
alcòli·co -ca *adj* (-ci -che) alcoholic || *m* alcoholic beverage
alcolismo *m* alcoholism
alcolizzare [ddzz] *tr* to intoxicate || *ref* to become intoxicated
alcolizza·to -ta [ddzz] *adj* intoxicated || *mf* alcoholic
alcool *m* (alcool) var of alcole
alcoolici·tà *f* (-tà) var of alcolicità
alcoòli·co -ca (-ci -che) *adj & m* var of alcolico
alcoolismo *m* var of alcolismo
alcoolizzare [ddzz] *tr* var of alcolizzare

alcoolizza·to -ta [ddzz] *adj & mf* var of alcolizzato
alcòva *f* bedroom; bed; alcove
alcunché *pron* something, anything
alcu·no -na *adj & pron* some; alcu·ni -ne some; quite a few, several, a good many
aldilà *m* life beyond, afterlife
àlea *f* chance, hazard; correre l'alea to try one's luck
aleggiare §290 (aléggio) *intr* to flutter; to flap the wings; to hover
aleróne *m* var of alettone
alesàg·gio *m* (-gi) (mach) bore
alesare (alèso) *tr* (mach) to bore
alesatóre *m* reamer
alesatrice *s* boring machine
Alessandria d'Egitto *f* Alexandria
alessandri·no -na *adj & mf* Alexandrian || *m* Alexandrine (*verse*)
Alessandro *m* Alexander; Alessandro Magno Alexander the Great
alétta *f* small wing; fin (*of fish*); (aer) tab; aletta di compensazione trim tab; aletta parasole (aut) sun visor
alettóne *m* (aer) aileron, flap
Aleutì·no -na *adj*—Isole Aleutine Aleutian Islands
al·fa *m* (-fa) alpha || *f* esparto
alfabèti·co -ca *adj* (-ci -che) alphabetical
alfabetizzazióne [ddzz] *f* teaching to read; learning to read
alfabèto *m* alphabet; code (*e.g., Morse*)
alfière *m* flagbearer, standardbearer; (chess) bishop
alfine *adv* finally, at last
al·ga *f* (-ghe) alga; alga marina seaweed
àlgebra *f* algebra
algèbri·co -ca *adj* (-ci -che) algebraic
Algèri *f* Algiers
Algerìa, l' *f* Algeria
algeri·no -na *adj & mf* Algerian
aliante *m* (aer) glider
alianti·sta *mf* (-sti -ste) glider pilot
àli·bi *m* (-bi) alibi
alice *f* anchovy
alienàbile *adj* alienable
alienare (alièno) *tr* to alienate; to transfer, convey || *ref*—alienarsi dalla ragione to go out of one's mind
aliena·to -ta *adj* alienated || *mf* insane person; dispossessed person
alienazióne *f* alienation
alieni·sta *mf* (-sti -ste) alienist
alièno -na *adj* disinclined; (poet) foreign, alien
alimentare *adj* alimentary || alimentari *mpl* food, foodstuff || *v* (aliménto) *tr* to feed; to fuel
alimentari·sta *m* (-sti) food merchant; food-industry worker
alimenta·tóre -trice *mf* stoker || *m* (mach) stoker, feeder
alimentazióne *f* nourishment; feeding; (mil) loading; alimentazione artificiale intravenous feeding
aliménto *m* food, nourishment; feed; alimenti *almost* (*maintenance*)
alimònia *f* alimony
alìnea *f* (law) paragraph, section

alìquota *f* share; parcel, quota

aliscafo *m* hydrofoil

alìse·o -a *adj* trade (*wind*) ‖ *m* trade wind

alitare (àlito) *intr* to breathe; to blow gently; **non alitare** to not breathe a word

àlito *m* breath; (fig) breeze

alìvo·lo -la *adj* (poet) winged; (fig) swift

alla §4

allacciaménto *m* binding; connection; linking

allacciare §128 *tr* to bind, tie; to connect; to buckle; (fig) to deceive

allacciatura *f* lacing; buckling

allagare §209 *tr* to flood, overflow

allampana·to -ta *adj* tall and lean, lanky

allargare §209 *tr* to broaden, widen; **allargare la mano** to be lenient; to be liberal; **allargare il freno** to give free rein ‖ *ref* to widen, spread out; **mi si allarga il cuore** I feel relieved

allargatura *f* widening

allarmante *adj* alarming

allarmare *tr* to alarm ‖ *ref* to worry, become alarmed

allarme *m* alarm; **allarme aereo** air-raid warning; **cessato allarme** all clear; **falso allarme** false alarm; **stare in allarme** to be alarmed

allascare §197 *tr* (naut) to ease, slacken (*a rope*)

allato *adv* (poet) near; **allato a** near; beside; in comparison with

allattaménto *m* nursing, feeding; **allattamento artificiale** bottle feeding

allattare *tr* to nurse (*at the breast*); to feed (*with a bottle*)

alle §4

alleanza *f* alliance

alleare (allèo) *tr* to ally ‖ *ref* to become allied; to be connected

allea·to -ta *adj* allied ‖ *mf* ally

allegare §209 (allégo) *tr* to enclose; to adduce; to allege; **allegare i denti** to set the teeth on edge ‖ *intr* (hort) to ripen

allega·to -ta *adj* enclosed ‖ *m* enclosure

alleggeriménto *m* lightening, easing

alleggerire §176 *tr* to lighten; to alleviate ‖ *ref* to put on lighter clothes; **alleggerirsi di** (naut) to jettison

allegoria *f* allegory

allegòri·co -ca *adj* (-ci -che) allegorical

allegraménte *adv* cheerfully, merrily; thoughtlessly

allegrézza *f* joy, cheerfulness

allegria *f* cheer, gaiety; **stare in allegria** to be merry ‖ *interj* good cheer!

allé·gro -gra *adj* cheerful, merry, gay ‖ *m* (mus) allegro

allelùia *m* hallelujah

allenaménto *m* training

allenare (alléno) *tr & ref* to train

allena·tóre -trice *adj* training ‖ *mf* trainer, coach

allentare (allènto) *tr* to loosen, slacken; to mitigate; (coll) to deliver (*a blow*); **essere allentato** to have a hernia ‖ *ref* to slow up; to loosen up; to diminish

allergìa *f* allergy

allèrgi·co -ca *adj* (-ci -che) allergic

alèrta *f* alert ‖ *adv* alert, on the alert

allessare (allésso) *tr* to boil

allés·so -sa *adj* boiled ‖ *m* boiled meat, boiled beef

allestire §176 *tr* to prepare, make ready; to rig (*e.g., a ship*); to produce (*e.g., a play*)

allettaménto *m* allure, fascination

allettante *adj* alluring, enticing

allettare (allètto) *tr* to allure, entice; to confine to bed; to bend (*plants*) to the ground ‖ *ref* to be confined to bed

allevaménto *m* raising, breeding; flock

allevare (allèvo) *tr* to raise, breed; to rear

alleva·tóre -trice *mf* raiser, breeder

alleviare §287 (allèvio) *tr* to alleviate, lighten

allibire §176 *intr* (ESSERE) to turn pale; to be astonished, be dismayed

allibraménto *m* registration, entry; booking (*of bets*)

allibrare *tr* to register, enter; to book (*a bet*) on a horse

allibratóre *m* bookmaker (*at races*)

allietare (allièto) *tr* to cheer, enliven

alliè·vo -va *mf* pupil, student; follower, disciple ‖ *m* trainee; **allievo ufficiale** cadet

alligatóre *m* alligator

allignare *intr* to take root; to do well, prosper

allineaménto *m* alignment; falling in line

allineare (allìneo) *tr* to align; (typ) to justify ‖ *ref* to align oneself, be aligned

allinea·to -ta *adj* aligned; **non allineato** nonaligned, uncommitted

allitterazióne *f* alliteration

allo §4

allòc·co *m* (-chi) horned owl; (fig) dolt, nincompoop

allocu·tóre -trice *mf* (poet) speaker

allocuzióne *f* (poet) speech, address

allòdola *f* lark, skylark

allogare §209 (allògo) *tr* to place; to let, lease; to find employment for; to invest (*money*); to marry off (*a daughter*)

allòge·no -na *adj* minority ‖ *mf* member of an ethnic minority

alloggiaménto *m* (mil) lodging, quarters; (carp, mach) housing

alloggiare §290 (allòggio) *tr* to lodge, put up ‖ *intr* to lodge, stay

allòg·gio *m* (-gi) lodging, living quarters; accommodations

allontanaménto *m* removal; estrangement

allontanare *tr* to remove; to send away; to exonerate; to dismiss; to alienate ‖ *ref* to go away; to withdraw; to become estranged

allóra *adj* then ‖ *adv* then; at that time; in that case; **da allora** ever since; **da allora in poi** from that time on; **fino allora** until then; **per allora** at that time

allorché *conj* when

allòro *m* laurel; **riposare sugli allori** to rest on one's laurels

allorquando *conj* (poet) when

àlluce *m* big toe

allucinante *adj* hallucinating; dazzling; deceptive

allucinare (**allùcino**) *tr* to hallucinate; to dazzle; to deceive

allucinazióne *f* hallucination

alludere §105 *intr* to allude

allume *m* alum

alluminare (**allùmino**) *tr* to illuminate (*a manuscript*); (poet) to light

alluminio *m* aluminum

allunàg·gio *m* (-gi) lunar landing; **allunaggio morbido** soft lunar landing

allunare *intr* to land on the moon

allunga *f* (mach) adapter

allungàbile *adj* extensible; extension (*table*)

allungaménto *m* lengthening

allungare §209 *tr* to lengthen; to stretch out (*e.g., the hand*); to dilute (*e.g., wine*); (coll) to deliver (*e.g., a slap*); (sports) to pass (*the ball*); **allungare il collo** to crane the neck; **allungare il passo** to walk faster || *ref* to grow longer; to stretch; to grow taller

allun·go *m* (-ghi) (sports) sprint; (sports) forward pass

allusióne *f* allusion

alluvióne *m* flood

almanaccare §197 *tr* to dream of || *intr* to dream, muse

almanac·co *m* (-chi) almanac

alméno *adv* at least; if only

alno *m* (bot) alder

àloe *m* & *f* aloe

alògeno *m* halogen

alogenuro *m* halide

alóne *m* halo

alòsa *f* (ichth) shad

alpacca *f* German silver

alpe *f* high mountain, alp || **le Alpi** the Alps

alpèstre *adj* mountainous; (fig) uncouth

alpìgia·no -na *adj* mountain, mountainous; (fig) uncouth || *mf* mountaineer

alpinismo *m* mountain climbing

alpini·sta *mf* (-sti -ste) mountain climber

alpinìsti·co -ca *adj* (-ci -che) mountain-climbing

alpi·no -na *adj* alpine; Alpine || *m* alpine soldier

alquan·to -ta *adj* & *pron* some; **alquanti -te** some; quite a few, several, a good many || **alquanto** *adv* somewhat, rather

Alsàzia, l' *f* Alsace

alsazia·no -na *adj* & *mf* Alsacian

alt *m* (alt) halt, stop || *interj* halt!, stop!

altaléna *f* seesaw; swing; (fig) ups and downs; **altalena a bilico** seesaw; **altalena sospesa** swing

altalenare (**altaléno**) *intr* to seesaw; to swing

altana *f* roof terrace

altare *m* altar

altarino *m* small altar; **svelare gli alta-** rini (joc) to expose the skeleton in the closet

altèa *f* marsh mallow

alterare (**àltero**) *tr* to alter; to falsify; to adulterate; to anger || *ref* to alter; to become adulterated; to get angry

altera·to -ta *adj* altered; adulterated; feverish; angry

alterazióne *f* change, alteration; adulteration; slight fever

altercare §197 (**altèrco**) *intr* to dispute, quarrel

altèr·co *m* (-chi) altercation; **venire a un alterco** to get into a quarrel

alterìgia *f* haughtiness

alternare (**altèrno**) *tr* & *ref* to alternate

alternatì·vo -va *adj* alternating || *f* alternative; choice

alterna·to -ta *adj* alternate; alternating (*current*)

alternatóre *m* (elec) alternator

altèr·no -na *adj* alternate

altè·ro -ra *adj* proud, haughty

altézza *f* height; width (*of cloth*); depth (*of water*); pitch (*of sound*); (astr, geom) altitude; (fig) loftiness, nobility; (naut) latitude; (typ) size; **essere all'altezza di** to be up to, be equal to; (naut) to be off || **Altezza** *f* Highness

altezzó·so -sa [s] *adj* haughty

altìc·cio -cia *adj* (-ci -ce) tipsy

altìmetro *m* altimeter

altipiano *m* var of **altopiano**

altiṣonante [s] *adj* high-sounding

altìssi·mo -ma *adj* very high, highest || **l'Altìssimo** *m* the Most High

altitùdine *f* altitude

al·to -ta *adj* high; tall; wide (*cloth*); deep (*water*); upper; full (*day*); late (*e.g., Easter*); deep (*sleep*); early (*Middle Ages*); loud (*voice*); lofty (*peak*) || *m* top; upper part; high quarters; **alti e bassi** ups and downs; **fare alto e basso** to be the undisputed boss; **guardare qlcu dall'alto in basso** to look down one's nose at s.o.; **in alto up** || **alto** *adv* up

altofórno *m* (altifórni) blast furnace

altoloca·to -ta *adj* high-placed, high-ranking

altoparlante *m* loudspeaker

altopiano *m* (altìpiani) plateau

altrettàn·to -ta *adj* & *pron* as much; the same; **altrettan·ti -te** as many || **altrettanto** *adv* as much; the same

altri *indef pron invar* someone; someone else; **non altri che** no one else but

altrièri *m* & *adv* day before yesterday

altriménti *adv* otherwise

al·tro -tra *adj* other; next (*world*); **altro ieri** day before yesterday; **chi altro?** who else?; **domani l'altro** the day after tomorrow; **fra l'altro** among other things; **ieri l'altro** the day before yesterday; **l'altro anno** last year; **l'altro giorno** the other day; **noi altri** we; **qualcun altro** somebody else; anybody else; **quest'altro (giorno, mese, anno)** next (day, month, year) || *pron* other; anything else; **altro che!** why yes! || **l'altro** §11 *correlative indef pron* || **l'altro** §12 *reciprocal pron*

altrónde *adv* (poet) somewhere else; **d'altronde** besides; on the other hand

altróve *adv* elsewhere, somewhere else

altrui *adj invar* somebody else's, other people's || *pron invar* somebody else || *m*—**l'altrui** what belongs to someone else

altrui·sta (-**sti** -**ste**) *adj* altruistic || *mf* altruist

altura *f* height; (naut) high seas

alun·no -**na** *mf* pupil, student

alveare *m* beehive

àlveo *m* bed (*of a river*)

alvèolo *m* alveolus; socket (*of tooth*); cell (*of honeycomb*)

alzabandiè·ra *m* (-**ra**) raising of the flag

alzacristal·li *m* (-**li**) (aut) crank (*to raise a window*)

alzàia *f* tow line; towpath

alzare *tr* to lift, raise; to cut (*cards*); to shrug (*one's shoulders*); to set (*sail*); **alzare al cielo** to praise to the sky; **alzare i tacchi** to show a clean pair of heels; **alzare la cresta** to get cocky || *ref* to rise; to get up; **alzarsi in piedi** to stand up

alzata *f* raising, lifting; shrugging (*of shoulders*); standing up; riser (*of step*); three-tier candy tray; **alzata di scudi** rebellion; **alzata di testa** whim, caprice

alzavàlvo·le *m* (-**le**) (aut) valve lifter

alzo *m* gunsight

amàbile *adj* amiable; sweetish (*wine*)

amabili·tà *f* (-**tà**) amiability, kindness

ama·ca *f* (-**che**) hammock

amàlga·ma *m* (-**mi**) amalgam

amalgamare (**amàlgamo**) *tr* to amalgamate || *ref* to amalgamate; to blend

amalgamazióne *f* amalgamation

amante *adj* loving, fond || *m* lover || *f* mistress

amanuènse *m* amanuensis, scribe

amare *tr* to love; to like || *ref* to love one another

amareggiare §290 (**amaréggio**) *tr* to make bitter; to sadden || *ref* to become bitter; to sadden

amarèna *f* sour cherry

amarétto *m* macaroon

amarézza *f* bitterness

ama·ro -**ra** *adj* bitter || *m* bitters; bitterness

amarógno·lo -**la** *adj* bitterish

amarra *f* (naut) hawser

amarrare *tr* & *intr* var of **ammarrare**

ama·tóre -**trice** *mf* lover; amateur

amató·rio -**ria** *adj* (-**ri** -**rie**) amatory, of love

amàzzone [ddzz] *f* horsewoman; female jockey; (obs) riding habit; **cavalcare all'amazzone** to ride sidesaddle || **Amazzone** *f* (myth) Amazon

ambage *f* winding path; **ambagi** circumlocutions; **senz'ambagi** without beating about the bush

ambasceria *f* embassy

ambà·scia *f* (-**sce**) shortness of breath; grief, sorrow

ambasciata *f* embassy; ambassadorship; errand, mission

ambasciatóre *m* ambassador

ambasciatrice *f* ambassadress

ambedùe *adj invar*—**ambedue i** or **le** both || *pron invar* both

ambiare §287 *intr* to amble, pace (*said of a horse*)

ambiatura *f* pacing (*said of a horse*)

ambidè·stro -**stra** *adj* ambidextrous

ambidùe *adj* & *pron invar* var of **ambedue**

ambientare (**ambiènto**) *tr* to accustom; to place (*a story in a certain period*) || *ref* to get accustomed to one's surroundings; to orient oneself

ambienta·tóre -**trice** *mf* interior decorator; (theat) decorator

ambiènte *adj* room, e.g., **temperatura ambiente** room temperature || *m* environment; habitat; milieu; room; **trovarsi fuori del proprio ambiente** to be out of one's element

ambigui·tà *f* (-**tà**) ambiguity

ambì·guo -**gua** *adj* ambiguous

àm·bio *m* (-**bi**) amble, pacing

ambire §176 *tr* to be eager for || *intr* to be ambitious; **ambire a** to be ambitious for

àmbito *m* range, circle; (mus) range; **nell'ambito di** within

ambizióne *f* ambition

ambizió·so -**sa** [s] *adj* ambitious || *mf* ambitious person

ambo or **am·bi** -**be** *adj pl*—**ambo i**, **ambo le**, **ambi i**, **ambe le** both

ambosèssi *adj invar* of both sexes, e.g., **giovani ambosessi** young people of both sexes

ambra *f* amber; **ambra grigia** ambergris

ambròsia *f* ambrosia; (bot) ragweed

ambulante *adj* itinerant; circulating; ambulant || *m* mail car

ambulanza *f* ambulance

ambulare (**àmbulo**) *intr* (coll) to ambulate

ambulatò·rio -**ria** (-**ri** -**rie**) *adj* ambulatory || *m* clinic, first-aid department

Amburgo *m* Hamburg

amèba *f* amoeba

a·men *m* (-**men**) amen || *interj* amen!

ameni·tà *f* (-**tà**) *f* amenity; pleasantry

amèno -**na** *adj* pleasant, agreeable; amusing (*fellow*)

Amèrica, l' *f* America; **l'America del Nord** North America; **l'America del Sud** South America

americana *f* bicycle race between pairs

americanismo *m* Americanism

americanizzare [ddzz] *tr* to Americanize || *ref* to become Americanized

america·no -**na** *adj* & *mf* American || *m* vermouth with bitters || *f* see **americana**

ametista *f* amethyst

amianto *m* asbestos

amicale *adj* (poet) friendly

amichévole *adj* friendly; (sports) noncompetitive

amicìzia *f* friendship; **stringere amicizia con** to make friends with

ami·co -ca (-ci -che) *adj* friendly ‖ *mf* friend; beloved ‖ *m* boy friend; lover, paramour; **amico del cuore** bosom friend ‖ *f* girl friend; mistress

amidàce·o -a *adj* starchy

amidatura *f* starching

àmido *m* starch

Amlèto *m* Hamlet

ammaccare §197 *tr* to crush; to pound; to bruise; to dent

ammaccatura *f* bruise; dent

ammaestraménto *m* instruction, teaching; training

ammaestrare (ammaèstro & ammaéstro) *tr* to teach, to educate; to train (*animals*)

ammainare (ammàino) *tr* to lower (*e.g., a flag*)

ammalare *intr* (ESSERE) to fall ill ‖ *ref* to fall ill; **ammalarsi di** to come down with

ammala·to -ta *adj* ill, sick ‖ *mf* patient

ammaliare §287 *tr* to cast a spell on; to charm, enchant, fascinate; to bewitch

ammalia·tóre -trice *adj* charming, enchanting ‖ *mf* charmer ‖ *m* enchanter, sorcerer ‖ *f* enchantress, sorceress

amman·co *m* (-chi) shortage

ammanettare (ammanétto) *tr* to handcuff

ammaniglia·to -ta *adj* shackled; (fig) closely bound, closely tied

ammannare *tr* to sheave (*grain*)

ammannire §176 *tr* to prepare (*a dish*); to dish up (*a meal*)

ammansare *tr* & *ref* var of **ammansire**

ammansa·tóre -trice *mf* (poet) tamer

ammansire §176 *tr* to tame; to calm ‖ *ref* to become tamed; to calm down

ammantare *tr* to mantle, clothe; to cover; to hide (*the truth*)

ammanto *m* mantle, cloak; (fig) authority

ammaràg·gio *m* (-gi) landing on water; splashdown (*of a space vehicle*)

ammaraménto *m* var of **ammaraggio**

ammarare *intr* (aer) to land on water; (rok) to splash down

ammarrare *tr* (naut) to moor

ammassare *tr* to amass ‖ *ref* to crowd, throng

ammasso *m* heap, pile; cluster (*of stars*); government stockpile

ammattiménto *m* worry, nuisance

ammattire §176 *intr* (ESSERE) to go crazy; **fare ammattire** to drive crazy

ammattonare (ammattóno) *tr* to floor with bricks

ammattona·to -ta *adj* floored with bricks ‖ *m* brick floor; bricklaying

ammazzare *tr* to kill ‖ *ref* to kill oneself; to get killed

ammazzasèt·te *m* (-te) braggart

ammazza·tóio *m* (-tói) slaughterhouse

ammènda *f* fine; satisfaction (*for injury*); **fare ammenda** to make amends

ammendaménto *m* emendation; improvement (*of land*)

ammendare (ammèndo) *tr* to emendate; to improve (*land*)

ammennìcolo *m* excuse; trifle; **ammennicoli** extras

ammés·so -sa *adj* admitted; **ammesso che** supposing that; **ammesso e non concesso** for the sake of argument

ammèttere §198 *tr* to admit; to accept, suppose

ammezzare [ddzz] (ammèzzo) *tr* to leave half-finished (*a piece of work*); to fill halfway; to empty halfway

ammezzato [ddzz] *m* mezzanine

ammiccare §197 *intr* to wink; to cock one's eye

amministrare *tr* to administer, manage

amministra·tóre -trice *mf* administrator, manager; **amministratore delegato** chairman of the board

amministrazióne *f* administration, management: **ordinaria amministrazione** run-of-the-mill business

ammiràbile *adj* admirable

ammiràglia *f* (nav) flagship

ammiragliato *m* admiralty

ammirà·glio *m* (-gli) admiral; **ammiraglio d'armata** admiral; **ammiraglio di divisione** rear admiral; **ammiraglio di squadra** vice admiral; **grande ammiraglio** admiral of the fleet

ammirare *tr* to admire ‖ *intr* to wonder

ammirati·vo -va *adj* admiring; exclamation (*mark*)

ammira·tóre -trice *mf* admirer ‖ *m* suitor

ammirazióne *f* admiration

ammirévole *adj* admirable

ammissibile *adj* admissible; permissible

ammissióne *f* admission; (mach) intake; **ammissione comune** consensus

ammobiliaménto *m* furnishing; furniture

ammobiliare §287 *tr* to furnish

ammodernare (ammodèrno) *tr* to modernize

ammòdo *adj invar* well-mannered, polite ‖ *adv* properly

ammogliare §280 **(ammóglio)** *tr* to marry, give in marriage ‖ *ref* to marry, get married

ammoglia·to *adj* married ‖ *m* married man

ammollare (ammòllo) *tr* to soften; to soak; to slacken (*e.g., a hawser*); to deliver (*a slap*) ‖ *ref* to get soaked

ammollire §176 *tr* to soften; to weaken ‖ *ref* to soften; to mellow

ammoniaca *f* ammonia

ammoniménto *m* warning

ammonire §176 *tr* to admonish, reprimand

ammoni·tóre -trice *adj* warning

ammonizióne *f* admonition, warning

ammontare *m* amount, total ‖ *v* **(ammónto)** *tr* to pile up ‖ *intr* (ESSERE) to amount

ammonticchiare §287 *tr* to pile up, heap up

ammorbare (ammòrbo) *tr* to infect, contaminate

ammorbidènte *m* softener

ammorbidire §176 *tr* to soften; to mitigate ‖ *ref* to soften

ammortaménto *m* amortization; payment, redemption (*of a loan*)

ammortare (ammòrto) *tr* to amortize
ammortire §176 *tr* to deaden; to weaken, soften
ammortizzaménto [ddzz] *m* amortization, amortizement
ammortizzare [ddzz] *tr* to amortize; (aut) to absorb (*shocks*)
ammortizzatóre [ddzz] *m* (aut) shock absorber
ammosciare §128 **(ammóscio)** *tr, intr* & *ref* var of **ammoscire**
ammoscia•to -ta *adj* (coll) downcast
ammoscire §176 *tr* to make sag; to make flabby || *intr* & *ref* to sag; to become flabby; to droop
ammucchiare §287 *tr* to heap up, pile up || *ref* to crowd together
ammuffire §176 *intr* (ESSERE) to become moldy
ammusare *tr* & *intr* to nuzzle
ammutinaménto *m* mutiny, riot
ammutinare (ammùtino & **ammutino)** *tr* to incite to riot || *ref* to mutiny
ammutinato *m* mutineer
ammutolire §176 *intr* (ESSERE) to become silent; to be dumbfounded
amnesìa *f* amnesia
amnistìa *f* amnesty
amnistiare §287 or §119 *tr* to amnesty
amo *m* hook; **abboccare all'amo** to bite, to swallow the hook
amorale *adj* immoral; amoral
amoralÌ•tà *f* (-tà) immorality; amorality
amóre *m* love; eagerness; **amor proprio** amour-propre, self-esteem; **con amore** with pleasure; **d'amore e d'accordo** in perfect agreement; **fare all'amore** to make love; **fare l'amore** to flirt; **per amor del cielo** for heaven's sake; **per amore di** for the sake of; **un amore di bambino** a charming child; **un amore di cappello** a darling hat
amoreggiare §290 **(amoréggio)** *intr* to flirt; to play around
amorévole *adj* loving; kindly
amòr•fo -fa *adj* amorphous; safety (*match*)
amorino *m* cupid; cute child; love seat; (bot) mignonette
amoró•so -sa [s] *adj* loving; kindly; amorous; love (*e.g., life*) || *mf* lover || *m* fiancé || *f* fiancée
amovìbile *adj* removable
amperàg•gio *m* (-gi) amperage
ampère *m* ampere
amperòmetro *m* ammeter
amperóra *m* ampere-hour
ampiézza *f* width, breadth; trajectory (*of a missile*); amplitude; **ampiezza di vedute** open-mindedness
àm•pio -pia *adj* (-pi -pie) ample; wide; roomy
amplèsso *m* (poet) embrace
ampliaménto *m* amplification, extension
ampliare §287 *tr* to enlarge, widen || *ref* to widen
amplificare §197 **(amplìfico)** *tr* to amplify; to widen; to exaggerate
amplifica•tóre *m* (rad & telv) amplifier
amplificazióne *f* amplification
amplitùdine *f* amplitude
ampólla *f* cruet; (eccl) ampulla
ampollièra *f* cruet stand

ampollosi•tà [s] *f* (-tà) grandiloquence, turgidity
ampolló•so -sa [s] *adj* grandiloquent, turgid
amputare **(àmputo)** *tr* to amputate
amputazióne *f* amputation
amulèto *m* amulet, charm
anabbagliante *m* (aut) low beam; **anabbaglianti** (aut) dimmers
anacàr•dio *m* (-di) cashew
ànace *m* var of **anice**
anacorè•ta *m* (-ti) anchorite, hermit
anacronismo *m* anachronism
anacronisti•co -ca *adj* (-ci -che) anachronistic(al)
anàgrafe *m* bureau of vital statistics; registry of births, deaths, and marriages
anagram•ma *m* (-mi) anagram
analcòli•co -ca (-ci -che) *adj* nonalcoholic; soft (*drink*) || *m* soft drink
analfabè•ta *mf* (-ti -te) illiterate
analfabèti•co -ca *adj* (-ci -che) unalphabetized, unalphabetic
analfabetismo *m* illiteracy
analgèsi•co -ca *adj* & *m* (-ci -che) analgesic
anàli•si *f* (-si) analysis; breakdown; **analisi grammaticale** parsing; **analisi dell'urina** urinalysis
anali•sta *mf* (-sti -ste) analyst; **analista finanziario** financial analyst; **analista tempi e metodi** efficiency expert, efficiency engineer
analìti•co -ca *adj* (-ci -che) analytic(al)
analizzare [ddzz] *tr* to analyze; to assay (*ores*); (telv) to scan
analogìa *f* analogy
anàlo•go -ga *adj* (-ghi -ghe) analogous; similar
anamnè•si *f* (-si) (med) case history
ananasso *m* pineapple
anarchìa *f* anarchy
anàrchi•co -ca (-ci -che) *adj* anarchical || *m* anarchist
anatè•ma or **anàte•ma** *m* (-mi) anathema
anatomìa *f* anatomy
anatòmi•co -ca *adj* (-ci -che) anatomic(al)
ànatra *f* duck; drake
anatròccolo *m* duckling
an•ca *f* (-che) hip; (coll) thigh (*e.g., of a chicken*); **dare d'anche** to run away; **menare anca** to walk
ancèlla *f* maidservant
ancestrale *adj* ancestral
anche *adv* also, too; even; (poet) yet; **anche a** + *inf* even if + *ind*
anchilosare **(anchilòso)** *tr* to paralyze || *ref* to become paralyzed
anchilòsto•ma *m* (-mi) hookworm
àn•cia *f* (-ce) (mus) reed
ancillare *adj* servant
ancòra *adv* still, yet; again; more e.g., **ancora cinque minuti** five minutes more
àncora *f* anchor; keeper (*of magnet*); armature (*of buzzer or electric bell*); **ancora di salvezza** last hope; **gettar l'ancora** to cast anchor; **salpare** or **levar l'ancora** to weigh anchor
ancoràg•gio *m* (-gi) anchorage, berth

ancorare (àncoro) *tr* to anchor; to tie (*e.g., a currency to gold*) ‖ *ref* to anchor; to hold fast

ancorché *conj* although

andalu·so -sa *adj & mf* Andalusian

andaménto *m* course, progress

andante *adj* ordinary, common; continuous

andare *m* going; gait; **a lungo andare** in the long run ‖ §106 *intr* (ESSERE) to go; to spread (*said of news*); to be (*e.g., proud*); to work (*said of machinery*); (with *dat*) to fit, e.g., **quel vestito non gli va** that suit does not fit him; (with *dat*) to please, e.g. **quel vestito non le va** that dress does not please her; **andare a cavallo** to go horseback riding; **andare a finire** to wind up; **andare a male** to spoil; **andare a picco** to sink; **andare d'accordo** to agree; **andare in cerca di** to seek; **andare in macchina** to be in press; **andare in onda** (rad & telv) to go on the air; **andare per i vent'anni** to be bordering on twenty years; **andare pazzo per** to be crazy about; **andare soldato** to be drafted; **andare via** to go away; **come va?** how are things?; **mi va il vino dolce** I like sweet wine; **ne va della vita** life is at stake; **va da sé** it goes without saying ‖ *ref*—**andarsene** to go away, leave

anda·to -ta *adj* gone, past; finished; (coll) spoiled (*e.g., meat*) ‖ *f* going; journey, trip; **a lunga andata** in the long run; **andata e ritorno** round trip; **dare l'andata a** to give the go-ahead to

andatura *f* gait; pace; **fare l'andatura** to set the pace

andazzo *m* bad practice, bad habit; fad

Ande, le the Andes

andicappare *tr* to handicap

andi·no -na *adj* Andean

andirivie·ni *m* (-ni) coming and going; maze; ado

àndito *m* corridor, hallway

andróne *m* hall, lobby

aneddòti·co -ca *adj* (-ci -che) anecdotal

anèddoto *m* anecdote

anelante *adj* panting

anelare (anèlo) *tr* to long for ‖ *intr* to yearn; (poet) to pant

anèlito *m* last breath; yearning; (poet) panting; **mandare l'ultimo anelito** to breathe one's last

anellino *m* ringlet

anèllo *m* ring; link (*of a chain*); traffic circle; segment (*of a worm*); (sports) track; **ad anello** ring-shaped; **anello di congiunzione** (fig) link; **anello di fidanzamento** engagement ring ‖ **anella** *fpl* (poet) ringlets; (archaic) rings

anemia *f* anemia

anèmi·co -ca *adj* (-ci -che) anemic

anestesìa *f* anesthesia

anestesi·sta *mf* (-sti -ste) anesthetist

anestèti·co -ca *adj & m* (-ci -che) anesthetic

anestetizzare [ddzz] *tr* to anesthetize

aneuri·sma *m* (-smi) aneurysm

anfi·bio -bia (-bi -bie) *adj* amphibian; (fig) ambiguous ‖ *m* amphibian

anfiteatro *m* amphitheater

anfitrióne *m* (lit) generous host

anfratto *m* ravine; narrow, winding, rugged spot

anfrattuosi·tà [s] *f* (-tà) rough broken ground; winding, rough spot

anfrattuó·so -sa [s] *adj* winding, rough, craggy

angariare §287 *tr* to pester, oppress

angèli·co -ca *adj* (-ci -che) angelic(al)

àngelo *m* angel; **angelo custode** guardian angel

angheria *f* vexation; outrage; imposition

angina *f* quinsy; **angina pectoris** angina pectoris

angipòrto *m* blind alley; narrow lane

anglica·no -na *adj & mf* Anglican

anglicismo *m* Anglicism

anglicizzare [ddzz] *tr* to Anglicize ‖ *ref* to become Anglicized

anglòfo·no -na *adj* English-speaking ‖ *m* English-speaking person

anglosàssone *adj & mf* Anglo-Saxon

angolare *adj* angular; corner (*stone*) ‖ *m* angle iron ‖ *v* (àngolo) *tr* to take an angle shot of; (sports) to kick (*the ball*) into the corner of the goal

angolazióne *f* (mov) angle shot

angolièra *f* corner shelving; corner cupboard

àngolo *m* angle; corner

angoló·so -sa [s] *adj* angular

àngora *f* Angora cat; Angora goat

angò·scia *f* (-sce) anxiety, distress, anguish

angosciare §128 (angòscio) *tr* to distress

angoscia·to -ta *adj* tormented, distressed

angosció·so -sa [s] *adj* agonizing

anguilla *f* eel

anguillé·sco -sca *adj* (-schi -sche) as slippery as an eel

angùria *f* watermelon

angùstia *f* narrowness; scarcity; **stare in angustia** to be worried

angustiare §287 *tr* to distress, grieve ‖ *ref* to worry

angu·sto -sta *adj* narrow

ànice *m* anise

anicino *m* anise cookie

anidride *f* anhydride

àni·dro -dra *adj* anhydrous

anilina *f* aniline

ànima *f* soul; life (*e.g., of the party*); core; kernel; bore (*of gun*); mold (*of button*); mind; enthusiasm; pith (*of fruit*); sounding post (*of violin*); web (*of rail*); **anima dannata** evil counselor; **anima mia!** darling!; **anima nera** villain; **anima viva** living soul; **buon'anima** late, e.g., **mio padre, buon'anima** my late father; **dannare l'anima** to lose patience; **la buon'anima di** the late; **rompere l'anima a** to annoy

animale *adj* animal; (poet) of the soul; (poet) animate ‖ *m* animal; (fig) boor, lout animalé•sco -sca *adj* (-schi -sche) ani-mal, bestial

animare (ànimo) *tr* to animate, to en-liven; to promote ‖ *ref* to become lively or heated

anima•to -ta *adj* animated (*cartoon*); animated, lively; animal

anima•tóre -trice *adj* animating ‖ *m* moving spirit; (mov) animator

animazióne *f* animation

animèlla *f* sweetbread

ànimo *m* mind; heart, affection; cour-age; aprire l'animo to open one's heart; avere in animo di to have a mind to; mal animo ill will; mettersi l'animo in pace to resign oneself; perdersi d'animo to lose heart; ser-bare nell'animo to keep in mind

animosi•tà [-tà] *f* (-tà) animosity, ill will

animó•so -sa [s] *adj* bold; spirited (*animal*); hostile

anióne *m* anion

anisétta *f* anisette

ànitra *f* var of anatra

anitròccolo *m* var of anatroccolo

annacquare (annàcquo) *tr* to water; to water down

annaffiare §287 *tr* to sprinkle; to water (*wine*)

annaffia•tóio *m* (-tói) sprinkling can

annaffia•tóre -trice *f* watering, sprin-kling

annali *mpl* annals *spl*

annaspare *tr* to reel ‖ *intr* to gesticu-late; to grope; to flounder

annata *f* year; year's activity; year's rent; year's issues (*of a magazine*)

annebbiare §287 (annèbbio) *tr* to befog; to dim ‖ *ref* to become foggy; to become dim

annegaménto *m* drowning

annegare §209 (annégo) *tr & intr* (ESSERE) to drown

anneriménto *m* blackening

annerire §176 *tr* to blacken ‖ *ref* to turn black

annessióne *f* annexation

annès•so -sa *adj* united, attached ‖ *m* annex; con tutti gli annessi e con-nessi everything included

annèttere §107 *tr* to annex; to attach, enclose; to unite; to ascribe (*impor-tance*)

annichilante *adj* annihilating; devastat-ing (*e.g., reply*)

annichilire (annìchilo) *tr* to annihilate ‖ *ref* to destroy oneself; (fig) to humble oneself

annichilìre §176 *tr & ref* var of annichi-lare

annidare *tr* to nest; (fig) to nourish, cherish ‖ *ref* to nest; to hide; (fig) to settle

annientaménto *m* annihilation

annientare (anniènto) *tr* to annihilate; to knock down, demolish; (fig) to crush ‖ *ref* to humble oneself

anniversà•rio -ria *adj & m* (-ri -rie) anniversary

anno *m* year; anno bisestile leap year; anno luce light-year; anno nuovo New Year; anno scolastico school year; avere . . . anni to be . . . years old; l'anno che viene next year; l'anno corrente this year; quest'al-tr'anno next year; un anno dopo l'altro year in, year out

annobilire §176 *tr* to ennoble

annodare (annòdo) *tr* to knot, tie; (fig) to tie up ‖ *ref* to get entangled

annoiare §287 (annòio) *tr* to bore ‖ *ref* to become bored

annòna *f* food; food-control agency

annonà•rio -ria *adj* (-ri -rie) food; ra-tioning (*card*)

annó•so -sa [s] *adj* old, aged

annotare (annòto) *tr* to jot down; to chalk up; to annotate; to comment

annotazióne *f* note; notation, annota-tion

annottare (annòtta) *impers* (ESSERE) & *ref* to grow dark, e.g., si annotta it's growing dark; è annottato it grew dark

annoverare (annòvero) *tr* to count, number

annuale *adj* annual ‖ *m* anniversary

annuà•rio *m* (-ri) annual, yearbook

annuire §176 *intr* to nod assent; to consent

annullaménto *m* nullification, annul-ment

annullare *tr* to annul, nullify; cancel; to call off ‖ *ref* to cancel one another

annunciare §128 *tr* var of annunziare

Annunciazióne *f* Annunciation

annunziare §287 *tr* to announce; (fig) to forecast, foreshadow

annunzia•tóre -trice *mf* announcer, newscaster

annùn•zio *m* (-zi) announcement, no-tice; annunzio economico classified ad; annunzio pubblicitario advertise-ment; annunzio pubblicitario radio-fonico (rad) commercial

ànnu•o -a *adj* yearly, annual

annusare [s] *tr* to smell; to snuff (*tobacco*)

annuvolaménto *m* cloudiness

annuvolare (annùvolo) *tr* to cloud, be-cloud ‖ *ref* to become cloudy; to turn somber

anòdi•no -na *adj* pain-relieving; ineffec-tive; weak, colorless (*person*)

ànodo *m* anode

anomalìa *f* anomaly

anòma•lo -la *adj* anomalous

anonimìa *f* anonymity

anòni•mo -ma *adj* anonymous ‖ *m* anonymous author; serbare l'ano-nimo to preserve one's anonymity

anormale *adj* abnormal ‖ *m* queer fellow

anormali•tà *f* (-tà) abnormality

ansa *f* handle (*of vase*); pretext; bend (*of a river*)

ansante *adj* panting

ansare *intr* to pant

ànsia *f* anxiety; essere in ansia to be worried

ansie•tà *f* (-tà) anxiety

ansìmare (ànsimo) *intr* to pant

ansió•so -sa [s] *adj* anxious

antagonismo *m* antagonism

antagoni·sta (-sti -ste) *adj* antagonistic || *mf* antagonist, opponent

antagonìsti·co -ca *adj* (-ci -che) antagonistic

antàrti·co -ca *adj* (-ci -che) antarctic || Antartico *m* Antarctic

antecedènte *adj* preceding || *m* antecedent

antecedènza *f* antecedence

antecessóre *m* predecessor

antefatto *m* background, antecedents

anteguèr·ra (-ra) *adj* prewar || *m* prewar period

anteluca·no -na *adj* (poet) predawn

antenato *m* ancestor

antènna *f* lance; (naut) yard; (rad & telv) aerial, antenna; (zool) antenna

antepórre §218 *tr* to prefer; to place before

anteprima *f* (mov & theat) preview

anterióre *adj* fore, front; previous; earlier

antesignano [s] *m* forerunner

anti- *pref adj* anti-, e.g., anticomunistico anticommunist; un-, e.g., antieconomico uneconomical || *pref mf* anti-, e.g., anticomunista anticomunist

antiabbagliante *adj* antiglare || *m* low beam

antiàci·do -da *adj & m* antacid

antiaère·o -a *adj* antiaircraft || *f* antiaircraft defense

antibattèri·co -ca (-ci -che) *adj* antibacterial || *m* bactericide

antibiòti·co -ca *adj & m* (-ci -che) antibiotic

anticà·glia *f* (-glie) antique, curio; rubbish, junk

anticàmera *f* waiting room, anteroom; fare anticamera to cool one's heels

anticarro *adj invar* antitank

antichi·tà *f* (-tà) antiquity; antichità *fpl* antiques

anticipare (antìcipo) *tr* to advance; to speed up; to pay in advance; to leak (*news*); to expect, anticipate || *intr* to be early

anticipa·to -ta *adj* in advance (*e.g., payment*)

anticipazióne *f* advance; collateral loan; expectation, anticipation

antìcipo *m* advance; loan (*on accounts receivable*); in anticipo in advance

anti·co -ca *adj* (-chi -che) antique, ancient, old; all'antica in the old-fashioned manner; gli antichi the ancients; the forefathers; in antico in olden times

anticoncezionale *adj & f* contraceptive

anticonformi·sta *mf* (-sti -ste) nonconformist

anticonformìsti·co -ca *adj* (-ci -che) unconventional

anticongelante *adj & m* antifreeze

anticongiunturale *adj* crisis, emergency

anticòrpo *m* antibody

anticristo *m* Antichrist

antidatare *tr* to predate

antiderapante *adj* nonskid

antidetonante *adj* antiknock || *m* antiknock compound

antidiluvia·no -na *adj* antediluvian

antidoto *m* antidote

antievanescènza *f* (rad) antifading device

antifecondati·vo -va *adj & m* contraceptive

antifona *f* antiphon; capire l'antifona (fig) to get the message

antifurto *adj invar* antitheft || *m* antitheft device

antigàs *adj invar* gas (*e.g., mask*)

antigièni·co -ca *adj* (-ci -che) unsanitary

antìlope *f* antelope

antimeridia·no -na *adj* antemeridian, A.M.

antimìssile *adj invar* antimissile

antimònio *m* antimony

antincèndio *adj invar* fire-fighting; fire, e.g., scala antincendio fire escape

antinéb·bia *adj invar* fog || *m* (-bia) fog light

antinéve *adj invar* snow, e.g., catena antineve snow chain

antiorà·rio -ria *adj* (-ri -rie) counterclockwise

antipatìa *f* antipathy, dislike

antipàti·co -ca *adj* (-ci -che) antipathetic; disagreeable; uncongenial

antipièga *adj invar* crease-resistant, wrinkle-proof

antìpodi *mpl* antipodes

antipòlio *adj invar* polio (*e.g., vaccine*)

antipòrta *f* stormdoor; corridor

antiquà·rio -ria *adj* (-ri -rie) *adj* antiquarian || *m* antiquary, antiquarian

antiqua·to -ta *adj* obsolete; antiquated

antireligió·so -sa [s] *adj* antireligious, irreligious

antirùggine *adj invar* antirust

antirumóre *adj invar* antinoise

antisala [s] *f* anteroom, waiting room

antisassi [s] *adj invar* protecting against falling stones

antischiavi·sta *adj & mf* (-sti -ste) abolitionist

antisemi·ta [s] (-ti -te) *adj* anti-Semitic || *mf* anti-Semite

antisemìti·co -ca [s] *adj* (-ci -che) anti-Semitic

antisemitìsmo [s] *m* anti-Semitism

antisètti·co -ca [s] *adj & m* (-ci -che) antiseptic

antisociale [s] *adj* antisocial

antisóle [s] *adj invar* sun (*glasses*); suntan (*lotion*)

antisommergìbile [s] *adj* antisubmarine

antistatale *adj* antigovernment

antitàrmi·co -ca *adj* (-ci -che) mothproof

antitèmpo *adv* early, prematurely

antìte·si *f* (-si) antithesis

antitèti·co -ca *adj* (-ci -che) antithetic(al)

antitossina *f* antitoxin

antiuòmo *adj invar* (mil) antipersonnel

antivigìlia *f*—l'antivigilia di two days before

antologìa *f* anthology

antònimo *m* antonym

antrace *m* anthrax

antracite *f* anthracite

antro *m* cave; den, hovel

antròpi·co -ca *adj* (**-ci -che**) human

antropofagìa *f* cannibalism

antropòfa·go -ga (**-gi -ghe**) *adj* cannibalistic ‖ *m* cannibal

antropòide *adj* anthropoid

antropologìa *f* anthropology

antropomòrfi·co -ca *adj* (**-ci -che**) anthropomorphic

antropomòr·fo -fa *adj* see **scimmia**

anulare *adj* ring-shaped, annular ‖ *m* ring finger

Anvèrsa *f* Antwerp

anzi *adv* on the contrary, rather; **anzi che no** rather ‖ *prep* (poet) before

anziani·tà *f* (**-tà**) seniority

anzia·no -na *adj* old, elderly; senior ‖ *m* senior

anziché *conj* rather than

anzidét·to -ta *adj* aforesaid

anzitutto *adv* above all, first of all

apatìa *f* apathy

apàti·co -ca *adj* (**-ci -che**) apathetic

ape *f* bee; **ape operaia** worker; **ape regina** queen bee

aperitivo *m* apéritif

apèr·to -ta *adj* open; frank, candid ‖ *m* open space; **all'aperto** in the open

apertura *f* opening; aperture; approach; **ad apertura di libro** at sight; **apertura alare** (*of a bird*) wingspread; (aer) wingspan

apià·rio *m* (**-ri**) apiary

àpice *m* apex, top; climax

apicol·tóre -trice *mf* beekeeper, apiarist

apicoltura *f* beekeeping, apiculture

Apocalisse *f* Apocalypse, Revelation

apocalìtti·co -ca *adj* (**-ci -che**) apocalyptic(al)

apòcri·fo -fa *adj* apocryphal

apofonìa *f* ablaut

apogèo *m* apogee

apòlide *adj* stateless ‖ *m* man without a country

apolìti·co -ca *adj* (**-ci -che**) nonpolitical, nonpartisan

apologè·ta *m* (**-ti**) apologist

apologèti·co -ca *adj* (**-ci -che**) apologetic

apologìa *f* apology

apòlo·go *m* (**-ghi**) apologue

apoplessìa *f* apoplexy

apoplètti·co -ca *adj & m* (**-ci -che**) apoplectic

apostasìa *f* apostasy

apòsta·ta *mf* (**-ti -te**) apostate

apostolato *m* apostolate

apostòli·co -ca *adj* (**-ci -che**) apostolic(al)

apòstolo *m* apostle

apostrofare (**apòstrofo**) *tr* to write with an apostrophe; to apostrophize

apòstrofe *f* apostrophe (*to a person*)

apòstrofo *m* (gram) apostrophe

apoteò·si *f* (**-si**) apotheosis

appagare §209 *tr* to satisfy, gratify ‖ *ref*—**appagarsi di** to be content with

appaiare §287 *tr* to pair, couple; to match ‖ *ref* to match (*said, e.g., of colors*)

appallottolare (**appallòttolo**) *tr* to crumple into a ball ‖ *ref* to become lumpy

appaltare *tr* to contract for

appalta·tóre -trice *mf* contractor

appalto *m* contract; state monopoly; **appalto di sali e tabacchi** tobacco shop

appannàg·gio *m* (**-gi**) appanage; (fig) prerogative

appannare *tr* to tarnish; to befog, becloud ‖ *ref* to become clouded (*said, e.g., of one's eyesight*)

apparato *m* decoration; display; appliance; leadership (*of political party*); (rad, telv) set

apparecchiare §287 (**apparécchio**) *tr* to prepare; to set (*the table*) ‖ *ref* to get ready

apparecchiatura *f* sizing (*of paper; of a wall*); preparation (*of a canvas*); apparatus

apparéc·chio *m* (**-chi**) apparatus; sizing; preparation; gadget; (rad, telv) set; airplane; **apparecchio da caccia** fighter plane; **apparecchio telefonico** telephone

apparentare (**apparènto**) *tr* to tie, unite (*through marriage*) ‖ *ref* to become related; to become intimate; (pol) to form a coalition

apparènte *adj* apparent, seeming

apparènza *f* appearance; **in apparenza** seemingly

apparigliare §280 *tr* to pair, team (*horses*)

apparire §108 *intr* (ESSERE) to appear, seem; to look

appariscènte *adj* showy, flashy, gaudy

apparizióne *f* apparition; appearance

appartaménto *m* apartment

appartare *tr* to set aside ‖ *ref* to withdraw, retire

apparta·to -ta *adj* secluded, solitary

appartenènza *f* belonging, membership; **appartenenze** accessories; annexes

appartenére §271 *intr* (ESSERE & AVERE) to belong; to pertain ‖ *impers* (ESSERE & AVERE)—**appartiene a** it behooves, it is up to

appassionaménto *m* excitement, interest, enthusiasm

appassionare (**appassióno**) *tr* to move; to interest; to excite ‖ *ref* to be deeply interested

appassiona·to -ta *adj* impassioned; deep, ardent ‖ *m* fan, amateur

appassire §176 *intr* (ESSERE) to wilt, wither; to decay; to dry up (*said, e.g., of grapes*)

appellare (**appèllo**) *tr* (law) to appeal; (poet) to call ‖ *ref* to appeal; **appellarsi da** or **contro** (law) to appeal

appèllo *m* call, roll call; **fare appello a** to summon (*e.g., one's strength*); **fare l'appello** to call the roll; **mancare all'appello** to be absent

appéna *adv* hardly, scarcely; only; just ‖ *conj* as soon as; **non appena as** soon as, no sooner

appèndere §109 *tr* to hang

appendice *f* appendix; feuilleton

appendicectomìa *f* appendectomy

appendicite *f* appendicitis

Appennino, l' *m* the Appennines

appesantire [s] §176 *tr* to make heavy; to burden, overwhelm || *ref* to get heavy; to get fat

appestare (appèsto) *tr* to infect; to stink up

appesta·to -ta *adj* plague-ridden || *m* plague victim ·

appetire §176 *tr* to crave, long for || *intr* (ESSERE & AVERE) to be appetizing

appetito *m* appetite

appetitó·so -sa [s] *adj* appetizing, tempting

appètto *adv* opposite; appetto a opposite; in comparison with

appezzaménto *m* plot, parcel (*of land*)

appianare *tr* to smooth, level; to settle (*a dispute*); to get around (*a difficulty*)

appiana·tóio *m* (-tói) road grader

appiattare *tr* & *ref* to hide

appiattiménto *m* leveling; equalization

appiattire §176 *tr* & *ref* to flatten, to level

appiccare §197 *tr* to hang; appiccare il fuoco a to set on fire; appiccare una lite to pick a fight

appicciare §128 *tr* (coll) to string together; (coll) to kindle, light

appiccicare §197 (appìccico) *tr* to stick, glue; appiccicare uno schiaffo a to slap || *ref* to stick, adhere

appiccicatíc·cio -cia *adj* (-ci -ce) sticky

appic·co *m* (-chi) grip; steep wall (*of mountain*); (fig) pretext

appiè *adv*—appiè di at the foot of; at the bottom of

appiedare (appièdo) *tr* to order (*a cavalryman*) off a horse; to order (*e.g., troops*) off a vehicle; to force out of a car (*said, e.g., of motor trouble*)

appièno *adv* (poet) fully

appigionare (appigióno) *tr* to rent || *ref*—appigionasi for rent

appigiónasi [s] *m* for-rent sign

appigliare §280 *ref* to cling, adhere; appigliarsi a un pretesto to seize a pretext

appì·glio *m* (-gli) grip; (fig) pretext

appiómbo *m* perpendicular || *adv* plumb, perpendicularly

appioppare (appiòppo) *tr* to plant with poplar trees; to tie (*a vine*) to a poplar tree; (coll) to deliver (*a blow*); (coll) to pass off (*e.g., inferior goods*)

appisolare (appisolo) *ref* to snooze, doze

applaudire §176 & (applàudo) *tr* to applaud || *intr* to applaud, clap the hands; (with *dat*) to applaud

applàuso *m* applause; applausi applause

applicàbile *adj* applicable

applicare §197 (applico) *tr* to apply; to attach; to give (*e.g., a slap*); to put into effect (*a law*); to assign || *ref* to apply oneself

applica·to -ta *adj* applied; appliqué || *m* clerk

applicazióne *f* application; appliqué

applique *m* (elec) wall fixture

appoggiaca·po *m* (-po) headrest; tidy (*on back of chair*)

appoggiagómi·ti *m* (-ti) elbowrest

appoggiama·no *m* (-no) mahlstick

appoggiare §290 (appòggio) *tr* to lean; to rest; to prop, support; to raise (*the tone of voice*); to give (*a slap*); to second (*a motion*); (fig) to back, support || *intr* to lean; to rest || *ref*—appoggiarsi a or su to lean on

appoggia·tóio *m* (-tói) support, rest; banister

appoggiatura *f* (mus) grace note

appòg·gio *m* (-gi) support, prop; backer; backing, support; grip; (mach) bearing

appollaiare §287 *ref* to roost

appórre §218 *tr* to affix, append

apportare (appòrto) *tr* to cause; to presage; (poet) to carry

appòrto *m* carrying; contribution; (law) share

appositaménte *adv* expressly, on purpose

appòsi·to -ta *adj* proper, fitting

apposizióne *f* apposition

appòsta *adj invar* suitable || *adv* on purpose, expressly, intentionally

appostaménto *m* ambush

appostare (appòsto) *tr* to ambush || *ref* to lie in ambush

apprèndere §220 *tr* to learn || *ref* (poet) to take hold

apprendi·sta *mf* (-sti -ste) apprentice

apprendistato *m* apprenticeship

apprensióne *f* apprehension, fear

apprensí·vo -va *adj* apprehensive

appressare (apprèsso) *tr* (poet) to approach || *ref* to come near

appresso *adj invar* next, following || *adv* near; later on; appresso a near; after

apprestare (apprèsto) *tr* to prepare; to supply, provide (*e.g., help*) || *ref* to prepare, get ready

apprettare (apprètto) *tr* to dress (*leather*); to size (*cloth*)

apprètto *m* tan (*for leather*); sizing (*for cloth*)

apprezzàbile *adj* appreciable

apprezzaménto *m* appreciation; estimation

apprezzare (apprèzzo) *tr* to appreciate

apprezza·to -ta *adj* esteemed

appròc·cio *m* (-ci) approach; approcci advances

approdare (appròdo) *intr* (ESSERE & AVERE) to land; (with *dat*) (poet) to benefit; approdare a to come to

appròdo *m* landing

approfittare *intr*—approfittare di to capitalize on || *ref*—approfittarsi di to take advantage of

approfondire §176 *tr* to make deep; to study thoroughly || *ref*—approfondirsi in to go deep into

approntare (apprónto) *tr* to prepare, make ready

appropriare §287 (appròprio) *tr* to adapt; to bestow || *ref*—appropriarsi a to befit; appropriarsi di to appropriate; to embezzle appròpria·to -ta *adj* appropriate

appropriazióne *f* appropriation; appropriazione indebita fraudulent conversion, embezzlement

approssimare (appròssimo) *tr* to bring near ‖ *ref* to approach, come near

approssimati·vo -va *adj* approximate

approssimazióne *f* approximation

approvàbile *adj* laudable

approvare (appròvo) *tr* to approve, countenance; to subscribe to (*an opinion*); to pass (*a student; a law*); to confirm

approvazióne *f* approval; confirmation; passage (*of a law*)

approvvigionaménto *m* supply

approvvigionare (approvvigióno) *tr* to supply ‖ *ref* to be supplied

appuntaménto *m* appointment; date; appuntamento amoroso assignation

appuntare *tr* to sharpen; to fasten, pin; to stick (*a pin*) in; to point; to jot down, take note of; to prick up (*one's ears*); (fig) to reproach ‖ *ref* to be turned; to aim

appunta·to -ta *adj* sharpened ‖ *m* corporal (*of Italian police*)

appuntellare (appuntèllo) *tr* to shore up, prop up

appuntellatura *f* shoring up, propping up

appuntino *adv* precisely, meticulously

appuntire §176 *tr* to sharpen

appunti·to -ta *adj* sharp, pointed

appunto *m* note; blame, charge; muovere un appunto a to blame; per l'appunto just, precisely ‖ *adv* exactly, precisely

appurare *tr* to ascertain

appuzzare *tr* to befoul, pollute

apribotti·glie *m* (-glie) bottle opener

apri·co -ca *adj* (-chi -che) (poet) sunny, bright

aprile *m* April

apripi·sta *m* (-sta) blade (*of bulldozer*); bulldozer

aprire §110 *tr* to open; to turn on; to dig (*e.g., a grave*) ‖ *ref* to open; to clear up (*said of the weather*); aprirsi con to open one's heart to; aprirsi il varco fra to press through

apriscàto·le *m* (-le) can opener

aquà·rio *m* (-ri) aquarium ‖ **Aquario** *m* (astr) Aquarius

aquàti·co -ca *adj* (-ci -che) aquatic

àquila *f* eagle; genius

aquili·no -na *adj* aquiline

aquilóne *m* north wind; kite

aquilòtto *m* eaglet; cadet (*in Italian Air Force Academy*)

Aquinate, l' *m* Saint Thomas Aquinas

ara *f* (poet) altar; are (*100 square meters*)

arabé·sca *f* (-sche) (mus) arabesque

arabesca·to -ta *adj* arabesque

arabé·sco -sca (-schi -sche) *adj* arabesque ‖ *m* arabesque; doodle ‖ *f* see arabesca

Aràbia, l' *f* Arabia

aràbi·co -ca *adj* (-ci -che) Arabic

aràbile *adj* tillable

àra·bo -ba *adj* Arabic, Arabian ‖ *mf* Arab (*person*) ‖ *m* Arabic (*language*)

aragonése [s] *adj & mf* Aragonese

aragósta *f* (*Palinurus vulgaris*) lobster

aràldi·co -ca (-ci -che) *adj* heraldic ‖ *f* heraldry

araldo *m* herald

arancéto *m* orange grove

aràn·cia *f* (-ce) orange

aranciata *f* orangeade

aràn·cio *adj invar* orange (*in color*) ‖ *m* (-ci) orange tree

arancióne *adj & m* orange (*color*)

arare *tr* to plow; (naut) to drag (*the anchor*)

aratro *m* plow

arazzo *m* tapestry, arras

arbitràg·gio *m* (-gi) (sports) umpiring; (com) arbitrage

arbitrale *adj* judge's, umpire's

arbitrare (àrbitro) *tr* to umpire, referee ‖ *intr* to arbitrate ‖ *ref*—arbitrarsi di to take the liberty to

arbitrà·rio -ria *adj* (-ri -rie) arbitrary; wanton

arbitrato *m* arbitration

arbì·trio *m* (-tri) will; abuse, violation; libero arbitrio free will

àrbitro *m* arbiter; judge, referee, umpire

arboscèllo *m* small tree

arbusto *m* shrub, bush

ar·ca *f* (-che) sarcophagus; ark; chest; arca di Noè Noah's Ark; arca di scienza (fig) fountain of knowledge

àrcade *adj & m* Arcadian

Arcàdia *f* Arcadia, Arcady

arcài·co -ca *adj* (-ci -che) archaic

arcaismo *m* archaism

arcàngelo *m* archangel

arca·no -na *adj* mysterious, arcane ‖ *m* mystery

arcata *f* arch; arcade

archeologìa *f* archaeology

archeològi·co -ca *adj* (-ci -che) archaeological

archeòlo·go -ga *mf* (-gi -ghe) archaeologist

archètipo *m* archetype

archétto *m* (archit) small arch; (elec) trolley pole; (mus) bow

archi- *pref adj* archi-, e.g., architettonico architectonic ‖ *pref m & f* archi-, e.g., architettura architecture

archibù·gio *m* (-gi) harquebus

Archimède *m* Archimedes

architettare (architétto) *tr* to plan (*a building*); (fig) to contrive, plot

architétto *m* architect

architettòni·co -ca *adj* (-ci -che) architectural

architettura *f* architecture

architetturale *adj* architectural

architrave *m* architrave; doorhead, lintel

archiviare §287 *tr* to file; to lay aside, shelve; (law) to throw out

archi·vio *m* (-vi) archives; record office; chancery, public records

archivi·sta *mf* (-sti -ste) archivist, file clerk

arci- *pref adj* archi-, e.g., **arcivescovile** archiepiscopal ‖ *pref m & f* arch-, e.g., **arciprete** archpriest
arcicontèn•to -ta *adj* (coll) very glad
arcidiàcono *m* archdeacon
arcidu•ca *m* (-**chi**) archduke
arciduchéssa *f* archduchess
arcière *m* archer, bowman
arci•gno -gna *adj* gruff, surly
arcióne *m* saddlebow; **montare in arcioni** to mount, to mount a horse
arcipèla•go *m* (-**ghi**) archipelago
arciprète *m* archpriest; dean
arcivescovado *m* archbishopric
arcivéscovo *m* archbishop
ar•co *m* (-**chi**) bow; (archit) arch; (geom, elec) arc; **arco rampante** flying buttress
arcobaléno *m* rainbow
arco•làio *m* (-**làI**) reel; **girare come un arcolaio** to spin like a top
arcuare (**àrcuo**) *tr* to arch; to bend; to camber
arcua•to -ta *adj* bent, curved; bow (*e.g., legs*); **avere le gambe arcuate** to be bowlegged
ardènte *adj* burning; hot; ardent, impassioned
àrdere §111 *tr* to burn ‖ *intr* to burn; to be in full swing (*said, e.g., of a war*)
ardèsia *f* slate
ardiménto *m* boldness, daring
ardire *m* boldness; presumption, impudence ‖ §176 *intr*—**ardire** + *inf* or **ardire di** + *inf* to dare to + *inf*
arditézza *f* daring; temerity
ardi•to -ta *adj* daring; rash ‖ *m* (hist) shock trooper
ardóre *m* intense heat; ardor
àr•duo -dua *adj* arduous
àrea *f* area, surface; group, camp; **area arretrata** backward area
àrem *m* (**àrem**) harem
arèna *f* arena; **scendere nell'arena** to throw one's hat in the ring
aréna *f* sand
arenare (**aréno**) *intr* (ESSERE) & *ref* to run aground
arenària *f* sandstone
arén•go *m* (-**ghi**) (hist) town meeting
arenile *m* sandy beach
arenó•so -sa [*s*] *adj* sandy
areòmetro *m* hydrometer
aeronàuti•co -ca *adj & f* (-**ci** -**che**) var of **aeronautico**
areoplano *m* var of **aeroplano**
areopòrto *m* var of **aeroporto**
areòstato *m* var of **aerostato**
àrgano *m* winch; (naut) capstan
argentare (**argènto**) *tr* to silver; to silver-plate; to back (*a mirror*) with foil
argenta•to -ta *adj* silver; silvery; silver-plated
argentatura *f* silver plating; silver plate; foil (*of mirror*)
argènte•o -a *adj* silver, silvery
argenteria *f* silverware
argentière *m* silversmith; jeweler
argenti•no -na *adj* silver, silvery; Argentine ‖ *mf* Argentine ‖ *f* high-necked sweater ‖ **l'Argentina** *f* Argentina

argènto *m* silver; (archaic) money; **argenti** silverware; **argento vivo** quicksilver
argentóne *m* German silver
argilla *f* clay
argilló•so -sa [*s*] *adj* clayey
arginare (**àrgino**) *tr* to dam, dike; to hold back, check
àrgine *m* embankment, dam; (fig) defense
ar•go *m* (-**ghi**) (chem) argon; (orn) grouse ‖ **Argo** *m* Argus
argomentare (**argoménto**) *tr & intr* to argue
argomentazióne *f* argumentation, discussion
argoménto *m* argument; pretext; subject; **fuori dell'argomento** beside the point
argonàu•ta *m* (-**ti**) Argonaut
arguire §176 *tr* to deduce, infer; (archaic) to denote
argutézza *f* wit; witty remark
argu•to -ta *adj* keen, acute; witty
argùzia *f* keenness; wit
ària *f* air; climate; look; mien; aria, tune; poem; **all'aria aperta** in the open air; **a mezz'aria** in midair; halfway; **andare all'aria** to fail; **aria condizionata** air conditioning; **avere l'aria di** to seem to; to look like; **dare aria a** to air; **in aria** in the air; **tira un'aria pericolosa** a mean wind is blowing
aria•no -na *adj & mf* Aryan
aridi•tà *f* (-**tà**) dryness, aridity; dearth
àri•do -da *adj* arid, dry, barren; (fig) dry
arieggiare §290 (**ariéggio**) *tr* to air; to imitate ‖ *ref*—**arieggiarsi a** to give oneself the airs of
ariète *m* ram; (mil) battering ram ‖ **Ariete** *m* (astr) Aries
ariétta *s* breeze; (mus) short aria
arin•ga *f* (-**ghe**) herring; **aringa affumicata** kippered herring, kipper
arin•go *m* (-**ghi**) assembly; field; joust; **scendere nell'aringo** to throw one's hat in the ring
arió•so -sa [*s*] *adj* airy, breezy; (fig) of wide scope
àrista *f* loin of pork
arista *f* (bot) awn
aristocràti•co -ca (-**ci** -**che**) *adj* aristocratic ‖ *mf* aristocrat
aristocrazìa *f* aristocracy
Aristòtele *m* Aristotle
aristotèli•co -ca *adj & m* (-**ci** -**che**) Aristotelian
aritmèti•co -ca (-**ci** -**che**) *adj* arithmetical ‖ *m* arithmetician ‖ *f* arithmetic
arlecchino *adj invar* harlequin; fiesta (*e.g., dishes*) ‖ **Arlecchino** *m* Harlequin
ar•ma *f* (-**mi**) arm, weapon; (fig) army; (mil) corps, service; **alle prime armi** at the beginning; **arma bianca** steel blade; **arma da taglio** cutting weapon; **arma delle trasmissioni** signal corps
armacòllo *m*—**ad armacollo** slung across the shoulders (*said of a rifle*)
armà•dio *m* (-**di**) cabinet; closet; **armadio a muro** built-in closet; **armadio**

d'angolo corner cupboard; **armadio farmaceutico** medicine cabinet; **armadio guardaroba** armoire

armaiòlo *m* gunsmith

armamentà·rio *m* (**-ri**) outfit, set (*of tools*)

armaménto *m* armament; crew; gun crew; crew (*of rowboat*); outfit, equipment

armare *tr* to arm; to dub (*s.o. a knight*); to outfit, commission (*a ship*); to cock (*a gun*); to brace, shore up (*a building*); (rr) to furnish with track || *ref* to arm oneself; to outfit oneself

arma·to -ta *adj* armed; reinforced (*concrete*) || *m* soldier || *f* army; navy; fleet; (nav) task force

arma·tóre -trice *adj* outfitting || *m* shipowner; (min) carpenter; (rr) trackwalker

armatura *f* armor; scaffold; framework, support; reinforcement (*for concrete*); (elec) plate (*of condenser*)

armeggiare §290 (**arméggio**) *intr* to fumble, fool around; to scheme; (archaic) to handle arms; (archaic) to joust

armeggì·o *m* (**-i**) fooling around; scheming, intriguing

arme·no -na *adj* & *mf* Armenian

arménto *m* herd

armerìa *f* armory

armière *m* (aer) gunner

armìge·ro -ra *adj* warlike, bellicose || *m* warrior; bodyguard

armistiziale *adj* armistice

armistì·zio *m* (**-zi**) *m* armistice

armonìa *f* harmony; **in armonia con** according to

armòni·co -ca (**-ci -che**) *adj* harmonic; resonant; harmonious || *f* harmònica; **armonica a bocca** mouth organ

armonió·so -sa [s] *adj* harmonious

armonizzare [ddzz] *tr* & *intr* to harmonize

arnése [s] *m* tool, implement; garb, dress; (coll) gadget; **bene in arnese** well-heeled; **male in arnese** down at the heels

àrnia *f* beehive

arò·ma *m* (**-mi**) aroma, odor; zest

aromàti·co -ca *adj* (**-ci -che**) aromatic

aromatizzare [ddzz] *tr* to flavor; to spice

arpa *f* harp

arpeggiare §290 (**arpéggio**) *intr* to play arpeggios; to play a harp; to strum

arpég·gio *m* (**-gi**) arpeggio

arpìa *f* Harpy; (coll) harpy

arpionare (**arpióno**) *tr* to harpoon

arpióne *m* hinge (*of door*); hook; harpoon; spike (*for mountain climbing*)

arpionismo *m* ratchet

arpì·sta *mf* (**-sti -ste**) harpist

arrabattare *ref* to exert oneself, to strive, to endeavor

arrabbiare §287 *intr* (ESSERE) to go mad (*said of dogs*) || *ref* to become angry (*said of people*)

arrabbià·to -ta *adj* mad (*dog*); angry; obstinate; confirmed

arrabbiatura *f* rage; **prendersi un'arrabbiatura** to burn up (*with rage*)

arraffare *tr* to snatch

arrampicare §197 (**arràmpico**) *ref* to climb, climb up

arrampicata *f* climbing

arrampica·tóre -trice *mf* climber; mountain climber; **arrampicatore sociale** social climber

arrancare §197 *intr* to hobble, limp; to struggle, work hard; to row hard

arrangiaménto *m* agreement; (mus) arrangement

arrangiare §290 *tr* to arrange; to fix; (coll) to steal || *ref* to manage, get along

arrecare §197 (**arrèco**) *tr* to cause; to carry, deliver

arredaménto *m* furnishing; furnishings; equipment

arredare (**arrèdo**) *tr* to furnish; to equip

arreda·tóre -trice *mf* interior decorator; upholsterer; (mov) property man

arrèdo *m* furnishings, furniture; piece of furniture; **arredi sacri** church supplies

arrembàg·gio *m* (**-gi**) boarding (*of a ship*)

arrenare (**arréno**) *tr* to sand

arrèndere §227 *tr* (archaic) to surrender || *ref* to surrender; **arrendersi a discrezione** to surrender unconditionally

arrendévole *adj* yielding, compliant, flexible

arrendevolézza *f* suppleness; compliance

arrestare (**arrèsto**) *tr* to stop; to arrest || *ref* to stop, stay

arrèsto *m* arrest; stop; pause; (mach) stop, catch; **arresti** (mil) house arrest; **in stato d'arresto** under arrest

arretrare (**arrètro**) *tr* to withdraw || *intr* (ESSERE & AVERE) & *ref* to withdraw

arretra·to -ta *adj* withdrawn; backward; back (*issue*); overdue || **arretrati** *mpl* arrears

arricchiménto *m* enrichment

arricchire §176 *tr* to enrich || *intr* (ESSERE) & *ref* to get rich

arricchì·to -ta *mf* nouveau riche

arricciacapél·li *m* (**-li**) curler

arricciare §128 *tr* to curl; to wrinkle; to screw up (*one's nose*); **arricciare il pelo** to bristle (*said of a person*); to bristle up (*said of an animal*) || *ref* to curl up

arriccia·to -ta *adj* curled up || *m* first coat (*of cement*)

arricciatura *f* curling (*of hair*); pleating (*of a skirt*); kink (*in a rope*)

arrìdere §231 *tr* (poet) to grant || *intr* to smile

arrìn·ga *f* (**-ghe**) harangue; (law) lawyer's plea

arringare §209 *tr* to harangue; (law) to plead

arrischiare §287 *tr* to endanger; to risk || *ref* to dare, venture

arrischia·to -ta *adj* risky; daring

arrivare *tr* to reach || *intr* (ESSERE) to arrive; to happen; to get along, be successful; **arrivare a** to reach; to succeed in

arriva·to -ta *adj* arrived; successful; **ben arrivato** welcome

arrivedér·ci *m* (-ci) good-bye || *interj* good-bye!, so long!

arrivedéria *interj* good-bye!

arrivismo *m* social climbing, ruthless ambition

arrivi·sta *mf* (-sti -ste) social climber

arrivo *m* arrival; (sports) goal line; (sports) finishing line

arroccare §197 (arròcco) *tr* to put (*e.g.*, flax) on the distaff || §197 (arròcco) *tr* to shelter; (chess) to castle || *ref* to seek shelter; (chess) to castle

arròc·co *m* (-chi) castling

arrochire §176 *tr* to make hoarse || *intr* (ESSERE) to become hoarse

arrogante *adj* arrogant, insolent

arroganza *f* arrogance, insolence

arrogare §209 (arrògo) *tr*—**arrogare a sé** to arrogate to oneself || *ref* to arrogate to oneself

arrolare §237 *tr* var of **arruolare**

arrossare (arrósso) *tr* to redden

arrossire §176 *intr* (ESSERE) to blush; to change color

arrostire §176 *tr* to roast; to toast; **arrostire allo spiedo** to barbecue on the spit || *intr* (ESSERE) & *ref* to roast

arrò·sto *m* (-sto & -sti) roast

arrotare (arròto) *tr* to grind, hone; to smooth; to strike, run over; to grit (*one's teeth*) || *ref* to grind (*to work hard*); to sideswipe

arrotatrice *f* floor sander

arrotatura *f* sharpening

arrotino *m* grinder

arrotolare (arròtolo) *tr* to roll

arrotondaménto *m* rounding; rounding out; increase (*in salary*)

arrotondare (arrotóndo) *tr* to make round; to round out; to supplement (*a salary*) || *ref* to round out, become plump

arrovellare (arrovèllo) *tr* to vex || *ref* to become angry; to strive, endeavor; **arrovellarsi il cervello** to rack one's brains

arroventare (arrovènto) *tr* to make red-hot || *ref* to become red-hot

arroventire §176 *tr* & *ref* var of **arroventare**

arruffapòpo·li *m* (-li) rabble-rouser

arruffare *tr* to tangle; to muss, rumple; to confuse

arruf·fío *m* (-fii) tangle; confusion, mess

arruffó·ne -na *mf* blunderer; swindler

arrugginire §176 *tr*, *intr* (ESSERE) & *ref* to rust

arruolaménto *m* enlistment; draft

arruolare (arruòlo) *tr* to recruit; to draft || *ref* to enlist

arruvidire §176 *tr* to make rough, roughen || *intr* (ESSERE) to become rough

arsenale *m* arsenal; navy yard

arsèni·co -ca (-ci -che) *adj* arsenic, arsenical || *m* arsenic

ar·so -sa *adj* burnt; dry, parched; **arso di** consumed with

arsura *f* sultriness; dryness

arte *f* art; ability; guile; **ad arte** on purpose; **arti e mestieri** arts and crafts

artefare §173 *tr* to adulterate

artefat·to -ta *adj* adulterated; artificial

artéfice *m* craftsman; creator

artèria *f* artery

arterioscleròsi *m* arteriosclerosis

arterió·so -sa [s] *adj* arterial

artesia·no -na *adj* artesian

àrti·co -ca *adj* (-ci -che) arctic || **Artico** *m* Arctic

articolare *adj* articular || *v* (**articolo**) *tr* & *ref* to articulate

articola·to -ta *adj* articulated; articulate; (gram) combined; jagged (*coastline*)

articolazióne *f* articulation

articoli·sta *mf* (-sti -ste) columnist; feature writer

artícolo *m* article; item; paragraph; **articolo di fondo** editorial; **articolo di spalla** comment

artificiale *adj* artificial

artificière *m* pyrotechnist; (mil) demolition expert

artifi·cio *m* (-ci) artifice; sophistication, affectation; **artificio d'illuminazione** (mil) flare

artificiosi·tà [s] *f* (-tà) artfulness, craftiness; artificiality

artifició·so -sa [s] *adj* artful, crafty; artificial, affected

artigianato *m* craftsmanship

artigia·no -na *adj* of craftsmen || *m* craftsman

artigliare §280 *tr* (poet) to claw

artiglière *m* artilleryman

artiglieria *f* artillery; **artiglieria a cavallo** mounted artillery

artí·glio *m* (-gli) claw; **cadere negli artigli di** to fall into the clutches of

arti·sta *mf* (-sti -ste) artist; actor

artìsti·co -ca *adj* (-ci -che) artistic

ar·to -ta *adj* (poet) narrow || *m* limb

artrite *f* arthritis

artríti·co -ca *adj* & *mf* (-ci -che) arthritic

arturia·no -na *adj* Arthurian

arzigogolare [dz] (arzigògolo) *intr* to muse; to cavil

arzigògolo [dz] *m* fantasy; cavil

arzil·lo -la [dz] *adj* lively, sprightly; (coll) sparkling (*wine*)

arzin·ga *f* (-ghe) tong (*of a blacksmith*)

asbèsto *m* asbestos

ascèlla *f* armpit

ascendènte *adj* ascendant || *m* upper hand, ascendancy; **ascendenti** forefathers

ascendènza *f* ancestry, lineage

ascéndere §245 *tr* to climb || *intr* (ESSERE & AVERE) to ascend, climb

ascensionale *adj* rising; lifting

ascensióne *f* ascent, climb || **Ascensione** *f* Ascension, Ascension Day

ascensóre *m* elevator

ascésa [s] *f* ascent

ascèsso *m* abscess

ascè·ta *mf* (-ti -te) ascetic

ascèti·co -ca *adj* (-ci -che) ascetic

ascetismo *m* asceticism

à·scia *f* (-sce) adze

asciugacapél·li *m* (**-li**) hair drier

asciugamano *m* towel; **asciugamano spugna** Turkish towel

asciugante *adj* drying; blotting; soaking ‖ *m* dryer

asciugare §209 *tr* to dry, dry up; to wipe; to drain (*e.g., a glass of wine*) ‖ *ref* to dry oneself; to dry, dry up

asciuga-tóio *m* (**-tói**) towel; bath towel

asciugatrice *f* dryer

asciut·to **-ta** *adj* dry; skinny; blunt (*in speech*) ‖ *m* dry land; dry climate; **all'asciutto** pennyless

ascoltare (**ascólto**) *tr* to listen to ‖ *intr* to listen

ascolta·tóre -trice *mf* listener

ascólto *m* listening; **stare in ascolto** to listen

ascòrbi·co -ca *adj* (**-ci -che**) ascorbic

ascrit·to -ta *adj* ascribed; belonging ‖ *m* member

ascrìvere §250 *tr* to inscribe, register; to ascribe, attribute

ascultare *tr* to sound (*s.o.'s chest*)

asèpsi [s] *f* asepsis

asètti·co -ca [s] *adj* (**-ci -che**) aseptic

asfaltare *tr* to tar, pave

asfalto *m* asphalt

asfissìa *f* asphyxia

asfissiante *adj* asphyxiating; poison (*gas*); boring

asfissiare §287 *tr* to asphyxiate; to bore ‖ *intr* (ESSERE) to be asphyxiated

asfodèlo *m* asphodel

Àsia, l' *f* Asia; **l'Asia Minore** Asia Minor

asiàti·co -ca *adj & mf* (**-ci -che**) Asian, Asiatic

asilo *m* shelter; asylum; home; **asilo di mendicità** poorhouse; **asilo infantile** kindergarten; **asilo per i vecchi** old-age home, nursing home

asimmetrìa [s] *f* asymmetry

asimmètri·co -ca [s] *adj* (**-ci -che**) asymmetric(al)

asinàggine [s] *f* stupidity, asininity

asi·nàio [s] *m* (**-nài**) donkey driver

asinata [s] *f* stupidity, folly

asinerìa [s] *f* asininity

asiné·sco -sca [s] *adj* (**-schi -sche**) asinine

asini·no -na [s] *adj* asinine

àsino [s] *m* ass, donkey; **fare l'asino a** (slang) to play up to; **qui casca l'asino** here is the rub

asma *f* asthma

asmàti·co -ca *adj & mf* (**-ci -che**) asthmatic

àsola *f* buttonhole; buttonhole hem

aspàra·go *m* (**-gi**) asparagus; piece of asparagus; **asparagi** asparagus (*as food*)

aspèrgere §112 *tr* to sprinkle

aspersióne *f* aspersing, sprinkling

aspettare (**aspètto**) *tr* to wait for, await; to expect; **aspettare al varco** to be on the lookout for ‖ *intr* to wait; **fare aspettare** to keep waiting ‖ *ref* to expect

aspettativa *f* expectancy, expectation; leave of absence without pay

aspètto *m* waiting; aspect, look; **al primo aspetto** at first sight

àspide *m* asp

aspirante *adj* suction (*pump*) ‖ *m* aspirant; applicant, candidate; suitor; upperclassman (*in naval academy*)

aspirapólve·re *m* (**-re**) vacuum cleaner

aspirare *tr* to inhale, breathe in; to suck (*e.g., air*); (phonet) to aspirate ‖ *intr* to aspire

aspiratóre *m* exhaust fan

aspirazióne *f* aspiration; (aut) intake

aspirina *f* aspirin

aspo *m* reel

asportàbile *adj* removable

asportare (**aspòrto**) *tr* to remove, take away

asportazióne *f* removal

asprézza *f* sourness; roughness, harshness

a·spro -spra *adj* sour; rough, harsh

assaggiare §290 *tr* to taste; to sample, test; **assaggiare il terreno** (fig) to see how the land lies

assaggia·tóre -trice *mf* taster

assàg·gio *m* (**-gi**) taste, sample; tasting; test, trial

assài *adj invar* a lot of ‖ *m* much ‖ *adv* enough; fairly; very

assale *m* axle

assalire §242 *tr* to attack, assail; (fig) to seize

assali·tóre -trice *mf* assailant

assaltare *tr* to assault; **assaltare a mano armata** to stick up

assalto *m* assault, attack; (law) battery; **cogliere d'assalto** to catch unawares; **prendere d'assalto** to assault

assaporare (**assapóro**) *tr* to taste; to relish, enjoy

assassinare *tr* to assassinate; (fig) to murder

assassì·nio *m* (**-ni**) assassination, murder

assassi·no -na *adj* murderous ‖ *mf* assassin, murderer

asse *m* axle; shaft, spindle; (geom, phys) axis; **asse ereditario** estate; **asse stradale** median strip ‖ *f* plank; **asse da stiro** ironing board

assecondare (**assecóndo**) *tr* to help; to second; to uphold

assediante *adj* besieging ‖ *m* besieger

assediare §287 (**assèdio**) *tr* to lay siege to, besiege

assè·dio *m* (**-di**) siege; **assedio economico** economic sanctions; **cingere d'assedio** to besiege

assegnaménto *m* awarding; allowance; faith, reliance; **fare assegnamento su** to rely upon

assegnare (**asségno**) *tr* to assign; to prescribe; to distribute; to award

assegnatà·rio -ria *mf* (**-ri -rie**) assignee

assegnazióne *f* assignment; awarding

asségno *m* allowance; check; **assegni fringe benefits; assegni familiari** family allowance; **assegno a copertura garantita** certified check; **assegno a vuoto** worthless check; **assegno di studio** (educ) stipend; **assegno turistico** traveler's check; **assegno vademecum** certified check; **contro asségno** C.O.D.

assemblàg·gio *m* (**-gi**) (mach) assembling, assembly

assemblèa *f* assembly

assembraménto *m* gathering

assembrare (**assémbro**) *tr* & *ref* to gather

assennatézza *f* good judgment, discretion

assenna·to -ta *adj* sensible, prudent

assènso *m* approval, consent

assentare (**assènto**) *ref* to be absent, to absent oneself

assènte *adj* absent || *mf* absentee

assenteismo *m* absenteeism

assentire (**assènto**) *tr* (poet) to grant || *intr* to assent, acquiesce; **assentire con un cenno** to nod assent

assènza *f* absence

assenziènte *adj* consenting, approving

assèn·zio *m* (**-zi**) absinthe; (bot) wormwood

asserire §176 *tr* to affirm, assert

asserragliare §280 *tr* to barricade || *ref* to barricade oneself

assèrto *m* (poet) assertion

asser·tóre -tríce *mf* advocate, supporter

asserviménto *m* enslavement

asservire §176 *tr* to enslave; to subjugate

asserzióne *f* assertion

assessóre *m* councilman; alderman

assestaménto *m* arrangement; settling (*of a building*)

assestare (**assèsto**) *tr* to arrange; to adapt, regulate; to deliver, deal (*a blow*) || *ref* to become organized; to settle (*said of a building*)

assesta·to -ta *adj* sensible, prudent

assetare (**assèto**) *tr* to make thirsty; (fig) to inflame

asseta·to -ta *adj* thirsty; parched; eager || *mf* thirsty person

assettare (**assètto**) *tr* to tidy, straighten up || *ref* to straighten oneself up

assetta·to -ta *adj* tidy

assètto *m* arrangement; order; (naut) trim; **assetto longitudinale** (aer) pitch, attitude; **in assetto di guerra** ready for war; **male in assetto** in poor shape

asseverare (**assèvero**) *tr* to asseverate, assert

assicèlla *f* roofing board, lath; batten

assicuràbile *adj* insurable

assicurare *tr* to assure; to insure; to protect; to fasten; to deliver (*e.g., a thief*) || *ref* to make sure; to take out insurance

assicura·to -ta *adj* & *mf* insured || *f* insured letter

assicura·tóre -tríce *mf* insurer

assicurazióne *f* assurance; insurance; **assicurazione contro gli infortuni sul lavoro** workman's compensation insurance; **assicurazione contro i danni** casualty insurance; **assicurazione incendio** fire insurance; **assicurazione infortuni** accident insurance; **assicurazione per la vecchiaia** old age insurance; **assicurazione sociale** social security; **assicurazione sulla vita** life insurance

assideraménto *m* freezing; frostbite

assiderare (**assìdero**) *ref* to freeze; to become frostbitten

assìdere §113 *ref* (poet) to take one's seat (*e.g., on the throne*)

assì·duo -dua *adj* assiduous, diligent

assième *m* ensemble || *adv* together; **assieme a** together with

assiepare (**assièpo**) *tr* & *ref* to crowd

assillante *adj* disturbing, troublesome

assillare *tr* to beset, trouble

assillo *m* gadfly; (fig) stimulus, goad

assimilare (**assìmilo**) *tr* to assimilate; to compare

assimilazióne *f* assimilation

assiòlo *m* horned owl

assiò·ma *m* (**-mi**) axiom

assiomàti·co -ca *adj* (**-ci -che**) axiomatic

assì·ro -ra *adj* & *mf* Assyrian

assisa *f* (poet) uniform, livery; (geol) layer; (archaic) duty, tax; **assise** criminal court; assembly, session; (hist) assises

assistènte *mf* assistant; **assistente sanitario** practical nurse; **assistente sociale** social worker || *m*—**assistente ai lavoro** foreman || *f*—**assistente di volo** (aer) hostess

assistènza *f* assistance, help; intervention; **assistenza pubblica** relief

assistenziale *adj* welfare, charity

assìstere §114 *tr* to assist, help || *intr*—**assistere a** to attend, be present at

assito *m* flooring, boarding

assiuòlo *m* var of **assiolo**

asso *m* ace; **asso del volante** speed king; **piantare in asso** to walk out on

associare §128 (**assòcio**) *tr* to associate; **associare alle carceri** to take to prison || *ref* to associate; to become a member; to subscribe; to participate

associa·to -ta *adj* associate || *mf* associate, partner

associazióne *f* association; union; subscription; membership

assodare (**assòdo**) *tr* to solidify; to strengthen; to ascertain || *ref* to solidify; to strengthen

assoggettare (**assoggètto**) *tr* to subject, subdue || *ref* to submit

assola·to -ta *adj* sunny, exposed to the sun

assolcare §197 (**assólco**) *tr* to furrow

assoldare (**assòldo**) *tr* to hire, recruit

assólo *m* (mus) solo

assolutismo *m* absolutism

assolutìsti·co -ca *adj* (**-ci -che**) absolutist, despotic

assolu·to -ta *adj* & *m* absolute

assoluzióne *f* absolution

assòlvere §115 *tr* to absolve; to fulfill

assomigliare §280 *tr* to compare; to make similar, make equal || *intr* (ESSERE & AVERE) (with *dat*) to resemble, to look like; to be like || *ref* to resemble each other, look alike; **assomigliarsi a** to resemble

assommare (**assómmo**) *tr* to add; to be the epitome of; (archaic) to complete || *intr* (ESSERE) to amount

assonna·to -ta *adj* sleepy

assopire §176 *tr* to lull to sleep; to

soothe || *ref* to drowse, to nod; to calm down

assorbènte *adj* absorbent || *m* sanitary napkin

assorbiménto *m* absorption

assorbire §176 & (**assòrbo**) *tr* to absorb

assorbi·to -ta *adj* absorbe**¢**; **assorbìto da** consumed with

assordare (**assórdo**) *tr* to deafen || *ref* to become deaf; to dim; to lessen

assortiménto *m* assortment; **avere in assortimento** (com) to carry, stock

assortire §176 *tr* to assort, sort out; to stock

assorti·to -ta *adj* assorted; **bene assortito** well matched

assòr·to -ta *adj* engrossed, absorbed

assottigliare §280 *tr* to thin; to sharpen; to reduce || *ref* to grow thinner

assuefare §173 *tr* to accustom || *ref* to become accustomed

assuefazióne *f* habit, custom

assùmere §116 *tr* to assume; to hire; to raise, elevate; (law) to accept in evidence

Assunta *f* Assumption

assunto *m* thesis, argument; (poet) task

assun·tóre -trice *mf* contractor

assunzióne *f* assumption; hiring; (law) examination || **Assunzione** *f* Assumption

assurdi·tà *f* (-**tà**) absurdity

assur·do -da *adj* absurd || *m* absurdity

assùrgere §117 *intr* (ESSERE) (poet) to rise

asta *f* staff; rod; arm (*e.g., of scale*); lance; leg (*of compass*); stroke (*in handwriting*); shaft (*of arrow*); auction; (naut) boom; (naut) mast; (elec) trolley pole; **a mezz'asta** half-mast; **vendere all'asta** to auction, auction off

astante *mf* bystander || *m* physician on duty (*in a hospital*)

astanterìa *f* receiving ward

astato *m* (chem) astatine

astè·mio -mia *adj* abstemious, temperate || *mf* teetotaler

astenére §271 *ref* to abstain

astensióne *f* abstention

astenuto *m* person who abstains from voting; abstention (*vote withheld*)

astèrgere §164 (*pp* **astèrso**) *tr* to wipe

asteri·sco *m* (-**schi**) asterisk

asticciòla *f* penholder; rib (*of umbrella*); temple (*of eyeglasses*)

àstice *m* (*Hommarus vulgaris*) lobster

asticèlla *f* (sports) bar

astinènte *adj* abstinent

astinènza *f* abstinence

à·stio *m* (-**sti**) grudge, rancor

astió·so -sa [s] *adj* full of malice, spiteful

astóre *m* goshawk

astràgalo *m* astragalus, anklebone

astrakàn *m* Persian lamb

astrarre §273 *tr* to abstract || *intr*—**astrarre da** to leave aside, overlook

astrat·to -ta *adj* abstract || *m* abstract

astrazióne *f* abstraction

astringènte *adj* & *m* astringent

-astro -astra *suf adj* -ish, e.g., **verdastro**

greenish || *suf mf* -aster, e.g., **poetastro** poetaster

astro *m* star, heavenly body; (bot) aster; (fig) star

astrologìa *f* astrology

astrològi·co -ca *adj* (-**ci -che**) astrological

astròlo·go *m* (-**gi** or **-ghi**) astrologer

astronàu·ta *mf* (-**ti -te**) astronaut

astronàuti·co -ca (-**ci -che**) *adj* astronautic(al) || *f* astronautics

astronautizzare [ddzz] *intr* (ESSERE) to be an astronaut

astronave *f* spaceship, spacecraft

astronomìa *f* astronomy

astrònomo *m* astronomer

astronòmi·co -ca *adj* (-**ci -che**) astronomic(al)

astruserìa *f* abstruseness

astrusi·tà *f* (-**tà**) abstruseness

astru·so -sa *adj* abstruse

astùc·cio *m* (-**ci**) case, box

astu·to -ta *adj* astute, crafty

astùzia *f* astuteness, craftiness

àta·vo -va *mf* ancestor

ateismo *m* atheism

atei·sta *mf* (-**sti -ste**) atheist

Atène *f* Athens

atenèo *m* athenaeum; university

ateniése [s] *adj* & *mf* Athenian

àteo -a *adj* atheistic || *mf* atheist

atlante *m* atlas || **Atlante** *m* Atlas

atlànti·co -ca *adj* (-**ci -che**) Atlantic || **Atlantico** *m* Atlantic

atlè·ta *mf* (-**ti -te**) athlete

atletéssa *f* female athlete

atlèti·co -ca (-**ci -che**) *adj* athletic || *f* athletics; **atletica leggera** track and field

atmosfèra *f* atmosphere

atmosfèri·co -ca *adj* (-**ci -che**) atmospheric

atòllo *m* atoll

atòmi·co -ca *adj* (-**ci -che**) atomic; (coll) stunning

atomizzare [ddzz] *tr* to atomize

atomizzatóre [ddzz] *m* atomizer

àtomo *m* atom

atòni·co -ca *adj* (-**ci -che**) (pathol) weak

àto·no -na *adj* (gram) atonic

atout *m* (atouts) trump

à·trio *m* (-**tri**) entrance hall, lobby

atróce *adj* atrocious

atroci·tà *f* (-**tà**) atrocity

atrofìa *f* atrophy

atròfi·co -ca *adj* (-**ci -che**) atrophied

atrofizzare [ddzz] *tr* & *ref* to atrophy

attaccabottó·ni *mf* (-**ni**) bore, pest, buttonholer

attaccabri·ghe *mf* (-**ghe**) (coll) quarrelsome person, scrapper

attaccaménto *m* attachment, affection

attaccapan·ni *m* (-**ni**) coathanger

attaccare §197 *tr* to attach; to bind, unite; to sew on; to stick; to hitch (*a horse*); to hang; to attack; to strike up (*a conversation*); to begin; to communicate (*a disease*); **attaccare un bottone a** (fig) to buttonhole || *intr* to stick; to gain a foothold, take root; to begin || *ref* to stick; to cling; to spread (*said of a disease*); (fig) to become attached

attaccatìc·cio -cia *adj* (**-ci -ce**) sticky

attacchino *m* billposter

attàc·co *m* (**-chi**) attachment; onslaught; fastening; beginning; seizure (*e.g., of epilepsy*); spell (*e.g., of coughing*); (elec) plug; (rad) jack; (sports) forward line; **attacco cardìaco** heart attack

attagliare §280 *ref*—**attagliarsi a** to fit, become

attanagliare §280 *tr* to grip; to seize; to hold (*e.g., with tongs*)

attardare *ref* to tarry, delay

attecchire §176 *intr* to take root; to take hold

atteggiaménto *m* attitude

atteggiare §290 (**attéggio**) *tr* to compose (*e.g., one's face*); to place || *ref* to pose; to strike an attitude

attempà·to -ta *adj* elderly

attendaménto *m* camping; jamboree (*of Boy Scouts*)

attendare (**attèndo**) *ref* to encamp; to pitch one's tent

attendènte *m* (mil) orderly

attèndere §270 *tr* to await; (archaic) to keep; **attendere l'ora propizia** to bide one's time || *intr*—**attendere a** to attend to

attendìbile *adj* reliable

attendismo *m* wait-and-see attitude

attendì·sta (**-sti -ste**) *adj* wait-and-see || *mf* fence-sitter

attenére §271 *tr* (poet) to keep (*a promise*) || *intr*—**attenere** (with *dat*) to concern, e.g., **ciò non gli attiene** this does not concern him || *ref*—**attenersi a** to conform to

attentare (**attènto**) *intr*—**attentare a** to attempt (*s.o.'s life*) || *ref* to make an attempt, dare

attentato *m* attempt

attenta·tóre -trice *mf* would-be murderer; attacker

attèn·ti *m* (**-ti**) attention || *interj* (mil) attention!

attèn·to -ta *adj* attentive; careful

attenuare (**attènuo**) *tr* to extenuate, play down; to attenuate; to mitigate

attenzióne *f* attention; **fare attenzione** to take care; **prestare attenzione** to pay attention

atterràg·gio *m* (**-gi**) landing; **atterraggio di fortuna** emergency landing; **atterraggio senza carrello** crash-landing

atterraménto *m* landing; pinning, pin (*in wrestling*); (boxing) knocking down; **atterramento frenato** (aer) arrested landing

atterrare (**attèrro**) *tr* to fell; to knock down; to pin (*in wrestling*); (fig) to humiliate || *intr* to land; **atterrare scassando** or **atterrare senza carrello** to crash-land

atterrire §176 *tr* to frighten, terrify || *ref* to become frightened

atté·so -sa [s] *adj* awaited, expected; **atteso che** considering that || *f* waiting; expectation; **in attesa (di)** waiting (for)

attestare (**attèsto**) *tr* to certify, attest; to prove; to join; (mil) to deploy || *ref* (mil) to take a stand

attestato *m* certificate

attestazióne *f* testimony; affidavit; attestation, proof

àtti·co -ca (-ci -che) *adj* & *mf* Attic || *m* attic

attì·guo -gua *adj* adjacent, contiguous

attillare *tr* & *ref* to preen

attillà·to -ta *adj* tight, close-fitting; tidy, all dressed up

àttimo *m* moment, split second; **di attimo in attimo** any moment

attinènte *adj* related, pertinent

attinènza *f* relation; **attinenze** appurtenances; annexes

attìngere §126 *tr* to draw (*water*); to get; (poet) to attain (*e.g., glory*)

attingi·tóio *m* (**-tói**) ladle

attirare *tr* to draw, attract

attitùdine *f* aptitude; attitude

attivare *tr* to activate; to expedite

attivazióne *f* activation; reassessment

attivi·tà *f* (**-tà**) activity; **attività** *fpl* assets

attì·vo -va *adj* active; profit-making || *m* assets

attizzare *tr* to stir, poke (*a fire*); (fig) to stir up

attizza·tóio *m* (**-tói**) poker

àt·to -ta *adj* apt, fit || *m* act, action; gesture; (law) instrument; **all'atto pratico** in reality; **atti** proceedings (*of a learned society*); **atti notarìli** legal proceedings; **atto di nascita** birth certificate; **fare atto di presenza** to put in a brief formal appearance; **atto di vendita** bill of sale; **nell'atto o sull'atto** in the act

attòni·to -ta *adj* astonished

attorcigliare §280 *tr* to twist || *ref* to wind; to coil up

attóre *m* actor; (law) plaintiff; **attore giovane** (theat) juvenile; **primo attore** (theat) lead

attorniare §287 (**attórnio**) *tr* to surround; (fig) to dupe

attórno *adv* around; **andare attorno** to walk around; **attorno a** around, near; **darsi d'attorno** to busy oneself; **levarsi qlcu d'attorno** to get rid of s.o.

attortigliare §280 *tr* to twist || *ref* to wind; to coil up

attraccare §197 *tr* & *intr* to moor, dock

attràc·co *m* (**-chi**) mooring, docking

attraènte *adj* attractive

attrarre §273 *tr* to attract, draw

attrattì·vo -va *adj* attractive; alluring || *f* attraction, charm

attraversaménto *m* crossing; **attraversamento pedonale** pedestrian crossing

attraversare (**attravèrso**) *tr* to cross; to go through; to thwart; **attraversare il passo a** to stand in the way of

attravèrso *adv* across; crosswise; **andare attraverso** to go down the wrong way (*said of food or drink*); (fig) to go wrong; **attraverso a** through, across || *prep* through, across

attrazióne *f* attraction

attrezzare (**attrézzo**) *tr* to outfit, equip

attrezzatura *f* outfit; gear, equipment; **attrezzatura di una nave** rigging; **attrezzatura facilities**

attrezzi‧sta (-sti -ste) *mf* gymnast || *m* toolmaker; (theat) property man

attrézzo *m* tool, utensil; **attrezzi** gymnastic equipment

attribuire §176 *tr* to award; to attribute; **attribuire qlco a qlcu** to credit s.o. with s.th || *ref* to ascribe to oneself, claim for oneself

attributo *m* attribute

attribuzióne *f* attribution

attrice *f* actress; (law) plaintiff; **prima attrice** (theat) lead

attristare *tr* (poet) to sadden || *ref* to become sad

attri‧to -ta *adj* worn, worn-out || *m* attrition; disagreement

attruppare *tr* to band, group || *ref* to mill about, throng

attuàbile *adj* feasible

attuale *adj* present; present-day, current

attuali‧tà *f* (-tà) timeliness; reality; **attualità** *fpl* current events; **di viva attualità** newsworthy; timely; in the news

attualizzare [ddzz] *tr* to bring up to date || *ref* to become a reality

attuare (àttuo) *tr* to carry out, make come true || *ref* to come true

attuà‧rio -ria (-ri -rie) *adj* (hist) transport (*e.g., ship*) || *m* actuary

attuazióne *f* realization

attutire §176 *tr* to mitigate; to deaden (*a sound, a blow*) || *ref* to diminish (*said of a sound*)

audace *adj* audacious

audàcia *f* audacity

audiofrequènza *f* audio frequency

audiovisí‧vo -va *adj* audio-visual

auditi‧vo -va *adj* var of **uditivo**

auditóre *m* var of **uditore**

auditò‧rio *m* (-ri) auditorium

audizióne *f* program; audition; (law) hearing

àuge *f* acme; **essere in auge** to enjoy a great reputation; to be in vogue; to be on top of the world

augurale *adj* well-wishing; salutatory

augurare (àuguro) *tr* to wish; to bid (*good day*) || *intr* to augur || *ref* to hope; to expect

àugure *m* augur

augù‧rio *m* (-ri) wish; augury, omen

augustè‧o -a *adj* Augustan

augu‧sto -sta *adj* august, venerable

àula *f* hall; classroom; (poet) chamber (*of a palace*)

àuli‧co -ca *adj* (-ci -che) courtly; noble, elevated

aumentare (auménto) *tr* to augment, increase || *intr* (ESSERE) to increase, rise

auménto *m* increase

àura *f* (poet) breeze; (poet) breath

àure‧o -a *adj* golden, gold

aurèola *f* halo

auricolare *adj* ear; first-hand || *m* (telp) receiver; (rad) earphone

auròra *f* dawn; (fig) aurora

ausiliare *adj* auxiliary || *m* collaborator, helper

ausilià‧rio -ria (-ri -rie) *adj* auxiliary; (mil) supply || *m* helper; (mil) reserve officer || *f* female member of the armed forces

ausì‧lio *m* (-li) (poet) help

auspicare §197 (àuspico) *tr* to wish, augur

àuspice *m* sponsor; (hist) augur

auspí‧cio *m* (-ci) sponsorship; (hist, poet) augury, omen; **sotto gli auspici di** under the auspices of

austeri‧tà *f* (-tà) austerity

austè‧ro -ra *adj* austere

australe *adj* austral, southern

Austràlia, l' *f* Australia

australia‧no -na *adj & mf* Australian

Austria, l' *f* Austria

austrì‧a‧co -ca *adj & mf* (-ci -che) Austrian

autarchìa *f* autarky; autonomy (*of an administration*)

autàrchi‧co -ca *adj* (-ci -che) autonomous, independent

autèntica *f* (-che) authentication of a signature or a document

autenticare §197 (autèntico) *tr* to authenticate

autentici‧tà *f* (-tà) authenticity

autènti‧co -ca (-ci -che) *adj* authentic, genuine || *f* see **autentica**

autière *m* (mil) driver

auti‧sta *mf* (-sti -ste) (aut) driver

au‧to *f* (-to) auto

autoabbronzante [dz] *adj* tanning || *m* tanning lotion

autoaffondaménto *m* scuttling

autoambulanza *f* ambulance

autobiografìa *f* autobiography

autobiogràfi‧co -ca *adj* (-ci -che) autobiographical

autoblinda‧to -ta *adj* armored

autoblin‧do *m* (-do) armored car

autobótte *f* tank truck

àuto‧bus *m* (-bus) bus

autocarro *m* truck, motor truck

autocèntro *m* (mil) motor pool

autocistèrna *f* tank truck

autocivétta *f* unmarked police car

autocolónna *f* row of cars

autocombustióne *f* spontaneous combustion

autocontròllo *m* self-control

autocorrièra *f* intercity bus, highway bus

autocrazìa *f* autocracy

autocrìti‧ca *f* (-che) self-criticism

autòcto‧no -na *adj* autochthonous, independent

autodecisióne *m* free will

autodeterminazióne *f* self-determination

autodidat‧ta *mf* (-ti -te) self-taught person

autodidàtti‧co -ca *adj* (-ci -che) self-instructional

autodifésa [s] *f* self-defense

autodisciplina *f* self-discipline

autòdromo *m* automobile race track

autoemotè‧ca *f* (-che) bloodmobile

autofilettante *adj* self-threading

autofurgóne *m* van; **autofurgone cellu-**

lare police van; **autofurgone funebre** hearse

autogiro m autogyro

autogovèrno m self-government

autògra·fo -fa adj autographic(al) ‖ m autograph

auto-grù f (-grù) tow truck

autolesioni·sta mf (-sti -ste) person who wounds himself to avoid the draft or collect insurance

autoletti·ga f (-ghe) ambulance

autolibro m bookmobile

autolìnea f bus line

autò·ma m (-mi) automaton, robot

automàti·co -ca (-ci -che) adj automatic ‖ m snap

automatizzare [ddzz] tr to automate

automazióne f automation

automèzzo [ddzz] m motor vehicle

automòbile f automobile, car; **automobile da corsa** racing car; **automobile di serie** stock car; **automobile fuori serie** custom-made car

automobilismo m motoring

automobili·sta mf (-sti -ste) motorist

automobilìsti·co -ca adj (-ci -che) car, automobile

automo·tóre -trice adj self-propelled ‖ f (rr) automotive rail car

autonolég·gio m (-gi) car rental agency

autonomìa f autonomy; (aer, naut) cruising radius

autonomi·sta adj (-sti -ste) autonomous

autòno·mo -ma adj autonomous, independent

autoparchég·gio m (-gi) parking; parking lot

autopar·co m (-chi) parking; parking lot

autopiano m player piano

autopilò·ta m (-ti) (aer) automatic pilot

autopómpa f fire engine

autopsìa f autopsy

autorà·dio f (-dio) car radio

autóre m author; perpetrator; creator, maker

autoreattóre m ramjet engine

autorespiratóre m aqualung

autorévole adj authoritative

autoriméssa f garage

autori·tà f (-tà) authority

autorità·rio -ria adj (-ri -rie) authoritarian

autoritratto m self-portrait

autorizzare [ddzz] tr to authorize

autorizzazióne [ddzz] f authorization

autoscala f hook and ladder; ladder (of hook and ladder)

autoscuòla f driving school

autoservì·zio m (-zi) bus service, bus line; self-service

autosilo m parking garage

autostazióne f bus station

autostèllo m roadside motel

auto·stòp m (-stòp) hitchhiking; **fare l'autostop** to hitchhike

autostoppi·sta mf (-sti -ste) hitchhiker

autostrada f highway, turnpike

autosufficiènte adj self-sufficient

autote·làio m (-lài) (aut) frame

autotrasportare (autotraspòrto) tr to truck

autotrasportatóre m trucker

autotreni·sta m (-sti) truck driver, teamster

autotrèno m tractor trailer

autoveìcolo m motor vehicle

autovettura f car, automobile

autrice f authoress

autunnale adj autumnal, fall

autunno m autumn, fall

avallare tr to endorse (a promissory note); to guarantee

avallo m endorsement (of a promissory note)

avambràc·cio m (-ci) forearm

avampósto m outpost

avancàrica f—**ad avancarica** muzzle-loading

avanguàrdia f vanguard; avant-garde

avanguardismo m avant-garde

avanguardi·sta m (-sti) avant-gardist; (hist) member of Fascist youth organization

avannòtto m small fry (young freshwater fish)

avanti adj preceding ‖ m forward ‖ adv forward, ahead; **andare avanti** to proceed, to go ahead; **andare avanti negli anni** to be up in years; **avanti a** in front of; **avanti che** rather than; **avanti di** before; **essere avanti** to be advanced (in work or study); **in avanti** ahead ‖ prep—**avanti Cristo** before Christ; **avanti giorno** before daybreak ‖ interj come in!

avantièri adv day before yesterday

avantrèno m (aut) front-axle assembly; (mil) limber

avanzaménto m advancement

avanzare tr to advance; to overcome; to be creditor for, e.g., **avanza cento dollari da suo fratello** he is his brother's creditor for one hundred dollars; to save ‖ intr (mil) to advance ‖ intr (ESSERE) to advance; to stick out; to be abundant; to be left over, e.g., **avanzano due polpette** two meatballs are left over; **avanzare negli anni** to grow older ‖ ref to advance, come forward

avanza·to -ta adj advanced; progressive ‖ f (mil) advance

avanzo m remainder; **avanzi** remains

avarìa f damage, breakdown; (naut) average

avariare §287 tr to damage, spoil ‖ intr to spoil

avaria·to -ta adj damaged, spoiled

avarìzia f avarice, greed

ava·ro -ra adj avaricious, stingy ‖ mf miser

avellana f filbert

avellano m filbert tree

avèllo m (poet) tomb

avéna f oats

avére m belongings, property; assets, credit; amount due ‖ §118 tr to have; to hold; to wear; to receive, get; to stand (a chance); to be, e.g., **avere . . . anni** to be . . . years old; **avere caldo** to be hot; to be warm; **avere fame** to be hungry; **avere freddo** to be cold; **avere fretta** to be in a hurry;

avere paura to be afraid; avere ragione to be right; avere sete to be thirsty; avere sonno to be sleepy; avere torto to be wrong; avere vergogna to be ashamed; avere voglia di to be anxious to; avere qlco da + inf to have s.th to + inf, e.g., ho molto lavoro da fare I have a lot of work to do; averla con to be angry at; non avere niente a che fare con to have nothing to do with ‖ impers—v'ha there is ‖ aux to have, e.g., ha letto il giornale he has read the newspaper; avere da + inf to have to + inf, e.g., avevo da lavorare I had to work; to be to + inf, e.g., ha da venire alle cinque he is to arrive at five o'clock

avià•rio -ria (-ri -rie) adj bird ‖ m aviary

avia•tóre m -trice f aviator ‖ f aviatrix

aviazióne f aviation

avicoltóre m bird raiser; poultry farmer

avidi•tà f (-tà) avidity, greediness

àvi•do -da adj avid, greedy

avière m airman

aviogètto m jet plane

aviolinea f airline

aviopista f (aer) airstrip

avioriméssa f (aer) hangar

aviotrasporta•to -ta adj airborne

avi•to -ta adj ancestral

a•vo -va m/ grandparent; ancestor ‖ m grandfather ‖ f grandmother

avocare §197 (àvoco) tr to demand (jurisdiction); to expropriate

avò•rio m (-ri) ivory

avul•so -sa adj (poet) torn, uprooted; (poet) separated

avvalére §278 ref—avvalersi di to avail oneself of

avvallaménto m sinking, settling

avvallare tr (poet) to lower (e.g., one's eyes) ‖ ref to sink; (lit) to humiliate oneself

avvalorare (avvalóro) tr to strengthen, confirm ‖ ref to gain strength

avvampare tr (poet) to inflame ‖ intr (ESSERE) to burn

avvantaggiare §290 tr to be profitable to; to benefit ‖ ref to profit; avvantaggiarsi su to overcome; to beat

avvedére §279 ref—avvedersi di to notice, become aware of

avvedutézza f discernment; shrewdness

avvedu•to -ta adj prudent; shrewd; fare qlcu avveduto di to inform s.o. of

avvelenaménto m poisoning

avvelenare (avveléno) tr to poison ‖ ref to take poison; to be poisoned

avveniménto m happening, event

avvenire adj invar future, to come ‖ m future; in avvenire in the future ‖ §282 intr (ESSERE) to happen, occur; avvenga quel che vuole come what may

avventare (avvènto) tr to hurl; to deliver (a blow); to venture (an opinion) ‖ ref to throw oneself

avventatézza f thoughtlessness, heedlessness

avventa•to -ta adj thoughtless, heedless; all'avventata heedlessly

avvènti•zio -zia adj (-zi -zie) outside, exterior; temporary, occasional

avvènto m advent; elevation, rise

avven•tóre -tóra m/ customer, consumer

avventura f adventure

avventurière•ro -ra adj adventurous ‖ m adventurer ‖ f adventuress

avventuró•so -sa [s] adj adventurous, adventuresome

avverare (avvéro) tr to make true ‖ ref to come true

avvèr•bio m (-bi) adverb

avversà•rio -ria (-ri -rie) adj opposing, contrary ‖ m/ adversary, opponent

avversióne f aversion

avversi•tà f (-tà) adversity

avvèr•so -sa adj adverse; (obs) opposite ‖ avverso prep (law) against

avvertènza f prudence, caution; advice; avvertenze instructions, directions

avvertiménto m caution, warning; advice

avvertire (avvèrto) tr to caution, warn; to notice

avvezzare (avvézzo) tr to accustom; to inure; to train; avvezzar male to spoil ‖ ref to get accustomed

avvéz•zo -za adj accustomed

avviaménto m starting; introduction; trade school; good shape (of a business); (mach) starting; (typ) adjustment (of printing press)

avviare §119 tr to start, set in motion; to introduce; to initiate; to begin ‖ ref to set out

avvia•to -ta adj going, thriving (concern)

avvicendaménto m alteration, rotation (of crops)

avvicendare (avvicènde) tr & ref to alternate

avvicinaménto m approach; rapprochement

avvicinare tr to bring near or closer; to approach, go or come near to ‖ ref to approach, come near; avvicinarsi a to come closer, approach

avviliménto m discouragment, dejection

avvilire §176 tr to degrade; to deject ‖ ref to become dejected, become discouraged

avviluppare tr to entangle, snarl; to wrap

avvinazza•to -ta adj & m/ drunk

avvincènte adj fascinating

avvincere §285 tr to fascinate, charm; (poet) to twine

avvinghiare §287 tr to claw; to clasp, clutch ‖ ref to grip one another

avvì•o m (-i) beginning

avvisàglia f skirmish; prime avvisaglie onset; first signs

avvisare tr to inform, advise; (archaic) to observe, notice

avvisa•tóre -trice m/ announcer, messenger ‖ m alarm; (theat) callboy; avvisatore acustico (aut) horn; avvisatore d'incendio fire alarm

avviso m advise; notice, poster; opinion; avviso di chiamata alle armi

notice of induction; **sull'avviso** on one's guard
avvistare *tr* to sight
avvitaménto *m* (aer) tailspin
avvitare *tr* to screw; to fasten || *ref* (aer) to go into a tailspin
avviticchiare §287 *tr* to entwine || *ref* to cling
avvivare *tr* to revive; to stir up
avvizzire §176 *tr* & *intr* (ESSERE) to wither
avvocatéssa *f* woman lawyer
avvocato *m* lawyer, attorney
avvocatura *f* law, legal profession
avvòlgere §289 *tr* to wind; to wrap up; to spread over, surround || *ref* to wind around; to wrap oneself up
avvolgiménto *m* winding; wrapping; (elec) coil; (mil) envelopment
avvol·tóio *m* (-tói) vulture
avvoltolare (avvòltolo) *tr* to roll up || *ref* to roll around, wallow
aziènda [dz] *f* business, firm
azionare (azióno) *tr* to start; to drive, propel
aziona·rio -ria *adj* (-ri -rie) (com) stock
azióne *f* action, act; (law) suit; (com) share (*of stock*); **azione legale** prosecution; **azione privilegiata** preferred stock
azioni·sta *mf* (-sti -ste) stockholder, shareholder

azòto [dz] *m* nitrogen
azoturo [dz] *m* nitride
aztè·co -ca *adj* & *mf* (-chi -che) Aztec
azzannare *tr* to seize with the fangs
azzardare [ddzz] *tr* to risk; to advance || *ref* to dare
azzardarsi *ref* to dare
azzardo [ddzz] *m* chance, hazard
azzardó·so -sa [ddzz] [s] *adj* hazardous, risky
azzeccagarbu·gli *m* (-gli) shyster
azzeccare §197 (azzécco) *tr* to hit; to deliver; to pass off (*counterfeit money*); **azzeccarla** (coll) to hit the mark
azzimare [ddzz] (àzzimo) *tr* & *ref* to spruce up
àzzi·mo -ma [ddzz] *adj* unleavened (*bread*)
azzittare & **azzittire** §176 *tr* to hush || *ref* to keep quiet
azzoppare (azzòppo) *tr* to cripple || *ref* to become lame or crippled
Azzòrre [ddzz] *fpl* Azores
azzuffare *ref* to come to blows; to scuffle
azzur·ro -ra [ddzz] *adj* blue || *m* blue; Italian athlete (*in international competition*)
azzurrógno·lo -la [ddzz] *adj* bluish

B

B, b [bi] *m* & *f* second letter of the Italian alphabet
ba·bàu *m* (-bàu) bogey, bugbear
babbè·o -a *adj* foolish || *mf* fool
babbo *m* (coll) daddy, father
babbù·cia *f* (-ce) babouche; bedroom slipper
babbuino *m* baboon
babèle *f* babel || **Babèle** *f* Babel
babilònia *f* confusion || **Babilònia** *f* Babylon
babórdo *m* (naut) port
bacare §197 *ref* to become worm-eaten
baca·to -ta *adj* worm-eaten; rotten
bac·ca *f* (-che) berry
bacca·là *m* (-là) dried codfish; (coll) skinny person; (coll) lummox
baccalaureato *m* baccalaureate, bachelor's degree
baccanale *m* bacchanal
baccano *m* noise, hubbub; **fare baccano** to carry on
baccante *f* bacchant
baccellière *m* (hist) bachelor
baccèllo *m* pod
baccellóne *m* simpleton, fool
bacchétta *f* rod, wand, baton; **bacchetta magica** magic wand; **bacchette del tamburo** drumsticks
bacchétto *m* stick; handle (*of a whip*)
bacchettó·ne -na *mf* bigot
bàcchi·co -ca *adj* (-ci -che) Bacchic
Bacco *m* Baccus

bachè·ca *f* (-che) showcase
bachelite *f* bakelite
bacheròzzo *m* worm; earthworm; (coll) cockroach
bachicoltura *f* silkworm raising
baciama·no *m* (-ni) kissing of the hand
baciapi·le *mf* (-le) bigot
baciare §128 *tr* to kiss; **baciare la polvere** to bite the dust || *ref* to kiss one another
bacia·to -ta *adj* kissed; rhymed (*couplet*)
bacile *m* basin
bacillo *m* bacillus
bacinèlla *f* small basin; (phot) tray
bacino *m* basin; reservoir; cove; (anat) pelvis; **bacino carbonifero** coal field; **bacino di carenaggio** drydock; **bacino fluviale** river basin
bà·cio *m* (-ci) kiss; **a bacio** with a northern exposure
baciucchiare §287 *tr* to keep on kissing || *ref* to pet
ba·co *m* (-chi) worm; **baco da seta** silkworm
bacuc·co -ca *adj* (-chi -che)—**vecchio bacucco** dotard
bada—**tenere a bada** to stave off; to delay
badare *intr* to tend, take care of || *intr* to attend; to take care; to pay attention; **badare a** to mind; to watch

over; to attend to; **badare alla salute** to take care of one's health

badéssa f abbess

badìa f abbey

badilata f shovelful

badile m shovel

baffo m whiskers; whisker; **baffi** mustache; whiskers; **baffo di gatto** (rad) cat's whiskers; **leccarsi i baffi** to lick one's chops; **sotto i baffi** up one's sleeve

baga·gliàio m (**-gliài**) (rr) baggage car; (rr) baggage room; (aut) baggage rack

bagagliéra f baggage room

bagagliére m baggage master

bagà·glio m (**-gli**) baggage, luggage; (of knowledge) fund

bagaglì·sta m (**-sti**) porter (in a hotel)

bagarinàg·gio m (**-gi**) profiteering; (theat) scalping

bagarino m profiteer; scalper

bagà·scia f (**-sce**) harlot, prostitute

bagattèlla f trifle, bauble

baggiano m nitwit, simpleton

bà·glio m (**-gli**) (naut) beam

baglióre m shine, gleam

bagnante mf bather, swimmer; vacationer at the seashore

bagnare tr to bathe; to wet; to soak; to water, sprinkle; to moisten; (fig) to celebrate || ref to bathe; to wet one another

bagnaròla f (coll) bathtub

bagnasciu·ga f (**-ghe**) (naut) waterline

bagnino m lifeguard

bagno m bath; bathroom; bathtub; **bagno di luce** diathermy; **bagno di schiuma** bubble bath; **bagno di sole** sun bath; **bagno di vapore** steam bath; **bagno turco** Turkish bath; **essere in un bagno di sudore** to be soaked with perspiration; **fare il bagno** to take a bath

bagnomarìa m (**bagnimarìa**) double boiler; bain-marie; **a bagnomaria** in a double boiler

bagórdo m carousal, revelry; **far bagordi** to carouse, revel

bàio bàia (**bài bàie**) adj & m bay || f bay; jest; trifle; **dare la baia a** to make fun of, tease

baionétta f bayonet; **baionetta in canna** with fixed bayonet

bàita f mountain hut

balaustrata f balustrade

balaùstro m baluster

balbettaménto m stammering

balbettare (**balbétto**) tr to stammer; to speak poorly (a foreign language) || intr to stammer; to babble (said of a baby)

balbettì·o m (**-i**) babble (of a baby); stammering

balbùzie f stammering

balbuziènte adj stammering || mf stammerer

Balcani, i the Balkans

balcàni·co -ca adj (**-ci -che**) Balkan

balconata f balcony; (theat) upper gallery

balcóne m balcony

baldacchino m canopy, baldachin

baldanza f boldness; aplomb, assurance

baldanzó·so -sa [s] adj bold; self-assured

bal·do -da adj bold; self-assured

baldòria f carousal, revelry; **fare baldoria** to carouse, revel

baldrac·ca f (**-che**) harlot, prostitute

baléna f whale

balenare (**baléno**) intr to stagger || intr (ESSERE) to flash, e.g., **gli balena un pensiero** a thought flashes through his mind || impers (ESSERE)—**balena**, it is lightning

balenièra f whaler, whaleboat

baléno m flash; flash of lightning; **in un baleno** in a flash

balenòttera f rorqual

balèstra f crossbow; (aut) spring, leaf spring

balestrière m crossbowman

bàlia f wet nurse; **balia asciutta** dry nurse; **prendere a balia** to wet-nurse

balìa f power; **in balia di** at the mercy of

balìsti·co -ca (**-ci -che**) adj ballistic || f ballistics

balla f bale; (vulg) lie

ballàbile adj dance || m dance tune

ballare tr to dance || intr to dance; to shake; to be loose; to wobble (said, e.g., of a chair)

ballata f ballad; (mus) ballade

balla·tóio m (**-tói**) gallery; perch (in birdcage)

ballerì·no -na adj dancing || m ballet dancer; dancer; dancing partner || f dancing girl; ballerina; chorus girl; ballet slipper; (orn) wagtail

ballétto m ballet; chorus

ballo m dance; chorus; ball; stake; **ballo di San Vito** Saint Vitus's dance; **ballo in maschera** masked ball; **in ballo** at stake; in question; **tirare in ballo** to drag in

ballonzolare (**ballónzolo**) intr to hop around

ballottàg·gio m (**-gi**) runoff

ballottare (**ballòtto**) tr to ballot (e.g., a candidate)

balneare adj bathing; water, watering

baloccare §197 (**balòcco**) tr to amuse with toys || ref to play; to trifle, to fool around

balòc·co m (**-chi**) toy; hobby

balordàggine f silliness

balór·do -da adj silly, foolish

balsàmi·co -ca adj (**-ci -che**) balmy; antiseptic

balsamina f balsam

bàlsamo m balsam, balsam

bàlti·co -ca adj (**-ci -che**) Baltic

baluardo m bastion, bulwark

baluginare (**balùgino**) intr (ESSERE) to flicker; to flash (through one's mind)

balza f crag, cliff; flounce (on dress); fringe (on curtains, bedspreads, etc.)

balza·no -na adj white-footed (horse); odd, funny || f flounce; fringe; white mark (on horse's foot)

balzare tr to throw (a rider; said of a horse) || intr (ESSERE) to jump, leap;

to bounce; **balzare in mente a** to suddenly dawn on

balzellare (balzèllo) *intr* to hop

balzèllo *m* hop; tribute; tax; toll; **stare a balzello** to lie in wait

balzellóni *adv*—**a balzelloni** leaping, skipping

balzo *m* leap; bounce; **pigliare la palla al balzo** to take time by the forelock

bambàgia *f* cotton wool

bambinàggine *f* childishness

bambinàia *f* nursemaid; **bambinaia ad ore** baby sitter

bambiné·sco -sca *adj* (**-schi -sche**) childish

bambi·no -na *adj* childish || *mf* child

bambòc·cio *m* (**-ci**) fat baby; doll; rag doll

bàmbola *f* doll; **bambola di pezza** rag-doll

bam·bù *m* (**-bù**) bamboo

banale *adj* banal, commonplace

banali·tà *f* (**-tà**) banality, commonplaceness, triviality

banana *f* banana; hair with curls shaped as rolls

baniéra *f* banana boat

banano *m* banana plant

ban·ca *f* (**-che**) bank; embankment

bancàbile *adj* negotiable

bancarèlla *f* cart, pushcart; stall

banca·rio -ria (**-ri -rie**) *adj* bank, banking || *m* bank clerk

bancaròtta *f* bankruptcy; **fare bancarotta** to go bankrupt

banchettare (banchétto) *intr* to feast, banquet

banchétto *m* banquet

banchière *m* banker

banchina *f* garden bench; bicycle path; sidewalk; shoulder (*of highway*); dock, pier; (rr) platform; (mil) banquette

ban·co *m* (**-chi**) bench; seat; bank; witness stand; school (*of fish*); **banco di coralli** coral reef; **banco di ghiaccio** ice pack; **banco di nebbia** fog bank; **banco di prova** (mach) bench; **banco di sabbia** sandbar; **banco d'ostriche** oyster bed; **banco lotto** lottery office

bancogiro *m* (com) transfer of funds

bancóne *m* counter; bench

banconòta *f* banknote

banda *f* band; **andare alla banda** (naut) to list; **da ogni banda** from every side; **mettere da banda** to put aside

bandèlla *f* hinge (*of door or window*); hinged leaf (*of table*)

banderuòla *f* banderole; weather vane

bandièra *f* flag; banner; **battere la bandiera** (e.g., **italiana**) to fly the (*e.g Italian*) flag; **mutar bandiera** to change sides

bandierare (bandièro) *tr* (aer) to feather

bandire §176 *tr* to announce (*e.g., a competitive examination*); to banish

bandìsti·co -ca *adj* (**-ci -che**) (mus) band

bandi·to -ta *adj* announced; open (*house*) || *m* bandit || *f* preserve (*for hunting or fishing*)

bandi·tóre -trice *mf* town crier; auctioneer; barker

bando *m* announcement; banishment; **bandi matrimoniali** (eccl) banns; **mandare in bando** to exile, banish

bandolièra *f* bandoleer; **a bandoliera** slung across the shoulders

bàndolo *m* end of a skein; **perdere il bandolo** to lose the thread (*e.g., of a story*)

bara *f* bier, coffin

barac·ca *f* (**-che**) hut, cabin; (fig) household; **fare baracca** to carouse around

baracca·to -ta *adj* lodged in a hut or a cabin; slum (*e.g., section*) || *m* dweller in a hut or a cabin; slum dweller

baraccóne *m* big circus tent

baraónda *f* hubbub; mess

barare *intr* to cheat (*e.g., at cards*)

bàratro *m* abyss, chasm

barattare *tr* to barter; **barattare le carte in mano a uno** to distort someone's words; **barattar parole** to chat, talk || *intr* to barter

barattière *m* grafter

baratto *m* barter

baràttolo *m* can, canister, jar

barba *f* beard; whiskers; barb, vane (*of feather*); (naut) line; **barba a punta** imperial, goatee; **fare la barba** (**a**) to shave; **farla in barba a qlcu** to act in spite of s.o.; to dupe s.o.; **mettere barbe** to take root; **radersi la barba** to shave

barbabiètola *f* beet; sugar beet

barbafòrte *m* horseradish

barbagian·ni *m* (**-ni**) owl; (fig) jackass

barbà·glio *m* (**-gli**) glitter, dazzle

barbaré·sco -sca (**-schi -sche**) *adj* Barbary || *m* inhabitant of the Barbary States

barbàri·co -ca *adj* (**-ci -che**) barbaric

barbà·rie *f* (**-rie**) barbarism, barbarity

barbarismo *m* barbarism

bàrba·ro -ra *adj* barbarous, barbaric || *m* barbarian

barbazzale *m* curb (*of bit*)

Barberìa, la Barbary States

barbétta *f* fetlock (*tuft of hair on horse*); goatee; (mil) barbette; (naut) painter

barbière *m* barber

barbierìa *f* barbershop

barbi·glio *m* (**-gli**) barb (*of arrow*)

barbi·no -na *adj* shoddy; botched; stingy

bàr·bio *m* (**-bi**) (ichth) barbel

barbiturato *m* barbiturate

barbitùri·co -ca (**-ci -che**) *adj* barbituric || *m* barbiturate

barbo *m* var of **barbio**

barbò·gio -gia *adj* (**-gi -gie**) senile

barbóne *m* long beard, thick beard; poodle; (coll) bum, hobo

barbó·so -sa [s] *adj* boring

barbugliare §280 *tr* to stutter (*e.g., a word*) || *intr* to stutter; to bubble, gurgle

barbu·to -ta *adj* bearded

bar·ca *f* (**-che**) boat; heap; (fig) family

affairs; **barca a motore** motorboat;
barca da pesca fishing boat; **barca a
remi** rowboat
barcàc•cia f (-ce) (theat) stage box
barcaiòlo m boatman
barcamenare (barcaméno) ref to manage, get along
barcarizzo m (naut) gangway
barcaròla f barcarole
barcata f boatful
barchéssa f tool shed
barchétta f small boat; (naut) log chip
barcollare (barcòllo) intr to totter,
stagger
barcollóni adv staggering, tottering
barcóne m barge
bardare tr to harness || ref to get
dressed
bardatura f harnessing; harness
bardo m bard
bardòsso m —**a bardosso** (archaic) bareback
barèlla f stretcher
barellare (barèllo) tr to carry on a
stretcher || intr to totter, stagger
barenatura f (mach) boring
bargèllo m (hist) chief of police; (hist)
police headquarters
bargi•glio m (-gli) wattle
baricèntro m center of gravity; (fig) essence, gist
barile m barrel, cask
barilòtto m keg
bàrio m barium
bari•sta mf (-sti -ste) bartender, bar-
keeper || m barman || f barmaid
baritonale adj baritone
barìto•no -na adj barytone || m bari-
tone
barlume m glimmer, gleam
baro m cheat, cardsharp
baròc•co -ca adj & m (-chi -che) baroque
baròmetro m barometer
baróne m baron
baronéssa f baroness
barra f bar; link; rod; sandbar; **andare
alla barra** to plead a case; **barra del
timone** (naut) tiller; **barra di torsione**
(aut) torsion bar; **barra spaziatrice**
space bar (of typewriter)
barrare tr to cross, draw lines across
(a check)
barrétta f bar (e.g., of chocolate)
barricare §197 **(bàrrico)** tr to barricade
|| ref to barricade oneself
barricata f barricade
barrièra f barrier; bar; **barriera corallina** barrier reef
barrire §176 intr to trumpet (said of
elephant)
barrito m trumpeting, cry of an elephant
barroc•ciàio m (-ciài) cart driver
barròc•cio m (-ci) cart
baruffa f fight, quarrel
barzellétta [dz] f joke
basale adj basal
basalto m basalt
basaménto m foundation (of building);
baseboard; base (of column)

basare tr to base || ref—**basarsi su** to be
based on; to rest on
ba•sco -sca adj & mf (-schi -sche)
Basque
basculla f balance, scale
base f base, foundation; (fig) basis; **a
base di** composed of, made of; **base
navale** naval base, naval station; **in
base a** according to
basétta f sideburns
bàsi•co -ca adj (-ci -che) (chem) basic
basilare adj basic, fundamental
Basilèa f Basel
basìli•ca f (-che) basilica
basìli•co m (-ci) basil
basilissa f (fig) queen bee
bàsolo m large paving stone
bassacórte f barnyard
bassézza f baseness
bas•so -sa adj low; shallow; late (e.g.,
date); (fig) base, vile; **basso di sta-
tura** short || m bottom; hovel (in
Naples); (mus) basso || **basso** adv
low; down; **a basso, da basso** or **in
basso** downstairs
bassofóndo m (bassifóndi) (naut) shal-
lows, shallow water; **bassifondi**
underworld, slums
bassopiano m lowland
bassorilièvo m bas-relief
bassòt•to -ta adj stocky || m basset
hound
bassotuba m bass horn
bassura f lowland; (fig) baseness
basta f hem; basting (with long stitches)
|| interj enough!
bastante adj sufficient, adequate; comfortable (income)
bastar•do -da adj bastard; irregular ||
m bastard
bastare intr to suffice, be enough;
basta! enough!; **basta che** + subj as
long as + ind; **bastare a sé stesso**
to be self-sufficient; **non basta che** +
subj not only + ind
bastévole adj sufficient
bastiménto m ship; shipload
bastióne m bastion; (fig) defense, rampart
basto m packsaddle; (fig) burden
bastonare (bastóno) tr to club, cudgel;
bastonare di santa ragione to give a
good thrashing to
bastonata f clubbing, cudgeling; **darsi
bastonate da orbi** to thrash one another soundly
bastoncino m small stick; roll; (anat)
rod
bastóne m stick, cane; pole; club;
baton; staff; French bread; **bastone
a leva** crowbar; **bastone animato**
sword cane; **bastone da golf** club;
bastone da montagna alpenstock;
bastone da passeggio walking stick;
bastone da sci ski pole; **bastoni** suit
in Neapolitan cards corresponding to
clubs; **mettere il bastone tra le ruote**
to throw a monkey wrench into the
machinery
batàc•chio m (-chi) clapper (of bell);
cudgel
batata f sweet potato

batisfèra *f* bathysphere
batista *f* batiste, cambric
batòsta *f* blow; (fig) blow
bàtrace or batrace *m* batrachian
battà·glia *f* (-glie) battle; campaign
battagliare §280 *intr* to fight
battagliè·ro -ra *adj* fighting, warlike
battà·glio *m* (-gli) clapper (*of bell*);
knocker
battagliòne *m* battalion
battèllo *m* boat; battello di salvataggio
lifeboat; battello pneumatico rubber
raft
battènte *m* leaf (*e.g., of door*); knocker;
tapper (*of alarm clock*)
bàttere *m*—in un batter d'occhio in the
twinkling of an eye || *tr* to beat; to
hit; to strike; to strike (*the hour;
said of a clock*); to click (*teeth,
heels*); to clap (*hands*); to stamp
(*one's foot*); to mint (*coins*); to fly
(*a flag*); to beat (*time*); to scour (*the
countryside*); to flap (*the wings*);
(sports) to beat; (sports) to kick (*a
penalty*); **battere a macchina** to type;
battere il naso in to chance upon;
battere la fiacca to goof off; **battere
la grancassa per** to ballyhoo; **battere
la strada** to be a streetwalker; **senza
batter ciglio** without batting an eye
|| *intr* (ESSERE) to beat down (*said,
e.g., of rain*); to beat (*said of the
heart*); to chatter (*said of teeth*); to
knock (*at the door*); **battere in ritirata** to beat a retreat; **battere in testa**
(aut) to knock
batteria *f* battery; set (*of utensils*);
(sports) heat
batterici·da (-di -de) *adj* bactericidal ||
m bactericide
battèri·co -ca *adj* (-ci -che) bacterial
battè·rio *m* (-ri) bacterium
batteriologìa *f* bacteriology
batteriòlo·go -ga *mf* (-gi -ghe) bacteriologist
batteri·sta *mf* (-sti -ste) jazz drummer
battesimale *adj* baptismal
battésimo *m* baptism; **tenere a battesimo** to christen
battezzare (battézzo) [ddzz] *tr* to chris-
ten || *ref* to receive baptism; to as-
sume the name of
battibaléno *m*—in un battibaleno in the
twinkling of an eye
battibéc·co *m* (-chi) squabble
batticuòre *m* palpitation; (fig) trepidation
battilò·ro *m* (-ro) goldsmith; silversmith
battimano *m* applause
battimuro *m*—giocare a battimuro to
pitch pennies (against a wall)
battipalo *m* pile driver
battipan·ni *m* (-ni) clothes beater
battira·me *m* (-me) coppersmith
battiscó·pa *m* (-pa) washboard, baseboard
batti·sta *adj & mf* (-sti -ste) Baptist
battistèro *m* baptistry
battistra·da *m* (-da) outrider; (sports)
leader; (aut) tread
battitappéto *m* carpet sweeper
bàttito *m* beating; palpitation; ticking;

wink; pitter-patter (*of rain*)
batti·tóio *m* (-tói) leaf (*e.g., of door*);
casement; cotton beater
battitóre *m* (hunt) beater; (baseball)
batter
battitrice *f* threshing machine
battitura *f* thrashing, whipping; threshing (*e.g., of wheat*)
battu·to -ta *adj* beaten; hammered ||
m pavement || *f* beat; stroke, key-
stroke; meter (*in poetry*); witticism,
quip; (hunt) battue; (mus) bar; (tennis) service; (theat) line; (theat) cue;
battuta d'aspetto (mus) pause; **dare
la battuta** to give the cue
batùffolo *m* wad; (fig) bundle
baule *m* trunk; **baule armadio** wardrobe
trunk; **fare i bauli** to be on one's
way; **fare il baule** to pack one's trunk
baulétto *m* small trunk; handbag; jewel
case
bava *f* slobber; foam, froth; burr (*on
metal edge*); **avere la bava alla bocca**
to be frothing at the mouth; **bava di
vento** breath of air, soft breeze
bavaglino *m* bib
bavà·glio *m* (-gli) gag
bavarése [*s*] *adj & mf* Bavarian || *f*
Bavarian cream; chocolate cream
bàvero *m* collar
bavièra *f* beaver (*of helmet*) || la Ba-
viera Bavaria
bavó·so -sa [*s*] *adj* slobbering, slobbery
bazza [ddzz] *f* protruding chin; windfall
bazzana [ddzz] *f* sheepskin
bazzècola [ddzz] *f* trifle, bauble
bazzicare §197 (bàzzico) *tr* to frequent
bazzòt·to -ta [ddzz] *adj* soft-boiled;
uncertain (*weather*)
beare (bèo) *tr* to delight || *ref* to be de-
lighted, be enraptured
beatificare §197 (beatìfico) *tr* to beatify
beatitùdine *f* beatitude, bliss
bea·to -ta *adj* blissful, happy; blessed
|| *mf* blessed
be·bè *m* (-bè) baby
beccàc·cia *f* (-ce) woodcock
beccaccino *m* snipe
beccafi·co *m* (-chi) figpecker, beccafico
bec·càio *m* (-cài) butcher
beccamòr·ti *m* (-ti) gravedigger
beccare §197 (bécco) *tr* to peck; to
pick; (coll) to catch || *ref* to peck
one another; to quarrel
beccata *f* peck
beccheggiare §290 (becchéggio) *intr*
(naut) to pitch
becchég·gio *m* (-gi) (naut) pitching
beccheria *f* butcher shop
becchime *m* food for poultry
becchino *m* gravedigger
béc·co *m* (-chi) beak, bill; tip, point;
nozzle (*e.g., of teapot*); billy goat;
(vulg) cuckold; **bagnarsi il becco**
(joc) to wet one's whistle; **mettere il
becco in** (coll; joc) to stick one's
nose into; **non avere il becco di un
quattrino** to not have a red cent
beccùc·cio *m* (-ci) small bill; lip, spout
beccuzzare *tr* to peck || *ref* to bill (*said
of doves*)

bécе·ro -ra *adj* (coll) boorish ‖ *m* (coll) boor

beduì·no -na *adj* & *m* Bedouin

befana *f* (coll) Epiphany; old hag

bèffa *f* jest, mockery; **farsi beffa di** to make fun of

beffar·do -da *adj* mocking

beffare (**bèffo**) *tr* to mock, deride ‖ *ref* —**beffarsi di** to make fun of

beffeggiare §290 (**befféggio**) *tr* to scoff at, deride

bè·ga *f* (**-ghe**) quarrel; trouble

beghìna *f* Beguine; bigoted woman

begònia *f* begonia

bèl *adj* apocopated form of **bello**, used only before masculine singular nouns beginning with a consonant except impure **s, z, gn, ps,** and **x,** e.g., **bel ragazzo**

belare (**bèlo**) *tr* to croon ‖ *intr* to bleat, baa; to moan

belato *m* bleat, baa

bèl·ga *adj* & *mf* (**-gi -ghe**) Belgian

Bèlgio, il Belgium

bèll' *adj* apocopated form of **bello,** used only before singular nouns of both genders beginning with a vowel, e.g., **bell'amico; bell'epoca**

bèlla *adj fem* of **bello** ‖ *f* belle; girlfriend; final draft; (sports) final game; (sports) rubber match; **alla bell'e meglio** the best one could; **bella di notte** (bot) four-o'clock

belladònna *f* belladonna

bellétto *m* rouge, makeup

bellézza *f* beauty; **che bellezza!** how lovely!; **la bellezza di** as much as

bellici·sta *adj* (**-sti -ste**) bellicose

bèlli·co -ca *adj* (**-ci -che**) war, warlike

bellicó·so -sa [s] *adj* bellicose

belligerante *adj* & *m* belligerent

belligeranza *f* belligerence

bellimbusto *m* fop, dandy, beau

bèl·lo -la (declined like **quello** §7) *adj* beautiful; lovely; handsome; good-looking; pleasing; fine; quite a, e.g., **una bella cifra** quite a sum; fair; pretty; **bell'e fatto** ready-made; taken care of; **farla bella** to start trouble; (coll) to do it, e.g., **l'hai fatta bella** you've done it; **farsi bello** to dress up; **farsi bello di** to appropriate ‖ *m* beauty; beautiful; climax; fine weather; beau; **il bello è** the funny thing is; **sul più bello** just then; **sul più bello che** just when ‖ *f* see **bella** ‖ **bello** *adv*—**bel bello** slowly

bellospìrito *m* (**begli spiriti**) wit, bel-esprit

bellui·no -na *adj* wild, fierce

bellumóre *m* (**begli umori**) jolly fellow

bel·tà *f* (**-tà**) beauty (*woman*); (lit) beauty

bélva *f* wild beast

belvedére *adj* (rr) observation (*car*) ‖ *m* belvedere; (naut) topgallant

Belzebù *m* Beelzebub

bemòlle *m* (mus) flat

benama·to -ta *adj* beloved

benarriva·to -ta *adj* welcome

benché *conj* although, albeit

bènda *f* bandage; band; blindfold; **benda gessata** cast, surgical dressing

bendàg·gio *m* (**-gi**) bandage

bendare (**bèndo**) *tr* to bandage; **bendare gli occhi a** to blindfold

bendispó·sto -sta *adj* well-disposed

bène *adj* well; well-born ‖ *m* goal, aim; good; love; sake; **bene dell'anima** profound affection; **beni** (econ) assets, goods; **beni di consumo** consumer goods; **beni immobili** real estate; **beni mobili** personal property, chattels; **beni rifugio** hedge (*e.g., against inflation*); **è un bene** it is a blessing; **fare del bene** to do good; **per il Suo bene** for your sake; **voler bene a** to love, like; to care for ‖ *adv* well; all right; properly; **ben bene** quite carefully; **star bene** to be well; **va bene** O.K., all right

benedetti·no -na *adj* & *m* Benedictine

benedét·to -ta *adj* blessed; holy

benedire §195 *tr* to bless; to praise; **andare a farsi benedire** (coll) to go to wrack and ruin; **mandare a farsi benedire** (coll) to get rid of, dump

benedizióne *f* benediction; boon

beneduca·to -ta *adj* well-behaved

benefattóre *m* benefactor

benefattrice *f* benefactress

beneficare §197 (**benèfico**) *tr* to benefit, help

beneficènza *f* welfare; charity, beneficence

beneficiale *adj* beneficial

beneficiare §128 *intr* to benefit

beneficià·rio -ria *adj* & *mf* (**-ri -rie**) beneficiary

beneficiata *f* benefit performance; streak of good luck; streak of bad luck

benefì·cio *m* (**-ci**) benefice; profit; favor; benefit

benèfi·co -ca *adj* (**-ci -che**) beneficial; beneficent

benemerènte *adj* deserving, well-deserving

benemèri·to -ta *adj* worthy, deserving ‖ *m*—**benemerito della patria** national hero ‖ *f*—**la Benemerita** the Carabinieri

beneplàcito *m* approval, consent; **a beneplacito di** at the pleasure of

benèssere *m* well-being, comfort; prosperity

benestante *adj* well-to-do ‖ *mf* well-to-do person

benestare *m* approval; prosperity; **dare il benestare a** to approve

benevolènte *adj* benevolent

benevolènza *f* benevolence

benèvo·lo -la *adj* well-meaning; benevolent

benfat·to -ta *adj* well-done; well-favored; shapely

benga·la *m* (**-li** & **-la**) fireworks

benga·li *adj* & *mf* (**-li**) Bengalese

beniami·no -na *mf* favorite child; favorite

benigni·tà *f* (**-tà**) benignity; graciousness; mildness (*of climate*)

beni·gno -gna *adj* benign; gracious; mild (*climate*)

benintenziona·to -ta *adj* well-meaning

benintéso [s] *adv* of course, naturally

bènna *f* bucket, scoop (*e.g., of dredge*)

benna·to -ta *adj* (lit) well-born

benpensante *m* sensible person; conformist

benportante *adj* well-preserved

benservito *m* testimonial, recommendation; **dare il benservito a** to dismiss, fire

bensì *adv* indeed || *conj* but

bentorna·to -ta *adj & m* welcome || *interj* welcome back!

benvenu·to -ta *adj & m* welcome; **dare il benvenuto a** to welcome

benvi·sto -sta *adj* well-thought-of

benvolére *tr*—**farsi benvolere da qlcu** to enter the good graces of s.o.; **prendere a benvolere qlcu** to be well-disposed toward s.o.

benvolu·to -ta *adj* liked, loved

benzina *f* gasoline, gas; benzine; **far benzina** (coll) to get gas

benzi·nàio *m* (**-nài**) gasoline dealer; gas-station attendant

benzòlo *m* benzene

beóne *m* drunkard, toper

bequadro *m* (mus) natural

berciare §128 (**bèrcio**) *intr* (coll) to yell

bére *m* drink, drinking || §120 *tr* to drink; (fig) to swallow; **bere come una spugna** to drink like a fish; **darla a bere** to make believe

bergamòt·to -ta *adj* bergamot || *m* bergamot orange || *f* bergamot pear

berillio *m* beryllium

berlina *f* pillory; berlin, coach; (aut) sedan; **mettere alla berlina** to pillory

berlinése [s] *adj* Berlin || *mf* Berliner

Berlino *m* Berlin

bermuda *mpl* Bermuda shorts || **le Bermude** Bermuda

bernòccolo *m* bump, protuberance; (fig) knack

berrétta *f* biretta

berrétto *m* cap; **berretto a sonagli** cap and bells; **berretto da notte** nightcap; **berretto gogliardico** student cap

bersagliare §280 *tr* to harass, pursue; to bomb, bombard

bersà·glio *m* (**-gli**) target; butt (*of a joke*); target (*of criticism*)

bèrta *f* pile driver; **dar la berta a** to ridicule

bertùc·cia *f* (**-ce**) Barbary ape; **fare la bertuccia di** to ape

bestémmia *f* blasphemy

bestemmiare §287 (**bestémmio**) *tr* to blaspheme, curse

bestemmia·tóre -trice *adj* blasphemous || *mf* blasphemer

béstia *f* beast, animal; **andare in bestia** to fly into a rage; **bestia da soma** beast of burden; **bestia nera** pet aversion, bête noire; **bestie grosse** cattle

bestiale *adj* beastly, bestial

bestiali·tà *f* (**-tà**) beastliness; blunder

bestiame *m* livestock; **bestiame da cortile** barnyard animals; **bestiame grosso** cattle

bestino *m* gamy odor; stench of perspiration

bestiòla *f* tiny animal; pet

bestsèl·ler *m* (**-ler**) best seller

Betlèmme *f* Bethlehem

betonièra *f* cement mixer

béttola *f* tavern

bettolière *m* tavern keeper

bettònica *f* betony; **conosciuto più della bettonica** very well-known

betulla *f* birch

bèuta *f* flask

bevanda *f* drink, beverage

beveràg·gio *m* (**-gi**) beverage, potion

bevìbile *adj* drinkable

bevi·tóre -trice *mf* drinker

bevuta *f* drink, drinking

bezzicare §197 (**bézzico**) *tr* to peck; to vex || *ref* to fight one another

biacca *f* white lead

biada *f* feed; **biade** harvest

bianca·stro -stra *adj* whitish

biancheria *f* laundry; linen; underwear; **biancheria da letto** bed linen; **biancheria da tavola** table linen; **biancheria di bucato** freshly laundered clothes; **biancheria intima** underclothes

bianchézza *f* whiteness

bianchire §176 *tr* to blanch; to bleach; to polish

bian·co -ca (**-chi -che**) *adj* white; clean; **bianco come un cencio lavato** as white as a ghost || *m* white; ... il **bianco a** to whitewash; **in bianco** blank (*paper*); **mangiare in bianco** to eat a bland or non-spicy ...et; **ricamare in bianco** to embroider

biancóre *m* whiteness

biancospino *m* hawthorn

biascicare §197 (**biàscico**) *tr* to chew with difficulty; to peck at (*one's food*); to mumble

biasimare (**biàsimo**) *tr* to blame

biasimévole *adj* blamable, censurable

biàsimo *m* blame, censure; **dare una nota di biasimo a** to censure

biauricolare *adj* binaural

Bibbia *f* Bible

bibe·rón *m* (**-rón**) nursing bottle

bìbita *f* soft drink

bìbli·co -ca *adj* (**-ci -che**) Biblical

biblio·bus *m* (**-bus**) bookmobile

bibliòfi·lo -la *mf* bibliophile

bibliografìa *f* bibliography

bibliotè·ca *f* (**-che**) library; bookshelf, stack; collection (*of books*); **biblioteca ambulante** walking encyclopedia

bibliotecà·rio -ria *mf* (**-ri -rie**) librarian

bìbu·lo -la *adj* absorbent (*e.g., paper*)

bi·ca *f* (**-che**) pile of sheaves

bicarbonato *m* bicarbonate; **bicarbonato di soda** bicarbonate of soda, baking soda

bicchierata *f* glassful; wine party

bicchière *m* glass

bicchierino *m* small glass, liquor glass; **bicchierino da rosolio** whiskey glass, jigger

biciclétta *f* bicycle

bicilìndri·co -ca *adj* (**-ci -che**) two-cylinder

bicìpite *adj* two-headed ‖ *m* biceps
bicòc·ca *f* (-che) castle built on a hill; shanty, hut
bicolóre *adj* two-color
bicòrno *m* two-cornered hat
bidèllo *m* school janitor, caretaker
bidènte *m* two-pronged pitchfork
bidimensionale *adj* two-dimensional
bidóne *m* can *(for milk)*; drum *(for gasoline or oil)*; jalopy; (slang) fraud
bidon·ville *f* (-ville) shantytown
biè·co -ca *adj* (-chi -che) awry; sullen; cross; fierce; **guardar bieco** to look askance (at)
bièlla *f* connecting rod
biennale *adj* biennial ‖ *f* biennial show
biènne *adj* biennial
bièn·nio *m* (-ni) biennium
biètola *f* Swiss chard
biétta *f* wedge, chock; (naut) batten
bifase *adj* diphase
biffa *f* (surv) rod
biffare *tr* to cross out; (surv) to level
bifi·do -da *adj* bifurcate
bifocale *adj* bifocal
bifól·co·m (-chi) ox driver; clodhopper, boor
biforcaménto *m* bifurcation
biforcare §197 (bifórco) *tr* to bifurcate
biforcazióne *f* bifurcation, branching off; fork *(of a road)*
biforcu·to -ta *adj* forked; cloven *(e.g., hoof)*
bifrónte *adj* two-faced
bi·ga *f* (-ghe) chariot
bigamìa *f* bigamy
bìga·mo -ma *adj* bigamous ‖ *mf* bigamist
bighellonare (bighellóno) *intr* to idle, dawdle, dally
bighelló·ne -na *mf* idler, dawdler
bigino *m* (slang) pony *(used to cheat)*
bì·gio -gia *adj* (-gi -gie) gray, grayish; (fig) undecided
bigiotterìa *f* costume jewelry; costume jewelry store
bigliardo *m* billiards
bigliet·tàio *m* (-tài) ticket agent; (rr) conductor
biglietterìa *f* ticket office; (theat) box office
bigliétto *m* note; card; ticket; **biglietto d'abbonamento** commutation ticket; season ticket; **biglietto d'andata e ritorno** round-trip ticket; **biglietto di banca** banknote; **biglietto di lotteria** lottery ticket, chance; **biglietto d'invito** invitation; **biglietto di visita** calling card; business card; **biglietto di Stato** banknote; **mezzo biglietto** half fare
bignè *m* (bigné) puff, creampuff
bigodino *m* curler; roller
bigón·cia *f* (-ce) vat; bucket; **a bigonce** abundantly
bigón·cio *m* (-ci) vat; tub; (theat) ticket box *(for stubs)*
bigottismo *m* bigotry
bigòt·to -ta *adj* bigoted ‖ *mf* bigot
bilàn·cia *f* (-ce) balance, scale; **bilancia commerciale** balance of trade; **bilan-**

cia dei pagamenti balance of payments ‖ **Bilancia** *f* (astr) Libra
bilanciare §128 *tr & ref* to balance
bilancière *m* balance; balance wheel; rope-walker's balancing rod
bilàn·cio *m* (-ci) balance; **bilancio consuntivo** balance sheet; **bilancio preventivo** budget; **fare il bilancio** to balance; to strike a balance
bile *f* bile; **rodersi dalla bile** to burn with anger
bìlia *f* billiard ball; marble; (billiards) pocket
biliardino *m* pocket billiards; pinball machine
biliardo *m* billiards
biliare *adj* bile; gall *(stone)*
bili·co *m* (-chi) balance, equipoise; **in bilico** in balance; **tenere in bilico** to balance
bilingue *adj* bilingual
bilióne *m* billion; trillion (Brit)
bilió·so -sa [s] *adj* bilious
bìm·bo -ba *mf* child
bimensile *adj* bimonthly
bimèstre *m* period of two months
bimotóre *adj* twin-engine ‖ *m* twin-engine plane
binà·rio -ria (-ri -rie) *adj* binary ‖ *m* (rr) track; **binario morto** (rr) siding; **uscire dai binari** (rr) to run off the track; (fig) to go astray
bina·to -ta *adj* binary; twin *(e.g., guns)*
binda *f* (aut) jack
binòcolo *m* binoculars; **binocolo da teatro** opera glasses
binò·mio -mia (-mi -mie) *adj* binomial ‖ *m* binomial; couple, pair
biòccolo *m* wad *(of cotton)*; flake *(of snow)*; flock *(of wool)*
biochìmi·co -ca (-ci -che) *adj* biochemical ‖ *m* biochemist ‖ *f* biochemistry
biodegradàbile *adj* biodegradable
biofisica *f* biophysics
biografìa *f* biography
biogràfi·co -ca *adj* (-ci -che) biographic(al)
biògra·fo -fa *mf* biographer
biologìa *f* biology
biòlo·go·m (-gi) biologist
biondeggiare §290 (biondéggio) *intr* to be or become blond; to ripen *(said of grain)*
bión·do -da *adj* blond, fair ‖ *m* blond; blondness ‖ *f* blonde
biopsìa *f* biopsy
biòssido *m* dioxide
bipartìti·co -ca *adj* (-ci -che) two-party, bipartisan
biparti·to -ta *adj* bipartite ‖ *m* two-party government
bìpede *adj* & *m* biped
bipènne *f* double-bitted ax
biplano *m* biplane
bipósto *adj* invar having seats for two ‖ *m* two-seater
birba *f* rascal, rogue
birbante *m* scoundrel, rascal; (joc) madcap, wild young fellow
birbanterìa *f* knavery; trick
birbonata *f* trick

birbó·ne -na *adj* wicked ‖ *mf* rascal, rogue, scoundrel
bireattóre *m* twin jet
birichinata *f* prank
birichi·no -na *adj* prankish; spirited ‖ *mf* rogue; urchin
birillo *m* pin; **birilli** ninepins; tenpins
Birmània, la Burma
birra *f* beer; **birra chiara** light beer; **birra scura** dark beer
bir·ràio *m* (**-rài**) brewer; beer distributor
birrería *f* brewery; tavern; beer saloon
bis *adj invar*—**treno bis** (rr) second section ‖ *m* (**bis**) encore ‖ *interj* encore!
bisàc·cia *f* (**-ce**) knapsack; saddlebag, bag (*of mendicant friar*)
Bisànzio *m* Byzantium
bisa·vo -va *mf* great-grandparent; ancestor ‖ *m* great-grandfather ‖ *f* great-grandmother
bisbèti·co -ca (**-ci -che**) *adj* shrewish; crotchety; cantankerous ‖ *f* (fig) shrew
bisbigliare §280 *tr & intr* to whisper
bisbì·glio *m* (**-gli**) whisper
bisbòccia *f*—**fare bisboccia** to revel
bisboccióne *m* reveler
bis·ca *f* (**-che**) gambling house
Biscàglia *f* Biscay, e.g., **Baia di Biscàglia** Bay of Biscay; **la Biscàglia** Biscay
biscaglina *f* (naut) Jacob's ladder
biscazzière *m* gaming-house operator; habitué of a gaming house; marker (*at billiards*)
bischero *m* (mus) peg
bi·scia *f* (**-sce**) snake; **biscia d'acqua** water snake
biscottare (**biscòtto**) *tr* to toast
biscotterìa *f* cookie factory; cookie store
biscottièra *f* cookie jar
biscottifì·cio *m* (**-ci**) cookie factory
biscòt·to -ta *adj* twice-baked ‖ *m* cookie
biscròma *f* (mus) demisemiquaver
bisdòsso *m*—**a bisdosso** bareback
bisecare [s] §197 (**biseco**) *tr* to bisect
bisènso *m* double meaning
bisessuale [s] *adj* bisexual
bisestile *adj* leap (*year*)
bisettimanale [s] *adj* biweekly
bisettrice [s] *f* bisector
bisezióne *f* bisection
bisìlla·bo -ba [s] *adj* disyllabic
bislac·co -ca *adj* (**-chi -che**) queer, extravagant
bislun·go -ga *adj* (**-ghi -ghe**) oblong
bismuto *m* bismuth
bisnòn·no -na *mf* great-grandparent; **bisnonni** ancestors ‖ *m* great-grandfather ‖ *f* great-grandmother
bisógna *f* (lit) task, job
bisognare (**bisógna**) *intr* (with *dat*) to need, e.g., **gli bisognavano tre litri di benzina** he needed three liters of gasoline ‖ *impers*—**bisogna** + *inf* it is necessary to, e.g., **bisogna partire** it is necessary to leave; **bisogna che** + *subj* must, to have to, e.g., **bisogna che me ne vada** I must go,

I have to go; **bisognando** if need be; **non bisogna** one should not; **più che non bisogna** more than necessary
bisognévole *adj* needy
bisógno *m* need; want, lack; **aver bisogno di** to need; **c'è bisogno di** there is need of; **se ci fosse bisogno** if need be
bisognó·so -sa *adj* needy ‖ **i bisognosi** the needy
bisolfato [s] *m* bisulfate
bisolfito [s] *m* bisulfite
bisolfuro [s] *m* bisulfide
bisónte *m* bison
bistec·ca *f* (**-che**) beefsteak, steak; **bistecca al sangue** rare steak
bisticciare §128 *intr & ref* to quarrel, bicker
bistìc·cio *m* (**-ci**) quarrel, bickering; play on words, pun
bistrattare *tr* to mistreat
bistu·ri *m* (**-ri**) bistouri, surgical knife
bisul·co -ca [s] *adj* (**-chi -che**) cloven
bisun·to -ta *adj* greasy
bitagliènte *adj* double-edged
bitòrzolo *m* wart (*on humans, plants, or animals*); pimple (*on human face*)
bitta *f* (naut) bollard
bitume *m* bitumen, asphalt
bituminó·so -sa [s] *adj* bituminous
bivaccare §197 *intr* to bivouac; to spend the night
bivac·co *m* (**-chi**) bivouac
bi·vio *m* (**-vi**) fork (*of road*); **essere al bivio** (fig) to be at the crossroads
bizanti·no -na [dz] *adj* Byzantine
bizza [ddzz] *f* tantrum; **fare le bizze** to go into a tantrum
bizzarrìa [ddzz] *f* extravagance, oddity
bizzar·ro -ra [ddzz] *adj* bizarre, odd; skittish (*e.g., horse*)
bizzèffe [ddzz] *adv*—**a bizzeffe** plenty, in abundance
bizzó·so -sa [ddzz] [s] *adj* irritable
blandire §176 *tr* to blandish, coax; to soothe, mitigate
blandìzie *fpl* blandishment
blan·do -da *adj* bland
blasfemare (**blasfèmo**) *tr & intr* to blaspheme
blasfè·mo -ma *adj* blasphemous
blasona·to -ta *adj* emblazoned
blasóne *m* coat of arms, blazon
blaterare (**blàtero**) *intr* to babble
blatta *f* water bug, cockroach
blenoraggìa *f* gonorrhea
blè·so -sa *adj* lisping
blindàg·gio *m* (**-gi**) armor
blindare *tr* to armor
bloccare §197 (**blòcco**) *tr* to block; to blockade; to stop; to jam; to close up; to freeze (*e.g., prices*); (sports) to block ‖ *intr*—**bloccare su** to vote as a block for ‖ *ref* to stop
blòc·co *m* (**-chi**) block; blockade; note-book, pad; freezing (*e.g., of wages*); **in blocco** in bulk
bloc-notes *m* (**-notes**) notebook ·
blu *adj invar & m* blue
blua·stro -stra *adj* bluish
bluffare *intr* to bluff
blusa *f* blouse; smock

bò·a *m* (-a) boa ‖ *f* buoy
boà·rio -ria *adj* (-ri -rie) cattle
boa·ro -ra *adj* ox ‖ *m* stable boy
boato *m* roar; **boato sonico** sonic boom
bobina *f* spool (*of thread*); coil (*of wire*); reel (*of movie film; of magnetic tape*); roll (*of film*); cylinder, bobbin; (elec) coil; **bobina d'accensione** spark coil
bóc·ca *f* (-che) mouth; nozzle; muzzle (*of gun*); pit (*of the stomach*); opening; straits; pass; **a bocca aperta** agape; **bocca da fuoco** cannon; **di buona bocca** easily pleased; **in bocca al lupo!** good luck!; **per bocca** orally; **rimanere a bocca asciutta** to be foiled; to be left high and dry; **tieni la bocca chiusa!** shut up!
boccaccé·sco -sca *adj* (-schi -sche) written by or in the style of Boccaccio; bawdy, licentious
boccàc·cia *f* (-ce) ugly mouth; grimace; **fare le boccacce** to make faces
boccà·glio *m* (-gli) nozzle (*of hose or pipe*); mouthpiece (*of megaphone*)
boccale *adj* oral ‖ *m* jug, tankard
boccapòrto *m* hatch; port; mouth (*of oven or furnace*); **chiudere i boccaporti** to batten the hatches
boccascè·na *m* (-na) proscenium, front (*of stage*)
boccata *f* mouthful; **andare a prendere una boccata d'aria** to go out for a breath of fresh air
boccétta *f* small bottle, vial; small billiard ball
boccheggiante *adj* gasping; moribund
boccheggiare §290 (bocchéggio) *intr* to gasp
bocchétta *f* nozzle (*of sprinkling can*); mouthpiece (*of wind instrument*); opening (*of drainage or ventilation system*); **bocchetta stradale** manhole
bocchino *m* cigarette holder; mouthpiece (*of cigarette or of musical instrument*)
bòc·cia *f* (-ce) decanter; ball (*for bowling*); **bocce** bowls
bocciare §128 (bòccio) *tr* to score (*at bowling*); to reject (*a proposal*); to flunk (*a student*)
bocciatura *f* failure
boccino *m* jack (*at bowls*)
bocciòlo *m* bud
bóccola *f* buckle; earring; (mach) bushing
bocconcino *m* morsel; (culin) stew
boccóne *m* mouthful; piece; morsel; **buttar giù un boccone amaro** to swallow a bitter pill; **levarsi il boccone di bocca** to take the bread out of one's mouth (to help someone); **mangiare un boccone** to have a bite ‖ **bocconi** *adv* flat on one's face
boè·mo -ma *adj* & *mf* Bohemian
boè·ro -ra *adj* & *m* Boer
bofonchiare §287 (bofónchio) *intr* to snort, grumble
bò·ia *m* (-ia) hangman, executioner
boiata *f* (slang) infamy; (slang) trash
boicottàg·gio *m* (-gi) boycott
boicottare (boicòtto) *tr* to boycott

bòl·gia *f* (-ge) pit (*in hell*)
bólide *m* (astr) bolide, fireball; (aut) racer; (joc) lummox; **andare come un bolide** to go like a flash
bolina *f* (naut) bowline; **di bolina** (naut) close-hauled
bolivia·no -na *adj* & *mf* Bolivian
bólla *f* bubble; blister; ticket; **bolla di consegna** receipt; **bolla di spedizione** delivery ticket; **bolla di sapone** soap bubble; **bolla papale** papal bull
bollare (bóllo) *tr* to stamp; to brand
bolla·to -ta *adj* stamped; sealed
bollatura *f* stamp; brand; postage
bollènte *adj* boiling, scalding hot
bollétta *f* ticket; receipt; bill; **essere in bolletta** (coll) to be broke
bollettà·rio *m* (-ri) receipt book
bollettino *m* bulletin; receipt; **bollettino dei prezzi correnti** price list; **bollettino di versamento** (com) deposit ticket; **bollettino meteorologico** weather forecast
bollire (bóllo) *tr* & *intr* to boil
bolli·to -ta *adj* boiled ‖ *m* boiled beef
bollitura *f* boiling
bóllo *m* mark, cancellation; revenue stamp; postmark; seal; **bollo a freddo** seal (*embossed*); **bollo postale** cancellation, postmark
bollóre *m* boiling; sultriness; (fig) passion, excitement; **alzare il bollore** to begin to boil
bolló·so -sa [s] *adj* blistery
bolscevi·co -ca *adj* & *mf* (-chi -che) Bolshevik
bolscevismo *m* Bolshevism
ból·so -sa *adj* broken-winded (*horse*); asthmatic
bòma *f* (naut) boom
bómba *f* bomb; bubble gum; fireworks; (aer) double loop; (journ) scandal; **bomba a idrogeno** hydrogen bomb; **bomba a mano** hand grenade; **bomba antisommergibile** depth charge; **bomba a orologeria** time bomb; **bomba atomica** atom bomb; **bomba H** (*acca*) H bomb; **tornare a bomba** (fig) to get back to the point
bombàggio *m* swelling (*of a spoiled can of food*)
bombardaménto *m* bombing, bombardment
bombardare *tr* to bomb, bombard; to besiege (*with questions*)
bombardière *m* (aer) bomber; (mil) artilleryman
bombétta *f* derby (*hat*)
bómbola *f* bottle, cylinder; **bombola d'ossigeno** oxygen tank
bombonièra *f* candy box
bomprèsso *m* (naut) bowsprit
bonàc·cia *f* (-ce) calm; calm sea; (fig) normalcy; (com) stagnation
bonacció·ne -na *adj* good-hearted, good-natured
bonarie·tà *f* (-tà) kindheartedness, good nature
bonà·rio -ria *adj* (-ri -rie) kindhearted, good-natured
boncinèllo *m* hasp
bonifi·ca *f* (-che) reclamation; re-

claimed land; improvement (e.g., of morals); clearing of mines; (metallurgy) hardening and tempering

bonificare §197 (**bonìfico**) tr to reclaim; to discount, make a reduction of; to clear of mines

bonìfi·co m (-ci) discount

bonomìa f good nature; simple-heartedness

bon·tà f (-tà) goodness; kindness; **avere la bontà di** to be kind enough to; be generous; **o la borsa o la vita!** your money or your life!; **pagare di borsa propria** to pay out of one's own pocket

bòra f northeast wind

borace m borax

borbogliare §280 (**borbóglio**) intr to gurgle; to rumble

borbòni·co -ca (-ci -che) adj Bourbon || m Bourbonist

borbottare (**borbòtto**) tr to mutter || intr to mutter; to gurgle; to rumble (said, e.g., of thunder)

borbottì·o m (-ì) mutter; gurgle; rumble

bòrchia f upholsterer's nail; boss, stud

bordare (**bórdo**) tr to border, hem

bordata f (naut) tack; (nav) broadside

bordatura f border, hem

bordeggiare §290 (**bordéggio**) intr (naut) to tack

bordèllo m brothel

borde·rò m (-rò) list; note; (theat) box office, receipts

bórdo m side (of ship); border, hem; edge, rim; (naut) tack; (naut) board; **a bordo on board**; **a bordo di** on board; on, in; **bordo d'entrata** (aer) leading edge; **bordo d'uscita** (aer) trailing edge; **d'alto bordo** (naut) big, sea-going; (fig) high-toned; **virare di bordo** (naut) to change course

bordóne m staff; bass stop (of organ); drone (of insect); **tener bordone a** (mus) to accompany; (fig) to hold the bag for

bordura f hem, edge; rim

boreale adj northern, boreal

borgata f hamlet, village

borghése [s] adj middle-class || mf bourgeois, person of the middle class; civilian; **in borghese** in civilian clothes; in plainclothes

borghesìa f bourgeosie, middle class; **alta borghesia** upper middle class

bór·go m (-ghi) borough; small town; suburb

borgógna m Burgundy (wine) || la **Borgogna** Burgundy

borgognóne m iceberg

borgomastro m burgomaster

bòria f haughtiness, vainglory

bòri·co -ca adj (-ci -che) boric

borió·so -sa [s] adj haughty, puffed-up; blustery

bòro m boron

borotal·co m (-chi) talcum powder

bórra f flock (for pillows); (fig) rubbish, filler

borràc·cia f (-ce) canteen (e.g., for carrying water)

bórro m gully

bórsa f bag; pouch; bourse, exchange; (sports) purse; **borsa da viaggio** traveling bag; **borsa dell'acqua** hot-water bag; **borsa della spesa** shopping bag; **borsa di ghiaccio** ice bag; **borsa di studio** scholarship; **borsa merci** commodity exchange; **borsa nera** black market; **borsa valori** stock exchange; **essere di borsa larga** to be generous;

borsaiòlo m pickpocket

borsanéra f black market

borsaneri·sta mf (-sti -ste) black marketeer

borseggiare §290 (**borséggio**) tr to pick the pocket of; to rob

borseggia·tóre -trice mf pickpocket

borség·gio m (-gi) theft

borsellino m purse

borsétta f handbag, pocketbook

borsétto m man's purse

borsi·sta mf (-sti -ste) recipient of a scholarship; stockbroker

borsìsti·co -ca adj (-ci -che) stock-exchange

borsite f bursitis

boscàglia f thicket, underbrush

boscaiòlo m woodcutter

boscheréc·cio -cia adj (-ci -ce) wood, woodland; rustic; pastoral

boschétto m coppice, copse

boschi·vo -va adj wooded, wood

bò·sco m (-schi) woods, forest; **bosco ceduo** or **da taglio** tree farm

boscó·so -sa [s] adj wooded, woody

bòsforo m (lit) straits || **Bosforo** m Bosphorus

bòsso m boxwood

bòssolo m box; cartridge case

botàni·co -ca (-ci -che) adj botanic(al) || m botanist || f botany

bòtola f trap door

bòtolo m small snarling dog

bòtta f hit; bump; rumble (e.g., of an explosion); thrust, lunging (in fencing); (fig) disaster; **botta dritta** (fencing) lunge; **botta e risposta** give-and-take; **botte da orbi** severe beating

bot·tàio m (-tài) cooper

bótte f barrel, cask, casket

botté·ga f (-ghe) store, shop; **chiudere bottega** to close up shop

botte·gàio -gàia (-gài -gàie) adj store, shop || mf storekeeper, shopkeeper

botteghino m box office; lottery agency

bottìglia f bottle; **bottiglia Molotov** Molotov cocktail

bottiglierìa f wine store, liquor store

bottino m booty, spoil; capture; cesspool; sewage

bòtto m hit, bump; explosion; noise; toll (of bell); **di botto** all of a sudden

bottoncino m small button; cuff button; **bottoncino di rosa** rosebud

bottóne m button; stud; bud; **attaccare un bottone a** (fig) to buttonhole; **botton d'oro** (bot) buttercup; **bottone automatico** snap; **bottone della**

luce (elec) pushbutton; **bottoni gemelli** cuff links; **bottoni gustativi**
taste buds
bottonièra f row of buttons; buttonhole; (elec) panel (*with buttons*)
bova·ro -ra adj & m var of **boaro**
bovile m ox stable
bovi·no -na adj cattle, cow; bovine ∥
m bovine
box m (**box**) locker (*e.g., in a station*);
box stall (*for a horse*); pit (*in auto
racing*); garage (*on the ground floor
of a split-level*); play pen
boxare (**bòxo**) intr to box
boxe f boxing
bòzza f stud, boss; bump (*caused by
blow*); rough copy, draft; **bozze** (typ)
galleys, galley proof
bozzèllo m (mach) block and tackle
bozzétto m sketch
bòzzolo m cocoon; lump (*of flour*)
bra·ca f (**-che**) safety belt; (naut) sling;
brache (archaic) breeches; (joc)
trousers
braccare §197 tr to stalk; to hunt out
braccétto—a braccetto arm in arm
bracciale m armlet, armband; arm rest
braccialétto m bracelet
bracciante m laborer
bracciata f armful; stroke (*in swimming*); **bracciata a rana** breaststroke;
bracciata sul dorso backstroke
bràc·cio m (**-cia** fpl) arm (*of body*);
unit of length (*about 60 centimeters*);
a braccia aperte with open arms;
avere le braccia legate to have one's
hands tied; **braccia** laborers; **braccio
destro** right-hand man; **braccio di
ferro** Indian wrestling; **fare a braccio
di ferro** to play at Indian wrestling;
sentirsi cascare le braccia to lose
courage ∥ m (**-ci**) arm (*e.g., of sea,
chair, lamp, etc.*); beam (*of balance*);
braccio diretto cutoff (*of river*)
bracciòlo m arm; arm rest; banister
brac·co m (**-chi**) hound, beagle
bracconàg·gio m (**-gi**) poaching
bracconière m poacher
brace f embers; (coll) charcoal; **farsi
di brace** to blush
brachétta f flap (*of trousers*); (bb) joint;
brachette shorts
brachière m truss (*for hernia*)
bracière m brazier
braciòla f chop, cutlet
bra·do -da adj wild, untamed
bra·go m (**-ghi**) (lit) mud, slime
brama f ardent desire; covetousness;
longing
bramare tr to desire intensely; to covet;
to long for
bramino m Brahmin
bramire §176 intr to roar; to bell (*said
of a deer*)
bramito m bell (*of deer*)
bramosia [s] f covetousness; greed
bramó·so -sa [s] adj (lit) covetous,
greedy
bran·ca f (**-che**) branch (*of tree*); flight
(*of stairs*); **branche** (poet) clutches
brànchia f gill
brancicare §197 (**bràncico**) tr to finger,
handle ∥ intr to grope

bran·co m (**-chi**) flock, herd; (pej)
crowd
brancolare (**bràncolo**) intr to grope
branda f cot
brandèllo m tatter, shred
brandire §176 tr to brandish
brando m (lit) sword
brano m shred, bit; excerpt; **cadere a
brani** to fall apart; **fare a brani** to
tear apart
brasare tr to braze (*to solder with
brass*); (culin) to braise
brasile m brazil (*nut*) ∥ **il Brasile**
Brazil
brasília·no -na adj & mf Brazilian
bravàc·cio m (**-ci**) braggart, swaggerer
bravare tr to challenge; to threaten ∥
intr to brag
bravata f swagger, bluster; boast; stunt
bra·vo -va adj good, able; honest; good-
hearted; brave; **alla brava** rapidly;
bravo ragazzo good boy; **fare il bravo**
to boast, be a braggart ∥ m mercenary soldier; bravo, hired assassin
∥ **bravo!** interj well done!, bravo!
bravura f ability; bravery; bravura
brèc·cia f (**-ce**) breach, gap; crushed
stone
brefotrò·fio m (**-fi**) foundling hospital
Bretagna, la Britanny
bretèlla f suspenders; strap, shoulder
strap
brètone adj Breton; Arthurian
brève adj brief, short; **in breve** in a nutshell; **per farla breve** in short ∥ m
(eccl) brief ∥ adv (lit) in short
brevettare (**brevétto**) tr to patent
brevétto m patent; (aer) license; (obs)
commission
brevià·rio m (**-ri**) compendium; handbook, vade mecum; (eccl) breviary
brevi·tà f (**-tà**) brevity
brézza [ddzz] f breeze
brezzare (**brézzo**) [ddzz] tr to winnow
∥ intr to blow gently
bricchétta f briquet
bric·co m (**-chi**) kettle, pot
bricconata f rascality
briccó·ne -na mf rascal
bricconeria f rascality
briciola f crumb; **ridurre in briciole** to
crumb, crumble
briciolo m bit, fragment; (fig) least bit;
andare in bricioli to crumble; **mandare in briciòli** to crumble
bri·ga f (**-ghe**) worry, trouble, attacar
briga to pick a fight; **darsi la briga di**
to worry about; **trovarsi in una briga**
to be in trouble
brigadière m noncommissioned officer
(*in carabinieri*); (hist) brigadier
brigantàg·gio m (**-gi**) brigandage
brigante m brigand
brigantino m (naut) brig, brigantine;
brigantino goletta (naut) brigantine
brigare §209 tr to plot; to scheme to get
∥ intr to plot, scheme
brigata f company; (mil) brigade
bri·glia f (**-glie**) bridle; harness (*for
holding baby*); (naut) bobstay; **a
briglia sciolta** at full speed; **tirare le
briglie a** to bridle
brillante adj brilliant ∥ m cut diamond

brillare *tr* to husk, hull (*rice*); to explode (*e.g., a mine*) || *intr* to shine, sparkle; far brillare to explode, blow up

brilli·o *m* (-i) shine, sparkle

bril·lo -la *adj* tipsy

brina *f* frost

brinare *tr* to frost; to turn (*e.g., hair*) gray || *impers* (ESSERE)—è brinato there was frost; brina there is frost

brinata *f* frost

brindare *intr* to toast; brindare alla salute di to toast

brìndisi *m* (-si) toast; pledge; fare un brindisi a to toast

brì·o *m* (-i) sprightliness, liveliness, verve, spirit

briò·scia *f* (-sce) brioche

briò·so -sa [s] *adj* sprightly, lively

briscola *f* briscola (*game*); trump (*card*)

britànni·co -ca *adj* (-ci -che) British, Britannic

britan·no -na *adj* British || *mf* Briton

brivido *m* shake, shiver; thrill; brivido di freddo chill, shiver

brizzola·to -ta *adj* grizzled

bròc·ca *f* (-che) pitcher; pitcherful; shoot, bud; hobnail

broccatèllo *m* brocatel

broccato *m* brocade

bròc·co *m* (-chi) twig; shoot; center pin (*of shield or target*); (coll) nag; dar nel brocco to hit the bull's eye

bròccolo *m* (bot) broccoli; broccoli broccoli (*as food*)

bròda *f* slop, thin or tasteless soup; mud

brodàglia *f* slop

brodétto *m* fish soup

bròdo *m* broth; andar in brodo di giuggiole (fig) to swoon with joy; brodo in dadi cube bouillon; brodo ristretto consommé

brodó·so -sa [s] *adj* thin, watery (*soup*)

brogliàc·cio *m* (-ci) (com) daybook, first draft; (naut) first draft of logbook

bròglio *m* (-gli) plot, intrigue; maneuver; broglio elettorale political maneuver

bròlo *m* (archaic) garden; (lit) garland

bromìdri·co -ca *adj* (-ci -che) hydrobromic

bròmo *m* bromine

bromuro *m* bromide

bronchite *f* bronchitis

brón·cio *m* (-ci) pout, pouting; fare il broncio to sulk; tenere il broncio a to harbor a grudge against

brón·co *m* (-chi) bronchial tube; thorny branch; ramification (*of antlers*)

brontolare (bróntolo) *tr* to grumble (*to express with a grumble*); to grumble at || *intr* to grumble, mutter; to rumble; to gurgle (*said of water*)

brontolì·o *m* (-i) grumble, mutter; rumble; gurgle

brontoló·ne -na *mf* grumbler; curmudgeon

bronzare [dz] (brónzo) *tr* to bronze

brónze·o -a [dz] *adj* bronze; tanned

bronzina [dz] *f* little bell; (mach) bearing; (mach) bushing

brónzo [dz] *m* bronze

brossura *f* brochure; in brossura paperback

brucare §197 *tr* to browse, graze

bruciacchiare §287 *tr* to singe

bruciante *adj* burning

bruciapélo *m*—a bruciapelo point-blank

bruciare §128 *tr* to burn; to burn down; to singe; to scorch; to cauterize (*a wound*); (sports) to overcome with a burst of speed; bruciare le tappe to go straight ahead; to press on || *intr* (ESSERE) to burn; to smart, sting || *ref* to burn (*e.g., one's fingers*); to get burnt; to blow (*one's brains*) out; to burn out (*said of an electric light or fuse*); bruciarsi i vascelli alle spalle to burn one's bridges behind one

bruciatíc·cio *m* (-ci) burnt material; sapere di bruciaticcio to taste burnt

brucia·to -ta *adj* burnt; burnt out || *f* burnt taste or smell || *f* roast chestnut

bruciatóre *m* burner; heater; bruciatore a gas gas burner; bruciatore a nafta oil burner

bruciatorì·sta *m* (-sti) oil burner mechanic

bruciatura *f* burn

brucióre *m* burning; burn; inflammation; bruciore agli occhi eye inflammation; bruciore di stomaco heartburn

bru·co *m* (-chi) caterpillar; worm

bruffolo *m* (coll) small boil

brughièra *f* waste land; heath

brulicare §197 (brùlico) *intr* to crawl; to swarm (*e.g., with bees*); to teem (*with people*)

brulichì·o *m* (-i) crawling; swarming; teeming

brul·lo -la *adj* barren, bare

bruma *f* shipworm; (lit) fog; (lit) winter

bruna·stro -stra *adj* brownish

brunire §176 *tr* to burnish

bru·no -na *adj* brown; dark (*bread; complexion*) || *m* brown; dark; brunet; vestire a bruno to dress in black || *f* brunette

bru·sca *f* (-sche) horse brush; con le brusche curtly

bruschézza *f* brusqueness

bruschino *m* scrub brush

bru·sco -sca (-schi -sche) *adj* sour; curt, gruff; sharp (*weather*); dangerous; sudden || *m* twig || *f* see brusca

brùscolo *m* speck, mote; fare di un bruscolo una trave to make a mountain out of a molehill

brusì·o *m* (-i) buzz, buzzing; (fig) whispering (*gossip*)

brutale *adj* brutal

brutali·tà *f* (-tà) brutality

brutalizzare [ddzz] *tr* to brutalize

bru·to -ta *adj & m* brute

brutta *f* rough copy

bruttare *tr* (lit) to soil

bruttézza *f* ugliness; (fig) lowliness

brut·to -ta *adj* ugly, homely; foul (*weather*); bad (*news*); alle brutte at the worst; con le brutte harshly; farla brutta a to play a mean trick on;

guardare **brutto** to look irritated; **vedersela brutta** to foresee trouble || *m* worst; bad weather || *f* see **brutta**

bruttura *f* ugliness

bùbbola *f* lie; trifle

bùbbolo *m* jingle bell (*on horse*)

bubbòni·co -ca *adj* (**-ci -che**) bubonic

bu·ca *f* (**-che**) hole; pit; hollow; **buca cieca** trap (*for hunting*); **buca del biliardo** pocket; **buca delle lettere** mailbox; **buca del suggeritore** prompter's box; **buca sepolcrale** grave

bucané·ve *m* (**-ve**) snowdrop

bucanière *m* buccaneer

bucare §197 *tr* to pierce; to prick; to puncture (*a tire*)

bucato *m* wash; laundry; **di bucato** freshly laundered; **fare il bucato in famiglia** (fig) to not air one's family affairs, to not wash one's dirty linen in public

bucatura *f* piercing; puncturing; puncture; **bucatura di una gomma** flat tire

bùc·cia *f* (**-ce**) rind, peel; skin (*of a person; of fruit and vegetables*); tender bark; **fare le bucce a** (coll) to thwart, frustrate

bucherellare (**bucherèllo**) *tr* to riddle

bu·co *m* (**-chi**) hole; **fare un buco nell'acqua** to fail miserably

bucòli·co -ca *adj* (**-ci -che**) bucolic, pastoral

Budda *m* Buddha

buddismo *m* Buddhism

buddi·sta *mf* (**-sti -ste**) Buddhist

budèl·lo *m* (**-la** *fpl*) bowel; **budella** bowels; guts || *m* (**-li**) casing (*for salami*); pipe; blind alley

budino *m* pudding

bùe *m* (**buòi**) ox (*for draft*); steer (*for meat*); **bue muschiato** musk ox

bùfalo *m* buffalo

bufèra *f* storm; **bufera di neve** snowstorm; **bufera di pioggia** rainstorm; **bufera di vento** windstorm

buffa *f* cowl; gust of wind; (archaic) trick, jest

buffare *tr* to huff (*at checkers*) || *intr* to joke; (archaic) to blow

buffetteria *f* (mil) accouterments

buffétto *m* tap, slight blow

buf·fo -fa *adj* funny, comical || *m* gust of wind; comic || *f* see **buffa**

buffonata *f* buffoonery; antics

buffóne *m* buffoon, clown; (hist) jester; **buffone di corte** court jester

buffonería *f* buffoonery

buffoné·sco -sca *adj* (**-schi -sche**) clownish

bugìa *f* lie; candlestick; **bugia ufficiosa** white lie

bugiar·do -da *adj* lying, false || *mf* liar

bugiàttolo *m* cubbyhole

bugna *f* ashlar; (naut) clew

bugnato *m* ashlar; (archit) boss

bù·io -ia (*pl* **-i -ie**) *adj* dark || *m* darkness; **buio pesto** pitch dark

bulbo *m* bulb

bùlga·ro -ra *adj & mf* Bulgarian || *m* Russian leather

bulinare *tr* to engrave

bulino *m* burin

bullétta *f* tack

bullonare (**bullóno**) *tr* to bolt

bullóne *m* bolt

buon *adj* apocopated form of **buono,** used before masculine singular nouns except those beginning with impure s, z, gn, ps, and x

buon' *adj* apocopated form of **buona** used before feminine singular nouns beginning with a vowel, e.g., **buon'ora**

buonagràzia *f* (**buonegràzie**) courtesy, good manners; **con Sua buonagrazia** with your permission

buonamano *f* (**buonemani**) tip, gratuity

buonànima *f* departed; **la buonanima di** the late lamented

buonavò·glia *m* (**-glia**) intern (*in a hospital*); (coll) lazybones || *f* good will

buoncostume *m* morals

buongu·stàio *m* (**-stài**) gourmet; connoisseur

buò·no -na *adj* good; kind; high (*society*); cheap (*price*); **alla buona** plainly; without ceremony; **buono a nulla** good-for-nothing; **con le buone** kindly, gently; **che Dio la mandi buona** a may God be kind with; **essere in buona con** to be on good terms with || *m* good person; bond; ticket; **buono a nulla** ne'er-do-well; **buono del tesoro** government bond; **buono di consegna** delivery order; **buono premio** trading stamp

buonsènso *m* common sense

buontempó·ne -na *adj* jolly || *m* playboy || *f* fun-loving girl; playgirl

buonumóre *m* good humor, good cheer

buonuscita *f* indemnity; bonus; severance pay

burattare *tr* to sift

buratti·nàio *m* (**-nài**) puppeteer; puppet maker

burattinata *f* clowning

burattino *m* puppet

buratto *m* sifter, sifting machine

burbanza *f* haughtiness, arrogance

burbanzó·so -sa [s] *adj* haughty, arrogant

bùrbe·ro -ra *adj* gruff, surly

bùr·chio *m* (**-chi**) (naut) lighter

burgun·do -da *adj & mf* Burgundian

burla *f* joke, jest; prank; **mettere in burla** to ridicule; **fuori di burla** joking aside

burlare *tr* to ridicule || *intr* to be joking || *ref* **—burlarsi di** to make fun of

burlé·sco -sca (**-schi -sche**) *adj* funny; mocking; burlesque; jocose || *m* burlesque; mock-heroic

burlétta *f* joke, jest; **mettere in burletta** to ridicule

burló·ne -na *mf* joker, jester

burócrate *m* bureaucrat

burocràti·co -ca *adj* (**-ci -che**) bureaucratic; clerical (*error*)

burocrazia *f* bureaucracy; red tape

burra·sca *f* (**-sche**) storm

burrascó·so -sa [s] *adj* stormy

burrièra *f* butter dish

burrifi·cio *m* (**-ci**) butter factory, dairy

burro *m* butter

burróne *m* canyon, ravine

burró·so -sa [s] *adj* buttery

buscare §197 *tr* to get; to catch ‖ *intr* to be damaged ‖ *ref*—**buscarsi un malanno** to catch a cold

busécchia *f* casing (*for sausage*)

busillis *m*—**qui sta il busillis** here's the rub, that's the trouble

bussa *f* hit, blow; **venire alle busse** to come to blows

bussare *intr* to knock; **bussare a quattrini** (fig) to hit somebody for a loan

bussata *f* knock (*at the door*)

bussa·tòio *m* (**-tòi**) knocker

bùssola *f* sedan chair; door; revolving door; swinging door; ballot box; (mach) bushing; (aer & naut) compass; **perdere la bussola** to lose one's bearings

bussolòtto *m* dice box

busta *f* envelope; briefcase; **busta a finestrella** window envelope; **busta primo giorno** first-day cover; **in busta a parte** under separate cover

bustapa·ga *f* (**-ga**) pay envelope

bustarèlla *f* bribery; kickback

bustina *f* powder, dose; small envelope; (mil) cap, fatigue cap

busto *m* chest, trunk; bust; corset

butirró·so -sa [s] *adj* buttery

buttafuò·ri *m* (**-ri**) bouncer (*in a night club*); (theat) callboy; (naut) outrigger

buttare *tr* to throw; to waste (*e.g., time*); to give off (*e.g., smoke*); **buttar giù** to demolish; to swallow; (fig) to discredit; to jot down; **buttar via** to throw away; to cast aside ‖ *intr* to secrete, ooze ‖ *ref* to throw oneself; to let oneself fall; **buttarsi giù** (fig) to become downcast

butterare (**bùttero**) *tr* to pock, pit

bùttero *m* pockmark; cowboy

buzzo [ddzz] *m* (vulg) belly; **di buzzo buono** with energy; willingly

C

C, c [t/i] *m & f* third letter of the Italian alphabet

càbala *f* cabala; cabal, intrigue

cabina *f* cabin, stateroom; car, cage (*of elevator*); cockpit (*of airplane*); booth (*of telephone*); cab (*of locomotive*)

cablàg·gio *m* (**-gi**) (elec) cable (*in auto or radio*)

cablare *tr* to cable

cablografare (**cablògrafo**) *tr* to cable

cablogram·ma *m* (**-mi**) cablegram, cable

cabotàg·gio *m* (**-gi**) coasting trade, coastal traffic

cabrare *intr* to zoom

cabrata *f* zoom

cacào *m* cocoa

cacasènno *m* (slang) wiseacre

cacatò·a *m* (**-a**) cockatoo

càc·cia -cia (**-cia**) pursuit plane, fighter; (nav) destroyer ‖ *f* chase, hunt; pursuit; **caccia alle streghe** witch hunt

cacciagióne *f* small game; venison; kill (*e.g., of game birds*)

cacciapiè·tre *m* (**-tre**) (rr) cowcatcher

cacciare §128 *tr* to hunt; to chase; to rout; to send out; to stick, thrust; to utter (*e.g., a cry*); **cacciar fuori** to pull out; **cacciar via** to chase away ‖ *ref* to hide; to intrude; to get; to wind up; to thrust oneself; **cacciarsi negli affari di** to butt into the affairs of

cacciasommergìbi·li *m* (**-li**) subchaser, submarine chaser

cacciata *f* hunting party; expulsion

cacciatóra *f* hunting jacket; **alla cacciatora** (culin) stewed with herbs

cacciatóre *m* hunter; (aer) fighter pilot; **cacciatore di frodo** poacher; **cacciatore di teste** headhunter

cacciatorpediniè·re *m* (**-re**) destroyer

cacciatrice *f* huntress

cacciavi·te *m* (**-te**) screwdriver

càccola *f* gum (*on edge of eyelid*); (slang) snot

caccoló·so -sa [s] *adj* gummy (*eyelid*); (slang) snotty

ca·chi (**-chi**) *adj* khaki ‖ *m* Japanese persimmon; khaki

cacic·co *m* (**-chi**) Indian chief; boss (*in Latin America*)

cà·cio *m* (**-ci**) cheese; **come il cacio sui maccheroni** (coll) at the right moment

cacofóni·co -ca *adj* (**-ci -che**) cacophonous

cac·tus *m* (**-tus**) cactus

cadau·no -na *adj* each ‖ *pron* each one

cadàvere *m* corpse, cadaver

cadavèri·co -ca *adj* (**-ci -che**) cadaverous

cadènte *adj* falling (*star*); rickety (*house*); run-down, decrepit (*person*)

cadènza *f* cadence, rhythm; accent (*peculiar to a region*)

cadére §121 *intr* (ESSERE) to fall; to sink; to slough (*said, e.g., of crust*); to fail; (gram) to end; **cadere a proposito** to come in handy; to come at the right moment; **cadere dalle nuvole** to be dumfounded

cadétto *m* cadet

càdmio *m* cadmium

caducità *f* transiency, brevity

cadu·co -ca *adj* (**-ci -che**) fleeting; deciduous

cadu·no -na *adj & pron* var of **cadauno**

cadu·to -ta *adj* fallen; lost, gone astray; **i caduti** the fallen, the dead ‖ *f* fall; crash (*of stock market*); slump (*of prices*)

caf·fè *m* (**-fè**) coffee; café

caffeina *f* caffeine

caffetteria *f* cafeteria

caffettièra *f* coffeepot

cafó·ne -na *adj* loud, gaudy || *m* boor, lout

cagionare (cagióno) *tr* to cause, produce

cagióne *f* cause, reason; a cagione di because of

cagionévole *adj* sickly, delicate

cagliare §280 *tr*, *intr* (ESSERE) & *ref* to curdle, curd

cagliata *f* curd

cà·glio *m* (-gli) rennet

cagna *f* bitch

cagnara *f* barking (*of dogs*); uproar, confusion

cagné·sco -sca (-schi -sche) *adj* dog-like, doggish || *m*—guardare in cagnesco to look askance at; stare in cagnesco con to be angry with

Caino *m* Cain

Càiro, il Cairo

cala *f* cove; (naut) hold

calabrése [s] *adj* & *mf* Calabrian

calabróne *m* hornet

calafatare *tr* (naut) to caulk

cala·màio *m* (-mài) inkwell

calamaro *m* squid

calamita *f* magnet; (*mineral*) loadstone; (fig) magnet, attraction

calami·tà *f* (-tà) calamity, disaster

calamitare *tr* to magnetize

calamitó·so -sa [s] *adj* calamitous

càlamo *m* reed, quill

calandra *f* calender; (aut) grille

calandrare *tr* to calender

calante *adj* waning (*moon*)

calàp·pio *m* (-pi) snare; noose

calapran·zi *m* (-zi) dumbwaiter

calare *tr* to lower; to strike (*sails*) || *intr* (ESSERE) to fall, sag (said, *e.g.*, *of prices*); to grow shorter (*said of days*); to come down; to shrink (*said, e.g., of meat*); to lose weight; to set (*said, e.g., of the sun*); to wane (*said of the moon*); (mus) to drop in pitch || *ref* to let oneself down; to dive

calata *f* lowering; descent; invasion; fall; wharf; (coll) intonation; calata del sole sunset

cal·ca *f* (-che) crowd, throng

calca·gno *m* (-gni) heel || *m* (-gna *fpl*) (fig) heel; alle calcagna di at the heels of

calcare *m* limestone || §197 *tr* to trample; to trace (*on paper*); to tread (*the boards*); to emphasize; calcare la mano to exaggerate; calcare le orme di to follow in the footsteps of

calce *m*—in calce at the foot of (*the page*); in calce a at the foot of || *f* lime; calce viva quicklime

calcedònio *m* chalcedony

calcestruzzo *m* concrete

calciare §128 *tr* & *intr* to kick

calciatóre *m* soccer player; football player

calcificare §197 (calcìfico) *tr* & *ref* to calcify

calcificazióne *f* calcification

calcina *f* mortar; lime

calcinàc·cio *m* (-ci) flake of plaster; calcinacci ruins, rubble

calci·nàio *m* (-nài) lime pit

calcinare *tr* to calcine; to lime (*e.g., a field*)

càl·cio *m* (-ci) kick; soccer; calcium; (*e.g., of rifle*) butt; calcio d'inizio (sports) kickoff

calciocianamide *m* calcium cyanamide

cal·co *m* (-chi) tracing; cast; imprint

calcografia *f* copper engraving

calcolare (càlcolo) *tr* to calculate; to estimate, reckon; to compute; to consider

calcola·tóre -trice *adj* calculating || *m* calculator; computer; schemer || *f* calculating machine, adding machine

càlcolo *m* calculation; estimate; planning; calculus; (pathol) calculus, stone; calcolo biliare gallstone; calcolo errato miscalculation; fare calcolo su to count upon

calcolò·si *f* (-si) (pathol) stones

calcomania *f* decalcomania

caldàia *f* boiler

cal·dàio *m* (-dài) cauldron, boiler

caldalléssa *f* boiled chestnut

caldana *f* flush

caldano *m* brazier

caldarròsta *f* roast chestnut

caldeggiare §290 (caldéggio) *tr* to favor, support; to recommend

càldo *m* calculation; estimate; planning; calculus; (pathol) calculus,

calde·ràio *m* (-rài) coppersmith; boiler-maker

calderóne *m* cauldron

cal·do -da *adj* warm; hot; rich (*voice*); caldo, caldo quite recent || *m* heat; warmth; aver caldo to be warm (*said of people*); tò be hot (*said of people*); fa caldo it is warm; it is hot; non mi fa nè caldo nè freddo it leaves me cold, it does not move me

calefazióne *f* heating

caleidoscò·pio *m* (-pi) kaleidoscope

calendà·rio *m* (-ri) calendar

calènde *fpl*—calende greche Greek calends

calendimàggio *m* May Day

calèsse *m* buggy, gig

calére *impers*—non mi cale (lit) I don't care

calettare (calétto) *tr* to dovetail, mortise || *intr* to fit

calibrare (càlibro) *tr* to gauge, calibrate

càlibro *m* caliber; (mach) calipers; (fig) quality, importance

càlice *m* wine cup; (bot) calyx; (eccl) chalice

cali·cò *m* (-cò) calico

califfo *m* caliph

caligine *f* fog, mist; (fig) darkness

caliginó·so -sa [s] *adj* foggy, misty; (fig) dark, gloomy

calla *f*—calla dei fioristi calla lily

calle *f* lane, alley

callifu·go *m* (-ghi) corn remedy

calligrafia *f* penmanship; handwriting

calli·sta *mf* (-sti -ste) chiropodist

callo *m* corn; callus; fare il callo a to get used to; pestare i calli a qlcu to step on s.o.'s feet

callosi·tà [s] *f* (-tà) callosity; callus

calló·so -sa [s] *adj* corny; callous; hard

calma *f* calm, tranquillity

calmante *adj* sedative, calming, soothing ‖ *m* sedative

calmare *tr* to calm, soothe, appease ‖ *ref* to calm down; to subside, abate

calmierare (calmièro) *tr* to fix the price of

calmière *m* ceiling price; price control

cal·mo -ma *adj* calm, quiet, still ‖ *f* see **calma**

calo *m* decrease; shrinkage

calomelano *m* calomel

calóre *m* heat; warmth; fervor, ardor; (pathol) rash, inflammation; (vet) rut, mating season

caloria *f* calorie

calòri·co -ca *adj* (-ci -che) caloric

calorifero *m* heater, radiator

caloró·so -sa [*s*] *adj* warm; hot; cordial; heated

calò·scia *f* (-sce) var of **galoscia**

calòtta *f* skullcap; case (*e.g., of watch*); (aut) hubcap; (mach) cap; **calotta cranica** skull

calpestare (calpésto) *tr* to trample

calpestìo *m* (-i) trampling

calùgine *f* down (*of bird*)

calùnnia *f* calumny, slander

calunniare §287 *tr* to calumniate, slander

calunnia·tóre -trice *mf* slanderer

calunnió·so -sa [*s*] *adj* slanderous

Calvàrio *m* (Bib) Calvary

calvìzie *f* baldness

cal·vo -va *adj* bald

calza *f* sock; stocking; wick; **calza da donna** stocking; **calze** hose, hosiery; **fare la calza** to knit

calzamàglia *f* tights

calzare *m* footwear ‖ *tr* to wear, put on (*shoes, gloves, or socks*) ‖ *intr* to fit (*said of any garment*); to suit

calzascar·pe *m* (-pe) shoehorn

calza·tóio *m* (-tói) shoehorn

calzatura *f* footwear; **calzature** footwear

calzaturière *m* shoe manufacturer

calzaturiè·ro -ra *adj* shoe (*e.g., industry*) ‖ *m* shoe worker

calzaturifì·cio *m* (-ci) shoe factory

calzeròtto *m* woolen sock

calzet·tàio *m* (-tài) hosier

calzettóne *m* knee-high woolen sock (*for mountain boots*)

calzifì·cio *m* (-ci) hosiery mill

calzino *m* sock; **calzini corti** socks; half hose; **calzini lunghi** knee-high socks

calzo·làio *m* (-lài) shoemaker; cobbler

calzolerìa *f* shoemaker's shop; shoe store

calzoncini *mpl* shorts

calzóne *m* trouser leg; **calzoni** trousers, pants; slacks; **calzoni a zampe d'elefante** bell-bottom trousers, flares

camaleònte *m* chameleon

camarilla *f* cabal, clique

cambiadi·schi *m* (-schi) record changer

cambiale *f* promissory note, IOU

cambiaménto *m* change, modification

cambiare §287 *tr* to change, exchange; to shift (*gears*) ‖ *intr* to change, switch ‖ *ref* to change (*clothing*); **cambiarsi in** to turn into

cambiavalu·te *m* (-te) moneychanger

càm·bio *m* (-bi) change; switch; rate of exchange; (mil) relief; **cambio a cloche** shift lever, stick; **cambio di velocità** gearshift; **in cambio di** in exchange for, in place of

cambrètta *f* staple (*to hold a wire*)

cam·brì *m* (-brì) cambric

cambusa *f* (naut) galley

cambusière *m* steward

càmera *f* room; bedroom; chamber; **camera ardente** funeral parlor; **Camera dei comuni** House of Commons; **Camera dei deputati** House of Representatives; **camera d'aria** inner tube; **camera di sicurezza** detention cell; vault (*of bank*)

camera·ta *m* (-ti) friend, comrade ‖ *f* dormitory; barracks; roomful (*of students or soldiers*)

cameratismo *m* comradeship

camerièra *f* waitress; maid, chambermaid

camerière *m* waiter; steward; valet

camerino *m* small room; toilet, lavatory; (nav) noncommissioned officer's quarters; (theat) dressing room

càmice *m* gown (*of physician*); smock (*of painter*); (eccl) alb

camiceria *f* shirt store; shirt factory

camicétta *f* blouse

camìcia *f* shirt; casing, jacket (*e.g., of boiler*); lining (*e.g., of furnace*); vest (*of sailor*); folder; **camicia da giorno** chemise; **camicia da notte** nightgown; **camicia di forza** strait jacket; **camicia di maglia** coat of mail; **camicia nera** black shirt (*Fascist*); **camicia rossa** red shirt (*Garibaldine*); **dare la camicia** to give the shirt off one's back; **essere nato con la camicia** to be born with a silver spoon in one's mouth; **perdere la camicia** to lose one's shirt

cami·ciàio -ciàia *mf* (-ciài -ciàie) shirtmaker, haberdasher

camiciòla *f* sport shirt; undershirt; T-shirt; (obs) vest

camiciòtto *m* smock (*of mechanic*); jumper; sport shirt

caminétto *m* small fireplace; fireplace

camino *m* fireplace; chimney, smokestack; shaft (*in mountain*); mouth (*of volcano*); (naut) funnel

cà·mion *m* (-mion) truck

camionale *f* highway

camioncino *m* small truck; panel truck; pickup truck

camionétta *f* small truck; van (*e.g., of police*)

camioni·sta *m* (-sti) truckdriver, teamster

camma *f* (mach) cam; (mach) wiper

cammellière *m* camel driver

cammèllo *m* camel

cammèo *m* cameo

camminaménto *m* (mil) communication trench

camminare *intr* to walk; to go, run

camminata *f* walk; gait; (obs) hall with fireplace

cammina·tóre -trice *mf* walker; runner

cammino *m* road, way, route; path (*e.g., of the moon*); course; journey; **cammin facendo** on the way; **cammino battuto** beaten path; **cammino coperto** (mil) covered way; **mettersi in cammino** to set out, start out

camomilla *f* camomile

camòrra *f* underworld

camò·scio *m* (**-sci**) chamois

campagna *f* country; countryside; country property; season (*for harvesting*); campaign; **andare in campagna** to go on vacation (in the country)

campagnò·lo -la *adj* country, rural || *mf* peasant

campale *adj* field (*artillery*); pitched, decisive (*battle*)

campana *f* bell; bell glass, bell jar; lamp shade; (archit) bell; **a campana** bell-bottomed; **campana a martello** alarm bell, tocsin; **campana di vetro** bell glass; **campana pneumatica** caisson

campanàc·cio *m* (**-ci**) cowbell

campanaro *m* bell ringer; (archaic) bell founder

campanèlla *f* small bell; door knocker; curtain ring; (bot) bluebell

campanèllo *m* bell; small bell; doorbell, chimes; **campanello d'allarme** alarm bell

campanile *m* steeple, belfry; native city or town

campanilismo *m* parochialism

campano *m* cowbell

campare *tr* to keep alive; to save; to bring out the details of || *intr* (ESSERE) to live; to survive; **si campa** one ekes out a living

campa·to *adj*—**campato in aria** without any foundation || *f* span

campeggiare §290 (**campéggio**) *intr* to camp, encamp; to stand out

campeggia·tóre -trice *mf* camper

campég·gio *m* (**-gi**) camping, outing; campground; (bot) logwood

campeggi·sta *mf* (**-sti -ste**) camper

campèstre *adj* field, country; (sports) cross-country

campidò·glio *m* (**-gli**) capitol || **Campidoglio** *m* Capitoline (*hill*); Capitol (*temple*)

campionare (**campióno**) *tr* to sample

campionà·rio -ria (**-ri -rie**) *adj* of samples; trade (*exposition*) || *m* sample book, catalogue, pattern book

campionato *m* championship, title

campióne *m* champion; sample; specimen; standard; **campione senza valore** uninsured parcel, sample post

campionéssa *f* championess

campionissimo *m* world champion, ace

campo *m* field; camp; ground; tennis court; golf course; center (*e.g., for refugees*); **campo addestramento** training camp; **campo d'aviazione** airfield, airport; **campo di battaglia** battlefield; **campo petrolifero** oil field; **lasciare il campo** to retreat; **mettere in campo** to bring up, adduce; **piantare il campo** to pitch camp

camposanto *m* cemetery, churchyard

camuffare *tr* to disguise, mask; to camouflage || *ref* to disguise oneself

camu·so -sa *adj* snub-nosed

Canadà, il Canada

canadése [s] *adj & mf* Canadian

canàglia *f* scoundrel; rabble

canagliata *f* knavery, mean trick

canale *m* canal; irrigation ditch; network (*of communications*); pipe, drain; (anat) duct, tract; (rad, telv) channel; (theat) aisle; **Canale della Manica** English Channel; **Canale di Panama** Panama Canal; **Canale di Suez** Suez Canal

canalizzare [ddzz] *tr* to channel; to install pipes in; (elec) to wire

canalizzazióne [ddzz] *f* channeling; piping; ductwork; (elec) wiring

canalóne *m* ravine

cànapa *f* hemp

cana·pè *m* (**-pè**) sofa, couch; (culin) canapé

cànapo *m* rope, cable

Canàrie, le the Canaries

canarino *m* canary

cancàn *m* noise, racket

cancellare (**cancèllo**) *tr* to cancel, erase; to obliterate; to write off (*a debt*); to scratch (*a horse*) || *ref* to vanish, fade

cancellata *f* railing

cancellatura *f* erasure

cancellazióne *f* cancellation; erasure (*of a tape*)

cancelleria *f* chancellery; stationery

cancellière *m* chancellor; court clerk; registrar, recorder

cancèllo *m* gate, railing, grating

canceró·so -sa [s] *adj* cancerous || *mf* cancer victim

cànchero *m* trouble; troublesome person; (coll) cancer

cancrèna *f* gangrene; **andare in cancrena** to become gangrenous

cancrenó·so -sa [s] *adj* gangrenous

cancro *m* cancer; (bot) canker || **Cancro** *m* (astr) Cancer

candeggiante *adj* bleaching || *m* bleaching agent, bleach

candeggiare §290 (**candéggio**) *tr* to bleach

candeggina *f* bleach

candég·gio *m* (**-gi**) bleaching

candéla *f* candle; candlestick; candle-power; (aut) spark plug; **studiare a lume di candela** to burn the midnight oil; **tenere la candela a** to favor the love affair of

candelabro *m* candelabrum

candelière *m* candlestick

candelóra *f* Candlemas

candelòtto *m* big wax candle; **candelotto lacrimogeno** tear-gas canister

candida·to -ta *mf* candidate

candidatura *f* candidature, candidacy

càndi·do -da *adj* white; candid

candire §176 *tr* to candy

candi·to -ta *adj* candied || *m* candied fruit

candóre *m* whiteness; candor

cane *m* dog; hound; hammer, cock (*of gun*); ham actor; **cane barbone**

poodle; **cane bastardo** mongrel; **cane da ferma** setter; **cane da guardia** watchdog; **cane da presa** retriever; **cane da punta** pointer; **cane grosso** big shot; **cane guida per ciechi** seeing eye dog; **cane sciolto** (pol) lone wolf; **come un cane** all alone; **come un cane in chiesa** as an unwelcome guest; **da cani** poorly; **menare il can per l'aia** to beat around the bush; **non c'è un cane** there is nobody there; **raddrizzare le gambe ai cani** to perform an impossible task

canèstro *m* basket

cànfora *f* camphor

cangiante *adj* changeable (*color*); changing, iridescent

canguro *m* kangaroo

canìcola *f* dog days

canile *m* doghouse, kennel

canino *adj* canine || *m* canine tooth

canìzie *f* gray hair; head of gray hair; old age

canna *f* cane, reed; rod (*for fishing or measuring*); pipe (*of organ*); barrel (*of gun*); **canna da zucchero** sugar cane; **canna di caduta** disposal chute; **canna fumaria** chimney; **canna della gola** (coll) windpipe

cannèlla *f* small tube; tap (*of barrel*); cinnamon

cannèllo *m* pipe, tube; stick (*e.g., of licorice*); (chem) pipette; **cannello ossiacetilenico** acetylene torch; **cannello ossidrico** oxyhydrogen blowpipe

cannellóni *mpl* cannelloni

cannéto *m* cane field

cannìbale *m* cannibal

cannìc·cio *m* (-ci) wicker frame; shade made out of rushes

cannocchiale *m* spyglass; **cannocchiale astronomico** telescope

cannonata *f* cannonade, cannon shot; (slang) hit

cannoncino *m* small gun; **cannoncino antiaereo** antiaircraft gun

cannóne *m* gun, cannon; pipe, stovepipe; box pleat; shin (*of cattle*); **è un cannone** (coll) he's the tops

cannoneggiare §290 (**cannonéggio**) *tr* to cannonade, shell

cannonièra *f* gunboat

cannonière *m* gunner, artilleryman; kicker (*in soccer*)

cannùc·cia *f* (-ce) reed; thin tube; stem (*e.g., of pipe*); straw (*for drinking*); (chem) pipette

canòa *f* canoe; launch

canòcchia *f* mantis shrimp

cànone *m* canon; rule; rent; fee, charge (*for use of radio*)

canonicato *m* canonry

canòni·co -ca (-ci -che) *adj* canonical, canon (*law*) || *m* canon; priest || *f* parsonage, rectory

canonizzare [ddzz] *tr* to canonize

canò·ro -ra *adj* song (*bird*); melodious

canottàg·gio *m* (-gi) boating, rowing

canottièra *f* undershirt, T-shirt; skimmer, boater

canottière *m* oarsman

canòtto *m* skiff, scull, shell

canovàc·cio *m* (-ci) dishcloth; embroidery cloth; plot (*of novel or play*)

cantàbile *adj* singable; songlike; cantabile || *m* song

cantamban·co *m* (-chi) jongleur, wandering minstrel; mountebank

cantante *adj* singing, song || *mf* singer

cantare *m* song; chant; laisse, epic strophe || *tr* to sing; to chant || *intr* to sing; to chant; (coll) to squeal

càntaride *f* Spanish fly

càntaro *m* urn

cantastò·rie *mf* (-rie) minstrel

canta·tóre -trice *adj* singing || *mf* singer

cantau·tóre -trice *mf* singer composer

canterano *m* chest of drawers

canterellare (**canterèllo**) *tr & intr* to sing in a low voice, hum

canteri·no -na *adj* singing, warbling; decoy (*bird*) || *mf* songster, singer

càntero *m* urinal

canticchiare §287 *tr & intr* to hum

cànti·co *m* (-ci) canticle

cantière *m* shipyard, dockyard; navy yard; undertaking, work in progress; **avere in cantiere** to have in hand, be working at; **cantiere edile** building site; builder's yard

cantilèna *f* singsong; **la stessa cantilena** the same old tune

cantimban·co *m* (-chi) var of **cantambanco**

cantina *f* cellar; wine cellar; wine shop, canteen

cantinière *m* cellarman; butler; wine-shop keeper; sommelier

canto *m* song, singing; chant; canto; crow (*of rooster*); chirping (*of grasshopper*); corner, edge; (mus) voice part; **canto del cigno** swan song; **dal canto mio** for my part; **d'altro canto** on the other hand; **da un canto** on the one hand

cantonata *f* corner (*of street*); **prendere una cantonata** to make a blunder

cantóne *m* corner (*of room or building*); canton

cantonièra *f* corner cupboard; (rr) section worker's house

cantonière *m* road laborer; (rr) section hand

cantóre *m* choir singer; cantor; (poet) singer

cantùc·cio *m* (-ci) nook, niche

canutézza *f* hoariness

canutìglia *f* gold thread

canu·to -ta *adj* gray-haired; white-haired; (poet) white

canzonare (**canzóno**) *tr* to mock, ridicule

canzonatò·rio -ria *adj* (-ri -rie) mocking

canzonatura *f* mockery, gibe

canzóne *f* song; canzone

canzonétta *f* canzonet; popular song

canzonetti·sta *mf* (-sti -ste) singer (*e.g., in a nightclub*) || *m* songster || *f* songstress

canzonière *m* songbook; collection of poems; song writer

caolino *m* kaolin

caos *m* chaos

caòti·co -ca *adj* (-ci -che) caotic

capace *adj* capacious; capable, intelligent; legally qualified; capace di with a capacity of (*e.g., fifty people*); essere capace di to be able to; fare capace di to convince of

capaci·tà *f* (-tà) capacity; capability

capacitare (capàcito) *tr* to persuade ‖ *ref* to become convinced

capanna *f* hut, cabin; thatched cottage; bathhouse

capannèllo *m* group, crowd

capanno *m* hunting box; cabana, bathhouse

capannóne *m* large shed; hangar

caparbiàggine *f* var of caparbietà

caparbie·tà *f* (-tà) obstinacy, stubborness

capàr·bio -bia *adj* (-bi -bie) stubborn, hard-headed

caparra *f* down payment, deposit; performance bond

capatina *f* short visit

capeggiare §290 (capéggio) *tr* to lead

capeggia·tóre -trice *mf* leader

capellini *mpl* small vermicelli

capéllo *m* hair; averne fin sopra i capelli to have one's fill; capelli hair; capelli a spazzola crew cut; c'è mancato un capello che + *subj* he came close to + *ger*; far rizzare i capelli a qlcu to make s.o.'s hair stand on end

capellóne *m* hippie, beatnik

capellu·to -ta *adj* hairy; long-haired

capelvènere *m* maidenhair

capèstro *m* halter; gallows

capezzale *m* bolster; (fig) bedside

capézzolo *m* nipple, teat; udder

capidò·glio *m* (-gli) var of capodoglio

capiènza *f* capacity (*e.g., of bus*)

capigliatura *f* head of hair

capillare *adj* capillary; (fig) far-reaching

capinéra *f* (orn) blackcap

capintè·sta *m* (-sta) boss; (sports) head, leader

capire §176 *tr* to understand; capire a volo to grasp immediately ‖ *intr—non capire dalla contentezza* to be bursting with joy ‖ *ref* to understand each other; to agree

capitale *adj* capital; mortal (*sin*) ‖ *m* capital; principal; capitale sociale capital stock ‖ *f* capital (*of country*)

capitalismo *m* capitalism

capitali·sta *m* (-sti -ste) capitalist

capitalìsti·co -ca *adj* (-ci -che) capitalistic

capitalizzare [ddzz] *tr* to capitalize; to compound (*interest*)

capitana *f* flagship

capitanare *tr* to lead, captain

capitanerìa *f* (hist) captaincy; capitaneria di porto harbor-master's office; coast guard office; port authority's office

capitano *m* captain; skipper, master (*of ship*); commander (*in air force*); capitano di corvetta or capitano di fregata (nav) lieutenant commander;

capitano di gran cabotaggio master; capitano di lungo corso master; capitano di porto harbor master; capitano di vascello (nav) commander

capitare (càpito) *intr* (ESSERE) to arrive; to happen, occur; to happen to get, e.g., capitò a casa mia alle tre he happened to get to my house at three; capitare bene to be lucky; dove capita at random

capitazióne *f* poll tax

capitèllo *m* (archit) capital; (bb) headband

capitolare *adj & m* capitular ‖ *v* (capìtolo) *intr* to capitulate, surrender

capitolato *m* (com) specifications

capitolazióne *f* capitulation

capitolo *m* chapter; article, paragraph (*of contract*)

capitombolare (capitómbolo) *intr* to tumble

capitómbolo *m* tumble; fare un capitómbolo (fig) to collapse

capitóne *m* big eel

capitozzare (capitòzzo) *tr* to poll (*a tree*)

capo *m* head; chief; boss, leader; top; (geog) cape; (nav) chief petty officer; a capo scoperto bareheaded; capo d'accusa (law) charge; capo del governo prime minister; capo dello stato president, chief of state; capo di vestiario garment; capo scarico scatterbrain; col capo nel sacco (fig) heedlessly; da capo all over (again); fare capo a to flow into; in capo a at the end of (*e.g., one month*); in capo al mondo at the end of the world; per sommi capi briefly; rompersi il capo to rack one's brain; scoprirsi il capo to take one's hat off; senza capo né coda without rhyme or reason; venire a capo di to come to the end of

capobanda *m* (capibanda) bandmaster; ringleader

capocameriere *m* headwaiter

capocannonière *m* (capicannonièri) petty gunnery officer; (soccer) leader in number of goals

capòcchia *f* head (*e.g., of a match*)

capòc·cia *m* (-ci & -cia) head of household; foreman, boss (*e.g., of roadworkers or farmers*)

capocòmi·co *m* (-ci) head of dramatic company

capocòr·da *m* (capicòrda) (elec) binding post, terminal

capocrònaca *m* (capicrònaca) leading article

capocronista *m* (capicronisti) city editor

capocuòco *m* (capocuòchi & capicuòchi) chef

capodanno *m* (capodanni & capi d'anno) New Year's Day

capodò·glio *m* (-gli) sperm whale

capofàbbrica *m* (capifàbbrica) foreman, superintendent

capofabbricato *m* (capifabbricato) airraid warden

capofamìglia *m* (capifamìglia) head of the family

capofila *m* (capifila) head of a line || *f* (capofila) head of a line

capofitto *adj invar*—a capofitto headlong

capogiro *m* vertigo, dizziness; da capogiro dizzying, e.g., prezzi da capogiro dizzying prices

capolavó·ro *m* (-ri) masterpiece

capolèttera *m* (capilèttera) letterhead; (typ) first large bold letter of a paragraph

capolìnea *m* (capilìnea) terminal, terminus

capolino *m*—fare capolino to peep

capolista *m* (capilista) first (*of a list*); (sports) leader || *f* (capolista) first (*of a list*)

capoluò·go *m* (-ghi) capital (*of province*); county seat

capomacchini·sta *m* (-sti) chief engineer

capomastro *m* (capomastri & capimastri) foreman; building contractor

capomùsica *m* (capimùsica) bandmaster

capoofficina *m* (capiofficina) superintendent (*of shop*)

capopàgina *m* (capipàgina) heading (*of newspaper*)

capopèzzo *m* (capipèzzo) gunnery sergeant

capopòpolo *m* (capipòpolo) demagogue

caporale *m* corporal

caporeparto *m* (capireparto) department manager, floor walker; shop foreman

caporióne *m* ringleader

caposaldo *m* (capisaldi) (fig) main point, basis; (mil) stronghold; (surv) datum

caposezióne *m* (capisezióne) department head

caposquadra *m* (capisquadra) group leader; (sports) team captain

capostazióne *m* (capistazióne) station master

capostìpite *m* founder (*of family*); prototype, archetype

capotaménto *m var of* cappottamento

capotare (capòto) *intr var of* cappottare

capotasto *m* nut (*of violin*)

capotàvola *m* (capitàvola) head of the table, honored guest

capòte *f* (aut) top

capotrèno *m* (capitrèno & capotrèni) (rr) conductor

capottaménto *m var of* cappottamento

capottare (capòtto) *intr var of* cappottare

capoufficio *m* (capiufficio) office manager

capovèrso *m* paragraph; (typ) indentation

capovòlgere §289 *tr* to overturn; (fig) to upset || *ref* to overturn; (fig) to be or become reversed

capovolgiménto *m* upset; (fig) reversal

capovòlta *f* overturn; turn (*in swimming*)

cappa *f* cape, cloak; mantle; letter K; shroud (*of clouds*); (naut) trysail;

cappa del cielo vault of heaven; navigare alla cappa (naut) to lay to

cappèlla *f* chapel; cappella mortuaria undertaker's parlor || Cappella Sistina Sistine Chapel

cappel·làio *m* (-lài) hatter, hat maker or dealer

cappellano *m* chaplain

cappellata *f* hatful

cappellerìa *f* hat store

cappellièra *f* hatbox

cappèllo *m* hat; bonnet; cap (*of mushroom*); head (*of nail*); cowl (*of chimney*); preamble (*of newspaper article*); cappello a cencio slouch hat; cappello a cilindro top hat; cappello a cono dunce cap; cappello a due punte cocked hat; cappello a tre punte three-cornered hat; cappello del lume lampshade; cappello di feltro felt hat; cappello di paglia straw hat; cappello floscio fedora; fare di cappello to take one's hat off; prendere cappello to take offense

cappellóne *adj invar* Western (*movie*) || *m* big hat; (coll) recruit; (mov) Western character

càppero *m* (bot) caper; capperi! (coll) wow!

càp·pio *m* (-pi) bow; noose; loop

capponàia *f* chicken coop

cappóne *m* capon

cappòtta *f* cape; navy coat; hood (*of car*)

cappottaménto *m* upset, rolling over

cappottare (cappòtto) *intr* to upset, roll over

cappottatura *f* (aer) cowl

cappòtto *m* overcoat; lurch (*at the close of game*); (cards) slam; cappotto da mezza stagione lightweight coat

cappuccino *m* espresso with cream; Capuchin (*friar*)

Cappuccétto *m*—Cappuccetto Rosso Little Red Ridinghood

cappùc·cio *m* (-ci) hood, cowl; cabbage; cap (*of fountain pen*)

capra *f* goat; nanny goat; tripod

ca·pràio -pràia *mf* (-prài -pràie) goatherd

caprét·to -ta *mf* kid

capriata *f* truss (*to support roof*)

capric·cio *m* (-ci) whim, fancy, caprice; tantrum; flirting; (mus) capriccio

capricció·so -sa [s] *adj* whimsical, capricious; naughty; fanciful, bizarre

Capricòrno *m* (astr) Capricorn

caprifò·glio *m* (-gli) honeysuckle

caprimul·go *m* (-gi) (orn) goatsucker

capri·no -na *adj* goatlike, goatish || *m* smell of goat

capriòla *f* female roe deer; caper, somersault; fare capriole to cut capers, to caper

capriòlo *m* roe deer; roebuck

capro *m* he-goat, billy goat; capro espiatorio scapegoat

capróne *m* he-goat, billy goat

càpsula *f* capsule; percussion cap; cap (*of bottle*); (rok) capsule

captare *tr* to captivate; to catch, intercept; to harness (a waterfall); (rad, telv) to pick up (a signal)

captazióne f undue influence (to secure an inheritance)

capzió·so -sa [s] adj insidious, treacherous

carabàttola f (coll) trifle

carabina f carbine

carabinière m carabineer; Italian military policeman, carabiniere; (hist) cavalryman

caracollare (caracòllo) intr to caracole, caper; (coll) to trot along

caracòllo m caracole, caper

caraffa f carafe, decanter

caràmbola f carom

carambolare (caràmbolo) intr to carom

caramèlla f piece of hard candy; taffy; (coll) monocle; caramelle hard candy

caramellare (caramèllo) tr to caramel; to candy

caramèllo m caramel (burnt sugar)

caraménte adv affectionately

carati·sta m (-sti) shareholder (in ship or business)

carato m carat; share (of ship)

caràttere m character; type; handwriting; characteristic; disposition; carattere corsivo (typ) italic; carattere maiuscolo capital; carattere minuscolo small letter, lower case; carattere neretto or grassetto (typ) boldface

caratteri·sta m (-sti) character actor || f (-ste) character actress

caratteristi·co -ca (-ci -che) adj & f characteristic

caratterizzare [ddzz] tr to characterize

caratura f share (in business or ship)

cara·vàn m (-vàn) trailer, mobile home

caravanserrà·glio m (-gli) caravansary

caravèlla f caravel; carpenter's glue

carbo·nàio -nàia (-nài -nàie) adj coal || m coal man, coal dealer || f charcoal pit; coalbin, bunker; coal yard

carbonato m carbonate

carbón·chio m (-chi) (agr) smut (on wheat); (jewelry) carbuncle

carboncino m charcoal (pencil and drawing)

carbóne m coal; charcoal; carbon (of arc light or primary battery); carbone bianco hydroelectric power; carbone dolce charcoal; carbone fossile coal; fare carbone to coal

carbòni·co -ca adj (-ci -che) carbonic

carbonièra f coal yard; (naut) collier; (rr) tender

carbonile m (naut) bunker

carbònio m (chem) carbon

carbonizzare [ddzz] tr to carbonize; to char

carbùncolo m boil, carbuncle; (archaic) ruby

carburante m fuel

carburatóre m carburetor

carburazióne f (aut) mixture

carburo m carbide

carcassa f carcass; framework; (aut) jalopy; (fig) wreck

carcerare (càrcero) tr to jail

carcerà·rio -ria adj (-ri -rie) jail, prison

carcera·to -ta adj imprisoned || mf prisoner

càrce·re m (-ri fpl) jail, prison

carcerière m jailer, prison guard

carciòfo m artichoke

cardàni·co -ca adj (-ci -che) universal (e.g., joint)

cardano m universal joint

cardatrice f carding machine

cardellino m goldfinch

cardìa·co -ca (-ci -che) adj heart, cardiac || m heart patient

cardinale adj cardinal || m (eccl, orn) cardinal

cardinali·zio -zia adj (-zi -zie) cardinal, cardinal's

càrdine m hinge; (fig) pivot, mainstay (e.g., of theory)

càr·dio m (-di) cockle (mollusk)

cardiochirurgìa f heart surgery

cardiogram·ma m (-mi) cardiogram

cardiòlo·go m (-gi) cardiologist

cardiopalmo m tachycardia

cardiopatìa f heart disease

cardo m (bot) thistle; (bot) cardoon

carèna f ship's bottom; (aer) outer cover (of airship); (bot) rib

carenàg·gio m (-gi) careening a ship; careen

carenare (carèno) tr to careen (a ship)

carenatura f streamlining; carenatura di fusoliera (aer) turtleback

carènza f lack, want

carestìa f famine; scarcity (e.g., of manpower)

carézza f caress; fare una carezza a to caress

carezzare (carézzo) tr to caress

carezzévole adj caressing, fondling; sweet, suave; blandishing

cariare §287 tr to cause (a tooth) to decay; to corrode || ref to decay; to rot

cariàtide f caryatid

caria·to -ta adj decayed

càri·ca f (-che) office, appointment; charge; (fig) insistence

caricaménto m loading

caricare §197 (càrico) tr to load; to burden; to wind (a watch); to fill (a pipe); to charge (a battery); to deepen (a color); caricare la mano to exceed; caricare le dosi to exaggerate || ref to burden oneself

carica·to -ta adj exaggerated, affected

carica·tóre -trice adj) loading || m clip, magazine (for rifle); loader (of gun); cassette (of tape recorder); charger (of battery); longshoreman; (phot) cartridge, cassette

caricatura f caricature, cartoon; mettere in caricatura to ridicule

caricaturi·sta mf (-sti -ste) cartoonist, caricaturist

càrice m (bot) sedge

càri·co -ca (-chi -che) adj loaded; burdened; vivid (color); strong (tea); charged (battery) || m loading; load, burden; charge; cargo || f see carica

càrie f caries, decay

cari·no -na adj nice, pretty, cute; questa è carina! this is funny!

cari·tà f (-tà) charity; alms; (poet) love; **per carità** please

caritatévole adj charitable

caritati·vo -va adj (obs) charitable

carlin·ga f (-ghe) fuselage

Carlo m Charles

Carlomagno m Charlemagne

carlóna f—**alla carlona** carelessly, haphazardly

carlòtta f charlotte || **Carlotta** Charlotte

carme' m poem, lyric poem

carmì·nio m (-nî) carmine

carnagióne f complexion

car·nàio m (-nài) carnage; slaughterhouse; mass of humanity

carnale adj carnal, sensual; full (e.g., brother, cousin)

carname m carrion

carne f flesh; meat; **bene in carne** plump; **carne da macello** cannon fodder; **carne suina** pork; **carne viva** open wound; **essere solo carne ed ossa** to be nothing but skin and bones; **in carne ed ossa** in person, in the flesh; **troppa carne al fuoco** too many irons in the fire

carnéfice m executioner

carneficina f slaughter, carnage

càrne·o -a adj fleshy, meaty; flesh-colored

carnet m (carnet) notebook; check-book; backlog

carnevale m carnival

carnièra f hunting jacket; gamebag

carnière m gamebag

carnì·voro -ra adj carnivorous || mpl carnivores; Carnivora

carnò·so -sa [s] adj fleshy

ca·ro -ra adj dear (beloved; high in price) || **caro** adv dear || m high price; beloved; **i miei cari** my parents; my relatives; my friends

carógna f carcass; cad, rotter; **carogne** carrion

carosèllo m tournament; carousel, merry-go-round

caròta f carrot; (fig) lie

caròtide f carotid artery

carovana f caravan; group, crowd; union of longshoremen; apprenticeship; (naut, nav) convoy; **far carovana** to join a tour; **fare la carovana** to be an apprentice

carovanie·ro -ra adj caravan || f desert trail

carovi·ta m (-ta) high cost of living; cost-of-living increase

carovìve·ri m (-ri) high cost of living; cost-of-living increase

carpa f (ichth) carp

carpentière m carpenter

carpire §176 tr to snatch, seize; to extract, worm (a secret)

carpóni adv on all fours; **avanzare carponi** to crawl

carradóre m cart maker, wheelwright

car·ràio -ràia (-rài -ràie) adj passable for vehicles || f cart road

carrarèc·cia f (-ce) country road; rut

carreggiata f paved road; track (of vehicles); (fig) right path

carrellare (carrèllo) intr (mov, telv) to dolly

carrellata f (mov) dolly shot, tracking shot

carrèllo m car (for narrow-gauge track); carriage (of typewriter); cart (for shopping); (aer) landing gear; (mach, rr) truck; (mov, telv) dolly; **carrello d'atterraggio** (aer) undercarriage, landing gear; **carrello elevatore** fork-lift truck

carrétta f cart; tramp steamer

carrettata f cartful; **a carrettate** abundantly

carrettière m cart driver, drayman; teamster

carrétto m small cart; **carretto a mano** pushcart

carriàg·gio m (-gi) wagon; **carriaggi** (mil) baggage train

carrièra f career; **di gran carriera** at top speed

carrieri·sta mf (-sti -ste) unscrupulous go-getter

carriòla f wheelbarrow

carro m wagon; cart; wagonload; cartload; carload; (rr) car; (astr) Plough; (poet) chariot; **carri armati** (mil) armor; **carro allegorico** float (in a pageant); **carro armato** (mil) tank; **carro attrezzi** (aut) tow truck, wrecker; **carro bestiame** (rr) cattle car; **carro botte** or **carro cisterna** (aut) tank truck; (rr) tank car; **carro di Tespi** traveling show; **carro funebre** hearse; **carro gru** (rr) wrecking crane; **carro marsupio** (rr) double decker (used to transport automobiles); **carro merci** (rr) freight car; **Gran Carro** (astr) Big Dipper; **mettere il carro innanzi ai buoi** to put the cart before the horse; **Piccolo Carro** (astr) Little Dipper || m (carra fpl) carload; wagonload; cartload

carròzza f wagon carriage; **carrozza letti** (rr) sleeping car; **carrozza ristorante** (rr) dining car; **carrozza salone** (rr) club car; **con la carrozza di S. Francesco** on shank's mare; **signori, in carrozza!** (rr) all aboard!

carrozzàbile adj open to vehicular traffic || f road open to vehicular traffic

carrozzèlla f small wagon; baby carriage; wheelchair; hackney

carrozzino m baby carriage; sidecar

carrozzóne m wagon; hearse; caravan (e.g., of gypsies); (rr) car

carruba f carob

carrubo m carob tree

carrùcola f pulley

carta f paper; document (e.g., of identification); **alla carta** à la carte; **carta assorbente** blotter; **carta astronomica** astronomical map; **carta bianca** carte blanche; **carta bollata** stamped paper (for official documents); **carta carbone** carbon paper; **carta catramata** tar paper; **carta da disegno** drawing paper; **carta da gioco** playing card; **carta da giornale** newsprint; **carta da imballaggio** or **da impacco** wrapping paper; **carta da lettera** or **da lettere** writing paper; **carta geografica** map, chart; **carta igienica** toilet paper; **carta oleata** wax paper; **carta torna-**

sole litmus paper; **carta velina** India paper; tissue paper; **carta vetrata** sandpaper; **carte** papers, writings; **carte francesi** cards in the four suits spades, hearts, diamonds, and clubs; **carte napoletane** cards in the four suits gold coins, cups, swords, and clubs; **fare le carte** to shuffle the cards; **fare le carte a qlcu** to tell s.o.'s fortune with cards

cartacarbóne *f* (**cartecarbóne**) carbon paper

cartàc·cia *f* (**-ce**) waste paper

cartàce·o -a *adj* (**-i -e**) paper

Cartàgine *f* Carthage

car·tàio *m* (**-tài**) papermaker; paper dealer; (cards) dealer

cartamonéta *f* paper money

cartapècora *f* parchment

cartapésta *f* papier-mâché

cartà·rio -ria *adj* (**-ri -rie**) paper

cartastràccia *f* (**cartestracce**) wrapping paper; wastepaper

cartég·gio *m* (**-gi**) correspondence; (aer, naut) reckoning

cartèlla *f* lottery ticket; card (*e.g., of bingo*); page of manuscript; Manila folder; schoolbag; briefcase; binding (*of book*); **cartella clinica** clinical chart; **cartella di rendita** government bond; **cartella esattoriale** tax bill; **cartella fondiaria** bond certificate

cartellino *m* label; nameplate (*on door*); file; (sports) contract; **cartellino di presenza** timecard; **cartellino signaletico** criminal record

cartèllo *m* poster; sign (*on store*); (com) cartel, trust; **cartello di sfida** challenge; **cartello stradale** traffic sign

cartellóne *m* show bill, theater poster; bill (*for advertising*); **tenere il cartellone** to find public favor, make a hit, be the rage

car·ter *m* (**-ter**) chain guard (*of bicycle*); (aut) crankcase

cartièra *f* papermill

cartilàgine *f* cartilage, gristle

cartina *f* dose; cigarette paper; small map

cartòc·cio *m* (**-ci**) paper cone; charge (*of gun*); cornhusk; (archit) scroll

cartògrafo *m* cartographer

carto·làio *m* (**-lài**) stationer

cartolerìa *f* stationery store

cartolina *f* card, post card; **cartolina precetto** induction notice

cartomante *mf* fortuneteller

cartoncino *m* light cardboard; calling card; **cartoncino natalizio** Christmas card

cartóne *m* cardboard, carton; **cartone animato** (mov) animated cartoon

cartùc·cia *f* (**-ce**) cartridge; shot, shell; **mezza cartuccia** (fig) half pint

cartuccièra *f* cartridge belt

casa [s] *f* house; dwelling; home; household; **andare a casa** to go home; **casa base** (baseball) home base; **casa colonica** farm house; **casa da gioco** gambling house; **casa del diavolo** faraway place; **casa di bambole** playhouse, doll's house; **casa di correzione** reform school; **casa di cura**

sanatorium, private clinic; **casa di riposo** convalescent home, nursing home; **casa di spedizione** shipping agency; **casa di tolleranza** bawdyhouse; **casa madre** home office, headquarters; **esser di casa** to be intimate; **fuori casa** (sports) away; **in casa** (sports) home; **metter su casa** to set up housekeeping; **sentirsi a casa** to feel at home; **stare a casa** to stay at home; **star di casa** to dwell, live

casac·ca *f* (**-che**) coat; **voltar casacca** to be a turncoat

casàccio *m*—**a casaccio** at random; heedlessly

casalin·go -ga (**-ghi -ghe**) [s] *adj* home, domestic; stay-at-home; homey; home-made ‖ **casalinghi** *mpl* household articles ‖ *f* housewife

casamatta [s] *f* casemate, bunker

casaménto [s] *m* apartment house, tenement; tenants

casata [s] *f* house, lineage

casato [s] *m* birth, family; (obs) family name

cascame *m* waste; remnants (*e.g., of silk*)

cascante *adj* flabby, loose; (poet) languid, dull

cascare §197 *intr* (ESSERE) to fall, droop; to fit (*said of clothes*); **cascare dalla noia** to be bored to death; **cascare dal sonno** to be overwhelmed with sleep; **cascare diritto** to escape unscathed; **non casca il mondo** the world is not coming to an end

cascata *f* fall, waterfall; necklace (*e.g., of pearls*); **a cascata** flood of, e.g., **telefonate a cascata** flood of telephone calls ‖ **le Cascate del Niagara** Niagara Falls

cascina *f* farm house; dairy barn

ca·sco *m* (**-schi**) helmet, crash helmet; electric hairdrier; cluster (*e.g., of bananas*)

caseggiato [s] *m* built-up zone; block, row of houses; apartment house

caseifi·cio *m* (**-ci**) dairy, creamery, cheese factory

casèlla [s] *f* pigeonhole; square (*of paper*); **casella postale** post-office box

caseliante [s] *mf* gatekeeper ‖ *m* (rr) trackwalker

casellà·rio [s] *m* (**-ri**) filing cabinet; row of post-office boxes; **casellario giudiziale** criminal file

casèllo [s] *m* tollgate (*on turnpike*); (rr) trackwalker's house

casèrma *f* barracks; fire station

casino [s] *m* country house; clubhouse; (slang) whorehouse; (slang) noise, racket

casisti·ca *f* (**-che**) case study; (eccl) casuistry

caso *m* case; chance; fate; vicissitude; opportunity; **a caso** inadvertently; **al caso** eventually; **caso fortuito** (law) act of God; **caso mai** assuming that, in the event that; **è il caso** it is the moment; **far caso a qlco** to notice s.th; **in ogni caso** in any event; **mettere il caso** to suppose; **mi fa caso** I am surprised; **non fare caso a** to make nothing of, pay no attention to; per caso perchance

casolare [s] *m* hut, hovel; isolated farmhouse

casòtto [s] *m* cabana, bathhouse; sentry box

Càspio *adj* Caspian

càspita *interj* you don't say!

cassa *f* box; chest; case; stock (*of rifle*); cash; cash register; desk (*e.g., in hotel*); check-out (*in a supermarket*); **a pronta cassa** by cash; **cassa acustica** loudspeaker; **cassa di risparmio** savings bank; **cassa malattia** health insurance; **cassa rurale** farmers' credit cooperative; **in cassa** in hand (*said of money*)

cassafórma *f* (**casseforme**) (archit) form (*for cement*)

cassafòrte *f* (**casseforti**) safe

cassapanca *f* (**cassapanche** & **cassepanche**) wooden chest

cassare *tr* to erase, cancel; to cross off; (law) to annull

cassata *f* Neapolitan ice cream with soft core; Sicilian cake

cassazióne *f* annulment, abolition; cancellation

casserétto *m* (naut) poop

càssero *m* (naut) quarterdeck; **cassero di poppa** (naut) cockpit

casseruòla *f* saucepan

cassétta *f* small box; coach box; (theat) box office; **cassetta dei ferri** workbox; **cassetta delle lettere** mail box; **cassetta di cottura** dish warmer; **cassetta di sicurezza** safe-deposit box; **cassetta per ugnature** miter box

cassettièra *f* chest of drawers

cassétto *m* drawer; **cassetto di distribuzione** (mach) slide valve

cassettóne *m* chest of drawers; (archit) coffer, caisson

cassiè·re -ra *mf* cashier; teller

cassóne *m* large case, large box; chest; caisson (*for underwater construction*); body (*of truck*); (mil) caisson

cassonétto *m* cornice

cast *m* cast (*of actors*)

casta *f* caste

castagna *f* chestnut; **castagna d'India** horse chestnut

castagnéto *m* chestnut grove

castagno *m* chestnut tree; chestnut (*lumber*); **castagno d'India** horse chestnut tree

casta·no -na *adj* chestnut (*color*)

castellana *f* chatelaine

castellano *m* lord of the castle, squire

castellétto *m* scaffold; (min) gallows, headframe

castèl·lo *m* castle; works (*e.g., of watch*); scaffold; jungle gym; hydraulic boom, bucket lift (*on truck*); (naut) forecastle; **castello di menzogne** pack of lies; **castello in aria** castle in Spain || *m* (**-la** *fpl*) (archaic) castle

castigare §209 *tr* to punish; (poet) to correct, castigate

castigatézza *f* purity (*e.g., of style*)

castiga·to -ta *adj* decent, modest; pure (*language*)

Castiglia, la Castile

castiglia·no -na *adj* & *mf* Castilian

casti·go *m* (**-ghi**) punishment; (fig) scourge; **mettere in castigo** (coll) to punish

casti·tà *f* (**-tà**) chastity; (fig) purity

ca·sto -sta *adj* chaste; pure, elegant (*language or style*)

castóne *m* setting (*of stone*)

castòro *m* beaver

castrare *tr* to castrate; to spay; (fig) to expurgate

castra·to -ta *adj* castrated; spayed; (fig) effeminate || *m* mutton (of castrated sheep); eunuch

castróne *m* wether (*sheep*); gelding (*horse*); (fig) nincompoop

castroneria *f* (vulg) stupidity

casuale *adj* fortuitous, casual; sundry (*e.g., expenses*)

casuali·tà *f* (**-tà**) chance, accident

casùpola [s] *f* hut, hovel

catacli·sma *m* (**-smi**) cataclysm

catacómba *f* catacomb

catafal·co *m* (**-chi**) catafalque

catafàscio *adv*—**a catafascio** topsy-turvy

catalès·si *f* (**-si**) catalepsy

catàli·si *f* (**-si**) catalysis

catalizza·tóre -trice [ddzz] *adj* catalytic || *m* catalyst

catalogare §209 (**catàlogo**) *tr* to catalogue

catàlo·go *m* (**-ghi**) catalogue

catapècchia *f* hovel

catapla·sma *m* (**-smi**) poultice, plaster; (fig) bore

catapulta *f* catapult

catapultare *tr* to catapult

cataratta *f* cataract; sluice (*of canal*)

catarro *m* catarrh

catar·si *f* (**-si**) catharsis

catàrti·co -ca *adj* (**-ci -che**) cathartic

catasta *f* pile, heap

catastale *adj* land (*office*)

catasto *m* real-estate register; land office

catàstrofe *f* catastrophe; wreck

catastròfi·co -ca *adj* (**-ci -che**) catastrophic

catechismo *m* catechism

catechizzare [ddzz] *tr* to catechize

categoria *f* category; weight (*in boxing*); (sports) class

categòri·co -ca *adj* (**-ci -che**) categorical; classified (*telephone directory*)

caténa *f* chain; range (*of mountains*); (archit) tie beam; **catene da neve** tire chains; **mordere la catena** to champ the bit

catenàc·cio *m* (**-ci**) bolt; (fig) jalopy; (journ) giant-size headline

catenèlla *f* chain

cateratta *f* var of **cataratta**

catèrva *f* great quantity, large number

catetère *m* catheter

cateterizzare [ddzz] *tr* to catheterize

catinèlla *f* water basin; **piovere a catinelle** (coll) to rain cats and dogs

catino *m* basin

càtodo *m* cathode

Catóne *m* Cato; **Catone il Maggiore** Cato the Elder

catòr·cio *m* (**-ci**) (coll) piece of junk

catramare tr to tar

catramatrice f asphalt-paving machine

catrame m tar, coal tar

càttedra f desk (of teacher); chair, professorship

cattedrale adj & f cathedral

cattedràti·co -ca (**-ci -che**) adj pedantic || m professor

catte·gu m (**-gù**) catgut

cattivare tr to captivate

cattivèria f wickedness; piece of wickedness

cattivi·tà f (**-tà**) captivity

catti·vo -va adj bad; wicked; vicious (animal); worthless; poor (reputation; condition); nasty; naughty; (archaic) cowardly || m bad person || m bad taste; **sapere di cattivo** to taste bad

cattolicità f catholicity

cattòli·co -ca (**-ci -che**) adj catholic || adj & mf Catholic

cattura f capture, seizure; arrest

catturare tr to capture, seize; to arrest

caucàsi·co -ca adj & mf (**-ci -che**) Caucasian

caucciù m (**caucciù**) rubber

càusa f cause, motive; fault; lawsuit, action; **a causa di** on account of; **causa civile** civil suit; **causa penale** criminal suit; **fare causa** to take legal action; **intentare causa a** to bring suit against

causale adj causal || f cause

causare (**càuso**) tr to cause

causìdi·co m (**-ci**) amicus curiae; (joc) pettifogger

càusti·co -ca adj (**-ci -che**) caustic

cautèla f caution; precaution, care

cautelare adj guaranteeing, protecting || v (**cautèlo**) tr to guarantee, protect || ref to take precautions

cauterizzare [ddzz] tr to cauterize

càu·to -ta adj cautious, prudent; cagey

cauzióne f security, bail; **dare cauzione** to give bail

cava f quarry; cave; (fig) mine

cavadènti m (**-ti**) (coll) tooth puller, poor dentist

cavagno m (coll) basket

cavalcare §197 tr to ride; to cross over (e.g., a river) || intr to ride; **cavalcare a bisdosso** to ride bareback; **cavalcare all'amazzone** to ride side-saddle

cavalcata f ride; cavalcade

cavalcatura f mount

cavalca·vìa m (**-vìa**) bridge (between two buildings); overpass

cavalcióni adj—**a cavalcioni (di)** astride

cavalierato m knighthood

cavalière m rider (on horseback); knight; cavalier; chevalier; **a cavaliere** astride; **cavaliere d'industria** adventurer; **cavaliere errante** knight errant; **essere a cavaliere di** to overlook (e.g., a valley); to stretch over (e.g., two centuries)

cavalla f mare

cavalleggièro m cavalryman

cavallere·sco -sca adj (**-schi -sche**) chivalrous, knightly

cavallerìa f cavalry; chivalry, knighthood; (fig) chivalry

cavallerizza f manège, riding school; horsemanship; horsewoman

cavallerizzo m horseman; riding master

cavallétta f grasshopper

cavallétto m tripod; easel; trestle (of ski lift); scaffold (e.g., of stonemason); sawhorse, sawbuck

cavalli·no -na adj horse, horse-like || m foal, colt || f foal, filly; **correre la cavallina** to be on the loose; to sow one's wild oats

cavallo m horse; knight (in chess); crotch (of pants); **a cavallo** on horse-back; **a cavallo di** astride; **andare col cavallo di San Francesco** to ride shank's mare; **cavallo a dondolo** hobbyhorse; **cavallo di battaglia** battle horse; (fig) specialty, forte; **cavallo da corsa** race horse; **cavallo da tiro** draft horse; **cavallo di Frisia** cheval-de-frise; **cavallo di ritorno** confirmed news; **cavallo vapore** metric horsepower; **essere a cavallo** (fig) to have turned the corner

cavallóne m big horse; billow

cavallùc·cio -cio m (**-ci**) little horse; **a cavalluccio** on one's shoulders; **cavalluccio marino** (ichth) sea horse

cavare tr to dig; to extract (e.g., a tooth); to pull out (e.g., money); to draw; **cavare il cuore a qlcu** to move s.o. to compassion; **cavare una spina dal cuore a qlcu** to ease s.o.'s mind || ref to take off (e.g., one's hat); **cavarsela** to overcome an obstacle; to get out of trouble; **cavarsi la camicia di dosso** to give the shirt off one's back; **cavarsi la fame** to eat one's fill; **cavarsi la voglia** to satisfy one's wishes

cavastiva·li m (**-li**) bootjack

cavatap·pi m (**-pi**) corkscrew

cavaturàccio·li m (**-li**) corkscrew

cavèrna f cave, cavern

cavernó·so -sa [s] adj cavernous; deep (voice)

cavézza f halter; (fig) check

càvia f guinea pig; **cavia umana** (fig) guinea pig

caviale m caviar

cavìc·chio·m (**-chi**) peg

cavì·glia f (**-glie**) ankle; bolt; pin, dowel, peg

caviglièra f ankle support

cavillare intr to cavil, quibble

cavillo m quibble

cavilló·so -sa [s] adj quibbling, captious

cavi·tà f (**-tà**) cavity

ca·vo -va adj hollow || m hollow; cable; trough (between two waves); (naut) hawser; **cavo di rimorchio** towline; **cavo telefonico** telephone cable || f see **cava**

cavolfióre m cauliflower

càvolo m cabbage; **cavolo di Bruxelles** Brussels sprouts (food); (bot) Brussels sprout; **non capire un cavolo** (vulg) to not understand a blessed thing

cazzòtto m (vulg) punch, sock

cazzuòla f trowel

ce §5
cecare §122 tr to blind
cèc·ca f (-che) magpie; fare cecca to misfire
cecchino m sniper
céce m chickpea
ceci·tà f (-tà) blindness
cè·co -ca adj & mf (-chi -che) Czech
Cecoslovàcchia, la Czechoslovakia
cecoslovac·co -ca adj & mf (-chi -che) Czechoslovak
cèdere §123 tr to cede; to give up; to sell at cost; cedere il passo to let s.o. through; cedere la strada to yield the right of way; non cederla to be second to none ‖ intr to give in, yield; to give way, succumb; to sag
cedévole adj yielding; soft; pliable
cedíglia f cedilla
cediménto m cave-in; (fig) yielding
cèdola f slip; coupon
cedri·no -na adj citron; citron-like; cedar, cedar-like
cédro m (Citrus medica) citron; (Cedrus) cedar; cedro del Libano cedar of Lebanon
CEE m (letterword) (Comunità Economica Europea) EEC (European Economic Community - Common Market)
cefalèa f slight headache; headache
cèfalo m (ichth) mullet
cèffo m snout; (pej) face; brutto ceffo ugly mug
ceffóne m slap in the face
celare (cèlo) tr to hide, conceal
cela·to -ta adj hidden ‖ f sallet
celebèrri·mo -ma adj very famous, renowned
celebrare (cèlebro) tr & intr to celebrate
celebrazióne f celebration
cèlebre adj famous, renowned, celebrated
celebri·tà f (-tà) celebrity
cèlere adj swift, rapid; express (train); short, quick; prompt ‖ Celere f special police
celeri·tà f (-tà) swiftness, rapidity; speed (e.g., of a machine gun)
celèste adj heavenly, celestial; blue, sky-blue ‖ m blue, sky blue; celesti heavenly spirits; (mythol) gods
celestiale adj celestial, heavenly
cèlia f jest; mettere in celia to deride; per celia in jest
celiare §287 (cèlio) intr to jest, joke
celibatà·rio -ria (-ri -rie) adj single ‖ m old bachelor
celibato m celibacy; bachelorhood
cèlibe adj single, unmarried ‖ m bachelor
cèlla f cell; cella frigorifera walk-in refrigerator; cella campanaria belfry
cèllofan or cellofàn m cellophane
cèllula f cell; cellula fotoelettrica photoelectric cell
cellulare adj cellular; ventilated (fabric); solitary (confinement)
cellulòide f celluloid
celluló·so -sa [s] adj cell-like, cellular ‖ f cellulose
cèl·ta mf (-ti -te) Celt

cèlti·co -ca adj (-ci -che) Celtic; venereal (disease)
cementare (ceménto) tr to cement
ceménto m cement, concrete; cemento armato reinforced concrete
céna f supper; Ultima Cena Last Supper
cenàcolo m cenacle
cenare (céno) intr to sup, have supper
cenciaió·lo -la mf ragpicker
cén·cio m (-ci) rag, duster (for cleaning)
cenció·so -sa [s] adj tattered, ragged
cénere adj ashen ‖ f ash; cinder; andare in cenere to go up in smoke; ceneri ashes (of a person); ridurre in cenere to burn to ashes ‖ le Ceneri Ash Wednesday
cenerèntola f (fig) Cinderella ‖ Cenerèntola f Cinderella (of the fable)
cén·gia f (-ge) ledge (of a mountain)
cénno m sign; wave (with hand); nod; wag; wink; gesture; hint; notice; al cenni di at the orders of; fare cenno a or di to mention; fare cenno di no to shake one's head; fare cenno di sì to nod assent
cenò·bio m (-bi) monastery
cenobi·ta m (-ti) monk, cenobite
censiménto m census
censire §176 tr to take the census of
cènso m wealth, income; census (in ancient Rome)
censóre m censor; faultfinder; (educ) proctor
censuà·rio -ria (-ri -rie) adj income; tax (register) ‖ m taxpayer
censura f censure; censorship; faultfinding
censurare tr to censure; to criticize, find fault with
centàuro m centaur
centellinare tr to sip; to take a nip of
centellino m sip, nip
centenà·rio -ria (-ri -rie) adj & mf centenary, centennial ‖ m centenary, centennial (anniversary)
centèsi·mo -ma adj hundredth ‖ m hundredth; centime; cent; penny
centigrado m centigrade
centigrammo m centigram
centìmetro m centimeter; tape measure
cèntina f (archit) centering; (aer) rib
centi·nàio m hundred; un centinaio di about a hundred ‖ m (-nàia fpl)—a centinaia by the hundreds
cènto adj, m & pron a hundred, one hundred; per cento per cent
centomila adj, m & pron a hundred thousand, one hundred thousand
centóne m cento
centopiè·di m (-di) centipede
centrale adj central ‖ f headquarters, home office; powerhouse, generating station; telephone exchange; centrale di conversione (elec) transformer station; centrale telefonica central
centralini·sta mf (-sti -ste) telephone operator
centralino m telephone exchange
centralizzare [ddzz] tr to centralize
centrare (cèntro) tr to center; to hit the center of

centrattac·co *m* (**-chi**) (sports) center forward

centrifu·go -ga *adj* (**-ghi -ghe**) centrifugal ‖ *f* centrifuge

centrino *m* centerpiece

centripe·to -ta *adj* centripetal

centri·sta *mf* (**-sti -ste**) (pol) centrist

cèntro *m* center; **al centro** downtown; **far centro** to hit the mark

centrocampo *m* (soccer) midfield

centuplicare §197 (**centùplico**) *tr* to multiply a hundredfold

cèntu·plo -pla *adj & m* hundredfold

céppo *m* trunk, stump; log; block (*for beheading*); brake shoe; stock (*of anchor*); **ceppi** stocks, fetters ‖ **il Ceppo** (coll) Christmas

céra *f* wax; face, aspect, air, look; **di cera** waxen; pale; **cera da scarpe** shoe polish; **avere buona cera** to look well; **fare buona cera a** to welcome

ceralac·ca *f* (**-che**) sealing wax

ceràmi·co -ca (**-ci -che**) *adj* ceramic ‖ *f* ceramics

cerare (**céro**) *tr* to wax

Cèrbero *m* Cerberus

cerbiatto *m* fawn

cerbottana *f* blowgun, peashooter

cer·ca *f* (**-che**) search, quest; **in cerca di** in search of

cercare §197 (**cérco**) *tr* to seek, look for; to desire, yearn for; **cercare il pelo nell'uovo** to be a faultfinder, to nitpick ‖ *intr* to try

cerca·tóre -trice *adj* seeking ‖ *mf* seeker; mendicant ‖ *m* prospector

cérchia *f* coterie; compass, limits (*of a wall*); circle (*of friends*)

cerchiare §287 (**cérchio**) *tr* to hoop (*a barrel*); to circle, encircle

cér·chio *m* (**-chi**) circle; hoop; loop; **fare il cerchio della morte** (aer) to loop the loop; **in cerchio** in a circle ‖ *m* (**-chia** *fpl*) (archaic) circle

cerchióne *m* rim; tire (*of metal*)

cereale *adj & m* cereal

cerebrale *adj* cerebral

cère·o -a *adj* waxen; wax-colored, pale

cerfò·glio *m* (**-gli**) chervil

cerimònia *f* ceremony; **fare cerimonie** to stand on ceremony; to make a fuss

cerimoniale *adj & m* ceremonial

cerimonière *m* master of ceremonies (*at court*)

cerimonió·so -sa [s] *adj* ceremonious

cerino *m* wax match; taper

cernéc·chio *m* (**-chi**) tuft (*of hair*)

cernièra *f* hinge; clasp (*of handbag*); **a cerniera** hinged; **cerniera lampo** zipper

cèrnita *f* sorting, selection, grading

céro *m* church candle; **offrire un cero** to light a candle

ceróne *m* make-up (*of actor*)

ceròtto *m* adhesive tape; (fig) bore; **cerotto per i calli** corn plaster

certame *m* (poet) combat; competition, contest (*of poets*)

certézza *f* certitude, assurance, conviction, certainty

certificare §197 (**certìfico**) *tr* to certify, certificate

certificato *m* certificate

cèr·to -ta *adj* such, some; convinced; certain; real, positive ‖ *m* certainty; **di certo** or **per certo** for certain ‖ **certi** *pron* some ‖ **certo** *adv* undoubtedly

certósa *f* Carthusian monastery, charterhouse

certosi·no *m* Carthusian monk; chartreuse (*liquor*); **da certosino** with great patience

certu·no -na *adj* (obs) some ‖ **certuni** *pron* some

cerùle·o -a *adj* cerulean

cerume *m* ear wax

cervellétto *m* cerebellum

cervelli·no -na *adj & mf* scatterbrain

cervèllo *m* (**cervèlli & cervèlla** *fpl*) brain; head; mind; **dare al cervello** to go to one's head

cervellòti·co -ca *adj* (**-ci -che**) queer, extravagant

cervice *f* (anat) cervix; (poet) nape of the neck

cerviè·ro -ra *adj* lynx-like; ‖ *m* lynx

cervi·no -na *adj* deer-like ‖ **Cervino** *m* Matterhorn

cèrvo *m* deer; (ent) stag beetle; **cervo volante** kite

Cèsare *m* Caesar

cesàre·o -a *adj* Caesarean; (poet) courtly

cesellare (**cesèllo**) *tr* to chase, chisel; to carve, engrave; to polish (*e.g., a poem*)

cesella·tóre -trice *mf* chaser, engraver, chiseler

cesellatura *f* chasing, engraving; polished writing

cesèllo *m* burin, graver

cesòia *f* shears, metal shears; **cesoie** shears (*for gardening*)

cesoiatrice *f* shearing machine

cèspite *m* source (*of income*); (poet) tuft

céspo *m* tuft

cespù·glio *m* (**-gli**) bush, shrub, thicket

cèssa *f*—**senza cessa** without letup

cessare (**cèsso**) *tr* to stop, interrupt ‖ *intr* to cease, stop; **cessare di** + *inf* to stop + *ger*

cessazióne *f* cessation, discontinuance; **cessazione d'esercizio** going out of business

cessionà·rio *m* (**-ri**) assignee

cèsso *m* (vulg) privy, outhouse

césta *f* basket, hamper

cestinare *tr* to throw into the wastebasket; to reject (*a book, article, etc.*)

césto *m* basket; tuft; head (*e.g., of lettuce*)

cesura *f* caesura

cetàceo *m* cetacean

cèto *m* class; **ceto medio** middle class

cétra *f* lyre; cither; inspiration

cetriolino *m* gherkin

cetriòlo *m* cucumber; (fig) dolt

che *adj* what; which; what a, e.g., **che bella giornata!** what a beautiful day! ‖ *pron interr* what ‖ *pron rel* who; whom; that; which; (coll) in which ‖ *m*—**essere un gran che** to be a big shot, to be somebody || *adv* how, e.g., **che bello!** how nice!; **non . . . che** only, e.g., **non venne che Luigi** only Luigi came; no one but, e.g., **non restò che mio cugino** no one but my cousin stayed || *conj* that; (*after comparatives*) than, as

ché *adv* (coll) why || *conj* (coll) because; (coll) so that

checché *pron* (lit) whatever, no matter what

checchessìa *pron* (lit) anything, everything

chèla *f* claw

che·pì *m* (-**pì**) kepi

cherubino *m* cherub

chetare (**chéto**) *tr* to quiet; to placate || *ref* to quiet down, become quiet

chetichèlla *f*—**alla chetichella** surreptitiously, stealthily

ché·to -ta *adj* quiet, still

chi *pron interr* who; whom || *pron rel* who; whom; **chi . . . chi** some . . . some

chiàcchiera *f* chatter, idle talk; gossip; glibness; **fare quattro chiacchiere** to have a chat

chiacchierare (**chiàcchiero**) *intr* to chat; to gossip

chiacchierata *f* talk, chat; **fare una chiacchierata** to visit

chiacchieri·no -na *adj* talkative, loquacious

chiacchierì·o *m* (-**i**) chattering, jabbering (*of a crowd*)

chiacchieró·ne -na *adj* talkative, loquacious || *mf* chatterbox

chiama *f* roll call; **fare la chiama** to call the roll; **mancare alla chiama** to be absent at the roll call

chiamare *tr* to call; to hail (*a cab*); to invoke, call upon; **chiamare al telefono** to call up; **esser chiamato a** to have the vocation for || *ref* to be named; **si chiama Giovanni** his name is John

chiamata *f* call; (law) designation (*of an heir*); (telp) ring; (theat) curtain call; (typ) catchword

chiappa *f* (vulg) buttock; (slang) catch (*e.g., of fish*)

chiarét·to -ta *adj & m* claret

chiarézza *f* clarity, clearness

chiarificare §197 (**chiarifico**) *tr* to clarify

chiarificazióne *f* clarification

chiariménto *m* explanation

chiarire §176 *tr* to clear up, explain; to unravel || *intr* (ESSERE) to clear, become clear || *ref* to make oneself clear; to assure oneself

chia·ro -ra *adj* clear; bright; light (*color*); honest; clear-cut; plain (*language*); illustrious, famous || *m* light; bright color; brightness; **chiaro di luna** moonlight; **con questi chiari di luna** in these troubled times; **mettere in chiaro** to clarify, explain || **chiaro** *adv* plainly; **chiaro e tondo** bluntly, frankly

chiaróre *m* light, glimmer

chiaroveggènte *adj & mf* clairvoyant

chiaroveggènza *f* clairvoyance

chiassata *f* uproar, disturbance, racket; noisy scene

chiasso *m* noise; uproar; alley; **fare chiasso** to cause a sensation

chiassó·so -sa [s] *adj* noisy; gaudy

chiatta *f* barge; pontoon

chiavarda *f* bolt

chiave *f* key; wrench; (archit) keystone; (mus) clef; **avere le chiavi di** to own; **chiave a rollino** adjustable wrench; **chiave a tubo** socket wrench; **chiave di volta** keystone; **chiave inglese** monkey wrench; **fuori chiave off** key; **sotto chiave** under lock and key

chiavétta *f* key; cock; cotter pin

chiàvi·ca *f* (-**che**) sewer

chiavistèlio *m* bolt

chiazza *f* spot, blotch

chiazzare *tr* to spot, blotch; to mottle

chiazza·to -ta *adj* spotted, mottled

chic·ca *f* (-**che**) sweet, candy

chìcchera *f* cup

chicchessìa *pron indef* anyone, anybody

chicchirichì *m* cock-a-doodle-doo

chic·co *m* (-**chi**) grain, seed; bead (*of rosary*); bean (*of coffee*); **chicco di grandine** hailstone; **chicco d'uva** grape

chièdere §124 *tr* to ask; to ask for; to beg (*pardon*); to require; to sue (*for damages or peace*); **chiedere a qlcu di + inf** to ask s.o. to + *inf*; **chiedere in prestito** to borrow; **chiedere qlco a qlcu** to ask s.o. for s.th || *ref* to wonder

chiéri·ca *f* (-**che**) tonsure; priesthood

chiéri·co *m* (-**ci**) clergyman; altar boy; (archaic) clerk

chièsa *f* church

chiesuòla *f* small church; clique, set (*e.g., of artists*); (naut) binnacle

chì·glia *f* (-**glie**) keel; **chiglia mobile** (naut) centerboard

chilo *m* kilo, kilogram; **fare il chilo** to take a siesta

chilociclo *m* kilocycle

chilogrammo *m* kilogram

chilohèrtz *m* kilohertz

chilomètràg·gio *m* (-**gi**) distance in kilometers

chilomètri·co -ca *adj* (-**ci -che**) kilometric; interminable (*e.g., speech*)

chilòmetro *m* kilometer

chilo·watt *m* (-**watt**) kilowatt

chimèra *f* chimera; daydream, utopia

chimèri·co -ca *adj* (-**ci -che**) chimerical

chìmi·co -ca (-**ci -che**) *adj* chemical || *m* chemist || *f* chemistry

chimòno *m* kimono

china *f* slope, decline; India ink; cinchona

chinare *tr* to bend; to lower (*one's eyes*); **chinare il capo** to nod assent; **chinare la fronte** to yield, give in || *ref* to bend, stoop

china·to -ta *adj* bent, lowered; bitter; with quinine, e.g., **vino chinato** wine with quinine

chincàglie *fpl* notions, knicknacks, sundries

chincaglière *m* notions or knicknack dealer

chincaglierìa *f* knicknack; chincaglierie knicknacks, notions

chinina *f* quinine (*alkaloid*)

chinino *m* quinine (*salt of the alkaloid*)

chi·no ·na *adj* bent, lowered ‖ *f* see china

chiòc·cia *f* (-ce) brooding hen

chiocciare §128 (chiòccio) *intr* to cluck; to sit, brood; to crouch

chiocciata *f* brood

chiòc·cio ·cia (-ci -ce) *adj* hoarse ‖ *f* see chioccia

chiòcciola *f* snail; (anat) cochlea; (mach) nut

chioccolì·o *m* (-ì) cackle (*of hen*); gurgle (*of water*)

chiodare (chiòdo) *tr* to nail

chioda·to ·ta *adj* nailed shut; hobnailed

chiòdo *m* nail; spike; obsession; craze; (coll) debt; chiodi climbing irons; chiodo a espansione expansion bolt; chiodo da cavallo horseshoe nail; chiodo di garofano clove; chiodo ribattino rivet

chiòma *f* hair; mane; foliage; (astr) coma

chioma·to ·ta *adj* hairy, long-haired; leafy

chiòsa *f* gloss

chiosare (chiòso) *tr* to gloss, comment on

chiò·sco *m* (-schi) kiosk, stand, newsstand; pavilion, bandstand

chiòstra *f* circular range (*of mountains*); (poet) enclosure; (poet) set (*of teeth*); (poet) zone, region

chiòstro *m* cloister

chiòt·to ·ta *adj* quiet, still; chiotto chiotto still as a mouse

chiromante *mf* palmist

chiromanzìa *f* palmistry

chiropràtica *f* chiropractice

chirurgìa *f* surgery

chirùrgi·co ·ca *adj* (-ci -che) surgical

chirur·go *m* (-ghi & -gi) surgeon

chissà *adv* maybe

chitarra *f* guitar; chitarra hawaiana ukulele

chitarri·sta *mf* (-sti -ste) guitar player

chiùdere §125 *tr* to shut, close; to lock; to turn off; to fasten; to block (*a road*); to fence in; to nail shut (*a box*); to strike (*a balance*); to conclude, wind up; chiudere a chiave to lock; chiudere bottega to go out of business; chiudere il becco (slang) to shut up ‖ *intr* to shut, close; to lock ‖ *ref* to shut, close; to lock; to withdraw; to cloud over

chiùnque *pron indef invar* anybody, anyone ‖ *pron rel invar* whoever, whomever; anyone who, anyone whom

chiurlo *m* (orn) curlew

chiusa [s] *f* fence; lock (*of canal*); end, conclusion (*e.g., of letter*)

chiusino [s] *m* manhole

chiu·so ·sa [s] *adj* shut, closed, locked; stuffy (*air*); high-bodiced (*dress*);

close (*vowel*) ‖ *m* enclosure, corral; close ‖ *f* see chiusa

chiusura [s] *f* closing, end; fastener; lock; chiusura lampo zipper, slide fastener

ci §5

ciabatta *f* slipper; old shoe

ciabat·tàio *m* (-tài) cobbler

ciabattare *intr* to shuffle along

ciabattino *m* cobbler, shoemaker

ciàc *f* (mov) clappers

cialda *f* wafer; thin waffle

cialdóne *m* cone (*for ice cream*)

cialtró·ne ·na *mf* rogue, scoundrel; slovenly person

ciambèlla *f* doughnut; ciambella di salvataggio life saver

ciambellano *m* chamberlain

ciampicare §197 (ciàmpico) *intr* to stumble along

ciana *f* (slang) fishwife

cianamide *f* cyanamide

ciàn·cia *f* (-ce) chatter, prattle, idle gossip

cianciare §128 (ciàncio) *intr* to chatter, prattle

cianciafrùscola *f* trifle, bagatelle

cianfrusà·glia *f* (-glie) trifle, trinket; rubbish, trash, junk

cianìdri·co ·ca *adj* (-ci -che) hydrocyanic

cianògeno *m* cyanogen

cianuro *m* cyanide

ciao *interj* (coll) hi!, hello!; (coll) goodbye!, so long!

ciarla *f* chatter, prattle, idle talk; gossip

ciarlare *intr* to chatter, prattle

ciarlatanata *f* charlatanism, quackery

ciarlatanerìa *f* charlatanism

ciarlatané·sco ·sca *adj* (-schi -sche) charlatan

ciarlatano *m* charlatan, quack

ciarliè·ro ·ra *adj* talkative, garrulous

ciarpame *m* rubbish, junk

ciaschedu·no ·na *adj indef* each ‖ *pron indef* each one, everyone

ciascu·no ·na *adj indef* each ‖ *pron indef* each one, everyone

cibare *tr* & *ref* to feed

cibà·rio ·ria (-ri -rie) *adj* alimentary ‖ cibarie *fpl* foodstuffs, victuals

cibo *m* food; meal; (fig) dish

cicala *f* cicada; grasshopper; locust; (fig) chatterbox; (naut) anchor ring

cicalare *intr* to prattle, babble; to chatter

cicaléc·cio *m* (-ci) prattle, babble; chatter

cicatrice *f* scar

cicatrizzare [ddzz] *tr* to heal (*a wound*) ‖ *intr* (ESSERE) & *ref* to heal, scar

cicatrizzazióne [ddzz] *f* closing, healing (*of a wound*)

cic·ca *f* (-che) butt (*of cigar or cigarette*); (slang) chewing gum

ciccare §197 *intr* to chew tobacco; (coll) to boil with anger

cicchettare (cicchétto) *tr* (slang) to prime (*a carburetor*); (slang) to dress down, reprimand ‖ *intr* to tipple

cicchétto *m* nip (*of liquor*); (slang) dressing down

cìc•cia f (-ce) (joc) flesh; (joc) fat

cicció•ne -na mf fatty

ciceróne m guide || Cicerone m Cicero

ciclàbile adj open to bicycles; bicycle, e.g., pista ciclabile bicycle trail

cìcli•co -ca adj (-ci -che) cyclic(al)

cicli•sta mf (-sti -ste) cyclist, bicyclist

ciclo m cycle; (coll) bicycle; ciclo operativo (econ) turnover

ciclomotóre m motorbike

ciclomotori•sta mf (-sti -ste) driver of motorbike

ciclóne m cyclone

ciclòpe m cyclops

ciclòpi•co -ca adj (-ci -che) cyclopean, gigantic

ciclopista f bicycle trail

ciclostilare tr to mimeograph

ciclostile or ciclostilo m mimeograph

ciclotróne m cyclotron

cicógna f stork

cicòria f chicory; endive

cicuta f hemlock

ciè•co -ca (-chi -che) adj blind; alla cieca blindly || mf blind person || m blind man; i ciechi the blind

cièlo m sky; heaven; weather, climate; roof (e.g., of wagon); a ciel sereno in the open air; cielo a pecorelle mackerel or fleecy sky; dal cielo from above; non stare né in cielo né in terra to be utterly absurd; per amor del cielo for heaven's sake; portare al cielo to praise to the skies; santo cielo! good heavens!; volesse il cielo che . . . ! I would that . . . !

cifra f number, figure; Arabic numeral; sum, total; digit; initial, monogram; cipher, code; cifra d'affari amount of business, turnover; cifra tonda round number

cifrare tr to cipher, code; to embroider (a monogram)

cifrà•rio m (-ri) code, cipher

cì•glio m (-glia fpl) eyelash; eyebrow; a ciglio asciutto with dry eyes; ciglia (zool) cilia; senza batter ciglio without batting an eye || m (-gli) (fig) edge, brow

ciglióne m bank, embankment

cigno m swan; cob

cigolante adj creaky, squeaky

cigolare (cigolo) intr to squeak, creak

cigolì•o m (-i) squeak, creak

Cile, il Chile

cilécca f—fare cilecca to misfire

cileccare §197 (cilécco) intr to goof, blunder; to fail

cilè•no -na adj & mf Chilean

cilè•stro -stra adj (poet) azure, blue

cilì•cio m (-ci) sackcloth

ciliè•gia f (-gie & -ge) cherry

cilié•gio m (-gi) cherry tree

cilindrare tr to calender (e.g., paper); to roll (a road)

cilindrata f (aut) cylinder capacity, piston displacement

cilìndri•co -ca adj (-ci -che) cylindric(al)

cilindro m cylinder; top hat; roll, roller

cima f top, summit; tip (e.g., of a pole); peak (of mountain); edge, end; rope, cable; head (e.g., of let-

tuce); (coll) genius; da cima a fondo from top to bottom

cimare tr to cut the tip off; to shear; (agr) to prune

cimasa f (archit) coping

cìmbalo m gong; (obs) cymbal; in cimbali tipsy; in a tizzy

cimè•lio m (-li) relic, souvenir, memento

cimentare (ciménto) tr to risk (e.g., one's life); to provoke; (archaic) to assay || ref to expose oneself; to venture

ciménto m risk, danger; (archaic) assay

cìmice f bug; bedbug; (coll) thumbtack

cimièro m crest; (poet) helmet

ciminièra f chimney (of factory); smokestack (of locomotive); funnel (of steamship)

cimitèro m cemetery, graveyard; (fig) ghosttown

cimósa [s] or cimóssa f selvage; blackboard eraser

cimurro m distemper; (joc) cold

Cina, la China

cinabro m cinnabar; crimson; red ink

cìn•cia f (-ce) titmouse

cinciallégra f great titmouse

cincilla f chinchilla

cincischiare §287 tr to shred; to wrinkle, crease; to waste (time); to mumble (words) || intr to wrinkle, crease

cine m (coll) cinema

cineamatóre m amateur movie maker

cine•asta m (-sti) motion-picture producer; movie fan; movie actor || f movie actress

cinecàmera f movie camera

cinedilettante mf amateur movie maker

cinegiornale m newsreel

cinelàndia f movieland

cìne•ma m (-ma) movies; movie house

cinematografare (cinematògrafo) tr to film, shoot

cinematografìa f cinema, motion pictures, movie industry

cinematogràfi•co -ca adj (-ci -che) movie, motion-picture; movie-like

cinematògrafo m motion picture; movie theater; (fig) hubbub; (fig) funny sight

cineparchég•gio m (-gi) drive-in movie

cinepar•co m (-chi) drive-in movie

cineprésa [s] f movie camera

cinère•o -a adj ashen

cinescò•pio m (-pi) kinescope, TV tube

cinése [s] adj & mf Chinese

cineteatro m movie house; cineteatro all'aperto outdoor movie

cinetè•ca f (-che) film library

cinèti•co -ca (-ci -che) adj kinetic || f kinetics

cingallégra f var of cinciallegra

cìngere §126 tr to surround; to gird (e.g., the head); to gird on (e.g., the sword); to gird cavaliere to dub a knight; cingere d'assedio to besiege

cìnghia f belt, strap; tirare la cinghia to tighten one's belt

cinghiale m wild boar

cinghiata f lash

cingola•to -ta adj track-driven, caterpillar

cìngolo *m* endless metal belt; track; girdle, belt (*of a priest*)

cinguettare (**cinguétto**) *intr* to chirp, twitter; to babble

cinguettì·o *m* (**-ì**) chirp, twitter; (fig) babble

cìni·co -ca (**-ci -che**) *adj* cynical || *m* cynic

ciniglia *f* chenille

cinismo *m* cynicism

cinòfilo *m* dog lover

cinquanta *adj, m & pron* fifty

cinquantenà·rio -ria (**-ri -rie**) *adj* fifty-year-old; occurring every fifty years || *m* fiftieth anniversary

cinquantènne *adj* fifty-year-old || *mf* fifty-year-old person

cinquantèn·nio *m* (**-ni**) period of fifty years, half century

cinquantèsi·mo -ma *adj, m & pron* fiftieth

cinquantina *f* about fifty; **sulla cinquantina** about fifty years old

cinque *adj & pron* five; **le cinque** five o'clock || *m* five; fifth (*in dates*)

cinquecenté·sco -sca *adj* (**-schi -sche**) sixteenth-century

cinquecènto *adj, m & pron* five hundred || *f* small car || **il Cinquecento** the sixteenth century

cinquina *f* set of five; five numbers (*drawn at Italian lotto*); (mil) pay

cinta *f* fence, wall; circuit, enclosure; circumference (*of a city*)

cintare *tr* to surround; to fence in; to hold (*in wrestling*)

cin·to -ta *adj* surrounded, girded || *m* belt; girdle; **cinto erniario** truss || *f* see **cinta**

cintola *f* waist; belt; **con le mani alla cintola** idling, loafing

cintura *f* belt; waist; waistband; lock (*in wrestling*); **cintura di salvataggio** life preserver; **cintura di sicurezza** safety belt

cinturare *tr* to surround

cinturino *m* strap (*of watch or shoes*); hem (*e.g., of cuffs*)

cinturóne *m* belt; Sam Browne belt

ciò *pron* this; that; **a ciò** for that purpose; **a ciò che** so that; **ciò nondimeno** or **ciò nonostante** though, nevertheless; **con tutto ciò** in spite of everything; **per ciò** therefore

ciòc·ca *f* (**-che**) lock (*of hair*); cluster (*e.g., of cherries*)

ciòc·co *m* (**-chi**) log; **dormire come un ciocco** to sleep like a log

cioccolata *adj invar* chocolate || *f* chocolate (*beverage*)

cioccolatino *m* chocolate candy

cioccolato *m* chocolate; **cioccolato al latte** milk chocolate

cioè *adv* that is to say, namely; to wit; rather

ciondolare (**cióndolo**) *tr* to dangle || *intr* to dawdle; to stroll, saunter

ciòndolo *m* pendant, charm

ciondolóne *m* idler || *adv* dangling

ciòtola *f* bowl

ciòttolo *m* pebble, small stone; cobblestone

ciottoló·so -sa [s] *adj* pebbly

cip *m* (**cip**) chip (*in gambling*)

cipì·glio *m* (**-gli**) frown

cipólla *f* onion; bulb (*e.g., of a lamp*); nozzle (*of sprinkling can*)

cippo *m* column; bench mark

ciprèsso *m* cypress

cipria *f* face powder; **cipria compatta** compact

ciprió·ta *adj & mf* (**-ti -te**) Cypriot

Cipro *m* Cyprus

circa *adv* about, nearly || *prep* concerning, regarding, as to

cìr·co *m* (**-chi**) circus; **circo equestre** circus; **circo glaciale** cirque; **circo lunare** walled plain

circolare *adj* circulating; lending (*library*) || *m* available cash (*of a corporation*)

circolare *adj* circular; cashier's (*check*) || *f* circular (*letter*); (rr) beltline || *v* (**cìrcolo**) *intr* to circulate

circolazióne *f* circulation; traffic; currency; **circolazione sanguigna** bloodstream; circulation of blood

cìrcolo *m* circle; circulation (*of blood*); reception (*e.g., at court*); club, set, group

circoncìdere §145 *tr* to circumcise

circoncisióne *f* circumcision

circonci·so -sa *adj* circumcised

circondare (**circóndo**) *tr* to surround, encircle; to overwhelm (*e.g., with kindness*) || *ref* to surround oneself; to be surrounded

circondà·rio *m* (**-ri**) district; surrounding territory

circonduzióne *f* rotation (*e.g., of the body in calisthenics*)

circonferènza *f* circumference

circonflès·so -sa *adj* circumflex

circonlocuzióne *f* circumlocution

circonvallazióne *f* city-line road; (rr) beltline

circonvenire §282 *tr* to circumvent; to outwit

circonvenzióne *f* circumvention

circonvici·no -na *adj* neighboring, nearby

circoscrìt·to -ta *adj* circumscribed

circoscrìvere §250 *tr* to circumscribe

circoscrizióne *f* district; circuit

circospèt·to -ta *adj* circumspect, cautious

circospezióne *f* circumspection

circostante *adj* neighboring, surrounding, nearby || **circostanti** *mpl* neighbors; bystanders, onlookers

circostanza *f* circumstance

circostanziale *adj* circumstantial

circostanziare §287 *tr* to describe in detail; to circumstanciate

circostanzia·to -ta *adj* detailed, circumstantial

circuire §176 *tr* to circumvent

circùito *m* circuit; race (*of automobiles or bicycles*); **circuito stampato** (rad, telv) printed circuit

circumnavigare §209 (**circumnàvigo**) *tr* to circumnavigate

circumnavigazióne *f* circumnavigation

cirìlli·co -ca *adj* (**-ci -che**) Cyrillic

Ciro m Cyrus
cirro m cirrus
cirrò·si f (-si) cirrhosis
cispa f gum (on edge of eyelids)
cisposità [s] f gum; gumminess
cispó·so -sa [s] adj gummy
ciste f cyst
cisterna f cistern; tank
cisti f cyst
cistifèllea f gall bladder
citante mf (law) plaintiff
citare tr to cite, quote; to mention; (law) to summon, subpoena
citazióne f citation, quotation; mention; (law) summons, subpoena; (mil) commendation
citillo m (zool) gopher
citòfono m intercom
citostàti·co -ca adj (-ci -che) (biochem) cancer-inhibiting
citrato m citrate
citri·co -ca adj (-ci -che) citric
citrul·lo -la adj simple, foolish || mf simpleton, fool
cit·tà f (-tà) city, town || Città del Capo Cape Town; Città del Messico Mexico City; Città del Vaticano Vatican City; città fungo boom town
cittadèlla f citadel
cittadinanza f citizenship
cittadi·no -na adj city, town, civic || mf citizen; city dweller, urbanite || m townsman
ciù·co m (-chi) (coll) donkey, ass
ciuffo m lock, forelock; tuft; (bot) tassel
ciuffolòtto m (orn) bullfinch
ciurlare intr—ciurlare nel manico to play fast and loose
ciurma f crew, gang, mob
ciurmare tr (archaic) to charm; (archaic) to trick, inveigle
ciurmatóre m swindler, charlatan
civètta f barn owl, little owl; unmarked police car; ship used as decoy; (fig) coquette, flirt
civettare (civétto) intr to flirt
civetteria f coquettishness, coquetry
civettuò·lo la adj coquettish; attractive
cìvi·co -ca adj (-ci -che) civic; town, city
civile adj civil; civilian || mf civilian
civili·sta mf (-sti -ste) attorney, solicitor
civilizzare [ddzz] tr to civilize || ref to become civilized
civilizzazióne [ddzz] f civilizing (e.g., of barbarians); civilization
civil·tà f (-tà) civilization; civility
civismo m good citizenship
clac·son m (-son) horn (of a car)
claire f (claire) grating (in front of a store window)
clamóre m clamor, uproar
clamoró·so -sa [s] adj noisy; clamorous
clan m (clan) clan; clique
clandesti·no -na adj clandestine
clangóre m clangor, clang
clarinetti·sta mf (-sti -ste) clarinet player
clarinétto m clarinet
clarino m clarion
classe f class

classicheggiante adj classicistic
classicismo m classicism
classici·sta mf (-sti -ste) classicist
classici·tà f (-tà) classical spirit; classical antiquity
clàssi·co -ca (-ci -che) adj classic(al) || m classic
classifi·ca f (-che) rank, rating (in competitive testing); classification; (sports) rating
classificare §197 (classìfico) tr to classify; to rate, rank || ref to score
classificazióne f classification
claudicante adj lame, limping
claudicare §197 (clàudico) intr to limp
clauné·sco -sca adj (-schi -sche) clownish
clàusola f provision, proviso; clause; close, conclusion (e.g., of a speech); clausola rossa instructions for payment (in bank-credit documents); clausola verde shipping instructions (in bank-credit documents)
clausura f (eccl) seclusion; (fig) secluded place
clava f club, bludgeon
clavicémbalo m harpsichord
clavìcola f clavicle, collarbone
clemàtide f clematis
clemènte adj clement, indulgent; mild (climate)
clemènza f clemency; mildness
cleptòmane adj & mf kleptomaniac
clericale adj clerical || m clericalist
clericalismo m clericalism
clèro m clergy
clessidra f water clock; sandglass
clicchetti·o m (-i) clicking, click-clack (e.g., of a typewriter)
cli·ché m (-ché) cliché; stereotype (plate)
cliènte m client, customer, patron
clientèla f clientele, customers; practice (of a professional man)
cli·ma m (-mi) climate
climatèri·co -ca adj (-ci -che) climacteric; crucial
climatè·rio m (-ri) climacteric; crucial period
climàti·co -ca adj (-ci -che) climatic
climatizzazióne [ddzz] f air conditioning
clìni·co -ca (-ci -che) adj clinic || m clinician; highly skilled physician || f clinic; private hospital
cli·sma m (-smi) enema
clistère m enema; clistere a pera fountain syringe
cloa·ca f (-che) sewer
cloche f (cloche) woman's wide-brimmed hat; (aer) stick; (aut) floor gearshift
clorare (clòro) tr to chlorinate
clorato m chlorate
clorìdri·co -ca adj (-ci -che) hydrochloric
clòro m chlorine
clorofilla f chlorophyll
clorofòr·mio m (-mi) chloroform
cloroformizzare [ddzz] tr to chloroform
cloruro m chloride

coabitare (coàbito) *intr* to live together; to cohabit

coabitazióne *f* sharing (*of an apartment*)

coaccusa·to -ta *adj* jointly accused ‖ *m* codefendant

coacèrvo *m* accumulation (*e.g., of interest*)

coadiutóre *m* coadjutor

coadiuvante *adj* helping ‖ *m* helper

coadiuvare (coàdiuvo) *tr* to assist, advise

coagulare (coàgulo) *tr & ref* to coagulate, clot

coagulazióne *f* coagulation, clotting

coàgulo *m* clot

coalescènza *f* coalescence

coalizióne *f* coalition

coalizzare [ddzz] *tr & ref* to unite, rally

coartare *tr* to coerce, force

coartazióne *f* coercion, forcing

coatti·vo -va *adj* forceful, compelling

coat·to -ta *adj* coercive

coautóre *m* coauthor

coazióne *f* coercion

cobalto *m* cobalt

cocaìna *f* cocaine

cocainòmane *mf* cocaine addict

coc·ca *f* (**-che**) notch (*of arrow*); corner, edge (*e.g., of a handkerchief*); three-mast galley

coccarda *f* cockade

cocchière *m* coachman, cab driver

còc·chio *m* (**-chi**) coach; chariot

cocchiume *m* bung

còc·cia *f* (**-ce**) sword guard; (coll) head, noggin

còccige *m* coccyx

coccinèlla *f* ladybug

cocciniglia *f* cochineal

còc·cio *m* (**-ci**) earthenware; broken piece of pottery

cocciutàggine *m* stubborness

cocciu·to -ta *adj* stubborn

còc·co *m* (**-chi**) coconut (*tree and nut*); (bact) coccus; (coll) egg; (coll) darling, favorite

cocco·dè *m* (**-dè**) cackle

coccodrillo *m* crocodile

còccola *f* berry (*of cypress*); darling girl

coccolare (còccolo) *tr* to fondle, cuddle ‖ *ref* to nestle, cuddle up; to bask

còcco·lo -la *adj* (coll) nice, darling ‖ *m* darling boy ‖ *f* see **coccola**

coccolóne or **coccolóni** *adv* squatting

cocènte *adj* burning

cocktail *m* (**cocktail**) cocktail; cocktail party

còclea *f* dredge; (anat) cochlea

cocòmero *m* watermelon; (coll) simpleton

cocorita *f* parakeet

cocuzza *f* (coll) pumpkin; (coll) head, noggin

cocùzzolo *m* crown (*of hat*); peak (*of mountain*)

còda *f* tail; train (*of skirt*); pigtail (*of hair*); **coda di paglia** (coll) uneasy conscience; **con la coda dell'occhio** out of the corner of the eye; **con la coda tra le gambe** with its tail between its legs; (fig) crestfallen; **di**

coda last; **fare la coda** to stand in line; **in coda** in a row; at the tail end

codardìa *f* (lit) cowardice

codar·do -da *adj* cowardly ‖ *mf* coward

codazzo *m* (pej) trail (*of people*)

codeina *f* codein

codé·sto -sta §7 *adj* ‖ **§8** *pron*

còdice *m* code; codex; **codice della strada** traffic laws; **codice di avviamento postale** zip code

codicillo *m* codicil

codificare §197 (codìfico) *tr* to codify

codi·no -na *adj* reactionary; conformist ‖ *m* pigtail (*of a man*); (fig) reactionary; conformist ‖ *f* small tail

códolo *m* tang, shank (*e.g., of knife*); handle (*of spoon or knife*); head (*of violin*)

coeducazióne *f* coeducation

coefficiènte *m* coefficient

coerciti·vo -va *adj* coercive

coercizióne *f* coercion

coerède *mf* coheir

coerènte *adj* coherent; consistent

coerènza *f* coherence; consistency

coesióne *f* cohesion

coesistènza *f* coexistence

coesìstere §114 *intr* to coexist

coesi·vo -va *adj* cohesive

coetàne·o -a *adj & m* contemporary

coè·vo -va *adj* contemporaneous, coeval

cofanétto *m* small chest, small coffer

còfano *m* chest, coffer; box, case (*for ammunition*); (aut) hood

còffa *f* masthead, crow's-nest

cofirmatà·rio -ria *adj & mf* (**-ri -rie**) cosigner

cogitabón·do -da *adj* (poet & joc) thoughtful, meditative

cogitare (còggito) *tr & intr* (poet & joc) to cogitate

cógli §4

cògliere §127 *tr* to gather; to hit (*the target*); to pluck (*flowers*); to grab, seize; (fig) to guess; **cogliere in fiagrante** to catch in the act; **cogliere la palla al balzo** to seize time by the forelock; **cogliere nel giusto** to hit the nail on the head; **cogliere qlcu alla sprovvista** to catch s.o. napping; **cogliere sul fatto** to catch in the act

coglióne *m* (vulg) testicle; (vulg) simpleton, fool

coglionerìa *f* (vulg) great stupidity

cognata *f* sister-in-law

cognato *m* brother-in-law

cògni·to -ta *adj* (poet & law) well-known

cognizióne *f* cognition, knowledge

cognóme *m* surname, family name

coguaro *m* cougar

cói §4

coibènte *adj* nonconducting ‖ *m* nonconductor

coincidènza *f* coincidence; harmony, identity; transfer (*from one streetcar or bus to another*); (rr) connection

coincìdere §145 *intr* to coincide

coinquilino *m* fellow tenant

cointeressare (cointerèsso) *tr* to give a share (*of profit*) to

cointeressa·to -ta *adj* jointly interested || *mf* party having a joint interest

cointeressènza *f* interest, share

coinvòlgere §289 *tr* to involve

còito *m* coitus, intercourse

cól §4

colà *adv* over there

colabròdo *m* colander, strainer

colàg·gio *m* (**-gi**) loss, leak

colapa·sta *m* (**-sta**) colander

colare (**cólo**) *tr* to filter, strain; to sift (*wheat*); to cast (*metals*); **colare a picco** to sink || *intr* to leak, drip; to flow (*said of blood*); **colare a picco** to sink

colata *f* casting (*of metal*); stream of lava; slide (*of snow or rocks*)

colatíc·cio *m* (**-ci**) drip, dripping

cola·tóio *m* (**-tói**) colander, strainer

colazióne *f* breakfast; lunch; **colazione al sacco** picnic; **prima colazione** breakfast; **seconda colazione** lunch

colbac·co *m* (**-chi**) busby

colèi §8 *pron dem*

colèn·do -da *adj* (archaic) honorable

colè·ra *m* (**-ra**) cholera

colesterina *f* cholesterol

coli·brì *m* (**-brì**) hummingbird

còli·co -ca *adj & f* (**-ci -che**) colic

colino *m* strainer

cólla §4

còlla *f* glue; paste; **colla di pesce** isinglass

collaborare (**collàboro**) *intr* to collaborate; to contribute (*to newspaper or magazine*)

collaboratóre *m* collaborator; contributor (*to newspaper or magazine*)

collaborazióne *f* collaboration

collaborazioni·sta *mf* (**-sti -ste**) collaborationist

collana *f* necklace; series, collection (*of literary works*)

collante *adj & m* adhesive

collare *m* collar || *v* (**còllo**) *tr* to lift or lower (*with a rope*)

collasso *m* collapse

collaterale *adj & m* collateral

collaudare (**collàudo**) *tr* to test; to approve; to pass

collauda·tóre -trice *mf* tester

collàudo *m* test

collazionare (**collazióno**) *tr* to collate

cólle §4

còlle *m* hill; low peak; mountain pass

collè·ga *mf* (**-ghi -ghe**) colleague, associate

collegaménto *m* connection, telephone connection; contact; (mil) liaison

collegare §209 (**collégo**) *tr* to join, connect || *intr* to agree, be in harmony || *ref* to become allied; to make contact, make connection (*e.g., by phone*)

collegiale *adj* collegiate || *mf* boarding-school student

collegiata *f* collegiate church

collè·gio *m* (**-gi**) college (*e.g., of surgeons*); boarding school, academy

còllera *f* anger, wrath; **montare in collera** to become angry

collèri·co -ca *adj* (**-ci -che**) hot-tempered, choleric

collètta *f* collection; collect (*in church*)

collettivismo *m* collectivism

collettivi·tà *f* (**-tà**) collectivity, community

colletti·vo -va *adj* collective || *m* party worker (*of leftist party*)

collétto *m* collar; flank (*of a tooth*)

collet·tóre -trice *adj* connecting; collecting (*pipe*) || *m* collector; tax collector; manifold; (elec) commutator (*of D.C. device*); (elec) collector (*of A.C. device*); **collettore d'ammissione** intake manifold; **collettore di scarico** exhaust manifold

collettoria *f* tax office; small post office

collezionare (**collezióno**) *tr* to collect (*e.g., stamps*)

collezióne *f* collection; collection, series (*of literary works*)

collezioni·sta *mf* (**-sti -ste**) collector

collìdere §135 *intr* to collide

collimare *tr* to point (*a telescope*) || *intr* to coincide, match; to dovetail

collina *f* hill; **in collina** in the hill country

collinó·so -sa [*s*] *adj* hilly

colli·rio *m* (**-ri**) eyewash

collisióne *f* collision; (fig) conflict: **entrare in collisione** to collide

cóllo §4

còllo *m* neck; piece (*of baggage*); package, parcel; **al collo** in a sling; (fig) downhill; **collo del piede** instep; **collo d'oca** crankshaft; **in collo** in one's arms (*said of a baby*)

collocaménto *m* placement, employment; **collocamento a riposo** retirement; **collocamento in aspettativa** leave of absence without pay; **collocamento in malattia** sick leave

collocare §197 (**còlloco**) *tr* to place; to find employment for; to sell; **collocare a riposo** to retire; **collocare in aspettativa** to give a leave of absence without pay; **collocare in malattia** to grant sick leave to

collocazióne *f* location (*of a book in a library*); catalogue card

colloidale *adj* colloidal

collòide *m* colloid

colloquiale *adj* colloquial

collò·quio *m* (**-qui**) talk, conference; colloquy; colloquium, symposium

collò·so -sa [*s*] *adj* gluey, sticky

collotòrto *m* (**collitòrti**) bigot, hypocrite

collòttola *f* nape or scruff of the neck

collùdere §105 *intr* to be in collusion

collusióne *f* collusion

collutó·rio *m* (**-ri**) mouthwash

collutare *intr* to scuffle, fight

colluttazióne *f* scuffle, fight

cólma *f* high-water level (*during high tide*)

colmare (**cólmo**) *tr* to fill, fill up; to fill in (*with dirt*); to overwhelm; **colmare una lacuna** to bridge a gap

colmata *f* silting; reclaimed land; sand bank

cól·mo -ma *adj* full, filled up || *m* top, peak, summit; (archit) ridgepole; (fig) acme; **al colmo di** at the height of; è il colmo that's the limit || f see colma

colofóne m colophon

colofònia f rosin

colombàia f dovecot

colombèlla f ingenue; a colombella vertically

colóm·bo -ba mf pigeon, dove || Colombo m Columbus

colònia f colony; cologne; settlement; summer camp; colonia penale penal colony; penitentiary || Colonia f Cologne

coloniale adj colonial || m colonial; colonist; coloniali imported foods

colòni·co -ca adj (-ci -che) farm (e.g., house)

colonizzare [ddzz] tr to colonize; to settle

colonizzazióne [ddzz] f colonization

colonna f column; row; colonna sonora sound track; Colonne d'Ercole Pillars of Hercules

colonnato m colonnade

colonnèllo m colonel

colonnétta f small column; gasoline pump

colò·no -na mf sharecropper; colonist; settler; (poet) farmer

colorante adj coloring || m dye; stain

colorare (colóro) tr & ref to color; to stain

colora·to -ta adj colored; stained (glass)

colorazióne f coloring

colóre m color; paint; suit (of cards); flush (at poker); shade; character (of a deal); di colore colored (man); farne di tutti i colori to be up to all kinds of deviltry; farsi di tutti i colori to change countenance

colorifi·cio m (-ci) paint factory; dye factory

colorire §176 tr to color

colori·to -ta adj colored, flushed; expressive || m color, complexion; (fig) expression

coloritura f coloring; characteristic; political complexion

colóro §8

colossale adj colossal

Colossèo m Coliseum

colòsso m colossus

cólpa f fault; sin; guilt; (law) injury; avere la colpa to be guilty; to be wrong; essere in colpa to be guilty

colpévole adj guilty || mf guilty person, culprit

colpevoli·sta mf (-sti -ste) person who prejudges s.o. guilty

colpire §176 tr to hit, strike; to harm; to impress; colpire nel segno to hit the mark

cólpo m hit, blow; strike; tip, rap; knock; shot; round (of gun); cut, slash (of knife); thrust (e.g., of spear); lash (of animal's tail); toot (of car's horn); andare a colpo sicuro to know where to hit; colpo apoplettico stroke; colpo da maestro master stroke; colpo d'aria draft; colpo d'ariete water hammer; colpo di fortuna stroke of luck; colpo di fulmine love at first sight; colpo di

grazia coup de grâce; colpo di mano surprise attack; colpo di scena dramatic turn of events; colpo di sole sunstroke; colpo di spugna wiping the slate clean; colpo di stato coup d'état; colpo di telefono telephone call; colpo di testa sudden decision, inconsiderate action; colpo di vento gust of wind; colpo d'occhio view; glance, look; di colpo at once; fallire il colpo to miss the mark; fare colpo to make a hit; sul colpo then and there; tutto in un colpo all at once

colpó·so -sa [s] adj unpremeditated; involuntary (e.g., manslaughter)

coltèlla f butcher knife; (elec) knife switch

coltellàc·cio m (-ci) hunting knife; butcher knife; (naut) studding sail

coltellata f stab, gash, slash; fare a coltellate to fight with knives

coltelleria f cutlery

coltelli·nàio m (-nài) cutler

coltèllo m knife; a coltello edgewise (said of bricks); avere il coltello per il manico to have the upper hand; coltello a serramanico switchblade knife; pocketknife

coltivare tr to cultivate

coltiva·to -ta adj cultivated

coltivatóre m farmer

coltivazióne f cultivation

cól·to -ta adj cultivated; learned (word) || m garden; (archaic) worship

cóltre f blanket; comforter; (fig) pall; coltri bedclothes

coltróne m quilt

coltura f cultivation; crop; culture (e.g., of silkworms, bacteria)

colubrina f culverin

colùi §8 pron dem

comandaménto m commandment

comandante m commanding officer; commandant; (nav) captain; comandante del porto harbor master; comandante in seconda (naut) first mate

comandare tr to command, order; to direct (employees); to register (a letter); (mach) to regulate; (mach) to control; (poet) to overlook, command the view of (e.g., a valley); comandare a bacchetta to command in a dictatorial manner || intr to command; comandi! (mil) at your orders!

comando m command, order

comare f godmother; (coll) friend, neighbor; (coll) gossip

combaciare §128 tr (archaic) to gather || intr to fit closely together; to tally, dovetail; to coincide

combattènte adj fighting || m combatant

combàttere tr & intr to combat || ref to fight one another

combattiménto m combat; fight; battle; fuori combattimento knockout, K.O.; fuori combattimento tecnico technical knockout, T.K.O.; mettere fuori combattimento to knock out; (fig) to weaken

combatti·vo -va *adj* pugnacious, combative

combattu·to -ta *adj* heated (*discussion*); overcome (*by doubt*); torn (*between two opposing feelings*)

combinàre *tr* to combine; to match (*e.g., colors*); to organize || *intr* to agree; **combinare a** to succeed in || *ref* to agree; to chance, happen; to combine

combinazióne *f* combination; chance; coverall (*for mechanics or flyers*)

combriccola *f* gang

combustibile *adj* combustible || *m* fuel, combustible

combustióne *f* combustion; (poet) upheaval

combutta *f* gang, band; **essere in combutta** to be in cahoots

cóme *m* manner, way; **il come e il perchè** the why and the wherefore || *adv* as; like; as for; how; **come mai?** why?; **e come!** and how!; **ma come?** what?, how is it? || *conj* as; as soon as; while; how; because; since; **come se** as if

comecchè *conj* (lit) although; (poet) wherever

comedóne *m* blackhead

comèta *f* comet

comici·tà *f* (-tà) comicalness

còmi·co -ca (-ci -che) *adj* comic(al) || *m* comic; author of comedies; comic actor

comìgnolo *m* chimney pot; ridge (*of roof*)

cominciare §128 *tr & intr* to begin, start, commence

comitato *m* committee

comitiva *f* group, party; (poet) retinue

comì·zio *m* (-zi) (pol) meeting, rally; (hist) comitia

còm·ma *m* (-mi) paragraph, article (*of law or decree*)

commèdia *f* comedy; play, drama; (fig) farce; **commedia di carattere** comedy of character; **commedia d'intreccio** comedy of intrigue; **far la commedia** to pretend, feign; **finire in commedia** to end ludicrously; **finire la commedia** to stop faking

commediante *mf* actor; comedian (*amusing person*); (fig) hypocrite

commediò·gra·fo -fa *mf* playwright, comedian

commemorare (commèmoro) *tr* to commemorate

commemorati·vo -va *adj* commemorative, memorial

commemorazióne *f* commemoration

commènda *f* commandership (*of an order*); (eccl) commendam

commendàbile *adj* commendable

commendare (commèndo) *tr* (lit) to commend, praise; (obs) to entrust

commendati·zio -zia (-zi -zie) *adj* introductory || *f* letter of introduction; recommendation

commendatóre *m* commander (*of an order*)

commendévole *adj* commendable

commensale *mf* guest; table companion

commensurare (commènsuro & commensuro) *tr* to compare; to proportion, prorate

commentare (comménto) *tr* to comment, comment on

commentà·rio *m* (-ri) commentary; diary, journal

commenta·tóre -trice *mf* commentator

comménto *m* comment; **fare commenti** to criticize; **non far commenti!** don't waste your time talking!

commerciàbile *adj* marketable

commerciale *adj* commercial; common, ordinary

commerciali·sta *mf* (-sti -ste) business-administration major; attorney specializing in commercial law

commerciante *mf* merchant, dealer

commerciare §128 (commèrcio) *tr* to deal in; to buy and sell || *intr* to deal

commèr·cio *m* (-ci) commerce, trade; illegal traffic; (poet) intercourse; **commercio all'ingrosso** wholesale (trade); **commercio al minuto** retail (trade); **fuori commercio** not for sale; **in commercio** for sale

commestibile *adj* edible || **commestibili** *mpl* staples, groceries; foodstuffs

comméttere §198 *tr* to join, connect; to commit; to charge, commission; to peg; (poet) to entrust || *intr* to join, fit

commettitura *f* joint, seam

commiato *m* leave; **dare commiato a** to dismiss; **prender commiato** to take one's leave

commilitóne *m* comrade, comrade in arms

comminare *tr* (law) to determine, fix (*a penalty*)

comminatò·rio -ria *adj* threatening

commiserare (commìsero) *tr* to pity, feel sorry for

commiserazióne *f* commiseration

commissariale *adj* commissioner's, e.g., **funzioni commissariali** commissioner's functions; commissar's functions

commissariato *m* commissary; inspector's office

commissà·rio *m* (-ri) commissary; inspector; commissioner; **commissario del popolo** commissar; **commissario di bordo** purser; **commissario di pubblica sicurezza** police inspector; **commissario tecnico** (sports) soccer commissioner

commissionare (commissióno) *tr* to commission, order

commissionà·rio -ria (-ri -rie) *adj* commission || *m* commission merchant

commissióne *f* commission, agency; order (*of merchandise*); committee; errand; commitment (*of an act*)

commisurare *tr* to proportion (*e.g., crime to punishment*)

committènte *mf* buyer, customer

commodòro *m* commodore

commòs·so -sa *adj* moved; moving

commovènte *adj* moving, touching

commozióne *f* commotion; emotion; commozione cerebrale (pathol) concussion

commuòvere §202 *tr* to move; to touch; to stir || *ref* to be moved; to be touched

commutare *tr* to commute; to switch || *ref* to turn

commuta·tóre -trice *adj* commutative || *m* (elec) change-over switch; (elec) commutator (*switch*); (telp) plugboard || *f* converter

commutatori·sta *mf* (-sti -ste) (telp) operator

commutazióne *f* commutation; (telp) selection; (elec) switchover

co·mò *m* (-mò) chest; chest of drawers

còmoda *f* commode

comodare (còmodo) *tr* to lend || *intr* (with *dat*) to please, e.g., **non le comoda** it doesn't please her

comodino *m* night table; (theat) bit player; **fare il comodino a** (coll) to follow sheepishly

comodi·tà *f* (-tà) comfort; convenience; opportunity

còmo·do -da *adj* comfortable; convenient; easy; loose-fitting; calm || *m* convenience; ease; advantage; comfort; opportunity; **a Suo comodo at your convenience; comodo di cassa** credit (*at the bank*); **con comodo** without hurrying; **fare comodo** to come in handy; (with *dat*) to please, e.g., **non gli fa comodo** it doesn't please him; **fare il proprio comodo** to think only of oneself; **stia comodo!** make yourself at home! || *f* see **comoda**

compaesa·no -na *mf* fellow citizen || *m* fellow countryman || *f* fellow countrywoman

compàgine *f* strict union; connection; assemblage; (fig) cohesion

compagna *f* companion, mate; (archaic) company

compagnia *f* company; **Compagnia di Gesù** Society of Jesus; **compagnia stabile** (theat) stock company

compa·gno -gna *adj* like, similar || *m* fellow; companion, comrade; mate; partner; **compagno d'armi** comrade in arms; **compagno di viaggio** fellow traveler || *f* see **compagna**

companàti·co *m* (-ci) food to eat with bread

comparàbile *adj* comparable

comparati·vo -va *adj* & *m* comparative

compara·to -ta *adj* comparative

comparazióne *f* comparison

compare *m* godfather; best man (*at wedding*); fellow; confederate

comparire §108 *intr* to appear; to be known; to cut a figure

comparizióne *f* appearance (*in court*)

comparsa *f* appearance; (theat) extra, supernumerary; (law) petition, brief; **far comparsa** to cut a figure

compartecipare (compartécipo) *intr* to share

compartecipazióne *f* sharing; **compartecipazione agli utili** profit sharing

compartécipe *adj* sharing

compartiménto *m* circle, clique; district; (naut, rr) compartment

compartire §176 & (**comparto**) *tr* to divide up, distribute

compassa·to -ta *adj* measured; stiff, formal; reserved; self-controlled

compassionare (compassióno) *tr* to pity

compassióne *f* compassion, pity

compassionévole *adj* compassionate; pitiful

compasso *m* compass; **compasso a grossezza** calipers

compatìbile *adj* excusable; compatible

compatiménto *m* compassion; condescension

compatire §176 *tr* to pity; to forgive, overlook; to bear with; **farsi compatire** to become an object of ridicule || *intr* to pity

compatriò·ta *mf* (-ti -te) compatriot

compattézza *f* compactness

compat·to -ta *adj* compact, tight

compendiare §287 (compèndio) *tr* to epitomize, summarize

compèn·dio *m* (-di) compendium, summary; **fare un compendio di** to abstract

compendió·so -sa [s] *adj* compendious, brief, succinct

compenetràbile *adj* penetrable

compenetrabilità *f* penetrability

compenetrare (compènetro) *tr* to penetrate; to permeate; to pervade || *ref* to be overcome; **compenetrarsi di** to be conscious of

compensare (compènso) *tr* to compensate, pay; to balance, offset; to clear (*checks*)

compensa·to -ta *adj* compensated; laminated || *m* laminate; plywood

compensazióne *f* compensation; offset; (com) clearing (*of checks*)

compènso *m* reward; retribution, pay; **in compenso** on the other hand

cómpera *f* var of **compra**

comperare (cómpero) *tr* & *intr* var of **comprare**

competènte *adj* competent

competènza *f* competence; jurisdiction; **competenze honoraria**

compètere §129 *intr* to compete; to concern; to have jurisdiction

competiti·vo -va *adj* competitive

competi·tóre -trice *mf* competitor, contender

competizióne *f* competition, contest

compiacènte *adj* complaisant, obliging

compiacènza *f* complaisance, kindness; pleasure

compiacére §214 *tr* to gratify || *intr* (with *dat*) to please, e.g., **non posso compiacere a tutti** I cannot please everybody || *ref* to be pleased; **compiacersi con** to congratulate; **compiacersi di** to be kind enough to

compiaciménto *m* pleasure; congratulation; approval

compiaciu·to -ta *adj* pleased, satisfied

compiàngere §215 *tr* to pity ǁ *ref* to feel sorry

compian·to -ta *adj* lamented (*departed person*) ǁ *m* sympathy; (poet) sorrow; (poet) lament

compiegare §209 (**compiègo**) *tr* to enclose (*in a letter*)

cómpiere §130 *tr* to complete, finish; to fulfill, accomplish; **compiere . . . anni** to be . . . years old; **compiere gli anni** to have a birthday ǁ *ref* to happen; to come true

compilare *tr* to compile

compila·tóre -trice *mf* compiler

compilazióne *f* compilation

compimento *m* fulfillment, accomplishment

compire §176 *tr* to complete, finish; to fulfill, accomplish; **per compir l'opera** as if it weren't enough ǁ *ref* to happen; to come true

compitare (**cómpito**) *tr* to syllabify; to read poorly; to spell, spell letter by letter

compitazióne *f* spelling letter by letter

compitézza *f* courtesy, politeness

cómpito *m* task; exercise; homework

compi·to -ta *adj* courteous, polite; (poet) adequate

compiu·to -ta *adj* accomplished

compleanno *m* birthday; **buon compleanno** happy birthday

complementare *adj* complementary; additional (*tax*) ǁ *f* graduated income tax

complemento *m* complement; (mil, nav) reserve

complessióne *f* build, physique

complessi·tà *f* (**-tà**) complexity

complessi·vo -va *adj* total, aggregate

complès·so -sa *adj* complex, complicated; compound (*fracture*) ǁ *m* whole; complex; **in complesso** in general

completare (**complèto**) *tr* to complete, carry through; to supplement, round off

complè·to -ta *adj* complete, full; overall, thoroughgoing; **al completo** full (*e.g., bus*) ǁ *m* set (*of matching items*); suit of clothes; **completo femminile** lady's tailor-made suit; **completo maschile** suit

complicare §197 (**còmplico**) *tr* to complicate ǁ *ref* to become complicated

complica·to -ta *adj* complicated, complex

complicazióne *f* complication

còmplice *mf* accomplice, accessory

complici·tà *f* (**-tà**) complicity

complimentare (**complimento**) *tr* to compliment ǁ *ref*—**complimentarsi con** to congratulate

complimento *m* compliment; congratulation; favor; **complimenti** regards; **complimenti!** congratulations!; **fare complimenti** to stand on ceremony; **senza complimenti** without ceremony; without any further ado

complimentó·so -sa [s] *adj* ceremonious; complimentary

complottare (**complòtto**) *intr* to plot

complòtto *m* plot, machination

complù·vio *m* (**-vi**) valley (*of roof*)

componènte *adj* component ǁ *mf* member ǁ *m* component (*component part*) ǁ *f* component (*force*)

componìbile *adj* sectional (*e.g., bookcase*)

componimento *m* composition, settlement (*of a dispute*)

compórre §218 *tr* to compose; to arrange; to settle (*a quarrel*); to lay out (*a corpse*); (typ) to set

comportamento *m* behavior

comportare (**compòrto**) *tr* to allow, tolerate; to entail ǁ *ref* to behave; to handle (*said, e.g., of a motor*); **comportarsi male** to misbehave

compòrto *m* (com) delay

compòsi·to -ta *adj* composite ǁ **composite** *fpl* (bot) Compositae

composi·tóio *m* (**-tói**) (typ) composing stick

composi·tóre -trice *mf* compositor, typesetter; composer ǁ *f* typesetting machine

composizióne *f* composition; settlement

compósta *f* compote; **composta di frutta** stewed fruit

compostézza *f* neatness, tidiness; good behavior; orderliness

compostièra *f* compote, compotier

compó·sto -sta *adj* compound; neat, tidy; well-behaved ǁ *m* compound ǁ *f* see **composta**

cómpra *f* purchase; shopping; **compre** shopping

comprare (**cómpro**) *tr* to buy, purchase; to buy off ǁ *intr* to buy, shop; to trade

compra·tóre -trice *mf* buyer, purchaser

compravéndere §281 *tr* to make a deal in, to transfer (*e.g., a house*)

compravéndita *f* transaction; transfer (*e.g., of real estate*)

comprèndere §220 *tr* to comprehend, include, comprise; to overwhelm; to understand; to forgive

comprendò·nio *m* (**-ni**) (joc) understanding

comprensìbile *adj* understandable, comprehensible

comprensióne *f* comprehension, understanding

comprensi·vo -va *adj* comprehensive; understanding

comprensò·rio *m* (**-ri**) land to be reclaimed; area, zone, e.g., **comprensorio turistico** tourist area

comprè·so -sa [s] *adj* comprised, included; understood; deeply touched; immersed

comprèssa *f* compress

compressióne *f* compression

comprès·so -sa *adj* compressed; (fig) repressed; (aut) supercharged ǁ *f* see **compressa**

compressóre *m* compressor; **compressore stradale** road roller

comprimà·rio *m* (**-ri**) (med) associate chief of staff; (theat) second lead

comprìmere §131 *tr* to compress; to repress, restrain; to tamp

compromés·so -sa *adj* jeopardized, in danger || *m* compromise; referral (*to arbitration*)

compromettènte *adj* compromising

comprométtere §198 *tr* to compromise; to endanger; to involve, commit; (law) to refer (*to arbitration*)

comproprie·tà *f* (-**tà**) joint ownership

comproprietà·rio -ria *mf* (-**ri -rie**) joint owner

compròva *f* confirmation

comprovare (**compròvo**) *tr* to confirm; to circumstantiate

compulsare *tr* to consult, peruse; to summon (*to appear in court*)

compulsì·vo -va *adj* compulsive

compun·to -ta *adj* contrite, repentant

compunzióne *f* compunction

computàbile *adj* computable

computare (**còmputo**) *tr* to compute

computi·sta *mf* (-**sti -ste**) bookkeeper

computisterìa *f* bookkeeping

còmputo *m* computation, reckoning

comunale *adj* municipal, town (*e.g., hall*); community-owned; (poet) common

comunanza *f* community; **in comunanza** in common

comune *adj* common || *m* normalcy; commune, municipality, town; town hall; (hist) guild; (nav) common seaman; **in comune** in common || *f* commune (*in communist countries*); (theat) main stage entrance; **andare per la comune** to follow the crowd; **per la comune** commonly

comunèlla *f* cabal, clique; passkey (*in a hotel*); (law) mutual insurance (*of cattlemen*); **fare comunella con** to consort with

comunicàbile *adj* communicable

comunicante *adj* communicant; communicating || *m* priest who gives communion

comunicare §197 (**comùnico**) *tr* to communicate; to administer communion to || *intr* to communicate || *ref* to spread; to receive communion, to commune

comunicatì·vo -va *adj* communicable, spreading; communicative

comunicato *m* communiqué; **comunicato commerciale** advertisement, ad; **comunicato stampa** press release

comunicazióne *f* communication; statement; (telp) connection; **comunicazioni** communications

comunióne *f* community; (law) community property || **Comunione** *f* Communion

comunismo *m* communism

comuni·sta (-**sti -ste**) *adj* communist || *mf* communist; (law) joint tenant

comunìsti·co -ca *adj* (-**ci -che**) communistic

comuni·tà *f* (-**tà**) community

comunità·rio -ria *adj* (-**ri -rie**) community, e.g., **interessi comunitari** community interests

comùnque *adv* however, nevertheless || *conj* however, no matter how

cón §4 *prep* with; by (*e.g., boat*); **con + art + inf** by **+ ger**, e.g., **col leggere** by reading

conato *m* effort, attempt

cón·ca *f* (-**che**) washbowl, washbasin; copper water jug; valley, hollow; (poet) shell; **conca idraulica** drydock

concatenaménto *m* (poet) concatenation

concatenare (**concaténo**) *tr* to link || *ref* to unfold, ensue

concatenazióne *f* concatenation

concàusa *f* joint cause; (law) aggravation

cònca·vo -va *adj* concave; hollow || *m* hollow

concèdere §132 *tr* to grant, concede; to stretch (*a point*) || *ref* to let oneself go, give oneself over

concènto *m* harmony; (fig) agreement

concentraménto *m* concentration

concentrare (**concèntro**) *tr* to concentrate; to center || *ref* to concentrate, focus; to center

concentra·to -ta *adj* concentrated; condensed (*e.g., milk*) || *m* purée (*e.g., of tomatoes*)

concentrazióne *f* concentration; (chem) condensation

concèntri·co -ca *adj* (-**ci -che**) concentric

concepìbile *adj* conceivable

concepiménto *m* conception; (fig) formulation

concepire §176 *tr* to conceive; (fig) to nurture

concerìa *f* tannery

concèrnere §133 *tr* to concern

concertare (**concèrto**) *tr* to scheme, concert; (mus) to orchestrate, arrange || *ref* to agree

concerta·to -ta *adj* agreed upon; (mus) with accompaniment || *m* ensemble (*of orchestra, soloists, and chorus*)

concerta·tóre -trice *mf* arranger || *m* plotter, schemer

concertazióne *f* (mus) arrangement

concerti·sta *mf* (-**sti -ste**) concert performer, soloist

concèrto *m* concert; concerto; (fig) choir

concessionà·rio *m* (-**ri**) sole agent, concessionaire; dealer; lessee (*of business establishment*)

concessióne *f* concession; dealership; admission

concessì·vo -va *adj* concessive

concès·so -sa *adj* granted, admitting

concètto *m* concept; opinion

concettó·so -sa [*s*] *adj* concise; full of ideas; full of conceits

concettuale *adj* conceptual

concezióne *f* conception; formulation

conchìglia *f* shell, conch; (sports) jock guard, protective cup

conchiùdere §125 *tr, intr & ref* var of **concludere**

cón·cia *f* (-**ce**) tanning

conciapèl·li *m* (-**li**) tanner

conciare §128 (**cóncio**) *tr* to tan; to cure (*e.g., tobacco*); to arrange; to straighten up; to reduce; to cut (*a precious stone*); **conciare per le feste** (coll) to give a good beating to || *ref* to get messed up, get dirty

conciatét·ti *m* (-ti) roofer

conciató·re -trice *mf* tanner

conciliàbile *adj* reconcilable

conciliàbolo *m* conventicle, secret meeting

conciliante *adj* conciliatory

conciliare *adj* council || *m* member of an ecclesiastical council || §287 *tr* to conciliate, reconcile; to settle (*a fine*); to promote (*e.g., sleep*); to obtain (*a favor*) || *ref* to become reconciled

concilia·tóre -trice *adj* conciliatory || *mf* conciliator, peacemaker || *m* justice of the peace

conciliazióne *f* conciliation || la Conciliazione the Concordat (*of 1929 between Italy and the Vatican*)

conci·lio *m* (-li) council; church council

concimàia *f* manure pit

concimare *tr* to manure

concimazióne *f* spreading of manure; chemical fertilization

concime *m* manure; fertilizer

cón·cio -cia (-ci -ce) *adj* tanned || *m* ashlar; dung, manure; (archaic) agreement; **concio di scoria** cinder block || *f* see **concia**

conciofossecosaché *conj* (archaic) since

concionare (concióno) *intr* (archaic) to harangue

concióne *f* (archaic) harangue; (archaic) assembly

conciossiacosaché *conj* (archaic) since

concisióne *f* concision, brevity

conci·so -sa *adj* concise, brief

concistòro *m* consistory; (fig) assembly

concitare (cóncito) *tr* to excite, stir up

concita·to -ta *adj* excited; (poet) decisive

concitazióne *f* impetus; excitement

concittadi·no -na *mf* fellow citizen

conclave *m* conclave

conclùdere §105 *tr* to conclude || *intr* to conclude; to be convincing || *ref* to conclude, end; **concludersi con** to end with; to result in

conclusionale *adj* (law) summary

conclusióne *f* conclusion; **conclusioni** (law) summation

conclusi·vo -va *adj* conclusive

conclu·so -sa *adj* concluded; terminated; (poet) closed

concomitante *adj* concomitant

concordanza *f* concordance, agreement; (gram) concord; **concordanze** concordance (*e.g., to the Bible*)

concordare (concòrdo) *tr* to agree on; to make agree || *intr* & *ref* to come to an agreement

concordato *m* agreement; concordat; settlement (*with creditors*)

concòrde *adj* in agreement

concòrdia *f* concord, harmony

concorrènte *adj* competitive || *m* (com) competitor; (sports) contestant

concorrènza *f* competition

concorrenziale *adj* competitive (*e.g., price*)

concórrere §139 *intr* to converge; to concur; to compete

concórso *m* attendance; concurrence; combination (*of circumstances*); competition; competitive examination; contest; **concorso di bellezza** beauty contest; **concorso di pubblico** turnout; **fuori concorso** not entering the competition; in a class by itself

concretare (concrèto) *tr* to realize (*e.g., a dream*); to conclude, accomplish || *ref* to come true

concretézza *f* concreteness, consistency

concrè·to -ta *adj* concrete, real; practical || *m* practical matter; **in concreto** really, in reality

concubina *f* concubine

concubinàg·gio *m* (-gi) concubinage

concubinato *m* var of **concubinaggio**

conculcare §197 *tr* (lit) to trample under foot; (lit) to violate

concupire §176 *tr* (poet) to lust for

concupiscènza *f* concupiscence, lust

concussióne *f* extortion, shakedown; **concussione cerebrale** (pathol) concussion

condanna *f* conviction; sentence; (fig) blame, condemnation

condannare *tr* to condemn; to find guilty, convict; to sentence; to damn (*to eternal punishment*); to declare incurable; to wall up

condanna·to -ta *adj* condemned || *m* convict

condensare (condènso) *tr* & *ref* to condense

condensa·to -ta *adj* condensed (*e.g., milk*)

condensatóre *m* condenser

condensazióne *f* condensation

condiménto *m* condiment, seasoning

condire §176 *tr* to season

condiret·tóre -trice *mf* associate manager

condiscendènte *adj* condescending

condiscendènza *f* condescension

condiscéndere §245 *intr* to condescend

condiscépo·lo -la *mf* schoolmate, school companion

condividere §158 *tr* to share

condizionale *adj* & *m* conditional || *f* (law) suspended sentence

condizionare (condizióno) *tr* to condition; to treat (*to prevent spoilage*)

condizionatóre *m* air conditioner

condizióne *f* condition; term (*of sale*); **a condizione che** provided that; **condizioni** condition, shape (*e.g., of a shipment*); **essere in condizione di** to be in a position to

condoglianza *f* condolence; **fare le condoglianze a** to extend one's sympathy to

condolére §159 *ref* to condole

condomì·nio *m* (-ni) condominium

condòmi·no -na *mf* joint owner (*of real estate*)

condonare (condóno) *tr* to condone; to remit

condóno *m* pardon, parole

condót·to -ta *adj* country (*doctor*) || *m* duct, canal; conduit || *f* behavior, conduct; district (of country doctor); transportation; pipeline; (theat) baggage; **condotta forzata** flume

conducènte m driver; bus driver; motorman

condù‧plex mf (-plex) (telp) party-line user

condurre §102 tr to lead; to drive (a car); to round up (cattle); to pipe (e.g., gas); to conduct; to trace (a line); to take; to bring; to manage; **condurre a termine** to bring to fruition, realize ‖ intr to lead ‖ ref to behave; to betake oneself, go; **condursi** (a poet) to be reduced to (e.g., poverty)

conduttivi‧tà f (-tà) conductivity

condutti‧vo -va adj conductive

condut‧tóre -trice adj guiding, leading ‖ m operator (of a bus); driver (of a car); (rr) engineer; (rr) ticket collector; (phys) conductor

conduttura f conduit, pipeline

conduzióne f conduction; leasing

conestàbile m constable (keeper of a castle)

confabulare (confàbulo) intr to confabulate, commune; to connive, scheme

confacènte adj suitable, appropriate; helpful

confare §173 ref—**confarsi a** to agree with, e.g., **le uova non gli si confanno** eggs do not agree with him

confederare (confèdero) tr & ref to confederate

confedera‧to -ta adj & m confederate

confederazióne f confederation

conferènza f conference; lecture; **conferenza illustrata** chalk talk; **conferenza stampa** press conference

conferenzie‧re -ra mf speaker, lecturer

conferimento m conferring, bestowal

conferire §176 tr to confer, bestow; to add; to contribute ‖ intr to confer; to contribute; **conferire alla salute** to be healthful

confèrma f confirmation; **a conferma di** (com) in reply to, confirming

confermare (confèrmo) tr to confirm; to verify; to retain (in office) ‖ ref to become more sure of oneself; to prove to be; to remain (in the conclusion of a letter)

confessare (confèsso) tr & ref to confess

confessionale adj confessional; church; church-related, parochial (e.g., school) ‖ m confessional

confessióne f confession

confès‧so -sa adj acknowledged, self-admitted; **confesso e comunicato** having made one's confession and taken communion

confessóre m confessor

confetterìa f candy store, confectioner's shop

confettièra f candy box

confettière m candy maker; candy dealer, confectioner

confètto m sugar-covered nut, sweetmeat; losenge, drop

confettura f candy; preserves, jam; **confetture** confectionery

confezionare (confezióno) tr to make; to tailor (a suit)

confezióne f preparation, manufacturing; packaging; **confezioni** ready-made clothes

confezioni‧sta mf (-sti -ste) ready-made clothier

conficcare §197 tr to drive (a nail); to thrust (a knife) ‖ ref to become embedded

confidare tr to trust (a secret) ‖ intr to trust ‖ ref to confide

confidènte adj confident ‖ mf confident; informer

confidènza f confidence; secret; familiarity

confidenziale adj confidential; friendly

configgere §104 tr to plunge, thrust

configurazióne f configuration

confinante adj bordering ‖ mf neighbor

confinare tr to exile; to confine ‖ intr to border

confinà‧rio -ria adj (-ri -rie) border (e.g., zone)

Confindùstria f (acronym) **Confederazione Nazionale degli Industriali** National Confederation of Industrialists

confine m border, boundary line; boundary mark, landmark

confino m exile (in a different town)

confi‧sca f (-sche) confiscation

confiscare §197 tr to confiscate

confit‧to -ta adj nailed; bound; tied; **confitto in croce** nailed to the cross

conflagrazióne f conflagration

conflitto m conflict

conflittualità f confrontation; belligerent attitude

confluènte m confluent

confluènza f confluence

confluire §176 intr to flow together, join; to converge

confóndere §178 tr to confuse; to overwhelm (with kindness); to humiliate; **confondere con** to mistake for ‖ ref to mix; to become confused

conformare (confórmo) tr to shape; to conform ‖ ref to conform

conformazióne f conformation

confórme adj faithful, exact; in agreement; true (copy)

conformeménte adv in conformity

conformi‧sta mf (-sti -ste) conformist

conformi‧tà f (-tà) conformity; **in conformità di** in conformity with, in accord with

confortante adj comforting

confortare (confòrto) tr to comfort

confortévole adj comforting, consoling; comfortable

confòrto m comfort, solace; convenience; corroboration; **conforti religiosi** last rites

confratèllo m brother, confrere

confratèrnita f brotherhood

confricare §197 tr to rub

confrontare (confrónto) tr to compare, confront; to consult ‖ intr to correspond

confrónto *m* comparison; (law) cross examination; **a confronto di** or **in confronto a** in comparison with; with regard to

confusaménte *adv* vaguely, hazily

confusionale *adj* confusing; confused

confusionà·rio -ria (-ri -rie) *adj* blundering; scatterbrain || *mf* blunderer; scatterbrain

confusióne *f* confusion, disorder; noise; error; embarrassment; shambles

confu·so -sa *adj* confused, mixed; vague, hazy; **in confuso** indistinctly

confutare (cònfuto) *tr* to confute

confutazióne *f* confutation

congedare (congèdo) *tr* to dismiss; to let (*a tenant*) go; (mil) to discharge || *ref* to take leave

congedà·to -ta *adj* discharged || *m* discharged soldier

congèdo *m* dismissal; leave; permission to leave; (mil) discharge; envoy, envoi; **congedo per motivi di salute** sick leave; **dare il congedo a** to discharge; **prender congedo** to take leave

congegnare (congégno) *tr* to assemble (*machinery*); to contrive, cook up

congégno *m* contrivance, gadget; mechanism; design (*of a play*)

congelaménto *m* freezing; frostbite

congelare (congèlo) *tr & ref* to freeze, congeal

congela·tóre -trice *adj* freezing || *m* freezer; freezer unit; freezing compartment (*of a refrigerator*)

congènere *adj* similar, alike

congeniale *adj* congenial

congèni·to -ta *adj* congenital

congèrie *f* congeries

congestionare (congestióno) *tr* to congest

congestióne *f* congestion

congettura *f* conjecture

congetturare *tr* to conjecture

congiùngere §183 *tr & ref* to unite, join

congiuntiva *f* (anat) conjunctiva

congiuntivite *f* (pathol) conjunctivitis

congiunti·vo -va *adj* conjunctive; subjunctive || *m* subjunctive || *f* see congiuntiva

congiun·to -ta *adj* joined; joint || *m* relative

congiuntura *f* juncture; joint; circumstance, situation; **bassa congiuntura** (econ) unfavorable circumstance; (econ) crisis

congiunzióne *f* conjunction

congiura *f* conspiracy, plot

congiurare *intr* to conspire, plot

congiura·to -ta *adj & m* conspirator

conglobare (conglòbo) *tr* to lump together

conglomerare (conglòmero) *tr & ref* to pile up, conglomerate

conglomera·to -ta *adj & m* conglomerate

congratulare (congràtulo) *intr* to rejoice || *ref*—**congratularsi con** to congratulate

congratulazióne *f* congratulation

congrèga *f* gang; cabal; religious brotherhood

congregare §209 (congrègo) *tr & ref* to congregate

congregazióne *f* congregation

congressi·sta *mf* (-sti -ste) delegate || *m* congressman || *f* congresswoman

congrèsso *m* congress, assembly; conference; convention

congruènte *adj* congruous

congruènza *f* congruence

còn·gruo -grua *adj* congruous; congruent

conguagliare §280 *tr* to adjust; to make up (*what is owed*)

conguà·glio *m* (-gli) balance; adjustment (*of wages*)

coniare §287 (cònio) *tr* to mint, coin

coniatura *f* mintage, coinage

còni·co -ca (-ci -che) *adj* conic(al) || *f* conic section

conìfera *f* conifer

coniglièra *f* warren, rabbit hutch

conì·glio *m* (-gli) rabbit

cò·nio *m* (-ni) die (*to mint coins*); mintage; wedge; **dello stesso conio** (fig) of the same feather; **di nuovo conio** newly-minted; new-fangled

coniugale *adj* conjugal

coniugare §209 (còniugo) *tr* to conjugate || *ref* to marry, get married

coniuga·to -ta *adj* coupled, paired || *mf* spouse, consort

coniugazióne *f* conjugation

còniuge *mf* spouse; **coniugi** *mpl* husband and wife

connaturale *adj* inborn, innate

connatura·to -ta *adj* deep-seated, deep-rooted; congenital

connazionale *mf* fellow countryman

connessióne *f* connection

connés·so -sa & connès·so -sa *adj* connected, tied

connéttere & connèttere §107 *tr* to connect, link || *ref* to refer

connetti·vo -va *adj* connective

connivènte *adj* conniving

connivènza *f* connivance

connotare (connòto) *tr* to connote

connotato *m* personal characteristic

connù·bio *m* (-bi) wedding, union

còno *m* cone

conòcchia *f* distaff

conoscènte *mf* acquaintance

conoscènza *f* knowledge; acquaintance; understanding; consciousness; **conoscenza di causa** full knowledge; **essere a conoscenza di** to be acquainted with; **prendere conoscenza di** to take cognizance of

conóscere §134 *tr* to know; to recognize; **conoscere i propri polli** to know one's onions; **conoscere per filo e per segno** to know thoroughly; **conoscere ragioni** to listen to reason; **darsi a conoscere** to make oneself known; to reveal oneself || *intr* to reason || *ref* to acknowledge oneself to be; to know one another

conoscìbile *adj* knowable

conosci·tóre -trice *mf* connoisseur; expert

conosciu·to -ta *adj* known, well-known; proven

conquìdere §135 *tr* (poet) to conquer

conquista *f* conquest
conquistare *tr* to conquer, win
conquista·tóre -trice *adj* conquering ‖ *m* conqueror; lady killer
consacrare *tr* to consecrate ‖ *ref* to dedicate oneself
consacrazióne *f* consecration
consanguineità *f* consanguinity
consanguíne·o -a *adj* consanguineous; **fratello consanguineo** half brother on the father's side ‖ *m* kin
consapévole *adj* aware, conscious
consapevolézza *f* awareness, consciousness
còn·scio -scia *adj* (**-sci -sce**) conscious
consecuti·vo -va *adj* consecutive
conségna *f* delivery; (mil) order; (mil) confinement (*to barracks*); **in consegna** (com) on consignment
consegnare (**conségno**) *tr* to deliver; to entrust; (mil) to confine (*to barracks*)
consegnatà·rio *m* (**-ri**) consignee
conseguènte *adj* consequent; consistent; **conseguente a** resulting from; consistent with
conseguènza *f* consequence; consistency; **in conseguenza di** as a result of
conseguìbile *adj* attainable
conseguiménto *m* attainment
conseguire (**conséguo**) *tr* to attain; to obtain ‖ *intr* to ensue, result
consènso *m* consent, approval; consensus
consensuale *adj* mutual-consent (*e.g., agreement*)
consentiménto *m* consent
consentire (**consènto**) *tr* to allow, permit ‖ *intr* to agree, consent; to yield; to admit
consenziènte *adj* consenting
consèr·to -ta *adj* intertwined; folded (*arms*); **di conserto** in agreement
consèrva *f* preserve; purée (*e.g., of tomatoes*); tank (*for water*); sauce (*e.g., of cranberries*); **conserve alimentari** canned goods; **di conserva** together, in a group; **far conserva di** to preserve
conservare (**consèrvo**) *tr* to preserve; to keep; to cure (*e.g., meat*); to cherish (*a memory*) ‖ *ref* to keep; to remain; to keep in good health
conservati·vo -va *adj* preserving; conservative ‖ *m* conservative
conserva·tóre -trice *adj* preserving; conservative ‖ *mf* keeper, curator; conservative
conservatoria *f* registrar's office (*in a court house*)
conservatò·rio *m* (**-ri**) conservatory; girl's boarding school (*run by nuns*)
conservatorismo *m* conservatism
conservazióne *f* conservation; preservation; self-preservation; canning
consèsso *m* assembly
consideràbile *adj* considerable; large, important
considerare (**considero**) *tr* to consider; to rate; (law) to provide for
considera·to -ta *adj* considered; **siderato che** considering that, since;

tutto considerato all in all, considering
considerazióne *f* consideration
considerévole *adj* considerable
consigliare *adj* council, councilmanic ‖ §280 *tr* to advise, counsel ‖ *ref* to consult
consigliè·re -ra *mf* counselor, advisor ‖ *m* chancellor (*of embassy*); councilman; **consigliere delegato** chairman of the board
consì·glio *m* (**-gli**) advice, counsel; will (*of God*); decision, idea; council; **consiglio d'amministrazione** (com) board of directors; **consiglio dei ministri** cabinet; **consiglio municipale** city council; **l'eterno consiglio** the will of God; **venire a più miti consigli** to become more reasonable
consìmile *adj* similar
consistènte *adj* consistent, solid; trustworthy
consistènza *f* consistency, resistance; foundation, grounds
consistere §114 *intr* to consist; **consistere in** to consist of
consociare §128 (**consòcio**) *tr* to syndicate, unite
consocia·to -ta *adj* syndicated, united
consociazióne *f* syndicate, association, group
consò·cio -cia *mf* (**-ci -cie**) fellow shareholder; associate, partner
consolare *adj* consular ‖ *v* (**consòlo**) *tr* to console, cheer, comfort ‖ *ref* to rejoice; to take comfort
consolato *m* consulate
consola·tóre -trice *adj* comforting ‖ *mf* comforter
consolazióne *f* consolation
cònsole *m* consul
consò·le *f* (**-le**) console
consòlida *f—*consolida maggiore comfrey; **consolida reale** field larkspur
consolidaménto *m* consolidation
consolidare (**consòlido**) *tr* to consolidate ‖ *ref* to consolidate; to harden
consolida·to -ta *adj* consolidated; joint (*e.g., balance sheet*); hardened ‖ *m* funded public debt; government bonds
consonante *adj* & *f* consonant
consonànti·co -ca *adj* (**-ci -che**) consonant
consonanza *f* consonance; agreement; (mus) harmony
cònso·no -na *adj* consonant
consorèlla *adj* sister (*e.g., company*) ‖ *f* sister of charity; sister branch; sister firm
consòrte *adj* (poet) equally fortunate; (poet) united ‖ *mf* consort, mate, spouse
consorteria *f* political clique
consòr·zio *m* (**-zi**) syndicate, consortium; (poet) society
constare (**cònsto**) *intr* to consist ‖ *impers* to be known; to be proved; to understand, e.g., **gli consta che Lei ha torto** he understands that you are wrong
constatare (**constato** & **cònstato**) *tr* to verify, ascertain, establish

constatazióne f ascertainment, verification

consuè·to **-ta** adj usual, customary; **consueto a** accustomed to, used to ‖ m manner, custom; **di consueto** generally

consuetudinà·rio **-ria** adj (**-ri** **-rie**) customary; common (law)

consuetùdine f custom; common law; (poet) familiarity

consulènte adj advising, consulting ‖ mf adviser, expert

consulènza f expert advice

consulta f council

consultare tr to consult ‖ ref to take counsel; to counsel with one another; **consultarsi con** to take counsel with

consultazióne f consultation; reference; **consultazione popolare** referendum

consulti·vo **-va** adj advisory

consulto m consultation (of physicians); legal conference

consul·tóre **-trice** mf adviser, expert ‖ m councilman

consultò·rio m (**-ri**) clinic, dispensary

consumare tr to consume; to perform, to consummate ‖ ref to be consumed, to waste away

consuma·to **-ta** adj consummate, accomplished; consummated (marriage); consumed, worn out

consuma·tóre **-trice** adj consuming ‖ mf consumer; customer (of a restaurant)

consumazióne f consummation (e.g., of a crime); consumption (of food); food or drink

consumismo m consumerism

consumo m consumption; wear

consunti·vo **-va** adj end-of-year (e.g., report); (econ) consumption ‖ m balance sheet

consun·to **-ta** adj worn-out

consunzióne f consumption

contàbile adj bookkeeping ‖ mf accountant; bookkeeper, clerk; **esperto contabile** certified public accountant

contabili·tà f (**-tà**) accounting, bookkeeping; accounts

contachilòme·tri m (**-tri**) odometer; (coll) speedometer

contadiné·sco **-sca** adj (**-schi** **-sche**) farm, farmer; rustic

contadi·no **-na** adj rustic ‖ mf peasant, farmer

contado m country, countryside

contagiare §290 tr to infect

contà·gio m (**-gi**) contagion

contagió·so **-sa** [s] adj contagious

contagi·ri m (**-ri**) tachometer

contagóc·ce m (**-ce**) dropper, eyedropper

contaminare (**contàmino**) tr to contaminate; to pollute

contaminazióne f contamination; pollution

contante adj & m cash; **in contanti** cash

contare (**cónto**) tr to count; to limit; to regard, value; to propose; **contarle grosse** (coll) to tell tall tales ‖ intr to count; **contare su** to count on

contasecón·di m (**-di**) watch with second hand

conta·to **-ta** adj limited; numbered (e.g., days)

conta·tóre **-trice** adj counting ‖ mf counter ‖ m meter; **contatore dell'acqua** water meter; **contatore della luce** electric meter

contattare tr to contact

contatto m contact

cónte m count

contèa f county

conteggiare §290 (**contéggio**) tr to charge (e.g., a bill) ‖ intr to count

contég·gio m (**-gi**) reckoning, calculation; (sports) count; **conteggio alla rovescia** countdown

contégno m behavior; reserve, reserved attitude; air

contegnó·so **-sa** [s] adj reserved, dignified

contemperare (**contèmpero**) tr to adapt; to mitigate, moderate

contemplare (**contèmplo**) tr to contemplate

contemplati·vo **-va** adj contemplative

contemplazióne f contemplation

contèmpo m—**nel contempo** meanwhile

contemporaneaménte adv at the same time

contemporàne·o **-a** adj contemporaneous ‖ mf contemporary

contendènte adj fighting ‖ m contender, fighter; (law) contestant

contèndere §270 tr to contest, oppose ‖ intr to contend, fight ‖ ref to fight

contenére §271 tr to contain ‖ ref to restrain oneself; to behave

conteniménto m containment

contenitóre m container

contentare (**contènto**) tr to satisfy, content ‖ ref to be satisfied

contentézza f gladness, contentedness, contentment

contentino m gratuity, makeweight, gift to a customer

contèn·to **-ta** adj contented, glad, happy; satisfied ‖ m (poet) happiness, contentedness

contenuto m content; contents

contenzióne f contention

contenzióso [s] m legal matter; legal department (of a corporation)

conterìe fpl beads, sequins

conterrà·neo **-nea** adj from the same country ‖ m fellow countryman ‖ f fellow countrywoman

conté·so **-sa** [s] adj coveted ‖ f contest; dispute; **venire a contesa** to dispute

contéssa f countess

contestare (**contèsto**) tr to serve (e.g., a summons); to deny; to challenge, contest; **contestare qlco a qlcu** to charge s.o. with s.th

contestazióne f notification, summons; dispute, confrontation; challenge

contè·sto **-sta** adj (poet) intertwined ‖ m context

contì·guo **-gua** adj contiguous

continentale adj continental

continènte adj & m continent

continènza f continence

contingentaménto m import quota

contingentare (**contingènto**) tr to assign a quota to (imports)

contingènte *adj* possible, contingent; (obs) due ‖ *m* contingent; import quota; **contingente di leva** draft quota

contingènza *f* contingency

continuare (continuo) *tr* to continue ‖ *intr* to last, continue; **continuare a** + *inf* to keep on + *ger*

continuazióne *f* continuation

continui·tà *f* (-tà) continuity

contì·nuo -nua *adj* continuous; direct (*current*); **di continuo** continuously

cón·to -ta *adj* (archaic) well-known; (poet) gentle; (poet) narrated ‖ *m* figuring; account; bill, invoice; check (*in a restaurant*); opinion; worth, value; **a conti fatti** everything considered; **chiedere conto di** to call to account; **conto all'indietro** countdown; **di conto** valuable; **estratto conto** (com) statement; **fare conto di** + *inf* to intend to + *inf*; **fare conto su** to count on; **fare di conto** to count; **fare i conti senza l'oste** to reckon without one's host; **il conto non torna** the sums do not jibe; **in conto** on account; **in conto di** in one's position as; **per conto di** in the name of; **per conto mio** as far as I am concerned; **render conto di** to give an account of; **rendersi conto di** to realize, be aware of; **tener conto di** to reckon with; **tener di conto** to treat with care; **torna conto** it is worthwhile

contòrcere §272 *tr* to twist ‖ *ref* to writhe

contorciménto *m* contortion, writhing

contornare (contórno) *tr* to surround

contórno *m* outline; contour; circle (*of people*); side dish (*of vegetables*)

contorsióne *f* contorsion; gyration (*e.g., of a dancer*); squirm

contòr·to -ta *adj* twisted (*e.g., face*)

contrabbandare *tr* to smuggle

contrabbandiè·re -ra *adj* smuggling ‖ *mf* smuggler; bootlegger

contrabbando *m* contraband; smuggling; **di contrabbando** by smuggling; (fig) without paying

contrabbasso *m* contrabass, bass viol

contraccambiare §287 *tr* to reciprocate, return ‖ *intr* to reciprocate

contraccàm·bio *m* (-bi) exchange; **in contraccambio di** in exchange for, in return for

contraccólpo *m* shock, rebound; recoil (*of a rifle*); backlash (*of a machine*)

contrada *f* road; (poet) region

contraddire §151 (*impv sg* **contraddici**) *tr* to contradict ‖ *ref* to contradict oneself; to contradict one another

contraddistinguere §156 *tr* to earmark ‖ *ref* to stand out

contraddittò·rio -ria (-ri -rie) *adj* contradictory; incoherent ‖ *m* open discussion, debate

contraddizióne *f* contradiction

contraènte *adj* contracting; acting ‖ *mf* contractor (*person who makes a contract*); (law) party

contraère·o -a *adj* antiaircraft

contraffare §173 *tr* to counterfeit; to

fake, sham ‖ *intr* (archaic) to disobey ‖ *ref* to camouflage oneself, disguise oneself

contraffat·to -ta *adj* counterfeit; adulterated; apocryphal

contraffat·tóre -trice *mf* counterfeiter; falsifier

contraffazióne *f* forgery; fake; imitation; piracy (*of book*); mockery (*of justice*)

contrafforte *m* spur (*of mountain*); crossbar (*to secure door*); (archit) buttress

c o n t r a g g è n i o *m*—**a contraggenio** against one's will

contral·to (-to) *adj* alto ‖ *m* contralto (*voice*) ‖ *f* contralto (*singer*)

contrammirà·glio *m* (-gli) rear admiral

contrappasso *m* retributive justice

contrappesare [s] (**contrappéso**) *tr* to counterweight, counterbalance

contrappéso [s] *m* counterweight, counterpoise

contrappórre §218 *tr* to oppose; to compare ‖ *ref*—**contrapporsi a** to oppose

contrappó·sto -sta *adj* opposing ‖ *m* opposite, antithesis

contrappunto *m* counterpoint

contrare (cóntro) *tr* (boxing) to counter; (bridge) to double

contrariare §287 *tr* to oppose, counter; to thwart; to contradict; to bother, vex

contrarie·tà *f* (-tà) contrariety, vexation; setback

contrà·rio -ria (-ri -rie) *adj* contrary, opposite ‖ *m* opposite; **al contrario** on the contrary; **al contrario di** unlike; **avere qlco in contrario** to have some objection, object

contrarre §273 *tr & ref* to contract

contrassegnare (contrasségno) *tr* to earmark, mark

contrasségno *m* earmark; proof

contrastare *tr* to oppose; to obstruct; to prevent ‖ *intr* to contrast; to disagree; (poet) to quarrel ‖ *ref* to contend

contrasto *m* contrast; fight, dispute; (telv) contrast knob

contrattàbile *adj* negotiable

contrattaccare §197 *tr* to counterattack

contrattac·co *m* (-chi) counterattack

contrattare *tr* to contract for, negotiate a deal for ‖ *intr* to bargain

contrattèmpo *m* mishap

contrat·to -ta *adj* contracted ‖ *m* contract

contrattuale *adj* contractual

contravveléno *m* antidote

contravvenire §282 *intr* (with *dat*) to contravene; **contravvenire a** to infringe upon

contravvenzióne *f* violation; ticket, fine; **in contravvenzione** in the wrong; **intimare una contravvenzione a** to give a ticket to

contrazióne *f* contraction

contribuènte *mf* taxpayer

contribuire §176 *intr* to contribute

contributo *m* contribution

contribu·tóre -trice *mf* contributor

contribuzióne *f* contribution
contristare *tr & ref* to sadden
contri·to -ta *adj* contrite
contrizióne *f* contrition
cóntro *m* con, contrary opinion ‖ *adv* —contro di against, versus; dar contro a to oppose; di contro opposite, facing; per contro on the other hand ‖ *prep* against, versus; at; contro pagamento upon payment; contro vento into the wind; contro voglia unwillingly
controbàttere *tr* (mil) to counterattack; (fig) to contest
controbilanciare §128 *tr* to counterpoise, counterbalance
controcanto *m* (mus) counterpoint
controcarro *adj invar* antitank
controchìglia *f* keelson
controcorrènte *f* countercurrent; undertow; (fig) undercurrent ‖ *adv* upstream
controdado *m* lock nut
controffensìva *f* counteroffensive
controfigura *f* (mov) stand-in; (mov) stuntman
controfilo *m*—a controfilo against the grain
controfinèstra *f* storm window
controfirma *f* countersign
controfirmare *tr* to countersign
controfòdera *f* inner facing (*of a suit, between lining and cloth*)
controfuò·co *m* (-chi) backfire (*to check the advance of a forest fire*)
controindicare §197 (controìndico) *tr* to contraindicate
controllare (contròllo) *tr* to control, check ‖ *ref* to control oneself
contròllo *m* control, check; restraint; (rad, telv) knob
controllóre *m* (com) comptroller; (rr) ticket collector, conductor
controluce *f* picture taken against the light ‖ *adv* against the light
contromano *adv* against traffic
contromar·ca *f* (-che) check, stub (*e.g., of ticket*)
contromàr·cia *f* (-ce) countermarch; (aut) reverse, reverse gear
contromezzana [ddzz] *f* (naut) topsail
contronòta *f* countermanding note
contropalo *m* strut
controparte *f* (law) opponent
contropedale *m* foot brake (*of a bicycle*)
contropélo *m* close shave (*in the opposite direction of hair's growth*) ‖ *adv* against the grain; the wrong way (*said of the hair*); against the nap; accarezzare contropelo to stroke the wrong way
contropiède *m* counterattack; cogliere in contropiede to catch off balance
contropòrta *f* storm door
controproducènte *adj* counterproductive, self-defeating
contropropósta *f* counterproposition
contropròva *f* proof; second balloting
contròrdine *m* countermand
controrèplica *f* retort; (law) rejoinder
controrifórma *f* Counter Reformation

controrivoluzióne *f* counterrevolution
controsènso *m* nonsense; mistranslation
controspallina *f* (mil) epaulet
controspionàg·gio *m* (-gi) counterespionage
controvalóre *m* equivalent
controvènto *m* (archit) strut; (archit) crossbrace ‖ *adv* windward
controvèrsia *f* controversy
controvèr·so -sa *adj* controversial, moot
controvòglia *adv* unwillingly
contumace *adj* (archaic) contumacious; (law) absent from court; (law) guilty of nonappearance
contumàcia *f* quarantine; (archaic) contumacy; (law) nonappearance; in contumacia (law) in absentia
contumèlia *f* contumely
contundènte *adj* blunt
conturbante *adj* disturbing, upsetting
conturbare *tr* to disturb, upset ‖ *ref* to become perturbed
contusióne *f* bruise, contusion
contu·so -sa *adj* bruised
contuttoché *conj* although
contuttociò *conj* although
convalescènte *adj* convalescent
convalescènza *f* convalescence
convalescenzià·rio *m* (-ri) convalescent home
convàlida *f* validation; confirmation
convalidare (convàlido) *tr* to validate; to confirm; to strengthen (*e.g., a suspicion*)
convégno *m* meeting, convention
conveniènte *adj* convenient; adequate; useful; profitable (*business*); cheap, reasonable
conveniènza *f* convenience; suitability; fitness; propriety; profit; convenienze conventions
convenire §282 *tr* to fix (*e.g., a price*); (law) to summon ‖ *intr* (ESSERE) to convene; to agree; to fit, be appropriate; (poet) to flow together ‖ *ref* to be proper; (with *dat*) to behoove, befit, e.g., gli si conviene it behooves him ‖ *impers*—conviene it is necessary
convènto *m* convent; monastery
convenu·to -ta *adj* agreed upon ‖ *m* agreement; (law) defendant; convenuti conventioners, delegates
convenzionale *adj* conventional
convenzióne *f* convention
convergènte *adj* converging, convergent
convergènza *f* convergence
convèrgere §137 *intr* to converge
convèrsa *f* lay sister; flashing (*on a roof*)
conversare (convèrso) *intr* to converse
conversazióne *f* conversation
conversióne *f* conversion; change of heart; (mil) wheeling
convèrso *m* lay brother
convertìbile *adj* convertible ‖ *m* (aer) fighter-bomber ‖ *f* (aut) convertible
convertibili·tà *f* (-tà) convertibility
convertire §138 *tr* to convert, change; to translate ‖ *ref* to convert, change; (poet) to address oneself

converti·to -ta *adj* converted ‖ *mf* convert

convertitóre *m* converter

convès·so -sa *adj* convex

convincènte *adj* convincing

convìncere §285 *tr* to convince; to convict ‖ *ref* to become convinced

convinciménto *m* conviction

convin·to -ta *adj* convinced, confirmed; convicted

convinzióne *f* conviction

convita·to -ta *adj* invited ‖ *mf* guest (*at a banquet*)

convito *m* banquet

convitto *m* boarding school

convit·tóre -trice *mf* boarding-school student

convivènte *adj* living together

convivènza *f* living together; **convivenza illecita** cohabitation; **convivenza umana** human society

convìvere §286 *intr* to live together; to cohabit

conviviale *adj* convivial

convì·vio *m* (-**vi**) banquet

convocare §197 (cònvoco) *tr* to summon, convoke; to convene

convocazióne *f* convocation

convogliare §280 (convòglio) *tr* to convoy, escort; to convey, carry

convò·glio *m* (-**gli**) convoy; cortege; (rr) train

convolare (convólo) *intr*—**convolare a nozze** to get married

convòlvolo *m* (bot) morning-glory

convulsióne *f* convulsion

convul·so -sa *adj* convulsive; convulsed; choppy (*style*)

coonestare (coonèsto) *tr* to justify, palliate

cooperare (coòpero) *intr* to cooperate

cooperati·vo -va *adj & f* cooperative

coopera·tóre -trice *adj* coadjutant, cooperating ‖ *m* coadjutor

cooperazióne *f* cooperation

coordinaménto *m* coordination

coordinare (coórdino) *tr* to coordinate; to collect (*ideas*)

coordinati·vo -va *adj* (gram) coordinate

coordina·to -ta *adj & f* coordinate

coordinazióne *f* coordination

coòrte *f* cohort

copèr·chio *m* (-**chi**) lid, cover; top (*of box*)

copertina *f* small blanket, child's blanket; cover (*of book*)

copèr·to -ta *adj* covered; protected; cloudy; obscure ‖ *m* cover; shelter; **al coperto** under cover; indoors; secure ‖ *f* blanket, cover; seat cover; case, sheath; (naut) deck; **coperta da viaggio** steamer rug, lap robe; **far coperta a** to cover up for

copertóne *m* canvas; casing, shoe (*of tire*); **copertone cinturato** belted tire

copertura *f* covering; cover; coverage; whitewash; (boxing) defensive stance; (archit) roof

còpia *f* copy; (poet) abundance; (archaic) opportunity; **brutta copia** first draft; **copia a carbone** carbon copy; **copia dattiloscritta** typescript; **per**

copia conforme certified copy (*formula appearing on a document*)

copialètte·re *m* (-**re**) letter file; copying press

copiare §287 (còpio) *tr* to copy

copiati·vo -va *adj* indelible; copying

copiatura *f* copying; copy; plagiarism

copiglia *f* cotterpin

copilò·ta *mf* (-**ti -te**) copilot

copióne *m* (theat) script

copiosi·tà [s] *f* (-**tà**) copiousness

copió·so -sa [s] *adj* copious

copi·sta *mf* (-**sti -ste**) scribe; copyist

copisterìa *f* copying office; public typing office

còppa *f* cup, goblet; bowl; pan (*of balance*); trophy; (aut) crankcase; (aut) housing; **coppe** suit of Neapolitan cards corresponding to hearts

coppàia *f* chuck (*of lathe*)

còppia *f* couple; pair; **a coppie** two by two; **far coppia fissa** to go steady

coppière *m* cupbearer

coppìglia *f* var of **copiglia**

cóppo *m* earthenware jar (*for oil*); roof tile

cepribu·sto *m* (-**sto**) bodice

copricapo *m* headgear

copricaté·na *m* (-**na**) chain guard (*on bicycle or motorcycle*)

coprifuò·co *m* (-**chi**) curfew

coprinu·ca *m* (-**ca**) havelock

coprire §110 *tr* to cover; to occupy (*a position*); to coat (*e.g., a wall*); to drown (*a noise*) ‖ *ref* to cover oneself; (econ) to hedge

copriteiè·ra *m* (-**ra**) cozy

coprivivan·de *m* (-**de**) dish cover

cò·pto -pta *adj* Coptic ‖ *mf* Copt

còpula *f* copulation; (gram) copula

coque *f* see **uovo**

coràg·gio *m* (-**gi**) courage; effrontery; (obs) heart; **fare coraggio a** to hearten, encourage; **prendere il coraggio a quattro mani** to screw up one's courage

coraggió·so -sa [s] *adj* courageous

corale *adj* choral; (archaic) cordial; (fig) unanimous ‖ *m* chorale

coralli·no -na *adj* coral

corallo *m* coral

corame *m* engraved leather

coramèlla *f* razor strop

Corano *m* Koran

corata *f* haslet

coratèlla *f* giblets

corazza *f* breastplate, cuirass; shoulder pad (*in football*); armor plate; carapace, shell

corazzare *tr* to armor ‖ *ref* to armor, protect oneself

corazza·to -ta *adj* armor-plated, armored; plated; protected ‖ *f* battleship, dreadnought

corazzière *m* cuirassier; mounted carabineer

còrba *f* basket

corbellerìa *f* (coll) blunder

corbèllo *m* basket; basketful

corbézzolo *m* (bot) arbutus; **corbezzoli!** gosh!

còrda *f* rope; tightrope; string (*of an*

instrument); chord; woof; cord; plumbline; **dare la corda a** to wind (*a clock*); **essere con la corda al collo** to have a rope around one's neck; **mostrare la corda** to be threadbare; **tagliare la corda** to take off, leave; **tenere sulla corda** to keep in suspense

cordame *m* cordage

cordata *f* group of climbers tied together

cordellina *f* (mil) braided cord, braid; (mil) lanyard

cordiale *adj & m* cordial

cordiali•tà *f* (-tà) cordiality

cordièra *f* (mus) tailpiece

cordò•glio *m* (-gli) sorrow, grief

cordonata *f* gradient

cordóne *m* cordon; (anat, elec) cord; curbstone; **cordone litorale** sandbar; **cordone sanitario** sanitary cordon

corèa *f* St. Vitus's dance ǁ **Corea** *f* Korea

corea•no -na *adj & mf* Korean

coréggia *f* leather strap

coreografia *f* choreography

coreògrafo *m* choreographer

coriàce•o -a *adj* tough, leathery

coriàndolo *m* (bot) coriander; **coriandoli** confetti

coricare §197 (**còrico**) *tr* to put to bed ǁ *ref* to lie down, go to bed

corindóne *m* corundum

corìn•zio -zia *adj & mf* (-zi -zie) Corinthian

cori•sta *mf* (-sti -ste) choir singer, choirmaster ǁ *m* chorus man; (mus) tuning fork; (mus) pitch pipe

coriza [dz] or **corizza** [ddzz] *f* coryza

cormorano *m* cormorant

cornàcchia *f* rook, crow

cornamusa *f* bagpipe

cornata *f* butt; hook, goring (*by bull*)

còrne•o -a *adj* horn, horn-like ǁ *f* cornea

cornétta *f* (mus) cornet; (mus) cornet player; (telp) receiver; (hist) pennon (*of cavalry*)

cornétto *m* little horn; amulet (*in shape of horn*); crescent (*bread*); ear trumpet

cornice *f* cornice; frame; (typ) box; (archit) pediment

cornicióne *m* (archit) ledge; (archit) cornice

cornificare §197 (**cornìfico**) *tr* (joc) to cuckold

corniòla *f* carnelian

corniola *f* (bot) dogberry

còrniolo *m* (bot) dogwood

còrno *m* horn; wing (*of army*); edge, end; (mus) horn; **corno da caccia** hunting horn; **corno da scarpe** shoe horn; **corno dell'abbondanza** horn of plenty; **corno dogale** (hist) Doge's hat; **corno inglese** (mus) English horn; **non capire un corno** to not understand a blessed thing; **non valere un corno** to not be worth a fig; **un corno!** (slang) heck no! ǁ *m* (**còrna** *fpl*) horn (*of animal*); **alzare le corna** to raise one's head; to be-

come rambunctious; **dire corna di** to speak evil of; **fare le corna** to make horns, to touch wood (*to ward off the evil eye*); **mettere le corna a** to cuckold (*one's husband*); to be unfaithful to (*one's wife*); **portare le corna** to be cuckolded; **rompersi le corna** to get the worst of it

cornu•to -ta *adj* horny; horn-shaped; (vulg) cuckolded

còro *m* choir; chorus; chancel

corollà•rio *m* (-ri) corollary

coróna *f* crown; coronet; wreath, garland; range (*of mountains*); collection (*e.g., of sonnets*); stem (*of watch*); felloe (*of wheel*); (astr) corona; (rel) string (*of beads*); (mus) pause; **fare corona a** to surround

coronaménto *m* crowning; (archit) capstone; (naut) taffrail

coronare (**coróno**) *tr* to crown; to top, surmount

coronà•rio -ria *adj* (-ri -rie) coronary; (hist) rewarded with a garland

corpétto *m* baby's shirt; waistcoat, vest

corpino *m* bodice; vest

còrpo *m* body; substance; staff (*of teachers*); (mil) corps; (typ) em quad; **a corpo a corpo** hand-to-hand (*fight*); (sports) in a clinch; **a corpo morto** heavily; doggedly; **andare di corpo** to have a bowel movement; **avere in corpo** (fig) to have inside; **corpo del reato** corpus delicti; **corpo di Bacco!** good Heavens!; **corpo di ballo** ballet; **corpo di commissariato** (mil) supply corps; **corpo di guardia** guard, guardhouse; **corpo semplice** (chem) simple substance; **prendere corpo** to materialize

corporale *adj* bodily, body ǁ *m* (eccl) corporal, Communion cloth

corporativismo *m* corporatism (*e.g., of Fascist Italy*)

corporati•vo -va *adj* corporative, corporate

corpora•to -ta *adj* corporate

corporatura *f* size, build

corporazióne *f* corporation

corpòre•o -a *adj* corporeal

corpó•so -sa [s] *adj* heavy-bodied

corpulèn•to -ta *adj* corpulent

corpùscolo *m* particle; (phys) corpuscle

Corpus Dòmini *m* (eccl) Corpus Christi

corredare (**corrèdo**) *tr* to provide, furnish; to annotate, accompany

corredino *m* layette

corrèdo *m* trousseau; outfit, garb; actor's kit; furniture; equipment; apparatus (*e.g., footnotes*)

corrèggere §226 *tr* to correct; to straighten (*e.g., a road*); to rewrite, revise (*news*); to touch up the flavor of ǁ *ref* to reform

corrég•gia *f* (-ge) leather strap

corregionale *adj* fellow ǁ *mf* person of the same section of the country

correità *f* complicity

correlare (**corrèlo**) *tr* to correlate

correlati•vo -va *adj* correlative

correla•tóre -trice *mf* second reader (*of a doctoral dissertation*)

correlazióne *f* correlation; (gram) sequence

corrènte *adj* current; running; fluent; recurring; run-of-the-mill ‖ *m*—**essere al corrente di** to be acquainted with; to be abreast of; **mettere al corrente di** to acquaint with ‖ *f* current; draft (*of air*); stream (*of water*); mass (*of lava*); (elec) current; (fig) tide; **contro corrente** upstream; **corrente alternata** (elec) alternating current; **corrente continua** (elec) direct current; **corrente di rete** (elec) house current

córrere §139 *tr* to travel; to run (*a risk; a race*); **correre la cavallina** to sow one's wild oats ‖ *intr* (ESSERE & AVERE) to run; to speed; to race; to flow; to fly (*said of time*); to elapse; to be (*e.g., the year 1820*); to be current (*said of coins*); to spread (*said of gossip*); to mature (*said of interest*); to intervene (*said of distance*); to have dealings; **ci corre!** there is quite a difference!; **ci corre poco che cadesse** he narrowly escaped falling; **correre a gambe levate** to run at breakneck speed; **corre l'uso** it is the fashion; **corrono parole grosse** they are having words; **non corre buon sangue fra loro** there is bad blood between them

corresponsàbile *adj* jointly responsible

corresponsióne *f* payment; (fig) gratitude

correttézza *f* correctness

corretti·vo -va *adj* corrective ‖ *m* flavoring

corrèt·to -ta *adj* correct; flavored; spiked

corret·tóre -trice *mf* corrector; **correttore di bozze** proofreader

correzionale *adj* correctional

correzióne *f* correction

còrri còrri *m* rush

corri·dóio *m* (**-dói**) corridor; hallway; (tennis) alley; (theat) aisle

corridóre *adj* running ‖ *m* racer; runner (*in baseball*)

corrièra *f* mail coach; bus

corrière *m* courier; mail; carrier (*of merchandise*)

corrispetti·vo -va *adj* equivalent, proportionate ‖ *m* requital, compensation

corrispondènte *adj* corresponding, equivalent ‖ *mf* correspondent

corrispondènza *f* correspondence

corrispóndere §238 *tr* to pay, compensate ‖ *intr* to correspond

corri·vo -va *adj* rash; indulgent

corroborante *adj* corroborating ‖ *m* tonic

corroborare (**corròboro**) *tr* to corroborate; to invigorate

corroborazióne *f* corroboration

corródere §239 *tr* to corrode; to erode

corrómpere §240 *tr* to corrupt; to suborn ‖ *ref* to putrefy, rot

corrosióne *f* corrosion

corrosi·vo -va *adj* & *m* corrosive

corró·so -sa *adj* corroded; eroded

corrót·to -ta *adj* corrupted, corrupt; putrefied, rotten ‖ *m* (archaic) lament

corrucciare §128 *tr* to anger, vex ‖ *ref* to get angry

corrùc·cio *m* (**-ci**) anger, vexation

corrugaménto *m* wrinkling; (geol) fold

corrugare §209 *tr* to wrinkle, knit (*one's brow*) ‖ *ref* to frown

corruscare §197 *intr* (poet) to shine

corruttèla *f* corruption

corruttibile *adj* corruptible

corrut·tóre -trice *adj* corrupting, depraving ‖ *m* seducer; briber

corruzióne *f* corruption; putrefaction, decomposition

córsa *f* race; run; trip; fare; (mach) stroke; (hist) privateering; **a tutta corsa** at full speed; **corsa al galoppo** flat race; **corsa al trotto** harness racing; **corsa semplice** one-way ticket; **corse** horse racing; **da corsa** race, for racing, e.g., **cavallo da corsa** race horse; **di corsa** running, in a hurry; **fare una corsa** to run an errand; **prendere la corsa** to begin to run

corsalétto *m* corselet

corsa·ro -ra *adj* privateering ‖ *m* privateer, corsair, pirate

corsétto *m* corset

corsìa *f* aisle; ward (*in hospital*); runner (*of carpet*); lane (*of highway*); **corsia d'accesso** entrance lane; **corsia d'uscita** exit lane

Còrsica, la Corsica

corsivi·sta *mf* (**-sti -ste**) (journ) political writer

corsi·vo -va *adj* cursive; (poet) running; (poet) current ‖ *m* cursive handwriting; (typ) italics

córso *m* course; navigation (*by sea*); path (*of stars*); parade; large street; boulevard; tender (*of currency*); current rate, current price (*of stock at the exchange*); **corso d'acqua** watercourse; **fuori corso** (*coin*) no longer in circulation; **in corso** in circulation; in progress; **in corso di** in the course of; **in corso di stampa** in press

còr·so -sa *adj* & *mf* Corsican

cor·sólo -sóia (**-sói -sóie**) *adj* running (*knot*); (mach) on rollers ‖ *m* slide (*of slide rule*); (mach) slide

córte *f* court; **corte bandita** open house; **Corte d'appello** appellate court; **Corte di cassazione** Supreme Court; **fare la corte a** to pay court to, woo

cortéc·cia *f* (**-ce**) bark; crust (*of bread*); (fig) appearance; (anat) cortex

corteggiaménto *m* courtship

corteggiatóre *m* wooer, suitor

cortég·gio *m* (**-gi**) retinue; cortege

cortèo *m* procession; parade; funeral train; wedding party

cortése *adj* courteous, polite; (lit) liberal; (poet & hist) courtly

cortesìa *f* courtesy, politeness; (lit) liberality; (poet & hist) courtliness; **per cortesìa** please

còrtice *f* cortex

cortigia·no -na *adj* flattering; courtly ‖ *mf* courtier; flatterer ‖ *f* courtesan

cortile *m* courtyard; barnyard

cortina f curtain; **cortina di ferro** iron curtain; **cortina di fumo** smoke screen; **oltre cortina** behind the iron curtain

cortisóne m cortisone

cór·to -ta adj short; close (haircut); **alle corte** in short; **essere a corto di** to be short of; **per farla corta** in short

cortocircùito m short circuit

cortometràg·gio m (-gi) (mov) short

cor·vè f (-vè) tiresome task, drudgery; **corvè di cucina** kitchen police

corvétta f corvette

corvi·no -na adj raven-black

còrvo m raven; crow

còsa [s] f thing; **belle cose!** or **buone cose!** regards!; **che cosa** what; **cosa da nulla** a mere trifle, nothing at all; **cos'ha?** what's the matter with you (him, her)?; **cosa pubblica** commonweal; **cosa strana** no wonder; **cose belongings; per la qual cosa** wherefore; **per prima cosa** first of all; **sopra ogni cosa** above all; **tante belle cose!** best regards!; **una cosa** something; **una cosa nuova** a piece of news

cosac·co -ca (-chi -che) adj Cossack's || mf Cossack

cò·scia f (-sce) thigh; haunch; leg (of gun); (archit) abutment; **coscia di montone** leg of lamb

cosciènte adj conscious; sensible; aware

cosciènza f conscience; consciousness; conscientiousness; awareness

coscienzió·so -sa [s] adj conscientious

cosciòtto m leg; leg of lamb

coscrit·to -ta adj conscript || m conscript, recruit, draftee

coscrìvere §250 tr to conscript

coscrizióne f conscription, draft

così [s] adj invar—**un così... or un... così** such a || adv thus; like this; so; **così . . . come** as . . . as; **così così** so so; **e così via** and so on, and so forth; **per così dire** so to speak

cosicché [s] conj so that

cosiddét·to -ta [s] adj so-called

cosiffat·to -ta [s] adj such, similar

cosino [s] m (coll) little fellow

cosmèti·co -ca adj & m (-ci -che) cosmetic

còsmi·co -ca adj (-ci -che) cosmic; outer (space)

còsmo m cosmos; outer space

cosmòdromo m space center

cosmologia f cosmology

cosmonàu·ta mf (-ti -te) cosmonaut, astronaut

cosmopòli·ta adj & mf (-ti -te) cosmopolitan

còso [s] m (coll) thing, what-d'you-call-it

cospàrgere §261 tr to spread; to sprinkle

cospèrgere §112 tr (poet) to wet, sprinkle

cospètto m presence; **al cospetto di** in the presence of

cospì·cuo -cua adj distinguished, outstanding; huge, immense; (poet) conspicuous

cospirare intr to conspire, plot

cospira·tóre -trice mf conspirator

cospirazióne f conspiracy, plot

còsta f side; rib; coast, seashore; slope; welt (along seam); wale (in fabric); (naut) frame

costà adv there; over there

costaggiù adv down there

costante adj & f constant

Costantinòpoli f Constantinople

costanza f constancy || **Costanza** f Constance

costare (còsto) intr (ESSERE) to cost; to be expensive; **costare caro** to cost dear; **costare un occhio della testa** to cost a fortune

costarica·no -na or **costaricènse** adj & mf Costa Rican

costassù adv up there

costata f rib roast; side

costeggiare §290 (costéggio) tr to sail along; to run along; to border on || intr to coast

costèi §8 pron dem

costellare (costèllo) tr to stud, star

costellazióne f constellation

costernare (costèrno) tr to dismay, cause consternation to

costernazióne f consternation

costì adv there

costiè·ro -ra adj coast, coastal; offshore || f coastline; gentle slope

costipare tr to constipate; to heap, pile || ref to become constipated

costipazióne f constipation

costituènte adj constituent; constituting || m member of constituent assembly; (chem) constituent

costituire §176 tr to constitute; to form || ref to form; to become; to appoint oneself; to give oneself up (to justice); **costituirsi in giudizio** (law) to sue (in civil court); **costituirsi parte civile** (law) to appear as a plaintiff (in civil court)

costituto m (law) pact, agreement; (naut) master's declaration (to health authorities)

costituzionale adj constitutional

costituzióne f constitution; charter; composition; (law) appearance; surrender (to justice)

còsto m cost; **a costo di** at the price of; **ad ogni costo** at any cost; **a nessun costo** by no means; **a tutti i costi** at any cost, in any event; **costo della vita** cost of living; **sotto costo** below cost

còstola f rib; spine (of book); back (of knife); **avere qlcu alle costole** to have s.o. at one's heels; **rompere le costole a** (fig) to break the bones of; **stare alle costole di** to be at the back of

costolétta f chop, cutlet

costolóne m (archit) groin

costóro §8 pron dem

costó·so -sa [s] adj costly

costrìngere §265 tr to force, constrain; (poet) to compress

costritti·vo -va adj constrictive

costrizióne f constriction

costruire §140 tr to construct, build

costrut·to -ta *adj* constructed || *m* profit; sense; (gram) construction; **dov'è il costrutto?** what's the point?

costruttóre *m* builder

costruzióne *f* construction; building

costùi §8 *pron dem*

costumanza *f* custom

costumare *intr* (+ *inf*) to be in the habit of (+ *ger*) || *intr* (ESSERE) to be the custom; to be in use

costumatézza *f* good manners

costuma·to -ta *adj* polite, well-bred

costume *m* custom, manner; costume, dress; bathing suit

costumi·sta *mf* (-sti -ste) (theat) costumer

costura *f* seam

cotale *adj & pron* such || *adv* (archaic) thus

cotan·to -ta *adj & pron* (poet) so much || **cotanto** *adv* (poet) such a long time

còte *f* flint

coténna *f* pigskin; rind; (coll) hide, skin

coté·sto -sta §7 *adj dem* || §8 *pron dem*

cóti·ca *f* (-che) (coll) hide, skin (*of porker*)

cotógna *f* quince (*fruit*)

cotognata *f* quince jam

cotógno *m* quince (*tree*)

cotolétta *f* chop, cutlet

cotóne *m* cotton; thread; **cotone fulminante** guncotton; **cotone idrofilo** absorbent cotton; **cotone silicato** mineral wool

cotonière *m* cotton manufacturer

cotoniè·ro -ra *adj* cotton || *mf* cotton worker

cotonifi·cio *m adj* (-ci) cotton mill

cotonó·so -sa [s] *adj* cotton; cottony

còtta *f* cooking; baking; drying (*of bricks*); (sports) exhaustion; (coll) drunkenness; (joc) infatuation, love; (eccl) surplice; **cotta d'armi** coat of mail

cottimi·sta *mf* (-sti -ste) pieceworker

còttimo *m* piecework

còt·to -ta *adj* cooked; baked; burnt; suntanned; (joc) half-baked; (joc) in love; (sports) exhausted || *m* brick || *f* see **cotta**

cottura *f* cooking; **a punto di cottura** (culin) done just right

coutènte *mf* (law) joint user; (telp) party-line user

cóva *f* brooding; nest

covare (**cóvo**) *tr* to brood, to hatch; to harbor or nurse (*an enmity*); to nurture (*a disease*); **covare con gli occhi** to look fondly at; **covare le lenzuola** to loll around || *intr* to smolder (*said of fire or passion*)

covata *f* brood, covey

covile *m* doghouse; den

cóvo *m* shelter; den, lair; **farsi il covo** (fig) to gather a nestegg; **uscire dal covo** to stick one's nose out of the house

covóne *m* sheaf; cock (*of hay*)

còzza *f* cockle

cozzare (**còzzo**) *tr* to hit; to butt (*one's head*) || *intr* to butt; (fig) to clash;

cozzare contro to bump into || *ref* to hit one another; to fight

còzzo *m* butt; clash, conflict

crac *m* crash

crampo *m* cramp

cràni·co -ca *adj* (-ci -che) cranial

crà·nio *m* (-ni) cranium, skull

cràpula *f* excess (*in eating and drinking*)

cras·so -sa *adj* crass, gross; large (*intestine*)

cratère *m* crater; bomb crater

cràuti *mpl* sauerkraut

cravatta *f* tie, necktie; **cravatta a farfalla** bow tie; **fare cravatte** to be a usurer

creanza *f* politeness; **buona creanza** good manners

creare (**crèo**) *tr* to create; to name, elect

creati·vo -va *adj* creative

crea·to -ta *adj* created || *m* creation, universe

crea·tóre -trice *adj* creative || *mf* creator

creatura *f* creature; baby; **povera creatura!** poor thing!

creazióne *f* creation; (poet) election

credènte *adj* believing || *mf* believer

credènza *f* credence, faith, belief; sideboard, buffet; (coll) credit

credenziale *f* letter of credit; **credenziali** credentials

credenzière *m* butler

crédere §141 *tr* to believe; to think; **lo credo bene!** I should say so! || *intr* to believe; to trust; **credere a** to believe in; **credere in Dio** to believe in God || *ref* to believe oneself to be

credìbile *adj* credible

credibilità *f* credibility

crédito *m* credit

credi·tóre -trice *mf* creditor

crèdo *m* credo, creed

credulità *f* credulity

crèdu·lo -la *adj* credulous

crèma *f* cream; custard; **crema da scarpe** shoe polish; **crema di bellezza** beauty cream; **crema di pomodoro** cream of tomato soup; **crema evanescente** vanishing cream; **crema per barba** shaving cream

cremaglièra *f* rack; cogway, cograil

cremare (**crèmo**) *tr* to cremate

crema·tóio *m* (-tói) crematory

cremató·rio *m* (-ri) crematory

cremazióne *f* cremation

cremerìa *f* creamery

crèmisi *adj & m* crimson

Cremlino *m* Kremlin

cremlinologìa *f* Kremlinology

cremortàrtaro *m* cream of tartar

cremó·so -sa [s] *adj* creamy

crèn *m* horseradish

creolina *f* creolin

crèo·lo -la *adj & mf* Creole

creosòto *m* creosote

crèpa *f* crack, crevice; rift

crepàc·cio *m* (-ci) crevasse; fissure

crepacuòre *m* heartbreak

crepapància *m*—**mangiare a crepapancia** to burst from eating too much

crepapèlle *m*—**ridere a crepapelle** to split one's sides laughing

crepare (crèpo) *intr* to burst; to crack; to chip; (slang) to croak; **crepare dalla sete** to die of thirst; **crepare dalle risa** to die laughing; **crepare d'invidia** to be green with envy

crepitare (crèpito) *intr* to crackle (*said of fire or weapons*); to rustle (*said of leaves*)

crepiti·o *m* (**-i**) crackle; rustle; pitter-patter (*of rain*)

crepuscolare *adj* twilight; (fig) dim

crepùscolo *m* twilight

crescènte *adj* rising, growing; crescent (*moon*) ‖ *m* (astr & heral) crescent

crescènza *f* growth

créscere §142 *tr* to grow, raise; to increase ‖ *intr* (ESSERE) to grow; to increase; to rise (*said, e.g., of prices*); to wax (*said of the moon*); **farsi crescere** to grow (*a beard*)

crescióne *m* watercress

créscita *f* growth; outgrowth; rise (*of water*)

crèsima *f* confirmation

cresimare (crèsimo) *tr* to confirm

Crèso *m* (mythol) Croesus

cré·spo -spa *adj* crispy, kinky; (archaic) wrinkled ‖ *m* crepe ‖ *f* wrinkle; ruffle

crésta *f* comb (*of chicken*); crest; **abbassare la cresta** to come down a peg or two; **alzare la cresta** to become insolent

crestàia *f* (coll) milliner

créta *f* clay

cretése [s] *adj & mf* Cretan

cretinerìa *f* idiocy

creti·no -na *adj & mf* idiot, cretin

cribro *m* (poet) sieve

cric·ca *f* (**-che**) clique, gang; group; crevice

cric·co *m* (**-chi**) (aut) jack

cricéto *m* hamster

cri cri *m* chirping (*of crickets*)

criminale *adj* criminal; (law) penal ‖ *mf* criminal

criminali·sta *mf* (**-sti -ste**) penal lawyer, criminal lawyer

criminalità *f* criminality

crìmine *m* crime

criminologìa *f* criminology

criminòlo·go *m* (**-gi**) criminologist

criminó·so -sa [s] *adj* criminal

crinale *adj* (poet) hair ‖ *m* ridge (*of mountains*)

crine *m* horsehair; (poet) hair; (poet) sunbeam

crinièra *f* mane

crinolina *f* crinoline

cripta *f* crypt

criptocomuni·sta *mf* (**-sti -ste**) fellow traveler

crisàlide *f* chrysalis

crisantèmo *m* chrysanthemum

cri·si *f* (**-si**) crisis; shortage (*of houses*); attack (*e.g., of fever*); outburst (*of tears*); (econ) slump; **crisi ancillare** or **domestica** servant problem; **in crisi** in difficulties

cristallerìa *f* glassware; crystal service; glassware shop; glassworks

cristallièra *f* china closet

cristalli·no -na *adj* crystalline ‖ *m* crystalline lens

cristallizzare [ddzz] *tr & ref* to crystallize

cristallo *m* crystal; glass; pane (*of glass*); windshield; **cristallo di rocca** rock crystal; **cristallo di sicurezza** (aut) safety glass

cristianaménte *adv* in a Christian manner, like a Christian; (coll) decently; **morire cristianamente** to die in the faith

cristianésimo *m* Christianity

cristianità *f* Christendom

cristia·no -na *adj & mf* Christian

Cristo *m* Christ; **avanti Cristo** before Christ (B.C.); **dopo Cristo** after Christ (A.D.); **un povero cristo** (slang) a poor guy

critè·rio *m* (**-ri**) criterion; judgment

crìti·ca *f* (**-che**) criticism; critique; slur

criticare §197 (**crìtico**) *tr* to criticize, censure; to find fault with

crìti·co -ca (**-ci -che**) *adj* critical ‖ *mf* critic; (coll) faultfinder ‖ *f* see **critica**

crittografìa *f* cryptography

crittogram·ma *m* (**-mi**) cryptogram

crivellare (crivèllo) *tr* to riddle

crivèllo *m* sieve, riddle

croa·to -ta *adj & mf* Croatian

Croàzia, la Croatia

croccante *adj* crisp, crunchy ‖ *m* almond brittle, peanut brittle

crocchétta *f* croquette

cròcchia *f* chignon, topknot

crocchiare §287 (**cròcchio**) *intr* to crackle; to sound cracked or broken; to cluck (*said of a hen*); to crack (*said of joints*)

cròc·chio *m* (**-chi**) group (*of people*); **far crocchio** to gather around

eróce *f* cross; x (*mark made by illiterate person*); tail (*of coin*); (fig) trial; **Croce del Sud** Southern Cross; **croce di Malta** Maltese cross; **Croce Rossa** Red Cross; **croce uncinata** swastika; **fare una croce sopra** to forget about; **gettare la croce addosso** (fig) to put the blame on; **mettere in croce** to crucify

crocefisso *m* crucifix

crocerossina *f* Red Cross worker

croceségno *m* cross, x (*mark made instead of signature*)

crocétta *f* (naut) crosstree

croce·via *m* (**-via**) crossroads, intersection

crocia·to -ta *adj* crossed; crusading; see **parola** ‖ *m* crusader ‖ *f* crusade

crocièra *f* cruise; (archit) cross (*vault*); (mach) cross (*of universal joint*)

crocière *m* (orn) crossbill

crocifìggere §104 *tr* to crucify

crocifissióne *f* crucifixion

crocifis·so -sa *adj* crucified ‖ *m* crucifix

crò·co *m* (**-chi**) crocus

crogiolare (crògiolo) *tr* to cook on a low fire; to simmer; to temper (*glass*) ‖ *ref* to bask; to snuggle (*e.g., in bed*)

crogiolo *m* cooking on a low fire; simmering; tempering (*of glass*)

crogiòlo *m* crucible; (fig) melting pot

crollare (cròllo) *tr* to shake (*e.g., one's head*) ‖ *intr* (ESSERE) to fall down, collapse ‖ *ref* to shake

cròllo *m* shake; fall, collapse
cròma *f* (mus) quaver
cromare (cròmo) *tr* to plate with chromium
croma·to -ta *adj* chromium-plated; chrome || *m* chrome yellow
cromatura *f* chromium plating
cròmo *m* chrome, chromium
cromosfèra *f* chromosphere
cromosò·ma [s] *m* (-mi) chromosome
cròna·ca *f* (-che) chronicle; report, news; **cronaca bianca** news of the day; **cronaca giudiziaria** court news; **cronaca mondana** social column; **cronaca nera** police and accident report; **cronaca rosa** wedding column; **stork news**
cròni·co -ca (-ci -che) *adj* chronic || *mf* incurable
croni·sta *mf* (-sti -ste) reporter; chronicler
cronistòria *f* chronicle
cronologìa *f* chronology
cronològi·co -ca *adj* (-ci -che) chronologic(al)
cronometrare (cronòmetro) *tr* to time
cronomètri·co -ca *adj* (-ci -che) chronometric(al); split-second
cronometri·sta *m* (-sti) (sports) timekeeper
cronòmetro *m* stopwatch; chronometer
crosciare §128 **(cròscio)** *tr* (archaic) to heave, throw || *intr* to rustle (*said of dry leaves*); to pitter-patter (*said of rain*)
cròsta *f* crust; bark (*of tree*); scab; slough; shell (*of crustacean*); poor painting
crostàceo *m* crustacean
crostata *f* pie
crostino *m* toast
crostó·so -sa [s] *adj* crusty
croupier *m* **(croupier)** croupier
crucciare §128 *tr* to worry, vex; to chagrin || *ref* to worry; to become angry
cruccia·to -ta *adj* afflicted; worried; angry; chagrined
cruc·cio *m* (-ci) sorrow; (obs) anger; **darsi cruccio** to fret
cruciale *adj* crucial
crucivèr·ba *m* (-ba) crossword puzzle
crudèle *adj* cruel
crudel·tà *f* (-tà) cruelty
crudézza *f* crudity; harshness
cru·do -da *adj* raw; rare (*meat*); (poet) cruel
cruèn·to *adj* (lit) bloody
crumiro *m* scab (*in strikes*)
cruna *f* eye (*of a needle*)
cru·sca *f* (-sche) bran; (coll) freckles
cruscante *adj* Della-Cruscan; affected || *m* member of the Accademia della Crusca
cruschèllo *m* middlings
cruscòtto *m* (aut) dashboard; (aer) instrument panel
cuba·no -na *adj* & *mf* Cuban
cubatura *f* volume
cùbi·co -ca *adj* (-ci -che) cubic; cube (*root*)
cubitale *adj* very large (*handwriting or type*)

cùbito *m* cubit; (poet) elbow
cubo *m* cube
cuccagna *f* plenty; windfall; Cockaigne
cuccétta *f* berth
cucchiàia *f* large spoon; ladle; trowel; bucket (*of power shovel*); **cucchiaia bucata** skimmer
cucchiaiàta *f* spoonful; tablespoonful
cucchiaino *m* teaspoon; teaspoonful; spoon (*lure*)
cuc·chiàio *m* (-chiài) spoon; spoonful; tablespoon; **cucchiaio da minestra** soupspoon
cucchiaióne *m* ladle
cùc·cia *f* (-ce) dog's bed; **a cuccia!** lie down!
cucciare §128 *intr* (ESSERE) & *ref* to lie down (*said of a dog*)
cucciolata *f* litter (*e.g., of puppies*)
cùcciolo *m* puppy; cub; (fig) greenhorn
cuc·co *m* (-chi) cuckoo; simpleton; darling (*child*)
cuccuru·cù *m* (-cù) cock-a-doodle-doo
cucina *f* kitchen; cuisine; kitchen range; **cucina componibile** kitchen with sectional cabinets; **cucina economica** kitchen range; **fare da cucina** to prepare a meal
cucinare *tr* to cook; (fig) to fix
cucinétta *f* kitchenette
cuciniè·re -ra *mf* cook
cucire §143 *tr* to sew; to stitch || *ref*— **cucirsi la bocca** to keep one's mouth shut
cucirino *m* sewing thread
cuci·tóre -trice *adj* sewing || *mf* sewing machine operator || *f* seamstress; sewing machine (*for bookbinding*); **cucitrice a grappe** stapler
cuci·to -ta *adj* sewn || *m* sewing; needlework
cucitura *f* seam; sewing; stitches
cu·cù *m* (-cù) cuckoo
cuculo or **cùculo** *m* cuckoo
cùffia *f* bonnet (*for baby*); coif; (rad) headset; (telp) headpiece; (theat) prompter's box
cugi·no -na *mf* cousin
cui *pron invar* whose; to which; whom; which; of whom; of which; **per cui** (coll) therefore
culatta *f* breech (*of a gun*)
culinà·rio -ria (-ri -rie) *adj* culinary || *f* gastronomy
culla *f* cradle
cullare *tr* to rock (*a baby*); (fig) to delude || *ref* to have delusions
culminante *adj* highest; culminating
culminare (cùlmino) *intr* to culminate
cùlmine *m* top, summit
culo *m* (vulg) behind; (slang) bottom (*of glass or bottle*): **culi di bicchiere** (coll) fake diamonds
cul·to -ta *adj* cultivated; learned (*e.g., word*) || *m* cult, worship
cul·tóre -trice *mf* devotee
cultura *f* culture; **cultura fisica** physical culture
culturale *adj* cultural
cumino *m* (bot) caraway seed; (bot) cumin
cumulati·vo -va *adj* cumulative

cùmulo *m* heap, pile; concurrence (*of penal sentences*); cumulus

cuna *f* cradle

cùneo *m* wedge; chock; (archit) voussoir

cunétta *f* ditch; gutter

cunìcolo *m* small tunnel; burrow

cuòcere §144a *tr* to cook; to bake (*bricks*); to burn, dry up; (fig) to stew || *intr* to cook; to burn; to dry up; (with *dat*) to grieve, to pain

cuò·co -ca *mf* (-chi -che) cook

cuòio *m* (cuòi) leather; avere il cuoio duro to have a tough hide; cuoio capelluto scalp || *m* (cuoia *fpl*) (archaic) leather; tirare le cuoia (slang) to croak, to kick the bucket

cuòre *m* heart; avere il cuore da coniglio to be chicken-hearted; avere il cuore da leone to be lion-hearted; cuori (cards) hearts; di cuore gladly; heartily; fare cuore a to encourage; stare a cuore to be important

cupidìgia *f* cupidity, greed, covetousness

Cupido *m* Cupid

cùpi·do -da *adj* greedy, covetous

cu·po -pa *adj* dark; deep (*color, voice*); sad, gloomy

cùpola *f* dome, cupola; crown (*of hat*)

cura *f* care; interest; cure; ministry; (poet) anxiety; a cura di edited by (*e.g., text*)

curare *tr* to take care of; to heed || *intr* to see to it || *ref* to take care of oneself; to care; to deign; curarsi di to care for

curatèla *f* (law) guardianship

curati·vo -va *adj* curative

cura·to -ta *adj* cured; healed || *m* curate

cura·tóre -trice *mf* curator; trustee; editor (*of critical edition*); receiver (*in bankruptcy*)

curculióne *m* (ent) weevil

cur·do -da *adj & mf* Kurd

cùria *f* curia; bar

curiale *adj* curia; legal

curiàle·sco -sca *adj* (-schi -sche) hairsplitting, legalistic

curiosare [s] (curióso) *intr* to pry around, snoop; to browse around

curiosi·tà [s] *f* (-tà) curiosity; whim; curio

curió·so -sa [s] *adj* curious; bizarre, quaint

curro *m* roller

cursóre *m* process server; court messenger; slide (*of slide ruler*)

curva *f* curve, bend; sweep; curva di livello contour line

curvare *tr* to curve, bend; curvare la fronte to bow down, yield || *intr* to curve (*said of a road*); to take a curve, negotiate a curve || *ref* to curve, bend; to bow; to become bent; to warp

curvatura *f* curving, bending; warp; stoop, curvature; camber

cur·vo -va *adj* bent, curved || *f* see curva

cuscinétto *m* small pillow; pad (*for ink*); buffer (*zone*); (mach) bearing; cuscinetto a rulli roller bearing; cuscinetto a sfere ball bearing

cuscino *m* pillow; cushion

cùspide *f* point (*e.g., of arrow*); (archit) steeple

custòde *adj* guardian (*angel*) || *m* custodian; janitor; warden; guard; (coll) policeman, cop

custòdia *f* safekeeping, custody; case (*e.g., of violin*); trust; (mach) housing

custodire §176 *tr* to keep; to protect, guard; to be in charge of (*prisoners*); to take care of; to cherish (*a memory*)

cutàne·o -a *adj* cutaneous

cute *f* (anat) skin

cuticagna *f* (joc) nape of the neck

cutìcola *f* epidermis; cuticle; dentine

cutireazióne *f* skin test (*for allergic reactions*)

cutréttola *f* (orn) wagtail

D

D, d [di] *m & f* fourth letter of the Italian alphabet

da *prep* from; to; at; on; through; between; since; with; by, e.g., è stato arrestato dalla polizia he was arrested by the police; worth, e.g., un libro da mille lire a book worth a thousand lire; worthy of, e.g., azione da gentiluomo action worthy of a gentleman; at the house, office, shop, etc., of, e.g., dal pittore at the house of the painter; da Giovanni at John's; dall'avvocato at the lawyer's office; d'altro lato on the other hand; d'ora in poi from now on

dabbasso *adv* downstairs; down below

dabbenàggine *f* simplicity, foolishness

dabbène *adj invar* honest, upright, e.g., un uomo dabbene an honest man;

simple, foolish, e.g., un dabben uomo a Simple Simon

daccanto *adv* near, nearby

daccapo *adv* again, all over again; andar daccapo to begin a new paragraph; daccapo a piedi from top to bottom

dacché *conj* since

dado *m* cube; pedestal (*of column*); (mach) nut; (mach) die (*to cut threads*); dadi dice; giocare ai dadi to shoot craps; il dado è tratto the die is cast

daffare *m* things to do; bustle; darsi daffare to bustle, bustle about

da·ga *f* (-ghe) dagger

dagli §4 || *interj*—dagli al ladro! stop thief!; e dagli! cut it out!

dài §4

dài·no -na *mf* fallow deer ‖ *m* fallow deer; buckskin

dal §4

dàlia *f* dahlia

dalla §4

dallato *adv* aside; sideways

dalle §4

dalli *interj*—**dalli al ladro!** stop thief!; **e dalli!** cut it out!

dallo §4

dàlma·ta *adj* & *mf* (**-ti -te**) Dalmatian

Dalmàzia, la Dalmatia

daltòni·co -ca *adj* (**-ci -che**) color-blind

daltonismo *m* color blindness

dama *f* lady; dancing partner; checkers; **andare a dama** (checkers) to be crowned; **dama di compagnia** companion; **dama di corte** lady-in-waiting

damare *tr* (checkers) to crown

damascare §197 *tr* to damask

damaschinare *tr* to damascene

dama·sco *m* (**-schi**) damask ‖ **Damasco** *f* Damascus

damerino *m* fop, dandy

damigèlla *f* (lit) damsel; (orn) demoiselle; **damigella d'onore** bridesmaid

damigiana *f* demijohn

danaro *m* var of **denaro**

danaró·so -sa [*s*] *adj* wealthy, rich

dande *fpl* leading strings

danése [*s*] *adj* Danish ‖ *mf* Dane ‖ *m* Danish (*language*); **Great Dane**

Danimarca, la Denmark

dannare *tr* to damn; to bedevil ‖ *ref* to be damned; to fret

danna·to -ta *adj* damned; wicked; terrible (*e.g., fear*) ‖ *m* damned soul

dannazióne *f* damnation

danneggiare §290 (**dannéggio**) *tr* to damage; to injure, impair

danneggia·to -ta *adj* damaged; injured, impaired ‖ *mf* victim

danno *m* damage; injury; (ins) loss; **chiedere i danni** to ask for indemnification; **far danni a** to damage; **rifare i danni a** to indemnify; **tuo danno** so much the worse for you

dannó·so -sa [*s*] *adj* damaging, harmful

dante *m*—**pelle di dante** buckskin

danté·sco -sca *adj* (**-schi -sche**) Dantean, Dantesque

danti·sta *mf* (**-sti -ste**) Dante scholar

Danùbio *m* Danube

danza *f* dance; dancing

danzare *tr* & *intr* to dance

danza·tóre -trice *mf* dancer

dappertutto *adv* everywhere

dappiè *adv*—**dappiè di** at the foot of

dappiù *adv*—**dappiù di** more than

dappòco *adj invar* worthless

dappói *adv* (obs) afterwards, after

dapprèsso *adv* near, nearby, close

dapprima *adv* first, in the first place

dapprincipio *adv* first, in the beginning; over again

dardeggiare §290 (**dardéggio**) *tr* to hurl darts at; to beat down on; to look daggers at ‖ *intr* to hurl darts; to beat down

dardo *m* dart, arrow; tip (*of blowtorch*)

da·re *m* (**-re**) (com) debit; **dare e avere**

debit and credit ‖ §144b *tr* to give; to set (*fire*); to hand over; to lay down (*one's life*); to render (*e.g., unto Caesar*); to give away (*a bride*); to take (*an examination*); to tender (*one's resignation*); to say (*good night*); to shed (*tears*); **dare acqua a** to water; **dare alla luce** to give birth to; to bring out (*e.g., a book*); **dare aria a** to air; **dare . . . anni a qlcu** to think that s.o. is . . . years old; **dare a ridire** to give rise to complaint; **dare da intendere** to lead to believe; **dare fastidio a** to bother, annoy; **dare fondo a** to use up; **dare gli otto giorni a** to dismiss, fire; **dare il benvenuto a** to welcome; **dare il via a** to start (*e.g., a race*); **dare la colpa a** to declare guilty; to put the blame on; **dare la mano a** to shake hands with; **dare l'assalto a** to assault; **dare luogo a** to give rise to; **dare noia a** to bother; **dare per certo a** to assure; **dare ragione a** to agree with; **dare torto a** to disagree with; **dare via** to give away ‖ *intr* to burst; to begin; to beat down (*said of the sun*); **dare a** to verge on; to face, overlook; **dare addosso a** to attack, persecute; **dare ai** or **sui nervi di** to irritate, irk; **dare alla testa a** to go to one's head, e.g., **il vino gli dà alla testa** wine goes to his head; **dare contro a** to disagree with; **dare del ladro a** to call (s.o.) a thief; **dare del Lei a** to address formally; **dare del tu a** to address familiarly; **dare di volta il cervello a** to go raving mad, e.g., **gli ha dato di volta il cervello** he went raving mad; **dare giù** to abate; **dare in** to hit; **dare in affitto** to rent, lease; **dare nell'occhio** to attract attention; to hit the eye; **dare nel segno** to hit the target ‖ *ref* to put on, e.g., **darsi la cipria** to put powder on; **darsela a gambe** to take to one's heels; **darsela per intesa** to become convinced; to take for granted; **darsele** to strike one another; **darsi a** to give oneself over to; **darsi delle arie** to put on airs; **darsi il vanto di** to boast of; **darsi un bacio** to kiss one another; **darsi la mano** to shake hands; **darsi la morte** to commit suicide; **darsi pace** to resign oneself; **darsi pensiero** to worry; **darsi per malato** to declare oneself ill; to fall ill; **darsi per vinto** to give in, submit; **può darsi** it's possible, maybe; **si dà il caso** it happens

dàrsena *f* dock; basin

data *f* date; deal (*of cards*); **a . . . data** (com) . . . days hence, on or before . . . days; **di fresca data** new (*e.g., friend*); **di vecchia data** old (*e.g., friend*)

datare *tr* to date ‖ *intr*—**a datare da** beginning with

datà·rio *m* (**-ri**) date stamp

dati·vo -va *adj* & *m* dative

da·to -ta *adj* inclined, bent; addicted; given; appointed (*date*); **dato e non concesso** assumed for the sake of argument; **dato che** since || *m* datum || *f* see **data**

da·tó·re -trice *mf* giver, donor; **datore di lavoro** employer; **datore di sangue** blood donor; **datori di lavoro** management

dàttero *m* date; (zool) date shell

dattilografare (dattilògrafo) *tr* to typewrite, type

dattilografia *f* typewriting

dattilògra·fo -fa *mf* typist

dattiloscopia *f* examination of fingerprints

dattiloscrit·to -ta *adj* typewritten || *m* typescript

dattórno *adv* near, nearby; **darsi dattorno** to strive; **stare dattorno a** to cling to; **togliersi dattorno qlcu** to get rid of s.o.

davanti *adj invar* fore, front || **davan·ti** *m* (**-ti**) front, face || *adv* ahead, in front; **davanti a** in front of; **levarsi davanti a qlcu** to get out of someone's way; **passare davanti a** to pass, outstrip

davanzale *m* window sill

davanzo *adv* more than enough

davvéro *adv* indeed; **dire davvero** to speak in earnest

daziare §287 *tr* to levy a duty on

dà·zio *m* (**-zi**) duty, custom; custom office

dèa *f* goddess

debellare (debèllo) *tr* (lit) to crush

debilitare (debìlito) *tr* to debilitate

debilitazióne *f* debilitation

débi·to -ta *adj* due || *m* debit; debt; **debito pubblico** national debt

debi·tóre -trice *mf* debtor

débole *adj* weak; faint; gentle (*sex*); **debole di mente** feeble-minded || *m* weakness, weak point; weakness, foible; weakling

debolézza *f* weakness, debility

debordare (debórdo) *intr* (ESSERE & AVERE) to overflow

debòscia *f* debauchery

deboscia·to -ta *adj* debauched || *mf* debauchee

debuttante *adj* beginning || *mf* beginner || *f* debutante

debuttare *intr* to come out, make one's debut; (theat) to perform for the first time; (theat) to open

debutto *m* debut; (theat) opening night, opening

dècade *f* ten; period of ten days; (mil) ten days' pay

decadènte *adj & m* decadent

decadènza *f* decadence; lapse (*of insurance policy*); (law) forfeiture

decadére §121 *intr* (ESSERE) to decline; to lose one's standing; (ins) to lapse; **decadere da** (law) to forfeit

decadiménto *m* decadence; (law) forfeiture

decadu·to -ta *adj* fallen upon hard times

decaffeinizzare [ddzz] *tr* to decaffeinate

decalcificatóre *m* water softener

decalcomanìa *f* decalcomania

decàlo·go *m* (**-ghi**) decalogue

decampare *intr* to decamp; **decampare da** to abandon (*a plan*)

decano *m* dean

decantare *tr* to praise, extol; to decant; (lit) to purify || *intr* to undergo decantation

decapàggio *m* (metallurgy) pickling

decapitare (decàpito) *tr* to behead, decapitate

decapitazióne *f* beheading

decappottàbile *adj & f* (aut) convertible

decèdere §123 *intr* (ESSERE) to die; to decease

decelerare (decèlero) *tr & intr* to decelerate

decennale *adj & m* decennial

decènne *adj & mf* ten-year-old

decèn·nio *m* (**-ni**) decade

decènte *adj* decent; proper

decentralizzare [ddzz] *tr* to decentralize

decentrare (decèntro) *tr* to decentralize

decènza *f* decency; propriety

decèsso *m* decease, demise

decidere §145 *tr* to decide; to persuade || *intr & ref* to decide; **deciditi!** make up your mind!

decifràbile *adj* decipherable

decifrare *tr* to decipher, decode; (fig) to puzzle out (*e.g., somebody's intentions*); (mus) to sight-read

dècima *f* tithe

decimale *adj & m* decimal

decimare (dècimo) *tr* to decimate

decìmetro *m* decimeter; **doppio decimetro** ruler

dèci·mo -ma *adj, m & pron* tenth || *f* see **decima**

decisionale *adj* decision-making

decisióne *f* decision

decisì·vo -va *adj* decisive, conclusive

deci·so -sa *adj* determined, resolute; appointed (*time*)

declamare *tr* to declaim || *intr* to declaim; to inveigh

declamazióne *f* declamation

declaratò·rio -ria *adj* (**-ri -rie**) declarative

declinare *tr* to decline; to declare, show; (gram) to decline; (lit) to bend || *intr* to set (*said, e.g., of a star*); to slope; to diminish

declinazióne *f* declination; (gram) declension

declino *m* decline

declì·vio *m* (**-vi**) declivity, slope

decollàg·gio *m* (**-gi**) take-off; lift-off

decollare (decòllo) *tr* to decapitate || *intr* (aer) to take off; (rok) to lift off

decòllo *m* take-off; lift-off

decolorante *adj* bleaching || *m* bleach

decompórre §218 *tr, intr & ref* to decompose

decomposizióne *f* decomposition

decompressióne *f* decompression

decongelare (decongèlo) *tr* to thaw; (com) to unfreeze

decontaminare (decontàmino) *tr* to decontaminate

decorare (decòro) *tr* to decorate

decoratì·vo -va *adj* decorative

decora·tóre -trice *mf* decorator

decorazióne f decoration
decòro m decorum, propriety; decor; dignity; decoration
decoró·so -sa [s] adj fitting, decorous, proper; dignified
decorrènza f beginning, effective date; lapse
decórrere §139 intr (ESSERE) to elapse; to begin; (lit) to run; **a decorrere da** effective, beginning with
decòr·so -sa adj past || m period, span; course; development; **nel decorso di** in the course of
decòt·to -ta adj (com) insolvent || m decoction
decozióne f (com) insolvency
decrèpi·to -ta adj decrepit
decréscere §142 intr (ESSERE) to decrease
decretare (**decréto**) tr to decree
decréto m decree; **decreto legge** decree law
decùbito m recumbency
decuplicare §197 (**decùplico**) tr to multiply tenfold
dècu·plo -pla adj tenfold || m tenfold part
decurtare tr to diminish, decrease
decurtazióne f decrease
dèda·lo -la adj (lit) ingenious || m maze, labyrinth
dèdi·ca f (-che) dedication; inscription (in a book)
dedicare §197 (**dèdico**) tr to dedicate; to inscribe (a book) || ref to devote oneself
dèdi·to -ta adj devoted; addicted
dedizióne f devotion; (obs) surrender
dedurre §102 tr to deduce; to deduct; to derive; (hist) to found (a colony)
deduzióne f deduction
defalcàbile adj deductible
defalcare §197 tr to deduct, withhold
defal·co m (-chi) deduction, withholding
defecare §197 (**defèco**) tr (chem) to purify || intr to defecate
defenestrare (**defenèstro**) tr to throw out of the window; (fig) to fire; (pol) to unseat
defenestrazióne f defenestration; (fig) firing, dismissal
deferènte adj deferential; (anat) deferent
deferènza f deference
deferire §176 tr to submit; (law) to commit; **deferire il giuramento a qlcu** to put s.o. under oath || intr to defer
defezionare (**defezióno**) intr to desert, defect
defezióne f defection
deficiènte adj deficient, lacking || mf idiot
deficiènza f deficiency; idiocy
dèfi·cit m (-cit) deficit
deficità·rio -ria adj (-ri -rie) lacking; deficit (e.g., budget)
defilare tr to defilade || ref to protect oneself
denfinìbile adj definable
definire §176 tr to define; to settle (an argument)

definiti·vo -va adj definitive; **in definitiva** after all
defini·to -ta adj definite
definizióne f definition; settlement (of an argument)
deflagrare intr to burst into flame; (fig) to burst out
deflazionare (**deflazióno**) tr (com) to deflate
deflazióne f deflation
deflèttere §177 intr to deflect
deflettóre m (aut) vent window; (mach) baffle
deflorare (**deflòro**) tr to deflower
defluire §176 intr (ESSERE) to flow down; (fig) to pour out
deflusso m flow; outflow, outpour; ebbtide
deformare (**defórmo**) tr to deform; to cripple; to alter (a word)
defórme adj deformed, crippled
deformi·tà f (-tà) deformity
defraudare (**defràudo**) tr to defraud, bilk
defun·to -ta adj dead; deceased; defunct; late || mf dead person, deceased || m deceased; **i defunti** the deceased
degenerare (**degènero**) intr (ESSERE & AVERE) to degenerate; to worsen
degenera·to -ta adj degenerate, perverted || mf degenerate, pervert
degenerazióne f degeneracy, degeneration
degènere adj degenerate
degènte adj bedridden; hospitalized || mf patient; inpatient
degènza f confinement; hospitalization
dégli §4
deglutire §176 tr to swallow
degnare (**dégno**) tr to honor || ref to deign, condescend
degnazióne f condescension
dé·gno -gna adj worthy; **degno di nota** noteworthy
degradante adj degrading
degradare tr to degrade; to downgrade; (mil) to break || ref to become degraded
degradazióne f degradation
degustare tr to taste
degustazióne f tasting
dèh interj oh!
déi §4
deiezióne f excrement; (geol) detritus
deificare §197 (**deìfico**) tr to deify
dei·tà f (-tà) deity
dél §4
dela·tóre -trice mf informer
delazióne f informing; (law) administration of an oath
dèle·ga f (-ghe) proxy, power of attorney
delegare §209 (**dèlego**) tr to delegate
delega·to -ta adj delegated || m delegate; (eccl) legate
delegazióne f delegation
deletè·rio -ria adj (-ri -rie) deleterious
delfino m dolphin; (hist) dauphin
delibare tr to relish; to touch on; to ratify (a foreign decree)

delibazióne *f* ratification (*of a foreign decree*)

deliberare (delìbero) *tr* to deliberate; to decide; to award (*at auction*) || *intr* to deliberate

delibera·to -ta *adj* deliberate; resolved

deliberazióne *f* deliberation; decision

delicatézza *f* delicacy; gentleness; tactfulness; luxury

delica·to -ta *adj* delicate; gentle; tactful

delimitare (delìmito) *tr* to delimit

delineare (delìneo) *tr* to outline, sketch || *ref* to take shape; to appear

delinquènte *m* criminal

delinquènza *f* delinquency; delinquenza minorile juvenile delinquency

delinquere §146 *intr* to commit a crime

delì·quio *m* (-qui) fainting spell, swoon; cadere in deliquio to faint

delirare *intr* to be delirious; to rave; (lit) to stray

delì·rio *m* (-ri) delirium; frenzy; andare in delirio to go wild; cadere in delirio to become delirious

delitto *m* crime

delittuó·so -sa [s] *adj* criminal

delizia *f* delight; (hort) Delicious (*variety of apple*)

deliziare §287 *tr & ref* to delight

delizió·so -sa [s] *adj* delicious; delightful

délla §4

délle §4

déllo §4

dèl·ta *m* (-ta) delta

delucidare (delùcido) *tr* to elucidate; to remove the sheen from

delucidazióne *f* elucidation; removal of sheen

delùdere §105 *tr* to disappoint; to deceive; to foil

delusióne *f* disappointment; deception

delu·so -sa *adj* disappointed; deceived

demagnetizzare [ddzz] *tr* to demagnetize

demagogìa *f* demagogy

demagò·go *m* (-ghi) demagogue

demandare *tr* (law) to commit

demà·nio *m* (-ni) state land, state property

demarcare §197 *tr* to demarcate

demarcazióne *f* demarcation

demènte *adj* demented, crazy; idiotic || *mf* insane person; idiot

demènza *f* insanity, madness; idiocy

demèrito *m* demerit

demilitarizzare [ddzz] *tr* to demilitarize

democrà·ti·co -ca (-ci -che) *adj* democratic || *mf* democrat

democrazìa *f* democracy || Democrazia Cristiana Christian Democratic Party

democristia·no -na *adj* Christian Democratic || *mf* Christian Democrat

demogrà·fi·co -ca (-ci -che) demographic

demolire §176 *tr* to demolish

demoli·tóre -trice *adj* wrecking; destructive || *mf* wrecker

demolizióne *f* demolition

dèmone *m* demon

demonia·co -ca *adj* (-ci -che) fiendish; demoniacal

demò·nio *m* (-ni) demon; avere il demonio addosso to be full of the devil

demoralizzare [ddzz] *tr* to demoralize || *ref* to become demoralized

demoralizza·to -ta [ddzz] *adj* demoralized, dejected

denaro *m* money; denier (*of nylon thread*); avere il denaro contato to be short of money; denari suit of Neapolitan cards corresponding to diamonds

denatura·to -ta *adj* denatured

denegare §209 (dènego *or* denégo) *tr* to deny

denigrare *tr* to denigrate; to backbite

denominare (denòmino) *tr* to call, designate

denomina·tóre -trice *adj* designating || *m* denominator

denominazióne *f* denomination; designation

denotare (denòto) *tr* to denote

densi·tà *f* (-tà) density

dèn·so -sa *adj* dense, thick

dentale *adj & f* dental

dentare (dènto) *tr* to notch, scallop || *intr* to teethe

dentaruòlo *m* teething ring

denta·to -ta *adj* toothed

dentatura *f* set of teeth; teeth (*of gear*)

dènte *m* tooth; peak (*of mountain*); pang (*of jealousy*); fluke (*of anchor*); prong (*of fork*); battere i denti to shiver; dente canino canine tooth; dente del giudizio wisdom tooth; dente di latte baby tooth; dente di leone (bot) dandelion; mettere i denti to teethe

dentellare (dentèllo) *tr* to notch, scallop; to perforate (*stamps*)

dentellatura *f* notch; perforation (*of postage stamps*); (archit) denticulation

dentèllo *m* notch, scallop; lace; (archit) dentil

dentièra *f* denture, plate; cog

dentifrì·cio -cia (-ci -cie) *adj* tooth || *m* dentifrice

denti·sta *mf* (-sti -ste) dentist

dentizióne *f* teething

déntro *adv* inside, in; dentro di inside of; within; essere dentro (coll) to be behind bars; in dentro inward || *prep* inside of

denuclearizzare [ddzz] *tr* to denuclearize

denudare *tr* to denude; to strip; (lit) to unveil

denunciare §128 *tr* var of denunziare

denùnzia *f* denunciation; announcement; report

denunziare §287 *tr* to denounce; to accuse; to announce; to report

denutrì·to -ta *adj* undernourished

denutrizióne *f* undernourishment

deodorante *adj & m* deodorant

deodorare (deodóro) *tr* to deodorize

depauperare (depàupero) *tr* to impoverish

depennare (depénno) *tr* to strike out, expunge

deperìbile *adj* perishable

deperiménto m deterioration; decline
deperire §176 intr (ESSERE) to deteriorate; to perish; to decay
depilatò·rio -ria adj & m (-ri -rie) depilatory
deplorare (deplòro) tr to deplore; to reproach
deplorévole adj deplorable; reproachable
depolarizzare [ddzz] tr to depolarize
depórre §218 tr to lay; to lay down (crown, arms); to depose (e.g., a king); to take off (clothes); to give up (hope); to renounce; **deporre l'abito talare** to doff the cassock
deportare (depòrto) tr to deport
deporta·to -ta adj deported || mf deportee
deportazióne f deportation
depositare (depòsito) tr to deposit; to register, check || intr to settle (said, e.g., of sand)
deposità·rio -ria (-ri -rie) adj deposit || mf depositary
depòsito m deposit; checking (e.g., of a suitcase); registration; heap (e.g., of refuse); warehouse; morgue; receiving ward; (mil) depot; **deposito bagagli** baggage room
deposizióne f deposition; Descent from the Cross
deprava·to -ta adj depraved
depravazióne f depravation
deprecare §197 (deprèco) tr to deprecate
depredare (deprèdo) tr to plunder
depredazióne f depredation
depressióne f depression
près·so -sa adj depressed
deprezzaménto m depreciation
deprezzare (deprèzzo) tr to depreciate; to underestimate || intr (ESSERE) to depreciate
deprimènte adj depressing
deprimere §131 tr to humble, discourage; to depress
depurare tr to purify
deputare (dèputo) tr to deputize, delegate
deputa·to -ta mf deputy, delegate; representative
deputazióne f deputation, delegation
deragliaménto m derailment
deragliare §280 intr to be derailed, to run off the track
derapàg·gio m (-gi) skidding
derapare intr to skid
derelit·to -ta adj & mf derelict
derelizióne f dereliction
dereta·no -na adj & m posterior
deridere §231 tr to deride, mock
derisióne f derision, ridicule
derisò·rio -ria adj (-ri -rie) derisory, derisive
deriva f (aer) vertical stabilizer; (aer, naut) leeway; (naut) drift; **alla deriva** adrift
derivare tr to derive; to branch off (e.g., a canal) || intr (ESSERE) to be derived, arise; to drift
deriva·to -ta adj derivative || m derivative (word) || f (math) derivative

derivazióne f derivation; (elec) shunt; (telp) extension
dermatòlo·go m (-gi) dermatologist
dermòide f imitation leather
dèro·ga f (-ghe) exception; **in deroga a** deviating from
derogare §209 (dèrogo) intr to transgress; **derogare a** to deviate from
derrata f foodstuff; **derrate** foodstuff, produce
derubare tr to rob
dèr·vis m (-vis) or **dervì·scio** m (-sci)** dervish
desalazióne [s] f desalinization
desalificare [s] §197 (desalìfico) tr to desalt
dé·sco m (-schi) dinner table; meal
descritti·vo -va adj descriptive
descrivere §250 tr to describe
descrizióne f description
desegregazióne [s] f desegregation
desensibilizzare [s] [ddzz] tr to desensitize
desèrti·co -ca adj (-ci -che) desert, wild
desèr·to -ta adj deserted; **andare deserto** to be unattended || m desert
desideràbile [s] adj desirable
desiderare (desìdero) [s] tr to desire; **farsi desiderare** to make oneself scarce; to be dilatory
desidè·rio [s] m (-ri) desire; craving; lust; **lasciar desiderio di sé** to be greatly missed
desideró·so -sa [s] adj desirous
designare [s] tr to designate
designazióne [s] f designation
desinare m dinner || intr to dine
desinènza f (gram) ending
desì·o m (-i) (lit) desire
desistere [s] §114 intr to desist
desolante adj distressing
desolare (dèsolo) tr to distress; (lit) to devastate
desola·to -ta adj desolate; distressed
desolazióne f desolation; distress
dèspo·ta m (-ti) despot
despòti·co -ca adj (-ci -che) var of dispotico
despotismo m var of dispotismo
des·sèrt m (-sèrt) dessert
destare (désto) tr to awaken; to stir up || ref to wake up
destinare tr to destine; to assign; to address
destinatà·rio -ria mf (-ri -rie) consignee; addressee
destinazióne f destination; assignment
destino m destiny; (com) destination
destituire §176 tr to demote; to dismiss; to deprive
destituzióne f demotion; dismissal
dé·sto -sta adj awake; (fig) wide-awake
dèstra f right, right hand
destreggiare §290 (destréggio) intr to maneuver || ref to manage shrewdly
destrézza f skill, dexterity
destrière or **destrièro** m (lit) steed
dè·stro -stra adj right; skillful || f see **destra**
destror·so -sa adj clockwise; right-hand; (bot) dextrorse
destròsio m dextrose

desùmere [s] §116 *tr* to obtain; to infer
detecti·ve *m* (-ve) detective
detèc·tor *m* (-tor) (rad) detector
detenére §271 *tr* to hold; to detain
deten·tóre -trice *mf* holder; receiver (*of stolen goods*)
detenu·to -ta *mf* prisoner
detenzióne *f* illegal possession; detention
detergènte *adj & m* detergent
detèrgere §164 (*pp* **detèrso**) *tr* to cleanse; to wipe
deterioràbile *adj* perishable
deteriorare (**deterióro**) *tr* to spoil || *intr* (ESSERE) & *ref* to deteriorate, spoil
determinare (**detèrmino**) *tr* to determine; to fix; to decide; to cause || *ref* to decide; to happen
determinatézza *f* determination; precision
determinati·vo -va *adj* (gram) definite
determina·to -ta *adj* given; resolved, determined
determinazióne *f* determination
deterrènte *adj & m* deterrent
detersi·vo -va *adj* cleansing || *m* cleanser; detergent
detestàbile *adj* detestable
detestare (**detèsto**) *tr* to detest
detettóre *m* detector; **detettore di bugie** lie detector
detonare (**detòno**) *intr* to explode, detonate
detonatóre *m* blasting cap, detonator
detonazióne *f* detonation; report
detrarre §273 *tr* to take away; (lit) to detract
detrat·tóre -trice *mf* detractor
detrazióne *f* detraction; deduction
detriménto *m* detriment
detrito *m* debris; detritus; (fig) outcast, outlaw
detronizzare [ddzz] *tr* to dethrone
détta *f*—**a detta di** according to
dettagliante *m* retailer
dettagliare §280 *tr* to tell in detail; to itemize; to retail || *intr*—**pregasi dettagliare** please send detailed information
dettà·glio *m* (-gli) detail; retail
dettame *m* (lit) law, norm
dettare (**détto**) *tr* to dictate; (lit) to compose, write; **dettar legge** to impose one's will
dettato *m* dictation; (lit) style
dettatura *f* dictation
dét·to -ta *adj* called, named; **detto (e) fatto** no sooner said than done || *m* saying || *f* see **detta**
deturpare *tr* to disfigure, mar
deturpazióne *f* disfigurement, disfiguration
devalutazióne *f* devaluation
devastare *tr* to devastate, lay waste; (fig) to disfigure
devasta·tóre -trice *adj* devastating || *m* devastator
devastazióne *f* devastation
deviaménto *m* switching; derailment; (fig) straying
deviare §119 *tr* to turn aside; to lead astray; (rr) to switch; (rr) to derail

|| *intr* to deviate; to wander; to go astray; (rr) to run off the track
deviatóre *m* (rr) switchman; (elec) two-way switch
deviazióne *f* deviation; detour; curvature (*of the spine*); (phys) declination; (phys) deflection; (rr) switching
deviazionismo *m* deviationism
deviazioni·sta *mf* (-sti -ste) deviationist
devoluzióne *f* transfer
devòlvere §147 *tr* to transfer || *intr & ref* (lit) to roll down
devò·to -ta *adj* devoted; devout, pious || *m* devout person; worshiper
devozióne *f* devotion
di §4 *prep of*; in, e.g., **la più bella della famiglia** the prettiest one in the family; (*with definite article*) some, e.g., **mi occorrono dei fiammiferi** I need some matches; than, e.g., **più veloce del baleno** faster than lightning; from, e.g., **è di Milano** he is from Milan; off, e.g., **smontare di sella** to get off the saddle; about, e.g., **discutere di politica** to talk about politics; with, e.g., **ornare di fiori** to adorn with flowers; made of, e.g., **una casa di mattoni** a house made of bricks; by, e.g., **di notte** by night; for, e.g., **amor di patria** love for one's country; worth, e.g., **casa di dieci milioni** house worth ten million; in the amount of, e.g., **multa di mille lire** fine in the amount of one thousand lire; son of, e.g., **Carlo Giovannini di Filippo** Carlo Giovannini son of Philip; daughter of, e.g., **Anna Ponti di Antonio** Anna Ponti daughter of Anthony; **di corsa** running; **di gran lunga** greatly; by far; **di . . . in** from . . . to; **di là da** beyond; **di nascosto** stealthily; **di qua da** on this side of; **di quando in quando** from time to time; **di tre metri** three meters long or wide or high
dì *m* (dì) day; **a dì** (e.g., **ventisei**) this (e.g., twenty-sixth) day; **conciare per il dì delle feste** (coll) to beat up
diabète *m* diabetes
diabèti·co -ca *adj & mf* (-ci -che) diabetic
diaboli·co -ca *adj* (-ci -che) diabolic(al)
diàcono *m* deacon
diadè·ma *m* (-mi) diadem (*of king*); tiara (*of lady*)
diàfa·no -na *adj* diaphanous
diafonìa *f* (telp) cross talk
diafram·ma *m* (-mi) diaphragm; (fig) partition
diàgno·si *f* (-si) diagnosis
diagnosticare §197 (**diagnòstico**) *tr* to diagnose
diagonale *adj & f* diagonal
diagram·ma *m* (-mi) diagram; chart
diagrammare *tr* to diagram
dialettale *adj* dialectal
dialètti·co -ca (-ci -che) *adj* dialectic(al) || *m* dialectician || *f* dialectic; (philos) dialectics
dialètto *m* dialect
dialettòfo·no -na *adj* dialect-speaking || *m* dialect-speaking person

dialogare §209 (diàlogo) *intr* to carry on a dialogue

dialoga·to -ta *adj* written in the form of a dialogue || *m* dialogue

diàlo·go *m* (-ghi) dialogue

diamante *m* diamond; **diamante tagliavetro** glass cutter

diametrale *adj* diametric(al)

diàmetro *m* diameter

diàmine *interj* good heavens!; the devil!; sure!

diana *f* (mil) reveille || **Diana** *f* Diana

dianzi *adv* (lit) a short while ago

diàpa·son *m* (-son) (mus) pitch; (mus) tuning fork

diapositiva *f* (phot) slide, transparency

dià·rio -ria (-ri -rie) *adj* daily || *m* diary; journal; **diario scolastico** homework book || *f* per diem

diarrèa *f* diarrhea

diascò·pio *m* (-pi) slide projector

diaspro *m* jasper

diàstole *f* diastole

diatermìa *f* diathermy

diatriba *f* diatribe

diavolàc·cio *m* (-ci) devil; **buon diavolaccio** good fellow

diavolerìa *f* deviltry; devilment; evil plot

diavolè·rio *m* (-rì) hubbub, uproar

diavoléto *m* hubbub, uproar

diavolétto *m* little devil, imp

diàvolo *m* devil; **avere il diavolo in corpo** to be nervous; **avere un diavolo per capello** to be in a horrible mood; **buon diavolo** good fellow; **essere come il diavolo e l'acqua santa** to be at opposite poles; **fare il diavolo a quattro** to make a racket; to try very hard

dibàttere *tr* to debate || *ref* to struggle; to writhe

dibattimento *m* debate; (law) pleading, trial

dibàttito *m* debate

dicastèro *m* department, ministry

dicèmbre *m* December

dicerìa *f* rumor, gossip

dichiarare *tr* to declare, state; to find (*guilty*); to proclaim; to nominate, name || *ref* to declare oneself to be; to declare one's love; to plead (*e.g., guilty*)

dichiarazióne *f* declaration; avowal (*of love*); return (*of income tax*); **dichiarazioni** representations

diciannòve *adj & pron* nineteen; **le diciannove** seven P.M. || *m* nineteen; nineteenth (*in dates*)

diciannovèsi·mo -ma *adj, m & pron* nineteenth

diciassètte *adj & pron* seventeen; **le diciassette** five P.M. || *m* seventeen; seventeenth (*in dates*)

diciassettèsi·mo -ma *adj, m & pron* seventeenth

diciottèsi·mo -ma *adj, m & pron* eighteenth

diciòtto *adj & pron* eighteen; **le diciotto** six P.M. || *m* eighteen; eighteenth (*in dates*)

dici·tóre -trice *mf* reciter

dicitura *f* caption, legend; (lit) wording, language

dicotomìa *f* dichotomy

didascalìa *f* note, notice; caption; legend (*e.g., on coin*); (mov) subtitle

didascàli·co -ca *adj* (-ci -che) didactic

didàtti·co -ca (-ci -che) *adj* didactic; elementary school (*director, principal*) || *f* didactics

didéntro *m* (coll) inside

didiètro *m* behind; back (*of house*) || *adv* behind

dièci *adj & pron* ten; **le dieci** ten o'clock || *m* ten; tenth (*in dates*)

diecimila *adj, m & pron* ten thousand

diecina *f* about ten

dière·si *f* (-si) dieresis

diè·sis *m* (-sis) (mus) sharp

dièta *f* diet; **dieta idrica** fluid diet

dietèti·co -ca (-ci -che) *adj* dietetic || *f* dietetics

dieti·sta *mf* (-sti -ste) dietitian

diètro *adj invar* back, rear || *m* back, rear || *adv* back, behind; **dal di dietro** from behind; **di dietro** hind (*legs*); back (*side*); behind, back (*e.g., of cupboard*) || *prep* behind; beyond; after; upon; **dietro a** behind; beyond; after; according to; **dietro consegna** on delivery; **dietro domanda** upon application; **dietro versamento** upon payment; **essere dietro a** to be in the process of

dietrofrónt *m* (mil) about face

difatti *adv* indeed

difèndere §148 *tr* to defend, protect || *ref* to protect oneself; (coll) to get along

difensi·vo -va *adj & f* defensive

difen·sóre -sóra or **difenditrice** *adj* defense || *mf* defender

difésa [s] *f* defense; bulwark; protection; **legittima difesa** self-defense; **pigliare le difese di** to defend, back up; **venire in difesa di** to go to the defense of

difettare (difètto) *intr* to be lacking; to be defective; **difettare di** to lack

difetti·vo -va *adj* defective

difètto *m* lack; blemish; fault; defect; **essere in difetto** to be at fault; **far difetto a** to lack, e.g., **gli fa difetto il denaro** he lacks money

difettó·so -sa [s] *adj* defective

diffamare *tr* to defame, slander

diffama·tóre -trice *mf* defamer, slanderer

diffamazióne *f* defamation, slander

differènte *adj* different

differènza *f* difference; spread; variance; **a differenza di** unlike; **c'è una bella differenza** it's a horse of another color

differenziale *adj & m* differential

differenziare §287 (differènzio) *tr* to differentiate

differiménto *m* deferment

differire §176 *tr* to postpone, defer || *intr* to be different; to differ

difficile *adj* hard, difficult; awkward (*situation*); hard-to-please; unlikely

‖ *mf* hard-to-please person ‖ **m— fare il difficile** to be hard to please; **qui sta il difficile!** here's the trouble!

difficol·tà *f* (-**tà**) difficulty; defect; obstacle; objection

difficoltó·so -**sa** [s] *adj* difficult, troublesome; fastidious

diffida *f* notice; warning

diffidare *tr* to give notice to; to warn ‖ *intr* to mistrust

diffidènte *adj* distrustful

diffidènza *f* mistrust

diffóndere §178 *tr* to spread; to circulate; to broadcast ‖ *ref* to spread; to dwell at length

diffórme *adj* unlike; (obs) deformed

diffrazióne *f* diffraction

diffusióne *f* spreading; circulation (*of a newspaper*); diffusion; (rad) broadcast

diffu·so -**sa** *adj* diffuse; widespread

diffusóre *m* diffuser (*to soften light*); baffle (*of loudspeaker*); (mach) choke

difilato *adv* forthwith, right away

difrónte *adj invar* in front

difterite *f* diphtheria

di·ga *f* (-**ghe**) dike; dam

digerènte *adj* alimentary (*canal*), digestive (*tube*)

digeribile *adj* digestible

digerire §176 *tr* to digest; to tolerate, stand

digestióne *f* digestion

digesti·vo -**va** *adj* digestive

digèsto *m* digest

digitale *adj* digital ‖ *f* (bot) digitalis

digitalina *f* (pharm) digitalin

digiunare *intr* to fast

digiu·no -**na** *adj* without food; deprived; **digiuno di cognizioni** ignorant; **tenere digiuno** to keep in ignorance ‖ *m* fast; **a digiuno** on an empty stomach; **fare digiuno** to fast

digni·tà *f* (-**tà**) dignity; **dignità** *fpl* dignitaries

dignitó·so -**sa** [s] *adj* dignified

digradare *tr* to shade (*colors*) ‖ *intr* to slope; to fade

digredire §176 *intr* to digress

digressióne *f* digression

digrignare *tr* to show (*one's or its teeth*); to grit (*one's teeth*)

digrossare (**digròsso**) *tr* to rough-hew; to whittle down; (fig) to refine ‖ *ref* to become refined

diguazzare *tr* to beat (*a liquid*) ‖ *intr* to wallow; to splash

dilagare §209 *intr* to flood, to overflow; to spread abroad

dilaniare §287 *tr* to tear to pieces ‖ *ref* to slander one another

dilapidare (**dilàpido**) *tr* to squander

dilatare *tr* to expand; to dilate ‖ *ref* to expand; to spread

dilatazióne *f* expansion; dilation

dilatò·rio -**ria** *adj* (-**ri** -**rie**) delaying; dilatory

dilavare *tr* to wash away, erode

dilava·to -**ta** *adj* dull, flat; wan

dilazionare (**dilazióno**) *tr* to delay, put off; (com) to extend

dilazióne *f* delay; (com) extension

dileggiare §290 (**diléggio**) *tr* to mock

dilég·gio *m* (-**gi**) mockery, scoffing; **mettere in dileggio** to scoff at

dileguare (**diléguo**) *tr* to scatter ‖ *intr* (ESSERE) to disappear, vanish; to melt

dilèm·ma *m* (-**mi**) dilemma

dilettante *mf* amateur; dilettante

dilettanté·sco -**sca** *adj* (-**schi** -**sche**) amateurish

dilettare (**dilètto**) *tr* to delight ‖ *intr* to delight; **dilettarsi a** + *inf* to delight in + *ger*; **dilettarsi di** to pursue as a hobby, e.g., **si diletta di pittura** he pursues painting as a hobby

dilettévole *adj* delectable, delightful

dilèt·to -**ta** *adj* beloved ‖ *m* loved one; pleasure; hobby

diligènte *adj* diligent

diligènza *f* diligence; stagecoach

dilucidare (**dilùcido**) *tr* to elucidate

diluire §176 *tr* to dilute

dilungare §209 *tr* (archaic) to stretch ‖ *ref* to expatiate; to be ahead by several lengths (*said of a race horse*)

dilungo *m*—**a un dilungo** more or less

diluviare §287 *tr* to devour ‖ *intr* (ESSERE & AVERE) to rain (said, e.g., of bullets) ‖ *impers* (ESSERE)—**diluvia** it is pouring

dilù·vio *m* (-**vi**) deluge, flood; **diluvio universale** Flood

dimagrante *adj* reducing

dimagrare *tr* to thin down ‖ *intr* (ESSERE) to become thin; to lose weight; to become exhausted (*said of land*); (fig) to become meager

dimagrire §176 *intr* (ESSERE) to become thin; to lose weight, reduce

dimanda *f* var of **domanda**

dimane *adv* (coll) tomorrow

dimani *m* & *adv* var of **domani**

dimenare (**diméno**) *tr* to wag (*the tail*); to beat (*eggs*); to wave (*one's arms*); to stir up (*a question*) ‖ *ref* to toss; to busy oneself

dimensióne *f* dimension; (fig) nature

dimenticanza *f* oversight, neglect; **andare in dimenticanza** to be forgotten

dimenticare §197 (**diméntico**) *tr* to forget; to forgive ‖ *ref* to forget; **dimenticarsi di** to forget; to neglect

dimenticatóio *m*—**mettere nel dimenticatoio** (coll) to forget

diménti·co -**ca** *adj* (-**chi** -**che**) forgetful; neglectful

dimés·so -**sa** *adj* humble, modest (*demeanor*); low (*voice*); shabby (*clothes*)

dimestichézza *f* familiarity

diméttere §198 *tr* to dismiss; to release ‖ *ref* to resign

dimezzare [ddzz] (**dimèzzo**) *tr* to halve

diminuire §176 *tr* to lessen, reduce; to lower (*prices*) ‖ *intr* (ESSERE) to diminish

diminuti·vo -**va** *adj* & *m* diminutive

diminuzióne *f* diminution

dimissionare (**dimissióno**) *tr* to dismiss, discharge ‖ *ref* to resign

dimissionà·rio -**ria** *adj* (-**ri** -**rie**) resigning, outgoing

dimissióne *f* resignation; **dare le dimis-**
   sióni to resign

dimól·to -ta *adj & m* (coll) much ||
   dimolto *adv* (coll) much

dimòra *f* stay; residence; (lit) delay;
   mettere a dimora to install; to plant
   (*trees*); **senza dimora** (lit) without
   delay; **senza fissa dimora** vagrant

dimorare (dimòre) *intr* to stay; to reside; (lit) to delay

dimostràbile *adj* demonstrable

dimostrante *m* demonstrator

dimostrare (dimóstro) *tr* to demonstrate; to register (*e.g., anger*); **dimo-**
   strare trent'anni to look thirty || *intr*
   to demonstrate || *ref* to prove oneself
   to be

dimostrati·vo -va *adj* demonstrative;
   (mil) diverting

dimostra·tóre -trice *mf* demonstrator

dimostrazióne *f* demonstration

dinàmi·co -ca (-ci -che) *adj* dynamic ||
   f dynamics

dinamismo *m* dynamism

dinamite *f* dynamite

dìna·mo *f* (-mo) generator, dynamo

dinanzi *adj invar* front, e.g., **la porta**
   dinanzi. the front door; preceding,
   e.g., **il mese dinanzi** the preceding
   month || *adv* ahead; beforehand; (lit)
   before; **dinanzi a** before, in front of

dina·sta *m* (-sti) dynast

dinastìa *f* dynasty

dinàsti·co -ca *adj* (-ci -che) dynastic

dindo *m* (coll) turkey

dindòn *m* ding-dong || *interj* ding-dong!

diniè·go *m* (-ghi) denial

dinoccola·to -ta *adj* gangling; clumsy
   (*gait*)

dinosàuro [s] *m* dinosaur

dintórno *m*—**dintorni** surroundings,
   neighborhood || *adv* around; **dintorno**
   a around

dì·o -a *adj* (-i -e) (poet) godly || *m*
   (**dèi**) god; **gli dei the gods** || **Dio** *m*
   God; **che Dio la manda** cats and
   dogs (*said of rain*); **come Dio volle**
   at long last; **come Dio vuole** botched
   (*piece of work*); **Dio ci scampi!** God
   forbid!; **Dio santo!** good heavens!;
   grazie a Dio God willing; thank God;
   voglia Dio God grant

diòce·si *f* (-si) diocese

diòdo *m* (electron) diode

diomedèa *f* (orn) albatross

diottrìa *f* (opt) diopter

dipanare *tr* to unravel, unwind

dipartiménto *m* department

dipartire §176 *tr* (archaic) to divide ||
   intr (**diparto**) (ESSERE) & *ref* (lit) to
   depart

dipartita *f* (lit) departure; (lit) demise

dipendènte *adj* dependent || *mf* em-
   ployee

dipendènza *f* dependence; employment;
   annex; (com) branch; **in dipendenza**
   di as a consequence of

dipèndere §150 *intr* (ESSERE) to depend;
   dipendere da to depend on

dipìngere §126 *tr* to paint; **dipingere a**
   olio to paint in oils; **dipingere a tem-**
   pera to distemper || *ref* to paint one-

self; to put make-up on; to appear,
   e.g., **gli si dipinse in volto la paura**
   fear appeared on his face

dipìn·to -ta *adj* painted || *m* painting,
   picture

diplomare (diplòmo) *tr* to grant a
   degree to; to graduate || *ref* to receive
   a degree; to graduate

diplomàti·co -ca (-ci -che) *adj* diplo-
   matic; true, faithful (*copy*) || *m*
   diplomat || *f* diplomatics

diploma·to -ta *adj* graduated || *mf*
   graduate || *m* alumnus || *f* alumna

diplomazìa *f* diplomacy

dipòi *adv* after, thereafter

diportare (dipòrto) *ref* (lit) to behave;
   (obs) to have a good time

dipòrto *m* recreation; (obs) sport; **an-**
   dare a diporto to go on an outing;
   to go for a walk

diprèsso *adv*—**a un dipresso** about, approximately

diradare *tr* to thin out (*vegetation*); to
   disperse; to space out (*one's visits*)
   || *intr* (ESSERE) & *ref* to diminish; to
   disperse

diramare *tr* to prune; to circulate
   (*notices*); to issue (*a communiqué*) ||
   ref to branch out; to spread

diramazióne *f* branch; ramification;
   issuance

dire *m* talk; **per sentito dire** by hearsay; **stando al dire** according to his
   words || §151 *tr & intr* to say; to tell;
   to call (*e.g., s.o. a genius*); to talk;
   detto (e) fatto no sooner said than
   done; **dica pure!** go ahead!; speak
   up!; **dire bene di** to speak well of;
   dire di no to say no; **dire di sì** to say
   yes; **direi quasi** I dare say; **dire la**
   sua to have one's say; **dire male di**
   to speak ill of; **dirla grossa** to make
   a blunder; to tell a tall tale; **dirlo**
   chiaro e tondo to speak bluntly;
   dirne un sacco e una sporta a to
   pour insults upon; **è tutto dire** that's
   all; **non c'è che dire** it's a fact; **non**
   fo per dire I do not want to boast;
   per così dire so to speak; **per meglio**
   dire rather; **trovarci a dire** to find
   fault with; **trovare da dire con** to
   have words with; **voler ben dire** to be
   sure; **voler dire** to mean || *ref*—**dir-**
   sela con to connive with; **si dice** it is
   said

dirètro *m & adv* (archaic) behind, back

direttìssima *f* (rr) high-speed line; **per**
   direttìssima straight up (*in mountain*
   climbing)

direttìssimo *m* express train

diretti·vo -va *adj* managerial || *m*
   board of directors || *f* directive;
   direction; guideline

dirèt·to -ta *adj* direct; **diretto a** ad-
   dressed to; directed at; bound for ||
   m through train

diret·tóre -trice *mf* manager; principal
   || *m* director; **direttore di macchina**
   (naut, nav) chief engineer; **direttore**
   di tiro (nav) gunnery officer; **direttore**
   di un giornale editor; **direttore d'or-**

chestra orchestra leader; **direttore responsabile** publisher; **direttore tecnico** (sports) manager ‖ *f* see **direttrice**

direttò·rio -ria (-ri -rie) adj directorial ‖ *m* directory

direttrice adj fem directing; guiding; front (wheels) ‖ *f* directress; line of action

direzionale adj directional; managerial

direzióne *f* direction; management; run (of events)

dirigènte adj leading; managerial ‖ *m* employer; boss; leader; executive

dirìgere §152 tr to direct; to turn; to lead ‖ ref to address oneself; **dirigersi verso** to head for

dirigìbile adj & *m* dirigible

dirimpètto adj invar & adv opposite; **dirimpetto a** opposite to; in comparison with

dirìt·to -ta adj straight; right; unswerving; (coll) smart ‖ *m* law; obverse, face (of coin); fee, dues; (fin) right; **a buon diritto** rightly so; **di diritto** by law; **diritti d'autore** copyright; **diritti di segreteria** registration fee; **diritti doganali** customs duty; **diritti speciali di prelievo** (econ) special drawing rights; **diritto canonico** canon law; **diritto consuetudinario** common law; **diritto internazionale** international law; **in diritto** according to law ‖ *f* right, right hand ‖ **diritto** adv straight; **tirare diritto** to go straight ahead

dirittura *f* direction; uprightness; (sports) straightaway, home stretch

dirizzóne *m* blunder

diroccare §197 (diròcco) tr to knock down ‖ intr (ESSERE) (archaic) to fall down

dirocca·to -ta adj dilapidated, rickety

dirompènte adj fragmentation (bomb)

dirottaménto *m* hijacking; skyjacking (of an airplane)

dirottare (diròtto) tr to detour (traffic); to hijack (e.g., a ship); to skyjack (an airplane) ‖ intr to change course

dirottatóre *m* hijacker; skyjacker (of a plane)

diròt·to -ta adj copious, heavy (rain, tears); (lit) craggy; **a dirotto** cats and dogs (said of rain)

dirozzare [ddzz] (diròzzo) tr to roughhew; to refine ‖ ref to become polished

dirugginire §176 tr to take the rust off; to limber up; to gnash (one's teeth); to clear (one's mind)

dirupa·to -ta adj rocky, craggy

dirupo *m* rock; crag, cliff

disabbigliare §280 tr & ref to undress, disrobe

disabita·to -ta adj uninhabited

disabituare (disabituo) tr to disaccustom ‖ ref to become unaccustomed

disaccenta·to -ta adj unaccented

disaccòrdo *m* disagreement

disadat·to -ta adj unfit

disadór·no -na adj unadorned, bare

disaffezionare (disaffezióno) tr to alien-

ate the affection of; to estrange ‖ ref to become estranged

disaffezióne *f* dislike

disagévole adj troublesome, uncomfortable

disagiare §290 tr to trouble, inconvenience

disagia·to -ta adj uncomfortable; needy

disà·gio *m* (-gi) discomfort; need

disalberare (disàlbero) tr to dismast

disambienta·to -ta adj bewildered, strange

disàmina *f* examination, scrutiny

disaminare (disàmino) tr to scrutinize; to weigh

disamorare (disamóro) tr to alienate the affection of; to estrange ‖ ref to become estranged

disancorare (disàncoro) intr to weigh anchor; to leave port ‖ ref to weigh anchor; (fig) to free oneself

disanimare (disànimo) tr to dishearten

disappetènza *f* loss of appetite

disapprovare (disappròvo) tr to disapprove

disapprovazióne *f* disapproval

disappunto *m* disappointment

disarcionare (disarrióno) tr to unsaddle, unhorse; to kick out

disarmare tr to disarm; to dismantle (a scaffold); to ship (oars); (naut) to unrig ‖ ref to disarm; (fig) to give up

disarma·to -ta adj unarmed, defenseless

disarmo *m* disarmament; dismantling; unrigging

disarmonìa *f* discord; contrast

disarmòni·co -ca adj (-ci -che) discordant

disarticolare (disartìcolo) tr to limber up; to disjoint ‖ ref to become dislocated

disassociare §128 (disassòcio) tr to dissociate

disastra·to -ta adj damaged ‖ *mf* victim

disastro *m* disaster, calamity; wreck

disastró·so -sa [s] adj disastrous

disattèn·to -ta adj inattentive; careless

disattenzióne *f* inattention; carelessness

disattivare tr to deactivate (e.g., a mine)

disavanzo *m* (com) deficit

disavvedu·to -ta adj heedless

disavventura *f* misfortune

disavvertènza *f* inadvertence

disavvezzare (disavvézzo) tr to break (s.o.) of a habit ‖ ref—**disavvezzarsi da** to give up or lose the habit of

disavvéz·zo -za adj unaccustomed

disbórso *m* disbursement, outlay

disboscare §197 (disbòsco) tr to deforest

disbrigare §209 tr to dispatch ‖ ref to extricate oneself

disbri·go *m* (-ghi) prompt execution, dispatch

discacciare §128 tr (lit) to chase away

discanto *m* (mus) harmonizing

discàpito *m* damage; **tornare a discapito di** to be detrimental to

discàri·ca *f* (-che) discharge (e.g., of pollutants); dumping (of refuse); unloading (of a ship)

discàri·co *m* (-chi) exculpation; a discarico di in defense of

discatóre *m* hockey player; discus thrower

discendènte *adj* descending; sloping; down (*train*) || *mf* descendant

discendènza *f* descent; pedigree

discéndere §245 *tr* to go down || *intr* (ESSERE & AVERE) to descend, go down; to slope; to fall (*said, e.g., of thermometer*); to get off; **discendere in picchiata** (aer) to nose-dive

discènte *mf* student, pupil

discépo·lo -la *mf* disciple

discèrnere §153 *tr* to discern

discerníbile *adj* discernible

discernimento *m* discernment

discésa [s] *f* descent; slope; drop

discettare (discètto) *tr* (lit) to discuss

dischiodare (dischiòdo) *tr* to take the nails out of

dischiùdere §125 *tr* to open; to reveal

discin·to -ta *adj* scantily dressed; untidy; in disarray

disciògliere §127 *tr* to dissolve, melt; (lit) to untie || *ref* to dissolve, melt

disciplina *f* discipline; whip, scourge

disciplinare *adj* disciplinary || *m* regulation || *tr* to discipline

disciplina·to -ta *adj* obedient

dì·sco *m* (-schi) disk; (phonograph) record; bob (*of pendulum*); (ice hockey) puck; (sports) discus; (rr) signal; (pharm) tablet; **disco combinatore** (telp) dial; **disco microsolco** microgroove record; **disco volante** flying saucer

discòfilo *m* record lover

discòide *m* (pharm) tablet, pill

dìsco·lo -la *adj* undisciplined, wild || *m* rogue, rascal

discolorare (discolóro) *tr* to discolor || *ref* to pale

discolorazióne *f* discoloration; paleness

discólpa *f* defense

discolpare (discólpo) *tr* to defend

disconnèttere §107 *tr* to disconnect

disconóscere §134 *tr* to ignore, to disregard; to be ungrateful for

discontinuare (discontìnuo) *tr* to perform sporadically || *intr* to lose continuity

discontì·nuo -nua *adj* uneven

disconvenire §282 *intr* (ESSERE) (lit) to disagree || *impers* (ESSERE) (lit) to be improper

discoprire §110 (discòpro) *tr* to discover

discordante *adj* discordant

discordare (discòrdo) *intr* (ESSERE) to disagree, differ

discòrde *adj* discordant; opposing

discòrdia *f* discord, dissension

discórrere §139 *intr* to talk, chat; (coll) to keep company; **discorrere del più e del meno** to make small talk; **e via discorrendo** and so forth

discórso *m* discourse; conversation; speech; **pochi discorsi!** (coll) cut it out!

discostare (discòsto) *tr* to remove || *ref* to withdraw; to differ

discò·sto -sta *adj* distant || **discosto** *adv* far

discotè·ca *f* (-che) record library; discotheque

discreditare (discrédito) *tr* to discredit

discrédito *m* discredit

discrepanza *f* discrepancy

discretaménte *adv* rather; fairly well

discré·to -ta *adj* discreet; fairly large; fair

discrezióne *f* discretion

discriminante *adj* discriminatory; extenuating || *m* (math) discriminant

discriminare (discrìmino) *tr* to discriminate; to extenuate

discriminazióne *f* discrimination

discussióne *f* discussion; argument

discus·so -sa *adj* controversial

discùtere §154 *tr* to discuss || *intr* to discuss; to argue

discutìbile *adj* moot, debatable

disdegnare (disdégno) *tr* to disdain, scorn || *ref* (obs) to be angry

disdégno *m* disdain, scorn

disdegnó·so -sa [s] *adj* disdainful

disdétta *f* ill luck; (law) notice

disdicévole *adj* unbecoming, unseemly

disdire §151 *tr* to retract; to belie; to cancel; to countermand; to terminate the contract of || *ref* to retract; disdire a to be unbecoming to

disdòro *m* shame; **tornare a disdoro di** to bring shame on

disegnare [s] (diségno) *tr* to draw; to sketch; to design; (obs) to elect

disegna·tóre -trice [s] *mf* cartoonist; designer || *m* draftsman

diségno [s] *m* drawing; sketch; outline; plan; design; **disegno animato** (mov) cartoon; **disegno di legge** (law) bill

disellare [s] (disèllo) *tr* var of **dissellare**

diserbante *adj* weed-killing || *m* weed-killer

diseredare (diserèdo) *tr* to disinherit

disereda·to -ta *adj* disinherited || **i diseredati** the underprivileged

disertare (disèrto) *tr* to desert; (lit) to lay waste || *intr* to desert

disertóre *m* deserter

diserzióne *f* desertion

disfaciménto *m* disintegration

disfare §173 *tr* to undo; to defeat; to melt; to unknit; to break up (*housekeeping*); **disfare il letto** to remove the bedclothes || *ref* to spoil (*said, e.g., of meat*); **disfarsi di** to get rid of

disfatta *f* defeat

disfattismo *m* defeatism

disfattì·sta *mf* (-sti -ste) defeatist

disfat·to -ta *adj* undone; defeated; melted; broken up; ravaged || *f* see **disfatta**

disfida *f* (lit) challenge

disfunzióne *f* malfunction

disgelare (disgèlo) *tr* & *intr* to thaw

disgèlo *m* thaw

disgiùngere §183 *tr* & *ref* to separate

disgiunti·vo -va *adj* disjunctive

disgràzia *f* disfavor; bad luck, misfortune; accident; **per disgrazia** unfortunately

disgrazia·to -ta *adj* unlucky; wretched
disgregaménto *m* disintegration
disgregare §209 **(disgrègo)** *tr & ref* to disintegrate
disgregazióne *f* disintegration
disguido *m* miscarriage, missending *(of a letter)*
disgustare *tr* to disgust, sicken || *ref* to become disgusted, sicken; to have a falling-out, to part company
disgusto *m* disgust, repugnance
disgustó·so -sa [s] *adj* disgusting
disidratare *tr* to dehydrate
disìlla·bo -ba *adj* disyllabic || *m* disyllable
disillùdere §105 *tr* to delude, deceive || *ref* to become disillusioned
disillusióne *f* disillusion
disimboscare §197 **(disimbòsco)** *tr* to put back in circulation
disimparare *tr* to unlearn, forget
disimpegnare (disimpégno) *tr* to release; to free, to open; to loosen; to redeem *(a pledge)*; to clear; to perform || *ref* to succeed
disimpégno *m* release; redemption; performance; disengagement; **di disimpegno** for every day *(e.g., a suit)*; main *(e.g., hallway)*
disimpiè·go *m* **(-ghi)** unemployment; (mil) withdrawal
disincagliare §280 *tr* to set afloat; (fig) to disentangle
disincantare *tr* disenchant
disinfestare (disinfèsto) *tr* to exterminate
disinfestazióne *f* extermination
disinfettante *adj & m* disinfectant
disinfettare (disinfètto) *tr* to disinfect
disingannare *tr* to disillusion || *ref* to become disillusioned
disinganno *m* disillusion
disinnescare §197 **(disinnésco)** *tr* to defuse
disinnestare (disinnèsto) *tr* to disconnect; to throw out, disengage
disinserire §176 *tr* (elec) to disconnect; (aut) to disengage
disintasare [s] *tr* to unclog
disintegrare (disìntegro) *tr & ref* to disintegrate
disintegrazióne *f* disintegration
disinteressare (disinterèsso) *tr* to make *(s.o.)* lose interest || *ref* to lose interest; to take no interest
disinteressa·to -ta *adj* selfless, unselfish
disinterèsse *m* disinterest; unselfishness
disintossicare §197 **(disintòssico)** *tr* to free of poison; (fig) to clean the air in || *ref* to shake the drug habit
disinvòl·to -ta *adj* free and easy; fresh, forward
disinvoltura *f* naturalness, ease of manners, offhandedness; freshness; impudence
disì·o *m* **(-i)** (poet) desire
disistima *f* scorn, low regard, disesteem
disistimare *tr* to scorn, hold in low regard
dislivèllo *m* difference of level; disparity
dislocaménto *m* transfer of troops; (naut) displacement

dislocare §197 **(dislòco)** *tr* to transfer *(troops)*; to post *(sentries)*; (naut) to displace
dislocazióne *f* (mil) transfer; (geog, naut, psychol) displacement
dismisura *f* excess; **a dismisura** excessively
disobbedire §176 *intr* var of **disubbidire**
disobbligare §209 **(disòbbligo)** *tr* to free from an obligation || *ref* to repay a favor
disoccupa·to -ta *adj* unemployed, jobless; idle; unoccupied || *m* unemployed person; **i disoccupati** the jobless
disoccupazióne *f* unemployment
disone·stà *f* **(-stà)** dishonesty; shamelessness
disonè·sto -sta *adj* dishonest; shameless; immoral
disonorante *adj* disgraceful
disonorare (disonóro) *tr* to dishonor, disgrace; to seduce
disonóre *m* dishonor, shame
disonorévole *adj* dishonorable; shameful
disoppilare (disòppilo) *tr* to clear of obstructions
disópra *adj invar* upper || *m* **(disópra)** upper part, top; **prendere il disopra** to have the upper hand || *adv* above; **al disopra di** above
disordinare (disórdino) *tr* to cancel, countermand; to confuse; to mess up || *intr* to indulge || *ref* to become disorganized
disordina·to -ta *adj* confused; messy; untidy; intemperate
disórdine *m* confusion; mess; disarray; disorder; intemperance
disorganizzare [ddzz] *tr* to disorganize; to disrupt
disorganizzazióne [ddzz] *f* disorganization, disorder; disruption
disorientaménto *m* disorientation; confusion, bewilderment
disorientare (disoriènto) *tr* to cause *(s.o.)* to lose his way; to confuse; to disorient || *ref* to be bewildered; to lose one's bearings
disorienta·to -ta *adj* disoriented; confused, bewildered; lost, astray
disormeggiare §290 **(disorméggio)** *tr* to unmoor
disossare (disòsso) *tr* to bone || *ref* (lit) to lose weight
disòtto [s] *adj invar* below || *m* **(disótto)** lower part, bottom || *adv* below; **al disotto di** below, underneath
disotturare *tr* to unclog
dispàc·cio *m* **(-ci)** dispatch; urgent letter; **dispaccio telegrafico** telegram
dispara·to -ta *adj* disparate
disparére *m* disagreement
dispari *adj invar* odd, uneven
dispari·tà *f* **(-tà)** disparity
dispàrte *adv*—**in disparte** apart, aside; **starsene in disparte** to keep aloof
dispèn·dio *m* **(-di)** expenditure; waste
dispendió·so -sa [s] *adj* expensive; wasteful

dispènsa f cupboard; pantry; distribution; number (of magazine); installment (of book); dispensation; (naut) storeroom; (coll) store

dispensare (dispènso) tr to exempt, free; to distribute || ref—**dispensarsi da** to get out of

dispensà·rio m (-ri) dispensary

dispensa·tóre -trice mf dispenser

dispensiè·re -ra mf dispenser || m steward

dispepsìa f dyspepsia

dispèpti·co -ca adj & mf (-ci -che) dyspeptic

disperare (dispèro) intr to despair; **fare disperare** to drive crazy || ref to despair

dispera·to -ta adj hopeless || m poor wretch; **come un disperato** desperately || f—**alla disperata** with all one's might

disperazióne f desperation, despair

dispèrdere §212 tr to scatter; to waste || ref to disperse; (fig) to waste one's energies

dispersióne f dispersion; loss; (elec) leakage

dispersività f tendency toward disorganization

dispersì·vo -va adj dispersive; disorganized

dispèr·so -sa adj scattered; lost; dispersed; missing in action

dispersóre m (elec) leakage conductor

dispètto m spite; (lit) haughtiness; **a dispetto di** in spite of; **far dispetto a** to provoke

dispettó·so -sa [s] adj pestiferous; spiteful, resentful

dispiacènte adj sorry; distressing

dispiacére m sorrow, displeasure || §214 intr (ESSERE) to be displeasing; to be sorry, e.g., **mi dispiace** I am sorry; (with dat) to displease; (with dat) to dislike, e.g., **le mie parole gli dispiacciono** he dislikes my words; **Le dispiace?** would you please?; **se non Le dispiace** if you don't mind

dispiegare §209 (dispiègo) tr to manifest; (lit) to unfurl || ref to spread out; to flow out

displù·vio m (-vi) divide, watershed; ridge (of roof)

disponìbile adj available; open-minded

disponibili·tà f (-tà) availability; inactive status; **disponibilità** fpl available funds

dispórre §218 tr to dispose; to prepare || intr to provide; to dispose; **disporre di** to have (available) || ref to get ready

dispositivo m gadget; device; (mil) deployment

disposizióne f arrangement; inclination, disposition; disposal; instruction; (law) provision

dispó·sto -sta adj arranged; disposed; provided; willing; **ben disposto** disposed || m (law) proviso

dispòti·co -ca adj (-ci -che) despotic

dispotìsmo m despotism

dispregiatì·vo -va adj disparaging; (gram) pejorative

disprè·gio m (-gi) contempt; disrepute

disprezzàbile adj contemptible; negligible

disprezzare (disprèzzo) tr to despise

disprèzzo m contempt, scorn

dìsputa f dispute; debate

disputàbile adj debatable

disputare (dìsputo) tr to contest; to discuss; to vie for (victory) || intr to dispute, debate; to vie || ref to vie for

disqualificare §197 (disqualìfico) tr to disqualify

disquisizióne f disquisition

dissacrare tr to desecrate

dissacrazióne f desecration

dissaldare tr to unsolder

dissanguare (dissànguo) tr to bleed || ref to bleed; to ruin oneself

dissangua·to -ta adj bled white; **morire dissanguato** to bleed to death

dissapóre m disagreement

disseccare §197 (dissécco) tr to dry || ref to dry; to dry up

disselciare §128 (dissélcio) tr to remove the cobblestones from

dissellare (dissèllo) tr to unsaddle

disseminare (dissèmino) tr to disseminate; to scatter

dissenna·to -ta adj foolish, unwise; crazy, mad

dissensióne f dissension

dissènso m dissent; disagreement

dissenterìa f dysentery

dissentire (dissènto) intr to dissent

dissenziènte adj dissenting || mf dissenter

disseppellire §176 tr to exhume

dissertare (dissèrto) intr to discourse

dissertazióne f dissertation

disservì·zio m (-zi) poor service

dissestare (dissèsto) tr to unsettle; to disarrange

dissesta·to -ta adj financially embarrassed; mentally deranged

dissèsto m financial embarrassment; mental derangement

dissetante adj thirst-quenching

dissetare (disséto) tr to quench the thirst of || ref to quench one's thirst

dissezióne f dissection

dissidènte adj & m dissident

dissidènza f dissent

dissì·dio m (-di) dissent; disagreement

dissigillare tr to unseal || ref (lit) to melt

dissìmile adj unlike

dissimulare (dissìmulo) tr to dissimulate, disguise || intr to dissimulate

dissimulazióne f dissimulation

dissipare (dissìpo) tr to dissipate; to squander; to clear up (a doubt) || ref to dissipate

dissipa·to -ta adj & mf profligate

dissipa·tóre -trice mf squanderer

dissipazióne f dissipation

dissociare §128 (dissòcio) tr to dissociate, disassociate || ref to dissociate or disassociate oneself

dissociazióne f dissociation

dissodare (dissòdo) *tr* to cultivate

dissolutézza *f* profligacy

dissolu·to -ta *adj* & *mf* profligate

dissoluzióne *f* dissolution

dissolvènza *f* (mov) fade-out; **dissolvenza incrociata** (mov) lap dissolve

dissòlvere §155 *tr* to dissolve; to clear up (*a doubt*); (obs) to untie || *ref* to dissolve

dissomiglianza *f* dissimilarity

dissonanza *f* dissonance

dissotterrare (dissottèrro) *tr* to exhume; to unearth

dissuadére §213 *tr* to dissuade

dissuè·to -ta *adj* (lit) unaccustomed

dissuggellare (dissuggèllo) *tr* to unseal

distaccaménto *m* (mil) detachment

distaccare §197 *tr* to detach; to remove; to transfer; to outdistance || *ref* to stand out; to withdraw, become separated

distacca·to -ta *adj* detached; branch (*office*)

distac·co *m* (**-chi**) detachment; separation; (sports) spread (*in points*)

distante *adj* distant; aloof; different || *adv* far away

distanza *f* distance; **mantenere le distanze** to keep one's distance; **tenere a distanza** to keep at arm's length

distanziare §287 *tr* to outdistance

distare *intr* to be distant

distèndere §270 *tr* to stretch; to spread; to unfurl; to relax; to knock down; to write || *ref* to stretch; to spread out; to relax

distensióne *f* relaxation; relaxation of tension

disté·so -sa [s] *adj* stretched out; full (*voice*); lank (*hair*) || *m*—**per disteso** in full || *f* expanse; row; **a distesa** with full voice; at full peal

distillare *tr* to distill; to exude; to pour; to trickle || *intr* (ESSERE) to trickle || *ref*—**distillarsi il cervello** to rack one's brain

distilla·to -ta *adj* distilled || *m* distillate

distilla·tóre -trice *mf* distiller || *m* still

distillerìa *f* distillery

distinguìbile *adj* distinguishable

distìnguere §156 *tr* to distinguish; to make out; to tell (*one thing from another*); to divide

distinta *f* note, list; **distinta di versamento** deposit slip

distintaménte *adj* distinctly; sincerely yours

distinti·vo -va *adj* distinctive || *m* emblem, insignia, badge

distìn·to -ta *adj* distinct; distinguished; sincere (*greetings*); reserved (*seat*); **Distinto Signor . . .** (*on an envelope*) **Mr. . . .** || *f* see **distinta**

distinzióne *f* distinction

distògliere §127 *tr* to dissuade; to deter; to distract; to turn (*one's eyes*) away

distòrcere §272 *tr* to distort; to twist || *ref* to become distorted; to sprain (*e.g., one's ankle*)

distorsióne *f* distortion; sprain; **distorsione acustica** wow

distrarre §273 *tr* to distract; to divert; to amuse; to pull (*a muscle*) || *ref* to become distracted; to relax

distrat·to -ta *adj* absent-minded

distrazióne *f* absent-mindedness; distraction; diversion (*of money*); pull (*of muscle*)

distrét·to -ta *adj* (obs) close; (obs) hard-pressed || *m* district; precinct (*e.g., of police*); circuit (*of court*); ward (*in city*); **distretto militare** draft board; **distretto postale** postal zone || *f* stricture; necessity

distrettuale *adj* district

distribuire §176 *tr* to distribute; to pass out; to allot; to deploy (*troops*); (theat) to cast (*roles*); (mov) to release; (mil) to issue (*e.g., clothing*)

distribu·tóre -trice *adj* distributing, dispensing || *mf* distributor, dispenser || *m* distributor; **distributore automatico** vending machine; **distributore di benzina** gasoline pump

distribuzióne *f* distribution; issue; delivery; (aut) timing gears; (mov) release; (fig) dispensation

districare §197 *tr* to unravel || *ref* to extricate oneself

distrofia *f* dystrophy

distrùggere §266 *tr* to destroy; to ruin

distrutti·vo -va *adj* destructive

distruzióne *f* destruction

disturbare *tr* to disturb, bother; **disturbo?** may I come in? || *ref* to bother; to go out of one's way

disturba·tóre -trice *mf* disturber; **disturbatore della quiete pubblica** disturber of the peace

disturbo *m* trouble, bother; disturbance; (rad) interference; **disturbi atmosferici** static, atmospherics; **togliere il disturbo a** to take leave of

disubbidiènte *adj* disobedient

disubbidiènza *f* disobedience

disubbidire §176 *intr* to disobey; (with *dat*) to disobey

disuguaglianza *f* inequality; disparity

disuguale *adj* uneven; unequal

disuma·no -na *adj* inhumane; unbearable

disunióne *f* disunion

disunire §176 *tr* to disunite

disusa·to -ta *adj* obsolete, out of use

disuso *m* disuse; **in disuso** obsolete

disùtile *adj* useless; burdensome || *m* worthless fellow; (com) loss

disvì·o *m* (**-i**) miscarriage, missending (*of a letter*)

ditale *m* thimble; fingerstall

ditata *f* poke with a finger; finger mark; dab (*with a finger*)

dito *m* (**dita** *fpl*) finger; toe; **avere le dita d'oro** to have a magic touch; **dita della mano** fingers; **dita del piede** toes; **legarsela al dito** to never forget || *m* (**diti**) finger, e.g., **dito indice** index finger; **dito anulare** ring finger; **dito medio** middle finger; **dito mignolo** little finger; **dito pollice** thumb

ditta *f* firm, house; office

dittàfono *m* intercom; dictaphone

dittatóre *m* dictator

dittatura *f* dictatorship

dittongare §209 (dittòngo) *tr* to diphthongize

dittòn·go *m* (-ghi) diphthong

diurèti·co -ca *adj* & *m* (-ci -che) diuretic

diur·no -na *adj* daily; daytime ǁ *f* (theat) matinée

diutur·no -na *adj* long-lasting

diva *f* diva; (mov) star; (lit) goddess

divagare §209 *tr* to amuse; to distract ǁ *intr* to digress ǁ *ref* to relax

divagazióne *f* distraction; digression; relaxation

divampare *intr* (ESSERE & AVERE) to blaze, flare

divano *m* divan; couch, sofa

divaricare §197 (divàrico) *tr* to spread (one's legs); to open up (an incision)

divà·rio *m* (-ri) difference

divèllere §267 *tr* to eradicate, uproot

diveni·re *m* (-re) (philos) becoming ǁ §282 *intr* (ESSERE) (lit) to become; (archaic) to come

diventare (divènto) *intr* (ESSERE) to become; **diventare di tutti i colori** to blush; to be embarrassed; **diventare grande** to grow up; **diventare matto** to go mad; **diventare pallido** to turn pale; **diventare piccolo** to grow smaller; **diventare rosso** to blush

divèr·bio *m* (-bi) argument; **venire a diverbio** to have an altercation

divergènza *f* divergency

divèrgere §157 *intr* to diverge

diversificare §197 (diversìfico) *tr* to diversify ǁ *ref* to be diversified; to differ

diversióne *f* diversion

diversi·tà *f* (-tà) diversity

diversi·vo -va *adj* diverting ǁ *m* diversion

diver·so -sa *adj* different; **diver·si -se** several, e.g., **diverse ragazze** several girls ǁ **diver·si -se** *pron* several

divertènte *adj* diverting, amusing

divertiménto *m* amusement, pastime; fun; (mus) divertimento

divertire (divèrto) *tr* to amuse, entertain; (lit) to turn aside ǁ *ref* to have fun, enjoy oneself; (lit) to go away

diverti·to -ta *adj* amused; amusing

divétta *f* starlet

divezzare (divèzzo) *tr* to wean ǁ *ref*— **divezzarsi da** to get out of the habit of

dividèndo *m* dividend

dividère §158 *tr* to divide; to partition; to split; to share in (e.g., s.o.'s grief) ǁ *ref* to be divided; to become separated; **dividersi fra** to divide one's time between

divièto *m* prohibition; **divieto d'affissione** post no bills; **divieto di parcheggio** no parking; **divieto di sosta** no stopping; **divieto di svolta** no turns; **divieto di transito** no thoroughfare

divinare *tr* (lit) to divine

divina·tóre -trice *adj* divining ǁ *m* diviner

divinazióne *f* divination

divincolare (divìncolo) *tr* & *ref* to wriggle

divini·tà *f* (-tà) divinity

divinizzare [ddzz] *tr* to deify

divi·no -na *adj* divine

divisa *f* uniform; motto; part (in hair); **divise** foreign exchange

divisare *tr* (lit) to intend

divisìbile *adj* divisible

divisióne *f* division; partition; (sports) league

divisionismo *m* (painting) divisionism; (pol) separatism

divismo *m* (mov) star system; (mov) adulation of stars

divisóre *m* (math) divisor

divisò·rio -ria (-ri -rie) *adj* dividing ǁ *m* partition; (math) divisor

di·vo -va *adj* (lit) divine ǁ *m* (theat, mov) star; (lit) god ǁ *f* see **diva**

divolgare §209 (divólgo) *tr* & *ref* var of **divulgare**

divorare (divóro) *tr* to devour; to gulp down; to consume; **divorare la via** to burn up the road

divora·tóre -trice *adj* consuming ǁ *mf* consumer (e.g., of food, books)

divorziare §287 (divòrzio) *intr* to become divorced; **divorziare da** to divorce

divorzia·to -ta *adj* divorced ǁ *m* divorcé ǁ *f* divorcée

divòr·zio *m* (-zi) divorce

divulgare §209 *tr* to divulge; to publicize; to popularize ǁ *ref* to spread; to become popular

divulga·tóre -trice *adj* popularizing ǁ *mf* popularizer; **divulgatore di calunnie** scandalmonger; **divulgatore di notizie** telltale

divulgazióne *f* publicizing; popularization

divulsióne *f* (surg) dilation

dizionà·rio *m* (-ri) dictionary; **dizionario geografico** gazetteer

dizióne *f* diction; reading (of poetry)

do [do] *m* (do) (mus) do; (mus) C

dóc·cia *f* (-ce) shower; gutter (on roof); spout; (fig) dash of cold water; **fare la doccia** to take a shower

docciare §128 (dóccio) *tr*, *intr* (ESSERE) & *ref* to shower

doccióne *m* trough, gutter; gargoyle

docènte *adj* teaching ǁ *m* teacher; **libero docente** certified university teacher

docènza *f* teaching post; **libera docenza** lectureship

dòcile *adj* docile; tame; amenable (person); workable (material)

documentare (documénto) *tr* to document ǁ *ref* to gather information

documentà·rio -ria *adj* & *m* (-ri -rie) documentary

documénto *m* document; paper; **documenti di bordo** ship's papers

dodecafonìa *f* twelve-tone system

dodecasilla·bo -ba *adj* twelve-syllable, dodecasyllable

dodicèsi·mo -ma *adj*, *m* & *pron* twelfth

dódici *adj* & *pron* twelve; **le dodici**

twelve o'clock || *m* twelve; twelfth (*in dates*)

dó·ga *f* (-ghe) stave

dogale *adj* (hist) of the doge

dogana *f* duty; customs; custom house

doganière *m* customs officer

dòge *m* (hist) doge

dò·glia *f* (-glie) (lit) pain, pang; **doglie** labor pains

dò·glio *m* (-gli) barrel; (lit) large jar

doglió·so **-sa** [*s*] *adj* (lit) sorrowful

dòg·ma *m* (-mi) dogma

dogmàti·co **-ca** (-ci -che) *adj* dogmatic || *mf* dogmatist

dogmatismo *m* dogmatism

dólce *adj* sweet; soft; gentle; fresh (*water*); mild (*climate*); delicate (*feet*); **dolce far niente** sweet idleness || *m* sweet; sweet dish; **dolci** candy

dolceama·ro **-ra** *adj* bittersweet

dolcézza *f* sweetness; mildness; gentleness

dolcia·stro **-stra** *adj* sweetish

dolcière *m* candy maker; pastry baker

dolcificare §197 (**dolcìfico**) *tr* to sweeten

dolciume *m* sweet; **dolciumi** candy

dolènte *adj* aching; sorrowful; sorry

dolére §159 *intr* (ESSERE & AVERE) to ache, e.g., **gli dolgono i denti** his teeth ache || *ref* to grieve || *impers* (ESSERE) to be sorry, e.g., **mi duole che Lei non possa venire** I am sorry that you won't be able to come

dolicònice *m* bobolink

dòllaro *m* dollar

dòlo *m* fraud, malice, guile

dolomite *f* dolomite || **Dolomìti** *fpl* Dolomites

dolorante *adj* aching

dolorare (**dolóro**) *intr* (lit) to ache

dolóre *m* ache; sorrow; contrition

doloró·so **-sa** [*s*] *adj* painful; sorrowful

dolό·so **-sa** [*s*] *adj* intentional, fraudulent; (law) felonious

domàbile *adj* tamable

domanda *f* question; application; appeal; (econ) demand; **domanda suggestiva** (com) leading question; **fare una domanda** to ask a question

domandare *tr* to ask; to ask for; **domandare la parola** to ask for the floor || *intr* to inquire || *ref* to wonder; (lit) to be called

doma·ni *m* (-ni) tomorrow || *adv* tomorrow; **a domani** until tomorrow; **domani a otto** a week from tomorrow; **domani l'altro** the day after tomorrow

domare (**dómo**) *tr* to tame; to extinguish; to quell

doma·tóre **-trice** *mf* tamer

domattina *adv* tomorrow morning

doméni·ca *f* (-che) Sunday

domenicale *adj* Sunday (*e.g., rest*)

domenica·no **-na** *adj* & *m* Dominican (*e.g., order*)

domesticare §197 (**domèstico**) *tr* to domesticate

domèsti·co **-ca** (-ci -che) *adj* family; household; familiar; domestic || *mf* domestic, servant || *f* maid; **alla**

domestica family style; **domestica a mezzo servizio** part-time domestic

domiciliare *adj* house || §287 *tr* (com) to draw || *ref* to dwell; to settle

domicìlia·to **-ta** *adj* residing

domicì·lio *m* (-li) domicile, residence; principal office; **domicilio coatto** imprisonment; **franco domicilio** free delivery

dominare (**dòmino**) *tr* to dominate, rule; to master; to overlook || *intr* to prevail; to reign || *ref* to control oneself

domina·tóre **-trice** *mf* ruler

dominazióne *f* domination; rule

domineddìo *m invar* (coll) the Lord God

dominica·no **-na** *adj* & *mf* Dominican (*e.g., Republic*)

domì·nio *m* (-ni) dominion; domain

dòmi·no *m* (-no) domino (*cloak*); dominoes (*game*)

dòn *m* (used only before singular Christian name) don (*Spanish title*); Don (*priest*); uncle (*familiar title of elderly man*)

donare (**dóno**) *tr* to donate; to give as a present || *intr*—**donare a** to be becoming to

dona·tóre **-trice** *mf* donor; **donatore di sangue** blood donor

donazióne *f* gift, donation

donchisciotté·sco **-sca** *adj* (-schi -sche) quixotic

dónde *adv* wherefrom, whence

dondolare (**dóndolo**) *tr* to swing, rock || *ref* to swing, rock; to loaf around

dondolì·o *m* (-i) swinging, rocking

dóndolo *m*—**a dondolo** rocking (*chair, horse*); **andare a dondolo** to loaf around

dondoló·ne **-na** *mf* idler, loafer

dongiovan·ni *m* (-ni) Don Juan

dònna *f* woman; ladyship; (lit) lady; (coll) Mrs.; (coll) maid; (cards) queen; **da donna** woman's, e.g., **scarpe da donna** woman's shoes; **donna cannone** fat lady (*of circus*); **donna di casa** housewife; **Nostra Donna** Our Lady

donnaiòlo *m* ladies' man, philanderer

donné·sco **-sca** *adj* (-schi -sche) womanly, feminine

dònnola *f* weasel

dóno *m* gift; **in dono** as a gift

donzèlla [*dz*] *f* (lit) damsel

donzèllo [*dz*] *m* (coll) doorman; (lit) page

dópo *adv* afterwards, later; **dopo che** after; **dopo di** after || *prep* after; **dopo + *pp*** after having + *pp*

dopobar·ba *adj invar* after-shaving || *m* (-ba) after-shaving lotion

dopodomani *m* & *adv* the day after tomorrow

dopoguèr·ra *m* (-ra) postwar era

dopolavóro *m* government office designed to organize workers' leisure time

dopopranzo *m* afternoon || *adv* in the afternoon

doppiàg·gio *m* (-gi) (mov) dubbing

doppiare §287 (**dóppio**) *tr* to double; (mov) to dub

doppière *m* candelabrum

doppiétta *f* double-barreled shotgun; (aut) double shift

doppièzza *f* duplicity

dóp·pio -pia (-pi -pie) *adj* double; coupled; double-dealing || *adv* twice, twofold || *m* double; twice as much; (tennis) doubles; (theat) understudy

doppióne *m* duplicate; (philol) doublet

doppiopèt·to *adj invar* double-breasted || *m* (-to) double-breasted suit

dorare (**dòro**) *tr* to gild; (culin) to brown; **dorare la pillola** to sugar-coat the pill

dora·to -ta *adj* gilt, golden

doratura *f* gilding

dormicchiare §287 *intr* to doze

dormiènte *adj* sleeping || *mf* sleeper

dormiglió·ne -na *mf* sleepyhead

dormire (**dòrmo**) *tr & intr* to sleep; **dormire a occhi aperti** to be overcome with sleep; **dormire della grossa** to sleep profoundly; **dormire tra due guanciali** to be safe and secure

dormita *f* long sleep; **fare una bella dormita** to have a long sleep

dormitò·rio *m* (-ri) dormitory

dormivé·glia *m* (-glia) drowsiness

dorsale *adj* dorsal; back (*bone*) || *m* head (*of bed*); back (*of chair*) || *f* (geog) ridge

dòrso *m* back; (sports) backstroke

dosàg·gio *m* (-gi) dosage

dosare (**dòso**) *tr* to dose

dosatura *f* dosage

dòse *f* dose

dòsso *m* back; (lit) summit; **levarsi di dosso** to take off; **mettersi in dosso** to put on

dotare (**dòto**) *tr* to provide with a dowry; to endow; to bless

dotazióne *f* dowry; endowment; supply

dòte *f* dowry; gift; endowment

dòt·to -ta *adj* learned, erudite || *m* scholar; (anat) duct

dottorale *adj* doctoral

dottó·re -réssa *mf* doctor

dottrina *f* doctrine; Christian doctrine

dóve *m* where; **per ogni dove** everywhere || *adv* where; **da dove** or **di dove** from where; which way; **fin dove** up to what point; **per dove** which way || *conj* where; whereas

dovére *m* duty, obligation; homework; **a dovere** properly; **doveri** regards; **farsi un dovere di** to feel duty-bound to; **mettere qlcu a dovere** to put s.o. in his place; **più del dovere** more than one should; **sentirsi in dovere di** to feel duty-bound to || §160 *tr & intr* to owe || *aux* (ESSERE & AVERE) must, e.g., **deve farlo** you must do it; to have to, e.g., **dovei partire I** had to leave; ought to, e.g., **dovrebbe lucidare la macchina** he ought to polish the car; should, e.g., **dovresti immaginarti** you should imagine; to be to, e.g., **il treno doveva arrivare alle sei** the train was to arrive at six; to be supposed to, e.g., **deve aver**

fatto un lungo viaggio he is supposed to have taken a long journey

doveró·so -sa [s] *adj* proper, right

dovìzia *f* (lit) abundance, wealth

dovunque *adv* wherever, anywhere; everywhere

dovu·to -ta *adj & m* due

dozzina [ddzz] *f* dozen; room and board; **da** or **di dozzina** common, ordinary; **tenere a dozzina** to board

dozzinale [ddzz] *adj* common, ordinary

dozzinante [ddzz] *mf* boarder

dra·ga *f* (-ghe) dredge

dragàg·gio *m* (-gi) dredging

dragami·ne *m* (-ne) minesweeper

dragare §209 *tr* to dredge

dràglia *f* (naut) stay

dra·go *m* (-ghi) dragon; **drago volante** kite

dragóna *f* sword strap

dragoncèllo *m* (bot) tarragon

dragóne *m* dragon; dragoon

dram·ma *m* (-mi) drama, play; **dramma musicale** (hist) melodrama || *f* drachma; dram

drammàti·co -ca (-ci -che) *adj* dramatic || *f* drama, dramatic art

drammatizzare [ddzz] *tr* to dramatize

drammatur·go *m* (-ghi) playwright, dramatist

drappég·gio *m* (-gi) drape; pleats

drappeggiare §290 (**drappéggio**) *tr* to drape || *ref* to be draped

drappèlla *f* pennon (*on bugler's trumpet*)

drappèllo *m* squad, platoon

drapperìa *f* dry goods; dry-goods store

drappo *m* cloth, silk cloth; (billiards) green cloth, baize

dràsti·co -ca *adj* (-ci -che) drastic

drenàg·gio *m* (-gi) drainage

drenare (**drèno**) *tr* to drain

dressàg·gio *m* (-gi) *m* training (*of animals*)

dribblare *tr & intr* (sports) to dribble

drit·to -ta *adj* straight; (lit) correct; **dritto come un fuso** straight as a ramrod || *m* (fig) old fox || *f* right; (naut) starboard

drizza *f* (naut) halyard

drizzare *tr* to straighten; to address; to erect; to cock (*the head*); to direct (*a blow*); **drizzare le gambe ai cani** to do the impossible; **drizzare le orecchie** to prick up one's ears || *intr* (naut) to hoist the halyard || *ref* to stand erect

drò·ga *f* (-ghe) drug; spice; seasoning

drogare §209 (**drògo**) *tr* to drug; to spice, season

drogheria *f* grocery (store)

droghière *m* grocer

dromedà·rio *m* (-ri) dromedary

dru·do -da *adj* (archaic) faithful; (lit) strong || *m* (obs) vassal; (lit) lover

drùi·da·m *m* (-di) druid

drupa *f* (bot) drupe, stone fruit

duale *adj & m* dual

dualismo *m* dualism

duali·tà *f* duality

dùb·bio -bia (-bi -bie) *adj* doubtful || *m* doubt; misgiving; **mettere in dub-**

bio to question; to risk; **senza dubbio** no doubt

dubbió·so -sa [s] *adj* dubious; doubtful; (lit) dangerous

dubitare (**dùbito**) *intr* to doubt; to suspect; **dubitare di** to mistrust; to doubt; **non dubitare!** don't worry!

du·ca *m* (**-chi**) duke; (lit) leader

ducato *m* duchy; ducat

duce *m* leader; duce

duchéssa *f* duchess

duchessina *f* young duchess

duchino *m* young duke

due *adj & pron* two; **le due** two o'clock || *m* two; second (*in dates*) || *f*—**fra le due** between two alternatives

duecentè·sco -sca *adj* (**-schi -sche**) thirteenth-century

duecentèsi·mo -ma *adj, m & pron* two hundredth

duecènto *adj, m & pron* two hundred || **il Duecento** the thirteenth century

duellante *adj* dueling || *m* duelist

duellare (**duèllo**) *intr* to duel

duèllo *m* duel; contest; debate; **sfidare a duello** to challenge to a duel

duemila *adj, m & pron* two thousand || **Duemila** *m* twenty-first century

duepèz·zi *m* (**-zi**) two-piece bathing suit

duétto *m* (mus) duet

dulcamara *f* (bot) bittersweet

dulcina *f* artificial sweetening

duna *f* dune

dunque *m*—**venire al dunque** to come

to the point || *adv* then || *conj* therefore, hence || *interj* well!

duodèno *m* (anat) duodenum

duòlo *m* (lit) grief

duòmo *m* cathedral; dome (*e.g., of a boiler*)

du·plex *m* (**-plex**) (telp) party line

duplicare §197 (**dùplico**) *tr* to duplicate

duplica·to -ta *adj & m* duplicate

duplicatóre *m* duplicator

dùplice *adj* twofold, double || *f* (racing) daily double

duplici·tà *f* (**-tà**) duplicity

duràbile *adj* durable, lasting

duràci·no -na *adj* clingstone || *f* clingstone peach

duralluminio *m* duralumin

durare *tr* to endure, bear || *intr* to last; **durare a** + *inf* to keep on + *ger*; **durare in carica** to remain in office

durata *f* duration; lasting quality; **di lunga durata** long-lasting

durante *prep* during; throughout

duratu·ro -ra *adj* enduring, lasting

durévole *adj* lasting, durable

durézza *f* hardness; toughness; rigidity

du·ro -ra *adj* hard; hard-boiled (*egg*); durum (*wheat*); tough (*skin*); harsh; (phonet) voiceless || *m* hard part; hard floor; hard soil; **il duro sta che . . .** the trouble is that . . . ; **tener duro** to hold out

duróne *m* callousness, callosity

dùttile *adj* ductile; tractable

E

E, e [e] *m & f* fifth letter of the Italian alphabet

e *conj* and

ebani·sta *m* (**-sti**) cabinetmaker

ebanisteria *f* cabinetmaking; cabinetmaker's shop

ebanite *f* ebonite, vulcanite

èbano *m* ebony

ebbène *interj* well!

ebbrézza *f* intoxication, drunkenness

èb·bro -bra *adj* intoxicated || *mf* drunk

ebdomadà·rio -ria *adj & m* (**-ri -rie**) weekly

èbete *adj* stupid, dull, dumb

ebollizióne *f* boil, boiling

ebrài·co -ca (**-ci -che**) *adj* Hebrew, Hebraic || *m* Hebrew (*language*)

ebrè·o -a *adj & mf* Hebrew || *m* Hebrew (*language*); Jew; **ebreo errante** Wandering Jew

è·bro -bra *adj & mf* var of **ebbro**

ebùrne·o -a *adj* (lit) ivory

ecatòmbe *f* hecatomb, slaughter

eccedènte *adj* exceeding || *m* excess

eccedènza *f* excess, surplus

eccèdere §123 *tr* to exceed || *intr* to go too far

eccellènte *adj* excellent

eccellènza *f* excellence || **Eccellenza** *f* Excellency

eccèllere §162 *intr* (ESSERE) to excel

eccèl·so -sa *adj* unexcelled; very high || **—l'Eccelso** *m* the Most High

eccentrici·tà *f* (**-tà**) eccentricity

eccèntri·co -ca (**-ci -che**) *adj* eccentric; suburban || *mf* vaudeville performer || *m* (mach) eccentric

eccepibile *adj* objectionable

eccepire §176 *tr* (law) to take exception to || *intr* (law) to object

eccessi·vo -va *adj* excessive; overweening (*opinion*)

eccèsso *m* excess; **all'eccesso** excessively; **andare agli eccessi** to go to extremes; **dare in eccessi** to fly into a rage; **eccesso di peso** excess weight

eccètera *adv* and so forth, et cetera

eccètto *prep* except, but; **eccetto che** except that; unless

eccettuare (**eccèttuo**) *tr* to except

eccettua·to -ta *adj* excepted || **eccettuato** *prep* except

eccezionale *adj* exceptional

eccezióne *f* exception; objection; **ad eccezione di** with the exception of; **d'eccezione** extraordinary; **sollevare un'eccezione** (law) to take exception

ecchimò·si *f* (**-si**) bruise

eccì·dio *m* (**-di**) massacre

eccitàbile *adj* excitable

eccitaménto *m* instigation; excitement

eccitante *adj* stimulating ‖ *m* stimulant

eccitare (**èccito**) *tr* to excite ‖ *ref* to become excited or aroused; (sports) to warm up

eccitazióne *f* excitement; (elec) excitation

ecclesiàsti·co -ca (**-ci -che**) *adj* ecclesiastical ‖ *m* clergyman

ècco *tr invar* here is (are), there is (are), **ecco che** here, e.g., **ecco che viene** he here comes; **eccoci** here we are; **ecco fatto** that's it; **eccola** here she is; here it is; **eccomi** here I am; **eccone** here are some ‖ *intr invar* here I am; here it is; **quand'ecco** suddenly ‖ *interj* look!

eccóme *interj* and how!, indeed!

echeggiare §290 (**echéggio**) *intr* (ESSERE & AVERE) to echo

eclètti·co -ca *adj & mf* (**-ci -che**) eclectic

eclissare *tr* to eclipse ‖ *ref* to be eclipsed; (coll) to vanish, sneak away

eclis·si *f* (**-si**) eclipse

eclìtti·ca *f* (**-che**) ecliptic

èclo·ga *f* (**-ghe**) var of **egloga**

è·co *m & f* (**-chi** *mpl*) echo; **far eco a** to echo

ecogoniòmetro *m* sonar

ecologìa *f* ecology

economato *m* comptroller's or administrator's office

economìa *f* administration; management; economy; economics; **economia aziendale** business management; **economia di mercato** free enterprise; **economia domestica** home economics; **economia politica** political economy; economics; **economie** savings; **fare economia** to save

econòmi·co -ca *adj* (**-ci -che**) economic(al); cheap

economi·sta *mf* (**-sti -ste**) economist

economizzare [ddzz] *tr & intr* to economize, save

ecòno·mo -ma *adj* thrifty ‖ *m* comptroller; administrator

ecosistè·ma [s] *m* (**-mi**) ecosystem

ecumèni·co -ca *adj* (**-ci -che**) ecumenical

eczè·ma [dz] *m* (**-mi**) eczema

édera *f* ivy

edìcola *f* shrine; newsstand

edificante *adj* edifying

edificare §197 (**edìfico**) *tr* to build; to edify ‖ *intr* to build

edifica·tóre -trice *adj* building ‖ *mf* builder

edificazióne *f* building; edification

edifì·cio *m* (**-ci**) building, edifice; pack (*e.g., of lies*); structure

edile *adj* building, construction ‖ *m* builder, construction worker

edilì·zio -zia (**-zi -zie**) *adj* building, construction ‖ *f* building trade

edìpi·co -ca *adj* (**-ci -che**) Oedipus (*e.g., complex*)

Edipo *m* Oedipus

èdi·to -ta *adj* published

edi·tóre -trice *adj* publishing ‖ *mf* publisher; editor (*e.g., of a text*)

editorìa *f* publishing; publishers

editoriale *adj* editorial; publishing ‖ *m* editorial

editoriali·sta *mf* (**-sti -ste**) editorial writer

editto *m* edict

edizióne *f* edition; performance; (fig) vintage

edonismo *m* hedonism

edoni·sta *mf* (**-sti -ste**) hedonist

edòt·to -ta *adj* (lit) informed, acquainted; **rendere qlcu edotto su qlco** (lit) to inform s.o. of s.th

edredóne *m* eider, eider duck

educanda *f* boarding-school girl; convent-school girl

educandato *m* (convent) boarding school for girls

educare §197 (**èduco**) *tr* to educate; to rear, bring up; to train; to accustom, inure; (lit) to grow

educatì·vo -va *adj* educational

educa·to -ta *adj* educated; polite, well-bred

educa·tóre -trice *mf* educator

educazióne *f* education; breeding, manners; **educazione civica** civics

edule *adj* edible

efèbo *m* (coll) sissy

efèlide *f* freckle

effeminatézza *f* effeminacy

effemina·to -ta *adj* effeminate; frivolous

efferatézza *f* savagery

effervescènte *adj* effervescent

effervescènza *f* effervescence

effettivaménte *adv* really

effettì·vo -va *adj* real, true; effective; full (*e.g., member*); regular (*e.g., army officer*) ‖ *m* effective; total amount; (mil) manpower

effètto *m* effect, result; (com) promissory note; (billiards) English; (sports) spin; **a questo effetto** for this purpose; **effetti** effects, belongings; **effetto di luce** play of light; **effetto ottico** optical illusion; **fare effetto** to make a sensation; **fare l'effetto di** to give the impression of; **in effetto** in fact; **mandare a effetto** to carry out; **porre in effetto** to put into effect

effettuàbile *adj* feasible

effettuare (**effèttuo**) *tr* to bring about; to contrive; to actuate; **effettuare** (*una corsa, un servizio*) to run, e.g., **l'autobus effettua una corsa ogni mezz'ora** the bus runs every half hour

efficace *adj* effective; forceful (*writer*)

efficà·cia *f* (**-cie**) effectiveness, efficacy; (law) validity

efficiènte *adj* efficient

efficiènza *f* efficiency; **in piena efficienza** in full working order; in top condition

effigiare §290 *tr* to portray, represent

effì·gie *f* (**-gie** or **-gi**) effigy; image

effìme·ro -ra *adj* ephemeral

efflusso *m* flow, outflow

efflù·vio *m* (**-vi**) effluvium; emanation (*e.g., of light*)

effrazióne *f* (law) burglary

effusióne *f* effusion; outflow; shedding (*of blood*); effusiveness

egemonìa *f* hegemony

egè·o -a *adj* Aegean
ègida *f* aegis
Egitto, l' *m* Egypt
egizia·no -na *adj & mf* Egyptian
eglantina *f* sweetbrier
eglefino *m* haddock
égli §5 *pron pers* he
ègło·ga *f* (**-ghe**) eclogue
egocèntri·co -ca *adj & mf* (**-ci -che**) egocentric
egoismo *m* egoism, selfishness
egoi·sta (**-sti -ste**) *adj* selfish || *mf* egoist
egoìsti·co -ca *adj* (**-ci -che**) egoistic(al)
egotismo *m* egotism
egoti·sta (**-sti -ste**) *adj* egotistic || *mf* egotist
egrè·gio -gia *adj* (**-gi -gie**) (lit) outstanding; **Egregio Signore** Mr. (*before a man's name in an address on a letter*); Dear Sir
eguaglianza *f* equality
eguale *adj* var of **uguale**
egualità·rio -ria *adj & m* (**-ri -rie**) equalitarian
éhi *interj* hey!
éi *pron* (lit) he; (archaic) they
eiaculazióne *f* ejaculation
eiettàbile *adj* ejection (*seat*)
eiezióne *f* ejection
él *pron* (archaic) he
elaborare (**elàboro**) *tr* to elaborate; to digest; to secrete
elabora·to -ta *adj* elaborate || *m* written exercise
elaboratóre *m* computer
elaborazióne *f* elaboration; data processing
elargire §176 *tr* to donate
elargizióne *f* donation
elastici·tà *f* (**-tà**) elasticity; agility; (com) oscillation; (com) range
elàsti·co -ca (**-ci -che**) *adj* elastic || *m* rubber band; bedspring
élce *m & f* holm oak
elefante *m* elephant; **elefante marino** sea elephant
elefantéssa *f* female elephant
elegante *adj* elegant, fashionable
elegantó·ne -na *mf* fashion plate || *m* dandy, dude
eleganza *f* elegance, stylishness
elèggere §193 *tr* to elect
eleggibile *adj* eligible
elegìa *f* elegy
elegìa·co -ca *adj* elegiac
elementare *adj* elementary || **elementari** *fpl* elementary schools
eleménto *m* element; rudiment; member; cell (*of battery*); **elementi** personnel, e.g., **elementi femminili** female personnel
elemòsina *f* alms; (eccl) collection; **chiedere l'elemosina** to beg; **vivere d'elemosina** to live on charity
elemosinare (**elemòsino**) *intr* to beg
Èlena *f* Helen
elencare §197 (**elènco**) *tr* to list; to enumerate
elèn·co *m* (**-chi**) list; **elenco telefonico** telephone directory
eletti·vo -va *adj* elective
elèt·to -ta *adj* elect; distinguished

(*audience*); precious (*metal*); chosen (*people*) || *mf* elect
elettorato *m* electorate, constituency
elet·tóre -trice *mf* voter; elector
elettràuto *m* automobile electrician; automotive electric shop
elettrici·sta *mf* (**-sti -ste**) electrician
elettrici·tà *f* (**-tà**) electricity
elèttri·co -ca (**-ci -che**) *adj* electrical || *m* electrical worker
elettrificare §197 (**elettrìfico**) *tr* to electrify
elettrizzare [ddzz] *tr* to electrify (*e.g., a person*) || *ref* to become electrified
ellètro *m* amber
elettrocalamita *f* electromagnet
elettrocardiògrafo *m* electrocardiograph
elettrocardiogram·ma *m* (**-mi**) electrocardiogram
elettrodinàmi·co -ca (**-ci -che**) *adj* electrodynamic || *f* electrodynamics
elèttrodo *m* electrode
elettrodomèsti·co -ca (**-ci -che**) *adj* electric household || *m* electric household appliance
elettroesecuzióne *f* electrocution
elettròge·no -na *adj* generating (*unit*)
elettròli·si *f* (**-si**) electrolysis
elettroliti·co -ca *adj* (**-ci -che**) electrolytic
elettròlito *m* electrolyte
elettromagnèti·co -ca *adj* (**-ci -che**) electromagnetic
elettromo·tóre -trice *adj* electromotive || *m* electric motor || *f* electric train; electric railcar
elettróne *m* electron
elettróni·co -ca *adj* (**-ci -che**) electronic || *f* electronics
elettropómpa *f* electric pump
elettrosquasso *m* electroshock
elettrostàti·co -ca *adj* (**-ci -che**) electrostatic || *f* electrostatics
elettrotècni·co -ca (**-ci -che**) *adj* electrotechnical || *m* electrician; electrical engineer || *f* electrical engineering
elettrotrèno *m* electric train
elevaménto *m* elevation
elevare (**èlevo & elèvo**) *tr* to lift, elevate; (math) to raise || *ref* to rise
elevatézza *f* loftiness, dignity
eleva·to -ta *adj* high, lofty
eleva·tóre -trice *adj* elevating || *m* elevator
elevazióne *f* elevation; (sports) jump; (math) raising
elezióne *f* election; choice
èlfo *m* elf
èli·ca *f* (**-che**) propeller; (geom) helix
elicoidale *adj* helicoidal
elicòttero *m* helicopter
elìdere §161 *tr* to annul; to elide || *ref* to neutralize one another
eliminare (**elìmino**) *tr* to eliminate
eliminatò·rio -ria (**-ri -rie**) *adj* eliminating || *f* (sports) heat
eliminazióne *f* elimination; extermination
èlio- *comb form adj* helio-, e.g., **eliocentrico** heliocentric || *comb form*

m & f helio-, e.g., **elioterapia** helio-therapy

èlio *m* helium

eliocèntri·co -ca *adj* (**-ci -che**) helio-centric

eliògrafo *m* heliograph

elioteràpi·co -ca *adj* (**-ci -che**) sunshine (*treatment*); sunbathing (*establish-ment*)

eliotrò·pio *m* (**-pi**) heliotrope; blood-stone

elipòrto *m* heliport

elisabettia·no -na *adj* Elizabethan

elì·sio -sia *adj* (**-si -sie**) Elysian

elisióne *f* elision

eli·sir *m* (**-sir**) elixir

èlitra *f* elytron, shard

élla *pron* (lit) she ‖ **Ella** *pron* (lit) you

ellèboro *m* hellebore

ellèni·co -ca *adj* (**-ci -che**) Hellenic

ellisse *f* ellipse

ellis·si *f* (**-si**) (gram) ellipsis

ellìtti·co -ca *adj* (**-ci -che**) elliptical

-èllo -èlla *suf adj* little, e.g., **poverello** poor little

elmétto *m* helmet; tin hat

élmo *m* helmet

elogiare §290 (**elògio**) *tr* to praise

elò·gio *m* (**-gi**) praise, encomium; write-up; **elogio funebre** eulogy

eloquènte *adj* eloquent

eloquènza *f* eloquence

elò·quio *m* (**-qui**) (lit) speech, diction

élsa *f* hilt

elucidare (**elùcido**) *tr* to elucidate

elùdere §105 *tr* to elude, evade

elusi·vo -va *adj* elusive

elvèti·co -ca *adj & mf* (**-ci -che**) Helvetian

elzevi·ro -ra [dz] *adj* Elzevir ‖ *m* Elzevir book; (journ) literary article

emacia·to -ta *adj* emaciated, lean

emanare *tr* to send forth; to issue ‖ *intr* (ESSERE) to emanate; to come forth

emanazióne *f* emanation; issuance

emancipare (**emàncipo**) *tr* to emanci-pate ‖ *ref* to become emancipated

emancipazióne *f* emancipation

emarginare (**emàrgino**) *tr* to note in the margin; (fig) to put aside, neglect

emarginato *m* marginal note

emàti·co -ca *adj* (**-ci -che**) blood, hematic

ematite *f* hematite

embàr·go *m* (**-ghi**) embargo

emblè·ma *m* (**-mi**) emblem

emblemàti·co -ca *adj* (**-ci -che**) em-blematic

embolìa *f* embolism

èmbrice *m* flat roof tile; shingle

embriologìa *f* embryology

embrionale *adj* embryonic

embrióne *m* embryo

emendaménto *m* emendation (*of a text*); amendment (*to a law*)

emendare (**emèndo**) *tr* to correct; to emend; to amend (*a law*) ‖ *ref* to reform

emergènza *f* emergence; emergency

emèrgere §162 *intr* (ESSERE) to emerge;

to surface (*said of a submarine*); to loom; to stand out

emèri·to -ta *adj* emeritus (*professor*); famous

emerotè·ca *f* (**-che**) periodical library

emersióne *f* emersion; surfacing

emèr·so -sa *adj* emergent

emèti·co -ca *adj & m* (**-ci -che**) emetic

eméttere §198 *tr* to emit, send forth; to utter (*a statement*); (com) to issue

emiciclo *m* hemicycle; floor (*of legis-lative body*)

emicrània *f* migraine, headache

emigrante *adj & mf* emigrant

emigrare *intr* (ESSERE & AVERE) to emi-grate

emigra·to -ta *adj & mf* emigrant

emigrazióne *f* emigration; migration (*e.g., of birds*)

eminènte *adj* eminent

eminènza *f* eminence; (eccl) Eminence

emisfèro *m* hemisphere

emissà·rio *m* (**-ri**) emissary; outlet (*river or lake*); drain

emissióne *f* emission; issuance; (rad) broadcast

emistì·chio *m* (**-chi**) hemistich

emittènte *adj* emitting; issuing; (rad) broadcasting ‖ *f* (rad) transmitting set; broadcasting station

emofilìa *f* hemophilia

emoglobìna *f* hemoglobin

emolliènte *adj & m* emollient

emoluménto *m* fee, emolument

emorragìa *f* hemorrhage

emorròidi *fpl* hemorrhoids, piles

emostàti·co -ca (**-ci -che**) *adj* hemo-static ‖ *m* hemostat

emotè·ca *f* (**-che**) blood bank

emotivi·tà *f* (**-tà**) emotionalism

emoti·vo -va *adj* emotional ‖ *mf* emo-tional person

emottìsi *f* (pathol) hemoptysis

emozionante *adj* emotional, moving

emozionare (**emozióno**) *tr* to move, stir; to thrill

emozióne *f* emotion

empiastro *m* var of **impiastro**

émpiere §163 *tr & ref* var of **empire**

empie·tà *f* (**-tà**) impiety; cruelty

ém·pio -pia *adj* (**-pi -pie**) impious; pitiless, wicked

empire §163 *tr* to fill; (lit) to fulfill; **empire qlcu di insulti** to heap insults on s.o. ‖ *ref* to get full

empìre·o -a *adj* heavenly, sublime ‖ *m* empyrean

empìri·co -ca *adj* (**-ci -che**) empirical ‖ *mf* empiricist

empirismo *m* empiricism

empìri·sta *mf* (**-sti -ste**) empiricist

émpito *m* (lit) rush; fury

empò·rio *m* (**-ri**) emporium, mart

emulare (**èmulo**) *tr* to emulate

emulazióne *f* emulation, rivalry; (law) evil intent

èmu·lo -la *adj* emulous ‖ *mf* emulator

emulsionare (**emulsióno**) *tr* to emulsify

emulsióne *f* emulsion

encefalite *f* encephalitis

encìcli·ca *f* (**-che**) encyclical

enciclopedìa *f* encyclopedia

enciclopèdi·co -ca *adj* (-ci -che) encyclopedic

enclave *f* enclave

enclìti·co -ca *adj & f* (-ci -che) enclitic

encomiàbile *adj* praiseworthy

encomiare §287 (encòmio) *tr* to praise

encò·mio *m* (-mi) encomium, praise

endecasìlla·bo -ba *adj* hendecasyllabic || *m* hendecasyllable

endemìa *f* endemic

endèmi·co -ca *adj* (-ci -che) endemic

èndice *m* nest egg; (obs) souvenir

endocàr·dio *m* (-di) (anat) endocardium

endocarpo *m* (bot) endocarp

endòcri·no -na *adj* endocrine

endourba·no -na *adj* inner-city

endovenó·so -sa [s] *adj* intravenous

energèti·co -ca (-ci -che) *adj* energy (*e.g., crisis*); (med) tonic || *m* (med) tonic

energìa *f* energy, power

enèrgi·co -ca *adj* (-ci -che) energetic

energùme·no -na *mf* wild or mad person

ènfa·si *f* (-si) emphasis; forcefulness

enfàti·co -ca *adj* (-ci -che) emphatic

enfiare §287 (énfio) *tr & ref* to swell

enfisè·ma *m* (-mi) emphysema

enfitèu·si *f* (-si) lease (*of land*)

enig·ma *m* (-mi) enigma, riddle, puzzle

enigmàti·co -ca *adj* (-ci -che) enigmatic, puzzling

-ènne *suf adj* -year-old, e.g., *ragazzo diciassettenne* seventeen-year-old boy || *suf mf* -year-old person, e.g., **diciassettenne** seventeen-year-old person

ennèsi·mo -ma *adj* nth

-èn·nio *suf m* (-nî) period of . . . years, e.g., **ventennio** period of twenty years

enòlo·go -ga *mf* (-gi -ghe) oenologist

enórme *adj* enormous

enormeménte *adv* enormously

enormi·tà *f* (-tà) enormity; outrage; absurdity

Enrico *m* Henry

ènte *m* being; entity; corporation; agency, body

enteroclìsma *m* (-smi) enema

enti·tà *f* (-tà) entity; value, importance

entomologìa *f* entomology

entram·bi -be *adj*—**entrambi i** both || *pron* both

entrante *adj* next (*e.g., week*)

entrare (éntro) *intr* (ESSERE) to enter; to go (*said of numbers*); to get (*into one's head*); **entrarci** to make it, e.g., **con questi soldi non c'entro I can't** make it with this money; **entrarci come i cavoli a merenda** to be completely out of line; **entrare a** to begin to; **entrare in** to enter (*e.g., a room*); to fit in; to go in (*said of a number*); to get into (*one's head*); **entrare in amore** to be in heat (*said of animals*); **entrare in ballo** to come into play; **entrare in carica** to take up one's duties; **entrare in collera** to get angry; **entrare in collisione** to collide; **entrare in contatto** to establish contact, **entrare in gioco** to come into play; **entrare in guerra** to go to war; **entrare in società** to make one's debut; **entrare nella parte di** (theat)

to play the role of; **entrare in vigore** to become effective; **Lei non c'entra** this is none of your business; **questo non c'entra** this is beside the point

entrata *f* entry; entrance; **entrata di favore** (theat) complimentary ticket; **entrate** income

entratura *f* entry; entrance; assumption (*of a position*); familiarity

éntro *adv* inside || *prep* within; **entro di** within, inside of

entrobórdo *m* inboard motorboat

entrotèrra *m* inland, hinterland

entusiasmare *tr* to carry away, enthuse || *ref* to be carried away, to become enthused

entusiasmo *m* enthusiasm

entusia·sta (-sti -ste) *adj* enthusiastic || *mf* enthusiast, devotee

entusiàsti·co -ca *adj* (-ci -che) enthusiastic

enucleare (enùcleo) *tr* to elucidate; (surg) to remove

enumerare (enùmero) *tr* to enumerate

enumerazióne *f* enumeration

enunciare §128 *tr* to enunciate, state

enunciatì·vo -va *adj* (gram) declarative

enunciazióne *f* enunciation, statement

enzi·ma [dz] *m* (-mi) enzyme

èpa *f* (lit) belly, paunch

epàti·co -ca *adj* (-ci -che) hepatic, liver

epatite *f* (pathol) hepatitis

epènte·si *f* (-si) epenthesis

eperlano *m* (ichth) smelt

èpi·co -ca *adj & f* (-ci -che) epic

epicurè·o -a *adj & m* epicurean

epidemìa *f* epidemic

epidèmi·co -ca *adj* (-ci -che) epidemic (al)

epidèrmi·co -ca *adj* (-ci -che) epidermal; (fig) superficial, skin-deep

epidèrmide *f* epidermis

Epifanìa *f* Epiphany

epiglòttide *f* (anat) epiglottis

epìgono *m* follower; descendant

epìgrafe *f* epigraph

epigram·ma *m* (-mi) epigram

epigrammàti·co -ca *adj* (-ci -che) epigrammatic

epilessìa *f* (pathol) epilepsy

epilètti·co -ca *adj & m* (-ci -che) epileptic

epìlo·go *m* (-ghi) epilogue; conclusion

episcopale *adj* episcopal

episcopalia·no -na *adj & mf* Episcopalian

episcopato *m* episcopate, bishopric

episòdi·co -ca *adj* (-ci -che) episodic

episò·dio *m* (-di) episode

epìstola *f* epistle

epistolà·rio *m* (-ri) letters, correspondence

epitàf·fio *m* (-fi) epitaph

epitè·lio *m* (-li) epithelium

epìteto *m* epithet; insult

epitomare (epìtomo) *tr* to epitomize

epìtome *f* epitome

èpo·ca *f* (-che) epoch; period; moment; **fare epoca** to be epoch-making

epopèa *f* epic

eppure *conj* yet, and yet

epsomite *f* Epsom salt

epurare *tr* to cleanse; to purge
epurazióne *f* purification; purge
equànime *adj* calm, composed; impartial
equanimità *f* equanimity; impartiality
equatóre *m* equator
equatoriale *adj & m* equatorial
equazióne *f* equation
equèstre *adj* equestrian
equilàte·ro -ra *adj* equilateral
equilibrare *tr* to balance; (aer) to trim || *ref* to balance one another
equilibra·to -ta *adj* level-headed
equilibra·tóre -trice *adj* stabilizing || *m* (aer) horizontal stabilizer
equilì·brio m (-bri) equilibrium, balance; (fig) proportion; **equilibrio politico** balance of power
equilibrì·sta *mf* **(-sti -ste)** acrobat, equilibrist
equi·no -na *adj & m* equine
equinoziale *adj* equinoctial
equinò·zio m (-zi) equinox
equipaggiaménto *m* equipment, outfit
equipaggiare §290 *tr* to equip, outfit; (naut) to fit out; (naut) to man
equipàg·gio m (-gi) equipage; (naut) crew, complement; (sports) team; (rowing) crew
equiparare *tr* to equalize (*e.g., salaries*)
équipe *f* team
equipollènte *adj* equivalent
equi·tà f (-tà) equity, fair-mindedness
equitazióne *f* horsemanship
equivalènte *adj & m* equivalent
equivalére §278 *intr* (ESSERE & AVERE) —**equivalere a** to be equivalent to || *ref* to be equal
equivocare §197 (equìvoco) *intr*—**equivocare su** to mistake, misunderstand
equìvo·co -ca (-ci -che) *adj* equivocal, ambiguous || *m* misunderstanding
è·quo -qua *adj* equitable, fair
èra *f* era, age; **era spaziale** space age
erà·rio m (-ri) treasury
èrba *f* grass; **erba limoncina** lemon verbena; **erba medica** alfalfa; **erbe** vegetables; **erbe aromatiche** herbs; **far l'erba** to cut the grass; **in erba** (fig) budding; **metter a erba** to put to pasture
erbàc·cia f (-ce) weed
erbaggi *mpl* vegetables
erbaiò·lo -la *mf* fresh vegetable retailer
erbici·da m (-di) weed-killer
erbivéndo·lo -la *mf* fresh fruit and vegetable retailer
erbìvo·ro -ra *adj* herbivorous
erbori·sta *mf* **(-sti -ste)** herbalist
erbó·so -sa [s] *adj* grassy
Èrcole *m* Hercules
ercùle·o -a *adj* Herculean
erède *m* heir || *f* heiress
eredi·tà f (-tà) inheritance; heredity
ereditare (eredìto) *tr* to inherit
eredità·rio -ria *adj* **(-ri -rie)** hereditary; crown (*prince*)
ereditièra *f* heiress
eremi·ta m (-ti) hermit
eremitàg·gio m (-gi) hermitage
èremo *m* hermitage
eresìa *f* heresy

eresiar·ca m (-chi) heretic
erèti·co -ca (-ci -che) *adj* heretical || *mf* heretic
erèt·to -ta *adj* erect, straight
erezióne *f* erection
ergastola·no -na *mf* lifer
ergàstolo *m* life imprisonment; prison for persons sentenced to life imprisonment
èrgere §164 *tr* (lit) to erect; (lit) to lift || *ref* to rise (*said, e.g., of a mountain*)
èrgo m *invar*—**venire all'ergo** to come to a conclusion || *adv* thus, hence
èri·ca f (-che) heather
erìgere §152 *tr* to erect, build || *ref* to rise; **erigersi a** to set oneself up as
eritrè·o -a *adj & mf* Eritrean
ermafrodi·to -ta *adj & m* hermafrodite
ermellino *m* ermine
ermèti·co -ca *adj* **(-ci -che)** airtight; watertight; hermetic
èrnia *f* hernia; **ernia del disco** (pathol) herniated disk
eródere §239 *tr* to erode
eròe *m* hero
erogare §209 (èrogo) *tr* to distribute; to bestow
erogazióne *f* distribution; bestowal
eròi·co -ca *adj* **(-ci -che)** heroic
eroicòmi·co -ca *adj* **(-ci -che)** mock-heroic
eroìna *f* heroine; (pharm) heroin
eroìsmo *m* heroism
erómpere §240 *intr* to erupt, burst out
erosióne *f* erosion
eròti·co -ca *adj* **(-ci -che)** erotic
erotìsmo *m* eroticism
èrpete *m* (pathol) herpes, shingles
erpicare §197 (èrpico) *tr* to harrow
érpice *m* harrow
errabón·do -da *adj* (lit) wandering
errante *adj* errant; wandering
errare (èrro) *intr* to wander; to err; (lit) to stray
erra·to -ta *adj* mistaken, wrong
erròne·o -a *adj* erroneous
erróre *m* error, mistake; fault; (lit) wandering; **errore di lingua** slip of the tongue; **errore di scrittura** slip of the pen; **errore di stampa** misprint; **errore giudiziario** miscarriage of justice; **salvo errore od omissione** barring error or omission
ér·to -ta *adj* arduous, steep; erect || *f* arduous ascent; **all'erta** on the alert
erudire §176 *tr* to educate, instruct
erudi·to -ta *adj* erudite, learned || *m* scholar, savant
erudizióne *f* erudition, learning
eruttare *tr* to belch forth (*e.g., lava*); to utter (*obscenities*) || *intr* to belch
erutti·vo -va *adj* eruptive
eruzióne *f* eruption
esacerbare (esacèrbo) *tr* to embitter; to exacerbate || *ref* to become embittered
esagerare (esàgero) *tr & intr* to exaggerate
esagera·to -ta *adj* exaggerated, excessive || *mf* exaggerator
esagerazióne *f* exaggeration

esagitare (esàgito) tr to perturb

esàgono m hexagon

esalare tr to exhale; esalare l'ultimo respiro to breathe one's last || intr to spread (said of odors)

esalazióne f exhalation; fume, vapor

esaltare tr to exalt; to excite || ref to glorify oneself; to become excited

esalta·to -ta adj frenzied, excited || mf hothead

esame m examination; checkup, test; dare gli esami to take an examination; esame attitudinale aptitude test; esame del sangue blood test; esame di riparazione make-up test; fare gli esami to prepare a test (for a student); prendere in esame to take in consideration

esàmetro m hexameter

esaminan·do -da mf candidate; examinee

esaminare (esàmino) tr to examine; to test

esamina·tóre -trice mf examiner

esàngue adj bloodless; (fig) pale

esànime adj lifeless

esasperante adj exasperating

esasperare (esàspero) tr to exasperate || ref to become exasperated

esasperazióne f exasperation

esattézza f exactness; punctuality

esat·to -ta adj exact; punctual

esattóre m tax collector; bill collector

esattoria f tax collector's office; bill collector's office

esaudire §176 tr to grant

esauriènte adj exhaustive; convincing

esauriménto m depletion (e.g., of merchandise); (pathol) exhaustion; (naut) drainage

esaurire §176 tr to exhaust; to play out (e.g., a hooked fish); to use up || ref to be exhausted; to be depleted; to be sold out

esauri·to -ta adj exhausted; depleted; sold out; out of print

esau·sto -sta adj exhausted; empty

esautorare (esàutoro) tr to deprive of authority; to discredit (a theory)

esazióne f exaction; collection

é·sca f (-sche) bait; punk (for lighting fireworks); tinder (for lighting powder): dare esca a to foment

escandescènza f—dare in escandescenze to fly off the handle

escava·tóre -trice mf excavator, digger || m excavator; escavatore a vapore steam shovel || f (mach) excavator

escavazióne f excavation

eschimése [s] adj & mf Eskimo

esclamare tr & intr to exclaim

esclamati·vo -va adj exclamatory; exclamation (mark)

esclùdere §105 tr to exclude; to keep or shut out

esclusióne f exclusion; a esclusione di with the exception of

esclusiva f sole right, monopoly; (journ) scoop

esclusivi·sta (-sti -ste) adj clannish; bigoted || mf bigot; (com) sole agent

esclusi·vo -va adj exclusive; intolerant, bigoted || f see esclusiva

esclu·so -sa adj excluded, excepted

escogitare (escògito) tr to think up, invent; to think out

escoriare §287 (escòrio) tr & ref to skin

escoriazióne f abrasion

escreménto m excrement

escrescènza f excrescence

escrè·to -ta adj excreted || m excreta

escursióne f excursion; (mach) sweep; (mil) transfer; escursione termica (meteor) temperature range

escursioni·sta mf (-sti -ste) excursionist, sightseer

escussióne f (law) examination, cross-examination

esecrare (esècro) tr to execrate

esecrazióne f execration

esecuti·vo -va adj & m executive

esecu·tóre -trice mf (mus) performer || m executor; esecutore di giustizia executioner || f executrix

esecuzióne f accomplishment, completion; performance; execution; esecuzione capitale capital punishment

esegè·si f (-si) exegesis

eseguire (eséguo) & §176 tr to execute, carry out; to perform

esèm·pio m (-pi) example; a mo' d'esempio as an illustration; dare il buon esempio to set a good example; per esempio for instance

esemplare adj exemplary || m copy; specimen || v (esèmplo) tr (lit) to copy

esemplificare §197 (esemplìfico) tr to exemplify

esentare (esènto) tr to exempt

esènte adj exempt, free

esenzióne f exemption

esèquie fpl obsequies, funeral rites

esercènte adj practicing || mf dealer, merchant

esercire §176 tr to practice; to run (a store)

esercitare (esèrcito) tr to exercise; to tax (e.g., s.o.'s patience); to practice, ply (a trade); to wield (e.g., power) || ref to practice

esercitazióne f exercise, training; esercitazioni militari drilling

esèrcito m army; (fig) flock; Esercito della Salvezza Salvation Army

esercì·zio m (-zi) exercise; practice; training; homework; occupation; drill; d'esercizio (com) administrative (expenses); esercizio finanziario fiscal year; esercizio provvisorio (law) emergency appropriation; esercizio pubblico establishment open to the public; esercizio spirituale (eccl) retreat

esibire §176 tr to exhibit || ref to show oneself, appear; esibirsi di to offer to

esibizióne f exhibition

esigènte adj demanding, exigent

esigènza f demand, requirement, exigency

esìgere §165 tr to demand; to require; to exact; to collect

esigìbile adj due; collectable

esigui·tà f (-tà) meagerness, scantiness

esì·guo -gua adj meager, scanty

esilarante *adj* exhilarating; laughing (*gas*)

esilarare (esìlaro) *tr* to amuse ‖ *ref* to be amused

èsile *adj* slender, thin; weak

esiliare §287 *tr* to exile ‖ *ref* to go into exile; to withdraw

esìlia·to -ta *adj* exiled ‖ *m* exile (*person*)

esì·lio *m* (**-li**) exile, banishment

esìmere §166 *tr* to exempt ‖ *ref—esìmersi da* to avoid (*an obligation*)

esì·mio -mia *adj* (**-mi -mie**) distinguished, eminent

-èsi·mo -ma *suf adj & pron* -eth, e.g., **ventesimo** twentieth; -th, e.g., **diciannovesimo** nineteenth

esistènte *adj* existent; extant

esistènza *f* existence

esistenzialismo *m* existentialism

esìstere §114 *intr* (ESSERE) to exist

esitante *adj* hesitant

esitare (èsito) *tr* to retail ‖ *intr* to hesitate; (med) to resolve itself

esitazióne *f* hesitation; haw (*in speech*)

èsito *m* result, outcome; sale; outlet; (philol) late form; **dare esito a** (com) to reply

esiziale *adj* ruinous, fatal

èsodo *m* exodus, flight

esòfa·go *m* (**-gi**) esophagus

esonerare (esònero) *tr* to exempt, release

esònero *m* exemption, release

Esòpo *m* Aesop

esorbitante *adj* exorbitant

esorbitare (esòrbito) *intr—esorbitare da* to go beyond

esorcismo *m* exorcism

esorcizzare [ddzz] *tr* to exorcise

esordiènte *adj* beginning, budding ‖ *mf* beginner ‖ *f* debutante

esòr·dio *m* (**-di**) beginning

esordire §176 *intr* to make a start; (theat) to debut; (theat) to open

esortare (esòrto) *tr* to exhort

esortazióne *f* exhortation

esò·so -sa *adj* greedy, avaricious; hateful; exorbitant (*price*)

esòti·co -ca *adj* (**-ci -che**) exotic

esotismo *m* exoticism; borrowing (*from a foreign language*)

espàndere §167 *tr* to expand ‖ *ref* to spread out; to confide

espansióne *f* expansion; effusiveness

espansionismo *m* expansionism

espansivi·tà *f* (**-tà**) effusiveness

espansi·vo -va *adj* expansive; effusive

espan·so -sa *adj* flared; expanded, dilated

espatriare §287 *intr* to emigrate

espà·trio *m* (**-tri**) emigration

espediènte *m* expedient, makeshift; ruse; **vivere di espedienti** to live by one's wits

espedire §176 *tr* to expedite ‖ *ref—espedirsi di* to get rid of

espèllere §168 *tr* to expel, eject

esperiènza *f* experience; experiment

esperimento *m* experiment; test

espèr·to -ta *adj & m* expert

espettorare (espèttoro) *tr & intr* to expectorate

espiare §119 *tr* to expiate; to placate (*the gods*); **espiare una pena** to serve a sentence

espiató·rio -ria *adj* (**-ri -rie**) expiatory

espiazióne *f* expiation

espirare *tr & intr* to breath out, to exhale

espirazióne *f* exhaling

espletare (esplèto) *tr* to dispatch, complete

esplicare §197 (**èsplico**) *tr* to carry out; (lit) to explain

esplicati·vo -va *adj* explanatory

esplìci·to -ta *adj* explicit

esplòdere §169 *tr* to shoot; to fire (*a shot*) ‖ *intr* (ESSERE & AVERE) to explode; to burst forth

esploditóre *m* blasting machine

esplorare (esplòro) *tr* to explore; to search, probe; (telv) to scan

esplora·tóre -trice *mf* explorer ‖ *m* (nav) gunboat; **giovane esploratore** boy scout

esplorazióne *f* exploration; (telv) scanning

esplosióne *f* explosion, blast; (fig) outburst

esplosi·vo -va *adj & m* explosive

esponènte *adj* (typ) superior ‖ *m* spokesman; dictionary entry; catchword (*of dictionary*); (math) exponent; (naut) net weight

espórre §218 *tr* to expose, show; to expound; to abandon (*a baby*); to lay out (*a corpse*); to lay open (*to danger*) ‖ *intr* to show, exhibit ‖ *ref* to expose oneself

esportare (espòrto) *tr* to export

esporta·tóre -trice *mf* exporter

esportazióne *f* export, exportation

esposìmetro *m* exposure meter

esposi·tóre -trice *mf* commentator; exhibitor

esposizióne *f* exposition; abandonment (*of a baby*); exhibit, fair; line (*of credit*); exposure (*of a house*); (phot) exposure

espó·sto -sta *adj* exposed; aforementioned ‖ *m* petition, brief; foundling

espressióne *f* expression; feeling

espressi·vo -va *adj* expressive

esprès·so -sa *adj* manifest; express; prepared on the spot ‖ *m* espresso; messenger; special-delivery letter; special-delivery stamp

esprìmere §131 *tr* to express; to convey (*an opinion*); (lit) to squeeze ‖ *ref* to express oneself

espropriare §287 (**espròprio**) *tr* to expropriate ‖ *ref* to deprive onself; **espropriarsi di** to divest oneself of

esprò·prio *m* (**-pri**) expropriation

espugnare *tr* to take by storm

espulsióne *f* expulsion; (mach) ejection

espulsóre *m* ejector

espurgare §209 *tr* to expurgate

éssa §5 *pron pers* she; it

ésse §5 *pron pers* they

essènza *f* essence

essenziale *adj* essential ‖ *m* main point

èssere *m* being; existence; condition; (coll) character; **in essere** in good shape ‖ §170 *intr* (ESSERE) to be;

c'è there is; ci sono there are; ci sono! I get it!; come sarebbe a dire? what do you mean?; come se nulla fosse as if nothing had happened; esserci to have arrived, to be there; essere di to belong to; essere per to be about to; può essere maybe; sarà maybe; sia . . . sia both . . . and; whether . . . or || *aux* (ESSERE) (to form passive) to be, e.g., fu investito da un tassametro he was run over by a taxi; (to form the compound tenses of certain intransitive verbs and all reflexive verbs) to have, e.g., sono arrivati they have arrived; mi sono appena alzato I have just got up || *impers* (ESSERE) to be, e.g., è giusto it is fair

éssi §5 *pron pers* they

essiccare §197 *tr* to dry || *ref* to dry up

essicca·tóio *m* (-tói) drier

essiccazióne *f* drying

èsso §5 *pron pers* he; it; chi per esso his representative

essudare *intr* to exude

èst *m* east

èsta·si *f* (-si) ecstasy; andare in estasi to become enraptured

estasiare §287 *tr* to enrapture, delight || *ref* to become enraptured

estate *f* summer

estàti·co -ca *adj* (-ci -che) ecstatic, enraptured

estemporàne·o -a *adj* extemporaneous

estèndere §270 *tr* to extend; to broaden (*e.g.*, one's knowledge); to draw up (*a document*) || *ref* to extend

estensìbile *adj* applicable; inviare saluti estensibili a to send greetings to be extended to (*e.g.*, another person)

estensióne *f* extension; extent; expanse (*e.g.*, of water); (mus) compass, range

estensi·vo -va *adj* extensive

estèn·so -sa *adj*—per esteso fully

estensóre *adj* extensible || *m* compiler (*e.g.*, of a dictionary); (sports) exerciser, chest expander

estenuante *adj* exhausting

estenuare (estènuo) *tr* to exhaust || *ref* to become exhausted

esterióre *adj* exterior || *m* outside appearance

esteriori·tà *f* (-tà) appearance

esternare (estèrno) *tr* to reveal, manifest || *ref* to confide

estèr·no -na *adj* external; outside; day (*student*) || *m* exterior, outside; (baseball) outfielder; all'esterno outside; in esterno (mov) on location

èste·ro -ra *adj* foreign || *m* foreign countries; all'estero abroad

esterrefat·to -ta *adj* terrified

esté·so -sa [s] *adj* extended, wide; per esteso in full

estè·ta *mf* (-ti -te) aesthete

estèti·co -ca (-ci -che) *adj* aesthetic || *f* aesthetics

esteti·sta *mf* (-sti -ste) beautician

estima·tóre -trice *mf* appraiser; admirer

èstimo *m* appraisal; assessment

estìnguere §156 *tr* to extinguish; to quench (*thirst*); to pay off (*a debt*) || *ref* to die out

estinguìbile *adj* extinguishable; payable

estìn·to -ta *adj* extinguished; extinct || *m* deceased, dead person

estintóre *m* fire extinguisher

estirpare *tr* to uproot; to eradicate; to pull (*a tooth*)

estirpa·tóre -trice *mf* eradicator || *m* (agr) weeder

estivare *tr & intr* to summer

esti·vo -va *adj* summer; summery

estòllere §171 *tr* to extol

èstone *adj & mf* Estonian

estòrcere §272 *tr* to extort; estorcere qlco a qlcu to extort s.th from s.o.

estorsióne *f* extortion

estradare *tr* (law) to extradite

estradizióne *f* extradition

estràne·o -a *adj* extraneous, foreign; aloof || *mf* outsider

estrapolare (estràpolo) *tr* to extrapolate

estrarre §273 *tr* to extract, draw; to pull (*a tooth*)

estrat·to -ta *adj* extracted || *m* extract; abstract; certified copy; (typ) offprint; estratto conto bank statement; estratto dell'atto di nascita copy of one's birth certificate

estrazióne *f* extraction; drawing (*of lottery*)

estrèma *f* (sports) wing, end

estremi·sta *adj & mf* (-sti -ste) extremist

estremi·tà *f* (-tà) end; tip, top; extremity; le estremità the extremities

estrè·mo -ma *adj* extreme; esalare l'estremo respiro to breath one's last || *m* extremity; end, extreme; essere agli estremi to be near the end; estremi essentials || *f see* estrema

estrìnse·co -ca *adj* (-ci -che) extrinsic

èstro *m* horsefly; whim, fancy; inspiration; estro venereo heat (*of female animal*)

estrométtere §198 *tr* to oust, expel

estró·so -sa [s] *adj* fanciful, whimsical; inspired

estrovèr·so -sa or estroverti·to -ta *adj & mf* extrovert

estrùdere §190 *tr* to extrude

estuà·rio *m* (-ri) estuary

esuberante *adj* exuberant; buoyant

esuberanza *f* exuberance; buoyancy; a esuberanza abundantly

esulare (èsulo) *intr* (ESSERE & AVERE) to go into exile; esulare da to be alien to

esulcerare (esùlcero) *tr* to ulcerate on the surface; (fig) to exacerbate

esulcerazióne *f* superficial ulceration; (fig) exasperation, exacerbation

èsule *mf* exile (*person*)

esultante *adj* exultant, jubilant

esultare *intr* to exult

esumare *tr* to exhume; to revive (*e.g.*, a custom)

esumazióne *f* exhumation; revival

e·tà *f* (-tà) age; che età ha? how old is he (or she)?; ha la sua età he (or she) is no longer a youngster; l'età di mezzo Middle Ages; maggiore età majority; mezza età middle age; minore età minority

etamine *f* cheesecloth

ètere *m* ether

etère·o -a *adj* ethereal
eternare (etèrno) *tr* to immortalize ‖ *ref* to become immortal
eterni·tà *f* (-tà) eternity
etèr·no -na *adj* eternal, everlasting ‖ *m* eternity; in eterno forever
eterodòs·so -sa *adj* heterodox
eterogène·o -a *adj* heterogeneous
èti·ca *f* (-che) ethics
etichétta *f* label; card (*e.g., of a library*); etiquette; etichetta gommata sticker
etichettare (etichétto) *tr* to label
èti·co -ca (-ci -che) *adj* ethical; consumptive ‖ *m* consumptive ‖ *f* see etica
etile *m* ethyl
etilène *m* ethylene
etìli·co -ca *adj* (-ci -che) ethyl
ètimo *m* etymon
etimologìa *f* etymology
etìope *adj* & *mf* Ethiopian
Etiòpia, l' *f* Ethiopia
etiòpi·co -ca *adj* (-ci -che) Ethiopian
etisìa *f* tuberculosis
ètni·co -ca *adj* (-ci -che) ethnic(al)
etnografìa *f* ethnography
etnologìa *f* ethnology
etru·sco -sca *adj* & *mf* (-schi -sche) Etruscan
ettàgono *m* heptagon
èttaro *m* hectare
ètte *m* (coll) particle, jot, whit, tittle
ètto or ettogrammo *m* hectogram
-étto -étta *suf adj* rather, e.g., piccoletto rather small; -ish, e.g., rotondetto roundish
ettòlitro *m* hectoliter
eucalipto *m* eucalyptus
eucaristìa *f* Eucharist
eufemismo *m* euphemism
eufonìa *f* euphony
eufòni·co -ca *adj* (-ci -che) euphonic
euforìa *f* euphoria
eufòri·co -ca *adj* (-ci -che) euphoric
eufuismo *m* euphuism
eugenèti·co -ca (-ci -che) *adj* eugenic ‖ *f* eugenics
eunu·co *m* (-chi) eunuch
europè·o -a *adj* & *mf* European
Euròpa, l' *f* Europe
eurovisióne *f* European television chain
eutanasìa *f* euthanasia
Èva *f* Eve
evacuaménto *m* evacuation
evacuare (evàcuo) *tr* to evacuate ‖ *intr* to evacuate; to have a bowel movement
evacuazióne *f* evacuation; bowel movement

evàdere §172 *tr* to evade; to complete (*a deal*); to answer (*a letter*); to execute (*orders*) ‖ *intr* (ESSERE) to flee, escape
evanescènza *f* evanescence; (rad) fading
evanescènte *adj* evanescent; vanishing
evangèli·co -ca *adj* (-ci -che) evangelic (al)
evangelì·sta *m* (-sti) evangelist
evangelizzare [ddzz] *tr* to evangelize; to campaign for; to subject to political propaganda
evaporare (evapóro) *tr* & *intr* to evaporate
evaporatóre *m* evaporator; humidifier
evaporazióne *f* evaporation
evasióne *f* evasion, escape; (com) reply; dare evasione a to complete (*an administrative matter*)
evasi·vo -va *adj* evasive
eva·so -sa *adj* escaped ‖ *m* escapee
evasóre *m* tax dodger
eveniènza *f* eventuality, contingency; nell'evenienza che in the event (that); per ogni evenienza just in case
evènto *m* event; eventi correnti current events; fausto or lieto evento happy event
eventuale *adj* contingent
eventuali·tà *f* (-tà) eventuality
eversi·vo -va *adj* upsetting; destructive
evidènte *adj* evident; clear
evidènza *f* evidence; clearness; mettersi in evidenza to make oneself conspicuous; tenere in evidenza (com) to keep active
evirare *tr* to emasculate
evitare (èvito) *tr* to avoid, shun; evitare qlco a qlcu to spare s.o. s.th, to save s.o. from s.th
èvo *m* age, era; evo antico ancient times; evo moderno modern times; medio evo Middle Ages
evocare §197 (èvoco) *tr* to evoke
evoluire §176 *intr* (aer, nav) to maneuver
evolu·to -ta *adj* developed; progressive; modern
evoluzióne *f* evolution
evòlvere §115 *tr* to develop ‖ *ref* to evolve
evvi·va *m* (-va) cheer ‖ *interj* long live!, hurrah for!
èx *adj invar* ex-, e.g., la sua ex moglie his ex-wife; ex, e.g., ex dividendo ex dividend
ex li·bris *m* (-bris) bookplate
extraconiugale *adj* extramarital
extraeuropè·o -a *adj* non-European
ex vó·to *m* (-to) votive offering
eziologìa *f* etiology

F

F, f ['ɛffe] *m* & *f* sixth letter of the Italian alphabet
fa *m* (fa) (mus) F, fa
fabbisógno *m invar* need; requirement
fàbbri·ca *f* (-che) building, construction; factory, plant

fabbricante *mf* builder, manufacturer
fabbricare §197 (fàbbrico) *tr* to manufacture; to fabricate
fabbrica·to -ta *adj* built ‖ *m* building
fabbricazióne *f* building; erection; manufacturing; fabrication (*invention*)

fabbro *m* blacksmith; locksmith; (fig) master; **fabbro ferraio** blacksmith
faccènda *f* business, matter; **faccende domestiche** household chores
faccendiè·re -ra *mf* operator, schemer
faccétta *f* small face; face, facet
facchinàg·gio *m* (**-gi**) porterage; (fig) drudgery
facchino *m* porter; **lavorare come un facchino** to work like a slave
fàc·cia *f* (**-ce**) face; countenance; **avere la faccia di** to have the gall to; **di faccia** opposite; **faccia da galeotto** (coll) gallows bird; **faccia tosta** cheek, gall; **in faccia a** in front of
facciale *adj* facial
facciata *f* façade; page; (fig) surface appearance
face *f* (lit) torch
facè·to -ta *adj* facetious
facèzia *f* pleasantry, banter; **scambiar facezie** to banter with each other
fachiro *m* fakir
fàcile *adj* easy; inclined; loose (*morals*); glib (*tongue*); **è facile** it is probable ‖ *m* something easy
facili·tà *f* (**-tà**) facility, ease; inclination; **facilità di pagamento** easy payments, easy terms; **facilità di parola** glibness
facilitare (**facìlito**) *tr* to facilitate; to grant (*credit*); to give (*easy terms*)
facilitazióne *f* facilitation; easy terms; cut rate
facinoró·so -sa [s] *adj* criminal ‖ *m* hoodlum, thug
facoltà *f* (**-tà**) faculty; power; school (*of a university*); **facoltà** *fpl* means, wealth
facoltati·vo -va *adj* optional
facoltó·so -sa [s] *adj* wealthy, affluent
facóndia *f* loquacity, gift of gab
facón·do -da *adj* loquacious
facsìmi·le *m* (**-le**) facsimile
faènza *f* faïence ‖ **Faenza** *f* Faenza
fàg·gio *m* (**-gi**) (bot) beech
fagia·no -na *mf* pheasant
falange *f* phalanx
fal·bo -ba *adj* tawny
falcata *f* step, stride; bucking
falce *f* scythe; crescent (*of moon*); **falce messoria** sickle
falcétto *m* sickle
falciare §128 *tr* to mow
falcia·tóre -trice *mf* mower ‖ *f* mowing machine
falcidiare §287 *tr* to reduce; to cut down
fal·co *m* (**-chi**) hawk; **falco pescatore** osprey
falcóne *m* falcon
falconeria *f* falconry

falconière *m* falconer
falda *f* band, strip; flake (*of snow*); gable (*of roof*); brim (*of hat*); foot (*of mountain*); slab (*of stone*); waist plate (*of armor*); hem (*of suit*); flounce (*of dress*); layer (*of rock*); flap, coattail; **falda della camicia** shirttail; **falde straps** (*to hold a baby*); **méttersi in falde** to wear tails
falegname *m* carpenter; cabinetmaker
falegnameria *f* carpentry; cabinetmaking; carpenter shop; woodworker shop
falèna *f* moth
falla *f* hole, leak; (archaic) fault
fallace *adj* fallacious, deceptive
fallà·cia *f* (**-cie**) fallacy
fallare *intr* & *ref* (lit) to be mistaken
fallìbile *adj* fallible
fallimentare *adj* bankrupt; ruinous
falliménto *m* bankruptcy; (fig) collapse, failure
fallire §176 *tr* to miss (*the target*) ‖ *intr* (ESSERE) to go bankrupt; to fail ‖ *intr* (AVERE) (lit) to be mistaken
falli·to -ta *adj* & *mf* bankrupt
fallo *m* error, fault; sin; flaw; phallus; (sports) penalty; (sports) foul; **cadere in fallo** to make the wrong move; to be mistaken; **cogliere in fallo** to catch in the act; **far fallo a** to fail, e.g., **gli faccio fallo** I fail him; **senza fallo** without fail
fa·lò *m* (**-lò**) bonfire
falpa·là *f* (**-là**) flounce, furbelow
falsare *tr* to falsify, alter; (lit) to forge
falsari·ga *f* (**-ghe**) guideline (*for writing*); model, pattern; **seguire la falsariga di** to follow in the footsteps of
falsà·rio *m* (**-ri**) forger; counterfeiter
falsétto *m* falsetto
falsificare §197 (**falsìfico**) to falsify; to forge, fake
falsificazióne *f* falsification; forgery; misrepresentation
falsi·tà *f* (**-tà**) falsehood; falsity
fal·so -sa *adj* false; wrong (*step*); assumed (*name*); bogus, counterfeit, fake (*money*); phony ‖ *m* falsehood; perjury; forgery; **committere un falso** to perjure oneself; to commit forgery; **giurare il falso** to bear false witness; to perjure oneself
fama *f* fame; reputation; **cattiva fama** notoriety
fame *f* hunger; dearth; **aver fame** to be hungry; **avere una fame da lupo** to be as hungry as a wolf, to be as hungry as a bear; **morire di fame** to starve to death; to be ravenous
famèli·co -ca *adj* (**-ci -che**) starving, famished
famigera·to -ta *adj* notorious
famìglia *f* family; community; **di famiglia** intimate; **in famiglia** at home
famì·glio *m* (**-gli**) beadle, usher; hired man
familiare *adj* family; familiar, intimate; homelike ‖ *m* member of the family
familiari·tà *f* (**-tà**) familiarity; **avere familiarità con** to be familiar with

familiarizzare [ddzz] *tr* to familiarize
famó·so -sa [s] *adj* famous, illustrious
fanale *m* lamp, lantern; (rr) headlight; **fanale di coda** taillight
fanalino *m* small light; (aut) parking light; (aut) tail light
fanàti·co -ca (**-ci -che**) *adj* fanatic, fanatical || *mf* fanatic
fanatismo *m* fanaticism
fanatizzare [ddzz] *tr* to make a fanatic of
fanciulla *f* girl; spinster; bride
fanciullè·sco -sca *adj* (**-schi -sche**) childish; children's
fanciullézza *f* childhood; (fig) infancy
fanciulo·lo -la *adj* childish; childlike || *mf* child || *m* boy || *f* see **fanciulla**
fandònia *f* fib, tale, yarn
fanèllo *m* (orn) linnet; (orn) finch
fanfara *f* military band; fanfare
fanfaróne *m* braggart
fangatura *f* mud bath
fanghiglia *f* mud, slush
fan·go *m* (**-ghi**) mud; **fare i fanghi** to take mud baths
fangó·so -sa [s] *adj* muddy
fannullo·ne -na *mf* idler, loafer
fanóne *m* whalebone
fantacino *m* infantryman, foot soldier
fantascientífi·co -ca *adj* (**-ci -che**) science-fiction
fantasciènza *f* science fiction
fantasia *f* fantasy, fancy, whim; (mus) fantasia; **di fantasia** fancy
fantasió·so -sa [s] *adj* fanciful; imaginative
fanta·sma *m* (**-smi**) ghost, spirit; phantom; **fantasma poetico** poetic fancy
fantasticare §197 (**fantástico**) *tr* to imagine, dream up || *intr* to daydream
fantasticherìa *f* imagination, daydreaming
fantàsti·co -ca *adj* (**-ci -che**) fantastic || **fantástico** *interj* unbelievable!
fante *m* infantryman, foot soldier; (cards) jack; (obs) youth
fanterìa *f* infantry
fantésca *f* (**-sche**) (joc, lit) housemaid
fantino *m* jockey
fantòc·cio *m* (**-ci**) puppet
fantomàti·co -ca *adj* (**-ci -che**) ghostly; mysterious
farabutto *m* scoundrel, heel
faraóna *f* guinea fowl
faraóne *m* Pharaoh; (cards) faro
farcire §176 *tr* to stuff
fardèllo *m* bundle; burden; **far fardello** to pack one's bags
fare *m* doing; break (*of day*); way (*of acting*); **sul far della sera** at nightfall || §173 *tr* to do; to make; to work; to take (*e.g., a walk, a step*); to give (*a sigh*); to deal (*cards*); to suffer (*hunger*); to lead (*a good or bad life*); to render (*service*); to log (*e.g., 15 m.p.h.*); to be, e.g., **tre volte tre fa nove** three times three is nine; to build (*e.g., a house*); to put together (*a collection*); to prepare (*dinner*); to say, utter (*a word*); to have (*a dream*); to give (*fruit*); to pay (*atten-*

tion); to play (*a role*); to stir up (*pity*); to mention (*a name*); **fare il** (or **la**) to be a (*e.g., carpenter*); **fare + inf** to have + **inf**, e.g., **gli ho fatto . . .** I had him . . . ; to make + **inf**, e.g., **il medico mi fece . . .** the doctor made me . . . ; to have + **pp**, e.g., **farò fare . . .** I shall have . . . done; **fare acqua** to leak, to take in water; to get a supply of water; (coll) to urinate; **fare a metà** to divide in half; **fare a pugni** to come to blows; **fare a tempo** to be on time; **fare benzina** to buy gasoline; **fare caldo** a to keep warm, e.g., **questa coperta gli fa caldo** this blanket keeps him warm; **fare carbone** to coal; **fare . . . che** to have been . . . since, e.g., **fanno tre mesi che siamo in questa città** it has been three months since we have been in this city; **fare che + subj** to see to it that + **inf**, e.g., **faccia che comincino a lavorare subito** see to it that they begin to work at once; **fare colpo** to make an impression; **fare corona** a to crown; **fare cuore** a to encourage; **fare del male** a to harm; **fare di + inf** to see to it that + **inf**; **fare di tutto** to do one's best; **fare festa** a to cheer; **fare fiasco** to fail; **fare finta di** to pretend to; **fare fronte** a to face, meet; **fare fuoco su** to fire upon; **fare il gioco di** to play into the hands of; **fare il pappagallo** to parrot, ape; **fare il pieno** to fill up (*with gasoline*); **fare la bocca** a to get used to; **fare la calza** to knit; **fare la coda** to queue up, line up; **fare la festa** a to kill; **fare la guardia** to stand guard; **fare la mano** a to get used to; **fare le cose in famiglia** to wash one's dirty linen at home; **fare le cose in grande stile** to splurge; **fare legna** to gather firewood; **fare l'occhio** to become accustomed; **fare mente** to pay attention; **fare onore** a to do honor to; **fare paura** a to frighten; **fare sangue** to bleed; **fare sapere** a **qlcu** to let s.o. know; **fare scalo** (aer, naut) to make a call; **fare sì che** to act in such a way that; to see to it that; **fare silenzio** to keep silent; **fare specie** a to amaze, e.g., **il tuo comportamento gli fa specie** your behavior amazes him; **fare tesoro di** to prize; **fare una bella figura** to look good; to make a fine appearance; **fare una mala figura** to look bad; to make a bad showing; **fare una malattia** (coll) to get sick; **fare vela** to set sail; **fare venire** to send for; **fare vigilia** to fast; **farla corta** to cut it short; **farla franca** to get off scot-free; **farla grossa** to commit a blunder; **farla in barba a** to outwit; **farne di cotte e di crude, farne di tutti i colori**, or **farne più di Carlo in Francia** to engage in all sorts of mischief; to paint the town red; **non fare che + ind** to do nothing but + **inf** || *intr*—**averla a che fare con** to have words with; to have to deal with; **fare a coltellate** to have a fight with knives; **fare a girotondo** to play ring-around-the-rosy; **fare al caso** to fit; to suit; **fare a meno di** to do without; **fare da** to serve as, e.g., **fare da cuscino** to serve as a pillow; **fare da cena** to fix dinner; **fare di cappello** to take one's hat off; **fare presto** to hurry; **fare per** to be just the thing for; **fare tardi** to be late || *ref* to become; to cut (*e.g.*, *one's hair*); to move, e.g., **farsi in là** to move farther; **farsi avanti** to come forward; **farsi beffe di** to make fun of; **farsi bello** to bedeck oneself; to dress up; **farsi bello di** to boast about; to appropriate; **farsi gioco di** to make fun of; **farsi le labbra** to put lipstick on; **farsi strada** to make one's way; **farsi una ragione di** to rationalize, explain to oneself; **farsi un baffo** to not give a hoot; **si fa giorno** it is getting light; **si fa tardi** it is getting late || *impers*—**che tempo fa?** what's the weather like?; **fa ago**, e.g., **alcune settimane fa** a few weeks ago; **fa estate** it is like summer; **fa fino** it is smart; **fa freddo** it is cold; **fa luna** there is moonlight, the moon is out; **fa nebbia** it is foggy; **fa notte** it is nighttime; it is dark; it is getting dark; **fa sole** it is sunny, the sun is out; **fa tipo** or **fa tono!** that's classy!; **non fa nulla** it doesn't matter, never mind

farètra *f* quiver
farfalla *f* butterfly; bow tie; (mach) butterfly valve; (coll) promissory note
farfallóne *m* large butterfly; blunder; Don Juan
farfugliare §280 *intr* to mumble, mutter
farina *f* flour; **farina d'avena** oatmeal; **farina di legno** sawdust; **farina di ossa** bone meal; **farina gialla** yellow corn meal
farinàce·o -a *adj* farinaceous || **farinacei** *mpl* flour-yielding cereals
farinata *f* porridge
faringe *f* pharynx
faringite *f* pharingitis
farinó·so -sa [s] *adj* floury; powdery (*snow*); crumbly, friable
farisèo *m* Pharisee; (fig) pharisee
farmacèuti·co -ca *adj* (-**ci -che**) pharmaceutical, drug
farmacìa *f* pharmacy; drugstore; medicine cabinet; **farmacia di guardia** or **di turno** drugstore open all night and Sunday
farmaci·sta *mf* (-**sti -ste**) pharmacist, druggist
fàrma·co *m* (-**ci** or -**chi**) remedy, medicine
farneticare §197 (**farnètico**) *intr* to rave
farnèti·co -ca (-**chi -che**) *adj* raving || *m* delirium; craze
faro *m* lighthouse, beacon; (aut) headlight; **faro retromarcia** (aut) back-up light
farràgine *f* hodgepodge
farraginó·so -sa [s] *adj* confused, mixed

farsa *f* farce; burlesque
farsè·sco -sca *adj* (-**schi -sche**) farcical, ludicrous
farsétto *m* sweater; (hist) doublet
fascétta *f* girdle; band; wrapper; clamp; **fascetta editoriale** advertising band (*of book*)
fà·scia *f* (-**sce**) band; belt; bandage; newspaper wrapper; **fascia del cappello** hatband; **fascia di garza** gauze bandage; **fascia elastica** abdominal supporter; (aut) piston ring; **fasce del neonato** swaddling clothes; **in fasce** newborn; **sotto fascia** in a wrapper
fasciame *m* (naut) planking; (naut) plating
fasciare §128 to bind; to bandage; to wrap; to surround
fasciatura *f* bandaging, dressing
fascicolo *m* number, issue; pamphlet; file, dossier; (bb) fasciculus
fascina *f* fagot
fascina·tóre -trice *mf* charmer
fàscino *m* fascination, charm
fà·scio *m* (-**sci**) bundle; sheaf; bunch (*of flowers*); pencil or beam (*of rays*); fascist party
fascismo *m* fascism
fasci·sta *adj & mf* (-**sti -ste**) fascist
fase *f* phase, stage; (aut) cycle; (astr, elec, mach) phase
fastèllo *m* bundle, fagot
fasti *mpl* records, annals; notable events; (hist) Roman calendar
fastì·dio *m* (-**dî**) annoyance; (coll) loathing, nausea; **avere in fastidio** to loathe; **dar fastidio a** to annoy; **fastidi** troubles, worries
fastidió·so -sa [s] *adj* annoying, irksome; irritable; (obs) disgusting
fastì·gio *m* (-**gi**) top, summit
fa·sto -sta *adj* (lit) propitious || *m invar* pomp, display || *mpl* see **fasti**
fastó·so -sa [s] *adj* pompous, ostentatious
fata *f* fairy; **buona fata** fairy godmother; **Fata Morgana** Fata Morgana (*mirage; Morgan le Fay*)
fatale *adj* fatal; inevitable; irresistible (*woman*)
fatalismo *m* fatalism
fatali·sta *mf* (-**sti -ste**) fatalist
fatali·tà *f* (-**tà**) fatality, fate
fatalóna *f* vamp
fata·to -ta *adj* fairy, enchanted; (lit) predestined
fati·ca *f* (-**che**) fatigue, weariness; labor; **a fatica** with difficulty; **da fatica** draft (*e.g.*, *horse*); of burden (*beast*); **durar fatica a** + *inf* to have trouble in + *ger*
faticare §197 *intr* to toil; **faticare a** to be hardly able to
fatic贸·so -sa [s] *adj* burdensome, heavy; (lit) weary
fatidi·co -ca *adj* (-**ci -che**) fatal
fato *m* fate, destiny
fatta *f* kind, sort; **essere sulla fatta di** to be on the trail of
fattàc·cio *m* (-**ci**) (coll) crime
fattézze *fpl* features

fattìbile adj feasible, possible

fattispècie f—**nella fattispecie** in this particular case

fat·to -ta adj made, e.g., **fatto a mano** handmade; broad (daylight); deep (night); ready-made (e.g., suit); **ben fatto** well-done; shapely; **esser fatto per** to be cut out for; **fatto di** made of; **venir fatto a** to happen, chance, e.g., **gli venne fatto d'incontrarmi** he happened to meet me || m fact; act, deed; feat; action; business, affair; **badare ai fatti propri** to mind one's own business; **cogliere sul fatto** to catch in the act; **dire a qlcu il fatto suo** to give s.o. a piece of one's mind; **fatto compiuto** fait accompli; **fatto d'arme** feat of arms; **fatto si è** the fact remains that; **in fatto di** concerning; as of; **sapere il fatto proprio** to know one's business; **venire al fatto** to come to the point || f see **fatta**

fat·tóre -tóra or **-toréssa** mf farm manager || m maker; factor; steward || f stewardess; manager's wife

fattorìa f farm; stewardship

fattorino m delivery boy, messenger boy; conductor (of streetcar)

fattrice f (zool) dam

fattucchiè·re -ra mf magician || m sorcerer || f sorceress, witch

fattura f preparation; workmanship; bill, invoice; (coll) witchcraft; (lit) creature

fatturare tr to adulterate; to invoice, bill

fattura·to -ta adj adulterated || m (com) turnover

fatturi·sta m (-sti -ste) billing clerk

fà·tuo -tua adj fatuous

fàuci fpl jaws; (fig) mouth

fàuna f fauna

fàuno m faun

fàu·sto -sta adj propitious, lucky

fau·tóre -trice mf supporter, promoter

fava f broad bean; **pigliare due piccioni con una fava** to catch two birds with one stone

favèlla f speech; (lit) tongue

favilla f spark; **far** or **mandare faville** to sparkle

favo m honeycomb

fàvola f fable; tale; **favola del paese** talk of the town

favoló·so -sa [s] adj fabulous; mythical

favóre m favor; help; cover (e.g., of night); **a favore di** for the benefit of; **di favore** special (price); complimentary (ticket); **favore politico** patronage; **per favore** please; **per favore di** courtesy of

favoreggiaménto m abetting, support

favoreggiare §290 (favoréggio) tr to abet, support

favoreggia·tóre -trice mf abettor, supporter, backer

favorévole adj favorable; propitious

favorire §176 tr to favor; to accept; to oblige, accommodate; **favorire qlcu di qlco** to oblige s.o. with s.th; **favorisca + inf** please + inf, be kind

enough to + inf; **favorisca alla cassa** please pay the cashier; **favorisca uscire!** please leave!; **tanto per favorire** just to keep you company; **vuol favorire?** won't you please join us (at a meal)?; please help yourself!

favorita f royal mistress

favoritismo m favoritism

favori·to -ta adj & mf favorite || m protegé; **favoriti** sideburns || f see **favorita**

faziòne f faction; **essere di fazione** to be on guard duty

faziò·so -sa [s] adj factious || m partisan

fazzolétto m handkerchief; **fazzoletto da collo** neckerchief

fé f var of **fede**

feb·bràio m (-brài) February

fèbbre f fever; fever blister; **febbre da cavallo** (coll) very high fever; **febbre da fieno** hay fever; **febbre dell'oro** gold fever

febbricitante adj feverish

febbrìle adj feverish

Fèbo m Phoebus

féc·cia f (-ce) dregs; (fig) dregs (of society); **fino alla feccia** to the bitter end

fèci fpl feces

fècola f starch

fecondare (fecóndo) tr to fecundate

fecondazióne f fecundation; **fecondazione artificiale** artificial insemination

fecondi·tà f (-tà) fecundity

fecón·do -da adj fecund, prolific

féde f faith; certificate; wedding ring; faithfulness; **far fede** to bear witness; **in fede di** or **in fede** in testimony whereof; **in fede mia!** upon my word! **prestar fede a** to put one's faith in; **tener fede alla parola data** to keep one's word

fedecommésso m fideicommissum; trusteeship

fedéle adj faithful, devoted || mf faithful person; **i fedeli** the faithful

fedel·tà f (-tà) faithfulness, allegiance; fidelity; **ad alta fedeltà** hi-fi

fèdera f pillowcase

federale adj federal

federali·sta mf (-sti -ste) federalist

federati·vo -va adj federative

federa·to -ta adj federate, federated

federazióne f federation; (sports) league

Federico m Frederick

fedìfra·go -ga adj (-ghi -ghe) unfaithful, treacherous

fedina f police record; **avere la fedina sporca** to have a bad record; **fedine** sideburns

fégato m liver; courage; **fegato d'oca** pâté de foie gras; **rodersi il fegato** to be consumed with rage

félce f fern

feldspato m feldspar

felice adj happy; blissful; glad; felicitous

felici·tà f (-tà) happiness; bliss

felicitare (felìcito) tr to make happy; **che Dio vi feliciti!** God bless you! ||

ref to rejoice; **felicitarsi con qlcu per qlco** to congratulate s.o. for or on s.th

felicitazióne *f* congratulation

feli·no -na *adj & m* feline

fellóne *m* (lit) traitor

félpa *f* plush

felpa·to -ta *adj* covered with plush; soft (*e.g., step*)

féltro *m* felt; felt hat

felu·ca *f* (-che) two-cornered hat; (naut) felucca

fémmina *adj & f* female

femminile *adj* feminine, female ‖ *m* feminine gender

femminili·tà *f* (-tà) femininity, womanliness

femminismo *m* feminism

fèmore *m* femur; thighbone

fendènte *m* slash with a sword

fèndere §174 *tr* to split, cleave; to plow (*water*); to rend (*air*); to make one's way through (*a crowd*) ‖ *ref* to split; to come apart

fenditura *f* split, breach, fissure

fenice *f* phoenix

feni·cio -cia (-ci -cie) *adj & mf* Phoenician ‖ **la Fenicia** Phoenicia

fèni·co -ca (-ci -che) carbolic

fenicòttero *m* flamingo

fenòlo *m* phenol

fenomenale *adj* phenomenal

fenòmeno *m* phenomenon; freak, monster; **essere un fenomeno** to be unbelievable

ferace *adj* (lit) fertile

ferale *adj* (lit) mortal, deadly

fèretro *m* bier, coffin

feriale *adj* working (*day*); weekday

fèrie *fpl* vacation; **ferie retribuite** vacation with pay

ferire §176 *tr* to wound; to strike; **senza colpo ferire** without striking a blow ‖ *ref* to wound oneself

feri·to -ta *adj* wounded, injured ‖ *m* wounded person; injured person; **i feriti** the wounded; the injured ‖ *f* wound, injury

feritóia *f* loophole; embrasure

feri·tóre -trice *mf* assailant

férma *f* setting (*of setter or pointer*); (mil) service; (mil) enlistment

fermacarro *m* (rr) buffer

fermacar·te *m* (-te) paperweight; large paper clip

fermacravat·ta *m* (-ta) tiepin

fermà·glio *m* (-gli) clasp; buckle; clip; brooch

fermare (**férmo**) *tr* to stop; to pay (*attention*); to fasten; to close, shut; to detain (*in police station*); to set (*game*); to reserve (*seats*) ‖ *ref* to stop; to stay

fermata *f* stop; **fermata a richiesta** or **facoltativa** stop on signal

fermentare (**ferménto**) *tr & intr* to ferment

fermentazióne *f* fermentation

ferménto *m* ferment

fermézza *f* firmness; steadfastness

fér·mo -ma *adj* firm; stopped; quiet (*water*); (fig) steadfast; **fermo in**

posta general delivery; **fermo restando che** seeing that; **stare fermo** to be quiet ‖ *m* stop; detention; **mettere il fermo a** to stop (*a check*)

fermopòsta *m* general delivery ‖ *adv* care of general delivery

feróce *adj* fierce; wild

feró·cia *f* (-cie) ferocity, ferociousness, fierceness

feròdo *m* (aut) brake lining

ferragósto *m* Assumption; mid-August holiday

ferrame *m* ironware

ferramén·to *m* (-ti) iron or metal bracket; iron or metal trimming ‖ *m* (-ta *fpl*)—**ferramenta** hardware

ferrare (**fèrro**) *tr* to shoe (*a horse*); to hoop (*a barrel*)

ferra·to -ta *adj* iron; ironclad; shod (*horse*); spiked (*shoe*); well-versed ‖ *f* pressing, ironing; mark or burn (*caused by ironing*); (coll) iron grate

ferravèc·chio *m* (-chi) scrap-iron dealer, junkman

fèrre·o -a *adj* iron; ironclad

ferrièra *f* ironworks; (obs) iron mine

fèrro *m* iron; tool; anchor; sword; **ai ferri** on the grill, broiled (*e.g., steak*); **essere sotto i ferri del chirurgo** to go under the knife; **ferri** shackles; **ferri del mestiere** tools of the trade; **ferro battuto** wrought iron; **ferro da arricciare** curling iron; **ferro da calza** knitting needle; **ferro da cavallo** horseshoe; **ferro da stiro** iron, flatiron; **ferro fuso** cast iron; **ferro grezzo** pig iron; **mettere a ferro e fuoco** to put to fire and sword; **venire ai ferri corti** to get into close quarters

ferromodellismo *m* hobby of model railroads

ferrotranvièri *mpl* transport workers

ferrovìa *f* railroad; **ferrovia a dentiera** rack railway; **ferrovia sopraelevata** elevated railroad

ferrovià·rio -ria *adj* (-ri -rie) railroad

ferrovière *m* railroader

fèrtile *adj* fertile

fertilizzante [ddzz] *adj* fertilizing ‖ *m* fertilizer

fertilizzare [ddzz] *tr* to fertilize

fervènte *adj* fervent

fèrvere §175 *intr* to be fervent; to rage (*said, e.g., of a battle*); to go full blast

fèrvi·do -da *adj* fervent

fervóre *m* fervor; (fig) heat

fervorino *m* lecture, sermon

fesserìa *f* (slang) stupidity, nonsense; (slang) trifle

fés·so -sa *adj* cracked; cleft; (slang) dumb ‖ *m* (lit) cranny; **fare fesso qlcu** (slang) to play s.o. for a sucker

fessura *f* crack; cranny

fèsta *f* feast; holiday; birthday; saint's day; **a festa** festively; **buone feste!** happy holiday!; **conciare per le feste** to drub the daylights out of; **fare festa a** to welcome; **fare le feste** to spend the holidays; **far festa** to celebrate; to take the day off; **far la festa**

a to do in, kill; **festa del ceppo** Christmas; **festa da ballo** or **danzante** dancing party; **festa della mamma** Mother's Day; **festa del papà** Father's Day; **festa di precetto** (eccl) day of obligation; **festa nazionale** national holiday; **mezza festa** half holiday

festante *adj* cheerful

festeggiaménto *m* celebration

festeggiare §290 (**festéggio**) *tr* to celebrate, fete; to cheer

festi·no -na *adj* (lit) rapid || *m* party

festivi·tà *f* (-**tà**) festivity

festi·vo -va *adj* festive, holiday

festóne *m* festoon

festó·so -sa [*s*] *adj* cheerful, merry

festu·ca *f* (-**che**) straw; (fig) mote

fetènte *adj* stinking; stink (*bomb*) || *mf* (fig) stinker, louse

fetìc·cio *m* (-**ci**) fetish

feticismo *m* fetishism

fèti·do -da *adj* stinking, fetid

fèto *m* fetus

fetóre *m* stench

fétta *f* slice; **tagliare a fette** to slice

fettina *f* thin slice; twist (*of lemon*); **fettina di vitello** veal cutlet

fettùc·cia *f* (-**ce**) tape, ribbon

fettuccine *fpl* noodles

feudale *adj* feudal

feudalismo *m* feudalism

feudatà·rio -ria (-**ri -rie**) *adj* feudatory || *m* feudal vassal

fèudo *m* fief

fiaba *f* fairy tale; tale, yarn

fiacca *f* tiredness; sluggishness; **batter la fiacca** to loaf, to goof off

fiaccare §197 *tr* to weaken; to weary; to break || *ref* to weaken; to break (*e.g., one's neck*)

fiacche·ràio *m* (-**rài**) (coll) hackman, cabman

fiacchézza *f* weakness; sluggishness

fiac·co -ca *adj* (-**chi -che**) weak; sluggish; slack || *f* see **fiacca**

fiàccola *f* torch; **fiaccola della discordia** firebrand

fiaccolata *f* torchlight procession

fiala *f* vial, phial

fiamma *f* flame; blaze; (mil) insignia; (nav) pennant; **alla fiamma** (culin) flaming; **dare alle fiamme** to set on fire; **diventare di fiamma** to blush; **in fiamme** afire

fiammante *adj* blazing; **nuovo fiammante** brand-new

fiammata *f* blaze; flare-up

fiammeggiante *adj* flaming, blazing; (archit) flamboyant

fiammeggiare §290 (**fiamméggio**) *tr* to singe || *intr* to flame, blaze

fiammìfero *m* match

fiammin·go -ga (-**ghi -ghe**) *adj* Flemish; Dutch (*e.g., master*) || *mf* Fleming || *m* Flemish (*language*); (orn) flamingo

fiancata *f* blow with one's hip; dig, sarcastic remark; side, flank; (nav) broadside

fiancheggiare §290 (**fianchéggio**) *tr* to flank; to border (*a road*); to support

fiancheggia·tóre -trice *mf* supporter, backer

fian·co *m* (-**chi**) flank, side; hip; **di fianco** sideways; **fianco a fianco** side by side; **fianco destr'!** (mil) right face!; **fianco destro** (naut) starboard; **fianco sinistr'!** (mil) left face!; **fianco sinistro** (naut) port; **prestare il fianco a** to leave oneself wide open to; **tenersi i fianchi dal ridere** to split one's sides laughing

Fiandre, le *fpl* Flanders

fia·sca *f* (-**sche**) flask

fiaschetterìa *f* tavern, wine shop

fia·sco *m* (-**schi**) straw-covered wine bottle; flask; fiasco

fiata *f* (archaic) time

fiatare *intr* to breathe; **senza fiatare** without breathing a word

fiato *m* breath; (archaic) stench; **avere il fiato grosso** to be out of breath; **bere d'un fiato** to gulp down; **col fiato sospeso** holding one's breath; **dare fiato a** to blow, sound (*a trumpet*); **d'un fiato** or **in un fiato** without interruption; in one gulp; **fiati** (mus) winds; **senza fiato** out of breath

fiatóne *m*—**avere il fiatone** to be out of breath

fibbia *f* clasp, buckle

fibra *f* fiber

fibró·so -sa [*s*] *adj* fibrous

ficcana·so [*s*] *mf* (-**si** *mpl* -**so** *fpl*) (coll) busybody, meddler; nosy person

ficcare §197 *tr* to stick; to drive (*e.g., a nail*); to push; **ficcare gli occhi addosso a** to gaze at, stare at; **ficcare il naso negli affari degli altri** to poke one's nose in other people's business || *ref* to hide; to butt in; to get involved

fi·co *m* (-**chi**) fig; fig tree

ficodìndia *m* (*pl* **fichidìndia**) prickly pear

fidanzaménto *m* engagement, betrothal

fidanzare *tr* to betroth || *ref* to become engaged

fidanza·to -ta *adj* engaged || *m* fiancé || *f* fiancée

fidare *tr* to entrust || *intr* to trust || *ref* to have confidence; **fidarsi a** (coll) to dare to; **fidarsi di** to trust, rely on

fida·to -ta *adj* trustworthy, reliable

fi·do -da *adj* (lit) faithful, trusted || *m* loyal follower; credit; **far fido** to extend credit

fidùcia *f* faith, confidence; (com) credit; **di fiducia** trustworthy

fiducià·rio -ria (-**ri -rie**) *adj* fiduciary || *mf* fiduciary, trustee

fidució·so -sa [*s*] *adj* confident, hopeful

fièle *m invar* gall, bile; acrimony

fienile *m* hayloft

fièno *m* hay

fierìsti·co -ca *adj* (-**ci -che**) of a fair, e.g., **attività fieristica** activity of a fair

fiè·ro -ra *adj* fierce; dignified; proud || *f* fair; exhibit; wild beast

fièvole adj feeble, weak

fifa f (coll) scare; **avere la fifa** (coll) to be chicken; **avere una fifa blu** (coll) to be scared stiff

fifó·ne -na mf (coll) scaredy-cat

figgere §104 tr (lit) to drive, thrust || ref—**figgersi in capo** to get into one's head

figlia f daughter; (com) stub; **figlia consanguinea** stepdaughter on the father's side

figliare §280 tr & intr to whelp (said of animals)

figlia·stro -stra mf stepchild || m stepson || f stepdaughter

figliata f litter (e.g., of pigs)

fi·glio -glia mf child, offspring || m son; **figli** children; **figlio consanguineo** stepson on the father's side || f see **figlia**

figlióc·cio -cia (-ci -ce) mf godchild || m godson || f goddaughter

figliolanza f children, offspring

figliò·lo -la mf child || m son, boy || f daughter, girl

figura f figure; illustration; figurehead; face card; **far bella figura** to make a good showing; **far cattiva figura** to make a poor showing; **far figura** to look good; **figura retorica** figure of speech

figurante mf (theat) extra, super

figurare tr to feign; to represent || intr to figure; to appear; to make a good showing || ref to imagine; **si figuri!** imagine!

figurati·vo -va adj (fa) figurative

figura·to -ta adj figurative (speech); transcribed (pronunciation); illustrated (book)

figurina f figurine; card, picture (of a series of athletes or entertainment celebrities)

figurini·sta mf (-sti -ste) dress designer; costume designer

figurino m fashion plate; fashion magazine

figuro m scoundrel; gangster

figurone m—**fare un figurone** to make a very good showing

fila f row; file, line; series; **di fila in a row**; **fare la fila** to wait in line; **file ranks**

filàc·cia f (-ce) lint

filacció·so -sa [s] or **filacció·so -sa** [s] adj thready, stringy

filaménto m filament

filamentó·so -sa [s] adj thready, stringy; thread-like

filanda f spinning mill; silk spinning mill

filante adj spinning; shooting (star); thready; flowing (e.g., line)

filantropia f philanthropy

filantròpi·co -ca adj (-ci -che) philanthropic

filàntro·po -pa mf philanthropist

filare m row, line || tr to spin; to drip, ooze; to rest on (one's oars); to make (e.g., ten knots); (naut) to pay out; (mus) to hold (a note); **filare l'amore** to be in love || intr to spin (said of a spider); to rope, thread (said of wine

or syrup); to make sense; to drip; **fare filare dritto qlcu** to keep s.o. in line; **filare a** to do (e.g., twenty miles an hour); **filare all'inglese** to take French leave; **fila via!** (coll) get out!

filarmòni·co -ca (-ci -che) adj philharmonic || f philharmonic society

filastròc·ca f (-che) rigmarole; nursery rhyme

filatelìa f philately

filatèli·co -ca (-ci -che) adj philatelic(al) || mf philatelist

fila·to -ta adj spun; well-constructed (speech) || m yarn

fila·tóio m (-tói) spinning wheel

filatura f spinning; spinning mill

filettare (filétto) tr to fillet; (mach) to thread

filettatura f stripe (on a cap); (mach) thread

filétto m fillet; stripe; snaffle (on a horse's bit); fine stroke (in handwriting); (mach) thread; (typ) ornamental line, headband; (typ) rule

filiale adj filial || f branch office

filiazióne f filiation

filibustière m filibuster, buccaneer; adventurer

filièra f (mach) drawplate; (mach) die (to cut threads)

filigrana f filigree; watermark (in paper)

filippi·no -na adj Philippine || m Filipino || **le Filippine** the Philippines

Filippo m Philip

filistè·o -a adj & m philistine; Philistine

Fillide f Phyllis

film m (film) film; movie, motion picture; **film parlato** or **sonoro** talking picture

filmare tr to film

filmina f filmstrip

filmìsti·co -ca adj (-ci -che) movie, motion-picture

filmotè·ca f (-che) film library

fi·lo m (-li) thread; wire; yarn; blade (of grass); breath (of air); string (of pearls); edge (of razor); **dare del filo da torcere** to cause trouble; **essere ridotto a un filo** to be only skin and bones; **fil di voce** thin voice; **filo a piombo** plumb line; **filo d'acqua** thin stream; **filo della schiena** or **delle reni** spine; **filo spinato** barbed wire; **passare a fil di spada** to put to the sword; **per filo e per segno** in detail; from beginning to end; **senza fili** wireless; **stare a filo** to stand upright; **tenere i fili** (fig) to pull wires; **tenere in filo** to keep in line; **un filo di** a bit of || m (-la fpl) string (e.g., of cooked cheese); (archaic) file, row

filo·bus m (-bus) trolley bus

filodiffusióne f wired wireless; cable TV

filodrammàti·co -ca adj & mf (-ci -che) (theat) amateur

filogovernati·vo -va adj on the government side

filologìa f philology

filòlo·go -ga (-gi -ghe) adj philologic(al) || m philologist

filóne m vein (of ore); ripple (of a cur-

rent); stream; loaf (*of bread*); (lit) mainstream; **fllone d'oro** gold lode

filó·so -sa [s] *adj* stringy

filosofia *f* philosophy

filosòfi·co -ca *adj* (**-ci -che**) philosophic(al)

filòso·fo -fa *mf* philosopher

filovìa *f* trolley bus line

filtrare *tr* to filter; to percolate (*coffee*) || *intr* to filter, permeate

filtrazióne *f* filtering, filtration

filtro *m* filter; philter

filugèllo *m* silkworm

filza *f* string (*of pearls*); series (*of errors*); row; dossier, file; basting (*of dress*)

finale *adj* final, last; consumer (*goods*) || *m* end, ending; (mus) finale; (sports) finish || *f* end, ending; (sports) finals

finali·sta *mf* (**-sti -ste**) finalist

finali·tà *f* (**-tà**) end, purpose

finanche *adv* even

finanza *f* finance

finanziaménto *m* financing

finanziare §287 *tr* to finance

finanzià·rio -ria (**-ri -rie**) *adj* finance, financial || *f* (com) holding company

finanzia·tóre -trice *mf* financial backer

finanzièra *f* frock coat; **alla finanziera** with giblet gravy

finanzière *m* financier; (coll) customs officer

fin·ca *f* (**-che**) column, row (*of ledger*)

finché *conj* until, as long as; **finché non** until

fine *adj* fine, thin; choice, nice || *m* end, purpose; conclusion; (lit) limit, border; **a fin di bene** to good purpose, for the best; **secondo fine** ulterior motive || *f* end, conclusion; **condurre a fine** to bring to fruition; **fine di settimana** weekend; **in fin dei conti** after all; **senza fine** endless

fine-settima·na *m* or *f* (**-na**) weekend

finèstra *f* window; (lit) gash, wound; **finestra a gangheri** casement window; **finestra a ghigliottina** sash window; **finestra panoramica** picture window; **finestre** (lit) eyes

finestrino *m* (aut, rr) window

finézza *f* thinness; delicacy; finesse; kindness

fingere §126 *tr* to feign, pretend; (lit) to invent || *intr* to feign, pretend || *ref* to pretend to be

finiménto *m* finishing touch; **finimenti** harness

finimóndo *m* fracas, uproar

finire §176 *tr* to end; to put an end to; **finiscila!** cut it out! || *intr* (ESSERE) to end, to be over; to abut; to wind up; **finire con** + *inf* to wind up + *ger*; **finire di** + *inf* to finish + *ger*, e.g., **ho finito di farmi la barba** I have finished shaving

fini·to -ta *adj* finished; accomplished; finite; exhausted; **aver finito** to be through; **falla finita!** cut it out! **farla finita con** to be through with; **farla finita con la vita** to end one's life

finitura *f* finishing touch

finlandése [s] *adj* Finnish || *mf* Finlander, Finn || *m* Finnish (*language*)

Finlàndia, la Finland

finni·co -ca *adj & mf* (**-ci -che**) Finnic

fi·no -na *adj* fine, thin; refined; pure; sheer; **fare fino** (coll) to be refined || *adv* even; **fin a quando?** till when?; **fin da domani** beginning tomorrow; **fin da ora** beginning right now; **fin dove?** how far?; **fin in cima** up to the top; **fino a** until; down to; up to; as far as; **fin qui** up to now; up to this point

finòc·chio *m* (**-chi**) fennel; (vulg) fairy, queer

finóra *adv* up to now, heretofore

finta *f* pretense; fly (*of trousers*); (sports) feint; **far finta di** + *inf* to pretend to + *inf*, to feign + *ger*

fintantoché *conj* until

fin·to -ta *adj* false (*teeth*); fake; fictitious; sham (*battle*) || *mf* hypocrite || *f* see **finta**

finzióne *f* pretense; fiction; figment

fio *m*—**pagare il fio** to pay the piper; **pagare il fio di** to pay the penalty for

fioccare §197 (fiòcco) *intr* (ESSERE) to fall (*said of snow*); to flow (*said, e.g., of complaints*) || *impers* (ESSERE) —**fiocca** it is snowing

fiòc·co *m* (**-chi**) bow, knot; flake (*of snow*); flock, tuft (*of wool*); (naut) jib; **coi fiocchi** excellent; made to perfection; **fiocco pallone** (naut) spinnaker

fioccó·so -sa [s] *adj* flaky

fiòcina *f* harpoon

fiò·co -ca *adj* (**-chi -che**) feeble, faint

fiónda *f* sling; slingshot

fio·ràio -ràia (**-rài -ràie**) *mf* florist || *f* flower girl

fiorami *mpl*—**a fiorami** with flower design

fiordaliso *m* fleur-de-lis; (bot) iris; (lit) lily

fiòrdo *m* fjord

fióre *m* flower; prime (*of life*); best, pick; bloom; **a fior d'acqua** on the surface; skimming the water; **a fior di labbra** in a low tone, sottovoce; **a fior di pelle** skin-deep, superficial; **fior di** (coll) a lot of; **fiore di latte** cream; **fiori** (cards) clubs; **primo fiore** down (*soft hairy growth*)

fiorènte *adj* flourishing, thriving

fiorenti·no -na *adj & mf* Florentine

fiorettare (fiorétto) *tr* (fig) to overembellish

fiorétto *m* little flower; choice, pick; overembellishment; choice passage (*from life of saint*); foil; button of foil

fioricoltóre *m* var of **floricoltore**

fioricoltura *f* var of **floricoltura**

fiorino *m* florin

fiorire §176 *tr* to cause to flower; to adorn with flowers || *intr* (ESSERE) to flower, bloom; to flourish; to break out (*said of skin eruption*); to get moldy

fiori·sta *mf* (**-sti -ste**) florist

fiori·to -ta *adj* flowering; flowery;

mottled; moldy; studded (*e.g., with errors*)

fioritura *f* flowering; flourish; mold; (pathol) eruption

fiorrancino *m* (orn) kinglet, firecrest

fiorràn·cio *m* (**-ci**) marigold

fiòtto *m* gush, surge; (obs) wave

Firènze *f* Florence

firma *f* signature; power of attorney; good reputation; (mil) enlisted man; **buona firma** famous writer; **farci la firma** (coll) to accept quite willingly; **firma di favore** guarantor's signature

firmaiòlo *m* (mil) enlisted man

firmaménto *m* firmament

firmare *tr* to sign

firmatà·rio -ria (**-ri -rie**) *adj* signatory || *mf* signer, signatory

fisarmòni·ca *f* (**-che**) accordion

fiscale *adj* fiscal, tax

fischiare §287 *tr* to whistle; to boo || *intr* to whistle; to ring (*said of ears*); to blow (*said, e.g., of a factory whistle*)

fischiettare (**fischiétto**) *tr & intr* to whistle

fischiétto *m* whistle (*instrument*)

fi·schio *m* (**-schi**) whistle; hiss, boo; blow (*of whistle*); ringing (*in the ears*)

fi·sciù *m* (**-sciù**) kerchief, fichu

fisco *m invar* treasury; internal revenue service

fìsi·co -ca (**-ci -che**) *adj* physical; bodily || *m* physicist; physique; (obs) physician || *f* physics

fìsima *f* whim, fancy, caprice

fisiologia *f* physiology

fisiològi·co -ca *adj* (**-ci -che**) physiological

fisionomìa or **fisonomìa** *f* physiognomy; countenance, face; appearance

fisionomi·sta *mf* (**-sti -ste**) person good at faces; physiognomist

fi·so -sa *adj* (lit) fixed

fissàg·gio *m* (**-gi**) (phot) fixing

fissare *tr* to fix; to fasten; to gaze at; to reserve; to hire; **fissare lo sguardo** to gaze || *ref* to gaze, stare; to become obsessed; to settle down

fissati·vo -va *adj* fixing

fissa·to -ta *adj* fixed; (coll) cracked || *mf* (coll) crackpot

fissa·tóre -trice *adj* (phot) fixing || *m* fixer; **fissatore per capelli** hair spray; hair dressing

fissazióne *f* fixation; fixed idea

fìssile *adj* fissionable

fissionàbile *adj* fissionable

fissióne *f* fission

fis·so -sa *adj* fixed; regular || *m* pay

fìstola *f* (pathol) fistula; (lit) pipe

fitta *f* pang, stitch; crowd; great amount; (coll) blow; (obs) quagmire

fittàvolo *m* tenant farmer

fittì·zio -zia *adj* (**-zi -zie**) fictitious

fit·to -ta *adj* fixed, dug in; thick, dense; pitch (*dark*) || *m* thick; rent; tenancy || *f* see **fitta**

fittóne *m* (bot) taproot

fiuma·no -na *adj* river; from Fiume || *m* person from Fiume || *f* flood, stream

fiumara *f* torrent

fiume *m* river; **a fiumi** like a river

fiutare *tr* to snuff, sniff; to smell

fiutata *f* snuff, sniff

fiuto *m* sense of smell; snuff; flair

flàcci·do -da *adj* flabby

flacóne *m* flacon

flagellare (**flagèllo**) *tr* to scourge, lash, flagellate

flagèllo *m* whip, scourge; pest, plague; (coll) mess

flagrante *adj* flagrant; **in flagrante** (*delitto*) in the act

flan *m* (flan) pudding; (typ) mat

flanèlla *f* flannel

flàn·gia *f* (**-ge**) flange

flato *m* gas, flatus

flatulènza *f* flatulence

flautino *m* flageolet

flauti·sta *mf* (**-sti -ste**) flutist

flàuto *m* flute; **flauto diritto** or **dolce** (mus) recorder

fla·vo -va *adj* (lit) blond, golden

flèbile *adj* mournful

flebite *f* phlebitis

flèmma *f* apathy; coolness; phlegm

flemmàti·co -ca *adj* (**-ci -che**) phlegmatic(al)

flessìbile *adj* flexible, pliable

flessióne *f* bending; (com) fall, drop; (gram) inflection

flessuó·so -sa [s] *adj* lithe, willowy; winding; flowing (*style*)

flèttere §177 *tr* to flex; (gram) to inflect

flirtare *intr* to flirt

flòra *f* flora

floreale *adj* floral

floricoltóre *m* floriculturist

floricoltura *f* floriculture

flòri·do -da *adj* florid; flourishing

flò·scio -scia *adj* (**-sci -sce**) flabby; soft (*hat*)

flòtta *f* fleet

flottante *adj* floating || *m* (com) floating stock

flottare (**flòtto**) *tr & intr* to float

flottìglia *f* flottilla

fluènte *adj* flowing

fluidità *f* fluidity

flùi·do -da *adj & m* fluid; fluent (*style*)

fluire §176 *intr* (ESSERE) to flow; to pour

fluitazióne *f* log driving

fluorescènte *adj* fluorescent

fluorescènza *f* fluorescence

fluorìdri·co -ca *adj* (**-ci -che**) hydrofluoric

fluorite *f* fluor, fluorite

fluorizzazióne [ddzz] *f* fluoridation

fluòro *m* fluorine

fluoruro *m* fluoride

flusso *m* flow; flood (*of tide*); high tide; (pathol) flow (*e.g., of blood*); (phys) flux

flutto *m* (lit) wave

fluttuare (**flùttuo**) *intr* to fluctuate; to bob, toss; to waver; to surge, stream

fluviale *adj* fluvial, river

fobìa *f* phobia

fò·ca *f* (**-che**) seal; sealskin

focàc·cia *f* (**-ce**) flat, rounded loaf; cake

focaccina *f* bun

fo·càia *adj fem* (-càie) flint

focale *adj* focal

fóce *f* mouth (*of river*)

focèna *f* porpoise

fochi·sta *m* (-sti) fireman, stoker; fireworks manufacturer

foco·làio *m* (-lài) (pathol) focus; (fig) hotbed

focolare *m* hearth; firebox; fireside, home

focó·so -sa [s] *adj* fiery, high-spirited

fòdera *f* lining (*of suit*); cover, case

foderare (fòdero) *tr* to line; to cover

fòdero *m* sheath, scabbard; raft

fó·ga *f* (-ghe) ardor, impetus

fòg·gia *f* (-ge) fashion, shape; **a foggia di** shaped like

foggiare §290 (fòggio) *tr* to shape, fashion

fòglia *f* leaf; petal; foil (*of gold*); **mangiare la foglia** (fig) to get wise, catch on

fogliame *m* foliage

fò·glio *m* (-gli) sheet; bill, banknote; folio; newspaper; permit; **foglio d'avviso** notice; **foglio di congedo** (mil) discharge; **foglio d'iscrizione** application; **foglio di via** (mil) travel orders; **foglio modello** blank form; **foglio rosa** (aut) permit; **foglio volante** flier, handbill

fógna *f* sewer, drain

fognatura *f* sewerage

fòla *f* tale, fable

fola·ga *f* (-ghe) (zool) coot

folata *f* gust; (lit) flight (*of birds*)

folclóre *m* folklore

folgorante *adj* striking; flashing; meteoric (*career*)

folgorare (fólgoro) *tr* to strike (with lightning) || *intr* to flash by || *impers* —folgora it is thundering

fólgore *m* (lit) thunderbolt || *f* flash of lightning; thunderbolt

fólla *f* crowd; (fig) flock

follare (fóllo) *tr* to full

fòlle *adj* mad, crazy; (aut) neutral; (mach) loose (*pulley*)

folleggiare §290 (folléggio) *intr* to act foolishly; to frolic

folleménte *adv* desperately, madly

follétto *m* elf; little imp

follìa *f* madness, lunacy; folly; **alla follia** madly; **far follie per** to be crazy about

follìcolo *m* follicle

fól·to -ta *adj* thick; beetle (*brow*); deep (*night*) || *m* depth (*e.g., of the night*); thick (*e.g., of the battle*)

fomentare (foménto) *tr* to foment

fòmite *m* (lit) instigation; impetus

fónda *f* anchorage; lowland; saddlebag; **alla fonda** at anchor

fónda·co *m* (-chi) (hist) warehouse

fondale *m* depth (*of river, sea*); (theat) backdrop

fondamentale *adj* fundamental, basic

fondamén·to *m* (-ti) ground, foundation; basis; **fare fondamento su** to count on; **fondamenti** elements; **senza fondamento** baseless; without getting anywhère || *m* (-ta *fpl*)—**fondamenta** foundations (*of a building*)

fondare (fóndo) *tr* to found; to build; to charter || *ref*—**fondarsi su** to rely on; to be based upon

fondatézza *f* basis, ground, foundation

fonda·to -ta *adj* well-founded

fonda·tóre -trice *mf* founder

fondazióne *f* foundation

fondèllo *m* bottom, base

fondènte *m* flux

fóndere §178 *tr* to smelt; to melt; to blow (*a fuse*); to cast (*a statue*); to blend (*colors*) || *intr* to melt; to blend || *ref* to melt; to blend; to burn out

fonderìa *f* foundry

fondià·rio -ria (-ri -rie) *adj* real-estate, land || *f* real-estate tax

fondìna *f* holster; (coll) soup dish

fondi·sta *mf* (-sti -ste) editorialist; (sports) long-distance runner

fóndita *f* (typ) font

fonditóre *m* smelter, founder

fón·do -da *adj* deep || *m* bottom; fund; innermost nature; seat; end; background; land, property; **a doppio fondo** with a false bottom; **a fondo** thoroughly; **a fondo perduto** as an outright grant; **dar fondo** (naut) to cast anchor; **dar fondo a** to exhaust; **di fondo** (journ) editorial; (sports) long-distance; **fondi** funds; lees; **fondi di bottega** remnants; **fondi di caffè** coffee grounds; **fondo comune d'investimento** mutual fund; **fondo d'ammortamento** sinking fund; **fondo di beneficenza** community chest; **fondo tinta** foundation (*in make-up*); **in fondo** in the end; at the bottom; after all

fonè·ma *m* (-mi) phoneme

fonèti·co -ca (-ci -che) *adj* phonetic || *f* phonetics

fonògeno *m* pickup (*of record player*)

fonògrafo *m* phonograph, Gramophone

fonogram·ma *m* (-mi) telegram delivered by telephone

fonologìa *f* phonology

fonorivelatóre *m* pickup (*of record player*)

fonovalìgia *f* portable phonograph

fontana *f* fountain; spring; source

fónte *m* (lit) spring, source; **fonte battesimale** font || *f* spring; fountain; source; **da fonte autorevole** on good authority

foraggiare §290 *tr* to subsidize || *intr* to forage

foràg·gio *m* (-gi) forage, provender, fodder

foràne·o -a *adj* rural; outer; (naut) outer (*dock*)

forare (fóro) *tr* to pierce; to bore; to puncture || *intr* to have a flat tire || *ref* to be punctured

foratura *f* puncture

fòrbice *f*—**a forbice** (sports) scissors (*e.g., kick*); **forbici** scissors; clippers; **forbici per le unghie** nail clippers

forbire §176 *tr* to wipe; to polish; to shine

fór·ca *f* (-che) fork; pitchfork; gallows; mountain pass; **fare la forca a qlcu** (slang) to betray s.o.; (slang) to do s.o. dirt; **fatto a forca** V-shaped

forcèlla *f* fork (*of bicycle or motorcycle*); mountain pass; fork-shaped pole; hairpin; cradle (*of handset*); (coll) wishbone (*of chicken*)

forchétta *f* fork; (coll) wishbone (*of chicken*); **alla forchetta** (culin) cold (*e.g., lunch*)

forchettata *f* forkful; blow with a fork

forchettóne *m* carving fork

forcina *f* hairpin

fòrcipe *m* forceps

forcóne *m* pitchfork

forellino *m* pinhole

forèsta *f* forest

forestale *adj* forest, park

foresterìa *f* guest quarters (*in college or monastery*)

forestierismo *m* borrowing (*from another language*)

forestiè·ro -ra *adj* foreign ‖ *mf* foreigner; stranger; outsider

forfettà·rio -ria *adj* (-ri -rie) job, e.g., **contratto forfettario** job contract; all-inclusive, e.g., **combinazione forfettaria** all-inclusive price agreement

fórfora *f* dandruff

fòr·gia *f* (-ge) forge; smithy

forgiare §290 (fòrgio) *tr* to forge

foriè·ro -ra *adj* forerunning ‖ *mf* forerunner, harbinger

fórma *f* shape; form; mold (*e.g., for cakes*); wheel (*of cheese*); (typ) form; **forma da cappelli** hat block; **forma da scarpe** shoe tree; shoe last (*used by shoemaker*); **forme** shape, body; good manners; **salvare le forme** to save face

formaggièra *f* dish for grated cheese

formàg·gio *m* (-gi) cheese

formaldèide *f* formaldehyde

formale *adj* formal; prim

formalismo *m* formality

formali·tà *f* (-tà) formality

formalizzare [ddzz] *tr* to scandalize ‖ *ref* to be shocked

formare (fórmo) *tr* & *ref* to form

forma·to -ta *adj* formed ‖ *m* format

formazióne *f* formation

fòrmica *f* (trademark) Formica

formì·ca *f* (-che) ant

formi·càio *m* (-cài) anthill; (fig) swarm

formichière *m* anteater

formicolare (formìcolo) *intr* to swarm; to crawl ‖ *intr* (ESSERE) to creep (*said, e.g., of a leg*)

formicolì·o *m* (-i) swarm; creeping sensation, numbness

formidàbile *adj* formidable

formó·so -sa [s] *adj* shapely, buxom

fòrmula *f* formula; (aut) category, class; **formula dubitativa** (law) lack of evidence; **formula piena** (law) acquittal

formulare (fòrmulo) *tr* to formulate

formulà·rio *m* (-ri) formulary; form

fornace *f* furnace, kiln

for·nàio -nàia *mf* (-nài -nàie) baker

fornèllo *m* stove, range; (*of boiler*) firebox; bowl (*of pipe*); (min) shaft; **fornello a gas** gas range; **fornello a spirito** kerosene stove; chafing dish

fornire §176 *tr* to furnish, supply

forni·tóre -trice *mf* supplier, purveyor

fornitura *f* supply; order; delivery

fórno *m* oven; furnace; kiln; bakery; (theat) empty house; **al forno** or **in forno** baked; **alto forno** blast furnace; **forno crematorio** crematorium; **far forno** (theat) to play before an empty house

fóro *m* hole

fòro *m* forum; (law) bar

forosétta [s] *f* (lit) peasant girl

fórse *m* doubt; **mettere in forse** to endanger; to put in doubt ‖ *adv* perhaps, maybe

forsenna·to -ta *adj* mad, insane ‖ *mf* lunatic

fòrte *adj* strong; firm; bad (*cold*); fat, hefty; fast (*color*); offensive (*joke*); hard (*smoker*); main (*dish*); (lit) thick ‖ *m* strong person; fortress; bulk, main body; forte; (lit) thick; **sapere di forte** to have a strong flavor; **farsi forte** to bear up; **farsi forte di** to appropriate, use; to be cocksure of ‖ *adv* hard, strong; much; loud; openly; a lot; fast; swiftly

fortézza *f* fortress; strength; fortitude

fortificare §197 (fortìfico) *tr* to fortify ‖ *ref* to be strengthened; to dig in

fortificazióne *f* fortification

fortino *m* blockhouse, redoubt

fortùi·to -ta *adj* fortuitous

fortuna *f* fortune; luck; good luck; fate, destiny; (lit) storm; **avere fortuna** to be lucky; to be a hit; **buona fortuna!** good luck!; **di fortuna** makeshift, emergency; **non aver la fortuna di** to not be fortunate enough to; **per fortuna** luckily

fortunale *m* storm, tempest

fortuna·to -ta *adj* fortunate, lucky

fortunó·so -sa [s] *adj* eventful

forùncolo *m* boil; pimple

forviare §119 *tr* to mislead, lead astray ‖ *intr* to go astray

fòrza *f* strength; force; power; police; (phys) force; **a forza di** by dint of; **a tutta forza** at full speed; **bassa forza** (mil) enlisted personnel; **di forza** by force; **di prima forza** first-rate; **far forza a** to encourage; to force; **fare forza a sé stesso** to restrain oneself; **forza!** courage!; **forza di corpo** (typ) height-to-paper; **forza maggiore** force majeure, act of God; **forza muscolare** brawn; **forza pubblica** police; **forza viva** kinetic energy; **per forza** of course; under duress

forzare (fòrzo) *tr* to force; to strain; to rape; to tamper with (*a lock*); **forzare il passo** to hasten one's step; **forzare la consegna** (mil) to violate orders

forza·to -ta *adj* forced; force (*e.g., feed*) ‖ *m* convict

forzière *m* chest, coffer

forzó·so -sa [s] *adj* compulsory; imposed by law

forzu·to -ta *adj* husky, robust

foschìa *f* smog; mist; haze

fó·sco -sca *adj* (**-schi -sche**) dark; gloomy; misty

fosfato *m* phosphate

fosforeggiare §290 (**fosforéggio**) *intr* to phosphoresce; to glow

fosforescènte *adj* phosphorescent

fòsforo *m* phosphorus

fòssa *f* grave; hollow; hole, ditch; moat; pit; den (*of lions*); **fossa biologica** sewage-treatment plant; **fossa di riparazione** (aut) pit; **fossa settica** septic tank

fossato *m* ditch; moat

fossétta *f* dimple

fòssile *adj & m* fossil

fossilizzare [**ddzz**] *tr* to fossilize || *ref* to become fossilized

fòsso *m* ditch; moat

fò·to *f* (**-to**) photo

fotocòpia *f* photocopy

fotocopiare §287 (**fotocòpio**) *tr* to photocopy

fotoelèttri·co -ca (**-ci -che**) *adj* photo-electric || *f* (mil) searchlight

fotogèni·co -ca *adj* (**-ci -che**) photogenic

fotogiornale *m* pictorial magazine

fotografare (**fotògrafo**) *tr* to photograph

fotografìa *f* photography; photograph

fotogràfi·co -ca *adj* (**-ci -che**) photographic

fotògrafo *m* photographer

fotogram·ma *m* (**-mi**) (phot) frame

fotoincisióne *f* photoengraving

fotolampo *m* flashlight

fotòmetro *m* exposure meter

fotomontàg·gio *m* (**-gi**) photomontage

fototubo *m* phototube

fra *m invar* brother, e.g., **fra Cristoforo** Brother Christopher || *prep* among; between; in, within

frac *m* (**frac**) swallow-tailed coat

fracassare *tr* to crash, smash || *ref* to crash

fracasso *m* crash; uproar; (coll) slew

fràdi·cio -cia (**-ci -cie**) *adj* rotten; soaked || *m* rotten part; decay; wet ground

fràgile *adj* fragile; brittle; frail

fragilità *f* fragility, frailty

fràgola *f* strawberry

fragóre *m* din; peal; roar

fragoró·so -sa [s] *adj* noisy

fragrante *adj* fragrant

fraintèndere §270 *tr* to misunderstand

frammassóne *m* Freemason

frammassonerìa *f* Freemasonry

frammentare (**framménto**) *tr* to fragment

frammentà·rio -ria *adj* (**-ri -rie**) fragmentary

framménto *m* fragment

framméttere §198 *tr* to interpose || *ref* to meddle; **frammettersi in** to intrude in, to butt into

frammèzzo [**ddzz**] *adv* in the middle || *prep* in the midst of

frammischiare §287 *tr* to mix || *ref* to concern oneself

frana *f* landslide; (fig) collapse

franare *intr* to slide; to collapse

francesca·no -na *adj & mf* Franciscan

francé·sco -sca (**-schi -sche**) *adj* (archaic) French || **Francesco** *m* Francis || **Francesca** *f* Frances

francése *adj* French || *m* French (*language*); Frenchman (*person*); **i francesi** the French || *f* Frenchwoman

francesismo *m* gallicism

francesizzare [**ddzz**] *tr* to Frenchify

franchézza *f* frankness

franchi·gia *f* (**-gie**) franchise; exemption; deductible insurance; (naut) shore leave; **franchigia postale** franking privilege

Frància, la France

fran·co -ca (**-chi -che**) *adj* free; frank; Frankish; **farla franca** to get off scot free; **franco di porto** prepaid, postpaid; **franco domicilio** home delivery, free delivery || *m* franc || **Franco** *m* Frank

francobóllo *m* postage stamp, stamp

frangènte *m* breaker, surf; **essere nei frangenti** to be in bad straits

fràngere §179 *tr* to crush; (lit) to break || *ref* to break, comb (*said of waves*)

frangétta *f* bangs

fràn·gia *f* (**-ge**) fringe; embellishment; shoreline; bangs; **frangia di corallo** coral reef

frangìbile *adj* breakable

frangiflut·ti *m* (**-ti**) breakwater

frangi·vènto *m* (**-vènto**) windbreak

frangizòl·le *m* (**-le**) disc harrow

Frankfur·ter *m* (**-ter**) hot dog

fran·tóio *m* (**-tói**) crusher; **frantoio a mascelle** jawbreaker

frantumare *tr* to crush; to break to pieces || *ref* to be crushed; to go to pieces

frantume *m* fragment; **andare in frantumi** to go to pieces

frappé *m* (**frappé**) shake; frappé; **frappé alla menta** mint julep; **frappé di latte** milk shake

frappórre §218 *tr* to interpose || *ref* to interfere; to intervene

frasà·rio *m* (**-ri**) language, speech

fra·sca *f* (**-sche**) branch; bush; ornament; whim; frivolous woman, flirt

frase *f* sentence; (mus) phrase; **frase fatta** cliché; **frase idiomatica** idiom; **frasi** words; **frasi di commiserazione** condolences

fraseggiare §290 (**fraséggio**) *intr* to use phrasing; to use big words; (mus) to phrase

fraseologìa *f* phraseology

fràssino *m* ash tree

frastagliare §280 *tr* to cut out (*e.g., paper*)

frastaglia·to -ta *adj* indented, jagged; ornamented

frastornare (**frastórno**) *tr* to disturb; (lit) to prevent

frastuòno *m* din, roar

frate *m* friar, monk, brother

fratellanza *f* brotherhood

fratellastro *m* stepbrother; half brother

fratèllo *m* brother; **fratelli** brothers and sisters; **fratello consanguineo** half brother on the father's side; **fratello**

di latte foster brother; **fratello ge-mello** twin
fraterni·tà f (**-tà**) fraternity
fraternizzare [ddzz] *intr* to fraternize
fratèr·no -na *adj* fraternal, brotherly
fratrici·da (-di -de) *adj* fratricidal ‖ *mf* fratricide
fratrici·dio m (-di) fratricide
fratta f brushwood; (coll) hedge
frattàglie *fpl* giblets, chitterlings, offal
frattanto *adv* meantime, meanwhile
frattèmpo m—**nel frattempo** meanwhile
frattura f fracture; break; breach
fratturare *tr & ref* to fracture, break
fraudolènto *adj* fraudulent
frazionare (frazióno) *tr* to fractionate; to break up
frazionà·rio -ria *adj* (**-ri -rie**) fractional
frazióne f fraction; hamlet; (eccl) breaking of the host
fréc·cia f (**-ce**) arrow, bolt; steeple; spire; clock (*on hosiery*); (archit) rise; (fig) aspersion; **freccia consen-siva** arrow (*on traffic light*); **freccia direzionale** (aut) turn signal
frecciata f arrow shot; taunt, gibe; **dare una frecciata a** to hit for a loan
freddare (fréddo) *tr* to chill; to kill
freddézza f chill; cold, coldness; cool-ness, cold shoulder; sang-froid
fréd·do -da *adj* cold; cool, chilly; frigid ‖ m cold, cold weather; chill; **a freddo** cold; cooly; **avere freddo** to be cold (*said of people*); **fare freddo** to be cold (*said of weather*); **freddo cane** biting cold; **sentire freddo** to feel cold; **sudare freddo** to be in a cold sweat
freddoló·so -sa [s] *adj* chilly (*person*)
freddura f joke, pun; cold weather
freddurì·sta *mf* (**-sti -ste**) punster
fregagióne f rubbing, rubdown, mas-sage
fregare §209 (frégo) *tr* to rub; to strike (*a match*); (slang) to steal; (slang) to cheat, dupe; (vulg) to make love with ‖ *ref* to rub (*e.g., one's hands*); **fregarsene di** (vulg) to not give a hoot about
fregata f rubbing; (nav) frigate; (orn) frigate bird; (slang) cheating
fregatura f (slang) cheating; (slang) hitch, halt
fregiare §290 (frégio) *tr* to decorate; to fret
fré·gio m (-gi) decoration; insignia (*on cap of officer*); (archit) frieze
fré·go m (-ghi) line, stroke
frégola f rut, heat; (slang) mania, craze
fremènte *adj* throbbing; thrilling
frèmere §123 *tr* (lit) to beg insistently ‖ *intr* to throb; to be thrilled; to shake, tremble, rustle; to shudder (*with horror*); (fig) to boil; (fig) to fret
frèmito m throb; thrill; shudder; roar; quiver
frenare (fréno) *tr* to brake, stop; to bridle (*a horse*); to curb (*passions*); to restrain (*e.g., laughter*); **frenare la corsa** to slow down ‖ *intr* to put the brakes on ‖ *ref* to control oneself

frenatóre m (**rr**) brakeman
frenesìa f frenzy; (fig) craze, fever; (lit) thought
frenèti·co -ca *adj* (**-ci -che**) frenzied; frantic; crazy, enthusiastic
fréno m bit, bridle; brake; (fig) check; (mach) lock; **freno ad aria compressa** air brake; **mordere il freno** to champ the bit; **senza freno** wild, unbridled; **tenere a freno** to keep in check
frenologìa f phrenology
frequentare (frequènto) *tr* to frequent; to attend ‖ *intr* to associate
frequenta·tóre -trice *mf* patron, cus-tomer; frequenter, habitué
frequènte *adj* frequent; rapid (*pulse*); (lit) crowded
frequènza f frequency; attendance; **fre-quenza ultraelevata** ultrahigh fre-quency
frèsa f milling cutter; burr (*of dentist's drill*)
fresatrice f milling machine
fresatura f (mach) milling
freschézza f freshness; coolness
fré·sco -sca (-schi -sche) *adj* fresh; cool; **fresco di malattia** just recov-ered; **fresco di stampa** fresh off the press; **fresco di studi** fresh out of school; **star fresco** to be in a fix; to be all wrong ‖ m cool weather; tropi-cal fabric; **di fresco** recently; **fare fresco** to be cool (*said of weather*); **mettere al fresco** (coll) to put in the clink; **per il fresco** in cool weather
frescó·ne -na *mf* (slang) dumbell
frescura f coolness, freshness
frétta f hurry, haste; **avere fretta** to be in a hurry; **in fretta** in a hurry; **in fretta e furia** in a rush
frettazzo m plasterer's wooden trowel; steel brush
frettoló·so -sa [s] *adj* hurried, hasty
freudismo m Freudianism
friàbile *adj* friable, crumbly
friabilità f friableness
fricassèa f fricassee
frìggere §180 *tr* to fry; **mandare qlcu a farsi friggere** to tell s.o. to go to the devil ‖ *intr* to fry; to sizzle; to fret
friggitorìa f fried-food shop
frigidézza f frigidity
frigidi·tà f (**-tà**) coldness; frigidity
frìgi·do -da *adj* cold; frigid
frì·gio -gia *adj* (**-gi -gie**) Phrygian
frignare *intr* to whimper
frigorìfe·ro -ra *adj* refrigerating ‖ m refrigerator; (journ) morgue
fringuèl·lo -la *mf* chaffinch, finch
frinire §176 *intr* to chirp
frisata f gunnel
frittata f omelet; **fare la frittata** (coll) to make a mess of it
frittèlla f fritter; pancake; (coll) grease spot
frit·to -ta *adj* fried; cooked, ruined ‖ m fry, fried platter
frittura f frying; fry, fried platter
frivolézza f frivolity
frìvo·lo -la *adj* frivolous; flighty
frizionare (frizióno) *tr* to massage

frizióne *f* friction; massage; (aut) clutch

frizzante [ddzz] *adj* crisp, brisk (*weather*); sparkling (*wine*)

frizzare [ddzz] *intr* to tingle; to sparkle, fizz (*said of wine*); (fig) to sting

frizzo [ddzz] *m* jest, witticism; gibe, dig

frodare (fròdo) *tr* to cheat, swindle

fròde *f* fraud; **frode fiscale** tax evasion or fraud

fròdo *m invar* customs evasion; **di frodo** smuggled

frò·gia *f* (-ge or -gie) nostril (*of horse*)

fròl·lo -la *adj* high (*meat*); soft, tender; (fig) weak

frónda *f* branch, bough; political opposition; **fronde** foliage; ornaments

frondó·so -sa [s] *adj* leafy

frontale *adj* front; frontal

frónte *m* (mil, pol) front; **far fronte a** to face; to face up to; to meet (*expenses*); **tenere fronte a** to face, resist ‖ *f* forehead, brow; countenance; title page; headline; (fig) face; **a fronte** opposite, facing; **a fronte di** (com) in reference to; **dietro front!** (mil) about face!; **di fronte a** in the face of; facing; **di fronte a tutti** in plain view; **fronte destr'!** (mil) right face!; **mettere a fronte** to compare; **tenere a fronte** to have in front of one's eyes

fronteggiare §290 (**frontéggio**) *tr* to face, front ‖ *ref* to face one another

frontespi·zio *m* (-zi) title page

frontièra *f* border, frontier

frontóne *m* (archit) pediment; (archit) gable

frónzolo *m* bauble, gewgaw; **fronzoli** finery, frippery

fròtta *f* crowd; swarm; flock

fròttola *f* fib; popular poem; **frottole** humbug

frugale *adj* frugal (*meal; life*); temperate (*in eating or drinking*)

frugare §209 *tr* to rummage through; to search (*a person*) ‖ *intr* to rummage, poke around

frùgo·lo -la *mf* restless child, imp

fruire §176 *tr* to enjoy ‖ *intr*—**fruire di** to enjoy

fruitóre *m* user

frullare *tr* to beat, whip ‖ *intr* to flutter; to spin; **frullare per il capo a** to get into the head of, e.g., **cosa gli è frullato per il capo?** what got into his head?

frulla·to -ta *adj* whipped ‖ *m* shake (*drink*)

frullatóre *m* electric beater

frullino *m* egg beater

fruménto *m* wheat

frumentóne *m* corn

frusciare §128 *intr* to rustle

frusci·o *m* (-i) rustle, rustling

frusta *f* whip; egg beater

frustare *tr* to whip, lash; (fig) to censure; (coll) to wear out (*clothes*)

frustata *f* lash; (fig) censure

frustino *m* whip, crop

fru·sto -sta *adj* worn out, threadbare ‖ *f* see **frusta**

frustrare *tr* to frustrate, baffle; to discomfit

frut·ta *f* (-ta & -te) fruit; **essere alle frutta** to be at the end of the meal, to be having one's dessert

fruttare *tr & intr* to yield

fruttéto *m* orchard

frutticoltóre *m* fruit grower

fruttièra *f* fruit dish

fruttife·ro -ra *adj* fruit-bearing; fruitful, profitable; (lit) fecund

fruttificare §197 (**fruttìfico**) *intr* to fructify; to yield

fruttivéndo·lo -la *mf* fruit dealer

frutto *m* fruit; **frutti di mare** shellfish; **mettere a frutto** to make yield

fruttuó·so -sa [s] *adj* fruitful, profitable

fu *adj invar* late (*deceased*); son of the late . . . ; daughter of the late . . .

fucilare *tr* to shoot

fucilata *f* rifle shot

fucilazióne *f* execution by a firing squad

fucile *m* rifle, gun; **fucile ad aria compressa** air gun; **fucile da caccia** shotgun; **un buon fucile** a good shot

fucilería *f* fusillade

fucilière *m* rifleman

fucina *f* forge, smithy

fu·co *m* (-chi) (bot) rockweed; (zool) drone

fùcsia *f* fuchsia

fu·ga *f* (-ghe) flight; leak; row (*e.g., of rooms*); spurt (*in bicycle race*); (mus) fugue; **di fuga** hastily; **prendere la fuga** to take flight; **volgere in fuga** to put to flight; to take flight

fugace *adj* passing, fleeting

fugare §209 *tr* (lit) to avoid; (lit) to put to flight; (lit) to dispel

fuggènte *adj* passing, fleeting

fuggévole *adj* fleeting

fuggia·sco -sca (-schi -sche) *adj* fleeing, fugitive ‖ *mf* fugitive; refugee

fuggi fug·gi *m* (-gi) stampede

fuggire *tr* to flee; to avoid ‖ *intr* (ESSERE) to flee, run away; (sports) to take the lead; **fuggire a** to flee from

fuggiti·vo -va *adj & mf* fugitive

fulcro *m* fulcrum; (fig) pivot

fulgènte *adj* (lit) resplendent

fùlgi·do -da *adj* resplendent

fulgóre *m* resplendency, radiance

fuliggine *f* soot

fuligginó·so -sa [s] *adj* sooty

fulmicotóne *m* guncotton

fulminante *adj* crushing (*illness*); withering (*look*); explosive ‖ *m* exploding cap; (coll) match

fulminare (**fùlmino**) *tr* to strike by lightning; to strike down; to confound, dumfound ‖ *ref* (elec) to burn out, to blow out ‖ *impers* (ESSERE)—**fulmina** it is lightning

fùlmine *m* lightning, thunderbolt; **fulmine a ciel sereno** bolt out of the blue

fulmìne·o -a *adj* swift, instant

ful·vo -va *adj* tawny

fumaiòlo *m* chimney; smokestack; (naut) funnel

fumante *adj* smoking; steaming; dusty
fumare *tr* to smoke; (lit) to exhale ‖ *intr* to smoke; to steam; to fume; **fumare come un turco** to smoke like a chimney
fumata *f* smoking; smoke signal; **fare una fumata** to have a smoke
fuma·tóre -trice *mf* smoker
fumetti·sta *mf* (**-sti -ste**) cartoonist
fumétto *m* cartoon; **fumetti** comics
fumigare §209 (**fùmigo**) *tr* (obs) to fumigate ‖ *intr* to steam, smoke
fumigazióne *f* fumigation
fumi·sta *m* (**-sti**) heater man; joker, hoaxer
fumisteria *f* fondness for practical jokes; bamboozling
fumo *m* smoke; vapor, steam; smoking; (coll) hot air; **andare in fumo** to go up in smoke; **fumi** vapors, fumes; **mandare in fumo** to squander; to thwart; **sapere di fumo** to taste smoky; **vedere qlcu come il fumo negli occhi** to not be able to stand s.o.; **vender fumo** to peddle influence
fumòge·no -na *adj* smoke, e.g., **cortina fumogena** smoke curtain
fumó·so -sa [s] *adj* smoky; obscure
funambolismo *m* tightrope walking; (fig) acrobatics
funàmbo·lo -la *mf* tightrope walker; (fig) acrobat
fune *f* rope, cable; **fune portante** suspension cable
fùnebre *adj* funeral; funereal, gloomy
funerale *adj & m* funeral
funerà·rio -ria *adj* (**-ri -rie**) funeral
funère·o -a *adj* funereal; funeral
funestare (**funèsto**) *tr* to afflict
funè·sto -sta *adj* baleful; mournful
fungàia *f* mushroom farm; mushroom bed; flock, swarm
fùngere §183 *intr*—**fungere da** to act as
fun·go *m* (**-ghi**) mushroom; fungus; **fungo atomico** mushroom cloud; **venir su come i funghi** to mushroom
fungó·so -sa [s] *adj* fungous
funicolare *adj* cable, cable-driven ‖ *f* funicular railway
funivìa *f* cableway
funzionale *adj* functional
funzionalità *f* functionalism
funzionaménto *m* working order; functioning
funzionare (**funzióno**) *intr* to work; to function; **funzionare da** to act as
funzionà·rio -ria *mf* (**-ri -rie**) functionary, official; public official
funzióne *f* function; office; duty; (eccl) service; **facente funzione** acting; **mettere in funzione** to make (*s.th*) work
fuò·co *m* (**-chi**) fire; burner (*of gas range*); focus; (fig) home; (lit) thunderbolt; **al fuoco!** fire! (*warning*); **andare per il fuoco** (culin) to boil over; **cuocere a fuoco lento** (culin) to simmer; **dar fuoco a** to set fire to; **di fuoco** fiery; blushing; **far fuoco** to fire; **fuochi artificiali** fireworks; **fuoco di fila** enfilade; **fuoco!** (mil) fire!; **fuoco di paglia** (fig) flash in the pan; **fuoco di segnalazione** flare; **fuoco fatuo** will-o'-the-wisp; **fuoco**

incrociato cross fire; **fuoco nutrito** drumfire; **mettere a fuoco** to focus; **mettere una mano sul fuoco** to be absolutely sure, to swear by it
fuorché *prep* except; **fuorché di** except to
fuòri *adv* outside, out; aside; e.g., **lasciar fuori** to leave aside; **andar di fuori** (culin) to boil over; **dar fuori** to do away with; to squander; **di fuori** outside; **far fuori** to publish; **fuori di** out of; outside of; beyond (*a doubt*); off (*the road*); beside (*oneself*); **fuori d'uso** out of style; obsolete; **il di fuori** the outside; **in fuori** protruding; forward; **mettere fuori** to throw out; to spread; to exhibit ‖ *prep* beyond; out of; outside; **fuori commercio** not for sale; **fuori concorso** in a class by itself (himself, etc.); **fuori luogo** untimely, out of place; **fuori (di) mano** far away; solitary; **fuori testo** inserted, tipped in
fuoribór·do *m* (**-do**) outboard; outboard motor
fuoricombattimén·to (**-to**) *adj* knocked out ‖ *m* knockout
fuorigiò·co *m* (**-co**) (sports) offside
fuorilég·ge *mf* (**-ge**) outlaw
fuorisè·rie (**-rie**) *adj* custom-built ‖ *m & f* custom model ‖ *f* custom-built car
fuoristra·da *m* (**-da**) land rover
fuoriusci·to -ta *adj* exiled ‖ *mf* political exile ‖ *f* leak; flow; protrusion
fuorvia·to -ta *adj* mislead, misguided
furbacchió·ne -na *mf* slippery person
furberia *f* slyness, cunning
fur·bo -ba *adj* sly, cunning ‖ *mf* knave; **furbo di tre cotte** slicker
furènte *adj* furious
fureria *f* (mil) company headquarters
furétto *m* ferret
furfante *m* sharper, scoundrel
furfanteria *f* rascality
furgoncino *m* small delivery van
furgóne *m* truck; patrol wagon; hearse; **furgone cellulare** prison van
furgoni·sta *mf* (**-sti -ste**) truck driver, teamster
fùria *f* fury; strength, violence; hurry; **a furia di** by dint of; **con furia** in a hurry; **far furia a** to urge; **montare in furia** to go berserk; to fly off the handle
furibón·do -da *adj* furious, wild
furière *m* soldier attached to company headquarters
furió·so -sa [s] *adj* furious; fierce; mad
furóre *m* furor, frenzy; violence; longing; **far furore** to be a hit, to be all the rage
furoreggiare §290 (**furoréggio**) *intr* to be a hit, be all the rage
furti·vo -va *adj* stealthy; furtive; stolen (*e.g., goods*)
furto *m* theft; stolen goods; **di furto** stealthily; **furto con scasso** burglary
fusa [s] *fpl*—**fare le fusa** to purr
fuscèllo *m* twig
fusciac·ca *f* (**-che**) sash (*around the waist*)

fusèllo [s] *m* spindle; axle, shaft
fusìbile *adj* fusible || *m* (elec) fuse
fusióne *f* fusion; melting; merger; blending (*of colors*)
fu·so -sa *adj* melted; molten
fuso [s] *m* spindle; shank (*of anchor*); shaft (*of column*); (aut) axle; **fuso orario** time zone
fusolièra *f* (aer) fuselage
fustagno *m* fustian
fustàia *f* adult forest, full-grown forest
fustèlla *f* (perforating) punch; (pharm) price stub

fustigare §209 (**fùstigo**) *tr* to whip
fusto *m* trunk (*of tree*); stalk; stem (*of key*); beam (*of balance*); butt (*of gun*); trunk, body; frame (*of armchair*); tank (*for holding liquids*); drum (*metal receptacle*); holding stick (*of umbrella*); shaft (*of column*); **d'alto fusto** full-grown (*tree*)
fùtile *adj* futile, trifling
futilità *f* futility
futurismo *m* futurism
futuri·sta *mf* (-**sti -ste**) futurist
futu·ro -ra *adj & m* future

G

G, g [dʒi] *m & f* seventh letter of the Italian alphabet
gabardi·ne *f* (-**ne**) gabardine; gabardine raincoat or topcoat
gabbamón·do *m* (-**do**) cheat, sharper
gabbanèlla *f* gown (*of physician or patient*); robe
gabbano *m* cloak; frock; **mutare gabbano** to be a turncoat
gabbare *tr* to dupe, cheat || *ref*—**gabbarsi di** to make fun of
gàbbia *f* cage; ox muzzle; dock (*in courtroom*); (mach) housing; (naut) top; (naut) topsail; **gabbia d'imballaggio** crate; **gabbia toracica** rib cage
gabbiano *m* sea gull
gabbo *m*—**farsi gabbo di** to make fun of; **prendere a gabbo** to make light of
gabèlla *f* (obs) customs, duty
gabellare (**gabèllo**) *tr* to palm off; to swallow (*e.g., a tall story*); (obs) to tax
gabinétto *m* office (*of doctor, dentist, lawyer*); cabinet; chamber (*of judge*); toilet; closet; laboratory; **gabinetto da bagno** bathroom; **gabinetto di decenza** toilet, bathroom
ga·gà *m* (**gà**) fop, dandy; lounge lizard
gaggia *f* acacia
gagliardétto *m* pennon; pennant
gagliardìa *f* (lit) vigor; (lit) prowess
gagliar·do -da *adj* vigorous; stalwart; hearty (*e.g., voice*)
gagliòf·fo -fa *adj* loutish; rascal || *mf* lout; rascal
gaiézza *f* gaiety, vivacity
gàio gàia *adj* (**gài gàie**) gay, vivacious
gala *m & f* gala; gala affair; **di gala** formal; **mettersi in gala** to dress up || *f* frill; bow tie (*for formal attire*); (naut) bunting
galalite *f* casein plastic, galalith
galante *adj* gallant, courtly; amorous; pretty, graceful
galanteria *f* gallantry, courtliness
galantuò·mo *m* (-**mini**) honest man; (coll) my good fellow
galàssia *f* galaxy
galatèo *m* good manners
galèna *f* (min) galena
galeóne *m* galleon
galeòt·to -ta *adj* (archaic) intermediary

(*in love affairs*) || *m* galley slave; convict; (archaic) procurer
galèra *f* galley; forced labor
gali·lèo -lèa (-**lèi -lèe**) *adj & m* Galilean
galla *f* (bot) gall; (pathol) blister; **a galla** afloat; **tenersi a galla** (fig) to keep alive; to manage; **venire a galla** to come to the surface
galleggiante *adj* floating || *m* float
galleggiare §290 (**galléggio**) *intr* to float
galleria *f* tunnel; gallery; balcony; mall, arcade; wind tunnel
Galles, il Wales
gallése [s] *adj* Welsh || *m* Welshman; Welsh (*language*) || *f* Welsh woman
gallétta *f* cracker; hardtack; (naut) ball on top of flagpole
gallétto *m* cockerel; (fig) gallant; (fig) whippersnapper; (mach) wing nut; **fare il galletto** to swagger
gàlli·co -ca *adj & m* (-**ci -che**) Gallic
gallina *f* hen; **gallina faraona** guinea fowl
gal·lo -la *adj* Gallic; (sports) Bantam (*weight*) || *m* rooster, cock; weathercock; Gaul; Gallic (*language*); **fare il gallo** to strut; **gallo cedrone** wood grouse; **gallo d'India** turkey
gallòc·cia *f* (-**ce**) (naut) cleat
gallóne *m* braid; stripe; chevron; gallon
galoppare (**galòppo**) *intr* to gallop; (fig) to rush around
galoppata *f* gallop
galoppa·tóio *m* (-**tói**) bridle path
galoppino *m* errand boy; **galoppino elettorale** ward heeler
galòppo *m* gallop; **andare al piccolo galoppo** to canter; **di gran galoppo** at full speed; **piccolo galoppo** canter
galò·scia *f* (-**sce**) overshoe, rubber
galvanizzare [ddzz] *tr* to electroplate; (fig) to galvanize
galvanoplàsti·ca *f* (-**che**) electroplating
gamba *f* leg; stem; (aer) shock strut; **a gambe all'aria** upside down; **a gambe levate** at top speed; upside down; **darsela a gambe** to take to one's heels; **essere in gamba** to be in good shape; to be on the ball; **essere male in gamba** to be in bad shape; **gamba di legno** peg leg; **gambe a ciambella** bowlegs; **le gambe mi fanno giacomo** my knees shake;

prendere qlcu sotto gamba to make light of s.o.; raddrizzare le gambe ai cani to try the impossible

gambale m legging, gaiter; boot last; leg (of boot)

gamberétto m shrimp

gàmbero m (Astacus, Cambarus) crawfish

gambétto m stumble; trip; (chess) gambit

gambo m stem

gamèlla f (mil) mess kit, mess tin

gamma f gamut; range; gamma d'onda (rad) wave band

ganà·scia f (-sce) jaw; (aut) brake shoe; mangiare a quattro ganasce to eat like a horse

gàn·cio m (-ci) hook; clasp; hanger

gan·ga f (-ghe) gang; (min) gangue

gànghero m hinge; clasp; uscire dai gangheri to fly off the handle

gàn·glio m (-gli) ganglion

ganzo [dz] m (slang) lover; (coll) slicker

gara f competition, match; fare a gara to compete; gara d'appalto competitive bidding

garagi·sta m (-sti) garage man

garante adj responsible ‖ m guarantor; farsi garante per to vouch for

garantire §176 tr to guarantee; to secure (a mortgage)

garanti·to -ta adj guaranteed, warranted; downright; absolute (liar)

garanzìa f guarantee, warranty; insurance, assurance

garbare tr (naut) to shape (a hull) ‖ intr (ESSERE) (with dat) to like, e.g., non gli garbano le Sue parole he does not like your words

garbatézza f politeness, courtesy

garba·to -ta adj polite, courteous

garbo m politeness, good manners; gesture; act; shape (of a hull); good cut (of clothes); elegance (in painting or writing); a garbo correctly

garbù·glio m (-gli) tangle, confusion; mess

gardènia f gardenia

gareggiare §290 (garéggio) intr to compete, vie

garétta f var of garitta

garétto m var of garretto

garganèlla f—bere a garganella to gulp down

gargarismo m gargling; gargle

gargarizzare [ddzz] intr & ref to gargle

gargaròzzo m throat, gullet

garitta f railroad-crossing box; (mil) sentry box; (rr) brakeman's box

garòfano m carnation, pink

garrése [s] m withers

garrétto m ankle (of man); hock (of horse)

garrire §176 intr to chirp, twitter; to flap; (archaic) to quarrel

garrito m chirp, twitter

garròtta f garrote

gàrru·lo ·la adj garrulous

garza f gauze

garzonato [dz] m apprenticeship

garzó·ne -na [dz] mf helper ‖ m helper, boy; apprentice; (archaic) bachelor; garzone di stalla stableboy

gas m (gas) gas; gasoline; gas assfisiante poison gas; gas delle miniere firedamp; gas esilarante laughing gas; gas illuminante illuminating gas; gas lacrimogeno tear gas

gasdótto m gas pipeline

gasificare §197 (gasìfico) tr var of gassificare

gasòlio m Diesel oil

gasòmetro m var of gassometro

gassificare §197 (gassìfico) tr to gasify

gassi·sta m (-sti) gasworker; gas fitter; gas-meter reader

gassòmetro m gasholder, gas tank

gassó·so -sa [s] adj gaseous, gassy ‖ f soda, pop

gastronomìa f gastronomy

gatta f she-cat, tabby; comprare la gatta nel sacco to buy a pig in a poke; gatta ci cova something is rotten in Denmark; pigliare una gatta da pelare to take on a heavy burden, to get a tiger by the tail

gattabùia f (coll) clink, lockup

gattamòrta f (gattemòrte) hypocrite

gattino m kitten; (bot) catkin

gat·to -ta mf cat ‖ m tomcat; tamper, pile driver; gatto a nove code cato'-nine-tails; gatto soriano tortoiseshell cat; quattro gatti a handful of people ‖ f see gatta

gattóni adv on all fours

gattopardo m (zool) serval; gattopardo americano ocelot

gattuè·cio m (-ci) compass saw; (ichth) small dotted dogfish

gaudènte adj jovial ‖ m bon vivant

gàu·dio m (-di) joy, happiness

gavazzare intr (lit) to revel

gavétta f mess kit, mess gear; venire dalla gavetta to come up through the ranks

gavitèllo m buoy

gazza [ddzz] f magpie

gazzarra [ddzz] f racket, uproar

gazzèlla [ddzz] f gazelle

gazzétta [ddzz] f newspaper; gazette; newsmonger; gossip; Gazzetta Ufficiale Official Gazette (in Italy); Congressional Record (U.S.A.)

gazzettino [ddzz] m small newspaper; column, gossip; gazzettino rosa social column; newsmonger; gossip

gazzósa [ddzz] f var of gassosa

gèl m gel

gelare (gèlo) tr to freeze; to nip ‖ intr (ESSERE) & ref to freeze ‖ impers (ESSERE & AVERE)—gela it is freezing

gelata f frost

gela·tàio ·tàia mf (-tài ·tàie) ice-cream dealer

gelaterìa f ice-cream parlor

gelatièra f ice-cream freezer

gelatière m ice-cream dealer

gelatina f gelatin; jelly; gelatina di frutta fruit jelly; gum drop

gelatinizzare [ddzz] tr & ref to gelatinize; to jell

gela·to ·ta adj frozen ‖ m ice-cream;

gelato da passeggio ice cream on a stick, popsicle

gèli·do -da *adj* icy, ice-cold

gèlo *m* frost; ice; cold; **diventare di gelo** to remain dumfounded; **farsi di gelo** to be cold or aloof; **sentirsi il gelo addosso** to get a chill

gelóne *m* chilblain

gelosìa [s] *f* jealousy; great care; shutter

geló·so -sa [s] *adj* jealous; solicitous

gèlso *m* mulberry

gelsomino *m* jasmine

gemebón·do -da *adj* (lit) moaning

gemellàggio *m* sisterhood (*of two cities*)

gemèl·lo -la *adj* twin; sister (*ship*) || *mf* twin || **gemelli** *mpl* cufflinks || **Gemelli** *mpl* (astr) Gemini

gèmere §123 *tr* (lit) to lament || *intr* (ESSERE & AVERE) to moan, groan; to suffer; to squeak (*said of a wheel*); to ooze; to coo (*said of a dove*)

gèmito *m* moan; howl (*of wind*)

gèmma *f* gem; (bot) bud

gemma·to -ta *adj* gemmate; jeweled

gendarme *m* gendarme, policeman

genealogìa *f* genealogy

generalato *m* generalship

generale *adj* general || *m* general; **generale d'armata** (mil) general; **generale di brigata** brigadier general; **generale di corpo d'armata** lieutenant general; **generale di divisione** major general || *f* (mil) assembly; **stare sulle generali** to speak in vague generalities

generali·tà *f* (-tà) generality; majority; **generalità** *fpl* personal data

generalizzare [ddzz] *tr* to generalize; to bring into general use || *intr* to generalize, deal in generalities

generare (gènero) *tr* to beget; to generate || *ref* to occur

genera·tóre -trice *adj* generating || *m* generator || *f* generatrix

generazióne *f* generation

gènere *m* genus; kind, type; genre; (gram) gender; **del genere** similar, alike; **farne di ogni genere** to commit all sorts of mischief; **genere umano** mankind; **generi alimentari** foodstuffs; **generi diversi** sundries, assorted articles; **in genere** generally

genèri·co -ca (-ci -che) *adj* generic; vague; all-round; general (*e.g., practitioner*) || *mf* (theat) actor playing bit parts || *m* vagueness, imprecision

gènero *m* son-in-law

generosi·tà [s] *f* (-tà) generosity

generó·so -sa [s] *adj* generous; rich (*wine*)

gène·si *f* (-si) genesis || **il Genesi** Genesis

genèti·co -ca (-ci -che) *adj* genetic(al) || *f* genetics

genetlìa·co -ca (-ci -che) *adj* birth || *m* birthday

gengiva *f* (anat) gum

genìa *f* set, gang; (lit) breed

geniale *adj* clever; genial; inspired, genius-like

geniali·tà *f* (-tà) cleverness, ingeniousness; genius; (lit) geniality

genière *m* (mil) engineer

gè·nio *m* (-ni) genius; (mil) corps of engineers; **andare a genio** (with *dat*) to like, e.g., **la musica moderna non gli va a genio** he does not like modern music; **fare qlco di genio** to do s.th willingly

genitale *adj* genital || **genitali** *mpl* genitals

geniti·vo -va *adj* & *m* genitive

geni·tóre -trice *mf* parent

gen·nàio *m* (-nài) January

genocìdio *m* genocide

Gènova *f* Genoa

genovése [s] *adj* & *mf* Genoese

gentàglia *f* riffraff, rabble, scum

gènte *adj* (archaic) gentle || *f* people; nation; family; (nav) crew; **gente d'arme** soldiers; **gente di mal affare** riffraff; **gente di mare** sailors

gentildònna *f* gentlewoman

gentile *adj* gentle; nice; genteel || **Gentili** *mpl* heathen

gentilézza *f* gentleness; kindness; **per gentilezza** kindly, please

gentilì·zio -zia *adj* (-zi -zie) of noble family; (lit) ancestral

gentiluò·mo *m* (-mini) gentleman, nobleman

genuflèttere §177 *ref* to kneel down

genuì·no -na *adj* genuine

genziana *f* gentian

geofisi·co -ca (-ci -che) *adj* geophysical || *f* geophysics

geografìa *f* geography

geogràfi·co -ca *adj* (-ci -che) geographic(al)

geògra·fo -fa *mf* geographer

geologìa *f* geology

geòlo·go -ga *mf* (-gi -ghe) geologist

geòme·tra *m* (-tri) geometrician; land surveyor

geometrìa *f* geometry

gerà·nio *m* (-ni) geranium

gerar·ca *m* (-chi) leader

gerarchìa *f* hierarchy

geràrchi·co -ca *adj* (-ci -che) hierarchical; **per via gerarchica** through proper channels

Geremìa *f* Jeremiah

geremìade *f* jeremiad

gerènte *m* manager, director; **gerente responsabile** (journ) managing editor

gèr·go *m* (-ghi) jargon

geriatrìa *f* geriatrics

Gèrico *f* Jericho

gèrla *f* pannier (*carried on the back*)

Germània, la Germany

germàni·co -ca *adj* (-ci -che) Germanic

germànio *m* germanium

germanizzare [ddzz] *tr* to Germanize

germa·no -na *adj* german, e.g., **fratello germano** brother-german; Germanic || *m* (lit) brother-german; **germano nero** (orn) coot; **germano reale** (orn) mallard

gèrme *m* germ; (lit) offspring

germici·da (-di) *adj* germicidal || *m* germicide

germinare (gèrmino) *intr* (ESSERE &
  AVERE) to germinate
germogliare §280 (germóglio) *tr* to put
  forth || *intr* (ESSERE & AVERE) to bud,
  sprout
germó·glio *m* (-gli) bud, sprout
geroglìfi·co -ca *adj & m* (-ci -che)
  hieroglyphic
Geròlamo *m* Jerome
gerontocò·mio *m* (-mi) or gerotrò·fio
  m (-fi) old people's home, nursing
  home
gerùn·dio *m* (-di) gerund
Gerusalèmme *f* Jerusalem
gessare (gèsso) *tr* to plaster; to lime
  (*a field*)
gèsso *m* gypsum; plaster; chalk; (sculp)
  plaster cast
gessó·so -sa [s] *adj* plastery, chalky;
  chalklike
gèsta *f* (archaic) army; gesta *fpl* deeds,
  exploits
gestante *f* pregnant woman
gestazióne *f* gestation
gesticolare (gestìcolo) *intr* to gesticu-
  late
gestióne *f* management, operation;
  data processing
gestire §176 *tr* to manage, operate ||
  intr to gesticulate; (theat) to make
  gestures
gèsto *m* gesture; attitude; act, deed
ge·stóre -strice *mf* manager, operator;
  gestore di stazione (rr) station agent
gestualità *f* bodily movements (*e.g., of
  an actor*)
Gesù *m* Jesus; Gesù Cristo Jesus Christ
gesuì·ta *m* (-ti) Jesuit
gesuìti·co -ca *adj* (-ci -che) Jesuitic(al)
gettare (gètto) *tr* to throw; to cast; to
  pour; to lay (*e.g., a floor*); to send
  forth; to yield; to broadcast (*seed*);
  to risk (*one's life*); gettare la colpa
  addosso a qlcu to lay the blame on
  s.o.; gettare le armi to lay down one's
  arms; gettar giù to fell, knock
  down; gettar sangue to bleed || *ref*
  to throw oneself; to plunge; to flow,
  empty (*said of a river*)
gettata *f* pour, pouring; jetty, shoot,
  sprout; cast; range (*of a gun*); gettata cardiaca (med) rate of flow of
  blood
gèttito *m* yield; waste; far gettito di to
  waste
gètto *m* throw; gush; shoot, sprout;
  cast; precast concrete slab; (aer) jet;
  a getto (aer) jet; a getto continuo
  continuously; di getto spontaneously;
  far getto di to waste; primo getto
  first draft
gettonare (gettóno) *tr* (coll) to call up
  from a pay station; (coll) to make
  the selection of (*a record in a juke-
  box*)
gettóne *m* counter, token; attendance
  fee; (cards) chip
gettopropulsióne *f* jet propulsion
ghepardo *m* cheetah
ghép·pio *m* (-pi) kestrel
gherì·glio *m* (-gli) kernel, meat (*of nut*)
gherlino *m* (naut) warp, line

gherminèlla *f* trick, sleight of hand;
  trickery
ghermire §176 *tr* to claw; to seize
gheróne *m* gusset
ghétta *f* gaiter; ghette spats
ghétto *m* ghetto
ghiacciàia *f* icebox, cooler
ghiac·ciàio *m* (-ciài) glacier; ghiacciaio
  continentale polar cap
ghiacciare §128 *tr* to freeze || *intr*
  (ESSERE) to freeze || *impers* (ESSERE)
  —ghiaccia it is freezing
ghiaccia·to -ta *adj* iced; ice-cold;
  frozen || *f* flavored crushed ice
ghiàc·cio -cia (-ci -ce) *adj* icy, ice-cold
  || *m* ice; ghiaccio secco dry ice
ghiacciò·lo -la *adj* crumbly, breakable
  || *m* icicle; popsicle
ghiàia *f* gravel, crushed stone
ghianda *f* fringe (*on a curtain*); (bot)
  acorn; ghiande mast (*for swine*)
ghiandàia *f* (orn) jay
ghiàndola *f* gland
ghibelli·no -na *adj & m* Ghibelline
ghièra *f* ferrule; ring
ghigliottina *f* guillotine; a ghigliottina
  sash (*window*)
ghigliottinare *tr* to guillotine
ghigna *f* (coll) grimace
ghignare *intr* to grimace; to sneer
ghigno *m* sneer, smirk; grin
ghinèa *f* guinea
ghìngheri *m invar*—in ghingheri dressed
  up
ghiót·to -ta *adj* fond; gluttonous; eager;
  dainty (*food*) || *f* (culin) dripping pan
ghiottó·ne -na *mf* glutton; (zool) glutton, wolverine
ghiottoneria *f* gluttony; tidbit; (fig)
  rarity
ghiòzzo [ddzz] *m* dolt; (ichth) gudgeon
ghirba *f* jar; (coll) skin, life
ghiribìzzo [ddzz] *m* (coll) whim, caprice
ghirigòro *m* doodle, curlicue
ghirlanda *f* garland, wreath
ghiro *m* dormouse; dormire come un
  ghiro to sleep like a log
ghisa *f* cast iron
già *adv* already; once upon a time;
  formerly || *interj* indeed!
giac·ca *f* (-che) jacket, coat; giacca a
  due petti double-breasted coat;
  giacca a vento windbreaker
giacché *conj* since
giacènte *adj* lying; idle (*capital*); unclaimed (*letter*); in abeyance
giacènza *f* lying; stay, abeyance; gia-
  cenze di capitali idle capital; gia-
  cenze di magazzino unsold stock of
  merchandise
giacére §181 *intr* (ESSERE) to lie; to be
  in abeyance; (lit) to be prostrate
giacì·glio *m* (-gli) pallet, cot
giaciménto *m* field, bed; giacimento
  petrolifero oil field
giacinto *m* hyacinth
Giàcomo *m* James
giaculatòria *f* ejaculation (*prayer*);
  litany (*monotonous account*); curse
giada *f* jade
giaggiòlo *m* (bot) iris

giaguaro *m* jaguar
giaiétto *m* jet (*black coal*)
gialappa *f* (pharm) jalap
gialla·stro -stra *adj* yellowish
gial·lo -la *adj* yellow; detective (*book or picture*); white (*with fear*) || *m* yellow; detective story, whodunit; suspense movie; **giallo dell'uovo** egg yolk
giamaica·no -na *adj & mf* Jamaican
giàmbi·co -ca *adj* (**-ci -che**) iambic
giambo *m* iamb
giammài *adv* never
giansenismo *m* Jansenism
Giappóne, il Japan
giapponése [s] *adj & mf* Japanese
giara *f* crock, jar
giardinàg·gio *m* (**-gi**) gardening
giardinétta *f* station wagon
giardinière -ra *mf* gardener || *f* jardiniere; mixed pickles; mixed salad; wagonette; station wagon
giardino *m* garden; **giardino d'infanzia** kindergarten; **giardino pensile** roof garden; **giardino zoologico** zoological garden
giarrettièra *f* garter
Giasóne *m* Jason
giavanése [s] *adj & mf* Javanese
giavellòtto *m* javelin
gibbó·so -sa [s] *adj* gibbous, humped; humpbacked; rough (*ground*)
gibèrna *f* cartridge box; cartridge belt
gi·bus *m* (**-bus**) opera hat
gi·ga *f* (**-ghe**) gigue, jig
gigante *adj & m* giant
gigante·sco -sca *adj* (**-schi -sche**) gigantic
gigantéssa *f* giantess
gigióne *m* ham actor
gi·glio *m* (**-gli**) Madonna lily; fleur-de-lys
gilda *f* guild
gi·lè *f* (**-lè**) vest, waistcoat
gimnòto *m* electric eel
ginecologia *f* gynecology
ginecò·lo·go -ga *mf* (**-gi -ghe**) gynecologist
gine·pràio *m* (**-prài**) juniper thicket; (fig) mess
ginépro *m* juniper
ginèstra *f* (bot) Spanish broom
Ginèvra *f* Geneva
ginevri·no -na *adj & mf* Genevan
gingillare *ref* to trifle; to idle
gingillo *m* trifle, bauble
ginnà·sio *m* (**-si**) secondary school; gymnasium
ginna·sta *mf* (**-sti -ste**) gymnast
ginnàsti·co -ca (**-ci -che**) *adj* gymnastic || *f* gymnastics; **ginnastica a corpo libero** or **ginnastica da camera** calisthenics
ginni·co -ca *adj* (**-ci -che**) gymnastic
ginocchiata *f* blow with the knee; blow on the knee
ginocchièra *f* kneepad; elastic bandage (*for knee*); kneepiece (*of armor*)
ginòc·chio *m* (**-chi**) knee; **avere il ginocchio valgo** to be bowlegged; **avere il ginocchio varo** to be knock-kneed; **in ginocchio** on one's knees

|| *m* (**-chia** *fpl*) knee; **fino alle ginocchia** knee-deep; **gettarsi alle ginocchia di** to go down on one's knees to; **mettere qlcu in ginocchio** to bring s.o. to his knees
ginocchióni *adv* on one's knees
giocare §182 *tr* to play; to stake, bet, risk, gamble; to make a fool of || *intr* to play; to gamble; to circulate (*said of air*); (fig) to play a role; **giocare** a to play; to wager; **giocare a mosca cieca** to play blindman's buff; **giocare con** to risk; **giocare d'armi** to fence; **giocare d'azzardo** to gamble; **giocare di** to use (*e.g., one's wits*); **giocare di gomiti** to elbow one's way; **giocare di mano** to steal; **giocare sulle parole** to play on words; to pun || *ref* to risk (*e.g., one's life*); to gamble away
giocata *f* wager, stake; game, play
gioca·tóre -trice *mf* player; gambler; speculator
giocàttolo *m* toy, plaything
giocherellare (giocherèllo) *intr* to play, trifle
giochétto *m* children's game; child's play; dirty trick
giò·co *m* (**-chi**) game; gambling; play; wager, stake; set; joke; (cards) hand; **entrare in gioco** to come into play; **fare gioco a** to come in handy to; **fare il doppio gioco** to be guilty of duplicity; **fare il gioco di** to play into the hands of; **giochi di equilibrio** balancing act; **gioco da ragazzi** child's play; **gioco d'azzardo** gambling; game of chance; **gioco del bussolotti** (fig) jugglery; **gioco di destrezza** game of skill; **gioco di parole** play on words, pun; **gioco di prestigio** sleight of hand; **gioco di società** parlor game; **metter in gioco** to risk; to stake; **per gioco** for fun; **prendersi gioco di** to make fun of
giocofòrza *m*—**è giocoforza** + *inf* it is necessary + *inf*
giocolière *m* juggler
giocón·do -da *adj* merry, joyful
giocó·so -sa [s] *adj* jocose, jolly
giogàia *f* dewlap; chain of mountains
gió·go *m* (**-ghi**) yoke; beam (*of balance*); rounded peak; pass
gioia *f* joy, happiness; darling; jewel; **darsi alla pazza gioia** to have a wild time
gioiellerìa *f* jewelry; jewelry store
gioiellière *m* jeweler
gioièllo *m* jewel
gioió·so -sa [s] *adj* joyful
gioire §176 (*pres part* missing) *intr* to rejoice
Giòna *m* Jonas
Giordània, la Jordan (*country*)
giorda·no -na *adj & mf* Jordanian || **Giordano** *m* Jordan (*river*)
Giórgio *m* George
giorna·làio -làia *mf* (**-lài -làie**) newsdealer
giornale *m* newspaper; magazine; (com) journal; **giornale di bordo** log, logbook; **giornale murale** poster; **giornale radio** newscast

giornaliè·ro -ra *adj* daily ‖ *mf* day laborer

giornalismo *m* journalism

giornali·sta *mf* (**-sti -ste**) journalist; **giornalista pubblicista** free-lance writer ‖ *m* newspaperman ‖ *f* news-paperwoman

giornalménte *adv* daily

giornata *f* day; day's work; birthday; pay, salary; battle; day's march; **giornata campale** pitched battle; **giornata della mamma** Mother's Day; **giornata lavorativa** workday; **vivere alla giornata** to live from hand to mouth

giórno *m* day; **a giorni** within the next few days; **a giorni . . . a giorni** some days . . . others; **a giorno** open, open-work (*needlework*); full (*light*); **al giorni nostri** nowadays; **al giorno d'oggi** nowadays; **buon giorno** good day; good morning; good-bye; **dare gli otto giorni a** to dismiss, fire; **di ogni giorno** everyday (*e.g., clothes*); **essere a giorno** to be up to date; **giorno dei morti** All Souls' Day; **giorno di lavoro** workday; **giorno di paga** payday; **giorno fatto** broad day-light; **giorno feriale** weekday; **giorno festivo** holiday; **mettere a giorno** to bring up to date; **otto giorni oggi** one week from today; **passare un brutto giorno** to have a bad time; **un giorno o l'altro** one of these days

giòstra *f* joust; merry-go-round

giostrare (**giòstro**) *intr* to joust; to get along, manage; to idle, loiter

Giosuè *m* Joshua

Giotté·sco -sca *adj* (**-schi -sche**) of the school of Giotto

giovaménto *m* benefit, advantage

gióvane *adj* young; youthful; fresh (*e.g., cheese*); Younger, e.g., **Plinio il Giovane** Pliny the Younger ‖ *m* young man; boy, apprentice; **i giovani** the young ‖ *f* young woman

giovanile *adj* youthful

Giovanni *m* John; **Giovanni Battista** John the Baptist

giovanòtta *f* young woman

giovanòtto *m* young man; (coll) bache-lor

giovare (**gióvo**) *tr* (lit) to help ‖ *intr* (with *dat*) to help, to be of use to ‖ *ref* to avail oneself ‖ *impers* (ESSERE) —**non giova** it's no use

Giòve *m* Jupiter

giove·dì *m* (**-dì**) Thursday; **giovedì santo** Maundy Thursday

giovèn·ca *f* (**-che**) heifer

gioventù *f* youth

giovévole *adj* helpful, beneficial

gioviale *adj* jovial

giovinézza *f* youth

gip *f* (**gip**) jeep

gippóne *m* large jeep, panel truck

giràbile *adj* endorsable

giradi·schi *m* (**-schi**) record player

giradito *m* (pathol) felon

giraffa *f* giraffe; (mov, telv) boom, crane

girafilièra *f* diestock

giramà·schio *m* (**-schi**) tap wrench

giraménto *m*—**giramento di testa** ver-tigo, dizziness

giramón·do *m* (**-do**) globetrotter

giràndola *f* girandole; pinwheel; (fig) weathercock

girandolare (**giràndolo**) *intr* to stroll, saunter

girante *mf* endorser ‖ *f* blade (*e.g., of fan*)

girare *tr* to turn; to tour; to go around, travel over; to switch (*the conversa-tion*); to film, shoot; to transfer (*a phone call*); to endorse; (mil) to surround ‖ *intr* to turn; to circulate; to spin (*said of one's head*) ‖ *ref* to turn; to toss and turn

girarrósto *m* turnspit; **girarrosto a mo-tore** rotisserie

girasóle *m* sunflower

girata *f* turn; walk, ramble; (com) endorsement; (cards) deal; (coll) tongue-lashing

giratà·rio -ria *mf* (**-ri -rie**) endorsee

giravòlta *f* turn, pirouette; bend; sud-den change of mind

girellare (**girèllo**) *intr* to stroll, wander around

girèllo *m* rump; go-cart, walker

girévole *adj* revolving

girino *m* tadpole; bicycle rider compet-ing on the Tour of Italy

giro *m* periphery; turn, revolution; ride; size (*of hat*); edge (*of glass*); round (*of a doctor*); (sports) tour; (sports) lap; (com) transfer; (cards) hand; (theat) tour; **a giro di posta** by return mail; **andare in giro** to poke along; **giro collo** neckline; **giro d'af-fari** volume of business, turnover; **giro di parole** circumlocution; **fare il giro di** to tour; **mettere in giro** to spread (*news, gossip*); **nel giro di** within (*a period*); **prendere in giro** to poke fun at

girobùssola *f* gyrocompass

girondolare (**giróndolo**) *intr* var of **girandolare**

giróne *m* (sports) conference; (sports) division; (sports) league; (archaic) circle

gironzolare [dz] (**girónzolo**) *intr* to stroll, saunter

giropilò·ta *m* (**-ti**) gyropilot

giroscò·pio *m* (**-pi**) gyroscope

girotóndo *m* ring-around-a-rosy

giròtta *f* weather vane

girovagare §209 (**giròvago**) *intr* to roam, wander

giròva·go -ga (**-ghi -ghe**) *adj* wandering; strolling (*player*) ‖ *m* vagrant, hobo

gita *f* trip, excursion, outing

gita·no -na *adj* & *mf* Gypsy

gitante *mf* excursionist, vacationist

gittata *f* range (*of gun*)

giù *adv* down; **andar giù** to go down; to deteriorate; to get worse; **buttar giù** to throw down; (culin) to start to cook, e.g., **buttar giù gli spaghetti** to start to cook the spaghetti; (fig) to jot down; **da . . . in giù** for the past . . . ; **dar giù** to look worse (*said* *of a sick person*); **esser giù** to be downcast; **giù di lì** thereabouts; **in giù** down; downstream; **mandar giù** to swallow; **non andar giù** to not be able to stomach or swallow, e.g., **non gli vanno giù i bugiardi** he cannot stomach liars; **venire giù** to come down; to crumble; to collapse

giubba *f* coat, jacket; mane

giubbétto *m* small coat; bodice; jerkin

giubbòtto *m* jacket (*e.g., of a motorcyclist*); **giubbotto salvagente** (aer, naut) life jacket

giubilare (**giùbilo**) *tr* to retire, to pension || *intr* to rejoice

giubilèo *m* jubilee

giùbilo *m* jubilation, exultation

giuda *m* Judas || **Giuda** *m* Judas

giudài·co -ca *adj* (**-ci -che**) Judaic

giudaismo *m* Judaism

giudè·o -a *adj* Judean; Jewish || *mf* Judean; Jew

giudicare §197 (**giùdico**) *tr* to judge; to find (*e.g., s.o. innocent*); to try (*a case*) || *intr* to judge, deem

giudicato *m* (hist) Sardinian region; **passare in giudicato** (law) to become final

giùdice *m* judge; magistrate, justice; **giudice conciliatore** justice of the peace; **giudice popolare** member of the jury

giudizià·rio -ria *adj* (**-ri -rie**) judicial, judiciary

giudì·zio *m* (**-zi**) judgment; wisdom; trial; sentence; **giudizio di Dio** (hist) ordeal; **giudizio finale** Last Judgment; **metter giudizio** to mend one's ways

giudizió·so -sa [*s*] *adj* judicious, wise

giùggiola *f* jujube; (joc) trifle; **andare in brodo di giuggiole** to swoon, become ecstatic

giugno *m* June

giugulare *adj* jugular || *v* (**giùgolo**) *tr* to cut the throat of

giulèbbe *m* julep

giuliana *f* (culin) julienne || **Giuliana** Juliana

giuli·vo -va *adj* gay

giullare *m* jongleur; (pej) mountebank

giumén·to -ta *mf* beast of burden || *f* female saddle horse

giun·ca *f* (**-che**) (naut) junk

giunchiglia *f* (bot) jonquil

giun·co *m* (**-chi**) (bot) rush

giùngere §183 *tr* to join (*e.g., one's hands*) || *intr* (ESSERE) to arrive; **giungere a** or **in** to arrive at, reach; **giungere a + inf** to succeed in + *ger*; **mi giunge nuovo** it's news to me

giungla *f* jungle

Giunóne *f* Juno

giunòni·co -ca *adj* (**-ci -che**) Junoesque

giunta *f* addition; makeweight; strip (*of cloth*); junta; committee; **di prima giunta** at the very beginning; **per giunta** in addition

giuntare *tr* to join

giuntatrice *f* (mov) splicer

giunto *m* (mach) joint, coupling;

giunto a sfere ball-and-socket joint; **giunto cardanico** universal joint

giuntura or **giunzióne** *f* joint; juncture, seam

giuò·co *m* (**-chi**) var of **gioco**

giuraménto *m* oath; **deferire il giuramento a** to put under oath

giurare *tr* to swear, pledge || *intr* to swear

giura·to -ta *adj* sworn || *m* juror

giurìa *f* committee; jury

giurìdi·co -ca *adj* (**-ci -che**) juridical

giurisdizióne *f* jurisdiction

giurisprudènza *f* jurisprudence

giurì·sta *mf* (**-sti -ste**) jurist

Giusèppe *m* Joseph

Giuseppina *f* Josephine

giusta *prep* according to; in accordance with

giustappórre §218 *tr* to juxtapose

giustézza *f* correctness, justness; (typ) measure

giustificàbile *adj* justifiable

giustificare §197 (**giustifico**) *tr* to justify || *ref* to excuse oneself

giustificazióne *f* justification

giustìzia *f* justice; **far giustizia a** to execute; **farsi giustizia da sé** to take the law into one's own hands; **render giustizia a** to do justice to

giustiziare §287 *tr* to execute

giustizière *m* executioner; (obs) judge

giu·sto -sta *adj* just; opportune || *m* just man; just price; rights, due || **giusto** *adv* just, justly

glà·bro -bra *adj* smooth (*face*)

glaciale *adj* glacial; (fig) icy

gladiatóre *m* gladiator

gladiòlo *m* gladiolus

glàndola *f* var of **ghiandola**

glassa *f* glaze, icing

glassare *tr* to glaze, ice

glèba *f* clod, lump of earth

gli §4 *art* || §5 *pers pron*

glicerina *f* glycerin

glìcine *m* wistaria

gliéla; gliéle; gliéli; gliélo; gliéne §5

globale *adj* total, aggregate

glòbo *m* globe; **globo oculare** eyeball

globulare *adj* globular, global

glòbulo *m* globule; (physiol) corpuscle

gloglottare (**gloglòtto**) *intr* to gobble; to gurgle

gloglottì·o *m* (**-i**) gobble, gobbling; gurgle

glòria *f* glory

gloriare §287 (**glòrio**) *tr* (lit) to exalt || *ref* to boast; to glory

glorificare §197 (**glorifico**) *tr* to glorify

glorió·so -sa [*s*] *adj* glorious; proud

glòssa *f* gloss

glossà·rio *m* (**-ri**) glossary

glòttide *f* glottis

glottòlo·go -ga *mf* (**-gi -ghe**) linguist

glucòsio *m* glucose

glùtine *m* gluten

gnòc·co *m* (**-chi**) potato dumpling

gnòmo *m* gnome

gnòrri *m invar*—**fare lo gnorri** to feign ignorance

gòb·bo -ba *adj* hunchbacked || *mf*

hunchback ‖ *f* hump; hunch; hump (*of gibbous moon*); hook (*of nose*)

góc·cia *f* (-ce) drop; bead; **avere la goccia al naso** to have a runny nose; **goccia d'acqua** raindrop

góc·cio *m* (-ci) drop, swallow

gócciola *f* drop; bead

gocciolare (**gócciolo**) *tr & intr* to drip

gocciola·tóio *m* (-tói) dripstone

gocciolì·o *m* (-i) drip, trickle

godére §184 *tr* to enjoy ‖ *intr* to take pleasure; to revel; to profit ‖ *ref* to enjoy; **godersela** to have a good time

godìbile *adj* enjoyable

godiménto *m* enjoyment, pleasure

goffàggine *f* clumsiness

gòf·fo -fa *adj* awkward; ill-fitting

gógna *f* pillory; **mettere alla gogna** to pillory

góla *f* throat; neck; gluttony; gorge (*of mountain*); mouth (*of cannon*); flue (*of chimney*); (archit) ogee; **far gola a** to tempt; **mentire per la gola** to lie shamelessly; **tornare a gola** to repeat (*said of food*)

golétta *f* neck (*of shirt*); (naut) schooner

gòlf *m* (**gòlf**) sweater, cardigan; (sports) golf

gólfo *m* gulf; **golfo mistico** orchestra pit ‖ **Golfo Persico** Persian Gulf

Gòlgota, il Golgotha

goliardo *m* goliard; university student

golosi·tà *f* (-tà) gluttony; tidbit

goló·so -sa [s] *adj* gluttonous; appetizing

gómena *f* hawser

gomitata *f* blow with the elbow; nudge

gómito *m* elbow; bend; **alzare il gomito** to crook the elbow; **dare di gomito a** to nudge

gomitolo *m* skein, clew

gómma *f* gum; rubber; eraser; tire; **bucare una gomma** to have a flat tire; **gomma arabica** gum arabic; **gomma a terra** flat tire; **gomma da masticare** chewing gum; **gomma lacca** shellac

gommapiuma *f* foam rubber

gomma·to -ta *adj* gummed; with tires

gommatura *f* gumming; (aut) tires

gommi·sta *m* (-sti) tire dealer; tire repairman

gommó·so -sa [s] *adj* gummy

góndola *f* gondola; (aer) pod

gonfalóne *m* gonfalon

gonfiare §287 (**gónfio**) *tr* to inflate, blow up; to bloat; to swell; to exaggerate; to puff up ‖ *intr* (ESSERE) to swell ‖ *ref* to swell; to puff up; to bulge, balloon

gonfiatura *f* inflation; exaggeration

gonfiézza *f* swelling; grandiloquence

gón·fio -fia (-fi -fie) *adj* inflated, swollen; conceited ‖ *m* swelling, bulge

gonfióre *m* swelling

gongolare (**góngolo**) *intr* to rejoice; to be elated

goniòmetro *m* goniometer; protractor

gònna *f* skirt; **gonna pantaloni** culottes

gonnèlla *f* skirt; (fig) petticoat

gonnellino *m* kilt; ballerina skirt

gón·zo -za [dz] *mf* simpleton, fool

gòra *f* millpond; marsh; (coll) spot

górbia *f* tip (*of umbrella*)

gorgheggiare §290 (**gorghéggio**) *tr & intr* to warble; to trill

gorghég·gio *m* (-gi) warbling; trill

gór·go *m* (-ghi) whirlpool; (lit) river

gorgogliare §280 (**gorgóglio**) *intr* to gurgle

gorgó·glio *m* (-gli) gurgle

gorgogli·o *m* (-i) gurgling

goril·la *m* (-la) gorilla

gòta *f* cheek; (lit) side

gòti·co -ca *adj & m* (-ci -che) Gothic

Gòto *m* Goth

gótta *f* (pathol) gout

gottazza *f* (naut) scoop

gottó·so -sa [s] *adj* gouty

governale *m* fin (*of bomb*); (obs) rudder

governante *adj* governing ‖ *m* ruler ‖ *f* governess; housekeeper

governare (**govèrno**) *tr* to rule, govern; to steer (*a ship*); to tend (*animals*); to wash and dry (*dishes*); to run (*e.g., a bank*) ‖ *intr* to steer

governatì·vo -va *adj* government

govèrno *m* government; tending (*e.g., of animals*); running (*of household*); cleaning (*of house*); blending (*of wine*); (archaic) steering

gózzo *m* crop, craw (*of bird*); (pathol) goiter

gozzovigliare §280 *intr* to go on a spree

gracchiare §287 *intr* to caw

gràc·chio *m* (-chi) caw; (orn) chough

gracidare (**gràcido**) *intr* to croak; to honk (*said, e.g., of a goose*)

gràcile *adj* weak, frail; thin, delicate

gradasso *m* swaggerer, braggadocio

grada·to -ta *adj* graded; gradual

gradazióne *f* gradation; alcoholic proof; **gradazione vocalica** (phonet) ablaut

gradévole *adj* pleasant

gradiménto *m* pleasure; acceptance (*of a product*); liking

gradinata *f* steps; tier (*of seats*)

gradino *m* step; (fig) stepping stone

gradire §176 *tr* to like; to welcome

gradì·to -ta *adj* agreeable; welcome (*guest*); kind (*letter*)

grado *m* degree; rank; (nav) rating; (archaic) step; **a buon grado o a mal grado** willy-nilly; **a grado a grado** little by little; **a Suo grado** according to your wishes; **di buon grado** willingly; **di secondo grado** secondary (*school*); **essere in grado di** to be in a position to; **saper grado a** (lit) to be grateful to

graduale *adj & m* gradual

graduare (**gràduo**) *tr* to graduate

gradua·to -ta *adj* graduated ‖ *m* noncommissioned officer

graduatòria *f* ranking; rank

graffa *f* clamp; brace, bracket

graffiare §287 *tr* to scratch; (coll) to swipe

grafflétto *m* tiny scratch; marking gage

gràf·fio *m* (-fi) scratch

grafìa *f* writing; spelling; (gram) graph

gràfi•co -ca (-ci -che) adj graphic || m graph, diagram; designer (for printing industry); member of printers' union || f graphic arts

grafite f graphite

grafologìa f graphology

gragnòla f hail

gramàglia f crepe; widow's weeds; **in gramaglie** in mourning

gramigna f couch grass; weed

grammàti•co -ca (-ci -che) adj grammatical || m grammarian || f grammar

grammo m gram

grammofòni•co -ca adj **(-ci -che)** phonograph, recording

grammòfono m phonograph, record player

gra•mo -ma adj poor, sad; wretched, miserable; frail, sickly

gran adj apocopated form of **grande**, used before singular and plural nouns beginning with a consonant sound other than gn, pn, ps, impure s, x, and z

gra•na m (-na) Parmesan cheese || f (-ne) cochineal; grain (of wood, metal, etc); (slang) dough; (coll) trouble

granàglie fpl grain, cereals

gra•nàio m (-nài) granary, barn

granata adj invar & m garnet (color) || f pomegranate (fruit); garnet; broom; grenade

granatière m grenadier

granatina f grenadine

Gran Bretagna, la Great Britain

grancassa f bass drum

grancèvola f spider crab

gràn•chio m (-chi) crab; claw (of hammer); (coll) cramp; **prendere un granchio** to make a blunder

grandangolare adj wide-angle

grande adj big, large; great; tall; high (mass; voice); long (time); capital (letter); full (speed); grown-up || m grownup; grandeur; grandee; **fare il grande** to show off; **i grandi** the great; **in grande** on a large scale; lavishly

grandézza f size; enormity; greatness; quantity; **in grandezza naturale** life-size; **grandezze** ostentatiousness

grandezzó•so -sa [s] adj ostentatious

grandiloquènza f grandiloquence

grandinare (gràndino) tr (obs) to hail || intr to hail || impers (ESSERE & AVERE)—**grandina** it is hailing

grandinata f hailstorm

gràndine f hail

grandiosi•tà [s] f (-tà) grandeur, magnificence

grandió•so -sa [s] adj grandiose, grand

grandu•ca m (-chi) grand duke

granduchéssa f grand duchess

granèllo m grain, seed; speck

grànfia f clutch

granìco•lo -la adj grain, wheat

granire §176 tr to grain; to stipple; (mus) to make (the notes) clear-cut || intr to teethe

granita f sherbet, water ice

granito m granite

granitura f knurl, milled edge

grano m wheat; grain of wheat; grain; speck; **grano duro** durum wheat; **grano saraceno** buckwheat; **grano turco** corn

granturco m corn

granulare adj granular || v **(grànulo)** tr to granulate

granulatóre m crusher

grànulo m granule, pellet, bud

granuló•so -sa [s] adj granular; lumpy; gritty; friable, crumbly

grappa f eau de vie; clamp, brace

grappétta f staple; crampon

grappino m (naut) grapnel

gràppolo m bunch, cluster

grassàg•gio m (-gi) (aut) lubrication

grassatóre m highwayman

grassazióne f holdup

grassétto m boldface

grassézza f fatness; richness

gras•so -sa adj fat; rich; greasy; risqué || m fat, suet; grease; shortening

grassòc•cio -cia adj **(-ci -ce)** pudgy, plump

grata f grate, grating

gratèlla f strainer; sieve; broiler

grati•cia f (-ce) (theat) gridiron

gratìc•cio m (-ci) lattice, trellis

graticola f gridiron; grating; graticule

gratìfi•ca f (-che) bonus

gratificare §197 (gratìfico) tr to give a bonus to; (fig) to pelt (with insults)

gratificazióne f bonus

gratis adv gratis, free, for nothing

gratitùdine f gratitude

gra•to -ta adj grateful, appreciative || f see **grata**

grattacapo m trouble, worry

grattacièlo m skyscraper

grattare tr to scratch; to scrape; to grate; (slang) to snitch || intr to scratch; to grate

grattùgia f grater

grattugiare §290 tr to grate

gratùi•to -ta adj gratuitous, free

gravame m burden; tax; (law) appeal; **fare gravame a qlcu di qlco** to impute s.th to s.o.

gravare tr to burden, oppress; (obs) to seize || intr (ESSERE & AVERE) to weigh; to lie; to be sorry, e.g., **gli grava d'avermi disturbato** he is sorry to have bothered me || ref—**gravarsi di** to take upon oneself

grave adj heavy; burdensome; grave, serious || m (phys) body; **stare sul grave** to put on airs

graveolènte adj stinking

gravézza f heaviness; burden; oppression; (obs) taxation

gravidanza f pregnancy

gràvi•do -da adj pregnant; fraught

gravi•tà f (-tà) gravity

gravitare (gràvito) intr to gravitate; to weigh, lie

gravitazióne f gravitation

gravó•so -sa [s] adj heavy; hard, burdensome; oppressive

gràzia f grace; pardon, mercy; delicacy; kindness; **di grazia!** please!;

essere nelle grazie di qlcu to be in s.o.'s good graces; fare grazia di qlco a qlcu to spare s.o. s.th; grazia di Dio abundance, bounty; grazie! thank you!; grazie tante! thanks a lot!; in grazia di thanks to; male grazie bad manners; per grazie as a favor; render grazia a to thank; saper grazia a to be thankful to

graziare §287 tr to pardon; graziare qlcu di qlco to grant s.th to s.o.

grazió·so -sa [s] adj graceful, pretty; gracious; (lit) free, gratuitous

Grècia, la Greece

grè·co -ca (-ci -che) adj & mf Greek ‖ f fret, fretwork; bullion (on Italian general's hat); tunic

gregà·rio -ria (-ri -rie) adj gregarious ‖ m private; follower

grég·ge m (-gi or -ge fpl) flock, herd

grég·gio -gia (-gi -ge) adj coarse; raw, unrefined ‖ m crude oil

gregoria·no -na adj Gregorian

grembiale m var of grembiule

grembiule m apron; frock; smock

grembiulino m pinafore

grèmbo m lap; womb; bosom

gremire §176 tr to crowd ‖ ref to become crowded

gremi·to -ta adj overcrowded

gréppia f manger, crib

gréto m dry gravel bed of a river

grettézza f stinginess; narrow-mindedness

grét·to -ta adj stingy; narrow-minded

grève adj heavy; uncouth; (lit) grievous

gréz·zo -za [ddzz] adj raw, crude; coarse

gridare tr to cry out; to cry for (help); (coll) to scold ‖ intr to cry out, shout

grido m cry (of animal) ‖ m (grida fpl) cry; scream; shout; yell; fame; di grido famous; grido di guerra war cry; ultimo grido latest fashion

grifa·gno -gna adj rapacious, fierce

griffa f hobnail; (mov, phot) sprocket

grifo m snout (of pig); (pej) snoot; (lit) griffin

grifóne m vulture; (mythol) griffin

grigia·stro -stra (-gi -gie) adj grayish

grì·gio -gia adj & m (-gi -gie) grey

grigiovérde adj invar olive-drab ‖ m olive-drab uniform

griglia f gridiron, broiler; grate, grille; (elec) grid (of vacuum tube)

grillare tr to grill, broil ‖ intr to sizzle; to bubble (said of fermenting wine); to have a sudden whim

grillétto m trigger

grillo m cricket; whim, fancy

grimaldèllo m picklock

grìnfia f claw, clutch; grinfie clutches

grinta f grim or forbidding face

grinza f wrinkle; crease; non fare una grinza to be perfect

grinzó·so -sa [s] adj wrinkled; creased

grippare intr & ref to bind, jam

grisèlla f (naut) ratline

grì·sou m (-sou) firedamp

grissino m breadstick

Groenlàndia, la Greenland

grómma f incrustation, deposit

grónda f eaves; slope (of ground)

grondàia f gutter (of roof)

grondare (gróndo) tr to drip ‖ intr (ESSERE) to ooze (said, e.g., of perspiration); to drip; grondare di sangue to stream with blood

gròppa f back (of animal); top (of mountain); restare sulla groppa a to be stuck with, e.g., gli sono restati sulla groppa cento esemplari he is stuck with one hundred copies

groppata f bucking (of horse)

gróppo m knot, tangle; lump (in throat); squall

groppóne m back, rump

gròssa f gross; dormire della grossa to sleep like a log

grossézza f bigness; thickness; density; swelling (of river); (fig) coarseness; grossezza d'udito hardness of hearing

grossi·sta mf (-sti -ste) wholesaler

gròs·so -sa adj big, large; thick; heavy (seas); swollen (river); hard (breathing); offensive (words); coarse (e.g., salt); pregnant; deep (voice); (coll) important; alla grossa approximately; di grosso a lot, very much; dirla grossa to talk nonsense; farla grossa to make a blunder; grosso d'udito hard of hearing; in grosso wholesale; spararle grosse to tell tall tales ‖ m bulk; main body (e.g., of an army) ‖ f see grossa

grossola·no -na adj coarse; boorish, uncouth; big (blunder)

gròtta f grotto; (coll) inn

grottè·sco -sca (-schi -sche) adj & m grotesque ‖ f (hist) grotesque painting

grovièra f Gruyère cheese

gróvi·glio m (-gli) tangle, snarl

gru f (gru) (orn, mach) crane

grùc·cia f (-ce) crutch; clothes hanger; (obs) wooden leg

grufolare (grùfolo) intr to nuzzle ‖ ref to wallow (in mud)

grugnire §176 tr & intr to grunt

grugnito m grunt

grugno m snout; (pej) snoot; fare il grugno to sulk

grui·sta m (-sti) crane operator

grulleria f foolishness

grul·lo -la adj silly, simple

gruma f deposit, incrustation

grumo m lump; clot

grùmolo m heart (e.g., of lettuce); small lump

grumó·so -sa [s] adj lumpy; incrusted, scaly

gruppo m group; main body (e.g., of runners); club; gruppo elettrogeno generating unit; gruppo motore (aut) power plant

grùzzolo m hoard, pile; farsi il gruzzolo to feather one's nest

guadagnare tr to earn; to win; to gain; to pick up (speed); to reach (port) ‖ intr to win; to look better ‖ ref to win; to win over; guadagnarsi il pane or la vita to earn one's living

guadagno m earnings; profit; a basso

guadagno (rad, telv) low-gain; **ad alto guadagno** (rad, telv) high-gain

guadare *tr* to wade, ford

guado *m* ford; (bot) woad; **passare a guado** to ford

guài *interj* woe!

guaina *f* case; scabbard, sheath; corset; (aut) seat cover

guàio *m* (**guài**) trouble || *interj* see **guài**

guaire §176 *intr* to yelp; to whine

guaito *m* yelp, whine

gualcire §176 *tr* to crumple

gualdrappa *f* saddlecloth

Gualtièro *m* Walter

guàn·cia *f* (-ce) cheek; moldboard; cheek side (*of gunstock*)

guanciale *m* pillow; **dormire tra due guanciali** to sleep safe and sound

guan·tàio -tàia *mf* (-tài -tàie) glove maker; glove merchant

guanterìa *f* glove factory

guantièra *f* glove case; tray

guanto *m* glove; **gettare il guanto** to fling down the gauntlet; **raccogliere il guanto** to take up the gauntlet; **trattare con i guanti gialli** to handle with kid gloves

guantóne *m* big glove; **guantoni da pugilato** boxing gloves

guardabarriè·re *m* (-re) (rr) gatekeeper, crossing watchman

guardabò·schi *m* (-schi) forester

guardacà·cia *m* (-cia) gamekeeper

guardacò·ste *m* (-ste) coast guard; coast-guard cutter

guardafi·li *m* (-li) (elec) lineman

guardali·nee *m* (-nee) (rr) trackwalker; (sports) linesman

guardama·no *m* (-no) guard (*of sabre or rifle*); work glove; (naut) handrail

guardapor·tó·ne *m* (-ne) doorman

guardare *tr* to look at; to protect, watch; to pay attention to; to face, overlook; (obs) to keep to (*one's bed*); (obs) to keep (*a holiday*); **guardare a vista** to keep under close watch; **guardare dall'alto in basso** to look down one's nose at; **guardare di sotto in su** to leer at || *intr* to look; to pay attention; **Dio guardi!** God forbid!; **guardare a** to face (*said, e.g., of a room*); **guardare di non + inf** to be careful not to + *inf*; **guardare in faccia** to face (*e.g., danger*); **stare a guardare** to keep on the sidelines || *ref* to look at one another; to look at oneself; **guardarsi da** to keep from; to guard against

guardaró·ba *m* (-ba) wardrobe; linen closet; checkroom, cloakroom

guardarobiè·re -ra *mf* checkroom attendant || *f* hatcheck girl

guardasigil·li *m* (-li) minister of justice (*in Italy*); (Brit) Lord Privy Seal; (U.S.A.) attorney general; (hist) keeper of the seals

guardaspal·le *m* (-le) bodyguard

guardata *f* quick look, glance

guarda·vìa *m* (-vìa) guardrail; median strip

guàrdia *f* watch; guard; top water level; flyleaf; **di guardia** on duty;

fare la guardia a to watch; **guardia campestre** forester; **guardia carceraria** prison guard; **guardia del corpo** guard, body guard; **guardia di finanza** customs officer; **guardia d'onore** honor guard; **guardia forestale** forester; park guard; **guardia giurata** private policeman; **guardia medica** emergency clinic; **guardia municipale** police officer; **guardia notturna** night watch; **mettere qlcu in guardia** to warn s.o.; **montare la guardia** to be on guard duty, keep guard; **stare in guardia** to be on one's guard

guardiamari·na *m* (-na) (nav) ensign

guardiano *m* keeper; warden; watchdog; (eccl) superior; **guardiano notturno** night watchman

guardina *f* lockup; **in guardina** in jail

guardinfante *m* bustle (*worn under the back of a woman's skirt*)

guardin·go -ga *adj* (-ghi -ghe) wary

guàrdolo *m* welt (*in shoe*)

guardóne *m* peeping tom

guarenti·gia *f* (-gie) guarantee

guaribile *adj* curable

guarigióne *f* cure, recovery

guarire §176 *tr* to cure; to heal || *intr* (ESSERE) to recover; to heal

guaritóre *m* healer; quack

guarnigióne *f* (mil) garrison

guarnire §176 *tr* to equip; to rig; to trim; (naut) to rig; (culin) to garnish || *intr* to add beauty

guarnizióne *f* decoration; trimming; lining; (culin) garniture; (mach) gasket; (mach) washer

Guascógna, la Gascony

guascó·ne -na *adj* & *mf* Gascon

guastafè·ste *mf* (-ste) kill-joy

guastare *tr* to ruin, spoil; to undo; to wreck; (obs) to lay waste; **guastare le uova nel paniere a** to spoil the plans of (*ref* to spoil; to worsen (*said, e.g., of the weather*); (mach) to break down; **guastarsi con qlcu** to quarrel with s.o.; **guastarsi il sangue** to blow one's top

guastatóre *m* commando

gua·sto -sta *adj* ruined, spoiled; wrecked || *m* breakdown; corruption; discord

guatare *tr* (lit) to look askance or with fear at

Guayana, la Guyana

guazza *f* dew

guazzabù·glio *m* (-gli) muddle, mess

guazzare *tr* to make (*an animal*) wade in a river || *intr* to wallow

guazzétto *m* stew, ragout

guazzo *m* puddle, pool; gouache

guèl·fo -fa *adj* & *mf* Guelph

guèr·cio -cia (-ci -ce) *adj* cross-eyed; one-eyed; almost blind || *mf* cross-eyed person; one-eyed person

guèrra *f* war; warfare; **guerra a coltello** internecine feud; **guerra di Troia** Trojan war; **guerra fredda** cold war; **guerra lampo** blitzkrieg; **guerra mondiale** world war

guerrafon·dàio -dàia (-dài -dàie) adj warmongering || mf warmonger

guerreggiare §290 **(guerréggio)** tr to fight, war against || intr to fight || ref to make war on one another

guerré·sco -sca adj **(-schi -sche)** warlike

guerriè·ro -ra adj war, warlike || mf fighter || m warrior

guerriglia f guerrilla

guerriglièro m guerrilla (soldier)

gufo m misanthrope; (orn) horned owl

giùglia f spire; peak

gugliata f needleful

Guglièlmo m William

guida f guide; guidance; driving; runner (rug); guidebook; manual (of instruction); (aut) steering; **guida a destra** right-hand drive; **guide** reins (of horse); (mach) slide

guidaiòlo m leader (among animals)

guidare tr to guide, lead; to steer; to drive || intr to drive || ref to restrain oneself

guida·tóre -trice mf driver

guiderdóne m (lit) premium, prize

guidóne m pennant, pennon

guidoslitta f bobsled

guidovìa f ski lift

Guinèa, la Guinea

guinzà·glio m **(-gli)** leash; (fig) fetter, shackle

guisa f way, manner; **in guisa che** so that; **in guisa di** under the guise of

guit·to -ta adj miserly, niggardly || m strolling player

guizzare intr to dart; to wriggle; to flash (said of lightning); (naut) to yaw || intr (ESSERE) to slip away

guizzo m dart; wriggle; flash

gù·scio m **(-sci)** shell; pod (of pea); tick (of mattress); **guscio di noce** nutshell; **guscio d'uovo** eggshell

gustare tr to taste; to relish || intr (ESSERE & AVERE) to please; to like, e.g., **gli gustano le gite in barca** he likes boat rides

gusto m taste; pleasure, fun; whim; style; **di cattivo gusto** tasteless; **di gusto** gladly, with gusto; **prendere gusto per** to take a liking for; **prendersi il gusto di** to relish; **provar gusto** to have fun

gustó·so -sa [s] adj tasty

guttapèrca f gutta-percha

gutturale adj & f guttural

H

H, h ['akka] m & f eighth letter of the Italian alphabet

handicappare tr var of **andicappare**

hangar m (hangar) hangar

havaia·no -na adj & mf Hawaiian

henné m henna

hertz m hertz

hertzia·no -na adj Hertzian

hi-fi f (coll) hi-fi

hockei·sta m **(-sti)** hockey player

hollywoodia·no -na adj Hollywood, Hollywood-like

hurrà interj hurrah!

I

I, i, [i] m & f ninth letter of the Italian alphabet

i §4 def art the

iarda f yard

iato m hiatus

iattanza f boasting, bragging

iattura f misfortune, calamity

ibèri·co -ca adj **(-ci -che)** Iberian

ibernare (ibèrno) intr to hibernate

ibi·sco m **(-schi)** hibiscus

ibridare (ìbrido) tr & intr to hybridize

ìbri·do -da adj & m hybrid

icàsti·co -ca adj **(-ci -che)** figurative; realistic

-ìccio -ìccia suf adj -ish, e.g., **gialliccio** yellowish

iconoclà·sta mf **(-sti -ste)** iconoclast

iconografia f iconography

iconoscò·pio m **(-pi)** iconoscope

iddì·o m **(-i)** god || **Iddio** m God

idèa f idea; goal, purpose; bit, touch; **avere idea di** to have a mind to; **dare l'idea di** to seem; **farsi un'idea di** to grasp the notion of; **idea fissa** fixed idea; **neanche per idea** not in the least

ideale adj & m ideal

idealismo m idealism

ideali·sta mf **(-sti -ste)** idealist

idealìsti·co -ca adj **(-ci -che)** idealistic

idealizzare [ddzz] tr to idealize

ideare (idèo) tr to conceive

idea·tóre -trice mf inventor

idem adv ditto

idènti·co -ca adj **(-ci -che)** identical

identificare §197 **(identìfico)** tr to identify || ref to resemble each other; **identificarsi con** to identify with

identificazióne f identification

identi·tà f **(-tà)** identity

ideologìa f ideology

idi mpl & fpl ides

idìllia·co -ca adj **(-ci -che)** idyllic

idìl·lio m **(-li)** idyll; romance

idiò·ma m **(-mi)** language, idiom

idiomàti·co -ca adj **(-ci -che)** idiomatic

idiosincrasìa *f* aversion; (med) idio-syncrasy
idiò·ta (-ti -te) *adj* idiotic || *mf* idiot
idiotismo *m* idiom; idiocy
idiozìa *f* idiocy
idolatrare *tr & intr* to idolize
idolatrìa *f* idolatry
idolo *m* idol
idonei·tà *f* (-tà) fitness, aptitude; quali-fication
idòne·o -a *adj* fit; qualified; opportune
idra *f* hydra
idrante *m* hydrant, fireplug
idratante *adj* moisturizing
idratare *tr & ref* to hydrate
idrato *m* hydrate
idràuli·co -ca (-ci -che) *adj* hydraulic || *m* plumber || *f* hydraulics
ìdri·co -ca *adj* (-ci -che) water, e.g., **forza idrica** water power
idrocarburo *m* hydrocarbon
idroelèttri·co -ca *adj* (-ci -che) hydro-electric
idròfi·lo -la *adj* absorbent
idrofobìa *f* hydrophobia, rabies
idròfo·bo -ba *adj* hydrophobic, rabid
idròfu·go -ga *adj* (-ghi -ghe) waterproof
idrogenare (idrògeno) *tr* to hydrogenate
idrògeno *m* hydrogen
idròpi·co -ca *adj* (-ci -che) *adj* dropsical || *mf* patient suffering from dropsy
idropisìa *f* dropsy
idroplano *m* hydroplane (*boat*)
idropòrto *m* seaplane airport
idrorepellènte *adj* water-repellent
idroscalo *m* seaplane airport
idro·scì m (-scì) water ski
idroscivolante *m* (naut) hydroplane
idrosilurante *m* torpedo plane
idròssido *m* hydroxide
idroterapìa *f* hydrotherapy
idrovìa *f* inland waterway
idrovolante *m* seaplane, hydroplane
idròvo·ro -ra *adj* suction (*pump*) || *f* suction pump
ièna *f* hyena
ièri *m & adv* yesterday; **ieri l'altro** the day before yesterday; **ieri notte** last night; **ieri sera** last evening, last night, yesterday evening
ietta·tóre -trice *mf* hoodoo
iettatura *f* evil eye; bad luck, jinx
igiène *f* hygiene; sanitation
igièni·co -ca *adj* (-ci -che) hygienic, sanitary
igname *m* yam
igna·ro -ra *adj* unaware; inexperienced
igna·vo -va *adj* (lit) slothful
ignizióne *f* ignition
ignòbile *adj* (lit) ignoble
ignomìnia *f* ignominy; outrage
ignominió·so -sa [s] *adj* ignominious
ignorante *adj* ignorant; illiterate || *mf* ignoramus
ignoranza *f* ignorance
ignorare (ignòro) *tr* to not know; to ignore
ignò·to -ta *adj & m* unknown
ignu·do -da *adj* (lit) naked || *m* (lit) naked person
il §4 *def art* the
ilare *adj* cheerful

ilari·tà *f* (-tà) cheerfulness; laughter
ìlice *f* (lit) ilex, holm oak
ìlio *m* (anat) ilium
illanguidire §176 *tr* to weaken || *intr* (ESSERE) to get weak
illazióne *f* inference
illéci·to -ta *adj* illicit, unlawful || *m* unlawful act
illegale *adj* illegal
illeggiadrire §176 *tr* to embellish
illeggìbile *adj* illegible
illegìtti·mo -ma *adj* illegitimate
illé·so -sa *adj* unhurt, unharmed
illetterà·to -ta *adj & mf* illiterate
illibà·to -ta *adj* spotless, pure
illimità·to -ta *adj* unlimited
illìri·co -ca *adj* (-ci -che) Illyrian
illògi·co -ca *adj* (-ci -che) illogical
illùdere §105 *tr* to delude
illuminare (illùmino) *tr* to illuminate; to brighten; to enlighten || *ref* to grow bright
illumina·to -ta *adj* illuminated; en-lightened; educated
illuminazióne *f* illumination; enlighten-ment
illuminismo *m* Age of Enlightenment
illusióne *f* illusion; delusion; **farsi illu-sioni** to indulge in wishful thinking
illusionismo *m* sleight of hand; magic
illusioni·sta *mf* (-sti -ste) magician
illu·so -sa *adj* deluded || *mf* deluded person
illusò·rio -ria *adj* (-ri -rie) illusory, illusive
illustrare *tr* to illustrate; to explain, elucidate || *ref* to become famous
illustra·to -ta *adj* illustrated, pictorial
illustra·tóre -trice *mf* illustrator
illustrazióne *f* illustration; illustrious person
illustre *adj* illustrious, famous
illustrìssi·mo -ma *adj* distinguished; honorable; **Illustrissimo Signore** Dear Sir; Mr. (*addressing a letter*)
imbacuccare §197 *tr & ref* to muffle up; to wrap up
imbaldanzire §176 *tr* to embolden || *intr* (ESSERE) & *ref* to grow bold
imballàg·gio *m* (-gi) wrapping, packag-ing
imballare *tr* to wrap up, package; to bale; to race (*the motor*); **imballarsi in una gabbia** to crate || *ref* to race (*said of a motor*)
imballa·tóre -trice *mf* packer
imballo *m* packing; packaging, wrap-ping; racing (*of motor*)
imbalsamare (imbàlsamo) *tr* to em-balm; to stuff (*animals*)
imbambola·to -ta *adj* gazing, staring; stunned, dumfounded; sleepy-eyed; sluggish
imbandierare (imbandièro) *tr* to bedeck with flags
imbandire §176 *tr* to prepare {*food, a meal, a table*} lavishly
imbarazzante *adj* embarrassing, awk-ward
imbarazzare *tr* to embarrass; to en-cumber, hamper; to upset (*the stomach*)

imbarazza·to -ta *adj* embarrassed, perplexed; upset (*stomach*); ill-at-ease
imbarazzo *m* embarrassment; annoyance; **imbarazzo di stomaco** upset stomach
imbarbarire §176 *tr* & *ref* to make barbarous; to corrupt (*a language*)
imbarcadèro *m* landing pier
imbarcare §197 *tr* to ship; to load, embark; to ship (*water*) ‖ *ref* to sail; to embark; to curve (*said of furniture*)
imbarca·tóio *m* (**-tói**) landing pier
imbarcazione *f* boat; **imbarcazione di salvataggio** lifeboat
imbar·co *m* (**-chi**) embarkation; port of embarkation
imbardare *intr* & *ref* (aer) to yaw; (aut) to swerve, lurch
imbardata *f* (aer) yaw; (aut) swerve, lurch
imbarilare *tr* to barrel
imbastardire §176 *tr* to corrupt ‖ *ref* to become corrupt
imbastire §176 *tr* (sew) to baste; (fig) to sketch out
imbastitura *f* (sew) basting
imbàttere *ref*—**imbattersi bene** to be lucky; **imbattersi in** to come across; **imbattersi male** to have bad luck
imbattìbile *adj* unbeatable
imbavagliare §280 *tr* to gag
imbeccare §197 (**imbécco**) *tr* to feed (*a fledgling*); (fig) to prompt
imbeccata *f* beakful; (fig) prompting
imbecillàggine *f* imbecility
imbecille *adj* & *mf* imbecile
imbecilli·tà *f* (**-tà**) imbecility
imbèlle *adj* unwarlike; cowardly
imbellettare (**imbellétto**) *tr* to apply rouge to, apply make-up on ‖ *ref* to put on make-up
imbellire §176 *tr* to embellish
imbèrbe *adj* beardless; callow
imbestialire §176 *tr* to enrage ‖ *intr* (ESSERE) & *ref* to become enraged
imbévere §185 *tr* to soak; to soak up; to imbue ‖ *ref* to become soaked; to become imbued
imbiancare §197 *tr* to whiten; to bleach; to whitewash ‖ *intr* (ESSERE) & *ref* to turn white (*said, e.g., of hair*); to clear up (*said of weather*)
imbiancatura *f* bleaching (*of laundry*); whitening; whitewashing
imbianchimento *m* bleaching
imbianchino *m* whitewasher; house painter; (pej) dauber
imbianchire §176 *tr* to whiten; to bleach ‖ *ref* to turn white
imbiondire §176 *tr* to bleach (*hair*) ‖ *intr* to become blond; to ripen (*said of wheat*)
imbizzarrire [ddzz] *intr* (ESSERE) & *ref* to become skittish (*said of a horse*); to become infuriated
imbizzire [ddzz] §176 *intr* (ESSERE) to get angry
imboccare §197 (**imbócco**) *tr* to feed by mouth; to put (*an instrument*) in one's mouth; to take, enter (*a road*); to prompt ‖ *intr* (ESSERE) to

flow; to open (*said of a road*); (mach) to fit
imboccatura *f* entrance (*of street*); inlet; opening, top (*e.g., of bottle*); bit (*of bridle*); (mus) mouthpiece; **avere l'imboccatura a** to be experienced in
imbóc·co *m* (**-chi**) entrance; inlet; opening
imbonimento *m* claptrap
imbonire §176 *tr* to lure, entice (*s.o. to buy or enter*)
imbonitóre *m* barker
imborghesire §176 *tr* to render middle-class ‖ *intr* (ESSERE) to become middle-class
imboscare §197 (**imbòsco**) *tr* to hide; to hide (*s.o.*) underground ‖ *ref* to shirk; to be a slacker
imbosca·to -ta *adj* (mil) shirking, draft-dodging ‖ *m* (mil) slacker; (mil) goldbrick ‖ *f* ambush; **tendere un'imboscata** to set an ambush
imboscatóre *m* accomplice of a draft dodger; hoarder (*of scarce items*)
imboschire §176 *tr* to forest
imbottare (**imbótto**) *tr* to barrel
imbottigliare §280 *tr* to bottle; to bottle up ‖ *ref* to get bottled up (*said of traffic*)
imbottire §176 *tr* to pad, fill; to stuff; to pad (*a speech*)
imbottita *f* bedspread, quilt
imbottitura *f* padding
imbra·ca *f* (**-che**) breeching strap (*of harness*); safety belt; (naut) sling
imbracare §197 *tr* to sling
imbracciare §128 *tr* to fasten (*shield*); to level (*gun*)
imbrancare §197 *tr* & *ref* to herd
imbrattacar·te *mf* (**-te**) scribbler
imbrattamu·ri *mf* (**-ri**) dauber
imbrattare *tr* to soil, dirty; to smudge, smear
imbrattaté·le *mf* (**-le**) dauber
imbratto *m* dirt; smudge, smear; daub; scribble; swill
imbrigliare §280 *tr* to bridle
imbroccare §197 (**imbròcco**) *tr* to hit (*the target*); to guess right
imbrodare (**imbròdo**) *tr* to soil
imbrogliare §280 (**imbròglio**) *tr* to cheat; to mix up; to tangle; to confuse; **imbrogliare le vele** (naut) to take in the reef ‖ *ref* to get tangled up; to get confused; to turn bad (*said of weather*)
imbrò·glio *m* (**-gli**) cheat; tangle; (naut) reef; **cacciarsi in un imbroglio** to get involved in a mess
imbroglió·ne -na *mf* swindler
imbronciare §128 (**imbróncio**) *intr* (ESSERE) & *ref* to pout, sulk ‖ *ref* to lower (*said of the weather*)
imbroncia·to -ta *adj* sulky, surly; cloudy, overcast
imbrunire *m*—**sull'imbrunire** at nightfall ‖ §176 *intr* (ESSERE) to turn brown ‖ *impers* (ESSERE)—**imbrunisce** it is growing dark
imbruttire §176 *tr* to mar; to make ugly ‖ *intr* (ESSERE) & *ref* to grow ugly
imbucare §197 *tr* to mail; to put in a hole ‖ *ref* to hide

imburrare *tr* to butter
imbuto *m* funnel
imène *m* (anat) hymen, maidenhead
imitare (ìmito) *tr* to imitate
imita·tóre -trice *mf* imitator; (theat) mimic
imitazióne *f* imitation
immacola·to -ta *adj* immaculate
immagazzinare [ddzz] *tr* to store, store up
immaginare (immàgino) *tr* to imagine; to guess; to invent || *ref*—si immagini! of course!; not at all!
immaginà·rio -ria *adj* (-ri -rie) imaginary
immaginativa *f* imagination
immaginazióne *f* imagination
immàgine *f* image; picture
immaginó·so -sa [s] *adj* imaginative
immalinconire §176 *tr* to sadden || *intr* (ESSERE) & *ref* to become melancholy
immancàbile *adj* unfailing; certain
immane *adj* monstrous; gigantic
immangiàbile *adj* uneatable, inedible
immantinente *adv* (lit) immediately
immarcescìbile *adj* incorruptible
immateriale *adj* immaterial
immatricolare (immatrìcolo) *tr* to matriculate
immatricolazióne *f* matriculation
immatu·ro -ra *adj* immature; premature
immedesimare (immedésimo) *tr* to identify; to blend || *ref* to identify oneself
immediataménte *adv* immediately
immediatézza *f* immediacy
immedia·to -ta *adj* immediate
immemoràbile *adj* immemorial
immèmore *adj* forgetful
immèn·so -sa *adj* immense, huge
immèrgere §162 *tr* to immerse; to plunge || *ref* to plunge; to become absorbed
immerita·to -ta *adj* undeserved
immeritévole *adj* undeserving
immersióne *f* immersion; submersion (of a submarine); (naut) draft
imméttere §198 *tr* to let in; immettere qlcu nel possesso di (law) to grant s.o. possession of
immigrante *adj* & *mf* immigrant
immigrare *intr* (ESSERE) to immigrate
immigrazióne *f* immigration; (biol) migration
imminènte *adj* imminent
imminènza *f* imminence
immischiare §287 *tr* to involve || *ref* to meddle; to become involved
immiserire §176 *tr* to impoverish || *intr* (ESSERE) & *ref* to become impoverished; to become debased
immissà·rio *m* (-ri) tributary
immissióne *f* letting in, introduction; intake; insertion (in lunar orbit)
immòbile *adj* motionless, immobile; real (property) || immobili *mpl* real estate
immobiliare *adj* real, e.g., proprietà immobiliare real estate; real-estate, e.g., imposta immobiliare real-estate tax
immobilizzare [ddzz] *tr* to immobilize; to pin down; to tie up (capital)

immodè·sto -sta *adj* indecent; immodest
immolare (immòlo) *tr* to immolate
immondézza *f* filth; impurity
immondez·zàio *m* (-zài) rubbish heap, dump; garbage can
immondìzia *f* trash; garbage; filth
immón·do -da *adj* filthy, dirty; unclean
immorale *adj* immoral
immorali·tà *f* (-tà) immorality
immortalare *tr* to immortalize
immortale *adj* immortal
immortalità *f* immortality
immò·to -ta *adj* (lit) motionless
immune *adj* immune
immunizzare [ddzz] *tr* to immunize
immutàbile *adj* immutable
immuta·to -ta *adj* unchanged
i·mo -ma *adj* (lit) bottom, lowest || *m* (lit) bottom; (lit) depth
impaccare §197 *tr* to pack, wrap up
impacchettare (impacchétto) *tr* to pack, bundle
impacciare §128 *tr* to hamper; to embarrass || *ref* to meddle
impaccia·to -ta *adj* hampered; clumsy
impàc·cio *m* (-ci) embarrassment; hindrance; trouble; essere d'impaccio to be in the way
impac·co *m* (-chi) wrapping; (med) compress
impadronire §176 *ref*—impadronirsi di to seize; to take possession of; to master (a language)
impagàbile *adj* invaluable, priceless
impaginare (impàgino) *tr* (typ) to make up (in pages), paginate
impaginato *m* (typ) page proof
impagliare §280 *tr* to cane (a chair); to stuff (an animal; a doll); to pack in straw
impalare *tr* to impale; to tie to a pole or stake || *ref* to stiffen up
impala·to -ta *adj* stiff, rigid
impalcatura *f* scaffold; frame, framework
impallidire §176 *intr* to turn pale; to blanch; to grow dim (said of a star); (fig) to wane
impalmare *tr* (lit) to wed
impalpàbile *adj* impalpable
impaludare *tr* to make swampy or marshy || *intr* to become marshy
impanare *tr* to bread; to thread (a screw) || *intr* to screw in
impaniare §287 *tr* to trap, ensnare || *ref* to fall into the trap
impantanare *tr* to turn into a swamp || *ref* to get stuck, to sink (in vice)
impaperare (impàpero) *ref* to fluff, make a slip
impappinare *tr* to confuse || *ref* to blunder; to stammer
imparare *tr* to learn; imparare a memoria to learn by heart || *intr* imparare a to learn to, to learn how to
impareggiàbile *adj* peerless, unmatched
imparentare (imparènto) *tr* to bring into the family || *ref*—imparentarsi con to marry into
ìmpari *adj* odd, uneven
imparrucca·to -ta *adj* bewigged
impartire §176 *tr* to impart
imparziale *adj* impartial

impasse *f* blind alley; deadlock; (cards) finesse

impassìbile *adj* impassible, impassive

impastare *tr* to knead; to mix; to smear with paste

impasta·to -ta *adj* kneaded; smeared; **impastato di** tainted with; overwhelmed with (*sleep*)

impasto *m* paste; pastiche

impastoiare §287 (**impastóio**) *tr* to fetter, hamstring

impataccare §197 *tr* to besmear, soil

impattare *tr* to even up; to tie (*a game*); **impattarla con** to tie (*a person*)

impatto *m* impact

impaurire §176 *tr* to scare ‖ *ref* to get scared

impàvi·do -da *adj* fearless

impaziènte *adj* impatient

impazientire §176 *intr* (ESSERE) & *ref* to get impatient

impaziènza *f* impatience

impazzare *intr* (ESSERE) to be wild with excitement; to go mad; (culin) to curdle

impazzata *f*—**all'impazzata** at top speed; berserk

impazzire §176 *intr* (ESSERE) to go crazy; **fare impazzire** to drive crazy

impeccàbile *adj* impeccable

impeciare §128 (**impécio**) *tr* to tar

impedènza *f* impedance

impediménto *m* hindrance, obstacle, impediment

impedire §176 *tr* to impede, hinder; to obstruct ‖ *intr* to prevent; **impedire** (with *dat*) **di** + *inf* or **che** + *subj* to prevent from + *ger*

impegnare (**impégno**) *tr* to pawn; to reserve (*a room*); to engage (*the enemy*); to keep occupied; to pledge ‖ *ref* to obligate oneself; to go all out; to become entangled

impegnati·vo -va *adj* demanding (*activity*); binding (*promise*)

impegna·to -ta *adj* pawned; pledged; occupied; committed

impégno *m* commitment; obligation; task; zeal; **senza impegno** without promising

impegolare (**impégolo**) *tr* to tar ‖ *ref* to become entangled

impelagare §209 (**impèlago**) *ref* to bog down; to become entangled

impellicciare §128 *tr* to fur; to veneer

impenetràbile *adj* impenetrable

impenitènte *adj* impenitent; confirmed

impennàg·gio *m* (-**gi**) (aer) empennage

impennare (**impénno**) *tr* to feather; (fig) to give wings to ‖ *ref* to rear (*said of a horse*); to take umbrage; (aer) to zoom

impennata *f* rearing (*of horse*); (aer) zoom

impensàbile *adj* unthinkable

impensa·to -ta *adj* unexpected

impensierire §176 *tr* & *ref* to worry

imperante *adj* prevailing

imperare (**impèro**) *intr* to rule, reign; to prevail; **imperare su** to rule over

imperati·vo -va *adj* & *m* imperative

imperatóre *m* emperor

imperatrice *f* empress

impercettìbile *adj* imperceptible

imperdonàbile *adj* unforgivable

imperfèt·to -ta *adj* & *m* imperfect

imperfezióne *f* imperfection

imperiale *adj* imperial ‖ *m* upper deck (*of bus or coach*); **imperiali** imperial troops

imperiali·sta *adj* & *mf* (-**sti** -**ste**) imperialist

impè·rio *m* (-**ri**) empire; rule

imperió·so -sa [s] *adj* imperious; imperative

imperì·to -ta *adj* (lit) inexperienced

imperitu·ro -ra *adj* immortal; everlasting, imperishable

imperìzia *f* inexperience

imperlare (**imperlo**) *tr* to bead; to cover with beads (*of perspiration*)

impermalire §176 *tr* to provoke ‖ *ref* to become provoked

impermeàbile *adj* waterproof ‖ *m* raincoat

imperniare §287 (**impèrnio**) *tr* to pivot; (fig) to base

impèro *adj invar* Empire ‖ *m* empire; control, sway

imperscrutàbile *adj* inscrutable

impersonale *adj* impersonal

impersonare (**impersóno**) *tr* to impersonate ‖ *ref*—**impersonarsi in** to be the embodiment of; (theat) to impersonate

impertèrri·to -ta *adj* undaunted

impertinènte *adj* impertinent, pert

impertinènza *f* impertinence

imperturbàbile *adj* imperturbable

imperturba·to -ta *adj* unperturbed

imperversare (**impervèrso**) *intr* to storm, rage; to be the rage

impèr·vio -via *adj* (-**vi** -**vie**) impassable

ìmpeto *m* impetus; onslaught; violence; outburst; **d'impeto** rashly

impetrare (**impètro**) *tr* to beg for; to obtain by entreaty ‖ *intr* (ESSERE) (lit) to turn to stone

impetti·to -ta *adj* puffed up with pride

impetuó·so -sa [s] *adj* impetuous

impiallacciare §128 *tr* to veneer

impiallacciatura *f* veneer, veneering

impiantare *tr* to install (*a machine*); to set up (*a business*); to open (*an account*)

impiantito *m* floor, flooring

impianto *m* installation; plant; system

impiastrare *tr* to plaster; to dirty

impiastricciare §128 *tr* to plaster; to daub; to soil

impiastro *m* (med) plaster; (fig) bore

impiccagióne *f* hanging

impiccare §197 *tr* to hang

impicciare §128 *tr* to hinder; to bother ‖ *ref* to meddle, butt in; **impicciarsi degli affari propri** to mind one's own business

impìc·cio *m* (-**ci**) hindrance; trouble; **essere d'impiccio** to be in the way

impicciolire §176 *tr* to reduce in size ‖ *ref* to shrink in size

impiegare §209 (**impiègo**) *tr* to employ;

to use; to devote (*one's energies*); to spend (*time*); to invest (*capital*); to take (*time*) || *ref* to have a job

impiegati·zio -zia *adj* (*-zi -zie*) employee, white-collar

impiega·to -ta *mf* employee; clerk

impiè·go *m* (*-ghi*) employment; use; job; place of business; investment

impietosire [s] §176 *tr* to move to pity || *ref* to be moved to pity

impietrire §176 *tr*, *intr* (ESSERE) & *ref* to turn to stone

impigliare §280 *tr* to entangle || *ref* to become entangled

impigrire §176 *tr* to make lazy || *intr* (ESSERE) & *ref* to get lazy

impinguare (**impìnguo**) *tr* & *ref* to fatten

impinzare *tr* to stuff || *ref* to stuff oneself; **impinzarsi il cervello** to stuff one's brain (*with knowledge*)

impiombare (**impiómbo**) *tr* to lead; to plumb, seal with lead; to fill (*a tooth*); (naut) to splice (*a cable*)

impiombatura *f* seal; filling (*of tooth*); (naut) splicing

impipare *ref*—**impiparsi di** (slang) to not give a hoot about

implacàbile *adj* implacable

implicare §197 (**implico**) *tr* to implicate; to imply

implici·to -ta *adj* implicit, implied

implorare (**implòro**) *tr* to implore

implume *adj* unfledged, featherless

impoliti·co -ca *adj* (*-ci -che*) unpolitical; impolitic, injudicious

impollinare (**impollìno**) *tr* to pollinate

impoltronire §176 *tr* to make lazy || *ref* to get lazy

impolverare (**impólvero**) *tr* to cover with dust || *ref* to get covered with dust

impomatare *tr* to pomade; to smear with pomade

imponderàbile *adj* imponderable; weightless

imponderabilità *f* imponderability; weightlessness

imponènte *adj* imposing; stately

imponìbile *adj* taxable || *m* taxable income

impopolare *adj* unpopular

impopolarità *f* unpopularity

impórre §218 *tr* to place, put; to impose; to order; to compel; to give (*a name*) || *intr* (ESSERE) to be imposing; (with *dat*) to order, command || *ref* to command respect; to win favor; to be necessary

importante *adj* important; sizable || *m* important thing

importanza *f* importance; size; **darsi importanza** to assume an air of importance

importare (**impòrto**) *tr* to import; to imply; to involve || *intr* (ESSERE) to be of consequence || *impers* (ESSERE) —**importa** it matters; **non importa** never mind

importa·tóre -trice *mf* importer

importazióne *f* importation; import

impòrto *m* amount

importunare *tr* to bother, importune

importu·no -na *adj* importunate, bothersome || *mf* bore

imposizióne *f* imposition; giving (*of a name*); order, command; taxation

impossessare (**impossèsso**) *ref*—**impossessarsi di** to seize; to master (*a language*)

impossìbile *adj* & *m* impossible

impossibili·tà *f* (*-tà*) impossibility

impossibilitare (**impossibilito**) *tr* to make impossible; to make unable or incapable

impossibilita·to -ta *adj* unable

impòsta *f* tax; shutter; (archit) impost; **imposta complementare** surtax; **imposta sul valore aggiunto** value-added tax

impostare (**impòsto**) *tr* to start, begin; to state (*a problem*); to mail; to lay (*a stone*); to open (*an account*); to attune (*one's voice*); to lay the keel of (*a ship*) || *ref* to take one's position, get ready

impostazióne *f* beginning, starting; laying; mail, mailing; (com) posting

impo·stóre -stóra *mf* impostor

impostura *f* imposture

impotènte *adj* weak; impotent

impotènza *f* impotence

impoverimén to *m* impoverishment

impoverire §176 *tr* to impoverish || *intr* (ESSERE) & *ref* to become impoverished

impraticàbile *adj* impracticable; impassable

impratichire §176 *tr* to train, familiarize || *ref* to become familiar (*e.g., with a task*)

imprecare §197 (**imprèco**) *tr* to wish (*e.g., s.o.'s death*) || *intr* to curse

imprecazióne *f* imprecation, curse

imprecisàbile *adj* undefinable

imprecisióne *f* inexactness, inaccuracy

impreci·so -sa *adj* vague, inexact

impregnare (**imprégno**) *tr* to impregnate

impremedita·to -ta *adj* unpremeditated

imprendìbile *adj* impregnable

imprendi·tóre -trice *mf* contractor || *m*—**imprenditore di pompe funebri** undertaker

imprenditoriale *adj* managerial

imprepara·to -ta *adj* unprepared

impreparazióne *f* unpreparedness

imprésa [s] *f* enterprise; undertaking; achievement; firm, concern; (theat) management; **impresa (di) pompe funebri** undertaking establishment

impresà·rio [s] *m* (*-ri*) manager; (theat) impresario

imprescindìbile *adj* essential, indispensable; unavoidable

impresentàbile *adj* unpresentable

impressionàbile *adj* impressionable

impressionante *adj* striking, impressive; frightening

impressionare (**impressióno**) *tr* to impress; (phot) to expose || *ref* to become frightened; (phot) to be exposed

impressióne *f* impression

imprestare (**imprèsto**) *tr* (coll) to lend

imprèstito *m* (philol) borrowing
imprevedíbile *adj* unforeseeable
imprevedu·to -ta *adj* unforeseen
imprevidènte *adj* improvident
imprevi·sto -sta *adj* unforeseen, unexpected ‖ imprevisti *mpl* unforeseen events
imprigionare (imprigióno) *tr* to imprison
imprimere §131 *tr* to impress; to imprint; to impart (*e.g., motion*)
improbàbile *adj* improbable, unlikely
ìmpro·bo -ba *adj* dishonest; laborious
improdutti·vo -va *adj* unproductive
imprónta *f* print, imprint; mark; impronta digitale fingerprint
improntare (imprónto) *tr* to impress, imprint; to mark
improntitúdine *f* audacity, impudence
impronunziàbile *adj* unpronounceable
impropè·rio *m* (-ri) insult
improprie·tà *f* (-tà) impropriety; error
imprò·prio -pria *adj* (-pri -prie) improper, inappropriate; (math) improper
improrogàbile *adj* unextendible
immprovvi·do -da *adj* improvident
improvvisare *tr* to improvise ‖ *ref* to suddenly decide to become
improvvisa·to -ta *adj* improvised; impromptu ‖ *f* surprise; surprise party
improvvisazióne *f* improvisation
improvvi·so -sa *adj* sudden ‖ *m* (mus) impromptu; all'improvviso or d'improvviso suddenly
imprudènte *adj* imprudent; rash
imprudènza *f* imprudence; rashness
impudènte *adj* shameless; brazen; impudent
impudènza *f* shamelessness; impudence
impudicizia *f* immodesty
impudi·co -ca *adj* (-chi -che) immodest, indecent
impugnare *tr* to grip, seize; to take up (*arms*); to impugn, contest
impugnatura *f* handle; grip, hold; hilt, haft
impulsi·vo -va *adj* impulsive
impulso *m* impulse; dare impulso a to promote, foment
impuneménte *adv* with impunity
impunità *f* impunity
impuni·to -ta *adj* unpunished
impuntare *intr* to stumble, trip; to stutter ‖ *ref* to stutter; to balk; to be stubborn; impuntarsi a or di + *inf* to stubbornly insist on + *ger*
impuntigliare §280 *ref* to persist, insist
impuntire §176 *tr* to tuft (*e.g., a pillow*)
impuntura *f* backstitch
impuri·tà *f* (-tà) impurity; unchastity
impu·ro -ra *adj* impure; unchaste
imputàbile *adj* attributable
imputare (imputo) *tr* to impute; to charge, accuse; (com) to post
imputa·to -ta *mf* accused, defendant
imputazióne *f* imputation; charge, accusation; (com) posting
imputridire §176 *tr* & *intr* (ESSERE) to rot
in *prep* in; at; into; to; on; upon; through; during; married to, e.g.,

Maria Roberti in Bianchi Marie Roberti married to Bianchi; as, e.g., in premio as a prize; by, e.g., in automobile by car; of, e.g., studente in legge student of law; essere in quattro to be four; in alto up; in breve soon; in a word; in giù down; in là there; in qua here; in realtà really; in seguito a because of
-ina *suf fem* about, e.g., cinquantina about fifty
inabbordàbile *adj* unapproachable
inàbile *adj* unfit; ineligible; awkward
inabili·tà *f* (-tà) unfitness; awkwardness; inability
inabilitare (inabílito) *tr* to incapacitate; to render unfit; to disqualify
inabilitazióne *f* disqualification
inabissare *tr* to plunge ‖ *ref* to sink
inabitàbile *adj* uninhabitable
inabita·to -ta *adj* uninhabited
inaccessìbile *adj* inaccessible; unfathomable
inaccettàbile *adj* unacceptable
inacerbire §176 *tr* to exacerbate ‖ *ref* to grow bitter
inacidire §176 *tr* & *ref* to sour
inadattàbile *adj* unadaptable; maladjusted
inadat·to -ta *adj* inadequate
inadegua·to -ta *adj* inadequate
inadempiènte *adj* not fulfilling; inadempiente agli obblighi di leva draft-dodging
inafferràbile *adj* that cannot be caught or captured; incomprehensible; elusive
inalare *tr* to inhale
inalatóre *m* inhaler
inalberare (inàlbero) *tr* to hoist ‖ *ref* to rear; to fly into a rage
inalteràbile *adj* unalterable
inamidare (inàmido) *tr* to starch
inamida·to -ta *adj* starched; pompous, starchy
inammissìbile *adj* inadmissible
inamovìbile *adj* irremovable
inamovibili·tà *f* (-tà) irremovability; tenure
inane *adj* inane; futile
inanella·to -ta *adj* curly; beringed
inanima·to -ta *adj* inanimate; lifeless
inanizióne *f* starvation
inappagàbile *adj* unquenchable
inappaga·to -ta *adj* unsatisfied
inappellàbile *adj* definitive, final
inappetènza *f* lack of appetite
inapprezzàbile *adj* inappreciable, imperceptible; inestimable
inappuntàbile *adj* faultless, impeccable
inarcare §197 *tr* to arch; to raise (*one's eyebrows*)
inargentare (inargènto) *tr* to silver
inaridire §176 *tr* to dry; to parch ‖ *ref* to dry up
inarrestàbile *adj* irresistible
inarrivàbile *adj* unattainable; inimitable
inarticola·to -ta *adj* indistinct, inarticulate
inascolta·to -ta *adj* unheeded
inaspetta·to -ta *adj* unexpected
inaspriménto *m* exacerbation

inasprire §176 *tr* to aggravate || *ref* to sour; to become embittered; to become sharper; to become fierce or furious

inastare *tr* to hoist (*flag*); to fix (*bayonets*)

inattaccàbile *adj* unattackable; unassailable; inattaccàbile da resistant to

inattendìbile *adj* unreliable

inatté·so -sa [s] *adj* unexpected

inatti·vo -ta *adj* inactive

inaudi·to -ta *adj* unheard-of

inaugurale *adj* inaugural; maiden (*voyage*)

inaugurare (inàuguro) *tr* to inaugurate; to usher in (*the New Year*); to open (*e.g., an exhibit*); to unveil (*a statue*); to sport for the first time

inaugurazióne *f* inauguration

inauspica·to -ta *adj* (lit) inauspicious

inavvedu·to -ta *adj* careless, rash

inavvertènza *f* inadvertence, oversight

inavverti·to -ta *adj* unnoticed; inadvertent, thoughtless

inazióne *f* inaction

incagliare §280 *tr* to hamper; to run aground || *intr* (ESSERE) & *ref* to run aground; (fig) to get stuck

incà·glio *m* (-gli) running aground; hindrance, obstacle

incalcinare *tr* to whitewash; to lime (*a field*)

incalcolàbile *adj* incalculable

incallire §176 *tr* to make callous || *intr* (ESSERE) to become callous; to become inured

incalli·to -ta *adj* callous; inveterate

incalzante *adj* pressing

incalzare *tr* to press, pursue || *intr* to be imminent; to be pressing || *ref* to follow one another in rapid succession

incamerare (incàmero) *tr* to confiscate

incamminare *tr* to launch; to guide, direct || *ref* to set out; to be on one's way

incanagli·to -ta *adj* vile, despicable

incanalare *tr* to channel || *ref* to flow

incancrenire §176 *tr* to affect with gangrene || *ref* to become gangrenous; (fig) to become callous

incandescènte *adj* incandescent; (fig) red-hot

incandescènza *f* incandescence

incannare *tr* to reel, wind

incantare *tr* to bewitch; to auction off || *ref* to become enraptured; to be spellbound; to jam, get stuck (*said of machinery*)

incanta·tóre -trice *adj* enchanting || *m* enchanter || *f* enchantress

incantésimo *m* enchantment, spell

incantévole *adj* enchanting, charming

incanto *m* enchantment; bewitchery; auction; d'incanto marvelously well

incanutire §176 *tr*, *intr* (ESSERE) & *ref* to turn gray-headed, to turn gray (*said of a person*)

incanuti·to -ta *adj* hoary

incapace *adj* incapable; (law) incompetent || *mf* oaf; (law) incompetent

incapaci·tà *f* (-tà) incapacity; (law) incompetence

incaparbire §176 *intr* (ESSERE) & *ref* to be obstinate; to be determined

incaponire §176 *ref* to get stubborn; to be determined

incappare *intr* (ESSERE) to stumble

incappottare (incappòtto) *tr* to cover with a coat || *ref* to wrap oneself in a coat

incappucciare §128 *tr* to cover with a hood

incapricciare §128 *ref*—incapricciarsi di to take a fancy to; to become infatuated with

incapsulare (incàpsulo) *tr* to encapsulate; to cap

incarcerare (incàrcero) *tr* to jail, incarcerate; (fig) to confine

incaricare §197 (incàrico) *tr* to charge || *ref*—incaricarsi di to take charge of; to take care of

incarica·to -ta *adj* in charge; visiting (*professor*) || *mf* deputy; incaricato d'affari chargé d'affaires

incàri·co *m* (-chi) task; appointment, position; per incarico di on behalf of

incarnare *tr* to incarnate, embody

incarna·to -ta *adj* incarnate || *m* pink complexion

incarnazióne *f* incarnation

incarnire §176 *intr* (ESSERE) & *ref* to grow in (*said of a toenail*)

incarni·to -ta *adj* ingrown (*toenail*)

incartaménto *m* file, dossier

incartapecori·to -ta *adj* shriveled up

incartare *tr* to wrap up (*in paper*)

incasellare [s] (incasèllo) *tr* to file; to sort out

incasellatóre [s] *m* post-office file clerk

incassare *tr* to box up; to put (*a watch*) in a case; to mortise (*a lock*); to channel (*a river*); to cash (*a check*); (fig) to take (*e.g., blows*) || *intr* to fit; to take it

incasso *m* receipts

incastellatura *f* scaffolding

incastonare (incastóno) *tr* to set, mount (*a gem*); incastonare citazioni in un discorso to stud a speech with quotations

incastrare *tr* to insert; to mortise; (fig) to corner || *intr* to fit || *ref* to fit; to become imbedded; to telescope (*said, e.g., of a train in a collision*)

incastro *m* joint; insertion; (carp) tenon; (carp) mortise

incatenare (incaténo) *tr* to chain, put in chains; to tie down, restrain

incatramare *tr* to tar

incàu·to -ta *adj* unwary, careless

incavallatura *f* truss (*to support roof*)

incavare *tr* to hollow out; to groove

incava·to -ta *adj* hollow

incavatura *f* hollow

incavicchiare §287 *tr* to peg

incavigliare §280 *tr* to peg

incavo *m* hollow; cavity; incavo dell'ascella armpit

incazzottare (incazzòtto) *tr* (naut) to furl

incèdere *m* stately walk || §123 *intr* to walk stately

incendiare §287 (**incèndio**) *tr* to set on fire; (fig) to inflame || *ref* to catch fire

incendià·rio -ria *adj* & *mf* (**-ri -rie**) incendiary

incèn·dio *m* (**-di**) fire; **incendio doloso** arson

incenerire §176 *tr* to reduce to ashes; to wither (*e.g., with a look*) || *ref* to turn to ashes

inceneritóre *m* incinerator

incensare (**incènso**) *tr* (eccl) to incense; (fig) to flatter

incensa·tóre -trice *mf* incense burner; (fig) flatterer

incensière *m* incense burner

incènso *m* incense

incensura·to -ta *adj* uncensured; (law) having no previous record

incentivo *m* incentive

inceppare (**incéppo**) *tr* to hinder; to shackle || *ref* to jam (*said of firearm*)

incerare (**incéro**) *tr* to wax

incerata *f* oilcloth; (naut) raincoat

incernierare (**incernièro**) *tr* to hinge

incertézza *f* uncertainty, incertitude

incèr·to -ta *adj* uncertain; irresolute || *m* uncertainty; **incerti** extras; **incerti del mestiere** cares of office, occupational annoyances, occupational hazards

incespicare §197 (**incéspico**) *intr* to stumble

incessàbile *adj* (lit) ceaseless

incessante *adj* unceasing, incessant

incèsto *m* incest

incestuó·so -sa [s] *adj* incestuous

incètta *f* cornering (*of market*)

incettare (**incètto**) *tr* to corner (*market*)

incetta·tóre -trice *mf* monopolizer

inchiavardare *tr* to key, bolt

inchièsta *f* probe, inquest; (journ) inquiry

inchinare *tr* to bend; to bow (*the head*) || *intr* (lit) to go down (*said of stars*) || *ref* to bow; to yield

inchi·no -na *adj* bent; bowing || *m* bow; curtsy

inchiodare (**inchiòdo**) *tr* to nail; to spike; to rivet; to tie, bind; to stop (*a car*) suddenly; to transfix || *ref* to freeze (*said, e.g., of brakes*); (fig) to be tied down; (fig) to go into debt

inchiostrare (**inchiòstro**) *tr* (typ) to ink

inchiòstro *m* ink; **inchiostro di china** India ink, Chinese ink

inciampare *intr* to trip, stumble

inciampo *m* stumbling block, obstacle; **essere d'inciampo a** to be in the way of

incidentale *adj* incidental

incidènte *adj* incidental || *m* incident; accident; argument, question

incidènza *f* incidence

incidere §145 *tr* to engrave; to cut; to record (*a record, a tape; a song*); **incidere all'acqua forte** to etch || *intr*—**incidere su** to weigh heavily on (*expenses, a budget*); to leave a mark on

incinerazióne *f* incineration; cremation

incinta *adj fem* pregnant

incipiènte *adj* incipient

incipriare §287 *tr* to powder || *ref* to powder oneself

incirca *adv* about; **all'incirca** more or less

incisióne *f* engraving; cutting (*of a record*); recording (*of a tape; of a song*); incision; **incisione all'acquaforte** etching

incisi·vo -va *adj* incisive; sharp (*photograph*) || *m* incisor

inciso *m* (gram) parenthetical clause; (mus) theme; **per inciso** incidentally

incisóre *m* engraver, etcher

incitare *tr* to incite, provoke

incivile *adj* uncivilized; uncouth

incivilire §176 *tr* to civilize || *ref* to become civilized

inclemènte *adj* inclement, harsh

inclemènza *f* inclemency, harshness

inclinare *tr* to tilt; to bow, bend; to incline || *intr* (fig) to lean || *ref* to bend

inclinazióne *f* inclination; slope; **inclinazione laterale** (aer) bank; **inclinazione magnetica** magnetic dip

incline *adj* inclined

incli·to -ta *adj* famous; noble

inclùdere §105 *tr* to enclose, include

inclusi·vo -va *adj* including; **inclusivo di** including

inclu·so -sa *adj* enclosed; included; inclusive || *f* enclosed letter

incoerènte *adj* incoherent

incògliere §127 *tr* (lit) to catch in the act || *intr*—**incogliere a** to happen to

incògni·to -ta *adj* unknown || *m* incognito; unknown; **in incognito** incognito || *f* (math) unknown quantity; (fig) puzzle

incollare (**incòllo**) *tr* to glue, paste; to size (*paper*) || *intr* to stick || *ref* to stick; to take on one's shoulders

incollatura *f* neck (*of horse*); glueing, sticking

incollerire §176 *intr* & *ref* to get angry

incolloca·to -ta *adj* unemployed

incolonnare (**incolónno**) *tr* to set up in columns

incolonnatóre *m* tabulator

incolóre *adj* colorless

incolpàbile *adj* blamable; (lit) guiltless

incolpare (**incólpo**) *tr*—**incolpare di** to charge with

incól·to -ta *adj* uncultivated; unkempt

incòlume *adj* unharmed, unhurt

incolumità *f* safety, security

incombènte *adj* (*danger*) impending; (*duty*) incumbent

incombènza *f* task, charge, incumbency

incómbere §186 *intr* (ESSERE) to be impending; to be incumbent

incombustibile *adj* incombustible

incominciare §128 *tr* & *intr* (ESSERE) to begin

incommensuràbile *adj* immeasurable; (math) incommensurable

incomodare (**incòmodo**) *tr* to bother, disturb || *ref* to bother; **non s'incomodi!** don't bother!

incòmo·do -da *adj* bothersome, inconvenient || *m* inconvenience; ailment;

levare l'incomodo a to get out of the way of

incomparàbile *adj* incomparable

incompatìbile *adj* incompatible; unforgivable

incompetènte *adj & mf* incompetent

incompiu·to -ta *adj* unfinished

incomplè·to -ta *adj* incomplete

incompó·sto -sta *adj* untidy; unkempt; unbecoming (*behavior*)

incomprensìbile *adj* incomprehensible

incomprensióne *f* lack of understanding

incompré·so -sa [s] *adj* misunderstood

incomprimìbile *adj* irrepressible; incompressible

inconcepìbile *adj* inconceivable

inconciliàbile *adj* irreconcilable

inconcludènte *adj* inconclusive; insignificant

inconcus·so -sa *adj* (lit) unshaken

incondiziona·to -ta *adj* unconditional

inconfessàbile *adj* unspeakable, vile

inconfessa·to -ta *adj* unavowed

inconfondìbile *adj* unmistakable

inconfutàbile *adj* irrefutable

incongruènte *adj* inconsistent

incòn·gruo -grua *adj* incongruous

inconoscìbile *adj* unknowable

inconsapévole *adj* unaware, unconscious

incòn·scio -scia *adj & m* (**-sci -sce**) unconscious

inconseguènte *adj* inconsistent, inconsequential

inconsidera·to -ta *adj* inconsiderate

inconsistènte *adj* flimsy; inconsistent

inconsistènza *f* flimsiness; inconsistency

inconsolàbile *adj* inconsolable

inconsuè·to -ta *adj* unusual

inconsul·to -ta *adj* ill-advised, rash

incontamina·to -ta *adj* uncontaminated

incontenìbile *adj* irrepressible

incontentàbile *adj* insatiable; hard to please; exacting

incontinènza *f* incontinence

incontrare (**incóntro**) *tr* to meet; to encounter, meet with || *intr* (ESSERE) to catch on (*said, e.g., of fashions*) || *ref* to meet; to agree || *impers* (ESSERE) to happen

incontrastàbile *adj* indisputable

incontrasta·to -ta *adj* undisputed

incóntro *m* meeting; encounter; success; meet; game, fight, match; occasion, opportunity; **all'incontro** on the other hand; opposite; **andare incontro a** to go towards; to go to meet; to face; to meet (*expenses*); to accommodate; **farsi incontro a** to advance toward

incontrollàbile *adj* uncontrollable

incontrolla·to -ta *adj* unchecked

incontrovertìbile *adj* incontrovertible

inconveniènte *adj* inconvenient || *m* inconvenience, disadvantage

incoraggiante *adj* encouraging

incoraggiare §290 *tr* to encourage

incorare §257 (**incuòro**) *tr* to hearten

incordare (**incòrdo**) *tr* to string (*e.g., a racket*); to tie up (*with a cord*) || *ref* to stiffen (*said of a muscle*)

incornare (**incòrno**) *tr* (taur) to gore

incorniciare §128 *tr* to frame; (journ) to border; (slang) to cuckold

incoronare (**incoróno**) *tr* to crown

incoronazióne *f* coronation

incorporàbile *adj* absorbable; adaptable

incorporare (**incòrporo**) *tr* to incorporate; to absorb || *ref* to incorporate

incorpòre·o -a *adj* incorporeal

incorreggìbile *adj* incorrigible

incórrere §139 *intr* (ESSERE)—**incorrere in** to incur

incorrót·to -ta *adj* uncorrupt

incosciènte *adj* unconscious; unaware; irresponsible || *mf* irresponsible person

incosciènza *f* unconsciousness; irresponsibility; madness

incostante *adj* inconstant, fickle

incredìbile *adj* incredible, unbelievable

incrèdu·lo -la *adj* incredulous || *mf* disbeliever; doubter

incrementare (**increménto**) *tr* to increase, boost

increménto *m* increase, increment, boost

incresció·so -sa [s] *adj* disagreeable, unpleasant

increspare (**incréspo**) *tr* to ripple; to wrinkle; to knit (*the brow*); to pleat || *ref* to ripple

incretinire §176 *tr* to make stupid; (fig) to deafen || *intr* (ESSERE) to become stupid; to lose one's mind

incriminare (**incrìmino**) *tr* to incriminate

incrinare *tr* to flaw; to ruin

incrinatura *f* crack, flaw

incrociare §128 (**incròcio**) *tr* to cross || *intr* (naut) to cruise || *ref* to cross one another; to interbreed

incrociatóre *m* (nav) cruiser

incró·cio *m* (**-ci**) crossing; cross; crossroads; crossbreed

incrollàbile *adj* unshakable

incrostare (**incròsto**) *tr* to incrust; to inlay (*e.g., with mosaic*) || *ref* to become incrusted

incrostazióne *f* incrustation

incrudelire §176 *tr* to enrage || *intr* to commit cruelties || *intr* (ESSERE) to become cruel; **incrudelire su** to commit cruelties upon

incruèn·to -ta *adj* bloodless

incubare (**ìncubo & incubo**) *tr* to incubate

incubatrice *f* incubator; brooder

incubazióne *f* incubation; **in incubazione** brewing (*said of an infectious disease*)

ìncubo *m* nightmare

incùdine *f* anvil; **essere tra l'incudine e il martello** to be between the devil and the deep blue sea

inculcare §197 *tr* to inculcate

incunàbolo *m* incunabulum

incuneare (**incùneo**) *tr & ref* to wedge

incuràbile *adj & mf* incurable

incurante *adj* careless, indifferent

incùria *f* malpractice; neglect

incuriosire [s] §176 *tr* to intrigue || *ref* to be intrigued

incursióne *f* incursion; **incursione aerea** air raid

incurvare *tr* to bend; (lit) to lower ‖ *intr* (ESSERE) & *ref* to bend; to warp
incurvatura *f* bend, curve
incustodi·to -ta *adj* unguarded, unwatched
incùtere §154 *tr* to inspire; **incutere terrore a** to strike with terror
ìndaco *adj* & *m* indigo
indaffara·to -ta *adj* busy
indagare §209 *tr* & *intr* to investigate; **indagare su** to investigate
indaga·tóre -trice *adj* probing, searching ‖ *mf* investigator
indàgine *f* investigation, inquiry
indarno *adv* (lit) in vain
indebitare (indébito) *tr* to burden with debts ‖ *ref* to run into debt
indebita·to -ta *adj* indebted
indébi·to -ta *adj* undue; unjust; fraudulent (*conversion*) ‖ *m* what one does not owe; excess payment
indebolimènto *m* weakening
indebolire §176 *tr, intr* (ESSERE) & *ref* to weaken
indecènte *adj* indecent
indecènza *f* indecency; outrage
indecifràbile *adj* indecipherable
indecisióne *f* indecision
indeci·so -sa *adj* uncertain; undecided; indecisive
indecoró·so -sa [s] *adj* indecorous, unseemly
indefès·so -sa *adj* indefatigable
indefinìbile *adj* indefinable
indefini·to -ta *adj* indefinite; undefined
indegni·tà *f* (-tà) indignity
indé·gno -gna *adj* unworthy; disgraceful
indelèbile *adj* indelible
indelica·to -ta *adj* indelicate
indemagliàbile *adj* runproof
indemonia·to -ta *adj* possessed by the devil; restless
indènne *adj* undamaged, unscathed; **tener indenne** to guarantee against harm or damage
indenni·tà *f* (-tà) indemnity; indemnification; **indennità di carica** special emolument; bonus; **indennità di carovita** cost-of-living allowance; **indennità di preavviso** severance pay; **indennità di trasferta** per diem
indennizzare [ddzz] *tr* to indemnify
indennizzo [ddzz] *m* indemnification; indemnity
inderogàbile *adj* inescapable
indescrivìbile *adj* indescribable
indesideràbile *adj* undesirable
indesidera·to -ta *adj* unwished-for; undesirable
indeterminati·vo -va *adj* indefinite
indetermina·to -ta *adj* indeterminate; (gram) indefinite
indi *adv* (lit) then; (lit) thence; **da indi innanzi** (lit) from that moment on
India, l' *f* India; **le Indie Occidentali** the West Indies; **le Indie Orientali** the East Indies
india·no -na *adj* & *mf* Indian; **fare l'indiano** to feign ignorance ‖ *f* printed calico
indiavola·to -ta *adj* devilish, fierce; impish (*child*)

indicare §197 (**ìndico**) *tr* to indicate; to show
indicati·vo -va *adj* & *m* indicative
indica·to -ta *adj* appropriate, fitting; recommended, advisable
indica·tóre -trice *adj* indicating, pointing ‖ *m* indicator; **indicatore di direzione** (aut) turn signal; **indicatore di livello** gauge; **indicatore di pressione** pressure gauge; **indicatore di velocità** (aut) speedometer; **indicatore stradale** road sign; **indicatore telefonico** telephone directory
indicazióne *f* indication; direction; **indicazioni per l'uso** instructions
ìndice *m* index finger; pointer; gauge; indicator; sign, indication; index; (typ) fist; **indice delle materie** table of contents ‖ **Indice** *m* Index; **mettere all'Indice** to put on the Index; to ban, index
indicìbile *adj* inexpressible, unspeakable
indietreggiare §290 (**indietréggio**) *intr* (ESSERE & AVERE) to withdraw
indiètro *adv* back; behind; **all'indietro** backwards; **dare indietro** to return, give back; **domandare indietro** to ask back; **essere indietro** to be slow (*said of a watch*); to be behind; to be backward, be slow; **tirarsi indietro** to withdraw; to step back
indifendìbile *adj* indefensible
indifé·so -sa [s] *adj* defenseless
indifferènte *adj* indifferent; **essere indifferente a** to be the same to; **lasciare indifferente** to leave cold
indifferènza *f* indifference
indìge·no -na *adj* indigenous ‖ *m* native
indigènte *adj* indigent, poor
indigestìbile *adj* indigestible
indigestióne *f* indigestion
indigè·sto -sta *adj* indigestible; (fig) dull, boring
indignare *tr* to anger, shock ‖ *ref* to be aroused, be indignant
indigna·to -ta *adj* indignant, outraged
indignazióne *f* indignation
indigni·tà *f* (-tà) indignity
indimenticàbile *adj* unforgettable
indipendènte *adj* & *m* independent
indipendènza *f* independence
indire §151 *tr* to announce publicly; (lit) to declare (*war*)
indirèt·to -ta *adj* indirect
indirizzare *tr* to direct; to address
indirizzà·rio m (-ri) mailing list
indirizzo *m* address; direction
indiscernìbile *adj* indiscernible
indisciplina *f* lack of discipline
indisciplina·to -ta *adj* undisciplined
indiscré·to -ta *adj* indiscreet; tactless
indiscrezióne *f* indiscretion; gossip; news leak
indiscus·so -sa *adj* unquestioned
indiscutìbile *adj* indisputable
indispensàbile *adj* indispensable ‖ *m* essential
indispettire §176 *tr* to annoy ‖ *ref* to get annoyed
indisponènte *adj* vexing, irritating

indispórre §218 *tr* to indispose; to disgust
indisposizióne *f* indisposition
indispó•sto -sta *adj* indisposed
indissolùbile *adj* indissoluble
indistìn•to -ta *adj* indistinct
indistruttìbile *adj* indestructible
indisturba•to -ta *adj* undisturbed
indìvia *f* endive
individuàbile *adj* distinguishable
individuale *adj* individual
individuali•tà *f* (-tà) individuality
individuare (indivìduo) *tr* to individuate; to outline; to single out
indivìduo *m* individual; fellow
indivisìbile *adj* indivisible
indivi•so -sa *adj* undivided
indiziare §287 *tr* to cast suspicion on
indizià•rio -ria *adj* (-ri -rie) circumstancial
indì•zio *m* (-zi) clue; token; symptom
indòcile *adj* indocile, unteachable
Indocìna, l' *f* Indochina
indocinése [s] *adj* & *mf* Indochinese
indoeuropè•o -a *adj* & *m* Indo-European
indolcire §176 *tr* to sweeten ‖ *ref* to become sweet
ìndole *f* temper, disposition; nature
indolènte *adj* indolent
indoleniménto *m* soreness, stiffness; numbness
indolenzire §176 *tr* to make sore or stiff; to benumb ‖ *ref* to become sore or stiff
indolenzì•to -ta *adj* sore, stiff; numb
indolóre *adj* painless
indomàbile *adj* indomitable
indoma•ni *m* (-ni) morrow, next day; **l'indomani di . . .** the day after . . .
indoma•to -ta *adj* (lit) indomitable, untamed
indòmi•to -ta *adj* (lit) indomitable, untamed
Indonèsia l' *f* Indonesia
indonesia•no -na *adj* & *mf* Indonesian
indorare (indòro) *tr* to gild; (culin) to brown; (fig) to sugar-coat
indoratura *f* gilding
indossare (indòsso) *tr* to wear; to put on
indossatrice *f* mannequin, model
indòsso *adv* on, on one's back; **avere indosso** to have on, wear
Indostàn, l' *m* Hindustan
indosta•no -na *adj* & *mf* Hindustani
indòtto *m* (elec) armature (*of motor*)
indottrinare *tr* to indoctrinate
indovinare *tr* to guess; **indovinarla** to guess right; **non indovinarne una** to never hit the mark
indovina•to -ta *adj* felicitous
indovinèllo *m* puzzle, riddle
indovi•no -na *mf* soothsayer, fortune-teller
indù *adj invar* & *mf* Hindu
indùb•bio -bia *adj* (-bi -bie) undoubted, undisputed
indubita•to -ta *adj* undeniable
indugiare §290 *tr* to delay ‖ *intr* to linger; to hesitate ‖ *ref* to linger
indù•gio *m* (-gi) delay; **rompere gli indugi** to come to a decision; **senza ulteriore indugio** without further delay
indulgènte *adj* indulgent
indulgènza *f* indulgence
indùlgere §187 *tr* to grant; to forgive ‖ *intr* to be indulgent; **indulgere a** to indulge; to yield to
indulto *m* (law) pardon
induménto *m* garment; **indumenti ìntimi** undergarments, unmentionables
indurire §176 *tr* to harden ‖ *intr* (ESSERE) to harden; to get stiff
indurre §102 *tr* to induce
indùstria *f* industry; **grande indùstria** heavy industry
industriale *adj* industrial ‖ *m* industrialist
industrializzare [ddzz] *tr* to industrialize
industriare §287 *ref* to try, try hard; **industriarsi a** or **per + *inf*** to try to + *inf*, to do one's best to + *inf*
industrió•so -sa [s] *adj* industrious
indut•tóre -trice *adj* inducing, provoking ‖ *m* (elec) field (*of motor*)
induzióne *f* induction
inebetire §176 *tr* to dull; to stun ‖ *intr* (ESSERE) & *ref* to become dull; to be stunned
inebriare §287 (inèbrio) *tr* to intoxicate ‖ *ref* to get drunk
inebriante *adj* intoxicating
ineccepìbile *adj* unexceptionable
inèdia *f* starvation, inanition; boredom
inèdi•to -ta *adj* unpublished; new, novel
ineduca•to -ta *adj* uneducated; ill-mannered
ineffàbile *adj* ineffable
inefficace *adj* ineffectual, ineffective
inefficàcia *f* inefficacy
inefficiènte *adj* inefficient
ineguale *adj* unequal; uneven
inelegante *adj* inelegant; shabby
ineleggìbile *adj* ineligible
ineluttàbile *adj* inevitable, inescapable
inenarràbile *adj* unspeakable
inerènte *adj* inherent
inèrme *adj* unarmed, defenseless
inerpicare §197 (inérpico) *ref* to clamber
inèrte *adj* inert
inèrzia *f* inertia; inactivity
inesattézza *f* inaccuracy
inesat•to -ta *adj* inaccurate, inexact; uncollected
inesaudì•to -ta *adj* unanswered
inesaurìbile *adj* inexhaustible
inescusàbile *adj* inexcusable
inesigìbile *adj* uncollectable
inesistènte *adj* inexistent
inesoràbile *adj* inexorable
inesperiènza *f* inexperience
inespèr•to -ta *adj* inexperienced; unskilled
inesplicàbile *adj* inexplicable
inesplica•to -ta *adj* unexplained
inesplora•to -ta *adj* unexplored
inesplò•so -sa *adj* unexploded
inespressì•vo -va *adj* inexpressive
inesprimìbile *adj* inexpressible

inespugnàbile *adj* impregnable; incorruptible

inespugna•to -ta *adj* unconquered

inestimàbile *adj* priceless, invaluable

inestinguìbile *adj* inextinguishable

inestirpàbile *adj* ineradicable

inestricàbile *adj* inextricable

inèt•to -ta *adj* inept

ineva•so -sa *adj* unfinished (*business*); unanswered (*mail*)

inevitàbile *adj* unavoidable, inevitable

inèzia *f* trifle, bagatelle

infagottare (infagòtto) *tr* & *ref* to bundle up

infallìbile *adj* infallible

infamante *adj* shameful, disgraceful

infamare *tr* to disgrace; to slander

infame *adj* infamous; villainous; (coll) horrible || *mf* villain

infàmia *f* infamy; (coll) botch, bungle

infangare §209 *tr* to splash with mud; (fig) to stain, spot

infante *adj* & *mf* infant, baby || *m* infante || *f* infanta

infantile *adj* infantile, childish

infànzia *f* infancy, childhood

infarcire §176 *tr* to cram; (culin) to stuff

infarinare *tr* to sprinkle with flour; to powder; (fig) to cram || *ref* to be covered with flour

infarinatura *f* sprinkling with flour; (fig) smattering

infastidire §176 *tr* to annoy || *ref* to be annoyed, lose one's patience

infaticàbile *adj* indefatigable, tireless

infatti *adv* indeed; really

infatuare (infàtuo) *tr* to infatuate || *ref* to become infatuated

infatua•to -ta *adj* infatuated

infàu•sto -sta *adj* unlucky, fatal

infecón•do -da *adj* barren

infedéle *adj* unfaithful; inaccurate || *mf* infidel

infedel•tà *f* (-tà) unfaithfulness; inaccuracy; infidelity

infelice *adj* unhappy, unfortunate; unfavorable || *mf* wretch

infelici•tà *f* (-tà) unhappiness

inferióre *adj* inferior; lower; **inferiore a** a lower than; less than; smaller than

inferiorità *f* inferiority

inferire §188a *tr* to inflict; to infer; (naut) to bend (*a sail*)

infermare (inférmo) *tr* (lit) to weaken || *intr* (ESSERE) to get sick

infermerìa *f* infirmary

infermiè•re -ra *adj* nursing || *m* male nurse || *f* nurse; **infermiera diplomata** trained nurse

infermierìsti•co -ca *adj* (-ci -che) nursing

infermi•tà *f* (-tà) infirmity

infér•mo -ma *adj* infirm; sick || *m* patient

infernale *adj* infernal

infèr•no -na *adj* (lit) lower (*region*) || *m* hell; inferno

inferocire §176 *tr* to infuriate || *intr*— **inferocire su** to be pitiless to || *intr* (ESSERE) to become infuriated

inferriata *f* grating, grill

infervorare (infèrvoro & infervóro) *tr* to excite, stir up || *ref* to get excited; to become absorbed

infestare (infèsto) *tr* to infest

infettare (infètto) *tr* to infect

infetti•vo -va *adj* infectious

infèt•to -ta *adj* infected; corrupted

infezióne *f* infection

infiacchire §176 *tr* to weaken || *intr* (ESSERE) & *ref* to grow weak

infiammàbile *adj* inflammable

infiammare *tr* to inflame; to ignite || *ref* to catch fire, ignite

infiamma•to -ta *adj* burning; aflame; inflamed, excited

infiammazióne *f* inflammation

infi•do -da *adj* untrustworthy

infierire §176 *intr* to become cruel; to be merciless to; to rage (said, e.g., of a disease)

infievolire §176 *tr* to weaken

infìggere §103 *tr* to thrust, stick, sink || *ref*—**infiggersi in** to creep in; to work in

infilare *tr* to thread (*a needle*); to insert (*a key*); to transfix (*with a sword*); to put on (*e.g., a coat*); to pull on (*one's pants*); to slip on (*a dress*); to slip (*e.g., one's arm into a sleeve*); to string (*beads*); to hit (*the target*); to take (*a road*); to enter through (*a door*); **infilare l'uscio** to slip away; **infilarle tutte** to succeed all the time; **non infilarne mai una** to never succeed || *ref* to slip; to sink; to slide (*e.g., through a crowd*)

infilata *f* row; string (*e.g., of insults*); (mil) enfilade; **d'infilata** lengthwise

infiltrare *ref* to infiltrate; to seep; (fig) to creep

infilzare *tr* to pierce; to string; (sew) to baste

infilzata *f* string (*of pearls, of lies, etc.*)

infi•mo -ma *adj* lowest, bottom

infine *adv* finally

infingar•do -da *adj* lazy, slothful

infini•tà *f* (-tà) infinity

infinitèsi•mo -ma *adj* & *m* infinitesimal

infiniti•vo -va *adj* (gram) infinitive

infini•to -ta *adj* infinite || *m* infinite; infinity; (gram) infinitive; (math) infinity; **all'infinito** ad infinitum

infino *adv* (lit)—**infino a** until; as far as; **infino a che** as long as

infinocchiare §287 (infinòcchio) *tr* (coll) to fool, bamboozle

infioccare §197 (infiòcco) *tr* to adorn with tassels

infiorare (infióro) *tr* to adorn with flowers; (fig) to sprinkle; (fig) to embellish || *ref* to be covered with flowers

infiorescènza *f* inflorescence

infirmare *tr* to weaken; to invalidate

infischiare §287 *ref*—**infischiarsi di** to not care a hoot about

infisso *m* frame (*e.g., of door*); fixture

infittire §176 *tr*, *intr* (ESSERE) & *ref* to thicken

inflazionare (inflaziòno) *tr* to inflate

inflazióne *f* inflation

inflessìbile *adj* inflexible

inflessióne *f* inflection
inflèttere §177 *tr* (lit) to inflect
infliggere §104 *tr* to inflict
influènte *adj* influential
influènza *f* influence; (pathol) influenza
influenzare (influènzo) *tr* to influence, sway
influire §176 *intr* to have an influence; **influire su** to influence || *intr* (ESSERE) —**influire in** to flow into
influsso *m* influence; (lit) plague
infocare §182 *tr* to make glow with heat || *ref* to catch fire; to get excited
infoca·to -ta *adj* red-hot; sultry
infognare (infógno) *ref* (coll) to sink (*e.g., in vice*); (coll) to get stuck (*e.g., in debt*)
infoltire §176 *tr* & *intr* (ESSERE) to thicken
infonda·to -ta *adj* unfounded, groundless
infóndere §178 *tr* to infuse, instill
inforcare §197 **(infórco)** *tr* to pitch (*hay*); to bestride; to mount (*a horse or bicycle*); to put on (*one's eyeglasses*)
inforcatura *f* pitching with a fork; crotch
informare (infórmo) *tr* to inform; (fig) to mold || *ref* to conform; to inquire; **informarsi da** to seek or get information from; **informarsi di** or **su** to inquire about; to find out about
informati·vo -va *adj* informative, informational
informa·tóre -trice *adj* underlying || *mf* informer; (journ) reporter || *m* informant (*of a foreign language*)
informazióne *f* piece of information; **chiedere informazioni sul conto di** to inquire about; **informazioni** information
infórme *adj* shapeless
informicolire §176 *ref* to tingle; **informicolirsi a** to go to sleep, *e.g.,* **gli si è informicolita la gamba** his leg went to sleep
infornare (infórno) *tr* to put in the oven; to bake
infornata *f* batch (*of bread*); (coll) flock
infortunare *ref* to get hurt
infortuna·to -ta *adj* injured || *mf* casualty, victim
infortù·nio *m* **(-ni)** accident, mishap; **infortunio sul lavoro** job-connected injury
infossare (infòsso) *tr* to bury || *ref* to cave in, settle; to become sunken (*said of eyes or cheeks*)
infracidare (infràcido) *tr* var of **infradiciare**
infracidire §176 *intr* to rot
infradiciare §128 **(infràdicio)** *tr* to drench || *ref* to get drenched; to rot (*said of fruit*)
inframmettènza *f* interference, meddling
inframméttere §198 *tr* to interpose || *ref* to meddle, interfere
inframmezzare [ddzz] **(inframmèzzo)** *tr* to intersperse

infràngere §179 *tr* & *ref* to break
infrangìbile *adj* unbreakable
infran·to -ta *adj* broken, shattered
infrarós·so -sa *adj* & *m* infrared
infrascrit·to -ta *adj* mentioned below
infrastruttura *f* underpinning; infrastructure; (rr) roadbed
infrazióne *f* infraction, breach
infreddatura *f* mild cold
infreddolire §176 *ref* to feel cold, to be chilled
infrenàbile *adj* irrepressible
infrequènte *adj* infrequent
infrollire §176 *tr* to make (*meat*) high || *intr* (ESSERE) & *ref* to get high (*said of meat*); (fig) to soften
infruttuó·so -sa [s] *adj* unprofitable
infuòri *adv* out; **all'infuori** outward; **all'infuori di** except
infuriare §287 *tr* to infuriate, enrage || *intr* to get blustery; to rage || *intr* (ESSERE) to lose one's temper
infusióne *f* infusion; sprinkling (*of holy water*)
infuso *m* infusion
ingabbiare §287 *tr* to cage; to jail; to corner; to build the framework of
ingabbiatura *f* frame, framework
ingaggiare §290 *tr* to hire; to engage || *ref* to sign up; to get tangled up
ingàg·gio *m* **(-gi)** engagement; (sports) bonus (*for signing up*)
ingagliardire §176 *tr* to strengthen || *ref* to become strong
ingannare *tr* to deceive; to cheat; to elude; to beguile || *ref* to be mistaken
inganna·tóre -trice *adj* deceptive || *mf* impostor
ingannévole *adj* deceitful; deceptive
inganno *m* deception; illusion
ingarbugliare §280 *tr* to entangle; to jumble || *ref* to get mixed up; to become embroiled
ingegnare (ingégno) *ref* to manage; to scheme
ingegnère *m* engineer
ingegneria *f* engineering; **ingegneria civile** civil engineering; **ingegneria meccanica** mechanical engineering
ingégno *m* brain, intelligence; talent; genius; expediency; (lit) machinery
ingegnosità [s] *f* ingeniousness
ingegnó·so -sa [s] *adj* ingenious; euphuistic
ingelosire [s] §176 *tr* to make jealous || *intr* (ESSERE) & *ref* to become jealous
ingemmare (ingèmmo) *tr* to adorn or stud with gems
ingenerare (ingènero) *tr* to engender
ingèni·to -ta *adj* inborn
ingènte *adj* huge, vast
ingentilire §176 *tr* to refine
ingenui·tà *f* **(-tà)** ingenuousness; ingenuous act
ingè·nuo -nua *adj* ingenuous, artless || *m* (theat) artless character || *f* (theat) ingénue
ingerènza *f* interference
ingerire §176 *tr* to ingest, swallow || *ref* to meddle

ingessare (ingèsso) *tr* to put in a plaster cast; to plaster up

ingessatura *f* (surg) plaster cast

inghiaiare §287 *tr* to gravel, cover with gravel

Inghilterra, l' *f* England; **la Nuova Inghilterra** New England

inghiottire (inghiótto) & §176 *tr* to swallow; to swallow up; to pocket (*one's pride*)

inghirlandare *tr* to bedeck with garlands; (lit) to encircle

ingiallire §176 *tr* & *intr* (ESSERE) to turn yellow

ingigantire §176 *tr* to exaggerate || *intr* (ESSERE) to grow larger, increase

inginocchiare §287 (**inginòcchio**) *ref* to kneel down

inginocchia·tóio *m* (-**tói**) prie-dieu

ingioiellare (ingioièllo) *tr* to bejewel; (fig) to stud

ingiù *adv* down; **all'ingiù** downwards

ingiùngere §183 *tr* to order, command || *intr* (with *dat*) to order, command, e.g., **il giudice ingiunse all'imputato di rispondere** the judge ordered the accused to answer

ingiunzióne *f* order; (law) injunction

ingiùria *f* insult, abuse; damage, wear

ingiuriare §287 *tr* to insult

ingiurió·so -sa [*s*] *adj* insulting

ingiustificàbile *adj* unjustifiable

ingiustifica·to -ta *adj* unjustified

ingiustizia *f* injustice

ingiu·sto -sta *adj* unjust, unfair || *m* unjust person

inglése [*s*] *adj* English; **all'inglese** in the English fashion; **andarsene all'inglese** to take French leave || *m* Englishman; English (*language*) || *f* Englishwoman

ingoiare §287 (**ingóio**) *tr* to swallow; to gulp down; **ingoiare un rospo** (fig) to swallow one's pride

ingolfare (ingólfo) *tr* (aut) to flood || *ref* to form a gulf; to get involved; (aut) to flood

ingollare (ingóllo) *tr* to swallow, gulp down

ingolosire [*s*] §176 *tr* to make the mouth of (*s.o.*) water || *intr* (ESSERE) & *ref* to have a craving

ingombrante *adj* cumbersome

ingombrare (ingómbro) *tr* to clutter

ingóm·bro -bra *adj* encumbered, cluttered || *m* encumbrance; **essere d'ingombro** to be in the way

ingommare (ingómmo) *tr* to glue

ingordìgia *f* greed

ingór·do -da *adj* greedy, covetous

ingorgare §209 (**ingórgo**) *ref* to get clogged up

ingór·go *m* (-**ghi**) blocking, congestion; **ingorgo stradale** traffic jam

ingovernàbile *adj* uncontrollable

ingozzare (ingózzo) *tr* to gobble, gulp down; to swallow; to cram (*e.g., a goose for fattening*)

ingranàg·gio *m* (-**gi**) gear, gearwheel; (fig) meshes; **ingranaggio di distribuzione** (aut) timing gear; **ingranaggio elicoidale** worm gear

ingranare *tr* to engage (*a gear*); **ingranare la marcia** to throw into gear || *intr* to be in gear; to succeed

ingrandiménto *m* enlargement; increase

ingrandire §176 *tr* to enlarge; to increase; || *intr* (ESSERE) & *ref* to increase, get larger

ingrassare *tr* to fatten; to lubricate || *intr* (ESSERE) & *ref* to get fat; to get rich

ingrassa·tóre -trice *mf* greaser, lubricator || *f* grease gun; lubricating machine

ingratitùdine *f* ingratitude

ingra·to -ta *adj* ungrateful; thankless || *mf* ingrate

ingraziare §287 *ref* to ingratiate oneself with

ingrediènte *m* ingredient

ingrèsso *m* entrance; admittance, entry; **ingressi** hallway furniture; **primo ingresso** debut

ingrossaménto *m* enlargement; swelling

ingrossare (ingròsso) *tr* to enlarge; to swell; to make bigger; to dull (*the mind*); to raise (*one's voice*) || *intr* (ESSERE) & *ref* to swell; to thicken; to become fat; to become pregnant; to become important

ingròsso *m*—**all'ingrosso** wholesale; approximately, more or less

ingrullire §176 *tr* to drive crazy || *intr* (ESSERE) & *ref* to become silly; **fare ingrullire** to drive crazy

inguadàbile *adj* not fordable

inguainare (inguaìno) *tr* to sheathe

ingualcibile *adj* wrinkle-free, wrinkleproof

inguanta·to -ta *adj* with gloves on; **con le mani inguantate** with gloves on

inguarìbile *adj* incurable

inguine *f* (anat) groin

ingurgitare (ingùrgito) *tr* to swallow, gulp down

inibire §176 *tr* to inhibit

inibi·tóre -trice *adj* inhibiting || *m* inhibitor

inidòne·o -a *adj* unfit, unqualified

iniettare (iniètto) *tr* to inject || *ref* to become bloodshot; **iniettarsi di sangue** to become bloodshot

iniezióne *f* injection

inimicare §197 *tr* to make an enemy of; to alienate || *ref*—**inimicarsi con** to fall out with

inimicizia *f* enmity

inimitàbile *adj* inimitable, matchless

ininterrót·to -ta *adj* uninterrupted

iniqui·tà *f* (-**tà**) injustice; iniquity

inì·quo -qua *adj* unjust; wicked

iniziale *adj* & *f* initial

iniziare §287 *tr* to initiate || *ref* to begin

iniziativa *f* initiative; sponsorship; **iniziativa privata** private enterprise

inizia·tóre -trice *adj* initiating || *mf* initiator, promoter

iniziazióne *f* initiation

inì·zio *m* (-**zi**) beginning, start

innaffiare §287 *tr* var of **annaffiare**

innaffia·tóio *m* (-**tói**) var of **annaffiatoio**

innalzaménto *m* elevation

innalzare *tr* to raise; to elevate; **innalzare al cielo** to praise to the sky ‖ *ref* to rise; to tower

innamorare (innamóro) *tr* to charm, fascinate; to inspire with love ‖ *ref* to fall in love

innamora·to -ta *adj* in love, enamored; fond ‖ *mf* sweetheart ‖ *m* boyfriend ‖ *f* girl friend

innanzi *adj invar* previous, prior (*e.g., day*) ‖ *adv* ahead, before; **innanzi a** in front of; **innanzi di** + *inf* before + *ger*; **mettere innanzi** to prefer; to place before; to advance (*an excuse*); **per l'innanzi** before, in the past; **tirare innanzi** to get along ‖ *prep* before; above; **innanzi tempo** ahead of time; **innanzi tutto** above all

innà·rio *m* (-ri) hymnal

inna·to -ta *adj* inborn, innate

innegàbile *adj* undeniable

inneggiare §290 **(innéggio)** *intr*—**inneggiare a** to sing the praises of

innervosire [s] §176 *tr* to make nervous

innescare §197 **(innésco)** *tr* to bait (*a hook*); to prime (*a bomb*)

inné·sco *m* (-schi) primer; detonator

innestare (innèsto) *tr* (hort & surg) to graft; (surg) to implant; (med) to inoculate (*a vaccine*); (mach) to engage; (elec) to plug in (*e.g., a plug*); **innestare la marcia** (aut) to throw into gear ‖ *ref* to be grafted; **innestarsi in** to merge with; **innestarsi su** to connect with

innèsto *m* (hort & surg) graft; (surg) implant; (med) inoculation; (mach) engagement; (mach) coupling; (elec) plug

inno *m* hymn; **inno nazionale** national anthem

innocènte *adj* innocent ‖ *m* innocent; **innocenti** foundlings

innocènza *f* innocence

innò·cuo -cua *adj* innocuous, harmless

innominàbile *adj* unmentionable

innomina·to -ta *adj* unnamed

innovare (innòvo) *tr* to innovate

innovazióne *f* innovation

innumerévole *adj* countless, innumerable

-ino -ina *suf adj* little, e.g., **poverino** poor little; hailing from, e.g., **fiorentino** hailing from Florence, Florentine ‖ *suf f* see **-ina**

inoccupa·to -ta *adj* unoccupied ‖ *m* person looking for his first job

inoculare (inòculo) *tr* to inoculate

inoculazióne *f* inoculation

inodó·ro -ra *adj* odorless

inoffensi·vo -va *adj* inoffensive

inoltrare (inóltro) *tr* (com) to forward (*e.g., a request*) ‖ *ref* to advance

inóltre *adv* besides, in addition

inóltro *m* (com) forwarding

inondare (inóndo) *tr* to inundate, flood; to swamp

inondazióne *f* flood, inundation

inoperosità [s] *f* idleness

inoperó·so -sa [s] *adj* idle

inopina·to -ta *adj* (lit) unexpected

inopportu·no -na *adj* inopportune, untimely

inoppugnàbile *adj* incontestable; indisputable

inorgàni·co -ca *adj* (-ci -che) inorganic

inorgoglire §176 *tr* to make proud ‖ *intr* (ESSERE) & *ref* to grow proud

inorridire §176 *tr* to horrify ‖ *intr* (ESSERE) to be horrified

inospitale *adj* inhospitable

inosservante *adj* unobservant

inosserva·to -ta *adj* unnoticed; unperceived

inossidàbile *adj* stainless

inquadrare *tr* to frame; to arrange

inquadratura *f* framing; (mov, phot) frame

inqualificàbile *adj* unspeakable

inquietante *adj* disquieting

inquietare (inquièto) *tr* to worry ‖ *ref* to worry; to get angry

inquiè·to -ta *adj* worried; restless; angry; (lit) stormy

inquietùdine *f* worry; restlessness; preoccupation

inquili·no -na *mf* tenant

inquinaménto *m* pollution

inquinare *tr* to pollute

inquirènte *adj* investigating

inquisi·tóre -trice *adj* inquiring ‖ *m* inquisitor

inquisizióne *f* inquisition

insabbiare §287 *tr* to cover with sand; to pigeonhole; to shelve ‖ *ref* to get covered with sand; to bury oneself in sand; to get stuck

insaccare §197 *tr* to bag; to stuff (*e.g., salami*); (mil) to hem in; (fig) to bundle up; (coll) to gulp down ‖ *ref* to be packed in; to crumple up; to disappear behind a thick bank of clouds (*said, e.g., of the sun*)

insaccato *m* participant in a sack race; **insaccati** cold cuts, lunch meat

insalata *f* salad; (fig) mess

insalatièra *f* salad bowl

insalubre *adj* unhealthy

insalsa·to -ta *adj* unsalted; **andarsene insalutato** ospite to take French leave

insanàbile *adj* incurable; implacable

insanguinare (insànguino) *tr* to bloody; to cover with blood; to bathe in blood

insa·no -na *adj* insane

insaponare (insapóno) *tr* to soap; to lather; (fig) to soft-soap

insaporire §176 *tr* to flavor ‖ *intr* (ESSERE) to become tasty

insaputa *f*—**all'insaputa di** without the knowledge of, unbeknown to

insaziàbile *adj* insatiable

insazia·to -ta *adj* insatiate, unsatisfied

inscatolare (inscàtolo) *tr* to can

inscenare (inscèno) *tr* to stage

inscindìbile *adj* inseparable

inscrìvere §250 *tr* (geom) to inscribe

inscrutàbile *adj* inscrutable

inscurire §176 *tr, intr* (ESSERE) & *ref* to darken

insecchire §176 *tr* to dry ‖ *intr* (ESSERE) & *ref* to dry up insediaménto *m* installation (*into an office*); assumption (*of an office*)

insediare §287 (insèdio) *tr* to install || *ref* to be installed; to take one's seat; to settle

inségna *f* badge, insignia, emblem; ensign, flag; coat of arms; motto; sign (*e.g., on a restaurant*); traffic sign

insegnaménto *m* education, instruction

insegnante *adj* teaching || *mf* teacher

insegnare (inségno) *tr* to teach; to show || *intr* to teach

inseguiménto *m* pursuit

inseguire (inséguo) *tr* to pursue, chase; to chase after

insellare (insèllo) *tr* to saddle; to put on (*e.g., one's glasses*); to bend

insellatura *f* saddling; bending

insenatura *f* inlet, cove

insensatézza *f* nonsense, folly

insensa·to -ta *adj* nonsensical, foolish || *mf* scatterbrain

insensibile *adj* insensible; unresponsive; insensitive

inseparàbile *adj* inseparable || *m* (orn) lovebird

insepól·to -ta *adj* unburied

inserire §176 *tr* to insert; to plug in || *ref* to slip in; to butt in

inseri·tóre -trice *adj* (elec) connecting || *m* (elec) connector, plug || *f* sorter (*of punch cards*)

insèrto *m* file, folder; insert; spliced film

inservìbile *adj* useless, worthless

inserviènte *m* attendant, porter; (eccl) server

inserzionare (inserzióno) *intr* to advertise

inserzióne *f* insertion; advertisement

inserzioni·sta (-sti -ste) *adj* advertising || *mf* advertiser

insettici·da *adj* & *m* (-di -de) insecticide

insettìfu·go *m* (-ghi) insect repellent

insètto *m* insect; insetti vermin

insidia *f* trap, ambush; insidie lure

insidiare §287 *tr* to ensnare; to try to trap; to try to seduce; to attempt (*someone's life*)

insidió·so -sa [s] *adj* insidious

insième *m* whole, entirety; harmony; ensemble; set; d'insieme general, comprehensive; nell'insieme as a whole || *adv* together

insigne *adj* famous; notable; arrant (*knave*)

insignificante *adj* insignificant; petty

insignire §176 *tr* to decorate; insignire qlcu di un titolo to bestow a title upon s.o.

insignorire §176 *tr* (lit) to invest with a fief || *intr* (ESSERE) to enrich oneself || *ref* to enrich oneself; insignorirsi di to seize; to take possession of

insilare *tr* to silo, ensile

insilato *m* ensilage

insincè·ro -ra *adj* insincere

insindacàbile *adj* final, indisputable

insino *adv* (lit)—insino a until; as far as; insino a che as long as

insinuante *adj* insinuating

insinuare (insìnuo) *tr* to stick, thrust;

to insinuate; (law) to register || *ref* to creep, filter; to ingratiate oneself; insinuarsi in to worm one's way into

insinuazióne *f* insinuation, hint

insìpi·do -da *adj* insipid, vapid

insistènte *adj* insistent

insìstere §114 *intr* to insist

ìnsi·to -ta *adj* inborn, inherent

insociévole *adj* unsociable

insoddisfat·to -ta *adj* dissatisfied

insofferènte *adj* intolerant

insoffrìbile *adj* unbearable, insufferable

insolazióne *f* sunning; sun bath; sun-stroke; sunny exposure

insolènte *adj* insolent

insolentire §176 *tr* to insult, abuse || *intr* to be insolent

insolènza *f* insolence; insult

insòli·to -ta *adj* unusual

insolùbile *adj* insoluble

insolu·to -ta *adj* unsolved; not dis-solved; unpaid

insolvènza *f* insolvency

insolvìbile *adj* insolvent; bad (*debt*)

insómma *adv* in conclusion || *interj* well!

insommergìbile *adj* unsinkable

insondàbile *adj* unfathomable

insònne *adj* sleepless

insònnia *f* insomnia

insonnoli·to -ta *adj* sleepy, drowsy

insonorizzazióne [ddzz] *f* soundproof-ing

insopportàbile *adj* unbearable

insorgènte *adj* appearing || *mf* insur-gent

insorgènza *f* appearance (*of illness*)

insórgere §258 *intr* (ESSERE) to rise up, revolt; to appear

insormontàbile *adj* unsurmountable, in-surmountable

insòr·to -ta *adj* & *m* insurgent

insospettàbile *adj* above suspicion; un-expected

insospetta·to -ta *adj* not suspect; un-expected

insospettire §176 *tr* to make suspicious || *intr* (ESSERE) & *ref* to become suspicious

insostenìbile *adj* indefensible; unbear-able

insostituìbile *adj* irreplaceable

insozzare (insózzo) *tr* to soil, sully

inspera·to -ta *adj* unexpected; unhoped-for

inspiegàbile *adj* unexplainable

inspirare *tr* to inhale, breathe in

inspirazióne *f* inhalation

instàbile *adj* unstable

installare *tr* to install; to set up, settle; to induct (*in an office*) || *ref* to settle

installatóre *m* plumber; erector

installazióne *f* installation; plumbing

instancàbile *adj* untiring

instante *adj* insistent; impending || *m* petitioner

instare (*pp* missing) *intr* to insist; to threaten, be imminent

instaurare (instàuro) *tr* to establish

instaurazióne *f* establishment

instigare §209 *tr* var of istigare

instillare *tr* var of istillare

instituire §176 *tr* var of istituire

instruire §176 *tr* var of **istruire**
instrumento *m* var of **istrumento**
instupidire §176 *tr* var of **istupidire**
insù *adv* up; **all'insù** up
insubordina•to -ta *adj* insubordinate
insuccèsso *m* failure
insudiciare §128 **(insùdicio)** *tr* to soil, dirty; to sully ‖ *ref* to get dirty
insufficiènte *adj* insufficient; failing (*in school*)
insufficiènza *f* insufficiency; failure (*in school*)
insulare *adj* insular
insulina *f* insulin
insulsàggine *f* silliness, nonsense
insul•so -sa *adj* insipid; simple, silly
insultante *adj* insulting
insultare *tr* to insult ‖ *intr* (with *dat*) to insult
insulto *m* insult; (pathol) attack
insuperàbile *adj* insuperable; unparalleled
insupera•to -ta *adj* unsurpassed
insuperbire §176 *tr, intr* (ESSERE) & *ref* to swell with pride
insurrezióne *f* insurrection
insussistènte *adj* nonexistent, unfounded
intabarrare *tr* to wrap up
intaccare §197 *tr* to notch; to corrode; to scratch; to attack (*said of a disease*); to damage (*e.g., a reputation*); to cut into (*capital*) ‖ *intr* to stutter
intaccatura *f* notch; (carp) mortise
intagliare §280 *tr* to carve; to engrave
intà•glio *m* (-gli) carving; intaglio
intanare *ref* to hide
intangìbile *adj* intangible; inviolable
intanto *adv* meanwhile; (coll) yet; (coll) finally; **intanto che** while; **per intanto** at present; in the meantime
intarsiare §287 *tr* to inlay; (fig) to stud
intarsia•to -ta *adj* inlaid
intàr•sio *m* (-si) inlay; inlaid work
intasare [s] *tr* to clog; to tie up (*traffic*); to stop up ‖ *ref* to be clogged up; to be tied up; to be stopped up (*said of nose*)
intascare §197 *tr* to pocket
intat•to -ta *adj* intact, untouched
intavolare **(intàvolo)** *tr* to start (*a conversation*); to broach (*a subject*); to launch (*negotiations*)
intavolato *m* boarding, planking
integèrri•mo -ma *adj* of the utmost honesty
integrale *adj* integral; whole; wholewheat (*bread*); built-in ‖ *m* integral
integralismo *m* policy of the complete absorption of the body politic by an ideology
integrante *adj* constituent, integral
integrare **(intègro)** *tr* to integrate ‖ *ref* to complement each other
integrazióne *f* integration
integrità *f* integrity
ìnte•gro -gra *adj* whole, complete; honest, upright; intact
intelaiatura *f* frame; framework
intellètto *m* intellect, mind; understanding
intellettuale *adj* & *mf* intellectual

intellettuali•tà *f* (-tà) intellectuality; intelligentsia
intellettualòide *mf* highbrow
intelligènte *adj* intelligent; clever
intelligènza *f* intelligence; understanding; **essere d'intelligenza con** to be in collusion with
intellighènzia *f* intelligentsia
intelligìbile *adj* intelligible
intemera•to -ta *adj* pure, spotless ‖ *f* reprimand, scolding; long, boring speech
intemperante *adj* intemperate
intemperanza *f* intemperance
intempèrie *fpl* inclement weather
intempesti•vo -va *adj* untimely
intendènte *m* district director; **intendente di finanza** director of customs office; **intendente militare** commissary, quartermaster
intendènza *f* office of the district director; intendance; **intendenza militare** quartermaster corps
intèndere §270 *tr* to understand; to hear; to intend; to turn (*e.g., one's eyes*); to mean; **dare ad intèndere a** to lead (*s.o.*) to believe (*s.th*); **far intendere** to give to understand; **farsi intendere** to force obedience; to make oneself understood; **intènder dire che** to hear that; **intèndere a rovescio** to misunderstand; **intendere a volo** to catch on quickly (to); **intèndere ragione** to listen to reason; **lasciare intèndere** to give to understand ‖ *intr* to aim (*toward a goal*) ‖ *ref* to come to an agreement; **intèndersela con** to be in collusion with; to have an affair with; **intèndersi di** to be a good judge of; to be an expert in
intendiménto *m* understanding, comprehension; aim, goal
intendi•tóre -trice *mf* connoisseur, expert; **a buon intenditore poche parole** a word to the wise is sufficient
intenerire §176 *tr* to soften; (fig) to move ‖ *ref* to soften; (fig) to be moved
intensificare §197 **(intensìfico)** *tr* & *ref* to intensify
intensi•tà *f* (-tà) intensity
intensi•vo -va *adj* intensive
intèn•so -sa *adj* intense
intentare **(intènto)** *tr* (law) to bring (*action*)
intenta•to -ta *adj* unattempted
intèn•to -ta *adj* intent ‖ *m* intent, goal; **coll'intento di** with the purpose of
intenzionale *adj* intentional
intenziona•to -ta *adj*—**bene intenzionato** well-meaning; **essere intenzionato di** to intend to
intenzióne *f* intention; purpose; **con intenzione** on purpose
intepidire §176 *tr* & *ref* var of **intiepidire**
interbase *f* (baseball) shortstop
intercalare *m* refrain; pet word or phrase ‖ *tr* to intercalate; to inset
intercalazióne *f* intercalation; inset
intercapèdine *f* air space
intercèdere §123 *tr* to seek, get (*a par-*

don for s.o.) || *intr* to intercede || *intr* (ESSERE)—**intercedere tra** to intervene or elapse between; to extend between; to exist between

intercettare (**intercètto**) *tr* to intercept; to tap (*a phone*)

intercetta·tóre **-trice** *mf* interceptor

intercettóre *m* (aer) interceptor

intercomunale *adj* long-distance (*call*)

intercórrere §139 *intr* (ESSERE) to elapse; to happen; to be, to stand

interdét·to **-ta** *adj* dumfounded; forbidden || *m* interdict; (coll) dumbell

interdire §151 *tr* to prohibit; (eccl) to interdict; (law) to disqualify

interessaménto *m* interest, concern

interessante *adj* interesting; **in stato interessante** in the family way

interessare (**interèsso**) *tr* to interest; to concern || *intr* to be of interest || *ref*—**interessarsi a** to take an interest in; **interessarsi di** to concern oneself with

interessa·to **-ta** *adj* interested; selfish || *m* interested party

interèsse *m* interest; self-interest

interessènza *f* (com) share, interest

interferènza *f* interference

interferire §176 *intr* to interfere

interfogliare §280 (**interfòglio**) *tr* to interleave

interiezióne *f* interjection

interinato *m* temporary office or tenure

interi·no **-na** *adj* acting || *m* temporary appointee

interióra *fpl* entrails

interióre *adj* interior || **interiori** *mpl* entrails

interlinea *f* interlining; (typ) leading

interlineare *adj* interlinear || *v* (**interlineo**) *tr* (typ) to lead

interlocu·tóre **-trice** *mf* participant (*in a discussion*); person speaking

interloquire §176 *intr* to take part in a discussion; to chime in

interlù·dio *m* (**-di**) interlude

intermedià·rio **-ria** (**-ri -rie**) *adj & mf* intermediary || *m* middleman

intermè·dio **-dia** (**-di -die**) *adj* intermediate || *mf* supervisor

intermèzzo [ddzz] *m* intermezzo; entr'acte; interval

interminàbile *adj* interminable, endless

intermissióne *f* intermission

intermittènte *adj* intermittent

internaménto *m* internment

internare (**intèrno**) *tr* to intern; to confine; to commit (*an insane person*) || *ref* to go deep (*into a problem*)

interna·to **-ta** *adj* interned || *m* internee; inmate; boarder; boarding school

internazionale *adj* international

internazionalizzare [ddzz] *tr* to internationalize

interni·sta *mf* (**-sti -ste**) internist

intèr·no **-na** *adj* inside, internal; inland; interior; boarding (*student*) || *m* inside; interior; (med) intern; lining (*of coat*); **all'interno** inside; **interni** (mov) indoor shots || **gli Interni** the Italian Ministry of Internal Affairs

inté·ro **-ra** *adj* entire, whole; full (*price*); (lit) upright, honest || *m* whole; **per intero** completely

interpellare (**interpèllo**) *tr* to interpellate; to question; to consult

interpetrare (**intèrpetro**) *tr* var of **interpretare**

interplanetà·rio **-ria** *adj* (**-ri -rie**) interplanetary

interpolare (**intèrpolo**) *tr* to interpolate

interpolazióne *f* interpolation

interpónte *m* (naut) between-deck

interpórre §218 *tr* to interpose || *ref* to intervene

interpretare (**intèrpreto**) *tr* to interpret

interpretazióne *f* interpretation

intèrprete *mf* interpreter

interpunzióne *f* punctuation

interrare (**intèrro**) *tr* to bury, inter; to fill in (*e.g., a marsh*) || *ref* to become silted

interra·to **-ta** *adj* underground; **piano interrato** basement

interrogare §209 (**intèrrogo**) *tr* to question; to interrogate

interrogati·vo **-va** *adj* interrogative || *m* why; question

interrogatò·rio **-ria** (**-ri -rie**) *adj* questioning || *m* (law) interrogatory; **interrogatorio di terzo grado** third degree

interrogazióne *f* interrogation; quiz, examination; **interrogazione retorica** rhetorical question

interrómpere §240 *tr* to interrupt

interruttóre *m* (elec) switch; **interruttore di linea** (elec) controller

interruzióne *f* interruption

interscàm·bio *m* (**-bi**) interchange

interscolàsti·co **-ca** *adj* (**-ci -che**) interscholastic; intercollegiate

intersecare §197 (**intèrseco**) *tr & ref* to intersect

intersezióne *f* intersection

interstellare *adj* interstellar

interstì·zio *m* (**-zi**) interstice

interurba·no **-na** *adj* interurban, intercity; (telp) long-distance || *f* (telp) long-distance call

intervallo *m* interval; pause; (educ) recess; (theat) intermission

intervenire §282 *intr* (ESSERE) to intervene; (surg) to operate; **intervenire a** to take part in

interventi·sta *mf* (**-sti -ste**) interventionist

intervènto *m* intervention; attendance; (surg) operation

intervenzióne *f* intervention

intervista *f* interview; **fare un'intervista a** to interview

intervistare *tr* to interview

inté·so **-sa** [s] *adj* understood; intended, designed; **bene inteso** of course; **non darsene per inteso** to not pay attention; **rimanere inteso** to agree || *f* understanding, agreement; entente

intèssere (**intèsso**) *tr* to interweave; to wreathe (*a garland*)

intestardire §176 *ref* to get obstinate; to be determined

intestare (intèsto) *tr* to caption; to label; (typ) to head (*a page*); **intestare qlco a qlcu** to register s.th in the name of s.o.; **intestare una fattura a** to issue a bill in the name of || *ref* to become obstinate; to take it into one's head

intesta·to -ta *adj* headed; registered (*stock*); obstinate; (law) intestate

intestazióne *f* heading; registration (*of stock*)

intestinale *adj* intestinal

intesti·no -na *adj & m* intestine; **intestino crasso** large intestine; **intestino tenue** small intestine

intiepidìre §176 *tr & ref* to warm up; to cool off

intiè·ro -ra *adj & m* var of **intero**

intimare (ìntimo & intìmo) *tr* to intimate; to order, command; to declare (*war*); to impose (*a fine*); (law) to enjoin

intimazióne *f* intimation; order; (law) injunction

intimidazióne *f* intimidation

intimidìre §176 *tr* to intimidate; to threaten || *ref* to become bashful

intimi·tà *f* (**-tà**) intimacy; privacy

inti·mo -ma *adj* intimate; inmost; **biancheria intima** underwear, lingerie || *m* intimate friend; depth (*of one's heart*)

intimorìre §176 *tr* to frighten

intìngere §126 *tr* to dip || *intr*—**intingere in** to dip in || *ref*—**intingersi in un affare** to have a finger in the pie

intìngolo *m* sauce, gravy; fancy dish

intirizzìre [ddzz] §176 *tr* to benumb || *intr* (ESSERE) & *ref* to become numb or stiff; to become stiff and frostbitten

intirizzì·to -ta [ddzz] *adj* numb

intisichìre §176 *tr* to make tubercular; (fig) to weaken || *intr* (ESSERE) to become tubercular; to wither

intitolare (intìtolo) *tr* to title; to dedicate || *ref* to be named; to assume the title of

intoccàbile *adj & m* untouchable

intolleràbile *adj* intolerable

intollerante *adj* intolerant

intonacare §197 (**intònaco**) *tr* to plaster; to whitewash; to cover (*e.g., with tar*) || *ref*—**intonacarsi la faccia** (joc) to put on one's warpaint

intòna·co m (**-chi**) plaster; roughcast

intonare (intòno) *tr* to intone; to harmonize; (mus) to tune || *ref* to harmonize, go

intonazióne *f* intonation; harmony

intòn·so -sa *adj* uncut; (lit) unsheared

intontìre §176 *tr* to stun || *intr* (ESSERE) & *ref* to become stunned

intoppare (intòppo) *tr* to stumble upon || *intr* (ESSERE) & *ref* to stumble

intòppo *m* obstacle, hindrance

intorbidare (intórbido) *tr* to cloud; to muddy; to obfuscate; to upset (*friendship*); to stir up (*passions*) || *ref* to become cloudy or muddy; to become obfuscated

intorbidìre §176 *tr & ref* to cloud; to muddy

intormentìre §176 *tr* to benumb || *intr* (ESSERE) to become numb

intórno *adv* around, about; **all'intorno** all around; **intorno a** around; about; **levarsi qlcu d'intorno** to get rid of s.o.

intorpidìre §176 *tr* to benumb || *ref* to become numb

intossicare §197 (**intòssico**) *tr* to poison, intoxicate

intossicazióne *f* poisoning, intoxication

intraducìbile *adj* untranslatable; inexpressible

intrafèrro *m* spark gap; air gap

intralciare §128 *tr* to hamper; to intertwine || *ref* to become hampered

intràl·cio m (**-ci**) hindrance; **essere d'intralcio** to be in the way; **intralcio del traffico** traffic congestion

intralicciatura *f* lattice truss (*of high-tension tower*)

intrallazzare *intr* to deal in the black market

intrallazza·tóre -trice *mf* black marketeer

intrallazzo *m* black-market dealing; kickback

intramezzare [ddzz] (**intramèzzo**) *tr* to alternate

intramontàbile *adj* undying, immortal

intransigènte *adj & mf* intransigent, die-hard

intransitàbile *adj* impassable

intransiti·vo -va *adj* intransitive

intrappolare (intràppolo) *tr* to entrap

intraprendènte *adj* enterprising

intraprendènza *f* enterprise, initiative

intraprèndere §220 *tr* to undertake

intrattàbile *adj* unmanageable, intractable

intrattenére §271 *tr* to entertain || *ref* to linger; **intrattenersi su** to dwell upon

intrattenimén到 *m* entertainment

intravedére §279 *tr* to glimpse, catch a glimpse of; to foresee

intravenó·so -sa [s] *adj* intravenous

intrecciare §128 (**intréccio**) *tr* to braid; to twine; to cross (*one's fingers*); (fig) to weave; to begin (*a dance*) || *ref* to become embroiled; to become intertwined; to crisscross

intréc·cio m (**-ci**) knitting; intertwining; plot (*of novel*); (theat) intrigue

intrepidézza *f* intrepidness, intrepidity

intrèpi·do -da *adj* intrepid

intricare §197 *tr* (lit) to entangle

intrica·to -ta *adj* tangled; intricate

intrì·co m (**-chi**) tangle, jumble

intrìdere §189 *tr* to soak; to knead

intrigante *adj* intriguing || *mf* schemer

intrigare §209 *tr* to tangle || *intr* to intrigue || *ref* (coll) to meddle

intrì·go m (**-ghi**) intrigue; trouble

intrìnse·co -ca (**-ci -che**) *adj* intrinsic; intimate || *m* intimate nature, core

intrì·so -sa *adj* soaked || *m* mash

intristìre §176 *intr* (ESSERE) to wither; to waste away

introdót·to -ta *adj* introduced; well-known; knowledgeable, expert

introdurre §102 *tr* to introduce; to insert; to open (*a speech*); to show in || *ref* to slip in

introdutti·vo -va *adj* introductory

introduzióne *f* introduction

introitare (intròito) *tr* to collect, take in

intròito *m* receipts, collection; (eccl) introit

introméttere §198 *tr* to insert; to introduce; to involve || *ref* to meddle; to pry

intromissióne *f* meddling; intrusion; intervention

intronare (intròno) *tr* to deafen; to stun

intronizzare [ddzz] *tr* to enthrone

introspetti·vo -va *adj* introspective

introspezióne *f* introspection

introvàbile *adj* unobtainable; inaccessible

introvèr·so -sa *adj & mf* introvert

intrùdere §190 *tr* (lit) to slip in || *ref* to intrude; to trespass

intrufolare (intrùfolo) *tr* (coll) to slip (*e.g., one's hand into somebody's pocket*) || *ref* to slip in, intrude

intrù·glio *m* (-gli) concoction, brew; hodgepodge; imbroglio; mess

intrusióne *f* intrusion

intru·so -sa *adj* intrusive || *mf* intruder

intuire §176 *tr* to know by intuition; to guess; to sense

intuiti·vo -va *adj* intuitive; obvious

intùito *m* intuition; insight

intuizióne *f* intuition

inturgidire §176 *intr* (ESSERE) & *ref* to swell

inuma·no -na *adj* inhuman; inhumane

inumare *tr* to bury, inhume

inumazióne *f* burial, inhumation

inumidire §176 *tr* to moisten || *ref* to get wet

inurbaménto *m* migration to the city

inurba·no -na *adj* uncouth, unmannerly

inurbare *ref* to move into the city; to become citified

inusa·to -ta *adj* unused; unusual

inusita·to -ta *adj* unusual; out-of-the-way

inùtile *adj* useless; worthless

inutilizzàbile [ddzz] *adj* unusable

inutilizzare [ddzz] *tr* to waste (*e.g., time*)

inutilizza·to -ta [ddzz] *adj* unused

inutilménte *adv* needlessly, to no purpose || *interj* no use!

invadènte *adj* meddlesome, intrusive

invàdere §172 *tr* to invade; to encroach on; to spread over; to overcome

invaghire §176 *tr* to charm || *ref* to fall in love

invalére §278 *intr* (ESSERE) to become established; to prevail

invalicàbile *adj* impassable, unsurmountable

invalidàbile *adj* voidable

invalidaménto *m* invalidity; invalidation

invalidare (invàlido) *tr* to void, invalidate; to negate (*e.g., evidence*)

invalidi·tà *f* (-tà) invalidity; invalidation; sickness, disability

invàli·do -da *adj* void, invalid; sick, disabled || *m* disabled person; invalid

inval·so -sa *adj* prevailing

invano *adv* in vain, vainly

invariàbile *adj* invariable

invaria·to -ta *adj* unchanging; unchanged

invasare *tr* to pot (*a plant*); to fill up (*a reservoir*); to possess, obsess

invasa·to -ta *adj* possessed, obsessed

invasióne *f* invasion

inva·so -sa *adj* invaded || *m* potting (*of plant*); capacity (*of reservoir*)

inva·sóre -ditrice *adj* invading || *m* invader

invecchiaménto *m* aging

invecchiare §287 **(invècchio)** *tr & intr* (ESSERE) to age

invéce *adv* on the contrary, instead; **invece di** instead of

inveire §176 *intr* to inveigh, rail

invelenire §176 *tr* to envenom; to embitter || *intr* (ESSERE) & *ref* to grow bitter

invendìbile *adj* unsalable

invendica·to -ta *adj* unavenged

invendu·to -ta *adj* unsold

inventare (invènto) *tr* to invent

inventariare §287 *tr* to inventory

inventà·rio *m* (-ri) inventory

inventi·vo -va *adj* inventive || *f* inventiveness

inven·tóre -trice *adj* inventive || *mf* inventor

invenzióne *f* invention; (lit) find

inverdire §176 *intr* (ESSERE) to turn green

inverecóndia *f* immodesty

inverecón·do -da *adj* immodest

invernale *adj* winter; wintry

inverniciare §128 *tr* to paint; to varnish

invèrno *m* winter

invéro *adv* (lit) truly, indeed

inverosimiglianza [s] *f* unlikelihood

inverosìmile [s] *adj* unlikely

inversióne *f* inversion

invèr·so -sa *adj* inverse, opposite; (coll) cross || *m* inverse

inversóre *m* inverter; **inversore di spinta** (aer) thrust reverser

invertebra·to -ta *adj & m* invertebrate

invertire §176 & (invèrto) *tr* to invert; to reverse

inverti·to -ta *adj* inverted || *m* invert

investigare §209 **(invèstigo)** *tr* to investigate

investiga·tóre -trice *adj* investigating || *mf* investigator; detective

investigazióne *f* investigation

investiménto *m* investment; collision

investire (invèsto) *tr* to invest; to collide with; **investire di insulti** to cover with insults || *ref*—**investirsi di** to become conscious of (*e.g., one's authority*); (theat) to become identified with (*a character*)

investi·tóre -trice *mf* investor

investitura *f* investiture

invetera·to -ta *adj* inveterate, confirmed

invetria·to -ta *adj* glazed || *f* window; window pane

invettiva *f* invective

inviare §119 *tr* to send

invia·to -ta *mf* envoy; correspondent

invidia *f* envy

invidiàbile *adj* enviable

invidiare §287 *tr* to envy; to begrudge; **non aver niente da invidiare a** to be just as good as

invidió·so -sa [s] *adj* envious

invigorire §176 *tr* to strengthen, invigorate || *intr* (ESSERE) & *ref* to grow stronger

invilire §176 *tr* to dishearten; to vilify; to lower (*prices*) || *intr* (ESSERE) & *ref* to lose heart; to lose one's reputation

inviluppare *tr* to envelop; to wrap up

invincibile *adj* invincible

invi·o *m* (-*i*) dispatch; shipment; remittance; envoy (*of a poem*)

inviolàbile *adj* inviolable

inviperire §176 *ref* to become enraged

invischiare §287 *tr* to smear with birdlime; to ensnare || *ref* to become ensnared

invisibile *adj* invisible

invi·so -sa *adj* disliked, hated

invitante *adj* attractive, inviting

invitare *tr* to invite; to summon; (*cards*) to bid; (*cards*) to open; (*mach*) to screw (*e.g., a light bulb*) in; to screw (*e.g., a lid*) on

invita·to -ta *adj* invited || *m* guest

invito *m* invitation; inducement; bottom of stairway; (*cards*) opening

invit·to -ta *adj* unvanquished

invocare §197 (invòco) *tr* to invoke

invocazióne *f* invocation

invogliare §280 (invòglio) *tr* to induce, entice || *ref* to yearn, long

involare (invólo) *tr* to steal; to abduct || *intr* (ESSERE) (aer) to take off || *ref* to disappear; to fly away

invòlgere §289 *tr* to wrap, envelop; to involve || *ref* to become entangled

invólo *m* (aer) take-off

involontà·rio -ria *adj* (-*ri* -*rie*) involuntary

invòlto *m* bundle; wrapper

invòlucro *m* wrapping; shell (*of boiler*); (aer) envelope

involu·to -ta *adj* (fig) involved; (lit) enveloped

invòlvere §147 (*pret* missing; *pp* also invòlto) *tr* (lit) to envelop

invulneràbile *adj* invulnerable

inzaccherare (inzàcchero) *tr* to bespatter

inzeppare (inzéppo) *tr* to cram, stuff

inzuccherare (inzùcchero) *tr* to sweeten

inzuppare *tr* to soak || *ref* to get drenched

io *m* ego; self || §5 *pron pers*

iòdio *m* iodine

iodìdri·co -ca *adj* (-*ci* -*che*) hydriodic

ioduro *m* iodide

iògurt *m* yogurt

iò·le *f* (-*le*) (naut) yawl; (sports) shell

ióne *m* ion

iòni·co -ca *adj* & *m* (-*ci* -*che*) Ionic

ionizzare [ddzz] *tr* to ionize

iòsa [s] *f*—a iosa in abundance

iperacidità *f* hyperacidity

ipèrbole *f* (geom) hyperbola; (rhet) hyperbole

iperbòli·co -ca *adj* (-*ci* -*che*) hyperbolic(al)

ipereccita·to -ta *adj* overexcited

ipermercato *m* shopping center

ipersensibile *adj* hypersensitive; supersensitive

ipersostentatóre *m* landing flap

ipertensióne *f* hypertension

ipnò·si *f* (-*si*) hypnosis

ipnòti·co -ca *adj* & *m* (-*ci* -*che*) hypnotic

ipnotismo *m* hypnotism

ipnotizzare [ddzz] *tr* to hypnotize

ipnotizza·tóre -trice [ddzz] *adj* hypnotizing || *m* hypnotizer

ipocondrìa·co -ca *adj* & *mf* (-*ci* -*che*) hypochondriac

ipocrisìa *f* hypocrisy

ipòcri·ta (-*ti* -*te*) *adj* hypocritical || *mf* hypocrite

ipodèrmi·co -ca *adj* (-*ci* -*che*) hypodermic

iposolfito [s] *m* hyposulfite

ipotè·ca *f* (-*che*) mortgage

ipotecare §197 (ipotèco) *tr* to mortgage

ipotecà·rio -ria *adj* (-*ri* -*rie*) mortgage

ipotenusa *f* hypotenuse

ipòte·si *f* (-*si*) hypothesis; **nella miglior delle ipotesi** at best; **nell'ipotesi che** in the event; **per ipotesi** by supposition

ipotèti·co -ca *adj* (-*ci* -*che*) hypothetic(al)

ipotizzare [ddzz] *tr* to hypothesize

ìppi·co -ca (-*ci* -*che*) *adj* horse, horse-racing || *f* horse racing

ippocampo *m* sea horse

ippocastano *m* horse chestnut tree

ippòdromo *m* race track

ippoglòsso *m* (ichth) halibut

ippopòtamo *m* hippopotamus

iprite *f* mustard gas

ira *f* wrath, anger, ire

irachè·no -na *adj* & *mf* Iraqi

iracóndia *f* wrath, anger

iracón·do -da *adj* wrathful

iranià·no -na *adj* & *mf* Iranian

irascìbile *adj* irascible

ira·to -ta *adj* irate, angry

ire §191 *intr* (ESSERE) (lit) to go

irida·to -ta *adj* rainbow-hued || *m* world bicycle champion

iride *f* rainbow; (anat, bot) iris

Irlanda, l' *f* Ireland

irlandése [s] *adj* Irish || *m* Irishman; Irish (*language*) || *f* Irishwoman

ironìa *f* irony

iròni·co -ca *adj* (-*ci* -*che*) ironic(al)

iró·so -sa [s] *adj* angry, wrathful

irradiare §287 *tr* to illuminate; to irradiate, radiate; to brighten; (rad) to broadcast || *intr* to radiate || *ref* to radiate; to spread

irraggiare §290 *tr* to illuminate; to irradiate, radiate, beam; to brighten; (rad) to broadcast || *intr* to radiate || *ref* to radiate; to spread

irraggiungìbile *adj* unattainable
irragionévole *adj* unreasonable
irrancidire §176 *intr* (ESSERE) & *ref* to get rancid
irrazionale *adj* irrational
irreale *adj* unreal
irreconciliàbile *adj* irreconcilable
irrecuperàbile *adj* irretrievable, irrecoverable
irredentismo *m* irredentism
irredenti·sta *mf* (-sti -ste) irredentist
irredèn·to -ta *adj* not yet redeemed
irredimìbile *adj* irredeemable
irrefrenàbile *adj* unrestrainable
irrefutàbile *adj* irrefutable
irregimentare (irregiménto) *tr* to regiment
irregolare *adj* irregular
irregolari·tà *f* (-tà) irregularity
irreligió·so -sa [s] *adj* irreligious
irremovìbile *adj* irremovable; obstinate
irreparàbile *adj* irreparable; unavoidable
irreperìbile *adj* not to be found; unaccounted for (*e.g.*, *soldier*)
irreprensìbile *adj* irreproachable
irreprimìbile *adj* irrepressible
irrequiè·to -ta *adj* restless, restive
irresistìbile [s] *adj* irresistible
irresolùbile [s] *adj* unbreakable (*bond*; *contract*); insoluble; unsolvable
irresolu·to -ta [s] *adj* irresolute
irrespiràbile *adj* unbreathable
irresponsàbile *adj* irresponsible
irrestringìbile *adj* unshrinkable
irretire §176 *tr* to ensnare, entrap
irrevocàbile *adj* irrevocable
irriconoscìbile *adj* unrecognizable
irriducìbile *adj* irreducible; stubborn
irriflessi·vo -va *adj* thoughtless, rash
irrigare §209 *tr* to irrigate
irrigazióne *f* irrigation
irrigidire §176 *tr* to chill || *intr* & *ref* to stiffen, harden; to get cool
irri·guo -gua *adj* well-watered; irrigating
irrilevante *adj* irrelevant
irrilevanza *f* irrelevance
irrimediàbile *adj* irremediable
irripetìbile *adj* unrepeatable
irrisióne *f* (lit) derision, mockery
irrisò·rio -ria *adj* (-ri -rie) mocking; paltry
irritàbile *adj* peevish; irritable
irritante *adj* irritating || *m* irritant
irritare (ìrrito) *tr* to irritate; to anger; to chafe || *ref* to become irritated
irritazióne *f* irritation
irriverènte *adj* irreverent
irrobustire §176 *tr* & *ref* to strengthen
irrómpere §240 (*pp* missing) *intr* to burst
irrorare (irròro) *tr* to sprinkle; to bathe, wet; to spray
irroratrice *f* sprayer; irroratrice a zaino portable sprayer
irruènte *adj* impetuous, rash
irruzióne *f* foray, raid; irruption
irsu·to -ta *adj* hairy, bristling
ir·to -ta *adj* prickly; shaggy (*hair*); irto di bristling with
iscrìvere §250 *tr* to inscribe; to register || *ref* to register; to sign up

iscrizióne *f* inscription; registration
Islam, l' *m* Islam
Islanda, l' *f* Iceland
islandése [s] *adj* Icelandic || *mf* Icelander || *m* Icelandic (*language*)
ìsola *f* island; block; isola spartitraffico traffic island
isolaménto *m* isolation; (elec) insulation
isola·no -na *adj* island || *mf* islander
isolante *adj* insulating || *m* (elec) insulation
isolare (ìsolo) *tr* to isolate; (elec) to insulate || *ref* to keep apart
isola·to -ta *adj* isolated; (elec) insulated || *m* city block; (sports) independent
isolatóre *m* (elec) insulator
isolazionismo *m* isolationism
isolazioni·sta *mf* (-sti -ste) isolationist
isolétta *f* isle
isòscele *adj* isosceles
isòto·po -pa *adj* isotopic || *m* isotope
ispani·sta *mf* (-sti -ste) Hispanist
ispa·no -na *adj* Hispanic
ispanoamerica·no -na *adj* & *mf* Spanish-American
ispessire §176 *tr* & *ref* to thicken
ispettorato *m* inspectorship
ispet·tóre -trice *mf* inspector; ispettore di produzione (mov) production manager
ispezionare (ispezióno) *tr* to inspect
ispezióne *f* inspection
ispi·do -da *adj* bristly
ispirare *tr* to inspire || *ref* to be inspired
ispirazióne *f* inspiration
Israèle *m* Israel
israelia·no -na *adj* & *mf* Israeli
israeli·ta *adj* & *mf* (-ti -te) Israelite
issare *tr* to hoist
issòpo *m* hyssop
istallare *tr* & *ref* var of installare
istantàne·o -a *adj* instantaneous || *f* snapshot
istante *m* instant, moment; petitioner
istanza *f* petition; request, application; (law) instance; in ultima istanza as a final decision
istèri·co -ca (-ci -che) *adj* hysteric(al) || *mf* hysteric
isterilire §176 *tr* to make barren || *ref* to become barren
isterismo *m* hysteria, hysterics
istigare §209 *tr* to instigate, prompt
istiga·tóre -trice *mf* instigator
istillare *tr* to instill, implant; istillare il collirio negli occhi to put drops in the eyes
istinti·vo -va *adj* instinctive
istinto *m* instinct
istituire §176 *tr* to institute, found; (lit) to decide
istituto *m* institute; institution; bank; istituto di bellezza beauty parlor
istitu·tóre -trice *mf* founder; teacher, instructor || *m* tutor || *f* governess; nurse
istituzionalizzare [ddzz] *tr* to institutionalize
istituzióne *f* institution
istmo *m* isthmus
istologìa *f* histology

istoriare §287 (istòrio) *tr* to adorn with historical figures

istradare *tr* to direct || *ref* to wend one's way

istrice *m & f* (European) porcupine

istrióne *m* ham actor; buffoon

istriòni·co -ca *adj* (-ci -che) histrionic

istrionismo *m* histrionics

istruire §176 *tr* to instruct; to train; (law) to draw up, prepare (*a case*) || *ref* to learn

istruí·to -ta *adj* learned, educated

istruménto *m* (law) instrument

istrutti·vo -va *adj* instructive

istrut·tóre -trice *mf* instructor; (sports) coach

istruttò·rio -ria (-ri -rie) *adj* investigating, preliminary || *f* (law) preliminary investigation

istruzióne *f* instruction; (law) prelimi-

nary investigation; istruzioni instructions; directions

istupidire §176 *tr* to make dull; to stupefy

Itàlia, l' *f* Italy

italia·no -na *adj & mf* Italian

itàli·co -ca *adj* (-ci -che) italic; Italic; (lit) Italian || *m* italics

italòfo·no -na *adj* Italian-speaking || *m* Italian-speaking person

itinerante *adj* itinerant

itinerà·rio *m* (-ri) itinerary

ittèri·co -ca *adj* (-ci -che) jaundiced

itterizia *f* jaundice

ittiologia *f* ichthiology

Iugoslàvia, la Yugoslavia

iugosla·vo -va *adj & mf* Yugoslav

iugulare *adj & tr* var of giugulare

iuta *f* jute

ivi *adv* (lit) there

J
K
L

L, l ['elle] *m & f* tenth letter of the Italian alphabet

la §4 *def art* the || *m* (mus) la, A; dare il la to set the tone || §5 *pers pron*

là *adv* there; al di là da venire to come, future; al di là (di) beyond; andare di là to go in the next room; andare troppo in là to go too far; farsi in là to move aside; in là con gli anni advanced in years; l'al di là the life beyond; più in là further; più in là di beyond; va' là! come on!

lab·bro *m* (-bri) edge (*of wound*); (lit) lip || *m* (-bra *fpl*) lip; labbro leporino harelip

labiale *adj & f* labial

làbile *adj* (coll) weak; (lit) fleeting

labiolettura *f* lip reading

labirinto *m* labyrinth, maze

laboratò·rio *m* (-ri) laboratory; workshop; laboratorio linguistico language laboratory

laborió·so -sa [s] *adj* hard-working, laborious; labored (*e.g., digestion*)

laburi·sta (-sti -ste) *adj* Labour || *mf* Labourite

lac·ca *f* (-che) lacquer

laccare §197 *tr* to lacquer; to japan; to polish (*nails*)

lac·chè *m* (-chè) lackey

lac·cio *m* (-ci) lasso; snare; noose; string; (fig) bond; laccio delle scarpe shoelace; laccio emostatico tourniquet

lacciòlo *m* snare

lacerare (làcero) *tr* to lacerate; to tear || *ref* to tear

làce·ro -ra *adj* torn; tattered

lacèrto *m* (lit) shred of flesh; (lit) biceps

lacòni·co -ca *adj* (-ci -che) laconic

làcrima *f* tear; drop

lacrimare (làcrimo) *tr* (lit) to weep

over || *intr* to water (*said of the eyes*); (lit) to weep

lacrima·to -ta *adj* (lit) lamented

lacrimévole *adj* pitiful

lacrimòge·no -na *adj* tear (*e.g., gas*)

lacrimó·so -sa [s] *adj* teary, watery (*eyes*); tearful; lachrymose

lacuna *f* gap, lacuna; blank (*in one's mind*); colmare una lacuna to bridge a gap

lacustre *adj* lake

laddóve *conj* while, whereas

ladré·sco -sca *adj* (-schi -sche) thievish

la·dro -dra *adj* thieving; foul (*weather*); bewitching (*eyes*) || *mf* thief; ladro di strada highwayman || *f* inside pocket (*of suit*)

ladróne *m* thief; highwayman; ladrone di mare pirate

ladrùncolo *m* petty thief, pilferer

laggiù *adv* down there

lagnanza *f* complaint

lagnare *ref* to complain; to moan

lagno *m* complaint, lament

la·go *m* (-ghi) lake; pool (*of blood*)

làgrima *f* var of lacrima

laguna *f* lagoon

lai *m* (lai) lay; lai *mpl* (lit) lamentations

laicato *m* laity

lài·co -ca *adj* (-ci -che) lay || *m* layman

lài·do -da *adj* foul; obscene

la·ma *m* (-ma) llama; lama || *f* (-me) blade (*of knife*); marsh; (lit) lowland

lambiccare §197 *tr* to distill || *ref* to strive; lambiccarsi il cervello to rack one's brains

lambic·co *m* (-chi) still

lambire §176 *tr* to lap; to graze, to touch lightly

lamèlla *f* thin sheet

lamentare (laménto) *tr* to bemoan, lament || *ref* to moan; to complain

lamentazióne *f* lamentation

lamentévole *adj* plaintive; lamentable
laménto *m* complaint, lament; moan
lamentó·so -sa [s] *adj* plaintive, doleful
lamétta *f* razor blade
lamièra *f* plate; armor plate
lamierino *m* sheet metal, lamina
làmina *f* sheet, lamina
laminare (làmino) *tr* to laminate; to roll (*steel*)
lamina·tóio *m* (**-tói**) rolling mill
làmpada *f* lamp, light; **lampada al neon** neon lamp; **lampada a petrolio** oil lamp; **lampada a stelo** pole lamp; **lampada di sicurezza** (min) safety lamp; **lampada fluorescente** fluorescent lamp; **lampada lampo** (phot) flash bulb
lampadà·rio *m* (**-ri**) chandelier
lampadina *f* bulb; **lampadina tascabile** flashlight
lampante *adj* shiny; clear; lamp (*oil*)
lampeggiare §290 (**lampéggio**) *tr* (lit) to flash (*a smile*) ‖ *intr* to flash; (aut) to blink; (coll) to flash the turn signals ‖ *impers* (ESSERE & AVERE)— **lampeggia** it lightens, it is lightning
lampeggiatóre *m* (aut) turn signal; (phot) flashlight
lampio·nàio *m* (**-nài**) lamplighter
lampióne *m* street lamp
lampiride *f* glowworm
lampo *m* lightning; flash of lightning; (fig) flash
lampóne *m* raspberry
lana *f* wool; **buona lana** (coll) rogue, rascal; **lana d'acciaio** steel wool; **lana di vetro** fiberglass, glass wool
lancétta *f* lancet; hand (*of watch*); pointer (*of instrument*)
làn·cia *f* (**-ce**) lance, spear; nozzle (*of fire hose*); launch; **lancia di salvataggio** lifeboat
lanciabóm·be *m* (**-be**) trench mortar
lanciafiam·me *m* (**-me**) flamethrower
lanciamissi·li (**-li**) *adj* missile-launching ‖ *m* missile launcher
lanciaraz·zi [ddzz] *m* (**-zi**) rocket launcher
lanciare §128 *tr* to throw, hurl; to drop (*from an airplane*); to launch (*e.g., an advertising campaign*) ‖ *ref* to hurl oneself; (rok) to blast off; **lanciarsi col paracadute** to parachute, bail out
lanciasilu·ri *m* (**-ri**) torpedo tube
lancia·to -ta *adj* hurled, flung; flying, e.g., **partenza lanciata** flying start
lancia·tóre -trice *mf* hurler, thrower; (baseball) pitcher
lancière *m* lancer
lancinante *adj* piercing
làn·cio *m* (**-ci**) throw; publicity campaign; (aer) drop; (aer) release (*of bombs*); (baseball) pitch; (rok) launch; **lancio del peso** shot put
landa *f* moor; wasteland
lanerie *fpl* woolens
languidézza *f* languidness, languor
làngui·do -da *adj* languid; sad (*eyes*)
languire (lànguo) & §176 *intr* to languish
languóre *m* languor; languishing; weakness; tenderness

laniè·ro -ra *adj* wool (*industry*)
lanifi·cio *m* (**-ci**) woolen mill
lanó·so -sa [s] *adj* woolly; kinky (*hair*); bushy (*face*)
lantèrna *f* lantern
lanùgine *f* down
lanzichenéc·co *m* (**-chi**) landsknecht
laónde *conj* (lit) wherefore
laotia·no -na *adj* & *mf* Laotian
lapalissia·no -na *adj* self-evident
lapidare (làpido) *tr* to stone (to death); (fig) to pick to pieces
làpide *f* stone tablet; tombstone
lapillo *m* lapillus
là·pis *m* (**-pis**) pencil
lappare *intr* to lap
làppola *f* (bot) burdock; (bot) bur
lappóne *adj* Lappish ‖ *mf* Lapp ‖ *m* Lapp (*language*)
Lappónia, la Lapland
lardellare (lardèllo) *tr* to lard; to stuff with bacon
lardo *m* lard; **nuotare nel lardo** to live on easy street
largheggiare §290 (**larghéggio**) *intr* to be liberal; to be lavish
larghézza *f* width; liberality; abundance; **larghezza di vedute** broadmindedness
largire §176 *tr* (lit) to bestow liberally
largizióne *f* bestowal; donation
lar·go -ga (**-ghi -ghe**) *adj* broad, wide; ample; liberal; abundant; (phonet) open; **prenderla larga** to keep away ‖ *m* width; open sea; square; (mus) largo; **al largo di** (naut) off; **fare largo a** to open the way to; **farsi largo** to elbow one's way; **prendere il largo** to run away; (naut) to put to sea; **tenersi al largo** to keep at a distance ‖ *interj* **—alla larga!** keep away! ‖ *largo adv*—**girare al largo** to keep away
làrice *m* larch
laringe *f* larynx
laringite *f* laryngitis
laringoia·tra *mf* (**-tri -tre**) laryngologist
laringoscò·pio *m* (**-pi**) laryngoscope
larva *f* (ent) larva; (lit) ghost; (lit) skeleton; (lit) sham
lasagne *fpl* lasagne
lasciapassa·re *m* (**-re**) safe-conduct; permit
lasciare §128 *tr* to leave; to let; to let go of; **lasciar cadere** to drop; **lasciarci le penne** (coll) to die; (coll) to be skinned alive; **lasciar correre** to let go; **lasciar detto** to leave word; **lasciar fare** to leave alone; **lasciare in pace** to leave alone; **lasciare libero** to let go; **lasciare scritto** to leave in writing ‖ *ref* to abandon oneself; to abandon one another
làscito *m* (law) bequest
lascìvia *f* lasciviousness
lascì·vo -va *adj* lascivious
lassati·vo -va *adj* mildly laxative ‖ *m* mild laxative
lassismo *m* laxity
las·so -sa *adj* lax ‖ *m* lasso; **lasso di tempo** period of time
lassù *adv* up there, up above
lastra *f* slab; paving stone; (phot)

plate; exposed X-ray film; **farsi le lastre** (coll) to be X-rayed

lastricare §197 (**làstrico**) *tr* to pave

lastricato *m* paving, pavement

làstri·co *m* (**-ci** or **-chi**) pavement; roadway; **ridursi sul lastrico** to fall into abject poverty

lastróne *m* slab; plate glass

latènte *adj* latent

laterale *adj* lateral ǁ *m* (soccer) half-back

later·zio -zia (**-zi -zie**) *adj* brick ǁ **laterizi** *mpl* bricks, tiles

làtice *m* latex

latifondi·sta *mf* (**-sti -ste**) rich landowner

latifóndo *m* large landed estate

lati·no -na *adj* Latin; lateen (*sail*) ǁ *m* Latin

latitante *adj* hiding ǁ *mf* fugitive

latitanza *f* flight from justice

latitùdine *f* latitude

la·to -ta *adj* wide; broad (*meaning*) ǁ *m* side; **d'altro lato** on the other hand

la·tóre -trice *mf* bearer

latrare *intr* to bark

latrato *m* bark

latrina *f* toilet, lavatory, washroom

latta *f* tin; can

lattàia *f* milkmaid

lat·tàio *m* (**-tài**) milkman, dairyman

lattante *adj* & *m* suckling

latte *m* milk; **latte detergente** cleansing cream; **latte di gallina** flip; (bot) star-of-Bethlehem; **latte in polvere** powdered milk; **latte magro** or **scremato** skim milk

lattemièle *m* whipped cream

làtte·o -a *adj* milky

latterìa *f* dairy; creamery

làttice *m* var of **latice**

latticèllo *m* buttermilk

lattici·nio *m* (**-ni**) dairy product

lattiginó·so -sa [s] *adj* milky

lattonière *m* tinsmith

lattu·ga *f* (**-ghe**) lettuce; head of lettuce; frill

làudano *m* paregoric, laudanum

laudati·vo -va *adj* laudatory

làurea *f* wreath; doctorate; doctoral examination

laurean·do -da *mf* candidate for the doctorate

laureare (**làureo**) *tr* to confer the doctorate on; to award (*s.o.*) the title of; (lit) to wreathe ǁ *ref* to receive the doctorate; (sports) to get the tile of

laurea·to -ta *adj* laureate ǁ *m* alumnus, graduate

làuro *m* laurel

làu·to -ta *adj* sumptuous, rich

lava *f* lava

lavabianche·rìa *f* (**-rìa**) washing machine

lavàbile *adj* washable

lavabo *m* washstand; lavatory

lavacristallo *m* windshield washer

lavacro *m* washing; font; purification; **santo lavacro** baptism

lavàg·gio *m* (**-gi**) washing; **lavaggio a secco** dry cleaning; **lavaggio del cervello** brainwashing

lavagna *f* slate; blackboard; **lavagna di panno** felt board; **lavagna luminosa** overhead projector

lavama·no *m* (**-no**) washstand

lavanda *f* washing; pumping (*of stomach*); lavender

lavandàia *f* laundrywoman; **lavandaia stiratrice** laundress (*woman who washes and irons*)

lavan·dàio *m* (**-dài**) laundryman; **lavandaio stiratore** launderer

lavanderìa *f* laundry; **lavanderia a gettone** laundromat; **lavanderia a secco** dry-cleaning establishment

lavandino *m* sink

lavapiat·ti *mf* (**-ti**) dishwasher (*person*)

lavare *tr* to wash; to cleanse; **lavare a secco** to dry-clean; **lavare il capo a** to scold ǁ *ref* to wash oneself; **lavarsi le mani** to wash one's hands

lavastovi·glie *mf* (**-glie**) dishwasher ǁ *m* & *f* dishwasher (*machine*)

lavata *f* washing; **lavata di capo** scolding

lavativo *m* (coll) enema; (coll) bore; (coll) goldbricker

lava·tóio *m* (**-tói**) laundry room; washtub

lava·tóre -trice *mf* washer ǁ *m* washerman; (mach) purifier ǁ *f* washerwoman; washing machine

lavatura *f* washing; **lavatura a secco** dry cleaning; **lavatura di piatti** dishwater; washing of dishes; (fig) watery soup

lavèllo *m* wash basin; sink

lavoràbile *adj* workable

lavorante *mf* helper, apprentice

lavorare (**lavóro**) *tr* to work; to till ǁ *intr* to work; to perform; to be busy; to trade; **lavorare ai ferri** to knit; **lavorare di fantasia** to daydream; **lavorare di ganasce** to eat voraciously; **lavorare di gomiti** to elbow one's way; **lavorare di mano** to pilfer; **lavorare di traforo** to work with a jig saw

lavorati·vo -va *adj* working; workable

lavora·to -ta *adj* wrought; tilled

lavora·tóre -trice *mf* worker ǁ *m* workman; workingman ǁ *f* workingwoman

lavorazióne *f* working; manufacturing; tilling

lavorì·o *m* (**-i**) bustle; steady work; scheming

lavóro *m* work; labor; steady work; homework; piece of work; (coll) trouble; **a lavori ultimati** when the work is finished; **lavori forzati** hard labor; **lavori in economìa** time and material contract work; **lavori teatrali** theatrical productions; **lavoro a cottimo** piecework; **lavoro a maglia** knitting; **lavoro di cucito** needlework; **mettere al lavoro** to press into service

lazzarétto [ddzz] *m* lazaretto

lazzaróne [ddzz] *m* cad; (coll) goldbricker

le §4 *def art* the ǁ §5 *pers pron*

leale *adj* loyal; sincere

leali·sta *mf* (**-sti -ste**) loyalist

leal·tà *f* (**-tà**) loyalty; sincerity

lébbra *f* leprosy
lebbró·so -sa [s] *adj* leprous || *mf* leper
lécca-léc·ca *m* (-ca) (coll) lollypop
leccapiat·ti *m* (-ti) glutton; sponger
leccapiè·di *mf* (-di) bootlicker
leccarda *f* dripping pan
leccare §197 (lécco) *tr* to lick; to fawn on; (fig) to polish || *ref* to make one-self up
lecca·to -ta *adj* affected; polished || *f* licking
léc·cio *m* (-ci) holm oak
leccornia *f* dainty morsel, delicacy
léci·to -ta *adj* licit, permissible; **mi sia lecito** may I || *m* right
lèdere §192 *tr* to damage, injure
lé·ga *f* (-ghe) league; alloy; **di bassa lega** poor, in poor taste; **fare lega** to unite
legale *adj* legal; lawyer's; official || *m* lawyer
legali·tà *f* (-tà) legality, lawfulness
legalità·rio -ria *adj* (-ri -rie) (pol) observing the rule of law
legalizzare [ddzz] *tr* to legalize; to authenticate
legame *m* bond; connection; relationship
legaménto *m* tie, bond; ligament; (phonet) liaison
legare §209 (légo) *tr* to tie; to bind; to unite; to set (*a stone*); to bequeath; to alloy; (bb) to bind || *intr* to bond; to mix (*said of metals*); to go together || *ref* to unite; **legàrsela al dito** to never forget
legatà·rio -ria *mf* (-ri -rie) legatee
lega·to -ta *adj* muscle-bound || *m* legate; bequest; (mus) legato
lega·tóre -trice *mf* bookbinder
legatoria *f* bookbindery
legatura *f* typing; binding; ligature; bookbinding; (mus) tie
legazióne *f* legation
légge *f* law; act; **dettar legge** to lay down the law; **è fuori della legge** he is an outlaw; **legge stralcio** emergency law
leggènda *f* legend; story, tall tale; (journ) caption
leggendà·rio -ria *adj* (-ri -rie) legendary
lèggere §193 *tr, intr & ref* to read
leggerézza *f* lightness; nimbleness; thoughtlessness; fickleness
leggè·ro -ra *adj* light; nimble; thoughtless; slight; fickle; **alla leggera** lightly || **leggero** *adv* lightly
leggia·dro -dra *adj* graceful, lovely
leggibile *adj* legible, readable
leggì·o *m* (-i) lectern; music stand
legiferare (legìfero) *intr* to legislate
legionà·rio -ria *adj & m* (-ri -rie) legionary
legióne *f* legion
legislati·vo -va *adj* legislative
legisla·tóre -trice *mf* legislator
legislatura *f* legislature
legittimare (legìttimo) *tr* to legitimize
legittimi·tà *f* (-tà) legitimacy
legìtti·mo -ma *adj* legitimate; pure; just, right || *f* (law) legitim
lé·gna *f* (-gna & -gne) firewood; (fig) fuel

legnàia *f* woodpile; woodshed
legname *m* timber, lumber
legnata *f* clubbing, thrashing
légno *m* wood; stick; ship; coach; timber; **legno compensato** plywood; **legno dolce** softwood; **legno forte** hardwood
legnòlo *m* ply (*e.g., of a cable*)
legnó·so -sa [s] *adj* wooden; tough (*meat*); dry (*style*)
legu·lèio *m* (-lèi) pettifogger
legume *m* legume; **legumi vegetables**; legumes
leguminósa [s] *f* leguminous plant; **leguminose** legumes
lèi §5 *pron pers*; **dare del Lei a** to address formally
lémbo *m* edge, border; patch (*of land*)
lèm·ma *m* (-mi) entry (*in a dictionary*)
léna *f* energy; enthusiasm; (lit) breath
lèndine *m* nit
lène *adj* (lit) light, soft, gentle; (phonet) voiced
lenire §176 *tr* to soothe, assuage
lenóne *m* panderer, procurer
lenóna *f* procuress
lènte *f* lens; bob, pendulum bob; **lente d'ingrandimento** magnifying glass; **lenti** glasses
lentézza *f* slowness
lenticchia *f* lentil
lentìggine *f* freckle
lentigginó·so -sa [s] *adj* freckly
lèn·to -ta *adj* slow; slack; (lit) loose (*hair*); (lit) loose-fitting (*garment*) || **lento** *adv* slowly
lènza *f* fishline
lenzuò·lo *m* (-li) sheet; (fig) blanket; **lenzuolo a due piazze** double sheet; **lenzuolo funebre** winding sheet, shroud || *m* (-la *fpl*) sheet; **lenzuola** pair of sheets (*in a bed*)
leoncino *m* lion cub
leóne *m* lion; **leone d'America** cougar; **leone marino** sea lion || **Leone** *m* (astr) Leo
leonéssa *f* lioness
leopardo *m* leopard
lepidézza *f* wit; witticism
lèpi·do -da *adj* witty, facetious
lepisma *f* (ent) silverfish
lèpre *adj invar* rendezvous, e.g., **razzo lepre** rendezvous rocket || *f* hare
lepròtto *m* leveret, young hare
lèr·cio -cia *adj* (-ci -ce) filthy
lerciume *m* filth, dirt
lèsbi·co -ca (-ci -che) *adj & mf* Lesbian || *f* Lesbian (*female homosexual*)
lésina *f* awl; stinginess; miser
lesinare (lésino & lèsino) *tr* to begrudge || *intr* to be miserly
lesionare (lesióno) *tr* to damage; to crack open
lesióne *f* damage; injury; lesion
lé·so -sa *adj* damaged; injured
lessare (lésso) *tr* to boil
lessicale *adj* lexical
lèssi·co *m* (-ci) lexicon
lessicografìa *f* lexicography
lessicogràfi·co -ca *adj* (-ci -che) lexicographic(al)
lessicògrafo *m* lexicographer

lessicologìa *f* lexicology
lés·so -sa *adj* boiled || *m* boiled meat; soup meat
lè·sto -sta *adj* swift; nimble; quick; **alla lesta** hastily; **lesto di lìngua** ready-tongued; **lesto di mano** lightfingered
lestofante *m* swindler
letale *adj* lethal, deadly
leta·màio *m* (-mài) dunghill
letame *m* manure, dung
letàrgi·co -ca *adj* (-ci -che) lethargic
letar·go *m* (-ghi) lethargy; hibernation
letìzia *f* happiness, joy
lèttera *f* letter; **alla lèttera** literally; **lettera morta** unheeded, e.g., **le sue parole rimasero lettera morta** his words remained unheeded; **lèttere** literature; **lèttere credenziali** credentials; **scrivere in tutte lèttere** to spell out
letterale *adj* literal
letterà·rio -ria *adj* (-ri -rie) literary; learned (*word*)
lettera·to -ta *adj* literary; literate || *m* man of letters; (coll) literate, learned person
letteratura *f* literature
lettièra *f* litter, bedding
letti·ga *f* (-ghe) sedan chair; stretcher
lètto *m* bed; bedding; **di primo letto** born of the first marriage; **letti gemelli** twin beds; **letto a castello** bunk bed; **letto a due piazze** double bed; **letto a scomparsa** Murphy bed; **letto a una piazza** single bed; **letto bastardo** oversize bed; **letto caldo** hotbed; **letto di morte** deathbed; **letto operatorio** operating table
lettóne or **lettòne** *adj* Lettish || *mf* Lett || *m* Lett, Lettish (*language*)
Lettònia, La Latvia
let·tóre -trice *mf* reader; lecturer; meter reader || *m* reader (*e.g., for microfilm*); **lettore perforatore** reader (*of punch cards*)
lettura *f* reading; lecture; **lettura del pensiero** mind reading
letturi·sta *m* (-sti) meter reader
leucemìa *f* leukemia
leucorrèa *f* leucorrhea
lèva *f* lever; (mil) draft; (mil) class; **essere di leva** to be of draft age; **fare leva su** to use (*s.o.'s emotions*)
levachio·di *m* (-di) claw hammer
levante *adj* rising || *m* east; Levant
levanti·no -na *adj* & *mf* Levantine
levare (**lèvo**) *tr* to lift, raise; to weigh (*anchor*); to pull (*a tooth*); to break (*camp*); to collect (*mail*); to remove, take away; to subtract; **levare alle stelle** to praise to the sky; **levare il disturbo** *a* to take leave of || *ref* to arise; to get up; to take off; to satisfy (*e.g., one's hunger*); to rise (*said of wind*); **levarsi dai piedi** to get out of the way; **levarsi dai piedi** or **di mezzo** *qlcu* to get rid of s.o.
levata *f* rise; reveille; collection (*of mail*); withdrawal (*of merchandise from warehouse*); **levata di scudi** uprising
levatàc·cia *f* (-ce) getting up at an im-

---

possible hour; **ho dovuto fare una levataccia** I had to get up way too early
leva·tóio -tóia *adj* (-tói -tóie)—**ponte levatoio** drawbridge
levatrice *f* midwife
levatura *f* intellectual breadth
leviatano *m* leviathan
levigare §209 (**lèvigo**) *tr* to polish
levigatrice *f* sander; buffer
levi·tà *f* (-tà) (lit) levity
levitazióne *f* levitation
levrière *m* greyhound
lezióne *f* lesson; lecture; reading
lezió·so -sa [s] *adj* affected, mincing
lézzo [ddzz] *m* stench; filth
lì *def art masc plur* (obs) the; **li tre novembre** the third of November (*in official documents*) || §5 *pers pron*
lì *adv* there; **di lì** that way; **di lì a un anno** a year hence; **essere lì lì per** to be about to; **fin lì** up to that point; **giù di lì** more or less; **lì per lì** on the spot
libanése [s] *adj* & *mf* Lebanese
Libano, il Lebanon
libare *tr* to toast; to taste || *intr* to toast
libazióne *f* libation
libbra *f* pound
libéc·cio *m* (-ci) southwest wind
libèllo *m* libel; (law) brief
libèllula *f* dragonfly
liberale *adj* & *m* liberal
liberali·tà *f* (-tà) liberality
liberare (**lìbero**) *tr* to free; to pay in full for; to open into (*said, e.g., of a hall opening into a room*); to clear, empty (*a room*) || *ref*—**liberarsi da** or **di** to get rid of
libera·tóre -trice *adj* liberating || *mf* liberator
liberismo *m* free trade
lìbe·ro -ra *adj* free; vacant; without a revenue stamp (*document*); open (*syllable; heart*); outspoken
liber·tà *f* (-tà) freedom; release (*e.g., from mortgage*); **libertà provvisoria** bail, parole; **libertà vigilata** probation; **mettersi in libertà** to put comfortable house clothes on; **rimettere in libertà** to set free
liberti·no -na *adj* & *mf* libertine
Libia, la Libya
lìbi·co -ca *adj* & *mf* (-ci -che) Libyan
libidine *f* lust; greed
libidinó·so -sa [s] *adj* lustful
libido *f* libido
li·bràio *m* (-brài) bookseller
librare *ref* to balance; to soar; (aer) to glide
libratóre *m* (aer) glider
librerìa *f* bookstore; library (*room*); bookshelf; book collection
libré·sco -sca *adj* (-schi -sche) bookish
libretto *m* booklet; card; (mus) libretto; **libretto di banca** passbook; **libretto degli assegni** checkbook; **libretto di circolazione** car registration; **libretto ferroviario** railroad pass; **libretto di risparmio** passbook (*of savings bank*)
libro *m* book; ledger; register (*e.g., of births*); **a libro** folding; **libro di**

bordo log; **libro in brossura** paperback; **libro mastro** ledger; **libro paga** (com) payroll

liceale adj high-school || mf high-school student

licènza f permit; license; diploma; (mil) leave; **con licenza parlando!** excuse my language!; **dar licenza a** to dismiss; **prender licenza da** to take leave of

licenziaménto m dismissal; **licenziamento in tronco** firing on the spot

licenziare §287 (licènzio) tr to dismiss; to O.K. (a book to be published); to graduate || ref to take leave; to give notice, resign; to graduate

licenzió·so -sa [s] adj licentious

licèo m high school; lycée

lichène m lichen

licitazióne f auction; (bridge) bidding

lido m shore; coast

liè·to -ta adj glad; blessed (event)

liève adj light; slight

lievitare (lièvito) tr to leaven || intr (ESSERE & AVERE) to rise; to ferment

lièvito m yeast; leaven; **lievito in polvere** baking powder

li·gio -gia adj (-gi -gie) devoted

lignà·gio m (-gi) ancestry, lineage

ligustro m privet

lil·la (-la) adj invar & m lilac

lilliputia·no -na adj & mf Lilliputian

lima f file; **lima per le unghie** nail file

limaccró·so -sa [s] adj miry, muddy

limare tr to file; to polish (e.g., a speech); to gnaw, plague

limatura f filing; filings

limbo m (lit) edge; (fig) limbo || **Limbo** m (theol) Limbo

limétta f nail file; (bot) lime

limitare m threshold || v (límito) tr to limit; to bound

limitazióne f limitation

limite m limit; boundary; check; (soccer) penalty line; **limite di carico** maximum weight; **limite di età** retirement age; **limite di velocità** speed limit; **senza limiti** limitless

limítro·fo -fa adj neighboring (country)

limo m mud, mire

limonare (limóno) intr (coll) to spoon

limonata f lemonade; (med) citrate of magnesia

limóne m lemon tree; lemon

limó·so -sa [s] adj slimy

límpi·do -da adj limpid, clear

lince f lynx, wildcat

lincià·gio m (-gi) lynching

linciare §128 tr to lynch

lin·do -da adj neat; clean

línea f line; degree (of temperature); **conservare la linea** to keep one's figure; **in linea** abreast; (telp) connected; **in linea d'aria** as the crow flies; **linea del fuoco** firing line; **linea del cambiamento di data** international date line; **linea di circonvallazione** (rr) beltline; **linea di condotta** policy; **linea di partenza** starting line; **linea laterale** (sports) side line

lineaménti mpl lineaments; elements

lineare adj linear || v (líneo) tr to delineate

lineétta f dash; hyphen

linfa f (anat) lymph; (bot) sap; **dar linfa** (bot) to bleed

lingòtto m (metallurgy) pig, ingot; **lingotto d'oro** bullion

lingua f tongue; language; strip (of land); **essere di due lingue** to speak with a forked tongue; **in lingua** in the correct language; **lingua di gatto** ladyfinger; **lingua lunga** backbiter; **lingua sciolta** glib tongue; **mala lingua** wicked tongue

linguacciu·to -ta adj talkative; sharp-tongued

linguàg·gio m (-gi) language

linguèlla f (philately) gummed strip

linguétta f tongue (of shoe); (mach) pin; (mus) reed

linguísti·co -ca (-ci -che) adj linguistic || f linguistics

linifí·cio m (-ci) flax-spinning mill

liniménto m liniment

lino m flax; linen

linósa [s] f flaxseed, linseed

linotipí·sta mf (-sti -ste) linotypist

liocòrno m unicorn

liofilizzare [ddzz] tr to freeze-dry

liquefare §194 tr & ref to liquefy

liquefazióne f liquefaction

liquidare (líquido) tr to liquidate; to close out; to dismiss; to settle

liquidazióne f liquidation; clearance; **liquidazione del danno** (ins) adjustment

liquidità f liquidity

líqui·do -da adj liquid; (com) due || m liquid; cash || f liquid

liqui·gàs m (-gàs) liquid gas

liquirízia f licorice

liquóre m liqueur; (pharm) liquor

liquorí·sta mf (-sti -ste) liqueur manufacturer or dealer

lira f lira; pound; (mus) lyre || **Lira** f (astr) Lyra

lìri·co -ca (-ci -che) adj lyric; (mus) operatic || m lyric poet || f lyric; lyric poetry; opera

lirismo m lyricism

Lisbóna f Lisbon

li·sca f (-sche) fishbone; lisp

lisciare §128 tr to smooth; **lisciare il pelo a** to butter up, flatter; to beat up || ref to preen

li·scio -scia adj (-sci -sce) smooth; straight (drink); black (coffee); **passarla liscia** to get away scot-free

liscívia f lye; bleach

lisciviatrice f washing machine

li·so -sa adj worn-out, threadbare

lista f list; strip, band; stripe; **lista delle spese** shopping list; **lista delle vivande** bill of fare; **lista elettorale** slate (of candidates)

listare tr to border; to stripe

listèllo m lath; (archit) listel

listino m price list; market quotation

litanìa f litany

lite f quarrel; lawsuit

litigante adj quarreling || mf quarreler; (law) litigant

litigare §209 (**lìtigo**) *tr*—**litigare qlco a qlcu** to fight with s.o. for s.th || *intr* to quarrel; to litigate || *ref*— **litigarsi qlco** to strive for s.th
lìti·gio *m* (-**gi**) quarrel, litigation
litigió·so -sa [*s*] *adj* quarrelsome
lìtio *m* lithium
litografìa *f* lithography
litògrafo *m* lithographer
litorale *adj* littoral || *m* seashore, coastline
litro *m* liter
Lituània, la Lithuania
litua·no -na *adj* & *mf* Lithuanian || *m* Lithuanian (*language*)
liturgìa *f* liturgy
litùrgi·co -ca *adj* (-**ci** -**che**) liturgical
liu·tàio *m* (-**tài**) lute maker
liuto *m* lute
livèlla *f* level; **livella a bolla d'aria** spirit level
livellaménto *m* leveling; equalization
livellare (**livèllo**) *tr* to level; to equalize; to survey || *intr* (ESSERE) & *ref* to become level
livella·tóre -trice *adj* leveling || *mf* surveyor || *f* bulldozer
livellazióne *f* leveling
livèllo *m* level; **livello delle acque** sea level
lìvi·do -da *adj* livid, black-and-blue || *m* bruise
lividóre *m* bruise
livóre *m* grudge; hatred
Livórno *f* Leghorn
livrèa *f* livery
lizza *f* tilting ground; **entrare in lizza** to enter the lists
lo §4 *def art* the || §5 *pers pron*
lòb·bia *m* & *f* (-**bia** *mpl* & *fpl*) homburg
lòbo *m* lobe
locale *adj* local || *m* room; place (*of business*); (naut) compartment; **locale notturno** night spot
locali·tà *f* (-**tà**) locality, spot
localizzare [*ddzz*] *tr* to localize; to locate || *ref* to become localized
localizzazióne [*ddzz*] *f* localization; **localizzazione dei guasti** troubleshooting
locanda *f* inn
locandiè·re -ra *mf* innkeeper
locandina *f* playbill; flyer; small poster
locare §197 (**lòco**) *tr* to rent, lease
locatà·rio -ria *mf* (-**ri** -**rie**) lessee, renter
loca·tóre -trice *mf* lessor
locazióne *f* rent; lease; **dare in locazione** to rent
locomotiva *f* locomotive, engine
locomo·tóre -trice *adj* locomotive || *m* & *f* (rr) electric locomotive
locomotorì·sta *m* (-**sti**) (rr) engineer
locomozióne *f* locomotion; transportation
lòculo *m* burial niche
locusta *f* locust
locuzióne *f* locution, expression; phrase; idiom
lodàbile *adj* praiseworthy
lodare (**lòdo**) *tr* to praise || *ref* to praise oneself, brag; **lodarsi di** (poet) to be pleased with

lodatì·vo -va *adj* laudatory
lòde *f* praise; **con la lode** cum laude; **con lode** plus (*on a report card*)
lodévole *adj* praiseworthy, commendable
lòdo *m* arbitration
logarìtmo *m* logarithm
lòg·gia *f* (-**ge**) lodge; (archit) loggia
loggióne *m* (theat) upper gallery
lògi·co -ca (-**ci** -**che**) *adj* logical; **esser logico** to think logically || *m* logician || *f* logic
logìsti·co -ca (-**ci** -**che**) *adj* logistic || *f* logistics
lò·glio *m* (-**gli**) cockle
logoraménto *m* wear; attrition
logorare (**lógoro**) *tr* to wear out; to fray || *ref* to wear away; to become threadbare
logorì·o *m* (-**i**) wear and tear
lógo·ro -ra *adj* worn out; threadbare
lòlla *f* chaff
lombàggine *f* lumbago
lombar·do -da *adj* & *mf* Lombard
lombata *f* loin, sirloin
lómbo *m* loin; hip; (lit) ancestry
lombrì·co *m* (-**chi**) earthworm
londinése [*s*] *adj* London || *mf* Londoner
Lòndra *f* London
longànime *adj* patient, forbearing
longanimi·tà *f* (-**tà**) patience, forbearance
longevità *f* longevity
longè·vo -va *adj* long-lived
longherina *f* beam, girder
longheróne *m* (aer) longeron; (aer) spar; (aut) main frame member
longitùdine *f* longitude
longobar·do -da *adj* & *mf* Lombard
lontananza *f* distance
lonta·no -na *adj* distant, remote; vague; indirect || *m* (lit) far-away place || *f*—**alla lontana** from a distance; vaguely; distant (*e.g., relative*) || **lontano** *adv* far; **da lontano** from afar; **lontano da** away from; far from; **rifarsi da lontano** to start from the very beginning
lóntra *f* otter
lónza *f* pork loin; (poet) leopard
lòppa *f* chaff; skin (*of plant*); slag, dross
loquace *adj* loquacious; (fig) eloquent
loquèla *f* (lit) tongue; (lit) style
lordare (**lórdo**) *tr* to soil, dirty
lór·do -da *adj* soiled, dirty; gross (*weight*)
lordume *m* dirt, filth
lordura *f* dirt, filth; soil
lóro §5 *pron pers* || §6 *adj poss* & *pron*
losan·ga *f* (-**ghe**) rhombus; (herald) lozenge
ló·sco -sca *adj* (-**schi** -**sche**) squint-eyed; cross-eyed; (fig) shady
lóto *m* mud
lòto *m* lotus
lòtta *f* fight; struggle; wrestling; **essere in lotta** to be at war; **lotta libera** catch-as-catch-can
lottare (**lòtto**) *intr* to fight; to quarrel; to struggle; to wrestle

lotta·tóre -trice *mf* fighter; wrestler

lotteria *f* lottery

lottizzare [ddzz] *tr* to divide into lots

lòtto *m* lotto; parcel, lot

lozióne *f* lotion

lùbri·co -ca *adj* (-ci -che) lewd; (*lit*) slippery

lubrificante *adj* & *m* lubricant

lubrificare §197 (**lubrìfico**) *tr* to lubricate

lucchétto *m* padlock

luccicare §197 (**lùccico**) *intr* to sparkle; to shine

luccichì·o *m* (-**i**) glittering; shining; sparkle

luccicóne *m* big tear

lùc·cio *m* (-**ci**) pike

lùcciola *f* firefly; usherette (*in movie*); **prendere lucciole per lanterne** to make a blunder; to be seeing things

luce *f* light; sunlight; opening; glass (*of mirror*); leaf (*e.g., of door*); (*archit*) span; (*coll*) electricity; **alla luce del sole** in plain view; **fare luce** to shed light; **luce degli occhi** eyesight; **luce del giorno** daylight; **luce della luna** moonlight; **luce di arresto** (*aut*) stoplight; **luce di incrocio** (*aut*) dimmer, low beam; **luce di posizione** (*aut*) parking light; **luce di profondità** (*aut*) high beam; **luci** (*poet*) eyes; **luci della ribalta** (*fig*) stage, boards; **mettere alla luce** to give birth to; **mettere in luce** to reveal; to publish; **venire alla luce** to be born; to come to light

lucènte *adj* shiny, shining

lucentézza *f* brightness; sheen

lucèrna *f* lamp; light; **lucerne** (*lit*) eyes ‖ **Lucerna** *f* Lucerne

lucernà·rio *m* (-**ri**) skylight

lucèrtola *f* lizard

lucherino *m* (*orn*) siskin

Lucìa *f* Lucy

lucidare (**lùcido**) *tr* to shine, polish; to trace (*a figure*)

lucida·tóre -trice *mf* polisher (*person*) ‖ *f* (*mach*) floor polisher

lucidatura *f* polish; tracing (*on paper*)

lucidi·tà *f* (-**tà**) polish; lucidity

lùci·do -da *adj* bright; lucid ‖ *m* shine; tracing; **lucido per le scarpe** shoe polish

lucìfe·ro -ra *adj* (*poet*) light-bringing ‖ **Lucìfero** *m* Lucifer, morning star

lucìgnolo *m* wick

lucrare *tr* to win, acquire

lucrati·vo -va *adj* lucrative

lucro *m* gain, earnings, lucre; **lucro cessante** (*law*) loss of earnings

lucró·so -sa [s] *adj* lucrative

ludì·brio *m* (-**bri**) mockery; laughingstock

lù·glio *m* (-**gli**) July

lùgubre *adj* gloomy, dismal

lui §5 *pron pers*

luìgi *m* louis ‖ **Luìgi** *m* Louis

luma·ca *f* (-**che**) snail

lume *m* light; lamp; **lume degli occhi** eyesight; **lume delle stelle** starlight; **lumi** eyesight; **lumi di luna** hard times; **perdere il lume degli occhi** to lose one's self-control; **reggere il lume a** to close one's eyes to; **studiare al lume di candela** to burn the midnight oil

lumeggiare §290 (**luméggio**) *tr* to illuminate, to shed light on

lumicino *m* faint light; **essere al lumicino** to be on one's last legs

luminare *m* star; luminary

luminària *f* illumination

lumino *m* night light; votive light; rush light

luminó·so -sa [s] *adj* luminous; bright (*idea*)

luna *f* moon; **andare a lune** to be fickle; **avere la luna di traverso** to be in a bad mood; **luna calante** waning moon; **luna crescente** crescent moon; **luna di miele** honeymoon

lunare *adj* lunar, moon

lunària *f* (min) moonstone; (bot) honesty

lunà·rio *m* (-**ri**) almanac; **sbarcare il lunario** to live from hand to mouth

lunàti·co -ca *adj* (-**ci -che**) moody; whimsical

lune·dì *m* (-**dì**) Monday

lunétta *f* lunette; fanlight

lunga *f*—**alla lunga** in the long run; **alla più lunga** at the latest; **andare per le lunghe** to last a long time, drag on; **di gran lunga** by far; **farla lunga** to dillydally

lungàggine *f* delay, procrastination

lunghézza *f* length; **lunghezza d'onda** wave length; **prendere la lunghezza di** to measure

lungi *adv* (*lit*) far

lungimirante *adj* (fig) far-sighted

lun·go -ga (-**ghi -ghe**) *adj* long; sharp (*tongue*); nimble (*fingers*); tall; thin (*soup*); (*coll*) slow; **a lungo** for a long time; at length; **a lungo andare** in the long run; **lungo disteso** sprawling ‖ *m* length; **in lungo e in largo** far and wide; **per il lungo** lengthwise ‖ *f* see **lunga** ‖ **lungo** *prep* along; during

lungofiume *m* river road

lungola·go *m* (-**ghi**) lakeshore road

lungomare *m* seashore road

lungometràg·gio *m* (-**gi**) full-length movie, feature film

lunòtto *m* (aut) rear window

luò·go *m* (-**ghi**) place; passage; site; (geom) locus; **aver luogo** to take place; **aver luogo in** to be laid in (*e.g., a certain place*); **dar luogo a** to give rise to; **del luogo** local; **far luogo** to make room; **fuori luogo** inopportune(ly); **in alto luogo** highplaced; **in luogo di** instead of; **luogo comune** commonplace; **luogo di decenza** toilet; **luogo di nascita** birthplace; **luogo di pena** penitentiary; **non luogo a procedere** (law) no ground for prosecution; (law) **nolle prosequi**; **sul luogo** on the spot; on the premises

luogotenènte *m* lieutenant

lupa *f* she-wolf

lupanare *m* (lit) brothel

lupé·sco -sca *adj* (-schi -sche) wolfish
lupétto *m* young wolf; cub (*in Boy Scouts*)
lupinèlla *f* sainfoin
lupi·no -na *adj* wolfish
lu·po -pa *mf* wolf; lupo cerviero lynx; lupo di mare seadog; lupo mannaro werewolf ‖ *f* see lupa
lùppolo *m* hops
lùri·do -da *adj* filthy, dirty
lusco *m*—tra il lusco e il brusco at twilight
lusin·ga *f* (-ghe) flattery; illusion
lusingare §209 *tr* to flatter ‖ *ref* to be flattered; to hope
lusinghiè·ro -ra *adj* flattering; promising
lussare *tr* to dislocate
lussazióne *f* dislocation

lusso *m* luxury; di lusso de luxe; lusso di abundance of
lussuó·so -sa [s] *adj* luxurious, sumptuous
lussureggiante *adj* luxuriant
lussùria *f* lust
lussurió·so -sa [s] *adj* lustful, lecherous
lustrare *tr* to polish, shine; to lick (*s.o.'s boots*) ‖ *intr* to shine, be shiny
lustrascar·pe *m* (-pe) bootblack
lustrino *m* sequin; tinsel
lu·stro -stra *adj* shiny, polished ‖ *m* shine, polish; period of five years; dare il lustro a to shine, polish
lutto *m* mourning; bereavement; a lutto black-edged (*e.g., stationery*); lutto stretto deep mourning
luttuó·so -sa [s] *adj* mournful

M

M, m ['ɛmme] *m & f* eleventh letter of the Italian alphabet
ma *m* but; ma e se ifs and buts ‖ *conj* but; yet ‖ *interj* who knows?; too bad!
màca·bro -bra *adj* macabre
maca·co *m* (-chi) macaque; (fig) dumbell
macadàm *m* macadam
macadamizzare [ddzz] *tr* to macadamize
mac·ca *f* (-che) abundance; a macca (coll) abundantly; (coll) without paying
maccarèllo *m* mackerel
maccheróni *mpl* macaroni
màcchia *f* spot, stain; brushwood; thicket; (fig) blot; alla macchia clandestinely; (painting) done in pointillism; darsi alla macchia to join the underground; to escape the law; macchia solare sunspot; senza macchia spotless
macchiare §287 *tr* to stain, soil ‖ *ref* to become stained; macchiarsi d'infamia to soil one's reputation
macchiétta *f* caricature; comedian; fare la macchietta di to impersonate, to parody
macchiettare (macchiétto) *tr* to speckle
macchietti·sta *mf* (-sti -ste) cartoonist; comedian; impersonator
màcchina *f* machine; engine; car, automobile; machination; andare in macchina to go to press; fatto a macchina machine-made; macchina da presa (mov) camera; macchina da proiezione projector; macchina fotografica camera; macchina per or da cucire sewing machine; macchina per or da scrivere typewriter; scrivere a macchina to typewrite
macchinale *adj* mechanical
macchinare (màcchino) *tr* to plot
macchinà·rio *m* (-ri) machinery
macchinazióne *f* machination

macchinétta *f* gadget; macchinetta del caffè coffee maker
macchini·sta *m* (-sti) engineer; (theat) stagehand
macchinó·so -sa [s] *adj* heavy, ponderous; complicated
macedònia *f* fruit salad, fruit cup
macel·làio *m* (-lài) butcher
macellare (macèllo) *tr* to butcher
macellerìa *f* butcher shop
macèllo *m* slaughterhouse; butchering; carnage; disaster
macerare (màcero) *tr* to soak; to mortify (*the flesh*) ‖ *ref* to waste away
macèria *f* low wall; macerie ruins
màce·ro -ra *adj* emaciated; skinny ‖ *m* soaking vat (*for papermaking*)
machiavèlli·co -ca *adj* (-ci -che) Machiavellian
macigno *m* boulder
macilèn·to -ta *adj* emaciated, pale, wan
màcina *f* millstone; (coll) grind
macinacaf·fè *m* (-fè) coffee grinder
macinapé·pe *m* (-pe) pepper mill
macinare (màcino) *tr* to grind, mill; to burn up (*e.g., the road*)
macina·to -ta *adj* ground ‖ *m* grindings; ground meat ‖ *f* grinding
macinino *m* grinder; (coll) jalopy
mà·cis *m & f* (-cis) mace (*spice*)
maciste *m* strong man (*in circus*)
maciullare *tr* to brake (*flax or hemp*); to crush
macrocòsmo *m* macrocosm
màdia *f* bread bin; kneading trough
màdi·do -da *adj* wet, perspiring
madònna *f* lady ‖ Madonna *f* Madonna
madornale *adj* huge; gross (*error*)
madre *f* mother; stub; mold; madre nubile unwed mother
madreggiare §290 (madréggio) *intr* to take after one's mother
madrelìngua *f* mother tongue
madrepàtria *f* mother country
madrepèrla *f* mother-of-pearl
madresélva *f* (coll) honeysuckle

madrevite f (mach) nut; die; **madrevite a palette** wing nut

madrigna f stepmother

madrina f godmother; **madrina di guerra** war mother

mae·stà f (-stà) majesty; **lesa maestà** lese majesty

maestó·so -sa [s] adj majestic, stately

maèstra f teacher; (fig) master; **maestra giardiniera** kindergarten teacher

maestrale m northwest wind (in Mediterranean)

maestranze fpl workmen

maestrìa f skill, mastery

maè·stro -stra adj masterly; main ‖ m teacher; master; instructor; northwester (in Mediterranean); **maestro di cappella** choirmaster ‖ f see maestra

mafló·so -sa [s] adj Mafia ‖ mf member of the Mafia; gaudy dresser

ma·ga f (-ghe) sorceress

magagna f fault, weak spot

magagna·to -ta adj spoiled (fruit)

magari adv even, maybe ‖ conj even if ‖ interj would that . . . !

magazzinàg·gio [ddzz] m (-gi) storage

magazziniè·re -ra [ddzz] mf stockroom attendant ‖ m warehouseman

magazzino [ddzz] m warehouse; store; inventory; (phot, journ) magazine; **grandi magazzini** department store

maggése [s] adj May ‖ m (agr) fallow

màg·gio m (-gi) May; May Day

maggiolino m cockchafer

maggiorana f sweet marjoram

maggioranza f majority

maggiorare (**maggióro**) tr to increase

maggiorazione f increase, appreciation

maggiordòmo m butler; majordomo

maggióre adj bigger, greater; major; main; higher (bidder); older, elder; (mil) master (e.g., sergeant); biggest, greatest; highest; oldest, eldest; **andare per la maggiore** to be all the rage; **maggiore età** majority ‖ m (mil) major; oldest one; **maggiori ancestors**

maggiorènne adj of age ‖ mf grown-up, adult

maggiorènte mf notable

maggiori·tà f (-tà) (mil) C.O.'s office

maggioritàrio -ria adj (-rì -rie) majority

magìa f magic

màgi·co -ca adj (-ci -che) magic

Magi mpl Magi, Wise Men

magióne f (lit) home, dwelling

magistèro m education, teaching; mastery; (chem) precipitation

magistrale adj teacher's; masterly ‖ f teacher's college

magistrato m magistrate

magistratura f judiciary

màglia f knitting; stitch; link; undershirt; sports shirt; (hist) mail; (fig) web; **lavorare a maglia** to knit

maglierìa f knitting mill; yarn shop; knitwear store

magliétta f polo shirt, T-shirt; buckle (to secure rifle strap); picture hook; buttonhole

maglifi·cio m (-ci) knitwear factory

mà·glio m (-gli) sledge hammer; mallet; drop hammer

magliòne m heavy sweater, jersey

magnàni·mo -ma adj magnanimous

magnano m (coll) locksmith

magnate m (lit) magnate, tycoon

magnèsio m magnesium

magnète m magnet; magneto

magnèti·co -ca adj (-ci -che) magnetic

magnetismo m magnetism

magnetite f loadstone

magnetizzare [ddzz] tr to magnetize

magnetòfono m tape recorder

magnificare §197 (**magnìfico**) tr to extol, praise; to magnify (to exaggerate)

magnificènza f magnificence

magnìfi·co -ca adj (-ci -che) magnificent; munificent; wonderful, splendid

ma·gno -gna adj (lit) great; the Great, e.g., **Alessandro Magno** Alexander the Great

magnòlia f magnolia

ma·go m (-ghi) magician; wizard

magóne m (coll) gizzard; (coll) grief; **avere il magone** (coll) to be in the dumps

magra f low water; (fig) dearth, want

magrézza f leanness; scarcity

ma·gro -gra adj lean, thin; meager ‖ m lean meat; meatless day ‖ f see magra

mài adv never; ever; **non . . . mai** never, not ever; **come mai?** how come?

maià·le -le -la mf pig; hog ‖ m pork ‖ f sow

maialé·sco -sca adj (-schi -sche) piggish

maiòli·ca f (-che) majolica

maionése [s] f mayonnaise

mà·is m (-is) corn, maize

maiuscolétto m (typ) small capital

maiùsco·lo -la adj capital ‖ m—**scrivere in maiuscolo** to capitalize ‖ f capital letter

Malacca, la Malay Peninsula

malaccèt·to -ta adj unwelcome

malaccòr·to -ta adj imprudent; awkward

malacreanza f (**malecreanze**) instance of bad manners; **malecreanze** bad manners

malafatta f (**malefatte**) defect; **malefatte** evildoings

malaféde f (**malefédi**) bad faith

malaffare m—**donna di malaffare** prostitute; **gente di malaffare** underworld

malagévole adj rough (road); hard (work)

malagràzia f (**malegràzie**) rudeness, uncouthness

malalìngua f (**malelìngue**) slanderer, backbiter

malanda·to -ta adj run-down; shabby

malandri·no -na adj dishonest; bewitching (eyes) ‖ m highwayman

malànimo m ill will; **di malanimo** reluctantly

malanno m misfortune; illness; (joc) menace

malaparata f (coll) danger, dangerous situation

malapéna f—**a malapena** hardly

malària f malaria

malàtic·cio -cia adj (-ci -ce) sickly

mala·to -ta adj sick, ill; essere malato agli occhi to have sore eyes; fare il malato to play sick || mf patient; i malati the sick

malattìa f sickness; illness; disease; malattie del lavoro occupational diseases

malaugura·to -ta adj unfortunate; ill-omened

malaugù·rio m (-ri) ill omen

malavita f underworld

malavòglia f (malevòglie) unwillingness; di malavoglia reluctantly

malcapita·to -ta adj unlucky || m unlucky person

malcàu·to -ta adj rash, heedless

malcón·cio -cia adj (-ci -ce) battered

malcontèn·to -ta adj dissatisfied, malcontent || mf malcontent || m dissatisfaction

malcostùme m immorality; bad practice

malcrea·to -ta adj ill-bred

maldè·stro -stra adj clumsy, awkward

maldicènte adj gossipy, slanderous || mf gossip, slanderer, backbiter

maldicènza f gossip, slander

male m evil; ill; trouble; andare a male to go to pot; aversela a male to take offense; di male in peggio from bad to worse, worse and worse; fare del male to do ill; fare male to be in error; fare male a to hurt; farsi male to get hurt; to hurt oneself; far venire il mal di mare a to make seasick; (fig) to nauseate; Lei fa male you should not; mal d'aereo airsickness; mal di capo headache; mal di cuore heart disease; mal di denti toothache; mal di gola sore throat; mal di mare sea-sickness; mal di montagna mountain sickness; mal di pancia bellyache; mal di schiena backache; mandare a male to spoil; mettere male to sow discord; prendere a male to take amiss; voler male a to bear a grudge against || adv badly, poorly; male educato ill-bred; meno male! fortunately!; restar male to be disappointed; sentirsi male to feel sick; stare male to be ill; star male a to not fit, e.g., questo vestito gli sta male this suit does not fit him; veder male qlco to disapprove of s.th; veder male qlcu to dislike s.o.

maledettaménte adv (coll) damned

maledét·to -ta adj cursed, damned

maledìre §195 tr to curse

maledizióne f malediction, curse || interj damn it!, confound it!

maleduca·to -ta adj ill-bred || mf boor

malefatta f var of malafatta

malefi·cio m (-ci) curse, spell; witchcraft; wickedness

malèfi·co -ca adj (-ci -che) maleficent

maleolènte adj (lit) malodorous

malèrba f weed, weeds

malése adj & mf Malay

Malésia, la Malaysia

malèssere m malaise; uneasiness; worry

malevolènza f malevolence; malice

malèvo·lo -la adj malevolent; malicious

malfama·to -ta adj ill-famed; notorious

malfat·to -ta adj botched; misshapen || m misdeed

malfat·tóre -trìce mf malefactor

malfér·mo -ma adj wobbly, unsteady

malfì·do -da adj untrustworthy

malgarbo m bad manners, rudeness

malgovèrno m misrule; mismanagement; neglect

malgrado prep in spite of; mìo malgrado in spite of me || conj although

malìa f spell, charm

maliar·do -da adj enchanting, charming || mf magician || f enchantress, witch

malignare intr to gossip

maligni·tà f (-tà) maliciousness; malevolence; malignancy

malì·gno -gna adj malicious, evil; unhealthy; malignant || il Maligno the Evil One

malinconìa f melancholy; melancholia

malincòni·co -ca adj (-ci -che) melancholy, wistful

malincuòre m—a malincuore unwillingly, against one's will

malintenziona·to -ta adj evil-minded || mf evildoer

malinté·so -sa [s] adj misunderstood; misapplied || m misunderstanding

malió·so -sa [s] adj malicious; cunning; mischievous; bewitching

malìzia f malice; trick; mischief

maliziò·so -sa [s] adj malicious; clever, artful; mischievous

malleàbile adj malleable; manageable

malleva·dóre -drìce mf guarantor

mallevería f surety

mallo m hull, husk

mallòppo m bundle; (aer) trail cable; (coll) lump (in one's throat); (slang) swag, booty

malmenare (malméno) tr to manhandle

malmés·so -sa adj shabby, seedy; tasteless

malna·to -ta adj uncouth; unfortunate; harmful

malnutri·to -ta adj undernourished

malnutrizióne f malnutrition

ma·lo -la adj (lit) bad

malòc·chio m (-chi) evil eye

malóra f ruin; mandare in malora to ruin; va in malora! go to the devil!

malóre m malaise; fainting spell

malpràti·co -ca adj (-ci -che) inexperienced

malsa·no -na adj unhealthy; unsound

malsìcu·ro -ra adj unsafe; insecure

malta f mortar; plaster; (obs) mud

maltèmpo m bad weather

malto m malt

maltòlto m ill-gotten gains

maltrattaménto m mistreatment

maltrattare tr to mistreat, maltreat

malumóre m bad humor; di malumore in a bad mood

malva f mallow

malvà·gio -gia (-gi -gie) adj wicked || mf wicked person || il Malvagio the Evil One

malversare (**malvèrso**) *tr* to embezzle; to misappropriate

malversazióne *f* embezzlement; misappropriation

malvesti·to -ta *adj* shabby, seedy

malvi·sto -sta *adj* disliked; unpopular

malvivènte *mf* criminal; (lit) profligate

malvolentièri *adv* unwillingly

malvolére *m* malevolence; indolence || §196 *tr* to dislike

mamma *f* mother, mom; (lit) breast; **mamma mia** dear me!

mammaluc·co *m* (**-chi**) simpleton

mammèlla *f* breast; udder

mammife·ro -ra *adj* mammalian || *m* mammal

màmmola *f* violet; (fig) shrinking violet

mam·mùt *m* (**-mut**) mammoth

manata *f* slap; handful; **dare una manata a** to slap

man·ca *f* (**-che**) left hand, left

mancante *adj* missing, lacking; unaccounted for

mancanza *f* lack; absence; defect; mistake; **in mancanza di** for lack of

mancare §197 *tr* to miss || *intr* (AVERE) to be at fault; **mancare a** to break (*e.g.*, *one's word*); **mancare di** to be wanting; to lack; **mancare di parola** to break one's word || *intr* (ESSERE) to fail (*said, e.g., of electric power*); to be lacking, e.g., **manca il sale nell'arrosto** salt is lacking in the roast; to be missing; to be absent, e.g., **mancano tre soci** three members are absent; to be, e.g., **mancano dieci minuti alle quattro** it is ten minutes to four; (with *dat*) to lack, e.g., **gli mancano le forze** he lacks the strength; to miss, e.g., **mi manca la sua compagnia** I miss his company; **mancare a** to be absent from (*e.g.*, *the roll call*); to be . . . from, e.g., **mancano dieci chilometri all'arrivo** we are ten kilometers from the journey's end; **mancare ai vivi** (lit) to pass away; **sentirsi mancare** to feel faint || *impers*—**mancare poco che** + *subj* to narrowly miss + *ger*, e.g., **ci mancò poco che fosse investito da un'automobile** he narrowly missed being hit by a car; **non ci mancherebbe altro!** that would be the last straw!, I should say not!

manca·to -ta *adj* unsuccessful; missed (*opportunity*); abortive (*attempt*), e.g., **omicidio mancato** abortive attempt to murder; manqué, e.g., **un poeta mancato** a poet manqué

manchévole *adj* faulty

manchevolézza *f* fault, shortcoming

màn·cia *f* (**-ce**) tip, gratuity; **mancia competente** reward

manciata *f* handful

manci·no -na *adj* left-handed; underhanded || *mf* left-handed person || *f* left hand, left; (mach) floating crane

man·co -ca (**-chi -che**) *adj* left; (lit) sinister, ill-omened; (lit) lacking || *m* (lit) lack; **senza manco** (coll) without fail || **manco** *adv*—**manco male!**

(coll) at least!; **manco per idea!** (coll) not at all! || *f* see **manca**

mandaménto *m* jurisdiction

mandante *m* (law) principal

mandare *tr* to send; to condemn (*to death*); to commit (*to memory*); to send forth (*e.g.*, *smoke, buds*); to operate (*a machine*); **che Dio ce la mandi buona!** may God help us!; **mandare ad effetto** to carry out; **mandare all'altro mondo** to dispatch, kill; **mandare a monte** to ruin; **mandare a picco** to sink; **mandare a quel paese** to send to the devil; **mandare a spasso** to fire, dismiss; to get rid of; **mandar giù** to swallow; **mandare in malora** to ruin; **mandare in pezzi** to break to pieces; **mandare per le lunghe** to delay || *intr*—**mandare a chiamare** to send for; **mandare a dire** to send word

mandarino *m* mandarin; (*Citrus nobilis*) tangerine; (*Citrus reticulata*) mandarin orange

mandata *f* sending; delivery (*of merchandise*); group; gang (*e.g.*, *of thieves*); turn (*of key*); **chiudere a doppia mandata** to double-lock

mandatà·rio *m* (**-ri**) mandatary, trustee

mandato *m* mandate; order; **mandato di cattura** arrest warrant; **mandato di comparizione** subpoena; **mandato di perquisizione** search warrant

mandìbola *f* jaw

mandolino *m* mandolin

màndorla *f* almond; kernel (*of fruit*)

mandorla·to -ta *adj* almond || *m* nougat

màndorlo *m* almond tree

mandràgola *f* mandrake

màndria *f* herd

mandriano *m* herdsman

mandrillo *m* mandrill

mandrino *m* (mach) mandrel; (mach) driftpin

mandritta *f*—**a mandritta** to the right

mane *f*—**da mane a sera** from morning till night

maneggévole *adj* usable; manageable; accessible to small craft (*sea*)

maneggiare §290 (**manéggio**) *tr* to work (*e.g.*, *clay*); to handle; to wield (*a sword*); to knead (*dough*); to manage; (equit) to train

manég·gio *m* (**-gi**) handling; intrigue; horsemanship; management; riding school; manège

mané·sco -sca *adj* (**-schi -sche**) readyfisted; hand (*e.g.*, *weapons*)

manétta *f* throttle (*on a motorcycle*); **manette** handcuffs, manacles

manfòrte *f*—**dar manforte a** to help

manganèllo *m* bludgeon, cudgel

manganése [s] *m* manganese

màngano *m* calender; mangle

mangeréc·cio -cia *adj* (**-ci -ce**) edible

mangerìa *f* graft, peculation

mangiàbile *adj* edible

mangiana·stri *m* (**-stri**) tape recorder

mangia·pane *m* (**-pane**) idler

mangia·prèti *m* (**-prèti**) priest hater

mangiare *m* eating; food || *v* §290 *tr*

to eat; to bite, gnaw; to erode; to embezzle, graft; (cards, chess) to take; **mangiar la foglia** to get wise || *intr* to eat; **mangiare alle spalle di qlcu** to eat at the expense of s.o. || *ref* to eat up; **mangiarsi il fegato** to be green with envy; **mangiarsi la parola** to break one's promise; **mangiarsi le unghie** to bite one's nails; **mangiarsi una promessa** to break one's promise

mangiasòldi *adj invar* money-eating, e.g., **macchina mangiasòldi** money-eating contraption

mangiata *f* (coll) fill, hearty meal, bellyful

mangiatóia *f* manger, crib

mangia-tóre -trice *mf* eater

mangime *m* fodder; feed; poultry feed

mangimisti-co -ca *adj* (-ci -che) feed, e.g., **attrezzatura mangimistiche** feed machinery

mangió-ne -na *mf* great eater, glutton

mangiucchiare §287 (**mangiùcchio**) *tr* to nibble

mangusta *f* mongoose

mania *f* mania, craze; complex; whim; **mania di grandezza** delusions of grandeur

mania-co -ca (-ci -che) *adj* maniacal; enthusiastic || *m* maniac; fan, enthusiast

màni-ca *f* (-che) sleeve; hose; (coll) crowd, bunch; **essere di manica larga** to be broad-minded; **essere nelle maniche di qlcu** to be in the favor of s.o.; **è un altro paio di maniche** this is a horse of another color; **in maniche di camicia** in shirt sleeves; **manica a vento** air sleeve, windsock; **manica per l'acqua** hose || **la Manica** the English Channel

manicarétto *m* dainty, delicacy

manichino *m* mannequin; cuff; (obs) handcuff; **fare il manichino** to model

màni-co *m* (-chi & -ci) handle; stock (of rifle); shaft (of golf club); stem (of spoon); (mus) neck; **manico di scopa** broomstick

manicò-mio *m* (-mi) insane asylum, madhouse

manicòtto *m* muff; (mach) collar; (mach) nipple; (mach) sleeve

manicu-re *mf* (-re) manicure, manicurist (person) || *f* (-re) manicure (treatment)

manicuri-sta *mf* (-sti -ste) manicurist

maniera *f* manner, fashion, way; **belle maniere** good manners; **di maniera** (lit, painting) Manneristic; **di maniera che** so that; **in nessuna maniera** by no means; **maniere bad** manners

maniera-to -ta *adj* mannered, affected; genteel

maniè-ro -ra *adj* tame, gentle || *m* manor house, mansion || *f* see **maniera**

manieró-so -sa [s] *adj* genteel; mannered

manifattura *f* manufacture; factory; product; ready-made wear

manifestare (**manifèsto**) *tr* to manifest

|| *intr* to demonstrate || *ref* to turn out to be

manifestazióne *f* manifestation; demonstration

manifestino *m* leaflet, handbill

manifè-sto -sta *adj* manifest, clear || *m* poster, placard; manifest; (pol) manifesto; **manifesto di carico** (naut) manifest

maniglia *f* handle; knob; (naut) link (of chain)

manigóldo *m* criminal; scoundrel

manipolare (**manìpolo**) *tr* to concoct; to adulterate; (telg) to transmit

manipola-tóre -trice *mf* schemer || *m* telegraph key

manìpolo *m* sheaf; (eccl; hist) maniple; (fig) handful

maniscal-co *m* (-chi) blacksmith

manna *f* manna; godsend

mannàia *f* axe; knife (of guillotine)

mano *f* hand; way (in traffic); coat (of paint); (lit) handful; (fig) finger; fingertip; **alla mano** plain, affable; **a mani nude** barehanded; **a mano** by hand; **a mano a mano** little by little; **a mano armata** armed (e.g., robbery); **at gunpoint**; **andare contro mano** to buck traffic; **a quattro mani** four-handed; **avere le mani bucate** to be a spendthrift; **avere le mani in pasta** to have one's fingers in the pie; **avere le mani lunghe** to be light-fingered; **battere le mani** to clap; **con le mani in mano** idle; **dare la mano a** to shake hands with; **dare man forte a** to help; **dare una mano** to pitch in; **dare una mano a** to lend a hand to; **di lunga mano** beforehand; **essere colto con le mani nel sacco** to be caught red-handed; **essere svelto di mano** to be light-fingered; **far man bassa** (su) to plunder; **fuori mano** out of the way; **mani di burro** butterfingers; **mani in alto!** hands up!; **man mano** (che) as; **mettere mano a** to begin; **mettere le mani sul fuoco** to guarantee; to swear; **per mano di** at the hands of; **prendere la mano** to balk; to get out of hand; **tenere la mano a** to abet; **venire alle mani** to come to blows

manodòpera *f* labor, manpower; **manodopera qualificata** skilled labor

manòmetro *m* manometer

manométtere §198 *tr* to tamper with

manomissióne *f* tampering

manomòrta *f* (law) mortmain

manòpola *f* mitten; handgrip; strap (to hold on to); (rad, telv) knob; (hist) gauntlet

manoscrit-to -ta *adj* & *m* manuscript

manoscrivere §250 *intr* to write in one's own handwriting

manovale *m* laborer, helper; hod carrier

manovèlla *f* handle, crank; lever

manòvra *f* maneuver; (rr) shifting; **fare manovra** to maneuver; (rr) to shift

manovrare (**manòvro**) *tr* to maneuver; to handle, drive; (rr) to shift || *intr* to maneuver; (rr) to shunt, shift; (fig) to plot

manovratóre *m* motorman; driver; (rr) brakeman; (rr) flagman

manrovè·scio *m* (-sci) backhanded slap

mansalva *f*—rubare a mansalva to help oneself freely (*e.g., to the till*)

mansarda *f* mansard

mansióne *f* duty, function

mansuè·to -ta *adj* tame; meek

mansuetùdine *f* tameness; meekness

mantèlla *f* coat; (mil) cape

mantellina *f* (mil) cape

mantèllo *m* woman's coat; coat (*of animal*); (fig) cloak; (mil) cape; (mach) casing

mantenére §271 *tr* to keep; to maintain; to hold (*e.g., a position*) || *ref* to stay alive; to last; to remain, stay, continue

mantenimento *m* keeping; maintenance

mantenu·to -ta *adj* kept || *m* gigolo || *f* kept woman

màntice *m* bellows; folding top (*of carriage*); (aut) convertible top

manto *m* mantle; coat; cloak

Màntova *f* Mantua

mantovana *f* valance

manuale *adj* & *m* manual

manualizzare [ddzz] *tr* to make (*e.g., a machine*) hand-operated; to include in a manual; to prepare a manual of

manù·brio *m* (-bri) handlebar; handle; dumbbell

manufat·to -ta *adj* manufactured || *m* manufactured product; manufacture

manutèngolo *m* accomplice

manutenzióne *f* maintenance, upkeep

manza [dz] *f* heifer

manzo [dz] *m* steer; beef

maomettà·no -na *adj* & *mf* Mahometan, Mohammedan

maomettismo *m* Mahometanism, Mohammedanism

Maométto *m* Mahomet

maóna *f* barge

mappa *f* map; bit (*of key*)

mappamóndo *m* globe; map of the world

marachèlla *f* mischief

maramèo *m*—fare marameo to thumb one's nose

mara·sma *m* (-smi) utter confusion; (pathol) decreptitude, feebleness

maratóna *f* marathon

maratonè·ta *m* (-ti) Marathon runner

mar·ca *f* (-che) mark, label; make, brand; token; ticket; (hist, geog) march; **di marca** of quality; **marca da bollo** revenue stamp; **marca di fabbrica** trademark

marcare §197 *tr* to mark; to label; to brand; to keep the score of; to score (*e.g., a goal*); to accentuate

marcatèm·po *m* (-po) timekeeper

marca·to -ta *adj* marked, pronounced

marchésa *f* marchioness, marquise

marchése *m* marquess, marquis

marchia·no -na *adj* gross (*error*)

marchiare §287 *tr* to brand

màr·chio *m* (-chi) brand; initials; characteristic; trademark

màr·cia *f* (-ce) march; operation; pus; (aut) gear, speed; (mil) hike; (sports) walk; **far marcia indietro** to back up; (naut) to back water; **marcia indietro** (aut) reverse; **marcia nuziale** wedding march

marciapiède *m* sidewalk; (rr) platform

marciare §128 *intr* to march; (mil) to advance; (sports) to walk; (coll) to function; **far marciare qlcu** to keep s.o. in line

màr·cio -cia (-ci -ce) *adj* rotten; infected; corrupt || *m* rotten part; decayed part; corruption || *f* see marcia

marcire §176 *intr* (ESSERE) to rot

marciume *m* rot; pus; decay

mar·co *m* (-chi) mark

marconigram·ma *m* (-mi) radiogram

marconi·sta *mf* (-sti -ste) radio operator

mare *m* sea; bunch, heap; **al mare** at the seashore; **alto mare** high sea; **fa mare** the sea is rough; **gettare a mare** to throw overboard; **mare grosso** rough sea; **mare territoriale** territorial waters; **promettere mari e monti** to promise the moon; **tenere il mare** to be seaworthy

marèa *f* tide; sea (*e.g., of mud*); **alta marea** high tide; **bassa marea** low tide; **marea di quadratura** neap tide; **marea di sizigia** spring tide

mareggiata *f* coastal storm

maremòto *m* seaquake

mareògrafo *m* tide-level gauge

maresciallo *m* marshall; warrant officer

marétta *f* choppy sea; instability

margarina *f* margarine

margherita *f* daisy; **margherite** beads

marginale *adj* marginal

marginatóre *m* margin stop (*of typewriter*); (typ) try square

màrgine *m* margin; edge; **margine a scaletta** thumb index

marijuana *f* marijuana, marihuana

marina *f* seashore; seascape; navy; **marina mercantile** merchant marine

mari·nàio *m* (-nài) seaman, sailor

marinara *f* middy blouse

marinare *tr* to marinate; **marinare la scuola** to cut school, play truant

marinarè·sco -sca *adj* (-schi -sche) sailor, seamanlike

marina·ro -ra *adj* sea, sailor; seamanlike; nautical || *m* (coll) sailor || *f* see marinara

mari·no -na *adj* marine, nautical || *f* see marina

mariòlo *m* rascal

marionétta *f* puppet, marionette

maritale *adj* marital

maritare *tr* to marry || *ref* to get married

marito *m* husband

maritti·mo -ma *adj* maritime, sea || *m* merchant seaman

marmàglia *f* riffraff, rabble

marmellata *f* jam, preserves; **marmellata di arancia** orange marmalade

marmi·sta *m* (-sti) marble worker; marble cutter

marmitta *f* pot, kettle; (aut) muffler

marmittóne *m* (coll) sad sack

marmo *m* marble

marmòc·chio *m* (-chi) brat

marmòre·o -a *adj* marble

marmorizzare [ddzz] *tr* to marble

marmòtta *f* marmot; woodchuck; (fig) sluggard; (rr) switch signal

marmottina *f* salesman's sample case

marna *f* marl

marnare *tr* to marl

marocchi·no -na *adj & mf* Moroccan || *m* morocco leather

Maròcco, il Morocco

maróso [s] *m* billow, surge

marra *f* hoe; fluke (*of anchor*)

marrano *m* Marrano; (fig) scoundrel; (lit) traitor

marronata *f* (coll) blunder, boner

marróne *adj invar* maroon, tan || *m* chestnut; (coll) blunder

Marsiglia *f* Marseille

marsigliése [s] *adj* Marseilles || *m* native or inhabitant of Marseilles || *f* Marseillaise

marsina *f* swallow-tailed coat

Marte *m* Mars

marte·dì *m* (-dì) Tuesday; martedì grasso Shrove Tuesday

martellare (martèllo) *tr* to hammer; to pester (*with questions*) || *intr* to throb; (fig) to insist

martellata *f* hammer blow

martellétto *m* hammer (*of piano or bell*); lever (*of typewriter*)

martèllo *m* hammer; martello dell'uscio knocker; martello perforatore jackhammer

martinétto *m* jack; martinetto a vite screw jack

martingala *f* half belt (*sewn in back of sports jacket*); martingale (*of harness*)

martinic·ca *f* (-che) wagon brake

martin pescatóre *m* kingfisher

màrtire *m* martyr

martì·rio *m* (-ri) martyrdom

martirizzare [ddzz] *tr* to martyrize

màrtora *f* marten

martoriare §287 (martòrio) *tr* to torment

marxi·sta *adj & mf* (-sti -ste) Marxist

marzapane *m* marzipan

marziale *adj* martial

marzia·no -na *adj & mf* Martian

marzo *m* March

mas *m* (mas) torpedo boat

mascalzóne *m* cad, rascal

mascèlla *f* jaw; jawbone

màschera *mf* usher || *f* mask; masque; maschera antigas gas mask; maschera di bellezza beauty pack; maschera respiratoria oxygen mask; maschera subacquea diving helmet

mascheraménto *m* camouflage

mascherare (màschero) *tr, intr & ref* to mask; to camouflage

mascherata *f* masquerade

mascherina *f* little mask, loup; tip (*of shoe*); (aut) grille; (phot) mask

maschiare §287 *tr* (mach) to tap

maschiétta *f* tomboy; alla maschietta bobbed (*hair*); tagliare i capelli alla maschietta to bob the hair

maschiétto *m* baby boy; pintle

maschile *adj* masculine; manly; men's;

male (*sex*); boys' (*school*) || *m* masculine

mà·schio -schia *adj* manly, virile; male || *m* male; keep, donjon; tenon; (mach) tap; (carp) tongue

mascolinizzare [ddzz] *tr* to make masculine or mannish || *ref* to act like a man

mascoli·no -na *adj* masculine; mannish (*woman*)

masnada *f* mob, gang; (obs) group

masnadière *m* highwayman

massa *f* mass; body (*of water*); (elec) ground; mettere a massa (elec) to ground; in massa in a body; massa ereditaria (law) estate

massacrante *adj* killing, fatiguing

massacrare *tr* to massacre; to ruin; to wear out, fatigue

massacro *m* massacre

massaggiare §290 *tr* to massage

massaggiatóre *m* masseur

massaggiatrice *f* masseuse

massàg·gio *m* (-gi) massage

massàia *f* housewife

massèllo *m* block (*of stone*); (metallurgy) pig, ingot

masseria *f* farm

masserìzie *fpl* household goods

massicciata *f* roadbed; (rr) ballast

massìc·cio -cia (-ci -ce) *adj* massive; bulky; heavy; (fig) gross || *m* massif

màssi·mo -ma *adj* maximum; top || *m* maximum; limit; al massimo at the most || *f* maxim; maximum temperature

massi·vo -va *adj* massive

masso *m* rock, boulder

Massóne *m* Mason

Massoneria *f* Masonry

mastèllo *m* washtub

masticare §197 (màstico) *tr* to chew, masticate; to mumble (*words*); to speak (*a language*) poorly; masticare amaro to grumble

masticazióne *f* mastication

màstice *m* mastic; glue; putty

mastino *m* mastiff

mastodònti·co -ca *adj* (-ci -che) mammoth

ma·stro -stra *adj* master || *m* ledger; master, e.g., mastro meccanico master mechanic

masturbare *tr & ref* to masturbate

matassa *f* skein; trouble

matemàti·co -ca (-ci -che) *adj* mathematical || *m* mathematician || *f* mathematics

materassino *m* (sports) mat; materassino pneumatico air mattress

materasso *m* mattress; (boxing) sparring partner

matèria *f* matter; substance; subject; (coll) pus; dare materia a to give ground for; materia grigia gray matter; materie coloranti dyestuffs; materie prime raw materials

materiale *adj* material; rough, bulky || *m* material; equipment, supplies; (fig) makings, stuff; materiale ferroviario (rr) rolling stock; materiale stabile (rr) permanent way

materni·tà *f* (**-tà**) maternity; maternity hospital; maternity ward

matèr·no -na *adj* maternal; mother (*tongue, country*)

matita *f* pencil; **matita per gli occhi** eye-shadow pencil; **matita per le labbra** lipstick; cosmetic pencil

matrice *f* matrix; stub

matrici·da *mf* (**-di -de**) matricide

matrici·dio *m* (**-di**) matricide

matrìcola *f* register, roll; registration (*number*); registry; beginner, novice; freshman (*in university*); **far la matricola** a to haze

matrìcola·to -ta *adj* notorious, arrant

matrigna *f* stepmother

matrimoniale *adj* matrimonial; double (*bed*); married (*life*)

matrimonialménte *adv* as husband and wife

matrimò·nio *m* (**-ni**) matrimony, marriage; wedding

matròna *f* matron

matronale *adj* matronly

matta *f* joker, wild card

mattacchió·ne -na *mf* jester, prankster

mattana *f* tantrum; fit of laughter

matta·tóio -m (**-tói**) slaughterhouse

matterèllo *m* rolling pin

mattina *f* morning; **di prima mattina** early in the morning; **la mattina in** the morning

mattinale *adj* morning ‖ *m* morning report

mattinata *f* morning; (theat) matinée

mattiniè·ro -ra *adj* early-rising

mattino *m* morning; **di buon mattino** early in the morning

mat·to -ta *adj* crazy; whimsical; dull; false (*jewelry*); wild (*desire*); **andare matto per** to be crazy about; **da matti** unbelievable; **fare il matto** to cut a caper; **matto da legare** raving mad ‖ *f* see **matta**

mattòide *adj & mf* madcap

mattonare (**mattóno**) *tr* to pave with bricks

mattonato *m* brick floor; **restare sul mattonato** to be utterly destitute

mattóne *m* brick; (fig) bore

mattonèlla *f* tile; cushion (*of billiard table*)

mattuti·no -na *adj* morning ‖ *m* matins

maturan·do -da *mf* lycée student who has to take the baccalaureate examination

maturare *tr* to ripen; to ponder; to pass (*a lycée pupil*) ‖ *intr* (ESSERE) to ripen, mature; to fall due

maturazióne *f* ripening

maturi·tà *f* (**-tà**) maturity; ripening; lycée final

matu·ro -ra *adj* ripe; mature; due

Matusalèmme *m* Methuselah

mausolèo *m* mausoleum

mazza *f* club; mallet; sledge hammer; cane; mace; golf club; (baseball) bat

mazzacavallo *m* well sweep

mazzapic·chio *m* (**-chi**) mallet; sledge

mazzata *f* heavy blow, wallop (*with club*)

mazzeran·ga *f* (**-ghe**) (mach) tamper

mazzière *m* macer; (cards) dealer

mazzo *m* bunch; bouquet; deck (*of cards*); **fare il mazzo** to shuffle the cards

mazzuòla *f* sledge hammer

mazzuòlo *m* sledge; mallet; wedge (*of golf club*); drumstick (*for bass drum*)

me §5 *pron pers*

meandro *m* meander; labyrinth

MEC *m* (letterword) (**Mercato Europeo Comune**) European Economic Community, Common Market

Mècca, la Mecca; (fig) the Mecca

meccàni·co -ca (**-ci -che**) *adj* mechanical ‖ *m* mechanic ‖ *f* mechanics; process (*e.g., of digestion*); machinery

meccanismo *m* machinery; mechanism; movement (*of watch*)

meccanizzare [ddzz] *tr* to mechanize ‖ *ref* to become mechanized

mecenate *m* patron (*of the arts*)

méco §5 *prep phrase* (lit) with me

medàglia *f* medal

medaglióne *m* medallion; locket; biographical sketch

medési·mo -ma *adj & pron* same; -self, e.g., **egli medesimo** he himself; very e.g., **la verità medesima** the very truth

mèdia *f* average; secondary school, middle school; (math) mean; **media oraria** average speed ‖ **mèdia** *mpl* media (*of communication*)

mediana *f* median; (soccer) middle line

mediàni·co -ca *adj* (**-ci -che**) medium

media·no -na *adj* median ‖ *m* (sports) halfback ‖ *f* see **mediana**

mediante *prep* by means of

mediare §287 (**mèdio**) *tr & intr* (ESSERE) to mediate

media·to -ta *adj* indirect

media·tóre -trice *adj* mediating ‖ *mf* mediator; broker; commission merchant

mediazióne *f* mediation; brokerage; broker's fee, commission

medicamento *m* medicine

medicamentó·so -sa [s] *adj* medicinal

medicare §197 (**mèdico**) *tr* to medicate; to treat

medicastro *m* quack

medicazióne *f* medication; dressing

medichéssa *f* (pej) lady doctor

medicina *f* medicine

medicinale *adj* medicinal ‖ *m* medicine

mèdi·co -ca (**-ci -che**) *adj* medical ‖ *m* doctor, physician; healer; **fare il medico** to practice medicine; **medico chirurgo** surgeon; **medico condotto** board-of-health doctor; country doctor; **medico curante** family physician

medievale *adj* medieval

medievali·sta *mf* (**-sti -ste**) medievalist

mè·dio -dia (**-di -die**) *adj* average; median; middle; secondary (*school*); medium ‖ *m* middle finger ‖ *f* see **media**

mediòcre *adj* mediocre

mediocri·tà *f* (**-tà**) mediocrity

medioèvo *m* Middle Ages

medioleggèro *m* welterweight

mediomàssimo *m* light heavyweight
meditabón·do -da *adj* meditative
meditare (**mèdito**) *tr & intr* to meditate
medita·to -ta *adj* considered
meditazióne *f* meditation
mediterrà·neo -nea *adj* inland (*sea*) ‖
　Mediterraneo *adj & m* Mediterranean
mè·dium *m* (**-dium**) medium
medusa *f* jellyfish
mefistofèli·co -ca *adj* (**-ci -che**) Mephis-
　tophelian
mefiti·co -ca *adj* (**-ci -che**) mephitic
megaciclo *m* megacycle
megàfono *m* megaphone
megalomanìa *f* megalomania
megalòpo·li *f* (**-li**) megalopolis
mega·òhm *m* (**-òhm**) megohm
megèra *f* hag, termagant, vixen
mèglio *adj invar* better; (coll) best ‖
　m—**il meglio** the best; **nel meglio di**
　(coll) in the middle of ‖ *f*—**avere la**
　meglio to get the upper hand; **avere**
　la meglio di to get the better of
　‖ *adv* better; best; rather; **stare**
　meglio to feel better; to be becom-
　ing; to fit better; **stare meglio a** to
　be becoming to; to fit; **tanto meglio!**
　so much the better!
méla *f* apple; nozzle (*of sprinkling*
　can); **mela cotogna** quince (*fruit*);
　mela renetta pippin
melagrana *f* pomegranate
melanzana [dz] *f* eggplant
melassa *f* molasses, treacle
mela·to -ta *adj* honey, honeyed
melèn·so -sa *adj* dull, silly
melissa *f* (bot) balm
mellìflu·o -a *adj* mellifluous
mélma *f* mud, slime
melmó·so -sa [s] *adj* muddy, slimy
mélo *m* apple tree
melodìa *f* melody
melòdi·co -ca *adj* (**-ci -che**) melodic
melodió·so -sa [s] *adj* melodious
melodram·ma *m* (**-mi**) melodrama;
　lyric opera; (fig) melodrama
melodrammàti·co -ca *adj* (**-ci -che**)
　melodramatic
melograno *m* pomegranate tree
melóne *m* melon; cantaloupe; **melone**
　d'acqua watermelon
membrana *f* membrane; parchment;
　diaphragm (*of telephone*); (zool) web
membratura *f* frame
mèm·bro *m* (**-bri,** *considered individ-*
　ually) limb; member; penis ‖ *m*
　(**-bra** *fpl,* *considered collectively*)
　limb (*of human body*)
membru·to -ta *adj* burly, husky
memoràbile *adj* memorable
memoràn·dum *m* (**-dum**) memorandum;
　agenda, calendar; note; note paper
mèmore *adj* (lit) mindful, grateful
memòria *f* memory; souvenir; memoir;
　dissertation; (law) brief
memoriale *m* memoir; memorial
memorizzare [ddzz] *tr* to memorize
ména *f* intrigue
mena·bò *m* (**-bò**) (typ) layout, dummy
menadito *m*—**a menadito** at one's
　fingertips; perfectly
menare (**méno**) *tr* to lead; to bring

(*luck*); to wag (*the tail*); to deliver
(*a blow*); (coll) to hit; **menare a**
effetto to carry out; **menare buono di**
to approve of; **menare il can per l'aia**
to beat around the bush; **menare per**
le lunghe to delay; **menare vanto** to
boast
mènda *f* (lit) fault, flaw
mendace *adj* lying, false, mendacious
mendà·cio *m* (**-ci**) (law) falsehood
mendicante *adj & m* mendicant
mendicare §197 (**méndico**) *tr & intr* to
beg
mendici·tà *f* (**-tà**) indigence, poverty
mendi·co -ca *adj & mf* (**-chi -che**)
mendicant
menefreghismo *m* I-don't-care attitude
menestrèllo *m* minstrel
méno *adj invar* less ‖ *m* less; least;
minus (*sign*); **i meno** the few; **per lo**
meno at least ‖ *adv* less; least;
minus; **a meno che** unless; **da meno**
inferior; **fare a meno di** to do without; to spare; **meno . . . di** less . . .
than; **meno male** fortunately; **meno**
. . . meno the less . . . the less; **non**
poter fare a meno di + *inf* to not be
able to help + *ger*, e.g., **la confe-**
renza non poteva fare a meno di
essere un successo the conference
could not help being a success;
quanto meno at least; **senza meno**
without fail; **venir meno** to swoon,
pass out; to fail; to lose, e.g., **gli**
venne meno il cuore he lost his
courage; **venir meno di** to break
(*one's word*) ‖ *prep* except; less;
minus; of, e.g., **le sette meno dieci**
ten minutes of seven
menomare (**mènomo**) *tr* to lessen, diminish; (fig) to hurt, damage
mèno·mo -ma *adj* least
menopàusa *f* menopause
mènsa *f* (prepared) table; mess, mess
hall; (eccl) altar; communion table;
(poet) mass; (poet) altar; **mensa**
aziendale company cafeteria
mensile *adj* monthly ‖ *m* monthly salary or allowance
mensili·tà *f* (**-tà**) monthly installment
mènsola *f* bracket; corner shelf; neck
(*of harp*); mantel (*of chimney*); console
ménta *f* mint
mentale *adj* mental; (anat) chin
mentali·tà *f* (**-tà**) mentality, mind
ménte *f* mind; **a mente di** according to;
avere in mente to mean; to intend;
di mente mental; **mente direttiva**
mastermind; **scappare di mente a**
qlcu to escape s.o.'s mind, e.g., **gli è**
scappato di mente it escaped his
mind; **uscire di mente** to go out of
one's mind; **venire in mente a qlcu**
to remember, e.g., **non gli è venuto**
in mente di spedire la lettera he did
not remember to mail the letter
mentecat·to -ta *adj & mf* lunatic
mentina *f* mint; **mentina digestiva**
after-dinner mint
mentire §176 & (**mènto**) *intr* to lie;

mentire per la gola to lie through one's teeth
menti·to -ta adj false; disguised
menti·tóre -trice adj lying || mf liar
ménto m chin
mentòlo m menthol
méntre m—**in quel mentre** at that very moment; **nel mentre che** at the time when || conj while; whereas
me·nù m (-nù) menu
menzionare (menzióno) tr to mention
menzióne f mention
menzógna f lie
menzognè·ro -ra adj false, deceptive; lying, untruthful
meraviglia f marvel, wonder; **a meraviglia** wonderfully; **destare le meraviglie di** to amaze; **dire meraviglie di** to praise to the skies; **fare meraviglia** (with dat) to amaze; **far meraviglie** to work wonders
meravigliare §280 (meraviglio) tr to amaze; to astonish || ref to be astonished
meraviglió·so -sa [s] adj marvelous, wonderful || m (lit) supernatural
mercan·te -téssa mf merchant, dealer
mercanteggiare §290 (mercantéggio) tr to sell || intr to deal; to haggle
mercantile adj mercantile; merchant (marine) || m cargo boat, freighter
mercanzìa f merchandise; (coll) junk
mercato m market; trafficking; **a buon mercato** cheap; **far mercato di** to traffic in; **sopra mercato** besides; into the bargain
mèrce f merchandise, goods; commodity
mercé f favor, grace; mercy; **alla mercé di** at the mercy of; **mercé a** thanks to; **mercé sua** thanks to him (her, etc.)
mercéde f pay; (lit) reward
mercenà·rio -ria adj & m (-ri -rie) mercenary
merceria f notions store; **mercerie** notions
mercerizzare [ddzz] tr to mercerize
mèr·ci adj invar freight (train, car, etc.) || m (-ci) freight train
mer·ciàio -ciàia mf (-ciài -ciàie) notions store owner
merciaiòlo m small businessman; **merciaiolo ambulante** peddler
mercole·dì m (-dì) Wednesday
mercuriale f market report; price ceiling
mercùrio m mercury || **Mercurio** m Mercury
merènda f afternoon snack, bite
meretrice f harlot
meridia·no -na adj & m meridian || f sundial
meridionale adj meridional, southern || mf southerner
meridióne m south; South
merìg·gio m (-gi) noon
merin·ga f (-ghe) meringue
meritare (mèrito) tr to deserve; to win || intr (eccl) to merit; **bene meritare di** to deserve the gratitude of || impers—**merita** it is worth while to
meritévole adj deserving, worthy

mèrito m merit; **in merito a** concerning; **per merito di** thanks to; **render merito a** to reward
merito·rio -ria adj (-ri -rie) meritorious
merlan·go m (-ghi) whiting
merlatura f battlement
merlétto m lace, needlepoint
mèrlo m blackbird; merlon; (fig) simpleton
merluzzo m cod
mè·ro -ra adj bare, mere; (poet) pure
merovìngi·co -ca -ci -che) adj Merovingian || f Merovingian script
mesata [s] f month's wages
méscere (pp mesciuto) tr to pour (e.g., wine); (poet) to mix
meschini·tà f (-tà) pettiness; narrow-mindedness; meanness, stinginess
meschi·no -na adj petty; narrowminded; wretched; puny || mf wretch
méscita f pouring; counter; bar
mescolanza f mixture, blend
mescolare (méscolo) tr to mix, blend; to shuffle (cards); to stir (e.g., coffee) || ref to mix, blend; to mingle; to consort; **mescolarsi in** to mind (somebody else's business)
mescolatrice f mixer, blender
mése [s] m month; month's pay
mesétto [s] m short month
mesóne m (phys) meson
méssa f (eccl & mus) Mass; **messa a fuoco** (phot) focusing; **messa a punto** adjustment; clear statement, outline of a problem; (aut) tune-up; **messa a terra** (elec) grounding; **messa cantata** high mass; **messa in marcia** or **in moto** (mach) starting; **messa in orbita** (rok) orbiting; **messa in piega** waving (of hair); **messa in scena** staging; **messa in vendita** putting up for sale
messaggerìe fpl delivery service
messaggè·ro -ra mf messenger; postal clerk
messàg·gio m (-gi) message
messale m missal
mèsse f harvest; crop
Messìa m Messiah
messiàni·co -ca adj (-ci -che) Messianic
messica·no -na adj & mf Mexican
Mèssico, il Mexico
messinscèna f staging; faking
mésso m clerk; (poet) messenger
mestare (mésto) tr to stir || intr to intrigue
mesta·tóre -trice mf ringleader; schemer
mèstica f (painting) filler
mesticare §197 (mèstico) tr to prime (a canvas); to mix (colors)
mestierante mf potboiler (person); tradesman, craftsman
mestière m trade, craft; (archaic) task; **di mestiere** by trade; habitual; **essere del mestiere** to be up in one's line
mestièri m—**essere di** or **far mestieri** to be necessary
mestìzia f sadness
mè·sto -sta adj sad
méstola f ladle; trowel
méstolo m kitchen spoon; **avere il mestolo in mano** to be the boss
mèstruo m menses, menstruation

mèta f goal, aim; (rugby) goal line

méta f heap, stack (e.g., of hay)

me•tà f (-tà) half; middle; halfway; better half; **a metà** halfway, in the middle; **aver qlco a metà con qlcu** to go half and half with s.o.

metabolismo m metabolism

metafisi•co -ca (-ci -che) adj metaphysical || m metaphysician || f metaphysics

metafonèsi f umlaut, metaphony

metafonìa f umlaut, metaphony

metàfora f metaphor

metafòri•co -ca adj (-ci -che) metaphoric(al)

metàlli•co -ca adj (-ci -che) metallic

metallizzare [ddzz] tr to cover with metal

metallo m metal; timbre (of voice); (poet) metal object; **il vile metallo** filthy lucre

metallòide m nonmetal

metallurgìa f metallurgy

metallùrgi•co -ca (ci -che) adj metallurgic(al) || m metalworker

metalmeccàni•co -ca (-ci -che) adj metallurgic(al) and mechanical || m metalworker

metamòrfo•si f (-si) metamorphosis

metanizzare [ddzz] tr to provide with methane

metano m methane

metanodótto m natural gas pipeline

metàte•si f (-si) metathesis

metèora f meteor; atmospheric phenomenon

meteorite m & f meteorite

meteorologìa f meteorology

meteorològi•co -ca adj (-ci -che) meteorologic(al); weather (forecast)

meteoròlo•go -ga mf (-gi -ghe) meteorologist

metic•cio -cia adj & mf (-ci -ce) half-breed

meticoló•so -sa [s] adj meticulous

metìli•co -ca adj (-ci -che) methyl

metòdi•co -ca (-ci -che) adj methodical; subject (e.g., index) || mf methodical person || f methodology

metodi•sta adj & mf (-sti -ste) Methodist

mètodo m method

metràg•gio m (-gi) length in meters; **corto metraggio** short; **lungo metraggio** full-length movie, feature film

metratura f length in meters

mètri•co -ca (-ci -che) adj metric(al) || f metrics, prosody

mètro m meter; (fig) yardstick; (lit) words

métro m (coll) subway

metrònomo m (mus) metronome

metronòt•te m (-te) night watchman

metròpo•li f (-li) metropolis

metropolità•no -na adj metropolitan || m policeman, traffic cop || f subway

metrovìa f subway

méttere §198 tr to put, place; to set (e.g., foot); to run (e.g., a nail into a board); to cause (fear; fever); to employ; to admit; to put forth; to give out; (coll) to charge; (coll) to install; (aut) to engage (a gear); **metterci** to take (e.g., an hour); **mettere a confronto** to compare; **mettere a freno** to check; **mettere a fuoco** (phot) to focus; **mettere al bando** to banish; **mettere all'asta** to auction off; **mettere al mondo** to give birth to; **mettere a nudo** to lay bare; **mettere fuori** to pull out; to give out (news); to throw (s.o.) out; **mettere giù** to lower; **mettere in onda** to broadcast; **mettere in pericolo** to endanger; **mettere la pulce nell'orecchio** a to put a bug in the ear of; **mettere qlcu alla porta** to show s.o. the door; **mettere su** to set up; (coll) to put (e.g., a coat) on; **mettere su qlcu contro qlcu** to excite s.o. against s.o. || intr to sprout; to lead (said, e.g., of a road) || ref to put on, to don; to place oneself, put oneself; to take shape; **mettersi a** to begin to; **mettersi al bello** to clear up (said of weather); **mettersi a letto** to go to bed; **mettersi a sedere** to sit down; **mettersi con** to start to work with; **mettersi in ferie** to take one's vacation; **mettersi in malattia** to fall ill; **mettersi in mare** to put to sea; **mettersi in maschera** to wear a masked costume; **mettersi in salvo** to get out of danger; to save oneself; **mettersi in viaggio** to set out on a journey; **mettersi in vista** to make oneself conspicuous || impers—**mette conto** it is worth while

mettima•le mf (-le) troublemaker

mezzadrìa [ddzz] f sharecropping

mezza•dro -dra [ddzz] mf sharecropper

mezzaluna [ddzz] f (mezzelune) half-moon; crescent (symbol of Turkey and Islam); curved chopping knife; lunette (of fortification)

mezzana [ddzz] f procuress; (naut) mizzen

mezzanave [ddzz] f—**a mezzanave** amidships

mezzanino [ddzz] m mezzanine

mezza•no -na [ddzz] adj median; medium; middle || m procurer || f see mezzana

mezzanòtte [ddzz] f (mezzenòtti) midnight

mezzatinta [ddzz] f (mezzetinte) halftone

méz•zo -za adj overripe, rotten

mèz•zo -za [ddzz] adj half; middle || m half; middle; medium; means; vehicle; **a mezzo** (di) by (e.g., messenger); **andar di mezzo** to suffer the consequences; to be the loser; **entrare di mezzo** to interpose oneself; **esserci di mezzo** to be present; to be at stake; **giusto mezzo** happy medium; **in mezzo a** among; in the lap of, e.g., **in mezzo alle delicatezze** in the lap of luxury; **in quel mezzo** meanwhile; **levar di mezzo** to get rid of; **mezzi** means; facilities; **mezzi di comunicazione di massa** mass media; **per mezzo di** by means of

mezzobusto [ddzz] m (mezzibusti) (sculp) bust; **a mezzobusto** half-length (e.g., portrait)

mezzo·dì [ddzz] *m* (**-dì**) noon; south; South

mezzogiórno [ddzz] *m* noon; south; South

mezzùc·cio [ddzz] *m* (**-ci**) expedient

mi §5 *pron*

miagolare (miàgolo) *intr* to meow

miagolì·o *m* (**-i**) meow, mew

mi·ca *f* (**-che**) mica; (obs) crumb || *adv*—**mica male** (coll) not too bad!; **non . . . mica** not . . . ever; not at all

mìc·cia *f* (**-ce**) fuse

michelàc·cio *m* (**-ci**) (coll) lazy bum

micidiale *adj* deadly; (fig) unbearable

mì·cio -cia *mf* (**-ci -cie**) (coll) pussy cat

micrò·bio *m* (**-bi**) microbe

microbiologìa *f* microbiology

mìcrobo *m* microbe

microfà·rad *m* (**-rad**) microfarad

microferrovìa *f* model railroad

micro·film *m* (**-film**) microfilm

microfilmare *tr* to microfilm

micròfono *m* microphone

microlettóre *m* microfilm reader

micromotóre *m* small motor; motor-cycle

microónda *f* microwave

microschèda *f* microcard

microscòpi·co -ca *adj* (**-ci -che**) microscopic(al)

microscò·pio *m* (**-pi**) microscope

microsól·co *adj invar* microgroove || *m* (**-chi**) microgroove; microgroove, long-playing record

microtelèfono *m* French telephone, handset

midólla *f* crumb; (coll) marrow

midól·lo *m* (**-la** *fpl*) marrow; (bot & fig) pith; **midollo spinale** (anat) spinal cord

miéle *m* honey

miètere (mièto) *tr* to reap; (lit) to kill

mietitrebbiatrice *f* combine

mieti·tóre -trice *mf* reaper, harvester

mietitura *f* harvesting

mi·gliàio *m* (**-gliàia** *fpl*) thousand

mì·glio *m* (**-glia** *fpl*) mile; milestone; **miglio marino** nautical mile; **miglio terrestre** mile || *m* (**-gli**) millet

miglioraménto *m* improvement

migliorare (miglióro) *tr, intr* (ESSERE & AVERE) & *ref* to improve

miglióre *adj* better; best

migliorìa *f* improvement (*e.g., of real estate*)

mignatta *f* leech

mìgnolo *adj masc* little (*finger or toe*) || *m* little finger; little toe

migrare *intr* to migrate

migra·tóre -trice *adj* & *m* migrant

migrazióne *f* migration

Milano *f* Milan

miliardà·rio -ria *adj* & *mf* (**-ri -rie**) billionaire

miliardo *m* billion

milionà·rio -ria *adj* & *mf* (**-ri -rie**) millionaire

milióne *m* million

milionèsi·mo -ma *adj* & *m* millionth

militante *adj* & *m* militant

militare *adj* military || *m* soldier || *v* (**milito**) *intr* to be a member; to mili-

tate; to be in the armed forces; **militare in** to be a member of (*e.g., a party*)

militaré·sco -sca *adj* (**-schi -sche**) military, soldierly

militarismo *m* militarism

militari·sta (**-sti -ste**) *adj* militaristic || *mf* militarist

militarizzare [ddzz] *tr* to militarize; to fortify

mìlite *m* militiaman; soldier; **milite del fuoco** fireman; **Milite Ignoto** Unknown Soldier

militesènte *adj* exempt from military service || *m* man exempt from military service

milìzia *f* militia; (mil) service; struggle; **milizie celesti** heavenly host

miliziano *m* militiaman

millantare *tr* to boast of || *ref* to brag, boast

millanta·tóre -trice *mf* braggart

millanterìa *f* bragging

mille *adj, m* & *pron* (**mila**) thousand, a thousand, one thousand || **il Mille** the eleventh century; the year one thousand

millecènto *m* eleven hundred || *f* car with a 1100 cc. motor

millefò·glie *m* (**-glie**) puff-paste cake

millenà·rio -ria *adj* millennial || *m* millennium

millèn·nio *m* (**-ni**) millennium

millepiè·di *m* (**-di**) millipede

millèsi·mo -ma *adj* & *m* thousandth

milliam·père *m* (**-père**) milliampere

milligrammo *m* milligram

millimetra·to -ta *adj* divided into squares of one millimeter square

millìmetro *m* millimeter

milli·vòlt *m* (**-vòlt**) millivolt

milza *f* spleen

mimare *tr* & *intr* to mime

mimetizzare [ddzz] *tr* (mil) to camouflage

mimetizzazióne [ddzz] *f* (mil) camouflage

mìmi·co -ca (**-ci -che**) *adj* mimic; sign (*language*) || *f* mimicry; (theat) gestures; (theat) miming

mì·mo -ma *mf* mime || *m* (orn) mockingbird

mina *f* lead (*of pencil*); (mil) mine; **mina anticarro** antitank mine; **mina antiuomo** antipersonnel mine

minaccévole *adj* (lit) threatening

minàc·cia *f* (**-ce**) threat, menace

minacciare §128 *tr* to threaten, menace

minacció·so -sa [s] *adj* threatening

minare *tr* to mine; to undermine

minaréto *m* minaret

minatóre *m* miner

minatò·rio -ria *adj* (**-ri -rie**) threatening

minchionare (minchióno) *tr* (slang) to make a sucker of

minchióne *m* (slang) sucker

minerale *adj* mineral || *m* mineral; ore

mineralogìa *f* mineralogy

minerà·rio -ria *adj* (**-ri -rie**) mining

minèr·va *m* (**-va**) safety match

minèstra *f* vegetable soup

minestróne *m* minestrone; hodgepodge

mìngere §199 *intr* to urinate

mìngherli·no -na *adj* frail, thin

miniare §287 *tr* to paint in miniature; to illuminate

miniatura *f* miniature

miniaturizzare [ddzz] *tr* to miniaturize

miniaturizzazióne [ddzz] *f* miniaturization

minièra *f* mine

mini·gòlf *m* (-gòlf) miniature golf

minigònna *f* miniskirt

mìnima *f* lowest temperature; (mus) minim

minimizzare [ddzz] *tr* to minimize

mìni·mo -ma *adj* smallest, least; minimum || *m* minimum; **al mìnimo** at the least; **girare al minimo** or **tenere il minimo** (aut) to idle || *f* see **mìnima**

mìnio *m* red lead; rouge

ministeriale *adj* ministerial

ministèro *m* ministry; cabinet; department; **pubblico ministero** public prosecutor

ministra *f* (joc) wife of minister; (joc) female minister; (poet) minister

ministro *m* minister; secretary; administrator; **ministro degli Esteri** foreign minister; (U.S.A.) Secretary of State

minoranza *f* minority

minorare (minóro) *tr* to lessen; to disable

minora·to -ta *adj* disabled || *mf* disabled person

minorazióne *f* reduction; disability

minóre *adj* smaller, lesser; minor; smallest, least; younger; youngest || *m* minor

minorènne *adj* underage || *mf* minor

minorìle *adj* juvenile (*e.g., court*)

minori·tà *f* (-tà) minority

minuétto *m* minuet

minù·gia *f* (-gia & -gie) (mus) catgut

minùsco·lo -la *adj* small (*letter*); diminutive || *m* & *f* small letter

minuta *f* first draft, rough copy

minutàglia *f* trifles; small fry

minutante *m* secretary; retailer

minuterìa *f* trinkets, notions

minu·to -ta *adj* minute; small (*change*); common (*people*) || *m* minute; **al minuto** retail; **di minuto in minuto** at any moment; **minuto secondo** second; **nel minuto** in detail; **per minuto** minutely || *f* see **minuta**

minùzia *f* trifle; **minuzie** minutiae

minuzió·so -sa [s] *adj* meticulous

minùzzolo *m* scrap, crumb; small boy

mìo mìa §6 *adj* & *pron poss* (mièi mìe)

mìope *adj* nearsighted || *mf* nearsighted person

miopìa *f* nearsightedness

mira *f* aim; sight; target, goal; **prendere di mira** to aim at; to torment

miràbile *adj* admirable || *m* wonder

mirabìlia *fpl* wonders; **far mirabilia** to perform wonders; **dir mirabilia di** to speak highly of

mirabolante *adj* amazing, astonishing

miracola·to -ta *adj* miraculously cured || *mf* miraculously cured person

mirácolo *m* miracle; wonder; **dir mira-**

coli di to praise to the skies; **per miracolo** by mere chance

miracoló·so -sa [s] *adj* miraculous; wonderful

miràg·gio *m* (-gi) mirage

mirare *tr* (lit) to look at; (lit) to aim at || *intr* to aim; **mirare a** to aim at; **mirare a + inf** to aim to + *inf*; to intend to + *inf*

mirìade *f* myriad

mirino *m* sight (*of gun*); (phot) finder

mirra *f* myrrh

mirtìllo *m* blueberry; whortleberry, huckleberry

mirto *m* myrtle

misantropìa *f* misanthropy

misàntro·po -pa *adj* misanthropic || *mf* misanthrope

miscèla *f* mixture, blend

miscelare (miscèlo) *tr* to mix, blend

miscellàne·o -a *adj* miscellaneous || *f* miscellany

mìschia *f* fight; (sports) scrimmage

mischiare §287 *tr* to mix, blend; to shuffle (*cards*) || *ref* to mix

misconóscere §134 *tr* to not appreciate, undervalue

miscredènte *adj* misbelieving || *mf* misbeliever

miseràbile *adj* pitiful, miserable; poor, wretched

miseran·do -da *adj* pitiable

miserère *m* Miserere; **essere al miserere** to be in one's last hours

miserévole *adj* pitiful; pitiable

misèria *f* destitution, misery; wretchedness; lack, want; trifle; **piangere miseria** to cry poverty

misericòrdia *f* mercy

misericordió·so -sa [s] *adj* merciful

mìse·ro -ra *adj* unhappy, wretched; poor; meager; mean; too small, too short

misfatto *m* misdeed, misdoing

misìriz·zi [s] *m* (-zì) tumbler (*toy*); (fig) chameleon

misògi·no -na *adj* misogynous || *m* misogynist

missile *adj* & *m* missile; **missile antimissile** antimissile missile; **missile intercontinentale** I.C.B.M.; **missile teleguidato** guided missile

missilìsti·co -ca *adj* (-ci -che) missile

missionà·rio -ria *adj* & *m* (-ri -rie) missionary

missióne *f* mission

missiva *f* missive

misterió·so -sa [s] *adj* mysterious

mistèro *m* mystery

mìstica *f* mysticism; mystical literature

misticismo *m* mysticism

mìsti·co -ca (-ci -che) *adj* & *mf* mystic || *f* see **mìstica**

mistificare §197 (mistìfico) *tr* to hoax

mistificazióne *f* hoax

mi·sto -sta *adj* mixed || *m* mixture; mixed train

mistura *f* mixture

misura *f* measure; size; bounds; fitting; **a misura che** in proportion as; **di**

misura (sports) with a narrow margin; su misura made-to-order

misuràbile *adj* measurable

misurare *tr* to measure; to deliver (*e.g.*, *a slap*); to budget (*expenses*); to try on (*clothes*); to weigh (*the outcome*) || *intr* to measure || *ref* to compete; to limit oneself; misurarsi con to try conclusions with

misura·to -ta *adj* moderate; scanty

misurino *m* measuring spoon or cup

mite *adj* mild; tame; low (*price*)

miti·co -ca *adj* (-ci -che) mythical

mitigare §209 (mìtigo) *tr* to mitigate; to assuage, allay || *ref* to abate

mìtilo *m* mussel

mito *m* myth

mitologìa *f* mythology

mitològi·co -ca *adj* (-ci -che) mytho-logic(al)

mitòmane *mf* compulsive liar

mi·tra *m* (-tra) submachine gun || *f* miter

mitràglia *f* grapeshot; scrap iron; (coll) machine gun

mitragliare §280 (mitràglio) *tr* to machine-gun

mitragliatrice *f* machine gun

mitraglièra *f* heavy machine gun

mitraglière *m* machine gunner

mittènte *mf* sender; shipper

mo' *m*—apocopated form of modo by way of; a mo' d'esempio as an illustration

mòbile *adj* movable; personal (*property*); (fig) fickle; (rr) rolling (*stock*) || *m* piece of furniture; cabinet; (phys) body; mobili furniture

mobilia *f* furniture

mobiliare *adj* (fin) security; (law) movable || §287 (mobìlio) *tr* to furnish

mobilière *m* furniture maker; furniture dealer

mobilità *f* mobility

mobilitare (mobìlito) *tr & intr* to mobilize

mobilitazióne *f* mobilization

mò·ca *m* (-ca) mocha; caffè moca Mocha coffee

mocassino *m* mocassin

moccicare §197 (móccico) *intr* (slang) to snivel; (slang) to run (*said of the nose*); (slang) to whimper

moccicó·so -sa [s] *adj* (slang) snotty

móc·cio *m* (-ci) snot, snivel

mocció·so -sa [s] *adj* snotty || *m* brat

mòccolo *m* end of candle, snuff; (joc) snot; (slang) curse word; reggere il moccolo a qlcu to be a third party to a couple's necking

mòda *f* fashion, vogue; andar di moda to be fashionable; to be all the rage; fuori moda outdated

modali·tà *f* (-tà) modality; method

modanatura *f* molding

mòdano *m* mold

modèlla *f* model

modellare (modèllo) *tr* to model; to mold || *ref* to pattern oneself

modella·tóre -trice *mf* pattern maker; molder

modellino *m* (archit) model, maquette

modèllo *adj invar* model || *m* model; fashion; style; pattern

moderare (mòdero) *tr* to moderate, control

moderatézza *f* moderation

modera·to -ta *adj* moderate; (mus) moderato || *m* middle-of-the-roader

modera·tóre -trice *adj* moderating || *m* moderator

modernizzare [ddzz] *tr & ref* to modernize

modèr·no -na *adj & m* modern

modèstia *f* modesty; scantiness, mea-gerness

modè·sto -sta *adj* modest; humble

mòdi·co -ca *adj* (-ci -che) reasonable

modìfica *f* (-che) modification; alteration

modificare §197 (modìfico) *tr* to modify; to change; to alter

modiglióne *m* (archit) modillion

modista *f* milliner

modisterìa *f* millinery; millinery shop

mòdo *m* manner, mode, way; custom; idiom; (gram) mood; (mus) mode; ad ogni modo anyhow; nevertheless; ad un modo equally; a bel modo proper; properly; a suo modo in his own way; bei modi good manners; di modo che so that; in malo modo poorly; in modo da so as to; in nessun modo by no means; in ogni modo anyhow; in qualche modo somehow; modo di dire idiom; turn of phrase; modo di fare behavior; modo di vedere opinion; per modo di dire so to speak

modulare (mòdulo) *tr* to modulate

modulazióne *f* modulation; modulazione d'ampiezza amplitude modulation; modulazione di frequenza frequency modulation

mòdulo *m* module; blank, form

moffétta *f* skunk

mògano *m* mahogany

mòg·gio *m* (-gi) bushel

mò·gio -gia *adj* (-gi -gie) downcast, crestfallen

móglie *f* (-gli) wife

moìne *fpl* blandishments

mòla *f* grindstone; (coll) millstone

molare *adj* grinding; molar || *m* molar || *v* (mòlo) *tr* to grind

molassa *f* molasse, sandstone

molatóre *m* grinder (*person*); sander (*person*)

molatrice *f* grinder (*machine*); sander (*machine*); molatrice di pavimenti floor sander

mòle *f* size; pile; bulk, mass; huge structure

molècola *f* molecule

molestare (molèsto) *tr* to bother, annoy

molèstia *f* bother, trouble, annoyance

molè·sto -sta *adj* bothersome, trouble-some

molibdèno *m* molybdenum

molinétto *m* (naut) winch

mòlla *f* spring; (fig) mainspring; molla a balestra leaf spring; molle tongs; molle del letto bedspring; prendere

qlco con le molle to keep at a reasonable distance from s.th

mollare (**mòllo**) *tr* to let go; to slacken; to drop (*anchor*); (coll) to soak ‖ *intr* to give up; (coll) to soak; **molla!** (coll) cut it out!

mòlle *adj* wet, soaked; soft; mild; easy (*life*); weak (*character*); flexible ‖ *m* softness; soft ground; **tenere a molle** to soak

mollécca *f* soft-shell crab

molleggiaménto *m* suspension; springiness

molleggiare §290 (**molléggio**) *tr* to provide with springs, to make elastic; (aut) to provide with suspension ‖ *intr* to be springy, to have bounce ‖ *ref* to bounce along

mollég·gio *m* (**-gi**) springs; (aut) suspension; springiness

mollétta *f* hairpin; clothespin; **mollette** sugar tongs

mollettièra *f* puttee

mollettóne *m* swansdown

mollézza *f* softness

molli·ca *f* (**-che**) crumb (*soft inner portion of bread*); **molliche** crumbs

mollificare §197 (**mollìfico**) *tr* & *ref* to mollify; to soften

mòl·lo -la *adj* soft ‖ *m*—**mettere a mollo** to soak ‖ *f* see **molla**

mollu·sco *m* (**-schi**) mollusk

mòlo *m* pier, wharf

moltéplice *adj* multiple, manifold

moltilaterale *adj* multilateral, many-sided

moltìpli·ca *f* (**-che**) front sprocket (*of bicycle*)

moltiplicare §197 (**moltìplico**) *tr* & *ref* to multiply

moltitùdine *f* multitude, crowd

mól·to -ta *adj* much, a lot of; very, e.g., **ho molta sete** I am very thirsty ‖ *pron* much; a lot; **a dir molto** mostly; **ci corre molto** there is a great difference ‖ **mol·ti -te** *adj* & *pron* many ‖ **molto** *adv* very; quite; much; a lot; widely; long; **fra non molto** before long; **non . . . molto** (coll) not . . . at all

momentàne·o -a *adj* momentary

moménto *m* moment; opportune time; (slang) trifle; (phys) momentum; **dal momento che** since; **per il momento** for the time being; **sul momento** this very moment

mòna·ca *f* (**-che**) nun

monacale *adj* monachal, conventual

monacato *m* monkhood

monachésimo *m* monachism, monasticism

monachina *f* little nun; **monachine** sparks

mòna·co *m* (**-ci**) monk; (archit) king post ‖ **Monaco** *m* Monaco ‖ *f* Munich

monar·ca *m* (**-chi**) monarch

monarchìa *f* monarchy

monàrchi·co -ca *adj* (**-ci -che**) monarchical; monarchist(ic) (*advocating a monarch*) ‖ *mf* monarchist

monastèro *m* monastery

monàsti·co -ca *adj* (**-ci -che**) monastic(al)

moncherino *m* stump (*without hand*)

món·co -ca *adj* (**-chi -che**) one-handed; one-armed; incomplete ‖ *mf* cripple

moncóne *m* stump

mondana *f* prostitute

mondani·tà *f* (**-tà**) worldliness

monda·no -na *adj* mundane; worldly; society; fashionable ‖ *m* playboy ‖ *f* see **mondana**

mondare (**móndo**) *tr* to peel, pare; to thresh; to weed; to prune; (fig) to cleanse

mondari·so *mf* (**-so**) rice weeder

mondez·zàio *m* (**-zài**) dump

mondiale *adj* world, world-wide; (coll) stupendous

mondìglia *f* chaff; trash; refuse

mondina *f* rice weeder

món·do da *adj* clean-peeled; (lit) pure ‖ *m* world; hopscotch; (coll) heap, bunch; **bel mondo** smart set; **cascasse il mondo!** (coll) come what may!; **da che mondo è mondo** since the world began; **essere nel mondo della luna** to be absent-minded; **mandare all'altro mondo** (coll) to send packing; **mettere al mondo** to give birth to; **mondo della luna** world of fancy; **un mondo a lot**; **venire al mondo** to be born ‖ **Mondo** *m*—**Terzo Mondo** Third World

monega·sco -sca *adj* & *mf* (**-schi -sche**) Monacan

monellerìa *f* prank

monèl·lo -la *mf* urchin, brat ‖ *f* romp

monéta *f* money; coin; piece of money; purse (*in horse races*); change; **batter moneta** to mint money; **moneta sonante** cash

monetà·rio -ria (**-ri -rie**) *adj* monetary ‖ *m*—**falso monetario** counterfeiter

monetizzare [ddzz] *tr* to express in money; to transform into cash

mòngo·lo -la *adj* & *mf* Mongolian

monile *m* necklace; jewel

mònito *m* admonition, warning

monitóre *m* monitor

mònna *f* (obs) lady; (coll) monkey

monoàlbero *adj* invar (aut) single-camshaft, valve-in-head (*distribution*)

monoaurale *adj* monaural

monoblòc·co (**-co**) *adj* single-block ‖ *m* (aut) cylinder block

monocilìndri·co -ca *adj* (**-ci -che**) (mach) single-cylinder

monòco·lo -la *adj* one-eyed ‖ *m* monocle

monocolóre *adj* invar one-color; one-party

monofa·se *adj* (**-si** & **-se**) single-phase

monogamìa *f* monogamy

monòga·mo -ma *adj* monogamous ‖ *m* monogamist

monografìa *f* monograph

monogram·ma *m* (**-mi**) monogram

monolìti·co -ca *adj* (**-ci -che**) monolithic

monolito *m* monolith

monòlo·go *m* (**-ghi**) monologue

monomanìa *f* monomania

monò·mio *m* (-mi) monomial
monopàttino *m* scooter
monopèt·to (-to) *adj* single-breasted ‖ *m* single-breasted suit
monoplano *m* (aer) monoplane
monopò·lio *m* (-li) monopoly
monopolizzare [ddzz] *tr* to monopolize
monopósto *adj invar* one-man ‖ *m* single-seater
monorotàia *adj invar* single-track ‖ *f* monorail
monoscò·pio *m* (-pi) (telv) test pattern
monosìlla·bo -ba *adj* monosyllabic ‖ *m* monosyllable
monòssido *m* monoxide
monoteìsti·co -ca *adj* (-ci -che) monotheistic
monotipìa *f* monotype
monotipo *m* monotype
monotonìa *f* monotony
monòto·no -na *adj* monotonous
monsignóre *m* monsignor
monsóne *m* monsoon
mónta *f* horseback riding; stud; jockey
montacàri·chi *m* (-chi) freight elevator
montàg·gio *m* (-gi) (mach) assembly; (mov) editing; (mov) montage
montagna *f* mountain; **montagna di ghiaccio** iceberg; **montagne russe** roller coaster
montagnó·so -sa [s] *adj* mountainous
montana·ro -ra *adj* mountain ‖ *mf* mountaineer
monta·no -na *adj* mountain
montante *adj* rising ‖ *m* riser, upright; (football) goal post; (aer) strut; (boxing) uppercut; (com) aggregate amount
montare (mónto) *tr* to mount; to go up (*the stairs*); to set (*jewels*); to frame (*a painting*); to whip (*e.g., eggs*); to excite; to exaggerate (*news*); to decorate (*a house*); to cover (*said of a male animal*); (mach) to assemble; (mov) to edit; **montare la testa a** to excite; **to give a swell head to** ‖ *intr* (ESSERE) to jump; to climb; to go up; to rise; to swell; **montare alla testa a** to go to the head of; **montare in collera** to get angry ‖ *impers*—**non monta** it doesn't matter, never mind
monta·tóre -trice *mf* (mach) assembler; (mov) editor
montatura *f* assembly; frame (*of glasses*); appliqué; setting (*of gem*); (journ) ballyhoo; (mov) editing; **montatura pubblicitaria** publicity stunt
montavivan·de *m* (-de) dumbwaiter
mónte *m* mountain; bank; mount (*in palmistry*); (cards) discard; **a monte** uphill; upstream; **andare a monte** to fail; **mandare a monte** to cause to fail; **monte di pietà** pawnbroker's; **monte di premi** pot (*in a lottery*)
montenegri·no -na *adj* & *mf* Montenegrin
montessoria·no -na *adj* Montessori
montóne *m* ram; mutton; rounded stone
montuó·so -sa [s] *adj* mountainous
montura *f* uniform

monumentale *adj* monumental
monuménto *m* monument
moquètte *f* (moquètte) wall-to-wall carpeting
mòra *f* mulberry; blackberry; brunette; Moorish woman; arrears; penalty (*for arrears*); (archaic) heap of stones
morale *adj* moral ‖ *m* morale; **giù di morale** downcast; **su di morale** in high spirits ‖ *f* morals, ethics; moral (*of a fable*)
moraleggiare §290 (moraléggio) *intr* to moralize
moralismo *m* moralism
morali·tà *f* (-tà) morality; morals
moralizzare [ddzz] *tr* & *intr* to moralize
moratòria *f* moratorium
morbidézza *f* softness
mòrbi·do -da *adj* soft; sleek; pliable ‖ *m* soft ground
morbillo *m* measles
mòrbo *m* disease; plague
morbó·so -sa [s] *adj* morbid
mòrchia *f* sediment; dregs of oil
mordace *adj* biting, mordacious
mordènte *adj* biting; (chem) mordant; (mach) interlocking ‖ *s* strength; (chem) mordant
mòrdere §200 *tr* to bite; to grab; to corrode; **mordere il freno** to champ the bit
mordicchiare §287 (mordìcchio) *tr* to nibble
morè·sco -sca (-schi -sche) *adj* Moresque, Moorish ‖ *f* Moorish dance
morét·to -ta *adj* brunet ‖ *m* Negro boy; dark-skinned boy; chocolate-covered ice-cream bar ‖ *f* Negro girl; dark-skinned girl; mask; (orn) scaup duck
morfè·ma *m* (-mi) morpheme
morfina *f* morphine
morfinòmane *mf* morphine addict
morfologìa *f* morphology
morìa *f* pestilence; high mortality
moribón·do -da *adj* moribund
morìgera·to -ta *adj* temperate, moderate
morire §201 *intr* (ESSERE) to die; to die out; to end (*said of a street*); **morire di noia** to be bored to death
moritu·ro -ra *adj* about to die, doomed
mormóne *mf* Mormon
mormorare (mórmoro) *tr* to murmur; to whisper ‖ *intr* to murmur; to whisper; to babble (*said of a brook*); to rustle; to gossip
mormorì·o *m* (-i) whisper; murmur
mò·ro -ra *adj* Moorish; dark-skinned; dark-brown ‖ *mf* Moor ‖ *m* mulberry tree ‖ *f* see **mora**
morosi·tà [s] *f* (-tà) delinquency (*in paying one's bills*)
moró·so -sa [s] *adj* delinquent (*in paying one's bills*) ‖ *m* (coll) boyfriend; **i morosi** (coll) the lovers ‖ *f* (coll) girl friend
mòrsa *f* vise; (archit) toothing
morsétto *m* clamp; (elec) binding post

morsicare §197 (mòrsico) tr to bite

morsicatura f bite

morsicchiare §287 (morsìcchio) tr to nibble

mòrso m bite; bit

mor·tàio m (-tài) mortar

mortale adj mortal; deadly ‖ m mortal

mortali·tà f (-tà) mortality

mortarétto m firecracker

mòrte f death; end; averla a morte con to harbor hatred for; morte civile (law) attainder, loss of civil rights

mortèlla f myrtle

mortificare §197 (mortìfico) tr to mortify ‖ ref to feel ashamed

mòr·to -ta adj dead; still (life); morto di fame dying of hunger; morto di paura scared to death ‖ mf dead person, deceased ‖ m hidden treasure; (cards) dummy, widow; fare il morto to float on one's back; to play possum; morto di fame ne'er-do-well, good-for-nothing; suonare a morto to toll

mortò·rio m (-ri) funeral

mortuà·rio -ria adj (-ri -rie) mortuary

mosài·co -ca (-ci -che) adj Mosaic ‖ m mosaic

mó·sca f (-sche) fly; imperial (beard); mosca bianca one in a million; mosca cieca blindman's buff; fare venire la mosca al naso a to make angry ‖ Mosca f Moscow

moscaiòla f fly netting; flytrap

moscardino m dandy; (zool) dormouse

moscatèl·lo -la adj muscat ‖ m muscatel

moscato m muscat grape; muscat wine

moscerino m gnat

moschèa f mosque

moschettière m musketeer; Italian National soccer player

moschétto m musket

moschettóne m snap hook

moschici·da adj (-di -de) fly-killing

mó·scio -scia adj (-sci -sce) flabby, soft

moscóne m big fly; pesky suitor

moscovi·ta adj & mf (-ti -te) Muscovite

Mosè m Moses

mòssa f gesture; movement; move; fake; post; fare la mossa to sprout (said of plants); mossa di corpo bowel movement; prendere le mosse to begin; stare sulle mosse to be about to begin; to be eager to take off (said of a horse)

mossière m starter (in a race)

mòs·so -sa adj moved; in motion; plowed; rough (sea); blurred (picture); wavy (hair; ground) ‖ f see mossa

mostarda f mustard; candied fruit

mósto m must

móstra f show; pretense, simulation; exhibit; display window; lapel; face (of watch); sample; (mil) insignia; (obs) military parade; far mostra di sé to show off; mettersi in mostra to show off

mostrare (móstro) tr to show; to put on; mostrare a dito to point to;

mostrare la corda to be threadbare ‖ ref to show up; to show oneself

mostreggiatura f lapel; cuff

mostrina f (mil) insignia

móstro m monster

mostruó·so -sa [s] adj monstruous

mòta f mud, mire

mo·tèl m (-tèl) motel

motivare tr to cause; to justify

motivazióne f justification, reason

motivo m motive, reason; motif; theme; (coll) tune; a motivo di because of; motivo per cui wherefore

mò·to m (-ti) motion; movement; emotion; riot; mettere in moto to start ‖ f (-to) (coll) motorcycle

motobar·ca f (-che) motorboat

motocannonièra f gunboat

motocarro m three-wheeler (truck)

motocarrozzétta f three-wheeler (vehicle with sidecar)

motociclétta f motorcycle

motocicli·sta mf (-sti -ste) motorcyclist

motocorazza·to -ta adj armored, panzer

motofalciatrice f power mower

motofurgóne m delivery truck

motolàn·cia f (-ce) motorboat, speedboat

motonàuti·co -ca (-ci -che) adj motorboat ‖ f motorboating

motonave f motor ship

motopescheréc·cio m (-ci) motor fishing boat

mo·tóre -trice adj motive (power); (mach) drive ‖ m motor; engine; car; a motore motorized, motor; motore rotativo (aut) rotary engine; primo motore prime mover ‖ f see motrice

motorétta f motor scooter

motorino m small motor; motor bicycle; motorino d'avviamento (aut) starter

motori·sta m (-sti) mechanic

motoristi·co -ca adj (-ci -che) motor

motorizzare [ddzz] tr to motorize

motoscafo m motorboat; motoscafo da corsa speedboat

motosé·ga f (-ghe) chain saw

motosilurante f torpedo boat

motoveicolo m motor vehicle

motovelièro m motor sailer

motrice f (rr) engine, motor; (aut) tractor; motrice a vapore steam engine

motteggiare §290 (mottéggio) tr to mock, jeer at ‖ intr to jest

mottég·gio m (-gi) mockery, jest

mòtto m witticism; motto; (lit) word

movènte m stimulus, motive

movènza f bearing, carriage; flow (of a sentence); cadence

movìbile adj movable

movimenta·to -ta adj lively; eventful

moviménto m motion, movement; traffic; movimento di cassa cash turnover

moviòla f (mov) viewer and splicer

mozióne f motion; (lit) movement

mozzare (mózzo) tr to lop off; to sever; mozzare la testa a to cut off the head of

mozzicóne *m* stump; butt (*e.g., of cigar*)

móz·zo -za *adj* cut off; truncated; cropped (*ears*); docked (*tail*); hard (*breathing*) || *m* cabin boy; **mozzo di stalla** stable boy

mòzzo [ddzz] *m* hub

muc·ca *f* (-**che**) milch cow

mùc·chio *m* (-**chi**) pile, heap; bunch

mucillàgine *f* mucilage

mu·co *m* (-**chi**) mucus, phlegm

mucó·so -sa [s] *adj* mucous || *f* mucous membrane

muda *f* molt

muffa *f* mold; mildew; **fare la muffa** to be musty

muffire §176 *intr* (ESSERE) to be musty

mùffola *f* mitten; muffle (*of furnace*)

muflóne *m* mouflon

mugghiare §287 (**mùgghio**) *intr* to bellow; to roar

mùggine *m* (ichth) mullet

muggire §176 & (**muggo**) *intr* to moo, low; to roar; to howl

muggito *m* bellow; moo, low; roar

mughétto *m* lily of the valley

mu·gnàio -gnàia *mf* (-**gnài -gnàie**) miller

mugolare (**mùgolo**) *intr* to yelp; to moan

mugolí·o *m* (-**i**) yelp; moan

mugò·lio *m* (-**li**) pine tar

mugugnare *intr* (coll) to mumble; (coll) to grumble

mugugno *m* (coll) grumble

mulattière *m* mule driver, muleteer

mulattiè·ro -ra *adj* mule || *f* mule track

mulat·to -ta *adj* & *mf* mulatto

muliebre *adj* womanly, feminine

mulinare *tr* to twirl; to scheme || *intr* to whirl; to muse; to buzz (*in the mind*)

mulinèllo *m* twirl; whirlpool; whirlwind; fishing reel; whirligig; **fare mulinello con** to twirl

mulino *m* mill; **mulino ad acqua** water mill; **mulino a vento** windmill

mu·lo -la *mf* mule; (slang) bastard

multa *f* penalty, fine

multare *tr* to fine

multilaterale *adj* multilateral, many-sided

mùlti·plo -pla *adj* & *m* multiple

mùmmia *f* mummy

mummificare §197 (**mummìfico**) *tr* to mummify

mùngere §183 *tr* to milk

mungi·tóre -trice *mf* milker || *f* milking machine; milk maid

mungitura *f* milking

municipale *adj* municipal, city

municipalizzazióne [ddzz] *f* municipalization; city management

munici·pio *m* (-**pi**) municipality; city council; city hall

munificènza *f* munificence

munìfi·co -ca *adj* (-**ci -che**) munificent

munire §176 *tr* to fortify; to provide; **munire di** to equip with || *ref* to provide oneself

munizióne *f* (obs) fortification; **munizioni** ammunition; building supplies

muòvere §202 *tr* to move; to wag; to propel, run; to lift (*one's finger*); to take (*a step*); to pose (*a question*); to stir up (*laughter*); to institute (*a lawsuit*); **muovere accusa a** to reproach || *intr* (ESSERE) to begin; to move, start || *ref* to move; to travel; to stir; to set out; to be moved; **muoviti!** hurry up!

mura *fpl* see **muro**

muràglia *f* wall; (fig) obstacle; **muraglia cinese** Chinese Wall

muraglióne *m* high wall, rampart

murale *adj* & *m* mural

murare *tr* to wall; to wall in || *intr* to build a wall; **murare a secco** to build a dry wall || *ref* to close oneself in

murata *f* (naut) bulwark

muratóre *m* bricklayer, mason

muratura *f* bricklaying, stonework

muriàti·co -ca *adj* (-**ci -che**) muriatic

mu·ro *m* (-**ri**) wall; **muro del pianto** Wailing Wall; **muro del suono** sound barrier || *m* (-**ra** *fpl*)—**mura** walls (*of a city*)

musa *f* muse

muschia·to -ta *adj* musk (*e.g., ox*)

mù·schio *m* (-**schi**) musk; (coll) moss

mu·sco *m* (-**schi**) moss

mùscolo *m* muscle; (fig) sinew; (coll) mussel

muscoló·so -sa [s] *adj* muscular

muscó·so -sa [s] *adj* (lit) mossy

musèo *m* museum

museruòla *f* muzzle

musétta *f* nose bag

mùsi·ca *f* (-**che**) music; band; **cambiare musica** to change one's tune

musicale *adj* musical

musicante *adj* music-playing (*angels*) || *mf* band player; second-rate musician

musicare §197 (**mùsico**) *tr* to set to music

musicassétta *f* cassette, tape cartridge

music-hall *m* (-**hall**) *m* vaudeville, burlesque

musici·sta *mf* (-**sti -ste**) musician

musicologìa *f* musicology

musicòlo·go m (-**gi**) musicologist

muso *m* muzzle, snout; (coll) mug; (fig) nose; **avere il muso lungo** to make a long face; **mettere il muso** to pout

musó·ne -na *mf* pouter, sulker

mussare *tr* to publish with great fanfare (*a piece of news*) || *intr* to foam (*said of wine*)

mùssola or **mussolina** *f* muslin

mussolinia·no -na *adj* of Mussolini

mùssolo *m* mussel

mustàc·chio *m* (-**chi**) shroud (*of bowsprit*); **mustacchi** moustache

musulma·no -na [s] *adj* & *mf* Moslem

muta *f* change; shift; molt; set (*of sails*); pack (*of hounds*); (mil) watch

mutàbile *adj* changeable

mutande *fpl* shorts, briefs, drawers

mutandine *fpl* panties; **mutandine da bagno** trunks

mutare *tr, intr* (ESSERE) & *ref* to change

mutazióne *f* mutation; (biol) mutation, sport

mutévole *adj* changeable; fickle

mutilare (**mùtilo**) *tr* to mutilate, maim
mutila·to -ta *adj* mutilated || *mf* cripple; amputee; **mutilato di guerra** disabled veteran
mutismo *m* silence, willful silence; (pathol) dumbness
mu·to -ta *adj* mute; dumb; silent (*movie*); unexpressed || *mf* mute || *f* see **muta**
mùtria *f* sulking attitude; proud demeanor

mùtua *f* mutual benefit society; medical insurance; **mettersi in mutua** to go on sick leave
mutuali·tà *f* (**-tà**) mutuality; mutual benefit institutions
mutuare (**mùtuo**) *tr* to borrow; to lend
mutua·to -ta *mf* person insured by mutual benefit society; person insured by medical insurance
mù·tuo -tua *adj* mutual; borrowing || *m* loan || *f* see **mutua**

N

N, n ['ɛnne] *m & f* twelfth letter of the Italian alphabet
nababbo *m* nabob
Nabucodònosor *m* Nebuchadnezzar
nàcchera *f* castanet
nafta *f* crude oil; naphta; Diesel oil
naftalina *f* naphthalene
nàia *f* cobra; (slang) army discipline; (slang) military service
nàiade *f* naiad
nàilon *m* nylon
nanna *f* sleep (*of child*); **fare la nanna** to sleep (*said of child*)
na·no -na *adj & mf* dwarf
nàpalm *m* napalm
napoleòne *m* napoleon (*gold coin*) || **Napoleone** *m* Napoleon
napoleòni·co -ca *adj* (**-ci -che**) Napoleonic
napoleta·no -na *adj & mf* Neapolitan || *f* espresso coffee machine
Nàpoli *f* Naples
nappa *f* tassel; tuft; kid (*leather*)
narciso *m* narcissus
narcòti·co -ca *adj & m* (**-ci -che**) narcotic
narcotizzare [ddzz] *tr* to drug, dope; to anesthetize
narghi·lè *m* (**-lè**) hookah
narice *f* nostril
narrare *tr* to narrate, tell, recount
narrati·vo -va *adj* narrative; fictional || *f* narrative; fiction
narra·tóre -trice *mf* narrator, storyteller
narrazióne *f* narration; tale, story; narrative
nasale [s] *adj & f* nasal
nascènte *adj* nascent; budding; rising (*sun*); dawning (*day*)
nàscere *m* beginning, origin || §203 *intr* (ESSERE) to be born; to bud; to shoot; to dawn; to rise; to spring up; **nascere con la camicia** to be born with a silver spoon in one's mouth
nàscita *f* birth; birthday; origin
nascitu·ro -ra *adj* unborn, future || *mf* unborn child
nascóndere §204 *tr* to hide; **nascondere a** to hide from || *ref* to hide; to lurk
nascondì·glio *m* (**-gli**) hiding place; hideout; cache
nascondino *m* hide-and-seek; **giocare a nascondino** to play hide-and-seek
nascó·sto -sta *adj* hidden, concealed; secret; **di nascosto** secretly

nasèllo [s] *m* catch (*of latch*); (ichth) hake
nasièra [s] *f* nose ring
naso [s] *m* nose; (fig) face; **aver buon naso** to have a keen sense of smell; **ficcare il naso negli affari degli altri** to pry into the affairs of others; **menare per il naso** to lead by the nose; **naso adunco** hooknose; **restare con un palmo di naso** to be duped
nassa *f* pot (*for fishing*); **nassa per aragoste** lobster pot
nastrino *m* ribbon; badge
nastro *m* ribbon; band; tape; streamer; tape measure; **nastro del cappello** hatband; **nastro isolante** friction tape; **nastro per capelli** hair ribbon
nastùr·zio *m* (**-zi**) nasturtium
natale *adj* native, natal || **natali** *mpl* birth; birthday; **dare i natali a** to be the birthplace of || **Natale** *m* Christmas
natali·tà *f* (**-tà**) birth rate
natalì·zio -zia (**-zi -zie**) *adj* natal; Christmas || *m* birthday
natante *adj* swimming; floating || *m* craft
natatóia *f* fin
natató·rio -ria *adj* (**-ri -rie**) swimming
nàti·ca *f* (**-che**) buttock
natì·o -a *adj* (**-i -e**) (poet) native
nativi·tà *f* (**-tà**) birth, nativity || **Nativi·tà** *f* Nativity
nati·vo -va *adj* native; natural, inborn || *mf* native
N.A.T.O. *f* (acronym) (**North Atlantic Treaty Organization**)—**la N.A.T.O.** NATO
na·to -ta *adj* born; **nata née**; **nato e sputato** the spit and image of; **nato morto** stillborn || *mf* child
natura *f* nature; **natura morta** still life; **in natura** in kind
naturale *adj* natural || *m* nature, disposition; **al naturale** life-size
naturalézza *f* naturalness; spontaneity
naturalismo *m* naturalism
naturali·sta *mf* (**-sti -ste**) naturalist
naturali·tà *f* (**-tà**) naturalization
naturalizzare [ddzz] *tr* to naturalize || *ref* to become naturalized
naturalizzazióne [ddzz] *f* naturalization
naturalménte *adv* naturally; of course
naufragare §209 (**nàufrago**) *intr* (ESSERE

& AVERE) to be shipwrecked; to sink, to fail

naufrà•gio *m* (-**gi**) shipwreck; failure

nàufra•go -**ga** (-**ghi** -**ghe**) *adj* shipwrecked || *mf* shipwrecked person; (fig) outcast

nàusea *f* nausea; disgust; **avere la nausea** to be sick at one's stomach

nauseabón•do -**da** *adj* sickening, nauseating; (fig) unsavory

nauseante (*adj*) sickening, nauseous

nauseare (**nàuseo**) *tr* to nauseate, sicken

nausea•to -**ta** *adj* sickened, disgusted

nàuti•co -**ca** (-**ci** -**che**) *adj* nautical || *f* sailing, navigation

navale *adj* naval, navy, sea

navata *f* nave; **navata centrale** nave; **navata laterale** aisle

nave *f* ship, vessel, boat; craft; **nave ammiraglia** flagship; **nave a motore** motorboat; **nave appoggio** tender; **nave a vela** sailboat; **nave da carico** freighter; **nave da guerra** warship; **nave petroliera** tanker; **nave portaerei** aircraft carrier; **nave rompighiaccio** icebreaker; **nave traghetto** ferryboat

navétta *f* shuttle; **fare la navetta** to shuttle

navicèlla *f* nacelle, cabin (*of airship*); car (*of balloon*)

navigàbile *adj* navigable

navigabili•tà *f* (-**tà**) navigability; seaworthiness

navigante *adj* sailing || *m* sailor

navigare §209 (**nàvigo**) *tr* & *intr* to navigate, to sail

naviga•to -**ta** *adj* seawise; wordly-wise

naviga•tóre -**trice** *mf* navigator

navigazióne *f* navigation

navì•glio *m* (-**gli**) ship, craft, boat; fleet; navy; canal; **naviglio mercantile** merchant marine

nazionale *adj* national || *f* national team

nazionalismo *m* nationalism

nazionali•sta *mf* (-**sti** -**ste**) nationalist

nazionalisti•co -**ca** *adj* (-**ci** -**che**) nationalistic

nazionali•tà *f* (-**tà**) nationality

nazionalizzare [ddzz] *tr* to nationalize

nazionalizzazióne [ddzz] *f* nationalization

nazióne *f* nation

nazi•sta *adj* & *mf* (-**sti** -**ste**) Nazi

nazzarè•no -**na** [ddzz] *adj* & *mf* Nazareno || **il Nazzareno** the Nazarene

ne §5 *pron* & *adv*

né *conj* neither, nor; **né . . . né** neither . . . nor

neanche *adv* not even; nor; not . . . either

nébbia *f* fog, haze, mist; **fa nebbia** it is foggy; **nebbia artificiale** smoke screen

nebbióne *m* thick fog, pea soup

nebbió•so -**sa** [s] *adj* foggy, hazy, misty

nebulare *adj* nebular

nebulizzare [ddzz] *tr* to atomize

nebulizzatóre [ddzz] *m* atomizer

nebulósa [s] *f* nebula

nebulosi•tà [s] *f* (-**tà**) fogginess, haziness, mistiness

nebuló•so -**sa** [s] *adj* foggy, hazy, misty || *f* see **nebulosa**

néces•saire *m* (-**saire**) vanity case; sewing kit

necessariaménte *adv* necessarily

necessà•rio -**ria** (-**ri** -**rie**) *adj* necessary, needed; essential || *m* necessity; necessities (*of life*)

necessi•tà *f* (-**tà**) necessity; need, want; **di necessità** necessarily

necessitare (**necèssito**) *tr* to require; to force || *intr* to be in want; to be necessary; **necessitare di** to need

necrologìa *f* necrology, obituary

necrològi•co -**ca** *adj* (-**ci** -**che**) obituary

necromanzìa *f* necromancy

necròsi *f* necrosis, gangrene

nefan•do -**da** *adj* heinous, nefarious

nefa•sto -**sta** *adj* ill-fated; ominous

nefrite *f* nephritis

negare §209 (**négo** & **nègo**) *tr* to deny, negate; to refuse

negati•vo -**va** *adj* & *f* negative

nega•to -**ta** *adj* unfit, unsuited

negazióne *f* negation, denial; (gram) negative

neghittó•so -**sa** [s] *adj* lazy, slothful

neglèt•to -**ta** *adj* neglected; untidy

négli §4

negligènte *adj* negligent, careless

negligènza *f* negligence, carelessness; dereliction (*of duty*)

negligere §205 *tr* to neglect

negoziàbile *adj* negotiable

negoziante *mf* merchant, shopkeeper; dealer; **negoziante all'ingrosso** wholesaler; **negoziante al minuto** retailer; shopkeeper, storekeeper

negoziare §287 (**negòzio**) *tr* to negotiate, transact || *intr* to negotiate, deal

negoziati *mpl* negotiations

negozia•tóre -**trice** *mf* negotiator

negò•zio *m* (-**zi**) business; transaction; store, shop; **negozio di cancelleria** stationery store

negrière *m* slave trader; slave driver

negriè•ro -**ra** *adj* slave || *m* slave trader; slave driver

né-gro -**gra** *adj* & *mf* Negro

negromante *m* sorcerer

néi §4

nél §4

nélla §4

nélle §4

néllo §4

némbo *m* rain cloud; cloud (*e.g., of dust*)

Nembròd *m* Nimrod

nèmesi *f invar* nemesis || **Nèmesi** *f* Nemesis

nemi•co -**ca** (-**ci** -**che**) *adj* inimical, hostile, unfriendly; enemy; (fig) adverse || *mf* enemy, foe; **Il Nemico** the Evil One

nemméno *adv* not even; nor; not . . . either

nènia *f* funeral dirge; lamentation

nenùfaro *m* water lily

nèo *m* mole (*on the skin*); flaw, blemish; neon; beauty spot

neoclassicheggiante *adj* in the direction of the neoclassical

neòfi·ta *mf* (**-ti -te**) neophite
neolati·no -na *adj* Neo-Latin, Romance
neologismo *m* neologism
neomicina *f* neomycin
nèon *m* neon
neona·to -ta *adj* newborn || *mf* infant, baby; newborn child
neozelandése [dz][s] *adj* New Zealand || *mf* New Zealander
nepènte *f* nepenthe
Nepóte *m* Nepos
neppure *adv* not even; nor; not . . . either
nequìzia *f* iniquity, wickedness
nera·stro -stra *adj* blackish
nerbata *f* heavy blow
nèrbo *m* whip; sinew; bulk; strength (*of an opposing force*)
nerboru·to -ta *adj* muscular, sinewy
nereggiare §290 (**neréggio**) *intr* to look black; to be blackish
nerétto *m* (*typ*) boldface
né·ro -ra *adj* black; dark; gloomy; dark-red (*wine*) || *mf* black; Negro || *m* black
nerofumo *m* lampblack
Neróne *m* Nero
nervatura *f* ribbing
nervi·no -na *adj* nerve (*gas*); nervine (*medicine*)
nèrvo *m* nerve; sinew; **avere i nervi** to be in a bad mood
nervosismo [s] *m* nervousness, irritability
nervó·so -sa [s] *adj* nervous, irritable; sinewy, vigorous (*style*) || *m* bad mood; **avere il nervoso** to be in a bad mood
nèsci *m*—**fare il nesci** to feign ignorance
nèspola *f* medlar; **nespole** (coll) blows
nèspolo *m* medlar tree
nèsso *m* connection, link; **avere nesso** to cohere
nessu·no -na *adj* no, not any || **nessuno** *pron* nobody, no one; none; not anybody; not anyone; **nessuno dei due** neither one
nettapén·ne *m* (**-ne**) penwiper
nettare (**nétto**) *tr* to clean, to cleanse
nèttare *m* nectar
nettézza *f* cleanness, cleanliness; neatness; **nettezza urbana** department of sanitation; garbage collection
nét·to -ta *adj* clean; clear; sharp; net || **netto** *adv* clearly, distinctly
nettùnio *m* neptunium
Nettuno *m* Neptune
netturbino *m* street cleaner
neurologia *f* neurology
neurò·si *f* (**-si**) neurosis
neuròti·co -ca *adj* (**-ci -che**) neurotic
neutrale *adj* & *mf* neutral
neutrali·sta *adj* & *mf* (**-sti -ste**) neutralist
neutrali·tà *f* (**-tà**) neutrality
neutralizzare [ddzz] *tr* to neutralize
nèu·tro -tra *adj* neuter; neutral
neutróne *m* neutron
ne·vàio *m* (**-vài**) snowfield; snowdrift
néve *f* snow; **neve carbonica** dry ice
nevicare §197 (**névica**) *impers* (ESSERE)
   —nevica it is snowing

nevicata *f* snowfall
nevischio *m* sleet
nevó·so -sa [s] *adj* snowy
nevralgìa *f* neuralgia
nevrastèni·co -ca *adj* & *mf* (**-ci -che**) neurasthenic
nevvéro (i.e., **n'è vero** for **non è vero**) see **non**
niacina *f* niacin
nìb·bio *m* (**-bi**) (orn) kite
nìcchia *f* niche; nook, recess
nicchiare §287 (**nìcchio**) *intr* to waver
nìc·chio *m* (**-chi**) shell; nook
nichel *m* nickel
nichelare (**nìchelo**) *tr* to ·nickel, to nickel-plate
nichelatura *f* nickel-plating
nichelino *m* nickel (*coin*)
nichèlio *m* var of **nichel**
Nicòla *m* Nicholas
nicotina *f* nicotine
nidiata *f* nestful; brood
nidificare §197 (**nidìfico**) *intr* to build a nest, to nest
nido *m* nest; home; nursery; den (*of thieves*)
niènte *m* nothing; nothingness; **dal niente** from scratch; **di niente** you're welcome || *pron* nothing; not . . . anything; **quasi niente** next to nothing
nientediméno *adv* no less, nothing less
Nilo *m* Nile
ninfa *f* nymph
ninfèa *f* white water lily
ninnananna *f* lullaby, cradlesong
nìnnolo *m* toy; trinket
nipóte *mf* grandchild || *m* grandson; nephew; **nipoti** descendants || *f* granddaughter; niece
nippòni·co -ca *adj* (**-ci -che**) Nipponese
nirvana, il nirvana
nìti·do -da *adj* clear, distinct
nitóre *m* brightness; elegance
nitrato *m* nitrate
nitrire §176 *intr* to neigh
nitrito *m* neigh; (chem) nitrite
nitro *m* niter; **nitro del Cile** Chile saltpeter
nitroglicerina *f* nitroglycerin
nitruro *m* nitride
niu·no -na *adj* (poet) var of **nessuno**
nìve·o -a *adj* snow-white
Nizza *f* Nice •
no *adv* no; not; **come no?** why not; certainly; **dire di no** to say no; **no?** is it not so?; **non dir di no** to consent; **proprio no** certainly not
nòbile *adj* noble; second (*floor*) || *m* nobleman || *f* noblewoman
nobiliare *adj* noble, of nobility
nobilitare (**nobìlito**) *tr* to ennoble
nobil·tà *f* (**-tà**) nobility
nòc·ca *f* (**-che**) knuckle
nocchière *m* or **nocchièro** *m* petty officer; (poet) pilot, helmsman
nocchieru·to -ta *adj* knotty
nòc·chio *m* (**-chi**) knot (*in wood*)
nocciòla *adj invar* hazel (*in color*) || *f* hazelnut; filbert
nocciolina *f* little nut; **nocciolina americana** peanut; roasted peanut
nòcciolo *m* stone, pit, kernel; **il noc-**

ciolo della questione the crux of the matter

nocciòlo m hazel (tree); filbert (tree)

nóce m walnut tree || f walnut (fruit); **noce del collo** Adam's apple; **noce di cocco** coconut; **noce di vitello** filet of veal; **noce moscata** nutmeg

nocévole adj harmful

noci·vo -va adj harmful, detrimental

nòdo m knot; crux, gist (of a question); junction; lump (in one's throat); (naut) knot; (phys) node; **lì è il nodo** there's the rub; **nodo d'amore** true-love knot; **nodo ferroviario** rail center, junction; **nodo scorsoio** noose; **nodo stradale** highway center, crossroads

nodó·so -sa [s] adj knotty

Noè m Noah

noi §5 pron pers we; us; **noi altri** we, e.g., **noi altri italiani** we Italians

nòia f boredom; bother, trouble; bug (in a motor); **venire a noia** (with dat) to weary; **dar noia** (with dat) to bother

noial·tri -tre pron we; us; **noialtri italiani** we Italians

noió·so -sa [s] adj boring, annoying

noleggiare §290 (noléggio) tr to rent; to hire, to charter || ref—**si noleggia, si noleggiano** for rent

noleggiatóre m hirer; lessor (e.g., of a car)

nolég·gio m (-gi) rent, lease; car rental; chartering; freightage

nolènte adj unwilling

nòlo m rent, hire; **a nolo** for hire

nòmade adj nomad, nomadic || mf nomad

nóme m name; fame; reputation; (gram) noun; **a nome di** on behalf of; **in nome di** in the name of; **nome commerciale** firm name; **nome depositato** registered name; **nome di battesimo** Christian name; **nome e cognome** full name

nomèa f name, reputation; notoriety

nomìgnolo m nickname; **affibbiare un nomignolo a** to nickname

nòmina f appointment; **di prima nomina** newly appointed

nominale adj nominal; noun

nominare (nòmino) tr to name, call; to mention; to elect; to appoint

nominati·vo -va adj nominative; with names in alphabetical order; (fin) registered || m nominative; name; model number

non adv no, not; none, e.g., **non troppo presto** none too soon; **non appena** as soon as; **non c'è di che** you are welcome; **non . . . che** but, only; **non è vero?** is it not so?, isn't it so? La traduzione in inglese di questa domanda dipende generalmente dalla proposizione che la precede. Se la proposizione è affermativa, l'interrogazione sarà negativa, p.es. **Lei mi scriverà, non è vero?** You will write me. Won't you? Se la proposizione è negativa, l'interrogazione sarà positiva, p.es. **Lei non beve birra, non è**

vero? You do not drink beer. Do you? Se il soggetto della proposizione è un nome sostantivo, sarà rappresentato nell'interrogazione da un pronome personale, p.es. **Giovanni ha finito, non è vero?** John has finished. Hasn't he?

nonagenà·rio -ria adj & mf (-ri -rie) nonagenarian

nonagèsi·mo -ma adj, pron & m ninetieth

nonconformi·sta mf (-sti -ste) nonconformist

noncurante adj careless, indifferent

noncuranza f carelessness, indifference

nondiméno conj yet, nevertheless

nòn·no -na mf grandparent || m grandfather || f grandmother

nonnulla m invar nothing, trifle

nò·no -na adj, m & pron ninth

nonostante prep in spite of, notwithstanding; **nonostante che** although, even though

nonpertanto adv nevertheless, still, yet

non plus ultra m ne plus ultra, acme

nonsènso m nonsense

non so che adj invar indefinable || m invar something indefinable

nontiscordardi·mé m (-mé) forget-me-not

nòrd m north

nòrdi·co -ca (-ci -che) adj Nordic; northern, north || mf northerner

nòrma f rule, regulation; **a norma di legge** according to law; **per Sua norma** for your guidance

normale adj normal; normative; perpendicular || f perpendicular line

normali·tà f (-tà) normality, normalcy

normalizzare [ddzz] tr to normalize, to standardize

Normandìa, la Normandy

norman·no -na adj & mf Norman || m Norseman

normati·vo -va adj normative || f normativeness

normògrafo m stencil

norvegése [s] adj & mf Norwegian

Norvègia, la Norway

nosocò·mio m (-mi) hospital

nossignóra (i.e., no signora) adv no, Madam

nossignóre (i.e., no signore) adv no, Sir

nostalgìa f nostalgia, longing; homesickness

nostàlgi·co -ca (-ci -che) adj nostalgic; homesick || m worshiper of the good old days (esp. of Fascism)

nostra·no -na adj domestic, national; home-grown; regional

nò·stro -stra §6 adj & pron poss

nostròmo m boatswain

nòta f mark; score; memorandum; list; bill, invoice; report (on a subordinate); (mus) note; **note caratteristiche** personal folder, efficiency report (of an employee); **prender nota di** to take down

notàbile adj notable, noteworthy || m notable

no·tàio m (-tài) notary (public); lawyer

notare (nòto) *tr* to mark, check; to note, to jot down; to observe; to bring out; **farsi notare** to attract attention, make oneself conspicuous; **nota bene** note well, take notice

notariale or **notarile** *adj* notarial

notazióne *f* notation; annotation; observation

nò·tes *m* (-tes) notebook

notévole *adj* noteworthy, remarkable

notìfi·ca *f* (-che) notification, notice; service (*e.g., of a summons*)

notificare §197 (**notìfico**) *tr* to report; to serve (*a summons*); to declare . . (*e.g., one's income*)

notificazióne *f* notification, notice; service (*e.g., of a summons*)

notizia *f* knowledge; report; piece of news; **aver notizie di** to hear from; **notizie** news; **una notizia** a news item

notizià·rio *m* (-ri) news; news report, news bulletin; (*rad*) newscast; **notiziario sportivo** sports page; (*rad, telv*) sports news

nò·to -ta *adj* known, well-known ‖ *m* south wind; (*coll*) swimming ‖ *f* see **nota**

notorie·tà *f* (-tà) general knowledge; affidavit; notoriety

notò·rio -ria *adj* (-ri -rie) well-known

nottàmbu·lo -la *adj* nighttime; night-wandering ‖ *mf* nightwalker; night owl

nottata *f* night; **far nottata bianca** to spend a sleepless night

nòtte *f* night; **buona notte** good night; **di notte** at night, by night, in the nighttime; **la notte di lunedì** Sunday night; Monday night; **lunedì notte** Monday night; **notte bianca** sleepless night; **notte di San Silvestro** New Year's Eve; watch night

nottetèmpo *adv*—**di nottetèmpo** at night, in the nighttime

nòttola *f* wooden latch; (zool) bat

nottolino *m* small wooden latch; ratchet, catch

nottùr·no -na *adj* nocturnal, night ‖ *m* nocturne

novanta *adj, m & pron* ninety

novantènne *adj* ninety-year-old ‖ *mf* ninety-year-old person

novantèsi·mo -ma *adj, m & pron* ninetieth

novantina *f* about ninety; **sulla novantina** about ninety years old

nòve *adj & pron* nine; **le nove** nine o'clock ‖ *m* nine; ninth (*in dates*)

novecentismo *m* twentieth-century arts and letters

novecenti·sta (-sti -ste) *adj* twentieth-century ‖ *mf* artist of the twentieth century

novecènto *adj, m & pron* nine hundred ‖ **il Novecento** the twentieth century

novèlla *f* short story; (poet) news

novelliè·re -ra *mf* storyteller; short-story writer

novelli·no -na *adj* early, tender, inexperienced, green

novellìstica *f* storytelling; fiction

novèl·lo -la *adj* fresh, young, tender; new ‖ *f* see **novella**

novèmbre *m* November

novenà·rio -ria *adj* (-ri -rie) nine-syllable

noverare (nòvero) *tr* to count; to enumerate; (poet) to remember

nòvero *m* number; class

novilù·nio *m* (-ni) new moon

novissi·mo -ma *adj* (lit) last, newest

novi·tà *f* (-tà) newness, originality; novelty, innovation; latest idea; late news

noviziato *m* novitiate; apprenticeship

novì·zio -zia (-zi -zie) *mf* novice; apprentice ‖ *f* novice (*in a convent*)

novocaina *f* novocaine

nozióne *f* notion, conception

nòzze *fpl* wedding, marriage; **nozze d'argento** silver wedding; **nozze d'oro** golden wedding

nube *f* cloud

nubifrà·gio *m* (-gi) cloudburst

nùbile *adj* unmarried, single (*woman*); marriageable ‖ *f* unmarried girl

nu·ca *f* (-che) nape of the neck, scruff

nucleare *adj* nuclear

nùcleo *m* nucleus; group; (elec) core

nudismo *m* nudism

nudi·sta *adj & mf* (-sti -ste) nudist

nudi·tà *f* (-tà) nudity, nakedness

nu·do -da *adj* naked, bare; barren; simple; **mettere a nudo** to lay bare; **nudo e crudo** stark-naked; destitute ‖ *m* nude

nùgolo *m* cloud; throng, swarm

nulla *pron* nothing ‖ *m invar* nothing; nothingness

nulla òsta *m* permission; visa

nullatenènte *adj* poor ‖ *mf* have-not

nullificare §197 (**nullìfico**) *tr* to nullify

nulli·tà *f* (-tà) nothingness; nonentity; invalidity (*of a document*)

nul·lo -la *adj* void, worthless ‖ **nullo** *pron* (poet) none, no one ‖ **nulla** *m & pron* see **nulla**

nume *m* divinity, deity

numerare (nùmero) *tr* to number

numeratóre *m* numerator; numbering machine

numèri·co -ca *adj* (-ci -che) numerical

nùmero *m* number; lottery ticket; size (*of shoes*); **numero dispari** odd number; **numero legale** quorum; **numero pari** even number

numeró·so -sa [s] *adj* numerous, large; harmonious

nùn·zio *m* (-zi) nuncio; (poet) news

nuòcere §206 *intr* to be harmful; (with *dat*) to harm

nuòra *f* daughter-in-law

nuotare (nuòto) *intr* to swim; to float; to wallow (*in wealth*)

nuotata *f* swim, dip, plunge

nuota·tóre -trice *mf* swimmer

nuòto *m* swimming; **gettarsi a nuoto** to jump into the water; **traversare a nuoto** to swim across

nuòva *f* news; late news

Nuòva York f New York
Nuòva Zelanda, la [dz] New Zealand
nuòvo -va *adj* new; **di nuovo** again; **nuovo di zecca** brand-new; **nuovo fiammante** brand-new; **nuovo venuto** new arrival || *m*—**il nuovo** the new || *f* see **nuova**
nùtria f coypu
nutrice f wet nurse; (lit) provider
nutriènte *adj* nourishing
nutriménto *m* nourishment
nutrire §176 & (**nútro**) *tr* to nourish;
to nurture; to harbor (*e.g., hatred*) || *ref*—**nutrirsi di** to feed on or upon
nutriti·vo -va *adj* nutritious, nutritive
nutri·to -ta *adj* well-fed; strong; rich (*food*); brisk, heavy (*gunfire*)
nutrizióne f nutrition; food
nùvo·lo -la *adj* cloudy || *m* cloudy weather; (lit) cloud; (fig) swarm || *f* cloud
nuvoló·so -sa [s] *adj* cloudy
nuziale *adj* wedding, nuptial
nuzialità f marriage rate

O

O, o [o] *m* & f thirteenth letter of the Italian alphabet
o *conj* or; now; **o . . . o** either . . . or; whether . . . or || *interj* oh!
òa·si f (-si) oasis
obbediènte *adj* var of **ubbidiente**
obbediènza f obedience
obbedire §176 *tr* & *intr* var of **ubbidire**
obbiettare (**obbiètto**) *tr* & *intr* var of **obiettare**
obbligare §209 (**òbbligo**) *tr* to oblige; to compel, to force || *ref* to obligate oneself
obbligatìssi·mo -ma *adj* much obliged
obbligatò·rio -ria *adj* (-rì -rie) compulsory, obligatory
obbligazióne f obligation; burden; (com) debenture, bond
obbligazioni·sta *mf* (-sti -ste) bondholder
òbbli·go *m* (-ghi) obligation; duty; **d'obbligo** obligatory, mandatory; **fare d'obbligo a qlcu** + *inf* to be necessary for s.o. to + *inf, e.g.,* **gli fa d'obbligo lavorare** it is necessary for him to work
obbrò·brio *m* (-bri) opprobrium, disgrace; **obbrobri** insults
obbrobrió·so -sa [s] *adj* opprobrious, disgraceful
obeli·sco *m* (-schi) obelisk
obera·to -ta *adj* overburdened
obesità f obesity
obè·so -sa *adj* obese, stout
òbice *m* howitzer
obiettare (**obiètto**) *tr* & *intr* to argue; to object
obietti·vo -va *adj* & *m* objective
obiettóre *m* objector; **obiettore di coscienza** conscientious objector
obiezióne f objection
obitò·rio *m* (-ri) morgue
oblare (**òblo**) *tr* to willingly pay (*a fine*)
obla·tóre -**trice** *mf* donor
oblazióne f donation; (eccl) oblation; (law) payment of a fine
obliare §119 *tr* (lit) to forget
oblì·o *m* (-i) (lit) oblivion
oblì·quo -qua *adj* oblique
obliterare (**oblìtero**) *tr to* obliterate, cancel
o·blò *m* (-blò) (naut) porthole; **oblò di accesso** door (*of space capsule*)
oblun·go -**ga** *adj* (-ghi -ghe) oblong
òbo·e *m* (-e) oboe
oboi·sta *mf* (-sti -ste) oboist
òbolo *m* mite
ò·ca f (-che) goose; gander
ocarina f ocarina, sweet potato
occasionale *adj* chance; immediate (*cause*)
occasionare (**occasióno**) *tr* to occasion
occasióne f occasion; opportunity; ground, pretext; bargain; **all'occasione** on occasion; **d'occasione** second-hand; occasional (*verses*)
occhiàia f eye socket; **occhiaie** rings under the eyes
occhia·làio *m* (-lài) optician
occhiale *adj* eye, ocular || **occhiali** *mpl* glasses; goggles; **occhiali antisole** sunglasses; **occhiali a stringinaso** nose glasses
occhialétto *m* lorgnon; monocle
occhiata f glance
occhieggiare §290 (**occhiéggio**) *tr* to eye || *intr* to peep
occhièllo *m* buttonhole; boutonniere; eyelet; half title; subhead
occhièra f eyecup
òc·chio *m* (-chi) eye; speck of grease (*in soup*); handle (*of scissors*); ring (*of stirrup*); (typ) face; (fig) bit; **a occhio e croce** at a rough guess; **a quattr'occhi** in private; **battere gli occhi** to blink; **cavarsi gli occhi** to strain one's eyes; **dar nell'occhio** to attract attention; **di buon occhio** favorably; **fare l'occhio a** to get used to; **fare tanto d'occhio** to be amazed, to open one's eyes wide; **lasciare gli occhi su** to covet; **non chiudere un occhio** not to sleep a wink; **occhio!** watch out!; **occhio della testa** outrageous price; **occhio di bue** (naut) porthole; **occhio di cubia** (naut) hawsehole; **occhio di pavone** (zool) peacock butterfly; **occhio di triglia** sheep's eyes; **occhio pesto** black eye; **occhio pollino** corn (*on toes*); **tenere d'occhio** to keep an eye on
occhiolino *m* small eye; **far l'occhiolino** to wink
occidentale *adj* western, occidental
occidènte *adj* (poet) setting (*sun*) || *m* west, occident

occìpite *m* occipital bone

occlusióne *f* occlusion

occlusì·vo -va *adj & f* occlusive

occlu·so -sa *adj* occluded

occorrènte *adj* necessary || *m* necessary; (lit) occurrence

occorrènza *f* necessity; all'occorrenza if need be

occórrere §139 *intr* (ESSERE) to happen; (with *dat*) to need, e.g., gli occorre dell'olio he needs oil || *impers* (ESSERE)—occorre it is necessary

occultaménto *m* concealment

occultare *tr & ref* to hide

occul·to -ta *adj* occult; (lit) hidden

occupante *adj* occupying || *m* occupant

occupare (òccupo) *tr* to occupy; to employ || *ref* to take employment; occuparsi di to busy oneself with, to mind; to attend to

occupa·to -ta *adj* occupied; busy

occupazionale *adj* occupational

occupazióne *f* occupation

oceàni·co -ca *adj* (-ci -che) oceanic

ocèano *m* ocean

òcra *f* ocher

oculare *adj* ocular; see testimone || *m* eyepiece

oculatézza *f* circumspection, prudence

ocula·to -ta *adj* circumspect, prudent

oculì·sta *mf* (-sti -ste) oculist

od *conj* or

odalì·sca *f* (-sche) odalisque

òde *f* ode

odepòri·co -ca (-ci -che) *adj* (lit) travel || *m* (lit) travelogue

odiare §287 (òdio) *tr* to hate

odièr·no -na *adj* today's, current

ò·dio *m* (-di) hatred; avere in odio to hate; essere in odio a to be hated by; odió·so -sa [*s*] *adj* hateful, odious

odissèa *f* odyssey || Odissea *f* Odyssey

Odissèo *m* Odysseus

odontoìa·tra *mf* (-tri -tre) doctor of dental surgery, dentist

odontoiatrìa *f* odontology, dentistry

odorare (odóro) *tr & intr* to smell

odora·to -ta *adj* (poet) fragrant || *m* smell

odóre *m* smell, odor, scent; cattivo odore bad odor; odori herbs, spice

odoró·so -sa [*s*] *adj* odorous, fragrant

offèndere §148 *tr & intr* to offend || *ref* to take offense

offensì·vo -va *adj & f* offensive

offensóre *m* offender

offerènte *mf* bidder; miglior offerente highest bidder

offèrta *f* offer; offering, donation; (at an auction) bid; (com) supply

offésa [*s*] *f* offense; wrongdoing; ravage (of time); da offesa (mil) offensive; recarsi a offesa qlco to regard s.th as offensive

officìna *f* shop, workshop; officina meccanica machine shop

offició·so -sa [*s*] *adj* helpful, obliging

offrire §207 *tr* to offer; to sponsor (a radio or TV program); to dedicate (a book); to bid (at an auction); (com) to tender || *ref* to offer oneself, to volunteer

offuscare §197 *tr* to darken, obscure; to obfuscate; to dim (mind; eyes) || *ref* to grow dark; to grow dim

oftàlmi·co -ca *adj* (-ci -che) opthalmic

oftalmòlo·go -ga *mf* (-gi -ghe) ophthalmologist

oggettività *f* objectivity

oggettì·vo -va *adj & m* objective

oggètto *m* object; subject, argument; article; oggetti preziosi valuables

òggi *m* today; dall'oggi al domani suddenly; overnight || *adv* today; d'oggi in poi henceforth; oggi a otto a week hence; oggi come oggi at present; oggi è un anno one year ago

oggidì *m invar & adv* nowadays

oggigiórno *m invar & adv* nowadays

ogiva *f* ogive, pointed arch; nose cone

ógni *adj indef invar* each; every, e.g., ogni due giorni every two days; ogni cosa everything; ogni tanto every now and then; per ogni dove (lit) everywhere

ogniqualvòlta *conj* whenever

Ognissan·ti *m* (-ti) All Saints' Day

ognitèmpo *adj invar* all-weather

-ógno·lo -la *suf adj* -ish, e.g., giallognolo yellowish

ognóra *adv* (lit) always

ognu·no -na *adj* (obs) each || *pron* each one, everyone

oh *interj* oh!

òhi *interj* ouch!

ohibò *interj* fie!

ohimè *interj* alas!

ohm *m* (ohm) ohm

olanda *f* Dutch linen || l'Olanda *f* Holland

olandése [*s*] *adj* Dutch || *m* Dutch (language); Dutchman; Dutch cheese || *f* Dutch woman

oleandro *m* oleander

oleà·rio -ria *adj* (-ri -rie) oil

olea·to -ta *adj* oiled

oleifì·cio *m* (-ci) oil mill

oleodótto *m* pipeline

oleó·so -sa [*s*] *adj* oily

olezzare [ddzz] (olézzo) *intr* (lit) to smell sweet

olézzo [ddzz] *m* perfume, fragrance

olfatto *m* smell

oliare §287 (òlio) *tr* to oil

oliatóre *m* oiler, oil can

olìbano *m* frankincense

olièra *f* cruet

oligarchìa *f* oligarchy

olimpìade *f* Olympiad

olìmpi·co -ca *adj* (-ci -che) Olympic; Olympian

olimpiòni·co -ca *adj* (-ci -che) Olympic || *mf* Olympic athlete

ò·lio *m* (-li) oil; ad olio oil, e.g., quadro ad olio oil painting; olio di fegato di merluzzo cod-liver oil; olio di lino linseed oil; olio di ricino castor oil; olio solare sun-tan lotion

oliva *f* olive

oliva·stro -stra *adj* livid; swarthy || *m* wild olive (tree)

olivéto *m* olive grove

Olivièro *m* Oliver

olivo *m* olive tree

ólmo *m* elm tree
olocàu·sto -sta *adj* (lit) burnt; (lit) sacrificed || *m* holocaust; sacrifice
ològra·fo -fa *adj* holographic
olóna *f* sailcloth, canvas
oltracciò *adv* besides
oltraggiare §290 *tr* to outrage; to insult
oltràg·gio *m* (-gi) outrage; offense; ravages (*of time*); **oltraggio al pudore** offense to public morals; **oltraggio al tribunale** contempt of court
oltraggió·so -sa [s] *adj* outrageous
oltranza *f*—a oltranza to the bitter end
oltranzí·sta *mf* (-sti -ste) (pol) extremist
óltre *adv* beyond; ahead; further; **oltre a** apart from; in addition to; **troppo oltre** too far || *prep* beyond; past; more than
oltrecortina *adj invar* beyond-the-iron-curtain || *m* country beyond the iron curtain
oltremare *m invar* country overseas || *adv* overseas
oltremisura *adv* (lit) beyond measure
oltremòdo *adv* (lit) exceedingly
oltrepassare *tr* to overstep; to cross (*a river*); to be beyond (. . . *years old*); (sports) to overtake
oltretómba *m*—**l'oltretomba** the life beyond
omàg·gio *m* (-gi) homage; compliment; **in omaggio** complimentary; **rendere omaggio a** to pay tribute to
òmaro *m* Norway lobster
ombelì·co *m* (-chi) navel
ómbra *f* shade; shadow; umbrage; form, mass; **nemmeno per ombra** not in the least
ombreggiare §290 (ombréggio) *tr* to shade
ombrèlla *f* shade (*of trees*); (bot) umbel; (coll) umbrella
ombrel·làio *m* (-lài) umbrella maker
ombrellino *m* parasol
ombrèllo *m* umbrella
ombrellóne *m* beach umbrella
ombró·so -sa [s] *adj* shady; touchy; skittish (*horse*)
omelette *f* (omelette) omelet
omelìa *f* homily
omeopàti·co -ca (-ci -che) *adj* homeopathic || *m* homeopathist
omèri·co -ca *adj* (-ci -che) Homeric
òmero *m* (anat) humerus; (lit) shoulder
omertà *f* code of silence of underworld
ométtere §198 *tr* to omit
ométto *m* little man; (coll) clothes hanger; (billiards) pin; (archit) king post
omicì·da (-di -de) *adj* homicidal, murderous || *mf* homicide, murderer
omicì·dio *m* (-di) homicide, murder; **omicidio colposo** (law) manslaughter; **omicidio doloso** (law) first-degree murder
ominó·so -sa [s] *adj* (lit) ominous
omissióne *f* omission
òmni·bus *m* (-bus) omnibus; way train
omnisciènte *adj* all-knowing, omniscient
omogène·o -a *adj* homogeneous
omologare §209 (omòlogo) *tr* to con-

firm, ratify; to probate (*a will*); (sports) to validate
omòni·mo -ma *adj* of the same name || *m* namesake; homonym
omosessuale [s] *adj* & *mf* homosexual
ón·cia *f* (-ce) ounce; **oncia a oncia** little by little
ónda *f* wave; **a onde** wavy; wavily; **essere in onda** (rad, telv) to be on the air; **farsi le onde** to have one's hair waved; **mettere in onda** (rad, telv) to put on the air; **onda crespa** whitecap; **onda portante** (rad, telv) carrier wave
ondata *f* wave, billow; gust (*e.g., of smoke*); rush (*of blood*); wave (*of cold weather*)
ondatra *f* muskrat
ónde *pron* from which; of which || *adv* whereof; hence; (poet) wherefrom || *prep* **onde + inf** in order to || *conj* **onde + subj** so that
ondeggiante *adj* waving, swaying
ondeggiare §290 (ondéggio) *intr* to wave, sway; to waver
ondìna *f* mermaid; (mythol) undine; (mythol) mermaid
ondó·so -sa [s] *adj* wavy
ondulare (óndulo & òndulo) *tr* to wave; to corrugate (*e.g., metal*) || *intr* to sway
ondula·to -ta *adj* wavy (*hair*); corrugated (*e.g., metal*); bumpy (*road*)
ondulazióne *f* undulation; **ondulazione permanente** permanent wave
-óne -óna *suf mf* big, e.g., **librone** big book; **dormigliona** big sleeper || **-óne** *suf m* (applies to both sexes) big, e.g., **donnone** *m* big woman
ònere *m* (lit) onus, burden
oneró·so -sa [s] *adj* onerous, burdensome
onestà *f* honesty; (poet) modesty
onè·sto -sta *adj* honest; fair; (poet) modest || *m* moderate amount; honest gain; honest person
ònice *m* onyx
onnipossènte & **onnipotènte** *adj* almighty, omnipotent
onnisciènte *adj* omniscient
onniveggènte *adj* all-seeing
onnìvo·ro -ra *adj* omnivorous
onomàsti·co -ca (-ci -che) *adj* onomastic || *m* name day || *f* study of proper names
onomatopèi·co -ca *adj* (-ci -che) onomatopeic
onoràbile *adj* honorable
onoranza *f* honor; **onoranze** homage; **onoranze funebri** obsequies
onorare (onóro) *tr* to honor || *ref* to deem it an honor
onorà·rio -ria (-ri -rie) *adj* honorary || *m* fee, honorarium
onora·to -ta *adj* honored; honest; honorable
onóre *m* honor; **d'onore** honest, e.g., **uomo d'onore** honest man; **estremi onori** last rites; **fare gli onori di casa** to receive guests; **fare onore a** to honor; **onore al merito** credit where

credit is due; **onor del mento** (lit) beard

onorévole *adj* honorable || *m* honorable member (*of parliament*)

onorificènza *f* dignity; decoration

onorìfi·co -ca *adj* (**-ci -che**) honorific; honorary (*e.g., title*)

ónta *f* dishonor, shame; **a onta di** in spite of; **avere onta** to be ashamed; **fare onta a** to bring shame upon; **in onta a** against

ontano *m* alder

O.N.U. (acronym) *f* (**Organizzazione delle Nazioni Unite**) United Nations, U.N.

onu·sto -sta *adj* (poet) laden·

opa·co -ca *adj* (**-chi -che**) opaque

opale *m* opal

opali·no -na *adj* opaline || *f* shiny cardboard; luster (*fabric*)

òpera *f* work; organization, foundation; day's work; (mus) opera; **mettere in opera** to install; to start work on; to make ready; to begin using; **opera di consultazione** reference work; **opera morta** (naut) upper works; **opera viva** (naut) quickwork; **per opera di** thanks to

ope·ràio -ràia (**-ràl -ràie**) *adj* workman's, worker's; working || *m* workman, worker; **operaio a cottimo** pieceworker; **operaio a giornata** day laborer; **operaio specializzato** craftsman, skilled workman || *f* workwoman

operante *adj* actively engaged; operative

operare (**òpero**) *tr* to operate; to work (*a miracle*); (surg) to operate on || *intr* to operate; to be actively engaged || *ref* to be operated on; to occur, take place

operatì·vo -va *adj* operative; operations, e.g., **ricerca operativa** operations research

opera·to -ta *adj* operated; embossed || *m* behavior; patient operated on

opera·tóre -trice *mf* operator || *m* (mov) cameraman

operatò·rio -ria *adj* (**-ri -rie**) surgical (*operation*); operating (*room*); (math) operational

operazióne *f* operation; transaction

operétta *f* short work; (mus) operetta

operìsti·co -ca *adj* (**-ci -che**) operatic

operosi·tà [*s*] *f* (**-tà**) industry

operó·so -sa [*s*] *adj* industrious; active

opi·mo -ma *adj* (lit) fat; rich, fertile

opinare *intr* to opine, deem

opinióne *f* opinion

opòs·sum *m* (**-sum**) opossum

oppia·to -ta *adj* opiate (*mixed with opium*); dulled by drugs || *m* opiate (*medicine containing opium*)

òppio *m* opium

oppiòmane *adj* opium-eating; opium-smoking || *mf* opium addict

oppórre §218 *tr* to oppose; to offer, put up (*resistance*) || *ref* to be opposite; **opporsi a** to oppose, to be against

opportuni·sta *mf* (**-sti -ste**) opportunist

opportuni·tà *f* (**-tà**) opportunity; opportuneness

opportu·no -na *adj* opportune

opposi·tóre -trice *mf* opponent

opposizióne *f* opposition; (law) appeal; **fare opposizione a** to object to

oppó·sto -sta *adj* opposite; contrary || *m* opposite; **all'opposto** on the contrary

oppressióne *f* oppression

oppressì·vo -va *adj* oppressive

opprès·so -sa *adj* oppressed; overcome, overwhelmed || **oppressi** *mpl* oppressed people

oppressóre *m* oppressor

opprimènte *adj* oppressive

opprìmere §131 *tr* to oppress; to overcome, overwhelm; to weigh down

oppugnare *tr* to refute, contradict

oppure *adv* otherwise || *conj* or else; or rather

optare (**òpto**) *intr* to choose; (com) to exercise an option

optometrì·sta *mf* (**-sti -ste**) optometrist

opulèn·to -ta *adj* opulent

opùscolo *m* booklet, brochure, pamphlet; **opuscolo d'informazioni** instruction manual

opzióne *f* option

ór *adv* now; **or ora** right now; **or sono** ago

óra *f* hour; time; period (*in school*); **alla buon'ora!** finally!; **a ore by the** hour; **a tarda ora** late; **che ora è?** or **che ore sono?** what time is it?; **da un'ora all'altra** from one moment to the next; **dell'ultima ora** up-to-date (*news*); **di buon'ora** early; early in the morning; **di ora in ora** at any moment; **d'ora in avanti** from this moment on; **d'ora in poi** from now on; **far l'ora** to kill time; **fin ora** until now; **non vedere l'ora di** + *inf* to be hardly able to wait until + *ind*; **ora di cena** suppertime; **ora di punta** rush hour, peak hour; **ora legale** daylight-saving time; **ore piccole** late hours; **un'ora di orologio** one full hour || *adv* now

oràcolo *m* oracle

òra·fo -fa *adj* goldsmith's || *m* goldsmith

orale *adj* & *m* oral

oralménte *adv* orally; by word of mouth

oramài *adv* now; already

oran·go *m* (**-ghi**) orangutan

orà·rio -ria *adj* (**-ri -rie**) hourly; per hour; clockwise || *m* timetable; schedule; roster; **essere in orario** to be on time; **orario di lavoro** working hours; **orario d'ufficio** office hours

ora·tóre -trice *mf* orator

oratò·rio -ria *adj* (**-ri -rie**) oratorical || *m* (eccl) oratory; (mus) oratorio || *f* oratory, public speaking

orazióne *f* oration; prayer; **orazione domenicale** Lord's Prayer

orbare (**òrbo**) *tr* (lit) to bereave; (lit) to deprive

òrbe *f* (lit) orb; (lit) world

orbène *adv* well

òrbita *f* orbit; (fig) sphere
orbitare (**òrbito**) *intr* to orbit
orbitazióne *f* orbiting
òr·bo -ba *adj* bereaved; deprived; blind ‖ *m* blind man
òrca *f* killer whale
Òrcadi *fpl* Orkney Islands
orchèstra *f* orchestra; band; orchestra pit
orchestrale *adj* orchestral ‖ *mf* orchestra player, orchestra performer
orchestrare (**orchèstro**) *tr* to orchestrate; (fig) to organize
orchestrina *f* dance band; dance-band music
orchidèa *f* orchid
ór·cio *m* (**-ci**) jar, jug, crock
orciòlo *m*—a orciolo puckered up (*lips*)
òr·co *m* (**-chi**) ogre
òrda *f* horde
ordàlia *f* (hist) ordeal
ordigno *m* gadget, contrivance; tool; **ordigno esplosivo** infernal machine
ordinale *adj* & *m* ordinal
ordinaménto *m* disposition; regulation
ordinanza *f* ordinance; (mil) orderly; **d'ordinanza** regulation (*e.g., uniform*); **in ordinanza** (mil) in formation
ordinare (**órdino**) *tr* to order; to straighten up; to range; to regulate; to ordain; to trim
ordinà·rio -ria (**-ri -rie**) *adj* ordinary; plain; inferior; workday (*suit*) ‖ *m* ordinary; full professor; **d'ordinario** ordinarily, usually
ordina·to -ta *adj* orderly, tidy; ordained ‖ *f* ordinate; straightening up; (aer) frame; (naut) bulkhead
ordinazióne *f* order; ordination
órdine *m* order; row; tier; series (*e.g., of years*); college (*e.g., of surgeons*); nature (*of things*); (law) warrant, writ; **in ordine a** concerning; **ordine del giorno** order of the day; **ordine d'idee** train of thought
ordire §176 *tr* to warp (*cloth*); to hatch (*a plot*)
ordi·to -ta *adj* plotted ‖ *m* warp (*of fabric*)
orécchia *f* ear; dog-ear; **con le orecchie tese** all ears
orecchiale *m* earphone (*of sonar equipment*)
orecchiétta *f* (anat) auricle
orecchino *m* earring
oréc·chio *m* (**-chi**) ear; hearing; dog-ear; moldboard; **fare orecchio da mercante** to turn a deaf ear ‖ *m* (**orécchia** *fpl*) (archaic) ear
orecchióne *m* long-eared bat; (mil) trunnion; **orecchioni** (pathol) mumps
oréfice *m* goldsmith; jeweler
oreficerìa *f* goldsmith shop; jewelry shop
orfanézza *f* orphanage (*condition*)
òrfa·no -na *adj* orphaned ‖ *mf* orphan
orfanotrò·fio *m* (**-fi**) orphanage (*institution*)
Orfèo *m* Orpheus
organdì *m* organdy
organétto *m* hand organ; mouth organ; **organetto di Barberia** hand organ

orgàni·co -ca (**-ci -che**) *adj* organic ‖ *m* personnel, staff ‖ *f* (mil) organization
organigram·ma *m* (**-mi**) organization chart
organino *m* hand organ, barrel organ
organismo *m* organism
organi·sta *mf* (**-sti -ste**) organist
organizzare [ddzz] *tr* to organize
organizza·tóre -trice [ddzz] *mf* organizer
organizzazióne [ddzz] *f* organization; **Organizzazione delle Nazioni Unite** United Nations
òrgano *m* organ; part (*of a machine*); **organo di stampa** mouthpiece
orgasmo *m* orgasm; agitation, excitement
òr·gia *f* (**-ge**) orgy
orgó·glio *m* (**-gli**) pride
orgoglió·so -sa [s] *adj* proud
orientale *adj* & *mf* oriental; Oriental
orientaménto *m* orientation; bearing; trend; trim (*of sail*); **orientamento scolastico e professionale** aptitude test; vocational guidance
orientare (**oriènto**) *tr* to orient; to guide; to trim (*a sail*) ‖ *ref* to find one's bearings
oriènte *m* orient; grand'oriente grand lodge ‖ **Oriente** *m* Orient, East; **Estremo Oriente** Far East; **Medio Oriente** Middle East; **Vicino Oriente** Near East
orifi·zio *m* (**-zi**) orifice, opening
orìgano *m* wild marjoram
originale *adj* original; odd ‖ *mf* queer character, odd person ‖ *m* original; copy (*for printer*)
originare (**orìgino**) *tr* to originate ‖ *intr* (ESSERE) & *ref* to originate
originà·rio -ria *adj* (**-ri -rie**) originating; native; original
orìgine *f* origin; source; extraction
origliare §280 *intr* to eavesdrop
origlière *m* (lit) pillow
orina *f* var of urina
orinale *m* chamber pot, urinal
orinare *tr* & *intr* to urinate
orina·tóio *m* (**-tói**) urinal, comfort station
oriòlo *m* (orn) oriole
oriun·do -da *adj* native ‖ *m* (sports) native son
orizzontale [ddzz] *adj* horizontal ‖ **orizzontali** *fpl* horizontal words (*in crossword puzzle*)
orizzontare [ddzz] (**orizzónto**) *tr* to orient ‖ *ref* to get one's bearings
orizzónte [ddzz] *m* horizon
Orlando *m* Roland
orlare (**órlo**) *tr* to hem, border; **orlare a zigzag** to pink
órlo *m* edge; brim; hem, border; (fig) brink; **orlo a giorno** hemstitch
órma *f* footprint; **orme** remains, vestiges; **calcare le orme di** to follow the footsteps of
ormeggiare §290 (**orméggio**) *tr* & *ref* (naut) to moor
ormég·gio *m* (**-gi**) mooring; **mollare gli ormeggi** (naut) to cast off
ormóne *m* hormone

ornamentale *adj* ornamental

ornaménto *m* ornament

ornare (órno) *tr* to adorn

orna·to -ta *adj* adorned; ornate ‖ *m* ornament; ornamental design

ornitòlo·go -ga *mf* (**-gi -ghe**) ornithologist

òro *m* gold; (fig) money; **d'oro** gold, golden; **ori** gold objects; jewels; suit of Neapolitan cards corresponding to diamonds; **oro zecchino** pure gold; **per tutto l'oro del mondo** for all the world

orologeria *f* watchmaking; clockmaking; watchmaker's shop

orolo·giàio *m* (**-giài**) watchmaker; clockmaker

orolò·gio *m* (**-gi**) watch; clock; **orologio a pendolo** clock; **orologio a polvere** sandglass; **orologio a scatto** digital clock; **orologio da polso** wristwatch; **orologio della morte** deathwatch; **orologio solare** sundial

oròscopo *m* horoscope

orpèllo *m* Dutch gold; (fig) tinsel

orrèndo *m* horrible

orribile *adj* horrible

òrri·do -da *adj* horrid ‖ *m* horridness; gorge, ravine

orripilante *adj* bloodcurdling, hair-raising

orróre *m* horror; awe; **aver in** or **per orrore** to loath; **fare orrore a** to horrify

órsa *f* she-bear ‖ **Orsa** *f*—**Orsa maggiore** Great Bear; **Orsa minore** Little Bear

orsacchiòtto *m* bear cub; Teddy bear

ór·so -sa *mf* bear; **orso bianco** polar bear; **orso grigio** grizzly bear ‖ *f* see **orsa**

orsù *interj* come on!

ortàg·gio *m* (**-gi**) vegetable

ortàglia *f* vegetable garden; vegetable

ortènsia *f* hydrangea

orti·ca *f* (**-che**) nettle; hives

orticària *f* hives, nettle rash

orticoltóre *m* truck gardener; horticulturist

òrto *m* garden, vegetable garden; (lit) sunrise; **orto botanico** botanical garden; **orto di guerra** Victory garden

ortodòs·so -sa *adj* orthodox ‖ *m* Greek Catholic

ortografia *f* orthography; spelling

ortola·no -na *adj* garden ‖ *m* truck farmer, gardener

ortopèdi·co -ca (**-ci -che**) *adj* orthopedic ‖ *m* orthopedist

òrza *f* bowline; windward; **andare all'orza** to sail close to the wind

orzaiòlo [dz] *m* (pathol) sty

orzare (òrzo) *intr* to sail close to the wind; to luff

orzata [dz] *f* orgeat

orzata *f* (naut) luff

òrzo [dz] *m* barley

osannare *intr* to cry or sing hosanna; **osannare a** to acclaim, applaud

osare (òso) *intr* to dare

osceni·tà *f* (**-tà**) obscenity

oscè·no -na *adj* obscene; (coll) horrible

oscillante *adj* oscillating

oscillare *intr* to oscillate; to swing; to wobble; to waver, hesitate

oscillazióne *f* oscillation; fluctuation

oscuraménto *m* darkening, dimming; blackout

oscurare *tr* to darken; to blot out; to dim ‖ *ref* to get dark; **oscurarsi in volto** to frown

oscuri·tà *f* (**-tà**) obscurity; darkness; ignorance

oscu·ro -ra *adj* obscure, dark; opaque (*style*) ‖ *m* obscurity, darkness; **essere all'oscuro di** to be in the dark about

osmòsi *f* osmosis

ospedale *m* hospital

ospedalière *m* hospital worker

ospedalière -ra *adj* hospital ‖ *m* hospitaler

ospedalizzare [ddzz] *tr* to hospitalize

ospitale *adj* hospitable ‖ *m* hospital

ospitali·tà *f* (**-tà**) hospitality

ospitare (òspito) *tr* to lodge, shelter, accommodate; to entertain; (sports) to play (*an opposing team*) at home

òspite *mf* host; guest; **andarsene insalutato ospite** to take French leave; **ospiti** company (*guests at home*)

ospì·zio *m* (**-zi**) hospice; hostel; (lit) hospitality; **ospizio dei vecchi** nursing home; **ospizio di mendicità** poorhouse

ossatura *f* frame, framework; skeleton

òsse·o -a *adj* bony

ossequènte *adj* (lit) respectful; (lit) reverent

ossequiare §287 (**ossèquio**) *tr* to pay one's respects to; to honor

ossè·quio *m* (**-qui**) respect; reverence; **i miei ossequi** my best regards; **in ossequio a** in conformity with; **porgere i propri ossequi a** to pay one's respects to

ossequió·so -sa [s] *adj* obsequious; respectful

osservante *adj* & *m* observant

osservanza *f* observance; deference

osservare (ossèrvo) *tr* to observe

osserva·tóre -trice *adj* observing, observant ‖ *mf* observer

osservatò·rio *m* (**-ri**) observatory

osservazióne *f* observation; rebuke

ossessionare (ossessióno) *tr* to obsess; to harass, bedevil

ossessióne *f* obsession

ossès·so -sa *adj* possessed ‖ *mf* person possessed

ossìa *conj* or; to wit

ossidante *adj* oxidizing ‖ *m* oxidizer

ossidare (òssido) *tr* & *ref* to oxidize

òssido *m* oxide; **ossido di carbone** carbon monoxide

ossìdulo *m* protoxide; **ossidulo di azoto** nitrous oxide

ossificare §197 (ossìfico) *tr* & *ref* to ossify

ossigenare (ossìgeno) *tr* to oxygenate; to bleach (*the hair*); to infuse strength into ‖ *ref* to bleach (*the hair*)

ossìgeno *m* oxygen; (fig) transfusion, shot in the arm

ossìto·no -na *adj* & *m* oxytone

òs•so m (-si) bone (of animal); stone (of fruit); osso di balena whalebone; osso di seppia cuttlebone; osso duro da rodere hard nut to crack; osso sacro sacrum; rimetterci l'osso del collo to be thoroughly ruined; rompersi l'osso del collo to break one's neck || m (-sa fpl) bone (of a person); avere le ossa rotte to be dead-tired

ossu•to -ta adj bony; scrawny

ostacolare (ostàcolo) tr to hinder; to obstruct; ostacolare l'azione (sports) to interfere

ostàcolo m obstacle; obstruction; (golf) hazard; (sports) hurdle

ostàg•gio m (-gi) hostage

ostare (òsto) intr (lit) to be in the way; (with dat) to hinder; nulla osta no objection, permission granted

òste ostéssa mf innkeeper || oste m & f (lit) army in the field || m (poet) enemy

ostèllo m hostel; (poet) abode

ostentare (ostènto) tr to show, display; to affect, feign

ostenta•to -ta adj affected, ostentatious

ostentazióne f show, ostentation

osteopatìa f osteopathy

osteria f tavern, inn, taproom

ostéssa f see oste

ostètri•ca f (-che) midwife

ostetricia f obstetrics

ostètri•co -ca (-ci -che) adj obstetrical || m obstetrician || f see ostetrica

òstia f wafer; Host; sacrificial victim

òsti•co -ca adj (-ci -che) hard; (lit) repugnant, distasteful

ostile adj hostile

ostili•tà f (-tà) hostility

ostinare ref to be stubborn; to persist

ostina•to -ta adj obstinate; persistent

ostinazióne f obstinacy

ostracismo m ostracism; dare l'ostracismo a to ostracize

ostracizzare [ddzz] tr (poet) to ostracize

òstri•ca f (-che) oyster; ostrica perlifera pearl oyster

ostri•càio m (-cài) oyster bed; oysterman

ostruire §176 tr to obstruct; to stop up

ostruzióne f obstruction

Otèllo m Othello

otorinolaringoia•tra mf (-tri -tre) ear, nose, and throat specialist, otorhinolaryngologist

ótre f wineskin; otre di vento windbag (person)

ottàni•co -ca adj (-ci -che) octane

ottano m octane

ottanta adj, m & pron eighty

ottantènne adj eighty-year-old || mf eighty-year-old person

ottantèsi•mo -ma adj, m & pron eightieth

ottantina f about eighty; essere sull'ottantina to be about eighty years old

ottava f octave

Ottaviano m Octavian

ottavino m (mus) piccolo; (com) commission of ⅛ of 1%

otta•vo -va adj & pron eighth || m eighth; octavo || f see ottava

ottemperare (ottèmpero) intr (with dat) to obey; ottemperare a to comply with

ottenebrare (ottènebro) tr to becloud

ottenére §271 tr to obtain, get

ottétto m octet

òtti•co -ca (-ci -che) adj optic(al) || m optician || f optics

ottimismo m optimism

ottimi•sta mf (-sti -ste) optimist

ottimìsti•co -ca adj (-ci -che) optimistic

òtti•mo -ma adj very good, excellent || m best; highest rating

òtto adj & pron eight; le otto eight o'clock || m eight; eighth (in dates); (sports) racing shell with eight oarsmen; otto giorni a week; otto volante roller coaster

ottóbre m October

ottocenté•sco -sca adj (-schi -sche) nineteenth-century

ottocènto adj, m & pron eight hundred || l'Ottocento the nineteenth century

ottoma•no -na adj & m Ottoman || m ottoman (fabric) || f ottoman (sofa)

ottomila adj, m & pron eight thousand

ottoname m brassware

ottonare (ottóno) tr to coat with brass

ottóne m brass; ottoni (mus) brasses || Ottone m Otto

ottuagenà•rio -ria adj & mf (-ri -rie) octogenerian

ottùndere §208 tr (fig) to deaden; (lit) to blunt

otturare tr to fill; to plug; to stop; to obstruct, stop up (e.g., a channel) || ref to clog up

otturatóre m breechblock; (phot, mov) shutter; (mach) cutoff (of cylinder)

otturazióne f filling (of tooth)

ottu•so -sa adj obtuse; blunt

ovàia f ovary

ovale adj oval || m oval; oval face

ovatta f wadding; absorbent cotton

ovattare tr to pad, wad; to muffle

ovazióne f ovation

óve adv (lit) where || conj (lit) if; (poet) while

òvest m west

Ovìdio m Ovid

ovile m sheepcote, fold

ovi•no -na adj ovine || ovini mpl sheep

òvo m var of uovo

ovoidale adj egg-shaped

òvulo m pill shaped like an egg; (biol) ovum; (bot) ovule

ovùnque adv (lit) wherever; (lit) everywhere

ovvéro conj or; to wit

ovvìa interj come on!

ovviare §119 intr—(with dat) to obviate

òv•vio -via adj (-vi -vie) obvious

oziare §287 (òzio) intr to idle, loiter

ò•zio m (-zi) idleness; leisure

oziosi•tà [s] f (-tà) idleness

ozió•so -sa [s] adj idle; useless, vain

ozòno [dz] m ozone

P, p [pi] *m & f* fourteenth letter of the Italian alphabet

pacare §197 *tr* (poet) to placate

pacatézza *f* tranquillity, serenity

paca·to -ta *adj* serene, tranquil

pac·ca *f* (-che) slap

pacchétto *m* parcel, package; book (*of matches*); pack (*of cigarettes*)

pàcchia *f* (coll) hearty meal; (coll) godsend, windfall

pacchia·no -na *adj* boorish, uncouth || *mf* boor

pacciamantura *f* mulching

pacciame *m* mulch

pac·co *m* (-chi) package; **pacchi postali** parcel post (*service*); **pacco dono** gift package; **pacco postale** parcel by mail

paccottìglia *f* shoddy goods, junk; trinkets

pace *f* peace; **lasciare in pace** to leave alone; **mettersi il cuore in pace** to resign oneself

pachidèr·ma *m* (-mi) pachyderm

pachista·no -na *adj & mf* Pakistani

paciè·re -ra *mf* peacemaker

pacificare §197 (**pacìfico**) *tr* to pacify; to appease; to mediate || *ref* to make one's peace

pacifica·tóre -trice *adj* pacifying || *mf* peacemaker

pacificazióne *f* pacification; appeasement

pacìfi·co -ca (-ci -che) *adj* peaceful, pacific; **è pacifico che** it goes without saying that || *m* peaceable person || **Pacifico** *adj & m* Pacific

pacifismo *m* pacifism

pacifi·sta *mf* (-sti -ste) pacifist

paciocco·ne -na *mf* chubby, easygoing person

padèlla *f* frying pan; bedpan; **cadere dalla padella nella brace** to jump from the frying pan into the fire

padiglióne *m* pavilion; hunting lodge; roof (*of car*); ward (*of a hospital*); (naut) rigging, tackle; **padiglione auricolare** (anat) auricle of the ear

Pàdova *f* Padua

padre *m* father; sire; **padre di famiglia** provider; (law) head of household; **Padre Eterno** Heavenly Father

padreggiare §290 (**padréggio**) *intr* to resemble one's father

padrino *m* godfather; second (*in duel*)

padrona *f* owner, boss, mistress; **padrona di casa** lady of the house

padronale *adj* proprietary; private (*e.g., car*)

padronanza *f* command; **padronanza di sé stesso** self-control

padróne *m* owner, boss, master; **essere padrone di** + *inf* to have the right to + *inf*; **padrone di casa** landlord; **padrone di sé** cool and collected

padroneggiare §290 (**padronéggio**) *tr* to master, control

paesàg·gio *m* (-gi) landscape

paesaggi·sta *mf* (-sti -ste) landscapist

paesa·no -na *adj* country || *mf* villager || *m* countryman || *f* countrywoman; **alla paesana** according to local tradition

paése *m* country; village; **i Paesi Bassi** the Netherlands; (hist) the Low Countries; **mandare a quel paese** to send to blazes

paesi·sta *mf* (-sti -ste) landscapist

paffu·to -ta *adj* chubby, plump

pa·ga *f* (-ghe) salary; wages; repayment; **mala paga** poor pay (*person*)

pagàbile *adj* payable

pagàia *f* paddle

pagaménto *m* payment; **pagamento alla consegna** c.o.d.

paganésimo *m* paganism

paga·no -na *adj & mf* pagan, heathen

pagare §209 *tr* to pay; to pay for; **far pagare** to charge; **pagare di egual moneta** to repay in kind; **pagare il fio per** to pay (the penalty) for; **pagare in natura** to pay in kind; **pagare salato** to pay dearly; **pagare un occhio della testa** to pay through the nose || *intr* to pay

paga·tóre -trice *mf* payer

pagèlla *f* report card

pàg·gio *m* (-gi) page (*boy attendant*)

paghe·rò *m* (-rò) promissory note, I.O.U.

pàgina *f* page (*e.g., of book*)

paginatura *f* pagination

pàglia *f* straw; thatch (*for roof*); **paglia di ferro** steel wool; **paglia di legno** excelsior

pagliacce·sco -sca *adj* (-schi -sche) clownish

pagliaccétto *m* rompers

pagliacciata *f* buffoonery, antics

pagliàc·cio *m* (-ci) clown, buffoon; **fare il pagliaccio** to clown

pa·gliàio *m* (-gliài) heap of straw; haystack

paglieric·cio *m* (-ci) straw mattress

paglieri·no -na *adj* straw-colored

pagliétta *f* skimmer, boater; steel wool; (coll) pettifogger

pagnòtta *f* loaf of bread; (coll) bread

pa·go -ga *adj* (-ghi -ghe) satisfied || *f* see paga

paguro *m* (zool) hermit crab

pà·io *m* (-ia *fpl*) pair, couple; **è un altro paio di maniche** this is a horse of another color; **fare il paio** to match perfectly

paiòlo *m* caldron, kettle; (mil) platform

Pakistan, il Pakistan

pala *f* shovel; blade (*e.g., of turbine*); paddle (*of waterwheel*); peel (*of baker*); **pala d'altare** altarpiece

paladi·no -na *mf* champion || *m* paladin; **farsi paladino di** to champion

palafitta *f* pile dwelling; piles (*to support a structure*)

palafrenière *m* groom

palafréno *m* palfrey

palan·ca *f* (-che) beam, board; (naut)

gangplank; copper coin; **palanche** (coll) money

palanchino *m* palanquin; (naut) pulley

palandrana *f* (joc) long, full coat

palata *f* shovelful; stroke (*of oar*); **a palate** by the bucketful

palatale *adj* & *f* palatal

palati·no -na *adj* palatine; (anat) palatal

palato *m* palate

palazzina *f* villa

palazzo *m* palace; large office or government building; mansion; **palazzo dello sport** sports arena; **palazzo di città** city hall; **palazzo di giustizia** courthouse

palchetti·sta (-sti -ste) *mf* (theat) boxholder ǁ *m* person who lays floors

palchétto *m* shelf; (theat) small box; (journ) box

pal·co *m* (-chi) flooring; scaffold; stand, platform; (theat) box; (theat) stage

palcoscèni·co *m* (-ci) (theat) stage

palesare (**paléso**) *tr* to reveal, manifest ǁ *ref* to show oneself

palése *adj* plain, manifest; **fare palese** to manifest, reveal

palèstra *f* gymnasium; palestra

palétta *f* small shovel, scoop; blade (*of turbine*)

palettata *f* shovelful

palétto *m* stake; bolt (*of door*)

palificazióne *f* pile work (*in the ground for foundation*); line of telephone poles

pà·lio *m* (-lii) embroidered cloth (*given as prize*); **metter in palio** to offer as a prize; **palio di Siena** colorful horserace at Siena

palissandro *m* Brazilian rosewood

palizzata *f* palisade; picket fence

palla *f* ball; bullet; sphere; **dar palla nera a** to blackball; **palla da cannone** cannon ball; **palla di neve** snowball; **prendere la palla al balzo** to seize the opportunity

pallabase *f* baseball

pallacanè·stro *f* (-stro) basketball

pallamuro *m* handball

pallanuòto *f* water polo

pallavó·lo *f* (-lo) volleyball

palleggiare §290 (**palléggio**) *tr* to toss (*e.g., a javelin*); to shift from one hand to another ǁ *intr* (tennis) to knock a few balls; (soccer) to dribble ǁ *ref*—**palleggiarsi la responsabilità** to shift the responsibility

pallég·gio *m* (-gi) (tennis) knocking back and forth; (soccer) dribbling

palliati·vo -va *adj* & *m* palliative

pallidézza *f* paleness

pàlli·do -da *adj* pale; faint

pallina *f* marble; small ball; **pallina antitarmica** mothball

pallino *m* little ball; (bowling) jack; bullet; **a pallini** polka-dot; **avere il pallino di** to be crazy about; **pallini** buckshot; polka dots

palloncino *m* child's balloon; Chinese lantern

pallóne *m* (soccer) ball; (aer) balloon;

pallone di sbarramento barrage balloon; **pallone gonfiato** (fig) stuffed shirt; **pallone sonda** trial balloon

pallonétto *m* (tennis) lob

pallóre *m* pallor, paleness

pallòttola *f* pellet; ball; bullet

pallottolière *m* abacus

pallovale *f* rugby

palma *f* palm; **tenere in palma di mano** to hold in the highest esteem

palmare *adj* evident, plain

palménto *m* millstone; **mangiare a quattro palmenti** (coll) to stuff oneself eating

palméto *m* palm grove

palmipede *adj* palmate, web-footed

palmi·zio *m* (-zi) palm

palmo *m* span; palm (*of hand*); foot (*measure*); **a palmo a palmo** little by little; **restare con un palmo di naso** to be disappointed

palo *m* pole (*of wood or metal*); beam; pile; (soccer, football) goal post; **fare il palo** to be on the lookout (*said of thieves*); **palo indicatore** signpost; **saltare di palo in frasca** to digress

palombaro *m* diver

palómbo *m* dogfish

palpàbile *adj* palpable

palpare *tr* to touch; to palpate

pàlpebra *f* eyelid; **battere le palpebre** to blink

palpeggiare §290 (**palpéggio**) *tr* to finger, touch repeatedly

palpitante *adj* throbbing; burning (*question*); fluttering (*e.g., with love*)

palpitare (**pàlpito**) *intr* to palpitate, pulsate; (fig) to pine

palpitazióne *f* palpitation

pàlpito *m* heartbeat; (fig) throb

pal·tò *m* (-tò) overcoat

paltoncino *m* child's winter coat; lady's topcoat

paludaménto *m* (joc) array, attire

palude *f* marsh, bog

paludó·so -sa [s] *adj* marshy

palustre *adj* marshy

pàmpino *m* grape leaf

panacèa *f* panacea, cure-all

pàna·ma *m* (-ma) Panama hat

panamé·gno -gna *adj* & *mf* Panamenian

panamènse *adj* & *mf* Panamenian

panare *tr* (culin) to bread

pan·ca *f* (-che) bench; **scaldare le panche** (coll) to loaf around; (coll) to waste one's time at school

pancétta *f* potbelly; bacon

panchétto *m* footstool

panchina *f* bench

pàn·cia *f* (-ce) belly; **a pancia all'aria** on one's back; **mangiare a crepa pancia** to stuff oneself like a pig; **mettere su pancia** to grow a potbelly; **salvar la pancia per i fichi** to not take any chances; **tenersi la pancia dalle risate** to split one's side laughing

panciata *f* belly flop

pancièra *f* bellypiece; body girth

panciòlle *m*—**in panciolle** frittering one's time away

panciòtto *m* waistcoat; vest; **panciotto a maglia** cardigan

panciu·to -ta *adj* potbellied

pàncre·as *m* (-as) pancreas

pandemò·nio *m* (-nì) pandemonium

pane *m* bread; thread (*of screw*); cake (*e.g., of butter*); loaf (*of sugar*); (metallurgy) pig; **a pane di zucchero** conic(al); **dire pane al pane e vino al vino** to call a spade a spade; **essere come pane e cacio** to be hand and glove; **essere pane per i propri denti** to be a match for s.o.; **guadagnarsi il pane** to earn one's living; **pane a cassetta** sandwich bread; **pane azzimo** unleavened bread, matzoth; **pan di Spagna** angel food cake, sponge cake; **pane integrale** graham bread; **render pan per focaccia** to give tit for tat

panegìri·co *m* (-ci) panegyric

panetterìa *f* bakery

panettière *m* baker

panétto *m* pat (*e.g., of butter*)

pànfilo *m* yacht

panfrutto *m* plum cake

pangrattato *m* bread crumbs

pània *f* birdlime; **cadere nella pania** to fall into the trap

pàni·co -ca (-ci -che) *adj* panicky ‖ *m* panic

pani·co *m* (-chi) Italian millet

panièra *f* basket; basketful

panière *m* basket; basketful

panificazióne *f* breadmaking

panifì·cio *m* (-cì) bakery

panino *m* roll, bun; **panino imbottito** sandwich

panna *f* cream, heavy cream; **essere in panna** (naut) to lie to; (aut) to have a breakdown; **mettere in panna** (naut) to heave to; **panna montata** whipped cream

panne *f* (aut) breakdown; **essere in panne** (aut) to have a breakdown

pannèllo *m* linen cloth; pane; panel (*of machine*); (archit; elec) panel

pannìcolo *m* (anat) membrane, tissue

panno *m* cloth; woolen cloth; film, membrane; **bianco come un panno** as white as a ghost; **mettersi nei panni di** to put oneself in the boots of; **non stare più nei propri panni** to be beside oneself with joy; **panni** clothes; **panno verde** baize

pannòcchia *f* ear (*of corn*)

pannolino *m* linen cloth; diaper; sanitary napkin

panòplia *f* panoply

panora·ma *m* (-mi) panorama

panoràmi·co -ca *adj* (-ci -che) panoramic ‖ *f* panoramic view; (mov) panoramic scene

pantaloncini *mpl* trunks

pantalóni *mpl* trousers; **pantaloni da donna** slacks

pantano *m* bog, quagmire

panteismo *m* pantheism

pànteon *m* pantheon

pantèra *f* panther; (slang) police car

pantòfola *f* slipper

pantomìma *f* pantomine, mimicry

panzana *f* (lit) fib, lie

Pàolo *m* Paul

paonaz·zo -za *adj* & *m* purple

pa·pa *m* (-pi) pope; **ad ogni morte di papa** once in a blue moon; **morto un papa se ne fa un altro** nobody is indispensable

pa·pà *m* (-pà) daddy, papa

papàbile *adj* likely to be elected ‖ *mf* front runner ‖ *m* cardinal likely to be elected to the papacy

papale *adj* papal (*e.g., benediction*); Papal (*States*)

papali·no -na *adj* papal ‖ *m* advocate of papal temporal power ‖ *f* skullcap

paparazzo *m* freelance photographer

papato *m* papacy

papàvero *m* poppy; **alto papavero** (fig) big shot

pàpera *f* young goose; slip of the tongue; spoonerism; **fare una papera** to make a boner

pàpero *m* gander

papiro *m* papyrus

pappa *f* bread soup, farina, pap; **pappa molla** (fig) jellyfish

pappafì·co *m* (-chi) (naut) topgallant; (slang) goatee

pappagallo *m* parrot; bedpan; (slang) masher

pappagòr·gia *f* (-ge) double chin, jowl

pappare *tr* (coll) to gulp; (fig) to gobble up fraudulently

pappata·ci *m* (-ci) gnat

pappina *f* light pap; poultice

pàpri·ca *f* (-che) paprika

para *f* crepe rubber

paràbola *f* parable; (geom) parabola

parabórdo *m* (naut) fender

parabréz·za [ddzz] *m* (-za) windshield

paracadutare *tr* to parachute, airdrop ‖ *ref* to parachute

paracadu·te *m* (-te) parachute

paracadutismo *m* parachute jumping; (sports) sky diving

paracaduti·sta *mf* (-sti -ste) parachutist; skydiver ‖ *m* paratrooper

paracarro *m* spur stone

paracól·pi *m* (-pi) doorstop

paràcqua *m* (**paràcqua**) umbrella

paradèn·ti *m* (-ti) (sports) mouthpiece

paradisì·a·co -ca *adj* (-ci -che) heavenly

paradiso *m* paradise

paradossale *adj* paradoxical

paradòsso *m* paradox

parafa *f* initials

parafan·go *m* (-ghi) fender, mudguard

parafare *tr* to initial

paraffina *f* paraffin

parafiam·ma *m* (-ma) fire-proof partition

parafrasare (**paràfraso**) *tr* to paraphrase

paràfra·si *f* (-si) paraphrase

parafùlmine *m* lightning rod

parafuò·co *m* (-co) screen, fender (*in front of fireplace*)

paràg·gio *m* (-gi) lineage; **paraggi** neighborhood, vicinity

paragonàbile *adj* comparable

paragonare (**paragóno**) *tr* to compare

paragóne *m* comparison; **a paragone di**

in comparison with; **mettere a paragone** to compare; **senza paragone** beyond compare

paragrafare (**paràgrafo**) *tr* to paragraph

paràgrafo *m* paragraph

paraguaia·no -na *adj & mf* Paraguayan

paràli·si *f* (**-si**) paralysis

paralìti·co -ca *adj & mf* (**-ci -che**) paralytic

paralizzare [ddzz] *tr* to paralyze

parallè·lo -la *adj & m* parallel || *f* (geom) parallel line; **parallele** (sports) parallel bars

paralume *m* lamp shade

paramano *m* cuff, wristband; (archit) facing brick

paraménto *s* facing (*of a wall*); (eccl) vestment

parami·ne *m* (**-ne**) (nav) paravane

paramó·sche *m* (**-sche**) fly net

paran·co *m* (**-chi**) tackle

paranin·fo -fa *mf* matchmaker

paranòi·co -ca *adj & mf* (**-ci -che**) paranoiac

paraòc·chi *m* (**-chi**) blinker (*on horse*)

parapètto *m* parapet

parapì·glia *m* (**-glia**) hubbub

parapiòg·gia *m* (**-gia**) umbrella

parare *tr* to adorn; to hang; to protect; to parry (*a thrust*); to offer; to drive (*e.g., cattle*) || *intr*—**dove va a parare?** what are you driving at? || *ref* to protect oneself; (eccl) to don the vestments; **pararsi dinanzi a** to loom up in front of

parasóle *m* parasol; (aut) sun visor

paraspal·le *m* (**-le**) (sports) shoulder pad

parassi·ta (**-ti -te**) *adj* parasitic || *m* parasite

parassità·rio -ria *adj* (**-ri -rie**) parasitic(al)

parassiti·co -ca *adj* (**-ci -che**) parasitic(al)

parastatale *adj* government-controlled || *mf* employee of government-controlled agency

parastin·chi *m* (**-chi**) (sports) shin guard

parata *f* fence, bar; (fencing) parry; (soccer) catch; (mil) parade; **mala parata** dangerous situation

paratìa *f* bulkhead

parato *m* hangings; **parati** hangings; (naut) bilgeways

paratóia *f* sluice gate

paraur·ti *m* (**-ti**) (aut) bumper; (rr) buffer

paravènto *m* screen

Par·ca *f* (**-che**) Fate

parcare §197 *tr & intr* to park

parcèlla *f* bill, fee, honorarium; parcel, lot (*of land*)

parcheggiare §290 (**parchéggio**) *tr & intr* to park

parchég·gio *m* (**-gi**) parking; parking lot

parchìmetro *m* parking meter

par·co -ca (**-chi -che**) *adj* frugal; parsimonious || *m* park; parking; parking lot; **parco dei divertimenti** amusement park

paréc·chio -chia (**-chi -chie**) *adj indef*

a good deal of, a lot of; **parecchi** several || *pron* a good deal, a lot; **parecchi** several || **parecchio** *adv* a lot; rather

pareggiare §290 (**paréggio**) *tr* to level; to equal; to match; to balance; to recognize || *intr* (sports) to tie

pareggia·to -ta *adj* accredited (*school*)

parég·gio *m* (**-gi**) leveling; matching; (sports) tie; **pareggio del bilancio** balancing of the budget

parentado *m* kinsfolk, kindred; relationship; **concludere il parentado di** to arrange for the wedding of

parènte *mf* relative; (lit) parent; **parenti** kin

parentèla *f* relationship; relations

parènte·si *f* (**-si**) parenthesis; break, interval; **fra parentesi** parenthetically; in parentheses; **parentesi quadra** bracket

parére *m* opinion, mind; advice; **a mio parere** in my opinion || §210 *intr* (ESSERE) to seem; **che Le pare?** what is your opinion?; **ma Le pare!** not at all!; **mi pare che** + *subj* it seems to me that + *ind;* I guess that + *ind;* **non Le pare?** don't you think so?; **non mi pare vero** I can't believe it

paréte *f* wall; **tra le pareti domestiche** within the four walls of the home

pargolét·to -ta *adj* (poet) infantile || *mf* (poet) child

pàrgo·lo -la *adj* (poet) infantile || *mf* (poet) child

pari *adj invar* equal, even; **camminare di pari passo** to walk at the same rate; **essere pari** to be quits; **essere pari al proprio compito** to be equal to the task; **fare un salto a piè pari** to jump with feet together; **pari pari** verbatim; **rimanere pari con** (sports) to be tied with; **saltare a piè pari** to skip (*e.g., a page*); to dodge (*a difficulty*); **trattare da pari a pari** to treat as an equal || *m* peer; **al pari di** as, like; **del pari** also; **in pari** even, leveled; **senza pari** matchless, peerless || *f*—**stare alla pari con** to be an even match for

parìa *f* peerage

pà·ria *m* (**-ria**) pariah

parificare §197 (**parìfico**) *tr* to level; to match; to accredit (*a school*); to balance

Parigi *f* Paris

parigi·no -na *adj & mf* Parisian || *f* slow-burning stove; Parisian woman; (rr) switching spur

parìglia *f* pair, couple; team (*of horses*); (cards) two of a kind; **rendere la pariglia** to give tit for tat

pariménti *adv* likewise

pari·tà *f* (**-tà**) parity

paritèti·co -ca *adj* (**-ci -che**) joint (*e.g., committee*)

parlamentare *adj* parliamentary || *mf* member of parliament || *m* (mil) envoy || *v* (**parlaménto**) *intr* to parley

parlaménto *m* parliament

parlante *adj* talking; life-like || *mf* speaker

parlantina *f* glibness

parlare *m* talk, speech; dialect || *tr* to speak (*a language*) || *intr* to speak, talk; to discuss; **chi parla?** (telp) hello!; **far parlare di sé** to be talked about; **parlare chiaro** to speak bluntly; **parlare del più e del meno** to make small talk; **parlare tra sé e sé** to talk to oneself || *ref* to talk to one another

parla·to -ta *adj* spoken; current (*speech*); talking (*movie*) || *m* talkie; (mov) sound track; (theat) dialogue || *f* speech, talk; dialect

parla·tóre -trice *mf* speaker

parlatò·rio *m* (-**ri**) visting room (*e.g., in jail*)

parlottare (parlòtto) *intr* to whisper in secret

parmigia·no -na *adj & mf* Parmesan || *m* Parmesan cheese

parnaso *m* Parnassus (*poetry, poets*) || **il Parnaso** Mount Parnassus

paro *m*—**in un par d'ore** in a couple of hours || *adv*—**andare a paro** to keep abreast; **mettere a paro** to compare

parodìa *f* parody; **fare la parodia di** to parody

parodiare §287 (**paròdio**) *tr* to parody

paròla *f* word; speech; **avere parole con** to have words with; **buttare la mezza parola** to make an allusion; **dare la parola a** to give the floor to; **di poche parole** of few words; **domandare la parola a** to ask for the floor; **essere di parola** to keep one's word; **essere in parola con** to have dealings with; **mangiarsi la parola** to break one's word; **mangiarsi le parole** to slur one's words; **non far parola** to not breathe a word; **parola crociata** crossword puzzle; **parola d'ordine** password; **parola macedonia** acronym **parola sdrucciola** proparoxytone; **parole** lyrics; **parole di circostanza** occasional words; **prendere la parola** to take the floor; **rivolgere la parola a** to address; **venire a parole** to begin to quarrel

parolàc·cia *f* (-**ce**) dirty word; swear-word

paro·làio -làia (-lài -làie) *adj* wordy, verbose || *mf* windbag

parolière *m* lyricist

parossismo *m* paroxysm; climax

parossìto·no -na *adj* paroxytone

parotìte *f* (pathol) parotitis; **parotite epidemica** (pathol) mumps

parrici·da *mf* (-**di -de**) patricide

parrocchétto *m* parakeet; (naut) fore-topsail; (naut) fore-topmast

parròcchia *f* parish

parrocchia·no -na *mf* parishioner

pàrro·co *m* (-**ci**) rector, parson

parruc·ca *f* (-**che**) wig; (fig) old fogey

parsimònia *f* parsimony

parsimonió·so -sa [s] *adj* parsimonious

partàc·cia *f*—**fare una partaccia** to break one's word; **fare una partaccia a** to make a scené in front of; to rebuke loudly

parte *f* part; share; section; side; party; partiality; (theat) role; **a parte sepa-** rately; (theat) aside; **d'altra parte** on the other hand; **da parte** aside; **da parte mia** as for me; **fare le parti** to divide in shares; **gran parte di** a great deal of; **in parte** partially; **la maggior parte di** most of; **parte civile** (law) plaintiff; **parte . . . parte** some . . . some; **part . . . part; prendere in mala parte** to take amiss

partecipante *adj* participating || *mf* participant; (sports) contestant

partecipare (partécipo) *tr* to announce; (lit) to share in || *intr*—**partecipare a** to share in; to participate in; **partecipare di** to partake of (*e.g., the nature of an animal*)

partécipe *adj* sharing, partaking

partecipazióne *f* announcement; card; announcement (*of a wedding*); share in a business); participation (*in some action*)

parteggiare §290 (**partéggio**) *intr* to side; **parteggiare per** to side with

Partenóne *m* Parthenon

partènte *adj* departing || *mf* person departing, traveler; (sports) starter

partènza *f* departure; sailing; (sports) start; **di partenza** or **in partenza** about to leave; **partenza lanciata** (sports) running start

particèlla *f* particle

partici·pio *m* (-**pi**) participle

particolare *adj* particular; private; **in particolare** especially || *m* detail

particolareggiare §290 (**particolaréggio**) *tr* to detail

particolarismo *m* regionalism, particularism

particolaristi·co -ca *adj* (-**ci -che**) particularistic; individualistic

particolari·tà *f* (-**tà**) peculiarity; detail

partigianerìa *f* partisanship, factionalism

partigia·no -na *adj & mf* partisan

partire §176 *tr* (lit) to divide || *v* (**parto**) *intr* to depart; (fig) to arise; **a partire da** beginning with; **far partire** to start (*e.g., a car*) || *ref* to depart, leave

parti·to -ta *adj* parted || *m* match (*in marriage*); (pol) party; **ridotto a mal partito** in bad shape; **mettere la testa a partito** to reform; **partito preso** parti pris; **prendere partito** to take sides; to make up one's mind; **trarre il miglior partito da** to make the best of || *f* panel (*e.g., of door*); lot (*of goods*); game; match; party; round (*of golf*); (com) entry; **partita di caccia** hunting party; **partita doppia** (com) double entry; **partita semplice** (com) single entry

partitura *f* (mus) score

partizióne *f* partition, division

parto *m* birth, childbirth

partorire §176 *tr* to bear, bring forth

parvènza *f* (lit) appearance

parziale *adj* partial, one-sided

parziali·tà *f* (-**tà**) partiality

pàscere §211 *tr, intr & ref* to pasture, graze

pa·scià *m* (-**scià**) pasha

pasciu·to -ta *adj* well-fed

pascolare (pàscolo) *tr & intr* to pasture

pàscolo *m* pasture

Pàsqua *f* Easter; **contento come una Pasqua** as happy as a lark; **Pasqua fiorita** Palm Sunday

pasquale *adj* paschal (*e.g., lamb*)

passàbile *adj* passable, tolerable

passàg·gio *m* (-gi) passage; transfer; crossing; traffic; passageway; ride; promotion; (sports) pass; **aprirsi il passaggio** to make one's way; **di passaggio** in passing; transient (*visitor*); **essere di passaggio** to be passing by; **passaggio a livello** railroad crossing; **passaggio zebrato** zebra crossing; **vietato il passaggio** no thoroughfare

passamano *m* passing from hand to hand; ribbon; (coll) railing, handrail

passante *adj* passing (*shot*) ‖ *mf* passer-by ‖ *m* strap

passapòrto *m* passport

passare *tr* to cross; to pass; to undergo (*a medical examination*); to move; to hand; to pay; to send (*word*); to pierce; to spend (*time*); to strain; to go over; to let have (*e.g., a slap*); to overstep (*the bounds*); **passare in rassegna** to pass in review; **passare per le armi** to execute; **passare un brutto quarto d'ora** to have a bad ten minutes; **passare un guaio** to have a hard time; **passarla a qlcu** (coll) to forgive s.o.; **passarla liscia** (coll) to get off unscathed; **passarsela bene** (coll) to have a good time ‖ *intr* (ESSERE) to pass; to go; to filter (*said of air, light*); to move; to spoil (*said of food*); to be overcooked; to be promoted; to become; to enter; (lit) to be over; **fare passare qlcu** to let s.o. come in; **passare a nozze** to get married; **passare a seconde nozze** to remarry; **passare avanti a** to overcome; **passare di mente a** to forget, e.g., **gli è passata di mente la riunione** he forgot the meeting; **passare di moda** to go out of style; **passare in giudicato** (law) to be no longer appealable; **passare per** to pass; **passare per il rotto della cuffia** to barely make it; **passare sopra qlco** to overlook s.th; **passi!** come in!; **passo!** (rad) over!; **passo** (cards) pass

passata *f* purée; **dare una passata a** to glance at; **dare una passata di straccio a** to rub lightly with a rag; to give a lick and a promise to; **di passata** hurriedly

passatèmpo *m* pastime; hobby

passati·sta *mf* (-sti -ste) traditionalist

passa·to -ta *adj* past; last; overcooked; **essere passato** (coll) to be no longer in one's prime; **passato di moda** out of fashion ‖ *m* past; purée; **passato prossimo** present perfect; **passato remoto** preterit ‖ *f* see **passata**

passatóia *f* runner (*rug*)

passa·tóio *m* (-tói) stepping stone

passeggè·ro -ra *adj* passing ‖ *mf* passenger; **pàsseggero clandestino** stow-away

passeggiare §290 (passéggio) *tr* to walk (*e.g., a horse*) ‖ *intr* to walk, promenade

passeggiata *f* promenade; walk; drive, ride; drive, road; **fare una passeggiata** to take a walk; to take a ride

passeggiatrice *f* streetwalker

passég·gio *m* (-gi) walk; promenade; **andare a passeggio** to take a walk

passerèlla *f* gangway; catwalk; footbridge

pàsse·ro -ra *mf* sparrow ‖ *f*—**passera di mare** (ichth) flounder

passìbile *adj*—**passibile di** subject to, liable to

passiflòra *f* passionflower

passino *m* colander, strainer

passióne *f* passion

passivi·tà *f* (-tà) passivity; (com) deficit

passi·vo -va *adj* passive ‖ *m* (com) liabilities; (com) debit side; (gram) passive

pas·so -sa *adj*—see **uva** ‖ *m* step; passage; pass (*in mountain*); pace; footstep; pitch (*of screw, helix, etc.*); (aut) wheelbase; (phot) tread; (phot) size (*of roll*); **a grandi passi** with great strides; **andare al passo** to march in step; to walk (*said of a horse*); **a passi di gigante** by leaps and bounds; **a passo di corsa** running; **a passo d'uomo** walking, at a walk; **aprire il passo** to open the way; **di buon passo** at a good clip; **di pari passo** at the same rate; **fare quattro passi** to take a stroll; **passo doppio** paso doble; **passo d'uomo** manhole; step; **passo falso** misstep; (fig) stumble; **sbarrare il passo** to block the way; **seguire i passi di** to walk in the footsteps of ‖ *interj* (cards) pass!; over!

pasta *f* paste; dough; **di pasta grossa** uncouth, coarse; **pasta alimentare** pasta, macaroni products; **pasta all'uovo** egg noodles; **pasta asciutta** pasta with sauce and cheese; **pasta dentifricia** toothpaste; **una pasta d'uomo** a good natured man

pastasciutta *f* pasta with sauce and cheese

pasteggiare §290 (pastéggio) *intr* to dine

pastèllo *adj invar & m* pastel ‖ *m* crayon

pastétta *f* batter; (coll) trickery

pastìc·ca *f* (-che) lozenge, tablet; **pasticche per la tosse** cough drops

pasticcerìa *f* pastrymaking; pastry; pastry shop

pasticciare §128 (pasticcio) *tr & intr* to bungle; to scribble

pasticciè·re -ra *mf* pastry cook; confectioner

pasticcino *m* cookie; patty

pastìc·cio *m* (-ci) pie (*of meat, macaroni, etc*); bungle; mess; **cacciarsi nei pasticci** to wind up in the soup

pasticció·ne -na *mf* bungler

pastifì·cio *m* (-ci) spaghetti and macaroni factory

pastìglia *f* lozenge, tablet; **pastiglia per la tosse** cough drop

pastina·ca *f* (**-che**) parsnip
pa·sto -sta *adj* (archaic) fed || *m* meal; **pasto a prezzo fisso** table d'hôte || *f* see **pasta**
pastóia *f* hobble; (fig) shackle
pastóne *m* mash
pastóra *f* shepherdess
pastorale *adj* pastoral
pastóre *m* shepherd; pastor
pastorì·zio -zia (**-zi -zie**) *adj* shepherd || *f* sheep raising
pastorizzare [ddzz] *tr* to pasteurize
pastó·so -sa [s] *adj* pasty; mellow
pastrano *m* overcoat
pastura *f* pasture; hay; fodder
patac·ca *f* (**-che**) large, worthless coin; fake; (coll) medal; (coll) spot
patata *f* potato
patatràc *m* (**patatràc**) crash
patèlla *f* kneecap; (zool) limpet
patè·ma *m* (**-mi**) affliction; **patema d'animo** anxiety
patenta·to -ta *adj* licensed; (coll) well-known
patènte *adj* patent || *f* license; driver's license; **patente sanitaria** (naut) bill of health
patentino *m* (aut) permit
paterèc·cio *m* (**-ci**) whitlow
paternale *adj* (obs) paternal || *f* reprimand
paterni·tà *f* (**-tà**) paternity; authorship
patèr·no -na *adj* paternal; fatherly
paternòstro *m* Lord's Prayer; **è vero come il paternostro** it is the gospel truth
patèti·co -ca (**-ci -che**) *adj* pathetic; mawkish || *m* pathos; mawkishness
pathos *m* pathos
patìbile *adj* endurable
patibolare *adj* gallows
patìbolo *m* executioner's instrument; scaffold
patiménto *m* suffering
pàtina *f* patina; coating (*on paper*); varnish; fur (*on tongue*)
patinare (**pàtino**) *tr* to gloss, glaze (*e.g., paper*)
patire §176 *tr* to suffer; (gram) to be the recipient of (*an action*) || *intr* to suffer
patì·to -ta *adj* suffering, sickly || *mf* fan || *m* boyfriend *f* girlfriend
patòge·no -na *adj* pathogenic
patologìa *f* pathology
patològi·co -ca (**-ci -che**) pathologic(al)
patos *m* var of **pathos**
patrasso *m*—**andare a patrasso** to die; to go to ruin; **mandare a patrasso** to kill; to ruin
pàtria *f* fatherland, native land
patriar·ca *m* (**-chi**) patriarch
patriarcale *adj* patriarchal
patrigno *m* stepfather
patrimoniale *adj* patrimonial; property (*tax*); capital (*e.g., transaction*)
patrimò·nio *m* (**-ni**) patrimony; estate; fortune; (fig) heritage
pà·trio -tria (**-tri -trie**) *adj* paternal; of one's country (*e.g., love*) || *f* see **patria**

patriò·ta *mf* (**-ti -te**) patriot; (coll) fellow citizen
patriòtti·co -ca *adj* (**-ci -che**) patriotic
patriottismo *m* patriotism
patrì·zio -zia (**-zi -zie**) *adj & m* patrician || **Patrizio** *m* Patrick
patrocinante *adj* pleading (*lawyer*)
patrocinare *tr* to favor, sponsor; to plead
patrocina·tóre -trice *mf* defender; pleader
patroci·nio *m* (**-ni**) support; sponsorship; (law) defense; **patrocinio gratuito** public defense
patronato *m* patronage; charitable institution, foundation; **patronato scolastico** state aid fund
patronéssa *f* sponsor; trustee (*of charitable institution*)
patròno *m* patron saint; patron; sponsor; trustee (*of charitable institution*); (law) counsel
patta *f* flap (*of garment*); bill (*of anchor*); (coll) potholder; **essere** or **far patta** to be even, tie
patteggiaménto *m* negotiation
patteggiare §290 (**pattéggio**) *tr & intr* to negotiate
pattinàggio *m* skating
pattinare (**pàttino**) *intr* to skate; to skid (*said of a car*)
pattina·tóio *m* (**-tói**) skating rink
pattina·tóre -trice *mf* skater
pàttino *m* skate; guide block (*of an elevator*); (aer) skid, runner; **pattino a rotelle** roller skate
pattino *m* racing shell with outrigger floats
patto *m* pact; **a nessun patto** by no means; **a patto che** provided (that); **patto sociale** social contract; **venire a patti** to come to terms
pattùglia *f* patrol
pattugliare §280 *tr & intr* to patrol
pattuire §176 *tr & intr* to negotiate
pattuì·to -ta *adj* agreed || *m* agreement
pattume *m* litter, garbage
pattumièra *f* dustpan; trash bin
patùrnie *fpl*—**avere le paturnie** (coll) to be in the dumps
paura *f* fear; **aver paura di** to be afraid of; **da far paura** frightful; **dar** or **metter paura a** to frighten; **per paura che** for fear that, lest
pauró·so -sa [s] *adj* fearful
pàusa *f* pause
pausare (**pàuso**) *tr* (lit) to interrupt || *intr* (lit) to pause
paventare (**pavènto**) *tr & intr* to fear
pavesare (**pavéso**) *tr* to deck with flags; to dress (*a ship*)
pavése [s] *adj*—see **zuppa** || *m* pavis (*shield*); (naut) bunting
pàvi·do -da *adj* cowardly, timid
pavimentare (**paviménto**) *tr* to pave
pavimentazióne *f* paving, pavement
paviménto *m* floor; bottom (*of sea*); paving (*of street*)
pavoncèlla *f* lapwing
pavó·ne -na or **-néssa** *mf* peacock
pavoneggiare §290 (**pavonéggio**) *ref* to swagger, strut
pazientare (**paziènto**) *intr* to be patient

paziènte *adj* & *mf* patient

paziènza *f* patience; fare scappare la pazienza a to drive mad; pazienza! too bad!

pazzé·sco -sca *adj* (-schi -sche) crazy, wild

pazzìa *f* madness, insanity; folly; fare pazzie to act like a fool

paz·zo -za *adj* crazy, insane; andar pazzo per to be crazy about || *mf* crazy person

pèc·ca *f* (-che) imperfection

peccaminó·so -sa [s] *adj* sinful

peccare §197 (pècco) *intr* to sin; to be lacking; to be at fault

peccato *m* sin; che peccato! what a pity!; è un peccato it's a shame

pecca·tóre -trice *mf* sinner

pécchia *f* bee

pecchióne *m* drone

péce *f* pitch; pece greca rosin

pechinése [s] *adj* & *mf* Pekingese

Pechino *f* Peking

pècora *f* sheep

peco·ràio *m* (-rài) shepherd

pecorèlla *f* small sheep, lamb

pecori·no -na *adj* sheep; sheepish || *m* sheep-milk cheese || *f* sheep manure

peculato *m* embezzlement, peculation

peculiare *adj* peculiar

peculiari·tà *f* (-tà) peculiarity

pecù·lio *m* (-li) nest egg, savings; (obs) cattle

pecùnia *m* (lit) money

pecunià·rio -ria *adj* (-ri -rie) pecuniary

pedàg·gio *m* (-gi) toll

pedagogìa *f* pedagogy, pedagogics

pedagògi·co -ca *adj* (-ci -che) pedagogic(al)

pedagò·go -ga *mf* (-ghi -ghe) pedagogue

pedalare *intr* to pedal

pedale *m* trunk (*of tree*); pedal; treadle (*e.g., of sewing machine*)

pedalièra *f* pedals, pedal keyboard; (aer) rudder bar

pedalino *m* (coll) sock, short stocking

pedana *f* footrest; platform; bedside rug; hem (*of skirt*); (aut) running board; (sports) springboard

pedante *adj* pedantic || *m* pedant

pedanterìa *f* pedantry

pedanté·sco -sca *adj* (-schi -sche) pedantic

pedata *f* kick; footprint; tread (*of step*)

pedèstre *adj* pedestrian

pedia·tra *mf* (-tri -tre) pediatrician

pediatrìa *f* pediatrics

pedicu·re *mf* (-re) pedicure

pedicu·ro -ra *mf* var of pedicure

pedilù·vio *m* (-vi) foot bath

pedina *f* (checkers) checker, man; (chess) pawn

pedinare *tr* to shadow, follow about

pedisse·quo -qua *adj* servile

pedivèlla *f* pedal crank

pedóne *m* pedestrian; (chess) pawn

pedule *m* stocking foot || *fpl* climbing shoes, sneakers

pedùncolo *m* (anat, bot, zool) peduncle

pegamòide *f* imitation leather

pèggio *adj invar* worse; il peggio the worst, e.g., il peggio ragazzo the worst boy; || *m* worst; andare per il peggio to be getting worse || *f* worst; alla peggio if worst comes to worst; averne la peggio to get the worst of it || *adv* worse; worst; at worst; peggio + *pp* less + *pp*; least + *pp*; tanto peggio so much the worse

peggioraménto *m* deterioration, worsening

peggiorare (peggióro) *tr* & *intr* to worsen

peggió·re (-ri) *adj* worse; worst || *m* worst

pégli §4

pégno *m* pledge, pawn

pégola *f* pitch; (coll) bad luck

péi §4

péi §4

pèla·go *m* (-ghi) (poet) open sea; (coll) mess; pelago di guai sea of trouble

pelame *m* hair, coat

pelandróne *m* (coll) shirker, do-nothing

pelapata·te *m* (-te) potato peeler

pelare (pélo) *tr* to fleece; to pluck; to pare, peel; to clear (*land*); (fig) to strip; to scald, burn || *ref* (coll) to shed; to become bald

pela·to -ta *adj* peeled; hairless, bald; barren || *m* (coll) baldy; pelati peeled tomatoes || *f* fleecing, plucking; (joc) baldness, bald spot

pélla §4

pellàc·cia *f* (-ce) tough hide

pellame *m* skins, hides

pèlle *f* skin, hide; a fior di pelle slightly, superficially; essere nella pelle di to be in the boots of; fare la pelle a to bump off; non stare più nella pelle to be beside oneself with joy; pelle di dante buckskin; pelle d'oca goose skin, goose flesh; pelle d'uovo mull; pelle pelle skin-deep, superficial

pélle §4

pellegrinàg·gio *m* (-gi) pilgrimage

pellegrinare *intr* (lit) to go on a pilgrimage

pellegri·no -na *adj* wandering; (lit) foreign; (lit) strange, quixotic || *mf* pilgrim, traveler

pelleróssa *mf* (pellirosse) redskin

pelletterìa *f* leather goods; leather goods store

pellicano *m* pelican

pelliccerìa *f* furrier's store; furrier's trade, fur industry

pellìc·cia *f* (-ce) fur

pellic·ciàio -ciàia *mf* (-ciài -ciàie) furrier

pelliccióne *m* fur jacket

pellicola *f* film; pellicola in rotolo roll film; pellicola piana film pack; pellicola sonora sound film; pellicola vergine unexposed film

pellirós·sa *mf* (-se) var of pellerossa

pélo *m* hair (*of beard*); pile (*of carpet*); fur; avere pelo sul cuore not to be easily moved; cercare il pelo nell'uovo to split hairs; di primo pelo green, inexperienced; non avere peli sulla lingua to not mince one's words; pelo dell'acqua water surface; per un pelo by a hair's breadth

peloponnesìa·co -ca *adj* (-ci -che) Peloponnesian

peló·so -sa [s] *adj* hairy; self-serving (*e.g., charity*)

péltro *m* pewter

pelùria *f* down, soft hair

péna *f* penalty; concern; compassion; pain, suffering; grief; **a mala pena** barely; **essere in pena per** to worry about; **fare pena** to arouse compassion; **pena infamante** degrading punishment; loss of civil rights; **sotto pena di** under penalty of; **valere la pena** to be worthwhile

penale *adj* penal || *f* penalty

penali·sta *mf* (-sti -ste) criminal lawyer

penali·tà *f* (-tà) penalty

penalizzare [ddzz] *tr* (sports) to penalize

penare (**péno**) *intr* to suffer; to find it difficult

pencolare (**pèncolo**) *intr* to totter; to waver

pendà·glio *m* (-gli) pendant; **pendaglio da forca** gallows bird

pendènte *adj* leaning; hanging; pending || *m* pendant

pendènza *f* inclination, pitch; controversy; balance; **in pendenza** pending

pèndere §123 *intr* to hang; to lean; to slope; to pitch

pendice *f* slope, declivity

pen·dìo *m* (-dìi) slant; slope

pèndola *f* clock

pendolare (**pèndolo**) *adj* pendulum-like; commuting; transient (*tourist*) || *mf* commuter || *v* (**pèndolo**) *intr* to sway back and forth; to waver; (nav) to cruise back and forth

pèndolo *m* pendulum; clock

pèndu·lo -la *adj* (lit) hanging

penetrante *adj* penetrating, piercing

penetrare (**pènetro**) *tr* to penetrate, pierce || *intr* to penetrate || *ref*—**penetrarsi di** to be convinced of; to become aware of

penicillina *f* penicillin

peninsulare *adj* peninsular

penìsola *f* peninsula

penitènte *adj* & *mf* penitent

penitènza *f* penitence; punishment

penitenzià·rio -ria *adj* & *mf* (-ri -rie) penitentiary

pénna *f* feather; pen; peen (*of hammer*); (mus) plectrum; **penna a sfera** ball-point pen; **penna d'oca** quill; **penna stilografica** fountain pen

pennàc·chio *m* (-chi) panache; plume, tuft; cloud (*of smoke*)

pennaiòlo *m* hack writer

pennarèllo *m* felt-tip pen

pennellare (**pennèllo**) *intr* to brush; (med) to pencil

pennellata *f* brush stroke

pennèllo *m* brush; (naut) signal flag; (naut) kedge; **pennello per la barba** shaving brush; **stare a pennello** to fit to a T

pennino *m* pen; penpoint, nib

pennóne *m* flagpole; (naut) yard; (mil) pennant

pennu·to -ta *adj* feathered || **pennuti** *mpl* birds

penómbra *f* penumbra; semidarkness; faint light; **vivere in penombra** to live in obscurity

penó·so -sa [s] *adj* painful

pensàbile *adj* thinkable

pensante *adj* thinking

pensare (**pènso**) *tr* to think; to think of || *intr* to think; to worry; **dar da pensare a** to cause worry to, *e.g.,* **suo figlio gli dà da pensare** his son causes him worry; **pensa ai fatti tuoi** (coll) mind your own business; **pensa alla salute** (coll) don't worry!; **pensare a** to think of; **pensare di** to plan, intend to

pensata *f* bright idea, brainstorm

pensa·tóre -trice *mf* thinker

pensièro *m* thought; **dare pensiero a** to cause worry to; **darsi pensiero per** to worry about; **essere sopra pensiero** to be absorbed in thought

pensieró·so -sa [s] *adj* thoughtful, pensive

pènsile *adj* hanging, overhead

pensilina *f* marquee

pensionaménto *m* retirement

pensionante *mf* boarder, paying guest

pensionare (**pensióno**) *tr* to pension

pensiona·to -ta *adj* pensioned || *m* pensioner || *m* boarding school

pensióne *f* pension; boarding house; **in pensione** retired; **tenere a pensione** to board (*a lodger*); **vivere a pensione** to board (*said of a lodger*)

pensó·so -sa [s] *adj* thoughtful, pensive

pentàgono *m* pentagon

pentagram·ma *m* (-mi) (mus) staff, stave

pentàmetro *m* pentameter

Pentecòste, la Pentecost, Whitsunday

pentiménto *m* repentance; correction (*e.g., in a manuscript*); change of heart

pentire (**pènto**) *ref* to repent; to change one's mind; **pentirsi di** to repent

penti·to -ta *adj* repentant, repenting; **pentito e contrito** in sackcloth and ashes

péntola *f* pot, kettle; potful; **pentola a pressione** pressure cooker

penùlti·mo -ma *adj* next to the last || *f* penult

penùria *f* shortage, scarcity

penzolare (**pènzolo**) [dz] *intr* to dangle, hang down

penzolóni [dz] *adv* dangling

peònia *f* peony

pepaiòla *f* pepper shaker; pepper mill

pepare (**pépo**) *tr* to pepper

pepa·to -ta *adj* peppered; peppery

pépe *m* pepper; **pepe della Giamaica** allspice; **pepe di Caienna** red pepper, cayenne pepper

peperóne *m* (bot) pepper

pepita *f* nugget

per *prep* by; through; throughout; for; because of; to, in order to; in favor of; considering; **essere per** to be about to; **per + *adj* or *adv* + che + *subj*** however + *adj* or *adv* + *ind*, e.g., **per intelligente che sia** however intelligent he is; **per caso** perchance; **per che cosa?** what for?; **per l'appunto** exactly, just; **per lungo** lengthwise; **per me** as for me; **per ora** now; **per parte mia** as for me; **per poco** hardly, scarcely, **per quanto** + *adj* or *adv* + *subj* however + *adj* or *adv* + *pres ind*, e.g., **per quanto disperatamente provi** however desperately he attempts; **per tempo** early; **per traverso** diagonally; **per via che** (coll) because; **stare per** to be about to

péra *f* pear (*fruit*); bulb, light bulb; (joc) head

peraltro *adv* besides, moreover

peranco *adv* yet

perbacco *interj* by Jove!

perbène *adj invar* nice, well brought up

percalle *m* percale

percènto *m* percent; percentage

percentuale *adj* percentage || *f* percent; commission, bonus

percepíbile *adj* collectable

percepire §176 *tr* to perceive; to receive (*a salary*)

percettíbile *adj* perceptible

percetti·vo -va *adj* perceptive

percezióne *f* perception

perché *m* why, reason; **il perché e il percome** the why and the wherefore || *pron rel* for which || *adv* why || *conj* because; so that

perciò *conj* therefore, accordingly

percóme *m* & *conj* wherefore

percorrènza *f* stretch, distance

percórrere §139 *tr* to cross; to cover, go through

percórso *m* crossing, distance

percòssa *f* hit, blow; contusion

percuòtere §251 *tr* to hit, beat; (fig) to shake || *intr* to strike

percussióne *f* percussion

percussóre *m* firing pin

perdènte *adj* losing || *mf* loser

pèrdere §212 *tr* to lose; to waste; to miss (*e.g., a train*); to ruin; to leak || *intr* to lose; to leak; to be inferior || *ref* to get lost; to waste one's time; **perdersi d'animo** to lose heart; **perdersi in un bicchier d'acqua** to become discouraged for nothing

perdifiato *m*—**a perdifiato** at the top of one's lungs

perdigiór·no *mf* (**-no**) idler

perdinci *interj* good Heavens!

pèrdita *f* loss; leak; **a perdita d'occhio** as far as the eye can see; **perdite** (mil) casualties

perditèm·po *mf* (**-po**) idler || *m* waste of time

perdizióne *f* perdition

perdonàbile *adj* pardonable

perdonare (**perdóno**) *tr* to forgive; to spare; **perdonare a qlcu qlco** or **perdonare qlco a qlcu** to forgive s.o. for s.th || *intr* (with *dat*) to pardon

perdóno *m* forgiveness, pardon

perdurare *intr* (ESSERE & AVERE) to last; to persevere

perdu·to -ta *adj* lost; **andar perduto** to be desperately in love; to get lost

peregrinare *intr* to wander

peregrinazióne *f* wandering

peregri·no -na *adj* far-fetched, outlandish

perènne *adj* everlasting; perennial

perentò·rio -ria *adj* (**-ri -rie**) peremptory

perequare (**perèquo**) *tr* to equalize

perequazióne *f* equalization

perfèt·to -ta *adj* & *m* perfect

perfezionaménto *m* improvement; (educ) specialization

perfezionare (**perfezióno**) *tr* to improve, polish up; to perfect || *ref* to improve; (educ) to specialize

perfezióne *f* perfection; **a** or **alla perfezione** to perfection

perfidia *f* perfidy

pèrfi·do -da *adj* perfidious, treacherous; (coll) foul, nasty

perfini·re *m* (**-re**) punch line

perfino *adv* even

perforante *adj* piercing, perforating

perforare (**perfóro**) *tr* to pierce; to perforate; to punch; to bore

perfora·tóre -trice *mf* key-punch operator || *m* drill || *f* punch; drill; pneumatic drill, rock drill

perforazióne *f* perforation

pergamèna *f* parchment, vellum

pèrgamo *m* (lit) pulpit

pèrgola *f* bower, pergola

pergolato *m* arbor, pergola; grape arbor

pericolante *adj* tottering, unsafe

perícolo *m* danger; **non c'è pericolo** don't worry

pericoló·so -sa [s] *adj* dangerous

periferia *f* periphery; suburbs

perifèri·co -ca *adj* (**-ci -che**) peripheral

perífra·si *f* (**-si**) periphrasis

perímetro *m* perimeter

periodare *m* writing style || *v* (**periodo**) *intr* to turn a phrase

periòdi·co -ca *adj* (**-ci -che**) periodic(al) || *m* periodical

período *m* period; age; (gram) sentence; (phys) cycle; **il periodo delle feste** holiday time

peripezia *f* vicissitude

pèriplo *m* circumnavigation

perire §176 *intr* (ESSERE) to perish

periscò·pio *m* (**-pi**) periscope

peritale *adj* expert

peritare (**pèrito**) *ref* (lit) to hesitate

peri·to -ta *adj* expert, skilled || *mf* expert; **perito agrario** land surveyor; **perito calligrafo** handwriting expert; **perito chimico** chemist; **perito industriale** industrial engineer

peritonèo *m* peritoneum

perizia *f* skill; survey; appraisal

periziare §287 (**perizio**) *tr* to estimate, appraise

pèrla *f* pearl; (med) capsule

perlàce·o -a *adj* pearly

perla·to -ta *adj* pearly, smooth

perlífe·ro -ra *adj* pearl-producing

perlina *f* bead

perlomèno *adv* at least

perlopiù *adv* mostly, generally

perlustrare *tr* to patrol

perlustrazióne *f* patrol, patrolling

permaló·so -sa [s] *adj* touchy, grouchy

permanènte *adj* permanente ‖ *f* permanent wave

permanènza *f* permanence; stay; continuance (*in office*); duration (*of a disease*); **in permanenza** permanent (*employee*); **buona permanenza!** may your stay be happy!

permanére §235 (*pp* **permaso**) *intr* (ESSERE) to remain, stay

permeàbile *adj* permeable

permeare (**pèrmeo**) *tr* to permeate

permés·so -sa *adj* permitted, allowed; **è permesso?** may I come in? ‖ *m* permit; (mil) pass, leave

perméttere §198 *tr* to permit, allow, let; **permette?** do you mind? ‖ *ref* to take the liberty; to afford

permissìbile *adj* permissible

pèrmuta *f* barter; exchange

permutàbile *adj* tradable, exchangeable

permutare (**pèrmuto**) *tr* to barter; (math) to permute

pernàcchia *f* (vulg) raspberry

pernice *f* partridge

pernició·so -sa [s] *adj* pernicious ‖ *f* pernicious malaria

pèr·nio *m* (-ni) var of **perno**

pèrno *m* pivot; pin; kingbolt; swivel; heart (*of the matter*); kernel (*of the story*); support (*of the family*); (mach) journal; **fare perno** to pivot

pernottare (**pernòtto**) *intr* to spend the night, stay overnight

péro *m* pear tree

però *conj* but, yet; however, nevertheless; **e però** (lit) therefore

peróne *m* fibula

peronòspora *f* downy mildew

perorare (**pèroro**) *tr & intr* to perorate; (law) to plead

perorazióne *f* peroration; (law) pleading

peròssido *m* peroxide; **perossido d'idrogeno** hydrogen peroxide

perpendicolare *adj & f* perpendicular

perpendìcolo *m* plumb line; **a perpendicolo** perpendicularly

perpetrare (**pèrpetro & perpètro**) *tr* (lit) to perpetrate

perpètua *f* priest's housekeeper

perpetuare (**perpètuo**) *tr* to perpetuate

perpè·tuo -tua *adj* perpetual, life ‖ *f* see **perpetua**

perplessi·tà *f* (-tà) perplexity

perplès·so -sa *adj* perplexed; (lit) ambiguous

perquisire §176 *tr* to search

perquisizióne *f* search

persecu·tóre -trice *mf* persecutor, oppressor

persecuzióne *f* persecution

perseguire (**perséguo**) *tr* to pursue; to persecute; to pester

perseguitare (**perséguito**) *tr* to persecute; to pursue; to pester

perseveranza *f* perseverance

perseverare (**persèvero**) *intr* to persevere

persia·no -na *adj* Persian ‖ *m* Persian; Persian lamb ‖ *f* slatted shutter; **persiana avvolgibile** Venetian blind

pèrsi·co -ca (**-ci -che**) *adj* Persian ‖ *m* (ichth) perch; (obs) peach ‖ *f* (coll) peach

persino *adv* var of **perfino**

persistènte *adj* persistent

persistènza *f* persistence

persìstere §114 *intr* to persist

pèr·so -sa *adj* lost, wasted; (archaic) reddish-brown; **a tempo perso in** one's spare time

persóna *f* person; **per persona** apiece; per capita; **persona di servizio** servant; **persone** people

personàg·gio *m* (-gi) personage; character

personale *adj* personal ‖ *m* figure, body; personnel, staff; crew ‖ *f* one-man show

personali·tà *f* (-tà) personality; personage

personificare §197 (**personìfico**) *tr* to personify

perspicace *adj* perspicacious; far-sighted

perspicàcia *f* perspicacity

perspì·cuo -cua *adj* perspicuous

persuadére §213 *tr* to persuade ‖ *ref* to become convinced

persuasióne *f* persuasion

persuasi·vo -va *adj* persuasive; pleasing ‖ *f* persuasiveness

persua·so -sa *adj* convinced; resigned

pertanto *conj* therefore; **non pertanto** nevertheless

pèrti·ca *f* (-che) perch; pole

pertinace *adj* pertinacious, persistent

pertinà·cia *f* (-cie) pertinacity, obstinacy

pertinènte *adj* pertinent, relevant

pertinènza *f* pertinence; competence

pertósse *f* whooping cough

pertù·gio *m* (-gi) hole

perturbare *tr* to perturb ‖ *ref* to be perturbed

perturbazióne *f* perturbation; disturbance

Perù, il Peru; **valere un Perù** to be worth a king's ransom

peruvia·no -na *adj & mf* Peruvian

pervàdere §172 *tr* (lit) to pervade

pervenire §282 *intr* (ESSERE) to arrive; to come; **pervenire a** to reach

perversióne *f* perversion

perversi·tà *f* (-tà) perversity

pervèr·so -sa *adj* perverse; wicked

pervertiménto *m* perversion

pervertire (**pervèrto**) *tr* to pervert ‖ *ref* to become perverted

perverti·to -ta *adj* perverted ‖ *mf* pervert

pervicace *adj* (lit) obstinate

pervìn·ca *f* (-che) periwinkle

pésa [s] *f* weighing; scale

pesage *m* (pesage) weigh-in; place for weighing in jockeys

pesalètte·re [s] *m* (-re) postal scale

pesante [s] *adj* heavy

pesantézza [s] *f* heaviness; weight

pesare (**péso**) [s] *tr* to weigh ‖ *intr* to weigh; **pesare a qlcu** to weigh upon s.o.

pesa·tóre -trice [s] *mf* scale or weighbridge operator; **pesatore pubblico** inspector for the department of weights and measures

pesatura [s] *f* weighing

pé·sca *f* (-sche) fishing; catch (*of fish*) **pesca alla traina** trawling; **pesca d'altura** deep-sea fishing; **pesca di beneficenza** benefit lottery

pè·sca *f* (-sche) peach

pescàg·gio *m* (-gi) (naut) draft

pescàia *f* dam, weir

pescare §197 (**pésco**) *tr* to fish; to draw (*a card*); to dig up (*a piece of news*); to dive for (*pearls*); **pescare con la lenza** to angle for (*fish*) ‖ *intr* to fish; (naut) to displace; **pescare con la lenza** to angle; **pescare di frodo** to poach; **pescare nel torbido** to fish in troubled waters

pesca·tóre -trice *mf* fisher; **pescatore di canna** angler; **pescatore di frodo** poacher

pésce *m* fish; (typ) omission; (coll) biceps; **a pesce** headlong; **non sapere che pesci pigliare** to not know which way to turn; **pesce d'aprile** April fool; **pesce gatto** catfish; **pesce martello** hammerhead ‖ **Pesci** *mpl* (astr) Pisces

pescecane *m* (**pescecani** & **pescicani**) shark; (fig) war profiteer

pescheréc·cio -cia (-ci -ce) *adj* fishing ‖ *m* fishing boat

pescheria *f* fish market

peschiera *f* fishpond; fishpound (*net*)

pescivéndo·lo -la *mf* fishmonger, fish dealer ‖ *f* fishwife, fishwoman

pè·sco *m* (-schi) peach tree

pesi·sta [s] *m* (-sti) (sports) weight lifter

péso -sa [s] *adj* (coll) heavy ‖ *m* weight; burden; bob (*of clock*); (racing) weigh-in; (sports) shot; **di peso** bodily; **peso lordo** gross weight; **peso massimo** (sports) heavyweight; **peso specifico** specific gravity; **rubare sul peso** to give short weight; **usare due pesi e due misure** to have a double standard ‖ *f* see **pesa**

pessimismo *m* pessimism

pessimi·sta *mf* (-sti -ste) pessimist

pessimìsti·co -ca *adj* (-ci -che) pessimistic

pèssi·mo -ma *adj* very bad, very poor

pésta *f* track, footprint; **lasciar nelle peste** to leave in the lurch; **seguir le peste di** to follow in the footsteps of

pestàggio *m* beating, clubbing

pestare (**pésto**) *tr* to pound; to trample; to step on; **pestare le orme di** to follow in the footsteps of; **pestare i piedi** to stamp the feet; **pestare sodo** to beat up

pèste *f* plague, pest

pestèllo *m* pestle

pestífe·ro -ra *adj* pestiferous

pestilènza *f* pestilence; stench

pestilenziale *adj* pestilential; pernicious

pé·sto -sta *adj* crushed; thick (*darkness*) ‖ *m* Genoese sauce ‖ *f* see **pesta**

pètalo *m* petal

petardo *m* petard, firecracker

petènte *mf* petitioner

petizióne *f* petition; **petizione di principio** begging the question

péto *m* wind, gas

Petrarca *m* Petrarch

petrarché·sco -sca *adj* (-schi -sche) Petrarchan

petrolièra *f* (naut) tanker

petrolière *adj* incendiary ‖ *m* petroleum-industry worker; incendiary; oilman (*producer*)

petrolífe·ro -ra *adj* oil-yielding

petrò·lio *m* (-li) petroleum; coal oil, kerosene

petró·so -sa [s] *adj* (lit) stony

pettegolare (**pettègolo**) *intr* to gossip

pettegolézzo [ddzz] *m* gossip, rumor

pettégo·lo -la *adj* gossipy ‖ *mf* gossip

pettinare (**pèttino**) *tr* to comb; to card; (coll) to scold

pettinatóre *m* carder

pettinatrice *f* hairdresser; carding machine

pettinatura *f* coiffure, hairstyling

pèttine *m* comb; (zool) scallop; **a pettine perpendicular** (*parking*)

pettino *m* dickey; bib (*of an apron*); plastron

pettirósso *m* robin redbreast

pètto *m* breast, chest; bust; bosom; **a un petto** single-breasted; **avere al petto** to feed at the breast; **a due petti** or **a doppio petto** double-breasted; **stare a petto** to be equal

pettorale *adj* pectoral ‖ *m* pectoral; breast collar (*of horse*)

pettorina *f* var of **pettino**

pettoru·to -ta *adj* strutting, haughty

petulante *adj* importunate; impertinent

petulanza *f* importunity; impertinence

petùnia *f* petunia

pèzza *f* piece (*of cloth*); diaper; patch (*in suit or tire*); bolt (*of paper or cloth*); **pezza d'appoggio** supporting document, voucher; **trattare come una pezza da piedi** to wipe one's boots on

pezza·to -ta *adj* spotted, dappled

pezzatura *f* dapple (*on a horse*); size (*e.g., of a loaf of bread*)

pezzènte *mf* beggar

pezzétto *m* little bit; scrap, snip

pèzzo *m* piece; cut (*of meat*); coin; (journ) article; **andare** or **cadere a pezzi** to fall apart; **a pezzi e bocconi** by fits and starts; **fare a pezzi** to break to pieces; to blow to bits; **pezzo di ricambio** spare part; **pezzo d'uomo** hunk of a man; **pezzo duro** brick ice cream; **pezzo forte** forte; **pezzo fuso** cast, casting; **un bel pezzo** a good while; **un pezzo grosso** a big shot

pezzuòla *f* small piece of cloth; (coll) handkerchief

phy·lum *m* (-lum) phylum

piacènte *adj* attractive, pleasant

piacére *m* pleasure; **a piacere** at will; **a Suo piacere** as you please; **fare piacere a** to do a favor for; to please; **per piacere** please; **piacere!**

pleased to meet you! || §214 *intr*
(ESSERE) to please; to be pleasing;
(with *dat*) to please, e.g., **come piace
a Dio** as it pleases God; to like, e.g.,
gli piace il ballo he likes dancing

piacévole *adj* pleasant, pleasing

piacevolézza *f* pleasantness; off-color
joke

pia‧ga *f* (-**ghe**) sore; ulcer; wound;
plague; (joc) bore; **piaga di decubito**
bedsore

piagare §209 *tr* to make sore, injure

piàg‧gia *f* (-**ge**) (archaic) declivity; (lit)
clime, country

piaggiare §290 *tr* (lit) to flatter, blan-
dish || *intr* (archaic) to coast

piagnistèo *m* whining

piagnó‧ne -**na** *mf* (coll) weeper, crybaby

piagnucolare (**piagnùcolo**) *intr* to
whimper, whine

piagnucoló‧ne -**na** *mf* whimperer, crybaby

piagnucoló‧so -**sa** [s] *adj* whimpering,
whining

pialla *f* (carp) plane

piallàc‧cio *m* (-**ci**) veneer

piallare *tr* (carp) to plane

piallatrice *f* (carp) planer

piallatura *f* (carp) planing

piana *f* plain; wide table

pianale *m* plain; platform; (rr) flatcar,
platform car

pianeggiante *adj* plane, level

pianèlla *f* mule (*slipper*); tile

pianeròttolo *m* landing (*of stairs*);
ledge

piané‧ta *m* (-**ti**) planet; horoscope
|| *f* (eccl) chasuble

piàngere §215 *tr* to shed (*tears*); to
mourn, lament; **piangere miseria** to
cry poverty || *intr* to cry, weep

piangimisè‧ria *mf* (-**ria**) poverty-crying
penny pincher

piangiucchiare §287 *intr* to whimper

pianificare §197 (**pianìfico**) *tr* to level;
(econ) to plan

pianifica‧tóre -**trice** *mf* planner

pianino *m* (coll) barrel organ

piani‧sta *mf* (-**sti** -**ste**) pianist

pia‧no -**na** *adj* plane; plain, flat || *m*
plain; plane; floor; plateau; plan;
map; (mus) piano; **di primo piano**
first-class; **in piano** horizontal; **piano
di coda** (aer) tail assembly; **piano di
studio** curriculum; **piano regolatore**
building plan; **piano terra** ground
floor; **primo piano** (phot) close-up;
(theat) foreground || *f* see **piana** ||
piano *adv* slowly; softly

pianofòrte *m* piano; **pianoforte a coda**
grand piano

pianòla *f* player piano

pianòro *m* plateau

pianotèr‧ra *m* (-**ra**) ground floor

pianta *f* plant; sole (*of foot*); plan,
map; floor plan; **di sana pianta**
wholly; **in pianta stabile** permanent
(*employee*); **pianta rampicante** (bot)
climber

piantagióne *f* plantation

piantana *f* scaffolding

piantare *tr* to plant; to set up (*e.g., a
gun emplacement*); to pitch (*a tent*);
piantala! (slang) cut it out!; **piantare
baracca e burattini** (coll) to clear
out; **piantar chiodi** (coll) to go into
debt; **piantare gli occhi addosso a**
to stare at; **piantare in asso** to leave
in the lurch || *ref* to place oneself;
to abandon one another

pianta‧to -**ta** *adj* planted; stuck; driven;
bien piantato well-built (*person*)

pianta‧tóre -**trice** *mf* planter

pianterréno *m* ground floor

piantito *m* (coll) floor

pianto *m* weeping, tears; sadness; (bot)
sap; (coll) sight, mess

piantonare (**piantóno**) *tr* to watch,
guard

piantóne *m* watchman; (mil) orderly;
(mil) sentry; (bot) cutting, shoot;
piantone di guida (aut) steering
wheel column

pianura *f* plain

piastra *f* plate; plaster (*coin*)

piastrèlla *f* tile; small flat stone; bounce
(*of an airplane on landing*)

piastrellaménto *m* bump, bounce (*of
motorboat or airplane*)

piastrelli‧sta *m* (-**sti**) tiler, tile layer

piastrina *f* or **piastrino** *m* small plate;
(mil) dog tag; (biol) platelet

piatire §176 *intr* (lit) to argue; (coll) to
beg insistingly

piattafórma *f* platform; roadbed (*of
highway*); (rr) turntable; (pol) plank;
piattaforma di lancio launching pad

piattèllo *m* small dish; bobèche; clay
pigeon

piattina *f* electric cord; metal band;
(min) wagon

piattino *m* saucer

piat‧to -**ta** *adj* flat || *m* dish, plate; pan
(*of scale*); pot (*in gambling*); course
(*of meal*); cover (*of book*); flat (*e.g.,
of blade*); **piatti** (mus) cymbals;
piatto del grammofono turntable;
piatto del giorno plat du jour; **piatto
di lenticchie** (Bib & fig) mess of pot-
tage; **piatto fondo** soup dish; **piatto
forte** pièce de résistance

piàttola *f* (zool) crab louse; (coll) cockroach; (vulg) bore

piazza *f* square; plaza; crowd; market;
fortress; **andare in piazza** (coll) to
become bald; **da piazza** common,
ordinary; **di piazza** for hire (*e.g.,
cab*); **fare la piazza** (com) to canvass
for customers; **far piazza pulita di**
to get rid of; to clean out; **mettere in
piazza** to noise abroad; **piazza d'armi**
parade ground; **scendere in piazza**
to take to the streets

piazzafòrte *f* (**piazzefòrti**) stronghold,
fortress

piazzale *m* large square, esplanade,
plaza

piazzaménto *m* placement; (sports) position (*of a team*)

piazzare *tr* to place; to sell || *ref* to
place; to show (*said of a racing
horse*)

piazza·to -ta *adj* placed; arrived (*at a high position*) || *f* row, brawl

piazzi·sta *m* (*-sti*) salesman; traveling salesman

piazzòla *f* court, place; rest area (*off a highway*); (mil) emplacement; **piazzola di partenza** (golf) tee

pi·ca *f* (*-che*) (orn) magpie

picaré·sco -sca *adj* (*-schi -sche*) picaresque

pic·ca *f* (*-che*) pike; pique; **per picca** out of spite; **picche** (cards) spades; **rispondere picche** (fig) to answer no

piccante *adj* piquant, racy

piccare §197 *tr* (obs) to prick || *ref* to become angry; **piccarsi di** to pride oneself on

pic·chè *f* (*-chè*).piqué

picchettaménto *m* picketing

picchettare (picchétto) *tr* to stake out; to picket

picchétto *m* stake; picket; (mil) detail

picchiare §287 *tr* to hit, strike || *intr* to knock; to strike; to tap (*said, e.g., of rain*); (aer) to nose-dive; **picchiare in testa** (aut) to knock || *ref* to hit one another

picchiata *f* hit, blow; (aer) nose dive

picchia·tóre -trice *mf* hitter || *m* (boxing) puncher

picchierellare (picchierèllo) *tr* & *intr* to tap

picchiettare (picchiétto) *tr* to tap; to scrape; to speckle || *intr* to tap

picchiet·tìo *m* (*-tìi*) patter (*e.g., of rain*)

pìc·chio *m* (*-chi*) knock; (orn) woodpecker; **di picchio** all of a sudden

picchiòtto *m* knocker (*on door*)

piccineria *f* pettiness

picci·no -na *adj* little, tiny; petty || *mf* child; baby

picciòlo *m* stem (*e.g., of cherry*); leaf-stalk, petiole

piccionàia *f* dovecote; loft; attic; (theat) upper gallery

piccióne -na *mf* pigeon; **pigliare due piccioni con una fava** to hit two birds with one stone

pic·co *m* (*-chi*) peak; (naut) gaff; andare a picco to sink; to go to ruin; **a picco** vertically; **picco di carico** (naut) derrick

piccolézza *f* smallness; trifle

picco·lo -la *adj* small; low (*speed*); short (*distance*); young; petty; **da piccolo** when young; **in piccolo** on a small scale; **nel mio piccolo** with my modest abilities || *mf* child

piccóne *m* pick

piccòzza *f* mattock (*for mountain climbing*)

pidocchieria *f* stinginess; meanness

pidòc·chio *m* (*-chi*) louse; **pidocchio rifatto** (slang) parvenu

pidocchió·so -sa [*s*] *adj* lousy; stingy

piè *m* (*piè*) (lit) foot; **ad ogni piè sospinto** on every occasion; **saltare a piè pari** to skip with the feet together; (fig) to skip over

piède *m* foot; leg (*of table*); stalk (*of salad*); bottom (*of column*); trunk (*of tree*); footing; **alzarsi in piedi** to stand up; **a piede libero** free; **a piedi**

on foot; **a piedi nudi** barefooted; **con i piedi di piombo** cautiously; **essere in piedi** to be up and around; **fare con i piedi** to botch; **mettere un piede in fallo** to stumble; **piede di porco** crowbar; **prendere piede** to take hold; **puntare i piedi** to balk; **su due piedi** offhand; **tenere il piede in due staffe** to carry water on both shoulders

piedestallo or **piedistallo** *m* pedestal

piedritto *m* buttress

piè·ga *f* (*-ghe*) bend; crease; pleat; crimp; wrinkle; (fig) turn; **prendere una cattiva piega** to take a turn for the worse

piegare §209 *tr* to bend; to wave (*hair*); to fold; to pleat; to bow (*head*) || *intr* to turn || *ref* to bow; to bend; to buckle; to yield

piega·tóre -trice *mf* folder || *f* folding machine

piegatura *f* fold, crease

pieghettare (pieghétto) *tr* to pleat

pieghévole *adj* folding; pliant; (fig) versatile || *m* folder

pieghevolézza *f* flexibility

piè·go *m* (*-ghi*) folder; bundle of papers

pièna *f* flood; rise (*of river*); crowd; (fig) overflow; **in piena** overflowing

pienézza *f* plenitude, fullness

piè·no -na *adj* full; solid; broad (*daylight*); full (*honors*); **a pieno** or **in pieno** to the full; **colpire nel pieno** to hit the bull's eye; **pieno di** alive with; **pieno di sé** conceited; **pieno zeppo** replete, chock-full || *m* fullness; height (*e.g., of winter*); **fare il pieno** (aut) to fill up || *f* see **piena**

pie·tà *f* (*-tà*) mercy; pity; (lit) piety

pietanza *f* main course

pietó·so -sa [*s*] *adj* pitiful, piteous; merciful

piètra *f* stone; rock; **pietra angolare** cornerstone; **pietra da affilare** whetstone; **pietra da sarto** French chalk; **pietra dello scandalo** source of scandal; **pietra di paragone** touchstone; **pietra focaia** flint; **pietra miliare** milestone; **pietra tombale** tombstone; **posare la prima pietra** to lay the cornerstone

pietrificare §197 (**pietrìfico**) *tr* & *ref* to petrify

pietrina *f* flint (*for lighter*)

pietri·sco *m* (*-schi*) rubble; (rr) ballast

Piètro *m* Peter

pietró·so -sa [*s*] *adj* (lit) stony

piè·vano *m* parish priest

pìffero *m* pipe, fife

pigia *m*—**pigia pigia** crowd, throng

pigìa·ma *m* (*-ma* & *-mi*) pajamas

pigiare §290 *tr* to squeeze, press || *intr* to insist || *ref* to squeeze

pigia·tóre -trice *mf* presser (*of grapes*) || *f* wine press

pigiatura *f* pressing, squeezing

pigionante *mf* tenant

pigióne *f* rent, rental; **dare a pigione** to rent; to grant the possession of; **prendere a pigione** to rent; to hold for payment

pigliamó·sche *m* (-sche) flypaper; fly-trap; (orn) flycatcher

pigliare §280 *tr* to take, catch; to mistake; che Le piglia? what's the matter with you? || *ref*—pigliarsela (con) to get angry (at)

pi·glio *m* (-gli) hold; countenance; dar di piglio a to grab

pigménto *m* pigment

pigmè·o -a *adj* & *mf* pygmy; Pygmy

pigna *f* strainer (*at the end of a suction pipe*); bunch (*of grapes*); (bot) pine cone

pignatta *f* pot

pignò·lo -la *adj* finicky, fussy || *m* pine nut

pignóne *m* pinion; embankment

pignoraménto *m* (law) seizure

pignorare (pìgnoro) *tr* (law) to seize

pigolare (pìgolo) *intr* to peep (*said, e.g., of young birds*)

pigolí·o *m* (-ìi) peep (*e.g., of a young bird*)

pigrìzia *f* laziness

pi·gro -gra *adj* lazy; (lit) sluggish

pila *f* pier; buttress (*of bridge*); heap; sink; font; (elec) cell; (elec) battery; pila atomica atomic pile

pilastro *m* pier, pillar

pillàcchera *f* mud splash; (fig) fault

pillola *f* pill; (slang) bullet; addolcire la pillola to sugar-coat the pill

pilóne *m* pier; pylon

pilò·ta (-ti -te) *adj* pilot || *mf* pilot; (aut) driver

pilotàg·gio *m* (-gi) piloting; steering

pilotare (pilòto) *tr* to pilot; to drive

pilotina *f* (naut) pilot boat

piluccare §197 *tr* to pluck (*e.g., grapes one by one*); to nibble, pick at; to scrounge; (lit) to consume

piménto *m* allspice

pinacotè·ca *f* (-che) picture gallery

pinéta *f* pine grove

pìngue *adj* fat; rich

pinguèdine *f* fatness, corpulence

pinguino *m* penguin

pinna *f* fin (*of fish*); flipper; (zool) pen shell (*mussel*)

pinnàcolo *m* pinnacle

pino *m* pine tree; pino marittimo pinaster; pino silvestre Scotch fir

pinòlo *m* pine nut

pinta *f* pint

pinza *f* claw (*of lobster*); pinza emostatica hemostat; pinza tagliafili wire cutter; pinze clippers; pliers; pincers

pinzatrice *f* stapler

pinzétte *fpl* tweezers, pliers

pinzòche·ro -ra *mf* bigot

pì·o -a *adj* (-i -e) pious; charitable || Pio *m* Pius

piòg·gia *f* (-ge) rain

piòlo *m* peg; rung (*of ladder*); picket, stake

piombàggine *f* graphite

piombare (piómbo) *tr* to lead; to seal; to knock down; to fill (*a tooth*) || *intr* to fall; to swoop down

piombatura *f* leading; filling (*of tooth*)

piombino *m* weight; seal; plumb; plumb bob

piómbo *m* lead; a piombo perpendicularly; di piombo suddenly

pionerìsti·co -ca *adj* (-ci -che) pioneering

pionière *m* pioneer

piòppo *m* poplar; pioppo tremolo aspen

piorrèa *f* pyorrhea

piotare (piòto) *tr* to sod

piova·no -na *adj* rain (*water*)

piova·sco *m* (-schi) rain squall

piovènte *m* pitch, slope

piòvere §216 *intr* (ESSERE) to rain; to pour; to flock (*said of people*); piovere addosso a to rain down on; piovere su to flow down over || *impers* (ESSERE & AVERE)—piove it is raining; it is leaking (*from rain*); piove a catinelle or a dirotto it is raining cats and dogs

piovigginare (piovìggina) *impers* (ESSERE & AVERE)—piovìggina it is drizzling

piovigginó·so -sa [s] *adj* drizzling, drizzly

piovór·no -na *adj* (lit) var of piovoso

piovosi·tà [s] *f* (-tà) raininess; rainfall

piovó·so -sa [s] *adj* rainy

piòvra *f* octopus; (fig) leech

pipa *f* pipe; non valere una pipa di tabacco to not be worth a tinker's dam

pipare *intr* to smoke a pipe

pipata *f* pipe, pipeful

pipistrèllo *m* (zool) bat

pipita *f* hangnail; (vet) pip

pira *f* (lit) pyre

piràmide *f* pyramid

pira·ta *adj invar* pirate || *m* (-ti) pirate; pirata dell'aria skyjacker; pirata della strada hit-and-run driver

pirateggiare §290 (piratéggio) *intr* to pirate

piraterìa *f* piracy; piratería letteraria piracy of literary works

Pirenèi *mpl* Pyrenees

pìri·co -ca *adj* (-ci -che) fireworks; polvere pirica gunpowder

pirite *f* pyrite

piroétta *f* pirouette

pirò·ga *f* (-ghe) pirogue

pirolisi *f* (chem) cracking

piróne *m* (mus) tuning pin

piròscafo *m* steamship; piroscafo da carico (naut) freighter; piroscafo da passeggeri passenger ship

piroscissióne *f* (chem) cracking

pirotècni·co -ca (-ci -che) *adj* pyrotecnic || *m* pyrotecnist || *f* fireworks, pyrotechnics

pisciare §128 *intr* (vulg) to urinate

piscia·tóio *m* (-tói) (vulg) street urinal

piscina *f* swimming pool

pisèllo [s] *m* pea; pisello odoroso sweet pea

pisolare (pìsolo) *intr* (coll) to doze

pìsolo *m* (coll) nap; schiacciare un pisolo (coll) to take a nap

pìsside *f* (eccl) pyx; (bot) pyxidium

pista *f* track; ring (*of circus*); race track, speedway (*for car races*); ski run; (aer) runway; pista ciclabile bicycle trail; pista da ballo dance floor; **seguire una pista** to follow a clue

pistàc·chio m (-chi) pistachio

pistillo m (bot) pistil

pistòla f pistol

pistolettata f pistol shot

pistolòtto m lecture, talking-to; theatrical peroration

pistóne m piston; plunger

pitagòri·co -ca adj & m (-ci -che) Pythagorean

pitale m (coll) chamber pot

pitoccare §197 (pitòcco) intr to beg

pitòc·co m (-chi) beggar; miser

pitóne m python

pittima f plaster; (fig) bore

pit·tóre -trice mf painter

pittoré·sco -sca adj (-schi -sche) picturesque

pittòri·co -ca adj (-ci -che) pictorial

pittura f painting; picture; (coll) paint

pitturare tr to paint; to varnish || ref to put on make-up

più adj invar more; several || m (più) plus; most; **credersi da più** to believe oneself superior; **dal più al meno** about, more or less; **i più** most, the majority; **parlare del più e del meno** (coll) to make small talk || adv more; again; **a più non posso** to the very utmost; **in più** besides; **mai più** never again; **non poterne più** to be exhausted; **per di più** besides; **per lo più** for the most part; **più o meno** more or less; **tanto più** moreover; **tutt'al più** mostly

piuma f feather, plume; **piume** (fig) bed

piumàc·cio m (-ci) feather pillow

piumàg·gio m (-gi) plumage

piumino m down; comforter; puff, powder puff; feather duster

piuttòsto adv rather; somewhat

piva f bagpipe; **tornare con le pive nel sacco** to return bitterly disappointed

pivèllo m greenhorn; whippersnapper

pivière m (orn) plover

pizza f pizza; (mov) canister; (coll) bore

pizzaiò·lo -la mf owner of pizzeria || m pizza baker || f—**alla pizzaiola** prepared with tomato and garlic sauce

pizzardóne m (coll) cop, officer

pizzicàgno·lo -la mf grocer; sausage dealer

pizzicare §197 (pìzzico) tr to pinch; to pluck; to bite, burn; (mus) to pick, twang

pizzicherìa f delicatessen, grocery

pìzzi·co m (-chi) pinch

pizzicóre m itch

pizzicòtto m pinch; **dar pizzicotti a** to pinch

pizzo m peak (of mountain); goatee; lace

placare §197 tr to placate || ref to calm down

plac·ca f (-che) plate; plaque; tag, badge; (elec, rad) plate; (pathol) blotch, spot

placcare §197 tr to plate; (sports) to tackle

plàci·do -da adj placid

plafond m (plafond) ceiling; (aer) ceiling; (com) top credit

pla·ga f (-ghe) (lit) clime, region

plagiare §290 tr to plagiarize

plagià·rio -ria (-ri -rie) adj plagiaristic || mf plagiarist

plà·gio m (-gi) plagiarism

planare intr (aer) to glide

planata f (aer) gliding

plàn·cia f (-ce) (naut) gangplank; (naut) bridge

planetà·rio -ria (-ri -rie) adj planetary || m planetarium; (aut) planetary gear

plantare m arch support

pla·sma m (-smi) plasma

plasmare tr to mold, shape

plàsti·ca f (-che) plastic art; plastics; plastic surgery; plastic

plasticare §197 (plàstico) tr to mold, shape; to cover with plastic

plàsti·co -ca (-ci -che) adj plastic || m relief map; maquette; plastic bomb || f see **plastica**

plastilina f modeling clay

plastron m (plastron) ascot

plàtano m plane tree; **platano americano** buttonwood tree

platèa f audience; (theat) orchestra; (archit) foundation

plateale adj obvious; plebeian

plàtina f (typ) platen

platinare (plàtino) tr to platinize; to bleach (hair)

plàtino m platinum

Platóne m Plato

plaudènte adj enthusiastic

plàudere (plàudo) & **plaudire** (plàudo)** intr to applaud; (with dat) to applaud, e.g., **plaudere alla generosità** to applaud the generosity

plausìbile adj plausible

plàuso m (lit) applause, praise

plebàglia f rabble

plèbe f populace; (lit) crowd

plebè·o -a adj & mf plebeian

plebiscito m plebiscite

plenà·rio -ria adj (-ri -rie) plenary

pleniù·nio m (-ni) full moon

plenipotenzià·rio -ria adj & m (-ri -rie) plenipotentiary

plètora f plethora

plèttro m (mus) pick, plectrum

pleurite f (pathol) pleurisy

pli·co m (-chi) sealed document; bundle of papers; **in plico a parte** or **in plico separato** under separate cover

plotóne m platoon; **plotone d'esecuzione** firing squad

plùmbe·o -a adj lead, leaden

plurale adj & m plural; **al plurale** in the plural

plurilìngue adj multilingual

plurimotóre adj multimotored || m multimotor

pluristàdio adj invar (rok) multistage

plusvalènza f unearned increment

plusvalóre m; surplus value (in Marxist economics)

Plutarco m Plutarch

plutocrazìa f plutocracy

Plutóne m Pluto

plutònio m plutonium

pluviale adj rain || m waterspout

pneumàti·co -ca (-ci -che) adj pneumatic, air || m tire; **pneumatico da neve** snow tire

po' m see **poco**

pochézza f lack, scarcity

pò·co -ca (-chi -che) adj little; short (distance); poor (health; memory); (with collective nouns) few, e.g., **poca gente** few people; (with plural nouns) a few, e.g., **fra pochi mesi** in a few months; (with plural nouns having singular meaning in English) little, e.g., **pochi quattrini** little money || m invar little; short distance; short time; **a ogni poco** often; **da poco** a little while ago; of no account; **da un bel po'** quite a while; quite a while ago; **fra poco** in a little while; **manca poco a** it won't be long till; **manca poco che** (e.g., il ragazzo) **non + subj** (e.g., the boy) almost + ind; **per poco non** almost; **poco di buono** good-for-nothing; **poco fa** a little while ago; **saper di poco** to taste flat; **un poco di** or **un po' di** a little || f—**poca di buono** hussy || **poco** adv little; **poco bene** poorly; **poco dopo** shortly after; **poco male** not too poorly

podagra f gout

podére m farm, country property

poderó·so -sa [s] adj powerful

pode·stà m (-stà) (hist) mayor; (hist) podesta

podia·tra mf (-tri -tre) chiropodist

pò·dio m (-di) podium; platform; (archit) base

podismo m foot racing

podi·sta mf (-sti -ste) foot racer

poè·ma m (-mi) long poem

poesìa f poetry; poem

poè·ta m (-ti) poet

poetéssa f poetess

poèti·co -ca (-ci -che) adj poetic(al) || f poetics

pòg·gia f (-ge) leeward

poggiare §290 (pòggio) tr to lean || intr to be based; (mil) to move; (naut) to sail before the wind; (archaic) to rise

poggiatè·sta m (-sta) headrest; (aut) head restrainer

pòg·gio m (-gi) hillock, knoll

poggiòlo m balcony

pòi m future || adv then; later; **a poi** until later; **poi dopo** later on

poiana f buzzard

poiché conj since, as; (lit) after

pòker m poker (game); four of a kind; **poker di re** four kings

polàc·co -ca (-chi -che) adj Polish || mf Pole || f (mus) polonaise

polare adj pole, polar

polarizzare [ddzz] tr to polarize

pòl·ca f (-che) polka

polèmi·co -ca (-ci -che) adj polemical || f polemics

polemizzare [ddzz] intr to engage in polemics

polèna f (naut) figurehead

polènta f corn mush

polentina f poultice

poliambulanza f clinic, emergency ward

policlìni·co m (-ci) polyclinic

polifonìa f polyphony

polìga·mo -ma adj polygamous || m polygamist

poliglòt·ta adj & mf (-ti -te) polyglot

poliglòt·to -ta adj & mf polyglot

poligono m polygon; **poligono di tiro** shooting range

polìgrafo m author skilled in many subjects; multigraph

polinesia·no -na adj & mf Polynesian

polinò·mio m (-mi) polynomial

pòlio f (coll) polio

poliomielite f poliomielitis, infantile paralysis

pòlipo m (pathol, zool) polyp

polisìlla·bo -ba adj polysyllabic || m polysyllable

poli·sta m (-sti) polo player

politea·ma m (-mi) theater

politècni·co -ca (-ci -che) adj polytechnic || m polytechnic institute

politeì·sta (-sti -ste) adj polytheistic || mf polytheist

politeìsti·co -ca adj (-ci -che) polytheistic

politézza f smoothness

politi·ca f (-che) politics; policy

politicante mf petty politician

politi·co -ca (-ci -che) adj political || m politician || f see **politica**

politti·co m (-ci) polyptych

polizìa f police; **polizia sanitaria** health department; **polizia stradale** highway patrol; **polizia tributaria** income-tax investigation department

polizié·sco -sca adj (-schi -sche) police (car); detective (story)

poliziòtto adj masc police (dog) || m policeman; detective; **poliziotto in borghese** plain-clothes man

pòlizza f policy; ticket (e.g., of pawnbroker); **polizza di carico** bill of lading

pólla f spring (of water)

pol·làio m (-lài) chicken coop

pollaiò·lo -la mf chicken dealer

pollame m poultry

pollastra f pullet; (coll) chick

pollerìa f poultry shop

pòllice m thumb; big toe; inch

pollicoltura f poultry raising

pòlline m pollen

pollivéndo·lo -la mf poultry dealer

póllo m chicken; (fig) sucker; **conoscere i propri polli** (fig) to know one's onions; **pollo d'India** turkey

pollóne m (bot) shoot; (fig) offspring

polmóne m lung; **a pieni polmoni** at the top of one's lungs; **polmone d'acciaio** iron lung

polmonìte f pneumonia

pòlo m pole; polo shirt; (sports) polo

Polònia, la Poland

pólpa f meat; pulp; flesh (of fruit); (fig) gist; **in polpe** (hist) in knee breeches

polpàc·cio m (-ci) calf (of leg); cut of meat; ball of thumb

polpastrèllo *m* finger tip

polpétta *f* meat ball; meat patty, cutlet

polpettóne *m* meat loaf; (fig) hash

pólpo *m* (zool) octopus

polpó·so -sa [s] *adj* pulpy, fleshy

polpu·to -ta *adj* meaty

polsino *m* cuff

pólso *m* pulse; wrist; cuff, wristband; strong hand, energy; **di polso** energetic

poltiglia *f* mash; slush

poltrire §176 *intr* to idle; to loll in bed

poltróna *f* armchair; (theat) orchestra seat; **poltrona a orecchioni** wing chair; **poltrona a sdraio** chaise longue; **poltrona letto** day bed

poltroncina *f* parquet-circle seat

poltró·ne -na *mf* lazybones, sluggard ‖ *f* see poltrona

poltronerìa *f* laziness

poltronìssima *f* (theat) first-row seat

pólvere *f* dust; powder; **in polvere** powdered; **polvere da sparo** gunpowder; **polvere di stelle** stardust; **polvere nera** or **pirica** gunpowder; **polveri** gunpowder

polverièra *f* powder magazine; (fig) tinderbox, trouble spot

polverifi·cio *m* (-ci) powder works

polverina *f* (pharm) powder

polverino *m* pounce, sand

polverizzare [ddzz] *tr* to crush, powder; to atomize; to pulverize

polverizza·to -ta [ddzz] *adj* powdered (*sugar*)

polverizzatóre [ddzz] *m* atomizer

polveróne *m* dust cloud

polveró·so -sa [s] *adj* dusty; powdery (*snow*)

pomata *f* ointment; pomade

pomella·to -ta *adj* dapple-grey

pomèllo *m* cheek; cheekbone; pommel, knob

pomeridia·no -na *adj* afternoon, P.M.

pomerìg·gio *m* (-gi) afternoon

pomiciare §128 (pómicio) *tr* to pumice ‖ *intr* (slang) to spoon

pomicióne *m* (slang) spooner

pomidòro *m* var of pomodoro

pómo *m* apple; knob; pommel (*of saddle*); **pomo della discordia** apple of discord; **pomo di Adamo** Adam's apple; **pomo di terra** potato

pomodòro *m* tomato; **pomodoro di mare** (zool) sea anemone

pómolo *m* (coll) knob, handle

pómpa *f* pump; pomp; state; **in pompa magna** all dressed up; **pompa aspirante** suction pump; **pompa premente** force pump; see imprenditore and impresa

pompare (pómpo) *tr* to pump; to pump up

pompèlmo *m* grapefruit

pompière *m* fireman

pompó·so -sa [s] *adj* pompous

pòn·ce *m* (-ci) punch

ponderare (póndero) *tr* to weigh, ponder; to weight ‖ *intr* to think it over

pondera·to -ta *adj* considerate, careful

ponderó·so -sa [s] *adj* ponderous

ponènte *m* west; west wind; West; West Wind

pónte *m* bridge; metal scaffolding; (aut) axle; (naut) deck; **fare il ponte** to take the day off between two holidays; **fare ponti d'oro** a to offer a good way out to; **ponte aereo** airlift; **ponte delle segnalazioni** (rr) gantry; **ponte di chiatte** pontoon bridge; **ponte di comando** (naut) bridge; **ponte di volo** flight deck; **ponte levatoio** drawbridge; **ponte radio** radio communication; **ponte sospeso** suspension bridge

pontéfice *m* pontiff; (hist) pontifex

pontéggio *m* scaffolding

ponticèllo *m* small bridge; nosepiece (*of eyeglasses*); (mus) bridge

pontière *m* (mil) engineer

pontificale *adj* pontifical ‖ *m* pontifical mass

pontifi·cio -cia *adj* (-ci -cie) papal

pontile *m* pier

pontóne *m* pontoon, barge

ponzare (pónzo) *tr* (coll) to strain to accomplish ‖ *intr* (coll) to rack one's brains

popeli·ne *f* (-ne) broadcloth

popola·no -na *adj* popular ‖ *mf* commoner

popolare *adj* popular ‖ *v* (pòpolo) *tr* to people, populate ‖ *ref* to be inhabited

popolarità *f* popularity

popola·to -ta *adj* peopled; crowded

popolazióne *f* population

pòpolo *m* people; crowd; **popolo grasso** (hist) rich bourgeoisie; **popolo minuto** (hist) artisans, common people

popoló·so -sa [s] *adj* populous

popóne *m* (coll) melon

póppa *f* breast; (naut) stern; (lit) ship; **a poppa** astern, aft

poppante *adj* & *mf* suckling

poppare (póppo) *tr* to suckle

poppa·tóio *m* (-tói) nursing bottle

poppavìa *f*—**a poppavia** astern, aft

pòr·ca *f* (-che) ridge (*between furrows*); sow

porcacció·ne -na *m* cad, rake ‖ *f* slut

por·càio *m* (-cài) swineherd; pigsty

porcellana *f* porcelain, china; (bot) purslane

porcellino *m* piggy; **porcellino d'India** guinea pig

porcherìa *f* dirt; (coll) dirty trick; (coll) botch

porchétta *f* roast suckling pig

po·cile *m* pigsty

porci·no -na *adj* pig ‖ *m* (bot) boletus

pòr·co -ca *mf* (-ci -che) pig, hog, swine; pork; **porco mondo!** (slang) heck! ‖ *f* see porca

porcospino *m* porcupine

pòrfido *m* porphyry

pòrgere §217 *tr* to hand, offer; to relate; **porgere l'orecchio** to lend an ear ‖ *intr* to declaim ‖ *ref* to appear, show up

pornografìa *f* pornography

pòro *m* pore

poró·so -sa [s] *adj* porous

pórpora *f* purple

porpora·to -ta adj purple ‖ m purple; cardinal

porpori·no -na adj purple

pórre §218 tr to put; to repose (trust); to set (a limit; one's foot); to lay (a stone); to pose (a question); to pay (attention); to suppose; to advance (the candidacy); **porre gli occhi addosso a** to lay one's eyes on; **porre in dubbio** to cast doubt on; **porre mano a** to set to work at; **porre termine a** to put an end to; **posto che** since, provided ‖ ref to place oneself; **porsi in cammino** to set out or forth; **porsi in salvo** to reach safety

pòrro m wart; (bot) leek

pòrta f door; gate; (cricket) wicket; (sports) goal; **di porta in porta** door-to-door; **fuori porta** outside the city limits; **mettere alla porta** to dismiss, fire; **porta di servizio** delivery entrance; **porta scorrevole** sliding door; **porta stagna** (naut; theat) safety door

portabagà·gli m (-gli) porter; baggage rack

portabandiè·ra m (-ra) standard-bearer

portàbile adj portable

portàbi·ti m (-ti) coat hanger

portabotti·glie m (-glie) bottle rack

portacar·te adj invar & m (-te) folder

portacati·no adj invar washstand-supporting ‖ m (-no) washstand

portacéne·re m (-re) ashtray

portachia·vi m (-vi) key ring

portacì·pria m (-pria) compact

portadi·schi m (-schi) record cabinet, record rack; turntable

portadól·ci m (-ci) candy dish

portaère·i f (-i) aircraft carrier

portaferì·ti m (-ti) (mil) stretcher bearer

portafinèstra f (portefinèstre) French window

portafió·ri m (-ri) flower vase

portafò·gli m (-gli) or **portafò·glio** m (-gli) billfold, wallet; pocketbook; portfolio

portafortu·na m (-na) charm, amulet

portafrut·ta m (-ta) fruit dish

portafusìbi·li m (-li) fuse box

portagiò·ie m (-ie) jewel box

portaimmondì·zie m (-zie) trash can, garbage can

portainsé·gna m (-gna) standard-bearer

portalàmpa·da m (-da) (elec) socket

portale m portal

portalètte·re (-re) mf letter carrier ‖ m postman, mailman

portamaz·ze m (-ze) caddie

portaménto m posture; gait; (fig) behavior

portami·na m (-na) mechanical pencil

portamìssi·li (-li) adj invar missile-carrying ‖ m missile carrier

portamoné·te m (-te) purse

portamùsi·ca m (-ca) music stand

portante adj carrying; (archit) weight-bearing; (aer) lifting; (rad) carrier ‖ m amble

portantina f sedan chair; stretcher

portantino m bearer (of sedan chair); stretcher bearer

portanza f (archit) capacity; (aer) lift

portaombrèl·li m (-li) umbrella stand

portaórdi·ni m (-ni) (mil) messenger

portapac·chi m (-chi) parcel delivery man; basket (on bicycle)

portapén·ne m (-ne) penholder

portapiat·ti m (-ti) dish rack

portaposa·te [s] m (-te) silverware chest

portapran·zi [dz] m (-zi) dinner pail

portaraz·zi (-zi) [ddzz] adj invar missile-carrying ‖ m missile carrier

portare (pòrto) tr to carry; to bring; to take; to carry along; to lead; to herald; to praise; to wear; to drive (car); to run (a candidate); to adduce; to nurture (hatred); (aut) to hold (e.g., five people); **portare a conoscenza di** to let know; **portare avanti** to carry forward; **portare in alto** to lift; **portare via** to steal; to take away ‖ intr to carry (said of a gun) ‖ ref to move; to behave; to be (a candidate)

portaritrat·ti m (-ti) picture frame

portasapó·ne m (-ne) soap dish

portasigarét·te m (-te) cigarette case

portasìga·ri m (-ri) cigar case; humidor

portaspil·li m (-li) pincushion

portata f course (of a meal); capacity; flow (of river); compass (of voice); range (of voice or gun); importance; (naut) burden; (naut) tonnage; **a portata di mano** within reach; **a portata di voce** within call, within earshot

portatès·se·re m (-re) card case

portàtile adj portable

porta·to -ta adj worn; **portato a** leaning toward ‖ m result, effect ‖ f see **portata**

porta·tóre -trice mf bearer

portatovagliòlo m napkin ring

portauò·vo m (-vo) eggcup

portavó·ce m (-ce) megaphone; (fig) mouthpiece

porte-enfant m (porte-enfant) baby bunting

portèllo m wicket; leaf (of cabinet door); (naut) porthole

portènto m portent

portica·to -ta adj arcaded ‖ m arcade

pòrti·co m (-ci) portico, arcade, colonnade; shed

portiè·re -ra mf concierge ‖ m janitor, doorman; (sports) goalkeeper ‖ f portiere (in church door); (aut) door

porti·nàio -nàia (-nài -nàie) adj door, door-keeping ‖ mf doorkeeper, concierge

portinerìa f janitor's quarters

pòrto m port, harbor; transportation charge; port wine; goal; **condurre a buon porto** to carry to fruition; **franco di porto** prepaid, postpaid; **porto a carico del mittente** postage prepaid; **porto assegnato** charges to be paid by addressee; **porto d'armi** permit to carry arms; **porto franco** free port

Portogallo, il Portugal

portoghése [s] adj & mf Portuguese;

fare il portoghese (theat) to crash the gate

portóne *m* portal

portorica•no -na *adj & mf* Puerto Rican

Portorico *m* Puerto Rico

portuale *adj* port, harbor || *m* dock worker, longshoreman

porzióne *f* portion

pòsa [s] *f* laying (*e.g., of cornerstone*); posing (*for portrait*); posture, affectation, pose; dregs; (phot) exposure; (lit) rest; **senza posa** relentless; relentlessly

posami•ne (-ne) [s] *adj invar* mine-laying || *f* minelayer

posare [s] (**pòso**) *tr* to lay, put down || *intr* to lie; to settle; to pose; **posare a** to pose as || *ref* to settle; to alight; (lit) to rest

posata [s] *f* cover, place (*at table*); table utensil (*knife, fork or spoon*); **posate** knife, fork and spoon

posatería [s] *f* service (*of knives, forks, and spoons*)

posa•to -ta [s] *adj* sedate, quiet; placed || *f see* **posata**

posa•tóre -trice [s] *mf* poseur || *m* layer, installer (*of cables or pipes*)

pòscia *adv* then, afterwards; **poscia che** after

poscritto *m* postscript

posdatare *tr* var of **postdatare**

posdomani *adv* (lit) day after tomorrow

positivamente *adv* for sure

positi•vo -va *adj* positive || *f* (phot) positive, print

posizióne *f* position; status; (fig) stand

posporre §218 *tr* to put off, postpone; to put last; **posporre qlco a qlco** to put or place s.th after s.th

pòssa *f* (lit) strength, vigor

possanza *f* (lit) power

possedére §252 *tr* to possess; to own; to master (*a language*); **essere posseduto da** to be enthralled with; to be possessed by

possedimento *m* possession, property

possedítrice *f* owner, possessor

possènte *adj* (lit) powerful

possessióne *f* possession

possessi•vo -va *adj* possessive

possèsso *m* possession

possessóre *m* owner, possessor

possibile *adj* possible || *m*—**fare il possibile** to do one's best

possibili•sta (-sti -ste) *adj* pragmatically flexible || *mf* pragmatically flexible person, possibilist

possibili•tà *f* (-**tà**) possibility; opportunity; **possibilità** *fpl* means

possidènte *mf* proprietor, owner; **possidente terriero** landowner

pòsta *f* post; mail; post office; box (*in stable*); ambush; bet; **a giro di posta** by return mail; **a posta** on purpose; **darsi la posta** to set up an appointment; **fare la posta a** to have under surveillance; **fermo in posta** general delivery; **levare la posta** to pick up the mail; **posta aerea** air mail; **posta dei lettori** (journ) letters to the editor; **poste** postal department

pósta *f* (archaic) planting; (archaic) footprint

postagi•ro *m* (-**ro &** -**ri**) postal transfer of funds

postale *adj* postal, mail || *m* mail; mail train (boat, bus, or plane)

postare (**pòsto**) *tr* (mil) to post || *ref* (mil) to take a position

postazióne *f* (mil) emplacement

postbèlli•co -ca *adj* (-**ci** -**che**) postwar

postbruciatóre *m* (aer) afterburner

postdatare *tr* to postdate

posteggiare §290 (**postéggio**) *tr & intr* to park

posteggia•tóre -trice *mf* parking-lot attendant; customer (*in a parking lot*); (coll) outdoor merchant; **posteggiatore abusivo** parking violator

postég•gio *m* (-**gi**) parking lot; stand (*in outdoor market*); **posteggio di tassì** cabstand

posterióre *adj* back; subsequent, later

posteri•tà *f* (-**tà**) posterity

pòste•ro -ra *adj* later, subsequent || **posteri** *mpl* posterity, descendants

postíc•cio -cia (-ci -ce) *adj* artificial; false (*e.g., tooth*); temporary || *m* wiglet, ponytail || *f* row of trees

posticipare (**posticípo**) *tr* to postpone

posticipa•to -ta *adj* deferred

postièrla *f* postern

postiglióne *m* postilion

postilla *f* marginal note

postillare *tr* to annotate

posti•no -na *mf* letter carrier || *m* mailman, postman

pósto *m* place; room; seat; job, position; spot; (mil) post; **a posto in** order; orderly; **al posto di** instead of; **essere a posto** to have a good job; **mettere a posto** to find a good job for; (coll) to keep quiet; **quel posto** (coll) seat of the pants; (coll) toilet; **posto a sedere** seat; **posto di blocco** road block; (rr) signal tower; **posto di guardia** (mil) guardhouse; **posto di medicazione** or **di pronto soccorso** first-aid station; **posto in piedi** standing room; **posto letto** bed (*e.g., in hospital*); **posto telefonico pubblico** public telephone, pay station; **rimettere a posto** to fix, repair; **saper stare al proprio posto** to know one's place; **sul posto** on the spot

postrè•mo -ma *adj* (lit) last

postríbolo *m* (lit) brothel

postulante *adj* petitioning || *mf* petitioner, applicant; (eccl) postulant

postulare (**pòstulo**) *tr* to postulate

pòstu•mo -ma *adj* posthumous || **postumi** *mpl* sequel; (pathol) sequelae

potàbile *adj* drinkable

potare (**póto**) *tr* to trim, prune

potassa *f* potash

potàssio *m* potassium

potatura *f* pruning, polling

potentato *m* (lit) potentate

potènte *adj* powerful; influential || **i potenti** the powers that be

potènza *f* power, might; (math) power; **all'ennesima potenza** (math) to the nth power; (fig) to the nth degree; **in potenza** potential; potentially

potenziale *adj & m* potential

potére *m* ability; authority, power; **in potere di** in the hands of; **potere d'acquisto** purchasing power; **potere esecutivo** executive; **potere giudiziario** judiciary; **quarto potere** fourth estate || §219 *intr* to be powerful; **non ne posso più** I am at the end of my rope; **ma è può?** may I come in? || *aux* (ESSERE & AVERE) to be able; **non posso fare a meno di** + *inf* I can't help + *ger*; **non potere fare a meno di** to not be able to do without; **posso**, etc. I can; I may, etc.; **potrei**, etc. I could; I might, etc.

potestà *f* (-stà) power, authority

poveràc·cio -cia *mf* (-ci -ce) poor guy, poor soul

pòve·ro -ra *adj* poor; needy, wretched; lean *(gasoline mixture)*; **povero in canna** as poor as a church mouse || *mf* pauper; beggar; poor devil || **i poveri** the poor

pover·tà *f* (-tà) poverty; paucity, scantiness

poveruòmo *m* (used only in *sg*) poor devil

pozióne *f* potion, brew

pózza *f* pool, puddle

pozzànghera *f* puddle

pozzétto *m* small well; manhole; forecastle *(in small boat)*

pózzo *m* well; shaft; **pozzo artesiano** artesian well; **pozzo delle catene** (naut) chain locker; **pozzo di scienza** fountain of knowledge; **pozzo di ventilazione** (min) air shaft; **pozzo nero** cesspool; **pozzo petrolifero** oil well; **pozzo trivellato** deep well; **un pozzo di** (fig) a barrel of

Praga *f* Prague

prammàti·co -ca (-ci -che) *adj* pragmatic || *f* social custom; **di prammatica** obligatory, de rigueur

pranzare [dz] *intr* to dine

pranzo [dz] *m* dinner; **dopo pranzo** afternoon

pras·si *f* (-si) practice, praxis

pratería *f* prairie

pràti·ca *f* (-che) practice; knowledge; matter; file, dossier; business; experience; (naut) pratique; **aver pratica con** to be familiar with *(people)*; **aver pratica di** to be familiar with *(things)*; **far pratica** to be an apprentice; **fare le pratiche** to make an application; **in pratica** practically; **insabbiare una pratica** to pigeonhole a matter

praticàbile *adj* practicable; passable || *m* (theat) raised platform

praticante *adj* practicing || *mf* apprentice; novice; churchgoer

praticare §197 (pràtico) *tr* to practice; to frequent; to be familiar with; to make *(e.g., a hole)*; to grant *(a discount)* || *intr* to practice; **praticare in** to frequent

pratici·tà *f* (-tà) utility; practicality

pràti·co -ca (-ci -che) *adj* practical; experienced || *f* see pratica

praticó·ne -na *mf* (pej) old hand

prato *m* meadow

pratolina *f* daisy

pra·vo -va *adj* (lit) wicked

preaccennare (preaccénno) *tr* to mention in advance

preaccenna·to -ta *adj* aforementioned

preallarme *m* early warning

Prealpi *fpl* foothills of the Alps

preàmbolo *m* preamble

preannunziare §287 (preannùnzio) *tr* to foretell, forebode

preannùn·zio *m* (-zi) advance information; foreboding

preaunnale *adj* pre-fall

preavvertire (preavvèrto) *tr* to forewarn

preavvisare *tr* to give advance notice to; to forewarn

preavviso *m* forewarning; notification of dismissal

prebèlli·co -ca *adj* (-ci -che) prewar

prebènda *f* prebend; (fig) easy money, sinecure

precà·rio -ria *adj* (-ri -rie) precarious

precauzióne *f* precaution

precedènte *adj* preceding || *m* precedent; **precedenti** background; **precedenti penali** previous offenses, record

precedènza *f* precedence; (aut) right of way; (fig) priority

precèdere §123 *tr & intr* to precede

precettare (precètto) *tr* (mil) to call back from furlough

precètto *m* precept; (eccl) obligation

precettóre *m* tutor

precipitare (precìpito) *tr* to precipitate; to hasten; (chem) to precipitate || *intr* (ESSERE) to fall; to fail; to rush *(said of events)*; (chem) to precipitate || *ref* to rush

precipitó·so -sa [s] *adj* hasty, headlong

precipì·zio *m* (-zi) precipice, cliff; ruin; **a precipizio** headlong

precì·puo -pua *adj* chief, principal, primary

precisare *tr* to say exactly, specify, clarify; to fix *(a date)*

precisazióne *f* clarification

precisióne *f* precision

precì·so -sa *adj* precise, exact; punctilious; identical, same; sharp, e.g., **alle sette precise** at seven o'clock sharp

preclà·ro -ra *adj* (lit) illustrious

preclùdere §105 *tr* to preclude

precòce *adj* precocious, premature

preconcèt·to -ta *adj* preconceived || *m* preconception; prejudice, bias

preconizzare [dzz] *tr* to foretell, forecast; (eccl) to preconize

precórrere §139 (lit) *tr* to precede || *intr* (lit) to occur before

precursóre *m* precursor

prèda *f* booty, prize; prey

predace *adj* (lit) preying, predatory

predare (prèdo) *tr* to pillage; to prey upon

preda·tóre -trice *adj* predacious, rapacious || *mf* plunderer

predecessóre *m* predecessor

predèlla *f* dais; altar step; platform

predellino *m* footboard

predestinare (predestino & predèstino) *tr* to predestine

predét•to -ta *adj* aforementioned
prediale *adj* field, rural || *f* land tax
prèdi•ca *f* (-che) sermon
predicare §197 (prèdico) *tr & intr* to preach
predicato *m* predicate; essere in predicato di + *inf* to be rumored to + *inf*; essere predicato per to be considered for
predica•tóre -trice *mf* preacher
predicazióne *f* preaching; sermon
predicòzzo *m* (coll) lecture, scolding
predilèt•to -ta *adj & m* favorite
predilezióne *f* predilection
predilìgere §149 (*pres part* missing) *tr* to prefer; to like best
predire §151 *tr* to foretell
predispórre §218 *tr* to predispose, prearrange || *ref* to prepare oneself
predisposizióne *f* predisposition
predizióne *f* prediction
predominare (predòmino) *tr* to overcome || *intr* to predominate; to prevail
predomì•nio *m* (-ni) predominance
predóne *m* marauder; predone del mare pirate
preesistere §114 *intr* (ESSERE) to preexist
prefabbricare §197 (prefàbbrico) *tr* to prefabricate
prefazióne *f* preface
preferènza *f* preference; a preferenza rather; usar preferenze a to favor
preferìbile *adj* preferable
preferire §176 *tr* to prefer
preferì•to -ta *adj* preferred, favored || *mf* favorite; pet
prefètto *m* prefect
prefettura *f* prefecture
prèfi•ca *f* (-che) professional mourner, paid mourner; (coll) crybaby
prefìggere §103 *tr* to set, fix; (gram) to prefix || *ref* to plan
prefìs•so -sa *adj* appointed; prefixed || *m* (gram) prefix; (telp) area code
prefissòide *m* prefixed combining form
pregare §209 (prègo) *tr* to beg, pray; to ask, request; farsi pregare to take a lot of asking; La prego please; prego! please!; beg your pardon!; you are welcome!
pregévole *adj* valuable
preghièra *f* entreaty; prayer
pregiare §290 (prègio) *tr* (lit) to praise, esteem || *ref* to be honored, to have the pleasure
pregia•to -ta *adj* precious; esteemed; la Sua pregiata (lettera) your favor, your kind letter; pregiatìssimo Signore (com) dear Sir; pregiato Signore (com) dear Sir
prè•gio *m* (-gi) value, worth; esteem; avere in pregio to value
pregiudicare §197 (pregiùdico) *tr* to damage, harm, jeopardize
pregiudica•to -ta *adj* prejudged; prejudiced; compromised; bound to fail || *m* previous offender
pregiudiziévole *adj* prejudicial, detrimental

pregiudì•zio *m* (-zi) prejudice, bias; harm, damage
pregnante *adj* pregnant
pré•gno -gna *adj* pregnant; saturated
prè•go *m* (-ghi) (lit) prayer || *interj* please!; beg your pardon!; you are welcome!
pregustare *tr* to foretaste, anticipate with pleasure
preistòri•co -ca *adj* (-ci -che) prehistoric(al)
prelato *m* prelate
prelazióne *f* (law) preemption; (obs) privilege
prelevaménto *m* (com) withdrawal
prelevare (prelèvo) *tr* to withdraw (*money*); to capture
prelìba•to -ta *adj* excellent, delicious
prelièvo *m* withdrawal; (med) specimen
preliminare *adj* preliminary || preliminari *mpl* preliminary negotiations
prelùdere §105 *intr* to make an introductory statement; (with *dat*) to precede, usher in
prelù•dio *m* (-di) prelude; (*of an opera*) overture
prematu•ro -ra *adj* premature
premeditare (premèdito) *tr* to premeditate
premeditazióne *f* premeditation; con premeditazione (law) with malice prepense
prèmere §123 *tr* to press; to push; to squeeze || *intr* (ESSERE & AVERE) to press; to be urgent; premere a to matter to, e.g., gli preme it matters to him; premere su to press, put pressure on
preméssa *f* premise; introduction (*to a book*)
preméttere §198 *tr* to state at the onset; to place at the beginning
premiare §287 (prèmio) *tr* to award a prize to, reward
premiazióne *f* awarding of prizes
preminènte *adj* prominent, preeminent
prè•mio *m* (-mi) prize; premium; bonus; award
prèmito *m* straining (*to defecate*)
premolare *adj & m* premolar
premonìre §176 *tr* (lit) to foretell
premonizióne *f* premonition
premorire §201 *intr* (ESSERE) (with *dat*) to predecease
premunire §176 *tr* to fortify || *ref*—premunirsi contro to provide against; premunirsi di to provide oneself with
premura *f* haste; attention, care; aver premura (di) to be in a hurry (to); di premura hastily; far premura (with *dat*) to urge
premuró•so -sa [s] *adj* attentive, careful
prèndere §220 *tr* to take; to catch; to lift; to pick up; to fetch; to get; to receive; prendere a calci to kick; prendere a pugni to punch; prendere a servizio to employ, hire; prendere commiato to take leave; prendere con le buone to treat with kid gloves; prendere in castagna to catch in the act; prendere il sole to sun oneself; prendere la fuga to take flight;

prendere la mano to run away (*said of a horse*); **prendere le mosse** to begin (*said, e.g., of a story*); **prendere lucciole per lanterne** to commit a gross error; **prender paura** to get scared; **prendere per** to take for; **prendere per il naso** to lead by the nose; **prendere quota** (aer) to gain altitude; **prendere sonno** to fall asleep; **prendere un granchio** to make a blunder || *intr* to take root; to set (*said of cement*); to catch (*said of fire*); to turn (*left or right*); **prendere a** + *inf* to begin to + *inf* || *ref* to grab one another; to get along together; **prendersela con** to become angry with; to lay the blame on; **prendersi a** to take hold of

prendi·tóre -trice *mf* receiver; payee (*of a note*); margin buyer || *m* (baseball) catcher

prenóme *m* first name, given name

prenotare (prenòto) *tr* to reserve, book || *ref* to register

prenotazióne *f* reservation, booking

preoccupare *adj* worrisome

preoccupare (preòccupo) *tr* to pre-occupy; **preoccupare la mente di** to win the favor of || *ref* to worry

preoccupazióne *f* preoccupation, worry

preordinare (preòrdino) *tr* to fore-ordain; to prearrange

preparare (prepàro) *tr* to prepare; to prime; to steep, brew || *ref* to be prepared; to brew (*said, e.g., of a storm*)

peparati·vo -va *adj* preparatory || **preparativi** *mpl* preparations

prepara·to -ta *adj* prepared; well-equipped || *m* patent medicine; (med) preparation; **preparato anatomico** dissection, anatomical specimen

preparatò·rio -ria *adj* (-ri -rie) prepar-atory

preparazióne *f* preparation

preponderante *adj* preponderant, pre-vailing

preponderanza *f* preponderance

prepórre §218 *tr* to prefix; to place before; to prefer; **preporre (qlcu) a** to place (*s.o.*) at the head of

preposizióne *f* preposition

prepósto *m* chief; (eccl) provost

prepotènte *adj* arrogant, overbearing; urgent (*desire*) || *m* bully

prepotènza *f* arrogance; outrage; **di prepotenza** by force

prerogativa *f* prerogative

présa [s] *f* hold, grip; handle; cot-holder; capture; pinch (*e.g., of salt*); setting (*of cement*); intake; (cards) trick; (elec) jack; (mov) take; **a pronta presa** quick-setting (*cement*); **dar presa a** to give rise to; **essere alle prese** to come to grips; **far presa** to stick (*said of glue*); to set (*said of cement*); to take root; **far presa su** to impress; **mettere alle prese** to pit (*e.g., animals*); **presa d'acqua** spigot, faucet; **presa d'aria** outlet (*of air hose*); air shaft; **presa di corrente** (elec) wall socket, outlet, receptacle; **presa di terra** (elec) ground; **presa**

in giro kidding, joke; **venire alle prese** to come to grips

presà·gio *m* (-gi) forecast; portent

presagire §176 *tr* to forecast; to portend

presalà·rio [s] *m* (-ri) (educ) stipend

prèsbite *adj* far-sighted || *mf* far-sighted person

presbiteria·no -na *adj* & *mf* Presby-terian

prescégliere §244 *tr* to choose, select

prescìndere §247 (*pret* prescindéi & prescissi) *intr*—**a prescindere da** except for; **prescindere da** to leave out

prescolàsti·co -ca *adj* (-ci -che) pre-school

prescrit·to -ta *adj* prescribed

prescrivere §250 *tr* to prescribe || *intr* (ESSERE) (law) to prescribe, to lapse

prescrizióne *f* prescription; (law) ex-tinctive prescription

presegnale [s] *m* warning sign

presentàbile *adj* presentable

presentare (presènto) *tr* to present; to introduce; **presentare la candidatura di** to nominate; **presentat'arm!** pre-sent arms! || *ref* to show up, appear; to come, arise (*said, e.g., of an opportunity*)

presenta·tóre -trice *mf* presenter; (rad, telv) announcer || *m* master of cere-monies

presentazióne *f* presentation; introduc-tion

presènte *adj* present; **avere presente** to have in mind; **fare presente qlco a qlcu** to bring s.th to s.o.'s attention; **tenere presente** to keep in mind || *m* present; bystander, onlooker; **al pre-sente** at present; **di presente** imme-diately || *interj* here!

presentimènto [s] *m* presentiment, foreboding

presentire [s] **(presènto)** *tr* to have a presentiment of

presènza *f* presence; attendance; **di presenza** in person; **presenza di spi-rito** presence of mind

presenziare §287 **(presènzio)** *tr* to at-tend; to witness || *intr*—**presenziare a** to be present at; to witness

presè·pio *m* (-pi) Nativity, crèche

preservare [s] **(presèrvo)** *tr* to pre-serve, protect

preservati·vo -va [s] *adj* & *m* pro-phylactic

prèside [s] *m* principal (*of secondary school*); **preside di facoltà** dean

presidènte [s] *m* president; chairman; **presidente del Consiglio** premier

presidentéssa [s] *f* president; chair-woman

presidènza [s] *f* presidency; chairman-ship

presi·dio [s] *m* (-di) garrison; (fig) defense, help; **presidi medical aids**

presièdere [s] §141 **(presièdo)** *tr* to preside over || *intr* to preside; **pre-siedere a** to preside over

prèssa *f* crowd; haste; (mach) press; **far pressa** (poet) to urge

pressacar·te *m* (-te) paperweight

pressaforàg·gio *m* (-gio) baler, hay baler

pressante *adj* pressing, urgent
pressappòco *adv* more or less
pressare (prèsso) *tr* to press; to urge
pressióne *f* pressure; **far pressione su** to put pressure on; **pressione sanguigna** blood pressure; **sotto pressione** under steam
prèsso *m*—**nei pressi di** in the neighborhood of || *adv* near, nearby; **a un di presso** approximately; **da presso** close; **press'a poco** more or less || *prep* near; about; at; according to; at the house of; at the office of; care of; with, e.g., **godere fama presso** to enjoy popularity with
pressoché *adv* almost, about, nearly
pressurizzare [ddzz] *tr* to pressurize
prestabilire §176 *tr* to preestablish
prestabili·to -ta *adj* appointed
prestanó·me *m* (-me) straw man, figurehead
prestante *adj* strong, vigorous; comely
prestanza *f* vigor; (lit) comeliness
prestare (prèsto) *tr* to lend; to loan; to give (*ear; help*); to pay (*attention*); to render (*obedience*); to take (*oath*); to keep (*faith*); **prestar man forte** to give aid; **prestar servizio** to work || *ref* to lend oneself; to be suitable; to be willing; to volunteer
presta·tóre -trice *mf* lender; **prestatore d'opera** worker; **prestatori d'opera** labor
prestazióne *f* service; performance
prestigia·tóre -trice *mf* magician, juggler
presti·gio *m* (-gi) prestige; spell, influence; ledgerdemain
prestigió·so -sa [s] *adj* captivating, spellbinding; illusory
prèstito *m* loan; (philol) borrowing; **dare a prestito** to lend; **prendere a prestito** to borrow
prè·sto -sta *adj* (archaic) quick || *m* (mus) presto || **presto** *adv* soon; fast; quick, quickly; early; **al più presto** at the earliest possible time; **ben presto** soon; **far presto** to hurry; **più presto che può** as soon as you can; **presto detto** easy to say
presùmere §116 *tr & intr* to presume
presunti·vo -va *adj* presumptive; budgeted, estimated (*expenditure*)
presun·to -ta *adj* alleged, supposed; estimated (*expenditure*)
presuntuó·so -sa [s] *adj* presumptuous; bumptious
presunzióne *f* presumption; conceit
presuppórre [s] §218 *tr* to presuppose
presuppósto [s] *m* assumption
prète *m* priest; minister; wooden frame (*to hold bed warmer*)
pretendente *m* suitor; pretender
pretèndere §270 *tr* to demand, claim; **pretenderla a** to pretend to be || *intr*—**pretendere a** to be a suitor for; to claim (*e.g., a throne*)
pretensióne *f* demand; pretention; pretense
pretensió·so -sa [s] or **pretenzió·so -sa** [s] *adj* pretentious
preterintenzionale *adj* (law) unintentional; (law) justifiable

pretèri·to -ta *adj & m* preterit
preté·so -sa [s] *adj* alleged, ostensible; assumed (*name*) || *f* pretense; pretension
pretèsto *m* pretext, excuse; **sotto il pretesto di** under pretense of
pretòni·co -ca *adj* (-ci -che) pretonic
pretóre *m* judge, magistrate (*of lower court*)
prèt·to -ta *adj* pure, genuine
pretura *f* lower court
prevalènte *adj* prevalent, prevailing
prevalènza *f* prevalence; **essere in prevalenza** to be in the majority; **in prevalenza** for the most part
prevalére §278 *intr* (ESSERE & AVERE) to prevail || *ref* to take advantage
prevaricare §197 (prevàrico) *intr* to transgress; to graft
prevarica·tóre -trice *mf* grafter
prevedére §279 *tr* to foresee; to provide for (*said of a statute*)
prevedìbile *adj* foreseeable
prevenire §282 *tr* to precede; to anticipate; to forewarn; to prejudice
preventivi·sta *mf* (-sti -ste) estimator
preventi·vo -va *adj* preventive; prior; estimated (*budget*) || *m* estimate
prevenu·to -ta *adj* forewarned; biased, prejudiced || *m* defendant
prevenzióne *f* prevention; prejudice, bias
previdènte *adj* provident, prudent
previdènza *f* providence; foresight; **previdenza sociale** social security
previdenziale *adj* social (*e.g., responsibility*); social-security (*e.g., contribution*)
prè·vio -via *adj* (-vi -vie) with previous, e.g., **previo accordo** with previous agreement
previsióne *f* foresightedness; **in previsione di** anticipating; **previsioni del tempo** weather forecast
previ·sto -sta *adj* foreseen, expected || *m* expected time; estimated amount
prezió·so -sa [s] *adj* precious, valuable; affected; **fare il prezioso** (coll) to play hard to get || **preziosi** *mpl* valuables, jewels
prezzare (prèzzo) *tr* to care about; to price
prezzémolo *m* parsley
prèzzo *m* price; cost; **mettere a prezzo** (fig) to sell; **prezzo di favore** special price; **prezzo d'ingresso** admission; **tenere in gran prezzo** to value highly, to esteem highly; **ultimo prezzo** rock-bottom price
prezzolare (prèzzolo) *tr* to hire (*e.g., a gunman*); to bribe
prigióne *f* prison, jail; (naut) brig
prigionia *f* imprisonment; bondage
prigioniè·ro -ra *adj* imprisoned || *mf* prisoner || *m* stud bolt
prillare *intr* to spin, whirl
prima *f* first grade (*in school*); (rr) first class; (theat) first night; (aut) first (gear); **alla prima** or **sulle prime** at the outset || *adv* before; first; prior; ahead; **di prima** previous; **prima che** before; **prima di** ahead of; before;

prima o poi sooner or later; **quanto prima** as soon as possible

primàrio -ria (**-ri -rie**) *adj* primary || *m* (elec) primary; (med) chief of staff

primati·sta *mf* (**-sti -ste**) (sports) record holder

primato *m* primacy; (sports) record

primavèra *f* spring; springtime; (bot) primrose

primaverile *adj* spring; spring-like

primeggiare §290 (**priméggio**) *intr* to excel

primiè·ro -ra *adj* (lit) prior; (lit) pristine || *f* (cards) meld

primiti·vo -va *adj & m* primitive

primìzia *f* first fruits; scoop, beat

pri·mo -ma *adj* first; early (*dawn*); prime (*cost*); raw (*material*); **sulle prime** at first || *m* first; minute; **primo arrivato** first comer || *f* see **prima**

primogèni·to -ta *adj* first-born; (fig) beloved || *mf* first-born child

primòrdi *mpl* beginning, origin

primordiale *adj* primordial, primeval

primula *f* primrose || **Primula** *f*—**la Primula Rossa** the Scarlet Pimpernel

principale *adj* principal, main || *m* (coll) boss, chief

principalménte *adv* chiefly, mainly

principato *m* principality

principe *adj* princeps || *m* prince; **il principe di Galles** the Prince of Wales; **principe ereditario** crown prince

principé·sco -sca *adj* (**-schi -sche**) princely

principéssa *f* princess

principiante *adj* beginning || *mf* beginner

principiare §287 *tr & intr* (ESSERE & AVERE) to begin; **a principiare da** beginning with

princi·pio *m* (**-pi**) beginning; principle; **in principio** at the beginning, at first

princisbécco *m* pinchbeck; **restare o rimanere di princisbecco** to be dumbfounded

prióre *m* prior

priori·tà *f* (**-tà**) priority

priorità·rio -ria *adj* (**-ri -rie**) priority, e.g., **progetto prioritario** priority project

pri·sma *m* (**-smi**) prism

privare *tr* to deprive; to remove

privativa *f* government monopoly; salt and tobacco store; patent

priva·to -ta *adj* private || *m* private individual

privazióne *f* privation, loss

privilegiare §290 (**privilègio**) *tr* to privilege; (fig) to endow

privilegia·to -ta *adj* privileged; preferred (*stock*) || *m* privileged person

privilè·gio *m* (**-gi**) privilege

pri·vo -va *adj* deprived; **privo di** lacking

prò *m* (**pro**) profit, advantage; **a che pro?** what's the use?; **buon pro!** good appetite!; **far pro** to be good for the health; **il pro e il contro** the pros and the cons || *prep* pro, in favor of

probàbile *adj* probable

probabili·tà *f* (**-tà**) probability; chance; odds

probante *adj* proving; evidential

probatò·rio -ria *adj* (**-ri -rie**) probative, evidential

problè·ma *m* (**-mi**) problem

prò·bo -ba *adj* (lit) honest

procàc·cia *mf* (**-cia**) messenger; mail carrier

procacciare §128 *tr* to get, procure || *ref* to eke out (*a living*); to get into (*trouble*)

procace *adj* buxom, sexy; saucy, petulant

procèdere §123 (**procèdo**) *intr* to proceed, take action || *intr* (ESSERE) to proceed, go ahead

procediménto *m* procedure; behavior

procedura *f* procedure

procèlla *f* (lit) storm, tempest

procellària *f* (orn) petrel

processare (**procèsso**) *tr* to try, prosecute

processióne *f* procession

procèsso *m* process; trial; **processo verbale** minutes

processuale *adj* trial

procinto *m*—**in procinto di** on the point of

procióne *m* raccoon

procla·ma *m* (**-mi**) proclamation

proclamare *tr* to proclaim

proclamazióne *f* proclamation

proclìti·co -ca *adj & f* (**-ci -che**) proclitic

proclive *adj* inclined, disposed

proclivi·tà *f* (**-tà**) proclivity

procrastinare (**procràstino**) *tr* to procrastinate, put off || *intr* to procrastinate

procreare (**procrèo**) *tr* to procreate

procura *f* agency; power of attorney; **Procura della Repubblica** attorney general's office; district attorney's office

procurare *tr* to procure, to get; to cause; **procurare che** to see to it that; **procurare di** to try to || *ref* to get, acquire

procura·tóre -trice *mf* proxy; agent; attorney-at-law; (sports) manager; **Procuratore della Repubblica** district attorney

pròda *f* shore, bank; (archaic) prow

pròde *adj* brave || *m* brave person, hero

prodézza *f* prowess; accomplishment

prodiè·ro -ra *adj* prow, e.g., **cannone prodiero** prow gun; preceding (*in a row of ships*)

prodigare §209 (**pròdigo**) *tr* to squander, lavish || *ref* to do one's best

prodi·gio *m* (**-gi**) prodigy; wonder

prodigió·so -sa [s] *adj* prodigious; wonderful

pròdi·go -ga *adj* (**-ghi -ghe**) lavish, prodigal; **prodigo di** profuse in

proditò·rio -ria *adj* (**-ri -rie**) traitorous

prodótto *m* product; result; **prodotti in scatola** canned goods; **prodotti (ortofrutticoli)** produce

produrre §102 *tr* to produce; to turn out; to yield; to breed; to cause; (lit) to prolong; (law) to exhibit || *ref* (theat) to perform, appear

produtti·vo -va *adj* productive

produttivísti·co -ca *adj* (**-ci -che**) productivity, e.g., **fine produttivístico** productivity policy

produt·tóre -trice *adj* producing || *mf* producer; agent; manufacturer's representative || *m* salesman || *f* saleswoman

produzióne *f* production; output; **produzione in massa** or **in serie** mass production

proè·mio *m* (**-mi**) preamble, proem

profanare *tr* to profane, desecrate

profanazióne *f* profanation, desecration

profa·no -na *adj* profane; lay, uninformed || *m* layman; **il profano** the profane

proferire §176 *tr* (lit) to utter; (lit) to proffer

professare (professo) *tr* to profess; to practice (*e.g., law*) || *intr* to practice || *ref* to profess oneself to be

professionale *adj* professional; occupational (*disease*); trade (*school*)

professióne *f* profession; **fare il ladro di professione** to be a confirmed thief; **fare qlco di professione** to pursue the trade of s.th, e.g., **fa il falegname di professione** he pursues the trade of carpenter

professioní·sta *mf* (**-sti -ste**) professional

professorale *adj* professorial; pedantic

profes·sóre -soréssa *mf* professor; teacher; **professore d'orchestra** orchestra member

profè·ta *m* (**-ti**) prophet

profetéssa *f* prophetess

profèti·co -ca *adj* (**-ci -che**) prophetic

profetizzare [ddzz] *tr* to prophesy

profezìa *f* prophecy

profferire §176 (*pp* **profferto**; *pret* **profferìi & proffèrsi**) *tr* to offer; (lit) to utter

profi·cuo -cua *adj* profitable

profilare *tr* to outline; to sketch; to hem; (mach) to shape || *ref* to be outlined; to loom

profilàs·si *f* (**-si**) prophylaxis

profila·to -ta *adj* outlined; hemmed; (mach) shaped || *m* structural piece

profilàtti·co -ca *adj* (**-ci -che**) prophylactic

profilatura *f* hemming; (mach) shaping

profilo *m* profile; sketch; outline

profittare *intr* to profit, benefit

profitta·tóre -trice *mf* profiteer

profittévole *adj* (lit) profitable

profitto *m* profit; progress; **profitti e perdite** profit and loss

proflù·vio *m* (**-vi**) overflow; (pathol) discharge

profondare (profóndo) *tr & intr* to sink

profóndere §178 *tr* to squander, lavish || *ref* to be profuse

profondi·tà *f* (**-tà**) depth

profón·do -da *adj* deep; profound; searching (*e.g., investigation*) || *m* bottom; depth; subconscious

pro fórma *adj invar* pro forma; perfunctory || *m* (coll) formality

pròfu·go -ga (**-ghi -ghe**) *adj* fugitive || *mf* refugee

profumare *tr* to perfume || *intr* to smell

profumataménte *adv* lavishly

profuma·to -ta *adj* perfumed, fragrant

profumerìa *f* perfumery; perfume shop

profumo *m* perfume; bouquet (*of wine*)

profusióne *f* profusion; **a profusione** in profusion

profu·so -sa *adj* profuse

progè·nie *f* (**-nie**) progeny, offspring; (pej) breed

progeni·tóre -trice *mf* ancestor

progettare (progètto) *tr* to plan; to design

progettí·sta *mf* (**-sti -ste**) planner; designer; wild dreamer

progètto *m* project; plan; draft (*of law*); **far progetti** to plan; **progetto di scala reale** (cards) possible straight flush

prògno·si *f* (**-si**) prognosis

program·ma *m* (**-mi**) program; plan; curriculum; cycle (*of washing machine*); (mov) feature; (theat) playbill; **programma politico** platform

programmare *tr* to program; to plan

programma·tóre -trice *mf* programmer

programmazióne *f* programming

progredire §176 *intr* (ESSERE & AVERE) to progress, advance

progredi·to -ta *adj* advanced

progressióne *f* progression

progressí·sta *adj & mf* (**-sti -ste**) progressive

progressí·vo -va *adj* progressive

progrèsso *m* progress; progression, advance; **fare progressi** to progress

proibire §176 *tr* to prohibit; to prevent

proibi·to -ta *adj* forbidden; **è proibito entrare** no admission; **è proibito fumare** no smoking

proibizióne *f* prohibition

proibizionismo *m* prohibition

proiettare (proiètto) *tr* to project; to cast (*a shadow*) || *intr* to project || *ref* to be projected, project

proièttile *m* projectile, missile

proiettóre *m* projector, projection machine; searchlight; (aut) headlight; **proiettore acustico** sonar projector

proiezióne *f* projection; **proiezione rallentata** slow motion

pròle *f invar* offspring, progeny

proletariato *m* proletariat

proletà·rio -ria *adj & mf* (**-ri -rie**) proletarian

proliferare (prolifero) *intr* to proliferate

prolificare §197 (**prolifico**) *intr* to proliferate

prolifi·co -ca *adj* (**-ci -che**) prolific

prolís·so -sa *adj* prolix, long-winded; long (*e.g., beard*)

pròlo·go *m* (**-ghi**) prologue; preface

prolun·ga *f* (**-ghe**) extension

prolungaménto *m* prolongation, extension

prolungare §209 *tr* to prolong, extend || *ref* to extend; to speak at great length

prolunga·to -ta *adj* extended, protracted

prolusióne *f* inaugural lecture

promemò·ria or **pro memò·ria** *m* (-ria) reminder

promés·so -sa *adj* promised || *mf* betrothed || *f* promise; promising individual

promettènte *adj* promising

prométtere §198 *tr* to promise; to threaten (*e.g., a storm*) || *intr* to promise; **promettere bene** to be very promising || *ref*—**promettersi a Dio** to make a vow to God; **promettersi in matrimonio** to become engaged

prominènte *adj* prominent

promi·scuo -scua *adj* promiscuous; coeducational; mixed (*marriage; races*); (gram) epicene

promontò·rio *m* (-ri) promontory, cliff

promo·tóre -trice *adj* promoting || *mf* promoter

promozióne *f* promotion

promulgare §209 *tr* to promulgate

promuòvere §202 *tr* to promote; to pass (*a student*); to initiate (*legal suit*); to induce (*e.g., perspiration*)

pronipóte *mf* great-grandchild || *m* great-grandson; grandnephew; **pronipoti** descendants || *f* great-granddaughter; grandniece

prò·no -na *adj* (lit) prone

pronóme *m* pronoun

pronominale *adj* (gram) pronominal; (gram) reflexive (*verb*)

pronosticare §197 (**pronòstico**) *tr* to prognosticate, forecast

pronòsti·co·m (-ci) prognostication, forecast; sign, omen

prontézza *f* readiness; quickness, promptness

prón·to -ta *adj* ready; first (*aid*); quick; prompt; ready (*cash*) || **pronto** *interj* (telp) hello!

prontuà·rio *m* (-ri) handbook

pronùn·cia *f* (-cie) or **pronunzia** *f* pronunciaton; (law) judgment

pronunziare §287 *tr* to pronounce; to utter; to pass (*sentence*); to make (*a speech*) || *ref* to pass judgment

pronunzia·to -ta *adj* pronounced, marked; prominent (*nose, chin, beard*) || *m* (law) sentence

propaganda *f* propaganda; advertisement; advertising

propagandi·sta *mf* (-sti -ste) propagandist; advertiser; agent; detail man

propagandìsti·co -ca *adj* (-ci -che) advertising

propagare §209 *tr* to propagate; to spread || *ref* to spread

propàggine *f* offspring; (geog) spur, counterfort; (hort) layer

propalare *tr* (lit) to spread, divulge

propellènte *adj* & *m* propellent

propèllere §168 *tr* to propel

propèndere §123 (*pp* **propènso**) *intr* to incline, tend

propensióne *f* propensity, inclination

propèn·so -sa *adj* inclined, bent

propinare *tr* to administer (*e.g., poison*); **propinare qlco a qlcu** to put s.th over on s.o.

propìn·quo -qua *adj* (lit) near; (lit) related

propiziare §287 *tr* to propitiate, appease

propì·zio -zia *adj* (-zi -zie) propitious, favorable

proponiménto *m* intention, plan

propórre §218 *tr* to propose, present; to propound; **proporre come candidato** to nominate || *ref*—**proporsi di** to propose to, resolve to

proporzionare (**proporzióno**) *tr* to proportion, prorate

proporzióne *f* proportion

propòsito *m* purpose; **a proposito** opportune; opportunely; proper; by the way; **a proposito di** on the subject of; **di proposito** deliberately; **fuor di proposito** out of place; **parlare a proposito** to speak to the point

proposizióne *f* proposition; (gram) clause; **proposizione subordinata** dependent clause

propósta *f* proposal; **proposta di legge** bill

propriaménte *adv* exactly; properly

proprie·tà *f* (-tà) propriety; ownership; property; **la proprietà** property owners; **proprietà immobiliare** real estate; **proprietà letteraria** copyright; **sulla proprietà** on the premises

proprietà·rio -ria *mf* (-ri -rie) owner, proprietor

prò·prio -pria (-pri -prie) *adj* peculiar, characteristic; proper (*e.g., name*); own, e.g., **il mio proprio libro** my own book || *m* one's own; **i propri** one's folks; **lavorare in proprio** to work for oneself || **proprio** *adv* just, really, exactly; **non . . . proprio** not . . . at all; **proprio adesso** just, just now

propugnare *tr* to advocate; (lit) to fight for

propugna·tóre -trice *mf* (lit) advocate

propulsare *tr* to propel; (lit) to repulse

propulsióne *f* propulsion

propulsóre *m* propeller, motor

pròra *f* prow, bow

proravìa *f*—**a proravia** (naut) fore

pròro·ga *f* (-ghe) delay, extension

prorogare §209 (**pròrogo**) *tr* to extend; to put off, delay

prorómpere §240 *intr* to overflow; to burst (*into tears*)

prosa *f* prose

prosài·co -ca *adj* (-ci -che) prose; prosaic

prosàpia *f* (lit) ancestry

prosa·tóre -trice *mf* prose writer

proscè·nio *m* (-ni) forestage

prosciògliere §127 *tr* to free; to exonerate

prosciugare §209 *tr* to drain, reclaim || *ref* to dry up

prosciutto *m* ham; **prosciutto cotto** boiled ham; **prosciutto crudo** prosciutto

proscrìvere §250 *tr* to proscribe, outlaw

prosecuzióne [s] *f* prosecution, pursuit

proseguiménto [s] *m* prosecution, pursuit

proseguire [s] (**proséguo**) *tr* to follow, pursue || *intr* (ESSERE & AVERE) to continue

prosèlito m proselyte

prosodìa f prosody

prosopopèa f conceit

prosperare (pròspero) intr to prosper, thrive

prosperi·tà f (-tà) prosperity || interj gesundheit!

pròspe·ro -ra adj prosperous, thriving; flourishing; successful || m. (coll) match

prosperó·so -sa [s] adj flourishing; healthy; buxom

prospettare (prospètto) tr to face, overlook; to outline || intr—prospettare su to face || ref to look; to appear; to loom up

prospetti·vo -va adj prospective || f perspective; prospect; view

prospètto m prospect, view; front (of building); diagram; outline; prospectus

prospettóre m prospector

prospiciènte adj facing

prossimaménte adv shortly

prossimi·tà f -tà proximity, nearness; **in prossimità di** near

pròssi·mo -ma adj near, close; next; immediate (cause) || m neighbor, fellow man

pròstata f prostate

prosternare (prostèrno) ref to prostrate oneself

prostituire §176 tr to prostitute

prostituta f prostitute

prostituzióne f prostitution

prostrare (pròstro) ref to prostrate oneself

prostrazióne f prostration

protagoni·sta mf (-sti -ste) protagonist

protèggere §193 tr to protect; to help, defend; to favor, promote

proteìna f protein

protèndere §270 tr & ref to stretch

pròte·si f (-si) (philol) prothesis; (surg) prosthesis

protèsta f protest, protestation

protestante adj & mf protestant; Protestant

protestare (protèsto) tr to protest; to reject (faulty merchandise) || intr & ref to protest

protestatà·rio -ria (-rì -rie) adj protesting || m protester

protèsto m (com) protest

protèt·to -ta adj protected || m protegé || f protegée

protettorato m protectorate

protet·tóre adj patron || mf protector, guardian || m patron || f patroness

protezióne f protection; patronage

pròto m (typ) foreman

protocòllo adj invar commercial (size) || m protocol; **mettere a protocollo** to register, record

protopla·sma m (-smi) protoplasm

protòtipo m prototype; (fig) epitome

protozòl [dz] mpl protozoa

protrarre §273 tr to protract, extend || ref to continue

protrùdere §190 intr to protrude (said, e.g., of a broken bone)

protuberante adj protruding, bulging

pròva f test, examination; proof; try, attempt; probationary period (of employment); trial; token (e.g., of friendship); (sports) competition, event; (theat) rehearsal; **a prova di bomba** bombproof; foolproof; **a tutta prova** thoroughly tested; **in prova** on approval; **mettere a dura prova** to test (e.g., one's patience); **mettere alla prova** to test (e.g., one's ability); **mettere in prova** to fit (a suit); **prova del fuoco** trial by fire; **prova dell'acido** acid test; **prova generale** dress rehearsal; **prova indiziaria** circumstantial evidence

provare (pròvo) tr to test; to try; to try on; to try out; to taste; to prove; to feel (e.g., anger); (theat) to rehearse || intr to try || ref to compete

proveniènza f origin

provenire §282 intr (ESSERE) to stem, originate

provènto m income, proceeds

provenzale adj & mf Provençal

provèr·bio m (-bi) proverb; byword

provétta f test tube

provèt·to -ta adj (lit) masterful

provìn·cia f (-ce) province; **in provincia** outside of the big cities

provinciale adj provincial || mf smalltown person || f provincial highway, state highway

provino m gauge; (mov) screen test

provocare §197 (pròvoco) tr to provoke; to bring about, cause; to arouse; to entice

provoca·tóre -trice adj provoking || mf provoker

provocatò·rio -ria adj (-rì -rie) provoking, provocative

provocazióne f provocation; challenge

provvedére §221 tr to prepare; to supply; **provvedere che** to see to it that || intr to take the necessary steps; **provvedere a** to provide for; **provvedere a + inf** to provide for + ger; **provvedere nei confronti di** to take steps against

provvediménto m measure, step

provvedi·tóre -trice mf provider || m superintendent; **provveditore agli studi** superintendent of schools

provvedu·to -ta adj supplied; careful

provvidènza f providence; windfall; **provvidenze** provisions, help

provvidenziale adj providential

pròvvi·do -da adj (lit) provident

provvigióne f (com) commission

provvisò·rio -ria adj (-rì -rie) provisional, temporary

provvi·sto -sta adj supplied || f supply, provision; **fare le provviste** to shop

prozìa f grandaunt

prozì·o m (-ì) granduncle

prua f bow, prow

prudènte adj prudent, cautious

prudènza f prudence, discretion

prùdere §222 intr to itch; **sentirsi prudere le mani** to feel like giving s.o. a beating

prugna f plum; **prugna secca** prune

prugno *m* plum tree
prùgnola *f* sloe
prùgnolo *m* sloe, blackthorn
pruno *m* thorn
prurito *m* itch
pseudònimo *m* pseudonym; alias; pen name
psicanàlisi *f* psychoanalysis
psicanali•sta *mf* (-sti -ste) psychoanalyst
psicanalizzare [ddzz] *tr* to psychoanalyze
psiche *f* psyche; cheval glass
psichia•tra *mf* (-tri -tre) psychiatrist
psichiatrìa *f* psychiatry
psìchi•co -ca *adj* (-ci -che) psychic
psicologìa *f* psychology
psicològi•co -ca *adj* (-ci -che) psychological
psicòlo•go -ga *mf* (-gi -ghe) psychologist
psicopàti•co -ca (-ci -che) *adj* psychopathic || *mf* psychopath
psicò•si *f* (-si) psychosis
psicosomàti•co -ca *adj* (-ci -che) psychosomatic
psicotècni•co -ca (-ci -che) *adj* psychotechnical || *m* industrial psychologist || *f* industrial psychology
psicòti•co -ca *adj* (-ci -che) psychotic
pubblicare §197 (pùbblico) *tr* to publish
pubblicazióne *f* publication; pubblicazioni di matrimonio marriage banns
pubblicìsmo *m* communications; advertising
pubblici•sta *mf* (-sti -ste) free-lance newspaper writer; publicist
pubblicìsti•co -ca (-ci -che) *adj* advertising; political-science || *f* newspaper business
pubblicità *f* publicity; advertising
pubblicità•rio -ria (-ri -rie) *adj* advertising || *mf* advertising agent
publicizzare [ddzz] *tr* to publicize
publicizzazióne [ddzz] *f* publicizing
pùbbli•co -ca *adj* & *m* (-ci -che) public; mettere in pubblico to publish
pubertà *f* puberty
pudibón•do -da *adj* (lit) modest, bashful; (lit) prudish
pudicìzia *f* prudery
pudi•co -ca *adj* (-chi -che) modest, chaste; bashful; (lit) reserved
pudóre *m* modesty; decency; shame
puericoltóre *m* pediatrician
puerile *adj* puerile, childish
puerili•tà *f* (-tà) puerility, childishness
puèrpera *f* lying-in patient
pugilato *m* boxing
pugilatóre *m* boxer, prize fighter
pùgile *m* boxer, prize fighter
pugili•sta *m* (-sti) boxer, prize fighter
pù•glia *f* (-glie) stake (*in gambling*)
pugnace *adj* (lit) pugnacious
pugnalare *tr* to stab
pugnalata *f* stab
pugnale *m* dagger
pugno *m* fist; fistful; punch; avere in pugno to have in one's grasp; di proprio pugno in one's own hand; fare a pugni to fight; to clash

pula *f* chaff
pulce *f* flea; mettere una pulce nell'orecchio di to put a bug in the ear of; pulce tropicale jigger, chigger
pulcèlla *f* maid, maiden
pulcinèlla *f*—pulcinella di mare (orn) Atlantic puffin || Pulcinel•la *m* (-la) buffoon; Punch, Punchinello
pulcino *m* chick
pulédra *f* filly
pulédro *m* colt, foal
puleg•gia *f* (-ge) pulley
pulire §176 *tr* to clean; to shine (*shoes*); to wipe; to polish
puliscipiè•di *m* (-di) doormat
puli•to -ta *adj* clean; polished; clear (*conscience*) || *f*—dare una pulita a to give a lick and a promise to
pulitura *f* cleaning; pulitura a secco dry cleaning
pulizìa *f* cleaning; cleanliness; fare le pulizie to clean house
pullulare (pùllulo) *intr* to swarm
pùlpito *m* pulpit
pulsante *m* knob; push button
pulsare *intr* to throb; to pulsate
pulvìscolo *m* fine dust; haze
pulzèlla *f* var of pulcella
pu•ma *m* (-ma) cougar
pungènte *adj* pungent; bitter (*cold*)
pùngere §183 *tr* to sting; (fig) to goad
pungiglióne *m* stinger (*of bee*); (fig) sting; (obs) goad
pungitòpo *m* (bot) butcher's broom
pungolare (pùngolo) *tr* to goad, prod
punire §176 *tr* to punish
punizióne *f* punishment; penalty
punta *f* point, tip; prong; brad; bit, trifle; needle (*of phonograph*); avantgarde; point (*of dog*); (lit) wound; (fig) peak; (mach) broach; averne fino alla punta dei capelli to be sick and tired; fare la punta a to sharpen; in punta di penna elegantly; prendere di punta to treat roughly; to face up to; punta delle dita fingertip; punta di piedi tiptoe
puntale *m* tip, ferrule
puntaménto *m* aiming
puntare *tr* to aim; to aim at; to point; to thrust; to dot; to bet; to stare at; to fix (*one's eyes*); puntare i piedi to stiffen up; (fig) to balk || *intr* to aim; to point; to pin; to bet; puntare su to count on; puntare verso to march on; to sail toward
puntaspil•li *m* (-li) pincushion
puntata *f* jab (*with weapon*); excursion; bet; issue, number (*of magazine*); installment (*of story*); (mil) incursion
punteggiare §290 (puntéggio) *tr* to dot; (gram) to punctuate
punteggiatura *f* dotting; punctuation
puntég•gio *m* (-gi) score
puntellare (puntèllo) *tr* to prop, brace; to support
puntèllo *m* prop, brace; support
punterìa *f* aiming; aiming gear; (aut) tappet
punteruòlo *m* punch; awl
punti•glio *m* (-gli) obstinacy, stubbornness; punctilio

puntiglió·so -sa [s] *adj* punctilious, scrupulous; obstinate, stubborn

puntina *f* brad; needle; thumbtack

puntino *m* small dot; G-string; **a puntino** to a T

punto *m* point; period; dot; place, spot; extent; stitch; **dare dei punti a** to be superior to; **di punto in bianco** all of a sudden; **di tutto punto** thoroughly; **due punti** colon; **essere a buon punto** to be well advanced; **essere sul punto di** + *inf* to be about to + *inf*; **fare il punto** (fig; naut) tc take one's bearings; **in punto** on the dot; **in punto franco in bond**; **in un punto** together; **mettere a punto** to get in working order; (aut) to tune up; **mettere i punti sulle i** to dot one's i's; **punto assistenza** service agency; **punto di partenza** starting point; **punto di vista** viewpoint; **punto esclamativo** exclamation point; **punto e virgola** semicolon; **punto fermo** full stop; **punto interrogativo** question mark; **punto morto** (mach) dead center; **punto stimato** (naut) dead reckoning; **qui sta il punto!** here's the rub!; **vincere ai punti** (boxing) to win by points, win by decision || **punto né punto né poco** not at all; **non . . . punto** not at all

puntóne *m* rafter

puntuale *adj* punctual, prompt

puntuali·tà *f* (-tà) punctuality, promptness

puntura *f* sting; stitch (*sharp pain*); (coll) injection; **puntura lombare** spinal anesthesia

punzecchiare §287 (punzécchio) *tr* to keep on stinging; to tease, torment

punzecchiatura *f* sting, bite

punzonare (punzóno) *tr* to mark or stamp with a punch

punzonatrice *f* punch press

punzóne *m* punch; nailset

pupa *f* doll; (zool) pupa

pupazzetti·sta *mf* (-sti -ste) cartoonist

pupazzétto *m* caricature; cartoon; **pupazzetto di carta** paper doll

pupazzo *m* puppet; **pupazzo di stoffa** rag doll

pupil·lo -la *mf* pupil; ward, protégé || *f* pupil (*of eye*); protégée

pupo *m* (coll) baby

purché *conj* provided, providing

pure *adv* too, also; indeed; (lit) only; **pur di** only in order to; **quando pure** even if; **se pure** even if || *conj* though, although; but, yet

pu·rè *m* (-rè) purée; **purè di patate** mashed potatoes

purézza *f* purity

pur·ga *f* (-ghe) laxative; purification; purge

purgante *adj* purging || *m* laxative

purgare §209 *tr* to purge; to purify; to expurgate || *ref* to take a laxative

purgati·vo -va *adj* laxative

purgatò·rio *m* (-ri) purgatory

purificare §197 (purìfico) *tr* to purify

purismo *m* purism

purità *f* purity

purita·no -na *adj & m* puritan; Puritan

pu·ro -ra *adj* pure; clear; simple, mere

purosàn·gue *adj invar & m* (-gue) thoroughbred

purpùre·o -a *adj* (lit) purple

purtròppo *adv* unfortunately

purulèn·to -ta *adj* purulent

pus *m* pus

pusillànime *adj* pusillanimous

pùstola *f* pustule; pimple

puta caso *adv* possibly, maybe

putifè·rio *m* (-ri) hubbub

putrefare §173 *intr* (ESSERE) *& ref* to putrefy, rot

putrefazióne *f* putrefaction

putrèlla *f* I beam

pùtri·do -da *adj* putrid || *m* corruption

putta *f* (coll) girl; (lit) prostitute

puttana *f* (vulg) whore

put·to -ta *adj* (archaic) meretricious || *m* figure of a child || *f* see **putta**

puzza *f* var of **puzzo**

puzzare *intr* to stink, smell

puzzo *m* stench, smell, bad odor

pùzzola *f* polecat, skunk

puzzolènte *adj* stinking, smelly

puzzonata *f* (coll) contemptible action; (coll) botch, bungle

puzzóne *m* (coll) skunk (*person*)

Q

Q, q [ku] *m & f* fifteenth letter of the Italian alphabet

qua *adv* here; **da un (giorno, mese, anno) in qua** for the past (day, month, year); **di qua da** on this side of; **in qua** on this side; here

quàcche·ro -ra or **quàcque·ro -ra** *adj & mf* Quaker; **alla quacquera** in a plain fashion

quadèrno *m* copybook; **quaderno di cassa** cash book

quadràngo·lo -la *adj* quadrangular || *m* quadrangle

quadrante *m* quadrant; dial; face (*of watch*); **quadrante solare** sundial

quadrare *tr* to square || *intr* (ESSERE & AVERE) to square; **quadrare a** to be satisfactory to; **quadrare con** to fit

quadra·to -ta *adj* square; sound (*mind*) || *m* square; diaper; (boxing) ring; (nav) wardroom

quadratura *f* squaring; concreteness; (astr) quadrature

quadrèl·lo *m* (-li) square ruler; square tile || *m* (-la *fpl*) (lit) bolt, arrow

quadreria *f* picture gallery; collection

quadretta·to -ta *adj* checkered

quadrétto *m* small painting; checker, small square; (fig) picture

quadriennale *adj* four-year ‖ *f* quadrennial

quadrifò·glio *m* (-gli) four-leaf clover; **a quadrifoglio** cloverleaf

quadri·glio *m* (-gli) (cards) quadrille

quadrimensionale *adj* four-dimensional

quadrimestrale *adj* four-month

quadrimèstre *m* four-month period; four-month payment

quadrimotóre *adj* four-motor ‖ *m* four-motor plane

quadrireattóre *m* four-motor jet

qua·dro -dra *adj* square; (fig) solid ‖ *m* picture; painting; sight; square; table, summary; panel, switchboard; (theat) scene; **quadri** bulletin board; (mil) cadres; (cards) diamonds

quadrùmane *adj* quadrumanous ‖ *m* monkey; ape

quadruplicare §197 **(quadrùplico)** *tr* & *ref* to quadruple

quadrùplice *adj* quadruple; **in quadruplice copia** in four copies

quàdru·plo -pla *adj* & *m* quadruple

quaggiù *adv* down here

quàglia *f* quail

quagliare §280 *tr, intr* (ESSERE) & *ref* var of **cagliare**

qualche *adj invar* some, e.g., **qualche giorno** some day; some, e.g., **qualche elefante è bianco** some elephants are white; any, e.g., **ha qualche libro da vendere?** do you have any books to sell?; a few, e.g., **qualche giorno** a few days

qualchedu·no -na *pron indef* var of **qualcuno**

qualcòsa [s] *m* (fig) something; (fig) somebody ‖ *pron indef* something; anything; **qualcosa di buono** something good

qualcu·no -na *pron indef* some; any; somebody; anybody ‖ *m* somebody

quale *adj* which, what; what a, e.g., **quale onore!** what an honor!; as, e.g., **il pane, quale vedi, è fresco** the bread, as you can see, is fresh; **quale che sia** regardless of ‖ *pron* which; what; (archaic) who; **il quale** who, whom; **per la quale** o.k.; well-bred; commendable; terrific; **quale . . . quale** some . . . some ‖ *prep* as, e.g., **quale ministro** as a minister

qualifi·ca *f* (-che) rating; position; quality, qualification

qualificare §197 **(qualifico)** *tr* to qualify; to classify; to rate, give a rating to ‖ *ref* to introduce oneself; to qualify

qualifica·to -ta *adj* aggravated (*assault*); qualified (*personnel*); specialized (*worker*)

quali·tà *f* (-tà) quality; capacity

qualóra *conj* if; (lit) whenever

qualsìasi [s] *adj invar* any; whatever; ordinary

qualunque *adj invar* any; whatever; common, ordinary; **in qualunque modo** anyway, anyhow; **qualunque altro** anybody else; **qualunque cosa** anything; no matter what

qualvòlta *conj* (lit) whenever

quando *m* when ‖ *adv* when; **di quando in quando** from time to time; **quando . . . quando** sometimes . . . sometimes ‖ *conj* when; whenever; while; **da quando** since

quantisti·co -ca *adj* (-ci -che) quantum

quanti·tà *f* (-tà) quantity; number

quantitativo *m* quantity

quan·to -ta *adj* how much; as much; how great; how great a; what a; **quan·ti -te** how many; as many ‖ *m* quantum ‖ *pron* how much; as much; how great; how long; that which; what; whatever; **a quanto si dice** according to what is rumored; **da quanto** from what; for how long; **fra quanto** how soon; **per quanto io ne sappia** as far as I know; **quanto più (or meno) . . . tanto più (or meno)** the more (or the less) . . . the more· (or the less); **quan·ti -te** how many; all those; as many as; **quanti ne abbiamo?** what's the date? ‖ **quanto** *adv* how much; as much as; **in quanto** as; **in quanto che** inasmuch as; **per quanto** although; no matter; nevertheless; **quanto a** as to, as for; **quanto mai** as never before; **quanto meno** at least; **quanto prima** as soon as possible

quantunque *conj* although, though

quaranta *adj*, *m* & *pron* forty; **gli anni quaranta** the forties; **i quaranta** the forties (*in age*)

quarantèna *f* quarantine

quarantènne *adj* forty-year-old ‖ *mf* forty-year-old person

quarantèsi·mo -ma *adj*, *m* & *pron* fortieth

quarantina *f* about forty; **essere sulla quarantina** to be about forty years old

quarantòtto *adj* forty-eight ‖ *m* forty-eight; (coll) hubbub, uproar

quarésima *f* Lent

quartabuòno *m* triangle (*in drafting*); **tagliare a quartabuono** to miter

quartétto *m* quartet; **quartetto d'archi** string quartet

quartière *m* quarter, district; (mil) quarters; (coll) apartment; **quartier generale** headquarters; **senza quartiere** (*fight*) without quarter

quar·to -ta *adj* & *pron* fourth ‖ *m* fourth; quarter; quarter of a kilo; quarter of a liter; (naut) watch; **l'una e un quarto** a quarter after one; **l'una meno un quarto** a quarter to one

quarzo *m* quartz

quasi *adv* almost, nearly; **quasi che** as if; **quasi mai** hardly ever; **senza quasi** without any ifs and buts

quassù *adv* up here

quat·to -ta *adj* crouching; squatting; **quatto quatto** stealthy, silent; **starsene quatto quatto** to not make a sound

quattordicènne *adj* fourteen-year-old ‖ *mf* fourteen-year-old person

quattordicèsi·mo -ma *adj*, *m* & *pron* fourteenth

quattórdici *adj* & *pron* fourteen; **le**

quattordici two P.M. ‖ *m* fourteen; fourteenth (*in dates*)

quattrino *m* penny; (fig) bit; **quattrini** money

quattro *adj* four; a few, e.g., **quattro gatti** a few people; **a quattro mani** (mus) for four hands ‖ *pron* four; **dirne quattro a** to upbraid; **farsi in quattro** to go all out; **in quattro e quattr'otto** in a few minutes; **le quattro** four o'clock ‖ *m* four; fourth (*in dates*); racing shell with four oarsmen

quattrocènto *adj, m & pron* four hundred ‖ **il Quattrocento** the fifteenth century

quattromila *adj, m & pron* four thousand

quégli §7 *adj* ‖ §8 *pron*

quéi §7 *adj*

quél §7 *adj* ‖ §8 *pron*

quéll' §7 *adj*

quél·lo -la §7 *adj* ‖ §8 *pron*—**per quello che so io** as far as I know

quèr·cia *f* (-ce) oak tree

querci·no -na *adj* oaken

querèla *f* complaint

querelante *adj* complaining ‖ *mf* plaintiff

querelare (**querèlo**) *tr* to sue ‖ *ref* (law) to sue; (lit) to complain

querela·to -ta *adj* accused ‖ *mf* defendant

quèru·lo -la *adj* (lit) plaintive

quesito *m* question; problem; (lit) request

quésti §7 *pron*

questionare (**questióno**) *intr* to quarrel

questionà·rio *m* (-ri) questionnaire

questióne *f* question; (coll) quarrel; **questione di gabinetto** call for a vote of confidence; **venire a questione** to quarrel

qué·sto -sta §7 *adj* ‖ §8 *pron*—**e con questo?** so what?; **per questo** therefore; **questa this matter; questo · · · quello** the former . . . the latter

questóre *m* police commissioner; sergeant at arms (*of congress*)

quèstua *f* begging; collection of alms; **andare alla questua** to go begging; **vietata la questua** no begging

questura *f* police department; police headquarters

questurino *m* (coll) policeman

què·to -ta *adj* var of **quieto**

qui *adv* here; **di qui** hence, from here; this way; **di qui a un anno** one year hence; **di qui in avanti** from now on; **qui vicino** nearby

quiescènza *f* quiescence; retirement

quietanza *f* receipt

quietanzare *tr* to receipt

quietare (**quièto**) *tr* to quiet, calm; to satisfy (*e.g., thirst*) ‖ *ref* to quiet down

quiète *f* quiet, calmness

quiè·to -ta *adj* quiet, calm; still; **stia quieto!** don't worry! ‖ *m* quiet life

quindi *adv* then; therefore; (archaic) thence, from there

quindicènne *adj* fifteen-year-old ‖ *mf* fifteen-year-old person

quindicèsi·mo -ma *adj, m & pron* fifteenth

quindici *adj & pron* fifteen; **le quindici** three P.M. ‖ *m* fifteen; fifteenth (*in dates*)

quindicina *f* about fifteen; two weeks, fortnight; semimonthly pay

quindicinale *adj* fortnightly

quinquennale *adj* five-year

quinta *f* (theat) wing; (mus) fifth; **dietro le quinte behind the scenes**

quintale *m* quintal (*100 kilos*)

quintèrno *m* signature of five sheets; (bb) quire

quintessènza *f* quintessence

quintétto *m* quintet

quin·to -ta *adj, m & pron* fifth ‖ *f* see **quinta**

quisquìlia *f* trifle

quivi *adv* (lit) over there; (lit) then

quòrum *m* quorum

quòta *f* quota; share; altitude; elevation; level (*of stock market*); market average; odds (*in betting*); subscription (*to club*); **quota zero** (fig) point of departure

quotare (**quòto**) *tr* to quote (*a price*); to value, esteem ‖ *ref* to sign up for, e.g., **si quotò duemila lire** he signed up for two thousand lire

quotazióne *f* quotation

quotidia·no -na *adj & m* daily

quoziènte *m* quotient; (sports) percentage; **quoziente d'intelligenza** I.Q.

R

R, r ['erre] *m & f* sixteenth letter of the Italian alphabet

rabàrbaro *m* rhubarb

rabberciare §128 (**rabbèrcio**) *tr* (coll) to patch up

ràbbia *f* rage, anger; rabies

rabbino *m* rabbi

rabbió·so -sa [s] *adj* furious; rabid

rabbonire §176 *tr* to pacify ‖ *ref* to calm down

rabbrividire §176 *intr* (ESSERE) to shiver, shudder

rabbuffare *tr* to rebuke; to dishevel

rabbuffo *m* rebuke; **fare un rabbuffo a** to rebuke

rabbuiare §287 *ref* to darken, turn dark

rabdomante *m* dowser, diviner

rabé·sco *m* (-schi) arabesque; scrawl, scribble

ràbi·do -da *adj* rabid

raccapezzare (**raccapézzo**) *tr* to put together; to gather (*news*); to find (*one's way*); to make out (*what is* *meant)* || *ref*—**non raccapezzarsi** to not be able to get one's bearings

raccapricciante *adj* bloodcurdling

raccapríc·cio *m* (**-ci**) horror

raccartocciare §128 (**raccartòccio**) *tr & ref* to shrivel

raccattare *tr* to pick up; to gather

racchétta *f* racket; **racchetta da neve** snowshoe; **racchetta da sci** ski pole

ràc·chio -chia *adj* (**-chi -chie**) (coll) ugly, homely

racchiùdere §125 *tr* to contain, hold

raccògliere §127 *tr* to pick up; to gather; to collect (*e.g., stamps*); to take up (*the gauntlet*); to receive; to reap; to furl (*sail*); to draw in (*a net*); to fold (*the wings*); to shelter (*e.g., foundlings*); **raccogliere i passi** to stop walking || *ref* to gather; to concentrate

raccoglimento *m* concentration; meditation

raccogli·tóre -trice *mf* collector, compiler || *m* folder

raccòl·to -ta *adj* crouched; collected; engrossed; snug, intimate || *m* harvest || *f* harvest; collection; **chiamare a raccolta** to rally

raccomandàbile *adj* recommendable; **poco raccomandàbile** unreliable

raccomandare *tr* to recommend; to secure (*e.g., a boat*); to register (*mail*); to exhort || *ref* to recommend oneself; to entreat; **mi raccomando** please; **raccomandarsi a** to beg, implore; **raccomandarsi alle gambe** to take to one's heels

raccomanda·to -ta *adj* recommended; registered || *m* protégé || *f* protégée; registered letter

raccomandazióne *f* recommendation; registration (*of mail*); exhortation

raccomodare (**raccòmodo**) *tr* to fix; to mend

racconciare §128 (**raccóncio**) *tr* to fix; to mend || *ref* to clear up (*said of the weather*); to tidy oneself up

raccontare (**raccónto**) *tr* to tell; **raccontarla bene** to be good at telling lies

raccónto *m* tale; story; narrative

raccorciaménto *m* shortening

raccorciare §128 (**raccòrcio**) *tr* to shorten

raccordare (**raccòrdo**) *tr* to link, connect

raccòrdo *m* link, connection; **raccordo a circolazione rotatoria** traffic circle; **raccordo anulare** (rr) belt line; **raccordo ferroviario** junction; spur; siding; **raccordo stradale** connecting road

raccostare (**raccòsto**) *tr & ref* to draw near

raccozzare (**raccòzzo**) *tr* to scrape together

ràchide *m & f* backbone; midrib (*of leaf*); shaft (*of feather*)

rachíti·co -ca *adj* (**-ci -che**) stunted; weak; (pathol) rickety

rachitismo *m* rickets

racimolare (**racìmolo**) *tr* to glean; to scrape together

rada *f* roadstead; cove

ràdar *m* radar

addobbare (**raddòbbo**) *tr* (naut) to refit

raddolcire §176 *tr & ref* to sweeten; to mellow

raddoppiare §287 (**raddóppio**) *tr, intr* (ESSERE) *& ref* to double, redouble

raddrizzare *tr* to straighten; (elec) to rectify || *ref* to straighten up

raddrizzatóre *m* (elec) rectifier

ràdere §223 *tr* to shave; to raze; to graze, skim || *ref* to shave

radézza *f* rarity, rareness; thinness; sparsity (*of vegetation*); space, distance (*e.g., between trees*)

radiante *adj* radiating

radiare §287 *tr* to strike off; to expel; to condemn (*a ship*); **radiare dall'albo degli avvocati** to disbar

radiatóre *m* radiator

radiazióne *f* radiation; expulsion

ràdi·ca *f* (**-che**) brier; (coll) root

radicale *adj & mf* radical || *m & j* (philol) radical, root || *m* (chem, math) radical

radicare §197 (**ràdico**) *tr & intr* to root

radíce *f* root; base or foot (*e.g., of a mountain or tower*); **mettere radice** to take root; **svellere dalle radici** to pull up by the roots; to eradicate

rà·dio *adj invar* radio || *m* (**-di**) (anat) radius; (chem) radium || *f* (**-dio**) radio; **radio fante** (mil) grapevine

radioabbonato *m* (rad) subscriber (*to radio broadcasting*)

radioama·tóre -trice *mf* radio fan; radio ham

radioannunciatóre *m* radio announcer

radioascolta·tóre -trice *mf* radio listener

radioatti·vo -va *adj* radioactive

radiobùssola *f* radio compass

radiocanale *m* radio channel

radiocoman·do -ta *adj* radio-controlled

radiocròna·ca *f* (**-che**) newscast

radiocroni·sta *mf* (**-sti -ste**) newscaster

radiodiffóndere §178 *tr* to broadcast

radiodiffusióne *f* broadcasting

radiofaro *m* radio beacon

radiofòni·co -ca *adj* (**-ci -che**) radio

radiofonògrafo *m* radiophonograph

radiofò·to *f* (**-to**) radiophoto

radiofrequenza *f* radiofrequency

radiologia *f* radiology

radiomontatóre *m* radio assembler

radioónda *f* radio wave; **radioonde** airwaves

radioricevènte *adj* radio || *f* radio set; radio station

radioriparatóre *m* radio repairman

radiosegnale *m* radio signal

radiosentièro *m* range of a radio beacon

radió·so -sa [s] *adj* radiant

radiosorgènte *f* quasar

radiostazióne *f* radio station

radiostélla *f* quasar

radiotas·sì *m* (**-sì**) radio-dispatched taxi

radiotelescò·pio *m* (**-pi**) radiotelescope

radiotrasméttere §198 *tr & intr* to broadcast, radio

radiotrasmissióne *f* broadcast

radiotrasmittènte *adj* broadcasting || *f* broadcasting station

ra·do -da *adj* rare; thin; sheer; sparse, scattered; **di rado** seldom, rarely

radunare *tr & ref* to assemble, gather

radunata *f* gathering; (mil) assembly; **radunata sediziosa** unlawful assembly

raduno *m* assembly, gathering

radura *f* clearing, glade

ràfano *m* (bot) radish

raffazzonare (raffazzóno) *tr* to mend, patch up

raffazzonatura *f* patchwork, hodge-podge

rafférma *f* confirmation; stay (*in office*); return to office; (mil) reenlistment

raffermare (raffèrmo) *tr* to reaffirm; to secure; (coll) to reconfirm; to reappoint, reelect; to return (*e.g., a mayor*) to office || *intr* (ESSERE) & *ref* to reenlist; (coll) to harden

raffér·mo -ma *adj* stale (bread) || *f see* rafferma

ràffi·ca *f* (-che) gust; blast; burst (*e.g., of machine gun*); **a raffiche** gusty

raffigurare *tr* to represent; to symbolize

raffinare *tr* to refine; to polish || *intr* (ESSERE) to become refined

raffinatézza *f* refinement, polish

raffinatura *f* refinement (*of oil*)

raffinazióne *f* refining

raffinerìa *f* refinery

ràf·fio *m* (-fi) hook; grappling iron

rafforzare (rafforzo) *tr* to strengthen

raffreddaménto *m* cooling

raffreddare (raffréddo) *tr* to make cold; to cool; **raffreddare gli spiriti di qlcu** to dampen s.o.'s enthusiasm || *intr* (ESSERE) & *ref* to get cold; to cool

raffreddóre *m* cold

raffrontare (raffrónto) *tr* to compare; (law) to bring face to face

raffrónto *m* comparison; confrontation

ràfia *f* raffia

raganèlla *f* rattle; (zool) tree frog

ragazza *f* girl; spinster; (coll) girl friend; **ragazza copertina** cover girl; **ragazza squillo** call girl

ragazzata *f* boyish prank

ragaz·zo -za *mf* youth, young person || *m* boy; (coll) boyfriend || *f see* ragazza

raggelare (raggèlo) *intr* (ESSERE) to freeze

raggiante *adj* radiant; beaming

raggiare §290 *tr & intr* to radiate

raggièra *f* rayed halo; **a raggiera** radially

ràg·gio *m* (-gi) ray; beam; spoke; (geom) radius; **raggio d'azione** radius, range of action; **raggio di sole** sunbeam

raggiornare (raggiórno) *tr* (coll) to bring up to date || *intr* (ESSERE) to dawn || *impers* (ESSERE)—**raggiorna** it is dawning

raggirare *tr* to trick, swindle || *ref* to roam, wander; **raggirarsi su** to turn on (*e.g., a certain subject*)

raggiro *m* trickery, swindle

raggiungere §183 *tr* to reach; to catch up with, rejoin

raggiungìbile *adj* attainable

raggomitolare (raggomìtolo) *tr* to roll up || *ref* to curl up; to cuddle

raggranellare (raggranèllo) *tr* to gather; to scrape together

raggrinzire §176 *tr & ref* to crease, wrinkle

raggrumare *tr & ref* to clot, coagulate

raggruppaménto *m* grouping; group

raggruppare *tr & ref* to group, assemble

ragguagliare §280 *tr* to compare; to balance; to inform in detail; to level

ragguà·glio *m* (-gli) comparison; detailed report

ragguardévole *adj* considerable, notable

ragionaménto *m* reasoning; discussion

ragionare (ragióno) *intr* to reason; to discuss || *impers ref*—**si ragiona** it is rumored

ragióne *f* reason; account; rate; justice; (math) ratio; **a maggior ragione** with all the more reason; **a ragione** within reason; **aver ragione** to be right; **aver ragione di** to get the best of; **dar ragione a qlcu** to admit that s.o. is right; **di santa ragione** hard, a great deal; **farsi ragione** to be resigned; **in ragione di** at the rate of; **ragion per cui** and therefore; **ragione sociale** (com) trade name; **rendere di pubblica ragione** to publicize

ragionerìa *f* accounting; bookkeeping

ragio·niè·re -ra *mf* accountant; book-keeper

ragliare §280 *intr* to bray

rà·glio *m* (-gli) bray

ragnatéla *f* spider web

ragno *m* spider

ra·gù *m* (-gù) meat gravy; stew

ràion *m* rayon

rallegraménto *m* congratulation, act of congratulating; **rallegramenti** congratulations

rallegrare (rallégro) *tr* to cheer up; to rejoice, gladden || *ref* to cheer up; to rejoice; **rallegrarsi con** to congratulate

rallentare (rallènto) *tr, intr & ref* to slow down; to lessen

rallentatóre *m* slow-motion projector; **al rallentatore** slow-motion

ra·màio *m* (-mài) tinker, coppersmith

ramaiòlo *m* ladle

ramanzina [dz] *f* reprimand

ramare *tr* to copperplate; (agr) to spray with copper sulfate

ramarro *m* green lizard

ramazza *f* broom; (mil) cleaning detail; (mil) soldier on cleaning detail

rame *m* copper; etching

ram·erino *m* (coll) rosemary

ramificare §197 (ramìfico) *intr & ref* to branch; to branch off; to branch out, ramify

ramìn·go -ga *adj* (-ghi -ghe) wandering

ramino *m* copper pot; rummy (*card game*)

rammagliare §280 *tr* to reknit; to mend a run in (*a stocking*)

rammaricare §197 (rammàrico) *tr* to afflict || *ref* to be sorry, regret; **rammaricarsi di** to be sorry for

rammàri•co *m* (-chi) regret
rammendare (rammèndo) *tr* to darn
rammèndo *m* darn
rammentare (ramménto) *tr* to remember; to remind || *ref*—**rammentarsi di** to remember
rammenta•tóre -trice *mf* prompter
rammollire §176 *tr & ref* to soften
rammolli•to -ta *adj* soft; soft-headed || *m* dodo, jellyfish
ramo *m* branch; bough; point (*of antler*); **ramo di pazzia** streak of madness
ramoscèllo *m* twig; **ramoscello d'olivo** olive branch
rampa *f* ramp; flight (*of stairs*); launching platform
rampicante *adj* climbing || *m* (ichth) perch; (orn) climber
rampino *m* hook; tine, prong; pretext
rampógna *f* (lit) reprimand
rampóllo *m* spring (*of water*); scion, shoot (*of a plant*); (joc) offspring
rampóne *m* harpoon; crampon
rana *f* frog
rànci•do -da *adj* rancid
ràn•cio -cia (-ci -ce) *adj* (poet) orange || *m* (mil) mess
rancóre *m* rancor; grudge; **serbar rancore** to bear malice
randa *f* (naut) spanker; (obs) edge
randà•gio -gia *adj* (-gi -gie) wandering, stray
randellare (randèllo) *tr* to cudgel; to bludgeon; to blackjack
randèllo *m* cudgel; bludgeon
ran•go *m* (-ghi) rank; station
rannicchiare §287 *tr* to cause to curl up || *ref* to crouch; to cower; to cuddle up
ranno *m* lye; **buttar via il ranno e il sapone** to waste one's time and effort
rannuvolare (rannùvolo) *tr & ref* to cloud; to darken
ranòcchia *f* frog
ranòc•chio *m* (-chi) frog
rantolare (ràntolo) *intr* to wheeze
ràntolo *m* wheezing; death rattle
ranùncolo *m* buttercup
rapa *f* turnip; **valere una rapa** to be not worth a fig
rapace *adj* rapacious || **rapaci** *mpl* birds of prey
rapare *tr* to shave (*s.o.'s head*) || *ref* to shave one's head; to have one's head shaved
rapidi•tà *f* (-tà) rapidity, swiftness
ràpi•do -da *adj* rapid, swift || *m* (rr) express || **rapide** *fpl* rapids
rapiménto *m* rape, abduction; rapture
rapina *f* pillage, plunder; misappropriation; prey; (lit) fury; **rapina a mano armata** armed robbery
rapinare *tr* to rob, plunder; to hold up; **rapinare qlco a qlcu** to rob s.o. of s.th
rapina•tóre -trice *mf* robber, plunderer
rapire §176 *tr* to rape, abduct; to kidnap; to enrapture
rapi•tóre -trice *mf* kidnaper
rappacificare §197 (rappacìfico) *tr* to reconcile || *ref* to become reconciled
rappezzare (rappèzzo) *tr* to patch; to

piece; **rappezzarla** to get out of trouble
rappèzzo *m* patch; patchwork
rapportare (rappòrto) *tr* to report; to transfer (*a design*) || *ref* to refer
rapporta•tóre -trice *mf* reporter || *m* protractor
rappòrto *m* report; relation; relationship; (math) ratio; **chiamare a rapporto** to summon; **chiedere di mettersi a rapporto** to ask for a hearing; **fare rapporto** to report; **in rapporto a** concerning; **mettersi a rapporto** to report; **sotto ogni rapporto** in every respect
rapprèndere §220 *tr & ref* to coagulate
rappresàglia [s] *f* reprisal; retaliation
rappresentante *adj* representing; representative || *mf* representative; agent; **rappresentante di commercio** agent
rappresentanza *f* delegation; proxy; agency; representation
rappresentare (rappresènto) *tr* to represent; to play; to portray
rappresentati•vo -va *adj* representative
rappresentazióne *f* representation; description; (theat) performance; **rappresentazione teatrale diurna** matinée; **sacra rappresentazione** (theat) mystery, miracle play
rapsodìa *f* rhapsody
raraménte *adv* seldom, rarely
rarefare §173 *tr* to rarefy || *ref* to become rarefied
rari•tà *f* (-tà) rarity
ra•ro -ra *adj* rare; **di raro** seldom
rasare [s] *tr* to shave; to mow; to trim; to smooth || *ref* to shave
raschiare §287 (ràschio) *tr* to scrape; to scratch || *intr* to clear one's throat
raschiétto *m* scraper; erasing knife; footscraper
rà•schio *m* (-schi) clearing one's throat; hoarseness; frog in the throat
rasentare (rasènto) *tr* to graze; to scrape; to border on; to come close to
rasènte *adv* close; **rasente a** close to || *prep* close to
ra•so -sa [s] *adj* shaved; trimmed; brimful; disreputable (*clothes*); flush || *m* satin || *adv*—**raso terra** down-to-earth; **volare raso terra** to skim the ground; to hedgehop
ra•sóio [s] *m* (-sói) razor; **rasoio a mano libera** straight razor; **rasoio di sicurezza** safety razor
raspa *f* rasp
raspare *tr* to rasp; to irritate; to stamp, paw; (coll) to steal || *intr* to rasp; to scratch (*said of a chicken*); to scrawl
raspo *m* grape stalk; scraper; (vet) mange
rasségna *f* review; exposition
rassegnare (rasségno) *tr* to resign; **rassegnare le dimissioni** to resign || *ref* to resign oneself; to submit
rassegnazióne *f* resignation
rasserenare (rasseréno) *tr & ref* to brighten; to cheer up
rassettare (rassètto) *tr & ref* to tidy up

rassicurare *tr* to reassure ‖ *ref* to be reassured

rassodare (rassòdo) *tr* to harden; to strengthen ‖ *intr* (ESSERE) & *ref* to harden

rassomigliare §280 **(rassomìglio)** *tr* to compare ‖ *intr* (ESSERE) (with *dat*) to resemble ‖ *ref* to resemble each other

rastrellaménto *m* roundup; mop-up operation

rastrellare (rastrèllo) *tr* to rake; to round up; to mop up; to drag (*e.g.*, *the bottom*)

rastrellièra *f* rack; crib

rastrèllo *m* rake

rastremare (rastrèmo) *tr* to taper

rata *f* installment; quota; **a rate** on time; by installments

rateale *adj* installment

rateizzare [ddzz] *tr* to prorate; to divide (*a payment*) into installments

ratìfi·ca *f* (**-che**) ratification

ratificare §197 **(ratìfico)** *tr* to ratify

rat·to -ta *adj* (lit) swift ‖ *m* rat; (lit) rape ‖ **ratto** *adv* (lit) swiftly

rattoppare (rattòppo) *tr* to patch, patch up

rattrappire §176 *tr* to cramp; to make numb, benumb ‖ *ref* to become cramped; to become numb

rattristare *tr* & *ref* to sadden

raucèdine *f* hoarseness

ràu·co -ca *adj* (**-chi -che**) hoarse, raucous

ravanèllo *m* radish

ravizzóne *m* (bot) rape

ravvedére §279 (*fut* **ravvedrò** & **ravvederò**; *pp* **ravveduto**) *ref* to repent; to mend one's ways

ravvedu·to -ta *adj* repentant; reformed

ravviare §119 *tr* to arrange, adjust; to poke (*fire*) ‖ *ref* to tidy up; (lit) to reform

ravvicinaménto *m* approach; reconciliation; rapprochement

ravvicinare *tr* to bring up; to reconcile ‖ *ref* to approach; to become reconciled; **ravvicinarsi a** to approach

ravviluppare *tr* to wrap up; to wind up; to bamboozle ‖ *ref* to become tangled

ravvisare *tr* to recognize

ravvivare *tr* to revive; to enliven; to brighten; to stir (*fire*) ‖ *ref* to revive

ravvòlgere §289 *tr* to wrap up

razioci·nio *m* (**-nî**) reasoning; reason; common sense

razionale *adj* rational

razionalizzare [ddzz] *tr* (com, math) to rationalize

razionaménto *m* rationing

razionare (razióno) *tr* to ration

razióne *f* ration; portion

razza *f* race; breed; kind; **dì razza** purebred; **far razza** to reproduce; **passare a razza** to go to stud

razza [ddzz] *f* (ichth) ray; **razza cornuta** manta ray

razzìa *f* raid; foray; insect powder

razziale *adj* racial

razziare §119 *tr* & *intr* to foray

razzismo *m* racism

razzi·sta *mf* (**-sti -ste**) racist

razzo [ddzz] *m* rocket; (coll) spoke; (mil) flare

razzolare (ràzzolo) *intr* to scratch (*said of chickens*); (coll) to rummage

re [e] *m* (**re**) king

re [e] *m* (**re**) (mus) re

reagènte *m* reagent

reagire §176 *intr* to react

reale *adj* real, actual; royal, regal

realismo *m* realism; royalism

reali·sta *mf* (**-sti -ste**) realist; royalist

realìsti·co -ca *adj* (**-ci -che**) realistic

realizzare [ddzz] *tr* to carry out; to realize; to build ‖ *ref* to come true

realizzazióne [ddzz] *f* realization; **realizzazione scenica** production

realizzo [ddzz] *m* conversion into cash; profit taking; forced sale

realménte *adv* really, indeed

real·tà *f* (**-tà**) reality; actuality; **realtà romanzesca** truth stranger than fiction

reato *m* crime

reatti·vo -va *adj* reactive

reattóre *m* reactor; jet plane; jet engine

reazionà·rio -ria (**-rî -rie**) *adj* & *mf* reactionary

reazióne *f* reaction; (mach) backlash; **a reazione** jet-propelled

réb·bio *m* (**-bî**) prong

recalcitrante *adj* balky, restive; **essere recalcitrante a** to be opposed to, to resist

recalcitrare (recàlcitro) *intr* to be balky; to kick; (with *dat*) to buck, resist

recapitare (recàpito) *tr* to deliver

recàpito *m* address; delivery; **far recapito in** to be domiciled in; **recapiti** (com) notes

recare §197 **(rèco)** *tr* to bring; to cause; **recare ad effetto** to carry out; **recare qlco alla memoria di qlcu** to remind s.o. of s.th; **recare qlco a lode di qlcu** to praise s.o. for s.th ‖ *ref* to go, betake oneself

recèdere §123 *intr* (ESSERE & AVERE) to recede

recensióne *f* book review; collation

recensire §176 *tr* to review; to collate

recensóre *m* reviewer

recènte *adj* recent; **dì recente** recently

recessióne *f* recession

recèsso *m* recess; subsiding (*of fever*); ebb tide

recìdere §145 *tr* to cut off; to chop off

recidìva *f* relapse; second offense

recìngere §126 *tr* to enclose, pen in

recìnto *m* enclosure; pen, yard; compound; playpen; paddock; **recinto delle grida** floor of the exchange

recipiènte *m* container

reciprocità *f* reciprocity

reciprò·co -ca *adj* (**-ci -che**) reciprocal

reci·so -sa *adj* cut off; abrupt

rècita *f* show, performance

recitare (rècito) *tr* to recite; to portray, play; **recitare la commedia** to put on an act ‖ *intr* to perform, play; **recitare a soggetto** (theat) to improvise

recitazióne *f* recitation; diction; acting

reclamare *tr* to claim, demand || *intr* to complain

récla·me *f* (**-me**) advertising; advertisement; **fare réclame a** to advertise; to boost

reclami·sta *mf* (**-sti -ste**) advertising agent; show-off || *m* advertising man

reclamisti·co -ca *adj* (**-ci -che**) advertising

reclamo *m* complaint; **fare reclamo a** complain

reclinare *tr* to bow || *intr* to recline

reclusióne *f* seclusion; imprisonment

reclu·so -sa *adj* recluse || *mf* recluse; prisoner

reclusò·rio *m* (**-ri**) penitentiary

rècluta *f* recruit; rookie

reclutaménto *m* recruitment

reclutare (**rècluto**) *tr* to recruit

recòndi·to -ta *adj* concealed; inmost; recondite

recriminare (**recrìmino**) *intr* to recriminate

recuperare (**recùpero**) *tr* see **ricuperare**

redarguire §176 *tr* to berate

redat·tóre -trice *mf* compiler; newspaper editor; **redattore capo** managing editor; **redattore pubblicitario** copywriter; **redattore responsabile** publisher; **redattore viaggiante** correspondent

redazionale *adj* editorial, editor's (*e.g., policy*)

redazióne *f* writing; draft; version; (*journ*) city room

redazza *f* mop; (*naut*) swab

redditi·zio -zia *adj* (**-zi -zie**) lucrative

rèddito *m* income, revenue; yield; **reddito nazionale** gross national product

redèn·to -ta *adj* redeemed, set free

reden·tóre -trice *mf* redeemer || **Redentore** *m*—**il Redentore** the Redeemer

redenzióne *f* redemption

redìgere §224 *tr* to compile; to write up, compose

redìmere §225 *tr* to redeem; to ransom; to save

rèdine *f* rein

redivì·vo -va *adj* come back to life

rèduce *adj* back (*from war*) || *mf* veteran

réfe *m* thread

referèn·dum *m* (**-dum**) referendum; **referendum postale** mail questionnaire

referènza *f* reference

referenziare (**referènzio**) *tr* to give references to; to write references for || *intr* to have good references

referenzia·to -ta *adj* with good references, e.g., **impiegato referenziato** employee with good references

refèrto *m* report (*of a physician*)

refettò·rio *m* (**-ri**) refectory

refezióne *f* lunch, light meal; **refezione scolastica** school lunch

refrattà·rio -ria *adj* (**-ri -rie**) refractory

refrigerante *adj* cooling || *m* refrigerator; (*chem*) condenser

refrigerare (**refrìgero**) *tr* to refrigerate; to cool || *ref* to cool off

refrigè·rio *m* (**-ri**) relief, comfort

refurtiva *f* stolen goods

refuso *m* misprint

regalare *tr* to present; to deliver (*a slap*); to throw away (*money*); **è regalato** it's a steal

regale *adj* regal; royal; imposing

regalìa *f* gratuity; bonus

regalità *f* regality, royalty

regalo *m* present, gift

regata *f* regatta

reggènte *adj & m* regent

reggènza *f* regency

règgere §226 *tr* to hold, hold up; to stand, withstand; to guide; (*gram*) to govern; **reggere il sacco a** to connive with; **reggere l'animo di** + *inf* to bear or stand + *ger*, e.g., **non gli regge l'animo di vederla piangere** he cannot stand seeing her cry || *intr* to hold; to be valid; to last, hold out (*said of weather*); **reggere** (with *dat*) to withstand (*e.g., the cold*); **reggere al paragone** to bear comparison || *ref* to stand up; to hold; to be ruled; **reggersi a** to hold on to; to be governed as (*e.g., a republic*); **reggersi a galla** to float

règ·gia *f* (**-ge**) royal palace

reggical·ze *m* (**-ze**) girdle

reggilibro *m* book end

reggimentale *adj* regimental

reggiménto *m* regiment

reggipètto *m* brassiere

reggisé·no *m* (**-ni & -no**) brassiere

regìa *f* monopoly; (*mov*) direction; (*theat*) production

regici·da *mf* (**-di -de**) regicide

regicì·dio *m* (**-di**) regicide

regime *m* regime; diet; flow (*e.g., of river*); government; authoritarian government; (*mach*) rate; **regime secco** total abstinence

regina *f* queen; **regina claudia** greengage; **regina madre** queen mother

reginétta *f* young queen; queen (*of a beauty contest*)

rè·gio -gia *adj* (**-gi -gie**) royal || **i regi** the king's soldiers

regióne *f* region

regi·sta *mf* (**-sti -ste**) coordinator; (*theat*) producer; (*mov*) director

registrare *tr* to register, record; to enter; to tally, log; to adjust; to tune up (*a musical instrument*) || *ref* to register

registra·tóre -trice *mf* registrar || *m* recorder; **registratore di cassa** cash register

registrazióne *f* registration; record, entry; adjustment; (*aut*) tune-up; (*telv*) videotaping; (*telv*) video-taping studio; (*telv*) video-taped program

registro *m* register; registration; classbook; regulator (*of watch*); stop (*of organ*); **cambiar registro** to change one's tune; **dar registro a** to regulate (*a watch*)

regnante *adj* reigning; prevailing || **i regnanti** the rulers

regnare (**régno**) *intr* to reign, rule; to prevail; to take hold (*said of a root*)

régno *m* kingdom; reign

règola *f* rule; regulation; moderation; **a regola d'arte** to a T; **di regola as a rule**; **in regola** in good order; **mettere in regola** to put in order; **regole** menstruation; **secondo le regole** by the book

regolamentare *adj* regulation || *v* (**regolaménto**) *tr* to regulate

regolaménto *m* regulation; settlement; **regolamento edilizio** building code

regolare *adj* regular; steady (*employment*); stock (*material*) || *v* (**règolo**) *tr* to regulate; to adjust; to set (*a watch*); to focus (*a lens*); to settle (*an account*) || *ref* to behave; to control oneself

regolari·tà *f* (**-tà**) regularity

regolarizzare [ddzz] *tr* to regularize

regolatézza *f* regularity; moderation

regola·to -ta *adj* regular, orderly

regola·tóre -trice *adj* regulating; see **piano** || *m* ruler; regulator (*of watch*); (mach) governor; **regolatore dell'aria** register; **regolatore di volume** (rad, telv) volume control

regolazióne *f* regulation

regolìzia *f* (coll) licorice

règolo *m* ruler; slat; (orn, hist) kinglet; **regolo calcolatore** slide rule

regredire §176 (*pres participle* **regrediènte**; *pp* **regredito** & **regrèsso**) *intr* (ESSERE & AVERE) to retrogress

regrèsso *m* regression; abatement (*of fever*); (com) recourse

reièt·to -ta *adj* rejected || *mf* outcast

reimbarcare §197 *tr* & *ref* to reship; to transship

reimbar·co *m* (**-chi**) reshipment; transshipment

reincarnare *tr* to reincarnate || *ref* to become reincarnated

reincarnazióne *f* reincarnation

reinseriménto *m* integration

reintegrare (**reìntegro**) *tr* to restore; to reinstate; to indemnify

reità *f* guilt

reiterare (**reìtero**) *tr* to reiterate

relativi·tà *f* (**-tà**) relativity

relati·vo -va *adj* relative

rela·tóre -trice *adj* reporting || *mf* relator (*of proceedings*); presenter (*of a bill*); dissertation supervisor

relazióne *f* relation; relationship; report; **relazione amorosa** affair; **relazioni** relations; connections

re-lè *m* (**-lè**) (elec) relay

relegare §209 (**rèlego**) *tr* to banish; to store away

religióne *f* religion

religió·so -sa [s] *adj* religious || *m* clergyman || *f* nun

relìquia *f* relic

relìt·to -ta *adj* residual || *m* shipwreck; air crash; derelict; shoal, bar

remare (**rèmo** & **rémo**) *intr* to row

rema·tóre -trice *mf* rower || *m* oarsman

reminiscènza *f* reminiscence

remissióne *f* submissiveness; remission

remissi·vo -va *adj* submissive

rèmo *m* oar; **remo alla battana** paddle

rèmora *f* hindrance; (lit) delay

remò·to -ta *adj* remote; **passato remoto** (gram) preterit

réna *f* sand

Renània, la the Rhineland

Renata *f* Renée

rèndere §227 *tr* to return, give back; to give (*thanks*); to render (*justice*); to yield; to translate; to make (*known*); **render conto di** to give an account of; **rendere di pubblica ragione** to publicize; **rendere l'anima a Dio** to give up the ghost; **rendere pan per focaccia** to give tit for tat || *intr* to pay, yield || *ref* to make oneself; to betake oneself; to become; (lit) to surrender; **rendersi conto di** to realize

rendicónto *m* account; report; **rendiconti** proceedings

rendiménto *m* rendering; yield; output; (mech) efficiency

rèndita *f* private income; yield; Italian Government bond

rène *m* kidney

renèlla *f* (pathol) gravel

renétta *f* pippin

réni *fpl* loins; **spezzare le reni a** to break the back of

renitènte *adj* opposed || *m*—**renitente alla leva** draft dodger

rènna *f* reindeer; reindeer skin

Rèno *m* Rhine

rè·o -a *adj* guilty; (lit) wicked || *m* guilty person; accused

reòstato *m* (elec) rheostat

reparto *m* department; (mil) unit; **reparto d'assalto** shock troops

repèllere §168 *tr* to repel

repentàglio *m* jeopardy; **mettere a repentaglio** to jeopardize

repènte *adj*—**di repente** suddenly

repenti·no -na *adj* sudden

reperìbile *adj* available

reperiménto *m* finding

reperire §176 *tr* to find

repèrto *m* (archeol) find; (law) evidence; (law) exhibit; (med) report

repertò·rio *m* (**-ri**) repertory; catalogue

rèpli·ca *f* (**-che**) repetition; replica; (law) rebuttal; (theat) repeat performance; **in replica** in reply

replicare §197 (**rèplico**) *tr* to repeat; to reply, answer; (theat) to repeat (*a performance*)

reportàg·gio *m* (**-gi**) news coverage; reporting

repòr·ter *m* (**-ter**) reporter

repressióne *f* repression; constraint

repressi·vo -va *adj* repressive; controlling, checking (*e.g., a disease*)

reprimere §131 *tr* to repress; to hold back (*tears*) || *ref* to restrain oneself

rèpro·bo -ba *adj* & *m* reprobate

repùbbli·ca *f* (**-che**) republic

repubblica·no -na *adj* & *mf* republican

repulisti *m*—**fare repulisti** (coll) to make a clean sweep

repulsióne *f* repulsion

repulsi·vo -va *adj* var of **ripulsivo**

reputare (**rèputo**) *tr* to think, esteem, repute

reputazióne *f* reputation

rèquie *m* & *f* (eccl) requiem || *f* rest, respite

Rèquiem *m* & *f* Requiem

requisire §176 *tr* to requisition, commandeer

requisito *m* requisite, requirement

requisitòria *f* scolding, reproach; (law) summation

requisizióne *f* requisition

résa [s] *f* surrender; rendering (*of an account*); delivery (*of merchandise*); return (*e.g., of newspapers*); yield; **resa a discrezione** unconditional surrender

rescìndere §247 *tr* to rescind

resezióne [s] *f* (surg) resection

residènte [s] *adj & mf* resident

residènza [s] *f* residence

residenziale [s] *adj* residential

residua·to -ta [s] *adj* residual

resì·duo -dua [s] *adj* residual ‖ *m* residue; remainder; balance

rèsina *f* resin

resipiscènza [s] *f* (lit) repentance

resistènte [s] *adj* resistant; strong; fast (*color*) ‖ *mf* member of the Resistance

resistènza [s] *f* resistance ‖ **Resistenza** *f* Resistance

resìstere [s] §114 *intr* to resist; (with *dat*) to withstand; (with *dat*) to endure; (with *dat*) to resist

rèso [s] *m* rhesus

resocónto [s] *m* report, relation

respingènte *m* (rr) bumper, buffer

respìngere §126 *tr* to drive back, beat off; to reject; to fail (*a student*); to vote down

respìn·to -ta *adj* rejected ‖ *mf* failure (*pupil*)

respirare *tr & intr* to breathe, respire

respiratò·rio -ria *adj* (-ri -rie) respiratory

respirazióne *f* breathing

respiro *m* breath; breathing; respite

responsàbile *adj* responsible; **responsabile di** responsible for

responsabili·tà *f* (-tà) responsibility

respònso *m* decision (*of an oracle*); report (*of a physician*); return (*of an election*); (lit) response

rèssa *f* crowd; **far ressa** to crowd

rèsta *f* string (*of garlic or onions*); awn (*e.g., of wheat*); (coll) fishbone; (*for a lance*) (hist) rest

restante *adj* remaining ‖ *m* remainder

restare (**rèsto**) *intr* (ESSERE) to remain; to stay; to be located; (lit) to stop; **non restare a...che** to have no alternative but to, e.g., **non gli resta che andarsene** he has no alternative but to go; **non restare a qlcu qlco da** + *inf* to not have s.th + to + *inf*, e.g., **non gli resta molto da finire** he does not have much to finish; **resta a vedere** it remains to be seen; **restare qlco a qlcu** to have s.th left, e.g., **gli restano tre dollari** he has three dollars left; **restare sul colpo** to die on the spot; **resti comodo** please don't get up!

restaurare (**restàuro**) *tr* to restore, renovate

restaurazióne *f* restoration

restàuro *m* restoration (*of a building*)

restì·o -a (-ì -e) *adj* balky, restive ‖ *m* balkiness

restituire §176 *tr* to give back; return; (lit) to restore ‖ *ref* (lit) to return

restituzióne *f* restitution, return

rèsto *m* remainder; change; balance; **del resto** besides, after all; **resti** remains

restrìngere §265 (*pp* **ristrétto**) *tr* to narrow down; to shrink; to take in (*a suit*); to limit (*expenses*); to tighten (*a knot*); to bind (*the bowels*); to restrict ‖ *ref* to contract; to narrow

restrizióne *f* restriction

retàg·gio *m* (-gi) (lit) heritage

retata *f* haul; (fig) roundup

réte *f* net; network; (soccer) goal; **rete a strascico** trawl; **rete da pesca** fishing net; **rete del letto** bedspring; **rete metallica** wire mesh; window screen; **rete per i capelli** hair net; **rete viaria** highway network

reticèlla *f* small net; hair net; mantle (*of gas jet*)

reticènte *adj* secretive, dissembling; evasive, noncommittal

reticènza *f* secretiveness; evasiveness

reticolato *m* grid (*on map*); wire entanglement

reticolo *m* grid

retina *f* small net

rètina *f* (anat) retina

retino *m* small net; (typ) screen

retòri·co -ca (-ci -che) *adj* rhetorical ‖ *m* rhetorician ‖ *f* rhetoric

retràttile *adj* retractile

retribuire §176 *tr* to remunerate

retributì·vo -va *adj* retributive; salary (*e.g., conditions*)

retrì·vo -va *adj* backward

rètro *m* back; verso; back of store ‖ *adv* (lit) behind; **retro a** (lit) behind

retroattì·vo -va *adj* retroactive

retrobottè·ga *m & f* (-ga *mpl* -ghe *fpl*) back of store

retrocàmera *f* back room

retrocàrica —a retrocarica breech-loading

retrocèdere §228 *tr* to demote; (com) to return; (com) to give a discount to ‖ *intr* (ESSERE & AVERE) to retreat

retrocessióne *f* demotion; (sports) assignment to a lower division

retrodatare *tr* to antedate, predate

retrògra·do -da *adj* backward; retrograde

retroguàrdia *f* rearguard

retromàr·cia *f* (-ce) (aut) reverse

retrorazzo [ddzz] *m* retrorocket

retrosapóre *m* aftertaste

retroscè·na *m* (-na) intrigue, maneuver ‖ *f* backstage

retrospettì·vo -va *adj* retrospective

retrotèr·ra *m* (-ra) hinterland; (fig) background

retrotrèno *m* rear end (*of vehicle*); (aut) rear assembly

retroversióne *f* retroversion; retranslation

retrovìe *fpl* zone behind the front

retrovisì·vo -va *adj* rear-view, e.g., **specchietto retrovisivo** rear-view mirror retrovisóre *m* rear-view mirror

rètta *f* board and lodging; straight line; dar retta a to pay attention to

rettangolare *adj* rectangular

rettàngolo *m* rectangle

rettifi·ca *f* (-che) straightening; rectification; (mach) grinding; (mach) reboring

rettificare §197 (rettífico) *tr* to straighten; to rectify; (mach) to grind; (mach) to rebore

rettifica·tóre -trice *adj* rectifying || *mf* rectifier (*person*) || *m* rectifier (*apparatus*)

rettifilo *m* straightaway

rèttile *m* reptile

rettili·neo -nea *adj* rectilinear || *m* straightaway || *f* straight line

rettitúdine *f* straightness; uprightness, rectitude

rèt·to -ta *adj* straight; correct; upright; (geom) right || *m* right; recto; (anat) rectum || *f* see retta

rettóre *m* rector; president (*of university*)

reumàti·co -ca *adj* (-ci -che) rheumatic

reumatismo *m* rheumatism

reverèn·do -da *adj* & *m* reverend

reverènte *adj* var of riverente

reverènza *f* var of riverenza

revisióne *f* revision; (mach) overhaul

revisionismo *m* revisionism

revisóre *m* inspector; revisore dei conti auditor; revisore di bozze proofreader

reviviscènza *f* rebirth

rèvo·ca *f* (-che) revocation; recall; repeal

revocare §197 (rèvoco) *tr* to revoke; to recall; to repeal

revòl·ver *m* (-ver) revolver

revolverata *f* gun shot

revulsióne *f* (med) revulsion

ri- *pref* re-, e.g., rivívere to relive; again, e.g., rifare to do again; back, e.g., riandare to go back

riabbonare (riabbòno) *tr* to renew the subscription of || *ref* to renew one's subscription

riabbracciare §128 (riabbràccio) *tr* to embrace again; to greet again

riabilitare (riabìlito) *tr* to rehabilitate || *ref* to reestablish one's good name

riaccèndere §101 *tr* to rekindle || *ref* to become rekindled

riaccompagnare *tr* to take home

riaccostare (riaccòsto) *tr* to bring near; to bring together || *ref* to draw near

riacquistare *tr* to buy back; to recover

riaddormentare (riaddorménto) *tr* to put back to sleep || *ref* to go back to sleep

riaffacciare §128 (riaffàccio) *tr* to present again || *ref* to reappear

riaffermare (riaffèrmo) *tr* to reaffirm

riaggravare *tr* to make worse || *ref* to get worse again

rialesare (rialèso) *tr* to rebore

riallacciare §128 (riallàccio) *tr* to tie again || *ref* to be tied or connected

rialto *m* knoll, height; fare rialto (coll) to eat better than usual

rialzare *tr* to lift, raise; to increase || *ref* to rise

rialzi·sta *mf* (-sti -ste) bull (*in stock market*)

rialzo *m* rise; raise; knoll, height; giocare al rialzo to bull the market

riammobiliare §287 *tr* to refurnish

rianimare (riànimo) *tr* to revive; to encourage || *ref* to revive; to recover one's spirits, to rally

riapertura *f* reopening

riapparire §108 *intr* (ESSERE) to reappear

riapparizióne *f* reappearance

riaprire §110 *tr* & *ref* to reopen

riarmare *tr* to rearm; to reinforce; to refit || *intr* & *ref* to rearm

riarmo *m* rearmament

riar·so -sa *adj* dry, parched

riassaporare (riassapóro) *tr* to relish again

riassettare (riassètto) *tr* to tidy up

riassicurare *tr* to reinsure; to fasten again; to reassure

riassorbire §176 & (riassòrbo) *tr* to reabsorb

riassùmere §116 *tr* to hire again; to summarize, sum up

riassunto *m* précis, abstract; résumé

riassunzióne *f* rehiring; resumption

riattaccare §197 *tr* to attach again; (coll) to begin again; (telp) to hang up

riattare *tr* to repair, fix

riattivare *tr* to reactivate

riavére §229 *tr* to get again; to recover; to get back || *ref* to recover

riavvicinaménto *m* var of ravvicinamento

riavvicinare *tr* & *ref* var of ravvicinare

ribadire §176 *tr* to clinch (*a nail*); to rivet; to drive home (*an idea*); to back up (*a statement*)

ribaldo *m* scoundrel, rogue

ribalta *f* lid with hinge; trap door; (theat) footlights; (theat) forestage; (fig) limelight; a ribalta hinged

ribaltàbile *adj* collapsable (*e.g., seat*) || *m* dump-truck lift; dump truck

ribaltare *tr* & *ref* to upset, turn over

ribassare *tr* & *intr* (ESSERE) to lower

ribassi·sta *mf* (-sti -ste) bear (*in stock market*)

ribasso *m* fall, decline; discount, rebate; giocare al ribasso to be a bear

ribàttere *tr* to clinch (*a nail*); to return (*a ball*); to iron smooth; to belabor (*a point*) || *intr* to answer back

ribattezzare [ddzz] (ribattézzo) *tr* to rebaptize

ribattino *m* rivet

ribellare (ribèllo) *tr* to rouse to rebellion || *ref* to rebel; ribellarsi a to rebel against

ribèlle *adj* rebellious || *mf* rebel

ribellióne *f* rebellion

ri·bes *m* (-bes) currant; gooseberry

ribobinazióne *f* rewind (*of a tape*)

riboccare §197 (ribócco) *intr* (ESSERE) & AVERE) to overflow

ribollire (ribóllo) *tr* to boil again ||

intr to boil over; to simmer; to ferment

ribrézzo [ddzz] *m* repugnance, disgust

ributtare *tr* to return (*a ball*); to throw up; to reject; to push back ‖ *intr* to sprout; (with *dat*) to disgust, nauseate

ricacciare §128 *tr* to drive back ‖ *intr* to sprout ‖ *ref* to sneak away, disappear

ricadére §121 *intr* (ESSERE) to fall back; to fall down; to relapse; **ricadere su** to devolve upon

ricaduta *f* relapse

ricalcare §197 *tr* to transfer (*a design*); to imitate; **ricalcare le orme di** follow in the footsteps of

rical·co *m* (**-chi**) copy, copying; **a ricalco** multiple-copy

ricamare *tr* to embroider

ricambiare §287 *tr* to return; to repay ‖ *ref* to change clothes

ricàm·bio *m* (**-bi**) exchange; spare part; refill; metabolism; **di ricambio** spare (*part*)

ricamo *m* embroidery; needlework; **ricami** (*fig*) embellishments

ricapitolare (**ricapìtolo**) *tr* to recapitulate

ricaricare §197 (**ricàrico**) *tr* to reload; to wind (*a watch*); to charge (*a battery*)

ricattare *tr* to blackmail

ricatta·tóre -trice *mf* blackmailer

ricatto *m* blackmail

ricavare *tr* to draw, extract; to obtain, derive

ricavato *m* proceeds; (fig) fruit, yield

ricavo *m* proceeds

ricchézza *f* wealth; **ricchezza mobile** income from personal property; **ricchezze** riches

ric·cio -cia (**-ci -ce**) *adj* curly ‖ *m* curl; shaving; burr; scroll (*of violin*); crook (*of crozier*); (zool) hedgehog; **riccio di mare** (zool) sea urchin

ricciolo *m* curl

ricciolu·to -ta *adj* curly

ricciu·to -ta *adj* curly

ric·co -ca *adj* (**-chi -che**) rich ‖ **i ricchi** the rich

ricér·ca *f* (**-che**) search; research; **ricerca operativa** operations research

ricercare §197 (**ricérco**) *tr* to search for again; to seek; to investigate; (poet) to pluck (*a musical instrument*)

ricercatézza *f* affectation; sophistication

ricerca·to -ta *adj* sought after, wanted; affected; sophisticated

ricetrasmettitóre *m* two-way radio

ricètta *f* prescription; recipe

ricettàcolo *m* receptacle; depository

ricettare (**ricètto**) *tr* to receive (*stolen goods*); to prescribe

ricettà·rio *m* (**-ri**) recipe book; prescription pad

ricetta·tóre -trice *mf* fence, receiver of stolen goods

ricetti·vo -va *adj* receptive

ricètto *m* (poet) refuge

ricévere §141 *tr* to receive; to get; to contain; to withstand

riceviménto *m* reception; receipt

ricevi·tóre -trice *mf* addressee ‖ *m* receiver; collector; registrar of deeds; **ricevitore postale** postmaster

ricevitoria *f* collection office; **ricevitoria postale** post office

ricevuta *f* receipt; **accusare ricevuta di** to acknowledge receipt of

ricezióne *f* (rad, telv) reception; **accusare ricezione** to acknowledge receipt

richiamare *tr* to call back; to recall; to call (*e.g., attention*); to quote; to chide ‖ *ref* to refer

richiamato *m* soldier recalled to active duty

richiamo *m* call; recall; admonition; cross reference; advertisement

richièdere §124 *tr* to ask again; to demand; to require; to apply for ‖ *ref* to be required

richiè·sto -sta *adj*—**essere richiesto** to be in demand ‖ *f* request; demand; petition, application

richiùdere §125 *tr & ref* to shut again

riciclare *tr* to recycle (*e.g., in the chemical industry*)

ricino *m* castor-oil plant

ricognitóre *m* scout; reconnaissance plane; (law) recognition

ricognizióne *f* recognition; (mil) reconnaissance

ricollegare §209 (**ricollégo**) *tr* to connect ‖ *ref* to be connected; to refer

ricolmare (**ricólmo**) *tr* to fill to the brim; to overwhelm

ricominciare §128 *tr & intr* (ESSERE) to begin again, resume

ricomparire §108 *intr* (ESSERE) to reappear

ricomparsa *f* reappearance

ricompènsa *f* compensation, recompense; reward; (mil) award

ricompensare (**ricompènso**) *tr* to compensate, recompense; to reward

ricomperare (**ricómpero**) *tr* var of ricomprare

ricompórre §218 *tr* to recompose; to plan again ‖ *ref* to regain one's composure

ricomprare (**ricómpro**) *tr* to buy again; to buy back

riconcentrare (**riconcèntro**) *tr* to concentrate again; to gather (*one's thoughts*) ‖ *ref* to be withdrawn

riconciliare §287 (**riconcìlio**) *tr* to reconcile ‖ *ref* to become reconciled

ricondurre §102 *tr* to bring back; to take back ‖ *ref* to go back

riconfermare (**riconfèrmo**) *tr* to reconfirm

riconfortare (**riconfòrto**) *tr* to comfort

ricongiùngere §183 *tr & ref* to reunite

riconoscènte *adj* grateful

riconoscènza *f* gratitude

riconóscere §134 *tr* to recognize; (mil) to reconnoiter

riconosciménto *m* recognition; **in riconoscimento di** in recognition of

riconquistare *tr* to reconquer

riconsegnare (**riconségno**) *tr* to give back, to return

riconsiderare (riconsìdero) *tr* to reconsider

ricontare (ricónto) *tr* to recount, count again

riconversióne *f* reconversion

riconvertire §138 *tr* to reconvert; to recycle

ricopèr·to -ta *adj* covered; coated

ricopertura *f* covering; seat cover

ricopiare §287 **(ricòpio)** *tr* to make a fair copy of; to recopy; to copy

ricoprire §110 *tr* to cover; to coat; to hide ‖ *ref* to become covered

ricordanza *f* (poet) memory

ricordare (ricòrdo) *tr* to remember; to remind; to mention ‖ *ref* to remember; **ricordarsi di** to remember

ricòrdo *m* memory; souvenir; **ricordo marmoreo** marble statue

ricorrènte *adj* recurrent, recurring

ricorrènza *f* recurrence; anniversary

ricórrere §139 *intr* (ESSERE & AVERE) to run again; to run back; to resort; to recur; (law) to appeal; **ricorrere a** to have recourse to

ricórso *m* recurrence; recourse; appeal

ricostituènte *adj* invigorating ‖ *m* tonic

ricostituire §176 *tr* to reconstitute, to reform; to reinvigorate

ricostruire §140 *tr* to rebuild; to reconstruct

ricostruzióne *f* rebuilding; reconstruction

ricòtta *f* Italian cottage cheese; **di ricotta** weak

ricoverare (ricóvero) *tr* to shelter ‖ *ref* to take shelter

ricóvero *m* shelter; nursing home; (med) admission; **ricovero antiaereo** air-raid shelter

ricreare (ricrèo) *tr* to recreate; to refresh ‖ *ref* to relax

ricreati·vo -va *adj* refreshing; recreational

ricreatò·rio -ria (-ri -rie) *adj* recreation, recreational ‖ *m* recreation room; playground

ricreazióne *f* recreation; recess

ricrédere §141 *intr*—**far ricredere qlcu** to make s.o. change his mind ‖ *ref* to change one's mind

ricréscere §142 *intr* (ESSERE) to grow again; to swell

ricucire §143 *tr* to sew up

ricuòcere §144a *tr* to cook again; to anneal

ricuperare (ricùpero) *tr* to recover; (naut) to salvage; (sports) to make up for (*rained-out game*)

ricùpero *m* recovery; salvage; rally; making up (*for lost time or postponed game*)

ricur·vo -va *adj* bent; bent over

ricusare *tr* to refuse

ridacchiare §287 *intr* to titter, giggle

ridancia·no -na *adj* prone to laughter; amusing

ridare §230 (*1st sg pres ind* **ridò**) *tr* to give back; to give again; **ridare fuori** to vomit ‖ *intr* (coll) to reappear, e.g., **gli ha ridato il foruncolo** his boil has reappeared ‖ *intr*

(ESSERE)—**ridare giù** to have a relapse

ridda *f* round; confusion; throng

ridènte *adj* laughing; bright, pleasant

ridere §231 *tr* (poet) to laugh at ‖ *intr* to laugh; (poet) to shine; **far ridere i polli** to be utterly ridiculous; **ridere sotto i baffi** to laugh up one's sleeve ‖ *ref*—**ridersi di** to laugh at

ridestare (ridésto) *tr & ref* to reawaken

ridicolizzare [ddzz] *tr* to ridicule; to twit

ridìco·lo -la *adj* ridiculous ‖ *m* ridicule; ridiculousness

ridipìngere §126 *tr* to paint again

ridire §151 *tr* to tell again; to repeat; to tell (*to express*); **avere** or **trovare a** or **da ridire (su)** to find fault (with)

ridistribuzióne *f* redistribution

ridivenire §282 or **ridiventare (ridivènto)** *intr* (ESSERE) to become again

ridonare (ridóno) *tr* to give back

ridondante *adj* redundant

ridondare (ridóndo) *intr* (ESSERE & AVERE) (fig) to overflow; **ridondare a** or **in** to redound to

ridòsso *m* back; shelter; **a ridosso** sheltered; as a shelter; behind, close behind

ridót·to -ta *adj* reduced; **mal ridotto** down at the heel ‖ *m* lounge; (theat) foyer ‖ *f* (mil) redoubt

ridurre §102 *tr* to reduce; to adapt; to translate; to lead; to curtail; (mus) to arrange ‖ *ref* to be reduced; to retire

riduttóre *m* (mach) reduction gear

riduzióne *f* reduction; (mus) arrangement

riecheggiare §290 **(riechéggio)** *tr & intr* to echo

riedificare §197 **(riedìfico)** *tr* to rebuild

rieducare §197 **(rièduco)** *tr* to reeducate

rielèggere §193 *tr* to reelect

rielezióne *f* reelection

riemèrgere §162 *intr* to resurface

riempiménto *m* fill

riempire §163 *tr* to fill; to stuff

riempiti·vo -va *adj* expletive ‖ *m* expletive; fill-in

rientrante *adj* hollow (*cheeks*); (mil) reentrant

rientranza *f* recess

rientrare (riéntro) *intr* (ESSERE) to reenter; to come back; to recede; (coll) to shrink; **rientrare in** to recover (*one's expenses*); **rientrare in sé** to come to one's senses

riéntro *m* reentry

riepilogare §209 **(riepìlogo)** *tr* to sum up, recapitulate

riepìlo·go *m* (-ghi) recapitulation

riesame *m* reexamination

riesaminare (riesàmino) *tr* to reexamine

riesumare *tr* to exhume; (fig) to dig up; (fig) to bring back

rievocare §197 **(rièvoco)** *tr* to recall

rifaciménto *m* adaptation; recasting

rifare §173 (*3d sg* **rifà**) *tr* to do again, redo; to remake; to imitate; to indemnify; to prepare again; to repeat;

to make (*a bed*) || *ref* to recover; to become again; to recoup one's losses; to begin; **rifarsi con** to get even with; **rifarsi da** to begin with

rifasciare §128 *tr* to rebind

riferimento *m* reference

riferire §176 *tr* to wound again; to refer; to relate || *ref*—**riferirsi a** to refer to; to concern

riffa *f* raffle; lottery; (coll) violence; **di riffa o di raffa** by hook or crook

rifilare *tr* to trim; (coll) to reel off (*a list of names*); (coll) to deal (*a blow*); (coll) to palm off

rifinire §176 *tr* to give the finishing touch to; to wear out || *intr* to stop || *ref* to wear oneself out

rifiorire §176 *tr* (lit) to revive || *intr* to bloom again || *intr* (ESSERE) to flourish; to grow better; to reappear

rifischiare §287 *tr* to whistle again; (coll) to report || *intr* to talk, gossip

rifiutare *tr* to refuse; (lit) to reject || *intr* (cards) to renege, renounce || *ref* to refuse, deny

rifiuto *m* refusal; refuse, rubbish; rejection; rebuff, spurn; (fig) wreck; (cards) renege; **di rifiuto** waste, e.g., **materiale di rifiuto** waste material

riflessióne *f* reflexion

riflessi•vo -va *adj* thoughtful; (gram) reflexive

riflès•so -sa *adj* reflex, e.g., **azione riflessa** reflex action || *m* reflection; (physiol) reflex; **di riflesso** vicarious

riflèttere §177 (*pp* riflettuto & riflèsso) *tr* & *intr* to reflect || *ref* to be reflected

riflettóre *m* searchlight; reflector

rifluire §176 *intr* (ESSERE & AVERE) to flow; to flow back

riflusso *m* flow; ebb, ebb tide

rifocillare *tr* to refresh (*with food*) || *ref* to take refreshment

rifóndere §218 *tr* to melt again; to recast; to refund; to reedit

rifórma *f* reform; (mil) rejection || **Riforma** *f*—**la Riforma** the Reformation

riformare (**rifórmo**) *tr* to reform; to amend; (mil) to reject

riformati•vo -va *adj* reformatory

riforma•tóre -trice *adj* reforming || *mf* reformer

riformatò•rio *m* (-**ri**) reform school, reformatory

rifornimento *m* supply; refueling; **fare rifornimento di** to fill up with; **rifornimenti** supplies

rifornire §176 *tr* to supply; to restock; **rifornire di benzina** to refuel

rifràngere §179 *tr* to crush || *ref* to break (*said of waves*) || §179 (*pp* **rifratto**) *tr* to refract || *ref* to be refracted

rifrat•tóre -trice *adj* refracting || *m* refractor

rifrazióne *f* refraction

rifriggere §180 *tr* to fry again; to rehash || *intr* to fry too long or in too much oil

rifrit•to -ta *adj* fried again; (fig) hack-

neyed || *m* taste of stale fat; (fig) rehash

rifuggire *tr* to avoid || *intr*—**rifuggire da** to abhor || *intr* (ESSERE) to take refuge

rifugiare §290 *ref* to take refuge, take shelter

rifugiato *m* refugee

rifù•gio *m* (-**gi**) refuge; **rifugio alpino** mountain hut; **rifugio antiaereo** air-raid shelter; **rifugio antiatomico** fall-out shelter

rifùlgere §233 *intr* (ESSERE & AVERE) to shine

rifusióne *f* recast; refund, reimbursement

ri•ga *f* (-**ghe**) line; row; rank; ruler; part (*in hair*); stripe; (fig) quality

rigàglie *fpl* giblets

rigàgnolo *m* rivulet; gutter (*at the side of a road*)

rigare §209 *tr* to rule, line; to stripe; to mark; to rifle (*gun*) || *intr*—**rigare diritto** to toe the line

rigatino *m* gingham

rigattière *m* second-hand dealer

rigatura *f* ruling; rifling (*of gun*)

rigenerare (**rigènero**) *tr* to regenerate; to reclaim; to recycle || *ref* to become regenerate

rigenera•tóre *m*—**rigeneratore per i capelli** hair restorer

rigettare (**rigètto**) *tr* to throw back; to reject; to recast; (slang) to throw up || *intr* to sprout

rigètto *m* rejection

righèllo *m* ruler

rigidi•tà *f* (-**tà**) rigidity; rigor; stiffness; **rigidità cadaverica** rigor mortis

rìgi•do -da *adj* rigid, stiff; severe

rigirare *tr* to keep turning; to dupe; to invest; to encircle || *intr* to ramble || *ref* to turn around; to tumble

ri•go *m* (-**ghi**) line; **rigo musicale** (mus) staff

rigò•glio *m* (-**gli**) luxuriance; bloom; gurgling

rigonfiare §287 (**rigónfio**) *tr* to inflate || *intr* (ESSERE) & *ref* to swell up

rigóre *m* rigor; severity; precision; **a rigor di termini** strictly speaking; **di rigore** de rigueur; (sports) penalty (*e.g., kick*)

rigorismo *m* rigorism, strictness, severity

rigori•sta *mf* (-**sti -ste**) rigorist || *m* (soccer) kicker of penalty goal

rigoró•so -sa [*s*] *adj* rigorous, strict

rigovernare (**rigovèrno**) *tr* to clean, wash (*dishes*); to groom, tend (*animals*)

riguadagnare *tr* to regain

riguardare *tr* to look again; to look back; to examine; to consider; to take care of; to concern || *intr*—**riguardare a** to look out for; to face (*said of a window*) || *ref* to take care of oneself; **riguardarsi da** to keep away from

riguardo *m* care; esteem; regard; **a questo riguardo** in this regard; **ri-**

guardo a as far as . . . is concerned; senza riguardo a irrespective of

riguardó·so -sa [s] *adj* considerate

rigurgitare (rigùrgito) *tr* & *intr* to regurgitate

rilanciare §128 *tr* to toss back; to re-establish (*e.g., fashions*); (poker) to raise

rilasciare §128 *tr* to free, let go; to relax; to grant || *ref* to relax

rilà·scio *m* (**-sci**) release; delivery; granting, issue (*of a document*)

rilassante *adj* relaxing

rilassare *tr* & *ref* to relax

rilassatézza *f* laxity

rilegare §209 (**rilégo**) *tr* to tie again; to bind, rebind (*a book*); to set (*a stone*)

rilega·tóre -trice *mf* binder

rilegatura *f* binding

rilèggere §193 *tr* to reread

rilènto *m*—**a rilento** slowly

rilevaménto *m* survey; (naut) bearing

rilevare (**rilièvo**) *tr* to lift again; to observe; to draw; to bring out; to survey; to take over; to pick up; (mil) to relieve || *ref* to be delineated; to be of import || *ref* to rise again; to recover

rilevatà·rio *m* (**-ri**) successor; (law) assignee

rilièvo *m* relief; survey; remark; assumption (*of debts*); taking over (*of business*); **mettere in rilievo** to bring out; to set off

rilò·ga *f* (**-ghe**) traverse rod

rilucènte *adj* shiny, shining

rilùcere §234 *intr* to shine

riluttante *adj* reluctant

riluttanza *f* reluctance

rima *f* rhyme; slit; crevice; **rispondere per le rime** to answer in kind, to retort

rimandare *tr* to send back; to refer; to dismiss; to put off, postpone; to refer; **rimandare a ottobre** to condition (*a student*)

rimando *m* delay; reference; footnote; repartee; postponement; (sports) return

rimaneggiare §290 (**rimanéggio**) *tr* to rearrange; to reshuffle; to shake up (*personnel*); to rewrite (*news*)

rimanènte *adj* remaining || *m* remainder; remnant; **i rimanenti** the rest

rimanènza *f* remainder

rimanére §235 *intr* (ESSERE) to remain, stay; to be in agreement; to have left, e.g., **mi sono rimasti solo tre dollari** I only have three dollars left; to be located; (poet) to stop; **rimanerci** (coll) to be killed; (coll) to be duped; **rimanere da** to depend on, e.g., **questo rimane da Lei** this depends on you

rimangiare §290 *tr* to eat again || *ref*—**rimangiarsi la parola** to go back on one's word

rimarcare §197 *tr* to mark again; to point out

rimar·co *m* (**-chi**) remark, notice

rimare *tr* & *intr* to rhyme

rimarginare (rimàrgino) *tr, intr* & *ref* to heal

rimaritare *tr* & *ref* to marry again

rimasù·glio *m* (**-gli**) leftover

rima·tóre -trice *mf* poet; rhymster

rimbalzare *intr* (ESSERE & AVERE) to bounce back, rebound

rimbalzo *m* rebound

rimbambire §176 *intr* (ESSERE) & *ref* to become feeble-minded (*from old age*)

rimbambi·to -ta *adj* feeble-minded || *mf* dotard

rimbeccare §197 (**rimbécco**) *tr* to peck; to retort

rimbecilli·to -ta *adj* feeble-minded

rimboccare §197 (**rimbócco**) *tr* to tuck up; to tuck in; to fill to the brim

rimbombare (**rimbómbo**) *intr* (ESSERE & AVERE) to thunder, boom

rimbómbo *m* thunder, boom

rimborsare (**rimbórso**) *tr* to reimburse, pay back

rimbórso *m* repayment

rimboscare §197 (**rimbòsco**) *tr* to re-forest || *ref* to take to the woods

rimboschiménto *m* reforestation

rimboschire §176 *tr* to reforest || *intr* (ESSERE) to become wooded

rimbrottare (**rimbròtto**) *tr* to scold

rimbròtto *m* scolding

rimediare §287 (**rimèdio**) *tr* (coll) to scrape together; (coll) to patch up || *intr* (with *dat*) to remedy; to make up (*lost time*)

rimè·dio *m* (**-di**) remedy

rimembranza *f* remembrance

rimeritare (**rimèrito**) *tr* to reward

rimescolare (**riméscolo**) *tr* to stir; to shuffle (*cards*)

riméssa *f* remittance; shipment; harvest; store; loss; sprout; carriage house; garage; (sports) return; (sports) putting in play; **rimessa del tram** carbarn

rimestare (**rimésto**) *tr* to stir

riméttere §198 *tr* to remit; to put back; to set back; to sprout; to postpone, defer; to ship; to vomit; to recover; to deliver; to straighten up; (sports) to return; **rimetterci** to lose; **rimettere a nuovo** to renovate; **rimettere in ordine** to tidy up; **rimettere in piedi** to rebuild, restore || *intr* (coll) to sprout; (coll) to grow; (lit) to abate || *ref* to recover; to quiet down; to defer; to be clearing (*said of weather*); **rimettersi a** to go back to (*e.g., bed*); **rimettersi a** + *inf* to start + *ger* + again; **rimettersi in cammino** to start off again

rimirare *tr* to stare at

rìmmel *m* mascara

rimodellare (**rimodèllo**) *tr* to remodel

rimodernare (**rimodèrno**) *tr* to modernize; to remodel; to bring up to date || *ref* to become modern

rimónta *f* reassembly; return (*of migratory birds*); revamping (*of shoes*); (mil) remount

rimontare (**rimónto**) *tr* to rewind; to go up (*a stream*); to vamp (*shoes*); to renovate; to regain; to reassemble (*a machine*); (mil) to remount ‖ *intr* (ESSERE & AVERE) to climb again; to go back (*in time*)

rimorchiare §287 (**rimòrchio**) *tr* to tow; to drag along

rimorchiatóre *m* tugboat; tow car

rimòr·chio *m* (**-chi**) tow; trailer; **prendere a rimorchio** to take in tow

rimórdere §200 *tr* to bite again; to prick (*said, e.g., of conscience*)

rimòrso *m* remorse

rimostranza *f* remonstrance

rimostrare (**rimóstro**) *tr* to show again ‖ *intr* to remonstrate; **rimostrare a** to remonstrate with

rimozióne *f* removal; demotion

rimpannucciare §128 *tr* to outfit better ‖ *ref* to be better dressed; to be better off

rimpastare *tr* to knead again; to reshuffle, remake

rimpasto *m* reshuffling, rearrangement

rimpatriare §287 *tr* to repatriate ‖ *intr* to be repatriated

rimpà·trio *m* (**-tri**) repatriation

rimpètto *adv* opposite; **di rimpetto a** opposite to; in comparison with

rimpiàngere §215 *tr* to regret; to mourn

rimpianto *m* regret

rimpiattare *tr* & *ref* to hide; **giocare a rimpiattarsi** to play hide-and-seek

rimpiattino *m* hide-and-seek

rimpiazzare *tr* to replace

rimpiazzo *m* replacement, substitute

rimpiccolire §176 *tr* to make smaller ‖ *intr* (ESSERE) to get smaller

rimpinzare *tr* to stuff, cram

rimproverare (**rimpròvero**) *tr* to chide, reproach; **rimproverare qlco di qlco** or **rimproverare qlco a qlcu** to reproach s.o. for s.th

rimpròvero *m* reproach, rebuke

rimuginare (**rimùgino**) *tr* & *intr* to rummage; to stir; to ruminate

rimunerare (**rimùnero**) *tr* to reward ‖ *intr* to pay

rimunerati·vo -va *adj* remunerative; rewarding

rimunerazióne *f* remuneration

rimuòvere §202 *tr* to remove; to demote; to move

rinàscere §203 *intr* (ESSERE) to be born again; to grow again; to revive; **far rinascere** to revive

rinascimento *m* rebirth ‖ **Rinascimento** *m* Renaissance

rinàscita *f* rebirth

rincagna·to -ta *adj* snub (*nose*)

rincalzare *tr* to hill (*plants*); to underpin; to tuck in

rincalzo *m* reinforcement; support

rincantucciare §128 *tr* & *ref* to hide in a corner

rincarare *tr* to raise the price of; to raise; **rincarare la dose** to add insult to injury ‖ *intr* (ESSERE) to rise, go up (*said of prices*)

rincasare [s] *intr* (ESSERE) to return home

rinchiùdere §125 *tr* to enclose, shut in

rinchiu·so -sa [s] *adj* shut in; musty ‖ *m*—**saper di rinchiuso** to smell musty

rincitrullire §176 *intr* (ESSERE) to grow stupid

rincóntro *m*—**a rincontro** opposite

rincorare §236 *tr* to encourage ‖ *ref* to take heart

rincórrere §139 *tr* to pursue, chase

rincórsa *f*—**prendere la rincorsa** to take off (*for a jump*); to get a running start

rincréscere §142 *intr* (ESSERE) (with *dat*) to displease; to be sorry, e.g., **gli rincresce** he is sorry; to mind, **Le rincresce?** do you mind?

rincrescimento *m* regret

rincrudire §176 *tr* to sharpen; to embitter ‖ *intr* (ESSERE) to become bitter; to get worse

rinculare *intr* (ESSERE & AVERE) to back up; to recoil

rinculo *m* recoil

rinfacciare §128 *tr* to throw in one's face

rinfarcire §176 *tr* to stuff

rinfiancare §197 *tr* to support

rinfocolare (**rinfòcolo**) *tr* to rekindle; to revive

rinfoderare (**rinfòdero**) *tr* to sheathe

rinforzare (**rinfòrzo**) *tr* to reinforce; strengthen ‖ *intr* (ESSERE) & *ref* to become stronger

rinforzo *m* reinforcement

rinfrancare §197 *tr* to reassure ‖ *ref* to buck up

rinfrescante *adj* refreshing ‖ *m* mild laxative

rinfrescare §197 (**rinfrésco**) *tr* to refresh; to restore; to renew ‖ *intr* (ESSERE & AVERE) to cool off (*said of the weather*) ‖ *ref* to have some refreshments; to cool off

rinfré·sco *m* (**-schi**) refreshment

rinfusa *f*—**alla rinfusa** at random; pell-mell; in bulk

ringalluzzire §176 *tr* & *ref* to perk up

ringhiare §287 *intr* to growl, to snarl

ringhièra *f* railing

rìn·ghio *m* (**-ghi**) growl, snarl

ringiovanimento *m* rejuvenation

ringiovanire §176 *tr* to rejuvenate ‖ *intr* (ESSERE) to grow or look younger

ringraziamento *m* thanks

ringraziare §287 *tr* to thank; to dismiss

ringuainare (**ringuaìno**) *tr* to sheathe

rinnegare §209 (**rinnègo** & **rinnégo**) *tr* to forswear; to repudiate

rinnega·to -ta *adj* & *m* renegade

rinnovamento *m* renewal; reawakening

rinnovare (**rinnòvo**) *tr* to renew; to renovate; to restore; to replace ‖ *ref* to occur again; to renew

rinnovellare (**rinnovèllo**) *tr* to repeat; (poet) to renew ‖ *intr* (ESSERE) & *ref* to change; to renew

rinnòvo *m* renewal

rinocerónte *m* rhinoceros

rinomanza *f* renown

rinoma·to -ta *adj* renowned, famous

rinsaldare *tr* to starch; (fig) to strengthen ‖ *ref* to become confirmed (*in one's opinion*)

rinsanguare (rinsànguo) *tr* to give new strength to ‖ *ref* to regain strength; to recover

rinsavire §176 *intr* (ESSERE) to return to reason

rintanare *ref* to burrow; to hide

rintóc·co *m* (**-chi**) toll (*of bell*)

rintontire §176 *tr* to stun, to daze

rintracciare §128 *tr* to track down

rintronare (rintròno) *tr* to deafen; to make rumble ‖ *intr* (ESSERE & AVERE) to thunder; to rumble

rintuzzare *tr* to dull, blunt; to repel; to repress

rinùn·cia *f* (**-ce**) or **rinùnzia** *f* renunciation

rinunziare §287 *tr* to renounce ‖ *intr* (with *dat*) to give up, renounce, e.g., **rinunziò al trono** he renounced the throne

rinvangare §209 *tr* & *intr* var of **rivangare**

rinvenire §282 *tr* to find ‖ *intr* (ESSERE) to come to; **far rinvenire** to bring to, revive

rinviare §119 *tr* to send back; to postpone; to refer; to adjourn; to remit (*to a lower court*)

rinvigorire §176 *tr* to strengthen ‖ *intr* (ESSERE) & *ref* to regain strength

rinvì·o *m* (**-i**) return; postponement; adjournment; reference; (law) continuance

rì·o *m* (**-i**) (lit) sin; (lit) brook; (coll) canal

rioccupare (riòccupo) *tr* to reoccupy

rioccupazióne *f* reoccupation

rionale *adj* neighborhood

rióne *m* district; neighborhood

riordinare (riórdino) *tr* to rearrange; to reorganize; to order again

riorganizzare [ddzz] *tr* to reorganize

riottó·so -sa *adj* (lit) quarrelsome; (lit) unruly, rebellious

ripa *f* (lit) bank (*of river*); (lit) escarpment

ripagare §209 *tr* to repay; to pay again

riparare *tr* to protect; to mend, fix, repair; to make up (*an exam*) ‖ *intr* —**riparare a** to make up for ‖ *intr* (ESSERE) & *ref* to take refuge; to betake oneself

riparazióne *f* repair; reparation; redress; (educ) make-up

riparlare *intr* to speak again; **ne riparleremo!** you will see!

riparo *m* repair; shelter

ripartire §176 *tr* to divide; to distribute; to share ‖ (**riparto**) *intr* (ESSERE) to leave again; to start again ‖ §176 *ref* to split up

ripartizióne *f* division; distribution

riparto *m* division; distribution; allotment

ripassare *tr* to cross again; to brush up, review; to repass; to sift again; to check; to read over; (mach) to overhaul ‖ *intr* (ESSERE) to go by; to come by

ripassata *f* checkup; review; (coll) rebuke

ripassa·tóre -trice *mf* checker

ripasso *m* return (*of birds*); (coll) review

ripensare (ripènso) *intr* to keep thinking; **ripensare a** to think of again; to think over again

ripentire (ripènto) *ref* to repent; **ripentirsi di** to repent

ripercórrere §139 *tr* to retrace

ripercuòtere §251 *tr* to reflect; to strike again ‖ *ref* to reverberate

ripescare §197 (**ripésco**) *tr* to fish again; (fig) to dig up

ripètere *tr* & *intr* to repeat ‖ *ref* to be repeated

ripeti·tóre -trice *mf* repeater; coach; tutor ‖ *m* (rad, telv) rebroadcasting station; (rad) relay

ripetizióne *f* repetition; review; tutoring; **a ripetizione** repeating (*firearm*)

ripiano *m* terrace; ledge; shelf; landing; (com) balancing

ripic·co *m* (**-chi**) pique; spite

ripi·do -da *adj* steep

ripiegaménto *m* bend; (mil) withdrawal, retreat

ripiegare §209 (**ripiègo**) *tr* to fold, fold over ‖ *intr* to do better; (mil) to fall back ‖ *ref* to bend over; to withdraw into oneself

ripiè·go *m* (**-ghi**) expedient

ripiè·no -na *adj* full; stuffed ‖ *m* stuffing; (culin) filling

ripigliare §280 *tr* to reacquire; to catch again; to begin again ‖ *intr* to recover ‖ *ref* to renew a quarrel

ripiombare (ripiómbo) *tr* to make plumb; (fig) to plunge back ‖ *intr* (ESSERE) (fig) to plunge back

ripopolare (ripòpolo) *tr* to repopulate; to restock (*e.g., a pond*)

ripórre §218 *tr* to put back; to place (*one's hope*); to repose (*one's trust*) ‖ *ref* to back down; **riporsi a** + *inf* to start + *ger* again

riportare (ripòrto) *tr* to bring back; to report; to get; to transfer (*a design*); (com) to carry forward; (hunt) to retrieve; (math) to carry ‖ *ref* to go back

ripòrto *m* filler; retrieving; (com) balance carried forward; (math) number carried

riposante [s] *adj* restful

riposare [s] (**ripòso**) *tr*, *intr* & *ref* to rest

ripòso [s] *m* rest; repose; Requiem; retirement; **buon ripòso!** sleep well!; **mettere a riposo** to retire; **riposo!** (mil) at ease

riposti·glio *m* (**-gli**) closet

ripó·sto -sta *adj* innermost ‖ *m* (coll) pantry

riprèndere §220 *tr* to take back; to take up again; to get back; to take in (*a garment*); to catch (*s.th thrown in the air*); to take up (*arms*); to get; to reconquer; to start again, resume; to reprehend; to recover; (mov, telv) to shoot; **riprendere moglie** to remarry ‖ *intr* to start again; to recover, improve; to pick up (*said of a* *motor*) || *ref* to recover; to catch oneself up

riprésa [s] *f* resumption; (aut) pickup; (theat) revival; (mov) shooting, take; (boxing) round; (soccer) second half; (mus, pros) refrain; **a più riprese** several times

ripresentare (riprosènto) *tr* to present again

ripristinare (ripristino) *tr* to restore; to reestablish

ripristino *m* revival, restoration

riprodurre §102 *tr* to reproduce; to express || *ref* to reproduce; to occur

riprodut·tóre -trice *adj* reproducing || *mf* reproducer || *m* reproducer (*e.g.*, *of sound*)

riproduzióne *f* reproduction; playback (*e.g.*, *of tape*)

ripronéttere §198 *tr* to promise again || *ref* to hope; to propose; to hope for

ripròva *f* new proof; confirmation

riprovare (ripròvo) *tr* to try again; to try on again; to feel, experience again; to flunk; to censure || *ref* to try again

riprovazióne *f* disapproval

ripudiare §287 *tr* to repudiate

ripugnante *adj* repugnant, repulsive

ripugnanza *f* repugnance; aversion

ripugnare *intr* (with *dat*) to disgust, revolt, be repugnant to

ripulire §176 *tr* to clean again; to tidy up; to clean up; to polish || *ref* to be dressed up; to become polished

ripulita *f*—**dare una ripulita a** to give a lick and a promise to; **fare una ripulita** (fig) to clean house

ripulsi·vo -va *adj* repulsive

riquadrare *tr* to square; to decorate (*a room*) || *intr* to measure; to square

riquadro *m* square

risac·ca [s] *f* (-che) undertow; backwash

risàia [s] *f* rice field

risalire [s] §242 *tr* to go up again; to stem (*the tide*); **risalire la corrente** to go upstream || *intr* (ESSERE) to climb again; to reascend; (com) to appreciate; to date back

risaltare [s] *tr* to jump again || *intr* (ESSERE & AVERE) to rebound || *intr* to stand out; **far risaltare** to emphasize

risalto [s] *m* emphasis; prominence; relief; foil

risanare [s] *tr* to heal; to reclaim (*land*); to redevelop (*urban areas*); to reorganize || *intr* (ESSERE) to heal; to improve

risapére [s] §243 *tr* to find out

risapu·to -ta [s] *adj* well-known

risarcimento [s] *m* indemnification, redress

risarcire [s] §176 *tr* to indemnify; to compensate

risata [s] *f* outburst of laughter

risatina [s] *f* chuckle

riscaldamento *m* heating; inflammation

riscaldare *tr* to heat; to warm up; to inflame || *ref* to warm up; to go in heat; to perspire; to get excited

riscaldo *m* inflammation; prickly heat; padding (*for clothes*)

riscattare *tr* to ransom; to redeem || *intr* (ESSERE) to click again (*said, e.g., of a ratchet*)

riscatto *m* ransom; redemption

rischiarare *tr*, *intr* (ESSERE) & *ref* to clear, clear up

rischiare §287 *tr* to risk || *intr* to run a risk

ri·schio *m* (-schi) risk

rischió·so -sa [s] *adj* risky

risciacquare (risciàcquo) *tr* to rinse

risciacquatura *f* rinse; swill

risciàcquo *m* rinsing (*of mouth*); mouthwash

riscónto *m* (com) discount

riscontrare (riscóntro) *tr* to compare, collate; to check; to reply to || *intr* to reply; to tally || *ref* to tally

riscóntro *m* comparison; check, control; draft; correspondence; reply; **far riscontro** to correspond; **far riscontro con** to correspond to; **far riscontro di** to check; **mettere a riscontro** to compare; **riscontri** drafts (*of air*); parts (*that fit together*)

riscoprire §110 *tr* to rediscover

riscòssa *f* insurrection; recovery, reconquest; (mil) counterattack

riscossióne *f* collection

riscrìvere §250 *tr* to rewrite; to write back

riscuòtere §251 *tr* to shake; to wake up; to collect; to get; to redeem || *ref* to wake up; to come to one's senses

risecentire [s] §197 (risécco) *tr*, *intr* (ESSERE) & *ref* to dry up

risecchire [s] §176 *intr* (ESSERE) & *ref* to dry up

risentimento [s] *m* resentment, pique

risentire [s] (risènto) *tr* to hear again; to feel || *intr*—**risentire di** to feel the effects of || *ref* to take offense; to wake up; to come to one's senses; (telp) to talk again; **a risentirci!** (telp) until we talk again!; **risentirsi con** to resent (*a person*); **risentirsi di** to feel the effects of; **risentirsi per** to resent (*an act*)

risenti·to -ta [s] *adj* heard again; resentful; strong; swift; incisive

riserbare [s] (risèrbo) *tr* var of riservare

risèrbo [s] *m* var of risèrvo

risèrva [s] *f* preservation; exclusive rights; preserve; reserve; supply; backlog; reservation; circumspection; vintage

riservare [s] (risèrvo) *tr* to reserve

riservatézza [s] *f* reservedness

riserva·to -ta [s] *adj* reserved; private; classified

riservista [s] *m* (-sti) reservist

risèrvo [s] *m* discretion

risguardo *m* end paper

risièdere [s] *intr* to reside

risma *f* ream; (fig) type

riso [s] *m* rice || *m* (risa *fpl*) laugh; laughter; jest; cheer; (lit) smile

risolare [s] §257 *tr* to resole

risolino [s] *m* smile; giggle

risollevare [s] **(risollèvo)** *tr* to raise again; to lift ‖ *ref* to rise

risolutézza [s] *f* resoluteness

risolu·to -ta [s] *adj* resolved, determined

risoluzióne [s] *f* resolution; resolve; dissolution

risòlvere [s] §256 (*pret ind* **risolvéi** or **risolvètti** or **risòlsi;** *pp* **risòlto**) *tr* to resolve; to solve; to dissolve; to persuade ‖ *ref* to dissolve; to resolve

risolvibile [s] *adj* solvable

risonante [s] *adj* resounding

risonanza [s] *f* resonance; (fig) sensation

risonare [s] §257 *tr* to ring again; (lit) to repeat ‖ *intr* (ESSERE & AVERE) to resonate; to resound; to ring again; to echo

risórgere [s] §258 *intr* (ESSERE) to rise again; to revive, to come back to life; to recover

risorgiménto [s] *m* renaissance; resurgence ‖ **Risorgimento** *m* Risorgimento

risórsa [s] *f* resource

risór·to -ta [s] *adj* arisen; reborn

risòtto [s] *m* risotto, rice cooked with broth

risparmiare §287 *tr* to save; to spare

rispàr·mio *m* (-mi) saving; sparing; savings; **risparmi** savings; **senza risparmio** lavishly

rispecchiare §287 **(rispècchio)** *tr* to reflect

rispedire §176 *tr* to send back; to forward; to reship

rispedizióne *f* reshipment

rispettàbile *adj* respectable

rispettare (rispètto) *tr* to respect; **farsi rispettare** to command respect; **rispettare sé stesso** to have self-respect

rispetti·vo -va *adj* respective

rispètto *m* respect; observance; restriction (*e.g., in building*); comparison; regard; **con rispetto parlando** excuse the word; **di rispetto** (naut) spare (*e.g., parts*); **rispetti** regards; **rispetto di sé medesimo** self-respect; **rispetto umano** fear of what people will say

rispettó·so -sa [s] *adj* respectful; respectable (*distance*)

risplendènte *adj* resplendent

risplèndere §281 *intr* (ESSERE & AVERE) to shine

rispóndere §238 *tr* to answer; **risponder picche** (coll) to say no ‖ *intr* to answer; **rispondere a** to answer (*e.g., a letter*); **rispondere con un cenno del capo** to nod assent; **rispondere di** to be responsible for; **rispondere in** to face, overlook

risposare (rispòso) *tr & ref* to marry again, remarry

rispósta *f* answer, reply, response

rissa *f* scuffle, brawl

rissó·so -sa [s] *adj* quarrelsome

ristabilire §176 *tr* to reestablish ‖ *ref* to recover

ristagnare *tr* to tin; to solder ‖ *intr* to stagnate

ristampa *f* reprint

ristampare *tr* to reprint

ristorante *m* restaurant

ristorare (ristòro) *tr & ref* to refresh

ristora·tóre -trice *adj* refreshing ‖ *m* restaurant

ristòro *m* refreshment; compensation

ristrettézza *f* narrowness; scarcity; **ristrettezza d'idee** narrow-mindedness

ristrét·to -ta *adj* narrow; limited; in straitened circumstances; concentrated, condensed (*e.g., broth*)

ristrutturazióne *f* restructuring

risùc·chio [s] *m* (-chi) whirlpool

risultante [s] *adj* resulting ‖ *m & f* resultant; (phys) resultant

risultare [s] *intr* (ESSERE) to result; to prove to be, turn out to be; to appear

risultato [s] *m* result

risurrezióne [s] *f* resurrection

risuscitare (risùscito) *tr* to resurrect; to revive ‖ *intr* to be resurrected; to be revived

risvegliare §280 **(risvéglio)** *tr & ref* to awaken; to reawaken

risvé·glio *m* (-gli) awakening, reawakening

risvòlto *m* cuff; lapel; inside flap (*of book*); minor aspect (*of a question*)

ritagliare §280 *tr* to cut again; to clip; to trim

rità·glio *m* (-gli) clipping (*of paper*); scrap (*of meat*); cutting (*of fabric*); bit (*of time*); **al ritaglio** retail

ritappezzare (ritappézzo) *tr* to repaper

ritardare *tr* to delay; to slow down, retard; ‖ *intr* to tarry; to be late; to be slow (*said of a watch*)

ritardatà·rio -ria *mf* (-ri -rie) latecomer; (com) delinquent

ritardo *m* delay; retard; lateness; **essere in ritardo** to be late

ritégno *m* reservation; discretion; **senza ritegno** shamelessly

ritemprare (ritèmpro) *tr* to temper again; to invigorate ‖ *ref* to harden

ritenére §271 *tr* to retain; to hold; to withhold; to believe, think ‖ *ref* to restrain oneself; to consider oneself; to be considered

ritentare (ritènto) *tr* to try again; (law) to retry

ritirare *tr* to withdraw; to pay (*a note*); to throw back; to shoot again; to accept delivery of; to take back (*a promise*) ‖ *intr* to shrink ‖ *ref* to shrink; to withdraw; to fall back, retreat; to retire

ritirata *f* toilet; (mil) retreat

ritiro *m* withdrawal; retreat; retirement; shrinkage; (metallurgy) shrinking

ritma·to -ta *adj* measured (*step*)

ritmi·co -ca *adj* (-ci -che) rhythmic(al)

ritmo *m* rhythm; **a ritmo serrato** at a quick pace

rito *m* rite; (fig) ritual, ceremony; **di rito** customary

ritoccare §197 **(ritócco)** *tr* to retouch; to brush up

ritóc·co *m* (-chi) retouch; improvement; change

ritòrcere §272 *tr* to twist, twine; to wring; to retort

ritornare (ritórno) *tr* to return, give back ‖ *intr* (ESSERE) to return, go back, come back; **ritornare in sé** to come back to one's senses

ritornèllo *m* refrain; chorus (*of song*)

ritórno *m* return; reoccurrence; **di ritorno** reoccurring; **essere di ritorno** to be back; **far ritorno** to return; **ritorno di fiamma** backfire

ritòr·to -ta *adj* twisted ‖ *m* twist

ritrarre §273 *tr* to retract; to draw; to portray ‖ *intr*—**ritrarre da** to look like ‖ *ref* to retreat; to portray oneself

ritrasméttere §198 *tr* (rad, telv) to retransmit, rebroadcast

ritrattare *tr* to treat again; to retract; (coll) to portray ‖ *ref* to recant

ritrattazióne *f* retraction

ritratti·sta *mf* (-sti -ste) portrait painter

ritratto *m* portrait, picture; photograph; **ritratto parlante** spit and image

ritri·to -ta *adj* (fig) stale, trite

ritrósa [s] *f* (coll) cowlick

ritrosia [s] *f* coyness, shyness

ritró·so -sa [s] *adj* coy, shy; **a ritroso** backwards ‖ *f* see **ritrosa**

ritrovare (ritròvo) *tr* to discover; to find; to regain; to meet again ‖ *ref* to meet again; to find oneself; to find one's bearings; **non ritrovarcisi** to be out of sorts

ritrovato *m* discovery, find

ritròvo *m* meeting; nightspot; **ritrovo estivo** summer resort; **ritrovo notturno** night club

rit·to -ta *adj* upright; straight; right ‖ *m* face (*of medal*); prop; (sports) post ‖ *f* (lit) right hand

rituale *adj* & *m* ritual

riunióne *f* reunion; meeting; assembly; **riunione alla sommità** summit conference

riunire §176 *tr* to assemble; to reunite; to reconcile ‖ *ref* to gather together; to meet; to be reunited; to rally

riuscire §277 *intr* (ESSERE) to go out again; to turn out, turn out to be; to lead (*said, e.g., of a door*); to succeed; **riuscire a** + *inf* to succeed in + *ger* ‖ *impers*—**riesce** (with *dat*) **di** + *inf* to succeed in + *ger*, e.g., **non gli è riuscito di farsi ricevere** he did not succeed in being received

riuscita *f* success; result; outlet

riva *f* shore; bank; (naut) board

rivale *adj* & *mf* rival

rivaleggiare §290 (rivaléggio) *intr* to compete; **rivaleggiare con** to rival

rivalére §278 *ref*—**rivalersi di** to use; **rivalersi su qlcu** to resort to s.o. for compensation; to fall back on s.o., to have recourse to s.o.

rivali·tà *f* (-tà) rivalry

rivalsa *f* compensation; revenge; (com) recourse

rivalutare (rivàluto & rivaluto) *tr* to revalue

rivalutazióne *f* reassessment

rivangare §209 *tr* to rake up; to mull over ‖ *intr* to reminisce

rivedére §279 *tr* to see again; to review; to check; to reread; to revise; to read (*proof*) ‖ *ref* to see one another; **a rivederci!** good-bye!, au revoir!

rivedìbile *adj* deferred (*for draft*)

rivelare (rivélo) *tr* to reveal; to detect; (phot) to develop

rivela·tóre -trice *adj* revealing ‖ *m* (phot) developer; (rad) detector; **rivelatore di mine** mine detector

rivelazióne *f* revelation

rivéndere §281 *tr* to resell; (fig) to surpass

rivendicare §197 (rivéndico) *tr* to demand; to claim

rivendicazióne *f* demand; claim

rivéndita *f* resale; shop; **rivendita sali e tabacchi** cigar store

rivendi·tóre -trice *mf* seller, dealer, retailer

rivendùgliolo *m* peddler; huckster

rivèrbero *m* reverberation; reflection; glare; echo

riverènte *adj* reverent

riverènza *f* reverence; curtsy, bow

riverire §176 *tr* to revere; to pay one's respects to

riversare (rivèrso) *tr* to pour again; to transfer ‖ *ref* to overflow

rivèr·so -sa *adj* on one's back

rivestiménto *m* coating; covering; lining

rivestire (rivèsto) *tr* to dress again; to coat; to line; to cover; to wear; to have (*importance*); to hold (*a rank*) ‖ *ref* to get dressed again; to wear; to be covered

rivièra *f* coast ‖ **Riviera** *f* Riviera

riviera·sco -sca *adj* (-schi -sche) coastal; riverside

rivincere §285 *tr* to win back

rivincita *f* revenge; return match; **prendersi la rivincita** to get even

rivista *f* review; parade; magazine; journal; revue; proofreading

rivìvere §286 *tr* to relive ‖ *intr* (ESSERE) to live again; to revive

rivo *m* (lit) rivulet, brook

rivolare (rivólo) *intr* (ESSERE & AVERE) to fly again

rivolére §288 *tr* to want back

rivòlgere §289 *tr* to turn again; to revolve; to overturn; to train (*a weapon*); to address; to deter ‖ *ref* to turn; to turn around; **rivolgersi a** to apply to

rivolgiménto *m* turn; revolution; upheaval

rivòlta *f* revolt; cuff

rivoltante *adj* revolting

rivoltare (rivòlto) *tr* to overturn; to turn inside out; to toss (*salad*); to upset ‖ *ref* to turn around; to revolt; to toss

rivoltèlla *f* revolver; spray gun

rivoltellata *f* revolver shot

rivoltó·so -sa [s] *adj* rebellious ‖ *m* rioter; rebel

rivoluzionare (rivoluzióno) *tr* to revolutionize

rivoluzionà·rio -ria *adj* & *mf* (**-ri -rie**) revolutionary

rivoluzióne *f* revolution

rizza *f* (naut) rigging

rizzare *tr* to raise; to hoist; to pay (*attention*); to build; (naut) to lash || *ref* to rise; to bristle (*said of hair*); to rear up (*said of a horse*)

ròba *f* things, stuff; property

robìnia *f* locust tree

robivèc·chi *m* (**-chi**) junk dealer

robu·sto -sta *adj* robust; burly

róc·ca *f* (**-che**) distaff

ròc·ca *f* (**-che**) fortress

roccafòrte *f* (**rocchefòrti**) stronghold

rocchétto *m* spool; reel; coil; roll (*of film*); pinion, rear sprocket wheel; (eccl) rochet; **rocchetto d'accensione** ignition coil; **rocchetto d'induzione** induction coil

ròc·cia *f* (**-ce**) rock; crag; cliff

rocció·so -sa [*s*] *adj* rocky

ròc·co -ca *adj* (**-chi -che**) hoarse; (poet) faint

rodàg·gio *m* (**-gi**) breaking in, running in; adjustment period (*to a new situation*); **in rodaggio** (aut) being run in

Ròdano *m* Rhone

rodare (**ròdo**) *tr* to break in; (aut) to run in

ródere §239 *tr* to gnaw; to bite; to corrode || *ref* to worry, to fret

Ròdi *f* Rhodes

rodì·o *m* (**-i**) gnawing

rodi·tóre -trice *adj* gnawing || *mf* rodent

rodomónte *m* braggart

rogare §209 (**rògo**) *tr* to draw up (*a contract*); (law) to request

rògito *m* (law) instrument, deed

rógna *f* mange; itch

rognóne *m* (culin) kidney

rognó·so -sa [*s*] *adj* scabby, mangy

** rò·go** *m* (**-ghi**) pyre; stake

rollì·o *m* (**-i**) roll (*of ship*)

Róma *f* Rome

romané·sco -sca *adj* (**-schi -sche**) Roman (*dialect*)

Romanìa, la Rumania

romàni·co -ca *adj* & *m* (**-ci -che**) Romanesque

roma·no -na *adj* & *mf* Roman; **pagare alla romana** to go Dutch

romanticismo *m* romanticism

romànti·co -ca (**-ci -che**) *adj* romantic || *mf* romanticist

romanza *f* romance; ballad

romanzare *tr* to fictionalize

romanzé·sco -sca *adj* (**-schi -sche**) romantic; of chivalry; novelistic

romanzière *m* novelist

roman·zo -za *adj* Romance (*language*) || *m* novel; story; romance; fiction; **romanzi** fiction; **romanzo a fumetti** comic strip; comic book; **romanzo d'appendice** serial story, feuilleton; **romanzo giallo** whodunit; **romanzo rosa** love story

rombare (**rómbo**) *intr* to thunder

rómbo *m* thunder, roar

romè·no -na *adj* & *mf* Rumanian

romì·to -ta *adj* (lit) lonely || *m* (coll) hermit

rómpere §240 *tr* to break; to bust; **rompere la testa a** to annoy, pester || *intr* to overflow; to be wrecked; to break; **rompere in pianto** to burst out crying || *ref* to fly to pieces; **rompersi la testa** to rack one's brains

rompicapo *m* annoyance; puzzle; jigsaw puzzle

rompicòllo *m* madcap; **a rompicollo** headlong, rashly; at breakneck speed

rompighiàc·cio *m* (**-cio**) icebreaker; ice pick

rompiscàto·le *m* (**-le**) bore, pest

ronci·glio *m* (**-gli**) (poet) hook

róncola *f* pruning hook

rónda *f* patrol; beat (*of policeman*)

rondèlla *f* (mach) washer

róndine *f* swallow

rondóne *m* European swift

ronfare (**rónfo**) *intr* (coll) to snore; (coll) to purr

ronzare [*dz*] (**rónzo**) *intr* to buzz; to hum

ronzino [*dz*] *m* jade, nag

ronzì·o [*dz*] *m* (**-i**) buzzing; humming

ròsa *adj invar* & *m* pink || *f* rose; group; rosette; **rosa dei venti** compass card; **rosa del Giappone** (bot) camelia; **rosa delle Alpi** (bot) rhododendron; **rosa di tiro** (mil) dispersion

ro·sàio *m* (**-sài**) rosebush

rosà·rio *m* (**-ri**) rosary; **recitare il rosario** to count one's beads

rosa·to -ta *adj* rosy

ròse·o -a *adj* rosy

roséto *m* rose garden

rosétta *f* rosette; hard roll; (mach) washer

rosicanti [*s*] *mpl* rodents

rosicchiare §287 *tr* to gnaw; to pick (*a bone*); to bite (*one's fingernails*)

rosmarino *m* (bot) rosemary

rosolare (**ròsolo**) *tr* (culin) to brown

rosolìa *f* German measles

rosóne *m* (archit) rosette; (archit) rose window

ròspo *m* toad; ugly person; unsociable person; **ingoiare un rospo** to swallow a bitter pill

rossa·stro -stra *adj* reddish

rossétto *m* rouge; **rossetto per le labbra** lipstick

rós·so -sa *adj* red; red-headed; Red; **diventare rosso** to blush || *mf* red-head; Red (*Communist*) || *m* red

rossóre *m* redness; blush

rosticcerìa *f* grill; rotisserie

rotàbile *adj* open to vehicular traffic (*road*); (rr) rolling (*stock*) || *f* road open to vehicular traffic

rotàia *f* rail; rut; **uscire dalle rotaie** to jump the track; (fig) to go astray

rotare §257 *tr* & *intr* to rotate; to circle

rotativa *f* (typ) rotary press

rotazióne *f* rotation

roteare (**ròteo**) *tr* to roll (*the eyes*); to flourish (*a sword*) || *intr* to circle

rotèlla *f* small wheel; caster; roller; kneecap; disk (*of ski pole*); **gli**

manca una rotella he has a screw loose

rotocal·co *m* (**-chi**) rotogravure

rotolare (**ròtolo**) *tr & intr* (ESSERE) to roll || *ref* to turn over; to wallow

ròtolo *m* roll; bolt; coil; **a rotoli** to rack and ruin

rotolóne *m* tumble; **a rotoloni** falling down; to rack and ruin

rotón·do -da *adj* round; rotund || *f* rotunda; terrace

ròtta *f* break; rout; (aer, naut) course; **a rotta di collo** at breakneck speed; **mettere in rotta** to rout

rottame *m* fragment; wreck; **rottami** scraps, debris; wreckage; **rottami di ferro** scrap iron

ròt·to -ta *adj* broken; shattered; inured || *m* break, tear; **e rotti** odd, e.g., **duecento e rotti** two hundred odd; **per il rotto della cuffia** hardly; just about || *f* see **rotta**

rottura *f* break; breakage; rupture; breakdown (*of relations*); crack

ròtula *f* kneecap

rovèllo *m* (lit) anger

rovènte *adj* red-hot

róvere *m & f* oak tree || *m* oak (*lumber*)

rovè·scia *f* (**-sce**) cuff; **alla rovescia** inside out; upside down; the wrong way

rovesciaménto *m* upset; overturn

rovesciare §128 (**rovèscio**) *tr* to overturn; to upset; tó throw back (*one's head*); to spill (*liquid*); to pour; to hurl (*insults*); to turn inside out || *intr* to throw up || *ref* to spill; to pour; to upset

rovè·scio -scia (**-sci -sce**) *adj* reverse; inverse; inside out; upside down; backwards || *m* reverse; wrong side; downpour; upset; (com) crash; (tennis) backhand; **a rovescio** upside down; backwards || *f* see **rovescia**

rovéto *m* bramble; brier patch

rovina *f* ruin; blight; **andare in rovina** to go to ruin; **mandare in rovina** to ruin; **rovine** ruins

rovinare *tr* to ruin || *intr* (ESSERE) to collapse || *ref* to go to ruin

rovinì·o *m* (**-i**) clatter; crash

rovinó·so -sa [s] *adj* ruinous

rovistare *tr* to rummage through

róvo *m* bramble

ròzza [ddzz] *f* nag

róz·zo -za [ddzz] *adj* rough; coarse

ruba *f*—**andare a ruba** to sell like hot-cakes; **mettere a ruba** to plunder

rubacchiare §287 *tr* to pilfer

rubacuò·ri (**-ri**) *adj* ravishing || *m* lady-killer || *f* vamp

rubare *tr* to steal; **rubare a man salva** to pillage, loot || *intr* to steal; **rubare sul peso** to give short measure

rubería *f* thieving, stealing

rubicón·do -da *adj* rubicund

rubinétto *m* faucet; cock

rubino *m* ruby; jewel (*of watch*)

rubiz·zo -za *adj* well-preserved (*person*)

rubri·ca *f* (**-che**) title, heading; directory; (journ) section

rude *adj* (lit) rough; (lit) rude

rùdere *m* ruin

rudimentale *adj* rudimentary

rudiménto *m* rudiment

ruffia·no -na *mf* go-between || *m* pimp, panderer || *f* bawd, procuress

ru·ga *f* (**-ghe**) wrinkle; (bot) rocket

rùggine *f* rust; ill-will; (bot) blight

rugginó·so -sa [s] *adj* rusty

ruggire §176 *tr & intr* to roar

ruggito *m* roar

rugiada *f* dew

rugó·so -sa [s] *adj* wrinkled, wrinkly

rullàg·gio *m* (**-gi**) (aer) taxiing

rullare *tr* to roll || *intr* to roll; to taxi

rullì·o *m* (**-i**) roll; rub-a-dub

rullo *m* roll; platen (*of typewriter*); pin (*in tenpins*); **rullo compressore** road roller

rumè·no -na *adj & mf* var of **romeno**

ruminare (**rùmino**) *tr & intr* to ruminate

rumóre *m* noise; rumor; ado; **far molto rumore** to create a stir

rumoreggiare §290 (**rumoréggio**) *intr* to rumble

rumoró·so -sa [s] *adj* noisy; rumbling; controversial

ruolino *m* roster

ruòlo *m* roll; role; list; **di ruolo** regular, full-time; **fuori ruolo** temporary, part-time

ruòta *f* wheel; paddle wheel; revolving server (*in convent*); **a quattro ruote** four-wheel; **dar la ruota a** to sharpen; **esser l'ultima ruota del carro** to be the fifth wheel to a wagon; **fare la ruota** to spread its tail, strut (*said, e.g., of a peacock*); to turn cartwheels (*said, e.g., of an acrobat*); **ruota dentata** cog, cogwheel; **ruota idraulica** water wheel; **seguire a ruota** to follow closely

rupe *f* cliff

rurale *adj* rural, farm, farmer

ruscèllo *m* brook

ruspa *f* road grader

ruspante *m* barnyard chicken

russare *intr* to snore

Rùssia, la Russia

rus·so -sa *adj & mf* Russian

rustica·no -na *adj* rustic, boorish

rùsti·co -ca (**-ci -che**) *adj* rustic; coarse || *m* tool shed; cottage; (lit) peasant

rutilante *adj* (lit) shiny

ruttare *tr* (lit) to belch || *intr* (vulg) to belch

rutto *m* (vulg) belch

ruttóre *m* (elec) contact breaker

ruvidézza *f* or **ruvidi·tà** *f* (**-tà**) coarseness; roughness

rùvi·do -da *adj* coarse; rough

ruzzare [ddzz] *intr* to romp

ruzzolare (**rùzzolo**) *tr* to roll || *intr* (ESSERE) to tumble down; to roll

ruzzolóne *m* tumble; **a ruzzoloni** tumbling down

S

S, s ['ɛsse] *m & f* seventeenth letter of the Italian alphabet

s- *pref* dis-, e.g., **sleale** disloyal; e.g., **sconto** discount; un-, e.g., **scatenare** to unchain, unleash

sàbato *m* Saturday; (*of Jews*) Sabbath; **sabato inglese** Saturday afternoon off

sabbàti·co -ca *adj* (**-ci -che**) sabbatical

sàbbia *f* sand; **sabbia mobile** quicksand

sabbiatura *f* sand bath; sandblast

sabbièra *f* (rr) sandbox

sabbió·so -sa [s] *adj* sandy

sabotàg·gio *m* (**-gi**) sabotage

sabotare (**sabòto**) *tr* to sabotage

sac·ca *f* (**-che**) bag; satchel; (mil) pocket; **sacca d'aria** (aer) air pocket; **sacca da viaggio** traveling bag; duffel bag

saccarina *f* saccharine

saccènte *mf* wiseacre, know-it-all

saccheggiare §290 (**sacchéggio**) *tr* to pillage, plunder

sacchég·gio *m* (**-gi**) pillage, plunder

sacchétto *m* little bag, pouch

sac·co *m* (**-chi**) bag; sack; sackcloth; pouch; (boxing) punching bag; (fig) heap, lot; **fare sacco** to sag; **mettere a sacco** to sack; **mettere nel sacco** to outwit; **sacco alpino** knapsack; **sacco a pelo** or **a piuma** sleeping bag; **sacco postale** mailbag

saccòc·cia *f* (**-ce**) (coll) pocket

sacerdòte *m* priest; (fig) devotee

sacerdotéssa *f* priestess

sacerdòzio *m* priesthood; ministry

sacramentale *adj* sacramental; (joc) habitual, ritual

sacraménto *m* sacrament

sacrà·rio *m* (**-ri**) memorial; sanctuary, shrine

sacrestìa *f* var of **sagrestia**

sacrificare §197 (**sacrìfico**) *tr* to sacrifice; to waste; to force || *ref* to sacrifice oneself

sacrifì·cio *m* (**-ci**) sacrifice

sacrilè·gio *m* (**-gi**) sacrilege

sacrile·go -ga *adj* (**-ghi -ghe**) sacrilegious

sacri·sta *m* (**-sti**) sexton

sacristìa *f* var of **sagrestia**

sa·cro -cra *adj* sacred

sacrosan·to -ta *adj* sacrosanct; sacred (*truth*)

sàdi·co -ca (**-ci -che**) *adj* sadistic || *mf* sadist

sadismo *m* sadism

saétta *f* stroke of lightning; hand (*of watch*); (mach) bit; (lit) arrow

saettare (**saétto**) *tr* to shoot; **saettare sguardi a** to look daggers at

saettóne *m* (archit) strut

sagace *adj* sagacious, shrewd

sagà·cia *f* (**-cie**) sagacity

saggézza *f* wisdom

saggiare §290 *tr* to assay; to test; (dial) to taste

saggia·tóre -trice *mf* assayer || *m* assay balance

saggina *f* sorghum

sàg·gio -gia (**-gi -ge**) *adj* wise || *m* sage; assay; sample; proof; theme; test; rate (*of interest*); display; **di saggio** examination (*copy*)

saggi·sta *mf* (**-sti -ste**) essayist

sagittària *f* (bot) arrowhead

sagittà·rio *m* (**-ri**) (obs) archer || **Sagittario** *m* Sagittarius

sàgola *f* (naut) halyard

sàgoma *f* outline; target; model, pattern; (joc) character

sagomare (**sàgomo**) *tr* to outline; to mold; to shape

sagomato *m* billboard

sagra *f* anniversary consecration (*of church*); festival

sagrato *m* elevated square in front of a church; churchyard; (coll) curse

sagrestano *m* sexton, sacristan

sagrestìa *f* sacristy, vestry

sàla *f* serge

sàio *m* (**sài**) habit (*of monk or nun*); doublet; frock coat

sala *f* axletree; hall, room; (bot) cattail, reed mace; **sala da ballo** dance hall; **sala da pranzo** dining room; **sala d'aspetto** waiting room; anteroom; **sala operatoria** operating room

salac·ca *f* (**-che**) (coll) sardine; (coll) shad

salace *adj* salacious; pungent

salamandra *f* salamander

salame *m* salami

salamelèc·co *m* (**-chi**) salaam

salamòia *f* brine

salare *tr* to salt; (coll) to cut (*school*)

salaria·to -ta *adj* wage-earning || *m* wage earner

salà·rio *m* (**-ri**) pay, wages

salassare *tr* to bleed

salasso *m* bloodletting

sala·to -ta *adj* salted; salty; dear, expensive; (fig) sharp || *m* salt pork; cold cuts || *f* salting

salda *f* starch solution (*used in laundering*)

saldacón·ti *m* (**-ti**) bookkeeping department; credit department; ledger; bookkeeping ma hine

saldare *tr* to solder; to set (*a bone*); to weld; to pay, settle || *ref* to knit (*said of a bone*); (lit) to heal

saldatóre *m* solderer; welder; soldering iron

saldatura *f* soldering; setting (*of bones*); joint; continuity; **saldatura autogena** welding

saldézza *f* firmness

sal·do -da *adj* firm; valid (*reason*); flawless || *m* balance; clearance sale; job lot; payment; **saldi** remnants || *f* see **salda**

saldobrasatura *f* soldering

sale *m* salt; wit; (lit) sea; **restare di sale** to be dumbfounded; **sale inglese** Epsom salts; **sali aromatici** smelling salts; **sali da bagno** bath salts

salgèmma *f* rock salt

sàlice *m* willow tree; **salice piangente** weeping willow

salicilato *m* salicylate

saliènte *adj* projecting; (fig) salient || *m* projection

salièra *f* saltcellar, salt shaker

salini·tà *f* (-tà) salinity

sali·no -na *adj* saline; salty || *f* salt bed

salire §242 *tr* to climb || *intr* (ESSERE) to climb; to go up; to rise; **salire in** or **su** to get on (*e.g., a train*)

saliscén·di *m* (-di) latch; **saliscendi** *mpl* ups and downs

salita *f* climbing; ascent, rise; slope; **in salita** uphill

saliva *f* saliva

salma *f* corpse, body

salma·stro -stra *adj* briny; saltish || *m*—**sapere di salmastro** to smell or taste salty

salmerìe *fpl* wagon train; (mil) supplies

salmì *m*—**in salmì** (culin) in a stew

salmo *m* psalm

salmodiare §287 (**salmòdio**) *intr* to chant, sing hymns, intone

salmóne *m* salmon

salnitro *m* saltpeter

Salomóne *m* Solomon

salóne *m* hall; salon, drawing room; (naut) saloon; **salone da barbiere** barber shop; **salone dell'automobile** auto show

salòtto *m* drawing room; living room, parlor; reception room

salpare *tr* to weigh (*anchor*) || *intr* (ESSERE) to weigh anchor

salsa *f* sauce

salsapariglia *f* sarsaparilla

salsèdine *f* saltiness

salsìc·cia *f* (-ce) sausage

salsièra *f* gravy boat

sal·so -sa *adj* salty; saline || *m* saltiness || *f* see salsa

saltabeccare §197 (**saltabécco**) *intr* to hop

saltaléone *m* coil spring

saltare *tr* to jump; to skip; to sauté; (sports) to vault, hurdle; **far saltare** to kick out; to blow up (*e.g., a mine*); **saltare la sbarra** (coll) to go A.W.O.L. || *intr* (ESSERE & AVERE) to jump; to pop off, e.g., **mi è saltato un bottone** one of my buttons has popped off; to blow out (*said of a fuse*); **saltare agli occhi** to be self-evident; **saltare a piè pari** to skip with both feet; **saltar fuori** to pop out (*said of the eyes*); to appear suddenly; **saltare in mente a** to come to the mind of; **saltare il ticchio a** (qlcu) di to feel like + *ger*, e.g., **gli è saltato il ticchio di ca**·tare he felt like singing; **saltare la mosca al** ·aso **a** (qlcu) to blow one's top, e.g., **le è saltata la mosca al naso** she blew her top; **saltare per aria** to blow up; **saltare su** to start (*to make a sudden jerk*); **saltare su a** + *inf* to begin suddenly to + *inf*

salta·tóre -trice *mf* jumper, hurdler

saltellare (**saltèllo**) *intr* to skip, hop

saltellóni *adv*—**a saltelloni** skipping, hopping

saltimban·co *m* (-chi) acrobat, tumbler; mountebank

salto *m* jump; leap; fall; skip; (*of animals*) mating; (fig) step; **a salti** skipping, jumping; **al salto** sauté; **fare quattro salti** to dance; **fare un salto** to hop, hurry; **salto a pesce** jackknife (*dive*); **salto coll'asta** pole vaulting; **salto in altezza** high jump; **salto in lunghezza** broad jump; **salto mortale** somersault; **salto nel vuoto** leap in the dark

saltua·rio -ria *adj* (-ri -rie) desultory, occasional

salubre *adj* salubrious, healthy, healthful

salume *m* pork product

salumeria *f* pork butcher shop

salumiè·re -ra *mf* pork butcher

salutare *adj* healthful || *tr* to greet; to salute; (lit) to proclaim

salute *f* health; salvation; safety || *interj* good luck; to your health!; gesundheit!

saluto *m* salute; greeting; salutation; **distinti saluti** sincerely yours

salva *f* salvo; outburst; **a salve** with blank cartridges, with blanks

salvacondótto *m* safe-conduct

salvada·nàio *m* (-nài) piggy bank

salvagèn·te *m* (-te & -ti) life preserver; fender (*of trolley car*) || *m* (-te) safety island

salvaguardare *tr* to safeguard

salvaguàrdia *f* safeguard

salvaménto *m* safety

salvamotóre *m* circuit breaker; fuse box

salvapun·te *m* (-te) pencil cap; tap (*on sole of shoe*)

salvare *tr* to save; to spare (*a life*); to rescue || *ref* to save oneself; to be rescued; **si salvi chi può!** every man for himself!

salvatàg·gio *m* (-gi) rescue

salvatóre *m* savior, rescuer || **il Salvatore** the Saviour

salvazióne *f* salvation

salve *interj* hello!, hail!

salvézza *f* salvation; safety

sàlvia *f* (bot) sage

salviétta *f* napkin; paper napkin; paper towel

sal·vo -va *adj* safe; saved; secure || *m*—**mettere in salvo** to put in a safe place; **mettersi in salvo** to reach safety || *f* see salva || *salvo prep* except; **salvo che** unless; **salvo il vero** unless I am mistaken

samarita·no -na *adj & mf* Samaritan

sambu·co *m* (-chi) elder tree

san *adj* apocopated and unstressed form of santo

sanàbile *adj* curable

sanare *tr* to heal; to remedy; to reclaim (*land*); to normalize

sanatò·rio *m* (-ri) sanatorium

sancire §176 *tr* to ratify, sanction; to establish

sàndalo *m* sandal; sandalwood; flatbottom boat

sandolino *m* canoe, skiff, kayak

sangue *m* blood; **agitarsi il sangue** to fret; **all'ultimo sangue** (*duel*) to the death; **al sangue rare** (*meat*); **a sangue freddo** in cold blood; cold-blooded; **cavar sangue da una rapa** to draw blood from a stone; **farsi cattivo sangue** to get angry; **il sangue non è acqua** blood is thicker than water; **puro sangue** thoroughbred; **sangue dal naso** nosebleed; **sangue freddo** calmness, composure

sangui·gno -gna *adj* blood (*circulation*); bloody; sanguine, ruddy || *m* (lit) color of blood

sanguinante *adj* bloody, bleeding

sanguinare (**sànguino**) *intr* to bleed; to be rare (*said of meat*)

sanguinà·rio -ria *adj* (**-ri -rie**) sanguinary

sanguinó·so -sa [s] *adj* bloody; bleeding; (fig) stinging

sanguisu·ga [s] *f* (**-ghe**) leech

sani·tà *f* (**-tà**) health; healthfulness; soundness (*of body*); sanity; health department

sanità·rio -ria (**-ri -rie**) *adj* health; sanitary || *m* physician

sa·no -na *adj* healthy; sound; **sano e salvo** safe and sound

sant' *adj* apocopated form of **santo** and **santa**

santa *f* saint

santabàrbara *f* (**santebàrbare**) (nav) powder magazine

santarellina *f* goody-goody girl

santificare §197 (**santìfico**) *tr* to sanctify

santìssi·mo -ma *adj* most holy || *m* Eucharist

santi·tà *f* (**-tà**) sanctity, holiness; sainthood, saintliness

san·to -ta *adj* saintly, holy; sacred; blessed, livelong, e.g., **tutto il santo giorno** all the livelong day || *m* saint; name day; (fig) someone || *f* see **santa**

santorég·gia *f* (**-ge**) (bot) savory

santuà·rio *m* (**-ri**) sanctuary

sanzionare (**sanzióno**) *tr* to sanction; to ratify

sanzióne *f* sanction

sapére *m* knowledge; **sapere fare** savoir-faire || §243 *tr* to know; to find out; to know how to; **far sapere** to let know; **saperla lunga** to know a thing or two; **un certo non so che** a certain something, something vague || *intr*— **sapere di** to know; to taste; to smell; to smack of; **mi sa che** I think that; **non voler più saperne di** to not want to have anything to do with; **sapere male** (with *dat*) to feel sorry, e.g., **gli sa male** he feels sorry || *ref*—**che io mi sappia** as far as I know

sàpido -da *adj* savory; witty

sapiènte *adj* wise; talented; trained (*dog*) || *m* wise man

sapientó·ne -na *mf* wiseacre, know-it-all

sapiènza *f* wisdom; knowledge

saponària *f* (bot) soapwort

saponata *f* soapsuds; lather; (fig) soft soap

sapóne *m* soap; **sapone da toletta** toilet soap; **sapone per la barba** shaving soap

saponétta *f* cake of soap

saponière *m* soap maker

saponifì·cio *m* (**-ci**) soap factory

saponó·so -sa [s] *adj* soapy

sapóre *m* taste; savor; flavor

saporire §176 *tr* to savor

saporitaménte *adv* heartily; soundly

sapori·to -ta *adj* tasty; flavorful; salty; expensive

saporó·so -sa [s] *adj* savory; witty

saputèl·lo -la *adj* cocksure || *m* smart aleck

sarac·co *m* (**-chi**) hand saw

saracè·no -na *adj* Saracen, Saracenic || *m* Saracen; quintain

saraciné·sca *f* (**-sche**) metal shutter (*of store*); sluice gate; (hist) portculis

sarcasmo *m* sarcasm

sarcàsti·co -ca *adj* (**-ci -che**) sarcastic

sarchiare §287 *tr* to weed

sarchia·tóre -trice *mf* weeder || *f* (agr) cultivator

sarchièllo *m* weeding hoe

sàr·chio *m* (**-chi**) hoe

sarcòfa·go *m* (**-gi & -ghi**) sarcophagus

sarcràuti *mpl* sauerkraut

Sardégna, la Sardinia

sardèlla *f* pilchard; sardine

sardina *f* pilchard; sardine

sar·do -da *adj & mf* Sardinian

sardòni·co -ca *adj* (**-ci -che**) sardonic

sarménto *m* vine shoot, running stem

sarta *f* dressmaker

sàrtie *fpl* (naut) shrouds

sarto *m* tailor

sartorìa *f* dressmaker's shop; tailor shop; dressmaking; tailoring

sassaiòla *f* shower of stones

sassata *f* blow with a stone

sasso *m* stone, rock; pebble; (poet) tombstone; **di sasso** stony; **restare di sasso** to be taken aback; **tirare sassi in colombaia** to cut one's nose to spite one's face

sassòforo *m* saxophone

sàssone *adj & mf* Saxon

sassó·so -sa [s] *adj* stony

Sàtana *m* Satan

satarasso *m* Satan; devil

satèllite *m* satellite

sa·tin *m* (**-tin**) sateen

satinare *tr* to gloss

sàtira *f* satire

satireggiare §290 (**satiréggio**) *tr* to satirize, lampoon || *intr* to compose satires

satìri·co -ca *adj* (**-ci -che**) satiric(al) || *m* satirist

sàtiro *m* satyr

satól·lo -la *adj* sated, full

saturare *tr* (**sàturo**) *tr* to saturate; to steep; (fig) to fill; (com) to glut (*a market*)

saturni·no -na *adj* Saturnian; saturnine

Saturno *m* (astr) Saturn

sàtu·ro -ra *adj* saturated; (fig) full; (lit) sated

sàu·ro -ra *adj* & *m* sorrel (*horse*)

Savèrio *m* Xavier

sà·vio -via (**-vi -vie**) *adj* wise || *m* wise man, sage

savoiar·do -da *adj* & *mf* Savoyard || *m* ladyfinger

saxòfono *m* saxophone

saziare §287 *tr* to satisfy; to cloy, satiate

sazietà *f* satiety, surfeit; **mangiare a sazietà** to eat one's fill

sà·zio -zia *adj* (**-zi -zie**) sated; full; satisfied

sbaciucchiare §287 (**sbaciùcchio**) *tr* to kiss again and again || *ref* to neck

sbadatàggine *f* carelessness; oversight

sbada·to -ta *adj* careless; heedless

sbadigliare §280 *intr* to yawn

sbadì·glio *m* (**-gli**) yawn

sbafa·tóre -trice *mf* sponger

sbafo *m*—**a sbafo** sponging; **mangiare a sbafo** to sponge

sbagliare §280 *tr* to miss; to mistake; **sbagliarla** to be sadly mistaken || *intr* & *ref* to be mistaken; to make a mistake

sbaglia·to -ta *adj* wrong; mistaken

sbà·glio *m* (**-gli**) error, mistake

sbalestrare (**sbalèstro**) *tr* to fling with the crossbow; to send (*an employee*) far away || *intr* to speak amiss; to ramble; to blunder

sbalestra·to -ta *adj* unbalanced; ill-at-ease

sballare *tr* to unpack; **sballarle grosse** to tell tall tales || *intr* to overbid

sballa·to -ta *adj* unpacked; absurd, wild

sballottare (**sballòtto**) *tr* to toss

sbalordire §176 *tr* to stun; to amaze; to bewilder || *intr* to lose consciousness; to be dumfounded

sbalorditi·vo -va *adj* amazing

sbalzare *tr* to upset; to send far away; to overthrow; to emboss || *intr* (ESSERE) to bounce

sbalzo *m* leap, jump; climb; embossment, relief; **a sbalzi** by leaps and bounds; **di sbalzo** all of a sudden

sbancare §197 *tr* to clear (*ground*) of rocks; to ruin; (*cards*) to break (*the bank*)

sbandaménto *m* skid; swerve; disbandment; breaking up; (naut) list

sbandare *tr* to disband; (naut) to cause to list || *intr* to list; to skid; to swerve; to deviate || *ref* to disband; to break up

sbanda·to -ta *adj* disbanded; stray; alienated || *mf* alienated person || *m* straggler || *f* listing (*of ship*); skidding (*of vehicle*); **prendere una sbandata per** to get a crush on

sbandierare (**sbandièro**) *tr* to wave (*a flag*); to display

sbaragliare §280 *tr* to rout; to crush

sbaràglio *m*—**mettere allo sbaraglio** to endanger

sbarazzare *tr* to clear out; to free || *ref* —**sbarazzarsi di** to get rid of

sbarazzi·no -na *adj* mischievous || *mf* scamp; **alla sbarazzina** cocked, at an angle (*said of a hat*)

sbarbare *tr* to shave; to uproot || *ref* to shave

sbarbatèllo *m* greenhorn, fledgling

sbarcare §197 *tr* to unload; to discharge; to disembark; to pass; to strew (*fodder*); **sbarcare il lunario** to make ends meet || *intr* (ESSERE) to come ashore, land

sbarca·tóio *m* (**-tói**) landing pier

sbar·co *m* (**-chi**) unloading; landing

sbarra *f* bar; (typ) dash

sbarraménto *m* barrage; obstacle

sbarrare *tr* to bar; to block (*the way*); to open (*one's eyes*) wide, e.g., **sbarrò gli occhi** he opened his eyes wide

sbarrétta *f* bar; **sbarrette verticali** (typ) parallels

sbatacchiare §287 *tr* to slam; to flap || *intr* to slam

sbatàc·chio *m* (**-chi**) shore, prop

sbàttere *tr* to flap; to fling; to slam; to beat; to toss; to send away; to beat pale; **sbatter fuori** to throw out || *intr* to flap; to slam

sbattighiàc·cio *m* (**-cio**) cocktail shaker

sbattitóre *m* electric mixer

sbattiuò·va *m* (**-va**) egg beater

sbattu·to -ta *adj* haggard; downcast

sbavare *tr* to slobber over; (mach) to trim || *intr* to drivel, slobber; to run (*said of colors*)

sbavatura *f* drivel; run (*of colors*); burr (*of metal*); deckle edge; verbosity

sbeccare §197 (**sbécco**) *tr* & *ref* to chip

sbeffeggiare §290 (**sbeffèggio**) *tr* to make fun of

sbellicare §197 *ref*—**sbellicarsi dalle risa** to burst with laughter

sbèrla *f* (coll) slap

sberlèffo *m* scar; grimace; **fare gli sberleffi a** to make faces at

sbevazzare *intr* to guzzle

sbevucchiare §287 *intr* to tipple

sbiadire §176 *tr* & *intr* (ESSERE) to fade

sbiadi·to -ta *adj* faded; dull

sbiancare §197 *tr* to whiten || *ref* to become white; to pale

sbianchire §176 *tr* (culin) to blanch

sbiè·co -ca (**-chi -che**) *adj* oblique; **di sbieco** on the bias; **guardare di sbieco** to look askance at || *m* cloth cut diagonally

sbigottire §176 *tr* to terrify, dismay || *intr* (ESSERE) & *ref* to be dismayed

sbilanciare §128 *tr* to unbalance; to upset || *intr* to lose one's balance || *ref* to commit oneself

sbilàn·cio *m* (**-ci**) disequilibrium; (com) deficit

sbilèn·co -ca *adj* (**-chi -che**) twisted, crooked

sbirciare §128 *tr* to leer at, ogle; to eye closely

sbir·ro -ra *adj* (coll) smart || *m* (pej) cop

sbizzarrire [ddzz] §176 *tr* to cure the whims of || *ref* to indulge one's whims

sbloccare §197 (**sblòcco**) *tr* to unblock; to raise the blockade of; to free

sbòbba *f* slop, dishwater

sboccare §197 (**sbócco**) *tr* to break the

mouth of (*a bottle*); to remove a few drops from (*a bottle*) || *intr* (ESSERE) to flow; to open (*said of a street*); **sboccare in** to turn out to be

sbocca·to -ta *adj* foulmouthed; foul (*language*); chipped at the mouth (*said of a bottle*)

sbocciare §128 (**sbòccio**) *intr* (ESSERE) to bud, burgeon, bloom

sbóc·co *m* (**-chi**) outlet; **avere uno sbocco di sangue** to spit blood

sbocconcellare (**sbocconcèllo**) *tr* to nibble at; to chip, nick

sbollentare (**sbollènto**) *tr* to blanch

sbollire §176 *intr* to stop boiling; to calm down

sbolognare (**sbológno**) *tr* (coll) to palm off; (coll) to get rid of

sbòrnia *f* (coll) drunk, jag; **smaltire la sbornia** to sober up

sborsare (**sbórso**) *tr* to pay out, disburse

sbórso *m* disbursement, outlay

sbottare (**sbòtto**) *intr*—**sbottare a + inf** to burst out + *ger*

sbottonare (**sbottóno**) *tr* to unbutton || *ref* (fig) to unbosom oneself

sbozzare (**sbòzzo**) *tr* to rough-hew; to sketch, outline

sbraca·to -ta *adj* without pants; slovenly; vulgar

sbracciare §128 *intr* to gesticulate || *ref* to roll up one's sleeves; to wear sleeveless clothes; to gesticulate; to do one's best

sbraccia·to -ta *adj* bare-armed

sbraitare (**sbràito**) *intr* to scream

sbraitó·ne -na *mf* bigmouth

sbranare *tr* to tear to pieces

sbrano *m* tear, rent

sbrattare *tr* to clean; to clear

sbreccare §197 (**sbrécco**) *tr* to chip, nick

sbrecciare §128 (**sbréccio**) *tr* to open a gap in

sbréndolo *m* tatter, rag

sbriciolare (**sbrìciolo**) *tr* to crumb || *ref* to crumble

sbrigare §209 *tr* to transact; to take care of || *ref* to hasten, hurry; **sbrigarsela** to get out of trouble; **sbrigarsi di** to get rid of; **sbrigati! make it snappy!, hurry up!**

sbrigativ·o -va *adj* quick, brisk; businesslike

sbrigliare §280 *tr* to unbridle; to reduce (*a hernia*); to lance (*an infected wound*) || *ref* to cut loose

sbrinare *tr* to defrost

sbrindella·to -ta *adj* tattered

sbrodolare (**sbròdolo**) *tr* to soil; (fig) to drag out || *ref* to slobber

sbrogliare §280 (**sbròglio**) *tr* to untangle; to clean up || *ref* to extricate oneself; **sbrogliarsela** to get out of a tight spot

sbronzare (**sbrónzo**) *ref* (coll) to get drunk

sbruffare *tr* to squirt out of the mouth; to spatter; to bribe || *intr* to tell tall tales

sbruffo *m* sprinkle, squirt; bribe

sbruffó·ne -na *mf* braggart

sbucare §197 *intr* (ESSERE) to pop out, come out

sbucciare §128 *tr* to peel; to skin || *ref* to slough (*said of snakes*); **sbucciarsela** (coll) to goldbrick

sbucciatura *f* slight abrasion

sbudellare (**sbudèllo**) *tr* to disembowel || *ref*—**sbudellarsi dalle risa** to burst with laughter, split one's sides laughing

sbuffare *tr & intr* to puff

sbuffo *m* puff; gust (*of wind*); **a sbuffo** puffed (*sleeve*)

sbullonare (**sbullóno**) *tr* to unbolt

sc- *pref* dis-, e.g., **sconto** discount; es-, e.g., **scalare** to escalate; ex-, e.g., **scusare** to excuse

scàbbia *f* scabies

scabró·so -sa [s] *adj* scabrous

scabro·ni *m & f* (**-ni**) rough; stony; tight (*style*)

scacchièra *f* checkerboard; chessboard

scacchière *m* (mil) sector; (obs) checkerboard; exchequer

scacciaca·ni *m & f* (**-ni**) toy gun; gun shooting only blanks

scacciamó·sche *m* (**-sche**) fly swatter

scacciapensiè·ri *m* (**-ri**) jew's-harp

scacciare §128 *tr* to chase away, drive away; to expel

scaccino *m* sexton, sacristan

scac·co *m* (**-chi**) chessman; checker; check; square; **a scacchi** checkered; **dare scacco matto a** to checkmate; **in scacco** or **sotto scacco** in check; **scacchi** chess; **scacco matto** checkmate

scàccoli *mpl* cement piles

scaccomatto *m* checkmate

scadènte *adj* inferior, poor, shoddy

scadènza *f* term, maturity; obligation; **a breve scadenza** short-term; **a lunga scadenza** long-term

scadére §121 *intr* (ESSERE) to decay, to decline; to fall due; to expire; (naut) to drift

scafandro *m* diving suit; **scafandro astronautico** space suit

scaffale *m* bookcase; shelf

scafo *m* hull

scagionare (**scagióno**) *tr* to exonerate, exculpate

scàglia *f* scale (*of fish*); chip; plate (*of medieval armor*); flake (*of soap*); tile (*of slate roof*)

scagliare §280 *tr* to hurl, fling, throw; to scale (*fish*) || *ref* to dash, to rush; to flake

scaglionare (**scaglióno**) *tr* to echelon; to stagger (*e.g., payments*)

scaglióne *m* terrace (*of mountain*); echelon; scale; **a scaglioni** graded (*e.g., income tax*)

scala *f* stairs; ladder; scale; (cards) straight; (rad) dial; **a scale** scaled, graded; **fare le scale** to climb the stairs; **scala a chiocciola** spiral stairway; **scala a gradini** or **a libretto** stepladder; **scala mobile** escalator; (econ) sliding scale; **scala porta** aerial ladder; **scala reale** (poker) straight flush; **su larga scala** large-scale; **su scala nazionale** on a national scale

scalandróne *m* (naut) gangway

scalare *adj* graded, scaled; gradual || *m* (com) running balance || *tr* to climb, ascend; to scale, grade; to reduce

scalata *f* climb, ascent; **dar la scalata a** to climb; to climb up to

scalcagna·to -ta *adj* down-at-the-heel

scalcare §197 *tr* to slice, carve

scalciare §128 *intr* to kick

scalcina·to -ta *adj* (wall or plaster) that is peeling off; worn-out; down-at-the-heels

scalda-acqua *m* (-acqua) hot-water heater

scaldaba·gno m (-gno) hot-water heater; **scaldabagno a gas** gas heater

scaldalèt·to m (-ti & -to) bedwarmer

scaldare *tr* to warm, warm up; to heat, heat up || *intr* (mach) to become hot || *ref* to warm up; to heat up; **scaldarsi la testa** to get excited

scaldavivan·de m (-de) hot plate

scaldino *m* hand warmer

scalèa *f* flight of stairs, stairway

scalèo *m* stepladder

scalétta *f* small ladder; small stairs; (mov) rough draft

scalfire §176 *tr* to graze, scratch; to cut (e.g., glass)

scalfittura *f* graze, scratch

scalinata *f* stairway, perron

scalino *m* step (of a stair); (fig) ladder

scalmana *f* chill; flush; **prendere una scalmana per** to take a fancy to

scalmanare *ref* to hustle, bustle; to fuss

scalmana·to -ta *adj* panting; hotheaded

scalmo *m* (naut) oarlock

scalo *m* pier, dock; (naut) ways; (naut) port of call; **fare scalo** (naut) to call, stop; (aer) to land; **scalo di alaggio** (naut) slip; **scalo merci** (rr) freight yard; **senza scalo** (aer, naut) nonstop

scalógna *f* (coll) bad luck

scalógno *m* (bot) scallion

scalòppa *f* veal chop

scaloppina *f* veal cutlet, scallop

scalpellare (scalpèllo) *tr* to chisel

scalpellino *m* stone cutter

scalpèllo *m* chisel; (surg) scalpel; **scalpello a taglio obliquo** skew chisel

scalpicciare §128 *tr* & *intr* to shuffle

scalpitare (scàlpito) *intr* to paw the ground

scalpóre *m* scene; **fare scalpore** to raise a fuss

scaltrézza *f* shrewdness, cunning

scaltrire §176 *tr* to polish, refine; to sharpen the wits of || *ref* to catch on; to improve

scal·tro -tra *adj* shrewd, smart

scalzare *tr* to take the shoes or stockings off of; to undermine || *ref* to take off one's shoes or stockings

scal·zo -za *adj* barefoot

scambiare §287 *tr* to exchange; to mistake || *ref* to exchange (presents)

scambiévole *adj* mutual

scàm·bio m (-bi) exchange; (rr) switch;

libero scambio free trade; **scambio di persona** mistaken identity

scamicia·to -ta *adj* in shirt sleeves; extremist || *m* extremist; tunic, waist

scamoscia·to -ta *adj* chamois, suede

scampagnata *f* excursion, outing

scampanare *intr* to peal, chime; to flare (said of a garment)

scampanellare (scampanèllo) *intr* to ring loud and clear

scampani·o m (-i) toll, peal

scampare *tr* to save, rescue; **scamparla bella** to have a narrow escape || *intr* (ESSERE)—**scampare a** to escape from; to take refuge in

scampo *m* escape; safety; (zool) Norway lobster; **non c'è scampo** there is no way out

scàmpolo *m* remnant; **scampoli di tempo** free moments

scanalare *tr* to channel, groove, rabbet || *intr* to overflow

scanalatura *f* channel, groove, rabbet

scandagliare §280 *tr* to sound

scandà·glio m (-gli) sounding lead; **fare uno scandaglio** to make a sounding or survey

scandalismo *m* scandalmongering, yellow journalism

scandalizzare [ddzz] *tr* to scandalize, shock || *ref* to be scandalized

scàndalo *m* scandal

scandalo·so -sa [s] *adj* scandalous

scandina·vo -va *adj* & *mf* Scandinavian

scandire §176 *tr* to scan; to syllabize; (telv) to scan

scàndola *f* wood shingle

scannare *tr* to slaughter, butcher

scanna·tóio m (-tói) slaughterhouse; gyp joint

scanno *m* bench; seat; sand bar

scansafati·che mf (-che) loafer

scansare *tr* to move; to avoid || *ref* to get out of the way

scansia *f* shelf; bookcase

scansióne *f* scansion; (telv) scanning

scanso *m*—**a scanso di** in order to avoid

scantinare *intr* to make a blunder; (mus) to be out of tune

scantinato *m* basement

scantonare (scantóno) *tr* to round (a corner) || *intr* to duck around the corner

scanzona·to -ta *adj* flippant; unconventional

scapaccióne *m* clout; **dare uno scapaccione a** to clout, slap

scapa·to -ta *adj* scatterbrained || *m* scatterbrain

scapestra·to -ta *adj* & *m* libertine

scapigliare §280 *tr* to dishevel || *ref* to be disheveled

scapiglia·to -ta *adj* disheveled; libertine; unconventional; free and easy

scapitare (scàpito) *intr* to lose

scàpito *m* damage; loss; **a scapito di** to the detriment of

scàpola *f* shoulder blade

scapolare *m* scapular || *v* (scàpolo) *tr* (coll) to escape, avoid || *intr*—**scapolare da** to get out of (danger)

scàpo·lo -la *adj* unmarried ‖ *m* bachelor ‖ *f* see **scapola**

scappaménto *m* escapement (*of watch, of piano*); (aut) exhaust

scappare *tr*—**scapparla bella** to have a narrow escape ‖ *intr* (ESSERE) to flee; to abscond; to run; to get away; to escape; to stick out; to burst out (*said, e.g., of sun*); **far scappare la pazienza a qlcu** to make s.o. lose his patience, to tax s.o.'s patience; **scappare a gambe levate** to run away, beat it; **scappare da** to burst out, e.g., **gli è scappato da ridere** he burst out laughing; **scappar detto di** to blurt out that, e.g., **gli scappò detto di non poterne più** he blurted out that he could not hold out; **scappare di mente** to escape one's mind; **scappar fuori con** to come out with

scappata *f* excursion; sally; escapade; bolt (*of horse*); **fare una scappata** to take a run; **scappata spiritosa** witticism

scappatóia *f* subterfuge; loophole

scappellare (**scappèllo**) *ref* to tip one's hat

scappellòtto *m* smack, slap (on the head); **entrare a scappellòtto** (coll) to squeeze in; **passare a scappellòtto** (coll) to squeeze through with influence

scapricciare §128 *tr* to satisfy the whims of

scarabèo *m* beetle; scarab (*stone*); **scarabeo sacro** scarab; **scarabeo stercorario** dung beetle

scarabocchiare §287 (**scarabòcchio**) *tr* to scribble; to blot (*with ink*)

scarabòc·chio *m* (**-chi**) ink blot; scribble; scrawl

scarafàg·gio *m* (**-gi**) cockroach

scaramanzìa *f* exorcism; **per scaramanzia** to ward off the evil eye, for good luck

scaramazza *adj fem* irregular (*pearl*)

scaramùc·cia *f* (**-ce**) skirmish

scaraventare (**scaravènto**) *tr* to hurl, chuck; to transfer suddenly

scarcerare (**scàrcero**) *tr* to release from jail

scardinare (**scàrdino**) *tr* to unhinge

scàri·ca *f* (**-che**) discharge; volley; evacuation; (elec) discharge; (fig) shower

scaricabarili *m*—**giocare a scaricabarili** (fig) to pass the buck

scaricare §197 (**scàrico**) *tr* to unload; to discharge; to hurl (*insults*); to wreak (*anger*); to free (*from responsibility*) ‖ *ref* to unburden oneself; to flow (*said of a river*); to discharge; to run down (*said of a battery or a watch*)

scaricatóre *m* longshoreman; (elec) lightning arrester

scàri·co -ca (**-chi -che**) *adj* empty, unloaded; discharged; clear (*sky*); free; run-down (*e.g., clock*) ‖ *m* unloading; discharge; exhaust; waste, refuse; **a mio (tuo, etc.) scarico** in my (your, etc.) defense ‖ *f* see **scarica**

scarlattina *f* scarlet fever

scarlat·to -ta *adj & m* scarlet

scarmigliare §280 *tr* to dishevel

scarnificare §197 (**scarnìfico**) or **scarnire** §176 *tr* to bone, take the flesh off; to make thin; to wear down to the bone

scarni·to -ta or **scar·no -na** *adj* boned; meager; skinny

scaròla *f* escarole, endive

scarpa *f* shoe; wedge, skid; scarp; **fare le scarpe a** to undercut; **scarpe al sole** violent death; **scarpe da sci** ski boots

scarpata *f* escarp, escarpment; slope (*of embankment*); blow with a shoe; **scarpata continentale** continental slope

scarpétta *f* small shoe; low shoe; **scarpette chiodate** spikes; **scarpette da ginnastica** gym shoes

scarpinare *intr* to trudge

scarpóne *m* heavy boot; clodhopper

scarròc·cio *m* (**-ci**) (aer, naut) leeway

scarrozzare (**scarròzzo**) *tr* to take for a ride ‖ *intr* to go for a ride; to go for a walk

scarrozzata *f* ride, drive

scarseggiare §290 (**scarséggio**) *intr* (ESSERE) to be scarce, be in short supply; **scarseggiare di** to be short of

scarsèlla *f* pocket; (obs) purse

scarsézza *f* or **scarsi·tà** *f* (**-tà**) scarcity, dearth, lack

scar·so -sa *adj* short; scarce; scanty, scant; weak (*wind*); **scarso a** short of

scartabellare (**scartabèllo**) *tr* to leaf through (*a book*)

scartafàc·cio *m* (**-ci**) note pad, notebook; poorly-bound copybook

scartaménto *m* (rr) gauge; **a scartamento ridotto** narrow-gauge; small-size; small-scale

scartare *tr* to unpack, unwrap; to discard (*cards*); to remove; to scrap (*e.g., a machine*); (mil) to reject ‖ *intr* to swerve; to side-step

scartata *f* unwrapping; side step; swerving; (fig) scolding

scartina *f* discard

scarto *m* discard; reject; swerve; (mil) rejected soldier; (sports) difference; **di scarto inferiore**

scartocciare §128 (**scartòccio**) *tr* to unwrap; to unfold; to husk (*corn*)

scartòffie *fpl* old papers, trash

scassare *tr* to uncrate; to plow up; (coll) to ruin, bust ‖ *ref* (coll) to break down

scassinare *tr* to pick (*a lock*); to burglarize; to break open

scassina·tóre -trice *mf* burglar; **scassinatore di casseforti** safe-cracker

scasso *m* plowing, tilling; burglary

scatenare (**scateno**) *tr* to unchain; to trigger; to excite, stir up ‖ *ref* to break loose

scàtola *f* box; can; **a scatola chiusa** sight unseen; **in scatola** canned; **rompere le scatole a** (vulg) to bug, pester; **scatola armonica** music box; **scatola a sorpresa** jack-in-the-box;

scatola cranica cranium, skull; **scatola del cambio** (aut) transmission, gear box

scatolame *m* boxes; canned food

scatolifi·cio *m* (**-ci**) box factory

scattare *tr* to take (*a picture*) ‖ *intr* (ESSERE & AVERE) to jump, spring; to go off (*said of a trap*); to go up (*said of the cost of living*); to go into action, begin

scatto *m* click (*of camera, gun*); outburst; sprint; automatic increase (*in salary*); shutter release; **a scatti** in jerks; **di scatto** suddenly

scaturire §176 *intr* (ESSERE) to spring; to pour, gush; to stem

scavalcare §197 *tr* to jump over; to pass over; to unsaddle; to skip (*a stitch*) ‖ *intr* (ESSERE) to dismount ‖ *ref* (coll) to rush

scavallare *intr* to caper, cavort

scavare *tr* to dig; to dig up, unearth

scava·tóre -trice *adj* excavating ‖ *m* digger ‖ *f* digger, excavator

scavezzacollo *m* scamp; daredevil; **a scavezzacollo** headlong, at breakneck speed

scavezzare (**scavézzo**) *tr* to lop; to burst; to break; to take the halter off (*a horse*)

scavo *m* digging, excavation

scazzottare (**scazzòtto**) *tr* to beat up

scégliere §244 *tr* to choose; to pick out

sceic·co *m* (**-chi**) sheik

scellerATÀggine *f* or **scellerATÉZza** *f* wickedness, villainy

scellera·to -ta *adj* wicked ‖ *m* villain

scellino *m* shilling

scél·to -ta *adj* choice; selected; (mil) first-class ‖ *f* choice; pick; selection; **di prima scelta** choice

scemare (**scémo**) *tr* to diminish, reduce; to lower the level of ‖ *intr* (ESSERE) & *ref* to lessen, diminish

scemènza *f* foolishness, stupidity

scé·mo -ma *adj* silly, foolish ‖ *mf* simpleton, fool

scempiàggine *f* silliness, foolishness

scém·pio -pia (**-pi -pie**) *adj* simple; single; (lit) wicked ‖ *m* ruination; (lit) slaughter; **fare scempio di** to ruin; (lit) to slaughter

scèna *f* scene; stage; acting; scenery; **esser di scena** (theat) to be on; **mettere in scena** (theat) to stage; **scene di prossima programmazione** (mov) coming attractions

scenà·rio *m* (**-ri**) scenery; scenario, setting

scenari·sta *mf* (**-sti -ste**) scenarist; script writer

scenata *f* scene (*outbreak of anger*)

scéndere §245 *tr* to descend, go down; to bring down ‖ *intr* (ESSERE) to descend, go down; to get off; to come (*to an agreement*); to step (*into the ring*); to put up (*at a hotel*); to check in (*at a hotel*)

scendilèt·to *m* (**-to**) scatter rug; bathrobe

sceneggiare §290 (**scenéggio**) *tr* to write a scenario for; to adapt for the stage

sceneggia·tóre -trice *mf* scenarist

sceneggiatura *f* (mov) screenplay; (rad, telv) continuity

scenètta *f* (theat) sketch

scenògrafo *m* scene designer

scenotècni·ca *f* (**-che**) stagecraft

·ceriffo *m* sheriff

scèrnere §246 *tr* to discern; to distinguish; to select

scervellare (**scervèllo**) *ref* to rack one's brains

scervella·to -ta *adj* scatterbrained

scésa [s] *f* discent; slope

scespiria·no -na *adj* Shakesperean

scetticismo *m* skepticism

scètti·co -ca (**-ci -che**) *adj* skeptic(al) ‖ *m* skeptic

scèttro *m* scepter

sceverare (**scévero**) *tr* (lit) to distinguish

scé·vro -vra *adj* (lit) free, exempt

schèda *f* card; slip, form; **scheda elettorale** ballot; **scheda perforata** punch card

schedare (**schèdo**) *tr* to file

schedà·rio *m* (**-ri**) card index, card catalogue; file cabinet

schég·gia *f* (**-ge**) splinter; chip

scheggiare §290 (**schéggio**) *tr* & *ref* to splinter

schelètri·co -ca *adj* (**-ci -che**) skeleton, skeletal; succint

schèletro *m* skeleton

schè·ma *m* (**-mi**) diagram; draft; model; scheme; **schema di montaggio** (electron) hookup

schérma *f* fencing

schermàglia *f* argument

schermare (**schérmo**) *tr* to screen; (elec) to shield

schermire §176 *tr* to protect; (obs) to fence with ‖ *ref*—**schermirsi da** to ward off, parry; to protect oneself from

schermi·tóre -trice *mf* fencer

schérmo *m* screen; protection; (elec) shield; **farsi schermo di** to use as protection; **farsi schermo delle mani** to ward off a blow with one's hands

schernire §176 *tr* to deride

schérno *m* derision, ridicule, mockery

scherzare (**schérzo**) *tr* (coll) to mock ‖ *intr* to play; to joke, trifle

schérzo *m* play; joke, jest; freak (*of nature*); child's play; trick; **neppure per scherzo** under no circumstances; **per scherzo** in jest; **stare allo scherzo** to take a joke

scherzó·so -sa [s] *adj* joking; playful

schiacciaménto *m* crushing; flattening

schiaccianó·ci *m* (**-ci**) nutcracker

schiacciante *adj* crushing

schiacciapata·te *m* (**-te**) ricer

schiacciare §128 *tr* to crush; to take (*a nap*); to squelch (*a rumor*); to subdue (*the details of a painting*); to mash (*potatoes*); to tread on, step on (*s.o.'s foot*); to flatten; to run (*s.o.*) over; to make (*s.o.'s figure*) look squatty; to crack (*nuts*); to flunk; (tennis) to smash

schiacciata *f* hot cake; (tennis) smash

schiaffare *tr* (coll) to fling, clap
schiaffeggiare §290 (schiaffèggio) *tr* to slap; to buffet
schiaffo *m* slap, box
schiamazzare *intr* to squawk, cackle; to honk; to make a racket
schiamazzo *m* squawking, cackle; honk; hubbub
schiantare *tr* to crush, burst || *intr* (ESSERE) (coll) to burst; (coll) to croak || *ref* to break, crack, split
schianto *m* break, crack; crash; bang; knockout (*extraordinary, attractive person or thing*); di schianto all of a sudden; schianto al cuore heartache
schiappa *f* splinter; (coll) good-for-nothing
schiarimènto *m* elucidation
schiarire §176 *tr* to make clearer; to make (*the hair*) light; to clear; to explain; to elucidate || *intr* (ESSERE) to become light || *ref* to clear up (*said of the weather*); to clear (*one's throat*); to fade || *impers* (ESSERE) —schiarisce it is getting light
schiarita *f* clearing (*of weather*); improvement (*in relations*)
schiatta *f* race, stock
schiattare *intr* (ESSERE) to burst
schiavi·sta (-sti -ste) *adj* slave (*e.g., state*) || *mf* antiabolitionist
schiavi·tù *f* (-tù) slavery; bondage
schia·vo -va *adj* enslaved || *mf* slave
schiccherare (schìcchero) *tr* to scribble; to soil; to sketch; to dash off; to blurt out; (coll) to clean out
schidionare (schidióno) *tr* to put on the spit
schidióne *m* spit
schièna *f* back; divide; crown (*of road*); giocare di schiena to buck
schienale *m* back (*of chair; cut of meat*)
schièra *f* crowd; flock; herd; (mil) rank
schieramènto *m* alignment
schierare (schièro) *tr* to line up || *ref* to line up; schierarsi dalla parte di to side with
schièt·to -ta *adj* pure; frank, honest
schifare *tr* to loathe; to disgust || *ref*—schifarsi di to feel disgusted with
schifa·to -ta *adj* disgusted
schifiltó·so -sa [s] *adj* fastidious; squeamish
schifo *m* disgust, loathing; skiff; shell; fare schifo a to disgust; to make sick
schifó·so -sa [s] *adj* disgusting; sickening; (slang) tremendous
schioccare §197 (schiòcco) *tr* to snap (*the fingers*); to click (*the tongue*); to smack (*the lips*); to crack (*a whip*) || *intr* to crack
schiòc·co *m* (-chi) crack, snap; click; smack
schiodare (schiòdo) *tr* to take the nails out of
schioppettata *f* gunshot; earshot
schiòppo *m* gun, shotgun; a un tiro di schioppo within earshot
schiùdere §125 *tr* & *ref* to open
schiuma *f* foam, froth; lather; head (*of beer*); dregs, scum; meerschaum;

avere la schiuma alla bocca to froth at the mouth
schiumaiòla *f* skimmer
schiumare *tr* to scum; to skim || *intr* to foam, froth; to lather
schiumó·so -sa [s] *adj* foamy
schivare *tr* to avoid; to avert || *ref* to shy
schi·vo -va *adj* averse; bashful, shy
schizzare *tr* to spray; to sprinkle; to ooze (*venom*); to sketch; schizzare fuoco dagli occhi to have fire in one's eyes || *intr* (ESSERE) to gush; to squirt; to dart; gli occhi gli schizzano dall'orbita his eyes are popping out of his head
schizzétto *m* sprayer; syringe; water pistol
schizzinó·so -sa [s] *adj* finicky, fastidious
schizzo *m* spray; splash; sketch; survey (*e.g., of literature*)
sci *m* (sci) ski
scia *f* wake; track; trail; scia di condensazione contrail
sciàbola *f* saber
sciabordare (sciabórdo) *tr* to shake, agitate || *intr* to break (*said of waves*)
sciacallo *m* jackal
sciacquadi·ta *m* (-ta) finger bowl
sciacquare (sciàcquo) *tr* to rinse
sciacquatura *f* rinse
sciacquì·o *m* (-i) splash, dash
sciàcquo *m* rinsing (*of the mouth*); mouthwash
sciagura *f* calamity, misfortune
sciagura·to -ta *adj* unfortunate; wretched
scialacquare (scialàcquo) *tr* to squander
scialare *tr* to squander || *intr* to be well off; to live it up
scial·bo -ba *adj* pale, faded; wan
scialle *m* shawl; scialle da viaggio traveling blanket
scialo *m* squandering; opulence; a scialo lavishly
scialuppa *f* launch; lifeboat
sciamanna·to -ta *adj* slovenly
sciamannó·ne -na *mf* slovenly person || *f* slattern
sciamare *intr* (ESSERE & AVERE) to swarm
sciame *m* swarm; flock
sciampagna *f* champagne
scianca·to -ta *adj* cripple, lame; wobbly (*table*)
sciangài *m* pick-up-sticks || Sciangài *f* Shanghai
sciarada *f* charade
sciare §119 *intr* to ski; to back water
sciarpa *f* scarf; sash (*e.g., of an officer or of a mayor*)
scias·sì *m* (-sì) chassis
sciàtica *f* (pathol) sciatica
scia·tóre -trice *mf* skier
sciatterìa *f* or sciattézza *f* slovenliness
sciat·to -ta *adj* slovenly, sloppy
scibile *m* knowledge
sciènte *adj* conscious; knowing
scientìfi·co -ca *adj* (-ci -che) scientific
sciènza *f* science; knowledge

scienzia·to -ta *mf* scientist
scilinguàgnolo *m* frenum (*of tongue*);
avere lo scilinguagnolo sciolto to
have a loose tongue
Scilla *f* Scylla; fra Scilla e Cariddi
between Scylla and Charibdis
scimitarra *f* scimitar
scimmia *f* monkey; (coll) drunk; fare
la scimmia a to ape; scimmia antro-
pomorfa anthropoid ape
scimmié·sco -sca *adj* (-schi -sche)
monkeyish; apish
scimmiottare (scimmiòtto) *tr* to ape
scimpan·zé *m* (-zé) chimpanzee
scimuni·to -ta *adj* idiotic || *mf* idiot
scìndere §247 *tr* (lit) to split; to separate
scintilla *f* spark; sparkle; (fig) scintilla;
scintilla elettrica jump spark
scintillare *intr* to spark; to sparkle
scintillì·o *m* (-i) sparkle, brilliance
scioccare §197 *tr* to shock
sciocchézza *f* silliness; trifle
sciòc·co -ca (-chi -che) *adj* silly, foolish
|| *mf* fool, blockhead
sciògliere §127 *tr* to loosen; to release;
to unfasten, untie; to solve; to disperse; to dissolve; to limber; to fulfill
(*a promise*); to unfurl (*sails*) || *ref*
to loosen up; to get loose; to dissolve; to melt (*into tears*)
scioglilin·gua *m*(-gue) tongue twister
scioglimento *m* melting; dissolution;
fulfillment; denouement
sciolina *f* ski wax
scioltézza *f* nimbleness, agility, freedom (*of movement*); ease
sciòl·to -ta *adj* loose; glib; free; blank
(*verse*)
scioperante *adj* striking || *m* striker
scioperare (sciòpero) *intr* to strike
sciopera·to -ta *adj* loafing; lazy || *m*
loafer
sciòpero *m* strike; walkout; sciopero a
singhiozzo slowdown strike; sciopero
bianco sit-down strike; sciopero della
fame hunger strike; sciopero di solidarietà sympathy strike; sciopero
pignolo slowdown
sciorinare *tr* to display; to tell (*lies*);
to air (*laundry*)
sciovìa *f* ski lift
sciovinismo *m* chauvinism, jingoism
scipi·to -ta *adj* insipid
scippo *m* snatching (*e.g., of a bag*)
sciròc·co *m* (-chi) sirocco; southeast
sciròppo *m* syrup
sci·sma *m* (-smi) schism
scismàti·co -ca *adj* (-ci -che) schismatic
scissióne *f* split; (biol, phys) fission
scis·so ·sa *adj* split, rent
scisto *m* schist
sciupare *tr* to spoil; to wear out; to
waste; to rumple || *ref* to wear; to
run down (*said of health*); to get
rumpled
sciupa·to -ta *adj* ruined; worn out;
wasted; run down
sciupì·o *m* (-i) waste
sciupó·ne -na *mf* waster, squanderer
sciu·scià *m* (-scià) bootblack; urchin
scìvola *f* chute

scivolare (scìvolo) *intr* (ESSERE & AVERE)
to slide, glide; to steal; scivolare
d'ala (aer) to sideslip
scivolata *f* slide, glide; scivolata d'ala
(aer) sideslip
scìvolo *m* chute; (aer) slip (*for sea-
planes*)
scivolóne *m* slip, slide
scivoló·so ·sa [s] *adj* slippery
scoccare §197 (scòcco) *tr* to shoot (*an
arrow*); to give (*a buss*); to strike
(*the hour*) || *intr* (ESSERE) to dart; to
spring; to strike (*said of a clock*);
to shoot
scocciare §128 (scòccio) *tr* (coll) to
break; (coll) to bother; (naut) to
unhook || *ref* to be bored
scoccia·tóre -trice *mf* (coll) nuisance
scocciatura *f* (coll) bother, annoyance
scòc·co *m* (-chi) darting; stroke (*e.g.,
of three*); (naut) hook; scocco di
baci bussing, kissing
scodèlla *f* bowl; soup plate
scodellare (scodèllo) *tr* to dish out
scodellino *m* small bowl; (mil) pan (*of
musket lock*)
scodinzolare (scodìnzolo) *intr* to wag
its tail; to waddle (*said of a woman*)
scoglièra *f* reef (*of rocks*); scogliera
corallina coral reef
scò·glio *m* (-gli) rock; reef; cliff; stumbling block
scoiare §248 *tr* to skin
scoiàttolo *m* squirrel
scolabrò·do *m* (-do) colander, strainer
scolafrit·to *m* (-to) strainer
scolapa·sta *m* (-sta) (coll) colander
scolare (scólo) *tr* to drain; (fig) to
polish off || *intr* (ESSERE) to drip ||
ref to melt
scolaré·sco -sca (-schi -sche) *adj* school
|| *f* schoolchildren; student body
scola·ro -ra *mf* pupil; student
scolàsti·co -ca (-ci -che) *adj* school;
scholastic || *m* scholastic, schoolman
|| *f* scholasticism
scola·tóio *m* (-tói) drain; strainer
scolatura *f* drip, drippings; dregs
scollaccia·to -ta *adj* low-necked; wearing a low-cut dress; dirty, obscene
scollare (scòllo) *tr* to cut off at the
neck; to unglue || *ref* to wear a low-
necked dress; to come unglued
scollatura *f* neckline; ungluing; scollatura a barchetta low neck; scollatura
a punta V neck
scòllo *m* neck, neckline
scólo *m* drain; drainage; (slang) clap
scolopèndra *f* centipede
scolorare (scolóro) *tr*, *intr* (ESSERE), &
ref to fade, discolor; to pale
scolorire §176 *tr*, *intr* (ESSERE), & *ref*
to fade, discolor
scolpare (scólpo) *tr* to excuse
scolpire §176 *tr* to sculpture; to engrave; to emphasize
scòlta *f* (lit) sentry; fare la scolta to
stand guard
scombaciare §128 *tr* to pull apart,
separate
scombinare *tr* to disarrange; to upset
scómbro *m* mackerel

scombù·glio *m* (**-gli**) (coll) disorder

scombussolare (**scombùssolo**) *tr* to upset

scomméssa *f* bet, wager

scomméttere §198 *tr* to bet; to separate

scommetti·tóre -trice *mf* bettor

scomodare (**scòmodo**) *tr* to trouble, disturb ǁ *ref* to take the trouble

scomodi·tà *f* (**-tà**) trouble, inconvenience

scòmo·do -da *adj* awkward, unwieldy; uncomfortable ǁ *m* inconvenience

scompaginare (**scompàgino**) *tr* to upset; (typ) to pi

scompagna·to -ta *adj* odd

scomparire §108 *intr* (ESSERE) to disappear; to make a bad showing

scompar·so -sa *adj* disappeared; extinct ǁ *mf* deceased ǁ *f* disappearance; death

scompartiménto *m* compartment; partition

scompènso *m* lack of compensation; imbalance

scompigliare §280 *tr* to disarray; to trouble, upset

scompì·glio *m* (**-gli**) disarray; upset

scompisciare §128 *tr* (vulg) to piss on ǁ *ref* (vulg) to wet oneself; **scompisciarsi dalla risa** (coll) to split one's sides laughing

scomplè·to -ta *adj* incomplete

scompórre §218 *tr* to decompose, disintegrate; to rumple; to dishevel; to upset; to dismantle, take apart; (typ) to pi ǁ *ref* to lose one's composure

scompó·sto -sta *adj* unseemly

scomùni·ca *f* (**-che**) excommunication

scomunicare §197 (**scomùnico**) *tr* to excommunicate; (joc) to ostracize

sconcertare (**sconcèrto**) *tr* to upset; to disconcert ǁ *ref* to become disconcerted

sconcézza *f* obscenity, indecency

scón·cio -cia (**-ci -ce**) *adj* dirty, filthy, obscene ǁ *m* obscenity; shame

sconclusiona·to -ta *adj* inconsequential; incoherent; rambling

sconcordanza *f* disagreement; (gram) lack of agreement

scondi·to -ta *adj* unseasoned

sconfessare (**sconfèsso**) *tr* to disavow; to retract

sconfessióne *f* disavowal

sconfiggere §104 *tr* to defeat, rout; to pull (*a nail*); to unfasten

sconfinare *intr* to cross the border; **sconfinare da** to stray from

sconfina·to -ta *adj* boundless, unlimited

sconfitta *f* defeat, rout

sconfortante *adj* discouraging

sconfortare (**sconfòrto**) *tr* to discourage; to distress ǁ *ref* to become discouraged

sconfòrto *m* depression; distress

scongelare (**scongèlo**) *tr* to thaw

scongiurare *tr* to conjure; to implore

scongiuro *m* conjuration; entreaty

sconnès·so -sa *adj* disconnected; incoherent

sconnèttere §107 *tr* to disconnect; to take apart ǁ *intr* to be incoherent

sconoscènte *adj* unappreciative

sconosciu·to -ta *adj* unknown ǁ *mf* stranger

sconquassare *tr* to smash, shatter

sconquassa·to -ta *adj* broken-down; upset

sconquasso *m* destruction; confusion; smash-up

sconsacrare *tr* to desecrate

sconsideratézza *f* thoughtlessness

sconsidera·to -ta *adj* inconsiderate

sconsigliare §280 *tr* to dissuade, discourage

sconsiglia·to -ta *adj* thoughtless

sconsola·to -ta *adj* disconsolate

scontare (**scónto**) *tr* to expiate; to discount; to serve (*time in jail*)

scontentare (**scontènto**) *tr* to dissatisfy

scontèn·to -ta *adj* & *m* discontent

scónto *m* discount; part payment; (fig) partial remission

scontrare (**scóntro**) *tr* to meet; (naut) to turn (*the wheel*) sharply ǁ *ref* to clash; to collide; to come to blows

scontrino *m* check, ticket

scóntro *m* collision; battle, encounter; clash; ward (*of key*)

scontró·so -sa [s] *adj* peevish, cross

sconveniènte *adj* unfavorable; unseemly, unbecoming; indecent

sconvenire §282 *intr* (ESSERE) to be unseemly or unbecoming

sconvòlgere §289 *tr* to upset; to disconcert

sconvolgiménto *m* upsetting; **sconvolgimento di stomaco** stomach upset; **sconvolgimento tellurico** upheaval

sconvòl·to -ta *adj* upset; disconcerted; distracted

scópa *f* broom; **scopa per lavaggio** mop

scopare (**scópo**) *tr* to sweep

scopata *f* sweep

scoperchiare §287 (**scopèrchio**) *tr* to uncover; to take the lid off

scopèr·to -ta *adj* uncovered; open; bare; exposed; unpaid ǁ *m* open ground; open air; overdraft; (econ) short sale; (com) balance; **allo scoperto** in the open; overdrawn (*check*); short (*sale*) ǁ *f* discovery; **alla scoperta** openly

scòpo *m* purpose, goal, aim

scoppiare §287 (**scòppio**) *tr* to uncouple ǁ *intr* (ESSERE) to burst; to blow; to explode; to break (*said, e.g., of news*); (fig) to die (*e.g., of overeating*); **scoppiare a** to burst out (*laughing or crying*)

scoppiettare (**scoppiétto**) *intr* to crackle

scoppiettì·o *m* (**-i**) crackle

scòp·pio *m* (**-pi**) burst; explosion; outbreak; outburst; blowout (*of tire*); **a scoppio** internal-combustion (*engine*); **scoppio di tuono** clap of thunder

scòppola *f* drop (*of plane in air pocket*); (coll) rabbit punch

scopriménto *m* uncovering; unveiling

scoprire §110 *tr* to uncover; to unveil; to discover; to expose ǁ *ref* to take off one's clothes; to take one's hat off; to reveal oneself

scopri·tóre -trice *mf* discoverer
scoraggiaménto *m* discouragement
scoraggiante *adj* discouraging
scoraggiare §290 *tr* to discourage, dishearten ‖ *ref* to be or become discouraged
scoraménto *m* (lit) discouragement
scorbuto *m* scurvy
scorciare §128 (**scórcio**) *tr* to shorten; to foreshorten ‖ *intr* (ESSERE) to shorten, grow shorter; to look foreshortened ‖ *ref* to shorten, grow shorter
scorciatóia *f* shortcut, cutoff
scór·cio *m* (-**ci**) foreshortening; end, close (*of a period*); **di scorcio** foreshortened
scordare (**scòrdo**) *tr* to forget; to put out of tune ‖ *ref* to forget; to get out of tune
scorég·gia *f* (-**ge**) (vulg) fart
scoreggiare §290 (**scoréggio**) *intr* (vulg) to fart
scòrgere §249 *tr* to perceive, to discern
scòria *f* slag, dross; (fig) scum, dregs; **scorie atomiche** atomic waste
scorna·to -ta *adj* humiliated, ridiculed; hornless
scòrno *m* humiliation, ridicule
scorpacciata *f* bellyful; **fare una scorpacciata di** to stuff oneself with
scorpióne *m* scorpion ‖ **Scorpione** *m* (astrol) Scorpio
scorrazzare *tr* to wander over ‖ *intr* to run around; to move about; (fig) to ramble; (mil) to raid
scórrere §139 *tr* to raid; to glance over ‖ *intr* (ESSERE) to flow; to run; to glide
scorrerìa *f* raid, foray, incursion
scorrettézza *f* imprecision; impropriety
scorrèt·to -ta *adj* incorrect; improper
scorrévole *adj* sliding; flowing, fluent ‖ *m* slide (*of slide rule*)
scorribanda *f* raid, foray, incursion
scór·so -sa *adj* past, last ‖ *m* error, slip ‖ *f* glance; short stay
scor·sólo -sóla *adj* (-**sói -sóle**) slip (*knot*)
scòrta *f* escort; provision, stock; **di scorta** spare (*tire*); **fare di scorta a** to escort; **scorta d'onore** (mil) honor guard; **scorte** (com) stockpile; (com) supplies; **scorte morte** agricultural supplies; **scorte vive** livestock
scortare (**scòrto**) *tr* to escort; to foreshorten
scortecciare §128 (**scortéccio**) *tr* to strip the bark from; to peel off; to scrape ‖ *ref* to peel off
scortése *adj* discourteous, impolite
scortesìa *f* discourtesy, impoliteness
scorticare §197 (**scórtico**) *tr* to skin; to be overdemanding with (*students*); to fleece ‖ *ref* to skin (*e.g., one's arm*)
scòrza *f* bark; skin, hide; (fig) appearance; **scorza di limone** lemon peel
scoscendiménto *m* landslide; cliff
scoscé·so -sa [s] *adj* sloping, steep
scòssa *f* shake; jerk; **scossa di pioggia** downpour; **scossa di terremoto** earth tremor; **scossa elettrica** electric shock; **scossa tellurica** earthquake
scossóne *m* jolt, jerk
scostaménto *m* removal; separation
scostare (**scòsto**) *tr* to move away; to try to avoid ‖ *intr* (ESSERE) to stand away ‖ *ref* to step aside; to stray
scostuma·to -ta *adj* dissolute, debauched
scotennare (**scoténno**) *tr* to scalp; to skin (*an animal*)
scòtta *f* whey; (naut) sheet
scottante *adj* burning (*question*); outrageous (*offense*)
scottare (**scòtto**) *tr* to burn; to scald; to sear; to boil (*eggs*); (fig) to sting ‖ *intr* to burn; to be hot (*said of stolen goods*) ‖ *ref* to get burnt
scottatura *f* burn; (fig) blow, jolt
scòt·to -ta *adj* overcooked, overdone ‖ *m*—**pagare lo scotto** to foot the bill; **pagare lo scotto di** to expiate ‖ *f* see **scotta**
scoutismo *m* scouting
scovare (**scóvo**) *tr* to rouse (*game*); to find, discover
scovolino *m* pipe cleaner; (mil) small swab
scóvolo *m* (mil) swab
scòzia *f* (archit) scotia ‖ **la Scozia** Scotland
scozzése [s] *adj* Scotch, Scottish ‖ *m* Scotch, Scottish (*language*); Scotchman ‖ *f* Scotchwoman
scozzonare (**scozzóno**) *tr* to break in (*a horse*); to train
scranna *f* (hist) seat
screanza·to -ta *adj* ill-mannered, rude
screditare (**scrédito**) *tr* to discredit
scremare (**scrèmo**) *tr* to cream
scrematrice *f* cream separator
screpolare (**scrèpolo**) *tr*, *intr* (ESSERE), & *ref* to crack; to chap
screpolatura *f* crack; chap (*of skin*)
screziare §287 (**scrèzio**) *tr* to mottle, variegate
scrè·zio *m* (-**zi**) tiff
scri·ba *m* (-**bi**) scribe (*Jewish scholar*)
scribacchiare §287 *tr* to scribble, scrawl
scribacchino *m* scribbler; hack
scricchiolare (**scrìcchiolo**) *intr* to crack, creak
scricchiolì·o *m* (-**i**) crack, creak
scricciolo *m* wren
scrigno *m* jewel box
scriminatura *f* part (*in hair*)
scrit·to -ta *adj* written ‖ *m* writing ‖ *f* sign; inscription; contract; **scritta luminosa** electric sign
scrit·tóio *m* (-**tói**) writing desk
scrit·tóre -trice *mf* writer
scrittura *f* handwriting; penmanship; writing; contract; entry; (theat) booking; **Sacra Scrittura** Holy Scripture; **scrittura privata** contract; **scrittura pubblica** deed, indenture; **scrittura a macchina** typing
scritturale *adj* scriptural ‖ *m* clerk; copyist; fundamentalist
scritturare *tr* (theat) to book, engage
scrivanìa *f* desk

scrivano *m* clerk, copyist, typist

scrivere §250 *tr & intr* to write; **scrivere a macchina** to type

scroccare §197 (scròcco) *tr* to sponge (*a meal*); to manage to get (*a prize*) || *intr* to sponge

scrocca·tóre -trice *mf* sponger

scròc·co *m* (-chi) sponging; creaking; **a scrocco** sponging; spring (*lock*); switchblade (*knife*)

scroccó·ne -na *mf* sponger

scròfa *f* sow; slut

scrollare (scròllo) *tr* to shake; to shrug (*one's shoulders*) || *ref* to get into action; to pull oneself together

scrollata *f* shake; **scrollata di spalle** shrug

scrosciare §128 (scròscio) *intr* (ESSERE & AVERE) to pelt down; (fig) to thunder

scrò·scio *m* (-sci) thunder, roar; **scroscio di pioggia** downpour; **scroscio di tuono** thunderclap

scrostare (scròsto) *tr* to pick (*a scab*); to scrape; to peel off || *ref* to peel off

scrosta·to -ta *adj* peeling; scaly

scròto *m* scrotum

scrùpolo *m* scruple; scrupulousness

scrupoló·so -sa [s] *adj* scrupulous

scrutare *tr* to scan, scrutinize

scruta·tóre -trice *adj* inquisitive || *mf* teller (*of votes*)

scrutina·tóre -trice *mf* teller (*of votes*)

scruti·nio *m* (-ni) poll, vote; evaluation (*of an examination*); count (*of votes*); **scrutinio segreto** secret ballot

scucire §143 *tr* to unstitch; (coll) to cough up || *ref* to come unstitched

scucitura *f* unstitching; rip

scuderia *f* stable

scudétto *m* badge; escutcheon; (sports) badge of victory

scudièro *m* esquire

scudisciare §128 *tr* to whip

scudi·scio *m* (-sci) whip

scudo *m* shield; escutcheon; **far scudo a** to shield

scùffia *f* (coll) load (*intoxication*); **fare scuffia** to capsize; **prendersi una scuffia per** to fall for, to fall in love with

scugnizzo *m* Neapolitan urchin

sculacciare §128 *tr* to spank

sculacciata *f* spank, spanking

sculacció·ne *m* spank, spanking

sculettare (sculétto) *intr* to waddle

scul·tóre -trice *mf* sculptor || *f* sculptress

scultura *f* sculpture

scuòla *f* school; **scuola allievi ufficiali** military academy; officers' candidate school; **scuola dell'obbligo** mandatory education; **scuola di danza** dancing school; **scuola di dressaggio** obedience school (*for dogs*); **scuola di guerra** war college; **scuola di guida** driving school; **scuola di perfezionamento per laureati** postgraduate school; **scuola di taglio** sewing school; **scuola materna** kindergarten; **scuola mista** coeducational school

scuòla·bus *m* (-bus) school bus

scuòtere §251 *tr* to shake; to shake up; **scuotere di dosso** to shake off

scure *f* ax; cleaver

scurire §176 *tr, intr* (ESSERE), & *ref* to darken

scu·ro -ra *adj* dark || *m* darkness; dark; shutter; **essere allo scuro** to be in the dark

scurrile *adj* scurrilous

scusa *f* excuse; apology; pretext; **chiedere scusa** to apologize

scusare *tr* to excuse; to pardon; to apologize for; **scusi!** pardon me! || *ref* to apologize; to beg off

sdaziare §287 *tr* to clear through customs

sdebitare (sdébito) *tr* to free from debt || *ref* to become free of debt; **sdebitarsi con** to repay a favor to

sdegnare (sdégno) *tr* to scorn; to arouse, enrage || *ref* to get mad

sdégno *m* indignation, anger; (lit) scorn

sdegnó·so -sa [s] *adj* indignant; haughty

sdenta·to -ta *adj* toothless

sdilinquire §176 *tr* to weaken || *intr* (ESSERE) & *ref* to swoon; to become mawkish

sdoganare *tr* to clear through customs

sdolcina·to -ta *adj* mawkish

sdolcinatura *f* mush, slobber

sdoppiare §287 (sdóppio) *tr & ref* to split

sdoppiaménto *m* splitting

sdottoreggiare §290 (sdottoréggio) *intr* to pontificate

sdràia *f* chaise longue; deck chair

sdraiare §287 *tr* to lay down || *ref* to stretch out (*e.g., on the ground*)

sdràio *m* (sdrài) stretching out; **mettersi a sdraio** to lie down

sdrucciolare (sdrùcciolo) *intr* (ESSERE & AVERE) to slip, slide

sdrucciolévole *adj* slippery

sdrùccio·lo -la *adj* proparoxytone || *m* slip; slope; proparoxytone

sdruccioló·ni *adv* slipping, sliding

sdrucire (sdrùcio) & §176 *tr* to tear, rend, rip

sdrucitura *f* tear, rend, rip

se *m* (se) if || §5 *pron* || *conj* if; whether; **se mai** in the event; **se no** otherwise; **se non tu** (lui, lei, etc.) nobody else but you (him, her, etc.), e.g., **non puoi essere stato se non tu** it could not have been anyone else but you; **se non altro** at least; **se non che** but; **se pure** even if

sé §5 *pron* himself; herself; itself; yourself; themselves; yourselves; oneself; **di per sé stesso** by itself; **fuori di sé** beside oneself; **rientrare in sé** to come back to one's senses; **uscire di sé** to be beside oneself

sebbène *conj* although, though

sèbo *m* sebum, tallow

séc·ca *f* (-che) sand bank, shoal; drought; **dare in secca** to run aground; **in secca** hard up

seccante *adj* drying; annoying

seccare §197 (sécco) *tr* to dry; to bore;

to bother, annoy || *intr* (ESSERE) to dry up || *ref* to dry up; to be annoyed

secca·tóio *m* (-tói) drying room; squeegee (*to remove water from wet decks*)

secca·tóre -trice *mf* bore, pest

seccatura *f* drying; trouble, nuisance

sécchia *f* bucket, pail; **piovere a secchie** to rain cats and dogs

secchièllo *m* little bucket

séc·chio *m* (-chi) bucket, pail; bucketful; **secchio dell'immondezza** trash can

séc·co -ca (-chi -che) *adj* dry; lanky; sharp || *m* dryness; dry land; drought; **a secco dry** (*cleaning*); **dare in secco** to run aground; **in secco** hard up; **lavare a secco** to dry-clean || *f* see **secca**

secenté·sco -sca -sca *adj* (-schi -sche) seventeenth-century

secentèsi·mo -ma *adj, m & pron* six hundredth

secèrnere §153 (*pp* **secrèto**) *tr* to secrete

secessióne *f* secession

séco §5 *prep phrase* (lit) with oneself; along, e.g., **portare seco** to bring along

secolare *adj* secular; century-old; worldly || *m* layman

sècolo *m* century; age; world

secónda *f* second; second-year class; **a seconda** with the wind; **a seconda di** according to; **in seconda** (aut) in second; (mil) second in command

secondare (**secóndo**) *tr* to second

secondà·rio -ria *adj* (-ri -rie) secondary

secondino *m* prison guard, turnkey

secón·do -da *adj* second; (lit) favorable || *m* second; second course; (nav) executive officer || *f* see **seconda** || *pron* second || **secondo** *prep* according to; **secondo me** (**te**, *etc.*) in my (your, etc.) opinion

secondogèni·to -ta *adj* second-born

secrezióne *f* secretion

sèdano *m* celery

sedare (**sèdo**) *tr* to calm, placate

sedatí·vo -va *adj & m* sedative

sède *f* seat; branch; residence; period; (gram) syllable; (rr) right of way; **in separata sede** in private; (law) with change of venue; **Santa Sede** Holy See; **sede centrale** main office, home office

sedentà·rio -ria *adj* (-ri -rie) *adj* sedentary || *m* sedentary person

sedére *m* sitting; rear, backside || *v* §252 *intr* (ESSERE) to sit, to be seated; to be in session; to be located || *ref* to sit down

sèdia *f* chair; seat; see; **sedia a braccioli** armchair; **sedia a dondolo** rocking chair; **sedia a pozzetto** bucket seat; **sedia a sdraio** deck chair; **sedia da posta** (hist) mail coach; **sedia di vimini** wicker chair; **sedia elettrica** electric chair; **sedia girevole** swivel chair

sedicènne *adj* sixteen-year-old || *mf* sixteen-year-old person

sedicènte *adj* so-called, self-styled

sedicèsi·mo -ma *adj, m & pron* sixteenth

sédici *adj & pron* sixteen; **le sedici** four P.M. || *m* sixteen; sixteenth (*in dates*)

sedile *m* seat; bench; bottom (*of chair*); (aut) bucket seat

sediménto *m* sediment

sediòlo *m* sulky

sedizióne *f* sedition

sedizió·so -sa [s] *adj* seditious

seducènte *adj* seductive; alluring

sedurre §102 *tr* to seduce; to allure; to lead astray; to charm, captivate

seduta *f* sitting; session, meeting; **seduta fiume** (pol) uninterrupted session; **seduta stante** on the spot

sedut·tóre -trice *adj* seductive; alluring; charming || *mf* seducer

seduzióne *f* seduction; allurement; charm

sefardi·ta (-ti -te) *adj* Sephardic || *mf* Sephardi

sé·ga *f* (-ghe) saw; **a sega** serrated; **sega a nastro** band saw; **sega circolare** buzz saw; **sega da carpentiere** lumberman's saw; **sega intelaiata a lama** hacksaw; **sega meccanica** power saw

ségala *f* rye

segali·gno -gna *adj* rye; lean, wiry

segare §209 (**ségo**) *tr* to saw; to cut

segatrice *f* power saw; **segatrice a disco** circular saw; **segatrice a nastro** band saw

segatura *f* cutting; sawdust

seggétta *f* commode

sèg·gio *m* (-gi) seat (*e.g., in congress*); **seggio elettorale** voting commission

sèggiola *f* chair; **seggiola a sdraio** deck chair

seggiolino *m* child's chair; stool; bucket seat; **seggiolino eiettabile** (aer) ejection seat

seggiolóne *m* highchair; easy chair

seggiovia *f* chair lift

segheria *f* sawmill

seghetta·to -ta *adj* serrated

seghétto *m* hacksaw; **seghetto da traforo** coping saw

segménto *m* segment; **segmento elastico** (aut) piston ring

segnaccénto *m* accent mark

segnàcolo *m* (lit) symbol, sign

segnalare *tr* to signal; to point out || *ref* to distinguish oneself

segnalazióne *f* signaling; sign, signal; nomination; recommendation; **dare la segnalazione a** to notify; **fare segnalazioni** to signal; **segnalazioni stradali** road signs

segnale *m* sign; signal; bookmark; **segnale di allarme** (mil) alarm; **segnale di occupato** (telp) busy signal; **segnale di via libera** (telp) dial tone; **segnale orario** (rad, telv) time signal; **segnali stradali** road signs

segnalèti·co -ca *adj* (-ci -che) identification (*mark*) || *f* road signs

segnalibro *m* bookmark

segnalìne·e *m* (-e) lineman

segnapósto *m* place card

segnapun·ti *m* (-ti) scorekeeper

segnare (ségno) *tr* to mark; to underscore, underline; to jot down; to say
(*e.g., five o'clock, said of a watch*);
to brand; (sports) to score; **segnare
a dito** to point to || *ref* to cross one-
self

segnàtas·se *m* (-se) postage-due stamp

segnatura *f* signing; signature; library
number; (eccl) chancery; (sports)
final score; (typ) signature

segnavèn·to *m* (-to) weather vane

ségno *m* mark; bookmark; symbol;
sign; signal; boundary; (mus) signature; **a segno che** so that; **a tal segno
to such a point;** **essere fatto segno di**
to be the target of; **in segno di** as a
token of; **mettere a segno** to check,
control; **segno della Croce** sign of the
Cross; **segno di croce** cross (*mark*);
segno d'interpunzione, or **di punteggiatura,** or **grafico** punctuation mark;
segno di riconoscimento identification mark

ségo *m* tallow, suet

segregare §209 (sègrego) *tr* to segre-
gate; to secrete || *ref* to withdraw

segregazióne *f* segregation; **segregazione cellulare** solitary confinement

segregazioni·sta *mf* (-sti -ste) segregationist

segretariato *m* secretariat

segretà·rio -ria *mf* secretary; clerk

segreteria *f* secretary's office; secretary-
ship

segretézza *f* secrecy

segré·to -ta *adj* secret; secretive || *m*
secret; secrecy; **segreto d'alcova**
boudoir secret; **segreto di Pulcinella**
open secret

seguace *mf* follower

seguènte *adj* following, next

segù·gio *m* (-gi) bloodhound; (fig) private eye

seguire (séguo) *tr* to follow; to attend
|| *intr* (ESSERE) to continue; to follow,
ensue; (with *dat*) to follow

seguitare (séguito) *intr*—**seguitare a +
inf** to keep on + *ger*, e.g., **seguitare
a parlare** to keep on talking; **seguiti!**
go ahead!

séguito *m* following; retinue; followers; sequence; sequel; pursuit; **di
seguito** in succession; **far seguito a**
to refer to; **in seguito** thereafter; **in
seguito a** as a consequence of

sèi *adj & pron* six; **le sei** six o'clock ||
m six; sixth (*in dates*)

seicènto *adj, m & pron* six hundred ||
f car with a motor displacing 600
cubic centimeters || **il Seicento** the
seventeenth century

seimila *adj, m, & pron* six thousand

sélce *f* silica; flint; (lit) stone; **selci**
paving blocks

selciare §128 (sélcio) *tr* to pave

selcia·to -ta *adj* paved || *m* paving

seletti·vo -va *adj* selective

selezionare (selezióno) *tr* to select, sort
out

selezióne *f* selection; choice

sèlla *f* saddle

sel·làio *m* (-lài) saddler

sellare (sèllo) *tr* to saddle

selleria *f* saddler's shop; saddlery; (aut)
upholstery

sélva *f* woods, forest

selvaggina *f* game

selvàg·gio -gia (-gi -ge) *adj* savage;
vicious (*horse*) || *m* savage; unsocia-
ble person

selvàti·co -ca *adj* (-ci -che) wild

selvicoltura *f* forestry

sèlz *m* (sèlz) seltzer, club soda

semàforo *m* traffic light; semaphore

semànti·co -ca (-ci -che) *adj* semantic
|| *f* semantics

sembiante *m* (lit) look; **fare sembianti
di** to pretend

sembianza *f* look; (lit) similarity

sembrare (sémbro) *intr* (ESSERE) to
seem, look, appear || *impers*—**sembra**
it seems

séme *m* seed; stone (*of fruit*); (cards)
suit

seménta *f* sowing season; (lit) seed

seménte *f* seed

semènza *f* seed; brads (*used in upholstery*)

semenzà·io *m* (-zài) hotbed, seedbed

semestrale *adj* semiannual, semiyearly

semèstre *m* semester; half year

sèmi- *pref adj* semi-, e.g., **semicircolare**
semicircular; half-, e.g., **semichiuso**
half-closed || *pref mf* semi-, e.g.,
semicerchio semicircle; half, e.g.,
semitono half tone; demi-, e.g., **semidio** demigod

semiapèr·to -ta *adj* half-open; ajar

semiasse *m* (mach) axle (*on each side
of differential*)

semicér·chio *m* (-chi) semicircle

semichiu·so -sa [s] *adj* half-closed

semicingola·to -ta *adj & m* half-track

semicircolo *m* semicircle

semiconduttóre *m* semiconductor

semiconvit·tóre -trice *mf* day student

semicù·pio *m* (-pi) sitz bath

semi·dìo *m* (-dèi) demigod

semidòt·to -ta *adj* semilearned

semifinale *f* semifinal

sémina *f* sowing; sowing season

seminare (sémino) *tr* to sow, seed; to
plant; (coll) to leave behind

seminà·rio *m* (-ri) seminary; seminar

seminari·sta *m* (-sti) seminarian

semina·to -ta *adj* sown, seeded || *m*
sown land; **uscire dal seminato** to
digress

semina·tóre -trice *mf* sower || *f* (mach)
seeder, seeding machine

seminterrato *m* basement

seminu·do -da *adj* half-naked

semioscurità *f* partial darkness

semirigi·do -da *adj* semirigid; inelastic

semirimòr·chio *m* (-chi) semitrailer

semisè·rio -ria [s] *adj* (-ri -rie) serio-
comic

semisfèra *f* (geom) hemisphere

semi·ta (-ti -te) *adj* Semitic || *mf* Semite

semitòno *m* (mus) semitone, half tone

semmài *conj* if ever; in the event that

sémola *f* bran; (coll) freckles

semolino *m* semolina

semovènte *adj* self-propelled

sempitèr·no -na *adj* (lit) everlasting
sémplice *adj* simple; single; plain; mere; (mil) private; (nav) ordinary || *m* medicinal herb; **semplici** simple folk
semplició·ne -na *adj* simple || *mf* simpleton
semplici·tà *f* (-tà) simplicity
semplificare §197 (**semplìfico**) *tr* to simplify || *ref* to become easier or simpler
sèmpre *adv* always; ever; yet; **da sempre** from time immemorial; **di sempre** same, same old; **e poi sempre** ever and ever; **ma sempre** but only; **per sempre** forever; **sempre che** provided; **sempre meglio** better and better; **sempre meno** less and less; **sempre però** but only; **sempre vostro** very truly yours
semprevérde *adj*, *m* & *f* evergreen
sènape *f* mustard
senapismo *m* mustard plaster
senato *m* senate
sena·tóre -trice *mf* senator
senése [s] *adj* & *mf* Sienese
senile *adj* old; of old age
senilismo *m* (pathol) senility
senilità *f* old age
senióre *adj* & *m* elder, senior
Sènna *f* Seine
sénno *m* wisdom; **far senno** to come back to one's senses; **senno di poi** hindsight; **uscir di senno** to go out of one's mind
séno *m* chest; breast, bosom; cove; (anat) sinus; (math) sine; (fig) heart; **in seno a** within
senonché or **se non che** *conj* but
sensale *m* broker; commission merchant
sensa·to -ta *adj* sensible, reasonable; sane
sensazionale *adj* sensational
sensazióne *f* sensation
sensìbile *adj* sensible; perceptible; appreciable; sensitive; responsive (*e.g., to affection*) || *m* world of the senses
sensibili·tà *f* (-tà) sensitivity; sensibility
sensibilizzare [ddzz] *tr* to sensitize
sensiti·vo -va *adj* sensitive || *m* medium
sènso *m* sense; feeling; meaning; aspect; tone, fashion; direction; **ai sensi di legge** according to law; **a senso** free (*translation*); **doppio senso** double entendre; **in senso contrario** in the opposite direction; **perdere i sensi** to lose consciousness; **riprendere i sensi** to come to; **sensi carnali** appetite, flesh; **senso unico** one-way; **senso vietato** no entry, one-way
sensò·rio -ria *adj* (-ri -rie) sensory
sensuale *adj* sensual, carnal; sensuous
sensualità *f* sensuality
sentènza *f* sentence; maxim
sentenziare §287 (**sentènzio**) *tr* to pass sentence upon, sentence || *intr* to pontificate
sentenzió·so -sa [s] *adj* sententious
sentièro *m* path, pathway
sentimentale *adj* sentimental; mawkish
sentimentalismo *m* sentimentalism
sentiménto *m* feeling; sentiment; sense;

uscire di sentimento (coll) to go out of one's mind
sentina *f* bilge; sink (*of vice*)
sentinèlla *f* sentry, sentinel
sentire *m* feeling || *v* (**sènto**) *tr* to feel; to hear; to listen to; to consult (*a doctor*); to smell; to taste **farsi sentire** to make oneself heard || *intr* to feel; to listen; to smell; to taste; **non sentirci** di quell'orecchio to turn a deaf ear; **sentirci bene** to have keen hearing || *ref* to feel; **non sentirsela di** to not have the courage to; **sentirsela** to feel up to it
senti·to -ta *adj* heartfelt
sentóre *m* inkling, feeling; sign; (lit) smell
sènza *prep* without; beyond (*e.g., comparison*); **senza** + *inf* without + *ger*; **senza che** + *subj* without + *ger*; **senza di** + *pron* without + *pron*, e.g., **senza di lui** without him; **senz'altro** without any doubt, of course
senza·dìo *m* (-dìo)—i **senzadio** the godless
senzapà·tria *m* (-tria) man without a country; renegade
senzatét·to *m* (-to) homeless person; **i senzatetto** the homeless
separare *tr* & *ref* to separate
separazióne *f* separation
sepolcrale *adj* sepulchral
sepolcréto *m* cemetery
sepólcro *m* sepulcher, grave
sepoltura *f* burial; grave
seppellire §253 *tr* to bury
séppia *adj invar* sepia || *f* cuttlefish
seppure *conj* even if
sè·psi *f* (-psi) sepsis
sequèla *f* series
sequènza *f* sequence
sequestrare (**sequèstro**) *tr* to seize, confiscate; to kidnap; to confine; to quarantine; (law) to attach, sequester
sequèstro *m* seizure; attachment; **sequestro di persona** unlawful detention
séra *f* evening; night; **da mezza sera** cocktail (*dress*); dark (*suit*); **da sera** evening (*gown*); formal (*attire*)
serac·co *m* (-chi) serac
serafino *m* seraph
serale *adj* evening; night
seralménte *adv* in the evening; every evening
serata *f* evening; soiree, evening party; **serata d'addio** (theat) farewell performance; **di beneficenza** benefit performance
serbare (**sèrbo**) *tr* to keep; to save (*e.g., a place*); to bear (*a grudge*) || *ref* to keep oneself; to stay
serba·tóio *m* (-tói) tank; reservoir; cartridge clip
sèr·bo -ba *adj* & *mf* Serbian || *m*—**in serbo** in store
serbocroa·to -ta *adj* & *mf* Serbo-Croatian
serenata *f* serenade
serenìssi·mo -ma *adj* Serene (*Highness*)
sereni·tà *f* (-tà) serenity

seré•no -na *adj* serene; clear, fair (*weather*)

sergènte *m* sergeant; carpenter's clamp; sergente maggiore first sergeant

sèri•co -ca *adj* (-ci -che) silk

sè•rie *f* (-rie) series; (sports) division; fuori serie (aut) custom-built; in serie (aut) standard; (elec) in series

serietà *f* seriousness; gravity

serigrafia *f* silkscreen process

sè•rio -ria *adj* (-ri -rie) *adj* serious; stern; poco serio unreliable (*man*); loose (*woman*) || *m* seriousness; sul serio in earnest; really, e.g., bello sul serio really beautiful

sermonare (sermóno) *tr & intr* (lit) to sermonize

sermóne *m* sermon

sermoneggiare §290 (sermonéggio) *intr* to preach; to lecture

seròti•no -na *adj* late; (lit) evening

sèrpa *f* coach box

sèrpe *f* snake, serpent; a serpe coiled, in a coil; nutrirsi or scaldarsi la serpe in seno to nourish a viper in one's bosom

serpeggiare §290 (serpéggio) *intr* to zigzag; to wind; to creep, spread

serpènte *m* snake, serpent; serpente a sonagli rattlesnake

serpenti•no -na *adj* serpentine || *m* serpentine; coil (*of pipe*) || *f* zigzag, turn (*of winding road*); coil (*of pipe*)

sérqua *f* dozen; lot, large number

sèrra *f* dike, levee; hothouse; sierra; un serra serra a milling crowd

serrafi•la *m* (-le) rear-guard soldier || *f* rear ship (*of convoy*)

serrafilo *m* electrician's pliers; (elec) binding post

serrà•glio *m* (-gli) menagerie; seraglio

serramànico *m*—a serramanico clasp (*knife*); switchblade (*knife*)

serrame *m* lock

serraménto *m* closing, bolting || serramén•ti *m* & -ta *fpl* closing devices, doors, windows, and shutters

serranda *f* shutter (*of store*)

serrare (sèrro) *tr* to shut, close; to pursue (*the enemy*); to increase (*tempo*); to furl (*sails*); to lock; to clench (*one's teeth, one's fists*); to shake (*hands*) || *intr* to shut; to be tight || *ref* to be wrenched, e.g., gli si serrò il cuore his heart was wrenched; serrarsi addosso a to press (*the enemy*)

serrata *f* lockout

serrate *m*—serrate finale (sports) finish

serra•to -ta *adj* shut (*e.g., door*); concise (*style*); tight (*game*); rapid (*gallop*); closed (*ranks*); thick (*crowd*) || *f* see serrata

serratura *f* lock

sèrto *m* (poet) crown, wreath

sèrva *f* (pej) maidservant, maid

servènte *adj* (*gentleman*) in waiting || *m* gunner; (obs) servant

servìbile *adj* usable

serviènte *m* (eccl) server

servì•gio *m* (-gi) service; favor

servile *adj* servile; menial; modal (*auxiliary*)

servire (sèrvo) *tr* to serve; to wait on; in che posso servirLa? what can I do for you?; may I help you?; per servirLa at your service || *intr* to serve || *intr* (ESSERE & AVERE) to serve; to answer the purpose; to last; (with *dat*) (coll) to need, e.g., gli serve il martello he needs the hammer; non servire a nulla to be of no use; servire da to act as || *ref* to help oneself; servirsi da to patronize, deal with; servirsi di to avail oneself of, use

servitóre *m* servant; tea wagon; servitor suo umilissimo your humble servant

servi•tù *f* (-tù) servitude; captivity; servants, help; servitù di passaggio (law) easement

serviziévole *adj* obliging, accommodating

servi•zio *m* (-zi) service; favor; turn; a mezzo servizio part-time (*domestic help*); di servizio delivery (*entrance*); for hire (*car*); domestic (*help*); fuori servizio out of commission; in servizio in commission; servizi kitchen and bath; facilities; servizi pubblici public services; public works; servizio attivo active duty; servizio permanente effettivo service in the regular army

sèr•vo -va *adj* (lit) enslaved || *m* slave; servant; servo della gleba serf || *f* see serva

servoassisti•to -ta *adj* servocontrolled

servofréno *m* (aut) power brake

servomotóre *m* servomotor

servostèrzo *m* (aut) power steering

sèsamo *m* sesame; apriti sesamo! open sesame!

sessanta *adj, m & pron* sixty

sessantènne *adj* sixty-year-old || *mf* sixty-year-old person

sessantèsi•mo -ma *adj, m & pron* sixtieth

sessantina *f* about sixty

sessióne *f* session

sèsso *m* sex; il sesso debole the fair sex

sessuale *adj* sexual

sestante *m* sextant

sestétto *m* sextet

sestière *m* district, section

sè•sto -sta *adj & pron* sixth || *m* sixth; curve (*of an arch*); fuori sesto out of sorts; mettere in sesto to arrange; to set in order; sesto acuto (archit) ogive

sèt *m* (sèt) set; set all'aperto (mov) location

séta *f* silk; seta artificiale rayon

setacciare §128 *tr* to sift, sieve

setàc•cio *m* (-ci) sieve

setàce•o -a *adj* silky

séte *f* thirst; aver sete to be thirsty; to lust after; sete di thirst for

seteria *f* silk mill; seterie silk goods

setifi•cio *m* (-ci) silk mill

sètola *f* bristle; (joc) stubble

sètta *f* sect

settanta *adj, m & pron* seventy

settantènne *adj* seventy-year-old || *mf* seventy-year-old person

settantèsi•mo -ma *adj, m & pron* seventieth

settantina *f* about seventy

settà·rio -ria *adj* & *mf* (**-ri -rie**) sectarian

sètte *adj* & *pron* seven; **le sette** seven o'clock || *m* seven; seventh (*in dates*); V-shaped tear (*in clothing*)

settecentèsi·mo -ma *adj, m* & *pron* seven hundredth

settecènto *adj, m* & *pron* seven hundred || **il Settecento** the eighteenth century

settèmbre *m* September

settennale *adj* seven-year (*e.g., plan*)

settènne *adj* seven-year-old || *mf* seven-year-old child

settentrionale *adj* northern || *mf* northerner

settentrióne *m* north; (astr) Little Bear

setticemìa *f* septicemia

sètti·co -ca *adj* (**-ci -che**) septic

settimana *f* week; week's wages; **settimana corta** five-day week

settimanale *adj* & *m* weekly

settimi·no -na *adj* premature (*baby*) || *m* (mus) septet

sètti·mo -ma *adj, m* & *pron* seventh

sètto *m* septum

settóre *m* sector; section, branch; dissector, anatomist; coroner's pathologist

sevè·ro -ra *adj* severe, stern

seviziare §287 *tr* to torture

sevìzie *fpl* cruelty

sezionale *adj* sectional

sezionare (**sezióno**) *tr* to cut up; to divide up; to dissect

sezióne *f* section; dissection; chapter (*of club*); department (*of agency*); (geom) cross section

sfaccenda·to -ta *adj* loafing || *mf* loafer

sfaccettare (**sfacétto**) *tr* to facet

sfacchinare *intr* (coll) to toil, drudge

sfacchinata *f* (coll) drudgery, grind

sfacciatàggine *f* brazenness, impudence

sfaccia·to -ta *adj* brazen, impudent; loud, gaudy; **fare lo sfacciato** to be fresh

sfacèlo *m* breakdown, collapse

sfà·glio *m* (**-gli**) swerve (*e.g., of horse*); (cards) discard

sfaldare *tr* to exfoliate; to cut into slices || *ref* to flake, scale; (fig) to collapse, crumble

sfamare *tr* to feed (*the hungry; the family*) || *ref* to get enough to eat

sfare §173 *tr* to undo || *ref* to spoil (*said, e.g., of meat*)

sfarzo *m* pomp, display; luxury

sfarzó·so -sa [s] *adj* sumptuous, luxurious

sfasare *tr* to throw out of phase; (coll) to depress || *intr* (ESSERE) (aut) to misfire; (elec) to be out of phase

sfasciare §128 *tr* to remove the bandage from; to unswathe; to smash, shatter || *ref* to go to pieces; to lose one's figure

sfatare *tr* to discredit; to unmask

sfatica·to -ta *adj* lazy || *mf* loafer

sfat·to -ta *adj* overdone; overripe; undone (*bed*); ravaged (*by age*)

sfavillare *intr* to spark, sparkle

sfavóre *m* disfavor

sfavorévole *adj* unfavorable

sfebbra·to -ta *adj* free of fever

sfegata·to -ta *adj* (coll) rabid, fanatical

sfèra *f* sphere; (coll) hand (*of clock*); **a sfera** ball-point (*pen*); **a sfere** ball (*bearing*); **sfera di cuoio** (sports) pigskin

sfèri·co -ca *adj* (**-ci -che**) spherical

sferrare (**sfèrro**) *tr* to unshoe (*a horse*); to unchain; to draw (*a weapon from a wound*); to deliver (*a blow*) || *ref* to hurl oneself

sfèrza *f* whip, scourge

sferzare (**sfèrzo**) *tr* to whip, scourge

sfiancare §197 *tr* to break open; to tire out; to fit (*clothes*) too tight || *ref* to burst open; to get worn out

sfiatare *intr* to leak (*said, e.g., of a tire*) || *intr* (ESSERE) to leak (*said of air or gas*) || *ref* to waste one's breath

sfiata·tóio *m* (**-tói**) vent

sfibbiare §287 *tr* to unbuckle, unfasten; to untie (*a knot*)

sfibrante *adj* exhausting

sfibrare *tr* to grind (*wood*) into fibers; to shred (*rags*) into fibers; to weaken, wear out

sfida *f* challenge

sfidare *tr* to challenge, dare; to brave, defy; to endure (*the challenge of time*); **sfidare che** to bet that

sfidù·cia *f* (**-cie**) mistrust; (pol) no confidence

sfiducia·to -ta *adj* downcast, depressed

sfigurare *tr* to disfigure || *intr* to make a bad impression; to lose face

sfilacciare §128 *tr* & *ref* to ravel, fray

sfilare *tr* to unstring; to take off (*one's shoes*); to count (*beads*); to unthread; to dull (*a blade*); to ravel || *intr* (ESSERE) to march, parade; to follow one another || *ref* to become unthreaded; to become frayed; to run (*said of knitted work*); to break one's back

sfilata *f* parade; row; **sfilata di moda** fashion show

sfilza *f* row, sequence

sfinge *f* sphinx

sfiniménto *m* exhaustion

sfinire §176 *tr* to exhaust, wear out || *ref* to be worn out

sfintère *m* sphincter

sfiorare (**sfióro**) *tr* to graze; to barely touch (*a subject*); to skim; (lit) to barely reach

sfioratóre *m* spillway

sfiorire §176 *intr* (ESSERE) to wither, fade

sfit·to -ta *adj* not rented

sfocare §197 (**sfòco**) *tr* to put out of focus; to blur

sfociare §128 (**sfócio**) *tr* to dredge (*the mouth of a river*) || *intr* (ESSERE) to flow; **sfociare in** (fig) to lead to

sfoderare (**sfòdero**) *tr* to unsheathe; to show off, sport, display; to take the cover or lining off || *intr* to be drawn out

sfogare §209 (**sfógo**) *tr* to vent, give vent to || *intr* (ESSERE) to flow; to pour out; **sfogare in** to turn into || *ref*—**sfogarsi a** + *inf* to have one's

fill of + *ger*; **sfogarsi con** to unburden oneself to; **sfogarsi su qlcu**
to take it out on s.o.

sfoga‧tóio *m* (**-tói**) vent

sfoggiare §290 (**sfòggio**) *tr* to display,
sport; to show off

sfòg‧gio *m* (**-gi**) display, ostentation

sfòglia *f* foil; skin (*of onion*); layer of
puff paste; (ichth) sole

sfogliare §280 (**sfòglio**) *tr* to pluck (*a
flower*); to defoliate (*a tree*); to leaf
through (*a book*); to deal (*cards*);
to husk (*corn*); to press (*dough*) into
layers || *ref* to shed its leaves; to
flake

sfogliata *f* defoliation; puff paste; **dare
una sfogliata a** to glance through

sfó‧go *m* (**-ghi**) exhaust; outlet; vent;
(coll) eruption (*of skin*)

sfolgorare (**sfólgoro**) *intr* (ESSERE &
AVERE) to shine, blaze

sfolgorì‧o *m* (**-i**) glittering, blazing

sfollagèn‧te *m* (**-te**) billy

sfollaménto *m* evacuation; layoff

sfollare (**sfòllo**) *tr* to clear; to cut the
staff of || *intr* (ESSERE & AVERE) to
disperse, evacuate; to cut down the
staff

sfolla‧to -ta *adj* driven from home ||
mf evacuee

sfoltire §176 *tr* to thin out

sfondare (**sfóndo**) *tr* to stave in; to
break through; to be heavy on (*the
stomach*) || *intr* to give || *ref* to
break open

sfóndo *m* background

sfondó‧ne *m* (coll) blunder, error

sforbiciare §128 (**sfòrbicio**) *tr* to clip,
shear

sforbiciata *f* clipping; (sports) scissors;
(sports) scissors kick

sformare (**sfórmo**) *tr* to pull out of
shape; to take out of the mold ||
intr to get mad

sforma‧to -ta *adj* out of shape || *m*
pudding

sfornare (**sfórno**) *tr* to take out of the
oven

sfornire §176 *tr* to deprive; to strip

sfortuna *f* bad luck, misfortune

sfortuna‧to -ta *adj* unsuccessful; unlucky, unfortunate

sforzare (**sfòrzo**) *tr* to strain; to force
|| *ref* to strive, endeavor

sforza‧to -ta *adj* forced, unnatural

sfòrzo *m* effort; strain; stretch (*of
imagination*); **senza sforzo** effort-
lessly

sfóttere *tr* (vulg) to make fun of

sfracassare *tr* to smash, crash

sfracellare (**sfracèllo**) *tr* & *ref* to shatter, smash

sfrangiare §290 *tr* to ravel

sfrattare *tr* to evict; to deport || *intr*
to be evicted

sfratto *m* eviction; notice of eviction

sfrecciare §128 (**sfréccio**) *intr* (ESSERE
& AVERE) to speed by

sfregaménto *m* rubbing

sfregare §209 (**sfrégo**) *tr* to rub; to
scrape; to strike (*a match*)

sfregiare §290 (**sfrégio** & **sfrègio**) *tr* to
disfigure, slash

sfregia‧to -ta *adj* disfigured, slashed ||
m scarface

sfré‧gio or **sfrè‧gio** *m* (**-gi**) slash, scar,
gash; insult

sfrenare (**sfréno** & **sfrèno**) *tr* to take
the brake off; to give free rein to ||
ref to kick over the traces

sfriggere §180 *intr* to sizzle

sfrigolì‧o *m* (**-i**) sizzle

sfrondare (**sfróndo**) *tr* to defoliate; to
lop off; to trim down || *ref* to lose
leaves

sfrontatézza *f* effrontery, impudence

sfronta‧to -ta *adj* brazen, impudent

sfrusciare §128 *intr* to rustle

sfruttare *tr* to exploit; to exhaust (*e.g.,
a mine*); to take advantage of

sfrutta‧tóre -trice *mf* exploiter, developer (*e.g., of an invention*)

sfuggènte *adj* fleeting; receding (*forehead*); shifty (*glance*)

sfuggire *tr* to avoid, flee || *intr* (ESSERE)
to flee, escape, get away; (with *dat*)
to escape, e.g., **nulla gli sfugge** nothing escapes him; to break, e.g.,
sfuggì a una promessa he broke a
promise; **lasciarsi sfuggire** to let slip

sfuggita *f*—**di sfuggita** hastily; incidentally; **dare una sfuggita** to run
down (*e.g., to the post office*)

sfumare *tr* to shade down; to tone
down; to trim (*hair*) || *intr* (ESSERE)
to vanish; to shade

sfumatura *f* nuance, shade; razor clipping

sfumino *m* stump (*in drawing*)

sfuriare §287 *tr* to vent (*one's anger*) ||
intr to rave

sfuriata *f* outburst of anger; gust (*of
wind*); **fare una sfuriata a** to give a
scolding to

sgabèllo *m* stool, footstool

sgabuzzino *m* cubbyhole

sgambettare (**sgambétto**) *tr* to trip ||
intr to toddle; to kick (*said of a
baby*); to scamper

sgambétto *m* trip, stumble; **dare lo
sgambetto a** to trip

sganasciare §128 *tr* to dislocate the jaw
of; to break the jaw of; to tear apart
|| *intr* to steal right and left || *ref* to
break one's jaw; **sganasciarsi dalle
risa** to split one's sides laughing

sganciare §128 *tr* to unhook; to lay out
(*money*); to drop (*bombs*) || *intr* to
drop bombs; (coll) to go away || *ref*
to get unhooked; (mil) to disengage
oneself; **sganciarsi da** to get rid of

sgangherare (**sgànghero**) *tr* to unhinge;
to burst || *ref*—**sgangherarsi dalle
risa** to split one's sides laughing

sganghera‧to -ta *adj* unhinged; broken
down; rickety; coarse (*laughter*)

sgarbatéz‧za *f* rudeness, incivility;
clumsiness

sgarba‧to -ta *adj* rude; clumsy

sgarberìa *f* var of **sgarbatezza**

sgarbo *m*—**fare uno sgarbo a** to be rude
to

sgargiante *adj* loud, flashy, showy

sgarrare *intr* to go wrong

sgattaiolare (**sgattàiolo**) *intr* (ESSERE)
to slip away; to wriggle out

sgelare (sgèlo) *tr* & *intr* to thaw, melt

sgèlo *m* thaw

sghém·bo -ba *adj* crooked; a sghembo askew || sghembo *adv* askew; sideways

sghèrro *m* hired assassin; gendarme

sghiacciare §128 *tr* to thaw

sghignazzare *intr* to guffaw

sghignazzata *f* guffaw

sghimbè·scio -scia *adj*—a or di sghimbescio askew, crooked

sghiribizzo [ddzz] *m* whim, fancy

sgobbare (sgòbbo) *intr* to drudge, plod, plug

sgobbó·ne -na *mf* plugger, plodder, drudge

sgocciolare (sgócciolo) *tr* to let drip || *intr* to drip (*said of container*) || *intr* (ESSERE) to drip (*said of liquid*)

sgocciola·tóio *m* (-tói) dish rack; drip pan

sgocciolatura *f* dripping; drippings

sgócciolo *m* last drop; essere agli sgoccioli to be coming to an end

sgolare (sgólo) *ref* to shout oneself hoarse

sgomberare (sgómbero) *tr* & *intr* var of sgombrare

sgómbero *m* moving

sgombrané·ve *m* (-ve) snowplow (*truck*)

sgombrare (sgómbro) *tr* to clear; to vacate || *intr* to move, vacate

sgóm·bro -bra *adj* clear || *m* moving; (ichth) mackerel

sgomentare (sgoménto) *tr* to frighten; to dismay

sgomén·to -ta *adj* dismayed || *m* dismay; rimanere di sgomento to be dismayed

sgominare (sgòmino) *tr* to rout

sgomma·to -ta *adj* unglued; without tires; with poor tires

sgonfiare §287 (sgónfio) *tr* to deflate; to damn with faint praise (*e.g., a play*); (coll) to bore || *intr* (ESSERE) to boast; to balloon || *ref* to go down (*said of swelling*); to go flat (*said of a tire*); (fig) to collapse

sgón·fio -fia *adj* deflated, flat

sgonfiòtto *m* jelly doughnut; puff (*in clothing*)

sgórbia *f* (carp) gouge

sgorbiare §287 (sgòrbio) *tr* to scribble; (carp) to gouge

sgòr·bio *m* (-bi) ink spot; scribble, scrawl

sgorgare §209 (sgórgo) *tr* to unclog || *intr* (ESSERE) to gush

sgottare (sgótto) *tr* to bail out (*a boat*)

sgozzare (sgózzo) *tr* to slaughter; to slit the throat of; (fig) to bleed, fleece

sgradévole *adj* disagreeable, unpleasant

sgradire §176 *tr* to refuse || *intr* to be displeasing

sgradi·to -ta *adj* unpleasant; unwelcome

sgraffignare *tr* to snitch, snatch

sgrammatica·to -ta *adj* ungrammatical

sgranare *tr* to shell (*e.g., peas*); to count (*one's beads*); to seed (*grapes*); to open (*one's eyes*) wide; (mach) to disengage || *ref* to crumble; to scratch oneself

sgranchire §176 *tr* to stretch (*e.g., one's legs*)

sgranocchiare §287 (sgranòcchio) *tr* to crunch, munch

sgrassare *tr* to remove the grease from; to skim (*broth*); to scour (*wool*)

sgravare *tr* to relieve, lighten || *ref* to be relieved; to give birth

sgrà·vio *m* (-vi) lightening, lessening; a sgravio di coscienza to ease one's conscience

sgrazia·to -ta *adj* gawky, clumsy

sgretolare (sgrétolo) *tr* & *ref* to crumble

sgretola·to -ta *adj* crumbling, falling down

sgridare *tr* to scold, chide

sgridata *f* scolding, reprimand

sgrondare (sgróndo) *tr* to cause to drip || *intr* to drip, trickle

sgroppare (sgròppo) *tr* to wear (*a horse*) out || *intr* to buck (*said of a horse*)

sgroppare (sgróppo) *tr* to untie

sgrossare (sgròsso) *tr* to rough-hew; (fig) to refine

sgrovigliare §280 *tr* to untangle

sguaiatàggine *f* uncouthness

sguaia·to -ta *adj* crude, vulgar; uncouth || *mf* vulgar person; uncouth person

sguainare *tr* to unsheathe; to show (*one's nails*)

sgualcire §176 *tr* to crumple || *ref* to become crumpled

sgualdrina *f* trollop, strumpet

sguardo *m* glance, look; eyes

sguarnire §176 *tr* to untrim; (mil) to strip, dismantle

sguàtte·ro -ra *mf* dishwasher, scullion || *f* kitchenmaid, scullery maid

sguazzare *tr* to waste, squander || *intr* to splash; to wallow; to be lost (*in shoes too big or clothes too loose*)

sguinzagliare §280 *tr* to unleash, let loose

sgusciare §128 *tr* to shell, hull || *intr* (ESSERE) to slip; sgusciare di soppiatto to slip away

shòp·ping *m* (-ping) shopping; shopping bag; fare lo shopping to go shopping

shràpnel *m* (shràpnel) shrapnel

si *m* (-si) (mus) si || §5 *pron*

sì *m* (-sì) yes; yea; stare tra il sì e il no to not be able to make up one's mind; un . . . sì e l'altro no every other (*e.g., day*)

sìa *conj* see essere

siamése [s] *adj* & *mf* Siamese

siberia·no -na *adj* & *mf* Siberian

sibilante *adj* & *f* sibilant

sibilare (sìbilo) *intr* to hiss

sibilla *f* sibyl

sìbilo *m* hiss, hissing

sicà·rio *m* (-ri) hired assassin

sicché *conj* so that

siccità *f* drought

siccóme *adv* as || *conj* since; as; how

Sicilia, la Sicily

sicilia·no -na *adj* & *mf* Sicilian

sicomòro *m* sycamore

sicumèra *f* cocksureness, overconfidence

sicura *f* safety lock (*on gun*)

sicurézza _f_ security; assurance; safety; certainty; reliability; **di sicurezza** safety; **sicurezza sociale** social security

sicu·ro -ra _adj_ sure; safe; steady; **di sicuro** certainly || _m_ safety; **camminare sul sicuro** to take no chances || **sicuro** _adv_ certainly || _f_ see **sicura**

sicur·tà _f_ (-tà) insurance

siderale _adj_ sidereal

sidère·o -a _adj_ sidereal

siderùrgi·co -ca (-ci -che) _adj_ iron-and-steel || _m_ iron-and-steel worker

sidro _m_ cider, hard cider

sièpe _f_ hedge; (fig) wall

sièro _m_ serum

sièsta _f_ siesta; **fare la siesta** to take a nap, take a siesta

siffat·to -ta _adj_ such

sifìlide _f_ syphilis

sifóne _m_ siphon; siphon bottle; trap

siga·ràio -ràia (-rài -ràie) _mf_ cigar maker || _m_ (ent) grape hopper; || _f_ cigarette girl

sigarétta _f_ cigarette

sìgaro _m_ cigar

sigillare _tr_ to seal

sigillo _m_ seal; **avere il sigillo alle labbra** to have one's lips sealed; **sigillo sacramentale** seal of confession

sigla _f_ acronym; initials; abbreviation; letterword; **sigla musicale** theme song

siglare _tr_ to initial

significare §197 (signìfico) _tr_ to mean; to signify; **significare qlco a qlcu** to inform s.o. of s.th

significati·vo -va _adj_ significant; meaningful

significato _m_ meaning; **senza significato** meaningless

signóra _f_ Madam, Mrs.; lady; mistress, owner; wife || **Nostra Signora** Our Lady

signóre _m_ sir, Mr.; gentleman; rich man; lord, master, owner; man; **il signore desidera?** what is your pleasure?; **per signori** stag || **Signore** _m_ Lord

signoreggiare §290 (signoréggio) _tr_ to rule over; to master; to tower over; to overshadow || _intr_ to be the master

signorìa _f_ seigniory; rule; **La Signoria Vostra** your Honor; **Sua Signoria** his Lordship; your Lordship

signorìle _adj_ seigniorial; gentlemanly; ladylike; elegant, refined

signorìna _f_ miss; Miss; young lady; spinster

signorìno _m_ master, young gentleman

signorò _adv_ no, Sir

signoró·ne -na _mf_ (coll) rich person

signoròtto _m_ lordling

signorsì _adv_ yes, Sir

silenziatóre _m_ silencer (_of firearm_); (aut) muffler

silèn·zio _m_ (-zi) silence; (mil) taps; **fare silenzio** to be silent; **ridurre al silenzio** (mil) to silence

silenzió·so -sa [s] _adj_ silent; noiseless

sìlfide _f_ sylphid

silfo _m_ sylph

silhouèt·te _f_ (-te) silhouette

sìlice _f_ silica

silìcio _m_ silicon

silicóne _m_ silicone

siliquastro _m_ redbud

sìllaba _f_ syllable

sillabare (sìllabo) _tr_ to syllabify; to spell

sillabà·rio _m_ (-ri) reader, primer

sìllabo _m_ syllabus

silo _m_ silo

silòfono _m_ xylophone

siluétta _f_ silhouette

silurante _adj_ torpedoing, torpedo || _f_ destroyer; torpedo boat

silurare _tr_ to torpedo; (fig) to fire, dismiss; (fig) to undermine

siluro _m_ torpedo

silva·no -na _adj_ sylvan

silvèstre _adj_ (lit) sylvan; (lit) wild; (lit) hard, arduous

simboleggiare §290 (simboléggio) _tr_ to symbolize

simbòli·co -ca _adj_ (-ci -che) symbolic

simbolismo _m_ symbolism

sìmbolo _m_ symbol

similari·tà _f_ (-tà) similarity

sìmile _adj_ similar; such || _m_ like; **i propri simili** fellow men

similòro _m_ tombac

simmetrìa _f_ symmetry

simmètri·co -ca _adj_ (-ci -che) symmetrical

simonìa _f_ simony

simpamina _f_ benzedrine

simpatèti·co -ca _adj_ (-ci -che) sympathetic

simpatìa _f_ like, liking; **cattivarsi la simpatìa di** to make oneself well liked by

simpàti·co -ca (-ci -che) _adj_ nice, pleasant, congenial || _m_ (anat) sympathetic system

simpatizzante [ddzz] _adj_ sympathizing || _mf_ sympathizer

simpatizzare [ddzz] _intr_ to sympathize; to become friends

simpò·sio _m_ (-si) symposium

simulare (sìmulo) _tr_ to simulate

simula·tóre -trice _mf_ faker, impostor || _m_ simulator

simultàne·o -a _adj_ simultaneous

sin- _pref adj_ syn-, e.g., **sinonimo** synonymous || _pref m & f_ syn-, e.g., **sinonimo** synonym

sin _adv_—**sin da** ever since

sinagò·ga _f_ (-ghe) synagogue

sincerare (sincèro) _tr_ (lit) to convince || _ref_—**sincerarsi di** to ascertain

sincè·ro -ra _adj_ sincere; pure

sinché _conj_ until

sìncope _f_ fainting spell; (phonet) syncope; (mus) syncopation

sincronìsmo _m_ syncronism; **sincronismo orrizzontale** (telv) horizontal hold; **sincronismo verticale** (telv) vertical hold

sincronizzare [ddzz] _tr_ to syncronize

sìncro·no -na _adj_ syncronous

sindacale _adj_ mayoral; union

sindacalismo _m_ trade unionism

sindacalì·sta _mf_ (-sti -ste) union member; union leader

sindacare §197 (sìndaco) *tr* to criticize; to scrutinize

sindaca·to -ta *adj* controlled, scrutinized || *m* control; labor union; syndicate; **sindacato giallo** company union

sìnda·co *m* (**-ci**) mayor; controller; auditor

sinecura *f* sinecure

sinfonìa *f* symphony; (*of an opera*) overture; (coll) racket (*noise*)

sinfòni·co -ca *adj* (**-ci -che**) symphonic

singhiozzare (singhiózzo) *intr* to sob; to hiccup; to jerk

singhiózzo *m* sob; hiccups; **a singhiozzo** in jerks; by fits and spurts

singolare *adj* singular || *m* singular; (tennis) singles

sìngo·lo -la *adj* single || *m* individual; shell for one oarsman; (rr) roomette; (telp) private line; (tennis) singles

singulto *m* hiccups; sob

sinistra *f* left hand; left

sinistrare *tr* to ruin; to damage

sinistra·to -ta *adj* injured, damaged, ruined || *mf* victim (*of bombing or flood*)

sinistrismo *m* leftism

sinistri·sta *adj* (**-sti -ste**) leftish, leftist

sini·stro -stra *adj* left; sinister || *m* accident; (boxing) left || *f* see **sinistra**

sinistròide *adj & mf* leftist

sino *adv* var of **fino**

sinologìa *f* Sinology

sinòni·mo -ma *adj* synonymous || *m* synonym

sinò·psi *f* (**-psi**) (mov) synopsis

sinóra *adv* var of **finora**

sinòs·si *f* (**-si**) synopsis

sinòtti·co -ca *adj* (**-ci -che**) synoptic(al)

sintas·si *f* (**-si**) syntax

sìnte·si *f* (**-si**) synthesis

sintèti·co -ca *adj* (**-ci -che**) synthetic(al); concise

sintetizzare [ddzz] *tr* to synthesize

sintogram·ma *m* (**-mi**) (rad) dial

sìntomo *m* symptom

sintonìa *f* harmony; (rad) tuning

sintonizzare [ddzz] *tr* (rad) to tune

sintonizzatóre [ddzz] *m* (rad) tuner

sinuó·so -sa [s] *adj* sinuous, winding

sionismo *m* Zionism

sipà·rio *m* (**-ri**) curtain; **sipario di ferro** iron curtain

sirèna *f* siren; mermaid; **sirena da nebbia** foghorn

Sìria, la Syria

siria·no -na *adj & mf* Syrian

sirìn·ga *f* (**-ghe**) panpipe; syringe; catheter; grease gun; (orn) syrinx

siringare §209 *tr* to catheterize

siròcchia *f* (obs) sister

sì·sma *m* (**-smi**) earthquake

sismògrafo *m* seismograph

sismologìa *f* seismology

sissignóre *adv* yes, Sir!

sistè·ma *m* (**-mi**) system

sistemare (sistèmo) *tr* to arrange; to put in order; to systematize; to settle; to find a job for; to find a husband for; (coll) to fix || *ref* to settle; to get married

sistemazióne *f* arrangement; settlement; job, position

sìstole *f* systole

sitibón·do -da *adj* (lit) thirsty

sì·to -ta *adj* (lit) located || *m* (lit) site, spot, location; (mil) sight; (coll) musty odor

situare (sìtuo) *tr* to locate, place, situate

situazióne *f* situation; condition

slabbrare *tr* to chip; to open (*a wound*) || *intr* to overflow || *ref* to become chipped; to reopen (*said of a cut*)

slacciare §128 *tr* to untie; to unfasten; to unbutton || *ref* to get undone; to get unbuttoned

sladinare *tr* (sports) to train; (mach) to run in, break in

slanciare §128 *tr* to hurl, throw || *ref* to hurl oneself; to rise (*said, e.g., of a tower*)

slancia·to -ta *adj* slender; soaring

slàn·cio *m* (**-ci**) leap; outburst (*of feeling*); momentum; **di slancio** with a rush; **prendere lo slancio** to get a running start

slargare §209 *tr* to widen; to warm (*the heart*) || *ref* to widen, spread out

slattare *tr* to wean

slava·to -ta *adj* pale, washed out

sla·vo -va *adj* Slav, Slavic || *mf* Slav || *m* Slavic (*language*)

sleale *adj* disloyal; unfair (*competition*)

sleal·tà *f* (**-tà**) disloyalty

slegare §209 (slégo) *tr* to untie

slega·to -ta *adj* untied; disconnected

slip *m* (slip) briefs; tank suit, bathing suit (*for men*)

slitta *f* sled, sleigh; (mach) carriage

slittaménto *m* skid; slide

slittare *intr* to sled; to skid; to slide

slogare §209 (slògo) *tr* to dislocate || *ref* to become dislocated; to dislocate (*e.g., an arm*)

slogatura *f* dislocation

sloggiare §290 (slòggio) *tr* to dislodge; to evict || *intr* to vacate

slòg·gio *m* (**-gi**) moving; eviction

slovac·co -ca *adj & mf* (**-chi -che**) Slovak

smacchiare §287 *tr* to clean; to deforest

smacchia·tóre -trice *mf* cleaner || *m* cleaning fluid; spot remover

smac·co *m* (**-chi**) letdown; slap in the face

smagliante *adj* dazzling, shining

smagliare §280 *tr* to break the links of; to undo the meshes of; to remove (*a fish*) from the net || *intr* to shine, dazzle || *ref* to run (*said, e.g., of knitted fabric*); to free itself from the net

smagliatura *f* run (*in stockings*); (fig) break

smagrire §176 *tr* to impoverish || *intr* (ESSERE) & *ref* to become thin or lean

smaliziare §287 *tr* to make wiser || *ref* to get wiser

smaltare *tr* to enamel; to glaze

smaltire §176 *tr* to digest; to sleep off (*a drunk*); to swallow (*an offense*);

to sell off; to get rid of; to drain off (*water*)

smalti·tóio *m* (-tól) drain, sewer

smalto *m* enamel; **smalto per le unghie** nail polish

smancerìe *fpl* affectation; mawkishness

smanceró·so -sa [s] *adj* prissy

smangiare §290 *tr* to erode, eat away || *ref* to be consumed (*e.g., by hatred*)

smània *f* frenzy; craze, yearning; **dare in smanie** to be in a frenzy

smaniare §287 *intr* to be delirious; to yearn, crave

smanió·so -sa [s] *adj* eager; disturbing

smantellare (**smantèllo**) *tr* to dismantle; to demolish; to disable (*a ship*)

smargias·so -sa *mf* braggart, boaster

smarrimento *m* loss; bewilderment; discouragement

smarrire §176 *tr* to lose || *ref* to get lost; to get discouraged

smascellare (**smascèllo**) *ref*—**smascellarsi dalle risa** to split one's sides laughing

smascherare (**smàschero**) *tr & ref* to unmask

smazzata *f* (cards) deal; (cards) hand

smembramento *m* dismemberment

smembrare (**smèmbro**) *tr* to dismember

smemoratàggine *f* forgetfulness

smemora·to -ta *adj* absent-minded; forgetful || *mf* absent-minded or forgetful person

smentire §176 *tr* to belie; to refute; to retract; to be untrue to || *ref* to not be consistent, to contradict oneself

smentita *f* denial; retraction

smeraldo *m* emerald

smerciare §128 (**smèrcio**) *tr* to sell, sell out

smèr·cio *m* (-cl) sale

smèr·go *m* (-ghi) (zool) merganser

smerigliare §280 *tr* to grind, polish; to sand

smeriglia·to -ta *adj* polished; sand (*paper*); emery (*cloth*); frosted (*glass*)

smerì·glio *m* (-gli) emery; (orn) merlin; (ichth) porbeagle

smerlare (**smèrlo**) *tr* to scallop

smèrlo *m* scallop (*along the edge of a garment*)

smés·so -sa *adj* hand-me-down, castoff

sméttere §198 *tr* to stop; to stop wearing; to break up (*housekeeping*); **smetterla** to cut it out || *intr*—**smettere di** + *inf* to stop + *ger*

smezzare [ddzz] (**smèzzo**) *tr* to halve

smidollare (**smidóllo**) *tr* to remove the marrow from; (fig) to emasculate

militarizzare [ddzz] *tr* to demilitarize

smil·zo -za *adj* slender; poor, worthless

sminare *tr* to remove mines from

sminuire §176 *tr* to belittle

sminuzzare *tr* to crumble; to mince; to expatiate on || *ref* to crumble

smistamento *m* sorting (*of mail*); (rr) shunting, shifting

smistare *tr* to sort; (rr) to shift; (soccer) to pass; (rad) to unscramble

smisura·to -ta *adj* immense, huge

smitizzante [ddzz] *adj* debunking, demythologizing

smitizzare [ddzz] *tr* to debunk; to demythologize

smobiliare §287 *tr* to remove the furniture from

smobilitare (**smobìlito**) *tr* to demobilize

smobilitazióne *f* demobilization

smoccolare (**smòccolo & smóccolo**) *tr* to snuff (*a candle*) || *intr* (slang) to swear, curse

smoda·to -ta *adj* excessive, immoderate

smòg *m* smog

smóking *m* (**smóking**) dinner jacket, tuxedo

smontàbile *adj* dismountable

smontàg·gio *m* (-gi) disassembling, dismantling

smontare (**smónto**) *tr* to take apart; to dismantle; to cause (*e.g., whipped cream*) to fall; to take (*a precious stone*) out of its setting; to dishearten; to dissuade; to drop (*s.o.*) off; **smontare la guardia** to come off guard duty || *intr* (ESSERE) to dismount; to get off or out (*of a conveyance*); to fade; to drop (*said, e.g., of beaten eggs*) || *ref* to become downcast

smòrfia *f* grimace; mawkishness; **fare le smorfie a** to make faces at

smorfió·so -sa [s] *adj* mawkish, prissy

smòr·to -ta *adj* pale, wan; faded

smorzare (**smòrzo**) *tr* to attenuate; to lessen; to tone down; to turn off (*light*); (phys) to dampen

smorzatóre *m* (mus) damper

smòs·so -sa *adj* moved; loose

smottamento *m* mud slide

smozzicare §197 (**smózzico**) *tr* to crumble; to mince; to clip, mince (*one's words*)

smun·to -ta *adj* emaciated, pale, wan

smuòvere §202 *tr* to budge; to till; (fig) to move || *ref* to budge; to move away; **smuoviti!** get going!

smussare *tr* to blunt; to bevel; (fig) to soften

snaturalizzare [ddzz] *tr* to denaturalize; to denationalize

snaturare *tr* to change the nature of; to distort, misrepresent

snatura·to -ta *adj* distorted; monstrous, unnatural

snebbiare §287 (**snébbio**) *tr* to drive the fog from; to clear (*e.g., one's mind*)

snellézza *f* slenderness; nimbleness

snellire §176 *tr & ref* to slenderize

snèl·lo -la *adj* slender; nimble; lively

snervante *adj* enervating

snervare (**snèrvo**) *tr* to enervate, prostrate || *ref* to become enervated

snidare *tr* to drive out, flush

snob *adj* invar snobbish || *mf* (**snòb**) snob

snobbare (**snòbbo**) *tr* to snub, slight

snobismo *m* snobbishness, snobbery

snobìsti·co -ca *adj* (-ci -che) snobbish

snocciolare (**snòcciolo**) *tr* to spill (*a secret*); to peel off (*sums of money*); to pit, stone (*fruit*)

snodare (**snòdo**) *tr* to untie; to limber up; to exercise; to loosen up (*e.g.,* *s.o.'s tongue*) || *ref* to become loose; to wind (*said, e.g., of a road*)

snòdo *m* (mach) joint; **a snodo** flexible

soave *adj* sweet, gentle

sobbalzare *intr* to jerk, jolt

sobbalzo *m* jerk, jolt; **di sobbalzo** with a jolt

sobbarcare §197 *tr* to overburden || *ref* —**sobbarcarsi a** to take it upon oneself to

sobbór·go *m* (-**ghi**) suburb

sobillare *tr* to instigate, stir up

sobilla·tóre -trice *mf* instigator

sobrietà *f* sobriety, temperance

sò·brio -bria *adj* sober, temperate; plain

socchiùdere §125 *tr* to half-shut; to leave ajar

socchiu·so -sa [s] *adj* ajar

soccómbere §186 *intr* to succumb

soccórrere §139 *tr* to help || *intr* (lit) to occur

soccórso *m* help, succor; **mancato soccorso** failure to render assistance; hit-and-run driving

sociale *adj* social; company (*e.g., outing*)

socialismo *m* socialism

sociali·sta (-sti -ste) *adj* socialistic || *mf* socialist

sociali·tà *f* (-**tà**) gregariousness; social responsibility

socie·tà *f* (-**tà**) company; **in società** in partnership; **società anonima** corporation; **società a responsabilità limitata** limited company; **Società delle Nazioni** League of Nations; **società finanziaria** holding company; **società in accomandita** limited partnership; **società per azioni** corporation

sociévole *adj* sociable; gregarious

sò·cio *m* (-**ci**) member; cardholder; partner; shareholder; **socio fondatore** charter member; **socio sostenitore** patron, sustaining member

sociologìa *f* sociology

sociòlo·go -ga *mf* (-**gi -ghe**) sociologist

sòda *f* soda

sodali·zio *m* (-**zi**) society; brotherhood, fraternity; friendship

soddisfacènte *adj* satisfying, satisfactory

soddisfare §173 (*2d sg pres ind* **soddisfài** or **soddisfi**; *3d pl pres* **soddisfanno** or **soddìsfano**; *1st, 2d & 3d sg pres subj* **soddisfaccia** or **soddisfi**; *3d pl pres subj* **soddisfàcciano** or **soddìsfino**) *tr* to satisfy || *intr* (with *dat*) to satisfy || *ref* to be satisfied

soddisfat·to -ta *adj* satisfied

soddisfazióne *f* satisfaction

sòdi·co -ca *adj* (-**ci -che**) sodium

sòdio *m* sodium

sò·do -da *adj* hard; hard-boiled; stubborn; solid; **prenderle sode** to get a good thrashing || *m* hard ground; untilled soil; solid foundation; **venire al sodo** to come to the point; **mettere in sodo** to ascertain || *f* see **soda** || **sodo** *adv* hard

sodomìa *f* sodomy

so·fà *m* (-**fà**) couch, sofa; **sofà a letto** sofa bed

sofferènte *adj* sickly, ailing; (lit) long-suffering

sofferènza *f* suffering, pain; bad debt; **in sofferenza** overdue

soffermare (sofférmo) *tr*—**soffermare il passo** to come to a stop || *ref* to linger, pause

soffiare §287 (**sóffio**) *tr* to blow; to whisper; (checkers) to huff; (coll) to steal || *intr* to blow; to bellow; (slang) to squeal (*about somebody's offense*); **soffiare sul fuoco** to stir up trouble || *ref* to blow (*one's nose*)

soffia·to -ta *adj* blown || *m* soufflé || *f* (slang) squealing, **darsi una soffiata di naso** to blow one's nose

soffiatóre *m* glass blower

sòffice *adj* soft

soffierìa *f* glass factory; blower

soffiétto *m* bellows; hood (*of carriage*); (journ) puff, ballyhoo

sóf·fio *m* (-**fi**) blow; breath; **in un soffio** in a jiffy; **soffio al cuore** heart murmur

soffióne *m* blowpipe; fumarole; (bot) dandelion; (coll) spy

soffitta *f* attic, garret

soffitto *m* ceiling

soffocaménto *m* choking

soffocante *adj* stifling; oppressive

soffocare §197 (**sòffoco**) *tr* to choke; to stifle; to suffocate; to smother; to repress

sòffo·co *m* (-**chi**) sultriness

soffóndere §178 *tr* (lit) to suffuse

soffregare §209 (**soffrégo**) *tr* to rub lightly

soffriggere §180 *tr* to fry lightly || *intr* to mutter

soffrire §207 *tr* to suffer; to endure; **non poter soffrire** to not be able to stand || *intr* to suffer; to ail; **soffrire di** to be troubled with

soffritto *m* fried onions and bacon

sofistica·to -ta *adj* adulterated; sophisticated, studied

sofisti·co -ca *adj* (-**ci -che**) sophistic; faultfinding || *f* sophistry

soggetti·sta *mf* (-**sti -ste**) scriptwriter

soggetti·vo -va *adj* subjective

soggèt·to -ta *adj* subject || *m* subject; (coll) character; (law) person; **cattivo soggetto** hoodlum; **recitare a soggetto** to improvise

soggezióne *f* subjection; awe, embarrassment; **mettere a soggezione** to awe

sogghignare *intr* to sneer

soggiacére §181 *intr* (ESSERE & AVERE) to be subject; to succumb

soggiogare §209 (**soggiógo**) *tr* to subjugate, subdue

soggiornare (soggiórno) *intr* to sojourn, stay

soggiórno *m* sojourn, stay; living room; sitting room (*in hotel*)

soggiùngere §183 *tr* to add

soggólo *m* wimple (*of nun*); throat-latch (*on horse*); (mil) chin strap

sòglia *f* doorsill; threshhold

sògliola *f* sole

sognare (sógno) *tr* to dream of || *intr*

to dream; **sognare ad occhi aperti** to daydream

sogna·tóre -trice *adj* dreaming ‖ *mf* dreamer

sógno *m* dream; **nemmeno per sogno** (coll) by no means

sòia *f* (bot) soy

sòl *m* (sòl) (mus) sol

so·làio *m* (-lài) attic, loft; (agr) crib

solare *adj* solar; bright; clear ‖ *v* §257 *tr* to sole

solàr·rio *m* (-rì) solarium

solati·o -a (-ì -e) *adj* sunny ‖ *m—a* **solatìo** with a southern exposure

solcare §197 (sólco) *tr* to furrow; to plow (*the waves*)

sól·co *m* (-chi) furrow; rut; groove (*of phonograph record*); (fig) path; (naut) wake

solcòmetro *m* (naut) log

soldaté·sco -sca (-schi -sche) *adj* soldier ‖ *f* soldiery; soldiers; undisciplined troops

soldatino *m* toy soldier

soldato *m* soldier; **andare soldato** to enlist; **soldato di ventura** soldier of fortune; **soldato scelto** private first class; **soldato semplice** private

sòldo *m* soldo (*Italian coin*); coin; money; (mil) pay; (fig) penny; **a soldo a soldo** a penny at a time; **al soldo di** in the pay of; **tirare al soldo** to be a tightwad

sóle *m* sun; sunshine; (fig) day, day-time; **sole artificiale** sun lamp; **sole a scacchi** (joc) hoosegow, calaboose

soleggia·to -ta *adj* sunny

solènne *adj* solemn; (joc) first-class

solenni·tà *f* (-tà) solemnity

solennizzare [ddzz] *tr* to solemnize

solére §255 *intr* (ESSERE) + *inf* to be accustomed to + *inf*, *e.g.*, **suole arrivare alle sette** he is accustomed to arrive at seven ‖ *impers* (ESSERE) —**suole** + *inf* it generally + *3d sg ind*, *e.g.*, **suole nevicare** it generally snows

solèrte *adj* (lit) diligent, industrious

solèrzia *f* (lit) diligence

solét·to -ta *adj* (lit) alone, lonely ‖ *f* sole; inner sole; (archit) slab, cement slab

sòlfa *f* (mus) solfeggio; **la solita solfa** the same old story

solfanèllo *m* var of **zofanello**

solfara *f* sulfur mine

solfato *m* sulfate

solfeggiare §290 (solféggio) *tr* to sol-fa

solfiè·ro -ra *adj* sulfur

solfito *m* sulfite

sólfo *m* var of **zolfo**

solfòri·co -ca *adj* (-ci -che) sulfuric

solforó·so·sa [s] *adj* sulfurous

solfuro *m* sulfide

solidale *adj* solidary; (law) joint; (law) jointly responsible; (mach) built-in; **solidale con** integral with

solidarie·tà *f* (-tà) solidarity; (law) joint liability

solidarizzare [ddzz] *intr* to make common cause, become united

solidificare §197 (solidìfico) *tr* to solidify; to settle

solidi·tà *f* (-tà) solidity; (fig) soundness

sòli·do -da *adj* solid; (law) joint ‖ *m* solid; **in solido** jointly

solilò·quio *m* (-qui) soliloquy

solin·go -ga *adj* (-ghi -ghe) (lit) lonely; (lit) solitary (*enjoying solitude*)

solino *m* detachable collar; **solino duro** stiff collar

soli·sta *mf* (-sti -ste) soloist

solità·rio -ria (-ri -rie) *adj* solitary, lonely ‖ *m* solitaire; solitary

sòli·to -ta *adj* usual, customary; **esser solito** to be accustomed to ‖ *m* habit, custom; **come il solito** as usual; **di solito** usually

solitùdine *f* solitude, loneliness

sollazzare *tr* to amuse ‖ *ref* to have a good time, amuse oneself

sollazzo *m* (lit) amusement; **essere il sollazzo di** to be the laughingstock of

sollecitare (sollécito) *tr* to solicit; to urge; to induce; (mach) to stress ‖ *intr & ref* to hasten

sollecitazióne *f* solicitation; urging; (mach) stress

solléci·to -ta *adj* quick, prompt; diligent; solicitous, anxious ‖ *m* (com) solicitation, urging

sollecitùdine *f* solicitude; promptness; diligence; **cortese sollecitudine** (com) prompt attention

solleóne *m* dog days

solleticare §197 (solletico) *tr* to tickle; (fig) to flatter

solléti·co *m* (-chi) tickling; stimulation; **fare il solletico a** to tickle

sollevaménto *m* lifting; **sollevamento di pesi** weight lifting

sollevare (sollèvo) *tr* to lift; to relieve; to pick up; to raise (*e.g.*, *a question*); to excite; to elevate ‖ *ref* to rise; to lift oneself; to pick up (*said of courage or health*)

sollevazióne *f* uprising

solliè·vo *m* relief

sollùchero *m*—**andare in solluchero** to become ecstatic; **mandare in solluchero** to thrill

só·lo -la *adj* lone, lonely, alone; only; single; **fare da solo** to operate all by oneself; **solo soletto** all by myself (yourself, himself, etc.); within oneself; **un solo** only one ‖ *m* (mus) solo ‖ **solo** *adv* only ‖ **solo** *conj* only; **solo che** provided that

solsti·zio *m* (-zi) solstice

soltanto *adv* only

solùbile *adj* soluble

soluzióne *f* solution; installment; **soluzione di comodo** compromise; **soluzione provvisoria** stopgap

solvènte *adj & m* solvent

solvènza *f* solvency

solvìbile *adj* collectable; solvent

sòma *f* burden, load

Somàlia, la Somaliland

sòma·lo -la *adj & mf* Somali

soma·ro -ra *mf* donkey, ass

someggia·to -ta *adj* carried by pack animal; carried on mule back

somigliante *adj* similar; **essere somigliante a** to look like ‖ *m* same thing

somiglianza *f* similarity, resemblance

somigliare §280 *tr* to resemble; (lit) to compare || *intr* (ESSERE & AVERE) (with *dat*) to resemble; to seem to be || *ref* to resemble each other

sómma *f* addition: sum; summary

sommare (**sómmo**) *tr* to add; to consider; **tutto sommato** all in all || *intr* to amount

summà·rio -ria (-ri -rie) *adj* summary || *m* summary; abstract; (journ) subheading

sommèrgere §162 *tr* to submerge; (fig) to plunge; (fig) to flood (*with insults*) || *ref* to submerge

sommergibile *adj* & *m* submarine

summés·so -sa *adj* submissive; subdued (*voice*)

somministrare *tr* to administer; to provide; to deliver (*a blow*); to adduce (*proof*)

somministrazióne *f* administration; provision

summi·tà *f* (**-tà**) summit

sóm·mo -ma *adj* highest; supreme || *m* top; peak, summit || *f* see **somma**

summòssa *f* insurrection, riot

summovimento *m* tremor (*of earth*); arousal (*of passions*); riot

summozzatóre *m* skin diver; (nav) frogman

summuòvere §202 *tr* (lit) to agitate; (lit) to stir up, excite

sonaglièra *f* collar with bells

sonà·glio *m* (**-gli**) bell; rattle; raindrop; pitter-patter (*of the rain*)

sonante *adj* ringing, sounding; ready (*cash*)

sonare §257 *tr* to sound; to play; to strike (*the hour*); to ring (*a bell*); (coll) to dupe, cheat; (coll) to give a sound thrashing to; **sonare le campane a distesa** to ring a full peal || *intr* (ESSERE & AVERE) to play; to ring (*said of a bell*); to sound; (lit) to spread (*said of reputation*)

sona·to -ta *adj* played; past, e.g., **le tre sonate** past three o'clock; **cinquant'anni sonati** past fifty years of age || *f* rung (*of bell*); (mus) sonata; (coll) thrashing; (coll) cheating

sona·tóre -trice *mf* (mus) player

sónda *f* sound; probe; drill

sondàg·gio *m* (**-gi**) sounding; probe; drilling; **sondaggio d'opinioni** opinion survey, public opinion poll

sondare (**sóndo**) *tr* to sound; to probe; to drill; to survey (*public opinion*)

sonerìa *f* alarm (*of clock*)

sonétto *m* sonnet

sonnacchió·so -sa [s] *adj* sleepy, drowsy

sonnàmbu·lo -la *mf* sleepwalker

sonnecchiare §287 (**sonnécchio**) *intr* to drowse, take a nap; to nap; to nod

sonnellino *m* nap

sonnife·ro -ra *adj* soporific; narcotic || *m* sleeping medicine; narcotic

sónno *m* sleep; (lit) dream; **aver sonno** to be sleepy; **far venir sonno a** to bore; **prender sonno** to fall asleep

sonnolèn·to -ta *adj* sleepy; lazy

sonnolènza *f* drowsiness; laziness

sonori·tà *f* (**-tà**) sonority; acoustics

sonorizzare [ddzz] *tr* to voice; (mov) to dub || *ref* to voice

sonò·ro -ra *adj* sound (*wave*); sonorous; (phonet) sonant, voiced

sontuó·so -sa [s] *adj* sumptuous

sopèr·chio -chia *adj* & *m* (**-chi -chie**) var of **soverchio**

sopire §176 *tr* to appease, calm

sopóre *m* drowsiness

soporife·ro -ra *adj* soporific

soppanno *m* interlining; lining (*of shoes*)

sopperire §176 *intr*—**sopperire a** to provide for; to make up for

soppesare [s] (**soppéso**) *tr* to heft; (fig) to weigh

soppiantare *tr* to supplant by scheming; to kick out; to replace; to trick

soppiatto *m*—**di soppiatto** stealthily

sopportàbile *adj* bearable, tolerable

sopportare (**soppòrto**) *tr* to bear, support; to suffer, endure

sopportazióne *f* forbearance, endurance

soppressióne *f* suppression, abolition

sopprìmere §131 *tr* to suppress, do away with

sópra *adj invar* upper; above, preceding || *m* upper, upper part; **al di sopra** above; **al di sopra di** above, over; beyond; **di sopra** upper || *adv* above; up; on top || *prep* on; upon; on top of; over; beyond; above; versus; **sopra pensiero** absorbed in thought

sopràbito *m* overcoat, topcoat

sopraccàri·co -ca (**-chi -che**) *adj* overburdened || *m* overload; overweight; (naut) supercargo

sopraccenna·to-ta *adj* above-mentioned

sopracci·glio *m* (**-gli** & **-glia** *fpl*) brow, eyebrow; window frame

sopraccita·to -ta *adj* above-mentioned

sopraccopèrta *f* bedspread; book jacket, dust jacket || *adv* (naut) on deck

sopraddét·to -ta *adj* above-mentioned

sopraffare §173 *tr* to overcome, overpower

sopraffazióne *f* overpowering; abuse

sopraffinèstra *f* transom window

sopraffi·no -na *adj* first-class; superfine

sopraggitto *m* (sew) overcasting

sopraggiùngere §183 *intr* (ESSERE) to arrive; to happen

sopraintèndere §270 *tr* var of **soprintendere**

sopralluò·go *m* (**-ghi**) inspection, investigation on the spot

sopralzo *m* var of **soprelevazione**

soprammercato *m*—**per soprammercato** in addition, to boot

soprammòbile *m* knickknack

soprannaturale *adj* & *m* supernatural

soprannóme *m* nickname

soprannominare (**soprannòmino**) *tr* to nickname

soprannùmero *adj invar* in excess; overtime || *m* —**in soprannumero** extra; in excess

sopra·no -na *adj* upper; (lit) supreme

|| **sopra·no** *mf* (**-ni -ne**) soprano (*person*) || *m* soprano (*voice*)

soprappensièro *adj invar & adv* immersed in thought

soprappéso [s] *m*—**per soprappeso** besides, into the bargain

soprap·più *m* (**-più**) plus, extra; **in soprappiù** besides, into the bargain

soprapprèzzo *m* extra charge, surcharge

soprascarpa *f* overshoe

soprascrit·to -ta *adj* written above || *f* address

soprassalto *m* start, jump; **di soprassalto** with a start

soprassedére §252 *intr* to wait; (with *dat*) to postpone

soprassòldo *m* extra pay; (mil) warzone indemnity

soprastare §263 *intr* (ESSERE) to be the boss

soprattac·co *m* (**-chi**) rubber heel

soprattassa *f* surtax; surcharge

soprattutto *adv* above all, especially

sopravanzare *tr* to overcome || *intr* (ESSERE) to be left over

sopravanzo *m* surplus

sopravvalutare *tr* to overrate

sopravvenire §282 *tr* (lit) to overrun || *intr* (ESSERE) to arrive; to happen, occur; (with *dat*) to befall

sopravvènto *m* windward; **avere il sopravvento** to have the upper hand || *adv* windward

sopravvissu·to -ta *adj* surviving || *mf* survivor

sopravvivènza *f* survival

sopravvìvere §286 *intr* (ESSERE) to survive; (with *dat*) to survive, to outlive

soprelevare (**soprelèvo**) *tr* to elevate (*e.g., a railroad*); to increase the height of (*building*)

soprelevazióne *f* elevation; addition of one or more floors

soprintendènte *m* superintendent

soprintendènza *f* superintendency

soprintèndere §270 *tr* to oversee

sopròsso *m* (coll) bony outgrowth

sopruso *m* abuse of power

soqquadro *m*—**a soqquadro** upside down, topsy-turvy

sòrba *f* sorb apple; (coll) hit, blow

sorbettièra *f* ice-cream freezer

sorbétto *m* ice cream; sherbet

sorbire §176 *tr* to sip; (fig) to swallow, endure

sòrbo *m* sorb; service tree

sór·cio *m* (**-ci**) mouse

sòrdi·do -da *adj* sordid; dirty

sordina *f* (mus) sordino, mute; (mus) soft pedal; **in sordina** quietly; stealthily; **mettere in sordina** (mus) to muffle

sór·do -da *adj* deaf; dull (*pain*); deepseated (*hatred*); hollow (*sound*); (phonet) surd, voiceless; **sordo come una campana** stone-deaf || *mf* deaf person

sordomu·to -ta *adj* deaf and dumb || *mf* deafmute

sorèlla *f* sister

sorellastra *f* stepsister

sorgènte *adj* rising || *f* spring; well (*of oil*); (fig) source; **sorgente del fiume** riverhead

sórgere §258 *intr* (ESSERE) to rise; to arise; to spring forth; **sorgere su un'ancora** (naut) to lie at anchor

sorgi·vo -va *adj* spring (*water*)

sór·go *m* (**-ghi**) sorghum

sormontare (**sormónto**) *tr* to surmount; to overcome || *intr* to fit

sornió·ne -na *adj* cunning, sly || *m* sneak

sorpassare *tr* to get ahead of; to surpass; to overstep; to go above

sorpasso *m* (aut) passing

sorprendènte *adj* surprising, astonishing

sorprèndere §220 *tr* to surprise; to catch; **sorprendere la buona fede di** to take advantage of || *ref* to be surprised

sorprésa [s] *f* surprise; surprise investigation; **di sorpresa** suddenly; unprepared; by surprise

sorrèggere §226 *tr* to sustain, support; to bolster

sorrìdere §231 *tr* (lit) to say with a smile || *intr* to smile; **sorridere a** to appeal to, e.g., **le sorride l'idea di questa gita** the idea of this trip appeals to her; to smile upon, e.g., **gli sorrideva la vita** life was smiling upon him

sorriso [s] *m* smile

sorsata *f* gulp, draught

sorseggiare §290 (**sorséggio**) *tr* to sip

sórso *m* sip; **a sorso a sorso** sipping

sòrta *f* kind, sort

sòrte *f* luck, lot, fate; chance; kind; (com) principal; **per sorte** of each kind; by chance; **tirare a sorte** to cast lots

sorteggiare §290 (**sortéggio**) *tr* to choose by lot; to raffle; **sorteggiare un premio** to draw a prize

sortég·gio *m* (**-gi**) drawing

sortilè·gio *m* (**-gi**) sortilege; sorcery, magic

sortire §176 *tr* (lit) to get by lot; (lit) to have (*results*); (lit) to allot || (**sòrto**) *intr* (ESSERE) to come out (*said, e.g., of a newspaper*); (coll) to be drawn (*by lot*); (coll) to go out; (mil) to make a sally

sortita *f* witticism; (mil) sally, sortie; (theat) appearance

sorvegliante *adj* watchful || *mf* overseer, caretaker; guardian || *m* watchman; foreman

sorveglianza *f* surveillance; supervision

sorvegliare §280 (**sorvéglio**) *tr* to oversee, watch over; to check, control

sorvolare (**sorvólo**) *tr* to fly over; to overfly; (fig) to avoid, skip

sorvólo *m* overflight

sò·sia *m* (**-sia**) double, counterpart

sospèndere §259 *tr* to hang; to suspend; (chem) to prepare a suspension of; (law) to stay

sospensióne *f* suspension; suspense; (law) stay; **sospensione cardanica** gimbals sospensò·rio *m* (-ri) jockstrap, supporter

sospé·so -sa [s] *adj* suspended; suspension (*bridge*); in sospeso in suspense; in abeyance ‖ *m* employee who has been disciplined by suspension; (com) pending item

sospettare (sospètto) *tr* to suspect ‖ *intr*—sospettare di to suspect; to fear

sospèt·to -ta *adj* suspected; suspicious ‖ *m* dash; suspicion

sospettó·so -sa [s] *adj* suspicious

sospìngere §126 *tr* (fig) to drive; (lit) to push

sospirare *tr* to long for, crave; fare sospirare to keep waiting ‖ *intr* to sigh

sospiro *m* sigh; longing; (lit) breath; a sospiri little by little

sossópra *adv* upside down

sòsta *f* stop; reprieve; (rr) demurrage

sostantì·vo -va *adj & m* substantive

sostanza *f* substance; sostanza grigia gray matter

sostanziale *adj* substantial

sostanzió·so -sa [s] *adj* substantial

sostare (sòsto) *intr* to stop, pause

sostégno *m* prop; (fig) support

sostenére §271 *tr* to support; to sustain; to take (*an examination*); to defend (*a thesis*); to prop up; to stand (*alcohol*); to play (*a role*) ‖ *ref* to support oneself; to hold up (*said, e.g., of a theory*); to take nourishment

sosteni·tóre -trice *mf* backer, supporter

sostentaménto *m* sustenance, support

sostentare (sostènto) *tr* to support, keep ‖ *ref* to feed, eat

sostenu·to -ta *adj* reserved, austere; rising (*prices*); bullish (*market*); starchy (*manner*)

sostituìbile *adj* replaceable

sostituire §176 *tr* to replace, substitute for, take the place of; sostituire (qlco or qlcu) a to substitute (s.th or s.o.) for

sostitu·to -ta *adj* acting; associate, assistant ‖ *m* replacement, substitute

sostituzióne *f* replacement, substitution

sostrato *m* substratum

sottàbito *m* slip

sottacére §268 *tr* (lit) to withhold

sottacéto *adj invar* pickled ‖ sottaceti *mpl* pickles

sott'àcqua *adv* underwater

sotta·no -na *adj* lower (*town*) ‖ *f* skirt; petticoat; (eccl) cassock; gettare la sottana alle ortiche to doff the cassock

sottécchi *adv*—di sottecchi stealthily, secretly; guardare di sottecchi to peep, look furtively (at)

sottentrare (sotténtro) *intr* (ESSERE) (with *dat*) to replace

sotterfù·gio *m* (-gi) subterfuge

sottèrra *adv* underground

sotterràne·o -a *adj* subterranean, underground; secret, clandestine ‖ *m* cave, vault; dungeon; underground passage ‖ *f* (rr) subway, underground

sotterrare (sottèrro) *tr* to bury

sottigliézza *f* thinness; subtlety

sottile *adj* thin; subtle; (naut) lightweight ‖ *m*—guardare troppo per il sottile to split hairs

sottilizzare [ddzz] *intr* to quibble

sottintèndere §270 *tr* to understand ‖ *ref* to be understood, be implied

sottinté·so -sa [s] *adj* understood, implied ‖ *m* innuendo

sótto *adj invar* lower ‖ *m* lower part ‖ *adv* under; underneath; al di sotto below; al di sotto di under, below; di sotto lower; underneath; downstairs; di sotto a under, below; farsi sotto to sneak up; metter sotto to run over (*with a vehicle*); sotto a under; sotto di under ‖ *prep* under; beneath; below; just before; prendere sotto gamba to underestimate; sotto braccio arm in arm; sotto carico (naut) being loaded; sotto i baffi up one's sleeve; sotto le armi in the service; sotto mano within reach; sotto voce under one's breath, sotto voce

sottoascèl·la *m* (-la) underarm pad

sottobanco *adv* under the counter

sottobicchière *m* coaster

sottobò·sco *m* (-schi) underbrush, thicket

sottobràccio *adv* arm in arm

sottòcchio *adv* under one's eyes

sottoccupà·to -ta *adj* underemployed

sottochiave *adv* under lock and key

sottocó·da *m* (-da) crupper

sottocommissióne *f* subcommittee

sottocopèrta *adv* (naut) below decks

sottocòp·pa *m* (-pa) mat; coaster; (aut) oil pan

sottocòsto *adj invar & adv* below cost

sottocutàne·o -a *adj* subcutaneous

sottofà·scia *m* (-scia) wrapper; spedire sottofascia to mail (*a newspaper*) in a wrapper ‖ *f* (-sce) wrapper (*for cigars*)

sottogamba *adv* lightly; prendere sottogamba to underestimate

sottogó·la *m & f* (-la) chin strap; throatlatch (*of harness*)

sottolineare (sottolìneo) *tr* to underline, underscore; to emphasize

sott'òlio *adv* in oil

sottomano *m* writing pad ‖ *adv* underhand; within reach

sottomari·no -na *adj & m* submarine

sottomés·so -sa *adj* conquered; subdued; submissive

sottométtere §198 *tr* to subdue, crush; to defer, postpone; to present (*a bill*); to subject ‖ *ref* to submit, yield

sottomissióne *f* submission

sottopan·cia *m* (-cia) bellyband, girth

sottopassàg·gio *m* (-gi) underpass; lower level (*of highway*)

sottopiatto *m* saucer

sottopórre §218 *tr* to subject; to submit ‖ *ref* to submit; sottoporsi a to submit to; to undergo (*e.g., an operation*)

sottopó·sto -sta *adj* subject; exposed ‖ *m* subordinate

sottoprèzzo *adj invar* cut-rate || *adv* at a cut rate

sottoprodótto *m* by-product

sottórdine *m* suborder; **in sottordine** secondary

sottosca·la *m* (-**la**) space under the stairs; closet under the stairs

sottoscrit·to -ta *adj & mf* undersigned

sottoscrit·tóre -trice *mf* subscriber

sottoscrìvere §250 *tr* to subscribe; to sign, undersign; to underwrite || *intr* to subscribe

sottoscrizióne *f* subscription

sottosegretà·rio *m* (-**ri**) undersecretary

sottosópra *adj invar* upset; **mettere sottosopra** to upset; to turn upside down || *m* confusion, disorder || *adv* upside down

sottostante *adj* lower; subordinate || *m* subordinate

sottostare §263 *intr* (ESSERE) to be located below; to be subject; to yield, submit; (with *dat*) to undergo (*e.g., an examination*)

sottosuòlo *m* subsoil; cellar

sottosviluppa·to -ta *adj* underdeveloped

sottotenènte *m* second lieutenant; **sottotenente di vascello** (nav) lieutenant j.g.

sottotèr·ra *m* (-**ra**) basement || *adv* underground

sottotétto *m* attic, garret

sottotìtolo *m* subtitle; (mov) caption

sottovalutare *tr* to underrate

sottovènto *m & adv* leeward

sottovèste *f* slip (*undergarment*)

sottovóce *adv* sotto voce, under one's breath

sottrarre §273 *tr* to subtract; **sottrarre a** to take away from, steal from || *ref*—**sottrarsi a** to avoid; to escape from

sottrazióne *f* subtraction

sottufficiale *m* noncommissioned officer

sovènte *adv* often

soverchiante *adj* overwhelming

soverchiare §287 (sovèrchio) *tr* to overwhelm; to excel; to bully; (lit) to overflow || *intr* to be in excess

sovèr·chio -chia (-chi -chie) *adj* excessive; overbearing || *m* overbearing action

sovè·scio *m* (-sci) plowing under (*of green manure*)

sovièti·co -ca (-ci -che) *adj* Soviet || *mf* Soviet citizen

sovrabbondante *adj* superabundant

sovrabbondare (sovrabbóndo) *intr* (ESSERE & AVERE) to be superabundant; to go to excesses

sovraccaricare §197 (sovraccàrico) *tr* to overload

sovraccàri·co -ca (-chi -che) *adj* overburdened || *m* overload; overweight

sovraespó·sto -sta *adj* overexposed

sovraggiùngere §183 *intr* (ESSERE) var of sopraggiungere

sovralimentazióne *f* (aut) supercharging

sovrani·tà *f* (-tà) sovereignty

sovra·no -na *adj & mf* sovereign

sovrappopolare (sovrappòpolo) *tr* to overpopulate

sovrappórre §218 *tr* to overlay; to superimpose; **sovrapporre qlco a** to lay s.th on || *ref* to be superimposed; to be added; **sovrapporsi a** to put oneself above

sovrapproduzióne *f* overproduction

sovrastampa *f* overprint

sovrastante *adj* overlooking, overhanging; impending

sovrastare *tr* to tower over; to hang over; to surpass; to excel || *intr* (ESSERE & AVERE)—**sovrastare a** to tower over; to overlook; to hang over; to surpass; to excel

sovratensióne *f* (elec) surge

sovreccitare (sovrèccito) *tr* to overexcite

sovrespórre §218 *tr* to overexpose

sovrimpòsta *f* surtax

sovrimpressióne *f* double exposure

sovruma·no -na *adj* superhuman

sovvenire §282 *tr* (lit) to help || *intr* (with *dat*) (lit) to help || *impers* (ESSERE)—**sovviene** (with *dat*) **di** remember, *e.g.*, **gli sovviene spesso dei suoi cari** he often remembers his dear ones || *ref*—**sovvenirsi di** to remember

sovvenzionare (sovvenzióno) *tr* to subsidize, grant a subvention to

sovvenzióne *f* subsidy, subvention

sovversi·vo -va *adj & m* subversive

sovvertire (sovvèrto) *tr* to subvert

sóz·zo -za *adj* dirty, filthy, foul

sozzura *f* dirt, filth

spaccalé·gna *m* (-gna) woodcutter

spaccamón·ti *m* (-ti) braggart

spaccós·sa *m* (-sa) butcher's cleaver

spaccare §197 *tr* to break, burst; to crack; to unpack; to chop; to split || *ref* to crack; to break; to split

spacca·to -ta *adj* broken; split; (coll) identical; (coll) true || *f* (sports, theat) splits

spaccatura *f* break; crack; cleavage; split

spacchétto *m* vent (*in jacket*)

spacciare §128 *tr* to sell out; to palm off; to spread (*reports*); to expedite; to abandon (*as hopeless*); (slang) to push (*e.g., dope*) || *ref*—**spacciarsi per** to pretend to be, pass oneself off as

spaccia·to -ta *adj* (coll) cooked, done for; (coll) hopeless

spaccia·tóre -trice *mf* passer (*of bad currency or stolen goods*); **spacciatore di notizie false** gossipmonger

spàc·cio *m* (-ci) sale; passing (*of counterfeit money*); spreading (*of false news*); post exchange; tobacco shop

spac·co *m* (-chi) break; split; tear; crack; vent (*in jacket*)

spacconata *f* brag, braggadocio

spaccó·ne -na *mf* braggart, braggadocio

spada *f* sword; **a spada tratta** doggedly; **spade suit** of Neapolitan cards corresponding to spades

spadaccino *m* swordsman; swashbuckler

spadóne *m* two-handed sword

spadroneggiare §290 (**spadronéggio**) *intr* to be domineering or bossy

spaesa·to -ta *adj* out-of-place

spaghétto *m* (coll) fear, jitters; **avere lo spaghetto** (coll) to be scared stiff; **spaghetti** spaghetti

Spagna, la Spain

spagnòla *f* Spanish woman; Spanish influenza

spagnolétta *f* espagnolette; spool; (coll) cigarette; (coll) peanut

spagnò·lo -la *adj* Spanish || *m* Spaniard (*individual*); Spanish (*language*); **gli spagnoli** the Spanish || *f* see **spagnola**

spa·go *m* (**-ghi**) string, twine; (coll) fear, jitters

spaiare §287 *tr* to break a pair of

spaia·to -ta *adj* unmatched

spalancare §197 *tr* to open wide || *ref* to open up; to gape

spalare *tr* to shovel; to feather (*oar*)

spalla *f* shoulder; back; abutment (*of bridge*); (theat) stooge, straight man; **alle spalle di qlcu** behind s.o.'s back; **a spalla** on one's back; **fare spalla a** to help; **lavorare di spalle** to elbow one's way; (fig) to worm one's way up; **vivere alle spalle di** to sponge on

spallàrm *interj* (mil) shoulder arms!

spallata *f* push with the shoulder; shrug of the shoulders

spalleggiare §290 (**spalléggio**) *tr* to back, support; (mil) to carry on one's back

spallétta *f* parapet, retaining wall; jamb

spallièra *f* back (*of chair*); head (*of bed*); foot (*of bed*); espalier

spallina *f* epaulet; shoulder strap

spallùccia *f*—**fare spallucce** to shrug one's shoulders

spalmare *tr* to spread; to smear

spalto *m* glacis; **spalti** seats (*of a stadium*)

spanare *tr* to strip the thread of || *ref* to be stripped (*said, e.g., of the thread of a nut*)

spanciare §128 *tr* to disembowel, gut || *intr* to belly-flop; to bulge (*said of a wall*) || *ref*—**spanciarsi dalle risa** to split one's sides laughing

spanciata *f* belly flop; bellyful; **fare una spanciata** to stuff oneself

spàndere §260 *tr* to spread; to spill; to shed (*tears*); to squander || *ref* to spread

spanna *f* span

spannare *tr* to skim (*milk*)

spannocchiare §287 (**spannòcchio**) *tr* to husk (*corn*)

spappolare (**spàppolo**) *tr* to crush, squash || *ref* to become mushy

sparadrappo *m* adhesive tape; (obs) plaster, poultice

sparagnare *tr* (coll) to save

sparare *tr* to gut, disembowel; to shoot; to let go with (*a kick*); to remove

the hangings from; **spararne delle grosse** to tell tall tales

sparato·le *m* shirt front, dickey

sparatòria *f* shooting

sparecchiare §287 (**sparécchio**) *tr* to clear (*the table*); to clear away (*one's tools*); to eat up

sparég·gio *m* (**-gi**) disparity; deficit; (sports) play-off

spàrgere §261 *tr* to spread; to shed; to spill || *ref* to spread

spargiménto *m* spreading; **spargimento di sangue** bloodshed

spargisa·le [s] *m* (**-le**) salt shaker

sparigliare §280 *tr* to break a pair of; to break (*a set*)

spariglia·to -ta *adj* unmatched

sparire §176 *intr* (ESSERE) to disappear

sparlare *intr* to backbite; **sparlare di** to backbite, slander

sparo *m* shot

sparpagliare §280 *tr* & *intr* to scatter

spar·so -sa *adj* scattered; dotted; speckled; hanging loosely (*e.g., hair*)

sparta·no -na *adj* & *mf* Spartan

spartiàc·que *m* (**-que**) watershed

spartiné·ve *m* (**-ve**) snowplow

spartire §176 *tr* to divide, share; to separate; **non aver nulla da spartire con** to have nothing to do with

spartito *m* (mus) score; (mus) arrangement

spartitràffi·co *m* (**-co**) median strip

spar·to -ta *adj* (lit) spread || *m* esparto grass

sparu·to -ta *adj* lean, wan; meager

sparvière *m* sparrow hawk; mortarboard

spasimante *m* (joc) lover, wooer

spasimare (**spàsimo**) *intr* to writhe; **spasimare per** to long for; to be madly in love with

spàsimo *m* pang; severe pain; longing

spasmo *m* spasm

spasmòdi·co -ca *adj* (**-ci -che**) spasmodic

spassare *tr* to amuse || *ref*—**spassarsela** to have a good time

spassiona·to -ta *adj* dispassionate, unbiased

spasso *m* fun, amusement; walk; (coll) funny guy; **andare a spasso** to go out for a walk; **essere a spasso** to be out of a job; **mandare a spasso** to fire, dismiss; to get rid of; **per spasso** for fun; **portare a spasso** to lead by the nose; **prendersi spasso di** to make fun of

spassó·so -sa [s] *adj* amusing, droll

spàsti·co -ca *adj* & *mf* spastic

spato *m* spar

spatofluòre *m* fluorspar

spàtola *f* spatula; putty knife; slapstick (*of harlequin*)

spauràc·chio *m* (**chi**) scarecrow; bugaboo, bugbear

spaurare *tr* & *ref* (lit) var of **spaurire**

spaurire §176 *tr* to frighten || *ref* to be scared

spaval·do -da *adj* bold, swaggering

spaventapàs·seri *m* (**-ri**) scarecrow

spaventare (spavènto) *tr* to scare, frighten ‖ *ref* to be scared

spaventévole *adj* frightening, dreadful

spavènto *m* fright, fear

spaventó·so -sa [s] *adj* frightful, fearful

spaziale *adj* space

spaziare §287 *tr* (typ) to space ‖ *intr* to soar; to range, rove (*said, e.g., of eye*)

spazia·tóre -trice *adj* spacing ‖ *f* space bar (*of typewriter*)

spaziatura *f* spacing

spazientire §176 *tr* to make (*s.o.*) lose his patience ‖ *intr* (ESSERE) & *ref* to lose patience

spà·zio *m* (-zi) space; (fig) room; **spazio aereo** air space; **spazio cosmico** outer space

spazió·so -sa [s] *adj* spacious, roomy; wide

spazzacamino *m* chimney sweep

spazzami·ne *m* (-ne) mine sweeper

spazzané·ve *m* (-ve) snowplow

spazzare *tr* to sweep; to plow (*snow*); to clean up

spazzata *f*—**dare una spazzata a** to give a lick and a promise to

spazzatrice *f* street sweeper

spazzatura *f* sweeping; sweepings; rubbish, trash

spazzatu·ràio *m* (-rài) or **spazzino** *m* street cleaner; trashman, garbage collector, trash collector

spàzzola *f* brush; **capelli a spazzola** crew cut

spazzolare (spàzzolo) *tr* to brush

spazzolino *m* little brush; (elec) brush; **spazzolino da denti** toothbrush; **spazzolino per le unghie** nailbrush

spazzolóne *m* push broom

specchiare §287 (spècchio) *tr* (lit) to reflect ‖ *ref* to look at oneself (*in a mirror*); to be reflected; **specchiarsi in qlcu** to model oneself on s.o.

specchièra *f* mirror; dressing table; full-length mirror

specchiétto *m* mirror; synopsis; **specchietto retrovisivo** (aut) rear-view mirror

spèc·chio *m* (-chi) mirror; synopsis; shore (*of lake or river*); panel (*of door or window*); sheet (*of water*); (sports) goal line; (sports) board; **specchio di poppa** (naut) transom; **specchio ustorio** burning glass

speciale *adj* special

speciali·sta *mf* (-sti -ste) specialist

speciali·tà *f* (-tà) specialty; (mil) special services; **specialità farmaceutica** patent or proprietary medicine

specializzare [ddzz] *tr* & *ref* to specialize

spè·cie *f* (-cie) species; kind, sort; appearance, semblance; **fare specie** (with *dat*) (coll) to be surprised, e.g., **gli fa specie** he is surprised; **in specie** especially; **sotto specie di** under pretext of

specìfi·ca *f* (-che) itemized list; specification

specificare §197 (specìfico) *tr* to specify; to itemize

specìfi·co -ca (-ci -che) *adj* & *m* specific ‖ *f* see **specifica**

speclllo *m* (med) probe

specló·so -sa [s] *adj* specious

spè·co *m* (-chi) (lit) cave

spècola *f* observatory

spèculo *m* (med, surg) speculum

speculare (spèculo) *tr* to observe; to meditate on ‖ *intr* to speculate

speculu·tóre -trice *adj* speculating ‖ *mf* speculator; **speculatore al rialzo** bull; **speculatore al ribasso** bear

speda·to -ta *adj* footworn

spedire §176 *tr* to expedite; to prepare; to ship, send, forward; (law) to deliver

spedì·to -ta *adj* rapid; free, easy

spedi·tóre -trice *mf* shipper, sender; shipping clerk

spedizióne *f* shipment, shipping; sending, forwarding; expedition; (naut) papers; **di spedizione** expeditionary

spedizionière *m* shipper, forwarder, forwarding agent

spègnere §262 *tr* to extinguish, put out; to turn off; to slake (*lime*); to kill; to mix (*flour*) with water or milk; to quench; to obliterate (*a memory*) ‖ *ref* to burn out; to go out (*said of a light*); to fade, die away; to die

spegni·tóio *m* (-tói) snuffer

spegnitura *f* (theat) blackout

spelacchiare §287 *tr* to strip of hair ‖ *ref* to shed hair or fur

spelacchia·to -ta *adj* mangy; (pej) baldy

spelare (spélo) *tr* to strip of hair; to pluck (*e.g., a chicken*); (fig) to fleece ‖ *ref* to shed hair or fur; to get bald

spellare (spèllo) *tr* to skin; (fig) to skin, fleece

spelón·ca *f* (-che) cave; hovel, den

spème *f* (poet) hope

spendacció·ne -na *mf* spendthrift

spèndere §220 *tr* to spend

spenderéc·cio -cia *adj* (-ci -ce) spendthrift, prodigal

spennacchiare §287 *tr* to pluck; (fig) to fleece ‖ *ref* to lose its feathers

spennare (spénno) *tr* & *ref* var of **spennacchiare**

spennellare (spennèllo) *tr* to dab

spensieratézza *f* thoughtlessness

spensiera·to -ta *adj* thoughtless, careless; carefree, happy-go-lucky

spèn·to -ta *adj* extinguished; turned off; slaked (*lime*); dull (*color*); low (*tone*)

spenzolare [dz] (spènzolo) *tr* & *intr* to hang ‖ *ref*—**spenzolarsi da** to hang out of

speranza *f* hope; prospect, expectation

speranzó·so -sa [s] *adj* hopeful

sperare (spèro) *tr* to candle (*eggs*); to hope for; to expect ‖ *intr* to hope; to trust

spèrdere §212 *tr* (lit) to scatter; (lit) to lose (*one's way*) ‖ *ref* to lose one's way, get lost

sperdu·to -ta *adj* lost, astray; godforsaken (*place*)

sperequazióne *f* disproportion; inequality; unjust distribution

spergiurare *tr & intr* to swear falsely; **giurare e spergiurare** to swear over and over again

spergiu·ro -ra *adj* perjured ‖ *mf* perjurer ‖ *m* perjury

spericola·to -ta *adj* reckless, daring

sperimentale *adj* experimental

sperimentare (speriménto) *tr* to test, try out; to experience

sperimenta·to -ta *adj* experienced

spèr·ma *m* (**-mi**) sperm

speronare (speróno) *tr* (naut) to ram

speróne *m* spur; abutment; (nav) ram

sperperare (spèrpero) *tr* to squander

spèrpero *m* squandering

spèr·so -sa *adj* lost, stray

spertica·to -ta *adj* too long; too tall; exaggerated, excessive

spésa [s] *f* expense; shopping; buy, purchase; **fare la spesa** to shop; **fare le spese di** to be the butt of; **lavorare per le spese** to work for one's keep; **pagare le spese** to bear the charges; **spese** expenses; room and board; **spese di manutenzione** upkeep; **spese minute** petty expenses; **spese processuali** (law) costs

spesare [s] (**spéso**) *tr* to support

spesa·to -ta [s] *adj* with all expenses paid

spés·so -sa *adj* thick; many (*times*) ‖ **spesso** *adv* often; **spesso spesso** again and again

spessóre *m* thickness

spettàbile *adj* esteemed; **Spettàbile Ditta** (com) Gentlemen

spettàcolo *m* spectacle, show; sight; **dar spettacolo di sé** to make a show of oneself; **spettacolo all'aperto** outdoor performance

spettacoló·so -sa [s] *adj* spectacular; (coll) exceptional; (coll) sensational

spettanza *f* concern; pay

spettare (spètto) *intr* (ESSERE)—**spettare a** to belong to ‖ *impers* (ESSERE) —**spetta a** it behooves, it is up to

spetta·tóre -trice *mf* spectator, bystander; **spettatori** public, audience

spettegolare (spettégolo) *intr* to gossip

spettinare (spèttino) *tr* to muss the hair of

spettrale *adj* ghost-like; spectral

spèttro *m* specter, ghost; spectrum

speziale *m* dealer in spices; (coll) pharmacist

spèzie *fpl* spices

spezieria *f* grocery; (coll) drug store, pharmacy; **spezierie** spices

spezzare (spèzzo) *tr* to break; to smash; to interrupt ‖ *ref* to break

spezzatino *m* stew; **spezzatini** change

spezza·to -ta *adj* broken; fragmentary; interrupted ‖ *m* stew; (theat) set piece; **spezzati** change

spezzettare (spezzétto) *tr* to mince

spezzóne *m* small aerial bomb; fragmentation bomb; fragment

spia *f* spy; indication; peephole; (aut) gauge; (aut) pilot light; **fare la spia** to be an informer

spiaccicare §197 (**spiàccico**) *tr* to squash, crush ‖ *ref* to be squashed

spiacènte *adj* sorry; (lit) disliked

spiacére §214 *intr* (ESSERE) (with *dat*) to dislike, e.g., **queste parole gli spiacciono** he dislikes these words; to mind, e.g., **se non Le spiace** if you don't mind ‖ *ref*—**spiacersi di** to be sorry for ‖ *impers* (ESSERE) (with *dat*)—**gli spiace** he is sorry

spiacévole *adj* unpleasant

spiàg·gia *f* (**-ge**) beach, shore

spianare *tr* to grade (*land*); to roll (*dough*); to pave (*the way*); to iron (*pleats*); to raze, demolish; to level (*a gun*); **spianare la fronte** to smooth one's brow ‖ *intr* (ESSERE) to be level

spianata *f* esplanade; **dare una spianata a** to level

spianatóia *f* board (*for rolling dough*)

spiana·tóio *m* (**-tói**) rolling pin

spianatrice *f* grader

spiano *m* leveling; esplanade; **a tutto spiano** at full blast; continuously

spiantare *tr* to uproot; to raze, level; to ruin (*financially*) ‖ *ref* to ruin oneself

spianta·to -ta *adj* ruined ‖ *m* pauper

spiare §119 *tr* to spy on; to keep an eye on

spiattellare (spiattèllo) *tr* to blurt out

spiazzo *m* square; plain; clearing

spiccare §197 *tr* to detach; to pick; to enunciate; to begin; to draw up (*a commercial paper*); to issue (*a warrant*); **spiccare il volo** (aer) to take off ‖ *intr* to stand out ‖ *ref* to separate (*said, e.g., of the stone of a peach*)

spicca·to -ta *adj* clear, distinct; typical; outstanding

spìc·chio *m* (**-chi**) section (*of fruit*); clove (*of garlic*); slice (*e.g., of apple*); arm (*of cross*)

spicciare §128 *tr* to clear up; to wait on; to dispatch (*business*) ‖ *intr* (ESSERE) to flow forth, gush out ‖ *ref* to hurry up, make haste

spicciati·vo -va *adj* expeditious, quick; straightforward; gruff

spiccicare §197 (**spiccico**) *tr* to unglue; to enunciate; to utter ‖ *ref* to come unglued; **spiccicarsi di** to get rid of

spìc·cio -cia (**-ci -ce**) *adj* expeditious, quick; unhampered; small (*change*) ‖ **spicci** *mpl* change

spicciolata *adj* *fem*—**alla spicciolata** little by little; a few at a time

spìcciolo -la *adj* small (change); (coll) plain ‖ **spiccioli** *mpl* small change

spìc·co -ca (**-chi -che**) *adj* freestone (*e.g., peach*) ‖ *m*—**fare spicco** to stand out

spidocchiare §287 (**spidòcchio**) *tr* to delouse

spièdo *m* spit; **allo spiedo** barbecued

spiegàbile *adj* explainable

spiegaménto *m* (mil) array; (mil) deployment

spiegare §209 (**spiègo**) *tr* to unfold; to let go (*with one's voice*); to unfurl; to spread (*wings*); to deploy (*troops*); to explain; to show, demonstrate; **spiegare il volo** (aer) to take off ‖ *ref* to become unfurled or unfolded;

to make oneself understood; to come to an understanding; to realize

spiega·to -ta adj open; full (voice)

spiegazióne f explanation

spiegazzare tr to crumple, rumple

spieta·to -ta adj pitiless, ruthless

spifferare (spìffero) tr (coll) to blurt out || intr to blow in (said of wind)

spìffero m (coll) draft

spì·ga f (ghe) panicle (of oats); (bot) ear, spike; **a spiga** herringbone

spiga·to -ta adj herringbone

spighétta f braid; (bot) spikelet

spigionare (spigióno) ref to be or become vacant

spiglia·to -ta adj easy, free and easy

spì·go m (-ghi) lavender

spigolare (spìgolo) tr to glean

spigola·tóre -trice mf gleaner

spìgolo m corner; edge; (archit) arris

spilla f brooch, pin; **spilla da cravatta** tiepin; **spilla di sicurezza** safety pin

spillare tr to draw off, tap; to wheedle, worm (money) || intr to leak (said of container) || intr (ESSERE) to leak (said of liquid)

spillàti·co m (-ci) (law) pin money (for one's wife)

spillo m pin; gimlet; trifle; **a spillo** spikelike; **spillo da balia or di sicurezza** safety pin

spillóne m hatpin; bodkin

spilluzzicare §197 (spilluzzico) tr to pick at, nibble; to scrape together

spilorcerìa f stinginess

spilòr·cio -cia (-ci -ce) adj stingy || mf miser, tightwad

spilungó·ne -na mf lanky person

spina f thorn; quill, spine (of porcupine); bone (of fish); (fig) preoccupation, worry; **alla spina** (beer) on tap; **a spina di pesce** herringbone (fabric); **con una spina nel cuore** sick at heart; **essere sulle spine** to be on pins and needles; **spina della botte** tap; bunghole; **spina dorsale** spinal column; (fig) backbone; **spina elettrica** plug

spinà·cio -cia (-ci) spinach (plant); **spinaci** spinach (as food)

spinapésce m—**a spinapesce** herringbone

spina·to -ta adj barbed (wire); herringbone (fabric)

spìngere §126 tr to push, press; to prod, goad || ref to push; to reach

spì·no -na adj thorny || m thorn || f see spina

spinóne m griffon

spinó·so -sa [s] adj thorny

spinòtto m wrist pin

spinta f push; pressure; poke, prod; stress

spinterògeno m (aut) distributor unit, ignition system

spin·to -ta adj pushed; bent, inclined; (coll) risqué; (coll) far-out, offbeat || f see spinta

spintóne m (coll) push, shove

spionàg·gio m (-gi) espionage, spying

spioncino m peephole

spió·ne -na mf spy, stool pigeon

spiovènte adj drooping; sloping; falling || m slope; drainage area (of a mountain)

spiòvere §216 intr to fall, to hang down (said, e.g., of hair); to flow down || impers (ESSERE)—**è spiovuto** it stopped raining

spira f turn (of a coil); coil (of serpent); **a spire** spiral

spirà·glio m (-gli) small opening; gleam (of light or hope)

spirale adj spiral || f spiral; hairspring; wreath (of smoke); **spirale di fumo** smoke ring

spirare tr to send forth; (lit) to inspire, infuse; (lit) to show (kindness) || intr to blow; to emanate; to die; to expire

spirita·to -ta adj possessed; wild, mad

spìriti·co -ca adj (-ci -che) spiritual; spiritualistic

spiritismo m spiritualism

spìrito m spirit; wit; mind; spirits, alcohol; sprite; **bello spirito** wit (person); **fare dello spirito** to be witty; to crack jokes; **l'ultimo spirito** (lit) one's last breath; **spirito di corpo** esprit de corps; **spirito di parte** partisanship; **spirito sportivo** sportsmanship

spiritosàggine [s] f witticism

spiritó·so -sa [s] adj witty; alcoholic

spirituale adj spiritual

spìzzi·co m (-chi)—**a spizzico** or **a spizzichi** little by little; **a little at a time**

splendènte adj resplendent, shining

splèndere §281 intr (ESSERE & AVERE) to shine

splèndi·do -da adj splendid; gorgeous; bright || m—**fare lo splendido** to be a big spender

splendóre m splendor; brightness; beauty

splène m (anat) spleen

spòcchia f haughtiness

spodestare (spodèsto) tr to dispossess; to dethrone; to oust

spoetizzare [ddzz] tr to disillusion

spòglia f slough (of snake); skin (of onion); husk (of corn); (lit) body; (lit) outer garment; **sotto mentite spoglie** under false pretense; **spoglie** spoils

spogliare §280 (spòglio) tr to undress, strip; to strip of armor; to defraud, deprive; to free; to check, examine; to husk (corn); to go through (e.g., correspondence) || ref to undress; to slough (said, e.g., of a snake); **spogliarsi di** to get rid of; to divest oneself of; to shake (a habit)

spogliarelli·sta f (-ste) stripteaser

spogliarèllo m striptease

spoglia·tóio m (-tói) dressing room; locker room

spò·glio -glia (-gli -glie) adj stripped, bare; free || m cast-off clothing; sorting; scrutiny; counting (of votes); **di spoglio** second-hand (material) || f see spoglia

spòla f bobbin; shuttle; **fare la spola** to shuttle

spolétta *f* bobbin, spool; (mil) fuse

spolmonare (spolmóno) *ref* (coll) to talk, sing, or shout oneself hoarse

spolpare (spólpo) *tr* to gnaw (*a bone*); to eat up (*fruit*); (fig) to fleece

spolverare (spólvero) *tr* to dust off, whisk; to powder, dust; to pounce

spolveratura *f* dusting; powdering; sprinkling, smattering (*of knowledge*); **dare una spolveratura a** to brush up on

spolverina *f* (coll) duster

spolverino *m* duster, smock; powder-sugar duster; pounce; (coll) whisk broom

spolverizzaménto [ddzz] *m* sprinkling (*with powder*)

spolverizzare [ddzz] *tr* to dust, powder, pounce

spólvero *m* dusting; powdering; pounce; smattering, sprinkling (*of knowledge*); display

spónda *f* bank (*of river*); side; cushion (*of billiard table*)

sponsale *adj* (lit) wedding ‖ **sponsali** *mpl* (lit) wedding

spontàne·o -a *adj* spontaneous; artless

spopolare (spòpolo) *tr* to depopulate ‖ *intr* to be a hit; to become depopulated or deserted

spoppare (spóppo) *tr* to wean

sporàdi·co -ca *adj* (-ci -che) sporadic

sporcaccio·ne -na *adj* filthy ‖ *mf* filthy person; (fig) dirty mouth

sporcare (spórco) *tr* to dirty; to soil ‖ *ref* to get dirty; to soil oneself; **sporcarsi la fedina** (coll) to get a black mark on one's record

sporcizia *f* dirt, filth

spòr·co -ca (-chi -che) *adj* dirty, filthy; foul; **farla sporca** to pull a dirty trick ‖ *m* dirt, filth

sporgènte *adj* leaning; protruding; beetle (*brow*)

sporgènza *f* prominence, projection

spòrgere §217 *tr* to stick out; to stretch out; to lodge (*a complaint*) ‖ *intr* (ESSERE) to project, jut out ‖ *ref* to lean out

spòrt *m* (spòrt) sport; game; **per sport** for fun, for pleasure

spòrta *f* shopping bag; bagful; basket; basketful; shopping; **a sporta** wide-brimmed (*hat*)

sportèllo *m* door; panel; window (*in bank, station, etc.*); wicket; branch (*of a bank*); (theat) box office

sportivi·tà *f* (-tà) sportsmanship

sporti·vo -va *adj* sporting; sportsman-like; athletic ‖ *m* sportsman

spòr·to -ta *adj* projecting; jutting out ‖ *m* projection; removable shutter (*on store door or window*) ‖ *f* see **sporta**

spòsa *f* bride; wife; **andare in sposa a** to get married to; **sposa promessa** fiancée

sposali·zio -zia (-zi -zie) *adj* (lit) nuptial ‖ *m* wedding

sposare (spòso) *tr* to marry; to unite; to embrace (*a cause*); to fit perfectly; to give in marriage ‖ *ref* to get married, marry

spòso *m* bridegroom; **sposi** newlyweds

spossare (spòsso) *tr* to exhaust ‖ *ref* to become worn out

spossatézza *f* exhaustion

spostaménto *m* shift; movement; displacement; change

spostare (spòsto) *tr* to move; to change, shift; to upset ‖ *ref* to move; to shift; to get out of place; to be upset

sposta·to -ta *adj* ill-adjusted, out of place ‖ *mf* misfit

spran·ga *f* (-ghe) bar, crossbar

sprangare §209 *tr* to bar, bolt

sprazzo *m* spray; flash; burst

sprecare §197 (sprèco) *tr* to waste; to miss (*an opportunity*) ‖ *ref* to waste one's efforts

sprè·co *m* (-chi) waste; squandering

sprecó·ne -na *adj* & *mf* spendthrift

spregévole *adj* contemptible, despicable

spregiare §290 (sprègio) *tr* to despise

sprè·gio *m* (-gi) contempt, scorn

spregiudica·to -ta *adj* open-minded, unbiased ‖ *m* open-minded person

sprèmere §123 *tr* to squeeze, press; **spremere le lacrime a** to move to tears ‖ *ref*—**spremersi il cervello** to rack one's brain

spremifrut·ta *m* (-ta) squeezer

spremilimó·ni *m* (-ni) lemon squeezer

spremuta *f* squeezing; **spremuta d'arancia** orange juice

spretare (sprèto) *ref* to doff the cassock

sprezzante *adj* contemptuous, haughty

sprezzare (sprèzzo) *tr* (lit) to despise

sprèzzo *m* disdain, contempt

sprigionare (sprigióno) *tr* to exhale, emit; to free from prison ‖ *ref* to free oneself; to escape, come forth, issue (*said, e.g., of steam*)

sprimacciare §128 *tr* to beat, fluff (*e.g., a pillow*)

sprizzare *tr* to spout; to sparkle with (*joy, health*) ‖ *intr* (ESSERE) to spurt; to fly (*said of sparks*); to sparkle

sprizzo *m* sprinkle; spurt; spark

sprofondare (sprofóndo) *tr* to send to the bottom; to destroy, ruin; to sink ‖ *intr* (ESSERE) to sink; to founder; to cave in; to be sunk (*e.g., in meditation*)

sprolò·quio *m* (-qui) long rigmarole

spronare (spróno) *tr* to spur, goad

spróne *m* spur; prodding; example; guimpe; buttress; abutment (*of bridge*); **a spronе battuto** at full speed; at once; **dar di sprone a** to spur on; **sprone di cavaliere** (bot) rocket larkspur

sproporziona·to -ta *adj* out of proportion, disproportionate

sproporzióne *f* disproportion

sproposita·to -ta *adj* out of proportion; excessive; gross (*error*)

spropòsito *m* blunder, gross error; excessive amount; **a sproposito** out of place; inopportunely

sprovvedu·to -ta *adj* deprived; brainless, witless

sprovvi·sto -sta *adj* deprived; devoid, lacking; **alla sprovvista** suddenly; unawares, off guard

spruzzabianche·rìa *m* (-rìa) sprinkler (*to sprinkle clothes*)

spruzzare *tr* to sprinkle, spray; to powder (*sugar*)

spruzzatóre *m* sprayer; (aut) nozzle (*of carburetor*)

spruzzo *m* spray; splash (*of mud*)

spudora·to -ta *adj* shameless; impudent

spugna *f* sponge; dare un colpo di spugna to wipe the slate clean; gettare la spugna to throw in the towel

spugnare *tr* to sponge; to swab

spugnatura *f* sponge bath

spugnó·so -sa [s] *adj* spongy

spulciare §128 *tr* to pick the fleas off; to scrutinize, examine minutely

spuma *f* foam, froth

spumante *adj* sparkling ‖ *m* sparkling wine; champagne

spumare *intr* to froth

spumeggiante *adj* sparkling; vaporous, foamy

spumeggiare §290 (spuméggio) *intr* to foam

spumóne *m* spumoni

spumó·so -sa [s] *adj* foamy, frothy

spunta *f* check; check list; check mark

spuntare *tr* to blunt; to unpin; to overcome; to clip, trim; to check off; spuntarla to come out on top; to overcome ‖ *intr* (ESSERE) to appear; to sprout; to rise; to well up (*said of tears*); to pop out; to break through ‖ *ref* to become blunt; to die down

spuntino *m* bite, snack; fare uno spuntino to have a bite

spunto *m* sourness (*of wine*); (theat) cue; (sports) sprint; (fig) starting point, origin

spuntóne *m* spike; pike; crag

spurgare §209 *tr* to purge, clear; to clean up ‖ *ref* to expectorate

spur·go *m* (-ghi) discharge; reject (*e.g., book*)

spù·rio -ria *adj* (-ri -rie) spurious

sputacchiare §287 *tr* to spit upon ‖ *intr* to sputter

sputacchièra *f* spittoon, cuspidor

sputare *tr* to spit; to cough up; (fig) to spew (*venom*); sputare sangue to spit blood; (fig) to sweat blood ‖ *intr* to spit

sputasentènze *mf* (-ze) wiseacre

sputo *m* spit, sputum; spitting

squadernare (squadèrno) *tr* to leaf through; squadernare qlco a qlcu to put s.th under the nose of s.o. ‖ *ref* to come apart (*said of a book*)

squadra *f* square (*for measuring right angles*); squad, group; (mil) squadron; (sports) team; a squadra at right angles; fuori squadra out of kilter; squadra di pompieri fire company; squadra mobile flying squad

squadrare *tr* to square; (fig) to examine, study

squadrìglia *f* (aer, nav) squadron

squadróne *m* squadron (*of cavalry*)

squagliare §280 *tr* to melt ‖ *ref* to melt; squagliarsela to take French leave

squalìfi·ca *f* (-che) disqualification

squalificare §197 (squalìfico) *tr* to disqualify ‖ *ref* to disqualify oneself; to prove to be unqualified

squàlli·do -da *adj* wretched, dreary, gloomy; faint (*smile*); (lit) emaciated

squallóre *m* wretchedness, dreariness, gloominess

squalo *m* shark

squama *f* scurf (*shed by the skin*); (bot, pathol, zool) scale

squamare *tr & ref* to scale

squamó·so -sa [s] *adj* scaly

squarciagóla *adv*—a squarciagola at the top of one's voice

squarciare §128 *tr* to rend, tear apart; to dispel (*a doubt*) ‖ *ref* to become torn; to open

squàr·cio *m* (-ci) tear, rip; passage (*of book*)

squartare *tr* to quarter

squartatura *f* quartering

squassare *tr* to shake violently; to wreck

squattrina·to -ta *adj* penniless ‖ *m* pauper

squilibra·to -ta *adj* unbalanced, deranged ‖ *mf* mad or insane person

squilì·brio *m* (-bri) lack of balance; squilibrio mentale insanity; unbalanced mental condition

squillante *adj* ringing, shrill; sharp

squillare *intr* to ring; to ring out; to blare

squillo *m* ring; peal; blare, blast (*of horn*); ‖ *f* call girl

squinternare (squintèrno) *tr* to tear (*a book*) to pieces; (fig) to upset

squisi·to -ta *adj* exquisite

squittire §176 *intr* to squeak; to squeal

sradicare §197 (sràdico) *tr* to uproot; to eradicate; to pull (*a tooth*)

sragionare (sragióno) *intr* to talk nonsense

sregola·to -ta *adj* intemperate; dissolute

srotolare (sròtolo) *tr* to unroll

stàb·bio *m* (-bi) pen; manure, dung

stabbiòlo *m* pigpen

stàbile *adj* stable; real (*estate*); permanent; stock (*company*) ‖ *m* building

stabiliménto *m* plant, factory; establishment; settlement, colony; conclusion (*of a deal*)

stabilire §176 *tr* to establish; to decide ‖ *ref* to settle

stabili·tà *f* (-tà) stability, steadiness

stabilito *m* (law) agreement of sale (*drawn up by a broker*)

stabilizzare [ddzz] *tr & ref* to stabilize

stabilizza·tóre -trice [ddzz] *mf* stabilizing person ‖ *m* (aer) stabilizer; (elec) voltage stabilizer

staccare §197 *tr* to detach; to unhitch; to outdistance; to draw (*a check*); to tear off; to take (*one's eyes*) away; to begin; to enunciate (*words*) ‖ *intr* to stand out; (coll) to stop working ‖ *ref* to come off; staccarsi da to come off (*e.g., the wall*); to leave (*one's home; the shore*); (aer) to take off from

stacciare §128 *tr* to sift, sieve

stàc·cio m (-ci) sieve
staccionata f fence; hurdle; stockade
stac·co m (-chi) tearing off; cut of cloth (*for a suit*); interval; **fare stacco** to stand out
stadèra f steelyard; **stadera a ponte** weighbridge
stàdia f leveling rod
stà·dio m (-di) stadium; stage
staffa f stirrup; heel (*of sock*); gaiter strap; clamp; (mach) bracket; **perdere le staffe** to lose one's nerve
staffétta f courier, messenger; pilot (*car*); **a staffetta** relay
staffière m groom, footman; servant
staffilare tr to whip, belt, lash
staffilata f lash
staffile m stirrup strap; whip
stàg·gio m (-gi) stay, upright
stagionale adj seasonal || mf seasonal worker
stagionare (**stagióno**) tr to season, cure
stagiona·to -ta adj seasoned, ripe
stagióne f season; **da mezza stagione** spring-and-fall (*coat*); **di fine stagione** year-end (*sale*)
stagliare §280 tr to hack || ref to stand out
staglia·to -ta adj sheer (*cliff*)
sta·gnàio m (-gnài) tinsmith; plumber
stagnante adj stagnant
stagnare tr to tin; to solder; to stanch || intr to stagnate
stagnaro m var of **stagnaio**
stagnina f tin can
stagnino m (coll) var of **stagnaio**
sta·gno -gna adj watertight; airtight || m tin; pond, pool
stagnòla f tin foil; tin can
stàio m (stài) bushel (*container*); **a staio** (coll) top (*hat*) || m (stàia fpl) bushel (*measure*); **a staia** in abundance
stalla f stable
stallìa f (com) lay day
stallière m stableman, stableboy
stallo m seat; stall; (chess) stalemate
stallóne m stallion
stamane, stamani or **stamattina** adv this morning
stambéc·co m (-chi) ibex
stambèr·ga f (-ghe) hovel
stambù·gio m (-gi) hole, hovel
stamburare tr to puff up, to boast about || intr to drum
stame m (bot) stamen; thread, yarn
stamigna f cheesecloth
stampa f printing; print; (fig) print; (fig) mold; **stampe** printed matter
stampàg·gio m (-gi) (mach) stamping
stampare tr to stamp; to print; to impress; to publish || ref (fig) to be ingraved
stampatèllo m—**in stampatello** in block letters; **scrivere in stampatello** to print (*with pen or pencil*)
stampa·to -ta adj printed; impressed || m printed form; **stampati** printed matter
stampa·tóre -trice mf printer
stampèlla f crutch
stamperìa f print shop

stampìglia f rubber stamp; billboard; overprint
stampigliare §280 tr to stamp; to overprint
stampinare tr to stencil
stampino m stencil
stampo m mold; stencil; stamp, kind; decoy
stanare tr to flush (*game*); (fig) to dig up
stancare §197 tr to tire, fatigue; to bore || ref to tire, weary
stanchézza f tiredness, weariness
stan·co -ca adj (-chi -che) tired; tired out; (lit) left (*hand*)
standardizzare [ddzz] tr to standardize
stan·ga f (-ghe) bar; shaft (*of cart*); beam (*of plow*)
stangata f blow
stanghétta f small bar; bolt (*of lock*); temple (*of spectacles*); (mus) bar
stanòtte adv tonight; last night
stante adj being; standing; **a sé stante** by itself, independent || prep because of; **stante che** since
stan·tìo -tìa adj (-tìi; -tìe) stale; musty
stantuffo m piston; plunger
stanza f room; stanza; **essere di stanza** (mil) to be stationed; **stanza da bagno** bath room; **stanza di compensazione** clearing house; **stanza di soggiorno** living room
stanziare §287 tr to allocate; to appropriate; to budget || ref to settle
stanzino m small room; closet
stappare tr to uncork
stare §263 intr (ESSERE) to stay; to stand; to live; to be; to be located; to linger; to last; to stick (*e.g., to a rule*); (poker) to stand pat; **come sta?** how are you?; **lasciar stare** to leave alone; **lasciar stare che** to leave aside that; **non stare in sé dalla gioia** to be beside oneself with joy; **sta bene!** O.K.!; **starci** to fit, e.g., **ci stanno trecento persone** three hundred people fit there; **starci di** to be in favor of, e.g., **io ci starei d'andare al cine** I would be in favor of going to the movies; **stare + ger** to be + ger, e.g., **stava leggendo** he was reading; **stare a** to be up to; to stand on (ceremony); to base oneself on; to take (*a joke*); to cost, e.g., **quanto sta il prosciutto?** how much does the ham cost?; **stare a + inf** to keep + ger, e.g., **stai sempre a sognare** you always keep dreaming; **to take + inf**, e.g., **stette poco a decidere** he took little time to decide; **stare a cuore** (with *dat*) to deem important, e.g., **gli sta a cuore il lavoro** he deems his work important; **stare a pancia all'aria** to not do a stroke of work; **stare al proprio posto** to keep one's place; **stare a segno** to behave properly; **stare a vedere** to be possible, e.g., **sta a vedere che non viene?** could it be possible that he won't come?; **stare bene** to be well; to be well-off; (with *dat*) to fit, to become, e.g., **questo vestito gli sta**

bene this suit fits him well, this suit becomes him; **to serve right**, e.g., **gli sta bene!** it serves him right!; **stare comodo** to be at ease; **to remain seated**; **stare con** (fig) to be on the side of; **starsene** to stay apart, e.g., **se ne sta solo soletto** he stays apart or all alone; **stare fermo** to be quiet; to not move; **stare in forse** to doubt; to be doubtful; **stare sulle proprie** to stand aloof; **stare su** to stand erect; **stare su tardi** to stay up late; **stia comodo!** remain seated!

starna f gray partridge

starnazzare intr to flap its wings; to flutter; to cackle

starnutare intr to sneeze

starnuto m sneeze

stasare [s] tr to unplug, unblock

staséra [s] adv tonight, this evening

sta·si f (-si) (com) stagnation; (pathol) stasis

statale adj government; state || mf government employee

stàti·co -ca (-ci -che) static || f statics

stati·no -na adj (coll) migratory || m itemized list; (educ) registration form

stati·sta m (-sti) statesman

statìsti·co -ca (-ci -che) adj statistical || m statistician || f statistics; **fare una statistica (di)** to survey; **statistiche statistics** (data)

stati·vo -va adj nonmigratory; permanent || m stand (of microscope)

stato m state; condition; plight; frame (of mind); status; estate (social class); **di stato** public (e.g., school); **essere in stato di arresto** to be under arrest; **stati extracts** from vital statistics; **Stati Pontifici** Papal States; **Stati Uniti** United States; **stato civile** marital status; vital statistics; **stato confessionale** state under ecclesiastical rule; **stato cuscinetto** buffer state; **stato di preallarme** state of emergency; **stato di previsione** preliminary budget; **stato interessante** pregnancy; **stato maggiore** (mil) general staff

statoreattóre m ramjet engine

stàtua f statue

statuà·rio -ria (-ri -rie) adj statuary; statuesque || m sculptor

statunitènse adj & mf American (U.S.A.)

statura f stature; height

statuto m statute

stavòlta adv (coll) this time

stazionaménto m parking; **stazionamento vietato** no parking

stazionare (stazióno) intr to park

stazionà·rio -ria adj (-ri -rie) stationary

stazióne f station; bearing, posture; **stazione balneare** shore resort; **stazione climatica** health resort; spa; **stazione di rifornimento** service station; **stazione di tassametri** cab stand; **stazione estiva** summer resort; **stazione generatrice** power plant; **stazione orbitale** orbiting station; **stazione sanitaria** clinic

stazza f tonnage; (naut) displacement

stazzare tr (naut) to gauge; (naut) to displace

stazzonare (stazzóno) tr to crumple

steatite f French chalk

stéc·ca f (-che) small stick; slat (of shutter); rib (of umbrella); bone (of whale); carton (of cigarettes); rail (of fence); letter opener; chisel (of sculptor); (billiards) cue; (billiards) miscue; (surg) splint; **fare una stecca** (billiards) to miscue; (mus) to sing or play a sour note

steccadèn·ti m (-ti) (coll) toothpick

steccare §197 (stécco) tr to fence; to put in a splint || intr to play or sing a sour note; (billiards) to miscue

steccato m fence; (racing) inside track

stecchétto m small stick; **tenere a stecchetto** to keep on a strict diet; to keep short of money

stecchino m toothpick

stecchi·to -ta adj stiff; lean, lank; dry (twig); dumfounded

stéc·co m (-chi) stick, twig

stecconata f stockade; fence

stélla f star; rowel (of spur); speck of fat (in soup); (fig) sky; a **stella** star-shaped; stellar; **montare alle stelle** to be sky-high (said, e.g., of prices); **portare alle stelle** to praise to the skies; **stella alpina** edelweiss; **stella cadente** shooting star; **stella di mare** starfish; **stella filante** shooting star; confetti; **stella polare** polestar, lodestar

stellare adj stellar; (mach) radial || v (stéllo) tr to spangle with stars; to stud

stella·to -ta adj starry; star-spangled; star-shaped; studded

stellétta f (mil) star; (typ) asterisk; **guadagnarsi le stellette** (mil) to earn a promotion; **portare le stellette** (mil) to be in the service

stellina f starlet

stelloncino m (journ) short paragraph

stèlo m stem, stalk

stèm·ma m (-mi) coat of arms; genealogy (of a manuscript)

stemperare (stèmpero) tr to dilute; to blunt; to untemper; (lit) to waste || ref to melt; to become dull or blunt

stendardo m banner, standard

stèndere §270 tr to stretch; to hang up (laundry); to spread; to draw up (a document); (mil) to deploy; **stendere a terra** to knock down || ref to stretch out

stendibianche·rìa m (-rìa) clothes rack, clotheshorse

stenodattilògra·fo -fa mf shorthand typist

stenografare (stenògrafo) tr to take down in shorthand

stenografìa f shorthand, stenography

stenogràfi·co -ca adj (-ci -che) stenographic, shorthand

stenògra·fo -fa mf stenographer

stenòsi f (pathol) stricture

stenotipìa f stenotypy

stentare (stènto) tr to eke out (a living)

|| *intr* to barely make ends meet; **stentare a** to hardly be able to; to find it hard to

stenta·to -ta *adj* hard; stunted; strained (*smile*)

stènto *m* privation; hardship; **a stento** hardly; with difficulty; **senza stento** without any trouble

stèr·co *m* (**-chi**) dung

stereofòni·co -ca *adj* (**-ci -che**) stereo, stereophonic

stereoscópi·co -ca *adj* (**-ci -che**) stereoscopic

stereoscò·pio *m* (**-pi**) stereoscope

stereotipà·to -ta *adj* stereotyped

sterilizzare [ddzz] *tr* to sterilize

sterlina *f* pound sterling

sterminare (**stèrmino**) *tr* to exterminate

stermina·to -ta *adj* immense, boundless

stermì·nio *m* (**-ni**) extermination; (coll) large amount, lots

stèrno *m* breastbone

sterpàglia *f* brushwood; undergrowth

stèrpo *m* dry twig; bramble

sterrare (**stèrro**) *tr* to excavate

sterratóre *m* digger

sterzare (**stèrzo**) *tr* to diminish by one third; to thin out (*woodland*); (aut) to steer || *intr* to swerve

sterzata *f* swerve

stèrzo *m* handle bar; (aut) steering gear; (aut) steering wheel

stésa [s] *f* coat (*of paint*); string (*of clothes on line*)

stés·so -sa *adj* same, e.g., **lo stesso mese** the same month; very, e.g., **tuo fratello stesso** your very brother; **essere alle stesse** to be just the same; **io stesso** I myself; **lui stesso he himself**, etc.; **per sé stesso** by himself; by itself || *pron* same; same thing; **fa lo stesso** it's all the same, it makes no difference

stesura [s] *f* drawing up (*of a contract*); **prima stesura** first draft

stetoscò·pio *m* (**-pi**) stethoscope

stìa *f* chicken coop

Stige *m* Styx

sti·gio -gia *adj* (**-gi -gie**) Stygian

sfigmate *fpl* stigmata

stilare *tr* to draft properly

stile *m* style

stilè *adj invar* stylish

stilétto *m* dagger, stiletto

stilizzare [ddzz] *tr* to stylize

stilla *f* (lit) drop, droplet

stillare *tr* to exude; to distill || *intr* (ESSERE) to ooze, drip, exude || *ref*— **stillarsi il cervello** to rack one's brains

stillici·dio *m* (**-di**) dripping; repetition

stilo *m* stylus; arm (*of steelyard*); dagger; gnomon (*of sundial*); (poet) style || *f* (coll) fountain pen

stilogràfi·ca *f* (**-che**) fountain pen

stima *f* appraisal; esteem; (naut) dead reckoning; **a stima d'occhio** more or less

stimare *tr* to estimate; to deem; to esteem || *ref* (coll) to think a lot of oneself

stima·tóre -trice *mf* appraiser; admirer

stìmmate *fpl* var of **stigmate**

stimolante *adj* & *m* stimulant

stimolare (**stìmolo**) *tr* to stimulate

stìmolo *m* influence; stimulus

stin·co *m* (**-chi**) shinbone; shin; **stinco di santo** saintly person, saint; **rompere gli stinchi a** to annoy

stìngere §126 *tr*, *intr* (ESSERE) & *ref* to fade

stipa *f* kindling wood, brushwood

stipare *tr* & *ref* to crowd, jam

stipendiare §287 (**stipèndio**) *tr* to employ, hire; to pay a salary to

stipendià·to -ta *adj* salaried || *mf* salaried person

stipèn·dio *m* (**-di**) pay, salary

stipétto *m* (naut) closet, cabinet

stìpite *m* jamb; stock, family; (bot) trunk (*of palm tree*)

stipo *m* cabinet

stipulare (**stìpulo**) *tr* to draw up (*a contract*); to stipulate

stiracchiare §287 *tr* to stretch; to eke out (*a living*); to twist (*a meaning*); to haggle over || *intr* to haggle; to economize || *ref* to stretch out

stirare *tr* to stretch; to iron, press || *intr* to iron || *ref* to stretch out

stira·tóre -trice *mf* ironer, presser

stiratura *f* ironing; stretching

stirerìa *f* ironing shop

stiro *m*—**ferro da stiro** see **ferro**

stirpe *f* family; birth, origin

stitichézza *f* constipation

stìti·co -ca *adj* (**-ci -che**) constipated; (fig) tight

stiva *f* (naut) hold; (lit) beam (*of plow*)

stivàg·gio *m* (**-gi**) stowage

stivale *m* boot; **dei miei stivali** good-for-nothing; **lustrare gli stivali a qlcu** to lick s.o.'s boots

stivalétto *m* high shoe

stivalóne *m* boot; **stivaloni da equitazione** riding boots; **stivaloni da palude** hip boots

stivare *tr* to stow

stivatóre *m* stevedore

stizza *f* anger; irritation

stizzire §176 *tr* to anger, vex || *ref* to get angry

stizzó·so -sa [s] *adj* peevish, irritable

stoccafisso *m* stockfish

stoccata *f* thrust (*with dagger or rapier*); dig, sarcastic remark; touch (*for money*)

stòc·co *m* (**-chi**) dagger; rapier; stalk (*of corn*)

Stoccólma *f* Stockholm

stòffa *f* cloth, material; (fig) stuff, makings

stoicismo *m* stoicism

stòi·co -ca (**-ci -che**) *adj* stoic, stoical || *m* stoic; Stoic

stoino *m* doormat

stòla *f* stole

stòli·do -da *adj* foolish, silly

stoltézza *f* foolishness, silliness

stól·to -ta *adj* silly || *mf* fool

stomacare §197 (**stòmaco**) *tr* to disgust; to nauseate

stomachévole *adj* disgusting, sickening

stòma·co *m* (**-ci** *or* **-chi**) stomach; maw (*of animal*); **dare di stomaco** to vomit

stonare (**stòno**) *tr* to sing or play out of tune; to upset ‖ *intr* to sing or play out of tune; to be out of place; to not harmonize

stona·to **-ta** *adj* out-of-tune; upset; clashing (*color*)

stonatura *f* jarring sound; clash (*of colors*); lack of harmony

stóppa *f* tow; oakum; **di stoppa** flaxen; weak, trembling; **stoppa incatramata** oakum

stoppàc·cio *m* (**-ci**) wad

stóppie *fpl* stubble

stoppino *m* wick

stoppó·so **-sa** [s] *adj* stubby; stringy

stórcere §272 *tr* to twist; to twitch; to wrench (*one's ankle*); to roll (*one's eyes*) ‖ *ref* to twist; to writhe; to bend

stordimento *m* bewilderment; dizziness

stordire §176 *tr* to bewilder; to daze ‖ *intr* to be bewildered ‖ *ref* to dull one's senses

stordità·ggine *f* carelessness; mistake, blunder

stordi·to **-ta** *adj* careless; bewildered; amazed; dizzy ‖ *mf* scatterbrain

stòria *f* history; story, tale; fact; **fare storie** to stand on ceremony; **un'altra storia** a horse of another color

stòri·co **-ca** (**-ci** **-che**) *adj* historical ‖ *m* historian

storièlla *f* tale, short story; joke

storiografìa *f* historiography

storióne *m* sturgeon

stormire §176 *intr* to rustle

stórmo *m* swarm, flock; (aer) group

stornare (**stórno**) *tr* to ward off; to dissuade; to divert (*funds*); to write off (*as noncollectable*)

stornèllo *m* Italian folksong; (orn) starling

stór·no **-na** *adj* dapple-gray ‖ *m* (com) transfer; (orn) starling

storpiare §287 (**stòrpio**) *tr* to cripple; to clip (*one's words*)

stòr·pio **-pia** (**-pi** **-pie**) *adj* crippled ‖ *m* cripple

stòr·to **-ta** *adj* twisted; crooked; crippled ‖ *f* twist; dislocation; retort

stoviglie *fpl* dishes; **lavare le stoviglie** to wash the dishes

stra- *pref adj* extra-, e.g., **straordinario** extraordinary; over-, e.g., **stracarico** overloaded

stràbi·co **-ca** *adj* (**-ci** **-che**) crosseyed

strabiliante *adj* astonishing, amazing

strabiliare §287 *tr* to amaze ‖ *intr & ref* to be amazed

strabismo *m* strabismus, squint

straboccare §197 (**strabócco**) *intr* to overflow

strabocchévole *adj* overflowing

strabuzzare [ddzz] *tr* (coll) to roll (*one's eyes*)

stracàri·co **-ca** *adj* (**-chi** **-che**) overloaded, overburdened

stracca *f*—**pigliare una stracca** to be dead tired

straccale *m* breeching (*of harness*); **straccali** (coll) suspenders

straccare §197 *tr* (coll) to tire

stracciaiò·lo **-la** *mf* ragpicker

stracciare §128 *tr* to tear, rend; to comb (*natural silk*)

stràc·cio **-cia** (**-ci** **-ce**) *adj* torn, in rags; waste (*paper*) ‖ *m* rag, tatter; tear, rend; combed silk

stracció·ne **-na** *mf* tatterdemalion

straccivéndo·lo **-la** *mf* ragpicker; rag dealer

strac·co **-ca** *adj* (**-chi** **-che**) tired; wornout; **alla stracca** lazily ‖ *f* see **stracca**

stracòt·to **-ta** *adj* overcooked, overdone ‖ *m* stew

stracuòcere §144a *tr* to overcook, overdo

strada *f* roadway; street; **da strada** vulgar, common; **divorare la stráda** to burn up the road; **essere in mezzo a una strada** to be in a bad way; **fare strada a** to pave the way for; **farsi strada** to make one's way; **prender la strada** to set forth; **strada carrozzabile** carriage road; **strada dell'orto** easy way out; **strada ferrata** railroad; **strada maestra** main road; **tagliare la strada a** to stand in the way of; (aut) to cut in front of

stradale *adj* road; street; traffic (*e.g., accident*); highway (*police*) ‖ *m* avenue ‖ *f* highway patrol

stradà·rio *m* (**-ri**) street directory

strafalcióne *m* blunder, gross error

strafare §173 *tr* to overdo; to overcook

strafóro *m* drilled hole; **di straforo** stealthily

strafottènte *adj* unconcerned, nonchalant; arrogant, impudent

strafottènza *f* nonchalance, unconcern; arrogance, impudence

strage *f* butchery, massacre, carnage; (coll) multitude, lot

stragrande *adj* enormous, huge

stralciare §128 *tr* to prune, trim (*grapevines*); to eliminate, remove; (com) to liquidate

stràl·cio *adj invar* interim; emergency (*e.g., law*); liquidating ‖ *m* (**-ci**) excerpt; clearance sale; **a stralcio** at a bargain

strale *m* (lit) arrow

strallo *m* (naut) stay

stralunare *tr* to roll (*one's eyes*)

straluna·to **-ta** *adj* upset; wild-eyed

stramazzare *tr* to fell ‖ *intr* (ESSERE) to fall down

stramazzo *m* sluice; (coll) straw mattress

stramberìa *f* eccentricity

stram·bo **-ba** *adj* odd, queer, eccentric; crooked (*legs*); squint (*eyes*)

strame *m* litter; fodder

strampala·to **-ta** *adj* strange; preposterous, absurd

stranézza *f* strangeness; oddity

strangolare (**stràngolo**) *tr* to strangle; (naut) to furl

strangola·tóre **-trice** *mf* strangler

straniare §287 *tr* (lit) to draw away ‖ *ref* to become estranged

straniè·ro -ra *adj* foreign, alien; (lit) strange || *mf* foreigner, alien

stra·no -na *adj* strange, odd; (lit) estranged

straordinà·rio -ria (**-ri -rie**) *adj* extraordinary; extra || *mf* temporary employee || *m* overtime

strapagare §209 *tr* to overpay; to pay too much for

strapazzare *tr* to rebuke, upbraid; to mishandle; to bungle || *ref* to overwork oneself

strapazza·to -ta *adj* crumpled; bungled; scrambled (*eggs*); overworked || *f* upbraiding, rebuke; fatigue

strapazzo *m* misuse; fatigue; excess; **da strapazzo** working (*clothes*); hackneyed, second-rate

straperdere §212 *tr* & *intr* to lose hopelessly || *intr* to be wiped out

straplè·no -na *adj* chock-full

straplombare (**straplómbo**) *intr* to overhang, jut out

straplómbo *m* overhang; **a straplombo** sheer (*cliff*)

strapotènte *adj* overpowerful

strappare *tr* to pull; to tear, rend; to wring (*s.o.'s heart*); **strappare le lacrime a qlcu** to move s.o. to tears; **strappare qlco a qlcu** to pry s.th out of s.o.; to snatch s.th from s.o. || *ref* to tear (*e.g., one's hair*)

strappata *f* pull, tug, snatch

strappo *m* pull; tear, rip; infraction, breach; pulling away (*on a bicycle*); patch (*of sky*); **a strappi** in jerks; **strappo muscolare** pulled muscle; sprain

strapuntino *m* folding seat, jump seat; bucket seat; (naut) mattress

straric·co -ca *adj* (**-chi -che**) (coll) immensely rich

straripare *intr* (ESSERE & AVERE) to overflow

strascicare §197 (**stràscico**) *tr* to drag; to shuffle; **strascicare le parole** to drawl

strascichi·o *m* (**-i**) shuffle (*of feet*)

stràsci·co *m* (**-chi**) train (*of skirt*); trail; sequel, aftermath; **a strascico** dragging

strascinare (**stràscino**) *tr* to drag || *ref* to drag oneself, drag

strascinì·o *m* (**-i**) shuffle

stràscino *m* dragnet, trawl

stratagèm·ma *m* (**-mi**) stratagem

strategìa *f* strategy

stratègi·co -ca *adj* (**-ci -che**) strategic

stratè·go *m* (**-ghi**) strategist; general, commander

stratificare §197 (**stratìfico**) *tr* to stratify

strato *m* layer; coat, coating; stratum; (meteor) stratus

stratosfèra *f* stratosphere

strattóne *m* jerk, tug

stravagante *adj* extravagant; whimsical, capricious || *mf* eccentric

stravèc·chio -chia *adj* (**-chi -chie**) aged (*cheese, wine, etc.*); very old

stravìncere §285 *tr* to overpower

straviziare §287 *intr* to be intemperate

stravìzio *m* (**-zi**) intemperance, excess

stravòlgere §289 *tr* to roll (*the eyes*); to distort; to derange

straziante *adj* heartbreaking; excruciating (*pain*); horrible

straziare §287 *tr* to torture; to dismay; to mangle; to murder (*a language*)

strazia·to -ta *adj* torn, stricken

strà·zio *m* (**-zi**) suffering, pain; torture; shame; boredom; **fare strazio di** to squander

stré·ga *f* (**-ghe**) witch; sorceress

stregare §209 (**strégo**) *tr* to bewitch

stregóne *m* sorcerer; witch doctor

stregonerìa *f* witchcraft; sorcery

strègua *f* standard, criterion; **alla strègua di** on the basis of

strema·to -ta *adj* exhausted

strènna *f* Christmas gift, New Year's gift; special New Year's issue

strè·nuo -nua *adj* strenuous

strepitare (**strèpito**) *intr* to make a noise; to shout, make a racket

strèpito *m* noise, racket; **fare strepito** to make a hit

strepitó·so -sa [s] *adj* loud, noisy; resounding (*success*)

streptomicina *f* streptomycin

stressa·to -ta *adj* under stress

strétta *f* grasp, clench; tightening (*of brakes*); hold; press, crush; pang; mountain pass; **mettere alle strette** to drive into a corner; **stretta dei conti** rendering of accounts; **stretta di mano** handshake; **stretta finale** climax

strettézza *f* narrowness; **strettezze** straits, hardship

strét·to -ta *adj* narrow; tight; bare (*necessities*); pure (*e.g., dialect*); strict; clenched (*fist*); heavy (*heart*); minimum (*price*); (phonet) close || *m* straits, narrows || *f* see stretta || **stretto** *adv* tightly

strettóia *f* narrow stretch; hardship; bandage

strìa *f* stripe, streak

striare §119 *tr* to stripe, streak

stricnina *f* strychnine

stridènte *adj* jarring; clashing (*colors*); strident (*sound*)

strìdere §264 *tr* to grit (*one's teeth*) || *intr* to shriek; to squeak; to creak; to clash (*said of colors*); to croak (*said of raven*); to hoot (*said of owl*); to howl (*said of wind*) || *ref* (coll) to be resigned

strido *m* (**-di** & **-da** *fpl*) shriek; squeak

stridóre *m* shriek; creak, squeak; gnashing (*of teeth*)

strìdu·lo -la *adj* shrill

strigare §209 *tr* to disentangle || *ref* to extricate oneself

strìglia *f* currycomb

strigliare §280 *tr* to curry; to upbraid || *ref* to groom oneself

strillare *tr* to shout; (coll) to scold; (coll) to hawk (*newspapers*) || *intr* to scream

strillo *m* shriek; shout, scream

strilló·ne -na *mf* loud-mouthed person || *m* newsdealer; newsboy, paperboy

striminzi·to -ta *adj* shrunken; tight; stunted; skinny

strimpellare (strimpèllo) *tr* to thrum; to thrum on

strinare *tr* to singe; to burn (*with a flatiron*)

strin·ga *f* (-ghe) lace; shoelace

stringa·to -ta *adj* terse, concise

stringere §265 *tr* to tighten; to grip; to shake, clasp (*a hand*); to drive into a corner; to squeeze; to embrace; to close (*an alliance, a deal*); to wring (*one's heart*); to clench (*the fist*); (lit) to gird (*a sword*); (mus) to accelerate; **stringere d'assedio** to besiege; **stringere i freni** to put the brakes on || *intr* to be tight; **il tempo stringe** time is running short; **stringi, stringi** at the very end, in conclusion || *ref* to squeeze close together; to shrink; to coagulate; to draw close; **stringersi a** to snuggle up to; **stringersi addosso a** to attack; **stringersi nelle spalle** to shrug one's shoulders

stringina·so [s] *m* (-so) pince-nez

strì·scia *f* (-sce) strip, band; trail; stripe; line; **a strisce** striped; **striscia d'atterramento** airstrip; **striscia di cuoio** strop

strisciante *adj* crawling; (fig) fawning

strisciare §128 *tr* to shuffle (*feet*); to graze; **strisciare una riverenza** to curtsy || *intr* to creep, crawl; to graze by || *ref* to fawn; **strisciarsi a** to rub one's back against

strisciata or **strisciatura** *f* sliding; trail

strì·scio *m* (-sci) rubbing; shuffling; **ballare di striscio** to shuffle; **da** or **di striscio** superficial (*wound*)

striscióne *m* festoon; festooned sign; flatterer; **striscione d'arrivo** landing (*in gymnastics*); **striscione del traguardo** (sports) tape

striscióni *adv* crawling

stritolare (stritolo) *tr* to crush, smash

strizzalimó·ni *m* (-ni) lemon squeezer

strizzare *tr* to squeeze, press; to wink (*the eye*); **strizzare l'occhio a** to wink

strizza·tóio *m* (-tói) wringer

strò·fa or **strò·fe** *f* (-fe) strophe

strofinàc·cio *m* (-ci) dust cloth

strofinare *tr* to rub; to polish || *ref* to rub oneself; to fawn

strofinata *f*—**dare una strofinata a** to give a lick and a promise to

strofinì·o *m* (-i) rubbing; wiping

strò·la·ga *f* (-ghe) (orn) loon

strombatura *f* embrasure

strombazzare *tr* to glorify; **strombazzare i propri meriti** to toot one's own horn || *intr* to blast away on the trumpet

strombazza·tóre -trice *mf* show-off

strombettare (strombétto) *tr* to trumpet, toot

stroncare §197 (**strónco**) *tr* to break off; to break down; to eliminate; (fig) to criticize severely

stroncatura *f* devastating criticism

strònzio *m* strontium

strónzo *m* (vulg) turd

stropicciare §128 *tr* to rub (*hands*); to

drag, shuffle (*feet*); (coll) to crumple || *ref*—**stropicciarsene** (coll) to not give a hoot

stropicci·o *m* (-i) rubbing; shuffling

stròzza *f* (coll) gullet, throat

strozzare (stròzzo) *tr* to strangle; to stop up; to fleece, swindle || *ref* to choke; to narrow

strozza·to -ta *adj* choked; choking; strangulated (*hernia*)

strozzatura *f* narrowing

strozzinàg·gio *m* (-gi) usury

strozzino *m* usurer, loan shark

strùggere §266 *tr* to melt; to consume || *ref* to melt; to pine away; to be upset; **struggersi di** to be consumed by

struggiménto *m* melting; longing; torment

strumentale *adj* instrument (*flying*); capital (*goods*); instructional (*language, in multi-lingual regions*); (gram, mus) instrumental

strumentali·sta *mf* (-sti -ste) instrumentalist

strumentalizzare [ddzz] *tr* to use, take advantage of

strumentare (struménto) *tr* to orchestrate

struménto *m* instrument; tool, implement; **strumento a corda** stringed instrument; **strumento a fiato** wind instrument; **strumento di bordo** (aer) flight recorder

strusciare §128 *tr* to rub; to shuffle (*feet*); to crumple; to wear out || *ref*—**strusciarsi a** to fawn on

strutto *m* lard, shortening

struttura *f* structure

strutturare *tr* to organize, structure

struzzo *m* ostrich

stuccare §197 *tr* to putty; to stucco; to surfeit || *ref* to grow weary

stucchévole *adj* sickening

stuc·co -ca (-chi -che) *adj* bored; **stucco e ristucco** sick and tired || *m* putty; stucco; plaster of Paris; **rimanere di stucco** to be taken aback

studèn·te -téssa *mf* student

studenté·sco -sca (-schi -sche) *adj* student; student-like || *f* student body

studiare §287 *tr* to study; **studiarle tutte** to consider every angle || *intr* to study; to try || *ref* to try; to gaze at oneself

studia·to -ta *adj* affected, studied

stù·dio *m* (-di) study; school district; office (*of professional man*); studio; (hist) university; (lit) wish; (mus) étude; **a studio** on purpose; **essere allo studio** to be under consideration

studió·so -sa [s] *adj* studious || *m* scholar

stufa *f* stove, heater; hothouse

stufare *tr* to warm up, heat up; to stew; (coll) to bore

stufato *m* stew

stu·fo -fa *adj* (coll) bored, sick and tired || *f* see **stufa**

stuòia *f* mat; matting

stuòlo *m* throng, crowd; flock; (lit) army

stupefacènte *adj* amazing; habit-forming ‖ *m* dope

stupefare §173 *tr* to amaze, astonish

stupefazióne *f* amazement, astonishment; stupefaction

stupèn·do ‑da *adj* stupendous

stupidàggine *f* stupidity; silliness; child's play, cinch

stùpi·do ‑da *adj* stupid; silly; (lit) amazed

stupire §176 *tr* to amaze ‖ *ref* to be amazed

stupóre *m* amazement

stuprare *tr* to rape

stura *f* tapping; uncorking; **dar la stura a** to begin (*a speech*)

sturabottì·glie *m* (**-glie**) bottle opener

sturalavandì·ni *m* (**-ni**) plunger (*to open up clogged sink*)

sturare *tr* to uncork; to take the wax out of (*ears*); to open up (*clogged line*)

stuzzicadèn·ti *m* (**-ti**) toothpick

stuzzicare §197 (**stùzzico**) *tr* to pick (*e.g., one's teeth*); to bother; to excite, arouse; to tease; to sharpen (*appetite*)

su *adv* up; on top; upstairs; **da . . . in su** from . . . on, e.g., **dal mese scorso in su** from last month on; **di su** from upstairs; **in su up; metter su** to put on the fire; to instigate; **metter su bottega** to set up shop; **metter su casa** to set up housekeeping; **più su** higher; further up; **su! come on!**; **let's go!; su di on; su e giù** back and forth; up and down; **su per giù** more or less; **tirarsi su** to lift oneself up; to sit up; to get better, recover; **tirar su** to pick up; to grow, raise; **venir su** to grow; to come up ‖ §4 *prep* on, upon; up; towards; over, above; onto; against; at, e.g., **sul far del giorno** at daybreak; **on top of**; out of, e.g., **due volte su tre** two times out of three; **mettere su superbia** to become proud; **stare sulle sue** to be reserved; **sul serio** in earnest; **su misura** made to order

suaccenna·to ‑ta *adj* above-mentioned

sub *m* (**sub**) (coll) skindiver

subàcque·o ‑a *adj* submarine

subaffittare *tr* to sublet

subaffitto *m* subletting, sublet; **prendere in subaffitto** to sublet

subaltèr·no ‑na *adj & m* subaltern; subordinate

subastare *tr* to auction off

sùbbia *f* stonecutter's chisel

subbù·glio *m* (**-gli**) turmoil, hubbub

subcosciènte *adj & m* subconscious

sùbdo·lo ‑la *adj* treacherous, deceitful

subentrare (**subéntro**) *intr* (ESSERE) (with *dat*) to succeed, follow

subire §176 *tr* to suffer; to undergo

subissare *tr* to ruin; to sink; to overwhelm ‖ *intr* (ESSERE) to sink; to go to rack and ruin

subisso *m* ruin; (coll) lots, plenty

subitàne·o ‑a *adj* sudden

sùbi·to ‑ta *adj* (lit) sudden ‖ *m*—**d'un subito** all of a sudden ‖ **subito** *adv*

rapidly; immediately; right away; **subito al principio** at the very beginning; **subito dopo** right after; **subito prima** right before ‖ *interj* right away!

sublima·to ‑ta *adj* sublimated ‖ *m* **sublimato corrosivo** corrosive sublimate

sublime *adj & m* sublime

subodorare (**subodóro**) *tr* to suspect; to get wind of

subordinare (**subórdino**) *tr* to subordinate

subordina·to ‑ta *adj & m* subordinate ‖ *f* subordinate clause

subornare (**subórno**) *tr* to bribe

substrato *m* substratum

suburba·no ‑na *adj* suburban

subùr·bio *m* (**-bi**) suburb

succedàne·o ‑a *adj & m* substitute

succèdere §132 (*pp* **succeduto** or **succèsso**) *intr* (ESSERE) (with *dat*) to succede, to follow ‖ *ref* to follow one another, follow one after the other ‖ (*pret* **succèssi**; *pp* **succèsso**) *intr* (ESSERE) to happen, to come to pass; (with *dat*) to happen to, to come over, e.g., **che gli è successo?** what happened to him?

successióne *f* succession; **in successione** in succession; in a row

successi·vo ‑va *adj* successive; next

succèsso *m* success; outcome

successóre *m* successor

successò·rio ‑ria *adj* (**-ri ‑rie**) inheritance (*tax*)

succhiare §287 *tr* to suck

succhièllo *m* gimlet

succhiétto *m* pacifier

sùc·chio *m* (**-chi**) suck, sucking; (bot) sap; (coll) gimlet

succiaca·pre *m* (**-pre**) goatsucker, whippoorwill

succin·to ‑ta *adj* scanty (*clothing*); succinct, concise

suc·co *m* (**-chi**) juice; (fig) gist

succó·so ‑sa [s] *adj* juicy; pithy

succursale *f* branch, branch office

sud *m* south

sudafrica·no ‑na *adj & mf* South African

sudamerica·no ‑na *adj & mf* South American

sudàmina *f* prickly heat

sudare *tr* to sweat; to ooze; **sudare il pane** to earn one's living by the sweat of one's brow; **sudare sette camicie** to toil very hard ‖ *intr* to perspire, sweat; to reek

sudà·rio *m* (**-ri**) shroud

suda·to ‑ta *adj* wet with perspiration; hard-earned ‖ *f* sweat, sweating

suddét·to ‑ta *adj* aforesaid, above

sùddi·to ‑ta *adj & mf* subject

suddivìdere §158 *tr* to subdivide

sud-èst *m* southeast

sudicerìa *f* filth, filthiness; smut

sùdi·cio ‑cia (**-ci ‑cie**) *adj* dirty, filthy ‖ *m* dirt, filth

sudiciume *m* dirt, filth

sudi·sta *mf* (**-sti ‑ste**) Southerner

sudóre *m* sweat, perspiration

sud-òvest m southwest

sufficiènte adj sufficient, adequate; self-sufficient || m sufficient

sufficiènza f sufficiency; self-sufficiency; (educ) minimum passing grade

suffisso m suffix

suffragare §209 tr to support; to pray for

suffragétta f suffragette

suffrà·gio m (-gi) suffrage

suffumicare §197 (suffùmico) tr to fumigate

suffumi·gio m (-gi) treatment by inhalation; fumigation

suggellare (suggèllo) tr to seal

suggèllo m seal

suggeriménto m suggestion

suggerire §176 tr to suggest; to prompt

suggeri·tóre -trice mf prompter || m (baseball) coach

suggestionàbile adj suggestible

suggestionare (suggestióno) tr to influence by suggestion || ref—suggestionarsi a + inf to talk oneself into + ger

suggestióne f suggestion; fascination

suggesti·vo -va adj suggestive; fascinating; (law) leading (question)

sùghero m cork

sugli §4

sugna f fat; lard

su·go m (-ghi) juice; gravy; gist, pith; non c'è sugo it's no fun; there's nothing to it; senza sugo pointless, dull

sugó·so -sa [s] adj juicy

sui §4

suici·da (-di -de) adj suicidal || mf suicide (person)

suicidare ref to commit suicide

suici·dio m (-di) suicide (act)

sui·no -na adj swinish; see carne || m swine

sul §4

sulfamìdi·co -ca (-ci -che) adj sulfa || m sulfa drug

sulla §4

sulle §4

sulli §4

sullo §4

sulloda·to -ta adj above-mentioned

sultano m sultan

summentova·to -ta, summenziona·to -ta, sunnomina·to -ta adj above-mentioned

sunteggiare §290 (suntéggio) tr to summarize

sunto m résumé, summary

suo sua §6 adj & pron poss (suòi sue)

suòcera f mother-in-law

suòcero m father-in-law; i suoceri the in-laws

suòla f sole (of shoe); share (of plow); (naut) sliding ways; (rr) flange (of rail)

suòlo m ground; soil; floor || m (suòla fpl) (coll) layer; (coll) sole (of shoe)

suonare (suòno) tr & intr var of sonare

suòno m sound; (fig) ring; a suon di bastonate with a sound thrashing; a suon di fischi with loud boos; suono armonico (mus) overtone

suòno·stère·o m (-o) stereo tape player

suòra f nun, sister

super- pref adj & mf super-, e.g., supersonico supersonic; over-, e.g., superallenamento overtraining

superaffollaménto m overcrowding

superare (sùpero) tr to surpass; to cross; to overcome; to pass; to exceed; (cards) to trump

supera·to -ta adj out-of-date, passé

supèrbia f pride, haughtiness; montare in superbia to get a swelled head

superbió·so -sa [s] adj proud, haughty

supèr·bo -ba adj proud, haughty; superb; spirited || i superbi the haughty ones

supercarburante m high-octane gas

supercolòsso m supercolossal film

superdònna f—si da arie di superdonna she thinks she's hot stuff

supereterodina f superheterodyne

superficiale adj superficial; surface; cursory, perfunctory || m superficial fellow

superfì·cie f (-ci & cie) surface; area; superficie portante airfoil

supèr·fluo -flua adj superfluous || m surplus

super-io m (-io) superego

superióra f (eccl) mother superior

superióre adj superior; upper; higher; above; superiore a higher than; more than; larger than || m superior

superlati·vo -va adj & m superlative

superlavóro m overwork

supermercato m supermarket

supersòni·co -ca adj (-ci -che) supersonic

supèrstite adj surviving; remaining || mf survivor

superstizióne f superstition

superstizió·so -sa [s] adj superstitious

superstrada f superhighway

superuòmo m superman

supervisióne f supervision

supervisóre m supervisor; (mov) director

supi·no -na adj supine; on one's back

suppellèttile f furnishings; equipment; fixtures; fund (of knowledge)

supplementare adj supplementary

suppleménto m supplement; (mil) reinforcement

supplènte adj & mf substitute

supplènza f substitute assignment

suppleti·vo -va adj additional; (gram) suppletive

sùppli·ca f (-che) supplication; plea; petition

supplicante mf supplicant

supplicare §197 (sùpplico) tr to beseech; to plead with; to appeal to

supplichévole adj beseeching, imploring

supplire §176 tr to replace || intr (with dat) to supplement, make up for

suppliziare §287 tr to torture; to execute

suppli·zio m (-zi) torture, torment; estremo supplizio capital punishment

suppórre §218 tr to suppose

suppòrto m support, prop

suppositò·rio m (-ri) suppository

supposizióne f supposition; presumption

suppó·sto -sta adj alleged || m supposition || f suppository

suppurare intr (ESSERE & AVERE) to suppurate

supremazìa f supremacy

suprè·mo -ma adj supreme

surclassare tr to outclass

surgelare (surgèlo) tr to quick-freeze

surreali·sta mf (-sti -ste) surrealist

surrenale adj adrenal (gland)

surrène m (anat) adrenal gland

surriscaldare tr to overheat

surrogare §209 (surrògo) tr to replace

surroga·to -ta adj replaceable || m makeshift, substitute, ersatz

suscettibile adj susceptible; touchy

suscitare (sùscito) tr to rouse; to give rise to; to provoke

susina f plum

susino m plum tree

susseguènte adj subsequent, following

susseguire (sussèguo) intr (ESSERE) (with dat) to follow || ref to follow one after the other

sussidiare §287 tr to subsidize

sussidià·rio -ria (-ri -rie) adj subsidiary; (nav) auxiliary || m supplementary text book; subsidiary

sussi·dio m (-di) subsidy; assistance, relief; **sussidi audiovisivi** audio-visual aids; **sussidi didattici** teaching aids; **sussidio di disoccupazione** unemployment compensation

sussiè·go m (-ghi) stiffness, haughtiness

sussistènza f substance; subsistence; (mil) quartermaster corps

sussistere §114 intr (ESSERE & AVERE) to subsist; to be, exist

sussultare intr to start, jump; to quake

sussulto m start, jump; **sussulto di terremoto** earth tremor

sussurrare tr to whisper; to murmur, mutter || intr to whisper; to rustle || ref—si sussurra it is rumored

sussurra·tóre -trice mf whisperer; grumbler

sussurrì·o m (-i) whispering; murmur; rustle

sussurro m whisper; murmur

susta f temple (of spectacles); (coll) spring

suvvìa interj come!, come on!

svagare §209 tr to entertain; to distract || ref to have a good time; to relax

svaga·to -ta adj absent-minded; inattentive

sva·go m (-ghi) entertainment, diversion; avocation, hobby

svaligiare §290 tr to ransack; to rob; to pirate

svaligia·tóre -trice mf thief, robber

svalutare (svàluto & svaluto) tr to devaluate; to depreciate; to belittle || ref to depreciate

svalutazióne f depreciation

svanire §176 intr (ESSERE) to evaporate; to vanish

svani·to -ta adj faded, evaporated; vanished; enfeebled

svantàg·gio m (-gi) disadvantage

svantaggió·so -sa [s] adj disadvantageous

svaporare (svapóro) intr (ESSERE) to evaporate; to vanish

svaria·to -ta adj varied; **svaria·ti** -te several

svarióne m blunder, gross error

svasare tr to transplant from a pot; to make (e.g., a gown) flare

svasa·to -ta adj bell-mouthed, flaring

svecchiare §287 (svècchio) tr to renew; to rejuvenate; to modernize

svedése [s] adj Swedish; safety (match) || mf Swede || m Swedish

svéglia f awakening; reveille; alarm clock; **dare la sveglia a** to wake up

svegliare §280 tr & ref to wake up

svegliarino m alarm clock; (coll) rebuke

své·glio -glia adj (-gli -glie) awake; alert || f see **sveglia**

svelare (svélo) tr to reveal; to unveil || ref to reveal oneself; **svelarsi per** to reveal oneself to be

svèllere §267 tr (lit) to eradicate

sveltézza f quickness; slenderness

sveltire §176 tr to make shrewd; to quicken, accelerate || ref to become smart

svèl·to -ta adj quick; slender; brisk; quick-witted; **alla svelta** quickly; **svelto di lingua** loose-tongued; **svelto di mano** light-fingered || **svelto** interj quick!

svenare (svéno) tr to bleed to death; (fig) to bleed || ref to bleed to death; (fig) to bleed oneself white

svéndere §281 tr to sell below cost; to undersell

svéndita f clearance sale

svenévole adj maudlin, mawkish

svenevolézza f maudlinness, mawkishness

sveniménto m faint, swoon

svenire §282 intr (ESSERE) to faint

sventagliare §280 tr to fan; to flash, display

sventagliata f blow with a fan; volley

sventare (svènto) tr to foil, thwart; (naut) to spill (a sail)

sventa·to -ta adj careless, thoughtless

svèntola f fan (to kindle fire); (coll) box, slap; **a sventola** (ears) that stick out

sventolare (svèntolo) tr to wave; to fan; to winnow || intr to flutter || ref to fan oneself

sventolì·o m (-i) fluttering, flutter

sventraménto m demolition; disembowelment; hernia

sventrare (svèntro) tr to demolish; to disembowel; to draw (a fowl)

sventura f misfortune, mishap; bad luck

sventura·to -ta adj unfortunate, unlucky

sverginare (svérgino) tr to deflower

svergognare (svergógno) tr to put to shame; to unmask

svergogna·to -ta adj shameless

svergolare (svérgolo) *tr* & *ref* to warp; (mach) to twist

svernare (svèrno) *intr* to winter

svérza [dz] *f* big splinter

sverzino [dz] *m* lash, whipcord

svestire (svèsto) *tr* to undress; to hull (*rice*); (fig) to strip || *ref* to undress; **svestirsi di** to shed (*e.g., leaves*)

svettare (svétto) *tr* to pollard, top || *intr* to stand out; to sway (*said of a tree*)

Svè·vo -va *adj* & *m* Swabian

Svèzia, la Sweden

svezzaménto *m* weaning

svezzare (svézzo) *tr* to wean; **svezzare da** to break (*s.o.*) of (*e.g., a habit*)

sviare §119 *tr* to turn aside; to lead astray || *intr* & *ref* to go astray; to straggle; (rr) to run off the track

svignare *intr* (ESSERE) to slip away || *ref*—**svignarsela** to sneak away

svilire §176 *tr* to devaluate

svillaneggiare §290 (svillanéggio) *tr* to insult, abuse

sviluppare *tr* to develop; to cause; (lit) to uncoil || *intr* (ESSERE & AVERE) & *ref* to develop; to break out (*said of fire*)

sviluppo *m* development; puberty

svincolare (svìncolo) *tr* to free; to clear (*at customs*)

svincolo *m*—**svincolo autostradale**

interchange; **svincolo doganale** customs clearance

svirilizzare [ddzz] *tr* (fig) to emasculate

svisare *tr* to alter, distort

sviscerare (svìscero) *tr* to eviscerate; to examine thoroughly || *ref*—**sviscerarsi per** to be crazy about; to bow and scrape to

svìscera·to -ta *adj* ardent, passionate; obsequious

svista *f* slip, error, oversight

svitare *tr* to unscrew

svìzze·ro -ra *adj* & *mf* Swiss || **la Svizzera** Switzerland

svocia·to -ta *adj* hoarse

svogliatézza *f* laziness; listlessness

svoglia·to -ta *adj* lazy; listless

svolazzare *intr* to flutter, flit

svolazzo *m* flutter; short flight; curlicue, flourish

svòlgere §289 *tr* to unwrap; to unfold; to unwind; to develop; to pursue (*an activity*); to dissuade || *ref* to unwind; to free oneself; to develop; to take place; to unfold

svolgiménto *m* development; composition

svòlta *f* turn; curve; turning point

svoltare (svòlto) *tr* to unwrap || *intr* to turn

svotare §257 or **svuotare** (svuòto) *tr* to empty

T

T, t [ti] *m* & *f* eighteenth letter of the Italian alphabet

tabac·càio -càia *mf* (-cài -càie) tobacconist

tabaccare §197 *intr* to take snuff

tabaccheria *f* cigar store

tabacchièra *f* snuffbox

tabac·co *m* (-chi) tobacco; **tabacco da fiuto** snuff

tabarro *m* winter coat; cloak

tabèlla *f* tablet; list; schedule; (coll) clapper, noisemaker; **tabella di marcia** timetable

tabellare *adj* (typ) on wooden blocks; scheduled

tabellóne *m* board; bulletin board; (basketball) backboard

tabernàcolo *m* tabernacle

ta·bù *adj invar* & *m* (-bù) taboo

tàbula *f*—**far tabula rasa di** to make a clean sweep of

tabulare (tàbulo) *tr* to tabulate

tabulatóre *m* tabulator

tabulatrice *f* printer (*of computer*)

tac·ca *f* (-che) notch; size; kind; tally; blemish; (typ) nick; **di mezza tacca** middle-sized; mediocre; **tacca di mira** rear sight (*of firearm*)

tacca·gno -gna *adj* stingy, closefisted || *mf* miser

taccheggia·tóre -trice *mf* shoplifter || *f* prostitute, streetwalker

taccheggiatura *f* or **tacchég·gio** *m* (-gi) shoplifting

tacchétto *m* high heel; cleat (*on soccer or football shoe*)

tacchina *f* turkey hen

tacchino *m* turkey

tàc·cia *f* (-ce) notoriety

tacciare §128 *tr*—**tacciare di** to accuse of, charge with

tac·co *m* (-chi) heel; block; (typ) underlay; **battere i tacchi** to take to one's heels

taccóne *m* (coll) patch; (coll) hobnail; **battere il taccone** to take to one's heels

taccuino *m* pocketbook; notebook

tacére *m* silence; **mettere a tacere** to silence || §268 *tr* to conceal, withhold; to imply, understand || *intr* to keep quiet; to stop playing; to quiet down; to be silent; **far tacere** to silence; **taci!** (coll) shut up!

tachìmetro *m* tachometer; (aut) speedometer

tacitare (tàcito) *tr* to silence, satisfy (*a creditor*); to pay off

tàci·to -ta *adj* silent; tacit

tacitur·no -na *adj* taciturn

tàfano *m* horsefly, gadfly

tafferù·glio *m* (-gli) scuffle

taffe·tà *m* (-tà) taffeta; **taffetà adesivo**

or **inglese** adhesive plaster, court plaster

tàglia *f* ransom, reward; size; build; tally; (mach) tackle

tagliabór·se *m* (**-se**) pickpocket

tagliabò·schi *m* (**-schi**) woodcutter, woodsman

tagliacar·te *m* (**-te**) letter opener, paper knife

tagli·àcque *m* (**-àcque**) cutwater (*of bridge*)

tagliaèrba *adj invar* grass-cutting

tagliafèr·ro *m* (**-ro**) cold chisel

taglialé·gna *m* (**-gna**) woodcutter

tagliama·re *m* (**-re**) cutwater (*of ship*)

tagliando *m* coupon

tagliapiè·tre *m* (**-tre**) stonecutter

tagliare §280 *tr* to cut; to cut down; to cut off; to pick (*a pocket*); to cross (*finish line*); to tailor (*a suit*); to blend (*wine*); to turn off (*e.g., water*); **tagliare a fette** to slice; **tagliare in due** to split; **tagliare i panni addosso a qlcu** to slander s.o.; **tagliare i ponti con** to sever relations with; **tagliare i viveri a** to cut off supplies from; **tagliare la corda** to run away; **tagliare la strada a** to stand in the way of; (aut) to cut in front of; **tagliare le gambe a** to make wobbly (*said of wine*) || *intr* to cut; to bite (*said of cold*); **tagliare per una scorciatoia** to take a shortcut || *ref* to cut oneself; to tear (*said of material*)

tagliasiga·ri *m* (**-ri**) cigar cutter

tagliata *f* cut; clearing; (mil) abatis; **tagliata ai capelli** haircut

tagliatèlle *fpl* noodles

taglia·to -ta *adj* cut; fashioned; **essere tagliato per** to be cut out for; **tagliato all'antica** old-fashioned; **tagliato con l'accetta** rough-hewn || *v* see **tagliata**

taglia·tóre -trice *mf* cutter

tagliènte *adj* cutting || *m* edge

taglière *m* carving board

taglierina *f* paper cutter

tà·glio *m* (**-gli**) cut; cutting; dressmaking; cutting edge; sharpness; blending (*of wines*); size; denomination (*of paper money*); crossing (*of t*); (bb) fore edge; **a due tagli** double-edged; **a tagli** by the slice; **dare un taglio a** to chop; **di taglio** edgewise; **rifare il taglio a** to sharpen; **taglio cesareo** Caesarean section; **taglio d'abito** suiting; **taglio dei capelli** haircut; **venire in taglio** to come in handy

tagliòla *f* trap

tagliuzzare *tr* to shred, cut into shreds

tailandése [s] *adj & mf* Thai

Tailàndia, la Thailand

tailleur *m* (**tailleur**) woman's tailored costume

talal·tro -tra *pron indef* another, some other

tàlamo *m* (lit) nuptial bed

talare *adj* ankle-length || *f* soutane, cassock

talché *conj* so that

talco *m* talcum; talcum powder

tale *adj* such; such a; that; **il tale** such and such a; **un tale** such a; a certain; **un tal quale** such a; a certain || *pron* so-and-so; **il tal dei tali** so-and-so; Mr. so-and-so; **il tale** that fellow; that guy; **quel tale** that fellow, that guy; **tale e quale** like; **tali e quali** exactly, word for word; **un tale** someone, a certain person

talèa *f* (hort) cutting

talènto *m* talent; inclination; **a proprio talento** gladly, willingly; **di mal talento** grudgingly; **andare a talento a** to suit, e.g., **non gli va a talento nulla** nothing suits him

talismano *m* talisman

tallire §176 *intr* (ESSERE & AVERE) to sprout

tallonare (tallóno) *tr* (sports) to be at the heels of

talloncino *m* coupon, stub

tallóne *m* heel; coupon, stub; tang (*of knife*); **tallone d'Achille** Achilles heel

talménte *adv* so, so much

talóra *adv* sometimes

talpa *f* mole

talu·no -na *pron indef* some; someone, somebody || **talu·ni -ne** *adj & pron indef* some

talvòlta *adv* sometimes

tamarindo *m* tamarind

tambureggiare §290 *intr* to drum; to beat down (said, *e.g.,* of hail)

tamburèllo *m* tambour (*for embroidering*); (mus) tambourine

tamburino *m* drummer

tamburo *m* drum; barrel (*of watch; of windlass*); **a tamburo battente** on the spot

tamerice *f* tamarisk

Tamigi *m* Thames

tampòco *adv*—**né tampoco** (archaic) nor . . . either

tamponaménto *m* stopping, plugging; rear-end collision

tamponare (tampóno) *tr* to tampon, plug; to collide with; to hit from the rear; (surg) to tampon

tampóne *m* plug, tampon; pad; (mus) drumstick; (rr) buffer; (surg) tampon; **tampone di vapore** vapor lock

tana *f* burrow; den; hole; hovel; base (*in children games*)

tanàglie *fpl* var of **tenaglie**

tan·ca *f* (**-che**) can, jerry can; tank

tanfo *m* musty or stuffy smell

tangènte *adj* tangent || *f* tangent; (com) commission

tàngere §269 *tr* (lit) to touch

Tàngeri *f* Tangier

tànghero *m* boor, lout

tangìbile *adj* tangible

tàni·ca *f* (**-che**) var of **tanca**

tantino *m*—**un tantino** a little, e.g., **è un tantino arrabbiato** he is a little angry; a little bit, e.g., **un tantino di dolce** a little bit of cake

tan·to -ta *adj & pron indef* such, such a; so much; as much; **a dir tanto** or **a far tanto** at the most; **ai tanti**

(*del mese*) on such and such a day (*of the month*); **a tanto** to such a point; to such a level; **e tanto** odd, e.g., **mille dollari e tanto** a thousand odd dollars; **è tanto** it has been a long time, e.g., **è tanto che lo conosco** it has been a long time since I made his acquaintance; **fra tanto** meanwhile; **senza tanto chiasso** without any noise; **tan·ti -te** many; so many; as many; a lot, e.g., **grazie tante!** thanks a lot! **tanti . . . che** so many . . . that; **tanti . . . quanti** as many . . . as; **tanto di guadagnato** so much the better || **tanto** *adv* so much; so; only, e.g., **tanto per passare il tempo** only to pass the time; anyhow; anyway; **nè tanto nè quanto** at all; **tant'è** it's the same; **tanto che** so much that, e.g., **mi ha annoiato tanto che l'ho mandato via** he bothered me so much that I dismissed him; **tanto . . . che** both . . . and, e.g., **tanto Maria che Roberto** both Mary and Robert; so much . . . that; **tanto fa** or **vale** it's all the same; **tanto meglio** so much the better; **tanto meno** so much the less; **tanto per cambiare** as usual; **tanto più . . . quanto più** the more . . . the more; **tanto . . . quanto** as . . . as || **s—** ascoltare con tanto d'orecchie** to be all ears; **di tanto in tanto** from time to time

tapi·no -na *adj* (*lit*) wretched || *mf* (*lit*) wretch

tappa *f* stopping place; stop; stage, leg; (*sports*) lap; **bruciare le tappe** to press on, keep going; **fare tappa** to stop

tappabu·chi *mf* (**-chi**) makeshift, pinch hitter, substitute

tappare *tr* to cork, plug; to shut up tight || *ref* to shut oneself in; to plug (*e.g., one's ears*)

tapparèlla *f* (coll) inside rolling shutter

tappéto *m* rug, carpet; (sports) canvas, mat; **mettere al tappeto** (boxing) to knock out; **tappeto erboso** lawn, green; **tappeto verde** gambling table

tappezzare (tappèzzo) *tr* to paper (*a wall*); to upholster

tappezzerìa *f* wallpaper; upholstery; upholsterer's shop; tapestry; wallflower

tappezzière *m* paperhanger; upholsterer

tappo *m* cork, stopper; cap; plug; **tappo a corona** bottle cap; **tappo a vite** screw cap

tara *f* tare

taràntola *f* tarantula

tarare *tr* to tare; to set, adjust

tara·to -ta *adj* net (*weight*); calibrated (*instrument*); sickly, weak

tarchia·to -ta *adj* stocky, sturdy

tardare *tr* to delay || *intr* to delay; to be late

tardi *adv* late; **al più tardi** at the latest; **a più tardi!** see you later!; **fare tardi** to be late; **più tardi** later; later on; **sul tardi** in the late afternoon

tardi·vo -va *adj* late; retarded, slow; belated

tar·do -da *adj* slow; late; **di età tarda** of advanced years; **tardo d'ingegno** slow-witted

tardó·ne -na *adj* slow-moving || *mf* slowpoke || *f* old dame, middle-aged vamp

tar·ga *f* (**-ghe**) plate; nameplate; shield; (aut) license plate; (sports) trophy

targare §209 *tr* (aut) to register

targatura *f* (aut) registration

targhétta *f* nameplate

tariffa *f* tariff; rate; rates

tariffà·rio -ria (-rì -rie) *adj* tariff; rate || *m* price list; rate book

tarlare *tr* to eat (*said of woodworms or moths*) || *intr* (ESSERE) & *ref* to become worm-eaten; to become moth-eaten

tarlo *m* woodworm; moth; bookworm; (fig) gnawing

tarma *f* moth; clothes moth

tarmare *tr* to eat (*said of moths*) || *intr* (ESSERE) & *ref* to become moth-eaten

tarmici·da (-di -de) *adj* moth-repelling || *m* moth repellent

taròc·co *m* (**-chi**) tarot; tarok

tarpare *tr* to clip; **tarpare le ali a** to clip the wings of

tartagliare §280 *tr & intr* to stutter, stammer

tàrta·ro -ra *adj* Tartar || *m* tartar; Tartar || **Tartaro** *m* Tartarus

tartaru·ga *f* (**-ghe**) turtle, tortoise; tortoise shell

tartassare *tr* to ill-treat; to harass

tartina *f* slice of bread and butter; canapé

tartufo *m* truffle; (fig) tartuffe, hypocrite

ta·sca *f* (**-sche**) pocket; briefcase; **aver le tasche piene di** to be sick and tired of; **da tasca** pocket; **rompere le tasche a** (vulg) to bother, annoy; **tasca in petto** inside pocket

tascàbile *adj* pocket; vest-pocket

tascapane *m* knapsack, rucksack

tascata *f* pocketful

taschino *m* vest pocket, small pocket

tassa *f* tax; (coll) duty, fee; tassa complementare** surtax; **tassa di circolazione** road-use tax; **tassa di registro** registration fee; **tassa scolastica** tuition

tassàbile *adj* taxable

tassàmetro *m* taximeter; **tassametro di parcheggio** parking meter

tassare *tr* to tax; to assess || *ref* to pledge money

tassati·vo -va *adj* positive; specific; peremptory

tassazióne *f* taxation; tax

tassèllo *m* dowel; inlay; plug; patch; reinforcement

tas·sì *m* (**-sì**) taxi, taxicab

tassì·sta *m* (**-sti**) taxi driver

tasso *m* stake (*anvil*); yew tree; (com) rate (*e.g., of interest*); (zool) badger; **tasso valutario fluttuante** (econ) fluctuation of currency rate

tastare *tr* to touch; to feel; to probe; **tastare il terreno** (fig) to see how the land lies

tastièra *f* keyboard; manual (*of organ*)

tasto *m* touch, feeling, feel; plug (*e.g.*, *in watermellon*); key (*of piano or typewriter*); sample (*in drilling*); **tasto bianco** white key, natural; **toccare un tasto falso** to strike a sour note

tastóni *adv*—**a tastoni** gropingly

tàtti·co -ca (-ci -che) *adj* tactical; tactful || *m* tactician || *f* tactics; prudence; tactfulness

tatto *m* touch; tact

tatuàg·gio *m* (**-gi**) tattoo

tatuare (tàtuo) *tr* to tattoo

taumatur·go *m* (**-gi & -ghi**) wonderworker

tauri·no -na *adj* taurine, bull-like; bull

tavèrna *f* tavern, inn

tavernière *m* tavernkeeper

tàvola *f* board, plank; slab; table; tablet; bookplate; list; **tavola a ribalta** drop-leaf table; **tavola armonica** (mus) sound board; **tavola calda** cafeteria, snack bar; **tavola da stirare** ironing board; **tavola di salvezza** (fig) last recourse, lifesaver; **tavola imbandita** open house; **tavola nera** blackboard; **tavola operatoria** operating table; **tavola pitagorica** multiplication table; **tavola reale** backgammon; **tavole di fondazione** charter (*of a charitable institution*)

tavolàc·cio *m* (**-ci**) wooden board (*on which soldiers on guard and prisoners used to sleep*)

tavolare (tàvolo) *tr* to board up

tavolata *f* tableful

tavolato *m* planking; plateau

tavolétta *f* small table; tablet; bar (*e.g.*, *of chocolate*)

tavolière *m* chessboard table; card table; plateau, tableland

tavolino *m* small table; desk

tàvolo *m* table; desk; **tavolo di gioco** gambling table; **tavolo d'ufficio** office desk

tavolòzza *f* palette

tazza *f* cup; bowl

tazzina *f* demitasse

tazzóna *f* mug

te §5 *pron pers*

tè *m* (**tè**) tea; **tè danzante** tea dance, thé dansant

tèa *adj fem*—**rosa tea** tea rose

teatrale *adj* theatrical

teatro *m* theater; performance; drama; stage; (fig) scene; **che teatro!** what fun!; **teatro dell'opera** or **teatro lirico** opera house; **teatro di posa** (mov) studio; **teatro di prosa** legitimate theater

teatróne *m* large theater; (coll) excellent box office

Tèbe *f* Thebes

tè·ca *f* (**-che**) case; (eccl) reliquary

tecnicismo *m* technicality

tècni·co -ca (-ci -che) *adj* technical || *m* technician; engineer || *f* technique; technics

téco §5 *prep phrase* (lit) with you

tedé·sco -sca *adj & mf* (**-schi -sche**) German

tediare §287 **(tèdio)** *tr* to bore || *ref* to get bored

tè·dio *m* (**-di**) dullness, tedium, boredom; **recare tedio a** to annoy, bother

tedió·so -sa [s] *adj* dull, tedious

tegame *m* pan; **al tegame** fried (*e.g.*, *eggs*)

tegamino *m* small pan; **uova al tegamino** fried eggs

téglia *f* pan; baking pan

tégola *f* tile; (fig) blow

tégolo *m* tile

teièra *f* teapot, teakettle

tèk *m* teak

téla *f* linen; cloth; material; canvas, oil painting; (fig) plot, trap; (lit) weft; (theat) curtain; **far tela** (coll) to beat it; **tela batista** batiste; **tela cerata** oilcloth; **tela da imballaggio** burlap; **tela di ragno** cobweb; **tela di sacco** sackcloth; **tela greggia** gunny, burlap; **tela smeriglio** emery cloth

te·làio *m* (**-lài**) loom; frame; embroidery frame; sash; stretcher (*for oil painting*); (aut) chassis; **telaio di finestra** window sash

teleama·tóre -trice *mf* TV viewer

telear·ma *f* (**-mi**) guided missile

telecabina *f* cable car

telecàmera *f* TV camera

telecomanda·to -ta *adj* remote-control

telecomando *m* remote control

telecommentatóre *m* TV newscaster

telecròna·ca *f* (**-che**) TV broadcast; **telecronaca diretta** live broadcast

telecroni·sta *mf* (**-sti -ste**) TV news announcer, TV newscaster

telediffusióne *f* TV broadcasting

teledram·ma *m* (**-mi**) teleplay

telefèri·ca *f* (**-che**) cableway, telpherage

telefonare (telèfono) *tr & intr* to telephone || *ref* to call one another

telefonata *f* telephone call

telefòni·co -ca *adj* (**-ci -che**) telephone

telefoni·sta *mf* (**-sti -ste**) telephone operator, central; telephone installer

telèfono *m* telephone; **telefono a gettone** pay telephone (*operated by tokens*); **telefono a moneta** pay telephone; **telefono interno** intercommunication system, intercom

telegèni·co -ca *adj* (**-ci -che**) telegenic, videogenic

telegiornale *m* TV newscast

telegrafare (telègrafo) *tr & intr* to telegraph

telegràfi·co -ca *adj* (**-ci -che**) telegraphic

telegrafi·sta *mf* (**-sti -ste**) telegrapher; telegraph installer

telègrafo *m* telegraph; **telegrafo di macchina** (naut) engine-room telegraph; **telegrafo ottico** heliograph; **telegrafo senza fili** wireless

telegram·ma *m* (**-mi**) telegram

teleguida *f* remote control

teleguidare *tr* to control from a distance, to operate by remote control

Telèmaco *m* Telemachus

telèmetro *m* telemeter; range finder

teleobbiettivo *m* (phot) telephoto lens

telepatìa *f* telepathy

teleproiètto *m* guided missile

telericévere §141 *tr* to receive by TV; to teleview

teleschérmo *m* television screen

telescò·pio m (-pi) telescope

telescrivènte f teletypewriter; ticker

telescriventi·sta mf (-sti -ste) teletype operator

teleselezióne f (telp) direct distance dialing

telespetta·tóre -trice mf televiewer

teletrasméttere §198 tr to televise, telecast

teletrasmissióne f telecast

televisióne f television, TV

televisi·vo -va adj television, TV

televisóre m television set

tellina f sunset shell or clam

télo m piece of cloth; yardage, length of material; (mil) side (of tent)

tèlo m (lit) dart, arrow

telóne m canvas; (theat) curtain

tè·ma m (-mi) theme; (gram) stem

téma f (lit) fear; per tema di (lit) for fear of

temerarie·tà f (-tà) recklessness, rashness

temerà·rio -ria adj (-ri -rie) reckless, rash; ill-founded

temére (témo & tèmo) tr to fear; to respect || intr to fear; temere di to be afraid to

temeri·tà f (-tà) temerity

temìbile adj frightening

tèmpera f tempera, distemper

temperala·pis m (-pis) or temperamati·te m (-te) pencil sharpener

temperaménto m middle course, compromise; temper, temperament

temperante adj temperate, moderate

temperanza f temperance

temperare (tèmpero) tr to mitigate; to temper; to sharpen (a pencil)

tempera·to -ta adj temperate; tempered (metal); watered (wine)

temperatura f temperature; temperatura ambiente room temperature

temperino m penknife, pocketknife

tempèsta f tempest, storm; tempesta in un bicchier d'acqua tempest in a teapot

tempestare (tempèsto) tr to pound; to pepper, pelt; to pester || intr to storm

tempesta·to -ta adj studded, spangled

tempesti·vo -va adj timely

tempestó·so -sa [s] adj stormy, tempestuous

tèmpia f temple (side of forehead); tempie (lit) head

tempiale m temple (in loom; of spectacles)

tempière m Templar

tèm·pio m (-pi & -pli) temple (edifice)

tempi·sta mf (-sti -ste) person or athlete showing good timing; (mus) rhythmist

tèmpo m time; weather; age; period, stage; cycle (of internal-combustion engine); (gram) tense; (mus) tempo, (mus) movement; (sports) period; (theat, mov) part; ad un tempo at the same time; al tempo che Berta filava long ago; a suo tempo in due time; long ago; a tempo debito in due time; a tempo e luogo at the opportune time; a tempo perso in

one's spare time; aver fatto il proprio tempo to be outdated; c'è sempre tempo we are still in time; col tempo in time; dare tempo al tempo to allow time to heal things; darsi del bel tempo to have a good time; da tempo for a long time; del tempo di from the time of; è scaduto il tempo utile the time is up; è tanto tempo it's been a long time; fa bel tempo the weather is fine; il Tempo Father Time; lasciare il tempo che trova to have no effect; molto tempo dopo long afterward; nel tempo che while; per tempo early; prima del tempo formerly; quanto tempo how long; sentire il tempo to feel the weather in one's bones; senza por tempo in mezzo without any delay; tempi che corrono present times; tempo fa some time ago; tempo legale legal time limit; tempo libero leisure time; tempo supplementare (sports) overtime; tempo un . . . within (e.g., one month); un tempo long ago

temporale adj temporal || m storm

temporàne·o -a adj temporary, provisional

temporeggiare §290 (tempORéggio) intr to temporize

tèmpra f (metallurgy) tempering, temper; (mus) timbre; (fig) fiber, timber

temprare (tèmpro) tr to temper (metal); to harden, inure || ref to become hardened or inured

tenace adj tenacious; tough

tenàcia f tenacity

tenaci·tà f (-tà) strength, resistance; tenacity

tenàglie fpl nippers, pincers, pliers; tongs; a tenaglie (mil) pincers (e.g., action)

tènda f curtain; awning; tent

tendènza f tendency; trend

tendenzió·so -sa [s] adj tendentious

tèn·der m (-der) (rr) tender

tèndere §270 tr to stretch; to tighten; to draw (a bow); to cast (nets); to lay (snares); to reach out (one's hand); to prick up (one's ears); to draw (s.o.'s attention); to set (sail) || intr to aim; to lean; to tend; to tend to be

tendina f curtain, blind

tèndine m (anat) tendon

tendiscar·pe m (-pe) shoetree

tenditóre m turnbuckle; tenditore della racchetta (tennis) press

tendóne m big curtain; canvas; tent (of circus); (theat) curtain

tendòpo·li f (-li) tent city

tènebre fpl darkness

tenebró·so -sa [s] adj dark, gloomy

tenènte m lieutenant; (mil) first lieutenant; (nav) lieutenant junior grade; tenente colonnello (mil) lieutenant colonel; tenente di vascello (nav) lieutenant senior grade

tenére §271 tr to hold; to have; to keep; to stand (e.g., rough sea); to wear; to make (a speech); to follow (*a course*); **tenere a battesimo** to stand for, sponsor; **tenere al corrente** to keep informed; **tenere a memoria** to remember; **tenere da conto** to hold in high esteem; to take good care of (*s.th*); **tenere d'occhio** to keep an eye on; **tenere la destra** to keep to the right; **tenere la strada** (aut) to hug the road; **tenere la testa a partito** to mend one's ways; **tenere le distanze** to keep aloof; **tenere mano a** to connive with; **tenere presente** to bear in mind; **tenere qlco a conto** to take good care of s.th ‖ *intr* to hold; to take root; **tenerci che** to be anxious for, e.g., **ci tengo che vinca le elezioni** I am anxious for him to win the elections; **tenere a destra** to keep to the right; **tenere alle apparenze** to stand on ceremony; to keep up appearances; **tenere da** to hail from; to take after; **tenere dietro a** to follow; to keep abreast of; **tenere duro** to hold fast; **tenere per** (sports) to be a fan of ‖ *ref* to hold; to hold on; to keep; to keep (*e.g., ready*); to regard oneself; **tenersi a** to adhere to (*e.g., a treaty*); to hold on to; to stick to; to follow; **tenersi a galla** to stay afloat; **tenersi al largo** (naut) to keep to the open sea; **tenersi al vento** (naut) to sail to leeward; (fig) to follow a safe course; **tenersi in piedi** to stand up; **tenersi per mano** to hold hands; **tenersi sulle proprie** to keep aloof

tenerézza *f* tenderness; fondness, endearment

tène·ro -ra *adj* tender ‖ *m* tender portion

tènia *f* tapeworm

teni·tóre -trice *mf* keeper

tènnis *m* tennis; **tennis da tavolo** table tennis, ping-pong

tenni·sta *mf* (**-sti -ste**) tennis player

tennìsti·co -ca *adj* (**-ci -che**) tennis

tenóne *m* tenon

tenóre *m* character, tone; tenor; alcoholic content; manner (*of living*); **tenore di vita** way of life; standard of living

tensióne *f* tension; **alta tensione** high tension; **tensione sanguigna** blood pressure

tentàcolo *m* tentacle

tentare (**tènto**) *tr* to try, attempt; to assay; to tempt; (lit) to touch

tentativo *m* attempt; **tentativo di furto** attempted robbery

tenta·tóre -trice *adj* tempting ‖ *m* tempter ‖ *f* temptress

tentazióne *f* temptation

tentennare (**tenténno**) *tr* to shake; to rock ‖ *intr* to shake; to wobble; to hesitate; to stagger

tentóne or **tentóni** *adv* blindly; gropingly; at random

tènue *adj* small (*intestine*); (lit) tenuous, thin

tenu·to -ta *adj* bound, obliged ‖ *f* capacity, volume; estate, farm; uniform; outfit; (sports) endurance,

resistance; **a tenuta d'acqua** watertight; **a tenuta d'aria** airtight; **tenuta dei libri** bookkeeping; **tenuta di gala** (mil, nav) full-dress uniform; **tenuta di servizio** (mil) fatigues; **tenuta di strada** (aut) roadability

tenzóne *f* combat; poetic contest

teologìa *f* theology

teòlo·go m (**-gi**) theologian

teorè·ma *m* (**-mi**) theorem

teorèti·co -ca *adj* (**-ci -che**) theoretic(al)

teorìa *f* theory; (lit) series, row

teòri·co -ca (**-ci -che**) *adj* theoretical ‖ *m* theoretician

tèpi·do -da *adj* var of **tiepido**

tepóre *m* warmth

tèppa *f* underworld, rabble

teppi·sta *m* (**-sti**) hoodlum, hooligan

terapèuti·co -ca (**-ci -che**) *adj* therapeutic ‖ *f* therapeutics

terapìa *f* therapy; **terapia convulsivante** or **terapia d'urto** shock therapy

Terèsa *f* Theresa

tèrgere §162 *tr* (lit) to wipe

tergicristallo *m* windshield wiper

tergiversare (**tergivèrso**) *intr* to stall; to beat around the bush

tèr·go m (**-ghi**) back (*of a coin*); **a tergo** on the reverse side ‖ *m* (**-ga** *fpl*) (lit) back; **volgere le terga** (lit) to turn one's back

termale *adj* thermal (*e.g., waters*)

tèrme *fpl* spa, hot spring

tèrmi·co -ca *adj* (**-ci -che**) thermal; heat, heating

terminale *adj* & *m* terminal

terminare (**tèrmino**) *tr* to border; to end, terminate ‖ *intr* (ESSERE) to end, terminate

terminazióne *f* termination; completion; (gram) ending

tèrmine *m* border; marker; term; deadline; end; goal; boundary, bounds; (fig) point; **a termini di legge** according to law; **avere termine** to end; **in altri termini** in other words; **mezzo termine** half measure; **porre termine a** to put an end to; **portare a termine** to put through

terminologìa *f* terminology

termistóre *m* (elec) thermistor

tèrmite *f* termite

termoconvettóre *m* baseboard radiator

termocòppia *f* thermocouple

termodinàmi·co -ca (**-ci -che**) *adj* thermodynamic ‖ *f* thermodynamics

termòforo *m* heating pad

termòmetro *m* thermometer

termonucleare *adj* thermonuclear

tèr·mos m (**-mos**) thermos bottle

termosifóne *m* radiator; hot-water heating system; steam heating system

termòstato *m* thermostat

termovisièra *f* electric defroster

tèrno *m* tern (*in lotto*); **vincere un terno al lotto** to hit the jackpot

tèrra *f* earth; land; ground; world; city, town; dirt; soil; clay; **essere a terra** to be downcast; to be broke; to be flat (*said of a tire*); **rimanere a terra** to miss the boat; **sotto terra** underground; **terra bruciata** scorched earth; **terra di nessuno** no man's land; **terra di Siena** sienna; **terra ferma** terra firma; mainland; **terra** skimming the ground; (naut) close to the shore; (fig) mediocre, second-rate

terracòtta f (**terrecòtte**) terra cotta; earthenware

terraférma f mainland (*as distinguished from adjacent islands*); terra firma (*dry land, not air or water*)

terràglia f crockery; **terraglie** earthenware

terranò•va m (**-va**) Newfoundland (*dog*) || **Terranova** f Newfoundland

terrapièno m embankment

terrazza f terrace; **a terrazza** terraced

terrazza•no -na mf villager

terrazzo m balcony; terrace; ledge, shelf; terrazzo

terremota•to -ta adj hit by an earthquake || mf earthquake victim

terremòto m earthquake

terré•no -na adj terrestrial, earthly; ground-floor; first-floor || m ground floor; first floor; ground; soil; land, plot of ground; combat zone, terrain; **preparare il terreno** to work the soil; (fig) to pave the way; **scendere sul terreno** to fight a duel; **tastare il terreno** to feel one's way; **terreno di gioco** (sports) field

tèrre•o -a adj wan, sallow

terrèstre adj terrestrial; ground, land || m earthling

terribile adj terrible; awesome, awful

terríc•cio m (**-ci**) soil; top soil

terriè•ro -ra adj land; landed

terrificare §197 (**terrífico**) tr to terrify

terrina f tureen

territò•rio m (**-ri**) territory

terróre m terror

terrorismo m terrorism

terrori•sta mf (**-sti -ste**) terrorist

terrorizzare [ddzz] tr to terrorize

terró•so -sa [s] adj dirty (*e.g., spinach*); dirty-earth (*color*); (chem) rare-earth (*metal*)

tèr•so -sa adj clear

tèrza f third grade; (aut) third; (eccl) tierce; (rr) third class

terzaforzí•sta (**-sti -ste**) adj of the third force || m partisan of the third force

terzaròlo m (naut) reef

terzétto m trio

terzià•rio -ria adj (**-ri -rie**) tertiary

terzina f tercet

terzino m (soccer) back

tèr•zo -za adj & pron third || m third; third party || f see **terza**

terzùlti•mo -ma adj third from the end

tésa [s] f brim (*of hat*); snare, net

tesare [s] (**téso**) tr to pull taut

tè•schio m (**-schi**) skull

tè•si f (**-si**) thesis; dissertation

té•so -sa [s] adj taut, tight; strained; outstretched (*hand*); **con le orecchie tese** all ears || f see **tesa**

tesorería f treasury; liquid assets

tesorière m treasurer

tesòro m treasure; treasury; thesaurus; bank vault; **far tesoro di** to treasure, prize; **tesoro mio!** my darling!

Tèspi m Thespis

tèssera f card; domino (*piece*); tessera (*of mosaic*)

tessera•to -ta adj card-carrying; rationed || mf card-carrying member; holder of ration card

tèssere tr to weave; to spin

tèssile adj textile || m textile; **tessili** textile workers

tessilsac•co m (**-chi**) garment bag

tessi•tóre -trice mf weaver

tessitura f weaving; spinning mill; (mus) range; (fig) plot

tessuto m cloth, fabric; tissue

tèsta f head; mind; bulb (*of garlic*); spindle (*of wheel*); warhead (*of torpedo*); row (*of bricks*); **a testa** apiece; per capita; **a testa a testa** neck and neck; **fare di testa propria** to act on one's own; **fare la testa grossa a** to stun; to annoy; **levarsi di testa** to forget about; **mettersi in testa di** to get it into one's head to; **non avere testa di** + *inf* to not feel like + *ger*; **non sapere dove battere la testa** to not know which way to turn; **per una corta testa** by a neck; **rompersi la testa** to rack one's brains; **tenere testa a** to face up to; **testa coda** (aut) spin; **testa di ponte** (mil) bridgehead; **testa di sbarco** beachhead; **testa e croce** head or tails

testaménto m will, testament || **Antico** or **Vecchio Testamento** Old Testament; **Nuovo Testamento** New Testament

testardàggine f stubborness

testar•do -da adj stubborn

testata f headboard (*of bed*); top; end (*e.g., of beam*); heading (*of newspaper*); butt with the head; nose (*of rocket*)

tèste m witness

testé adv (lit) a short time ago; (lit) presently, in a little while

testícolo m testicle

testièra f headboard; crown (*of harness*); battering ram

testimòne m witness; **testimone di nozze** best man; **testimone di veduta** or **testimone oculare** eyewitness

testimonianza f testimony

testimoniare §287 (**testimònio**) tr to attest; to depose, testify; **testimoniare il falso** to bear false witness || *intr* to bear witness

testimò•nio m (**-ni**) (coll) witness

testina f small head; whimsical person; boiled head of veal; head (*e.g., of tape recorder*)

tèsto m text; pie dish; (coll) flower vase; **fare testo** to serve as a model

testó•ne -na mf dolt; stubborn person

testuale adj textual; word-for-word

testùggine f turtle; tortoise

tétano m tetanus

tè•tro -tra adj (lit) gloomy, dark

tétta f (coll) teat

tettarèlla f nipple

tétto m roof; ceiling price; home; **senza tetto** homeless; **tetto a capanna** gable roof; **tetto a padiglione** hip roof; **tetto a una falda** lean-to roof; **tetto di paglia** thatched roof

tettóia *f* shed; pillared roof

tettóia-garage *f* (**tettóie-garage**) carport

tettùc·cio *m* (**-ci**) (aut) roof; (aut) top; **tettuccio a bulbo** dome; **tettuccio rigido** (aut) convertible top

ti §5 *pron*

tìbia *f* tibia, shinbone

tic *m* (**tic**) twitch; habit

ticchettì·o *m* (**-ì**) click (*of typewriter*); patter (*of rain*); tick (*of clock*)

tìc·chio *m* (**-chi**) whim; tic; viciousness (*of animal*); blemish

tièpi·do -da *adj* tepid, lukewarm

tifo *m* typhus; **fare il tifo per** to root for; to be a fan of

tifoidèa *f* typhoid fever

tifóne *m* typhoon

tifó·so -sa [s] *adj* rooting || *mf* fan, rooter

ti·glio *m* (**-gli**) linden, lime; bast; fiber

tiglió·so -sa [s] *adj* tough, fibrous

tigna *f* ringworm; (coll) tightwad

tignòla *f* clothes moth

tìgra·to -ta *adj* striped; tabby

tigre *f* tiger

timballo *m* pie, meat pie; timbale; (lit) drum

timbrare *tr* to stamp; to cancel (*stamps*)

timbro *m* stamp; character (*of a writer*); (mus) timbre; **timbro di gomma** rubber stamp; **timbro postale** postmark

timidézza *f* shyness, bashfulness; timidity

tìmi·do -da *adj* shy, bashful; timid || *mf* shy person

timo *m* (anat) thymus; (bot) thyme

timóne *m* rudder, helm; shaft, pole (*of cart*); **timone di direzione** (aer) rudder; **timone di profondità** (aer) elevator; (nav) diving plane (*of submarine*)

timonièra *f* (naut) pilot house

timonière *m* helmsman, steersman; coxswain

timoniè·ro -ra *adj* rudder; tail (*feather*) || *f* see **timoniera**

timora·to -ta *adj* conscientious; **timorato di Dio** God-fearing

timóre *m* fear; awe; **avere timore di** to fear

timoró·so -sa [s] *adj* timorous

tìmpano *m* (archit) tympanum; (anat) eardrum; (mus) kettledrum; **rompere i timpani a** to deafen

tin·ca *f* (**-che**) (ichth) tench

tinèllo *m* pantry; breakfast room

tìngere §126 *tr* to dye; to dirty, soil; to color || *ref* to dye (*e.g., one's hair*); to put on make-up; to become colored

tino *m* tub, vat

tinòzza *f* tub, washtub

tinta *f* paint; color; dye; shade; stain; **calcare le tinte** to exaggerate; **mezza tinta** halftone, shade; **vedere qlco a fosche tinte** to take a dim view of s.th; **vedere qlco a tinte rosee** to see s.th through rose-colored glasses

tintarèlla *f* (coll) suntan

tinteggiare §290 (**tintéggio**) *tr* to calci-

mine; to whitewash; to tint; to paint (*e.g., a house*)

tintinnare *intr* (ESSERE & AVERE) to jingle; to clink

tintìnni·o *m* (**-i**) jingling; clink

tin·to -ta *adj* dyed; tinged; soiled; (lit) dark || *f* see **tinta**

tintó·re -ra *mf* dyer; dry cleaner

tintorìa *f* dyeworks; dry cleaning establishment; dyeing

tintura *f* dyeing; dyestuff; tincture; smattering; **tintura di iodio** iodine

tìpi·co -ca *adj* (**-ci -che**) typical

tipificare §197 (**tipìfico**) *tr* to standardize

tipizzare [ddzz] *tr* to standardize

tipo *adj invar* typical, *e.g.*, **famiglia tipo** typical family || *m* type; standard, model; fellow, guy; phylum (*in taxonomy*); **bel tipo** (coll) character, card; **coi tipi di** printed in the shop of; **sul tipo di** similar to; **vero tipo** prototype, epitome

tipografìa *f* typography; print shop

tipogràfi·co -ca *adj* (**-ci -che**) typographical

tipògrafo *m* typographer; owner of print shop; printer

tipòmetro *m* (typ) line gauge

tiptologìa *f* table rapping (*during séance*); tapping in code (*among jailbirds*)

tiraba·ci *m* (**-ci**) (coll) spitcurl

tiràg·gio *m* (**-gi**) draft; **a tiraggio forzato** forced-draft

tiralìne·e *m* (**-e**) ruling pen

tirannìa *f* tyranny

tirànni·co -ca *adj* (**-ci -che**) tyrannical

tiran·no -na *adj* tyrannical || *mf* tyrant

tirante *m* brace; rod; strap; trace (*of harness*); **tirante degli stivali** bootstrap

tirapiè·di *m* (**-di**) hangman's assistant; underling

tirapu·gni *m* (**-gni**) brass knuckles

tirare *tr* to pull; to draw; to tug; to suck; to haul in (*nets*); to deserve (*a slap*); to pluck; to throw; to give (*blows*); to utter (*oaths*); to shoot (*arrows, bullets*); to stretch; to tighten (*one's belt*); to print; to make (*an addition*); (sports) to force (*the pace*); **tirare a lucido** to polish; **tirare a sé** to attract; **tirare a sorte** to draw lots for; **tirare fuori** to draw out; to pull out; to get out; **tirare giù** to lower; to jot down; (coll) to gulp down; **tirare gli orecchi** a to punish by yanking the ears of; **tirare il collo a** to wring the neck of; **tirare in ballo** to bring up (*a subject*); **tirare l'acqua al proprio mulino** to look out for number one; **tirare l'anima coi denti** to be at the end of one's rope; **tirare l'aria** to draw (*said of a chimney*); **tirare le cuoia** (slang) to kick the bucket; **tirare per i capelli** to drag by the hair; to drag in; to push, coerce; **tirare per le lunghe** to stretch out; **tirare su** to lift; to raise (*children*); to pull up || *intr* to be too tight (*said of clothes*); to shoot; to blow (*said of wind*); to draw (*said, e.g., of chimney*); **tirare a** to tend toward, lean toward; **tirare a** + *inf* to try to + *inf*; **tirare a campare** (coll) to goldbrick; **tirare avanti** to go ahead; to manage to get along; **tirare di boxe** to box; **tirare diritto** to go straight ahead; **tirare di scherma** to fence; **tirare in lungo** to delay, linger; to dillydally; **tirare innanzi** to keep on going; to go ahead; **tirare sul prezzo** to haggle; **tirare via** to hurry along || *ref*—**tirarsi addosso** (coll) to bring upon oneself; **tirarsi dietro** to drag along; **tirarsi fuori da** to get out of (*e.g., trouble*); **tirarsi gente in casa** to keep open house; **tirarsi indietro** to move back; **tirarsi in là** to move aside; **tirarsi su** to get up; to recover; to roll up (*one's sleeves*); **tirarsi un colpo di rivoltella** to shoot oneself

tirastiva·li m (-**li**) bootjack

tirata f pull; stretch; tirade

tirati·ra m (-**ra**) (coll) yen; **fare a tira-tira per** (coll) to scramble for

tira·to -**ta** adj taut; forced (*smile*); drawn (*face*); tight, closefisted; **tirato con** short of || f see **tirata**

tira·tóre -**trice** mf shot; tiratore scelto sharpshooter; **franco tiratore** sniper

tiratura f printing

tirchieria f stinginess

tìr·chio -**chia** (-**chi** -**chie**) adj stingy, closefisted || mf miser

tirèlla f trace (*of harness*)

tirétto m (coll) drawer

tiritèra f rigmarole

tiro m pull; pair, brace (*e.g., of oxen*); throw; fire, shot; trick; **a tiro** within reach; **a un tiro di schioppo** within gunshot; **da tiro** draft; **fuori del tiro dell'orecchio** out of earshot; **tiro alla fune** tug of war; **tiro al piattello** trapshooting; **tiro a quattro** four-in-hand; **tiro a segno** rifle range; shooting gallery

tiroci·nio m (-**ni**) apprenticeship; internship; **tirocinio didattico** practice teaching

tiròide f thyroid

tirolése [s] adj & mf Tyrolean

tirrèni·co -**ca** adj (-**ci** -**che**) Tyrrhenian **Tirrèno** m Tyrrhenian Sea

tisana f tea, infusion

tisi f consumption, tuberculosis

tisi·co -**ca** (-**ci** -**che**) adj consumptive; stunted || mf consumptive

titàni·co -**ca** adj (-**ci** -**che**) titanic

titànio m titanium

titillare tr to tickle

titolare adj titular; regular; full-time || m owner, boss; incumbent || v (**titolo**) tr to name, call

titolo m title; heading; name; caption; entry (*in dictionary*); grade; fineness (*of gold*); (chem) titer; (educ) credit; **avere titolo a** to have a right to; **a titolo di** as, by way of; **titoli di testa** (mov) credits; **titolo al portatore** security payable to bearer; **titolo azionario** share; **titolo corrente** subtitle; **titolo di credito** instrument of

credit; certificate; deed; conveyance; **titolo di studio** degree, diploma; credits; **titolo di trasporto** travel document

titubare (**tìtubo**) intr to hesitate; to waver

tiziané·sco -**sca** adj (-**schi** -**sche**) titian; Titian

tì·zio m (-**zi**) fellow, guy

tizzo or **tizzóne** m brand, firebrand

to' interj here!; well!

tobò·ga m (-**ga**) toboggan

toccafèrro m tag (*game*)

toccamano m handshake (*to close a deal*); bribe, under-the-table tip

toccante adj touching, moving

toccare §197 (**tócco**) tr to touch; to reach; to concern; to push (*a button*); to play (*an instrument*); to feel; to hit (*the target*); to border on (*e.g., the age of forty*); **toccare con mano** to make sure of; **toccare il cielo col dito** to be in seventh heaven; **toccare nel vivo** to touch to the quick; **toccare terra** to land; **toccarne molte** to get a good thrashing; **toccato!** touché! || intr (ESSERE) to be touching; **toccare a** to be up to, e.g., **tocca a lui** it's up to him; to have to, e.g., **le tocca partire domani** she has to leave tomorrow; to deserve, e.g., **gli è toccato il premio** he deserved the prize || *ref* to meet, e.g., **gli estremi si toccano** extremes meet

toccasa·na [s] m (-**na**) cure-all, panacea

tocca·to -**ta** adj touché; touched in the head, nutty; **già toccato** above-mentioned || f (mus) toccata

tóc·co -**ca** (-**chi** -**che**) adj touched, nutty; spoiled (*fruit*) || m touch; knock; one o'clock (*P.M.*); (coll) stroke

tòc·co m (-**chi**) chunk, piece; mortar-board; toque; **un bel tocco di ragazza** a buxom lass

tò·ga f (-**ghe**) gown, academic gown; (hist) toga

tògliere §127 tr to remove, take away; to take; to cut (*telephone connection*); to deduct; to take off; to preclude, prevent; **togliere a** to take away from; **togliere al cielo** (lit) to praise to the skies; **togliere di mezzo** to remove; to do away with; **togliere la parola a** to take the floor from; **togliere l'onore a** to dishonor; **togliere una spina dal cuore a** to relieve the heart and mind of || intr—**tolga Dio!** God forbid! || *ref* to take off (*e.g., one's coat*); to have (*e.g., a tooth*) pulled; to satisfy (*a whim*); **togliersi di mezzo** to get out of the way; **togliersi la vita** to take one's life; **togliersi qlcu dai piedi** to get rid of s.o.

tòlda f (naut) deck

tolemài·co -**ca** adj (-**ci** -**che**) Ptolemaic

tolétta f dressing table; dressing room; toilet, washroom; dress, gown; **fare toletta** or **farsi la toletta** to make one's toilet

tolleràbile adj tolerable

tollerante *adj* tolerant; liberal
tolleranza *f* tolerance; leeway
tollerare (**tòllero**) *tr* to tolerate; to bear, stand
tòl·to -ta *adj* taken; except, leaving out, e.g., **tolta sua figlia** leaving his daughter out ‖ *m*—**il mal tolto** ill-gotten goods
to·màio *m* (**-mài** & **-màia** *fpl*) or **to·màia** *f* (**-màie**) upper (*of shoe*)
tómba *f* tomb, grave
tombale *adj* grave (*e.g., stone*)
tombino *m* sewer inlet
tómbola *f* bingo; (coll) tumble
tombolare (**tómbolo**) *tr* (coll) to tumble down (*the steps*) ‖ *intr* (ESSERE) to fall headlong; (coll) to go to rack and ruin; (aer) to tumble
tómbolo *m* fall, tumble; bolster; lace pillow; (coll) fatso; **fare un tombolo** to go to rack and ruin; to lose one's position
Tommaso *m* Thomas
tòmo *m* volume; (coll) character
tòna·ca *f* (**-che**) (eccl) frock; (eccl) soutane; **gettare la tonaca alle ortiche** to doff the cassock
tonare §257 *intr* to peal; to thunder ‖ *impers* (ESSERE & AVERE)—**tuona** it is thundering
tondeggiante *adj* round; rounded; chubby; curvaceous
tondino *m* coaster; iron rod (*for reinforced concrete*); (archit) molding (*at top or bottom of column*); (archit) astragal
tón·do -da *adj* round; (typ) roman ‖ *m* round; circle; plate, dish; (typ) roman; **in tondo** around
tónfo *m* splash; thump
tòni·co -ca (**-ci -che**) *adj* tonic ‖ *m* tonic (*medicine*) ‖ *f* (mus) tonic
tonificare §197 (**tonìfico**) *tr* to invigorate
tonnara *f* tuna nets
tonnellàg·gio *m* (**-gi**) tonnage
tonnellata *f* ton; **tonnellata di stazza** displacement ton
tónno *m* tuna
tòno *m* tone; tune; hue; style; (mus) pitch; (mus) key; **darsi tono** to put on airs; **di tono** stylish; **fuori di tono** out of tune
tonsilla *f* tonsil
tonsura *f* tonsure
tón·to -ta *adj* (coll) dumb, stupid
topàia *f* rat's nest; hovel
topà·zio *m* (**-zi**) topaz
tòpi·co -ca (**-ci -che**) *adj* topical ‖ *f* topic; (coll) blunder
tòpo *m* mouse; rat; **topo campagnolo** field mouse; **topo d'acqua** water rat; **topo d'albergo** hotel thief; **topo d'auto** car thief; **topo di biblioteca** bookworm
topografia *f* topography
topolino *m* little mouse ‖ **Topolino** *m* Mickey Mouse
toporagno *m* shrew
tòppa *f* patch; keyhole
tòppo *m* stump; headstock (*of lathe*)
torace *m* thorax

tórba *f* peat
tórbi·do -da *adj* cloudy; murky ‖ *m* trouble; **pescare nel torbido** to fish in troubled waters; **torbidi** disorder
torbièra *f* peatbog
tòrcere §272 *tr* to twist; to wring; to bend, curve; to curl (*the lips*); to lead astray ‖ *intr* (ESSERE) to bend, curve ‖ *ref* to writhe; to bend over; **torcersi dalle risa** to split with laughter
torchiare §287 (**tòrchio**) *tr* to press
tòr·chio *m* (**-chi**) press; printing press
tòr·cia *f* (**-ce**) torch
torcicòllo *m* stiff neck; (orn) wryneck
torcinaso [s] *m* (vet) twitch
tórdo *m* thrush; simpleton
torèllo *m* young bull; (naut) garboard
torèro *m* bullfighter
tórlo *m* yolk
tórma *f* crowd, throng; herd
torménta *f* blizzard
tormentare (**torménto**) *tr* to torture, torment; to pester, nag ‖ *ref* to worry
torménto *m* torture, torment; pang; bore, pest, annoyance
tornacónto *m* interest, advantage
tornante *m* curve
tornare (**tórno**) *tr* (lit) to restore; (obs) to turn ‖ *intr* (ESSERE) to return; to go back; (coll) to jibe, agree, square; **tornare a** to be profitable to; **tornare a** + *inf* verb + again, e.g., **tornare a essere** to become again; **tornare a fare** to do again; **tornare a bomba** to return to the point; **tornare a galla** to come back to the surface; **tornare a gola** to repeat (*said of food*); **tornare a onore a qlcu** to do credit to s.o.; **tornare a pennello** to fit to a T; **tornare in sé** to come to; **tornare opportuno** or **utile a** to suit, e.g., **non gli tornó opportuno vendere la casa** it did not suit him to sell the house; **tornare utile** to come in handy; **tornare sulle proprie decisioni** to change one's mind
tornasóle *m* litmus
tornèllo *m* turnstile
tornèo *m* tournament, tourney
tór·nio *m* (**-ni**) lathe
tornire §176 *tr* to turn, turn up (*on a lathe*); to polish
tornitóre *m* lathe operator
tórno *m* turn; period (*of time*); **levarsi di torno** to get rid of; **torno torno** all around
tòro *m* bull; (archit, geom) torus; (lit) marital bed ‖ **Toro** *m* (astrol) Taurus
torpèdine *f* torpedo
torpedinièra *f* destroyer escort; torpedo-boat destroyer
torpè·do *f* (**-do**) (aut) touring car
torpedóne *m* bus, motor coach
tòrpi·do -da *adj* torpid, sluggish; numb
torpóre *m* torpor, sluggishness; numbness
tórre *f* tower; (chess) castle; (nav) turret; **torre campanaria** bell tower; **torre d'avorio** ivory tower; **torre di**

lancio (rok) gantry; **torre pendente** leaning tower

torrefare §173 *tr* to roast (*coffee*)

torreggiante *adj* towering

torreggiare §290 (**torréggio**) *intr* to tower

torrènte *m* torrent

torrenziale *adj* torrential

torrétta *f* turret; (nav) conning tower (*of submarine*); (archit) bartizan

tòrri·do -da *adj* torrid

torrióne *m* donjon; (nav) conning tower (*of battleship*)

torróne *m* nougat

torsióne *f* torsion

tórso *m* stalk; core (*of fruit*); torso, trunk; **a torso nudo** bare-chested

tórsolo *m* core; stalk; stem; **non vale un torsolo** it's not worth a fig

tórta *f* pie; cake, tart; **torta di mele** apple pie

tòrta *f* twist

tortièra *f* baking pan

tòr·to -ta *adj* twisted; crooked; gloomy (*face*) || *m* wrong; **a torto** unjustly; **avere torto** to be wrong; **avere torto marcio** to be dead wrong; **dar torto a** to lay the blame on; **fare torto a** to wrong, e.g., **fece torto al proprio fratello** he wronged his own brother; to bring discredit upon || *f* see **tòrta** || **torto** *adv* askance

tórtora *f* turtledove

tortuó·so -sa [s] *adj* winding; ambiguous; (fig) devious

tortura *f* torture

torturare *tr* to torture; to pester || *ref* to torment oneself; **torturarsi il cervello** to rack one's brain

tosare (tóso) *tr* to clip, crop; to shear; (fig) to fleece

tosa·tóre -trice *mf* clipper, shearer || *f* clippers; lawn mower

tosatura *f* sheepshearing; clip (*of wool*)

tosca·no -na *adj & mf* Tuscan || *m* stogy || **Toscana, la** Tuscany

tósse *f* cough; **tosse asinina** or **canina** whooping cough

tòssi·co -ca (-ci -che) toxic || *m* (archaic) poison

tossicòmane *mf* drug addict

tossicomanìa *f* drug addiction

tossina *f* toxin

tossire (tósso) & §176 *intr* to cough

tostapa·ne *m* (-ne) toaster

tostare (tòsto) *tr* to toast; to roast (*e.g., coffee*)

tò·sto -sta *adj* (lit) prompt; (lit) impudent; (lit) brazen (*face*) || **tosto** *adv* (lit) soon; **ben tosto** (lit) very soon; **tosto che** (lit) as soon as

tòt *adj pl invar* so many, that many || *pron invar* so much, that much

totale *adj & m* total

totalità·rio -ria *adj* (-ri -rie) total, complete; totalitarian

totalizzare [ddzz] *tr* to add up; to make (*so many points*)

totalizzatóre [ddzz] *m* pari-mutuel; betting window; (mach) totalizator

tòtano *m* squid; (orn) tattler

totocàlcio *m* soccer pool

tovàglia *f* tablecloth

tovagliòlo *m* napkin

tra *prep* among; between

trabàccolo *m* small fishing boat

traballare *intr* to shake; to totter; to wobble; to stagger; to toddle

trabìccolo *m* frame for bedwarmer; jalopy; hulk

traboccante *adj* overflowing

traboccare §197 (**trabócco**) *tr* to knock down || *intr* to overflow (*said of container*) || *intr* (ESSERE) to overflow (*said of liquid*) || *intr* (ESSERE & AVERE) to tip (*said of scales*); **far traboccare la macchina** (*the scales*) tip

trabocchétto *m* pitfall; trapdoor

trabóc·co m (-chi)—trabocco di sangue internal hemorrhage

tracagnòt·to -ta *adj* stubby, stocky || *mf* stocky person

tracannare *tr* to gulp down

tracchég·gio *m* (-gi) delay; (fencing) feint

tràc·cia *f* (-ce) track; trace, clue; trail; outline, plan; (lit) line, row; **buona traccia** right track; **fare la traccia a** to open the way for; **in** or **sotto traccia** concealed (*e.g., wiring*); **tracce** tinge; (chem) traces

tracciante *adj* tracer (*bullet*)

tracciare §128 *tr* to trace; to pave (*the way*); to outline; (lit) to track

tracciato *m* tracing, drawing; outline; map; layout

trachèa *f* trachea, windpipe

tracòlla *f* baldric; shoulder strap; **a tracolla** slung across the shoulders

tracòllo *m* collapse, debacle

tracotanza *f* arrogance

tradiménto *m* treason; treachery; **a tradimento** unawares, unexpectedly; treacherously

tradire §176 *tr* to betray; to fail (*a person; said of memory*) || *ref* to give oneself away

tradi·tóre -trice *adj* charming, seductive; treacherous; deceitful, faithless || *mf* traitor; betrayer || *f* traitress

tradizionale *adj* traditional

tradizióne *f* tradition

tradótta *f* military train

tradurre §102 *tr* to translate

tradut·tóre -trice *mf* translator

traduzióne *f* translation

traènte *mf* (com) drawer

trafela·to -ta *adj* breathless, out of breath

traférro *m* (elec) air gap; (elec) spark gap

trafficante *m* dealer, trader; trafficker

trafficare §197 (**tràffico**) *tr* to sell; to traffic in || *intr* to trade, deal; to hustle

tràffi·co m (-ci) traffic

trafficó·ne -na *mf* hustler

trafiggere §104 *tr* to pierce, stab, transfix; to wound

trafila *f* routine; red tape; (mach) drawplate

trafilare *tr* to wiredraw

trafilétto m (journ) short feature, special item; (journ) notice

trafitta f stab wound; shooting pain

trafittura f stab; shooting pain

traforare (**trafóro** & **trafóro**) tr to bore; to pierce; to carve (*wood*); to pink (*leathe-*); to embroider with open work

trafóro m boring; tunnel; open work

trafugare §209 tr to purloin; to sneak off with

tragèdia f tragedy; **far tragedie** (coll) to make a fuss

traghettare (**traghétto**) tr to ferry

traghétto m ferry; **traghetto spaziale** space shuttle

tràgi·co -ca (-ci -che) adj tragic || m tragedian; **il tragico** (fig) the tragic

tragitto m journey; (obs) ferry

traguardo m sight; aim; goal; finish line; (phot) viewfinder; (sports) tape

traiettòria f trajectory; path

tràina f towline; **pescare alla traina** to troll

trainare (**tràino**) tr to drag, tug, pull

tràino m drag; load; trailer

tralasciare §128 tr to interrupt; to omit; **non tralasciare di** to not fail to

tràl·cio m (-ci) stem (*of vine*)

tralic·cio m (-ci) ticking, bedtick; trellis; tower (*of high-tension line*)

tralice m—**in tralice** askance

tralignare intr (ESSERE & AVERE) to degenerate

tram m (tram) streetcar

trama f woof, weft; plot (*of play*); texture (*of cloth*)

tramà·glio m (-gli) trammel net

tramandare tr to hand down

tramare tr & intr to weave; to plot

trambusto m bustle

tramesti·o m (-i) bustle, confusion

tramèzza [ddzz] f partition

tramezzare (**tramèzzo**) [ddzz] tr to interpose; to partition

tramezzino [ddzz] m small partition; sandwich; sandwich man

tramèzzo [ddzz] m partition; side dish; (sew) insertion || adv in between; **tramezzo a** among

tràmite m intermediary; (lit) pass; **per tramite di** through || prep (coll) by; by means of

tramòg·gia f (-ge) hopper

tramontana f north wind; **perdere la tramontana** to lose one's bearings

tramontare (**tramónto**) intr (ESSERE) to set (*said, e.g., of sun*); to end

tramónto m setting; sunset; decline

tramortire §176 tr to stun || intr (ESSERE) to faint, swoon

trampolière m wading bird; (orn) stilt

tràmpoli mpl stilts

trampolino m diving board; springboard; ski jump; (fig) springboard

tramutare tr to transfer; to transform

tràn·cia f (-ce) slice; (mach) shears

tranèllo m trap, snare

trangugiare §290 tr to swallow; to gulp down

tranne prep except, save; **tranne che** unless

tranquillante m tranquilizer

tranquillare tr & ref (lit) to tranquilize; to calm down

tranquilli·tà f (-tà) tranquillity

tranquillizzare [ddzz] tr to tranquilize; to reassure || ref to become reassured

tranquìl·lo -la adj tranquil, calm; clear (*conscience*)

transatlànti·co -ca adj & m (-ci -che) transatlantic

transazióne f compromise

transènna f bar, barrier

transètto m (archit) transept

trànsfu·ga m (-ghi) (lit) deserter

transìgere §165 tr to settle || intr to compromise

transistóre m transistor

transitàbile adj passable

transitare (**trànsito**) intr to move; to walk

transiti·vo -va adj transitive

trànsito m passage; traffic; (lit) passing; **di transito** transient

transitò·rio -ria adj (-ri -rie) temporary; transitory; transitional

transizióne f transition

transoceàni·co -ca adj (-ci -che) transoceanic

transòni·co -ca adj (-ci -che) transonic

transunto m abstract, summary (*of a document*)

trantràn m routine

tran·vài m (-vài) (coll) streetcar

tranvìa f streetcar line

tranvià·rio -ria adj (-ri -rie) streetcar

tranvière m streetcar conductor; motorman

trapanare (**tràpano**) tr to drill; (surg) to trephine

tràpano m drill; (surg) trephine; **trapano a vite** automatic drill

trapassare tr to pierce; (fig) to grieve; (poet) to cross; (lit) to pass, spend || intr (ESSERE) to go through; to pass (*said of an inheritance*); (lit) to pass away; **trapassare da, per o al di là di** to come through (*said, e.g., of a nail, light*)

trapassato m (lit) deceased; **trapassato prossimo** past perfect

trapasso m crossing; transfer; transition; (lit) passing, death

trapelare (**trapélo**) intr (ESSERE) to ooze; to trickle out; to leak through; (fig) to leak out

trapè·zio m (-zi) trapeze; (geom) trapezoid

trapezòide adj trapezoidal || m trapezoid

trapiantare tr to transplant || ref to transfer

trapianto m transplantation; transplant; **trapianto cardiaco** heart transplant

tràppola f trap; (coll) gadget; (fig) lie; **trappola esplosiva** booby trap

trapunta f quilt

trapuntare tr to quilt; to embroider

trapun·to -ta adj quilted; embroidered; studded || m embroidery || f see **trapunta**

trarre §273 tr to pull; to drag; to draw; to bring; to deduct; to lead; to unsheathe (*a sword*); to heave (*a sigh*); to spin (*silk, wool*, etc.); **il dado è tratto** the die is cast; **trarre dalla prigione** to free from prison; **trarre d'impaccio** to get (*s.o.*) out of trouble; **trarre fuori** to extract; **trarre in inganno** to deceive; **trarre in rovina** to ruin; **trarre per mano** to lead by the hand || *intr* to kick (*said of a mule*); (lit) to run; (lit) to blow (*said of the wind*) || *ref* to take off (*e.g., one's hat*); **trarsi d'impaccio** to get out of trouble; **trarsi indietro** to pull back; **trarsi in disparte** to move aside

trasalire [s] §176 *intr* (ESSERE & AVERE) to start, jump

trasanda·to -ta *adj* untidy, slovenly

trasbordare (**trasbórdo**) *tr* to transfer, transship

trasbórdo *m* transfer, transshipment

trascéndere §245 *tr* to transcend || *intr* (ESSERE) to go to excesses

trascinare *tr* to drag; to stir; to enthrall; to lead astray; **trascinare la vita** to barely make ends meet || *ref* to drag oneself; to drag on

trascolorare (**trascolóro**) *tr* to discolor; to change the color of || *intr* (ESSERE) & *ref* to discolor; to change color

trascórrere §139 *tr* to pass (*time*); to skim through (*e.g., a book*); (lit) to go through || *intr* to go to excesses || *intr* (ESSERE) to elapse, pass

trascórso *m* slip (*e.g., of pen*); peccadillo

trascrìvere §250 *tr* to transcribe

trascrizióne *f* transcription; registration (*e.g., of a deed*)

trascuràbile *adj* negligible

trascurare *tr* to neglect; to fail; to disregard || *ref* to not take care of oneself

trascuratézza *f* negligence, neglect; carelessness; slovenliness

trascura·to -ta *adj* neglected; careless; slovenly

trasecolare (**trasècolo**) [s] *intr* (ESSERE & AVERE) to marvel, be astonished

trasferìbile *adj* transferable

trasferiménto *m* transfer; conveyance

trasferire §176 *tr* to transfer; to assign, convey || *ref* to move

trasfèrta *f* business trip; traveling expenses, per diem

trasfigurare *tr* to transfigure; to distort (*the truth*) || *ref* to be transfigured; to change countenance

trasfocatóre *m* (phot) zoom lens

trasfóndere §178 *tr* to transfuse; (fig) to instill

trasformàbile *adj* transformable; (aut) convertible

trasformare (**trasfórmo**) *tr* to transform; to alter || *ref* to transform oneself; to be converted

trasformati·vo -va *adj* (gram) transformational

trasformatóre *m* transformer

trasformazióne *f* transformation

trasformi·sta *mf* (-sti -ste) quick-change artist

trasfusióne *f* transfusion

trasgredire §176 *tr* & *intr* to transgress

trasgressióne *f* transgression

trasgressóre *m* transgressor

trasla·to -ta *adj* figurative; metaphorical; (lit) transferred || *m* figure of speech; metaphor

traslitterare (**traslìttero**) *tr* to transliterate

traslocare §197 (**traslòco**) *tr* to transfer; to move || *intr* & *ref* to move

traslò·co *m* (-chi) moving

traslùci·do -da *adj* translucent

trasméttere §198 *tr* to transmit; (rad) to broadcast

trasmetti·tóre -trice *mf* transmitter || *m* (naut) engine-room telegraph; (telg) sender

trasmigrare *intr* (ESSERE & AVERE) to transmigrate || *intr* (ESSERE) to pass, pass on

trasmissióne *f* transmission; conveyance; broadcast; telecast; **trasmissione del pensiero** thought transference

trasmittènte *adj* transmitting; broadcasting || *f* broadcasting station

trasmutare *tr* to transmute; to change

trasogna·to -ta [s] *adj* dreamy; daydreaming; dazed

trasparènte *adj* transparent || *m* transparency

trasparènza *f* transparence; **in trasparenza** against the light

trasparire §108 *intr* (ESSERE) to appear; to shine; to show through; to show, be revealed (*said of feelings*); **far trasparire** to reveal

traspirare *intr* to perspire || *intr* (ESSERE) to show, be revealed

traspirazióne *f* perspiration

traspórre §218 *tr* to transpose

trasportare (**traspòrto**) *tr* to transport; to carry away; to transfer; to translate; to postpone; (mus) to transpose; **lasciarsi trasportare** to be carried away || *ref* to move; (fig) to go back

trasporta·tóre -trice *mf* carrier || *m* (mach) conveyor belt; (phot) sprocket

traspòrto *m* transportation; transport; transfer; eagerness; moving; (mus) transposition; **trasporto funebre** funeral procession

trasposi·tóre -trice *mf* (mus) transposer

trassa·to -ta *adj* paying || *m* drawee

trastullare *tr* to amuse; to entice || *ref* to have a good time; to loiter

trastullo *m* play, game; fun; plaything

trasudare [s] *tr* to ooze; (fig) to exude || *intr* to ooze (*said of a wall*) || *intr* (ESSERE) to drip (*said of perspiration*)

trasversale *adj* transverse, cross || *f* crossroad

trasvèr·so -sa *adj* transverse || *m* transverse beam

trasvolare (**trasvólo**) *tr* to fly over, cross by air || *intr*—**trasvolare su** to skip over

trasvolata *f* non-stop flight

tratta *f* tug, pull; (rr) stretch; (com)

draft; (lit) crowd; **tratta dei neri** slave trade; **tratta delle bianche** white slavery

trattàbile adj negotiable; friendly, sociable

trattaménto m treatment; working conditions; food, spread; reception, welcome; **trattamento di favore** special treatment; **trattamento di quiescenza** retirement benefits

trattare tr to treat; to deal with; to transact; to wield; to play (an instrument); to work (e.g., iron); to deal in; **trattare qlcu da bugiardo** to call s.o. a liar; **trattare da cane** to treat like a dog || intr to bargain; **trattare di** to deal with; to take care of; to treat, handle || ref to take good care of oneself || impers (ESSERE) **si tratta di** it's question of

trattà·rio -ria mf (-ri -rie) drawee

trattativa f negotiation

trattato m treatise; treaty

trattazióne f treatment

tratteggiare §290 (**trattéggio**) tr to sketch; to outline; to hatch

trattég·gio m (-gi) hatching

trattenére §271 tr to keep; to entertain; to withhold; to hold back; to detain || ref to stop; to refrain; to remain

trattenimónto m entertainment, party; delay

trattenuta f withholding; checkoff

trattino m dash; hyphen

trat·to -ta adj drawn, extracted || m stretch; span; passage; tract; gesture; throw (of dice); stroke (of pen); bearing; section; (chess) move; **a larghi tratti** in broad outline; **a tratti** from time to time; **a un tratto** all of a sudden; at the same time; **dare un tratto alla bilancia** to tip the scales; **tratti features**; **tratti del volto** features; **tratto di corda** strappado; **tratto di unione** hyphen; **tutto d'un tratto** all of a sudden; **un bel tratto** quite a while

trat·tóre -trice mf innkeeper; restaurateur || m tractor; **trattore a cingoli** caterpillar tractor || f tractor (vehicle)

trattoria f inn, restaurant

tratturo m cow path

traumatizzare [ddzz] tr to traumatize

travagliare §280 tr to torment; to molest || intr & ref to toil, labor

travà·glio m (-gli) suffering; toil; trave (to inhibit horse being shod); **travaglio di parto** labor pains; **travaglio di stomaco** upset stomach

travasare tr to pour off; to decant; to transfer || ref to spill

travaso m pouring off; transfer; **travaso di bile** gall bladder attack; **travaso di sangue** hemorrhage

travatura f roof timbers; **travatura maestra** ridgepole

trave f beam; joist; **fare una trave d'un fuscello** to make a mountain out of a molehill

travedére §279 tr to glimpse || intr to be mistaken

travéggole fpl—**avere le traveggole** to see things; to see one thing for another

travèrsa f crossbar; crossroad; crosspiece; rung; bar (of goalpost); dam; rail (of fence); transom; slat (to hold bedspring); rubber pad; (rr) tie

traversare (**travèrso**) tr to cross

traversata f passage, crossing

traversìa f strong wind; **traversìe** misfortunes

traversina f (rr) tie

travèr·so -sa adj cross; devious || m width; crossbar; (naut) beam; (naut) side; **a traverso** (naut) on the beam; **capire a traverso** to misunderstand; **di traverso** askance; crosswise; the wrong way || f see **traversa**

traversóne m large crossbar; westerly gale; side blow with saber

travestiménto m disguise; travesty

travestire (**travèsto**) tr to disguise; to travesty, parody || ref to disguise oneself

traviare §119 tr to lead astray || intr & ref to go astray

travicèllo m joist

travisare tr to distort

travolgènte adj impetuous; fascinating; sweeping

travòlgere §289 tr to overwhelm; to overturn; to sweep away

trazióne f traction

tre [e] adj & pron three; **le tre** three o'clock || m three; third (in dates)

trébbia f thresher; threshing

trebbiare §287 (**trébbio**) tr & intr to thresh

trebbiatrice f thresher, threshing machine

trebbiatura f threshing

tréc·cia f (-ce) plait; braid; **treccia a ciambella** bun, knot

trecentèsi·mo -ma adj, m & pron three hundredth

trecènto adj, m & pron three hundred || **il Trecento** the fourteenth century

tredicèsi·mo -ma adj, m & pron thirteenth || f Xmas bonus

trédici adj & pron thirteen; **le tredici** one P.M. || m thirteen; thirteenth (in dates)

trégua f truce; respite; **tregua atomica** nuclear test ban; **senza tregua** without letup

tremare (**trèmo**) intr to shake, tremble; to quiver; **far tremare** to shake

tremarèlla f—**avere la tremarèlla** (coll) to shake in one's boots

tremebón·do -da adj (lit) shaky

tremèn·do -da adj tremendous

trementina f turpentine

tremila adj, m & pron three thousand

trèmito m trembling; quivering

tremolare (**trèmolo**) intr to shake; to quiver; to flicker

trèmo·lo -la adj tremulous || m (bot) aspen; (mus) tremolo

trèno m train; quarter (of animal); set (of tires); threnody, lamentation; **treno accelerato** local; **treno di lusso** Pullman train; **treno direttissimo** express; **treno di vita** mode of life; mode of living; **treno merci** freight train; **treno stradale** tractor-trailer

trenodìa f threnody

trénta adj & pron thirty || m thirty; thirtieth (in dates)

trentèsi·mo -ma adj, m & pron thirtieth

trentina f about thirty

Trènto f Trent

trepidare (**trèpido**) intr to fear; to worry

trepidazióne f fear, trepidation

treppiède m tripod; trivet

tré·sca f (-sche) intrigue; liaison

tréspolo m stool; pedestal; stand, perch; (coll) jalopy

triàngolo m triangle; **triangolo rettangolo** right triangle

tribolare (**trìbolo**) tr to torment, afflict || intr to suffer

tribolazióne f tribulation, ordeal

tribórdo m (naut) starboard

tri·bù f (-bù) tribe

tribuna f rostrum, platform; (sports) grandstand; **tribuna stampa** press box

tribunale m court, tribunal; courthouse; **tribunale dei minorenni** juvenile court; **tribunale di prima istanza** court of first instance

tributare tr to bestow

tributà·rio -ria (-ri -rie) adj tributary; tax || m tributary

tributo m tribute; tax

trichè·co m (-chi) walrus

triciclo m tricycle

tricolóre adj & m tricolor

tricórno m cocked hat, tricorn

tricromìa f three-color printing; three-color print

tridènte m trident

trifase adj three-phase

trifocale adj trifocal

trifò·glio m (-gli) clover; three-leaf clover

trìfola f (coll) truffle

trìglia f red mullet

trigonometrìa f trigonometry

trilióne m trillion

trillare intr to trill; to vibrate

trillo m trill; ringing

trilogìa f trilogy

trimestrale adj quarterly

trimèstre m quarter; quarterly dues; quarterly payment; (educ) quarter, trimester

trimotóre m three-engine plane

trina f lace

trin·ca f (-che) (naut) gammoning; **di trinca** clearly, cleanly; **nuovo di trinca** brand-new

trincare §197 tr (coll) to gulp down, swill

trincèa f trench

trincerare (**trincèro**) tr to dig trenches in || ref to entrench oneself

trincétto m shoemaker's blade

trinchétto m (naut) foremast; (naut) foresail

trinciante adj cutting || m carving knife

trinciapóllo m meat shears

trinciare §128 tr to carve; to shred; to advance (rash opinions); to cut up

trinciato m smoking tobacco

trinciatrice f shredder; slicer

Trinità f Trinity

trionfale adj triumphal

trionfante adj triumphant

trionfare (**triónfo**) intr to triumph

triónfo m triumph; center piece; tidbit dish with three or four tiers; trump (in game of tarot)

triparti·to -ta adj tripartite

triplicare §197 (**trìplico**) tr & ref to triple

triplice adj threefold

tri·plo -pla adj & m triple

tripode m tripod

trippa f tripe; (coll) belly

tripudiare §287 intr to exult

tripù·dio m (-di) exultation

tris m (tris) (poker) three of a kind

trisàvola f great-great-grandmother

trisàvolo m great-great-grandfather; **trisavoli** great-great-grandparents

trisma m lockjaw

triste adj sad; gloomy, bleak

tristézza f sadness

tri·sto -sta adj wicked; wretched; poor (figure); (lit) sad

tritacar·ne m (-ne) meat grinder

tritaghiàc·cio m (-cio) ice crusher

tritare tr to chop; to grind; to mince, hash; to pound

tri·to -ta adj minced, hashed; worn, trite

tritòlo m T.N.T.

tritóne m (zool) newt; (fig) merman || **Tritone** m Triton

trìtti·co m (-ci) triptych; export document in triplicate; trilogy

trittòn·go m (-ghi) triphthong

triturare tr to mince, hash

trivèlla f auger, drill; post-hole digger

trivellare (**trivèllo**) tr to drill, bore

triviale adj vulgar

trivialì·tà f (-tà) vulgarity

tri·vio m (-vi) crossroads; trivium; **da trivio** vulgar

trofèo m trophy; (mil) insignia (on headpiece)

ttrògolo m trough

tròia f sow; slut || **Troia** f Troy

troia·no -na adj & m Trojan

trómba f trumpet; bugle, clarion; trunk (of elephant); leg (of boot); (anat) tube; (aut, rad) horn; **con le trombe nel sacco** crestfallen, dejected; **tromba d'aria** whirlwind; tornado; **tromba marina** waterspout; **tromba delle scale** stairwell

trombétta f trumpet

trombettière m (mil) trumpeter

trombetti·sta m (-sti) trumpet player

trombóne m trombone; blunderbuss

trombò·si f (-si) thrombosis

troncare §197 (**trónco**) tr to chop; to cut off; to clip (words); to break, sever; to block (s.o.'s progress); to apocopate

tronchése [s] m wire cutter

trón·co -ca (-chi -che) adj truncate; oxytone; apocopated; exhausted, dead-tired; incomplete; **in tronco** in the middle; (dismissal) on the spot || m trunk; stub (of receipt book);

section (*of highway*); log; strain (*of a family*); (rr) branch; **tronco di cono** truncated cone; **tronco maggiore** (naut) lower mast

troncóne *m* stump

troneggiare §290 (tronéggio) *intr* to tower; to hold forth; **troneggiare su** to lord it over

trón·fio -fia *adj* (-fi -fie) haughty; bombastic

tròno *m* throne

tropicale *adj* tropical

tròpi·co *m* (-ci) tropic

troposfèra *f* troposphere

tròp·po -pa *adj & pron* too much; **trop·pi -pe** too many || *m* too much; **questo è troppo!** enough is enough! || **troppo** *adv* too; too much; **essere di troppo** to be in the way

tròta *f* trout

trottare (tròtto) *intr* to trot

trotterellare (trotterèllo) *intr* to trot along; to toddle

tròtto *m* trot; **piccolo trotto** jog trot

tròttola *f* top

trovare (tròvo) *tr* to find; to visit; **trovare a** or **da ridire** (su) to find fault (with); **trovi!** don't you think so? || *ref* to find oneself; to meet; to be; to be located; to happen, e.g., **mi trovai a passare di fronte a casa sua** I happened to pass in front of his house

trovaró·be *m* (-be) (theat) property man || *f* (theat) dresser

trovata *f* find; trick, gimmick

trovatèl·lo -la *mf* foundling, waif

trovatóre *m* troubadour

trovièro *m* trouvère

truccare §197 *tr* to make up; to falsify; (aut) to soup up || *ref* to put on make-up

truccatura *f* make-up; trick, gimmick

truc·co *m* (-chi) make-up; trick, gimmick

truce *adj* fierce, cruel; menacing

trucidare (trùcido) *tr* to massacre

trùciolo *m* chip, shaving

truculènto *adj* truculent

truffa *f* cheat, fraud, swindle; **truffa all'americana** confidence game

truffare *tr* to cheat, swindle

truffa·tóre -trice *mf* cheat, swindler

truismo *m* truism

truògolo *m* var of **trogolo**

truppa *f* troop; soldiers; **di truppa** (mil) enlisted (*man or woman*); **in truppa** in a flock

tu §5 *pron pers*; **a tu per tu** face to face; **dare del tu a** to address in the familiar form

tuba *f* tuba; (hist) horn, trumpet; (joc) top hat, stovepipe; (anat) tube

tubare *intr* to coo

tubatura *f* piping, tubing; pipe, tube; pipeline

tubazióne *f* tubes, pipes

tubèrcolo *m* tubercle

tubercolosà·rio [s] *m* (-ri) tuberculosis sanitarium

tubercoló·si *f* (-si) tuberculosis

tubercoló·so -sa [s] *adj* tuberculous || *mf* T.B. patient

tùbero *m* tuber

tubétto *m* tube (*for pills or toothpaste*); spool

tubino *m* small tube; derby (hat)

tubo *m* tube; pipe; (anat) canal, duct; **a tubo** tubular; **tubo di scarico** exhaust pipe; **tubo di troppopieno** overflow; **tubo di ventilazione** air shaft

tubolare *adj* tubular || *m* tire (*for racing bicycle*)

tuffare *tr* to dip; to plunge || *ref* to plunge; to dive

tuffa·tóre -trice *mf* diver || *m* dive bomber

tuffétto *m* (orn) dabchick, grebe

tuffo *m* dive; plunge; throb; **a tuffo** (aer) diving; **scendere a tuffo** (aer) to dive; **tuffo ad angelo** (sports) swan dive; **tuffo d'acqua** downpour

tufo *m* tufa

tu·ga *f* (-ghe) (naut) deckhouse

tugù·rio *m* (-ri) hovel

tulipano *m* tulip

tumefare §173 *tr & ref* to swell

tumefazióne *f* swelling

tùmi·do -da *adj* tumid

tumóre *m* tumor

tùmulo *m* tomb; tumulus

tumulto *m* tumult, riot; commotion

tumultuó·so -sa [s] *adj* tumultuous

tùni·ca *f* (-che) tunic

Tùnisi *f* Tunis

Tunisia, la Tunisia

tunisi·no -na *adj & mf* Tunisian

tuo tua §6 *adj & pron poss* (**tuòi tue**)

tuòno *m* thunder

tuòrlo *m* yolk

turàcciolo *m* cork, stopper

turare *tr* to plug, stop; to cork

turba *f* crowd; mob; (pathol) upset

turbaménto *m* commotion, perturbation; disturbance, breach (*of law and order*)

turbante *m* turban

turbare *tr* to muddy; to disturb; to upset || *ref* to become cloudy; to become upset

turba·to -ta *adj* upset; disturbed; distracted

tùrbi·do -da *adj* turbid

turbina *f* turbine

turbinare (tùrbino) *tr* to separate in a centrifuge || *intr* to whirl

tùrbine *m* whirlwind; swarm; tumult

turbinó·so -sa [s] *adj* whirling; tumultuous

turboèli·ca *m* (-ca) turboprop

turbogètto *m* turbojet

turbolèn·to -ta *adj* turbulent

turbolènza *f* turbulence

turbomotrice *f* (rr) turbine engine

turboreattóre *m* turbojet

turcasso *m* quiver

turchése [s] *m* turquoise

Turchìa, la Turkey

turchinétto *m* bluing

turchi·no -na *adj* dark-blue || *m* dark blue

tur·co -ca (-chi -che) *adj* Turkish; **sedere alla turca** to sit cross-legged || *mf* Turk || *m* Turkish (*language*); **bestemmiare come un turco** to swear like a trooper; **fumare come un turco** to smoke like a steam engine

tùrgi·do -da *adj* turgid

turibolo *m* thurible, censer

turismo *m* tourism

turi·sta *mf* (**-sti -ste**) tourist

turìsti·co -ca *adj* (**-ci -che**) tourist; travel (*e.g.*, *bureau*); traveler's (*check*)

turlupinare *tr* to hoodwink, swindle

turlupinatura *f* swindle, confidence game

turno *m* turn; shift; **a turno** in turn; **di turno** on duty; **fare a turno** to take turns

turpe *adj* base, abject; (*lit*) ugly

turpilò·quio *m* (**-qui**) foul language

turpitùdine *f* turpitude

tuta *f* overalls; **tuta antigravità** anti-G suit; **tuta da bambini** jumpers; **tuta spaziale** spacesuit

tutèla *f* guardianship; defense, protection

tutelare *adj* tutelary || *v* (**tutèlo**) *tr* to protect, defend

tùtolo *m* corncob

tu·tóre -trice *mf* guardian; protector

tuttavìa *adv* yet, nevertheless; (*lit*) always, continuously

tut·to -ta *adj* whole; all; full; **con tutto** in spite of, *e.g.*, **con tutto quello che ho fatto per lui** in spite of all I have done for him; **del tutto** fully, completely; **è tutt'uno** it's all the same; **tutt'altro** completely different; on the contrary; **tutt'altro che** anything but; **tutti** every, *e.g.*, **tutti gli scolari** every pupil; **tutti e due** both || *m* everything; whole; **con tutto che** although; **fare di tutto** to do everything possible; **in tutto** altogether || *pron* **tut·ti -te** all, everybody (*of a group*); **tutti** everybody || **tutto** *adv* quite; **tutt'a un tratto** all of a sudden; **tutto al contrario** quite the opposite

tuttofa·re *adj invar* of all trades; of all work || *m* (**-re**) factotum, jack-of-all-trades || *f* (**-re**) maid of all work

tuttóra *adv* yet, still

tzìga·no -na *adj & mf* var of zigano

U

U, u [u] *m & f* nineteenth letter of the Italian alphabet

ubbìa *f* prejudice, bias; complex; whim

ubbidiènte *adj* obedient

ubbidire §176 *tr* to obey || *intr* to obey; to respond (*said of a car*); (*with dat*) to obey, *e.g.*, **gli ubbedì** he obeyed him

ubertó·so -sa [s] *adj* fruitful; fertile

ubicazióne *f* location

ubiquità *f* ubiquity; **non ho il dono dell'ubiquità** I can't be everywhere at the same time

ubi·quo -qua *adj* ubiquitous

ubriacare §197 *tr* to make drunk, intoxicate || *ref* to get drunk

ubriacatura or **ubriachézza** *f* drunkenness, intoxication

ubria·co -ca (**-chi -che**) *adj* drunk; **ubriaco fradicio** dead drunk || *mf* drunkard

ubriacó·ne -na *mf* drunkard

uccellare (**uccèllo**) *tr* to take in, cajole || *intr* to snare; to fowl; to hunt birds

uccèllo *m* bird; **uccello di bosco** fugitive; **uccello di galera** gallows bird; **uccello di passo** bird of passage

uccella·tóre -trice *mf* live-bird catcher

uccellièra *f* aviary; large birdcage

uccìdere §274 *tr* to kill || *ref* to kill oneself; to get killed; to kill one another

-ùccio -ùccia (**-ucci -ucce**) *suf adj* not very, *e.g.*, **calduccio** not very hot; rather, *e.g.*, **magruccio** rather thin; poor little, *e.g.*, **caruccio** poor little darling || *suf m & f* small *e.g.*, **cappelluccio** small hat

uccisióne *f* killing; murder

uccì·so -sa *adj* killed || *mf* victim

ucci·sóre -ditrice *mf* killer

ucraì·no -na *adj & mf* Ukrainian || **l'Ucraina** *f* the Ukraine

udìbile *adj* audible

udiènza *f* audience; hearing; **l'udienza è aperta!** the court is now in session!

udire §275 *tr* to hear; to listen to

udìto *m* hearing

uditòfono *m* hearing aid

udi·tóre -trice *mf* hearing || *mf* (*educ*) auditor || *m* magistrate

udìtò·rio -ria (**-ri -rie**) *adj* auditory || *m* audience

ufficiale *adj* official || *m* official; officer; **primo ufficiale** (*naut*) first officer, mate; **ufficiale di giornata** (*mil*) officer of the day; **ufficiale di rotta** (*aer*, *naut*) navigator; **ufficiale giudiziario** clerk of the court; process server, bailiff; **ufficiale medico** (*mil*) medical officer

ufficiare §128 *tr* to officiate

uffì·cio *m* (**-ci**) duty; office; bureau; department (*of agency*); **d'ufficio** ex-officio; public, *e.g.*, **avvocato d'ufficio** public defender; **ufficio di collocamento** placement bureau; **ufficio di compensazione** clearing house; **ufficio d'igiene** board of health

uffició·so -sa [s] *adj* unofficial; kindly; white (*lie*)

uffì·zio *m* (**-zi**) (*eccl*) office

ufo *m*—**a ufo** gratis, without paying

ugèllo *m* nozzle

ùg·gia *f* (**-ge**) darkness; gloom; dislike; **avere in uggia** to dislike

uggiolare (**ùggiolo**) *intr* to whine (*said of a dog*)

uggió·so -sa [s] *adj* gloomy; boring

ugnare *tr* to bevel; to miter

ugnatura f bevel; miter
ògola f uvula; bagnarsi l'ugola (coll) to wet one's whistle
ugonòtto m Huguenot
uguaglianza f equality
uguagliare §280 tr to equal; to make equal; to equalize; to level; to compare || ref to compare oneself; to be equal; to be compared
uguale adj equal; same; even; level; per me è uguale it's the same to me || m equal; (math) equal sign
òlcera f ulcer; sore
ulcerare (úlcero) tr & ref to ulcerate
uliva f var of oliva
ulterióre adj further, subsequent, ulterior
òltima f latest news; last straw
ultimare (último) tr to complete, finish
ultimato m ultimatum
ultimíssima f latest edition (of newspaper); ultimíssime late news
òlti·mo- ma adj last; final; latest; latter; farthest; ultimate; least; top (floor); all'ultimo, dall'ultimo, nell'ultimo or sull'ultimo lately; finally, at the end || f see ultima
ultimogèni·to -ta adj last-born || mf last-born child
ultra- pref adj & m & f ultra-, e.g., ultraelevato ultrahigh; super-, e.g., ultrasonico supersonic (speed)
ultracór·to -ta adj ultrashort
ultraróṣ·ṣo -sa adj & m infrared
ultraterré·no -na adj ultramundane; unearthly
ultraviolét·to -ta adj & m ultraviolet
ululare (ùlulo) intr to howl
ululato m howl
umanésimo m humanism
umani·sta mf (-sti -ste) humanist
umani·tà f (-tà) humanity; umanità fpl humanities
umanità·rio -ria adj & mf (-ri -rie) humanitarian
uma·no -na adj human; humane || m human nature; umani human beings
um·bro -bra adj & m Umbrian
umettare (umétto) tr to moisten, dampen
umidìc·cio -cia adj (-ci -ce) dampish
umidi·tà f (-tà) humidity, dampness
òmi·do -da adj humid, damp || m humidity, dampness; in umido stewed (e.g., meat)
ùmile adj humble || gli umili mpl the meek
umiliare §287 tr to humiliate, humble || ref to humble oneself
umiliazióne f humiliation
umiltà f humility
umóre m humor, mood, temper; whim; (bot) sap; un bell'umore (coll) quite a character
umorismo m humor
umori·sta mf (-sti -ste) humorist
umorìsti·co -ca adj (-ci -che) humorous; amusing, comic, funny
un (apocopated form of uno) §9 indef art a, an || §9 numeral adj one || §12 reciprocal indef pron—l'un l'altro each other, one another

unànime adj unanimous
unanimità f unanimity
unàni·mo -ma adj unanimous
uncinare tr to hook, grapple
uncinétto m small hook; crochet hook
uncino m hook; grapnel; clasp; pothook; (fig) pretext; a uncino hooked
undicèṣi·mo -ma adj, m & pron eleventh
ùndici adj & pron eleven; le undici eleven o'clock || m eleven; eleventh (in dates); (soccer) squad
ùngere §183 tr to grease; to oil; to smear; to anoint; to flatter || ref to smear oneself
Ungheria, l' f Hungary
ungheré·ṣe [s] adj & mf Hungarian
ùnghia f nail; fingernail; claw; hoof; fluke (of anchor); (fig) hairbreadth; avere le unghie lunghe to be lightfingered; unghia del piede toenail; unghie (fig) clutches
unghiata f nail scratch
unguènto m unguent, ointment
ùni·co -ca adj (-ci -che) only, sole; unique; single (copy); complete (text) || f—l'unica the only solution
unicòrno m unicorn
unificare §197 (unìfico) tr to unify; to standardize
unificazióne f unification; standardization
uniformare (unifórmo) tr to make uniform, standardize || ref—uniformarsi a to conform to; to comply with
unifórme adj uniform; standard || f uniform; alta uniforme (mil) full dress
unilaterale adj unilateral
unióne f union; agreement; unione libera free love
unire §176 tr & ref to unite
unìsono [s] m unison; all'unisono in unison
uni·tà f (-tà) unity; unit; unità di misura unit of measurement
unità·rio -ria (-ri -rie) adj unit (e.g., price); united || m Unitarian
uni·to -ta adj united; joined; compact; plain (color); consolidated
universale adj universal; last (judgment)
universi·tà f (-tà) university
università·rio -ria (-ri -rie) adj university; college || mf university or college student; university or college professor
univer·so -sa adj universal || m universe
unno m Hun
u·no -na §9 indef art a, an || §9 numeral adj one || m one || §10 pron indef one; le una, la una, or l'una one o'clock; l'uno e l'altro both; l'uno o l'altro either, either one; per uno in single file; uno per uno one by one; each other || §11 correlative pron one
un·to -ta adj greasy || m grease, fat; flattery; anointed one
untuoṣità [s] f greasiness; unction, unctuousness
untuó·ṣo -sa [s] adj greasy; unctuous

unzióne *f* unction

uò·mo *m* (-mini) man; **come un sol uomo** to a man; **uomo d'affari** businessman; **uomo del giorno** man of the hour; **uomo della strada** man of the street; **uomo di chiesa** churchman; **uomo di fatica** laborer; **uomo di fiducia** trusted man; **uomo di mare** seaman; **uomo di paglia** straw man; **uomo di parola** man of his word; **uomo in mare!** man overboard!; **uomo meccanico** automaton; **uomo morto** (rr) deadman brake; **uomo nuovo** nouveau riche; **uomo rana** frogman

uòpo *m*—**all'uopo** if need be; **essere d'uopo** (lit) to be necessary

uòse [s] *fpl* leggings

uò·vo *m* (-va *fpl*) egg; **meglio un uovo oggi che una gallina domani** a bird in a hand is worth two in the bush; **rompere le uova nel paniere a qlcu** to spoil s.o.'s plans; **uovo affogato** poached egg; **uovo alla coque** soft-boiled egg; **uovo all'occhio di bue** fried egg; **uovo da tè** tea ball; **uovo strapazzato** scrambled egg

uragano *m* hurricane; storm (*of applause*); **uragano di neve** blizzard

Urali *mpl* Ural Mountains

uranìfe·ro -ra *adj* uranium-bearing

urànio *m* uranium

urbanésimo *m* urbanization, migration toward the cities

urbanìsti·co -ca (-ci -che) *adj* city-planning ǁ *f* city planning

urbani·tà *f* (-tà) urbanity, civility; city population

urbanizzare [ddzz] *tr* to urbanize

urba·no -na *adj* urban; urbane

urètra *f* urethra

urgènte *adj* urgent, pressing

urgènza *f* urgency; **d'urgenza** urgent; emergency (*e.g., operation*); **fare urgenza a** to urge

ùrgere §276 *tr* to urge, press ǁ *intr* to be urgent

urina *f* urine

urinà·rio -ria *adj* (-ri -rie) urinary

urlare *tr* to shout; to shout down ǁ *intr* to howl; to shout, yell

urla·tóre -trice *adj* screaming ǁ *mf* screamer; loud singer

ur·lo *m* howl ǁ *m* (-la *fpl*) yell, scream

urna *f* urn; ballot box; (poet) grave; **urne** polls

-uro *suf m* (chem) -ide, e.g., **cloruro** chloride

urologìa *f* urology

urrà *interj* hurrah!

ursóne *m* Canada porcupine

urtare *tr* to hit; to bump; to annoy ǁ *intr*—**urtare contro** to hit, strike against; **urtare in** to hit; to stumble into ǁ *ref* to get annoyed; to clash; to bump into one another

urto *m* hit; bump; collision; onslaught; clash, disagreement; **urto di nervi** huff

Uruguai, l' *m* Uruguay

uruguaia·no -na *adj* & *mf* Uruguayan

usanza *f* usage, custom; habit, practice

usare *tr* to use, employ; to wear out;

(lit) to frequent; **usare** + *inf* to be accustomed to + *ger* ǁ *intr* to be fashionable; **usare di** to use, employ ǁ *ref* to become accustomed; **si usa** + *inf* it is customary to + *inf*

usa·to -ta *adj* used, second-hand; worn; worn-out; (lit) usual ǁ *m* usage, custom; norm; second-hand goods

usbèr·go *m* (-ghi) hauberk; (fig) shield, protection

uscènte *adj* ending, terminating; retiring

uscière *m* receptionist; office boy, errand boy; (coll) court clerk; (coll) bailiff; (coll) tipstaff

ù·scio *m* (-sci) door; **infilar l'uscio** to take French leave; **metter tra l'uscio e il muro** (fig) to corner

uscire §277 *intr* (ESSERE) to go out, leave; to come out; to flow out; to escape; to turn out, ensue; **essere uscito** to be out; **uscire da** to leave; to run off (*the track*); **uscire dai gangheri** to get mad; **uscire dal comune** to be out of the ordinary; **uscire dal segno** to go too far; **uscire dal seminato** to go astray; **uscire di mente a** to escape one's mind, e.g., **gli è uscito di mente** it escaped his mind; **uscire di sentimento** to pass out; **uscire di vita** to die; **uscire in** to lead into; **uscire per il rotto della cuffia** to barely make it

uscita *f* exit; outlay; quip, sally; gate (e.g., *in an airport*); (gram) ending; **all'uscita** on the way out; **buona uscita** severance pay; bonus; **libera uscita** day off (*of servant*); (mil) pass; **uscita di sicurezza** emergency exit

usignòlo *m* nightingale

u·so -sa *adj* (lit) accustomed ǁ *m* practice; usage; use; wear; faculty; power (e.g., *of hearing*); (lit) intimate relations; **all'uso di** in the fashion of; **avere per uso di** to be wont to; **come d'uso** as usual; **farci l'uso** to get used to it!; **fuori d'uso** worn-out, out of commission; **uso esterno!** (pharm) not to be taken internally!

ustionare (ustióno) *tr* to burn, scorch

ustióne *f* burn

usuale *adj* usual; ordinary, common

usufruire §176 *intr*—**usufruire di** to have the use of; to enjoy

usura *f* usury; (mach) wear and tear; **ad usura** abundantly

usu·ràio -ràia (-rài -ràie) *adj* usurious ǁ *mf* usurer, loanshark

usurpare *tr* to usurp

utensile *adj* tool, e.g., **macchina utensile** machine tool ǁ *m* utensil; tool

utènte *m* user; customer, consumer

ùtero *m* uterus, womb

ùtile *adj* useful; usable; workable; legal, prescribed (e.g., *time*); **essere utile a** to help; **venire utile** to come in handy ǁ *m* usefulness; profit, gain

utili·tà *f* (-tà) utility, usefulness; profit, gain

utilitària *f* economy car, compact

utilizzare [ddzz] *tr* to utilize

utopìa *f* utopia
utopi·sta *mf* (-sti -ste) utopian
utopìsti·co -ca *adj* (-ci -che) utopian
uva *f* grapes; un grano di uva passa a raisin; uva passa raisins

uxorici·da *m* (-di) uxoricide || *f* (-de) murderer of one's husband
uxorìci·dio *m* (-di) uxoricide; murder of one's husband
ùzzolo [ddzz] *m* whim, fancy, caprice

V

V, v [vu] *m & f* twentieth letter of the Italian alphabet
V. *abbr* (vostro) your
vacante *adj* vacant
vacanza *f* vacancy; vacation; fare vacanza to be on vacation; vacanze vacation
vacanzière *m* vacationer
vac·ca *f* (-che) cow
vac·càio *m* (-cài) cowboy; stable boy
vaccherìa *f* dairy farm
vacchétta *f* cowhide
vaccìna *f* cow manure; cow
vaccinare *tr* to vaccinate
vaccinazióne *f* vaccination
vaccì·no -na *adj* cow; bovine || *m* vaccine || *f see* vaccìna
vacillante *adj* vacillating
vacillare *intr* to totter; to vacillate; to shake; to flicker; to fail, e.g., la memoria gli vacilla his memory is failing; far vacillare to rock
vacui·tà *f* (-tà) vacuity
và·cuo -cua *adj* empty || *m* vacuum
vademè·cum *m* (-cum) almanac, ready-reference handbook
vagabondàg·gio *m* (-gi) vagrancy; wandering; rambling
vagabondare (vagabóndo) *intr* to wander, rove
vagabón·do -da *adj* wandering; vagabond || *mf* vagrant, bum, tramp; rover
vagare §209 *intr* to wander, ramble, rove
vagheggiare §290 (vaghéggio) *tr* to gaze fondly at; to cherish
vagire §176 *intr* to cry, whimper
vagito *m* cry, whimper
và·glia *m* (-glia) money order || *f* —di vaglia worthy, capable
vagliare §280 *tr* to sift, bolt
và·glio *m* (-gli) sieve; mettere al vaglio to scrutinize
va·go -ga (-ghi -ghe) *adj* vague; vacant (stare); (lit) beautiful; (lit) roving; (poet) desirous || *m* vagueness; (lit) rover; (anat) vagus
vagonata *f* carload
vagóne *m* (rr) car; vagone frigorifero (rr) refrigerator car; vagone letto (rr) sleeping car, sleeper; vagone ristorante (rr) dining car; vagone volante (aer) flying boxcar
vàio vàia (vài vàie) *adj* dark-grey || *m* dark grey; (heral) vair; (zool) Siberian squirrel
vaiòlo *m* smallpox
valan·ga *f* (-ghe) avalanche
valènte *adj* capable, skillful; clever
valentìa *f* skill; cleverness

valentino *m* Valentine (*sweetheart*)
valènza *f* (chem) valence
valére §278 *tr* to win, get (*e.g., an honor for s.o.*); che vale? what's the use?; valere la pena to be worthwhile; valere un Perù to be worth a king's ransom || *intr* (ESSERE & AVERE) to be worth; to be of avail; to be valid; to mean; to be the equivalent; far valere to enforce; farsi valere to assert oneself; tanto vale it's all the same; vale a dire that is to say; valere meglio to be better || *ref*—valersi di to avail oneself of; to play on; to employ
valévole *adj* valid, good
valicare §197 (vàlico) *tr* to cross, pass
vàli·co *m* (-chi) mountain pass; passage; opening (*in a hedge*)
validi·tà *f* (-tà) validity
vàli·do -da *adj* valid; able, able-bodied; strong
valigerìa *f* luggage; luggage store
valigétta *f* valise; valigetta diplomatica attaché case
valì·gia *f* (-ge) suitcase; traveling bag; fare le valige to pack one's bags; valigia diplomatica diplomatic pouch; attaché case; valigia per abiti suit carrier
vallata *f* valley
valle *f* valley; a valle downhill; downstream
vallétta *f* (telv) assistant
vallétto *m* valet; page; (telv) assistant
valló·ne -na *adj & mf* Walloon || *m* narrow valley
valóre *m* value; valor, bravery; force; (fig) jewel; (math) variable; mettere in valore to raise the value of; valore di mercato market value; valore facciale face value; valore locativo rental value; valori valuables; securities; valori mobiliari securities
valorizzare [ddzz] *tr* to enhance the value of
valoró·so -sa [s] *adj* brave, valiant
valuta *f* currency; (com) effective date; (com) value (*of promissory note*)
valutare *tr* to estimate, appraise; to value, prize; to count, reckon; to take into consideration
valutazióne *f* estimation, appraisal; evaluation
valva *f* (bot, zool) valve
vàlvola *f* (anat, mach) valve; (elec) fuse; (rad, telv) tube, valve; valvola a galleggiante ball cock; valvola di sicurezza safety valve; valvola in testa overhead valve
vàl·zer *m* (-zer) waltz

vamp f (vamp) vamp
vampa f flame; blaze; flash; flush
vampata f burst (of heat); blast (of hot air); flash, flush
vampiro m vampire
vanàdio m vanadium
vanaglòria f vainglory, boastfulness
vanaglorió·so -sa [s] adj vainglorious
vandalismo m vandalism
vànda·lo -la adj & m vandal || **Vandalo** m Vandal
vaneggiare §290 (vanéggio) intr to rave; to be delirious; (lit) to open, yawn
vanè·sio -sia adj (-si -sie) vain
van·ga f (-ghe) spade
vangare §209 tr to spade up; to dig with a spade
vangèlo m gospel. || **Vangelo** m Gospel
vanghétto m spud
vaniglia f vanilla
vanilò·quio m (-qui) empty talk
vani·tà f (-tà) vanity
vanitó·so -sa [s] adj vain, conceited
va·no -na adj vain; (lit) empty, hollow; **in vano** in vain || m empty space; room
vantàg·gio m (-gi) advantage; profit; odds, handicap; discount; (coll) extra; (typ) galley; **a vantaggio di** on behalf of
vantaggió·so -sa [s] adj advantageous
vantare tr to boast of; to set up (a claim) || ref to boast; **vantarsi di** to brag about, vaunt
vanteria f brag, boast, vaunt
vanto m brag, boast; **aver vanto su** (lit) to overcome
vànvera f—**a vanvera** at random
vapóre m vapor; steam; locomotive; steamship; **a tutto vapore** at full speed
vaporétto m small river boat; vaporetto (in Venice)
vaporizzare [ddzz] tr to vaporize; to spray || intr (ESSERE) & ref to evaporate
vaporizzatóre [ddzz] m vaporizer; sprayer
vaporó·so -sa [s] adj vaporous
varaménto m assemblage (of prefab pieces)
varano m monitor lizard
varare tr to launch; to pass (a law); (coll) to back, promote (a candidate)
varcare §197 tr to cross || intr (poet) to pass (said of time)
var·co m (-chi) opening; mountain pass; breach; **attendere al varco** to lie in wait for; **cogliere al varco** to catch unawares; **fare varco in** to breach
varechina f (laundry) bleach
variàbile adj & f variable
variante f variant; detour; (aut) model
variare §287 tr & intr (ESSERE & AVERE) to vary
variazióne f variation
varicèlla f chicken pox
varicó·so -sa [s] adj varicose
variega·to -ta adj variegated
varie·tà m (-tà) (theat) vaudeville || f variety

và·rio -ria (-ri -rie) adj varied; various; variable; different; **va·ri -rie** several || m variety || **varie** fpl miscellanies || **va·ri -rie** pron indef several
variopin·to -ta adj multicolored
varo m (naut) launch
vas m (vas) subchaser
va·sàio m (-sài) potter
va·sca f (-sche) tub; basin; pool; **vasca da bagno** bathtub; **vasca dei pesci** aquarium; **vasca navale** (naut) basin
vascèllo m vessel, ship
vaselina or **vasellina** f vaseline
vasellame m dishes; set of dishes; **vasellame da cucina** kitchen ware; **vasellame d'argento** silverware; **vasellame di porcellana** chinaware
vasèllo m (lit) vessel
vasi·stas [s] m (-stas) transom
vaso m vase; vessel; jar, pot; nave (of church); hall (of building); (naut) shipway; (poet) cup; **vasi vinari** wine containers; **vaso da fiori** flowerpot; **vaso da notte** chamber pot; **vaso d'elezione** (eccl) chosen vessel (viz., Saint Paul)
vassallo m vassal; (obs) helper
vas·sóio m (-sói) tray; mortarboard
vasti·tà f (-tà) vastness
va·sto -sta adj spacious; vast; (fig) deep
vate m (lit) prophet, poet
vatica·no -na adj Vatican || **Vaticano** m Vatican
vaticinare (vaticino & vaticino) tr to prophesy
vaticì·nio m (-ni) prophecy
ve §5 pron
V.E. abbr (Vostra Eccellenza) Your Excellency
vècchia f old woman
vecchiàia f old age
vecchiézza f old age
vèc·chio -chia (-chi -chie) adj old; elder; **vecchio come il cucco** as old as the hills || m old man; **vecchi** old people; **vecchio del mestiere** old hand || f see **vecchia**
véc·cia f (-ce) vetch
véce f stead, e.g., **in vece mia** in my stead; (lit) vicissitude; **fare le veci di** to act for or as
vedére m seeing; looks; view, opinion || §279 tr to see; to review; to look over; **chi s'è visto s'è visto!** good-by and good luck!; **dare a vedere** to make believe; **stare a vedere** to watch; observe; **non poter vedere** to not be able to stand; **non vedere l'ora di** to be hardly able to wait for; **vedere male qlcu** to be ill-disposed toward s.o. || intr—**stare a vedere** to wait and see; **vederci bene** to see (e.g., in the dark); **vederci chiaro** to look into it; **vedere di** to try to || ref to see oneself; to see each other; **vedersela brutta** to anticipate trouble
vedétta f lookout; (nav) vedette
védova f widow
vedovanza f widowhood
vedovile adj widow's; widower's || m dower

védo·vo -va *adj* widowed || *m* widower || *f* see **vedova**
veduta *f* view; (lit) eyesight; **di corte vedute** narrowminded; **di larghe vedute** broadminded
veemènte *adj* vehement; violent; impassioned
veemènza *f* vehemence; violence
vegetale *adj* vegetable || *m* plant, vegetable
vegetare (vègeto) *intr* to vegetate
vegetaria·no -na *adj & mf* vegetarian
vegetazióne *f* vegetation
vège·to -ta *adj* vigorous, spry
veggènte *adj* (obs) seeing || *mf* fortuneteller || *m* seer, prophet; **i veggenti** people having eyesight || *f* seeress, prophetess
véglia *f* vigil, watch; wakefulness; evening party, soirée; party, crowd; **a veglia** unbelievable (*tale*); **veglia danzante** dance; **veglia funebre** wake
vegliardo *m* old man
vegliare §280 (véglio) *tr* to keep watch over || *intr* to stay awake; to keep watch; to stay up
vegli óne *m* masked ball
veicolo *m* vehicle; carrier (*of disease*)
véla *f* sail; sailing; **alzare le vele** to set sail; **ammainare le vele** to take in sail; **a vela** under sail; **far vela** to set sail; **vela aurica** lugsail; **vela bermudiana** or **Marconi** jib; **vela maestra** mainsail
ve·làio *m* (-lài) sailmaker
velare *adj & f* (phonet) velar || *v* (vélo) *tr* to veil; to cover; to muffle (*sound*); to attenuate, reduce (*a shock*); to dim, cloud; to conceal; (phot) to fog || *ref* to cover oneself with a veil; to take the veil; to get dim, e.g., **gli si è velata la vista** his eyesight got dim
velà·rio *m* (-ri) (hist) velarium; (theat) curtain
vela·to -ta *adj* veiled; sheer (*hosiery*)
velatura *f* coating; (aer) airfoil; (naut) sails
veleggiare §290 (veléggio) *tr* (lit) to sail over (*the sea*) || *intr* to sail; (aer) to glide
veleggiatóre *m* sailboat; (aer) glider
veléno *m* poison; (fig) venom
veléno·so -sa [s] *adj* poisonous; (fig) venomous
velétta *f* veil; (naut) topgallant
vèli·co -ca *adj* (-ci -che) sail, sailing
velièro *m* sailing ship
veli·no -na *adj* thin (*paper*) || *f* carbon copy; onionskin; slant (*given to a news item*)
velívo·lo -la *adj* (lit) gliding; (lit) sailing || *m* (lit) airplane, aircraft
velleità *f* (-tà) wild ambition, dream
vellicare §197 (vèllico) *tr* to tickle
vèllo *m* (lit) fleece; **vello d'oro** Golden Fleece
velló·so -sa [s] *adj* hairy
velluta·to -ta *adj* velvety
vellutino *m* thin velvet; velvet ribbon; **vellutino di cotone** velveteen
vellu·to -ta *adj* (lit) hairy || *m* velvet; **velluto a coste** corduroy

vélo *m* veil; coating; film; skin (*e.g., of onion*); (anat, bot) velum; (fig) body; **fare velo a** to becloud; to fog
velóce *adj* speedy, quick, fast; fleeting
velocipedastro *m* poor or reckless bicycle rider
veloci·sta *mf* (-sti -ste) (sports) sprinter
veloci·tà *f* (-tà) velocity; speed; (aut) speed; **a grande velocità** by express; **a piccola velocità** by freight; **velocità di crociera** cruising speed; **velocità di fuga** (rok) escape velocity
velòdromo *m* bicycle ring or track
véna *f* vein; grain (*in wood or stone*); mood; streak (*of madness*); **di vena** willingly; **essere in vena di** to be in the mood to
venale *adj* venal
venare (véno) *tr* to vein
vena·to -ta *adj* veined; streaked; suffused; **venato di sangue** bloodshot
venatura *f* veining; (fig) streak
vendémmia *f* vintage
vendemmiare §287 (vendémmio) *tr* to harvest (*grapes*) || *intr* to gather grapes; (fig) to make a killing
vendemmia·tóre -trice *mf* vintager
véndere §281 *tr* to sell; **da vendere** plenty, more than enough; **vendere allo scoperto** (fin) to sell short; **vendere fumo** to peddle influence || *intr* to sell; **vendere allo scoperto** (fin) to sell short || *ref* to sell; **si vende for sale**
vendétta *f* vengeance; revenge; **gridare vendetta** to cry out for retribution
vendicare §197 (véndico) *tr* to avenge || *ref* to get revenge
vendicati·vo -va *adj* vengeful, vindictive
vendica·tóre -trice *adj* avenging || *mf* avenger
vendifu·mo *mf* (-mo) influence peddler
véndita *f* sale; shop; **in vendita** for sale; **vendita allo scoperto** (fin) short sale; **vendita per corrispondenza** catalogue sale
vendi·tóre -trice *mf* seller; clerk (*in store*) || *m* salesman; **venditore ambulante** peddler; **venditore di fumo** influence peddler || *f* saleslady
venefi·cio *m* (-ci) poisoning
venèfi·co -ca (-ci -che) *adj* poisonous; unhealthy || *m* (lit) poisonmaker
veneràbile or **veneràndo** *adj* venerable
venerare (vènero) *tr* to venerate, revere; to worship
venerazióne *f* veneration; worship
vener·dì *m* (-dì) Friday || **Venerdì Santo** Good Friday
Vènere *m* (astr) Venus || *f* (mythol & fig) Venus
venè·reo -rea *adj* (-rei -ree) venereal
Venèzia *f* Venice; Venetia (*province*)
venezia·no -na *adj & mf* Venetian || *f* Venetian blind
venezola·no -na *adj & mf* Venezuelan
vènia *f* (lit) forgiveness, pardon
venire §282 *intr* (ESSERE) to come; to turn out (*well or badly*); to turn out to be; **che viene** next, e.g., **il mese che viene** next month; **come viene as it is; far venire** to send for; to

give, cause; **un va e vieni a back-ward-and-forward** motion; **venire +
ger** to keep + *ger*; **venire + pp** to be
+ *pp, e.g.,* **il portone viene aperto
alle tre** the gate is opened at three;
venire a capo di to solve; **venire ai
ferri corti** to come into open conflict; **venire al dunque** or **al fatto** to
come to the point; **venire alle corte**
to get down to brass tacks; **venire
alle mani** or **alle prese** to come to
blows; **venire a parole** to have
words; **venire a patti con** to come to
terms with; **venire a proposito** to
come in handy; **venire incontro a** to
go to meet; **venire in possesso di**
to come into possession of (*s.th*); to
come into the hands of (*s.o.*); **venire
meno** to faint; **venir meno a** to fail
to keep (*one's word*); **venir su** to
grow, come up; **venire via** to give
way || *ref*—**venirsene** to stroll along
|| *impers* (with *dat*)—**viene da** feel
the urge to, *e.g.,* **gli venne da star-
nutire** he felt the urge to sneeze;
gli è venuto da ridere he felt the urge
to laugh; **viene detto** blurt out, *e.g.,*
**gli è venuto detto che non gli pia-
ceva quel tipo** he blurted out that he
did not like that fellow; **viene fatto
di +** *inf* succeed in + *ger, e.g.,* **le venne
fatto di convincerli** she succeeded in
convincing them; happen to + *inf,
e.g.,* **gli venne fatto di incontrarmi
per istrada** he happened to meet me
on the way

ventà·glio *m* (-**gli**) fan; (fig) spread;
a ventaglio fanlike; **diramarsi a ventaglio** to fan out

ventaròla *f* weather vane

ventata *f* gust of wind; (fig) wave

venténne *adj* twenty-year-old || *mf*
twenty-year-old person

ventèsi·mo -ma *adj, m & pron* twentieth

vénti *adj & pron* twenty; **le venti** eight
P.M. || *m* twenty; twentieth (*in
dates*)

ventidue *adj & pron* twenty-two **le
ventidue** ten P.M. || *m* twenty-two;
twenty-second (*in dates*)

ventilare (**vèntilo**) *tr* to air, ventilate;
to winnow (*grain*); to discuss mi-
nutely; to air (*a subject*); to broach
(*a subject*); to unfurl (*a flag*) ||
ref to fan oneself

ventilatóre *m* fan, ventilator; vent;
(min) ventilation shaft; (naut) funnel

ventilazióne *f* ventilation; winnowing

ventina *f* score; **una ventina (di)** twenty,
about twenty

ventino *m* twenty-cent coin

ventiquattro *adj & pron* twenty-four;
le ventiquattro twelve P.M. || *m*
twenty-four; twenty-fourth (*in dates*)

ventiquattró·re *f* (-**re**) overnight bag;
twenty-four-hour race; **ventiquat-
trore** *fpl* period of twenty-four hours

ventitré *adj & pron* twenty-three; **le
ventitré** eleven P.M.; **portare il cappello alle ventitré** to wear one's hat
cocked || *m* twenty-three; twenty-
third (*in dates*)

vènto *m* wind; air; guy wire; **presentarsi al vento** to sail into the wind;
farsi vento to fan oneself; **a vento**
windproof; wind-propelled; **col vento
in prora** downwind; **col vento in
poppa** upwind; favorably, famously

ventola *f* fireside fan; lampshade; candle sconce; blade (*of fan*)

ventó·so -sa [s] *adj* windy || *f* cupping
glass; suction cup; (zool) sucker

vèntre *m* belly; **a ventre a terra** on
one's belly; on one's face; at full
speed (*said of a horse*)

ventricolo *m* ventricle

ventrièra *f* abdominal band or belt

ventrìloquia *f* ventriloquism

ventrìlo·quo -qua *mf* ventriloquist

ventuno *adj & pron* twenty-one; **le
ventuno** nine P.M. || *m* twenty-one;
twenty-first (*in dates*); (cards) blackjack

ventu·ro -ra *adj* next || *f* (lit) luck, for-
tune; (lit) good fortune; **alla ventura**
at random, a venture; **di ventura**
of fortune, *e.g.,* **soldato di ventura**
soldier of fortune

venustà *f* (lit) pulchritude

venu·to -ta *mf*—**nuovo venuto** new-
comer; **primo venuto** firstcomer || *f*
coming, arrival

véra *f* curbstone (*of well*); (coll) wedding ring

verace *adj* true; truthful, veracious

veraci·tà *f* (-**tà**) veracity, truthfulness

veranda *f* veranda; porch

verbale *adj* verbal || *m* minutes; ticket
(*given by a policeman*); **mettere a
verbale** to enter into the record

verbèna *f* verbena

vèrbo *m* verb; (lit) word || **Verbo** *m*
(theol) Word

verbosità [s] *f* verbiage, verbosity

verbó·so -sa [s] *adj* windy, long-
winded, verbose

verda·stro -stra *adj* greenish

vérde *adj* green; young, youthful || *m*
green; **al verde** (coll) broke, penniless; **nel verde degli anni** in the
prime of life

verdeggiante *adj* verdant

verderame *m* blue vitriol; verdigris

verdét·to -ta *adj* greenish || *m* verdict

verdógno·lo -la *adj* greenish; sallow
(*face*)

verdura *f* vegetables

verecóndia *f* modesty, bashfulness

verecón·do -da *adj* modest, bashful

vér·ga *f* (-**ghe**) switch; rod; ingot, bar;
pole; penis; (eccl) staff, crosier;
(naut) yard; **tremare a verga a verga**
to shake like a leaf

vergare §209 (**vérgo**) *tr* to switch; to
rule (*paper*); to stripe; to write

vergati·no -na *adj* thin (*paper*) || *m*
striped cloth

verga·to -ta *adj* striped; watermarked
with stripes || *m* (obs) serge

verginale *adj* maidenly, virginal

vérgine *adj & f* virgin || **Vergine** *f*
(eccl) Virgin; (astr) Virgo

verginità *f* virginity, maidenhood

vergógna *f* shame; **aver vergogna** to be

ashamed; **vergogne** privates || *interj* for shame!

vergognare (vergógno) *ref* to be ashamed; to feel cheap; **vergognatí!** shame on you!

vergognó·so -sa [s] *adj* ashamed; bashful; shameful

veridici·tà *f* (**-tà**) veracity

verídi·co -ca *adj* (**-ci -che**) veracious

verífi·ca *f* (**-che**) verification; control; **verifica fiscale** auditing (*of tax return*)

verificare §197 (**verífico**) *tr* to verify; to control, check; to audit || *ref* to come true; to happen

verifica·tóre -trice *mf* checker, inspector

verismo *m* verism (*as developed in Italy*)

veri·sta *adj & mf* (**-sti -ste**) verist

veri·tà *f* (**-tà**) truth; **in verità** truthfully, verily

veritiè·ro -ra *adj* truthful

vèrme *m* worm; (mach) thread; **verme solitario** tapeworm

vermí·glio -glia (**-gli -glie**) *adj* vermilion; ruby (*lips*) || *m* vermilion

vèr·mut *m* (**-mut**) vermouth

vernàcolo *m* vernacular

vernice *f* varnish; paint; polish; patina; (painting) private viewing; (fig) veneer; **scarpe di vernice** patent-leather shoes; **vernice a olio** oil paint; **vernice a spruzzo** spray paint; **vernice da scarpe** shoe polish

verniciare §128 *tr* to varnish; to paint

vé·ro -ra *adj* true; real; right; pure; **non è vero?** isn't that so? La traduzione precedente è generalmente rimpiazzata da molte altre frasi. Se la prima espressione è negativa, la domanda equivalente a **non è vero?** sarà affermativa, per esempio, **Lei non lavora, non è vero?** You are not working, are you? Se la prima espressione è affermativa, la domanda sarà negativa, per esempio, **Lei lavora, non è vero?** You are working, are you not? or aren't you? Se la prima espressione contiene un ausiliare, la domanda conterrà l'ausiliare stesso senza infinito o senza participio passato, per esempio, **Arriveranno domani, non è vero?** They will arrive tomorrow, won't they? **Ha finito il compito, non è vero?** He has finished his homework, hasn't he? Se la prima espressione non contiene né un ausiliare, né una delle forme del verbo "to be" in funzione di copula, la domanda conterrà l'ausiliare "do" o "did" senza l'infinito del verbo, per esempio, **Lei è vissuto a Milano, non è vero?** You lived in Milano, did you not? **Lei non va mai al parco, non è vero?** You never go to the park, do you?; **non mi par vero** it seems unbelievable || *m* truth; actuality; **a dire il vero** to tell the truth, as a matter of fact; **dal vero** from nature; **salvo il vero** if I am not mistaken || *f* see **vera**

veróne *m* (lit) balcony

verosimiglianza *f* verisimilitude; probability, likelihood

verosímile *adj* verisimilar; probable, likely

verricèllo *m* winch, windlass

vèrro *m* boar

verru·ca *f* (**-che**) wart

versaménto *m* spilling; payment; deposit

versante *m* depositor; slope, side

versare (vèrso) *tr* to pour; to spill; to shed; to pay; to deposit || *intr* to overflow; **versare in gravi condizioni** to be in a bad way || *ref* to spill; to pour (*said of people*); to empty (*said of a river*)

versàtile *adj* versatile; fickle

versa·to -ta *adj* versed; gifted; fully subscribed to (e.g., stock of a corporation)

verseggia·tóre -trice *mf* verse writer

versétto *m* verse (*of Bible*)

versificare §197 (**versífico**) *tr & intr* to versify

versificazióne *f* versification

versióne *f* version; translation

vèrso *adj invar*—**pollice verso** (hist) thumbs down || *m* verse; local accent; voice, cry; reverse (*of coin*); verso (*of page*); line (*of poetry*); singsong; gesture; direction, way, manner; respect; **andare a verso** (with *dat*) to suit, e.g., **le sue maniere non gli vanno a verso** her manners do not suit him; **a verso** properly; **contro verso** against the grain; **fare un verso** to make faces; **per un verso** on one hand; **rifare il verso** (with *dat*) to mimick; **senza verso** without rhyme or reason; **verso sciolto** blank verse || *prep* toward; near, around; about; for, toward; upon, in return for; as compared with; **verso di** toward

vèrtebra *f* vertebra

vertebrale *adj* vertebral; spinal

vertebra·to -ta *adj & m* vertebrate

vertènza *f* quarrel, dispute; **vertenza sindacale** labor dispute

vèrtere §283 *intr*—**vertere su** to deal with, to turn on

verticale *adj & f* vertical

vèrtice *m* top, summit; vertex; summit conference

vertígine *f* vertigo, dizziness; **avere le vertigini** to feel dizzy

vertiginó·so -sa [s] *adj* dizzy; breathtaking

vérza [dz] *f* cabbage

verzière [dz] *m* (lit) fruit, vegetable, and flower garden; (coll) produce market

verzura [dz] *f* verdure

vescí·ca *f* (**-che**) bladder; blister; **vescica di vento** (fig) windbag; **vescica gonfiata** swellhead; **vescica natatoria** air bladder

vescichétta *f* blister; vescicle; **vescichetta biliare** gall bladder

vescícola *f* blister

vescovado *m* bishopric

véscovo *m* bishop

vè·spa *f* wasp, yellowjacket || *f* (-spe & -spa) motor scooter

ve·spàio *m* (-spài) wasp's nest; (fig) hornet's nest

vespasiano *m* public urinal

Vèspero *m* Vesper

vesperti·no -na *adj* (lit) evening

vèspro *m* (eccl) vespers; (lit) vespertide

vessare (vèsso) *tr* (lit) to oppress

vessatò·rio -ria *adj* (-ri -rie) vexatious

vessazióne *f* oppression

vessillo *m* flag

vestàglia *f* negligee, dressing gown; vestaglia da bagno bathrobe

vèste *f* dress; cover; (lit) body; in veste di in the quality of; as; in the guise of; veste da camera negligee, dressing gown; bathrobe; veste talare (eccl) long vestment; vesti clothes

vestià·rio *m* (-ri) wardrobe

vestìbolo *m* vestibule, lobby

vestì·gio *m* (-gi & -gia *fpl*) vestige, trace; (lit) footprint

vestire (vèsto) *tr* to dress; to don; to wear; to clothe; to cover, bedeck || *intr* to dress; to fit || *ref* to get dressed; to dress; to dress oneself; to buy one's own clothes

vestì·to -ta *adj* dressed; covered || *m* dress; suit; clothing; vestiti clothes; vestito da donna dress; vestito da festa Sunday best; vestito da sera evening clothes, formal suit; evening gown; vestito da uomo suit

Vesùvio, il Vesuvius

vetera·no -na *adj* & *mf* veteran

veterinà·rio -ria *adj* (-ri -rie) veterinary || *m* veterinarian || *f* veterinary medicine

vèto *m* veto; porre il veto a to veto

ve·tràio *m* (-trài) glass manufacturer; glass dealer; glass blower

vetra·to -ta *adj* glass, glass-enclosed; sand (*paper*) || *m* glare ice, glaze || *f* glass door; glass window; glass enclosure; vetrata a colori or vetrata istoriata stained-glass window

vetrerìa *f* glassworks; vetrerie glassware

vetria·to -ta *adj* glassy; glass-covered

vetrificare §197 (vetrifico) *tr* to vitrify || *ref* to become vitrified

vetrina *f* show window; showcase, glass cabinet; mettersi in vetrina to show off; vetrine (coll) eyeglasses

vetrini·sta *mf* (-sti -ste) window dresser

vetri·no -na *adj* glass-like; brittle, fragile || *m* slide (*of microscope*) || *f* see vetrina

vetriòlo *m* vitriol

vétro *m* glass; glassware; window pane; piece of glass; vetro aderente contact lens; vetro infrangibile (aut) safety glass; vetro smerigliato ground glass, frosted glass

vetrorèsina *f* fiberglass

vetró·so -sa [s] *adj* vitreous, glassy

vétta *f* peak; top, tip; limb (*of tree*); (naut) end (*of hawser*); tremare come una vetta to shake like a leaf

vet·tóre -trice *adj* leading, guiding; spreading, carrying || *m* carrier; (math, phys) vector

vettovagliare §280 *tr* to supply with food

vettovàglie *fpl* victuals, food; supplies

vettura *f* forwarding; coach; car; freight; in vettura! (rr) all aboard!; prendere in vettura to hire (*a conveyance*); vettura belvedere (rr) observation car; vettura da turismo (aut) pleasure car; vettura di piazza hack, hackney; vettura letto (rr) sleeping car; vettura ristorante (rr) diner

vetturétta *f* economy car, compact

vetturino *m* hackman, cab driver

vetu·sto -sta *adj* old, ancient

vezzeggiare §290 (vezzéggio) *tr* to coddle || *intr* (lit) to strut

vezzeggiati·vo -va *adj* endearing || *m* endearing expression; diminutive

vézzo *m* habit; caress; necklace; bad habit; vezzi fondling, petting; mawkish behavior; charms

vezzó·so -sa [s] *adj* graceful, charming; affected, mincing

vi §5

via *m* (via) starting signal; dare il via a to give the go-ahead to || *f* street; road, way; route; career; dare la via a to open the way to; in via confidenziale in confidence; in via eccezionale as an exception; per via di via, through; (coll) because of; per via gerarchica through administrative channels; per via orale orally; per via rettale rectally; prendere la via to be on one's way; venire a vie di fatto to come to blows; Via Crucis Way of the Cross; via d'acqua waterway; via di scampo (fig) way out; via d'uscita way out; Via Lattea Milky Way; vie di fatto assault and battery; vie legali legal steps || *adv* away; (math) times, by; e così via and so on; e via dicendo and so on; tirar via to hurry along; via via che as || *prep* via, by way of

viadótto *m* viaduct

viaggiare §290 *intr* to travel; (com) to deal

viaggia·tóre -trice *adj* traveling; homing (*pigeon*) || *mf* traveler || *m* traveling salesman

viàg·gio *m* (-gi) travel; journey, trip; buon viaggio! bon voyage!; viaggio d'andata e ritorno round trip; viaggio di prova (naut) trial run, shakedown cruise

viale *m* boulevard

viandante *mf* (lit) wayfarer

vià·rio -ria *adj* (-ri -rie) road, highway

viàti·co *m* (-ci) viaticum

viavài *m* coming and going; hustle and bustle

vibrante *adj* vibrant; wiry; (phonet) vibrant || *f* (phonet) trill, vibrant

vibrare *tr* to jar; to deliver (*a blow*); to vibrate; (lit) to hurl || *intr* to vibrate

vibra·to -ta *adj* vibrant; resolute, vigorous || *m* vibrating sound

vibrazióne *f* vibration

vicariato *m* vicarage

vicà·rio *m* (-ri) vicar

vice- *pref adj* vice-, e.g., **vicereale** viceroyal ‖ *pref m & f* vice-, e.g., **viceammiraglio** vice-admiral; assistant, e.g., **vicegovernatore** assistant governor; deputy, e.g., **vicesindaco** deputy mayor

vicediret·tóre -trice *mf* assistant manager

vicènda *f* vicissitude; rotation (*of crops*); **a vicenda** in turn

vicendévole *adj* mutual, reciprocal

vicepresidènte [s] *mf* vice president

vice·ré *m* (**-ré**) viceroy

vicevèrsa *adv* vice versa; (coll) instead, on the contrary

vichin·go -ga *adj & mf* (**-ghi -ghe**) Viking

vicinanza *f* nearness; **in vicinanza di** in the neighborhood of; **vicinanze** vicinity, neighborhood

vicinato *m* neighborhood

vici·no -na *adj* near; neighboring; next; close (*relative*) ‖ *mf* neighbor ‖ **vicino** *adv* nearby, near; **da vicino** closely; at close quarters; **vicino a** near; next to, close to

vicissitùdine *f* vicissitude

vi·co *m* (**-chi**) alley, lane; village; (lit) region

vìcolo *m* alley, court, place; **vicolo cieco** blind alley, dead end

videocassétta *f* video cassette

vidimare (**vìdimo**) *tr* to validate, visa; to sign

vidimazióne *f* validation, visa; signature

viennése [s] *adj & mf* Viennese

viepiù *adv* (lit) more and more

vietare (**vièto**) *tr* to forbid, prohibit

vieta·to -ta *adj* forbidden; **senso vietato** one way; **sosta vietata** no parking; no stopping; **vietato fumare** no smoking

Vietnam, il Vietnam

vietnami·ta *adj & mf* (**-ti -te**) Vietnamese

viè·to -ta *adj* (lit) old-fashioned; (coll) musty-smelling, rancid

vigènte *adj* current, in force

vìgere §284 *intr* to be in force

vigèsi·mo -ma *adj* twentieth

vigilante *adj* watchful, vigilant ‖ *m* watchman

vigilanza *f* vigilance; surveillance

vigilare (**vìgilo**) *tr* to watch; to watch over; to police ‖ *intr* to watch; **vigilare che** to see to it that

vigila·tóre -trice *mf* inspector ‖ *f* camp counselor; **vigilatrice sanitaria** child health inspector

vìgile *adj* (lit) watchful ‖ *m* watch; **vigile del fuoco** fireman; **vigile urbano** policeman

vigìlia *f* fast; vigil; **la vigilia di** on the eve of, the night before

vigliacchería *f* cowardice

vigliac·co -ca (**-chi -che**) *adj* cowardly ‖ *m* coward

vigna *f* vineyard

vignaiòlo *m* vine dresser

vignéto *m* vineyard

vignétta *f* vignette; **vignetta umoristica** cartoon

vignetti·sta *mf* (**-sti -ste**) cartoonist

vigógna *f* vicuña

vigóre *m* vigor; **in vigore** in force

vigorìa *f* vigor

vigoró·so -sa [s] *adj* vigorous

vile *adj* cowardly; vile, low, cheap; base (*metal*)

vilificare §197 (**vilìfico**) *tr* to vilify

vilipèndere §148 *tr* to despise; to show scorn for

villa *f* villa; country house; one-family detached house; (lit) country

villàg·gio *m* (**-gi**) village; **villaggio del fanciullo** boys' town

villanata *f* boorishness

villanìa *f* boorishness, rudeness; insult

villa·no -na *adj* rude, churlish ‖ *mf* boor, churl; (lit) peasant

villanzó·ne -na *mf* boor, uncouth person

villeggiante *mf* vacationist

villeggiare §290 (**villéggio**) *intr* to vacation

villeggiatura *f* vacation, summer vacation

villétta *f* or **villino** *m* bungalow

villó·so -sa [s] *adj* hairy

vil·tà *f* (**-tà**) baseness; cowardice

viluppo *m* tangle, twist

vìmine *m* withe, wicker, osier

vinàcce *fpl* pressed grapes

vi·nàio *m* (**-nài**) wine merchant

vincènte *adj* winning ‖ *mf* winner

vìncere §285 *tr* to overcome; to win; to convince; to check; to defeat; **vincere per un pelo** to nose out; **vincerla** to come out on top ‖ *ref* to control oneself

vincetòssi·co *m* (**-ci**) swallowwort, tame poison

vincipèr·di *m* (**-di**) giveaway

vìncita *f* gain; winnings

vinci·tóre -trice *adj* conquering, victorious ‖ *mf* winner; conqueror; victor

vincolare *adj* binding; bound ‖ *v* (**vìncolo**) *tr* to tie; to bind, obligate; to restrict the use of (*real-estate property*)

vìncolo *m* tie, bond; (law) entail; (law) restriction (*in a real-estate deed*)

vinìco·lo -la *adj* wine, wine-producing

vinile *m* vinyl

vino *m* wine; **vin caldo** mulled wine; **vino da pasto** table wine; **vino di marca** vintage wine; **vino di mele** cider

vin·to -ta *adj* vanquished, overcome, defeated; victorious (*battle*); **averla vinta su** to overcome; **darla vinta a qlcu** to let s.o. get away with murder; **darsi per vinto** to give in, yield ‖ *m* vanquished person; **i vinti** the vanquished

viò·la *adj invar* violet ‖ *m* (**-la**) violet (*color*) ‖ *f* violet; (mus) viola; **viola del pensiero** pansy; **viola mammola** sweet violet

violacciòc·ca *f* (**-che**) (bot) wallflower

violà·ceo -cea *adj* violet

violare (**vìolo**) *tr* to violate; to run (*a blockade*)

violazióne *f* violation; **violazione di**

domicilio housebreaking, burglary; violazione di proprietà trespass

violentare (violènto) tr to violate, force; to do violence to; to rape

violèn·to -ta adj violent || m violent person

violènza f violence; violenza carnale rape

violét·to -ta adj & m violet || f (bot) violet

violini·sta mf (-sti -ste) violinist

violino m violin; primo violino concertmaster

violoncelli·sta mf (-sti -ste) violoncellist

violoncèllo m violoncello, cello

viòttolo m path

vìpera f viper, adder

viràg·gio m (-gi) turn; (aer) banking; (naut) tacking; (phot) toning

virare tr to veer; to turn (a winch); (aer) to bank; (phot) to tone || intr to veer, steer; virare di bordo (naut) to put about; (naut) to tack

virata f turn, veer; (aer) banking; (naut) tacking

virginale adj var of verginale

virgi·nia m (-nia) Virginia tobacco || f (-nia) Virginia cigarette

vìrgola f comma; (used in Italian to set off the decimal fraction from the integer) decimal point; doppia virgola quotation mark

virgolétta f quotation mark

virgulto m (lit) shoot; (lit) shrub

virile adj virile

virilità f virility

viròla f (mach) male piece

virologia f virology

vir·tù f (-tù) virtue; (lit) valor

virtuale adj virtual

virtualménte adv virtually, to all intents and purposes

virtuosismo [s] m virtuosity; showing off

virtuosità [s] f virtuosity

virtuó·so -sa [s] adj virtuous || mf virtuoso

virulèn·to -ta adj virulent

virulènza f virulence

vi·rus m (-rus) virus

vìsce·re m (-ri) internal organ; visceri entrails, viscera || viscere fpl entrails, viscera; (fig) heart, feeling; (fig) bowels (of the earth)

vì·schio m (-schi) mistletoe; birdlime; (fig) trap

vischió·so -sa [s] adj sticky, viscous; (com) steady

vìsci·do -da adj viscid; clammy; (fig) unctuous

vìsciola f sour cherry

vìsciolo m sour cherry tree

viscónte m viscount

viscontéssa f viscountess

viscó·so -sa [s] adj viscous, sticky || f viscose

visétto m small face; baby face

visìbile adj visible; obvious

visibì·lio m (-lì) (coll) crowd; (coll) bunch; andare in visibilio to become ecstatic; mandare in visibilio to throw into ecstasy, enrapture

visibilità f visibility

visièra f visor; fencing mask; eyeshade; visiera termica (aut) electric defroster

visigò·to -ta adj Visigothic || mf Visigoth

visionà·rio -ria adj & mf (-ri -rie) visionary

visióne f vision; sight; (mov, telv) showing; in visione gratuita for free examination; mandare qlco a qlcu in visione to send s.th to s.o. for his (or her) opinion; prendere visione di to examine; to peruse

vi·sìr m (-sìr) vizier

vìsita f visit; visitation; fare una visita to pay a visit; marcare visita (mil) to report sick; visita doganale customs inspection

visitare (visito) tr to visit; to inspect

visita·tóre -trice mf visitor || f social worker

visitazióne f visitation

visì·vo -va adj visual

viso m face; far buon viso a cattivo gioco to grin and bear it

visóne m mink

visóre m (phot) viewer; (phot) viewfinder

vi·spo -spa adj brisk, lively

vissu·to -ta adj wordly-wise

vista f sight, eyesight; view; vista; glance; (poet) window; a vista exposed, visible; a vista d'occhio as far as the eye can see; essere in vista to be expected; to be imminent; to be in the limelight; far vista di to pretend to; in vista di in view of; mettere in vista to show off; vista a volo d'uccello bird's-eye view; vista corta poor eyesight

vistare tr to validate, visa

vi·sto -sta adj—visto che seeing that, inasmuch as || m visa; approval || f see vista

vistó·so -sa [s] adj showy, flashy; (fig) considerable

visuale adj visual || f view; line of sight

visualizzare [ddzz] tr to visualize

vita f life; livelihood; living; waist; avere breve vita to be short-lived; fare la vita to be a prostitute; vita natural durante for life; during one's lifetime

vitaiòlo m man about town; playboy, bon vivant

vitale adj vital

vitalità f vitality

vitalì·zio -zia (-zi -zie) adj life, lifetime || m life annuity

vitamina f vitamin

vite f (bot) grapevine; (mach) screw; a vite threaded; (aer) in a tailspin; vite autofilettante self-tapping screw; vite del Canadà woodbine, Virginia creeper; vite per legno wood screw; vite per metallo machine screw; vite perpetua (mach) endless screw, worm gear; vite prigioniera stud bolt

vitèllo m calf; veal

vitìc·cio m (-ci) tendril

vìtre·o -a adj vitreous; glassy (eyes)

vìttima f victim

vitto m food; diet; vitto e alloggio room and board

vittòria f victory; cantar vittoria to crow; to crow too soon

vittorió•so -sa [s] adj victorious

vituperare (vitùpero) tr to vituperate

vituperévole adj contemptible, shameful

vitupè•rio m (-ri) shame, infamy; insult; (lit) blame

viuzza f narrow street, lane

viva interj long live!

vivacchiare §287 intr (coll) to get along || ref—si vivacchia (coll) so, so

vivace adj lively, brisk; brilliant; vivacious

vivacità f liveliness, briskness; brilliancy, brightness; vivacity

vivaddío interj yes, of course!; by Jove!

vivagno m selvage; edge

vi•vàio m (-vài) fishpond; fish tank; tree nursery; (fig) seedbed

vivanda f food

vivandiè•re -ra mf (mil) sutler

vivere m life; living; cost of living; viveri food, provisions; allowance || §286 tr to live; vivere un brutto momento to spend an uncomfortable moment || intr (ESSERE) to live; vive (typ) stet; vivere alla giornata to live from hand to mouth

vivézza f liveliness

vivi•do -da adj vivid, lively

vivificare §197 (vivìfico) tr to vivify

vivisezionare (vivisezióno) tr to vivisect; to scrutinize

vivisezióne f vivisection

vi•vo -va adj alive; living; live, vivacious; lively; vivid; high (flame); bright (light); raw (flesh); sharp, acute (pain); hearty (thanks); outright (expense); gross (weight); brute (strength); modern (language); kinetic (energy); running (water) || m living being; heart (of a question); al vivo lively; lifelike; i vivi e i morti the quick and the dead; toccare nel vivo to sting to the quick || viva interj see viva

viziare §287 tr to spoil; to ruin; (law) to vitiate || ref to become spoiled

vizia•to -ta adj spoiled; ruined; stale (air)

vi•zio m (-zi) vice; defect; flaw; (law) vitiation

vizió•so -sa [s] adj vicious; defective || mf profligate

viz•zo -za adj withered

vocabolà•rio m (-ri) dictionary; vocabulary

vocàbolo m word

vocale adj vocal; (lit) sonorous || f vowel

vocalizzare [ddzz] tr & ref to vocalize

vocativo m vocative

vocazióne f vocation

vóce f voice; noise, roar; word; rumor; entry; tone; ad alta voce aloud; a bassa voce in a low voice; a viva voce by word of mouth; a voce orally; dare una voce a (coll) to call; dare sulla voce a to rebuke; to con-

tradict; fare la voce grossa to raise one's voice; non avere voce in capitolo to have no say; schiarirsi la voce to clear one's throat; senza voce hoarse; sotto voce in a low tone; voce bianca child's voice (in singing)

vociare m bawl || §128 (vócio) intr to bawl

vociferare (vocìfero) intr to vociferate, shout || ref—si vocifera it is rumored

vó•ga f (-ghe) fashion, vogue; energy, enthusiasm; rowing

vogare §209 (vógo) tr & intr to row

voga•tóre -trice mf rower || m oarsman; rowing machine

vòglia f wish; whim, fancy; willingness; birthmark; aver voglia di to feel like, have a notion to; di buona voglia willingly; di mala voglia unwillingly

voglió•so -sa [s] adj fanciful; (lit) desirous

vói §5 pron pers you; voi altri you, e.g., voi altri americani you Americans

voialtri •tre pron pl you, e.g., voialtri americani you Americans

volano m shuttlecock; (mach) flywheel

volante adj flying; loose (sheet); free (agent) || m steering wheel; (mach) hand wheel; shuttlecock

volantino m leaflet; fringe; (mach) hand wheel

volare (vólo) tr (soccer) to overthrow || intr (ESSERE & AVERE) to fly

volata f flight; sprint; run; mouth (of gun); (tennis) volley; di volata in a hurry

volàtile adj volatile; flying (animal) || volatili mpl birds

volatilizzare [ddzz] tr & intr (ESSERE) to volatilize

volènte adj—Dio volente God willing; volente o nolente willy-nilly

volentieri adv gladly, willingly

volére m will, wish; al volere di at the bidding of || §288 tr to will; to want, desire; (lit) to believe, affirm; l'hai voluto tu it's your fault; non vuol dire! never mind!; qui ti voglio here's the rub, that's the trouble; senza volere without meaning to; voglia Dio! may God grant!; voler bene (with dat) to like; volerci to take, e.g., ci vorranno due anni per finire questo palazzo it will take two years to complete this building; ce ne vogliono ancora tre it takes three more of them; voler dire to mean; to try, e.g., vuole piovere it is trying to rain; volere che + subj to want + inf, e.g., vuole che vengano he wants them to come; volere piuttosto to prefer; volere è potere where there is a will there is a way; voler male (with dat) to dislike; volerne a to bear a grudge against; vorrei I should like, I'd like; vuoi . . . vuoi either . . . or

volgare adj vernacular, popular, common; vulgar || m vernacular

volgari•tà f (-tà) vulgarity

volgarizzare [ddzz] *tr* to popularize

vòlgere §289 *tr* to turn; (lit) to translate ‖ *intr* to turn; (lit) to go by; **volgere a** to turn toward; to draw near, to approach; **volgere in fuga** to take to flight ‖ *ref* to turn; to devote oneself

vól·go *m* (-ghi) (lit) crowd, mob

volièra *f* aviary

voliti·vo -va *adj* volitional; strong-minded, strong-willed

vólo *m* flight; fall; **al volo** on the spot; on the wing; **a volo d'uccello** as the crow flies; bird's-eye (*e.g., view*); **di volo** at top speed, immediately; **in volo** aloft, in the air; **prendere il volo** to take flight; **volo a vela** or **volo planato** gliding; **volo strumentale** instrument flying; **volo veleggiato** gliding

volon·tà *f* (-tà) will; **di spontanea volontà** of one's own volition; **pieno di buona volontà** eager to please; **ultime volontà** last will and testament

volontariato *m* volunteer work; apprenticeship without pay; (mil) volunteer service

volontà·rio -ria (-ri -rie) *adj* voluntary ‖ *m* volunteer

volonteró·so -sa [s] *adj* willing, well-disposed

volpacchiòtto *m* fox cub; (fig) sly fox

vólpe *f* fox; (agr) smut; **volpe argentata** silver fox

volpi·no -na *adj* fox; fox-colored; foxy ‖ *m* Pomeranian

volpó·ne -na *mf* sly fox

vòlt *m* (vòlt) (elec) volt

vòl·ta *m* (-ta) (elec) volt ‖ *f* turn; time; vault; roof (*of mouth*); **alla volta di** toward; **a volta di corriere** by return mail; **a volte** sometimes; **c'era una volta** once upon a time there was; **certe volte** sometimes; **dare di volta il cervello a** to go crazy, e.g., **gli ha dato di volta il cervello** he went crazy; **dar la volta** to turn sour (*said of wine*); **due volte** twice; **molte volte** often; **per una volta** tanto only once; **poche volte** seldom; **tante volte** often; **tutto in una volta** at one swoop, at one stroke; in one gulp, in one swallow; **una volta** once; **una volta che** (coll) inasmuch as; **una volta per sempre** once and for all; **una volta tanto** for once; **volta a crociera** cross vault; **volta per volta** little by little; **volte** (math) times, e.g., **cinque volte cinque** five times five

voltafàc·cia *m* (-cia) volte-face; **fare voltafaccia** to wheel around (*said of a horse*)

voltagabba·na *mf* (-na) turncoat

voltàg·gio *m* (-gi) voltage

voltài·co -ca *adj* (-ci -che) voltaic

voltare (vòlto) *tr*, *intr* & *ref* to turn

voltastòma·co *m* (-chi) (coll) nausea; **fare venire il voltastomaco a qlcu** (coll) to turn s.o.'s stomach

voltata *f* turn; curve

volteggiare §290 (voltéggio) *tr* to put (*a horse*) through its paces ‖ *intr* to hover; to flit, flutter; (sports) to vault (*e.g., on horseback or trapeze*)

voltég·gio *m* (-gi) (sports) vaulting

vòltmetro *m* voltmeter

vólto *m* (lit) face

voltura *f* (com, law) transfer

volùbile *adj* fickle

volubilità *f* fickleness

volume *m* volume; bulk; mass

voluminó·so -sa [s] *adj* voluminous, bulky

volu·to -ta *adj* desired; intentional ‖ *f* (archit) volute, scroll

volut·tà *f* (-tà) pleasure, enjoyment; voluptuousness

voluttuà·rio -ria *adj* (-ri -rie) luxury (*goods*)

voluttuó·so -sa [s] *adj* voluptuous, sensuous

vòmere *m* plowshare; trail spade (*of gun*)

vòmi·co -ca *adj* (-ci -che) emetic

vomitare (vòmito) *tr* & *intr* to vomit

vomitati·vo -va *adj* & *m* emetic

vòmito *m* vomit

vóngola *f* clam

vorace *adj* voracious

voraci·tà *f* (-tà) voracity

voràgine *f* chasm, gulf, abyss

vòrtice *m* vortex, whirlpool; whirlwind

vorticó·so -sa [s] *adj* whirling, swirling

vò·stro -stra §6 *adj* & *pron poss*

votare (vóto) *tr* to devote; to vote ‖ *intr* to vote ‖ *ref* to devote oneself

votazióne *f* vote, voting, poll; (educ) grades

voti·vo -va *adj* votive

vóto *m* vow; wish; votive offering; vote, ballot; grade, mark; **a pieni voti** with highest honors; **fare un voto** to make a vow; **pronunciare i voti** to take vows; **voto di fiducia** vote of confidence; **voto preferenziale** write-in vote; preferential ballot

vudù *m* voodoo

vudui·sta *mf* (-sti -ste) voodoo (*person*)

vulcàni·co -ca *adj* (-ci -che) volcanic

vulcanizzare [ddzz] *tr* to vulcanize

vulcano *m* volcano

vulga·to -ta *adj* disseminated ‖ **Vulgata** *f* Vulgate

vulneràbile *adj* vulnerable

vuotare (vuòto) *tr* to empty; **vuotare il sacco** to speak one's mind, unburden oneself ‖ *ref* to empty

vuò·to -ta *adj* empty; devoid ‖ *m* vacuum; emptiness; empty space; empty seat; empty feeling; empty (*e.g., container*); **a vuoto** in vain; wide of the mark; (check) without sufficient funds; **andare a vuoto** to fail; (mach) to idle; **cadere nel vuoto** to fall on deaf ears; **mandare a vuoto** to thwart; **sotto vuoto** in a vacuum; **vuoto d'aria** (aer) air pocket; **vuoto di cassa** deficit; **vuoto di potere** power vacuum

W

W, w ['doppjo 'vu] *m & f*
wà•fer *m* (-fer) wafer
water-clòset *m* (-clòset) flush toilet
watt *m* (watt) watt

watt•óra *m* (-óra) watt-hour
wèstern *m* (wèstern) (mov) western
whisky *m* (whisky) whiskey
wìgwam *m* (wìgwam) wigwam

X

X, x [ɪks] *m & f*
xèno *m* xenon
xenòfo•bo -ba *mf* xenophobe

xè•res *m* (-res) sherry
xerografìa *f* xerography
xeròfito *m* xerophyte

Y

Y, y ['ɪpsɪlon] *m & f*
yacht *m* (yachts) yacht
yak *m* (yak) yak

yànkee *m* (yànkees) Yankee
yìddish *adj invar & m* Yiddish

Z

Z, z ['dzeta] *m & f* twenty-first letter
of the Italian alphabet
zabaióne [dz] *m* eggnog
zàcchera *f* splash of mud
zaffare *tr* to plug; to bung
zaffata *f* unpleasant whiff, stench; gust
zafferano [dz] *m* saffron
zaffiro [dz] *m* sapphire
zaffo *m* plug; bung; tampon
zàgara [dz] *f* orange blossom
zàino [dz] *m* knapsack; (mil) pack
zampa *f* paw; (culin) leg; **a quattro
zampe** on all fours; **zampa di gallina**
crow's-foot; illegible scrawl; **zampa
di porco** crowbar
zampare *intr* to paw; to stamp
zampettare (zampétto) *intr* to toddle;
to scamper
zampillare *intr* (ESSERE & AVERE) to
spurt, gush, spring
zampillo *m* spurt, gush, spring
zampino *m* little paw; **metterci lo zampino** to put one's finger in the pie
zampiróne *m* slow-burning mosquito
repellent; foul-smelling cigarette
zampógna *f* bagpipe
zampognare (zampógno) *intr* to pipe,
play the bagpipe
zampóne *m* Modena salami (*stuffed
forepaw of a hog*)
zanèlla *f* gully
zàngola *f* butter churn
zanna *f* tusk; fang; **mostrare le zanne**
to show one's teeth
zanzara [dz] [dz] *f* mosquito
zanzarièra [dz] [dz] *f* mosquito net;
window screen
zappa *f* hoe; **darsi la zappa sui piedi**

to cut one's nose off to spite one's
face
zappare *tr* to hoe
zappatóre *m* hoer, digger; (mil) sapper
zar *m* (zar) czar
zàttera *f* raft; **zattera di salvataggio** life
raft
zatterière *m* log driver
zavòrra [dz] *f* ballast; (fig) deadwood
zavorrare [dz] (zavòrro) *tr* to ballast
zàzzera *f* mop (*of hair*)
zèbra [dz] *f* zebra; **zebre** zebra crossing
zebra•to -ta [dz] *adj* zebra-striped
ze•bù [dz] *m* (-bù) zebu
zéc•ca *f* (-che) mint; (ent) tick; **nuovo
di zecca** brand-new
zecchino *m* sequin, gold coin
zèfiro [dz] *m* zephyr
zelante [dz] *adj* zealous; studious ǁ *mf*
zealot; eager beaver
zèlo [dz] *m* zeal; **zelo pubblico** public
spirit
zènit [dz] *m* zenith
zénzero [dz] [dz] *m* ginger
zép•po -pa *adj* crammed, jammed ǁ *f*
wedge; (fig) padding
zerbino [dz] *m* doormat; dandy
zerbinòtto [dz] *m* dandy, sporty fellow
zèro [dz] *m* zero
zìa *f* aunt
zibaldóne [dz] *m* notebook; collection
of thoughts; (pej) hodgepodge
zibellino [dz] *m* sable
zibétto [dz] *m* civet cat; civet (*substance used in perfumery*)
zibibbo [dz] *m* raisin
ziga•no -na *adj & mf* gypsy
zigomo [dz] *m* cheekbone

zigrinare [dz] *tr* to grain (*leather*); to mill, knurl (*metal*)

zigrina·to -ta [dz] *adj* shagreened, grained (*leather*); knurled

zigzàg [dz] [dz] *m* (**zigzàg**) zigzag; **andare a zigzag** to zigzag

zigzagare §209 [dz] [dz] *intr* to zigzag

zimarra [dz] *f* cassock; (obs) overcoat

zimbèllo *m* decoy (*bird*); laughingstock

zincare §197 *tr* to zinc

zinco *m* zinc

zingaré·sco -sca (**-schi -sche**) *adj & mf* gypsy

zìnga·ro -ra *mf* gypsy

zìnnia [dz] *f* zinnia

zìo *m* uncle; **zio d'America** rich uncle

zìpolo *m* peg, bung

zircóne [dz] *m* zircon

zircònio [dz] *m* zirconium

zirlare *intr* to warble; to squeak (*said of mouse*)

zitèlla *f* old maid

zittire §176 *tr & intr* to hoot, hiss

zit·to -ta *adj* silent; **far stare zitto** to hush up; **stare zitto** to keep quiet || *m* whisper || **zitto** *interj* quiet!; hush!; shut up!

zizzània [dz] [ddzz] *f* (bot) darnel; **seminar zizzania** to sow discord

zòccolo *m* clog, sabot; clump, clod; clodhopper; base (*of column*); pedestal; wide baseboard; (zool) hoof

zodìaco [dz] *m* zodiac

zolfanèllo *m* sulfur match

zolfara *f* var of **solfara**

zólfo *m* sulfur

zòlla *f* clod, clump; turf; lump, cube (*of sugar*)

zollétta *f* lump, cube (*of sugar*)

zòna [dz] *f* zone; area; girdle; band, stripe; ticker tape; (pathol) shingles; (telg) tape; **zona glaciale** frigid zone; **zona tropicale** tropics, tropical zone

zónzo [dz] [dz] *m*—**andare a zonzo** to stroll, loiter along

zoòfito [dz] *m* zoophite

zoologìa [dz] *f* zoology

zoològi·co -ca [dz] *adj* (**-ci -che**) zoological

zoòlo·go -ga [dz] *mf* (**-gi -ghe**) zoologist

zootecnìa [dz] *f* animal husbandry

zootècni·co -ca [dz] (**-ci -che**) *adj* livestock || *m* livestock specialist

zoppicante *adj* limping; halting; shaky

zoppicare §197 (**zòppico**) *intr* to limp; to be shaky (*in one's studies*); to wobble

zoppicatura *f* limp; wobble

zòp·po -pa *adj* crippled; lame; wobbly || *mf* cripple; lame person

zòti·co -ca [dz] (**-ci -che**) *adj* uncouth, boorish || *m* churl, boor

zuc·ca *f* (**-che**) pumpkin; (joc) pate; (coll) empty head

zuccata *f* bump with the head

zuccherare (**zùcchero**) *tr* to sweeten, sugar

zuccherièra *f* sugar bowl

zuccherifì·cio *m* (**-ci**) sugar refinery

zuccheri·no -na *adj* sugary || *m* candy; sugar plum; sugar-coated pill

zùcchero *m* sugar; **zucchero filato** cotton candy; **zucchero in polvere** powdered sugar

zuccheró·so -sa [s] *adj* sugary

zucchétto *m* scull cap; zucchetto

zucchi·no -na *m & f* zucchini

zuccó·ne -na *mf* dunce, dumbbell

zuffa *f* brawl, fight

zufolare (**zùfolo**) *tr & intr* to whistle

zùfolo *m* (mus) whistle, pipe

zu·lù (-lù) [dz] *adj & mf* Zulu

zumare [dz] *tr & intr* (mov, telv) to zoom

zumata [dz] *f* (mov, telv) zoom

zuppa *f* soup; (fig) mess; **zuppa inglese** cake with brandy and whipped cream; **zuppa pavese** consommé with toast and eggs

zuppièra *f* tureen

zup·po -pa *adj* drenched, soaked || *f* see **zuppa**

Zurigo *f* Zurich

zuzzurulló·ne -na [dz] [ddzz] *mf* overgrown child, just a big kid

PART TWO

Inglese-Italiano

La pronunzia dell'inglese

I simboli seguenti rappresentano approssimativamente tutti i suoni della lingua inglese.

VOCALI

SIMBOLO	SUONO	ESEMPIO
[æ]	Più chiuso della a in caso.	hat [hæt]
[ɑ]	Come la a in basso.	father ['fɑðər] proper ['prɑpər]
[ɛ]	Come la e in sella.	met [mɛt]
[e]	Più chiuso della e in ché. Specialmente in posizione finale, si pronunzia come se fosse seguita da [ɪ].	fate [fet] they [ðe]
[ə]	Come la seconda e nella parola francese gouvernement.	heaven ['hevən] pardon ['pɑrdən]
[i]	Come la i in nido.	she [ʃi] machine [mə'ʃin]
[ɪ]	Come la i in ritto.	fit [fɪt] beer [bɪr]
[o]	Più chiuso della o in sole. Specialmente in posizione finale, si pronunzia come se fosse seguito da [ʊ].	nose [noz] road [rod] row [ro]
[ɔ]	Meno chiuso della o in torre.	bought [bɔt] law [lɔ]
[ʌ]	Piuttosto simile alla eu nella parola francese peur	cup [kʌp] come [kʌm] mother ['mʌðər]
[ʊ]	Meno chiuso della u in insulto.	pull [pʊl] book [bʊk] wolf [wʊlf]
[u]	Come la u in acuto.	rude [rud] move [muv] tomb [tum]

DITTONGHI

SIMBOLO	SUONO	ESEMPIO
[aɪ]	Come ai in laico.	night [naɪt] eye [aɪ]
[aʊ]	Come au in causa.	found [faʊnd] cow [kaʊ]
[ɔɪ]	Come oi in poi.	voice [vɔis] oil [ɔɪl]

3

CONSONANTI

SIMBOLO	SUONO	ESEMPIO
[b]	Come la **b** in **bambino**. Suono bilabiale occlusivo sonoro.	**bed** [bed] **robber** [ˈrɑbər]
[d]	Come la **d** in **caldo**. Suono dentale occlusivo sonoro.	**dead** [ded] **add** [æd]
[dʒ]	Come la **g** in **gente**. Suono palatale affricato sonoro.	**gem** [dʒem] **jail** [dʒel]
[ð]	Come la **d** nella pronuncia castigliana di **nada**. Suono interdentale fricativo sonoro.	**this** [ðɪs] **father** [ˈfɑðər]
[f]	Come la **f** in **fare**. Suono labiodentale fricativo sordo.	**face** [fes] **phone** [fon]
[g]	Come la **g** in **gatto**. Suono velare occlusivo sonoro.	**go** [go] **get** [get]
[h]	Come la **c** aspirata nella pronuncia toscana di **casa**.	**hot** [hɑt] **alcohol** [ˈælkə͵hɔl]
[j]	Come la **i** in **ieri** o la **y** in **yo-yo**. Semiconsonante di suono palatale sonoro.	**yes** [jes] **unit** [ˈjunɪt]
[k]	Come la **c** in **casa** ma accompagnato da un'aspirazione. Suono velare occlusivo sordo.	**cat** [kæt] **chord** [kɔrd] **kill** [kɪl]
[l]	Come la **l** in **latino**. Suono alveolare fricativo laterale sonoro.	**late** [let] **allow** [əˈlɑu]
[m]	Come la **m** in **madre**. Suono bilabiale nasale sonoro.	**more** [mor] **command** [kəˈmænd]
[n]	Come la **n** in **notte**. Suono alveolare nasale sonoro.	**nest** [nest] **manner** [ˈmænər]
[ŋ]	Come la **n** in **manca**. Suono velare nasale sonoro.	**king** [kɪŋ] **conquer** [ˈkɑŋkər]
[p]	Come la **p** in **patto** ma accompagnato da un'aspirazione. Suono bilabiale occlusivo sordo.	**pen** [pen] **cap** [kæp]
[r]	La **r** più comune in molte parti dell'Inghilterra e nella maggior parte degli Stati Uniti e del Canadà è un suono semivocalico articolato con la punta della lingua elevata verso la volta del palato. Questa consonante è debolissima in posizione intervocalica o alla fine di una sillaba, e può appena percepirsi. L'articolazione di questa consonante ha la tendenza di influenzare il suono delle vocali contigue. La **r**, preceduta dai suoni [ʌ] o [ə], dà il proprio colorito a questi suoni e sparisce completamente come suono consonantico.	**run** [rʌn] **far** [fɑr] **art** [ɑrt] **carry** [ˈkæri] **burn** [bʌrn] **learn** [lʌrn] **weather** [ˈweðər]
[s]	Come la **s** in **sette**. Suono alveolare fricativo sordo.	**send** [send] **cellar** [ˈselər]
[ʃ]	Come **sc** in **lasciare**. Suono palatale fricativo sordo.	**shall** [ʃæl] **machine** [məˈʃin]
[t]	Come la **t** in **tavolo** ma accompagnato da un'aspirazione. Suono dentale occlusivo sordo.	**ten** [ten] **dropped** [drɑpt]
[tʃ]	Come **c** in **cibo**. Suono palatale affricato sordo.	**child** [tʃaɪld] **much** [mʌtʃ] **nature** [ˈnetʃər]
[θ]	Come la **z** castigliana in **zapato**. Suono interdentale fricativo sordo.	**think** [θɪŋk] **truth** [truθ]
[v]	Come la **v** in **vento**. Suono labiodentale fricativo sonoro.	**vest** [vest] **over** [ˈovər] **of** [ɑv]

4

SIMBOLO	SUONO	ESEMPIO
[w]	Come la **u** in **quadro.** Suono labiovelare fricativo sonoro.	**work** [wʌrk] **tweed** [twid] **queen** [kwin]
[z]	Come la **s** in **asilo.** Suono alveolare fricativo sonoro.	**zeal** [zil] **busy** ['bɪzi] **his** [hɪz]
[ʒ]	Come la seconda **g** nella parola francese **garage.** Suono palatale fricativo sonoro.	**azure** ['eʒər] **measure** ['meʒər]

ACCENTO

L'accento tonico principale, indicato col segno grafico ', e l'accento secondario, indicato col segno grafico „ precedono la sillaba sulla quale cadono, per es., **fascinate** ['fæsɪ ˌnet].

La pronunzia delle parole composte

Nella parte inglese-italiano di questo Dizionario la pronunzia figurata di tutte le parole inglesi semplici è indicata in parentesi quadre che seguono immediatamente l'esponente, secondo un nuovo adattamento dell'alfabeto fonetico internazionale.

Vi sono tre generi di parole composte in inglese: (1) le parole in cui gli elementi componenti si sono uniti per formare una parola solida, come per es., **steamboat** vapore; (2) la parole in cui gli elementi componenti sono uniti da un trattino, come per es., **high'-grade'** di qualità superiore; (3) le parole in cui gli elementi componenti rimangono graficamente indipendenti gli uni da gli altri, per es., **post card** cartolina postale. La pronunzia delle parole inglesi composte non è indicata in questo Dizionario qualora gli elementi componenti appaiono come esponenti indipendenti nella loro normale posizione alfabetica e mostrano quindi la loro pronunzia figurata. Solo gli accenti principali e secondari di tali parole sono indicati, come per es., **steam'boat'**, **high'-grade'**, **post' card'**. Se i due membri di una parola composta inglese solida non sono separati da un accento grafico, si usa un punto leggermente elevato sopra il rigo per indicarne la divisione, come per es., **la'dy·like'**.

Nei nomi in cui l'accento secondario cade sul membro **-man** o **-men,** le vocali di tali membri si pronunziano come nelle parole semplici **man** e **men,** come per es., **mailman** ['mel ˌmæn] e **mailmen** ['mel ˌmen]. Nei nomi in cui tali membri componenti non sono accentati, le loro vocali si pronunziano come se fossero un'e muta francese, come per es., **policeman** [pə'lismən] e **policemen** [pə'lismən]. In questo Dizionario la trascrizione fonetica di tali nomi non è stata indicata qualora il primo membro componente appaia come esponente con la sua pronunzia in alfabeto fonetico internazionale. Gli accenti sono ciò nondimeno indicati:

mail'man' s (-men')
police'man s (-men)

La pronunzia dei participi passati

La pronunzia di una parola la cui desinenza è **-ed** (o **-d** dopo una e muta) non è indicata nel presente Dizionario, purché la pronunzia della parola stessa senza tale suffisso appaia con il suo esponente nella sua posizione alfabetica. In tale caso la pronunzia segue le regole indicate qui sotto. Si osservi che il raddoppiamento della vocale finale dopo una semplice vocale tonica non muta la pronunzia del suffisso **-ed,** per es.: **batted** ['bætɪd], **dropped** [drɑpt], **robbed** [rɑbd].

La desinenza **-ed** (o **-d** dopo una e muta) del preterito, del participio passato e di certi aggettivi ha tre pronunzie differenti, che dipendono dal suono in cui il tema termina:

1) Se il tema termina in suono consonantico sonoro (che non sia [d]), cioè [b], [g], [l], [m], [n], [ŋ], [r], [v], [z], [ð], [ʒ] o [dʒ] o in un suono vocalico, l'**-ed** è pronunziato [d]:

SUONO IN CUI TERMINA IL TEMA	INFINITO	PRETERITO E PARTICIPIO PASSATO
[b]	**ebb** [ɛb] **rob** [rɑb] **robe** [rob]	**ebbed** [ɛbd] **robbed** [rɑbd] **robed** [robd]

5

SUONO IN CUI TERMINA IL TEMA	INFINITO	PRETERITO E PARTICIPIO PASSATO
[g]	egg [ɛg] sag [sæg]	egged [ɛgd] sagged [sægd]
[l]	mail [mel] scale [skel]	mailed [meld] scaled [skeld]
[m]	storm [stɔrm] bomb [bɑm] name [nem]	stormed [stɔrmd] bombed [bɑmd] named [nemd]
[n]	tan [tæn] sign [saɪn] mine [maɪn]	tanned [tænd] signed [saɪnd] mined [maɪnd]
[ŋ]	hang [hæŋ]	hanged [hæŋd]
[r]	fear [fɪr] care [kɛr]	feared [fɪrd] cared [kɛrd]
[v]	rev [rɛv] save [sev]	revved [rɛvd] saved [sevd]
[z]	buzz [bʌz] fuze [fjuz]	buzzed [bʌzd] fuzed [fjuzd]
[ð]	smooth [smuð] bathe [beð]	smoothed [smuðd] bathed [beðd]
[ʒ]	massage [məˈsɑʒ]	massaged [məˈsɑʒd]
[dʒ]	page [pedʒ]	paged [pedʒd]
suono vocalico	key [ki] sigh [saɪ] paw [pɔ]	keyed [kid] sighed [saɪd] pawed [pɔd]

2) Se il tema termina in un suono consonantico sordo (che non sia [t]), cioè [f], [k], [p], [s], [θ], [ʃ] o [tʃ], l'-ed si pronunzia [t]:

SUONO IN CUI TERMINA IL TEMA	INFINITO	PRETERITO E PARTICIPIO PASSATO
[f]	loaf [lof] knife [naɪf]	loafed [loft] knifed [naɪft]
[k]	back [bæk] bake [bek]	backed [bækt] baked [bekt]
[p]	cap [kæp] wipe [waɪp]	capped [kæpt] wiped [waɪpt]
[s]	hiss [hɪs] mix [mɪks]	hissed [hɪst] mixed [mɪkst]
[θ]	lath [læθ]	lathed [læθt]
[ʃ]	mash [mæʃ]	mashed [mæʃt]
[tʃ]	match [mætʃ]	matched [mætʃt]

3) Se il tema termina in un suono dentale, cioè [t] o [d], l'-ed si pronunzia [ɪd] o [əd]:

SUONO IN CUI TERMINA IL TEMA	INFINITO	PRETERITO E PARTICIPIO PASSATO
[t]	wait [wet] mate [met]	waited [ˈwetɪd] mated [ˈmetɪd]
[d]	mend [mɛnd] wade [wed]	mended [ˈmɛndɪd] waded [ˈwedɪd]

L'-ed di alcuni aggettivi aggiunto ad un tema che termina in suono consonantico (oltre a quelli che terminano in [d] o [t]), è ciò nonostante talvolta pronunziato [ɪd] e tale fenomeno è idicato con la piena pronunzia della parola in simboli dell'alfabeto fonetico internazionale, per es., blessed [ˈblɛsɪd], crabbed [ˈkræbɪd].

6

A, a [e] *s* prima lettera dell'alfabeto inglese

a [e] *art indef* un, uno, una, un'

aback [ə'bæk] *adv* all'indietro; **taken aback** colto alla sprovvista, sconcertato

aba·cus ['æbəkəs] *s* (**-cuses** or **-ci** [,saɪ]) pallottoliere *m*; (archit) abaco

abaft [ə'bæft] or [ə'baft] *adv* a poppa || *prep* dietro a

abandon [ə'bændən] *s* disinvoltura || *tr* abbandonare

abase [ə'bes] *tr* umiliare, degradare

abash [ə'bæ/] *tr* imbarazzare; sconcertare

abate [ə'bet] *tr* ridurre; omettere; (law) terminare || *intr* diminuire, calmarsi

aba·tis ['æbətɪs] or [ə'bætɪs] *s* (**-tis** or **-tises**) (mil) tagliata

abattoir ['æbə,twar] *s* macello

abba·cy ['æbəsi] *s* (**-cies**) abbazia

abbess ['æbɪs] *s* badessa

abbey ['æbi] *s* badia, abbazia

abbot ['æbət] *s* abate *m*

abbreviate [ə'brivɪ,et] *tr* abbreviare, raccorciare

abbreviation [ə,brivɪ'e/ən] *s* (*abbreviated form*) abbreviazione; (*shortening*) abbreviamento

A B C [,e,bi'si] *s* (letterword) abbicci *m*; **A B C's** abbecedario

abdicate ['æbdɪ,ket] *tr* abdicare a || *intr* abdicare

abdomen ['æbdəmən] or [æb'domən] *s* addome *m*

abduct [æb'dʌkt] *tr* rapire

abed [ə'bed] *adv* a letto

abet [ə'bet] *v* (*pret & pp* **abetted;** *ger* **abetting**) *tr* favoreggiare

abeyance [ə'be·əns] *s* sospensione; **in abeyance** in sospeso

ab·hor [æb'hor] *v* (*pret & pp* **-horred;** *ger* **-horring**) *tr* aborrire

abhorrent [æb'harənt] or [æb'horənt] *adj* detestabile

abide [ə'baɪd] *v* (*pret & pp* **abode** or **abided**) *tr* aspettare; tollerare || *intr* —**to abide by** attenersi a; rimanere fedele a

abili·ty [ə'bɪlɪti] *s* (**-ties**) abilità *f*, bravura

abject ['æbdʒekt] or [æb'dʒekt] *adj* abietto, turpe

abjure [æb'dʒur] *tr* abiurare

ablative ['æblətɪv] *adj & s* ablativo

ablaut ['æblaut] *s* apofonia

ablaze [ə'blez] *adj* in fiamme; risplendente

able ['ebəl] *adj* abile, esperto; **to be able to** + *inf* potere + *inf*

able-bodied ['ebəl'badid] *adj* sano; forte

abloom [ə'blum] *adj & adv* in fiore

abnormal [æb'nɔrməl] *adj* anormale

aboard [ə'bord] *adv* a bordo; **all aboard!** (rr) signori, in vettura!; **to go aboard** imbarcarsi; **to take aboard** imbarcare || *prep* a bordo di; (*a bus, train, etc.*) in, su

abode [ə'bod] *s* abitazione, dimora

abolish [ə'balɪ/] *tr* abolire

A-bomb ['e,bam] *s* bomba atomica

abominable [ə'bamənəbəl] *adj* abominevole

abomination [ə,bamɪ'ne/ən] *s* abominazione

aborigenes [,æbə'rɪdʒɪ,niz] *spl* aborigeni *mpl*

abort [ə'bort] *tr* terminare prematuramente; provocare un aborto in || *intr* abortire

abortion [ə'bor/ən] *s* aborto

abound [ə'baund] *intr* abbondare; **to abound in** or **with** abbondare di

about [ə'baut] *adv* circa, press'a poco; qua intorno; qua e là; in direzione opposta; (coll) quasi; **to be about to** star sul punto di || *prep* intorno a; circa a; addosso a; tutt'intorno a; riguardo a

about-face' *interj* (mil) dietro front!

about-face' or **about-'face'** *s* voltafaccia; (mil) dietro front *m* || **about-'face'** *intr* fare dietro front

above [ə'bʌv] *adj* soprammenzionato; superiore || *s*—from above dal cielo; dall'alto || *adv* in alto; su; più sopra || *prep* sopra, sopra a; più di; al di là di, oltre; **above all** soprattutto

above-mentioned [ə'bʌv'men/ənd] *adj* summenzionato, sunnominato

abrasive [ə'bresɪv] or [ə'brezɪv] *adj & s* abrasivo

abreast [ə'brest] *adj & adv* in fila, in linea; **to keep abreast of** tenersi alla pari con; essere al corrente di

abridge [ə'brɪdʒ] *tr* compendiare; ridurre

abroad [ə'brod] *adv* all'estero; all'aria aperta; **to be abroad** (*said of news*) circolare

abrupt [ə'brʌpt] *adj* brusco, improvviso; (*very steep*) scosceso

abscess ['æbses] *s* ascesso

abscond [æb'skand] *intr* scappare; **to abscond with** svignarsela con

absence ['æbsəns] *s* assenza; **in the absence of** in mancanza di

absent ['æbsənt] *adj* assente || [æb-,sent] *tr*—**to absent oneself** assentarsi

absentee [,æbsən'ti] *s* assente *mf*

absent-minded ['æbsənt'maindid] *adj* distratto, assente

absinth ['æbsɪnθ] *s* assenzio

absolute ['æbsə,lut] *adj & s* assoluto

absolutely ['æbsə,lutli] *adv* assolutamente, certamente || [,æbsə'lutli] *interj* certamente!

absolve [æb'salv] *tr* assolvere

absorb [æb'sorb] *tr* assorbire; **to be** or **become absorbed** essere assorto

absorbent [æb'sorbənt] *adj* assorbente; (*cotton*) idrofilo || *s* sostanza assorbente

absorbing [æb'sorbɪŋ] *adj* interessantissimo

abstain [æb'sten] *intr* astenersi

abstemious [æb'stimɪ·əs] *adj* astemio

abstention [æb'sten/ən] *s* astensione; astenuto (*vote withheld*)

abstinent ['æbstɪnənt] *adj* astinente

abstract ['æbstrækt] *adj* astratto ‖ *s* compendio, sommario ‖ *tr* compendiare ‖ [æb'strækt] *tr* astrarre; (*to steal*) sottrarre

abstruse [æb'strus] *adj* astruso

absurd [æb'sʌrd] or [æb'zʌrd] *adj* assurdo

absurdi·ty [æb'sʌrditi] or [æb'zʌrditi] *s* (-ties) assurdità *f*

abundant [ə'bʌndənt] *adj* abbondante

abuse [ə'bjus] *s* (*misuse*) abuso; maltrattamento; insulto ‖ [ə'bjuz] *tr* (*to misuse, take unfair advantage of*) abusare di; maltrattare; insultare

abusive [ə'bjusɪv] *adj* abusivo; insultante

abut [ə'bʌt] *v* (*pret & pp* **abutted; ger abutting**) *intr*—**to abut on** confinare con

abutment [ə'bʌtmənt] *s* rinfianco; (*at either end of bridge*) spalla; (*of buttresses of bridge*) sprone *m*

abysmal [ə'bɪzməl] *adj* abissale; (*e.g., ignorance*) spropositato

abyss [ə'bɪs] *s* abisso

academic [,ækə'dɛmɪk] *adj* accademico

ac'ademic cos'tume *s* toga accademica

academician [ə,kædə'mɪʃən] *s* accademico

ac'adem'ic year' *s* anno scolastico

acade·my [ə'kædəmi] *s* (-mies) accademia

accede [æk'sid] *intr* accedere; **to accede to** salire a; accedere a

accelerate [æk'sɛlə,ret] *tr & intr* accelerare

accelerator [æk'sɛlə,retər] *s* acceleratore *m*

accent ['æksɛnt] *s* accento ‖ ['æksɛnt] or [æk'sɛnt] *tr* accentare; (*to accentuate*) accentuare

ac'cent mark' *s* segnaccento, accento grafico

accentuate [æk'sɛntʃu,et] *tr* accentuare

accept [æk'sɛpt] *tr* accettare

acceptable [æk'sɛptəbəl] *adj* accettabile

acceptance [æk'sɛptəns] *s* accettazione

access ['æksɛs] *s* accesso

accessible [æk'sɛsɪbəl] *adj* accessibile; (*person*) abbordabile

accession [æk'sɛʃən] *s* accessione, acquisto; (*e.g., to the throne*) adito

accesso·ry [æk'sɛsəri] *adj* accessorio ‖ *s* (-ries) accessorio; (*to a crime*) complice *m*

accident ['æksɪdənt] *s* accidente *m*; **by accident** accidentalmente, per caso

accidental [,æksɪ'dɛntəl] *adj* accidentale ‖ *s* (mus) accidente *m*

acclaim [ə'klem] *s* acclamazione, applauso ‖ *tr & intr* acclamare, applaudire

acclimate ['æklɪ,met] *tr* acclimatare ‖ *intr* acclimatarsi

accolade [,ækə'led] *s* accollata; (fig) elogio

accommodate [ə'kɑmə,det] *tr* (*to adjust, make fit*) accomodare; (*to pro-*

vide with a loan) venire incontro a; (*to supply with lodging*) alloggiare; (*to oblige*) favorire; (*to have room for*) aver posto per

accommodating [ə'kɑmə,detɪŋ] *adj* servizievole, compiacente

accommodation [ə,kɑmə'deʃən] *s* (*favor*) favore *m*; (*loan*) prestito; (*adaptation*) adattamento; (*reconciliation*) conciliazione; (*compromise*) accomodamento; **accommodations** (*traveling space*) posto; (*in a hotel*) alloggio

accommoda'tion train' *s* treno accelerato

accompaniment [ə'kʌmpənɪmənt] *s* accompagnamento

accompanist [ə'kʌmpənɪst] *s* accompagnatore *m*

accompa·ny [ə'kʌmpəni] *v* (*pret & pp* -nied) *tr* accompagnare

accomplice [ə'kɑmplɪs] *s* complice *mf*

accomplish [ə'kɑmplɪʃ] *tr* compiere

accomplished [ə'kɑmplɪʃt] *adj* (*completed*) compiuto, terminato; (*skilled*) finito, compiuto

accomplishment [ə'kɑmplɪʃmənt] *s* (*completion*) esecuzione, realizzazione; (*something accomplished*) opera; (*acquired ability*) talento; (*military achievement*) prodezza; (*social skill*) compitezza

accord [ə'kɔrd] *s* accordo; **in accord with** in conformità con; **of one's own accord** spontaneamente; **with one accord** di comune accordo ‖ *tr* concedere ‖ *intr* accordarsi

accordance [ə'kɔrdəns] *s* accordo; **in accordance with** in conformità con

according [ə'kɔrdɪŋ] *adv*—**according as** a seconda che; **according to** secondo, a seconda di

accordingly [ə'kɔrdɪŋli] *adv* per conseguenza, perciò; in conformità

accordion [ə'kɔrdɪ·ən] *s* fisarmonica

accost [ə'kɔst] or [ə'kɑst] *tr* accostare, abbordare

accouchement [ə'kuʃmənt] *s* parto

account [ə'kaunt] *s* (*explanation*) versione; (*report*) resoconto; conto; (*statement*) estratto conto; **by all accounts** secondo la voce comune; **of account** d'importanza; **of no account** senza importanza; **on account** in acconto; **on account of** a causa di; per l'amor di; **on all accounts** in ogni modo; **on no account** in nessuna maniera; **to call to account** chiedere conto di; **to give a good account of oneself** comportarsi bene; **to take account of** prendere in considerazione; **to turn to account** trarre profitto da ‖ *intr*—**to account for** render conto di; essere responsabile per

accountable [ə'kauntəbəl] *adj* responsabile; (*explainable*) spiegabile

accountant [ə'kauntənt] *s* contabile *mf*, ragioniere *m*

accounting [ə'kauntɪŋ] *s* contabilità *f*, ragioneria

accouterments [ə'kutərmənts] *spl* (mil)

buffetterie *fpl;* (*trappings*) ornamenti *mpl*

accredit [ə'krɛdɪt] *tr* accreditare; **to accredit s.o. with s.th** ascrivere qlco a credito di qlcu

accrue [ə'kru] *intr* accumularsi; (*said of interest*) maturare

acculturation [ə,kʌltʃə're/ən] *s* acculturazione

accumulate [ə'kjumjə,let] *tr* accumulare || *intr* accumularsi

accuracy ['ækjərəsɪ] *s* esattezza, precisione; fedeltà *f*

accurate ['ækjərɪt] *adj* esatto, preciso; fedele

accursed [ə'kʌrsɪd] or [ə'kʌrst] *adj* maledetto

accusation [,ækjə'zeʃən] *s* accusa

accusative [ə'kjuzətɪv] *adj & s* accusativo

accuse [ə'kjuz] *tr* accusare

accustom [ə'kʌstəm] *tr* abituare

ace [es] *s* asso; **to be within an ace of** essere quasi sul punto di

ace' in the hole' *s* asso nella manica

acetate ['æsɪ,tet] *s* acetato

ace'tic ac'id [ə'sitɪk] *s* acido acetico

aceti•fy [ə'sɛtɪ,faɪ] *v* (*pret & pp* -**fied**) *tr* acetificare || *intr* acetificarsi

acetone ['æsɪ,ton] *s* acetone *m*

acetylene [ə'sɛtɪ,lin] *s* acetilene *m*

acet'ylene torch' *s* cannello ossiacetilenico

ache [ek] *s* dolore *m* || *intr* dolere, e.g., **my tooth aches** mi duole il dente

Acheron ['ækə,rɑn] *s* Acheronte *m*

achieve [ə'tʃiv] *tr* compiere, conseguire

achievement [ə'tʃɪvmənt] *s* compimento; successo; (*exploit*) impresa, prodezza

Achil'les heel' [ə'kɪliz] *s* tallone *m* d'Achille

acid ['æsɪd] *adj & s* acido

acidi•fy [ə'sɪdɪ,faɪ] *v* (*pret & pp* -**fied**) *tr & intr* acidificare

acidity [ə'sɪdɪtɪ] *s* acidità *f*

acid' test' *s* prova del fuoco

ack-ack ['æk'æk] *s* (slang) cannone antiaereo

acknowledge [æk'nɑlɪdʒ] *tr* riconoscere; (*receipt of a letter*) accusare; (*a claim*) ammettere; mostrare la gratitudine per; (law) certificare

acknowledgment [æk'nɑlɪdʒmənt] *s* riconoscimento; (*of receipt of a letter*) accusa, cenno

acme ['ækmi] *s* acme *f*

acolyte ['ækə,laɪt] *s* accolito

acorn ['ekərn] or ['ekərn] *s* ghianda

acoustic [ə'kustɪk] *adj* acustico || **acoustics** *s* acustica

acquaint [ə'kwent] *tr* mettere al corrente; **to be acquainted with** conoscere; essere al corrente di; **to become acquainted** (*with each other*) conoscersi

acquaintance [ə'kwentəns] *s* conoscenza; (*person*) conoscente *mf*, conoscenza

acquiesce [,ækwɪ'ɛs] *intr* acconsentire, accondiscendere

acquiescence [,ækwɪ'ɛsəns] *s* accondiscendenza

acquire [ə'kwaɪr] *tr* acquistare

acquisition [,ækwɪ'zɪʃən] *s* acquisto

acquit [ə'kwɪt] *v* (*pret & pp* **acquitted;** *ger* **acquitting**) *tr* (*to pay*) ripagare; (*to declare not guilty*) assolvere; **to acquit oneself** condursi

acquittal [ə'kwɪtəl] *s* assoluzione

acre ['ekər] *s* acro

acrid ['ækrɪd] *adj* acrido, pungente

acrobat ['ækrə,bæt] *s* acrobata *mf*

acrobatic [,ækrə'bætɪk] *adj* acrobatico || **acrobatics** *ssg* (*e.g., of a stunt pilot*) acrobazie *fpl;* **acrobatics** *spl* (*gymnastics*) acrobatica

acronym ['ækrənɪm] *s* acronimo, parola macedonia

acropolis [ə'krɑpəlɪs] *s* acropoli *f*

across [ə'krɔs] or [ə'krɑs] *adv* dall'altra parte; **to get an idea across to** farsi capire da || *prep* attraverso; (*on the other side of*) al di là di, dall'altra parte di; **to come across** (*a person*) imbattersi in; **to go across** attraversare

across'-the-board' *adj* generale

act [ækt] *s* atto; legge *f;* rappresentazione; **in the act** in flagrante || *tr* (*a drama*) rappresentare; (*a role*) recitare || *intr* (*on the stage*) recitare; (*to behave*) comportarsi; (*to perform special duties; to reach a decision*) agire; (*to have an effect*) reagire; **to act as** fungere da; **to act for** rimpiazzare; **to act on** eseguire; **to act up** (coll) fare il matto; non funzionare bene (*said, e.g., of a motor*); **to act up to** (coll) fare festa a

acting ['æktɪŋ] *adj* facente funzione, interino || *s* recita

action ['ækʃən] *s* azione; (*moving parts*) meccanismo; **to take action** iniziare azione; (law) intentare causa

activate ['æktɪ,vet] *tr* attivare

active ['æktɪv] *adj & s* attivo

activi•ty [æk'tɪvɪtɪ] *s* (-**ties**) attività *f*

act' of God' *s* forza maggiore

actor ['æktər] *s* attore *m*

actress ['æktrɪs] *s* attrice *f*

actual ['æktʃuəl] *adj* reale

actually ['æktʃu əli] *adv* realmente, in realtà

actuar•y ['æktʃu,ɛri] *s* (-**ies**) attuario

actuate ['æktʃu,et] *tr* attuare, mettere in azione; (*to motivate*) stimulare

acuity [ə'kju·ɪti] *s* acuità *f*

acumen [ə'kjumən] *s* acume *m*

acupuncture ['ækju,pʌnktʃər] *s* agopuntura

acute [ə'kjut] *adj* acuto

ad [æd] *s* (coll) inserzione pubblicitaria

Adam ['ædəm] *s* Adamo; **not to know from Adam** non conoscere affatto

adamant ['ædəmənt] *adj* saldo, inflessibile

Ad'am's ap'ple *s* pomo d'Adamo

adapt [ə'dæpt] *tr* adattare

adaptation [,ædæp'teʃən] *s* adattamento; (*e.g., of a play*) rifacimento

add [æd] *tr* aggiungere; (*numbers*)

sommare ‖ *intr* aggiungere; far di conto; **to add up to** ammontare a; (coll) voler dire

adder ['ædər] *s* vipera

addict ['ædɪkt] *s (to drugs)* tossicomane *mf*; *(to a sport)* tifoso ‖ [ə'dɪkt] *tr* abituare; rendere propenso alla tossicomania; **to addict oneself to** darsi a, abbandonarsi a

addiction [ə'dɪkʃən] *s* dedizione; *(to drugs)* tossicomania; *(to sports)* tifo

add'ing machine' *s* calcolatrice *f*

addition [ə'dɪʃən] *s* addizione; *(building)* annessi *mpl;* **in addition** inoltre, per di più; **in addition to** oltre a

additive ['ædɪtɪv] *adj & s* additivo

address [ə'dres] or ['ædres] *s (speech)* discorso; *(place and destination of mail)* indirizzo; *(skill)* destrezza; *(formal request)* petizione; **to deliver an address** pronunciare un discorso ‖ [ə'dres] *tr* indirizzare; *(to speak to)* rivolgere la parola a

addressee [‚ædre'si] *s* destinatario

address'ing machine' *s* macchina per indirizzi

adduce [ə'djus] or [ə'dus] *tr* addurre

adenoids ['ædə‚nɔɪdz] *spl* vegetazioni *fpl* adenoidi, adenoidi *fpl*

adept [ə'dept] *adj & s* esperto

adequate ['ædɪkwɪt] *adj* sufficiente; *(suitable)* conveniente

adhere [æd'hɪr] *intr* aderire

adherence [æd'hɪrəns] *s* aderenza

adherent [æd'hɪrənt] *adj & s* aderente

adhesion [æd'hiʒən] *s* adesione; *(pathol)* aderenza

adhesive [æd'hisɪv] or [æd'hizɪv] *adj & s* adesivo

adhe'sive tape' *s* tela adesiva, cerotto

adieu [ə'dju] or [ə'du] *s (adieus or adieux)* addio ‖ *interj* addio!

adjacent [ə'dʒesənt] *adj* adiacente

adjective ['ædʒɪktɪv] *adj* aggettivale; accessorio, secondario ‖ *s* aggettivo

adjoin [ə'dʒɔɪn] *tr* confinare con ‖ *intr* essere confinanti

adjoining [ə'dʒɔɪnɪŋ] *adj* confinante; vicino, attiguo

adjourn [ə'dʒʌrn] *tr* aggiornare, rinviare ‖ *intr* rinviarsi

adjournment [ə'dʒʌrnmənt] *s* aggiornamento, rinvio

adjust [ə'dʒʌst] *tr* accomodare; regolare; (ins) liquidare ‖ *intr* abituarsi

adjustable [ə'dʒʌstəbəl] *adj* regolabile

adjustment [ə'dʒʌstmənt] *s* aggiustamento; accomodamento; (ins) liquidazione del danno

adjutant ['ædʒətənt] *s* aiutante *mf*

ad-lib [ˌæd'lɪb] *v (pret & pp -libbed; ger -libbing) tr & intr* improvvisare

administer [æd'mɪnɪstər] *tr* amministrare; *(medicine)* somministrare; *(an oath)* dare ‖ *intr*—**to administer to** ministrare, prestare aiuto a

administrator [æd'mɪnɪs‚tretər] *s* amministratore *m*

admirable ['ædmɪrəbəl] *adj* ammirabile, ammirevole

admiral ['ædmɪrəl] *s* ammiraglio

admiral•ty ['ædmɪrəlti] *s (-ties)* ammiragliato

admire [æd'maɪr] *tr* ammirare

admirer [æd'maɪrər] *s* ammiratore *m*

admissible [æd'mɪsɪbəl] *adj* ammissibile

admission [æd'mɪʃən] *s* ammissione; confessione; *(entrance fee)* prezzo d'ingresso; **to gain admission** arrivare a entrare

ad•mit [æd'mɪt] *v (pret & pp -mitted; ger -mitting) tr* ammettere; confessare ‖ *intr* dare l'ingresso; **to admit of** permettere, ammettere; consentire

admittance [æd'mɪtəns] *s* ammissione; permesso di entrare; **no admittance** divieto d'ingresso

admonish [æd'mɑnɪʃ] *tr* ammonire

ado [ə'du] *s* confusione, trambusto; **much ado about nothing** molto rumore per nulla; **to make a big ado** fare cerimonie

adobe [ə'dobi] *s* mattone crudo

adolescence [‚ædə'lesəns] *s* adolescenza

adolescent [‚ædə'lesənt] *adj & s* adolescente *mf*

adopt [ə'dɑpt] *tr* adottare

adoption [ə'dɑpʃən] *s* adozione

adorable [ə'dorəbəl] *adj* adorabile

adore [ə'dor] *tr* adorare

adorn [ə'dɔrn] *tr* adornare

adornment [ə'dɔrnmənt] *s* ornamento

adre'nal gland' [æd'rinəl] *s* glandola surrenale

Adriatic [‚edrɪ'ætɪk] or [‚ædrɪ'ætɪk] *adj* adriatico ‖ *adj & s* Adriatico

adrift [ə'drɪft] *adj & adv* alla deriva

adroit [ə'drɔɪt] *adj* destro

adult [ə'dʌlt] or ['ædʌlt] *adj & s* adulto

adulterate [ə'dʌltə‚ret] *tr* adulterare

adulterer [ə'dʌltərər] *s* adultero

adulteress [ə'dʌltərɪs] *s* adultera

adulter•y [ə'dʌltərɪ] *s (-ies)* adulterio

advance [æd'væns] or [æd'vɑns] *adj* avanzato ‖ *s* avanzata; *(increase in price)* aumento; *(of money)* anticipo; **advances** approcci *mpl;* **in advance** in anticipo ‖ *tr* avanzare; aumentare; *(to make earlier)* anticipare; *(money)* anticipare; *(a clock)* mettere avanti ‖ *intr* avanzare; *(said, e.g., of prices)* aumentare

advanced [æd'vænst] or [æd'vɑnst] *adj* avanzato, progredito

advanced' stand'ing *s* trasferimento di voti scolastici

advancement [æd'vænsmənt] or [æd'vɑnsmənt] *s* progresso; promozione; (mil) avanzata

advance' public'ity *s* pubblicità *f* di lancio

advantage [æd'væntɪdʒ] or [æd'vɑntɪdʒ] *s* vantaggio; **to advantage** in maniera favorevole; **to take advantage of** approfittarsi di; abusare di ‖ *tr* avantaggiare

advantageous [‚ædvən'tedʒəs] *adj* vantaggioso

advent ['ædvɛnt] *s* avvento

adventure [æd'vɛntʃər] s avventura || tr avventurare || intr avventurarsi

adventurer [æd'vɛntʃərər] s avventuriero

adventuresome [æd'vɛntʃərsəm] adj avventuroso

adventuress [æd'vɛntʃərɪs] s avventuriera

adventurous [æd'vɛntʃərəs] adj avventuroso

adverb ['ædvʌrb] s avverbio

adversar·y ['ædvər,sɛri] s (-ies) avversario

adverse [æd'vʌrs] or ['ædvʌrs] adj avverso, contrario

adversi·ty [æd'vʌrsɪti] s (-ties) avversità f

advertise ['ædvər,taɪz] or [,ædvər'taɪz] tr propagandare; reclamizzare || intr fare la pubblicità; inserire un annunzio; inserzionare

advertisement [,ædvər'taɪzmənt] or [æd'vʌrtɪsmənt] s annuncio pubblicitario, inserzione

advertiser ['ædvər,taɪzər] or [,ædvər'taɪzər] s inserzionista mf

advertising ['ædvər,taɪzɪŋ] s pubblicità f, pubblicismo

ad'vertising a'gent s pubblicista mf

ad'vertising campaign' s campagna pubblicitaria

ad'vertising man' s agente m di pubblicità, reclamista m

advice [æd'vaɪs] s consiglio; **a piece of advice** un consiglio

advisable [æd'vaɪzəbəl] adj consigliabile

advise [æd'vaɪz] tr consigliare; informare || intr—to advise with chiedere il consiglio di; avere una conferenza con

advisement [æd'vaɪzmənt] s considerazione; **to take under advisement** prendere in considerazione

adviser [æd'vaɪzər] s consigliere m

advisory [æd'vaɪzəri] adj consultivo

advocate ['ædvə,ket] s difensore m; (lawyer) avvocato || tr sostenere, propugnare

adze [ædz] s ascia

Aege'an Sea' [ɪ'dʒi·ən] s mare Egeo

aegis ['idʒɪs] s egida

Aeneid [i'ni·ɪd] s Eneide f

aerate ['ɛret] or ['e·ə,ret] tr aerare

aerial ['ɛrɪ·əl] or ['ɪrɪ·əl] adj aereo || ['ɛri·əl] s (rad & telv) antenna

aer'ial pho'tograph s aerofotogramma m

aerodrome ['ɛrə,drom] s aerodromo

aerodynamic [,ɛrodaɪ'næmɪk] adj aerodinamico || **aerodynamics** ssg aerodinamica

aeronaut ['ɛrə,nɔt] s aeronauta m

aeronautic [,ɛrə'nɔtɪk] adj aeronautico || **aeronautics** ssg aeronautica

aerosol ['ɛrə,sɔl] s aerosol m

aerospace ['ɛro,spes] adj aerospaziale || s aerospazio

Aesop ['isap] s Esopo

aesthete ['ɛsθit] s esteta mf

aesthetic [ɛs'θɛtɪk] adj estetico || **aesthetics** ssg estetica

afar [ə'fɑr] adv lontano; **from afar** da lontano

affable ['æfəbəl] adj affabile

affair [ə'fɛr] s affare m; (romance) relazione amorosa

affect [ə'fɛkt] tr influenzare; (to touch the heart of) commuovere; (to pretend to have) affettare

affectation [,æfɛk'teʃən] s affettazione

affected [ə'fɛktɪd] adj affettato

affection [ə'fɛkʃən] s affezione

affectionate [ə'fɛkʃənɪt] adj affettuoso, affezionato

affidavit [,æfɪ'devɪt] s affidavit m, dichiarazione sotto giuramento

affiliate [ə'fɪlɪ,et] adj & s affiliato || tr affiliare || intr affiliarsi

affini·ty [ə'fɪnɪti] s (-ties) affinità f

affirm [ə'fʌrm] tr affermare; confermare

affirmative [ə'fʌrmətɪv] adj affermativo || s affermativa

affix ['æfɪks] s affisso || [ə'fɪks] tr affiggere; (a signature) apporre; (e.g., blame) attribuire

afflict [ə'flɪkt] tr affliggere

affliction [ə'flɪkʃən] s afflizione

affluence ['æflu·əns] s opulenza, abbondanza

affluent ['æflu·ənt] adj opulento, abbondante; ricco || s affluente m

afford [ə'ford] tr permettersi il lusso di; (to furnish) provvedere; (to give) dare

affray [ə'fre] s rissa

affront [ə'frʌnt] s affronto || tr fare un affronto a

afghan ['æfgən] or ['æfgæn] s coperta di lana all'uncinetto || **Afghan** adj & s afgano

afield [ə'fild] adv sul campo; **far afield** lontano

afire [ə'faɪr] adj ardente; in fuoco, in fiamme

aflame [ə'flem] adj in fiamme

afloat [ə'flot] adj & adv a galla; a bordo; (drifting) alla deriva; (said of a rumor) in circolazione

afoot [ə'fut] adj & adv a piedi; in movimento, in moto

aforementioned [ə'for,mɛnʃənd] or **aforesaid** [ə'for,sɛd] adj suddetto

afoul [ə'faul] adj & adv in collisione; **to run afoul of** finire nelle mani di, impigliarsi con

afraid [ə'fred] adj impaurito, spaventato; **to be afraid (of)** aver paura (di)

African ['æfrɪkən] adj & s africano

aft [æft] or [ɑft] adv a poppa; indietro

after ['æftər] or ['ɑftər] adj seguente; di poppa || adv dopo; (behind) dietro || prep dopo; dopo di; (in the manner of) secondo; **to run after** correre dietro a || conj dopo che

afterburner ['æftər,bʌrnər] or ['ɑftər,bʌrnər] s (aer) postbruciatore m

af'ter-din'ner adj dopo la cena

aftereffect ['æftərɪ,fɛkt] or ['ɑftərɪ,fɛkt] s conseguenza

af'ter-hours' adj dopo le ore di ufficio

af'ter-life' s aldilà m; vita susseguente

aftermath ['æftər,mæθ] or ['ɑftər-,mæθ] s conseguenze fpl; gravi conseguenze fpl

af'ter·noon' adj pomeridiano || s pomeriggio

after-shaving ['æftər,ʃevɪŋ] or ['ɑftər-,ʃevɪŋ] adj dopobarba

af'ter·taste' s retrosapore m

af'ter·thought' s pensiero tardivo

afterward ['æftərwərd] or ['ɑftərwərd] adv dopo; **long afterward** molto tempo dopo

af'ter·while' adv fra un po'

again [ə'gen] adv di nuovo; ancora; un'altra volta; **again and again** ripetutamente; **as much again** due volte tanto, altrettanto; **to** + inf + **again** tornare a + inf, e.g., **to cook again** tornare a cuocere

against [ə'genst] prep contro; (opposite) in faccia a; **to be against** opporsi a; **to go against the grain** ripugnare

agape [ə'gep] adj & adv a bocca aperta

age [edʒ] s età f; (old age) vecchiaia; (full term of life) vita; (historical or geological period) evo; generazione; **of age** maggiorenne; **to come of age** diventare maggiorenne; **under age** minorenne || tr & intr invecchiare

aged [edʒd] adj dell'età di || ['edʒɪd] adj vecchio, invecchiato

ageless ['edʒlɪs] adj eternamente giovane, che non invecchia mai

agen·cy ['edʒənsɪ] s (-cies) azione; agenzia; mediazione; (of government) ente m

agenda [ə'dʒendə] s agenda, ordine m del giorno

agent ['edʒənt] s agente m; (coll) commesso viaggiatore, agente m di commercio; (rr) gestore m

Age' of Enlight'enment s illuminismo

agglomeration [ə,glɑmə're/ən] s agglomerazione

aggrandizement [ə'grændɪzmənt] s aumento, innalzamento

aggravate ['ægrə,vet] tr aggravare; (coll) irritare, esasperare

aggregate ['ægrɪ,get] adj & s aggregato, totale m; **in the aggregate** nel complesso || tr aggregare; ammontare a

aggression [ə'gre/ən] s aggressione

aggressive [ə'gresɪv] adj aggressivo, attivo

aggressor [ə'gresər] s aggressore m

aggrieve [ə'griv] tr affliggere

aghast [ə'gæst] or [ə'gɑst] adj atterrito

agile ['ædʒɪl] adj agile

agitate ['ædʒɪ,tet] tr agitare || intr agitarsi

agitator ['ædʒɪ,tetər] s agitatore m

aglow [ə'glo] adj splendente

agnostic [æg'nɑstɪk] adj & s agnostico

ago [ə'go] adv fa, e.g., **a year ago** un anno fa; **long ago** molto tempo fa

agog [ə'gɑg] adj & adv ansioso; **to set agog** riempire di ansietà

agonize ['ægə,naɪz] intr soffrire straziantemente; (to struggle) dibattersi

ago·ny ['ægənɪ] s (-nies) agonia

agrarian [ə'grerɪ·ən] adj agrario || s membro del partito agrario

agree [ə'gri] intr aderire, andar d'accordo; (to consent) acconsentire; (gram) concordare; **to agree with** confarsi a, e.g., **eggs do not agree with him** le uova non gli si confanno

agreeable [ə'gri·əbəl] adj gentile; gradevole; (willing to agree) consenziente

agreement [ə'grimənt] s accordo; **in agreement** d'accordo

agriculture ['ægrɪ,kʌltʃər] s agricoltura

agriculturist [,ægrɪ'kʌltʃərɪst] s (farmer) agricoltore m; perito in agricoltura, agronomo

agronomy [ə'grɑnəmɪ] s agronomia

aground [ə'graund] adv alla riva; **to run aground** andare o dare in secca

ague ['egju] s (chill) brivido; febbre f

ahead [ə'hed] adv davanti, avanti; **to get ahead** (coll) andare avanti, aver successo; **to get ahead of** sorpassare; **to go ahead** avanzare; continuare

ahoy [ə'hɔɪ] interj—**ship ahoy!** ehi della barca!

aid [ed] s aiuto; assistente m; (mil) aiutante m di campo || tr aiutare; **to aid and abet** essere complice di

aide [ed] s assistente m

aide-de-camp ['eddə'kæmp] s (aides-de-camp) aiutante m di campo

ail [el] tr affliggere; **what ails you?** che ha? || intr soffrire, essere malato

aileron ['elə,rɑn] s alerone m

ailing ['elɪŋ] adj ammalato

ailment ['elmənt] s malattia, indisposizione; (chronic) acciacco

aim [em] s mira; intento || tr (a gun) puntare; (words) dirigere || intr mirare; **to aim to** cercare di, aver l'intenzione di

air [er] adj (pocket) d'aria; (e.g., show) aeronautico || s aria; **by air** per via aerea; **in the open air** all'aria aperta; **to be in the air** circolare; **to be on the air** (rad, telv) essere in onda; **to go on the air** (rad, telv) andare in onda; **to put on airs** darsi delle arie; **to take the air** andar fuori; **up in the air** incerto; (slang) arrabbiato || tr aerare, ventilare

airborne ['er,bɔrn] or ['er,born] adj aerosostentato; aerotrasportato

air' brake' s freno ad aria compressa

air' cas'tle s castello in aria

air'-condi'tion tr climatizzare

air' condi'tioner s condizionatore m

air' condi'tioning s aria condizionata, climatizzazione

air'-cool' tr raffreddare con aria

air' corps' s aviazione, arma aeronautica

air'craft' s (-craft) aeromobile m

air'craft car'rier s portaerei f

airdrome ['er,drom] s aerodromo

air'drop' tr paracadutare

air'field' s campo d'aviazione

air'foil' s superficie f portante, velatura

air' force' s forza aerea

air' gap' s (elec) intraferro

airing ['erɪŋ] s aerazione; passeggiata all'aria aperta; pubblica discussione

air' jack'et s (aer, naut) giubbotto salvagente

air' lane' s aerovia

air'lift' s ponte aereo, aerotrasporto || tr aerotrasportare

air'line' s linea aerea; tubo dell'aria

air' mail' s posta aerea

air'-mail' adj per via aerea || s lettera per posta aerea || adv per posta aerea || tr spedire per posta aerea

air'-mail let'ter s lettera per posta aerea

air'-mail stamp' s francobollo posta aerea

air'man s (-men) aviatore m, aviere m

air' mat'tress s materassino pneumatico

air'plane' s aeroplano, aereo

air'plane car'rier s portaerei f

air' pock'et s vuoto d'aria

air' pollu'tion s contaminazione atmosferica, inquinamento atmosferico

air' port' s aeroporto

air' pump' s pompa pneumatica

air' raid' s incursione aerea

air'-raid shel'ter s rifugio antiaereo

air'-raid warn'ing s allerta

air' ri'fle s fucile m ad aria compressa

air' serv'ice s aeroservizio

air' shaft' s tubo di ventilazione

air'ship' s aeronave f

airsickness ['er,sɪknɪs] s male m d'aria

air' sleeve' s manica a vento

airspace ['er,spes] s aerospazio

air'strip' s aviopista

air' ter'minal s aerostazione

air'tight' adj impermeabile all'aria, ermetico

air'waves' spl onde fpl, radioonde fpl

air'way' s aerovia; airways (rad) onda, onde fpl

air·y ['eri] adj (-ier; -iest) arioso; leggero; aereo

aisle [aɪl] s (between rows of seats) corsia; (of a church) navata laterale; (theat) canale m

ajar [ə'dʒar] adj socchiuso; in disaccordo

akimbo [ə'kɪmbo] adj & adv—with arms akimbo con le mani sui fianchi

akin [ə'kɪn] adj affine; congiunto

alabaster ['ælə,bæstər] or ['ælə,bastər] s alabastro

à la carte [,alɑ'kɑrt] adv alla carta

à la mode [,alə'mod] or [,ælə'mod] adv alla moda; servito con gelato

alarm [ə'lɑrm] s allarme m || tr allarmare

alarm' clock' s sveglia

alas [ə'læs] or [ə'lɑs] interj ahimé!; povero me!

Albanian [æl'beni·ən] adj & s albanese mf

albatross ['ælbə,trɔs] or ['ælbə,trɑs] s albatro, diomedea

album ['ælbəm] s album m

albumen [æl'bjumən] s albume m

alchemy ['ælkəmi] s alchimia

alcohol ['ælkə,hɔl] or ['ælkə,hɑl] s alcole m

alcoholic [,ælkə'hɔlɪk] or [,ælkə'hɑlɪk] adj alcolico || s alcolizzato

alcove ['ælkov] s (recess) alcova; (in a garden) chiosco, padiglione m; cameretta attigua

alder ['ɔldər] s ontano, alno

al'der·man s (-men) assessore m municipale, consigliere m municipale

ale [el] s birra amara

alembic [ə'lɛmbɪk] s alambicco

alert [ə'lʌrt] adj attento; vispo || s allerta; **to be on the alert** stare allerta || tr dare l'allerta a

Aleu'tian Is'lands [ə'luʃən] spl Isole Aleutine

Alexander [,ælɪg'zændər] or [,ælɪg'zandər] s Alessandro

Alexan'der the Great' s Alessandro Magno

Alexandrine [,ælɪg'zændrɪn] adj & s alessandrino

alfalfa [æl'fælfə] s (bot) erba medica

algae ['ældʒi] spl alghe fpl

algebra ['ældʒɪbrə] s algebra

algebraic [,ældʒɪ'bre·ɪk] adj algebrico

Algeria [æl'dʒɪrɪ·ə] s l'Algeria

Algerian [æl'dʒɪrɪ·ən] adj & s algerino

Algiers [æl'dʒɪrz] s Algeri f

alias ['elɪ·əs] s pseudonimo || adv alias

ali·bi ['ælɪ,baɪ] s (-bis) alibi m

alien ['eljən] or ['elɪ·ən] adj straniero; (strange) strano || s straniero; (outsider) estraneo

alienate ['eljə,net] or ['elɪ·ə,net] tr alienare

alight [ə'laɪt] v (pret & pp alighted or alit [ə'lɪt]) intr scendere; **to alight on** or **upon** posarsi su

align [ə'laɪn] tr allineare || intr allinearsi

alike [ə'laɪk] adj uguali; **to look alike** assomigliarsi || adv nello stesso modo

alimen'tary canal' [,ælɪ'mɛntəri] s tubo digestivo

alimony ['ælɪ,moni] s alimonia

alive [ə'laɪv] adj vivo, in vita; (lively) vivace; **alive to** conscio di; **alive with** brulicante di, pieno zeppo di; **look alive!** fa presto!

alka·li ['ælkə,laɪ] s (-lis or -lies) alcali m

alkaline ['ælkə,laɪn] or ['ælkəlɪn] adj alcalino

all [ɔl] adj indef tutto, tutto il, ogni || s tutto || pron tutto, tutti; **all of** tutti || adv completamente; **all but** quasi; **all in** (slang) stanco morto; **all in all** tutto considerato; **all the better** tanto meglio; **all the worse** tanto peggio; **far all that** per quello che, e.g., **for all that I know** per quello che io ne sappia; **in all** tutto contato; **it's all right!** va bene!; **not at all** niente affatto; prego

allay [ə'le] tr calmare, mitigare

all' clear' s fine f dell'allarme, cessato allarme

allegation [,ælɪ'geʃən] s asserzione, affermazione

allege [ə'lɛdʒ] tr asserire, affermare; addurre

allegiance [ə'lidʒəns] s fedeltà f, lealtà f

allegoric(al) [ˌælɪˈgɑrɪk(əl)] or [ˌælɪˈgɔrɪk(əl)] *adj* allegorico

allego·ry [ˈælɪˌgori] *s* (-ries) allegoria

aller·gy [ˈælərdʒɪ] *s* (-gies) allergia

alleviate [əˈlivɪˌet] *tr* alleviare

alley [ˈælɪ] *s* vicolo, calle *f*; (*for bowling*) pista; (*tennis*) corridoio

All' Fools' Day' *s* primo d'aprile

all' fours' *spl*—**on all fours** a quattro gambe

alliance [əˈlaɪ-əns] *s* alleanza

alligator [ˈælɪˌgetər] *s* alligatore *m*

alliteration [əˌlɪtəˈreʃən] *s* allitterazione

all-knowing [ˈɔlˈno·ɪŋ] *adj* onnisciente

allocate [ˈæləˌket] *tr* assegnare; (*funds*) stanziare; (*to fix the place of*) allogare

allot [əˈlɑt] *v* (*pret & pp* allotted; *ger* allotting) *tr* distribuire, assegnare

all'-out' *adj* completo; (*ruthless*) acerrimo

allow [əˈlaʊ] *tr* permettere; ammettere; concedere ‖ *intr* **to allow for** prendere in considerazione

allowance [əˈlaʊ-əns] *s* (*limited share*) assegno; concessione; (*reduction in price*) sconto; tolleranza; **to make allowance for** prendere in considerazione

alloy [ˈælɔɪ] or [əˈlɔɪ] *s* lega; impurezza ‖ [əˈlɔɪ] *tr* far lega di, legare; adulterare

all-powerful [ˈɔlˈpaʊ-ərfəl] *adj* onnipotente

all' right' *adj* esatto; bene; in buona salute; (*slang*) dabbene

All' Saints'' Day' *s* Ognissanti *m*

All' Souls'' Day' *s* giorno dei morti

all'spice' *s* pimento, pepe *m* della Giamaica

all'-star game' *s* partita sportiva in cui tutti i giocatori sono scelti fra i migliori

allude [əˈlud] *intr* alludere

allure [əˈlʊr] *s* fascino, incanto ‖ *tr* affascinare, incantare

alluring [əˈlʊrɪŋ] *adj* affascinante, seducente

allusion [əˈluʒən] *s* allusione

al·ly [ˈælaɪ] or [əˈlaɪ] *s* (-lies) alleato ‖ [əˈlaɪ] *v* (*pret & pp* -lied) *tr* allearc; associare; **to become allied** allearsi; imparentarsi ‖ *intr* allearsi

almanac [ˈɔlmə‚næk] *s* almanacco

almighty [ɔlˈmaɪtɪ] *adj* onnipotente

almond [ˈɑmənd] or [ˈæmənd] *s* (*nut*) mandorla; (*tree*) mandorlo

al'mond brittle' *s* croccante *m*

almost [ˈɔlmost] or [ɔlˈmost] *adv* quasi

alms [ɑmz] *s* elemosina

aloe [ˈælo] *s* aloe *m*

aloft [əˈlɔft] or [əˈlɑft] *adv* in alto, sopra; (*aer*) in volo; (*naut*) nell'alberatura

alone [əˈlon] *adj* solo; **let alone** senza menzionare; **to leave alone** non disturbare ‖ *adv* solo, solamente

along [əˈlɔŋ] or [əˈlɑŋ] *adv* (*lengthwise*) per il lungo; (*onward*) avanti; **all along** tutto il tempo; **along with**

con; **to get along** andar d'accordo; andarsene; avanzare; aver successo; **to take along** prendere con sè ‖ *prep* lungo

along'side' *adv* a lato; **alongside of** a lato di ‖ *prep* a lato di, vicino a

aloof [əˈluf] *adj* riservato, freddo; **to keep or stand aloof from** tenersi a distanza‚da ‖ *adv* lontano; da solo

aloud [əˈlaʊd] *adv* ad alta voce

alphabet [ˈælfəˌbet] *s* alfabeto

alpine [ˈælpaɪn] *adj* alpino

Alps [ælps] *spl* Alpi *fpl*

already [ɔlˈredɪ] *adv* già

Alsace [ælˈses] or [ˈælsæs] *s* l'Alsazia

Alsatian [ælˈseʃən] *adj & s* alsaziano

also [ˈɔlso] *adv* anche

altar [ˈɔltər] *s* altare *m*

al'tar boy' *s* accolito, chierico

al'tar-piece' *s* pala d'altare

alter [ˈɔltər] *tr* alterare; (*a male animal*) castrare ‖ *intr* diventare differente, cambiare

alteration [ˌɔltəˈreʃən] *s* alterazione, modifica

alternate [ˈɔltərnɪt] or [ˈæltərnɪt] *s* sostituto, supplente *mf* ‖ [ˈɔltərˌnet] or [ˈæltərˌnet] *tr* alternare ‖ *intr* alternarsi, avvicendarsi

al'ternating cur'rent *s* corrente alternata

alternator [ˈɔltərˌnetər] or [ˈæltərˌnetər] *s* alternatore *m*

although [ɔlˈðo] *conj* benchè, per quanto, malgrado

altimeter [ælˈtɪmɪtər] or [ˈæltəˌmitər] *s* altimetro

altitude [ˈæltɪˌtjud] or [ˈæltɪˌtud] *s* altitudine *f*

al·to [ˈælto] *s* (-tos) contralto

altogether [ˌɔltəˈgeðər] *adv* completamente, affatto, tutt'insieme

altruist [ˈæltru·ɪst] *s* altruista *mf*

altruistic [ˌæltruˈɪstɪk] *adj* altruistico

alum [ˈæləm] *s* allume *m*

aluminum [əˈlumɪnəm] *s* alluminio

alum·na [əˈlʌmnə] *s* (-nae [ni]) diplomata, laureata

alum·nus [əˈlʌmnəs] *s* (-ni [nai]) diplomato, laureato

always [ˈɔlwɪz] or [ˈɔlwez] *adv* sempre

amalgam [əˈmælgəm] *s* amalgama *m*

amalgamate [əˈmælgəˌmet] *tr* amalgamare ‖ *intr* amalgamarsi

amass [əˈmæs] *tr* ammassare

amateur [ˈæmətʃər] *adj* da dilettante ‖ *s* amatore *m*, dilettante *mf*

amaze [əˈmez] *tr* stupire, meravigliare

amazing [əˈmezɪŋ] *adj* straordinario

Amazon [ˈæməˌzɑn] or [ˈæməzən] *s* rio delle Amazzoni; (*myth*) Amazzone *f*

ambassador [æmˈbæsədər] *s* ambasciatore *m*

ambassadress [æmˈbæsədrɪs] *s* ambasciatrice *f*

amber [ˈæmbər] *s* ambra

ambigu·ty [ˌæmbɪˈgju·ɪtɪ] *s* (-ties) ambiguità *f*

ambiguous [æmˈbɪgju·əs] *adj* ambiguo

ambition [æmˈbɪ/ən] *s* ambizione
ambitious [æmˈbɪ/əs] *adj* ambizioso
amble [ˈæmbəl] *s* ambio ‖ *intr* ambiare
ambulance [ˈæmbjələns] *s* ambulanza
ambush [ˈæmbu/] *s* imboscata; **to lie in ambush** tendere un'imboscata ‖ *tr* appostare ‖ *intr* appostarsi
amelioration [ə‚miljəˈre/ən] *s* miglioramento
amen [ˈeˈmen] or [ˈɑˈmen] *s* amen *m* ‖ *interj* amen!
amenable [əˈminəbəl] or [əˈmenəbəl] *adj* docile, aperto; (*accountable*) responsabile
amend [əˈmend] *tr* emendare ‖ **amends** *spl* ammenda, contravvenzione; **to make amends for** fare ammenda per
amendment [əˈmendmənt] *s* emendamento
ameni·ty [əˈmɪnɪti] or [əˈmenɪti] *s* (**-ties**) amenità *f*
American [əˈmerɪkən] *adj* & *s* americano
Americanize [əˈmerɪkə‚naɪz] *tr* americanizzare
amethyst [ˈæmɪθɪst] *s* ametista
amiable [ˈemɪ·əbəl] *adj* amabile
amicable [ˈæmɪkəbəl] *adj* amichevole
amid [əˈmɪd] *prep* in mezzo a, fra, tra
amidship [əˈmɪd/ɪp] *adv* a mezzanave
amiss [əˈmɪs] *adj* erroneo, sbagliato ‖ *adv* erroneamente; **to take amiss** offendersi, prendere in mala parte
ami·ty [ˈæmɪti] *s* (**-ties**) amicizia
ammeter [ˈæm‚mitər] *s* amperometro
ammonia [əˈmonɪ·ə] *s* ammoniaca; acqua ammoniacale
ammunition [‚æmjəˈnɪ/ən] *s* munizione, munizioni *fpl*
amnes·ty [ˈæmnɪsti] *s* (**-ties**) amnistia ‖ *v* (*pret* & *pp* **-tied**) *tr* amnistiare
amoeba [əˈmibə] *s* ameba
among [əˈmʌŋ] *prep* fra, tra, in mezzo a
amorous [ˈæmərəs] *adj* amoroso; erotico
amortize [ˈæmər‚taɪz] *tr* ammortare
amount [əˈmaunt] *s* ammontare *m* ‖ *intr*—**to amount to** ammontare a
ampere [ˈæmpɪr] *s* ampere *m*
am'pere-hour' *s* amperora *m*
amphibious [æmˈfɪbɪ·əs] *adj* anfibio
amphitheater [ˈæmfɪ‚θi·ətər] *s* anfiteatro
ample [ˈæmpəl] *adj* ampio
amplifier [ˈæmplɪ‚faɪ·ər] *s* amplificatore *m*
ampli·fy [ˈæmplɪ‚faɪ] *v* (*pret* & *pp* **-fied**) *tr* amplificare
amplitude [ˈæmplɪ‚tjud] or [ˈæmplɪ‚tud] *s* ampiezza
am'plitude modula'tion *s* modulazione d'ampiezza
amputate [ˈæmpjə‚tet] *tr* amputare
amputee [‚æmpjəˈti] *s* chi ha subito l'amputazione di un arto
amuck [əˈmʌk] *adv* freneticamente; **to run amuck** dare in un accesso di pazzia; attaccare alla cieca
amulet [ˈæmjəlɪt] *s* amuleto
amuse [əˈmjuz] *tr* divertire

amusement [əˈmjuzmənt] *s* divertimento
amuse'ment park' *s* parco dei divertimenti, luna park *m*
amusing [əˈmjuzɪŋ] *adj* divertente
an [æn] or [ən] *art indef* var of **a**, used before words beginning with vowel or mute *h*
anachronism [əˈnækrə‚nɪzəm] *s* anacronismo
anaemia [əˈnimɪ·ə] *s* var of **anemia**
anaesthesia [‚ænɪsˈθiʒə] *s* anestesia
anaesthetic [‚ænɪsˈθetɪk] *adj* & *s* anestetico
anaesthetize [æˈnesθɪ‚taɪz] *tr* anestetizzare
analogous [əˈnæləgəs] *adj* analogo
analo·gy [əˈnælədʒi] *s* (**-gies**) analogia
analy·sis [əˈnælɪsɪs] *s* (**-ses** [‚siz]) analisi *f*
analyst [ˈænəlɪst] *s* analista *mf*
analytic(al) [‚ænəˈlɪtɪk(əl)] *adj* analitico
analyze [ˈænə‚laɪz] *tr* analizzare
anarchist [ˈænərkɪst] *s* anarchico
anarchy [ˈænərki] *s* anarchia
anathema [əˈnæθɪmə] *s* anatema *m*
anatomic(al) [‚ænəˈtɑmɪk(əl)] *adj* anatomico
anato·my [əˈnætəmi] *s* (**-mies**) anatomia
ancestor [ˈænsestər] *s* antenato
ances·try [ˈænsestri] *s* (**-tries**) lignaggio, prosapia
anchor [ˈæŋkər] *s* ancora; **to cast anchor** gettare l'ancora; **to ride at anchor** stare all'ancora; **to weigh anchor** salpare l'ancora, salpare ‖ *tr* ancorare ‖ *intr* ancorarsi, stare all'ancora
ancho·vy [ˈæntʃovi] *s* (**-vies**) acciuga
ancient [ˈen/ənt] *adj* antico ‖ *s* vecchio, anziano; **the ancients** gli antichi
ancillary [ˈænsɪ‚leri] *adj* dipendente; ausiliario, ausiliare
and [ænd] or [ənd] *conj* e, ed; **and so on, and so forth** e così via
Andean [ænˈdi·ən] or [ˈændɪ·ən] *adj* andino ‖ *s* abitante *mf* della regione andina
Andes [ˈændiz] *spl* Ande *fpl*
andiron [ˈænd‚aɪ·ərn] *s* alare *m*
anecdote [ˈænɪk‚dot] *s* aneddoto
anemia [əˈnimɪ·ə] *s* anemia
anemic [əˈnimɪk] *adj* anemico
an'eroid barom'eter [ˈænə‚rɔɪd] *s* barometro aneroide
anesthesia [‚ænɪsˈθiʒə] *s* anestesia
anesthetic [‚ænɪsˈθetɪk] *adj* & *s* anestetico
anesthetize [æˈnesθɪ‚taɪz] *tr* anestetizzare
aneurysm [ˈænjə‚rɪzəm] *s* aneurisma *m*
anew [əˈnju] or [əˈnu] *adv* di nuovo, nuovamente
angel [ˈendʒəl] *s* angelo; (*financial backer*) (coll) finanziatore *m*
angelic(al) [ænˈdʒelɪk(əl)] *adj* angelico
anger [ˈæŋgər] *s* ira, collera ‖ *tr* adirare ‖ *intr* adirarsi, incollerirsi
angle [ˈæŋgəl] *s* angolo; punto di vista

|| *intr* intrigare; **to angle for** darsi da fare per

an'gle i'ron *s* cantonale *m*, angolare *m*

angler ['æŋglər] *s* pescatore *m* alla lenza; (fig) intrigante *m*

Anglo-Saxon [æŋglo'sæksən] *adj* & *s* anglosassone *mf*

an·gry ['æŋgrɪ] *adj* (**-grier; -griest**) arrabbiato; (pathol) infiammato; **to become angry** at incollerirsi per; **to become angry with** adirarsi con

anguish ['æŋgwɪʃ] *s* angoscia, pena

angular ['æŋgjələr] *adj* angolare

anhydrous [æn'haɪdrəs] *adj* anidro

aniline ['ænɪlɪn] *or* ['ænɪ‚laɪn] *s* anilina

animal ['ænɪməl] *adj* & *s* animale *m*

an'imated cartoon' ['ænɪ‚metɪd] *s* cartone animato

animation [‚ænɪ'meʃən] *s* animazione

animosi·ty [‚ænɪ'mɑsɪti] *s* (**-ties**) animosità *f*

animus ['ænɪməs] *s* odio, malanimo

anion ['æn‚aɪ-ən] *s* anione *m*

anise ['ænɪs] *s* anice *f*

anisette [‚ænɪ'zet] *s* anisetta

ankle ['æŋkəl] *s* caviglia

an'kle·bone' *s* malleolo

an'kle support' *s* cavigliera

anklet ['æŋklɪt] *s* calzino corto; bracciale *m* da caviglia

annals ['ænəlz] *spl* annali *mpl*

annex ['æneks] *s* annesso, dipendenza || [ə'neks] *tr* annettere, appropriarsi di

annihilate [ə'naɪ-ɪ‚let] *tr* annientare

anniversa·ry [‚ænɪ'vɑrsəri] *adj* anniversario || *s* (**-ries**) anniversario

annotate ['ænə‚tet] *tr* annotare

announce [ə'naʊns] *tr* annunciare

announcement [ə'naʊnsmənt] *s* annuncio, partecipazione

announcer [ə'naʊnsər] *s* annunziatore *m*

annoy [ə'nɔɪ] *tr* annoiare, seccare

annoyance [ə'nɔɪ-əns] *s* fastidio, seccatura

annoying [ə'nɔɪ-ɪŋ] *adj* noioso

annual ['ænjʊ-əl] *adj* annuale || *s* annuario; pianta annuale

annui·ty [ə'nju-ɪti] *or* [ə'nu-ɪti] *s* (**-ties**) annualità *f*; (*for life*) vitalizio

an·nul [ə'nʌl] *v* (*pret & pp* **-nulled; *ger* -nulling**) *tr* annullare, cassare

annunciation [ə‚nʌnsɪ'eʃən] *s* annunzio || **Annunciation** *s* Annunciazione

anode ['ænod] *s* anodo

anoint [ə'nɔɪnt] *tr* ungere

anomalous [ə'nɑmələs] *adj* anomalo

anoma·ly [ə'nɑməli] *s* (**-lies**) anomalia

anonymi·ty [‚ænə'nɪmɪti] *s* (**-ties**) anonimia; **to preserve one's anonymity** serbare l'anonimo

anonymous [ə'nɑnɪməs] *adj* anonimo

another [ə'nʌðər] *adj* & *pron indef* un altro

answer ['ænsər] *or* ['ɑnsər] *s* risposta; (*to a problem*) soluzione || *tr* rispondere a; **this will answer your purpose** questo fa per Lei; **to answer back** (slang) dare una rispostaccia a; **to answer the door** andare a rispondere

|| *intr* rispondere; corrispondere; essere responsabile; **to answer back** (slang) dare una rispostaccia

ant [ænt] *s* formica

antagonism [æn'tægə‚nɪzəm] *s* antagonismo

antagonize [æn'tægə‚naɪz] *tr* opporsi a; creare antagonismo in

antarctic [ænt'ɑrktɪk] *adj* antartico || **the Antarctic** la regione antartica

anteater ['ænt‚itər] *s* formichiere *m*

antecedent [‚æntɪ'sidənt] *adj* & *s* antecedente *m*; **antecedents** antenati *mpl*

antechamber ['æntɪ‚tʃembər] *s* anticamera

antedate ['æntɪ‚det] *tr* antidatare; (*to happen before*) antecedere

antelope ['æntɪ‚lop] *s* antilope *f*

anten·na [æn'tenə] *s* (**-nae** [ni]) (*of insect*) antenna || *s* (**-nas**) (rad, telv) antenna

antepenult [‚æntɪ'pinʌlt] *s* terzultima sillaba

anteroom ['æntɪ‚rum] *or* ['æntɪ‚rʊm] *s* anticamera, sala d'aspetto

anthem ['ænθəm] *s* inno

ant'hill' *s* formicaio

antholo·gy [æn'θɑlədʒi] *s* (**-gies**) antologia

anthracite ['ænθrə‚saɪt] *s* antracite *f*

anthrax ['ænθræks] *s* antrace *m*

anthropoid ['ænθrə‚pɔɪd] *adj* antropoide, antropomorfo

anthropology [‚ænθrə'pɑlədʒi] *s* antropologia

antiaircraft [‚æntɪ'er‚kræft] *or* [‚æntɪ'er‚krɑft] *adj* antiaereo

antibiotic [‚æntɪbaɪ'ɑtɪk] *adj* & *s* antibiotico

antibod·y ['æntɪ‚bɑdi] *s* (**-ies**) anticorpo

anticipate [æn'tɪsɪ‚pet] *tr* anticipare, prevedere; ripromettersi

anticipation [æn‚tɪsɪ'peʃən] *s* anticipazione, previsione

antics ['æntɪks] *spl* pagliacciate *fpl*, buffonate *fpl*

antidote ['æntɪ‚dot] *s* antidoto

antifreeze ['æntɪ‚friz] *s* anticongelante *m*

antiglare [‚æntɪ'gler] *adj* antiabbagliante

anti-G' suit' *s* tuta antigravità

antiknock [‚æntɪ'nɑk] *adj* antidetonante

antimissile [‚æntɪ'mɪsɪl] *adj* antimissile

antimony ['æntɪ‚moni] *s* antimonio

antinoise [‚æntɪ'nɔɪz] *adj* antirumore

antipa·thy [æn'tɪpəθi] *s* (**-thies**) antipatia

antipersonnel [‚æntɪ‚pɑrsə'nel] *adj* (*e.g., mine*) antiuomo

antiquarian [‚æntɪ'kweri-ən] *adj* & *s* antiquario

antiquar·y ['æntɪ‚kweri] *s* (**-ies**) antiquario

antiquated ['æntɪ‚kwetɪd] *adj* antiquato

antique [æn'tik] *adj* antico, vecchio; antiquato || *s* oggetto d'epoca, antichità *f*

antique' deal'er s antiquario
antique' store' s negozio d'antiquariato
antiqui·ty [æn'tıkwıtı] s (-ties) antichità f
anti-Semitic [,æntısı'mıtık] adj antisemita
antiseptic [,æntı'septık] adj & s antisettico
antislavery [,æntı'sleveri] adj antischiavista
antitank [,æntı'tæŋk] adj anticarro
antitheft [,æntı'θeft] adj antifurto
antithe·sis [æn'tıθısıs] s (-ses [,siz]) antitesi f
antitoxin [,æntı'taksın] s antitossina
antitrust [,æntı'trʌst] adj antitrust
antler ['æntlər] s corno di cervo
antonym ['æntənım] s antonimo
Antwerp ['æntwərp] s Anversa
anvil ['ænvıl] s incudine m
anxie·ty [æŋ'zaı·əti] s (-ties) ansietà f; (psychol) angoscia
anxious ['æŋk/əs] adj ansioso; anxious about sollecito di; anxious for desideroso di
any ['eni] adj indef ogni, qualunque, qualsiasi; qualche, e.g., do you know any boy who could help me? conosce qualche ragazzo che possa aiutarmi?; di + art, e.g., do you want any cheese? vuole del formaggio?; not . . . any non . . . nessuno, e.g., he does not read any newspaper non legge nessun giornale || adv un po', e.g., do you want any? ne vuole un po'?; not . . . any longer non . . . più; not . . . any more non . . . più || pron ne, e.g., do you want any? ne vuole?
an'y·bod'y pron indef chiunque; (in interrogative sentences) qualcuno; not . . . anybody non . . . nessuno
an'y·how' adv in qualunque modo, comunque; in ogni caso; (haphazardly) alla rinfusa
an'y·one' pron indef chiunque; (in interrogative sentences) qualcuno; not . . . anyone non . . . nessuno
an'y·thing' s qualunque cosa || pron indef qualcosa; qualunque cosa; tutto quanto; checchessia; anything at all qualunque cosa; not . . . anything non . . . niente; not . . . anything at all non . . . niente affatto, non . . . nulla; not . . . anything else non . . . nient'altro
an'y·way' adv in qualunque modo, comunque; in ogni caso; (haphazardly) alla rinfusa
an'y·where' adv dovunque, in qualsiasi luogo; not . . . anywhere non . . . in nessun luogo
apace [ə'pes] adv presto, rapidamente
apart [ə'part] adv a parte, a pezzi; separatamente; apart from a parte da; oltre a; to come apart andare a pezzi, cadere a pezzi; to set apart mettere in disparte; to take apart smontare; to tear apart fare a pezzi; to tell apart distinguere
apartment [ə'partmənt] s appartamento; (single room) stanza

apart'ment house' s casa d'appartamenti
apathetic [,æpə'θetık] adj apatico
apathy ['æpəθı] s apatia
ape [ep] s scimmia antropomorfa; scimmia || tr imitare, scimmiottare
Apennines ['æpə ,naınz] spl Appennini mpl
aperture ['æpərt/ər] s apertura
apex ['epeks] s (apexes or apices ['æpı ,siz]) apice m
apheresis [ə'ferısıs] s aferesi f
aphorism ['æfə ,rızəm] s aforisma m
aphrodisiac [,æfrə'dızı ,æk] adj & s afrodisiaco
apiar·y ['epı ,eri] s (-ies) apiario
apiece [ə'pis] adv a testa, per persona; ciascuno
apish ['epı/] adj scimmiesco; da scimmia
aplomb [ə'plam] s disinvoltura, baldanza
apocalypse [ə'pakə ,lıps] s apocalisse f
apogee ['æpə ,dʒi] s apogeo
apologetic [ə ,palə'dʒetık] adj pieno di scuse
apologize [ə'palə ,dʒaız] intr chiedere scusa, scusarsi
apolo·gy [ə'palədʒi] s (-ies) scusa; (makeshift) surrogato
apoplectic [,æpə'plektık] adj & s apoplettico
apoplexy ['æpə ,pleksi] s apoplessia
apostle [ə'pasəl] s apostolo
apostrophe [ə'pastrəfi] s (mark) apostrofo; (rhet) apostrofe f
apothecar·y [ə'paθı ,keri] s (-ies) farmacista mf
appall [ə'pɔl] tr sgomentare, sbigottire
appalling [ə'pɔlıŋ] adj sconcertante
appara·tus [,æpə'retəs] or [,æpə'ratəs] s (-tus or -tuses) apparato
apparel [ə'pærəl] s confezioni fpl, vestiario
apparent [ə'pærənt] or [ə'perənt] adj apparente; chiaramente visibile
apparition [,æpə'rı/ən] s apparizione
appeal [ə'pil] s appello; (attraction) attrattiva, fascino || tr (a sentence) appellare contro || intr dare nell'occhio; to appeal from (law) appellarsi contro; to appeal to supplicare, pregare; piacere a, e.g., his idea appeals to me la sua idea mi piace
appear [ə'pır] intr apparire; (to seem) sembrare; (said of a book) uscire; (before the public) presentarsi; (law) comparire
appearance [ə'pırəns] s apparizione; (of a book) pubblicazione; (outward look) apparenza; (law) comparizione; to keep up appearances salvare le apparenze
appease [ə'piz] tr pacificare, placare; (a desire) soddisfare
appeasement [ə'pizmənt] s pacificazione, tranquillizzazione
appel'late court' [ə'pelıt] s corte f d'appello
appellation [,æpə'le/ən] s denominazione, nome m
append [ə'pend] tr allegare, aggiungere

appendage [ə'pendɪdʒ] s appendice f
appendicitis [ə‚pendɪ'saɪtɪs] s appendicite f
appen-dix [ə'pendɪks] s (-dixes or -dices [dɪ‚siz]) appendice f
appertain [‚æpər'ten] intr spettare, riferirsi
appetite ['æpɪ‚taɪt] s appetito
appetizer ['æpɪ‚taɪzər] s (drink) aperitivo; (food) stimulante m dell'appetito
appetizing ['æpɪ‚taɪzɪŋ] adj appetitoso
applaud tr applaudire, applaudire (with dat) ‖ intr applaudire
applause [ə'plɔz] s applauso, applausi mpl
apple ['æpəl] s mela, pomo; (tree) melo, pomo
ap'plejack' s acquavite f di mele
ap'ple of dis'cord s pomo della discordia
ap'ple of one's eye' s pupilla degli occhi di qlcu, beniamino di qlcu
ap'ple pie' s torta di mele
ap'ple pol'isher s leccapiedi mf
ap'ple-sauce' s marmellata di mele; (slang) scemenza
appliance [ə'plaɪ-əns] s apparecchio, apparato; (complicated instrument) congegno; (for domestic chores) utensile m; (act of applying) applicazione
applicant ['æplɪkənt] s postulante mf, aspirante m, candidato
application [‚æplɪ'keʃən] s applicazione; uso; richiesta, domanda
ap-ply [ə'plaɪ] v (pret & pp -plied) tr applicare; (the brakes) mettere; (e.g., a nickname) affibbiare ‖ intr (said of a rule) essere applicabile; fare richiesta; **to apply for** sollecitare
appoint [ə'pɔɪnt] tr nominare; assegnare; (to furnish) ammobiliare
appointee [‚æpɔɪn'ti] s persona nominata a una carica
appointive [ə'pɔɪntɪv] adj a nomina
appointment [ə'pɔɪntmənt] s nomina; (position) ufficio; (agreement to meet) appuntamento; **appointments** mobilia, arredamento; **by appointment** previo appuntamento
apportion [ə'pɔrʃən] tr spartire, dividere proporzionatamente
appraisal [ə'prezəl] s stima, valutazione; (of real estate) estimo
appraise [ə'prez] tr stimare, valutare
appreciable [ə'priʃɪ-əbəl] adj apprezzabile, notevole
appreciate [ə'priʃɪ‚et] tr apprezzare, valutare; (to be grateful for) gradire; (to be aware of) rendersi conto di; (to raise in value) valorizzare ‖ intr aumentare di valore
appreciation [ə‚priʃɪ'eʃən] s apprezzamento, valutazione; (grateful recognition) gradimento, riconoscenza; valorizzazione
appreciative [ə'priʃɪ‚etɪv] adj grato, riconoscente
apprehend [‚æprɪ'hend] tr (to fear) temere; (to understand) comprendere; (to arrest) arrestare

apprehension [‚æprɪ'henʃən] s timore m, apprensione; comprensione; arresto
apprehensive [‚æprɪ'hensɪv] adj apprensivo
apprentice [ə'prentɪs] s apprendista mf, novizio ‖ tr mettere in apprendistato; accettare in apprendistato
apprenticeship [ə'prentɪs‚ʃɪp] s apprendistato, carovana
apprise or **apprize** [ə'praɪz] tr avvertire, avvisare; stimare, valutare
approach [ə'protʃ] s (a coming near) avvicinamento; (of night) avvicinarsi m, far m; approssimazione; (access) via d'accesso; (to a problem) impostazione; **approaches** approcci mpl ‖ tr avvicinarsi a, avvicinare; fare approcci con ‖ intr avvicinarsi, approssimarsi
approbation [‚æprə'beʃən] s approvazione
appropriate [ə'proprɪ-ɪt] adj appropriato, acconcio ‖ [ə'proprɪ‚et] tr (to take) appropriarsi di; (to set aside for some specific use) stanziare
approval [ə'pruvəl] s approvazione, consenso; **on approval** in prova
approve [ə'pruv] tr & intr approvare
approximate [ə'praksɪmɪt] adj approssimato, approssimativo ‖ [ə'praksɪ‚met] tr approssimarsi a ‖ intr approssimarsi
apricot ['eprɪ‚kɑt] or ['æprɪ‚kɑt] adj color albicocca ‖ s (fruit) albicocca; (tree) albicocco
April ['eprɪl] s aprile m
A'pril fool' s pesce m d'aprile
A'pril Fools' Day' s primo d'aprile
apron ['eprən] s grembiale m, grembiule m; **tied to the apron strings of** attaccato alle sottane di
apropos [‚æprə'po] adj opportuno ‖ adv—**apropos of** a proposito di
apse [æps] s abside f
apt [æpt] adj atto, appropriato; (quick) pronto; **to be apt to** essere propenso a, portato a
aptitude ['æptɪ‚tjud] or ['æptɪ‚tud] s attitudine f
ap'titude test' s esame m attitudinale
Apulia [ə'pjulɪ-ə] s la Puglia
aqualung ['ækwə‚lʌŋ] s autorespiratore m
aquamarine [‚ækwəmə'rin] s acquamarina
aquaplane ['ækwə‚plen] s acquaplano ‖ intr andare in acquaplano
aquari-um [ə'kwerɪ-əm] s (-ums or -a [ə]) acquario, vasca dei pesci
Aquarius [ə'kwerɪ-əs] s (astr) Acquario
aquatic [ə'kwætɪk] or [ə'kwɑtɪk] adj acquatico ‖ s animale acquatico; pianta acquatica; **aquatics** sport acquatici
aqueduct ['ækwə‚dʌkt] s acquedotto
aqueous ['ekwɪ-əs] or ['ækwɪ-əs] adj acquoso
aq'uiline nose' ['ækwɪ‚laɪn] s naso aquilino
Arab ['ærəb] adj & s arabo
Arabic ['ærəbɪk] adj & s arabo

arbiter [ˈɑrbɪtər] s arbitro

arbitrary [ˈɑrbɪˌtreri] adj arbitrario

arbitrate [ˈɑrbɪˌtret] tr arbitrare || intr fare l'arbitro

arbitration [ˌɑrbɪˈtreʃən] s arbitrato

arbitrator [ˈɑrbɪˌtretər] s arbitro

arbor [ˈɑrbər] s pergola, pergolato; (mach) albero, asse m

arbore·tum [ˌɑrbəˈritəm] s (-tums or -ta [tə]) arboreto

arbutus [ɑrˈbjutəs] s (Arbutus unedo) corbezzolo

arc [ɑrk] s arco; (elec) arco voltaico || intr (elec) formare un arco

arcade [ɑrˈked] s arcata, portico

arch [ɑrtʃ] adj malizioso || s arco; (anat) arco del piede || tr attraversare; arcuare; intr inarcarsi

archaeology [ˌɑrkɪˈɑlədʒi] s archeologia

archaic [ɑrˈke‧ɪk] adj arcaico

archaism [ˈɑrke‧ˌɪzəm] or [ˈɑrkiˌɪzəm] s arcaismo

archangel [ˈɑrkˌendʒəl] s arcangelo

archbishop [ˈɑrtʃˈbɪʃəp] s arcivescovo

archduke [ˈɑrtʃˈdjuk] or [ˈɑrtʃˈduk] s arciduca m

archene·my [ˈɑrtʃˈenɪmi] s (-mies) nemico giurato

archer [ˈɑrtʃər] s arciere m

archery [ˈɑrtʃəri] s tiro con l'arco

archetype [ˈɑrkɪˌtaɪp] s archetipo, prototipo

archipela·go [ˌɑrkɪˈpelego] s (-gos or -goes) arcipelago

architect [ˈɑrkɪˌtekt] s architetto

architectural [ˌɑrkɪˈtektʃərəl] adj architetturale, architettonico

architecture [ˈɑrkɪˌtektʃər] s architettura

archives [ˈɑrkaɪvz] spl archivio

arch′way′ s arcata

arc′ lamp′ s lampada ad arco

arctic [ˈɑrktɪk] adj artico || the Arctic la regione artica

arc′ weld′ing s saldatura ad arco

ardent [ˈɑrdənt] adj ardente

ardor [ˈɑrdər] s ardore m

arduous [ˈɑrdʒu‧əs] or [ˈɑrdju‧əs] adj arduo

area [ˈɛrɪ‧ə] s area

ar′ea code′ s prefisso

Argentina [ˌɑrdʒənˈtinə] s l'Argentina

Argentine [ˈɑrdʒənˌtin] or [ˈɑrdʒənˌtaɪn] adj & s argentino || the Argentine l'Argentina

Argonaut [ˈɑrgəˌnɔt] s argonauta m

argue [ˈɑrgju] tr dibattere; (to indicate) indicare, provare; to argue out of dissuadere da; to argue s.o. into s.th persuadere qlcu di qlco || intr argomentare, discutere

argument [ˈɑrgjəmənt] s discussione, argomentazione; (theme) soggetto

argumentative [ˌɑrgjəˈmentətɪv] adj litigioso

aria [ˈɑrɪ‧ə] or [ˈɛrɪ‧ə] s aria

arid [ˈærɪd] adj arido

aridity [əˈrɪdɪti] s aridità f

Aries [ˈɛriz] or [ˈɛriˌiz] s (astr) Ariete m

aright [əˈraɪt] adv correttamente; to set aright rettificare

arise [əˈraɪz] v (pret arose [əˈroz]; pp arisen [əˈrɪzən]) intr alzarsi; (to originate) provenire, trarre origine; (to occur) succedere, avvenire; (to be raised, as objections) avanzarsi

aristocra·cy [ˌærɪsˈtɑkrəsi] s (-cies) aristocrazia

aristocrat [əˈrɪstəˌkræt] s aristocratico

aristocratic [əˌrɪstəˈkrætɪk] adj aristocratico

Aristotelian [ˌærɪstəˈtilɪ‧ən] adj & s aristotelico

Aristotle [ˈærɪˌstɑtəl] s Aristotele m

arithmetic [əˈrɪθmətɪk] s aritmetica

arithmetical [ˌærɪθˈmetɪkəl] adj aritmetico

arithmetician [əˌrɪθməˈtɪʃən] or [əˌrɪθməˈtɪʃən] s aritmetico

ark [ɑrk] s arca

ark′ of the cov′enant s arca dell'alleanza

arm [ɑrm] s braccio; (e.g., of a bear) zampa; (of a chair) bracciolo; (weapon) arma; arm in arm a braccetto; to be up in arms essere in armi; essere indignato; to lay down one's arms deporre le armi; to rise up in arms levarsi in armi; with open arms a braccia aperte || tr armare || intr armarsi

armament [ˈɑrməmənt] s armamento

armature [ˈɑrməˌtʃər] s (of an animal) corazza; (of motor or dynamo) indotto; (of a buzzer or electric bell) ancora

arm′chair′ s poltrona

Armenian [ɑrˈminɪ‧ən] adj & s armeno

armful [ˈɑrmˌful] s bracciata

armistice [ˈɑrmɪstɪs] s armistizio

armlet [ˈɑrmlɪt] s bracciale m

armor [ˈɑrmər] s armatura, corazza || tr corazzare, blindare

ar′mored car′ s carro armato

ar′mor plate′ s lamiera di corazza

armor·y [ˈɑrməri] s (-ies) armeria; arsenale m

arm′pit′ s ascella

arm′rest′ s bracciolo

ar·my [ˈɑrmi] adj dell'esercito, militare || s (-mies) esercito; (two or more army corps) armata

ar′my corps′ s corpo d'armata

aromatic [ˌærəˈmætɪk] adj aromatico

around [əˈraund] adv intorno; all'intorno; dappertutto; to turn around voltarsi || prep intorno a; (coll) vicino a; (approximately) (coll) circa

arouse [əˈrauz] tr eccitare, incitare; svegliare

arpeg·gio [ɑrˈpedʒo] s (-gios) arpeggio

arraign [əˈren] tr citare, portare in giudizio; accusare

arrange [əˈrendʒ] tr disporre, sistemare; (a dispute) comporre, accomodare; (mus) ridurre, arrangiare

arrangement [əˈrendʒmənt] s disposizione, sistemazione; composizione; accomodamento; (mus) riduzione,

arrangiamento; **arrangements** prepara-
razione, preparativi *mpl*

array [ə're] *s* ordine *m*; *(clothes)*
abbigliamento; (mil) spiegamento,
schiera || *tr* disporre; abbigliare,
adornare; (mil) spiegare, schierare

arrears [ə'rɪrz] *spl* arretrati *mpl*; **in
arrears** in arretrato

arrest [ə'rest] *s* arresto; **under arrest**
in arresto || *tr* arrestare; *(the atten-
tion)* attrarre

arresting [ə'restɪŋ] *adj* interessante,
che fa colpo

arrival [ə'raɪvəl] *s* arrivo; persona ar-
rivata

arrive [ə'raɪv] *intr* arrivare

arrogance ['ærəgəns] *s* arroganza

arrogant ['ærəgənt] *adj* arrogante

arrogate ['ærə‚get] *tr* (*to take without
right*) arrogare per sé, arrogarsi; *(to
claim for another)* attribuire ingiusta-
mente

arrow ['æro] *s* freccia, saetta

ar'row‐head' *s* punta di freccia, (bot)
sagittaria

arsenal ['ɑrsənəl] *s* arsenale *m*

arsenic ['ɑrsɪnɪk] *s* arsenico

arson ['ɑrsən] *s* incendio doloso

art [ɑrt] *s* arte *f*

arter‐y ['ɑrtəri] *s* (-ies) arteria

artful ['ɑrtfəl] *adj* artificioso; *(clever)*
destro; *(crafty)* astuto

arthritic [ɑr'θrɪtɪk] *adj* & *s* artritico

arthritis [ɑr'θraɪtɪs] *s* artrite *f*

artichoke ['ɑrtɪ‚t/ok] *s* carciofo

article ['ɑrtɪkəl] *s* articolo

articulate [ɑr'tɪkjəlɪt] *adj* articolato;
facile di parola || [ɑr'tɪkjə‚let] *tr*
articolare || *intr* pronunziare in modo
articolato

articulation [ɑr‚tɪkjə'le/ən] *s* articola-
zione

artifact ['ɑrtɪ‚fækt] *s* manufatto

artifice ['ɑrtɪfɪs] *s* artificio

artificial [‚ɑrtɪ'fɪ/əl] *adj* artificiale

artillery [ɑr'tɪləri] *s* artiglieria

artil'lery‐man *s* (-men) artigliere *m*,
cannoniere *m*

artisan ['ɑrtɪzən] *s* artigiano

artist ['ɑrtɪst] *s* artista *mf*

artistic [ɑr'tɪstɪk] *adj* artistico

artistry ['ɑrtɪstri] *s* abilità artistica

artless ['ɑrtlɪs] *adj* ingenuo, naturale;
ignorante; *(clumsy)* grossolano

arts' and crafts' *spl* arti *fpl* e mestieri
mpl

art‐y ['ɑrti] *adj* (-ier; -iest) (coll) interessato nell'arte con ostentazione

Aryan ['ɛrɪ‐ən] *or* ['ɑrjən] *adj* & *s*
ariano

as [æz] *or* [əz] *pron rel* che; **the same
as** lo stesso che || *adv* come; per
esempio; **as . . . as** così . . . come;
as far as fino a; **as far as I know** per
quanto mi consta; **as for** in quanto a,
per quanto concerne; **as is** (slang)
com'è, nelle condizioni in cui si
trova; **as long as** tanto che, mentre
che; **as per** secondo; **as soon as** appena, non appena, non appena che;
as to per non quanto concerne; **as well**
pure, anche; **as yet** ancora || *prep*
come; da; **as a rule** come regola ||

conj come; mentre; dato che; per
quanto; **as if** come se; **as it were** per
così dire; **as though** come se

asbestos [æs'bestəs] *s* asbesto, amianto

ascend [ə'send] *tr* ascendere, scalare ||
intr ascendere, salire

ascension [ə'sen/ən] *s* ascensione, sca-
lata || **Ascension** *s* Ascensione

ascent [ə'sent] *s* scalata; salita; *(slope)*
erta

ascertain [‚æsər'ten] *tr* sincerarsi di,
verificare

ascertainable [‚æsər'tenəbəl] *adj* verificabile

ascetic [ə'setɪk] *adj* ascetico || *s* asceta
m

ascor'bic ac'id [ə'skɔrbɪk] *s* acido
ascorbico

ascribe [ə'skraɪb] *tr* attribuire, imputare

aseptic [ə'septɪk] *or* [e'septɪk] *adj*
asettico

ash [æʃ] *s* cenere *f*; (bot) frassino

ashamed [ə'/emd] *adj* vergognoso; **to
be or feel ashamed** vergognarsi

ash'can' *s* pattumiera; (coll) bomba
antisommergibile

ashen ['æ/ən] *adj* cinereo

ashlar ['æ/lər] *s* bugna, bugnato

ashore [ə'/or] *adv* a terra; **to come
ashore** andare a terra, sbarcare; **to
run ashore** arenarsi

ash'tray' *s* portacenere *m*

Ash' Wednes'day *s* le Ceneri

Asia ['eʒə] *or* ['e/ə] *s* l'Asia *f*

A'sia Mi'nor *s* l'Asia *f* Minore

Asian ['eʒən] *or* ['e/ən] *or* **Asiatic**
[‚eʒɪ'ætɪk] *or* [‚e/ɪ'ætɪk] *adj* & *s*
asiatico

aside [ə'saɪd] *s* parola detta a parte;
(theat) a parte *m* || *adv* da parte; a
parte; **aside from** (coll) eccetto; separato da; **to step aside** farsi da un
lato

asinine ['æsɪnaɪn] *adj* *(like an ass)*
asinino; *(stupid)* asinesco

ask [æsk] *or* [ɑsk] *tr* chiedere (with
dat), domandare (with *dat*); invitare;
(a question) fare; **to ask s.o. for s.th**
chiedere or domandare qlco a qlcu;
to ask s.o. to + *inf* chiedere a qlcu
di + *inf* || *intr* chiedere; **to ask about**
chiedere informazioni di; **to ask for**
chiedere, domandare; **to ask for it**
(coll) andare in cerca di disgrazie;
(coll) volerlo, e.g., **he asked for it**
l'ha voluto

askance [ə'skæns] *adv* di traverso, di
sbieco; (fig) con sospetto

asleep [ə'slip] *adj* addormentato; **to
fall asleep** addormentarsi

asp [æsp] *s* aspide *m*

asparagus [ə'spærəgəs] *s* asparago; *(as
food)* asparagi *mpl*

aspect ['æspekt] *s* aspetto; *(direction
anything faces)* esposizione

aspen ['æspən] *s* pioppo tremolo, tremolo

aspersion [ə'spʌrʒən] *or* [ə'spʌr/ən] *s*
diffamazione, calunnia; (eccl) aspersione

asphalt ['æsfɔlt] *or* ['æsfælt] *s* asfalto
|| *tr* asfaltare

asphyxiate [æs'fıksı ,et] *tr* asfissiare
aspirant [ə'spaırənt] *or* ['æspırənt] *s* aspirante *mf*
aspire [ə'spaır] *intr* aspirare
aspirin ['æspırın] *s* aspirina
ass [æs] *s* asino
assail [ə'sel] *tr* assalire, assaltare
assassin [ə'sæsın] *s* assassino
assassinate [ə'sæsı ,net] *tr* assassinare
assassination [ə ,sæsı'ne/ən] *s* assassinio
assault [ə'səlt] *s* assalto ‖ *tr* assaltare
assault' and bat'tery *s* vie *fpl* di fatto
assay [ə'se] *or* ['æse] *s* saggio, esame *m* ‖ [ə'se] *tr* saggiare
assemblage [ə'semblıdʒ] *s* assemblea; (mach) montaggio
assemble [ə'sembəl] *tr* riunire; (mach) montare, mettere insieme ‖ *intr* assembrarsi, riunirsi
assembler [ə'semblər] *s* montatore *m*
assem·bly [ə'semblı] *s* (-blies) assemblea, riunione; (mach) montaggio
assem'bly hall' *s* sala di riunioni
assem'bly line' *s* catena di montaggio
assem'bly·man *s* (-men) membro dell'assemblea legislativa
assent [ə'sent] *s* assenso ‖ *intr* assentire
assert [ə'sart] *tr* asserire; **to assert oneself** far valere i propri diritti
assertion [ə'sar/ən] *s* asserzione
assess [ə'ses] *tr* stimare, valutare; (*for taxation or fine*) tassare
assessment [ə'sesmənt] *s* valutazione; tassazione
assessor [ə'sesər] *s* agente *m* delle tasse
asset ['æsət] *s* vantaggio; persona di valore; **assets** (com) attivo; (law) beni *mpl*
assiduous [ə'sıdʒʊ-əs] *or* [ə'sıdjʊ-əs] *adj* assiduo
assign [ə'saın] *s* cessionario ‖ *tr* assegnare; (*e.g., a date*) fissare; (*a right*) trasferire
assignation [,æsıg'ne/ən] *s* assegnazione; trasferimento; (*date*) appuntamento amoroso
assignment [ə'saınmənt] *s* assegnamento; (*of rights*) trasferimento; (*schoolwork*) compito
assimilate [ə'sımı ,let] *tr* assimilare ‖ *intr* essere assimilato; assimilarsi
assist [ə'sıst] *s* aiuto ‖ *tr* aiutare, assistere
assistance [ə'sıstəns] *s* assistenza, aiuto
assistant [ə'sıstənt] *adj & s* assistente *m*
associate [ə'so/ı·ıt] *or* [ə'so/ı ,et] *adj* associato ‖ *s* associato; membro limitato ‖ [ə'so/ı ,et] *tr* associare ‖ *intr* associarsi
association [ə ,so/ı'e/ən] *s* associazione
assort [ə'sort] *tr* assortire ‖ *intr* associarsi
assortment [ə'sortmənt] *s* assortimento
assuage [ə'swedʒ] *tr* alleviare
assume [ə'sum] *or* [ə'sjum] *tr* assumere; (*to appropriate*) usurpare; (*to pretend*) fingere; (*to suppose*) supporre
assumed [ə'sumd] *or* [ə'sjumd] *adj* supposto, immaginario

assumption [ə'sʌmp/ən] *s* (*arrogance*) aria, arroganza; (*thing taken for granted*) supposizione; (*of an undertaking*) assunzione
assurance [ə'/ʊrəns] *s* assicurazione, certezza; baldanza, fiducia in sè; (*too much boldness*) sicumera
assure [ə'/ʊr] *tr* assicurare
assuredly [ə'/ʊrıdlı] *adv* sicuramente
astatine ['æstə ,tin] *s* astato
asterisk ['æstə ,rısk] *s* asterisco, stelloncino
astern [ə'starn] *adv* a poppa, a poppavia
asthma ['æzmə] *or* ['æsmə] *s* asma
astonish [ə'stanı/] *tr* meravigliare, stupefare
astonishing [ə'stanı/ıŋ] *adj* stupefacente, sorprendente
astound [ə'staund] *tr* stupefare, sbalordire
astounding [ə'staundıŋ] *adj* stupefacente
astraddle [ə'strædəl] *adv* a cavaliere, a cavalcioni
astray [ə'stre] *adv* sulla cattiva via; **to go astray** traviarsi; **to lead astray** traviare
astride [ə'straıd] *adj & adv* a cavaliere; (*said of a person*) a cavalcioni ‖ *prep* a cavaliere di; a cavalcioni di
astrology [ə'stralədʒı] *s* astrologia
astronaut ['æstrə ,nɔt] *s* astronauta *mf*
astronautic [,æstrə'nɔtık] *adj* astronautico ‖ **astronautics** *ssg* astronautica
astronomer [ə'stranəmər] *s* astronomo
astronomic(al) [,æstrə'namık(əl)] *adj* astronomico
astronomy [ə'stranəmı] *s* astronomia
astute [ə'stjut] *or* [ə'stut] *adj* astuto
asunder [ə'sʌndər] *adv* a pezzi; **to tear asunder** separare, fare a pezzi
asylum [ə'saıləm] *s* asilo
asymmetry [ə'sımıtrı] *s* asimmetria
at [æt] *or* [ət] *prep* a; in; a casa di, e.g., **at John's** a casa di Giovanni; da, e.g., **at Mary's** da Maria; di, e.g., **to be surprised at** essere sorpreso di; **to laugh at** ridersi di
atheist ['eθı·ıst] *s* ateista *mf*
Athenian [ə'θinı·ən] *adj & s* ateniese *mf*
Athens ['æθınz] *s* Atene *f*
athirst [ə'θʌrst] *adj* assetato
athlete ['æθlit] *s* atleta *mf*
athletic [æθ'letık] *adj* atletico ‖ **athletics** *ssg & spl* atletica
Atlantic [æt'læntık] *adj* atlantico ‖ *adj & s* Atlantico
atlas ['ætləs] *s* atlante *m* ‖ **Atlas** *s* Atlante *m*
atmosphere ['ætməs ,fır] *s* atmosfera
atmospheric [,ætməs'ferık] *adj* atmosferico ‖ **atmospherics** *spl* disturbi atmosferici
atom ['ætəm] *s* atomo
at'om bomb' *s* bomba atomica
atomic [ə'tamık] *adj* atomico
atom'ic age' *s* era atomica
atom'ic sub'marine *s* sommergibile *m* nucleare
atomize ['ætə ,maız] *tr* atomizzare

atomizer ['ætə ,maɪzər] s nebulizzatore *m*

at'om smash'er s acceleratore *m* di particelle

atone [ə'ton] *intr*—**to atone for** espiare

atonement [ə'tonmənt] s riparazione; espiazione

atop [ə'tɑp] *adv* in cima ‖ *prep* in cima a

atrocious [ə'troʃəs] *adj* atroce

atroci•ty [ə'trɑsɪti] s (**-ties**) atrocità *f*

atro•phy ['ætrəfi] s atrofia ‖ *v* (*pret & pp* **-phied**) *tr* atrofizzare ‖ *intr* atrofizzarsi

attach [ə'tæt/] *tr* attaccare; (*to affix*) apporre; (*to attribute*) attribuire; (law) sequestrare; **to be attached to** essere legato a; fare parte di ‖ *intr*—**to attach to** essere pertinente a

attaché [,ætə'/e] or [ə'tæ/e] s attaché *m.*, addetto

attaché' case' s valigetta diplomatica

attachment [ə'tæt/mənt] s attacco, unione; affezione; (mach) accessorio; (law) sequestro

attack [ə'tæk] s attacco ‖ *tr & intr* attaccare

attain [ə'ten] *tr* raggiungere ‖ *intr*—**to attain to** raggiungere, conseguire

attainder [ə'tendər] s morte *f* civile

attainment [ə'tenmənt] s raggiungimento, realizzazione; (*accomplishment*) dote *f*

attempt [ə'tempt] s tentativo; (*attack*) attentato ‖ *tr* tentare; (*s.o.'s life*) attentare a

attend [ə'tend] *tr* (*to be present at*) presenziare, presenziare a, assistere a; (*to accompany*) accompagnare; (*to take care of; to pay attention to*) assistere ‖ *intr*—**to attend to** occuparsi di, attendere a

attendance [ə'tendəns] s (*attending*) presenza; (*company present*) concorso; **to dance attendance** essere al servizio completo

attendant [ə'tendənt] *adj* assistente; (*accompanying*) concomitante ‖ s (*servant*) inserviente *mf*; presente *m*

attention [ə'ten/ən] s attenzione; (mil) attenti *m*; **attentions** attenzioni *fpl*; **to call s.o.'s attention to s.th** fare presente qlco a qlcu; **to stand at attention** stare sull'attenti ‖ *interj* attenti!

attentive [ə'tentɪv] *adj* attento, premuroso

attenuate [ə'tenju ,et] *tr* attenuare

attest [ə'test] *tr* attestare ‖ *intr*—**to attest to** attestare, testimoniare

attic ['ætɪk] s attico, solaio ‖ **Attic** *adj & s* attico

attire [ə'taɪr] s vestiti *mpl*, vestiario ‖ *tr* vestire

attitude ['ætɪ ,tjud] or ['ætɪ ,tud] s atteggiamento, attitudine *f*; **to strike an attitude** atteggiarsi

attorney [ə'tʌrni] s avvocato; (*proxy*) procuratore *m*

attor'ney gen'eral s (**attor'neys gen'eral** or **attor'ney gen'erals**) procuratore

m generale ‖ **Attorney General** s (U.S.A.) ministro di grazia e giustizia

attract [ə'trækt] *tr* attrarre; (*attention*) chiamare

attraction [ə'træk/ən] s attrazione

attractive [ə'træktɪv] *adj* attrattivo

attribute ['ætrɪ ,bjut] s attributo ‖ [ə'trɪbjut] *tr* attribuire

attrition [ə'trɪ/ən] s attrito; diminuzione di numero

auburn ['ɔbərn] *adj & s* biondo fulvo, rosso tizianesco

auction ['ɔk/ən] s asta, incanto ‖ *tr* vendere all'asta

auctioneer [,ɔk/ə'nɪr] s banditore *m* ‖ *tr & intr* vendere all'asta

audacious [ɔ'de/əs] *adj* audace

audaci•ty [ɔ'dæsɪti] s (**-ties**) audacia

audience ['ɔdɪ-əns] s (*hearing*) udienza; uditorio, pubblico

au'dio fre'quency ['ɔdɪ ,o] s audiofrequenza

au'dio-vis'ual aids' *spl* sussidi audiovisivi

audit ['ɔdɪt] s verifica or esame *m* dei conti ‖ *tr* esaminare i conti di; (*a class*) assistere a, come uditore ‖ *intr* assistere a una classe come uditore

audition [ɔ'dɪ/ən] s audizione ‖ *tr* dare un'audizione a

auditor ['ɔdɪtər] s revisore *m* dei conti; (educ) uditore *m*

auditorium [,ɔdɪ'tɔrɪ-əm] s auditorio

auger ['ɔgər] s succhiello, trivella

aught [ɔt] s zero; **for aught I know** per quanto ne so ‖ *adv* affatto

augment [ɔg'mɛnt] *tr & intr* aumentare

augur ['ɔgər] s augure *m* ‖ *tr & intr* vaticinare

augu•ry ['ɔgəri] s (**-ries**) augurio

august [ɔ'gʌst] *adj* augusto ‖ **August** ['ɔgəst] s agosto

aunt [ænt] or [ɑnt] s zia

aurora [ə'rɔrə] s aurora

auspice ['ɔspɪs] s auspicio; **under the auspices of** sotto gli auspici di

austere [ɔs'tɪr] *adj* austero

Australia [ə'streljə] s l'Australia *f*

Australian [ə'streljən] *adj & s* australiano

Austria ['ɔstrɪ-ə] s l'Austria *f*

Austrian ['ɔstrɪ-ən] *adj & s* austriaco

authentic [ɔ'θɛntɪk] *adj* autentico

authenticate [ɔ'θɛntɪ ,ket] *tr* autenticare

author ['ɔθər] s autore *m*

authoress ['ɔθərɪs] s autrice *f*

authoritarian [ə ,θɑrɪ'tɛrɪ-ən] or [ɔ ,θɔrɪ'tɛrɪ-ən] *adj* autoritario ‖ s persona autoritaria

authoritative [ə'θɑrɪ ,tetɪv] or [ə'θɔrɪ ,tetɪv] *adj* autorevole; autoritario

authori•ty [ə'θɑrɪti] or [ə'θɔrɪti] s (**-ties**) autorità *f*; **on good authority** da buona fonte, da fonte autorevole

authorize ['ɔθə ,raɪz] *tr* autorizzare

authorship ['ɔθər ,/ɪp] s paternità letteraria

au•to ['ɔto] s (**-tos**) (coll) auto *f*

autobiogra•phy [,ɔtobaɪ'ɑgrəfi] or [,ɔtobɪ'ɑgrəfi] s (**-phies**) autobiografia

autobus ['ɔto ,bʌs] *s* autobus *m*

autocratic(al) [,ɔtə'krætɪk(əl)] *adj* autocratico

autograph ['ɔtə ,græf] *or* ['ɔtə ,graf] *adj & s* autografo || *tr* porre l'autografo su, firmare con firma autografa

automat ['ɔtə ,mæt] *s* ristorante *m* self-service a distribuzione automatica

automate ['ɔtə ,met] *tr* automatizzare

automatic [,ɔtə'mætɪk] *adj* automatico || *s* pistola automatica

automat'ic transmis'sion *s* trasmissione automatica

automation [,ɔtə'meʃən] *s* automazione

automa·ton [ə'tɑmə ,tɑn] *s* (-tons *or* -ta [tə]) automa *m*

automobile [,ɔtəmo'bil] *or* [,ɔtə'mo-bil] *adj & s* automobile *f*

automobile' show' *s* salone *m* dell'automobile

automotive [,ɔtə'motɪv] *adj* (*self-propelled*) automotore; automobilistico

autonomous [ə'tɑnəməs] *adj* autonomo

autonomy [ə'tɑnəmi] *s* autonomia

autop·sy ['ɔtɑpsi] *s* (-sies) autopsia

au'to trans'port rig' *s* autotreno per trasporto di automobili

autumn ['ɔtəm] *s* autunno

autumnal [ə'tʌmnəl] *adj* autunnale

auxilia·ry [ɔg'zɪljəri] *adj & s* (-ries) ausiliare *m*

avail [ə'vel] *s* utilità *f*; **of no avail** che non serve a nulla || *tr* servire (with *dat*); **to avail oneself of** servirsi di; approfittare di || *intr* servire

available [ə'veləbəl] *adj* disponibile; **to make available to** mettere alla disposizione di

avalanche ['ævə ,læntʃ] *or* ['ævə ,lantʃ] *s* valanga

avant-garde [əvã'gard] *adj* d'avanguardia

avant-gardism [ə'vã'gardɪzəm] *s* avanguardismo

avarice ['ævərɪs] *s* avarizia

avaricious [,ævə'rɪ/əs] *adj* avaro

avenge [ə'vendʒ] *tr* vendicare; **to avenge oneself on** vendicarsi di

avenue ['ævə ,nju] *or* ['ævənu] *s* viale *m*, corso

aver [ə'vʌr] *v* (*pret & pp* **averred;** *ger* **averring**) *tr* asserire, affermare

average ['ævərɪdʒ] *adj* medio || *s* media; (naut) avaria; (*e.g., of goals*) (sports) quoziente *m*; **on the average** di media || *tr* fare la media di; fare . . . di media, e.g., **he averages one hundred dollars a week** fa cento dollari di media alla settimana

averse [ə'vʌrs] *adj* avverso

aversion [ə'vʌrʒən] *s* avversione

avert [ə'vʌrt] *tr* (*to ward off*) evitare; (*to turn away*) distogliere

aviar·y ['əvi ,eri] *s* (-ies) aviario, voliera

aviation [,evi'eʃən] *s* aviazione

aviator ['evi ,etər] *s* aviatore *m*

avid ['ævɪd] *adj* avido

avidity [ə'vɪdɪti] *s* avidità *f*

avocation [,ævə'keʃən] *s* svago, passatempo

avoid [ə'vɔɪd] *tr* evitare

avoidable [ə'vɔɪdəbəl] *adj* evitabile

avow [ə'vau] *tr* confessare, ammettere

avowal [ə'vau·əl] *s* confessione, ammissione

await [ə'wet] *tr* aspettare, attendere

awake [ə'wek] *adj* sveglio || *v* (*pret & pp* **awoke** [ə'wok] *or* **awaked**) *tr* svegliare || *intr* svegliarsi

awaken [ə'wekən] *tr* svegliare || *intr* svegliarsi

awakening [ə'wekənɪŋ] *s* risveglio

award [ə'wɔrd] *s* (*prize*) premio; (*decision by judge*) sentenza || *tr* aggiudicare

aware [ə'wer] *adj* conscio, consapevole; **to become aware of** rendersi conto di

awareness [ə'wernɪs] *s* coscienza

awash [ə'waʃ] *or* [ə'wɔʃ] *adj & adv* a fior d'acqua

away [ə'we] *adj* distante, assente || *adv* lontano; via; continuamente; **away back** (coll) molto tempo fa; **away from** lontano da; **to do away with** disfarsi di, sopprimere; **to get away** scappare, sfuggire; **to go away andarsene; to run away** fuggire; **to send away** mandar via; **to take away** portar via

awe [ɔ] *s* estremo rispetto; sacro timore || *tr* infondere rispetto a; infondere un sacro timore a

aweigh [ə'we] *adj* (*anchor*) levato

awesome ['ɔsəm] *adj* grandioso, imponente

awestruck ['ɔ ,strʌk] *adj* pieno di sacro timore

awful ['ɔfəl] *adj* terribile; imponente || *adv* (coll) terribilmente

awfully ['ɔfəli] *adv* tremendamente, terribilmente; (coll) molto

awhile [ə'hwaɪl] *adv* un po', un po' di tempo

awkward ['ɔkwərd] *adj* (*clumsy*) goffo, maldestro; (*unwieldly*) scomodo; (*embarrassing*) imbarazzante

awl [ɔl] *s* punteruolo

awning ['ɔnɪŋ] *s* tenda; (*in front of a store*) tendone *m*

awry [ə'raɪ] *adv*—**to go awry** andare a capovesci; **to look awry** guardare di sbieco

ax *or* **axe** [æks] *s* scure *f*; **to have an axe to grind** (coll) avere un interesse speciale

axiom ['æksɪ·əm] *s* assioma *m*

axiomatic [,æksɪ·ə'mætɪk] *adj* assiomatico

axis ['æksɪs] *s* (axes ['æksiz]) asse *m*

axle ['æksəl] *s* assale *m*, asse *m*

ax'le·tree' *s* assale *m*

ay [aɪ] *s & adv* sì *m*

Azores [ə'zorz] *or* ['ezorz] *spl* Azzorre *fpl*

azure ['æʒər] *or* ['eʒər] *adj & s* azzurro, blu *m*

B

B, b [bi] s seconda lettera dell'alfabeto inglese

baa [bɑ] s belato || intr belare

babble ['bæbəl] s (*murmuring sound*) mormorio; (*senseless prattle*) balbettio || tr (*e.g., a secret*) divulgare || intr mormorare; balbettare; (*to talk idly*) parlare a vanvera

babe [beb] s bebè m, bambino; persona inesperta; (slang) ragazza

baboon [bæ'bun] s babbuino

ba·by ['bebi] s (-bies) bebè m, neonato; bambino; (*the youngest child*) piccolo || v (*pret & pp* -bied) tr coccolare, ninnare

ba'by car'riage s carrozzella

ba'by grand' s piano a mezza coda

babyhood ['bebi‚hʊd] s infanzia

babyish ['bebi·ɪʃ] adj infantile

Babylon ['bæbɪlən] or ['bæbɪ‚lɑn] s Babilonia

ba'by sit'ter s bambinaia ad ore

ba'by teeth' spl denti mpl di latte

baccalaureate [‚bækə'lɔrɪ·ɪt] s baccalaureato; servizio religioso prima del baccalaureato

bacchanal ['bækənəl] adj bacchico || s baccanale m; (*person*) ubriacone m, bisboccione m

bachelor ['bætʃələr] s (*unmarried man*) scapolo, celibe m; (*holder of bachelor's degree*) diplomato; (*apprentice knight*) bacelliere m

bachelorhood ['bætʃələr‚hʊd] s celibato

bacil·lus [bə'sɪləs] s (-li [laɪ]) bacillo

back [bæk] adj di dietro, posteriore, arretrato; contrario || s dorso, schiena; parte f posteriore, didietro; (*of a sheet or coin*) tergo; (*of a knife*) costola; (*of a room*) fondo; (*of a book*) fine f; (*of a chair*) schienale m; **behind one's back** dietro le spalle di uno; **to turn one's back on** volgere la schiena a || adv dietro; indietro; **a few weeks back** alcune settimane fa; **as far back as** sino da; **back of** di dietro, dietro a; **to go back on one's word** mancare di parola; **to go back to** ritornare a; **to pay back** ripagare; **to send back** restituire || tr appoggiare; far indietreggiare || intr indietreggiare; rinculare; **to back down** rinunciarci; **to back off** or **out** ritirarsi; **to back up** (*said of a car*) fare marcia indietro

back'ache' s mal m di schiena

back'bite' v (*pret* -bit; *pp* -bitten or -bit) tr sparlare di || intr sparlare

back'bit'er s maldicente mf

back'board' s (basketball) tabellone m

back'bone' s spina dorsale; (*of a book*) costola, dorso; (fig) fermezza

back'break'ing adj sfiancante

back'door' adj segreto, clandestino

back' door' s porta di dietro; (fig) mezzo clandestino

back'drop' s (theat) fondale m

backer ['bækər] s sostenitore m, difensore m; (com) finanziatore m

back'fire' s (*for firefighting*) controfuoco; (aut) ritorno di fiamma || intr (aut) avere un ritorno di fiamma; (fig) raggiungere l'effetto opposto

back'ground' s fondo, sfondo; precedenti mpl; origine f

back'ground mu'sic s musica di fondo

backhand ['bæk‚hænd] adj obliquo || s scrittura inclinata a sinistra; (tennis) rovescio

back'hand'ed adj obliquo; sarcastico; insincero

backing ['bækɪŋ] s appoggio; sostegno; (bb) dorso

back'ing light' s (aut) faro retromarcia; (theat) luce f per il fondale

back'lash' s reazione; contraccolpo; (mach) gioco

back'log' s ceppo; (fig) riserva

back' num'ber s numero arretrato; (coll) persona all'antica

back' pay' s paga arretrata, arretrati mpl

back' scratch'er s manina per grattare la schiena; (coll) leccapiedi m

back' seat' s (aut) sedile m posteriore; (fig) posizione secondaria

back'side' s dorso; didietro

back'slide' v (*pret & pp* -slid [‚slɪd]) intr ricadere

back'spac'er s tasto ritorno

back'spin' s effetto

back'stage' adj dietro alle quinte || s retroscena m || adv a retroscena, dietro alle quinte

back'stairs' adj indiretto, segreto

back' stairs' spl scala di servizio

back'stitch' s impuntura || tr & intr impunturare

back'stroke' s (swimming) bracciata sul dorso

back'swept wing' s ala a freccia

back' talk' s risposta impertinente

back'track' intr ritornare sulle proprie tracce; (fig) fare macchina indietro

back'up light' s (aut) faro retromarcia

backward ['bækwərd] adj ritroso; poco progredito, retrogrado || adv a ritroso, all'indietro; verso il passato; alla rovescia; **backward and forward** (coll) completamente, perfettamente; **to go backward and forward** andare avanti e indietro

back'wash' s risacca

back'wa'ter s gora, ristagno; (fig) eremo

back'woods' spl zona boscosa lontana dai centri popolati

back'yard' s cortile m posteriore

bacon ['bekən] s pancetta

bacteria [bæk'tɪrɪ·ə] spl batteri mpl

bacterial [bæk'tɪrɪ·əl] adj batterico

bacteriologist [bæk‚tɪrɪ'alədʒɪst] s batteriologo

bacteriology [bæk‚tɪrɪ'alədʒi] s batteriologia

bad [bæd] adj (worse [wʌrs]; worst [wʌrst]) cattivo; (*coin*) falso; (*weather*) brutto; (*debt*) insolvibile; severo || s male m; **from bad to**

worse da male in peggio || *adv* male; **to be too bad** essere peccato; **to feel bad** esser spiacente; sentirsi male; **to look bad** aver brutta cera

bad' breath' *s* fiato cattivo

bad' egg' *s* (slang) cattivo soggetto

badge [bædʒ] *s* divisa; decorazione; simbolo, placca

badger ['bædʒər] *s* tasso || *tr* molestare

badly ['bædli] *adv* male; gravemente; molto

bad'ly off' *adj* in cattive condizioni

badminton ['bædmɪntən] *s* badminton *m*

baffle ['bæfəl] *s* (mach) deflettore *m*; (rad) schermo acustico || *tr* frustrare, confondere

baffling ['bæflɪŋ] *adj* sconcertante

bag [bæg] *s* sacco, borsetta; (*of a marsupial*) borsa; (hunt) presa; **bag and baggage** con armi e bagagli; **to be in the bag** (slang) averlo nel sacco; **to be left holding the bag** (coll) essere piantato in asso || *v* (*pret & pp* **bagged**; *ger* **bagging**) *tr* insaccare; (hunt) pigliare || *intr* (*to hang loosely*) far pieghe

baggage ['bægɪdʒ] *s* bagaglio

bag'gage car' *s* bagagliaio

bag'gage check' *s* scontrino del bagaglio

bag'gage room' *s* deposito bagagli

bag-gy ['bægi] *adj* (**-gier; -giest**) come un sacco

bag'pipe' *s* cornamusa, zampogna

bag'pip'er *s* zampognaro

bail [bel] *s* cauzione; libertà provvisoria sotto cauzione; (*bucket*) sassola || *tr* liberare sotto cauzione; **to bail out** (*a boat*) sgottare || *intr*—**to bail out** (aer) gettarsi col paracadute

bailiwick ['belɪwɪk] *s* (fig) sfera di competenza

bait [bet] *s* esca; (fig) allettamento || *tr* adescare; (fig) allettare

baize [bez] *s* panno verde

bake [bek] *tr* cuocere al forno || *intr* cuocersi al forno; abbrustolirsi

bakelite ['bekə,laɪt] *s* bachelite *f*

baker ['bekər] *s* fornaio, panettiere *m*

bak'er's doz'en *s* tredici per ogni dozzina

baker-y ['bekəri] *s* (**-ies**) panetteria

bak'ing pan' ['bekɪŋ] *s* tortiera

bak'ing pow'der *s* lievito in polvere

bak'ing so'da *s* bicarbonato di soda

balance ['bæləns] *s* (*scales*) bilancia; equilibrio; armonia; (*of watch*) bilanciere *m*; (*remainder; amount due*) resto; (*of budget*) pareggio; **in the balance** in bilico; **to lose one's balance** perdere l'equilibrio; **to strike a balance** fare il bilancio || *tr* bilanciare, pesare; (com) bilanciare, pareggiare || *intr* bilanciarsi

bal'ance of pay'ments *s* bilancia dei pagamenti

bal'ance of pow'er *s* equilibrio politico

bal'ance of trade' *s* bilancia commerciale

bal'ance sheet' *s* bilancio

balco-ny ['bælkəni] *s* (**-nies**) balcone *m*; (theat) galleria

bald [bɔld] *adj* calvo; (*bare*) nudo; (*unadorned*) semplice

bald' ea'gle *s* aquila col capo bianco dell'America del Nord

baldness ['bɔldnɪs] *s* calvizie *f*

baldric ['bɔldrɪk] *s* tracolla

bale [bel] *s* balla; collo || *tr* imballare

baleful ['belfəl] *adj* minaccioso, funesto

balk [bɔk] *tr* ostacolare || *intr* intestarsi, impuntarsi

Balkan ['bɔlkən] *adj* balcanico || **the Balkans** i Balcani

balk-y ['bɔki] *adj* (**-ier; -iest**) caparbio, ostinato

ball [bɔl] *s* palla; pallone *m*; sfera; (*of the thumb*) polpastrello; (*of wool*) gomitolo; (*projectile*) palla, pallottola; (*dance*) ballo; **on the ball** (slang) capace, efficiente; (slang) in gamba; **to play ball** giocare alla palla; **to play ball with** essere in cooperazione con || *tr*—**to ball up** (slang) confondere

ballad ['bæləd] *s* ballata

ball' and chain' *s* palla di piombo; (fig) impedimento; (slang) moglie *f*

ball'-and-sock'et joint' ['bɔlən'sɑkɪt] *s* giunto a sfere

ballast ['bæləst] *s* zavorra; (rr) pietrisco || *tr* zavorrare

ball' bear'ing *s* cuscinetto a sfere

ballet ['bæle] *s* balletto

ballistic [bə'lɪstɪk] *adj* balistico || **ballistics** *ssg* balistica

balloon [bə'lun] *s* pallone *m*; (*for children*) palloncino; (*in comic strip*) fumetto

ballot ['bælət] *s* scheda elettorale; voto || *intr* votare, ballottare

bal'lot box' *s* bussola, urna

ball'play'er *s* giocatore *m* di palla, giocatore *m* di baseball

ball'-point pen' *s* penna a sfera

ball'room' *s* salone *m* da ballo

ballyhoo ['bælɪ,hu] *s* chiasso; montatura || *tr* far chiasso a favore di

balm [bɑm] *s* balsamo

balm-y ['bɑmi] *adj* (**-ier; -iest**) balsamico; salubre; (slang) pazzo

balsam ['bɔlsəm] *s* balsamo; (*plant*) balsamina

Baltic ['bɔltɪk] *adj* baltico

baluster ['bæləstər] *s* balaustro

balustrade [,bæləs'tred] *s* balaustrata

bamboo [bæm'bu] *s* bambù *m*

bamboozle [bæm'buzəl] *tr* ingannare, raggirare

bamboozler [bæm'buzlər] *s* raggiratore *m*

ban [bæn] *s* bando; (*of marriage*) pubblicazione matrimoniale; (eccl) interdetto, scomunica || *v* (*pret & pp* **banned**; *ger* **banning**) *tr* proibire

banal ['benəl] *or* [bə'næl] *adj* banale

banana [bə'nænə] *s* banana, (*tree*) banano

band [bænd] *s* banda, striscia; (*of thin cloth*) benda; (*of metal, rubber*) fascia, nastro; (*of hat*) nastro; (mus) banda, fanfara; **to beat the band** fortemente; abbondantemente || *tr* unire || *intr*—**to band together** unirsi

bandage ['bændɪdʒ] *s* benda, bendaggio ‖ *tr* fasciare

bandanna [bæn'dænə] *s* fazzolettone colorato

band'box' *s* cappelliera

bandit ['bændɪt] *s* bandito

band'mas'ter *s* capomusica *m*

bandoleer [ˌbændə'lɪr] *s* bandoliera

band' saw' *s* sega a nastro

band'stand' *s* chiosco della banda

band'wag'on *s* carrozzone *m* da circo; **to jump on the bandwagon** prendere le parti del vincitore

baneful ['benfəl] *adj* nocivo; funesto

bang [bæŋ] *s* rumore *m*, scoppio; (coll) energia; (*pleasure*) piacere *m*, eccitazione; **bangs** frangetta ‖ *adv* tutto d'un colpo ‖ *tr* sbattere ‖ *intr* rimbombare ‖ *interj* bum!

bang'-up' *adj* (slang) eccellente, di prim'ordine

banish ['bænɪʃ] *tr* sbandire, mettere al bando

banishment ['bænɪʃmənt] *s* bando, esilio

banister ['bænɪstər] *s* balaustra; **banisters** balaustrata

bank [bæŋk] *s* (*of fish; of fog*) banco; (*of a river*) sponda; (*for coins*) salvadanaio; (*financial institution*) banca, banco; (*of earth, snow*) mucchio, banco; (*of clouds*) cumulo; (aer) inclinazione laterale; (billiards) sponda ‖ *tr* (*a fire*) coprire di cenere; (*to pile up*) ammonticchiare; (*a curve*) soprelevare; (*money*) depositare ‖ *intr* depositare denaro; (aer) inclinarsi lateralmente; **to bank on** (coll) contare su (di)

bank'book' *s* libretto bancario, libretto di deposito

banker ['bæŋkər] *s* banchiere *m*

banking ['bæŋkɪŋ] *adj* bancario ‖ *s* attività bancaria; professione di banchiere

bank' note' *s* biglietto di banca

bank'roll' *s* rotolo di carta moneta; soldi *mpl* ‖ *tr* (slang) finanziare

bankrupt ['bæŋkrʌpt] *adj* & *s* fallito; **to go bankrupt** andare in fallimento ‖ *tr* dichiarare in fallimento; far fallire

bankrupt•cy ['bæŋkrʌptsi] *s* (-cies) fallimento

banner ['bænər] *adj* importante ‖ *s* bandiera, stendardo; (journ) titolo in grassetto

banns [bænz] *spl* bandi *mpl* matrimoniali

banquet ['bæŋkwɪt] *s* banchetto ‖ *tr* dar un banchetto a ‖ *intr* banchettare

bantam ['bæntəm] *adj* piccolo ‖ *s* pollo nano

ban'tam-weight' *s* peso gallo, bantam *m*

banter ['bæntər] *s* scherzo, facezia ‖ *intr* scherzare, celiare

baptism ['bæptɪzəm] *s* battesimo

baptismal [bæp'tɪzməl] *adj* battesimale; (*certificate*) di battesimo

Baptist ['bæptɪst] *adj* & *s* battista *mf*

baptister•y ['bæptɪstəri] *s* (-ies) battistero

baptize [bæp'taɪz] *or* ['bæptaɪz] *tr* battezzare

bar [bɑr] *s* barra; sbarra; (*of soap*) saponetta; (*of chocolate*) tavoletta; (*of sand*) banco; (*obstacle*) barriera; bar *m*; (*of public opinion*) tribunale *m*; (*legal profession*) avvocatura; (*of door or window*) spranga; (*of lead*) (typ) lingotto; (mus) battuta; **behind bars** in guardina; **to be admitted to the bar** diventare avvocato; **to tend bar** fare il barista ‖ *prep* eccetto, salvo; **bar none** senza eccezione ‖ *v* (*pret* & *pp* **barred;** *ger* **barring**) *tr* sbarrare; sprangare; bloccare; escludere

bar' associa'tion *s* associazione dell'ordine degli avvocati

barb [bɑrb] *s* (*of arrow*) barbiglio

barbarian [bɑr'berɪ·ən] *s* barbaro

barbaric [bɑr'bærɪk] *adj* barbaro

barbarism ['bɑrbəˌrɪzəm] *s* barbarismo

barbari•ty [bɑr'bærɪti] *s* (-ties) barbarie *f*

barbarous ['bɑrbərəs] *adj* barbaro, crudele

Bar'bary ape' ['bɑrbəri] *s* bertuccia

barbecue ['bɑrbɪˌkju] *s* arrosto allo spiedo ‖ *tr* arrostire allo spiedo

barbed [bɑrbd] *adj* irto di punte; mordace, pungente

barbed' wire' *s* filo spinato

barber ['bɑrbər] *s* barbiere *m*; (*who cuts and styles hair*) parrucchiere *m*

bar'ber-shop' *s* barbieria, negozio di barbiere; negozio di parrucchiere

barbiturate [bɑr'bɪtʃəˌret] *s* barbiturato, barbiturico

bard [bɑrd] *s* bardo, poeta *m*

bare [ber] *adj* nudo; (*head*) a capo scoperto; (*unconcealed*) palese; (*empty*) vuoto; (*wire*) senza isolante; (*unadorned*) semplice; **to lay bare** mettere a nudo ‖ *tr* denudare, scoprire

bare'back' *adj* & *adv* senza sella

barefaced ['ber,fest] *adj* impudente, sfacciato, spudorato

bare'foot' *adj* scalzo

barehanded ['ber,hændɪd] *adj* & *adv* a mani nude

bareheaded ['ber,hedɪd] *adj* a capo scoperto

barelegged ['ber,legɪd] *adj* a gambe nude

barely ['berli] *adv* appena, soltanto

bargain ['bɑrgɪn] *s* affare *m*, buon affare *m*; contrattazione; **at a bargain** a buon prezzo; **into the bargain** in soprappiù ‖ *tr*—**to bargain away** vendere a buonissimo prezzo ‖ *intr* contrattare, mercanteggiare; **to bargain for** aspettarsi

bar'gain sale' *s* vendita sottoprezzo

barge [bɑrdʒ] *s* barcone *m*, chiatta ‖ *intr*—**to barge in** entrare senza chiedere permesso

baritone ['bærɪˌton] *adj* di baritono ‖ *s* baritono *m*

barium ['berɪ·əm] *s* bario

bark [bɑrk] *s* corteccia, scorza; (*of dog*) abbaiamento, latrato ‖ *tr* (e.g., *insults*) lanciare || *intr* abbaiare, latrare

bar'keep'er *s* barista *mf*

barker ['barkər] *s* banditore *m*, imbonitore *m*

barley ['barli] *s* orzo

bar' mag'net *s* calamita a forma di barra allungata

bar'maid' *s* barista *f*

bar'man *s* (-men) barista *m*

barn [barn] *s* granaio; (*for hay*) fienile *m*; (*for livestock*) stalla

barnacle ['barnəkəl] *s* cirripede *m*

barn' owl' *s* civetta

barn'yard' *s* bassacorte *f*, aia

barn'yard fowl' *s* animale *m* da cortile || *spl* animali *mpl* da cortile

barometer [bə'ramitər] *s* barometro

baron ['bærən] *s* barone *m*; (*industrialist*) cavaliere *m* d'industria

baroness ['bærənɪs] *s* baronessa

baroque [bə'rok] *adj* & *s* barocco

bar'rack-room' *adj* da caserma || *s* camerata

barracks ['bærəks] *spl* caserma; camerata

barrage [bə'raʒ] *s* (mil) fuoco di sbarramento

barrel ['bærəl] *s* barile *m*, botte *f*; (*of gun*) canna; (mach) cilindro

bar'rel or'gan *s* organetto di Barberia

barren ['bærən] *adj* sterile; (*without vegetation*) brullo

barricade [,bærɪ'ked] *s* barricata || *tr* barricare

barrier ['bærɪ-ər] *s* barriera

bar'rier reef' *s* barriera corallina

barring ['barɪŋ] *prep* eccetto, salvo

barrister ['bærɪstər] *s* (Brit) avvocato

bar'room' *s* bar *m*, cantina, mescita

bar'tend'er *s* barista *mf*, barman *m*

barter ['bartər] *s* baratto || *tr* & *intr* barattare, permutare

basalt [bə'səlt] *s* basalto

base [bes] *adj* basale; basso; servile; (*morally low*) turpe; (*metal*) vile, non prezioso || *s* base *f*; (*in children's games*) tana; (*of a word*) radice *f* basale || *tr* basare

base'ball' *s* baseball *m*, pallabase *f*

base'board' *s* basamento; (*of wall*) zoccolo

Basel ['bazəl] *s* Basilea

baseless ['beslɪs] *adj* infondato

basement ['besmənt] *s* scantinato, piano interrato

bashful ['bæʃəl] *adj* timido

basic ['besɪk] *adj* fondamentale; (chem) basico

ba'sic commod'ities *spl* articoli *mpl* di prima necessità

basilica [bə'sɪlɪkə] *s* basilica

basin ['besɪn] *s* catino; vasca; (*of balance*) piatto; (*of river*) bacino; (*of harbor*) darsena

ba·sis ['besɪs] *s* (-ses [siz]) base *f*

bask [bæsk] *or* [bask] *intr* crogiolarsi

basket ['bæskɪt] *or* ['baskɪt] *s* cesta; (sports) cesto

bas'ket-ball' *s* pallacanestro *f*

Basque [bæsk] *adj* & *s* basco

bas-relief [,barɪ'lif] *or* [,bærɪ'lif] *s* bassorilievo

bass [bes] *adj* & *s* (mus) basso || [bæs] *s* (ichth) pesce persico

bass' drum' *s* grancassa

bass' horn' *s* bassotuba *m*

bassinet ['bæsə,net] *or* [,bæsə'net] *s* culla a forma di cesto; carrozzina a forma di cesto

bas·so ['bæso] *or* ['baso] *s* (-sos *or* -si [si]) basso

bassoon [bə'sun] *s* fagotto

bass' vi'ol ['vaɪ-əl] *s* contrabbasso

bastard ['bæstərd] *adj* & *s* bastardo

baste [best] *tr* (*to sew*) imbastire; (*meat*) inumidire con acqua o grasso

bastion ['bæstʃən] *or* ['bæstɪ-ən] *s* bastione *m*

bat [bæt] *s* mazza; (*in cricket*) maglio; (coll) colpo; (zool) pipistrello || *v* (*pret & pp* batted; *ger* batting) *tr* colpire con la mazza; **without batting an eye** (coll) senza batter ciglio

batch [bætʃ] *s* (*of bread*) infornata; gruppo, numero

bath [bæθ] *or* [baθ] *s* bagno; **to take a bath** fare il bagno

bathe [beð] *tr* bagnare, lavare || *intr* bagnarsi, fare il bagno

bather ['beðər] *s* bagnante *mf*

bath'house' *s* (*individual*) cabina; spogliatoio

bath'ing beau'ty *s* bellezza in costume da bagno

bath'ing cap' *s* cuffia da bagno

bath'ing resort' *s* stazione balneare

bath'ing suit' *s* costume *m* da bagno

bath'ing trunks' *spl* mutandine *fpl* da bagno

bath'robe' *s* accappatoio

bath'room' *s* stanza da bagno

bath' salts' *spl* sali *mpl* da bagno

bath'tub' *s* bagno, vasca da bagno

baton [bæ'tɑn] *or* ['bætən] *s* bastone *m*; (mus) bacchetta

battalion [bə'tæljən] *s* battaglione *m*

batten ['bætən] *tr* assicella; piccola traversa; (naut) bietta || *tr*—**to batten down the hatches** chiudere ermeticamente i boccaporti

batter ['bætər] *s* pasta, farina pastosa; (baseball) battitore *m* || *tr* battere, tempestare di colpi; (*to wear out*) logorare

bat'tering ram' *s* ariete *m*

batter·y ['bætəri] *s* (-ies) (*primary cell*) pila; (*secondary cell*) accumulatore *m*; (*group of batteries*) batteria; (law) assalto; (mil & mus) batteria

battle ['bætəl] *s* battaglia; **to do battle** dar battaglia || *tr* combattere contro || *intr* combattere

bat'tle cry' *s* grido di guerra

battledore ['bætəl,dor] *s* racchetta; **battledore and shuttlecock** gioco del volano

bat'tle-field' *s* campo di battaglia

bat'tle-front' *s* fronte *m* di combattimento

battlement ['bætəlmənt] *s* merlatura

bat'tle roy'al *s* baruffa generale, zuffa generale

bat'tle-ship' *s* corazzata

battue [bæ'tu] *or* [bæ'tju] *s* (hunt) battuta

bat·ty ['bætɪ] *adj* (-tier; -tiest) (slang) pazzo, eccentrico

bauble ['bɔbəl] *s* bazzecola, gingillo

Bavaria [bə'vɛrɪ-ə] *s* la Baviera

Bavarian [bə'vɛrɪ-ən] *adj* & *s* bavarese *mf*

bawd [bɔd] *s* ruffiano; ruffiana

bawd·y ['bɔdɪ] *adj* (-ier; -iest) indecente, osceno

bawd'y-house' *s* casa di malaffare

bawl [bɔl] *s* grido; (coll) pianto || *tr*—to bawl out (slang) fare una ramanzina a || *intr* strillare; (coll) piangere

bay [be] *adj* baio || *s* baia; vano, alcova; *(recess in wall)* apertura nel muro; finestra sporgente; *(of dog)* latrato; cavallo baio; (bot) lauro; at bay in una posizione disperata || *intr* latrare

bayonet ['be-ənɪt] *s* baionetta || *tr* dare baionettate a || *intr* dare baionettate

bay' win'dow *s* finestra sporgente; (slang) pancia

bazooka [bə'zukə] *s* bazooka *m*

be [bi] *v* (*pres* am [æm], is [ɪz], are [ar]; *pret* was [wɑz] or [wʌz], were [wʌr]; *pp* been [bɪn]) *intr* essere; fare, e.g., to be a mason far il muratore; fare, e.g., 3 times 3 is 9 tre volte tre fa nove; be as it may be comunque sia; here is or here are ecco; there are ci sono; there is c'è; to be futuro, e.g., my wife to be la mia futura sposa; to be ashamed aver vergogna; to be cold aver freddo; to be hot aver caldo; to be hungry aver fame; to be in stare a casa; to be in a hurry aver fretta; to be in with (coll) essere amico intimo di; to be off andarsene; to be out essere fuori; to be out of (coll) non aver più; to be right aver ragione; to be sleepy aver sonno; to be thirsty avere sete; to be up essere alzato; to be up to essere all'altezza di; toccare, e.g., it's up to you tocca a Lei; to be warm avere caldo; to be wrong avere torto; sbagliarsi; to be . . . years old avere . . . anni || *aux* stare, e.g., to be waiting stare aspettando; essere, e.g., the murder has been committed l'omicidio è stato commesso; dovere, e.g., he is to clean the stables tomorrow domani deve pulire la stalla || *impers* essere, e.g., it is necessary è necessario; fare, e.g., it is cold fa freddo; it is hot fa caldo

beach [bitʃ] *s* spiaggia || *tr* (*a boat*) arenare || *intr* arenarsi

beach'comb' *intr* raccogliere relitti sulla spiaggia

beach'comb'er *s* girellone *m* di spiaggia

beach'head' *s* testa di sbarco

beach' robe' *s* accappatoio

beach' shoe' *s* sandalo da spiaggia

beach' umbrel'la *s* ombrellone *m* da spiaggia

beacon ['bikən] *s* faro || *tr* rischiarare; fare da guida a || *intr* brillare

bead [bid] *s* perlina; grano, chicco; *(drop)* goccia; beads *(in a necklace or rosary)* conterie *fpl*; to count one's beads recitare il rosario

beagle ['bigəl] *s* segugio, bracco

beak [bik] *s* becco; promontorio

beam [bim] *s* trave *f*; *(of balance)* braccio; *(of light)* raggio; *(ship's breadth)* larghezza; *(smile)* sorriso; *(radio signal)* fascio direttore; *(course indicated by radio beam)* aerovia; (naut) traverso || *tr* (*a radio signal*) dirigere; (e.g., light) irraggiare || *intr* raggiare

bean [bin] *s* fagiolo; *(of coffee)* chicco; (slang) testa

beaner·y ['binərɪ] *s* (-ies) (slang) gargotta, taverna di secondo ordine

bean'pole' *s* puntello per i fagioli; (coll) palo del telegrafo

bear [bɛr] *s* orso; (astr) orsa; (com) ribassista *m*, giocatore *m* al ribasso || *v* (*pret* bore [bor]; *pp* borne [born]) *tr* (*to carry*) portare; (*to give birth to*) partorire; (*to sustain*) sostenere; (*to withstand*) sopportare; (*a grudge*) serbare; (*in mind*) tenere; (*interest*) produrre; (*to pay*) pagare; to bear the date aver la data; to bear out confermare; to bear witness testimoniare || *intr* (*to be productive*) fruttificare; (*to move*) dirigersi; (*to be oppressive*) fare pressione; to bear down on fare pressione su; avvicinarsi a; to bear up resistere; to bear with tollerare

bearable ['bɛrəbəl] *adj* tollerabile

beard [bɪrd] *s* barba; (e.g., *in wheat*) arista

bearded *adj* barbuto

beardless ['bɪrdlɪs] *adj* imberbe

bearer ['bɛrər] *s* portatore *m*

bearing ['bɛrɪŋ] *s* portamento; relazione; importanza; (mach) bronzina, cuscinetto; bearings orientamento; to lose one's bearings perdere la bussola; perdere l'orientamento

bearish ['bɛrɪʃ] *adj* (*like a bear*) orsino; (e.g., *prices*) in ribasso; *(market)* al ribasso; *(speculator)* ribassista

bear'skin' *s* pelle *f* dell'orso; (mil) colbacco

beast [bist] *s* bestia

beast·ly ['bistlɪ] *adj* (-lier; -liest) bestiale || *adv* (coll) malissimo

beast' of bur'den *s* bestia da soma

beast' of prey' *s* animale *m* da rapina

beat [bit] *s* (*of heart*) battito; *(of policeman)* ronda; *(stroke)* colpo; *(habitual route)* cammino battuto; (mus) tempo; (phys) battimento || *v* (*pret* beat; *pp* beat or beaten) *tr* battere; percuotere; (*eggs*) frullare; (*to whip*) frustare; (coll) confondere; beat it! (slang) vattene!; to beat a retreat battere in ritirata; to beat back respingere; to beat down sopprimere; to beat off respingere; to beat up (*eggs*) frullare; (*people*) dargliene a || *intr* battere; pulsare; to beat around the bush (coll) menare il can per l'aia

beat'en path' ['bitən] *s* cammino battuto

beater ['bitər] *s* frullino

beati·fy [bɪ'ætɪ‚faɪ] *v* (*pret* & *pp* -fied) *tr* beatificare

beating ['bitɪŋ] s battitura; (*whipping*) frustatura; (*throbbing*) pulsazione, battito; (*defeat*) sconfitta

beau [bo] s (**beaus** or **beaux** [boz]) (*dandy*) bellimbusto; (*girl's sweetheart*) spasimante m

beautician [bju'tɪ/ən] s estetista mf

beautiful ['bjutɪfəl] adj bello

beauti•fy ['bjutɪ‚faɪ] v (pret & pp -fied) tr abbellire

beau•ty ['bjuti] s (-ties) bellezza

beau'ty con'test s concorso di bellezza

beau'ty par'lor s istituto di bellezza

beau'ty sleep' s primo sonno

beau'ty spot' s neo; posto pittoresco

beaver ['bivər] s castoro; pelle f di castoro; cappello a cilindro

because [bɪ'kɔz] conj perchè; **because of** a causa di

beck [bɛk] s gesto; **at the beck and call of** agli ordini di

beckon ['bɛkən] s gesto || tr fare gesto a || intr fare gesto

becloud [bɪ'klaud] tr annebbiare; oscurare

be•come [bɪ'kʌm] v (pret -came; pp -come) tr convenire a; stare bene a, e.g., **this hat becomes you** questo cappello Le sta bene || intr diventare; farsi; convertirsi, e.g., **water became wine** l'acqua si convertì in vino; succedere, e.g., **what became of my coat?** che è successo del mio cappotto? che è successo del mio pastrano?; essere, e.g., **what will become of me?** che sarà di me?; **to become accustomed** abituarsi; **to become angry** entrare in collera; **to become crazy** impazzire; **to become ill** ammalarsi

becoming [bɪ'kʌmɪŋ] adj conveniente; appropriato; acconcio; **this is very becoming to you** questo Le sta molto bene

bed [bɛd] s letto; (*layer*) strato; giacimento; **to go to bed** andare a letto; **to take to one's bed** mettersi a letto

bed' and board' s vitto e alloggio; pensione completa

bed'bug' s cimice f

bed'clothes' spl lenzuola fpl e coperte fpl, biancheria da letto

bed'cov'er s coperta da letto

bedding ['bɛdɪŋ] s lenzuola fpl e coperte fpl; (*litter*) lettiera; (*foundation*) fondamenta fpl

bedeck [bɪ'dɛk] tr ornare, adornare

bedev•il [bɪ'dɛvɪl] v (pret & pp -iled or -illed; ger -iling or -illing) tr tormentare diabolicamente; confondere

bed'fast' adj confinato a letto

bed'fel'low s compagno di letto; compagno di stanza; compagno

bedlam ['bɛdləm] s manicomio; pandemonio

bed' lin'en s biancheria da letto

bed'pan' s padella

bedridden ['bɛd‚rɪdən] adj degente a letto

bed'room' s stanza da letto, camera da letto

bed'room slip'per s babbuccia, pantofola

bed'side' s capezzale m

bed'side man'ner s maniera di fare coi pazienti

bed'sore' s piaga da decubito

bed'spread' s coperta da letto

bed'spring' s rete f del letto; molla del letto

bed'stead' s fusto del letto

bed'tick' s traliccio

bed'time' s ora di coricarsi

bed'warm'er s scaldaletto

bee [bi] s ape f

beech [bit/] s faggio

beech'nut' s faggiola

beef [bif] s bue m, manzo; carne f di manzo; (coll) forza; (slang) lamentela || tr—**to beef up** (coll) rinforzare || intr (slang) lamentarsi

beef' cat'tle s manzi mpl da carne

beef'steak' s bistecca

beef' stew' s stufato di manzo

bee'hive' s alveare m

bee'keep'er s apicoltore m

bee'line' s—**to make a beeline for** (coll) andare direttamente verso

beer [bɪr] s birra

beer' saloon' s birreria

beeswax ['biz‚wæks] s cera d'api

beet [bit] s barbabietola

beetle ['bitəl] adj sporgente, folto || s scarafaggio

bee'tle-browed' adj dalle sopracciglia folte

beet' su'gar s zucchero di barbabietola

be•fall [bɪ'fɔl] v (pret -fell ['fɛl]; pp -fallen ['fɔlən]) tr succedere a || intr succedere

befitting [bɪ'fɪtɪŋ] adj appropriato

before [bɪ'for] adv prima, prima d'ora || prep (in time) prima di; (in place) dinnanzi a, davanti a; **before Christ** avanti Cristo || conj prima che

before'hand' adv in anticipo; precedentemente

befriend [bɪ'frɛnd] tr diventare amico di, proteggere, favorire; aiutare

befuddle [bɪ'fʌdəl] tr confondere

beg [bɛg] v (pret & pp begged; ger begging) tr chiedere; implorare; (alms) mendicare; **I beg your pardon** Le chiedo scusa; **to beg s.o. for s.th** chiedere qlco a qlcu || intr chiedere la carità; **to beg for** sollecitare; **to beg off** scusarsi; **to go begging** rimanere invenduto

beget [bɪ'gɛt] v (pret -got ['gɑt]; pp -gotten or -got; ger -getting) tr generare

beggar ['bɛgər] s accattone m, mendicante m

be•gin [bɪ'gɪn] v (pret -gan ['gæn]; pp -gun ['gʌn]; ger -ginning) tr & intr cominciare, iniziare; **beginning with** a partire da; **to begin with** per cominciare

beginner [bɪ'gɪnər] s principiante mf

beginning [bɪ'gɪnɪŋ] s inizio, origine f, principio, esordio

begrudge [bɪ'grʌdʒ] tr invidiare; concedere con riluttanza

beguile [bɪ'gaɪl] tr ingannare; sedurre; (to delight) divertire

behalf [bɪ'hæf] or [bɪ'hɑf] s—**on behalf of** nell'interesse di; a nome di

behave [bɪ'hev] *intr* comportarsi; comportarsi bene

behavior [bɪ'hevjər] *s* comportamento, condotta; funzionamento

behead [bɪ'hed] *tr* decapitare

behest [bɪ'hest] *s* ordine *m*, comando

behind [bɪ'haɪnd] *s* didietro; (slang) sedere *m* || *adv* dietro; (*in arrears*) in arretrato; **from behind** dal didietro || *prep* dietro a, dietro di; **behind time** in ritardo

be·hold [bɪ'hold] *v* (*pret & pp* **-held** ['held]) *tr* contemplare; ammirare || *interj* guarda!

behoove [bɪ'huv] *impers*—**it behooves** him to gli conviene di

being ['bi·ɪŋ] *adj* esistente; **for the time being** per ora || *s* essere *m*, ente *m*

belabor [bɪ'lebər] *tr* attaccare; (fig) ribattere, confutare; (fig) insistere su

belated [bɪ'letɪd] *adj* tardivo

belch [bɛltʃ] *s* rutto || *tr* eruttare, vomitare || *intr* ruttare

beleaguer [bɪ'ligər] *tr* assediare

bel·fry ['belfri] *s* (-fries) (*tower*) campanile *m*; (*site of bell*) cella campanaria; (slang) testa

Belgian ['beldʒən] *adj & s* belga *mf*

Belgium ['beldʒəm] *s* il Belgio

be·lie [bɪ'laɪ] *v* (*pret & pp* **-lied** ['laɪd]; *ger* **-lying** ['laɪ·ɪŋ]) *tr* (*to misrepresent*) tradire; (*to prove false*) smentire

belief [bɪ'lif] *s* fede *f*, credenza

believable [bɪ'livəbəl] *adj* credibile

believe [bɪ'liv] *tr* credere || *intr* credere, aver fede; **to believe in** credere in

believer [bɪ'livər] *s* credente *mf*

belittle [bɪ'lɪtəl] *tr* menomare

bell [bel] *s* campana; (*for a door*) campanello; (*sound*) rintocco; (*on cattle*) campanaccio; (*of deer*) bramito || *intr* bramire

belladonna [,belə'dɑnə] *s* belladonna

bell'-bot'tom *adj* a campana

bell'boy' *s* cameriere *m*, ragazzo

belle [bel] *s* bella

belles-lettres [,bel'letrə] *spl* belle lettere

bell' glass' *s* campana di vetro

bell'hop' *s* cameriere *m*, ragazzo

bellicose ['belɪ,kos] *adj* bellicoso

belligerent [bə'lɪdʒərənt] *adj & s* belligerante *m*

bellow ['belo] *s* muggito; **bellows** mantice *m*; (*of camera*) soffietto || *tr* gridare || *intr* muggire

bell' ring'er ['rɪŋər] *s* campanaro

bellwether ['bel,weðər] *s* pecora guida

bel·ly ['beli] *s* (-lies) ventre *m*, pancia || *v* (*pret & pp* **-lied**) *intr* far pancia

bel'ly·ache' *s* (coll) mal *m* di pancia || *intr* (slang) lamentarsi

bel'ly·but'ton *s* (coll) ombelico

bel'ly dance' *s* (coll) danza del ventre

bel'ly flop' *s* panciata

bellyful ['belɪ,ful] *s*—**to have a bellyful** (slang) averne fino agli occhi

bel'ly·land' *intr* (aer) atterrare sul ventre

belong [bɪ'lɔŋ] or [bɪ'lɑŋ] *intr* appartenere; stare bene, e.g., **this chair belongs in this room** questa sedia sta bene in questa stanza

belongings [bɪ'lɔŋɪŋz] or [bɪ'lɑŋɪŋz] *spl* effetti *mpl* personali

beloved [bɪ'lʌvɪd] or [bɪ'lʌvd] *adj & s* diletto, amato

below [bɪ'lo] *adv* sotto; più sotto; sotto zero, e.g., **ten below** dieci gradi sotto zero || *prep* sotto, sotto di

belt [belt] *s* cintura, cinghia; (mach) nastro; (mil) cinturone *m*; (geog) fascia, zona; **to tighten one's belt** far cintura || *tr* cingere; (slang) staffilare

belt'ed tire' *s* copertone cinturato

belt' line' *s* linea di circonvallazione

beltway ['belt,we] *s* raccordo anulare

bemoan [bɪ'mon] *tr* lamentare; compiangere

bench [bentʃ] *s* banco, panca; tribunale *m*; (mach) banco di prova; **to be on the bench** (law) essere giudice

bend [bend] *s* curva; (e.g., *of pipe*) gomito, angolo || *v* (*pret & pp* **bent** [bent]) *tr* curvare; piegare; far piegare || *intr* deviare; piegare, piegarsi; **to bend over** inchinarsi

beneath [bɪ'niθ] *adv* sotto; più sotto || *prep* sotto, sotto di

benediction [,benɪ'dɪkʃən] *s* benedizione

benefactor ['benɪ,fæktər] or [,benɪ'fæktər] *s* benefattore *m*

benefactress ['benɪ,fæktrɪs] or [,benɪ'fæktrɪs] *s* benefattrice *f*

beneficence [bɪ'nefɪsəns] *s* beneficenza

beneficent [bɪ'nefɪsənt] *adj* caritatevole; benefico

beneficial [,benɪ'fɪʃəl] *adj* benefico

beneficiar·y [,benɪ'fɪʃɪ,eri] *s* (-ies) beneficiario

benefit ['benɪfɪt] *s* beneficio; festa di beneficenza; **for the benefit of** a beneficio di || *tr & intr* beneficiare

ben'efit perfor'mance *s* beneficiata

benevolence [bɪ'nevələns] *s* benevolenza; carità *f*

benevolent [bɪ'nevələnt] *adj* benevolo; (*institution*) benefico

benign [bɪ'naɪn] *adj* benigno

bent [bent] *adj* curvo; **bent on** deciso a || *s* curva; tendenza, propensità *f*

Benzedrine ['benzɪ,drin] (trademark) *s* benzedrina

benzene ['benzin] *s* benzolo

benzine ['ben'zin] *s* benzina

bequeath [bɪ'kwiθ] or [bɪ'kwið] *tr* legare, lasciare in eredità

bequest [bɪ'kwest] *s* legato, lascito

berate [bɪ'ret] *tr* redarguire

be·reave [bɪ'riv] *v* (*pret & pp* **-reaved** or **-reft** ['reft]) *tr* spogliare

bereavement [bɪ'rivmənt] *s* lutto, perdita

beret [bə're] or ['bere] *s* berretto

Berlin [bər'lɪn] *adj* berlinese || *s* Berlino

Berliner [bər'lɪnər] *s* berlinese *mf*

Bermuda [bər'mjudə] *s* le Bermude

ber·ry ['beri] *s* (-ries) (*dry seed*) chicco; (*fruit*) bacca

berserk [bʌr'sʌrk] adj infuriato || adv —to go berserk impazzire

berth [bʌrθ] s (for a ship) posto di ormeggio; (bed) cuccetta; (coll) posto

beryllium [bə'rɪlɪ-əm] s berillio

be·seech [bɪ'sitʃ] v (pret & pp -sought ['sɔt] or -seeched) tr supplicare

be·set [bɪ'sɛt] v (pret & pp -set; ger -setting) tr assediare, circondare; (e.g., with problems) assillare

beside [bɪ'saɪd] adv oltre, inoltre || prep vicino a; in confronto di; oltre a; beside oneself fuori di sé; beside the point fuori del seminato

besides [bɪ'saɪdz] adv inoltre; d'altronde || prep oltre a

besiege [bɪ'sidʒ] tr assediare; (with questions) bombardare

besmear [bɪ'smɪr] tr imbrattare, sgorbiare; sporcare

besmirch [bɪ'smʌrtʃ] tr insudiciare

bespatter [bɪ'spætər] tr inzaccherare

be·speak [bɪ'spik] v (-spoke ['spok]; -spoken) tr chiedere anticipatamente a; (to show) dimostrare

best [bɛst] adj super (il) migliore, ottimo || s meglio; at best nella miglior delle ipotesi; to do one's best fare del proprio meglio; to get the best of avere la meglio di; to make the best of adattarsi a || adv super meglio; had best, e.g., I had best dovrei || tr battere, riuscire superiore a

bestial ['bɛstjəl] or ['bɛstʃəl] adj bestiale

be·stir [bɪ'stʌr] v (pret & pp -stirred; ger -stirring) v eccitare; to bestir oneself darsi da fare

best' man' s testimone m di nozze

bestow [bɪ'sto] tr accordare; conferire

best' sell'er s best-seller m

bet [bɛt] s scommessa || v (pret & pp bet or betted; ger betting) tr & intr scommettere; I bet ci scommetto; you bet (coll) evidentemente

be·take [bɪ'tek] v (pret -took ['tuk]; pp -taken) tr—to betake oneself andare, dirigersi

be·think [bɪ'θɪŋk] v (pret & pp -thought ['θɔt]) tr to bethink oneself pensare; ricordarsi

Bethlehem ['bɛθlɪ-əm] or ['bɛθlɪ,hɛm] s Betlemme f

betide [bɪ'taɪd] tr accadere a || intr accadere

betoken [bɪ'tokən] tr indicare, presagire

betray [bɪ'tre] tr tradire, ingannare; (to reveal) rivelare

betroth [bɪ'troð] or [bɪ'trɔθ] tr promettere in matrimonio a

betrothal [bɪ'troðəl] or [bɪ'trɔθəl] s fidanzamento

betrothed [bɪ'troðd] or [bɪ'trɔθt] adj fidanzato || s promesso sposo, fidanzato

better ['bɛtər] adj comp migliore; to grow better migliorare || s—betters superiori mpl; ottimati mpl; to get the better of avere la meglio di || adv meglio; had better dovere, e.g., I had

better dovrei; to be better off stare meglio; to think better of riconsiderare; you ought to know better dovrebbe vergognarsi || tr sorpassare; migliorare; to better oneself migliorare la propria situazione

bet'ter half' s metà f

betterment ['bɛtərmənt] s miglioramento

bettor ['bɛtər] s scommettitore m

between [bɪ'twin] adv in mezzo; in between in mezzo, fra i piedi || prep fra, tra

between'-decks' s interponte m

bev·el ['bɛvəl] s (instrument) falsa squadra; (sloping part) augnatura || v (pret & pp -eled or -elled; ger -eling or -elling) tr augnare

beverage ['bɛvərɪdʒ] s bevanda

bev·y ['bɛvi] s (-ies) (of women) gruppo; (of birds) stormo

bewail [bɪ'wel] tr lamentare

beware [bɪ'wɛr] tr fare attenzione a, guardarsi da || intr fare attenzione, guardarsi

bewilder [bɪ'wɪldər] tr lasciar perplesso, confondere, disorientare

bewilderment [bɪ'wɪldərmənt] s perplessità f, disorientamento

bewitch [bɪ'wɪtʃ] tr stregare

beyond [bɪ'jɑnd] s—the beyond l'aldilà m || adv più lontano || prep al di là di; oltre a; più tardi di; beyond a doubt fuori dubbio; beyond repair irreparabile

bias ['baɪ-əs] s linea diagonale; pregiudizio; on the bias diagonalmente || tr prevenire

bib [bɪb] s bavaglino

Bible ['baɪbəl] s Bibbia

Biblical ['bɪblɪkəl] adj biblico

bibliogra·phy [,bɪblɪ'ɑgrəfɪ] s (-phies) bibliografia

bibliophile ['bɪblɪ-ə,faɪl] s bibliofilo

bicarbonate [baɪ'kɑrbə,net] s bicarbonato

biceps ['baɪsɛps] s bicipite m

bicker ['bɪkər] s bisticcio, disputa || intr bisticciare, disputare

bicycle ['baɪsɪkəl] s bicicletta

bid [bɪd] s offerta; (cards) dichiarazione; (coll) invito || v (pret bade [bæd] or bid; pp bidden ['bɪdən] or bid; ger bidding) tr & intr offrire; comandare; (cards) dichiarare

bidder ['bɪdər] s offerente mf; (cards) dichiarante mf; the highest bidder il miglior offerente

bidding ['bɪdɪŋ] s ordine m; offerte fpl; (cards) dichiarazione

bide [baɪd] tr—to bide one's time attendere l'ora propizia

biennial [baɪ'ɛnɪ-əl] adj biennale

bier [bɪr] s catafalco

bifocal [baɪ'fokəl] adj bifocale || bifocals spl occhiali mpl bifocali

big [bɪg] adj (bigger; biggest) grande; (coll) importante; (coll) stravagante; big with child incinta || adv—to talk big (coll) parlare con iattanza

bigamist ['bɪgəmɪst] s bigamo

bigamous ['bɪgəməs] adj bigamo

big-bellied ['bɪg ,belid] *adj* panciuto

Big' Dip'per *s* Gran Carro

big' game' *s* caccia grossa

big-hearted ['bɪg ,hɑrtɪd] *adj* magnanimo, generoso

big' mouth' *s* (slang) sbraitone *m*

bigot ['bɪgət] *s* bigotto, bacchettone *m*

bigoted ['bɪgətɪd] *adj* (*in religion*) bigotto; intransigente

bigot·ry ['bɪgətri] *s* (-ries) bigottismo; intransigenza

big' shot' *s* (slang) pezzo grosso, (un) qualcuno

big' slam' *s* (bridge) grande slam *m*

big-time op'erator *s* (slang) grosso trafficante

big' toe' *s* alluce *m*

big' wheel' *s* (slang) pezzo grosso

bike [baɪk] *s* (coll) bicicletta

bile [baɪl] *s* bile *f*

bilge [bɪldʒ] *s* sentina; (*of barrel*) ventre *m*

bilge'ways' *spl* parati *mpl*

bilingual [baɪ'lɪŋgwəl] *adj* bilingue

bilious ['bɪljəs] *adj* bilioso

bilk [bɪlk] *tr* defraudare

bill [bɪl] *s* (*of bird*) becco; (*statement of charges*) conto; (*e.g., for electricity*) bolletta; (*menu*) lista; (*money*) biglietto; (*proposed law*) disegno di legge; (*handbill*) annunzio; (*law*) atto; (theat) cartellone *m*; **to fill the bill** (coll) riempire i requisiti; **to foot the bill** (coll) pagare lo scotto || *tr* fare una lista di; mettere in conto a || *intr* (*said of doves*) beccuzzarsi; (*said of lovers*) baciucchiarsi

bill'board' *s* cartellone *m*; (rad, telv) titolo di testa

billet ['bɪlɪt] *s* (mil) alloggiamento; (mil) ordine *m* d'alloggiamento || *tr* (mil) alloggiare, accasermare

bill'fold' *s* portafoglio

bill'head' *s* intestazione di fattura

billiards ['bɪljərdz] *s* bigliardo

bil'ling clerk' *s* fatturista *mf*

billion ['bɪljən] *s* (U.S.A.) miliardo; (Brit) bilione *m*

bill' of exchange' *s* tratta

bill' of fare' *s* menu *m*, lista delle vivande

bill' of lad'ing ['ledɪŋ] *s* polizza di carico

bill' of rights' *s* dichiarazione dei diritti

bill' of sale' *s* atto di vendita

billow ['bɪlo] *s* ondata, cavallone *m*

bill'post'er *s* attacchino

bil·ly ['bɪli] *s* (-lies) manganello

bil'ly goat' *s* capro, caprone *m*

bimonthly [baɪ'mʌnθli] *adj* (*occurring every two months*) bimestrale; (*occurring twice a month*) bimensile

bin [bɪn] *s* cassone *m*; (*for bread*) madia; (*for coal*) deposito

binaural [baɪ'nɔrəl] *adj* biauricolare

bind [baɪnd] *v* (*pret & pp* bound [baʊnd]) *tr* legare; allacciare; (*to bandage*) fasciare; (*to constipate*) costipare; (*a book*) rilegare; (*to oblige*) obbligare; (mach) grippare

binder ['baɪndər] *s* rilegatore *m*; (*cover*) cartella

binder·y ['baɪndəri] *s* (-ies) rilegatoria

binding ['baɪndɪŋ] *adj* obbligatorio || *s* (*of book*) rilegatura; legatura; fasciatura

bind'ing post' *s* (elec) capocorda; (*e.g., of battery*) (elec) serrafilo

binge [bɪndʒ] *s*—**to go on a binge** (coll) far baldoria

bingo ['bɪngo] *s* tombola

binnacle ['bɪnəkəl] *s* abitacolo

binoculars [bɪ'nakjələrz] or [baɪ'nakjələrz] *spl* binocolo

biochemical [,baɪ·ə'kemɪkəl] *adj* biochimico

biochemist [,baɪ·ə'kemɪst] *s* biochimico

biochemistry [,baɪ·ə'kemɪstri] *s* biochimica

biodegradable [,baɪ·odɪ'gredəbəl] *adj* biodegradabile

biographer [baɪ'agrəfər] *s* biografo

biographic(al) [,baɪ·ə'græfɪk(əl)] *adj* biografico

biogra·phy [baɪ'agrəfi] *s* (-phies) biografia

biologist [baɪ'alədʒɪst] *s* biologo

biology [baɪ'alədʒi] *s* biologia

biophysics [,baɪ·ə'fɪzɪks] *s* biofisica

biop·sy ['baɪ ,apsi] *s* (-sies) biopsia

bipartisan [baɪ'partɪzən] *adj* (*system*) bipartitico; (*government*) bipartito

biped ['baɪped] *adj & s* bipede *m*

birch [bʌrtʃ] *s* betulla || *tr* scudisciare

bird [bʌrd] *s* uccello; **a bird in the hand is worth two in the bush** un uovo oggi vale meglio di una gallina domani; **birds of a feather** gente *f* della stessa risma; **to kill two birds with one stone** pigliare due piccioni con una fava

bird' cage' *s* gabbia

bird' call' *s* richiamo

birdie ['bʌrdi] *s* uccellino; (golf) giocata di un colpo sotto la media

bird'lime' *s* pania

bird' of pas'sage *s* uccello di passo

bird' of prey' *s* uccello da preda

bird'seed' *s* becchime *m*

bird's'-eye view' *s* vista a volo d'uccello

bird' shot' *s* pallini *mpl* da caccia

birth [bʌrθ] *s* nascita; **to give birth to** dare i natali a; mettere alla luce

birth' certif'icate *s* certificato di nascita

birth' control' *s* limitazione delle nascite

birth'day' *s* natalizio, compleanno; (*of an event*) anniversario

birth'mark' *s* voglia

birth'place' *s* patria; (*e.g., city*) luogo di nascita; **to be the birthplace of** dare i natali a

birth' rate' *s* natalità *f*

birth'right' *s* diritto acquisito sin dalla nascita

biscuit ['bɪskɪt] *s* panino soffice; (Brit) biscotto

bisect [baɪ'sekt] *tr* bisecare || *intr* (*said of roads*) incrociarsi

bisection [baɪ'sekʃən] *s* bisezione

bishop ['bɪʃəp] *s* vescovo; (chess) alfiere *m*

bishopric ['bɪʃəprɪk] *s* vescovado

bismuth ['bɪzməθ] s bismuto
bison ['baɪsən] or ['baɪzən] s bisonte m
bisulfate [baɪ'sʌlfet] s bisolfato
bisulfite [baɪ'sʌlfaɪt] s bisolfito
bit [bɪt] s (of bridle) morso; (of key) mappa; (tool) punta, trivella; (small piece) bricciolo; **a bit un po'**; (coll) un momento; **a good bit** una buona quantità; **bit by bit** poco a poco; **to blow to bits** fare a pezzi; **to champ the bit** mordere il freno; **two bits** (slang) quarto di dollaro, cinque soldi
bitch [bɪtʃ] s cagna; (vulg) donnaccia || intr (slang) lamentarsi
bite [baɪt] s morso; (mouthful) boccone m; **to take a bite** fare uno spuntino; mangiare un boccone || v (pret **bit** [bɪt]; pp **bit** or **bitten** ['bɪtən]) tr mordere, addentare; pungere; (the dust) baciare || intr mordere; (said of insects) pungere; (said of fish) abboccare
biting ['baɪtɪŋ] adj mordace; pungente
bitter ['bɪtər] adj amaro; (e.g., fight) accanito; (cold) pungente || s amaro; **bitters** amaro
bit'ter end' s—**to the bitter end** fino alla fine; fino alla morte
bit·ten·der [bɪ'zɑr] (coll) intransigente mf
bitterness ['bɪtərnɪs] s amarezza
bit'ter-sweet' adj dolceamaro; (fig) agrodolce || s dulcamara
bitumen [bɪ'tjumən] or [bɪ'tumən] s bitume m
bivou·ac ['bɪvu‚æk] or ['bɪvwæk] s bivacco || v (pret & pp -acked; ger -acking) intr bivaccare
biweekly [baɪ'wiklɪ] adj bisettimanale; quindicinale || adv ogni due settimane
biyearly [baɪ'jɪrlɪ] adj semestrale || adv semestralmente
bizarre [bɪ'zɑr] adj bizzarro
blab [blæb] s chiacchierone m || v (pret & pp **blabbed**; ger **blabbing**) tr rivelare || intr chiacchierare
black [blæk] adj nero; (without light) buio || s nero; **to wear black** vestire a lutto, vestire di nero || intr—**to black out** perdere i sensi
black'-and-blue' adj livido e pesto
black'-and-white' adj in bianco e nero
black'ball' s palla nera, voto contrario || tr dare la palla nera a
black'ber'ry s (-ries) mora
black'bird' s merlo
black'board' s lavagna, tavola nera
black'cap' s capinera
black'damp' s putizza
Black' Death' s peste bubbonica
blacken ['blækən] tr annerire; (shoes) lucidare; (reputation) sporcare
black' eye' s occhio pesto; (fig) cattiva reputazione
blackguard ['blægɑrd] s canaglia
black'head' s comedone m
blackish ['blækɪʃ] adj nerastro
black'jack' s randello; (cards) ventuno || tr randellare
black' mag'ic s magia nera

black'mail' s ricatto || tr ricattare
blackmailer ['blæk ‚melər] s ricattatore m
Black' Mari'a [mə'raɪ·ə] s (coll) furgone m cellulare
black' mar'ket s borsa nera
black' marketeer' [‚mɑrkɪ'tɪr] s borsanerista mf
blackness ['blæknɪs] s nerezza
black'out' s oscuramento; (theat) spegnitura; (pathol) svenimento passeggero
black' sheep' s (fig) pecora nera
black'smith' s fabbro
black' tie' s cravatta da smoking; smoking m
bladder ['blædər] s vescica
blade [bled] s (of a leaf) pagina; (of grass) stelo, filo; (of oar) pala; (of turbine) paletta; (of fan) ventola; (of knife) lama; (coll) caposcarico
blame [blem] s colpa; **to be to blame for** aver la colpa di; **to put the blame on s.o. for s.th** attribuire a qlcu la colpa di qlco; **you are to blame** è colpa Sua || tr biasimare, incolpare
blameless ['blemlɪs] adj innocente, senza colpa
blanch [blæntʃ] or [blɑntʃ] tr bianchire || intr impallidire
bland [blænd] adj blando; (weather) mite
blandish ['blændɪʃ] tr blandire
blank [blæŋk] adj (not written on) in bianco; (e.g., stare) vuoto; (utter) completo || s (printed form) modulo; (cartridge) cartuccia a salve; (of the mind) lacuna; **to draw a blank** (coll) non avere alcun successo || tr—**to blank out** cancellare
blank' check' s assegno in bianco; (fig) carta bianca
blanket ['blæŋkɪt] adj generale, combinato || s coperta; (of snow) cappa || tr coprire con una coperta; oscurare
blank' verse' s verso sciolto
blare [bler] s squillo || tr proclamare; fare echeggiare || intr squillare; echeggiare
blaspheme [blæs'fim] tr & intr bestemmiare
blasphemous ['blæsfɪməs] adj bestemmiatore
blasphe·my ['blæsfɪmi] s (-mies) bestemmia
blast [blæst] or [blɑst] s (of air) raffica; (of a horn) squillo; (blight) rovina; scoppio, esplosione; **at full blast** a piena velocità || tr rovinare; fare scoppiare, far saltare || intr—**to blast off** (rok) lanciarsi
blast' fur'nace s altoforno
blast'off' s lancio di missile or di nave spaziale
blatant ['bletənt] adj (noisy) rumoroso; (obtrusive) palmare; (flashy) chiassoso
blaze [blez] s fiammata; splendore m; (on a horse's head) stella; **in a blaze** in fiamme || tr proclamare; **to blaze a**

trail marcare il cammino ‖ *intr* divampare

bleach [blit∫] *s* candeggio, candeggina ‖ *tr* imbiancare, candeggiare

bleachers ['blit∫ərz] *spl* posti *mpl* allo scoperto or di gradinata

bleak [blik] *adj* nudo, deserto; (*cold*) freddo; (*gloomy*) triste

blear·y ['bliri] *adj* (-ier; iest) (*sight*) cisposo; confuso; offuscato

bleat [blit] *s* belato ‖ *intr* belare

bleed [blid] *v* (*pret & pp* **bled** [bled]) *tr* (*to draw blood from*) salassare; (*a tree*) estrare linfa da; (coll) sfruttare ‖ *intr* sanguinare; (*said of a tree*) dar linfa; **to bleed to death** morire dissanguato

blemish ['blemi∫] *s* difetto; macchia ‖ *tr* danneggiare; macchiare

blend [blend] *s* mescolanza, miscuglio; (*of gasoline*) miscela ‖ *v* (*pret & pp* **blended** or **blent** [blent]) *tr* mescolare, miscelare ‖ *intr* mescolarsi, mischiarsi; armonizzare; fondersi

bless [bles] *tr* benedire; (*to endow*) dotare; (*to make happy*) allietare

blessed ['blesid] *adj* benedetto; beato; fortunato; dotato

bless'ed event' *s* lieto evento

blessing ['blesiŋ] *s* benedizione

blight [blait] *s* (*insect; disease*) piaga; rovina; (*fungus*) ruggine *f* ‖ *tr* rovinare, guastare

blimp [blimp] *s* piccolo dirigibile

blind [blaind] *adj* cieco; (slang) ubriaco ‖ *s* persiana; tendina; (*decoy*) mascheratura; pretesto ‖ *adv* alla cieca ‖ *tr* accecare

blind' al'ley *s* vicolo cieco

blinder ['blaindər] *s* paraocchi *m*

blind' fly'ing *s* (aer) volo senza visibilità

blind'fold' *adj* bendato, cogli occhi bendati ‖ *s* benda ‖ *tr* bendare gli occhi a

blindly ['blaindli] *adv* alla cieca

blind' man' *s* cieco

blind'man's buff' *s* mosca cieca

blindness ['blaindnis] *s* cecità *f*

blind' spot' *s* (anat) punto cieco; (rad) zona di silenzio; (fig) debole *m*

blink [bliŋk] *s* batter *m* di ciglio; (*glimpse*) occhiata; (*glimmer*) barlume *m*; **on the blink** (slang) fuori servizio ‖ *tr*—**to blink one's eyes** batter il ciglio ‖ *intr* occhieggiare; (*to wink*) ammiccare; (*to flash on and off*) lampeggiare; **to blink at** ignorare; far finta di non vedere

blinker ['bliŋkər] *s* (*at a crossing*) luce *f* intermittente; (*on a horse*) paraocchi *m*

blip [blip] *s* guizzo sullo schermo radar

bliss [blis] *s* beatitudine *f*, felicità *f*

blissful ['blisfəl] *adj* beato, felice

blister ['blistər] *s* vescica, bolla ‖ *tr* coprire di vesciche; (fig) bollare ‖ *intr* coprirsi di vesciche

blithe [blaið] *adj* gaio, giocondo

blitzkrieg ['blits‚krig] *s* guerra lampo

blizzard ['blizərd] *s* tormenta, ventoneve *m*

bloat [blot] *tr* gonfiare ‖ *intr* gonfiarsi

blob [blɑb] *s* (*lump*) zolla; (*of liquid*) macchia

block [blɑk] *s* (*e.g., of wood*) blocco; (*for chopping*) ceppo; (*pulley*) puleggia; ostacolo; (*of houses*) isolato; (typ) cliché *m* ‖ *tr* bloccare; (*a hat*) mettere in forma; **to block up** tappare

blockade [blɑ'ked] *s* blocco; **to run a blockade** forzare il blocco ‖ *tr* bloccare

block' and tack'le *s* bozzello

block'bust'er *s* (coll) superbomba

block'head' *s* imbecille *mf*

block' let'ter *s* carattere *m* stampatello

block' sig'nal *s* (rr) segnale di blocco

blond [blɑnd] *adj & s* biondo

blonde [blɑnd] *s* bionda

blood [blʌd] *s* sangue *m*; **in cold blood** a sangue freddo; **to draw blood** ferire, fare sanguinare

blood' bank' *s* emoteca

bloodcurdling ['blʌd‚kʌrdliŋ] *adj* orripilante

blood' do'nor *s* donatore *m* di sangue

blood'hound' *s* segugio

bloodless ['blʌdlis] *adj* esangue; (*e.g., revolution*) senza effusione di sangue

blood'mobile' [mo‚bil] *s* autoemoteca

blood' poi'soning *s* avvelenamento del sangue

blood' pres'sure *s* pressione sanguigna

blood' rela'tion *s* consanguineo

blood'shed' *s* spargimento di sangue, carneficina

blood'shot' *adj* iniettato di sangue

blood'stained' *adj* macchiato di sangue

blood'stream' *s* circolazione sanguigna

blood'suck'er *s* sanguisuga

blood' test' *s* esame *m* del sangue

blood'thirst'y *adj* assetato di sangue

blood' transfu'sion *s* trasfusione di sangue

blood' type' *s* gruppo sanguigno

blood' ves'sel *s* vaso sanguigno

blood·y ['blʌdi] *adj* (-ier; -iest) sanguinoso; (*bloodthirsty*) avido di sangue ‖ *v* (*pret & pp* -ied) *tr* macchiare di sangue

bloom [blum] *s* fiore *m*; (*state of having open buds*) sboccio; (*youthful glow*) incarnato ‖ *intr* fiorire; sbocciare

bloomers ['blumərz] *spl* pantaloni *mpl* femminili larghi fermati sotto il ginocchio

blossom ['blɑsəm] *s* fiore *m*; sboccio ‖ *intr* sbocciare

blot [blɑt] *s* macchia ‖ *v* (*pret & pp* **blotted**; *ger* **blotting**) *tr* macchiare; (*with blotting paper*) asciugare; **to blot out** cancellare; oscurare ‖ *intr* macchiarsi; (*to be absorbent*) essere assorbente; (*said of a pen*) fare macchie

blotch [blɑt∫] *s* chiazza, macchia ‖ *tr* chiazzare

blotter ['blɑtər] *s* carta asciugante, carta assorbente; (*book*) registro

blouse [blaus] *s* blusa

blow [blo] *s* colpo; (*blast*) folata; (*of*

horn) squillo; (*sudden reverse*) batosta; **at one blow** d'un sol colpo; **to come to blows** venire alle mani; **without striking a blow** senza colpo ferire || *v* (*pret* **blew** [blu]; *pp* **blown**) *tr* soffiare, soffiare su; (*an instrument*) suonare; (*one's nose*) soffiarsi; **to blow in** sfondare; **to blow one's brains out** bruciarsi le cervella; **to blow open** aprire completamente; **to blow out** (*e.g., a candle*) spegnere; (*a fuse*) fondere; **to blow up** (*e.g., a mine*) far brillare; (phot) ingrandire || *intr* soffiare; (*to pant*) ansimare; (*with an instrument*) suonare; (*to puff*) sbuffare; (slang) andarsene; **to blow hot and cold** cambiare d'opinione ogni cinque minuti; **to blow in** (coll) arrivare inaspettatamente; **to blow out** (*said, e.g., of a candle*) spegnersi; (*said of a fuse*) saltare, fondersi; (*said of a tire*) scoppiare; **to blow over** passare; **to blow up** saltar per aria; (*said of a storm*) scoppiare; (coll) perdere la pazienza, scoppiare d'ira

blow'out' *s* scoppio di un pneumatico

blow'pipe' *s* (*tube*) soffione *m*; (*peashooter*) cerbottana

blow'torch' *s* saldatrice *f* a benzina

blubber ['blʌbər] *s* grasso di balena || *intr* piangere, lamentarsi

bludgeon ['blʌdʒən] *s* randello || *tr* randellare

blue [blu] *adj* blu, azzurro; (*gloomy*) triste; (*e.g., laws*) puritanico || *s* blu *m*, azzurro; **out of the blue** inaspettatamente; **the blues** la malinconia; (mus) **blues** *m*; **to have the blues** essere giù di morale || *tr* tingere di azzurro; (*a metal*) brunire

blue'ber'ry *s* (-ries) mirtillo

blue'bird' *s* uccello azzurro

blue' blood' *s* sangue *m* blu

blue' cheese' *s* gorgonzola americano

blue' chip' *s* (fin) azione di prim'ordine

blue' jay' *s* ghiandaia azzurra

blue' moon' *s*—**once in a blue moon** ad ogni morte di papa

blue'-pen'cil *v* (*pret & pp* -ciled or -cilled; *ger* -ciling or -cilling) *tr* correggere col lapis blu

blue'print' *s* riproduzione cianografica; (*plan*) piano || *tr* riprodurre in cianografia; preparare dettagliatamente

blue'stock'ing *s* saccente *f*, sapientona

blue' streak' *s*—**like a blue streak** (coll) come un razzo

bluff [blʌf] *adj* scosceso; brusco, burbero || *s* promontorio scosceso; bluff *m*; bluffatore *m* || *intr* bluffare

bluing ['bluɪŋ] *s* turchinetto

bluish ['bluɪʃ] *adj* bluastro

blunder ['blʌndər] *s* errore *m* madornale || *intr* pigliare un granchio

blunt [blʌnt] *adj* ottuso; (*plain-spoken*) franco || *tr* rendere ottuso

bluntness ['blʌntnɪs] *s* ottusità *f*; franchezza

blur [blʌr] *s* macchia; offuscamento; confusione || *v* (*pret & pp* **blurred**;

ger **blurring**) *tr* macchiare; (*the view*) offuscare

blurb [blʌrb] *s* annuncio pubblicitario

blurt [blʌrt] *tr*—**to blurt out** prorompere a dire, lasciarsi sfuggire

blush [blʌʃ] *s* rossore *m*; (*pinkish natural tinge*) incarnato || *intr* arrossire; **to blush at** vergognarsi di

bluster ['blʌstər] *s* frastuono; (fig) boria || *intr* (*said of the wind*) infuriare; fare il bravaccio

blustery ['blʌstəri] *adj* tempestuoso; violento; (*swaggering*) borioso

boar [bor] *s* verro; (*wild hog*) porco selvatico, cinghiale *m*

board [bord] *s* asse *m*; (*notice*) cartello; (*pasteboard*) cartone *m*; (*table*) tavola; (*meals*) vitto; (*group of administrators*) consiglio; (naut) bordo; **above board** franco; **in boards** rilegato; **on board** a bordo; (rr) in vettura; **to go by the board** andare in rovina; **to tread the boards** fare l'attore || *tr* chiudere con assi; (*to provide with meals*) dare pensione a, tenere a dozzina; (*a ship*) salire a bordo di; (*a train*) salire su; (naut) abbordare || *intr* essere a pensione

board' and lodg'ing *s* pensione completa

boarder ['bordər] *s* pensionante *mf*

board'ing house' *s* pensione di famiglia

board'ing school' *s* collegio di pensionanti

board' of direc'tors *s* consiglio d'amministrazione

board' of health' *s* ufficio d'igiene

board' of trade' *s* camera di commercio

board'walk' *s* passeggiata a mare

boast [bost] *s* millanteria, vanteria || *intr* vantarsi

boastful ['bostfəl] *adj* millantatore

boat [bot] *s* nave *f*, battello; (*small ship*) barca, imbarcazione; (*dish*) salsiera; **in the same boat** nella stessa situazione

boat' hook' *s* alighiero

boat'house' *s* capannone *m* per i canotti

boating ['botɪŋ] *s* escursione in barca

boat'man *s* (-men) barcaiolo

boat' race' *s* regata

boatswain ['bosən] or ['bot,swen] *s* nostromo

bob [bab] *s* (*plumb*) piombino; (*short haircut*) taglio alla bebè; coda mozza (*di cavallo*); (*jerky motion*) strattone *m*; (*on pendulum of clock*) lente *f*; (*on fishing line*) sughero || *v* (*pret & pp* **bobbed**; *ger* **bobbing**) *tr* tagliare alla bebè; far muovere a scatti || *intr* muoversi a scatti; fare mossa; **to bob up** apparire

bobbin ['babɪn] *s* bobina

bob'by pin' ['babi] *s* forcina

bob'by·socks' *spl* (coll) calzini *mpl* da ragazza

bobbysoxer ['babi,saksər] *s* (coll) ragazzina

bobolink ['babə,lɪŋk] *s* dolicònice *m*

bob'sled' *s* guidoslitta

bode [bod] *tr & intr* presagire

bodice ['badɪs] *s* giubbetto, copribusto

bodily ['bɑdɪlɪ] *adj* fisico, corporeo ‖ *adv* fisicamente, corporeamente; di persona; in massa

bodkin ['bɑdkɪn] *s* punteruolo; (*for lady's hair*) spillone *m*

bod·y ['bɑdɪ] *s* (-**ies**) corpo; (*corpse*) cadavere *m*; (*of water*) massa; (*of people*) gruppo; (*of a liquid*) sostanza; (*of truck*) cassone *m*; (*of car*) carrozzeria; (*of tree*) tronco; (*coll*) persona; **in a body** in massa

bod'y·guard' *s* (*of a high official*) guardia del corpo; (*e.g., of a movie star*) guardaspalle *m*

bod'y suit' *s* calzamaglia

bog [bɑg] *s* pantano, palude *m* ‖ (*pret & pp* **bogged**; *ger* **bogging**) *intr*—**to bog down** impelagarsi

bogey·man ['bogɪ,mæn] *s* (-**men** [men]) babau *m*

bogus ['bogəs] *adj* (coll) falso, finto

Bohemian [bo'himɪ·ən] *adj* boemo; da bohémien ‖ *s* boemo; (fig) bohémien *m*

boil [bɔɪl] *s* bollore *m*, ebollizione; (pathol) foruncolo; **to come to a boil** cominciare a bollire ‖ *tr* bollire; **to boil down** condensare ‖ *intr* bollire; **to boil away** evaporare completamente; **to boil down** condensarsi; **to boil over** andare per il fuoco

boiled' ham' *s* prosciutto cotto

boiler ['bɔɪlər] *s* caldaia; (*for cooking*) caldaio

boil'er·mak'er *s* calderaio

boiling ['bɔɪlɪŋ] *adj* bollente ‖ *s* bollore *m*, ebollizione

boisterous ['bɔɪstərəs] *adj* (*storm*) violento; (*loud*) rumoroso

bold [bold] *adj* (*daring*) coraggioso; (*impudent*) sfacciato; (*steep*) scosceso; (*clear, sharp*) netto

bold'face' *s* (typ) neretto, grassetto

boldness ['boldnɪs] *s* coraggio, audacia; sfacciataggine *f*, impudenza

boll' wee'vil [bol] *s* antonomo del cotone

bologna [bə'lonə] or [bə'lonjə] *s* mortadella

Bolshevik ['bɑlʃəvɪk] or ['bolʃəvɪk] *adj & mf* bolscevico

bolster ['bolstər] *s* cuscino; cuscinetto; (*support*) sostegno ‖ *tr* sorreggere; **to bolster up** sostenere

bolt [bolt] *s* (*arrow*) freccia; (*of lightning*) fulmine *m*; (*sliding bar*) chiavistello; (*threaded rod*) bullone *m*; (*of paper or cloth*) pezza, rotolo ‖ *adv*—**bolt upright** dritto come un fuso ‖ *tr* (*to swallow hurriedly*) ingollare; (*to fasten, e.g., a door*) sprangare; (*to fasten, e.g., two metal parts*) bullonare; (*e.g., a political party*) abbandonare ‖ *intr* (*said of people*) spiccare un salto; (*said of a horse*) prendere la mano; precipitarsi

bolt' from the blue' *s* fulmine *m* a ciel sereno

bomb [bɑm] *s* bomba; (*e.g., for spraying*) bombola ‖ *tr* bombardare

bombard [bɑm'bɑrd] *tr* bombardare; (*with questions*) bersagliare

bombardment [bɑm'bɑrdmənt] *s* bombardamento

bombast ['bɑmbæst] *s* ampollosità *f*

bombastic [bɑm'bæstɪk] *adj* ampolloso

bomb' cra'ter *s* cratere *m*

bomber ['bɑmər] *s* bombardiere *m*

bomb'proof' *adj* a prova di bomba

bomb'shell' *s* bomba; (fig) colpo di bomba, colpo di sorpresa

bomb' shel'ter *s* rifugio antiaereo

bomb'sight' *s* traguardo aereo

bona fide ['bonə,faɪdə] *adj* sincero ‖ *adv* in buona fede

bonanza [bə'nænzə] *s* (min) ricca vena; (coll) fortuna

bond [bɑnd] *s* legame *m*, vincolo; (*contractual obligation*) obbligazione; (*interest-bearing certificate*) buono, obbligazione; (*surety*) cauzione; **bonds** catene *fpl;* **in bond** sotto cauzione; (*said of goods*) in punto franco ‖ *tr* unire, connettere

bondage ['bɑndɪdʒ] *s* schiavitù *f*

bond'ed ware'house *s* deposito in punto franco

bond'hold'er *s* obbligazionista *mf*

bonds'man *s* (-**men**) garante *m*

bone [bon] *s* osso; (*of fish*) spina; (*of whale*) stecca; **bones** ossa *fpl;* **to have a bone to pick with** avere un conto da regolare con; **to make no bones about** (coll) ammettere; (coll) parlare esplicitamente ‖ *tr* dissossare; cavare le spine a ‖ *intr*—**to bone up on** (coll) ripassare

bone'head' *s* (coll) testa dura

boneless ['bonlɪs] *adj* senz'osso; (*fish*) senza spine

boner ['bonər] *s* (slang) errore *m* madornale

bonfire ['bɑn,faɪr] *s* falò *m*

bonnet ['bɑnɪt] *s* cappello da donna; (*of child*) berrettino

bonus ['bonəs] *s* gratifica; indennità *f*; (*to an outgoing employee*) buonuscita

bon·y ['bonɪ] *adj* (-**ier; -iest**) (*having bones*) osseo; (*emaciated*) scarno; (*fish*) spinoso

boo [bu] *s* fischio, urlaccio ‖ *tr & intr* fischiare, disapprovare

boo·by ['bubɪ] *s* (-**bies**) stupido

boo'by hatch' *s* (naut) portello; (slang) manicomio; (slang) prigione *f*

boo'by prize' *s* premio dato al peggior giocatore

boo'by trap' *s* (mil) trappola esplosiva; (fig) tranello

boogie-woogie ['bugɪ'wugɪ] *s* bughi-bughi *m*

book [bʊk] *s* libro; (*e.g., of matches*) pacchetto; (mus) libretto; (fig) regole *fpl;* **the Book** la Bibbia; **to be in one's book** essere nelle grazie di; **to bring s.o. to book** fare una ramanzina a ‖ *tr* registrare; (*e.g., on a horse*) allibrare; (*e.g., a room*) prenotare; (*an actor*) scritturare

book'bind'er *s* rilegatore *m*

book'bind'er·y *s* (-**ies**) rilegatoria

book'bind'ing *s* rilegatura

book'case' *s* scaffale *m*

book' end' *s* reggilibri *m*

bookie ['buki] s (coll) allibratore m

booking ['bukɪŋ] s (of a trip) prenotazione; (of an actor) scrittura

book'ing clerk' s impiegato alla biglietteria

bookish ['bukɪʃ] adj studioso; libresco

book'keep'er s contabile mf

booklet ['buklɪt] s libretto; (pamphlet) opus olo

book'keep'ing s contabilità f

book'mak'er s (one who accepts bets) allibratore m

book'mi rk' s segnalibro

bookmobile ['bukmo ,bil] s bibliobus m

book'plate' s ex libris m

book' review' s rassegna, recensione

book'sell'er s libraio

book'shelf' s (-shelves) scaffale m

book'stand' s (rack) scansia; (stall) edi ola

book'store' s libreria

book'worm' s (zool) tarlo dei libri; (t,g) topo da biblioteca

boom [bum] s (of crane) braccio; (barrier) barriera galleggiante; (noise) bum m; (fin) boom m; (naut) boma; (mov, telv) giraffa || intr rimbombare; essere in condizioni floride

boomerang ['bumə ,ræŋ] s bumerang m

boom' town' s città f fungo

boon [bun] s fortuna, benedizione

boon' compan'ion s compagnone m

boor [bur] s bifolco, zotico

boorish ['burɪʃ] adj grossolano

boost [bust] s aumento; (coll) spinta || tr spingere in su; sostenere; (prices) alzare; parlare a favore di

booster ['bustər] s (backer) sostenitore m; propulsore m a razzo; (rok) propulsore m del primo stadio; (med) seconda iniezione

boot [but] s stivale m; (kick) calcio; (patch) (aut) pezza; the boot is on the other foot la situazione è rovesciata; to be in the boots of essere nella pelle di; to boot per di più; to get the boot (coll) essere messo sulla strada; to lick the boots of leccare i piedi a; to wipe one's boots on trattare come una pezza da piedi || tr dare un calcio a; to boot out (slang) buttar fuori

boot'black' s lustrascarpe m

booth [buθ] s (stall) banco da mercato; (for telephoning, voting) cabina

boot'jack' s tirastivali m

boot'leg' adj di contrabbando || s liquore m di contrabbando || v (pret & pp -legged; ger -legging) tr vendere di contrabbando || intr vendere alcol di contrabbando

bootlegger ['but ,legər] s contrabbandiere m di liquori

boot'lick'er [,lɪkər] s (coll) leccapiedi mf

boot'strap' s tirante m degli stivali

boo-ty ['buti] s (-ties) bottino

booze [buz] s (coll) bevanda alcolica || intr (coll) ubriacarsi

borax ['boræks] s borace m

border ['bordər] adj confinario, con-

finante || s bordo, margine m; (between two countries) confine m || tr bordare; confinare con || intr con-linare

bor'der clash' s incidente m ai confini

bor der-line' adj incerto || s frontiera

bore [bor] s (drill hole) buco, foro; (hollow part of gun) anima; (caliber) calibro; (dull person) seccatore m; (annoyance) seccatura; (mach) alesaggio || tr bucare, forare, seccare; (ma h) alesare

boreom ['bordəm] s noia, tedio

boring ['borɪŋ] adj noioso || s trivellazione

born [born] adj nato, partorito; to be born a scere; to be born again rinascere; to be born with a silver spoon in one's mouth nascere con la camicia

borough ['bʌro] s borgata, comune m

borrow ['baro] or ['boro] tr chiedere a or in prestito; prendere a or in prestito; ricevere a or in prestito; (to adopt) adottare; to borrow trouble preo uparsi per nulla

borrower ['baro-ər] or ['boro-ər] s chi riceve a prestito; (law) comodatario, prestatario

borrowing ['baro-ɪŋ] or ['boro-ɪŋ] s prestito; prestito linguistico, forestierismo

bosom ['buzəm] s petto, seno; (e.g., of the family) grembo, seno; (of shirt) pettorina

bos'om friend' s amico del cuore

Bosporus ['baspərəs] s Bosforo

boss [bos] or [bas] s (coll) padrone m; (coll) direttore m; (coll) capintesta m; (coll) principale m; (archit) bugna, bozza || tr fare da padrone a || intr fare da padrone

boss-y ['bosi] or ['basi] adj (-ier; -iest) autoritario

botanical [bə'tænɪkəl] adj botanico

botanist ['batənɪst] s botanico

botany ['batəni] s botanica

botch [batʃ] s abborracciatura || tr abborracciare

both [boθ] adj entrambi i, tutti e due i || pron entrambi, tutti e due || conj del pari, al medesimo tempo; both . . . and tanto . . . quanto

bother ['baðər] s (worry) noia, seccatura; (person) seccatore m || tr dar noia a, seccare || intr preoccuparsi; to bother about or with occuparsi di; to bother to + inf molestarsi di + inf

bothersome ['baðərsəm] adj incomodo

bottle ['batəl] s bottiglia, fiasco || tr imbottigliare; to bottle up imbottigliare

bot'tle cap' s tappo a corona

bot'tle-neck' s collo di bottiglia; (of traffic) congestione, imbottigliamento

bot'tle o'pener ['opənər] s apribottiglie m

bottom ['batəm] adj basso; (price, dollar) ultimo; infimo || s fondo; (of chair) sedile m; base f; (of bottle) culo; (of ship) scafo; at bottom in realtà; to begin at the bottom cominciare dalla gavetta; **to get at the bottom of** andare a fondo di; **to go to the bottom** andare a picco

bottomless [ˈbatəmlɪs] *adj* senza fondo

boudoir [buˈdwar] *s* gabinetto di toletta (da signora)

bough [bau] *s* ramo

bouillon [ˈbujan] *s* brodo schietto

boulder [ˈboldər] *s* masso, roccia

boulevard [ˈbulə‿vard] *s* corso

bounce [bauns] *s* balzo; salto; elasticità *f*; (*of boat or plane*) piastrellamento; (*fig*) spirito; **to get the bounce** (slang) essere licenziato || *tr* far balzare; (slang) buttar fuori || *intr* rimbalzare; saltare; (aer, naut) piastrellare

bouncer [ˈbaunsər] *s* (*in night club*) (slang) buttafuori *m*

bouncing [ˈbaunsɪŋ] *adj* forte, vigoroso; grande, rumoroso

bound [baund] *adj* legato; collegato; obbligato; (bb) rilegato; (coll) risoluto; **bound for** destinato a, diretto per; **bound up in** or **with** in strette relazioni con; assorto in || *s* salto; rimbalzo; limite *m*; **bounds** zona limitrofa; **out of bounds** fuori limiti; al di là delle convenienze || *tr* delimitare

bounda·ry [ˈbaundəri] *s* (**-ries**) confine *m*, limite *m*

bound'ary stone' *s* pietra di confine

boundless [ˈbaundlɪs] *adj* illimitato, sconfinato

bountiful [ˈbauntɪfəl] *adj* generoso; abbondante

boun·ty [ˈbaunti] *s* (**-ties**) dono generoso; generosità *f*, abbondanza; (*reward*) premio

bouquet [buˈke] or [boˈke] *s* mazzo, mazzolino; profumo, aroma *m*

bourgeois [ˈburʒwa] *adj & s* borghese *mf*

bourgeoisie [‿burʒwaˈzi] *s* borghesia

bout [baut] *s* lotta, contesa; (*of illness*) attacco

bow [bau] *s* inchino, riverenza; (naut) prua; **to take a bow** ricevere gli applausi || *tr* chinare, piegare || *intr* inchinarsi; sottomettersi; **to bow and scrape** fare riverenza || [bo] *s* (*weapon*) arco; (*knot*) nodo; (mus) archetto; (*stroke of bow*) (mus) arcata || *tr & intr* (mus) suonare con l'archetto

bowdlerize [ˈbaudlə‿raɪz] *tr* espurgare

bowel [ˈbau‿əl] *s* budello; **bowels** viscere *fpl*

bow'el move'ment *s* evacuazione; **to have a bowel movement** andar di corpo

bower [ˈbau‿ər] *s* pergolato

bowery [ˈbau‿əri] *adj* frondoso

bowknot [ˈbo‿nat] *s* nodo scorsoio

bowl [bol] *s* (*dish*) ciotola; (*cup*) tazza; (*of pipe*) fornello; (*basin*) catino; (*amphitheater*) arena; (*ball*) boccia; (*delivery of ball*) bocciata; **bowls** bocce *fpl* || *tr* bocciare; **to bowl down** or **over** abbattere || *intr* giocare alle bocce

bowlegged [ˈbo‿legd] or [ˈbo‿legɪd] *adj* con le gambe storte

bowler [ˈbolər] *s* giocatore *m* di bocce

bowling [ˈbolɪŋ] *s* bocce *fpl*; bowling *m*, birilli *mpl*

bowl'ing al'ley *s* pista per il bowling; bowling *m*

bowl'ing green' *s* campo di bocce erboso

bowshot [ˈbo‿ʃat] *s* tiro d'arco

bowsprit [ˈbausprit] or [ˈbosprit] *s* (naut) bompresso

bow' tie' [bo] *s* cravatta a farfalla

bowwow [ˈbau‿wau] *interj* bau bau!

box [baks] *s* scatola; cassa; (*for jury*) banco; (*for sentry*) garitta; (*on coach*) cassetta; (*in stable*) posta; (*slap*) ceffone *m*; (*with fist*) pugno; (bot) bosso; (theat) palco, barcaccia; (baseball) posto del battitore; (typ) riquadratura || *tr* mettere in scatola; (*to slap*) schiaffeggiare; (*to hit with fist*) fare a pugilato con; **to box in** or **up** rinchiudere || *intr* fare a pugni; combattere

box'car' *s* vagone *m* merci coperto

boxer [ˈbaksər] *s* pugile *m*

box'hold'er *s* palchettista *mf*

boxing [ˈbaksɪŋ] *s* pugilato

box'ing gloves' *spl* guantoni *mpl* da pugilato

box' of'fice *s* sportello, biglietteria; (theat) incasso; (theat) successo

box'-of'fice hit' *s* grande successo

box' pleat' *s* (*of skirt*) cannone *m*

box' seat' *s* posto in palco

box'wood' *s* bosso

boy [bɔɪ] *s* ragazzo, giovane *m* || *interj* accidempoli!

boycott [ˈbɔɪkat] *s* boicottaggio || *tr* boicottare

boy'friend' *s* innamorato, amico

boyhood [ˈbɔɪhud] *s* fanciullezza

boyish [ˈbɔɪ‿ɪʃ] *adj* giovanile

boy' scout' *s* giovane esploratore *m*

bra [bra] *s* (coll) reggiseno

brace [bres] *s* (*couple*) paio; (*device for maintaining tension*) tirante *m*; (*prop*) sostegno; (*tool*) trapano; (typ) graffa; **braces** (Brit) bretelle *fpl* || *tr* legare; serrare; puntellare; sostenere; invigorare; **to brace oneself** pigliare animo || *intr*—**to brace up** (coll) pigliare animo

brace' and bit' *s* menarola, trapano

bracelet [ˈbreslɪt] *s* braccialetto

bracer [ˈbresər] *s* (coll) bicchierino

bracket [ˈbrækɪt] *s* mensola; (*for lamp*) braccio; angolo; classifica; (typ) parentesi quadra || *tr* sostenere con mensola; mettere tra parentesi quadra; classificare

brackish [ˈbrækɪʃ] *adj* salmastro

brad [bræd] *s* chiodino, punta

brag [bræg] *s* vanto || *v* (*pret & pp* **bragged;** *ger* **bragging**) *intr* vantare

braggart [ˈbrægərt] *s* millantatore *m*

Brah·man [ˈbramən] *s* (**-mans**) bramino

braid [bred] *s* treccia; (*strip of cloth*) spighetta; (mil) cordellina || *tr* intrecciare; decorare con spighette

brain [bren] *s* cervello; **brains** cervello, intelligenza; **to rack one's brains** rompersi la testa || *tr* far saltare le cervella di

brain'child' *s* (coll) parto dell'ingegno, idea geniale

brain' drain' *s* (coll) fuga di cervelli

brainless ['brenlɪs] *adj* senza testa

brain' pow'er *s* intelligenza

brain'storm' *s* (coll) ispirazione

brain' trust' *s* consiglio d'esperti

brain'wash'ing *s* lavaggio del cervello

brain' wave' *s* onda encefalica; (coll) idea geniale

brain'work' *s* lavoro intellettuale

brain•y ['breni] *adj* (**-ier; -iest**) intelligente

braise [brez] *tr* (culin) brasare

brake [brek] *s* freno; (*thicket*) macchia || *tr & intr* frenare

brake' drum' *s* tamburo del freno

brake' lin'ing *s* ferodo

brake'man *s* (**-men**) frenatore *m*

brake' shoe' *s* ganascia

bramble ['bræmbəl] *s* rovo

bran [bræn] *s* crusca

branch [bræntʃ] *s* (*of tree*) branca, ramo; (*of river*) braccio; (*of a family*) ramo; (*of business*) filiale *f*; (rr) diramazione || *intr* biforcarsi; **to branch off** *or* **out** ramificarsi, diramarsi

branch' line' *s* ferrovia di diramazione

branch' of'fice *s* succursale *f*

brand [brænd] *s* (*burning stick*) tizzone *m*; (*mark; stigma*) marchio; (*label; make*) marca || *tr* (*to mark with a brand*) marchiare; (*to put a stigma on*) bollare; **to brand as** tacciare di

brandied ['brændid] *adj* conservato in acquavite

brand'ing i'ron *s* ferro da marchio

brandish ['brændɪʃ] *tr* brandire

brand'-new' *adj* nuovo fiammante

bran•dy ['brændi] *s* (**-dies**) cognac *m*, acquavite *f*

brash [bræʃ] *adj* (*too hasty*) avventato; (*insolent*) impudente || *s* frammenti *mpl*; attacco (di malattia), indigestione

brass [bræs] *or* [brɑs] *s* ottone *m*; (coll) faccia tosta; (slang) alti ufficiali; **brasses** (mus) ottoni *mpl*

brass' band' *s* fanfara

brassiere [brə'zir] *s* reggiseno

brass' knuck'les *spl* tirapugni *m*

brass' tack' *s* chiodino *or* borchia d'ottone; **to get down to brass tacks** (coll) venire al sodo

brass•y ['bræsi] *or* ['brɑsi] *adj* (**-ier; -iest**) fatto d'ottone, sfacciato, impudente

brat [bræt] *s* marmocchio, monello

brava•do [brə'vɑdo] *s* (**-does** *or* **-dos**) bravata

brave [brev] *adj* coraggioso || *s* persona coraggiosa; guerriero indiano || *tr* (*to defy*) sfidare; (*to meet with courage*) affrontare

bravery ['brevəri] *s* coraggio

bra•vo ['brɑvo] *s* (**-vos**) bravo; applauso || *interj* bravo!

brawl [brɔl] *s* zuffa, rissa || *intr* azzuffarsi, rissare

brawn [brɔn] *s* forza muscolare

brawn•y ['brɔni] *adj* (**-ier; -iest**) muscoloso

bray [bre] *s* raglio || *intr* ragliare

braze [brez] *s* brasatura || *tr* brasare

brazen ['brezən] *adj* d'ottone; (*shameless*) sfrontato; (*sound*) penetrante || *tr*—**to brazen out** *or* **through** affrontare sfacciatamente

brazier ['breʒər] *s* caldano, braciere *m*; (*workman*) ottonaio

Brazil [brə'zɪl] *s* il Brasile

Brazilian [brə'zɪljən] *adj & s* brasiliano

Brazil' nut' *s* noce *f* del Brasile

breach [britʃ] *s* (*gap*) breccia; (*failure to observe a law*) infrazione || *tr* fare breccia su, fare varco in

breach' of faith' *s* abuso di confidenza

breach' of prom'ise *s* rottura di promessa di matrimonio

breach' of the peace' *s* violazione dell'ordine pubblico

bread [brɛd] *s* pane *m*; **to break bread with** sedersi a tavola con || *tr* impannare

bread' and but'ter *s* pane *m* e burro; (coll) pane quotidiano

bread' crumbs' *spl* pangrattato

breaded ['brɛdɪd] *adj* impannato

bread' knife' *s* coltello da pane

bread' line' *s* coda del pane

bread' stick' *s* grissino

breadth [brɛdθ] *s* (*width*) larghezza; (*scope*) ampiezza

bread'win'ner *s* sostegno della famiglia

break [brek] *s* interruzione; intervallo; omissione; (*breaking*) rottura; (*of bones*) frattura; (*of day*) fare *m*, spuntare *m*; (*sudden change*) mutamento; (*from jail*) evasione; (*luck*) (coll) fortuna; **to give s.o. a break** dare a qlcu l'opportunità || *v* (*pret* **broke** [brok]; *pp* **broken**) *tr* (*to smash*) rompere, spezzare; (*to tame*) domare; (*to demote*) destituire; (*a record*) superare; (*to violate*) violare; (*to make bankrupt*) mandare al fallimento; (*to interrupt*) interrompere; (*to reduce the effects of*) attutire; (*to disclose*) rivelare; (*to bring to an end by force*) battere; (*a banknote*) cambiare; (*one's word*) mancare (with *dat*); (*a law*) rompere; **to break asunder** separare; **to break down** analizzare; **to break in** forzare; **to break open** forzare, scassinare; **to break up** dissolvere || *intr* (*to divide*) rompersi; (*to burst*) scoppiare; (*said of voice of youngster*) cambiare; (*said of voice*) indebolirsi; (*said of a crowd*) disperdersi; (*said of weather*) rischiararsi; (*said of prices*) ribassare; (*to come into being*) scoppiare; (boxing) separarsi; **to break asunder** separarsi; **to break away** scappare; **to break down** abbattersi; (aut) essere *or* rimanere in panna; **to break even** fare patta; **to break in** irrompere; interrompere; **to break into** forzare; **to break into a run** incominciare a correre; **to break loose** liberarsi; (said of a storm) scatenarsi; **to break off** interrompere; **to break out** (said of the skin) avere un'eruzione; (said, e.g., of war) scoppiare; **to break through** aprirsi il varco; **to break up** disperdersi; **to break with** rompere le relazioni con

breakable ['brekəbəl] adj fragile

breakage ['brekɪdʒ] s rottura

break'down' s (in negotiations) rottura; (aut) panna; (chem) analisi f; (pathol) colasso

breaker ['brekər] s (wave) frangente m

breakfast ['brɛkfəst] s prima colazione || intr fare prima colazione

break'neck' adj pericoloso; **at breakneck speed** a rotta di collo, a rompicollo

break' of day' s alba

break'through' s (mil) penetrazione; (fig) scoperta sensazionale

break'up' s dispersione; dissoluzione; (of a friendship) rottura

break'wa'ter s diga, frangiflutti m

breast [brɛst] s petto; (of female) seno; (source of emotions) animo; **to make a clean breast of** fare una piena confessione di

breast'bone' s sterno

breast' drill' s trapano da petto

breast'feed' v (pret & pp -fed [fɛd]) tr allattare

breast'pin' s spilla

breast'stroke' s bracciata a rana

breath [brɛθ] s respiro, respirazione; (odor) alito; (breeze) soffio; (whisper) sussurro; (fig) vita; **out of breath** ansimante; **short of breath** corto di respiro; **to gasp for breath** respirare affannosamente; **under one's breath** sottovoce

breathe [brɪð] tr respirare; (to whisper) sussurrare; **to breathe one's last** esalare l'ultimo sospiro; **to not breathe a word** non dire una parola || intr respirare; **to breathe in** inspirare; **to breathe out** espirare

breath'ing spell' s attimo di respiro

breathless ['brɛθlɪs] adj senza fiato, ansimante; soffocante

breath'tak'ing s emozionante, commovente

breech [britʃ] s (buttocks) natiche fpl; (rear part) parte f posteriore; (of gun) culatta; **breeches** ['brɪtʃɪz] pantaloni mpl al ginocchio; pantaloni mpl da cavallo; **to wear the breeches** (coll) portare le brache

breed [brid] s razza; tipo; (stock) origine f || v (pret & pp bred [brɛd]) tr produrre; (to raise) allevare

breeder ['bridər] s allevatore m; riproduttore m

breeding ['bridɪŋ] s (e.g., of livestock) allevamento; educazione

breeze [briz] s brezza

breez·y ['brizi] adj (-ier; -iest) ventilato; (brisk) vivace, brioso

brethren ['brɛðrɪn] spl fratelli mpl

brevi·ty ['brɛvɪti] s (-ties) brevità f

brew [bru] s pozione; bevanda || tr (beer) fabbricare; (to steep) preparare; (to plot) complottare || intr (said of beer) fermentare; (said of a storm) prepararsi

brewer ['bru·ər] s birraio

brew'er's yeast' s lievito di birra

brewer·y ['bru·əri] s (-ies) birreria, fabbrica di birra

bribe [braɪb] s subornazione, bustarella || tr subornare, dare la bustarella a

briber·y ['braɪbəri] s (-ies) subornazione, corruzione

bric-a-brac ['brɪkə‚bræk] s bric-a-brac m, cianfrusaglia, cianfrusaglie fpl

brick [brɪk] s mattone m || tr mattonare

brick'bat' s pezzo di mattone; (coll) insulto

brick'kiln' s fornace f per mattoni

bricklayer ['brɪk‚le·ər] s muratore m

brick'yard' s deposito di mattoni

bridal ['braɪdəl] adj nuziale, da sposa

brid'al wreath' s serto nuziale

bride [braɪd] s sposa

bride'groom' s sposo

bridesmaid ['braɪdz‚med] s damigella d'onore

bridge [brɪdʒ] s ponte m; (of violin) ponticello; (on a ship) ponte m di comando || tr gettare un ponte su; congiungere; **to bridge a gap** colmare una lacuna

bridge'head' s testa di ponte

bridle ['braɪdəl] s briglia || tr mettere la briglia a; (fig) frenare || intr drizzare il capo, insuperbirsi

bri'dle path' s strada cavalcabile

brief [brif] adj breve || s sommario; (law) esposto; (eccl) breve m; **briefs** slip m || tr dare istruzioni a, mettere al corrente

brief' case' s cartella, borsa d'avvocato

brier ['braɪ·ər] s radica; pipa di radica

brig [brɪg] s (naut) brigantino; (naut) prigione

brigade [brɪ'ged] s brigata

brigadier [‚brɪgə'dir] s (coll) brigadier generale m, generale m di brigata

brigand ['brɪgənd] s brigante m

brigantine ['brɪgən‚tin] or ['brɪgən‚taɪn] s (naut) brigantino goletta

bright [braɪt] adj (shining) lucido; (light) brillante; (lively) vivo; intelligente; famoso; (idea) luminoso

brighten ['braɪtən] tr illuminare; ravvivare || intr illuminarsi; ravvivarsi; rischiararsi

bright' lights' spl luci fpl abbaglianti; (aut) fari mpl abbaglianti

brilliance ['brɪljəns] or **brilliancy** ['brɪljənsi] s splendore m, scintillio

brilliant ['brɪljənt] adj brillante

brim [brɪm] s (e.g., of cup) orlo, bordo; (of hat) ala, tesa || v (pret & pp brimmed; ger brimming) intr essere pieno sino all'orlo

brim'stone' s zolfo

brine [braɪn] s salamoia; acqua di mare

bring [brɪŋ] v (pret & pp **brought**

[brɔt]) *tr* far venire; provocare; (*to carry along*) portare con sè; **to bring about** causare; **to bring around** persuadere; **to bring back** restituire; **to bring down** far abbassare; (fig) umiliare; **to bring forth** dare alla luce; **to bring forward** (*an excuse*) addurre; (math) riportare; **to bring in** introdurre; far entrare; **to bring off** compiere; **to bring on** causare; **to bring oneself to** rassegnarsi a; **to bring out** (*to expose*) rivelare; (*to offer to the public*) presentare al pubblico; (*a book*) far uscire; **to bring to** far rinvenire; (*a ship*) fermare; **to bring together** riunire; **to bring up** (*children*) allevare, tirar su; (*to introduce*) allegare; (*to cough up*) rigettare

bringing-up ['brɪŋɪŋ,ʌp] *s* educazione
brink [brɪŋk] *s* orlo
briquet [brɪ'ket] *s* bricchetta
brisk [brɪsk] *adj* (*quick*) svelto; (*sharp*) acuto; (*invigorating*) frizzante; (*gunfire*) nutrito
bristle ['brɪsəl] *s* setola || *intr* (*to be stiff*) irrigidirsi; (*said of hair*) rizzarsi; (*with anger*) adirarsi
bris·tly ['brɪsli] *adj* (-tlier; -tliest) irto di setole
British ['brɪtɪʃ] *adj* britannico || **the British** i britannici, gl'inglesi
Britisher ['brɪtɪʃər] *s* britannico
Briton ['brɪtən] *s* britannico
Brittany ['brɪtəni] *s* la Bretagna
brittle ['brɪtəl] *adj* fragile, friabile; (*crisp*) croccante
broach [brotʃ] *s* (*pin*) spilla; (*spit*) spiedo; (mach) alesatore *m* || *tr* perforare; (*a subject*) intavolare
broad [brɔd] *adj* largo; tollerante, liberale; (*daylight*) pieno; (*story*) grossolano; (*extensive*) lato; (*accent*) pronunciato
broad'cast' *s* disseminazione; (rad) radiodiffusione || *v* (*pret & pp* -cast) *tr* disseminare, diffondere || (*pret & pp* -cast or -casted*) *tr* radiodiffondere
broad'casting sta'tion *s* stazione radiotrasmittente
broad'cloth' *s* (*wool*) panno di lana; (*cotton*) popeline *f*
broaden ['brɔdən] *tr* allargare, estendere || *intr* allargarsi, estendersi
broad' jump' *s* salto in lunghezza
broadloom ['brɔd,lum] *adj* tessuto su telaio largo
broad-minded ['brɔd'maɪndɪd] *adj* di ampie vedute, liberale
broad-shouldered ['brɔd'ʃoldərd] *adj* largo di spalle
broad'side' *s* (nav) bordo; (nav) bordata; (*verbal criticism*) (coll) sfuriata; (*written criticism*) (coll) attacco violento
broad'sword' *s* spada da taglio
brocade [bro'ked] *s* broccato
broccoli ['brɑkəli] *s* broccolo; (*as food*) broccoli *mpl*
brochure [bro'ʃur] *s* opuscolo, libriccino

brogue [brog] *s* accento irlandese; scarpa forte e comoda
broil [brɔɪl] *s* cottura alla graticola; carne *f* cotta alla graticola; (*quarrel*) rissa, zuffa || *tr* cucinare alla graticola; bruciare || *intr* cucinare alla graticola; (*to quarrel*) rissare, azzuffarsi
broiler ['brɔɪlər] *s* graticola, gratella; (*chicken*) pollo da cucinare alla gratella or allo spiedo
broke [brok] *adj* (coll) al verde
broken ['brokən] *adj* rotto; fratturato; (*e.g., English*) parlato male; (*tamed*) domato
bro'ken-down' *adj* avvilito; rovinato
broken-hearted ['brokən'hɑrtɪd] *adj* affranto
broker ['brokər] *s* sensale *m*; (*on the stock exchange*) agente *m* di cambio
brokerage ['brokərɪdʒ] *s* mediazione
bromide ['bromaɪd] *s* bromuro; (coll) banalità *f*
bromine ['bromin] *s* bromo
bronchitis [brɑŋ'kaɪtɪs] *s* bronchite *f*
bron·co ['brɑŋko] *s* (-cos) puledro brado
broncobuster ['brɑŋko,bʌstər] *s* domatore *m* di puledri bradi
bronze [brɑnz] *adj* bronzeo || *s* bronzo || *tr* bronzare || *intr* abbronzarsi
brooch [brotʃ] or [brutʃ] *s* spilla
brood [brud] *s* covata, nidiata || *tr* covare || *intr* chiocciare; meditare; **to brood on or over** meditare con tristezza (su)
brook [bruk] *s* ruscello || *tr*—**to brook no** non sopportare
broom [brum] or [brum] *s* scopa; (*shrub*) saggina
broom'corn' *s* sorgo
broom'stick' *s* manico di scopa
broth [brɔθ] or [brɑθ] *s* brodo
brothel ['brɑθəl] or ['brɔðəl] *s* postribolo, bordello
brother ['brʌðər] *s* fratello
brotherhood ['brʌðər,hud] *s* fratellanza; (*association*) confraternita
broth'er-in-law' *s* (**brothers-in-law**) cognato
brotherly ['brʌðərli] *adj* fraterno || *adv* fraternamente
brow [brau] *s* ciglio; (*forehead*) fronte *f*; **to knit one's brow** aggrottare la fronte
brow'beat' *v* (*pret* -beat; *pp* -beaten) *tr* intimidire, intimorire
brown [braun] *adj* bruno; (*tanned*) abbronzato || *s* color bruno || *tr* colorare di bruno; abbronzare; (*metal*) brunire; (culin) dorare || *intr* colorarsi di bruno; abbronzarsi; brunirsi; (culin) dorarsi
brownish ['braunɪʃ] *adj* brunastro
brown' stud'y *s*—**in a brown study** assorto in fantasticherie
brown' sug'ar *s* zucchero greggio
browse [brauz] *intr* (*said of cattle*) brucare; sfogliare; **to browse around** curios.re
bruise [bruz] *s* ammaccatura, contu-

sione || *tr* ammaccare || *intr* ammaccarsi

brunet [bru'net] *adj* bruno

brunette [bru'net] *adj & s* bruna

brunt [brʌnt] *s* forza; scontro; peso

brush [brʌʃ] *s* pennello; spazzola; (*stroke*) pennellata; (*light touch*) tocco; (*brushwood*) macchia; (*brief encounter*) scaramuccia; (elec) spazzola || *tr* spazzolare; pennellare; to **brush aside** rigettare; **to brush up** ritoccare || *intr*—**to brush by** passar vicino; **to brush up on** ripassare

brush'-off' *s* (slang) scortesia; **to give the brush-off to** (slang) snobbare

brush'wood' *s* macchia, fratta

brusque [brʌsk] *adj* brusco

brusqueness ['brʌsknɪs] *s* bruschezza

Brussels ['brʌsəlz] *s* Bruxelles *f*

Brus'sels sprouts' *spl* cavolini *mpl*

brutal ['brutəl] *adj* brutale

brutali•ty [bru'tælɪti] *s* (**-ties**) brutalità *f*

brute [brut] *adj & s* bruto

brutish ['brutɪʃ] *adj* bruto

bubble ['bʌbəl] *s* bolla; (fig) chimera || *intr* bollire; (*to make a bubbling sound*) barbugliare; **to bubble over** traboccare

bub'ble bath' *s* bagno di schiuma

buccaneer [ˌbʌkə'nɪr] *s* bucaniere *m*

buck [bʌk] *s* (*deer*) cervo; (*goat*) caprone *m*; (*sawhorse*) cavalletto; (*rabbit*) coniglio maschio; (*bucking*) groppata; (*dandy*) damerino; (slang) dollaro; **to pass the buck** (coll) giocare a scaricabarile || *tr* resistere accanitamente || *intr* (*said of a horse*) fare salti da caprone; **to buck for** (slang) cercare di ottenere; **to buck up** (coll) rianimarsi, prender animo

bucket ['bʌkɪt] *s* secchio; bigoncia; (*e.g., of dredge*) benna; **to kick the bucket** (slang) tirare le cuoia

buck'et seat' *s* sedile *m*, strapuntino

buckle ['bʌkəl] *s* (*clasp*) fibbia, boccola; piega || *tr* affibbiare || *intr* piegarsi, curvarsi; **to buckle down to** (coll) mettersi di buzzo buono a

buck' pri'vate *s* (slang) soldato semplice

buckram ['bʌkrəm] *s* tela da fusto

buck'saw' *s* cavalletto

buck'shot' *s* pallini *mpl* da caccia

buck'tooth' *s* (**-teeth**) dente *m* in fuori, dente *m* sporgente

buck'wheat' *s* grano saraceno

bud [bʌd] *s* bocciolo, gemma; **to nip in the bud** troncare sul nascere || *v* (*pret & pp* **budded**; *ger* **budding**) *intr* sbocciare; nascere

Buddhism ['budɪzəm] *s* buddismo

bud•dy ['bʌdi] *s* (**-dies**) (coll) amico, compare *m*

budge [bʌdʒ] *tr* smuovere || *intr* muoversi

budget ['bʌdʒɪt] *s* bilancio || *tr* stanziare, preventivare; (*to schedule*) anticipare; (*time*) calcolare in anticipo

budgetary ['bʌdʒɪ ˌteri] *adj* preventivo, di bilancio

buff [bʌf] *adj* bruno giallastro; di pelle || *s* (*leather*) pelle gialla; dilet-

tante *m*; (mil) giacca di pelle gialla; (coll) pelle nuda || *tr* lucidare; (*to reduce the force of*) ammortizzare

buffa•lo ['bʌfəˌlo] *s* (**-loes** or **-los**) bufalo || *tr* (coll) intimidire

buffer ['bʌfər] *s* ammortizzatore *m*; cuscinetto; (*worker*) lucidatore *m*; (mach) lucidatrice *f*; (rr) respingente *m*

buff'er state' *s* stato cuscinetto

buffet [bu'fe] *s* (*piece of furniture*) credenza; (*counter*) buffet *m* || ['bʌfɪt] *s* pugno; schiaffo || *tr* dar pugni a; schiaffeggiare; lottare con; (*to push about*) sballottare

buffet' car' [bu'fe] *s* vagone *m* ristorante

buffoon [bə'fun] *s* buffone *m*

buffoner•y [bə'funəri] *s* (**-ies**) buffoneria

bug [bʌg] *s* insetto; (coll) germe *m*; (*in motor*) (slang) noia; (slang) pazzo; **to put a bug in the ear of** mettere una pulce nell'orecchio di || *v* (*pret & pp* **bugged**; *ger* **bugging**) *tr* (slang) installare un sistema d'ascolto nel telefono di; (*to annoy*) (slang) seccare || *intr*—**to bug out** (slang) andarsene

bug'bear' *s* spauracchio

bug•gy ['bʌgi] *adj* (**-gier; -giest**) pieno di cimici; (slang) pazzo || *s* (**-gies**) carrozzino

bug'house' *adj* (slang) pazzo || *s* (slang) manicomio

bugle ['bjugəl] *s* tromba, cornetta

bugler ['bjuglər] *s* trombettiere *m*

build [bɪld] *s* corporatura, taglia || *v* (*pret & pp* **built** [bɪlt]) *tr* costruire, edificare; fondare, basare; **to build up** sviluppare

builder ['bɪldər] *s* costruttore *m*; costruttore *m* edile

building ['bɪldɪŋ] *s* edificio, stabile *m*; costruzione; edilizia

build'ing and loan' associa'tion *s* società *f* di credito fondiario

build'ing lot' *s* (coll) terreno da costruzioni

build'ing trades' *spl* edilizia

build'-up' *s* concentrazione; sviluppo; processo di preparazione; propaganda favorevole

built'-in' *adj* (*in a wall*) murato; (*in a cabinet*) incassato, incorporato

built'-in clos'et *s* armadio a muro

built'-up' *adj* armato; popolato

bulb [bʌlb] *s* bulbo; (*lamp*) lampadina; (*of a lamp*) globo, cipolla

Bulgarian [bʌl'geri•ən] *adj & s* bulgaro

bulge [bʌldʒ] *s* protuberanza, sporgenza || *intr* sporgere, gonfiarsi

bulk [bʌlk] *s* volume *m*, massa; **in bulk** in blocco; sciolto || *intr* avere importanza; aumentare d'importanza

bulk'head' *s* diga; (naut) paratia

bulk•y ['bʌlki] *adj* (**-ier; -iest**) voluminoso

bull [bul] *s* toro; (*in the stockmarket*) rialzista *mf*; (slang) scemenza; (eccl) bulla || *tr*—**to bull the market** giocare al rialzo

bull'dog' *s* molosso

bulldoze ['bul,doz] *tr* intimidire; (*land*) livellare

bulldozer ['bul,dozər] *s* livellatrice *f*, apripista *m*

bullet ['bulɪt] *s* palla, pallottola

bulletin ['bulətɪn] *s* bollettino; (*of a school*) albo; (journ) comunicato

bul'letin board' *s* tabellone *m*

bul'let-proof' *adj* blindato

bull'fight' *s* corrida

bull'fight'er *s* torero

bull'finch' *s* (orn) ciuffolotto

bull'frog' *s* rana americana

bull-headed ['bul,hedɪd] *adj* testardo

bullion ['buljən] *s* lingotti *mpl* d'oro or d'argento; frangia d'oro; (*on an Italian general's hat*) greca

bullish ['bulɪʃ] *adj* ostinato; (*market*) al rialzo; (*speculator*) rialzista

bullock ['bulək] *s* manzo

bull'ring' *s* arena

bull's-eye ['bulz,aɪ] *s* centro, tiro in pieno sul bersaglio; **to hit the bull's-eye** fare centro

bul-ly ['bulɪ] *adj* (coll) eccellente || *s* (-lies) bravaccio || *v* (*pret & pp* -lied) *tr* intimidire

bulrush ['bul,rʌʃ] *s* giunco; (Bibl) papiro

bulwark ['bulwərk] *s* baluardo; protezione || *tr* proteggere

bum [bʌm] *adj* (slang) pessimo || *s* (slang) vagabondo; **on the bum** (slang) rotto, fuori servizio || *v* (*pret & pp* **bummed**) *ger* **bumming**) *tr* (slang) scroccare || *intr* (slang) oziare; (slang) vivere d'elemosina; (slang) fare lo scroccatore

bumble ['bʌmbəl] *tr* abborracciare || *intr* abborracciare; (*to stagger*) barcollare; (*to stumble*) balbettare; (*said of a bee*) ronzare

bum'blebee' *s* calabrone *m*

bump [bʌmp] *s* botta, botto; (*collision*) colpo, urto; (*swelling*) bernoccolo || *tr* urtare; **to bump off** (slang) uccidere || *intr* urtare, cozzare; **to bump into** incontrarsi con; cozzare contro

bumper ['bʌmpər] *adj* (coll) abbondante || *s* bicchiere pieno fino all'orlo; (aut) paraurti *m;* (rr) respingente *m*

bumpkin ['bʌmpkɪn] *s* beota *m*

bumptious ['bʌmpʃəs] *adj* vanitoso, presuntuoso

bump·y ['bʌmpɪ] *adj* (-ier; -iest) (*road*) irregolare, ondulato; (*air*) agitato

bun [bʌn] *s* panino; (*of hair*) crocchia, treccia a ciambella

bunch [bʌntʃ] *s* (*of grapes*) grappolo; (*of keys*) mazzo; (*of grass*) ciuffo; (*of people*) gruppo; (*of twigs*) fastello; (*of animals*) branco || *tr* (*things*) ammonticchiare; (*people*) raggruppare || *intr* raggrupparsi

bundle ['bʌndəl] *s* fascio, fastello; (*package*) pacco; (*large package*) collo; (*bunch*) mucchio || *tr* affastellare; impacchettare; ammucchiare; **to bundle off** or **out** c cci· re precipitosamente; **to bundle up** inf ugottare || *intr*—**to bundle up** infagottarsi

bung [bʌŋ] *s* spina, cannella

bungalow ['bʌŋgə,lo] *s* casetta, villino, bungalow *m*

bung'hole' *s* spina, foro della botte

bungle ['bʌŋgəl] *s* abborracciatura || *tr* abborracciare || *intr* lavorare alla carlona

bungler ['bʌŋglər] *s* abborraccione *m*

bungling ['bʌŋglɪŋ] *adj* goffo; mal fatto || *s* abborracciatura

bunion ['bʌnjən] *s* gonfiore *m* dell'alluce

bunk [bʌŋk] *s* letto a castello; (nav) cuccetta; (slang) sciocchezza || *intr* dormire in cuccetta

bunk' bed' *s* letto a castello

bunker ['bʌŋkər] *s* (bin) carbonile *m;* (mil) casamatta; (golf) ostacolo

bun·ny ['bʌnɪ] *s* (-nies) coniglietto

bunting ['bʌntɪŋ] *s* ornamento di bandiere; (nav) gala; (orn) zigolo

buoy [bɔɪ] or ['bu·i] *s* boa; (*life preserver*) salvagente *m* || *tr*—**to buoy up** tenere a galla; (fig) rincuorare

buoyancy ['bɔɪ·ənsi] or ['bujənsi] *s* galleggiabilità *f;* (*cheerfulness*) allegria, esuberanza

buoyant ['bɔɪ·ənt] or ['bujənt] *adj* galleggiante; allegro, esuberante

bur [bʌr] *s* riccio, aculeo

burble ['bʌrbəl] *s* gorgoglio || *intr* gorgogliare

burden ['bʌrdən] *s* carico, peso, fardello; (*of a speech*) tema *m;* (*chorus*) ritornello; (naut) portata || *tr* caricare

bur'den of proof' *s* onere *m* della prova

burdensome ['bʌrdənsəm] *adj* oneroso

burdock ['bʌrdɑk] *s* lappa, lappola

bureau ['bjuro] *s* comò *m;* (*agency*) ufficio, servizio

bureaucra·cy [bju'rɑkrəsi] *s* (-cies) burocrazia

bureaucrat ['bjurə,kræt] *s* burocrate *m*

burglar ['bʌrglər] *s* scassinatore *m*

bur glar alarm' *s* campanello antifurto

burglarize ['bʌrglə,raɪz] *tr* scassinare

bur'glar-proof' *adj* a prova di furto

burgla·ry ['bʌrglərɪ] *s* (-ries) furto con s·asso, scassinatura

Burgundy ['bʌrgəndɪ] *s* la Borgogna; (*wine*) borgogna *m*

burial ['berɪ·əl] *s* sepoltura

bur'ial ground' *s* cimitero

burin ['bjurɪn] *s* burino, cesello

burlap ['bʌrlæp] *s* tela di iuta

burlesque [bʌr'lesk] *adj* burlesco || *s* farsa, burlesque *m* || *tr* parodiare

burlesque' show' *s* spettacolo di varietà, musi.-hall *m*

bur·ly ['bʌrlɪ] *adj* (-lier; -liest) membruto, robusto

Burma ['bʌrmə] *s* la Birmania

burn [bʌrn] *s* bruciatura, scottatura || *v* (*pret & pp* **burned** or **burnt** [bʌrnt]) *tr* bruciare; (*to set on fire*) dar fuoco a; (*bricks*) cuocere; **to burn down** radere al suolo; **to burn up** consumare; (*the road*) divorare; (coll) fare arrabbiare || *intr* bruciare, bruciarsi; (*said of lights*) essere acceso, e.g., **the lights were burning** la luce era accesa; **to burn out** (*said of an electric bulb or a fuse*) bruciarsi;

to burn to (fig) agognare di; **to burn up** (coll) essere arrabiato; **to burn with** (e.g., envy) ardere di

burner ['bʌrnər] s (of gas fixture or lamp) becco; (of furnace) bruciatore m

burning ['bʌrnɪŋ] adj bruciante, scottante ‖ s incendio; (ceramic) cottura finale

burn'ing ques'tion s questione di attualità palpitante

burnish ['bʌrnɪʃ] s lucidatura ‖ tr brunire

burnt' al'mond [bʌrnt] s mandorla tostata

burp [bʌrp] s (coll) rutto ‖ intr (coll) ruttare

burr [bʌr] s riccio, aculeo; (rough edge) bava; (dentist's drill) fresa

burrow ['bʌro] s tana, buca ‖ intr imbucarsi, rintanarsi

bursar ['bʌrsər] s tesoriere universitario

burst [bʌrst] s esplosione; (e.g., of machine gun) raffica; (break) crepa; (of passion) accesso; (of speed) slancio ‖ tr far scoppiare ‖ intr scoppiare, esplodere; **to burst into** (e.g., a room) irrompere in; (e.g., angry words) esplodere in; **to burst out crying** scoppiare in lacrime; **to burst with laughter** scoppiare dalle risa

bur·y ['beri] v (pret & pp -ied) tr sotterrare; **to be buried in thought** essere immerso nel pensiero; **to bury the hatchet** fare la pace

bus [bʌs] s (buses or busses) bus m, autobus m ‖ v (pret & pp bused or bussed; ger busing or bussing) tr trasportare con autobus

bus'boy' s secondo cameriere

bus·by ['bʌzbi] s (-bies) colbacco

bus' driv'er s conducente mf di autobus

bush [buʃ] s cespuglio, arbusto; **to beat around the bush** menare il can per l'aia

bushed [buʃt] adj (coll) stanco morto

bushel ['buʃəl] s staio

bushing ['buʃɪŋ] s (mach) bronzina

bush·y ['buʃi] adj (-ier; -iest) ricco di arbusti; (face) barbuto

business ['bɪznɪs] adj commerciale ‖ s occupazione; commercio; affare m, negozio; faccenda; impiego; **it is not your business** non è affare Suo; **to know one's business** sapere il fatto proprio; **to make it one's business to** proporsi di; **to mean business** (coll) farla sul serio; **to mind one's own business** impicciarsi degli affari propri

businesslike ['bɪznɪs,laɪk] adj metodico; serio; efficace

busi'ness·man' s (-men') commerciante m, uomo d'affari

busi'ness suit' s abito da passeggio

busi'ness·wom'an s (wom'en) commerciante f

bus'man s (-men) guidatore m d'autobus

buss [bʌs] s (coll) bacione sonoro ‖ tr (coll) baciare sonoramente

bus' stop' s fermata degli autobus

bust [bʌst] s busto; petto; (slang) fallimento; (slang) pugno ‖ tr (slang) rompere; (slang) far fallire; (slang) colpire, dare pugni a; (mil) degradare

buster ['bʌstər] s (coll) ragazzo; (coll) rompitore m

bustle ['bʌsəl] s (on a dress) guardinfante m; attività f ‖ intr affrettarsi

bus·y ['bɪzi] adj (-ier; -iest) occupato ‖ v (pret & pp -ied) tr occupare, tenere occupato; **to busy oneself with** occuparsi di

bus'y·bod'y s (-ies) ficcanaso

bus'y sig'nal s (telp) segnale m d'occupato

but [bʌt] s ma m ‖ adv solo, solamente; **but for** se non . . . per ‖ prep eccetto, ad eccezione di, meno, se non; **all but** quasi ‖ conj ma; che non, e.g., **I never go out in the rain but I catch a cold** non esco mai con la pioggia che non mi pigli un raffreddore

butcher ['butʃər] s macellaio ‖ tr macellare; massacrare

butch'er knife' s coltello da cucina, coltella

butch'er shop' s macelleria

butcher·y ['butʃəri] s (-ies) macello; carneficina

butler ['bʌtlər] s cantiniere m, credenziere m

butt [bʌt] s (butting) cornata; (of rifle or gun) calcio; (of cigar) mozzicone m; (target) bersaglio; (end) estremità f; (of ridicule) zimbello; (cask) botte f ‖ tr dare cornate a; cozzare contro ‖ intr—**to butt into** (slang) intromettersi in

butter ['bʌtər] s burro ‖ tr imburrare; **to butter up** (coll) adulare

but'ter·cup' s (bot) bottone m d'oro, ranuncolo

but'ter dish' s piattino per il burro, burriera

but'ter·fat' s grasso nel latte

but'ter·fly' s (-flies) farfalla

but'ter knife' s coltello per il burro

but'ter·milk' s latticello

but'ter sauce' s burro fuso

but'ter·scotch' s caramella al burro

buttocks ['bʌtəks] spl chiappe fpl, natiche fpl

button ['bʌtən] s bottone m ‖ tr abbottonare

but'ton·hole' s occhiello, asola ‖ tr attaccare un bottone a

but'ton·hook' s allacciabottoni m

buttress ['bʌtrɪs] s contrafforte m; piedritto ‖ tr rinforzare

buxom ['bʌksəm] adj avvenente, procace

buy [baɪ] s compra ‖ v (pret & pp bought [bɔt]) tr comprare; **to buy off** corrompere; **to buy out** comprare la parte di

buyer ['baɪər] s compratore m

buzz [bʌz] s brusio, ronzio ‖ tr volare a bassa quota sopra; (coll) fare una telefonata a ‖ intr ronzare

buzzard ['bʌzərd] s (hawk) poiana; avvoltoio americano

buzzer ['bʌzər] s suoneria ronzante

buzz' saw' s sega circolare, segatrice f a disco

by [bai] adv oltre, e.g., **to speed by** correre velocemente oltre; **by and by** fra poco; **by and large** generalmente || prep vicino a; di, durante, e.g., **by night** di notte, durante la notte; a, e.g., **they work by the hour** lavorano all'ora; (not later than, through) per; (past) in fronte a; (through the agency of) da; (according to) secondo; (math) per, volte; **by far** di molto; **by the way** a proposito

bygone ['bai ˌgɒn] or ['bai ˌgɔn] adj & s passato; **to let bygones be bygones** dimenticare il passato

bylaw ['bai ˌlɔ] s legge f locàle, regolamento di una società

by'-line' s (journ) firma

by'pass' s linea secondaria; (detour) deviazione || tr fare una deviazione oltre a; (a difficulty) evitare

by'path' s sentiero secondario; sentiero privato

by'prod'uct s sottoprodotto

bystander ['bai ˌstændər] s astante m, spettatore m

byway ['bai ˌwe] s via traversa

byword ['bai ˌwʌrd] s proverbio; oggetto di obbrobrio

Byzantium [bɪˈzænʃɪ-əm] or [bɪˈzæntɪ-əm] s Bisanzio

C

C, c [si] s terza lettera dell'alfabeto inglese

cab [kæb] s vettura di piazza; tassì m; (of truck or locomotive) cabina

cabbage ['kæbɪdʒ] s cavolo, verza

cab' driv'er s autista m di piazza; (of horse-drawn cab) vetturino

cabin ['kæbɪn] s (shed) capanna; (hut) baracca; (aer, naut) cabina

cab'in boy' s mozzo

cabinet ['kæbɪnɪt] s (piece of furniture) vetrina; (for a radio) armadietto; (small room; ministry of a government) gabinetto

cab'inet-mak'er s ebanista m

cab'inet-mak'ing s ebanisteria

cable ['kebəl] s cavo; cablogramma; (elec) cablaggio || tr cablare, mandare un cablogramma a

ca'ble address' s indirizzo telegrafico

ca'ble car' s funicolare f, teleferica

cablegram ['kebel ˌgræm] s cablogramma m

caboose [kəˈbus] s (rr) vagone m di coda

cab'stand' s stazione di tassametri

cache [kæʃ] s nascondiglio || tr mettere in un nascondiglio

cachet [kæˈʃe] s sigillo; (distinguishing feature) impronta

cackle ['kækəl] s (of chickens) coccodè m; (of people) chiaccherio || intr fare coccodè; ciarlare

cac·tus ['kæktəs] s (-tuses or -ti [tai]) cactus m

cad [kæd] s mascalzone m

cadaver [kəˈdævər] s cadavere m

cadaverous [kəˈdævərəs] adj cadaverico

caddie ['kædi] s portamazze m

cadence ['kedəns] s cadenza

cadet [kəˈdet] s cadetto

cadmium ['kædmɪ-əm] s cadmio

cadres ['kædriz] spl (mil) quadri mpl

Caesar'ean sec'tion [sɪˈzɛrɪ-ən] s taglio cesareo

café [kæˈfe] s caffè m, bar m, ristorante m

ca'fé soci'ety s bel mondo

cafeteria [ˌkæfəˈtɪrɪ-ə] s mensa, tavola calda, caffetteria

caffeine [kæˈfin] or ['kæfi-ɪn] s caffeina

cage [kedʒ] s gabbia; (of elevator) cabina || tr ingabbiare

ca·gey ['kedʒi] adj (-gier; -giest) (coll) astuto, cauto

cahoots [kəˈhuts] s—**to be in cahoots** (slang) far lega, essere in combutta; **to go cahoots** (slang) dividere in parti eguali

Cain [ken] s Caino; **to raise Cain** (slang) arrabbiarsi; (slang) fare una sfuriata

Cairo ['kairo] s il Cairo

caisson ['kesən] s cassone m; (archit) cassettone m

cajole [kəˈdʒol] tr lusingare; persuadere con lusinghe

cajoler·y [kəˈdʒoləri] s (-ies) lusinga

cake [kek] s dolce m; torta, pasta; (with bread-like dough) focaccia; (of soap) saponetta; (of earth) zolla; **to take the cake** (coll) essere il colmo || tr incrostare || intr indurirsi; incrostarsi

calabash ['kælə ˌbæʃ] s zucca a fiasca

calaboose ['kælə ˌbus] s (coll) gattabuia

calamitous [kəˈlæmɪtəs] adj calamitoso

calami·ty [kəˈlæmɪti] s (-ties) calamità f

calci·fy ['kælsɪ ˌfai] v (pret & pp -fied) tr calcificare || intr calcificarsi

calcium ['kælsɪ-əm] s calcio

calculate ['kælkjə ˌlet] tr calcolare || intr calcolare; **to calculate on** contare su

cal'culating machine' s (macchina) calcolatrice

calcu·lus ['kælkjələs] s (-luses or -li [ˌlai]) (math, pathol) calcolo

calendar ['kæləndər] s calendario; (agenda) ordine m del giorno

calf [kæf] or [kɑf] s (calves [kævz] or [kɑvz]) vitello; (of shoes or binding) pelle f di vitello; (of the leg) polpaccio

calf'skin' s pelle f di vitello

caliber ['kælɪbər] s calibro

calibrate ['kælɪ ‚bret] tr calibrare

cali·co ['kælɪ ‚ko] s (-coes or -cos) cotone stampato, calico

California [‚kælɪ'fɔrnɪ-ə] s la California

calipers ['kælɪpərz] spl compasso a grossezze, calibro

caliph ['kelɪf] or ['kælɪf] s califfo

calisthenic [‚kælɪs'θenɪk] adj ginnastico || **calisthenics** spl ginnastica a corpo libero

calk [kɔk] tr var of **caulk**

call [kɔl] s chiamata; visita; (shout) grido, richiamo; (of bugle) squillo; (of telephone) colpo; (of ship) scalo; obbligo; vocazione; (com) richiesta; **on call** disponibile; **within call** a portata di voce || tr chiamare; convocare; (to awaken) svegliare; **to call back** richiamare; **to call in** (e.g., an expert) fare venire; (e.g., currency) domandare, esigere; **to call off** annullare; **to call out** chiamare; **to call together** convocare; **to call up** chiamare per telefono || intr chiamare; visitare; **to call at** passare per la casa di; (naut) fare scalo a; **to call for** venire a prendere; **to call out** gridare; **to go calling** andare a fare visite

cal'la lil'y ['kælə] s (Zantedeschia aethiopica) calla dei fioristi

call'boy' s (in a hotel) fattorino; (theat) buttafuori m

caller ['kɔlər] s visitatore m

call' girl' s ragazza squillo

calling ['kɔlɪŋ] s appello; professione

call'ing card' s biglietto da visita

call' num'ber s numero telefonico; numero di biblioteca

callous ['kæləs] adj calloso, insensibile

callow ['kælo] adj inesperto, immaturo

call' to arms' s chiamata alle armi

call' to the col'ors s chiamata sotto la bandiera

callus ['kæləs] s callo

calm [kɑm] adj calmo, tranquillo || s calma || tr calmare, tranquillizzare || intr—**to calm down** calmarsi; (said of weather) abbonacciarsi

calmness ['kɑmnɪs] s calma, placidità f, tranquillità f

calomel ['kælə ‚mel] s calomelano

calorie ['kæləri] s caloria

calum·ny ['kæləmnɪ] s (-nies) calunnia

Calvary ['kælvəri] s (Bib) Calvario

cam [kæm] s camma

camber ['kæmbər] s curvatura; convessità f || tr arcuare || intr curvarsi

cambric ['kembrɪk] s cambrì m

camel ['kæməl] s cammello

came·o ['kæmɪ ‚o] s (-os) cammeo

camera ['kæmərə] s macchina fotografica; (mov) cinepresa

cam'era·man' s (-men') operatore m

camomile ['kæmə ‚maɪl] s camomilla

camouflage ['kæmə ‚flɑʒ] s mascheramento || tr mascherare, camuffare

camp [kæmp] s accampamento, campo || intr accamparsi

campaign [kæm'pen] s campagna || intr fare una campagna

campaigner [kæm'penər] s veterano; (pol) propagandista mf

camp' bed' s letto da campo, branda

camper ['kæmpər] s campeggiatore m, campeggista mf

camp'fire' s fuoco di accampamento

camp'ground' s terreno per campeggio

camphor ['kæmfər] s canfora

camp'stool' s seggiolino pieghevole

campus ['kæmpəs] s campo, terreno dell'università

cam'shaft' s albero di distribuzione, albero a camme

can [kæn] s lattina, barattolo; (of gasoline or oil) bidone m || v (pret & pp canned; ger canning) tr inscatolare; (slang) licenziare || v (pret & cond could) aux I can speak English so parlare inglese; **can he go now?** se ne può andare ora?

Canada ['kænədə] s il Canadà

Canadian [kə'nedɪ-ən] adj & s canadese mf

canal [kə'næl] s canale m

canar·y [kə'nerɪ] s (-ies) canarino || **Can·ries** spl Canarie fpl

can·cel ['kænsəl] v (pret & pp -celed or -celled; ger -celing or -celling) tr cancellare; annullare; revocare; (stamps) timbrare, annullare

cancellation [‚kænsə'leʃən] s cancellazione, annullamento; cassazione; (of a stamp) bollo

cancer ['kænsər] s cancro || **Cancer** s Cancro

cancerous ['kænsərəs] adj canceroso

candela·brum [‚kændə'lɑbrəm] s (-bra [brə] or -brums) candelabro

candid ['kændɪd] adj candido; sincero, franco

candida·cy ['kændɪdəsɪ] s (-cies) candidatura

candidate ['kændɪ ‚det] s candidato; (for a degree) laureando

can'did cam'era s camera fotografica indiscreta

candied ['kændɪd] adj candito

candle ['kændəl] s candela || tr (eggs) sperare

can'dle·hold'er s var of candlestick

can'dle·light' s luce f or lume m di candela

can'dle·pow'er s (phys) candela

can'dle·stick' s (ornate) candeliere m; (plain) bugia

candor ['kændər] s candore m; ingenuità f

can·dy ['kændɪ] s (-dies) dolciumi mpl; **a piece of candy** un bombon || v (pret & pp -died) tr candire

can'dy box' s bomboniera

can'dy dish' s bomboniera; (three-tier-high) alzata

can'dy store' s confetteria

cane [ken] s canna, giunco; (for walking) bastone m || tr bastonare; (chairs) impagliare

cane' seat' s sedia impagliata

cane' sug'ar s zucchero di canna

canine ['kenaɪn] adj canino || s (tooth) canino; (dog) cane m

canister ['kænɪstər] s barattolo

canned' goods' *spl* conserve *fpl* alimentari; prodotti *mpl* in scatola

canned' mu'sic *s* (slang) musica su dischi

canner·y ['kænəri] *s* (-ies) fabbrica di conserve alimentari

cannibal ['kænɪbəl] *adj & s* cannibale *mf*, antropofago

canning ['kænɪŋ] *s* conservazione

cannon ['kænən] *s* cannone *m*

cannonade [,kænə'ned] *s* cannonata || *tr* cannoneggiare

can'non·ball' *s* palla da cannone

can'non fod'der *s* carne *f* da cannone

can·ny ['kænɪ] *adj* (-nier; -niest) astuto, fino; malizioso

canoe [kə'nu] *s* canoa, piroga

canon ['kænən] *s* canone *m*; (*priest*) canonico

canonical [kə'nɑnɪkəl] *adj* canonico || **canonicals** *spl* paramenti liturgici

canonize ['kænə,naɪz] *tr* canonizzare

can'on law' *s* diritto canonico

canon·ry ['kænənrɪ] *s* (-ries) canonicato

can' o'pener ['opənər] *s* apriscatole *m*

cano·py ['kænəpɪ] *s* (-pies) tenda; baldacchino; (*of sky*) (fig) volta

cant [kænt] *adj* ipocrita || *s* linguaggio ipocrita; gergo; (*slope*) inclinazione

cantaloupe ['kæntə,lop] *s* melone *m*

cantankerous [kæn'tæŋkərəs] *adj* bisbetico, attaccabrighe

canteen [kæn'tin] *s* cantina, spaccio; (*metal bottle*) borraccia

canter ['kæntər] *s* piccolo galoppo || *intr* andare al piccolo galoppo

cantiliver ['kæntɪ,lɪvər] *adj* a cantiliver || *s* trave *f* a sbalzo; (archit) trave *f* a mensola

cantle ['kæntəl] *s* arcione *m* posteriore

canton [kæn'tɑn] *s* cantone *m*; regione || *tr* accantonare

cantonment [kæn'tɑnmənt] *s* accantonamento

cantor ['kæntər] or ['kæntər] *s* cantore *m*

canvas ['kænvəs] *s* (*cloth*) olona; (*e.g. on open truck*) copertone *m*; (*painting*) tela; (naut) vela; **under canvas** (naut) a vele spiegate

canvass ['kænvəs] *s* discussione; dibattito; (pol) sollecitazione di voti || *tr* discutere; (*votes*) sollecitare; (*to investigate*) indagare; (com) fare la piazza a || *intr* discutere; sollecitare voti; indagare; (com) fare la piazza

canyon ['kænjən] *s* cañon *m*

cap [kæp] *s* berretto; cuffia; (*of academic costume*) berrettone *m*; (*of bottle*) tappo, capsula; (*e.g., of fountain pen*) cappuccio || *v* (*pret & pp* **capped;** *ger* **capping**) *tr* (*a person*) coprire il capo di; (*s.o.'s head*) coprire con il berretto; (*a bottle*) mettere il tappo a; terminare; **to cap the climax** essere il colmo

capabili·ty [,kepə'bɪlɪtɪ] *s* (-ties) capacità *f*, abilità *f*

capable ['kepəbəl] *adj* capace, abile

capacious [kə'peʃəs] *adj* ampio, capace

capaci·ty [kə'pæsɪtɪ] *s* (-ties) capacità

f; **filled to capacity** pieno zeppo; **in the capacity of** in veste di

cap' and bells' *spl* berretto a sonagli; scettro di buffone

cap' and gown' *s* costume accademico, toga e tocco

caparison [kə'pærɪsən] *s* bardatura || *tr* bardare

cape [kep] *s* cappa, mantello; (mil) mantella; (geog) capo

Cape' of Good' Hope' *s* Capo di Buona Speranza

caper ['kepər] *s* capriola; (bot) cappero; **to cut capers** far capriole; (fig) fare monellerie || *intr* fare capriole; saltellare

Cape' Town' *s* Città *f* del Capo

capital ['kæpɪtəl] *adj* capitale || *s* (*money*) capitale *m*; (*city*) capitale *f*; (*of column*) capitello

cap'ital expen'ditures *spl* spese *fpl* d'impianto

cap'ital goods' *spl* beni *mpl* strumentali

capitalism ['kæpɪtə,lɪzəm] *s* capitalismo

capitalize ['kæpɪtə,laɪz] *tr* capitalizzare; scrivere con la maiuscola || *intr*—**to capitalize on** approfittare di

cap'ital let'ter *s* lettera maiuscola

cap'ital pun'ishment *s* pena capitale

cap'ital stock' *s* capitale *m* sociale

capitol ['kæpɪtəl] *s* campidoglio

capitulate [kə'pɪtʃə,let] *intr* capitolare

capon ['kepən] *s* cappone *m*

caprice [kə'pris] *s* capriccio, ghiribizzo

capricious [kə'prɪʃəs] *adj* capriccioso, estroso

Capricorn ['kæprɪ,kɔrn] *s* Capricorno

capsize ['kæpsaɪz] *tr* capovolgere || *intr* capovolgersi

capstan ['kæpstən] *s* argano

cap'stone' *s* (archit) coronamento

capsule ['kæpsəl] *adj* in miniatura; riassuntivo || *s* capsula

captain ['kæptən] *s* capitano; (naut) comandante *m*; || *tr* capitanare

caption ['kæpʃən] *s* titolo; (mov) didascalia; (journ) leggenda

captivate ['kæptɪ,vet] *tr* cattivare, affascinare

captive ['kæptɪv] *adj & s* prigioniero

captivi·ty ['kæp'tɪvɪtɪ] *s* (-ties) cattività *f*, prigionia

captor ['kæptər] *s* persona che cattura

capture ['kæptʃər] *s* cattura, presa; (*person*) prigioniero; (*thing*) bottino || *tr* catturare; prendere

car [kɑr] *s* (*of train*) vagone *m*, vettura; (*automobile*) automobile *m &* *f*, macchina, vettura; (*of elevator*) cabina; (*of balloon*) navicella; (*for narrow-gauge track*) carrello

carafe [kə'ræf] *s* caraffa

caramel ['kærəməl] or ['kɑrməl] *s* (*burnt sugar*) caramello; (*candy*) caramella appicciaticcia

carat ['kærət] *s* carato

caravan ['kærə,væn] *s* carovana; (*covered vehicle*) furgone *m*

caravansa·ry [,kærə'vænsərɪ] *s* (-ries) caravanserraglio

caraway ['kærə,we] *s* cumino

car'barn' *s* rimessa del tram

carbide ['kɑrbaɪd] *s* carburo
carbine ['kɑrbaɪn] *s* carabina
carbol'ic ac'id [kɑr'bɑlɪk] *s* acido fenico
carbon ['kɑrbən] *s* (*in arc light, battery, auto cylinder*) carbone *m;* carta carbone; (chem) carbonio
car'bon cop'y *s* copia a carbone, velina
car'bon diox'ide *s* anidride carbonica
car'bon monox'ide *s* ossido di carbonio, monossido di carbonio
car'bon pa'per *s* carta carbone
carbuncle ['kɑrbʌŋkəl] *s* (*stone; boil*) carbonchio; (*boil*) foruncolo
carburetor ['kɑrbə ‚retər] *or* ['kɑrbjə ‚retər] *s* carburatore *m*
carcass ['kɑrkəs] *s* carcassa; (*in state of decay*) carogna
card [kɑrd] *s* (*file*) scheda; (*post card*) cartolina; (*personal card*) biglietto; (*announcement*) partecipazione; (*playing card*) carta da gioco; (coll) tipo divertente, bel tipo
card'board' *s* cartone *m*
card'-car'rying mem'ber *s* tesserato
card' case' *s* portatessere *m*
card' cat'alogue *s* schedario
card'hold'er *s* socio, tesserato
cardiac ['kɑrdɪ ‚æk] *adj & s* cardiaco
cardigan ['kɑrdɪgən] *s* panciotto a maglia
cardinal ['kɑrdɪnəl] *adj* cardinale, fondamentale || *s* cardinale *m*
card' in'dex *s* schedario
cardiogram ['kɑrdɪ‚o‚græm] *s* cardiogramma *m*
card' par'ty *s* riunione per giocare a carte
card'sharp' *s* baro
card' ta'ble *s* tavoliere *m*, tavolino da gioco
card' trick' *s* gioco di prestigio colle carte
care [ker] *s* cura, custodia; inquietudine *f*, preoccupazione; cautela; **care of** presso, e.g., **R. Smith care of Jones** R. Smith presso Jones; **to take care** fare attenzione; **to take care of** prendersi cura di, badare a; **to take care of oneself** badare alla salute || *intr* curarsi, badare; **I don't care** non m'importa; **to care about** preoccuparsi di; **to care for** voler bene a; curarsi di; **to care to** volere
careen [kə'rin] *s* carenaggio || *intr* sbandare
career [kə'rir] *adj* di carriera || *s* carriera
care'free' *adj* spensierato
careful ['kerfəl] *adj* attento; diligente; premuroso; **careful!** faccia attenzione!
careless ['kerlɪs] *adj* trascurato; imprudente; indifferente
carelessness ['kerlɪsnɪs] *s* trascuratezza; imprudenza; indifferenza
caress [kə'rɛs] *s* carezza || *tr* carezzare, accarezzare
caretaker ['ker‚tekər] *adj* interinale, provvisorio || *s* custode *m;* guardiano; (*of school*) bidello
care'taker gov'ernment *s* governo interinale

care'worn' *adj* accasciato dalle preoccupazioni
car'fare' *s* passaggio, denaro per il tram; (*small sum of money*) spiccioli *mpl*
car-go ['kɑrgo] *s* (-goes *or* -gos) carico mercantile
car'go boat' *s* battello da carico
Caribbean [‚kærɪ'bi‚ən] *or* [kə'rɪbɪ‚ən] *s* Mare *m* dei Caraibi
caricature ['kærɪkət‚ʃər] *s* caricatura || *tr* mettere in caricatura
carillon ['kærɪ ‚lɑn] *or* [kə'rɪljən] *s* carillon *m* || *intr* suonare il carillon
car'load' *s* vagone completo, vagonata
carnage ['kɑrnɪdʒ] *s* carnaio, carneficina
carnal ['kɑrnəl] *adj* carnale
carnation [kɑr'neʃən] *adj* incarnato || *s* garofano; (*color*) incarnato
carnival ['kɑrnɪvəl] *adj* carnevalesco || *s* carnevale *m;* festa, spettacolo all'aperto
carob ['kærəb] *s* (*fruit*) carruba; (*tree*) carrubo
car-ol ['kærəl] *s* canzone *f* popolare; pastorella di Natale || *v* (*pret & pp* -oled *or* -olled; *ger* -oling *or* -olling) *tr* cantare
carom ['kærəm] *s* carambola || *intr* carambolare
carousal [kə'rauzəl] *s* baldoria, gozzoviglia
carouse [kə'rauz] *intr* fare baldoria, gozzovigliare
carousel [‚kærə'zɛl] *or* [‚kæru'zɛl] *s* giostra, carosello
carp ['kɑrp] *s* carpa || *intr* lagnarsi, criticare
carpenter ['kɑrpəntər] *s* falegname *m*
carpentry ['kɑrpəntri] *s* falegnameria
carpet ['kɑrpɪt] *s* tappeto || *tr* coprire con un tappeto, tappetare
carpetbagger ['kɑrpɪt‚bægər] *s* avventuriero; (hist) politicante *m*
car'pet sweep'er *s* spazzolone elettrico per tappeti
car'port' *s* tettoia-garage *f*
car'-ren'tal serv'ice *s* servizio di autonoleggi
carriage ['kærɪdʒ] *s* carrozza; (*of gun*) affusto; (*of typewriter*) carrello; (*bearing*) portamento; (mach) slitta
carrier ['kærɪ‚ər] *s* portatore *m;* (*person or organization in business of carrying goods*) spedizioniere *m;* (*mail*) postino; (*e.g., on top of station wagon*) portabagagli *m;* (*of a disease*) veicolo
car'rier pig'eon *s* piccione *m* viaggiatore
car'rier wave' *s* (rad) onda portante
carrion ['kærɪ‚ən] *s* carogne *fpl*
carrot ['kærət] *s* carota
car-ry ['kæri] *v* (*pret & pp* -ried) *tr* portare; trasportare; (*a burden*) sopportare; (*an election*) guadagnare; (*to keep in stock*) avere in assortimento; **to carry along** portare con sé; **to carry away** trasportare; entusiasmare; **to carry forward** riportare; **to carry out** eseguire; **to carry**

through completare; **to carry weight** aver importanza || *intr* avere la portata (di), e.g., **this gun carries two miles** questo cannone ha la portata di due miglia; **to carry on** continuare; (coll) fare baccano

cart [kɑrt] *s* carro, carretto; (*for shopping*) carrello; **to put the cart before the horse** mettere il carro davanti ai buoi || *tr* trasportare col carro

carte blanche ['kɑrt'blɑnʃ] *s* carta bianca

cartel [kɑr'tɛl] *s* cartello

Carthage ['kɑrθɪdʒ] *s* Cartagine *f*

cart' horse' *s* cavallo da tiro

cartilage ['kɑrtɪlɪdʒ] *s* cartilagine *f*

carton ['kɑrtən] *s* cartone *m;* scatola di cartone; (*of cigarettes*) stecca

cartoon [kɑr'tun] *s* disegno; caricatura; (*comic strip*) fumetto; (*mov*) disegno animato || *tr* fare caricature di

cartoonist [kɑr'tunɪst] *s* disegnatore *m;* caricaturista *mf*

cartridge ['kɑrtrɪdʒ] *s* cartuccia; (*e.g., of camera*) caricatore *m*

car'tridge belt' *s* cartucciera; (mil) giberna

car'tridge clip' *s* serbatoio

cart'wheel' *s* ruota di carro; **to turn cartwheels** fare la ruota

carve [kɑrv] *tr* (*meats*) trinciare; scolpire, intagliare

carv'ing knife' *s* trinciante *m*

car' wash'er *s* lavamacchine *m*

cascade [kæs'ked] *s* cascata || *intr* cadere a mo' di cascata

case [kes] *s* (*box*) cassetta; (*of watch*) calotta; (*outer covering*) astuccio; (*instance*) caso; (gram) caso; (law) causa; (typ) cassa; **in case** in caso, nel caso; **in no case** in nessun modo || *tr* rinchiudere; (*to package*) impaccare; (slang) ispezionare

casement ['kesmənt] *s* telaio di finestra; finestra a gangheri

case' stud'y *s* casistica

cash [kæʃ] *s* contante *m; **cash on delivery** spedizione contro assegno; **for cash** in contanti; a pronta cassa || *tr* (*a check*) cambiare, incassare || *intr* **—to cash in on** (coll) trarre profitto da

cash' box' *s* cassa

cashew ['kæʃu] *s* (*tree*) anacardio; (*nut*) mandorla indiana

cashier [kæ'ʃɪr] *s* cassiere *m* || *tr* (*to dismiss*) silurare

cashier's' check' *s* assegno circolare

cash' reg'ister *s* registratore *m* cassa

casing ['kesɪŋ] *s* rivestimento; tubo di rivestimento; (*for salami*) budello; (*of tire*) copertone *m*

cask [kæsk] *or* [kɑsk] *s* barile *m,* botte *f*

casket ['kæskɪt] *or* ['kɑskɪt] *s* scrigno, cofanetto; (*coffin*) bara, cassa da morto

casserole ['kæsə,rol] *s* tegame *m* di terracotta o vetro; (*food*) pasticcio, timballo

cassette [kə'sɛt] *s* (mus) musicassetta; (mus & phot) caricatore *m*

cassock ['kæsək] *s* sottana, tonaca; **to doff the cassock** gettar la tonaca alle ortiche

cast [kæst] *or* [kɑst] *s* getto; lancio; forma; (mach) pezzo fuso; (surg) gesso; (theat) complesso artistico, cast *m* || *v* (*pret & pp* **cast**) *tr* gettare; fondere; (*a ballot*) dare; (*the roles*) distribuire; (*actors*) scegliere; **to cast aside** abbandonare; **to cast down** deprimere; **to cast lots** tirare a sorte; **to cast off** abbandonare; **to cast out** buttar fuori || *intr* tirare i dadi; **to cast off** (naut) mollare gli ormeggi

castanets [,kæstə'nɛts] *spl* nacchere *fpl*

cast'a-way' *adj & s* naufrago; (fig) reprobo

caste [kæst] *or* [kɑst] *s* casta; **to lose caste** perdere prestigio

caster ['kæstər] *or* ['kɑstər] *s* ampollina, saliera, pepaiola; (*roller*) rotella per i mobili

castigate ['kæstɪ,get] *tr* castigare, punire; correggere

Castile [kæs'til] *s* (la) Castiglia

Castilian [kæs'tɪljən] *adj & s* castigliano

casting ['kæstɪŋ] *or* ['kɑstɪŋ] *s* getto, getto fuso; (*in fishing*) pesca a getto

cast' i'ron *s* ghisa

cast'-i'ron *adj* fatto di ghisa; (*e.g., stomach*) fatto d'acciaio, di struzzo

castle ['kæsəl] *or* ['kɑsəl] *s* castello; (chess) torre *f* || *tr & intr* (chess) arroccare

cas'tle in Spain' *or* **cas'tle in the air'** *s* castello in aria

cast'off' *adj* abbandonato || *s* rigetto; persona abbandonata; (typ) stima

cas'tor oil' ['kæstər] *or* ['kɑstər] *s* olio di ricino

castrate ['kæstret] *tr* castrare

casual ['kæʒu·əl] *adj* casuale, fortuito; (*clothing*) semplice, sportivo

casually ['kæʒu·əli] *adv* con disinvoltura; (*by chance*) fortuitamente

casual·ty ['kæʒu·əlti] *s* (**-ties**) accidente *m,* disastro; vittima; **casualties** (*in war*) perdite *fpl*

casuist·ry ['kæʒu·ɪstri] *s* (**-ries**) (*specious reasoning*) speciosità *f;* (philos) casistica

cat [kæt] *s* gatto; donna perfida; **to let the cat out of the bag** lasciarsi scappare il segreto

cataclysm ['kætə,klɪzəm] *s* cataclisma *m*

catacomb ['kætə,kom] *s* catacomba

catalogue ['kætə,lɔg] *or* ['kætə,lɑg] *s* catalogo || *tr* catalogare

cat'alogue sale' *s* vendita per corrispondenza

catalyst ['kætəlɪst] *s* catalizzatore *m*

catapult ['kætə,pʌlt] *s* catapulta || *tr* catapultare

cataract ['kætə,rækt] *s* cataratta

catarrh [kə'tɑr] *s* catarro

catastrophe [kə'tæstrəfi] *s* catastrofe *f,* disastro

cat'call' s urlo di disapprovazione

catch [kætʃ] s presa; cattura; (of door) paletto; (in marriage) partito; (trick) inganno; (of fish) pesca; (mach) nottolino ‖ v (pret & pp caught [kɔt]) tr prendere, acchiappare; (a cold) pigliare, buscarsi; to catch hold of afferrare; to catch it (coll) prendersele; to catch oneself contenersi; to catch up sorprendere sul fatto ‖ intr agganciarsi; (said of a disease) trasmettersi; to catch on capire l'antifona; to catch up mettersi al corrente; to catch up with raggiungere

catch'-as-catch'-can' s lotta libera americana

catch' ba'sin s ricettacolo di fogna

catcher ['kætʃər] s ricevitore m, catcher m

catching ['kætʃɪŋ] adj (alluring) seducente; (infectious) contagioso

catch'word' s slogan m; (typ) chiamata; (typ) esponente m in testa di pagina

catch-y ['kætʃi] adj (-ier; -iest) attraente, vivo; (tricky) insidioso

catechism ['kætɪ,kɪzəm] s catechismo

catego-ry ['kætɪ,gori] s (-ries) categoria

cater ['ketər] intr provvedere cibo; to cater to servire

cater-cornered ['kætər,kɔrnərd] adj diagonale ‖ adv diagonalmente

caterer ['ketərər] s provveditore m

caterpillar ['kætər,pɪlər] s bruco

cat'erpillar trac'tor s trattore m a cingoli

cat'fish' s pesce m gatto

cat'gut' s (mus) corda di minugia; (surg) catgut m, cattegù m

cathartic [kə'θɑrtɪk] adj & s catartico

cathedral [kə'θidrəl] s cattedrale f

catheter ['kæθɪtər] s catetere m

catheterize ['kæθɪtə,raɪz] tr cateterizzare

cathode ['kæθod] s catodo

catholic ['kæθəlɪk] adj cattolico; (e.g., mind) liberale ‖ Catholic adj & s cattolico

catkin ['kætkɪn] s (bot) amento, gattino

cat'nap' s corta siesta, sonnellino

cat-o'-nine-tails [,kætə'naɪn,telz] s gatto a nove code

cat's'-paw' s gonzo; (breeze) brezzolina

catsup ['kætsəp] or ['ketʃəp] s salsa piccante di pomodoro, ketchup m

cat'tail' s stiancia

cattle ['kætəl] s bestiame grosso

cat'tle-man s (-men) allevatore m di bestiame

cat-ty ['kæti] adj (-tier; -tiest) malizioso, maligno; felino, gattesco

cat'walk' s passerella, ballatoio

Caucasian [kɔ'keʒən] or [kɔ'keʃən] adj & s caucasico

caucus ['kɔkəs] s comitato elettorale; conciliabolo politico

cauldron ['kɔldrən] s calderone m

cauliflower ['kɔlɪ,flaʊ·ər] s cavolfiore m

caulk [kɔk] tr calafatare, stoppare

cause [kɔz] s causa, cagione ‖ tr causare, cagionare; to cause to + inf

fare + inf, e.g., she caused him to fall l'ha fatto cadere

cause'way' s strada rialzata, scarpata

caustic ['kɔstɪk] adj caustico

cauterize ['kɔtə,raɪz] tr cauterizzare

caution ['kɔ/ən] s cautela, prudenza; ammonizione ‖ tr ammonire

cautious ['kɔ/əs] adj prudente

cavalcade ['kævəl,ked] or [,kævəl-'ked] s cavalcata

cavalier [,kævə'lir] or ['kævə,lir] adj altero, sdegnoso; disinvolto ‖ s cavaliere m

caval-ry ['kævəlri] s (-ries) cavalleria

cav'alry-man or cav'alry-man s (-men or -men) cavalleggero, soldato di cavalleria

cave [kev] s caverna, grotta ‖ intr— to cave in sprofondarsi; (to give in) (coll) cedere; (to become exhausted) (coll) diventare spossato

cave'-in' s sprofondamento

cave' man' s troglodita m

cavern ['kævərn] s caverna

caviar ['kævɪ,ɑr] or [,kævɪ'ɑr] s caviale m

cav-il ['kævɪl] v (pret & pp -iled or -illed; ger -iling or -illing) intr cavillare

cavi-ty ['kævɪti] s (-ties) cavità f; (in tooth) carie f

cavort [kə'vɔrt] intr far capriole

caw [kɔ] s gracchiamento ‖ intr gracchiare

cease [sis] tr cessare, interrompere ‖ intr cessare, interrompersi; to cease + ger cessare di + inf

cease'-fire' s sospensione delle ostilità

ceaseless ['sislɪs] adj incessante

cedar ['sidər] s cedro; legno di cedro

cede [sid] tr cedere, trasferire

ceiling ['silɪŋ] s soffitto; (aer) altezza massima; to hit the ceiling (slang) uscire dai gangheri

ceil'ing price' s calmiere m, tetto

celebrate ['selɪ,bret] tr celebrare ‖ intr celebrare; far festa

celebrated ['selɪ,bretɪd] adj celebre, famoso

celebration [,selɪ'breʃən] s celebrazione

celebri-ty [sɪ'lebrɪti] s (-ties) celebrità f

celery ['seləri] s sedano

celestial [sɪ'lestʃəl] adj celestiale, celeste

celibacy ['seləbəsi] s celibato

celibate ['selə,bet] or ['seləbɪt] adj & s celibe m; nubile f

cell [sel] s (e.g., of jail) cella; (of electric battery) elemento; (biol, phys, pol) cellula

cellar ['selər] s cantina; (partly above ground) seminterrato

cellist or 'cellist ['tʃelɪst] s violoncellista mf

cel-lo or 'cel-lo ['tʃelo] s (-los) violoncello

cellophane ['selə,fen] s cellofan m

celluloid ['seljə,lɔɪd] s celluloide f

Celtic ['seltɪk] or ['keltɪk] adj celtico ‖ s lingua celtica

cement [sɪ'ment] *s* cemento || *tr* cementare

cemete·ry ['semɪ‚teri] *s* (-ries) cimitero

censer ['sensər] *s* turibolo

censor ['sensər] *s* censore *m* || *tr* censurare

censure ['senʃər] *s* censura, critica || *tr* censurare, criticare

census ['sensəs] *s* censo, censimento

cent [sent] *s* centesimo di dollaro, cent *m*; **not to have a red cent to one's name** non avere il becco di un quattrino

centaur ['sentər] *s* centauro

centennial [sen'tenɪ-əl] *adj* & *s* centenario

center ['sentər] *s* centro || *tr* centrare, concentrare || *intr*—**to center on** concentrarsi su

cen'ter·board' *s* chiglia mobile

cen'ter·piece' *s* centro tavola

cen'ter punch' *s* punzone *m*, punteruolo

centigrade ['sentɪ‚gred] *adj* centigrado

centimeter ['sentɪ‚mitər] *s* centimetro

centipede ['sentɪ‚pid] *s* centopiedi *m*

cento ['sento] *s* centone *m*

central ['sentrəl] *adj* centrale || *s* centrale *f*, centrale telefonica; (*operator*) telefonista *mf*

Cen'tral Amer'ica *s* l'America Centrale

centralize ['sentrə‚laɪz] *tr* centralizzare || *intr* centralizzarsi

centu·ry ['sentʃəri] *s* (-ries) secolo

ceramic [sɪ'ræmɪk] *adj* ceramico || **ceramics** *ssg* ceramica; *spl* oggetti *mpl* di ceramica

cereal ['sɪrɪ-əl] *adj* cerealicolo || *s* (*grain*) cereale *m*; (*uncooked breakfast food, e.g., cornflakes*) fiocchi *mpl*; (*breakfast food to be cooked*) farina

cerebral ['serɪbrəl] *adj* cerebrale

ceremonious [‚serɪ'monɪ-əs] *adj* cerimonioso

ceremo·ny ['serɪ‚moni] *s* (-nies) cerimonia; **to stand on ceremony** fare cerimonie

certain ['sʌrtən] *adj* certo; **for certain** di or per certo; **to be certain to** + *inf* non mancare di + *inf*

certainly ['sʌrtənli] *adv* certamente; (*gladly*) con piacere

certain·ty ['sʌrtənti] *s* (-ties) certezza

certificate [sər'tɪfɪkɪt] *s* certificato; (com) titolo || [sər'tɪfɪ‚ket] *tr* certificare

cer'tified check' *s* assegno a copertura garantita

cer'tified cop'y *s* estratto; (*as a formula on a document*) per copia conforme

cer'tified pub'lic account'ant *s* esperto contabile

certi·fy ['sʌrtɪ‚faɪ] *v* (*pret* & *pp* -fied) *tr* certificare, garantire

cervix ['sʌrvɪks] *s* (**cervices** (sər'vaɪsiz]) cervice *f*

cessation [se'seʃən] *s* cessazione

cesspool ['ses‚pul] *s* pozzo nero

Ceylo·nese [‚silə'niz] *adj* & *s* (-nese) singalese *mf*

chafe [tʃef] *s* irritazione || *tr* (*the hands*) strofinare; irritare; (*to wear*

away) logorare || *intr* irritarsi; logorarsi

chaff [tʃæf] or [tʃɑf] *s* lolla; pula; (*joke*) buria; (fig) loppa

chaf'ing dish' *s* fornello a spirito

cha·grin [ʃə'grɪn] *s* cruccio, dispiacere *m* || *v* (*pret* -grined or -grinned; *ger* -grining or -grinning) *tr* crucciare, affliggere

chain [tʃen] *s* catena; (*e.g., for necklace*) catenella || *tr* incatenare

chain' gang' *s* catena di forzati

chain' reac'tion *s* reazione a catena

chain' saw' *s* motosega

chain'-smoke' *intr* fumare come un turco

chain' store' *s* negozio a catena

chair [tʃer] *s* sedia, seggiola; (*of important person*) seggio; (*at a university*) cattedra; (*chairman*) presidente *m*, presidenza; **to take the chair** cominciare una riunione || *tr* (*a meeting*) presiedere

chair' lift' *s* seggiovia

chair'man *s* (-men) presidente *m*

chair'man·ship' *s* presidenza

chair wom'an *s* (-wom'en) presidentessa

chalice ['tʃælɪs] *s* calice *m*

chalk [tʃɔk] *s* gesso || *tr* marcare or scrivere col gesso; **to chalk up** prendere ppunti di; tribuire

chalk' talk' *s* conferenza illustrata

chalk·y ['tʃɔki] *adj* (-ier; -iest) gessoso

challenge ['tʃælɪndʒ] *s* sfida; (law) ricusazione; (mil) chi va là *m* || *tr* sfidare; (*a juror*) (law) ricusare; (mil) dare il chi va là a

chamber ['tʃembər] *s* camera, stanza; (*of a palace*) aula; (*of a judge*) gabinetto

chamberlain ['tʃembərlɪn] *s* ciambellano

cham'ber·maid' *s* cameriera

cham'ber of com'merce *s* camera di commercio

cham'ber pot' *s* orinale *m*

chameleon [kə'milɪ-ən] *s* camaleonte *m*

cham·ois ['ʃæmi] *s* (-ois) camoscio

champ [tʃæmp] *s* (slang) campione *m* || *tr* masticare rumorosamente; (*the bit*) mordere || *intr* masticare rumorosamente

champagne [ʃæm'pen] *s* champagne *m*, spumante *m*

champion ['tʃæmpɪ-ən] *s* campione *m* || *tr* difendere; farsi paladino di

championship ['tʃæmpɪ-ən ‚ʃɪp] *s* campionato

chance [tʃæns] or [tʃɑns] *adj* casuale, fortuito || *s* occasione; caso; probabilità *f*; rischio; biglietto di lotteria; **by chance** per caso; **not to stand a chance** non avere la probabilità di riuscita; **to take one's chances** arrischiarsi; **to wait for a chance** attendere l'opportunità || *intr* succedere; **to chance upon** imbattersi in

chancel ['tʃænsəl] or ['tʃɑnsəl] *s* presbiterio, coro

chanceller·y ['tʃænsələri] or ['tʃɑnsələri] *s* (-ies) cancelleria

chancellor ['tʃænsələr] or ['tʃɑnsələr] *s* cancelliere *m*

chandelier [ˌʃændə'lir] *s* lampadario

change [tʃendʒ] *s* cambiamento; (*of clothes*) muta; (*of currency*) cambio; (*coins*) spiccioli *mpl*; **for a change** tanto per cambiare; **to keep the change** tenere il resto || *tr* cambiare, rimpiazzare; (*clothes*) cambiare, cambiarsi di || *intr* cambiare, mutare

changeable ['tʃendʒəbəl] *adj* mutevole, variabile, incostante

change' of heart' *s* pentimento, conversione

change' of life' *s* menopausa

chan·nel ['tʃænəl] *s* canale *m*; tubo, passaggio; stretto; (*of river*) alveo; (*groove*) solco; (rad, telv) canale *m*; **through channels** per via gerarchica || *v* (*pret & pp* **-neled** or **-nelled;** *ger* **-neling** or **-nelling**) *tr* incanalare; (*a river*) incassare || **the Channel** il Canale della Manica

chant [tʃænt] or [tʃɑnt] *s* canto; salmodia; canzone *f* || *tr & intr* cantare

chanticleer ['tʃæntɪˌklɪr] *s* il gallo

chaos ['ke·ɑs] *s* caos *m*

chaotic [ke'ɑtɪk] *adj* caotico

chap [tʃæp] *s* (*fellow*) individuo, tipo; (*of skin*) screpolatura; **chaps** pantaloni *mpl* di cuoio || *v* (*pret & pp* **chapped;** *ger* **chapping**) *tr* screpolare || *intr* screpolarsi

chapel ['tʃæpəl] *s* cappella

chaperon or **chaperone** ['ʃæpəˌron] *s* accompagnatrice *f* (di signorina) || *tr* accompagnare

chaplain ['tʃæplɪn] *s* cappellano

chaplet ['tʃæplɪt] *s* (*wreath*) corona, ghirlanda; rosario

chapter ['tʃæptər] *s* capitolo; (*of a club*) sezione

chap'ter and verse'—**to give chapter and verse** citare le autorità

char [tʃɑr] *v* (*pret & pp* **charred;** *ger* **charring**) *tr* carbonizzare; bruciare

character ['kærɪktər] *s* carattere *m*; lettera, scrittura; indole *f*; (theat) personaggio; (coll) tipo; **in character** caratteristico di lui (lei, loro, etc.)

char'acter ac'tor *s* caratterista *m*

char'acter ac'tress *s* caratterista *f*

char'acter assassina'tion *s* linciaggio morale

characteristic [ˌkærɪktə'rɪstɪk] *adj* caratteristico || *s* caratteristica

characterize ['kærɪktəˌraɪz] *tr* caratterizzare

char'coal' *s* carbone *m* di legna, carbone *m* dolce; (*for sketching*) carboncino; (*sketch*) disegno al carboncino

charge [tʃɑrdʒ] *s* carica; incarico; responsabilità *f*; (*indictment*) accusa; costo; prezzo; debito; **in charge** in comando; **in charge of** a cura di; **to take charge of** prendersi cura di || *tr* caricare; comandare; accusare; (*a price*) fare pagare; mettere in conto; **to charge s.o. with s.th** addebitare q!co a q!cu; accusare q!cu di q!co || *intr* fare una carica

charge' account' *s* conto corrente

chargé d'affaires [ʃɑr'ʒe dɛ'fɛr] *s* (**chargés d'affaires**) incaricato d'affari

charger ['tʃɑrdʒər] *s* cavallo di battaglia; (*of a battery*) caricatore *m*

chariot ['tʃærɪ·ət] *s* cocchio

charioteer [ˌtʃærɪ·ə'tɪr] *s* auriga *m*

charis·ma [kə'rɪzmə] *s* (**-mata** [mətə]) fascino personale; (theol) carisma *m*

charitable ['tʃærɪtəbəl] *adj* (*person*) caritatevole; (*institution*) caritativo

char·i·ty ['tʃærɪtɪ] *s* (**-ties**) carità *f*; associazione di beneficenza

charlatan ['ʃɑrlətən] *s* ciarlatano

charlatanism ['ʃɑrlətənˌɪzəm] *s* ciarlataneria

Charlemagne ['ʃɑrləˌmen] *s* Carlomagno

Charles [tʃɑrlz] *s* Carlo

char'ley horse' ['tʃɑrlɪ] *s* (coll) crampo

charlotte ['ʃɑrlət] *s* charlotte *f* || **Charlotte** *s* Carlotta

charm [tʃɑrm] *s* fascino; amuleto; portafortuna *m* || *tr* incantare, stregare

charming ['tʃɑrmɪŋ] *adj* affascinante

charnel ['tʃɑrnəl] *adj* orribile || *s* ossario

chart [tʃɑrt] *s* carta geografica; lista; diagramma *m* || *tr* tracciare

charter ['tʃɑrtər] *s* statuto; privilegio || *tr* (*a company*) fondare; (*a conveyance*) noleggiare

char'ter mem'ber *s* socio fondatore

char'wom·an *s* (**-wom'en**) domestica per la pulizia

chase [tʃes] *s* inseguimento; caccia; (typ) telaio || *tr* inseguire; cacciare; (*to chisel*) cesellare; **to chase away** scacciare || *intr*—**to chase after** inseguire

chaser ['tʃesər] *s* cacciatore *m*; (coll) bibita da bersi dopo un liquore

chasm ['kæzəm] *s* abisso, baratro

chas·sis ['tʃæsi] *s* (**-sis** [siz]) telaio

chaste [tʃest] *adj* casto

chasten ['tʃesən] *tr* castigare

chastise [tʃæs'taɪz] *tr* castigare

chastity ['tʃæstɪtɪ] *s* castità *f*

chat [tʃæt] *s* chiacchierata || *v* (*pret & pp* **chatted;** *ger* **chatting**) *intr* chiacchierare

chatelaine ['ʃætəˌlen] *s* castellana

chattels ['tʃætəlz] *spl* beni *mpl* mobili

chatter ['tʃætər] *s* cicaleccio; balbettio; (*of teeth*) battito || *intr* cicalare; balbettare; (*said of teeth*) battere

chat'ter·box' *s* chiacchierone *m*

chauffeur ['ʃofər] or [ʃo'fʌr] *s* autista *mf* || *intr* fare l'autista

cheap [tʃip] *adj* a buon mercato, economico; (*of poor quality*) scadente; **to feel cheap** vergognarsi || *adv* a buon mercato

cheapen ['tʃipən] *tr* deprezzare; avvilire; rendere di cattivo gusto

cheapness ['tʃipnəs] *s* buon mercato, prezzo basso

cheat [tʃit] *s* truffa; truffatore *m* || *tr* imbrogliare, truffare || *intr* truffare; (*at cards*) barare

check [tʃɛk] *s* arresto, pausa; ostacolo;

esame *m;* verifica, controllo; (*of bank*) assegno; (*for baggage*) tagliando, scontrino; (*square pattern*) quadretto; (*fabric in squares*) tessuto a scacchi; (*in a restaurant*) conto; in check controllato, sotto controllo; (chess) sotto scacco ‖ *tr* fermare; confrontare; ispezionare; marcare; (*e.g., a coat*) depositare; disegnare a quadretti; (chess) dare scacco a; to check off controllare marcando; to check on controllare, verificare ‖ *intr* fermarsi; corrispondere perfettamente; to check in scendere (a un albergo); to check out andar via; pagare il conto; to check up on controllare

check·book' *s* libretto d'assegni

checker ['tʃɛkər] *s* ispettore *m;* quadretto; (*in game of checkers*) pedina; checkers dama ‖ *tr* variegare; marcare a quadretti

check'er·board' *s* scacchiera

check'ered *adj* (*e.g., career*) pieno di vicissitudini; (*marked with squares*) a scacchi; (*in color*) variegato

check'ing account' *s* conto corrente

check'mate' *s* scacco matto ‖ *tr* dare scacco matto a ‖ *interj* scacco matto!

check'off' dues' *spl* trattenute *fpl* sindacali

check'-out' *s* (*from hotel room*) partenza; (*time*) ora della partenza; (*examination*) esame *m* di controllo; (*in a supermarket*) cassa

check'point' *s* punto di ispezione

check'room' *s* guardaroba *m*

check'up' *s* (*of car*) ispezione; (*of patient*) esame *m* (fisico)

cheek [tʃik] *s* guancia, gota; (coll) faccia tosta

cheek'bone' *s* zigomo

cheek·y ['tʃiki] *adj* (-ier; -iest) (coll) impudente, sfacciato

cheer [tʃɪr] *s* gioia, allegria; applauso; of good cheer di buon umore ‖ *tr* riempire di gioia, rallegrare; applaudire; ricevere con applausi ‖ *intr* rallegrarsi; cheer up! animo, coraggio!

cheerful ['tʃɪrfəl] *adj* allegro, di buon umore; (*willing*) volonteroso

cheerless ['tʃɪrlɪs] *adj* tetro, triste

cheese [tʃiz] *s* formaggio ‖ *intr*—cheese it! (slang) scappa via!

cheese' cake' *s* torta di formaggio; (slang) pin-up girl *f*

cheese'cloth' *s* etamine *f,* stamigna

chees·y ['tʃisi] *adj* (-ier; -iest) di formaggio; come il formaggio; (slang) meschino, di cattiva qualità

chef [ʃef] *s* chef *m,* capocuoco

chemical ['kɛmɪkəl] *adj* chimico ‖ *s* prodotto chimico

chemise [ʃə'miz] *s* sottoveste *f*

chemist ['kɛmɪst] *s* chimico

chemistry ['kɛmɪstri] *s* chimica

cherish ['tʃɛrɪʃ] *tr* accarezzare; (*a memory*) custodire; (*a hope*) nutrire

cher·ry ['tʃɛri] *s* (-ries) (*tree*) ciliegio; (*fruit*) ciliegia

cher·ub ['tʃɛrəb] *s* (-ubim [əbɪm] & -ubs) cherubino

chess [tʃes] *s* scacchi *mpl*

chess'board' *s* scacchiera

chess'man' or chess'man *s* (-men' or -men) scacco

chest [tʃest] *s* petto; (*box*) cassapanca; (*furniture with drawers*) cassettone *m;* (*for money*) forziere *m*

chestnut ['tʃesnət] *s* (*tree, wood, color*) castagno; (*nut*) castagna

chest' of drawers' *s* cassettone *m*

cheval' glass' [ʃə'væl] *s* psiche *f*

chevalier [ˌʃɛvə'lɪr] *s* cavaliere *m*

chevron ['ʃɛvrən] *s* gallone *m*

chew [tʃu] *tr* masticare; to chew the cud ruminare; to chew the rag (slang) chiacchierare ‖ *intr* masticare

chew'ing gum' *s* gomma da masticare

chic [ʃik] *adj & s* chic

chicaner·y [ʃɪ'kenəri] *s* (-ies) trucco, rigiro

chick [tʃɪk] *s* pulcino; (slang) ragazza

chicken ['tʃɪkən] *s* pollo, pollastro; (coll) giovane *mf;* to be chicken (slang) avere la fifa ‖ *intr*—to chicken out (coll) indietreggiare

chick'en coop' *s* pollaio

chick'en feed' *s* (slang) spiccioli *mpl*

chicken-hearted ['tʃɪkən,hɑrtɪd] *adj* timido, fifone

chick'en pox' *s* varicella

chick'en store' *s* polleria

chick'en wire' *s* rete metallica esagonale

chick'pea' *s* cece *m*

chico·ry ['tʃɪkəri] *s* (-ries) cicoria

chide [tʃaɪd] *v* (*pret* chided or chid [tʃɪd]; *pp* chided, chid, or chidden ['tʃɪdən]) *tr & intr* rimproverare, correggere

chief [tʃif] *adj* principale, sommo, supremo ‖ *s* capo, comandante supremo; (slang) padrone *m*

chief' exec'utive *s* capo del governo

chief' jus'tice *s* presidente *m* di una corte; presidente *m* della corte suprema

chiefly ['tʃifli] *adv* principalmente

chief' of staff' *s* capo di stato maggiore

chief' of state' *s* capo dello stato

chieftain ['tʃiftən] *s* capo

chiffon [ʃɪ'fɑn] *s* velo trasparente, chiffon *m;* chiffons trine *fpl*

chiffonier [ˌʃɪfə'nɪr] *s* mobile *m* a cassettini, chiffonier *m*

chilblain ['tʃɪl,blen] *s* gelone *m*

child [tʃaɪld] *s* (children ['tʃɪldrən]) bebè *mf,* bambino; figlio; discendente *mf;* with child incinta

child'birth' *s* parto

childhood ['tʃaɪldhʊd] *s* infanzia

childish ['tʃaɪldɪʃ] *adj* infantile

childishness ['tʃaɪldɪnɪs] *s* puerilità *f,* infanzia

child' la'bor *s* lavoro dei minorenni

childless ['tʃaɪldlɪs] *adj* senza figli

child'like' *adj* infantile, innocente

child's' play' *s* un gioco

child' wel'fare *s* protezione dell'infanzia

Chile ['tʃɪli] *s* il Cile

Chilean ['tʃɪlɪ·ən] *adj* cileno

chil′i sauce′ [′tʃɪli] *s* salsa di pomodoro con peperoni

chill [tʃɪl] *adj* freddo; brivido di freddo; freddezza; (*depression*) abbattimento ‖ *tr* raffreddare; (*a metal*) temprare; (fig) scoraggiare ‖ *intr* raffreddarsi

chill·y [′tʃɪli] *adj* (**-ier; -iest**) fresco, freddiccio; (*reception*) freddo

chime [tʃaɪm] *s* scampanio; **chimes** campanello ‖ *intr* scampanare; **to chime in** cominciare a cantare all'unisono; (coll) intromettersi

chime′ clock′ *s* orologio con carillon

chimney [′tʃɪmni] *s* camino; (*of factory*) ciminiera; **to smoke like a chimney** fumare come un turco

chim′ney flue′ *s* tubo di stufa, canna del camino

chim′ney pot′ *s* testa della canna fumaria, comignolo

chim′ney sweep′ *s* spazzacamino

chimpanzee [tʃɪm′pænzi] *or* [ˌtʃɪm-pæn′zi] *s* scimpanzé *m*

chin [tʃɪn] *s* mento; **to keep one's chin up** (coll) non perdersi di coraggio; **to take it on the chin** (slang) subire una sconfitta ‖ *v* (*pret & pp* **chinned;** *ger* **chinning**) *tr*—**to chin oneself** sollevarsi fino al mento (ai manubri) ‖ *intr* (slang) chiacchierare

china [′tʃaɪnə] *s* porcellana ‖ **China** *s* la Cina

chi′na clos′et *s* armadio per le stoviglie

chi′na·ware′ *s* porcellana, stoviglie *fpl*

Chi·nese [tʃaɪ′niz] *adj* cinese ‖ *s* (-nese) cinese *mf*

Chi′nese lan′tern *s* lampioncino alla veneziana

Chi′nese puz′zle *s* rebus *m*

chink [tʃɪŋk] *s* fessura

chin′ strap′ *s* sottogola

chintz [tʃɪnts] *s* chintz *m*

chip [tʃɪp] *s* scheggia; frammento; (*in card games*) gettone *m*; (*of wood*) truciolo; **chip off the old block** vero figlio di suo padre (di sua madre); **chip on one's shoulder** propensità *f* a attaccar brighe ‖ *v* (*pret & pp* **chipped;** *ger* **chipping**) *tr* scheggiare; **to chip in** contribuire ‖ *intr* scheggiarsi

chipmunk [′tʃɪpˌmʌŋk] *s* tamia

chipper [′tʃɪpər] *adj* (coll) allegro, vivo

chiropodist [kaɪ′rɑpədɪst] *or* [kɪ′rɑpə-dɪst] *s* callista *mf*, pedicure *mf*

chiropractic [′kaɪrəˌpræktɪs] *s* chiropratica

chirp [tʃʌrp] *s* (*of birds*) cinguettio; (*of crickets*) cri cri *m* ‖ *intr* cinguettare; fare cri cri

chis·el [′tʃɪzəl] *s* (*for wood and metal*) scalpello; (*for metal*) cesello ‖ *v* (*pret & pp* **-eled** *or* **-elled;** *ger* **-eling** *or* **-elling**) *tr* scalpellare; cesellare; (slang) imbrogliare ‖ *intr* (slang) imbrogliare, fare l'imbroglione

chiseler [′tʃɪzələr] *s* scalpellino; cesellatore *m*; (slang) imbroglione *m*

chit-chat [′tʃɪtˌtʃæt] *s* chiacchierata

chivalrous [′ʃɪvəlrəs] *adj* cavalleresco

chivalry [′ʃɪvəlri] *s* cavalleria

chive [tʃaɪv] *s* cipolla porraia

chloride [′klɔraɪd] *s* cloruro

chlorine [′klɔrin] *s* cloro

chloroform [′klɔrəˌfɔrm] *s* cloroformio ‖ *tr* cloroformizzare

chlorophyll [′klɔrəfɪl] *s* clorofilla

chock [tʃak] *s* (*wedge*) bietta, cuneo

chock-full [′tʃak′ful] *adj* colmo, pieno zeppo

chocolate [′tʃɔkəlɪt] *or* [′tʃakəlɪt] *s* (*candy*) cioccolato; (*drink*) cioccolata

choc′olate bar′ *s* barretta di cioccolato

choice [tʃɔɪs] *adj* di prima scelta, superiore ‖ *s* scelta; (*variety*) assortimento

choir [kwaɪr] *s* coro

choir′boy′ *s* ragazzo cantore

choir′ loft′ *s* coro

choir′mas′ter *s* maestro di cappella

choke [tʃok] *s* strozzatura; (aut) farfalla del carburatore ‖ *tr* strozzare; ostruire; (*an internal-combustion engine*) arricchire la miscela di; **to choke back** trattenere; **to choke up** tappare, ostruire ‖ *intr* soffocarsi; **to choke up** tapparsi; (coll) soffocarsi

choker [′tʃokər] *s* (*necklace*) (coll) collana; (*scarf*) (coll) foulard *m*

cholera [′kalərə] *s* colera *m*

choleric [′kalərɪk] *adj* collerico

cholesterol [kə′lestəˌrol] *or* [kə′lestə-ˌrɑl] *s* colesterina

choose [tʃuz] *v* (*pret* **chose** [tʃoz]; *pp* **chosen** [′tʃozən]) *tr* scegliere ‖ *intr* —**to choose to** decidere di

choos·y [′tʃuzi] *adj* (**-ier; -iest**) (coll) di difficile contentatura

chop [tʃap] *s* colpo; (*of meat*) cotoletta; **chops** labbra *fpl*, bocca ‖ *v* (*pret & pp* **chopped;** *ger* **chopping**) *tr* tagliare; (*meat*) tritare; **to chop off** troncare; **to chop up** sminuzzare

chopper [′tʃapər] *s* (*man*) tagliatore *m*; interruttore automatico; coltello da macellaio; (slang) elicottero; **choppers** (slang) i denti

chop′ping block′ *s* tagliere *m*

chop·py [′tʃapi] *adj* (**-pier; -piest**) (*wind*) variabile; (*sea*) agitato; (*style*) instabile

choral [′kɔrəl] *adj & s* corale *m*

chorale [ko′ral] *s* corale *m*

chord [kɔrd] *s* corda; (mus) accordo

chore [tʃor] *s* lavoro; lavoro spiacevole; **chores** faccende domestiche

choreography [ˌkɔri′agrəfi] *s* coreografia

chorine [ko′rin] *s* (slang) ballerina

chorus [′kɔrəs] *s* coro; (*group of dancers*) corpo di ballo; (*of a song*) ritornello

cho′rus girl′ *s* ballerina

cho′rus man′ *s* (**men′**) corista *m*

chow [tʃau] *s* (*dog*) chow chow *m*; (slang) cibo, pappa

chowder [′tʃaudər] *s* zuppa di vongole; zuppa di pesce

Christ [kraɪst] *s* Cristo

christen [′krɪsən] *tr* battezzare

Christendom [′krɪsəndəm] *s* cristianità *f*

christening ['krɪsənɪŋ] s battesimo
Christian ['krɪstʃən] adj & s cristiano
Christianity [,krɪstʃɪ'ænɪtɪ] s (Christendom) cristianità f; (religion) cristianesimo
Chris'tian name' s nome m di battesimo
Christmas ['krɪsməs] adj natalizio || s Natale m; **Merry Christmas!** Buon Natale!
Christ'mas card' s cartoncino natalizio
Christ'mas car'ol s pastorella di Natale
Christ'mas Eve' s vigilia di Natale
Christ'mas gift' s strenna natalizia
Christ'mas tree' s albero di Natale
chrome [krom] adj cromato || s cromo || tr cromare
chromium ['kromɪ-əm] s cromo
chromosome ['kromə,som] s cromosoma m
chronic ['krɑnɪk] adj cronico
chronicle ['krɑnɪkəl] s cronaca || tr fare la storia di
chronicler ['krɑnɪklər] s cronista mf
chronolo·gy [krə'nɑlədʒɪ] s (-gies) cronologia
chronometer [krə'nɑmɪtər] s cronometro
chrysanthemum [krɪ'sænθɪməm] s crisantemo
chub·by ['tʃʌbɪ] adj (-bier; -biest) paffuto
chuck [tʃʌk] s buffetto sotto il mento; (cut of meat) reale m; (of lathe) coppaia || tr accarezzare sotto il mento; (to throw) (coll) gettare
chuckle ['tʃʌkəl] s risatina || intr ridacchiare
chum [tʃʌm] s (coll) amico intimo; (coll) compagno di stanza || v (pret & pp chummed; ger chumming) intr (coll) essere amico intimo; essere compagno di stanza
chum·my ['tʃʌmɪ] adj (-mier; -miest) (coll) intimo, amicone
chump [tʃʌmp] s ciocco, ceppo; (coll) sciocco
chunk [tʃʌŋk] s grosso pezzo
church [tʃʌrtʃ] s chiesa
churchgoer ['tʃʌrtʃ,go·ər] s praticante mf
church'man s (-men) parrocchiano; (clergyman) sacerdote m
Church' of Eng'land s chiesa anglicana
church'yard' s camposanto
churl [tʃʌrl] s zotico, villano
churlish ['tʃʌrlɪʃ] adj villano
churn [tʃʌrn] s zangola || tr agitare violentemente, sbattere || intr (said of water) ribollire
chute [ʃut] s piano inclinato, canna; (in a river) cascata, rapida; paracadute m; (into a swimming pool) toboga m
Cicero ['sɪsə,ro] s Cicerone m
cider ['saɪdər] s sidro
cigar [sɪ'gɑr] s sigaro
cigar' case' s portasigari m
cigar' cut'ter s tagliasigari m
cigarette [,sɪgə'rɛt] s sigaretta
cigarette' butt' s cicca
cigarette' case' s portasigarette m
cigarette' hold'er s bocchino

cigarette' light'er s accendisigaro, accendino
cigarette' pa'per s cartina da sigarette
cigar' store' s tabaccheria, rivendita di sali e tabacchi
cinch [sɪntʃ] s (on a horse) sottopancia m; (hold) (coll) presa; (slang) giochetto || tr legare con una cinghia; (slang) agguantare
cinder ['sɪndər] s tizzone m; (slag) scoria; **cinders** cenere f
cin'der block' s concio di scoria
Cinderella [,sɪndə'rɛlə] s (la) Cenerentola
cinema ['sɪnəmə] s cine m, cinema m
cinnabar ['sɪnə,bɑr] s cinabro
cinnamon ['sɪnəmən] s cannella
cipher ['saɪfər] s zero; cifra; codice m; monogramma m || tr calcolare; (to write in code) cifrare
circle ['sʌrkəl] s cerchio; (of theater) prima galleria; (of friends) cerchia || tr cerchiare, compiere una rotazione intorno a
circuit ['sʌrkɪt] s circuito; (district) circoscrizione
circuitous [sər'kju·ɪtəs] adj tortuoso
circuitry ['sʌrkɪtrɪ] s (plan) schema m di montaggio; (components) elementi mpl di un circuito
circular ['sʌrkjələr] adj & s circolare f
circulate ['sʌrkjə,let] tr mettere in circolazione, diffondere || intr circolare
cir'culating li'brary s biblioteca circolante
circulation [,sʌrkjə'leʃən] s circolazione; (of newspaper) diffusione
circumcise ['sʌrkəm,saɪz] tr circoncidere
circumference [sər'kʌmfərəns] s circonferenza
circumflex ['sʌrkəm,flɛks] adj circonflesso || s accento circonflesso
circumscribe [,sʌrkəm'skraɪb] tr circoscrivere
circumspect ['sʌrkəm,spɛkt] adj circospetto
circumstance ['sʌrkəm,stæns] s circostanza; (fact) dettaglio; solennità f; **circumstances** condizioni fpl; dettagli mpl; condizioni economiche; **under no circumstances** a nessuna condizione; **under the circumstances** le cose essendo come sono
circumstantial [,sʌrkəm'stænʃəl] adj circostanziale, indiziario; (incidental) secondario; (complete) circostanziato
cir'cumstan'tial ev'idence s prova indiziaria
circumstantiate [,sʌrkəm'stænʃɪ,et] tr (to support with particulars) comprovare; (to describe in detail) circonstanziare
circumvent [,sʌrkəm'vɛnt] tr (to surround) accerchiare; (to outwit) circuire; (a difficulty) eludere, scansare
circus ['sʌrkəs] s circo equestre
cistern ['sɪstərn] s cisterna, serbatoio
citadel ['sɪtədəl] s cittadella
citation [saɪ'teʃən] s citazione

cite [saɪt] *tr* citare

cither ['sɪðər] *s* cetra

citizen ['sɪtɪzən] *s* cittadino; (*civilian*) civile *mf*

citizenship ['sɪtɪzən‚ʃɪp] *s* cittadinanza

citric ['sɪtrɪk] *adj* citrico

citron ['sɪtrən] *s* cedro; cedro candito

cit'rus fruit' ['sɪtrəs] *s* agrumi *mpl*

cit·y ['sɪti] *s* (-ies) città *f*

cit'y coun·cil *s* consiglio municipale

cit'y ed'itor *s* capocronista *m*

cit'y fa'thers *spl* maggiorenti *mpl;* consiglieri *mpl* municipali

cit'y hall' *s* municipio

cit'y plan'ning *s* urbanistica

cit'y room' *s* (journ) redazione

civic ['sɪvɪk] *adj* civico || civics *s* educazione civica

civil ['sɪvɪl] *adj* civile

civ'il engineer'ing *s* genio civile

civilian [sɪ'vɪljən] *adj & s* civile *mf,* borghese *mf*

civili·ty [sɪ'vɪlɪti] *s* (-ties) cortesia; civilities ossequi *mpl*

civilization [‚sɪvɪlɪ'zeʃən] *s* civilizzazione, civiltà *f*

civilize ['sɪvɪ‚laɪz] *tr* civilizzare

civ'il law' *s* diritto civile

civ'il serv'ant *s* impiegato statale

civ'il war' *s* guerra civile || Civil War *s* (*of the U.S.A.*) guerra di secessione

claim [klem] *s* pretesa; richiesta; (min) concessione || *tr* (*one's rights*) rivendicare; (*one's property*) richiedere; dichiarare; **to claim to be** pretendere d'essere

claim' check' *s* tagliando

clairvoyance [kler'vɔɪ-əns] *s* chiaroveggenza

clairvoyant [kler'vɔɪ-ənt] *adj* chiaroveggente || *s* veggente *mf,* chiaroveggente *mf*

clam [klæm] *s* vongola || *intr*—to clam up (coll) essere muto come un pesce

clamber ['klæmər] *intr* arrampicarsi

clam·my ['klæmi] *adj* (-mier; -miest) coperto di sudore freddo; morbido

clamor ['klæmər] *s* clamore *m* || *intr* fare clamore

clamorous ['klæmərəs] *adj* clamoroso

clamp [klæmp] *s* graffa, morsetto; (*e.g., to hold a hose*) fascetta || *tr* assicurare con graffa, aggrappare; (*a tool*) montare || *intr*—to clamp down on (coll) fare pressione su, mettere i freni a

clan [klæn] *s* clan *m*

clandestine [klæn'destɪn] *adj* clandestino

clang [klæŋ] *s* clangore *m* || *intr* risonare con clangore

clannish ['klænɪʃ] *adj* esclusivista, partigiano

clap [klæp] *s* applauso; (*of thunder*) scoppio || *v* (*pret & pp* clapped; *ger* clapping) *tr* (*the hands*) battere; (*e.g., in jail*) sbattere; **to clap shut** sbattere || *intr* applaudire

clapper ['klæpər] *s* applauditore *m;* (*of bell*) batacchio

clap'trap' *s* imbonimento

claret ['klærɪt] *adj & s* chiaretto

clari·fy ['klærɪ‚faɪ] *v* (*pret & pp* -fied) *tr* chiarificare, chiarire

clarinet [‚klærɪ'net] *s* clarinetto

clarion ['klærɪ-ən] *adj* chiaro e metallico || *s* tromba, clarino

clash [klæʃ] *s* cozzo, urto; conflitto di opinioni || *intr* cozzare, urtarsi; essere in conflitto

clasp [klæsp] or [klɑsp] *s* gancio, fermaglio; (*hold*) presa; (*grip*) stretta || *tr* agganciare; (*to hold in the arms*) abbracciare; (*to grip*) stringere

class [klæs] or [klɑs] *s* classe *f* || *tr* classificare

class'book' *s* registro

classic ['klæsɪk] *adj & s* classico

classical ['klæsɪkəl] *adj* classico

classicism ['klæsɪ‚sɪzəm] *s* classicismo

classicist ['klæsɪsɪst] *s* classicista *mf*

classified ['klæsɪ‚faɪd] *adj* segreto

clas'sified ad' *s* annunzio economico

classi·fy ['klæsɪ‚faɪ] *v* (*pret & pp* -fied) *tr* classificare

class'mate' *s* compagno di scuola

class'room' *s* aula scolastica

class' strug'gle *s* lotta di classe

class·y [klæsi] *adj* (-ier; -iest) (slang) di lusso, di prim'ordine

clatter ['klætər] *s* (*of dishes*) acciottolio; vocio, schiamazzo || *tr* acciottolare || *intr* fare schiamazzo

clause [klɔz] *s* clausola; (gram) proposizione

clavicle ['klævɪkəl] *s* clavicola

claw [klɔ] *s* artiglio; (*of lobster*) pinza; (*tool*) raffio; (*of hammer*) granchio; (coll) dita *fpl* || *tr* aggraffiare; artigliare

claw' ham'mer *s* levachiodi *m*

clay [kle] *s* argilla, creta

clay' pipe' *s* pipa di terracotta

clean [klin] *adj* pulito; (*precise*) netto; (*e.g., break*) completo || *adv* completamente || *tr* pulire; **to clean out** pulire, fare repulisti di; (slang) ripulire; **to clean up** pulire completamente; mettere in ordine || *intr* pulirsi, fare pulizia

clean' bill' of health' *s* patente sanitaria; (fig) esonero completo

clean'-cut' *adj* ben delineato, deciso

cleaner ['klinər] *s* pulitore *m,* smacchiatore *m;* (*machine*) pulitrice *f,* smacchiatrice *f;* **to send to the cleaners** (slang) spolpare

clean'ing fluid' *s* smacchiatore *m*

clean'ing wom'an *s* donna di servizio per fare la pulizia

clean·ly ['klenli] *adj* (-lier; -liest) pulito, netto

cleanse [klenz] *tr* pulire; detergere; purificare

cleanser ['klenzər] *s* detergente *m*

clean'-sha'ven *adj* sbarbato di fresco

clean'up' *s* pulizia; (slang) guadagno enorme

clear [klɪr] *adj* chiaro; evidente; completo; innocente; (*profit*) netto; **clear of** libero da || *s* posto libero; **in the clear** libero; esonerato; non in codice || *adv* chiaramente; completamente || *tr* (*e.g., trees*) rischiarare; (*e.g., peo-*

ple) sgombrare; (*the table*) sparecchiare; (*an obstacle*) superare; (*from guilt*) discolpare; (*a profit*) guadagnare; (*goods at customs*) svincolare; (*a ship through customs*) dichiarare il carico di; (*checks*) compensare; **to clear away or off** liberare; **to clear out** sgombrare, sbarazzare; **to clear up** spiegare; (*a doubt*) dissipare ‖ *intr* rasserenarsi; (*said of a ship*) partire; **to clear away or off** sparire; **to clear out** (coll) andarsene; **to clear up** rasserenarsi

clearance ['klɪrəns] *s* liberazione; (*of a ship*) partenza; (*of goods through customs*) sdoganamento; (*of checks*) compensazione; (*of goods*) liquidazione; (*mach*) gioco

clear'ance sale' *s* liquidazione

clear'-cut' *adj* chiaro, distinto

clearing ['klɪrɪŋ] *s* (*open space*) radura; (*of checks*) compensazione

clear'ing house' *s* stanza di compensazione

cleat [klit] *s* bietta, cuneo; (*on the sole of shoe*) tacchetto; (naut) galloccia

cleavage ['klivɪdʒ] *s* divisione; fessura

cleave [kliv] *v* (*pret & pp* **cleft** [kleft] *or* **cleaved**) *tr* dividere, fendere ‖ *intr* aderire, essere fedele

cleaver ['klivər] *s* scure *f*, accetta; (*of butcher*) spaccaossa *m*, fenditoio

clef [klef] *s* (mus) chiave *f*

cleft [kleft] *adj* diviso, fesso ‖ *s* fessura, crepaccio

cleft' pal'ate *s* palato spaccato, gola lupina

clematis ['klemətɪs] *s* clematide *f*

clemen·cy ['klemənsi] *s* (-cies) clemenza

clement ['klemənt] *adj* clemente

clench [klentʃ] *s* stretta ‖ *tr* stringere; afferrare

clergy ['klɜrdʒi] *s* clero

cler'gy·man *s* (-men) ecclesiastico

cleric ['klɛrɪk] *s* ecclesiastico, sacerdote *m*

clerical ['klɛrɪkəl] *adj* da impiegato; (*error*) burocratico; (*of clergy*) clericale ‖ *s* ecclesiastico; **clericals** abiti ecclesiastici

cler'ical work' *s* lavoro d'ufficio

clerk [klɑrk] *s* impiegato, commesso; (*accountant*) contabile *mf*; (*e.g., in a record office*) ufficiale *m*; cancelliere *m*; (*copyist, typist*) scrivano

clever ['klevər] *adj* intelligente; bravo, abile; destro

cleverness ['klevərnɪs] *s* intelligenza; bravura, abilità *f*

clew [klu] *s* indizio, traccia; (*of yarn*) gomitolo; (naut) bugna

cliché [kli'ʃe] *s* cliché *m*, luogo comune

click [klɪk] *s* (*of camera or gun*) scatto; (*of typewriter*) battito, ticchettio ‖ *tr* (*the tongue*) schioccare; (*the heels*) battere ‖ *intr* ticchettare; (slang) andare d'accordo; (slang) avere fortuna

client ['klaɪ·ənt] *s* cliente *mf*

clientele [,klaɪ·ən'tɛl] *s* clientela

cliff [klɪf] *s* rupe *f*, precipizio

climate ['klaɪmɪt] *s* clima *m*

climax ['klaɪmæks] *s* apice *m*; (*acute phase*) parossismo

climb [klaɪm] *s* salita; (*of a mountain*) scalata, ascensione ‖ *tr* (*the stairs*) salire; (*a mountain*) scalare, ascendere ‖ *intr* salire, arrampicarsi; **to climb down** discendere a carponi; (coll) ritirarsi

climber ['klaɪmər] *s* scalatore *m*; pianta rampicante; (*ambitious person*) (coll) arrampicatore *m*

clinch [klɪntʃ] *s* stretta, presa; (*boxing*) corpo a corpo *m* ‖ *tr* (*nails*) ribattere, ribadire

clincher ['klɪntʃər] *s* chiodo per ribaditura; argomento decisivo

cling [klɪŋ] *v* (*pret & pp* **clung** [klʌŋ]) *intr* avviticchiare, attaccarsi; aderire, rimanere attaccato

cling'stone' peach' *s* pesca duracino

clinic ['klɪnɪk] *s* clinica

clinical ['klɪnɪkəl] *adj* clinico

clinician [klɪ'nɪʃən] *s* clinico

clink [klɪŋk] *s* tintinnio; (slang) gattabuia ‖ *tr* (*glasses*) toccare ‖ *intr* tintinnare

clinker ['klɪŋkər] *s* clinker *m*; mattone vetrificato; (slang) sbaglio

clip [klɪp] *s* (*of hair*) taglio; (*of wool*) tosatura; (*speed*) passo rapido; clip *f*, fermaglio; (*large clip*) fermacarte *m*; (*for cartridges*) caricatore *m*; (coll) colpo ‖ *v* (*pret & pp* **clipped**) *ger* **clipping**) *tr* tagliare, tosare; (*words*) mangiare, storpiare; (*paper*) ritagliare; ritenere; (coll) battere ‖ *intr* andare di buon passo

clipper ['klɪpər] *s* tagliatore *m*; (aer, naut) clipper *m*; **clippers** (*for hair*) tosatrice *f*; (*for nails*) pinze *fpl* per le unghie

clipping ['klɪpɪŋ] *s* taglio; (*from newspaper*) ritaglio

clique [klik] *s* cricca, chiesuola

cloak [klok] *s* mantello, manto; (fig) velo, maschera ‖ *tr* ammantare, velare

cloak'-and-dag'ger *adj* d'avventura

cloak'-and-sword' *adj* di cappa e spada

cloak'room' *s* guardaroba *m*

clock [klɑk] *s* orologio; (*with pendulum*) pendolo, pendola; (*on stocking*) freccia ‖ *tr* registrare, cronometrare

clock'mak'er *s* orologiaio

clock' tow'er *s* torre *f* dell'orologio

clock'wise' *adj & adv* nella direzione delle lancette dell'orologio

clock'work' *s* movimento d'orologeria; **like clockwork** come un orologio

clod [klɑd] *s* zolla; (fig) tonto

clod'hop'per *s* (*shoe*) scarpone *m*; (fig) villano, bifolco

clog [klɑg] *s* intoppo; (*to impede movement*) pastoia; scarpone *m*, zoccolo ‖ *v* (*pret & pp* **clogged**; *ger* **clogging**) *tr* intoppare; (*to hold back*) impastoiare ‖ *intr* otturarsi, ostruirsi

cloister ['klɔɪstər] *s* chiostro ‖ *tr* rinchiudere in un chiostro

close [klos] *adj* vicino; (*translation*)

fedele; (*air in room*) male arieggiato; (*weather*) soffocante; (*stingy*) avaro; limitato, senza gioco; (*haircut*) corto; (*friend*) intimo; (*hit*) preciso; (*enclosed*) chiuso; (*narrow*) stretto || *adv* da vicino; **close to** vicino a || [kloz] *s* fine *f*, conclusione; **to bring to a close** concludere || *tr* chiudere; otturare; concludere; **to close down** chiudere completamente; **to close out** vendere in liquidazione; **to close up** bloccare || *intr* chiudersi; serrarsi; **to close down** chiudersi completamente; **to close in on** venire alle prese con; **to close up** bloccarsi; (*said of a wound*) rimarginarsi

close' call' [klos] *s* rischio scampato per miracolo

closed' chap'ter *s* affare chiuso

closed' cir'cuit *s* circuito chiuso

closed' sea'son *s* periodo di caccia o pesca vietata

closefisted ['klos'fɪstɪd] *adj* taccagno

close'-fit'ing [klos] *adj* attillato

close-lipped ['klos'lɪpt] *adj* riservato

closely ['klosli] *adv* da vicino; strettamente; fedelmente; attentamente

close' quar'ters [klos] *spl* (*cramped space*) pigia pigia *m*; **at close quarters** a corpo a corpo

close' quote' [kloz] *s* fine *f* della citazione

close' shave' [klos] *s*—**to have a close shave** farsi fare la barba a contropelo; (coll) scamparla per un pelo

closet ['klɑzɪt] *s* armadio a muro; (*small private room*) gabinetto; (*for keeping clothing*) ripostiglio || *tr*—**to be closeted with** essere in concialabolo con

close'-up' [klos] *s* (mov) primo piano

closing ['klozɪŋ] *s* fine *f*, conclusione

clos'ing price' *s* ultimo corso

clot [klɑt] *s* grumo, coagulo || *v* (*pret & pp* **clotted;** *ger* **clotting**) *intr* raggrumarsi, coagularsi

cloth [klɔθ] *or* [klɑθ] *s* panno, tessuto, stoffa; abito; (*for binding books*) tela; **the cloth** il clero

clothe [kloð] *v* (*pret & pp* **clothed** *or* **clad** [klæd]) *tr* vestire, rivestire, coprire

clothes [kloz] *or* [kloðz] *spl* vestiti *mpl*, abiti *mpl*; (*for a bed*) coltre *f*; **to change clothes** cambiarsi

clothes'bas'ket *s* cesto della biancheria

clothes'brush' *s* spazzola per vestiti

clothes' dry'er *s* asciugatrice *f*

clothes' hang'er *s* attaccapanni *m*

clothes'horse' *s* cavalletto per stendere il bucato; elegantone *m*

clothes'line' *s* corda per stendere il bucato

clothes' moth' *s* tarma, tignola

clothes'pin' *s* molletta

clothes' tree' *s* attaccapanni *m*

clothier ['kloðjər] *s* negoziante *m* di confezioni; mercante *m* di panno

clothing ['kloðɪŋ] *s* vestiti *mpl*, vestiario

cloud [klaud] *s* nuvola, nube *f*; (*great number*) nuvolo; macchia; sospetto

|| tr annuvolare; offuscare || *intr* annuvolarsi; offuscarsi

cloud' bank' *s* banco di nubi

cloud'burst' *s* acquazzone *m*, nubifragio

cloud'-capped' *adj* coperto di nubi

cloudless ['klaudlɪs] *adj* senza nubi

cloud·y ['klaudi] *adj* (-ier; -iest) nuvoloso, annuvolato; confuso; tenebroso

clout [klaut] *s* (coll) schiaffo || *tr* (coll) schiaffeggiare

clove [klov] *s* chiodo di garofano; (*of garlic*) spicchio

cloven-hoofed ['klovən'huft] *adj* dal piede biforcuto; demoniaco

clover ['klovər] *s* trifoglio; **in clover** come un papa

clo'ver·leaf' *s* (-leaves [ˌlivz]) foglia di trifoglio; incrocio stradale a quadrifoglio

clown [klaun] *s* pagliaccio, buffone *m* || *intr* fare il pagliaccio

clownish ['klaunɪʃ] *adj* buffonesco, clownesco, claunesco

cloy [klɔɪ] *tr* saziare fino alla nausea

club [klʌb] *s* bastone *m*; circolo, società *f*; (*playing card*) fiore *m* || *v* (*pret & pp* **clubbed;** *ger* **clubbing**) *tr* bastonare || *intr*—**to club together** unirsi

club' car' *s* vagone *m* con servizio di buffet

club'house' *s* sede *f* di un circolo

club'man' *s* (-men') frequentatore *m* di circoli

club'room' *s* sala delle riunioni

club' sand'wich *s* sandwich *m* a tre fette di pane con insalata

club'wom'an *s* (-wom'en) frequentatrice *f* di circoli

cluck [klʌk] *s* (il) chiocciare || *intr* chiocciare

clue [klu] *s* traccia, indizio

clump [klʌmp] *s* gruppo, massa; (*of earth*) zolla || *intr* camminare con passo pesante

clum·sy ['klʌmzi] *adj* (-sier; -siest) goffo, malaccorto, sgraziato

cluster ['klʌstər] *s* gruppo; (*of grapes*) grappolo; (*of bees*) sciame *m*; (*of stars*) ammasso; (*of people*) folla || *tr* raggruppare || *intr* raggrupparsi

clutch [klʌtʃ] *s* presa; (*claw*) grinfia; (*of chickens*) covata; (mach) innesto; (aut) frizione; **clutches** grinfie *fpl*; **to throw the clutch in** innestare la marcia; **to throw the clutch out** disinnestare la marcia || *tr* afferrare, aggrappare || *intr*—**to clutch at** aggrapparsi a

clutter ['klʌtər] *tr*—**to clutter up** ingombrare alla rinfusa

coach [kotʃ] *s* carrozza, vettura; vagone *m*; (*automobile*) berlina; autobus *m*; (*trainer*) allenatore *m*; (*teacher*) ripetitore *m* || *tr* allenare; preparare

coach' house' *s* rimessa

coaching ['kotʃɪŋ] *s* suggerimento; (*in school*) ripetizione; (sports) allenamento

coach'man *s* (-men) cocchiere *m*

coagulate [koˈægjə‿ˌlet] *tr* coagulare ‖ *intr* coagularsi

coal [kol] *s* carbone *m;* (*piece of burning wood*) tizzone *m;* **to call** or **haul over the coals** rimproverare ‖ *tr* rifornire di carbone ‖ *intr* rifornirsi di carbone; (*naut*) fare carbone

coal′bin′ *s* carbonaia

coal′ deal′er *s* (*wholesale*) negoziante *m* di carbone; (*retail*) carbonaio

coal′ field′ *s* bacino carbonifero

coal′ gas′ *s* gas *m* illuminante

coalition [ˌko‿əˈlɪʃən] *s* coalizione

coal′ mine′ *s* miniera di carbone

coal′ oil′ *s* cherosene *m*

coal′ scut′tle *s* secchio del carbone

coal′ tar′ *s* catrame *m*

coal′ yard′ *s* carbonaia, carboniera

coarse [kors] *adj* (*manners*) volgare, ordinario; (*unrefined*) greggio; (*lacking refinement in manners*) rozzo, grossolano

coast [kost] *s* costa; discesa a ruota libera; **the coast is clear** la via è libera ‖ *tr* costeggiare ‖ *intr* costeggiare; scendere a ruota libera

coastal [ˈkostəl] *adj* costiero

coaster [ˈkostər] *s* nave *f* di cabotaggio; (*amusement*) otto volante, montagna russa; (*small tray*) sottobicchiere *m*

coast′er brake′ *s* freno a contropedale

coast′ guard′ *s* guardacoste *m*

coast′-guard cut′ter *s* guardacoste *m*

coast′ing trade′ *s* cabotaggio

coast′land′ *s* costa

coast′line′ *s* linea costiera, litorale *m*

coast′wise′ *adv* lungo la costa

coat [kot] *s* soprabito; cappotto; (*jacket*) giacca; (*hide of man and animals*) mantello; (*of paint*) mano *f;* (*layer*) strato ‖ *tr* vestire, proteggere; ricoprire, coprire

coat′ed [ˈkotɪd] *adj* rivestito; (*tongue*) patinato

coat′ hang′er *s* attaccapanni *m*

coating [ˈkotɪŋ] *s* rivestimento; (*of paint*) mano *f;* (*of cement*) strato; (*cloth*) tessuto per abiti

coat′ of arms′ *s* scudo, stemma *m*

coat′room′ *s* guardaroba *m*

coat′tail′ *s* falda

coax [koks] *tr* blandire; ottenere con lusinghe

cob [kɑb] *s* spiga di granturco; (*horse*) cavallo da tiro; (*swan*) cigno maschio

cobalt [ˈkobɔlt] *s* cobalto

cobble [ˈkɑbəl] *s* ciottolo ‖ *tr* acciottolare; (*to mend*) raccomodare, riparare

cobbler [ˈkɑblər] *s* calzolaio, ciabattino; (*pie*) torta di frutta

cob′ble-stone′ *s* ciottolo

cob′web′ *s* tela di ragno, ragnatela

cocaine [koˈken] *s* cocaina

cock [kɑk] *s* gallo; (*faucet*) rubinetto; (*of gun*) cane *m;* (*of the eye*) ammicco; (*of nose*) angolo (del naso) rivolto all'insù; (*of hay*) covone *m* ‖ *tr* (*a gun*) armare; (*the head*) drizzare

cockade [kɑˈked] *s* coccarda

cock-a-doodle-doo [ˈkɑkə‿ˌdudəlˈdu] *s* chicchirichì *m*

cock′-and-bull′ sto′ry *s* racconto incredibile

cocked′ hat′ *s* tricorno, cappello tricorno; **to knock into a cocked hat** (*slang*) distruggere completamente

cockeyed [ˈkɑkˌaɪd] *adj* strabico; (*slang*) sbilenco; (*slang*) sciocco, scemo

cockle [ˈkɑkəl] *s* (*mollusk*) cardio; (*weed*) loglio; (*boat*) barchetta; (*wrinkle*) grinza; **to warm the cockles of one's heart** far bene al cuore ‖ *intr* raggrinzirsi

cock′ of the walk′ *s* gallo del pollaio

cock′pit′ *s* (*of boat*) cabina; (*aer*) carlinga; (*naut*) cassero di poppa

cock′roach′ *s* scarafaggio, blatta

cocks′comb′ *s* cresta di gallo; berretto da buffone

cock′sure′ *adj* ostinato; troppo sicuro di sé stesso

cock′tail′ *s* cocktail *m*

cock′tail par′ty *s* cocktail *m*

cock•y [ˈkɑki] *adj* (*-ier; -iest*) impudente, presuntuoso

cocoa [ˈkoko] *s* (*bean*) cacao; (*drink*) cioccolata; (*tree*) cocco

coconut [ˈkokəˌnʌt] *s* noce *f* di cocco

co′conut palm′ or **tree′** *s* cocco

cocoon [kəˈkun] *s* bozzolo

cod [kɑd] *s* merluzzo

C.O.D. [ˈsiˈoˈdi] *s* (letterword) (**Collect on Delivery**) contro assegno

coddle [ˈkɑdəl] *tr* vezzeggiare

code [kod] *s* codice *m*, cifra; **in code** in codice, in cifra ‖ *tr* mettere in codice or in cifra; cifrare

codex [ˈkodeks] *s* (**codices** [ˈkodɪˌsiz] or [ˈkɑdɪˌsiz]) codice *m*

cod′fish′ *s* merluzzo

codger [ˈkɑdʒər] *s*—**old codger** (coll) vecchietto

codicil [ˈkɑdɪsɪl] *s* codicillo

codi•fy [ˈkɑdɪˌfaɪ] or [ˈkodɪˌfaɪ] *v* (*pret & pp* -**fied**) *tr* codificare

cod′-liver oil′ *s* olio di fegato di merluzzo

coed [ˈcoˌed] *s* studentessa di scuola mista

coeducation [ˌkoˌedʒəˈkeʃən] *s* coeducazione

co′educa′tional school′ [ˌko‿edʒəˈkeʃənəl] *s* scuola mista

coefficient [ˌko‿ɪˈfɪʃənt] *s* coefficiente *m*

coerce [koˈʌrs] *tr* forzare, costringere

coercion [koˈʌrʃən] *s* coercizione

coexist [ˌko‿ɪɡˈzɪst] *intr* coesistere

coffee [ˈkɔfi] or [ˈkɑfi] *s* caffè *m;* **ground coffee** caffè macinato; **roasted coffee** caffè torrefatto

cof′fee bean′ *s* chicco di caffè

cof′fee-cake′ *s* pasticcino (da mangiarsi con il caffè)

cof′fee grind′er *s* macinino da caffè, macinacaffè *m*

cof′fee grounds′ *spl* fondi *mpl* di caffè

cof′fee house′ *s* caffè *m*

cof′fee mak′er *s* macchinetta del caffè

cof'fee mill' s macinino del caffè, macinacaffè m

cof'fee·pot' s caffettiera

cof'fee shop' s caffè m

coffer ['kɔfər] or ['kafər] s forziere m; (ceiling) soffitto a cassettoni; (archit) cassettone m; coffers tesoro

coffin ['kɔfɪn] or ['kafɪn] s bara

cog [kɑg] s dente m d'ingranaggio; ruota dentata; to slip a cog fare un errore

cogent ['kodʒənt] adj convincente, persuasivo

cogitate ['kadʒɪ,tet] tr & intr cogitare, ponzare

cognac ['konjæk] or ['kanjæk] s cognac m

cognate ['kɑgnet] adj consanguineo, parente, affine || s parola dello stesso ceppo linguistico; consanguineo, parente mf

cognizance ['kɑgnɪzəns] or ['kɑnɪzəns] s conoscenza; to take cognizance of prendere conoscenza di

cognizant ['kɑgnɪzənt] or ['kɑnɪzənt] adj informato, al corrente

cog'wheel' s ruota dentata

cohabit [ko'hæbɪt] intr convivere; (archaic) coabitare

coheir [ko'ɛr] s coerede mf

cohere [ko'hɪr] intr aderire; (fig) avere nesso

coherent [ko'hɪrənt] adj coerente

coiffeur [kwɑ'fʌr] s parrucchiere m per signora; (Brit) parrucchiere m

coiffure [kwɑ'fjur] s pettinatura || tr pettinare

coil [kɔɪl] s (of rope) rotolo; (of pipe) serpentino; (of wire) bobina, avvolgimento || tr arrotolare || intr arrotolarsi

coil' spring' s molla a spirale, molla elicoidale

coin [kɔɪn] s moneta; to pay back in one's own coin pagare della stessa moneta; to toss a coin giocare a testa o croce || tr (money) coniare, battere; (words) inventare, creare; to coin money battere moneta; (coll) fare soldoni

coincide [,ko·ɪn'saɪd] intr coincidere

coincidence [ko'ɪnsɪdəns] s coincidenza

coke [kok] s coke m, carbone m coke

colander ['kʌləndər] or ['kʌləndər] s colabrodo, colapasta m

cold [kold] adj freddo; it is cold (said of weather) fa freddo; to be cold (said of a person) avere freddo || s freddo; (ailment) raffreddore m; out in the cold solo soletto; to catch cold pigliare freddo, pigliarsi un raffreddore

cold' blood' s—in cold blood a sangue freddo

cold'-blood'ed adj insensibile; (sensitive to cold) freddoloso; (animal) a sangue freddo

cold' chis'el s tagliaferro

cold' com'fort s magra consolazione

cold' cream' s crema emolliente

cold' cuts' spl salumi mpl, affettato

cold' feet' spl—to get cold feet (coll) perdersi d'animo

cold'-heart'ed adj—to be coldhearted avere il cuore duro

coldness ['koldnɪs] s freddezza

cold' shoul'der s—to get the cold shoulder (coll) essere trattato con freddezza; to turn a cold shoulder on (coll) trattare con freddezza

cold' snap' s freddo breve e improvviso

cold' stor'age s conservazione a freddo

cold' war' s guerra fredda

cold' wave' s ondata di freddo

coleslaw ['kol,slɔ] s insalata di cavolo cappuccio

colic ['kɑlɪk] adj colico || s colica

coliseum [,kɑlɪ'si·əm] s stadio, arena || Coliseum s Colosseo

collaborate [kə'læbə,ret] intr collaborare

collaborationist [kə,læbə're/ənɪst] s collaborazionista mf

collaborator [kə'læbə,retər] s collaboratore m

collapse [kə'læps] s (of business) fallimento; (e.g., of a roof) caduta; (of a person) collasso || tr piegare || intr (to shrink) restringersi, sgonfiarsi; (said of a business) fallire; (said of health) venir meno; (said, e.g., of a roof) cadere, crollare

collapsible [kə'læpsɪbəl] adj pieghevole, smontabile

collar ['kɑlər] s (of shirt) colletto; (for dog or horse) collare m; (ring) anello; (short piece of pipe) manicotto || tr afferrare per il collo, catturare

col'lar·band' s cinturino della camicia

col'lar·bone' s clavicola

collate [kə'let] or ['kɑlet] tr collazionare, confrontare

collateral [kə'lætərəl] adj collaterale; accessorio, addizionale || s collaterale m

colleague ['kɑlig] s collega mf

collect ['kɑlekt] s (eccl) colletta || [kə'lekt] adv contro assegno; (telp) tr raccogliere, riunire; (e.g., stamps) collezionare; (mail) levare; (bills) incassare; (ideas) coordinare; (thoughts) riordinare; (e.g., classroom papers) raccogliere; (taxes) riscuotere; to collect oneself riprendersi, riprendere il controllo di sé stesso || intr (for the poor) fare la colletta; riunirsi, raccogliersi

collected [kə'lektɪd] adj raccolto; equilibrato, padrone di sè

collection [kə'lek/ən] s collezione; (for the poor) colletta; (of mail) levata; (heap) deposito; (of taxes) esazione; (of bills) riscossione

collec'tion a'gency s agenzia di riscossione

collective [kə'lektɪv] adj collettivo

collector [kə'lektər] s (of stamps) collezionista mf; (of taxes) esattore m; (of tickets) controllore m

college ['kɑlɪdʒ] s scuola superiore,

università *f*; (*e.g.*, *of medicine*) facoltà *f*; (*electoral*) collegio

collide [kə'laɪd] *intr* collidere, scontrarsi

collie ['kɑli] *s* collie *m*

collier ['kaljər] *s* (*ship*) carboniera; (min) minatore *m* di carbone

collier•y ['kaljəri] *s* (**-ies**) miniera di carbone

collision [kə'lɪʒən] *s* collisione

colloid ['kaloɪd] *adj* colloidale ‖ *s* colloide *m*

colloquial [kə'lokwɪ-əl] *adj* familiare, colloquiale

colloquialism [kə'lokwɪ-ə,lɪzəm] *s* espressione familiare

collo•quy ['kaləkwi]•*s* (**-quies**) colloquio

collusion [kə'luʒən] *s* collusione; **to be in collusion with** essere d'intelligenza con

cologne [kə'lon] *s* acqua di colonia, colonia ‖ **Cologne** *s* Colonia

colon ['kolən] *s* (anat) colon *m*; (gram) due punti *mpl*

colonel ['kʌrnəl] *s* colonnello

colonist ['kalənɪst] *s* colono, coloniale *m*

colonize ['kalə,naɪz] *tr & intr* colonizzare

colonnade [,kalə'ned] *s* colonnato

colo•ny ['kaləni] *s* (**-nies**) colonia

color ['kʌlər] *s* colore *m*; **off color** sbiadito, scolorito; (slang) sporco, volgare; **the colors** i colori, la bandiera; **to call to the colors** chiamare in servizio militare; **to change color** cambiar colore; arrossire; impallidire; **to give or lend color to** far parere probabile; **to lose color** impallidire; **to show one's colors** mostrarsi come si è; **under color of** sotto il pretesto di ‖ *tr* colorare; (fig) colorire ‖ *intr* arrossire

col'or-blind' *adj* daltonico

colored ['kʌlərd] *adj* colorato; (*person*) di colore; esagerato

colorful ['kʌlərfəl] *adj* colorito, espressivo

col'or guard' *s* guardia d'onore alla bandiera

coloring ['kʌlərɪŋ] *s* colorazione; colore *m*; pigmento; (fig) specie *f*

colorless ['kʌlərlɪs] *adj* incolore, incoloro

col'or photog'raphy *s* fotografia a colori

col'or ser'geant *s* sergente *m* portabandiera

col'or tel'evision *s* televisione a colori

colossal [kə'lasəl] *adj* colossale

colossus [kə'lasəs] *s* colosso

colt [kolt] *s* puledro

Columbus [kə'lʌmbəs] *s* Colombo

column ['kaləm] *s* colonna

columnist ['kaləmɪst] *s* giornalista incaricato di una colonna speciale; articolista *mf*

coma ['komə] *s* coma *m*

comb [kom] *s* pettine *m*; (*for horse*) striglia; (*of hen or wave*) cresta; (*honeycomb*) favo ‖ *tr* pettinare;

(fig) esaminare minuziosamente ‖ *intr* (*said of waves*) frangersi

com•bat ['kambæt] *s* combattimento ‖ ['kambæt] or [kəm'bæt] *v* (*pret & pp* **-bated** or **-batted**; *ger* **-bating** or **-batting**) *tr & intr* combattere

combatant ['kambətənt] *s* combattente *mf*

com'bat du'ty *s* servizio in zona di guerra

combination [,kambɪ'neʃən] *s* combinazione

combine ['kambaɪn] *s* consorzio; (pol) coalizione; mieto-trebbiatrice *f* ‖ [kəm'baɪn] *tr* combinare ‖ *intr* combinarsi

combin'ing form' *s* membro di parola composta

combo ['kambo] *s* orchestrina

combustible [kəm'bʌstɪbəl] *adj & s* combustibile *m*

combustion [kəm'bʌstʃən] *s* combustione

come [kʌm] *v* (*pret* **came** [kem]; *pp* **come**) *intr* venire; arrivare; (*to become*) diventare; (*to amount*) ammontare; **come!** macchè!; **come along!** andiamo!; **come in!** avanti, entri!; **come on!** andiamo!, avanti, coraggio!; **to come about** accadere, succedere; **to come across** incontrarsi con; (slang) pagare; **to come around** cedere; mettersi d'accordo; (*said of health*) rimettersi; **to come at** raggiungere; (*to attack*) attaccare; **to come back** ritornare; **to come between** mettersi fra; **to come by** ottenere; **to come down** scendere; decadere; essere trasmesso; **to come down with** ammalarsi di; **to come forward** farsi avanti; **to come in** entrare, passare; **to come in for** ricevere; **to come into** ricevere; ereditare; **to come off** succedere; riuscire; **to come on** mostrarsi; migliorare; incontrarsi; **to come out** uscire; debuttare in società; andare a finire; **to come out with** uscire con; mostrare; **to come over** succedere a, *e.g.*, **what came over him?** che gli è successo?; **to come through** riuscire; **to come to** riprendere i sensi; **to come under** essere di competenza di; appartenere a; **to come up** salire; **to come up to** salire fino a; avvicinarsi a; **to come up with** raggiungere; produrre, fornire; proporre

come'back' *s* (coll) ritorno; (slang) pronta risposta; **to stage a comeback** (coll) ritornare in auge

comedian [kə'midɪ·ən] *s* attore comico; (*author*) commediografo; (*amusing person*) commediante *mf*

comedienne [kə,midɪ'en] *s* attrice comica

come'down' *s* (coll) rovescio di fortuna

come•dy ['kamədi] *s* (**-dies**) commedia

come•ly ['kʌmli] *adj* (**-lier; -liest**) bello, grazioso

comet ['kamɪt] *s* cometa

comfort ['kʌmfərt] *s* conforto, sollievo;

(ease) benessere *m* ‖ *tr* confortare, alleviare

comfortable ['kʌmfərtəbəl] *adj* comodo, agiato; *(e.g., income)* (coll) bastante ‖ *s* coltre *f*

comforter ['kʌmfərtər] *s* consolatore *m;* *(bedcover)* coltre *f;* sciarpa di lana ‖ **the Comforter** lo Spirito Santo, lo Spirito Consolatore

comforting ['kʌmfərtɪŋ] *adj* confortante

com'fort sta'tion *s* latrina pubblica

comic ['kɑmɪk] *adj* comico ‖ *s (actor)* comico; comicità *f;* **comics** fumetti *mpl*

comical ['kɑmɪkəl] *adj* comico

com'ic book' *s* libretto a fumetti

com'ic op'era *s* opera buffa

com'ic strip' *s* racconto umoristico a fumetti

coming ['kʌmɪŋ] *adj* venturo, prossimo; promettente ‖ *s* venuta

com'ing out' *s* debutto in società; *(e.g., of stock)* emissione

comma ['kɑmə] *s* virgola

command [kə'mænd] *or* [kə'mɑnd] *s* comando; *(e.g., of a language)* padronanza *f* ‖ *tr* comandare, ordinare; *(to overlook)* dominare; *(to be able to have)* disporre di ‖ *intr* avere il comando

commandant [,kɑmən'dænt] *or* [,kɑmən'dɑnt] *s* comandante *m*

commandeer [,kɑmən'dɪr] *tr* requisire

commander [kə'mændər] *or* [kə'mɑndər] *s (of knighthood)* commendatore *m;* (mil) comandante *m;* (nav) capitano di vascello

command'er in chief' *s* comandante *m* in capo

command'ing of'ficer *s* comandante *m*

commandment [kə'mændmənt] *or* [kə'mɑndmənt] *s* comandamento

command' mod'ule *s* (rok) modulo di comando

commando [kə'mændo] *s* guastatore *m*

commemorate [kə'mɛmə,ret] *tr* commemorare, celebrare

commence [kə'mɛns] *tr & intr* cominciare

commencement [kə'mɛnsmənt] *s* inizio, esordio; *(in a school)* cerimonia per la distribuzione dei diplomi

commend [kə'mɛnd] *tr* lodare; *(to entrust)* raccomandare, affidare

commendable [kə'mɛndəbəl] *adj (person)* lodevole; *(act)* commendevole

commendation [,kɑmən'deʃən] *s* lode *f;* raccomandazione; (mil) citazione

comment ['kɑmɛnt] *s* commento ‖ *tr* commentare ‖ *intr* fare commenti; **to comment on** fare commenti su

commentary ['kɑmən,teri] *s (-ies)* commentario

commentator ['kɑmən,tetər] *s* commentatore *m*

commerce ['kɑmərs] *s* commercio

commercial [kə'mɛrʃəl] *adj* commerciale ‖ *s* (rad, telv) programma *m* di pubblicità; (rad, telv) annunzio pubblicitario

commiserate [kə'mɪzə,ret] *intr—to*

commiserate with commiserare, compiangere

commissar ['kɑmɪ,sɑr] *or* [,kɑmɪ'sɑr] *s* commissario del popolo

commissary ['kɑmɪ,seri] *s (-ies)* *(store)* economato; *(deputy)* commissario; *(in army)* intendente *m*

commission [kə'mɪʃən] *s* commissione; *(e.g., in army)* nomina, brevetto; autorità *f;* *(of a crime)* perpetrazione; *(il)* fare; **in commission** in servizio, in uso; **out of commission** fuori servizio ‖ *tr* nominare, dare un brevetto a; autorizzare; *(a ship)* armare

commis'sioned of'ficer *s* (mil, nav) ufficiale *m*

commissioner [kə'mɪʃənər] *s* commissario; membro di una commissione

commis'sion mer'chant *s* sensale *m*

commit [kə'mɪt] *v (pret & pp -mitted; ger -mitting)* *tr* commettere, perpetrare; *(to deliver)* affidare, consegnare; *(to imprison)* mandare in prigione; *(an insane person)* internare; *(to refer)* rinviare; *(to involve)* compromettere; **to commit oneself** compromettersi; **to commit to memory** imparare a memoria; **to commit to writing** mettere in iscritto

commitment [kə'mɪtmənt] *s (act of committing)* commissione; *(to an asylum)* internamento; promessa; (law) mandato

committal [kə'mɪtəl] *s* consegna; promessa

committee [kə'mɪti] *s* comitato, commissione

commode [kə'mod] *s (chest of drawers)* cassettone *m;* *(washstand)* lavabo; seggetta, comoda

commodious [kə'modɪ-əs] *adj* spazioso; conveniente

commodity [kə'mɑdɪti] *s (-ties)* merce *f;* articolo di prima necessità

commod'ity exchange' *s* borsa merci

common ['kɑmən] *adj* comune ‖ *s* fondo comunale; pascolo comune; **commons** gente *f* non nobile; refettorio; **in common** in comune ‖ **the Commons** la Camera dei Comuni

commoner ['kɑmənər] *s* plebeo, borghese *m;* membro della Camera dei Comuni

com'mon law' *s* consuetudine *f,* diritto consuetudinario

com'mon-law mar'riage *s* matrimonio basato sulla mera convivenza

commonly ['kɑmənli] *adv* generalmente

com'mon-place' *adj* banale, ordinario ‖ *s* banalità *f,* cosa ordinaria

com'mon sense' *s* senso comune

com'mon-sense' *adj* giudizioso

com'mon stock' *s* azione ordinaria; azioni ordinarie

commonweal ['kɑmən,wil] *s* bene pubblico

com'mon-wealth' *s (citizens of a state)* cittadinanza; repubblica; *(one of the*

50 states of the U.S.A.) stato; comunità *f*, federazione

commotion [kə'moʃən] *s* agitazione

commune [kə'mjun] *s* comune *m* || *intr* confabulare; (eccl) comunicarsi

communicate [kə'mjunɪ,ket] *tr & intr* comunicare

communicating [kə'mjunɪ,ketɪŋ] *adj* comunicante

communication [kə,mjunɪ'keʃən] *s* comunicazione; **communications** sistema *m* di comunicazione; mezzi *mpl* di comunicazione

communicative [kə'mjunɪ,ketɪv] *adj* comunicativo

Communion [kə'mjunjən] *s* Comunione; **to take Communion** comunicarsi

communiqué [kə,mjunɪ'ke] *or* [kə'mjunɪ,ke] *s* comunicato

communism ['kamjə,nɪzəm] *s* comunismo

communist ['kamjənɪst] *s* comunista *mf*

communi·ty [kə'mjunɪti] *s* (**-ties**) (*people living together*) comunità *f*; (*sharing together*) comunanza; (*neighborhood*) circondario

commu'nity cen'ter *s* centro sociale

commu'nity chest' *s* fondo di beneficenza

commuta'tion tick'et [,kamjə'teʃən] *s* biglietto d'abbonamento

commutator ['kamjə,tetər] *s* (*switch*) commutatore *m*; (*of dynamo or motor*) collettore *m*

commute [kə'mjut] *tr* commutare || *intr* commutare; fare il pendolare

commuter [kə'mjutər] *s* pendolare *mf*

compact [kəm'pækt] *adj* compatto || ['kampækt] *s* (*small case for face powder*) portacipria *m*; (*agreement*) accordo; (*small car*) utilitaria

companion [kəm'pænjən] *s* compagno; (*one of two items*) pendant *m*; (*lady*) dama di compagnia

compan'ion·ship' *s* cameratismo

compan'ion·way' *s* (naut) scaletta per andare sottocoperta

compa·ny ['kampəni] *s* (**-nies**) compagnia; (coll) ospite *m* or ospiti *mpl*; (naut) equipaggio; **to bear company** accompagnare; **to be good company** essere simpatico; **to keep company** (*said of a couple*) andare insieme; **to keep company with** accompagnare; (coll) fare la corte a; **to part company** separarsi

comparable ['kampərəbəl] *adj* comparabile, paragonabile

comparative [kəm'pærətɪv] *adj* comparativo; (*e.g., anatomy*) comparato || *s* (gram) comparativo

compare [kəm'per] *s*—**beyond compare** incomparabile || *tr* confrontare; **compared to** a confronto di, in confronto a

comparison [kəm'pærɪsən] *s* confronto; (gram) comparazione; **in comparison with** in confronto a, a confronto di

compartment [kəm'partmənt] *s* compartimento; (naut) compartimento stagno; (rr) compartimento

compass ['kʌmpəs] *s* (*instrument for showing direction*) bussola; (*boundary*) limite *m*; (*range*) ambito; (*range of voice*) portata; (*of a wall*) cerchia; (*circuit*) circuito; (*drawing instrument*) compasso; **compasses** (*drawing instrument*) compasso || *tr* girare intorno a; comprendere; **to compass about** accerchiare

com'pass card' *s* rosa dei venti

compassion [kəm'pæʃən] *s* compassione

compassionate [kəm'pæʃənɪt] *adj* compassionevole

com'pass saw' *s* gattuccio

com·pel [kəm'pel] *v* (*pret & pp* **-pelled;** *ger* **-pelling**) *tr* forzare, obbligare

compelling [kəm'pelɪŋ] *adj* imperioso, coercitivo

compendious [kəm'pendɪ·əs] *adj* compendioso, conciso

compensate ['kampən,set] *tr & intr* compensare

compensation [,kampən'seʃən] *s* compensazione; (*pay*) pagamento; (*something given to offset a loss*) risarcimento, indennità *f*

compete [kəm'pit] *intr* competere

competence ['kampɪtəns] *or* **competency** ['kampɪtənsi] *s* (*fitness*) abilità *f*; (*money*) agiatezza; (*authority*) competenza

competent ['kampɪtənt] *adj* abile; competente

competition [,kampɪ'tɪʃən] *s* competizione, gara; (*in business*) concorrenza

competitive [kəm'petɪtɪv] *adj* competitivo; (*based on competition*) di concorso

compet'itive pric'es *spl* prezzi *mpl* di concorrenza

competitor [kəm'petɪtər] *s* competitore *m*, concorrente *mf*; rivale *mf*

compilation [,kampɪ'leʃən] *s* compilazione

compile [kəm'paɪl] *tr* compilare

complacence [kəm'plesəns] *or* **complacency** [kəm'plesənsi] *s* compiacenza; compiacenza di sé stesso

complacent [kəm'plesənt] *adj* compiaciuto or soddisfatto con sé stesso

complain [kəm'plen] *intr* lagnarsi

complainant [kəm'plenənt] *s* (law) querelante *mf*

complaint [kəm'plent] *s* lagnanza, reclamo; (*sickness*) malattia; (law) querela

complaisance [kəm'plezəns] *or* ['kamplɪ,zæns] *s* compiacenza

complaisant [kəm'plezənt] *or* ['kamplɪ,zænt] *adj* compiacente, cortese

complement ['kamplɪmənt] *s* complemento; (naut) equipaggio || ['kamplɪ,ment] *tr* completare

complete [kəm'plit] *adj* completo; (*done*) finito || *tr* completare, finire

completion [kəm'pliʃən] *s* completamento, compimento

complex [kəm'pleks] *or* ['kampleks]

adj complesso, complicato || ['kɑm-pleks] *s* complesso

complexion [kəm'plekʃən] *s (of skin)* carnagione; *(appearance)* aspetto; *(viewpoint)* punto di vista

compliance [kəm'plaɪəns] *s* condiscendenza, arrendevolezza; in compliance with in conformità di

complicate ['kɑmplɪ‚ket] *tr* complicare

complicated ['kɑmplɪ‚ketɪd] *adj* complicato

complici·ty [kəm'plɪsɪti] *s* (-ties) complicità *f*

compliment ['kɑmplɪmənt] *s* complimento, omaggio || ['kɑmplɪ‚ment] *tr*—to compliment s.o. on s.th felicitarsi con qlcu per qlco; to compliment s.o. with s.th regalare qlco a qlcu

complimentary [‚kɑmplɪ'mentəri] *adj* complimentoso, lusinghiero; *(free)* in omaggio, gratis; *(ticket)* di favore

com·ply [kəm'plaɪ] *v (pret & pp -plied) intr* acconsentire, accondiscendere; to comply with accedere a

component [kəm'ponənt] *adj* componente, costituente || *s (component part)* componente *m; (force)* componente *f*

compose [kəm'poz] *tr* comporre; to be composed of essere composto di; to compose oneself calmarsi

composed [kəm'pozd] *adj* calmo, tranquillo

composer [kəm'pozər] *s (peacemaker)* conciliatore *m; (mus)* compositore *m*

compos'ing stick' *s* (typ) compositoio

composite [kɑm'pazɪt] *adj & s* composto, composito

composition [‚kɑmpə'zɪʃən] *s* composizione; *(agreement)* compromesso

compositor [kəm'pazɪtər] *s* compositore *m*

compost ['kɑmpost] *s* concime *m* naturale

composure [kəm'poʒər] *s* calma

compote ['kɑmpot] *s (stewed fruit)* composta; *(dish)* compostiera

compound ['kɑmpaʊnd] *adj* composto; *(fracture)* complesso; *(archit, bot)* composito || *s* composto; parola composta; *(yard)* recinto || [kɑm'paʊnd] *tr (to mix)* combinare; *(to settle)* comporre; *(interest)* capitalizzare

comprehend [‚kɑmprɪ'hend] *tr* comprendere

comprehensible [‚kɑmprɪ'hensɪbəl] *adj* comprensibile

comprehension [‚kɑmprɪ'henʃən] *s* comprensione

comprehensive [‚kɑmprɪ'hensɪv] *adj* comprensivo

compress ['kɑmpres] *s* compressa || [kəm'pres] *tr* comprimere

compressed' air' *s* aria compressa

compression [kəm'preʃən] *s* compressione

comprise [kəm'praɪz] *tr* comprendere, includere; to be comprised of consistere di

compromise ['kɑmprə‚maɪz] *s* com-

promesso || *tr (a dispute)* transigere, comporre; *(to put in danger)* compromettere || *intr* transigere, fare un compromesso

comptroller [kən'trolər] *s* economo, amministratore *m*, controllore *m*

compulsive [kəm'pʌlsɪv] *adj* obbligatorio, coercitivo; (psychol) compulsivo

compulsory [kəm'pʌlsəri] *adj* obbligatorio

compute [kəm'pjut] *tr & intr* computare, calcolare

computer [kəm'pjutər] *s* calcolatore *m*; elaboratore *m*

comrade ['kɑmræd] or ['kɑmrɪd] *s* camerata *m*, compagno

com'rade in arms' *s* compagno d'armi

con [kɑn] *s* contro || *v (pret & pp conned; ger conning) tr* imparare a memoria; (slang) imbrogliare

concave ['kɑnkev] or [kɑn'kev] *adj* concavo

conceal [kən'sil] *tr* nascondere; *(to keep secret)* celare

concealment [kən'silmənt] *s* occultamento; *(place)* nascondiglio

concede [kən'sid] *tr* concedere

conceit [kən'sit] *s (high opinion of oneself)* presunzione; *(fanciful notion)* concetto sottile

conceited [kən'sitɪd] *adj* vanitoso

conceivable [kən'sivəbəl] *adj* concepibile

conceive [kən'siv] *tr & intr* concepire

concentrate ['kɑnsən‚tret] *s* concentrato || *tr* concentrare || *intr* concentrarsi; to concentrate on concentrarsi in

concentra'tion camp' [‚kɑnsən'treʃən] *s* campo di concentrazione

concept ['kɑnsept] *s* concetto

conception [kən'sepʃən] *s* concezione

concern [kən'sʌrn] *s* interesse *m; (worry)* ansietà *f; (firm)* ditta, compagnia; of concern d'interesse || *tr* concernere; as concerns circa; to concern oneself interessarsi; to whom it may concern a chiunque possa averne interesse

concerning [kən'sʌrnɪŋ] *prep* riguardo a

concert ['kɑnsərt] *s* concerto || [kən'sʌrt] *tr & intr* concertare

con'cert·mas'ter *s* primo violino

concer·to [kən'tʃɛrto] *s* (-tos or -ti [ti]) concerto

concession [kən'seʃən] *s* concessione

conciliate [kən'sɪli‚et] *tr* conciliare, conciliarsi con

concise [kən'saɪs] *adj* conciso

conclude [kən'klud] *tr* concludere || *intr* concludersi, terminare

conclusion [kən'kluʒən] *s* conclusione; in conclusion per finire; to try conclusions with misurarsi con

conclusive [kən'klusɪv] *adj* decisivo, convincente

concoct [kən'kɑkt] *tr* preparare, confezionare; *(a story)* inventare

concoction [kɑn'kɑkʃən] *s* preparazione, mescolanza; (unpleasant in taste) intruglio

concomitant [kən'kɑmɪtənt] adj concomitante || s fatto or sintomo concomitante

concord ['kɑŋkɔrd] s concordia, armonia; (treaty) accordo; (gram) concordanza

concourse ['kɑŋkors] s confluenza; (crowd) affluenza, concorso; (boulevard) viale m; (rr) salone m principale

concrete ['kɑnkrit] or [kɑn'krit] adj concreto; fatto di cemento; solido || s cemento, calcestruzzo || tr (e.g., a sidewalk) cementare

con'crete mix'er s betoniera

con·cur [kən'kʌr] v (pret & pp -curred; ger -curring) intr (to work together) concorrere; (to agree) essere d'accordo, aderire

concurrence [kən'kʌrəns] s concorso; (agreement) accordo

concurrent [kən'kʌrənt] adj concomitante, simultaneo; cooperante; armonioso

concussion [kən'kʌʃən] s scossa, urto; (of brain) commozione cerebrale

condemn [kən'dem] tr condannare; (to take for public use) espropriare

condemnation [,kɑndem'neʃən] s condanna

condense [kən'dens] tr condensare || intr condensarsi

condescend [,kɑndɪ'send] intr condiscendere, degnarsi

condescending [,kɑndɪ'sendɪŋ] adj condiscendente

condescension [,kɑndɪ'senʃən] s condiscendenza, degnazione

condiment ['kɑndɪmənt] s condimento

condition [kən'dɪʃən] s condizione; clausola; **on condition that** a condizione che || tr condizionare; mettere in buone condizioni fisiche

conditional [kən'dɪʃənəl] adj & s condizionale m

condole [kən'dol] intr condolersi

condolence [kən'doləns] s condoglianza

condone [kən'don] tr condonare

conduce [kən'djus] or [kən'dus] intr contribuire, indurre

conducive [kən'djusɪv] or [kən'dusɪv] adj contribuente

conduct ['kɑndʌkt] s condotta; direzione || [kən'dʌkt] tr condurre; (an orchestra) dirigere; **to conduct oneself** condursi, comportarsi || intr dirigere

conductor [kən'dʌktər] s direttore m; (of a streetcar) fattorino, conduttore m; (phys) conduttore m; (rr) capotreno

conduit ['kɑndɪt] or ['kɑndu·ɪt] s condotto

cone [kon] s cono; (bot) pigna

Con'estoga wag'on ['kɑnɪ'stogə] s carriaggio coperto

confectioner [kən'fekʃənər] s confettiere m, pasticcere m

confec'tioners' sug'ar s zucchero in polvere finissimo

confectioner·y [kən'fekʃə,neri] s (-ies) confetteria, pasticceria; (candies) confetture fpl

confedera·cy [kən'fedərəsi] s (-cies) confederazione; lega

confederate [kən'fedərɪt] s alleato; (in crime) complice mf || [kən'fedə,ret] tr confederare || intr confederarsi

con·fer [kən'fʌr] v (pret & pp -ferred; ger -ferring) tr conferire || intr conferire, abboccarsi

conference ['kɑnfərəns] s conferenza

confess [kən'fes] tr confessare, ammettere || intr confessare, confessarsi

confession [kən'feʃən] s confessione

confessional [kən'feʃənəl] s confessionale m

confes'sion of faith' s professione di fede

confessor [kən'fesər] s confessore m

confetti [kən'feti] s coriandoli mpl

confide [kən'faɪd] tr confidare; (to entrust) affidare || intr confidarsi

confidence ['kɑnfɪdəns] s fiducia; sicurezza di sé; (boldness) baldanza; (secrecy) confidenza

confident ['kɑnfɪdənt] adj fiducioso; baldanzoso || s confidente mf

confidential [,kɑnfɪ'denʃəl] adj confidenziale

confine ['kɑnfaɪn] s confine m || [kən'faɪn] tr limitare; confinare; **to be confined** essere in altro stato; **to be confined to bed** dover stare a letto

confinement [kən'faɪnmənt] s confino; (childbirth) parto; (imprisonment) prigionia

confirm [kən'fʌrm] tr confermare; (eccl) cresimare

confirmed [kən'fʌrmd] adj (e.g., piece of news) confermato; (bachelor; drunkard) impenitente; inveterato; (e.g., invalid) cronico

confiscate ['kɑnfɪs,ket] tr confiscare

conflagration [,kɑnflə'greʃən] s conflagrazione

conflict ['kɑnflɪkt] s conflitto || [kən'flɪkt] intr lottare; essere in conflitto

conflicting [kən'flɪktɪŋ] adj contrastante; contraddittorio

confluence ['kɑnflu·əns] s confluenza

conform [kən'fɔrm] tr conformare || intr conformarsi

conformi·ty [kən'fɔrmɪti] s (-ties) conformità f; **in conformity with** in conformità di

confound [kən'faund] tr confondere || ['kɑn'faund] tr maledire; **confound it!** accidenti!

confounded [kən'faundɪd] or ['kɑn'faundɪd] adj maledetto; (hateful) odioso

confront [kən'frʌnt] tr affrontare, opporsi a; (to bring face to face) raffrontare; (to compare) confrontare

confrontation [,kɑnfrən'teʃən] s contestazione

confuse [kən'fjuz] tr confondere; **to get confused** confondersi

confusion [kən'fjuʒən] s confusione

congeal [kən'dʒil] *tr* congelare; coagulare ‖ *intr* congelarsi; (*said, e.g., of blood*) coagularsi

congenial [kən'dʒinjəl] *adj* (*agreeable*) simpatico; (*having similar tastes*) affine; (*suited to one's needs or tastes*) congeniale

congenital [kən'dʒenɪtəl] *adj* congenito

con'ger eel' ['kəŋgər] *s* grongo

congest [kən'dʒest] *tr* congestionare ‖ *intr* essere congestionarsi

congestion [kən'dʒestʃən] *s* congestione

conglomerate [kən'glamərɪt] *adj & s* conglomerato ‖ [kən'glamə,ret] *tr* conglomerare ‖ *intr* conglomerarsi

congratulate [kən'grætʃə,let] *tr* congratularsi con

congratulation [kən,grætʃə'leʃən] *s* congratulazione, felicitazione

congregate ['kaŋgrɪ,get] *intr* congregarsi

congregation [,kaŋgrɪ'geʃən] *s* congregazione; fedeli *mpl* di una chiesa

congress ['kaŋgrɪs] *s* parlamento; congresso

con'gress-man *s* (**-men**) deputato al congresso degli S.U.

con'gress-wom'an *s* (**-wom'en**) deputatessa al congresso degli S.U.

conical ['kanɪkəl] *adj* conico

conjecture [kən'dʒektʃər] *s* congettura ‖ *tr & intr* congetturare

conjugate ['kandʒə,get] *tr* coniugare

conjugation [,kandʒə'geʃən] *s* coniugazione

conjunction [kən'dʒʌŋkʃən] *s* congiunzione

conjure [kən'dʒur] *tr* (*to entreat*) scongiurare ‖ ['kandʒər] or ['kʌndʒər] *tr* evocare, stregare; **to conjure up** evocare ‖ *intr* fare delle stregonerie

conk [kaŋk] *intr*—**to conk out** (slang) essere in panna; (slang) svenire

connect [kə'nekt] *tr* connettere, unire ‖ *intr* connettersi, essere associato; (*said of public conveyances*) operare in coincidenza

connect'ing rod' [kə'nektɪŋ] *s* (mach) biella

connection [kə'nekʃən] *s* connessione; unione, associazione; (*of trains*) coincidenza; (*relative*) parente *mf*; (*e.g., of a water pipe*) allacciamento; **in connection with** rispetto a

con'ning tow'er ['kanɪŋ] *s* (nav) torretta

conniption [kə'nɪpʃən] *s* (slang) attacco di rabbia

connive [kə'naɪv] *intr* essere connivente; **to connive at** chiudere un occhio su

connote [kə'not] *tr* indicare, suggerire

conquer ['kaŋkər] *tr & intr* conquistare

conqueror ['kaŋkərər] *s* conquistatore *m*

conquest ['kaŋkwest] *s* conquista

conscience ['kanʃəns] *s* coscienza; **in all conscience** a prezzo onesto; certamente

conscientious [,kanʃɪ'enʃəs] *adj* coscienzioso

conscien'tious objec'tor [ab'dʒektər] *s* obiettore *m* di coscienza

conscious ['kanʃəs] *adj* (*aware of one's existence*) cosciente; (*aware*) conscio, consapevole; (*lie*) consapevole; **to become conscious** riprendere i sensi

consciousness ['kanʃəsnɪs] *s* coscienza, conoscenza; **to lose consciousness** perdere la conoscenza

conscript ['kanskrɪpt] *s* coscritto ‖ [kən'skrɪpt] *tr* coscrivere, arruolare

conscription [kən'skrɪpʃən] *s* coscrizione

consecrate ['kansɪ,kret] *tr* consacrare

consecutive [kən'sekjɪtɪv] *adj* consecutivo; di seguito

consensus [kən'sensəs] *s* consenso

consent [kən'sent] *s* consenso; **by common consent** per comune consenso ‖ *intr* consentire

consequence ['kansɪ,kwens] *s* conseguenza

consequential [,kansɪ'kwenʃəl] *adj* conseguente; importante, d'importanza; pomposo, pieno di sé

consequently ['kansɪ,kwentli] *adv* conseguentemente, per conseguenza

conservation [,kansər've ʃən] *s* conservazione; preservazione delle foreste

conservatism [kən'sʌrvə,tɪzəm] *s* conservatorismo

conservative [kən'sʌrvətɪv] *adj* conservatore; (*cautious*) cauto; (*preserving*) conservativo; (*free from fads*) tradizionale ‖ *s* conservatore *m*

conservato·ry [kən'sʌrvə,tori] *s* (**-ries**) (*greenhouse*) serra; (mus) conservatorio

conserve [kən'sʌrv] *tr* conservare

consider [kən'sɪdər] *tr* considerare

considerable [kən'sɪdərəbəl] *adj* (*fairly large*) considerevole; (*worth thinking about*) considerabile

considerate [kən'sɪdərɪt] *adj* riguardoso, premuroso

consideration [kən,sɪdə'reʃən] *s* considerazione; (*reason*) motivo; (*money*) pagamento; **in consideration of** a cagione di; in cambio di; **on no consideration** in nessuna maniera, mai; **under consideration** in considerazione, sotto esame; **without consideration** senza riflessione, alla leggera

considering [kən'sɪdərɪŋ] *adv* tutto considerato ‖ *prep* per, visto ‖ *conj* considerando che, visto che

consign [kən'saɪn] *tr* consegnare; (*to send*) inviare; (*to set apart*) assegnare

consignee [,kansaɪ'ni] *s* consegnatario

consignment [kən'saɪnmənt] *s* consegna; **on consignment** in conto consegna

consist [kən'sɪst] *intr*—**to consist in** consistere in; **to consist of** consistere in, constare di

consisten·cy [kən'sɪstənsi] *s* (**-cies**) (*firmness, amount of firmness*) consistenza; (*logical connection*) coerenza

consistent [kən'sɪstənt] *adj* (*holding firmly together*) consistente; (*agree-*

ing with itself or oneself) conseguente, coerente; compatibile

consolation [ˌkɑnsəˈleʃən] s consolazione

console [ˈkɑnsol] s (*table*) console f; (*rad, telv*) mobile m; (*mus*) console f || [kənˈsol] tr consolare

consonant [ˈkɑnsənənt] adj consonante, armonioso; (*gram*) consonantico || s consonante f

consort [ˈkɑnsort] s consorte mf || [kənˈsort] intr associarsi; (*to agree*) concordarsi

conspicuous [kənˈspɪkjʊ-əs] adj visibile, manifesto; notevole; (*too noticeable*) appariscente; **to make oneself conspicuous** farsi notare

conspira•cy [kənˈspɪrəsi] s (-cies) cospirazione, congiura

conspire [kənˈspaɪr] intr cospirare, congiurare; (*to act together*) cooperare

constable [ˈkɑnstəbəl] or [ˈkʌnstəbəl] s poliziotto; (*keeper of a castle*) conestabile m

constancy [ˈkɑnstənsi] s costanza

constant [ˈkɑnstənt] adj & s costante f

constellation [ˌkɑnstəˈleʃən] s costellazione

constipate [ˈkɑnstɪˌpet] tr costipare

constipation [ˌkɑnstɪˈpeʃən] s costipazione

constituen•cy [kənˈstɪtʃʊ-ənsi] s (-cies) (*voters*) elettorato; (*district*) circoscrizione elettorale

constituent [kənˈstɪtʃʊ-ənt] adj costituente || s (*component*) parte f costituente; (*voter*) elettore m; (*of a chemical substance*) costituente m

constitute [ˈkɑnstɪˌtjut] or [ˈkɑnstɪˌtut] tr costituire

constitution [ˌkɑnstɪˈtjuʃən] or [ˌkɑnstɪˈtuʃən] s costituzione

constrain [kənˈstren] tr (*to force*) costringere; (*to restrain*) restringere, comprimere

constrict [kənˈstrɪkt] tr stringere, comprimere

construct [kənˈstrʌkt] tr costruire

construction [kənˈstrʌkʃən] s costruzione; (*meaning*) interpretazione

construe [kənˈstru] tr (*to interpret*) interpretare; (*to translate*) tradurre; (*gram*) analizzare

consul [ˈkɑnsəl] s console m

consular [ˈkɑnsələr] or [ˈkɑnsjələr] adj consolare

consulate [ˈkɑnsəlɪt] or [ˈkɑnsjəlɪt] s consolato

consult [kənˈsʌlt] tr consultare || intr consultarsi

consultation [ˌkɑnsəlˈteʃən] s consultazione, conferenza

consume [kənˈsum] or [kənˈsjum] tr consumare; distruggere; **consumed with** (*passion*) arso di; (*curiosity*) assorbito da

consumer [kənˈsumər] or [kənˈsjumər] s consumatore m

consum'er goods' spl beni mpl di consumo

consumerism [kənˈsumər ˌɪzem] s consumismo

consummate [kənˈsʌmɪt] adj consumato || [ˈkɑnsəˌmet] tr consumare

consumption [kənˈsʌmpʃən] s (*decay*) consunzione; (*using up*) consumo; (*pathol*) consunzione

consumptive [kənˈsʌmptɪv] adj tubercolotico, tisico; (*wasteful*) logorante || s tisico, etico

contact [ˈkɑntækt] s contatto; (*elec*) contatto; (*elec*) presa di corrente || tr (*coll*) mettersi in contatto con || intr (*coll*) mettersi in contatto

con'tact break'er s ruttore m

con'tact lens' s lente f a contatto

contagion [kənˈtedʒən] s contagio

contagious [kənˈtedʒəs] adj contagioso

contain [kənˈten] tr contenere; **to contain oneself** frenarsi

container [kənˈtenər] s recipiente m, contenitore m

contaminate [kənˈtæmɪˌnet] tr contaminare

contamination [kənˌtæmɪˈneʃən] s contaminazione

contemplate [ˈkɑntəmˌplet] tr contemplare; (*to think about*) meditare; (*to have in mind*) progettare, avere in mente || intr meditare

contemplation [ˌkɑntəmˈpleʃən] s contemplazione; (*intention*) intenzione

contemporaneous [kənˌtempəˈreni-əs] adj contemporaneo, coevo

contemporar•y [kənˈtempəˌreri] adj contemporaneo, coevo || s (-ies) contemporaneo

contempt [kənˈtempt] s (*despising*) disprezzo; (*condition of being despised*) dispregio; (*of the law*) disprezzo

contemptible [kənˈtemptɪbəl] adj disprezzabile, spregevole

contempt' of court' s (law) offesa alla magistratura, oltraggio al tribunale

contemptuous [kənˈtemptʃʊ-əs] adj sprezzante, sdegnoso

contend [kənˈtend] tr dichiarare || intr (*to argue*) disputare, contendere; (*to fight*) lottare

contender [kənˈtendər] s competitore m, concorrente m

content [kənˈtent] adj contento; (*willing*) pronto || s contentezza || [ˈkɑntent] s contenuto; **contents** contenuto || [kənˈtent] tr contentare

contented [kənˈtentɪd] adj soddisfatto

contention [kənˈtenʃən] s disputa, litigio; contenzione

contentious [kənˈtenʃəs] adj litigioso

contentment [kənˈtentmənt] s contentezza

contest [ˈkɑntest] s contesa, controversia; (*game*) gara || [kənˈtest] tr disputare, contestare || intr combattere, fare resistenza

contestant [kənˈtestənt] s concorrente m; (law) contendente m

context [ˈkɑntekst] s contesto

contiguous [kənˈtɪgjʊ-əs] adj contiguo

continence [ˈkɑntɪnəns] s continenza

continent [ˈkɑntɪnənt] adj & s continente *m*; **on the Continent** nel continente europeo

continental [ˌkɑntɪˈnɛntəl] *adj & s* continentale *mf*

contingen·cy [kənˈtɪndʒənsi] *s* (**-cies**) contingenza, congiuntura; (*chance*) eventualità *f*

contingent [kənˈtɪndʒənt] *adj* eventuale; imprevisto; (philos) contingente; **to be contingent upon** dipendere da

continual [kənˈtɪnju·əl] *adj* continuo

continuance [kənˈtɪnjuəns] *s* continuazione; (*in office*) permanenza; (law) rinvio

continue [kənˈtɪnju] *tr* continuare; (*to cause to remain*) mantenere; (law) rinviare || *intr* continuare; rimanere

continui·ty [ˌkɑntɪˈnju·ɪti] or [ˌkɑntɪˈnu·ɪti] *s* (**-ties**) continuità *f*; (mov & telv) sceneggiatura; (rad) copione *m*

continuous [kənˈtɪnju·əs] *adj* continuo

contin'uous show'ing *s* (mov) spettacolo permanente

contortion [kənˈtɔrʃən] *s* contorsione; (*of facts*) distorsione

contour [ˈkɑntur] *s* contorno

con'tour line' *s* curva di livello, isoipsa

contraband [ˈkɑntrəˌbænd] *adj* di contrabbando || *s* contrabbando

contrabass [ˈkɑntrəˌbes] *s* contrabbasso

contraceptive [ˌkɑntrəˈsɛptɪv] *adj & s* antifecondativo

contract [ˈkɑntrækt] *s* contratto || [ˈkɑntrækt] or [kənˈtrækt] *tr* (*a business deal*) contrattare; (*marriage*) contrarre || *intr* (*to shrink*) contrarsi; **to contract for** contrattare, appaltare

contraction [kənˈtrækʃən] *s* contrazione

contractor [kənˈtræktər] *s* (*person who makes a contract*) contraente *m*; (*person who contracts to supply material*) appaltatore *m*, imprenditore *m*; (*in building*) capomastro

contradict [ˌkɑntrəˈdɪkt] *tr* contraddire

contradiction [ˌkɑntrəˈdɪkʃən] *s* contraddizione

contradictory [ˌkɑntrəˈdɪktəri] *adj* contr. ddittorio

contrail [ˈkɑnˌtrel] *s* (aer) scia di condensazione

contral·to [kənˈtrælto] *s* (**-tos**) (*person*) contralto *mf*; (*voice*) contralto *m*

contraption [kənˈtræpʃən] *s* (coll) aggeggio

contra·ry [ˈkɑntreri] *adj* contrario || [kənˈtreri] *adj* ostinato, capriçio || [ˈkɑntreri] *s* (**-ries**) contrario; **on the contrary** al contrario || *adv* contrariamente

contrast [ˈkɑntræst] *s* contrasto || [kənˈtræst] *tr* confrontare || *intr* contrastare

contravene [ˌkɑntrəˈvin] *tr* contraddire; (*a law*) contravvenire (with dat)

contribute [kənˈtrɪbjut] *tr* contribuire || *intr* contribuire; (*to a newspaper*) collaborare

contribution [ˌkɑntrɪˈbjuʃən] *s* contribuzione; (*to a newspaper*) collaborazione

contributor [kənˈtrɪbjutər] *s* contributore *m*; (*to a newspaper*) collaboratore *m*

contrite [kənˈtraɪt] *adj* contrito

contrition [kənˈtrɪʃən] *s* contrizione

contrivance [kənˈtraɪvəns] *s* dispositivo, congegno; (*faculty*) invenzione; (*scheme*) artificio, piano

contrive [kənˈtraɪv] *tr* inventare; (*to scheme up*) macchinare; (*to bring about*) effettuare; **to contrive to** trovare il modo di

con·trol [kənˈtrol] *s* controllo; (*check*) freno; **controls** comandi *mpl*; **to get under control** riuscire a controllare || *v* (*pret & pp* **-trolled**; *ger* **-trolling**) *tr* controllare

controller [kənˈtrolər] *s* controllore *m*; analista *mf* di gestione; economo; (mach) regolatore *m*; (elec) interruttore *m* di linea

control'ling in'terest *s* maggioranza delle ioni

control' stick' *s* leva di comando

controversial [ˌkɑntrəˈvʌrʃəl] *adj* controverso, polemico, discusso

controver·sy [ˈkɑntrəˌvʌrsi] *s* (**-sies**) controversia

controvert [ˈkɑntrəˌvʌrt] or [ˌkɑntrəˈvʌrt] *tr* contraddire

contumacious [ˌkɑntjuˈmeʃəs] or [ˌkɑntuˈmeʃəs] *adj* ribelle, contumace

contuma·cy [ˈkɑntjuməsi] or [ˈkɑntuməsi] *s* (**-cies**) contumacia

contusion [kənˈtjuʒən] or [kənˈtuʒən] *s* ontusione

conundrum [kəˈnʌndrəm] *s* indovinello

conva·lesce [ˌkɑnvəˈles] *intr* essere convalescente

convalescence [ˌkɑnvəˈlesəns] *s* convales.enza

convalescent [ˌkɑnvəˈlesənt] *adj & s* convalescente *mf*

con'vales'cent home' *s* convalescenziario

convene [kənˈvin] *tr* convocare || *intr* convenire

convenience [kənˈvinjəns] *s* convenienza; (*comfort*) agio; (*anything that saves work*) conforto; **at your earliest convenience** quanto prima

convenient [kənˈvinjənt] *adj* conveniente, adatto; comodo; **convenient to** (*near*) (coll) vicino a

convent [ˈkɑnvənt] *s* convento di religiose

convention [kənˈvɛnʃən] *s* convenzione, assemblea; **conventions** (*customs*) convenzioni *fpl*

conventional [kənˈvɛnʃənəl] *adj* convenzionale

converge [kənˈvʌrdʒ] *intr* convergere

conversant [kənˈvʌrsənt] *adj* versato, esperto, dotto

conversation [ˌkɑnvərˈseʃən] *s* conversazione

converse [ˈkɑnvʌrs] *adj & s* contrario || [kənˈvʌrs] *intr* conversare

conversion [kən'vʌrʒən] *s* conversione; (*unlawful appropriation*) malversazione

convert ['kɑnvʌrt] *s* convertito || [kən'vʌrt] *tr* convertire; misappropriare || *intr* convertirsi

convertible [kən'vʌrtɪbəl] *adj & s* convertibile *f*; (aut) trasformabile *f*, decappottabile *f*

convex ['kɑnveks] *or* [kɑn'veks] *adj* convesso

convey [kən've] *tr* (*to carry*) trasportare; (*liquids*) convogliare; (*sounds*) trasmettere; (*to express*) esprimere; (*e.g., property*) trasferire

conveyance [kən've·əns] *s* trasporto; veicolo; comunicazione; (*of property*) trasferimento; (*deed*) titolo di proprietà

convey'or belt' [kən've·ər] *s* trasportatore *m*

convict ['kɑnvɪkt] *s* condannato || [kən'vɪkt] *tr* convincere, condannare

conviction [kən'vɪkʃən] *s* condanna; (*belief*) convinzione, convincimento

convince [kən'vɪns] *tr* convincere

convincing [kən'vɪnsɪŋ] *adj* convincente

convivial [kən'vɪvɪ·əl] *adj* (*festive*) conviviale; gioviale, bonaccione

convocation [ˌkɑnvə'keʃən] *s* convocazione, assemblea

convoke [kən'vok] *tr* convocare

convoy ['kɑnvɔɪ] *s* (*of ships*) convoglio; (*of vehicles*) carovana || *tr* convogliare

convulse [kən'vʌls] *tr* (*to shake*) scuotere; (*to throw into convulsions*) mettere in convulsioni; (*to cause to shake with laughter*) far torcere dalle risa

coo [ku] *intr* tubare, gemere

cook [kʊk] *s* cuoco || *tr* cuocere; **to cook up** (coll) preparare, macchinare || *intr* (*said of food*) cuocere; (*said of a person*) fare il cuoco

cook'book' *s* libro di cucina

cookie ['kʊki] *s var of* **cooky**

cooking ['kʊkɪŋ] *s* culinaria

cook'out' *s* picnic *m*, spuntino all'aperto

cook'stove' *s* cucina economica

cook·y ['kʊki] *s* (-ies) pasticcino, biscotto

cool [kul] *adj* fresco; calmo; (*not cordial*) freddo; (*bold*) sfacciato || *s* fresco || *tr* rinfres are; **to cool one's heels** fare anticamera || *intr* rinfrescarsi; **to cool off** rinfrescarsi; calmarsi

coolant ['kulənt] *s* miscela refrigerante

cooler ['kulər] *s* ghiacciaia; (slang) prigione

cool'-head'ed *adj* calmo, imperturbabile

coolish ['kulɪʃ] *adj* freschetto

coon [kun] *s* procione *m*

coop [kup] *s* pollaio; conigliera; **to fly the coop** (slang) scapparsene || *tr*— **to coop up** rinchiudere tra quattro mura

cooper ['kupər] *s* bottaio

cooperate [ko'ɑpə‚ret] *intr* cooperare

cooperation [ko‚ɑpə'reʃən] *s* cooperazione

cooperative [ko'ɑpə‚retɪv] *adj* cooperativo || *s* cooperativa

coordinate [ko'ɔrdɪnɪt] *adj* coordinato; (gram) coordinativo || *s* (math) coordinata || [ko'ɔrdɪ‚net] *tr & intr* coordinare

coot [kut] *s* (zool) folaga; (slang) vecchio pazzo

cootie ['kuti] *s* (slang) pidocchio

cop [kɑp] *s* (slang) poliziotto || *v* (*pret & pp* **copped**; *ger* **copping**) *tr* (slang) rubare

copartner [ko'pɑrtnər] *s* consocio, socio

cope [kop] *intr*—**to cope with** tener testa a

cope'stone' *s* pietra da cimasa

copier ['kɑpɪ·ər] *s* (*person*) copista *mf*; imitatore *m*; (*machine*) duplicatore *m*

copilot ['ko‚paɪlət] *s* copilota *mf*

coping ['kopɪŋ] *s* coronamento, cimasa

cop'ing saw' *s* seghetto da traforo

copious ['kopɪ·əs] *adj* copioso

copper ['kɑpər] *s* rame *m*; (*coin*) soldo; (*boiler*) calderone *m*; (slang) poliziotto

cop'per·head' *s* vipera (*Ancistrodon contortrix*)

cop'per·smith' *s* battirame *m*, calderaio

coppice ['kɑpɪs] *or* **copse** [kɑps] *s* boschetto

copulate ['kɑpjə‚let] *intr* copularsi, congiungersi carnalmente

cop·y ['kɑpi] *s* (-ies) copia; modello; manoscritto || *v* (*pret & pp* -ied) *tr* copiare, imitare || *intr* copiare; **to copy after** imitare

cop'y·book' *s* quaderno

copyist ['kɑpɪ·ɪst] *s* copista *mf*; imitatore *m*

cop'y·right' *s* copyright *m*, diritto di proprietà letteraria || *tr* registrare; proteggere con copyright

cop'y·writ'er *s* copy-writer *m*, redattore *m* pubblicitario

coquet·ry ['kokətri] *or* [ko'ketri] *s* (-ries) civetteria

coquette [ko'ket] *s* civetta

coquettish [ko'ketɪʃ] *adj* civettuolo

coral ['kɑrəl] *or* ['kɔrəl] *adj* corallino || *s* corallo

cor'al reef' *s* banco di coralli

cord [kɔrd] *s* corda, fune *f*; (*corduroy*) tessuto cordonato; (elec) cordone *m* || *tr* legare con corda

cordial ['kɔrdʒəl] *adj & s* cordiale *m*

corduroy ['kɔrdə‚rɔɪ] *s* velluto a coste; **corduroys** pantaloni *mpl* alla cacciatora

core [kor] *s* (*of fruit*) torsolo; (*central part*) centro; (*of problem*) nocciolo; (*of earth*) barisfera, nucleo centrale; (phys) nucleo; **rotten to the core** guasto nelle ossa

corespondent [‚korɪs'pɑndənt] *s* coimputato in un processo di divorzio

cork [kɔrk] *s* (*bark*) sughero; (*stopper*) tappo, tappo di sughero || *tr* tappare

cork' oak' *s* sughero

cork'screw' s cavatappi m
cormorant ['kɔrmərənt] s cormorano
corn [kɔrn] s granturco, mais m; (kernel) chicco; (thickening of skin) callo; (whiskey) whisky m di granturco; (Brit) grano; (Scot) avena; (slang) banalità f
corn' bread' s pane m di farina gialla
corn' cake' s omelette f di granturco
corn'cob' s tutolo
corn'cob pipe' s pipa fatta di un tutolo di pannocchia
corn'crib' s granaio per le pannocchie
corn' cure' s callifugo
cornea ['kɔrnɪə] s cornea
corner ['kɔrnər] s angolo; (of street) cantonata; situazione difficile; (of the eye) coda dell'occhio; (com) accaparramento, incetta, bagarinaggio; to cut corners t gli re le spese; to turn the corner p ss re il punto più pericoloso || tr mettere in una situazione difficile; (the market) incettare, accaparrare
cor'ner cup'board s cantoniera, armadio d'angolo
cor'ner stone' s pietra angolare; (of new building) prima pietra
cornet ['kɔrnɛt] s cornetta
corn' exch nge' s borsa dei cereali
corn'field' s (in U.S.A.) campo di granturco; (in England) campo di grano; (in Scotland) campo di avena
corn'flakes' spl fiocchi mpl di granturco
corn' flour' s farina di granturco
corn'flow'er s nordaliso
corn'husk' s brattea, cartoccio
cornice ['kɔrnɪs] s (of house) cornicione m; (of room) cornice f
corn' liq'uor s whisky m di granturco
corn' meal' s farina di granturco
corn' on the cob' s granturco servito in pannocchia
corn' plas'ter s cerotto per i calli
corn' silk' s barba del granturco
corn'stalk' s fusto di granturco
corn'starch' s amido di granturco
corn·y ['kɔrni] adj (-ier; -iest) (slang) banale, trito, triviale
coronation [,kɔrə'neʃən] or [,kɔrə'neʃən] s incoronazione
coroner ['kɔrənər] or ['kɔrənər] s magistrato inquirente
cor'oner's in'quest s inchiesta giudiziaria dinanzi a giuria
coronet ['kɔrə,nɛt] or ['kɔrə,nɛt] s corona (non reale); diadema m
corporal ['kɔrpərəl] adj caporalesco || s caporale m
corporation [,kɔrpə'reʃən] s società anonima
corps [kɔr] s (corps [kɔrz]) corpo
corps' de bal'let s corpo di ballo
corpse [kɔrps] s cadavere m
corpulent ['kɔrpjələnt] adj corpulento
corpuscle ['kɔrpəsəl] s (anat) globulo; (phys) corpuscolo
cor·ral [kə'ræl] s recinto per bestiame || v (pret & pp -ralled; ger -ralling) tr mettere in un recinto; catturare
correct [kə'rɛkt] adj corretto || tr correggere
correction [kə'rɛkʃən] s correzione

corrective [kə'rɛktɪv] adj & s correttivo
correctness [kə'rɛktnɪs] s correttezza
correlate ['kɔrə,let] or ['kɔrə,let] tr correlare || intr essere in correlazione
correlation [,kɔrə'leʃən] or [,kɔrə'leʃən] s correlazione
correspond [,kɔrɪ'spand] or [,kɔrɪ'spand] intr corrispondere
correspondence [,kɔrɪ'spandəns] or [,kɔrɪ'spandəns] s corrispondenza
correspond'ence school' s scuola per corrispondenza
correspondent [,kɔrɪ'spandənt] or [,kɔrɪ'spandənt] adj & s corrispondente mf
corridor ['kɔrɪdər] or ['kɔrɪdər] s corridoio
corroborate [kə'rabə,ret] tr corroborare
corrode [kə'rod] tr corrodere || intr corrodersi
corrosion [kə'roʒən] s corrosione
corrosive [kə'rosɪv] adj & s corrosivo
corrugated ['kɔrə,getɪd] or ['kɔrə,getɪd] adj ondulato
corrupt [kə'rʌpt] adj corrotto || tr corrompere; (a language) imbarbarire || intr corrompersi
corruption [kə'rʌpʃən] s corruzione
corsage [kɔr'saʒ] s (bodice) corpetto; (bouquet) mazzolino di fiori da appuntarsi al vestito
corsair ['kɔr,ser] s corsaro
corset ['kɔrsɪt] s corsetto
Corsic·an ['kɔrsɪkən] adj & s corso
cortege [kɔr'teʒ] s corteggio
cor·tex ['kɔr,tɛks] s (-tices [tɪ,siz]) ortice f
cortisone ['kɔrtɪ,son] s cortisone m
corvette [kɔr'vɛt] s corvetta
cosmetic [kaz'mɛtɪk] adj & s cosmetico
cosmic ['kazmɪk] adj cosmico
cosmonaut ['kazmə,nɔt] s cosmonauta mf
cosmopolitan [,kazmə'palɪtən] adj & s cosmopolita mf
cosmos ['kazməs] s cosmo
cost [kɔst] or [kast] s costo, prezzo; at all costs or at any cost ad ogni costo; costs (law) spese fpl processuali || v (pret & pp cost) intr costare
cost·ly ['kɔstli] or ['kastli] adj (-lier; -liest) costoso; (sumptuous) lussuoso
cost' of liv'ing s costo della vita
costume ['kastjum] or ['kastum] s costume m
cos'tume ball' s ballo in costume
cos'tume jew'elry s gioielli falsi
cot [kat] s (narrow bed) branda; (cottage) capanna, cabina
coterie ['kɔtəri] s gruppo; (clique) chiesuola
cottage ['katɪdʒ] s casetta, villino
cot'tage cheese' s ricotta americana
cot'ter pin' ['katər] s copiglia, coppiglia
cotton [katən] s cotone m || intr—to cotton up to (coll) cominciare a provare della simpatia per; (coll) andare d'accordo con
cot'ton can'dy s zucchero filato

cot'ton gin' *s* sgranatrice *f*

cot'ton pick'er ['pɪkər] *s* chi raccoglie il cotone; macchina che raccoglie il cotone

cot'tonseed oil' *s* olio di semi di cotone

cot'ton waste' *s* cascame *m* di cotone

cot'ton·wood' *s* pioppo deltoide

couch [kautʃ] *s* canapè *m*, sofà *m*, divano ‖ *tr* esprimere

couch' grass' *s* gramigna

cougar ['kugər] *s* puma *m*

cough [kɔf] *or* [kaf] *s* tosse *f* ‖ *tr*—to cough up sputare, sputare tossendo; (slang) dare, pagare ‖ *intr* tossire

cough' drop' *s* pastiglia per la tosse

cough' syr'up *s* sciroppo per la tosse

could [kud] *v aux*—I could not come yesterday non ho potuto venire ieri; I could not see you tomorrow non potrei vederLa domani; it could not be so non potrebbe essere così

council ['kaunsəl] *s* consiglio; (eccl) concilio

coun'cil·man *s* (-men) consigliere *m or* assessore *m* municipale

coun·sel ['kaunsəl] *s* consiglio; (lawyer) avvocato; to keep one's counsel essere riservato; to take counsel with consultarsi con ‖ *v* (pret & pp -seled or -selled; ger -seling or -selling) *tr* consigliare ‖ *intr* consigliare; consigliarsi

counselor ['kaunsələr] *s* consigliere *m*; avvocato

count [kaunt] *s* conto; (nobleman) conte *m*; (law) capo d'accusa ‖ *tr* contare; to count off by (twos, threes) contare per (due, tre); to count out escludere; (boxing) contare ‖ *intr* contare; (to be worth) valere; to count on contare su

count'down' *s* conteggio alla rovescia

countenance ['kauntɪnəns] *s* espressione; (face) faccia; (approval) approvazione ‖ *tr* approvare, incoraggiare

counter ['kauntər] *adj* contrario ‖ *s* contatore *m*; (token) gettone *m*; (table in store) banco; (opposite) contrario ‖ *adv* contro, contrariamente ‖ *tr* contrariare, opporre ‖ *intr* (boxing) rispondere

coun'ter·act' *tr* contrariare, neutralizzare

coun'ter·attack' *s* contrattacco ‖ coun'ter·attack' *tr & intr* contrattaccare

coun'ter·bal'ance *s* contrappeso ‖ coun'ter·bal'ance *tr* controbilanciare

coun'ter·clock'wise' *adj* antiorario ‖ *adv* in senso antiorario

coun'ter·es'pionage' *s* controspionaggio

counterfeit ['kauntərfɪt] *adj* contraffatto ‖ *s* contraffazione; moneta falsa ‖ *tr & intr* contraffare

counterfeiter ['kauntər,fɪtər] *s* contraffattore *m*

coun'ter·feit mon'ey *s* moneta falsa

countermand ['kauntər,mænd] *or* ['kauntər,mand] *tr* (troops) dare un contrordine a; (an order; a payment) cancellare

coun'ter·march' *s* contromarcia ‖ *intr* fare contromarcia

coun'ter·offen'sive *s* controffensiva

coun'ter·pane' *s* sopraccoperta

coun'ter·part' *s* copia; (person) sosia

coun'ter·point' *s* (mus) contrappunto; (mus) controcanto

Coun'ter Reforma'tion *s* controriforma

coun'ter·rev'olu'tion *s* controrivoluzione

coun'ter·sign' *s* (password) parola d'ordine; (signature) controfirma ‖ *tr* controfirmare

coun'ter·sink' *v* (pret & pp -sunk) *tr* incassare, accecare

coun'ter·spy' *s* (-spies) membro del controspionaggio

coun'ter·stroke' *s* contraccolpo

coun'ter·weight' *s* contrappeso

countess ['kauntɪs] *s* contessa

countless ['kauntlɪs] *adj* innumerevole

countrified ['kʌntrɪ,faɪd] *adj* rustico, rurale

coun·try ['kʌntri] *s* (-tries) (land) terreno; (nation) paese *m*; (land of one's birth) patria; (rural region) campagna

coun'try club' *s* circolo privato sportivo situato nei sobborghi

coun'try cous'in *s* campagnolo

coun'try estate' *s* tenuta

coun'try·folk' *s* campagnoli *mpl*

coun'try gen'tleman *s* proprietario terriero, signorotto di campagna

coun'try house' *s* casa di campagna

coun'try jake' *s* (coll) zoticone *m*

coun'try life' *s* vita rustica

coun'try·man *s* (-men) paesano, compaesano

coun'try·peo'ple *s* gente *f* di campagna

coun'try·side' *s* campagna

coun'try·wide' *adj* nazionale

coun'try·wom'an *s* (-wom'en) paesana, compaesana

coun·ty ['kaunti] *s* (-ties) contea, distretto

coun'ty seat' *s* capoluogo di contea

coup [ku] *s* colpo; colpo di stato

coup de grâce [ku də 'gras] *s* colpo di grazia

coup d'état [ku de'ta] *s* colpo di stato

coupe [kup] *or* coupé [ku'pe] *s* coupé *m*

couple ['kʌpəl] *s* (of people or animals) paio, coppia; (of things) paio; (link) unione ‖ *tr* accoppiare; (to link) unire, agganciare ‖ *intr* accoppiarsi

couplet ['kʌplɪt] *s* coppia di versi; (mus) couplet *m*

coupling ['kʌplɪŋ] *s* unione; (mach) giunto

coupon ['kupan] *or* ['kjupan] *s* coupon *m*, tagliando

courage ['kʌrɪdʒ] *s* coraggio; to have the courage of one's convictions avere il coraggio delle proprie opinioni

courageous [kə'redʒəs] *adj* coraggioso

courier ['kʌrɪ·ər] *or* ['kurɪ·ər] *s* corriere *m*

course [kors] *s* corso; (part of meal) portata; (place for games) campo;

(*row*) fila; **in due course** a tempo debito; **in the course of** durante, nel corso di; **of course** certamente, senza dubbio

court [kort] *s* (*uncovered place surrounded by walls*) corte *f*, cortile *m*; (*royal residence; courtship*) corte *f*; (*short street*) vicolo; (*playing area*) campo; (*law*) corte *f* || *tr* corteggiare; (*e.g., disaster*) andare in cerca di

courteous ['kʌrtɪ·əs] *adj* cortese

courtesan ['kʌrtɪzən] or ['kortɪzən] *s* cortigiana, meretrice *f*

courte·sy ['kʌrtɪsɪ] *s* (**-sies**) cortesia, gentilezza; **through the courtesy of** con il gentile permesso di

court'house' *s* palazzo di giustizia

courtier ['kortɪ·ər] *s* cortigiano

court' jest'er *s* buffone *m* di corte

court·ly ['kortlɪ] *adj* (**-lier; -liest**) cortese, cortigiano; ossequioso

court'-mar'tial *s* (**courts-martial**) corte *f* marziale || *v* (*pret & pp* **-tialed** or **-tialled**) *ger* **-tialing** or **-tialling**) *tr* sottomettere a corte marziale

court' plas'ter *s* taffettà *m*

court'room' *s* aula di giustizia

courtship ['kortʃɪp] *s* corte *f*, corteggiamento

court'yard' *s* corte *f*, cortile *m*

cousin ['kʌzɪn] *s* cugino

cove [kov] *s* piccola baia, cala

covenant ['kʌvənənt] *s* convenzione, patto || *tr* promettere solennemente

cover ['kʌvər] *s* (*lid*) coperchio; (*tablecloth; shelter*) coperto; (*of book*) copertina; **to take cover** nascondersi; **under cover** in segreto, segret.mente; **under cover of** sotto la protezione di; **under separate cover** in busta a parte, in plico a parte || *tr* coprire; puntare un'arma verso; (*journ*) riferire, riportare; **to cover up** coprire completamente || *intr* (*said of paint*) spandersi

coverage ['kʌvərɪdʒ] *s* copertura; (*journ*) servizio giornalistico; (*rad, telv*) raggio di udibilità

coveralls ['kʌvər ˌɔlz] *spl* tuta

cov'er charge' *s* coperto

cov'ered wag'on *s* carro coperto da tendone

cov'er girl' *s* ragazza-copertina

covering ['kʌvərɪŋ] *s* copertura; involucro

covert ['kʌvərt] *adj* nascosto, segreto

cov'er-up' *s* dissimulazione; sotterfugio

covet ['kʌvɪt] *tr* desiderare, agognare

covetous ['kʌvɪtəs] *adj* cupido

covey ['kʌvɪ] *s* covata

cow [kau] *s* vacca; (*of seal, elephant, etc.*) femmina || *tr* spaventare, intimidire

coward ['kau·ərd] *s* codardo, vile *m*

cowardice ['kau·ərdɪs] *s* codardia, viltà *f*

cowardly ['kau·ərdlɪ] *adj* codardo, vile || *adv* vilmente

cow'bell' *s* campano, campanaccio

cow'boy' *s* cowboy *m*

cow'catch'er *s* (rr) cacciapietre *m*

cower ['kau·ər] *intr* rannicchiarsi

cow'herd' *s* guardiano d'armenti

cow'hide' *s* pelle *f* di vacca

cowl [kaul] *s* (*hood*) cappuccio; (*monk's cloak*) cappa; (*of car*) sostegno del cofano; (*of chimney*) cappello; (aer) cappottatura

cow'lick' *s* ritrosa

cow'pox' *s* (vet) vaiolo bovino

coxcomb ['kaks ˌkom] *s* zerbinotto

coxwain ['kaksən] or ['kak ˌswen] *s* timoniere *m*

coy [kɔɪ] *adj* timido, ritroso

co·zy ['kozi] *adj* (**-zier; -ziest**) comodo || *s* (**-zies**) copriteiera *m*

C.P.A. ['si'pi'e] *s* (letterword) (**certified public accountant**) esperto contabile

crab [kræb] *s* granchio; (aer) scarroccio; (*complaining person*) (coll) scontroso || *v* (*pret & pp* **crabbed**) *ger* **crabbing**) *intr* (coll) lamentarsi

crab' apple' *s* mela selvatica; (*tree*) melo selvatico

crabbed ['kræbɪd] *adj* sgarbato; (*handwriting*) da gallina; (*style*) oscuro, ermetico

crab' louse' *s* piattola

crab·by ['kræbɪ] *adj* (**-bier; -biest**) scontroso, sgarbato

crack [kræk] *adj* (slang) di prim'ordine, eccellente || *s* (*noise*) schiocco; (*break*) rottura, screpolatura, crepa; (*opening*) fessura; (slang) tentativo; (slang) barzelletta || *tr* (*e.g., a whip*) schioccare; (*to break*) rompere, screpolare; (*oil*) ridurre con distillazione; (coll) risolvere; (*a safe*) (slang) forzare; (*a joke*) (slang) dire; **cracked up to be** (slang) avendo fama di || *intr* (*to make a noise*) scricchiolare; (*to break*) rompersi, screpolarsi; (*said of voice*) diventare fesso; (slang) avere un esaurimento nervoso; **to crack down** (slang) essere severo; **to crack up** (slang) andare a pezzi

cracked [krækt] *adj* rotto, spezzato; (*voice*) fesso; (coll) pazzo

cracker ['krækər] *s* cracker *m*, galletta

crack'er-bar'rel *adj* in piccolo, alla buon˙

crack'er-jack' *adj* (slang) di prim'ordine || *s* (slang) persona di prim'ordine

cracking ['krækɪŋ] *s* piroscissione

crackle ['krækəl] *s* crepitio, crepito || *intr* crepitare

crack'pot' *adj & s* (coll) mattoide *mf*

crack'-up' *s* accidente *m*; collisione; (*breakdown in health or in relations*) (coll) colasso; (aer) accidente *m* d'atterraggio

cradle ['kredəl] *s* culla; (*of handset*) forcella || *tr* cullare

crad'le-song' *s* ninnananna

craft [kræft] or [krɑft] *s* (*skill*) abilità *f*; (*trade*) mestiere *m*; (*guile*) astuzia, furberia; (*ship*) nave *f*; aeronave

craftiness ['kræftɪnɪs] or ['krɑftɪnɪs] *s* astuzia, furberia

crafts'man *s* (**-men**) operaio specializzato, artigiano

craft' un·ion *s* artigianato, sindacato artigiano

craft·y ['kræfti] or ['krɑfti] *adj* (-ier; -iest) astuto, furbo

crag [kræg] *s* roccia scoscesa, rupe *f*

cram [kræm] *v* (*pret & pp* **crammed;** *ger* **cramming**) *tr* (*to pack full*) riempire fino all'orlo; (*to stuff with food*) rimpinzare || *intr* rimpinzarsi; (coll) preparare un esame alla svelta

cramp [kræmp] *s* (*painful contraction*) crampo; (*bar with hooks*) grappa; (fig) ostacolo || *tr* ostacolare, restringere

cran·ber·ry ['kræn,beri] *s* (-ries) mirtillo

crane [kren] *s* (orn, mach) gru *f*; (*boom*) (telv, mov) giraffa || *tr* (*one's neck*) allungare || *intr* allungare il collo

crani·um ['krenɪ·əm] *s* (-a [ə]) cranio

crank [kræŋk] *s* manovella; (aut) alza-cristalli *m*; (coll) eccentrico || *tr* girare con la manovella; mettere in moto con la manovella

crank'case' *s* coppa dell'olio, carter *m*

crank'shaft' *s* albero a gomito

crank·y ['kræŋki] *adj* (-ier; -iest) irritabile; eccentrico

cran·ny ['kræni] *s* (-nies) (*crevice*) crepaccio; (*crack*) fessura

crape [krep] *s* crespo

crape'hang'er *s* (slang) pessimista uggioso, guastafeste *mf*

craps [kræps] *s* gioco dei dadi; **to shoot craps** giocare ai dadi

crash [kræʃ] *adj* (coll) d'emergenza || *s* (*noise*) scoppio, schianto; accidente *m*; (*collapse of business*) crac *m*, rovescio; (*bad landing*) atterraggio senza carrello || *tr* fracassare; **to crash the gate** (coll) entrare senza invito || *intr* fracassarsi; (com) fallire; **to cash into** investire, cozzare contro; **to cash through** sfondare

crash' dive' *s* immersione rapida di un sottomarino

crash' hel'met *s* casco

crass [kræs] *adj* crasso

crate [kret] *s* gabbia d'imballaggio || *tr* imballare in una gabbia

crater ['kretər] *s* cratere *m*

cravat [krə'væt] *s* cravatta

crave [krev] *tr* anelare; (*to beg*) implorare || *intr*—**to crave for** desiderare ardentemente

craven ['krevən] *adj & s* codardo

craving ['krevɪŋ] *s* anelito, desiderio

craw [krɔ] *s* gozzo

crawl [krɔl] *s* strisciamento, avanzata striscioni; (sports) crawl *m* || *intr* strisciare, avanzare striscioni; (*said of worms*) brulicare; (*said of insects*) formicolare; (*to feel creepy*) sentirsi il formicolio

crayfish ['krefɪʃ] *s* (*Palinurus vulgaris*) aragosta; (*Astacus; Cambarus*) gambero

crayon ['kre·ən] *s* pastello; disegno a pastello || *tr* disegnare a pastello

craze [krez] *s* mania, moda || *tr* fare impazzire

cra·zy ['krezi] *adj* (-zier; -ziest) pazzo, matto; **to be crazy about** (coll) esser matto per; **to drive crazy** fare impazzire

cra·zy bone' *s* osso rabbioso (del gomito)

creak [krik] *s* scricchiolio, cigolio || *intr* scricchiolare, cigolare

creak·y ['kriki] *adj* (-ier; -iest) stridente, cigolante

cream [krim] *s* crema, panna; (*finest part*) fior fiore *m* || *tr* rendere di consistenza cremosa; (*to remove cream from*) scremare; prendere il meglio di

creamer·y ['krimərɪ] *s* (-ies) (*factory*) caseificio; (*store*) cremeria

cream' puff' *s* bignè *m*

cream·y ['krimi] *adj* (-ier; -iest) cremoso; butirroso

crease [kris] *s* piega, grinza || *tr* piegare, raggrinzire || *intr* piegarsi, raggrinzirsi, far pieghe

crease'-resis'tant *adj* antipiega

create [kri'et] *tr* creare

creation [kri'eʃən] *s* creazione; **the Creation** il creato

creative [kri'etɪv] *adj* creativo

creator [kri'etər] *s* creatore *m*

creature ['kritʃər] *s* creatura

credence ['kridəns] *s* credenza

credentials [krɪ'denʃəlz] *spl* lettere *fpl* credenziali; documento d'autorizzazione

credible ['krɛdɪbəl] *adj* credibile

credit ['krɛdɪt] *s* credito; (*in a school*) unità *f* di promozione; (com) avere *m*; **credits** (mov, telv) titoli *mpl* di testa || *tr* accreditare; **to credit s.o. with s.th** attribuire qlco a qlcu

creditable ['krɛdɪtəbəl] *adj* lodevole

cred'it card' *s* carta di credito

creditor ['krɛdɪtər] *s* creditore *m*

cre·do ['krido] or ['kredo] *s* (-dos) credo

credulous ['krɛdʒələs] *adj* credulo

creed [krid] *s* credo

creek [krik] *s* fiumicello

creep [krip] *v* (*pret & pp* **crept** [krept]) *intr* strisciare, avanzare striscioni; (*to grow along a wall*) arrampicarsi; (*to feel creepy*) sentirsi il formicolio

creeper ['kripər] *s* strisciante *m*; (*plant*) rampicante *f*

creeping ['kripɪŋ] *adj* lento; (*plant*) rampicante

cremate ['krimet] *tr* cremare

cremato·ry ['krimə,tori] *adj* crematorio || *s* (-ries) forno crematorio

Creole ['kri·ol] *adj & s* creolo

crescent ['krɛsənt] *s* (*of Islam*) mezzaluna; (*of moon*) crescente *m*; (*roll*) cornetto

cress [krɛs] *s* crescione *m*

crest [krɛst] *s* cresta; (heral) stemma *m*, insegna

crestfallen ['krɛst,fɔlən] *adj* depresso

Cretan ['kritən] *adj & s* cretese *mf*

cretin ['kritən] *s* cretino

crevice ['krɛvɪs] *s* fessura, fenditura

crew [kru] *s* (*group working together*) personale *m*; (*group of workmen;*

mob) ciurma; (*of a ship or racing boat*) equipaggio; (sports) canottaggio

crew' cut' *s* capelli *mpl* a spazzola

crib [krɪb] *s* (*bed*) lettino; (*rack*) rastrelliera; (*building*) capanna, granaio; (coll) bigino ‖ *v* (*pret & pp* **cribbed;** *ger* **cribbing**) *tr* (coll) usare un bigino in ‖ *intr* (coll) usare un bigino; (coll) commettere un plagio

cricket [ˈkrɪkɪt] *s* grillo; (sports) cricket *m*, palla a spatola

crier [ˈkraɪ·ər] *s* banditore *m*

crime [kraɪm] *s* delitto, crimine *m*

criminal [ˈkrɪmɪnəl] *adj* criminale; (*code*) penale ‖ *s* delinquente *mf*

crimp [krɪmp] *s* piega, pieghettatura; **to put a crimp in** (slang) mettere i bastoni fra le ruote a ‖ *tr* pieghettare; (*the hair*) arricciare

crimson [ˈkrɪmzən] *adj & s* cremisi *m* ‖ *intr* imporporarsi

cringe [krɪndʒ] *intr* rannicchiarsi; (*to fawn*) umiliarsi

crinkle [ˈkrɪŋkəl] *tr* arricciare ‖ *intr* (*to rustle*) sfrusciare

cripple [ˈkrɪpəl] *s* zoppo, sciancato ‖ *tr* storpiare; (*e.g., business*) paralizzare

cri·sis [ˈkraɪsɪs] *s* (-ses [siz]) crisi *f*

crisp [krɪsp] *adj* (*brittle*) croccante, friabile; (*air*) frizzante; (*sharp and clear*) acuto

criteri·on [kraɪˈtɪrɪ·ən] *s* (-a [ə] or -ons) criterio

critic [ˈkrɪtɪk] *s* critico

critical [ˈkrɪtɪkəl] *adj* critico

criticism [ˈkrɪtɪˌsɪzəm] *s* critica

criticize [ˈkrɪtɪˌsaɪz] *tr & intr* criticare

critique [krɪˈtik] *s* critica

croak [krok] *s* (*of frogs*) gracidio; (*of crows*) gracchiamento ‖ *intr* gracidare; gracchiare; (slang) crepare

Croat [ˈkro·æt] *s* croato

Croatian [kroˈeʃən] *adj & s* croato

cro·chet [kroˈʃe] *s* lavoro all'uncinetto ‖ *v* (*pret & pp* **-cheted** [ˈʃed]; *ger* **-cheting** [ˈʃe·ɪŋ]) *tr & intr* lavorare all'uncinetto

crock [krɑk] *s* vaso di terracotta, giara, orcio

crockery [ˈkrɑkəri] *s* vasellame *m* di terracotta, terracotta

crocodile [ˈkrɑkəˌdaɪl] *s* coccodrillo

croc'odile tears' *spl* lacrime *fpl* di coccodrillo

crocus [ˈkrokəs] *s* croco

crone [kron] *s* vecchia incartapecorita

cro·ny [ˈkroni] *s* (-nies) amicone *m*, compare *m*

crook [kruk] *s* (*hook*) uncino; (*staff*) pastorale *m*; (*bend*) curva; (*bend of pipe*) gomito; (coll) imbroglione *m* ‖ *tr* piegare ‖ *intr* piegarsi

crooked [ˈkrukɪd] *adj* uncinato; curvo, piegato; (coll) disonesto

croon [krun] *intr* canterellare; cantare in modo sentimentale

crop [krɑp] *s* (*of bird*) gozzo; (*agricultural product, growing or harvested*) messe *f*; (*agricultural product harvested*) raccolto; (*riding whip*) fru-

stino; (*hair cut close*) capelli corti; gruppo ‖ *v* (*pret & pp* **cropped;** *ger* **cropping**) *tr* (*to cut the ends off of*) spuntare; (*to reap*) raccogliere; (*to cut short*) tosare ‖ *intr*—**to crop out** or **up** apparire inaspettatamente

crop'-dust'ing *s* fumigazione aerea

cropper [ˈkrɑpər] *s* mietitore *m*; (*sharecropper*) mezzadro; **to come a cropper** (coll) fare una cascataccia; (coll) andare in rovina

croquet [kroˈke] *s* croquet *m*, pallamaglio *m & f*

croquette [kroˈket] *s* crocchetta

crosier [ˈkroʒər] *s* pastorale *m*

cross [krɔs] or [krɑs] *adj* trasversale, contrario, obliquo; (*irritable*) bisbetico, di cattivo umore; (*of mixed breed*) incrociato ‖ *s* croce *f*; (*crossing of breeds*) incrocio; **to take the cross** farsi crociato ‖ *tr* crociare, segnare con una croce; (*the street*) attraversare; (*e.g., the legs*) incrociare; (*to draw a line across*) barrare; (*to thwart*) ostacolare; **to cross oneself** farsi il segno della croce; **to cross one's mind** venire in mente a uno; **to cross out** cancellare ‖ *intr* incrociarsi

cross'bones' *spl* teschio e tibie incrociate (*simbolo della morte*)

cross'bow' *s* balestra

cross'breed' *v* (*pret & pp* **-bred** [ˌbred]) *tr* incrociare, ibridare

cross'-coun'try *adj* campestre; attraverso il paese

cross'-examina'tion *s* (law) confronto, interrogatorio in contraddittorio

cross-eyed [ˈkrɔsˌaɪd] or [ˈkrɑsˌaɪd] *adj* guercio, strabico

crossing [ˈkrɔsɪŋ] or [ˈkrɑsɪŋ] *s* incrocio; ostacolo; (*of the sea*) traversata; (*of a river*) guado; (rr) passaggio a livello

cross'patch' *s* (coll) bisbetico

cross'piece' *s* traversa

cross' ref'erence *s* richiamo, rimando

cross'road' *s* strada trasversale; **at the crossroads** al bivio; **crossroads** crocicchio

cross' sec'tion *s* sezione trasversale

cross' street' *s* traversa

cross' talk' *s* conversazione; (telp) diafonia

cross'word puz'zle *s* cruciverba *m*, parole incrociate

crotch [krɑtʃ] *s* inforcatura; (*of pants*) cavallo

crotchety [ˈkrɑtʃɪti] *adj* bisbetico

crouch [krautʃ] *intr* accocolarsi

croup [krup] *s* (pathol) crup *m*

crouton [ˈkrutɑn] *s* crostino

crow [kro] *s* corvo, cornacchia; (*cry of rooster*) chicchirichì *m*; **as the crow flies** in linea retta, a volo d'uccello; **to eat crow** (coll) rimangiarsi le parole ‖ *intr* fare chicchirichì; **to crow over** vantarsi di, esultare per

crow'bar' *s* bastone *m* a leva

crowd [kraud] *s* folla; (*common people*) masse *fpl*; (coll) gruppo ‖ *tr*

affollare; (to push) spingere ‖ intr
affollarsi; (to press forward) spin-
gersi

crowded ['kraudɪd] adj affollato

crown [kraun] s corona; (of hat) cupola; (highest point) sommo ‖ tr
coronare; (checkers) damare; **to
crown s.o.** (coll) battere qlcu sulla
testa

crown′ prince′ s principe ereditario

crown′ prin′cess s principessa ereditaria

crow′s′-foot′ s (-feet) zampa di gallina

crow′s′-nest′ s coffa, gabbia

crucial ['kruʃəl] adj cruciale, critico

crucible ['krusɪbəl] s crogiolo

crucifix ['krusɪfɪks] s crocefisso

crucifixion [,krusɪ'fɪkʃən] s crocifis-
sione

cruci·fy ['krusɪ,faɪ] v (pret & pp -fied)
tr crocifiggere

crude [krud] adj (raw) grezzo; (unripe) acerbo; (roughly made; uncultured) rozzo

crudi·ty ['krudɪti] s (-ties) rozzezza

cruel ['kru·əl] adj crudele

cruel·ty ['kru·əlti] s (-ties) crudeltà f

cruet ['kru·ɪt] s oliera

cruise [kruz] s crociera ‖ tr navigare
‖ intr andare in crociera; andare
avanti e indietro

cruiser ['kruzər] s (nav) incrociatore
m

cruising ['kruzɪŋ] adj di crociera

cruis′ing ra′dius s autonomia di crociera

cruller ['krʌlər] s frittella

crumb [krʌm] s briciola ‖ tr sbriciolare; (e.g., a cutlet) impannare ‖
intr sbriciolarsi

crumble ['krʌmbəl] tr sbriciolare, polverizzare ‖ intr andare a pezzi, polverizzarsi, sbriciolarsi

crum·my ['krʌmi] adj (-mier; -miest)
(slang) sporco; (miserable) (slang)
schifoso; (e.g., joke) (slang) povero

crumple ['krʌmpəl] tr sgualcire, spiegazzare; **to crumple into a ball** appallottolare ‖ intr spiegazzarsi

crunch [krʌntʃ] s crocchio; (coll)
stretta, morsa ‖ tr sgranocchiare ‖
intr crocchiare

crusade [kru'sed] s crociata ‖ intr
crociarsi; (to take up a cause) farsi
paladino

crusader [kru'sedər] s crociato; (of a
cause) paladino

crush [krʌʃ] s pigiatura, schiacciatura;
(crowd) calca; (coll) infatuazione ‖
tr schiacciare; (to grind) frantumare;
(to subdue) sottomettere; (to extract
by squeezing) pigiare

crust [krʌst] s crosta; (slang) faccia
tosta ‖ tr incrostare ‖ intr incrostare,
incrostarsi

crustacean [krʌs'teʃən] s crostaceo

crust·y ['krʌsti] adj (-ier; -iest) crostoso; duro; rude

crutch [krʌtʃ] s gruccia, stampella;
(fig) sostegno

crux [krʌks] s difficoltà f, busillis m;
(crucial point) punto cruciale

cry [kraɪ] s (cries) (shout) grido; (fit
of weeping) pianto; (entreaty) richiamo; (of animal) urlo; **a far cry**
ben lontano, ben distinto; **to have a
good cry** sfogarsi, piangere a calde
lacrime ‖ tr gridare; (to proclaim)
bandire; **to cry down** disprezzare; **to
cry one's heart out** piangere a calde
lacrime; **to cry out** proclamare; **to
cry up** elogiare ‖ intr gridare, urlare;
piangere; **to cry for** implorare

cry′ba′by s (-bies) piagnucolone m

crypt [krɪpt] s cripta

cryptic(al) ['krɪptɪk(əl)] adj segreto,
occulto, misterioso

crystal ['krɪstəl] s cristallo

crys′tal ball′ s globo di cristallo

crystalline ['krɪstəlɪn] or ['krɪstə,laɪn]
adj cristallino

crystallize ['krɪstə,laɪz] tr cristallizzare ‖ intr cristallizzarsi

cub [kʌb] s cucciolo; (of lion) leoncino; (of fox) volpicino, volpac-
chiotto

cubbyhole ['kʌbɪ,hol] s sgabuzzino,
bugigattolo

cube [kjub] adj cubico ‖ s cubo; (of
sugar) zolla ‖ tr elevare al cubo; (to
shape) tagliare in quadretti

cubic ['kjubɪk] adj cubico

cub′ report′er s giornalista novello

cuckold ['kʌkəld] adj & s cornuto,
becco ‖ tr cornificare

cuckoo ['kuku] adj (slang) pazzo ‖ s
cuculo

cuck′oo clock′ s orologio a cucù

cucumber ['kjukʌmbər] s cetriolo

cud [kʌd] s mangime masticato; **to
chew the cud** ruminare

cuddle ['kʌdəl] tr abbracciare affet-
tuosamente ‖ intr (to lie close) gia-
cere vicino; (to curl up) rannicchiarsi, raggomitolarsi

cudg·el ['kʌdʒəl] s manganello, ran-
dello; **to take up the cudgels for** farsi
palà dino di ‖ v (pret & pp -eled or
-elled) ger -eling or -elling) tr bastonare, randellare; **to cudgel one's
brains** rompersi la testa

cue [kju] s suggerimento, imbeccata;
(billiards) stecca; **to miss a cue**
(theat) mancare la battuta; (coll)
non capire l'antifona ‖ tr—**to cue
s.o. (in) on** (coll) dare a qlcu informazioni su

cuff [kʌf] s (of shirt) polsino; (of
trousers) risvolto; (slap) schiaffo ‖
tr schiaffeggiare

cuff′ links′ spl bottoni doppi, gemelli
mpl

cuirass [kwɪ'ræs] s corazza

cuisine [kwɪ'zin] s cucina

culinary ['kjulɪ,nɛri] adj culinario

cull [kʌl] s scarto ‖ tr (to gather,
pluck) cogliere; selezionare, scegliere

culminate ['kʌlmɪ,net] intr culminare

culottes [ku'lɑts] spl gonna pantaloni

culpable ['kʌlpəbəl] adj colpevole

culprit ['kʌlprɪt] s colpevole m, imputato

cult [kʌlt] s culto

cultivate ['kʌltɪ,vet] tr coltivare

cultivated ['kʌltɪ ‚vetɪd] *adj* colto, coltivato

cultivation [‚kʌltɪ'veʃən] *s* coltivazione, cultura

culture ['kʌltʃər] *s* cultura

cultured ['kʌltʃərd] *adj* colto

cul'tured pearl' *s* perla coltivata

culvert ['kʌlvərt] *s* chiavica

cumbersome ['kʌmbərsəm] *adj* ingombrante, incomodo; (*clumsy*) goffo

cumulative ['kjumjə ‚letɪv] *adj* cumulativo

cunning ['kʌnɪŋ] *adj* (*sly*) astuto; (*skillful*) abile; (*pretty*) bello; (*created with skill*) ben fatto, fine || *s* astuzia; abilità *f*, destrezza

cup [kʌp] *s* tazza; (*mach, sports*) coppa; (*eccl*) calice *m*; **in one's cups** ubriaco || *v* (*pret & pp* **cupped**) *ger* **cupping**) *tr* mettere ventose a; **to cup one's hands** foggiare le mani a mo' di conca

cupboard ['kʌbərd] *s* armadio a muro, dispensa; (*buffet*) credenza

Cupid ['kjupɪd] *s* Cupido

cupidity [kju'pɪdɪti] *s* cupidigia

cup' of tea' *s* tazza di tè; (coll) forte *m*, e.g., **physics is not my cup of tea** la fisica non è il mio forte

cupola ['kjupələ] *s* cupola

cur [kʌr] *s* cane bastardo; (*despicable fellow*) canaglia, gaglioffo

curate ['kjurɪt] *s* curato

curative ['kjurətɪv] *adj* curativo

curator [kju'retər] *s* conservatore *m*

curb [kʌrb] *s* (*of bit*) barbazzale *m*; (*of pavement*) orlo del marciapiede; (*check*) freno || *tr* frenare

curb'stone' *s* cordone *m*; (*of well*) sponda del pozzo

curd [kʌrd] *s* cagliata || *tr* cagliare || *intr* cagliarsi

curdle ['kʌrdəl] *tr* cagliare; (*the blood*) far gelare || *intr* cagliarsi; (*said of custard*) impazzare

cure [kjur] *s* cura || *tr* curare; (*e.g., meat*) conservare; (*wood*) stagionare

cure'-all' *s* panacea

curfew ['kʌrfju] *s* coprifuoco

curi-o ['kjurɪ ‚o] *s* (*-os*) curiosità *f*

curiosi-ty [‚kjurɪ'ɑsɪti] *s* (*-ties*) curiosità *f*

curious ['kjurɪ-əs] *adj* curioso

curl [kʌrl] *s* (*of hair*) ricciolo; (*anything curled*) rotolo, spirale *f* || *tr* arricciare; arrotolare; (*the lips*) torcere || *intr* arricciarsi; arrotolarsi; **to curl up** raggomitolarsi

curlicue ['kʌrlɪ ‚kju] *s* ghirigoro

curl'ing i'ron *s* ferro da arricciare

curl'pa'per *s* bigodino

curl-y ['kʌrli] *adj* (*-ier; -iest*) ricciuto

curmudgeon [kər'mʌdʒən] *s* bisbetico

currant ['kʌrənt] *s* (*seedless raisin*) uva passa di Corinto, uva sultanina; (*shrub and berry of genus Ribes*) ribes *m*

curren-cy ['kʌrənsi] *s* (*-cies*) (*circulation*) circolazione; (*money*) denaro circolante; (*general use*) corso

current ['kʌrənt] *adj & s* corrente *f*

cur'rent account' *s* conto corrente

cur'rent events' *spl* attualità *fpl*, eventi *mpl* correnti

curricu•lum [kə'rɪkjələm] *s* (*-lums* or *-la* [lə]) programma *m*; piano educativo

cur•ry ['kʌri] *s* (*-ries*) (*spice*) curry *m* || *v* (*pret & pp -ried*) *tr* (*a horse*) strigliare; (*leather*) conciare; **to curry favor** cercare di compiacere

cur'ry-comb' *s* striglia || *tr* strigliare

curse [kʌrs] *s* maledizione; bestemmia || *tr* maledire || *intr* imprecare, bestemmiare

cursed ['kʌrsɪd] or [kʌrst] *adj* maledetto; (*hateful*) odiato

cursive ['kʌrsɪv] *adj & s* corsivo

cursory ['kʌrsəri] *adj* rapido, superficiale

curt [kʌrt] *adj* (*rude*) brusco, sgarbato; (*short*) breve, conciso

curtail [kər'tel] *tr* ridurre, restringere

curtain ['kʌrtən] *s* (*in front of stage*) sipario; (*for window*) tendina; (fig) cortina || *tr* coprire con tenda; separare con tenda; coprire, nascondere

cur'tain call' *s* (theat) chiamata

cur'tain rais'er ['rezər] *s* (theat) avanspettacolo; (sports) incontro preliminare

cur'tain ring' *s* campanella

cur'tain rod' *s* bastone *m* su cui si fissano le tende

curt-sy ['kʌrtsi] *s* (*-sies*) riverenza, inchino || *v* (*pret & pp -sied*) *intr* fare la riverenza, inchinarsi

curve [kʌrv] *s* curva || *tr* curvare || *intr* curvarsi

curved [kʌrvd] *adj* curvo, curvato

cushion ['kʊʃən] *s* cuscino; (*of billiard table*) mattonella || *tr* proteggere, ammortizzare, attutire

cuspidor ['kʌspɪ ‚dər] *s* sputacchiera

cuss [kʌs] *s* (coll) bestemmia; (coll) tipo perverso || *tr* maledire || *intr* bestemmiare

custard ['kʌstərd] *s* crema

custodian [kəs'todɪ-ən] *s* (*caretaker*) custode *m*, guardiano *m*; (*person who is entrusted with s.th*) conservatore *m*; (*janitor of school*) bidello

custo-dy ['kʌstədi] *s* (*-dies*) custodia; (*imprisonment*) arresto; **in custody** in prigione; **to take into custody** arrestare

custom ['kʌstəm] *s* costume *m*; (*customers*) clientela; **customs** dogana; diritti *mpl* doganali

customary ['kʌstə ‚meri] *adj* consueto, abituale

custom-built ['kʌstəm'bɪlt] *adj* fatto su misura; (*car*) fuori serie

customer ['kʌstəmər] *s* cliente *mf*

cus'tom-house' *adj* doganale || *s* dogana

custom-made ['kʌstəm'med] *adj* fatto su misura

cus'toms inspec'tion *s* visita doganale

cus'toms of'ficer *s* doganiere *m*

cus'tom work' *s* lavoro fatto su misura

cut [kʌt] *adj* (*prices*) ridotto; **to be cut out for** essere tagliato per || *s* taglio; (*reduction*) ribasso; (typ) cliché *m*;

(*snub*) (coll) affronto; (coll) assenza non autorizzata; (coll) parte *f*; **a cut above** (coll) un po' meglio di ‖ *tr* tagliare; (*cards*) alzare; (*prices*) ridurre; (coll) far finta di non riconoscere; (coll) marinare; **cut it out!** basta!; **to cut back** ridurre; **to cut off** tagliare; diseredare; (surg) amputare; **to cut short** interrompere; **to cut teeth** fare i denti; **to cut up** sminuzzare; criticare ‖ *intr* tagliare, tagliarsi; **to cut across** attraversare; **to cut in** interrompere; **to cut under** vendere sottoprezzo; **to cut up** (slang) fare il pagliaccio

cut-and-dried ['kʌtən'draɪd] *adj* monotono, stantio; bell'e fatto, fatto in anticipo

cutaneous [kju'teni·əs] *adj* cutaneo

cut'away' coat' ['kʌtə,we] *s* marsina da giorno

cut'back' *s* riduzione; eliminazione; (mov) ritorno dell'azione a un'epoca anteriore

cute [kjut] *adj* (coll) carino, grazioso; (*shrewd*) (coll) furbo

cut' glass' *s* cristallo intagliato

cuticle ['kjutɪkəl] *s* cuticola

cutlass ['kʌtləs] *s* sciabola

cutler ['kʌtlər] *s* coltellinaio

cutlery ['kʌtləri] *s* coltelleria

cutlet ['kʌtlɪt] *s* cotoletta; (*flat croquette*) polpetta

cut'off' *s* taglio; (*road*) scorciatoia; (*of cylinder*) otturatore *m*, chiusura dell'ammissione; (*of river*) braccio diretto

cut'out' *s* ritaglio; (aut) valvola di scappamento libero

cut'-rate' *adj* a prezzo ridotto

cutter ['kʌtər] *s* tagliatore *m*; (naut) cutter *m*

cut'throat' *adj* spietato; (*relentless*) senza posa ‖ *s* assassino

cutting ['kʌtɪŋ] *adj* tagliente ‖ *s* taglio; (*from a newspaper*) ritaglio;

(*e.g., of prices*) riduzione; (hort) talea

cut'ting board' *s* tagliere *m*; (*of dishwasher*) piano d'appoggio

cut'ting edge' *s* taglio

cuttlefish ['kʌtəl,fɪʃ] *s* seppia

cut'wat'er *s* (*of bridge*) tagliacque *m*; (*of boat*) tagliamare *m*

cyanamide [saɪ'ænə,maɪd] *s* cianamide *f*; cianamide *f* di calcio

cyanide ['saɪ-ə,naɪd] *s* cianuro

cycle ['saɪkəl] *s* ciclo; bicicletta; (*of internal combustion engine*) tempo; (phys) periodo ‖ *intr* andare in bicicletta

cyclic(al) ['saɪklɪk(əl)] or ['sɪklɪk(əl)] *adj* ciclico

cyclone ['saɪklon] *s* ciclone *m*

cyclops ['saɪklaps] *s* ciclope *m*

cyclotron ['saɪklo,tran] or ['sɪklo,tran] *s* ciclotrone *m*

cylinder ['sɪlɪndər] *s* cilindro; (*container*) bombola

cyl'inder block' *s* monoblocco

cyl'inder bore' *s* alesaggio

cyl'inder head' *s* testa

cylindric(al) [sɪ'lɪndrɪk(əl)] *adj* cilindrico

cymbals ['sɪmbəls] *spl* piatti *mpl*

cynic ['sɪnɪk] *adj* & *s* cinico

cynical ['sɪnɪkəl] *adj* cinico

cynicism ['sɪnɪ,sɪzəm] *s* cinismo

cynosure ['saɪnə,ʃʊr] or ['sɪnə,ʃʊr] *s* centro dell'attenzione

cypress ['saɪprəs] *s* cipresso

Cyprus ['saɪprəs] *s* Cipro

Cyrus ['saɪrəs] *s* Ciro

cyst [sɪst] *s* ciste *f*, cisti *f*

czar [zar] *s* zar *m*

czarina [zɑ'rinə] *s* zarina

Czech [tʃɛk] *adj* & *s* ceco

Czecho-Slovak ['tʃɛko'slovæk] *adj* & *s* cecoslovacco

Czecho-Slovakia [,tʃɛkoslo'vækɪ-ə] *s* la Cecoslovacchia

D

D, d [di] *s* quarta lettera dell'alfabeto inglese

dab [dæb] *s* tocco; (*of mud*) schizzo; (*e.g., of butter*) spalmata ‖ *v* (*pret & pp* **dabbed;** *ger* **dabbing**) *tr* toccare leggermente; (*to apply a substance to*) spennellare

dabble ['dæbəl] *tr* spruzzare ‖ *intr* diguazzare; **to dabble in** occuparsi di; (*stocks*) speculare in

dad [dæd] *s* (coll) papà *m*

dad-dy ['dædi] *s* (**-dies**) (coll) papà *m*

daffodil ['dæfədɪl] *s* trombone *m*

daff·y ['dæfi] *adj* (**-ier; -iest**) (coll) pazzo

dagger ['dægər] *s* daga, pugnale *m*; (typ) croce *f*; **to look daggers at** fulminare con lo sguardo

dahlia ['dæljə] *s* dalia

dai·ly ['deli] *adj* quotidiano, diurno ‖ *s* (**-lies**) quotidiano ‖ *adv* giornalmente

dai'ly dou'ble *s* duplice *f*, accoppiata

dain·ty ['denti] *adj* (**-tier; -tiest**) delicato ‖ *s* (**-ties**) manicaretto

dair·y ['deri] *s* (**-ies**) (*store*) latteria; (*factory*) caseificio

dair'y farm' *s* vaccheria

dair'y-man *s* (**-men**) lattaio

dais ['de·ɪs] *s* predella

dai·sy ['dezi] *s* (**-sies**) margherita

dal·ly ['dæli] *v* (*pret & pp* **-lied**) *intr* (*to loiter*) bighellonare; (*to trifle*) scherzare

dam [dæm] *s* diga; (*for fishing*) pescaia; (zool) fattrice *f* ‖ *v* (*pret & pp* **dammed;** *ger* **damming**) *tr* arginare; ostruire; tappare

damage ['dæmɪdʒ] *s* danno, scapito; (fig) menomazione; (com) avaria; **damages** danni *mpl* || *tr* danneggiare, ledere; sinistrare

damascene ['dæmə,sin] or [,dæmə'sin] *adj* damasceno || *s* damaschinatura || *tr* damaschinare

dame [dem] *s* dama, signora; (slang) donna

damn [dæm] *s*—I don't give a damn (slang) me ne impipo; that's not worth a damn (slang) non vale un fico || *tr* dannare, condannare || *intr* maledire || *interj* maledizione!

damnation [dæm'neʃən] *s* dannazione; (theol) condanna

damned [dæmd] *adj* dannato, maledetto || the damned *s* i dannati || *adv* maledettamente

damp [dæmp] *adj* umido || *s* umidità *f*; (firedamp) grisou *m* || *tr* inumidire; umettare; (to muffle) smorzare; (waves) (elec) smorzare; to damp s.o.'s enthusiasm *r*: ffreddare gli spiriti di qlcu; scoraggiare qlcu

dampen ['dæmpən] *tr* inumidire; umettare; smorzare; (s.o.'s enthusiasm) raffreddare

damper ['dæmpər] *s* (of chimney) valvola di tiraggio; (fig) doccia fredda; (mus) smorzatore *m*; (mus) sordina

damsel ['dæmzəl] *s* damigella

dance [dæns] or [dɑns] *s* ballo, danza || *tr & intr* ballare, danzare

dance' band' *s* orchestrina

dance' floor' *s* pista da ballo

dance' hall' *s* sala da ballo

dancer ['dænsər] or ['dɑnsər] *s* danzatore *m*; (expert or professional) ballerino

danc'ing part'ner *s* cavaliere *m*; dama

danc'ing par'ty *s* festa da ballo

dandelion ['dændɪ,laɪ·ən] *s* dente *m* di leone, soffione *m*

dandruff ['dændrəf] *s* forfora

dan-dy ['dændɪ] *adj* (-di-er; -diest) (coll) eccellente, magnifico || *s* (-dies) damerino, elegantone *m*

Dane [den] *s* danese *mf*

danger ['dendʒər] *s* pericolo

dangerous ['dendʒərəs] *adj* pericoloso

dangle ['dæŋgəl] *tr* dondolare || *intr* penzolare, ciondolare

Danish ['denɪʃ] *adj* & *s* danese *m*

dank [dæŋk] *adj* umido

Danube ['dænjub] *s* Danubio

dapper ['dæpər] *adj* azzimato

dapple ['dæpəl] *adj* pezzato || *tr* chiazzare

dap'ple-gray' *adj* storno

dare [dɛr] *s* sfida || *tr* sfidare || *intr* osare; I dare say oserei dire; forse, e.g., I dare say we will be done at seven forse avremo finito alle sette; to dare to (to have the courage to) osare di, fidarsi a

dare'dev'il *s* scavezzacollo

daring ['dɛrɪŋ] *adj* temerario, spericolato || *s* audacia, temerarietà *f*

dark [dɑrk] *adj* scuro; (complexion) bruno; oscuro, segreto; (gloomy) tetro, fosco || *s* oscurità *f*, scuro; tenebre *fpl*; in the dark al buio

Dark' Ag'es *spl* alto medio evo

dark-complexioned ['dɑrkkəm'plekʃənd] *adj* b uno

darken ['dɑrkən] *tr* scurire, oscurare || *intr* s urirsi, oscurarsi

dark' horse' *s* vincitore imprevisto, outsider *m*

darkly ['dɑrkli] *adv* oscuramente; segretamente

dark' meat' *s* gamba o anca (di pollo o tacchino)

darkness ['dɑrknɪs] *s* oscurità *f*

dark'room' *s* camera oscura

darling ['dɑrlɪŋ] *adj* & *s* caro, amato

darn [dɑrn] *s* rammendo || *tr* rammendare || *interj* (coll) accidenti!

darned [dɑrnd] *adj* (coll) maledetto || *adv* maledettamente; (coll) tremendamente

darnel ['dɑrnəl] *s* zizzania

darning ['dɑrnɪŋ] *s* rammendo

darn'ing nee'dle *s* ago da rammendo

dart [dɑrt] *s* freccia, dardo; (game) frecciolo || *intr* dardeggiare; lanciarsi, precipitarsi

dash [dæʃ] *s* sciacquio; piccola quantità, sospetto; (spirit) brio; (typ, telg) trattino, lineetta || *tr* lanciare; mescolare; (s.o.'s hopes) frustrare; deprimere; to dash off gettar giù; to dash to pieces fare a pezzi || *intr* precipitarsi; to dash against gettarsi contro; to dash by passare a gran velocità; to dash in entrare come un razzo; to dash off or out andarsene in frett ; l nci rsi fuori

dash'board' *s* cruscotto; (in an open carriage) parafango

dashing ['dæʃɪŋ] *adj* impetuoso; vistoso || *s* (of waves) sciacquio

dastard ['dæstərd] *adj* & *s* vile *mf*, codardo

da'ta proc'essing *s* elaborazione

date [det] *s* (time) data; (palm) palma da datteri; (fruit) dattero; (appointment) (coll) appuntamento; out of date fuori mod ; to date sinora; up to date a giorno || *tr* datare; (coll) avere un appuntamento con || *intr*— to date from p rtire da

date' line' *s* linea del cambiamento di data

dative ['detɪv] *adj* & *s* dativo

datum ['detəm] or ['dætəm] *s* (data ['detə] or ['dætəl) dato

daub [dɔb] *s* imbratto || *tr* imbrattare

daughter ['dɔtər] *s* figlia, figliola

daughter-in-law ['dɔtərɪn,lɔ] *s* (daughters-in-law) nuora

daunt [dɔnt] *tr* spaventare; intimidire

dauntless ['dɔntlɪs] *adj* intrepido

dauphin ['dɔfɪn] *s* delfino

davenport ['dævən,port] *s* sofà *m*, sofà *m* letto

davit ['dævɪt] *s* gru *f* per lancia

daw [dɔ] *s* cornacchia

dawdle ['dɔdəl] *intr* bighellonare

dawn [dɔn] *s* alba || *intr* (said of the day) farsi, nascere, spuntare; to dawn on cominciare a apparire nella mente di

day [de] *adj* diurno; (student) esterno || *s* giorno; (of travel, work, etc.)

giornata; **a few days ago** giorni fa;
any day now da un giorno all'altro;
by day di giorno; **the day after** il
giorno dopo; **the day after tomorrow**
dopodomani; **the day before yesterday** ieri l'altro; **to call it a day** (coll)
finire di lavorare
day' bed' s sofà m letto
day'book' s brogliaccio
day'break' s far m del giorno
day'dream' s fantasticheria || intr fan-
tasticare
day' la'borer s giornaliero
day'light' s luce f del giorno; alba; **in
broad daylight** alla luce del sole; **to
see daylight** comprendere; vedere la
fine
day'light-sav'ing time' s ora legale, ora
estiva
day' nurs'ery s asilo infantile
day' off' s giorno di vacanza; (of servant) libera uscita
day' of reck'oning s giorno di rendi-
conto; (last judgment) giorno del
giudizio
day' shift' s turno diurno
day'time' adj diurno || s giornata
daze [dez] s stordimento; **in a daze**
stordito || tr stordire
dazzle ['dæzəl] s abbagliamento || tr
abbagliare
dazzling ['dæzliŋ] adj abbagliante
deacon ['dikən] s diacono
dead [ded] adj morto || s—**in the dead
of** (e.g., night) nel pieno di; **the dead**
i morti || adv (coll) completamente;
(abruptly) (coll) di colpo
dead' beat' adj (coll) stanco morto
dead'beat' s (coll) scroccone m
dead' cen'ter s punto morto
dead'drunk' adj ubriaco fradicio
deaden ['dedən] tr attutire; (e.g., s.o.'s
senses) ottundere
dead' end' s vicolo cieco
dead' let'ter s lettera morta; lettera non
reclamata
dead'line' s termine m
dead'lock' s punto morto || tr portare
al punto morto || intr giungere al
punto morto
dead·ly ['dedli] adj (-lier; -liest) mortale; insopportabile
dead' pan' s (slang) faccia senza
espressione
dead'pan' adj senza espressione
dead' reck'oning s (naut) stima
dead'wood' s legna secca; (fig) zavorra
deaf [def] adj sordo; **to turn a deaf ear**
fare orecchio di mercante
deaf'-and-dumb' adj sordomuto
deafen ['defən] tr assordare, intronare
deafening ['defəniŋ] adj assordante
deaf'-mute' s sordomuto
deafness ['defnis] s sordità f
deal [dil] s accordo; quantità f; (cards)
mano, girata; (coll) affare m; (coll)
trattamento; **a good deal (of)** or **a
great deal (of)** moltissimo || v (pret
& pp **dealt** [delt]) tr (a blow) menare; (cards) fare, sfogliare; **to deal
s.o. in** (coll) includere || intr mer-
canteggiare, commerciare; fare le

carte; **to deal with** trattare con; trattare di
dealer ['dilər] s commerciante mf,
esercente mf; (cards) mazziere m
dean [din] s decano
dear [dir] adj (beloved; expensive)
caro; **dear me!** povero me!; **Dear
Sir** egregio Signore || s caro
dearie ['diri] s (coll) caro
dearth [dʌrθ] s scarsezza; insufficienza
death [deθ] s morte f; **to bleed to death**
morire dissanguato; **to burn to death**
morire bruciato; **to choke to death**
morire di soffocazione; **to freeze to
death** morire di gelo; **to put to death**
dare la morte a; **to shoot to death**
uccidere a fucilate; **to stab to death**
scannare; **to starve to death** far
morire di fame; morire di fame
death'bed' s letto di morte
death'blow' s colpo mortale
deathless ['deθlis] adj immortale,
eterno
deathly ['deθli] adj mortale || adv mor-
talmente; assolutamente
death' pen'alty s pena di morte
death' rate' s mortalità f
death' rat'tle s rantolo della morte
death' ray' s raggio della morte
death' sen'tence s pena di morte
death' war'rant s pena di morte; fine f
di ogni speranza
death'watch' s veglia mortuaria; (zool)
orologio della morte
debacle [de'bakəl] s disastro; (down-
fall) tracollo; (in a river) sgelo re-
pentino
de·bar [dɪ'bar] v (pret & pp -barred;
ger -barring) tr escludere; proibire
(with dat)
debark [dɪ'bark] tr & intr sbarcare
debarkation [,dibar'keʃən] s sbarco
debase [dɪ'bes] tr degradare; adulterare
debatable [dɪ'betəbəl] adj discutibile
debate [dɪ'bet] s discussione || tr &
intr discutere
debauch [dɪ'bɔtʃ] s dissolutezza, cor-
ruzione || tr corrompere
debauchee [,debɔ'ʃi] or [,debɔ't'ʃi] s
degenerato, vizioso
debaucher·y [dɪ'bɔtʃəri] s (-ies) dissolutezza, corruzione
debenture [dɪ'bentʃər] s (bond) obbligazione; (voucher) buono
debilitate [dɪ'bɪlɪ,tet] tr debilitare
debili·ty [dɪ'bɪlɪti] s (-ties) debolezza
debit ['debit] s debito; (debit side)
(com) dare m || tr addebitare
debonair [,debə'ner] adj gioviale; cortese
debris [de'bri] s detrito, rottami mpl
debt [det] s debito; **to run into debt**
indebitarsi
debtor ['detər] s debitore m
debut [de'bju] or ['debju] s debutto;
to make one's debut debuttare || intr
debuttare
debutante [,debju'tant] or ['debjə-
,tænt] s debuttante f, esordiente f
decade ['deked] s decennio
decadence [dɪ'kedəns] s decadenza

decadent [dɪˈkedənt] *adj & s* decadente *mf*

decanter [dɪˈkæntər] *s* boccia

decapitate [dɪˈkæpɪˌtet] *tr* decapitare

decay [dɪˈke] *s (decline)* decadimento; *(rotting)* marciume *m*, putredine *f*; *(of teeth)* carie *f* ‖ *tr* imputridire ‖ *intr* imputridire, marcire; *(said of teeth)* cariarsi

decease [dɪˈsis] *s* decesso ‖ *intr* decedere

deceased [dɪˈsist] *adj & s* defunto

deceit [dɪˈsit] *s* inganno, frode *f*

deceitful [dɪˈsitfəl] *adj* ingannatore, menzognero, subdolo

deceive [dɪˈsiv] *tr & intr* ingannare

decelerate [dɪˈseləˌret] *tr & intr* decelerare

December [dɪˈsembər] *s* dicembre *m*

decen·cy [ˈdisənsi] *s* (-cies) decenza, pudore *m*; **decencies** convenienze *fpl*

decent [ˈdisənt] *adj* decente; *(proper)* conveniente

decentralize [dɪˈsentrəˌlaɪz] *tr* decentrare

deception [dɪˈsepʃən] *s* inganno

deceptive [dɪˈseptɪv] *adj* ingannevole

decide [dɪˈsaɪd] *tr* decidere ‖ *intr* decidere, decidersi

decimal [ˈdesɪməl] *adj & s* decimale *m*

dec'imal point' *s (in Italian the comma is used to separate the decimal fraction from the integer)* virgola

decimate [ˈdesɪˌmet] *tr* decimare

decipher [dɪˈsaɪfər] *tr* decifrare

decision [dɪˈsɪʒən] *s* decisione

decisive [dɪˈsaɪsɪv] *adj* decisivo; *(resolute)* fermo

deck [dek] *s (of cards)* mazzo; *(naut)* coperta, tolda, ponte *m*; **on deck** *(coll)* pronto; *(coll)* prossimo ‖ *tr*— **to deck out** adornare; *(with flags)* imbandierare

deck' chair' *s* sedia a sdraio

deck' hand' *s* marinaio di coperta

deck'house' *s* (naut) tuga

deck'le edge' [ˈdekəl] *s* sbavatura

declaim [dɪˈklem] *tr & intr* declamare

declaration [ˌdeklɪˈreʃən] *s* dichiarazione

declarative [dɪˈklærətɪv] *adj* declaratorio; *(gram)* enunciativo

declare [dɪˈkler] *tr* dichiarare ‖ *intr* dichiararsi

declension [dɪˈklenʃən] *s* declinazione

declination [ˌdeklɪˈneʃən] *s* declinazione

decline [dɪˈklaɪn] *s* decadenza; *(in prices)* ribasso; *(in health)* deperimento; *(of sun)* tramonto ‖ *tr* declinare ‖ *intr* declinare; decadere, scadere

declivi·ty [dɪˈklɪvɪti] *s* (-ties) declivio, pendice *f*

decode [diˈkod] *tr* decifrare

décolleté [ˌdekalˈte] *adj* scollato

decompose [ˌdikəmˈpoz] *tr* decomporre ‖ *intr* decomporsi

decomposition [ˌdikampəˈzɪʃən] *s* decomposizione

décor [deˈkɔr] *s* decorazione; *(of a room)* stile *m*; (theat) scenario

decorate [ˈdekəˌret] *tr* decorare

decoration [ˌdekəˈreʃən] *s* decorazione

decorator [ˈdekəˌretər] *s* decoratore *m*

decorous [ˈdekərəs] *or* [dɪˈkorəs] *adj* corretto, decoroso

decorum [dɪˈkorəm] *s* decoro, correttezza

decoy [dɪˈkɔɪ] *or* [ˈdikɔɪ] *s* richiamo; *(for birds)* zimbello; *(person)* adescatore *m* ‖ *tr (to lure)* adescare; *(to deceive)* abbindolare

decrease [ˈdikrɪs] *or* [dɪˈkrɪs] *s* diminuzione; *(of salary)* decurtazione ‖ [dɪˈkrɪs] *tr* decurtare ‖ *intr* diminuire

decree [dɪˈkri] *s* decreto ‖ *tr* decretare

de·cry [dɪˈkraɪ] *v (pret & pp* -**cried**) *tr* denigrare, screditare

dedicate [ˈdedɪˌket] *tr* dedicare

dedication [ˌdedɪˈkeʃən] *s* dedizione; *(inscription in a book)* dedica

deduce [dɪˈdjus] *or* [dɪˈdus] *tr* dedurre

deduct [dɪˈdʌkt] *tr* dedurre, defalcare

deductible [dɪˈdʌktɪbəl] *adj* defalcabile ‖ *s* (ins) franchigia

deduction [dɪˈdʌkʃən] *s* deduzione

deed [did] *s* fatto; *(exploit)* prodezza; *(law)* titolo ‖ *tr* trasferire legalmente

deem [dim] *tr & intr* credere, giudicare

deep [dip] *adj* profondo; basso; *(woods)* folto; *(friendship)* intimo; **deep in debt** carico di debiti; **deep in thought** assorto in pensieri ‖ *adv* profondamente; **deep into the night** a notte fatta; **to go deep into** approfondirsi in

deepen [ˈdipən] *tr* approfondire ‖ *intr* approfondirsi

deep'-freeze' *tr (pret* -**froze** [froz]; *pp* -**frozen** [ˈfrozən]) *tr* surgelare

deep-laid [ˈdipˌled] *adj* preparato astutamente

deep' mourn'ing *s* lutto stretto

deep-rooted [ˈdipˌrutɪd] *adj* profondo

deep'-sea' fish'ing *s* pesca d'alto mare or d'altura

deep-seated [ˈdipˌsitɪd] *adj* profondo, connaturato

Deep' South' *s* Profondo Sud

deer [dɪr] *s* cervo

deer'skin' *s* pelle *f* di daino

deface [dɪˈfes] *tr* sfigurare

defamation [ˌdefəˈmeʃən] *or* [ˌdifəˈmeʃən] *s* diffamazione

defame [dɪˈfem] *tr* diffamare

default [dɪˈfɔlt] *s* mancanza; *(failure to act)* inadempienza; **in default of** per mancanza di; **to lose by default** dichiarare forfeit ‖ *tr* essere inadempiente a ‖ *intr* essere inadempiente; *(sports)* dichiarare forfeit

defeat [dɪˈfit] *s* sconfitta, disfatta ‖ *tr* sconfiggere, vincere

defeatism [dɪˈfitɪzəm] *s* disfattismo

defeatist [dɪˈfitɪst] *adj & s* disfattista *mf*

defecate [ˈdefɪˌket] *intr* defecare

defect [dɪˈfekt] *or* [ˈdifekt] *s* vizio, difetto ‖ [dɪˈfekt] *intr* defezionare

defection [dɪˈfekʃən] *s* defezione

defective [dɪˈfektɪv] *adj* difettivo, difettoso

defend [dɪ'fɛnd] *tr* difendere, proteggere

defendant [dɪ'fɛndənt] *s* (law) imputato, querelato

defender [dɪ'fɛndər] *s* difensore *m*

defense [dɪ'fɛns] *s* difesa

defenseless [dɪ'fɛnslɪs] *adj* indifeso

defensive [dɪ'fɛnsɪv] *adj* difensivo ‖ *s* difensiva

de·fer [dɪ'fʌr] *v* (*pret & pp* **-ferred;** *ger* **-ferring**) *tr* differire, rinviare ‖ *intr* rimettersi

deference ['dɛfərəns] *s* deferenza

deferential [,dɛfə'rɛnʃəl] *adj* deferente

deferment [dɪ'fʌrmənt] *s* differimento

defiance [dɪ'faɪəns] *s* opposizione; sfida; **in defiance of** a dispetto di

defiant [dɪ'faɪ·ənt] *adj* provocante, ostile

deficien·cy [dɪ'fɪʃənsi] *s* (**-cies**) deficienza; (com) ammanco

deficient ['fɪʃənt] *adj* deficiente

deficit ['dɛfɪsɪt] *adj* deficitario ‖ *s* deficit *m*, disavanzo

defile [dɪ'faɪl] or ['difaɪl] *s* gola, passo ‖ [dɪ'faɪl] *tr* profanare ‖ *intr* marciare in fila

define [dɪ'faɪn] *tr* definire

definite ['dɛfɪnɪt] *adj* definito; (gram) determinativo, determinato

definition [,dɛfɪ'nɪʃən] *s* definizione

definitive [dɪ'fɪnɪtɪv] *adj* definitivo

deflate [dɪ'flet] *tr* sgonfiare; (*s.o.'s hopes*) deprimere; (*e.g., currency*) deflazionare

deflation [dɪ'fleʃən] *s* sgonfiamento; (*of prices*) deflazione

deflect [dɪ'flɛkt] *tr* far deflettere ‖ *intr* deflettere

deflower [di'flaʊ·ər] *tr* privare dei fiori; (*a woman*) deflorare

deforest [di'fɔrɛst] or [di'fɔrɛst] *tr* disboscare, smacchiare

deform [dɪ'fɔrm] *tr* deformare

deformed [dɪ'fɔrmd] *adj* deforme

deformi·ty [dɪ'fɔrmɪti] *s* (**-ties**) deformità *f*

defraud [dɪ'frɔd] *tr* defraudare

defray [dɪ'fre] *tr* pagare

defrost [di'frɔst] or [di'frɑst] *tr* sgelare, sbrinare

defroster [di'frɔstər] or [di'frɑstər] *s* (aut) visiera termica

deft [dɛft] *adj* destro, lesto

defunct [dɪ'fʌŋkt] *adj* defunto

de·fy [dɪ'faɪ] *v* (*pret & pp* **-fied**) *tr* sfidare, provocare

degeneracy [dɪ'dʒɛnərəsi] *s* degenerazione

degenerate [dɪ'dʒɛnərɪt] *adj & s* degenerato ‖ [dɪ'dʒɛnə,ret] *intr* degenerare, tralignare

degrade [dɪ'gred] *tr* degradare

degrading [dɪ'gredɪŋ] *adj* degradante

degree [dɪ'gri] *s* grado; titolo accademico; **by degrees** a grado a grado; **to a degree** fino a un certo punto; troppo; **to take a degree** ricevere un titolo di studio

dehydrate [di'haɪdret] *tr* disidratare

deice [di'aɪs] *tr* sgelare

dei·fy ['di·ɪ ,faɪ] *v* (*pret & pp* **-fied**) *tr* deificare

deign [den] *intr* degnarsi

dei·ty ['di·ɪti] *s* (**-ties**) deità *f;* **the Deity** Dio

dejected [dɪ'dʒɛktɪd] *adj* demoralizzato

dejection [dɪ'dʒɛkʃən] *s* (*in spirits*) demoralizzazione; (*evacuation*) deiezione

delay [dɪ'le] *s* ritardo, proroga; dilazione; **without further delay** senza ulteriore indugio ‖ *tr* tardare; (*to put off*) differire ‖ *intr* tardare, ritardare

delayed'-ac'tion *adj* a azione differita

delectable [dɪ'lɛktəbəl] *adj* dilettevole

delegate ['dɛlɪ,get] or ['dɛlɪgɪt] *s* delegato, incaricato; (*to a convention*) congressista *mf* ‖ ['dɛlɪ,get] *tr* delegare, incaricare

delegation [,dɛlɪ'geʃən] *s* delegazione

delete [dɪ'lit] *tr* cancellare, sopprimere

deletion [dɪ'liʃən] *s* cancellazione

deliberate [dɪ'lɪbərɪt] *adj* meditato; (*slow in deciding*) cauto; (*slow in moving*) lento ‖ [dɪ'lɪbə,ret] *tr & intr* deliberare

deliberately [dɪ'lɪbərɪtli] *adv* (*on purpose*) deliberatamente; (*without hurrying*) con ponderatezza

delica·cy ['dɛlɪkəsi] *s* (**-cies**) delicatezza; (*choice food*) leccornia

delicatessen [,dɛlɪkə'tɛsən] *s* negozio di salumerie ‖ *spl* salumerie *fpl*, articoli alimentari scelti

delicious [dɪ'lɪʃəs] *adj* delizioso

delight [dɪ'laɪt] *s* gioia, delizia ‖ *tr* dilettare ‖ *intr* dilettarsi

delightful [dɪ'laɪtfəl] *adj* delizioso

delinquen·cy [dɪ'lɪŋkwənsi] *s* (**-cies**) colpa; (*offense*) delinquenza; (*in payment of a debt*) morosità *f*

delinquent [dɪ'lɪŋkwənt] *adj* colpevole; (*in payment*) moroso; non pagato ‖ *s* delinquente *m;* debitore moroso

delirious [dɪ'lɪrɪ·əs] *adj* in delirio

deliri·um [dɪ'lɪrɪ·əm] *s* (**-ums** or **-a** [ə]) delirio

deliver [dɪ'lɪvər] *tr* consegnare; (*a blow*) affibbiare; (*a speech*) fare; (*a letter*) recapitare; (*electricity or gas*) erogare; (*said of a pregnant woman*) partorire; (*said of a doctor*) assistere durante il parto

deliver·y [dɪ'lɪvəri] *s* (**-ies**) consegna; (*of mail*) distribuzione; (*of merchandise*) fornitura; (*of a speech*) dizione; (*childbirth*) parto; (sports) lancio

deliv'ery·man' *s* (**-men'**) fattorino

deliv'ery room' *s* sala parto

deliv'ery truck' *s* furgoncino

dell [dɛl] *s* valletta

delouse [di'laʊs] or [di'laʊz] *tr* spidocchiare

delude [dɪ'lud] *tr* illudere, ingannare

deluge ['dɛljudʒ] *s* diluvio, inondazione ‖ **the Deluge** il diluvio universale ‖ *tr* inondare

delusion [dɪ'luʒən] *s* illusione, inganno; (*psychopath*) allucinazione;

(psychopath) idea fissa; **delusions of grandeur** mania di grandezza

de luxe [dɪ'lʊks] or [dɪ'lʌks] *adj* di lusso || *adv* in gran lusso

delve [delv] *intr* frugare; **to delve into** approfondirsi in

demagnetize [di'mægnɪ,taɪz] *tr* smagnetizzare

demagogue ['demə,gɑg] *s* demagogo

demand [dɪ'mænd] or [dɪ'mɑnd] *s* esigenza; (com) richiesta, domanda; **to be in demand** essere in richiesta || *tr* esigere

demanding [dɪ'mændɪŋ] or [dɪ'mɑnd-ɪŋ] *adj* esigente, impegnativo

demarcate [dɪ'mɑrket] or ['dimɑr-,ket] *tr* demarcare

démarche [de'mɑrʃ] *s* progetto, piano

demean [dɪ'min] *tr* degradare; **to demean oneself** comportarsi; degradarsi

demeanor [dɪ'minər] *s* condotta, contegno

demented [dɪ'mentɪd] *adj* demente

demigod ['demɪ,gɑd] *s* semidio

demijohn ['demɪ,dʒɑn] *s* damigiana

demilitarize [dɪ'mɪlɪtə,raɪz] *tr* smilitarizzare

demimonde ['demɪ,mɑnd] *s* donne *fpl* della società equivoca

demise [dɪ'maɪz] *s* decesso

demitasse ['demɪ,tæs] or ['demɪ,tɑs] *s* tazzina da caffè; (*contents*) caffè nero

demobilize [di'mobɪ,laɪz] *tr* smobilitare

democra-cy [dɪ'mɑkrəsi] *s* (**-cies**) democrazia

democrat ['demə,kræt] *s* democratico

democratic [,demə'krætɪk] *adj* democratico

demolish [dɪ'mɑlɪʃ] *tr* demolire

demolition [,demə'lɪʃən] or [,dimə-'lɪʃən] *s* demolizione

demon ['dimən] *s* demonio

demoniacal [,dimə'naɪ-əkəl] *adj* demoniaco

demonstrate ['demən,stret] *tr* & *intr* dimostrare

demonstration [,demən'streʃən] *s* dimostrazione

demonstrative [dɪ'mɑnstrətɪv] *adj* dimostrativo; (*giving open exhibition of emotion*) espansivo

demonstrator ['demən,stretər] *s* (*of a product*) dimostratore *m*; (*in a public gathering*) dimostrante *m*; (*product*) prodotto usato da dimostratori

demoralize [dɪ'mɑrə,laɪz] or [dɪ-'mɔrə,laɪz] *tr* demoralizzare

demote [dɪ'mot] *tr* retrocedere

demotion [dɪ'moʃən] *s* retrocessione

de-mur [dɪ'mʌr] *v* (*pret & pp* **-murred**; *ger* **-murring**) *intr* sollevare obiezioni

demure [dɪ'mjʊr] *adj* modesto; sobrio

demurrage [dɪ'mʌrɪdʒ] *s* (com) controstallie *fpl*; (rr) sosta

den [den] *s* (*of animals, thieves*) tana; (*little room*) bugigattolo; (*little room for studying or writing*) studiolo; (*of lions*) (Bib) fossa

denaturalize [di'nætʃərə,laɪz] *tr* snaturare; privare della nazionalità

denatured al'cohol [di'netʃərd] *s* alcole denaturato

denial [dɪ'naɪ-əl] *s* diniego; (*disavowal*) smentita

denim ['denɪm] *s* tessuto di cotone per tuta; **denims** tuta; (*trousers*) jeans *mpl*

deni·zen ['denɪzən] *s* abitante *mf*

Denmark ['denmɑrk] *s* la Danimarca

denomination [dɪ,nɑmɪ'neʃən] *s* denominazione; categoria; (com) taglio; (eccl) confessione

denote [dɪ'not] *tr* denotare, significare

denouement [denu'mɑ̃] *s* scioglimento

denounce [dɪ'naʊns] *tr* denunziare

dense [dens] *adj* denso; stupido

densi·ty ['densɪti] *s* (**-ties**) densità *f*

dent [dent] *s* ammaccatura; (*in a gearwheel*) tacca, dente *m*; **to make a dent** fare progresso; fare impressione || *tr* ammaccare; (fig) ferire

dental ['dentəl] *adj* dentale, dentario || *s* dentale *f*

den'tal floss' *s* filo cerato dentario

dentifrice ['dentɪfrɪs] *s* dentifricio

dentist ['dentɪst] *s* dentista *mf*

dentistry ['dentɪstri] *s* odontoiatria

denture ['dentʃər] *s* dentiera

denunciation [dɪ,nʌnsɪ'eʃən] or [,nʌn,rɪ'eʃən] *s* denunzia

de-ny [dɪ'naɪ] *v* (*pret & pp* **-nied**) *tr* (*to declare not to be true*) negare; (*to refuse*) rifiutare; **to deny oneself to callers** sottrarsi alle visite || *intr* negare; rifiutare

deodorant [di'odərənt] *adj* & *s* deodorante *m*

deo'dorant spray' *s* deodorante *m* spray

deodorize [di'odə,raɪz] *tr* deodorare

depart [dɪ'pɑrt] *intr* partire, andarsene; (*to diverge*) dipartire

departed [dɪ'pɑrtɪd] *adj* morto, defunto || **the departed** i defunti

department [dɪ'pɑrtmənt] *s* dipartimento; (*of government*) ministero; (*e.g., of a hospital*) reparto; (*of agency*) sezione, ufficio

depart'ment store' *s* grandi magazzini *mpl*

departure [dɪ'pɑrtʃər] *s* partenza; divergenza, deviazione

depend [dɪ'pend] *intr* dipendere; **to depend on** (*to rely on*) contare su; dipendere da

dependable [dɪ'pendəbəl] *adj* sicuro, fidato

dependence [dɪ'pendəns] *s* dipendenza; (*trust*) fiducia

dependen-cy [dɪ'pendənsi] *s* (**-cies**) dipendenza; (*territory*) possessione

dependent [dɪ'pendənt] *adj* dipendente; a carico; **to be dependent on** dipendere da || *s* persona a carico

depend'ent clause' *s* proposizione subordinata

depict [dɪ'pɪkt] *tr* descrivere, dipingere

deplete [dɪ'plit] *tr* esaurire

depletion [dɪ'pliʃən] *s* esaurimento

deplorable [dɪ'plorəbəl] *adj* deplorevole

deplore [dɪ'plor] *tr* deplorare

deploy [dɪ'plɔɪ] *tr* (mil) spiegare, stendere

deployment [dɪ'plɔɪmənt] s (mil) dispositivo, spiegamento

depolarize [di'poləˌraɪz] tr depolarizzare

depopulate [di'pɑpjəˌlet] tr spopolare

deport [dɪ'port] tr deportare; **to deport oneself** comportarsi

deportation [ˌdiporˈteʃən] s deportazione

deportee [ˌdiporˈti] s deportato

deportment [dɪ'portmənt] s condotta, comportamento

depose [dɪ'poz] tr & intr deporre

deposit [dɪ'pɑzɪt] s deposito; (down payment) caparra || tr depositare || intr depositarsi

depos'it account' s conto corrente

depositor [dɪ'pɑzɪtər] s versante mf; (to the credit of an established account) orrentista mf

deposito·ry [dɪ'pɑzɪˌtori] s (-ries) deposito; (person) depositario

depos'it slip' s distinta di versamento

depot ['dipo] or ['depo] s magazzino; (mil) deposito; (rr) stazione

depraved [dɪ'prevd] adj depravato

depravi·ty [dɪ'prævɪti] s (-ties) depravazione

deprecate ['depriˌket] tr deprecare

depreciate [dɪ'priʃɪˌet] tr svalutare, deprezzare || intr deprezzarsi

depreciation [dɪˌpriʃɪˈeʃən] s (drop in value) deprezzamento; (disparagement) disprezzo

depredation [ˌdepriˈdeʃən] s depredazione

depress [dɪ'pres] tr deprimere; avvilire; (prices) far abbassare

depression [dɪ'preʃən] s depressione; (gloom) sconforto; (slump) crisi f

deprive [dɪ'praɪv] tr privare; **to deprive oneself** espropriarsi

depth [depθ] s profondità f; (of a house or room) lunghezza; (of sea) fondale m; (fig) vastità f; **in the depth of** nel cuor di; **to go beyond one's depth** non toccare più; (fig) andare oltre le proprie possibilità

depth' bomb' s (aer) bomba antisommergibile

depth' charge' s (nav) granata antisommergibile

depth' of hold' s (naut) puntale m

deputation [ˌdepjəˈteʃən] s deputazione

deputize ['depjəˌtaɪz] tr deputare

depu·ty ['depjəti] s (-ties) deputato

derail [dɪ'rel] tr far deragliare || intr deragliare, deviare

derailment [dɪ'relmənt] s deragliamento, deviamento

derange [dɪ'rendʒ] tr (to disarrange) dissestare; (to make insane) squilibrare, render pazzo

derangement [dɪ'rendʒmənt] s (disorder) disordine m; (insanity) squilibrio mentale, pazzia

der·by ['dʌrbi] s (-bies) bombetta; (race) derby m

derelict ['derɪlɪkt] adj derelitto; negligente || s derelitto; (naut) relitto

dereliction [ˌderɪˈlɪkʃən] s (in one's duty) negligenza; (law) derelizione

deride [dɪ'raɪd] tr deridere, schernire, farsi beffe di

derision [dɪ'rɪʒən] s derisione, scherno

derisive [dɪ'raɪsɪv] adj derisorio

derivation [ˌderɪˈveʃən] s derivazione

deriv·tive [dɪ'rɪvətɪv] adj & s derivato

derive [dɪ'raɪv] tr & intr derivare

dermatology [ˌdʌrməˈtɑlədʒi] s dermatologia

deroga·tory [dɪ'rɑgəˌtori] adj spregiativo

derrick ['derɪk] s gru f; (naut) picco di carico

dervish ['dʌrvɪʃ] s dervis m

desalinization [diˌselɪnɪˈzeʃən] s desalazione

desalt [di'sɔlt] tr desalificare

descend [dɪ'send] tr discendere || intr discendere; **to descend on** calare su, gett rsi su

descendant [dɪ'sendənt] adj & s discendente mf

descendent [dɪ'sendənt] adj discendente

descent [dɪ'sent] s (slope) china; (decline) declino; (descesa; (lineage) stirpe f, discendenza; (sudden raid) calata

Descent' from the Cross' s Deposizione dalla Croce

describe [dɪ'skraɪb] tr descrivere

description [dɪ'skrɪpʃən] s descrizione

descriptive [dɪ'skrɪptɪv] adj descrittivo

de·scry [dɪ'skraɪ] v (pret & pp -scried) tr avvistare

desecrate ['desɪˌkret] tr profanare, disscrare

desecration [ˌdesɪˈkreʃən] s profanazione, dissacrazione

desegregate [di'segrɪˌget] intr sopprimere la segregazione razziale

desegregation [diˌsegrɪˈgeʃən] s desegregazione

desensitize [di'sensɪˌtaɪz] tr desensibilizzare

desert ['dezərt] adj & s deserto || [dɪ'zɜrt] s merito; **he received his just deserts** ricevette quanto meritava || tr & intr disertare

deserter [dɪ'zɜrtər] s disertore m

deserted [dɪ'zɜrtɪd] adj (person) abbandonato; (place) deserto

desertion [dɪ'zɜrʃən] s diserzione; abbandono del coniuge

deserve [dɪ'zɜrv] tr & intr meritare

deservedly [dɪ'zɜrvɪdli] adv meritatamente, meritevolmente

design [dɪ'zaɪn] s disegno; (of a play) congegno; **to have designs on** aver mire su || tr disegnare; progettare || intr disegnare; **designed for** destinato a

designate ['dezɪgˌnet] tr designare

designer [dɪ'saɪnər] s disegnatore m

designing [dɪ'zaɪnɪŋ] adj intrigante, macchinatore || s disegnazione

desirable [dɪ'zaɪrəbəl] adj desiderabile

desire [dɪ'zaɪr] s desiderio || tr desiderare

desirous [dɪ'zaɪrəs] adj desideroso

desist [di'zɪst] intr desistere

desk [desk] s scrittoio; tavolo d'ufficio;

(*lectern*) leggio; (*of professor*) cattedra; (*of pupil*) banco; (com) cassa

desk'bound' *adj* sedentario; legato al tavolino

desk' pad' *s* blocco da tavolo; blocco per appunti

desolate ['desəlɪt] *adj* desolato, deserto; (*hopeless*) disperato; (*dismal*) lugubre ‖ ['desə,let] *tr* desolare; devastare

desolation [,desə'leʃən] *s* desolazione; devastazione

despair [dɪ'sper] *s* disperazione; **to be in despair** disperarsi ‖ *intr* disperare, disperarsi

despairing [dɪ'sperɪŋ] *adj* disperato

despera-do [,despə'redo] *or* [,despə'rɑdo] *s* (**-does** *or* **-dos**) fuorilegge disposto a tutto

desperate ['despərɪt] *adj* disposto a tutto; (*hopeless*) disperato; (*very bad*) atroce, terribile; (*bitter, excessive*) accanito; (*remedy*) estremo

desperation [,despə'reʃən] *s* disperazione

despicable ['despɪkəbəl] *adj* spregevole, incanaglito

despise [dɪ'spaɪz] *tr* sprezzare, disprezzare, vilipendere

despite [dɪ'spaɪt] *prep* malgrado

despoil [dɪ'spɔɪl] *tr* spogliare

despondency [dɪ'spɑndənsi] *s* (**-cies**) scoraggiamento, abbattimento

despondent [dɪ'spɑndənt] *adj* scoraggiato, abbattuto

despot ['despɑt] *s* despota *m*

despotic [des'pɑtɪk] *adj* dispotico

despotism ['despə,tɪzəm] *s* dispotismo

dessert [dɪ'zʌrt] *s* dessert *m*

dessert' spoon' *s* cucchiaio *or* cucchiaino da dessert

destination [,destɪ'neʃən] *s* destinazione

destine ['destɪn] *tr* destinare

desti-ny ['destɪni] *s* (**-nies**) destino

destitute ['destɪ,tjut] *or* ['destɪ,tut] *adj* (*poverty-stricken*) indigente; (*lacking*) privo

destitution [,destɪ'tjuʃən] *or* [,destɪ'tuʃən] *s* indigenza, miseria

destroy [dɪ'strɔɪ] *tr* distruggere

destroyer [dɪ'strɔɪ·ər] *s* (nav) cacciatorpediniere *m*

destruction [dɪ'strʌkʃən] *s* distruzione

destructive [dɪ'strʌktɪv] *adj* distruttivo

desultory ['desəl,tori] *adj* saltuario, sconnesso

detach [dɪ'tætʃ] *tr* staccare, distaccare; (mil) distaccare

detachable [dɪ'tætʃəbəl] *adj* staccabile; separabile

detached [dɪ'tætʃt] *adj* (*e.g., stub*) staccato; (*e.g., house*) discosto; (*aloof*) riservato, freddo; imparziale

detachment [dɪ'tætʃmənt] *s* distacco; imparzialità *f*; (mil) distaccamento

detail [dɪ'tel] *or* ['ditel] *s* dettaglio, ragguaglio; (mil) distaccamento *f* [dɪ'tel] *tr* dettagliare; (mil) distaccare

detain [dɪ'ten] *tr* detenere, trattenere

detect [dɪ'tekt] *tr* scoprire, discernere; (rad) rivelare

detection [dɪ'tekʃən] *s* scoperta; (rad) rivelazione

detective [dɪ'tektɪv] *s* detective *m*

detec'tive sto'ry *s* romanzo poliziesco, romanzo giallo

detector [dɪ'tektər] *s* (rad) detector *m*, rivelatore *m*

detention [dɪ'tenʃən] *s* detenzione

de-ter [dɪ'tʌr] *v* (*pret & pp* **-terred**; *ger* **-terring**) *tr* distogliere, impedire

detergent [dɪ'tʌrdʒənt] *adj & s* detergente *m*

deteriorate [dɪ'tɪrɪ·ə,ret] *tr* deteriorare ‖ *intr* deteriorarsi, andar giù

determination [dɪ,tʌrmɪ'neʃən] *s* determinazione

determine [dɪ'tʌrmɪn] *tr* determinare

determined [dɪ'tʌrmɪnd] *adj* determinato, risoluto

deterrent [dɪ'tʌrənt] *s* deterrente *m*

detest [dɪ'test] *tr* detestare, odiare

dethrone [dɪ'θron] *tr* detronizzare

detonate ['detə,net] *or* ['ditə,net] *tr* far scoppiare ‖ *intr* detonare

detonator ['detə,netər] *s* innesco

detour ['ditur] *or* [dɪ'tur] *s* deviazione ‖ *tr* far deviare ‖ *intr* deviare

detract [dɪ'trækt] *tr* detrarre ‖ *intr—* **to detract from** diminuire

detractor [dɪ'træktər] *s* detrattore *m*

detriment ['detrɪmənt] *s* detrimento; **to the detriment of** a danno di

detrimental [,detrɪ'mentəl] *adj* pregiudizievole

deuce [djus] *or* [dus] *s* (cards) due *m*; **the deuce!** diavolo!

devaluate [di'vælju,et] *tr* svalutare

devaluation [di,vælju'eʃən] *s* devalutazione, svalutazione

devastate ['devəs,tet] *tr* devastare

devastating ['devəs,tetɪŋ] *adj* devastatore, devastante; (*e.g., reply*) schiacciante, annichilante

devastation [,devəs'teʃən] *s* devastazione

develop [dɪ'veləp] *tr* sviluppare; (phot) sviluppare, rivelare ‖ *intr* svilupparsi; manifestarsi

developer [dɪ'veləpər] *s* (*e.g., of a new engine*) sfruttatore *m*; (*in real estate*) specialista *mf* in lottizzazione; (phot) sviluppatore *m*, rivelatore *m*

development [dɪ'veləpmənt] *s* sviluppo; valorizzazione; sfruttamento; (phot) rivelazione

deviate ['divɪ,et] *tr* sviare ‖ *intr* deviare, sviarsi

deviation [,divɪ'eʃən] *s* deviazione

deviationism [,divɪ'eʃə,nɪzəm] *s* deviazionismo

deviationist [,divɪ'eʃənɪst] *s* deviazionista *mf*

device [dɪ'vaɪs] *s* dispositivo, congegno; (*trick*) stratagemma *m*; (*motto*) divisa, emblema *m*; **to leave s.o. to his own devices** lasciare che qlcu faccia come gli pare e piace

dev-il ['devəl] *s* diavolo; **between the devil and the deep blue sea** fra l'incudine e il martello; **to raise the devil** (slang) fare diavolo a quattro ‖ *v* (*pret & pp* **-iled** *or* **-illed**; *ger*

-iling or **-illing** *tr* condire con spezie o con pepe; (coll) infastidire

devilish ['devəlɪʃ] *adj* diabolico

devilment ['devəlmənt] *s (mischief)* diavoleria; *(evil)* cattiveria

devil·try ['devəltri] *s (-tries)* malvagità *f*, crudeltà *f*; *(mischief)* diavoleria

devious ['dɪvɪ·əs] *adj (tricky)* traverso; *(roundabout)* tortuoso

devise [dɪ'vaɪz] *tr* ideare, inventare; (law) legare, disporre per testamento

devoid [dɪ'vɔɪd] *adj* sprovvisto

devolve [dɪ'vɑlv] *intr*—**to devolve on** ricadere su

devote [dɪ'vot] *tr* dedicare

devoted [dɪ'votɪd] *adj* devoto; dedito, dedicato

devotee [͵devə'ti] *s* devoto; *(fan)* fanatico, tifoso, entusiasta *mf*

devotion [dɪ'voʃən] *s* devozione; *(e.g., to work)* dedizione; **devotions** orazioni *mpl*, preghiere *fpl*

devour [dɪ'vaʊr] *tr* divorare

devout [dɪ'vaʊt] *adj* devoto; sincero

dew [dju] or [du] *s* rugiada

dew'drop' *s* goccia di rugiada

dew'lap' *s* giogaia

dew·y ['dju·i] or ['du·i] *adj (-ier; -iest)* rugiadoso

dexterity [deks'terɪti] *s* destrezza

diabetes [͵daɪ·ə'bitɪs] or [͵daɪ·ə'bitiz] *s* diabete *m*

diabetic [͵daɪ·ə'betɪk] or [͵daɪ·ə'bitɪk] *adj & s* diabetico

diabolic(al) [͵daɪ·ə'bɑlɪk(əl)] *adj* diabolico

diadem ['daɪ·ə͵dem] *s* diadema *m*

diaere·sis [daɪ'erɪsɪs] *s (-ses* [͵siz]) dieresi *f*

diagnose [͵daɪ·əg'nos] or [͵daɪ·əg'noz] *tr* diagnosticare

diagno·sis [͵daɪ·əg'nosɪs] *s (-ses* [siz]) diagnosi *f*

diagonal [daɪ'ægənəl] *adj & s* diagonale *f*

dia·gram ['daɪ·ə͵græm] *s* diagramma *m*; *(drawing)* schema *m*; *(plan)* prospetto *m* ‖ *v (pret & pp* -gramed or -grammed; *ger* -graming or -gramming) *tr* diagrammare

dial ['daɪ·əl] *s (of watch)* quadrante *m*; (rad) tabella graduata, sintogramma *m*; (telp) disco combinatore ‖ *tr* (rad) sintonizzare; *(a person)* (telp) chiamare; *(a number)* (telp) comporre; *(the phone)* (telp) comporre il numero de ‖ *intr* (telp) comporre il numero

dialect ['daɪ·ə͵lekt] *s* dialetto

dialing ['daɪ·əlɪŋ] *s* composizione del numero

dialogue ['daɪ·ə͵lɔg] or ['daɪ·ə͵lɑg] *s* dialogo

di'al tel'ephone *s* telefono automatico

di'al tone' *s* (telp) segnale *m* di via libera

diameter [daɪ'æmɪtər] *s* diametro

diametric(al) [͵daɪ·ə'metrɪk(əl)] *adj* diametrico, diametrale

diamond ['daɪmənd] *s* diamante *m*; *(figure of a rhombus)* losanga; (baseball) diamante *m*; **diamonds** (cards) quadri *mpl*

diaper ['daɪ·pər] *s* pannolino

diaphanous [daɪ'æfənəs] *adj* diafano

diaphragm ['daɪ·ə͵fræm] *s* diaframma *m*; (telp) membrana

diarrhea [͵daɪ·ə'ri·ə] *s* diarrea

dia·ry ['daɪ·əri] *s (-ries)* diario

diastole [daɪ'æstəli] *s* diastole *f*

diathermy ['daɪ·ə͵θ͵ɑrmi] *s* diatermia

dice [daɪs] *spl* dadi *mpl*; *(small cubes)* cubetti *mpl*; **no dice** (slang) niente da fare; (slang) risposta a picche

dice' cup' *s* bussolotto

dichloride [daɪ'klɔraɪd] *s* bicloruro

dichoto·my [daɪ'kɑtəmi] *s (-mies)* dicotomia

dickey ['dɪki] *s* camiciola; *(starched insert)* sparato; *(bib)* bavaglino

dictaphone ['dɪktə͵fon] *s* dittafono

dictate ['dɪktet] *s* dettato ‖ ['dɪktet] or [dɪk'tet] *tr* dettare

dictation [dɪk'teʃən] *s* dettato; *(act of ordering)* ordine *m;* **to take dictation** scrivere sotto dettatura

dictator ['dɪktetər] or [dɪk'tetər] *s* dittatore *m*

dictatorship ['dɪktetər͵ʃɪp] or [dɪk'tetər͵ʃɪp] *s* dittatura

diction ['dɪkʃən] *s* dizione

dictionar·y ['dɪkʃən͵eri] *s (-ies)* dizionario, vocabolario

dic·tum ['dɪktəm] *s (-ta* [tə]) detto, sentenza

didactic(al) [daɪ'dæktɪk(əl)] or [dɪ'dæktɪk(əl)] *adj* didattico

die [daɪ] *s (dice* [daɪs]) dado; **the die is cast** il dado è tratto ‖ *s (dies) (for stamping coins, medals,* etc.) stampo; *(for cutting threads)* filiera ‖ *v (pret & pp* died; *ger* dying) *intr* morire; **to die hard** morire lentamente; morire lottando; **to die laughing** morire dalle risa; **to die off** morire uno per uno

die'-hard' *adj & s* intransigente *m*

die'sel oil' ['dizəl] *s* nafta, gasolio

die'stock' *s* girafiliera

diet ['daɪ·ət] *s* dieta, regime *m* ‖ *intr* stare a dieta

dietetic [͵daɪ·ə'tetɪk] *adj* dietetico ‖ **dietetics** *ssg* dietetica

dietitian [͵daɪ·ə'tɪʃən] *s* dietista *mf*

differ ['dɪfər] *intr (to be different)* differire, differenziarsi; **to differ with** dissentire da

difference ['dɪfərəns] *s* differenza; **to make no difference** fare lo stesso; **to split the difference** dividere la differenza; (fig) venire a un compromesso

different ['dɪfərənt] *adj* differente

differential [͵dɪfə'ren[ə]l] *adj & s* differenziale *m*

differentiate [͵dɪfə'ren[ɪ͵et] *tr* differenziare ‖ *intr* differenziarsi

difficult ['dɪfr͵kʌlt] *adj* difficile

difficul·ty ['dɪfr͵kʌlti] *s (-ties)* difficoltà *f*

diffident ['dɪfɪdənt] *adj* timido, imbarazzato

diffuse [dɪ'fjus] *adj* diffuso ‖ [dɪ'fjuz] *tr* diffondere ‖ *intr* diffondersi

dig [dɪg] *s (poke)* botta, spintone *m*; *(jibe)* stoccata, fiancata ‖ *v (pret & pp* dug [dʌg]; *ger* digging) *tr* scavare, sterrare; **to dig up** dissodare; (*to uncover*) dissotterrare ‖ *intr* scavare; **to dig in** (mil) fortificarsi; **to dig into** (coll) sprofondarsi in

digest ['daɪdʒɛst] *s* compendio; digesto ‖ [dɪ'dʒɛst] or [daɪ'dʒɛst] *tr & intr* digerire

digestible [dɪ'dʒɛstɪbəl] or [daɪ'dʒɛstɪbəl] *adj* digeribile, digestibile

digestion [dɪ'dʒɛstʃən] or [daɪ'dʒɛstʃən] *s* digestione

digestive [dɪ'dʒɛstɪv] or [daɪ'dʒɛstɪv] *adj* (*tube*) digerente ‖ *s* digestivo

digit ['dɪdʒɪt] *s* cifra, unità *f*; (*finger*) dito; (*toe*) dito del piede

dig'ital clock' *s* orologio a scatto

digitalis [ˌdɪdʒɪ'tælɪs] or [ˌdɪdʒɪ'telɪs] *s* (bot) digitale *f*; (pharm) digitalina

dignified ['dɪgnɪˌfaɪd] *adj* dignitoso, fiero, contegnoso

digni•fy ['dɪgnɪˌfaɪ] *v* (*pret & pp* **-fied**) *tr* (*to ennoble*) nobilitare; onorare, esaltare; dare la dignità a

dignitar•y ['dɪgnɪˌteri] *s* (**-ies**) dignitario; **dignitaries** dignità *fpl*

digni•ty ['dɪgnɪti] *s* (**-ties**) dignità *f*, decoro; **to stand on one's dignity** mantenere la propria dignità

digress [dɪ'grɛs] or [daɪ'grɛs] *intr* digredire, divagare

digression [dɪ'grɛʃən] or [daɪ'grɛʃən] *s* digressione, divagazione

dike [daɪk] *s* diga; (*in a river*) argine *m*; (*ditch*) fosso; scarpata

dilapidated [dɪ'læpɪˌdetɪd] *adj* dilapidato, decrepito

dilate [daɪ'let] *tr* dilatare ‖ *intr* dilatarsi

dilatory ['dɪləˌtori] *adj* lento, tardivo; (*e.g., strategy*) dilatorio

dilemma [dɪ'lɛmə] *s* dilemma *m*

dilettan•te [ˌdɪlə'tænti] *adj* dilettantesco ‖ *s* (**-tes** or **-ti** [ti]) dilettante *mf*

diligence ['dɪlɪdʒəns] *s* diligenza

diligent ['dɪlɪdʒənt] *adj* diligente

dill [dɪl] *s* (bot) aneto

dillydal•ly ['dɪlɪˌdæli] *v* (*pret & pp* **-lied**) *intr* farla lunga

dilute [dɪ'lut] or [daɪ'lut] *adj* diluito ‖ [dɪ'lut] *tr* diluire ‖ *intr* diluirsi

dilution [dɪ'luʃən] *s* diluizione

dim [dɪm] *adj* (**dimmer; dimmest**) (*light*) fioco; (*sight*) debole; (*memory*) vago; (*color*) smorzato; (*sound*) sordo; **to take a dim view of** avere una visione pessimistica di ‖ *v* (*pret & pp* **dimmed**; *ger* **dimming**) *tr* (*lights*) smorzare; **to dim the headlights** abbassare i fari

dime [daɪm] *s* moneta di dieci centesimi di dollaro

dimension [dɪ'mɛnʃən] *s* dimensione

diminish [dɪ'mɪnɪʃ] *tr & intr* diminuire, scemare

diminutive [dɪ'mɪnjətɪv] *adj* (*tiny*) minuscolo; (gram) diminutivo ‖ *s* diminutivo

dimly ['dɪmli] *adv* indistintamente

dimmer ['dɪmər] *s* smorzatore *m*; (aut) luce *f* di incrocio; **dimmers** fari *mpl* antiabbaglianti

dimple ['dɪmpəl] *s* fossetta

dimwit ['dɪmˌwɪt] *s* (slang) stupido, cretino

din [dɪn] *s* fragore *m*, frastuono ‖ *v* (*pret & pp* **dinned**; *ger* **dinning**) *tr* assordare; **to din s.th into s.o.'s ears** rintronare qlco nelle orecchie di qlcu

dine [daɪn] *tr* offrire un pranzo a; offrire una cena a ‖ *intr* pasteggiare; cenare; **to dine out** mangiare fuori di casa

diner ['daɪnər] *s* commensale *m*; (rr) vettura ristorante; (U.S.A.) ristorante *m* a forma di vagone

ding-dong ['dɪŋˌdɔŋ] or ['dɪŋˌdɑŋ] *s* dindon *m*

din•gy ['dɪndʒi] *adj* (**-gier; -giest**) sporco, sbiadito

din'ing car' *s* vagone *m* ristorante

din'ing room' *s* sala da pranzo

dinner ['dɪnər] *s* cena; pranzo; (*formal meal*) banchetto

din'ner coat' or **jack'et** *s* smoking *m*

din'ner knife' *s* coltello da tavola

din'ner set' *s* servizio da tavola

din'ner ta'ble *s* desco

din'ner time' *s* ora di pranzo o di cena

dinosaur ['daɪnəˌsɔr] *s* dinosauro

dint [dɪnt] *s* tacca, ammaccatura; **by dint of** a forza di ‖ *tr* ammaccare

diocese ['daɪəˌsɪs] or ['daɪəsɪs] *s* diocesi *f*

diode ['daɪod] *s* diodo

dioxide [daɪ'ɑksaɪd] *s* biossido

dip [dɪp] *s* immersione; (*brief swim*) tuffo, nuotata; (*in a road*) depressione; inclinazione magnetica ‖ *v* (*pret & pp* **dipped**; *ger* **dipping**) *tr* immergere, tuffare; (*the flag*) abbassare; (*bread*) inzuppare ‖ *intr* immergersi, tuffarsi; inclinarsi; (*to drop down*) sparire subitamente; **to dip into** (*a book*) sfogliare; (*business*) mettersi in; (*a container of liquids*) intingere; **to dip into one's purse** spendere soldi

diphtheria [dɪf'θɪrɪə] *s* difterite *f*

diphthong ['dɪfθɔŋ] or ['dɪfθɑŋ] *s* dittongo

diphthongize ['dɪfθɔŋˌgaɪz] or ['dɪfθɑŋˌgaɪz] *tr & intr* dittongare

diploma [dɪ'plomə] *s* diploma *m*

diploma•cy [dɪ'ploməsi] *s* (**-cies**) diplomazia

diplomat ['dɪpləˌmæt] *s* diplomatico

diplomatic [ˌdɪplə'mætɪk] *adj* diplomatico

dip'lomat'ic pouch' *s* valigia diplomatica

dipper ['dɪpər] *s* mestolo

dip'stick' *s* asta di livello

dire [daɪr] *adj* terribile, orrendo

direct [dɪ'rɛkt] or [daɪ'rɛkt] *adj* diretto; sincero ‖ *tr* dirigere; ordinare

direct' cur'rent *s* corrente continua

direct' dis'course *s* discorso diretto

direct' dis'tance di'aling *s* (telp) teleselezione *f*

direct' hit' *s* colpo centrato

direction [dɪ'rɛkʃən] or [daɪ'rɛkʃən] *s* direzione; **directions** istruzioni *fpl*; (*for use*) indicazioni *fpl* per l'uso

directional [dɪ'rek/ənəl] or [daɪ-'rek/ənəl] *adj* direzionale

directive [dɪ'rektɪv] or [daɪ'rektɪv] *s* direttiva

direct' ob'ject *s* (gram) complemento diretto, complemento oggetto

director [dɪ'rektər] or [daɪ'rektər] *s* direttore *m*, gerente *m*; (*member of a governing body*) consigliere *m*

directorship [dɪ'rektər‚/ɪp] or [daɪ-'rektər‚/ɪp] *s* direzione; amministrazione

directo·ry [dɪ'rektəri] or [daɪ'rektəri] *s* (**-ries**) (*board of directors*) direzione, direttorio; (*list of names and addresses*) rubrica, elenco; (telp) elenco dei telefoni, guida telefonica

dirge [dʌrdʒ] *s* canto funebre

dirigible ['dɪrɪdʒɪbəl] *adj* & *s* dirigibile *m*

dirt [dʌrt] *s* (*soil*) terra, suolo; (*dust*) polvere *m*; (*mud*) fango; (*accumulation of dirt*) sudiciume *m*, lerciume *m*; (*moral filth*) porcheria, sozzura; (*gossip*) pettegolezzi *mpl*; **to do s.o. dirt** (slang) calunniare qlcu

dirt'-cheap' *adj* a prezzo bassissimo

dirt' road' *s* strada di terra battuta

dirt·y ['dʌrti] *adj* (**-ier; -iest**) sporco, sudicio; fangoso; polveroso; (*e.g.*, *spinach*) terroso; (*obscene*) sconcio, lurido; immondo ‖ *v* (*pret & pp* -**ied**) *tr* sporcare, insudiciare, imbrattare

dir'ty lin'en *s* roba sporca; **to air one's dirty linen in public** mettere i panni al sole

dir'ty trick' *s* brutto tiro

disabili·ty [‚dɪsə'bɪlɪti] *s* (**-ties**) incapacità *f*, invalidità *f*

disabil'ity insur'ance *s* assicurazione invalidità

disable [dɪs'ebəl] *tr* mutilare, storpiare; (*a ship*) smantellare; (law) invalidare

disabuse [‚dɪsə'bjuz] *tr* disingannare

disadvantage [‚dɪsəd'væntɪdʒ] or [‚dɪsəd'vɑntɪdʒ] *s* svantaggio

disadvantageous [dɪs‚ædvən'tedʒəs] *adj* svantaggioso

disagree [‚dɪsə'gri] *intr* discordare, disconvenire; (*to quarrel*) litigare, altercare; **to disagree with** non essere del parere di

disagreeable [‚dɪsə'gri·əbəl] *adj* sgradevole

disagreement [‚dɪsə'grimənt] *s* sconcordanza, dissidio, dissenso

disallow [‚dɪsə'lau] *tr* non permettere, rifiutare

disappear [‚dɪsə'pɪr] *intr* sparire, scomparire

disappearance [‚dɪsə'pɪrəns] *s* scomparsa

disappoint [‚dɪsə'pɔɪnt] *tr* deludere, disilludere; **to be disappointed** rimanere deluso

disappointment [‚dɪsə'pɔɪntmənt] *s* delusione, disinganno, disappunto

disapproval [‚dɪsə'pruvəl] *s* disapprovazione, riprova

disapprove [‚dɪsə'pruv] *tr & intr* disapprovare

disarm [dɪs'ɑrm] *tr* disarmare ‖ *intr* disarmare, disarmarsi

disarmament [dɪs'ɑrməmənt] *s* disarmo

disarming [dɪs'ɑrmɪŋ] *adj* ingraziante, simpatico

disarray [‚dɪsə're] *s* disordine *m*, scompiglio; (*of apparel*) sciatteria ‖ *tr* scomporre, scompigliare

disassemble [‚dɪsə'sɛmbəl] *tr* smontare, sconnettere

disassociate [‚dɪsə'soʃɪ‚et] *tr* dissociare, disassociare

disaster [dɪ'zæstər] or [dɪ'zɑstər] *s* disastro, sinistro

disastrous [dɪ'zæstrəs] or [dɪ'zɑstrəs] *adj* disastroso

disavow [‚dɪsə'vau] *tr* sconfessare

disavowal [‚dɪsə'vau·əl] *s* sconfessione

disband [dɪs'bænd] *tr* (*an assembly*) sciogliere; (*troops*) congedare; (*any group*) sbandare ‖ *intr* sbandarsi

dis·bar [dɪs'bɑr] *v* (*pret & pp* -**barred**; *ger* -**barring**) *tr* (law) radiare dall'albo degli avvocati

disbelief [‚dɪsbɪ'lif] *s* incredulità *f*

disbelieve [‚dɪsbɪ'liv] *tr* rifiutarsi di credere a ‖ *intr* rifiutarsi di credere

disburse [dɪs'bʌrs] *tr* sborsare

disbursement [dɪs'bʌrsmənt] *s* sborso, disborso

discard [dɪs'kɑrd] *s* scarto, scartina; **to put into the discard** scartare ‖ *tr* scartare

discern [dɪ'zʌrn] or [dɪ'sʌrn] *tr* scernere, discernere, sceverare

discernible [dɪ'zʌrnɪbəl] or [dɪ'sʌrnɪbəl] *adj* discernibile

discerning [dɪ'zʌrnɪŋ] or [dɪ'sʌrnɪŋ] *adj* perspicace, oculato

discernment [dɪ'zʌrnmənt] or [dɪ-'sʌrnmənt] *s* discernimento

discharge [dɪs'tʃɑrdʒ] *s* (*of a load*) scarico; (*of a gun; of electricity*) scarica; (*of a prisoner*) liberazione; (*of a duty*) adempimento; (*of a debt*) pagamento; (*from a job*) licenziamento; (mil) foglio di congedo; (pathol) spurgo ‖ *tr* scaricare; (*a duty*) adempiere; (*a prisoner*) liberare; (*a debt*) pagare; (*an employee*) licenziare; (*a patient*) lasciar uscire; (*a passenger from a ship*) sbarcare; (*a battery*) scaricare; (mil) congedare ‖ *intr* (*said, e.g., of a liquid*) sboccare; (*said of a gun or a battery*) scaricarsi

disciple [dɪ'saɪpəl] *s* discepolo

disciplinarian [‚dɪsɪplɪ'nɛrɪ·ən] *s* disciplinatore *m*; partigiano di una forte disciplina

disciplinary ['dɪsɪplɪ‚nɛri] *adj* disciplinare

discipline ['dɪsɪplɪn] *s* disciplina; castigo ‖ *tr* disciplinare; castigare

disclaim [dɪs'klem] *tr* non riconoscere, negare

disclose [dɪs'kloz] *tr* rivelare, scoprire

disclosure [dɪs'kloʒər] *s* rivelazione, s operta; divulgazione

discolor [dɪs'kʌlər] *tr* scolorare, scolorire ‖ *intr* scolorirsi

discoloration [dɪs‚kʌlə'reʃən] *s* discolorazione

discomfit [dɪsˈkʌmfɪt] *tr* sconcertare, turbare; frustrare, battere, mettere in fuga

discomfiture [dɪsˈkʌmfɪt/ər] *s* sconcerto, turbamento; frustrazione; disfatta

discomfort [dɪsˈkʌmfərt] *s* disagio ‖ *tr* incomodare

disconcert [ˌdɪskənˈsɑrt] *tr* sconcertare

disconnect [ˌdɪskəˈnekt] *tr* sconnettere; (elec) disinserire

disconsolate [dɪsˈkɑnsəlɪt] *adj* sconsolato, desolato

discontent [ˌdɪskənˈtent] *adj* & *s* scontento ‖ *tr* scontentare

discontented [ˌdɪskənˈtentɪd] *adj* scontento

discontinue [ˌdɪskənˈtɪnju] *tr* cessare, interrompere

discord [ˈdɪskɔrd] *s* discordia, dissidio

discordance [dɪsˈkɔrdəns] *s* discordanza

discotheque [ˌdɪskoˈtek] *s* discoteca

discount [ˈdɪskaʊnt] *s* sconto ‖ [ˈdɪskaʊnt] or [dɪsˈkaʊnt] *tr* scontare; (news) fare la tara a

dis′count rate′ *s* tasso di sconto

discourage [dɪsˈkʌrɪdʒ] *tr* scoraggiare, sconfortare; (to dissuade) sconsigliare

discouragement [dɪsˈkʌrɪdʒmənt] *s* scoraggiamento; disapprovazione

discourse [ˈdɪskɔrs] or [dɪsˈkɔrs] *s* discorso ‖ [dɪsˈkɔrs] *intr* discorrere

discourteous [dɪsˈkʌrtɪ-əs] *adj* scortese

discourte•sy [dɪsˈkʌrtəsi] *s* (-sies) scortesia

discover [dɪsˈkʌvər] *tr* scoprire

discover•er [dɪsˈkʌvərər] *s* scopritore *m*

discover•y [dɪsˈkʌvəri] *s* (-ies) scoperta

discredit [dɪsˈkredɪt] *s* discredito ‖ *tr* screditare

discreditable [dɪsˈkredɪtəbəl] *adj* indegno, disonorevole

discreet [dɪsˈkrit] *adj* discreto

discrepan•cy [dɪsˈkrepənsi] *s* (-cies) discrepanza, divario

discretion [dɪsˈkreʃən] *s* discrezione

discriminate [dɪsˈkrɪmɪˌnet] *tr* discriminare ‖ *intr*—to discriminate against fare delle discriminazioni contro

discrimination [dɪsˌkrɪmɪˈneʃən] *s* discriminazione

discriminatory [dɪsˈkrɪmɪnəˌtori] *adj* discriminante

discuss [dɪsˈkʌs] *tr* & *intr* discutere

discussion [dɪsˈkʌʃən] *s* discussione

discus thrower [ˈdɪskəs ˈθro-ər] *s* discobolo

disdain [dɪsˈden] *s* disdegno ‖ *tr* disdegnare, sdegnare

disdainful [dɪsˈdenfəl] *adj* sdegnoso

disease [dɪˈziz] *s* malattia

diseased [dɪˈzizd] *adj* malato

disembark [ˌdɪsemˈbɑrk] *tr* & *intr* sbarcare

disembarkation [dɪsˌembɑrˈkeʃən] *s* sbarco

disembowel [ˌdɪsemˈbaʊ-əl] *tr* sbudellare, sventrare

disenchant [ˌdɪsenˈtʃænt] or [ˌdɪsenˈtʃɑnt] *tr* disincantare

disenchantment [ˌdɪsenˈtʃæntmənt] or [ˌdɪsenˈtʃɑntmənt] *s* disinganno

disengage [ˌdɪsenˈgedʒ] *tr* (from a pledge) svincolare; (to disconnect) sgranare, disinnestare; (mil) sganciare

disengagement [ˌdɪsenˈgedʒmənt] *s* liberazione; disinnesto; svincolamento

disentangle [ˌdɪsenˈtæŋgəl] *tr* disincagliare, districare

disentanglement [ˌdɪsenˈtæŋgəlmənt] *s* districamento

disestablish [ˌdɪsesˈtæblɪʃ] *tr* (the Church) separare dallo Stato

disfavor [dɪsˈfevər] *s* disfavore *m*

disfigure [dɪsˈfɪgjər] *tr* sfigurare, deturpare

disfigurement [dɪsˈfɪgjərmənt] *s* deturpazione

disfranchise [dɪsˈfræntʃaɪz] *tr* privare dei diritti civili

disgorge [dɪsˈgɔrdʒ] *tr* vomitare; (something illicitly obtained) restituire; (said of a river) scaricare ‖ *intr* vomitare; scaricarsi

disgrace [dɪsˈgres] *s* vergogna; disgrazia ‖ *tr* disonorare; privare del favore

disgraceful [dɪsˈgresfəl] *adj* infamante, disonorante

disgruntle [dɪsˈgrʌntəl] *tr* scontentare, irritare

disgruntled [dɪsˈgrʌntəld] *adj* irritato, di cattivo umore

disguise [dɪsˈgaɪz] *s* travestimento ‖ *tr* travestire, dissimulare

disgust [dɪsˈgʌst] *s* disgusto, schifo ‖ *tr* disgustare, fare schifo a

disgusting [dɪsˈgʌstɪŋ] *adj* disgustoso, schifoso

dish [dɪʃ] *s* piatto, dishes vasellame *m*; to wash the dishes fare i piatti ‖ *tr* scodellare; (to defeat) (slang) sconfiggere; to dish out (slang) distribuire

dish′cloth′ *s* canovaccio, strofinaccio

dishearten [dɪsˈhɑrtən] *tr* scoraggiare, disanimare, desolare

dishev•el [dɪˈʃevəl] *v* (pret & pp -eled or -elled; ger -eling or -elling) *tr* scomporre, scarmigliare, scapigliare

dishonest [dɪsˈɑnɪst] *adj* disonesto

dishones•ty [dɪsˈɑnɪsti] *s* (-ties) disonestà *f*

dishonor [dɪsˈɑnər] *s* disonore *m* ‖ *tr* disonorare; (com) rifiutare di pagare

dishonorable [dɪsˈɑnərəbəl] *adj* disonorevole, disonorante

dish′pan′ *s* bacinella per lavare i piatti

dish′rack′ *s* portapiatti *m*, sgocciolatoio

dish′rag′ *s* canovaccio, strofinaccio

dish′towel′ *s* canovaccio per le stoviglie

dish′wash′er *s* (person) sguattero, lavapiatti *m*; (machine) lavastoviglie *m* & *f*

dish′wa′ter *s* lavatura di piatti

disillusion [ˌdɪsɪˈluʒən] *s* disillusione ‖ *tr* disilludere

disillusionment [ˌdɪsɪˈluʒənmənt] *s* disillusione

disinclination [dɪsˌɪnklɪˈneʃən] *s* riluttanza, avversione

disinclined [dɪsɪnˈklaɪnd] *adj* riluttante, avverso

disinfect [,dɪsɪn'fekt] *tr* disinfettare
disinfectant [,dɪsɪn'fektənt] *adj* & *s* disinfettante *m*
disingenuous [,dɪsɪn'dʒɛnju·əs] *adj* poco schietto, insincero
disinherit [,dɪsɪn'herɪt] *tr* diseredare
disintegrate [dɪs'ɪntɪ ,gret] *tr* disintegrare, disgregare || *intr* disintegrarsi, disgregarsi
disintegration [dɪs ,ɪntɪ'greʃən] *s* disintegrazione, disgregamento
disin·ter [,dɪsɪn'tʌr] *v* (*pret* & *pp* **-terred**; *ger* **-terring**) *tr* dissotterrare
disinterested [dɪs'ɪntə ,restɪd] or [dɪs'ɪntrɪstɪd] *adj* disinteressato
disjunctive [dɪs'dʒʌŋktɪv] *adj* disgiuntivo
disk [dɪsk] *s* disco; (*of ski pole*) rotella
disk' jock'ey *s* presentatore *m* di un programma radiodiffuso di dischi
dislike [dɪs'laɪk] *s* antipatia, avversione; **to take a dislike for** prendere in uggia || *tr* non piacere (with *dat*), e.g., **he dislikes wine** non gli piace il vino
dislocate [dɪslo ,ket] *tr* spostare, mettere fuori posto; (*a bone*) slogare
dislodge [dɪs'lɑdʒ] *tr* sloggiare
disloyal [dɪs'lɔɪ·əl] *adj* sleale
disloyal·ty [dɪs'lɔɪ·əltɪ] *s* (**-ties**) slealtà *f*
dismal ['dɪzməl] *adj* tetro, triste; cattivo, orribile
dismantle [dɪs'mæntəl] *tr* smontare, smantellare; (*a fortress*) sguarnire
dismay [dɪs'me] *s* costernazione || *tr* costernare
dismember [dɪs'membər] *tr* smembrare
dismiss [dɪs'mɪs] *tr* congedare; (*to fire*) licenziare; (*a subject*) scartare; (*from the mind*) scacciare
dismissal [dɪs'mɪsəl] *s* congedo; licenziamento
dismount [dɪs'maunt] *tr* disarcionare || *intr* scendere, smontare
disobedience [,dɪsə'bidɪ·əns] *s* disubbidienza
disobedient [,dɪsə'bidɪ·ənt] *adj* disubbidiente
disobey [,dɪsə'be] *tr* disubbidire (with *dat*) || *intr* disubbidire
disorder [dɪs'ɔrdər] *s* disordine *m* || *tr* disordinare, confondere
disorderly [dɪs'ɔrdərlɪ] *adj* disordinato, confuso; (*unruly*) turbolento
disor'derly con'duct *s* contegno contrario all'ordine pubblico
disor'derly house' *s* bordello, lupanare *m*
disorganize [dɪs'ɔrgə ,naɪz] *tr* disorganizzare
disoriented [dɪs'ɔrɪ ,entɪd] *adj* disorientato
disown [dɪs'on] *tr* disconoscere
disparage [dɪs'pærɪdʒ] *tr* svilire, deprezzare
disparagement [dɪs'pærɪdʒmənt] *s* discredito, deprezzamento
disparate ['dɪspərɪt] *adj* disparato
dispari·ty [dɪs'pærɪtɪ] *s* (**-ties**) disparità *f*, spareggio
dispassionate [dɪs'pæʃənɪt] *adj* spassionato

dispatch [dɪs'pætʃ] *s* dispaccio || *tr* spedire; (*to dismiss*) congedare; uccidere; (*a meal*) (coll) liquidare
dis·pel [dɪs'pel] *v* (*pret* & *pp* **-pelled**; *ger* **-pelling**) *tr* dissipare
dispensa·ry [dɪs'pensərɪ] *s* (**-ries**) dispensario
dispensation [,dɪspen'seʃən] *s* (*dispensing*) distribuzione, dispensa; (*exemption*) dispensa
dispense [dɪs'pens] *tr* (*medicines*) distribuire; (*justice*) amministrare; (*to distribute*) dispensare; (*to exempt*) esimere || *intr*—**to dispense with** fare a meno di; esimersi da
dispenser [dɪ'spensər] *s* dispensatore *m*; (*automatic*) distributore *m*
disperse [dɪs'pʌrs] *tr* disperdere || *intr* dispersi
dispersion [dɪ'spʌrʒən] or [dɪ'sper/ən] *s* dispersione
dispersive [dɪ'spʌrsɪv] *adj* dispersivo
dispirit [dɪ'spɪrɪt] *tr* scoraggiare
displace [dɪs'ples] *tr* muovere; costringere a lasciare il proprio paese; (*to supplant*) rimpiazzare; (naut) dislocare
displaced' per'son *s* rifugiato politico
displacement [dɪs'plesmənt] *s* spostamento; sostituzione; (*of a piston*) cilindrata; (naut) dislocamento
display [dɪs'ple] *s* sfoggio, mostra || *tr* mostrare; (*e.g., in a store window*) mettere in mostra; (*to unfold*) spiegare; (*to show ostentatiously*) sfoggiare, ostentare; (*ignorance*) rivelare
display' cab'inet *s* bacheca
display' win'dow *s* mostra, vetrina
displease [dɪs'pliz] *tr* dispiacere (with *dat*)
displeasing [dɪs'plizɪŋ] *adj* spiacevole
displeasure [dɪs'pleʒər] *s* dispiacere *m*; sfavore *m*
disposable [dɪs'pozəbəl] *adj* (*available*) disponibile; (*made to be thrown away after use*) scartabile, da gettarsi via, usa e getta
disposal [dɪs'pozəl] *s* disposizione; eliminazione; **to have at one's disposal** disporre di
dispose [dɪs'poz] *tr* disporre; **to dispose of** disporre di; (*to get rid of*) sbarazzarsi di; vendere
disposed [dɪs'spozd] *adj*—**to be disposed to** essere disposto a
disposition [,dɪspə'zɪʃən] *s* disposizione; (*mental outlook*) indole *f*; tendenza; (mil) ordinamento
dispossess [,dɪspə'zes] *tr* spodestare, bandire; (*to evict*) sfrattare
disproof [dɪs'pruf] *s* confutazione
disproportionate [,dɪsprə'porʃənɪt] *adj* sproporzionato
disprove [dɪs'pruv] *tr* confutare
dispute [dɪs'pjut] *s* disputa; **beyond dispute** incontestabile; **in dispute** in discussione || *tr* & *intr* disputare
disquali·fy [dɪs'kwɑlɪ ,faɪ] *v* (*pret* & *pp* **-fied**) *tr* squalificare
disquiet [dɪs'kwaɪ·ət] *s* inquietudine *f* || *tr* inquietare, turbare
disquisition [,dɪskwɪ'zɪʃən] *s* disquisizione

disregard [ˌdɪsrɪ'gɑrd] *s* (*of a rule*) inosservanza; (*of danger*) disprezzo, noncuranza || *tr* non fare attenzione a

disrepair [ˌdɪsrɪ'per] *s* cattivo stato, rovina

disreputable [dɪs'rɛpjətəbəl] *adj* malfamato; disonorevole; (*in bad condition*) raso, logoro

disrepute [ˌdɪsrɪ'pjut] *s* cattiva fama; **to bring into disrepute** rovinare la reputazione di

disrespect [ˌdɪsrɪ'spɛkt] *s* mancanza di rispetto || *tr* mancare di rispetto a

disrespectful [ˌdɪsrɪ'spɛktfəl] *adj* non rispettoso, irriverente

disrobe [dɪs'rob] *tr* svestire || *intr* svestirsi, spogliarsi

disrupt [dɪs'rʌpt] *tr* disorganizzare; interrompere

disruption [dɪs'rʌpʃən] *s* rottura; disorganizzazione

dissatisfaction [ˌdɪsætɪs'fækʃən] *s* scontento, malcontento

dissatisfied [dɪs'sætɪs.faɪd] *adj* scontento, malcontento; insoddisfatto

dissatis·fy [dɪs'sætɪs.faɪ] *v* (*pret & pp* -fied*) *tr* scontentare

dissect [dɪ'sɛkt] *tr* sezionare

dissemble [dɪ'sɛmbəl] *tr & intr* dissimulare

disseminate [dɪ'sɛmɪ.net] *tr* disseminare, divulgare

dissension [dɪ'sɛnʃən] *s* dissensione

dissent [dɪ'sɛnt] *s* dissenso; (*nonconformity*) dissidio || *intr* dissentire

dissenter [dɪ'sɛntər] *s* dissenziente *m*

dissertation [ˌdɪsər'teʃən] *s* dissertazione

disservice [dɪs'sʌrvɪs] *s* danno; cattivo servizio

dissidence ['dɪsɪdəns] *s* dissidenza

dissident ['dɪsɪdənt] *adj & s* dissidente *m*

dissimilar [dɪ'sɪmɪlər] *adj* dissimile

dissimilate [dɪ'sɪmɪ.let] *tr* dissimilare || *intr* dissimilarsi

dissimulate [dɪ'sɪmjə.let] *tr & intr* dissimulare

dissipate ['dɪsɪ.pet] *tr* dissipare || *intr* dissiparsi; (*to indulge oneself*) darsi alla dissipatezza

dissipated ['dɪsɪ.petɪd] *adj* dissipato

dissipation [ˌdɪsɪ'peʃən] *s* dissipazione

dissociate [dɪ'soʃɪ.et] *tr* dissociare || *intr* dissociarsi

dissolute ['dɪsə.lut] *adj* dissoluto

dissolution [ˌdɪsə'luʃən] *s* dissoluzione

dissolve [dɪ'zɑlv] *tr* sciogliere, disciogliere || *intr* sciogliersi, disciogliersi

dissonance ['dɪsənəns] *s* dissonanza

dissuade [dɪ'swed] *tr* dissuadere

dissyllabic [ˌdɪsɪ'læbɪk] *adj* disillabo

dissyllable [dɪ'sɪləbəl] *s* disillabo

distaff ['dɪstæf] *or* ['dɪstɑf] *s* rocca

dis'taff side' *s* ramo femminile di una famiglia

distance ['dɪstəns] *s* distanza; **a long distance** (fig) moltissimo; **in the distance** in lontananza; **to keep at a distance** *or* **to keep one's distance** mantenere le distanze || *tr* distanziare

distant ['dɪstənt] *adj* distante; (*relative*) lontano; (*aloof*) freddo, riservato

distaste [dɪs'test] *s* ripugnanza

distasteful [dɪs'testfəl] *adj* ripugnante, sgradevole

distemper [dɪs'tɛmpər] *s* cimurro; (*painting*) tempera || *tr* dipingere a tempera

distend [dɪs'tɛnd] *tr* stendere, distendere; gonfiare || *intr* stendersi, distendersi; gonfiarsi

distension [dɪs'tɛnʃən] *s* distensione; gonfiamento

distill [dɪs'tɪl] *tr* distillare

distillation [ˌdɪstɪ'leʃən] *s* distillazione

distiller·y [dɪs'tɪlərɪ] *s* (-ies) distilleria

distinct [dɪs'tɪŋkt] *adj* distinto, chiaro; (*not blurred*) nitido

distinction [dɪs'tɪŋkʃən] *s* distinzione

distinctive [dɪs'tɪŋktɪv] *adj* distintivo

distinguish [dɪs'tɪŋgwɪʃ] *tr* distinguere

distinguished [dɪs'tɪŋgwɪʃt] *adj* distinto

distort [dɪs'tɔrt] *tr* distorcere; (*the truth*) svisare, snaturare

distortion [dɪs'tɔrʃən] *s* deformazione; (*of the truth*) alterazione, svisamento; (rad) distorsione

distract [dɪs'trækt] *tr* distrarre

distracted [dɪs'træktɪd] *adj* distratto; (*irrational*) turbato, sconvolto

distraction [dɪs'trækʃən] *s* distrazione

distraught [dɪs'trɔt] *adj* turbato, stordito

distress [dɪs'tres] *s* pena, dispiacere *m*; pericolo; (naut) difficoltà *f* || *tr* sconfortare, affliggere

distressing [dɪs'tresɪŋ] *adj* penoso

distress' mer'chandise *s* merce *f* sotto costo

distress' sig'nal *s* segnale *m* di soccorso

distribute [dɪs'trɪbjut] *tr* distribuire

distribution [ˌdɪstrɪ'bjuʃən] *s* distribuzione, erogazione

distributor [dɪs'trɪbjətər] *s* distributore *m*; (aut) distributore *m* d'accensione

district ['dɪstrɪkt] *s* regione; (*of a city*) rione *m*, quartiere *m*; (*administrative division*) distretto || *tr* dividere in distretti

dis'trict attor'ney *s* procuratore *m* generale

distrust [dɪs'trʌst] *s* diffidenza || *tr* diffidare di

distrustful [dɪs'trʌstfəl] *adj* diffidente

disturb [dɪs'tʌrb] *tr* disturbare, turbare; disordinare

disturbance [dɪs'tʌrbəns] *s* disturbo, turbamento, perturbazione; disordine *m*

disuse [dɪs'jus] *s* disuso

ditch [dɪtʃ] *s* fossa, fossato || *tr* scavare un fosso in; (rr) far deragliare; (slang) piantare in asso || *intr* fare un ammaraggio forzato

dither ['dɪðər] *s* agitazione; **to be in a dither** (coll) essere agitato

dit·to ['dɪto] *s* (-tos*) lo stesso; (*ditto symbol*) virgolette *fpl* || *adv* ugualmente, idem || *tr* copiare, duplicare

dit'to marks' *spl* virgolette *fpl*

dit·ty [ˈdɪti] *s* (**-ties**) canzonetta
diva [ˈdivɑ] *s* (mus) diva
divan [ˈdaɪvæn] or [dɪˈvæn] *s* divano
dive [daɪv] *s* tuffo; (*of a submarine*)
immersione; (aer) picchiata; (coll)
taverna; (com) discesa ‖ *v* (*pret &
pp* **dived** or **dove** [dov]) *intr* tuffarsi;
(*said of submarine*) immergersi; (*to
plunge*) lanciarsi; (aer) scendere in
picchiata; **to dive for** (*e.g., pearls*)
pescare
dive'-bomb' *tr* bombardare in picchiata
‖ *intr* scendere a tuffo
dive' bomb'ing *s* bombardamento in
picchiata
diver [ˈdaɪvər] *s* tuffatore *m*; (*person
who works under water*) palombaro;
(orn) tuffetto
diverge [dɪˈvʌrdʒ] or [daɪˈvʌrdʒ] *intr*
divergere
divers [ˈdaɪvərz] *adj* diversi, vari
diverse [dɪˈvʌrs], [daɪˈvʌrs] or [ˈdaɪ-
vʌrs] *adj* (*different*) diverso; (*of various kinds*) multiforme
diversification [dɪˌvʌrsɪfɪˈkeʃən] or
[daɪˌvʌrsɪfɪˈkeʃən] *s* diversificazione
diversi·fy [dɪˈvʌrsɪ ˌfaɪ] or [daɪˈvʌrsɪ-
ˌfaɪ] *v* (*pret & pp* **-fied**) *tr* diversificare ‖ *intr* diversificarsi
diversion [dɪˈvʌrʒən] or [daɪˈvʌrʒən]
s diversione; (*pastime*) svago
diversi·ty [dɪˈvʌrsɪti] or [daɪˈvʌrsɪti]
s (**-ties**) diversità *f*
divert [dɪˈvʌrt] or [daɪˈvʌrt] *tr* deviare; (*to entertain*) divertire;
(*money*) stornare, distrarre
diverting [dɪˈvʌrtɪŋ] or [daɪˈvʌrtɪŋ]
adj divertente
divest [dɪˈvest] or [daɪˈvest] *tr* spogliare; spossessare; **to divest oneself
of** spogliarsi di, espropriarsi di
divide [dɪˈvaɪd] *s* spartiacque *m* ‖ *tr*
dividere ‖ *intr* dividersi
dividend [ˈdɪvɪ ˌdend] *s* dividendo
dividers [dɪˈvaɪdərz] *spl* compasso a
punte fisse
divination [ˌdɪvɪˈneʃən] *s* divinazione
divine [dɪˈvaɪn] *adj* divino ‖ *s* sacerdote *m*, prete *m* ‖ *tr* divinare
diviner [dɪˈvaɪnər] *s* divinatore *m*
diving [ˈdaɪvɪŋ] *s* tuffo, immersione
div'ing bell' *s* campana da palombaro
div'ing board' *s* trampolino
div'ing suit' *s* scafandro
divin'ing rod' [dɪˈvaɪnɪŋ] *s* bacchetta
rabdomantica
divini·ty [dɪˈvɪnɪti] *s* (**-ties**) divinità *f*;
teologia; **the Divinity** Dio
divisible [dɪˈvɪsɪbəl] *adj* divisibile
division [dɪˈvɪʒən] *s* divisione
divisor [dɪˈvaɪzər] *s* divisore *m*
divorce [dɪˈvors] *s* divorzio; **to get a
divorce** divorziare ‖ *tr* (*a married
couple*) divorziare; (*one's spouse*) divorziare da ‖ *intr* divorziare
divorcé [dɪvorˈse] *s* divorziato
divorcee [dɪvorˈsi] *s* divorziata
divulge [dɪˈvʌldʒ] *tr* divulgare
dizziness [ˈdɪzɪnɪs] *s* vertigine *f*, stordimento; confusione
diz·zy [ˈdɪzi] *adj* (**-zier; -ziest**) (*causing
dizziness*) vertiginoso; (*suffering diz-*

ziness) preso da vertigine, stordito;
(coll) stupido
do [du] *v* (*3rd pers* **does** [dʌz]; *pret*
did [dɪd]; *pp* **done** [dʌn]; *ger* **doing**
[ˈdu·ɪŋ]) *tr* fare; (*a problem*) risolvere; (*a distance*) percorrere; (*to
study*) studiare; (*to explore*) attraversare; (*to tire*) stancare; **to do one's
best** fare del proprio meglio; **to do
over** tornare a fare; ripetere; **to do
right by** trattare bene; **to do s.o. out
of s.th** (coll) portare via qlco a qlcu;
to do to death mettere a morte; **to do
up** (coll) impacchettare; stancare;
(*one's hair*) farsi; vestire; (*a shirt*)
lavare e stirare; **to have done** far fare
‖ *intr* fare; agire; comportarsi; servire; bastare; stare; succedere; **how
do you do?** come sta?; **that will do**
basta; è sufficiente; **to have done with**
non aver più nulla a che fare con; **to
have nothing to do with** non aver
nulla a che vedere con; **to have to do
with** aver a che fare con, trattarsi di;
to do away with togliere di mezzo;
to do for servire da; **to do well** crescere bene; **to do without** fare a
meno di ‖ *v aux* used 1) in interrogative sentences: **Do you speak Italian?**
Parla italiano?; 2) in negative sentences: **I do not speak Italian** Non
parlo italiano; 3) to avoid repetition
of a verb or full verbal expression:
**Did you go to church this morning?
Yes, I did.** È stato in chiesa questa
mattina? Sì, ci sono stato; 4) to lend
emphasis to a principal verb: **I do
believe what you told me** Ci credo a
quello che mi ha detto; 5) in inverted
constructions after certain adverbs:
Seldom does he come to see me Mi
viene a vedere di raro; 6) in a sup-
plicating tone with imperatives: **Do
come in** entri per favore
docile [ˈdɑsɪl] *adj* docile
dock [dɑk] *s* (*wharf*) molo; (*waterway
between two piers*) darsena; (*area
including piers and waterways*) scalo
portuario; (law) gabbia degli impu-
tati ‖ *tr* (*to deduct from the wages
of*) fare una deduzione a; (*to deduct
s.o.'s salary*) dedurre da; (*an animal*)
scodare; (naut) attaccare ‖ *intr*
(aer) agganciarsi; (naut) attaccare
dockage [ˈdɑkɪdʒ] *s* attacco; (*charges*)
diritti *mpl* di porto
docket [ˈdɑkɪt] *s* ordine *m* del giorno;
(law) ruolo delle sentenze; **on the
docket** (coll) pendente, in sospeso
dock' hand' *s* portuale *m*
docking [ˈdɑkɪŋ] *s* (aer) aggancio;
(naut) attacco
dock'yard' *s* cantiere *m* navale
doctor [ˈdɑktər] *s* dottore *m*; (*physician*) medico ‖ *tr* curare; aggiustare;
falsificare; adulterare ‖ *intr* esercitare la medicina; (coll) curarsi, prendere medi ine
doctorate [ˈdɑktərɪt] *s* dottorato
doctrine [ˈdɑktrɪn] *s* dottrina
document [ˈdɑkjəmənt] *s* documento ‖
[ˈdɑkjə ˌment] *tr* documentare

documenta·ry [ˌdɑkjə'mentəri] *adj &
s* (-ries) documentario
documentation [ˌdɑkəmen'teʃən] *s* do-
cumentazione
doddering ['dɑdərɪŋ] *adj* tremante,
rimbambito
dodge [dɑdʒ] *s* scarto, schivata; (fig)
stratagemma *m* ‖ *tr* schivare, evitare
‖ *intr* schivarsi; (fig) rispondere eva-
sivamente; **to dodge around the corner** scantonare
do·do ['dodo] *s* (-dos *or* -does) (coll)
rimbecillito
doe [do] *s* (*of deer*) cerva; (*of goat*)
capretta; (*of rabbit*) coniglia
doeskin ['do ˌskɪn] *s* pelle *f* di daino,
pelle *f* di dante; lana finissima
doff [dɑf] *or* [dɔf] *tr* (*one's hat*) togliersi; (*clothing*) deporre
dog [dɔg] *or* [dag] *s* cane *m*; **to go to
the dogs** (coll) andare in malora; **to
put on the dog** (coll) darsi delle arie
‖ *v* (*pret & pp* **dogged;** *ger* **dogging**)
tr seguire; perseguitare
dog'catch'er *s* accalappiacani *m*
dog' days' *s* solleone *m*, canicola
doge [dodʒ] *s* doge *m*
dog'-ear' *s* orecchia, orecchio
dog'fight' *s* duello aereo
dogged ['dɔgɪd] *or* ['dagɪd] *adj* accanito
doggerel ['dɔgərəl] *or* ['dagərəl] *s*
versi *mpl* da colascione
dog·gy ['dɔgi] *or* ['dagi] *adj* (-gier;
-giest) vistoso; canino ‖ *s* (-gies)
cagnolino
dog'house' *s* canile *m*; **to be in the doghouse** (slang) essere in disgrazia
dog' Lat'in *s* latino maccheronico
dogma ['dɔgmə] *or* ['dagmə] *s* dogma
m
dogmatic [dɔg'mætɪk] *or* [dag'mætɪk]
adj dogmatico
dog' rac'ing *s* corse *fpl* dei cani
dog' show' *s* mostra canina
dog's' life' *s* vita da cani
Dog' Star' *s* canicola
dog' tag' *s* (mil) piastrina, piastrino
dog'-tired' *adj* (coll) stanco morto
dog'tooth' *s* (-teeth [ˌtiθ]) canino
dog' track' *s* cinodromo
dog'watch' *s* (naut) quarto di solo due
ore, gaettone *m*
dog'wood' *s* corniolo
doi·ly ['dɔili] *s* (-lies) centrino
doings ['du·ɪŋz] *spl* azioni *fpl*, fatti
mpl
do'-it-your·self' *s* il fare tutto da sé
doldrums ['dɑldrəmz] *spl* calma equatoriale; inattività *f*; depressione
dole [dol] *s* elemosina; (*to the jobless*)
sussidio di disoccupazione ‖ *tr*—**to
dole out** distribuire parsimoniosa-
mente
doleful ['dolfəl] *adj* lugubre, triste
doll [dɑl] *s* bambola ‖ *intr*—**to doll up**
(slang) agghindarsi
dollar ['dɑlər] *s* dollaro
dol'lar-wise' *adv* in termini finanziari
dol·ly ['dɑli] *s* (-lies) pupattola; (*low,
wheeled frame for moving heavy
loads*) carrello; (mov, telv) carrello

‖ *v* (*pret & pp* -lied) *intr* (mov, telv)
carrellare
dol'ly shot' *s* (mov, telv) carrellata
dolphin ['dɑlfɪn] *s* delfino
dolt [dolt] *s* gonzo, balordo
doltish ['doltɪʃ] *adj* gonzo, balordo
domain [do'men] *s* dominio; (law) proprietà *f*; (fig) campo, orbita
dome [dom] *s* cupola
dome' light' *s* lampadario
domestic [də'mestɪk] *adj & s* domestico
domesticate [də'mestɪ ˌket] *tr* domesticare
domicile ['dɑmɪsɪl] *or* ['dɑmɪ ˌsaɪl] *s*
domicilio ‖ *tr* domiciliare
dominance ['dɑmɪnəns] *s* dominio
dominant ['dɑmɪnənt] *adj & s* domi-
nante *f*
dominate ['dɑmɪ ˌnet] *tr & intr* dominare
domination [ˌdɑmɪ'neʃən] *s* domina-
zione
domineer [ˌdɑmɪ'nɪr] *intr* spadroneggiare
domineering [ˌdɑmɪ'nɪrɪŋ] *adj* dispotico, tirannico
Dominican [də'mɪnɪkən] *adj & s* do-
minicano; (*eccl*) domenicano
dominion [də'mɪnjən] *s* dominio
domi·no ['dɑmɪ ˌno] *s* (-noes *or* -nos)
(*costume and person*) domino;
(*piece*) tessera di domino; **dominoes**
(*game*) domino
don [dɑn] *s* signore *m*; don *m*; membro
di un collegio universitario inglese ‖
v (*pret & pp* **donned;** *ger* **donning**)
tr (*clothes*) mettersi, vestire
donate ['donet] *tr* donare, dare
donation [do'neʃən] *s* donazione
done [dʌn] *adj* fatto; finito; stanco;
(culin) ben cotto, ben rosolato
done' for' *adj* (coll) stanco morto;
(coll) rovinato; (coll) fuori combattimento; (coll) morto
donjon ['dʌndʒən] *or* ['dandʒən] *s* torrione *m*, maschio
Don Juan [dɑn 'wɑn] *or* [dən 'hwɑn]
s Don Giovanni
donkey ['dɑŋki] *or* ['dʌŋki] *s* asino,
somaro
donnish ['dɑnɪʃ] *adj* pedante
donor ['donər] *s* donatore *m*
doodle ['dudəl] *tr & intr* scarabocc-
chiare, riempire di ghirigori
doom [dum] *s* destino; morte *f*, rovina;
sentenza di morte; giudizio finale ‖
tr destinare; condannare; condannare
a morte
doomsday ['dumz ˌde] *s* giorno del
giudizio
door [dor] *s* porta; (*of a carriage or
automobile*) portiera, sportello; (*one
part of a double door*) battente *m*;
behind closed doors a porte chiuse;
to see to the door accompagnare alla
porta; **to show s.o. the door** mettere
qlcu alla porta
door'bell' *s* campanello della porta
door' check' *s* chiusura automatica di
porta, scontro
door'frame' *s* cornice *f*

door'head' s architrave m

door'jamb' s stipite m

door'keep'er s portinaio

door'knob' s maniglia della porta

door' knock'er s battente m

door' latch' s paletto

door'man' s (-men') portiere m, portinaio; (of large apartment house) guardaportone m

door'mat' s stoino, zerbino

door'nail' s borchione m; dead as a doornail morto e ben morto

door'post' s stipite m

door' scrap'er s raschietto

door'sill' s soglia

door'step' s gradino davanti la porta

door'stop' s paracolpi m

door'-to-door' adj (shipment) diretto; (selling) di porta in porta

door'way' s vano della porta; porta

dope [dop] s lubrificante m; (aer) vernice f; (slang) stupido, scemo; (slang) informazioni fpl; (slang) narcotico || tr (slang) narcotizzare; to dope out (slang) indovinare, decifrare, immaginare

dope' fiend' s (slang) tossicomane mf

dope'sheet' s giornaletto con le previsioni della corse ippiche

dormant ['dɔrmənt] adj dormente; latente

dor'mer win'dow ['dɔrmər] s abbaino

dormito·ry ['dɔrmɪ,tori] s (-ries) dormitorio

dor·mouse ['dɔr,maʊs] s (-mice [,maɪs]) ghiro

dosage ['dosɪdʒ] s dosatura

dose [dos] s dose f; (coll) boccone amaro || tr dosare; somministrare

dossier ['dɑsɪ,e] s incartamento

dot [dɑt] s punto; on the dot (coll) in punto || v (pret & pp dotted; ger dotting) tr punteggiare; to dot one's i's mettere i punti sulle i

dotage ['dotɪdʒ] s rimbecillimento; to be in one's dotage essere rimbambito

dotard ['dotərd] s vecchio rimbambito

dote [dot] intr rimbambirsi; to dote on essere pazzo per

doting ['dotɪŋ] adj che ama alla follia; (from old age) rimbambito, rimbecillito

dots' and dash'es spl (telg) punti mpl e tratti mpl

dot'ted line' s linea punteggiata; to sign on the dotted line firmare inconsideratamente

double ['dʌbəl] adj doppio || s doppio; (bridge) contre m; doubles (tennis) doppio || tr raddoppiare; (bridge) contrare || intr raddoppiarsi; (bridge) contrare; (mov, theat) sostenere due ruoli; (mov) doppiare; to double up (said of two people) dividere la stessa camera, dividere lo stesso letto; piegarsi in due

double-barreled ['dʌbəl'bærəld] adj a due canne; (fig) a doppio fine

dou'ble bass' s contrabbasso

dou'ble bed' s letto matrimoniale

dou'ble boil'er s bagnomaria m

double-breasted ['dʌbəl'brestɪd] adj a doppio petto, doppiopetto

dou'ble chin' s pappagorgia

dou'ble-cross' tr (coll) tradire

dou'ble date' s (coll) appuntamento amoroso di due coppie

dou'ble-deal'ing adj doppio

dou'ble-deck'er s (bed) letto a castello; (sandwich) tramezzino doppio; autobus m a due piani; (naut) nave f due ponti; (aer) aereo due ponti

double-edged ['dʌbəl'edʒd] adj a due tagli, a doppio taglio

dou'ble en'try s (com) partita doppia

dou'ble fea'ture s (mov) programma m di due lungometraggio

double-header ['dʌbəl'hedər] s treno con due locomotive; due partite di baseball giocate successivamente

double-jointed ['dʌbəl'dʒɔɪntɪd] adj snodato

dou'ble-park' tr & intr parcheggiare in doppia fila

dou'ble-quick' adj & adv a passo di carica

dou'ble stand'ard s—to have a double standard usare due pesi e due misure

doublet ['dʌblɪt] s (close-fitting jacket) farsetto; (philol) doppione m

dou'ble-talk' s discorso incomprensibile; to give s.o. double-talk parlare evasivamente a qlcu || intr parlare evasivamente

dou'ble time' s paga doppia; (mil) passo di carica

doubleton ['dʌbəltən] s doppio

doubly ['dʌblɪ] adv doppiamente

doubt [daʊt] s dubbio; beyond doubt senza dubbio; if in doubt in caso di dubbio; no doubt senza dubbio || tr dubitare di || intr dubitare

doubter ['daʊtər] s incredulo

doubtful ['daʊtfəl] adj incerto; dubbioso

doubtless ['daʊtlɪs] adj indubitabile || adv senza dubbio; probabilmente

douche [duʃ] s irrigazione f; (instrument) irrigatore m || tr irrigare || intr fare irrigazioni

dough [do] s pasta di pane; (money) (slang) soldi mpl, quattrini mpl

dough'boy' s fantaccino americano

dough'nut' s ciambella; (with filling) sgonfiotto

dough·ty ['daʊti] adj (-tier; -tiest) forte, coraggioso

dough·y ['do·i] adj (-ier; -iest) pastoso, molle

dour [daʊr] or [dʊr] adj triste, severo

douse [daʊs] tr immergere; bagnare; (the light) (coll) spegnere

dove [dʌv] s colomba, tortora

dovecote ['dʌv,kot] s piccionaia

dove'tail' s coda di rondine || tr calettare a coda di rondine; (to make fit) adattare, far combaciare || intr (to fit) combaciare; corrispondere

dowager ['daʊ·ədʒər] s vedova titolata; vecchia signora austera; queen dowager regina madre

dow·dy ['daʊdi] adj (-dier; -diest) trasandato

dowel 94 drastic

dow·el ['dau·əl] *s* caviglia, tassello ||
v (*pret & pp* **-eled** or **-elled;** *ger*
-eling or **-elling**) *tr* tassellare
dower ['dau·ər] *s* (*widow's portion*)
legittima, vedovile *m;* (*marriage por-*
tion; natural gift) dote *f* || *tr* dotare;
assegnare un vedovile a
down [daun] *adj* che discende; basso;
(*train*) che va al centro; depresso;
finito; (*money, payment*) anticipato;
(*storage battery*) esaurito || *s* (*of*
fruit and human body) lanugine *f;*
(*of birds*) piumino; (*upset*) rovescio;
discesa; (*sandhill*) duna || *adv* giù;
all'ingiù, in giù; dabbasso; a terra; al
sud; (*in cash*) a contanti; **down and**
out rovinato; senza una soldo; **down**
from da; down on one's knees in
ginocchio; **down a fino a; down**
under agli antipodi; down with . . . !
abasso . . . !; **to get down to work**
mettersi seriamente al lavoro; **to go**
down scendere; **to lie down** sdraiarsi;
andare a letto; **to sit down** sedersi ||
prep giù per; **down the river a valle;**
down the street giù per la strada || *tr*
abbattere; (coll) buttar giù, tracannare
down'cast' *adj* mogio, sfiduciato
down'fall' *s* rovina, rovescio
down'grade' *adj & adv* in declivio, a
valle || *s* discesa; **to be on the down-**
grade essere in declino || *tr* attribuire
minor importanza a; degradare
downhearted ['daun·hɑrtɪd] *adj* scoraggiato, abbattuto
down'hill' *adj & adv* in declivio; **to go**
downhill declinare
down' pay'ment *s* acconto
down'pour' *s* acquazzone *m*, rovescio
down'right' *adj* assoluto; completo;
franco, diretto || *adv* completamente
down'stairs' *adj* del piano di sotto || *s*
il piano di sotto; i piani di sotto ||
adv dabbasso, di sotto, giù
down'stream' *adv* a valle
down'stroke' *s* corsa discendente
down'town' *adj* centrale || *s* centro
della città || *adv* al centro della città
down' train' *s* treno discendente, treno
che va al centro
down'trend' *s* tendenza al ribasso
downtrodden ['daun·trɑdən] *adj* cal-
pestato, oppresso
downward ['daunwərd] *adj & adv* al-
l'ingiù
down·y ['dauni] *adj* (**-ier; -iest**) piu-
moso, lanuginoso; (*soft*) molle, morbido
dow·ry ['dauri] *s* (**-ries**) dote *f*
doze [doz] *s* pisolo || *intr* dormic-
chiare; **to doze off** appisolarsi
dozen ['dʌzən] *s* dozzina
dozy ['dozi] *adj* sonnolento
drab [dræb] *adj* (**drabber; drabbest**)
grigiastro; (*dull*) scialbo || *s* colore
grigiastro; (*fabric*) tela naturale;
donna di malaffare
drach·ma ['drækmə] *s* (**-mas** or **-mae**
[mi]) dramma
draft [dræft] or [drɑft] *s* corrente *f*
d'aria; (*pulling*) tiro; (*in a chimney*)

tiraggio; (*sketch, outline*) schizzo;
(*first form of a writing*) prima stesura; (*drink*) sorso, bicchiere *m;*
(com) tratta, lettera di credito; (law)
progetto, disegno; (naut) pesca; (mil)
coscrizione *f*, leva; **on draft** alla
spina || *tr* disegnare; fare uno schizzo
di; (*a document*) stendere; (mil) coscrivere; **to be drafted** essere di leva,
andar coscritto
draft' age' *s* età *f* di leva
draft' beer' *s* birra alla spina
draft' board' *s* consiglio di leva
draft' dodg'er ['dɑdʒər] *s* renitente *m*
alla leva, imboscato
draftee [,dræf'ti] or [,drɑf'ti] *s* coscritto
draft' horse' *s* cavallo da tiro
drafts'man *s* (**-men**) disegnatore *m;*
(*man who draws up documents*) redattore *m*
draft' trea'ty *s* progetto di trattato
draft·y ['dræfti] or ['drɑfti] *adj* (**-ier;**
-iest) pieno di correnti d'aria
drag [dræg] *s* (*sledge for conveying*
heavy bodies) traino, treggia; (*on a*
cigarette) boccata; (aer) resistenza
aerodinamica; (naut) pressione idro-
statica; (naut) draga; (fig) noia; (*in-*
fluence) (slang) aderenze *fpl;* (*a*
bore) (slang) rompiscatole *m* || *v*
(*pret & pp* **dragged;** *ger* **dragging**) *tr*
strascinare, strascicare; (naut) ra-
strellare || *intr* strascicare, strasci-
carsi; dilungarsi; **to drag on** andare
per le lunghe
drag'net' *s* paranza; (fig) retata
dragon ['drægən] *s* drago, dragone *m*
drag'on·fly' *s* (**-flies**) libellula
dragoon [drə'gun] *s* (mil) dragone *m*
|| *tr* forzare, costringere
drain [dren] *s* scolo; prosciugamento;
(geog) spiovente *m;* (surg) drenaggio;
(fig) salasso || *tr* (*a liquid*) scolare;
prosciugare; (*humid land; a wound*)
drenare || *intr* scolare; prosciugarsi;
(geog) defluire
drainage ['drenɪdʒ] *s* drenaggio; (geog)
displuvio, spartiacque *m*
drain'board' *s* scolatoio per le stoviglie
drain' cock' *s* rubinetto di scarico
drain'pipe' *s* tubo di scarico
drake [drek] *s* anatra maschio
dram [dræm] *s* dramma; bicchierino di
liquore
drama ['drɑmə] or ['dræmə] *s*
dramma *m;* (*art and genre*) dramm-
matica
dramatic [drə'mætɪk] *adj* drammatico
|| **dramatics** *ssg* drammatica; *spl* rap-
presentazione dilettantesca; comportamento drammatico
dramatist ['dræmətɪst] *s* drammaturgo
dramatize ['dræmə ,taɪz] *tr* drammatizzare
drape [drep] *s* tenda, cortina; (*of a*
curtain) drappeggio; (*of a skirt*) ta-
glio || *tr* drappeggiare
draper·y ['drepəri] *s* (**-ies**) drapperia;
negozio di tessuti; **draperies** tendaggi
mpl
drastic ['dræstɪk] *adj* drastico

draught [dræft] or [drɑft] *s & tr* var of **draft**

draught' beer' *s* birra alla spina

draw [drɔ] *s* (*in a game*) patta; (*in a lottery*) sorteggio; (*act of drawing*) tiro; (*of chimney*) tiraggio; (*attraction*) attrazione; (*of a drawbridge*) ala ‖ *v* (*pret* drew [dru]; *pp* drawn [drɔn]) *tr* (*a line*) tirare; (*to attract*) richiamare; (*butter*) fondere; (*a sword*) sguainare; (*a nail*) estrarre; (*people*) attrarre; (*a sigh*) emettere; (*a curtain*) far scorrere; (*a salary*) pigliare; (*a prize*) ricevere; (*a game*) impattare; (*in card games*) pescare; (*a drawbridge*) sollevare; (*said of a ship*) pescare; (*a comparison*) fare; (*a profit*) ricavare; (*a chicken*) sventrare; (*e.g., a picture*) disegnare, ritrarre; (*to sketch in words*) descrivere; (*a contract*) stipulare; (*interest*) ricevere; (*com*) spiccare, staccare; **to draw forth** far uscire; **to draw off** estrarre; (*a liquid*) spillare; **to draw** (*shoes*) **on** mettersi; **to draw** (*money*) **on** ritirare da; **to draw** (*a draft*) **on** domiciliare presso; **to draw oneself up** raddrizzarsi; **to draw out** (*to persuade to talk*) far parlare, tirar fuori le parole a; **to draw up** (*a document*) estendere; (*mil*) schierare ‖ *intr* (*said of chimney*) tirare; impattare; sorteggiare un premio; aver attrazione; disegnare; **to draw aside** scostarsi; **to draw back** retrocedere, ritirarsi; **to draw near** avvicinarsi; volgere a; **to draw to a close** essere quasi finito; **to draw together** unirsi

draw'back' *s* inconveniente *m*

draw'bridge' *s* ponte levatoio

drawee [ˌdrɔ'i] *s* trattario, trassato

drawer [ˈdrɔ·ər] *s* disegnatore *m*; (*com*) traente *m* ‖ [drɔr] *s* cassetto; **drawers** mutande *fpl*

drawing [ˈdrɔ·ɪŋ] *s* disegno; (*in a lottery*) sorteggio

draw'ing board' *s* tavolo da disegno

draw'ing card' *s* attrazione

draw'ing room' *s* salotto, salottino

draw'knife' *s* (**-knives** [ˌnaɪvz]) coltello a petto

drawl [drɔl] *s* accento strascicato ‖ *tr* dire con accento strascicato ‖ *intr* strascicare le parole

drawn' but'ter *s* burro fuso

drawn' work' *s* lavoro a giorno

dray [dre] *s* carro pesante; slitta, treggia; autocarro

drayage [ˈdre·ɪdʒ] *s* carreggio

dray'man *s* (**-men**) carrettiere *m*

dread [dred] *adj* spaventoso, terribile ‖ *s* spavento, terrore *m* ‖ *tr & intr* temere

dreadful [ˈdredfəl] *adj* spaventevole, terribile; (*coll*) orribile

dread'nought' *s* corazzata

dream [drim] *s* sogno; illusione, fantasticheria; **dream come true** sogno fatto realtà ‖ *v* (*pret & pp* dreamed or dreamt [dremt]) *tr* sognare; **to dream up** (*coll*) immaginare, fantasticare ‖ *intr* sognare

dreamer [ˈdrimər] *s* sognatore *m*

dream'land' *s* paese *m* dei sogni

dream·y [ˈdrimi] *adj* (**-ier; -iest**) sognante; (*visionary*) trasognato; vago

drear·y [ˈdrɪri] *adj* (**-ier; -iest**) squallido; triste; (*boring*) noioso

dredge [dredʒ] *s* draga ‖ *tr* dragare; (*culin*) infarinare

dredger [ˈdredʒər] *s* (*boat*) draga; (*container*) spolverino

dredging [ˈdredʒɪŋ] *s* dragaggio

dregs [dregz] *spl* feccia

drench [drentʃ] *tr* infradiciare, inzuppare

dress [dres] *s* vestito; vestiti *mpl*; vestito da donna; abito; abito da cerimonia; (*of a bird*) piumaggio ‖ *tr* vestire; adornare, decorare; (*hair*) pettinare; (*a wound*) medicare; (*leather*) conciare; (*food*) condire; (*a boat*) pavesare; **to dress down** (*coll*) rimproverare; **to get dressed** vestirsi ‖ *intr* vestire; vestirsi; (*mil*) schierarsi; **to dress up** vestirsi da sera; farsi bello, mettersi in gala

dress' ball' *s* ballo di gala

dress' coat' *s* frac *m*

dresser [ˈdresər] *s* toletta; (*sideboard*) credenza; **to be a good dresser** vestire con eleganza

dress' goods' *spl* stoffa per abiti

dressing [ˈdresɪŋ] *s* ornamento; (*for food*) condimento, salsa; (*stuffing for fowl*) ripieno; (*fertilizer*) concime *m*; (*for a wound*) medicazione

dress'ing down' *s* ramanzina

dress'ing gown' *s* vestaglia

dress'ing room' *s* spogliatoio, toletta; (*theat*) camerino

dress'ing sta'tion *s* posto di pronto soccorso

dress'ing ta'ble *s* toletta, specchiera

dress'mak'er *s* sarta, sarto per donna

dress'mak'ing *s* taglio, sartoria

dress' rehears'al *s* prova generale

dress' shirt' *s* camicia inamidata

dress' suit' *s* marsina

dress' u'niform *s* (*mil*) alta uniforme

dress·y [ˈdresi] *adj* (**-ier; iest**) (*coll*) elegante, ricercato

dribble [ˈdrɪbəl] *s* goccia ‖ *tr* (*sports*) palleggiare, dribblare ‖ *intr* gocciolare; (*at the mouth*) sbavare; (*sports*) dribblare

driblet [ˈdrɪblɪt] *s* piccola quantità; **in driblets** col contagocce

dried' beef' [draɪd] *s* carne seccata

dried' fruit' *s* frutta secca

drier [ˈdraɪ·ər] *s* (*for hair*) asciugacapelli *m*; (*for clothes*) asciugatrice *f*

drift [drɪft] *s* movimento; (*of sand, snow, etc.*) cumulo; (*snowdrift*) neve accumulata dal vento; tendenza, corrente *f*; intenzione; (*aer, naut*) deriva; (*rad, telv*) deviazione ‖ *intr* andare alla deriva; (*said of snow*) accumularsi; (*aer, naut*) derivare, scadere

drift' ice' *s* ghiaccio alla deriva

drift'pin' *s* (*mach*) mandrino

drift'wood' *s* legname andato alla deriva

drill [drɪl] *s* esercizio; (*fabric*) tela cruda; (*agr*) seminatrice *f*; (*mach*) trapano, trivella; (*mil*) esercitazioni *fpl* militari ‖ *tr* trivellare; istruire; (*mil*) insegnare gli esercizi militari a ‖ *intr* addestrarsi; (*mil*) fare gli esercizi militari

drill'mas'ter *s* istruttore *m*

drill' press' *s* trapano a colonna

drink [drɪŋk] *s* bevanda; **the drinks are on the house!** pagata il proprietario! ‖ *v* (*pret* **drank** [dræŋk]; *pp* **drunk** [drʌŋk]) *tr* bere; assorbire; **to drink down** tracannare; **to drink in** bere, assorbire; (*air*) aspirare ‖ *intr* bere; **to drink out of** bere da; **to drink to the health of** bere alla salute di

drinkable ['drɪŋkəbəl] *adj* bevibile, potabile

drinker ['drɪŋkər] *s* bevitore *m*

drinking ['drɪŋkɪŋ] *s* (il) bere

drink'ing foun'tain *s* fontanella pubblica

drink'ing song' *s* canzone bacchica

drink'ing straw' *s* cannuccia

drink'ing trough' *s* abbeveratoio

drink'ing wa'ter *s* acqua potabile

drip [drɪp] *s* sgocciolo, sgocciolatura ‖ *v* (*pret* & *pp* **dripped**) *ger* **dripping**) *intr* sgocciolare, stillare; (*said of perspiration*) trasudare

drip' cof'fee *s* caffè fatto con la macchinetta

drip'-dry' *adj* non-stiro

drip' pan' *s* (culin) ghiotta; (mach) coppa

dripping ['drɪpɪŋ] *s* gocciolio; **drippings** grasso che cola dall'arrosto

drive [draɪv] *s* scarrozzata; strada; passeggiata; impulso; forza, iniziativa; urgenza; spinta; campagna; (aut) trazione; (mach) trasmissione ‖ *v* (*pret* **drove** [drov]; *ger* **driven** ['drɪvən]) *tr* (*a nail*) ficcare, piantare; (*e.g., cattle*) condurre, parare; (*s.o. in a carriage or auto*) condurre, portare; spingere; stimulare; forzare; spingere a lavorare; (*sports*) colpire molto forte; **to drive away** scacciare; **to drive back** respingere; **to drive mad** far impazzire; **to drive out** scacciare ‖ *intr* fare una scarrozzata; **to drive at** parare a; voler dire; **to drive hard** lavorare sodo; **to drive in** entrare in automobile; (*a place*) entrare in automobile in; **to drive on the right** guidare a destra; **to drive out** uscire in macchina; **to drive up** arrivare in macchina

drive'-in' mov'ie the'ater *s* cineparco

drive'-in' res'taurant *s* ristorante *m* con servizio alla portiera

driv-el ['drɪvəl] *s* (*slobber*) bava; (*non-sense*) scemenza ‖ *v* (*pret* **-eled** or **-elled**; *ger* **-eling** or **-elling**) *intr* sbavare; dire scemenze

driver ['draɪvər] *s* guidatore *m*; (*of a carriage*) cocchiere *m*; (*of a locomotive*) macchinista *m*; (*of pack animals*) carrettiere *m*, mulattiere *m*

driv'er's li'cense *s* patente automobilistica

driv'er's seat' *s* posto di guida

drive' shaft' *s* albero motore

drive'way' *s* strada privata d'accesso; carrozzabile *f*

drive' wheel' *s* ruota motrice

driv'ing school' ['draɪvɪŋ] *s* autoscuola, scuola guida

drizzle ['drɪzəl] *s* pioviggine *f* ‖ *intr* piovigginare

droll [drol] *adj* buffo, spassoso

dromedar·y ['drɑmə,dɛri] *s* (-ies) dromedario

drone [dron] *s* fuco, pecchione *m*; (*hum*) ronzio; (*of bagpipe*) bordone *m*; areoplano teleguidato ‖ *tr* dire in tono monotono ‖ *intr* (*to live in idleness*) fare il fannullone; (*to buzz, hum*) ronzare

drool [drul] *s* (*slobber*) bava; (slang) scemenza ‖ *intr* sbavare; (slang) dire scemenze

droop [drup] *s* accasciamento ‖ *intr* (*to sag*) pendere; (*to lose spirit*) accasciarsi; (*said, e.g., of wheat*) avvizzire

drooping ['drupɪŋ] *adj* (*eyelid*) abbassato; (*shoulder*) spiovente; (fig) accasciato

drop [drɑp] *s* goccia; (*slope*) pendenza; (*earring*) pendente *m*; (*in temperature*) discesa; (*from an airplane*) lancio; (*trap door*) botola; (*gallows*) trabocchetto della forca; (*lozenge*) pastiglia; (*slit for letters*) buca; (*curtain*) tela; (*in prices*) calo; **a drop in the bucket** una goccia nell'oceano ‖ *v* (*pret* & *pp* **dropped**; *ger* **dropping**) *tr* lasciar cadere; (*a letter*) imbucare; (*a curtain*) abbassare; (*a remark*) lasciar scappare; (*a note*) scrivere; omettere; abbandonare; (*anchor*) gettare; (*from an airplane*) lanciare; (*from an automobile*) lasciare; (*from a list*) cancellare ‖ *intr* cadere; lasciarsi cadere; terminare; **to drop dead** cader morto; **to drop in** entrare un momento; **to drop off** sparire; addormentarsi; morire improvvisamente; **to drop out** scomparire; ritirarsi; dare le dimissioni

drop' cur'tain *s* telone *m*

drop' ham'mer *s* maglio

drop'-leaf' ta'ble *s* tavola a ribalta

drop'light' *s* lampada sospesa

drop'out' *s* studente *m* che abbandona permanentemente la scuola media

dropper ['drɑpər] *s* contagocce *m*

dropsical ['drɑpsɪkəl] *adj* idropico

dropsy ['drɑpsi] *s* idropisia

dross [drɔs] or [drɑs] *s* scoria; (fig) feccia

drought [draʊt] *s* siccità *f*; (*shortage*) mancanza

drove [drov] *s* branco; folla; **in droves** in massa

drover ['drovər] *s* mandriano

drown [draʊn] *tr* & *intr* affogare, annegare

drowse [draʊz] *intr* sonnecchiare

drow·sy ['draʊzi] *adj* (-sier; -siest) sonnolento, insonnolito

drub [drʌb] *v* (*pret* & *pp* **drubbed**; *ger* **drubbing**) *tr* bastonare; battere

drudge [drʌdʒ] *s* sgobbone *m* ‖ *intr* sgobbare, sfacchinare

drudg•y ['drʌdʒəri] *s* (-ies) lavoro ingrato, sfacchinata

drug [drʌg] *s* droga, medicina; narcotico; **drug on the market** merce *f* invendibile ‖ *v* (*pret* & *pp* **drugged;** *ger* **drugging**) *tr* drogare, narcotizzare

drug' ad'dict *s* tossicomane *mf*

drug' addic'tion *s* tossicomania

druggist ['drʌgɪst] *s* farmacista *mf*

drug' hab'it *s* tossicomania

drug'store' *s* farmacia

drug' traf'fic *s* traffico in stupefacenti

druid ['druːɪd] *s* druida *m*

drum [drʌm] *s* (*cylinder; instrument*) tamburo; (*container*) fusto ‖ *v* (*pret* & *pp* **drummed;** *ger* **drumming**) *tr* stamburare; **to drum up** (*customers*) farsi; (*enthusiasm*) creare ‖ *intr* tambureggiare; (*with the fingers*) tamburellare

drum'beat' *s* rullo di tamburi

drum' corps' *s* banda di tamburi

drum'fire' *s* fuoco nutrito

drum'head' *s* membrana del tamburo

drum' ma'jor *s* tamburo maggiore

drummer ['drʌmər] *s* (*salesman*) agente *m* viaggiatore; (*mus*) tamburo; (*mil*) tamburino

drum'stick' *s* bacchetta del tamburo; (*of cooked fowl*) coscia

drunk [drʌŋk] *adj* ubriaco; **to get drunk** ubriacarsi ‖ *s* ubriaco; (*spree*) sbornia; **to go on a drunk** (coll) ubriacarsi

drunkard ['drʌŋkərd] *s* ubriacone *m*

drunken ['drʌŋkən] *adj* ubriaco

drunk'en driv'ing *s*—**to be arrested for drunken driving** esser arrestato per aver guidato in stato di ubriachezza

drunkenness ['drʌŋkənnɪs] *s* ubriachezza, ebbrezza

dry [draɪ] *adj* (**drier;** **driest**) secco; (*boring*) arido; **to be dry** aver sete ‖ *s* (**drys**) abolizionista *mf* ‖ *v* (*pret* & *pp* **dried**) *tr* seccare; (*to wipe dry*) asciugare ‖ *intr* seccarsi; **to dry up** prosciugarsi, essiccarsi; (slang) star zitto

dry' bat'tery *s* pila a secco; (*group of dry cells*) batteria a secco

dry' cell' *s* pila a secco

dry'-clean' *tr* lavare a secco, pulire a secco

dry' clean'er *s* tintore *m*

dry' clean'ing *s* lavaggio a secco, pulitura a secco

dry'-clean'ing estab'lishment *s* tintoria

dry' dock' *s* bacino di carenaggio

dryer ['draɪ•ər] *s* var of **drier**

dry'-eyed' *adj* a occhi asciutti

dry' farm'ing *s* coltivazione di terreno arido

dry' goods' *spl* tessuti *mpl*; aridi *mpl*

dry'-goods store' *s* drapperia, negozio di tessuti

dry' ice' *s* neve carbonica, ghiaccio secco

dry' law' *s* legge *f* proibizionista

dry' meas'ure *s* misura per solidi

dryness ['draɪnɪs] *s* siccità *f*; (*e.g., of a speaker*) aridità *f*

dry' nurse' *s* balia asciutta

dry' run' *s* esercizio di prova; (mil) esercitazione senza munizioni

dry' sea'son *s* stagione arida

dry' wash' *s* roba lavata e asciugata ma non stirata

dual ['djuː•əl] or ['duː•əl] *adj* & *s* duale *m*

duali•ty [dju'ælɪti] or [du'ælɪti] *s* (-ties) dualità *f*

dub [dʌb] *s* (slang) giocatore inesperto ‖ *v* (*pret* & *pp* **dubbed;** *ger* **dubbing**) *tr* chiamare, affibbiare il nome di; (*a knight*) armare; (mov) doppiare

dubbing ['dʌbɪŋ] *s* doppiaggio

dubious ['djubɪ•əs] or ['dubɪ•əs] *adj* dubbioso; incerto

ducat ['dʌkət] *s* ducato

duchess ['dʌtʃɪs] *s* duchessa

duch•y ['dʌtʃi] *s* (-ies) ducato

duck [dʌk] *s* anatra; mossa rapida; (*in the water*) tuffo; (*dodge*) schivata; **ducks** pantaloni *mpl* di tela cruda ‖ *tr* (*one's head*) abbassare rapidamente; (*in water*) tuffare; (*a blow*) schivare ‖ *intr* tuffarsi; **to duck out** (coll) svignarsela

duckling ['dʌklɪŋ] *s* anatroccolo

ducks' and drakes' *s*—**to play ducks and drakes with** buttar via, sperperare

duck' soup' *s* (slang) cosa facilissima

duct [dʌkt] *s* tubo, condotto

ductile ['dʌktɪl] *adj* duttile

duct'less gland' ['dʌktlɪs] *s* ghiandola a secrezione interna

duct'work' *s* condotto, canalizzazione

dud [dʌd] *s* (slang) bomba inesplosa; (*person*) (slang) fallito; (*enterprise*) (slang) fallimento; **duds** (coll) vestito; roba

dude [djud] or [dud] *s* elegantone *m*

due [dju] or [du] *adj* dovuto; atteso, debito; pagabile; **due to** dovuto a; **to fall due** scadere; **when is the train due?** a che ora arriva il treno? ‖ *s* spettanza; debito; **dues** (*of a member*) quota sociale; **to get one's due** ricevere quanto uno merita; **to give the devil his due** trattare ognuno con giustizia ‖ *adv* in direzione, e.g., **due north** in direzione nord

duel ['djuː•əl] or ['duː•əl] *s* duello; **to fight a duel** battersi a duello ‖ *v* (*pret* & *pp* **dueled** or **duelled;** *ger* **dueling** or **duelling**) *intr* duellare

duelist or **duellist** ['djuː•əlɪst] or ['duː•əlɪst] *s* duellante *mf*

dues-paying ['djuz,pe•ɪŋ] or ['duz,pe•ɪŋ] *adj* regolare, effettivo

duet [dju'et] or [du'et] *s* duetto

duf'fel bag' ['dʌfəl] *s* sacca da viaggio

duke [djuk] or [duk] *s* duca *m*

dukedom ['djukdəm] or ['dukdəm] *s* ducato

dull [dʌl] *adj* (*not sharp*) spuntato, senza filo; (*color*) spento, sbiadito; (*sound, pain*) sordo; (*stupid*) ebete, tonto; (*business*) inattivo; (*boring*) noioso, melenso; (*flat*) opaco, appannato ‖ *tr* spuntare; sbiadire; inebetire; ottundere; (*enthusiasm*) raffreddare; (*pain*) alleviare ‖ *intr* spuntarsi; sbiadirsi; inebetirsi; raffreddarsi

dullard ['dʌlərd] s stupido

duly ['djuli] or ['duli] adv debitamente

dumb [dʌm] adj (lacking the power to speak) muto; (coll) tonto, stupido

dumb'bell' s manubrio; (slang) zuccone m, stupido

dumb' crea'ture s animale m, bruto

dumb' show' s pantomima

dumb'wai'ter s montavivande m

dumfound [ˌdʌm'faʊnd] tr interdire, lasciare esterrefatto

dum·my ['dʌmi] adj copiato; falso || s (-mies) (dress form) manichino; (in card games) morto; (figurehead) uomo di paglia, prestanome m; (skeleton copy of a book) menabò m; copia; (slang) stupido, tonto

dump [dʌmp] s immondezzaio; mucchio di spazzature; (mil) deposito munizioni; (min) montagnetta di scarico; to be down in the dumps (coll) avere le paturnie || tr scaricare; (to tip over) rovesciare; (com) scaricare sul mercato; (com) vendere sottocosto

dumping ['dʌmpɪŋ] s scarico; (com) dumping m

dumpling ['dʌmplɪŋ] s gnocco

dump' truck' s ribaltabile m

dump·y ['dʌmpi] adj (-ier; -iest) grassoccio, tarchiato

dun [dʌn] adj bruno grigiastro || s creditore importuno; (demand for payment) sollecitazione di pagamento || v (pret & pp dunned) ger dunning) tr sollecitare

dunce [dʌns] s ignorante mf, zuccone m

dunce' cap' s berretto d'asino

dune [djun] or [dun] s duna

dung [dʌŋ] s sterco, letame m || tr concimare con il letame

dungarees [ˌdʌŋgə'riz] spl tuta di cotone blu

dungeon ['dʌndʒən] s carcere sotterraneo; (fortified tower) torrione m, maschio

dung'hill' s letamaio

dunk [dʌŋk] tr inzuppare

du·o ['dju·o] or ['du·o] s (-os) duo

duode·num [ˌdju·ə'dinəm] or [ˌdu·ə'dinəm] s (-na [nə]) duodeno

dupe [djup] or [dup] s gonzo || tr gabbare, ingannare

du'plex house' ['djupleks] or ['dupleks] s casa di due appartamenti

duplicate ['djuplɪkɪt] or ['duplɪkɪt] adj & s duplicato ['djuplɪˌket] or ['duplɪˌket] tr duplicare

du'plicating machine' s duplicatore m

duplici·ty [dju'plɪsɪti] or [du'plɪsɪti] s (-ties) duplicità f, doppiezza

durable ['djurəbəl] or ['durəbəl] adj durabile, duraturo

du'rable goods' spl beni mpl durevoli

duration [dju're∫ən] or [du're∫ən] s durata

during ['djurɪŋ] or ['durɪŋ] prep durante

du'rum wheat' ['djurəm] or ['durəm] s grano duro

dusk [dʌsk] s crepuscolo

dust [dʌst] s polvere f || tr (to free of dust) spolverare; (to sprinkle with dust) spolverizzare; to dust off (slang) rimettere in uso; (slang) spolverare le spalle a

dust' bowl' s regione polverosissima

dust'cloth' s strofinaccio

dust' cloud' s polverone m

duster ['dʌstər] s (cloth) cencio; (light overgarment) spolverino

dust' jack'et s sopraccoperta

dust'pan' s pattumiera

dust' rag' s strofinaccio

dust·y ['dʌsti] adj (-ier; -iest) polveroso; grigiastro

Dutch [dʌt∫] adj olandese; (slang) tedesco || s (language) olandese m; (language) (slang) tedesco m; in Dutch (slang) in disgrazia; (slang) nei pasticci; the Dutch gli olandesi; (slang) i tedeschi; to go Dutch (coll) pagare alla romana

Dutch'man s (-men) olandese m; (slang) tedesco

Dutch' treat' s invito alla romana

dutiable ['djutɪ·əbəl] or ['dutɪ·əbəl] adj soggetto a dogana

dutiful ['djutɪfəl] or ['dutɪfəl] adj obbediente, doveroso

du·ty ['djuti] or ['duti] s (-ties) dovere m; (task) funzione; dazio, dogana; off duty libero; in libera uscita; on duty in servizio; di guardia; to do one's duty fare il proprio dovere; to take up one's duties entrare in servizio

du'ty-free' adj esente da dogana

dwarf [dwɔrf] adj & s nano || tr rimpiccolire || intr rimpiccolire; apparire più piccolo

dwarfish ['dwɔrfɪ∫] adj nano, da nano

dwell [dwel] v (pret & pp dwelled or dwelt [dwelt]) intr dimorare, abitare; to dwell on or upon intrattenersi su

dwelling ['dwelɪŋ] s abitazione, residenza

dwell'ing house' s casa d'abitazione

dwindle ['dwɪndəl] intr diminuire; restringersi, consumarsi

dye [daɪ] s tinta, colore m || v (pret & pp dyed; ger dyeing) tr tingere

dyed-in-the-wool ['daɪdɪnðəˌwʊl] adj tinto prima della tessitura; completo, intransigente

dyeing ['daɪ·ɪŋ] s tintura

dyer ['daɪ·ər] s tintore m

dye'stuff' s tintura, materia colorante

dying ['daɪ·ɪŋ] adj morente

dynamic [daɪ'næmɪk] or [dɪ'næmɪk] adj dinamico

dynamite ['daɪnəˌmaɪt] s dinamite f || tr far saltare con la dinamite

dyna·mo ['daɪnəˌmo] s (-mos) dinamo f

dynast ['daɪnæst] s dinasta m

dynas·ty ['daɪnəsti] s (-ties) dinastia f

dysentery ['dɪsənˌteri] s dissenteria

dyspepsia [dɪs'pepsɪ·ə] or [dɪs'pep∫ə] s dispepsia

E

E, e [i] *s* quinta lettera dell'alfabeto inglese

each [itʃ] *adj indef* ogni || *pron indef* ognuno, ciascuno; **each other** ci; vi; si; l'un l'altro || *adv* l'uno; a testa

eager ['igər] *adj* (*enthusiastic*) ardente; **eager to** avido di; **eager to** + *inf* desideroso di + *inf*

ea'ger bea'ver *s* zelante *mf*

eagerness ['igərnıs] *s* ardore *m;* brama

eagle ['igəl] *s* aquila

ea'gle owl' *s* gufo reale

eaglet ['iglıt] *s* aquilotto

ear [ir] *s* orecchio; (*of corn*) pannocchia; (*of wheat*) spiga; **to be all ears** essere tutt'orecchi; **to prick up one's ears** tendere l'orecchio; **to turn a deaf ear** far l'orecchio di mercante

ear'ache' *s* mal *m* d'orecchi

ear'drop' *s* pendente *m*

ear'drum' *s* timpano

ear'flap' *s* paraorecchi *m*

earl [ʌrl] *s* conte *m*

earldom ['ʌrldəm] *s* contea

ear·ly ['ʌrli] (**-lier; -liest**) *adj* (*occurring before customary time*) di buon'ora; (*first in a series*) primo; (*far back in time*) remoto, antico; (*occurring in near future*) prossimo || *adv* presto; per tempo, di buon'ora; **as early as** (*a certain time of day*) già a; (*a certain time or date*) fin da, già in; **as early as possible** quanto prima possibile; **early in** (*e.g., the month*) all'inizio di; **early in the morning** di mattina presto, di buon mattino; **early in the year** all'inizio dell'anno

ear'ly bird' *s* persona mattiniera

ear'ly mass' *s* prima messa

ear'ly ris'er *s* persona mattiniera

ear'mark' *s* contrassegno || *tr* contrassegnare; assegnare a s copo speciale

ear'muff' *s* paraorecchi *m*

earn [ʌrn] *tr* guadagnare, guadagnarsi; (*to get one's due*) meritarsi; (*interest*) (com) produrre || *intr* trarre profitto, rendere

earnest ['ʌrnıst] *adj* serio; fervente; **in earnest** sul serio || *s* caparra

ear'nest mon'ey *s* caparra

earnings ['ʌrnıŋz] *s* guadagno; salario

ear'phone' *s* (*of sonar*) orecchiale *m;* (rad, telp) cuffia

ear'piece' *s* (*of eyeglasses*) susta; (telp) ricevitore *m*

ear'ring' *s* orecchino

ear'shot' *s* tiro dell'orecchio; **within earshot** a portata di voce

ear'split'ting *adj* assordante

earth [ʌrθ] *s* terra; **to come back to** or **down to earth** scendere dalle nuvole

earthen ['ʌrθən] *adj* di terra; di terracotta

ear'then·ware' *s* coccio, terraglie *fpl,* terracotta

earthling ['ʌrθlıŋ] *s* terrestre *mf*

earthly ['ʌrθli] *adj* terreno, terrestre;

to be of no earthly use non servire assolutamente a niente

earthmover ['ʌrθ‚muvər] *s* ruspa

earth'quake' *s* terremoto

earth'work' *s* terrapieno

earth'worm' *s* lombrico

earth·y ['ʌrθi] *adj* (**-ier; -iest**) terroso; (*coarse*) rozzo; pratico; sincero, diretto

ear' trum'pet *s* corno acustico

ear'wax' *s* cerume *m*

ease [iz] *s* facilità *f;* (*naturalness*) spigliatezza, disinvoltura; (*comfort*) benestare *m;* tranquillità *f;* **at ease!** (mil) riposo!; **with ease** con facilità || *tr* facilitare; (*a burden*) alleggerire; (*to let up on*) rallentare; mitigare; **to ease out** licenziare con le buone maniere || *intr* alleviarsi, mitigarsi, diminuire; rallentare

easel ['izəl] *s* cavalletto

easement ['izmənt] *s* attenuamento; (law) servitù *f*

easily ['izıli] *adv* facilmente; senza dubbio; probabilmente

easiness ['izınıs] *s* facilità *f;* disinvoltura; grazia, agilità *f;* indifferenza

east [ist] *adj* orientale, dell'est || *s* est *m* || *adv* verso l'est

Easter ['istər] *s* Pasqua

East'er egg' *s* uovo di Pasqua

East'er Mon'day *s* lunedì *m* di Pasqua

eastern ['istərn] *adj* orientale

East'er-tide' *s* tempo pasquale

eastward ['istwərd] *adv* verso l'est

eas·y ['izi] *adj* (**-ier; -iest**) facile; (*conducive to ease*) comodo, agiato; (*free from worry*) tranquillo; (*easygoing*) disinvolto, spigliato; (*not tight*) ampio; (*not hurried*) lento, moderato || *adv* (coll) facilmente; (coll) tranquillamente; **to take it easy** (coll) riposarsi; (coll) non prendersela; (coll) andar piano

eas'y chair' *s* poltrona

eas'y·go'ing *adj* (*person*) comodone; (*horse*) sciolto nell'andatura

eas'y mark' *s* (coll) gonzo

eas'y mon'ey *s* denaro fatto senza fatica; soldi rubati

eas'y terms' *spl* facilitazioni *fpl* di pagamento

eat [it] *v* (*pret* **ate** [et]; *pp* **eaten** ['itən]) *tr* mangiare; **to eat away** smangiare; **to eat up** mangiarsi || *intr* mangiare

eatable ['itəbəl] *adj* mangiabile || **eatables** *spl* commestibili *mpl*

eaves [ivz] *spl* gronda

eaves'drop' *v* (*pret & pp* **-dropped;** *ger* **-dropping**) *intr* origliare

ebb [eb] *s* riflusso; decadenza || *intr* (*said of the tide*) ritirarsi; decadere

ebb' and flow' *s* flusso e riflusso

ebb' tide' *s* riflusso, deflusso

ebon·y ['ebəni] *s* (**-ies**) ebano

ebullient [ı'bʌljənt] *adj* bollente

eccentric [ek'sentrık] *adj & s* eccentrico

e:centrici·ty [‚eksen'trısıtı] s (-ties) eccentricità f, originalità f

ecclesiastic [ı ‚klizı'æstık] adj & s ecclesiastico

echelon ['eʃə‚lan] s scaglione m; (mil) scaglione m || tr scaglionare

ech·o ['eko] s (-oes) eco || tr far eco a || intr echeggiare, riecheggiare

éclair [e'kler] s dolce ripieno di crema

eclectic [ek'lektık] adj & s eclettico

eclipse [ı'klıps] s eclisse f, eclissi f || tr eclissare

eclogue ['eklɔg] or ['eklɑg] s egloga

ecology [ı'kɑlədʒı] s ecologia

economic(al) [‚ikə'namık(əl)] or [‚ekə'namık(əl)] adj economico

economics [‚ikə'namıks] or [‚ekə-'namıks] s economia (politica)

economist [ı'kɑnəmıst] s economista mf

economize [ı'kɑnə‚maız] tr & intr economizzare

econo·my [ı'kɑnəmi] s (-mies) economia

ecosystem ['eko‚sıstəm] s ecosistema m

ecsta·sy ['ekstəsi] s (-sies) estasi f

ecstatic [ek'stætık] adj estatico

ecumenic(al) [‚ekjə'menık(əl)] adj ecumenico

eczema ['eksımə] or [eg'zimə] s eczema m

ed·dy ['edı] s (-dies) turbine m || v (pret & pp -died) tr & intr turbinare

edelweiss ['edəl‚vaıs] s stella alpina

edge [edʒ] s (of knife, sword, etc) filo, tagliente m; (border at which a surface terminates) orlo, bordo; (of a wound) labbro, margine m; (of a book) taglio; (of a tumbler) giro; (of clothing) vivagno; (of a table) spigolo; (slang) vantaggio; on edge nervoso; to have the edge on (coll) avere il vantaggio su; to set the teeth on edge far allegare i denti || tr affilare, aguzzare; orlare, bordare; to edge out riuscire ad eliminare || intr avanzare lentamente

edgeways ['edʒ‚wez] adv di taglio; to not let s.o. get a word in edgeways non lasciar dire una parola a qlcu

edging ['edʒıŋ] s orlo, bordo

edg·y ['edʒı] adj (-ier; -iest) acuto, angolare; nervoso, ansioso

edible ['edıbəl] adj mangereccio, mangiabile || edibles spl commestibili mpl

edict | 'idıkt] s editto

edification [‚edıfı'keʃən] s edificazione f

edifice ['edıfıs] s edificio

edi·fy ['edı‚faı] v (pret & pp -fied) tr edificare

edifying ['edı‚faı·ıŋ] adj edificante

edit ['edıt] tr redigere; (e.g., a manuscript) correggere; (an edition) curare; (a newspaper) dirigere; (mov) montare

edition [ı'dıʃən] s edizione f

editor ['edıtər] s (of a newspaper or magazine) direttore m, gerente mf; (of an editorial) redattore m, cronista mf; (of a critical edition) editore m; (of a manuscript) revisore m

editorial [‚edı'torı·əl] adj editoriale || s capocronaca m, articolo di fondo

ed'ito'rial staff' s redazione

ed'itor in chief' s gerente mf responsabile

educate ['edʒu‚ket] tr educare, erudire

education [‚edʒu'keʃən] s educazione; istruzione, insegnamento

educational [‚edʒu'keʃənəl] adj educativo

educa'tional institu'tion s istituto di magistero

educator ['edʒu‚ketər] s educatore m

eel [il] s anguilla; to be as slippery as an eel guizzare di mano come un'anguilla

ee·rie or ee·ry ['ırı] adj (-rier; -riest) spettrale, pauroso

efface [ı'fes] tr cancellare; to efface oneself eclissarsi, mettersi in disparte

effect [ı'fekt] s effetto; (main idea) tenore m; in effect in vigore; in realtà; to go into effect or to take effect andare in vigore; to put into effect mandare ad effetto || tr effettuare

effective [ı'fektıv] adj efficace; (actually in effect) effettivo; (striking) che colpisce; to become effective entrare in vigore

effectual [ı'fektʃu·əl] adj efficace

effectuate [ı'fektʃu‚et] tr effettuare

effeminacy [ı'femınəsi] s effemminatezza

effeminate [ı'femınıt] adj effemminato

effervesce [‚efər'ves] intr essere in effervescenza

effervescence [‚efər'vesəns] s effervescenza

effervescent [‚efər'vesənt] adj effervescente

effete [ı'fit] adj esausto, sterile

efficacious [‚efı'keʃəs] adj efficace

effica·cy [efıkəsı] s (-cies) efficacia

efficien·cy [ı'fıʃənsı] s (-cies) efficienza; (mech) rendimento, efficienza

effi'ciency engineer' s analista mf tempi e metodi

efficient [ı'fıʃənt] adj efficiente; (person) abile; (mech) efficiente

effi·gy ['efıdʒı] s (-gies) effigie f

effort ['efərt] s sforzo

effronter·y [ı'frʌntərı] s (-ies) sfrontatezza, sfacciataggine f

effusion [ı'fjuʒən] s effusione

effusive [ı'fjusıv] adj espansivo

egg [eg] s uovo; (slang) bravo ragazzo || tr—to egg on incitare

egg'beat er s frullino, sbattiuova m

egg cup' s portauovo

egg'head' s (coll) intellettuale mf

eggnog ['eg ‚nɑg] s zabaione m

egg'plant' s melanzana, petonciano

egg'shell' s guscio d'uovo

egoism ['ego ‚ızəm] or ['igo ‚ızəm] s egoismo

egoist ['ego·ıst] or ['igo·ıst] s egoista mf

egotism ['ego ‚tızəm] or ['igo ‚tızəm] s egotismo

egotist ['egotıst] or ['igotıst] s egotista mf

egregious [ɪ'gridʒəs] *adj* gigantesco, tremendo, marchiano

egress ['igres] *s* uscita

Egypt ['idʒɪpt] *s* l'Egitto

Egyptian [ɪ'dʒɪp/ən] *adj* & *s* egiziano

ei'der down' ['aɪdər] *s* piumino

ei'der duck' *s* edredone *m*

eight [et] *adj* & *pron* otto ‖ *s* otto; **eight o'clock** le otto

eighteen ['et'tin] *adj*, *s* & *pron* diciotto

eighteenth ['et'tinθ] *adj*, *s* & *pron* diciottesimo ‖ *s* (*in dates*) diciotto

eighth [etθ] *adj* & *s* ottavo ‖ *s* (*in dates*) otto

eight' hun'dred *adj*, *s* & *pron* ottocento

eightieth ['etɪ-ɪθ] *adj*, *s* & *pron* ottantesimo

eight·y ['eti] *adj* & *pron* ottanta ‖ *s* (-ies) ottanta *m*; **the eighties** gli anni ottanta

either ['iðər] *or* ['aɪðər] *adj* l'uno o l'altro; l'uno e l'altro; ciascuno; entrambi i, tutti e due i ‖ *pron* l'uno o l'altro; l'uno e l'altro; entrambi ‖ *adv*—**not either** nemmeno ‖ *conj*—**either . . . or** o . . . o

ejaculate [ɪ'dʒækjə,let] *tr* esclamare; (*physiol*) emettere ‖ *intr* esclamare; (*physiol*) avere un'eiaculazione

eject [ɪ'dʒekt] *tr* espellere, gettar fuori; (*to evict*) sfrattare

ejection [ɪ'dʒek/ən] *s* espulsione; (*of a tenant*) sfratto

ejec'tion seat' *s* sedile *m* eiettabile

eke [ik] *tr*—**to eke out a living** sbarcare il lunario

elaborate [ɪ'læbərɪt] *adj* (*done with great care*) elaborato; (*detailed*) minuzioso; (*ornate*) ornato ‖ [ɪ'læbə-,ret] *tr* elaborare ‖ *intr*—**to elaborate on** or **upon** circonstanziare, particolareggiare

elapse [ɪ'læps] *intr* passare, trascorrere

elastic [ɪ'læstɪk] *adj* & *s* elastico

elasticity [ɪ,læs'tɪsɪti] *or* [,ilæs'tɪsɪti] *s* elasticità *f*

elated [ɪ'letɪd] *adj* esultante, gongolante

elation [ɪ'le/ən] *s* esultanza, gaudio

elbow ['elbo] *s* gomito; (*in a river*) ansa; (*of a chair*) braccio; **at one's elbow** sotto mano; **out at the elbows** coi gomiti logori; **to crook the elbow** alzare il gomito; **to rub elbows** stare gomito a gomito; **up to the elbows** fino al collo ‖ *tr*—**to elbow one's way** aprirsi il passo a gomitate ‖ *intr* dar gomitate

el'bow grease' *s* (coll) olio di gomiti

el'bow patch' *s* toppa al gomito

el'bow rest' *s* bracciolo

el'bow·room' *s* spazio sufficiente; libertà *f* d'azione

elder ['eldər] *adj* seniore, maggiore ‖ *s* (bot) sambuco; (eccl) maggiore *m*

el'der·ber'ry *s* (-ries) sambuco; (*fruit*) bacca del sambuco

elderly ['eldərli] *adj* attempato, anziano

eld'er states'man *s* uomo di stato esperto

eldest ['eldɪst] *adj* (il) maggiore; (il) più vecchio

elect [ɪ'lekt] *adj* & *s* eletto; **the elect** gli eletti ‖ *tr* eleggere

election [ɪ'lek/ən] *s* elezione

electioneer [ɪ,lek/ə'nɪr] *intr* fare una campagna elettorale

elective [ɪ'lektɪv] *adj* elettivo ‖ *s* corso facoltativo

electorate [ɪ'lektərɪt] *s* elettorato

electric(al) [ɪ'lektrɪk(əl)] *adj* elettrico

elec'tric blend'er *s* frullatore *m*

elec'tric chair' *s* sedia elettrica

elec'tric cord' *s* piattina, filo elettrico

elec'tric eel' *s* gimnoto

elec'tric eye' *s* occhio elettrico

electrician [ɪ,lek'trɪ/ən] *or* [,elek-'trɪ/ən] *s* elettricista *m*

electricity [ɪ,lek'trɪsɪti] *or* [,elek-'trɪsɪti] *s* elettricità *f*

elec'tric me'ter *s* contatore *m* della luce

elec'tric per'cola'tor *s* caffettiera elettrica

elec'tric shav'er *s* rasoio elettrico

elec'tric shock' *s* scossa elettrica, elettrosquasso

elec'tric tape' *s* nastro isolante

elec'tric train' *s* elettrotreno

electri·fy [ɪ'lektrɪ,faɪ] *v* (*pret* & *pp* -fied) *tr* (*to provide with electric power*) elettrificare; (*to communicate electricity to; to thrill*) elettrizzare

electrocute [ɪ'lektrə,kjut] *tr* fulminare con la corrente; far morire sulla sedia elettrica

electrode [ɪ'lektrod] *s* elettrodo

electrolysis [ɪ,lek'trɑlɪsɪs] *or* [,elek-'trɑlɪsɪs] *s* elettrolisi *f*

electrolyte [ɪ'lektrə,laɪt] *s* elettrolito

electromagnet [ɪ,lektrə'mægnɪt] *s* elettrocalamita

electromagnetic [ɪ,lektrəmæg'netɪk] *adj* elettromagnetico

electromotive [ɪ,lektrə'motɪv] *adj* elettromotore

electron [ɪ'lektrɑn] *s* elettrone *m*

electronic [ɪ,lek'trɑnɪk] *or* [,elek-'trɑnɪk] *adj* elettronico ‖ **electronics** *s* elettronica

electroplating [ɪ'lektrə,pletɪŋ] *s* galvanostegia

electrostatic [ɪ,lektrə'stætɪk] *adj* elettrostatico

electrotype [ɪ'lektrə,taɪp] *s* stereotipia ‖ *tr* stereotipare

eleemosynary [,elɪ'mɑsɪ,neri] *adj* caritatevole, di beneficenza

elegance ['eligəns] *s* eleganza

elegant ['eligənt] *adj* elegante

elegiac [,elɪ'dʒaɪ-æk] *adj* elegiaco

ele·gy ['elɪdʒi] *s* (-gies) elegia

element ['elimənt] *s* elemento; **to be out of one's element** essere fuori del proprio ambiente

elementary [,elɪ'mentəri] *adj* elementare

elephant ['elɪfənt] *s* elefante *m*

elevate ['elɪ,vet] *tr* elevare, innalzare

elevated ['elɪ,vetɪd] *adj* elevato ‖ *s* ferrovia soprelevata, metropolitana soprelevata

elevation [,elɪ've/ən] *s* elevazione; (surv) quota

elevator ['elɪ,vetər] *s* ascensore *m*;

(*for freight*) montacarichi *m;* (*for hoisting grain*) elevatore *m* di grano; (*warehouse for storing grain*) deposito granaglie; (aer) timone *m* di profondità

eleven [ɪ'lɛvən] *adj & pron* undici ‖ *s* undici *m;* **eleven o'clock** le undici

eleventh [ɪ'lɛvənθ] *adj, s & pron* undicesimo ‖ *s* (*in dates*) undici *m*

elev'enth hour' *s* ultimo momento

elf [ɛlf] *s* (**elves** [ɛlvz]) elfo

elicit [ɪ'lɪsɪt] *tr* cavare, sottrarre

elide [ɪ'laɪd] *tr* elidere

eligible ['ɛlɪdʒɪbəl] *adj* eleggibile; accettabile

eliminate [ɪ'lɪmɪ ,net] *tr* eliminare

elision [ɪ'lɪʒən] *s* elisione

elite [e'lit] *adj* eletto, scelto ‖ *s*—**the elite** l'élite *f*

elk [ɛlk] *s* alce *m*

ellipse [ɪ'lɪps] *s* (geom) ellisse *f*

ellip·sis [ɪ'lɪpsɪs] *s* (**-ses** [siz]) (gram) ellissi *f*

elliptic(al) [ɪ'lɪptɪk(əl)] *adj* ellittico

elm [ɛlm] *s* olmo

elongate [ɪ'lɔŋget] *or* [ɪ'lɑŋget] *tr* allungare, prolungare

elope [ɪ'lop] *intr* fuggire con un amante

elopement [ɪ'lopmənt] *s* fuga con un amante

eloquence ['ɛləkwəns] *s* eloquenza

eloquent ['ɛləkwənt] *adj* eloquente

else [ɛls] *adj*—**nobody else** nessun altro; **nothing else** nient'altro; **somebody else** qualcun altro; **something else** qualcosa d'altro; **what else** che altro; **who else** chi altro; **whose else** di che altra persona ‖ *adv*—**how else** in che altra maniera; **or else** se no; altrimenti; **when else** in che altro momento; in che altro periodo; **where else** dove mai, da che parte

else'where' *adv* altrove

elucidate [ɪ'lusɪ ,det] *tr* dilucidare

elude [ɪ'lud] *tr* eludere

elusive [ɪ'lusɪv] *adj* elusivo; (*evasive*) fugace, sfuggente

emaciated [ɪ'meʃɪ ,etɪd] *adj* smunto, emaciato, macilento

emanate ['ɛmə ,net] *tr & intr* emanare

emancipate [ɪ'mænsɪ ,pet] *tr* emancipare

embalm [ɛm'bɑm] *tr* imbalsamare

embankment [ɛm'bæŋkmənt] *s* terrapieno

embar·go [ɛm'bɑrgo] *s* (**-goes**) embargo ‖ *tr* mettere l'embargo a

embark [ɛm'bɑrk] *intr* imbarcarsi

embarkation [,ɛmbɑr'keʃən] *s* imbarco

embarrass [ɛm'bærəs] *tr* imbarazzare, mettere a disagio; (*to impede*) imbarazzare, impacciare; mettere in difficoltà economiche

embarrassing [ɛm'bærəsɪŋ] *adj* sconcertante; imbarazzante

embarrassment [ɛm'bærəsmənt] *s* imbarazzo, disagio, confusione; impaccio; difficoltà finanziaria, dissesto

embas·sy ['ɛmbəsi] *s* (**-sies**) ambasciata

em·bed [ɛm'bɛd] *s* (*pret & pp* **-bedded;** *ger* **-bedding**) *tr* incastrare, incassare

embellish [ɛm'bɛlɪʃ] *tr* imbellire

embellishment [ɛm'bɛlɪʃmənt] *s* abbellimento; (fig) fioretto

ember ['ɛmbər] *s* brace *f;* **embers** braci *fpl*

Em'ber days' *spl* tempora *fpl*

embezzle [ɛm'bɛzəl] *tr* appropriare, malversare ‖ *intr* appropriarsi

embezzlement [ɛm'bɛzəlmənt] *s* appropriazione indebita, malversazione; (*of public funds*) peculato

embezzler [ɛm'bɛzlər] *s* malversatore *m*

embitter [ɛm'bɪtər] *tr* amareggiare

emblazon [ɛm'blezən] *tr* blasonare; celebrare

emblem ['ɛmbləm] *s* emblema *m*

emblematic(al) [,ɛmblə'mætɪk(əl)] *adj* emblematico

embodiment [ɛm'bɑdɪmənt] *s* incarnazione, personificazione

embod·y [ɛm'bɑdi] *v* (*pret & pp* **-ied**) *tr* incarnare, personificare; incorporare

embolden [ɛm'boldən] *tr* imbaldanzire

embolism ['ɛmbə ,lɪzəm] *s* embolia

emboss [ɛm'bɔs] *or* [ɛm'bɑs] *tr* (*metal*) sbalzare; (*paper*) goffrare

embrace [ɛm'bres] *s* abbraccio ‖ *tr* abbracciare ‖ *intr* abbracciarsi

embrasure [ɛm'breʒər] *s* (archit) strombatura; (mil) feritoia

embroider [ɛm'brɔɪdər] *tr* ricamare, trapuntare

embroider·y [ɛm'brɔɪdəri] *s* (**-ies**) ricamo, trapunto

embroil [ɛm'brɔɪl] *tr* ingarbugliare; (*to involve in contention*) coinvolgere

embroilment [ɛm'brɔɪlmənt] *s* imbroglio; (*in contention*) disaccordo

embry·o ['ɛmbrɪ ,o] *s* (**-os**) embrione *m*

embryology [,ɛmbrɪ'ɑlədʒi] *s* embriologia

embryonic [,ɛmbrɪ'ɑnɪk] *adj* embrionale

emcee ['ɛm'si] *s* presentatore *m* ‖ *tr* presentare

emend [ɪ'mɛnd] *tr* emendare

emendation [,imɛn'deʃən] *s* emendamento

emerald ['ɛmərəld] *s* smeraldo

emerge [ɪ'mʌrdʒ] *intr* emergere

emergence [ɪ'mʌrdʒəns] *s* emergenza

emergen·cy [ɪ'mʌrdʒənsi] *s* (**-cies**) emergenza

emer'gency brake' *s* freno a mano

emer'gency ex'it *s* uscita di sicurezza

emer'gency land'ing *s* atterragio di fortuna

emer'gency ward' *s* sala d'urgenza

emeritus [ɪ'mɛrɪtəs] *adj* emerito

emersion [ɪ'mʌrʒən] *or* [ɪ'mʌrʃən] *s* emersione

emery ['ɛməri] *s* smeriglio

em'ery cloth' *s* tela smeriglio

em'ery wheel' *s* mola a smeriglio

emetic [ɪ'mɛtɪk] *adj & s* emetico

emigrant ['ɛmɪgrənt] *adj & s* emigrante *mf*

emigrate ['ɛmɪ ,gret] *intr* emigrare

émigré [emi'gre] *or* ['ɛmɪ ,gre] *s* emigrato

eminence ['ɛmɪnəns] s eminenza; (eccl) Eminenza

eminent ['ɛmɪnənt] adj eminente

emissar·y ['ɛmɪ‚sɛri] s (-ies) emissario

emission [ɪ'mɪʃən] s emissione

emit [ɪ'mɪt] v (pret & pp emitted; ger emitting) tr emettere

emolument [ɪ'mɑljəmənt] s emolumento

emotion [ɪ'moʃən] s emozione

emotional [ɪ'moʃənəl] adj emotivo

emperor ['ɛmpərər] s imperatore m

empha·sis ['ɛmfəsɪs] s (-ses [‚siz]) enfasi f. risalto

emphasize ['ɛmfə‚saɪz] tr dar rilievo a, sottolineare

emphatic [ɛm'fætɪk] adj enfatico

emphysema [‚ɛmfɪ'simə] s enfisema m

empire ['ɛmpaɪr] s impero

empiric(al) [ɛm'pɪrɪk(əl)] adj empirico

empiricist [ɛm'pɪrɪsɪst] s empirista mf

emplacement [ɛm'plesmənt] s piazzola, postazione

employ [ɛm'plɔɪ] s impiego ǁ tr impiegare, usare; valersi di

employee [ɛm'plɔɪ·i] or [‚ɛmplɔɪ'i] s impiegato, dipendente mf

employer [ɛm'plɔɪ·ər] s dirigente mf, datore m di lavoro

employment [ɛm'plɔɪmənt] s impiego, occupazione

employ'ment a'gency s agenzia di collocamento

empower [ɛm'pau·ər] tr autorizzare; permettere

empress ['ɛmprɪs] s imperatrice f

emptiness ['ɛmptɪnɪs] s vuoto

emp·ty ['ɛmpti] adj (-tier; -tiest) vuoto; (gun) scarico; (hungry) (coll) digiuno; (fig) esausto ǁ v (pret & pp -tied) tr vuotare ǁ intr vuotarsi

empty-handed ['ɛmpti'hændɪd] adj a mani vuote

empty-headed ['ɛmpti'hɛdɪd] adj dalla testa vuota, balordo

empyrean [‚ɛmpɪ'ri·ən] adj & s empireo

emulate ['ɛmjə‚let] tr emulare

emulator ['ɛmjə‚letər] s emulo

emulous ['ɛmjələs] adj emulo

emulsi·fy [ɪ'mʌlsɪ‚faɪ] v (pret & pp -fied) tr emulsionare

emulsion [ɪ'mʌlʃən] s emulsione

enable [ɛn'ebəl] tr abilitare; permettere (with dat)

enact [ɛn'ækt] tr decretare; (a role) rappresentare

enactment [ɛn'æktmənt] s legge f; (of a law) promulgazione; (of a play) rappresentazione

enam·el [ɪn'æməl] s smalto ǁ v (pret & pp -eled or -elled; ger -eling or -elling) tr smaltare

enam'el·ware' s utensili mpl di cucina di ferro smaltato

enamor [ɛn'æmər] tr innamorare; to become enamored of innamorarsi di

encamp [ɛn'kæmp] tr accampare ǁ intr accamparsi

encampment [ɛn'kæmpmənt] s campeggio; (mil) accampamento

encase [ɛn'kes] tr incassare

encephalitis [ɛn‚sɛfə'laɪtɪs] s encefalite f

enchain [ɛn't/en] tr incatenare

enchant [ɛn't/ænt] or [ɛn't/ɑnt] tr incantare

enchantment [ɛn't/æntmənt] or [ɛn-'t/ɑntmənt] s incanto, malia

enchanting [ɛn't/æntɪŋ] or [ɛn't/ɑnt-ɪŋ] adj incantatore, incantevole

enchantress [ɛn't/æntrɪs] or [ɛn't/ɑn-trɪs] s incantatrice f, maliarda

enchase [ɛn't/es] tr incastonare

encircle [ɛn'sʌrkəl] tr rigirare, girare intorno a; (mil) circondare

enclave ['ɛnklev] s enclave f

enclitic [ɛn'klɪtɪk] adj enclitico ǁ s enclitica

enclose [ɛn'kloz] tr rinchiudere; (in a letter) accludere, includere; to enclose herewith accludere alla presente

enclosure [ɛn'klozər] s (land surrounded by fence) recinto, chiuso; (e.g., letter) allegato

encomi·um [ɛn'komi·əm] s (-ums or -a [ə]) encomio, elogio

encompass [ɛn'kʌmpəs] tr circondare; racchiudere, contenere

encore ['ɑŋkor] s bis m ǁ tr (a performance) chiedere il bis di; (a performer) chiedere il bis a ǁ interj bis!

encounter [ɛn'kauntər] s (casual meeting) incontro; (combat) scontro ǁ tr incontrare ǁ intr scontrarsi

encourage [ɛn'kʌrɪdʒ] tr incoraggiare; (to foster) favorire

encouragement [ɛn'kʌrɪdʒmənt] s incoraggiamento; favoreggiamento

encroach [ɛn'krot/] intr—to encroach on or upon invadere; usurpare; occupare il territorio di

encumber [ɛn'kʌmbər] tr imbarazzare; ingombrare; (to load with debts, etc) gravare

encumbrance [ɛn'kʌmbrəns] s imbarazzo; ingombro; gravame m

encyclical [ɛn'sɪklɪkəl] or [ɛn'saɪklɪ-kəl] s enciclica

encyclopedia [ɛn‚saɪklə'pidɪ·ə] s enciclopedia

encyclopedic [ɛn‚saɪklə'pidɪk] adj enciclopedico

end [ɛnd] s (extremity; concluding part) fine f; (e.g., of the week) fine f; (purpose) fine m; (part adjacent to an extremity) lembo; (small piece) pezza, avanzo; (of a beam) testata; (sports) estrema; at the end of in capo a; in fondo a; in the end alla fine, all'ultimo; no end (coll) moltissimo; no end of (coll) un mucchio di; to make both ends meet sbarcare il lunario; to no end senza effetto; to stand on end mettere in piedi, drizzare; mettersi diritto; (said of hair) drizzarsi; to the end that affinché ǁ tr finire, terminare; to end up andare a finire ǁ intr finire, terminare; to end up finire

endanger [ɛn'dendʒər] tr mettere in pericolo

endear [en'dɪr] *tr* affezionare; **to endear oneself to** rendersi caro a

endeavor [en'devər] *s* tentativo, sforzo || *intr* tentare, sforzarsi

endemic [en'dɛmɪk] *adj* endemico || *s* endemia

ending ['endɪŋ] *s* fine *f*, conclusione; (gram) terminazione, desinenza

endive ['endaɪv] *s* indivia

endless ['endlɪs] *adj* interminabile; sterminato; (mach) senza fine

end'most' *adj* estremo, ultimo

endorse [en'dɔrs] *tr* girare; (fig) approvare, confermare

endorsee [,endɔr'si] *s* giratario

endorsement [en'dɔrsmənt] *s* girata; approvazione, conferma

endorser [en'dɔrsər] *s* girante *mf*

endow [en'dau] *tr* dotare

endowment [en'daumənt] *adj* dotale || *s* (*of an institution*) dotazione; (*gift, talent*) dote *f*

end' pap'er *s* risguardo

endurance [en'djurəns] or [en'durəns] *s* sopportazione, tolleranza; (*ability to hold out*) resistenza, forza; (*lasting time*) durata

endure [en'djur] or [en'dur] *tr* sopportare, tollerare; resistere (with *dat*) || *intr* durare, resistere

enduring [en'djurɪŋ] or [en'durɪŋ] *adj* duraturo, durevole; paziente

enema ['enəmə] *s* clistere *m*

ene•my ['enəmi] *adj* nemico || *s* (-mies) nemico

en'emy al'ien *s* straniero nemico

energetic [,enər'dʒɛtɪk] *adj* energetico, vigoroso

ener•gy ['enərdʒi] *s* (-gies) energia

enervate ['enər,vet] *tr* snervare

enfeeble [en'fibəl] *tr* indebolire

enfold [en'fold] *tr* avvolgere; abbracciare

enforce [en'fors] *tr* far osservare; ottenere per forza; (*e.g., obedience*) imporre; (*an argument*) far valere

enforcement [en'forsmənt] *s* imposizione; (*of a law*) esecuzione

enfranchise [en'fræntʃaɪz] *tr* liberare; concedere il diritto di voto a

engage [en'gedʒ] *tr* occupare; riservare; (*s.o.'s attention*) attrarre; (*a gear*) ingranare; (*the enemy*) ingaggiare; (*to hire*) assumere; (*theat*) scritturare; **to be engaged, to be engaged to be married** essere fidanzato; **to engage s.o. in conversation** intavolare una conversazione con qlcu || *intr* essere occupato; essere impiegato; assumere un'obbligazione; (mil) impegnarsi; (mach) ingranare, incastrarsi

engaged [en'gedʒd] *adj* fidanzato; occupato, impegnato; (*column*) murato

engagement [en'gedʒmənt] *s* accordo; fidanzamento; impegno, contratto; (*appointment*) appuntamento; (mil) azione; (mach) innesto

engage'ment ring' *s* anello di fidanzamento

engaging [en'gedʒɪŋ] *adj* attrattivo

engender [en'dʒendər] *tr* ingenerare

engine ['endʒɪn] *s* macchina; (aut) motore *m*; (rr) locomotiva, motrice *f*

engineer [,endʒə'nɪr] *s* ingegnere *m*; (rr) macchinista *m*; (mil) zappatore *m*, geniere *m* || *tr* costruire; progettare

engineering [,endʒə'nɪrɪŋ] *s* ingegneria

en'gine house' *s* stazione dei pompieri

en'gine•man' *s* (-men) (rr) macchinista *m*

en'gine room' *s* sala macchine

en'gine-room' tel'egraph *s* (naut) telegrafo di macchina, trasmettitore *m*

England ['ɪŋglənd] *s* l'Inghilterra

Englander ['ɪŋgləndər] *s* nativo dell'Inghilterra

English ['ɪŋglɪʃ] *adj* inglese || *s* inglese *m*; (billiards) effetto; **the English** gli inglesi

Eng'lish Chan'nel *s* Canale *m* della Manica

Eng'lish dai'sy *s* margherita

Eng'lish horn' *s* (mus) corno inglese

Eng'lish•man *s* (-men) inglese *m*

Eng'lish-speak'ing *adj* di lingua inglese, anglofono

Eng'lish•wom'an *s* (-wom'en) inglese *f*

engraft [en'græft] or [en'graft] *tr* (hort) innestare; (fig) inculcare

engrave [en'grev] *tr* incidere

engraver [en'grevər] *s* incisore *m*

engraving [en'grevɪŋ] *s* incisione

engross [en'gros] *tr* preoccupare, assorbire; redigere ufficialmente, scrivere a grandi caratteri; monopolizzare

engrossing [en'grosɪŋ] *adj* assorbente

engulf [en'gʌlf] *tr* sommergere, inondare

enhance [en'hæns] or [en'hans] *tr* valorizzare; far risaltare

enigma [ɪ'nɪgmə] *s* enigma *m*

enigmatic(al) [,ɪnɪg'mætɪk(əl)] *adj* enigmatico

enjambment [en'dʒæmmənt] or [en'dʒæmbmənt] *s* inarcatura

enjoin [en'dʒɔɪn] *tr* ingiungere, intimare

enjoy [en'dʒɔɪ] *tr* godere; **to enjoy +** *ger* provar piacere in + *inf*; **to enjoy oneself** divertirsi

enjoyable [en'dʒɔɪəbəl] *adj* gradevole

enjoyment [en'dʒɔɪmənt] *s* (*pleasure*) piacere *m*; (*pleasurable use*) godimento

enkindle [en'kɪndəl] *tr* infiammare

enlarge [en'lardʒ] *tr* aumentare; ingrossare; (phot) ingrandire || *intr* aumentare; **to enlarge on** or **upon** dilungarsi su

enlargement [en'lardʒmənt] *s* aumento; ingrossamento; (phot) ingrandimento

enlighten [en'laɪtən] *tr* illustrare, illuminare

enlightenment [en'laɪtənmənt] *s* spiegazione, schiarimento || **Enlightenment** *s* illuminismo

enlist [en'lɪst] *tr* (*e.g., s.o.'s favor*) guadagnarsi; (*the help of a person*) ottenere; (mil) ingaggiare || *intr* (mil) ingaggiarsi, arruolarsi; **to enlist**

in (*a cause*) dare il proprio appoggio a

enlistment [ɛnˈlɪstmənt] *s* arruolamento, ingaggio

enliven [ɛnˈlaɪvən] *tr* ravvivare

enmesh [ɛnˈmɛʃ] *tr* irretire

enmi·ty [ˈɛnmɪtɪ] *s* (**-ties**) inimicizia

ennoble [ɛnˈnobəl] *tr* nobilitare

ennui [ˈɑnwi] *s* noia, tedio

enormous [ɪˈnɔrməs] *adj* enorme

enormously [ɪˈnɔrməslɪ] *adv* enormemente

enough [ɪˈnʌf] *adj* abbastanza || *s* il sufficiente || *adv* abbastanza || *interj* basta!

enounce [ɪˈnaʊns] *tr* enunciare; (*to declare*) affermare

enrage [ɛnˈredʒ] *tr* infuriare, irritare

enrapture [ɛnˈræptʃər] *tr* mandare in visibilio, estasiare

enrich [ɛnˈrɪtʃ] *tr* arricchire

enroll [ɛnˈrol] *tr* arruolare, ingaggiare; (*a student*) iscrivere || *intr* arruolarsi, ingaggiarsi; (*said of a student*) iscriversi

enrollment [ɛnˈrolmənt] *s* arruolamento, ingaggio; (*of a student*) iscrizione

en route [ɑnˈrut] *adv* in cammino; **en route to** in via per

ensconce [ɛnˈskɑns] *tr* nascondere; **to esconce oneself** rannicchiarsi, istallarsi comodamente

ensemble [ɑnˈsɑmbəl] *s* insieme *m*; (*mus*) concertato

ensign [ˈɛnsaɪn] *s* (*standard*) bandiera, insegna; (*badge*) distintivo || [ˈɛnsən] or [ˈɛnsaɪn] *s* guardamarina *m*

ensilage [ˈɛnsəlɪdʒ] *s* (*preservation of fodder*) insilamento; (*preserved fodder*) insilato

ensile [ˈɛnsaɪl] or [ɛnˈsaɪl] *tr* insilare

enslave [ɛnˈslev] *tr* fare schiavo, asservire

enslavement [ɛnˈslevmənt] *s* asservimento

ensnare [ɛnˈsnɛr] *tr* irretire

ensue [ɛnˈsu] or [ɛnˈsju] *intr* risultare; seguire, conseguire

ensuing [ɛnˈsu·ɪŋ] or [ɛnˈsju·ɪŋ] *adj* risultante, conseguente; seguente

ensure [ɛnˈʃʊr] *tr* assicurare, garantire

entail [ɛnˈtel] *s* (*law*) obbligo || *tr* provocare, comportare; (*law*) obbligare

entangle [ɛnˈtæŋgəl] *tr* intricare, imbrogliare, impigliare

entanglement [ɛnˈtæŋgəlmənt] *s* groviglio, garbuglio

enter [ˈɛntər] *tr* (*a house*) entrare in; (*in the customhouse*) dichiarare; (*to make a record of*) registrare; (*a student*) iscrivere; iscriversi a; fare membro; (*to undertake*) intraprendere; **to enter s.o.'s head** passare per la testa a qlcu || *intr* entrare; (*theat*) entrare in scena; **to enter into** entrare in; (*a contract*) impegnarsi in; **to enter on** or **upon** intraprendere

enterprise [ˈɛntər ˌpraɪz] *s* (*undertak-*

ing) impresa; (*spirit, push*) intraprendenza

enterprising [ˈɛntər ˌpraɪzɪŋ] *adj* intraprendente

entertain [ˌɛntərˈten] *tr* divertire, intrattenere; (*guests*) ospitare; (*a hope*) accarezzare; (*a proposal*) considerare || *intr* ricevere

entertainer [ˌɛntərˈtenər] *s* (*host*) ospite *mf*; (*in public*) attore *m*, cantante *mf*, fine dicitore *m*

entertaining [ˌɛntərˈtenɪŋ] *adj* divertente

entertainment [ˌɛntərˈtenmənt] *s* trattenimento, svago; spettacolo, attrazione; buon trattamento

enthrall [ɛnˈθrɔl] *tr* affascinare, incantare; (*to subjugate*) asservire, soggiogare

enthrone [ɛnˈθron] *tr* mettere sul trono, intronizzare; esaltare, innalzare

enthuse [ɛnˈθuz] or [ɛnˈθjuz] *tr* (coll) entusiasmare || *intr* (coll) entusiasmarsi

enthusiasm [ɛnˈθuzɪ ˌæzəm] or [ɛnˈθjuzɪ ˌæzəm] *s* entusiasmo

enthusiast [ɛnˈθuzɪ ˌæst] or [ɛnˈθjuzɪ ˌæst] *s* entusiasta *mf*, maniaco

enthusiastic [ɛn ˌθuzɪˈæstɪk] or [ɛn ˌθjuzɪˈæstɪk] *adj* entusiastico

entice [ɛnˈtaɪs] *tr* attrarre, provocare; tentare

enticement [ɛnˈtaɪsmənt] *s* attrazione, provocazione; tentazione

entire [ɛnˈtaɪr] *adj* intero

entirely [ɛnˈtaɪrlɪ] *adv* interamente; (*solely*) solamente

entire·ty [ɛnˈtaɪrtɪ] *s* (**-ties**) interezza; totalità *f*

entitle [ɛnˈtaɪtəl] *tr* dar diritto a; (*to give a name to*) intitolare

enti·ty [ˈɛntɪtɪ] *s* (**-ties**) (*something real; organization, institution*) ente *m*; (*existence*) entità *f*

entomb [ɛnˈtum] *tr* seppellire

entombment [ɛnˈtummənt] *s* sepoltura

entomology [ˌɛntəˈmɑlədʒɪ] *s* entomologia

entourage [ˌɑntuˈrɑʒ] *s* seguito

entrails [ˈɛntrelz] or [ˈɛntrəlz] *spl* visceri *mpl*

entrain [ɛnˈtren] *tr* far salire sul treno || *intr* imbarcarsi sul treno

entrance [ˈɛntrəns] *s* entrata, ingresso || [ɛnˈtræns] or [ɛnˈtrɑns] *tr* ipnotizzare, incantare

en'trance exam'ina'tion *s* esame *m* d'ammissione

entrancing [ɛnˈtrænsɪŋ] or [ɛnˈtrɑnsɪŋ] *adj* incantatore

entrant [ˈɛntrənt] *s* nuovo membro; (sports) concorrente *mf*

en·trap [ɛnˈtræp] *v* (*pret & pp* **-trapped**; *ger* **-trapping**) *tr* intrappolare, irretire

entreat [ɛnˈtrit] *tr* implorare

entreat·y [ɛnˈtritɪ] *s* (**-ies**) implorazione, supplica

entree [ˈɑntre] *s* entrata, ingresso; (culin) prima portata

entrench [ɛnˈtrɛntʃ] *tr* trincerare || *intr* **—to entrench on** or **upon** violare

entrust [ɛn'trʌst] *tr* affidare, confidare
en·try ['ɛntri] *s* (**-tries**) entrata; (*item*) partita, registrazione; (*in a dictionary*) lemma, esponente *m;* (sports) concorrente *mf*
entwine [ɛn'twaɪn] *tr* intrecciare ‖ *intr* intrecciarsi
enumerate [ɪ'njumə,ret] or [ɪ'numə,ret] *tr* enumerare
enunciate [ɪ'nʌnsɪ,et] or [ɪ'nʌnʃɪ,et] *tr* enunciare, staccare
envelop [ɛn'vɛləp] *tr* involgere
envelope ['ɛnvə,lop] or ['ɑnvə,lop] *s* (*for a letter*) busta; (*wrapper*) involucro
envenom [ɛn'vɛnəm] *tr* avvelenare
enviable ['ɛnvɪ·əbəl] *adj* invidiabile
envious ['ɛnvɪ·əs] *adj* invidioso
environment [ɛn'vaɪrənmənt] *s* ambiente *m;* condizioni *fpl* ambientali
environs [ɛn'vaɪrənz] *spl* dintorni *mpl,* sobborghi *mpl*
envisage [ɛn'vɪzɪdʒ] *tr* considerare, immaginare
envoi ['ɛnvɔɪ] *s* (pros) congedo
envoy ['ɛnvɔɪ] *s* inviato; (mil) parlamentare *m;* (pros) congedo
en·vy ['ɛnvi] *s* (**-vies**) invidia ‖ *v* (*pret & pp* **-vied**) *tr* invidiare
enzyme ['ɛnzaɪm] or ['ɛnzɪm] *s* enzima *m*
epaulet or **epaulette** ['ɛpə,lɛt] *s* spallina
epenthe·sis [ɛ'pɛnθɪsɪs] *s* (**-ses** [,siz]) epentesi *f*
ephemeral [ɪ'fɛmərəl] *adj* effimero
epic ['ɛpɪk] *adj* epico ‖ *s* epica
epicure ['ɛpɪ,kjur] *s* epicureo
epicurean [,ɛpɪkju'ri·ən] *adj & s* epicureo
epidemic [,ɛpɪ'dɛmɪk] *adj* epidemico ‖ *s* epidemia
epidermis [,ɛpɪ'dʌrmɪs] *s* epidermide *f*
epiglottis [,ɛpɪ'glɑtɪs] *s* epiglottide *f*
epigram ['ɛpɪ,græm] *s* epigramma *m*
epilepsy ['ɛpɪ,lɛpsi] *s* epilessia
epileptic [,ɛpɪ'lɛptɪk] *adj & s* epilettico
epilogue ['ɛpɪ,lɔg] or ['ɛpɪ,lɑg] *s* epilogo
Epiphany [ɪ'pɪfəni] *s* Epifania
Episcopalian [ɪ,pɪskə'pelɪ·ən] *adj & s* episcopaliano
episode ['ɛpɪ,sod] *s* episodio
epistle [ɪ'pɪsəl] *s* epistola
epitaph ['ɛpɪ,tæf] *s* epitaffio
epithet ['ɛpɪ,θɛt] *s* epiteto
epitome [ɪ'pɪtəmi] *s* epitome *f;* (fig) prototipo, personificazione
epitomize [ɪ'pɪtə,maɪz] *tr* epitomare; (fig) incarnare, personificare
epoch ['ɛpək] or ['ipɑk] *s* epoca
epochal ['ɛpəkəl] *adj* memorabile
ep'och-mak'ing *adj*—**to be epoch-making** fare epoca
Ep'som salt' ['ɛpsəm] *s* sale *m* inglese
equable ['ɛkwəbəl] or ['ikwəbəl] *adj* uniforme; tranquillo
equal ['ikwəl] *adj* uguale; **equal to** pari a, all'altezza di ‖ *s* uguale *m* ‖ *v* (*pret & pp* **equaled** or **equalled**); *ger* **equaling** or **equalling**) *tr* uguagliare

equali·ty [ɪ'kwɑlɪti] *s* (**-ties**) uguaglianza
equalize ['ikwə,laɪz] *tr* uguagliare; (*to make uniform*) perequare, pareggiare
equally ['ikwəli] *adv* ugualmente
equanimity [,ikwə'nɪmɪti] *s* equanimità *f*
equate [ɪ'kwet] *tr* mettere in forma di equazione; considerare uguale or uguali
equation [ɪ'kweʒən] or [ɪ'kweʃən] *s* equazione
equator [ɪ'kwetər] *s* equatore *m*
equatorial [,ikwə'tori·əl] *adj* equatoriale
equer·ry ['ɛkwəri] or [ɪ'kwɛri] *s* (**-ries**) scudiero
equestrian [ɪ'kwɛstrɪ·ən] *adj* equestre ‖ *s* cavallerizzo
equilateral [,ikwɪ'lætərəl] *adj* equilatero
equilibrium [,ikwɪ'lɪbrɪ·əm] *s* equilibrio
equinoctial [,ikwɪ'nɑkʃəl] *adj* equinoziale
equinox ['ikwɪ,nɑks] *s* equinozio
equip [ɪ'kwɪp] *v* (*pret & pp* **equipped**; *ger* **equipping**) *tr* equipaggiare; **to equip** (*e.g., a ship*) **with** munire di
equipment [ɪ'kwɪpmənt] *s* equipaggiamento; (*skill*) attitudine *f,* capacità *f*
equipoise ['ikwɪ,pɔɪz] or ['ɛkwɪ,pɔɪz] *s* equilibrio ‖ *tr* equilibrare
equitable ['ɛkwɪtəbəl] *adj* equo
equi·ty ['ɛkwɪti] *s* (**-ties**) (*fairness*) equità *f;* valore *m* al netto; (*in a corporation*) interessenza azionaria
equivalent [ɪ'kwɪvələnt] *adj* equivalente ‖ *s* equivalente *m;* (com) controvalore *m*
equivocal [ɪ'kwɪvəkəl] *adj* equivoco
equivocate [ɪ'kwɪvə,ket] *intr* giocare sulle parole, parlare in maniera equivoca
equivocation [ɪ,kwɪvə'keʃən] *s* equivocità *f;* equivoco
era ['ɪrə] or ['irə] *s* era, evo
eradicate [ɪ'rædɪ,ket] *tr* sradicare
erase [ɪ'res] *tr* cancellare
eraser [ɪ'resər] *s* gomma da cancellare; (*for blackboard*) spugna
erasure [ɪ'reʃər] or [ɪ'reʒər] *s* cancellatura; (*of a tape*) cancellazione
ere [ɛr] *prep* (lit) prima di ‖ *conj* (lit) prima che
erect [ɪ'rɛkt] *adj* dritto, eretto; (*hair*) irto ‖ *tr* (*to set in upright position*) drizzare; (*a building*) erigere, costruire; (*a machine*) montare
erection [ɪ'rɛkʃən] *s* erezione
ermine ['ʌrmɪn] *s* ermellino; (fig) carica di giudice, toga, magistratura
erode [ɪ'rod] *tr* erodere ‖ *intr* corrodersi, consumarsi
erosion [ɪ'roʒən] *s* erosione
erotic [ɪ'rɑtɪk] *adj* erotico
err [ʌr] *intr* errare; (*to be incorrect*) sbagliarsi
errand ['ɛrənd] *s* corsa, commissione; **to run an errand** fare una commissione
er'rand boy' *s* fattorino, galoppino

erratic [ɪˈrætɪk] *adj* erratico; strano, eccentrico

erra·tum [ɪˈretəm] or [ɪˈrɑtəm] *s* (**-ta** [tə]) errore *m* di stampa

erroneous [ɪˈronɪ·əs] *adj* erroneo

error [ˈɛrər] *s* errore *m*, sbaglio

erudite [ˈɛrʊ ˌdaɪt] or [ˈɛrjʊ ˌdaɪt] *adj* erudito, dotto

erudition [ˌɛrʊˈdɪʃən] or [ˌɛrjʊˈdɪʃən] *s* erudizione

erupt [ɪˈrʌpt] *intr* (*said of a volcano*) eruttare; (*said of a skin rash*) fiorire; (*said of a tooth*) spuntare; (fig) erompere

eruption [ɪˈrʌpʃən] *s* eruzione

escalate [ˈɛskə ˌlet] *tr & intr* aumentare

escalation [ˌɛskəˈleʃən] *s* aumento

escalator [ˈɛskə ˌletər] *s* scala mobile

escallop [ɛˈskæləp] *s* (*on edge of cloth*) dentellatura, festone *m*; (*mollusk*) pettine *m* ‖ *tr* cuocere in conchiglia; cuocere al forno con salsa e pane grattugiato

escapade [ˌɛskəˈped] *s* scappatella

escape [ɛsˈkep] *s* (*getaway*) fuga; (*from responsibility, duties, etc.*) scampo ‖ *tr* sottrarsi a, eludere; **to escape s.o.** scappar da qlcu; scappar di mente a qlcu ‖ *intr* scappare; sprigionarsi; **to escape from** (*a person*) sfuggire a; (*jail*) evadere da

escapee [ˌɛskəˈpi] *s* evaso

escape' lit'erature' *s* letteratura di evasione

escapement [ɛsˈkepmənt] *s* scappamento

escape' veloc'ity *s* (rok) velocità *f* di fuga

escarpment [ɛsˈkɑrpmənt] *s* scarpata

eschew [ɛsˈtʃu] *tr* evitare, rifuggire da

escort [ˈɛskɔrt] *s* scorta; (*of a woman or girl*) compagno, cavaliere *m* ‖ [ɛsˈkɔrt] *tr* scortare

escutcheon [ɛsˈkʌtʃən] *s* scudo; (*plate in front of lock on door*) bocchetta

Esk·imo [ˈɛskɪ ˌmo] *adj* eschimese ‖ *s* (**-mos** or **-mo**) eschimese *mf*

esophagus [iˈsɑfəgəs] *s* (**-gi** [ˌdʒaɪ]) esofago

espalier [ɛsˈpæljər] *s* spalliera

especial [ɛsˈpɛʃəl] *adj* speciale

espionage [ˈɛspɪ·ənɪdʒ] or [ˌɛspɪ·əˈnɑʒ] *s* spionaggio

esplanade [ˌɛspləˈned] or [ˌɛspləˈnɑd] *s* spianata, piazzale *m*

espousal [ɛsˈpauzəl] *s* sposalizio; (*of a cause*) adozione

espouse [ɛsˈpauz] *tr* sposare; (*to advocate*) abbracciare, adottare

esquire [ɛsˈkwaɪr] or [ˈɛskwaɪr] *s* scudiero ‖ **Esquire** *s* titolo di cortesia usato generalmente con persone di riguardo

essay [ˈɛse] *s* saggio

essayist [ˈɛse·ɪst] *s* saggista *mf*

essence [ˈɛsəns] *s* essenza

essential [ɛsˈɛnʃəl] *adj & s* essenziale *m*

establish [ɛsˈtæblɪʃ] *tr* stabilire

establishment [ɛsˈtæblɪʃmənt] *s* stabilimento; fondazione; **the Establishment** l'autorità costituita

estate [ɛsˈtet] *s* stato; condizione sociale; (*landed property*) tenuta; (*a*

person's possessions) patrimonio; (*left by a decedent*) massa ereditaria

esteem [ɛsˈtim] *s* stima ‖ *tr* stimare

esthete [ˈɛsθit] *s* esteta *mf*

esthetic [ɛsˈθɛtɪk] *adj* estetico ‖ **esthetics** *ssg* estetica

estimable [ˈɛstɪmǝbǝl] *adj* stimabile

estimate [ˈɛstɪ ˌmet] or [ˈɛstɪmɪt] *s* stima, valutazione; (*statement of cost of work to be done*) preventivo ‖ [ˈɛstɪ ˌmet] *tr* stimare, valutare; preventivare

estimation [ˌɛstɪˈmeʃən] *s* stima; **in my estimation** a mio parere

estimator [ˈɛstɪ ˌmetər] *s* preventivista *mf*

estrangement [ɛsˈtrendʒmənt] *s* alienazione, disaffezione

estuar·y [ˈɛstʃʊ ˌɛri] *s* (**-ies**) estuario

etch [ɛtʃ] *tr & intr* incidere all'acquaforte

etcher [ˈɛtʃər] *s* acquafortista *mf*

etching [ˈɛtʃɪŋ] *s* acquaforte *f*

eternal [ɪˈtʌrnəl] *adj* eterno

eterni·ty [ɪˈtʌrnɪti] *s* (**-ties**) eternità *f*

ether [ˈiθər] *s* etere *m*

ethereal [ɪˈθɪrɪ·əl] *adj* etereo

ethical [ˈɛθɪkəl] *adj* etico

ethics [ˈɛθɪks] *ssg* etica

Ethiopian [ˌiθɪˈopɪ·ən] *adj & s* etiope *mf*

ethnic(al) [ˈɛθnɪk(əl)] *adj* etnico

ethnography [ɛθˈnɑgrəfi] *s* etnografia

ethnology [ɛθˈnɑlədʒi] *s* etnologia

ethyl [ˈɛθɪl] *s* etile *m*

ethylene [ˈɛθɪ ˌlin] *s* etilene *m*

etiquette [ˈɛtɪ ˌkɛt] *s* etichetta

étude [eˈtjud] *s* (mus) studio

etymology [ˌɛtɪˈmɑlədʒi] *s* etimologia

ety·mon [ˈɛtɪ ˌmɑn] *s* (**-mons** or **-ma** [mə]) etimo

eucalyp·tus [ˌjukəˈlɪptəs] *s* (**-tuses** or **-ti** [taɪ]) eucalipto

Eucharist [ˈjukərɪst] *s* Eucaristia

eugenics [juˈdʒɛnɪks] *ssg* eugenetica

eulogistic [ˌjuləˈdʒɪstɪk] *adj* elogiativo

eulogize [ˈjulə ˌdʒaɪz] *tr* elogiare

eulo·gy [ˈjulədʒi] *s* (**-gies**) elogio; elogio funebre

eunuch [ˈjunək] *s* eunuco

euphemism [ˈjufɪ ˌmɪzəm] *s* eufemismo

euphemistic [ˌjufɪˈmɪstɪk] *adj* eufemistico

euphonic [juˈfɑnɪk] *adj* eufonico

eupho·ny [ˈjufəni] *s* (**-nies**) eufonia

euphoria [juˈforɪ·ə] *s* euforia

euphuism [ˈjufju ˌɪzəm] *s* eufuismo

Europe [ˈjurəp] *s* l'Europa

European [ˌjurəˈpi·ən] *adj & s* europeo

euthanasia [ˌjuθəˈneʒə] *s* eutanasia

evacuate [ɪˈvækju ˌet] *tr & intr* evacuare

evacuation [ɪ ˌvækjuˈeʃən] *s* evacuazione

evacuee [ɪˈvækju ˌi] or [ɪ ˌvækjuˈi] *s* sfollato

evade [ɪˈved] *tr* eludere ‖ *intr* evadere

evaluate [ɪˈvælju ˌet] *tr* valutare

evaluation [ɪ ˌvæljuˈeʃən] *s* valutazione

Evangel [ɪˈvændʒəl] *s* Vangelo

evangelic(al) [ˌivænˈdʒɛlɪk(əl)] or [ˌɛvənˈdʒɛlɪk(əl)] *adj* evangelico

Evangelist [ɪ'vændʒəlɪst] s evangelista m

evaporate [ɪ'væpə‚ret] tr & intr evaporare

evasion [ɪ'veʒən] s evasione; (subterfuge) scappatoia

evasive [ɪ'vesɪv] adj evasivo

eve [iv] s vigilia; **on the eve of** la vigilia di

even ['ivən] adj (smooth) piano, regolare; (number) pari; uguale, uniforme; (temperament) calmo, placido; **even with** a livello di; **to be even** mettersi in pari; **to get even** prendersi la rivincita ‖ adv anche; fino, perfino; pure; esattamente; magari; **even as** proprio mentre; **even if** anche se, quando pure; **even so** anche se così; **even though** quantunque; **even when** anche quando; **not even** neppure, nemmeno; **to break even** impattare ‖ tr spianare; **to even up** bilanciare

evening ['ivnɪŋ] adj serale ‖ s sera, serata; **all evening** tutta la sera; **every evening** tutte le sere; **in the evening** la sera

eve'ning clothes' spl vestito da sera

eve'ning gown' s vestito da sera da signora

eve'ning star' s espero

e'ven-song' s (eccl) vespro

event [ɪ'vɛnt] s avvenimento; (outcome) evenienza; (public function) manifestazione; (sports) prova; **at all events** or **in any event** in ogni caso; **in the event that** in caso che, se mai

eventful [ɪ'vɛntfəl] adj ricco di avvenimenti; movimentato

eventual [ɪ'vɛntʃʊ‚əl] adj finale

eventuali-ty [ɪ‚vɛntʃʊ'ælɪti] s (-ties) eventualità f, evenienza

eventually [ɪ'vɛntʃʊ‚əli] adv finalmente, alla fine

eventuate [ɪ'vɛntʃʊ‚et] intr risultare; accadere

ever ['ɛvər] adv (at all times) sempre; (at any time) mai; **as ever** come sempre; **as much as ever** tanto come prima; **ever since** (since that time) sin da; da allora in poi; **ever so** molto; **ever so much** moltissimo; **hardly ever** or **scarcely ever** quasi mai; **not . . . ever** non . . . mai

ev'er-glade' s terreno paludoso coperto di erbe

ev'er-green' adj & s sempreverde m & f; **evergreens** decorazione di sempreverdi

ev'er-last'ing adj eterno; incessante; (lasting indefinitely) duraturo; (wearisome) noioso ‖ s eternità f; (bot) sempreviyo

ev'er-more' adv eternamente; **for evermore** per sempre

every ['ɛvri] adj tutti i; (each) ogni, ciascuno; (being each in a series) ogni, e.g., **every three days** ogni tre giorni; **every bit** (coll) in tutto e per tutto, e.g., **every bit a man** un uomo in tutto e per tutto; **every now and then** di quando in quando; **every once in a while** una volta ogni tanto;

every other day ogni secondo giorno; **every which way** (coll) da tutte le parti; (coll) in disordine

ev'ery-bod'y pron indef ognuno, tutti

ev'ery-day' adj di ogni giorno; quotidiano; ordinario

ev'ery-man' s l'uomo qualunque ‖ pron chiunque

ev'ery-one' or **ev'ery one'** pron indef ciascuno, tutti

ev'ery-thing' pron indef tutto, ogni cosa, tutto quanto

ev'ery-where' adv dappertutto, dovunque

evict [ɪ'vɪkt] tr sfrattare,‚sloggiare

eviction [ɪ'vɪkʃən] s sfratto, sloggio

evidence ['ɛvɪdəns] s evidenza; (law) prova

evident ['ɛvɪdənt] adj evidente

evil ['ivəl] adj cattivo, malvagio ‖ s male m; disgrazia

evildoer ['ivəl‚du·ər] s malfattore m, malvagio

e'vil-do'ing s malafatta, malvagità f

e'vil eye' s iettatura, malocchio

evil-minded ['ivəl'maɪndɪd] adj malintenzionato

e'vil one', the il nemico

evince [ɪ'vɪns] tr mostrare, manifestare

evoke [ɪ'vok] tr evocare

evolution [‚ɛvə'luʃən] s evoluzione

evolve [ɪ'vɑlv] tr sviluppare ‖ intr evolversi

ewe [ju] s pecora

ewer ['ju·ər] s brocca

ex [ɛks] prep senza includere

exacerbation [ɪg‚zæsər'beʃən] s esulcerazione, esacerbazione

exacerbate [ɪg'zæsər‚bet] tr esacerbare, esulcerare

exact [ɛg'zækt] adj esatto ‖ tr esigere

exacting [ɛg'zæktɪŋ] adj esigente

exaction [ɛg'zækʃən] s esazione

exactly [ɛg'zæktli] adv esattamente; (sharp, on the dot) in punto

exactness [ɛg'zæktnɪs] s esattezza

exaggerate [ɛg'zædʒə‚ret] tr esagerare

exalt [ɛg'zɔlt] tr elevare, esaltare

exam [ɛg'zæm] s (coll) esame m

examination [ɛg‚zæmɪ'neʃən] s esame m; **to take an examination** sostenere un esame

examine [ɛg'zæmɪn] tr esaminare

examiner [ɛg'zæmɪnər] s esaminatore m

example [ɛg'zæmpəl] or [ɛg'zɑmpəl] s esempio; (precedent) precedente m; (of mathematics) problema m; **for example** per esempio

exasperate [ɛg'zæspə‚ret] tr esasperare

excavate ['ɛkskə‚vet] tr scavare

exceed [ɛk'sid] tr eccedere

exceedingly [ɛk'sidɪŋli] adv estremamente, sommamente

ex-cel [ɛk'sɛl] v (pret & pp -celled; ger -celling) tr sorpassare ‖ intr eccellere

excellence ['ɛksələns] s eccellenza

excellen-cy ['ɛksələnsi] s (-cies) eccellenza; **Your Excellency** Sua Eccellenza

excelsior [ɛk'sɛlsɪ·ər] s trucioli mpl per imballaggio

except [ɛk'sɛpt] prep eccetto; **except**

for tranne, ad eccezione di; **except that** eccetto che || *tr* eccettuare

exception [ɛk'sɛpʃən] *s* eccezione; **to take exception** obiettare; scandalizzarsi; **with the exception of** a esclusione di, eccetto

exceptional [ɛk'sɛpʃənəl] *adj* eccezionale

excerpt ['ɛksʌrpt] or [ɛk'sʌrpt] *s* brano, selezione || [ɛk'sʌrpt] *tr* scegliere, selezionare

excess ['ɛksɛs] or [ɛk'sɛs] *adj* eccedente || [ɛk'sɛs] *s* (*amount or degree by which one thing exceeds another*) eccedente *m*, eccedenza; (*excessive amount; immoderate indulgence*); **in excess of** più di

ex′cess bag′gage *s* bagaglio eccedente

ex′cess fare′ *s* (rr) supplemento

excessive [ɛk'sɛsɪv] *adj* eccessivo

ex′cess-prof′its tax′ *s* tassa sui soprapprofitti

exchange [ɛks'tʃendʒ] *s* scambio; (*place for buying and selling*) borsa; (*transactions in the currencies of two different countries*) cambio; (telp) centrale *f*, centralino; **in exchange for** in cambio di || *tr* scambiare, scambiarsi; **to exchange blows** venire alle mani; **to exchange greetings** salutarsi

exchequer [ɛks'tʃɛkər] or ['ɛkstʃɛkər] *s* erario, tesoro

ex′cise tax′ [ɛk'saɪz] or ['ɛksaɪz] *s* imposta sul consumo

excitable [ɛk'saɪtəbəl] *adj* eccitabile

excite [ɛk'saɪt] *tr* eccitare

excitement [ɛk'saɪtmənt] *s* eccitazione

exciting [ɛk'saɪtɪŋ] *adj* emozionante; (*stimulating*) eccitante

exclaim [ɛks'klem] *tr & intr* esclamare

exclamation [ˌɛksklə'meʃən] *s* esclamazione

exclama′tion mark′ or **point′** *s* punto esclamativo

exclude [ɛks'klud] *tr* escludere

excluding [ɛks'kludɪŋ] *prep* a esclusione di, senza contare

exclusion [ɛks'kluʒən] *s* esclusione; **to the exclusion of** tranne, salvo

exclusive [ɛks'klusɪv] *adj* esclusivo; **exclusive of** escluso, senza contare || *s* (journ) esclusiva

excommunicate [ˌɛkskə'mjunɪˌket] *tr* scomunicare

excommunication [ˌɛkskə,mjunɪ'keʃən] *s* scomunica

excoriate [ɛks'korɪ,et] *tr* criticare aspramente, vituperare

excrement ['ɛkskrəmənt] *s* escremento

excruciating [ɛks'kruʃɪ,etɪŋ] *adj* (*e.g., pleasure*) estremo; (*e.g., pain*) atroce, lancinante, straziante

exculpate ['ɛkskʌl,pet] or [ɛks'kʌlpet] *tr* scolpare, scagionare

excursion [ɛks'kʌrʒən] or [ɛks'kʌrʃən] *s* escursione, gita

excursionist [ɛks'kʌrʒənɪst] or [ɛks-'kʌrʃənɪst] *s* escursionista *m*

excusable [ɛks'kjuzəbəl] *adj* scusabile

excuse [ɛks'kjus] *s* scusa || [ɛks'kjuz] *tr* scusare; esentare; (*a debt*) rimettere

execute ['ɛksɪ,kjut] *tr* (*to carry out; to produce*) eseguire; (*to put to death*) giustiziare; (law) rendere esecutorio

execution [ˌɛksɪ'kjuʃən] *s* esecuzione; (*e.g., of a criminal*) esecuzione capitale

executioner [ˌɛksɪ'kjuʃənər] *s* giustiziere *m*, boia *m*, carnefice *m*

executive [ɛg'zɛkjətɪv] *adj* esecutivo || *s* esecutivo; (*of a school, business, etc.*) dirigente *mf*

Exec′utive Man′sion *s* palazzo del governatore; residenza del capo del governo statunitense

executor [ɛg'zɛkjətər] *s* (law) esecutore testamentario

executrix [ɛg'zɛkjətrɪks] *s* (law) esecutrice testamentaria

exemplary [ɛg'zɛmplərɪ] or ['ɛgzəm-,plɛrɪ] *adj* esemplare

exempli-fy [ɛg'zɛmplɪ,faɪ] *v* (*pret & pp* -**fied**) *tr* esemplificare

exempt [ɛg'zɛmpt] *adj* esente || *tr* esimere, esentare

exemption [ɛg'zɛmpʃən] *s* esenzione

exercise ['ɛksər,saɪz] *s* esercizio; cerimonia; **to take exercise** fare del moto || *tr* esercitare; (*care*) usare; (*to worry*) preoccupare || *intr* esercitarsi

exert [ɛg'zʌrt] *tr* (*e.g., power*) esercitare; **to exert oneself** sforzarsi

exertion [ɛg'zʌrʃən] *s* sforzo, tentativo; (*active use*) uso, esercizio

exhalation [ˌɛks-hə'leʃən] *s* (*of gas, vapors*) esalazione; (*of air from lungs*) espirazione

exhale [ɛks'hel] or [ɛg'zel] *tr* (*gases, vapors, etc.*) esalare; (*air from lungs*) espirare || *intr* esalare; espirare

exhaust [ɛg'zɔst] *s* scarico, scappamento; tubo di scarico or scappamento || *tr* (*to wear out*) spossare, finire; (*to use up*) esaurire, dar fondo a; vuotare

exhaust′ fan′ *s* aspiratore *m*

exhaustion [ɛg'zɔstʃən] *s* esaurimento; estenuazione; (sports) cotta

exhaustive [ɛg'zɔstɪv] *adj* esauriente

exhaust′ man′ifold *s* collettore *m* di scarico

exhaust′ pipe′ *s* tubo di scarico

exhaust′ valve′ *s* valvola di scappamento

exhibit [ɛg'zɪbɪt] *s* esposizione; (law) documento in giudizio || *tr* esibire

exhibition [ˌɛksɪ'brɪʃən] *s* esibizione

exhibitor [ɛg'zɪbɪtər] *s* espositore *m*

exhilarating [ɛg'zɪlə,retɪŋ] *adj* esilarante

exhort [ɛg'zɔrt] *tr* esortare

exhume [ɛks'hjum] or [ɛg'zjum] *tr* esumare, dissotterrare

exigen-cy ['ɛksɪdʒənsɪ] *s* (-**cies**) esigenza

exigent ['ɛksɪdʒənt] *adj* esigente

exile ['ɛgzaɪl] or ['ɛksaɪl] *s* esilio; (*person*) esule *mf* || *tr* esiliare

exist [ɛg'zɪst] *intr* esistere

existence [ɛg'zɪstəns] *s* esistenza

existing [ɛg'zɪstɪŋ] *adj* esistente

exit ['ɛgzɪt] or ['ɛksɪt] *s* uscita || *intr* uscire

exodus ['eksədəs] s esodo
exonerate [eg'zɑnə‚ret] tr (from an obligation) esonerare; (from blame) scagionare
exorbitant [eg'zɔrbɪtənt] adj esorbitante
exorcise ['eksɔr‚saɪz] tr esorcizzare
exotic [eg'zɑtɪk] adj esotico
expand [eks'pænd] tr (a metal) dilatare; (gas) espandere; (to enlarge) allargare, ampliare; (to unfold) spiegare; (math) svolgere, sviluppare || intr dilatarsi; espandersi; allargarsi, ampliarsi; spiegarsi, estendersi
expanse [eks'pæns] s vastità f
expansion [eks'pænʃən] s espansione
expansive [eks'pænsɪv] adj espansivo
expatiate [eks'peʃɪ‚et] intr dilungarsi
expatriate [eks'petrɪ‚ɪt] adj esiliato || s esule mf || [eks'petri‚et] tr esiliare; **to expatriate oneself** espatriare
expect [eks'pekt] tr aspettare, attendere; (coll) credere, supporre; **to expect it** aspettarselo, aspettarsela
expectan·cy [eks'pektənsi] s (-cies) aspettativa, aspettazione
expect'ant moth'er [eks'pektənt] s futura madre
expectation [‚ekspek'teʃən] s aspettativa
expectorate [eks'pektə‚ret] tr & intr espettorare
expedien·cy [eks'pidɪ‚ənsi] s (-cies) industria, ingegno; opportunismo, vantaggio personale
expedient [eks'pidɪ‚ənt] adj conveniente; vantaggioso; (acting with self-interest) opportunista || s espediente m
expedite ['ekspɪ‚daɪt] tr sbrigare, accelerare; (a document) dar corso a
expedition [‚ekspɪ'dɪʃən] s spedizione; (speed) celerità f
expeditionary [‚ekspɪ'dɪʃən‚eri] adj (e.g., corps) di spedizione
expeditious [‚ekspɪ'dɪʃəs] adj spicciativo, spiccio
ex·pel [eks'pel] v (pret & pp -pelled; ger -pelling) tr espellere, scacciare
expend [eks'pend] tr spendere, consumare
expendable [eks'pendəbəl] adj spendibile; da buttarsi via; (mil) da sacrificare
expenditure [eks'pendɪtʃər] s spesa
expense [eks'pens] s spesa; **at the expense of** al costo di; **expenses** spese fpl; **to meet expenses** far fronte alle spese
expense' account' s conto delle spese risarcibili
expensive [eks'pensɪv] adj caro, costoso
experience [eks'pɪrɪ‚əns] s esperienza || tr sperimentare, provare
experienced [eks'pɪrɪ‚ənst] adj esperto, sperimentato
experiment [eks'perɪmənt] s esperimento || [eks'peri‚ment] intr sperimentare
expert ['ekspərt] adj & s esperto
expertise [‚ekspər'tiz] s maestria

expiate ['ekspɪ‚et] tr espiare
expiation [‚ekspɪ'eʃən] s espiazione
expire [eks'paɪr] tr espirare || intr (to breathe out) espirare; (said of a contract) scadere; (to die) morire
explain [eks'plen] tr spiegare; **to explain away** giustificare; dar ragione di || intr spiegare, spiegarsi
explainable [eks'plenəbəl] adj spiegabile
explanation [‚eksplə'neʃən] s spiegazione, delucidazione
explanatory [eks'plænə‚tori] adj esplicativo
explicit [eks'plɪsɪt] adj esplicito
explode [eks'plod] tr far scoppiare; (a theory) smontare || intr scoppiare
exploit [eks'plɔɪt] or ['eksplɔɪt] s impresa, prodezza || [eks'plɔɪt] tr utilizzare, sfruttare
exploitation [‚eksplɔɪ'teʃən] s utilizzazione, sfruttamento
exploration [‚eksplə'reʃən] s esplorazione
explore [eks'plor] tr esplorare
explorer [eks'plorər] s esploratore m
explosion [eks'ploʒən] s esplosione, scoppio; (of a theory) confutazione
explosive [eks'plosɪv] adj & s esplosivo
exponent [eks'ponənt] s esponente m
export ['eksport] adj di esportazione || s esportazione, articolo di esportazione || [eks'port] or ['eksport] tr & intr esportare
exportation [‚ekspor'teʃən] s esportazione
exporter ['eksportər] or [eks'portər] s esportatore m
expose [eks'poz] tr esporre; (to unmask) smascherare
exposé [‚ekspo'ze] s rivelazione scandalosa, smascheramento
exposition [‚ekspə'zɪʃən] s esposizione; interpretazione, commento
expostulate [eks'pɑstʃə‚let] intr protestare; **to expostulate with** lagnarsi con
exposure [eks'poʒər] s (disclosure) rivelazione; (situation with regard to sunlight) esposizione; (phot) esposizione
expo'sure me'ter s (phot) fotometro, esposimetro
expound [eks'paund] tr esporre
express [eks'pres] adj espresso || s (rr) celere m, rapido, direttissimo; **by express** per espresso, a grande velocità || adv per espresso, a grande velocità || tr esprimere; mandare per espresso; (to squeeze out) spremere; **to express oneself** esprimersi
ex'press com'pany s servizio corriere
expression [eks'preʃən] s espressione
expressive [eks'presɪv] adj espressivo
expressly [eks'presli] adv espressamente
express'man s (-men) fattorino di servizio corriere
express'way' s autostrada
expropriate [eks'propri‚et] tr espropriare
expulsion [eks'pʌlʃən] s espulsione

expunge [ɛks'pʌndʒ] tr espungere

expurgate ['ɛkspər ‚get] tr espurgare

exquisite ['ɛkskwɪzɪt] or [ɛks'kwɪzɪt] adj squisito; intenso

ex'serv'ice-man' s (-men') ex combattente m

extant ['ɛkstənt] or [ɛks'tænt] adj ancora esistente

extemporaneous [ɛks ‚tɛmpə'renɪ·əs] adj estemporaneo; (made for the occasion) improvvisato

extempore [ɛks'tɛmpəri] adj improvvisato || adv senza preparazione

extemporize [ɛks'tɛmpə ‚raɪz] tr & intr improvvisare

extend [ɛks'tɛnd] tr allungare; estendere; (e.g., aid) offrire; (payment of a debt) dilazionare || intr estendersi

extended [ɛks'tɛndɪd] adj esteso; prolungato

extension [ɛks'tɛnʃən] s estensione; prolungamento; (com) proroga; (telp) derivazione

exten'sion lad'der s scala porta, scala a prolunga

exten'sion ta'ble s tavola allungabile

exten'sion tel'ephone' s telefono interno

extensive [ɛks'tɛnsɪv] adj (wide) vasto; (lengthy) lungo; (characterized by extention) estensivo

extent [ɛks'tɛnt] s estensione; to a certain extent fino a un certo punto; to a great extent in larga misura; to the full extent all'estremo limite

extenuate [ɛks'tɛnju ‚et] tr (to make seem less serious) attenuare; (to underrate) sottovalutare

exterior [ɛks'tɪrɪ·ər] adj & s esteriore m

exterminate [ɛks'tʌrmɪ ‚net] tr sterminare

external [ɛks'tʌrnəl] adj esterno || externals spl esteriorità f, di fuori m

extinct [ɛks'tɪŋkt] adj estinto

extinction [ɛks'tɪŋkʃən] s estinzione

extinguish [ɛks'tɪŋgwɪʃ] tr estinguere

extinguisher [ɛks'tɪŋgwɪʃər] s estintore m

extirpate ['ɛkstər ‚pɛt] or [ɛks'tʌrpɛt] tr estirpare

ex·tol [ɛks'tol] or [ɛks'tal] v (pret & pp -tolled) ger -tolling) tr inneggiare

extort [ɛks'tɔrt] tr estorcere

extortion [ɛks'tɔrʃən] s estorsione

extra ['ɛkstrə] adj extra; (spare) di scorta || s (of a newspaper) edizione straordinaria; (something additional) soprappiù m; (theat) figurante mf || adv straordinariamente

ex'tra charge' s supplemento

extract ['ɛkstrækt] s estratto || [ɛks-'trækt] tr (to pull out) estrarre; (to take from a book) scegliere, selezionare

extraction [ɛks'trækʃən] s estrazione

extracurricular [‚ɛkstrəkə'rɪkjələr] adj fuori del programma normale

extradition [‚ɛkstrə'dɪʃən] s estradizione

ex'tra-dry' adj molto secco, brut

ex'tra fare' s supplemento al biglietto

ex'tra·mar'ital adj extraconiugale

extramural [‚ɛkstrə'mjurəl] adj fuori della scuola, interscolastico; fuori delle mura

extraneous [ɛks'trenɪ·əs] adj estraneo

extraordinary [‚ɛkstrə'ɔrdɪ ‚nɛri] or [ɛks'trɔrdɪ ‚nɛri] adj straordinario

extrapolate [ɛks'træpə ‚let] tr & intr estrapolare

extrasensory [‚ɛkstrə'sɛnsəri] adj extrasensoriale

extravagance [ɛks'trævəgəns] s prodigalità f; (wildness, folly) stravaganza

extravagant [ɛks'trævəgənt] adj prodigo; (wild, foolish) stravagante

extreme [ɛks'trim] adj & s estremo; in the extreme in massimo grado; to go to extremes andare agli estremi

extremely [ɛks'trimli] adv estremamente, in sommo grado

extreme' unc'tion s Estrema Unzione

extremist [ɛks'trimɪst] adj & s estremista mf

extremi·ty [ɛks'trɛmɪti] s (-ties) estremità f; (great want) estrema necessità; extremities estremi mpl; (hands and feet) estremità fpl

extricate ['ɛkstrɪ ‚ket] tr districare

extrinsic [ɛks'trɪnsɪk] adj estrinseco

extrovert ['ɛkstrə ‚vʌrt] s estroverso

extrude [ɛks'trud] tr estrudere || intr protrudere

exuberant [ɛg'zubərənt] or [ɛg'zjubərənt] adj esuberante

exude [ɛg'zud] or [ɛk'sud] tr & intr trasudare, stillare

exult [ɛg'zʌlt] intr esultare, tripudiare

exultant [ɛg'zʌltənt] adj esultante

eye [aɪ] s occhio; (of hook and eye) occhiello; to catch one's eye attirare l'attenzione di qlcu; to feast one's eyes on deliziarsi la vista con; to lay eyes on riuscire a vedere; to make eyes at fare gli occhi dolci a; to roll one's eyes stralunare gli occhi; to see eye to eye andare perfettamente d'accordo; to shut one's eyes to chiudere un occhio a; far finta di non vedere; without batting an eye senza batter ciglio || v (pret & pp eyed; ger eying or eyeing) tr occhieggiare; to eye up and down guardare da capo a piedi

eye'ball' s globo oculare

eye'bolt' s bullone m ad anello

eye'brow' s sopracciglio; to raise one's eyebrows inarcare le sopracciglia

eye'cup' s occhiera

eye'drop'per s contagocce m

eyeful ['aɪ ‚ful] s vista, colpo d'occhio; (coll) bellezza

eye'glass' s (of optical instrument) lente f, oculare m; (eyecup) occhiera; eyeglasses occhiali mpl

eye'lash' s ciglio

eyelet ['aɪlɪt] s occhiello, maglietta, asola; (hole to look through) feritoia

eye'lid' s palpebra

eye' o'pener ['opənər] s affare m che apre gli occhi; (coll) bicchierino bevuto di mattina presto

eye'piece' s oculare m
eye'shade' s visiera
eye' shad'ow s rimmel m
eye'shot' s—within eyeshot a portata di vista
eye'sight' s vista; (range) capacità visiva
eye' sock'et s occhiaia, orbita
eye'sore' s pugno in un occhio

eye'strain' s vista affaticata
eye'-test chart' s tabella optometrica
eye'tooth' s (-teeth) dente canino; to cut one's eyeteeth (coll) fare esperienza; to give one's eyeteeth for (coll) dare un occhio della testa per
eye'wash' s (flattery) burro, lusinga; (pharm) collirio; (slang) balla
eye' wit'ness s testimone m oculare

F

F, f [εf] s sesta lettera dell'alfabeto inglese
fable ['febəl] s favola
fabric ['fæbrɪk] s stoffa, tessuto; fabbrica, struttura
fabricate ['fæbrɪ‚ket] tr fabbricare
fabrication [‚fæbrɪ'keʃən] s fabbricazione; falsificazione, invenzione
fabulous ['fæbjələs] adj favoloso
façade [fə'sad] s facciata
face [fes] s volto, viso, faccia; (surface) superficie f; (of coin) diritto; (of precious stone) faccetta; (of watch) mostra; (grimace) smorfia; (of building) facciata; (typ) occhio; in the face of di fronte a; to have a long face fare il muso lungo; to keep a straight face contenere le risa; to show one's face farsi vedere || tr far fronte a, frontegggiare; (a wall) ricoprire; (a suit) foderare; facing di fronte a || intr—to face about voltarsi, fare dietro front; to face on dare a; to face up to guardare in faccia
face' card' s figura
face' lift'ing s plastica facciale
face' pow'der s cipria
facet ['fæsɪt] s faccetta; (fig) faccia
facetious [fə'siʃəs] adj faceto
face' val'ue s valore m facciale
facial ['feʃəl] adj facciale || s massaggio facciale
fa'cial tis'sue s velina detergente
facilitate [fə'sɪlɪ‚tet] tr facilitare
facili-ty [fə'sɪlɪti] s (-ties) facilità f; facilities (installations) attrezzature fpl; (for transportation) mezzi mpl; (services) servizi mpl
facing ['fesɪŋ] s rivestimento
facsimile [fæk'sɪmɪli] s facsimile m
fact [fækt] s fatto; in fact in realtà; the fact is that il fatto si è che
faction ['fækʃən] s fazione; discordia
factional ['fækʃənəl] adj fazioso; (partisan) partigiano
factionalism ['fækʃənə‚lɪzəm] s partigianeria; parzialità f
factor ['fæktər] s fattore m || tr scomporre in fattori
facto-ry ['fæktəri] s (-ries) fabbrica
factual ['fæktʃʊ‚əl] adj effettivo, reale
facul-ty ['fækəlti] s (-ties) facoltà f
fad [fæd] s moda passeggera
fade [fed] tr stingere || intr (said of colors) stingersi, sbiadire; (said of

sounds, sight, radio signals, memory, etc.) svanire, affievolirsi; (said of beauty) sfiorire
fade'-out' s affievolimento, affievolirsi m; (mov) chiusura in dissolvenza; (rad, telv) evanescenza
fading ['fedɪŋ] s affievolimento; (mov) dissolvenza; (rad, telv) evanescenza
fag [fæg] s schiavo del lavoro; (coll) sigaretta || tr—to fag out stancare
fagot ['fægət] s fascina, fastello
fail [fel] s—without fail senza meno || tr mancare (with dat); (a student) riprovare; (an examination) farsi bocciare in || intr fallire, venire a meno; (said of a student) farsi riprovare; (said of a motor) rompersi, fermarsi; (com) cadere in fallimento; to fail to mancare di
failure ['feljər] s insuccesso; insufficienza; (student) bocciato; (com) fallimento
faint [fent] adj debole; to feel faint sentirsi mancare || s svenimento || intr svenire
faint-hearted ['fent'hartɪd] adj codardo, timido
fair [fɛr] adj giusto, onesto; (moderately large) discreto; (even) liscio; (civil) gentile; (hair) biondo; (complexion) chiaro; (sky, weather) sereno || s (exhibition) fiera; (carnival) sagra || adv direttamente; to play fair agire onestamente
fair'ground' s terreno dell'esposizione, campo della fiera
fairly ['fɛrli] adv giustamente, imparzialmente; discretamente, abbastanza; completamente
fair-minded ['fɛr'maɪndɪd] adj equanime, equo, giusto
fairness ['fɛrnɪs] s giustizia, imparzialità f; bellezza; (of complexion) bianchezza
fair' play' s comportamento leale
fair' sex' s bel sesso
fair'-weath'er adj—a fair-weather friend un amico del tempo felice
fair-y ['fɛri] adj fatato || s (-ies) fata; (slang) finocchio
fair'y god'mother's buona fata
fair'y-land' s terra delle fate
fair'y tale' s fantasia, racconto delle fate
faith [feθ] s fede f; to break faith with venir meno alla parola data a; to keep faith with tener fede alla parola

data a; **to pin one's faith on** porre tutte le proprie speranze su; **upon my faith!** in fede mia!

faithful ['feθfəl] *adj* fedele || **the faithful** i fedeli

faithless ['feθlɪs] *adj* infedele, sleale

fake [fek] *adj* falso, finto || *s* contraffazione; (*person*) imbroglione *m* || *tr &* *intr* contraffare, falsificare

faker ['fekər] *s* (coll) imbroglione *m*

falcon ['fɔkən] or ['fɔlkən] *s* falcone *m*

falconer ['fɔkənər] or ['fɔlkənər] *s* falconiere *m*

falconry ['fɔkənrɪ] or ['fɔlkənrɪ] *s* falconeria

fall [fɔl] *adj* autunnale || *s* caduta; (*of water*) cataratta, cascata; (*of prices*) ribasso; (*autumn*) autunno; **falls** cataratta, cascate *fpl* || *v* (*pret* **fell** [fɛl]; *pp* **fallen** ['fɔlən]) *intr* cadere; discendere; **to fall apart** farsi a pezzi; **to fall back** (mil) ripiegare; **to fall behind** rimanere indietro; **to fall down** cadere; stramazzare; **to fall due** scadere; **to fall flat** stramazzare; essere un insuccesso; **to fall for** (slang) lasciarsi abbindolare da; (slang) innamorarsi di; **to fall in** (*said of a building*) crollare; (mil) allinearsi; **to fall in with** imbattersi in; mettersi d'accordo con; **to fall off** ritirarsi; diminuire; **to fall out** accadere; essere in disaccordo; (mil) rompere i ranghi; **to fall out of** cadere da; **to fall out with** inimicarsi con; **to fall over** cadere; (coll) adulare; **to fall through** fallire; **to fall to** cominciare; (coll) cominciare a mangiare; (*said, e.g., of an inheritance*) ricadere su; **to fall under** rientrare in

fallacious [fə'leʃəs] *adj* fallace

falla·cy ['fæləsɪ] *s* (-cies) fallacia

fall' guy' *s* (slang) testa di turco

fallible ['fælɪbəl] *adj* fallibile

fall'ing star' *s* stella cadente

fall'out' *s* pulviscolo radioattivo

fall'out shel'ter *s* rifugio antiatomico

fallow ['fælo] *adj* incolto; **to lie fallow** rimanere incolto || *s* maggese *m* || *tr* maggesare

false [fɔls] *adj* falso; (*hair, teeth, etc.*) posticcio, finto || *adv* falsamente; **to play false** tradire

false' bot'tom *s* doppio fondo

false' col'ors *spl* apparenze mentite

false' face' *s* maschera; (*ugly false face*) mascherone *m*

false'-heart'ed ['fɔls'hɑrtɪd] *adj* perfido

falsehood ['fɔls·hʊd] *s* falsità *f*, falso

false' pretens'es *spl* falso, impostura; **under false pretenses** allegando ragioni false

falset·to [fɔl'sɛto] *s* (-tos) (*voice*) falsetto; (*person*) cantante *m* in falsetto

falsi·fy ['fɔlsɪ ,faɪ] *v* (*pret & pp* **-fied**) *tr* falsificare; (*to disprove*) smentire || *intr* mentire

falsi·ty ['fɔlsɪtɪ] *s* (-ties) falsità *f*

falter ['fɔltər] *s* vacillamento; (*in*

speech) balbettio || *intr* vacillare; balbettare

fame [fem] *s* fama

famed [femd] *adj* famoso

familiar [fə'mɪljər] *adj* familiare; intimo; **to be familiar with** (*people*) aver pratica con; (*things*) aver pratica di

familiari·ty [fə ,mɪlɪ'ærɪtɪ] *s* (-ties) familiarità *f*, dimestichezza

familiarize [fə'mɪljə ,raɪz] *tr* far conoscere

fami·ly ['fæmɪlɪ] *adj* familiare; **in the family way** (coll) in altro stato || *s* (-lies) famiglia

fam'ily man' *s* (**men'**) padre *m* di famiglia

fam'ily name' *s* cognome *m*

fam'ily tree' *s* albero genealogico

famine ['fæmɪn] *s* carestia

famished ['fæmɪʃt] *adj* famelico; **to be famished** avere una fame da lupo

famous ['feməs] *adj* famoso; (coll) eccellente

fan [fæn] *s* ventaglio; (elec) ventilatore *m*; (coll) tifoso, patito || *v* (*pret & pp* **fanned**; *ger* **fanning**) *tr* sventagliare; (*to winnow*) vagliare; (*fire, passions*) attizzare || *intr* sventagliarsi; **to fan out** (*said of a road*) diramarsi a ventaglio

fanatic [fə'nætɪk] *adj & s* fanatico

fanatical [fə'nætɪkəl] *adj* fanatico

fanaticism [fə'nætɪ ,sɪzm] *s* fanatismo

fan' belt' *s* (aut) cinghia del ventilatore

fancied ['fænsɪd] *adj* immaginario

fancier ['fænsɪ·ər] *s* maniaco, tifoso; (*of animals*) conoscitore *m*, allevatore *m*

fanciful ['fænsɪfəl] *adj* fantasioso, estroso; immaginario

fan·cy ['fænsɪ] *adj* (-cier; -ciest) immaginario; immaginativo; ornamentale; di lusso; fantasioso, estroso || *s* fantasia; (*whim*) grillo, estro; **to take a fancy to** prendere una passione per || *v* (*pret & pp* **-cied**) *tr* immaginare

fan'cy ball' *s* ballo in costume

fan'cy dress' *s* costume *m*

fan'cy foods' *spl* cibi *mpl* di lusso

fan'cy-free' *adj* libero dai lacci dell'amore

fan'cy skat'ing *s* pattinaggio artistico

fan'cy·work' *s* (sew) ricamo ornamentale

fanfare ['fænfer] *s* fanfara

fang [fæŋ] *s* zanna; (*of reptile*) dente velenoso

fan'light' *s* lunetta

fantastic(al) [fæn'tæstɪk(əl)] *adj* fantastico

fanta·sy ['fæntəzɪ] or ['fæntəsɪ] *s* (-sies) fantasia

far [fɑr] *adj* distante; **on the far side of** dall'altra parte di || *adv* lontano; **as far as** fino a; **as far as I am concerned** per quanto mi riguardi; **as far as I know** per quanto io sappia; **by far** di gran lunga; **far and near** in lungo e in largo; **far away** molto lontano; **far be it from me** Dio me ne scampi e liberi; **far better** molto meglio; molto migliore; **far different** molto differente; **far from** lontano da; **far from it** tutto al contrario; **far into** fino al fondo di; **far into the night** fino a tarda ora; **far more** molto più; **far off** lontanissimo; **how far** quanto lontano; **how far is it?** a che distanza è da qui?; **in so far as** in quanto; **thus far** sinora; **to go far towards** contribuire molto a

faraway ['fɑrəˌwe] adj distante, lontano; distratto

farce [fɑrs] s farsa

farcical ['fɑrsɪkəl] adj farsesco

fare [fer] s prezzo della corsa; passeggero; (food) vitto || intr andare, e.g., **how did you fare?** come Le è andata?

Far' East' s Estremo Oriente

fare'well' s congedo, commiato; **to bid farewell to** or **to take farewell of** prender commiato da || interj addio!

far-fetched ['fɑr'fɛt/t] adj peregrino, campato in aria

far-flung ['fɑr'flʌŋ] adj ampio; d'ampia distribuzione

farm [fɑrm] adj agricolo || s fattoria, tenuta || tr (land) coltivare || intr fare l'agricoltore or l'allevatore

farmer ['fɑrmər] s agricoltore m, contadino

farm' hand' s bracciante m

farm'house' s casa colonica, masseria

farming ['fɑrmɪŋ] s agricoltura, coltivazione

farm'yard' s aia

far'-off' adj lontano

far-reaching ['fɑr'rit/ɪŋ] adj di grande portata

far-sighted ['fɑr'saɪtɪd] adj lungimirante; perspicace; presbite

farther ['fɑrðər] adj più lontano; addizionale || adv più lontano, più in là; inoltre; **farther on** più oltre

farthest ['fɑrðɪst] adj (il) più lontano; ultimo || adv al massimo

farthing ['fɑrðɪŋ] s (Brit) quarto di centesimo

Far' West' s (U.S.A.) lontano Occidente

fascinate ['fæsɪˌnet] tr affascinare

fascinating ['fæsɪˌnetɪŋ] adj incantatore, affascinante

fascism ['fæsɪzəm] s fascismo

fascist ['fæsɪst] adj & s fascista mf

fashion ['fæʃən] s voga, moda; foggia, maniera; alta società; **after a fashion** in certo modo; **in fashion** di moda; **out of fashion** fuori moda; **to go out of fashion** passare di moda || tr fare, foggiare

fashionable ['fæʃənəbəl] adj elegante, alla moda

fash'ion design'ing s alta moda

fash'ion plate' s figurino

fash'ion show' s sfilata di moda

fast [fæst] or [fɑst] adj veloce; (clock) che corre, in anticipo; dissoluto; ben legato; (color) solido; (friend) fedele || s digiuno; **to break fast** rompere il digiuno || adv rapidamente; forte-mente; (asleep) profondamente; **to hold fast** tenersi saldo; **to live fast**

condurre una vita dissoluta || intr digiunare, fare vigilia

fast' day'_s giorno di magro

fasten ['fæsən] or ['fɑsən] tr fissare; attaccare; (a door) sbarrare; (a nick-name; blows) affibbiare; (a dress) allacciarsi || intr attaccarsi

fastener ['fæsənər] or ['fɑsənər] s legaccio, laccio; (snap, clasp) fermaglio; (for papers) fermacarte m

fastidious [fæs'tɪdɪ·əs] adj schizzinoso; meticoloso

fasting ['fæstɪŋ] or ['fɑstɪŋ] s digiuno

fat [fæt] adj (**fatter; fattest**) grasso; (productive) forte, ricco, pingue; **to get fat** ingrassare || s grasso, unto; (of pork) sugna

fatal ['fetəl] adj fatale

fatalism ['fetə,lɪzəm] s fatalismo

fatalist ['fetəlɪst] s fatalista mf

fatal·i·ty [fə'tælɪti] s (-ties) (in an accident) morte f; accidente m mortale; fatalità f

fate [fet] s fato; **the Fates** le Parche || tr predestinare

fated ['fetɪd] adj destinato

fateful ['fetfəl] adj fatidico, fatale

fat'head' s (coll) zuccone m

father ['fɑðər] s padre m; (male ancestor) antenato || tr procreare; creare; assumere la paternità di

fatherhood ['fɑðər,hud] s paternità f

fa'ther-in-law' s (**fathers-in-law**) suocero

fa'ther-land' s patria

fatherless ['fɑðərlɪs] adj orfano di padre; senza padre

fatherly ['fɑðərli] adj paterno

Fa'ther's Day' s festa del papà

Fa'ther Time' s il Tempo

fathom ['fæðəm] s braccio || tr sondare

fathomless ['fæðəmlɪs] adj senza fondo; imponderabile

fatigue [fə'tig] s fatica, strapazzo; (mil) comandata || tr stancare, affaticare

fatigue' clothes' spl (mil) tenuta di servizio, tenuta di fatica

fatten ['fætən] tr & intr ingrassare

fat·ty ['fæti] adj (**-tier; -tiest**) grasso; (pathol) adiposo || s (**-ties**) (coll) tombolo

fatuous ['fæt/u·əs] adj fatuo

faucet ['fɔsɪt] s rubinetto

fault [fɔlt] s (misdeed, blame) colpa; (defect) difetto, magagna; (geol) faglia; (sports) fallo; **it's your fault** è colpa Sua; **to a fault** all'eccesso; **to find fault with** trovare a ridire sul conto di

fault'find'er s ipercritico, criticone m

fault'find'ing adj criticone || s ipercritica

faultless ['fɔltlɪs] adj perfetto, inappuntabile

fault·y ['fɔlti] adj (**-ier; -iest**) manchevole, difettoso

faun [fɔn] s fauno

fauna ['fɔnə] s fauna

favor ['fevər] s favore m; (letter) pregiata; **do me the favor to** mi faccia il piacere di; **by your favor** col Suo permesso; **favors** regali *mpl* di festa; **to be in favor with** essere nelle grazie di; **to be out of favor** cadere in disgrazia ‖ *tr* favorire; (coll) assomigliare (with *dat*)

favorable ['fevərəbəl] *adj* favorevole

favorite ['fevərɪt] *adj & s* favorito

favoritism ['fevərɪ,tɪzəm] *s* favoritismo

fawn [fɔn] *s* cerbiatto ‖ *intr*—**to fawn on** adulare, strusciarsi a

faze [fez] *tr* (coll) perturbare

fear [fɪr] *s* paura; **for fear of** per paura di; **for fear that** per paura che; **no fear** non c'è pericolo; **to be in fear of** aver timore di ‖ *tr & intr* temere

fearful ['fɪrfəl] *adj* pauroso, timorato; (coll) spaventoso

fearless ['fɪrlɪs] *adj* impavido

feasible ['fizɪbəl] *adj* fattibile, possibile

feast [fist] *s* festa; (*sumptuous meal*) festino, banchetto ‖ *tr* intrattenere ‖ *intr* banchettare; **to feast on** rallegrarsi alla vista di

feat [fit] *s* fatto, prodezza

feather ['fɛðər] *s* penna; (*soft and fluffy structure covering bird*) piuma; (*type*) qualità *f*, conio; (*tuft*) pennacchio; **in fine feather** di buon umore; **in buona salute** ‖ *tr* impennare; coprire di piume; (naut) spalare; (aer) bandierare; **to feather one's nest** arricchirsi

feath'er bed' *s* letto di piume

feath'er-bed'ding *s* impiego di mano d'opera non necessaria richiesto da un sindacato operaio

feath'er-brain' *s* cervello di gallina

feath'er-edge' *s* (*of board*) augnatura; (*of sharpened tool*) filo morto

feath'er-weight' *s* peso piuma

feathery ['fɛðərɪ] *adj* piumato; leggero

feature ['fitʃər] *s* fattezza; caratteristica; (journ) articolo principale; (mov) attrazione; **features** fattezze *fpl* ‖ *tr* caratterizzare; mettere in evidenza; (coll) immaginare

fea'ture film' *s* lungometraggio

fea'ture sto'ry *s* articolo di spalla

February ['fɛbru,ɛrɪ] *s* febbraio

feces ['fisiz] *spl* feci *fpl*

feckless ['fɛklɪs] *adj* debole; inetto

federal ['fɛdərəl] *adj* federale ‖ *s* federalista *mf*

federate ['fɛdə,ret] *adj* federato ‖ *tr* federare ‖ *intr* federarsi

federation [,fɛdə're/ən] *s* federazione

federative ['fɛdə,retɪv] or ['fɛdərətɪv] *adj* federativo

fedora [fɪ'dorə] *s* cappello floscio di feltro

fed' up' [fɛd] *adj* stanco e stufo; **to be fed up with** averne fin sopra gli occhi di

fee [fi] *s* onorario; (*charge allowed by law*) diritto; (*tip*) mancia; (*for tuition*) tassa; (*for admission*) ingresso ‖ *tr* pagare

feeble ['fibəl] *adj* debole, fievole

feeble-minded ['fibəl'maɪndɪd] *adj* rimbecillito; debole, vacillante

feed [fid] *s* mangime *m;* (coll) mangiata; (mach) dispositivo d'alimentazione ‖ *v* (*pret & pp* **fed** [fɛd]) *tr* nutrire; (*a machine*) alimentare; (*cattle*) pascere; (theat) imbeccare ‖ *intr* mangiare; **to feed upon** nutrirsi di

feed'back' *s* (*of a computer*) ritorno d'informazioni; (electron) reazione

feed' bag' *s* musetta

feed' pump' *s* pompa di alimentazione

feed' trough' *s* (*for cattle*) vasca; (*for hogs*) trogolo

feed' wire' *s* cavo di alimentazione

feel [fil] *s* sensazione; (*touch*) tocco; (*vague mental impression*) senso ‖ *v* (*pret & pp* **felt** [fɛlt]) *tr* sentire; (*e.g., with the hands*) palpare, toccare; (*s.o.'s pulse*) tastare ‖ *intr* (*sick, tired, etc.*) sentire; **to feel bad** sentirsi male; (*to be unhappy*) essere spiacente; **to feel cheap** vergognarsi; **to feel comfortable** sentirsi a proprio agio; **to feel for** cercare di toccare; avere compassione per; **to feel like** aver voglia di; **to feel safe** sentirsi al sicuro; **to feel sorry** essere spiacente; **to feel sorry for** aver compassione di; pentirsi di

feeler ['filər] *s* (*hint*) sondaggio; **feelers** (*of insect*) antenne *fpl;* (*of mollusk*) tentacoli *mpl;* **to put out feelers** (fig) tastare il terreno

feeling ['filɪŋ] *s* (*with senses*) senso; (*impression, emotion*) sentimento, sensazione; opinione

feign [fen] *tr* fingere; inventare; imitare ‖ *intr* far finta; **to feign to be** fingersi

feint [fent] *s* finta ‖ *intr* fare una finta

feldspar ['fɛld,spɑr] *s* feldspato

felicitate [fə'lɪsɪ,tet] *tr* felicitarsi con

felicitous [fə'lɪsɪtəs] *adj* felice, indovinato; eloquente

fell [fɛl] *adj* crudele, mortale ‖ *tr* (*trees*) abbattere

felloe ['fɛlo] *s* cerchione *m;* (*part of the rim*) gavello

fellow ['fɛlo] *s* compagno; collega *m;* (*of a society*) membro, socio; (*holder of fellowship*) borsista *mf;* (coll) tipo, tizio; (coll) innamorato; **good fellow** buon diavolo; galantuomo

fel'low cit'izen *s* concittadino

fel'low coun'try-man *s* (-men) concittadino

fel'low crea'ture *s* prossimo

fel'low-man' *s* (-men') prossimo

fel'low mem'ber *s* consocio

fellowship ['fɛlo,ʃɪp] *s* compagnia; (*for study*) borsa di studio

fel'low trav'eler *s* simpatizzante *mf;* criptocomunista *mf;* compagno di viaggio

felon ['fɛlən] *s* criminale *mf;* (pathol) patereccio, giradito

felo-ny ['fɛlənɪ] *s* (-nies) delitto doloso

felt [fɛlt] *s* feltro

felt' board' *s* lavagna di panno

felt'-tip pen' *s* pennarello

female ['fimɛl] *adj* (*sex*) femminile;

(*animal, plant, piece of a device*) femmina || *s* femmina

feminine ['femɪnɪn] *adj* & *s* femminile *m*

feminism ['femɪ,nɪzəm] *s* femminismo

fence [fens] *s* steccato, staccionata; (*for stolen goods*) ricettatore *m*; (carp) squadra di guida; (sports) scherma; **on the fence** (coll) indeciso || *tr* recingere || *intr* tirare di scherma

fencing ['fensɪŋ] *s* scherma; (fig) schermaglia

fenc'ing mask' *s* visiera

fend [fend] *tr*—**to fend off** parare || *intr*—**to fend for oneself** (coll) badare a sé stesso

fender ['fendər] *s* (*of trolley car*) salvagente *m*; (*of fireplace*) parafuoco; (aut) parafango; (naut) parabordo

fennel ['fenəl] *s* finocchio

ferment ['fɑrment] *s* fermento || [fər-'ment] *tr* & *intr* fermentare

fern [fʌrn] *s* felce *f*

ferocious [fə'roʃəs] *adj* feroce

ferocity [fə'rɑsɪti] *s* ferocia

ferret ['ferɪt] *s* furetto || *tr*—**to ferret out** scovare || *intr* indagare

Fer'ris wheel' ['ferɪs] *s* ruota (del parco dei divertimenti)

fer·ry ['feri] *s* (-ries) traghetto; nave *f* traghetto || *v* (*pret* & *pp* -ried) *tr* traghettare || *intr* attraversare

fer'ry·boat' *s* nave *f* traghetto, ferryboat *m*

fertile ['fʌrtɪl] *adj* fertile

fertilize ['fʌrtɪ,laɪz] *tr* fertilizzare; (*to impregnate*) fecondare

fertilizer ['fʌrtɪ,laɪzər] *s* fertilizzante *m*; (*e.g., of flowers*) fecondatore *m*

fervent ['fʌrvənt] *adj* fervente, fervido

fervid ['fʌrvɪd] *adj* fervido

fervor ['fʌrvər] *s* fervore *m*

fester ['festər] *s* ulcera, piaga || *tr* corrompere || *intr* suppurare; (fig) corrompersi

festival ['festɪvəl] *adj* festivo || *s* festa; (*of music*) festival *m*

festive ['festɪv] *adj* festivo

festivi·ty [fes'tɪvɪti] *s* (-ties) festività *f*

festoon [fes'tun] *s* festone *m* || *tr* ornare di festoni

fetch [fetʃ] *tr* andare a prendere; (*a price*) fruttare, vendersi per

fetching ['fetʃɪŋ] *adj* (coll) cattivante, attraente

fete [fet] *s* festa || *tr* festeggiare

fetid ['fetɪd] or ['fitɪd] *adj* fetido

fetish ['fitɪʃ] or ['fetɪʃ] *s* feticcio

fetlock ['fetlɑk] *s* nocca; (*tuft of hair*) barbetta

fetter ['fetər] *s* ceppo, catena || *tr* mettere ai ceppi, incatenare

fettle ['fetəl] *s* stato, condizione; **in fine fettle** in buone condizioni

fetus ['fitəs] *s* feto

feud [fjud] *s* antagonismo; odio ereditario || *intr* essere in lotta

feudal ['fjudəl] *adj* feudale

feudalism ['fjudə,lɪzəm] *s* feudalismo

fever ['fivər] *s* febbre *f*

feverish ['fivərɪʃ] *adj* febbrile

few [fju] *adj* & *pron* pochi; **a few** alcuni; **quite a few** molti

fiancé [,fi·ɑn'se] *s* fidanzato

fiancée [,fi·ɑn'se] *s* fidanzata

fias·co [fi'æsko] *s* (-cos or -coes) fiasco

fib [fɪb] *s* menzogna, frottola || *v* (*pret* & *pp* fibbed; *ger* fibbing) *intr* raccontar frottole

fiber ['faɪbər] *s* fibra; (fig) tempra

fi'ber·glass' *s* vetroresina

fibrous ['faɪbrəs] *adj* fibroso

fickle ['fɪkəl] *adj* volubile, incostante, mobile

fiction ['fɪkʃən] *s* (*invention*) finzione; (*branch of literature*) novellistica

fictional ['fɪkʃənəl] *adj* immaginario

fictionalize ['fɪkʃənə,laɪz] *tr* romanzare

fictitious [fɪk'tɪʃəs] *adj* fittizio

fiddle ['fɪdəl] *s* violino; **fit as a fiddle** in perfetta salute || *tr* (coll) suonare sul violino; **to fiddle away** (coll) sprecare || *intr* (coll) suonare il violino; **to fiddle with** (coll) giocherellare con

fiddler ['fɪdlər] *s* (coll) violinista *mf*

fiddling ['fɪdlɪŋ] *adj* triviale, futile, insignificante

fideli·ty [faɪ'delɪti] or [fɪ'delɪti] *s* (-ties) fedeltà *f*

fidget ['fɪdʒɪt] *intr* agitarsi; **to fidget with** giocherellare con

fidgety ['fɪdʒɪti] *adj* irrequieto

fiduciar·y [fɪ'dju/ɪ,eri] or [fɪ'du/ɪ-,eri] *adj* fiduciario || *s* (-ies) fiduciario

fie [faɪ] *interj* vergogna!

fief [fif] *s* feudo

field [fild] *adj* (mil) da campagna || *s* campo; (sports) terreno; (min) giacimento; (*of motor or dynamo*) (elec) induttore *m*; (phys) campo

fielder ['fildər] *s* (*outfielder*) giocatore *m* del campo esterno

field' glass'es *spl* binocolo

field' hock'ey *s* hockey *m* su prato

field' mag'net *s* induttore *m*, calamita induttrice

field' mar'shal *s* (mil) maresciallo di campo

field' mouse' *s* topo di campagna

field'piece' *s* pezzo da campagna

fiend [find] *s* diavolo; (coll) addetto, tifoso

fiendish ['findɪʃ] *adj* diabolico

fierce [fɪrs] *adj* fiero, feroce; (*wind*) furioso; (coll) maledetto

fierceness ['fɪrsnɪs] *s* ferocia

fier·y ['faɪri] or ['faɪ·əri] *adj* (-ier; -iest) ardente, focoso

fife [faɪf] *s* piffero

fifteen ['fɪf'tin] *adj*, *s* & *pron* quindici *m*

fifteenth ['fɪf'tinθ] *adj*, *s* & *pron* quindicesimo || *s* (*in dates*) quindici *m*

fifth [fɪfθ] *adj*, *s* & *pron* quinto || *s* (*in dates*) cinque *m*

fifth' col'umn *s* quinta colonna

fiftieth ['fɪfti·ɪθ] *adj*, *s* & *pron* cinquantesimo

fif·ty ['fɪfti] *adj* & *pron* cinquanta || *s* (-ties) cinquanta *m*; **the fifties** gli anni cinquanta

fif'ty-fif'ty *adv*—**to go fifty-fifty** fare a metà

fig [fɪg] *s* fico

fight [faɪt] *s* lotta; baruffa; combattimento; spirito combattivo; (sports) incontro; **to pick a fight with** attaccar briga con || *v* (*pret & pp* **fought** [fɔt]) *tr* lottare con; combattere contro; opporsi a || *intr* lottare; combattere; **to fight shy of** cercar di evitare

fighter ['faɪtər] *s* lottatore *m*; (*warrior*) combattente *m*; (aer) caccia *m*

fig' leaf' *s* foglia di fico

figment ['fɪgmənt] *s* finzione

figurative ['fɪgjərətɪv] *adj* (fa) figurativo; (rhet) figurato

figure ['fɪgjər] *s* figura; numero; prezzo; **to be good at figures** far bene di conto; **to cut a figure** fare una buona figura; **to keep one's figure** conservare la linea || *tr* figurare; immaginare; raffigurare; supporre, calcolare; **to figure out** calcolare; decifrare || *intr* apparire; **to figure on** (coll) contare su

fig'ure·head' *s* uomo di paglia, prestanome *m*; (naut) polena

fig'ure of speech' *s* figura retorica

fig'ure skat'ing *s* pattinaggio artistico

figurine [,fɪgjə'rin] *s* figurina

filament ['fɪləmənt] *s* filamento

filbert ['fɪlbərt] *s* (*tree*) nocciolo, avellano; (*nut*) nocciola, avellana

filch [fɪltʃ] *tr* rubacchiare

file [faɪl] *s* (*row*) fila; (*tool*) lima; (*folder*) filza; (*room*) archivio; (*of cards*) schedario || *tr* mettere in fila; limare; archiviare, schedare; (journ) trasmettere || *intr* sfilare; **to file for** fare domanda di

file' clerk' *s* schedarista *mf*

filet [fɪ'le] *or* ['fɪle] *s* filetto || *tr* tagliare in filetti

filial ['fɪlɪ·əl] *or* ['fɪljəl] *adj* filiale

filiation [,fɪlɪ'eʃən] *s* filiazione

filibuster ['fɪlɪ,bʌstər] *s* (*tactics*) ostruzionismo; (*speech*) discorso ostruzionista; (*person making such a speech*) ostruzionista *mf*; (*buccaneer*) filibustiere *m* || *tr* fare ostruzionismo contro || *intr* fare dell'ostruzionismo

filigree ['fɪlɪ,gri] *adj* filigranato || *s* filigrana || *tr* lavorare in filigrana

filing ['faɪlɪŋ] *s* (*of documents*) schedatura; limatura; **filings** limatura

fil'ing cab'inet *s* schedario

fil'ing card' *s* cartellino, scheda

fill [fɪl] *s* sazietà *f*; (*place filled with earth*) terrapieno; **to have or get one's fill** mangiare a sazietà || *tr* riempire; (*an order*) eseguire; (*a hole*) otturare; (*a tooth*) piombare; (*a tire*) gonfiare; (*a place*) occupare; (*with sand*) interrare; **to fill out** (*a form*) riempire; **to fill up** (aut) fare il pieno di || *intr* riempirsi; **to fill in** prendere il posto; **to fill up** riempirsi

filler ['fɪlər] *s* ripieno; (*person*) riempitore *m*; (*painting*) mestica; (journ) articolo riempitivo

fillet ['fɪlɪt] *s* nastro, fascia; (*for hair*) nastro; (archit) listello || *tr* filettare

|| ['frɪle] *or* ['frɪlɪt] *s* (*of meat or fish*) filetto || *tr* tagliare a filetti

filling ['fɪlɪŋ] *s* (*of a tooth*) impiombatura; (*of turkey*) ripieno

fill'ing sta'tion *s* stazione di rifornimento

fillip ['fɪlɪp] *s* stimolo; colpetto col dito || *tr* dare un colpetto col dito a; (fig) stimulare

fil·ly ['fɪli] *s* (**-lies**) puledra

film [fɪlm] *s* pellicola; (mov, phot) pellicola, film *m* || *tr* filmare

film' li'brary *s* cineteca, filmoteca

film'strip' *s* filmina

film·y ['fɪlmi] *adj* (**-ier; -iest**) sottile, delicato; (*look*) annebbiato

filter ['fɪltər] *s* filtro || *tr & intr* filtrare

filtering ['fɪltərɪŋ] *s* filtrazione

fil'ter pa'per *s* carta da filtro

fil'ter tip' *s* filtro, bocchino filtro

filth [fɪlθ] *s* sporco, sporcizia

filth·y ['fɪlθi] *adj* (**-ier; -iest**) sporco, sudicio

filth'y lu'cre ['lukər] *s* il vile metallo

filtrate ['fɪltret] *s* liquido filtrato || *tr & intr* filtrare

fin [fɪn] *s* pinna; (slang) biglietto da cinque dollari

final ['faɪnəl] *adj* finale; (*last in a series*) ultimo; definitivo, insindacabile || *s* esame *m* finale; **finals** (sports) finale *f*

finale [fɪ'nɑli] *s* (mus) finale *m*

finalist ['faɪnəlɪst] *s* finalista *mf*

finally ['faɪnəli] *adv* finalmente

finance [fɪ'næns] *or* ['faɪnæns] *s* finanza; **finances** finanze *fpl* || *tr* finanziare

financial [fɪ'næn/əl] *or* [faɪ'næn/əl] *adj* finanziario

financier [,fɪnən'sɪr] *or* [,faɪnən'sɪr] *s* finanziere *m*

financing [fɪ'nænsɪŋ] *or* ['faɪnænsɪŋ] *s* finanziamento

finch [fɪntʃ] *s* fringuello

find [faɪnd] *s* trovata || *v* (*pret & pp* **found** [faʊnd]) *tr* trovare; rinvenire; (*s.o. innocent or guilty*) dichiarare; **to find out** venire a sapere || *intr* (law) sentenziare; **to find out about** informarsi su

finder ['faɪndər] *s* (phot) mirino; (astr) cannochiale cercatore

finding ['faɪndɪŋ] *s* scoperta; (law) sentenza

fine [faɪn] *adj* buono; bello; fino, fine || *s* multa || *adv* (coll) benissimo; **to feel fine** (coll) sentirsi benissimo || *tr* multare

fine' arts' *spl* belle arti

fineness ['faɪnnɪs] *s* finezza; (*of metal*) titolo

fine' print' *s* testo in caratteri minuti

finer·y ['faɪnəri] *s* (**-ies**) ornamenti *mpl*, fronzoli *mpl*; abito vistoso

fine-spun ['faɪn,spʌn] *adj* sottile

finesse [fɪ'nes] *s* finezza; (bridge) impasse *f* || *tr* fare l'impasse a || *intr* fare l'impasse

fine'-tooth comb' *s* pettine fitto; **to go over with a fine-tooth comb** esaminare minuziosamente

finger ['fɪŋɡər] s dito; **to have a finger in the pie** avere le mani in pasta; **to put one's finger on the spot** mettere il dito nella piaga; **to slip between the fingers** sfuggire di tra le dita; **to snap one's fingers at** infischiarsi di; **to twist around one's little finger** fare ciò che si vuole di || *tr* toccare con le dita; (*to pilfer*) rubacchiare; (slang) mostrare a dito

fin'ger board' s (mus) tastiera

fin'ger bowl' s sciacquadita m

fingering ['fɪŋɡərɪŋ] s palpeggiamento; (mus) diteggiatura

fin'ger mark' s ditata

fin'ger-nail' s unghia

fin'ger-print' s impronta digitale || *tr* prendere le impronte digitali di

fin'ger-tip' s polpastrello; **to have at one's fingertips** avere sulla punta delle dita, sapere a menadito

finical ['fɪnɪkəl] *or* **finicky** ['fɪnɪki] *adj* pignolo, schizzinoso

finish ['fɪnɪʃ] s fine *f*; finitura; (sports) finale m || *tr* finire; **to finish off** distruggere || *intr* finire; **to finish** + *ger* finire di + *inf*; **to finish by** + *ger* finire per + *inf*

fin'ishing school' s scuola di perfezionamento per signorine

fin'ishing touch' s ultimo tocco

finite ['faɪnaɪt] *adj* finito

Finland ['fɪnlənd] s la Finlandia

Finlander ['fɪnləndər] s finlandese *mf*

Finn [fɪn] s (*member of a Finnish-speaking group of people*) finnico; (*native or inhabitant of Finland*) finlandese *mf*

Finnic ['fɪnɪk] *adj & s* finnico

Finnish ['fɪnɪʃ] *adj* finlandese || *s* (*language*) finlandese m

fir [fʌr] s abete m

fire [faɪr] s fuoco; (*destructive burning*) incendio; **to be on fire** ardere; **to be under enemy fire** essere sotto tiro nemico; **to catch fire** infiammarsi; **to hang fire** essere in sospeso; **to open fire** aprire il fuoco; **to set on fire, to set fire to** dar fuoco a; **under fire** sotto fuoco nemico; accusato || *tr* accendere; (*an oven*) scaldare; (*bricks*) cuocere; (*a weapon*) sparare; (*the imagination*) riscaldare; (*an employee*) (coll) licenziare || *intr* accendersi; **to fire on** far fuoco su; **to fire up** attivare una caldaia

fire' alarm' s avvisatore m d'incendio

fire'arm' s arma da fuoco

fire'ball' s palla da cannone esplosiva; (*lightning*) lampo a forma di globo infocato; meteorite m a forma di globo infocato; globo infocato

fire'boat' s lancia dei pompieri

fire'box' s (*of a boiler*) fornello; (*to give alarm*) stazione d'allarme

fire'brand' s tizzone m; (fig) fiaccola della discordia

fire'brick' s mattone refrattario

fire' brigade' s corpo di pompieri volontari

fire'bug' s (coll) incendiario

fire' com'pany s corpo dei pompieri;

compagnia d'assicurazioni contro gli incendi

fire'crack'er s mortaretto

fire'damp' s grisou m

fire' depart'ment s corpo dei pompieri

fire'dog' s alare m

fire' drill' s esercitazione in caso d'incendio

fire' en'gine s autopompa

fire' escape' s scala di sicurezza

fire' extin'guisher s estintore m

fire'fly' s (**-flies**) lucciola

fire'guard' s parafuoco

fire' hose' s manichetta

fire'house' s caserma dei pompieri

fire' hy'drant s bocca d'incendi

fire' insur'ance s assicurazione contro gli incendi

fire' i'rons *spl* arnesi *mpl* del camino

fire'man s (**-men**) (*man who extinguishes fires*) pompiere m, vigile m del fuoco; (*stoker*) fochista m

fire'place' s camino

fire'plug' s bocca da incendio, idrante m

fire'proof' *adj* incombustibile || *tr* rendere incombustibile

fire' sale' s vendita di merce avariata dal fuoco

fire' screen' s parafuoco

fire' ship' s brulotto

fire'side' s focolare m

fire'trap' s edificio senza mezzi adeguati per combattere incendi

fire' wall' s paratia antincendio

fire'wa'ter s (coll) acquavite *f*

fire'wood' s legna

fire'works' *spl* fuochi *mpl* artificiali

firing ['faɪrɪŋ] s (*of furnace*) alimentazione; (*of bricks*) cottura; (*of a gun*) sparo; (*of soldiers*) tiro; (*of an internal-combustion engine*) accensione; (*of an employee*) (coll) licenziamento

fir'ing line' s linea del fuoco

fir'ing or'der s (aut) ordine m d'accensione

fir'ing pin' s percussore m

fir'ing squad' s (*for saluting at a burial*) plotone m d'onore; (*for executing*) plotone m d'esecuzione

firm [fʌrm] *adj* forte, fermo || s ditta, compagnia

firmament ['fʌrməmənt] s firmamento

firm' name' s ragione *f* sociale

firmness ['fʌrmnɪs] s fermezza

first [fʌrst] *adj* primo || s primo; (aut) prima; (mus) voce *f* principale; **at first** sulle prime; **from the first** da bel principio || *adv* prima; **first of all** per prima cosa

first' aid' s pronto soccorso

first'-aid' kit' s cassetta farmaceutica d'urgenza

first'-aid' sta'tion s posto di pronto soccorso

first'-born' *adj & s* primogenito

first'-class' *adj* di prim'ordine, sopraffino || *adv* in prima classe

first' cous'in s cugino primo

first'-day cov'er s busta primo giorno

first' draft' s brutta copia

first' fin'ger s dito indice
first' floor' s pianoterra m
first' fruits' spl primizie fpl
first' lieuten'ant s tenente m
firstly ['fʌrstli] adv in primo luogo
first' mate' s (naut) primo ufficiale, comandante m in seconda, secondo
first' name' s nome m di battesimo
first' night' s (theat) prima
first' of'ficer s (naut) primo ufficiale, comandante m in seconda, secondo
first'-rate' adj di prima forza; eccellente || adv (coll) benissimo
first'-run' adj di prima visione
fiscal ['fɪskəl] adj (pertaining to public treasury) fiscale; finanziario || s avvocato fiscale
fis'cal year' s esercizio finanziario
fish [fɪʃ] s pesce m; **to be like a fish out of water** essere come un pesce fuor d'acqua; **to be neither fish nor fowl** non essere né carne né pesce; **to drink like a fish** bere come una spugna || tr pescare || intr pescare; **to fish for compliments** cercare di farsi fare dei complimenti; **to go fishing** andare alla pesca; **to take fishing** portare con sé alla pesca
fish'bone' s lisca, spina di pesce
fish'bowl' s vaschetta per i pesci rossi
fisher ['fɪʃər] s pescatore m; (zool) martora canadese
fish'er·man s (-men) pescatore m; (boat) peschereccio
fisher·y ['fɪʃəri] s (-ies) (activity) pesca; (business) pescheria; (grounds) riserva di pesca, luogo dove si pesca
fish' glue' s colla di pesce
fish'hook' s amo
fishing ['fɪʃɪŋ] adj da pesca || s pesca
fish'ing reel' s mulinello
fish'ing rod' s canna da pesca
fish'ing tack'le s attrezzatura da pesca
fish'line' s lenza
fish' mar'ket s pescheria
fish'pool' s peschiera
fish' spear' s fiocina
fish' sto'ry s (coll) fandonia; **to tell fish stories** sparare grosse
fish'tail' s (aut) imbardata (aer) spedalata || intr (aut) imbardare; (aer) compiere una spedalata
fish'wife' s (-wives') pescivendola; (foul-mouthed woman) ciana
fish'worm' s lombrico
fish·y ['fɪʃi] adj (-ier; -iest) che sa di pesce; (coll) dubbioso, inverosimile
fission ['fɪʃən] s (biol) scissione; (phys) fissione
fissionable ['fɪʃənəbəl] adj fissionabile
fissure ['fɪʃər] s fenditura; (in rock) crepaccio
fist [fɪst] s pugno; (typ) indice m; **to shake one's fist at** mostrare i pugni a
fist'fight' s scontro a pugni
fist'ful' s pugno, manciata
fisticuff ['fɪstɪ͵kʌf] s pugno; **fisticuffs** scontro a pugni
fit [fɪt] adj (fitter; fittest) indicato; idoneo, adatto; in buona salute; **fit to be tied** (coll) infuriato, arrabbia-

tissimo; **fit to eat** mangiabile; **to feel fit** sentirsi in buona salute; **to see fit** giudicare conveniente || s equipaggiamento; (of a suit) taglio; (of one piece with another) incastro; (of coughing) accesso; (of anger) attacco; **by fits and starts** a pezzi e a bocconi || v (pret & pp fitted; ger fitting) tr adattare; quadrare a; andar bene a; equipaggiare; preparare; servire a; esser d'accordo con; **to fit out** or **up** attrezzare, equipaggiare || intr stare; incastrare; (said of clothes) cascare; entrare; **to fit in** entrarci
fitful ['fɪtfəl] adj capriccioso; incostante, irregolare
fitness ['fɪtnɪs] s convenienza; idoneità f; buona salute
fitter ['fɪtər] s aggiustatore m; (of machinery) montatore m; (of clothing) sarto che mette in prova
fitting ['fɪtɪŋ] adj appropriato, adatto, conveniente || s adattamento; (of a garment) prova; tubo adattabile; (carp) incastro; **fittings** accessori mpl; utensili mpl; (iron trimmings) ferramenta fpl
five [faɪv] adj & pron cinque || s cinque m; **five o' clock** le cinque
five' hun'dred adj, s & pron cinquecento
five'-year plan' s piano quinquennale
fix [fɪks] s—**in a tight fix** (coll) nei pasticci; **to be in a fix** (coll) star fresco, essere nei guai || tr riparare; fissare; (a meal) preparare; (a bayonet) inastare; (attention) attrarre, fermare; (hair) mettere a posto; (coll) arrangiare || intr fissarsi, stabilirsi; **to fix on** scegliere
fixed [fɪkst] adj fisso; (time) improrogabile; (coll) arrangiato
fixing ['fɪksɪŋ] adj fissativo || s (fastening) attacco; (phot) fissaggio; **with all the fixings** (coll) con tutti i contorni
fix'ing bath' s bagno di fissaggio
fixture ['fɪkstʃər] s infisso; accessorio; (of a lamp) guarnizione; **fixtures** (e.g., of a store) suppellettili fpl
fizz [fɪz] s effervescenza; gazosa; (Brit) spumante m || intr frizzare
fizzle ['fɪzəl] s (coll) fiasco || intr crepitare; (coll) fare fiasco
flabbergast ['flæbər͵gæst] tr (coll) sbalordire, lasciare stupefatto
flab·by ['flæbi] adj (-bier; -biest) floscio, flaccido, cascante
flag [flæg] s bandiera || v (pret & pp flagged; ger flagging) tr imbandierare; segnalare; (rr) far fermare || intr ammosciarsi, afflosciarsi
flageolet [͵flædʒə'lɛt] s flautino
flag'man s (-men) (rr) manovratore m
flag' of truce' s bandiera parlamentaria
flag'pole' s pennone m
flagrant ['flegrənt] adj flagrante; scandaloso
flag'ship' s nave ammiraglia
flag'staff' s pennone m
flag' sta'tion s (rr) stazione facoltativa
flag'stone' s lastra di pietra

flag' stop' s (rr) fermata facoltativa
flail [flel] s correggiato ‖ tr battere col correggiato; battere
flair [fler] s fiuto, istinto
flak [flæk] s fuoco antiaereo
flake [flek] s falda; (of snow) fiocco, falda; (of cereal) fiocco; ‖ tr sfaldare; (fish) scagliare ‖ intr sfaldarsi
flak·y ['fleki] adj (-ier; -iest) a falde, faldoso
flamboyant [flæm'bɔɪ·ənt] adj sgargiante; (archit) fiammeggiante
flame [flem] s fiamma ‖ tr & intr fiammeggiare
flamethrower ['flem,θro·ər] s lanciafiamme m
flaming ['flemɪŋ] adj fiammeggiante; appassionato; (culin) alla fiamma
flamin·go [flə'mɪŋgo] s (-gos or -goes) fenicottero, fiammingo
flammable ['flæməbəl] adj infiammabile
Flanders ['flændərz] s le Fiandre
flange [flændʒ] s (e.g., on a pipe) flangia; (on I beam) bordo; (of a wheel) cerchione m
flank [flæŋk] s fianco ‖ tr fiancheggiare
flannel ['flænəl] s flanella
flap [flæp] s (in clothing) falda; (of hat) tesa; (of book) risvolto; (of pocket) patta; (of shoe) linguetta; (blow) colpo; (of a table) pannello; (of the counter in a store) ribalta; (of wings) alata ‖ v (pret & pp flapped; ger flapping) tr battere, sbattere; (to move violently) sbatacchiare ‖ intr penzolare
flare [fler] s vampa; scintillio; (of a dress) svasatura; (mil) fuoco di segnalazione; flares (trousers) calzoni mpl a zampe d'elefante ‖ tr svasare ‖ intr scintillare; (said of a garment) scampanare; to flare up divampare; (said of an illness) aggravarsi, infiammarsi
flare'-up' s vampa, fiammata; (of an illness) recrudescenza; scoppio d'ira, accesso di collera
flash [flæʃ] s (of light) sprazzo; (of lightning) lampo, baleno; (of hope) raggio; (of joy) accesso; (journ, phot) flash m; (fig) lampo; flash in the pan fuoco di paglia ‖ tr (powder) accendere; (a sword) brandire; (journ) diffondere; (e.g., money) (coll) ostentare ‖ intr lampeggiare, balenare, folgorare; to flash by passare come un lampo
flash'back' s flashback m　　　　•
flash' bulb' s lampada lampo
flash' cube' s cuboflash m
flash' flood' s inondazione torrenziale
flashing ['flæʃɪŋ] s metallo per coprire la conversa; commessura metallica fra tetto e comignolo
flash'light' s lampadina tascabile; (of a lighthouse) luce f intermittente; (phot) fotolampo, lampeggiatore m
flash'light bulb' s lampada per fotolampo
flash·y ['flæʃi] adj (-ier; -iest) sgargiante, chiassoso, vistoso

flask [flæsk] or [flɑsk] s fiasco, fiasca; (for laboratory use) beuta
flat [flæt] adj (flatter; flattest) piano; (nose) camuso; (boat) a fondo piatto; (surface) liscio; (beer) svanito; (tire) sgonfio; (denial) deciso; (mus) bemolle; (coll) al verde ‖ s (flat surface) piatto; (flat area) piano; (apartment) appartamento; (mus) bemolle m; (coll) gomma a terra ‖ adv—to fall flat fallire
flat'boat' s chiatta
flat'car' s (rr) pianale m
flat-footed ['flæt,fʊtɪd] adj dai piedi piatti; (coll) inflessibile
flat'head' s (of a bolt) testa piatta; (coll) testa di legno
flat'i'ron s ferro da stiro
flat' race' s corsa piana
flatten ['flætən] tr schiacciare; distendere ‖ intr appiattirsi; indebolirsi; to flatten out appiattirsi; (aer) porsi in linea orizzontale di volo
flatter ['flætər] tr adulare, lusingare; (to make seem more attractive) favorire ‖ intr adulare
flatterer ['flætərər] s adulatore m, lusingatore m
flattering ['flætərɪŋ] adj lusinghiero
flatter·y ['flætəri] s (-ies) lusinga
flat' tire' s gomma a terra
flat'top' s portaerei f
flatulence ['flætʃələns] s flatulenza
flat'ware' s argenteria, vasellame m
flaunt [flɔnt] or [flɑnt] tr sfoggiare, ostentare
flautist ['flɔtɪst] s flautista mf
flavor ['flevər] s sapore m, gusto; condimento ‖ tr insaporire; condire; aromatizzare, profumare
flavoring ['flevərɪŋ] s condimento, sapore m
flaw [flɔ] s difetto, menda, fallo; (crack) incrinatura
flawless ['flɔlɪs] adj senza difetti
flax [flæks] s lino
flaxen ['flæksən] adj di lino; biondo
flax'seed' s linosa
flay [fle] tr scorticare, scoiare
flea [fli] s pulce f
flea'bite' s morso di pulce; (fig) inezia, seccatura secondaria
fleck [flek] s macchia; (fig) efelide f ‖ tr chiazzare, macchiare
fledgling ['fledʒlɪŋ] s uccellino appena nato; (fig) pivello
flee [fli] v (pret & pp fled [fled]) tr & intr fuggire, sfuggire
fleece [flis] s vello; (e.g., of clouds) bioccolo ‖ tr tosare; (fig) pelare
fleec·y ['flisi] adj (-ier; -iest) lanoso; (sky) a pecorelle
fleet [flit] adj rapido ‖ s flotta
fleeting ['flitɪŋ] adj fugace, passeggero
Fleming ['flemɪŋ] s fiammingo
Flemish ['flemɪʃ] adj & s fiammingo
flesh [fleʃ] s carne f; (of fruit) polpa; in the flesh in carne ed ossa; to lose flesh dimagrire; to put on flesh ingrassare
flesh' and blood' s (relatives) carne f della carne, i miei, i suoi, etc.; il corpo umano

flesh-colored [ˈfleʃˌkʌlərd] *adj* color carne

fleshiness [ˈfleʃɪnɪs] *s* carnosità *f*

fleshless [ˈfleʃlɪs] *adj* scarno

flesh'pot' *s* piatto di carne; locale *m* di dissoluzione; **fleshpots** vita dissoluta

flesh' wound' *s* ferita superficiale

flesh·y [ˈfleʃi] *adj* (**-ier; -iest**) carnoso; polposo

flex [fleks] *tr* piegare ‖ *intr* piegarsi

flexible [ˈfleksɪbəl] *adj* flessibile; (*joint*) a snodo

flick [flɪk] *s* schiocco; (slang) pellicola cinematografica ‖ *tr* schioccare

flicker [ˈflɪkər] *s* fiamma tremolante; (*of eyelids*) battito; (*of hope*) bagliore *m* ‖ *intr* tremolare; vacillare

flier [ˈflaɪ·ər] *s* aviatore *m*; (*venture*) (coll) impresa rischiosa; (coll) foglio volante

flight [flaɪt] *s* fuga; (*of an airplane*) volo; (*of birds*) stormo; (*of stairs*) rampa; (*of fancy*) slancio; **to put to flight** mettere in fuga; **to take flight** prendere la fuga

flight' deck' *s* ponte *m* di volo

flight·y [ˈflaɪti] *adj* (**-ier; -iest**) frivolo; volubile

flim-flam [ˈflɪmˌflæm] *s* (coll) imbroglio, truffa ‖ *v* (*pret & pp* **-flammed;** *ger* **-flamming**) *tr* (coll) imbrogliare, truffare

flim·sy [ˈflɪmzi] *adj* (**-sier; -siest**) leggero; (*material*) di scarsa consistenza; (*excuse*) inconsistente

flinch [flɪntʃ] *intr* indietreggiare; **without flinching** senza scomporsi

fling [flɪŋ] *s* tiro; ballo scozzese; **to go on a fling** darsi alla pazza gioia; **to have a fling** at tentare di fare; **to have one's fling** correre la cavallina ‖ *v* (*pret & pp* **flung** [flʌŋ]) *tr* sbattere, scagliare; (*e.g., in jail*) schiaffare; **to fling open** spalancare; **to fling shut** chiudere improvvisamente

flint [flɪnt] *s* selce *f*, pietra focaia

flint'lock' *s* fucile *m* a pietra focaia

flint·y [ˈflɪnti] *adj* (**-ier; -iest**) pietroso; (*unmerciful*) spietato; duro come un macigno

flip [flɪp] *adj* (**flipper; flippest**) impertinente ‖ *s* buffetto; salto mortale ‖ *v* (*pret & pp* **flipped;** *ger* **flipping**) *tr* sbattere in aria; muovere d'un tratto; **to flip a coin** giocare a testa e croce; **to flip shut** (*e.g., a fan*) chiudere improvvisamente

flippancy [ˈflɪpənsi] *s* leggerezza

flippant [ˈflɪpənt] *adj* scanzonato, leggero

flirt [flʌrt] *s* (*woman*) civetta; (*man*) vagheggino ‖ *intr* (*said of a woman*) civettare; (*said of a man*) fare il damerino; **to flirt with** flirtare con; (*an idea*) accarezzare; (*death*) giocare con

flit [flɪt] *v* (*pret & pp* **flitted;** *ger* **flitting**) *intr* svolazzare, volteggiare; passare rapidamente, volare

flitch [flɪtʃ] *s* fetta di pancetta

float [flot] *s* (*raft*) galleggiante *m*; (*of mason*) cazzuola; carro allegorico ‖ *tr* far galleggiare; (*a business*) lan-

ciare; (*stocks, bonds*) emettere ‖ *intr* galleggiare, tenersi a galla

floating [ˈflotɪŋ] *adj* galleggiante

flock [flɑk] *s* (*of birds*) stormo; (*of sheep*) gregge *m*; (*of people*) stuolo; (*of wool*) fiocco; (fig) mucchio ‖ *intr* affollarsi, riunirsi, radunarsi

floe [flo] *s* tavola di ghiaccio

flog [flɑg] *v* (*pret & pp* **flogged;** *ger* **flogging**) *tr* battere, fustigare

flood [flʌd] *s* (*caused by rain*) diluvio; (*sudden rise of river*) piena, fiumana; (*of tide*) flusso ‖ *tr* inondare; (aut) ingolfare ‖ *intr* straripare; (aut) ingolfarsi ‖ **the Flood** il diluvio universale

flood'gate' *s* (*of a canal*) chiusa; (*of a dam*) saracinesca

flood'light' *s* riflettore *m*

flood' tide' *s* flusso

floor [flor] *s* (*inside bottom surface of room*) pavimento; (*story of building*) piano; (*of the sea, a swimming pool, etc.*) fondo; (*of the exchange*) recinto delle grida; (*of an assembly hall*) emiciclo; (naut) madiere *m*; **to ask for the floor** chiedere la parola; **to have the floor** avere la parola; **to take the floor** prendere la parola ‖ *tr* pavimentare; abbattere, gettare al suolo; (coll) confondere; (coll) vincere

flooring [ˈflorɪŋ] *s* palco, impiantito

floor' mop' *s* redazza

floor' plan' *s* pianta

floor' show' *s* spettacolo di caffè concerto

floor'walk'er *s* direttore *m* di sezione

floor' wax' *s* cera da pavimenti

flop [flɑp] *s* (coll) fiasco ‖ *v* (*pret & pp* **flopped;** *ger* **flopping**) *tr* lasciar cadere; sbattere ‖ *intr* lasciarsi cadere; (coll) fare fiasco; **to flop over** (*to change sides*) cambiare casacca

flora [ˈflorə] *s* flora

floral [ˈflorəl] *adj* floreale

Florence [ˈflorəns] *or* [ˈflɑrəns] *s* Firenze *f*

Florentine [ˈflɑrənˌtin] *or* [ˈflɔrənˌtin] *adj & s* fiorentino

florescence [floˈrɛsəns] *s* inflorescenza

florid [ˈflɑrɪd] *or* [ˈflɔrɪd] *adj* florido

florist [ˈflorɪst] *s* fiorista *mf*, fioraio

floss [flɔs] *or* [flɑs] *s* lanugine *f*; (*of corn*) barba

floss·y [ˈflɔsi] *or* [ˈflɑsi] *adj* (**-ier; -iest**) serico; (*downy*) lanuginoso; (coll) vistoso

flotsam [ˈflɑtsəm] *s* relitti gettati a mare

flot'sam and jet'sam *s* relitti *mpl* di naufragio; (*trifles*) cianfrusaglie *fpl*; gentaglia, vagabondi *mpl*

flounce [flauns] *s* balza, falda, falpalà *m* ‖ *tr* ornare di falpalà ‖ *intr*—**to flounce out** andarsene irosamente

flounder [ˈflaundər] *s* (ichth) passera ‖ *intr* dibattersi

flour [flaur] *adj* farinoso ‖ *s* farina ‖ *tr* infarinare

flourish [ˈflʌrɪʃ] *s* (*with the sword*) mulinello; (*with the pen*) ghirigoro; (*as part of signature*) svolazzo; (mus) fioritura || *tr* (*one's sword*) roteare || *intr* rifiorire, prosperare

flourishing ['flʌrɪʃɪŋ] *adj* prosperoso

flour' mill' *s* mulino per grano

floury ['flaurɪ] *adj* farinoso; infarinato

flout [flaut] *tr* burlarsi di || *intr* burlare, motteggiare

flow [flo] *s* flusso; (*of a river*) regime *m* || *intr* fluire; (*said of tide*) montare; (*said of hair in the air*) ondeggiare; **to flow into** gettarsi in, sfociare in; **to flow over** traboccare; **to flow with** abbondare di

flower ['flau·ər] *s* fiore *m* || *tr* infiorare ||*intr* fiorire

flow'er bed' *s* aiola fiorita

flow'er gar'den *s* giardino

flow'er girl' *s* fioraia; (*at a wedding*) damigella d'onore

flow'er pot' *s* vaso da fiori

flow'er shop' *s* negozio di fiori

flow'er show' *s* esposizione di fiori

flow'er stand' *s* portafiori *m*

flowery ['flau·ərɪ] *adj* fiorito

flowing ['flo·ɪŋ] *adj* (*water*) corrente; (*language*) scorrevole; (*e.g., hair*) fluente; (*e.g., lines of a dress*) filante

flu [flu] *s* influenza

fluctuate ['flʌktʃu,et] *intr* fluttuare, ondeggiare; (*said of prices*) oscillare

flue [flu] *s* gola, fumaiolo

fluency ['flu·ənsɪ] *s* facilità *f* di parola

fluent ['flu·ənt] *adj* (*speaker*) facondo; (*style*) fluido

fluently ['flu·əntlɪ] *adv* correntemente

fluff [flʌf] *s* lanugine *f*; vaporosità *f*; (*of an actor*) papera || *tr* sprimacciare || *intr* sprimacciarsi; (*coll*) impaperarsi

fluff·y ['flʌfɪ] *adj* (**-ier; -iest**) lanuginoso; vaporoso

fluid ['flu·ɪd] *adj & s* fluido

flu'id drive' *s* trasmissione idraulica

fluidity [flu'ɪdɪtɪ] *s* fluidità *f*

fluke [fluk] *s* (*of anchor*) marra, dente *m*; (*in billiards*) colpo fortunato; (*ichth*) passera

flume [flum] *s* gora; condotta forzata

flunk [flʌŋk] *s* (*coll*) bocciatura || *tr* (*coll*) bocciare; (*a course*) (*coll*) farsi bocciare in || *intr* (*coll*) fare fiasco; **to flunk out** (*coll*) farsi bocciare

flunk·y ['flʌŋkɪ] *s* (**-ies**) valletto; parassita *m*

fluor ['flu·ər] *s* fluorite *f*

fluorescence [,flu·ə'resəns] *s* fluorescenza

fluorescent [,flu·ə'resənt] *adj* fluorescente

fluoridation [,flu·ərɪ'deʃən] *s* fluorizzazione

fluoride ['flu·ə,raɪd] *s* fluoruro

fluorine ['flu·ə,rin] *s* fluoro

fluoroscope ['flu·ərə,skop] *s* schermo fluorescente

fluorspar ['flu·er,spar] *s* spatofluore *m*

flur·ry ['flʌrɪ] *s* (**-ries**) agitazione; (*of wind*) raffica; (*of rain*) acquazzone *m*; (*of snow*) turbine *m* || *v* (*pret & pp* **-ried**) *tr* agitare

flush [flʌʃ] *adj* livellato; contiguo; pro-

spero, ben provvisto; abbondante; vigoroso; (*full to overflowing*) rigurgitante; arrossito; **flush with** allo stesso livello che || *s* (*of water*) flusso improvviso; (*in the cheeks*) caldana, scalmana; (*of spring*) germogliare *m*; (*of joy*) ebbrezza; (*of youth*) rigoglio; (*in poker*) colore *m* || *adv* rasente, raso || *tr* (*to cause to blush*) far arrossire; lavare con un getto d'acqua; (*e.g., a rabbit*) snidare || *intr* essere accaldato; (*to blush*) arrossire; (*to gush*) zampillare

flush' tank' *s* sciacquone *m*

flush' toi'let *s* gabinetto a sciacquone

fluster ['flʌstər] *s* nervosismo, eccitazione || *tr* innervosire, eccitare

flute [flut] *s* (*of a column*) scanalatura; (*mus*) flauto || *tr* scanalare

flutist ['flutɪst] *s* flautista *mf*

flutter ['flʌtər] *s* svolazzo; agitazione; sensazione || *intr* frullare; svolazzare; agitarsi; (*said of the heart*) palpitare; (*said of the heartbeat*) essere irregolare

flux [flʌks] *s* (*flow*) flusso; (*for fusing metals*) fondente *m*

fly [flaɪ] *s* (*flies*) mosca; (*of trousers*) finta; (*for fishing*) mosca artificiale || *v* (*pret* **flew** [flu]; *pp* **flown** [flon]) *tr* (*an airplane*) pilotare, far volare; trasportare a volo; (*e.g., an ocean*) trasvolare; (*a flag*) battere || *intr* volare; fuggire, scappare; (*said of a flag*) ondeggiare; **to fly away** involarsi; **to fly into a rage** andare in eccessi; **to fly off** volare via; scappare; **to fly over** trasvolare; **to fly shut** chiudersi improvvisamente

fly'blow' *s* uovo di mosca

fly'-by-night' *adj* poco raccomandabile; di breve durata

fly'catch'er *s* (orn) pigliamosche *m*

flyer ['flaɪ·ər] *s* var of **flier**

fly'-fish' *intr* pescare con le mosche artificiali

flying ['flaɪ·ɪŋ] *adj* volante; rapido; in fuga; (*start*) lanciato || *s* volo

fly'ing boat' *s* idrovolante *m* a scafo centrale

fly'ing but'tress *s* contrafforte *m*

fly'ing col'ors *spl* successo; **with flying colors** a bandiere spiegate

fly'ing field' *s* campo d'aviazione

fly'ing sau'cer *s* disco volante

fly'ing sick'ness *s* male *m* d'aria

fly'ing squad' *s* squadra mobile

fly'ing time' *s* ore *fpl* di volo

fly'leaf' *s* (**-leaves'**) (bb) guardia

fly' net' *s* (*for a bed*) moschettiera; (*for a horse*) scacciamosche *m*

fly'pa'per *s* carta moschicida

fly'speck' *s* macchia di mosca; macchiolina

fly' swat'ter ['swatər] *s* scacciamosche *m*

fly'trap' *s* pigliamosche *m*

fly'wheel' *s* volano

foal [fol] *s* puledro || *intr* (*said of a mare*) figliare

foam [fom] *s* schiuma || *intr* schiumare

foam' rub'ber *s* gommapiuma

foamy   123   **foothill**

foam·y ['fomɪ] *adj* (**-ier; -iest**) spumoso, schiumeggiante
fob [fɑb] *s* taschino per l'orologio; (*chain*) catenina per l'orologio ‖ *v* (*pret & pp* **fobbed;** *ger* **fobbing**) *tr*— **to fob off s.th on s.o.** rifilare qlco a qlcu
f.o.b. or **F.O.B.** [,ɛf,o'bi] *adv* (letter-word) (**free on board**) franco
focal ['fokəl] *adj* focale
fo·cus ['fokəs] *s* (**-cuses** or **-ci** [saɪ]) fuoco; (*of a disease*) focolaio ‖ *v* (*pret & pp* **-cused** or **-cussed;** *ger* **-cusing** or **-cussing**) *tr* mettere a fuoco; (*attention*) concentrare ‖ *intr* convergere
fodder ['fɑdər] *s* foraggio
foe [fo] *s* nemico
fog [fɑg] or [fɔg] *s* nebbia; (phot) velo ‖ *v* (*pret & pp* **fogged;** *ger* **fogging**) *tr* annebbiare; (phot) velare ‖ *intr* annebbiarsi; (phot) velarsi
fog' bank' *s* banco di nebbia
fog'bound' *adj* avvolto nella nebbia
fog·gy ['fɑgɪ] or ['fɔgɪ] *adj* (**-gier; -giest**) annebbiato; nebbioso; (*idea*) vago; (phot) velato; **it is foggy** fa nebbia
fog'horn' *s* sirena da nebbia
foible ['fɔɪbəl] *s* debolezza, debole *m*
foil [fɔɪl] *s* (*thin sheet of metal*) foglia; (*of mirror*) argentatura; contrasto, risalto; (*sword*) fioretto ‖ *tr* sventare; (*a mirror*) argentare
foist [fɔɪst] *tr*— **to foist s.th on s.o.** rifilare qlco a qlcu
fold [fold] *s* piega; drappeggio; (*for sheep*) ovile *m*; (*of sheep; of the faithful*) gregge *m*; (geol) corrugamento ‖ *tr* piegare; (*the arms*) incrociare; **to fold up** ripiegare ‖ *intr* piegarsi; **to fold up** (coll) fare fallimento
folder ['foldər] *s* (*pamphlet*) pieghevole *m*; (*cover*) portacarte *m*
folding ['foldɪŋ] *adj* pieghevole
fold'ing cam'era *s* macchina fotografica a soffietto
fold'ing chair' *s* sedia pieghevole
fold'ing cot' *s* branda
fold'ing door' *s* porta a libro
fold'ing seat' *s* strapuntino
foliage ['folɪɪdʒ] *s* fogliame *m*
foli·o ['folɪ,o] *adj* in-folio ‖ *s* (**-os**) foglio; (*book*) in-folio ‖ *tr* numerare
folk [fok] *adj* popolare ‖ *s* (**folk** or **folks**) gente *f*; **your folks** i Suoi
folk'lore' *s* folclore *m*
folk' mu'sic *s* musica folcloristica
folk' song' *s* canzone *f* tradizionale
folk·sy ['foksɪ] *adj* (**-sier; -siest**) socievole; alla buona, alla mano
folk'ways' *spl* costumi *mpl* tradizionali
follicle ['fɑlɪkəl] *s* follicolo
follow ['fɑlo] *tr* seguire; (*to keep up with*) interessarsi di; **to follow suit** seguire l'esempio; (cards) rispondere al colore ‖ *intr* seguire; derivare; **as follows** come segue; **it follows** ne risulta
follower ['fɑlo·ər] *s* seguace *m*; discepolo; partigiano

following ['fɑlo·ɪŋ] *adj* susseguente ‖ *s* seguito; aderenti *mpl*
fol'low-up' *adj* susseguente; ricordativo; da continuarsi ‖ *s* prosecuzione; lettera ricordativa
fol·ly ['fɑlɪ] *s* (**-lies**) follia; **follies** rivista di varietà
foment [fo'mɛnt] *tr* fomentare
fond [fɑnd] *adj* appassionato; (*of food*) ghiotto; **to become fond of** appassionarsi di
fondle ['fɑndəl] *tr* accarezzare, vezzeggiare
fondness ['fɑndnɪs] *s* tenerezza; passione
font [fɑnt] *s* acquasantiera, pila; fonte *f* battesimale; (typ) fondita
food [fud] *adj* alimentare ‖ *s* cibo, vitto; (*for animals*) mangiare *m*; **food for thought** materia di che pensare
food' store' *s* negozio di commestibili
food'stuffs' *spl* commestibili *mpl*
fool [ful] *s* scemo, sciocco; (*jester*) buffone *m*; (*person imposed on*) vittima, zimbello; **to make a fool of** beffarsi di; **to play the fool** fare lo stupido ‖ *tr* infinocchiare, ingannare; **to fool away** sprecare ‖ *intr* giocare, fare per gioco; **to fool around** perdere il proprio tempo; **to fool with** giocherellare con
fooler·y ['fulərɪ] *s* (**-ies**) pazzia, buffonata
fool'har'dy *adj* (**-dier; -diest**) temerario
fooling ['fulɪŋ] *s* scherzo; **no fooling** senza scherzi, parlando sul serio
foolish ['fulɪʃ] *adj* sciocco; matto
fool'proof' *adj* a tutta prova; infallibile
fools'cap' *s* berretto a sonagli; carta formato protocollo
fool's' er'rand *s* impresa inutile
fool's' par'adise *s* felicità immaginaria
foot [fut] *s* (**feet** [fit]) piede *m*; (*of an animal*) zampa; (*of horse*) zoccolo; **to drag one's feet** procedere a passo di lumaca; **to put one's best foot forward** fare del proprio meglio; **to put one's foot down** farsi valere, imporsi; **to put one's foot in it** (coll) fare una topica; **to stand on one's own two feet** agire indipendentemente; **to tread under foot** calcare ‖ *tr* (*the bill*) pagare; **to foot it** andare a piedi; ballare
footage ['futɪdʒ] *s* distanza or lunghezza in piedi; (*of film measured in meters*) metraggio
foot'-and-mouth' disease' *s* (vet) afta epizootica
foot'ball' *s* (*ball*) pallone *m*; (*game*) pallovale *f*; (*soccer*) calcio, football *m*
foot'board' *s* (*support for foot*) predellino; (*of bed*) spalliera
foot' brake' *s* freno a pedale
foot'bridge' *s* passerella, ponte riservato ai pedoni
foot'fall' *s* passo
foot'hill' *s* collina ai piedi di una montagna

foot'hold' s stabilità f; **to gain a foot-hold** prender piede

footing ['fʊtɪŋ] s piede m, e.g., **he lost his footing** perse piede; **on a friendly footing** in relazioni amichevoli; **on an equal footing** su un piede di parità; **on a war footing** su un piede di guerra

foot'lights' spl luci fpl della ribalta; (fig) ribalta, scena

foot'loose' adj completamente libero

foot'man s (-men) staffiere m

foot'mark' s orma

foot'note' s rimando, rinvio

foot'path' s sentiero

foot'print' s orma, pesta

foot' race' s corsa podistica

foot'rest' s orma

foot' rule' s regolo di un piede

foot' soldier' s fante m, fantaccino

foot'sore' adj coi piedi stanchi

foot'step' s passo; **to follow in the footsteps of** seguire le orme di

foot'stone' s pietra tombale a piè di un sepolcro; (archit) pietra di sostegno

foot'stool' s sgabello

foot' warm'er s scaldino

foot'wear' s calzature fpl

foot'work' s allenamento delle gambe; (fig) manovra delicata

foot'worn' adj (road) battuto; (person) spedato

foozle ['fuzəl] s schiappinata || tr & intr mancare completamente

fop [fap] s bellimbusto, gagà m

for [fɔr] prep per; malgrado, e.g., **for all his wealth** malgrado tutta la sua ricchezza; come, e.g., **he uses his house for an office** adopera la casa come ufficio; di, e.g., **time for bed** ora di andare a letto; da, e.g., **he has been here for three days** è qui da tre giorni; per amor di; **to go for a walk** andare a fare una passeggiata || conj perchè, poichè

forage ['farɪdʒ] or ['fɔrɪdʒ] s foraggero || s foraggio || tr foraggiare || intr andare in cerca di foraggio

foray ['fare] or ['fɔre] s razzia, scorreria || intr razziare

for-bear [fɔr'ber] v (pret -bore ['bor]; pp -borne ['born] tr astenersi da || intr essere longanime

forbearance [fɔr'berəns] s longanimità f, tolleranza; astensione

for-bid [fɔr'bɪd] v (pret -bade ['bæd] or -bad ['bæd]; pp -bidden ['bɪdən]; ger -bidding) tr proibire, vietare || intr—**God forbid!** Dío ci scampi!

forbidding [fɔr'bɪdɪŋ] adj severo, sinistro

force [fɔrs] s forza; (staff of workers) forza, personale m; (phys) forza; **by force of** a forza di; **by main force** con tutte le sue forze; **in force** vigente; in gran numero; **to join forces** allearsi || tr forzare; obbligare; **to force back** respingere; **to force open** forzare; **to force s.th on s.o.** obbligare qlcu a accettare qlco

forced [fɔrst] adj forzato; studiato

forced' air' s aria sotto pressione

forced' draft' s tiraggio forzato

forced' land'ing s atterraggio forzato

forced' march' s marcia forzata

forceful ['fɔrsfəl] adj vigoroso, energico

for·ceps ['fɔrsəps] s (-ceps or -cipes [sɪ,piz]) (dent, surg) pinze fpl; (obstet) forcipe m

force' pump' s pompa premente

forcible ['fɔrsɪbəl] adj impetuoso, energico; efficace

ford [fɔrd] s guado || tr guadare

fore [fɔr] adj davanti; (naut) prodiero || s davanti m; (naut) prua; **to the fore** alla ribalta; d'attualità || adv prima; (naut) a proravia || interj attenzione!

fore' and aft' adv a poppa e a prua

fore'arm' s avambraccio || **fore·arm'** tr premunire; prevenire

fore'bears' spl antenati mpl

forebode [fɔr'bod] tr (to portend) preannunziare; (to have a presentiment of) presentire

foreboding [fɔr'bodɪŋ] s preannunzio; presentimento

fore'cast' s pronostico || v (pret & pp -cast or -casted) tr pronosticare

forecastle ['foksəl], ['fɔr,kæsəl] or ['fɔr,kasəl] s castello, pozzetto

fore-close' tr escludere, precludere; (a mortgage) (law) precludere il riscatto s

fore-doom' tr condannare all'insuccesso

fore' edge' s (bb) taglio

fore'fa'ther s antenato

fore'fin'ger s dito indice

fore'front' s—**in the forefront** all'avanguardia

fore-go' v (pret -went'; pp -gone') tr & intr precedere

fore-go'ing adj precedente, anteriore

fore'gone' conclu'sion s conclusione inevitabile; decisione già scontata

fore'ground' s primo piano

forehanded ['for'hændɪd] adj previdente; (thrifty) risparmiatore

forehead ['farɪd] or ['fɔrɪd] s fronte f

foreign ['farɪn] or ['fɔrɪn] adj straniero; (product; affairs) estero; **foreign to** estraneo a

for'eign affairs' spl affari esteri

for'eign-born' adj nato all'estero

foreigner ['farɪnər] or ['fɔrɪnər] s straniero, forestiero

for'eign exchange' s divise fpl; (money) valuta

for'eign min'ister s ministro degli affari esteri

for'eign of'fice s ministero degli affari esteri

for'eign serv'ice s servizio diplomatico e consolare; (Brit) servizio militare in paesi d'oltremare

fore'leg' s zampa anteriore

fore'lock' s ciuffo sulla fronte; **to take time by the forelock** acchiappare l'occasione

fore'man s (-men) sorvegliante m, capomastro; presidente m dei giurati

foremast ['formast], ['for,mæst] or ['for,mast] s trinchetto

foremost ['for,most] adj primo, principale, più importante

fore'noon' adj mattinale || s mattina
fore'part' s parte f anteriore; prima parte
fore'paw' s zampa anteriore
fore'quar'ter s quarto anteriore
fore'run'ner s precursore m, predecessore m, foriero
fore·sail ['fɔrsəl] or ['fɔrˌsel] s trinchetto
fore·see' v (pret -saw'; pp -seen') tr prevedere
foreseeable [for'si·əbəl] adj prevedibile
fore·shad'ow tr presagire
fore·short'en tr scorciare
fore'sight' s (prudence) previdenza; (foreknowledge) previsione
fore'sight'ed adj previdente
fore'skin' s prepuzio
forest ['fɑrɪst] or ['fɔrɪst] adj forestale || s foresta, bosco
fore·stall' tr prevenire; anticipare; (to buy up) accaparrare
for'est rang'er ['rendʒər] s guardaboschi m, guardia forestale
forestry ['fɑrɪstri] or ['fɔrɪstri] s selvicoltura
fore'taste' s pregustazione || tr pregustare
fore·tell' v (pret & pp -told') tr predire, presagire, preannunziare
fore'thought' s premeditazione; previdenza
forever [for'ɛvər] adv per sempre; continuamente
fore·warn' tr prevenire, preavvertire
fore'word' s avvertenza, prefazione
forfeit ['fɔrfɪt] adj perduto || s perdita, confisca; multa; (article deposited) pegno; **forfeits** (game) pegni mpl || tr decadere da
forfeiture ['fɔrfɪtʃər] s perdita di un pegno
forgather [fɔr'gæðər] intr riunirsi; incontrarsi
forge [fɔrdʒ] s fucina, forgia || tr forgiare; (a lie) inventare; (e.g., handwriting) falsificare || intr forgiare; commettere un falso; **to forge ahead** farsi strada
forger·y ['fɔrdʒəri] s (-ies) falsificazione, falso, contraffazione
for·get [fɔr'gɛt] v (pret -got ['gɑt]; pp -got or -gotten ['gɑtən]) tr dimenticare; **forget it!** non si preoccupi!; **to forget oneself** venir meno alla propria dignità; **to forget** to passare di mente a (qlcu) di, e.g., **he forgot to turn off the lights** gli è passato di mente di spegnere la luce
forgetful [fɔr'gɛtfəl] adj (apt to forget) smemorato; (neglectful) dimentico, immemore
forgetfulness [fɔr'gɛtfəlnɪs] s (inability to recall) smemorataggine f; (neglectfulness) dimenticanza
for·get'-me-not' s nontiscordardimé m
forgivable [fɔr'gɪvəbəl] adj perdonabile
for·give [fɔr'gɪv] v (pret -gave'; pp -giv'en) tr perdonare
forgiveness [fɔr'gɪvnɪs] s perdono
forgiving [fɔr'gɪvɪŋ] adj clemente
for·go [fɔr'go] v (pret -went; pp -gone) tr rinunciare (with dat)

fork [fɔrk] s (pitchfork) forca, forcone m; (of a bicycle) forcella; (for eating) forchetta; (of a tree or road) biforcazione, diramazione || tr muovere col forcone; inforcare; **to fork out** (slang) cacciar fuori || intr biforcarsi, diramarsi
forked [fɔrkt] adj biforcuto
fork'-lift truck' s carrello elevatore a forca
forlorn [fər'lɔrn] adj abbandonato; disperato; miserabile
forlorn' hope' s impresa disperata
form [fɔrm] s forma; (paper to be filled out) formulario; (construction to give shape to cement) cassaforma || tr formare || intr formarsi
formal ['fɔrmal] adj formale; di gala, da sera, da etichetta
for'mal attire' s vestito da cerimonia
for'mal call' s visita di prammatica
formali·ty [fɔr'mælɪti] s (-ties) formalità f; (excessive adherence to rules) formalismo
for'mal par'ty s ricevimento di gala
for'mal speech' s discorso ufficiale
format ['fɔrmæt] s formato
formation [fɔr'meʃən] s formazione
former ['fɔrmər] adj (preceding) anteriore; (long past) passato, antico; (having once been) già, ex; (of two) primo; **the former** quello
formerly ['fɔrmərli] adv già, prima, in tempi passati
form'fit'ting adj aderente al corpo
formidable ['fɔrmɪdəbəl] adj formidabile
formless ['fɔrmlɪs] adj informe
form' let'ter s lettera a formulario, stampato
formu·la ['fɔrmjələ] s (-las or -lae [ˌli]) formula
formulate ['fɔrmjəˌlet] tr formulare
for·sake [fɔr'sek] v (pret -sook ['sʊk]; pp -saken ['sekən]) tr abbandonare
fort [fɔrt] s forte m, fortezza
forte [fɔrt] s forte m
forth [fɔrθ] adv avanti; in avanti e così via; **from this day forth** da oggi in poi; **to go forth** uscire
forth'com'ing adj prossimo; immediatamente disponibile
forth'right' adj diretto || adv direttamente; senza ambagi; immediatamente
forth'with' adv immediatamente
fortieth ['fɔrti·ɪθ] adj, s & pron quarantesimo
fortification [ˌfɔrtɪfɪ'keʃən] s fortificazione
forti·fy ['fɔrtɪˌfaɪ] v (pret & pp -fied) tr fortificare; aumentare il livello alcolico di
fortitude ['fɔrtɪˌtjud] or ['fɔrtɪˌtud] s fortezza, fermezza
fortnight ['fɔrtnaɪt] or ['fɔrtnɪt] s quindicina, due settimane
fortress ['fɔrtrɪs] s fortezza, forte m
fortuitous [fɔr'tju·ɪtəs] or [fɔr'tu·ɪtəs] adj fortuito, occasionale
fortunate ['fɔrtʃənɪt] adj fortunato
fortune ['fɔrtʃən] s fortuna; **to make a fortune** farsi un patrimonio; **to tell**

s.o. his fortune leggere il futuro a qlcu

for'tune hunt'er s cacciatore m di dote

for'tune·tel'ler s indovino, cartomante mf

for·ty ['fortɪ] adj & pron quaranta || s (**-ties**) quaranta m; **the forties** gli anni quaranta

fo·rum ['forəm] s (**-rums** or **-ra** [rə]) foro

forward ['fɔrwərd] adj avanzato; precoce; impertinente || s (soccer) avanti m || adv avanti; **to bring forward** mettere in luce; riportare; **to come forward** avanzare; **to look forward to** anticipare il piacere di || tr inoltrare, trasmettere; promuovere

fossil ['fasɪl] adj & s fossile m

foster ['fastər] or ['fɔstər] adj adottivo; di latte || tr allevare; promuovere

fos'ter home' s famiglia adottiva

foul [faʊl] adj sporco; (air) viziato; (wind) contrario; (weather; breath) cattivo; (baseball) fuori linea di gioco || s (of boats) urto, collisione; (baseball) palla colpita fuori linea di gioco; (boxing) colpo basso; (sports) fallo || adv slealmente; (baseball) fuori linea di gioco; **to fall foul of** entrare in collisione con; urtarsi con; **to run foul of** avere una controversia con || tr sporcare; otturare; (baseball) colpire fuori linea di gioco || intr (said of two boats) entrare in collisione; (said, e.g., of a rope) imbrogliarsi

foul-mouthed ['faʊl'maʊðd] or ['faʊl-'maʊθt] adj sboccato, osceno

foul' play' s reato; (sports) gioco sleale

found [faʊnd] tr fondare; (to melt, to cast) fondere

foundation [faʊn'deʃən] s fondazione f; (endowment) dotazione; (charitable) patronato; (masonry support) platea, fondamenta fpl; (make-up) fondo tinta; (fig) fondatezza

founder ['faʊndər] s fondatore m; (of family) capostipite m; (of metals) fonditore m || intr (said of a ship) affondare; (said of a horse) azzopparsi; (to fail) fare fiasco

foundling ['faʊndlɪŋ] s trovatello

found'ling hos'pital s brefotrofio

found·ry ['faʊndrɪ] s (**-ries**) fonderia

found'ry·man s (**-men**) fonditore m

fount [faʊnt] s fonte f

fountain ['faʊntən] s fonte f, fontana; (of knowledge) pozzo

foun'tain·head' s sorgente f

foun'tain pen' s penna stilografica

foun'tain syringe' s clistere m a pera

four [for] adj & pron quattro || s quattro; **four o'clock** le quattro; **on all fours** gattoni, carponi

four'-cy'cle adj a quattro tempi

four'-cyl'inder adj a quattro cilindri

four'-flush' intr (coll) millantarsi

fourflusher ['for,flʌʃər] s (coll) millantatore m

four-footed ['for'fʊtɪd] adj quadrupede

four' hun'dred adj, s & pron quattro-

cento || **the Four Hundred** l'alta società

four'-in-hand' s cravatta a cappio; tiro a quattro

four'-lane' adj a quattro corsie

four'-leaf clo'ver s quadrifoglio

four-legged ['for'legɪd] or ['for'legd] adj a quattro zampe; (schooner) (coll) a quattro alberi

four'-letter word' s parolaccia di quattro lettere

four'-mo'tor plane' s quadrimotore m

four'-o'clock' s (bot) bella di notte

four' of a kind' s (cards) poker m

four'post'er s letto a baldacchino

four'score' adj ottanta

foursome ['forsəm] s gruppo di quattro giocatori

fourteen ['for'tin] adj, s & pron quattordici m

fourteenth ['for'tinθ] adj, s & pron quattordicesimo || s (in dates) quattordici m

fourth [forθ] adj, s & pron quarto || s (in dates) quattro

fourth' estate' s quarto potere

four'-way' adj a quattro orifizi; fra quattro persone; quadruplice

fowl [faʊl] s pollo || intr uccellare

fowl'ing piece' s fucile m da caccia

fox [faks] s volpe f || tr (coll) ingannare

fox'glove' s digitale f

fox'hole' s buca ricovero

fox'hound' s segugio

fox' hunt' s caccia alla volpe

fox' ter'rier s fox-terrier m

fox'-trot' s (of a horse) piccolo trotto; (dance) fox-trot m

fox·y ['faksɪ] adj (**-ier; -iest**) volpino, astuto

foyer ['fɔɪ·ər] s (of a private house) ingresso, vestibolo; (theat) ridotto

fracas ['frekəs] s lite f, tumulto

fraction ['frækʃən] s frazione f; frammento

fractional ['frækʃənəl] adj frazionario; insignificante

fractious ['frækʃəs] adj litigioso, permaloso; indisciplinato

fracture ['fræktʃər] s frattura || tr fratturare; (e.g., an arm) fratturarsi, rompersi || intr fratturarsi

fragile ['frædʒɪl] adj fragile

fragment ['frægmənt] s frammento; (e.g., of a movie) spezzone m || tr frammentare, spezzare

fragmenta'tion bomb' [,frægmən'teʃən] s bomba dirompente

fragrant ['fregrənt] adj fragrante

frail [frel] adj (not robust) gracile; (easily broken) fragile; (morally weak) debole || s canestro di giunco

frail·ty ['freltɪ] s (**-ties**) fragilità f; (of a person) debolezza

frame [frem] s (of picture) cornice f; (of glasses) montatura; (structure) ossatura; (of a building) ingabbiatura, impalcatura; (for embroidering) telaio; (of a window) intelaiatura; (of mind) stato; (of government) sistema m; (mov) inquadratura; (phot) fotogramma m; (aer) ordinata;

(naut) costa ‖ tr (to put in a frame) incorniciare; montare; costruire; inventare; esprimere; (slang) architettare un' accusa contro

frame' house' s casa con l'ossatura di legno

frame'-up' s (slang) complotto per incriminare un innocente

frame'work' s intelaiatura, impalcatura; palificazione

franc [fræŋk] s franco

France [fræns] or [frɑns] s la Francia

Frances ['frænsɪs] or ['frɑnsɪs] s Francesca

franchise ['frænt∫aɪz] s diritto di voto; concessione; (privilege) franchigia

Francis ['frænsɪs] or ['frɑnsɪs] s Francesco

Franciscan [fræn'sɪskən] adj & s francescano

frank [fræŋk] adj sincero, schietto ‖ s affrancatura postale; lettera affrancata; (franking privilege) franchigia postale ‖ tr affrancare ‖ **Frank** s (member of Frankish tribe) franco; (masculine name) Franco

frankfurter ['fræŋkfərtər] s salsiccia di Francoforte, Frankfurter m

frankincense ['fræŋkɪn,sɛns] s olibano

Frankish ['fræŋkɪ∫] adj & s franco

frankness ['fræŋknɪs] s franchezza

frantic ['fræntɪk] adj frenetico

frappé [fræ'pe] adj & s frappé m

frat [fræt] s (slang) associazione di studenti

fraternal [frə'tʌrnəl] adj fraterno

fraterni-ty [frə'tʌrnɪti] s (-ties) (brotherliness) fraternità f; sodalizio; (eccl) confraternita; (U.S.A.) associazione di studenti

fraternize ['frætər,naɪz] intr fraternizzare

fraud [frɔd] s truffa, frode f; (person) (coll) truffatore m

fraudulent ['frɔdjələnt] adj fraudolento; (conversion) indebito

fraught [frɔt] adj—fraught with carico di, gravido di

fray [fre] s zuffa, rissa, lotta ‖ intr sfilacciarsi, logorarsi

freak [frik] s (sudden fancy) capriccio, ticchio; (person, animal) fenomeno

freakish ['frikɪ∫] adj capriccioso; strano, grottesco

freckle ['frɛkəl] s lentiggine f, efelide f

freckle-faced ['frɛkəl,fest] adj lentigginoso

freckly ['frɛkli] adj lentigginoso

Frederick ['frɛdərɪk] s Federico

free [fri] adj (freer ['fri·ər]; freest ['fri·ɪst]) libero; gratis; franco; sciolto; esente; generoso; **to be free with** essere prodigo di; **to set free** liberare ‖ adv liberamente; in libertà; gratis ‖ v (pret & pp **freed** [frid]; ger **freeing** ['fri·ɪŋ]) tr liberare; (from customs) svincolare; esimere

freebooter ['fri,butər] s pirata m

free'born' adj nato in libertà; proprio di un popolo libero

freedom ['fridəm] s libertà f

free'dom of speech' s libertà f di parola

free'dom of the press' s libertà f di stampa

free'dom of the seas' s libertà f di navigazione

free'dom of wor'ship s libertà religiosa

free' en'terprise s economia libera

free'-for-all' s rissa, tafferuglio

free' hand' s libertà assoluta

free'-hand' adj a mano libera

freehanded ['fri'hændɪd] adj liberale, generoso

free' lance' s giornalista mf pubblicista; scrittore m che lavora senza contratto; soldato di ventura

free'load'er ['lodər] s (coll) mangiatore m a sbafo

free'man s (-men) uomo libero; cittadino

Free'ma'son s frammassone m

Free'ma'sonry s frammassoneria

free' of charge' adj gratis, senza spese

free' port' s porto franco

free' serv'ice s manutenzione gratuita

free'-spo'ken adj franco, aperto

free'stone' adj spiccagnolo ‖ s pesca spicca

free'think'er s libero pensatore

free' thought' s libero pensiero

free' trade' s libero scambio

free'trad'er s liberoscambista mf

free'way' s autostrada

free' will' s libero arbitrio

freeze [friz] s gelo, gelata; (e.g., of prices) blocco ‖ v (pret **froze** [froz]; pp **frozen**) tr gelare; (credits, rentals, etc.) bloccare ‖ intr gelarsi; (said of brakes) inchiodarsi; morire assiderato; (to become immobilized) irrigidirsi

freeze'-dry' v (pret & pp **-dried'**) tr liofilizzare

freezer ['frizər] s congelatore m; (for making ice cream) sorbettiera

freight [fret] s carico; (charge) porto; (naut) nolo; **by freight** come carico mercantile; (rr) a piccola velocità ‖ tr spedire come carico

freight' car' s vagone m or carro merci

freighter ['fretər] s speditore m; nave f da carico

freight' plat'form s (rr) banchina adibita al traffico merci

freight' sta'tion s (rr) stazione merci

freight' train' s treno merci, merci m

freight' yard' s (rr) scalo merci

French [frɛnt∫] adj & s francese m; **the French** i francesi

French' bread' s pane m a bastone

French' chalk' s pietra da sarto

French' door' s porta a vetri

French' dress'ing s salsa verde con aceto

French' fried' pota'toes spl patate fritte affettate

French' horn' s (mus) corno

French' leave' s—**to take French leave** andarsene all'inglese, filare all'inglese

French'man s (-men) francese m

French' tel'ephone s microtelefono

French' toast' s pane dorato al salto

French' win'dow s portafinestra

French'wom'an s (-wom'en) francese f

frenzied ['frɛnzid] *adj* frenetico

fren·zy ['frɛnzɪ] *s* (-zies) frenesia

frequen·cy ['frikwənsɪ] *s* (-cies) frequenza

fre′quency modula′tion *s* modulazione di frequenza

frequent ['frikwənt] *adj* frequente || [frɪ'kwɛnt] *or* ['frikwənt] *tr* frequentare, praticare

frequently ['frikwəntlɪ] *adv* frequentemente

fres·co ['frɛsko] *s* (-coes *or* -cos) affresco || *tr* affrescare

fresh [frɛʃ] *adj* fresco; (*water*) dolce; (*new*) nuovo; (*wind*) moderato; (*inexperienced*) novizio; (*cheeky*) (slang) sfacciato || *adv* recentemente, di recente; **fresh in** (coll) appena arrivato; **fresh out** (coll) appena esaurito

freshen ['frɛʃən] *tr* rinfrescare || *intr* rinfrescarsi

freshet ['frɛʃɪt] *s* piena, crescita

fresh′man *s* (-men) (*newcomer*) novizio; (educ) matricola

freshness ['frɛʃnɪs] *s* freschezza; (*of air*) frescura; (*cheek*) (slang) sfacciataggine *f*

fresh′-wa′ter *adj* d'acqua dolce; poco conosciuto; piccolo

fret [frɛt] *s* (*interlaced design*) fregio, greca; irritazione; (mus) tasto || *v* (*pret & pp* **fretted**; *ger* **fretting**) *tr* fregiare || *intr* fremere, trepidare, agitarsi

fretful ['frɛtfəl] *adj* irritabile, permaloso

fret′work′ *s* greca

Freudianism ['frɔɪdɪ·ə‚nɪzəm] *s* freudismo

friar ['fraɪ·ər] *s* frate *m*

friar·y ['fraɪ·ərɪ] *s* (-ies) convento di frati

fricassee [‚frɪkə'si] *s* fricassea

friction ['frɪkʃən] *s* frizione; disaccordo, dissenso

fric′tion tape′ *s* nastro isolante

Friday ['fraɪdɪ] *s* venerdì *m*

fried [fraɪd] *adj* fritto

fried′ egg′ *s* uovo al tegame, uovo occhio di manzo

friend [frɛnd] *s* amico; **to be friends with** essere amico di; **to make friends** allacciare amicizie; **to make friends with** fare l'amicizia di

friend·ly ['frɛndlɪ] *adj* (-lier; -liest) amico, amichevole

friendship ['frɛndʃɪp] *s* amicizia

frieze [friz] *s* (archit) fregio

frigate ['frɪgɪt] *s* fregata

fright [fraɪt] *s* spavento; **to take fright at** spaventarsi di

frighten ['fraɪtən] *tr* intimorire, spaventare; **to frighten away** mettere in fuga, sgomentare || *intr* spaventarsi

frightful ['fraɪtfəl] *adj* spaventevole, orribile; (coll) enorme

frightfulness ['fraɪtfəlnɪs] *s* spavento; terrorismo

frigid ['frɪdʒɪd] *adj* freddo; (*zone*) glaciale

frigidity [frɪ'dʒɪdɪtɪ] *s* (fig) frigidezza; (pathol) frigidità *f*

frill [frɪl] *s* pieghettatura; (*of birds and other animals*) collarino; (*in dress, speech, etc.*) affettazione

fringe [frɪndʒ] *s* frangia; (*in dressmaking*) volantino; (*on curtains*) balza; **on the fringe of** all'orlo di || *tr* orlare

fringe′ ben′efits *spl* assegni *mpl*, benefici *mpl* marginali

fripper·y ['frɪpərɪ] *s* (-ies) (*finery*) fronzoli *mpl*; ostentazione; (*trifles*) cianfrusaglie *fpl*

frisk [frɪsk] *tr* perquisire; (slang) derubare || *intr* fare capriole

frisk·y ['frɪskɪ] *adj* (-ier; -iest) gaio, vivace

fritter ['frɪtər] *s* frittella; frammento || *tr*—**to fritter away** sprecare

frivolous ['frɪvələs] *adj* frivolo

friz [frɪz] *s* (**frizzes**) ricciolo || *v* (*pret & pp* **frizzed**; *ger* **frizzing**) *tr* arricciare

frizzle ['frɪzəl] *s* ricciolo || *tr* arricciare || *intr* arricciarsi

friz·zly ['frɪzlɪ] *adj* (-zlier; -zliest) crespo, riccio

fro [fro] *adv*—**to and fro** avanti e indietro; **to go to and fro** andare e venire

frock [frɑk] *s* gabbano; (*smock*) grembiule *m*; blusa; (*of priest*) tonaca

frock′ coat′ *s* finanziera

frog [frɑg] *or* [frɔg] *s* rana; (*button and loop on a garment*) alamaro; (*in throat*) raschio

frog′man′ *s* (-men) sommozzatore *m*, uomo rana

frol·ic ['frɑlɪk] *s* scherzo, monelleria || *v* (*pret & pp* -**icked**; *ger* -**icking**) *intr* scherzare, folleggiare

frolicsome ['frɑlɪksəm] *adj* scherzoso

from [frʌm], [frɑm] *or* [frəm] *prep* da; di, e.g., **I am from New York** sono di New York; da parte di; a, e.g., **to take s.th away from s.o.** portar via qlco a qlcu

front [frʌnt] *adj* frontale, anteriore; di fronte || *s* fronte *m & f*; (*of a building*) prospetto; (*of a book*) principio; (*of a shirt*) sparato; (*e.g., of wealth*) apparenza; (theat) boccascena *m*; (mil) fronte *m*; **in front of** dinanzi a; **to put on a front** (coll) fare ostentazione; **to put up a bold front** (coll) farsi coraggio || *tr* (*to face*) fronteggiare; (*to confront*) affrontare; (*to supply with a front*) coprire; servire da facciata a || *intr*—**to front on** dare su

frontage ['frʌntɪdʒ] *s* facciata, veduta; terreno di fronte alla casa

front′ door′ *s* porta d'entrata

front′ drive′ *s* (aut) trazione anteriore

frontier [frʌn'tɪr] *adj* limitrofo || *s* frontiera

fron′tiers′man *s* (-men) pioniere *m*

frontispiece ['frʌntɪs‚pis] *s* (*of book*) pagina illustrata di fronte al frontispizio; (*of building*) facciata

front′ mat′ter *s* (*of book*) parte *f* preliminare

front′-page′ *tr* stampare in prima pagina

front′ porch′ *s* porticato

front' room' s stanza con vista sulla strada
front' row' s prima fila
front' seat' s posto in una delle file davanti; (aut) sedile m anteriore
front' steps' spl scalinata d'ingresso
front' view' s vista sulla strada
frost [frɔst] or [frɑst] s gelo, brina, gelata; (fig) freddezza; (slang) fiasco || tr agghiacciare; (with sugar) glassare; (glass) smerigliare
frost'bite' s congelamento
frost'ed glass' s vetro smerigliato
frosting ['frɔstɪŋ] or ['frɑstɪŋ] s glassatura; (of glass) smerigliatura
frost·y ['frɔstɪ] or ['frɑstɪ] adj (-ier; -iest) brinato; (hair) canuto; (fig) gelido
froth [frɔθ] or [frɑθ] s schiuma; (fig) frivolezza || intr schiumare; (at the mouth) avere la schiuma
froth·y ['frɔθɪ] or ['frɑθɪ] adj (-ier; -iest) spumoso; frivolo
froward ['frowərd] adj indocile
frown [fraʊn] s aggrottare m delle ciglia; (of disapproval) cipiglio || intr aggrottare le ciglia; **to frown at** or **on** disapprovare
frows·y or **frowz·y** ['fraʊzɪ] adj (-ier; -iest) sporco; puzzolente
fro'zen foods' ['frozən] spl cibi congelati; cibi surgelati
frugal ['frugəl] adj parsimonioso; (in food and drink) frugale
fruit [frut] adj (tree) fruttifero; (dish) da frutta || s (such as apple) frutto; (collectively) frutta, e.g., **I like fruit** mi piace la frutta; (fig) frutto
fruit' cake' s torta con noci e canditi
fruit' cup' s macedonia di frutta
fruit' dish' s fruttiera, portafrutta m
fruit' fly' s moscerino del vino
fruitful ['frutfəl] adj fruttuoso
fruition [fru'ɪʃən] s realizzazione; **to come to fruition** giungere a buon fine
fruit' jar' s vaso da frutta
fruit' juice' s sugo or spremuta di frutta
fruitless ['frutlɪs] adj infruttuoso
fruit' sal'ad s macedonia di frutta
fruit' stand' s bancarella da fruttivendolo
fruit' store' s negozio di frutta
frumpish ['frʌmpɪʃ] adj trasandato
frustrate ['frʌstret] tr frustrare
fry [fraɪ] s (fries) fritto || v (pret & pp fried) tr & intr friggere
fry'ing pan' s padella; **out of the frying pan into the fire** dalla padella nella brace
fudge [fʌdʒ] s dolce m di cioccolato
fuel ['fju·əl] s combustibile m; (fig) cibo || v (pret & pp fueled or fuelled; ger fueling or fuelling) tr rifornire di carburante || intr rifornirsi di carburante
fuel' cell' s cellula elettrogena
fu'el oil' s nafta, olio pesante
fu'el tank' s serbatoio del carburante
fugitive ['fjudʒɪtɪv] adj & s fuggiasco, fuggitivo
fugue [fjug] s (mus) fuga
ful·crum ['fʌlkrəm] s (-crums or -cra [krə]) fulcro

fulfill [fʊl'fɪl] tr (to carry out) eseguire; (an obligation) mantenere; (to bring to an end) completare
fulfillment [fʊl'fɪlmənt] s adempimento; realizzazione
full [fʊl] adj pieno; (speed) tutto; (garment) ampio; (voice) spiegato; (of food) sazio; (member) effettivo; **full of aches and pains** pieno d'acciacchi; **full of fun** divertentissimo; **full of play** pieno di vita || s pieno; colmo; **in full** per esteso, in pieno; **to the full** completamente || adv completamente; **full many (a)** moltissimi; **full well** perfettamente || tr follare
full-blooded ['fʊl'blʌdɪd] adj vigoroso; purosangue
full-blown ['fʊl'blon] adj completamente sbocciato; maturo
full-bodied ['fʊl'bɑdɪd] adj forte, ricco
full' dress' s vestito da sera; (mil) tenuta di gala, alta uniforme
full-faced ['fʊl'fest] adj paffuto; (view) intero; (typ) grassetto
full-fledged ['fʊl'fledʒd] adj completamente sviluppato; vero, autentico
full-grown ['fʊl'gron] adj completamente sviluppato, adulto
full' house' s (theat) piena; (poker) full m
full'-length' mir'ror s specchiera
full'-length mov'ie s lungometraggio
full' moon' s luna piena
full' name' s nome m e cognome m
full'-page' adj di tutta una pagina
full' pow'ers spl pieni poteri
full' sail' adv a vele spiegate
full'-scale' adj in grandezza naturale; completo
full-sized ['fʊl'saɪzd] adj in grandezza naturale
full' speed' adv a tutta velocità
full' stop' s fermata; (gram) punto
full' swing' s piena attività
full' tilt' adv a tutta forza
full'-time' adj a orario completo
fully ['fʊlɪ] or ['fʊlli] adv completamente, del tutto
fulsome ['fʊlsəm] or ['fʌlsəm] adj basso, volgare; nauseante
fumble ['fʌmbəl] tr (a ball) lasciar cadere || intr titubare; andare a tentoni; (in one's pocket) cercare alla cieca
fume [fjum] s fumo, vapore m, esalazione || tr affumicare || intr fumare, esalare fumo; (to show anger) irritarsi
fumigate ['fjumɪ,get] tr fumigare
fumigation [,fjumɪ'geʃən] s fumigazione
fun [fʌn] s divertimento, spasso; **to be fun** essere divertente; **to have fun** divertirsi; **to make fun of** prendersi gioco di
function ['fʌŋkʃən] s funzione || intr funzionare, marciare, camminare
functional ['fʌŋkʃənəl] adj funzionale
functionalism ['fʌŋkʃənəl,ɪzəm] s funzionalismo
functionar·y ['fʌŋkʃə,nerɪ] s (-ies) funzionario

fund [fʌnd] *s* fondo; *(of knowledge)* suppellettile *f* || *tr (debts)* consolidare

fundamental [ˌfʌndə'mentəl] *adj* fondamentale || *s* fondamento

fundamentalist [ˌfʌndə'mentəlɪst] *adj & s* scritturale *m*

funeral ['fjunərəl] *adj* funebre, funerario || *s* funerale *m*, trasporto funebre; **it's not my funeral** (slang) non sono affari miei

fu'neral direc'tor *s* imprenditore *m* di pompe funebri

fu'neral home' or **par'lor** *s* impresa di pompe funebri

fu'neral serv'ice *s* ufficio dei defunti

funereal [fju'nɪrɪ·əl] *adj* funebre

fungous ['fʌŋgəs] *adj* fungoso

fungus ['fʌŋgəs] *s* (**funguses** or **fungi** ['fʌndʒaɪ]) fungo

funicular [fju'nɪkjələr] *adj & s* funicolare *f*

funk [fʌŋk] *s* (coll) paura; (coll) codardo; **in a funk** (coll) con una paura matta

fun-nel ['fʌnəl] *s* imbuto; *(smokestack)* fumaiolo; *(for ventilation)* manica a vento || *v* (*pret & pp* **-neled** or **-nelled;** *ger* **-neling** or **-nelling**) *tr* incanalare

funnies ['fʌniz] *spl* pagine *fpl* fumetti

fun-ny ['fʌni] *adj* (**-nier; -niest**) comico, buffo; (coll) strano; **to strike as funny** parere strano o buffo a

fun'ny bone' *s* osso rabbioso (del gomito); **to strike s.o.'s funny bone** far ridere qlcu

fur [fʌr] *s* pelo; *(garment)* pelliccia; *(on the tongue)* patina

furbelow ['fʌrbə·lo] *s* falpalà *m*

furbish ['fʌrbɪʃ] *tr* lustrare; mettere a nuovo; **to furbish up** rinfrescare

furious ['fjʊrɪ·əs] *adj* furioso

furl [fʌrl] *tr (a flag)* incazzottare; (naut) raccogliere, strangolare

fur-lined ['fʌr‚laɪnd] *adj* foderato di pelliccia

furlong ['fʌrlɔŋ] or ['fʌrlɑŋ] *s* un ottavo di miglio terrestre

furlough ['fʌrlo] *s* licenza || *tr* licenziare

furnace ['fʌrnɪs] *s* fornace *f*; *(to heat a house)* caldaia del calorifero

furnish ['fʌrnɪʃ] *tr* fornire; ammobiliare

furnishings ['fʌrnɪʃɪŋz] *spl* mobilia; *(things to wear)* accessori *mpl* da uomo

furniture ['fʌrnɪtʃər] *s* mobili *mpl*, mobilia; (naut) attrezzatura; **a piece of furniture** un mobile

fur·ni·ture deal'er *s* mobiliere *m*

furor ['fjʊrər] *s* furore *m*

furrier ['fʌrɪ·ər] *s* pellicciaio

furrier·y ['fʌrɪ·əri] *s* (**-ies**) pellicceria

furrow ['fʌro] *s* solco || *tr* solcare

further ['fʌrðər] *adj* più lontano; ulteriore || *adv* oltre; più; inoltre || *tr* favorire, incoraggiare

furtherance ['fʌrðərəns] *s* avanzamento, incoraggiamento

furthermore ['fʌrðər‚mor] *adv* inoltre

furthest ['fʌrðɪst] *adj* (il) più lontano || *adv* al massimo

furtive ['fʌrtɪv] *adj* furtivo

fu·ry ['fjʊri] *s* (**-ries**) furia

furze [fʌrz] *s* ginestra spinosa

fuse [fjuz] *s (for igniting an explosive)* miccia; *(for detonating an explosive)* spoletta; (elec) fusibile *m;* **to burn out a fuse** bruciare un fusibile || *tr* fondere || *intr* fondersi; (elec) saltare

fuse' box' *s* valvoliera

fuselage ['fjuzəlɪdʒ] or [‚fjuzə'laʒ] *s* fusoliera

fusible ['fjuzɪbəl] *adj* fusibile

fusillade [‚fjuzɪ'led] *s* fucileria; (fig) gragnola || *tr* attaccare con fuoco di fucileria

fusion ['fjuʒən] *s* fusione

fuss [fʌs] *s* -agitazione inutile; (coll) alterco per nulla; **to make a fuss** accogliere festosamente; fare molte storie; **to make a fuss over** aver un alterco su || *tr* disturbare || *intr* agitarsi per un nonnulla

fuss·y ['fʌsi] *adj* (**-ier; -iest**) *(person)* pignolo, meticoloso; *(object)* carico di fronzoli; *(writing)* complicato

fustian ['fʌstʃən] *s* fustagno; (fig) verbosità *f*, magniloquenza

fust·y ['fʌsti] *adj* (**-ier; -iest**) ammuffito, che sa di muffa; antico, sorpassato

futile ['fjutɪl] *adj (unproductive)* sterile; *(unimportant)* futile

futil·i·ty [fju'tɪlɪti] *s* (**-ties**) sterilità *f;* futilità *f*

future ['fjutʃər] *adj* futuro || *s* futuro; **futures** contratto con consegna a termine; **in the near future** nel prossimo avvenire

fuze [fjuz] *s (for igniting an explosive)* miccia; *(for detonating an explosive)* spoletta; (elec) fusibile *m* || *tr* innestare la spoletta a

fuzz [fʌz] *s* lanugine *f*, peluria; *(in corners)* polvere *f;* (slang) poliziotto; (slang) polizia

fuzz·y ['fʌzi] *adj* (**-ier; -iest**) lanuginoso; coperto di polvere; *(indistinct)* confuso

G, g [dʒi] *s* settima lettera dell'alfabeto inglese

gab [gæb] *s* (coll) parlantina || *v* (*pret & pp* **gabbed;** *ger* **gabbing**) *intr* (coll) chiacchierare

gabardine ['gæbər‚din] *s* gabardine *f*

gabble ['gæbəl] *s* barbugliamento || *intr* barbugliare

gable ['gebəl] *s* (archit) timpano

ga'ble roof' *s* tetto a due falde, tetto a capanna

gad [gæd] *v* (*pret & pp* **gadded;** *ger* **gadding**) *intr* bighellonare

gad'about' *adj* ozioso || *s* vagabondo, bighellone *m;* fannullone *m*

gad'fly' *s* (**-flies**) tafano, moscone *m*

gadget ['gædʒɪt] *s* congegno, dispositivo, macchinetta

Gaelic ['gelɪk] *adj & s* gaelico

gaff [gæf] *s* arpione *m*; (naut) picco; **to stand the gaff** (slang) aver pazienza

gag [gæg] *s* bavaglio; (*joke*) barzelletta; (theat) battuta improvvisata || *v* (*pret & pp* **gagged;** *ger* **gagging**) *tr* imbavagliare; soffocare || *intr* sentirsi venire la nausea

gage [gedʒ] *s* (*pledge*) pegno; (*challenge*) sfida

gaie·ty ['ge·ɪti] *s* (-**ties**) gaiezza

gaily ['geli] *adv* allegramente

gain [gen] *s* profitto; (*increase*) aumento || *tr* guadagnare; (*to reach*) raggiungere; (*altitude*) prendere || *intr* (said of a patient) migliorare; (said of a watch) correre; **to gain on** guadagnare terreno su; sorpassare

gainful ['genfəl] *adj* rimunerativo

gain'say' *v* (*pret & pp* **-said** [,sed] or [,sɛd]) *tr* disdire, misconoscere; negare

gait [get] *s* portamento, andatura

gaiter ['getər] *s* ghetta

gala [ˈgelə] or [ˈgelə] *adj* di gala || *s* gala *m & f*, festa

galax·y ['gæləksi] *s* (-**ies**) galassia

gale [gel] *s* (*of wind*) bufera; (*of laughter*) scoppio; **to weather the gale** resistere alla tempesta

gall [gɔl] *s* fiele *m*; bile *f*; cistifellea; scorticatura; (*gallnut*) galla; (*audacity*) (coll) faccia tosta || *tr* irritare || *intr* irritarsi; (naut) logorarsi

gallant ['gælənt] or [gəˈlænt] *adj* galante || ['gælənt] *adj* (*brave*) valoroso; (*grand*) magnifico; (*showy*) festivo || *s* prode *m*; (*man attentive to women*) galante *m*

gallant·ry ['gæləntri] *s* (-**ries**) galanteria; valore *m*

gall' blad'der *s* vescichetta biliare

gall'-blad'der attack' *s* travaso di bile

galleon ['gælɪ·ən] *s* galeone *m*

galler·y ['gæləri] *s* (-**ies**) galleria; tribuna; (*cheapest seats in theater*) loggione *m*

galley ['gæli] *s* (*vessel*) galera; (*kitchen*) (aer) cucina; (*kitchen*) (naut) cambusa; (*galley proof*) (typ) bozza in colonna; (*tray*) (typ) vantaggio

gal'ley proof' *s* bozza in colonna

gal'ley slave' *s* galeotto

Gallic ['gælɪk] *adj* gallo, gallico

galling ['gɔlɪŋ] *adj* irritante

gallivant ['gælɪ,vænt] *intr* andare a spasso; fare il galante

gall'nut' *s* galla

gallon ['gælən] *s* gallone *m*

galloon [gəˈlun] *s* gallone *m*, nastro

gallop ['gæləp] *s* galoppo; **at a gallop** al galoppo || *tr* far galoppare || *intr* galoppare

gal·lows ['gæloz] *s* (-**lows** or -**lowses**) forca; (min) castelletto

gal'lows bird' *s* (coll) remo di galera, pendaglio da forca

gall'stone' *s* calcolo biliare

galore [gəˈlor] *adv* in abbondanza

galosh [gəˈlɑʃ] *s* stivaletto di gomma

galvanize ['gælvə,naɪz] *tr* galvanizzare

gal'vanized i'ron *s* ferro zincato

gambit ['gæmbɪt] *s* gambetto

gamble ['gæmbəl] *s* azzardo; (*game*) gioco d'azzardo || *tr* giocare; **to gamble away** giocarsi || *intr* giocare d'azzardo; (com) speculare

gambler ['gæmblər] *s* giocatore *m*; speculatore *m*

gambling ['gæmblɪŋ] *s* gioco (d'azzardo)

gam'bling den' *s* bisca

gam'bling house' *s* casa da gioco

gam·bol ['gæmbəl] *s* salto, capriola || *v* (*pret & pp* **-boled** or **-bolled;** *ger* **-boling** or **-bolling**) *intr* saltare, far capriole

gambrel ['gæmbrəl] *s* garretto

gam'brel roof' *s* tetto a mansarda

game [gem] *adj* da caccia; coraggioso; (*leg*) (coll) zoppo; (coll) pronto || *s* (*amusement*) gioco; (*contest*) partita; (*any sport*) sport *m*; (*wild animals hunted*) selvaggina; (*any pursuit*) attività *f*; (*object of pursuit*) bersaglio; (*bridge*) manche *f*; **the game is up** il gioco è fallito; **to make game of** farsi gioco di; **to play the game** giocare onestamente

game' bag' *s* carniere *m*

game'cock' *s* gallo da combattimento

game'keep'er *s* guardacaccia *m*

game' of chance' *s* gioco d'azzardo

game' preserve' *s* bandita di caccia

game' war'den *s* guardacaccia *m*

gamut ['gæmət] *s* (mus, fig) gamma

gam·y ['gemi] *adj* (-**ier, -iest**) coraggioso; (culin) che sa di selvatico

gander ['gændər] *s* papero, oca

gang [gæŋ] *adj* multiplo || *s* (*of workers*) ganga; (*of thugs*) cricca || *intr*—**to gang up** riunirsi; **to gang up against** or **on** (coll) gettarsi insieme contro

gangling ['gæŋglɪŋ] *adj* dinoccolato

gangli·on ['gæŋglɪ·ən] *s* (-**ons** or -**a** [ə]) ganglio

gang'plank' *s* palanca, plancia

gangrene ['gæŋgrin] *s* cancrena || *tr* far andare in cancrena || *intr* andare in cancrena

gangster ['gæŋstər] *s* gangster *m*

gang'way' *s* (*passageway*) corridoio; (*gangplank*) passerella, scalandrone *m*; (*in ship's side*) barcarizzo || *interj* lasciar passare!

gan·try ['gæntri] *s* (-**tries**) (*of crane*) cavalletto; (rr) ponte *m* delle segnalazioni; (rok) piattaforma verticale, torre *f* di lancio

gap [gæp] *s* (*pass*) passo; (*in a wall*) breccia; (*interval*) lacuna; (*between two points of view*) abisso; (mach) gioco

gape [gep] or [gæp] *s* apertura; (*yawn*) sbadiglio; sguardo di meraviglia || *intr* stare a bocca aperta; **to gape at** guardare a bocca aperta

garage [gəˈrɑʒ] *s* rimessa

garb [garb] *s* veste *f* || *tr* vestire

garbage ['garbɪdʒ] *s* pattume *m*, immondizia, immondizie *fpl*

gar'bage can' *s* portaimmondizie *m*

gar′bage collec′tor s spazzaturaio, spazzino, netturbino

garble ['gɑrbəl] tr falsare, mutilare

garden ['gɑrdən] s (of vegetables) orto; (of flowers) giardino

gardener ['gɑrdnər] s (of vegetables) ortolano; (of flowers) giardiniere m

gardenia [gɑr'dinɪ‧ə] s gardenia

gardening ['gɑrdnɪŋ] s orticoltura; giardinaggio

gar′den par′ty s trattenimento in giardino

gargle ['gɑrgəl] s gargarismo ‖ intr gargarizzare

gargoyle ['gɑrgɔɪl] s doccione m, gargolla

garish ['gerɪʃ] or ['gærɪʃ] adj appariscente; abbagliante

garland ['gɑrlənd] s ghirlanda ‖ tr inghirlandare

garlic ['gɑrlɪk] s aglio

garment ['gɑrmənt] s capo di vestiario

gar′ment bag′ s tessilsacco

garner ['gɑrnər] tr mettere in granaio; (to get) acquistarsi; (to hoard) incettare

garnet ['gɑrnɪt] adj & s granata

garnish ['gɑrnɪʃ] s guarnizione; ‖ tr guarnire; (law) sequestrare

garret ['gerɪt] s sottotetto, soffitta

garrison ['gærɪsən] s guarnigione, presidio ‖ tr presidiare

garrote [gə'rɑt] or [gə'rot] s strangolamento; garrotta ‖ tr strangolare; giustiziare con la garrotta

garrulous ['gærələs] or ['gærjələs] adj garrulo, loquace

garter ['gɑrtər] s giarrettiera

gas [gæs] s gas m; (coll) benzina; (slang) successo; (slang) chiacchiere fpl ‖ v (pret & pp **gassed;** ger **gassing**) tr fornire di gas; (mil) gassare; (slang) divertire ‖ intr emettere gas; (slang) chiacchierare; **to gas up** fare il pieno

gas′bag′ s involucro per il gas; (coll) chiacchierone m

gas′ burn′er s becco a gas; (on a stove) fornello a gas

Gascony ['gæskənɪ] s la Guascogna

gaseous ['gæsɪ‧əs] adj gassoso

gas′ fit′ter s gassista m

gash [gæʃ] s sfregio ‖ tr sfregiare

gas′ heat′ s calefazione a gas

gas′hold′er s gassometro

gas·i·fy ['gæsɪ‚faɪ] v (pret & pp -**fied**) tr gassificare ‖ intr gassificarsi

gas′ jet′ s fornello a gas; fiamma

gasket ['gæskɪt] s guarnizione

gas′light′ s luce f del gas

gas′ main′ s tubatura principale del gas

gas′ mask′ s maschera antigas

gas′ me′ter s contatore m del gas

gasoline ['gæsə‚lin] or [‚gæsə'lin] s benzina

gas′oline′ deal′er s benzinaio

gas′oline′ pump′ s colonnetta, distributore m di benzina

gasp [gæsp] or [gɑsp] s respirazione affannosa; (of death) rantolo ‖ tr dire affannosamente ‖ intr boccheggiare

gas′ range′ s cucina a gas, fornello a gas

gas′-sta′tion attend′ant s benzinaio

gas′ stove′ s cucina a gas

gas′ tank′ s gassometro; (aut) serbatoio di benzina

gastric ['gæstrɪk] adj gastrico

gastronomy [gæs'trɑnəmɪ] s gastronomia

gas′ works′ s officina del gas

gate [get] s porta; (in fence or wall) cancello; (of sluice) saracinesca; (in an airport or station) uscita; (rr) barriera; (sports, theat) incasso totale; **to crash the gate** (coll) fare il portoghese

gate′keep′er s portiere m; (rr) guardiabarriere m

gate′way′ s passaggio, entrata

gather ['gæðər] tr raccogliere, cogliere; (news) raccapezzare; (dust) coprirsi di; (e.g., a shawl) avvolgere; (speed) aumentare (di); concludere, dedurre; (signatures) (bb) riunire; (sew) increspare ‖ intr riunirsi; raccogliersi; accumularsi

gathering ['gæðərɪŋ] s riunione; (bb) raccolta e piegatura; (pathol) ascesso; (sew) pieghettatura

gaud·y ['gɔdɪ] adj (-ier; -iest) chiassoso, vistoso

gauge [gedʒ] s misura; calibro; (for liquids) indicatore m di livello; (of carpenter) graffietto; indice m; diametro; (aut) spia; (rr) scartamento ‖ tr misurare; calibrare; (naut) stazzare

Gaul [gɔl] s gallo

gaunt [gɔnt] or [gɑnt] adj magro, emaciato; (e.g., landscape) desolato

gauntlet ['gɔntlɪt] or ['gɑntlɪt] s guanto; guanto di ferro; guantone m, manopola; **to run the gauntlet** (fig) esporsi alla critica; **to take up the gauntlet** raccogliere il guanto; **to throw down the gauntlet** gettare il guanto

gauze [gɔz] s garza

gavel ['gævəl] s martello, martelletto

gavotte [gə'vɑt] s gavotta

gawk [gɔk] s sciocco ‖ intr guardare a bocca aperta

gawk·y ['gɔkɪ] adj (-ier; -iest) sgraziato, goffo

gay [ge] adj gaio; brillante; dissipato; (slang) omosessuale

gaye·ty ['ge‧ɪtɪ] s (-ties) gaiezza

gaze [gez] s sguardo fisso ‖ intr fissare lo sguardo

gazelle [gə'zel] s gazzella

gazette [gə'zet] s gazzetta

gazetteer [‚gæzə'tɪr] s dizionario geografico

gear [gɪr] s utensili mpl, attrezzi mpl; (mechanism) meccanismo, dispositivo; (aut) marcia; (mach) ingranaggio **out of gear** disingranato; (fig) disturbato; **to throw into gear** ingranare; **to throw out of gear** disingranare; (fig) disturbare ‖ tr adattare ‖ intr adattarsi

gear′ box′ s scatola del cambio

gear′shift′ s cambio di velocità

gear'shift lev'er s leva del cambio
gear'wheel s ruota dentata
gee [dʒi] *interj* oh!; che bellezza!; **gee up!** (*command to a draft animal*) arri!
Gei'ger count'er ['gaɪgər] s contatore *m* Geiger
gel [dʒɛl] s gel *m* || *v* (*pret & pp* **gelled**; *ger* **gelling**) *intr* gelatinizzarsi
gelatine ['dʒɛlətɪn] s gelatina
geld [gɛld] *v* (*pret & pp* **gelded** or **gelt** [gɛlt]) *tr* castrare
gem [dʒɛm] s gemma, gioia
Gemini ['dʒɛmɪ͵naɪ] *spl* i Gemelli
gender ['dʒɛndər] s (gram) genere *m*; (coll) sesso
gene [dʒin] s (biol) gene *m*
genealo•gy [͵dʒɛnɪ'ælədʒɪ] or [͵dʒini-'ælədʒi] s (**-gies**) genealogia
general ['dʒɛnərəl] *adj & s* generale *m*
gen'eral deliv'ery s fermo in posta, fermo posta *m*
generalissi•mo [͵dʒɛnərə'lɪsɪmo] s (**-mos**) generalissimo
generali•ty [͵dʒɛnə'rælɪtɪ] s (**-ties**) generalità *f*
generalize ['dʒɛnərə͵laɪz] *tr & intr* generalizzare
generally ['dʒɛnərəli] *adv* in genere, generalmente
gen'eral part'ner s accomandatario
gen'eral practi'tioner s medico generico
generalship ['dʒɛnərəl͵ʃɪp] s generalato; strategia, abilità *f* militare; abilità amministrativa
gen'eral staff' s stato maggiore
generate ['dʒɛnə͵ret] *tr* (*offspring*; *electricity*) generare; (math) originare
gen'erat'ing sta'tion s centrale elettrica
generation [͵dʒɛnə'reʃən] s generazione
generative ['dʒɛnə͵retɪv] *adj* generativo
gen'erative gram'mar s grammatica generativa
generator ['dʒɛnə͵retər] s generatore *m*; (elec) generatrice *f*
generic [dʒɪ'nɛrɪk] *adj* generico
generous ['dʒɛnərəs] *adj* generoso; abbondante, copioso
gene•sis ['dʒɛnɪsɪs] s (**-ses** [͵siz]) genesi *f* || **Genesis** s (Bib) Genesi *m*
genetic [dʒɪ'nɛtɪk] *adj* genetico || **genetics** *ssg* genetica
Geneva [dʒɪ'nivə] s Ginevra
Genevan [dʒɪ'nivən] *adj & s* ginevrino
genial ['dʒinɪ•əl] *adj* affabile, geniale
genie ['dʒini] s genio
genital ['dʒɛnɪtəl] *adj* genitale || **genitals** *spl* genitali *mpl*
genitive ['dʒɛnɪtɪv] *adj & s* genitivo
genius ['dʒinjəs] or ['dʒini•əs] s (**geniuses**) genio || s (**genii** ['dʒini-͵aɪ] (*spirit; deity*) genio
Genoa ['dʒɛno•ə] s Genova
genocide ['dʒɛnə͵saɪd] s (*act*) genocidio; (*person*) genocida *mf*
Geno•ese [͵dʒɛno'iz] *adj* genovese || s (**-ese**) genovese *mf*
genre ['ʒɑnrə] *adj* (*e.g., painting*) di genere || s genere *m*

genteel [dʒɛn'til] *adj* (*well-bred*) beneducato; (*affectedly polite*) manieroso, manierato
gentian ['dʒɛnʃən] s genziana
gentile ['dʒɛntɪl] or ['dʒɛntaɪl] *adj* gentilizio || ['dʒɛntaɪl] *adj & s* non circonciso; non ebreo; cristiano; (*pagan*) gentile
gentili•ty [dʒɛn'tɪlɪtɪ] s (**-ties**) distinzione, raffinatezza
gentle ['dʒɛntəl] *adj* (*e.g., manner*) gentile; (*e.g., wind*) dolce, soave; (*wellborn*) bennato; (*tap*) leggero
gen'tle-folk' s gente *f* per bene
gen'tle-man s (**-men**) signore *m*; (*attendant to a person of high rank*) gentiluomo; (*well-mannered man*) gentleman *m*
gen'tleman in wait'ing s gentiluomo di camera
gentlemanly ['dʒɛntəlmənlɪ] *adj* signorile
gen'tleman of the road' s brigante *m*; vagabondo
gen'tlemen's agree'ment s accordo fondato sulla buona fede
gen'tle sex' s gentil sesso
gentry ['dʒɛntrɪ] s gente *f* per bene
genuine ['dʒɛnjʊ•ɪn] *adj* genuino
genus ['dʒinəs] s (**genera** ['dʒɛnərə] or **genuses**) genere *m*
geographer [dʒɪ'ɑgrəfər] s geografo
geographic(al) [͵dʒɪ-ə'græfɪk(əl)] *adj* geografico
geogra•phy [dʒɪ'ɑgrəfɪ] s (**-phies**) geografia
geologic(al) [͵dʒɪ-ə'lɑdʒɪk(əl)] *adj* geologico
geologist [dʒɪ'ɑlədʒɪst] s geologo
geolo•gy [dʒɪ'ɑlədʒɪ] s (**-gies**) geologia
geometric(al) [͵dʒɪ-ə'mɛtrɪk(əl)] *adj* geometrico
geometrician [dʒɪ͵ɑmɪ'trɪʃən] s geometra *mf*
geome•try [dʒɪ'ɑmɪtrɪ] s (**-tries**) geometria
George [dʒɔrdʒ] s Giorgio
geranium [dʒɪ'renɪ•əm] s geranio
geriatrics [͵dʒɛrɪ'ætrɪks] *ssg* geriatria
germ [dʒʌrm] s germe *m*
German ['dʒʌrmən] *adj & s* tedesco
germane [dʒʌr'men] *adj* pertinente
Germanize ['dʒʌrmə͵naɪz] *tr* germanizzare
Ger'man mea'sles s rosolia, rubeola
Ger'man sil'ver s alpacca
Germany ['dʒʌrmənɪ] s la Germania
germ' car'rier s portatore *m* di germi
germ' cell' s cellula germinale
germicidal [͵dʒʌrmɪ'saɪdəl] *adj* germicida
germicide ['dʒʌrmɪ͵saɪd] s germicida *m*
germinate ['dʒʌrmɪ͵net] *intr* germinare
germ' war'fare s guerra batteriologica
gerontology [͵dʒɛrɑn'tɑlədʒɪ] s gerontologia
gerund ['dʒɛrənd] s gerundio
gestation [dʒɛs'teʃən] s gestazione
gesticulate [dʒɛs'tɪkjə͵let] *intr* gesticolare

gesticulation [dʒes‚tɪkjə'leʃən] s gesticolazione

gesture ['dʒest/ər] s gesto ‖ intr gestire, gesticolare

get [get] v (pret **got** [gɑt]; pp **got** or **gotten** ['gɑtən]; ger **getting**) tr ottenere; ricevere; prendere; andare a comprare; procacciare; riportare; procurarsi; riscuotere; guadagnare; **to get across** far capire; **to get back** riacquistare; **to get down** staccare; (to swallow) trangugiare; **to get off** togliere, cavare; **to get s.o. to** + inf indurre che qlcu + subj; **to get done** far fare; **to have got** (coll) avere; **to have got to** + inf (coll) dovere + inf ‖ intr (to become) diventare, farsi; (to arrive) arrivare, venire; **to get out** (said of a convalescent) alzarsi; **to get along** andarsene; andare avanti; tirare avanti, giostrare; aver successo; **to get along in years** essere avanti con gli anni; **to get along with** andare d'accordo con; **to get angry** arrabbiarsi; **to get around** uscire; divulgarsi; rigirare; **to get away** scappare, darsela a gambe; **to get away with** s.th scappare con qlco; (coll) farla franca; **to get back** ritornare, ricuperare; **to get back at** (coll) vendicarsi di; **to get behind** rimanere indietro; (to support) appoggiare, patrocinare; **to get better** migliorare; **to get by** passare oltre; (to succeed) arrivare a farcela; passare inosservato; **to get even with** rifarsi con, prendersi la rivincita con; **to get going** mettersi in moto; **to get in** entrare; rientrare; arrivare; **to get in deeper and deeper** cacciarsi nei pasticci; **to get in with** diventare amico di; **to get married** sposarsi; **to get off** andarsene; smontare da; **to get old** invecchiare; **to get on** andare avanti; andare d'accordo; **to get out** uscire; propagarsi; **to get out of** (a car) uscire da; (trouble) trarsi di; **to get out of the way** togliersi di mezzo; **to get run over** essere investito; **to get through** finire; arrivare; farsi capire; **to get to be** finire per essere; **to get under way** mettersi in cammino; **to get up** alzarsi; **to not get over it** (coll) non arrivare a rassegnarsi

get'a‧way' s fuga; (sports) partenza

get'-to‧geth'er s riunione, crocchio

get'up' s (coll) stile m, presentazione; (coll) costume m, abbigliamento

gewgaw ['gjugɔ] s cianfrusaglia

geyser ['gaɪzər] s geyser m

ghast‧ly ['gæstli] or ['gɑstli] adj (-lier; -liest) orribile, orrendo; spettrale

gherkin ['gʌrkɪn] s cetriolino

ghet‧to ['geto] s (-tos or -toes) ghetto

ghost [gost] s spettro, fantasma m; **not a ghost of** nemmeno l'ombra di; **to give up the ghost** rendere l'anima

ghost‧ly ['gostli] adj (-lier; -liest) spettrale, fantomatico

ghost' sto'ry s storia di fantasmi

ghost' town' s città morta

ghost' writ'er s collaboratore anonimo

ghoul [gul] s spirito necrofago; ladro di tombe

ghoulish ['gulɪʃ] adj demoniaco, macabro

GI ['dʒi'aɪ] (letterword) (**General Issue**) s (**GI's**) soldato degli Stati Uniti

giant ['dʒaɪ‧ənt] adj & s gigante m

giantess ['dʒaɪ‧əntɪs] s gigantessa

gibberish ['dʒɪbərɪʃ] or ['gɪbərɪʃ] s linguaggio inintelligibile

gibbet ['dʒɪbɪt] s forca ‖ tr impiccare sulla forca; (to hold up to scorn) mettere alla berlina

gibe [dʒaɪb] s scherno, frecciata ‖ intr schernire; **to gibe at** beffarsi di

giblets ['dʒɪblɪts] spl rigaglie fpl

giddiness ['gɪdɪnɪs] s vertigine f; frivolezza

gid‧dy ['gɪdi] adj (-dier; -diest) vertiginoso; preso dalle vertigini; frivolo

gift [gɪft] s regalo; (natural ability) dono, dote f; (for Christmas) strenna

gifted ['gɪftɪd] adj dotato

gift' horse' s—**never look a gift horse in the mouth** a caval donato non si guarda in bocca

gift' of gab' s (coll) facondia; **to have the gift of gab** (coll) avere la lingua sciolta

gift' pack'age s pacco-dono

gift' shop' s negozio di regali

gift'-wrap' v (pret & pp **-wrapped;** ger **-wrapping**) tr incartare in carta speciale per regali

gigantic [dʒaɪ'gæntɪk] adj gigantesco

giggle ['gɪgəl] s risolino ‖ intr ridere scioccamente, ridacchiare

gigo‧lo ['dʒɪgə‚lo] s (-los) gigolo

gild [gɪld] v (pret & pp **gilded** or **gilt** [gɪlt]) tr dorare, indorare

gilding ['gɪldɪŋ] s doratura

gill [gɪl] s (of fish) branchia ‖ [dʒɪl] s quarto di pinta

gilt [gɪlt] adj & s dorato

gilt-edged ['gɪlt‚edʒd] adj a bordo dorato; di primissima qualità

gimcrack ['dʒɪm‚kræk] adj di nessun valore ‖ s cianfrusaglia

gimlet ['gɪmlɪt] s succhiello

gimmick ['gɪmɪk] s (slang) trucco

gin [dʒɪn] s (liquor) gin m; (trap) trappola; (mach) arganello; (tex) sgranatrice f di cotone ‖ v (pret & pp **ginned**; ger **ginning**) tr ginnare, sgranare

ginger ['dʒɪndʒər] s zenzero; (coll) energia, vivacità f

gin'ger ale' s gazosa allo zenzero

gin'ger‧bread' s pan di zenzero; ornamento di cattivo gusto

gingerly ['dʒɪndʒərli] adj cauto ‖ adv con cautela

gin'ger‧snap' s biscotto allo zenzero

gingham ['gɪŋəm] s rigatino

giraffe [dʒɪ'ræf] or [dʒɪ'rɑf] s giraffa

girandole ['dʒɪrən‚dol] s girandola

gird [gʌrd] v (pret & pp **girt** [gʌrt] or **girded**) tr cingere; (to equip) dotare; (to prepare) preparare; (to surround) circondare

girder ['gʌrdər] s longherina

girdle ['gʌrdəl] *s* reggicalze *m*, zona, fascetta || *tr* fasciare; circondare

girl [gʌrl] *s* fanciulla; ragazza

girl' friend' *s* amica, innamorata

girlhood ['gʌrlhud] *s* adolescenza, giovinezza

girlish ['gʌrlɪʃ] *adj* fanciullesco; da ragazza

girl' scout' *s* giovane esploratrice *f*

girth [gʌrθ] *s* circonferenza; fascia; (*to hold a saddle*) sottopancia *m*

gist [dʒɪst] *s* sugo, nocciolo, essenza

give [gɪv] *s* elasticità *f* || *v* (*pret* **gave** [gev]; *pp* **given** ['gɪvən]) *tr* dare; (*trouble*) causare; (*a play*) rappresentare; (*a speech; fruit; a sigh*) fare; **to give away** distribuire gratuitamente; (*to reveal*) lasciarsi sfuggire; (*a bride*) accompagnare all'altare; (*coll*) tradire; **to give back** restituire; **to give forth** (*odors*) emettere; **to give oneself up** darsi; **to give up cedere**; (*a position*) abbandonare || *intr* dare; cedere; (*said, e.g., of a rope*) rompersi; **to give in** cedere; darsi per vinto; **to give out** esaurirsi; venir meno; **to give up** darsi per vinto

give'-and-take' *s* compromesso; conversazione briosa

give'a·way' *s* premio gratuito; rivelazione involontaria; (*game*) vinciperdi *m*; (*rad, telv*) programma *m* a premi

given ['gɪvən] *adj* dato; **given that** dato che, concesso che

giv'en name' *s* nome *m* di battesimo

giver ['gɪvər] *s* donatore *m*; dispensatore *m*

gizzard ['gɪzərd] *s* magone *m*

glacial ['gleʃəl] *adj* glaciale

glacier ['gleʃər] *s* ghiacciaio

glad [glæd] *adj* (**gladder; gladdest**) felice, lieto, contento; **to be glad (to)** essere felice (di)

gladden ['glædən] *tr* rallegrare

glade [gled] *s* radura

glad' hand' *s* (coll) accoglienza calorosa

gladiator ['glædɪˌetər] *s* gladiatore *m*

gladiola [ˌglædɪˈolə] or [gləˈdaɪ·ələ] *s* gladiolo

gladly ['glædli] *adv* volentieri, di buon grado

gladness ['glædnɪs] *s* contentezza

glad' rags' *s* (coll) panni *mpl* da festa; (coll) vestito da sera

glamorous ['glæmərəs] *adj* affascinante, attraente

glamour ['glæmər] *s* fascino, malia

glam'our girl' *s* ragazza sci-sci

glance [glæns] or [glɑns] *s* occhiata, guardata; **at first glance** a prima vista || *intr* lanciare uno sguardo; **to glance at** dare un'occhiata a; **to glance off** sorvolare su; deviare da; **to glance over** dare una scorsa a

gland [glænd] *s* ghiandola

glanders ['glændərz] *spl* morva

glare [gler] *s* splendore *m*, luce *f* abbagliante; sguardo minaccioso || *intr* risplendere; lanciare occhiatacce; **to glare at** fare la faccia feroce a

glare' ice' *s* vetrato

glaring ['glerɪŋ] *adj* risplendente, abbagliante; (*look*) torvo; evidente

glass [glæs] or [glɑs] *s* vetro; (*tumbler*) bicchiere *m;* (*mirror*) specchio; (*glassware*) cristalleria; **glasses** occhiali *mpl*

glass' blow'er ['blo·ər] *s* vetraio

glass' case' *s* vetrinetta

glass' cut'ter *s* tagliatore *m* di cristallo; (*tool*) diamante *m* tagliavetro

glass' door' *s* porta a vetri

glassful ['glæsful] or ['glɑsful] *s* bicchiere *m*

glass'house' *s* vetreria; (fig) casa di vetro

glass'ware' *s* vetreria, cristalleria

glass' wool' *s* vetro filato

glass'work'er *s* vetraio

glass'works' *s* vetreria, cristalleria

glass·y ['glæsi] or ['glɑsi] *adj* (**-ier; -iest**) vetriato, vetroso

glaze [glez] *s* vernice vitrea; smalto; (*of ice*) superficie invetriata; (culin) glassa || *tr* smaltare; invetriare; (culin) glassare

glazier ['gleʒər] *s* vetraio

gleam [glim] *s* barlume *m*, raggio || *intr* baluginare

glean [glin] *tr* spigolare, racimolare; (*to gather facts*) raccogliere

glee [gli] *s* gioia, esultanza

glee' club' *s* società *f* corale

glib [glɪb] *adj* (**glibber; glibbest**) loquace; (*tongue*) facile, sciolto

glide [glaɪd] *s* scivolata; (aer) volo a vela, volo planato; (mus) legamento || *intr* scivolare; (aer) librarsi, planare; **to glide away** scorrere

glider ['glaɪdər] *s* (aer) libratore *m*, veleggiatore *m*

glimmer ['glɪmər] *s* barlume *m* || *intr* brillare, luccicare; tralucere

glimmering ['glɪmərɪŋ] *adj* tenue, tremulo || *s* luce fioca; barlume *m*

glimpse [glɪmps] *s* occhiata; **to catch a glimpse of** intravedere || *tr* travedere

glint [glɪnt] *s* scintillio || *intr* scintillare

glisten ['glɪsən] *s* scintillio, luccichio || *intr* scintillare, luccicare

glitter ['glɪtər] *s* luccichio || *intr* rilucere, sfolgorare

gloaming ['glomɪŋ] *s* crepuscolo (vespertino)

gloat [glot] *intr* guardare con maligna soddisfazione; **to gloat over** godere di

global ['globəl] *adj* globale; universale; globulare

globe [glob] *s* globo; (*with map of earth*) mappamondo

globe-trotter ['glob,trotər] *s* giramondo

globule ['globjul] *s* globulo

glockenspiel ['glokən,ʃpil] *s* vibrafono

gloom [glum] *s* oscurità *f*; malinconia, uggia

gloom·y ['glumi] *adj* (**-ier; -iest**) lugubre, triste, tetro

glori·fy ['glorɪ,faɪ] *v* (*pret & pp* **-fied**) *tr* glorificare; (*to enhance*) esaltare

glorious ['glorɪ·əs] *adj* glorioso; magnifico, splendido

glo·ry ['glori] *s* (**-ries**) gloria; **to go to glory** morire || *v* (*pret & pp* **-ried**) *intr* gloriarsi

gloss [glɔs] *or* [glɑs] *s* lucentezza, patina; (*commentary*) glossa || *tr* satinare, patinare; (*to annotate*) glossare; **to gloss over** nascondere, discolpare

glossa·ry ['glɑsəri] *s* (**-ries**) glossario

gloss·y ['glɔsi] *or* ['glɑsi] *adj* (**-ier**; **-iest**) lucido; (*paper*) satinato

glottal ['glɑtəl] *adj* articolato alla glottide

glottis ['glɑtɪs] *s* glottide *f*

glove [glʌv] *s* guanto

glove' compart'ment *s* cassetto portaoggetti

glow [glo] *s* fuoco, incandescenza; splendore *m*, scintillio; calore *m*; colorito acceso || *intr* essere incandescente; (*said of cheeks*) avvampare; (*said of cat's eyes*) fosforeggiare

glower ['glau·ər] *s* sguardo torvo || *intr* guardare col viso torvo

glowing ['glo·ɪŋ] *adj* incandescente; acceso; entusiasta, entusiastico

glow'worm' *s* lucciola; lampiride *m*

glucose ['glukos] *s* glucosio

glue [glu] *s* colla, mastice *m* || *tr* incollare, ingommare

glue'pot' *s* pentolino per la colla

gluey ['glu·i] *adj* (**gluier; gluiest**) attaccaticcio; (*smeared with glue*) incollato

glum [glʌm] *adj* (**glummer; glummest**) tetro, accigliato

glut [glʌt] *s* abbondanza; eccesso; **there is a glut on the market** il mercato è saturo || *v* (*pret & pp* **glutted**; *ger* **glutting**) *tr* saziare; (*the market*) saturare; (*a channel*) otturare

glutton ['glʌtən] *adj & s* ghiottone *m*

gluttonous ['glʌtənəs] *adj* ghiotto

glutton·y ['glʌtəni] *s* (**-ies**) ghiottoneria, golosità *f*

glycerine ['glɪsərɪn] *s* glicerina

G'-man' *s* (**-men'**) agente *m* federale

gnarl [nɑrl] *s* nodo || *tr* torcere || *intr* ringhiare

gnarled [nɑrld] *adj* nodoso; (*wrinkled*) grinzoso

gnash [næʃ] *tr* digrignare || *intr* digrignare i denti

gnat [næt] *s* moscerino, pappataci *m*

gnaw [nɔ] *tr* rosicchiare, rodere || *intr* —**to gnaw at** (fig) rimordere

gnome [nom] *s* gnomo

go [go] *s* (**goes**) andata; energia; (*for traffic*) via libera; **it's a go** è un affare fatto; **it's all the go** (coll) è all'ultimo grido; **it's no go** (coll) è impossibile; **on the go** in continuo andare e venire; **to make a go of** (coll) aver successo con || *v* (*pret* **went** [wɛnt]; *pp* **gone** [gɔn] *or* [gɑn]) *tr* (coll) sopportare; (coll) scommettere; (coll) pagare; **to go it alone** fare da sé || *intr* andare; (*to operate*) camminare, funzionare; (*e.g., mad*) diventare; (*said of numbers*) entrare; **gone!** venduto!; **so it goes** così va il mondo; **to**

be going to + *inf* andare a + *inf*, e.g., **I am going to New York to see him** vado a New York a vederlo; (*to express futurity*) use *fut ind*, e.g., **I am going to stay home today** starò a casa oggi; **to be gone** essere andato; esser morto; **to go against** opporsi a; **to go ahead** andar avanti; tirare avanti; **to go around** andare in giro; **to go away** andarsene; **to go back** tornare; **to go by** passare per; regolarsi su; (*said of time*) passare; **to go down** discendere; (*said of a boat*) affondare; **to go fishing** andare a pescare; **to go for** vendersi per; andare a pigliare; attaccare; favorire; **to go get** andare a pigliare; **to go house hunting** andare in cerca di una casa; **to go hunting** andare a caccia; **to go in** entrare in; (*to fit in*) starci in; **to go in for** dedicarsi a; **to go into** investigare; darsi a, dedicarsi a; (*gear*) (aut) ingranare; **to go in with** associarsi con; **to go off** andarsene; aver luogo; (*said of a bomb*) esplodere; (*said of a rifle*) sparare; (*said of a trap*) scattare; **to go on** continuare, protrarsi; **to go on** + *ger* continuare a + *inf*; **to go out** uscire; passare di moda; (*said, e.g., of fire*) spegnersi; (*to strike*) mettersi in sciopero; **to go over** aver successo; leggere; esaminare; **to go over to** passare ai ranghi di; **to go skiing** andare a sciare; **to go swimming** andare a nuotare, andare al bagno; **to go through** esperimentare; (*to examine carefully*) rovistare; (*said, e.g., of a plan or a project*) aver successo; (*a fortune*) dissipare; **to go through a red light** passare la strada col semaforo rosso; **to go with** andare con, accompagnare; (*a girl*) essere l'amico di; **to go without** fare a meno di

goad [god] *s* pungolo || *tr* pungolare; (fig) spronare

go'-ahead' *adj* intraprendente || *s* via *m*

goal [gol] *s* meta; (football) gol *m*

goalie ['goli] *s* portiere *m*

goal'keep'er *s* portiere *m*

goal' line' *s* linea di porta

goal' post' *s* montante *m*

goat [got] *s* capra; (*male*) becco; (coll) capro espiatorio; **to get the goat of** (coll) irritare

goatee [go'ti] *s* barbetta, pizzo

goat'herd' *s* capraio

goat'skin' *s* pelle *f* di capra

goat'suck'er *s* caprimulgo

gob [gɑb] *s* massa informe; **gobs** (coll) mucchio, quantità *f* enorme

gobble ['gɑbəl] *tr* ingozzare; **to gobble up** (coll) tranguiare; (coll) impadronirsi di || *intr* tranguiare; (*said of a turkey*) gloglottare

gobbledegook ['gɑbəldɪ͵guk] *s* linguaggio oscuro

go'-between' *s* intermediario; (*pander*) mezzano; (poet) pronubo

goblet ['gɑblɪt] *s* coppa

goblin ['gɑblɪn] *s* folletto

go'-by' *s*—**to give s.o. the go-by** (coll) schivare qlcu

go'-cart' *s* carrettino; (*walker*) girello

god [gɑd] *s* dio; **God forbid** Dio ci scampi; **God grant** voglia Dio; **God willing** se Dio vuole

god'child' *s* (**-chil'dren**) figlioccio

god'daugh'ter *s* figlioccia

goddess ['gɑdɪs] *s* dea, diva

god'fa'ther *s* padrino

God'-fear'ing *adj* timorato di Dio

God'for-sak'en *adj* miserabile; (*place*) sperduto, fuori di mano

god'head' *s* deità *f* || **Godhead** *s* Ente Supremo, Dio

godless ['gɑdlɪs] *adj* ateo; malvagio || **the godless** i senza Dio

god·ly ['gɑdli] *adj* (**-lier; -liest**) devoto, pio

god'moth'er *s* madrina

God's' a'cre *s* camposanto

god'send' *s* manna, provvidenza

god'son' *s* figlioccio

God'speed' *s* successo, buona fortuna

go-getter ['go ˌgɛtər] *s* (coll) persona intraprendente

goggle ['gɑgəl] *intr* stralunare gli occhi

goggle-eyed ['gɑgəl ˌaɪd] *adj* dagli occhi sporgenti

goggles ['gɑgəlz] *spl* occhiali *mpl* da protezione

going ['go·ɪŋ] *adj* in moto, in funzione; **going on** quasi, e.g., **it is going on seven o'clock** sono quasi le sette || *s* andata; progresso

go'ings on' *s* (coll) comportamento, contegno; (coll) avvenimenti *mpl*

goiter ['gɔɪtər] *s* gozzo

gold [gold] *adj* aureo, d'oro || *s* oro

gold'beat'er *s* battiloro

gold'brick' *s* imitazione, frode *f*; (slang) fannullone *m*

gold' dig'ger ['dɪgər] *s* cercatore *m* d'oro; (coll) donna unicamente interessata nel denaro

golden ['goldən] *adj* aureo, d'oro; (*gilt*) dorato; (fig) splendido

gold'en age' *s* età *f* dell'oro

gold'en calf' *s* vitello d'oro

Gold'en Fleece' *s* vello d'oro

gold'en mean' *s* aurea mediocrità

gold'en-rod' *s* (bot) verga d'oro

gold'en rule' *s* regola della carità cristiana

gold'en wed'ding *s* nozze *fpl* d'oro

gold-filled ['gold ˌfɪld] *adj* otturato in oro

gold'finch' *s* cardellino

gold'fish' *s* pesce rosso

goldilocks ['goldɪ ˌlɑks] *s* bionda; (bot) ranuncolo

gold' leaf' *s* oro in foglia

gold' mine' *s* miniera d'oro

gold' plate' *s* vasellame *m* d'oro

gold'-plate' *tr* dorare

gold' rush' *s* febbre *f* dell'oro

gold'smith' *s* orefice *m*

gold' stand'ard *s* regime aureo

golf [gɑlf] *s* golf *m* || *intr* giocare a golf

golf' cart' *s* mini-auto *f* per campi da golf

golf' club' *s* mazza; associazione di giocatori di golf

golfer ['gɑlfər] *s* giocatore *m* di golf

golf' links' *spl* campo di golf

Golgotha ['gɑlgəθə] *s* il Golgota

gondola ['gɑndələ] *s* gondola

gondolier [ˌgɑndə'lɪr] *s* gondoliere *m*

gone [gɔn] *or* [gɑn] *adj* partito; rovinato; andato; morto; **gone on** (coll) innamorato di

gong [gɔŋ] *or* [gɑŋ] *s* gong *m*

goo [gu] *s* (coll) sostanza appicciaticcia

good [gud] *adj* (**better; best**) buono; **good and . . .** (coll) molto, e.g., **good and cheap** molto a buon mercato; **good for** buono per; responsabile per; (*equivalent*) valido per; **to be good at** esser bravo a; **to be no good** (coll) non servire a nulla; (coll) essere un perdigiorno; **to make good** avere successo; (*one's promise*) mantenere; (*a debt*) pagare; (*damages*) indennizzare || *s* bene *m*; utile *m*, profitto; **for good** per sempre; **for good and all** una volta per sempre; **goods** merce *f*, mercanzia; **the good** il bene; i buoni; **to catch with the goods** (coll) cogliere in flagrante; **to deliver the goods** (slang) mantenere le promesse; **to do good** fare del bene; **to the good** come profitto; come attivo; **what is the good of . . . ?** a che serve . . . ?

good' afternoon' *s* buon pomeriggio

good'-by' [ˌgud'baɪ] *s* addio || *interj* addio!; arrivederci!

good' day' *s* buon giorno

good' deed' *s* buona azione

good' egg' *s* (slang) bonaccione *m*, gran brava persona

good' eve'ning *s* buona sera; buona notte

good' fel'low *s* buon ragazzo

good'-fel'low-ship' *s* cameratismo

good'-for-noth'ing *adj* inutile, senza valore || *s* pelandrone *m*, inetto

Good' Fri'day *s* Venerdì Santo

good' grac'es *spl* buone grazie

good-hearted ['gud'hɑrtɪd] *adj* di buon cuore

good'-hum'ored *adj* di buon umore

good'-look'ing *adj* bello

good' looks' *s* bellezza

good·ly ['gudli] *adj* (**-lier; -liest**) bello; di buona qualità; ampio, considerevole

good' morn'ing *s* buon giorno

good-natured ['gud'netʃərd] *adj* bonaccione, affabile

goodness ['gudnɪs] *s* bontà *f*; **for goodness sake!** per amor di Dio!; **goodness knows!** chi sa mai! || *interj* Dio mio!

good' night' *s* buona notte

good'-sized' *adj* piuttosto grande

good' speed' *s* buona fortuna

good'-tem'pered *adj* di carattere mite, gioviale

good' time' *s* periodo gradevole; **to have a good time** divertirsi; **to make good time** andare di buon passo

good' turn' *s* favore *m*, servizio

good' will' *s* buona volontà; (com) reputazione; (com) clientela

good·y ['gudi] *adj* (coll) troppo buono || *s* (**-ies**) (coll) santerello; **goodies**

(coll) ghiottonerie *fpl* || *interj* (coll) bene!, benissimo!

gooey ['gu·i] *adj* (**gooier; gooiest**) (slang) attaccaticcio

goof [guf] *s* (slang) sciocco || *tr* (slang) rovinare; **to goof up** (*an opportunity*) (slang) mancare || *intr* (slang) pigliare un granchio; **to goof off** (slang) battere la fiacca; **to goof up** (slang) farla grossa

goof·y ['gufi] *adj* (**-ier; -iest**) (slang) sciocco

goon [gun] *s* (slang) sceno; (coll) crumiro, gaglioffo, terrorista *m*

goose [gus] *s* (**geese** [gis]) oca; **the goose hangs high** tutto va per il meglio; **to cook one's goose** rompere le uova nel paniere di qlcu; **to kill the goose that lays the golden eggs** uccidere la gallina delle uova d'oro || *s* (**gooses**) ferro da stiro per sarto

goose'ber'ry *s* (**-ries**) uva spina; (*berry*) bacca d'uva spina

goose' egg' *s* (slang) zero; (*lump on the head*) (coll) bernoccolo

goose' flesh' *s* pelle *f* d'oca

goose'neck' *s* collo d'oca

goose' pim'ples *spl* pelle *f* d'oca

goose' step' *s* passo dell'oca

gopher ['gofər] *s* scoiattolo di terra, citillo

gore [gor] *s* sangue coagulato; (*in a garment*) gherone *m* || *tr* (*with a horn*) incornare; inserire gheroni in

gorge [gɔrdʒ] *s* gola, burrone *m*; (*meal*) mangiata || *tr* rimpinzare || *intr* rimpinzarsi

gorgeous ['gɔrdʒəs] *adj* splendido, magnifico

gorilla [gə'rɪlə] *s* gorilla *m*

gorse [gɔrs] *s* gineprone *m*

gor·y ['gori] *adj* (**-ier; -iest**) sanguinolento

gosh [gaʃ] *interj* perbacco!

goshawk ['gas‚hɔk] *s* sparviere *m*, astore *m*

gospel ['gaspəl] *s* vangelo || **Gospel** *s* Vangelo

gos'pel truth' *s* santissima verità

gossamer ['gasəmər] *s* ragnatela; (*variety of gauze*) garza finissima; tessuto impermeabile finissimo

gossip ['gasɪp] *s* maldicenza; (*person*) pettegolo; **piece of gossip** maldicenza || *intr* spettegolare

gossipy ['gasɪpi] *adj* pettegolo

Goth [gaθ] *s* Goto

Gothic ['gaθɪk] *adj & s* gotico

gouge [gaudʒ] *s* (*cut made with a gouge*) scanalatura; (*tool*) sgorbia; (coll) truffa || *tr* sgorbiare; (coll) truffare

goulash ['gulaʃ] *s* gulasch *m*

gourd [gord] *or* [gʊrd] *s* zucca

gourmand ['gʊrmənd] *s* ghiottone *m*

gourmet ['gʊrme] *s* buongustaio

gout [gaʊt] *s* gotta, podagra

gout·y ['gaʊti] *adj* (**-ier; -iest**) gottoso

govern ['gʌvərn] *tr* governare; (gram) reggere

governess ['gʌvərnɪs] *s* governante *f*, istitutrice *f*

government ['gʌvərnmənt] *s* governo; (gram) reggenza

governmental [‚gʌvərn'mentəl] *adj* governativo

governor ['gʌvərnər] *s* governatore *m*; (mach) regolatore *m*

governorship ['gʌvərnər‚ʃɪp] *s* governatorato

gown [gaʊn] *s* (*of a woman*) vestito; (*academic*) toga; (*of a physician or patient*) gabbanella; (*of a priest*) veste *f* talare

grab [græb] *s* presa; **up for grabs** pronto a esser pigliato || *v* (*pret & pp* **grabbed;** *ger* **grabbing**) *tr* pigliare, afferrare

grace [gres] *s* (*charm; favor*) grazia; (*pardon*) mercé *f*; (*prayer*) benedicite *m*; (com) dilazione; **to say grace** recitare il benedicite; **with good grace** di buona voglia || *tr* adornare

graceful ['gresfəl] *adj* grazioso, vezzoso, leggiadro

grace' note' *s* (mus) appoggiatura

gracious ['greʃəs] *adj* grazioso; misericordioso || *interj* Dio buono!

gradation [gre'deʃən] *s* gradazione; (*step in a series*) passo

grade [gred] *s* grado; (*slope*) pendenza; (*mark in school*) voto; **to make the grade** raggiungere la meta || *tr* selezionare; (*a student*) dare un voto a; (*land*) spianare

grade' cros'sing *s* (rr) passaggio a livello

grade' school' *s* scuola elementare

gradient ['gredɪ·ənt] *adj* in pendenza || *s* pendenza; (phys) gradiente *m*

gradual ['grædʒu·əl] *adj* gràduale

graduate ['grædʒu·ɪt] *adj* graduato; superiore; (*student*) laureato; (*candidate for degree*) laureando || ['grædʒu‚et] *tr* graduare; laureare, diplomare || *intr* laurearsi, diplomarsi

grad'uate school' *s* facoltà *f* di studi avanzati

graduation [‚grædʒu'eʃən] *s* graduazione; laurea; cerimonia della consegna delle lauree

graft [græft] *or* [grɑft] *s* (hort) innesto; (surg) trapianto; (coll) prevaricazione || *tr* (hort) innestare; (surg) trapiantare || *intr* (coll) prevaricare

gra'ham bread' ['gre·əm] *s* pane *m* integrale

grain [gren] *s* chicco; (*of sand*) granello; (*cereal seeds*) granaglie *fpl*; (*in wood*) venatura; (*in stone*) grana; **against the grain** di cattivo verso || *tr* granulare; (*leather*) zigrinare; (*metal*) granire

grain' el'evator *s* elevatore *m* di grano; (*building*) deposito di cereali

graining ['grenɪŋ] *s* venatura

gram [græm] *s* grammo

grammar ['græmər] *s* grammatica

grammarian [grə'merɪ·ən] *s* grammatico

gram'mar school' *s* scuola elementare

grammatical [grə'mætɪkəl] *adj* grammatico

gramophone ['græmə,fon] *s* (trade-mark) grammofono

grana·ry ['grænəri] *s* (-ries) granaio

grand [grænd] *adj* grandioso; grande, famoso

grand'aunt' *s* prozia

grand'child' *s* (-chil'dren) nipote *mf*

grand'daugh'ter *s* nipote *f*

grand' duch'ess *s* granduchessa

grand' duke' *s* granduca *m*

grandee [græn'di] *s* grande *m*

grandeur ['grændʒər] or ['grændʒur] *s* grande *m*, grandiosità *f*

grand'fa'ther *s* nonno; (*forefather*) antenato

grand'father's clock' *s* grande orologio a pendolo

grandiose ['grændɪ,os] *adj* grandioso

grand' ju'ry *s* giuria investigativa

grand' lar'ceny *s* furto importante

grand' lodge' *s* grande oriente *m*

grandma ['grænd,ma], ['græm,ma] or ['græmə] *s* (coll) nonna

grand'moth'er *s* nonna

grand'neph'ew *s* pronipote *m*

grand'niece' *s* pronipote *f*

grand' op'era *s* opera, opera lirica

grandpa ['grænd,pa], ['græn,pa] or ['græmpə] *s* (coll) nonno

grand'par'ent *s* nonno, nonna

grand' pian'o *s* pianoforte *m* a coda

grand'son' *s* nipote *m*

grand'stand' *s* tribuna

grand' to'tal *s* somma totale; importo globale

grand'un'cle *s* prozio

grand' vizier' *s* gran visir *m*

grange [grendʒ] *s* (*farm*) fattoria; (*organization of farmers*) sindacato di agricoltori

granite ['grænɪt] *s* granito

grant [grænt] or [grɑnt] *s* concessione; (*sum of money*) sovvenzione; trapasso di proprietà || *tr* concedere; (*a wish*) esaudire; (*a permit*) rilasciare; (law) trasferire; **to take for granted** ammettere come vero; trattare con indifferenza

grantee [græn'ti] or [grɑn'ti] *s* concessionario; beneficiario

grant'-in-aid' *s* (grants'-in-aid') sussidio governativo a un ente pubblico; borsa di studio

grantor [græn'tor] or [grɑn'tor] *s* concedente *m*, concessore *m*

granular ['grænjələr] *adj* granulare

granulate ['grænjə,let] *tr* granulare || *intr* diventare granulato

gran'ulated sug'ar *s* zucchero cristallizzato

granule ['grænjul] *s* granulo

grape [grep] *s* chicco d'uva; (*vine*) vite *f*; **grapes** uva

grape' ar'bor *s* pergolato

grape'fruit' *s* pompelmo

grape' juice' *s* succo d'uva

grape'shot' *s* mitraglia

grape'vine' *s* vite *f*; **by the grapevine** di bocca in bocca; (mil) attraverso la radio fante

graph [græf] or [grɑf] *s* (*diagram*) grafico; (gram) segno grafico

graphic(al) ['græfɪk(əl)] *adj* grafico

graphite ['græfaɪt] *s* grafite *f*

graph' pa'per *s* carta millimetrata

grapnel ['græpnəl] *s* uncino; (*anchor*) grappino

grapple ['græpəl] *s* uncino; lotta corpo a corpo || *tr* uncinare || *intr* combattere; **to grapple with** lottare con

grap'pling i'ron *s* raffio, grappino

grasp [græsp] or [grɑsp] *s* impugnatura; (*power*) possesso; **to have a good grasp of** sapere a fondo; **within the grasp of** nei limiti della comprensione di || *tr* (*with hand*) impugnare; (*to get control of*) impadronirsi di; (fig) capire || *intr*—**to grasp at** cercare di afferrare

grasping ['græspɪŋ] or ['grɑspɪŋ] *adj* tenace; avido, cupido

grass [græs] or [grɑs] *s* erba; (*pasture land*) pastura; (*lawn*) tappeto erboso; **to go to grass** (*said of cattle*) andare al pascolo; andare in vacanza; ritirarsi; andare in rovina; morire; **to not let the grass grow under one's feet** non dormire in piuma

grass' court' *s* campo da tennis d'erba

grass'hop'per *s* cavalletta

grass'-roots' *adj* popolare

grass' seed' *s* semente *f* d'erba

grass' wid'ow *s* donna separata dal marito

grass·y ['græsi] or ['grɑsi] *adj* (-ier; -iest) erboso

grate [gret] *s* (*for cooking*) griglia; (*at a window*) grata || *tr* mettere una grata a; (*one's teeth*) digrignare; (*e.g., cheese*) grattugiare || *intr* stridere, cigolare; **to grate on one's nerves** dare sui nervi di qlcu

grateful ['gretfəl] *adj* riconoscente; (*pleasing*) piacevole, gradito

grater ['gretər] *s* grattugia

grati·fy ['grætɪ,faɪ] *v* (*pret & pp* -fied) *tr* gratificare, soddisfare

gratifying ['grætɪ,faɪ·ɪŋ] *adj* soddisfacente, piacevole

grating ['gretɪŋ] *adj* irritante; (*sound*) stridente || *s* inferriata

gratis ['gretɪs] or ['grætɪs] *adj* gratuito || *adv* gratis

gratitude ['grætɪ,tjud] or ['grætɪ,tud] *s* gratitudine *f*, riconoscenza

gratuitous [grə'tju·ɪtəs] or [grə'tu·ɪtəs] *adj* gratuito

gratui·ty [grə'tju·ɪti] or [grə'tu·ɪti] *s* (-ties) mancia, regalia

grave [grev] *adj* grave || *s* tomba, sepolcro, fossa

gravedigger ['grev,dɪgər] *s* becchino

gravel ['grævəl] *s* ghiaia; (pathol) renella

grav'en im'age ['grevən] *s* idolo

grave'stone' *s* pietra tombale

grave'yard' *s* cimitero, camposanto

gravitate ['grævɪ,tet] *intr* gravitare

gravitation [,grævɪ'te/ən] *s* gravitazione

gravi·ty ['grævɪti] *s* (-ties) gravità *f*

gravure [grə'vjur] or ['grevjur] *s* fotoincisione

gra·vy ['grevi] *s* (-vies) (*juice from*

cooking meat) sugo; (*sauce made with it*) salsa, intingolo; (slang) guadagni *mpl* facili

gra′vy boat′ *s* salsiera

gra′vy train′ *s* (slang) greppia, mangiatoia

gray [gre] *adj* grigio; (*gray-haired*) canuto ‖ *s* grigio; cavallo grigio ‖ *intr* incanutire

gray′beard′ *s* vecchio

gray-haired [′gre ˌherd] *adj* canuto

gray′hound′ *s* levriere *m*

grayish [′gre·ɪʃ] *adj* grigiastro

gray′ mat′ter *s* materia grigia

graze [grez] *tr* (*to touch lightly*) sfiorare; (*to scratch lightly*) scalfire; (*grass*) brucare; (*cattle*) pascere, pascolare ‖ *intr* pascere, brucare

grease [gris] *s* grasso, unto ‖ [gris] or [griz] *tr* ingrassare, ungere

grease′ cup′ [gris] *s* coppa dell'olio

grease′ gun′ [gris] *s* ingrassatore *m*

grease′ lift′ [gris] *s* piattaforma di lubrificazione

grease′ paint′ [gris] *s* cerone *m*

grease′ pit′ [gris] *s* fossa di riparazione

greas-y [′grisi] or [′grizi] *adj* (*-ier; -iest*) grasso, unto, untuoso

great [gret] *adj* grande; (coll) eccellente ‖ **the great** i grandi

great′-aunt′ *s* prozia

Great′ Bear′ *s* Orsa Maggiore

Great′ Brit′ain [′brɪtən] *s* la Gran Bretagna

Great′ Dane′ *s* danese *m*, alano

Great′er New York′ *s* Nuova York e i suoi sobborghi

great′-grand′child′ *s* (*-chil′dren*) pronipote *mf*

great′-grand′daught′er *s* pronipote *f*

great′-grand′fa′ther *s* bisnonno

great′-grand′moth′er *s* bisnonna

great′-grand′par′ent *s* bisnonno, bisnonna

great′-grand′son′ *s* pronipote *m*

greatly [′gretli] *adj* molto

great′-neph′ew *s* pronipote *m*

greatness [′gretnɪs] *s* grandezza

great′-niece′ *s* pronipote *f*

great′-un′cle *s* prozio

Grecian [′griʃən] *adj & s* greco

Greece [gris] *s* la Grecia

greed [grid] *s* avarizia, avidità *f*

greediness [′gridɪnɪs] *s* bramosia

greed-y [′gridi] *adj* (*-ier; -iest*) avaro, ingordo, bramoso

Greek [grik] *adj & s* greco

green [grin] *adj* verde; (fig) verde, inesperto ‖ *s* verde *m*; (*lawn*) tappeto erboso; **greens** verdura, insalata

green′back′ *s* (U.S.A.) biglietto di banca

green′ earth′ *s* verdaccio

greener-y [′grinəri] *s* (*-ies*) (*foliage*) vegetazione; (*hothouse*) serra

green′-eyed′ *adj* dagli occhi verdi; (coll) geloso

green′gage′ *s* regina claudia

green′horn′ *s* (slang) pivello, semplicotto

green′house′ *s* serra

greenish [′grinɪʃ] *adj* verdastro

Greenland [′grinlənd] *s* la Groenlandia

green′ light′ *s* semaforo verde; (coll) via *m*

greenness [′grinnɪs] *s* verdore *m*, verdezza; inesperienza

green′ pep′per *s* peperone *m* verde

greensward [′grin ˌswɔrd] *s* tappeto erboso

green′ thumb′ *s* abilità *f* speciale per il giardinaggio

green′ veg′etables *spl* verdura

green′wood′ *s* bosco verde

greet [grit] *tr* salutare; ricevere; (*e.g., one's ears*) offrirsi a

greeting [′gritɪŋ] *s* saluto; accoglienza ‖ **greetings** *interj* saluti!

greet′ing card′ *s* cartolina d'auguri

gregarious [grɪ′gɛrɪ·əs] *adj* (*living in the midst of others*) gregario; (*sociable*) sociale

Gregorian [grɪ′gorɪ·ən] *adj* gregoriano

grenade [grɪ′ned] *s* granata

grenadier [ˌgrɛnə′dɪr] *s* granatiere *m*

grenadine [ˌgrɛnə′din] *s* granatina

grey [gre] *adj, s & intr* var of **gray**

grid [grɪd] *s* (*network*) rete *f*; (*on map*) reticolato; (electron) griglia

griddle [′grɪdəl] *s* tegame *m*

grid′dle-cake′ *s* frittella cotta in teglia, crêpe *m*

grid′i′ron *s* griglia; campo di football; (theat) graticcia

grief [grif] *s* affanno, dolore *m*; disgrazia; **to come to grief** andare in rovina

grievance [′grivəns] *s* lagnanza; motivo di lagnanza

grieve [griv] *tr* affliggere ‖ *intr* affliggersi, dolersi; **to grieve over** soffrire per

grievous [′grivəs] *adj* doloroso, penoso; (*error*) grave; (*deplorable*) deplorevole

griffin [′grɪfɪn] *s* grifo, grifone *m*

grill [grɪl] *s* griglia ‖ *tr* mettere alla griglia; (coll) interrogare insistentemente

grille [grɪl] *s* inferriata; (aut) mascherina, calandra

grill′room′ *s* grill-room *m*, rosticceria

grim [grɪm] *adj* (*grimmer; grimmest*) (*stern*) acciagliato; (*fierce*) feroce; (*sinister*) sinistro; (*unyielding*) implacabile

grimace [′grɪməs] or [grɪ′mes] *s* smorfia, sberleffo ‖ *intr* fare le boccacce

grime [graɪm] *s* sporco; (*soot*) fuliggine *f*

grim-y [′graɪmi] *adj* (*-ier; -iest*) sporco; fuligginoso

grin [grɪn] *s* sorriso; (*malicious in intent*) ghigno ‖ *v* (*pret & pp* grinned; *ger* grinning) *intr* sorridere; ghignare

grind [graɪnd] *s* macinata; (*laborious work*) (coll) macina; (slang) sgobbone *m* ‖ *v* (*pret & pp* ground [graund]) *tr* macinare; (*to sharpen*) molare; (*lenses*) smerigliare; (*meat*) tritare; opprimere; (*a crank*) girare; (mach) rettificare ‖ *intr* macinare; frantumarsi; cigolare; (coll) sgobbare

grinder [′graɪndər] *s* (*to sharpen tools*) mola; (*to grind coffee*) macinino;

(*back tooth*) molare *m*; (*person*) molatore *m*

grind'stone' *s* mola; **to keep one's nose to the grindstone** lavorare senza posa

grin·go ['grɪŋgo] *s* (-**gos**) (*disparaging*) gringo

grip [grɪp] *s* (*grasp*) presa; (*with hand*) stretta; (*handle*) impugnatura; **to come to grips** venire alle prese ‖ *v* (*pret & pp* **gripped**; *ger* **gripping**) *tr* stringere; impugnare; attirare l'attenzione di

gripe [graɪp] *s* (coll) lamentela; (naut) rizza; **gripes** colica ‖ *intr* (coll) lamentarsi, brontolare

grippe [grɪp] *s* influenza

gripping ['grɪpɪŋ] *adj* interessantissimo, affascinante

gris·ly ['grɪzli] *adj* (-**lier**; -**liest**) orribile, spaventoso

grist [grɪst] *s* (*grain to be ground*) macinata; (*ground grain*) farina; (coll) mucchio; **to be grist to the mill of** (coll) fare comodo a

gristle ['grɪsəl] *s* cartilagine *f*

gris·tly ['grɪsli] *adj* (-**tlier**; -**tliest**) cartilaginoso

grist'mill' *s* mulino

grit [grɪt] *s* sabbia, arenaria; (fig) forza d'animo ‖ *v* (*pret & pp* **gritted**; *ger* **gritting**) *tr* (*one's teeth*) far stridere, digrignare

grit·ty ['grɪti] *adj* (-**tier**; -**tiest**) sabbioso, granuloso; (fig) forte, coraggioso

griz·zly ['grɪzli] *adj* (-**zlier**; -**zliest**) brizzolato, canuto ‖ *s* (-**zlies**) orso grigio

groan [gron] *s* gemito ‖ *intr* gemere; (*to be overburdened*) essere sovraccarico

grocer ['grosər] *s* droghiere *m*; pizzicagnolo; proprietario di negozio di generi alimentari

grocer·y ['grosəri] *s* (-**ies**) (*store selling spices, soap, etc.*) drogheria; (*store selling cheese, cold cuts, etc.*) negozio di pizzicagnolo; negozio di generi alimentari; **groceries** generi *mpl* alimentari, commestibili *mpl*

grog [grɑg] *s* grog *m*

grog·gy ['grɑgi] *adj* (-**gier**; -**giest**) (coll) groggy, intontito

groin [grɔɪn] *s* (anat) inguine *m*; (archit) costolone *m*

groom [grum] *s* mozzo di stalla; (*bridegroom*) sposo ‖ *tr* rassettare; (*horses*) rigovernare; (pol) preparare per le elezioni

grooms'man *s* (-**men**) compare *m* di nozze

groove [gruv] *s* scanalatura; (*of a pulley*) gola; (*of a phonograph record*) solco; (fig) routine *f* ‖ *tr* scanalare, incavare

grope [grop] *intr* brancicare; (*for words*) cercare; **to grope for** cercare a tastoni

gropingly ['gropɪŋli] *adv* a tastoni

gross [gros] *adj* (*thick*) spesso; (*coarse*) volgare; (*fat*) grosso; (*error*) mar-

chiano; (*without deductions*) lordo ‖ *s* grossa ‖ *tr* fare un incasso lordo di

grossly ['grosli] *adv* approssimativamente; totalmente

gross' na'tional prod'uct *s* reddito nazionale

grotesque [gro'tesk] *adj & s* grottesco

grot·to ['grɑto] *s* (-**toes** or -**tos**) grotta

grouch [graʊtʃ] *s* (coll) malumore *m*; (coll) persona stizzosa ‖ *intr* (coll) brontolare

grouch·y ['graʊtʃi] *adj* (-**ier**; -**iest**) (coll) stizzoso, brontolone

ground [graʊnd] *s* (*earth, soil, land*) terra; (*piece of land*) terreno; (*basis*) causa, fondatezza; (elec) terra, massa; (fig) occasione, motivo; **grounds** giardini *mpl*, terreno; (*of coffee*) fondi *mpl*; **on the ground of** per motivo di; **to break ground** dare la prima palata; (fig) mettere la prima pietra; **to fall to the ground** cadere al suolo; (fig) fallire; **to gain ground** guadagnar terreno; **to give ground** ceder terreno; **to lose ground** perder terreno; **to stand one's ground** non indietreggiare ‖ *tr* fondare; (elec) mettere a massa; **to be grounded** (*said of an airplane*) essere forzato di rimanere a terra; **to be well grounded** essere bene al corrente ‖ *intr* incagliarsi

ground' connec'tion *s* messa a terra

ground' crew' *s* (aer) personale *m* di servizio

ground' floor' *s* pianterreno

ground' glass' *s* vetro smerigliato

ground' hog' *s* marmotta americana

ground' lead' [lid] *s* (elec) collegamento a massa

groundless ['graʊndlɪs] *adj* infondato

ground' meat' *s* carne tritata

ground' plan' *s* progetto, pianta

ground' swell' *s* mareggiata

ground' wire' *s* filo di terra, filo di massa

ground'work' *s* fondamento, base *f*

group [grup] *adj* collettivo ‖ *s* gruppo; (aer) stormo ‖ *tr* raggruppare ‖ *intr* raggrupparsi

grouse [graʊs] *s* gallo cedrone; (slang) brontolio ‖ *intr* (slang) brontolare

grout [graʊt] *s* stucco ‖ *tr* stuccare

grove [grov] *s* boschetto

grov·el ['grʌvəl] or ['grɑvəl] *v* (*pret & pp* -**eled** or -**elled**; *ger* -**eling** or -**elling**) *intr* umiliarsi

grow [gro] *v* (*pret* **grew** [gru]; *pp* **grown** [gron]) *tr* (*plants*) coltivare; (*animals*) allevare; (*a beard*) farsi crescere ‖ *intr* crescere; svilupparsi; nascere; venir su; (*to become*) diventare; farsi; **to grow angry** arrabbiarsi; **to grow old** invecchiare; **to grow out of** (*fashion*) passare di; originare da; **to grow up** svilupparsi

growing ['gro·ɪŋ] *adj* crescente; (*pains*) di crescenza; (*child*) in crescita

growl [graʊl] *s* ringhio; brontolio ‖ *intr* (*said of animals*) ringhiare; brontolare

grown'-up' *adj* adulto, grande || *s* (grown-ups) adulto
growth [groθ] *s* crescita, sviluppo; aumento; (pathol) escrescenza
growth' stock' *s* azione *f* che promette di aumentare di valore
grub [grʌb] *s* (drudge) sgobbone *m*; larva di coleottero; (coll) mangiare *m* || *v* (pret & pp grubbed; ger grubbing) *tr* scavare, zappare, dissodare || *intr* cercare assiduamente; scavare; sgobbare
grub·by ['grʌbi] *adj* (-bier; -biest) sporco; bacato; infestato di larve
grudge [grʌdʒ] *s* rancore *m*; to have a grudge against nutrire rancore contro || *tr* (to spend unwillingly) lesinare; invidiare
grudgingly ['grʌdʒɪŋli] *adv* di cattiva voglia
gru·el ['gru·əl] *s* farinata d'avena || *v* (pret & pp -eled or -elled; ger -eling or -elling) *tr* estenuare
gruesome ['grusəm] *adj* raccapricciante
gruff [grʌf] *adj* brusco, burbero; (voice) rauco, roco
grumble ['grʌmbəl] *s* brontolio || *intr* brontolare, borbottare
grump·y ['grʌmpi] *adj* (-ier; -iest) di cattivo umore, scontroso
grunt [grʌnt] *s* grugnito || *intr* grugnire
G-string ['dʒi,strɪŋ] *s* (loincloth) perizoma *m*; (worn by a female entertainer) triangolino di stoffa; (mus) corda di sol
guarantee [,gærən'ti] *s* garanzia; (guarantor) garante *mf* || *tr* garantire
guarantor ['gærən,tɔr] *s* garante *mf*
guaran·ty ['gærənti] *s* (-ties) garanzia || *v* (pret & pp -tied) *tr* garantire
guard [gɑrd] *s* guardia; (safeguard) protezione; (in a prison) guardia carceraria; (of a sword) guardamano; (football) mediano; off guard alla sprovvista; on guard in guardia; di fazione; to mount a guard montare la guardia; under guard ben custodito || *tr* guardare || *intr* fare la sentinella; to guard against guardarsi da
guarded ['gɑrdɪd] *adj* (remark) prudente
guard'house' *s* locale *m* di detenzione; (mil) corpo di guardia
guardian ['gɑrdɪ·ən] *adj* tutelare || *s* guardiano; (law) tutore *m*
guard'ian an'gel *s* angelo custode
guardianship ['gɑrdɪ·ən,ʃɪp] *s* protezione; (law) tutela
guard'rail' *s* guardavia *m*; (naut) parapetto
guard'room' *s* (mil) corpo di guardia
guards'man *s* (-men) guardia
guerrilla [gə'rɪlə] *s* guerrigliero
guerril'la war'fare *s* guerriglia
guess [ges] *s* congettura, supposizione || *tr & intr* congetturare, supporre; (to estimate correctly) indovinare; (coll) credere; I guess so credo di sì
guess'work' *s* congettura
guest [gest] *s* invitato, ospite *m*; (of a hotel) cliente *mf*; (of a boarding house) pensionante *mf*

guest' book' *s* albo d'onore; (in a hotel) registro
guffaw [gə'fɔ] *s* sghignazzata || *intr* sghignazzare
Guiana [gɪ'ɑnə] or [gɪ'ænə] *s* la Guayana
guidance ['gaɪdəns] *s* guida, governo; for your guidance per Sua norma
guide [gaɪd] *s* guida || *tr* guidare
guide'board' *s* indicatore *m* stradale
guide'book' *s* guida
guid'ed mis'sile ['gaɪdɪd] *s* telearma, teleproietto, missile teleguidato
guide' dog' *s* cane *m* conduttore di un cieco
guide'line' *s* falsariga; corda fissa; linea di condotta, direttiva
guide'post' *s* indicatore *m* stradale
guide' word' *s* esponente *m* in testa di pagina
guidon ['gaɪdən] *s* guidone *m*
guild [gɪld] *s* associazione mutua; (hist) gilda
guild'hall' *s* palazzo delle corporazioni
guile [gaɪl] *s* astuzia, frode *f*
guileful ['gaɪlfəl] *adj* astuto, insidioso
guileless ['gaɪllɪs] *adj* sincero, innocente
guillotine ['gɪlə,tin] *s* ghigliottina || ['gɪlə'tin] *tr* ghigliottinare
guilt [gɪlt] *s* colpa, reità *f*
guiltless ['gɪltlɪs] *adj* innocente
guilt·y ['gɪlti] *adj* (-ier; -iest) colpevole, reo
guimpe [gɪmp] or [gæmp] *s* sprone *m*
guinea ['gɪni] *s* ghinea; gallina faraona || **Guinea** *s* la Guinea
guin'ea fowl' *s* gallina faraona
guin'ea pig' *s* porcellino d'India, cavia; (fig) cavia
guise [gaɪz] *s* aspetto; veste *f*; under the guise of in guisa di
guitar [gɪ'tɑr] *s* chitarra
guitarist [gɪ'tɑrɪst] *s* chitarrista *mf*
gulch [gʌltʃ] *s* burrone *m*
gulf [gʌlf] *s* golfo; abisso
Gulf' Stream' *s* corrente *f* del Golfo
gull [gʌl] *s* gabbiano; (coll) credulone *m* || *tr* darla da bere a
gullet ['gʌlɪt] *s* gargarozzo; esofago
gullible ['gʌlɪbəl] *adj* credulone
gul·ly ['gʌli] *s* (-lies) borro, zanella
gulp [gʌlp] *s* sorsata || *tr*—to gulp down (food) ingoiare; (drink) tracannare; (fig) ingoiare, tranguggiare
gum [gʌm] *s* gomma; (mucus on eyelids) cispa; gums (anat) gengive *fpl* || *v* (pret & pp gummed; ger gumming) *tr* ingommare; to gum up (slang) guastare || *intr* secernere gomma
gum' ar'abic *s* gomma arabica
gum' boil' *s* flemmone *m* gengivale
gum' boot' *s* stivale *m* da palude
gum'drop' *s* caramella alla gelatina di frutta, pasticca di gomma, drop *m*
gum·my ['gʌmi] *adj* (-mier; -miest) gommoso, vischioso; (eyelid) cisposo
gumption ['gʌmpʃən] *s* (coll) iniziativa; (coll) coraggio, fegato
gum'shoe' *s* caloscia; (slang) poliziotto || *v* (pret & pp -shoed; ger -shoeing)

intr (slang) camminare silenziosamente

gun [gʌn] *s* (*rifle*) fucile *m*; (*revolver*) revolver *m*; (*pistol*) rivoltella; (*e.g., for spraying*) rivoltella; **to stick to one's guns** tener duro ‖ *v* (*pret & pp* **gunned;** *ger* **gunning**) *tr* far fuoco su, freddare; (*a motor*) (slang) accelerare rapidamente ‖ *intr* andare a caccia; sparare; **to gun for** andare a caccia di

gun'boat' *s* cannoniera, esploratore *m*

gun' car'riage *s* affusto

gun'cot'ton *s* fulmicotone *m*

gun'fire' *s* fuoco, tiro

gun'man *s* (-men) bandito, sicario

gun' met'al *s* bronzo da cannoni; acciaio brunito

gunnel ['gʌnəl] *s* (naut) frisata

gunner ['gʌnər] *s* artigliere *m*, servente *m*

gunnery ['gʌnəri] *s* artiglieria, tiro

gunnysack ['gʌni͵sæk] *s* sacco di tela greggia

gunpoint ['gʌn͵pɔint] *s* mirino; **at gunpoint** a mano armata, *e.g.,* **he was held up at gunpoint** subì una rapina a mano armata

gun'pow'der *s* polvere nera o pirica

gun'run'ner *s* contrabbandiere *m* di armi da fuoco

gun'shot' *s* schioppettata; revolverata; **within gunshot** a tiro di schioppo

gun'shot' wound' *s* schioppettata

gun'smith' *s* armaiolo

gun'stock' *s* cassa del fucile

gunwale ['gʌnəl] *s* frisata

gup·py ['gʌpi] *s* (-pies) lebiste *m*

gurgle ['gʌrgəl] *s* gorgoglio, borboglio ‖ *intr* gorgogliare, borbogliare; (*said of a human being*) barbugliare

gush [gʌʃ] *s* getto, fiotto ‖ *intr* zampillare, sgorgare; (coll) dare in effusioni

gusher ['gʌʃər] *s* pozzo di petrolio; (coll) persona espansiva

gushing ['gʌʃiŋ] *adj* zampillante, sgorgante; (coll) espansivo ‖ *s* zampillo; (coll) espansione, effusione

gush·y ['gʌʃi] *adj* (-ier; -iest) (coll) espansivo, effusivo

gusset ['gʌsit] *s* gherone *m*

gust [gʌst] *s* (*of wind*) raffica; (*of smoke*) ondata, zaffata; (*of noise*) esplosione; (*of anger*) sfuriata

gusto ['gʌsto] *s* gusto; entusiasmo

gust·y ['gʌsti] *adj* (-ier; -iest) a raffiche, burrascoso

gut [gʌt] *s* budello; **guts** budello; (slang) fegato, coraggio ‖ *v* (*pret & pp* **gutted;** *ger* **gutting**) *tr* sparare, spanciare; distruggere l'interno di

gutta-percha ['gʌtə'pʌrt/ə] *s* guttaperca

gutter ['gʌtər] *s* (*on side of road*) cunetta; (*in street*) rigagnolo; (*of roof*) doccia, grondaia; (fig) bassifondi *mpl*

gut'ter·snipe' *s* monello

guttural ['gʌtərəl] *adj & s* gutturale *f*

guy [gai] *s* cavo di sicurezza; (coll) tipo, tizio ‖ *tr* burlarsi di

guzzle ['gʌzəl] *tr & intr* trincare, bere a garganella

guzzler ['gʌzlər] *s* ubriacone *m*

gym [dʒim] *s* (coll) palestra

gymnasi·um [dʒim'nezi·əm] *s* (-ums or -a [ə]) palestra

gymnast ['dʒimnæst] *s* ginnasta *mf*

gymnastic [dʒim'næstik] *adj* ginnastico ‖ **gymnastics** *spl* ginnastica

gynecologist [͵gainə'kalədʒist], [͵dʒainə'kalədʒist] or [͵dʒinə'kalədʒist] *s* ginecologo

gyp [dʒip] *s* (coll) imbroglio; (*person*) (coll) imbroglione *m* ‖ *v* (*pret & pp* **gypped;** *ger* **gypping**) *tr* imbrogliare

gypsum ['dʒipsəm] *s* gesso

gyp·sy ['dʒipsi] *adj* zingaresco, zingaro ‖ *s* (-sies) zingaro ‖ **Gypsy** *s* (*language*) zingaresco

gypsyish ['dʒipsi·iʃ] *adj* zingaresco

gyrate ['dʒairet] *intr* turbinare

gyrocompass ['dʒairo͵kʌmpəs] *s* girobussola

gyroscope ['dʒairə͵skop] *s* giroscopio

H

H, h [etʃ] *s* ottava lettera dell'alfabeto inglese

haberdasher ['hæbər͵dæʃər] *s* camiciaio; (*dealer in notions*) merciaio

haberdasher·y ['hæbər͵dæʃəri] *s* (-ies) camiceria; merceria

habit ['hæbit] *s* abitudine *f*; (*addiction*) vizio; (*garb*) saio; **to be in the habit of** aver l'usanza di

habitat ['hæbi͵tæt] *s* habitat *m*

habitation [͵hæbi'teʃən] *s* abitazione

habit-forming ['hæbit͵fɔrmiŋ] *adj* (*e.g., drugs*) stupefacente; (*e.g., T.V.*) assuefacente, che fa venire il vizio

habitual [hə'bit/u·əl] *adj* abituale

habitué [hə͵bit/u'e] *s* habitué *m*

hack [hæk] *s* (*cut*) taglio; (*notch*) tacca; (*cough*) tosse secca; cavallo da nolo; vettura di piazza; (*nag*) ronzino; (*poor writer*) scribacchino ‖ *tr* tagliare; stagliare

hack'man *s* (-men) vetturino

hackney ['hækni] *s* cavallo da sella; vettura di piazza

hackneyed ['hæknid] *adj* banale, trito

hack'saw' *s* seghetto per metalli

haddock ['hædək] *s* eglefino

haft [hæft] or [hɑft] *s* impugnatura

hag [hæg] *s* (*ugly old woman*) megera; (*witch*) strega

haggard ['hægərd] *adj* sparuto, macilento; (*wild-looking*) stralunato

haggle ['hægəl] *intr* mercanteggiare

hagiographer [ˌhægi'ɑgrəfər] or [ˌhedʒi'ɑgrəfər] *s* agiografo

hagiography [ˌhægi'ɑgrəfi] or [ˌhedʒi-'ɑgrəfi] *s* agiografia

Hague, The [heg] *s* L'Aia *f*

hail [hel] *s* (*precipitation*) grandine *f*; (*greeting*) saluto; **within hail** a portata di voce || *tr* salutare; accogliere; chiamare; (*e.g., blows*) far cadere || *intr* grandinare; **to hail from** venire da || *interj* salute!; salve!

hail'-fel'low *adj* gioviale

Hail' Mar'y *s* Ave Maria, avemaria

hail'stone' *s* chicco di grandine

hail'storm' *s* grandinata

hair [her] *s* capelli *mpl*; (*of animals*) pelame *m* or pelo; **a hair** (*a single filament*) un capello or un pelo; **to a hair** a perfezione; **to get in one's hair** (slang) dare sui nervi a qlcu; **to let one's hair down** (slang) parlare francamente; (slang) comportarsi alla buona; **to make one's hair stand on end** far rizzare i capelli a qlcu; **to not turn a hair** non scomporsi; **to split hairs** cercare il pelo nell'uovo

hair'breadth' *s* spessore *m* di un capello; **to escape by a hairbreadth** scamparla per un pelo

hair'brush' *s* spazzola per i capelli

hair'cloth' *s* cilicio

hair'cut' *s* taglio dei capelli; **to get a haircut** farsi tagliare i capelli

hair'do' *s* (-**dos**) acconciatura

hair'dress'er *s* parrucchiere *m* per signora; pettinatrice *f*

hair' dri'er *s* asciugacapelli *m*

hair' dye' *s* tintura per i capelli

hairless ['herlɪs] *adj* pelato, calvo

hair' net' *s* rete *f* per i capelli

hair'pin' *s* forcella, forcina, molletta

hair-raising ['her ˌrezɪŋ] *adj* orripilante

hair' re-mov'er *s* depilatorio

hair' restor'er [rɪ'storər] *s* rigeneratore *m* per i capelli

hair' rib'bon *s* nastro per i capelli

hairsplitting ['her ˌsplɪtɪŋ] *adj* meticoloso, pignolo

hair'spring' *s* spirale *f*

hair' styl'ing *s* pettinatura per signora

hair-y ['heri] *adj* (-**ier**; -**iest**) peloso, villoso, irsuto

hake [hek] *s* merluzzo, nasello

halberd ['hælbərd] *s* alabarda

halberdier [ˌhælbər'dɪr] *s* alabardiere *m*

halcyon ['hælsɪ-ən] *adj* calmo, pacifico

hale [hel] *adj* sano, robusto || *tr* trascinare a viva forza

half [hæf] or [hɑf] *adj* mezzo; **a half** or **half a** mezzo; **half the** la metà di || *s* (**halves** [hævz] or [hɑvz]) metà *f*; (*arith*) mezzo; **in half** a metà; **to go halves** fare a metà || *adv* mezzo, e.g., **half asleep** mezzo addormentato; a metà, e.g., **half finished** a metà finito; **half past** e mezzo or e mezza, e.g., **half past three** le tre e mezzo or le tre e mezza; **half . . . half** metà . . . metà

half'-and-half' *adj* mezzo e mezzo || *s* mezza crema e mezzo latte; mezza

birra chiara e mezza scura || *adv* a metà, in parti uguali

half'back' *s* (football) mediano; (soccer) laterale *m*

half-baked ['hæf ˌbekt] or ['hɑf ˌbekt] *adj* mezzo cotto; (*ideas*) infondato, inesperto

half' bind'ing *s* rilegatura in mezza pelle

half'-blood' *s* meticcio; fratellastro; sorellastra

half'-breed' *s* meticcio

half' broth'er *s* fratellastro

half-cocked ['hæf ˌkɑkt] or ['hɑf ˌkɑkt] *adj* immaturo, precipitato || *adv* (coll) precipitatamente

half' fare' *s* mezza corsa

half'-full' *adj* mezzo pieno

half-hearted ['hæf ˌhɑrtɪd] or ['hɑf-ˌhɑrtɪd] *adj* indifferente, freddo

half'-hol'iday *s* mezza festa

half' hose' *s* calzini *mpl* corti

half'-hour' *s* mezz'ora; **on the half-hour** ogni trenta minuti allo scoccare dell'ora e della mezz'ora

half'-length' *adj* a mezzo busto || *s* ritratto a mezzo busto

half'life' *s* (phys) vita media

half'-mast' *s*—**at half-mast** a mezz'asta

half'moon' *s* mezzaluna

half' mourn'ing *s* mezzo lutto

half' note' *s* (mus) minima

half' pay' *s* mezza paga

halfpen-ny ['hepəni] or ['hepni] *s* (-**nies**) mezzo penny

half' pint' *s* mezza pinta; (slang) mezza cartuccia, mezza calzetta

half-seas o'ver *adj*—**to be half-seas over** (slang) essere sbronzato

half' shell' *s*—**on the half shell** in conchiglia

half' sis'ter *s* sorellastra

half' sole' *s* mezza suola

half'-sole' *tr* mettere la mezza suola a

half'-staff' *s*—**at half-staff** a mezz'asta

half-timbered ['hæf ˌtɪmbərd] or ['hɑf-ˌtɪmbərd] *adj* in legno e muratura

half' ti'tle *s* occhiello, occhietto

half'tone' *s* mezzatinta

half'-track' *s* semicingolato

half'truth' *s* mezza verità, mezza bugia

half'way' *adj* a metà strada; parziale, mezzo || *adv* a metà strada; **halfway through** nel mezzo di; **to meet halfway** fare concessioni mutue

half-witted ['hæf ˌwɪtɪd] or ['hɑf-ˌwɪtɪd] *adj* mezzo scemo

halibut ['hælɪbət] *s* ippoglosso

halide ['hælaɪd] or ['helaɪd] *s* alogenuro

halitosis [ˌhælɪ'tosɪs] *s* alito cattivo, fiato puzzolente

hall [hɔl] *s* (*passageway*) corridoio; (*entranceway*) vestibolo; (*large meeting room*) salone *m*; (*assembly room of a university*) aula magna; (*building of a university*) edificio

halleluiah or **hallelujah** [ˌhælɪ'lujə] *s* alleluia *m* || *interj* alleluia!

hall'mark' *s* punzone *m* di garanzia; (fig) contrassegno, caratteristica

hal·lo [hə'lo] *s* (-**los**) grido || *interj* ehi!

hallow ['hælo] *tr* santificare

hallowed ['hælod] *adj* consacrato
Halloween or **Hallowe'en** [ˌhælo'in] *s* vigilia di Ognissanti
hallucination [həˌlusɪ'neʃən] *s* allucinazione
hall'way' *s* corridoio; entrata
ha·lo ['helo] *s* (**-los** or **-loes**) alone *m*
halogen ['hælədʒən] *s* alogeno
halt [hɔlt] *adj* zoppicante || *s* fermata; **to call a halt** dare ordine di fermarsi; **to come to a halt** fermarsi || *tr* fermare || *intr* fermarsi, esitare || *interj* altolà!
halter ['hɔltər] *s* (*for leading horse*) cavezza; (*noose*) capestro; (*hanging*) impiccagione; corpino bagno di sole
halting ['hɔltɪŋ] *adj* zoppicante; esitante
halve [hæv] or [hɑv] *tr* dimezzare
halyard ['hæljərd] *s* (naut) drizza
ham [hæm] *s* (*part of leg behind knee*) polpaccio; (*thigh and buttock*) coscia; (*cured meat from hog's kind leg*) prosciutto; (slang) istrione *m*; (slang) radioamatore *m*; **hams** natiche *fpl*
ham' and eggs' *spl* uova *fpl* col prosciutto
hamburger ['hæmˌbʌrgər] *s* hamburger *m*
hamlet ['hæmlɪt] *s* frazione, paese *m* || **Hamlet** *s* Amleto
hammer ['hæmər] *s* martello; (*of gun*) cane *m*; (*of piano*) martelletto; **under the hammer** all'asta pubblica || *tr* martellare; **to hammer out** battere; portare a fine faticosamente || *intr* martellare; **to hammer away** lavorare accanitamente
hammock ['hæmək] *s* amaca
hamper ['hæmpər] *s* cesta || *tr* imbarazzare, intralciare
hamster ['hæmstər] *s* criceto
ham-string ['hæmˌstrɪŋ] *v* (*pret & pp* **-strung**) *tr* azzoppare; tagliare i garretti a; (fig) impastoiare
hand [hænd] *adj* manuale; fatto a mano || *s* mano *f*; (*workman*) garzone *m*, operaio; (*way of writing*) scrittura; (*signature*) firma; (*clapping of hands*) applauso; (*of clock or watch*) lancetta; (*all the cards in one's hand*) gioco; (*a round of play*) smazzata, mano *f*; (*player*) giocatore *m*; (*skill*) destrezza; (*side*) lato; **all hands** (naut) tutto l'equipaggio; (coll) tutti *mpl*; **at first hand** direttamente; **at hand** a portata di mano; **hand in glove** in perfetta unione; **hand in hand** tenendosi per mano; **hands up!** le mani in alto!; **hand to hand** corpo a corpo; **in hand** tra le mani; **in his own hand** di proprio pugno; **on hands and knees** (*crawling*) a gattoni; (*beseeching*) in ginocchio; **on the one hand** da un canto; **on the other hand** per contro; **to change hands** cambiare di mano; **to clap hands** battere le mani; **to eat out of one's hand** essere sottomesso a qlcu; **to get out of hand** diventare incontrollabile; **to have a hand in** prender parte a; **to have one's hands**
full essere occupatissimo; **to hold hands** tenersi per mano; **to hold up one's hands** (*as a sign of surrender*) alzare le mani; **to join hands** darsi la mano; **to keep one's hands off** non mettere il naso in; **to lend a hand** dare una mano; **to live from hand to mouth** vivere alla giornata; **to not lift a hand** non alzare un dito; **to play into the hands of** fare il gioco di; **to shake hands** darsi la mano; **to show one's hand** scoprire il proprio gioco; **to take in hand** prendere in mano; (*a matter*) prendere in esame; **to throw up one's hands** darsi per vinto; **to try one's hand** mettere la propria abilità alla prova; **to turn one's hand to** dedicarsi a; **to wash one's hands of** lavarsi le mani di; **under my hand** di mia firma autografa; **under the hand and seal of** firmato di pugno da || *tr* dare, porgere; **to hand down** tramandare; **to hand in** consegnare; **to hand on** trasmettere; **to hand out** distribuire
hand'bag' *s* borsetta
hand' bag'gage *s* valigie *fpl* a mano
hand'ball' *s* palla a mano
hand'bill' *s* manifestino, foglio volante
hand'book' *s* manuale *m*; guida; (*of a particular field*) prontuario
hand'breadth' *s* palmo
hand'car' *s* (rr) carrello a mano
hand'cart' *s* carretto a mano
hand'cuffs' *spl* manette *fpl* || *tr* mettere le manette a
handful ['hændˌful] *s* manata, manciata
hand' glass' *s* lente *f* di ingrandimento; specchietto
hand' grenade' *s* bomba a mano
handi-cap ['hændɪˌkæp] *s* svantaggio; (sports) handicap *m* || *v* (*pret & pp* **-capped**; *ger* **-capping**) *tr* andicappare
handicraft ['hændɪˌkræft] or ['hændɪˌkrɑft] *s* destrezza manuale; artigianato
handiwork ['hændɪˌwʌrk] *s* lavoro fatto a mano; opera, lavoro
handkerchief ['hæŋkərtʃɪf] or ['hæŋkərˌtʃif] *s* fazzoletto
handle ['hændəl] *s* manico; (*of a sword*) impugnatura; (*of a door*) maniglia; (*of a drawer*) pomolo; (*of a hand organ*) manovella; espediente *m*; **to fly off the handle** (slang) uscire dai gangheri || *tr* maneggiare; manovrare, dirigere; commerciare in || *intr* comportarsi
handle'bar' *s* manubrio
handler ['hændlər] *s* (sports) allenatore *m*
hand'made' *adj* fatto a mano
hand'maid' or **hand'maid'en** *s* domestica, serva; (fig) ancella
hand'-me-down' *adj* smesso || *s* vestito smesso or di seconda mano
hand' or'gan *s* organetto, organino, organetto di Barberia
hand'out' *s* elemosina di cibo; articolo distribuito gratis; comunicato stampa
hand-picked ['hændˌpɪkt] *adj* colto a mano; scelto specialmente

hand'rail' s guardamano, passamano
hand'saw' s sega a mano
hand'set' s microtelefono
hand'shake' s stretta di mano
handsome ['hænsəm] adj bello; considerevole; generoso
hand'spring' s capriola, salto mortale fatto toccando il terreno con le mani
hand'-to-hand' adj corpo a corpo
hand'-to-mouth' adj precario, da un giorno all'altro
hand'work' s lavoro fatto a mano
hand'writ'ing s scrittura
hand'wrought' adj lavorato a mano
hand-y ['hændɪ] adj (-ier; -iest) (easy to handle) maneggevole; (within easy reach) vicino; (skillful) destro, abile; **to come in handy** tornare utile
hand'y-man' s (-men') factotum m
hang [hæŋ] s maniera di cadere; **to get the hang of** (coll) imparare a adoperare; **to not give a hang** (coll) non importare un fico a || v (pret & pp **hung** [hʌŋ]) tr sospendere; (laundry) stendere; (to attach) attaccare; (a door or window) mettere sui cardini; (one's head) abbassare; **hang it!** (coll) al diavolo!; **to hang up** appendere; sospendere il progresso di || intr pendere, penzolare; esitare; essere sospeso; essere attaccato; **to hang around** ciondolare, oziare, gironzolare; **to hang on** essere sospeso a; dipendere da; persistere; (s.o.'s words) pendere; **to hang out** sporgersi; (slang) raccogliersi; (slang) vivere; **to hang over** esser sospeso; (to threaten) minacciare; **to hang together** mantenersi uniti; **to hang up** (telp) riattaccare || v (pret **hanged** or **hung**) tr (to execute) impiccare || intr impiccarsi
hangar ['hæŋər] or ['hæŋgar] s rimessa; (aer) aviorimessa, hangar m
hanger ['hæŋər] s gancio, uncino; (for clothes) attaccapanni m
hang'er-on' s (hangers-on) seguace m/f; seccatore m; (sponger) parassita m/f
hanging ['hæŋɪŋ] adj pendente, pensile || s impiccagione; **hangings** parati mpl
hang'man s (-men) boia m
hang'nail' s pipita delle unghie
hang'out' s (coll) ritrovo abituale
hang'o'ver s mal m di testa dopo una sbornia
hank [hæŋk] s matassa
hanker ['hæŋkər] intr agognare
Hannibal ['hænɪbəl] s Annibale m
haphazard [,hæp'hæzərd] adj fortuito, a caso || adv a caso; alla carlona
hapless ['hæplɪs] adj sfortunato
happen ['hæpən] intr succedere; **to happen along** sopravvenire; **to happen on** incontrarsi per caso con; **to happen to + inf** per caso + ind, e.g., I happened to see her at the theater l'ho incontrata per caso a teatro
happening ['hæpənɪŋ] s avvenimento, fatto
happily ['hæpɪli] adv felicemente; fortunatamente

happiness ['hæpɪnɪs] s felicità f; gioia, piacere m
hap·py ['hæpi] adj (-pier; -piest) lieto, felice, contento; **to be happy to** avere il piacere di
hap'py-go-luck'y adj spensierato
hap'py me'dium s giusto mezzo
Hap'py New Year' interj buon anno!, felice anno nuovo!
harangue [hə'ræŋ] s arringa, concione || tr & intr arringare
harass ['hærəs] or [hə'ræs] tr bersagliare; tartassare, tormentare
harbinger ['harbɪndʒər] s foriero; annunzio || tr annunziare
harbor ['harbər] adj di porto, portuario || s porto || tr albergare; (love or hatred) nutrire; (e.g., a criminal) dare ricetto a
har'bor mas'ter s capitano di porto
hard [hard] adj duro; (difficult) difficile; (work) improbo; (solder) forte; (hearing or breathing) grosso; (drinker) impenitente; (liquor) fortemente alcolico; **to be hard on** essere severo con; (to wear out fast) logorare rapidamente || adv duro; forte; molto; **hard upon** subito dopo
hard'-and-fast' adj inflessibile
hard-bitten ['hard'bɪtən] adj duro, incallito
hard-boiled ['hard'bɔɪld] adj (egg) sodo; (coll) duro
hard' can'dy s caramelle fpl; **piece of hard candy** caramella
hard' cash' s denaro contante
hard' ci'der s sidro fermentato
hard' coal' s antracite f
hard'-earned' adj guadagnato a stento
harden ['hardən] tr indurire || intr indurirsi
hardening ['hardənɪŋ] s indurimento; (metallurgy) tempra
hard' facts' spl realtà f
hard-fought ['hard'fɔt] adj accanito
hard-headed ['hard'hedɪd] adj astuto; ostinato, caparbio
hard-hearted ['hard'hartɪd] adj dal cuore duro
hardihood ['hardɪ,hud] s forza, coraggio; insolenza
hardiness ['hardɪnɪs] s ardire m; vigore m, robustezza fisica
hard' la'bor s lavori forzati
hard' luck' s mala sorte
hard'-luck' sto'ry s storia delle proprie disgrazie
hardly ['hardli] adv appena, quasi no; (with great difficulty) a malapena, a fatica; **hardly ever** quasi mai
hardness ['hardnɪs] s durezza
hard'-of-hear'ing adj duro d'orecchio
hard-pressed ['hard'prest] adj oppresso; **to be hard-pressed for** essere a corto di
hard' rub'ber s ebanite f
hard' sauce' s miscela di burro e zucchero
hard'-shell crab' s granchio con la corazza
hardship ['hard/ɪp] s pena, privazione; **hardships** privazioni fpl, strettezze fpl

hard'tack' s galletta
hard' times' spl strettezze fpl
hard' to please' adj di difficile contentatura
hard' up' adj (coll) in urgente bisogno; **to be hard up for** (coll) essere a corto di
hard'ware' s ferramenta fpl; macchinario
hard'ware store' s negozio di ferramenta
hard-won ['hard,wʌn] adj (victory, battle) conquistato con molti sforzi; (money) acquistato con molti sforzi
hard'wood' s legno forte
hard'wood floor' s pavimento di legno, parquet m
har·dy ['hardi] adj (-dier; -diest) forte, resistente; (rash) temerario; (hort) resistente al freddo
hare [her] s lepre f
harebrained ['her,brend] adj scervellato, sventato
hare'lip' s labbro leporino
harem ['herəm] s arem m
hark [hark] intr ascoltare; **to hark back** (said of hounds) ritornare sulla pista; riandare col pensiero || interj ascolta!
harken ['harkən] intr ascoltare
harlequin ['harləkwɪn] s arlecchino
harlot ['harlət] s meretrice f, baldracca
harm [harm] s danno || intr rovinare; nuocere (with dat), fare del male (with dat)
harmful ['harmfəl] adj nocivo
harmless ['harmlɪs] adj innocuo
harmonic [har'manɪk] adj armonico || s (phys) armonica || **harmonics** ssg armonica; spl suoni armonici
harmonica [har'manɪkə] s armonica a bocca
harmonious [har'monɪ·əs] adj armonioso
harmonize ['harmə,naɪz] tr intonare; (mus) armonizzare || intr intonarsi; (mus) cantare all'unisono
harmo·ny ['harməni] s (-nies) armonia
harness ['harnɪs] s bardatura, finimenti mpl; (fig) routine f; **to die in the harness** morire sulla breccia || tr bardare, imbrigliare; (a waterfall) captare
har'ness mak'er s sellaio
har'ness race' s corsa al trotto, corsa di cavalli col sulky
harp [harp] s arpa || intr—**to harp on** ripetere ostinatamente
harpist ['harpɪst] s arpista mf
harpoon [har'pun] s rampone m || tr & intr arpionare
harpsichord ['harpsɪ,kɔrd] s arpicordo, clavicembalo
har·py ['harpi] s (-pies) arpia
harrow ['hæro] s erpice m || tr (agr) erpicare; (fig) tormentare
harrowing ['hæro·ɪŋ] adj straziante
har·ry ['hæri] v (pret & pp -ried) tr saccheggiare; tormentare
harsh [harʃ] adj (to touch) ruvido; (to taste or hearing) aspro; inclemente

harshness ['harʃnɪs] s ruvidezza; asprezza; inclemenza
hart [hart] s cervo
harum-scarum ['herəm'skerəm] adj & s scervellato
harvest ['harvɪst] s raccolta, mietitura || tr raccogliere, mietere
harvester ['harvɪstər] s (person) mietitore m; (machine) mietitrice f
har'vest home' s fine f della mietitura; festa dei mietitori; canzone f dei mietitori
har'vest moon' s luna di settembre
has-been ['hæz,bɪn] s (person) fallito; (thing) anticaglia
hash [hæʃ] s polpettone m || tr tritare
hash' house' s osteria di terz'ordine
hashish ['hæʃɪʃ] s ascisc m
hasp [hæsp] or [hasp] s boncinello
hassle ['hæsəl] s (coll) rissa, disputa
hassock ['hæsək] s cuscino poggiapiedi
haste [hest] s premura; **in haste** di premura; **to make haste** fare presto
hasten ['hesən] tr affrettare || intr affrettarsi
hast·y ['hesti] adj (-ier; -iest) frettoloso; precipitato
hat [hæt] s cappello; **to keep under one's hat** (coll) mantenere il segreto su; **to throw one's hat in the ring** (coll) dichiarare la propria candidatura
hat'band' s nastro del cappello
hat' block' s forma da cappelli
hat'box' s cappelliera
hatch [hætʃ] s (brood) nidiata; (shading line) tratteggio; (trap door) porta a ribalta; (lower half of door) mezza porta; (naut) boccaporto || tr (eggs) covare; (a drawing) tratteggiare; complottare, tramare || intr schiudersi
hat'check' girl' s guardarobiera
hatchet ['hætʃɪt] s accetta; **to bury the hatchet** fare la pace
hatch'way' s (trap door) porta a ribalta; (naut) boccaporto
hate [het] s odio || tr & intr odiare
hateful ['hetfəl] adj odioso
hat'pin' s spillone m
hat'rack' s attaccapanni m
hatred ['hetrɪd] s odio, livore m
hatter ['hætər] s cappellaio
haughtiness ['hotɪnɪs] s superbia
haugh·ty ['hoti] adj (-tier; -tiest) superbo, sprezzante
haul [hol] s (tug) tiro; (amount caught) retata; (distance transported) percorso, pezzo || tr trasportare; tirare; (naut) alare
haunch [hɔntʃ] or [hantʃ] s fianco; anca; (hind quarter of an animal) coscia; (same used for food) cosciotto
haunt [hont] or [hant] s ritrovo, nido || tr frequentare assiduamente; perseguitare
haunt'ed house' s casa frequentata dai fantasmi
haute couture [ot ku'tyr] s alta moda
have [hæv] s—**the haves and the have-nots** gli abbienti e i nullatenenti || v

(*pret & pp* had [hæd]) *tr* avere; (*a dream*) fare; (*to get, take*) prendere, ottenere, ricevere; **to have got** (coll) avere; **to have got to** + *inf* (coll) dovere + *inf*; **to have it in for** (coll) serbar rancore per; **to have it out with** avere a che dire con; **to have on** portare; **to have** (s.th) **to do with** avere (qlco) a che fare con, e.g., **I don't want to have anything to do with him** non voglio aver nulla a che fare con lui; **to have** + *inf* fare + *inf*, e.g., **I had him pay the bill** gli ho fatto pagare il conto; **to have** + *pp* fare + *inf*, e.g., **I had my watch repaired** ho fatto aggiustare l'orologio || *intr*—**to have at** attaccare, mettersi di buzzo buono con; **to have to** + *inf* dovere + *inf*; **to have to do with** avere a che fare con; trattare di, e.g., **this book has to do with superstition** questo libro tratta di superstizione || *v aux* avere, e.g., **he has studied his lesson** ha studiato la sua lezione

havelock ['hævlɑk] *s* coprinuca *m*

haven ['hevən] *s* porto; asilo

haversack ['hævər‚sæk] *s* bisaccia; (mil) zaino

havoc ['hævək] *s* rovina; **to play havoc with** rovinare; scompigliare

haw [hɔ] *s* (*of hawthorn*) bacca; (*in speech*) esitazione || *intr* voltare a sinistra || *interj* voltare a sinistra!

hawk [hɔk] *s* falco; (*mortarboard*) sparviere *m*; (coll) persona rapace || *tr* imbonire; (*newspapers*) strillare; **to hawk up** sputare raschiandosi la gola || *intr* fare il merciaiolo ambulante; schiarirsi la gola

hawker ['hɔkər] *s* merciaiolo ambulante

hawse [hɔz] *s* (naut) cubia; (*hole*) (naut) occhio di cubia; (naut) altezza di cubia

hawse'hole' *s* occhio di cubia

hawser ['hɔzər] *s* cavo, gomena

haw'thorn' *s* biancospino

hay [he] *s* fieno; **to hit the hay** (slang) andare a letto; **to make hay while the sun shines** battere il ferro fin ch'è caldo

hay' fe'ver *s* febbre *f* da fieno, raffreddore *m* da fieno

hay'field' *s* prato seminato a fieno

hay'fork' *s* forcone *m*; (mach) rastrello

hay'loft' *s* fienile *m*

haymow ['he‚mau] *s* fienile *m*

hay'rack' *s* rastrelliera

hay'ride' *s* gita notturna in carro da fieno

hay'seed' *s* semente *f* d'erba; (coll) semplicione *m*, campagnolo

hay'stack' *s* meta, pagliaio

hay'wire' *adj* (coll) disordinato, in confusione; (coll) impazzito || *s* filo per legare il fieno

hazard ['hæzərd] *s* pericolo; (*chance*) rischio; (golf) ostacolo || *tr* rischiare; (*an opinion*) arrischiare

hazardous ['hæzərdəs] *adj* pericoloso

haze [hez] *s* foschia; (fig) confusione || *tr* far la matricola a

hazel ['hezəl] *adj* nocciola || *s* (*tree*) nocciolo; (*fruit*) nocciola

ha'zel-nut' *s* nocciola

hazing ['hezɪŋ] *s* vessazione, angheria; (*at university*) matricola

ha·zy ['hezi] *adj* (-zier; -ziest) nebbioso; confuso

H-bomb ['etʃ‚bɑm] *s* bomba H

he [hi] *s* (hes) maschio || *pron pers* (they) lui, egli, esso

head [hɛd] *s* testa, capo; (*of bed*) testiera; (*caption*) testata; (*of a nail*) cappello; (*on a glass of beer*) schiuma; (*of a boil*) punta purulenta; (e.g., *of cattle*) capo; **at the head of** a capo di; **from head to foot** da capo a piedi; **head over heels** a gambe levate; completamente; **heads or tails** testa o croce; **over one's head** al di sopra della capacità intellettuale di qlcu; (*going to a higher authority*) al di sopra di qlcu; **to be out of one's head** (coll) esser matto; **to bring to a head** far giungere alla crisi; **to come into one's head** passar per la mente a qlcu; **to go to one's head** dare al cervello a qlcu; **to keep one's head** non perdere la testa; **to keep one's head above water** arrivare a sbarcare il lunario; **to not make head or tail of** non riuscire a raccappezzarsi su || *tr* dirigere, comandare; essere alla testa di || *intr*—**to head towards** dirigersi verso

head'ache' *s* mal di capo, emicrania

head'band' *s* fascia sul capo; (bb) capitello; (typ) filetto

head'board' *s* testiera del letto

head' cheese' *s* salame *m* di testa

head'dress' *s* acconciatura

header ['hɛdər] *s*—**to take a header** (coll) gettarsi a capofitto

head'first' *adv* a capofitto

head'gear' *s* copricapo; (*for protection*) casco

head'hunt'er *s* cacciatore *m* di teste

heading ['hɛdɪŋ] *s* intestazione; (*of a chapter of a book*) titolo; (journ) testata, capopagina *m*

headland ['hɛdlənd] *s* promontorio

headless ['hɛdlɪs] *adj* senza testa

head'light' *s* (naut, rr) fanale *m*; (aut) faro

head'line' *s* (*of a page of a book*) titolo; (journ) testata || *tr* intestare; fare pubblicità a

head'lin'er *s* (slang) attrazione principale

head'long' *adj* precipitoso || *adv* a precipizio; a capofitto

head'man *s* (-men) capo; giustizere *m*

head'mas'ter *s* direttore *m* di un collegio per ragazzi

head'most' *adj* primo, più avanzato

head' of'fice *s* sede *f* centrale

head' of hair' *s* capigliatura

head'-on' *adj* frontale || *adv* di fronte, frontalmente

head'phones' *spl* cuffia

head'piece' *s* (*any covering for the head*) copricapo; (*helmet*) elmo; (*brains, judgment*) testa; (*of bed*) spalliera; (*headset*) cuffia; (typ) testata

head'quar'ters *s* sede *f* centrale, direzione; (mil) quartier *m* generale

head'rest' *s* poggiatesta *m*, testiera

head'set' *s* cuffia

head'ship' *s* direzione

head'stone' *s* pietra angolare; (*on a grave*) pietra tombale

head'stream' *s* affluente *m* principale

head'strong' *adj* testardo, ostinato

head'wait'er *s* capocameriere *m*

head'wa'ters *spl* fonti *fpl* or sorgenti *fpl* d'un fiume

head'way' *s* progresso; to make headway progredire

head'wear' *s* copricapo

head'wind' *s* vento di prua

head'work' *s* lavoro intellettuale

head·y ['hedi] *adj* (-ier; -iest) eccitante; impetuoso; violento; (*clever*) astuto; intossicante

heal [hil] *tr* sanare, guarire; purificare || *intr* risanarsi, guarire; (*said of a wound*) rimarginare

healer ['hilər] *s* guaritore *m*

health [helθ] *s* salute *f*; to your health sprizzare salute da tutti i pori; to your health! alla Sua salute!

health' depart'ment *s* sanità *f*

healthful ['helθfəl] *adj* salutare

health' insur'ance *s* assicurazione malattia

health·y ['helθi] *adj* (-ier; -iest) sano; salubre

heap [hip] *s* mucchio; (coll) insalata, mare *m* || *tr* ammucchiare; to heap s.th upon s.o. colmare qlcu di qlco; to heap with colmare di

hear [hɪr] *v* (*pret & pp* heard [hʌrd]) *tr* udire; to hear it said sentirlo dire || *intr* udire; hear!, hear! bravo!; to hear about sentir parlare di; to hear from aver notizie di; to hear of sentir parlare di; to hear that sentir dire che

hearer ['hɪrər] *s* ascoltatore *m*

hearing ['hɪrɪŋ] *s* (*sense*) udito, orecchio; (*act*) udienza; in the hearing of in presenza di; within hearing a portata d'orecchio

hear'ing aid' *s* uditofono

hear'say' *s* diceria; by hearsay per sentito dire

hearse [hʌrs] *s* carro, carrozzone *m*, or furgone *m* funebre

heart [hɑrt] *s* cuore *m*; (*e.g., of lettuce*) grumolo; after one's heart di gusto di qlcu; by heart a memoria; heart and soul di tutto cuore; to break the heart of spezzare il cuore di; to die of a broken heart morire di crepacuore; to eat one's heart out piangere silenziosamente; to get to the heart of sviscerare il nocciolo di; to have one's heart in one's work lavorare di buzzo buono; to have one's heart in the right place essere buon intenzioni; to lose heart scoraggiarsi; to open one's heart to aprire il cuore a; to take heart prender coraggio; to take to heart prendersi a cuore; to

wear one's heart on one's sleeve parlare a cuore aperto; with one's heart in one's mouth col cuore in bocca

heart'ache' *s* angustia, angoscia

heart' attack' *s* attacco cardiaco

heart'beat' *s* battito del cuore

heart'break' *s* angoscia straziante

heart'break'er *s* rubacuori *m*

heartbroken ['hɑrt,brokən] *adj* col cuore spezzato

heart'burn' *s* bruciore *m* di stomaco

heart' disease' *s* mal *m* di cuore

hearten ['hɑrtən] *tr* rincuorare

heart' fail'ure *s* (*death*) arresto cardiaco; collasso cardiaco

heartfelt ['hɑrt,felt] *adj* sentito

hearth [hɑrθ] *s* focolare *m*

hearth'stone' *s* pietra del focolare

heartily ['hɑrtɪli] *adv* di cuore, cordialmente; saporitamente

heartless ['hɑrtlɪs] *adj* senza cuore, insensibile

heart' mur'mur *s* soffio al cuore

heart-rending ['hɑrt,rendɪŋ] *adj* da far male al cuore

heart'sick' *adj* afflitto, sconsolato

heart'strings' *spl* precordi *mpl*

heart'-to-heart' *adj* cuore a cuore

heart' trans'plant *s* trapianto cardiaco

heart'wood' *s* cuore *m* del legno

heart·y ['hɑrti] *adj* (-ier; -iest) cordiale, di cuore; abbondante; (*eater*) grande

heat [hit] *adj* termico || *s* calore *m*; (*of room, house, etc.*) riscaldamento; (zool) fregola; (sports) batteria; (fig) fervore *m*; in heat (zool) in amore || *tr* scaldare, riscaldare; (fig) eccitare || *intr* riscaldarsi; (fig) accalorarsi

heated ['hitɪd] *adj* accalorato

heater ['hitər] *s* riscaldatore *m*; (*for central heating*) calorifero; (to heat hands or bed) scaldino; (to heat water in tub) scaldabagno

heath [hiθ] *s* (*shrub*) brugo, erica; (*tract of land*) brughiera

hea·then ['hiðən] *adj* pagano; irreligioso || *s* (-then or -thens) pagano

heathendom ['hiðəndəm] *s* (*worship*) paganesimo; (*land*) pagania

heather ['heðər] *s* erica, brugo

heating ['hitɪŋ] *adj* di riscaldamento || *s* riscaldamento

heat'ing pad' *s* termoforo

heat' light'ning *s* lampo di caldo

heat' shield' *s* (rok) scudo termico

heat'stroke' *s* colpo di calore

heat' wave' *s* ondata di caldo

heave [hiv] *s* sollevamento, sforzo; heaves (vet) bolsaggine *f* || *v* (*pret & pp* heaved or hove [hov]) *tr* sollevare, alzare; rigettare; (*a sigh*) emettere || *intr* alzarsi e abbassarsi; (*said of one's chest*) palpitare; avere conati di vomito

heaven ['hevən] *s* cielo; for heaven's sake! or good heavens! per amor del cielo!; heavens (*firmament*) cielo || Heaven *s* cielo

heavenly ['hevənli] *adj* celeste

heav'enly bod'y *s* corpo celeste

heav·y ['hevi] *adj* (-ier; -iest) (*of great*

weight) pesante; (*liquid*) denso; (*cloth, sea*) grosso; (*traffic*) forte; (*serious*) grave; (*crop*) abbondante; (*rain*) dirotto; (*features*) grossolano; (*heart*) stretto; (*ponderous*) macchinoso; (*industry*) grande; (*stock market*) abbattuto ‖ *adv* (coll) pesantemente; **to hang heavy** (*said of time*) passar lentamente

heav'y-du'ty *adj* extraforte

heavy-hearted ['hɛvɪ'hɑrtɪd] *adj* afflitto, triste

heav'y-set' *adj* forte, corpulento

heav'y-weight' *s* peso massimo

Hebrew ['hibru] *adj & s* ebreo; (*language*) ebraico

hecatomb ['hɛkə,tom] or ['hɛkə,tum] *s* ecatombe *f*

heckle ['hɛkəl] *tr* interrompere con domande imbarazzanti

hectic ['hɛktɪk] *adj* febbrile

hedge [hɛdʒ] *s* barriera; (*of bushes*) siepe *f*; (*in stock market*) operazione controbilanciante ‖ *tr* circondare con siepe; **to hedge in** circondare ‖ *intr* evitare di compromettersi; (com) coprirsi

hedge'hog' *s* (zool) riccio; (*porcupine*) (zool) porcospino

hedge'hop' *v* (*pret & pp* -hopped; *ger* hopping) *intr* volare a volo radente

hedgehopping ['hɛdʒ,hɑpɪŋ] *s* volo radente

hedge'row' [ro] *s* siepe *f*

heed [hid] *s* attenzione; **to take heed** fare attenzione ‖ *tr* badare a ‖ *intr* fare attenzione, badare

heedless [hidlɪs] *adj* sbadato

heehaw ['hi,hɔ] *s* (*of donkey*) raglio d'asino; risata ‖ *intr* ragliare; ridere fragorosamente

heel [hil] *s* (*of shoe, of foot*) calcagno, tallone *m*; (*of stocking or shoe*) tallone *m*; (*raised part of shoe below heel*) tacco; (coll) farabutto; **down at the heel** mal ridotto; **to cool one's heels** aspettare a lungo; **to kick up one's heels** darsi alla pazza gioia; **to show a clean pair of heels** or **to take to one's heels** battere i tacchi

heeler ['hilər] *s* politicante *mf*

heft·y ['hɛftɪ] *adj* (-ier; -iest) (*heavy*) pesante; (*strong*) forte

hegemon·y [hɪ'dʒɛmənɪ] or ['hɛdʒɪ,monɪ] *s* (-ies) egemonia

hegira [hɪ'dʒaɪrə] or ['hɛdʒɪrə] *s* fuga

heifer ['hɛfər] *s* manza, giovenca

height [haɪt] *s* altezza; (*of a person*) altezza, statura; (*e.g., of folly*) colmo

heighten ['haɪtən] *tr* innalzare; (*to increase the amount of*) accrescere, aumentare ‖ *intr* aumentare

heinous ['henəs] *adj* nefando, odioso

heir [ɛr] *s* erede *m*

heir' appar'ent *s* (**heirs' appar'ent**) erede necessario

heirdom ['ɛrdəm] *s* eredità *f*

heiress ['ɛrɪs] *s* ereditiera, erede *f*

heirloom ['ɛr,lum] *s* cimelio di famiglia

Helen ['hɛlən] *s* Elena

helicopter ['hɛlɪ,kɑptər] *s* elicottero

heliport ['hɛlɪ,port] *s* eliporto

helium ['hilɪ·əm] *s* elio

helix ['hilɪks] *s* (**helixes** or **helices** ['hɛlɪ,siz]) spirale *f*; (geom) elica

hell [hɛl] *s* inferno

hell-bent ['hɛl'bɛnt] *adj* (coll) risoluto; **to be hell-bent on** (coll) avere un chiodo in testa di

hell'cat' *s* arpia, megera

hellebore ['hɛlɪ,bor] *s* elleboro

Hellene ['hɛlin] *s* greco

Hellenic [hɛ'lɛnɪk] or [hɛ'linɪk] *adj* ellenico

hell'fire' *s* fuoco dell'inferno

hellish ['hɛlɪʃ] *adj* infernale

hel-lo [hɛ'lo] *s* saluto ‖ *interj* ciao!; (*on telephone*) pronto!

helm [hɛlm] *s* barra del timone; ruota del timone; timone *m* ‖ *tr* dirigere

helmet ['hɛlmɪt] *s* (mil) elmetto; (sports) casco; (hist) elmo

helms'man *s* (-men) timoniere *m*

help [hɛlp] *s* aiuto; (*relief*) rimedio, e.g., **there's no help for it** non c'è rimedio; servitù *f*; impiegati *mpl*; operai *mpl*; **to come to the help of** venire in aiuto di ‖ *tr* aiutare; soccorrere, mitigare; (*to wait on*) servire; **it can't be helped** non c'è rimedio; **so help me God!** Dio mi sia testimonio!; **to help down** aiutare a scendere; **to help s.o. with his coat** aiutare qlcu a mettersi il cappotto; **to help oneself** servirsi da solo; **to help up** aiutare a salire; aiutare ad alzarsi; **to not be able to help** + *ger* non poter fare a meno di + *inf*, e.g., **he can't help laughing** non può fare a meno di ridere ‖ *intr* aiutare ‖ *interj* aiuto!

helper ['hɛlpər] *s* aiutante *m*; (*in a shop*) garzone *m*, lavorante *m*

helpful ['hɛlpfəl] *adj* utile, servizievole

helping ['hɛlpɪŋ] *s* (*of food*) razione

helpless ['hɛlplɪs] *adj* (*weak*) debole; (*powerless*) impotente; senza risorse; (*confused*) perplesso; (*situation*) irrimediabile

help'mate' *s* compagno; (*wife*) compagna

helter-skelter ['hɛltər'skɛltər] *adj & adv* in fretta e furia; alla rinfusa

hem [hɛm] *s* (*any edge*) orlo; (*of skirt*) basta, pedana; (*of suit*) falda ‖ *v* (*pret & pp* hemmed; *ger* hemming) *tr* orlare, bordare; **to hem in** insaccare ‖ *intr* esitare; **to hem and haw** esitare; essere evasivo

hemisphere ['hɛmɪ,sfɪr] *s* emisfero

hemistich ['hɛmɪ,stɪk] *s* emistichio

hem'line' *s* orlo della gonna

hem'lock' *s* (*herb and poison*) cicuta; (*Tsuga canadensis*) abete *m* del Canada

hemoglobin [,hɛmə'globɪn] or [,himə'globɪn] *s* emoglobina

hemophilia [,hɛmə'fɪlɪ·ə] or [,himə'fɪlɪ·ə] *s* emofilia

hemorrhage ['hɛmərɪdʒ] *s* emorragia

hemorrhoids ['hɛmə,rɔɪdz] *spl* emorroidi *fpl*

hemostat ['hɛmə,stæt] or ['himə,stæt] *s* pinza emostatica

hemp [hɛmp] *s* canapa

hemstitch ['hem,stɪtʃ] *s* orlo a giorno || *tr & intr* orlare a giorno

hen [hen] *s* gallina

hence [hens] *adv* di qui; da ora; quindi; di qui a, e.g., **three weeks hence** di qui a tre settimane

hence'forth' *adv* d'ora innanzi

hench•man ['hentʃmən] *s* (**-men** [mən]) accolito; politicante *m*

hen'house' *s* pollaio

henna ['henə] *s* henna || *tr* tingere con la henna

hen'peck' *tr* (*a husband*) trovare a ridire con

hen'pecked' hus'band *s* marito dominato dalla moglie

her [hʌr] *adj poss* suo, il suo || *pron pers* la, lei; **to her** le, a lei

herald ['herəld] *s* araldo; annunziatore *m* || *tr* annunziare

heraldic [he'rældɪk] *adj* araldico

herald•ry ['herəldri] *s* (**-ries**) (*office*) consulta araldica; (*science*) araldica; (*coat of arms*) blasone *m*

herb [ʌrb] *or* [hʌrb] *s* erba; erba medicinale

herbaceous [hʌr'beʃəs] *adj* erbaceo

herbage ['ʌrbɪdʒ] *or* ['hʌrbɪdʒ] *s* erba; (*law*) erbatico

herbalist ['hʌrbəlɪst] *or* ['ʌrbəlɪst] *s* erborista *mf*

herbari•um [hʌr'berɪ•əm] *s* (**-ums** *or* **-a** [ə]) erbario

herb' doc'tor *s* erborista *mf*

herculean [hʌr'kjulɪ•ən] *or* [,hʌrkju-'li•ən] *adj* erculeo

herd [hʌrd] *s* (*of sheep*) gregge *m*; (*of cattle*) mandria; (*of men*) torma || *tr & intr* imbrancare

herds'man *s* (**-men**) (*of cattle*) mandriano, vaccaio; (*of sheep*) pastore *m*

here [hɪr] *adj* presente || *s*—**the here and the hereafter** la vita presente e l'aldilà || *adv* qui, qua; **here and there** qua e là; **here is** *or* **here are** ecco; **that's neither here not there** ciò non ha nulla a che vedere || *interj* presente!

hereabouts ['hɪrə,bauts] *adv* qua vicino

here•af'ter *s* aldilà *m* || *adv* d'ora innanzi; nel futuro

here•by' *adv* con la presente

hereditary [hɪ'redɪ,teri] *adj* ereditario

heredi•ty [hɪ'redɪti] *s* (**-ties**) eredità *f*

here•in' *adv* qui; in questo posto

here•of' *adv* di questo

here•on' *adv* in questo; su questo

here•sy ['herəsi] *s* (**-sies**) eresia

heretic ['herətɪk] *adj & s* eretico

heretical [hɪ'retɪkəl] *adj* eretico

heretofore [,hɪrtu'for] *adv* sinora

here•u•pon' *adv* su questo; in questo; immediatamente dopo

here•with' *adv* accluso; con la presente

heritage ['herɪtɪdʒ] *s* eredità *f*

hermetic(al) [hʌr'metɪk(əl)] *adj* ermetico

hermit ['hʌrmɪt] *s* eremita *m*

hermitage ['hʌrmɪtɪdʒ] *s* eremitaggio

herni•a ['hʌrnɪ•ə] *s* (**-as** *or* **-ae** [,i]) ernia

he•ro ['hɪro] *s* (**-roes**) eroe *m*

heroic [hɪ'ro•ɪk] *adj* eroico || **heroics** *spl* linguaggio altisonante

heroin ['hero•ɪn] *s* (pharm) eroina

heroine ['hero•ɪn] *s* eroina

heroism ['hero,ɪzəm] *s* eroismo

heron ['herən] *s* airone *m*

herring ['herɪŋ] *s* aringa

her'ring-bone' *s* (*in fabric*) spina di pesce; (*in hardwood floors*) spiga

hers [hʌrz] *pron poss* il suo; **of hers** suo

herself [hʌr'self] *pron pers* lei stessa; sé stessa; si, e.g., **she enjoyed herself** si divertì; **with herself** con sé

hertz [hʌrts] *s* hertz *m*

hesitan•cy ['hezɪtənsi] *s* (**-cies**) titubanza, esitanza

hesitant ['hezɪtənt] *adj* esitante

hesitate ['hezɪ,tet] *intr* esitare, titubare; (*to stutter*) balbettare

hesitation [,hezɪ'teʃən] *s* esitazione

heterodox ['hetərə,daks] *adj* eterodosso

heterodyne ['hetərə,daɪn] *s* eterodina

heterogeneous [,hetərə'dʒini•əs] *adj* eterogeneo

hew [hju] *v* (*pret* **hewed**; *pp* **hewed** *or* **hewn**) *tr* tagliare; (*a passage*) aprirsi; (*a statue*) abbozzare; **to hew down** abbattere || *intr*—**to hew close to the line** (coll) filare diritto

hex [heks] *s* strega; incantesimo || *tr* stregare, incantare

hexameter [heks'æmɪtər] *s* esametro

hey [he] *interj* ehi!

hey'day' *s* apogeo

hia•tus [haɪ'etəs] *s* (**-tuses** *or* **-tus**) (*gap*) lacuna; (gram) iato

hibernate ['haɪbər,net] *intr* ibernare; (*said of people*) svernare

hibiscus [hɪ'bɪskəs] *or* [haɪ'bɪskəs] *s* ibisco

hic•cup ['hɪkəp] *s* singhiozzo || *v* (*pret & pp* **-cuped** *or* **-cupped**; *ger* **-cuping** *or* **-cupping**) *intr* singhiozzare

hick [hɪk] *adj & s* (coll) rustico

hicko•ry ['hɪkəri] *s* (**-ries**) hickory *m*

hidden ['hɪdən] *adj* nascosto

hide [haɪd] *s* cuoio, pelle *f*; **hides** cuoio; **neither hide nor hair** nemmeno una traccia; **to tan s.o.'s hide** (coll) dargliele sode a qlcu || *v* (*pret* **hid** [hɪd]; *pp* **hid** *or* **hidden** ['hɪdən]) *tr* nascondere || *intr* nascondersi; **to hide out** (coll) rintanarsi

hide'-and-seek' *s* rimpiattino; **to play hide-and-seek** giocare a rimpiattino *or* a nascondino

hide'bound' *adj* retrogrado, conservatore

hideous ['hɪdɪ•əs] *adj* orribile, brutto

hide'out' *s* nascondiglio

hiding ['haɪdɪŋ] *s* nascondere *m*; (*place*) nascondiglio; **in hiding** nascosto

hid'ing place' *s* nascondiglio

hie [haɪ] *v* (*pret & pp* **hied**; *ger* **hieing** *or* **hying**) *tr*—**hie thee home** affrettati a tornare a casa || *intr* affrettarsi

hierar•chy ['haɪ•ə,rɑrki] *s* (**-chies**) gerarchia

hieroglyphic [,haɪ•ərə'glɪfɪk] *adj & s* geroglifico

hi-fi ['haɪ'faɪ] *adj* di alta fedeltà || *s* alta fedeltà

higgledy-piggledy ['hɪgəldɪ'pɪgəldɪ] *adj* confuso || *adv* alla rinfusa

high [haɪ] *adj* alto; (*color*) forte; (*merry*) allegro; (*luxurious*) lussuoso; (coll) ubriaco; (culin) frollo; **high and dry** abbandonato; **high and mighty** (coll) arrogante || *adv* molto; riccamente; **to aim high** mirare in alto; **to come high** essere caro || *s* (aut) quarta, diretta; **on high** in cielo

high′ al′tar *s* altare *m* maggiore

high′ball′ *s* whiskey con ghiaccio e gazosa || *intr* (slang) andare di carriera

high′ blood′ pres′sure *s* ipertensione

high′born′ *adj* di nobile lignaggio

high′boy′ *s* cassettone alto

high′brow′ *s* intellettuale *mf*; (coll) intellettualoide *mf*

high′chair′ *s* seggiolino per bambini

high′ command′ *s* comando supremo

high′ cost′ of liv′ing *s* carovita *m*, caroviveri *m*

high′er educa′tion *s* insegnamento universitario, istruzione superiore

higher-up [,haɪ-ər'ʌp] *s* (coll) superiore *m*

high′ explo′sive *s* esplosivo ad alta potenza

highfalutin [,haɪfə'lutən] *adj* (coll) pomposo, pretenzioso

high′ fidel′ity *s* high fidelity, alta fedeltà

high′-fre′quency *adj* ad alta frequenza

high′ gear′ *s* (aut) presa diretta

high′-grade′ *adj* di qualità superiore

high-handed ['haɪ'hændɪd] *adj* arbitrario

high′ hat′ *s* cappello a cilindro

high′-hat′ (coll) snob *m* || *v* (*pret & pp* **-hatted**; *ger* **-hatting**) *tr* (coll) snobbare

high′-heeled′ shoe′ ['haɪ,hild] *s* scarpa coi tacchi alti

high′ horse′ *s* comportamento arrogante; **to get up on one's high horse** darsi delle grandi arie

high′ jinks′ [dʒɪŋks] *s* (slang) pagliacciata, gazzarra

high′ jump′ *s* salto in altezza

highland ['haɪlənd] *adj* montagnoso || **highlands** *spl* regione montagnosa

high′ life′ *s* high-life *f*, alta società

high′light′ *s* punto culminante || *tr* mettere in risalto

highly ['haɪlɪ] *adv* altamente, molto; (*paid*) profumatamente; **to speak highly of** parlar molto bene di

High′ Mass′ *s* messa cantata

high-minded ['haɪ'maɪndɪd] *adj* magnanimo

highness ['haɪnɪs] *s* altezza || **Highness** *s* Altezza

high′ noon′ *s* mezzogiorno in punto; (fig) sommo

high-pitched ['haɪ'pɪtʃt] *adj* acuto; intenso, emozionante

high-powered ['haɪ'pau-ərd] *adj* ad alta potenza; (*binoculars*) ad alto ingrandimento

high′pres′sure *adj* ad alta pressione || *tr* sollecitare con insistenza

high-priced ['haɪ'praɪst] *adj* caro, di alto prezzo

high′ priest′ *s* sommo sacerdote

high′ rise′ *s* edificio di molti piani

high′road′ *s* strada principale

high′school′ *s* scuola media; (*in Italy*) liceo

high′ sea′ *s* alto mare; **high seas** alto mare

high′ soci′ety *s* l'alta società

high′-sound′ing *adj* altisonante

high′-speed′ *adj* ad alta velocità

high-spirited ['haɪ'spɪrɪtɪd] *adj* fiero, vivace, focoso

high′ spir′its *spl* allegria, vivacità *f*

high-strung ['haɪ'strʌŋ] *adj* teso, nervoso

high′-test′ fuel′ *s* supercarburante *m*

high′ tide′ *s* alta marea; punto culminante

high′ time′ *s* ora, e.g., **it is high time for you to go** è proprio ora che Lei se ne vada; (coll) baldoria

high′ trea′son *s* (*against the sovereign*) lesa maestà; (*against the state*) alto tradimento

high′ wa′ter *s* alta marea; (*in a river*) straripamento

high′way′ *adj* autostradale || *s* autostrada

high′way′man *s* (**-men**) grassatore *m*

hijack ['haɪ,dʒæk] *tr* rubare; (*e.g., an airplane*) dirottare || *intr* effettuare un dirottamento

hijacker ['haɪ,dʒækər] *s* ladro a mano armata; (*e.g., of an airplane*) dirottatore *m*

hijacking ['haɪ,dʒækɪŋ] *s* furto a mano armata; dirottamento

hike [haɪk] *s* (*for pleasure*) gita, camminata; (*increase*) aumento; (mil) marcia || *tr* tirar su; aumentare || *intr* fare una gita; (mil) fare una marcia

hiker ['haɪkər] *s* camminatore *m*

hilarious [hɪ'lerɪ·əs] or [haɪ'lerɪ·əs] *adj* ilare; (*e.g., joke*) allegro, divertente

hill [hɪl] *s* collina || *tr* rincalzare

hillbil·ly ['hɪl,bɪlɪ] *s* (**-lies**) (coll) montanaro rustico

hillock ['hɪlək] *s* poggio, collinetta

hill′side′ *s* pendio

hill′top′ *s* cima

hill·y ['hɪlɪ] *adj* (**-ier**; **-iest**) collinoso; ripido

hilt [hɪlt] *s* impugnatura, elsa; **up to the hilt** completamente

him [hɪm] *pron pers* lo; lui; **to him** gli, a lui

himself [hɪm'self] *pron pers* lui stesso; sé stesso; si, e.g., **he enjoyed himself** si è divertito; **with himself** con sé

hind [haɪnd] *adj* posteriore, di dietro || *s* cerva

hinder ['hɪndər] *tr* ostacolare, impedire

hindmost ['haɪnd,most] *adj* ultimo

hind′quar′ter *s* quarto posteriore

hindrance ['hɪndrəns] *s* ostacolo, impedimento

hind'sight' *s* senno di poi

Hindu ['hɪndu] *adj & s* indù *mf*

hinge [hɪndʒ] *s* cardine *m;* (bb) cerniera; (philately) listello gommato; punto principale ‖ *tr* munire di cardini ‖ *intr*—**to hinge on** dipendere da

hin·ny ['hɪni] *s* (**-nies**) bardotto

hint [hɪnt] *s* insinuazione; **to take the hint** capire l'antifona ‖ *tr & intr* insinuare; **to hint at** alludere a

hinterland ['hɪntər,lænd] *s* retroterra *m*, entroterra *m*

hip [hɪp] *adj*—**to be hip to** (slang) essere al corrente di ‖ *s* anca, fianco; (*of a roof*) spigolo

hip'bone' *s* ileo, osso iliaco

hipped [hɪpt] *adj* (*livestock*) zoppicante; (*roof*) a padiglione; **hipped on** (coll) ossessionato per

hippie ['hɪpi] *s* capellone *m*

hip·po ['hɪpo] *s* (**-pos**) (coll) ippopotamo

hippodrome ['hɪpə,drom] *s* ippodromo

hippopota·mus [,hɪpə'pɑtəməs] *s* (**-muses** or **-mi** [,maɪ]) ippopotamo

hip' roof' *s* tetto a padiglione

hire [haɪr] *s* paga, salario; nolo; **for hire** a nolo ‖ *tr* (*help*) impiegare; (*a conveyance*) noleggiare ‖ *intr*—**to hire out** mettersi a servizio

hired' girl' *s* lavorante *f* di campagna

hired' hand' *s* lavorante *mf*

hired' man' *s* (**men'**) lavorante *m* di campagna

hireling ['haɪrlɪŋ] *adj* venale ‖ *s* persona prezzolata

his [hɪz] *adj poss* suo, il suo ‖ *pron poss* il suo

Hispanic [hɪs'pænɪk] *adj* ispano

Hispanist ['hɪspənɪst] *s* ispanista *mf*

hiss [hɪs] *s* (*of fire, wind, serpent, etc.*) sibilo; (*of disapproval*) fischio, zittio ‖ *tr* zittire ‖ *intr* zittire; sibilare; (*said of a kettle*) fischiare

histology [hɪs'talədʒi] *s* istologia

historian [hɪs'tori·ən] *s* storico

historic(al) [hɪs'tɑrɪk(əl)] or [hɪs'tɔrɪk(əl)] *adj* storico

histo·ry ['hɪstəri] *s* (**-ries**) storia

histrionic [,hɪstri'ɑnɪk] *adj* teatrale; (*artificial, affected*) istrionico, teatrale ‖ **histrionics** *s* istrionismo, teatralità *f*

hit [hɪt] *s* colpo; successo; (*sarcastic remark*) frecciata; **to be a hit** far furore; **to make a hit with** fare ottima impressione con ‖ *v* (*pret & pp* **hit;** *ger* **hitting**) *tr* colpire; (*to bump*) cozzare; (*the target*) toccare, imbroccare, infilare; (*with a car*) metter sotto; (*a certain speed*) andare a ‖ *intr* battere; **to hit on** (*s.th new*) imbroccare; **to hit out at** attaccare

hit'-and-run' *adj* (*driver*) colpevole di mancato soccorso

hit'-and-run' driv'er *s* pirata *m* della strada

hitch [hɪtʃ] *s* (*jerk*) strattone *m;* (*knot*) nodo; difficoltà *f*, ostacolo; ‖ *tr* (*to tie*) attaccare; (*oxen*) aggiogare; (slang) sposare

hitch'hike' *intr* fare l'autostop

hitch'hik'er *s* autostoppista *mf*

hitch'ing post' *s* palo per attaccare un cavallo

hither ['hɪðər] *adv* qua, qui; **hither and thither** qua e là

hith'er·to' *adv* sinora

hit'-or-miss' *adj* fatto alla carlona

hit' rec'ord *s* disco di grande successo

hive [haɪv] *s* (*box for bees*) alveare *m;* (*swarm*) sciame *m;* **hives** orticaria ‖ *tr* (*bees*) raccogliere

hoard [hord] *s* cumulo; (*of money*) gruzzolo ‖ *tr & intr* custodire gelosamente; tesaurizzare

hoarding ['hordɪŋ] *s* ammassamento, tesaurizzazione

hoarfrost ['hor,frɔst] *s* brina

hoarse [hors] *adj* rauco, svociato

hoarseness ['horsnɪs] *s* raucedine *f*

hoar·y ['hori] *adj* (**-ier; -iest**) canuto, incanutito

hoax [hoks] *s* mistificazione ‖ *tr* mistificare

hob [hɑb] *s* mensola del focolare; **to play hob with** (coll) mettere a soqquadro

hobble ['hɑbəl] *s* zoppicamento; (*to tie legs of animal*) pastoia ‖ *tr* far zoppicare; imbarazzare; mettere le pastoie a ‖ *intr* zoppicare

hob·by ['hɑbi] *s* (**-bies**) svago, passatempo; **to ride a hobby** dedicarsi troppo alla propria occupazione favorita

hob'by-horse' *s* cavallo a dondolo

hob'gob'lin *s* folletto

hob'nail' *s* brocca, bulletta

hob·nob ['hɑb,nɑb] *v* (*pret & pp* **-nobbed;** *ger* **-nobbing**) *intr* essere amiconi; **to hobnob with** essere intimo di

ho·bo ['hobo] *s* (**-bos** or **-boes**) girovago, vagabondo

Hob'son's choice' ['hɑbsənz] *s* scelta fra quanto viene offerto o niente

hock [hɑk] *s* garretto; (coll) pegno; **in hock** (coll) impegnato, al monte di pietà ‖ *tr* tagliare i garretti a; (coll) impegnare

hockey ['hɑki] *s* hockey *m*

hock'ey play'er *s* hockeista *m*, discatore *m*

hock'shop' *s* (coll) negozio di prestiti su pegno

hocus-pocus ['hokəs'pokəs] *s* (*meaningless formula*) abracadabra *m;* gherminella

hod [hɑd] *s* vassoio; secchio per il carbone

hod' car'rier *s* manovale *m*

hodgepodge ['hɑdʒ,pɑdʒ] *s* farragine *f*

hoe [ho] *s* marra, zappa ‖ *tr & intr* zappare

hog [hɑg] or [hɔg] *s* suino, porco, maiale *m* ‖ *v* (*pret & pp* **hogged;** *ger* **hogging**) *tr* (slang) mangiarsi il meglio di

hoggish ['hɑgɪʃ] or ['hɔgɪʃ] *adj* maialesco; egoista

hogs'head' *s* barilozzo di sessantatrè galloni

hog'wash' *s* broda da maiali

hoist [hɔɪst] *s* montacarichi *m; (lift)* spinta ‖ *(lift)* alzare, rizzare; *(a flag)* inastare; *(naut)* issare

hoity-toity [ˈhɔɪtɪˈtɔɪtɪ] *adj* arrogante, altezzoso

hokum [ˈhokəm] *s* (coll) fandonie *fpl;* (coll) sentimentalismo volgare

hold [hold] *s* presa, piglio; *(handle)* impugnatura; autorità *f*, ascendente *m; (wrestling)* presa; *(aer)* cabina bagagli; *(mus)* corona; *(naut)* cala, stiva; **to take hold of** afferrare; **impossessarsi di** ‖ *v (pret & pp* **held** [held]) *tr* tenere; *(to hold up)* sostenere; *(e.g., with a pin)* assicurare; *(a rank)* rivestire; contenere; *(a meeting)* avere; *(a note)* (mus) filare; **to hold back** trattenere; **to hold in** trattenere; **to hold one's own** non perdere terreno; **to hold over** differire; **to hold up** reggere, sostenere; *(to rob)* (coll) derubare, rapinare ‖ *intr* stare; *(to cling)* reggere; restare valido; **hold on!** un momento!; **to hold back** frenarsi; **to hold forth** fare un discorso; **to hold off** astenersi; mantenersi a distanza; **to hold on** continuare; **to hold on to** attaccarsi a; **to hold out** tener duro, resistere; **to hold out for** mantenersi fermo per

holder [ˈholdər] *s* possessore *m*, detentore *m; (e.g., for a cigar)* bocchino; *(e.g., for a pot)* manico, impugnatura

holding [ˈholdɪŋ] *s* possesso; **holdings** valori *mpl*, patrimonio

hold'ing com'pany *s* società finanziaria

hold'up' *s (delay)* interruzione *f;* (coll) rapina a mano armata; (fig) furto

hold'up man' *s* grassatore *m*

hole [hol] *s* buco; *(in cheese)* occhio; *(in a road)* buca; *(den)* tana; *(burrow)* fossa; **in a hole** in grane, in difficoltà; **to burn a hole in one's pocket** *(said of money)* scorrere attraverso le mani bucate di qlcu; **to pick holes in** trovare a ridire su ‖ *intr*—**to hole up** (coll) imbucarsi

holiday [ˈhɑlɪˌde] *s* giorno festivo, festa; vacanza

holiness [ˈholɪnɪs] *s* santità *f;* **his Holiness** sua Santità

Holland [ˈhɑlənd] *s* l'Olanda *f*

Hollander [ˈhɑləndər] *s* olandese *mf*

hollow [ˈhɑlo] *adj* vuoto; *(sound)* sordo; *(eyes, cheeks)* infossato; vano, futile ‖ *s* buca, cavità *f; (small valley)* valletta ‖ *adv*—**to beat all hollow** (coll) battere completamente ‖ *tr* scavare

hol·ly [ˈhɑli] *s* (-lies) agrifoglio

holly'hock' *s* altea, malvone *m*

holm' oak' [hom] *s* leccio

holocaust [ˈhɑləˌkɔst] *s* olocausto

holster [ˈholstər] *s* fondina

ho·ly [ˈholi] *adj* (-lier; -liest) santo; *(writing)* sacro; *(water)* benedetto

Ho'ly Ghost' *s* Spirito Santo

ho'ly or'ders *spl* ordini sacri; **to take holy orders** entrare in un ordine religioso

Ho'ly Rood' [rud] *s* Santa Croce

Ho'ly Scrip'ture *s* Sacra Scrittura

Ho'ly See' *s* Santa Sede

Ho'ly Sep'ulcher *s* Santo Sepolcro

Ho'ly Thurs'day *s* l'Ascensione; il giovedì santo

ho'ly wa'ter *s* acqua benedetta, acquasanta

Ho'ly Writ' *s* Sacra Scrittura

homage [ˈhɑmɪdʒ] or [ˈɑmɪdʒ] *s* omaggio

homburg [ˈhɑmbʌrg] *s* lobbia *m & f*

home [hom] *adj* casalingo, domestico; nazionale ‖ *s* casa, dimora; *(fatherland)* patria; *(for the sick, aged, etc.)* ricovero; *(sports)* meta, traguardo; **at home** a casa; *(at ease)* a proprio agio; *(sports)* nel proprio campo; **away from home** fuori di casa; **make yourself at home** stia comodo; **to be at home** *(to receive callers)* ricevere ‖ *adv* a casa; **to see home** accompagnare a casa; **to strike home** toccare nel vivo

home'bod'y *s* (-ies) persona casalinga

homebred [ˈhomˌbred] *adj* domestico; rozzo; semplice

home'brew' *s* bevanda fatta in casa

home-coming [ˈhomˌkʌmɪŋ] *s* ritorno a casa

home' coun'try *s* paese *m* natale

home' deliv'ery *s* trasporto a domicilio

home' front' *s* fronte domestico

home'land' *s* paese natio

homeless [ˈhomlɪs] *adj* senza tetto

home' life' *s* vita familiare

home-loving [ˈhomˌlʌvɪŋ] *adj* casalingo

home·ly [ˈhomli] *adj* (-lier; -liest) *(not goodlooking)* brutto; *(not elegant)* semplice, scialbo

homemade [ˈhomˈmed] *adj* fatto in casa

homemaker [ˈhomˌmekər] *s* casalinga

home' of'fice *s* sede *f* centrale ‖ **Home Office** *s* (Brit) ministero degli interni

homeopath [ˈhomɪˌ·pæθ] or [ˈhɑmɪ·ˌpæθ] *s* omeopatico

home' plate' *s* casa base

home' port' *s* porto d'iscrizione (nel registro marittimo)

home' rule' *s* autogoverno

home' run' *s* colpo che permette al battitore di percorrere tutte le basi del diamante fino alla casa base

home'sick' *adj* nostalgico; **to be homesick for** sentire la nostalgia per

home'sick'ness *s* nostalgia

homespun [ˈhomˌspʌn] *adj* filato a casa; semplice

home'stead *s* casa e terreno

home'stretch' *s* (sports) dirittura d'arrivo; (fig) fase *f* finale

home'town' *s* città *f* natale

homeward [ˈhomwərd] *adj* di ritorno ‖ *adv* verso casa; verso la patria

home'work' *s* lavoro a domicilio; *(of a student)* dovere *m*, esercizio

homey [ˈhomi] *adj* (homier; homiest) intimo, comodo

homicidal [ˌhɑmɪˈsaɪdəl] *adj* omicida

homicide [ˈhɑmɪˌsaɪd] *s (act)* omicidio; *(person)* omicida *mf*

homi·ly [ˈhɑmɪli] *s* (-lies) omelia

homing ['homɪŋ] *adj* (*pigeon*) viaggiatore; (*weapon*) cercatore del bersaglio

hominy ['hɑmɪnɪ] *s* granturco macinato

homogenei·ty [ˌhomədʒɪ'niːɪtɪ] or [ˌhɑmədʒɪ'niːɪtɪ] *s* (-**ties**) omogeneità *f*

homogeneous [ˌhomə'dʒɪnɪ·əs] or [ˌhɑmə'dʒɪnɪ·əs] *adj* omogeneo

homogenize [hə'mɑdʒə ˌnaɪz] *tr* omogeneizzare

homonym ['hɑmənɪm] *s* omonimo

homonymous [hə'mɑnɪməs] *adj* omonimo

homosexual [ˌhomə'sekʃʊ·əl] *adj & s* omosessuale *mf*

hone [hon] *s* cote *f* ‖ *tr* affilare

honest ['ɑnɪst] *adj* onesto; guadagnato onestamente; integro, schietto

honesty ['ɑnɪstɪ] *s* onestà *f*; (bot) lunaria

hon·ey ['hʌnɪ] *adj* melato, dolce ‖ *s* miele *m*; nettare *m*; (coll) caro ‖ *v* (*pret & pp* **-eyed** or **-ied**) *tr* dire parole melate a

hon'ey·bee' *s* ape domestica

hon'ey·comb' *s* favo ‖ *tr* crivellare

honeyed ['hʌnɪd] *adj* melato

hon'eydew mel'on *s* melone *m* dolce dalla scorza liscia

hon'ey lo'cust *s* acacia a tre spine

hon'ey·moon' *s* luna di miele ‖ *intr* andare in viaggio di nozze

honeysuckle ['hʌnɪ ˌsʌkəl] *s* caprifoglio

honk [hɑŋk] or [hɔŋk] *s* (of wild goose) schiamazzo; (of automobile horn) suono del clacson ‖ *tr* (aut) suonare ‖ *intr* schiamazzare; (aut) suonare

honkytonk ['hɑŋkɪ ˌtɑŋk] or ['hɔŋkɪ ˌtɔŋk] *s* (coll) locale notturno rumoroso

honor ['ɑnər] *s* onore *m* ‖ *tr* onorare; (com) accettare e pagare

honorable ['ɑnərəbəl] *adj* (*upright*) onorato; (*bringing honor; worthy of honor*) onorevole

honorari·um [ˌɑnə'rɛrɪ·əm] *s* (-**ums** or **-a** [ə]) onorario

honorary ['ɑnə ˌrɛrɪ] *adj* onorario

honorific [ˌɑnə'rɪfɪk] *adj* onorifico ‖ *s* titolo onorifico; formula di gentilezza

hon'or sys'tem *s* sistema scolastico basato sulla parola d'onore

hood [hʊd] *s* cappuccio; cappuccio di toga universitaria; (of carriage) soffietto; (aut) cofano; (slang) gangster *m* ‖ *tr* incappucciare

hoodlum ['hudləm] *s* (slang) facinoroso, gangster *m*, teppista *m*

hoodoo ['hudu] *s* (body of primitive rites) vuduismo; (bad luck) iettatura; (person who brings bad luck) iettatore *m* ‖ *tr* iettare

hood'wink' *tr* turlupinare, imbrogliare

hooey ['hu·ɪ] *s* (coll) sciocchezze *fpl*

hoof [hʊf] or [huf] *s* zoccolo, unghia; **on the hoof** (cattle) vivo ‖ *tr*—to **hoof it** (slang) camminare; ballare

hoof'beat' *s* rumore *m* degli zoccoli

hook [hʊk] *s* gancio; (for fishing) amo;

(to join two things) agganciamento; (for pulling) raffio, rampino; (curve) curva; (of hook and eye) uncinello; (boxing) hook *m*, gancio; by **hook** or by **crook** di riffa o di raffa; to **swallow the hook** abboccare all'amo ‖ *tr* agganciare; (to bend) curvare; (fish) pigliare; (to wound with the horns) incornare; to **hook up** agganciare; (e.g., a loudspeaking system) montare ‖ *intr* agganciarsi; curvarsi

hookah ['hukə] *s* narghilè *m*

hook' and eye' *s* uncinello e occhiello

hook' and lad'der *s* autoscala

hooked' rug' *s* tappeto fatto all'uncinetto

hook'nose' *s* naso gobbo

hook'up' *s* (electron) diagramma *m*, schema *m* di montaggio; (rad, telv) rete *f*

hook'worm' *s* anchilostoma *m*

hooky ['hukɪ] *s*—to **play hooky** marinare la scuola

hooligan ['hulɪgən] *s* teppista *m*

hooliganism ['hulɪgən ˌɪzəm] *s* teppismo

hoop [hup] or [hʊp] *s* cerchio ‖ *tr* cerchiare

hoop' skirt' *s* crinolina

hoot [hut] *s* grido della civetta; grido di derisione ‖ *tr* zittire ‖ *intr* stridere; to **hoot at** fischiare

hoot' owl' *s* allocco

hop [hɑp] *s* salto, saltello; (aer) breve volo; (bot) luppolo; (coll) corsa; **hops** (dried flowers of hop vine) luppolo ‖ *v* (pret & pp **hopped**) ger **hopping**) *tr* saltare su; (aer) trasvolare ‖ *intr* saltellare; saltellare su un piede; to **hop over** saltare su; fare una corsa a

hope [hop] *s* speranza ‖ *tr & intr* sperare; to **hope for** sperare

hope' chest' *s* corredo da sposa

hopeful ['hopfəl] *adj* (feeling hope) fiducioso; (giving hope) promettente

hopeless ['hoplɪs] *adj* disperato

hopper ['hɑpər] *s* tramoggia

hop'scotch' *s* gioco del mondo

horde [hord] *s* orda

horehound ['hor ˌhaund] *s* marrubio; pastiglie *fpl* per la tosse al marrubio

horizon [hə'raɪzən] *s* orizzonte *m*

horizontal [ˌhɑrɪ'zɑntəl] or [ˌhɔrɪ'zɑntəl] *adj & s* orizzontale *f*

hormone ['hɔrmon] *s* ormone *m*

horn [hɔrn] *s* corno; (aut) clacson *m*, avvisatore acustico; (mus) corno; (trumpet) (slang) tromba; to **blow one's horn** cantare le proprie lodi; to **lock horns** lottare, disputare; to **pull in one's horns** battere in ritirata ‖ *intr*—to **horn in** (slang) intromettersi (in)

horned' owl' ['hɔrnəd] *s* allocco

hornet ['hɔrnɪt] *s* calabrone *m*

hor'net's nest' *s* vespaio; to **stir up a hornet's nest** suscitare un vespaio

horn' of plen'ty *s* corno dell'abbondanza

horn'pipe' *s* clarinetto contadinesco inglese fatto di corno di bue

horn'-rimmed glass'es ['hɔrn'rɪmd] *spl* occhiali cerchiati di corno or con la montatura di corno

horn·y ['hɔrni] *adj* (**-ier; -iest**) corneo; (*callous*) calloso; (*having hornlike projections*) cornuto; (slang) preso da desiderio lussurioso

horoscope ['harə‚skop] *or* ['hɔrə‚skop] *s* oroscopo

horrible ['harɪbəl] *or* ['hɔrɪbəl] *adj* orrendo, orribile

horrid ['harɪd] *or* ['hɔrɪd] *adj* orrido, orribile

horri·fy ['harɪ‚faɪ] *or* ['hɔrɪ‚faɪ] *v* (*pret & pp* **-fied**) *tr* inorridire

horror ['harər] *or* ['hɔrər] *s* orrore *m*; **to have a horror of** provare orrore per

hors d'oeuvre [ɔr 'dʌrv] *s* (**hors d'oeuvres** [ɔr 'dʌrvz]) *s* antipasto

horse [hɔrs] *s* cavallo; (*of carpenter*) cavalletto; **hold your horses!** (coll) aspetti un momento!; **to back the wrong horse** (coll) puntare sul perdente; **to be a horse of another color** (coll) essere un altro paio di maniche ‖ **to horse around** (slang) giocherellare; (slang) fare tiri burloni

horse'back'—**on horseback** a cavallo ‖ *adv*—**to ride horseback** montare a cavallo

horse' block' *s* montatoio

horse'break'er *s* domatore *m* di cavalli

horse'car' *s* tram *m* a cavalli

horse' chest'nut *s* (*tree*) ippocastano; (*nut*) castagna d'India

horse' deal'er *s* mercante *m* di cavalli

horse' doc'tor *s* veterinario

horse'fly' *s* (**-flies**) tafano

horse'hair' *s* crine *m* di cavallo; (*fabric*) cilicio

horse'hide' *s* cuoio di cavallo

horse'laugh' *s* risataccia

horse'man *s* (**-men**) cavallerizzo

horsemanship ['hɔrsmən‚ʃɪp] *s* equitazione, maneggio

horse' meat' *s* carne equina

horse' op'era *s* western *m*

horse' pis'tol *s* pistola da sella

horse'play' *s* gioco violento, tiro burlone

horse'pow'er *s* cavallo vapore inglese

horse' race' *s* corsa ippica

horse'rad'ish *s* cren *m*, barbaforte *m*

horse' sense' *s* (coll) senso comune

horse'shoe' *s* ferro di cavallo

horse'shoe mag'net *s* calamita a ferro di cavallo

horse'shoe nail' *s* chiodo da cavallo

horse' show' *s* concorso ippico

horse' thief' *s* ladro di cavalli

horse'-trade' *intr* trafficare

horse'whip' *s* staffile *m* ‖ *v* (*pret & pp* **-whipped**); *ger* **-whipping**) *tr* staffilare

horse'wom'an *s* (**-wom'en**) amazzone *f*

hors·y ['hɔrsi] *adj* (**-ier; -iest**) equestre; (*interested in horses*) appassionato ai cavalli; (coll) goffo

horticulture ['hɔrtɪ‚kʌltʃər] *s* orticoltura

horticulturist [‚hɔrtɪ'kʌltʃərɪst] *s* orticoltore *m*

hose [hoz] *s* (*stocking*) calza; (*sock*) calzino corto; (*flexible tube*) manica ‖ **hose** *spl* calze *fpl*

hosier ['hoʒər] *s* calzettaio

hosiery ['hoʒəri] *s* calze *fpl*; calzificio

hospice ['haspɪs] *s* ospizio

hospitable ['haspɪtəbəl] *or* [has'pɪtəbəl] *adj* ospitale

hospital ['haspɪtəl] *s* ospedale *m*

hospitali·ty [‚haspɪ'tælɪti] *s* (**-ties**) ospitalità *f*

hospitalize ['haspɪtə‚laɪz] *tr* ospedalizzare

host [host] *s* ospite *m*; (*at an inn*) oste *m*; (*army*) milizia; (*crowd*) folla ‖ **Host** *s* (eccl) ostia

hostage ['hastɪdʒ] *s* ostaggio

hostel ['hastəl] *s* ostello della gioventù

hostel·ry ['hastəlri] *s* (**-ries**) albergo

hostess ['hostɪs] *s* ospite *f*, padrona di casa; (*e.g., on a bus*) accompagnatrice *f*, guida *f*; (aer) assistente *f* di volo

hostile ['hastɪl] *adj* ostile

hostili·ty [has'tɪlɪti] *s* (**-ties**) ostilità *f*

hostler ['haslər] *or* ['aslər] *s* stalliere *m*

hot [hat] *adj* (**hotter; hottest**) caldo; (*reception*) caloroso; (*e.g., pepper*) piccante; (*fresh*) fresco; (*pursuit*) impetuoso; (*in rut*) in calore; (coll) radioattivo; **to be hot** (*said of a person*) aver caldo; (*said of the weather*) fare caldo; **to make it hot for** (coll) dare del filo da torcere a

hot' air' *s* aria calda; (slang) fumo

hot'-air fur'nace *s* impianto di riscaldamento ad aria calda

hot' baths' *spl* terme *fpl*

hot'bed' *s* (*e.g., of revolt*) focolaio; (hort) semenzaio, letto caldo

hot'-blood'ed *adj* ardente; impetuoso

hot' cake' *s* frittella; **to sell like hot cakes** vendersi come se fosse regalato

hot' dog' *s* Frankfurter *m*, Würstel *m*

hotel [ho'tel] *adj* alberghiero ‖ *s* albergo

ho·tel'keep'er *s* albergatore *m*

hot'head' *s* testa calda

hotheaded ['hat‚hedɪd] *adj* esaltato, scalmanato

hot'house' *s* serra

hot' plate' *s* fornello elettrico, scaldavivande *m*

hot' springs' *spl* terme *fpl*

hot-tempered ['hat'tempərd] *adj* impulsivo, irascibile

hot' wa'ter *s*—**to be in hot water** (coll) essere nei guai

hot'-wa'ter boil'er *s* caldaia del termosifone

hot'-wa'ter bot'tle *s* borsa dell'acqua calda

hot'-wa'ter heat'er *s* scaldabagno

hot'-wa'ter heat'ing *s* riscaldamento a circolazione d'acqua calda

hound [haund] *s* bracco; **to follow the hounds** *or* **to ride to hounds** andare a caccia alla volpe ‖ *tr* perseguitare

hour [aur] *s* ora; **by the hour** a ore; **in an evil hour** in un brutto momento; **on the hour** ogni ora al suonar del-

l'ora; **to keep late hours** andare a
letto tardi
hour'glass' s clessidra
hour' hand' s lancetta delle ore
hourly ['aurli] adj orario || adv ogni
ora; spesso
house [haus] s (**houses** ['hauzɪz])
casa; (legislative body) camera; (size
of audience) concorso di pubblico;
teatro; **to keep house** fare le faccende domestiche; **to put one's house
in order** migliorare il proprio comportamento; accomodare le proprie
faccende || [hauz] tr allogare
house' arrest' s arresto a domicilio
house'boat' s casa galleggiante
house'break'er s scassinatore m
housebreaking ['haus,brekɪŋ] s violazione di domicilio, scasso
housebroken ['haus,brokən] adj (e.g.,
cat) che è stato addestrato a tenersi
pulito
house'clean'ing s pulizia della casa;
(fig) pulizia, repulisti m
house'coat' s vestaglia da casa
house' cur'rent s corrente f di rete
house'fly' s (-flies) mosca domestica
houseful ['haus,ful] s casa piena
house' fur'nishings spl arredi domestici
house'hold' adj domestico || s famiglia
house'hold'er s capo della famiglia
house'-hunt' intr—**to go house-hunting**
andare in cerca di casa
house'keep'er s governante f
house'keep'ing s faccende domestiche;
to set up housekeeping metter su
casa
house'keeping apart'ment s apparta-
mentino
house'maid' s domestica
house' me'ter s contatore domestico
house'moth'er s maestra in pensionato
per studenti
house' of cards' s castello di carte
house' of ill' repute' s casa di malaffare
house' paint'er s imbianchino
house' physi'cian s medico residente
house'top' s tetto; **to shout from the
housetops** proclamare ai quattro
venti
housewarming ['haus,wɔrmɪŋ] s festa
per l'inaugurazione di una casa
house'wife' s (-wives) donna di casa
house'work' s faccende domestiche
housing ['hauzɪŋ] s (of a horse) gualdrappa; (dwelling) abitazioni fpl;
(carp) alloggiamento; (mach) gabbia,
custodia; (aut) coppa; (of transmission) (aut) scatola
hous'ing short'age s crisi f degli alloggi
hovel ['hʌvəl] or ['hɑvəl] s catapec-
chia, stamberga; (shed) baracca
hover ['hʌvər] or ['hɑvər] intr librarsi,
(on the lips) trapelare; (fig) ondeggiare, esitare
how [hau] adv come; (at what price)
a quanto; **how early** quando, a che
ora; **how else** in che altro modo; **how
far** fino a dove; quanto, e.g., **how far
is it to the station?** quanto c'è da qui
alla stazione?; **how long** quanto
tempo; **how many** quanti; **how much**

quanto; **how often** quante volte; **how
old are you?** quanti anni ha?; **how
soon** quando, a che ora; **how** + adj
quanto + adj, e.g., **how beautiful she
is!** quanto è bella!
how·ev'er adv comunque; in qualunque
modo; per quanto . . . , e.g., **however
wrong he may be** per quanto torto
possa avere || conj come, e.g., **do it
however you want** lo faccia come
vuole
howitzer ['hau·ɪtsər] s obice m
howl [haul] s ululato, urlo; scoppio di
risa || tr gridare; **to howl down**
sopraffare a grida; || intr ululare,
urlare
howler ['haulər] s urlatore m; (coll)
strafalcione m, topica
hoyden ['hɔɪdən] s ragazzaccia
hub [hʌb] s mozzo; (fig) centro
hubbub ['hʌbəb] s putiferio, fracasso
hub'cap' s (aut) calotta della ruota
huckleber·ry ['hʌkəl,beri] s (-ries) s
mirtillo
huckster ['hʌkstər] s venditore m ambulante; trafficante m
huddle ['hʌdəl] s conferenza segreta ||
intr affollarsi, accalcarsi
hue [hju] s tono, tinta; **hue and cry**
grido d'indignazione
huff [hʌf] s stizza; **in a huff** di cattivo
umore || tr (checkers) buffare
hug [hʌg] s abbraccio || v (pret & pp
hugged; ger **hugging**) tr abbracciare;
(e.g., a wall) costeggiare || intr ab-
bracciarsi
huge [hjudʒ] adj smisurato, immane
huh [hʌ] interj ehi
hulk [hʌlk] s scafo, carcassa; (unwieldy object) trabiccolo
hulking ['hʌlkɪŋ] adj grosso e goffo
hull [hʌl] s (of ship or hydroplane)
scafo; (of dirigible) intelaiatura; (of
airplane) fusoliera; (e.g., of a nut)
guscio || tr sgusciare; (rice) brillare
hullabaloo ['hʌləbə,lu] or [,hʌləbə'lu]
s fracasso, baccano
hum [hʌm] s canterellio; (of bee, ma-
chine, etc.) ronzio || v (pret & pp
hummed; ger **humming**) tr canterel-
lare || intr canterellare; (to buzz)
ronzare; (coll) vibrare, essere attivo
human ['hjumən] adj umano
hu'man be'ing s essere umano
humane [hju'men] adj umano; compassionevole
humanist ['hjumənɪst] adj umanistico
|| s umanista mf
humanitarian [hju,mænɪ'terɪ·ən] adj &
s umanitario
humani·ty [hju'mænɪti] s (-ties) umanità f; **humanities** (of Greece and
Rome) studi umanistici; (literature,
art, philosophy) scienze umanistiche
hu'man·kind' s genere umano
humble ['hʌmbəl] or ['ʌmbəl] adj
umile || tr umiliare
hum'ble pie' s—**to eat humble pie** accettare un'umiliazione
hum'bug' s frottola; (person) impostore
m || v (pret & pp -**bugged;** ger

-bugging) *tr* imbrogliare ‖ *intr* fare l'imbroglione

hum'drum' *adj* noioso, monotono

humer·us ['hjumərəs] *s* (**-i** [‚aɪ]) omero

humid ['hjumɪd] *adj* umido

humidifier [hju'mɪdɪ‚faɪ·ər] *s* evaporatore *m*

humidi·fy [hju'mɪdɪ‚faɪ] *v* (*pret & pp* **-fied**) *tr* inumidire

humidity [hju'mɪdɪti] *s* umidità *f*

humiliate [hju'mɪlɪ‚et] *tr* umiliare

humiliating [hju'mɪlɪ‚etɪŋ] *adj* umiliante

humility [hju'mɪlɪti] *s* umiltà *f*

hummingbird ['hʌmɪŋ‚bʌrd] *s* colibrì *m*

humor ['hjumər] *or* ['jumər] *s* umore *m;* umorismo; **out of humor** di cattivo umore ‖ *tr* adattarsi alle fisime di, assecondare

humorist ['hjumərɪst] *or* ['jumərɪst] *s* umorista *mf*

humorous ['hjumərəs] *or* ['jumərəs] *adj* umoristico

hump [hʌmp] *s* gobba; (*in the ground*) monticello

hump'back' *s* gobba; (*person*) gobbo

humus ['hjuməs] *s* humus *m*

hunch [hʌntʃ] *s* gobba; (*premonition*) (coll) sospetto ‖ *tr* piegare ‖ *intr* accovacciarsi

hunch'back' *s* gobba; (*person*) gobbo

hundred ['hʌndrəd] *adj, s & pron* cento; **a hundred** *or* **one hundred** cento; **by the hundreds** a centinaia

hundredth ['hʌndrədθ] *adj, s & pron* centesimo

hun'dred·weight' *s* cento libbre

Hungarian [hʌŋ'gerɪ·ən] *adj & s* ungherese *mf*

Hungary ['hʌŋgəri] *s* l'Ungheria *f*

hunger ['hʌŋgər] *s* fame *f* ‖ *intr* aver fame; **to hunger for** aver un desiderio ardente di, agognare

hun'ger strike' *s* sciopero della fame

hun·gry ['hʌŋgri] *adj* (**-gri·er; -gri·est**) affamato; **to be hungry** aver fame; **to go hungry** andare digiuno

hunk [hʌŋk] *s* (coll) bel pezzo

hunt [hʌnt] *s* caccia; **on the hunt for** a caccia di ‖ *tr* cacciare; (*to look for*) cercare ‖ *intr* andare a caccia; cercare; **to go hunting** andare a caccia; **to hunt for** cercare

hunter ['hʌntər] *s* cacciatore *m*; (*dog*) cane *m* da caccia

hunting ['hʌntɪŋ] *adj* da caccia ‖ *s* caccia

hunt'ing box' *s* capanno

hunt'ing dog' *s* cane *m* da caccia

hunt'ing ground' *s* terreno di caccia

hunt'ing horn' *s* corno da caccia

hunt'ing jack'et *s* cacciatora

hunt'ing lodge' *s* (*hut*) capanno; villino da caccia

hunt'ing sea'son *s* stagione della caccia

huntress ['hʌntrɪs] *s* cacciatrice *f*

hunts'man *s* (**-men**) cacciatore *m*

hurdle ['hʌrdəl] *s* (*hedge*) siepe *f*; (*wooden frame*) barriera; (sports, fig) ostacolo; **hurdles** corsa ad ostacoli ‖ *tr* saltare, superare

hur'dle race' *s* corsa agli ostacoli

hurl [hʌrl] *s* lancio ‖ *tr* lanciare; **to hurl back** respingere

hurrah [hu'rɑ] *or* **hurray** [hu're] *s* viva *m* ‖ *tr* applaudire ‖ *intr* gridare urrà ‖ *interj* evviva!, urrà!; **hurrah for . . . !** viva . . . !

hurricane ['hʌrɪ‚ken] *s* uragano

hurried ['hʌrid] *adj* frettoloso

hur·ry ['hʌri] *s* (**-ries**) fretta; **to be in a hurry** avere fretta ‖ *v* (*pret & pp* **-ried**) *tr* affrettare, sollecitare ‖ *intr* affrettarsi; **to hurry after** correr dietro a; **to hurry away** andarsene di furia; **to hurry back** ritornare presto; **to hurry up** spicciarsi

hurt [hʌrt] *adj* (*injured*) ferito; (*offended*) risentito ‖ *s* (*harm*) danno; (*injury*) ferita; (*pain*) dolore *m* ‖ *v* (*pret & pp* **hurt**) *tr* (*to harm*) fare male a; (*to injure*) ferire; (*to offend*) offendere; (*to pain*) dolere (with *dat*) ‖ *intr* fare male, dolere; aver male, e.g., **my head hurts** ho male alla testa

hurtle ['hʌrtəl] *intr* sferrarsi, scagliarsi, precipitarsi

husband ['hʌzbənd] *s* marito ‖ *tr* amministrare con economia

hus'band·man *s* (**-men**) agricoltore *m*

husbandry ['hʌzbəndri] *s* agricoltura; (*management of domestic affairs*) governo, economia domestica

hush [hʌʃ] *s* silenzio ‖ *tr* far tacere; **to hush up** (*a scandal*) soffocare ‖ *intr* tacere ‖ *interj* zitto!

hushaby ['hʌ/ə‚baɪ] *interj* fa' la nanna!

hush'-hush' *adj* segretissimo

hush' mon'ey *s* prezzo del silenzio

husk [hʌsk] *s* guscio; (*of corn*) spoglia ‖ *tr* sgusciare; (*rice*) brillare; (*corn*) scartocciare, spogliare

husk·y ['hʌski] *adj* (**-ier; -iest**) forte; (*voice*) rauco

hus·sy ['hʌzi] *or* ['hʌsi] *s* (**-sies**) poca di buono; ragazza impudente

hustle ['hʌsəl] *s* vigore *m*; (slang) traffico ‖ *tr* forzare, spingere ‖ *intr* affrettarsi, scalmanarsi; (slang) trafficare; (*said of a prostitute*) (slang) accostare un cliente

hustler ['hʌslər] *s* (*go-getter*) persona intraprendente; (slang) trafficone *m*, imbroglione *m*; (slang) passeggiatrice *f*

hut [hʌt] *s* casolare *m*, casupola

hyacinth ['haɪ·əsɪnθ] *s* giacinto

hybrid ['haɪbrɪd] *adj & s* ibrido

hybridize ['haɪbrɪ‚daɪz] *tr & intr* ibridare

hy·dra ['haɪdrə] *s* (**-dras** *or* **-drae** [dri]) idra

hydrant ['haɪdrənt] *s* idrante *m*; (*water faucet*) rubinetto

hydrate ['haɪdret] *s* idrato ‖ *tr* idratare ‖ *intr* idratarsi

hydraulic [haɪ'drɔlɪk] *adj* idraulico ‖ **hydraulics** *s* idraulica

hydrau'lic ram' *s* pompa idraulica

hydriodic [‚haɪdrɪ'ɑdɪk] *adj* iodidrico

hydrobromic [‚haɪdrə'bromɪk] *adj* bromidrico

hydrocarbon [ˌhaɪdrəˈkɑrbən] s idro-carburo

hydrochloric [ˌhaɪdrəˈklorɪk] adj clo-ridrico

hydroelectric [ˌhaɪdro·ɪˈlektrɪk] adj idroelettrico

hydrofluoric [ˌhaɪdrəfluˈɑrɪk] or [ˌhaɪdrəfluˈɒrɪk] adj fluoridrico

hydrofoil [ˈhaɪdrəˌfɔɪl] s superficie idrodinamica; (winglike member) aletta idrodinamica; (vessel) ali-scafo, idroplano

hydrogen [ˈhaɪdrədʒən] s idrogeno

hy'drogen bomb' s bomba all'idrogeno

hy'drogen perox'ide s perossido d'idro-geno, acqua ossigenata

hy'drogen sul'fide s solfuro d'idrogeno

hydrometer [haɪˈdrɑmɪtər] s areome-tro

hydrophobia [ˌhaɪdrəˈfobɪ·ə] s idro-fobia

hydroplane [ˈhaɪdrəˌplen] s (aer) idro-volante m; (naut) idroscivolante m, idroplano

hydroxide [haɪˈdrɑksaɪd] s idrossido

hyena [haɪˈinə] s iena

hygiene [ˈhaɪdʒin] or [ˈhaɪdʒɪˌin] s igiene f

hygienic [ˌhaɪdʒɪˈenɪk] or [haɪˈdʒinɪk] adj igienico

hymn [hɪm] s inno

hymnal [ˈhɪmnəl] s innario

hyperacidity [ˌhaɪpərəˈsɪdɪti] s ipera-cidità f

hyperbola [haɪˈpʌrbələ] s (geom) iper-bole f

hyperbole [haɪˈpʌrbəli] s (rhet) iper-bole f

hyperbolic [ˌhaɪpərˈbɑlɪk] adj iper-bolico

hypersensitive [ˌhaɪpərˈsensɪtɪv] adj ipersensibile

hypertension [ˌhaɪpərˈtenʃən] s iper-tensione

hyphen [ˈhaɪfən] s trattino

hyphenate [ˈhaɪfəˌnet] tr unire con trattino; scrivere con trattino

hypno·sis [hɪpˈnosɪs] s (-ses [siz]) ipnosi f

hypnotic [hɪpˈnɑtɪk] adj & s ipnotico

hypnotism [ˈhɪpnəˌtɪzəm] s ipnotismo

hypnotize [ˈhɪpnəˌtaɪz] tr ipnotizzare

hypochondriac [ˌhaɪpəˈkɑndrɪˌæk] or [ˌhɪpəˈkɑndrɪˌæk] s ipocondriaco

hypocri·sy [hɪˈpɑkrəsi] s (-sies) ipo-crisia

hypocrite [ˈhɪpəkrɪt] s ipocrita mf

hypocritical [ˌhɪpəˈkrɪtɪkəl] adj ipo-crita

hypodermic [ˌhaɪpəˈdʌrmɪk] adj ipo-dermico

hyposulfite [ˌhaɪpəˈsʌlfaɪt] s iposolfito

hypotenuse [haɪˈpɑtɪˌnus] or [haɪˈpɑtɪˌnjus] s ipotenusa

hypothesis [haɪˈpɑθɪsɪs] s (-ses [ˌsiz]) ipotesi f

hypothesize [haɪˈpoθɪˌsaɪz] tr ipotiz-zare

hypothetic(al) [ˌhaɪpəˈθetɪk(əl)] adj ipotetico

hyssop [ˈhɪsəp] s issopo

hysteria [hɪsˈtɪrɪ·ə] s isterismo

hysteric [hɪsˈterɪk] adj isterico ‖ **hys-terics** s isterismo

hysterical [hɪsˈterɪkəl] adj isterico

I

I, i [aɪ] s nona lettera dell'alfabeto inglese

I [aɪ] pron pers (we [wi]) io; **it is I** sono io

iambic [aɪˈæmbɪk] adj giambico

iam·bus [aɪˈæmbəs] s (-bi [baɪ]) giambo

I'-beam' s putrella

Iberian [aɪˈbɪrɪ·ən] adj iberico ‖ s abi-tante mf dell'Iberia; lingua iberica

ibex [ˈaɪbeks] s (ibexes or ibices [ˈɪbɪˌsiz]) stambecco

ice [aɪs] s ghiaccio; **to break the ice** rompere il ghiaccio; **to cut no ice** (coll) non avere importanza; **to skate on thin ice** cacciarsi in una situazione delicata ‖ tr gelare; (to cover with icing) glassare ‖ intr gelarsi

ice' age' s epoca glaciale

ice' bag' s borsa di ghiaccio

iceberg [ˈaɪsˌbʌrg] s borgognone m, montagna di ghiaccio

ice'boat' s slitta a vela; (icebreaker) rompighiaccio

icebound [ˈaɪsˌbaund] adj chiuso dal ghiaccio

ice'box' s ghiacciaia

ice'break'er s rompighiaccio

ice' buck'et s secchiello da ghiaccio

ice'cap' s calotta glaciale

ice'-cold' adj gelido, ghiacciato

ice' cream' s gelato, sorbetto

ice'-cream cone' s cono gelato

ice'-cream freez'er s gelatiera

ice'-cream par'lor s gelateria

ice' cube' s cubetto di ghiaccio

ice' hock'ey s hockey m su ghiaccio

Iceland [ˈaɪslənd] s l'Islanda f

Icelander [ˈaɪsˌlændər] or [ˈaɪsləndər] s islandese mf

Icelandic [aɪsˈlændɪk] adj islandese ‖ s (language) islandese m

ice'man' s (-men') venditore m di ghiaccio

ice' pack' s banco di ghiaccio; (ice bag) borsa di ghiaccio

ice' pick' s rompighiaccio

ice' shelf' s tavolato di ghiaccio

ice' skate' s pattino da ghiaccio

ice' wa'ter s acqua gelata

ichthyology [ˌɪkθɪˈɑlədʒi] s ittiologia

icicle [ˈaɪsɪkəl] s ghiacciolo

icing [ˈaɪsɪŋ] s glassa; (meteor) gelo

iconoclast [aɪˈkɑnəˌklæst] s icono-clasta mf

iconoscope [aɪ'kɑnə‚skop] *s* (trademark) iconoscopio

icy ['aɪsi] *adj* (**icier; iciest**) ghiacciato; (*e.g., wind, hands*) gelido; (fig) glaciale

idea [aɪ'di·ə] *s* idea

ideal [aɪ'di·əl] *adj* & *s* ideale *m*

idealist [aɪ'di·əlɪst] *adj* & *s* idealista *mf*

idealistic [aɪ‚di·əl'ɪstɪk] *adj* idealistico

idealize [aɪ'di·ə‚laɪz] *tr* idealizzare

identic(al) [aɪ'dɛntɪk(əl)] *adj* identico

identification [aɪ‚dɛntɪfɪ'keʃən] *s* identificazione, riconoscimento

identifica'tion card' *s* carta d'identità

identifica'tion tag' *s* piastrina

identi·fy [aɪ'dɛntɪ‚faɪ] *v* (*pret* & *pp* **-fied**) *tr* identificare

identi·ty [aɪ'dɛntɪti] *s* (**-ties**) identità *f*

ideolo·gy [‚aɪdɪ'ɑlədʒi] or [‚ɪdɪ'ɑlədʒi] *s* (**-gies**) ideologia

ides [aɪdz] *spl* idi *mpl* & *fpl*

idio·cy ['ɪdɪ·əsi] *s* (**-cies**) idiozia

idiom ['ɪdɪ·əm] *s* (*expression that is contrary to the usual patterns of the language*) locuzione idiomatica, idiotismo; (*style of language*) lingua, idioma *m*; (*style of an author*) stile *m*; (*character of a language*) indole *f*

idiomatic [‚ɪdɪ·ə'mætɪk] *adj* idiomatico

idiosyncra·sy [‚ɪdɪ·ə'sɪnkrəsi] *s* (**-sies**) eccentricità *f*, originalità *f*; (med) idiosincrasia

idiot ['ɪdɪ·ət] *s* idiota *mf*

idiotic [‚ɪdɪ'ɑtɪk] *adj* idiota

idle ['aɪdəl] *adj* (*unemployed*) disoccupato; (*machine*) fermo; (*capital*) giacente; (*time*) perso; (*talk*) vano; (*lazy*) fannullone, ozioso; **to run idle** girare a vuoto ‖ *tr*—**to idle away** (*time*) sprecare ‖ *intr* poltrire, fare il fannullone; (aut) girare al minimo

idleness ['aɪdəlnɪs] *s* ozio

idler ['aɪdlər] *s* fannullone *m*

idling ['aɪdlɪŋ] *s* (*of motor*) minimo

idol ['aɪdəl] *s* idolo

idola·try [aɪ'dɑlətri] *s* (**-tries**) idolatria

idolize ['aɪdə‚laɪz] *tr* idolatrare

idyll ['aɪdəl] *s* idillio

idyllic [aɪ'dɪlɪk] *adj* idilliaco

if [ɪf] *conj* se; **as if** come se; **even if** anche se; **if so** se è così; **if true** se è vero

ignis fatuus ['ɪgnɪs'fætʃu·əs] *s* (**ignes fatui** ['ɪgniz'fætʃu‚aɪ]) fuoco fatuo

ignite [ɪg'naɪt] *tr* infiammare ‖ *intr* infiammarsi

ignition [ɪg'nɪʃən] *s* ignizione; (aut) accensione

igni'tion switch' *s* (aut) chiavetta dell'accensione

igni'tion sys'tem *s* (aut) apparecchiatura d'accensione

ignoble [ɪg'nobəl] *adj* ignobile

ignominious [‚ɪgnə'mɪnɪ·əs] *adj* ignominioso

ignoramus [‚ɪgnə'reməs] *s* ignorante *mf*

ignorance ['ɪgnərəns] *s* ignoranza

ignorant ['ɪgnərənt] *adj* ignorante; **to be ignorant of** ignorare

ignore [ɪg'nor] *tr* (*a person; a person's kindness*) ignorare

ill [ɪl] *adj* (**worse** [wʌrs]; **worst** [wʌrst]) malato; **to take ill** cadere malato ‖ *adv* male; **to take ill** prendere in mala parte

ill-advised ['ɪləd'vaɪzd] *adj* inconsulto, sconsiderato

ill-bred ['ɪl'brɛd] *adj* maleducato

ill-considered ['ɪlkən'sɪdərd] *adj* sconsiderato

ill-disposed ['ɪldɪs'pozd] *adj* maldisposto, malintenzionato

illegal [ɪ'ligəl] *adj* illegale

illegible [ɪ'lɛdʒɪbəl] *adj* illeggibile

illegitimate [‚ɪlɪ'dʒɪtɪmɪt] *adj* illegittimo

ill' fame' *s* pessima fama

ill-fated ['ɪl'fetɪd] *adj* infausto

ill-gotten ['ɪl'gɑtən] *adj* male acquistato

ill-humored ['ɪl'hjumərd] *adj* di cattivo umore

illicit [ɪ'lɪsɪt] *adj* illecito

illitera·cy [ɪ'lɪtərəsi] *s* (**-cies**) analfabetismo; (*mistake*) solecismo; ignoranza

illiterate [ɪ'lɪtərɪt] *adj* (*uneducated*) illetterato; (*unable to read or write*) analfabeta ‖ *s* analfabeta *mf*

ill-mannered ['ɪl'mænərd] *adj* screanzato, ineducato

illness ['ɪlnɪs] *s* malattia

illogical [ɪ'lɑdʒɪkəl] *adj* illogico

ill-spent ['ɪl'spɛnt] *adj* sprecato

ill-starred ['ɪl'stɑrd] *adj* nato sotto una cattiva stella; sfortunato, funesto

ill-tempered ['ɪl'tɛmpərd] *adj* di cattivo umore

ill-timed ['ɪl'taɪmd] *adj* inopportuno

ill-treat' *tr* maltrattare, tartassare

illuminate [ɪ'lumɪ‚net] *tr* illuminare; (*a manuscript*) miniare

illumination [ɪ‚lumɪ'neʃən] *s* illuminazione; (*in manuscript*) miniatura

illusion [ɪ'luʒən] *s* illusione

illusive [ɪ'lusɪv] *adj* illusorio

illusory [ɪ'lusəri] *adj* illusorio

illustrate ['ɪləs‚tret] or [ɪ'lʌstret] *tr* illustrare

illustration [‚ɪləs'treʃən] *s* illustrazione

illustrator ['ɪləs‚tretər] *s* illustratore *m*

illustrious [ɪ'lʌstrɪ·əs] *adj* illustre

ill' will' *s* astio, ruggine *f*, malevolenza

image ['ɪmɪdʒ] *s* immagine *f*; **the very image of** il ritratto parlante di

image·ry ['ɪmɪdʒri] or ['ɪmɪdʒəri] *s* (**-ries**) (*mental images*) fantasia; (*images collectively*) immagini *fpl*; (rhet) linguaggio figurato

imaginary [ɪ'mædʒɪ‚nɛri] *adj* immaginario

imagination [ɪ‚mædʒɪ'neʃən] *s* immaginazione

imagine [ɪ'mædʒɪn] *tr* & *intr* immaginare; (*to conjecture*) immaginarsi; **imagine!** si figuri!

imbalance [ɪm'bæləns] *s* scompenso

imbecile ['ɪmbɪsɪl] *adj* & *s* imbecille *mf*

imbecili·ty [ˌɪmbɪˈsɪlɪti] *s* (**-ties**) imbecillità *f*, imbecillaggine *f*
imbibe [ɪmˈbaɪb] *tr* (*to drink*) bere; assorbire ‖ *intr* bere
imbue [ɪmˈbju] *tr* imbevere
imitate [ˈɪmɪˌtet] *tr* imitare
imitation [ˌɪmɪˈteʃən] *adj* (*e.g., jewelry*) falso ‖ *s* imitazione
imitator [ˈɪmɪˌtetər] *s* imitatore *m*
immaculate [ɪˈmækjəlɪt] *adj* immacolato
immaterial [ˌɪmaˈtɪrɪ·əl] *adj* immateriale; poco importante; **it's immaterial to me** a me fa lo stesso
immature [ˌɪməˈtjur] or [ˌɪməˈtur] *adj* immaturo
immeasurable [ɪˈmɛʒərəbəl] *adj* incommensurabile, smisurato
immediacy [ɪˈmidɪ·əsi] *s* immediatezza
immediate [ɪˈmidɪ·ɪt] *adj* immediato
immediately [ɪˈmidɪ·ɪtli] *adv* immediatamente
immemorial [ˌɪmɪˈmorɪ·əl] *adj* immemorabile
immense [ɪˈmɛns] *adj* immenso
immerge [ɪˈmʌrdʒ] *intr* sommergersi
immerse [ɪˈmʌrs] *tr* immergere
immersion [ɪˈmʌrʃən] or [ɪˈmʌrʒən] *s* immersione
immigrant [ˈɪmɪgrənt] *adj* & *s* immigrante *mf*
immigrate [ˈɪmɪˌgret] *intr* immigrare
immigration [ˌɪmɪˈgreʃən] *s* immigrazione
imminent [ˈɪmɪnənt] *adj* imminente
immobile [ɪˈmobɪl] or [ɪˈmobɪl] *adj* immobile
immobilize [ɪˈmobɪˌlaɪz] *tr* immobilizzare
immoderate [ɪˈmɑdərɪt] *adj* smodato, sregolato
immodest [ɪˈmɑdɪst] *adj* immodesto
immoral [ɪˈmɑrəl] or [ɪˈmɔrəl] *adj* immorale
immortal [ɪˈmɔrtəl] *adj* & *s* immortale *mf*
immortalize [ɪˈmɔrtəˌlaɪz] *tr* eternare, immortalare
immune [ɪˈmjun] *adj* immune
immunize [ˈɪmjəˌnaɪz] or [ɪˈmjunaɪz] *tr* immunizzare
imp [ɪmp] *s* diavoletto; (*child*) frugolo
impact [ˈɪmpækt] *s* impatto
impair [ɪmˈpɛr] *tr* danneggiare; (*to weaken*) indebolire
impan·el [ɪmˈpænəl] *v* (*pret & pp* **-eled** or **-elled**; *ger* **-eling** or **-elling**) *tr* iscrivere nella lista dei giurati; (*a jury*) selezionare
impart [ɪmˈpɑrt] *tr* (*a secret*) far conoscere; (*knowledge*) impartire; (*motion*) imprimere
impartial [ɪmˈpɑrʃəl] *adj* imparziale
impassable [ɪmˈpæsəbəl] or [ɪmˈpɑsəbəl] *adj* impraticabile, intransitabile
impasse [ɪmˈpæs] or [ˈɪmpæs] *s* vicolo cieco, impasse *f*
impassible [ɪmˈpæsɪbəl] *adj* impassibile
impassioned [ɪmˈpæʃənd] *adj* caloroso, veemente
impassive [ɪmˈpæsɪv] *adj* impassibile

impatience [ɪmˈpeʃəns] *s* impazienza
impatient [ɪmˈpeʃənt] *adj* impaziente
impeach [ɪmˈpitʃ] *tr* accusare; (*a public official*) sottoporre a un'inchiesta; (*a statement*) mettere in dubbio
impeachment [ɪmˈpitʃmənt] *s* accusa; inchiesta
impeccable [ɪmˈpɛkəbəl] *adj* impeccabile
impecunious [ˌɪmpɪˈkjunɪ·əs] *adj* indigente
impedance [ɪmˈpidəns] *s* impedenza
impede [ɪmˈpid] *tr* impedire, intralciare
impediment [ɪmˈpɛdɪmənt] *s* impedimento; ostacolo
im·pel [ɪmˈpɛl] *v* (*pret & pp* **-peled** or **-pelled**; *ger* **-peling** or **-pelling**) *tr* spingere, forzare
impending [ɪmˈpɛndɪŋ] *adj* imminente, incombente
impenetrable [ɪmˈpɛnətrəbəl] *adj* impenetrabile
impenitent [ɪmˈpɛnɪtənt] *adj* impenitente ‖ *s* persona impenitente
imperative [ɪmˈpɛrɪtɪv] *adj* (*commanding*) imperativo; (*urgent*) imperioso ‖ *s* imperativo
imperceptible [ˌɪmpərˈsɛptɪbəl] *adj* impercettibile
imperfect [ɪmˈpʌrfɪkt] *adj* & *s* imperfetto
imperfection [ˌɪmpərˈfɛkʃən] *s* imperfezione
imperial [ɪmˈpɪrɪ·əl] *adj* imperiale ‖ *s* (*goatee*) barbetta, mosca; (*top of coach*) imperiale *m*
imperialist [ɪmˈpɪrɪ·əlɪst] *adj* & *s* imperialista *mf*
imper·il [ɪmˈpɛrɪl] *v* (*pret & pp* **-iled** or **-illed**; *ger* **-iling** or **-illing**) *tr* mettere in pericolo
imperious [ɪmˈpɪrɪ·əs] *adj* imperioso
imperishable [ɪmˈpɛrɪʃəbəl] *adj* imperituro, duraturo
impersonate [ɪmˈpʌrsəˌnet] *tr* (*to pretend to be*) spacciarsi per; (*on the stage*) impersonare
impertinence [ɪmˈpʌrtɪnəns] *s* impertinenza
impertinent [ɪmˈpʌrtɪnənt] *adj* impertinente
impetuous [ɪmˈpɛtʃʊ·əs] *adj* impetuoso
impetus [ˈɪmpɪtəs] *s* impeto, foga
impie·ty [ɪmˈpaɪ·əti] *s* (**-ties**) empietà *f*
impinge [ɪmˈpɪndʒ] *intr*—**to impinge on** or **upon** violare; (*said, e.g., of the sun*) ferire; (*the imagination*) colpire
impious [ˈɪmpɪ·əs] *adj* empio
impish [ˈɪmpɪʃ] *adj* indiavolato
implant [ɪmˈplænt] *tr* innestare; instillare, istillare
implement [ˈɪmplɪmənt] *s* utensile *m*, strumento ‖ [ˈɪmplɪˌment] *tr* completare, mettere in opera; (*to provide with implements*) attrezzare
implicate [ˈɪmplɪˌket] *tr* implicare
implicit [ɪmˈplɪsɪt] *adj* implicito; (*unquestioning*) assoluto, cieco
implied [ɪmˈplaɪd] *adj* implicito
implore [ɪmˈplor] *tr* (*a person; pardon*)

implorare; (to entreat) raccoman-
darsi a
im·ply [ɪm'plaɪ] v (pret & pp -plied)
tr voler dire, significare; implicare,
sottintendere
impolite [ˌɪmpə'laɪt] adj scortese
import ['ɪmport] s importazione; arti-
colo d'importazione; importanza ||
[ɪm'port] or ['ɪmport] tr importare;
significare || intr importare
importance [ɪm'portəns] s importanza
important [ɪm'portənt] adj importante
importation [ˌɪmpor'teʃən] s importazione
importer [ɪm'portər] s importatore m
importunate [ɪm'portʃənɪt] adj importuno
importune [ˌɪmpor'tjun] or [ˌɪmpor-
'tun] tr importunare
impose [ɪm'poz] tr imporre || intr—to
impose on or upon abusare di; abusare della gentilezza di
imposing [ɪm'pozɪŋ] adj imponente
imposition [ˌɪmpə'zɪʃən] s imposizione; abuso; abuso della gentilezza;
inganno
impossible [ɪm'pasɪbəl] adj impossibile
impostor [ɪm'pastər] s impostore m
imposture [ɪm'pastʃər] s impostura
impotence ['ɪmpətəns] s impotenza
impotent ['ɪmpətənt] adj impotente
impound [ɪm'paʊnd] tr rinchiudere,
recintare; (water) raccogliere; (law)
sequestrare, confiscare
impoverish [ɪm'pavərɪʃ] tr impoverire
impracticable [ɪm'præktɪkəbəl] adj impraticabile; (intractable) intrattabile
impractical [ɪm'præktɪkəl] adj poco
pratico
impregnable [ɪm'prɛgnəbəl] adj inespugnabile, imprendibile
impregnate [ɪm'prɛgnet] tr impregnare
impresari·o [ˌɪmprɪ'sarɪ ˌo] s (-os) impresario
impress [ɪm'prɛs] tr (to affect in mind
or feelings) impressionare; (to produce by pressure; to fix on s.o.'s
mind) imprimere; (mil) arruolare
impression [ɪm'prɛʃən] s impressione
impressionable [ɪm'prɛʃənəbəl] adj
impressionabile
impressive [ɪm'prɛsɪv] adj impressionante, imponente
imprint ['ɪmprɪnt] s impronta; (typ)
indicazione dell'editore || [ɪm'prɪnt]
tr imprimere
imprison [ɪm'prɪzən] tr imprigionare
imprisonment [ɪm'prɪzənmənt] s prigione, prigionia
improbable [ɪm'prabəbəl] adj improbabile
impromptu [ɪm'pramptju] or [ɪm-
'pramptu] adj improvvisato || s im-
provvisazione; (mus) impromptu m ||
adv all'improvviso
improper [ɪm'prapər] adj (erroneous)
improprio; (inappropriate; unseemly)
scorretto; (math) improprio
improve [ɪm'pruv] tr migliorare; (an
opportunity) approfittare di || intr
migliorare; to improve on or upon
perfezionare

improvement [ɪm'pruvmənt] s miglioramento, perfezionamento; (in real
estate) miglioria; (e.g., of time) buon
uso
improvident [ɪm'pravɪdənt] adj im-
provvido, imprevidente
improvise ['ɪmprə ˌvaɪz] tr & intr improvvisare
imprudence [ɪm'prudəns] s imprudenza
imprudent [ɪm'prudənt] adj imprudente
impudence ['ɪmpjədəns] s impudenza,
sfrontatezza, sfacciataggine f
impudent ['ɪmpjədənt] adj sfrontato,
sfacciato, spudorato
impugn [ɪm'pjun] tr impugnare
impulse ['ɪmpʌls] s impulso
impulsive [ɪm'pʌlsɪv] adj impulsivo
impunity [ɪm'pjunɪti] s impunità f
impure [ɪm'pjur] adj impuro
impuri·ty [ɪm'pjurɪti] s (-ties) impurità
f
impute [ɪm'pjut] tr imputare
in [ɪn] adj interno; (coll) moderno,
alla moda || s relazione; the ins and
outs tutti i dettagli || adv dentro; a
casa; in ufficio; in here qui dentro;
in there lì dentro; to be in essere a
casa; to be in for essere destinato a;
to be in with essere in intimità con ||
prep in; (within) dentro a; (over,
through) per; di, e.g., the best in the
class il migliore della classe; dressed
in vestito di; in so far as per quanto;
in that per quanto, dato che
inability [ˌɪnə'brlɪti] s inabilità f
inaccessible [ˌɪnæk'sɛsɪbəl] adj inac-
cessibile
inaccura·cy [ɪn'ækjərəsi] s (-cies) ine-
sattezza, imprecisione
inaccurate [ɪn'ækjərɪt] adj inesatto
inaction [ɪn'ækʃən] s inazione
inactive [ɪn'æktɪv] adj inattivo
inadequate [ɪn'ædɪkwɪt] adj inade-
guato, inadatto
inadvertent [ˌɪnəd'vʌrtənt] adj disattento; inavvertito
inadvisable [ˌɪnəd'vaɪzəbəl] adj poco
consigliabile
inane [ɪn'en] adj insensato, assurdo
inanimate [ɪn'ænɪmɪt] adj inanimato
inappreciable [ˌɪnə'priʃ/ɪ·əbəl] adj
inapprezzabile
inappropriate [ˌɪnə'propri·ɪt] adj non
appropriato, improprio
inarticulate [ˌɪnar'tɪkjəlɪt] adj
(sounds, words) inarticolato; (person) incapace di esprimersi
inasmuch as [ˌɪnəs'mætʃ ˌæz] conj dato
che, visto che, in quanto che
inattentive [ˌɪnə'tɛntɪv] adj disattento
inaugural [ɪn'ɔgjərəl] adj inaugurale ||
s discorso inaugurale
inaugurate [ɪn'ɔgjə ˌret] tr inaugurare
inauguration [ɪn ˌɔgjə'reʃən] s inaugurazione; (investiture of a head of
government) assunzione dei poteri
inborn ['ɪn ˌbɔrn] adj innato, ingenito
inbreeding ['ɪn ˌbridɪŋ] s incrocio fra
animali o piante affini
incandescent [ˌɪnkən'dɛsənt] adj incandescente

incapable [ɪn'kepəbəl] *adj* incapace
incapacitate [ˌɪnkə'pæsɪ ˌtet] *tr* inabilitare; (law) interdire
incapaci·ty [ˌɪnkə'pæsɪti] *s* (-ties) incapacità *f*
incarcerate [ɪn'kɑrsə ˌret] *tr* incarcerare
incarnate [ɪn'kɑrnɪt] or [ɪn'kɑrnet] *adj* incarnato || [ɪn'kɑrnet] *tr* incarnare
incarnation [ˌɪnkɑr'neʃən] *s* incarnazione
incendiarism [ɪn'sɛndɪ·ə ˌrɪzəm] *s* incendio doloso; (*agitation*) sobillazione
incendiar·y [ɪn'sɛndɪ ˌeri] *adj* incendiario || *s* (-ies) incendiario; (fig) sobillatore *m*
incense ['ɪnsɛns] *s* incenso || (*tr to burn incense for*) incensare || [ɪn'sɛns] *tr* irritare, esasperare
in'cense burn'er *s* (*person*) incensatore *m*; (*vessel*) incensiere *m*
incentive [ɪn'sɛntɪv] *adj* & *s* incentivo
inception [ɪn'sɛpʃən] *s* principio
incertitude [ɪn'sʌrtɪ ˌtjud] or [ɪn'sʌrtɪ ˌtud] *s* incertezza
incest ['ɪnsɛst] *s* incesto
incestuous [ɪn'sɛst/ʊ·əs] *adj* incestuoso
inch [ɪntʃ] *s* pollice *m*; to be within an inch of essere a due dita da || *intr*—to inch ahead spingersi avanti poco a poco
incidence ['ɪnsɪdəns] *s* incidenza
incident ['ɪnsɪdənt] *adj* incidente, incidentale || *s* incidente *m*
incidental [ˌɪnsɪ'dɛntəl] *adj* incidentale || *s* elemento incidentale; incidentals piccole spese
incidentally [ˌɪnsɪ'dɛntəli] *adv* incidentalmente, per inciso; a proposito
incinerator [ɪn'sɪnə ˌretər] *s* inceneritore *m*
incision [ɪn'sɪʒən] *s* incisione
incisive [ɪn'saɪsɪv] *adj* incisivo
incite [ɪn'saɪt] *tr* incitare, stimulare
inclemen·cy [ɪn'klɛmənsi] *s* (-cies) inclemenza
inclination [ˌɪnklɪ'neʃən] *s* inclinazione
incline ['ɪnklaɪn] or [ɪn'klaɪn] *s* declivio || [ɪn'klaɪn] *tr* inclinare || *intr* inclinarsi
inclose [ɪn'kloz] *tr* includere, accludere; to inclose herewith accludere alla presente
inclosure [ɪn'kloʒər] *s* (*land surrounded by fence*) recinto; (*e.g., letter*) allegato
include [ɪn'klud] *tr* includere; including incluso, e.g., three books including the grammar tre libri inclusa la grammatica
inclusive [ɪn'klusɪv] *adj* incluso, e.g., until next Friday inclusive fino a venerdì prossimo incluso; inclusive of inclusivo di, e.g., price inclusive of freight prezzo inclusivo delle spese di trasporto
incogni·to [ɪn'kɑgnɪ ˌto] *adj* incognito || *s* (-tos) incognito || *adv* in incognito

incoherent [ˌɪnko'hɪrənt] *adj* incoerente
incombustible [ˌɪnkəm'bʌstɪbəl] *adj* incombustibile
income ['ɪnkʌm] *s* reddito, provento
in'come tax' *s* imposta sul reddito
incoming ['ɪn ˌkʌmɪŋ] *adj* entrante; futuro; (*tide*) ascendente || *s* entrata
incomparable [ɪn'kɑmpərəbəl] *adj* incomparabile, impareggiabile
incompatible [ˌɪnkəm'pætɪbəl] *adj* incompatibile
incomplete [ˌɪnkəm'plit] *adj* incompleto, tronco, scompleto
incomprehensible [ˌɪnkɑmprɪ'hɛnsɪbəl] *adj* incomprensibile
inconceivable [ˌɪnkən'sivəbəl] *adj* inconcepibile
inconclusive [ˌɪnkən'klusɪv] *adj* inconcludente
incongruous [ɪn'kɑŋgru·əs] *adj* incongruo
inconsequential [ɪn ˌkɑnsɪ'kwɛnʃəl] *adj* (*lacking proper sequence of thought or speech*) inconseguente; (*trivial*) di poca importanza
inconsiderate [ˌɪnkən'sɪdərɪt] *adj* inconsiderato, sconsiderato
inconsisten·cy [ˌɪnkən'sɪstənsi] *s* (-cies) inconsistenza
inconsistent [ˌɪnkən'sɪstənt] *adj* inconsistente, inconseguente
inconsolable [ˌɪnkən'soləbəl] *adj* inconsolabile, sconsolato
inconspicuous [ˌɪnkən'spɪkju·əs] *adj* poco appariscente, poco apparente
inconstant [ɪn'kɑnstənt] *adj* incostante
incontinence [ɪn'kɑntɪnəns] *s* incontinenza
incontrovertible [ˌɪnkɑntrə'vʌrtɪbəl] *adj* incontrovertibile
inconvenience [ˌɪnkən'vini·əns] *s* scomodo, incomodo || *tr* scomodare
inconvenient [ˌɪnkən'vini·ənt] *adj* incomodo, inconveniente
incorporate [ɪn'kɔrpə ˌret] *tr* incorporare; costituire in società anonima || *intr* incorporarsi; costituirsi in società anonima
incorrect [ˌɪnkə'rɛkt] *adj* scorretto
increase ['ɪnkris] *s* aumento; crescita; to be on the increase essere in aumento || [ɪn'kris] *tr* aumentare; (*by propagation*) moltiplicare || *intr* aumentarsi; moltiplicarsi
increasingly [ɪn'krisɪŋli] *adv* sempre più
incredible [ɪn'krɛdɪbəl] *adj* incredibile
incredulous [ɪn'krɛdʒələs] *adj* incredulo
increment ['ɪnkrɪmənt] *s* aumento, incremento
incriminate [ɪn'krɪmɪ ˌnet] *tr* incriminare
incrust [ɪn'krʌst] *tr* incrostare
incubate ['ɪnkjə ˌbet] *tr* incubare || *intr* essere in incubazione; (*said, e.g., of a hen*) covare; (fig) covare
incubator ['ɪnkjə ˌbetər] *s* incubatrice *f*
inculcate [ɪn'kʌlket] or ['ɪnkʌl ˌket] *tr* inculcare

incumben·cy [ɪn'kʌmbənsi] s (-cies) incombenza

incumbent [ɪn'kʌmbənt] adj—**to be incumbent on** incombere a, spettare a || s titolare mf

incunabula [ˌɪnkju'næbjələ] spl (beginnings) origini fpl; (early printed books) incunaboli mpl

in·cur [ɪn'kʌr] v (pret & pp -curred; ger -curring) tr incorrere in; (a debt) assumere, contrarre

incurable [ɪn'kjurəbəl] adj & s incurabile mf

incursion [ɪn'kʌrʒən] or [ɪn'kʌrʃən] s incursione, scorreria

indebted [ɪn'detɪd] adj indebitato; obbligato

indecen·cy [ɪn'disənsi] s (-cies) indecenza, sconcezza

indecent [ɪn'disənt] adj indecente, sconveniente

indecisive [ˌɪndɪ'saɪsɪv] adj indeciso; (e.g., event) non decisivo

indeed [ɪn'did] adv difatti, infatti || interj davvero!

indefatigable [ˌɪndɪ'fætɪgəbəl] adj indefesso, infaticabile

indefensible [ˌɪndɪ'fensɪbəl] adj indifendibile, insostenibile

indefinable [ɪndɪ'faɪnəbəl] adj indefinibile

indefinite [ɪn'defɪnɪt] adj indefinito

indelible [ɪn'delɪbəl] adj indelebile

indemnification [ɪnˌdemnɪfɪ'keʃən] s indennità f, indennizzo

indemni·fy [ɪn'demnɪˌfaɪ] v (pret & pp -fied) tr indennizzare

indemni·ty [ɪn'demnɪti] s (-ties) indennità f, indennizzo

indent [ɪn'dent] tr frastagliare, dentellare; (typ) far rientrare

indentation [ˌɪnden'teʃən] s frastaglio, dentellatura; (typ) accapo

indenture [ɪn'dentʃər] s scrittura pubblica; contratto di apprendista || tr obbligare per contratto

independence [ˌɪndɪ'pendəns] s indipendenza

independent [ˌɪndɪ'pendənt] adj & s indipendente mf

indescribable [ˌɪndɪ'skraɪbəbəl] adj indescrivibile

indestructible [ˌɪndɪ'strʌktɪbəl] adj indistruttibile

indeterminate [ˌɪndɪ'tʌrmɪnɪt] adj indeterminato

index ['ɪndeks] s (indexes or indices ['ɪndɪˌsiz]) indice m; (typ) indice m indicatore || tr mettere un indice a; mettere all'indice || **Index** s Indice m

in'dex card' s scheda di catalogo

in'dex fin'ger s dito indice

India ['ɪndɪə] s l'India f

In'dia ink' s inchiostro di china

Indian ['ɪndɪən] adj & s indiano

In'dian club' s clava di ginnastica

In'dian corn' s granoturco

In'dian file' s fila indiana || adv in fila indiana

In'dian O'cean s Oceano Indiano

In'dian sum'mer s estate f di San Martino

In'dian wres'tling s braccio di ferro

In'dia pa'per s carta bibbia, carta d'India

In'dia rub'ber s cauccià m

indicate ['ɪndɪˌket] tr indicare

indication [ˌɪndɪ'keʃən] s indicazione

indicative [ɪn'dɪkətɪv] adj & s indicativo

indicator ['ɪndɪˌketər] s indicatore m, indice m

indict [ɪn'daɪt] tr accusare

indictment [ɪn'daɪtmənt] s accusa, atto d'accusa

indifferent [ɪn'dɪfərənt] adj indifferente; (not particularly good) passabile

indigenous [ɪn'dɪdʒɪnəs] adj indigeno

indigent ['ɪndɪdʒənt] adj indigente || **the indigent** gli indigenti

indigestion [ˌɪndɪ'dʒestʃən] s indigestione

indignant [ɪn'dɪgnənt] adj indignato

indignation [ˌɪndɪg'neʃən] s indignazione

indigni·ty [ɪn'dɪgnɪti] s (-ties) indignità f

indi·go ['ɪndɪˌgo] adj indaco || s (-gos or -goes) indaco

indirect [ˌɪndɪ'rekt] or [ˌɪndaɪ'rekt] adj indiretto

in'direct dis'course s discorso indiretto

indiscernible [ˌɪndɪ'zʌrnɪbəl] or [ˌɪndɪ'sʌrnɪbəl] adj indiscernibile

indiscreet [ˌɪndɪs'krit] adj indiscreto

indispensable [ˌɪndɪs'pensəbəl] adj indispensabile, imprescindibile

indispose [ˌɪndɪs'poz] tr indisporre

indisposed [ˌɪndɪs'pozd] adj (disinclined) mal disposto; (slightly ill) indisposto

indissoluble [ˌɪndɪ'saljəbəl] adj indissolubile

indistinct [ˌɪndɪs'stɪŋkt] adj indistinto

indite [ɪn'daɪt] tr redigere

individual [ˌɪndɪ'vɪdʒʊ·əl] adj individuale || s individuo

individuali·ty [ˌɪndɪˌvɪdʒʊ'ælɪti] s (-ties) individualità f; (person of distinctive character) individuo

Indochina ['ɪndo'tʃaɪnə] s l'Indocina f

Indo-Chi·nese ['ɪndoˈtʃaɪˈniz] adj indocinese || s (-nese) indocinese mf

Indo-European ['ɪndoˌjurə'pi·ən] adj & s indoeuropeo

indolent ['ɪndələnt] adj indolente

Indonesia [ˌɪndo'niʒə] or [ˌɪndo'niʒə] s l'Indonesia f

Indonesian [ˌɪndo'niʃən] or [ˌɪndo'niʒən] adj & s indonesiano

indoor ['ɪnˌdor] adj situato in casa; da farsi in casa

indoors ['ɪn'dorz] adv dentro, a casa, al coperto

indorse [ɪn'dɔrs] tr (com) girare; (fig) appoggiare, approvare

indorsee [ˌɪndɔr'si] s giratario

indorsement [ɪn'dɔrsmənt] s (com) girata; (fig) appoggio, approvazione

indorser [ɪn'dɔrsər] s girante mf

induce [ɪn'djus] or [ɪn'dus] tr indurre

inducement [ɪn'djusmənt] or [ɪn'dusmənt] s stimolo, incentivo

induct [ɪn'dʌkt] *tr* installare; iniziare; (mil) arruolare

induction [ɪn'dʌk/ən] *s* iniziazione; (elec & log) induzione; (mil) arruolamento

indulge [ɪn'dʌldʒ] *tr* indulgere (with *dat*) || *intr* cedere, lasciarsi andare; **to indulge in** abbandonarsi a; permettersi il lusso di

indulgence [ɪn'dʌldʒəns] *s* compiacenza; intemperanza, abbandono; (leniency) indulgenza

indulgent [ɪn'dʌldʒənt] *adj* indulgente

industrial [ɪn'dʌstrɪ-əl] *adj* industriale

industrialist [ɪn'dʌstrɪ-əlɪst] *s* industriale *m*

industrialize [ɪn'dʌstrɪ-ə,laɪz] *tr* industrializzare

industrious [ɪn'dʌstrɪ-əs] *adj* industrioso, laborioso

indus·try ['ɪndʌstrɪ] *s* (-tries) industria

inebriation [ɪn,ibrɪ'e/ən] *s* ubriachezza

inedible [ɪn'edɪbəl] *adj* immangiabile

ineffable [ɪn'ɛfəbəl] *adj* ineffabile

ineffective [,ɪnɪ'fektɪv] *adj* inefficace; (person) incapace

ineffectual [,ɪnɪ'fekt/ʊ-əl] *adj* inefficace

inefficient [,ɪnɪ'fɪ/ənt] *adj* inefficiente

ineligible [ɪn'elɪdʒɪbəl] *adj* ineleggibile

inequali·ty [,ɪnɪ'kwɑlɪtɪ] *s* (-ties) disuguaglianza

inequi·ty [ɪn'ekwɪtɪ] *s* (-ties) ingiustizia

ineradicable [,ɪnɪ'rædɪkəbəl] *adj* inestirpabile

inertia [ɪn'ʌr/ə] *s* inerzia

inescapable [,ɪnes'kepəbəl] *adj* ineluttabile, inderogabile

inevitable [ɪn'evɪtəbəl] *adj* inevitabile

inexact [,ɪneg'zækt] *adj* inesatto

inexcusable [,ɪneks'kjuzəbəl] *adj* inescusabile

inexhaustible [,ɪneg'zɔstɪbəl] *adj* inesauribile

inexorable [ɪn'eksərəbəl] *adj* inesorabile

inexpedient [,ɪnek'spidɪ-ənt] *adj* inopportuno

inexpensive [,ɪnek'spensɪv] *adj* poco costoso, a buon mercato

inexperience [,ɪnek'spɪrɪ-əns] *s* inesperienza

inexplicable [ɪn'eksplɪkəbəl] *adj* inesplicabile

inexpressible [,ɪnek'spresɪbəl] *adj* indicibile, inesprimibile

infallible [ɪn'fælɪbəl] *adj* infallibile

infamous ['ɪnfəməs] *adj* infame

infa·my ['ɪnfəmɪ] *s* (-mies) infamia

infan·cy ['ɪnfənsɪ] *s* (-cies) infanzia

infant ['ɪnfənt] *adj* infantile; (in the earliest stage) (fig) nascente || *s* neonato, bebè *m*

infantile ['ɪnfən,taɪl] or ['ɪnfəntɪl] *adj* infantile

infan·try ['ɪnfəntrɪ] *s* (-tries) fanteria

in'fantry·man *s* (-men) fante *m*

infatuated [ɪn'fæt/ʊ,etɪd] *adj* infatuato

infect [ɪn'fekt] *tr* infettare

infection [ɪn'fek/ən] *s* infezione

infectious [ɪn'fek/əs] *adj* infettivo

in·fer [ɪn'fʌr] *v* (*pret* & *pp* **-ferred;** *ger* **-ferring**) *tr* inferire; (coll) dedurre, supporre

inferior [ɪn'fɪrɪ-ər] *adj* & *s* inferiore *m*

inferiority [ɪn,fɪrɪ'ɑrɪtɪ] *s* inferiorità *f*

inferior'ity com'plex *s* complesso di inferiorità

infernal [ɪn'fʌrnəl] *adj* infernale

infest [ɪn'fest] *tr* infestare

infidel ['ɪnfɪdəl] *adj* & *s* infedele *mf*

infideli·ty [,ɪnfɪ'delɪtɪ] *s* (-ties) infedeltà *f*

in'field' *s* campo interno, diamante *m*

infiltrate [ɪn'fɪltret] or ['ɪnfɪl,tret] *tr* infiltrarsi in || *intr* infiltrarsi

infinite ['ɪnfɪnɪt] *adj* & *s* infinito

infinitive [ɪn'fɪnɪtɪv] *adj* infinitivo || *s* infinito

infini·ty [ɪn'fɪnɪtɪ] *s* (-ties) infinità *f*; (math) infinito

infirm [ɪn'fʌrm] *adj* infermo; (not firm) debole

infirma·ry [ɪn'fʌrmərɪ] *s* (-ries) infermeria

infirmi·ty [ɪn'fʌrmɪtɪ] *s* (-ties) infermità *f*

inflame [ɪn'flem] *tr* infiammare || *intr* infiammarsi

inflammable [ɪn'flæməbəl] *adj* infiammabile

inflammation [,ɪnflə'me/ən] *s* infiammazione

inflate [ɪn'flet] *tr* gonfiare; (currency, prices) inflazionare || *intr* gonfiarsi

inflation [ɪn'fle/ən] *s* inflazione; (of a tire) gonfiatura

inflect [ɪn'flekt] *tr* curvare; (voice) modulare; (gram) flettere

inflection [ɪn'flek/ən] *s* inflessione; (gram) flessione

inflexible [ɪn'fleksɪbəl] *adj* inflessibile

inflict [ɪn'flɪkt] *tr* infliggere, inferire

influence ['ɪnflu-əns] *s* influenza || *tr* influire su, influenzare

influential [,ɪnflu'en/əl] *adj* influente

influenza [,ɪnflu'enzə] *s* influenza

inform [ɪn'form] *tr* informare || *intr* dare informazioni; **to inform on** denunziare, fare la spia contro

informal [ɪn'forməl] *adj* non ufficiale, ufficioso; (unceremonious) alla buona, familiare

informant [ɪn'formənt] *s* informatore *m*; (informer) delatore *m*; (ling) fonte *f* orale, informatore *m*

information [,ɪnfər'me/ən] *s* informazioni *fpl*; conoscenze *fpl*

informational [,ɪnfər'me/ənəl] *adj* informativo

informed' sour'ces *spl* fonti *fpl* attendibili

informer [ɪn'formər] *s* (informant) informatore *m*; (spy) delatore *m*

infraction [ɪn'fræk/ən] *s* infrazione

infrared [,ɪnfrə'red] *adj* & *s* infrarosso

infrequent [ɪn'frikwənt] *adj* infrequente

infringe [ɪn'frɪndʒ] *tr* violare || *intr*— **to infringe on** or **upon** violare, contravvenire a

infringement [ɪn'frɪndʒmənt] *s* infrazione

infuriate [ɪnˈfjurɪ ˌet] *tr* infuriare

infuse [ɪnˈfjuz] *tr* infondere

infusion [ɪnˈfjuʒən] *s* infusione

ingenious [ɪnˈdʒinjəs] *adj* ingegnoso

ingenui·ty [ˌɪndʒɪˈnu·ɪti] or [ˌɪndʒɪ-ˈnju·ɪti] *s* (**-ties**) ingegnosità *f*

ingenuous [ɪnˈdʒɛnju·əs] *adj* ingenuo

ingenuousness [ɪnˈdʒɛnju·əsnɪs] *s* ingenuità *f*

ingest [ɪnˈdʒɛst] *tr* ingerire

ingoing [ˈɪn ˌgoɪŋ] *adj* entrante

ingot [ˈɪŋgət] *s* lingotto, massello

ingraft [ɪnˈgræft] or [ɪnˈgrɑft] *tr* (hort & surg) innestare; (fig) inculcare

ingrate [ˈɪngret] *s* ingrato

ingratiate [ɪnˈgreʃɪ ˌet] *tr*—**to ingratiate oneself with** ingraziarsi

ingratiating [ɪnˈgreʃɪ ˌetɪŋ] *adj* attraente, affascinante, insinuante

ingratitude [ɪnˈgrætɪ ˌtjud] or [ɪnˈgrætɪ ˌtud] *s* ingratitudine *f*

ingredient [ɪnˈgridɪ·ənt] *s* ingrediente *m*

in'grown nail' [ˈɪngron] *s* unghia incarnita

ingulf [ɪnˈgʌlf] *tr* sommergere, inondare

inhabit [ɪnˈhæbɪt] *tr* abitare, popolare

inhabitant [ɪnˈhæbɪtənt] *s* abitante *mf*

inhale [ɪnˈhel] *tr* & *intr* inspirare

inherent [ɪnˈhɪrənt] *adj* inerente

inherit [ɪnˈhɛrɪt] *tr* & *intr* ereditare

inheritance [ɪnˈhɛrɪtəns] *s* eredità *f*

inheritor [ɪnˈhɛrɪtər] *s* erede *mf*

inhibit [ɪnˈhɪbɪt] *tr* inibire

inhospitable [ɪnˈhɑspɪtəbəl] or [ˌɪn-hɑsˈpɪtəbəl] *adj* inospitale

inhuman [ɪnˈhjumən] *adj* inumano

inhumane [ˌɪnhjuˈmen] *adj* inumano

inimical [ɪˈnɪmɪkəl] *adj* nemico

iniqui·ty [ɪˈnɪkwɪti] *s* (**-ties**) iniquità *f*

ini·tial [ɪˈnɪʃəl] *adj* & *s* iniziale *f* ‖ *v* (*pret* **-tialed** or **-tialled**; *ger* **-tialing** or **-tialling**) *tr* siglare

initiate [ɪˈnɪʃɪ ˌet] *tr* iniziare

initiation [ɪ ˌnɪʃɪˈeʃən] *s* iniziazione

initiative [ɪˈnɪʃɪ·ətɪv] or [ɪˈnɪʃətɪv] *s* iniziativa

inject [ɪnˈdʒɛkt] *tr* iniettare; introdurre

injection [ɪnˈdʒɛkʃən] *s* iniezione

injudicious [ˌɪndʒuˈdɪʃəs] *adj* avventato, sconsiderato

injunction [ɪnˈdʒʌŋkʃən] *s* ingiunzione

injure [ˈɪndʒər] *tr* (*to harm*) danneggiare; (*to wound*) ferire; (*to offend*) offendere, ingiuriare

injurious [ɪnˈdʒurɪ·əs] *adj* dannoso, offensivo, ingiurioso

inju·ry [ˈɪndʒəri] *s* (**-ries**) (*harm*) danno; (*wound*) ferita, lesione; offesa, ingiuria

injustice [ɪnˈdʒʌstɪs] *s* ingiustizia

ink [ɪŋk] *s* inchiostro ‖ *tr* inchiostrare

inkling [ˈɪŋklɪŋ] *s* sentore *m*, indizio

ink'stand' *s* (*container*) calamaio; (*stand*) calamaiera

ink'well' *s* calamaio

ink·y [ˈɪŋki] *adj* (**-ier; -iest**) nero come l'inchiostro; nero d'inchiostro

inlaid [ˈɪn ˌled] or [ˌɪnˈled] *adj* intarsiato, incrostato

inland [ˈɪnlənd] *adj* & *s* interno ‖ *adv* verso l'interno

in'-law' *s* affine *mf*

in·lay [ˈɪn ˌle] *s* intarsio, tassello ‖ [ɪnˈle] or [ˈɪn ˌle] *v* (*pret* & *pp* **-laid**) *tr* intarsiare

in'let *s* (*of the shore*) insenatura; (*entrance*) ammissione

in'mate' *s* (*patient, e.g., in an insane asylum*) internato; (*in a jail*) prigioniero

inn [ɪn] *s* taverna, osteria

innate [ɪˈnet] or [ˈɪnet] *adj* innato

inner [ˈɪnər] *adj* interno, interiore; intimo, profondo

in'ner·spring' mat'tress *s* materasso a molle

in'ner tube' *s* camera d'aria

inning [ˈɪnɪŋ] *s* (baseball) turno

inn'keep'er *s* locandiere *m*, oste *m*

innocence [ˈɪnəsəns] *s* innocenza

innocent [ˈɪnəsənt] *adj* & *s* innocente *mf*

innovate [ˈɪnə ˌvet] *tr* innovare

innovation [ˌɪnəˈveʃən] *s* innovazione

innuen·do [ˌɪnjuˈɛndo] *s* (**-does**) sottinteso, insinuazione

innumerable [ɪˈnjumərəbəl] or [ɪˈnumərəbəl] *adj* innumerevole

inoculate [ɪnˈɑkjə ˌlet] *tr* inoculare; (*e.g., with hatred*) inoculare; permeare

inoculation [ɪn ˌɑkjəˈleʃən] *s* inoculazione

inoffensive [ˌɪnəˈfɛnsɪv] *adj* inoffensivo

inopportune [ɪn ˌɑpərˈtjun] or [ɪn ˌɑpərˈtun] *adj* inopportuno

inordinate [ɪnˈɔrdɪnɪt] *adj* smoderato

inorganic [ˌɪnɔrˈgænɪk] *adj* inorganico

in'pa'tient *s* degente *mf*

in'put' *s* entrata; (elec, mach) energia immessa

inquest [ˈɪnkwɛst] *s* inchiesta

inquire [ɪnˈkwaɪr] *tr* domandare, chiedere ‖ *intr*—**to inquire about, after,** or **for** chiedere di; **to inquire into** investigare

inquir·y [ɪnˈkwaɪri] or [ˈɪnkwɪri] *s* (**-ies**) indagine *f*, inchiesta

inquisition [ˌɪnkwɪˈzɪʃən] *s* inquisizione

inquisitive [ɪnˈkwɪzɪtɪv] *adj* indagatore, curioso

in'road' *s* incursione, invasione

insane [ɪnˈsen] *adj* pazzo, matto

insane' asy'lum *s* manicomio

insani·ty [ɪnˈsænɪti] *s* (**-ties**) pazzia, follia, demenza

insatiable [ɪnˈseʃəbəl] *adj* insaziabile

inscribe [ɪnˈskraɪb] *tr* iscrivere; (*a book*) dedicare; (geom) inscrivere

inscription [ɪnˈskrɪpʃən] *s* scritta, iscrizione; (*of a book*) dedica

inscrutable [ɪnˈskrutəbəl] *adj* imperscrutabile

insect [ˈɪnsɛkt] *s* insetto

insecticide [ɪnˈsɛktɪ ˌsaɪd] *adj* & *s* insetticida *m*

insecure [ˌɪnsɪˈkjur] *adj* malsicuro

inseparable [ɪnˈsɛpərəbəl] *adj* inseparabile

insert ['ɪnsʌrt] s inserzione; (*circular*) inserto || [ɪn'sʌrt] *tr* inserire

insertion [ɪn'sʌrʃən] s inserzione; (*in lunar orbit*) immissione; (*of lace*) tramezzo

in·set ['ɪn,set] s intercalazione || [ɪn-'set] or ['ɪn,set] v (*pret & pp* -**set**; *ger* -**setting**) *tr* intercalare

in'shore' *adj & adv* vicino alla spiaggia

in'side' *adj* interno; privato, confidenziale || s interno; **insides** (coll) interiora *fpl*; **to be on the inside** avere informazioni confidenziali || *adv* dentro; all'interno; **inside of** dentro, dentro a, dentro di; **to turn inside out** rovesciare, voltare il diritto al rovescio || *prep* dentro, dentro a

in'side flap' s (bb) risvolto

insider [,ɪn'saɪdər] s persona informata

in'side track' s (racing) steccato; **to have the inside track** (coll) trovarsi in una situazione vantaggiosa

insidious [ɪn'sɪdɪ·əs] *adj* insidioso

in'sight' s intuito, penetrazione

insigni·a [ɪn'sɪgnɪ·ə] s (-a or -as) distintivo; (*distinguishing sign*) segno

insignificant [,ɪnsɪg'nɪfɪkənt] *adj* insignificante

insincere [,ɪnsɪn'sɪr] *adj* insincero

insinuate [ɪn'sɪnju,et] *tr* insinuare

insist [ɪn'sɪst] *intr* insistere

insofar as [,ɪnso'fɑr,æz] *conj* per quanto

insolence ['ɪnsələns] s insolenza

insolent ['ɪnsələnt] *adj* insolente

insoluble [ɪn'sɑljəbəl] *adj* insolubile

insolven·cy [ɪn'sɑlvənsi] s (-cies) insolvenza

insomnia [ɪn'sɑmnɪ·ə] s insonnia

insomuch [,ɪnso'mʌtʃ] *adv* fino al punto; **insomuch as** giacché, visto che; **insomuch that** fino al punto che

inspect [ɪn'spekt] *tr* ispezionare

inspection [ɪn'spekʃən] s ispezione

inspector [ɪn'spektər] s ispettore *m*

inspiration [,ɪnspɪ'reʃən] s ispirazione

inspire [ɪn'spaɪr] *tr & intr* ispirare

install [ɪn'stɔl] *tr* istallare

installment [ɪn'stɔlmənt] s rata; (*of a book*) dispensa; **in installments** a rate

install'ment plan' s pagamento rateale; **on the installment plan** con facilitazioni di pagamento

instance ['ɪnstəns] s esempio; (law) istanza; **for instance** per esempio

instant ['ɪnstənt] *adj* istantaneo || s istante *m*; mese *m* corrente

instantaneous [,ɪnstən'tenɪ·əs] *adj* istantaneo

instantly ['ɪnstəntli] *adv* immediatamente, istantaneamente

instead [ɪn'sted] *adv* invece; **instead of** invece di

in'step' s collo del piede

instigate ['ɪnstɪ,get] *tr* istigare

instigation [,ɪnstɪ'geʃən] s istigazione

in·still [ɪn'stɪl] *tr* instillare, istillare

instinct ['ɪnstɪŋkt] s istinto

instinctive [ɪn'stɪŋktɪv] *adj* istintivo

institute ['ɪnstɪ,tjut] or ['ɪnstɪ,tut] s istituto || *tr* istituire

institution [,ɪnstɪ'tjuʃən] or [,ɪnstɪ-'tuʃən] s istituzione

institutionalize [,ɪnstɪ'tjuʃənə,laɪz] or [,ɪnstɪ'tuʃənə,laɪz] *tr* istituzionalizzare

instruct [ɪn'strʌkt] *tr* istruire

instruction [ɪn'strʌkʃən] s istruzione

instructive [ɪn'strʌktɪv] *adj* istruttivo

instructor [ɪn'strʌktər] s istruttore *m*

instrument ['ɪnstrəmənt] s strumento; (law) istrumento || ['ɪnstrə,ment] *tr* strumentare

instrumental [,ɪnstrə'mentəl] *adj* strumentale; **to be instrumental in** contribuire a

instrumentalist [,ɪnstrə'mentəlɪst] s strumentista *mf*

instrumentali·ty [,ɪnstrəmən'tælɪti] s (-ties) mediazione, aiuto

in'strument fly'ing s volo strumentale

in'strument pan'el s (aut) cruscotto

insubordinate [,ɪnsə'bɔrdɪnɪt] *adj* insubordinato

insufferable [ɪn'sʌfərəbəl] *adj* insoffribile

insufficient [,ɪnsə'fɪʃənt] *adj* insufficiente

insular ['ɪnsələr] or ['ɪnsjulər] *adj* insulare; (*e.g., attitude*) gretto

insulate ['ɪnsə,let] *tr* isolare

in'sulating tape' ['ɪnsəletɪŋ] s nastro isolante

insulation [,ɪnsə'leʃən] s isolamento

insulator ['ɪnsə,letər] s isolatore *m*

insulin ['ɪnsəlɪn] s insulina

insult ['ɪnsʌlt] s insulto || [ɪn'sʌlt] *tr* insultare, insolentire

insulting [ɪn'sʌltɪŋ] *adj* insultante

insurance [ɪn'ʃurəns] s assicurazione

insure [ɪn'ʃur] *tr* assicurare

insurer [ɪn'ʃurər] s assicuratore *m*

insurgent [ɪn'sʌrdʒənt] *adj & s* insorgente *mf*

insurmountable [,ɪnsər'mauntəbəl] *adj* insormontabile

insurrection [,ɪnsə'rekʃən] s insurrezione

insusceptible [,ɪnsə'septɪbəl] *adj* non suscettibile

intact [ɪn'tækt] *adj* intatto, integro

in'take' s (*place of taking in*) entrata; (*act of taking in*) ammissione; (mach) presa, immissione, aspirazione

in'take man'ifold' s collettore *m* d'ammissione

intangible [ɪn'tændʒɪbəl] *adj* intangibile; (fig) vago, inafferrabile

integer ['ɪntɪdʒər] s numero intero

integral ['ɪntɪgrəl] *adj* integrale; (*part of a whole*) integrante || s (math) integrale *m*

integration [,ɪntɪ'greʃən] s integrazione

integrity [ɪn'tegrɪti] s integrità *f*

intellect ['ɪntə,lekt] s intelletto

intellectual [,ɪntə'lekt/u·əl] *adj & s* intellettuale *mf*

intelligence [ɪn'telɪdʒəns] s intelligenza; informazione, conoscenza

intel'ligence bu'reau *s* ufficio spionaggi

intel'ligence quo'tient *s* quoziente *m* d'intelligenza

intelligent [ɪn'telɪdʒənt] *adj* intelligente

intelligentsia [ɪn,telɪ'dʒentsɪ-ə] or [ɪn-,telɪ'gentsɪ-ə] *s* intellighenzia, intellettualità *f*

intelligible [ɪn'telɪdʒɪbəl] *adj* intelligibile, comprensibile

intemperance [ɪn'tempərəns] *s* intemperanza, sregolatezza

intemperate [ɪn'tempərɪt] *adj* intemperante; (*climate*) rigoroso

intend [ɪn'tend] *tr* intendere, prefiggersi; (*to mean for a particular purpose*) destinare; (*to signify*) voler dire

intendance [ɪn'tendəns] *s* intendenza

intendant [ɪn'tendənt] *s* intendente *m*

intended [ɪn'tendɪd] *adj* & *s* (coll) promesso, promessa

intense [ɪn'tens] *adj* intenso

intensi·fy [ɪn'tensɪ,faɪ] *v* (*pret* & *pp* **-fied**) *tr* intensificare, rinforzare; (phot) rinforzare ‖ *intr* intensificarsi, rinforzarsi

intensi·ty [ɪn'tensɪti] *s* (**-ties**) intensità *f*

intensive [ɪn'tensɪv] *adj* intensivo

intent [ɪn'tent] *adj* intento, attento; **intent on** deciso a ‖ *s* (*purpose*) intento, scopo; (*meaning*) significato; **to all intents and purposes** virtualmente, in realtà

intention [ɪn'tenʃən] *s* intenzione

intentional [ɪn'tenʃənəl] *adj* intenzionale, deliberato

intentionally [ɪn'tenʃənəli] *adv* apposta, deliberatamente

in·ter [ɪn'tʌr] *v* (*pret* & *pp* **-terred**; *ger* **-terring**) *tr* interrare, inumare

interact [,ɪntər'ækt] *intr* esercitare un'azione reciproca

interaction [,ɪntər'ækʃən] *s* azione reciproca

inter·breed [,ɪntər'brid] *s* (*pret* & *pp* **-bred** ['bred]) *tr* incrociare ‖ *intr* incrociarsi

intercalate [ɪn'tʌrkə,let] *tr* intercalare

intercede [,ɪntər'sid] *intr* intercedere

intercept [,ɪntər'sept] *tr* intercettare

interceptor [,ɪntər'septər] *s* (*person*) intercettatore *m*; (aer) intercettore *m*

interchange ['ɪntər,tʃendʒ] *s* interscambio; (*on a highway*) svincolo autostradale ‖ [,ɪntər'tʃendʒ] *tr* scambiare ‖ *intr* scambiarsi

intercollegiate [,ɪntərkə'lidʒɪ-ɪt] *adj* interscolastico, fra università

intercom ['ɪntər,kɑm] *s* citofono

intercourse ['ɪntər,kors] *s* comunicazione; (*of products, ideas, etc.*) scambio; (*copulation*) copula, coito; **to have intercourse** accoppiarsi sessualmente

intercross [,ɪntər'krɔs] or [,ɪntər-'krɑs] *tr* incrociare ‖ *intr* incrociarsi

interdict [,ɪntər'dɪkt] *tr* interdetto ‖ [,ɪntər'dɪkt] *tr* interdire; **to interdict s.o. from** + *ger* interdire a qlcu di + *inf*

interest ['ɪntərɪst] or ['ɪntrɪst] *s* interesse *m;* **the interests** i potenti ‖ ['ɪntərɪst], ['ɪntrɪst] or ['ɪntə,rest] *tr* interessare

interested ['ɪntrɪstɪd] or ['ɪntə,restɪd] *adj* interessato

interesting ['ɪntrɪstɪŋ] or ['ɪntə-,restɪŋ] *adj* interessante

interfere [,ɪntər'fɪr] *intr* interferire; (sports) ostacolare l'azione; **to interfere with** interferire in

interference [,ɪntər'fɪrəns] *s* interferenza

interim ['ɪntərɪm] *adj* interino ‖ *s* interim *m;* **in the interim** frattanto

interior [ɪn'tɪrɪ-ər] *adj* & *s* interno

interject [,ɪntər'dʒekt] *tr* interporre ‖ *intr* interporsi

interjection [,ɪntər'dʒekʃən] *s* interposizione; esclamazione; (gram) interiezione

interlard [,ɪntər'lɑrd] *tr* infiorare, lardellare

interline [,ɪntər'laɪn] *tr* scrivere nell'interlinea di; (*a garment*) foderare con ovattina

interlining ['ɪntər,laɪnɪŋ] *s* soppanno

interlink [,ɪntər'lɪŋk] *tr* concatenare

interlock [,ɪntər'lɑk] *tr* connettere ‖ *intr* connettersi

interlope [,ɪntər'lop] *intr* intromettersi; trafficare senza permesso

interloper [,ɪntər'lopər] *s* intruso

interlude ['ɪntər,lud] *s* interludio; (theat) intermezzo

intermarriage [,ɪntər'mærɪdʒ] *s* matrimonio tra consanguinei; matrimonio fra membri di razze diverse

intermediar·y [,ɪntər'midɪ,ɛri] *adj* intermediario ‖ (**-ies**) *s* intermediario

intermediate [,ɪntər'midɪ-ɪt] *adj* intermedio

interment [ɪn'tʌrmənt] *s* inumazione

intermingle [,ɪntər'mɪŋgəl] *tr* mescolare ‖ *intr* mescolarsi

intermission [,ɪntər'mɪʃən] *s* interruzione; (theat) intervallo

intermittent [,ɪntər'mɪtənt] *adj* intermittente

intermix [,ɪntər'mɪks] *tr* mescolare ‖ *intr* mescolarsi

intern ['ɪntʌrn] *s* interno ‖ [ɪn'tʌrn] *tr* internare

internal [ɪn'tʌrnəl] *adj* interno

inter'nal-combus'tion en'gine *s* motore *m* a combustione interna, motore *m* a scoppio

inter'nal rev'enue *s* fisco

international [,ɪntər'næʃənəl] *adj* internazionale

in'terna'tional date' line' *s* linea del cambiamento di data

internationalize [,ɪntər'næʃənə,laɪz] *tr* internazionalizzare

internecine [,ɪntər'nisɪn] *adj* micidiale, sanguinario

internee [,ɪntər'ni] *s* internato

internist [ɪn'tʌrnɪst] *s* internista *mf*

internment [ɪn'tʌrnmənt] *s* internamento

internship ['ɪntʌrn,ʃɪp] *s* tirocinio in un ospedale, internato

interpellate [,ɪntər'pɛlet] or [ɪn'tʌrpɪ-
,let] *tr* interpellare
interplanetary [,ɪntər'plænə ,tɛri] *adj*
interplanetario
interplay ['ɪntər ,ple] *s* azione reciproca
interpolate [ɪn'tʌrpə ,let] *tr* interpolare
interpose [,ɪntər'poz] *tr* frapporre
interpret [ɪn'tʌrprɪt] *tr* interpretare
interpreter [ɪn'tʌrprətər] *s* interprete
mf
interrogate [ɪn'tɛrə ,get] *tr* & *intr* interrogare
interrogation [ɪn ,tɛrə'geʃən] *s* interrogazione
interroga'tion mark' or **point'** *s* punto
interrogativo
interrupt [,ɪntə'rʌpt] *tr* interrompere
interruption [,ɪntə'rʌpʃən] *s* interruzione
interscholastic [,ɪntərskə'læstɪk] *adj*
interscolastico
intersect [,ɪntər'sɛkt] *tr* intersecare ‖
intr intersecarsi
intersection [,ɪntər'sɛkʃən] *s* (*of
streets, roads, etc.*) crocevia *m*;
(geom) intersezione
intersperse [,ɪntər'spʌrs] *tr* cospargere, inframezzare
interstellar [,ɪntər'stɛlər] *adj* interstellare
interstice [ɪn'tʌrstɪs] *s* interstizio
intertwine [,ɪntər'twaɪn] *tr* intrecciare
‖ *intr* intrecciarsi
interval ['ɪntərvəl] *s* intervallo; **at in-
tervals** a intervalli; di tanto in tanto
intervene [,ɪntər'vin] *intr* intervenire;
(*to happen*) succedere
intervening [,ɪntər'vinɪŋ] *adj*—**in the
intervening time** nel frattempo
intervention [,ɪntər'vɛnʃən] *s* interven-
zione
interview ['ɪntər ,vju] *s* intervista ‖ *tr*
intervistare
inter·weave [,ɪntər'wiv] *v* (*pret* **-wove**
['wov] or **-weaved**; *pp* **-wove, -woven**
or **-weaved**) *tr* intessere
intestate [ɪn'tɛstet] or [ɪn'tɛstɪt] *adj*
intestato
intestine [ɪn'tɛstɪn] *s* intestino
inthrall [ɪn'θrɔl] *tr* affascinare, incantare; (*to subjugate*) asservire, soggiogare
inthrone [ɪn'θron] *tr* mettere sul trono,
intronizzare; esaltare, innalzare
intima·cy ['ɪntɪməsi] *s* (**-cies**) intimità
f
intimate ['ɪntɪmɪt] *adj* & *s* intimo ‖
['ɪntɪ ,met] *tr* insinuare
intimation [,ɪntɪ'meʃən] *s* insinuazione
intimidate [ɪn'tɪmɪ ,det] *tr* intimidire
into ['ɪntu] or ['ɪntʊ] *prep* in; verso;
contro
intolerant [ɪn'tɑlərənt] *adj* & *s* intollerante *mf*, insofferente *mf*
intomb [ɪn'tum] *tr* inumare, seppellire
intombment [ɪn'tummənt] *s* sepoltura
intonation [,ɪnto'neʃən] *s* intonazione
intone [ɪn'ton] *tr* intonare ‖ *intr* salmodiare
intoxicant [ɪn'tɑksɪkənt] *s* bevanda al-
coolica

intoxicate [ɪn'tɑksɪ ,ket] *tr* ubriacare;
esilarare; (*to poison*) avvelenare, intossicare
intoxication [ɪn ,tɑksɪ'keʃən] *s* ubriachezza; ebbrezza, allegria; (*poisoning*) avvelenamento, intossicazione
intractable [ɪn'træktəbəl] *adj* intrattabile
intransigent [ɪn'trænsɪdʒənt] *adj* & *s*
intransigente *mf*
intransitive [ɪn'trænsɪtɪv] *adj* intransitivo
intravenous [,ɪntrə'vinəs] *adj* intrave-
noso, endovenoso
intrench [ɪn'trɛntʃ] *tr* & *intr* var of
entrench
intrepid [ɪn'trɛpɪd] *adj* intrepido
intrepidity [,ɪntrɪ'pɪdɪti] *s* intrepi-
dezza
intricate ['ɪntrɪkɪt] *adj* intricato
intrigue [ɪn'trig] or ['ɪntrig] *s* intrigo;
tresca, intrigo amoroso; (theat) intreccio ‖ [ɪn'trig] *tr* incuriosire ‖
intr intrigare; trescare
intrinsic(al) [ɪn'trɪnsɪk(əl)] *adj* intrin-
seco
introduce [,ɪntrə'djus] or [,ɪntrə'dus]
tr introdurre; (*a product*) lanciare; (*a
person*) presentare
introduction [,ɪntrə'dʌkʃən] *s* introdu-
zione; presentazione
introductory [,ɪntrə'dʌktəri] *adj* intro-
duttivo
introit ['ɪntro-ɪt] *s* (eccl) introito
introspective [,ɪntrə'spɛktɪv] *adj* intro-
spettivo
introvert ['ɪntrə ,vʌrt] *adj* & *s* intro-
verso
intrude [ɪn'trud] *intr* intrudersi, intru-
folarsi
intruder [ɪn'trudər] *s* intruso; importuno
intrusion [ɪn'truʒən] *s* intrusione
intrusive [ɪn'trusɪv] *adj* invadente
intrust [ɪn'trʌst] *tr* affidare, confidare
intuition [,ɪntu'ɪʃən] or [,ɪntju'ɪʃən]
s intuizione, intuito
inundate ['ɪnən ,det] *tr* inondare
inundation [,ɪnən'deʃən] *s* inondazione
inure [ɪn'jur] *tr* indurire, assuefare ‖
intr entrare in vigore; **to inure to**
ridondare in favore di
invade [ɪn'ved] *tr* invadere
invader [ɪn'vedər] *s* invasore *m*
invalid [ɪn'vælɪd] *adj* (*non valid*) invalido ‖ ['ɪnvəlɪd] *adj* (*person*) invalido; (*thing*) povero; (*diet*) per malati
‖ ['ɪnvəlɪd] *s* invalido
invalidate [ɪn'vælɪ ,det] *tr* invalidare
invalidity [,ɪnvə'lɪdɪti] *s* invalidità *f*
invaluable [ɪn'væljʊ-əbəl] *adj* inestimabile, inapprezzabile
invariable [ɪn'vɛri-əbəl] *adj* invariabile
invasion [ɪn'veʒən] *s* invasione
invective [ɪn'vɛktɪv] *s* invettiva
inveigh [ɪn've] *intr*—**to inveigh against**
inveire contro
inveigle [ɪn'vegəl] or [ɪn'vigəl] *tr* sedurre, abbindolare
invent [ɪn'vɛnt] *tr* inventare
invention [ɪn'vɛnʃən] *s* invenzione

inventiveness [ɪn'vɛntɪvnɪs] *s* inventiva
inventor [ɪn'vɛntər] *s* inventore *m*
invento·ry ['ɪnvən,tori] *s* (-ries) inventario || *v* (*pret* & *pp* -ried) *tr* inventariare
inverse [ɪn'vʌrs] *adj* & *s* inverso
inversion [ɪn'vʌrʒən] *or* [ɪn'vʌrʃən] *s* inversione
invert ['ɪnvʌrt] *s* invertito || [ɪn'vʌrt] *tr* invertire
invertebrate [ɪn'vʌrtɪ,bret] *or* [ɪn'vʌrtɪbrɪt] *adj* & *s* invertebrato
invest [ɪn'vɛst] *tr* investire || *intr* fare un investimento; fare investimenti
investigate [ɪn'vɛstɪ,get] *tr* investigare
investigation [ɪn,vɛstɪ'geʃən] *s* investigazione
investigator [ɪn'vɛstɪ,getər] *s* investigatore *m*
investment [ɪn'vɛstmənt] *s* (*of money*) investimento; (*e.g., with an office*) investitura; (*siege*) assedio
investor [ɪn'vɛstər] *s* investitore *m*
inveterate [ɪn'vɛtərɪt] *adj* inveterato
invidious [ɪn'vɪdɪ·əs] *adj* irritante, odioso
invigorate [ɪn'vɪgə,ret] *tr* invigorire
invigorating [ɪn'vɪgə,retɪŋ] *adj* ritemprante, ricostituente, rinforzante
invincible [ɪn'vɪnsɪbəl] *adj* invincibile
invisible [ɪn'vɪzɪbəl] *adj* invisibile
invis'ible ink' *s* inchiostro simpatico
invitation [,ɪnvɪ'teʃən] *s* invito
invite [ɪn'vaɪt] *tr* invitare
inviting [ɪn'vaɪtɪŋ] *adj* invitante, attrattivo; (*food*) appetitoso; accogliente
invoice ['ɪnvɔɪs] *s* fattura; **as per invoice** secondo fattura || *tr* fatturare
invoke [ɪn'vok] *tr* invocare; (*a spirit*) evocare
involuntary [ɪn'vɑlən,tɛri] *adj* involontario
involve [ɪn'vɑlv] *tr* involvere, includere; occupare; (*to bring unpleasantness upon*) implicare, coinvolgere; complicare
invulnerable [ɪn'vʌlnərəbəl] *adj* invulnerabile
inward ['ɪnwərd] *adj* interno || *adv* al di dentro, verso l'interno
iodide ['aɪ·ə,daɪd] *s* ioduro
iodine ['aɪ·ə,daɪn] *s* iodio || ['aɪ·ə,daɪn] *s* tintura di iodio
ion ['aɪ·ən] *or* ['aɪ·ɑn] *s* ione *m*
ionize ['aɪ·ə,naɪz] *tr* ionizzare
IOU ['aɪ,o'ju] *s* (letterword) (**I owe you**) cambiale *f*, pagherò *m*
I.Q. ['aɪ'kju] *s* (letterword) (**intelligence quotient**) quoziente *m* d'intelligenza
Iranian [aɪ'renɪ·ən] *adj* & *s* iraniano
Ira·qi ['ɪraki] *adj* iracheno || *s* (-qis) iracheno
irate ['aɪret] *or* [aɪ'ret] *adj* irato
ire [aɪr] *s* ira, collera
Ireland ['aɪrlənd] *s* l'Irlanda *f*
iris ['aɪrɪs] *s* iride *f*
I'rish·man *s* (-men) irlandese *m*
I'rish stew' *s* stufato all'irlandese
I'rish·wom'an *s* (-wom'en) irlandese *f*
irk [ʌrk] *tr* infastidire, annoiare

irksome ['ʌrksəm] *adj* fastidioso
iron ['aɪ·ərn] *adj* ferreo || *s* ferro; (*to press clothes*) ferro da stiro; **irons** ferri *mpl*; **strike while the iron is hot** batti il ferro fin ch'è caldo || *tr* (*clothes*) stirare; **to iron out** (*a difficulty*) (coll) appianare
i'ron·bound' *adj* ferrato; (*unyielding*) ferreo, inflessibile; (*rock-bound*) roccioso, scabroso
ironclad ['aɪ·ərn,klæd] *adj* corazzato, blindato; inflessibile, ferreo
i'ron constitu'tion *s* salute *f* di ferro
i'ron cur'tain *s* cortina di ferro
i'ron horse' *s* locomotiva a vapore
ironic(al) [aɪ'rɑnɪk(əl)] *adj* ironico
ironing ['aɪ·ərnɪŋ] *s* stiratura; roba stirata; roba da stirare
i'roning board' *s* tavolo *or* asse *m* da stiro
i'ron lung' *s* polmone *m* d'acciaio
i'ron·ware' *s* ferrame *m*
i'ron will' *s* volontà *f* di ferro
i'ron·work' *s* lavoro in ferro; **ironworks** *ssg* ferriera
i'ron·work'er *s* ferraio; metalmeccanico, siderurgico
iro·ny ['aɪrəni] *s* (-nies) ironia
irradiate [ɪ'redɪ,et] *tr* irradiare || *intr* irradiare, irradiarsi
irrational [ɪ'ræʃənəl] *adj* irrazionale
irrecoverable [,ɪrɪ'kʌvərəbəl] *adj* irrecuperabile
irredeemable [,ɪrɪ'diməbəl] *adj* irredimibile
irrefutable [,ɪrɪ'fjutəbəl] *adj* irrefutabile
irregular [ɪ'rɛgjələr] *adj* irregolare || *s* (mil) irregolare *m*
irrelevance [ɪ'rɛləvəns] *s* irrilevanza
irrelevant [ɪ'rɛləvənt] *adj* irrilevante
irreligious [,ɪrɪ'lɪdʒəs] *adj* irreligioso
irremediable [,ɪrɪ'midɪ·əbəl] *adj* irrimediabile
irremovable [,ɪrɪ'muvəbəl] *adj* irremovibile, inamovibile
irreplaceable [,ɪrɪ'plesəbəl] *adj* insostituibile
irrepressible [,ɪrɪ'prɛsɪbəl] *adj* irreprimibile, incontenibile
irreproachable [,ɪrɪ'protʃəbəl] *adj* irreprensibile
irresistible [,ɪrɪ'zɪstɪbəl] *adj* irresistibile
irrespective [,ɪrɪ'spɛktɪv] *adj*—**irrespective of** senza riguardo a
irresponsible [,ɪrɪ'spɑnsɪbəl] *adj* irresponsabile
irretrievable [,ɪrɪ'trivəbəl] *adj* irrecuperabile
irreverent [ɪ'rɛvərənt] *adj* irriverente
irrevocable [ɪ'rɛvəkəbəl] *adj* irrevocabile
irrigate ['ɪrɪ,get] *tr* irrigare
irrigation [,ɪrɪ'geʃən] *s* irrigazione
irritant ['ɪrɪtənt] *adj* & *s* irritante *m*
irritate ['ɪrɪ,tet] *tr* irritare
irritation [,ɪrɪ'teʃən] *s* irritazione
irruption [ɪ'rʌpʃən] *s* irruzione
isinglass ['aɪzɪŋ,glæs] *or* ['aɪzɪŋ,glɑs] *s* (*gelatine*) colla di pes·e; mica
Islam ['ɪsləm] *or* [ɪs'lɑm] *s* l'Islam *m*

island ['aɪlənd] *adj* isolano ‖ *s* isola; *(for safety of pedestrians)* salvagente *m*

islander ['aɪləndər] *s* isolano

isle [aɪl] *s* isoletta

isolate ['aɪsə,let] or ['ɪsə,let] *tr* isolare

isolation [,aɪsə'leʃən] or [,ɪsə'leʃən] *s* isolamento

isolationist [,aɪsə'leʃənɪst] or [,ɪsə-'leʃənɪst] *s* isolazionista *mf*

isosceles [aɪ'sɑsə,liz] *adj* isoscele

isotope ['aɪsə,top] *s* isotopo

Israel ['ɪzrɪ-əl] *s* l'Israele *m*

Israe·li [ɪz'reli] *adj* israeliano ‖ *s* (-lis [liz]) israeliano

Israelite ['ɪzrɪ-ə,laɪt] *adj* & *s* israelita *mf*

issuance ['ɪʃu-əns] *s* (of stamps, stocks, bonds, etc.) emissione; (e.g., of clothes) distribuzione; (of a law) emanazione

issue ['ɪʃu] *s* (outlet) uscita; distribuzione; (result) conseguenza; (offspring) prole *f*; (of a magazine) puntata, fascicolo; (of a bond) emissione; (yield) prodotto; (of a law) promulgazione; (pathol) flusso; **at issue** in discussione; **to face the issue** affrontare la situazione; **to force the issue** forzare la soluzione; **to take issue with** non essere d'accordo con, dissentire da ‖ *tr* (e.g., a book) pubblicare; (bonds, orders) emettere; (a communiqué) diramare; (e.g., food) distribuire ‖ *intr* uscire; **to issue from** provenire da

isthmus ['ɪsməs] *s* istmo

it [ɪt] *pron pers* esso, essa; lo, la; **it is**

I sono io; **it is raining** piove; **it is four o'clock** sono le quattro

Italian [ɪ'tæljən] *adj* & *s* italiano

Ital'ian-speak'ing *adj* italofono

italic [ɪ'tælɪc] *adj* (typ) corsivo ‖ *italics* *s* (typ) corsivo ‖ **Italic** *adj* italico

italicize [ɪ'tælɪ,saɪz] *tr* stampare in carattere corsivo; sottolineare

Italy ['ɪtəli] *s* l'Italia *f*

itch [ɪtʃ] *s* prurito; (pathol) rogna; (eagerness) (fig) pizzicore *m* ‖ *tr* prudere, e.g., **his foot itches him** gli prude il piede ‖ *intr* (said of a part of body) prudere; (said of a person) avere il prurito; **to itch to** avere il pizzicore di

itch·y ['ɪtʃi] *adj* (-ier; -iest) che prude; (pathol) rognoso

item ['aɪtəm] *s* articolo; notizia; (on the agenda) questione; (slang) notizia scottante

itemize ['aɪtə,maɪz] *tr* dettagliare, specificare

itinerant [aɪ'tɪnərənt] or [ɪ'tɪnərənt] *adj* itinerante, ambulante ‖ *s* viaggiatore *m*, viandante *m*

itinerar·y [aɪ'tɪnə,reri] or [ɪ'tɪnə,reri] *adj* itinerario ‖ *s* (-ies) itinerario

its [ɪts] *adj* & *pron poss* il suo

itself [ɪt'self] *pron pers* sé stesso; si, e.g., **it opened itself** si è aperto

ivied ['aɪvid] *adj* coperto di edera

ivo·ry ['aɪvəri] *adj* d'avorio ‖ *s* (-ries) avorio; **ivories** (slang) tasti *mpl* del piano; (slang) palle *fpl* da bigliardo; (dice) (slang) dadi *mpl*; (slang) denti *mpl*

i'vory tow'er *s* torre *f* d'avorio

ivy ['aɪvi] *s* (ivies) edera

J

J, j [dʒe] *s* decima lettera dell'alfabeto inglese

jab [dʒæb] *s* puntata; (prick) puntura; (with elbow) gomitata ‖ *v* (pret & pp jabbed; ger jabbing) *tr* pugnalare; pungere; dare una gomitata a ‖ *intr* dare colpi

jabber ['dʒæbər] *s* borbottamento, ciarla ‖ *tr* & *intr* borbottare, ciarlare

jack [dʒæk] *s* (for lifting heavy objects) cricco, martinetto; (jackass) asino; (device for turning a spit) girarrosto; (to remove a boot) cavastivali *m*; (cards) fante *m*; (bowling) pallino; (rad & telv) jack *m*; (elec) presa; (slang) soldi *mpl*; **every man jack** ognuno, tutti *mpl* ‖ **Jack** *s* marinaio; (coll) buonuomo ‖ *tr*—**to jack up** alzare col cricco; (prices) (coll) alzare

jackal ['dʒækəl] *s* sciacallo

jack'ass' *s* asino

jack'daw' *s* cornacchia

jacket ['dʒækɪt] *s* giacca; (of boiled

potatoes) buccia; (of book) sopraccoperta; (metal casing) camicia

jack'ham'mer *s* martello perforatore

jack'-in-the-box' *s* scatola a sorpresa

jack'knife' *s* (-knives) coltello a serramanico; (sports) salto a pesce

jack'-of-all'-trades' *s* factotum *m*

jack-o'-lantern ['dʒækə,læntərn] *s* lanterna a forma di testa umana fatta con una zucca; fuoco fatuo

jack'pot' *s* monte *m* premi; **to hit the jackpot** (slang) vincere un terno al lotto

jack' rab'bit *s* lepre nordamericana di taglia grande

jack'screw' *s* cricco a verme

jack'-tar' *s* (coll) marinaio

jade [dʒed] *adj* di giada, come la giada ‖ *s* (ornamental stone) giada; (worn-out horse) ronzino; (disreputable woman) donnaccia ‖ *tr* logorare

jad'ed ['dʒedɪd] *adj* logoro, stanco; (appetite) stucco

jag [dʒæg] *s* slabbratura; **to have a jag on** (slang) avere la sbornia

jagged ['dʒægɪd] *adj* dentato, slabbrato

jaguar ['dʒægwɑr] *s* giaguaro

jail [dʒel] *s* prigione *f;* **to break jail** evadere dal carcere || *tr* carcerare

jail'bird' *s* galeotto, remo di galera

jail'break' *s* evasione *f* dal carcere

jailer ['dʒelər] *s* carceriere *m*

jalop·y [dʒə'lɑpi] *s* (-ies) carcassa, trespolo, trabiccolo

jam [dʒæm] *s* stretta, compressione; *(in traffic)* imbottigliamento; *(preserve)* marmellata, confettura; *(difficult situation)* (coll) pasticcio || *v* *(pret & pp* **jammed;** *ger* **jamming)** *tr* stipare; *(e.g., one's finger)* schiacciare, schiacciarsi; (rad) disturbare; **to jam on the brakes** bloccare i freni || *intr* schiacciarsi; *(said of firearms)* incepparsi; (mach) grippare

jamb [dʒæm] *s* stipite *m*

jamboree [,dʒæmbə'ri] *s* riunione nazionale di giovani esploratori; (coll) riunione

James [dʒemz] *s* Giacomo

jamming ['dʒæmɪŋ] *s* radiodisturbo

jam-packed ['dʒæm'pækt] *adj* gremito, pieno fino all'orlo

jangle ['dʒæŋgəl] *s* suono stridente; *(quarrel)* baruffa || *tr* fare suoni stridenti con || *intr* stridere; litigare

janitor ['dʒænɪtər] *s* portiere *m*

janitress ['dʒænɪtrɪs] *s* portinaia

January ['dʒænju,eri] *s* gennaio

ja·pan [dʒə'pæn] *s* lacca giapponese; oggetto di lacca || *v* *(pret & pp* **-panned)** *ger* **-panning)** *tr* laccare ||

Japan *s* il Giappone

Japa·nese [,dʒæpə'niz] *adj* giapponese || *s* (-nese) giapponese *mf*

Jap'anese bee'tle *s* scarabeo giapponese

Jap'anese lan'tern *s* lampioncino alla veneziana

Jap'anese persim'mon *s* cachi *m*

jar [dʒɑr] *s* barattolo; *(earthenware container)* orcio, giara; discordanza; *(jolt)* scossa; (fig) brutta sorpresa; **on the jar** *(said of a door)* socchiuso || *v* *(pret & pp* **jarred;** *ger* **jarring)** *tr* scuotere; far stridere || *intr* vibrare; stridere; essere in conflitto; **to jar on** irritare

jardiniere [,dʒɑrdɪ'nɪr] *s (pot)* vaso da fiori; giardiniera

jargon ['dʒɑrgən] *s* gergo

jasmine ['dʒæsmɪn] *or* ['dʒæzmɪn] *s* gelsomino

jasper ['dʒæspər] *s* diaspro

jaundice ['dʒɔndɪs] *or* ['dʒɑndɪs] *s* itterizia; (fig) invidia

jaundiced ['dʒɔndɪst] *or* ['dʒɑndɪst] *adj* itterico; (fig) invidioso

jaunt [dʒɔnt] *or* [dʒɑnt] *s* passeggiata, gita

jaun·ty ['dʒɔnti] *or* ['dʒɑnti] *adj* (-tier; -tiest) disinvolto; elegante

Java·nese [,dʒævə'niz] *adj* giavanese || *s* (-nese) giavanese *m*

javelin ['dʒævlɪn] *or* ['dʒævəlɪn] *s* giavellotto

jaw [dʒɔ] *s* mascella, mandibola; (mach) ganascia; **jaws** fauci *fpl;* gola, stretta || *tr* (slang) rimproverare ||

intr (slang) chiacchierare; (slang) fare la predica

jaw'bone' *s* mascella, mandibola

jaw'break'er *s* (coll) parola difficile da pronunciare; (coll) caramella durissima; (mach) frantoio a mascelle

jay [dʒe] *s* (orn) ghiandaia; (coll) sempliciotto

jay'walk' *intr* attraversare la strada contro la luce rossa del semaforo

jay'walk'er *s* (coll) pedone distratto che attraversa la strada contro la luce rossa del semaforo

jazz [dʒæz] *s* jazz *m;* (slang) spirito || *tr*—**to jazz up** (slang) dar vita a

jazz' band' *s* orchestra jazz

jealous ['dʒeləs] *adj* geloso; *(envious)* invidioso; vigilante

jealous·y ['dʒeləsi] *s* (-ies) gelosia; invidia; vigilanza

jean [dʒin] *s* tela cruda; **jeans** pantaloni *mpl* di tela cruda

jeep [dʒip] *s* gip *f,* jeep *f*

jeer [dʒɪr] *s* beffa || *tr* beffare || *intr* beffarsi; **to jeer at** motteggiare

Jeho'vah's Wit'nesses [dʒɪ'hovəs] *spl* Testimoni *mpl* di Geova

jell [dʒel] *s* gelatina || *intr (to congeal)* gelatinizzarsi; *(to become substantial)* cristallizzarsi

jel·ly ['dʒeli] *s* (-lies) gelatina || *v* *(pret & pp* **-lied)** *tr* gelatinizzare || *intr* gelatinizzarsi

jel'ly-fish' *s* medusa; *(weak person)* (coll) fiaccone *m*

jeopardize ['dʒepər,daɪz] *tr* compromettere, mettere a repentaglio

jeopardy ['dʒepərdi] *s* pericolo, repentaglio

jeremiad [,dʒerɪ'maɪ,æd] *s* geremiade *f*

Jericho ['dʒerɪ,ko] *s* Gerico *f*

jerk [dʒʌrk] *s* strattone *m,* scatto; tic *m;* *(stupid person)* scempio, sciocco; **by jerks** a scatti || *tr* tirare a strattoni; *(meat)* essiccare || *intr* sobbalzare

jerked' beef' *s* fetta di carne di bue essiccata

jerkin ['dʒʌrkɪn] *s* giubbetto

jerk'wa'ter *adj* di scarsa importanza

jerk·y ['dʒʌrki] *adj* (-ier; -iest) sussultante; *(style)* disuguale

Jerome [dʒə'rom] *s* Gerolamo

jersey ['dʒʌrzi] *s* jersey *m,* maglione *m*

Jerusalem [dʒɪ'rusələm] *s* Gerusalemme *f*

jest [dʒest] *s* scherzo, burla; **in jest** per celia || *intr* scherzare

jester ['dʒestər] *s* motteggiatore *m,* burlone *m;* (hist) buffone *m*

Jesuit ['dʒeʒu·ɪt] *or* ['dʒezju·ɪt] *adj & s* gesuita *m*

Jesuitic(al) [,dʒeʒu'ɪtɪk(əl)] *or* [,dʒezju'ɪtɪk(əl)] *adj* gesuitico

Jesus ['dʒizəs] *s* Gesù *m*

Je'sus Christ' *s* Gesù *m* Cristo

jet [dʒet] *adj* di giaietto || *s (of a fountain)* zampillo; *(stream shooting forth from nozzle)* getto; *(mineral; lustrous black)* giaietto; (aer) aereo a getto || *v* *(pret & pp* **jetted;** *ger* **jetting)** *tr* spruzzare || *intr* zampillare; volare in aereo a getto

jet′ age′ *s* era dell'aviogetto

jet′-black′ *adj* nero come il carbone

jet′ bomb′er *s* bombardiere *m* a reazione

jet′ coal′ *s* carbone *m* a lunga fiamma

jet′ en′gine *s* motore *m* a reazione

jet′ fight′er *s* caccia *m* a reazione

jet′lin′er *s* aviogetto da trasporto passeggeri

jet′ plane′ *s* aviogetto

jet′ propul′sion *s* gettopropulsione

jetsam ['dʒɛtsəm] *s* relitto

jet′ stream′ *s* corrente *f* a getto; scappamento di motore a razzo

jettison ['dʒɛtɪsən] *s* (naut) alleggerimento || *tr* (naut) alleggerirsi di; (fig) disfarsi di

jet·ty ['dʒɛti] *s* (**-ties**) gettata; (*wharf*) molo, imbarcadero

Jew [dʒu] *s* giudeo

jewel ['dʒu·əl] *s* pietra preziosa; (*valuable personal ornament*) gioia, gioiello; (*of a watch*) rubino; (*costume jewelry*) gioia finta; (fig) valore *m*, gioiello

jew′el case′ *s* scrigno, portagioie *m*

jeweler or **jeweller** ['dʒu·ələr] *s* gioielliere *m*, orefice *m*

jewelry ['dʒu·əlri] *s* gioielli *mpl*

jew′elry shop′ *s* gioielleria

Jewess ['dʒu·ɪs] *s* giudea

Jewish ['dʒu·ɪʃ] *adj* giudeo

jews′-harp or **jew′s-harp** ['dʒuz ,hɑrp] *s* scacciapensieri *m*

jib [dʒɪb] *s* (*of a crane*) (mach) braccio (di gru); (naut) fiocco, vela Marconi

jib′ boom′ *s* asta di fiocco

jibe [dʒaɪb] *s* burla, beffa || *intr* beffarsi; accordarsi; **to jibe at** beffarsi di

jif·fy ['dʒɪfi] *s*—**in a jiffy** (coll) in men che non si dica

jig [dʒɪg] *s* (*dance*) giga; **the jig is up** (slang) tutto è perduto

jigger ['dʒɪgər] *s* bicchierino di liquore d'un'oncia e mezza; (flea) pulce *f* tropicale; (*gadget*) (coll) aggeggio; (naut) bozzello; (min) crivello

jiggle ['dʒɪgəl] *s* scossa || *tr* scuotere, agitare || *intr* scuotersi

jig′ saw′ *s* sega da traforo

jig′saw puz′zle *s* gioco di pazienza, rompicapo

jilt [dʒɪlt] *tr* piantare

jim·my ['dʒɪmi] *s* (**-mies**) piccolo piede di porco || *v* (*pret & pp* **-mied**) *tr* scassinare; **to jimmy open** scassinare

jingle ['dʒɪŋgəl] *s* sonaglio, bubbolo; (*sound*) rumore *m* di sonagliera; cantilena, rima infantile || *tr* far suonare || *intr* tintinnare

jin·go ['dʒɪŋgo] *adj* sciovinista || *s* (**-goes**) sciovinista *mf*; **by jingo!** perbacco!

jingoism ['dʒɪŋgo ,ɪzəm] *s* sciovinismo

jinx [dʒɪŋks] *s* iettatura; (*person*) iettatore *m* || *tr* portare la iettatura a

jitters ['dʒɪtərz] *spl* (coll) nervosismo; **to have the jitters** (coll) essere nervoso

jittery ['dʒɪtəri] *adj* nervoso

job [dʒab] *s* (*piece of work*) lavoro; (*task*) mansione; (*employment*) posto, impiego; (slang) furto; **by the job** a cottimo; **on the job** (slang) attento, sollecito; **to be out of a job** essere disoccupato; **to lie down on the job** (slang) dormire sul lavoro

job′ anal′ysis *s* valutazione delle mansioni

jobber ['dʒabər] *s* grossista *mf*; (*pieceworker*) lavoratore *m* a cottimo; funzionario disonesto

job′hold′er *s* impiegato; (*in the government*) burocrate *m*

jobless ['jablɪs] *adj* disoccupato

job′ lot′ *s* (com) saldo

job′ print′er *s* piccolo tipografo non specializzato

job′ print′ing *s* piccolo lavoro tipografico

jockey ['dʒaki] *s* fantino || *tr* (*a horse*) montare; manovrare; (*to trick*) abbindolare

jockstrap ['dʒak ,stræp] *s* sospensorio

jocose [dʒo'kos] *adj* giocoso

jocular ['dʒakjələr] *adj* scherzoso

jog [dʒag] *s* spinta; piccolo trotto || *v* (*pret & pp* **jogged;** *ger* **jogging**) *tr* spingere leggermente; (*the memory*) rinfrescare || *intr* barcarellare; **to jog along** continuare col solito tran tran

jog′ trot′ *s* piccolo trotto; (fig) tran tran *m*

John [dʒan] *s* Giovanni *m*

John′ Bull′ *s* il tipico inglese; gli inglesi, il popolo inglese

John′ Han′cock ['hænkak] *s* (coll) la firma

johnnycake ['dʒani ,kek] *s* pane *m* di granturco

John′ny-come′-late′ly *s* (coll) ultimo arrivato

John′ny-jump′-up′ *s* violetta, viola del pensiero

John′ny-on-the-spot′ *s* (coll) persona sempre pronta

John′ the Bap′tist *s* San Giovanni Battista

join [dʒɔɪn] *tr* giungere, congiungere; associarsi a; unire; (*e.g., a party*) farsi membro di; (*the army*) arruolarsi in; (*battle*) ingaggiare; (*to empty into*) sfociare in || *intr* congiungersi, unirsi; (*said, e.g., of two rivers*) confluire

joiner ['dʒɔɪnər] *s* falegname *m*; membro di molte società

joint [dʒɔɪnt] *adj* congiunto || *s* (*in a pipe*) giuntura; (*of bones*) giuntura, articolazione; (*hinge of book*) brachetta; (*in woodwork*) incastro, commettitura; (*of meat*) taglio; (mach) snodo; (*gambling den*) (slang) bisca; (elec) innesto; (slang) bettola; **out of joint** slogato; (fig) fuori luogo; **to throw** (*e.g., one's arm*) **out of joint** slogarsi

joint′ account′ *s* conto in comune

joint′ commit′tee *s* commissione mista

jointly ['dʒɔɪntli] *adv* unitamente

joint′ own′er *s* con′omino

joint′-stock′ com′pany *s* società *f* per azioni a responsabilità illimitata

joist [dʒɔɪst] *s* trave *f*

joke [dʒok] *s* burla, barzelletta; *(trifling matter)* cosa da nulla; *(person laughed at)* zimbello; **to tell a joke** raccontare una barzelletta; **to play a joke on** fare uno scherzo a ‖ *tr*—**to joke one's way into** ottenere dicendo barzellette ‖ *intr* burlare, dire storielle; **joking aside** senza scherzi

joker ['dʒokər] *s* burlone *m*, fumista *m*; *(wise guy)* saputello; *(hidden provision)* clausola ingannatrice; *(cards)* matta

jol·ly ['dʒali] *adj* (**-lier; -liest**) allegro, gaio ‖ *adv* (coll) molto ‖ *v* (*pret & pp* **-lied**) *tr* (coll) prendersi gioco di

jolt [dʒolt] *s* scossa ‖ *tr* scuotere ‖ *intr* sobbalzare

Jonah ['dʒona] *s* Giona; (fig) uccello di mal augurio

jongleur ['dʒaŋglər] *s* giullare *m*

jonquil ['dʒaŋkwɪl] *s* giunchiglia

Jordan ['dʒordən] *s* *(country)* la Giordania; *(river)* Giordano

Jordanian [dʒor'denɪ·ən] *adj & s* giordano

josh [dʒaʃ] *tr & intr* (coll) canzonare

jostle ['dʒasəl] *s* spintone *m* ‖ *tr* spingere ‖ *intr* scontrarsi; farsi strada a gomitate

jot [dʒat] *s*—**I don't care a jot for** non mi importa un fico di ‖ *v* (*pret & pp* **jotted**; *ger* **jotting**) *tr*—**to jot down** notare, gettar giù

jounce [dʒauns] *s* scossa ‖ *tr* scuotere ‖ *intr* sobbalzare

journal ['dʒarnəl] *s* *(newspaper)* giornale *m*; *(magazine)* rivista; *(daily record)* diario; (com) giornale *m*; (mach) perno; (naut) giornale *m* di bordo

journalese [,dʒarnə'liz] *s* linguaggio giornalistico

journalism ['dʒarnə,lɪzəm] *s* giornalismo

journalist ['dʒarnəlɪst] *s* giornalista *mf*

journey ['dʒarni] *s* viaggio ‖ *intr* viaggiare

jour'ney·man *s* (**-men**) operaio specializzato

joust [dʒʌst] *or* [dʒust] *or* [dʒaust] *s* giostra ‖ *intr* giostrare

jovial ['dʒovɪ·əl] *adj* gioviale

jowl [dʒaul] *s* *(cheek)* guancia; *(jawbone)* mascella; *(of cattle)* giogaia; *(of fowl)* bargiglio; *(of fat person)* pappagorgia

joy [dʒɔɪ] *s* gioia, allegria; **to leap with joy** ballare dalla gioia

joyful ['dʒɔɪfəl] *adj* gioioso, festoso; **joyful over** lieto di

joyless ['dʒɔɪlɪs] *adj* senza gioia

joyous ['dʒɔɪ·əs] *adj* gioioso

joy' ride' *s* (coll) gita in auto; (coll) gita all'impazzata in auto

jubilant ['dʒubɪlənt] *adj* esultante

jubilation [,dʒubɪ'le/ən] *s* giubilo

jubilee ['dʒubɪ,li] *s* *(jubilation)* giubilo; (eccl) giubileo

Judaism ['dʒude,ɪzəm] *s* giudaismo

judge [dʒʌdʒ] *s* giudice *m* ‖ *tr & intr* giudicare; **judging by** a giudicare da

judge' ad'vocate *s* avvocato militare; avvocato della marina da guerra

judgeship ['dʒʌdʒ/ɪp] *s* carica di giudice

judgment ['dʒʌdʒmənt] *s* giudizio; *(legal decision)* sentenza

judg'ment day' *s* giorno del giudizio

judg'ment seat' *s* banco dei giudici; tribunale *m*

judicature ['dʒudɪkət/ər] *s* carica di giudice

judicial [dʒu'dɪ/əl] *adj* giudiziario; *(becoming a judge)* giudizioso

judiciar·y [dʒu'dɪ/ɪ,ɛri] *adj* giudiziario ‖ *s* (**-ies**) *(judges collectively)* magistratura; *(judicial branch)* potere giudiziario

judicious [dʒu'dɪ/əs] *adj* giudizioso

jug [dʒʌg] *s* brocca, boccale *m*; *(narrow-necked vessel)* orcio; *(jail)* (slang) prigione

juggle ['dʒʌgəl] *s* gioco di prestigio ‖ *tr* fare il giocoliere con; *(documents, facts)* alterare frodolentamente; **to juggle away** ghermire, trafugare ‖ *intr* fare il giocoliere; fare l'imbroglione

juggler ['dʒʌglər] *s* giocoliere *m*, prestigiatore *m*; impostore *m*

juggling ['dʒʌglɪŋ] *s* giochi *mpl* di prestigio

Jugoslav ['jugo'slav] *adj & s* iugoslavo, jugoslavo

Jugoslavia ['jugo'slavɪ·ə] *s* la Iugoslavia, la Jugoslavia

jugular ['dʒʌgjələr] *or* ['dʒugjələr] *adj & s* giugulare *f*

juice [dʒus] *s* sugo; *(natural fluid of an animal body)* succo; (slang) elettricità *f*; (slang) benzina; **to stew in one's own juice** (coll) annegarsi nel proprio sugo

juic·y ['dʒusi] *adj* (**-ier; -iest**) sugoso, succoso; *(spicy)* piccante

jukebox ['dʒuk,baks] *s* grammofono a gettone, juke-box *m*

julep ['dʒulɪp] *s* bibita di menta col ghiaccio; (pharm) giulebbe *m*

julienne [,dʒulɪ'ɛn] *s* giuliana

July [dʒu'laɪ] *s* luglio

jumble ['dʒʌmbəl] *s* intrico, garbuglio ‖ *tr* ingarbugliare

jum·bo ['dʒʌmbo] *adj* (coll) enorme ‖ *s* (**-bos**) *(person)* (coll) elefante *m*; *(thing)* (coll) oggetto enorme

jump [dʒʌmp] *s* salto; *(in a parachute)* lancio; *(of prices)* sbalzo; *(start)* soprassalto; **on the jump** in moto; **to get or to have the jump on** (coll) avere il vantaggio su ‖ *tr* saltare; *(a horse)* far saltare; *(prices)* alzare; uscire da, e.g., **the train jumped the track** il treno uscì dalle rotaie; *(to attack)* (coll) balzare su; *(checkers)* suffiare ‖ *intr* saltare; *(from surprise)* trasalire; *(said of prices)* salire; *(in a parachute)* lanciarsi; **to jump at** (e.g., *an offer*) afferrare; **to jump on** saltare su; (coll) sgridare, arrabbiarsi con; **to jump over** oltrepassare; *(a page)* saltare; **to jump to a conclusion** arrivare precipitosamente a una conclusione

jumper ['dʒʌmpər] *s* saltatore *m*; camiciotto; **jumpers** tuta da bambini

jump'ing jack' [ˈdʒʌmpɪŋ] s marionetta
jump'ing-off' place' s fine f del mondo;
(fig) trampolino, punto di partenza
jump' seat' s strapuntino
jump' spark' s scintilla elettrica; (of induction coil) (elec) scintilla d'intraferro
jump' wire' s filo elettrico di contatto
jump·y [ˈdʒʌmpi] adj (-ier; -iest) nervoso, eccitato
junction [ˈdʒʌŋkt/ən] s congiunzione;
(of two rivers) confluenza; (carp)
commettitura; (rr) raccordo ferroviario
juncture [ˈdʒʌŋkt/ər] s giuntura; (occasion) congiuntura; (moment) mo-
mento
June [dʒun] s giugno
jungle [ˈdʒʌŋgəl] s giungla
junglegym [ˈdʒʌŋgəl ˌdʒɪm] s (trademark) castello
junior [ˈdʒunjər] adj minore, di minore
età; giovane; (in American university) del penultimo anno; figlio, e.g.,
John H. Smith, Junior Giovanni H.
Smith, figlio || s minore m; socio
secondario; studente m del penultimo
anno
jun'ior col'lege s scuola universitaria
unicamente di primo biennio
jun'ior high' school' s scuola media;
ginnasio
juniper [ˈdʒunɪpər] s ginepro
ju'niper ber'ry s coccola di ginepro
junk [dʒʌŋk] s roba vecchia, ferro
vecchio; (Chinese ship) giunca;
(naut) carne salata || tr (slang) get-
tar via
junk' deal'er s robivecchi m
junket [ˈdʒʌŋkɪt] s budino di giun-
cata; (outing) viaggio di piacere;
viaggio pagato a spese del tesoro ||
intr far un viaggio di piacere; far un
viaggio a spese del tesoro
junk'man' s (-men') ferravecchio; rigattiere m
junk' room' s ripostiglio

junk' shop' s negozio di robivecchi
junk'yard' s cantiere m di ferravecchio
juridical [dʒuˈrɪdɪkəl] adj giuridico
jurisdiction [ˌdʒuːrɪsˈdɪkʃ/ən] s giurisdizione
jurisprudence [ˌdʒuːrɪsˈprudəns] s giu-
risprudenza
jurist [ˈdʒuːrɪst] s giurista mf
juror [ˈdʒuːrər] s giurato
ju·ry [ˈdʒuːri] s (-ries) giuria
ju'ry box' s banco della giuria
ju'ry·man s (-men) giurato
just [dʒʌst] adj giusto || adv giusta-
mente, giusto; appena; proprio; **just
as** come, proprio come; **just beyond**
un po' più in là (di); **just now** poco
fa, or ora; **just out** appena uscito,
appena pubblicato
justice [ˈdʒʌstɪs] s giustizia; (judge)
giudice m; **to bring to justice** arrestare e condannare; **to do justice to**
render giustizia a; apprezzare ba-
stantemente
jus'tice of the peace' s giudice m conciliatore
justifiable [ˈdʒʌstɪ ˌfaɪ·əbəl] adj giustificabile
justi·fy [ˈdʒʌstɪ ˌfaɪ] v (pret & pp
-fied) tr giustificare; (typ) giustificare
justly [ˈdʒʌstli] adj giustamente
jut [dʒʌt] v (pret & pp jutted; ger jutting) intr—to jut out strapiombare,
sporgere
jute [dʒut] s iuta || **Jute** s Juto
juvenile [ˈdʒuvənɪl] or [ˈdʒuvə ˌnaɪl]
adj giovanile; minorile || s giovane
mf; libro per la gioventù; (theat)
amoroso
ju'venile court' s tribunale m per i
minorenni
ju'venile delin'quency s delinquenza
minorile
juvenilia [ˌdʒuvəˈnɪlɪ·ə] spl opere fpl
giovanili; libri mpl per ragazzi
juxtapose [ˌdʒʌkstəˈpoz] tr giustap-
porre

K

K, k [ke] s undicesima lettera dell'alfabeto inglese
kale [kel] s verza; (slang) cocuzza
soldi mpl
kaleidoscope [kəˈlaɪdə ˌskop] s calei-
doscopio
kangaroo [ˌkæŋgəˈru] s canguro
katydid [ˈketidɪd] s grossa cavalletta
verde nordamericana
kedge [kedʒ] s (naut) ancorotto
keel [kil] s chiglia || intr—to keel over
(naut) abbattersi in carena, capovolgersi; (fig) svenire
keelson [ˈkelsən] or [ˈkɪlsən] s (naut)
controchiglia
keen [kin] adj (sharpened) affilato;
(wind; wit) tagliente, mordente;
(eyes) penetrante; (ears; mind) acuto;

fine; (eager) entusiasta; intenso,
vivo; (slang) meraviglioso; **to be
keen on** essere appassionato per
keep [kip] s mantenimento; (of medieval castle) torrione m, maschio; **for
keeps** (coll) seriamente; (coll) per
sempre; **to earn one's keep** guada-
gnarsi la vita || v (pret & pp kept
[kept]) tr mantenere; (watch) fare;
(one's word) mantenere; (to withhold) trattenere; (accounts) tenere;
(servants, guests) avere; (a garden)
coltivare; (a business) esercitare; (a
holiday) festeggiare; (to support) sostentare; (a secret; one's seat) ser-
bare; (to decide to purchase) prendere **to keep away** tener lontano; **to
keep back** trattenere; (a secret) man-

tenere; **to keep down** reprimere; (*expenses*) ridurre al minimo; **to keep s.o. from** + *ger* impedire a qlcu di + *inf*; **to keep in** tener chiuso; **to keep off** tenere a distanza; (*e.g., moisture*) non lasciar penetrare; **to keep s.o. informed about s.th** tenere qlcu al corrente di qlco; **to keep s.o. waiting** fare aspettare qlcu; **to keep up** mantenere, sostenere || *intr* **to keep** + *ger* continuare a + *inf*; **to keep away** tenersi lontano; **to keep from** + *ger* evitare di + *inf*; **to keep informed (about)** tenersi al corrente (di); **to keep in with** (coll) stare nelle buone grazie di; **to keep off** stare lontano (da); (*the grass*) non calpestare; **to keep on** + *ger* seguitare a + *inf*; **to keep out** star fuori, non entrare; **to keep out of** non entrare in; (*danger*) stare lontano da; non immischiarsi in; **to keep quiet** stare tranquillo; **to keep to** (*left or right*) tenere; **to keep to oneself** stare in disparte; **to keep up** continuare; **to keep up with** stare alla pari con; (*e.g., the news*) tenersi al corrente di

keeper ['kipər] *s* (*of a shop*) tenitore *m*; guardiano; (*of a game preserve*) guardacaccia *m*; (*of a magnet*) ancora

keeping ['kipɪŋ] *s* custodia; (*of a holiday*) celebrazione; **in keeping with** in armonia con; **in safe keeping** in luogo sicuro; **out of keeping with** in cattivo accordo con

keep'sake' *s* ricordo

keg [keg] *s* barilotto, botticella

ken [ken] *s* portata; **beyond the ken of** al di là dell'ambito di

kennel ['kenəl] *s* canile *m*

kep·i ['kepi] or ['kepi] *s* (-is) chepì *m*

kept' wo'man [kept] *s* (wom'en) mantenuta

kerchief ['kʌrtʃɪf] *s* fisciù *m*

kernel ['kʌrnəl] *s* (*of a nut*) gheriglio; (*of wheat*) chicco; (fig) nucleo

kerosene ['kerə,sin] or [,kerə'sin] *s* cherosene *m*, petrolio da illuminazione

kerplunk [kər'plʌŋk] *interj* patapum!

ketchup ['ketʃəp] *s* salsa piccante di pomodoro, ketchup *m*

kettle ['ketəl] *s* marmitta, paiolo; (*teakettle*) bricco, teiera

ket'tle·drum' *s* timpano

key [ki] *adj* a chiave; chiave || *s* chiave *f*; (*of piano, typewriter, etc.*) tasto; (*cotter pin*) chiavetta, coppiglia; (*reef*) isolotto; (*tone of voice*) tono; (fig, mus) chiave *f*; (bot) samara; (telg) tasto trasmettitore, manipolatore *m*; **off key** stonato || *tr* aggiustare; inchiavardare; **to key up** eccitare, portare al parossismo

key'board' *s* tastiera

key'hole' *s* toppa, buco della serratura; (*of a clock*) buco della chiave

key'note' *s* (mus) tono; (fig) principio informatore

key'note address' *s* discorso d'apertura

key'punch op'era'tor *s* perforatore *m*

key' ring' *s* portachiavi *m*

key'stone' *s* chiave *f* di volta

key' word' *s* parola chiave

kha·ki ['kɑki] or ['kæki] *adj* cachi || *s* (-kis) cachi *m*

khedive [kə'div] *s* kedivè *m*

kibitz ['kɪbɪts] *intr* (coll) dare consigli non richiesti

kibitzer ['kɪbɪtsər] *s* (*at a card game*) (coll) consigliere *m* importuno; (coll) ficcanaso *mf*

kibosh ['kaɪbɑʃ] or [kɪ'bɑʃ] *s* (coll) sciocchezza; **to put the kibosh on** (coll) impossibilitare

kick [kɪk] *s* calcio, pedata; (*of a gun*) rinculo; (*complaint*) (slang) protesta; (*of liquor*) (slang) forza; **to get a kick out of** (slang) pigliar piacere da || *tr* prendere a calci; (*a ball*) calciare; (*one's feet*) battere; **to kick out** (coll) sbatter fuori a pedate; **to kick up a row** scatenare un putiferio || *intr* calciare; (*said of an animal*) scalciare, trarre; (*said of a firearm*) rinculare; (coll) lamentarsi; **to kick against the pricks** dar calci al vento; **to kick off** (football) dare il calcio d'inizio

kick'back' *s* (coll) contraccolpo; (coll) intrallazzo, bustarella

kick'off' *s* calcio d'inizio

kid [kɪd] *s* capretto; (coll) piccolo; **kids** guanti *mpl* or scarpe *fpl* di capretto || *v* (*pret & pp* kidded; *ger* kidding) *tr* (coll) prendere in giro; **to kid oneself** (coll) farsi illusioni || *intr* (coll) dirlo per scherzo

kidder ['kɪdər] *s* (coll) burlone *m*

kid' gloves' *spl* guanti *mpl* di capretto; **to handle with kid gloves** trattare con la massima cautela

kid'nap' *v* (*pret & pp* -naped or -napped; *ger* -naping or -napping) *tr* rapire, sequestrare

kidnaper or **kidnapper** ['kɪd,næpər] *s* rapitore *m* a scopo d'estorsione

kidnaping or **kidnapping** ['kɪd,næpɪŋ] *s* rapimento a scopo di estorsione

kidney ['kɪdni] *s* rene *m*; (culin) rognone *m*; (*temperament*) carattere *m*; (*kind*) tipo

kid'ney bean' *s* fagiolo

kid'ney stone' *s* calcolo renale

kill [kɪl] *s* uccisione; (*game killed*) cacciagione; (coll) fiumicello; **for the kill** per il colpo finale || *tr* uccidere; eliminare; (*a bill*) bocciare; (fig) opprimere

killer ['kɪlər] *s* uccisore *m*

kill'er whale' *s* orca

killing ['kɪlɪŋ] *adj* mortale; (*exhausting*) opprimente; (coll) molto divertente || *s* uccisione; (*game killed*) cacciagione; (coll) fortuna; **to make a killing** (coll) fare una fortuna da un giorno all'altro

kill'-joy' *s* guastafeste *mf*

kiln [kɪl] or [kɪln] *s* forno, fornace *f*

kil·o ['kilo] or ['kilo] *s* (-os) chilogrammo; chilometro

kilocycle ['kɪlə,saɪkəl] *s* chilociclo

kilogram ['kɪlə,græm] *s* chilogrammo

kilo·hertz ['kɪlə,hɜrts] *s* (-hertz) chilohertz

kilometer ['kɪlə͵mitər] or [kɪ'lɑmɪtər] s chilometro

kilowatt ['kɪlə͵wɑt] s kilowatt m, chilowatt m

kilowatt-hour ['kɪlə͵wɑt'aʊr] s (**kilowatt-hours**) chilowattora m

kilt [kɪlt] s gonnellino

kilter ['kɪltər] s—**to be out of kilter** (coll) essere fuori squadra

kimo·no [kɪ'monə] or [kɪ'mono] s (**-nos**) chimono

kin [kɪn] s (*family relationship*) parentela; (*relatives*) parenti mpl; **of kin** parente, affine; **the next of kin** il parente più prossimo, i parenti più prossimi

kind [kaɪnd] adj gentile; **kind to** buono con || s genere m, specie f; **a kind of** una specie di; **all kinds of** (coll) ogni sorta di; **in kind** in natura; **kind of** (coll) quasi, piuttosto; **of a kind** dello stesso stampo; (*mediocre*) di poco valore

kindergarten ['kɪndər͵gɑrtən] s scuola materna, giardino d'infanzia

kindergartner ['kɪndər͵gɑrtnər] s allievo della scuola d'infanzia; (*teacher*) maestra giardiniera

kind-hearted ['kaɪnd'hɑrtɪd] adj gentile, di buon cuore

kindle ['kɪndəl] tr accendere || intr accendersi

kindling ['kɪndlɪŋ] s accensione; legna minuta

kin'dling wood' s legna minuta per accendere il fuoco

kind·ly ['kaɪndli] adj (**-lier; -liest**) gentile; (*climate*) benigno, favorevole || adv gentilmente; cordialmente; per gentilezza; **to not take kindly to** non accettare di buon grado

kindness ['kaɪndnɪs] s gentilezza; **have the kindness to** abbia la bontà di

kindred ['kɪndrɪd] adj imparentato; affine || s parentela; affinità f

kinescope ['kɪnɪ͵skop] s (trademark) cinescopio

kinetic [kɪ'nɛtɪk] or [kaɪ'nɛtɪk] adj cinetico || **kinetics** s cinetica

kinet'ic en'ergy s forza viva, energia cinetica

king [kɪŋ] s re m; (checkers) dama; (cards, chess) re m

king'bolt' s perno

kingdom ['kɪŋdəm] s regno

king'fish'er s martin pescatore m

king·ly ['kɪŋli] adj (**-lier; -liest**) reale; (*stately*) maestoso || adv regalmente

king'pin' s birillo centrale; (aut) perno dello sterzo; (fig) figura principale

king' post' s (archit) ometto, monaco

king's' e'vil s scrofola

kingship ['kɪŋʃɪp] s regalità f

king'-size' adj extra-grande

king's' ran'som s ricchezza di Creso

kink [kɪŋk] s (*in a rope*) arricciatura; (*in hair*) crespatura; (*soreness in neck*) torcicollo; (*flaw*) ostacolo; (*mental twist*) ghiribizzo || tr attorcigliare || intr attorcigliarsi

kink·y ['kɪŋki] adj (**-ier; -iest**) attorcigliato; (*hair*) crespo

kinsfolk ['kɪnz͵fok] s parentado

kinship ['kɪnʃɪp] s parentela; affinità f

kins'man s (**-men**) parente m

kins'wom'an s (**-wom'en**) parente f

kipper ['kɪpər] s aringa affumicata || tr (*herring or salmon*) affumicare

kiss [kɪs] s bacio; (billiards) rimpallo leggerissimo; (*confection*) meringa || tr baciare; **to kiss away** (*tears*) asciugare con baci || intr baciare, baciarsi; (billiards) rimpallare leggermente

kit [kɪt] s (*case*) cassetta dei ferri; (*tools*) ferri mpl del mestiere; (*set of supplies*) corredo; (*of small tools*) astuccio; (*of a traveler*) borsa da viaggio; (*pail*) secchio; **the whole kit and caboodle** (coll) tutti quanti

kitchen ['kɪtʃən] s cucina

kitchenette [͵kɪtʃə'nɛt] s cucinetta

kitch'en gar'den s orto

kitch'en-maid' s sguattera

kitch'en police' s (mil) corvè f di cucina

kitch'en range' s cucina economica

kitch'en sink' s acquaio

kitch'en-ware' s utensili mpl di cucina

kite [kaɪt] s cervo volante, aquilone m; (orn) nibbio

kith' and kin' [kɪθ] spl amici mpl e parenti mpl

kitten ['kɪtən] s gattino

kittenish ['kɪtənɪʃ] adj giocattolone; civettuolo

kit·ty ['kɪti] s (**-ties**) gattino; (cards) piatto || interj micio!

kleptomaniac [͵klɛptə'menɪ͵æk] s cleptomane mf

knack [næk] s abilità f, destrezza

knapsack ['næp͵sæk] s zaino

knave [nev] s furfante m; (cards) fante m

knaver·y ['nevəri] s (**-ies**) furfanteria

knead [nid] tr maneggiare, intridere; (*a muscle*) massaggiare

knee [ni] s ginocchio; (*of trousers*) ginocchiera; (mach) gomito; **to bring s.o. to his knees** ridurre qlcu all'obbedienza; **to go down on one's knees** (**to**) gettarsi in ginocchio (davanti a)

knee' breech'es [͵brɪtʃɪz] spl calzoni mpl al ginocchio

knee'cap' s rotula, patella; (*protective covering*) ginocchiera

knee'-deep' adj fino al ginocchio

knee'-high' adj fino al ginocchio

knee' jerk' s riflesso patellare

kneel [nil] v (pret & pp **knelt** [nɛlt] or **kneeled**) intr inginocchiarsi

knee'pad' s ginocchiera

knee'pan' s rotula, patella

knell [nɛl] s rintocco funebre, campana a morto; **to toll the knell of** annunciare la morte di || intr suonare a morte

knickers ['nɪkərz] spl knickerbockers mpl, calzoni mpl alla zuava

knickknack ['nɪk͵næk] s soprammobile m; gingillo, ninnolo

knife [naɪf] s (**knives** [naɪvz]) coltello; (*of a paper cutter*) mannaia; (*of a milling machine*) fresa; **to go under the knife** essere sulla tavola operatoria || tr accoltellare; mettere il coltello nella schiena di

knife' sharp'ener s affilatoio

knife' switch' s (elec) coltella
knight [naɪt] s cavaliere m; (chess) cavallo || tr armare cavaliere
knight-errant ['naɪt'ɛrənt] s (knights-errant) cavaliere m errante
knighthood ['naɪt‧hʊd] s cavalleria
knightly ['naɪtli] adj cavalleresco
knit [nɪt] v (pret & pp knitted or knit; ger knitting) tr lavorare a maglia; (to join) unire; (e.g., the brow) corrugare || intr lavorare a maglia; fare la calza; unirsi; (said of a bone) saldarsi
knitting ['nɪtɪŋ] s maglia, lavoro a maglia
knit'ting machine' s macchina per maglieria
knit'ting mill' s maglieria
knit'ting nee'dle s ferro da calza
knit'wear' s maglieria
knit'wear store' s maglieria
knob [nab] s (lump) bozza, protuberanza; (of a door) maniglia; (on furniture) pomolo; (hill) collinetta rotondeggiante; (rad, telv) manopola, pulsante m
knock [nak] s colpo; (on a door) tocco; (slang) attacco, critica || tr battere; (repeatedly) sbatacchiare; (slang) attaccare, criticare; to knock down (with a punch) stendere a terra; (a wall) diroccare; (to the highest bidder) aggiudicare; (e.g., a machine) smontare; to knock off (work) (slang) sospendere; (slang) terminare; (slang) uccidere; to knock out mettere fuori combattimento || intr battere; (aut) battere in testa; (slang) criticare; to knock about (slang) gironzolare; to knock against urtare contro; to knock at (e.g., a door) battere a, bussare a; to knock off (slang) cessare di lavorare
knock'down' adj (blow) knock down, che atterra; (dismountable) smontabile || s (blow) colpo che atterra; (discount) sconto
knocker ['nakər] s (on a door) battaglio, bussatoio; (coll) criticone m
knock-kneed ['nak‚nid] adj con le gambe a X [iks]
knock'out' s pugno che mette fuori combattimento; fuori combattimento; (coll) pezzo di giovane
knock'out drops' spl (slang) narcotico
knoll [nol] s poggio, rialzo
knot [nat] s nodo; (worn as an ornament) fiocco; (in wood) nocchio; gruppo; protuberanza; (tie) nodo;

(naut) nodo; to tie the knot (coll) sposarsi || v (pret & pp knotted; ger knotting) tr annodare; (the brow) corrugare || intr annodarsi
knot'hole' s buco lasciato da un nodo (nel legno)
knot‧ty ['nati] adj (-tier; -tiest) nodoso; (fig) spinoso
know [no] s—to be in the know (coll) essere al corrente || v (pret knew [nju] or [nu]; pp known) tr & intr (by reasoning or learning) sapere; (by the senses or by perception; through acquaintance or recognition) conoscere; as far as I know per quanto io ne sappia; to know about essere al corrente di; to know best essere il miglior giudice; to know how to + inf sapere + inf; to know it all (coll) sapere tutto; to know what's what (coll) saperla lunga; you ought to know better dovresti vergognarti
knowable ['no‧əbəl] adj conoscibile
know'-how' s sapere m, abilità f
knowingly ['no‧ɪŋli] adv con conoscenza di causa; (on purpose) apposta
know'-it-all' adj & s (coll) saputello
knowledge ['nalɪdʒ] s (faculty) scibile m, sapere m, sapienza; (awareness, acquaintance, familiarity) conoscenza; to have a thorough knowledge of conoscere a fondo; to my knowledge per quanto io ne sappia; with full knowledge con conoscenza di causa; without my knowledge a mia insaputa
knowledgeable ['nalɪdʒəbəl] adj intelligente, bene informato
knuckle ['nʌkəl] s nocca; foro del cardine, cardine m; knuckles pugno di ferro || intr—to knuckle down (coll) lavorare di impegno; to knuckle under (coll) darsi per vinto
knurl [nʌrl] s granitura || tr godranare, zigrinare
Koran [ko'ran] or [ko'ræn] s Corano
Korea [ko'ri‧ə] s la Corea
Korean [ko'ri‧ən] adj & s coreano
kosher ['koʃər] adj kasher, casher, puro secondo la legge giudaica; (coll) autentico
kowtow ['kau'tau] or ['ko'tau] intr inchinarsi servilmente
Kremlin ['krɛmlɪn] s Cremlino
Kremlinology [‚krɛmlɪ'nalədʒi] s Cremlinologia
kudos ['kjudas] or ['kudas] s (coll) gloria, fama, approvazione

L

L, l [ɛl] s dodicesima lettera dell'alfabeto inglese
la‧bel ['lebəl] s marca, etichetta; (descriptive word) qualifica || v (pret & pp -beled or -belled; ger -beling or -belling) tr etichettare; qualificare
labial ['lebɪ‧əl] adj & s labiale f

labor ['lebər] adj operaio || s lavoro; (toil) fatica; (childbirth) parto; (body of wage earners) manodopera; (class as contrasted with management) prestatori mpl d'opera, lavoro; labors fatiche fpl; to be in labor avere le doglie || intr lavorare; (to exert one-

self) travagliare; (*said of a ship*) rollare e beccheggiare; **to labor for** lottare per; **to labor under** soffrire di

labora·to·ry ['læbərə‚tori] *s* (**-ries**) laboratorio

la'bor dispute' *s* vertenza sindacale

labored ['lebərd] *adj* elaborato, artificiale; penoso, difficile

laborer ['lebərər] *s* lavoratore *m*; (*unskilled worker*) bracciante *m*, manovale *m*, uomo di fatica

laborious [lə'borɪ‚əs] *adj* laborioso

la'bor un'ion *s* sindacato

Labourite ['lebə‚raɪt] *s* laburista *mf*

labyrinth ['læbɪrɪnθ] *s* labirinto

lace [les] *s* (*cord or string*) stringa; (*netlike ornament*) trina, merletto; (*braid*) gallone *m* ‖ *tr* stringare; merlettare; (*coll*) fustigare

lace'work' *s* trina, merletto, pizzo

lachrymose ['lækrɪ‚mos] *adj* lacrimoso

lacing ['lesɪŋ] *s* stringa, cordone *m*; gallone *m*; (*coll*) battuta, frustata

lack [læk] *s* mancanza, scarsezza, difetto ‖ *tr* mancare di, scarseggiare di ‖ *intr* mancare, scarseggiare, difettare

lackadaisical [‚lækə'dezɪkəl] *adj* letargico, indifferente

lackey ['læki] *s* lacchè *m*

lacking ['lækɪŋ] *prep* privo di

lack'lus'ter *adj* smorto, spento

laconic [lə'kɑnɪk] *adj* laconico

lacquer ['lækər] *s* lacca ‖ *tr* laccare

lac'quer spray' *s* lacca spray

lac'quer ware' *s* oggetti *mpl* laccati

lacu·na [le'kjunə] *s* (**-nas** or **-nae** [ni]) lacuna

lac·y ['lesi] *adj* (**-ier; -iest**) simile al merletto

lad [læd] *s* ragazzo, fanciullo

ladder ['lædər] *s* scala; (*stepladder hinged on top*) scaleo; (*stepping stone*) (fig) scalino

lad'der truck' *s* autocarro di pompieri munito di scale

la'dies' man' *s* beato fra le donne

la'dies' room' *s* gabinetto per signore

ladle ['ledəl] *s* ramaiolo, mestolo; (*of tinsmith*) cucchiaio ‖ *tr* scodellare

la·dy ['ledi] *s* (**-dies**) signora, dama

la'dy·bug' *s* coccinella

la'dy·fin'ger *s* savoiardo, lingua di gatto

la'dy-in-wait'ing *s* (**ladies-in-waiting**) dama di corte

la'dy·kil'ler *s* rubacuori *m*

la'dy·like' *adj* signorile; **to be ladylike** comportarsi come una signora

la'dy·love' *s* amata

la'dy of the house' *s* padrona di casa

ladyship ['ledi‚ʃɪp] *s* signoria

la'dy's maid' *s* cameriera personale della signora

lag [læg] *s* ritardo ‖ *v* (*pret & pp* **lagged;** *ger* **lagging**) *intr* ritardare; **to lag behind** rimanere indietro

la'ger beer' ['lɑgər] *s* birra invecchiata

laggard ['lægərd] *s* tardo, pigro

lagoon [lə'gun] *s* laguna

laid' pa'per [led] *s* carta vergata

laid' up' *adj* messo da parte; (naut) disarmato; (coll) costretto a letto

lair [ler] *s* tana, covo

laity ['le·ɪti] *s* laicato

lake [lek] *adj* lacustre ‖ *s* lago

lamb [læm] *s* agnello

lambaste [læm'best] *tr* (*to thrash*) sferzare; (*to reprimand*) riprovare

lamb' chop' *s* cotoletta d'agnello

lambkin ['læmkɪn] *s* agnellino; (fig) innocente *mf*

lamb'skin' *s* (*leather*) pelle *f* d'agnello; (*skin with its wool*) agnello

lame [lem] *adj* zoppo; difettoso; (*disabled*) invalido; (*excuse*) debole ‖ *tr* azzoppare

lament [lə'ment] *s* lamento; lamento funebre ‖ *tr* lamentare ‖ *intr* lamentarsi

lamentable ['læməntəbəl] or [lə'mentəbəl] *adj* lamentevole

lamentation [‚læmən'teʃən] *s* lamentazione

laminate ['læmɪ‚net] *tr* laminare

lamp [læmp] *s* lampada

lamp'black' *s* nerofumo

lamp' chim'ney *s* tubo di vetro di lampada a petrolio

lamp'light' *s* luce *f* di lampada

lamp'light'er *s* lampionaio

lampoon [læm'pun] *s* satira ‖ *tr* satireggiare

lamp'post' *s* colonna del lampione

lamp'shade' *s* paralume *m*, ventola

lamp'wick' *s* lucignolo

lance [læns] or [lɑns] *s* lancia; (surg) lancetta ‖ *tr* (*with an oxygen lance*) tagliare col cannello ossidrico; (surg) sbrigliare, incidere col bisturi

lance' rest' *s* resta

lancet ['lænsɪt] or ['lɑnsɪt] *s* (surg) lancetta

land [lænd] *adj* terrestre; (*wind*) di terra ‖ *s* terra; **on land, on sea, and in the air** per mare, per terra e nel cielo; **to make land** toccare terra; **to see how the land lies** tastare terreno ‖ *tr* sbarcare; (aer) fare atterrare; (coll) pigliare ‖ *intr* sbarcare; (*to come to rest*) andare a finire; (naut) toccar terra; (aer) atterrare; **to land on one's feet** cadere in piedi; **to land on one's head** andare a gambe all'aria; **to land on the moon** allunare; **to land on the water** ammarare

land' breeze' *s* vento di terra

landed ['lændɪd] *adj* (*owning land*) terriero; (*real estate*) immobile

land'fall' *s* (*sighting land*) avvistamento; terra avvistata; (*landslide*) frana

land' grant' *s* terreno ricevuto in dono dallo stato

land'hold'er *s* proprietario terriero

landing ['lændɪŋ] *s* (*of passengers*) sbarco; (*place where passengers and goods are landed*) imbarcadero; (*of stairway*) pianerottolo; (aer, naut) atterraggio

land'ing bea'con *s* radiofaro d'atterraggio

land'ing card' *s* cartoncino di sbarco

land'ing craft' *s* imbarcazione da sbarco

land'ing field' *s* campo d'atterraggio

land'ing flap' *s* (aer) ipososteutatore *m*
land'ing gear' *s* (aer) carrello d'atterraggio
land'ing strip' *s* (aer) pista d'atterraggio
land'la·dy *s* (-dies) (*of an apartment*) padrona di casa; (*of a lodging house*) affittacamere *f*; (*of an inn*) ostessa
landlocked ['lænd͵lɑkt] *adj* circondato da terra
land'lord' *s* (*of an apartment*) padrone *m* di casa; (*of a lodging house*) affittacamere *m*; (*of an inn*) oste *m*
land-lubber ['lænd͵lʌbər] *s* marinaio d'acqua dolce
land'mark' *s* (*boundary stone*) pietra di confine; (*distinguishing landscape feature*) punto di riferimento; (fig) pietra miliare
land' of'fice *s* ufficio del catasto
land'-office busi'ness *s* (coll) sacco d'affari
land'own'er *s* proprietario terriero
landscape ['lænd͵skep] *s* paesaggio || *tr* abbellire
land'scape gar'dener *s* giardiniere *m* ornamentale
land'scape paint'er *s* paesista *mf*
landscapist ['lænd͵skepɪst] *s* paesista *mf*
land'slide' *s* frana; (fig) vittoria strepitosa
landward ['lændwərd] *adv* verso terra, verso la costa
land' wind' *s* vento di terra
lane [len] *s* (*narrow street*) vicolo, viuzza; (*of a highway*) corsia; (naut) rotta; (aer) corridoio
langsyne ['læŋ'saɪn] *s* (Scotch) tempo passato || *adv* (Scotch) molto tempo fa
language ['læŋgwɪdʒ] *s* lingua; (*style of language*) linguaggio; (*of a special group of people*) gergo
lan'guage lab'oratory *s* laboratorio linguistico
languid ['læŋgwɪd] *adj* languido
languish ['læŋgwɪʃ] *intr* languire; affettare languore
languor ['læŋgər] *s* languore *m*
languorous ['læŋgərəs] *adj* languido; (*causing languor*) snervante
lank [læŋk] *adj* scarnito, sparuto
lank·y ['læŋki] *adj* (-ier; -iest) scarnito, sparuto
lantern ['læntərn] *s* lanterna
lan'tern slide' *s* diapositiva
lanyard ['lænjərd] *s* (naut) drizza; (mil) aghetto, cordellina
lap [læp] *s* (*of human body or clothing*) grembo; (*with the tongue*) leccata; (*of the waves*) sciacquio; (sports) giro, tappa; **in the lap of** in mezzo a, e.g., **in the lap of luxury** in mezzo alle delicatezze || *v* (*pret & pp* **lapped**; *ger* **lapping**) *tr* lappare; (*said, e.g., of waves*) lambire; (*to fold*) piegare; (*to overlap*) sovrapporre; **to lap up** lappare; (coll) accettare con entusiasmo || *intr* sovrapporsi; **to lap against** (*said of the waves*) lambire; **to lap over** traboccare

lap'board' *s* tavolino da lavoro da tenersi sulle ginocchia
lap' dissolve' *s* (mov) dissolvenza incrociata
lap' dog' *s* cagnolino da salotto
lapel [lə'pɛl] *s* risvolto
Lap'land' *s* la Lapponia
Laplander ['læp͵lændər] *s* lappone *mf*
Lapp [læp] *s* lappone *mf*; (*language*) lappone *m*
lap' robe' *s* coperta da viaggio
lapse [læps] *s* (*interval*) spazio di tempo; (*fall, decline*) caduta; (*of memory*) perdita; errore *m*; (ins) risoluzione; (law) decadenza || *intr* cadere, ricadere; cadere in disuso; (*said of time*) passare; (ins) risolversi; (law) decadere
lap'wing' *s* pavoncella
larce·ny ['lɑrsəni] *s* (-nies) furto
larch [lɑrtʃ] *s* larice *m*
lard [lɑrd] *s* strutto || *tr* lardellare
larder ['lɑrdər] *s* dispensa
large [lɑrdʒ] *adj* grande, grosso || *s—* **at large** in libertà
large' intes'tine *s* intestino crasso
largely ['lɑrdʒli] *adv* in gran parte
large'-scale' *adj* su larga scala
lariat ['læri·ət] *s* lazo, laccio
lark [lɑrk] *s* allodola; (coll) burla; **to go on a lark** (coll) far festa
lark'spur' *s* (*rocket larkspur*) sprone *m* di cavaliere; (*field larkspur*) consolida reale
lar·va ['lɑrvə] *s* (-vae [vi]) larva
laryngitis [͵lærɪn'dʒaɪtɪs] *s* laringite *f*
laryngoscope [lə'rɪŋgə͵skop] *s* laringoscopio
larynx ['lærɪŋks] *s* (**larynxes** or **larynges** [lə'rɪndʒiz]) laringe *f*
lascivious [lə'sɪvɪ·əs] *adj* lascivo
lasciviousness [lə'sɪvɪ·əsnɪs] *s* lascivia
laser ['lesər] *s* (acronym) (*light amplification by stimulated emission of radiation*) laser *m*
lash [læʃ] *s* (*cord on end of whip*) sverzino; (*blow with whip; scolding*) staffilata; (*of animal's tail*) colpo; (*eyelash*) ciglio; (fig) assalto || *tr* (*to whip*) frustare; (*to bind*) legare; (*to shake*) agitare; (*to attack with words*) staffilare || *intr* lanciarsi; **to lash out** at attaccare violentemente
lashing ['læʃɪŋ] *s* legatura; (*severe scolding*) staffilata; (*fastening with a rope*) (naut) rizza
lass [læs] *s* ragazza, giovane *f*; innamorata
las·so ['læso] or [læ'su] *s* (-sos or -soes) lasso, lazo || *tr* pigliare col lasso
last [læst] or [lɑst] *adj* ultimo, passato; (*most recent*) scorso; **before last** ieraltro, e.g., **the night before last** ieraltro notte; **every last one** tutti senza eccezione; **last but one** penultimo || *s* ultima persona; ultima cosa; fine *f*; (*for holding shoes*) forma; **at last** alla fine; **at long last!** finalmente!; **stick to your last!** fa' il mestiere tuo!; **the last of the month** alla fine del mese; **to breathe one's last** dare l'ultimo sospiro; **to see the last of s.o.** vedere qlcu per l'ultima

volta; **to the last** fino alla fine || *adv* ultimo, per ultimo, alla fine || *intr* durare, continuare

lasting ['læstɪŋ] or ['lɑstɪŋ] *adj* duraturo, durevole

lastly ['læstli] or ['lɑstli] *adv* finalmente, in conclusione

last'-min'ute news' *s* notizie *fpl* dell'ultima ora

last' name' *s* cognome *m*

last' night' *adv* ieri sera; la notte scorsa

last' quar'ter *s* ultimo quarto

last' sleep' *s* ultimo sonno

last' straw' *s* ultima, colmo

Last' Sup'per *s* Ultima Cena

last will' and tes'tament *s* ultime volontà *fpl*

last' word' *s* ultima parola; (*latest style*) ultima novità, ultimo grido

latch [lætʃ] *s* saliscendi *m*; (*wooden*) nottola || *tr* chiudere col saliscendi

latch'key' *s* chiave *f* per saliscendi

latch'string' *s* **the latchstring is out** faccia come fosse a casa Sua

late [let] *adj* (*happening after the usual time*) tardo; (*person*) in ritardo; (*hour of the night*) avanzato; (*news*) dell'ultima ora, recente; (*incumbent of an office*) predecessore, ex, passato; (*coming toward the end of a period*) tardivo; (*deceased*) defunto, fu; **in the late 30's, 40's,** etc. verso la fine del decennio che va dal 1930, 1940, etc. al 1940, 1950, etc.; **of late** recentemente; **to be late in** + *ger* essere in ritardo a + *inf*; **to grow late** farsi tardi; **to keep late hours** fare le ore piccole || *adv* tardi; in ritardo; **late in** (*the week, the month, etc.*) alla fine di; **late in life** a un'età avanzata

latecomer ['let ,kʌmər] *s* ritardatario

lateen' sail' [læ'tin] *s* vela latina

lately ['letli] *adv* recentemente

latent ['letənt] *adj* latente

later ['letər] *adj comp* più tardi; (*event*) susseguente; **later than** posteriore a || *adv comp* più tardi; **later on** più tardi; **see you later** (coll) arrivederci, a ben presto

lateral ['lætərəl] *adj* laterale

lath [læθ] or [lɑθ] *s* listello, striscia di legno || *tr* mettere listelli su

lathe [leð] *s* tornio

lather ['læðər] *s* schiuma di sapone; schiuma || *tr* insaponare; (coll) bastonare || *intr* schiumare

lathery ['læðəri] *adj* schiumoso

lathing ['læθɪŋ] or ['lɑθɪŋ] *s* costruzione con listelli

Latin ['lætɪn] or ['lætən] *adj & s* latino

Lat'in Amer'ica *s* l'America latina

Lat'in-Amer'ican *adj* dell'America latina

Lat'in Amer'ican *s* abitante *mf* dell'America latina

latitude ['lætɪ ,tjud] or ['lætɪ ,tud] *s* latitudine *f*

latrine [lə'trin] *s* latrina militare

latter ['lætər] *adj* (*more recent*) posteriore; (*of two*) secondo; **the latter** questo; **the latter part of** la fine di

lattice ['lætɪs] *s* graticcio || *tr* munire di graticcio, graticciare

lat'tice gird'er *s* trave *f* a traliccio

lat'tice-work' *s* graticcio, traliccio

Latvia ['lætvɪ·ə] *s* la Lettonia

laud [lɔd] *tr* lodare

laudable ['lɔdəbəl] *adj* lodevole

laudanum ['lɔdənəm] or ['lɔdnəm] *s* laudano

laudatory ['lɔdə ,tori] *adj* lodativo

laugh [læf] or [lɑf] *s* riso || *tr*—**to laugh away** dissipare ridendo; **to laugh off** prendere sotto gamba, non dare importanza a || *intr* ridere, ridersi; **to laugh at** ridersi di; **to laugh up one's sleeve** ridere sotto i baffi

laughable ['læfəbəl] or ['lɑfəbəl] *adj* risibile

laughing ['læfɪŋ] or ['lɑfɪŋ] *adj* che ride; **to be no laughing matter** non esserci niente da ridere || *s* riso

laugh'ing gas' *s* gas *m* esilarante

laugh'ing-stock' *s* ludibrio, zimbello

laughter ['læftər] or ['lɑftər] *s* riso

launch [lɔntʃ] or [lɑntʃ] *s* (*of a ship*) varo; (*of a rocket*) lancio; (naut) lancia, scialuppa || *tr* (*to throw; to send forth*) lanciare; (naut) varare || *intr* lanciarsi

launching ['lɔntʃɪŋ] or ['lɑntʃɪŋ] *s* lancio; (*of a ship*) varo

launch'ing pad' *s* piattaforma di lancio

launder ['lɔndər] or ['lɑndər] *tr* lavare e stirare || *intr* riuscire dopo il lavaggio

launderer ['lɔndərər] or ['lɑndərər] *s* lavandaio stiratore *m*

laundress ['lɔndrɪs] or ['lɑndrɪs] *s* lavandaia stiratrice *f*

laundromat ['lɔndrə ,mæt] or ['lɑndrə- ,mæt] *s* (trademark) lavanderia a gettone

laun·dry ['lɔndri] or ['lɑndri] *s* (**-dries**) lavanderia; (*clothing*) bucato

laun'dry·man' *s* (**-men'**) lavandaio

laun'dry·wom'an *s* (**-wom'en**) lavandaia

laureate ['lɔrɪ·ɪt] *adj* laureato || *s* laureato; poeta laureato

lau·rel ['lɔrəl] or ['lɑrəl] *s* lauro, alloro; **laurels** (fig) alloro; **to rest or sleep on one's laurels** dormire sugli allori || *v* (*pret & pp* **-reled** or **-relled**; *ger* **-reling** or **-relling**) *tr* laureare

lava ['lɑvə] or ['lævə] *s* lava

lavato·ry ['lævə ,tori] *s* (**-ries**) (*room*) gabinetto da bagno; (*bowl*) lavabo; (*toilet*) gabinetto di decenza, cesso

lavender ['lævəndər] *s* lavanda

lavish ['lævɪʃ] *adj* prodigo || *tr* prodigare, profondere

law [lɔ] *s* (*of man, of nature, of science*) legge *f*; (*study, profession of law*) diritto; **to enter the law** farsi avvocato; **to go to law** ricorrere alla legge; **to lay down the law** dettar legge; **to maintain law and order** mantenere la pace interna; **to practice law** fare l'avvocato

law-abiding ['lɔ·ə ,bardɪŋ] *adj* osservante della legge

law'break'er *s* violatore *m* della legge

law' court' s tribunale m di giustizia
lawful ['lɔfəl] adj legale, legittimo
lawless ['lɔlɪs] adj illegale; (unbridled) sfrenato
law'mak'er s legislatore m
lawn [lɔn] s tappeto erboso; (fabric) batista
lawn' mow'er s tosatrice f
law' of'fice s ufficio d'avvocato
law' of na'tions s diritto delle genti
law' of the jun'gle s legge f della giungia
law' stu'dent s studente m di legge
law'suit' s causa, lite f, processo
lawyer ['lɔjər] s avvo ato, legale m
lax [læks] adj (not in morals) lasso, rilassato; (rope) lento; (negligent) trascurato; vago, indeterminato
laxative ['læksətɪv] adj purgativo || s purga, purgante m
lay [le] adj (not belonging to the clergy) laico, (not having special training) non dotto, profano || s configurazione, disposizione || v (pret & pp laid [led]) tr mettere, collocare; (snares) tendere; (one's eyes; a stone) porre; (blame) dare, gettare; (a bet) fare; (for consideration) presentare; (the table) imbandire; (said of a hen) deporre; (plans) impostare; (to locate) disporre; **to be laid in** (said of a scene) aver luogo in; **to lay aside** mettere da parte; **to lay down** dichiarare; (one's life) dare; (one's arms) deporre; **to lay low** abbattere, uccidere; **to lay off** (workers) licenziare; (to measure) marcare; (slang) lasciare in pace; **to lay open** rivelare; (to a danger) esporre; **to lay out** estendere; preparare, disporre; (a corpse) comporre; (money) (coll) sborsare; **to lay over** posporre; **to lay up** mettere da parte; obbligare a letto; (naut) disarmare || intr (said of a hen) fare le uova; **to lay about** dar botte da orbi; **to lay for** (slang) attendere al varco; **to lay off** (coll) cessare di lavorare; **to lay over** trattenersi, fermarsi; **to lay to** (naut) navigare alla cappa
lay' broth'er s frate m secolare; converso
lay' day' s (com) stallia
layer ['le·ər] s (of paint) mano f; (of bricks) testa; (e.g., of rocks) strato, falda; (anat) pannicolo; (hort) propaggine f || tr (hort) propagginare
lay'er cake' s dolce m a strati
layette [le'et] s corredino
lay' fig'ure s manichino
laying ['le·ɪŋ] s posa; (of eggs) deporre m; (of a wire) tendere m
lay'man s (-men) (member of the laity) laico, secolare m; (not a member of a special profession) laico, profano
lay'off' s (dismissal of workers) licenziamento; (period of unemployment) disoccupazione
lay' of the land' s andamento generale
lay'out' s piano; (sketch) tracciato; (of tools) armamentario; (coll) residenza; (typ) menabò m; (coll) banchetto, festino

lay'o'ver s fermata in un viaggio
lay' sis'ter s suora al secolo; conversa
la'iness ['lezɪnɪs] s pigrizia
la·zy ['lezi] adj (-zier; -ziest) pigro
la'zy-bones' s (coll) poltrone m
lea [li] s (fallow land) maggese m; (meadow) prato
lead [led] adj plumbeo || s piombo; (of lead pencil) mina; (for sounding depth) (naut) scandaglio; (typ) interlinea || [led] v (pret & pp leaded; ger leading) tr impiombare; (typ) interlineare || [lid] s (foremost place) primato; (guidance) guida, direzione; (leash) guinzaglio; (journ) testata; (cards) mano f, prima mano; (elec) conduttore m; (mach) passo; (min) filone m; (rad, telv) filo d'entrata; (theat) ruolo principale; (theat) primo attore; (theat) prima attrice; **to take the lead** prendere il comando || [lid] v (pret & pp led [led]) tr condurre, portare; (to command) comandare, essere alla testa di; (an orchestra) dirigere; (a good or bad life) fare; (s.o. into vice) trascinare; (cards) cominciare a giocare; (elec, mach) anticipare; **to lead astray** forviare || intr essere in testa, guidare; prendere l'offensiva; (said of a road) condurre; (cards) cominciare a giocare; **to lead to** risultare in; **to lead up to** andare a condurre a
leaden ['ledən] adj (of lead; like lead) plumbeo; (sluggish) tardo; (with sleep) carico; triste
leader ['lidər] s capo, comandante m; (ringleader) capobanda m; (of an orchestra) direttore m; (among animals) guidaiolo; (in a dance) ballerino guidaiolo; (sports) capintesta m; (journ) articolo di fondo
lead'er dog' s cane m guida di ciechi
leadership ['lidər ʃɪp] s comando, direzione; doti fpl di comando
leading ['lidɪŋ] adj principale; primo; dirigente, preeminente
lead'ing ar'ticle s articolo di fondo
lead'ing edge' s (aer) bordo d'attacco
lead'ing la'dy s prima attrice
lead'ing man' s (men') primo attore
lead'ing ques'tion s domanda suggestiva, domanda orientatrice
lead'ing strings' spl dande fpl
lead'-in wire' ['lid ˌɪn] s filo d'antenna
lead' pen'cil [led] s lapis m, matita
leaf [lif] s (leaves [livz]) (of plant) foglia; (of vine) pampino; (of paper) foglio; (of double door) battente m; (of table) asse m a ribalta; **to turn over a new leaf** ricominciare una nuova vita || intr fogliare; **to leaf through** sfogliare
leafless ['liflɪs] adj senza foglie
leaflet ['liflɪt] s manifestino, volantino; (of plant) foglietta
leaf' spring' s molla a balestra
leaf'stalk' s picciolo
leaf·y ['lifi] adj (-ier; -iest) foglioso, frondoso
league [lig] s lega || tr associare || intr associarsi

League' of Na'tions s Società f delle Nazioni

leak [lik] s (in a roof) stillicidio; (in a ship) falla; (of water, gas, steam) fuga; (of electricity) dispersione; buco, fessura; (of news) filtrazione; **to spring a leak** avere una perdita; (naut) cominciare a far acqua ‖ tr (gas, liquids) perdere, lasciar scappare; (news) lasciar trapelare ‖ intr (said of water, gas etc.,) perdere, scappare; (said of a barrel) spillare; (naut) fare acqua; **to leak away** (said of money) andarsene; **to leak out** (said of news) trapelare

leakage ['likɪdʒ] s perdita, fuoruscita, fuga; (elec) dispersione; (com) colaggio

leak·y ['liki] adj (-ier; -iest) che perde; (naut) che fa acqua; (coll) indiscreto

lean [lin] adj magro, secco; (gasoline mixture) povero ‖ v (pret & pp **leaned** or **leant** [lɛnt]) tr inclinare; appoggiare ‖ intr pendere, inclinarsi; (fig) inclinare, tendere; **to lean against** appoggiarsi a, addossarsi a; **to lean back** sdraiarsi; **to lean on** appoggiarsi su; **to lean out** (of) sporgersi (da); **to lean over backwards** fare di tutto; **to lean toward** (fig) tendere a, avere un'inclinazione per

leaning ['linɪŋ] adj inclinato, pendente ‖ s inclinazione

lean'ing tow'er s torre f pendente

lean'-to' s (-tos) tetto a una falda

leap [lip] s salto, balzo; **by leaps and bounds** a passi da gigante; **leap in the dark** salto nel vuoto ‖ v (pret & pp **leaped** or **leapt** [lɛpt]) tr saltare ‖ intr saltare; (said of one's heart) balzare

leap'frog' s cavallina; **to play leapfrog** giocare alla cavallina

leap' year' s anno bisestile

learn [lʌrn] s (pret & pp **learned** or **learnt** [lʌrnt]) tr imparare; imparare a memoria; (news) apprendere ‖ intr istruirsi, apprendere

learned ['lʌrnɪd] adj dotto; (word) colto

learn'ed jour'nal s rivista scientifica

learn'ed soci'ety s associazione di eruditi

learn'ed word' s parola dotta

learn'ed world' s mondo di dotti

learner ['lʌrnər] s apprendista mf; studente m; (beginner) principiante mf

learning ['lʌrnɪŋ] s istruzione; (scholarship) erudizione

lease [lis] s locazione, contratto d'affitto; **a new lease on life** nuove prospettive di felicità; vita nuova (dopo una malattia) ‖ tr locare; prendere in affitto ‖ intr affittare

lease'hold' adj affittato ‖ s beni mpl sotto locazione

leash [liʃ] s guinzaglio; **to strain at the leash** mordere il freno ‖ tr frenare, controllare

least [list] adj minore, menomo, minimo ‖ s (il) meno; **at least** or **at the least** per lo meno, quanto meno;

not in the least nient'affatto ‖ adv meno

leather ['lɛðər] s cuoio

leath'er·back tur'tle s tartaruga di mare

leath'er goods' store' s pelletteria

leathery ['lɛðəri] adj coriaceo

leave [liv] s (permission) permesso; (permission to be absent) licenza; (farewell) commiato; **on leave** in licenza; **to take French leave** andarsene all'inglese; **to take leave** (of) prender congedo (da) ‖ v (pret & pp **left** [lɛft]) tr (to go away from) lasciare, uscire da; (to let stay) lasciare; (to bequeath) lasciare in testamento; **leave it to me!** lasciami fare!; **to be left** restare, e.g., **the door was left open** la porta restò aperta; esserci, e.g., **there is no bread left** non c'è più pane; **to leave alone** lasciare in pace; **to leave no stone unturned** cercare ogni possibilità; **to leave off** abbandonare, lasciare; **to leave out** omettere; **to leave things as they are** lasciar stare le cose ‖ intr andarsene; (said of a conveyance) partire

leaven ['lɛvən] s lievito ‖ tr lievitare; (fig) impregnare, permeare

leavening ['lɛvənɪŋ] s lievito

leave' of ab'sence s licenza; (without pay) aspettativa

leave'-tak'ing s commiato

leavings ['livɪŋz] spl rifiuti mpl

Leba·nese [ˌlɛbəˈniz] adj libanese ‖ s (-nese) libanese mf

Lebanon ['lɛbənən] s il Libano

lecher ['lɛtʃər] s libertino

lecherous ['lɛtʃərəs] adj libidinoso

lechery ['lɛtʃəri] s lussuria

lectern ['lɛktərn] s leggio

lecture ['lɛktʃər] s conferenza; (tedious reprimand) pistolotto ‖ tr dare una conferenza a; sermoneggiare ‖ intr fare una conferenza; sermoneggiare

lecturer ['lɛktʃərər] s conferenziere m

ledge [lɛdʒ] s cornice f, cornicione m

ledger ['lɛdʒər] s (com) libro mastro

ledg'er line' s (mus) rigo supplementare

lee [li] s (shelter) rifugio; (naut) parte f sottovento; **lees** feccia

leech [litʃ] s mignatta, sanguisuga; **to stick like a leech** attaccarsi come una sanguisuga

leek [lik] s porro

leer [lɪr] s occhiata lussuriosa or maligna ‖ intr—**to leer at** guardare di sbieco, sbirciare

leer·y ['lɪri] adj (-ier; -iest) sospettoso

leeward ['liwərd] or ['luˌərd] adj di sottovento ‖ s sottovento, poggia ‖ adv sottovento

lee'way' s (aer, naut) deriva, scarroccio; (in time) (coll) tolleranza; (coll) libertà f d'azione

left [lɛft] adj sinistro; (pol) di sinistra ‖ s sinistra; (boxing) sinistro ‖ adv alla sinistra

left' field' s fuoricampo di sinistra

left'-hand' drive' s guida a sinistra

left-handed ['lɛft'hændɪd] adj (individual) mancino; (awkward) goffo;

(*compliment*) ambiguo; (*mach*) sinistrorso

leftish ['leftɪʃ] *adj* sinistrista

leftist ['leftɪst] *adj* di sinistra || *s* membro della sinistra

left'o'ver *adj* & *s* rimanente *m*; **leftovers** resti *mpl*

left'-wing' *adj* di sinistra

left-winger ['left'wɪŋər] *s* (coll) membro dell'estrema sinistra; (coll) membro della sinistra

leg [leg] *s* (*of man, animal, table, chair; of trousers*) gamba; (*of fowl; of lamb*) coscia; (*of boot*) gambale *m*; (*of a journey*) tappa; **to be on one's last legs** essere agli estremi, essere ridotto alla disperazione; **to not have a leg to stand on** (coll) non avere la minima giustificazione; **to pull the leg of** (coll) prendere in giro, burlarsi di; **to shake a leg** (coll) affrettarsi; (*to dance*) (coll) ballare; **to stretch one's legs** sgranchirsi le gambe

lega·cy ['legəsi] *s* (**-cies**) legato

legal ['ligəl] *adj* legale

legali·ty [lɪ'gælɪti] *s* (**-ties**) legalità *f*

legalize ['ligə,laɪz] *tr* legalizzare

le'gal ten'der *s* denaro a corso legale

legate ['legɪt] *s* legato

legatee [,legə'ti] *s* legatario

legation [lɪ'geʃən] *s* legazione

legend ['ledʒənd] *s* leggenda

legendary ['ledʒən,deri] *adj* leggendario

legerdemain [,ledʒərdɪ'men] *s* gioco di prestigio; (*trickery*) imbroglio

legging ['legɪŋ] *s* gambale *m*

leg·gy ['legi] *adj* (**-gier; -giest**) dalle gambe lunghe

leg'horn' *s* cappello di paglia di Firenze; gallina bianca livornese || **Leghorn** *s* Livorno

legible ['ledʒɪbəl] *adj* leggibile

legion ['lidʒən] *s* legione *f*

legislate ['ledʒɪs,let] *tr* ordinare per mezzo di legge || *intr* legiferare

legislation [,ledʒɪs'leʃən] *s* legislazione

legislative ['ledʒɪs,letɪv] *adj* legislativo

legislator ['ledʒɪs,letər] *s* legislatore *m*

legislature ['ledʒɪs,letʃər] *s* legislatura; corpo legislativo

legitimacy [lɪ'dʒɪtɪməsi] *s* legittimità *f*

legitimate [lɪ'dʒɪtɪmɪt] *adj* legittimo || [lɪ'dʒɪtɪ,met] *tr* legittimare

legit'imate dra'ma *s* teatro serio

legitimize [lɪ'dʒɪtɪ,maɪz] *tr* legittimare

leg' of lamb' *s* cosciotto d'agnello

legume ['legjum] or [lɪ'gjum] *s* (*pod*) legume *m*; (*table vegetables*) legumi *mpl*; (bot) leguminose *fpl*

leg'work' *s* lavoro che involve molto cammino

leisure ['liʒər] or ['leʒər] *s* ozio *m*; **at leisure** senza fretta; disoccupato; **at one's leisure** quando si abbia un po' di tempo libero

lei'sure class' *s* gente agiata

lei'sure hours' *spl* ore *fpl* d'ozio

leisurely ['liʒərli] or ['leʒərli] *adj* lento || *adv* lentamente, a tempo perso

lei'sure time' *s* tempo libero

lemon ['lemən] *s* limone *m*; (*car*) (coll) catorcio

lemonade [,lemə'ned] *s* limonata

lem'on squeez'er *s* spremilimoni *m*

lend [lend] *s* (*pret & pp* **lent** [lent]) *tr* prestare; (*a hand*) dare

lender ['lendər] *s* prestatore *m*

lend'ing li'brary *s* biblioteca circolante

length [lenθ] *s* lunghezza; (*of time*) durata; **at length** finalmente; **to go to any lengths** fare quanto è possibile; essere disposto a tutto; **to keep at arm's length** (*someone else*) tenere a distanza (qlcu); (*said of oneself*) tenere la distanza

lengthen ['leŋθən] *tr* allungare || *intr* allungarsi

length'wise' *adj* longitudinale || *adv* per il lungo

length·y ['leŋθi] *adj* (**-ier; -iest**) lungo, prolungato

lenien·cy ['linɪ·ənsi] *s* (**-cies**) indulgenza

lenient ['linɪ·ənt] *adj* indulgente, clemente

lens [lenz] *s* lente *f*; (*of the eye*) cristallino

Lent [lent] *s* quaresima

Lenten ['lentən] *adj* quaresimale

lentil ['lentəl] *s* lenticchia

Leo ['li·o] *s* (astr) il Leone

leopard ['lepərd] *s* leopardo

leotard ['li·ə,tard] *s* calzamaglia

leper ['lepər] *s* lebbroso

leprosy ['leprəsi] *s* lebbra

leprous ['leprəs] *adj* lebbroso; (*of an animal or plant*) squamoso

Lesbian ['lezbɪ·ən] *adj* lesbico || *s* lesbico; (*female homosexual*) lesbica

lesbianism ['lezbɪ·ə,nɪzəm] *s* lesbismo

lese majesty ['liz'mædʒɪsti] *s* delitto di lesa maestà

lesion ['liʒən] *s* lesione

less [les] *adj* minore || *adv* meno; **less and less** sempre meno; **less than** meno che; (*followed by numeral or personal pron*) meno di; (*followed by verb*) meno di quanto || *s* meno

lessee [les'i] *s* locatario; (*of business establishment*) concessionario

lessen ['lesən] *tr* diminuire, ridurre || *intr* diminuire, ridursi

lesser ['lesər] *adj comp* minore

lesson ['lesən] *s* lezione

lessor ['lesər] *s* locatore *m*

lest [lest] *conj* per paura che

let [let] *v* (*pret & pp* **let**; *ger* **letting**) *tr* permettere; (*to rent*) affittare; **let** + *inf* che + *subj*, e.g., **let him go** che vada; **let alone** tanto meno; senza menzionare; **let good enough alone** essere contento dell'onesto; **let us** + *inf* = *1st pl impv*, e.g., **let us sing** cantiamo; **to let** da affittare; **to let alone** lasciare in pace; **to let be** lasciar stare; **to let by** lasciar passare; **to let down** far scendere; deludere; tradire; abbandonare; **to let fly** (*insults*) lanciare; **to let go** lasciar libero; vendere; **to let in** fare entrare; **to let it go at that** non parlarne più; **to let know** far sapere; **to**

let loose sciogliere; **to let out** lasciar uscire; (*a secret*) divulgare; (*a scream*) lasciarsi scappare; (*to enlarge*) allargare; affittare; **to let through** lasciar passare; **to let up** lasciar salire; lasciar alzare || *intr* affittare; **to let down** diminuire gli sforzi; **to let go of** disfarsi di; **to let on** (coll) fare finta; **to not let on** (coll) non lasciar trapelare; **to let out** (said, *e.g., of school*) terminare; **to let up** (coll) cessare; (coll) diminuire

let'down' *s* diminuzione; smacco, umiliazione; delusione

lethal ['liθəl] *adj* letale

lethargic [lɪ'θɑrdʒɪk] *adj* letargico

lethar-gy ['lɛθərdʒi] *s* (**-gies**) letargo

Lett [lɛt] *s* lettone *mf*; (*language*) lettone *m*

letter ['lɛtər] *s* lettera; **letters** (*literature*) lettere *fpl*, letteratura; **to the letter** alla lettera || *tr* marcare con lettere

let'ter box' *s* cassetta delle lettere

let'ter car'rier *s* postino

let'ter drop' *s* buca delle lettere

let'ter-head' *s* capolettera *m*; (*paper with printed heading*) carta da lettera intestata

lettering ['lɛtərɪŋ] *s* iscrizione; lettere *fpl*

let'ter of cred'it *s* lettera di credito

let'ter o'pener ['opənər] *s* tagliacarte *m*

let'ter pa'per *s* carta da lettere

let'ter-per'fect *adj* alla lettera; che sa alla perfezione

let'ter-press' *s* stampato in tipografia || *adv* a stampa tipografica

let'ter scales' *spl* pesalettere *m*

let'ter-word' *s* sigla

Lettish ['lɛtɪʃ] *adj* & *s* lettone *m*

lettuce ['lɛtɪs] *s* lattuga

let'up' *s* (coll) pausa, sosta; (coll) tregua; **without letup** (coll) senza posa

leucorrhea [,lukə'ri-ə] *s* leucorrea

leukemia [lu'kimɪ-ə] *s* leucemia

Levant [lɪ'vænt] *s* levante *m*

levee ['lɛvi] *s* (*embankment*) argine *m*; (*reception*) ricevimento

lev·el ['lɛvəl] *adj* piano; livellato; equilibrato; **level with** a livello di; **one's level best** (coll) il proprio meglio || *s* (*instrument*) livella; (*degree of elevation*) livello; (*flat surface*) spianata, pianura; **on the level** (slang) onesto; onestamente; **to find one's level** trovare il proprio ambiente || *v* (*pret & pp* **-eled** or **-elled;** *ger* **-eling** or **-elling**) *tr* livellare; (*to flatten out*) spianare; (*e.g., prices*) pareggiare, ragguagliare; (*a gun*) puntare; (coll) gettare a terra; (fig) dirigere || *intr*— **to level off** (aer) volare orizzontalmente

level-headed ['lɛvəl'hɛdɪd] *adj* equilibrato

lev'eling rod' *s* stadia

lever ['livər] or ['lɛvər] *s* leva || *tr* far leva su || *intr* far leva

leverage ['livərɪdʒ] or ['lɛvərɪdʒ] *s* azione di una leva; (fig) potere *m*

leviathan [lɪ'vaɪ-əθən] *s* leviatano

levitation [,lɛvɪ'teʃən] *s* levitazione

levi-ty ['lɛvɪti] *s* (**-ties**) leggerezza

lev·y ['lɛvi] *s* (**-ies**) (*of taxes*) esazione; (*of money*) tributo; (*of troops*) leva || *v* (*pret & pp* **-ied**) *tr* (*a tax*) imporre; (*soldiers*) reclutare; (*war*) fare

lewd [lud] *adj* (*lustful*) lascivo; osceno

lexical ['lɛksɪkəl] *adj* lessicale

lexicographer [,lɛksɪ'kɑgrəfər] *s* lessicografo

lexicographic(al) [,lɛksɪko'græfɪk(əl)] *adj* lessicografico

lexicography [,lɛksɪ'kɑgrəfi] *s* lessicografia

lexicology [,lɛksɪ'kɑlədʒi] *s* lessicologia

lexicon ['lɛksɪkən] *s* lessico

liabili-ty [,laɪ-ə'bɪlɪti] *s* (**-ties**) svantaggio; responsabilità *f*; (*e.g., to disease*) tendenza; (com) passivo; **liabilities** debiti *mpl*; (com) passivo

liabil'ity insur'ance *s* assicurazione sulla responsabilità civile

liable ['laɪ-əbəl] *adj* (*e.g., to disease; e.g., to make mistakes*) soggetto; responsabile; probabile; (*e.g., to a fine*) passibile

liaison ['li-ə,zɑn] or [li'zɑn] *s* legame *m*; relazione illecita; (mil, nav) collegamento; (phonet) legamento

li'aison of'ficer *s* ufficiale *m* di collegamento

liar ['laɪ-ər] *s* bugiardo, mentitore *m*

libation [laɪ'beʃən] *s* (joc) libazione, bevuta

li·bel ['laɪbəl] *s* diffamazione; (*defamatory writing*) libello || *v* (*pret & pp* **-beled** or **-belled;** *ger* **-beling** or **-belling**) *tr* diffamare

libelous ['laɪbələs] *adj* diffamatorio

liberal ['lɪbərəl] *adj* liberale; (*translation*) libero || *s* liberale *mf*

liberali-ty [,lɪbə'rælɪti] *s* (**-ties**) liberalità *f*; (*breadth of mind*) ampiezza di vedute

liberal-minded ['lɪbərəl'maɪndɪd] *adj* liberale, tollerante

liberate ['lɪbə,ret] *tr* liberare

liberation [,lɪbə're(ə)n] *s* liberazione

liberator ['lɪbə,retər] *s* liberatore *m*

libertine ['lɪbər,tin] *adj* & *s* libertino

liber-ty ['lɪbərti] *s* (**-ties**) libertà *f*; **to take the liberty to** permettersi di

liberty-loving ['lɪbərti'lʌvɪŋ] *adj* amante della libertà

libidinous [lɪ'bɪdɪnəs] *adj* libidinoso

libido [lɪ'bido] or [lɪ'baɪdo] *s* libidine *f*; (psychoanal) libido *f*

Libra ['librə] or ['laɪbrə] *s* (astr) Bilancia

librarian [laɪ'brɛrɪ-ən] *s* bibliotecario

librar·y ['laɪ,brɛri] or ['laɪbrəri] *s* (**-ies**) biblioteca; (*room in a house; collection of books*) libreria

li'brary num'ber *s* segnatura

li'brary sci'ence *s* biblioteconomia

libret·to [lɪ'breto] *s* (**-tos**) (mus) libretto

Libya ['lɪbɪ-ə] *s* la Libia

license ['laɪsəns] *s* licenza; (aut) patente *f* || *tr* dare la licenza a

li'cense num'ber s numero di targa di circolazione

li'cense plate' or tag' s targa di circolazione

licentious [laɪ'senʃəs] adj licenzioso

lichen ['laɪkən] s lichene m

lick [lɪk] s leccata, leccatura; (coll) esplosione di energia; (coll) velocità f; (coll) battitura; (coll) ripulita; to give a lick and a promise to (coll) fare rapidamente e con poca attenzione || tr leccare; (said of waves, flames, etc.) lambire; (to defeat) (coll) battere, vincere; (e.g., with a stick) (coll) bastonare

licorice ['lɪkərɪs] s liquirizia

lid [lɪd] s coperchio; (eyelid) palpebra; (curb) (coll) restrizione, freno; (hat) (slang) cappello

lie [laɪ] s menzogna; to catch in a lie pigliare in castagna; to give the lie to smentire || v (pret & pp lied; ger lying) tr—to lie oneself out of or to lie one's way out of trarsi fuori da (un impaccio) con una menzogna || intr mentire || v (pret lay [le]; pp lain [len]; ger lying) intr essere sdraiato; trovarsi; (in the grave) giacere; to lie down sdraiarsi

lie' detec'tor s macchina della verità

lien [lin] or ['li-ən] s diritto di pegno, diritto di garanzia

lieu [lu] s—in lieu of in luogo di

lieutenant [lu'tenənt] s luogotenente m; (mil) tenente m; (nav) tenente m di vascello

lieuten'ant colo'nel s (mil) tenente m colonnello

lieuten'ant command'er s (nav) capitano di corvetta

lieuten'ant gen'eral s (mil) generale m di corpo d'armata

lieuten'ant gov'ernor s (USA) vicegovernatore m

lieuten'ant jun'ior grade' s (nav) sottotenente m di vascello

life [laɪf] adj (animate) vitale; (lifelong) perpetuo; (annuity) vitalizio; (working from nature) dal vero || s (lives [laɪvz]) vita; (of an insurance policy) forza; for life a vita; for the life of me per quanto io provi; the life and soul of (e.g., the party) l'anima di; to come to life tornare a sé; riprender vita; to depart this life passar a miglior vita; to run for one's life scappare a tutta corsa

life' annu'ity s rendita vitalizia

life' belt' s cintura di salvataggio

life'boat' s imbarcazione di salvataggio, lancia di salvataggio

life' buoy' s salvagente m

life' float' s zattera di salvataggio

life'guard' s bagnino

life' impris'onment s ergastolo

life' insur'ance s assicurazione sulla vita

life' jack'et s cintura or giubbotto di salvataggio

lifeless ['laɪflɪs] adj inanimato; (in a faint) esanime; senza vita

life'like' adj (e.g., portrait) parlante; naturale

life' line' s sagola di salvataggio; (fig) linea di comunicazioni vitale

life'long' adj perpetuo, a vita

life' of Ri'ley ['raɪli] s vita del michelaccio

life' of the par'ty s anima della festa

life' preserv'er [prɪ'zʌrvər] s salvagente m

lifer ['laɪfər] s (slang) ergastolano

life' raft' s zattera di salvataggio

life'sav'er s salvatore m della vita; (something that saves from a predicament) ancora di salvezza

life' sen'tence s condanna all'ergastolo

life'-size' adj in grandezza naturale

life'time' adj vitalizio || s corso della vita

life' vest' s (air, naut) giubbotto salvagente or di salvataggio

life'work' s lavoro di tutta una vita

lift [lɪft] s sollevamento; (act of helping) aiuto; (ride) passaggio; (apparatus) elevatore m; (aer) portanza || tr sollevare, alzare; (one's hat) levarsi; rimuovere; (coll) plagiare; (coll) rubare; (fire) (mil) sospendere || intr sollevare, sollevarsi; (said, e.g., of fog) dissiparsi

lift'-off' s (aer) decollo verticale

lift' truck' s carrello elevatore

ligament ['lɪgəmənt] s legamento

ligature ['lɪgətʃər] s legatura

light [laɪt] adj (in weight) leggero; (hair) biondo; (complexion) chiaro; (oil) fluido; (naut) con poco carico; (room) chiaro, illuminato; (beer) chiaro; light in the head (dizzy) allegro; (silly) scimunito; to make light of prendere sotto gamba || s luce f; (to light a cigarette) fuoco; (to control traffic) segnale m; (shining example) luminare m; (lighthouse) faro; (window) luce f; according to one's lights secondo l'intelligenza che il buon Dio gli (le) ha dato; against the light controluce; in this light sotto questo punto di vista; lights esempio; (of sheep) polmone m; to come to light venire alla luce; to shed or throw light on mettere in luce; to strike a light accendere un fiammifero || v (pret & pp lighted or lit [lɪt] tr (to furnish with illumination) illuminare; (to ignite) accendere; to light up illuminare || intr illuminarsi; accendersi; (said, e.g., of a bird) posarsi; (from a car) scendere; to light into (coll) gettarsi contro; to light out (slang) darsela a gambe; to light upon imbattersi in || adv senza bagagli; senza carico

light' bulb' s lampadina

light-complexioned ['laɪtkəm'plekʃənd] adj dal colorito chiaro

lighten ['laɪtən] tr alleggerire, sgravare; illuminare; (to cheer up) rallegrare || intr alleggerirsi; (to become less dark) illuminarsi; (to give off flashes of lightning) lampeggiare

lighter ['laɪtər] s accenditore m; (naut) burchio

light-fingered ['laɪt'fɪŋgərd] adj svelto di mano, con le mani lunghe

light-footed ['laɪt'futɪd] *adj* agile
light-headed ['laɪt'hedɪd] *adj* (*dizzy*) allegro; (*simple*) scemo
light-hearted ['laɪt'hɑrtɪd] *adj* allegro
light'house' *s* faro
lighting ['laɪtɪŋ] *s* illuminazione
lightly ['laɪtlɪ] *adv* alla leggera
light' me'ter *s* esposimetro
lightness ['laɪtnɪs] *s* (*in weight*) leggerezza; (*in illumination*) chiarezza
light'ning ['laɪtnɪŋ] *s* lampo, fulmine *m* || *v* (*ger -ning*) *intr* lampeggiare
light'ning arrest'er [ə'restər] *s* scaricatore *m*
light'ning bug' *s* lucciola
light'ning rod' *s* parafulmine *m*
light' op'era *s* operetta
light'ship' *s* battello faro
light-struck ['laɪt,strʌk] *adj* che ha preso luce
light'weight' *adj* leggero; da mezza stagione, e.g., **lightweight coat** cappotto da mezza stagione
light'-year' *s* anno luce
likable ['laɪkəbəl] *adj* simpatico
like [laɪk] *adj* uguale, simile; uguale a, simile a, e.g., **this hat is like mine** questo cappello è simile al mio; (*elec*) di segno uguale; **like father like son** tale il padre quale il figlio; **to feel like** + *ger* aver voglia di + *inf*; **to look like** assomigliare a; sembrare, e.g., **it looks like rain** sembra che pioverà || *s* (*liking*) preferenza; (*fellow man*) simile *m*; **and the like** e cose dello stesso genere; **to give like for like** rendere pane per focaccia || *adv* come; **like enough** (coll) probabilmente || *prep* come || *conj* (coll) come; come se; (coll) che, e.g., **it seems like he is afraid** sembra che abbia paura || *tr* voler bene (with *dat*), e.g., **I like her very much le voglio molto bene; trovar piacere in, e.g., I like music** trovo piacere nella musica; piacere (with *dat*), e.g., **John likes apples** le mele piacciono a Giovanni; **to like best** *or* **better** preferire; **to like it in** trovarsi a proprio agio in; **to like to** + *inf* piacere (with *dat*) + *inf*, e.g., **she likes to dance** le piace ballare; gradire che + *subj*, e.g., **I should like him to pay a visit to my parents** gradirei che facesse una visita ai miei genitori || *intr* volere, desiderare, e.g., **as you like** come ti desidera; **if you like** se vuole
likelihood ['laɪklɪ,hud] *s* probabilità *f*
like-ly ['laɪklɪ] *adj* (*-lier, -liest*) probabile; verosimile; a proposito; promettente; **to be likely to** + *inf* essere probabile che + *fut*, e.g., **Mary is likely to get married in the spring** è probabile che Maria si sposerà in primavera || *adv* probabilmente
like-minded ['laɪk'maɪndɪd] *adj* dello stesso parere, della stessa opinione
liken ['laɪkən] *tr* paragonare
likeness ['laɪknɪs] *s* (*picture*) ritratto; (*similarity*) rassomiglianza; apparenza
like'wise' *adv* ugualmente; inoltre; **to do likewise** fare lo stesso

liking ['laɪkɪŋ] *s* simpatia; **to be to the liking of** essere di gusto di; **to have a liking for** (*things*) prendere gusto per; (*people*) affezionarsi a
lilac ['laɪlək] *adj* & *s* lilla *m*
Lilliputian [,lɪlɪ'pjuʃən] *adj* & *s* lillipuziano
lilt [lɪlt] *s* canzone *f* a cadenza; movimento a cadenza; (*in verse*) cadenza
lil-y ['lɪlɪ] *s* (*-ies*) giglio; **to gild the lily** cercare di migliorare quanto è già perfetto
lil'y of the val'ley *s* mughetto
li'ma bean' ['laɪmə] *s* fagiolo bianco
limb [lɪm] *s* (*of body*) membro, arto; (*of tree*) ramo; (*of cross*) braccio; **to be out on a limb** (coll) essere nei guai
limber ['lɪmbər] *adj* agile || *intr*—**to limber up** sciogliersi i muscoli, sgranchirsi le gambe
lim-bo ['lɪmbo] *s* (*-bos*) esilio; dimenticatoio; (theol) limbo
lime [laɪm] *s* (*calcium oxide*) calce *f*; (*Citrus aurantifolia*) limetta agra; (*linden tree*) tiglio || *tr* gessare
lime'kiln' *s* fornace *f* da calce
lime'light' *s*—**to be in the limelight** essere in vista
limerick ['lɪmərɪk] *s* canzoncina umoristica di cinque versi
lime'stone' *s* calcare *m*
limit ['lɪmɪt] *s* limite *m*; (coll) colmo; **to go to the limit** andare agli estremi || *tr* limitare
limitation [,lɪmɪ'teʃən] *s* limitazione
lim'ited-ac'cess high'way ['lɪmɪtɪd] *s* autostrada, strada con corsia d'accesso
lim'ited com'pany *s* società *f* a responsabilità limitata
lim'ited mon'archy *s* monarchia costituzionale
limitless ['lɪmɪtlɪs] *adj* illimitato
limousine ['lɪmə,zin] *or* [,lɪmə'zin] *s* berlina
limp [lɪmp] *adj* floscio; debole || *s* zoppicatura || *intr* zoppicare
limpid ['lɪmpɪd] *adj* limpido
linage ['laɪnɪdʒ] *s* (typ) numero di linee
linchpin ['lɪntʃ,pɪn] *s* acciarino
linden ['lɪndən] *s* tiglio
line [laɪn] *s* linea; (*e.g., of people*) fila; (*of trees*) filare *m*; (*for fishing*) lenza; (*written or printed*) rigo, riga; (*wrinkle*) ruga; (*of goods*) ramo; (naut) gherlino; **all along the line** su tutta la linea; **in line** allineato; sotto controllo; **in line with** secondo; **out of line** fuori d'allineamento; (slang) in disaccordo; **to bring into line** far filare; **to draw the line at** fermarsi a; stabilire il limite a; **to fall in line** conformarsi; allinearsi; **to have a line on** (coll) aver informazioni su; **to read between the lines** leggere fra le righe; **to stand in line** fare la coda; **to toe the line** filare diritto; **to wait in line** fare la fila || *tr* rigare; (*e.g., the street*) schierare lungo; (*a suit*) foderare; (*a brake*) rivestire; **to line up** allineare; trovare, scovare || *intr*

—to line up mettersi in fila; fare la coda

lineage ['lɪnɪ‑ɪdʒ] s lignaggio

lineaments ['lɪnɪ‑əmənts] spl lineamenti mpl

linear ['lɪnɪ‑ər] adj lineare

line'man s (-men) (elec) guardafili m; (sports) guardalinee m; (surv) assistente geometra m

linen ['lɪnən] adj di tela di lino || s (fabric) tela di lino, lino; (yarn) filo di lino; biancheria

lin'en clos'et s guardaroba m per la biancheria

line' of fire' s (mil) linea di tiro

line' of least' resist'ance s principio del minimo sforzo; **to follow the line of least resistance** prendere la via più facile

line' of sight' s visuale f; (mil) linea di mira

liner ['laɪnər] s transatlantico

line'-up' s disposizione; (of prisoners) allineamento; (sports) formazione

linger ['lɪŋgər] intr indugiare, soffermarsi; (to be tardy) tardare; rimanere in vita; **to linger over** contemplare

lingerie [ˌlænʒə'ri] s biancheria intima

lingering ['lɪŋgərɪŋ] adj prolungato

lingual ['lɪŋgwəl] adj linguale || s suono linguale

linguist ['lɪŋgwɪst] s poliglotto; (specialist in linguistics) glottologo

linguistic [lɪŋ'gwɪstɪk] adj linguistico || **linguistics** s linguistica, glottologia

lining ['laɪnɪŋ] s (of a coat) fodera; (of auto brake) guarnizione; (of a furnace) rivestimento interno; (of wall) rivestimento

link [lɪŋk] s anello, maglia; unione; (of sausage) nocco; **links** campo di golf || tr connettere || intr connettersi

linnet ['lɪnɪt] s fanello

linotype ['laɪnəˌtaɪp] s linotype f || tr comporre in linotipia

lin'otype op'erator s linotipista mf

linseed ['lɪnˌsid] s linosa

lin'seed oil' s olio di lino

lint [lɪnt] s peluria, sfilacciatura; (for dressing wounds) filaccia

lintel ['lɪntəl] s architrave m

lion ['laɪ‑ən] s leone m; celebrità f; **to beard the lion in his den** affrontare l'avversario a casa sua; **to put one's head in the lion's mouth** cacciarsi nei pericoli

lioness ['laɪ‑ənɪs] s leonessa

lion-hearted ['laɪ‑ən ˌhɑrtɪd] adj cuor di leone, coraggioso

lionize ['laɪ‑əˌnaɪz] tr festeggiare come una celebrità

li'ons' den' s fossa dei leoni

li'on's share' s parte f del leone

lip [lɪp] s labbro; (of a jar) beccuccio; (slang) linguaggio insolente; **to smack one's lips** leccarsi le labbra

lip'read' v (pret & pp -read [ˌred]) tr leggere le labbra di || intr leggere le labbra

lip' read'ing s labiolettura

lip' serv'ice s omaggio non sentito

lip'stick' s rossetto per le labbra, matita per le labbra

lique-fy ['lɪkwɪˌfaɪ] v (pret & pp -fied) tr & intr liquefare

liqueur [lɪ'kʌr] s liquore m

liquid ['lɪkwɪd] adj liquido || s liquido; (phonet) liquida

liquidate ['lɪkwɪˌdet] tr & intr liquidare

liquidity [lɪ'kwɪdɪti] s liquidità f

liq'uid meas'ure s misura di capacità per liquidi

liquor ['lɪkər] s distillato alcolico, bevanda alcolica; (broth) brodo

Lisbon ['lɪzbən] s Lisbona

lisp [lɪsp] s pronuncia blesa || intr parlare bleso

lissome ['lɪsəm] adj flessibile, agile

list [lɪst] s lista, elenco; (border) orlo; (selvage) cimossa, vivagno; (naut) sbandamento; **lists** lizza; **to enter the lists** entrare in lizza || tr elencare, listare || intr (naut) sbandare, andare alla banda

listen ['lɪsən] intr ascoltare; obbedire; **to listen in** ascoltare una conversazione; (rad) captare una comunicazione; **to listen to** ascoltare; obbedire a, prestare attenzione a; **to listen to reason** intendere ragione

listener ['lɪsənər] s ascoltatore m; radioascoltatore m

lis'tening post' s (mil) posto di ascolto

listless ['lɪstlɪs] adj svogliato

list' price' s prezzo di catalogo

lita-ny ['lɪtəni] s (-nies) litania

liter ['litər] s litro

literacy ['lɪtərəsi] s abilità f di leggere e scrivere; istruzione

literal ['lɪtərəl] adj letterale

literary ['lɪtəˌreri] adj letterario; (individual) letterato

literate ['lɪtərɪt] adj che sa leggere e scrivere; (educated) istruito; (well-read) letterato || s persona che sa leggere e scrivere; letterato

literature ['lɪtərətʃər] s letteratura; (printed matter) opuscoli pubblicitari

lithe [laɪθ] adj flessibile, agile

lithium ['lɪθɪ‑əm] s litio

lithograph ['lɪθəˌgræf] or ['lɪθəˌgrɑf] s litografia || tr litografare

lithographer [lɪ'θɑgrəfər] s litografo

lithography [lɪ'θɑgrəfi] s litografia

Lithuania [ˌlɪθu'enɪ‑ə] s la Lituania

Lithuanian [ˌlɪθu'enɪ‑ən] adj & s lituano

litigant ['lɪtɪgənt] adj & s litigante mf

litigate ['lɪtɪˌget] tr & intr litigare

litigation [ˌlɪtɪ'geʃən] s litigio; (lawsuit) lite f, causa

litmus ['lɪtməs] s tornasole m

lit'mus pa'per s cartina al tornasole

litter ['lɪtər] s disordine m; (scattered rubbish) pattume m; (young brought forth at one birth) figliata; (of puppies) cucciolata; (bedding for animals) strame m; (stretcher; bed carried by men or animals) lettiga, portantina || tr mettere in disordine; spargere rifiuti per; coprire di strame || intr partorire

lit'ter·bug' s sparpagliatore m di rifiuti

littering ['lɪtərɪŋ] s—no littering vietato gettare rifiuti

little ['lɪtəl] adj (in size) piccolo; (in amount) poco, e.g., little salt poco sale; a little un po' di, e.g., a little salt un po' di sale; the little ones i piccini || s poco; a little un po'; to make little of farsi gioco di; non pigliar sul serio; to think little of non tener di conto || adv poco; little by little poco a poco, mano a mano

Lit'tle Bear' s Orsa minore

Lit'tle Dip'per s Piccolo Carro

lit'tle fin'ger s mignolo; to twist around one's little finger maneggiare come un fantoccio

lit'tle·neck' s piccola vongola (Venus mercenaria)

lit'tle owl' s civetta

lit'tle peo'ple spl fate fpl; folletti mpl

Lit'tle Red Rid'inghood' ['raɪdɪŋ ,hʊd] s Cappuccetto Rosso

lit'tle slam' s (bridge) piccolo slam

liturgic(al) [lɪ'tʌrdʒɪk(əl)] adj liturgico

litur·gy ['lɪtərdʒɪ] s (-gies) liturgia

livable ['lɪvəbəl] adj abitabile; socievole; tollerabile

live [laɪv] adj vivo; (flame) ardente; di attualità; (elec) sotto tensione; (telv) in diretta || [lɪv] tr vivere; to live down (one's past) far dimenticare; to live it up (oll) darsi alla bella vita, scialare; to live out (e.g., a war) sopravvivere (with dat) || intr vivere; to live from hand to mouth vivere alla giornata; to live high darsi alla bella vita; to live on continuare a vivere; (e.g., vegetables) vivere di; vivere alle spalle di; to live up to (one's promises) compiere; (one's earnings) spendere

live' coal' [laɪv] s brace f

livelihood ['laɪvlɪ ,hʊd] s vita; to earn one's livelihood guadagnarsi la vita

livelong ['lɪv ,lɔŋ] or ['lɪv ,lɑŋ] adj—all the livelong day tutto il santo giorno

live·ly ['laɪvlɪ] adj (-lier; -liest) vivo, vivace; (color) vivido; (resilient) elastico; (tune) brioso

liven ['laɪvən] tr animare || intr animarsi, rianimarsi

liver ['lɪvər] s abitante mf; (anat) fegato

liver·y ['lɪvərɪ] s (-ies) livrea

liv'ery·man s (-men) stalliere m

liv'ery sta'ble s stallaggio

livestock ['laɪv ,stɑk] adj zootecnico || s bestiame m

live' wire' [laɪv] s (elec) filo carico di corrente; (slang) persona energica

livid ['lɪvɪd] adj livido; (with anger) incollerito

living ['lɪvɪŋ] adj vivo; (conditions) abitativo || s vivere m; to earn a living guadagnarsi la vita

liv'ing quar'ters spl abitazione, alloggio

liv'ing room' s stanza di soggiorno

liv'ing wage' s salario sufficiente per vivere

lizard ['lɪzərd] s lucertola

load [lod] s peso, carico; loads of (coll) un mucchio di; to get a load of (slang) stare a vedere; (slang) stare a sentire; to have a load on (slang) essere ubriaco || tr caricare || intr caricarsi

loaded ['lodɪd] adj caricato; (slang) ubriaco fradicio; (slang) ricchissimo

load'ed dice' spl dadi truccati

load'stone' s magnetite f; (fig) calamita

loaf [lof] s (loaves [lovz]) pane m; (molded mass) forma; (of sugar) pane m; (long and thin loaf) filone m || intr batter fiacca, oziare

loafer ['lofər] s fannullone m

loam [lom] s ricca argilla sabbiosa; terra da fonderia

loan [lon] s prestito; to hit for a loan (coll) dare una stoccata a || tr prestare

loan' shark' s (coll) strozzino

loan' word' s (ling) prestito

loath [loθ] adj poco disposto; nothing loath molto volentieri

loathe [loð] tr detestare, aborrire

loathsome ['loðsəm] adj abominevole, disgustoso

lob [lab] s (tennis) pallonetto || v (pret & pp lobbed; ger lobbing) tr (tennis) dare un pallonetto a

lob·by ['labɪ] s (-bies) anticamera, vestibolo; sollecitazione di voti || v (pret & pp -bied) intr sollecitare voti, influenzare il voto dietro le quinte

lobbyist ['labɪ·ɪst] s politicante m che cerca di influenzare il voto dietro le quinte

lobe [lob] s lobo

lobster ['labstər] s (Palinurus vulgaris) aragosta; (Hommarus vulgaris) astice m

lob'ster pot' s nassa per aragoste

local ['lokəl] adj locale || s treno accelerato; notizia di interesse locale; (of a union) sezione

locale [lo'kæl] s località f

locali·ty [lo'kælɪtɪ] s (-ties) località f

localize ['lokə ,laɪz] tr localizzare

lo'cal op'tion s referendum m locale sulla vendita di alcolici

locate [lo'ket] or ['loket] tr (to discover the location of) lo alizzare; (to place, settle) situare, stabilire; (to ascribe a location to) individuare || intr stabilirsi

location [lo'keʃən] s localizzazione; posizione; sito; on location (mov) in esterno

lock [lak] s serratura; (of a canal) chiusa; (of hair) ciocca; (of a firearm) percussore m; (mach) freno; lock, stock, and barrel (oll) completamente; under lock and key sotto chiave || tr chiudere a hiave; (a boat) far passare per una chiusa; unire; abbracciare; to lock in chiudere sotto chiave; to lock out chiudere fuori; (workers) sbarrare dal lavoro; to lock up chiudere a chiave; incarcerare

locker ['lakər] s armadietto a chiave; (in the form of a chest) bauletto

lock′er room′ s spogliatoio
locket [′lɑkɪt] s medaglione m
lock′jaw′ s tetano, trisma m
lock′ nut′ s controdado
lock′out′ s serrata
lock′smith′ s magnano, fabbro
lock′ step′ s—**to march in lock step** marciare a passo serrato
lock′ stitch′ s punto a filo doppio
lock′ ten′der s guardiano di chiusa
lock′up′ s prigione; (typ) messa in forma
lock′ wash′er s rondella di sicurezza
locomotive [‚lokə′motɪv] s locomotiva
lo•cus [′lokəs] s (-ci [saɪ]) luogo
locust [′lokəst] s (ent) locusta; (cicada) (ent) cicala; (bot) robinia
lode [lod] s filone m, vena
lode′star′ s stella polare; guida
lodge [lɑdʒ] s casetta; padiglione m da caccia; albergo; (e.g., of Masons) loggia ‖ tr alloggiare, ospitare; depositare; contenere; (a complaint) sporgere ‖ intr alloggiare; essere contenuto, trovarsi; andar a finire
lodger [′lɑdʒər] s inquilino
lodging [′lɑdʒɪŋ] s alloggio
loft [lɔft] or [lɑft] s (attic) solaio; (hayloft) fienile m; (in theater or church) galleria
loft•y [′lɔftɪ] or [′lɑftɪ] adj (-ier; -iest) alto, elevato; (haughty) orgoglioso
log [lɔg] or [lɑg] s ceppo, ciocco; (naut) solcometro; (aer, naut) giornale m di bordo; **to sleep like a log** dormire della grossa ‖ v (pret & pp **logged**; ger **logging**) tr registrare; (a speed) fare; (a distance) percorrere
logarithm [′lɔgə‚rɪθəm] or [′lɑgə‚rɪθəm] s logaritmo
log′book′ s (aer, naut) libro di bordo
log′ cab′in s capanna di tronchi
log′ chip′ s palo barchetta
log′ driv′er s zatteriere m
log′ driv′ing [′draɪvɪŋ] s fluitazione
logger [′lɔgər] or [′lɑgər] s taglialegna m; trattore m per trasporto tronchi
log′ger•head′ s testone m; **at loggerheads** in lite
loggia [′lɔdʒə] s loggia
logic [′lɑdʒɪk] s logica
logical [′lɑdʒɪkəl] adj logico
logician [lo′dʒɪʃən] s logico
logistic(al) [lo′dʒɪstɪk(əl)] adj logistico
logistics [lo′dʒɪstɪks] s logistica
log′jam′ s ingorgo fluviale dovuto a ammasso di tronchi; (fig) ristagno
log′ line′ s (naut) sagola
log′roll′ intr barattare favori politici
log′wood′ s campeggio
loin [lɔɪn] s lombo; **to gird up one′s loins** prepararsi per l′azione
loin′cloth′ s perizoma m, copripudende m
loiter [′lɔɪtər] tr—**to loiter away** (time) sprecare in ozio ‖ intr bighellonare, trastullarsi
loiterer [′lɔɪtərər] s perdigiorno
loll [lɑl] intr sdraiarsi pigramente, adagiarsi pigramente; pendere
lollipop [′lɑlɪ‚pɑp] s caramella sullo stecchetto, lecca-lecca m

Lombard [′lɑmbərd] or [′lʌmbərd] adj & s lombardo; (hist) longobardo
Lom′bardy pop′lar s pioppo italico
London [′lʌndən] adj londinese ‖ s Londra
Londoner [′lʌndənər] s londinese mf
lone [lon] adj solo; solitario
loneliness [′lonlɪnɪs] s solitudine f
lone•ly [′lonlɪ] adj (-lier; -liest) solingo, solo, solitario
lonesome [′lonsəm] adj solitario
lone′ wolf′ s (coll) orso, solitario
long [lɔŋ] or [lɑŋ] (longer [′lɔŋgər] or [′lɑŋgər]; longest [′lɔŋgɪst] or [′lɑŋgɪst]) adj lungo; **three meters long** lungo tre metri ‖ adv molto, molto tempo; **as long as** mentre; (provided) fin tanto che; (inasmuch as) dato che; **before long** fra poco; **how long?** quanto?; **long ago** molto tempo fa; **long before** molto prima; **long since** molto tempo fa; **no longer** non più; **so long!** (coll) ciao!, arrivederci!; **so long as** fino a che, finché ‖ intr anelare; **to long for** sviscerarsi per, sospirare per
long′boat′ s (naut) lancia
long′-dis′tance adj (telp) interurbano, intercomunale; (sports) di fondo; (aer) a distanza
long′-drawn′-out′ adj prolungato
longeron [′lɑndʒərən] s longherone m
longevity [lɑn′dʒɛvɪtɪ] s longevità f
long′ face′ s (coll) faccia triste, muso lungo
long′hair′ adj & s (coll) intellettuale mf; (coll) musicomane mf
long′hand′ adj (scritto) a mano ‖ s scrittura a mano; **in longhand** scritto a mano
longing [′lɔŋɪŋ] or [′lɑŋɪŋ] adj bramoso, anelante ‖ s brama, anelito
longitude [′lɑndʒɪ‚tjud] or [′lɑndʒɪ‚tud] s longitudine f
long-lived [′lɔŋ′lɪvd], [′lɔŋ′laɪvd], [′lɑŋ′laɪvd] or [′lɑŋ′lɪvd] adj (person) longevo, di lunga vita; (e.g., rumor) di lunga durata
long′-play′ing rec′ord s disco di grande durata
long′-range′ adj a lunga portata
long′shore′man s (-men) portuale m, scaricatore m
long′stand′ing adj vecchio, che esiste da lungo tempo
long′-suf′fering adj paziente, longanime
long′ suit′ s (cards) serie lunga; (fig) forte m
long′-term′ adj a lunga scadenza
long′-wind′ed adj verboso; (speech) chilometrico
look [lʊk] s (appearance) aspetto; (glance) sguardo; (search) ricerca; **looks** aspetto, apparenza; **to take a look at** dare un′occhiata a ‖ tr guardare; (one′s age) mostrare; **to look daggers at** fulminare con lo sguardo; **to look up** (e.g., in a dictionary) cercare; andare a visitare; venire a visitare ‖ intr guardare; cercare; parere; **look out!** attenzione!; **to look after** badare a; occuparsi di; **to look at** guardare; **to look back** riguardare;

(fig) guardare al passato; **to look down on s.o.** guardare qlcu dall'alto in basso; **to look for** cercare; aspettarsi; **to look forward to** anticipare il piacere di; **to look ill** avere una brutta cera; **to look in on** passare per la casa di; **to look into** esaminare a fondo; **to look like** sembrare, parere; **to look out** fare attenzione; **to look out for** aver cura di; **to look out of** guardare da; **to look out on** dare su; **to look through** guardare per; (*a book*) sfogliare; **to look toward** dare su; **to look up to** ammirare, guardare con ammirazione; **to look well** avere una buona cera; fare figura

looker-on [ˌlukərˈɑn] or [ˌlukərˈɔn] s (**lookers-on**) astante m

look'ing glass' [ˈlukɪŋ] s specchio

look'out' s guardia; (*person; watch kept; place from which a watch is kept*) vedetta; (*concern*) (coll) affare m; **to be on the lookout** stare in guardia; **to be on the lookout for** essere in cerca di

loom [lum] s telaio || *intr* apparire indistintamente; pararsi dinanzi; apparire

loon [lun] s scemo; fannullone m; (orn) (*Gavia*) strolaga

loon·y [ˈluni] *adj* (**-ier; -iest**) (slang) pazzo || s (**-ies**) (slang) pazzo

loop [lup] s cappio; (*e.g., of a road*) tortuosità f; (*for fastening a button*) occhiello; (aer) cerchio or giro della morte; (phys) ventre m; || *tr* fare cappi in; annodare; **to loop the loop** (aer) fare il giro della morte || *intr* avanzare tortuosamente, girare

loop'hole' s (*narrow opening*) feritoia; (*means of evasion*) scappatoia

loose [lus] *adj* libero, sciolto; (*available*) disponibile; (*not firm*) rilasciato; (*tooth*) che balla; (*unchaste*) facile; (*garment*) ampio; (*soil*) smosso; (*translation*) libero; (*rein*) lento; **to become loose** sciogliersi; **to break loose** mettersi in libertà; **to have loose bowels** avere la diarrea; **to turn loose** liberare || s—**to be on the loose** (coll) essere in libertà; (coll) correre la cavallina || *tr* sciogliere; slegare; lanciare

loose' change' s spiccioli mpl

loose' end' s capo sciolto; **at loose ends** indeciso; disoccupato, senza nulla da fare

loose'-leaf' *adj* a fogli mobili

loosen [ˈlusən] *tr* snodare; rilasciare; smuovere; allentare; (*the bowels*) liberare dalla stitichezza || *intr* snodarsi; rilasciarsi; smuoversi; allentarsi

looseness [ˈlusnɪs] s scioltezza; (*in morals*) rilassamento

loose-tongued [ˈlusˈtʌŋd] *adj* sciolto di lingua; linguacciuto, maldicente

loot [lut] s bottino || *tr* saccheggiare

lop [lɑp] v (*pret & pp* **lopped**; *ger* **lopping**) *tr* lasciar cadere, lasciar penzolare; **to lop off** mozzare; (*a tree*) potare; (*a vine*) stralciare || *intr* penzolare

lopsided [ˈlɑpˈsaɪdɪd] *adj* che pende da una parte; asimmetrico, sproporzionato

loquacious [loˈkweʃəs] *adj* loquace

lord [lɔrd] s signore m; (Brit) lord m || *tr*—**to lord it over** signoreggiare su

lord·ly [ˈlɔrdli] *adj* (**-lier; -liest**) signorile, magnifico; altero, disdegnoso, arrogante

Lord's' Day', the la domenica, il giorno del Signore

lordship [ˈlɔrdʃɪp] s signoria

Lord's' Prayer' s paternostro

Lord's' Sup'per s Eucarestia; Ultima Cena

lore [lor] s tradizioni fpl popolari; cognizioni fpl

lorgnette [lɔrnˈjɛt] s occhialetto, lorgnette f; binocolo da teatro col manico

lor·ry [ˈlɑri] or [ˈlɔri] s (**-ries**) (rr) vagoncino; (Brit) camion m

lose [luz] v (*pret & pp* **lost** [lɔst] or [lɑst]) *tr* perdere; (*said of a physician*) non riuscire a salvare; **to lose heart** perdersi d'animo; **to lose oneself** perdersi, smarrirsi || *intr* perdere; (*said of a watch*) ritardare; **to lose out** rimettterci

loser [ˈluzər] s perdente mf

losing [ˈluzɪŋ] *adj* perdente || **losings** spl perdite fpl

loss [lɔs] or [lɑs] s perdita; **to be at a loss** essere perplesso; **to be at a loss to** + *inf* non saper come + *inf*; **to sell at a loss** vendere in perdita

loss' of face' s perdita di faccia

lost [lɔst] or [lɑst] *adj* perduto; **lost in thought** assorto in sè stesso; **lost to** perso per; insensibile a

lost'-and-found' depart'ment s ufficio degli oggetti smarriti

lost' sheep' s pecorella smarrita

lot [lɑt] s (*for building*) lotto; (*fate*) sorte f; (*parcel, portion*) partita; (*of people*) gruppo; (coll) grande quantità f; (coll) tipo, soggetto; **a lot (of)** or **lots of** (coll) molto, molti; **to cast** or **to throw in one's lot with** condividere la sorte di; **to draw** or **to cast lots** tirare a sorte

lotion [ˈloʃən] s lozione

lotter·y [ˈlɑtəri] s (**-ies**) lotteria, riffa

lotto [ˈlɑto] s tombola, lotto

lotus [ˈlotəs] s loto

loud [laud] *adj* forte; (*noisy*) rumoroso; (*voice*) alto; (*garish*) sgargiante, chiassoso, appariscente; (*foul-smelling*) puzzolente || *adv* a voce alta; rumorosamente

loud-mouthed [ˈlaudˈmauθt] or [ˈlaudˌmauðd] *adj* chiassone

loud'speak'er s altoparlante m

lounge [laundʒ] s divano, sofà m; sala soggiorno; ridotto || *intr* oziare, star senza far niente; bighellonare; **to lounge around** bighellonare

lounge' liz'ard s (slang) damerino, bellimbusto, gagà m

louse [laus] s (lice [laɪs]) pidocchio || *tr*—**to louse up** (slang) rovinare

lous·y [ˈlauzi] *adj* (**-ier; -iest**) pidocchioso; (*mean; bungling*) (coll) schifoso; (*filthy*) (coll) sporco; **lousy with** (*e.g., money*) (slang) pieno di

lout [laʊt] *s* gaglioffo, tanghero

louver ['luvər] *s* sportello girevole di persiana; (aut) feritoia per ventilazione

lovable ['lʌvəbəl] *adj* amabile

love [lʌv] *s* amore *m*; (tennis) zero; **not for love nor money** a nessun prezzo; **to be in love (with)** essere innamorato (di); **to make love to** fare l'amore con || *tr* amare; voler bene a; piacere (with *dat*), *e.g.,* **she loves short skirts** le piacciono le sottane corte

love' affair' *s* passione, amori *mpl*

love'bird' *s* (orn) inseparabile *m*; **love-birds** (slang) amanti appassionati

love' child' *s* figlio naturale

love' feast' *s* agape *f*

loveless ['lʌvlɪs] *adj* senza amore

lovelorn ['lʌv͵lɔrn] *adj* abbandonato dalla persona amata

love·ly ['lʌvli] *adj* (**-lier; -liest**) bello; (coll) delizioso

love' match' *s* matrimonio d'amore

love' po'tion *s* filtro d'amore

lover ['lʌvər] *s* amante *m*; (*e.g., of music*) amico, appassionato

love' seat' *s* amorino

love'sick' *adj* malato d'amore

love'sick'ness *s* mal *m* d'amore

love' song' *s* canzone *f* d'amore

loving ['lʌvɪŋ] *adj* affezionato, amoroso; **your loving son** il vostro affezionato figlio

lov'ing-kind'ness *s* tenera sollecitudine

low [lo] *adj* basso; (*deep*) profondo; (*diet*) magro; (*visibility*) cattivo; (*dress*) scollato; (*dejected*) abbattuto; (*fire*) lento; (*flame; speed*) piccolo; **to lay low** ammazzare; abbattere; **to lie low** rimanere nascosto; attendere || *s* punto basso; prezzo minimo; (*of cow*) muggito; (aut) prima velocità; (meteor) depressione || *adv* basso, a basso, in basso || *intr* (*said of a cow*) muggire

low'born' *adj* di umili origini

low'boy' *s* cassettone basso con le gambe corte

low'brow' *adj* & *s* (coll) ignorante *mf*

low'-cost hous'ing *s* case *fpl* popolari

Low' Coun'tries, the i Paesi Bassi

low'-down' *adj* (coll) basso, vile || **low'-down'** *s* (coll) semplice verità *f*, notizie *fpl* confidenziali

lower ['lo·ər] *adj* inferiore, disotto || *tr* abbassare; (*prices*) ribassare || *intr* diminuire; discendere || ['lau·ər] *intr* aggrottare le ciglia; (*said of the weather*) imbronciarsi

low'er berth' ['lo·ər] *s* cuccetta inferiore

low'er case' ['lo·ər] *s* (typ) cassa inferiore

lower-case ['lo·ər͵kes] *adj* (typ) minuscolo

low'er mid'dle class' ['lo·ər] *s* piccola borghesia

lowermost ['lo·ər͵most] *adj* (il) più basso, (l') infimo

low'-fre'quency *adj* a bassa frequenza

low' gear' *s* prima velocità, prima

lowland ['lolənd] *s* pianura || **Lowlands** *spl* Scozia meridionale, bassa Scozia

low·ly ['loli] *adj* (**-lier; -liest**) umile

Low' Mass' *s* messa bassa

low-minded ['lo'maɪndɪd] *adj* vile, basso

low-necked ['lo'nekt] *adj* scollato

low-pitched ['lo'pɪtʃt] *adj* (*sound*) basso, grave; (*roof*) poco inclinato

low'-pres'sure *adj* a bassa pressione

low-priced ['lo'praɪst] *adj* a buon mercato, a basso prezzo

low' shoe' *s* scarpa bassa

low'-speed' *adj* di piccola velocità

low-spirited ['lo'spɪrɪtɪd] *adj* depresso

low' tide' *s* bassa marea; (fig) punto più basso

low' visibil'ity *s* scarsa visibilità

low' wa'ter *s* (low tide) bassa marea; (*of a river*) magra

loyal ['lɔɪ·əl] *adj* leale

loyalist ['lɔɪ·əlɪst] *s* lealista *mf*

loyal·ty ['lɔɪ·əlti] *s* (**-ties**) lealtà *f*

lozenge ['lɑzɪndʒ] *s* losanga; (*candy cough drop*) pasticca, pastiglia

LP ['ɛl'pi] *s* (letterword) (trademark) disco di grande durata

lubricant ['lubrɪkənt] *adj* & *s* lubrificante *m*

lubricate ['lubrɪ͵ket] *tr* lubrificare; (*e.g., one's hands*) ungersi

lubrication [͵lubrɪ'keʃən] *s* lubrificazione

lubricous ['lubrɪkəs] *adj* lubrico; incerto, incostante

lucerne [lu'sʌrn] *s* erba medica

lucid ['lusɪd] *adj* lucido

Lucifer ['lusɪfər] *s* Lucifero

luck [lʌk] *s* (good or bad) sorte *f*; (good) sorte *f*, fortuna; **down on one's luck** in cattive condizioni; **in luck** fortunato; **out of luck** sfortunato; **to bring luck** portare (buona) fortuna; **to try one's luck** tentare la sorte; **worse luck** disgraziatamente

luckily ['lʌkɪli] *adv* fortunatamente

luckless ['lʌklɪs] *adj* sfortunato

luck·y ['lʌki] *adj* (**-ier; -iest**) fortunato; (supposed to bring luck) portafortuna; (foretelling good luck) di buon augurio; **to be lucky** aver fortuna

luck'y hit' *s* (coll) colpo di fortuna

lucrative ['lukrətɪv] *adj* lucrativo

ludicrous ['ludɪkrəs] *adj* ridicolo

lug [lʌg] *s* manico; (pull) tiro; **to put the lug on s.o.** (slang) batter cassa a qlcu || *v* (*pret & pp* **lugged**; *ger* **lugging**) *tr* tirarsi dietro; (coll) introdurre a sproposito

luggage ['lʌgɪdʒ] *s* (used in traveling) bagaglio; (found in a store) valigeria

lug'gage store' *s* valigeria

lugubrious [lu'gubrɪ·əs] or [lu'gjubrɪ·əs] *adj* lugubre

lukewarm ['luk͵wɔrm] *adj* tiepido

lull [lʌl] *s* momento di calma, calma || *tr* calmare, pacificare; addormentare

lulla·by ['lʌlə͵baɪ] *s* (**-bies**) ninna-nanna

lumbago [lʌm'bego] *s* lombaggine *f*

lumber ['lʌmbər] s legname m, legno da costruzione; cianfrusaglie fpl ‖ intr muoversi pesantemente

lum'ber-jack' s boscaiolo

lum'ber jack'et s giaccone m

lum'ber·man s (-men) (dealer) commerciante m in legname; (man who cuts down lumber) boscaiolo

lum'ber room' s ripostiglio

lum'ber·yard' s deposito legnami

luminar·y ['lumi,neri] s (-ies) luminare m

luminous ['luminəs] adj luminoso

lummox ['lʌməks] s (coll) scimunito

lump [lʌmp] s grumo; mucchio; cumulo; (swelling) bernoccolo; (of sugar) zolletta; (in one's throat) groppo; (coll) stupidone m; in the lump in blocco; nell'insieme ‖ tr mescolare; (to make into lumps) raggrumare; to lump it (coll) mandarla giù

lumpish ['lʌmpɪʃ] adj grumoso; goffo; balordo

lump' sum' s ammontare unico, somma globale

lump·y ['lʌmpi] adj (-ier; -iest) grumoso; (person) pesante, ottuso; (sea) agitato

luna·cy ['lunəsi] s (-cies) pazzia

lunar ['lunər] adj lunare

lu'nar land'ing s allunaggio

lu'nar mod'ule s modulo lunare

lu'nar rov'er s auto f lunare

lunatic ['lunətɪk] adj & s demente mf

lu'natic asy'lum s manicomio

lu'natic fringe' s estremisti mpl fanatici

lunch [lʌntʃ] s (regular midday meal) seconda colazione; (light meal) spuntino, merenda ‖ intr fare colazione; fare uno spuntino

lunch' bas'ket s portavivande m

luncheon ['lʌntʃən] s seconda colazione; pranzo ufficiale

luncheonette [,lʌntʃə'nɛt] s tavola calda

lunch'eon meat' s insaccati mpl

lunch'room' s tavola calda

lung [lʌŋ] s polmone m

lunge [lʌndʒ] s slancio; (fencing) affondo ‖ intr slanciarsi

lurch [lʌrtʃ] s barcollamento; (at close of a game) cappotto; (naut) sbandata; to leave in the lurch piantare

in asso ‖ intr barcollare; (naut) sbandare

lure [lur] s esca; (fig) insidie fpl ‖ tr adescare; to lure away distogliere, sviare

lurid ['lurɪd] adj (fiery) ardente, acceso; sensazionale; (gruesome) orripilante

lurk [lʌrk] intr stare in agguato, nascondersi; (fig) essere latente

luscious ['lʌʃəs] adj delizioso; lussuoso, lussureggiante; voluttuoso

lush [lʌʃ] adj lussureggiante, lussuoso

lust [lʌst] s desiderio sfrenato; libidine f, lussuria ‖ intr—to lust after or for aver sete di

luster ['lʌstər] s (gloss) lustro, lucentezza; (glory) lustro, onore m

lus'ter·ware' s ceramiche smaltate

lustful ['lʌstfəl] adj lussurioso

lustrous ['lʌstrəs] adj lucido

lust·y ['lʌsti] adj (-ier; -iest) vigoroso, gagliardo

lute [lut] s (mus) liuto; (chem) luto

Lutheran ['luθərən] adj & s luterano

luxuriance [lʌg'ʒuri·əns] s rigoglio

luxuriant [lʌg'ʒuri·ənt] adj lussureggiante; (imagery) ridondante

luxuriate [lʌg'ʒuri,et] or [lʌk'ʃuri,et] intr lussureggiare; trovare piacere

luxurious [lʌg'ʒuri·əs] or [lʌk'ʃuri·əs] adj lussuoso, fastoso

luxu·ry ['lʌkʃəri] or ['lʌgʒəri] s (-ries) lusso, sfarzo

lye [lai] s ranno, liscivia

lying ['lai·ɪŋ] adj menzognero ‖ s il mentire

ly'ing-in' hos'pital s clinica ostetrica, maternità f

lymph [lɪmf] s linfa

lymphatic [lɪm'fætɪk] adj linfatico

lynch [lɪntʃ] tr linciare

lynching ['lɪntʃɪŋ] s linciaggio

lynx [lɪŋks] s lince f

lynx-eyed ['lɪŋks,aid] adj dagli occhi di lince

lyonnaise [,lai·ə'nez] s (culin) alla maniera di Lione

lyre [lair] s lira

lyric ['lɪrɪk] adj lirico ‖ s lirica; (words of a song) parole fpl

lyrical ['lɪrɪkəl] adj lirico

lyricism ['lɪrɪ,sɪzəm] s lirismo

lyricist ['lɪrɪsɪst] s (writer of words for songs) paroliere m; (poet) lirico

M

M, m [ɛm] s tredicesima lettera dell'alfabeto inglese

ma'am [mæm] or [mɑm] s (coll) signora

macadam [mə'kædəm] s macadàm m

macadamize [mə'kædə,maiz] tr macadamizzare

macaroni [,mækə'roni] s maccheroni mpl

macaroon [,mækə'run] s amaretto

macaw [mə'kɔ] s ara

mace [mes] s mazza; (spice) macis m & f

mace' bear'er s mazziere m

machination [,mækɪ'neʃən] s macchinazione, macchina

machine [mə'ʃin] s macchina ‖ tr fare a macchina

machine' gun' s mitragliatrice f

machine'-gun' v (pret & pp -gunned; ger -gunning) tr mitragliare

machine'-made' adj fatto a macchina

machiner·y [mə'∫inəri] *s* (**-ies**) macchinario, meccanismo
machine' screw' *s* vite *f* per metallo
machine' shop' *s* officina meccanica
machine' tool' *s* macchina utensile
machinist [mə'∫inɪst] *s* meccanico; (*nav*) secondo macchinista
mackerel ['mækərəl] *s* maccarello
mack'erel sky' *s* cielo a pecorelle
mackintosh ['mækɪn,tɑ∫] *s* impermeabile *m*
mad [mæd] *adj* (**madder; maddest**) (*angry; rabid*) arrabbiato; (*insane; foolish*) pazzo, folle; furioso; **to be mad about** (coll) andar pazzo per; **to drive mad** far impazzire; **to go mad** impazzire; (*said of a dog*) diventare idrofobo
madam ['mædəm] *s* signora
mad'cap' *s* mattoide *m*, rompicollo
madden ['mædən] *tr* (*to make angry*) inferocire; (*to make insane*) fare impazzire
made-to-order ['medtə'ɔrdər] *adj* fatto apposta; (*clothing*) fatto su misura
made'-up' *adj* inventato; (*using cosmetics*) truccato
mad'house' *s* manicomio
mad'man' *s* (**-men'**) pazzo
madness ['mædnɪs] *s* rabbia; pazzia
Madonna lily [mə'dɑnə] *s* giglio
maelstrom ['melstrəm] *s* vortice *m*
magazine ['mægə,zin] or [,mægə'zin] *s* (*periodical*) rivista, giornale *m*; (*warehouse*) magazzino; (*for cartridges*) caricatore *m*; (*for powder*) polveriera; (*naut*) santabarbara; (*phot*) magazzino
maggot ['mægət] *s* larva di dittero
Magi ['medʒaɪ] *spl* Re Magi
magic ['mædʒɪk] *adj* magico ‖ *s* magia; illusionismo; **as if by magic** come per incanto
magician [mə'dʒɪ∫ən] *s* (*entertainer*) illusionista *mf*; (*sorcerer*) mago
magistrate ['mædʒɪs,tret] *s* magistrato
magnanimous [mæg'nænɪməs] *adj* magnanimo
magnesium [mæg'niʃɪ·əm] or [mæg'niʒɪ·əm] *s* magnesio
magnet ['mægnɪt] *s* calamita, magnete *m*
magnetic [mæg'nɛtɪk] *adj* magnetico
magnetism ['mægnɪ,tɪzəm] *s* magnetismo
magnetize ['mægnɪ,taɪz] *tr* calamitare, magnetizzare
magne·to [mæg'nito] *s* (**-tos**) magnete *m*
magnificent [mæg'nɪfɪsənt] *adj* magnifico
magni·fy ['mægnɪ,faɪ] *v* (*pret* & *pp* **-fied**) *tr* ingrandire; (*to exaggerate*) magnificare
mag'nifying glass' *s* lente *f* d'ingrandimento
magnitude ['mægnɪ,tjud] or ['mægnɪ,tud] *s* grandezza
magpie ['mæg,paɪ] *s* gazza
mahlstick ['mɑl,stɪk] or ['mɔl,stɪk] *s* appoggiamano
mahoga·ny [mə'hɑgəni] *s* (**-nies**) mogano

Mahomet [mə'hɑmɪt] *s* Maometto
maid [med] *s* (*girl*) ragazza; (*servant*) cameriera, domestica
maiden ['medən] *s* pulzella
maid'en·hair' *s* (bot) capelvenere *m*
maid'en·head' *s* imene *m*
maidenhood ['medən,hud] *s* verginità *f*
maid'en la'dy *s* zitella
maid'en name' *s* nome *m* da signorina
maid'en voy'age *s* viaggio inaugurale
maid'-in-wait'ing *s* (**maids-in-waiting**) (*of a princess*) damigella d'onore; (*of a queen*) dama d'onore
maid' of hon'or *s* (*attendant at a wedding; attendant of a princess*) damigella d'onore; (*attendant of a queen*) dama d'onore
maid'serv'ant *s* domestica, ancella
mail [mel] *s* posta; (*of armor*) maglia; **by return mail** a volta di corriere ‖ *tr* impostare
mail'bag' *s* sacco postale
mail'boat' *s* battello postale
mail'box' *s* cassetta or buca delle lettere
mail' car' *s* vagone *m* postale
mail' car'rier *s* postino, portalettere *m*
mail'ing list' *s* indirizzario
mail'ing per'mit *s* abbonamento postale
mail'man' *s* (**-men'**) portalettere *m*
mail' or'der *s* ordinazione per corrispondenza
mail'-order house' *s* ditta che fa affari unicamente per corrispondenza
mail'plane' *s* areoplano postale
mail' train' *s* treno postale
maim [mem] *tr* mutilare
main [men] *adj* principale, maggiore ‖ *s* condotta principale; **in the main** principalmente, per lo più
main' clause' *s* proposizione principale
main' course' *s* piatto forte
main' deck' *s* ponte *m* principale
mainland ['men,lænd] or ['menlənd] *s* terra ferma, continente *m*
main' line' *s* (rr) linea principale
mainly ['menli] *adv* principalmente
mainmast ['menmæst], ['men,mæst] or ['men,mɑst] *s* albero maestro
mainsail ['mensəl] or ['men,sel] *s* vela maestra
main'spring' *s* molla motrice; (fig) molla
main'stay' *s* (naut) strallo di maestra; (fig) cardine *m*
main' street' *s* strada principale
maintain [men'ten] *tr* mantenere
maintenance ['mentɪnəns] *s* mantenimento; (*upkeep*) manutenzione
maître d'hôtel [,metər do'tel] *s* (*butler*) maggiordomo; (*headwaiter*) capocameriere *m*
maize [mez] *s* mais *m*
majestic [mə'dʒɛstɪk] *adj* maestoso
majes·ty ['mædʒɪsti] *s* (**-ties**) maestà *f*
major ['medʒər] *adj* maggiore ‖ *s* (educ) specializzazione; (mil) maggiore *m* ‖ *intr* (educ) specializzarsi
major-do·mo [,medʒər'domo] *s* (**-mos**) maggiordomo
ma'jor gen'eral *s* generale *m* di divisione

majori•ty [məˈdʒɑrɪti] or [məˈdʒɔrɪti] adj maggioritario ‖ s (-ties) (being of full age) maggiore età f; (larger number or part) maggioranza; (mil) grado di maggiore

make [mek] s (brand) marca; (form) stile m; produzione; **on the make** (slang) tirando l'acqua al proprio mulino ‖ v (pret & pp made [med]) tr fare; (a train) pigliare; (a circuit) chiudere; essere, e.g., **she will make a good typist** sarà una buona dattilografa; **to make + inf** fare + inf, e.g., **she made him study** lo fece studiare; **to make for** sapere; **to make into** trasformare in; **to make known** far conoscere; **to make of** pensare di; **to make oneself known** darsi a conoscere; **to make out** decifrare; (a prescription) scrivere, preparare; (a check) riempire; **to make over** convertire; (com) trasferire; **to make up** preparare, comporre; (a story) inventare; (lost time) riguadagnare; (typ) impaginare; (theat) truccare ‖ intr essere fatto; **to make away with** rubare; disfarsi di; **to make believe that + ind** far finta di + inf, e.g., **he made believe (that) he was sleeping** fece finta di dormire; **to make for** avvicinarsi a; attaccare; (better relations) contribuire a cementare; **to make much of** (coll) fare le feste a; **to make off** andarsene; **to make off with** svignarsela con; **to make out** (coll) farcela; **to make toward** incamminarsi verso; **to make up** truccarsi; fare la pace; **to make up for** compensare per, supplire a; **to make up to** (coll) ingraziarsi; (coll) fare la corte a

make′-be•lieve′ adj immaginario ‖ s finzione, sembianza

maker [ˈmekər] s fabbricante mf, costruttore m ‖ **Maker** s Fattore m

make′shift′ adj improvvisato, di fortuna ‖ s espediente m, ripiego; (person) tappabuchi mf

make′-up′ s composizione, costituzione; truccatura, cosmetico; (typ) impaginazione; (journ) caratteristica

make′-up man′ s truccatore m

make′-up test′ s esame m di riparazione

make′weight′ s giunta, contentino; (fig) supplemento, di più m

making [ˈmekɪŋ] s fabbricazione; costituzione; causa del successo; **makings** materiale m; (potential) stoffa

maladjusted [ˌmælədˈʒʌstɪd] adj spostato

mala•dy [ˈmælədi] s (-dies) malattia

malaise [mæˈlez] s malessere m

malapropos [ˌmæləprəˈpo] adj inopportuno ‖ adv a sproposito

malaria [məˈlɛrɪ·ə] s malaria

Malay [ˈmele] or [məˈle] adj & s malese mf

malcontent [ˈmælkənˌtɛnt] adj & s malcontento

male [mel] adj & s maschio

malediction [ˌmælɪˈdɪkʃən] s maledizione

malefactor [ˈmælɪˌfæktər] s malfattore m

male′ nurse′ s infermiere m

malevolent [məˈlɛvələnt] adj malevolo

malfeasance [mælˈfizns] s reato di pubblico funzionario

malice [ˈmælɪs] s malizia; (law) dolo; **to bear malice** serbar rancore; **with malice prepense** (law) con premeditazione

malicious [məˈlɪʃəs] adj malizioso, maligno

malign [məˈlaɪn] adj maligno ‖ tr calunniare

malignan•cy [məˈlɪgnənsi] s (-cies) malignità f; (pathol) malignità f

malignant [məˈlɪgnənt] adj maligno

maligni•ty [məˈlɪgnɪti] s (-ties) malignità f

malinger [məˈlɪŋgər] intr fingersi ammalato, darsi malato (per sottrarsi al proprio dovere)

mall [mɔl] or [mæl] s viale m; (strip of land in a boulevard) aiola

mallet [ˈmælɪt] s maglio; (of a stone cutter) mazzuolo

mallow [ˈmælo] s malva

malnutrition [ˌmælnjuˈtrɪʃən] or [ˌmælnuˈtrɪʃən] s malnutrizione

malodorous [mælˈodərəs] adj puzzolente

malpractice [mælˈpræktɪs] s incuria, negligenza; (of physician or lawyer) negligenza colposa

malt [mɔlt] s malto

maltreat [mælˈtrit] tr maltrattare

mamma [ˈmɑmə] or [məˈmɑ] s (coll) mamma

mammal [ˈmæməl] s mammifero

mammalian [mæˈmelɪ·ən] adj & s mammifero

mammoth [ˈmæməθ] adj mastodontico ‖ s mammut m

man [mæn] s (men [mɛn]) uomo; (in chess) pedina; (in checkers) pezzo; **a man uno**, e.g., **a man can get lost in this town** uno può perdersi in questa città; **as one man** come un sol uomo; **man alive!** accidenti! **man and wife** marito e moglie; **to be one's own man** essere completamente indipendente ‖ v (pret & pp manned; ger manning) tr (a boat) equipaggiare; (a fortress) guarnire; (a cannon) maneggiare

man′ about town′ s vitaiolo

manacle [ˈmænəkəl] s—**manacles** manette fpl ‖ tr ammanettare

manage [ˈmænɪdʒ] tr (a business) gestire; (e.g., a tool) maneggiare ‖ intr sbrogliarsela; **to manage to** fare in modo di; ingegnarsi a; **to manage to get along** barcamenarsi

manageable [ˈmænɪdʒəbəl] adj maneggevole

management [ˈmænɪdʒmənt] s direzione, gestione; (executives collectively) classe f dirigente; direzione; (college course) economia aziendale

manager [ˈmænədʒər] s direttore m, gerente mf; (theat) impresario; (sports) procuratore m, manager m

managerial [ˌmænəˈdʒɪrɪ·əl] adj direttoriale, imprenditoriale

man'aging ed'itor *s* gerente *m* responsàbile, redattore *m* in capo

mandate ['mændet] *s* mandato || *tr* dare in mandato a

mandatory ['mændə‚tori] *adj* obbligatorio

mandolin ['mændəlın] *s* mandolino

mandrake ['mændrek] *s* mandragola

mandrel ['mændrəl] *s* (mach) mandrino

mane [men] *s* criniera

maneuver [mə'nuvər] *s* manovra || *tr* manovrare || *intr* manovrare; (aer, nav) evoluire; (fig) intrigare

manful ['mænfəl] *adj* maschile, risoluto

manganese ['mæŋgə‚nis] *or* ['mæŋgə‚niz] *s* manganese *m*

mange [mendʒ] *s* rogna

manger ['mendʒər] *s* presepio

mangle ['mæŋgəl] *tr* straziare, lacerare

man·gy ['mendʒi] *adj* (-gier; -giest) rognoso; (*squalid*) misero

man'han'dle *tr* malmenare, maltrattare

man'hole' *s* passo d'uomo, pozzetto

manhood ['mænhʊd] *s* virilità *f*; uomini *mpl*, umanità *f*

man'hunt' *s* caccia all'uomo

mania ['menɪ‚ə] *s* mania

maniac ['menɪ‚æk] *adj & s* maniaco

manicure ['mænɪ‚kjur] *s* (*treatment*) manicure *f*; (*manicurist*) manicure *mf* || *tr* (*a person*) curare le mani di; (*the hands*) curare

manicurist ['mænɪ‚kjurɪst] *s* manicurista *mf*, manicure *mf*

manifest ['mænɪ‚fest] *adj* manifesto || *s* (naut) manifesto di carico || *tr* manifestare

manifes·to [‚mænɪ'festo] *s* (-toes) manifesto

manifold ['mænɪ‚fold] *adj* molteplice || *s* copia; carta velina; (aut, mach) collettore *m*

manikin ['mænɪkɪn] *s* manichino; (*dwarf*) nano

man' in the moon' *s* faccia di uomo che appare nella luna piena

man' in the street' *s* uomo qualunque, uomo della strada

manipulate [mə'nɪpjə‚let] *tr* manipolare

man'kind' *s* genere umano || **man'kind'** *s* il sesso maschile

manliness ['mænlɪnɪs] *s* virilità *f*

man·ly ['mænli] *adj* (-lier; -liest) maschio, virile

manned' space'ship *s* astronave pilotata

mannequin ['mænɪkɪn] *s* (*figure*) manichino; (*person*) indossatrice *f*

manner ['mænər] *s* maniera; **by all manner of means** in tutti i modi; **in a manner of speaking** in una certa maniera; **in the manner of** alla moda di; **manners** maniere, *fpl*, educazione; **to the manner born** avvezzo sin dalla nascita

mannish ['mænɪʃ] *adj* maschile; (*woman*) mascolino

man' of God' *s* santo; profeta *m*; (*priest*) uomo al servizio di Dio

man' of let'ters *s* letterato

man' of means' *s* uomo danaroso

man' of parts' *s* uomo di talento

man' of straw' *s* uomo di paglia

man' of the world' *s* uomo di mondo

man-of-war [‚mænəv'wɔr] *s* (**men-of-war** [‚menəv'wɔr] *s* nave *f* da guerra

manor ['mænər] *s* maniero; feudo

man'or house' *s* maniero, palazzo

man' o'verboard *interj* uomo in mare!

man'pow'er *s* manodopera; (mil) effettivo

mansard ['mænsɑrd] *s* mansarda

man'serv'ant *s* (**men'serv'ants**) servo, servitore *m*

mansion ['mænʃən] *s* palazzo, palazzina; (*manor house*) maniero

man'slaugh'ter *s* omicidio colposo

mantel ['mæntəl] *s* parte *f* anteriore dei pilastri del camino; (*shelf above it*) mensola

man'tel·piece' *s* mensola del camino

man'tis shrimp' ['mæntɪs] *s* canocchia

mantle ['mæntəl] *s* mantello, cappa || *tr* ammantare; (*to conceal*) nascondere || *intr* (*to blush*) arrossire

manual ['mænju‚əl] *adj* manuale || *s* (*book*) manuale *m*; (mil) esercizio; (mus) tastiera d'organo

man'ual train'ing *s* istruzione nelle arti e mestieri

manufacture [‚mænjə'fæktʃər] *s* fabbricazione; (*thing manufactured*) manufatto || *tr* fabbricare

manufacturer [‚mænjə'fæktʃərər] *s* fabbricante *mf*, industriale *m*

manure [mə'njur] *or* [mə'nur] *s* letame *m* || *tr* concimare

manuscript ['mænjə‚skrɪpt] *adj & s* manoscritto

many ['meni] *adj & pron* molto; **a good many or a great many** un buon numero; **as many . . . as** tanti . . . quanti; **as many as** fino a, e.g., **they sell as many as five thousand dozen** vendono fino a cinquemila dozzine; **how many** quanti; **many a** molti, e.g., **many a day** molti giorni; **many another** molti altri; **many more** molti di più; **so many** tanti; **too many** troppi; **twice as many** altrettanti, il doppio

many-sided ['meni‚saɪdɪd] *adj* multilaterale; versatile

map [mæp] *s* mappa; (*of a city*) piano || *v* (*pret & pp* **mapped**; *ger* **mapping**) *tr* tracciare la mappa di; mostrare sulla mappa; **to map out** fare il piano di

maple ['mepəl] *s* acero

maquette [mɑ'ket] *s* plastico

mar [mɑr] *v* (*pret & pp* **marred**; *ger* **marring**) *tr* deturpare, sfigurare

maraud [mə'rɔd] *tr & intr* predare

marauder [mə'rɔdər] *s* predone *m*

marble ['mɑrbəl] *adj* marmoreo || *s* marmo; (*little ball of glass*) bilia; **marbles** bilie *fpl*; **to lose one's marbles** (slang) mancare una rotella a qlcu || *tr* marmorizzare

march [mɑrtʃ] *s* marcia; (hist) marca; **to steal a march on** guadagnare il vantaggio su || *tr* far marciare || *intr* marciare || **March** *s* marzo

marchioness ['marʃənis] *s* marchesa

mare [mer] *s* (*female horse*) cavalla; (*female donkey*) asina

margarine ['mɑrdʒərɪn] *s* margarina

margin ['mɑrdʒɪn] *s* margine *m;* (econ) scoperto

mar'gin stop' *s* marginatore *m*

marigold ['mærɪ ‚gold] *s* fiorrancio

marihuana or **marijuana** ['mɑrɪ- 'hwɑnə] *s* marijuana

marina [mə'rinə] *s* porto turistico di imbarcazioni, porticciolo turistico

marinate ['mærɪ ‚net] *tr* marinare

marine [mə'rin] *adj* marino, marittimo || *s* marina; soldato di fanteria da sbarco; **marines** fanteria da sbarco; **tell that to the marines!** (coll) va a raccontarlo ai frati!

mariner ['mærɪnər] *s* marinaio

marionette [‚mærɪ-ə'nɛt] *s* marionetta

mar'ital sta'tus ['mærɪtəl] *s* stato civile

maritime ['mærɪ ‚taɪm] *adj* marittimo

marjoram ['mɑrdʒərəm] *s* origano; (*sweet marjoram*) maggiorana

mark [mɑrk] *s* segno; (*brand*) marca; (*of punctuation*) punto; (*in an examination*) voto; (*sign made by illiterate person*) croce *f;* (*landmark*) segnale *m;* (*target*) bersaglio; (*spot*) macchia; (*starting point in a race*) linea di partenza; (*of confidence*) voto; (*coin*) marco; impronta; **to be beside the mark** essere fuori del seminato; **to hit the mark** colpire il bersaglio; **to leave one's mark** lasciare la propria impronta; **to make one's mark** raggiungere il successo; **to miss the mark** fallire il colpo; **to toe the mark** mettersi in fila; filare diritto || *tr* marcare, segnare, contrassegnare; (*a student*) dar il voto a; (*a test*) esaminare; improntare; notare, avvertire; **to mark down** mettere in iscritto; ribassare il prezzo di

mark'down' ['mɑrk ‚daʊn] *s* riduzione di prezzo

market ['mɑrkɪt] *s* mercato; **to bear the market** giocare al ribasso; **to bull the market** giocare al rialzo; **to play the market** giocare in borsa; **to put on the market** lanciare sul mercato || *tr* mettere sul mercato

marketable ['mɑrkɪtəbəl] *adj* commerciabile, vendibile

marketing ['mɑrkɪtɪŋ] *s* compravendita; marketing *m*

mar'ket-place' *s* piazza del mercato

mar'ket price' *s* prezzo corrente

mark'ing gauge' ['mɑrkɪŋ] *s* graffietto

marks'man *s* (**-men**) tiratore *m;* **a good marksman** un tiratore scelto

marksmanship ['mɑrksmən ‚ʃɪp] *s* qualità *f* di tiratore scelto

mark'up' *s* margine *m* di rivendita

marl [mɑrl] *s* marna || *tr* marnare

marmalade ['mɑrmə ‚led] *s* marmellata d'arance

marmot ['mɑrmət] *s* marmotta

maroon [mə'run] *adj* & *s* marrone *m* || *tr* abbandonare (*in un luogo deserto*)

marquee [mɑr'ki] *s* pensilina

marquess ['mɑrkwɪs] *s* marchese *m*

marque•try ['mɑrkətri] *s* (**-tries**) intarsio

marquis ['mɑrkwɪs] *s* marchese *m*

marquise [mɑr'kiz] *s* marchesa; (Brit) pensilina

marriage ['mærɪdʒ] *s* matrimonio

marriageable ['mærɪdʒəbəl] *adj* adatto al matrimonio; (*woman*) nubile

mar'riage por'tion *s* dote *f*

mar'riage rate' *s* nuzialità *f*

mar'ried life' *s* vita coniugale

marrow ['mæro] *s* midollo

mar•ry ['mæri] *v* (*pret & pp* **-ried**) *tr* sposare; **to get married to** sposarsi con || *intr* sposarsi; **to marry into** (*e.g., a noble family*) imparentarsi con; **to marry the second time** risposarsi

Mars [mɑrz] *s* Marte *m*

Marseilles [mɑr'selz] *s* Marsiglia

marsh [mɑrʃ] *s* palude *f,* lama

mar•shal ['mɑrʃəl] *s* direttore *m* di una sfilata; maestro di cerimonie; (mil) maresciallo; (U.S.A.) ufficiale *m* di giustizia || *v* (*pret & pp* **-shaled** or **-shalled**) *ger* **-shaling** or **-shalling**) *tr* introdurre cerimoniosamente; mettere in buon ordine

marsh' mal'low *s* (bot) altea

marsh'mal'low *s* dolce *m* di gelatina e zucchero

marsh•y ['mɑrʃi] *adj* (**-ier; -iest**) paludoso, palustre

marten ['mɑrtən] *s* (*Martes martes*) martora; (*Martes zibellina*) zibellino

martial ['mɑrʃəl] *adj* marziale

mar'tial law' *s* legge *f* marziale

Martian ['mɑrʃən] *adj* & *s* marziano

martin ['mɑrtɪn] *s* rondicchio

martinet [‚mɑrtɪ'nɛt] or ['mɑrtɪ ‚nɛt] *s* pignolo

martyr ['mɑrtər] *s* martire *mf*

martyrdom ['mɑrtərdəm] *s* martirio

mar•vel ['mɑrvəl] *s* meraviglia || *v* (*pret & pp* **-veled** or **-velled**; *ger* **-veling** or **-velling**) *intr* meravigliarsi; **to marvel at** stupirsi di, meravigliarsi di

marvelous ['mɑrvələs] *adj* meraviglioso

Marxist ['mɑrksɪst] *adj* & *s* marxista *mf*

mascara [mæs'kærə] *s* bistro, rimmel *m*

mascot ['mæskət] *s* mascotte *f*

masculine ['mæskjəlɪn] *adj* & *s* maschile *m*

mash [mæʃ] *s* (*crushed mass*) poltiglia; (*to form wort*) decotto d'orzo germinato; (*e.g., for poultry*) intriso || *tr* schiacciare; impastare

mashed' pota'toes *spl* purè *m* di patate

masher ['mæʃər] *s* utensile *m* per schiacciare; (slang) pappagallo

mask [mæsk] or [mɑsk] *s* maschera; (phot) mascherina || *tr* mascherare; (phot) mettere una mascherina a || *intr* mascherarsi

masked' ball' *s* ballo in maschera

mason ['mesən] *s* muratore *m* || **Mason** *s* massone *m*

mason•ry ['mesənri] *s* (**-ries**) arte *f* del

masquerade   198   **matter**

muratore; muratura || **Masonry** *s* massoneria

masquerade [,mæskə'red] or [,mɑskə-'red] *s* mascherata; *(disguise)* maschera; *(pretense)* finzione || *intr* mascherarsi; **to masquerade as** mascherarsi da; farsi passare per

mass [mæs] *s* massa; *(celebration of the Eucharist)* messa; **in the mass** nell'insieme; **the masses** le masse || *tr* ammassare || *intr* ammassarsi, accumularsi

massacre ['mæsəkər] *s* massacro, strage *f* || *tr* massacrare, trucidare

massage [mə'sɑʒ] *s* massaggio || *tr* massaggiare

masseur [mæ'sœr] *s* massaggiatore *m*

masseuse [mæ'sœz] *s* massaggiatrice *f*

massive ['mæsɪv] *adj* massiccio; *(e.g., dose)* massivo; solido

mass' me'dia ['midɪ-ə] *s* mezzi *mpl* di comunicazione di massa

mass' meet'ing *s* assemblea popolare; adunanza in massa

mass' produc'tion *s* produzione in serie

mast [mæst] or [mɑst] *s (post)* palo; *(agr)* ghiande *fpl*, faggiole *fpl*; *(naut)* albero; **before the mast** come marinaio semplice

master ['mæstər] or ['mɑstər] *s (employer)* padrone *m*; *(male head of household)* capo di casa; *(man who possesses some special skill)* maestro; *(title of respect for a boy)* signorino; *(naut)* capitano || *tr* dominare; *(a language)* possedere

mas'ter bed'room *s* camera da letto padronale

mas'ter blade' *s* foglia maestra (di una balestra)

mas'ter build'er *s* capomastro

masterful ['mæstərfəl] or ['mɑstərfəl] *adj* autoritario; provetto, magistrale

mas'ter key' *s* chiave maestra

masterly ['mæstərlɪ] or ['mɑstərlɪ] *adj* magistrale || *adv* magistralmente

mas'ter mechan'ic *s* mastro meccanico

mas'ter·mind' *s* mente direttiva || *tr* organizzare, dirigere

mas'ter of cer'emonies *s* maestro di cerimonia; *(in a night club, radio, etc.)* presentatore *m*

mas'ter·piece' *s* capolavoro

mas'ter ser'geant *s* (mil) sergente *m* maggiore

mas'ter stroke' *s* colpo da maestro

mas'ter·work' *s* capolavoro

master·y ['mæstərɪ] or ['mɑstərɪ] *s* (-ies) *(command of a subject)* dominio; *(skill)* maestria

mast'head' *s* (journ) titolo; (naut) testa d'albero

masticate ['mæstɪ,ket] *tr* masticare

mastiff ['mæstɪf] or ['mɑstɪf] *s* mastino

masturbate ['mæstər,bet] *tr* masturbare || *intr* masturbarsi

mat [mæt] *s (for floor)* tappeto, stuoia; *(under a dish)* tondo, sottocoppa, centrino; *(before a door)* stoino, zerbino; *(around a picture)* bordo di cartone; (sports) materas-

sino; (typ) flan *m;* flano || *v (pret & pp* matted; *ger* matting) *tr* coprire di stuoie; arruffare || *intr* arruffarsi

match [mætʃ] *s (counterpart)* uguale *m;* *(suitably associated pair)* paio; *(light)* fiammifero; *(wick)* miccia; *(prospective mate)* partito; (sports) partita, gara; **to be a match for** essere pari a, fare fronte a; **to meet one's match** trovare un degno rivale || *tr* uguagliare, pareggiare; *(colors)* combinare; *(in pairs)* appaiare; giocarsi, e.g., **to match s.o. for the drinks** giocarsi le bevande con qlcu || *intr* corrispondersi, fare il paio

match'box' *s* scatola di fiammiferi; *(of wax matches)* scatola di cerini

matchless ['mætʃlɪs] *adj* incomparabile, senza pari

match'mak'er *s* paraninfo

mate [met] *s* compagno; *(husband or wife)* consorte *mf;* *(to a female)* maschio; *(to a male)* femmina; (chess) scacco matto; (naut) primo ufficiale || *tr* appaiare; (chess) dar scacco matto a; **to be well mated** esser ben appaiato || *intr* accoppiarsi

material [mə'tɪrɪ-əl] *adj* materiale; importante || *s* materiale *m*, materia; *(cloth, fabric)* tela, stoffa; **materials** occorrente *m*

materialist [mə'tɪrɪ-əlɪst] *s* materialista *mf*

materialize [mə'tɪrɪ-ə,laɪz] *intr* materializzarsi

matériel [mə,tɪrɪ'ɛl] *s* materiale *m;* materiale bellico

maternal [mə'tʌrnəl] *adj* materno

maternity [mə'tʌrnɪti] *s* maternità *f*

mater'nity ward' *s* maternità *f*

mathematical [,mæθɪ'mætɪkəl] *adj* matematico

mathematician [,mæθɪmə'tɪʃən] *s* matematico

mathematics [,mæθɪ'mætɪks] *s* matematica

matinée [,mætɪ'ne] *s* mattinata, diurna

matins ['mætɪnz] *spl* mattutino

matriarch ['metrɪ,ɑrk] *s* matrona dignitosa; donna che possiede l'autorità matriarcale

matricidal [,metrɪ'saɪdəl] or [,mætrɪ-'saɪdəl] *adj* matricida

matricide ['metrɪ,saɪd] or ['mætrɪ-,saɪd] *s (act)* matricidio; *(person)* matricida *mf*

matriculate [mə'trɪkjə,let] *tr* immatricolare || *intr* immatricolarsi

matriculation [mə,trɪkjə'leʃən] *s* immatricolazione, iscrizione

matrimonial [,mætrɪ'monɪ-əl] *adj* matrimoniale

matrimo·ny ['mætrɪ,monɪ] *s* (-nies) *f* matrimonio

ma·trix ['metrɪks] or ['mætrɪks] *s* (-trices [trɪ,siz] or -trixes) matrice *f*

matron ['metrən] *s* matrona; direttrice *f;* guardiana

matronly ['metrənlɪ] *adj* matronale

matter ['mætər] *s (physical substance)* materia; *(pus)* materia; *(affair, busi-*

ness) faccenda; (*material of a book*) contenuto; (*reason*) motivo; (*copy for printer*) manoscritto; (*printed material*) stampati *mpl*; **a matter of** un caso di; **for that matter** per quanto riguarda ciò; **in the matter** al soggetto; **no matter** non importa; **no matter how** non importa come; **no matter when** non importa quando; **no matter where** non importa dove; **what is the matter?** cosa succede?; **what is the matter with you?** cosa ha? || *intr* importare

mat'ter of course' *s*—**as a matter of course** come se nulla fosse, come se fosse una cosa naturale

mat'ter of fact' *s*—**as a matter of fact** in realtà, a onor del vero

matter-of-fact ['mætərəv‚fækt] *adj* prosaico, pratico

mattock ['mætək] *s* piccone *m*

mattress ['mætrɪs] *s* materasso

mature [mə't/ur] or [mə'tur] *adj* maturo; (*due*) scaduto || *tr* maturare || *intr* maturare; (com) scadere

maturity [mə't/urɪti] or [mə'turɪti] *s* maturità *f*; (com) scadenza

maudlin ['mɔdlɪn] *adj* sentimentale, lagrimoso; piagnucoloso e ubriaco

maul [mɔl] *tr* maltrattare, bistrattare

maulstick ['mɔl‚stɪk] *s* appoggiamano

maundy ['mɔndi] *s* lavanda

Maun'dy Thurs'day *s* giovedì santo

mausole·um [‚mɔsə'li-əm] *s* (**-ums** or **-a** [ə]) mausoleo

maw [mɔ] *s* (e.g., *of a hog*) stomaco; (*of carnivorous mammal*) fauci *fpl*; (*of fowl*) gozzo; (fig) bocca, fauci *fpl*

mawkish ['mɔkɪ/] *adj* (*sickening*) nauseante; (*sentimental*) svenevole

maxim ['mæksɪm] *s* massima

maximum ['mæksɪməm] *adj* & *s* massimo

may [me] *v aux*—**it may be** può essere; **may I come in?** si può?; **may you be happy!** possa tu essere felice! || **May** *s* maggio

maybe ['mebi] *adv* forse

May' Day' *s* primo maggio; festa della primavera; (hist) calendimaggio (*in Florence*)

mayhem ['mehem] or ['me·əm] *s* mutilazione dolosa

mayonnaise [‚me·ə'nez] *s* maionese *f*

mayor ['me·ər] or [mer] *s* sindaco

mayoress ['me·ərɪs] or ['merɪs] *s* donna sindaco

May'pole *s* maio, maggio, palo per le danze di calendimaggio

May'pole dance' *s* ballo figurato con nastri per la festa di primavera

May' queen' *s* reginetta di maggio

maze [mez] *s* dedalo, labirinto

me [mi] *pron* me; mi; **to me** mi; **a me** mi

meadow ['medo] *s* prato

mead'ow·land' *s* prateria

meager ['migər] *adj* magro

meal [mil] *s* (*food*) pasto; (*unbolted grain*) farina

meal'time' *s* ora del pasto

mean [min] *adj* (*intermediate*) medio;

(*low in rank*) basso, umile; (*shabby*) misero; (*of poor quality*) inferiore; (*stingy*) taccagno; (*nasty*) villano; (*vicious, as a horse*) intrattabile; (coll) indisposto; (coll) vergognoso; (slang) splendido; **no mean** eccellente || *s* media, termine medio; **by all means** certamente, senza dubbio; **by means of** per mezzo di; **by no means** in nessuna maniera; **means** beni *mpl*; (*agency*) mezzo, maniera; **to live on one's means** vivere di rendita || *v* (*pret & pp* **meant** [ment]) *tr* significare, voler dire; **to mean to** pensare || *intr*—**to mean well** aver buone intenzioni

meander [mɪ'ændər] *s* meandro || *intr* serpeggiare, vagare

meaning ['minɪŋ] *s* senso, significato

meaningful ['minɪŋfəl] *adj* significativo

meaningless ['minɪŋlɪs] *adj* senza senso, senza significato

meanness ['minnɪs] *s* viltà *f*, bassezza; (*stinginess*) meschinità *f*; (*lowliness*) umiltà *f*, povertà

mean'time' *s*—**in the meantime** nel frattempo || *adv* frattanto, intanto

mean'while' *s* & *adv* var of **meantime**

measles ['mizəlz] *s* morbillo; (*German measles*) rosolia

mea·sly ['mizli] *adj* (**-slier**; **-sliest**) col morbillo; (coll) miserabile

measurable ['meʒərəbəl] *adj* misurabile

measure ['meʒər] *s* misura; (*legislative bill*) progetto di legge; (mus) battuta; **in a measure** in un certo senso; **to take the measure of** prendere le misure di; giudicare accuratamente || *tr* misurare; (*a distance*) percorrere; **to measure out** somministrare || *intr* misurare; **to measure up to** essere all'altezza di

measurement ['meʒərmənt] *s* misura; **to take s.o.'s measurements** prendere le misure di qlcu

meas'uring cup' *s* vetro graduato

meat [mit] *s* carne *f*; (*food in general*) cibo; (*of nut*) gheriglio; (fig) sostanza, midollo

meat'ball' *s* polpetta

meat' grind'er *s* tritacarne *m*

meat' loaf' *s* polpettone *m*

meat' mar'ket *s* macelleria

meat·y ['miti] *adj* (**-ier**; **-iest**) carnoso, polputo; (fig) sostanzioso

Mecca ['mekə] *s* la Mecca; **the Mecca** (fig) la Mecca

mechanic [mɪ'kænɪk] *s* meccanico; (aut) motorista *m*

mechanical [mɪ'kænɪkəl] *adj* meccanico; (*machinelike*) (fig) macchinale

mechan'ical engineer'ing *s* ingegneria meccanica

mechan'ical pen'cil *s* matita automatica

mechanics [mɪ'kænɪks] *s* meccanica

mechanism ['mekə‚nɪzəm] *s* meccanismo, congegno

mechanize ['mekə‚naɪz] *tr* meccanizzare

medal ['medəl] *s* medaglia

medallion [mɪ'dæljən] *s* medaglione *m*

meddle ['mɛdəl] *intr* intromettersi

meddler ['mɛdlər] *s* ficcanaso

meddlesome ['mɛdəlsəm] *adj* invadente, indiscreto

median ['midɪ·ən] *adj* medio, mediano || *s* punto medio, numero medio

me′dian strip′ *s* spartitraffico

mediate ['midɪ‚et] *tr* (*a dispute*) comporre; (*parties*) pacificare || *intr* (*to be in the middle*) mediare; fare da paciere

mediation [‚midɪ'eʃən] *s* mediazione

mediator ['midɪ‚etər] *s* mediatore *m*

medical ['mɛdɪkəl] *adj* medico; (*student*) di medicina

medicinal [mə'dɪsɪnəl] *adj* medicinale

medicine ['mɛdɪsɪn] *s* medicina

med′icine cab′inet *s* armadietto farmaceutico

med′icine kit′ *s* cassetta farmaceutica

med′icine man′ *s* (**men′**) stregone indiano

medieval [‚midɪ'ivəl] or [‚mɛdɪ'ivəl] *adj* medievale

medievalist [‚midɪ'ivəlɪst] or [‚mɛdɪ'ivəlɪst] *s* medievalista *mf*

mediocre ['midɪ‚okər] or [‚midɪ'okər] *adj* mediocre

mediocri·ty [‚midɪ'akrɪti] *s* (**-ties**) mediocrità *f*

meditate ['mɛdɪ‚tet] *tr & intr* meditare

meditation [‚mɛdɪ'teʃən] *s* meditazione

Mediterranean [‚mɛdɪtə'renɪ·ən] *adj & s* Mediterraneo

medi·um ['midɪ·əm] *adj* medio; (*heat*) moderato; (*meat*) cotto moderatamente || *s* (**-ums** or **-a** [ə]) (*middle state; mean*) media; mezzo; (*in spiritualism*) medium *m*; **media** (*of communication*) media *mpl*; **through the medium of** per mezzo di

medlar ['mɛdlər] *s* (*tree*) nespolo; (*fruit*) nespola

medley ['mɛdli] *s* farragine *f*, mescolanza; (*mus*) pot-pourri *m*

medul·la [mɪ'dʌlə] *s* (**-lae** [li]) midollo

meek [mik] *adj* mansueto, umile

meekness ['miknɪs] *s* mansuetudine *f*

meerschaum ['mɪrʃəm] or ['mɪrʃəm] *s* schiuma; pipa di schiuma

meet [mit] *adj* conveniente || *s* incontro || *v* (*pret & pp* **met** [mɛt]) *tr* incontrare, incontrarsi con; (*to become acquainted with*) fare la conoscenza di; riunirsi con; (*to cope with*) sopperire a; (*said of a public carrier*) fare coincidenza con; andar incontro a; (*one's obligations*) far fronte a; (*bad luck*) avere; **to meet the eyes of** presentarsi agli occhi di || *intr* incontrarsi; riunirsi; conoscersi; **till we meet again** arrivederci; **to meet with** incontrare, incontrarsi con; (*an accident*) avere; (*said of a public carrier*) fare coincidenza con

meeting ['mitɪŋ] *s* riunione, ritrovo; seduta, convegno; (*political*) comizio; (*e.g., of two rivers*) confluenza; duello

meet′ing of the minds′ *s* accordo, consonanza di voleri

meet′ing place′ *s* luogo di riunione

megacycle ['mɛgə‚saɪkəl] *s* megaciclo

megaphone ['mɛgə‚fon] *s* megafono, portavoce *m*

megohm ['mɛg‚om] *s* megaohm *m*

melancholia [‚mɛlən'kolɪ·ə] *s* melanconia, malinconia

melanchol·y ['mɛlən‚kɑli] *adj* malinconico || *s* (**-ies**) malinconia

melee ['mele] or ['méle] *s* (*fight*) mischia; confusione

mellow ['mɛlo] *adj* (*fruit*) maturo; (*wine*) pastoso; (*voice*) soave, melodioso || *tr* raddolcire || *intr* raddolcirsi

melodic [mɪ'lɑdɪk] *adj* melodico

melodious [mɪ'lodɪ·əs] *adj* melodioso

melodramatic [‚mɛlədrə'mætɪk] *adj* melodrammatico

melo·dy ['mɛlədi] *s* (**-dies**) melodia

melon ['mɛlən] *s* melone *m*, popone *m*

melt [mɛlt] *tr* sciogliere; (*metals*) fondere; (*fig*) intenerire || *intr* sciogliersi; fondersi; (*fig*) intenerirsi; **to melt away** svanire; **to melt into** convertirsi in, diventare; (*tears*) struggersi in

melt′ing pot′ *s* crogiolo

member ['mɛmbər] *s* membro

membership ['mɛmbər‚ʃɪp] *s* associazione; numero di membri

membrane ['mɛmbren] *s* membrana

memen·to [mɪ'mɛnto] *s* (**-tos** or **-toes**) oggetto ricordo

mem·o ['mɛmo] *s* (**-os**) (coll) memorandum *m*

memoir ['mɛmwɑr] *s* memoria, memoriale *m*; biografia; **memoirs** memorie *fpl*

memoran·dum [‚mɛmə'rændəm] *s* (**-dums** or **-da** [də]) memorandum *m*

memorial [mɪ'morɪ·əl] *adj* commemorativo || *s* sacrario; (*petition*) memoriale *m*

Memo′rial Day′ *s* giorno dei caduti

memorialize [mɪ'morɪ·ə‚laɪz] *tr* commemorare

memorize ['mɛmə‚raɪz] *tr* imparare a memoria

memo·ry ['mɛməri] *s* (**-ries**) memoria; **to commit to memory** imparare a memoria

menace ['mɛnɪs] *s* minaccia || *tr & intr* minacciare

ménage [me'naʒ] *s* casa; (*housekeeping*) economia domestica

menagerie [mə'næʒəri] or [mə'nædʒəri] *s* serraglio

mend [mɛnd] *s* riparo; **to be on the mend** migliorare || *tr* (*to repair*) raccomodare, riparare; (*to patch*) rammendare; (fig) correggere || *intr* correggersi

mendacious [mɛn'deʃəs] *adj* mendace

mendicant ['mɛndɪkənt] *adj & s* mendicante *mf*

menfolk ['mɛn‚fok] *spl* uomini *mpl*

menial ['minɪ·əl] *adj* basso, servile || *s* servitore *m*, servo

menses ['mɛnsiz] *spl* mestruazione, mestrui *mpl*

men′s′ fur′nishings *spl* articoli *mpl* d'abbigliamento maschile

men′s′ room′ *s* gabinetto per signori

menstruate ['menstru̇‚et] *intr* avere le mestruazioni

men'tal arith'metic ['mentəl] *s* calcolo mentale

men'tal hos'pital *s* manicomio

men'tal ill'ness *s* malattia mentale

men'tal reserva'tion *s* riserva mentale

men'tal test' *s* test *m* mentale

mention ['menʃən] *s* menzione || *tr* menzionare; **don't mention it** non c'è di che

menu ['menju] or ['menju] *s* menu *m*, lista

meow [mɪ'au] *s* miagolio || *intr* miagolare

Mephistophelian [‚mefɪstə'filɪ‚ən] *adj* mefistofelico

mercantile ['mʌrkən‚til] or ['mʌrkən‚tɪl] *adj* mercantile

mercenar·y ['mʌrsə‚neri] *adj* mercenario || *s* (**-ies**) mercenario

merchandise ['mʌrtʃən‚daɪz] *s* mercanzia, merce *f*

merchant ['mʌrtʃənt] *adj* mercantile || *s* mercante.*m*, commerciante *mf*

mer'chant-man *s* (**-men**) mercantile *m*

mer'chant marine' *s* marina mercantile

merciful ['mʌrsɪfəl] *adj* misericordioso

merciless ['mʌrsɪlɪs] *adj* spietato

mercu·ry ['mʌrkjəri] *s* (**-ries**) mercurio || **Mercury** *s* Mercurio

mer·cy ['mʌrsi] *s* (**-cies**) misericordia; **at the mercy of** alla mercé di

mere [mɪr] *adj* mero, puro

meretricious [‚merɪ'trɪʃəs] *adj* vistoso, chiassoso, sgargiante; artificiale, falso, finto

merge [mʌrdʒ] *tr* fondere || *intr* fondersi; (*said of two roads*) convergere; **to merge into** convertirsi lentamente in

merger ['mʌrdʒər] *s* fusione

meridian [mə'rɪdɪ‚ən] *adj* meridiano, culminante || *s* meridiano; apogeo

meringue [mə'ræŋ] *s* meringa

merit ['merɪt] *s* merito || *tr* meritare

meritorious [‚merɪ'torɪ‚əs] *adj* meritorio

merlon ['mʌrlən] *s* merlo

mermaid ['mʌr‚med] *s* sirena

mer'man' *s* (**-men'**) tritone *m*

merriment ['merɪmənt] *s* allegria

mer·ry ['meri] *adj* (**-rier; -riest**) allegro, giocondo; **to make merry** divertirsi

Mer'ry Christ'mas *interj* Buon Natale!

mer'ry-go-round' *s* giostra, carosello; (*of parties*) serie interrotta

mer'ry-mak'er *s* festaiolo

mesh [meʃ] *s* (*network*) rete *f*; (*each open space of net*) maglia; (*mach*) ingranaggio; **meshes** rete *f* || *tr* irretire; (*mach*) ingranare || *intr* irretirsi; (*mach*) ingranarsi

mess [mes] *s* (*dirty condition*) disordine *m*; (*meal for a group of people*) mensa, rancio; porzione; **to get into a mess** mettersi nei pasticci; **to make a mess of** rovinare || *tr* sporcare; disordinare; rovinare || *intr* mangiare in comune; **to mess around** (coll) perdersi in cose inutili

message ['mesɪdʒ] *s* messaggio

messenger ['mesəndʒər] *s* messaggero; (*person who goes on an errand*) fattorino; (mil) portaordini *m*

mess' hall' *s* mensa

Messiah [mə'saɪ‚ə] *s* Messia *m*

mess' kit' *s* gavetta, gamella

mess'mate' *s* compagno di rancio

mess' of pot'tage ['patɪdʒ] *s* (Bib & fig) piatto di lenticchie

Messrs. ['mesərz] *pl* of **Mr.**

mess·y ['mesi] *adj* (**-ier; -iest**) disordinato; sporco

metal ['metəl] *adj* metallico || *s* metallo

metallic [mɪ'tælɪk] *adj* metallico

metallurgy ['metə‚lʌrdʒi] *s* metallurgia

met'al pol'ish *s* lucido per metalli

met'al·work' *s* lavoro di metallo

metamorpho·sis [‚metə'mɔrfəsɪs] *s* **-ses** [‚siz]) metamorfosi *f*

metaphony [mə'tæfəni] *s* metafonia, metafonesi *f*

metaphor ['metəfər] or ['metə‚fɔr] *s* metafora

metaphorical [‚metə'fɑrɪkəl] or [‚metə'fɔrɪkəl] *adj* metaforico

metathe·sis [mɪ'tæθɪsɪs] *s* (**-ses** [‚siz]) metatesi *f*

mete [mit] *tr*—**to mete out** distribuire

meteor ['mitɪ‚ər] *s* meteora

meteoric [‚mitɪ'arɪk] or [‚mitɪ'ɔrɪk] *adj* meteorico; (fig) rapidissimo, folgorante

meteorite ['mitɪ‚ə‚raɪt] *s* meteorite *m* & *f*

meteorology [‚mitɪ‚ə'ralədʒi] *s* meteorologia

meter ['mitər] *s* (*unit of length; verse*) metro; (*instrument for measuring gas, water, etc.*) contatore *m*; (mus) tempo || *tr* misurare col contatore

me'ter read'er *s* lettore *m*, letturista *m*

methane ['meθen] *s* metano

method ['meθəd] *s* metodo

methodic(al) [mɪ'θadɪk(əl)] *adj* metodico

Methodist ['meθədɪst] *adj* & *s* metodista *mf*

Methuselah [mɪ'θuzələ] *s* Matusalemme *m*

meticulous [mɪ'tɪkjələs] *adj* meticoloso

metric(al) ['metrɪk(əl)] *adj* metrico

metronome ['metrə‚nom] *s* metronomo

metropolis [mɪ'trapəlɪs] *s* metropoli *f*

metropolitan [‚metrə'palɪtən] *adj* & *s* metropolitano

mettle ['metəl] *s* disposizione, temperamento; brio, animo; **to be on one's mettle** impegnarsi a fondo

mettlesome ['metəlsəm] *adj* brioso

mew [mju] *s* miagolio; (orn) gabbiano; **mews** scuderie *fpl*

Mexican ['meksɪkən] *adj* & *s* messicano

Mexico ['meksɪ‚ko] *s* il Messico

mezzanine ['mezə‚nin] *s* mezzanino

mica ['maɪkə] *s* mica

microbe ['maɪkrob] *s* microbio

microbiology [‚maɪkrəbaɪ'alədʒi] *s* microbiologia

microcard ['maɪkrə‚kard] *s* microscheda

microfarad [,maɪkrə'færæd] *s* micro-farad *m*

microfilm ['maɪkrə,fɪlm] *s* microfilm *m* || *tr* microfilmare

microgroove ['maɪkrə,gruv] *adj* micro-solco || *s* microsolco; disco micro-solco

microphone ['maɪkrə,fon] *s* microfono

microscope ['maɪkrə,skop] *s* micro-scopio

microscopic [,maɪkrə'skɑpɪk] *adj* mi-croscopico

microwave ['maɪkrə,wev] *s* microonda

mid [mɪd] *adj* mezzo, la metà di, e.g., **mid October** la metà di ottobre

mid'day' *adj* di mezzogiorno || *s* mez-zogiorno

middle ['mɪdəl] *adj* medio, mezzo || *s* mezzo, metà *f*; (*of human body*) cin-tura; **about the middle of** verso la metà di; **in the middle of** nel mezzo di

mid'dle age' *s* mezza età || **Middle Ages** *spl* Medio Evo

mid'dle class' *s* ceto medio, borghesia

Mid'dle East' *s* Medio Oriente

Mid'dle Eng'lish *s* inglese *m* medievale parlato fra il 1150 e il 1500

mid'dle fin'ger *s* dito medio

mid'dle-man' *s* (-**men**) intermediario

middling ['mɪdlɪŋ] *adj* mediocre, pas-sabile || *s* (*coarsely ground wheat*) farina grossa integrale; **middlings** articoli *mpl* di qualità mediocre || *adv* moderatamente

mid-dy ['mɪdi] *s* (-**dies**) aspirante *m* di marina

mid'dy blouse' *s* marinara

midget ['mɪdʒɪt] *s* nano

midland ['mɪdlənd] *adj* centrale, in-terno || *s* regione centrale

mid'night' *adj* di mezzanotte; **to burn the midnight oil** studiare a lume di candela || *s* mezzanotte *f*

midriff ['mɪdrɪf] *s* diaframma *m*; (*mid-dle part of body*) cintura, vita

mid'ship'man *s* (-**men**) aspirante *m* di marina

midst [mɪdst] *s* mezzo, centro; **in the midst of** in mezzo a

mid'stream' *s*—**in midstream** in mezzo al fiume

mid'sum'mer *s* cuore *m* dell'estate

mid'way' *adj* situato a metà strada || *s* metà strada; viale *m* principale di un' esposizione || *adv* a metà strada

mid'week' *s* mezzo della settimana

mid'wife' *s* (-**wives**) levatrice *f*

mid'win'ter *s* cuore *m* dell'inverno

mid'year' *adj* nel mezzo dell'anno || *s* mezzo dell'anno; **midyears** (coll) esami *mpl* nel mezzo dell'anno sco-lastico

mien [min] *s* aspetto, portamento

miff [mɪf] *s* (coll) battibecco || *tr* (coll) offendere

might [maɪt] *s* forza, potenza; **with might and main** a tutta forza || *v aux* used to form the potential, e.g., **he might change his mind** è possibile che cambi opinione

might·y ['maɪti] *adj* (-**ier; -iest**) po-tente; (*huge*) grandissimo || *adv* (coll) moltissimo, grandemente

migraine ['maɪgren] *s* emicrania

migrate ['maɪgret] *intr* migrare

migratory ['maɪgrə,tori] *adj* migratore

milch [mɪltʃ] *adj* lattifero

mild [maɪld] *adj* dolce, mite, gentile; (*disease*) leggero

mildew ['mɪl,dju] or ['mɪl,du] *s* (*mold*) muffa; (*plant disease*) perono-spora

mile [maɪl] *s* miglio terrestre; miglio marino

mileage ['maɪlɪdʒ] *s* distanza in miglia

mile'age tick'et *s* biglietto calcolato in miglia simile al biglietto chilometrag-gio

mile'post' *s* colonnina miliare

mile'stone' *s* pietra miliare

milieu [mɪl'ju] *s* ambiente *m*

militancy ['mɪlɪtənsi] *s* bellicismo; spirito militante

militant ['mɪlɪtənt] *adj* & *s* militante *mf*

militarism ['mɪlɪtə,rɪzəm] *s* milita-rismo

militarist ['mɪlɪtərɪst] *adj* & *s* mili-tarista *mf*

militarize ['mɪlɪtə,raɪz] *tr* militariz-zare

military ['mɪlɪ,teri] *adj* militare || *s*—**the military** le forze armate

mil'itary acad'emy *s* scuola allievi uffi-ciali, accademia militare

mil'itary police' *s* polizia militare

militate ['mɪlɪ,tet] *intr* militare

militia [mɪ'lɪʃə] *s* milizia

mili'tia-man *s* (-**men**) miliziano

milk [mɪlk] *adj* lattifero; di latte; **al latte** || *s* latte *m*; || *tr* mungere; (fig) spillare || *intr* dare latte

milk' can' *s* bidone *m* per il latte

milk' choc'olate *s* cioccolato al latte

milk' diet' *s* regime latteo

milking ['mɪlkɪŋ] *s* mungitura

milk'maid' *s* lattaia

milk'man' *s* (-**men**) lattaio

milk' of hu'man kind'ness *s* grande compassione

milk' pail' *s* secchio da latte

milk' shake' *s* frappé *m* or frullato di latte

milk'sop' *s* effeminato

milk'weed' *s* vincetossico

milk·y ['mɪlki] *adj* (-**ier; -iest**) latteo; (*whitish*) lattiginoso

Milk'y Way' *s* Via Lattea

mill [mɪl] *s* (*for grinding grain*) mu-lino; (*for making fabrics*) filanda; (*for cutting wood*) segheria; (*for re-fining sugar*) zuccherificio; (*for pro-ducing steel*) acciaieria; (*to grind coffee*) macinino; (*part of a dollar*) millesimo; **to put through the mill** mettere a dura prova || *tr* (*grains*) macinare; (*coins*) zigrinare; (*steel*) làminare; (*ore*) frantumare; (*with a milling machine*) fresare; (*chocolate*) frullare || *intr*—**to mill about** or **around** girare intorno

millennial [mɪ'lɛnɪ·əl] *adj* millenario

milleni·um [mɪ'lɛnɪ-əm] s (**-ums** or **-a** [ə]) millennio

miller ['mɪlər] s mugnaio; (ent) tignola notturna

millet ['mɪlɪt] s panico, miglio

milliampere [,mɪlɪ'æmpɪr] s milliampere m

milliard ['mɪljərd] or ['mɪljɑrd] s (Brit) miliardo, bilione m

milligram ['mɪlɪ,græm] s milligrammo

millimeter ['mɪlɪ,mitər] s millimetro

milliner ['mɪlɪnər] s modista

milliner·y ['mɪlɪ,nɛri] or ['mɪlɪnəri] s (**-ies**) cappelli mpl per signora; modisteria; articoli mpl di modisteria

mil′linery shop′ s modisteria

milling ['mɪlɪŋ] s (*of grain*) macinatura; (*of coins*) granitura; (mach) fresatura

mill′ing machine′ s fresatrice f

million ['mɪljən] adj milione di, milioni di || s milione m

millionaire [,mɪljən'ɛr] s milionario

millionth ['mɪljənθ] adj, s & pron milionesimo

millivolt ['mɪlɪ,volt] s millivolt m

mill′pond′ s gora

mill′race′ s corrente f che aziona il mulino; canale m di presa

mill′stone′ s mola, macina, palmento; (fig) peso, gravame m

mill′ wheel′ s ruota del mulino

mill′work′ s lavoro di falegnameria; lavoro di falegnameria fatto a macchina

mime [maɪm] s mimo || tr mimare

mimeograph ['mɪmɪə,græf] or ['mɪmɪə,grɑf] s (trademark) ciclostile m || tr ciclostilare

mim·ic ['mɪmɪk] s mimo, imitatore m || v (pret & pp **-icked**; ger **-icking**) tr imitare, scimmiottare

mimic·ry ['mɪmɪkri] s (**-ries**) mimica; (biol) mimetismo

minaret [,mɪnə'rɛt] or ['mɪnə,rɛt] s minareto

mince [mɪns] tr tagliuzzare, triturare; (*words*) pronunziare con affettazione; **to not mince one's words** non aver peli sulla lingua

mince′meat′ s carne tritata; **to make mincemeat of** annientare completamente

mince′ pie′ s torta di frutta secca e carne tritata

mind [maɪnd] s mente f; opinione; **to bear in mind** tener presente; **to be not in one's right mind** essere fuori di senno; **to be of one mind** essere d'accordo; **to be out of one's mind** essere impazzito; **to change one's mind** cambiare d'opinione; **to go out of one's mind** impazzire; **to have a mind to** aver voglia di; **to have in mind to** pensare a; **to have on one's mind** avere in mente; **to lose one's mind** uscire di mente; **to make up one's mind** decidersi; **to my mind** a mio modo di vedere; **to say whatever comes to one's mind** dire quanto salta in testa, e.g., **John always says whatever comes to his mind** Gio-

vanni dice sempre quanto gli salta in testa; **to set one's mind on** risolversi a; **to slip one's mind** scappare di mente (with *dat*), e.g., **it slipped his mind** gli è scappato di mente; **to speak one's mind** dire la propria opinione; **with one mind** unanimamente || tr (*to take care of*) occuparsi di; obbedire (with *dat*); **do you mind the smoke?** Le disturba il fumo?; **mind your own business** si occupi degli affari Suoi || intr osservare, fare attenzione; rincrescere, e.g., **do you mind if I go?** Le rincresce se vado?; **never mind** non si preoccupi

mindful ['maɪndfəl] adj memore

mind′ read′er s lettore m del pensiero

mind′ read′ing s lettura del pensiero

mine [maɪn] s (*e.g., of coal*) miniera; (mil & nav) mina || pron poss il mio; mio || tr minare; (*earth*) scavare; (*ore*) estrarre || intr lavorare una miniera; (mil & nav) minare

mine′ detec′tor s rivelatore m di mine

mine′field′ s campo minato

mine′lay′er s posamine m

miner ['maɪnər] s minatore m

mineral ['mɪnərəl] adj & s minerale m

mineralogy [,mɪnə'rælədʒi] s mineralogia

min′eral wool′ s cotone m or lana minerale

mine′ sweep′er s dragamine m

mingle ['mɪŋgəl] tr mescolare; unire || intr mescolarsi, associarsi

miniature ['mɪnɪ-ət/ər] or ['mɪnɪt/ər] s miniatura; **to paint in miniature** miniare, dipingere in miniatura

min′iature golf′ s minigolf m

miniaturization [,mɪnɪ-ət/ərɪ'ze/ən] or [,mɪnɪt/ərɪ'ze/ən] s miniaturizzazione

minimal ['mɪnɪməl] adj minimo

minimize ['mɪnɪ,maɪz] tr minimizzare

minimum ['mɪnɪməm] adj & s minimo

min′imum wage′ s salario minimo

mining ['maɪnɪŋ] adj minerario || s estrazione di minerali; (nav) posa di mine

minion ['mɪnjən] s servo; favorito, beniamino

min′ion of the law′ s poliziotto

miniskirt ['mɪnɪ,skʌrt] s minigonna

minister ['mɪnɪstər] s ministro; pastore m protestante || tr & intr ministrare

ministerial [,mɪnɪs'tɪrɪ-əl] adj ministeriale

minis·try ['mɪnɪstri] s (**-tries**) ministero; sacerdozio

mink [mɪŋk] s visone m

minnow ['mɪno] s pesciolino; (ichth) ciprino

minor ['maɪnər] adj minore || s minore m, minorenne mf; (educ) corso secondario

minori·ty [mɪ'nɑrɪti] or [maɪ'nɑrɪti] adj minoritario || s (**-ties**) (*smaller number or part; group differing in race, etc., from majority*) minoranza; (*under legal age*) minorità f

minstrel ['mɪnstrəl] s (hist) menestrello; **(U.S.A.)** comico vestito da nero

minstrel·sy [ˈmɪnstrəlsɪ] *s* (**-sies**) giulleria; poesia giullaresca

mint [mɪnt] *s* zecca; (*plant*) menta; (*losenge*) mentina; (fig) miniera d'oro ‖ *tr* coniare

minuet [ˌmɪnjuˈet] *s* minuetto

minus [ˈmaɪnəs] *adj* meno ‖ *s* meno, perdita ‖ *prep* meno, senza

minute [maɪˈnjut] or [maɪˈnut] *adj* minuto ‖ [ˈmɪnɪt] *adj* fatto in un minuto ‖ *s* minuto; momento; **minutes** processo verbale; **to write up the minutes** tenere i verbali; **up to the minute** al corrente; dell'ultima ora

min'ute hand' [ˈmɪnɪt] *s* sfera or lancetta dei minuti

minutiae [mɪˈnjuʃɪˌi] or [mɪˈnuʃɪˌi] *spl* minuzie *fpl*

minx [mɪŋks] *s* sfacciata, civetta

miracle [ˈmɪrəkəl] *s* miracolo

mir'acle play' *s* sacra rappresentazione

miraculous [mɪˈrækjələs] *adj* miracoloso

mirage [mɪˈrɑʒ] *s* miraggio

mire [maɪr] *s* limo, mota

mirror [ˈmɪrər] *s* specchio ‖ *tr* specchiare, riflettere

mirth [mʌrθ] *s* allegria, gioia

mir·y [ˈmaɪrɪ] *adj* (**-ier; -iest**) fangoso, limaccioso

misadventure [ˌmɪsədˈventʃər] *s* disavventura, contrattempo

misanthrope [ˈmɪsənˌθrop] *s* misantropo

misanthropy [mɪsˈænθrəpɪ] *s* misantropia

misapprehension [ˌmɪsæprɪˈhenʃən] *s* malinteso

misappropriation [ˌmɪsəˌproprɪˈeʃən] *s* malversazione

misbehave [ˌmɪsbɪˈhev] *intr* comportarsi male

misbehavior [ˌmɪsbɪˈhevɪˌər] *s* cattiva condotta

miscalculation [ˌmɪskælkjəˈleʃən] *s* calcolo errato

miscarriage [mɪsˈkærɪdʒ] *s* (*of justice*) errore *m*; (*of a letter*) disguido; (pathol) aborto

miscar·ry [mɪsˈkærɪ] *v* (*pret & pp* **-ried**) *intr* (*said of a project*) fallire; (*said of a letter*) smarrirsi; (pathol) abortire

miscellaneous [ˌmɪsəˈlenɪ·əs] *adj* miscellaneo

miscella·ny [ˈmɪsəˌlenɪ] *s* (**-nies**) miscellanea

mischief [ˈmɪstʃɪf] *s* (*harm*) danno; (*disposition to annoy*) malizia; (*prankishness*) birichinata

mis'chief-mak'er *s* mettimale *mf*

mischievous [ˈmɪstʃɪvəs] *adj* dannoso; malizioso; birichino

misconception [ˌmɪskənˈsepʃən] *s* concetto erroneo, fraintendimento

misconduct [mɪsˈkɑndəkt] *s* cattiva condotta; (*of a public official*) malgoverno ‖ [ˌmɪskənˈdʌkt] *tr* male amministrare; **to misconduct oneself** comportarsi male

misconstrue [ˌmɪskənˈstru] or [mɪsˈkɑnstru] *tr* fraintendere

miscount [mɪsˈkaunt] *s* conteggio erroneo ‖ *tr & intr* contare male

miscue [mɪsˈkju] *s* sbaglio; (*in billiards*) stecca ‖ *intr* steccare; (theat) sbagliarsi di battuta

mis·deal [ˈmɪsˌdil] *s* distribuzione sbagliata ‖ [mɪsˈdil] *v* (*pret & pp* **-dealt** [delt]) *tr & intr* distribuire erroneamente

misdeed [mɪsˈdid] or [ˈmɪsˌdid] *s* misfatto, malfatto

misdemeanor [ˌmɪsdɪˈminər] *s* cattiva condotta; (law) delitto colposo

misdirect [ˌmɪsdɪˈrekt] or [ˌmɪsdaɪˈrekt] *tr* dare un indirizzo sbagliato a; (*a letter*) mettere un indirizzo sbagliato su

misdoing [mɪsˈduˌɪŋ] *s* misfatto

miser [ˈmaɪzər] *s* avaro, spilorcio

miserable [ˈmɪzərəbəl] *adj* miserabile, miserevole; (coll) malissimo; (coll) schifoso

miserly [ˈmaɪzərlɪ] *adj* spilorcio

miser·y [ˈmɪzərɪ] *s* (**-ies**) miseria

misfeasance [mɪsˈfizəns] *s* infrazione della legge; abuso di autorità commesso da pubblico funzionario

misfire [mɪsˈfaɪr] *s* difetto di esplosione; (aut) difetto d'accensione ‖ *intr* (*said of a gun*) fare cilecca; (aut) dare accensione irregolare; (fig) fallire

mis·fit [ˈmɪsˌfɪt] *s* vestito che non va bene; (*person*) spostato, pesce *m* fuor d'acqua ‖ [mɪsˈfɪt] *v* (*pret & pp* **-fitted;** *ger* **-fitting**) *intr* andar male

misfortune [mɪsˈfɔrtʃən] *s* disgrazia

misgiving [mɪsˈgɪvɪŋ] *s* dubbio, timore *m*, cattivo presentimento

misgovern [mɪsˈgʌvərn] *tr* amministrare male

misguided [mɪsˈgaɪdɪd] *adj* fuorviato; (*e.g., kindness*) sconsigliato

mishap [ˈmɪshæp] or [mɪsˈhæp] *s* accidente *m*, infortunio

misinform [ˌmɪsɪnˈfɔrm] *tr* dare informazioni errate a

misinterpret [ˌmɪsɪnˈtɜrprɪt] *tr* interpretare male, trasfigurare

misjudge [mɪsˈdʒʌdʒ] *tr & intr* giudicare male

mis·lay [mɪsˈle] *v* (*pret & pp* **-laid** [ˌled]) *tr* (*e.g., tile*) applicare in maniera sbagliata; (*e.g., papers*) smarrire, mettere al posto sbagliato

mis·lead [mɪsˈlid] *v* (*pret & pp* **-led** [ˌled]) *tr* sviare, traviare

misleading [mɪsˈlidɪŋ] *adj* ingannatore

mismanagement [mɪsˈmænɪdʒmənt] *s* malgoverno

misnomer [mɪsˈnomər] *s* termine improprio

misplace [mɪsˈples] *tr* mettere fuori di posto; (*trust*) riporre erroneamente

misprint [ˈmɪsˌprɪnt] *s* errore *m* di stampa, refuso ‖ [mɪsˈprɪnt] *tr* stampare erroneamente

mispronounce [ˌmɪsprəˈnauns] *tr* pronunciare in modo erroneo

mispronunciation [ˌmɪsprəˌnʌnsɪ-

'e∫ən] or [,mɪsprə ,nʌn∫ɪ'e∫ən] s errore *m* di pronuncia

misquote [mɪs'kwot] *tr* citare incorrettamente

misrepresent [,mɪsreprɪ'zent] *tr* travisare, snaturare; (pol) rappresentare slealmente

miss [mɪs] *s* sbaglio, omissione; tiro fuori bersaglio; signorina ‖ *tr* (*a train, an opportunity*) perdere; (*the target*) fallire; (*an appointment*) mancare; (*the point*) non vedere, non capire; per poco, e.g., **the car missed hitting him** l'automobile non l'ha investito per poco ‖ *intr* sbagliare, fallire; mancare il bersaglio ‖ **Miss** *s* signorina, la signorina

missal ['mɪsəl] *s* messale *m*

misshapen [mɪs'∫epən] *adj* deforme, malfatto

missile ['mɪsɪl] *adj* missilistico ‖ *s* missile *m*

mis'sile launch'er *s* lanciamissili *m*

missing ['mɪsɪŋ] *adj* mancante; assente; (*in action*) disperso

mis'sing link' *s* anello di congiunzione

miss'ing per'son *s* disperso

mission ['mɪ∫ən] *s* missione

missionar·y ['mɪ∫ən ,erɪ] *adj* missionario ‖ *s* (-ies) (eccl) missionario; (dipl) incaricato in missione

missive ['mɪsɪv] *s* missiva

mis·spell [mɪs'spel] *v* (*pret & pp* -**spelled** or -**spelt** ['spelt]) *tr & intr* scrivere male

misspelling [mɪs'spelɪŋ] *s* errore *m* di ortografia

misspent [mɪs'spent] *adj* sprecato

misstatement [mɪs'stetmənt] *s* dichiarazione inesatta

misstep [mɪs'step] *s* passo falso

miss·y ['mɪsɪ] *s* (-ies) (coll) signorina

mist [mɪst] *s* caligine *f*, foschia; (*of tears*) velo; (*of smoke, vapors, etc.*) nuvola

mis·take [mɪs'tek] *s* errore *m*, sbaglio; **and no mistake** (coll) di sicuro; **by mistake** per sbaglio; **to make a mistake** sbagliarsi ‖ *v* (*pret* -**took** ['tʊk]; *pp* -**taken**) *tr* fraintendere; **to be mistaken for** essere preso per; **to mistake for** pigliare per

mistaken [mɪs'tekən] *adj* errato, sbagliato; **to be mistaken** essere in errore, sbagliarsi

mister ['mɪstər] *s* (mil, nav) signore *m;* (coll) marito ‖ *interj* (coll) signore!; (coll) Lei!; (coll) buonuomo! ‖ **Mister** *s* Signore *m*

mistletoe ['mɪsəl ,to] *s* vischio

mistreat [mɪs'trit] *tr* maltrattare

mistreatment [mɪs'tritmənt] *s* maltrattamento

mistress ['mɪstrɪs] *s* (*of a household*) signora, padrona; (*paramour*) amante *f*, ganza; (Brit) maestra di scuola

mistrial [mɪs'traɪ·əl] *s* processo viziato da errore giudiziario

mistrust [mɪs'trʌst] *s* diffidenza ‖ *tr* diffidare di ‖ *intr* diffidarsi

mistrustful [mɪs'trʌstfəl] *adj* diffidente

mist·y ['mɪstɪ] *adj* (-ier; -iest) fosco, brumoso; (fig) vago, confuso

misunder·stand [,mɪsʌndər'stænd] *v* (*pret & pp* -**stood** ['stʊd]) *tr* fraintendere, equivocare

misunderstanding [,mɪsʌndər'stændɪŋ] *s* malinteso

misuse [mɪs'jus] *s* abuso; (*of funds*) malversazione ‖ [mɪs'juz] *tr* abusare di; (*funds*) malversare

misword [mɪs'wʌrd] *tr* comporre male

mite [maɪt] *s* obolo; (ent) acaro

miter ['maɪtər] *s* (carp) ugnatura; (carp) giunto a quartabuono; (eccl) mitra ‖ *tr* tagliare a quartabuono, ugnare; giungere a quartabuono

mi'ter box' *s* cassetta per ugnature

mi'ter joint' *s* giunto a quartabuono

mitigate ['mɪtɪ ,get] *tr* mitigare

mitten ['mɪtən] *s* manopola, muffola

mix [mɪks] *tr* mescolare; (*colors*) mesticare; (*dough*) impastare; (*salad*) condire; **to mix up** confondere ‖ *intr* confondersi, mescolarsi

mixed [mɪkst] *adj* misto; (*candy*) assortito; (coll) confuso

mixed' com'pany *s* riunione *f* di ambo i sessi

mixed' drink' *s* miscela di liquori diversi

mixed' feel'ing *s* sentimento ambivalente

mixed' met'aphor *s* metafora incongruente

mixer ['mɪksər] *s* (mach) mescolatrice *f*; **to be a good mixer** essere socievole

mixture ['mɪkst∫ər] *s* mistura, mescolanza; (aut) miscela, carburazione

mix'-up' *s* confusione; (coll) baruffa

mizzen ['mɪzən] *s* mezzana

moan [mon] *s* gemito ‖ *intr* gemere

moat [mot] *s* fosso, fossato

mob [mɑb] *s* turba ‖ *v* (*pret & pp* **mobbed;** *ger* **mobbing**) *tr* assaltare; affollarsi intorno a; (*a place*) affollare

mobile ['mobɪl] or ['mobɪl] *adj* mobile

mo'bile home' *s* caravan *m*, roulotte *f*

mobility [mo'bɪlɪtɪ] *s* mobilità *f*

mobilization [,mobɪlɪ'ze∫ən] *s* mobilitazione

mobilize ['mobɪ ,laɪz] *tr & intr* mobilitare

mob' rule' *s* legge *f* della teppa

mobster ['mɑbstər] *s* gangster *m*

moccasin ['mɑkəsɪn] *s* mocassino

Mo'cha cof'fee ['mokə] *s* caffè *m* moca

mock [mɑk] *adj* finto, imitato ‖ *s* dileggio, burla ‖ *tr* deridere, canzonare; ingannare ‖ *intr* motteggiare; **to mock at** farsi gioco di

mocker·y ['mɑkərɪ] *s* (-ies) dileggio, scherno; (*subject of derision*) zimbello; (*poor imitation*) contraffazione

mock'-hero'ic *adj* eroicomico

mockingbird ['mɑkɪŋ ,bʌrd] *s* mimo

mock' or'ange *s* gelsomino selvatico

mock' tur'tle soup' *s* finto brodo di tartaruga

mock'-up' *s* modello dimostrativo

mode [mod] *s* modo, maniera; (*fashion*) moda; (gram) modo

mod·el ['mɑdəl] *adj* modello, e.g., **model student** studente modello ‖ *s* modello; (*woman serving as subject for artists*) modello *f*; (*woman wearing clothes at fashion show*) indossatrice *f* ‖ *v* (*pret & pp* **-eled** or **-elled**; *ger* **-eling** or **-elling**) *tr* modellare ‖ *intr* modellarsi; fare il manichino

mod'el air'plane *s* aeromodello

mo'del-air'plane build'er *s* aeromodellista *mf*

mod'eling clay' *s* plastilina

moderate ['mɑdərɪt] *adj* moderato ‖ ['mɑdə,ret] *tr* moderare; (*a meeting*) presiedere a ‖ *intr* moderarsi

moderator ['mɑdə,retər] *s* moderatore *m*; (*mediator*) arbitro; (*phys*) moderatore *m*

modern ['mɑdərn] *adj* moderno

modernize ['mɑdər,naɪz] *tr* modernizzare, rimodernare

modest ['mɑdɪst] *adj* modesto

modes·ty ['mɑdɪsti] *s* (**-ties**) modestia

modicum ['mɑdɪkəm] *s* piccola quantità

modi·fy ['mɑdɪ,faɪ] *v* (*pret & pp* **-fied**) *tr* modificare; (gram) determinare

modish ['modɪʃ] *adj* alla moda

modulate ['mɑdʒə,let] *tr & intr* modulàre

modulation [,mɑdʒə'leʃən] *s* modulazione

mohair ['mo,her] *s* mohair *m*

Mohammedan [mo'hæmɪdən] *adj & s* maomettano

Mohammedanism [mo'hæmɪdə,nɪzəm] *s* maomettismo

moist [mɔɪst] *adj* umido; lacrimoso

moisten ['mɔɪsən] *tr* inumidire ‖ *intr* inumidirsi

moisture ['mɔɪstʃər] *s* umidità *f*

molar ['molər] *s* molare *m*

molasses [mə'læsɪz] *s* melassa

mold [mold] *s* stampo, forma; (*fungus*) muffa; humus *m*; (fig) indole *f* ‖ *tr* plasmare, conformare; (*to make moldy*) fare ammuffire ‖ *intr* ammuffire

molder ['moldər] *s* modellatore *m* ‖ *intr* sgretolarsi; polverizzarsi

molding ['moldɪŋ] *s* modellato; (archit, carp) modanatura

mold·y ['moldi] *adj* (**-ier; -iest**) ammuffito

mole [mol] *s* (*pier*) molo; (*harbor*) darsena; (*spot on skin*) neo; (*small mammal*) talpa

molecule ['mɑlɪ,kjul] *s* molecola

mole'hill' *s* mucchio di terra sopra la tana di talpe

mole'skin' *s* pelle *f* di talpa; (*fabric*) fustagno di prima qualità

molest [mə'lest] *tr* molestare; fare proposte disoneste a

moll [mɑl] *s* (slang) ragazza della malavita; (slang) puttana

molli·fy ['mɑlɪ,faɪ] *v* (*pret & pp* **-fied**) *tr* pacificare, placare

mollusk ['mɑləsk] *s* mollusco

mollycoddle ['mɑlɪ,kɑdəl] *s* effeminato ‖ *tr* viziare, coccolare

Mo'lotov cock'tail ['mɑlə,tɔf] *s* bottiglia Molotov

molt [molt] *s* muda ‖ *intr* andare in muda

molten ['moltən] *adj* fuso

molybdenum [mə'lɪbdɪnəm] or [,mɑlɪb'dinəm] *s* molibdeno

moment ['momənt] *s* momento; **at any moment** da un momento all'altro

momentary ['momən,teri] *adj* momentaneo

momentous [mo'mentəs] *adj* grave, importante

momen·tum [mo'mentəm] *s* (**-tums** or **-ta** [tə]) slancio; (mech) momento

monarch ['mɑnərk] *s* monarca *m*

monarchic(al) [mə'nɑrkɪk(əl)] *adj* monarchico

monarchist ['mɑnərkɪst] *adj & s* monarchico

monar·chy ['mɑnərki] *s* (**-chies**) monarchia

monaster·y ['mɑnəs,teri] *s* (**-ies**) monastero

monastic [mə'næstɪk] *adj* monastico, monacale

monasticism [mə'næstɪ,sɪzəm] *s* monachesimo

Monday ['mʌndi] *s* lunedì *m*

monetary ['mʌnɪ,teri] *adj* monetario; pecuniario

money ['mʌni] *s* denaro; **to be in the money** esser carico di soldi; **to make money** far quattrini

mon'ey·bag' *s* borsa per denaro; **moneybags** (coll) riccone sfondato

moneychanger ['mʌnɪ,tʃendʒər] *s* cambiavalute *m*

moneyed ['mʌnid] *adj* danaroso

moneylender ['mʌnɪ,lendər] *s* prestatore *m* di denaro

mon'ey·mak'er *s* capitalista *mf*; affare vantaggioso

mon'ey or'der *s* vaglia *m*

Mongolian [mɑŋ'golɪ·ən] *adj & s* mongolo

mon·goose ['mɑŋgus] *s* (**-gooses**) mangusta

mongrel ['mʌŋgrəl] or ['mɑŋgrəl] *adj* ibrido ‖ *s* ibrido; cane bastardo

monitor ['mɑnɪtər] *s* (educ) capoclasse *mf*; (rad, telv) monitore *m* ‖ *tr* osservare; (*a signal*) controllare; (*a broadcast*) ascoltare

monk [mʌŋk] *s* monaco

monkey ['mʌŋki] *s* scimmia; **to make a monkey of** farsi gioco di ‖ *intr*—**to monkey around** (coll) oziare; **to monkey around with** (coll) giocherellare con

mon'key·shines' *spl* (slang) monellerie *fpl*, pagliacciate *fpl*

mon'key wrench' *s* chiave *f* inglese

monkhood ['mʌŋkhʊd] *s* monacato

monkshood ['mʌŋks,hʊd] *s* (bot) aconito

monocle ['mɑnəkəl] *s* monocolo

monogamy [mə'nɑgəmi] *s* monogamia

monogram ['mɑnə,græm] *s* monogramma *m*

monograph ['mɑnə,græf] or ['mɑnə,grɑf] *s* monografia

monolithic [,mɑnə'lɪθɪk] *adj* monolitico

monologue ['manə,lɔg] or ['manə-
,lag] s monologo
monomania [,manə'menɪ·ə] s monomania
monomial [mə'nomɪ·əl] s monomio
monopolize [mə'napə,laɪz] tr monopolizzare, accaparrare
monopo·ly [mə'napəli] s (-lies) mono-
polio, privativa
monorail ['manə ,rel] s monorotaia
monosyllable ['manə ,sɪləbəl] s mono-
sillabo
monotheist ['manə ,θi·ɪst] adj & s
monoteista mf
monotonous [mə'natənəs] adj monotono
monotype ['manə,taɪp] s (method)
monotipia; (typ) monotipo
monoxide [mə'naksaɪd] s monossido
monseigneur [,mansen'jœr] s monsignore m
monsignor [man'sinjər] s (-monsignors)
or **monsignori** [,mɒnsi'njori]) (eccl)
monsignore m
monsoon [man'sun] s monsone m
monster ['manstər] adj mostruoso ǁ s
mostro
monstrance ['manstrəns] s ostensorio
monstrosi·ty [man'strɑsɪti] s (-ties)
mostruosità f
monstrous ['manstrəs] adj mostruoso
month [mʌnθ] s mese m
month·ly ['mʌnθli] adj mensile ǁ s
(-lies) rivista mensile; **monthlies**
(coll) mestruazione ǁ adv mensil-
mente
monument ['manjəmənt] s monumento
moo [mu] s muggito ǁ intr muggire
mood [mud] s umore m, vena; (gram)
modo; **moods** luna, malumore m
mood·y ['mudi] adj (-ier; -iest) triste,
malinconico; lunatico, capriccioso
moon [mun] s luna; **once in a blue
moon** ad ogni morte di papa ǁ tr—
to moon away (time) (coll) sprecare
ǁ intr—**to moon about** (coll) gingil-
larsi, baloccarsi; (to daydream about)
(coll) sognarsi di
moon'beam' s raggio di luna
moon'light' s chiaro m di luna
moon'light'ing s secondo lavoro notturno
moon'shine' s chiaro di luna; (coll)
chiacchiere fpl, balle fpl; (coll) whisky m distillato illegalmente
moon'shot' s lancio alla luna
moon'stone' s lunaria
moor [mur] s brughiera, landa ǁ tr
ormeggiare ǁ intr ormeggiarsi ǁ
Moor s moro
Moorish ['murɪʃ] adj moresco
moor'land' s brughiera, landa
moose [mus] s (moose) alce americano
moot [mut] adj controverso, discutibile
mop [map] s scopa di filacce; (naut)
redazza; (of hair) zazzera ǁ v (pret &
pp **mopped**; ger **mopping**) tr (a floor)
pulire, asciugare; (one's brow) asciu-
garsi; **to mop up** rastrellare
mope [mop] intr andare rattristato
mopish ['mopɪʃ] adj triste, avvilito

moral ['marəl] or ['mɔrəl] adj morale
ǁ s (of a fable) morale f; **morals**
(ethics) morale f; (modes of conduct)
costumi mpl
morale [mə'ræl] or [mə'ral] s morale
m
morali·ty [mə'rælɪti] s (-ties) moralità
f
mor'als charge' s accusa di oltraggio al
pudore
morass [mə'ræs] s palude f
moratori·um [,marə'torɪ·əm] or
[,mɔrə'torɪ·əm] s (-ums or -a [ə])
moratoria
morbid ['mɔrbɪd] adj (gruesome) orribile; (feelings; curiosity; pertaining
to disease; pathologic) morboso
mordacious [mɔr'deʃəs] adj mordace
mordant ['mɔrdənt] adj & s mordente
m
more [mor] adj & s più m ǁ adv più;
more and more sempre più; **more
than** più di; (followed by verb) più
di quanto; **the more . . . the less**
tanto più . . . quanto meno
more·o'er adv per di più, inoltre
Moresque [mo'resk] adj moresco
morgue [mɔrg] s deposito, obitorio;
(journ) archivio di un giornale, frigorifero
moribund ['mɔrɪ,bʌnd] or ['marɪ-
,bʌnd] adj moribondo
morning ['mɔrnɪŋ] adj mattiniero ǁ s
mattina, mattino; **good morning** buon
giorno; **in the morning** di mattina
morn'ing coat' s giacca nera a code
morn'ing-glo'ry s (-ries) convolvolo;
(Ipomea) campanella; (Convolvulus
tricolor) bella di giorno
morn'ing sick'ness s vomito di gravidanza
morn'ing star' s Lucifero, stella del
mattino
Moroccan [mə'rakən] adj & s maroc-
chino
morocco [mə'rako] s (leather) maroc-
chino ǁ **Morocco** s il Marocco
moron ['morɑn] s deficiente mf
morose [mə'ros] adj tetro, imbronciato
morphine ['mɔrfin] s morfina
morphology [mɔr'falədʒi] s morfologia
morrow ['maro] or ['mɔro] s—**on the
morrow** l'indomani, il giorno seguente; domani
morsel ['mɔrsəl] s boccone m, bocconcino; pezzetto
mortal ['mɔrtəl] adj & s mortale m
mortality [mɔr'tælɪti] s mortalità f;
(death or destruction on a large
scale) moria
mortar ['mɔrtər] s (mixture of lime
or cement) malta, calcina; (bowl)
mortaio; (mil) mortaio, lanciabombe
m
mor'tar·board' s sparviere m; (cap)
tocco accademico
mortgage ['mɔrgɪdʒ] s ipoteca ǁ tr
ipotecare
mortgagee [,mɔrgɪ'dʒi] s creditore m
ipotecario
mortgagor ['mɔrgɪdʒər] s debitore m
ipotecario

mortician [mɔr'tɪʃ/ən] s impresario di pompe funebri

morti·fy ['mɔrtɪ,faɪ] v (pret & pp -fied) tr mortificare; **to be mortified** vergognarsi

mortise ['mɔrtɪs] s intaccatura, incastro || tr incassare, incastrare

mor'tise lock' s serratura incastrata

mortuar·y ['mɔrtʃu,ɛri] adj mortuario || s (-ies) camera mortuaria

mosaic [mo'ze·ɪk] s mosaico

Moscow ['maskau] or ['masko] s Mosca

Moses ['moziz] or ['mozɪs] s Mosè m

Mos·lem ['mazləm] or ['masləm] adj musulmano || s (-lems or -lem) musulmano

mosque [mask] s moschea

mosqui·to [məs'kito] s (-toes or -tos) zanzara

mosqui'to net' s zanzariera

moss [mɔs] or [mas] s musco

moss'back' s (coll) ultraconservatore m, fossile m

moss·y ['mɔsi] or ['masi] adj (-ier; -iest) muscoso

most [most] adj il più di, la maggior parte di || s la maggioranza, il più; **most of** la maggior parte di; **to make the most of** trarre il massimo da || adv più, maggiormente, al massimo

mostly ['mostli] adv per lo più, maggiormente, al massimo

motel [mo'tɛl] s motel m, autostello

moth [mɔθ] or [maθ] s falena; (clothes moth) tarma

moth'ball' s pallina antitarmica

moth-eaten ['mɔθ,itən] or ['maθ,itən] adj tarmato; antiquato

mother ['mʌðər] adj (love, tongue) materno; (country) natio; (church, company) madre || s madre f; (elderly woman) (coll) zia || tr fare da madre a; creare; procreare; assumere la maternità di

moth'er coun'try s madrepatria

Moth'er Goose' s supposta autrice di una raccolta di favole infantili

motherhood ['mʌðər,hud] s maternità f

moth'er-in-law' s (moth'ers-in-law') suocera

moth'er-land' s madrepatria

motherless ['mʌðərlɪs] adj orfano di madre, senza madre

mother-of-pearl ['mʌðərəv'pʌrl] adj madreperlaceo || s madreperla

motherly ['mʌðərli] adj materno

Moth'er's Day' s giorno della madre, festa della mamma

moth'er supe'rior s madre superiora

moth'er tongue' s madrelingua; (language from which another language is derived) lingua madre

moth'er wit' s intelligenza nativa

moth' hole' s tarlatura

moth·y ['mɔθi] or ['maθi] adj (-ier; -iest) tarmato

motif [mo'tif] s motivo

motion ['moʃən] s movimento; (e.g., of a dancer) movenza, mossa; (in parliamentary procedure) mozione; **in motion** in moto || intr fare cenno

motionless ['moʃənlɪs] adj immobile

mo'tion pic'ture s pellicola cinematografica; **motion pictures** cinematografia

mo'tion-picture' adj cinematografico

motivate ['motɪ,vet] tr animare, incitare

motive ['motɪv] adj motivo; (producing motion) motore || s motivo; (incentive) movente m

mo'tive pow'er s forza motrice; impianto motore; (rr) insieme m di locomotive

motley ['matli] adj eterogeneo; variato, variopinto

motor ['motər] adj motore; (operated by motor) motorizzato; (pertaining to motor vehicles) motoristico || s motore m; (aut) macchina || intr viaggiare in macchina

mo'tor·boat' s motobarca, motoscafo

mo'tor·bus' s torpedone m; autobus m

motorcade ['motər,ked] s carovana di automobili

mo'tor·car' s automobile f

mo'tor·cy'le s motocicletta

motorist ['motərɪst] s automobilista mf

motorize ['motə,raɪz] tr motorizzare

mo'torman ['motər-man] s guidatore m di tram; guidatore m di locomotore

mo'tor sail'er s motoveliero

mo'tor scoot'er s motoretta

mot'or ship' s motonave f

mo'tor truck' s autocarro, camion m

mo'tor ve'hicle s motoveicolo

mottle ['matəl] tr chiazzare, screziare

mot·to ['mato] s (-toes or -tos) motto, divisa

mould [mold] s, tr, & intr var of **mold**

mound [maund] s monticello, collinetta

mount [maunt] s monte m, montagna; (horse for riding) cavalcatura, monta; (setting for a jewel) montatura; supporto; (for a picture) incorniciatura || tr montare; (a wall) scalare; (theat) allestire || intr montare; (to climb) salire

mountain ['mauntən] s montagna; **to make a mountain out of a molehill** fare di un bruscolo una trave, fare d'una mosca un elefante

moun'tain climb'ing s alpinismo

mountaineer [,mauntə'nɪr] s montanaro

mountainous ['mauntənəs] adj montagnoso

moun'tain rail'road s ferrovia a dentiera

moun'tain range' s catena di montagne

moun'tain sick'ness s mal m di montagna

mountebank ['maunti,bæŋk] s ciarlatano

mounting ['mauntɪŋ] s (act) il montare, montaggio; (setting) montatura; (mach) supporto

mourn [morn] tr (the loss of s.o.) piangere; (a misfortune) lamentare || intr piangere; vestire a lutto

mourner ['mornər] s persona in lutto; (penitent sinner) penitente mf;

(woman hired to attend a funeral or funerals) prefica

mourn'er's bench' *s* banco dei penitenti

mournful ['mɔrnfəl] *adj* luttuoso, funesto; *(gloomy)* lugubre

mourning ['mɔrnɪŋ] *s* lutto; **to be in mourning** portare il lutto

mourn'ing band' *s* bracciale *m* a lutto

mouse [maʊs] *s* (**mice** [maɪs]) topo, sorcio

mouse'hole' *s* topaia; piccolo buco

mouser ['maʊzər] *s* cacciatore *m* di topi

mouse'trap' *s* trappola per topi

moustache [məs'tæʃ] or [məs'tɑʃ] *s* baffi *mpl*, mustacchi *mpl*

mouth [maʊθ] *s* (**mouths** [maʊðz]) bocca; **by mouth** per via orale; **to be born with a silver spoon in one's mouth** essere nato con la camicia; **to make one's mouth water** fare venire a qlcu l'acquolina in bocca

mouthful ['maʊθ,fʊl] *s* boccata

mouth' or'gan *s* armonica a bocca

mouth'piece' *s* *(of wind instrument)* bocchetta; *(of bridle)* imboccatura; *(of megaphone)* boccaglio; *(of cigarette)* bocchino; *(of telephone)* imboccatura; *(spokesman)* portavoce *m*

mouth'wash' *s* sciacquo, risciacquo

movable ['muvəbəl] *adj* mobile, movibile; *(law)* mobiliare

move [muv] *s* movimento; *(change of residence)* trasloco; *(step)* passo; *(e.g., in chess)* mossa; **on the move in** moto, in movimento; **to get a move on** (coll) affrettarsi ‖ *tr* muovere; *(the bowels)* provocare l'evacuazione di; *(to prompt)* spingere; *(to stir the feelings of)* emozionare, commuovere; *(law)* proporre; *(com)* svendere; **to move up** *(a date)* anticipare ‖ *intr* muoversi; passare; *(to another house)* traslocare; *(to another city)* trasferirsi; *(said of goods)* avere una vendita; *(said of the bowels)* evacuare; procedere; *(law)* presentare una mozione; *(coll)* andarsene; **to move away** andarsene; trasferirsi; **to move back** tirarsi indietro; **to move in** avanzare; *(society)* frequentare; **to move off** allontanarsi

movement ['muvmənt] *s* movimento; *(of a watch)* meccanismo; *(of the bowels)* evacuazione; *(mus)* movimento, tempo

movie ['muvi] *s* (coll) film *m*, pellicola

movie-goer ['muvi,go-ər] *s* frequentatore *m* del cinema

mov'ie house' *s* (coll) cinematografo

mov'ie-land' *s* (coll) cinelandia

moving ['muvɪŋ] *adj* commovente, emozionante ‖ *s* trasporto; *(from one house to another)* trasloco

mov'ing pic'ture *s* film *m*, pellicola

mov'ing stair'case *s* scala mobile

mow [mo] *v* *(pret* **mowed**; *pp* **mowed** or **mown**) *tr & intr* falciare

mower ['mo-ər] *s* falciatore *m*; *(mach)* falciatrice *f*

Mr. ['mɪstər] *s* (**Messrs.** ['mesərz]) Signore *m*

Mrs. ['mɪsɪz] *s* Signora

much [mʌtʃ] *adj & pron* molto; **as much . . . as** tanto . . . quanto; **too much** troppo ‖ *adv* molto; **however much** per quanto; **how much** quanto; **too much** troppo; **very much** moltissimo

mucilage ['mjusɪlɪdʒ] *s* colla; *(gummy secretion in plants)* mucillagine *f*

muck [mʌk] *s* letame *m*; *(dirt)* sudiciume *m*; *(min)* materiale *m* di scoria

muck'rake' *intr* (coll) sollevare scandali

mucous ['mjukəs] *adj* mucoso

mucus ['mjukəs] *s* muco

mud [mʌd] *s* fango, melma, limo; **to sling mud at** calunniare

muddle ['mʌdəl] *s* confusione, guazzabuglio ‖ *tr* confondere, intorbidire ‖ *intr*—**to muddle through** arrangiarsi; cavarsela alla meno peggio in

mud'dle·head' *s* (coll) semplicione *m*

mud-dy ['mʌdi] *adj* (**-dier; -diest**) fangoso, melmoso; *(obscure)* torbido ‖ *v* *(pret & pp* **-died**) *tr* turbare, intorbidare; *(to soil with mud)* infangare

mud'guard' *s* parafango

mud'hole' *s* pozzanghera, fangaia

mud' slide' *s* smottamento

mudslinger ['mʌd,slɪŋgər] *s* calunniatore *m*

muff [mʌf] *s* manicotto ‖ *tr* (coll) mancare; *(to handle badly)* (coll) abborracciare; *(sports)* mancare di pigliare

muffin ['mʌfɪn] *s* panino soffice

muffle ['mʌfəl] *tr* infagottare, imbacuccare; *(a sound)* velare, smorzare

muffler ['mʌflər] *s* sciarpa; *(aut)* silenziatore *m*, marmitta

mufti ['mʌfti] *s*—**in mufti** in borghese

mug [mʌg] *s* tazzona; *(slang)* muso, grugno ‖ *v* *(pret & pp* **mugged**; *ger* **mugging**) *tr* (slang) fotografare; *(slang)* attaccare proditoriamente ‖ *intr* fare le smorfie

mug-gy ['mʌgi] *adj* (**-gier; -giest**) afoso, opprimente

mulat·to [mju'læto] or [mə'læto] *s* (**-toes**) mulatto

mulber·ry ['mʌl,beri] *s* (**-ries**) *(tree)* gelso; *(fruit)* mora di gelso

mulct [mʌlkt] *tr* defraudare

mule [mjul] *s* mulo; *(slipper)* pianella

muleteer [,mjulə'tɪr] *s* mulattiere *m*

mulish ['mjulɪʃ] *adj* testardo

mull [mʌl] *tr* *(wine)* scaldare aggiungendo spezie ‖ *intr*—**to mull over** pensarci sopra, rinvangare

mulled' wine' *s* vino caldo

mullion ['mʌljən] *s* colonnina che divide una bifora

multigraph ['mʌltɪ,græf] or ['mʌltɪ,grɑf] *s* (trademark) poligrafo ‖ *tr* poligrafare

multilateral [,mʌltɪ'lætərəl] *adj* multilaterale

multimotor [,mʌltɪ'motər] *s* plurimotore *m*

multiple ['mʌltɪpəl] *adj & s* multiplo

multiplici·ty [,mʌltɪ'plɪsɪti] *s* (**-ties**) molteplicità *f*

multi-ply ['mʌltɪ,plaɪ] *v* *(pret & pp* **-plied**) *tr* moltiplicare ‖ *intr* moltiplicarsi

multistage [ˈmʌltɪ ˌstedʒ] *adj* (rok) pluristadio

multitude [ˈmʌltɪ ˌtjud] or [ˈmʌltɪ- ˌtud] *s* moltitudine *f*

mum [mʌm] *adj* zitto; **mum's the word!** acqua in bocca!; **to keep mum** stare zitto ‖ *interj* zitto!

mumble [ˈmʌmbəl] *tr* biascicare ‖ *intr* farfugliare

mummer·y [ˈmʌməri] *s* (**-ies**) buffonata, mascherata

mum·my [ˈmʌmi] *s* (**-mies**) mummia

mumps [mʌmps] *s* orecchioni *mpl*

munch [mʌnt∫] *tr* sgranocchiare

mundane [ˈmʌnden] *adj* mondano

municipal [mjuˈnɪsɪpəl] *adj* municipale

municipali·ty [mju ˌnɪsɪˈpælɪti] *s* (**-ties**) municipio

munificent [mjuˈnɪfɪsənt] *adj* munifico

munition [mjuˈnɪʃən] *s* munizione ‖ *tr* fornire di munizioni

muni′tion dump′ *s* deposito munizioni

mural [ˈmjurəl] *adj* murale ‖ *s* pittura murale

murder [ˈmʌrdər] *s* omicidio ‖ *tr* assassinare

murderer [ˈmʌrdərər] *s* omicida *m*

murderess [ˈmʌrdərɪs] *s* omicida *f*

murderous [ˈmʌrdərəs] *adj* omicida, crudele, sanguinario

murk·y [ˈmʌrki] *adj* (**-ier; -iest**) fosco, tenebroso; brumoso, nebbioso

murmur [ˈmʌrmər] *s* mormorio ‖ *tr & intr* mormorare

Mur′phy bed′ [ˈmʌrfi] *s* letto a scomparsa

muscle [ˈmʌsəl] *s* muscolo

muscular [ˈmʌskjələr] *adj* muscolare; (*having well-developed muscles*) muscoloso

muse [mjuz] *s* musa; **the Muses** le Muse ‖ *intr* meditare, rimuginare

museum [mjuˈzi·əm] *s* museo

mush [mʌ∫] *s* pappa, polentina; (fig) leziosaggine *f*, sdolcinatura

mush′room *s* fungo ‖ *intr* venir su come i funghi; **to mushroom into** diventare rapidamente

mush′room cloud′ *s* fungo atomico

mush·y [ˈmʌ∫i] *adj* (**-ier; -iest**) polposo, spappolato; (fig) sdolcinato, sentimentale

music [ˈmjuzɪk] *s* musica; **to face the music** (coll) affrontare le conseguenze; **to set to music** mettere in musica

musical [ˈmjuzɪkəl] *adj* musicale

mu′sical com′edy *s* operetta, commedia musicale

musicale [ˌmjuzɪˈkæl] *s* serata musicale

mu′sic box′ *s* scatola armonica

mu′sic cab′inet *s* scaffaletto per la musica

mu′sic hall′ *s* salone *m* da concerti; (Brit) teatro di varietà, music-hall *m*

musician [mjuˈzɪʃən] *s* musicista *mf*

musicianship [mjuˈzɪʃən ˌʃɪp] *s* abilità *f* musicale, virtuosismo

musicologist [ˌmjuzɪˈkɑlədʒɪst] *s* musicologo

musicology [ˌmjuzɪˈkɑlədʒi] *s* musicologia

mu′sic stand′ *s* portamusica *m*

musk [mʌsk] *s* muschio

musk′ deer′ *s* mosco

musket [ˈmʌskɪt] *s* moschetto

musketeer [ˌmʌskɪˈtɪr] *s* moschettiere *m*

musk′mel′on *s* melone *m*

musk′ ox′ *s* bue muschiato

musk′rat′ *s* ondatra, topo muschiato

muslin [ˈmʌzlɪn] *s* mussolina

muss [mʌs] *tr* (*the hair*) scompigliare, arruffare; (*clothing*) (coll) sciupare

mussel [ˈmʌsəl] *s* mussolo

Mussulman [ˈmʌsəlmən] *adj & s* musulmano

muss·y [ˈmʌsi] *adj* (**-ier; -iest**) (coll) arruffato, scompigliato

must [mʌst] *s* (*new wine*) mosto; (*mold*) muffa; (coll) cosa assolutamente indispensabile ‖ *v aux*—**I must go now** devo andarmene ora; **it must be Ann** deve essere Anna; **she must be ill** dev'essere malata; **they must have known it** devono averlo saputo

mustache [məsˈtæ∫], [məsˈta∫] or [ˈmʌstæ∫] *s* baffi *mpl*, mustacchi *mpl*

mustard [ˈmʌstərd] *s* mostarda

mus′tard plas′ter *s* senapismo

muster [ˈmʌstər] *s* adunata, rivista; **to pass muster** passar ispezione ‖ *tr* chiamare a raccolta; riunire; **to muster in** arruolare; **to muster out** congedare; **to muster up courage** prendere coraggio a quattro mani

mus′ter roll′ *s* ruolo; (naut) appello

mus·ty [ˈmʌsti] *adj* (**-tier; -tiest**) (*moldy*) ammuffito; (*stale*) stantio; (fig) ammuffito, stantio

mutation [mjuˈteʃən] *s* mutazione

mute [mjut] *adj & s* muto ‖ *tr* mettere la sordina a

mutilate [ˈmjutɪ ˌlet] *tr* mutilare

mutineer [ˌmjutɪˈnɪr] *s* ammutinato

mutinous [ˈmjutɪnəs] *adj* ammutinato

muti·ny [ˈmjutɪni] *s* (**-nies**) ammutinamento ‖ *v* (*pret & pp* **-nied**) *intr* ammutinarsi

mutt [mʌt] *s* (slang) cane bastardo; (slang) scemo

mutter [ˈmʌtər] *tr & intr* borbottare

mutton [ˈmʌtən] *s* montone *m*

mut′ton chop′ *s* cotoletta di montone

mutual [ˈmut∫ʊ·əl] *adj* mutuo, vicendevole

mu′tual aid′ *s* mutualità *f*

mu′tual fund′ *s* fondo comune di investimento

muzzle [ˈmʌzəl] *s* (*of animal*) muso; (*device to keep animal from biting*) museruola; (*of firearm*) bocca ‖ *tr* mettere la museruola a; (fig) imbavagliare

my [maɪ] *adj poss* mio, il mio ‖ *interj* (coll) corbezzoli!

myriad [ˈmɪrɪ·əd] *s* miriade *f*

myrrh [mʌr] *s* mirra

myrtle [ˈmʌrtəl] *s* mirto, mortella

myself [maɪˈsɛlf] *pron pers* io stesso; me, me stesso; mi, e.g., **I hurt myself** mi sono fatto male

mysterious [mɪsˈtɪrɪ-əs] *adj* misterioso

myster·y [ˈmɪstəri] *s* (-ies) mistero

mystic [ˈmɪstɪk] *adj & s* mistico

mystical [ˈmɪstɪkəl] *adj* mistico

mysticism [ˈmɪstɪ ˌsɪzəm] *s* misticismo

mystification [ˌmɪstɪfɪˈkeʃən] *s* mistificazione

mysti·fy [ˈmɪstɪ ˌfaɪ] *v* (*pret & pp -fied*) *tr* avvolgere nel mistero; (*to hoax*) mistificare

myth [mɪθ] *s* mito

mythical [ˈmɪθɪkəl] *adj* mitico

mythological [ˌmɪθəˈlɑdʒɪkəl] *adj* mitologico

mytholo·gy [mɪˈθɑlədʒi] *s* (-gies) mitologia

N

N, n [ɛn] *s* quattordicesima lettera dell'alfabeto inglese

nab [næb] *v* (*pret & pp* **nabbed;** *ger* **nabbing**) *tr* (slang) afferrare, agguantare

nag [næg] *s* ronzino || *v* (*pret & pp* **nagged;** *ger* **nagging**) *tr & intr* tormentare, infastidire

naiad [ˈne·æd] or [ˈnaɪ·æd] *s* naiade *f*

nail [nel] *s* (*of finger or toe*) unghia; (*of metal*) chiodo; **to hit the nail on the head** cogliere nel giusto || *tr* inchiodare

nail'brush' spazzolino per le unghie

nail' file' *s* lima per le unghie

nail' pol'ish *s* smalto per le unghie

nail' set' *s* punzone *m*

naïve [nɑˈiv] *adj* candido, ingenuo

naked [ˈnekɪd] *adj* nudo, ignudo; **to strip naked** denudare; denudarsi; **with the naked eye** a occhio nudo

name [nem] *s* nome *m;* (*first name*) nome *m;* (*last name*) cognome *m;* fama, reputazione; titolo; lignaggio; **in the name of** nel nome di; **to call s.o. names** coprire qlco di ingiurie; **to go by the name of** essere conosciuto sotto il nome di; **to make a name for oneself** farsi un nome; **what is your name?** come si chiama Lei? || *tr* nominare; menzionare; battezzare; (*a price*) fissare

name' day' *s* onomastico

nameless [ˈnemlɪs] *adj* senza nome, anonimo

namely [ˈnemli] *adv* cioè, vale a dire

name'plate' *s* targa, targhetta

namesake [ˈnem ˌsek] *s* omonimo; persona chiamata in onore di qualcun altro

nan'ny goat' [ˈnæni] *s* capra

nap [næp] *s* lanugine *f;* (*pile*) pelo; pisolino, sonnellino; **to take a nap** schiacciare un sonnellino || *v* (*pret & pp* **napped;** *ger* **napping**) *intr* sonnecchiare; **to catch napping** cogliere alla sprovvista

napalm [ˈnepɑm] *s* napalm *m*

nape [nep] *s* nuca

naphtha [ˈnæfθə] *s* nafta

napkin [ˈnæpkɪn] *s* tovagliolo

nap'kin ring' *s* portatovagliolo

Naples [ˈnepləz] *s* Napoli *f*

Napoleonic [nə ˌpolɪˈɑnɪk] *adj* napoleonico

narcissus [nɑrˈsɪsəs] *s* narciso

narcotic [nɑrˈkɑtɪk] *adj & s* narcotico

narrate [næˈret] *tr* narrare

narration [næˈreʃən] *s* narrazione

narrative [ˈnærətɪv] *adj* narrativo || *s* narrazione; (*genre*) narrativa

narrator [næˈretər] *s* narratore *m*

narrow [ˈnæro] *adj* stretto; limitato; (*illiberal*) meschino, ristretto || **narrows** *spl* stretti *mpl* || *tr* limitare, restringere || *intr* limitarsi, restringersi

nar'row escape' *s*—**to have a narrow escape** scamparla bella

nar'row-gauge' *adj* a scartamento ridotto

narrow-minded [ˈnæroˈmaɪndɪd] *adj* gretto, ristretto d'idee

nasal [ˈnezəl] *adj & s* nasale *f*

nasturtium [nəˈstʌrʃəm] *s* nasturzio

nas·ty [ˈnæsti] or [ˈnɑsti] *adj* (-tier; -tiest) brutto, cattivo; sgradevole, orribile; sudicio; (*foul*) perfido

natatorium [ˌnetəˈtorɪ-əm] *s* piscina

nation [ˈneʃən] *s* nazione

national [ˈnæʃənəl] *adj & s* nazionale *mf*

na'tional an'them *s* inno nazionale

na'tional debt' *s* debito pubblico

na'tional hol'iday *s* festa nazionale

nationalism [ˈnæʃənə ˌlɪzəm] *s* nazionalismo

nationali·ty [ˌnæʃənˈælɪti] *s* (-ties) nazionalità *f*

nationalize [ˈnæʃənə ˌlaɪz] *tr* nazionalizzare

na'tion-wide' *adj* su scala nazionale

native [ˈnetɪv] *adj* nativo, indigeno, oriundo; (*language*) materno || *s* indigeno, nativo

na'tive land' *s* patria, paese natio

nativi·ty [nəˈtɪvɪti] *s* (-ties) nascita, natività *f* || **Nativity** *s* Natività *f*

Nato [ˈneto] *s* (acronym) (**North Atlantic Treaty Organization**) la N.A.T.O.

nat·ty [ˈnæti] *adj* (-tier; -tiest) accurato, elegante

natural [ˈnætʃərəl] *adj* naturale || *s* imbecille *mf;* (mus) bequadro; (mus) tono naturale; (mus) tasto bianco; **a natural** (coll) proprio quello che ci vuole

naturalism [ˈnætʃərə ˌlɪzəm] *s* naturalismo

naturalist [ˈnætʃərəlɪst] *s* naturalista *mf*

naturalization [ˌnætʃərəlɪˈzeʃən] *s* naturalizzazione

nat'uraliza'tion pa'pers *spl* documenti *mpl* di naturalizzazione naturalize ['næt∫ərə‚laız] tr naturaliz- zare

naturally ['næt∫ərəli] adv naturalmente

nature ['net∫ər] s natura; from nature dal vero

naught [nɔt] s niente m; zero; to come to naught ridursi al nulla; to set at naught disprezzare

naugh·ty ['nɔti] adj (-tier; -tiest) cattivo, disubbidiente; (joke) di cattivo genere

nausea ['nɔ∫ɪ·ə] or ['nɔsɪ·ə] s nausea

nauseate ['nɔ∫ɪ‚et] or ['nɔsɪ‚et] tr nauseare || intr essere nauseato

nauseating ['nɔ∫ɪ‚etɪŋ] or ['nɔsɪ‚etɪŋ] adj nauseabondo, stomachevole

nauseous ['nɔ∫ɪ·əs] or ['nɔsɪ·əs] adj nauseabondo

nautical ['nɔtɪkəl] adj nautico, marittimo, marino

naval ['nevəl] adj navale

na'val acad'emy s accademia navale

na'val of'ficer s ufficiale m di marina

na'val sta'tion s base f navale

nave [nev] s navata centrale; (of a wheel) mozzo

navel ['nevəl] s ombelico

na'vel or'ange s arancia (con depressione alla sommità)

navigability [‚nævɪgə'bɪlɪti] s navigabilità f; (of a ship) manovrabilità f

navigable ['nævɪgəbəl] adj (river) navigabile; (ship) manovrabile

navigate ['nævɪ‚get] tr & intr navigare

navigation [‚nævɪ'ge∫ən] s navigazione

navigator ['nævɪ‚getər] s navigatore m; (in charge of navigating ship or plane) ufficiale m di rotta

na·vy ['nevi] adj blu marino || s (-vies) marina (da guerra)

na'vy bean' s fagiolo secco

na'vy blue' s blu marino

na'vy yard' s arsenale m

nay [ne] s no; voto negativo || adv no; anzi

Nazarene [‚næzə'rin] adj & s nazzareno; the Nazarene il Nazzareno

Nazi ['nɑtsi] or ['nætsi] adj & s nazista mf

N-bomb ['en‚bɑm] s bomba al neutrone

Neapolitan [‚ni·ə'pɑlɪtən] adj & s napoletano

neap' tide' [nip] s marea di quadratura

near [nɪr] adj vicino, prossimo; intimo; esatto || adv vicino, da vicino || prep vicino a, accanto a; to come near avvicinarsi a || tr avvicinarsi a || intr avvicinarsi

nearby ['nɪr‚baɪ] adj vicino || adv vicino, qui vicino

Near' East' s Medio Oriente

nearly ['nɪrli] adv quasi; (a little more or less) press'a poco; per poco non, e.g., he nearly died per poco non morì

near-sighted ['nɪr'saɪtɪd] adj miope

near'-sight'ed·ness s miopia

neat [nit] adj netto, pulito; elegante, accurato; puro

neat's'-foot oil' s olio di piede di bue

Nebuchadnezzar [‚nebjəkəd'nezər] s Nabucodonosor m

nebu·la ['nebjələ] s (-lae [‚li] or -las) nebulosa

nebular ['nebjələr] adj nebulare

nebulous ['nebjələs] adj nebuloso

necessary ['nesɪ‚seri] adj necessario

necessitate [nɪ'sesɪ‚tet] tr necessitare, esigere

necessitous [nɪ'sesɪtəs] adj bisognoso

necessi·ty [nɪ'sesɪti] s (-ties) necessità f

neck [nek] s collo; (of a horse) incollatura; (of violin) manico; (of mountain) gola, passo; neck and neck testa a testa; to stick one's neck out (coll) esporsi al pericolo; to win by a neck vincere per una corta testa || intr (slang) abbracciarsi, sbaciucchiarsi

neck'band' s colletto

neckerchief ['nekər‚t∫ɪf] s fazzoletto da collo

necklace ['neklɪs] s collana

neck'line' s giro collo, scollatura

necktie ['nek‚taɪ] s cravatta

neck'tie pin' s spilla da cravatta

necrolo·gy [ne'krɑlədʒi] s (-gies) necrologia

necromancy ['nekrə‚mænsi] s necromanzia

nectar ['nektər] s nettare m

née or nee [ne] adj nata

need [nid] s necessità f, bisogno; povertà f; if need be se ci fosse bisogno; in need in strettezze || tr aver bisogno di || intr necessitare, essere in necessità || v aux—to need (to) + inf dovere + inf

needful ['nidfəl] adj necessario

needle ['nidəl] s ago; (of phonograph) puntina; to look for a needle in a haystack cercare l'ago nel pagliaio || tr cucire; (fig) aguzzare, eccitare

nee'dle bath' s bagno a doccia filiforme

nee'dle-case' s agoraio

nee'dle-point' s merletto; ricamo su canovaccio

needless ['nidlɪs] adj inutile

nee'dle-work' s lavoro di cucito; (embroidery) ricamo; (needlepoint) merletto

needs [nidz] adv necessariamente; it must needs be dev'essere proprio così

need·y ['nidi] adj (-ier; -iest) bisognoso, indigente || the needy i bisognosi

ne'er-do-well ['nerdu‚wel] adj & s buono a nulla

negate ['neget] or [nɪ'get] tr invalidare; negare

negation [nɪ'ge∫ən] s negazione

negative ['negətɪv] adj negativo || s negativa; (elec) polo negativo; (gram) negazione || tr respingere, votare contro; neutralizzare

neglect [nɪ'glekt] s negligenza, trascuratezza || tr trascurare; to neglect to trascurare di; dimenticarsi di

neglectful [nɪ'glektfəl] adj negligente, trascurato

négligée or negligee [‚neglɪ'ʒe] s veste f da camera or vestaglia per signora

negligence ['neglɪdʒəns] s negligenza, trascuratezza

negligent ['neglɪdʒənt] *adj* negligente, trascurato

negligible ['neglɪdʒɪbəl] *adj* trascurabile, insignificante

negotiable [nɪ'goʃɪ‧əbəl] *adj* negoziabile; (*security*) al portatore; (*road*) transitabile

negotiate [nɪ'goʃɪ,et] *tr* negoziare; (*to overcome*) superare || *intr* negoziare

negotiation [nɪ,goʃɪ'e/ən] *s* negoziazione, negoziato

Ne·gro ['nigro] *adj* negro || *s* (**-groes**) negro, nero

neigh [ne] *s* nitrito || *intr* nitrire

neighbor ['nebər] *adj* vicino, adiacente || *s* vicino; (*fellow man*) prossimo || *tr* essere vicino a || *intr* essere vicino

neighborhood ['nebər,hʊd] *s* vicinanza, vicinato; **in the neighborhood of** nei pressi di; (coll) a un dipresso, all'incirca

neighboring ['nebərɪŋ] *adj* vicino, attiguo; (*country*) limitrofo

neighborly ['nebərli] *adj* da buon vicino, socievole

neither ['niðər] *or* ['naɪðər] *adj indef* nessuno dei due, e.g., **neither boy** nessuno dei due ragazzi || *pron indef* nessuno dei due, né l'uno né l'altro || *conj* neppure, nemmeno, e.g., **neither do I** nemmeno io; **neither . . . nor** nè . . . nè

neme·sis ['nemɪsɪs] *s* (**-ses** [,sɪz]) nemesi *f* || **Nemesis** *s* Nemesi *f*

neologism [nɪ'ɑlə,dʒɪzəm] *s* neologismo

neomycin [,ni‧ə'maɪsɪn] *s* neomicina

ne'on lamp' ['ni‧ɑn] *s* lampada al neon

neophyte ['ni‧ə,faɪt] *s* neofita *mf*

nepenthe [nɪ'pɛnθi] *s* nepente *f*

nephew ['nɛfju] *or* ['nɛvju] *s* nipote *m*

Nepos ['nipɑs] *or* ['nepɑs] *s* Nipote *m*

Neptune ['nɛpt/un] *or* ['nɛptjun] *s* Nettuno

neptunium [nɛp't/unɪ‧əm] *or* [nɛp-'tjunɪ‧əm] *s* (chem) nettunio

Nero ['nɪro] *s* Nerone *m*

nerve [nʌrv] *adj* nervoso || *s* nervo; (*courage*) coraggio; (*boldness*) (coll) faccia tosta; **to get on one's nerves** dare ai nervi di qlcu; **to lose one's nerve** perdere le staffe

nerve-racking ['nʌrv,rækɪŋ] *adj* irritante, esasperante

nervous ['nʌrvəs] *adj* nervoso

nerv'ous break'down *s* esaurimento nervoso

nervousness ['nʌrvəsnɪs] *s* nervosismo

nerv·y ['nʌrvi] *adj* (**-ier; -iest**) (*strong*) forte, vigoroso; audace; (coll) insolente, sfacciato

nest [nɛst] *s* nido; (*of hen*) cova; (*retreat*) rifugio; (*hangout*) tana; (*brood*) nidiata; **to feather one's nest** farsi il gruzzolo || *tr* (*e.g., tables*) mettere l'uno nell'altro || *intr* nidificare

nest' egg' *s* endice *m*; (fig) gruzzolo

nestle ['nɛsəl] *tr* annidare || *intr* annidarsi, nidificare; (*to cuddle up*) rannicchiarsi

net [nɛt] *adj* netto || *s* rete *f*; (*snare*) laccio, trappola; guadagno netto ||

tr prendere con la rete; (*a sum of money*) fare un guadagno netto di

nether ['nɛðər] *adj* inferiore, infero

Netherlander ['nɛðər,lændər] *or* ['nɛð-ərlændər] *s* olandese *mf*

Netherlands, The ['nɛðərləndz] *spl* i Paesi Bassi

netting ['nɛtɪŋ] *s* rete *f*

nettle ['nɛtəl] *s* ortica || *tr* irritare, provocare

net'work' *s* rete *f*

neuralgia [njʊ'rældʒə] *or* [nʊ'rældʒə] *s* nevralgia

neurology [njʊ'rɑlədʒi] *or* [nʊ'rɑlədʒi] *s* neurologia

neuro·sis [njʊ'rosɪs] *or* [nʊ'rosɪs] (**-ses** [sɪz]) *s* neurosi *f*

neurotic [njʊ'rɑtɪk] *or* [nʊ'rɑtɪk] *adj* & *s* neurotico

neuter ['njutər] *or* ['nutər] *adj* neutro || *s* genere neutro

neutral ['njutrəl] *or* ['nutrəl] *adj* neutro; (*not aligned*) neutrale || *s* neutrale *m*; (mach) folle *m*

neutralist ['njutrəlɪst] *or* ['nutrəlɪst] *adj* & *s* neutralista *mf*

neutrality [nju'trælɪti] *or* [nu'trælɪti] *s* neutralità *f*

neutralize ['njutrə,laɪz] *or* ['nutrə,laɪz] *tr* neutralizzare

neutron ['njutrɑn] *or* ['nutrɑn] *s* neutrone *m*

neu'tron bomb' *s* bomba al neutrone

never ['nɛvər] *adv* mai, giammai; non . . . mai; **never mind** non importa

nev'er·more' *adv* mai più

nevertheless [,nɛvərðə'lɛs] *adv* ciò nonostante, ciò nondimeno, tuttavia

new [nju] *or* [nu] *adj* nuovo; **what's new?** che c'è di nuovo?

new' arri'val *s* nuovo venuto; (*baby*) neonato

new'born' *adj* neonato; (*e.g., faith*) rinato

New'cas'tle *s*—**to carry coals to Newcastle** portare l'acqua al mare, portare vasi a Samo

newcomer ['nju,kʌmər] *or* ['nu-,kʌmər] *s* nuovo venuto

New' Eng'land *s* la Nuova Inghilterra

newfangled ['nju'fæŋgəld] *or* ['nu-,fæŋgəld] *adj* all'ultima moda; di nuovo conio, di nuova invenzione

Newfoundland ['njufənd,lænd] *or* ['nufənd,lænd] *s* la Terranova || [nju'faʊndlənd] *or* [nu'faʊndlənd] *s* (*dog*) terranova *m*

newly ['njuli] *or* ['nuli] *adv* di recente, di fresco

new'ly·wed' *s* sposino *or* sposina; **the newlyweds** gli sposi

new' moon' *s* luna nuova, novilunio

news [njuz] *or* [nuz] *s* notizie *fpl*; **a news item** una notizia; **a piece of news** una notizia

news' a'gency *s* agenzia d'informazioni

news'beat' *s* colpo giornalistico

news'boy' *s* strillone *m*

news'cast' *s* notiziario

news'cast'er *s* annunziatore *m*, radiocommentatore *m*, telecommentatore *m*

news' con'ference *s* conferenza stampa

news' cov'erage *s* reportaggio
news'deal'er *s* venditore *m* di giornali
news'man' *s* (**-men'**) (*reporter*) giornalista *m;* giornalaio
newsmonger ['njuz ,mʌŋgər] or ['nuz ,mʌŋgər] *s* persona pettegola, gazzettino
news'pa'per *adj* giornalistico || *s* giornale *m*
news'pa'per·man' *s* (**-men'**) giornalista *m*
news'print' *s* carta da giornale
news'reel' *s* cinegiornale *m*
news'stand' *s* chiosco, edicola
news'week'ly *s* (**-lies**) settimanale *m* d'informazione
news'wor'thy *adj* degno d'essere pubblicato, di viva attualità
news·y ['njuzi] or ['nuzi] *adj* (**-ier; -iest**) (coll) informativo
New' Tes'tament *s* Nuovo Testamento
New' Year's' card' *s* cartolina d'auguri di capodanno
New' Year's' Day' *s* il capo d'anno, il capodanno
New' Year's' Eve' *s* la vigilia di capodanno, la sera di San Silvestro
New' York' [jork] *adj* nuovayorchese || *s* New York *f,* Nuova York
New' York'er ['jorkər] *s* nuovayorchese *mf*
New' Zea'land ['ziland] *adj* neozelandese || *s* la Nuova Zelanda
New' Zea'lander ['zilandər] *s* neozelandese *mf*
next [nekst] *adj* prossimo, seguente; (*month*) prossimo, entrante || *adv* la prossima volta; dopo, in seguito; **next to** vicino a; **next to nothing** quasi nulla; **to come next** essere il prossimo
next'-door' *adj* della casa vicina || **next'-door'** *adv* nella casa vicina
next' of kin' *s* (**next' of kin'**) parente più prossimo
niacin ['naɪ·əsɪn] *s* niacina
Niag'ara Falls' [naɪ'ægərə] *spl* le Cascate del Niagara
nib [nɪb] *s* becco; punta; **his nibs** (slang & pej) sua eccellenza
nibble ['nɪbəl] *s* piccolo morso || *tr & intr* mordicchiare, sbocconcellare; (*said of a fish*) abboccare
nice [naɪs] *adj* (*pleasant*) simpatico, gentile; (*requiring skill*) buono, bello; (*fine*) sottile; (*refined*) raffinato, per bene; (*fussy*) esigente, difficile; rispettabile; (*weather*) bello; (*attractive*) bello; **nice . . . and** (coll) bello, e.g., **it is nice and warm** fa un bel caldo
nice-looking ['naɪs'lʊkɪŋ] *adj* bello, attraente
nicely ['naɪsli] *adv* precisamente, esattamente; (coll) benissimo
nice·ty ['naɪsəti] *s* (**-ties**) esattezza, precisione; **to a nicety** con la massima precisione
niche [nɪtʃ] *s* nicchia
Nicholas ['nɪkələs] *s* Nicola *m*
nick [nɪk] *s* intaccatura; (*of a dish*) slabbratura; **in the nick of time** al

momento giusto || *tr* intaccare; (*to cut*) tagliare; (*a dish*) slabbrare
nickel ['nɪkəl] *s* nichel *m;* moneta americana di cinque cents || *tr* nichelare
nick'el plate' *s* nichelatura
nick'el-plate' *tr* nichelare
nicknack ['nɪk,næk] *s* soprammobile *m;* gingillo, ninnolo
nick'name' *s* nomignolo, soprannome *m* || *tr* soprannominare
nicotine ['nɪkə,tin] *s* nicotina
niece [nis] *s* nipote *f*
nif·ty ['nɪfti] *adj* (**-tier; -tiest**) (coll) elegante; (coll) eccellente
niggard ['nɪgərd] *adj & s* spilorcio
night [naɪt] *adj* notturno || *s* notte *f;* **at** or **by night** di notte; **the night before last** l'altra notte; **to make a night of it** (coll) fare le ore piccole
night'cap' *s* berretto da notte; bicchierino di liquore che si beve prima di coricarsi
night' club' *s* night-club *m*
night' driv'ing *s* il guidare di notte
night'fall' *s* crepuscolo; **at nightfall** sul cader della notte, all'imbrunire
night'gown' *s* camicia da notte
nightingale ['naɪtən,gel] *s* usignolo
night' latch' *s* serratura a molla
night' let'ter *s* telegramma notturno
night'long' *adj* di tutta la notte || *adv* tutta la notte
nightly ['naɪtli] *adj* di notte; di ogni notte || *adv* di notte; ogni notte
night'mare' *s* incubo
nightmarish ['naɪt,merɪʃ] *adj* raccapricciante
night' owl' *s* (coll) nottambulo
night' school' *s* scuola serale
night'shirt' *s* camicia da notte
night'time' *s* notte *f*
night'walk'er *s* nottambulo; vagabondo notturno; (*prostitute*) passeggiatrice *f*
night' watch' *s* guardia notturna
night' watch'man *s* (**-men**) guardiano notturno
nihilist ['naɪ·ɪlɪst] *s* nichilista *mf*
nil [nɪl] *s* nulla *m,* niente *m*
Nile [naɪl] *s* Nilo
nimble ['nɪmbəl] *adj* agile, svelto
Nimrod ['nɪmrad] *s* Nembrod *m*
nincompoop ['nɪnkəm,pup] *s* babbeo, tonto, semplicione *m*
nine [naɪn] *adj & pron* nove || *s* nove *m;* **nine o' clock** le nove
nine' hun'dred *adj, s & pron* novecento
nineteen ['naɪn'tin] *adj, s & pron* diciannove *m*
nineteenth ['naɪn'tinθ] *adj & s* diciannovesimo; (*century*) decimonono || *s* (*in dates*) diciannove *m* || *pron* diciannovesimo
ninetieth ['naɪntɪ·ɪθ] *adj, s & pron* novantesimo
nine·ty ['naɪnti] *adj & pron* novanta || *s* (**-ties**) novanta *m;* **the gay nineties** il decennio scapestrato dal 1890 al 1900
ninth [naɪnθ] *adj, s & pron* nono || *s* (*in dates*) nove *m*
nip [nɪp] *s* morso, pizzicotto; freddo pungente; (*of liquor*) bicchierino,

sorso; **nip and tuck** testa a testa ‖ *v* (*pret* & *pp* **nipped; ger nipping**) *tr* pizzicare, mordere; (*to squeeze*) spremere; (*to freeze*) gelare; (*liquor*) sorseggiare; **to nip in the bud** arrestare di bel principio ‖ *intr* bere a sorsi

nipple ['nɪpəl] *s* capezzolo; (*of rubber*) tettarella; (*mach*) corto tubo filettato a entrambe le estremità, manicotto, cappuccio

Nippon [nɪ'pɑn] or ['nɪpɑn] *s* il Giappone

Nippon·ese [ˌnɪpə'niz] *adj* nipponico ‖ *s* (*-ese*) Giapponese *mf*

nip·py ['nɪpi] *adj* (*-pier; -piest*) mordente, pizzicante; gelato

nirvana [nɪr'vɑnə] *s* il nirvana

nit [nɪt] *s* lendine *m*; pidocchio

niter ['naɪtər] *s* nitro

nit'-pick' *intr* (coll) cercare il pelo nell'uovo

nitrate ['naɪtret] *s* nitrato; (agr) nitrato di soda; (agr) nitrato di potassio

ni'tric ac'id ['naɪtrɪk] *s* acido nitrico

nitride ['naɪtraɪd] *s* azoturo, nitruro

nitrogen ['naɪtrədʒən] *s* azoto

nitroglycerin [ˌnaɪtrə'glɪsərɪn] *s* nitroglicerina

ni'trous ox'ide ['naɪtrəs] *s* ossidulo di azoto

nitwit ['nɪtˌwɪt] *s* (slang) baggiano

no [no] *adj* nessuno; **no admittance** vietato l'ingresso; **no doubt** senza dubbio; **no matter** non importa; **no parking** divieto di sosta; **no smoking** vietato fumare; **no thoroughfare** divieto di transito; **no use** inutilmente; **with no senza** ‖ *s* no; voto negativo ‖ *adv* no; non; **no longer** non . . . più; **no sooner** non appena

Noah ['no-ə] *s* Noè *m*

nob·by ['nɑbi] *adj* (*-bier; -biest*) (slang) elegante; (slang) eccellente

nobili·ty [no'bɪlɪti] *s* (*-ties*) nobiltà *f*

noble ['nobəl] *adj* & *s* nobile *m*

no'ble·man *s* (*-men*) nobile *m*, nobiluomo

no'ble·wom'an *s* (*-wom'en*) nobile *f*, nobildonna

nobod·y ['no ˌbɑdi] or ['nobədi] *s* (*-ies*) nessuno, illustre sconosciuto ‖ *pron indef* nessuno; **nobody but** nessun altro che; **nobody else** nessun altro

nocturnal [nɑk'tʌrnəl] *adj* notturno

nod [nɑd] *s* cenno d'assenso, cenno del capo; (*of person going to sleep*) crollo del capo ‖ *v* (*pret* & *pp* **nodded**; *ger* **nodding**) *tr* (*one's head*) inclinare; **to nod assent** fare cenno di sì ‖ *intr* inclinare il capo; (*to drowse*) assopirsi

node [nod] *s* nodo; protuberanza; (phys) nodo

no'-good' *adj* & *s* (coll) buono a nulla

nohow ['no ˌhaʊ] *adv* (coll) in nessuna maniera

noise [nɔɪz] *s* rumore *m* ‖ *tr* divulgare

noiseless ['nɔɪzlɪs] *adj* silenzioso

nois·y ['nɔɪzi] *adj* (*-ier; -iest*) rumoroso, chiassoso

nomad ['nomæd] *adj* & *s* nomade *m*

no' man's' land' *s* terra di nessuno

nominal ['nɑmɪnəl] *adj* nominale; simbolico

nominate ['nɑmɪ ˌnet] *tr* presentare la candidatura di; (*to appoint*) nominare, designare

nomination [ˌnɑmɪ'neʃən] *s* candidatura; nomina

nominative ['nɑmɪnətɪv] *adj* & *s* nominativo

nominee [ˌnɑmɪ'ni] *s* candidato designato

nonbelligerent [ˌnɑnbə'lɪdʒərənt] *adj* & *s* non belligerante *m*

nonbreakable [nɑn'brekəbəl] *adj* infrangibile

nonce [nɑns] *s*—**for the nonce** per l'occasione

nonchalance ['nɑnʃələns] or [ˌnɑnʃə'lɑns] *s* disinvoltura, indifferenza

nonchalant ['nɑnʃələnt] or [ˌnɑnʃə'lɑnt] *adj* disinvolto, indifferente

noncom ['nɑn ˌkɑm] *s* (coll) sottufficiale *m*

noncombatant [nɑn'kɑmbətənt] *adj* non combattente ‖ *s* persona non combattente

non'commis'sioned of'ficer [ˌnɑnkə'mɪʃənd] *s* sottufficiale *m*

noncommittal [ˌnɑnkə'mɪtəl] *adj* ambiguo, evasivo

non compos mentis ['nɑn 'kɑmpəs 'mentɪs] *adj* pazzo; (law) incapace

nonconformist [ˌnɑnkən'fɔrmɪst] *s* anticonformista *mf*, nonconformista *mf*

nondelivery [ˌnɑndɪ'lɪvəri] *s* mancata consegna

nondescript ['nɑndɪ ˌskrɪpt] *adj* indefinibile, inclassificabile

none [nʌn] *pron indef* nessuno; **none of** nessuno di; **none other** nessun altro ‖ *adv* non; affatto, niente affatto; **none the less** ciò nonostante, nondimeno

nonenti·ty [nɑn'entɪti] *s* (*-ties*) inesistenza; (*person*) nullità *f*

nonfiction [nɑn'fɪkʃən] *s* letteratura non romanzesca

nonfulfillment [ˌnɑnfʊl'fɪlmənt] *s* mancanza di esecuzione

nonintervention [ˌnɑnɪntər'venʃən] *s* non intervento

nonmetal ['nɑn ˌmetəl] *s* metalloide *m*

nonpayment [nɑn'pemənt] *s* mancato pagamento

non·plus ['nɑnplʌs] or [nɑn'plʌs] *s* perplessità *f* ‖ *v* (*pret* & *pp* **-plussed** or **plused**; *ger* **-plussing** or **-plusing**) *tr* lasciare perplesso

nonprofit [nɑn'prɑfɪt] *adj* senza scopo lucrativo

nonrefillable [ˌnɑnrɪ'fɪləbəl] *adj* (*prescription*) non ripetibile; (*e.g., bottle*) non ricaricabile

nonresident [nɑn'rezɪdənt] *s* persona di passaggio, non residente *mf*

nonresidential [nɑn ˌrezɪ'denʃəl] *adj* commerciale, non residenziale

nonscientific [nɑn ˌsaɪ-ən'tɪfɪk] *adj* non scientifico

nonsectarian [,nɑnsek'tɛrɪ·ən] *adj* che non segue nessuna confessione religiosa

nonsense ['nɑnsens] *s* sciocchezza, assurdità *f*, nonsenso

nonsensical [nɑn'sensɪkəl] *adj* sciocco, assurdo, illogico

nonskid ['nɑn'skɪd] *adj* antiderapante

nonstop ['nɑn'stɑp] *adj & adv* senza scalo

nonsupport [,nɑnsə'port] *s* mancato pagamento degli alimenti

noodle ['nudəl] *s* (slang) scemo; (slang) testa; **noodles** tagliatelle *fpl*

noo'dle soup' *s* tagliatelle *fpl* in brodo

nook [nʊk] *s* angolo, cantuccio

noon [nun] *s* mezzogiorno; **at high noon** a mezzogiorno in punto

no one or **no-one** ['no ,wʌn] *pron indef* nessuno; **no one else** nessun altro

noontime ['nun ,taɪm] *s* mezzogiorno

noose [nus] *s* laccio, nodo scorsoio

nor [nɔr] *conj* nè

Nordic ['nɔrdɪk] *adj* nordico

norm [nɔrm] *s* norma, media, tipo

normal ['nɔrməl] *adj* normale || *s* condizione normale; norma; (geom) normale *f*

Norman ['nɔrmən] *adj & s* normanno

Normandy ['nɔrməndɪ] *s* la Normandia

Norse [nɔrs] *adj* norvegese; scandinavo || *s* (*ancient Scandinavian language*) scandinavo; (*language of Norway*) norvegese *m;* **the Norse** gli scandinavi; i norvegesi

Norse'man *s* (**-men**) normanno

north [nɔrθ] *adj* del nord, settentrionale || *s* nord *m* || *adv* al nord, verso il nord

North' Amer'ica *s* l'America del Nord

North' Amer'ican *adj & s* nordamericano

north'east' *adj* di nord-est || *s* nord-est *m* || *adv* al nord-est

north'east'er *s* vento di nord-est

northern ['nɔrðərn] *adj* settentrionale; (*Hemisphere*) boreale

North' Kore'a *s* la Corea del Nord

North' Pole' *s* polo nord

northward ['nɔrθwərd] *adv* verso il nord

north'west' *adj* di nord-ovest || *s* nord-ovest *m* || *adv* al nord-ovest

north' wind' *s* vento del nord, aquilone *m*

Norway ['nɔrwe] *s* la Norvegia

Norwegian [nɔr'widʒən] *adj & s* norvegese *mf* || *s* (*language*) norvegese *m*

nose [noz] *s* naso; (*of missile*) testata; **to blow one's nose** soffiarsi il naso; **to count noses** contare il numero dei presenti; **to follow one's nose** andare a lume di naso; **to lead by the nose** menare per il naso; **to look down one's nose at** (coll) guardare dall'alto in basso; **to pay through the nose** pagare un occhio della testa; **to pick one's nose** mettersi le dita nel naso; **to speak through the nose** parlare nel naso; **to thumb one's nose at** fare marameo a; **to turn up one's nose at** guardare dall'alto in basso, guardare

con dispregio || *tr* fiutare; **to nose out** vincere per un pelo || *intr* fiutare; **to nose about** curiosare

nose' bag' *s* musetta

nose'band' *s* museruola di cavallo

nose'bleed' *s* sangue *m* dal naso

nose' cone' *s* ogiva

nose' dive' *s* (*of prices*) subita discesa; (aer) discesa in picchiata

nose'-dive' *intr* discendere in picchiata

nosegay ['noz ,ge] *s* mazzolino di fiori

nose' glass'es *spl* occhiali *mpl* a stringinaso

nose' ring' *s* nasiera

nose'wheel' *s* (aer) ruota del carrello anteriore

no'-show' *s* (coll) passeggero che si è prenotato e non parte

nostalgia [nɑ'stældʒə] *s* nostalgia

nostalgic [nɑ'stældʒɪk] *adj* nostalgico

nostril ['nɑstrɪl] *s* narice *f*

nos·y ['nozi] *adj* (**-ier; -iest**) (coll) curioso

not [nɑt] *adv* no; non; **not at all** niente affatto; **not yet** non ancora; **to think not** credere di no; **why not?** come no?

notable ['notəbəl] *adj* notevole, notabile || *s* notabile *m*

notarize ['notə ,raɪz] *tr* munire di fede notarile

nota·ry ['notəri] *s* (**-ries**) notaio

notch [nɑtʃ] *s* tacca; (*in mountain*) passo; (coll) tantino; **notches** (coll) di gran lunga, e.g., **notches above** di gran lunga migliore || *tr* intaccare

note [not] *s* nota, annotazione; (*currency*) banconota; (*communication*) memorandum *m;* (*of bird*) canto; (*tone of voice*) tono; (*reputation*) riguardo; (*short letter*) biglietto, letterina; (mus) nota; (com) cambiale *f* || *tr* notare, annotare; osservare

note'book' *s* (*for school*) quaderno; taccuino, notes *m*

noted ['notɪd] *adj* ben noto, eminente

note' pa'per *s* carta da lettera

note'wor'thy *adj* notevole

nothing ['nʌθɪŋ] *s* niente *m*, nulla; **for nothing** gratis; inutilmente; **next to nothing** quasi niente || *pron indef* niente, nulla, non . . . niente, non . . . nulla; **nothing else** nient'altro; **to make nothing of** il non farne caso || *adv* per nulla; **nothing less** non meno

notice ['notɪs] *s* attenzione; notizia, notifica; annunzio, preavviso; (*in newspaper*) trafiletto; (law) disdetta; **on short notice** senza preavviso; (com) a breve scadenza; **to escape the notice of** passare inavvertito a; **to serve notice to** far sapere a, far constatare a || *tr* osservare, notare, prendere nota di

noticeable ['notɪsəbəl] *adj* notevole; (*e.g., difference*) percettibile

noti·fy ['notɪ ,faɪ] *v* (*pret & pp* **-fied**) *tr* informare, far sapere

notion ['noʃən] *s* nozione; (*whim*) capriccio; **notions** mercerie *fpl*; **to have a notion to** aver voglia di

notorie·ty [,notə'raɪ·ɪti] *s* (**-ties**) (*state*

of being well known) notorietà *f;* cattiva fama

notorious [no'tori·əs] *adj (generally known)* notorio; *(unfavorably known)* famigerato

no'-trump' *adj & s* senza atout *m*

notwithstanding [ˌnɑtwɪð'stændɪŋ] or [ˌnɑtwɪθ'stændɪŋ] *adv* ciò nonostante || *prep* malgrado || *conj* sebbene

nougat ['nugət] *s* torrone *m*

noun [naun] *s* nome *m,* sostantivo

nourish ['nɑrɪʃ] *tr* nutrire

nourishing ['nɑrɪʃɪŋ] *adj* nutriente

nourishment ['nɑrɪʃmənt] *s* nutrimento

novel ['nɑvəl] *adj* nuovo, novello, insolito, originale || *s* romanzo

novelist ['nɑvəlɪst] *s* romanziere *m*

novel·ty ['nɑvəlti] *s* (**-ties**) novità *f;* **novelties** chincaglierie *fpl*

November [no'vembər] *s* novembre *m*

novice ['nɑvɪs] *s* novizio

novitiate [no'vɪʃi·ɪt] *s* noviziato

novocaine ['novə‚ken] *s* novocaina

now [nau] *s* presente *m* || *adv* adesso; **from now on** d'ora in poi; **just now** un momento fa; **now and then** di tempo in tempo; **now that** visto che || *conj* visto che, dato che

nowadays ['nau·ə‚dez] *adv* al giorno d'oggi, oggidì

no'way' *adv* in nessun modo; nient'affatto

no'where' *adv* da nessuna parte; **nowhere else** da nessun'altra parte, in nessun altro luogo

noxious ['nɑkʃəs] *adj* nocivo

nozzle ['nɑzəl] *s (of hose or pipe)* boccaglio; *(of tea pot, gas burner)* becco; *(of gun)* bocca; *(of sprinkling can)* bocchetta; *(aut, mach)* becco; (slang) naso

nth [enθ] *adj* ennesimo; **to the nth degree** all'ennesima potenza

nuance [nju'ɑns] or ['nju·ɑns] *s* sfumatura

nub [nʌb] *s* protuberanza; *(of coal)* pezzo; (coll) nocciolo, cuore *m*

nuclear ['njukli·ər] or ['nukli·ər] *adj* nucleare

nu'clear fis'sion *s* fissione nucleare

nu'clear fu'sion *s* fusione nucleare

nu'clear test' ban' *s* accordo per la tregua atomica

nucle·us ['njukli·əs] or ['nukli·əs] *s* (**-i** [‚aɪ] or **-uses**) nucleo

nude [njud] or [nud] *adj* nudo || *s*—**in the nude** nudo

nudge [nʌdʒ] *s* gomitatina || *tr* dare di gomito a

nudist ['njudɪst] or ['nudɪst] *adj & s* nudista *mf*

nudi·ty ['njudɪti] or ['nudɪti] *s* (**-ties**) nudità *f*

nugget ['nʌgɪt] *s* pepita

nuisance ['njusəns] or ['nusəns] *s* noia, seccatura; *(person)* seccatore *m,* pittima *mf*

null [nʌl] *adj* nullo; **null and void** invalido

nulli·fy ['nʌlɪ‚faɪ] *v* (*pret & pp* **-fied**) *tr* annullare, invalidare

nulli·ty ['nʌlɪti] *s* (**-ties**) nullità *f*

numb [nʌm] *adj* intorpidito; *(from cold)* intirizzito; **to become numb** intorpidirsi || *tr* intorpidire

number ['nʌmbər] *s* numero; *(for sale)* articolo di vendita; *(publication)* fascicolo; *(of a serial)* dispensa, puntata; **a number of** parecchi; **beyond** or **without number** senza numero, infiniti || *tr* numerare, contare; **his days are numbered** i suoi giorni sono contati || *intr*—**to number among** essere tra

numberless ['nʌmbərlɪs] *adj* innumerevole

numeral ['njumərəl] or ['numərəl] *adj* numerale || *s* numero

numerical [nju'merɪkəl] or [nu'merɪkəl] *adj* numerico

numerous ['njumərəs] or ['numərəs] *adj* numeroso

numskull ['nʌm‚skʌl] *s* (coll) stupido

nun [nʌn] *s* monaca, religiosa

nuptial ['nʌpʃəl] *adj* nuziale || **nuptials** *spl* nozze *fpl*

nurse [nʌrs] *s* infermiera; *(to suckle a child)* nutrice *f;* *(to take care of a child)* bambinaia || *tr (to minister to)* curare; allattare; allevare; *(e.g., hatred)* covare || *intr* fare l'infermiera

nurser·y ['nʌrsəri] *s* (**-ies**) stanza dei bambini; *(shelter for children)* asilo infantile; (hort) vivaio

nurs'ery·man *s* (**-men**) orticoltore *m*

nurs'ery rhyme' *s* canzoncina per i più piccini

nurs'ery school' *s* scuola materna

nursing ['nʌrsɪŋ] *adj* infermieristico || *s* allattamento; professione d'infermiera

nurs'ing bot'tle *s* biberon *m,* poppatoio

nurs'ing home' *s* convalescenziario; ospizio dei vecchi, gerontocomio

nurture ['nʌrt/ər] *s* allevamento; nutrimento || *tr* allevare; alimentare; *(e.g., hope)* accarezzare

nut [nʌt] *s* noce *f;* *(eccentric)* (slang) esaltato, pazzoide *m;* (mus) capotasto; *(mach)* madrevite *f,* dado; **a hard nut to crack** un osso duro da rodere; **to be nuts for** (coll) essere pazzo per

nut'crack'er *s* schiaccianoci *m*

nutmeg ['nʌt‚meg] *s* noce moscata

nutrition [nju'trɪʃən] or [nu'trɪʃən] *s* *(process)* nutrizione; *(food)* nutrimento

nutritious [nju'trɪʃəs] or [nu'trɪʃəs] *adj* nutriente

nut'shell' *s* guscio di noce; **in a nutshell** in breve, in poche parole

nut·ty ['nʌti] *adj* (**-tier; -tiest**) che sa di noci; (slang) pazzo; **nutty about** (slang) pazzo per

nuzzle ['nʌzəl] *tr* toccare col muso, ammusare || *intr (said of swine)* grufolare; *(said of other animals)* stare muso a muso, ammusare; *(to snuggle)* rannicchiarsi

nylon ['naɪlɑn] *s* nailon *m*

nymph [nɪmf] *s* ninfa

O

O, o [o] *s* quindicesima lettera dell'alfabeto inglese

O *interj* o!, oh!

oaf [of] *s* balordo, scemo, imbecille *mf*

oak [ok] *s* quercia

oaken ['okən] *adj* di quercia, quercino

oakum ['okəm] *s* stoppa incatramata

oar [or] *s* remo; **to lie or rest on one's oars** dormire sugli allori; non lavorare più ‖ *tr* spingere coi remi ‖ *intr* remare

oar'lock' *s* scalmo

oars'man *s* (**-men**) rematore *m*

oa·sis [o'esɪs] *s* (**-ses** [siz]) oasi *f*

oat [ot] *s* avena; **oats** (*seeds*) avena; **to feel one's oats** (coll) essere pieno di vita; (coll) sentirsi importante; **to sow one's wild oats** correre la cavallina

oath [oθ] *s* giuramento; **on oath** sotto giuramento; **to take an oath** giurare, prestar giuramento

oat'meal' *s* (*breakfast food*) fiocchi *mpl* d'avena; farina d'avena

obdurate ['abdjərɪt] *adj* indurito, inesorabile; impenitente, incallito

obedience [o'bidɪ·əns] *s* obbedienza, ubbidienza

obedient [o'bidɪ·ənt] *adj* ubbidiente

obeisance [o'besəns] *or* [o'bisəns] *s* saluto rispettoso; omaggio

obelisk ['abəlɪsk] *s* obelisco

obese [o'bis] *adj* obeso

obesity [o'bisɪti] *s* obesità *f*

obey ['obe] *tr* ubbidire (with *dat*), ubbidire ‖ *intr* ubbidire

obfuscate [ab'fʌsket] *or* ['abfəs,ket] *tr* offuscare

obitu·ar·y [o'bɪtʃʊ,ɛri] *adj* necrologico ‖ *s* (**-ies**) necrologia

object [ab'dʒɪkt] *s* oggetto ‖ [ab'dʒɛkt] *tr* obiettare ‖ *intr* fare obiezioni, obiettare

objection [ab'dʒɛkʃən] *s* obiezione

objectionable [ab'dʒɛkʃənəbəl] *adj* reprensibile; (*e.g., odor*) sgradevole; offensivo

objective [ab'dʒɛktɪv] *adj & s* obiettivo

obligate ['ablɪ,get] *tr* obbligare

obligation [,ablɪ'geʃən] *s* obbligo, obbligazione

oblige [ə'blaɪdʒ] *tr* obbligare; favorire; **much obliged** obbligatissimo

obliging [ə'blaɪdʒɪŋ] *adj* compiacente, accomodante, servizievole

oblique [ə'blik] *adj* obliquo; indiretto

obliterate [ə'blɪtə,ret] *tr* obliterare; spegnere, distruggere

oblivion [ə'blɪvɪ·ən] *s* oblio

oblivious [ə'blɪvɪ·əs] *adj* (*forgetful*) dimentico; (*unaware*) ignaro

oblong ['ablɔŋ] *or* ['ablaŋ] *adj* oblungo

obnoxious [ab'nakʃəs] *adj* detestabile

oboe ['obo] *s* oboe *m*

oboist ['obo·ɪst] *s* oboista *mf*

obscene [ab'sin] *adj* osceno

obsceni·ty [ab'senɪti] *or* [ab'sɪnɪti] *s* (**-ties**) oscenità *f*, sconcezza

obscure [əb'skjʊr] *adj* oscuro ‖ *tr* oscurare

obscuri·ty [əb'skjʊrɪti] *s* (**-ties**) oscurità *f*

obsequies ['absɪkwiz] *spl* esequie *fpl*

obsequious [əb'sikwɪ·əs] *adj* ossequioso, servile

observance [əb'zʌrvəns] *s* osservanza; **observances** pratiche *fpl*; cerimonie *fpl*

observation [,abzər've∫ən] *s* osservazione; osservanza

observa'tion car' *s* (rr) vettura belvedere

observato·ry [əb'zʌrvə,tori] *s* (**-ries**) osservatorio

observe [əb'zʌrv] *tr* osservare

observer [əb'zʌrvər] *s* osservatore *m*

obsess [əb'ses] *tr* ossessionare

obsession [əb'seʃən] *s* ossessione

obsolescent [,absə'lesənt] *adj* che sta cadendo in disuso

obsolete ['absə,lit] *adj* disusato

obstacle ['abstəkəl] *s* ostacolo

obstetrical [ab'stetrɪkəl] *adj* ostetrico

obstetrics [ab'stetrɪks] *s* ostetricia

obstina·cy ['abstɪnəsi] *s* (**-cies**) ostinazione

obstinate ['abstɪnɪt] *adj* ostinato

obstreperous [ab'strepərəs] *adj* turbolento; rumoroso

obstruct [əb'strʌkt] *tr* ostruire

obstruction [əb'strʌkʃən] *s* ostruzione

obtain [əb'ten] *tr* ottenere ‖ *intr* prevalere, essere in voga

obtrusive [əb'trusɪv] *adj* intruso, importuno; sporgente

obtuse [əb'tjus] *or* [əb'tus] *adj* ottuso

obviate ['abvɪ,et] *tr* ovviare (with *dat*)

obvious ['abvɪ·əs] *adj* ovvio, palmare

occasion [ə'keʒən] *s* occasione; **on occasion** di quando in quando ‖ *tr* occasionare

occasional [ə'keʒənəl] *adj* saltuario; (*e.g., verses*) d'occasione

occasionally [ə'keʒənəli] *adv* occasionalmente, di tanto in tanto

occident ['aksɪdənt] *s* occidente *m*

occidental [,aksɪ'dɛntəl] *adj & s* occidentale *mf*

occlud'ed front' [ə'kludɪd] *s* fronte occluso

occlusion [ə'kluʒən] *s* occlusione

occlusive [ə'klusɪv] *adj* occlusivo ‖ *s* occlusiva

occult [ə'kʌlt] *or* ['akʌlt] *adj* occulto

occupancy ['akjəpənsi] *s* occupazione, presa di possesso; (*tenancy*) locazione

occupant ['akjəpənt] *s* occupante *m*; (*tenant*) inquilino

occupation [,akjə'peʃən] *s* occupazione

occupational [,akjə'peʃənəl] *adj* occupazionale; (*e.g., disease*) professionale, del lavoro

occu·py ['akjə,paɪ] *v* (*pret & pp* **-pied**) *tr* occupare; (*to dwell in*) abitare

oc·cur [ə'kʌr] *v* (*pret & pp* **-curred**;

ger -curring) *intr* accadere, succedere; incontrarsi; (*to come to mind*)
venir in mente, e.g., **it occurs to me**
mi viene in mente

occurrence [ə'kʌrəns] *s* evento, avvenimento; apparizione

ocean ['oʃən] *s* oceano

o'cean lin'er *s* transatlantico

o'clock [ə'klak] *adv* secondo l'orologio; **it is one o'clock** è la una; **it is
two o'clock** sono le due

octane ['ʌkten] *adj* ottanico || *s* ottano

octave ['ʌktɪv] or ['ʌktev] *s* ottava

Octavian [ʌk'tevɪ·ən] *s* Ottaviano

October [ʌk'tobər] *s* ottobre *m*

octo·pus ['ʌktəpəs] *s* (**-puses** or **-pi**
[,paɪ]) (*small*) polpo; (*large*) piovra;
(fig) piovra

ocular ['ʌkjələr] *adj & s* oculare *m*

oculist ['ʌkjəlɪst] *s* oculista *mf*

odd [ad] *adj* (*number*) dispari;
strambo, bizzarro; (*not matching*)
scompagnato, spaiato; strano; e rotti,
e.g., **three hundred odd** tre cento e
rotti || **odds** *ssg* or *spl* probabilità *f*;
(*advantage*) vantaggio, superiorità *f*;
at odds in disaccordo; **by all odds**
senza dubbio; **it makes no odds** fa lo
stesso; **the odds are** la quota è; **to
set at odds** seminare zizzania fra

oddi·ty ['ʌdɪti] *s* (**-ties**) stranezza

odd' jobs' *spl* lavori saltuari

odd' lot' *s* (fin) compravendita di meno
di cento unità

odds' and ends' *spl* un po' di tutto

odious ['odɪ·əs] *adj* odioso

odor ['odər] *s* odore *m*; **to be in bad
odor** aver cattiva fama

odorless ['odərlɪs] *adj* inodoro

odorous ['odərəs] *adj* odoroso

Odysseus [o'dɪsjus] or [o'dɪsɪ·əs] *s*
Odisseo

Odyssey ['ʌdɪsi] *s* Odissea

Oedipus ['ɛdɪpəs] or ['idɪpəs] *s* Edipo

of [ʌv] or [əv] *prep* di, e.g., **the lead
of the pencil** la mina della matita; a,
e.g., **to think of** pensare a; meno,
e.g., **a quarter of ten** le dieci meno
un quarto

off [ɔf] or [af] *adj* (*wrong*) sbagliato;
(*slightly abnormal*) matto, pazzo; inferiore; (*electricity*) tagliato; (*agreement*) sospeso; libero, in libertà; di-
stante; destro; (*season*) morto || *adv*
via; fuori, lontano, distante; **to be
off** mettersi in marcia || *prep* da;
fuori da; al disotto di; lontano da;
distolto da, e.g., **his eyes were off the
target** i suoi occhi erano distolti dal
bersaglio; (naut) al largo di

offal ['ʌfəl] or ['ɔfəl] *s* (*of butchered
animal*) frattaglie *fpl*; rifiuti *mpl*

off' and on' *adv* di tempo in tempo

off'beat' *adj* insolito, originale

off' chance' *s* possibilità remota

off'-col'or *adj* scolorito; indisposto;
(*joke*) di dubbio gusto

offend [ə'fɛnd] *tr & intr* offendere

offender [ə'fɛndər] *s* offensore *m*

offense [ə'fɛns] *s* offesa; **to take offense
(at)** offendersi (di)

offensive [ə'fɛnsɪv] *adj* offensivo || *s*
offensiva

offer ['ɔfər] or ['afər] *s* offerta || *tr*
offrire; (*thanks*) porgere; (*resistance*)
opporre || *intr* offrirsi

offering ['ɔfərɪŋ] or ['afərɪŋ] *s* offerta

off'hand' *adj* fatto all'improvviso; sbri-
gativo, alla buona || *adv* all'improv-
viso; bruscamente

office ['ɔfɪs] or ['afɪs] *s* ufficio; funzione, incombenza; (*of a doctor*) gabinetto; (*of a lawyer*) studio; (eccl)
uffizio; **through the good offices of**
per tramite di

of'fice boy' *s* fattorino

of'fice-hold'er *s* pubblico funzionario

of'fice hours' *spl* orario d'ufficio

officer ['ɔfɪsər] or ['afɪsər] *s* (*in a
corporation*) funzionario; (*policeman*) agente *m*; (mil, nav, naut)
ufficiale *m*; **officer of the day** (mil)
ufficiale *m* di giornata

of'fice seek'er ['sikər] *s* aspirante *m* a
un ufficio pubblico

of'fice supplies' *spl* articoli *mpl* di
cancelleria

official [ə'fɪʃəl] *adj* ufficiale || *s* fun-
zionario, ufficiale *m*

officiate [ə'fɪʃɪ,et] *intr* ufficiare

officious [ə'fɪʃəs] *adj* invadente, infra-
mettente; **to be officious** essere un
impiccione

offing ['ɔfɪŋ] or ['afɪŋ] *s*—**in the
offing** al largo; (fig) in preparazione,
probabile

off'-lim'its *adj* proibito; **off-limits to**
ingresso proibito a

off'-peak' heat'er *s* (elec) scaldabagno
azionato unicamente in periodi di
consumo minimo

off'-peak' load' *s* (elec) carico di consumo minimo

off'print' *s* estratto

off'set' *s* compensazione; (typ) offset *m*
|| **off'set'** *v* (*pret & pp* **-set**; *ger*
-setting) *tr* compensare; stampare in
offset

off'shoot' *s* (*of plant*) germoglio; (*of
family or race*) discendente *mf*;
(*branch*) ramo; (fig) conseguenza

off'shore' *adj*·(*wind*) di terra; (*fishing*)
vicino alla costa; (*island*) costiero ||
adv al largo

off'side' *adv* (sports) fuori gioco

off'spring' *s* discendente *m*; prole *f*;
figlio; figli *mpl*

off'stage' *adv* tra le quinte

off'-the-rec'ord *adj* confidenziale || *adv*
confidenzialmente

often ['ɔfən] or ['afən] *adv* sovente,
spesso; **how often?** quante volte?;
once too often una volta di troppo

ogive ['odʒaɪv] or [o'dʒaɪv] *s* ogiva

ogle ['ogəl] *tr* adocchiare, occhieggiare

ogre ['ogər] *s* orco

ohm [om] *s* ohm *m*

oil [ɔɪl] *adj* (*pertaining to edible oil*)
oleario; (*e.g., well*) di petrolio; (*e.g.,
lamp*) a olio; (*tanker*) petroliero;
(*field*) petrolifero || *s* olio; petrolio;
to burn the midnight oil studiare a
lume di candela; **to pour oil on troubled waters** pacificare; **to strike oil**
trovare petrolio || *tr* oliare; lubrifi-

care; ungere || *intr* (*said of a motor-ship*) fare petrolio

oil' burn'er s bruciatore *m* a gasolio

oil'can' s oliatore *m*

oil'cloth' s incerata, tela cerata

oil' field' s giacimento petrolifero

oil' lamp' s lampada a petrolio

oil'man s (**-men**) (*retailer*) mercante *m* di petrolio; (*operator*) petroliere *m*

oil' paint'ing s quadro a olio

oil' slick' s macchia d'olio

oil' tank'er s petroliera

oil' well' s pozzo di petrolio

oil-y ['ɔɪlɪ] *adj* (**-ier; -iest**) oleoso; untuoso

ointment ['ɔɪntmənt] s unguento

O.K. ['o'ke] *adj* (coll) corretto || *s* (coll) approvazione || *adv* (coll) benissimo, d'accordo || *v* (*pret & pp* **O.K.'d;** *ger* **O.K.'ing**) *tr* (coll) dare l'approvazione a || *interj* benissimo!

okra ['okrə] s (bot) ibisco esculento; (bot) baccello dell'ibisco esculento

old [old] *adj* vecchio; antico, vetusto; **how old is . . . ?** quanti anni ha . . . ?; **of old** anticamente; **to be . . . years old** avere . . . anni

old' age' s vecchiaia

old' boy' s vecchietto arzillo; (Brit) vecchio mio

old'-clothes'man' s (**-men'**) rigattiere *m*

old' coun'try s madre patria

old-fashioned ['old'fæ/ənd] *adj* all'antica; fuori moda

old' fo'gey or **old' fo'gy** ['fogi] s (**-gies**) uomo di idee antiquate, reazionario

Old' Glo'ry s la bandiera degli Stati Uniti

Old' Guard' s (U.S.A.) parte *f* più conservatrice di un partito

old' hand' s vecchio del mestiere

old' maid' s zitella

old' mas'ter s grande maestro; quadro di un gran maestro

old' moon' s luna calante

old' salt' s lupo di mare

old' school' s gente *f* all'antica

old' school' tie' s (Brit) cravatta coi colori della propria scuola; (fig) tradizionalismo

Old' Tes'tament s Antico Testamento

old'-time' *adj* all'antica; del tempo antico

old-timer ['old'taɪmər] s (coll) veterano; (coll) vecchio

old' wives'' tale' s superstizione da donnicciole; racconto di vecchie comari

Old' World' s mondo antico

oleander [,olɪ'ændər] s oleandro

oligar-chy ['ɑlɪ,gɑrki] s (**-chies**) oligarchia

olive ['ɑlɪv] *adj* oleario; (*color*) olivastro || s (*tree*) olivo; (*fruit*) oliva

ol'ive branch' s ramoscello d'olivo

ol'ive grove' s oliveto

ol'ive oil' s olio d'oliva

Oliver ['ɑlɪvər] s Oliviero

ol'ive tree' s olivo

Olympiad [o'lɪmpɪ,æd] s olimpiade *f*

Olympian [o'lɪmpɪ-ən] *adj* olimpico || s deità olimpica; giocatore olimpico

Olympic [o'lɪmpɪk] *adj* olimpico, olimpionico

omelet or **omelette** ['ɑmələt] or ['ɑmlɪt] s frittata, omelette *f*

omen ['omən] s augurio

ominous ['ɑmɪnəs] *adj* infausto, ominoso

omission [o'mɪ/ən] s omissione

omit [o'mɪt] *v* (*pret & pp* **omitted;** *ger* **omitting**) *tr* omettere

omnibus ['ɑmnɪ,bʌs] or ['ɑmnɪbəs] *adj* di interesse generale || s bus *m*; volume collettivo

omnipotent [ɑm'nɪpətənt] *adj* onnipotente

omniscient [ɑm'nɪ/ənt] *adj* onnisciente

omnivorous [ɑm'nɪvərəs] *adj* onnivoro

on [ɑn] or [ɔn] *adj* addosso, e.g., **with his hat on** col cappello addosso; in uso, in funzione; (*light*) acceso; (*deal*) fatto, concluso; (*e.g., game*) già cominciato; **what is on at the theater?** che cosa si dà al teatro? || *adv* su; avanti; dietro, e.g., **to drag on** tirarsi dietro; **and so on** e così via; **come on!** va via!; **farther on** più in là; **later on** più tardi; **to be on to s.o.** (coll) scoprire il gioco di qlcu; **to have on** avere addosso; **to . . . on** continuare a, e.g., **the band played on** la banda continuò a suonare; **to put on** mettersi || *prep* su, sopra; a, e.g., **on foot** a piedi; **on his arrival** al suo arrivo; sotto, e.g., **on my responsibility** sotto la mia responsabilità; contro, e.g., **an attack on the government** un attacco contro il governo; da, e.g., **on good authority** da buona fonte; **on all sides** da tutte le parti; verso, e.g., **to march on the capital** marciare verso la capitale; dopo, e.g., **victory on victory** vittoria dopo vittoria

on' and on' *adv* senza cessa

once [wʌns] s una volta; volta, e.g., **this once** questa volta || *adv* una volta; mai, e.g., **if this once becomes known** se questo si risapesse mai; all at once repentinamente; **at once** subito; allo stesso tempo; **for once** almeno una volta; **once and again** ripetutamente; **once in a blue moon** ad ogni morte di papa; **once in a while** di tanto in tanto; **once upon a time there was** c'era una volta || *conj* se appena; una volta che

once'-o'ver s (coll) occhiata rapida; **to give s.th** the once-over (coll) esaminare qlco rapidamente; (coll) pulire qlco superficialmente

one [wʌn] *adj* uno; un certo, e.g., **one Smith** un certo Smith; uno, e.g., **one price** prezzo unico || s uno || *pron* uno, e.g., **how can one live here?** come è possibile che uno viva qui?; sì, e.g., **how does one go to the museum?** come si va al museo?; **I for one** per lo meno io; **it's all one and the same** to me per me fa lo stesso; **my little one** piccolo mio; **one and all** tutti; **one another** sì, e.g., **they wrote one another** si scrissero;

l'un(o) l'altro, e.g., **they looked at one another** si guardarono l'un l'altro; **one o'clock** la una; **one's** il suo, il proprio; **the blue hat and the red one** il cappello blu e quello rosso; **the one and only** l'unico; **the one that** chi, quello che; **this one** questo; **that one** quello; **to make one** unire

one'-eyed' adj monocolo

one'-horse' adj a un solo cavallo; (coll) da nulla, poco importante

one'-man' show' s personale f

onerous ['anərəs] adj oneroso

one·self' pron sé stesso; se; si; **to be oneself** essere normale; comportarsi normalmente

one-sided ['wʌn'saɪdɪd] adj unilaterale; ingiusto, parziale

one'-track' adj a un solo binario; (coll) unilaterale, limitato

one'-way' adj a senso unico; (ticket) semplice, d'andata

onion ['ʌnjən] s cipolla; **to know one's onions** (coll) conoscere i propri polli

on'ion·skin' s carta pelle aglio, carta velina

on'look'er s presente m, spettatore m

only ['onlɪ] adj solo, unico || adv solo, soltanto, non . . . più di; **not only . . . but also** non solo . . . ma anche || conj ma; se non che

on'set' s attacco; (beginning) inizio; **at the onset** dapprincipio

onslaught ['ɑn,slɔt] or ['ɔn,slɔt] s attacco

on'to prep su, sopra a; **to be onto** (coll) rendersi conto del gioco di

onward ['ɑnwərd] or **onwards** ['ɑnwərdz] adv avanti, più avanti

onyx ['ɑnɪks] s onice m

ooze [uz] s trasudazione; liquido per concia || tr sudare || intr trasudare; (said, e.g., of blood) stillare; (said, e.g., of air) filtrare; (fig) trapelare

opal ['opəl] s opale m

opaque [o'pek] adj opaco; (writer's style) oscuro; stupido

open ['opən] adj aperto, scoperto; (job) vacante; (time) libero; (hunting season) legale; indeciso; manifesto; (hand) liberale; (needlework) a giorno; **to break** or **to crack open** forzare; **to throw open** aprire completamente || s apertura; (in the woods) radura; **in the open** all'aperto; all'aria aperta; in alto mare; apertamente || tr aprire; (an account) impostare; **to open up** spalancare; (one's eyes) sbarrare || intr aprire, aprirsi; (theat) esordire; **to open into** sboccare in; **to open on** darè su; **to open up** sbottonarsi

o'pen-air' adj all'aria aperta

open-eyed ['opən,aɪd] adj con gli occhi aperti; meravigliato; fatto con piena conoscenza

open-handed ['opən'hændɪd] adj generoso, liberale

open-hearted ['opən'hɑrtɪd] adj franco, sincero; gentile

o'pen house' s tavola imbandita; **to keep open house** aver sempre ospiti

opening ['opənɪŋ] s apertura; (of dress) giro collo; (e.g., of sewer) imbocco; (in the woods) radura; (vacancy) posto vacante; (beginning) inizio; (chance to say something) occasione

o'pening night' s debutto, prima

o'pening num'ber s primo numero

o'pening price' s prezzo d'apertura

open-minded ['opən'maɪndɪd] adj di larghe vedute; imparziale

o'pen se'cret s segreto di Pulcinella

o'pen shop' s officina che impiega chi non è membro del sindacato

o'pen-work' s traforo

opera ['ɑpərə] s opera

op'era glass'es spl binocolo da teatro

op'era hat' s gibus m

op'era house' s teatro dell'opera

operate ['ɑpə,ret] tr (a machine) far funzionare; (a shop) gestire; operare || intr funzionare; operare; **to operate on** (surg) operare

operatic [,ɑpə'rætɪk] adj operistico

op'erating expens'es spl spese fpl di ordinaria amministrazione

op'erating room' s sala operatoria

op'erating ta'ble s tavola operatoria

operation [,ɑpə're ʃən] s operazione; funzionamento, marcia

opera'tions research' s ricerca operativa

operator ['ɑpə,retər] s operatore m; (of a conveyance) conduttore m, conducente mf; (com) gestore m; (telp) telefonista mf; (surg) chirurgo operatore; (slang) faccendiere m

opiate ['opɪ·ɪt] or ['opɪ,et] adj & s oppiato

opinion [ə'pɪnjən] s opinione; **in my opinion** a mio modo di vedere; **to have a high opinion of** avere una grande stima di

opinionated [ə'pɪnjə,netɪd] adj ostinato, testardo, dogmatico

opium ['opɪ·əm] s oppio

o'pium den' s fumeria d'oppio

opossum [ə'pɑsəm] s opossum m

opponent [ə'ponənt] s avversario

opportune [,ɑpər'tjun] or [,ɑpər'tun] adj opportuno

opportunist [,ɑpər'tjunɪst] or [,ɑpər'tunɪst] s opportunista mf

opportuni·ty [,ɑpər'tjunɪti] or [,ɑpər'tunɪti] s (-ties) opportunità f, occasione

oppose [ə'poz] tr opporsi a

opposite ['ɑpəsɪt] adj opposto; di rimpetto, e.g., **the house opposite** la casa di rimpetto || s contrario || prep di faccia a, di rimpetto a

op'posite num'ber s persona di grado corrispondente

opposition [,ɑpə'zɪ ʃən] s opposizione

oppress [ə'pres] tr opprimere

oppressive [ə'presɪv] adj oppressivo; opprimente, soffocante

oppressor [ə'presər] s oppressore m

opprobrious [ə'probrɪ·əs] adj obbrobrioso

opprobrium [ə'probrɪ-əm] *s* obbrobrio
optic ['aptɪk] *adj* ottico || **optics** *ssg* ottica
optical ['aptɪkəl] *adj* ottico
optician [ap'tɪʃən] *s* ottico, occhialaio
optimism ['aptɪ ,mɪzəm] *s* ottimismo
optimist ['aptɪmɪst] *s* ottimista *mf*
optimistic [,aptɪ'mɪstɪk] *adj* ottimistico
option ['apʃən] *s* opzione
optional ['apʃənəl] *adj* facoltativo
optometrist [ap'tamɪtrɪst] *s* optometrista *mf*
opulent ['apjələnt] *adj* opulento
or [ɔr] *conj* o; (*or else*) oppure
oracle ['arəkəl] or ['ɔrəkəl] *s* oracolo
oracular [o'rækjələr] *adj* profetico; ambiguo; misterioso; sentenzioso
oral ['ɔrəl] *adj* orale
orange ['arɪndʒ] or ['ɔrɪndʒ] *adj* di arance; arancio || *s* arancia
orangeade [,arɪndʒ'ed] or [,ɔrɪndʒ-'ed] *s* aranciata
or'ange blos'som *s* zagara
or'ange grove' *s* aranceto
or'ange juice' *s* sugo d'arancia
or'ange squeez'er *s* spremiagrumi *m*
or'ange tree' *s* arancio
orang-outang [o'ræŋu,tæŋ] *s* orango
oration [o're ʃən] *s* orazione, discorso
orator ['arətər] or ['ɔrətər] *s* oratore *m*
oratorical [,arə'tarɪkəl] or [,ɔrə'tɔrɪ-kəl] *adj* oratorio
oratori·o [,arə'tɔrɪ ,o] or [,ɔrə'tɔrɪ ,o] *s* (*-os*) (mus) oratorio
orato·ry ['arə ,tɔri] or ['ɔrə ,tɔri] *s* (*-ries*) oratoria; (eccl) oratorio
orb [ɔrb] *s* orbe *m*
orbit ['ɔrbɪt] *s* orbita; **to go into orbit** entrare in orbita || *tr* mettere in orbita; orbitare intorno a || *intr* orbitare
or'biting sta'tion *s* stazione orbitale
orchard ['ɔrtʃərd] *s* frutteto
orchestra ['ɔrkɪstrə] *s* orchestra; (*parquet*) platea
orchestral [ɔr'kestrəl] *adj* orchestrale
or'chestra pit' *s* golfo mistico
or'chestra seat' *s* poltrona di platea
orchestrate ['ɔrkɪs ,tret] *tr* orchestrare
orchid ['ɔrkɪd] *s* orchidea
ordain [ɔr'den] *tr* predestinare; decretare; (eccl) ordinare
ordeal [ɔr'dil] or [ɔr'di-əl] *s* sfacchinata; (hist) ordalia
order ['ɔrdər] *s* ordine *m*; compito, e.g., **a big order** un compito difficile; (com) commessa, ordinazione; (mil) consegna; **in order that** affinché; **in order to** + *inf* per + *inf*; **made to order** fatto su misura; **to get out of order** guastarsi; **to give an order** dare un ordine; (com) fare una commessa || *tr* (*e.g., a drink*) ordinare; (*a person*) ordinare (with *dat*); (*e.g., a suit of clothes*) far fare; **to order around** mandare attorno; **to order s.o. away** mandar via qlcu
or'der blank' *s* cedola d'ordinazione
order·ly ['ɔrdərli] *adj* ordinato; disciplinato || *s* (*-lies*) (*in a hospital*) in-

serviente *mf;* (mil) ordinanza, attendente *m*
ordinal ['ɔrdɪnəl] *adj & s* ordinale *m*
ordinance ['ɔrdɪnəns] *s* ordinanza
ordinary ['ɔrdɪ ,neri] *adj* ordinario
ordnance ['ɔrdnəns] *s* artiglieria; bocche *fpl* da fuoco; munizionamento
ore [or] *s* minerale *m* (metallifero)
organ ['ɔrgən] *s* organo
organ·dy ['ɔrgəndi] *s* (*-dies*) organdì *m*
or'gan grind'er *s* suonatore *m* d'organetto
organic [ɔr'gænɪk] *adj* organico
organism ['ɔrgə ,nɪzəm] *s* organismo
organist ['ɔrgənɪst] *s* organista *mf*
organization [,ɔrgənɪ'zeʃən] *s* organizzazione
organize ['ɔrgə ,naɪz] *tr* organizzare
organizer ['ɔrgə ,naɪzər] *s* organizzatore *m*
or'gan loft' *s* palco, galleria per l'organo
orgasm ['ɔrgæzəm] *s* orgasmo
or·gy ['ɔrdʒi] *s* (*-gies*) orgia
orient ['ori·ent] *s* oriente *m* || **Orient** *s* Oriente *m* || **orient** ['orɪ ,ent] *tr* orientare, orizzontare
oriental [,orɪ'entəl] *adj* orientale || **Oriental** *s* orientale *mf*
orifice ['arɪfɪs] or ['ɔrɪfɪs] *s* orifizio
origin ['arɪdʒɪn] or ['ɔrɪdʒɪn] *s* origine *f*, provenienza
original [ə'rɪdʒɪnəl] *adj & s* originale *mf*
originate [ə'rɪdʒɪ ,net] *tr* originare || *intr* originare, originarsi
oriole ['orɪ ,ol] *s* oriolo, rigogolo
Ork'ney Is'lands ['ɔrkni] *spl* Orcadi *fpl*
ormolu ['ɔrmə'lu] *s* (*alloy*) similoro; (*gold powder*) polvere *f* d'oro; (*gilded metal*) bronzo dorato
ornament ['ɔrnəmənt] *s* ornamento || ['ɜrnə ,ment] *tr* ornamentare
ornamental [,ɔrnə'mentəl] *adj* ornamentale
ornate [ɔr'net] or ['ɔrnet] *adj* ornato; (*style*) elaborato
ornithologist [,ɔrnɪ'θɑlədʒɪst] *s* ornitologo
orphan ['ɔrfən] *adj & s* orfano || *tr* rendere orfano
orphanage ['ɔrfənɪdʒ] *s* (*institution*) orfanotrofio; (*condition*) orfananza
Orpheus ['ɔrfjus] or ['ɔrfɪ·əs] *s* Orfeo
orthodox ['ɔrθə ,daks] *adj* ortodosso
orthogra·phy [ɔr'θɑgrəfi] *s* (*-phies*) ortografia
oscillate ['asɪ ,let] *intr* oscillare
osier ['oʒər] *s* vimine *m*; (bot) vinco
osmosis [az'mosɪs] or [as'mosɪs] *s* osmosi *f*
osprey ['aspri] *s* falco pescatore
ossi·fy ['asɪ ,faɪ] *v* (*pret & pp* **-fied**) *tr* ossificare || *intr* ossificarsi
ostensible [as'tensɪbəl] *adj* apparente, preteso
ostentatious [,asten'teʃəs] *adj* ostentato
osteopathy [,astɪ'apəθi] *s* osteopatia
ostracism ['astrə ,sɪzəm] *s* ostracismo

ostracize ['astrɪ‚saɪz] tr dare l'ostracismo a, ostracizzare
ostrich ['astrɪtʃ] s struzzo
Othello [o'θɛlo] or [ə'θɛlo] s Otello
other ['ʌðər] adj & pron indef altro ||
adv—**other than** diversamente che
otherwise ['ʌðər‚waɪz] adv altrimenti;
differentemente
otter ['atər] s lontra
ottoman ['atəmən] s (fabric) otto-
mano; (sofa) ottomana; cuscino per i
piedi || **Ottoman** adj & s ottomano
ouch [autʃ] interj ahi!
ought [ɔt] s qualcosa; zero; **for ought
I know** per quanto io sappia || v aux
is rendered in Italian by the conditional of dovere, e.g., **you ought to
be ashamed** dovresti vergognarti
ounce [auns] s oncia
our [aur] adj poss nostro, il nostro
ours [aurz] pron poss il nostro
ourselves [aur'sɛlvz] pron pers noi
stessi; ci, e.g., **we enjoyed ourselves**
ci siamo divertiti
oust [aust] tr espellere; (a tenant)
sfrattare
out [aut] adj erroneo; esterno; fuori
pratica; svenuto; ubriaco; finito;
(book) pubblicato; (lights) spento;
fuori moda; introvabile; palmare; di
permesso, e.g., **my night out** la mia
serata di permesso; (e.g., at the
knees) frusto; (sports) fuori gioco ||
s via d'uscita; **to be on the outs** or
at outs with (coll) essere in disac-
cordo con || adv fuori, all'infuori;
all'aria libera; **out for** in cerca di;
out of fuori, fuori di; di; da; (e.g.,
money) a corto di, senza; su, e.g.,
two students out of three due stu-
denti su tre || prep fuori di; per,
lungo || interj fuori!
out' and away' adv di gran lunga
out'-and-out' adj perfetto, completo ||
adv perfettamente, completamente
out'bid' v (pret -bid; pp -bid or
-bidden; ger -bidding) tr fare un'offerta migliore di; (bridge) fare una
dichiarazione più alta di
out'board mo'tor s fuoribordo, motore
m fuoribordo
out'break' s insurrezione; (of hives)
eruzione; (of anger; of war) scoppio
out'build'ing s dipendenza
out'burst' s (of tears; of laughter) scoppio; (of energy) impeto, slancio
out'cast' s vagabondo reietto
out'come' s risultato
out'cry' s (-cries) grido, chiasso
out'dat'ed adj fuori moda
out'dis'tance tr distanziare
out'do' v (pret -did; pp -done) tr sorpassare; **to outdo oneself** sorpassare
sé stesso
out'door' adj all'aria aperta
out'doors' s aria libera, aperta cam-
pagna || adv all'aria aperta, fuori di
casa
out'er space' ['autər] s spazio cosmico
out'field' s (baseball) campo esterno
out'field'er s (baseball) esterno
out'fit' s equipaggiamento; (female cos-

tume) insieme m; (of bride) corredo;
(group) (coll) corpo; (com) compa-
gnia || v (pret & pp **-fitted; ger
-fitting**) tr equipaggiare
out'flow' s efflusso
out'go'ing adj in partenza; (tide) de-
crescente; (character) espansivo || s
efflusso
out'grow' v (pret -grew; pp -grown) tr
essere troppo grande per; sorpassare
in statura; perdere l'interesse per ||
intr protrudere
out'growth' s risultato, conseguenza;
crescita
outing ['autɪŋ] s gita, scampagnata
outlandish [aut'lændɪʃ] adj strano,
bizzarro; dall'aspetto straniero; (remote, far away) in capo al mondo
out'last' tr sopravvivere (with dat)
out'law' s fuorilegge mf || tr proscri-
vere; dichiarare illegale
out'lay' s disborso || **out·lay'** v (pret &
pp -laid) tr sborsare
out'let s uscita; (e.g., of river) sbocco;
(com) mercato; (elec) presa di corrente; (fig) sfogo
out'line' s contorno; traccia, tracciato;
sagoma, profilo; prospetto || tr de-
lineare; tracciare, tratteggiare; sagomare, profilare; prospettare
out'live' tr sopravvivere (with dat)
out'look' s prospettiva; (watch) guardia; (mental view) modo di vedere,
opinione
out'ly'ing adj lontano, fuori di mano;
periferico
outmoded [‚aut'modɪd] adj fuori
moda, antiquato
out'num'ber tr superare in numero
out'-of-date' adj fuori moda
out'-of-door' adj all'aria aperta
out'-of-doors' adj all'aria aperta || s
aria aperta || adv all'aria aperta;
fuori di casa
out'-of-print' adj esaurito
out'-of-the-way' adj appartato, fuori
mano; inusitato, strano
out' of tune' adj stonato || adv fuori di
tono
out' of work' adj disoccupato
out'pa'tient s paziente mf esterno
out'post' s (mil) posto avanzato
out'put' s produzione; (elec) uscita;
(mach) rendimento, potenza utile
out'rage s oltraggio, indecenza || tr
oltraggiare; (a woman) violare
outrageous [aut'redʒəs] adj oltrag-
gioso; (excessive) eccessivo; atroce,
feroce
out'rank' tr superare in grado
out'rid'er s battistrada m
out'right' adj completo, intero || adv
completamente; apertamente; sul
colpo, sull'istante
out'set' s inizio, principio
out'side' adj esterno; (unlikely) impro-
babile; (price) massimo || s esterno,
di fuori m; aspetto esteriore; vita
fuori del carcere || adv fuori, di
fuori; **outside of** fuori di || prep fuori
di; (coll) all'infuori di

outsider [,auˈtˈsaɪdər] s estraneo, intruso; (sports) outsider m

out'skirts' spl sobborghi mpl, periferia

out'spo'ken adj franco, esplicito

out'stand'ing adj saliente, eminente; (debt) arretrato, non pagato

outward [ˈautwərd] adj esterno, superficiale || adv al di fuori

out'weigh' tr pesare più di; eccedere in importanza

out'wit' v (pret & pp -witted; ger -witting) tr farla in barba di; (a pursuer) far perdere la traccia or la pista a

oval [ˈovəl] adj & s ovale m

ova·ry [ˈovəri] s (-ries) ovaia

ovation [oˈveʃən] s ovazione

oven [ˈʌvən] s forno

over [ˈovər] adj superiore; esterno; finito, concluso || adv su, sopra; dall'altra parte; dall'altra sponda; al rovescio; di nuovo; (at the bottom of a page) continua; qui, e.g., **hand over the money** dammi qui il denaro; **over again** di nuovo; **over against** contro; **over and over** ripetutamente; **over here** qui; **over there** là || prep su, sopra; dall'altra parte di; attraverso, per; (a certain number) più di; a causa di; **over and above** in eccesso di

o'ver·all' adj completo, totale || **over·alls** spl tuta

o'ver·bear'ing adj arrogante, prepotente

o'ver·board' adv in acqua; **man overboard!** uomo in mare!; **to go overboard** andare agli estremi

o'ver·cast' adj annuvolato || s cielo annuvolato || v (pret & pp -cast) tr coprire, annuvolare

o'ver·charge' s prezzo eccessivo; sovraccarico; (elec) carica eccessiva || **o'ver·charge'** tr far pagare eccessivamente; sovraccaricare

o'ver·coat' s soprabito, pastrano

o'ver·come' v (pret -came; pp -come) tr vincere, sopraffare; (e.g., passions) frenare; opprimere

o'vercon'fidence s sicumera

o'ver·crowd' tr gremire

o'ver·do' v (pret -did; pp -done) tr esagerare; strafare; esaurire; (meat) stracuocere || intr esaurirsi

o'ver·dose' s dose eccessiva

o'ver·draft' s assegno allo scoperto

o'ver·draw' v (pret -drew; pp -drawn) tr (a check) emettere allo scoperto; (a character) esagerare la descrizione di

o'ver·due' adj in ritardo; (com) in sofferenza, scaduto

o'ver·eat' v (pret -ate; pp -eaten) tr & intr mangiare troppo

o'ver·exer'tion s sforzo eccessivo

o'ver·expose' tr sovresporre

o'ver·expo'sure s sovresposizione

o'ver·flow' s (of a river) piena, straripamento; (excess) sovrabbondanza; (e.g., of a fountain) trabocco; (outlet) tubo di troppopieno || **o'ver·flow'** intr (said of a river) straripare; (said of a container) traboccare

o'ver·fly' v (pret -flew; pp -flown) tr sorvolare; (a target) oltrepassare

o'ver·grown' adj cresciuto troppo; coperto, denso

o'ver·hang' s strapiombo || **o'ver·hang'** v (pret & pp -hung) tr sovrastare (with dat); sovrastare; (to threaten) minacciare; pervadere, permeare || intr sovrastare, strapiombare

o'ver·haul' s riparazione; esame m, revisione || tr riparare; esaminare, ripassare, rivedere; raggiungere, mettersi alla pari con

o'ver·head' adj in alto, sopra la testa; aereo; elevato, pensile; generale || **o'ver·head'** adv in alto, di sopra || **o'ver·head'** s spese fpl generali

o'ver·head projec'tor s lavagna luminosa

o'ver·head valve' s valvola in testa

o'ver·hear' v (pret & pp -heard) tr sentire per caso, udire per caso

o'ver·heat' tr surriscaldare || intr surriscaldarsi; eccitarsi

overjoyed [,ovərˈdʒɔɪd] adj felicissimo; **to be overjoyed** non stare in sé dalla contentezza

overland [ˈovərˌlænd] or [ˈovərlənd] adj & adv per via di terra

o'ver·lap' v (pret & pp -lapped; ger -lapping) tr sovrapporre, estendersi sopra || intr sovrapporsi, estendersi; coincidere parzialmente

o'ver·load' s sovraccarico || **o'ver·load'** tr sovraccaricare, stracaricare

o'ver·look' tr sovrastare su, dominare; ispezionare, sorvegliare; passare sopra, trascurare; dare su, e.g., **the window overlooks the street** la finestra dà sulla strada

o'ver·lord' s dominatore m || tr dominare despoticamente

overly [ˈovərli] adv eccessivamente

o'ver·night' adj per la notte, per solo una notte || **o'ver·night'** adv durante la notte; la notte prima

o'vernight bag' s astuccio di toletta per la notte

o'ver·pass' s cavalcavia, viadotto

o'ver·pop'ulate' tr sovrappopolare

o'ver·pow'er tr sopraffare

o'ver·pow'ering adj schiacciante

o'ver·produc'tion s sovrapproduzione

o'ver·rate' tr sopravvalutare

o'ver·run' v (pret -ran; pp -run; ger -running) tr invadere, infestare; inondare; (one's time) oltrepassare, eccedere

o'ver·sea' or **o'ver·seas'** adj di oltremare || **o'ver·seas'** adv oltremare, al di là dei mari

o'ver·see' v (pret -saw; pp -seen) tr sorvegliare

o'ver·seer' s sorvegliante mf

o'ver·shad'ow tr oscurare, eclissare

o'ver·shoe' s soprascarpa

o'ver·shoot' v (pret & pp -shot) tr (the target) oltrepassare; (said of water) scorrere sopra; **to overshoot oneself** andare troppo in là || intr (aer) atterrare lungo e richiamare

o'ver·sight' s sbadataggine f, svista; sorveglianza, supervisione o'ver-sleep' v (pret & pp -slept) tr (a certain hour) dormire oltre || intr dormire troppo a lungo

o'ver-step' v (pret & pp -stepped; ger -stepping) tr eccedere, oltrepassare

o'ver-stock' tr riempire eccessivamente

o'ver-sup-ply' s (-plies) fornitura superiore alla richiesta || o'ver-sup-ply' v (pret & pp -plied) tr fornire in quantità superiore alla richiesta

overt ['ovʌrt] or [o'vʌrt] adj palmare, chiaro, manifesto

o'ver-take' v (pret -took; pp -taken) tr raggiungere, sorpassare; sorprendere

o'ver-the-count'er adj (securities) venduto direttamente al compratore

o'ver-throw' s rovesciamento; disfatta || o'ver-throw's v (pret -threw; pp -thrown) tr rovesciare, sconfiggere

o'ver-time' adj supplementare, fuori orario || s straordinario; (sports) tempo supplementare || adv fuori orario

o'ver-tone' s (mus) suono armonico; (fig) sottinteso

o'ver-trump' s taglio con atout più alto || o'ver-trump' tr & intr tagliare con atout più alto

overture ['ovʌrt/ər] s apertura; (mus) preludio, sinfonia

o'ver-turn' s rovesciamento || o'ver-turn' tr rovesciare, travolgere || intr rovesciarsi, ribaltarsi

overweening [,ovʌr'winɪŋ] adj presuntuoso, vanitoso; esagerato, eccessivo

o'ver-weight' adj troppo grasso; oltrepassante i limiti di peso || o'ver-weight' s sovraccarico; preponderanza; eccesso di peso

overwhelm [,ovʌr'hwelm] tr schiacciare, debellare; coprire; (e.g., with kindness) colmare, ricolmare

o'ver-work' s lavoro straordinario; superlavoro || o'ver-work' tr far lavorare eccessivamente || intr lavorare eccessivamente

Ovid ['avɪd] s Ovidio

ow [au] interj ahi!

owe [o] tr dovere || intr essere in debito

owing ['o-ɪŋ] adj dovuto; owing to a causa di

owl [aul] s gufo, barbagianni m

own [on] adj proprio, e.g., my own brother il mio proprio fratello || s il proprio; on one's own (coll) per proprio conto; (without anybody's advice) di testa propria; to come into one's own entrare in possesso del proprio; essere riconosciuto per quanto si vale; to hold one's own non perdere terreno; essere pari || tr possedere; riconoscere || intr—to own up to confessare

owner ['onər] s padrone m, proprietario, titolare m

ownership ['onər,ʃɪp] s proprietà f

own'er's li'cence s permesso di circolazione

ox [aks] s (oxen ['aksən]) bue m

ox'cart' s carro tirato da buoi

oxide ['aksaɪd] s ossido

oxidize ['aksɪ,daɪz] tr ossidare || intr ossidarsi

oxygen ['aksɪdʒən] s ossigeno

ox'ygen mask' s maschera respiratoria

ox'ygen tent' s tenda ad ossigeno

oxytone ['aksɪ,ton] adj tronco, ossitono || s ossitono

oyster ['ɔɪstər] adj di ostriche || s ostrica

oys'ter bed' s ostricaio, banco di ostriche

oys'ter cock'tail s ostriche fpl servite in valva

oys'ter fork' s forchettina da ostriche

oys'ter-house' s ristorante m per la vendita delle ostriche

oys'ter-knife' s coltello per aprire le ostriche

oys'ter-man s (-men) ostricaio

oys'ter shell' s conchiglia d'ostrica

oys'ter stew' s brodetto d'ostrica

ozone ['ozon] s ozono

P

P, p [pi] s sedicesima lettera dell'alfabeto inglese

pace [pes] s passo, andatura; (of a horse) ambio; to keep pace with andare di pari passo con; to put s.o. through his paces mettere qlcu a dura prova; to set the pace for fare l'andatura per; dare l'esempio a || tr misurare a passi, percorrere; to pace the floor andare avanti e indietro per la stanza || intr camminare lentamente; andare al passo; (said of a horse) ambiare

pace'mak'er s battistrada m; (in races) chi stabilisce il passo; (med) pacemaker m

pacific [pə'sɪfɪk] adj pacifico || Pacific adj & s Pacifico

pacifier ['pæsɪ,faɪ-ər] s paciere m; (teething ring) succhietto, tettarella

pacifism ['pæsɪ,fɪzəm] s pacifismo

pacifist ['pæsɪfɪst] adj & s pacifista mf

paci-fy ['pæsɪ,faɪ] v (pret & pp -fied) tr pacificare

pack [pæk] s fardello, pacco; (of merchandise) balla; (of lies) mucchio; (of cards) mazzo; (of thieves) banda; (of dogs) muta; (of animals) branco; (of birds) stormo; (of cigarettes) pacchetto; (of ice) banchiglia; (of people) turba || tr affardellare, impaccare; (to wrap) imballare, ammucchiare; (in cans) mettere in conserva; (people) stipare; (a trunk) fare; to pack in stipare; to pack off mandare via || intr ammucchiarsi, pigiarsi, accalcarsi; **to pack up** fare il baule

package ['pækɪdʒ] s pacco, collo; (*small*) pacchetto || *tr* impacchettare

pack' an'imal s bestia da soma

packer ['pækər] s imballatore m; (*of canned goods*) proprietario (di fabbrica di conserve alimentari)

packet ['pækɪt] s pacchetto; (*boat*) vapore m postale

packing ['pækɪŋ] s imballaggio; (*on shoulders of suit*) spallina; (*mach*) stoppa; (*ring*) (mach) guarnizione

pack'ing box' or **case'** s cassa d'imballaggio

pack'ing house' s fabbrica di conserve alimentari; fabbrica di carne in conserva

pack'ing slip' s foglio d'imballaggio

pack'sad'dle s basto

pack'thread' s spago d'imballaggio

pack'train' s fila di animali da soma

pact [pækt] s patto

pad [pæd] s cuscinetto, tampone m; imbottitura; (*of writing paper*) blocco da annotazioni; (*of an animal*) superficie f plantare, zampa; (*of a water lily*) foglia; (rok) piattaforma || v (*pret & pp* **padded**; *ger* **padding**) *tr* imbottire, ovattare; (*e.g., a speech*) infarcire || *intr* camminare pesantemente

pad'ding s imbottitura

paddle ['pædəl] s pagaia; (*of waterwheel*) pala || *tr* remare; (*to spank*) bastonare || *intr* remare; (*to splash*) diguazzare

pad'dle wheel' s ruota a pale

paddock ['pædək] s prato d'allenamento, paddock m

pad'lock' s lucchetto || *tr* chiudere col lucchetto

pagan ['pegən] adj & s pagano

paganism ['pegə,nɪzəm] s paganesimo

page [pedʒ] s (*of a book*) pagina; (*at court*) paggio; (*in hotels*) fattorino, valletto || *tr* impaginare; (*in hotels*) chiamare, far chiamare

pageant ['pædʒənt] s parata, corteo, spettacolo

pageant·ry ['pædʒəntri] s (**-ries**) pompa, fasto

paginate ['pædʒɪ,net] *tr* impaginare

pail [pel] s secchio

pain [pen] s dolore m; **on pain of** sotto pena di; **to take pains to** prendersi cura di; **to take pains not to** guardarsi da || *tr & intr* dolere

painful ['penfəl] adj doloroso, penoso

pain'kill'er s (coll) analgesico

painless ['penlɪs] adj indolore

painstaking ['penz,tekɪŋ] adj meticoloso

paint [pent] s (*for pictures*) colore m; (*for a house*) vernice f; (*make-up*) trucco || *tr* dipingere; (*a house*) verniciare, tinteggiare || *intr* (*with make-up*) dipingersi; essere pittore

paint'box' s scatola da colori

paint'brush' s pennello

painter ['pentər] s (*of pictures*) pittore m; (*of a house*) verniciatore m; (naut) barbetta

painting ['pentɪŋ] s pittura, dipinto

paint' remov'er [rɪ'muvər] s solvente m per levar la vernice

paint' thin'ner s diluente m

pair [per] s paio; (*of people*) coppia || *tr* appaiare, accoppiare || *intr* appaiarsi, accoppiarsi

pair' of scis'sors s forbici fpl

pair' of trou'sers s calzoni mpl

pajamas [pə'dʒaməz] or [pə'dʒæməz] spl pigiama m

Pakistan [,pɑkɪ'stɑn] s il Pakistan

Pakistani [,pɑkɪ'stɑni] adj & s pachistano

pal [pæl] s (coll) compagno || v (*pret & pp* **palled**; *ger* **palling**) *intr* (coll) essere compagni

palace ['pælɪs] s palazzo

palatable ['pælətəbəl] adj gustoso, appetitoso; accettabile

palatal ['pælətəl] adj & s palatale f

palate ['pælɪt] s palato

pale [pel] adj pallido || s palo; (*enclosure*) recinto; (fig) ambito || *intr* impallidire

pale'face' s faccia pallida

palette ['pælɪt] s tavolozza

palfrey ['pɔlfri] s palafreno

palisade [,pælɪ'sed] s palizzata; (*line of cliffs*) dirupo

pall [pɔl] s panno mortuario; (*of smoke*) cappa || *tr* saziare, infastidire || *intr* saziarsi, perdere l'appetito

pall'bear'er s chi accompagna il feretro; chi porta il feretro

palliate ['pælɪ,et] *tr* attenuare, alleviare

pallid ['pælɪd] adj pallido

pallor ['pælər] s pallore m

palm [pɑm] s (*tree and leaf*) palma; (*of hand; measure*) palmo; **to carry off the palm** riportare la palma; **to grease the palm of** ungere le ruote a || *tr* far sparire nella mano; nascondere; **to palm off s.th on s.o.** rifilare qlco a qlcu

palmet·to [pæl'meto] s (**-tos** or **-toes**) palmeto

palmist ['pɑmɪst] s chiromante mf

palmistry ['pɑmɪstri] s chiromanzia

palm' leaf' s palma, foglia di palma

palm' oil' s olio di palma

Palm' Sun'day s Domenica delle Palme

palpable ['pælpəbəl] adj palpabile

palpitate ['pælpɪ,tet] *intr* palpitare

pal·sy ['pɔlzi] s (**-sies**) paralisi f || v (*pret & pp* **-sied**) *tr* paralizzare

pal·try ['pɔltri] adj (**-trier; -triest**) vile, meschino, irrisorio

pamper ['pæmpər] *tr* viziare; (*the appetite*) saziare

pamphlet ['pæmflɪt] s opuscolo, libello

pan [pæn] s padella, casseruola; (*of a balance*) coppa, piatto; (phot) bacinella || v (*pret & pp* **panned**; *ger* **panning**) *tr* friggere; (*gold*) vagliare in padella; (*salt*) estrarre in salina; (coll) criticare || *intr* essere estratto; **to pan out** (coll) riuscire || **Pan** s Pan m

panacea [,pænə'si·ə] s panacea

Pan'ama Canal' ['pænə,mɑ] s Canale m di Panama

Pan'ama hat' s panama m
Panamanian [ˌpænəˈmɛnɪ·ən] or [ˌpænəˈmɑnɪ·ən] adj & s panamegno
pan'cake' s frittella || intr (aer) atterrare a piatto
pan'cake land'ing s atterraggio a piatto
pancreas [ˈpænkrɪ·əs] s pancreas m
pander [ˈpændər] s mezzano || intr ruffianeggiare; **to pander to** favorire, assecondare i desideri di
pane [pen] s pannello, vetro di finestra
pan·el [ˈpænəl] s pannello; gruppo che discute in faccia al pubblico, telequiz m; discussione pubblica; (of door or window) specchio; (law) lista di giurati || v (pret & pp -eled or -elled; ger -eling or -elling) tr coprire di pannelli
pan'el discus'sion s colloquio di esperti in faccia al pubblico
panelist [ˈpænəlɪst] s partecipante mf a una discussione in faccia al pubblico
pan'el lights' spl luci fpl del cruscotto
pan'el truck' s camioncino
pang [pæŋ] s (sharp pain) spasimo; (of remorse) tormento
pan'han'dle s manico della padella || intr accattare, mendicare
pan·ic [ˈpænɪk] adj & s panico || v (pret & pp -icked; ger -icking) tr riempire di panico || intr essere colto dal panico
pan'ic-strick'en adj morto di paura, in preda al panico
pano·ply [ˈpænəpli] s (-plies) panoplia; abbigliamento in pompa magna
panorama [ˌpænəˈræmə] or [ˌpænəˈrɑmə] s panorama m
pan·sy [ˈpænzi] s (-sies) viola del pensiero
pant [pænt] s anelito, affanno; **pants** pantaloni mpl, calzoni mpl; **to wear the pants** portare i calzoni || intr ansare; (said of heart) palpitare
pantheism [ˈpænθɪ·ɪzəm] s panteismo
pantheon [ˈpænθɪ·ən] or [ˈpænθɪ·ən] s panteon m, pantheon m
panther [ˈpænθər] s pantera
panties [ˈpæntiz] spl mutandine fpl
pantomime [ˈpæntəˌmaɪm] s pantomima
pan·try [ˈpæntri] s (-tries) dispensa
pap [pæp] s pappa
papa·cy [ˈpepəsi] s (-cies) papato
Pa'pal States' [ˈpepəl] spl Stati mpl pontifici
paper [ˈpepər] adj di carta, cartaceo || s carta; (newspaper) giornale m; (of a student) tema m, saggio; (of a scholar) dissertazione; **on paper** per iscritto || tr (a wall) tappezzare
pa'per·back' s libro in brossura
pa'per·boy' s giornalaio, strillone m
pa'per clip' s fermaglio per le carte, clip m
pa'per cone' s cartoccio
pa'per cut'ter s rifilatrice f
pa'per doll' s pupazzetto di carta
pa'per·hang'er s tappezziere m
pa'per knife' s tagliacarte m
pa'per mill' s cartiera
pa'per mon'ey s carta moneta

pa'per prof'its spl guadagni mpl non realizzati su valori non venduti
pa'per tape' s (of teletype) nastro di carta; (of computer) nastro perforato
pa'per·weight' s fermacarte m
pa'per work' s lavoro a tavolino
papier-mâché [ˌpepərməˈʃe] s cartapesta
paprika [pæˈprikə] or [ˈpæprɪkə] s paprica
papy·rus [pəˈpaɪrəs] s (-ri [raɪ]) papiro
par [par] adj alla pari, nominale; normale || s parità f, valore m nominale; **at par** alla pari
parable [ˈpærəbəl] s parabola
parabola [pəˈræbələ] s parabola
parachute [ˈpærəˌʃut] s paracadute m || intr lanciarsi col paracadute
par'a·chute jump' s lancio col paracadute
parachutist [ˈpærəˌʃutɪst] s paracadutista mf
parade [pəˈred] s parata, sfilata; ostentazione, sfoggio || tr ostentare, sfoggiare; disporre in parata || intr fare mostra di sé; (mil) sfilare
paradise [ˈpærəˌdaɪs] s paradiso
paradox [ˈpærəˌdaks] s paradosso
paradoxical [ˌpærəˈdaksɪkəl] adj paradossale
paraffin [ˈpærəfɪn] s paraffina
paragon [ˈpærəˌgan] s paragone m
paragraph [ˈpærəˌgræf] or [ˈpærəˌgraf] s paragrafo, capoverso; (in a newspaper) trafiletto; (of law) comma m
parakeet [ˈpærəˌkit] s parrocchetto
paral·lel [ˈpærəˌlel] adj parallelo || s (geog, fig) parallelo; (geom) parallela; **parallels** (typ) sbarrette fpl verticali || v (pret & pp -leled or -lelled; ger -leling or -lelling) tr collocare parallelamente; correre parallelo a; confrontare
par'allel bars' spl parallele fpl
paraly·sis [pəˈrælɪsɪs] s (-ses [ˌsiz]) paralisi f
paralytic [ˌpærəˈlɪtɪk] adj & s paralitico
paralyze [ˈpærəˌlaɪz] tr paralizzare
paramount [ˈpærəˌmaunt] adj capitale, supremo
paramour [ˈpærəˌmur] s amante mf
paranoiac [ˌpærəˈnɔɪ·æk] adj & s paranoico
parapet [ˈpærəˌpet] s parapetto
paraphernalia [ˌpærəfərˈnelɪ·ə] spl roba, cose fpl; attrezzi mpl, aggeggi mpl
parasite [ˈpærəˌsaɪt] s parassita m
parasitic(al) [ˌpærəˈsɪtɪk(əl)] adj parassitico, parassitario
parasol [ˈpærəˌsɔl] or [ˈpærəˌsal] s parasole m, ombrellino da sole
par'a·troop'er s paracadutista m
par'a·troops' spl truppe fpl paracadutiste
parboil [ˈparˌbɔɪl] tr bollire parzialmente; (fig) far bollire
parcel [ˈparsəl] s pacchetto; (of land) appezzamento || v (pret & pp -celed or -celled; ger -celing or -celling) tr

impacchettare; **to parcel out** dividere, distribuire

par'cel post' *s* servizio pacchi postali

parch [part∫] *tr* bruciare; (*land*) inaridire; (*e.g., beans*) essiccare; **to be parched** bruciare dalla sete ‖ *intr* arrostirsi; inaridire

parchment ['part∫mənt] *s* pergamena

pardon ['pardən] *s* perdono, grazia; **I beg your pardon** scusi ‖ *tr* perdonare; (*an offense*) graziare

pardonable ['pardənəbəl] *adj* perdonabile, veniale

par'don board' *s* ufficio per la decisione delle grazie

pare [per] *tr* (*fruit, potatoes*) sbucciare, pelare; (*nails*) tagliare; (*expenses*) ridurre

parent ['perənt] *adj* madre, principale ‖ *s* genitore *m* or genitrice *f*; (fig) origine *f*; **parents** genitori *mpl*

parentage ['perəntɪdʒ] *s* discendenza, lignaggio

parenthesis [pə'renθɪsɪs] *s* (**-ses** [ˌsiz]) parentesi *f*; **in parenthesis** tra parentesi

parenthetically [ˌpærən'θetɪkəli] *adv* tra parentesi

parenthood ['perənt ˌhʊd] *s* paternità *f* or maternità *f*

pariah [pə'raɪ·ə] or ['parɪ·ə] *s* paria *m*

pari-mutuel ['pærɪ'mjut/ʊ·əl] *s* totalizzatore *m*

par'ing knife' ['perɪŋ] *s* coltello per sbucciare

Paris ['pærɪs] *s* Parigi *f*

parish ['pærɪ∫] *s* parrocchia

parishioner [pə'rɪ/ənər] *s* parrocchiano

Parisian [pə'rɪʒən] *adj & s* parigino

parity ['pærɪti] *s* parità *f*

park [park] *s* parco ‖ *tr* parcare, parcheggiare ‖ *intr* parcare, parcheggiare, stazionare

parking ['parkɪŋ] *s* posteggio, parcheggio; **no parking** divieto di parcheggio

park'ing lights' *spl* luci *fpl* di posizione

park'ing lot' *s* posteggio, parcheggio

park'ing me'ter *s* parchimetro

park'ing tick'et *s* contravvenzione per parcheggio abusivo

park'way' *s* boulevard *m*

parlay ['parli] or ['par'le] *tr* rigiocare

parley ['parli] *s* trattativa, conferenza ‖ *tr* parlamentare

parliament ['parlɪmənt] *s* parlamento

parlor ['parlər] *s* salotto; (*of beautician or undertaker*) salone *m;* (*of convent*) parlatorio

par'lor car' *s* vettura salone

par'lor game' *s* gioco di società

par'lor pol'itics *s* politica da caffè

Parmesan [ˌparmɪ'zæn] *adj & s* parmigiano

Parnassus [par'næsəs] *s* (*poetry; poets*) parnaso; il Parnaso

parochial [pə'rokɪ·əl] *adj* parrocchiale; ristretto, limitato; (*school*) confessionale

paro·dy ['pærədi] *s* (**-dies**) parodia ‖ *v* (*pret & pp* **-died**) *tr* parodiare

parole [pə'rol] *s* parola d'onore; libertà *f* condizionale, condizionale *f* ‖ *tr* mettere in libertà condizionale

paroxytone [pær'aksɪ ˌton] *adj* parossitono ‖ *s* parola parossitona

par·quet [par'ke] *s* pavimento di legno tassellato, tassellato; (theat) platea ‖ *v* (*pret & pp* **-queted** ['ked]; *ger* **-queting** ['ke·ɪŋ]) *tr* pavimentare in legno tassellato

par'quet cir'cle *s* poltroncine *fpl*

parricide ['pærɪ ˌsaɪd] *s* (*act*) patricidio, parricidio; (*person*) patricida *mf*, parricida *mf*

parrot ['pærət] *s* pappagallo ‖ *tr* scimmiottare, fare il pappagallo a

par·ry ['pæri] *s* (**-ries**) parata ‖ *v* (*pret & pp* **-ried**) *tr* parare; (fig) evitare

parse [pars] *tr* (gram) analizzare grammaticalmente

parsimonious [ˌparsɪ'monɪ·əs] *adj* parsimonioso

parsley ['parsli] *s* prezzemolo

parsnip ['parsnɪp] *s* pastinaca

parson ['parsən] *s* parroco; pastore *m* protestante

part [part] *s* parte *f;* (*of a machine*) pezzo, organo; (*of hair*) riga; **for my part** per parte mia; **on the part of da** parte di; **part and parcel** parte *f* integrante; **parts** abilità *f*, dote *f;* regione *f*, paesi *mpl;* **to do one's part** fare il proprio dovere ‖ *adv* parzialmente, in parte ‖ *tr* dividere, separare; **to part company** separarsi; **to part one's hair** farsi la riga ‖ *intr* separarsi; **to part from** separarsi da, dividersi da; **to part with** rinunciare a

par·take [par'tek] *v* (*pret* **-took** ['tʊk]; *pp* **-taken**) *tr* condividere ‖ *intr*—**to partake in** partecipare a; **to partake of** condividere

parterre [par'ter] *s* aiola; (theat) platea

Parthenon ['parθɪ ˌnan] *s* Partenone *m*

partial ['par/əl] *adj* parziale

participate [par'tɪsɪ ˌpet] *intr* partecipare; **to participate in** partecipare a

participation [par ˌtɪsɪ'pe/ən] *s* partecipazione

participle ['partɪ ˌsɪpəl] *s* participio

particle ['partɪkəl] *s* particella

particular [pər'tɪkjələr] *adj* (*belonging to a single person*) particolare; (*exacting*) esigente, fastidioso ‖ *s* particolare *m;* **in particular** specialmente, particolarmente

part'ing *adj* (*words*) di commiato; (*last*) ultimo ‖ *s* commiato; separazione

partisan ['partɪzən] *adj & s* partigiano

partition [par'tɪ/ən] *s* partizione, divisione; (*of house*) tramezzo ‖ *tr* dividere; tramezzare

partner ['partnər] *s* (*in sports*) compagno; (*in dancing*) cavaliere *m*, dama; (*husband or wife*) consorte *mf;* (com) socio

partnership ['partnər ˌ∫ɪp] *s* associazione; (com) società *f*

part' of speech' *s* parte *f* del discorso

partridge ['partrɪdʒ] *s* pernice *f*

part'-time' *adj* a orario ridotto, a ore

par·ty ['parti] *adj* comune; di gala ‖ *s* (**-ties**) festa, ricevimento, trattenimento; (*of people*) gruppo; (*indi-*

vidual) persona; (pol) partito; (law) contraente *mf;* (mil) distaccamento; **to be a party to** prendere parte a; essere complice di

par'ty girl' *s* ragazza che fa la vita

par'ty-go'er *s* frequentatore *m* di trattenimenti

par'ty line' *s* (*boundary*) linea di confine; (*of Communist party*) politica del partito; (telp) linea in coutenza

pass [pæs] or [pɑs] *s* passaggio; (*state*) stato, situazione; (*free ticket*) ingresso gratuito; (*leave of absence given to a soldier*) congedo, permesso; (*of a hypnotist*) gesto; (*between mountains*) passo; (slang) tentativo d'abbraccio; **a pretty pass** (coll) un bell'affare || *tr* (*a course in school*) passare; (*to promote*) promuovere; (*a law*) approvare; (*a sentence*) pronunciare; (*an opinion*) esprimere, avanzare; (*to excrete*) evacuare; far muovere; **to pass by** non fare attenzione a; **to pass off** (*e.g., bogus money*) azzeccare; **to pass on** trasmettere; **to pass out** distribuire; **to pass over** omettere || *intr* (*to go*) passare; (*said of a law*) essere approvato; (*said of a student*) essere promosso; (*to be accepted*) farsi passare; (*said, e.g., of two trains*) incrociarsi; **to come to pass** accadere, succedere; **to pass as** passare per; **to pass away** morire; **to pass out** (slang) svenire; **to pass over** or **through** attraversare, passare per

passable ['pæsəbəl] or ['pɑsəbəl] *adj* praticabile; (*by boat*) navigabile; (*adequate*) passabile; (*law*) promulgabile

passage ['pæsɪdʒ] *s* passaggio; (*of a law*) approvazione, passaggio; (*ticket*) biglietto di passaggio; (*of the bowels*) evacuazione

pass'book' *s* libretto di banca; libretto della cassa di risparmio

passenger ['pæsəndʒər] *s* passeggero

passer-by ['pæsər'baɪ] or ['pɑsər'baɪ] *s* (**passers-by**) passante *mf*

passing ['pæsɪŋ] or ['pɑsɪŋ] *adj* (*fleeting*) fuggente; (*casual*) incidentale; (*grade*) che concede la promozione || *s* passaggio; (*death*) morte *f;* promozione

passion ['pæʃən] *s* passione

passionate ['pæʃənɪt] *adj* appassionato; (*hot-tempered*) collerico; veemente, ardente

passive ['pæsɪv] *adj* & *s* passivo

pass'key' *s* chiave maestra; (*for use of hotel help*) comunella

Pass'o'ver *s* Pasqua ebraica

pass'port' *s* passaporto

pass'word' *s* parola d'ordine

past [pæst] or [pɑst] *adj* passato, scorso; ex, e.g., **past president** ex presidente || *s* passato || *adv* oltre; al di fuori; al di là || *prep* oltre; al di là di; dopo (di); **past belief** incredibile; **past cure** incurabile; **past hope** senza speranza; **past recovery** incurabile; **past three o'clock** le tre passate

---

paste [pest] *s* (*dough*) pasta; (*adhesive*) colla; diamante *m* artificiale || *tr* incollare; (slang) dare pugni a

paste'board' *s* cartone *m*

pastel [pæs'tɛl] *adj* & *s* pastello

pasteurize ['pæstə,raɪz] *tr* pastorizzare

pastime ['pæs,taɪm] or ['pɑs,taɪm] *s* diversione, passatempo

pastor ['pæstər] or ['pɑstər] *s* pastore *m*, sacerdote *m*

pastoral ['pæstərəl] or ['pɑstərəl] *adj* pastorale || *s* (*poem, letter*) pastorale *f;* (*crosier*) pastorale *m*

pas·try ['pestri] *s* (**-tries**) pasticceria

pas'try cook' *s* pasticciere *m*

pas'try shop' *s* pasticceria

pasture ['pæstʃər] or ['pɑstʃər] *s* pastura, pascolo || *tr* condurre al pascolo || *intr* brucare

past·y ['pesti] *adj* (**-ier; -iest**) pastoso; flaccido

pat [pæt] *s* colpetto; (*of butter*) panetto || *v* (*pret* & *pp* **patted;** *ger* **patting**) *tr* accarezzare leggermente; battere leggermente; **to pat on the back** elogiare, incoraggiare battendo sulla spalla

patch [pætʃ] *s* (*on a suit or shoes*) toppa; (*in a tire*) pezza; (*on wound*) benda; (*of ground*) appezzamento; (*small area*) lembo || *tr* rammendare; **to patch up** (*an argument*) comporre; (*to produce crudely*) raffazzonare

patent ['petənt] *adj* patente, palmare || ['pætənt] *adj* brevettato || *s* (*of invention*) brevetto; (*sole right*) privativa || *tr* brevettare

pat'ent leath'er ['pætənt] *s* copale *m* & *f*, pelle *f* di vernice

pat'ent med'icine ['pætənt] *s* specialità *f* medicinale

pat'ent right' ['pætənt] *s* proprietà brevettata

paternal [pə'tʌrnəl] *adj* paterno

paternity [pə'tʌrnɪti] *s* paternità *f*

path [pæθ] or [pɑθ] *s* via battuta, sentiero; (fig) via

pathetic [pə'θɛtɪk] *adj* patetico

path'find'er *s* esploratore *m*

pathology [pə'θɑlədʒi] *s* patologia

pathos ['peθɑs] *s* patos *m*, pathos *m*

path'way' *s* sentiero, cammino

patience ['peʃəns] *s* pazienza

patient ['peʃənt] *adj* & *s* paziente *mf*

patriarch ['petri,ɑrk] *s* patriarca *m*

patrician [pə'trɪʃən] *adj* & *s* patrizio

patricide ['pætri,saɪd] *s* (*act*) parricidio; (*person*) parricida *mf*

Patrick ['pætrɪk] *s* Patrizio

patrimo·ny ['pætri,moni] *s* (**-nies**) patrimonio

patriot ['petri-ət] or ['pætri-ət] *s* patriota *mf*

patriotic [,petri'ɑtɪk] or [,pætri'ɑtɪk] *adj* patriottico

patriotism ['petri-ə,tɪzəm] or ['pætri-ə,tɪzəm] *s* patriottismo

pa·trol [pə'trol] *s* (*group*) pattuglia; (*individual*) soldato or agente *m* di pattuglia || *v* (*pret* & *pp* **-trolled;** *ger* **-trolling**) *tr* & *intr* pattugliare

patrol'man *s* (**-men**) agente *m*, poliziotto

patrol' wag'on s carrozzone m cellulare, cellulare m

patron ['petrən] or ['pætrən] s patrono, sostenitore m; (customer) cliente mf

patronize ['petrə ,naɪz] or ['pætrə ,naɪz] tr (to support) sostenere; trattare con condiscendenza; essere cliente abituale di

pa'tron saint' s patrono

patter ['pætər] s (e.g., of rain) battito; (of feet) scalpiccio; (speech) chiaccherio ‖ intr battere, picchiettare; chiaccherare

pattern ['pætərn] s modello; disegno; (of flight) procedura ‖ tr modellare

pat·ty ['pæti] s (-ties) pasticcino; (meat cake) polpetta

paucity ['pɔsɪti] s pochezza, scarsità f, insufficienza

Paul [pɔl] s Paolo

paunch [pɔntʃ] s pancia

paunch·y ['pɔntʃi] adj (-ier; -iest) panciuto

pauper ['pɔpər] s povero, indigente mf

pause [pɔz] s pausa; (of a tape recorder) arresto momentaneo; **to give pause (to)** dar di che pensare (a) ‖ intr far pausa, fermarsi; (to hesitate) esitare, vacillare

pave [pev] tr pavimentare, lastricare; **to pave the way (for)** aprire il cammino (a)

pavement ['pevmənt] s pavimentazione, lastricato; (sidewalk) marciapiede m

pavilion [pə'vɪljən] s padiglione m; (of circus) tendone m

paw [pɔ] s zampa ‖ tr (to touch with paws) dar zampate a; (to handle clumsily) maneggiare goffamente; (coll) palpeggiare ‖ intr zampare

pawn [pɔn] s (security) pegno; (tool of another person) pedina; (chess) pedina, pedone m; (fig) ostaggio ‖ tr dare in pegno, impegnare

pawn'bro'ker s prestatore m su pegno

pawn'shop' s agenzia di prestiti su pegno, monte m di pietà

pawn' tick'et s ricevuta di pegno, polizza del monte di pietà

pay [pe] s pagamento; (wages) paga, salario; (mil) soldo ‖ v (pret & pp **paid** [ped]) tr pagare; (wages) conguagliare; (one's respects) presentare; (a visit) fare; (a bill) saldare; (attention) fare, presentare; **to pay back** ripagare; (fig) pagare pan per focaccia a; **to pay for** pagare; **to pay off** liquidare; (in order to discharge) pagare e licenziare; **to pay up** saldare ‖ intr pagare; valere la pena; **pay as you enter** pagare all'ingresso; **pay as you go** pagare le tasse per trattenuta; **pay as you leave** pagare all'uscita

payable ['pe·əbəl] adj pagabile

pay'boost' s aumento di salario

pay'check' s assegno in pagamento del salario; salario, paga

pay'day' s giorno di paga

payee [pe'i] s beneficiario

pay' en'velope s bustapaga

payer ['pe·ər] s pagatore m

pay'load' s peso utile

pay'mas'ter s ufficiale m pagatore

payment ['pemənt] s pagamento

pay'off' s pagamento, regolamento; (coll) conclusione

pay' phone' s telefono a moneta

pay'roll' s lista degli impiegati; libro paga

pay' sta'tion s telefono pubblico

pea [pi] s pisello

peace [pis] s pace f; **to hold one's peace** tacere, stare zitto

peaceable ['pisəbəl] adj pacifico

peaceful ['pisfəl] adj pacifico

peace'mak'er s paciere m

peace' of mind' s serenità f d'animo

peace' pipe' s calumet m della pace

peach [pitʃ] s pesca; (coll) persona or cosa stupenda

peach' tree' s pesco

peach·y ['pitʃi] adj (-ier; -iest) (coll) stupendo

pea'cock' s pavone m

peak [pik] s picco; (of traffic) punta; (of one's career) sommo

peak' hour' s ora di punta

peak' load' s carico delle ore di punta, carico massimo

peal [pil] s (of bells) squillo; (of gun) rombo; (of laughter) scoppio; (of thunder) scroscio ‖ intr scampanare, squillare

pea'nut' s nocciolina americana; (plant) arachide f

pea'nut but'ter s pasta d'arachidi

pear [per] s (fruit) pera; (tree) pero

pearl [pʌrl] s perla; (mother-of-pearl) madreperla; colore perlaceo

pearl' oys'ter s ostrica perlifera

pear' tree' s pero

peasant ['pezənt] adj & s contadino

pea'shoot'er s cerbottana

pea' soup' s minestra di piselli; (coll) nebbione m

peat [pit] s torba

pebble ['pebəl] s ciottolo

peck [pɛk] s beccata; misura di due galloni; **a peck of trouble** un mare di guai ‖ tr beccare ‖ intr beccare; **to peck at** beccucciare

peculation [,pekjə'leʃən] s malversazione, peculato

peculiar [pɪ'kjuljər] adj peculiare; (odd) strano

pedagogue ['pedə ,gɑg] s pedagogo

pedagogy ['pedə ,godʒi] or ['pedə ,gɑdʒi] s pedagogia

ped·al ['pedəl] s pedale m ‖ v (pret & pp **-aled** or **-alled**; ger **-aling** or **-alling**) tr spingere coi pedali ‖ intr pedalare

pedant ['pedənt] s pedante mf

pedantic [pɪ'dæntɪk] adj pedantesco

pedant·ry ['pedəntri] s (-ries) pedanteria

peddle ['pedəl] tr vendere di porta in porta ‖ intr fare il venditore ambulante

peddler ['pedlər] s venditore m or merciaiolo ambulante

pedestal ['pedɪstəl] *s* piedistallo
pedestrian [pɪ'destrɪ·ən] *adj* pedestre || *s* pedone *m*
pediatrics [ˌpidɪ'ætrɪks] *or* [ˌpedɪ'ætrɪks] *s* pediatria
pedigree ['pedɪˌgri] *s* albero genealogico; discendenza, lignaggio
pediment ['pedɪmənt] *s* frontone *m*
peek [pik] *s* sbirciata || *intr* sbirciare
peel [pil] *s* scorza, buccia; (*of baker*) pala || *tr* sbucciare; **to keep one's eyes peeled** (slang) tenere gli occhi aperti || *intr* pelarsi
peep [pip] *s* sbirciata; (*sound*) pigolio || *intr* guardare attraverso una fessura; (*said of birds*) pigolare; (*to begin to appear*) fare capolino
peep'hole' *s* spioncino
Peep'ing Tom' *s* guardone *m*
peep' show' *s* cosmorama *m*
peer [pɪr] *s* pari *m*, uguale *m*; (Brit) pari *m* || *intr* guardare da vicino
peerless ['pɪrlɪs] *adj* senza pari
peeve [piv] *s* (coll) seccatura, irritazione || *tr* (coll) seccare, irritare
peevish ['pivɪʃ] *adj* irritabile
peg [peg] *s* (*to plug holes*) zipolo; (*pin*) cavicchio; (mus) bischero; (coll) grado; **to take down a peg** (coll) fare abbassare la testa a || *v* (*pret & pp* **pegged;** *ger* **pegging**) *tr* fissare con cavicchi; (*prices*) stabilizzare || *intr*—**to peg away** lavorare di lena
peg' leg' *s* gamba di legno
Peking ['pi'kɪŋ] *s* Pechino *f*
Peking·ese [ˌpikɪ'niz] *adj* pechinese || *s* (**-ese**) pechinese *mf*
pelf [pelf] *s* (pej) denaro rubacchiato, maltolto
pelican ['pelɪkən] *s* pellicano
pellet ['pelɪt] *s* pallottola; (*for shotgun*) pallino; (*pill*) pillola
pell-mell ['pel'mel] *adj* confuso, disordinato || *adv* alla rinfusa
Peloponnesian [ˌpeləpə'niʃən] *adj & s* peloponnesiaco
pelt [pelt] *s* pelle grezza; (*blow*) colpo || *tr* scagliare contro; (*to beat*) battere violentemente || *intr* battere, scrosciare
pen [pen] *s* (*enclosure*) recinto; (*for writing*) penna; (*pen point*) pennino || *v* (*pret & pp* **penned**); *ger* **penning**) *tr* scrivere a penna; (*to compose*) redigere || *v* (*pret & pp* **penned** *or* **pent**; *ger* **penning**) *tr* recintare
penalize ['pinəˌlaɪz] *tr* punire; (sports) penalizzare
penal·ty ['penəltɪ] *s* (**-ties**) punizione; (*fine*) multa; (*for late payment*) penale *f*; **under penalty of** sotto pena di
pen'alty goal' *s* calcio di rigore
penance ['penəns] *s* penitenza
penchant ['penʃənt] *s* propensione
pen·cil ['pensəl] *s* matita; (*of rays*) fascio || *v* (*pret & pp* **-ciled** *or* **-cilled;** *ger* **-ciling** *or* **-cilling**) *tr* scrivere a matita; (med) pennellare
pen'cil sharp'ener *s* temperalapis *m*
pendent ['pendənt] *adj* pendente, sospeso || *s* pendente *m*, ciondolo

pending ['pendɪŋ] *adj* imminente; in sospeso || *prep* durante; fino a
pendulum ['pendʒələm] *s* pendolo
pen'dulum bob' *s* lente *f*
penetrate ['penɪˌtret] *tr & intr* penetrare
penguin ['peŋgwɪn] *s* pinguino
pen'hold'er *s* portapenne *m*
penicillin [ˌpenɪ'sɪlɪŋ] *s* penicillina
peninsula [pe'nɪnsələ] *s* penisola
peninsular [pe'nɪnsələr] *adj & s* peninsulare
penitence ['penɪtəns] *s* penitenza
penitent ['penɪtənt] *adj & s* penitente *mf*
pen'knife' *s* (**-knives**) temperino
penmanship ['penmənˌʃɪp] *s* calligrafia
pen' name' *s* nome *m* di penna, pseudonimo
pennant ['penənt] *s* pennone *m*
penniless ['penɪlɪs] *adj* povero in canna, senza un soldo
pennon ['penən] *s* pennone *m*
pen·ny ['penɪ] *s* (**-nies**) (U.S.A.) centesimo || *s* (**pence** [pens]) (Brit) penny *m*
pen'ny pinch'er *s* ['pɪntʃər] *s* spilorcio
pen' pal' *s* amico corrispondente
pen'point' *s* pennino; (*of ball-point pen*) punta
pension ['penʃən] *s* pensione || *tr* pensionare, mettere in pensione
pensioner ['penʃənər] *s* pensionato
pensive ['pensɪv] *adj* pensieroso
Pentecost ['pentɪˌkɔst] *or* ['pentɪˌkast] *s* la Pentecoste
penthouse ['pentˌhaus] *s* appartamento di lusso sul tetto; tettoia
pent-up ['pent ˌʌp] *adj* represso
penult ['pinʌlt] *s* penultima
penum·bra [pɪ'nʌmbrə] *s* (**-brae** [bri] *or* **-bras**) penombra
penurious [pɪ'nurɪ·əs] *adj* taccagno, meschino; indigente
penury ['penjərɪ] *s* taccagneria; estrema povertà, miseria
pen'wip'er *s* nettapenne *m*
people ['pipəl] *spl* popolo, gente *f*; (*relatives*) famiglia; gente *f* del popolo; si, e.g., **people say** si dice || *ssg* (**peoples**) nazione, popolazione || *tr* popolare
pep [pep] *s* (coll) animo, brio || *v* (*pret & pp* **pepped;** *ger* **pepping**) *tr*—**to pep up** (coll) dar animo a
pepper ['pepər] *s* pepe *m* || *tr* pepare; (*to pelt*) tempestare
pep'per·box' *s* pepaiola
pep'per·mint' *s* menta piperita
per [pʌr] *prep* per; (*for each*) il, e.g., **three dollars per meter** tre dollari il metro; **as per** secondo
perambulator [pər'æmbjəˌletər] *s* carrozzella, carrozzino
per capita [pər 'kæpɪtə] per persona, a testa
perceive [pər'siv] *tr* percepire
percent [pər'sent] *s* percento, per cento
percentage [pər'sentɪdʒ] *s* percento, percentuale *f*; (coll) vantaggio
perception [pər'sepʃən] *s* percezione

perch [pʌrtʃ] s (*roost*) posatoio; (*horizontal rod*) ballatoio; (ichth) pesce persico ‖ *intr* appollaiarsi

percolator ['pʌrkə ˌletər] s caffettiera filtro a circolazione

percus'sion cap' [pər'kʌʃən] s capsula di percussione

per diem [pər 'daɪ·əm] s assegno giornaliero

perdition [pər'dɪʃən] s perdizione

perennial [pə'rɛnɪ·əl] *adj* perenne ‖ s pianta perenne

perfect ['pʌrfɪkt] *adj & s* perfetto ‖ [pər'fɛkt] *tr* perfezionare

perfidious [pər'fɪdɪ·əs] *adj* perfido

perfi·dy ['pʌrfɪdi] s (-dies) perfidia

perforate ['pʌrfə ˌret] *tr* perforare

perforation [ˌpʌrfə'reʃən] s perforazione; (*of postage stamp*) dentellatura

perforce [pər'fɔrs] *adv* per forza, necessariamente

perform [pər'fɔrm] *tr* (*a task*) eseguire; (*a promise*) adempiere; (*to enact*) rappresentare ‖ *intr* recitare; (*said, e.g., of a machine*) funzionare

performance [pər'fɔrməns] s esecuzione; (*of a machine*) funzionamento; (*deed*) atto di prodezza; (theat) rappresentazione

performer [pər'fɔrmər] s esecutore m; attore m; acrobata mf

perform'ing arts' spl arti fpl dello spettacolo

perfume ['pʌrfjum] s profumo ‖ [pər'fjum] *tr* profumare

perfumer·y [pər'fjuməri] s (-ies) profumeria

perfunctory [pər'fʌŋktəri] *adj* superficiale, pro forma; indifferente

perhaps [pər'hæps] *adv* forse

per·il ['pɛrəl] s pericolo ‖ v (*pret & pp* -iled or -illed; *ger* -iling or -illing) *tr* mettere in pericolo

perilous ['pɛrɪləs] *adj* pericoloso

period ['pɪrɪ·əd] s periodo; mestruazione; (*in school*) ora; (sports) tempo; (gram) punto

pe'riod cos'tume s costume m dell'epoca

periodic [ˌpɪrɪ'ɑdɪk] *adj* periodico

periodical [ˌpɪrɪ'ɑdɪkəl] *adj & s* periodico

peripher·y [pə'rɪfəri] s (-ies) periferia

periscope ['pɛrɪ ˌskop] s periscopio

perish ['pɛrɪʃ] *intr* perire

perishable ['pɛrɪʃəbəl] *adj* deteriorabile

periwig ['pɛrɪ ˌwɪg] s parrucca

perjure ['pʌrdʒər] *tr*—**to perjure oneself** spergiurare, giurare il falso

perju·ry ['pʌrdʒəri] s (-ries) spergiuro

perk [pʌrk] *tr* (*the head, the ears*) alzare; **to perk oneself up** agghindarsi ‖ *intr*—**to perk up** ringalluzzirsi

permanence ['pʌrmənəns] s permanenza

permanen·cy ['pʌrmənənsi] s (-cies) permanenza

permanent ['pʌrmənənt] *adj* permanente ‖ s permanente f, ondulazione permanente

per'manent fix'ture s cosa or persona permanente

per'manent ten'ure s inamovibilità f

per'manent way' s (rr) sede f stradale ed armamento

permeate ['pʌrmɪ ˌet] *tr* permeare ‖ *intr* permearsi

permissible [pər'mɪsɪbəl] *adj* permissibile

permission [pər'mɪʃən] s permesso

per·mit ['pʌrmɪt] s permesso; patente f, licenza ‖ [pər'mɪt] v (*pret & pp* -mitted; *ger* -mitting) *tr* permettere

permute [pər'mjut] *tr* permutare

pernicious [pər'nɪʃəs] *adj* pernicioso

pernickety [pər'nɪkɪti] *adj* (coll) incontentabile, meticoloso

perorate ['pɛrə ˌret] *intr* perorare

peroxide [pər'ɑksaɪd] s perossido; perossido d'idrogeno

perox'ide blonde' s bionda ossigenata

perpendicular [ˌpʌrpən'dɪkjələr] *adj & s* perpendicolare f

perpetrate ['pʌrpɪ ˌtret] *tr* (*a crime*) perpetrare; (*a blunder*) commettere

perpetual [pər'pɛtʃʊ·əl] *adj* perpetuo

perpetuate [pər'pɛtʃʊ ˌet] *tr* perpetuare

perplex [pər'plɛks] *tr* lasciare perplesso

perplexed [pər'plɛkst] *adj* perplesso

perplexi·ty [pər'plɛksɪti] s (-ties) perplessità f

per se [pər 'si] di per se

persecute ['pʌrsɪ ˌkjut] *tr* perseguitare

persevere [ˌpʌrsɪ'vɪr] *intr* perseverare

Persian ['pʌrʒən] *adj & s* persiano

Per'sian Gulf' s Golfo Persico

persimmon [pər'sɪmən] s diospiro virginiano; cachi m

persist [pər'sɪst] or [pər'zɪst] *intr* persistere

persistent [pər'sɪstənt] or [pər'zɪstənt] *adj* persistente

person ['pʌrsən] s persona; **no person** nessuno

personage ['pʌrsənɪdʒ] s personaggio; persona

personal ['pʌrsənəl] *adj* personale; (*goods*) mobile ‖ s inserzione personale; trafiletto di società

personali·ty [ˌpʌrsə'nælɪti] s (-ties) personalità f; offesa personale

personal'ity cult' s culto della personalità

per'sonal prop'erty s beni mpl mobili

personi·fy [pər'sɑnɪ ˌfaɪ] v (*pret & pp* -fied) *tr* personificare

personnel [ˌpʌrsə'nɛl] s personale m

per'son-to-per'son call' s (telp) chiamata con preavviso

perspective [pər'spɛktɪv] s prospettiva

perspicacious [ˌpʌrspɪ'keʃəs] *adj* perspicace

perspire [pər'spaɪr] *intr* sudare

persuade [pər'swed] *tr* persuadere

persuasion [pər'sweʒən] s persuasione; fede religiosa

pert [pʌrt] *adj* impertinente, sfacciato; vivace

pertain [pər'ten] *intr* appartenere; (*to have reference*) riferirsi

pertinacious [ˌpʌrtɪ'neʃəs] *adj* pertinace

pertinent [ˈpʌrtɪnənt] *adj* pertinente
perturb [pərˈtʌrb] *tr* perturbare
Peru [pəˈru] *s* il Perù
perusal [pəˈruzəl] *s* attenta lettura
peruse [pəˈruz] *tr* leggere attentamente
pervade [pərˈved] *tr* pervadere
perverse [pərˈvʌrs] *adj* perverso; (*obstinate*) ostinato
perversion [pərˈvʌrʒən] *s* perversione
perversi•ty [pərˈvʌrsɪti] *s* (**-ties**) perversità *f*; contrarietà *f*
pervert [ˈpʌrvərt] *s* pervertito, degenerato ‖ [pərˈvʌrt] *tr* pervertire, degenerare
pes•ky [ˈpeski] *adj* (**-kier; -kiest**) (coll) noioso, molesto
pessimism [ˈpesɪˌmɪzəm] *s* pessimismo
pessimist [ˈpesɪmɪst] *s* pessimista *mf*
pessimistic [ˌpesɪˈmɪstɪk] *adj* pessimistico
pest [pest] *s* peste *f*, pestilenza; insetto; animale nocivo; (*person*) peste *f*, seccatore *m*
pester [ˈpestər] *tr* seccare, annoiare
pest'house' *s* lazzaretto
pesticide [ˈpestɪˌsaɪd] *s* insetticida *m*
pestiferous [pestˈtɪfərəs] *adj* pestifero
pestilence [ˈpestɪləns] *s* pestilenza
pestle [ˈpesəl] *s* pestello
pet [pet] *s* animale favorito; beniamino ‖ *v* (*pret & pp* **petted**; *ger* **petting**) *tr* accarezzare ‖ *intr* (coll) pomiciare
petal [ˈpetəl] *s* petalo
petard [pɪˈtard] *s* petardo
pet'cock' *s* chiavetta
Peter [ˈpitər] *s* Pietro; **to rob Peter to pay Paul** fare un buco per tappare un altro ‖ *intr*—**to peter out** (coll) affievolirsi
petition [pɪˈtɪʃən] *s* petizione ‖ *tr* rivolgere un'istanza a
pet' name' *s* nomignolo vezzeggiativo
Petrarch [ˈpitrɑrk] *s* Petrarca *m*
petri•fy [ˈpetrɪˌfaɪ] *v* (*pret & pp* **-fied**) *tr* pietrificare ‖ *intr* pietrificarsi
petrol [ˈpetrəl] *s* (Brit) benzina
petroleum [pɪˈtroli•əm] *s* petrolio
pet' shop' *s* negozio di animali domestici
petticoat [ˈpetɪˌkot] *s* sottoveste *f*; (coll) sottana, gonnella
pet•ty [ˈpeti] *adj* (**-tier; -tiest**) insignificante, minore; meschino
pet'ty cash' *s* cassa delle piccole spese
pet'ty lar'ceny *s* furterello
pet'ty of'ficer *s* (nav) sottufficiale *m* di marina
petulant [ˈpetjələnt] *adj* stizzoso, irritabile
pew [pju] *s* banco di chiesa
pewter [ˈpjutər] *s* peltro; oggetti *mpl* di peltro
phalanx [ˈfelæŋks] *or* [ˈfælæŋks] *s* falange *f*
phantasm [ˈfæntæzəm] *s* fantasma *m*
phantom [ˈfæntəm] *s* fantasma *m*
Pharaoh [ˈfero] *s* Faraone *m*
pharisee [ˈfærɪˌsi] *s* fariseo ‖ **Pharisee** *s* fariseo
pharmaceutical [ˌfɑrməˈsutɪkəl] *adj* farmaceutico

pharmacist [ˈfɑrməsɪst] *s* farmacista *mf*
pharma•cy [ˈfɑrməsi] *s* (**-cies**) farmacia
pharynx [ˈfærɪŋks] *s* faringe *f*
phase [fez] *s* fase *f* ‖ *tr* mettere in fase; sincronizzare; **to phase in** mettere in operazione gradualmente; **to phase out** eliminare gradualmente
pheasant [ˈfezənt] *s* fagiano
phenobarbital [ˌfino•ˈbɑrbɪˌtæl] *s* acido fenil-etilbarbiturico, barbiturato
phenomenal [fɪˈnɑmɪnəl] *adj* fenomenale
phenome•non [fɪˈnɑmɪˌnɑn] *s* (**-na** [nə]) fenomeno
phial [ˈfaɪ•əl] *s* fiala
philanderer [fɪˈlændərər] *s* donnaiolo
philanthropist [fɪˈlænθrəpɪst] *s* filantropo
philanthro•py [fɪˈlænθrəpi] *s* (**-pies**) filantropia
philatelist [fɪˈlætəlɪst] *s* filatelico
philately [fɪˈlætəli] *s* filatelia
Philip [ˈfɪlɪp] *s* Filippo
Philippine [ˈfɪlɪˌpin] *adj* filippino ‖ **Philippines** *spl* isole *fpl* Filippine
Philistine [fɪˈlɪstin], [ˈfɪlɪˌstin] *or* [ˈfɪlɪˌstaɪn] *adj & s* filisteo
philologist [fɪˈlɑlədʒɪst] *s* filologo
philology [fɪˈlɑlədʒi] *s* filologia
philosopher [fɪˈlɑsəfər] *s* filosofo
philosophic(al) [ˌfɪləˈsɑfɪk(əl)] *adj* filosofico
philoso•phy [fɪˈlɑsəfi] *s* (**-phies**) filosofia
philter [ˈfɪltər] *s* filtro
phlebitis [flɪˈbaɪtɪs] *s* flebite *f*
phlegm [flem] *s* (*secretion*) muco, catarro; (*self-possession*) flemma; apatia
phlegmatic(al) [flegˈmætɪk(əl)] *adj* flemmatico
Phoebus [ˈfibəs] *s* Febo
Phoenician [fɪˈnɪʃən] *or* [fɪˈniʃən] *adj & s* fenicio
phoenix [ˈfinɪks] *s* fenice *f*
phone [fon] *s* (coll) telefono ‖ *tr & intr* (coll) telefonare
phone' call' *s* chiamata telefonica
phonetic [foˈnetɪk] *adj* fonetico ‖ **phonetics** *s* fonetica
phonograph [ˈfonəˌgræf] *or* [ˈfonəˌgrɑf] *s* fonografo
phonology [fəˈnɑlədʒi] *s* fonologia
pho•ny [ˈfoni] *adj* (**-nier; -niest**) (coll) falso ‖ *s* (**-nies**) (coll) frode *f*; (*person*) (coll) impostore *m*
phosphate [ˈfɑsfet] *s* fosfato
phosphorescent [ˌfɑsfəˈresənt] *adj* fosforescente
phospho•rus [ˈfɑsfərəs] *s* (**-ri** [ˌraɪ]) fosforo
pho•to [ˈfoto] *s* (**-tos**) (coll) foto *f*
photo•cop•y [ˈfotəˌkɑpi] *s* (**-ies**) fotocopia ‖ *tr* fotocopiare
pho'toelec'tric cell' [ˌfoto•ɪˈlektrɪk] *s* cellula fotoelettrica
photoengraving [ˌfoto•enˈgrevɪŋ] *s* fotoincisione
pho'to fin'ish *s* photofinish *m*, arrivo con fotografia

photogenic [ˌfoto'dʒɛnɪk] *adj* fotogenico

photograph ['fotəˌgræf] *or* ['fotəˌgraf] *s* fotografia || *tr* fotografare || *intr*—**to photograph well** riuscire in fotografia

photographer [fə'tɑgrəfər] *s* fotografo

photography [fə'tɑgrəfi] *s* fotografia

photojournalism [ˌfotə'dʒɝnəˌlɪzəm] *s* giornalismo fotografico

pho′to·play′ *s* dramma adattato per il cinematografo

photostat ['fotəˌstæt] *s* (trademark) copia fotostatica || *tr* riprodurre fotostaticamente

phototube ['fotəˌtjub] *or* ['fotəˌtub] *s* fototubo

phrase [frez] *s* (gram) locuzione; (mus) frase *f* || *tr* esprimere, formulare || *intr* (mus) fraseggiare

phrenology [frɪ'nɑlədʒi] *s* frenologia

Phyllis ['fɪlɪs] *s* Fillide *f*

phy·lum ['faɪləm] *s* (-la [lə]) phylum *m*, tipo

phys·ic ['fɪzɪk] *s* purgante *m* || *v* (pret & pp -icked; ger -icking) *tr* dare il purgante a, purgare

physical ['fɪzɪkəl] *adj* fisico

physician [fɪ'zɪʃən] *s* medico

physicist ['fɪzɪsɪst] *s* fisico

physics ['fɪzɪks] *s* fisica

physiognomy [ˌfɪzɪ'ɑgnəmi] *or* [ˌfɪzɪ'ɑnəmi] *s* fisionomia

physiological [ˌfɪzɪ·ə'lɑdʒɪkəl] *adj* fisiologico

physiology [ˌfɪzɪ'ɑlədʒi] *s* fisiologia

physique [fɪ'zik] *s* fisico

pi [paɪ] *s* (math) pi greco; (typ) tipi scartati || *v* (pret & pp **pied;** ger **piing**) *tr* (typ) scompaginare, scomporre

pian·o [pɪ'æno] *s* (-os) piano

picaresque [ˌpɪkə'rɛsk] *adj* picaresco

picayune [ˌpɪkə'jun] *adj* meschino, minore, di poca importanza

picco·lo ['pɪkəˌlo] *s* (-los) ottavino

pick [pɪk] *s* (tool) piccone *m*; (choice) scelta; (the best) fiore *m*; (mus) plettro || *tr* scavare; (to scratch at) grattare; (to gather) cogliere; (to pluck) spennare; (to pull apart) separare; (one's teeth) stuzzicarsi; (a bone) rosicchiare; (to choose) scegliere; (a lock) scassinare; (a pocket) tagliare, rubare; (mus) pizzicare; **to pick a fight** attaccare briga; **to pick faults** trovare a ridire; **to pick out** scegliere; distinguere; discriminare; **to pick s.o. to pieces** (coll) tagliare i panni addosso a qlcu; **to pick up** sollevare; (to find) trovare; (to learn) arrivare a sapere; (a radio signal) captare; (speed) acquistare || *intr* usare il piccone; **to pick at** (food) spilluzzicare; (coll) criticare; **to pick on** (coll) scegliere; (coll) criticare; **to pick up** (coll) migliorarsi

pick′ax′ *s* piccone *m*

picket ['pɪkɪt] *s* picchetto || *tr* rinchiudere con palizzata; (to hitch) legare; (to post) (mil) mettere di picchetto; (e.g., a factory) picchettare

pick′et fence′ *s* steccato

pick′et line′ *s* corteo di scioperanti; corteo di dimostranti

pickle ['pɪkəl] *s* salamoia, sottaceto; (cucumber) cetriolo sottaceto; **to get into a pickle** (coll) cacciarsi in un imbroglio || *tr* mettere sottaceto; (metallurgy) decapare

pick-me-up ['pɪkmiˌʌp] *s* (coll) spuntino; (coll) bevanda stimulante

pick′pock′et *s* borseggiatore *m*, borsaiolo

pick′up′ *s* sollevamento; (in speed) accelerazione; (of phonograph) pick-up *m*, fonorivelatore *m*; (aut) camioncino; (coll) persona conosciuta per caso; (coll) miglioramento

pick′-up-sticks′ *spl* sciangai *m*

pic·nic ['pɪknɪk] *s* picnic *m* || *v* (pret & pp -nicked; ger -nicking) *intr* fare merenda all'aperto

pictorial [pɪk'torɪ·əl] *adj* pittorico; illustrato; vivido || *s* rivista illustrata

picture ['pɪktʃər] *s* illustrazione, disegno; (painting) quadro, dipinto; (of a person) ritratto; fotografia; film *m*, pellicola || *tr* fare il ritratto di; disegnare; dipingere; fotografare; descrivere; immaginare, immaginarsi

pic′ture frame′ *s* cornice *f*

pic′ture gal′lery *s* pinacoteca, galleria di quadri, quadreria

pic′ture post′ card′ *s* cartolina illustrata

pic′ture show′ *s* cinematografo; mostra di quadri

picturesque [ˌpɪktʃə'rɛsk] *adj* pittoresco

pic′ture tube′ *s* tubo televisivo

pic′ture win′dow *s* finestra panoramica

piddling ['pɪdlɪŋ] *adj* insignificante

pie [paɪ] *s* (with fruit) torta; (with meat) timballo; (orn) pica || *v* (pret & pp **pied;** ger **pieing**) *tr* (typ) scompaginare, scomporre

piece [pis] *s* pezzo; (e.g., of cloth) pezza; **a piece of advice** un consiglio; **a piece of baggage** un collo; **a piece of furniture** un mobile *m*; **a piece of news** una notizia; **by the piece** a cottimo; **to break to pieces** frantumare; frantumarsi; **to cut to pieces** fare a pezzi; **to fall to pieces** cadere a pezzi; **to fly to pieces** rompersi in mille pezzi; **to give s.o. a piece of one's mind** dirne a qlcu di tutti i colori; **to go to pieces** perdere il controllo di sé stesso; **to take to pieces** confutare punto per punto || *tr* rappezzare, mettere insieme || *intr* (coll) mangiucchiare

piece′meal′ *adv* poco a poco

piece′work′ *s* lavoro a cottimo

piece′work′er *s* cottimista *mf*

pier [pɪr] *s* (of a bridge) pila; (over water) molo; (archit) pilastro, pilone *m*

pierce [pɪrs] *tr* forare, bucare; penetrare; (to stab) trapassare || *intr* penetrare

piercing ['pɪrsɪŋ] *adj* acuto; (eyes) penetrante; (pain) lancinante pier' glass' s specchiera

pie·ty ['paɪ·əti] s (-ties) pietà f

piffle ['pɪfəl] s (coll) fesserie fpl

pig [pɪg] s maiale m, porco; (metallurgy) lingotto, massello; **to buy a pig in the poke** comprare il gatto nel sacco

pigeon ['pɪdʒən] s piccione m

pi'geon-hole' s nicchia nella piccionaia; (for filing) casella || tr (to lay aside for later time) archiviare; (to shelve, e.g., an application) insabbiare

pi'geon house' s colombaia, piccionaia

piggish ['pɪgɪʃ] adj porcino, maialesco

pig'gy·back' ['pɪgɪ,bæk] adv sulle spalle, sulla schiena; (rr) su carrello stradale per trasporto carri

pig'head'ed adj ostinato, cocciuto

pig' i'ron s ghisa, ferro grezzo

pigment ['pɪgmənt] s pigmento || tr pigmentare || intr pigmentarsi

pig'pen' s porcile m

pig'skin' s pelle f di maiale; (coll) pallone m da football, sfera di cuoio

pig'sty' s (-sties) porcile m

pig'tail' s codino; (of girl) treccia; treccia di tabacco

pike [park] s (weapon) picca; (road) autostrada; (ichth) luccio

piker ['paɪkər] s (coll) uomo piccino

pile [paɪl] s (heap) pila; (for burning a corpse) pira; (large building) mole f; (beam) palo; (of carpet) pelo; (of money) (slang) gruzzolo; (coll) mucchio; **piles** emorroidi fpl || tr ammucchiare, accumulare; **to pile up** ammonticchiare || intr accumularsi; **to pile into** pigiarsi in; **to pile up** accumularsi

pile' driv'er s battipalo, berta

pilfer ['pɪlfər] tr & intr rubacchiare

pilgrim ['pɪlgrɪm] s pellegrino

pilgrimage ['pɪlgrɪmɪdʒ] s pellegrinaggio

pill [pɪl] s pillola; amara pillola; (coll) rompiscatole mf; **to sugar-coat the pill** addolcire la pillola

pillage ['pɪlɪdʒ] s saccheggio, rapina || tr & intr saccheggiare, rapinare

pillar ['pɪlər] s pilastro, colonna; **from pillar to post** da Erode a Pilato

pill'box' s scatoletta per le pillole; (mil) casamatta

pillo·ry ['pɪləri] s (-ries) gogna, berlina || v (pret & pp -ried) tr mettere alla berlina

pillow ['pɪlo] s cuscino, guanciale m

pil'low-case' s federa

pilot ['paɪlət] adj pilota || s pilota m; (of locomotive) respingente m || tr pilotare

pi'lot light' s fiammella automatica

pimp [pɪmp] s ruffiano, lenone m

pimple ['pɪmpəl] s bitorzolo

pim·ply ['pɪmpli] adj (-plier; -pliest) bitorzoluto

pin [pɪn] s (of metal) spillo; (peg) caviglia; (adornment) spilla; (linchpin) acciarino; (of key) mappa; (clothespin) molletta; (bowling pin) birillo; **to be on pins and needles** stare sulle spine || tr appuntare; (to hold) immobilizzare; **to pin s.o. down** forzare qlcu a rivelare i propri piani **to pin s.th on s.o.** (coll) dare la colpa a qlcu per qlco

pinafore ['pɪnə ,for] s grembiulino

pinaster [paɪ'næstər] s pino marittimo

pin'ball machine' s biliardino

pince-nez ['pæns ,ne] s occhiali mpl a stringinaso

pincers ['pɪnsərz] ssg or spl tenaglie fpl; (zool) pinze fpl

pinch [pɪntʃ] s (squeeze) pizzicotto; (of tobacco) presa; (of salt) pizzico; (hardship) strettoia; **in a pinch** in caso di necessità || tr stringere, pizzicare; (to press) comprimere; ridurre alle strettezze; (slang) rubare; (slang) arrestare || intr stringere; (to be stingy) fare l'avaro

pin'cush'ion s puntaspilli m

pine [paɪn] s pino || intr—**to pine away** struggersi; **to pine for** spasimare per

pine'ap'ple s ananas m

pine' cone' s pigna

pine' nee'dle s ago del pino

ping [pɪŋ] s rumore secco; rumore metallico || intr fare un rumore secco or metallico

pin'head' s capocchia di spillo; (slang) testa quadra

pin'hole' s forellino

pink [pɪŋk] adj rosa || s color m rosa; condizione perfetta; (bot) garofano || tr orlare a zig-zag; (to stab) perforare

pin' mon'ey s denaro per le piccole spese

pinnacle ['pɪnəkəl] s pinnacolo

pin'point' adj di precisione || s punta di spillo || tr mettere in rilievo

pin'prick' s puntura di spillo

pint [paɪnt] s pinta

pintle ['pɪntəl] s maschietto

pin'up' s pin-up-girl f

pin'wheel' s girandola

pioneer [,paɪ·ə'nɪr] s pioniere m || tr aprire la via a || intr fare il pioniere

pioneering [,paɪ·ə'nɪrɪŋ] adj pionieristico

pious ['paɪ·əs] adj pio, devoto

pip [pɪp] s (seed) seme m; (vet) pipita

pipe [paɪp] s tubo, canna; (of stove) cannone m; (for smoking) pipa; (mus) legno; (mus) cornamusa || tr suonare; cantare ad alta voce; fischiare; condurre in una tubatura; munire di tubatura || intr suonare la zampogna; **to pipe down** (slang) stare zitto

pipe' clean'er s scovolino

pipe' dream' s castello in aria

pipe' line' s oleodotto; (fig) fonte f (d'informazioni)

pipe' or'gan s organo a canne

piper ['paɪpər] s zampognaro; **to pay the piper** pagare lo scotto

pipe' wrench' s chiave f per tubi

piping ['paɪpɪŋ] adj (voice) acuto; (sound) di cornamusa || s tubatura; suono di cornamuse; suono acuto; (on cakes) fregio; (on garments) cordoncino ornamentale ‖ *adv*—**piping hot** scottante, bollente

pippin ['pɪpɪn] *s* mela renetta; (*seed*) seme *m*; (*fig*) gran brava persona

piquant ['pikənt] *adj* piccante

pique [pik] *s* picca, ripicco ‖ *tr* offendere, eccitare

pira·cy ['paɪrəsi] *s* (**-cies**) pirateria

pirate ['paɪrɪt] *s* pirata *mf* ‖ *tr* derubare; (*a book*) svaligiare, pubblicare illegalmente ‖ *intr* pirateggiare

pirouette [,pɪru'et] *s* piroetta ‖ *intr* piroettare

Pisces ['paɪsɪz] *or* ['pɪsɪz] *s* (astr) Pesci *mpl*

pistol ['pɪstəl] *s* pistola

piston ['pɪstən] *s* pistone *m*

pis'ton displace'ment *s* cilindrata

pis'ton ring' *s* segmento elastico

pis'ton rod' *s* (*of a steam engine*) biella d'accoppiamento; (*of a motor*) asta del pistone, biella

pis'ton stroke' *s* corsa dello stantuffo

pit [pɪt] *s* (*in the ground*) buca; (*trap*) trappola; (*of fruit*) nocciolo; (*of stomach*) bocca; (*scar*) buttero; (*in exchange*) recinto delle grida; (*for fights*) arena; (theat) platea; (min) miniera; (aut) fossa di riparazione ‖ *v* (*pret & pp* **pitted**; *ger* **pitting**) *tr* infossare; butterare; opporre; (*to remove pits from*) snocciolare

pitch [pɪtʃ] *s* (*black sticky substance*) pece *f*; (*throw*) lancio; (*of a roof*) pendenza, inclinazione; (*of a boat*) beccheggio; (*of a screw*) passo; (*of sound*) altezza ‖ *tr* lanciare; (*a tent*) rizzare ‖ *intr* beccheggiare; **to pitch in** (coll) mettersi al lavoro; (coll) cominciare a mangiare

pitch' ac'cent *s* accento di altezza

pitch' at'titude *s* assetto longitudinale

pitch'-dark' *adj* nero come la pece

pitched' bat'tle *s* battaglia campale

pitcher ['pɪtʃər] *s* brocca; (baseball) lanciatore *m*

pitch'fork' *s* forca, tridente *m*; **to rain pitchforks** (coll) piovere a dirotto

pitch' pipe' *s* (mus) corista *m*

pit'fall' *s* trappola, trabocchetto

pith [pɪθ] *s* midollo; (*strength*) (fig) forza; (fig) succo, essenza

pith·y ['pɪθi] *adj* (**-ier; -iest**) midolloso; succoso, essenziale

pitiful ['pɪtɪfəl] *adj* pietoso

pitiless ['pɪtɪlɪs] *adj* spietato

pit·y ['pɪti] *s* (**-ies**) pietà *f*; **it is a pity that** è un peccato che; **what a pity!** che peccato! ‖ *v* (*pret & pp* **-ied**) *tr* aver pietà di

Pius ['paɪəs] *s* Pio

pivot ['pɪvət] *s* asse *m*, perno; (fig) asse *m* ‖ *tr* imperniare ‖ *intr* imperniarsi; **to pivot on** fare perno su; dipendere da

placard ['plækɑrd] *s* manifesto, affisso ‖ *tr* affiggere

place [ples] *s* luogo; locale *m*; (*court*) piazzetta; (*short street*) vicolo; residenza; sito, luogo, località *f*; (*point*) punto; (*space occupied*) posto; (*office*) posto, impiego; **in no place**

da nessuna parte; **in place** a posto; **in place of** al posto di, invece di; **in the first place** in primo luogo; **in the next place** in secondo luogo; **to know one's place** saper stare al proprio posto; **to take place** aver luogo ‖ *tr* piazzare, mettere; (*to find employment for*) collocare; (*to identify*) ravvisare ‖ *intr* (sports) piazzarsi

place·bo [plə'sibo] *s* (**-bos** *or* **-boes**) rimedio fittizio

place' card' *s* segnaposto

placement ['plesmənt] *s* (*e.g., of furniture*) collocazione; (*employment*) collocamento

place' name' *s* toponimo

place' of busi'ness *s* ufficio, negozio

placid ['plæsɪd] *adj* placido

plagiarism ['pledʒə,rɪzəm] *s* plagio

plagiarize ['pledʒə,raɪz] *tr* plagiare

plague [pleg] *s* peste bubbonica; (*widespread affliction*) piaga, flagello ‖ *tr* infestare, appestare; tormentare

plaid [plæd] *s* tessuto scozzese

plain [plen] *adj* piano; aperto; evidente, esplicito; semplice; (*undyed*) naturale; comune, ordinario; **in plain English** senz'ambagi; **in plain view** di fronte a tutti ‖ *s* pianura

plain'-clothes' man' *s* (**-men'**) agente *m* in borghese

plains'man *s* (**-men**) abitante *m* della pianura

plaintiff ['plentɪf] *s* querelante *mf*

plaintive ['plentɪv] *adj* lamentevole

plan [plæn] *s* piano, progetto ‖ *v* (*pret & pp* **planned**; *ger* **planning**) *tr & intr* progettare

plane [plen] *adj* piano ‖ *m* piano; (*tool*) pialla; (aer) aeroplano; (aer) ala d'aeroplano; (bot) platano ‖ *tr* piallare ‖ *intr* andare in aeroplano

plane' sick'ness *s* male *m* d'aria

planet ['plænɪt] *s* pianeta *m*

plane' tree' *s* platano

plan'ing mill' *s* officina di piallatura

plank [plæŋk] *s* tavola, asse *m*; (*of political party*) piattaforma ‖ *tr* coprire d'assi; cucinare sulla graticola e servire sul tagliere; **to plank down** (*e.g., money*) (coll) snocciolare

plant [plænt] *or* [plɑnt] *s* (*factory*) impianto, stabilimento; (*e.g., of a college*) complesso di edifici; (bot) pianta; (mach) apparato motore; (slang) trappola ‖ *tr* (*e.g., a tree*) piantare; (*seeds*) seminare; (*to stock*) fornire

plantation [plæn'teʃən] *s* piantagione

planter ['plæntər] *s* piantatore *m*; (mach) piantatrice *f*

plaster ['plæstər] *or* ['plɑstər] *s* (*gypsum*) gesso; (*mixture to cover walls*) intonaco, malta; (*poultice*) impiastro ‖ *tr* ingessare; intonacare; impiastrare; (*with posters*) affiggere, ricoprire

plas'ter·board' *s* cartone *m* di gesso

plas'ter cast' *s* (sculp) gesso; (surg) ingessatura

plas'ter of Par'is *s* gesso, stucco

plastic ['plæstɪk] *adj & s* plastico

plate 237 plug

plate [plet] *s* (*dish*) piatto; (*sheet of metal*) placca, piastra; (*thin sheet of metal*) lamina; (*of vacuum tube*) placca; (*of auto license*) targa; (*of condenser*) armatura; (*tableware*) vasellame *m* d'argento, vasellame *m* d'oro; dentiera; (*baseball*) casa base; (phot) lastra; (typ) cliché *m* || *tr* (*with gold or silver*) placcare; (*with armor*) blindare, corazzare

plateau [plæˈto] *s* altipiano

plate' glass' *s* lastrone *m*

platen [ˈplætən] *s* rullo

platform [ˈplæt ˌfɔrm] *s* piattaforma; (*for speaker*) tribuna, palco; (*for passengers*) (rr) marciapiede *m;* (*at end of car*) (rr) piattaforma

plat'form car' *s* (rr) pianale *m*

platinum [ˈplætɪnəm] *s* platino

plat'inum blonde' *s* bionda platinata

platitude [ˈplætɪˌtjud] or [ˈplætɪˌtud] *s* trivialità *f,* banalità *f*

Plato [ˈpleto] *s* Platone *m*

platoon [pləˈtun] *s* plotone *m*

platter [ˈplætər] *s* piatto di portata; (slang) disco di grammofono

plausible [ˈplɔzɪbəl] *adj* plausibile; (*person*) credibile, attendibile

play [ple] *s* gioco; libertà *f* d'azione; recreazione; turno, volta; (theat) dramma *m;* (mach) gioco || *tr* giocare; giocare contro; causare, produrre; (*a drama*) rappresentare; (*a character*) fare la parte di; (*to wield*) esercitare; (mus) suonare; **to play back** (e.g., *a tape*) riprodurre; **to play down** diminuire l'importanza di; **to play one off against another** mettere uno contro l'altro; **to play up** dare importanza a || *intr* giocare; (*to act*) giocare, comportarsi; (theat) recitare; (mus) suonare; (mach) aver gioco; **to play on** continuare a giocare; continuare a suonare; valersi di; **to play safe** non prendere rischi; **to play sick** fare il malato; **to play up to** fare la corte a

play'back' *s* riproduzione; apparecchiatura di riproduzione

play'bill' *s* (theat) programma *m*

play'boy' *s* playboy *m,* gaudente *m*

player [ˈple·ər] *s* giocatore *m;* (theat) attore *m;* (mus) suonatore *m*

play'er pian'o *s* pianola

playful [ˈplefəl] *adj* giocoso

playgoer [ˈple ˌgo·ər] *s* frequentatore *m* del teatro

play'ground' *s* parco di ricreazione; (*resort*) posto di villeggiatura

play'house' *s* teatro; casa di bambole

play'ing card' [ˈple·ɪŋ] *s* carta da gioco

play'ing field' *s* campo da gioco

play'mate' *s* compagno di gioco

play'-off' *s* (sports) spareggio

play'pen' *s* recinto, box *m*

play'thing' *s* giocattolo

play'time' *s* ricreazione

playwright [ˈple ˌraɪt] *s* drammaturgo, commediografo

play'writ'ing *s* drammaturgia

plaza [ˈplæzə] or [ˈplazə] *s* piazzale *m*

plea [pli] *s* scusa; richiesta, domanda; (law) dichiarazione

plead [plid] *v* (*pret & pp* **pleaded** or **pled** [pled]) *tr* (*ignorance*) dichiarare; (*a case*) perorare || *intr* supplicare; argomentare; **to plead guilty** dichiararsi colpevole

pleasant [ˈplezənt] *adj* piacevole; (*person*) simpatico

pleasant·ry [ˈplezəntri] *s* (-ries) facezia, motto

please [pliz] *tr* piacere (with *dat*) || *intr* piacere; **as you please** come vuole; **if you please** per favore; **please** per cortesia; **to be pleased to** avere il piacere di; **to be pleased with** essere soddisfatto con; **to do as one pleases** fare come par e piace

pleasing [ˈplizɪŋ] *adj* piacevole

pleasure [ˈpleʒər] *s* piacere *m;* desiderio; **what is your pleasure?** cosa desidera?

pleas'ure car' *s* vettura da turismo

pleat [plit] *s* piega || *tr* piegare, pieghettare

plebeian [plɪˈbi·ən] *adj & s* plebeo

plebiscite [ˈplebɪ ˌsaɪt] *s* plebiscito

pledge [pledʒ] *s* pegno; promessa; voto; (*person*) ostaggio; (*toast*) brindisi *m;* **as a pledge** in pegno; **to take the pledge** giurare d'astenersi dal bere || *tr* dare in pegno; (*to bind*) far promettere a

plentiful [ˈplentɪfəl] *adj* abbondante

plenty [ˈplenti] *s* abbondanza || *adv* (coll) abbastanza

pleurisy [ˈplʊrɪsi] *s* pleurite *f*

pliable [ˈplaɪ·əbəl] *adj* flessibile, pieghevole, docile

pliers [ˈplaɪ·ərz] *ssg* or *spl* pinze *fpl*

plight [plaɪt] *s* condizione or situazione precaria || *tr*—**to plight one's troth** fidanzarsi

plod [plad] *v* (*pret & pp* **plodded;** *ger* **plodding**) *tr* percorrere pesantemente || *intr* camminare pesantemente; (*to drudge*) sgobbare

plot [plat] *s* (*of ground*) appezzamento; (*of a play*) trama, intreccio; (*evil scheme*) cospirazione, trama || *v* (*pret & pp* **plotted;** *ger* **plotting**) *tr* fare il piano di; macchinare; preparare la trama di; (aer, naut) fare il punto di || *intr* tramare, cospirare

plover [ˈplʌvər] or [ˈplovər] *s* piviere *m*

plow [plaʊ] *s* aratro; (*for snow*) spazzaneve *m* || *tr* arare; (e.g., *water*) solcare; (*snow*) spazzare; **to plow back** reinvestire || *intr* arare; aprirsi la via; camminare pesantemente

plow'man *s* (-men) aratore *m;* contadino

plow'share' *s* vomere *m*

pluck [plʌk] *s* strattone *m;* coraggio; (*giblets*) frattaglie *fpl* || *tr* (*to snatch*) svellere; (e.g., *fruit*) svellere; (*a fowl*) spennare; (mus) pizzicare || *intr* tirare; **to pluck up** farsi coraggio

pluck·y [ˈplʌki] *adj* (-ier; -iest) coraggioso

plug [plʌg] *s* tappo, zaffo; tavoletta di

tabacco; bocca da incendi; (elec) spina; (horse) (slang) ronzino; (slang) raccomandazione || v (pret & pp plugged; ger plugging) tr tappare, otturare; colpire; inserire; (slang) fare la pubblicità di; to plug in (elec) innestare, connettere || intr (coll) sgobbare

plum [plʌm] s (fruit) susina; (tree) susino; (slang) cosa bellissima; (slang) colpo di fortuna

plumage ['plumɪdʒ] s piumaggio

plumb [plʌm] adj appiombo || s piombino || adv appiombo; (coll) completamente || tr determinare la verticale col piombino; assodare

plumb' bob' s piombino

plumber ['plʌmər] s installatore m, idraulico

plumbing ['plʌmɪŋ] s impianto idraulico; mestiere m d'idraulico; sondaggio

plumb'ing fix'tures spl rubinetteria, impianti mpl sanitari

plumb' line' s filo a piombo

plum' cake' s panfrutto

plume [plum] s piuma; (tuft of feathers) pennacchio || tr coprire di piume; **to plume oneself on** piccarsi di; **to plume one's feathers** pulirsi le penne

plummet ['plʌmɪt] s piombino || intr cadere a piombo

plump [plʌmp] adj grassoccio, paffuto; franco || s caduta || adv francamente || intr cadere a piombo

plum' pud'ding s budino con uva passa

plum' tree' s susino

plunder ['plʌndər] s (act) saccheggio; (loot) bottino || tr & intr saccheggiare

plunge [plʌndʒ] s (fall) caduta; (dive) nuotata, tuffo || tr gettare; tuffare; (e.g., a knife) configgere || intr (to rush) precipitarsi; (to gamble) (coll) darsi al gioco; (fig) ripiombare

plunger ['plʌndʒər] s tuffatore m; (for clearing clogged drains) sturalavandini m; (mach) stantuffo; (coll) giocatore temerario

plunk [plʌŋk] adv (coll) proprio; (coll) con un colpo secco || tr (coll) gettare; lasciar cadere; (mus) pizzicare || intr (coll) lasciarsi cadere

plural ['plurəl] adj & s plurale m

plus [plʌs] adj superiore; (elec) positivo; (coll) con lode || s più m; soprappiù m || prep più

plush [plʌʃ] adj di lusso || s peluche f, felpa

Plutarch ['plutɑrk] s Plutarco

Pluto ['pluto] s Plutone m

plutonium [plu'tonɪəm] s plutonio

ply [plaɪ] s (plies) spessore m; (layer) strato; (of rope) legnolo || v (pret & pp plied) tr (a trade) esercitare; (a tool) maneggiare; (to assail) premere, incalzare || intr lavorare assiduamente; **to ply between** fare la spola tra

ply'wood' s legno compensato

pneumatic [nju'mætɪk] or [nu'mætɪk] adj pneumatico

pneumat'ic drill' s martello perforatore or pneumatico

pneumonia [nju'monɪ·ə] or [nu'monɪ·ə] s polmonite f

poach [potʃ] tr (eggs) affogare || intr cacciare or pescare di frodo

poacher ['potʃər] s bracconiere m; pescatore m di frodo

pock [pɑk] s buttero

pocket ['pɑkɪt] adj tascabile || s tasca; (billiards) buca; (aer) vuoto; (min) deposito || tr intascare; (e.g., one's pride) ingoiare

pock'et-book' s portafoglio; (woman's purse) borsetta

pock'et book' s libro tascabile

pock'et-hand'kerchief s fazzoletto

pock'et-knife' s (-knives) temperino

pock'et mon'ey s spiccioli mpl

pock'mark' s buttero

pod [pɑd] s baccello; (aer) contenitore m

poem ['po·ɪm] s poesia; (of some length) poema m

poet ['po·ɪt] s poeta m

poetess ['po·ɪtɪs] s poetessa

poetic [po'etɪk] adj poetico || **poetics** ssg poetica

poetry ['po·ɪtri] s poesia

pogrom ['pogrəm] s pogrom m

poignancy ['pɔɪnjənsi] or ['pɔɪnənsi] s strazio; intensità f

poignant ['pɔɪnjənt] or ['pɔɪnənt] adj straziante; intenso

point [pɔɪnt] s (sharp end) punta; (something essential) essenziale m; (hint) suggerimento; (dot, decimal point, spot, degree, instant, position of compass) punto; (coll) costrutto; **beside the point** fuori del seminato; **in point of** per quanto concerne; **to come to the point** venire al sodo; **to get the point** capire l'antifona; **to make a point of** dar importanza a; insistere di; **to stretch a point** fare un'eccezione, fare uno strappo alla regola; **to the point** a proposito || tr (e.g., a weapon) puntare; (to sharpen) aguzzare; (to dot) punteggiare; (to give force to) dare enfasi a; (with mortar) rinzaffare || intr puntare; **to point at** puntare il dito a; **to point to** mostrare a ditto

point'blank' adj & adv a bruciapelo

pointed ['pɔɪntɪd] adj appuntito; personale, diretto, acuto

pointer ['pɔɪntər] s (rod) bacchetta; indice m, indicatore m; cane m da punta, pointer m; (coll) direttiva

poise [pɔɪz] s equilibrio, stabilità f; dignità f || tr equilibrare || intr equilibrarsi, stare in equilibrio

poison ['pɔɪzən] s veleno || tr avvelenare

poi'son i'vy s edera del Canada, tossicodendro

poisonous ['pɔɪzənəs] adj velenoso

poke [pok] s spinta, urto; (with elbow) gomitata; (slang) polentone m || tr (to prod) spingere, urtare; (the head) sporgere; (the fire) attizzare; **to poke fun at** burlarsi di; **to poke one's nose into** ficcare il naso in || intr (to jab) urtare; (to thrust oneself) ficcarsi; (to pry) ficcare il naso; to poke around gironzolare; to poke out spuntare, protrudere

poker ['pokǝr] s (game) poker m; (bar) attizzatoio

pok'er face' s faccia impassibile

pok·y ['poki] adj (-ier; -iest) (coll) lento; (coll) meschino, modesto || (-ies) s (slang) gattabuia

Poland ['polǝnd] s la Polonia

po'lar bear' ['polǝr] s orso bianco

polarize ['polǝ,raɪz] tr polarizzare

pole [pol] s palo; (long rod) pertica; (of wagon) timone m; (for jumping) asta; (astr, biol, elec, geog, math) polo || tr (a boat) spingere con un palo || intr spingere una barca con un palo || **Pole** s polacco

pole'cat' s puzzola

pole' lamp' s lampada a stelo

pole' star' s stella polare

pole' vault' s salto coll'asta

police [pǝ'lis] s polizia || tr vigilare, proteggere; (mil) pulire

police'man s (-men) agente m di polizia, vigile urbano

police' state' s governo poliziesco

police' sta'tion s commissariato di polizia

poli·cy ['palɪsi] s (-cies) politica; (ins) polizza

polio ['polɪ,o] s (coll) polio f

polish ['palɪʃ] s lustro, lucentezza; (for shoes or furniture) cera; (fig) raffinatezza, eleganza || tr pulire; (e.g., a stone) levigare; to polish off (slang) finire; to polish up (slang) migliorare || intr pulirsi; diventar lucido || **Polish** ['polɪʃ] adj & s polacco

polisher ['palɪʃǝr] s lucidatore m; (mach) lucidatrice f

polite [pǝ'laɪt] adj raffinato, cortese

politeness [pǝ'laɪtnɪs] s cortesia

politic ['palɪtɪk] adj prudente; (expedient) diplomatico

political [pǝ'lɪtɪkǝl] adj politico

politician [,palɪ'tɪʃǝn] s politico; (pej) politicante m, politicastro

politics ['palɪtɪks] ssg or spl politica

poll [pol] s votazione; (registering of votes) scrutinio; lista elettorale; (analysis of public opinion) referendum m, sondaggio; (head) testa; to go to the polls andare alle urne; to take a poll fare un'inchiesta || tr ricevere i voti di; contare i voti di; (a tree) potare; fare un'inchiesta di

pollen ['palǝn] s polline m

pollinate ['palɪ,net] tr fecondare col polline

poll'ing booth' ['polɪŋ] s cabina elettorale

polliwog ['palɪ,wag] s girino

poll' tax' s capitazione

pollute [pǝ'lut] tr insudiciare; (to defile) desecrare, profanare; (e.g., the environment) inquinare, contaminare

pollution [pǝ'luʃǝn] s inquinamento, contaminazione

poll' watch'er s rappresentante m di lista

polo ['polo] s polo

po'lo play'er s giocatore m di polo, polista m

po'lo shirt' s maglietta, polo

polygamist [pǝ'lɪgǝmɪst] s poligamo

polygamous [pǝ'lɪgǝmǝs] adj poligamo

polyglot ['palɪ,glat] adj & s poliglotto

polygon ['palɪ,gan] s poligono

polynomial [,palɪ'nomɪ·ǝl] adj polinomiale || s polinomio

polyp ['palɪp] s (pathol, zool) polipo

polytheist ['palɪ,θi·ɪst] s politeista mf

polytheistic [,palɪθi'ɪstɪk] adj politeistico

pomade [pǝ'med] or [pǝ'mad] s pomata

pomegranate ['pam,grænɪt] s (shrub) melograno; (fruit) melagrana

pom·mel ['pʌmǝl] or ['pamǝl] s (of sword) pomello; (of saddle) arcione m || v (pret & pp -meled or -melled; ger -meling or -melling) tr prendere a pugni

pomp [pamp] s pompa

pompadour ['pampǝ,dor] or ['pampǝ,dur] s acconciatura a ciuffo

pompous ['pampǝs] adj pomposo

pon·cho ['pantʃo] s (-chos) poncho

pond [pand] s stagno

ponder ['pandǝr] tr & intr ponderare; to ponder over pensare sopra

ponderous ['pandǝrǝs] adj ponderoso

poniard ['panjǝrd] s pugnale m

pontiff ['pantɪf] s pontefice m

pontifical [pan'tɪfɪkǝl] adj pontificale

pontoon [pan'tun] s (boat) chiatta, pontone m; (aer) galleggiante m

po·ny ['poni] s (-nies) pony m; (glass and drink) bicchierino; (for cheating) (slang) bigino

poodle ['pudǝl] s barbone m, cane m barbone

pool [pul] s (pond) stagno; (puddle) pozza; (for swimming) piscina; (game) biliardo; (com) cartello, consorzio; (com) fondo comune || tr mettere in un fondo comune || intr formare un cartello or un consorzio

pool'room' s sala da biliardo

pool' ta'ble s tavolo da biliardo

poop [pup] s poppa; (deck) casseretto

poor [pur] adj povero; (inferior) scadente || **the poor** spl i poveri

poor' box' s cassetta per l'elemosina

poor'house' s asilo dei poveri

poorly ['purli] adv male

pop [pap] s scoppio; (soda) gazzosa || v (pret & pp popped; ger popping) tr far scoppiare; to pop the question (coll) fare la domanda di matrimonio || intr esplodere con fragore; to pop in fare una capatina; entrare all'improvviso

pop'corn' s pop-corn m

pope [pop] s papa m

popeyed ['pap,aɪd] adj con gli occhi sporgenti; con gli occhi fuori dalle orbite

pop'gun' s fucile m ad aria compressa

poplar ['paplǝr] s pioppo

pop·py ['papi] s (-pies) papavero

pop'py·cock' s (coll) scemenza

popsicle ['pɑpsɪkəl] *s* (trademark) gelato da passeggio

populace ['pɑpjələs] *s* gente *f*, popolino

popular ['pɑpjələr] *adj* popolare

popularize ['pɑpjələ ˌraɪz] *tr* divulgare, volgarizzare

populate ['pɑpjə ˌlet] *tr* popolare

population [ˌpɑpjə'leʃən] *s* popolazione

populous ['pɑpjələs] *adj* popoloso

porcelain ['pɔrsəlɪn] or ['pɔrslɪn] *s* porcellana

porch [pɔrtʃ] *s* portico

porcupine ['pɔrkjəˌpaɪn] *s* (*Hystrix cristata*) istrice *m* & *f*, porcospino; (*Erethizon dorsatum*) ursone *m*, porcospino americano

pore [por] *s* poro || *intr*—to pore over studiare minutamente

pork [pork] *s* carne *f* di maiale

pork' butch'er shop' *s* salumeria

pork'chop' *s* cotoletta di maiale

porous ['porəs] *adj* poroso

po'rous plas'ter *s* cataplasma *m*

porphy·ry ['pɔrfɪri] *s* (-ries) porfido

porpoise ['pɔrpəs] *s* focena; (*dolphin*) delfino

porridge ['pɑrɪdʒ] or ['pɔrɪdʒ] *s* pappa, farinata

port [port] *adj* portuario || *s* (*harbor; wine*) porto; (*naut*) babordo, sinistra; (*opening in side of ship*) portello; (*round opening*) (naut) oblò *m*

portable ['portəbəl] *adj* portabile

portal ['portəl] *s* portale *m*

portend [por'tend] *tr* presagire

portent ['portent] *s* presagio

portentous [por'tentəs] *adj* sinistro, funesto, premonitore; (*amazing*) portentoso

porter ['portər] *s* (*doorman*) portiere *m*; (*man who carries luggage*) facchino; (*of a sleeper*) conduttore *m*; (*in a store*) inserviente *mf*; (*beverage*) birra scura e amara

portfoli·o [port'folɪˌo] *s* (-os) cartella; (*office; holdings*) portafoglio

port'hole' *s* (*opening in side of ship*) portello; (*round opening*) (naut) oblò *m*

porti·co ['portɪˌko] *s* (-cos or -coes) portico

portion ['porʃən] *s* porzione; (*dowry*) dote *f* || *tr*—to portion out dividere, ripartire

port·ly ['portli] *adj* (-lier; -liest) obeso, corpulento

port' of call' *s* scalo

portrait ['portret] or ['portrɪt] *s* ritratto

portray [por'tre] *tr* ritrarre

portrayal [por'tre·əl] *s* delineazione; ritratto

Portugal ['portʃəgəl] *s* il Portogallo

Portu·guese ['portʃə ˌgiz] *adj* portoghese || *s* (-guese) portoghese *mf*

pose [poz] *s* posa || *tr* (*a question*) avanzare; (*a model*) mettere in posa || *intr* posare; **to pose as** posare a, atteggiarsi a

posh [pɑʃ] *adj* (coll) di lusso

position [pə'zɪʃən] *s* posizione; rango;

impiego, posto; **to be in a position to** essere in grado di

positive ['pɑzɪtɪv] *adj* positivo || *s* positivo; (phot) positiva

possess [pə'zɛs] *tr* possedere

possession [pə'zɛʃən] *s* possedimento; (*of mental faculties*) possesso; **possessions** (*wealth*) beni *mpl*

possessive [pə'zɛsɪv] *adj* possessivo; (*e.g., mother*) opprimente, soffocante

possible ['pɑsɪbəl] *adj* possibile

possum ['pɑsəm] *s* opossum *m*; **to play possum** (coll) fare il morto

post [post] *s* (*mail*) posta; (*pole*) palo; (*in horse racing*) linea di partenza; posizione, rango; (*job*) posto; (mil) presidio || *tr* mettere in una lista; impostare; tenere al corrente; **post no bills** divieto d'affissione

postage ['postɪdʒ] *s* affrancatura

post'age me'ter *s* affrancatrice *f*

post'age stamp' *s* francobollo

postal ['postəl] *adj* postale

post'al card' *s* cartolina postale

pos'tal per'mit *s* abbonamento postale

pos'tal sav'ings bank' *s* cassa di risparmio postale

post'al scale' *s* pesalettere *m*

post' card' *s* cartolina illustrata; cartolina postale

post'date' *tr* postdatare

poster ['postər] *s* cartellone *m*, manifesto pubblicitario

posterity [pɑs'tɛrɪti] *s* posterità *f*

postern ['postərn] *adj* posteriore || *s* postierla

post' exchange' *s* spaccio militare

post'haste' *adv* al più presto possibile

posthumous ['pɑst/uməs] *adj* postumo

post'man *s* (-men) portalettere *m*

post'mark' *s* bollo, timbro postale || *tr* bollare, timbrare

post'mas'ter *s* ricevitore *m* postale

post'master gen'eral *s* (postmasters general) ministro delle poste

post-mortem ['post'mortəm] *adj* postumo || *s* autopsia

post' of'fice *s* ufficio postale

post'-office box' *s* casella postale

postpaid ['post ˌped] *adj* franco di porto

postpone [post'pon] *tr* differire, posporre

postscript ['post ˌskrɪpt] *s* poscritto

postulant ['postʃələnt] *s* postulatore *m*, postulante *mf*

posture ['pɑstʃər] *s* portamento; posa || *intr* posare

post'war' *adj* del dopoguerra

po·sy ['pozi] *s* (-sies) fiore *m*; (*nosegay*) mazzolino di fiori

pot [pɑt] *s* pentola, pignatta; pitale *m*, orinale *m*; (*in gambling*) (coll) piatto; **to go to pot** andare a gambe all'aria

potash ['pɑt ˌæʃ] *s* potassa

potassium [pə'tæsɪ·əm] *s* potassio

pota·to [pə'teto] *s* (-toes) patata

pota'to om'elet *s* omelette *f* con patate

potbellied ['pɑt ˌbelɪd] *adj* panciuto

poten·cy ['potənsi] *s* (-cies) potenza

potent ['potənt] *adj* potente

potentate ['potən ‚tet] s potentato
potential [pə'tenʃəl] adj & s potenziale m
pot'hold'er s patta, presa
pot'hook' s uncino
potion ['poʃən] s pozione
pot'luck' s—**to take potluck** mangiare quello che passa il convento
pot' shot' s colpo sparato a casaccio
potter ['potər] s vasaio
pot'ter's clay' s argilla per stoviglie
pot'ter's field' s cimitero dei poveri
potter·y ['potəri] s (-ies) vasellame m; fabbrica di vasellame; ceramica
pouch [pautʃ] s sacchetto, borsa; (of kangaroo) borsa
poultice ['poltɪs] s cataplasma m
poultry ['poltri] s pollame m
poul'try·man s (-men) pollivendolo
pounce [pauns] intr—**to pounce on** balzare su
pound ['paund] s libbra; lira sterlina; (for stray animals) recinto || tr battere, picchiare; tempestare di colpi; (to crush) polverizzare || intr battere
pound' cake' s dolce m fatto con una libbra di burro, una di zucchero ed una di farina
pound' ster'ling s lira sterlina
pour [por] tr versare; (e.g., tea) servire; (wine) mescere; (stones upon an enemy) far piovere || intr fluire; (to rain) diluviare; **to pour in** affluire; **to pour out** uscire in massa
pout [paut] s broncio || intr tenere il broncio
poverty ['pavərti] s povertà f
POW ['pi'o'dʌb‚ju] s (letterword) (**prisoner of war**) prigioniero di guerra
powder ['paudər] s polvere f; (for the face) cipria; (med) polverina || tr incipriare; (to sprinkle with powder) spolverizzare
pow'dered sug'ar s zucchero in polvere
pow'der puff' s piumino
pow'der room' s toletta
powdery ['paudəri] adj polveroso; fragile; (snow) farinoso
power ['pau·ər] s (ability, authority) potere m; forza, energia; (nation) potenza; (math, phys) potenza; **in power** al potere; **the powers that be** i potenti || tr azionare
pow'er·boat' s barca a motore
pow'er brake' s (aut) servofreno
pow'er com'pany s compagnia di elettricità
pow'er drive' s picchiata
powerful ['pau·ərfəl] adj poderoso
pow'er·house' s centrale elettrica
powerless ['pau·ərlɪs] adj impotente
pow'er line' s elettrodotto
pow'er mow'er s motofalciatrice f
pow'er of attor'ney s procura legale
pow'er plant' s stazione f generatrice; (aut) gruppo motore
pow'er steer'ing s servosterzo
pow'er tool' s apparecchiatura a motore
pow'er vac'uum s vuoto di potere
practical ['præktɪkəl] adj pratico

prac'tical joke' s scherzo da prete
practically ['præktɪkəli] adv (in a practical manner; virtually, really) praticamente; più o meno, quasi
practice ['præktɪs] s pratica; (of a profession) esercizio; (e.g., of a doctor) clientela; (process of doing something) prassi f; (habitual performance) abitudine f || tr praticare, esercitare || intr esercitarsi, praticare; (to be active in a profession) esercitare; **to practice as** esercitare la professione di
practitioner [præk'tɪʃənər] s professionista mf
Prague [prɑg] or [preg] s Praga
prairie ['preri] s prateria
prai'rie dog' s cinomio
prai'rie wolf' s coyote m
praise [prez] s lode f, elogio || tr lodare, elogiare; **to praise to the skies** levare alle stelle
praise'wor'thy adj lodevole
pram [præm] s (coll) carrozzella
prance [præns] or [prans] s caracollo || intr caracollare; (to caper) ballonzolare
prank [præŋk] s burla, tiro
prate [pret] intr cianciare
prattle ['prætəl] s ciancia, chiacchierio || intr cianciare, parlare a vanvera
pray [pre] tr & intr pregare
prayer [prer] s preghiera
prayer' book' s libro di preghiere
preach [pritʃ] tr & intr predicare
preacher ['pritʃər] s predicatore m
preamble ['pri ‚æmbəl] s preambolo
precarious [prɪ'kɛrɪ·əs] adj precario
precaution [prɪ'koʃən] s precauzione
precede [prɪ'sid] tr & intr precedere
precedent ['presɪdənt] s precedente m
precept ['prisɛpt] s precetto
precinct ['prisɪŋkt] s distretto; circoscrizione elettorale; **precincts** dintorni mpl
precious ['preʃəs] adj prezioso || adv—**precious little** (coll) molto poco
precipice ['presɪpɪs] s precipizio
precipitate [prɪ'sɪpɪ ‚tet] adj precipitoso || s precipitato || tr & intr precipitare
precipitous [prɪ'sɪpɪtəs] adj precipitoso, a precipizio
precise [prɪ'saɪs] adj preciso
precision [prɪ'sɪʒən] s precisione
preclude [prɪ'klud] tr precludere; escludere
precocious [prɪ'koʃəs] adj precoce
predatory ['predə ‚tori] adj da preda, predatore
predicament [prɪ'dɪkəmənt] s situazione critica or imbarazzante
predict [prɪ'dɪkt] tr predire
prediction [prɪ'dɪkʃən] s predizione
predispose [‚prɪdɪs'poz] tr predisporre
predominant [prɪ'dɑmɪnənt] adj predominante
preeminent [prɪ'emɪnənt] adj preminente
preempt [prɪ'empt] tr occupare or acquistare in precedenza
preen [prin] tr (feathers, fur) lisciarsi;

to preen oneself agghindarsi, attillarsi

prefabricate [pri'fæbrɪ‚ket] *tr* prefabbricare

preface ['prefɪs] *s* prefazione || *tr* prefazionare; essere la prefazione di

pre-fer [prɪ'fʌr] *v* (*pret & pp -ferred; ger -ferring*) *tr* preferire; (*to advance*) promuovere; (law) presentare, avanzare

preferable ['prefərəbəl] *adj* preferibile

preference ['prefərəns] *s* preferenza

preferred' stock' *s* azioni *fpl* privilegiate

prefix ['prifɪks] *s* prefisso || *tr* prefiggere

pregnan·cy ['pregnənsi] *s* (**-cies**) gravidanza

pregnant ['pregnənt] *adj* incinta, gravida; (fig) gravido

prehistoric [‚prihɪs'tarɪk] or [‚prihɪs-'tɔrɪk] *adj* preistorico

prejudice ['predʒədɪs] *s* pregiudizio; preconcetto; **without prejudice** senza detrimento || *tr* (*to harm*) pregiudicare; predisporre; **to prejudice against** prevenire contro

prejudicial ['predʒə'dɪ/əl] *adj* pregiudizievole

prelate ['prelɪt] *s* prelato

preliminar·y [prɪ'lɪmɪ‚neri] *adj* preliminare || *s* (**-ies**) preliminare *m*

prelude ['preljud] or ['prilud] *s* preludio || *tr* preludere a || *intr* preludere

premeditate [pri'medɪ‚tet] *tr* premeditare

premier [prɪ'mɪr] or ['primɪ·ər] *s* primo ministro, presidente *m* del consiglio

premiere [prə'mjer or [prɪ'mɪr] *s* prima; prima attrice

premise ['premɪs] *s* premessa; **on the premises** nella proprietà, sul luogo; **premises** proprietà *f*

premium ['primɪ·əm] *s* premio; **at a premium** in gran richiesta; a prezzo altissimo

premonition [‚primə'nɪ/ən] *s* presentimento; indizio

preoccupation [pri‚akjə'pe/ən] *s* preoccupazione

preoccu·py [pri'akjə‚paɪ] *v* (*pret & pp -pied*) *tr* preoccupare; (*to occupy beforehand*) occupare prima

prepaid [pri'ped] *adj* pagato in anticipo; franco di porto

preparation [‚prepə're/ən] *s* preparazione; (*for a trip*) preparativo; (pharm) preparato

preparatory [prɪ'pærə‚tori] *adj* preparatorio

prepare [prɪ'per] *tr* preparare || *intr* prepararsi

preparedness [prɪ'perɪdnəs] or [prɪ-'perdnɪs] *s* preparazione; preparazione militare

pre·pay [pri'pe] *v* (*pret & pp -paid*) *tr* pagare anticipatamente

preponderant [prɪ'pandərənt] *adj* preponderante

preposition [‚prepə'zɪ/ən] *s* preposizione

prepossessing [‚pripə'zesɪŋ] *adj* simpatico, attraente, piacevole

preposterous [prɪ'pastərəs] *adj* assurdo, ridicolo

prep' school' [prep] *s* (coll) scuola preparatoria

prerecorded [‚priri'kɔrdɪd] *adj* (rad & telv) a registrazione differita

prerequisite [pri'rekwɪzɪt] *s* requisito

prerogative [prɪ'ragətɪv] *s* prerogativa

presage ['presɪdʒ] *s* presagio || [prɪ-'sedʒ] *tr* presagire

Presbyterian [‚prezbɪ'tɪrɪ·ən] *adj & s* presbiteriano; Presbiteriano

prescribe [prɪ'skraɪb] *tr & intr* prescrivere

prescription [prɪ'skrɪp/ən] *s* prescrizione; (pharm) ricetta

presence ['prezəns] *s* presenza; **in the presence of** alla presenza di

present ['prezənt] *adj* presente || *s* presente *m*, regalo || [prɪ'zent] *tr* presentare; **present arms!** presentat'arm!; **to present s.o. with s.th** regalare qlco a qlcu

presentable [prɪ'zentəbəl] *adj* presentabile

presentation [‚prezən'te/ən] or [‚prizən'te/ən] *s* presentazione; (theat) rappresentazione

presenta'tion cop'y *s* copia d'omaggio

presentiment [prɪ'zentɪmənt] *s* presentimento

presently ['prezəntli] *adv* fra poco; attualmente

preserve [prɪ'zʌrv] *s* (*for hunting*) riserva; **preserves** conserva, marmellata || *tr* preservare; conservare

preserved' fruit' *s* frutta in conserva

preside [prɪ'zaɪd] *intr* presiedere; **to preside over** presiedere, presiedere a

presiden·cy ['prezɪdənsi] *s* (**-cies**) presidenza

president ['prezɪdənt] *s* presidente *m*; (*of a university*) rettore *m*

press [pres] *s* pressione; (*crowd*) folla; (*closet*) armadio; (mach) pressa; (typ) stampa; **to go to press** andare in macchina || *tr* (*to push*) spingere, premere; (*to squeeze*) spremere; (*to embrace*) abbracciare; forzare; costringere; urgere, sollecitare; (*to iron*) stirare || *intr* premere; avanzare

press' a' gent *s* agente pubblicitario

press' con'ference *s* conferenza stampa

pressing ['presɪŋ] *adj* pressante, urgente || *s* (*of records*) incisione

press' release' *s* comunicato stampa

pressure ['pre/ər] *s* pressione; tensione; urgenza || *tr* pressare, incalzare con insistenza

pres'sure cook'er ['kukər] *s* pentola a pressione

pressurize ['pre/ə‚raɪz] *tr* pressurizzare

prestige [pres'tiʒ] or ['prestɪdʒ] *s* prestigio

prestigious [pres'stɪdʒɪ·əs] or [pre-'stɪdʒəs] *adj* onorato, stimato

presumably [prɪ'zuməbli] or [prɪ'zjuməbli] *adv* presumibilmente

presume [prɪ'zum] or [prɪ'zjum] *tr* presumere; **to presume to** prendersi la libertà di || *intr* assumere; **to presume on** or **upon** abusare di

presumption [prɪˈzʌmp/ən] *s* presunzione; supposizione

presumptuous [prɪˈzʌmpt/ʊ-əs] *adj* presuntuoso

presuppose [ˌprisəˈpoz] *tr* presupporre

pretend [prɪˈtɛnd] *tr* fingere, fare finta di || *intr* fingere; **to pretend to** (*e.g., the throne*) pretendere a

pretender [prɪˈtɛndər] *s* pretendente *mf;* impostore *m*

pretense [prɪˈtɛns] or [ˈpritɛns] *s* pretesa; finzione; **under false pretenses** allegando ragioni false; **under pretense of** sotto l'apparenza di

pretentious [prɪˈtɛn/əs] *adj* pretenzioso

preterit [ˈprɛtərɪt] *adj* passato, preterito || *s* passato remoto, preterito

pretext [ˈpritɛkst] *s* pretesto

pretonic [prɪˈtɑnɪk] *adj* pretonico

pret·ty [ˈprɪti] *adj* (**-tier; -tiest**) grazioso, carino; (*e.g., sum of money*) (coll) bello || *adv* abbastanza; molto; **sitting pretty** (slang) ben messo

prevail [prɪˈvel] *intr* prevalere; **to prevail on** or **upon** persuadere

prevailing [prɪˈvelɪŋ] *adj* prevalente

prevalent [ˈprɛvələnt] *adj* comune

prevaricate [prɪˈværɪˌket] *intr* mentire

prevent [prɪˈvɛnt] *tr* impedire; **to prevent from** + *ger* impedire (with *dat*) di + *inf* or che + *subj*

prevention [prɪˈvɛn/ən] *s* prevenzione

preventive [prɪˈvɛntɪv] *adj* preventivo || *s* rimedio preventivo

preview [ˈpriˌvju] *s* indizio; (*private showing*) (mov) anteprima; (*showing of brief scenes for advertising*) (mov) scene *fpl* di prossima programmazione

previous [ˈprivɪ-əs] *adj* previo, precedente || *adv* precedentemente; **previous to** prima di

prewar [ˈpriˌwɔr] *adj* anteguerra

prey [pre] *s* preda; **to be prey to** essere preda di || *intr* predare; **to prey on** or **upon** predare, sfruttare; preoccupare

price [praɪs] *s* prezzo; **at any price** a qualunque costo || *tr* chiedere il prezzo di; fissare il prezzo di

price′ control′ *s* calmiere *m*

price′ cut′ting *s* riduzione di prezzo

price′ fix′ing *s* regolamento dei prezzi

price′ freez′ing *s* congelamento dei prezzi

priceless [ˈpraɪslɪs] *adj* inestimabile; (coll) molto divertente

price′ list′ *s* listino prezzi

price′ tag′ *s* cartellino del prezzo

price′ war′ *s* guerra dei prezzi

prick [prɪk] *s* punta; puntura; **to kick against the pricks** tirare calci al vento || *tr* bucare, forare; pungere; (*to goad*) spronare; (*the ears*) ergere; (*said, e.g., of the conscience*) rimordere (with *dat*)

prick·ly [ˈprɪkli] *adj* (**-lier; -liest**) spinoso, pungente

prick′ly heat′ *s* sudamina

prick′ly pear′ *s* ficodindia *m*

pride [praɪd] *s* orgoglio; arroganza; **the**

pride of il fiore di || *tr*—**to pride oneself on** or **upon** inorgoglirsi di

priest [prist] *s* prete *m,* sacerdote *m*

priesthood [ˈpristˌhud] *s* sacerdozio

priest·ly [ˈpristli] *adj* (**-lier; -liest**) sacerdotale

prig [prɪg] *s* pedante *mf,* moralista *mf*

prim [prɪm] *adj* (**primmer; primmest**) formale, corretto, compito

prima·ry [ˈpraɪˌmɛri] or [ˈpraɪmərɪ] *adj* primario || *s* (**-ries**) elezione preferenziale; (elec) bobina primaria; (elec) primario

prime [praɪm] *adj* primo; originale; di prima qualità || *s* (*earliest part*) inizio; (*best period*) fiore *m;* (*choicest part*) fior fiore *m;* (math) numero primo; (*mark*) (math) primo || *tr* preparare; (*a pump*) adescare; (*a firearm*) innescare; (*a canvas*) mesticare; (*a wall*) dare la prima mano a; (*to supply with information*) istruire

prime′ min′ister *s* primo ministro

primer [ˈprɪmər] *s* sillabario, abbecedario || [ˈpraɪmər] *s* innesco, detonatore *m*

primeval [praɪˈmivəl] *adj* primordiale

primitive [ˈprɪmɪtɪv] *adj* primitivo

primp [prɪmp] *tr* agghindare || *intr* agghindarsi

prim′rose′ *s* primula

prim′rose path′ *s* sentiero dei piaceri

prince [prɪns] *s* principe *m;* **to live like a prince** vivere da principe

prince′ roy′al *s* principe ereditario

princess [ˈprɪnsɪs] *s* principessa

principal [ˈprɪnsɪpəl] *adj* principale || *s* (*chief*) padrone *m,* principale *m;* (*of school*) direttore *m,* preside *m;* (*actor*) primo attore; (com) capitale *m;* (law) mandante *mf*

principle [ˈprɪnsɪpəl] *s* principio; **on principle** per principio

print [prɪnt] *s* stampa; (*cloth*) tessuto stampato; (*printed matter*) stampato; (*newsprint*) giornale *m;* (*mark made by one's thumb*) impronta; (phot) positiva; **in print** stampato; disponibile; **out of print** esaurito || *tr* stampare, tirare; (*to write in print*) scrivere in stampatello; (*in the memory*) imprimere

print′ed cir′cuit *s* circuito stampato

print′ed mat′ter *s* stampati *mpl*

printer [ˈprɪntər] *s* stampatore *m;* (*of computer*) tabulatrice *f*

print′er's dev′il *s* apprendista *m* tipografo

print′er's ink′ *s* inchiostro da stampa

printing [ˈprɪntɪŋ] *s* stampa; stampato; tiratura, edizione; (*writing in printed letters*) stampatello

prior [ˈpraɪ·ər] *adj* anteriore, precedente || *s* priore *m* || *adv* prima; **prior to** prima di

priori·ty [praɪˈɔrɪti] or [praɪˈɔrɪti] *s* (**-ties**) priorità *f*

prism [ˈprɪzəm] *s* prisma *m*

prison [ˈprɪzən] *s* prigione, carcere *m*

prisoner [ˈprɪzənər] or [ˈprɪznər] *s* prigioniero

pris′on van′ *s* furgone *m* cellulare

pris•sy ['prɪsi] adj (-sier; -siest) smanceroso, smorfioso

priva•cy ['praɪvəsi] s (-cies) ritiro; segreto; **to have no privacy** non esser mai lasciato in pace

private ['praɪvɪt] adj privato, personale || s soldato semplice; **in private** privatamente; **privates** pudende fpl

pri'vate eye' s poliziotto privato

pri'vate first' class' s soldato scelto

pri'vate hos'pital s clinica

priv'ate view'ing s (mov) anteprima; (painting) vernice f

privet ['prɪvɪt] s ligustro

privilege ['prɪvɪlɪdʒ] s privilegio

priv•y ['prɪvi] adj privato; **privy to** segretamente a conoscenza di || s (-ies) latrina

prize [praɪz] s premio; (nav) preda || tr valutare, stimare

prize' fight' s incontro di pugilato

prize' fight'er s pugile m, pugilista m

prize' ring' s ring m, quadrato

pro [pro] s (pros) pro; voto favorevole; argomento favorevole; (coll) professionista m; **the pros and the cons** il pro e il contro

probabili•ty [,prabə'bɪlɪti] s (-ties) probabilità f

probable ['prabəbəl] adj probabile

probate ['probet] s omologazione di un testamento; copia autenti a di un testamento || tr (a will) omologare

probation [pro'beʃən] s prova; periodo di prova; (law) condizionale f, libertà vigilata; (educ) provvedimento disciplinare

probe [prob] s inchiesta; (surg) sonda || tr indagare; sondare

problem ['prabləm] s problema m

procedure [pro'sidʒər] s procedura

proceed [pro'sid] s—**proceeds** provento || [pro'sid] intr procedere

proceeding [pro'sidɪŋ] s procedimento; **proceedings** atti mpl; (law) procedimenti mpl

process ['proses] s processo; **in the process of time** in processo di tempo || tr trattare

procession [pro'seʃən] s processione

proc'ess serv'er s ufficiale giudiziario

proclaim [pro'klem] tr proclamare

proclitic [pro'klɪtɪk] adj proclitico || s parola proclitica

procrastinate [pro'kræstɪ,net] tr & intr procrastinare

procure [pro'kjur] tr ottenere || intr ruffianeggiare

prod [prad] s pungolo, stimolo || v (pret & pp prodded; ger prodding) tr stimulare, pungolare, incitare

prodigal ['pradɪgəl] adj & s prodigo

prodigious [pro'dɪdʒəs] adj prodigioso

prodi•gy ['pradɪdʒi] s (-gies) prodigio

produce ['prodjus] or ['produs] s produzione; prodotti mpl agricoli || [pro'djus] or [pro'dus] tr produrre; (theat) presentare

producer [pro'djusər] or [pro'dusər] s produttore m; (of a play) impresario; (mov) produttore m

product ['pradəkt] s prodotto

production [pro'dʌkʃən] s produzione

profane [pro'fen] adj profano; blasfemo || tr profanare

profani•ty [pro'fænɪti] s (-ties) bestemmia

profess [pro'fes] tr & intr professare

profession [pro'feʃən] s professione

professor [pro'fesər] s professore m

proffer ['prafər] s offerta || tr offrire

proficient [pro'frʃənt] adj abile, competente

profile ['profaɪl] s profilo || tr profilare

profit ['prafɪt] s profitto; vantaggio; **at a profit** con guadagno || tr avvantaggiare; giovare (with dat) || intr avvantaggiarsi; **to profit by** approfittare di

profitable ['prafɪtəbəl] adj vantaggioso

prof'it and loss' s profitti mpl e perdite fpl

profiteer [,prafɪ'tɪr] s profittatore m || intr fare il profittatore

prof'it shar'ing s cointeressenza, partecipazione agli utili

prof'it tak'ing s realizzo

profligate ['praflɪgɪt] adj & s dissoluto; prodigo

pro for'ma in'voice ['fɔrmə] s fattura fittizia

profound [pro'faund] adj profondo

profuse [prə'fius] adj profuso, abbondante; **profuse in** prodigo di

proge•ny ['pradʒəni] s (-nies) prole f

progno•sis [prag'nosɪs] s (-ses [siz]) prognosi f

prognostic [prag'nastɪk] s pronostico

prognosticate [prag'nastɪ,ket] tr pronostic are

pro•gram ['progræm] s programma m || v (pret & pp -gramed or -grammed; ger -graming or -gramming) tr programmare

programmer ['progræmər] s pannellista mf, programmatore m

progress ['pragres] s progresso; **in progress** in corso; **to make progress** fare dei progressi || [prə'gres] intr progredire; migliorare

progressive [prə'gresɪv] adj (proceeding step by step) progressivo; progressista || s progressista mf

prohibit [pro'hɪbɪt] tr proibire

prohibition [,pro•ə'bɪʃən] s proibizione; (hist) proibizionismo

project ['pradʒekt] s progetto || [prə'dʒekt] tr (to propose, plan) progettare; (light, a shadow, etc.) proiettare || intr sporgere, protrudere

projectile [prə'dʒektɪl] s proiettile m

projection [prə'dʒekʃən] s proiezione, sporgenza

projector [prə'dʒektər] s (apparatus) proiettore m; (person) progettista mf

proletarian [,prolɪ'tɛri•ən] adj & s proletario

proliferate [prə'lɪfə,ret] intr proliferare

prolific [prə'lɪfɪk] adj prolifico

prolix ['prolɪks] or [pro'lɪks] adj prolisso

prologue ['prolɔg] or ['prolɑg] s prologo

prolong [prɔ'lɔŋ] or [pro'lɑŋ] *tr* prolungare

promenade [,prɑmɪ'ned] or [,prɑmɪ'nɑd] *s* passeggiata; ballo di gala || *tr & intr* passeggiare

promenade' deck' *s* ponte *m* passeggiata

prominent ['prɑmɪnənt] *adj* prominente

promise ['prɑmɪs] *s* promessa || *tr & intr* promettere

prom'ising young' man' *s* giovane *m* di belle speranze

prom'issory note' ['prɑmɪ ,sori] *s* cambiale *f*, pagherò *m*

promonto·ry ['prɑmən ,tori] *s* (**-ries**) promontorio

promote [prə'mot] *tr* promuovere

promotion [prə'moʃən] *s* promozione

prompt [prɑmpt] *adj* pronto || *tr* incitare, istigare; (theat) suggerire

prompter ['prɑmptər] *s* suggeritore *m*, rammentatore *m*

prompt'er's box' *s* buca del suggeritore

promptness ['prɑmptnɪs] *s* prontezza

promulgate ['prɑməl ,get] or [pro'mʌl get] *tr* promulgare

prone [pron] *adj* prono

prong [prɔŋ] or [prɑŋ] *s* punta; (*of fork*) dente *m*; (*of pitchfork*) rebbio

pronoun ['pronaun] *s* pronome *m*

pronounce [prə'nauns] *tr* pronunziare

pronounced [prə'naunst] *adj* pronunziato, marcato

pronouncement [prə'naunsmənt] *s* dichiarazione ufficiale

pronunciamen·to [prə ,nʌnsɪ-ə'mento] *s* (**-tos**) pronunciamento

pronunciation [prə ,nʌnsɪ'eʃən] or [prə ,nʌnsɪ'eʃən] *s* pronunzia

proof [pruf] *adj*—**proof against** a prova di || *s* prova; (*of alcoholic beverages*) gradazione; (typ) bozza

proof'read'er *s* correttore *m* di bozze

prop [prɑp] *s* sostegno, puntello; (*pole*) palo; **props** attrezzi *mpl* teatrali || *v* (*pret & pp* **propped;** *ger* **propping**) *tr* sostenere, puntellare

propaganda [,prɑpə'gændə] *s* propaganda

propagate ['prɑpə ,get] *tr* propagare || *intr* propagarsi

pro·pel [prə'pel] *v* (*pret & pp* **-pelled;** *ger* **-pelling**) *tr* propulsare, spingere, azionare; (*a rocket*) propellere

propeller [prə'pelər] *s* elica

propensi·ty [prə'pensɪti] *s* (**-ties**) propensione

proper ['prɑpər] *adj* appropriato, corretto; decente, convenevole; (gram) proprio; **proper to** proprio di

proper·ty ['prɑpərti] *s* (**-ties**) proprietà *f*; **properties** attrezzi *mpl* teatrali

prop'erty man' *s* trovarobe *m*, attrezzista *m*

prop'erty own'er *s* proprietario fondiario

prophe·cy ['prɑfɪsi] *s* (**-cies**) profezia

prophe·sy ['prɑfɪ ,sai] *v* (*pret & pp* **-sied**) *tr* profetizzare

prophet ['prɑfɪt] *s* profeta *m*

prophetess ['prɑfɪtɪs] *s* profetessa

prophylactic [,profɪ'læktɪk] *adj* profilattico || *s* rimedio profilattico; preservativo

propitiate [prə'pɪʃɪ ,et] *tr* propiziare

propitious [prə'pɪʃəs] *adj* propizio

prop'jet' *s* turboelica *m*

proportion [prə'porʃən] *s* proporzione; **in proportion as** a misura che; **in proportion to** in proporzione a; **out of proportion** sproporzionato || *tr* proporzionare, commensurare

proportionate [prə'porʃənɪt] *adj* proporzionato

proposal [prə'pozəl] *s* proposta; proposta di matrimonio

propose [prə'poz] *tr* proporre || *intr* fare una proposta di matrimonio; **to propose to** chiedere la mano di; proporsi di + *inf*

proposition [,prɑpə'zɪʃən] *s* proposizione, proposta; (coll) progetto || *tr* fare delle proposte indecenti a

propound [prə'paund] *tr* proporre

proprietary [prə'praɪ-ə ,teri] *adj* padronale; esclusivo, patentato

proprietor [prə'praɪ-ətər] *s* proprietario

proprietress [prə'praɪ-ətrɪs] *s* proprietaria

proprie·ty [prə'praɪ-əti] *s* (**-ties**) correttezza, decoro; **proprieties** convenzioni *fpl* sociali

propulsion [prə'pʌlʃən] *s* propulsione

prorate [pro'ret] *tr* rateizzare

prosaic [pro'ze-ɪk] *adj* prosaico

proscribe [pro'skraɪb] *tr* proscrivere

prose [proz] *adj* prosaico || *s* prosa

prosecute ['prɑsɪ ,kjut] *tr* eseguire; (law) processare

prosecutor ['prɑsɪ ,kjutər] *s* esecutore *m*; (law) querelante *m*; (law) avvocato d'accusa

proselyte ['prɑsɪ ,laɪt] *s* proselito

prose' writ'er *s* prosatore *m*

prosody ['prɑsədi] *s* prosodia, metrica

prospect ['prɑspekt] *s* vista; prospettiva; candidato; probabile cliente *m*; **prospects** speranze *fpl* || *intr* fare il cercatore; **to prospect for** fare il cercatore di

prospectus [prə'spektəs] *s* prospetto

prosper ['prɑspər] *tr & intr* prosperare

prosperi·ty [prɑs'perɪti] *s* (**-ties**) prosperità *f*, benessere *m*

prosperous ['prɑspərəs] *adj* prospero

prostitute ['prɑstɪ ,tjut] or ['prɑstɪ ,tut] *s* prostituta || *tr* prostituire

prostrate ['prɑstret] *adj* prostrato || *tr* prostrare

prostration [prɑs'treʃən] *s* prostrazione

protagonist [pro'tægənɪst] *s* protagonista *mf*

protect [prə'tekt] *tr* proteggere

protection [prə'tekʃən] *s* protezione

protégé ['protə ,ʒe] *s* protetto, favorito

protégée ['protə ,ʒe] *s* protetta, favorita

protein ['proti-ɪn] or ['protin] *s* proteina

pro tempore [pro'tempə ,ri] *adj* provvisorio, interinale

protest ['protest] *s* protesta; (com)

protesto || [pro'test] *tr & intr* pro-
testare
Protestant ['pratɪstənt] *adj & s* protestante *mf*
protester [prə'testər] *s* protestatario
prothonotar·y [pro'θɑnə,tɛri] *s* (-ies)
(law) cancelliere *m* capo
protocol ['protə,kɑl] *s* protocollo
protoplasm ['protə,plæzəm] *s* proto-
plasma *m*
prototype ['protə,taɪp] *s* prototipo
proto·zoon [,protə'zo·ɑn] *s* (-zoa
['zo·ə]) protozoo
protract [pro'trækt] *tr* prolungare
protractor [pro'træktər] *s* rapportatore
m
protrude [pro'trud] *intr* sporgere
proud [praud] *adj* fiero; arrogante;
maestoso, magnifico
proud' flesh' *s* tessuto di granulazione
prove [pruv] *v* (*pret* **proved**; *pp* **proved**
or **proven**) *tr* provare; (*ore*) analizzare; (law) omologare; (math) fare
la prova di || *intr* risultare
proverb ['pravərb] *s* proverbio
provide [prə'vaɪd] *tr* provvedere ||
intr—**to provide for** provvedere a;
(*to be ready for*) prepararsi a
provided [prə'vaɪdɪd] *conj* a condizione che, purché; **provided that** a
condizione che, purché
providence ['pravɪdəns] *s* provvidenza
providential [,pravɪ'dɛn/əl] *adj* provvidenziale
providing [prə'vaɪdɪŋ] *conj* var of
provided
province ['pravɪns] *s* provincia; (fig)
pertinenza, competenza
provision [prə'vɪ/ən] *s* provvedimento;
clausola; **provisions** viveri *mpl*
provi·so [prə'vaɪzo] *s* (-sos or -soes)
stipulazione, clausola
provoke [prə'vok] *tr* provocare; contrariare, irritare
prow [prau] *s* prora, prua
prowess ['prau·ɪs] *s* prodezza; maestria
prowl [praul] *intr* andare in cerca di
preda; vagabondare
prowler ['praulər] *s* vagabondo; ladro
proximity [prak'sɪmɪti] *s* prossimità *f*
prox·y ['praksi] *s* (-ies) procura; (*person*) procuratore *m*
prude [prud] *s* pudibondo
prudence ['prudəns] *s* prudenza
prudent ['prudənt] *adj* prudente
pruder·y ['prudəri] *s* (-ies) attitudine
pudibonda
prudish ['prudɪ/] *adj* pudibondo
prune [prun] *s* prugna secca || *tr* potare
pry [praɪ] *v* (*pret & pp* **pried**) *tr*—**to
pry open** forzare con una leva; **to pry
s.th out of s.o.** strappare qlco a qlcu
|| *intr* intromettersi, cacciarsi
psalm [sɑm] *s* salmo
pseudo ['sudo] or ['sjudo] *adj* falso,
finto, sedicente
pseudonym ['sudənɪm] or ['sjudənɪm]
s pseudonimo
psychiatrist [saɪ'kaɪ·ətrɪst] *s* psichiatra
mf
psychiatry [saɪ'kaɪ·ətri] *s* psichiatria

psychic ['saɪkɪk] *adj* psichico || *s* me-
dium *mf*
psychoanalysis [,saɪko·ə'nælɪsɪs] *s*
psicanalisi *f*
psychoanalyze [,saɪko'ænə,laɪz] *tr* psicanalizzare
psychologic(al) [,saɪko'lɑdʒɪk(əl)] *adj*
psicologico
psychologist [saɪ'kɑlədʒɪst] *s* psicologo
psycholo·gy [saɪ'kɑlədʒi] *s* (-gies) psicologia
psychopath ['saɪkə,pæθ] *s* psicopatico
psycho·sis [saɪ'kosɪs] *s* (-ses [siz])
psicosi *f*
psychotic [saɪ'kɑtɪk] *adj* psicotico
pub [pʌb] *s* (Brit) taverna, bar *m*
puberty ['pjubərti] *s* pubertà *f*
public ['pʌblɪk] *adj & s* pubblico
pub'lic-address' sys'tem *s* sistema *m*
d'amplificazione per discorsi in pubblico
publication [,pʌblɪ'ke/ən] *s* pubblicazione
pub'lic convey'ance *s* veicolo di servizi
pubblici
publicity [pʌb'lɪsɪti] *s* pubblicità *f*
publicize ['pʌblɪ,saɪz] *tr* pubblicare,
divulgare
pub'lic li'brary *s* biblioteca comunale
pub'lic-opin'ion poll' *s* sondaggio
d'opinioni
pub'lic pros'ecutor *s* pubblico ministero
pub'lic school' *s* (U.S.A.) scuola del-
l'obbligo; (Brit) scuola privata, collegio
pub'lic serv'ant *s* funzionario pubblico
pub'lic speak'ing *s* oratoria
pub'lic spir'it *s* civismo
pub'lic toi'let *s* gabinetto pubblico
pub'lic util'ity *s* impresa di servizio
pubblico; **public utilities** azioni
emesse da imprese di servizi pubblici
publish ['pʌblɪ/] *tr* pubblicare
publisher ['pʌblɪ/ər] *s* editore *m;*
(journ) direttore *m* responsabile
pub'lishing house' *s* casa editrice
pucker ['pʌkər] *s* grinza || *tr* raggrin-
zire || *intr* raggrinzirsi
pudding ['pudɪŋ] *s* budino, torta
puddle ['pʌdəl] *s* pozza, pozzanghera
|| *intr* diguazzare
pudg·y ['pʌdʒi] *adj* (-ier; -iest) grassoccio
puerile ['pju·ərɪl] *adj* puerile
Puerto Rican ['pwerto'rikən] *adj & s*
portoricano
puff [pʌf] *s* soffio, sbuffo; (*e.g., of
cigar*) boccata; (*pad*) piumino; (*exaggerated praise*) pistolotto; (culin)
bignè *m* || *tr* sbuffare; gonfiare; adu-
lare || *intr* soffiare, sbuffare; (*to
breathe heavily*) ansimare, ansare;
gonfiarsi; tirare boccate
puff' paste' *s* pasta sfoglia
pugilist ['pjudʒɪlɪst] *s* pugile *m*
pug-nosed ['pʌg,nozd] *adj* camuso
puke [pjuk] *tr & intr* (slang) vomitare
pull [pul] *s* tiro; (*act of drawing in*)
tirata; (*handle*) tirante *m;* (slang)
influenza, appoggi *mpl* || *tr* tirare; (*a
tooth*) cavare; (*a muscle*) strappare;

(*a punch*) (coll) limitare la forza di; **to pull apart** fare a pezzi; **to pull down** abbattere; degradare; **to pull on** (*e.g., one's pants*) infilarsi; **to pull oneself together** ricomporsi; **to pull s.o.'s leg** beffarsi di qlcu || *intr* tirare; **to pull apart** andare a pezzi; **to pull at** tirare; **to pull away** andarsene; **to pull for** (coll) fare il tifo per; **to pull in** (*said of a train*) arrivare, entrare in stazione; **to pull out** (*said of a train*) partire; **to pull through** guarire, riuscire a cavarsela; **to pull up to** avanzare fino a

pullet ['pulɪt] *s* pollastra

pulley ['pulɪ] *s* puleggia, carrucola

pulp [pʌlp] *s* polpa; (*for making paper*) pasta

pulpit ['pulpɪt] *s* pulpito

pulsate ['pʌlset] *intr* pulsare

pulsation [pʌl'seʃən] *s* pulsazione

pulse [pʌls] *s* polso; **to feel or take the pulse of** tastare il polso a

pulverize ['pʌlvə,raɪz] *tr* polverizzare

pum'ice stone' *s* ['pʌmɪs] *s* pomice *f*, pietra pomice

pum·mel ['pʌməl] *v* (*pret & pp* -meled or -melled; *ger* -meling or -melling) *tr* prendere a pugni

pump [pʌmp] *s* pompa; (*slipper*) scarpina || *tr* pompare; (coll) cavare un segreto a; **to pump up** pompare

pumpkin ['pʌmpkɪn] or ['pʌŋkɪn] *s* zucca

pump-priming ['pʌmp,praɪmɪŋ] *s* stimolo governativo per sostenere l'economia

pun [pʌn] *s* gioco di parole || *v* (*pret & pp* punned; *ger* punning) *intr* fare giochi di parole

punch [pʌntʃ] *s* pugno; (*tool*) punteruolo, punzone *m*; (*drink*) ponce *m*; (coll) forza || *tr* dare un pugno a; (*metal*) punzonare; (*a ticket*) perforare || **Punch** *s* Pulcinella *m*; **pleased as Punch** soddisfattissimo

punch' bowl' *s* vaso per il ponce

punch' card' *s* scheda perforata

punch' clock' *s* orologio di controllo

punch'-drunk' *adj* stordito

punched' tape' *s* nastro perforato

punch'ing bag' *s* sacco

punch' line' *s* perfinire *m*, motto finale

punctilious [pʌŋk'tɪlɪ·əs] *adj* cerimonioso, pignolo

punctual ['pʌŋktʃu·əl] *adj* puntuale

punctuate ['pʌŋktʃu,et] *tr* punteggiare

punctuation [,pʌŋktʃu'eʃən] *s* punteggiatura

punctua'tion mark' *s* segno d'interpunzione

puncture ['pʌŋktʃər] *s* puntura; (*hole*) bucatura; **to have a puncture** avere una gomma a terra || *tr* bucare, perforare || *intr* essere bucato

punc'ture-proof' *adj* antiperforante

pundit ['pʌndɪt] *s* esperto, autorità *f*

pungent ['pʌndʒənt] *adj* pungente

punish ['pʌnɪʃ] *tr* punire

punishment ['pʌnɪʃmənt] *s* punizione, castigo

punk [pʌŋk] *adj* (slang) di pessima

qualità || *s* esca; (*decayed wood*) legno marcio; (slang) malandrino

punster ['pʌnstər] *s* freddurista *mf*

punt [pʌnt] *s* (football) calcio dato al pallone prima che tocchi il terreno

pu·ny ['pjuni] *adj* (-nier; -niest) insignificante, meschino; (*weak*) debole

pup [pʌp] *s* cucciolo

pupil ['pjupəl] *s* allievo, scolaro; (anat) pupilla

puppet ['pʌpɪt] *s* marionetta, burattino; (fig) fantoccio

puppeteer [,pʌpɪ'tɪr] *s* burattinaio

pup'pet gov'ernment *s* governo fantoccio or pupazzo

pup'pet show' *s* spettacolo di marionette

pup·py ['pʌpi] *s* (-pies) cucciolo

pup'py love' *s* amore m giovanile

purchase ['pʌrtʃəs] *s* compra, acquisto; (*grip*) presa, leva || *tr* comprare, acquistare

pur'chasing pow'er *s* potere *m* d'acquisto

pure [pjur] *adj* puro

purgative ['pʌrgətɪv] *adj* purgativo || *s* purga

purge [pʌrdʒ] *s* purga || *tr* purgare

puri·fy ['pjurɪ,faɪ] *v* (*pret & pp* -fied) *tr* purificare || *intr* purificarsi

puritan ['pjurɪtən] *adj & s* puritano || **Puritan** *adj & s* puritano

purity ['pjurɪti] *s* purezza

purloin [pər'lɔɪn] *tr & intr* rubare

purple ['pʌrpəl] *adj* purpureo || *s* porpora

purport ['pʌrport] *s* senso, significato || [pər'port] *tr* significare; **to purport to** + *inf* pretendere di + *inf*

purpose ['pʌrpəs] *s* scopo, fine *m*; **on purpose** apposta; **to good purpose** con buoni risultati; **to no purpose** inutilmente; **to serve one's purpose** fare al caso proprio

purposely ['pʌrpəsli] *adv* a bella posta, apposta

purr [pʌr] *s* ronfare *m* || *intr* fare le fusa

purse [pʌrs] *s* borsa; (*woman's handbag*) borsetta; (*for men*) borsetto || *tr* (*one's lips*) arricciare

purser ['pʌrsər] *s* commissario di bordo

purse' snatch'er ['snætʃər] *s* borsaiolo

purse' strings' *spl* cordini mpl della borsa; **to hold the purse strings** controllare le spese

purslane ['pʌrslen] or ['pʌrslɪn] *s* (bot) porcellana

pursue [pər'su] or [pər'sju] *tr* perseguire; (*to harass*) perseguitare; (*a career*) proseguire

pursuit [pər'sut] or [pər'sjut] *s* inseguimento, caccia; occupazione, esercizio

pursuit' plane' *s* caccia *m*

purvey [pər've] *tr* provvedere, fornire

pus [pʌs] *s* pus *m*

push [puʃ] *s* spinta; (*advance*) avanzata; (coll) impulso, energia || *tr* premere, spingere; (*a product*) promuovere la vendita di; dare impulso a; (*narcotics*) (slang) spacciare; **to**

push around (coll) dare spintoni a; (fig) fare pressione su; **to push back** ricacciare ‖ *intr* spingere; **to push ahead** avanzarsi a spintoni, avanzarsi; **to push on** avanzare

push' but'ton *s* pulsante *m*, bottone *m*

push'-button con'trol *s* controllo a pulsanti

push'cart' *s* carretto a mano

pusher ['puʃər] *adj* spingente; (aer) propulsivo ‖ *s* spingitore *m*; (aer) aeroplano a elica propulsiva; (slang) spacciatore *m* di stupefacenti

pushing ['puʃɪŋ] *adj* aggressivo, intraprendente

puss [pus] *s* micio

puss' in the cor'ner *s* gioco dei quattro cantoni

puss·y ['pusi] *s* (-ies) micio

puss'y wil'low *s* salice americano a gattini

pustule ['pʌstʃul] *s* pustola

put [put] *v* (*pret & pp* put; *ger* putting) *tr* mettere; (*to estimate*) stimare; (*a question*) rivolgere; (*to throw*) lanciare; imporre; **to put across** (slang) far accettare; **to put aside, away** or **by** mettere da parte; **to put down** annotare; (*to suppress*) reprimere; **to put off** differire; evadere; **to put on** (*clothes*) mettersi; (*a brake*) azionare; (*to assume*) fingere; (*airs*) darsi; **to put out** spegnere; imbarazzare; incomodare; deludere; annoiare, irritare; (*of a game*) espellere; **to put it over on s.o.** fargliela a qlcu; **to put off** rinviare; **to put over** mandare ad effetto; **to put to flight** mettere in fuga; **to put to shame** svergognare; **to put through** portare a

termine; **to put up** offrire; mettere in conserva; alloggiare; costruire; (*money*) contribuire; (coll) incitare ‖ *intr* dirigersi; **to put to sea** mettersi in mare; **to put up** prendere alloggio; **to put up with** tollerare

put'-out' *adj* sconcertato, seccato

putrid ['pjutrɪd] *adj* putrido

Putsch [putʃ] *s* tentativo di sollevazione, sollevazione

putter ['pʌtər] *intr* occuparsi di inezie; **to putter about** andare avanti e indietro

put·ty ['pʌti] *s* (-ties) stucco, mastice *m* ‖ *v* (*pret & pp* -tied) *tr* stuccare

put'ty knife' *s* spatola

put'-up' *adj* (coll) complottato

puzzle ['pʌzəl] *s* enigma *m*; (*toy*) indovinello ‖ *tr* rendere perplesso, confondere; **to puzzle out** decifrare ‖ *intr* essere perplesso

puzzler ['pʌzlər] *s* enigma *m*

puzzling ['pʌzlɪŋ] *adj* enigmatico

pyg·my ['pɪgmi] *s* (-mies) pigmeo

pylon *s* pilone *m*

pyramid ['pɪrəmɪd] *s* piramide *f* ‖ *tr* (*e.g., costs*) aumentare gradualmente; (*one's money*) aumentare giocando in margine

pyre [paɪr] *s* pira

Pyrenees ['pɪrɪ‚niz] *spl* Pirenei *mpl*

pyrites [paɪ'raɪtiz] or ['paɪraɪts] *s* pirite *f*

pyrotechnics [‚paɪrə'teknɪks] *spl* pirotecnica

python ['paɪθən] or ['paɪθən] *s* pitone *m*

pythoness ['paɪθənɪs] *s* pitonessa

pyx [pɪks] *s* (eccl) pisside *f*

Q

Q, q [kju] *s* diciassettesima lettera dell'alfabeto inglese

quack [kwæk] *adj* falso ‖ *s* medicastro; ciarlatano; qua qua *m* ‖ *intr* (*said of a duck*) fare qua qua

quacker·y ['kwækəri] *s* (-ies) ciarlataneria

quadrangle ['kwad ‚ræŋgəl] *s* quadrangolo

quadrant ['kwadrənt] *s* quadrante *m*

quadruped ['kwadru ‚ped] *adj & s* quadrupede *m*

quadruple ['kwadrupəl] or [kwa'drupəl] *adj* quadruplo; (*alliance*) quadruplice ‖ *s* quadruplo ‖ *tr* quadruplicare ‖ *intr* quadruplicarsi

quaff [kwaf] or [kwæf] *s* lungo sorso ‖ *tr & intr* bere a lunghi sorsi

quail [kwel] *s* quaglia ‖ *intr* sgomentarsi

quaint [kwent] *adj* strano, strambo, originale; all'antica ma bello

quake [kwek] *s* terremoto ‖ *intr* tremare, sussultare

Quaker ['kwekər] *adj & s* quacchero, quacquero

Quak'er meet'ing *s* riunione di quaccheri; (coll) riunione in cui si parla poco

quali·fy ['kwalɪ‚faɪ] *v* (*pret & pp* -fied) *tr* qualificare; (*for a profession*) abilitare ‖ *intr* qualificarsi; abilitarsi

quali·ty ['kwalɪti] *s* (-ties) qualità *f*; (*of a sound*) timbro

qualm [kwam] *s* scrupolo di coscienza; preoccupazione; nausea

quanda·ry ['kwandəri] *s* (-ries) incertezza, perplessità *f*

quanti·ty ['kwantɪti] *s* (-ties) quantità *f*

quan·tum ['kwantəm] *adj* quantistico ‖ *s* (-ta [tə]) quanto

quarantine ['kwarən‚tin] or ['kwɔrən‚tin] *s* quarantena ‖ *tr* mettere in quarantena

quar·rel ['kwarəl] or ['kwɔrəl] *s* litigio, diverbio; **to have no quarrel with** non essere in disaccordo con; **to pick a quarrel with** venire a diverbio con ‖ *v* (*pret & pp* -reled or -relled; *ger* -reling or -relling) *intr* litigare

quarrelsome [ˈkwɑrəlsəm] or [ˈkwɔrəl-səm] *adj* litigioso, rissoso

quar·ry [ˈkwɑri] or [ˈkwɔri] *s* (-ries) cava; (*game*) selvaggina, cacciagione || *v* (*pret & pp* -ried) *tr* cavare

quart [kwɔrt] *s* quarto di gallone

quarter [ˈkwɔrtər] *adj* quarto || *s* quarto; moneta di un quarto di dollaro; (*three months*) trimestre *m*; (*of town*) quartiere *m*; **a quarter after one** l'una e un quarto; **a quarter of an hour** un quarto d'ora; **a quarter to one** l'una meno un quarto; **at close quarters** corpo a corpo; **quarters** quartiere *m* || *tr* squartare; (*soldiers*) accasermare

quar'ter-deck' *s* cassero

quar'ter-hour' *s* quarto d'ora; **on the quarter-hour** ogni quindici minuti allo scoccare del quarto d'ora

quarter·ly [ˈkwɔrtərli] *adj* trimestrale || *s* (-lies) pubblicazione trimestrale || *adv* trimestralmente

quar'ter-mas'ter *s* (mil) intendente *m* militare; (nav) secondo capo

quartet [kwɔrˈtet] *s* quartetto

quartz [kwɔrts] *s* quarzo

quasar [ˈkwesɑr] *s* (astr) radiostella

quash [kwɑʃ] *tr* sopprimere; annullare

quaver [ˈkwevər] *s* tremito; (mus) tremolo; (mus) croma || *intr* tremare

quay [ki] *s* molo

queen [kwin] *s* regina; (*in cards*) donna; (chess) regina

queen' bee' *s* ape regina; (fig) basilessa

queen' dow'ager *s* regina vedova

queen·ly [ˈkwinli] *adj* (-lier; -liest) da regina; regio

queen' moth'er *s* regina madre

queen' post' *s* monaco

queen's' Eng'lish *s* inglese corretto

queer [kwɪr] *adj* strano, curioso; poco bene, indisposto; falso; (slang) omosessuale || *s* (slang) finocchio || *tr* rovinare, mettere in pericolo

quell [kwel] *tr* soffocare, domare; (*pain*) calmare

quench [kwentʃ] *tr* (*fire, thirst*) spegnere, estinguere; (*rebellion*) soffocare; (elec) ammortizzare

que·ry [ˈkwɪri] *s* (-ries) domanda; punto interrogativo; dubbio || *v* (*pret & pp* -ried) *tr* interrogare; (typ) apporre punto interrogativo a

quest [kwest] *s* ricerca; **in quest of** in cerca di

question [ˈkwestʃən] *s* domanda; problema *m*, quesito; (*matter*) questione; **beyond question** senza dubbio; **out of the question** impossibile; **this is beside the question** questo non c'entra; **to ask a question** fare una domanda; **to be a question of** trattarsi di; **to call in** or **into question** mettere in dubbio; **without question** senza dubbio || *tr* interrogare; mettere in dubbio; (pol) interpellare

questionable [ˈkwestʃənəbəl] *adj* discutibile

ques'tion mark' *s* punto interrogativo

questionnaire [ˌkwestʃənˈer] *s* questionario

queue [kju] *s* (*of hair*) codino; (*of people*) coda || *intr* fare la coda

quibble [ˈkwɪbəl] *intr* sottilizzare

quick [kwɪk] *adj* pronto, sollecito; sbrigativo; veloce, rapido; vivo || *s*— **the quick and the dead** i vivi e i morti; **to cut to the quick** toccare nel vivo

quicken [ˈkwɪkən] *tr* sveltire; animare; ravvivare

quick'lime' *s* calce viva

quick' lunch' *s* tavola calda

quickly [ˈkwɪkli] *adv* svelto, alla svelta; presto

quick'sand' *s* sabbia mobile

quick'-set'ting *adj* a presa rapida

quick'sil'ver *s* argento vivo

quick'work' *s* (naut) opera viva

quiet [ˈkwaɪ·ət] *adj* quieto; silenzioso; (com) calmo; **to keep quiet** stare zitto || *s* quiete *f*, tranquillità *f*; pace *f*, calma || *tr* quietare; calmare || *intr*— **to quiet down** quietarsi, calmarsi

quill [kwɪl] *s* penna d'oca; (*basal part of feather*) calamo; (*e.g., of porcupine*) aculeo

quilt [kwɪlt] *s* trapunta, imbottita || *tr* trapuntare

quince [kwɪns] *s* cotogna; (*tree*) cotogno

quinine [ˈkwaɪnaɪn] *s* (*alkaloid*) chinina; (*salt of the alkaloid*) chinino

quinsy [ˈkwɪnzi] *s* angina

quintessence [kwɪnˈtesəns] *s* quintessenza

quintet [kwɪnˈtet] *s* quintetto

quintuplet [kwɪnˈtjuplet] or [kwɪnˈtuplet] *s* gemello nato da un parto quintuplice

quip [kwɪp] *s* frizzo, uscita || *v* (*pret & pp* **quipped**; *ger* **quipping**) *tr & intr* uscire a dire, dire come battuta

quire [kwaɪr] *s* ventiquattro fogli; (bb) quinterno

quirk [kwʌrk] *s* stranezza, manierismo; (*quibble*) cavillo; (*sudden turn*) mutamento improvviso

quit [kwɪt] *adj* libero; **to be quits** esser pari; **to call it quits** finirla, farla finita || *v* (*pret & pp* **quit** or **quitted**; *ger* **quitting**) *tr* abbandonare || *intr* andarsene; abbandonare l'impiego; smettere (di + *inf*)

quite [kwaɪt] *adv* completamente; molto, del tutto

quitter [ˈkwɪtər] *s* persona che abbandona facilmente

quiver [ˈkwɪvər] *s* fremito; (*to hold arrows*) faretra, turcasso || *intr* fremere, tremare

quixotic [kwɪksˈɑtɪk] *adj* donchisciottesco

quiz [kwɪz] *s* (**quizzes**) esame *m*; interrogatorio || *v* (*pret & pp* **quizzed**; *ger* **quizzing**) *tr* esaminare; interrogare

quiz' game' *s* quiz

quiz' pro'gram *s* programma *m* di quiz

quiz' sec'tion *s* (educ) classe *f* a base di esercizi (e non di conferenze)

quizzical [ˈkwɪzɪkəl] *adj* strano, curioso; (*derisive*) canzonatore

quoin [kɔɪn] or [kwɔɪn] *s* cantone *m*,

pietra angolare; (*piece of wood*) zeppa; (typ) serraforme *m* || *tr* fissare con serraforme

quoit [kwɔɪt] *or* [kɔɪt] *s* anello di corda o di metallo da lanciarsi come gioco; **quoits** *ssg* gioco consistente nel lancio di anelli su di un piolo

quondam ['kwɑndæm] *adj* quondam

quorum ['kworəm] *s* quorum *m*

quota ['kwotə] *s* (*share*) quota; (*of

imports*) contingentamento; (*of persons*) contingente *m*

quotation [kwo'teʃən] *s* (*from a book*) citazione; (*of prices*) quotazione

quota'tion mark' *s* doppia virgola, virgoletta

quote [kwot] *s* citazione, richiamo || *tr & intr* citare, richiamare; (com) quotare; **quote cito**

quotient ['kwoʃənt] *s* quoziente *m*

R

R, r [ɑr] *s* diciottesima lettera dell'alfabeto inglese

rabbet ['ræbɪt] *s* scanalatura, incastro || *tr* scanalare, incastrare

rab·bi ['ræbaɪ] *s* (*-bis*) rabbino

rabbit ['ræbɪt] *s* coniglio

rab'bit ears' *spl* (telv) doppia antenna a stilo

rabble ['ræbəl] *s* gentaglia, marmaglia

rab'ble-rous'er ['rauzər] *s* arruffapopoli *m*

rabies ['rebiz] *or* ['rebɪ‚iz] *s* rabbia

raccoon [ræ'kun] *s* procione *m*

race [res] *s* (*branch of human stock*) razza; (*contest in speed*) corsa; (*contest of any kind*) gara; (*channel*) canale *m* di adduzione || *tr* far correre; gareggiare (in velocità) con; (*a motor*) imballare || *intr* correre; fare le corse; (*said of a motor*) imballarsi; (naut) fare le regate

race' horse' *s* cavallo da corsa

race' ri'ot *s* contestazione di razza

race' track' *s* pista

racial ['reʃəl] *adj* razziale

rac'ing car' *s* automobile *f* da corsa

rack [ræk] *s* (*to hang clothes*) attaccapanni *m*; (*framework to hold fodder, baggage, guns, etc.*) rastrelliera; (mach) cremagliera; **to go to rack and ruin** andare a rotoli || *tr* tormentare, torturare; **to rack off** (*wine*) travasare; **to rack one's brains** rompersi il capo, lambiccarsi il cervello

racket ['rækɪt] *s* racchetta; (*noise*) chiasso, gazzarra; (coll) racket *m*; **to raise a racket** fare gazzarra

racketeer [‚rækɪ'tɪr] *s* chi è nel racket; (*engaged in extortion*) ricattatore *m* || *intr* essere nel racket; fare il ricattatore

rack' rail'way *s* ferrovia a cremagliera

rac·y ['resi] *adj* (*-ier; -iest*) pungente, vigoroso; piccante

radar ['redɑr] *s* radar *m*

radiant ['redɪ‚ənt] *adj* raggiante, radioso

radiate ['redɪ‚et] *tr* irradiare || *intr* irradiarsi

radiation [‚redɪ'eʃən] *s* radiazione

radia'tion sick'ness *s* malattia causata da radiazione atomica

radiator ['redɪ‚etər] *s* radiatore *m*

ra'diator cap' *s* tappo del radiatore

radical ['rædɪkəl] *adj* radicale || *s

radicale *mf*; (chem, math) radicale *m*

radi·o ['redɪ‚o] *s* (*-os*) radio *f*; radiogramma *m* || *tr* radiotrasmettere

radioactive [‚redɪ·o'æktɪv] *adj* radioattivo

ra'dio am'ateur *s* radioamatore *m*

ra'dio announc'er *s* radioannunciatore *m*

ra'dio bea'con *s* radiofaro

ra'dio·broad'cast *s* radiodiffusione || *tr* radiodiffondere

ra'dio com'pass *s* radiobussola

ra'dio-fre'quency *s* radiofrequenza

ra'dio lis'tener *s* radioascoltatore *m*

radiology [‚redɪ'ɑlədʒi] *s* radiologia

ra'dio net'work *s* rete *f*

ra'dio news'caster *s* radiocronista *mf*

ra'dio·pho'to *s* (*-tos*) (coll) radiofoto *f*

ra'dio set' *s* radioricevente *f*

ra'dio sta'tion *s* stazione radio

radish ['rædɪʃ] *s* ravanello

radium ['redɪ·əm] *s* radio

radi·us ['redɪ·əs] *s* (*-i* [‚aɪ] *or* **-uses**) (anat) radio; (fig, geom) raggio; **within a radius of** entro un raggio di

raffle ['ræfəl] *s* riffa || *tr* sorteggiare

raft [ræft] *or* [rɑft] *s* zattera; (coll) mucchio

rafter ['ræftər] *or* ['rɑftər] *s* puntone *m*

rag [ræg] *s* straccio; **to chew the rag** (slang) chiacchierare

ragamuffin ['rægə‚mʌfɪn] *s* straccione *m*

rag' doll' *s* bambola di pezza

rage [redʒ] *s* rabbia; **to be all the rage** furoreggiare; **to fly into a rage** montare in bestia || *intr* infuriare

ragged ['rægɪd] *adj* cencioso; (*torn*) stracciato; (*edge*) rozzo, scabroso

ragpicker ['ræg‚pɪkər] *s* cenciaiolo, straccivendolo

rag'weed' *s* (bot) ambrosia

raid [red] *s* irruzione, razzia || *tr* scorrere || *intr* scorrazzare

rail [rel] *s* (*of fence*) stecca, traversa; (*fence*) stecconata; (*railing*) ringhiera; (rr) rotaia; **by rail** per ferrovia; **rails** titoli *mpl* ferroviari || *intr* inveire; **to rail at** inveire contro

rail'car' *s* automotrice *f*

rail' fence' *s* stecconata fatta di traverse piallate alla buona

rail'head' *s* fine *f* della linea ferroviaria
railing ['reliŋ] *s* ringhiera
rail'road' *adj* ferroviario ‖ *s* ferrovia ‖ *tr* trasportare in ferrovia; (*a bill*) far passare precipitosamente; (coll) imprigionare falsamente
rail'road cros'sing *s* passaggio a livello
rail'road'er *s* ferroviere *m*
rail'way' *s* ferrovia, strada ferrata
raiment ['remənt] *s* (lit) abbigliamento
rain [ren] *s* pioggia; **rain or shine** con qualunque tempo ‖ *tr* fare piovere; (lit) piovere; **to rain cats and dogs** piovere a catinelle; **to rain out** far sospendere per via della pioggia ‖ *intr* piovere
rainbow ['ren͵bo] *s* arcobaleno
rain'coat' *s* impermeabile *m*
rain'fall' *s* acquazzone *m;* piovosità *f*
rain·y ['reni] *adj* (-ier; -iest) piovoso, piovano
rain'y day' *s* giorno piovoso; (fig) tempi *mpl* difficili
raise [rez] *s* aumento ‖ *tr* levare, rialzare; (*children, animals*) allevare; (*to build*) tirare su; (*a question*) sollevare; (*the dead*) risollevare; (*to increase*) aumentare; (*money*) raccogliere; (*a siege*) togliere; (*at cards*) rilanciare; (*anchor*) salpare; (math) elevare
raisin ['rezən] *s* grano d'uva passa, grano d'uva secca; **raisins** uva passa, uva secca
rake [rek] *s* rastrello; (*person*) porcaccione *m*, libertino ‖ *tr* rastrellare; **to rake in money** far soldoni
rake'-off' *s* (coll) compenso illecito, bustarella; (coll) sconto
rakish ['rekɪ/] *adj* libertino; brioso, vivace; **to wear one's hat at a rakish angle** portare il cappello sulle ventitré
ral·ly ['ræli] *s* (-lies) riunione, comizio; adunata; ricupero ‖ *v* (*pret & pp* -lied) *tr* riunire, chiamare a raccolta; rianimare ‖ *intr* riunirsi; rianimarsi; (*said of stock prices*) rialzarsi; rimettersi in forze; **to rally to the side of** correre all'aiuto di
ram [ræm] *s* (*male sheep*) montone *m;* (mil) ariete *m;* (nav) sperone *m;* (mach) maglio del battipalo ‖ *v* (*pret & pp* **rammed**; *ger* **ramming**) *tr* battere, sbattere contro; cacciare, conficcare; forzare; (nav) speronare ‖ *intr*—**to ram into** sbattere contro
ramble ['ræmbəl] *s* girata ‖ *intr* (*to wander around*) gironzolare; vagare; (*said of a vine*) crescere disordinatamente; (*said, e.g., of a river*) serpeggiare; (fig) scorrazzare; divagare
rami·fy ['ræmɪ͵faɪ] *v* (*pret & pp* -fied) *tr* ramificare ‖ *intr* ramificarsi
ram'jet en'gine *s* statoreattore *m*
ramp [ræmp] *s* rampa
rampage ['ræmpedʒ] *s* stato d'eccitazione; **to go on a rampage** infierire, comportarsi furiosamente
rampart ['ræmpɑrt] *s* baluardo, muraglione *m*

ram'rod' *s* (*for ramming*) (mil) bacchetta; (*for cleaning*) (mil) scovolo
ram'shack'le *adj* cadente, in rovina
ranch [ræntʃ] *s* fattoria agricola
rancid ['rænsɪd] *adj* rancido
rancor ['ræŋkər] *s* rancore *m*
random ['rændəm] *adj* fortuito; **at random** alla rinfusa, a casaccio
range [rendʒ] *s* (*row*) fila; (*rank*) classe *f;* (*distance*) portata; campo di tiro a segno; raggio d'azione; (*scope*) gamma; (*for grazing*) pascolo; (*stove*) fornello, cucina economica; **within range of** alla portata di ‖ *tr* allineare; ordinare; passare attraverso; mandare al pascolo ‖ *intr* variare, fluttuare; estendersi; trovarsi; (mil) portare; **to range over** percorrere; (fig) trattare
range' find'er *s* telemetro
rank [ræŋk] *adj* esuberante; grossolano; denso, spesso; puzzolente; eccessivo; completo, assoluto ‖ *s* rango, grado; (*row*) fila, schiera; **ranks** truppe *fpl*, ranghi *mpl* ‖ *tr* arrangiare, allineare; classificare; avere rango superiore a ‖ *intr* avere il massimo rango; **to rank high** avere un'alta posizione; **to rank low** avere una posizione bassa; **to rank with** essere allo stesso livello di
rank' and file' *s* truppa; massa
rankle ['ræŋkəl] *tr* irritare ‖ *intr* inasprirsi
ransack ['rænsæk] *tr* (*to search thoroughly*) frugare, rovistare; (*to pillage*) svaligiare, saccheggiare
ransom ['rænsəm] *s* taglia, riscatto ‖ *tr* riscattare
rant [rænt] *intr* farneticare, parlare a vanvera
rap [ræp] *s* colpo, colpetto; **I don't care a rap** non m'importa un fico; **to take the rap** (slang) prendersi la colpa ‖ *v* (*pret & pp* **rapped**; *ger* **rapping**) *tr* dare colpi a; battere; **to rap out** (*e.g., a command*) lanciare ‖ *intr* dare colpi, bussare
rapacious [rə'peʃəs] *adj* rapace
rape [rep] *s* rapimento; (*of a woman*) stupro; (bot) ravizzone *m* ‖ *tr* rapire; forzare, violentare
rapid ['ræpɪd] *adj* rapido ‖ **rapids** *spl* rapide *fpl*
rap'id-fire' *adj* a tiro rapido
rapidity [rə'pɪdəti] *s* rapidità *f*
rapier ['repɪ·ər] *s* spada, stocco
rapt [ræpt] *adj* assorto; estatico
rapture ['ræptʃər] *s* rapimento, estasi *f*
rare [rer] *adj* raro; (*thinly distributed*) rado; (*gas*) rarefatto; (*meat*) al sangue; (*gem*) prezioso
rare'-earth' met'al *s* metallo delle terre rare
rare·fy ['rerɪ͵faɪ] *v* (*pret & pp* -fied) *tr* rarefare ‖ *intr* rarefarsi
rarely ['rerli] *adv* di rado, raramente
rascal ['ræskəl] *s* briccone *m*, birbante *m*
rash [ræʃ] *adj* temerario, precipitato ‖ *s* eruzione; (fig) mucchio
rasp [ræsp] *or* [rɑsp] *s* raspa; rumore

m di raspa ‖ *tr* raspare; irritare; dire con voce roca ‖ *intr* fare rumore raspante

raspber·ry ['ræz‚beri] *or* ['rɑz‚beri] *s* (**-ries**) lampone *m;* (slang) pernacchia

rat [ræt] *s* ratto; (*to give fullness to hair*) posticcio; (slang) traditore *m;* **to smell a rat** (coll) subodorare un inganno

ratchet ['rætʃɪt] *s* nottolino

rate [ret] *s* (*of interest*) saggio, tasso; prezzo; costo; velocità *f;* (*degree of action*) ragione; tariffa; **at any rate** ad ogni modo; **at the rate of** in ragione di ‖ *tr* valutare, classificare ‖ *intr* essere considerato; essere classificato

rate' of exchange' *s* corso del cambio

rather ['ræðər] *or* ['rɑðər] *adv* piuttosto; a preferenza; per meglio dire; bensì; discretamente; **rather than** piuttosto di ‖ *interj* e come!

rati·fy ['rætɪ‚faɪ] *v* (*pret & pp* **-fied**) *tr* ratificare, sancire

rating ['retɪŋ] *s* classifica; (nav) grado; (com) valutazione

ra·tio ['reʃo] *or* ['reʃɪ‚o] *s* (**-tios**) ragione, rapporto; proporzione

ration ['reʃən] *or* ['ræʃən] *s* razione ‖ *tr* razionare

rational ['ræʃənəl] *adj* razionale

ra'tion book' *s* tessera di razionamento

rat' poi'son *s* veleno per i topi

rat' race' *s* (coll) corsa dei barberi

rattle ['rætəl] *s* (*sharp sounds*) fracasso; (*child's toy*) sonaglio; (*noise-making device*) raganella; (*in throat*) rantolo ‖ *tr* scuotere; (*to confuse*) sconcertare; **to rattle off** dire rapidamente, snocciolare ‖ *intr* risuonare; scuotersi; cianciare

rat'tle-snake' *s* serpente *m* a sonagli

rat'trap' *s* trappola per topi; (*hovel*) topaia; (*jam*) (fig) frangente *m*

raucous ['rɔkəs] *adj* rauco

ravage ['rævɪdʒ] *s* distruzione; **ravages** (*of time*) oltraggio ‖ *tr* distruggere, disfare

rave [rev] *intr* farneticare, delirare; infuriare; andare in estasi; **to rave about** levare alle stelle

raven ['revən] *s* corvo

ravenous ['rævənəs] *adj* famelico

ravine [rə'vin] *s* canalone *m,* burrone *m*

ravish ['rævɪʃ] *tr* incantare, entusiasmare; rapire; (*a woman*) stuprare

raw [rɔ] *adj* crudo; (*e.g., silk*) grezzo; (*flesh*) vivo; inesperto

raw' deal' *s* trattamento brutale e ingiusto

raw'hide' *s* pelle greggia

raw' mate'rial *s* materia prima

ray [re] *s* raggio; (*fish*) razza

rayon ['re·ɑn] *s* raion *m*

raze [rez] *tr* radere al suolo

razor ['rezər] *s* rasoio

ra'zor blade' *s* lametta

ra'zor strop' *s* coramella

razz [ræz] *s* (slang) pernacchia ‖ *tr* (slang) prendere in giro

reach [ritʃ] *s* portata; estensione; **out**

of reach (of) fuori della portata (di); oltre alle possibilità (di); fuori tiro (di); **within reach of** alla portata di ‖ *tr* raggiungere; toccare; (*customers*) guadagnare ‖ *intr* estendere la mano; **to reach for** cercare di raggiungere

react [rɪ'ækt] *intr* reagire

reaction [rɪ'ækʃən] *s* reazione

reactionar·y [rɪ'ækʃə‚neri] *adj* reazionario ‖ *s* (**-ies**) reazionario

reactor [rɪ'æktər] *s* reattore *m*

read [rid] *v* (*pret & pp* **read** [red]) *tr* leggere; (*s.o.'s thoughts*) leggere in; **to read over** ripassare ‖ *intr* leggere; saper leggere; essere concepito, e.g., **your cable reads thus** il vostro telegramma è concepito così; leggersi, e.g., **this books reads easily** questo libro si legge facilmente; **to read on** continuare a leggere

reader ['ridər] *s* lettore *m;* libro di lettura, sillabo

readily ['redɪli] *adv* velocemente; facilmente; di buona voglia

reading ['ridɪŋ] *s* lettura; dizione

read'ing desk' *s* leggio

read'ing glass' *s* lente *f* d'ingrandimento; **reading glasses** occhiali *mpl* per la lettura

read'ing lamp' *s* lampada da scrittoio

read'ing room' *s* sala di lettura

read·y ['redi] *adj* (**-ier**; **-iest**) pronto; disponibile; **to make ready** preparare; prepararsi ‖ *v* (*pret & pp* **-ied**) *tr* preparare ‖ *intr* prepararsi

read'y cash' *s* denaro contante

read'y-made cloth'ing *s* confezioni *fpl*

read'y-made suit' *s* vestito già fatto

reaffirm [‚ri·ə'fʌrm] *tr* riaffermare

reagent [rɪ'edʒənt] *s* reagente *m*

real ['ri·əl] *adj* effettivo, reale

re'al estate' *s* beni *mpl* immobili, proprietà *f* immobiliare

re'al-estate' *adj* immobiliare, fondiario

realism ['ri·ə‚lɪzəm] *s* realismo

realist ['ri·əlɪst] *s* realista *mf*

realistic [‚ri·ə'lɪstɪk] *adj* realistico

reali·ty [rɪ'ælɪti] *s* (**-ies**) realtà *f*

realize ['ri·ə‚laɪz] *tr* rendersi conto di; concretare; realizzare ‖ *intr* convertire proprietà in contanti

realm [relm] *s* regno

realtor ['ri·əl‚tɔr] *or* ['ri·əltər] *s* (trademark) agente *m* d'immobili membro dell'associazione nazionale

realty ['ri·əlti] *s* proprietà *f* immobiliare

ream [rim] *s* risma; **reams** pagine *fpl* e pagine ‖ *tr* alesare

reamer ['rimər] *s* (mach) alesatore *m;* (dentistry) fresa

reap [rip] *tr & intr* (*to cut*) mietere; (*to gather*) raccogliere

reaper ['ripər] *s* (*person*) mietitore *m;* (mach) mietitrice *f*

reappear [‚ri·ə'pɪr] *intr* ricomparire, riapparire

reappearance [‚ri·ə'pɪrəns] *s* riapparizione, ricomparsa

reapportionment [‚ri·ə'pɔr/ənmənt] *s* ridistribuzione

rear [rɪr] *adj* posteriore, di dietro ‖ *s*

retro, di dietro; posteriore *m;* (mil) retroguardia || *tr* alzare, elevare; allevare, educare || *intr* (*said of a horse*) impennarsi

rear' ad'miral *s* contrammiraglio

rear' drive' *s* trazione posteriore

rear' end' *s* retro, di dietro; (coll) posteriore *m;* (aut) retrotreno

rearmament [ri'ɑrməmənt] *s* riarmo

rear'-view mir'ror *s* specchietto retrovisivo

rear' win'dow *s* (aut) lunetta posteriore

reason ['rizən] *s* ragione; **by reason of** per causa di; **to bring s.o. to reason** indurre qlcu alla ragione; **to stand to reason** esser logico || *tr* & *intr* ragionare

reasonable ['rizənəbəl] *adj* ragionevole

reassessment [,ri·ə'sɛsmənt] *s* rivalutazione

reassure [,ri·ə'ʃʊr] *tr* rassicurare, riassicurare

reawaken [,ri·ə'wekən] *tr* risvegliare || *intr* risvegliarsi

rebate ['ribet] *or* [rɪ'bet] *s* ribasso || *tr* ribassare

rebel ['rɛbəl] *adj* & *s* ribelle *mf* || **re·bel** [rɪ'bɛl] *v* (*pret* & *pp* **-belled;** *ger* **-belling**) *intr* ribellarsi

rebellion [rɪ'bɛljən] *s* ribellione

rebellious [rɪ'bɛljəs] *adj* ribelle

re·bind [ri'baɪnd] *v* (*pret* & *pp* **bound** ['baʊnd]) *tr* rifasciare; (bb) rilegare

rebirth ['ribʌrθ] *or* [ri'bʌrθ] *s* rinascita

rebore [ri'bor] *tr* rialesare, rettificare

rebound ['ri,baʊnd] *or* [ri'baʊnd] *s* rimbalzo || [ri'baʊnd] *intr* rimbalzare

rebroad'casting sta'tion *s* stazione ripetitrice

rebuff [rɪ'bʌf] *s* rifiuto || *tr* respingere, rifiutare

rebuild [ri'bɪld] *v* (*pret* & *pp* **-built** ['bɪlt]) *tr* ricostruire, riedificare

rebuke [rɪ'bjuk] *s* rabbuffo || *tr* rabbuffare

re·but [rɪ'bʌt] *v* (*pret* & *pp* **-butted;** *ger* **-butting**) *tr* confutare

rebuttal [rɪ'bʌtəl] *s* confutazione

recall [rɪ'kɔl] *or* ['rikɔl] *s* richiamo; revoca || [rɪ'kɔl] *tr* richiamare; ricordare, ricordarsi di; richiamare alla memoria

recant [rɪ'kænt] *tr* ritrattare || *intr* ritrattarsi

re·cap ['ri,kæp] *or* [ri'kæp] *v* (*pret* & *pp* **-capped;** *ger* **-capping**) *tr* ricapitolare, riepilogare; (*a tire*) rifare il battistrada a

recapitulation [,rikə,pɪtʃə'leʃən] *s* ricapitolazione, riepilogo

re·cast ['ri,kæst] *or* ['ri,kɑst] *s* rifusione || [ri'kæst] *or* [ri'kɑst] *v* (*pret* & *pp* **-cast**) *tr* rifondere

recede [rɪ'sid] *intr* ritirarsi, allontanarsi; recedere, retrocedere; (*said, e.g., of chin*) sfuggire

receipt [rɪ'sit] *s* ricevimento; (*acknowledgment of payment*) ricevuta; (*recipe*) ricetta; **receipts** incasso, introito || *tr* quietanzare

receive [rɪ'siv] *tr* ricevere; (*stolen goods*) ricettare; (*to have inflicted upon one*) subire || *intr* ricevere

receiver [rɪ'sivər] *s* ricevitore *m;* ricettatore *m;* (law) curatore *m* fallimentare; (telp) auricolare *m*

receiv'ing set' *s* apparecchio radioricevente

receiv'ing tell'er *s* cassiere *m* incaricato delle riscossioni

recent ['risənt] *adj* recente

recently ['risəntli] *adv* recentemente, di recente

receptacle [rɪ'sɛptəkəl] *s* recipiente *m;* (elec) presa

reception [rɪ'sɛpʃən] *s* accoglienza; (*function*) ricevimento

recep'tion desk' *s* ufficio informazioni, bureau *m*

receptionist [rɪ'sɛpʃənɪst] *s* accoglitrice *f;* (*male*) usciere *m*

receptive [rɪ'sɛptɪv] *adj* ricettivo

recess [rɪ'sɛs] *or* ['risɛs] *s* intermezzo, interludio; ora di ricreazione; (*in a line*) rientranza; (*in a wall*) nicchia, alcova; (fig) recesso || [rɪ'sɛs] *tr* aggiornare, dare vacanza a; incassare, mettere in una nicchia || *intr* aggiornarsi, prendersi vacanza

recession [rɪ'sɛʃən] *s* ritirata; processione finale; (com) recessione

recipe ['rɛsɪ,pi] *s* ricetta

reciprocal [rɪ'sɪprəkəl] *adj* reciproco

reciprocity [,rɛsɪ'prɑsɪti] *s* reciprocità *f*

recital [rɪ'saɪtəl] *s* narrazione; (*of music or poetry*) recital *m*

recite [rɪ'saɪt] *tr* raccontare; (*music or poetry*) recitare

reckless ['rɛklɪs] *adj* temerario, spericolato

reckon ['rɛkən] *tr* calcolare; considerare; (coll) supporre || *intr* contare; **to reckon with** prevedere, tener conto di

reclaim [rɪ'klem] *tr* (*land*) sanare, prosciugare; (*substances*) rigenerare; (fig) rigenerare

recline [rɪ'klaɪn] *tr* reclinare || *intr* reclinarsi, adagiarsi

recluse [rɪ'klus] *or* ['rɛklus] *adj* & *s* recluso

recognition [,rɛkəg'nɪʃən] *s* riconoscimento

recognize ['rɛkəg,naɪz] *tr* riconoscere

recoil [rɪ'kɔɪl] *s* indietreggiamento; (*of a firearm*) rinculo || *intr* indietreggiare; rinculare

recollect [,rɛkə'lɛkt] *tr* & *intr* ricordare

recollection [,rɛkə'lɛkʃən] *s* ricordo

recommend [,rɛkə'mɛnd] *tr* raccomandare

recompense ['rɛkəm,pɛns] *s* ricompensa || *tr* ricompensare

reconcile ['rɛkən,saɪl] *tr* riconciliare; **to reconcile oneself** rassegnarsi

reconnaissance [rɪ'kɑnɪsəns] *s* ricognizione

reconnoiter [,rɛkə'nɔɪtər] *or* [,rikə'nɔɪtər] *tr* & *intr* perlustrare

reconsider [,rikən'sɪdər] *tr* riconsiderare

reconstruct [ˌrikən'strʌkt] *tr* ricostruire

reconversion [ˌrikən'vʌrʒən] *s* riconversione

record ['rɛkərd] *s* registrazione; annotazione; (*official report*) verbale *m*, protocollo; (*criminal*) fedina sporca; (*of a phonograph*) disco; (*educ*) documenti *mpl* scolastici; (*sports*) record *m*, primato; **off the record** confidenziale; confidenzialmente; **records** annali *mpl*, documenti *mpl*; **to break a record** battere un record || [rɪ'kɔrd] *tr* registrare; mettere a verbale; (*e.g., a song*) incidere

rec'ord break'er *s* (sports) primatista *mf*

rec'ord chang'er [ˈtʃɛndʒər] *s* cambiadischi *m*

recorder [rɪ'kɔrdər] *s* (*apparatus*) registratore *m*; (law) cancelliere *m*; (mus) flauto a imboccatura a tubo

rec'ord hold'er *s* (sports) primatista *mf*

recording [rɪ'kɔrdɪŋ] *s* registrazione; (*of a record*) incisione; (*record*) disco

record'ing sec'retary *s* cancelliere *m*

rec'ord play'er *s* giradischi *m*

recount ['ri‿kaunt] *s* nuovo conteggio || [ri'kaunt] *tr* (*to count again*) ricontare || [rɪ'kaunt] *tr* (*to narrate*) raccontare

recourse [rɪ'kors] or ['rikors] *s* ricorso; (com) rivalsa; **to have recourse to** ricorrere a

recover [rɪ'kʌvər] *tr* ricuperare, riacquistare; (*a substance*) rigenerare; **to recover consciousness** riaversi, riprendere conoscenza || *intr* rimettersi; guadagnare una causa

recover·y [rɪ'kʌvəri] *s* (-ies) ricupero; guarigione; **past recovery** incurabile

recreant ['rɛkrɪ‿ənt] *adj* & *s* codardo; traditore *m*

recreation [ˌrɛkrɪ'eʃən] *s* ricreazione

recruit [rɪ'krut] *s* recluta || *tr* & *intr* reclutare

rectangle ['rɛk‿tæŋgəl] *s* rettangolo

rectifier ['rɛktə‿faɪ‿ər] *s* rettificatore *m*; (elec) raddrizzatore *m*

recti·fy ['rɛktɪ‿faɪ] *v* (*pret* & *pp* -fied) *tr* rettificare; (elec) raddrizzare

rectitude ['rɛktɪ‿tud] or ['rɛktɪ‿tjud] *s* rettitudine *f*

rec·tum ['rɛktəm] *s* (-tums or -ta [tə]) retto

recumbent [rɪ'kʌmbənt] *adj* sdraiato

recuperate [rɪ'kjupə‿ret] *tr* ricuperare || *intr* ristabilirsi, rimettersi

re·cur [rɪ'kʌr] *v* (*pret* & *pp* -curred; *ger* -curring) *intr* ricorrere; ritornare; tornare a mente

recurrent [rɪ'kʌrənt] *adj* ricorrente

recycle [ri'saɪkəl] *tr* riconvertire; (*e.g., in chemical industry*) riciclare

red [rɛd] *adj* (redder; reddest) rosso || *s* rosso; **in the red** in debito , in rosso || **Red** *adj* & *s* (*Communist*) rosso

red'bait' *tr* dare del comunista a

red'bird' *s* cardinale *m*

red-blooded ['rɛd‿blʌdɪd] *adj* sanguigno; vigoroso

red'breast' *s* pettirosso

red'bud' *s* siliquastro

red'cap' *s* (Brit) poliziotto militare; (U.S.A.) facchino

red' cell' *s* globulo rosso

red' cent' *s*—**to not have a red cent** (coll) non avere il becco di un quattrino

Red' Cross' *s* Croce Rossa

redden ['rɛdən] *tr* arrossare || *intr* arrossire

redeem [rɪ'dim] *tr* redimere; (*a promise*) disimpegnare

redeemer [rɪ'dimər] *s* redentore *m*

redemption [rɪ'dɛmpʃən] *s* redenzione; disimpegno

red-handed ['rɛd'hændɪd] *adj*—**to be caught red-handed** esser colto sul fatto or con le mani nel sacco

red'head' *s* persona dai capelli rossi

red' her'ring *s* argomento usato per sviare l'attenzione; aringa affumicata

red'-hot' *adj* rovente, incandescente; fresco fresco, appena uscito

rediscover [ˌridɪs'kʌvər] *tr* riscoprire

red'-let'ter *adj* memorabile

red'-light' dis'trict *s* quartiere *m* delle case di tolleranza

red' man' *s* pellerossa *m*

re·do ['ri'du] *v* (*pret* -did ['dɪd]; *pp* -done ['dʌn]) *tr* rifare

redolent ['rɛdələnt] *adj* fragrante, profumato; **redolent of** che sa di

redoubt [rɪ'daut] *s* (mil) ridotta

redound [rɪ'daund] *intr* ridondare

red' pep'per *s* pepe *m* di Caienna

redress [rɪ'drɛs] or ['ridrɛs] *s* riparazione, risarcimento || [rɪ'drɛs] *tr* riparare, risarcire

red'skin' *s* pellerossa *mf*

red' tape' *s* trafila, burocrazia

reduce [rɪ'djus] or [rɪ'dus] *tr* ridurre; diluire; (mil) retrocedere; (*a hernia*) (surg) sbrigliare || *intr* ridursi; (*to lose weight*) dimagrire

reducing [rɪ'djusɪŋ] or [rɪ'dusɪŋ] *adj* dimagrante; (chem) riducente

reduction [rɪ'dʌkʃən] *s* riduzione

redundant [rɪ'dʌndənt] *adj* ridondante

red'wood' *s* sequoia

reed [rid] *s* (*stalk*) calamo; (*plant*) canna; (mus) linguetta; (mus) strumento a linguetta

reedit [ri'ɛdɪt] *tr* rifondere

reef [rif] *s* scoglio, barriera; (naut) terzarolo; (min) vena, filone *m* || *tr* (*sail*) imbrogliare

reefer ['rifər] *s* giacchetta a doppio petto; (slang) sigaretta di marijuana

reek [rik] *intr* puzzare; sudare, evaporare, fumare

reel [ril] *s* (*spool*) bobina; (*sway*) vacillamento; (*for fishing*) mulinello; **off the reel** senza esitazione || *tr* bobinare; **to reel off** rifilare || *intr* barcollare

reelection [ˌri‿ɪ'lɛkʃən] *s* rielezione

reenlist [ˌri‿ɛn'lɪst] *tr* arruolare di nuovo || *intr* arruolarsi di nuovo

reen·try [rɪ'ɛntri] *s* (-tries) rientro

reexamination [ˌri‿ɛg‿zæmɪ'neʃən] *s* riesame *m*

re·fer [rɪ'fʌr] v (pret & pp **-ferred;** ger **-ferring**) tr riferire ‖ intr riferirsi

referee [‚refə'ri] s arbitro ‖ tr & intr arbitrare

reference ['refərəns] s riferimento; (testimonial) referenza; (e.g., in a book) rinvio, rimando

ref'erence book' s libro di consultazione

referen·dum [‚refə'rendəm] s (-dums or -da [də]) referendum m

refill ['rifɪl] s ricambio ‖ [rɪ'fɪl] tr riempire di nuovo

refine [rɪ'faɪn] tr raffinare

refinement [rɪ'faɪnmənt] s raffinatezza; (of oil) raffinatura

refiner·y [rɪ'faɪnəri] s (-ies) raffineria

reflect [rɪ'flekt] tr riflettere ‖ intr riflettere, riflettersi

reflection [rɪ'flekʃən] s riflessione

reflex ['rifleks] adj riflesso ‖ s riflesso; (camera) reflex m

reflexive [rɪ'fleksɪv] adj riflessivo

reforestation [‚rifarɪs'teʃən] or [‚rifɔrɪs'teʃən] s rimboschimento

reform [rɪ'fɔrm] s riforma ‖ tr riformare ‖ intr correggersi

reformation [‚refər'meʃən] s riforma ‖ **Reformation** s—**the Reformation** la Riforma

reformato·ry [rɪ'fɔrmə‚tori] adj riformativo ‖ s (-ries) riformatorio

reformer [rɪ'fɔrmər] s riformatore m

reform' school' s riformatorio

refraction [rɪ'frækʃən] s rifrazione

refrain [rɪ'fren] s ritornello, intercalare m ‖ intr astenersi

refresh [rɪ'freʃ] tr rinfrescare; ristorare ‖ intr ristorarsi

refreshing [rɪ'freʃɪŋ] adj rinfrescante; ristoratore; ricreativo

refreshment [rɪ'freʃmənt] s rinfresco

refrigerate [rɪ'frɪdʒə‚ret] tr refrigerare

refrigerator [rɪ'frɪdʒə‚retər] s refrigerante m, frigorifero

refrig'erator car' s vagone frigorifero

re·fuel [ri'fjul] v (pret & pp **-fueled** or **-fuelled;** ger **-fueling** or **-fuelling**) tr rifornire di carburante ‖ intr rifornirsi di carburante

refuge ['refjudʒ] s rifugio; scampo; **to take refuge (in)** rifugiarsi (in)

refugee [‚refju'dʒi] s rifugiato

refund ['rifʌnd] s rifusione ‖ [rɪ'fʌnd] tr (to repay) rifondere ‖ [ri'fʌnd] tr (bonds) consolidare; (to fund anew) rifondere

refurnish [ri'fʌrnɪʃ] tr riammobiliare

refusal [rɪ'fjuzəl] s rifiuto

refuse ['refjus] s rifiuto, spazzatura ‖ [rɪ'fjuz] tr rifiutare; **to refuse to** rifiutarsi di

refute [rɪ'fjut] tr smentire, confutare

regain [rɪ'gen] tr riguadagnare; **to regain consciousness** tornare in sé

regal ['rigəl] adj reale, regale

regale [rɪ'gel] tr intrattenere, rallegrare

regalia [rɪ'gelɪ·ə] spl (of royalty) prerogative fpl reali; alta uniforme

regard [rɪ'gard] s riguardo; (look)

sguardo; (esteem) rispetto; **in regard to** rispetto a; **regards** rispetti mpl; **warm regards** cordiali saluti mpl; **without regard to** senza considerare ‖ tr considerare; osservare; concernere; **as regards** per quanto concerne

regarding [rɪ'gardɪŋ] prep per quanto concerne

regardless [rɪ'gardlɪs] adj incurante ‖ adv ciò nonostante; costi quello che costi; **regardless of** malgrado

regatta [rɪ'gætə] s regata

regen·cy ['ridʒənsi] s (-cies) reggenza

regenerate [rɪ'dʒenə‚ret] tr rigenerare ‖ intr rigenerarsi

regent ['ridʒənt] s reggente mf

regicide ['redʒɪ‚saɪd] s (act) regicidio; (person) regicida mf

regiment ['redʒɪmənt] s reggimento ‖ ['redʒɪ‚ment] tr irreggimentare

regimental [‚redʒɪ'mentəl] adj reggimentale ‖ **regimentals** spl uniforme f reggimentale

region ['ridʒən] s regione

register ['redʒɪstər] s registro; (for controlling the flow of air) regolatore m dell'aria ‖ tr registrare; (e.g., a student) iscrivere; (e.g., anger) dimostrare; (a letter) raccomandare ‖ intr registrarsi; iscriversi; fare impressione

reg'istered let'ter s raccomandata

reg'istered nurse' s infermiera diplomata

registrar ['redʒɪs‚trar] s registratore m, archivista mf; (of deeds) ricevitore m

registration [‚redʒɪs'treʃən] s registrazione; (e.g., of a student) iscrizione; (of mail) raccomandazione

registra'tion fee' s diritto di segreteria

re·gret [rɪ'gret] s pentimento, rammarico; **regrets** scuse fpl ‖ v (pret & pp **-gretted;** ger **-gretting**) tr rimpiangere; **to regret to** essere spiacente di

regrettable [rɪ'gretəbəl] adj deplorevole

regular ['regjələr] adj regolare; (life) regolato; (coll) vero ‖ s cliente m abituale; (mil) effettivo

regularity [‚regju'lærɪti] s regolarità f

regularize ['regjələ‚raɪz] tr regolarizzare

regulate ['regjə‚let] tr regolare

regulation [‚regjə'leʃən] s regolazione; (rule) regolamento

rehabilitate [‚rihə'bɪlɪ‚tet] tr riabilitare

rehearsal [rɪ'hʌrsəl] s prova

rehearse [rɪ'hʌrs] tr provare ‖ intr fare le prove

rehiring [ri'haɪrɪŋ] s riassunzione

reign [ren] s regno ‖ intr regnare

reimburse [‚ri·ɪm'bʌrs] tr rimborsare

rein [ren] s redine f; **to give full rein to** dare briglia sciolta a ‖ tr guidare con le redini; frenare

reincarnation [‚ri·ɪnkar'neʃən] s reincarnazione

reindeer ['ren‚dɪr] s renna

reinforce [‚ri·ɪn'fors] tr rinforzare; (a wall) armare

re'inforced con'crete s cemento armato

reinforcement [ˌri·ɪnˈforsmənt] *s* rinforzo

reinstate [ˌri·ɪnˈstet] *tr* reintegrare

reiterate [riˈɪtəˌret] *tr* reiterare

reject [ˈridʒekt] *s* rigetto, rifiuto; **rejects** scarti *mpl* ‖ [rɪˈdʒekt] *tr* rigettare; (*to refuse*) rifiutare

rejection [rɪˈdʒekʃən] *s* rigetto; rifiuto

rejoice [rɪˈdʒɔɪs] *intr* rallegrarsi

rejoin [rɪˈdʒɔɪn] *tr* raggiungere; (*to reunite*) riunire; (*to reply*) rispondere

rejoinder [rɪˈdʒɔɪndər] *s* risposta; (law) controreplica

rejuvenation [rɪˌdʒuvɪˈneʃən] *s* ringiovanimento

rekindle [riˈkɪndəl] *tr* riaccendere

relapse [rɪˈlæps] *s* ricaduta ‖ *intr* ricadere

relate [rɪˈlet] *tr* mettere in relazione; (*to tell*) narrare

relation [rɪˈleʃən] *s* relazione; (*account*) resoconto; (*relative*) parente *mf*; (*kinship*) parentela; **in relation to** or **with** in relazione a

relationship [rɪˈleʃənˌʃɪp] *s* rapporto, relazione; (*kinship*) parentela

relative [ˈrelətɪv] *adj* relativo ‖ *s* congiunto, parente *mf*

relativity [ˌrelaˈtɪvɪti] *s* relatività *f*

relax [rɪˈlæks] *tr* rilasciare, rilassare ‖ *intr* rilasciarsi, rilassarsi

relaxation [ˌrilækˈseʃən] *s* distensione; (*entertainment*) ricreazione

relaxa'tion of ten'sion *s* distensione

relaxing [rɪˈlæksɪŋ] *adj* rilassante; divertente

relay [ˈrile] or [rɪˈle] *s* (elec) relè *m*; (rad) ripetitore *m*; (mil, sports) staffetta; (sports) corsa a staffetta ‖ *v* (*pret & pp* -**layed**) *tr* trasmettere, ritrasmettere ‖ [rɪˈle] *v* (*pret & pp* -**laid**) *tr* rimettere, porre di nuovo

re'lay race' *s* corsa a staffetta

release [rɪˈlis] *s* (*e.g., from jail*) liberazione; (*from obligation*) disimpegno; (*for publication*) autorizzazione; (mov) distribuzione; (journ) comunicato; (aer) lancio; (mach) scappamento ‖ *tr* liberare; disimpegnare; autorizzare la pubblicazione di; (mov) distribuire; (*a bomb*) (aer) lanciare; **to release s.o. from a debt** rimettere un debito a qlcu

relent [rɪˈlent] *intr* placarsi

relentless [rɪˈlentlɪs] *adj* implacabile

relevant [ˈreləvənt] *adj* pertinente

reliable [rɪˈlai·əbəl] *adj* (*person*) fidato; (*source*) attendibile

reliance [rɪˈlai·əns] *s* fiducia, fede *f*

relic [ˈrelɪk] *s* reliquia

relief [rɪˈlif] *s* sollievo; sussidio; (*prominence; projection*) rilievo; (mil) cambio; **in relief** in rilievo; **on relief** sotto sussidio

relieve [rɪˈliv] *tr* (*e.g., pain*) alleviare; (*e.g., a load*) sgravare; (mil) rilevare

religion [rɪˈlɪdʒən] *s* religione

religious [rɪˈlɪdʒəs] *adj* religioso

relinquish [rɪˈlɪŋkwɪʃ] *tr* abbandonare

relish [ˈrelɪʃ] *s* piacere *m*, gusto; sapore *m*, aroma *m*; (culin) condimento ‖ *tr* gustare, apprezzare; dare gusto a

reluctance [rɪˈlʌktəns] *s* riluttanza

reluctant [rɪˈlʌktənt] *adj* riluttante

re·ly [rɪˈlaɪ] *v* (*pret & pp* -**lied**) *intr* fare assegnamento; **to rely on** fidarsi di, fondarsi di

remain [rɪˈmen] *s*—**remains** resti *mpl*; resti *mpl* mortali ‖ *intr* restare, rimanere

remainder [rɪˈmendər] *s* resto, restante *m*; (*unsold books*) fondi *mpl* di libreria ‖ *tr* vendere come rimanenza

re-make [riˈmek] *v* (*pret & pp* -**made** [ˈmed]) *tr* rifare

remark [rɪˈmɑrk] *s* osservazione, rimarco ‖ *tr & intr* osservare; **to remark on** fare osservazioni su

remarkable [rɪˈmɑrkəbəl] *adj* notevole

remar·ry [riˈmæri] *v* (*pret & pp* -**ried**) *intr* riprendere moglie, risposarsi

reme·dy [ˈremɪdi] *s* (-**dies**) rimedio ‖ *v* (*pret & pp* -**died**) *tr* rimediare (with *dat*)

remember [rɪˈmembər] *tr* ricordarsi di; (*to send greetings to*) ricordare ‖ *intr* ricordare, ricordarsi

remembrance [rɪˈmembrəns] *s* rimembranza, ricordo

remind [rɪˈmaɪnd] *tr* rammentare

reminder [rɪˈmaɪndər] *s* promemoria

reminisce [ˌremɪˈnɪs] *intr* ricordare il passato

reminiscence [ˌremɪˈnɪsəns] *s* reminiscenza

remiss [rɪˈmɪs] *adj* negligente

re·mit [rɪˈmɪt] *v* (*pret & pp* -**mitted**; *ger* -**mitting**) *tr* rimettere; (*to a lower court*) (law) rinviare

remittance [rɪˈmɪtəns] *s* rimessa

remnant [ˈremnənt] *s* (*remaining quantity*) rimanente *m*; (*of cloth*) scampolo; vestigio; **remnants** (*of merchandise*) rimanenze *fpl*, fondi *mpl* di magazzino

remod·el [riˈmɑdəl] *v* (*pret & pp* -**eled** or -**elled**; *ger* -**eling** or -**elling**) *tr* rimodellare; ricostruire

remonstrance [rɪˈmɑnstrəns] *s* rimostranza

remonstrate [rɪˈmɑnstret] *intr* protestare, rimostrare; **to remonstrate with** rimostrare a

remorse [rɪˈmɔrs] *s* rimorso

remorseful [rɪˈmɔrsfəl] *adj* tormentato dal rimorso, pentito

remote [rɪˈmot] *adj* remoto

remote' control' *s* telecomando

removable [rɪˈmuvəbəl] *adj* amovibile

removal [rɪˈmuvəl] *s* rimozione; trasferimento; (*dismissal*) destituzione

remove [rɪˈmuv] *tr* rimuovere; (*one's jacket*) togliersi, cavarsi; (*from office*) destituire; eliminare ‖ *intr* trasferirsi; andarsene

remuneration [rɪˌmjunəˈreʃən] *s* rimunerazione

renaissance [ˌrenəˈsɑns] or [rɪˈnesəns] *s* rinascimento, rinascita ‖ **Renaissance** *s* Rinascimento

rend [rend] *v* (*pret & pp* **rent** [rent]) *tr* (*to tear*) stracciare; (*to split*) fendere, squarciare

render [ˈrendər] *tr* (*justice*) rendere;

(*a service*) fare; (*aid*) prestare; (*a bill*) presentare; (*to translate*) tradurre; (*a piece of music*) interpretare; (*e.g., fat*) struggere

rendez·vous [ˈrɑndə‚vu] *s* (**-vous** [‚vuz]) appuntamento; (*in space*) incontro ‖ *v* (*pret & pp* **-voused** [‚vud]; *ger* **-vousing** [‚vu·ɪŋ]) *intr* incontrarsi

rendition [rɛnˈdɪʃən] *s* restituzione, resa; traduzione; interpretazione

renege [rɪˈnɪg] *s* rifiuto ‖ *intr* rifiutare; (coll) venire meno

renew [rɪˈnju] *or* [rɪˈnu] *tr* rinnovare ‖ *intr* rinnovarsi

renewal [rɪˈnju·əl] *or* [rɪˈnu·əl] *s* rinnovo, rinnovamento

renounce [rɪˈnauns] *tr* rinunziare (with *dat*); ripudiare

renovate [ˈrɛnə‚vet] *tr* rinnovare; (*a building*) restaurare; (*a room*) rimettere a nuovo

renown [rɪˈnaun] *s* rinomanza

renowned [rɪˈnaund] *adj* rinomato

rent [rɛnt] *adj* scisso ‖ *s* fitto, pigione; (*tear*) squarcio ‖ *tr* locare, dare a pigione ‖ *intr* prendere a pigione

rental [ˈrɛntəl] *s* affitto

renter [ˈrɛntər] *s* affittuario, locatario

renunciation [rɪ‚nʌnsɪˈeʃən] *or* [rɪ‚nʌn/ɪˈeʃən] *s* rinunzia

reopen [riˈopən] *tr* riaprire ‖ *intr* riaprirsi

reopening [riˈopənɪŋ] *s* riapertura

reorganize [riˈɔrgə‚naɪz] *tr* riorganizzare ‖ *intr* riorganizzarsi

repair [rɪˈpɛr] *s* riparazione; **in good repair** in buono stato ‖ *tr* riparare ‖ *intr* riparare, dirigersi

repair′man *s* (**-men**) aggiustatore *m*

repaper [riˈpepər] *tr* ritappezzare

reparation [‚rɛpəˈreʃən] *s* riparazione

repartee [‚rɛpɑrˈti] *s* replica arguta, rimando

repast [rɪˈpæst] *or* [rɪˈpɑst] *s* pasto

repatriate [riˈpetrɪ‚et] *tr* rimpatriare

re·pay [rɪˈpe] *v* (*pret & pp* **-paid** [ˈped]) *tr* ripagare

repayment [rɪˈpemənt] *s* rimborso; risarcimento, compensazione

repeal [rɪˈpil] *s* revoca, abrogazione ‖ *tr* revocare, abrogare

repeat [rɪˈpit] *s* ripetizione ‖ *tr* ripetere ‖ *intr* ripetere; (*said of food*) tornare a gola

re·pel [rɪˈpɛl] *v* (*pret & pp* **-pelled**; *ger* **-pelling**) *tr* respingere, ricacciare; ripugnare (with *dat*)

repent [rɪˈpɛnt] *tr* pentirsi di ‖ *intr* pentirsi, ravvedersi

repentance [rɪˈpɛntəns] *s* pentimento

repentant [rɪˈpɛntənt] *adj* pentito

repercussion [‚ripərˈkʌʃən] *s* ripercussione

reper·to·ry [ˈrɛpər‚torɪ] *s* (**-ries**) (com) magazzino; (theat) repertorio

repetition [‚rɛpɪˈtɪʃən] *s* ripetizione

repine [rɪˈpaɪn] *intr* lamentarsi

replace [rɪˈples] *tr* (*to put back*) rimettere; (*to take the place of*) rimpiazzare

replaceable [rɪˈplesəbəl] *adj* sostituibile

replacement [rɪˈplesmənt] *s* rimpiazzo, sostituzione; **as a replacement for** al posto di

replenish [rɪˈplɛnɪʃ] *tr* rifornire

replete [rɪˈplit] *adj* pieno zeppo

replica [ˈrɛplɪkə] *s* replica

re·ply [rɪˈplaɪ] *s* (**-plies**) risposta ‖ *v* (*pret & pp* **-plied**) *tr & intr* rispondere

report [rɪˈport] *s* rapporto, informazione; voce *f*, rumore *m*; (*of a physician*) responso; (*of a firearm*) detonazione ‖ *tr* riportare, rapportare; denunziare ‖ *intr* fare un rapporto; fare il rapporto; presentarsi; **to report sick** (mil) marcare visita

report′ card′ *s* pagella

reportedly [rɪˈportɪdlɪ] *adv* secondo la voce comune

reporter [rɪˈportər] *s* cronista *mf*, reporter *m*

reporting [rɪˈportɪŋ] *s* reportage *m*

repose [rɪˈpoz] *s* riposo ‖ *tr* posare, riporre ‖ *intr* riposare

reprehend [‚rɛprɪˈhɛnd] *tr* riprovare, rimproverare

represent [‚rɛprɪˈzɛnt] *tr* rappresentare

representation [‚rɛprɪsɛnˈteʃən] *s* rappresentazione; protesta; **representations** dichiarazioni *fpl*

representative [‚rɛprɪˈzɛntətɪv] *adj* rappresentativo ‖ *s* rappresentante *mf;* (pol) deputato

repress [rɪˈprɛs] *tr* reprimere

repression [rɪˈprɛʃən] *s* repressione

reprieve [rɪˈpriv] *s* tregua temporanea; sospensione della pena capitale ‖ *tr* accordare una tregua a; sospendere l'esecuzione di

reprimand [ˈrɛprɪ‚mænd] *or* [ˈrɛprɪ‚mɑnd] *s* sgridata, ramanzina ‖ *tr* sgridare, rimproverare

reprint [ˈri‚prɪnt] *s* ristampa; (*offprint*) estratto ‖ [riˈprɪnt] *tr* ristampare

reprisal [rɪˈpraɪzəl] *s* rappresaglia

reproach [rɪˈprotʃ] *s* rimprovero; vituperio ‖ *tr* rimproverare; **to reproach s.o. for s.th** rimproverare qlco di qlco, rimproverare qlco a qlcu

reproduce [‚riprəˈdjus] *or* [‚riprəˈdus] *tr* riprodurre ‖ *intr* riprodursi

reproduction [‚riprəˈdʌkʃən] *s* riproduzione

reproof [rɪˈpruf] *s* rimprovero

reprove [rɪˈpruv] *tr* rimproverare; disapprovare

reptile [ˈrɛptɪl] *s* rettile *m*

republic [rɪˈpʌblɪk] *s* repubblica

republican [rɪˈpʌblɪkən] *adj & s* repubblicano

repudiate [rɪˈpjudɪ‚et] *tr* ripudiare; rinnegare

repugnant [rɪˈpʌgnənt] *adj* ripugnante

repulse [rɪˈpʌls] *s* rifiuto; sconfitta ‖ *tr* rifiutare; (*e.g., an enemy*) sconfiggere

repulsive [rɪˈpʌlsɪv] *adj* ripulsivo

reputation [‚rɛpjəˈteʃən] *s* reputazione

repute [rɪ'pjut] *s* reputazione, fama ‖ *tr* reputare

reputedly [rɪ'pjutɪdlɪ] *adv* secondo l'opinione corrente

request [rɪ'kwest] *s* domanda, richiesta; **at the request of** su domanda di ‖ *tr* richiedere

Requiem ['rikwɪ ,em] or ['rekwɪ ,em] *adj* di Requiem ‖ *s* Requiem *m* & *f*; Messa di Requiem

require [rɪ'kwaɪr] *tr* richiedere

requirement [rɪ'kwaɪrmənt] *s* requisito; richiesta, fabbisogno

requisite ['rekwɪzɪt] *adj* requisito, richiesto ‖ *s* requisito

requisition [,rekwɪ'zɪʃən] *s* requisizione

requital [rɪ'kwaɪtəl] *s* contraccambio

requite [rɪ'kwaɪt] *tr* (*e.g., an injury*) contraccambiare; (*a person*) contraccambiare (with *dat*)

re-read [ri'rid] *v* (*pret & pp* -**read** ['red]) *tr* rileggere

resale ['ri ,sel] or [ri'sel] *s* rivendita

rescind [rɪ'sɪnd] *tr* annullare, cancellare; (law) rescindere

rescue ['reskju] *s* salvataggio, liberazione; **to go to the rescue of** andare al soccorso di ‖ *tr* salvare, liberare, soccorrere

research [rɪ'sʌrtʃ] or ['risʌrtʃ] *s* ricerca, indagine *f* ‖ *intr* investigare

re-sell [ri'sel] *v* (*pret & pp* -**sold** ['sold]) *tr* rivendere

resemblance [rɪ'zembləns] *s* somiglianza

resemble [rɪ'zembəl] *tr* somigliare (with *dat*), rassomigliare (with *dat*); **to resemble one another** rassomigliarsi

resent [rɪ'zent] *tr* (*a remark*) risentirsi per; (*a person*) risentirsi con

resentful [rɪ'zentfəl] *adj* risentito

resentment [rɪ'zentmənt] *s* risentimento

reservation [,rezər've ʃən] *s* riserva; (*e.g., for a room*) prenotazione

reserve [rɪ'zʌrv] *s* riserva; (*self-restraint*) riserbo, contegno ‖ *tr* riservare; prenotare

reservist [rɪ'zʌrvɪst] *s* riservista *m*

reservoir ['rezər ,vwar] *s* serbatoio, cisterna; (*large storage place for supplying community with water*) bacino di riserva; (fig) pozzo

re-set [ri'set] *v* (*pret & pp* -**set**; *ger* -**setting**) *tr* rimettere a posto; (*a watch*) regolare; (*a gem*) incastonare di nuovo; (*a machine*) rimontare

re-ship [ri'ʃɪp] *v* (*pret & pp* -**shipped**; *ger* -**shipping**) *tr* rispedire; (*on a ship*) reimbarcare ‖ *intr* reimbarcarsi

reshipment [ri'ʃɪpmənt] *s* rispedizione; (*on a ship*) reimbarco

reside [rɪ'zaɪd] *intr* risiedere

residence ['rezɪdəns] *s* residenza

resident ['rezɪdənt] *adj* & *s* residente *mf*

residential [,rezɪ'den ʃəl] *adj* residenziale

residue ['rezɪ ,dju] or ['resɪ ,du] *s* residuo

resign [rɪ'zaɪn] *tr* rassegnare, abbandonare; **to be resigned to** rassegnarsi a ‖ *intr* dimettersi, rassegnare le dimissioni

resignation [,rezɪg'ne ʃən] *s* (*from a job*) dimissione; (*submission*) rassegnazione

resin ['rezɪn] *s* resina

resist [rɪ'zɪst] *tr* resistere (with *dat*) ‖ *intr* resistere

resistance [rɪ'zɪstəns] *s* resistenza

resole [ri'sol] *tr* risolare

resolute ['rezə ,lut] *adj* risoluto

resolution [,rezə'lu ʃən] *s* risoluzione; **good resolutions** buoni propositi

resolve [rɪ'zɒlv] *s* risoluzione ‖ *tr* risolvere ‖ *intr* risolversi

resonance ['rezənəns] *s* risonanza

resort [rɪ'zɔrt] *s* (*appeal*) ricorso; (*for vacation*) centro di villeggiatura ‖ *intr* ricorrere

resound [rɪ'zaund] *intr* risonare

resounding [rɪ'zaundɪŋ] *adj* risonante; (*success*) strepitoso

resource [rɪ'sors] or ['risors] *s* risorsa

resourceful [rɪ'sorsfəl] *adj* ingegnoso

respect [rɪ'spekt] *s* rispetto; **respects** rispetti *mpl*, ossequi *mpl*; **with respect to** rispetto a ‖ *tr* rispettare

respectable [rɪ'spektəbəl] *adj* rispettabile; onesto, per bene

respectful [rɪ'spektfəl] *adj* rispettoso

respecting [rɪ'spektɪŋ] *prep* rispetto a

respective [rɪ'spektɪv] *adj* rispettivo

respiratory ['respɪrə ,torɪ] or [rɪ-'spaɪrə ,torɪ] *adj* respiratorio

respire [rɪ'spaɪr] *tr* & *intr* respirare

respite ['respɪt] *s* tregua, requie *f*; (*reprieve*) proroga, dilazione

resplendent [rɪ'splendənt] *adj* risplendente

respond [rɪ'spand] *intr* rispondere

response [rɪ'spans] *s* risposta

responsibili-ty [,rɪ spansɪ'bɪlɪtɪ] *s* (-ties) responsabilità *f*

responsible [rɪ'spansɪbəl] *adj* responsabile; (*job*) di fiducia; **responsible for** responsabile di

responsive [rɪ'spansɪv] *adj* rispondente; (*e.g., to affection*) sensibile; (*e.g., motor*) che risponde

rest [rest] *s* riposo; (*what remains*) resto; (mus) pausa; **at rest** in riposo; tranquillo, in pace; (*dead*) morto; **the rest** il resto, gli altri; **to come to rest** andare a finire; **to lay to rest** sotterrare ‖ *tr* riposare; (*to direct one's eyes*) dirigere; (*faith*) porre ‖ *intr* riposarsi, riposare; appoggiarsi; **to rest assured** (that) esser sicuro (che); **to rest on** aver fiducia in; basarsi su; (*one's laurels*) dormire su

restaurant ['restərənt] or ['restə ,rant] *s* ristorante *m*

restful ['restfəl] *adj* riposante, tranquillo

rest' home' *s* casa di riposo

rest'ing place' *s* luogo di riposo; (*of a staircase*) pianerottolo; (*of the dead*) ultima dimora

restitution [,restɪ'tju ʃən] or [,restɪ-'tu ʃən] *s* restituzione

restive ['rɛstɪv] *adj* irrequieto; *(e.g., horse)* recalcitrante

restless ['rɛstlɪs] *adj* irrequieto; *(night)* insonne, in bianco

restock [ri'stɑk] *tr* rifornire; *(e.g., with fish)* ripopolare

restoration [ˌrɛstə'reʃən] *s* restaurazione

restore [rɪ'stor] *tr* restaurare, ripristinare

restrain [rɪ'stren] *tr* ritenere, frenare; limitare

restraint [rɪ'strent] *s* restrizione; controllo, ritegno; detenzione

restrict [rɪ'strɪkt] *tr* restingere, limitare

restriction [rɪ'strɪkʃən] *s* restrizione

rest' room' *s* toletta; gabinetto di decenza

restructuring [rɪ'strʌkt/ərɪŋ] *s* ristrutturazione

result [rɪ'zʌlt] *s* risultato || *intr* risultare; **to result in** risolversi in, concludersi con

resume [rɪ'zum] *or* [rɪ'zjum] *tr* riprendere || *intr* ricominciare

résumé [ˌrɛzu'me] *or* [ˈˌrɛzju'me] *s* sunto, riassunto

resumption [rɪ'zʌmpʃən] *s* ripresa

resurface [ri'sʌrfɪs] *tr* mettere copertura nuova a || *intr* riemergere

resurrect [ˌrɛzə'rɛkt] *tr* & *intr* risuscitare

resurrection [ˌrɛzə'rɛkʃən] *s* risurrezione

resuscitate [rɪ'sʌsɪˌtet] *tr* rendere alla vita

retail ['ritel] *adj* & *adv* al dettaglio, al minuto || *s* dettaglio || *tr* dettagliare, vendere al minuto || *intr* vendere *or* vendersi al minuto

retailer ['ritelər] *s* dettagliante *mf*

retain [rɪ'ten] *tr* ritenere; *(a lawyer)* assicurarsi i servizi di

retaliate [rɪ'tælɪˌet] *intr* fare rappresaglie; **to retaliate for** ricambiare

retaliation [ˌrɪtælɪ'eʃən] *s* rappresaglia

retard [rɪ'tard] *s* ritardo || *tr* ritardare

retch [rɛtʃ] *intr* avere sforzi di vomito

reticence ['rɛtɪsəns] *s* riservatezza

reticent ['rɛtɪsənt] *adj* riservato, taciturno

retina ['rɛtɪnə] *s* retina

retinue ['rɛtɪˌnju] *or* ['rɛtɪˌnu] *s* seguito, corteggio

retire [rɪ'taɪr] *tr* ritirare; *(an employee)* giubilare, mettere a riposo || *intr* ritirarsi; andare a riposo; *(to go to bed)* andare a letto

retired [rɪ'taɪrd] *adj* *(employee)* in pensione; *(officer)* a riposo

retirement [rɪ'taɪrmənt] *s* ritiro; *(of an employee)* pensionamento, quiescenza

retort [rɪ'tɔrt] *s* risposta per le rime; controreplica; *(chem)* storta || *tr* rispondere per le rime a || *intr* rispondere per le rime

retouch [rɪ'tʌtʃ] *tr* ritoccare

retrace [rɪ'tres] *tr* ripercorrere; **to retrace one's steps** ritornare sui propri passi

retract [rɪ'trækt] *tr* ritrattare, disdire || *intr* disdirsi

re·tread ['ri ˌtrɛd] *s* pneumatico col copertone ricostruito || [ri'trɛd] *v* (*pret* & *pp* **-treaded**) *tr* ricostruire il copertone di || *v* (*pret* **-trod** ['trɑd]; *pp* **-trod** *or* **-trodden**) *tr* ripercorrere || *intr* rimettere il piede

retreat [rɪ'trit] *s* *(seclusion)* ritiro; (mil) ritirata; (eccl) esercizio spirituale; **to beat a retreat** battere in ritirata || *intr* ritirarsi

retrench [rɪ'trɛntʃ] *tr* ridurre, tagliare; (mil) trincerare || *intr* ridurre le spese; (mil) trincerarsi

retribution [ˌrɛtrɪ'bjuən] *s* ricompensa; (theol) giudizio finale

retributive [rɪ'trɪbjətɪv] *adj* retributivo

retrieve [rɪ'triv] *tr* riguadagnare, riconquistare; *(to repair)* risarcire; (hunt) riportare || *intr* riportare la presa

retriever [rɪ'trivər] *s* cane *m* da presa

retroactive [ˌrɛtro'æktɪv] *adj* retroattivo

retrofiring [ˌrɛtro'faɪrɪŋ] *s* accensione dei retrorazzi

retrogress ['rɛtrəˌgrɛs] *intr* regredire; retrocedere

retrorocket [ˌrɛtro'rɑkɪt] *s* retrorazzo

retrospect ['rɛtrəˌspɛkt] *s* esame retrospettivo; **in retrospect** retrospettivamente

retrospective [ˌrɛtrə'spɛktɪv] *adj* retrospettivo

re·try [ri'traɪ] *v* (*pret* & *pp* **-tried**) *tr* *(a person)* riprocessare; *(a case)* ritentare

return [rɪ'tʌrn] *adj* di ritorno; ripetuto || *s* restituzione; ritorno; profitto; *(of income tax)* dichiarazione; risposta; rapporto ufficiale; *(of an election)* responso; (sports) rimando, rimessa; **in return (for)** in cambio (di); **many happy returns of the day!** cento di questi giorni!; **returns** *(of an election)* responso, risultato || *tr* tornare, ritornare restituire; *(a favor)* contraccambiare; *(a profit)* dare; *(thanks; a decision)* rendere; (sports) ribattere || *intr* tornare; rispondere

return' ad'dress *s* indirizzo del mittente

return' bout' *s* (boxing) rivincita

return' mail' *s*—**by return mail** a volta di corriere, a giro di posta

return' tick'et *s* biglietto di ritorno; (Brit) biglietto di andata e ritorno

reunification [ri ˌjunɪfɪ'keʃən] *s* riunione, unificazione

reunion [ri'junjən] *s* riunione

reunite [ˌrijə'naɪt] *tr* riunire || *intr* riunirsi

rev [rɛv] *s* (coll) giro || *v* (*pret* & *pp* **revved**; *ger* **revving**) *tr*—**to rev up** (coll) imballare || *intr* (coll) accelerare, imballarsi

revamp [ri'væmp] *tr* rinnovare, rappezzare

reveal [rɪ'vil] *tr* rivelare, svelare

reveille ['rɛvəli] *s* sveglia, levata

rev·el ['rɛvəl] *s* baldoria || *v* (*pret* &

pp **-eled** or **-elled;** *ger* **-eling** or **-elling**) *intr* gozzovigliare; bearsi

revelation [ˌrevəˈleʃən] *s* rivelazione || **Revelation** *s* (Bib) Apocalisse *f*

revel·ry [ˈrevəlri] *s* (**-ries**) baldoria

revenge [rɪˈvendʒ] *s* vendetta || *tr* vendicare

revengeful [rɪˈvendʒfəl] *adj* vendicativo

revenue [ˈrevəˌnju] or [ˈrevəˌnu] *s* entrata, profitto; (*government income*) entrate *fpl* erariali

rev'enue cut'ter *s* motobarca della guardia di finanza

rev'enue stamp' *s* marca da bollo

reverberate [rɪˈvʌrbəˌret] *intr* riverberarsi; (*said, e.g., of sound*) ripercuotersi, risonare; (*said of an echo*) rimbalzare

revere [rɪˈvɪr] *tr* venerare, riverire

reverence [ˈrevərəns] *s* riverenza || *tr* ossequiare

reverend [ˈrevərənd] *adj & s* reverendo

reverent [ˈrevərənt] *adj* reverente

reverie [ˈrevəri] *s* sogno, fantasticheria

reversal [rɪˈvʌrsəl] *s* inversione, cambio; (law) annullamento

reverse [rɪˈvʌrs] *adj* rovescio, contrario; (mach) di retromarcia || *s* contrario; (*rear*) dietro; (*misfortune; side of a coin not bearing principal design*) rovescio; (mach) retromarcia || *tr* invertire; rovesciare; mettere in marcia indietro; **to reverse oneself** cambiare d'opinione; **to reverse the charges** far pagare al destinatario; (telp) far pagare al numero chiamato || *intr* invertirsi

revert [rɪˈvʌrt] *intr* ritornare

review [rɪˈvju] *s* (*critical article*) recensione; (*magazine*) rivista; (educ) ripasso, ripetizione; (mil) rivista || *tr* recensire; rivedere; (*a lesson*) ripassare; (mil) passare in rassegna

revile [rɪˈvaɪl] *tr* insultare, offendere

revise [rɪˈvaɪz] *s* revisione; (typ) seconda bozza || *tr* rivedere; correggere

revision [rɪˈvɪʒən] *s* revisione

revisionism [rɪˈvɪʒəˌnɪzəm] *s* revisionismo

revival [rɪˈvaɪvəl] *s* ripresa delle forze; (*restoration*) ripristino; (*of learning*) rinascimento; risveglio religioso; (theat, mov) ripresa

revive [rɪˈvaɪv] *tr* ravvivare; (*a custom*) ripristinare; (theat) dare la ripresa di || *intr* ravvivarsi; risorgere

revoke [rɪˈvok] *tr* revocare

revolt [rɪˈvolt] *s* rivolta || *tr* rivoltare || *intr* rivoltarsi

revolting [rɪˈvoltɪŋ] *adj* rivoltante

revolution [ˌrevəˈluʃən] *s* rivoluzione

revolutionar·y [ˌrevəˈluʃəˌneri] *adj* rivoluzionario || *s* (**-ies**) rivoluzionario

revolve [rɪˈvalv] *tr* far rotare; (*in one's mind*) rivolgere || *intr* girare, rotare

revolver [rɪˈvalvər] *s* rivoltella

revolv'ing book'case *s* scaffale *m* girevole

revolv'ing cred'it *s* credito rotativo

revolv'ing door' *s* porta girevole

revolv'ing fund' *s* fondo rotativo

revue [rɪˈvju] *s* rivista

revulsion [rɪˈvʌlʃən] *s* ripugnanza, avversione; (med) revulsione

reward [rɪˈword] *s* premio, ricompensa; (*money offered for capture*) taglia; (*for return of articles lost*) mancia competente || *tr* premiare, ricompensare

rewarding [rɪˈwordɪŋ] *adj* rimunerativo; gradevole

re·wind [riˈwaɪnd] *s* (*of a tape*) ribobinazione || *v* (*pret & pp* **-wound** [ˈwaund]) *tr* ribobinare

re·write [riˈraɪt] *v* (*pret* **-wrote** [ˈrot]; *pp* **-written** [ˈrɪtən]) *tr* riscrivere; (*news*) rimaneggiare, correggere

rhapso·dy [ˈræpsədi] *s* (**-dies**) rapsodia

rheostat [ˈri·əˌstæt] *s* reostato

rhesus [ˈrisəs] *s* reso

rhetoric [ˈretərɪk] *s* retorica

rhetorical [rɪˈtɑrɪkəl] or [rɪˈtɔrɪkəl] *adj* retorico

rheumatic [ruˈmætɪk] *adj & s* reumatico

rheumatism [ˈruməˌtɪzəm] *s* reumatismo

Rhine [raɪn] *s* Reno

Rhineland [ˈraɪnˌlænd] *s* la Renania

rhine'stone' *s* gemma artificiale

rhinoceros [raɪˈnɑsərəs] *s* rinoceronte *m*

Rhodes [rodz] *s* Rodi *f*

Rhone [ron] *s* Rodano

rhubarb [ˈrubɑrb] *s* rabarbaro; (slang) baruffa

rhyme [raɪm] *s* rima; **without rhyme or reason** senza capo né coda || *tr & intr* rimare

rhythm [ˈrɪðəm] *s* ritmo

rhythmic(al) [ˈrɪðmɪk(əl)] *adj* ritmico

rial·to [rɪˈælto] *s* (**-tos**) mercato || **the Rialto** il ponte di Rialto; il centro teatrale di New York

rib [rɪb] *s* costola; (*cut of meat*) costata; (*of umbrella*) stecca; (*of leaf*) nervatura; (aer, archit) centina; (naut) costa || (*pret & pp* **ribbed;** *ger* **ribbing**) *tr* (slang) prendersi gioco di

ribald [ˈrɪbəld] *adj* volgare, indecente

ribbon [ˈrɪbən] *s* nastro; (*decoration*) nastrino; **ribbons** (*shreds*) brandelli *mpl*

rice [raɪs] *s* riso

rich [rɪtʃ] *adj* ricco; (*food*) nutrito, grasso; (*wine*) generoso; (*voice*) caldo; (*color*) vivo; (*odor*) forte; (coll) divertente; (coll) assurdo; **to strike it rich** trovare la miniera d'oro || **riches** *spl* ricchezze *fpl*; **the rich** i ricchi

rickets [ˈrɪkɪts] *s* rachitismo

rickety [ˈrɪkɪti] *adj* (*object*) sgangherato; (*person*) vacillante; (*suffering from rickets*) rachitico

rid [rɪd] *v* (*pret & pp* **rid;** *ger* **ridding**) *tr* liberare, sbarazzare; **to get rid of** liberarsi di, sbarazzarsi di

riddance [ˈrɪdəns] *s* liberazione; **good riddance!** che sollievo!

riddle [ˈrɪdəl] *s* enigma *m*, indovinello; (*sieve*) crivello ‖ *tr* crivellare; (*to sift*) vagliare; (*s.o.'s reputation*) rovinare; **to riddle with** crivellare di

ride [raɪd] *s* scarrozzata; cavalcata; gita ‖ *v* (*pret* **rode** [rod]; *pp* **ridden** [ˈrɪdən]) *tr* cavalcare, montare, montare su; (*e.g., a bus*) andare in; (*the waves*) galleggiare su; attraversare; tiranneggiare; farsi gioco di; **to ride down** travolgere; sorpassare; **to ride out** uscire felicemente da ‖ *intr* cavalcare; fare una passeggiata, fare una gita; (*to float*) galleggiare; **to let ride** lasciar correre; **to ride on** dipendere da

rider [ˈraɪdər] *s* cavallerizzo; ciclista *mf*; viaggiatore *m*, passeggero

ridge [rɪdʒ] *s* (*of mountains*) crinale *m*, dorsale *f*; (*of roof*) displuvio; (*agr*) porca

ridge′pole′ *s* trave maestra, colmo

ridicule [ˈrɪdɪ‚kjul] *s* ridicolo; **to expose to ridicule** porre in ridicolo ‖ *tr* ridicolizzare

ridiculous [rɪˈdɪkjələs] *adj* ridicolo

rid′ing boot′ *s* stivalone *m* d'equitazione

rid′ing school′ *s* maneggio

rife [raɪf] *adj* comune, prevalente; **rife with** pieno di

riffraff [ˈrɪf‚ræf] *s* gentaglia

rifle [ˈraɪfəl] *s* fucile *m*; cannone rigato ‖ *tr* (*a place*) svaligiare; (*a person*) derubare; (*a gun*) rigare

rifle′ range′ *s* tiro a segno

rift [rɪft] *s* crepa, fessura; disaccordo

rig [rɪg] *s* attrezzatura, equipaggio; impianto di sondaggio (per il petrolio); (*outfit*) tenuta ‖ *v* (*pret & pp* **rigged**; *ger* **rigging**) *tr* attrezzare, equipaggiare; guarnire; abbigliare in maniera strana

rigging [ˈrɪgɪŋ] *s* (naut) padiglione *m*; (*tackle*) (naut) rizza; (coll) vestiti *mpl*

right [raɪt] *adj* giusto; corretto; (*mind*) sano; destro, diritto; (geom) retto; (geom) perpendicolare; **right or wrong** a torto o a ragione; **to be all right** star bene di salute; **to be right** aver ragione ‖ *s* diritto; quanto è giusto, (il) giusto; (*in a company*) interessenza; (*right hand*) destra; (*turn*) giro a destra; (boxing) diritto; (tex) dritto; (pol) destra; **by right** in giustizia; **on the right** alla destra; **to be in the right** aver ragione ‖ *adv* direttamente; completamente; immediatamente; proprio, precisamente; correttamente, giustamente; bene; alla destra; (coll) molto; **all right** benissimo ‖ *tr* drizzare; correggere; rimettere a posto ‖ *intr* drizzarsi

righteous [ˈraɪtʃəs] *adj* retto; virtuoso

right′ field′ *s* (baseball) campo destro

rightful [ˈraɪtfəl] *adj* giusto; legittimo

right′-hand drive′ *s* guida a destra

right-handed [ˈraɪtˈhændɪd] *adj* che usa la destra; destrorso

right′-hand man′ *s* braccio destro

rightist [ˈraɪtɪst] *adj* conservatore ‖ *s* conservatore *m*, membro della destra

rightly [ˈraɪtli] *adv* correttamente; giustamente; **rightly or wrongly** a torto o a ragione

right′ mind′ *s*—**in one's right mind** nel pieno possesso delle proprie facoltà, con la testa a posto

right′ of way′ *s* precedenza; (law) servitù *f* di passaggio; (rr) sede *f*

rights′ of man′ *s* diritti *mpl* dell'uomo

right′-wing′ *adj* della destra

right-winger [ˈraɪtˈwɪŋər] *s* membro della destra, conservatore *m*

rigid ‖ [ˈrɪdʒɪd] *adj* rigido

rigmarole [ˈrɪgmə‚rol] *s* sproloquio

rigorous [ˈrɪgərəs] *adj* rigoroso

rile [raɪl] *tr* irritare, esasperare

rill [rɪl] *s* rigagnolo

rim [rɪm] *s* orlo, bordo; (*of a wheel*) cerchione *m*

rime [raɪm] *s* brina; (*in verse*) rima ‖ *tr* brinare; rimare ‖ *intr* rimare

rind [raɪnd] *s* (*of animals*) cotenna; (*of fruit or cheese*) scorza

ring [rɪŋ] *s* (*for finger*) anello; (*anything round*) cerchio; (*circular course*) pista; (*of people*) crocchio; (*of evildoers*) combriccola; (*of anchor*) anello; (*sound of bell*) squillo; (*loud sound of bell*) scampanellata; (*of small bell; of glassware*) tintinnio; (*act of ringing*) sonata; (telp) chiamata; (fig) suono; (boxing) quadrato; (mach) ghiera; (fig, taur) arena; **to run rings around** essere molto migliore di ‖ *v* (*pret & pp* **ringed**) *tr* accerchiare; mettere un anello a ‖ *intr* formare cerchi ‖ *v* (*pret* **rang** [ræŋ]; *pp* **rung** [rʌŋ]) *tr* sonare; squillare; tintinnare; chiamare al telefono; **to ring up** chiamare al telefono; (*a sale*) battere sul registratore di cassa ‖ *intr* sonare; squillare; tintinnare; chiamare; (*said of one's ears*) fischiare; **to ring for** chiamare col campanello; **to ring off** terminare una conversazione telefonica; **to ring up** chiamare al telefono

ring-around-a-rosy [ˈrɪŋə‚raʊndəˈrozi] *s* girotondo

ringing [ˈrɪŋɪŋ] *adj* alto, sonoro ‖ *s* accerchiamento; squillo; tintinnio; (*in the ears*) fischio

ring′lead′er *s* capobanda *m*

ringlet [ˈrɪŋlɪt] *s* anellino

ring′mas′ter *s* direttore *m* di circo equestre

ring′side′ *s* posto vicino al quadrato

ring′worm′ *s* tigna

rink [rɪŋk] *s* pattinatoio

rinse [rɪns] *s* risciacquatura ‖ *tr* risciacquare

riot [ˈraɪ‚ət] *s* sommossa, tumulto; profusione; **to be a riot** (coll) essere divertentissimo; **to run riot** sfrenarsi; (*said of plants*) crescere disordinatamente ‖ *intr* tumultuare; darsi alle gozzoviglie

rioter [ˈraɪ‚ətər] *s* rivoltoso

rip [rɪp] *s* sdrucitura; (*open seam*) scucitura ‖ *v* (*pret & pp* **ripped**; *ger* **ripping**) *tr* sdrucire; (*to open the* *seam of)* scucire ‖ *intr* sdrucirsi; scucirsi; **to rip out with insults** (coll) prorompere in improperi

ripe [raɪp] *adj* maturo; *(lips)* turgido; *(cheese)* stagionato; pronto

ripen ['raɪpən] *tr & intr* maturare

ripple ['rɪpəl] *s* increspatura; *(sound)* mormorio ‖ *tr* increspare ‖ *intr* incresparsi; mormorare

rise [raɪz] *s (of prices, temperature)* aumento; *(of a road)* salita; *(of ground)* elevazione; *(of a heavenly body)* levata; *(in rank)* ascesa; *(of a step)* alzata; *(of a stream)* sorgente *f; (of water)* crescita; **to get a rise out of** (coll) farsi rispondere per le rime da; **to give rise to** dar origine a ‖ *v (pret* **rose** [roz]; *pp* **risen** ['rɪzən]) *intr (said of the sun)* sorgere; rialzarsi; *(said of plants)* crescere; *(said of the wind)* alzarsi; *(said of a building)* ergersi; *(to return from the dead)* risorgere; *(to increase)* aumentare; **to rise above** alzarsi al di sopra di; essere al di sopra di; **to rise to** sorgere all'altezza di

riser ['raɪzər] *s (of step)* alzata; *(upright)* montante *m;* **early riser** persona mattiniera; **late riser** dormiglione *m*

risk [rɪsk] *s* rischio; **to run or take a risk** correre un rischio ‖ *tr* rischiare

risk·y ['rɪskɪ] *adj* (**-ier; -iest**) rischioso

risqué [rɪs'ke] *adj* audace, spinto

rite [raɪt] *s* rito; **last rites** riti *mpl* funebri

ritual ['rɪtʃʊ·əl] *adj & s* rituale *m*

ri·val ['raɪvəl] *s* rivale *mf* ‖ *v (pret & pp* **-valed** or **-valled;** *ger* **-valing** or **-valling**) *tr* rivaleggiare con

rival·ry ['raɪvəlrɪ] *s* (**-ries**) rivalità *f*

river ['rɪvər] *s* fiume *m;* **down the river** a valle; **up the river** a monte

riv'er ba'sin *s* bacino fluviale

riv'er·bed' *s* letto di fiume

riv'er front' *s* riva di fiume

riv'er·head' *s* sorgente *f* di fiume

riv'er·side' *adj* rivierasco ‖ *s* riva del fiume

rivet ['rɪvɪt] *s* ribattino; *(of scissors)* perno ‖ *tr* ribadire; *(s.o.'s attention)* concentrare

roach [rotʃ] *s* scarafaggio

road [rod] *adj* stradale ‖ *s* strada; via; (naut) rada; **to be in the road of** ostacolare il cammino a; **to burn up the road** divorare la strada; **to get out of the road** togliersi di mezzo

roadability [ˌrodə'bɪlɪtɪ] *s* tenuta di strada

road'bed' *s (of highway)* piattaforma; (rr) massicciata, infrastruttura

road'block' *s* (mil) barricata; (fig) impedimento

road'house' *s* taverna su autostrada

road' la'borer *s* cantoniere *m*

road' map' *s* carta stradale

road' roll'er *s* compressore *m* stradale, rullo compressore

road' serv'ice *s* servizio di assistenza stradale

road'side' *s* bordo della strada

road'side inn' *s* taverna posta su autostrada

road' sign' *s* indicatore *m* stradale

road'stead' *s* rada

road'way' *s* carreggiata; strada

roam [rom] *s* vagabondaggio ‖ *tr* girovagare per ‖ *intr* girovagare

roar [ror] *s* ruggito, muggito; boato, fragore *m* ‖ *intr* muggire; **to roar with laughter** fare una risata

roast [rost] *s* arrosto; torrefazione ‖ *tr* arrostire; *(coffee)* tostare, torrefare; (coll) farsi beffe di ‖ *intr* arrostirsi

roast' beef' *s* rosbif *m*

roast'ed pea'nut *s* nocciolina americana abbrustolita

roast' pork' *s* arrosto di maiale

rob [rɑb] *v (pret & pp* **robbed;** *ger* **robbing**) *tr & intr* derubare

robber ['rɑbər] *s* ladro, malandrino

robber·y ['rɑbərɪ] *s* (**-ies**) furto

robe [rob] *s (of a woman)* vestito; *(of a professor)* toga; *(of a priest)* abito talare; *(dressing gown)* vestaglia; *(for lap)* coperta da viaggio; **robes** vestiti *mpl* ‖ *tr* vestire ‖ *intr* vestirsi

robin ['rɑbɪn] *s* pettirosso

robot ['robɑt] *s* robot *m*

robust [ro'bʌst] *adj* robusto

rock [rɑk] *s* roccia; *(any stone)* pietra; *(sticking out of water)* scoglio; *(one that is thrown)* sasso; *(hill)* rocca; (slang) pietra preziosa; **on the rocks** (coll) in rovina; (coll) al verde; *(said, e.g., of whiskey)* sul ghiaccio ‖ *tr* far vacillare; dondolare ‖ *intr* vacillare; dondolare

rock'-bot'tom *adj* (l') ultimo; (il) minimo

rock' can'dy *s* zucchero candito

rock' crys'tal *s* cristallo di rocca

rocker ['rɑkər] *s (curved piece at bottom of rocking chair)* dondolo; sedia a dondolo; (mach) bilanciere *m;* **off one's rocker** (slang) matto

rocket ['rɑkɪt] *s* razzo ‖ *intr* partire come un razzo

rock'et launch'er ['lɔntʃər] or ['lɑntʃər] *s* lanciarazzo

rock' gar'den *s* giardino piantato fra le rocce

rock'ing chair' *s* sedia a dondolo

rock'ing horse' *s* cavallo a dondolo

rock' salt' *s* salgemma *m*

rock' wool' *s* cotone *m* or lana minerale

rock·y ['rɑkɪ] *adj* (**-ier; -iest**) roccioso; traballante; (coll) debole

rod [rɑd] *s* verga, bacchetta; scettro; punizione; *(bar)* asta; *(for fishing)* canna da pesca; (anat, biol) bastoncino; (mach) biella; (surv) biffa; (Bib) razza, tribù *f;* (slang) pistola; **spare the rod and spoil the child** la madre pietosa fa la piaga cancrenosa

rodent ['rodənt] *adj & s* roditore *m*

rod'man *s* (**-men**) *s* aiutante *m* geometra

roe [ro] *s* capriolo; *(of fish)* uova *fpl*

rogue [rog] *s* furfante *m; (scamp)* pícaro

rogues'' gal'lery s collezione di fotografie di malviventi

rôle or **role** [rol] s ruolo, parte f; **to play a role** fare la parte

roll [rol] s (of film, paper, etc.) rotolo, bobina; (of fat) strato; (roller) rotella; (of bread) panino; (ondulazione; (noise) rullio, rullo; (of a boat) rollio; (of thunder) rombo; (list) ruolo; (of money) (slang) fascio; **to call the roll** fare la chiama || tr far rotolare; (one's r's) arrotare; (one's eyes) stralunare; (e.g., dough) spianare; (steel) laminare; (to wrap) arrotolare; (a drum) rullare; **to roll back** (prices) ridurre; **to roll out** spianare; srotolare; **to roll up** (one's sleeves) arrotolarsi; accumulare; aumentare || intr rotolare; rullare; arrotolarsi; raggomitolarsi; **to roll on** passare; **to roll out** srotolarsi; (to get out of bed) (slang) alzarsi

roll' call' s chiama, appello

roller ['rolər] s rotella; (for hair) bigodino; rotolo; (wave) ondata lunga

roll'er bear'ing s cuscinetto a rotolamento

roll'er coast'er s montagne russe

roll'er skate' s pattino a rotelle

roll'er-skate' intr pattinare coi pattini a rotelle

roll'er tow'el s bandinella

roll'ing mill' ['rolɪŋ] s laminatoio

roll'ing pin' s matterello

roll'ing stock' s (rr) materiale m rotabile

roll'-top desk' s scrivania a piano scorrevole

roly-poly ['roli'poli] adj grassoccio

roman ['romən] adj (typ) romano, tondo || s (typ) carattere romano, tondo || **Roman** adj & s romano

Ro'man can'dle s candela romana

Ro'man Cath'olic Church' s Chiesa Cattolica Apostolica Romana

romance [ro'mæns] or ['romæns] s romanzo; sentimentalità f; idillio, intrigo amoroso; (mus) romanza || [ro'mæns] intr scrivere romanzi; raccontare romanzi; fare il romantico || **Romance** ['romæns] or [ro-'mæns] adj romanzo, neolatino

Ro'man Em'pire s Impero Romano

romanesque [,romən'ɛsk] adj romantico || **Romanesque** adj & s romanico

Ro'man nose' s naso aquilino

romantic [ro'mæntɪk] adj romantico

romanticism [ro'mæntɪ,sɪzəm] s romanticismo

romanticist [ro'mæntɪsɪst] s romantico

romp [ramp] intr ruzzare

rompers ['rampərz] spl pagliacetto

roof [ruf] or [ruf] s (of house) tetto; (of heaven) volta; (of car) tetto, padiglione m; **to hit the roof** (slang) andare fuori dai gangheri; **to raise the roof** (slang) fare molto chiasso; (slang) protestare violentemente || tr ricoprire con tetto

roofer ['rufər] or ['rufər] s conciatetti m

roof' gar'den s giardino pensile

rook [ruk] s (bird) cornacchia; (in chess) torre f || tr truffare

rookie ['ruki] s novizio; (mil) recluta

room [rum] or [rum] s stanza, camera; vano, locale m; posto, spazio; opportunità f; **to make room for** luogo || intr alloggiare

room' and board' s vitto e alloggio

room' clerk' s impiegato d'albergo assegnato alle prenotazioni

roomer ['rumər] or ['rumər] s inquilino

room'ing house' s casa con camere d'affittare

room'mate' s compagno di stanza

room·y ['rumi] or ['rumi] adj (-ier; -iest) ampio, spazioso

roost [rust] s (perch) ballatoio; (house for chickens) pollaio; (place for resting) posto di riposo; **to rule the roost** essere il gallo del pollaio || intr appollaiarsi; andare a dormire

rooster ['rustər] s gallo

root [rut] or [rut] s radice f; **to get to the root of** andare al fondo di; **to take root** metter radici || tr inchiodare, piantare || intr radicare; (said of swine) grufolare; **to root for** fare il tifo per

rooter ['rutər] or ['rutər] s tifoso

rope [rop] s fune f, corda; (of a hangman) capestro; laccio, lasso; **to know the ropes** (coll) conoscere la faccenda a fondo, saperla lunga || tr legare con fune; prendere al laccio; **to rope in** (slang) imbrogliare

rope'danc'er or **rope'walk'er** s funambolo

rosa·ry ['rozəri] s (-ries) rosario

rose [roz] adj & s rosa

rose'bud' s bottoncino di rosa

rose'bush' s rosaio

rose'-col'ored adj color di rosa

rose'-colored glass'es spl occhiali mpl rosa

rose' gar'den s roseto

rosemar·y ['roz,meri] s (-ies) rosmarino

rose' of Shar'on ['ʃærən] s altea

rosette [ro'zet] s rosetta; (archit) rosone m

rose' win'dow s rosone m

rose'wood' s palissandro

rosin ['razɪn] s colofonia

roster ['rastər] s ruolino; orario scolastico

rostrum ['rastrəm] s tribuna

ros·y ['rozi] adj (-ier; -iest) rosa, roseo

rot [rat] s marcio; (coll) stupidaggine f || v (pret & pp **rotted**; ger **rotting**) tr & intr imputridire

ro'tary en'gine ['rotəri] s motore rotativo

ro'tary press' s rotativa

rotate ['rotet] or [ro'tet] tr & intr rotare

rotation [ro'teʃən] s rotazione; **in rotation** in successione, a turno

rote [rot] s ripetizione macchinale; **by rote** a memoria

rot'gut' s (slang) acquavite f di infima qualità

rotisserie [ro'tɪsəri] *s* girarrosto a motore

rotten ['rɑtən] *adj* marcio, fradicio; corrotto

rotund [ro'tʌnd] *adj* (*plump*) rotondetto; (*voice*) profondo; (*speech*) enfatico

rouge [ruʒ] *s* belletto, rossetto || *tr* dare il belletto a || *intr* darsi il belletto

rough [rʌf] *adj* scabroso; (*sea*) agitato; (*crude*) rozzo, rude; (*road*) accidentato; approssimativo || *tr—to rough it* vivere primitivamente; **to rough up** malmenare

rough'cast' *s* intonaco; modello di sgrossato || *v* (*pret & pp* **-cast**) *tr* (*a wall*) intonacare; disgrossare, dirozzare

rough' cop'y *s* brutta copia

rough-hew ['rʌf'hju] *tr* digrossare, dirozzare

roughly ['rʌfli] *adv* aspramente; rozzamente; approssimativamente

round [raund] *adj* rotondo || *s* tondo; (*of applause*; *of guns*) salva; (*of a single gun*) colpo, tiro; (*of a chair*) piolo; (*of a doctor*) giro; (*of a policeman*) ronda; serie *f*; (*of golf*) partita; (*e.g., of bridge*) mano *f*; cerchio; (*boxing*) ripresa || *adv* intorno; dal principio alla fine || *prep* intorno a; attraverso || *tr* (*to make round*) arrotondare; circondare; (*a corner*) scantonare; **to round off** arrotondare; completare, perfezionare; **to round up** raccogliere; (*cattle*) condurre

roundabout ['raundə,baut] *adj* indiretto || *s* giacca attillata; via traversa; giro di parole; (Brit) giostra; (Brit) anello stradale

round'house' *s* rimessa per locomotive

round-shouldered ['raund'foldərd] *adj* dalle spalle spioventi

round'-trip tick'et *s* biglietto d'andata e ritorno

round'up' *s* (*of cattle*) riunione; (*of criminals*) retata; (*of facts*) riassunto

rouse [rauz] *tr* svegliare; suscitare; (*game*) scovare || *intr* svegliarsi

rout [raut] *s* sconfitta, rotta || *tr* sconfiggere, mettere in rotta || *intr* grufolare

route [rut] *or* [raut] *s* via, rotta; itinerario || *tr* istradare

routine [ru'tin] *adj* ordinario || *s* trafila, routine *f*

rove [rov] *intr* vagabondare, vagare

rover ['rovər] *s* vagabondo

row [rau] *s* piazzata, scenata; (*clamor*) (coll) baccano; **to raise a row** (coll) fare baccano || [ro] *s* fila; (*of figures*) finca; (*e.g., of trees*) filare *m*; **in a row** in continuazione, di seguito || *tr* vogare || *intr* remare, vogare

rowboat ['ro,bot] *s* barca a remi

row·dy ['raudi] *adj* (**-dier; -diest**) turbolento || *s* (**-dies**) attaccabrighe *mf*

rower ['ro·ər] *s* rematore *m*

rowing ['ro·ɪŋ] *s* (*action*) voga; (*sport*) canottaggio

royal ['rɔɪ·əl] *adj* reale, regio

royalist ['rɔɪ·əlɪst] *adj* sostenitore del re || *s* realista *mf*

royal·ty ['rɔɪ·əlti] *s* (**-ties**) regalità *f*; membro della famiglia reale; nobiltà *f*; diritto d'autore; diritto d'inventore; percentuale *f* sugli utili

rub [rʌb] *s* frizione; difficile *m*; **here's the rub** qui sta il busillis || *v* (*pret & pp* **rubbed**; *ger* **rubbing**) *tr* fregare; **to rub elbows with** stare giunto a gomiti con; **to rub out** cancellare con la gomma; (slang) togliere di mezzo || *intr* sfregare; **to rub off** venir via sfregando; cancellarsi

rubber ['rʌbər] *s* gomma, cauccìu *m*; gomma da cancellare; (*overshoe*) caloscia; (*in cards*) rubber *m*; (sports) bella

rub'ber band' *s* elastico

rub'ber·neck' *s* (coll) ficcanaso; (coll) turista curioso || *intr* (coll) allungare il collo

rub'ber plant' *s* albero del cauccìu

rub'ber stamp' *s* timbro di gomma; (coll) persona che approva inconsultamente

rub'ber-stamp' *tr* timbrare; (coll) approvare inconsultamente

rubbish ['rʌbɪʃ] *s* spazzatura; immondizia; (fig) detrito; (coll) sciocchezza

rubble ['rʌbəl] *s* (*broken stone*) pietrisco; (*masonry*) mistura di malta e pietrame; (*broken bits*) calcinacci *mpl*

rub'down' *s* fregagione

rube [rub] *s* (slang) contadino gonzo

ru·by ['rubi] *adj* vermiglio || (**-bies**) *s* rubino

rudder ['rʌdər] *s* timone *m*; (aer) timone *m* di direzione

rud·dy ['rʌdi] *adj* (**-dier; -diest**) rubicondo

rude [rud] *adj* rude, sgarbato

rudiment ['rudɪmənt] *s* rudimento

rue [ru] *tr* lamentare, rimpiangere

rueful ['ruful] *adj* lamentevole; triste

ruffian ['rʌfɪ·ən] *s* ribaldo

ruffle ['rʌfəl] *s* increspatura; (*of drum*) rullo; (sew) gala, crespa || *tr* increspare; arruffare; irritare; (*a drum*) far rullare; (sew) guarnire di gala or crespa

rug [rʌg] *s* tappeto

rugged ['rʌgɪd] *adj* aspro, irregolare; rugoso; rozzo; forte; tempestuoso

ruin ['ru·ɪn] *s* rovina || *tr* rovinare, mandare in rovina

rule [rul] *s* regola; dominazione; (*reign*) regno; (law) ordinanza; (typ) filetto; **as a rule** in generale || *tr* governare; dominare; (*with lines*) rigare; (law) deliberare; **to rule out** escludere || *intr* governare; regnare; **to rule over** governare

rule' of thumb' *s* regola basata sull'esperienza; **by rule of thumb** secondo la propria esperienza

ruler ['rulər] *s* governante *m*, dominatore *m*; (*for ruling lines*) riga, regolo

ruling ['rulɪŋ] *adj* dirigente || *s* (*ruled lines*) rigatura; (law) decisione

rum [rʌm] *s* rum *m*; (*any alcoholic drink*) acquavite *f*

Rumanian [ruˈmɛnɪ-ən] *adj & s* rumeno

rumble [ˈrʌmbəl] *s* rimbombo; (*of the intestines*) gorgoglio; (*slang*) rissa fra ganghe rivali ‖ *intr* rimbombare; gorgogliare

ruminate [ˈrumɪ ˌnet] *tr & intr* ruminare

rummage [ˈrʌmɪdʒ] *tr & intr* rovistare, frugare

rum'mage sale' *s* vendita di cianfrusaglie

rumor [ˈrumər] *s* voce *f*, diceria ‖ *tr* vociferare; **it is rumored that** corre voce che

rump [rʌmp] *s* anca; posteriore *m;* (*of beef*) quarto posteriore

rumple [ˈrʌmpəl] *s* piega ‖ *tr* spiegazzare, sgualcire ‖ *intr* sgualcirsi

rumpus [ˈrʌmpəs] *s* tumulto; rissa; **to raise a rumpus** fare baccano

run [rʌn] *s* corsa; percorso; produzione; (*e.g., in a stocking*) smagliatura; direzione; (*spell*) serie *f*; (*in cards*) scala; (*of goods*) richiesta; (*on a bank*) afflusso; **in the long run** a lungo andare; **on the run** (coll) di corsa; in fuga; **the common run of men** la media della gente; **to give s.o. a run for his money** dare a qlcu del filo da torcere; essere denaro ben speso per qlcu, e.g., **that sweater gave me a run for my money** quello sweater è stato denaro ben speso per me; **to have a long run** tenere il cartellone per lungo tempo; **to have the run of** avere la libertà di andare e venire per ‖ *v* (*pret* **ran** [ræn]; *pp* **run;** *ger* **running**) *tr* muovere; (*a horse*) far correre; (*the street*) vivere liberamente in; (*game*) inseguire; trasportare; (*a machine*) far camminare; (*a store*) esercire; (*a candidate*) portare; (*a risk*) correre; (*a blockade*) violare; mettere, ficcare; (*a line*) tirare; **to run down** cacciare; esaminare; trovare; (*a pedestrian*) investire; denigrare, criticare; **to run in** (*a machine*) rodare; (slang) schiaffare in prigione; **to run off** creare di getto; cacciare; (typ) tirare; **to run up** ammassare ‖ *intr* correre; scappare; (*in a race*) arrivare; (*said of a candidate*) portarsi; passare; (*said of knitted material*) smagliarsi; (*said of a liquid*) scorrere; (*said of a color*) sbavare; (*said of fish*) migrare; funzionare; (*to become*) diventare; (*to be worded*) essere del tenore di; (com) decorrere; (theat, mov) durare in cartellone; **to run across** imbattersi in; **to run aground** incagliarsi; **to run away** fuggire; (*said of a horse*) prendere la mano; **to run down** (*said of a liquid*) scorrere; (*said of a battery, a watch*) scaricarsi; (*in health*) sciuparsi; **to run for** presentarsi candidato per; **to run in the family** essere una caratteristica familiare; **to run into** imbattersi in; ammontare a; (*to follow*) succedersi a; **to run off the track** (rr) uscire dalle rotaie; **to run out** aver termine; scadere; esaurirsi; **to run out of** rimanere senza; **to run over** oltrepassare; (*e.g., with a car*) investire; **to run through** trapassare; (*a fortune*) dilapidare; esaminare rapidamente

run'a·way' *adj* fuggiasco; (*horse*) che ha preso la mano ‖ *s* fuggiasco; cavallo che ha preso la mano; fuga

run'-down' *adj* esausto; negletto, cadente; (*watch, battery*) scarico

rung [rʌŋ] *s* (*of chair or ladder*) piolo

runner [ˈrʌnər] *s* corridore *m*; messaggero; fattorino, messo; (*of sleigh*) pattino; (*of ice skate*) lama; (*rug*) guida; (*on a table*) striscia di pizzo; (*in stocking*) smagliatura

run'ner-up' *s* (**runners-up**) finalista *mf* secondo

running [ˈrʌnɪŋ] *adj* in corsa; da corsa; (*water*) corrente; (*vine*) rampicante; (*knot*) scorsoio; (*sore*) purulento; (*writing*) corsivo; consecutivo; (*start*) (sports) lanciato ‖ *s* corsa; (*of a business*) esercizio; direzione; funzionamento; **to be in the running** avere possibilità di vittoria

run'ning board' *s* (aut) pedana

run'ning head' *s* titolo corrente

run·ny [ˈrʌni] *adj* (**-nier; -niest**) (*liquid*) scorrevole; (*color*) sbavante; **to have a runny nose** avere la goccia al naso

run'off' *s* ballottaggio

run-of-the-mill [ˈrʌnəvðəˈmɪl] *adj* ordinario, corrente

run'proof' *adj* indemagliabile

runt [rʌnt] *s* nanerottolo; animale deperito

run'way' *s* pista; (*of a stream*) letto; (*for animals*) chiusa; (aut) corsia

rupture [ˈrʌptʃər] *s* rottura; (pathol) ernia ‖ *tr* rompere; causare un'ernia a ‖ *intr* rompersi; soffrire di ernia

ru'ral free' deliv'ery [ˈrurəl] *s* distribuzione postale campestre

ruse [ruz] *s* astuzia, stratagemma *m*

rush [rʌʃ] *adj* urgente ‖ *s* fretta; slancio, corsa; (*of blood*) ondata; (*rushing of persons to a new mine*) febbre *f*; (bot) giunco; **in a rush** in fretta e furia ‖ *tr* affrettare; portare di fretta; spingere; (coll) fare la corte a; **to rush through** fare di fretta; (*e.g., a bill through Congress*) far approvare di fretta ‖ *intr* lanciarsi; affrettarsi; passare velocemente; **to rush through** (*a book*) leggere velocemente; (*one's work*) fare in fretta; (*a town*) attraversare velocemente

rush'-bot'tomed chair' *s* sedia di giunchi

rush' can'dle *s* lumicino con lo stoppino fatto di midollo di giunco

rush' hour' *s* ora di punta

russet [ˈrʌsɪt] *adj* color cannella

Russia [ˈrʌʃə] *s* la Russia

Russian [ˈrʌʃən] *adj & s* russo

rust [rʌst] *s* ruggine *f*; (fig) torpore *m* ‖ *tr* arrugginire ‖ *intr* arrugginirsi

rustic [ˈrʌstɪk] *adj & s* rustico

rustle [ˈrʌsəl] *s* fruscio; (*of leaves*) stormire *m* ‖ *tr* far frusciare; far stormire; (*cattle*) (coll) rubare ‖ *intr* frusciare; stormire; (coll) lavorare di buzzo buono

rust•y ['rʌsti] *adj* (**-ier; -iest**) rugginoso; color ruggine; fuori pratica

rut [rʌt] *s* (*track*) solco, carrareccia; (*of animals*) fregola; (il) solito tran tran

ruthless ['ruθlɪs] *adj* spietato

rye [raɪ] *s* segala; whiskey *m* di segala

S

S, s [es] *s* diciannovesima lettera dell'alfabeto inglese

Sabbath ['sæbəθ] *s* (*of Jews*) sabato; (*of Christians*) domenica; **to keep the Sabbath** osservare il riposo domenicale

sabbat'ical year' [sə'bætɪkəl] *s* anno di congedo; (Bib) anno sabbatico

saber ['sebər] *s* sciabola

sa'ber rat'tling *s* minacce *fpl* di guerra

sable ['sebəl] *adj* nero ‖ *s* zibellino; **sables** vestiti di lutto

sabotage ['sæbə,taʒ] *s* sabotaggio ‖ *tr* & *intr* sabotare

saccharin ['sækərɪn] *s* saccarina

sachet ['sæʃe] or [sæ'ʃe] *s* sacchetto profumato (per la biancheria)

sack [sæk] *s* sacco; (*of an employee*) (slang) licenziamento; (slang) letto ‖ *tr* insaccare; (*to lay waste*) saccheggiare, mettere a sacco; (slang) licenziare

sack'cloth' *s* tela di sacco; (*for penitence*) sacco, cilicio; **in sackcloth and ashes** pentito e contrito

sacrament ['sækrəmənt] *s* sacramento

sacramental [,sækrə'mɛntəl] *adj* sacramentale

sacred ['sekrəd] *adj* sacro

sacrifice ['sækrɪ,faɪs] *s* sacrificio; **at a sacrifice** in perdita ‖ *tr* sacrificare; (com) svendere

sacrilege ['sækrɪlɪdʒ] *s* sacrilegio

sacrilegious [,sækrɪ'lɪdʒəs] or [,sækrɪ'lidʒəs] *adj* sacrilego

sacristan ['sækrɪstən] *s* sagrestano

sacris•ty ['sækrɪsti] *s* (**-ties**) sagrestia

sad [sæd] *adj* (**sadder; saddest**) triste; (*bad*) cattivo; (*color*) tetro

sadden ['sædən] *tr* rattristare ‖ *intr* rattristarsi

saddle ['sædəl] *s* sella ‖ *tr* insellare; **to saddle with** gravare di

saddle'bag' *s* fonda

saddlebow ['sædəl,bo] *s* arcione *m* anteriore

sad'dle•cloth' *s* gualdrappa

saddler ['sædlər] *s* sellaio

sad'dle•tree' *s* arcione *m*

sadist ['sædɪst] or ['sedɪst] *s* sadico

sadistic [sæ'dɪstɪk] or [se'dɪstɪk] *adj* sadico

sadness ['sædnɪs] *s* tristezza

sad' sack' *s* (coll) marmittone *m*

safe [sef] *adj* sicuro; cauto; (*distance*) rispettoso; **safe and sound** sano e salvo ‖ *s* cassaforte *f*

safe'-con'duct *s* salvacondotto

safe'-depos'it box' *s* cassetta di sicurezza

safe'guard' *s* salvaguardia ‖ *tr* salvaguardare

safe•ty ['sefti] *adj* di sicurezza ‖ *s* (**-ties**) sicurezza; (*of a gun*) sicura; **to reach safety** mettersi in salvo

safe'ty belt' *s* (*of a worker*) imbraca; (aer, aut) cintura di sicurezza; (naut) cintura di salvataggio

safe'ty glass' *s* vetro infrangibile

safe'ty is'land *s* salvagente *m*

safe'ty match' *s* fiammifero svedese

safe'ty pin' *s* spillo di sicurezza

safe'ty ra'zor *s* rasoio di sicurezza

safe'ty valve' *s* valvola di sicurezza

saffron ['sæfrən] *s* zafferano

sag [sæg] *s* cedimento; depressione; (*of a rope*) allentamento ‖ *v* (*pret* & *pp* **sagged; ger sagging**) *intr* curvarsi; cedere, afflosciarsi; allentarsi; (*said of prices*) calare

sagacious [sə'geʃəs] *adj* sagace

sage [sedʒ] *adj* saggio, savio ‖ *s* saggio, savio; (bot) salvia

sage'brush' *s* artemisia

Sagittarius [,sædʒɪ'teri-əs] *s* Sagittario

sail [sel] *s* vela; (*of windmill*) ala; gita a vela; **to set sail** far vela; **under full sail** a piena velatura ‖ *tr* veleggiare, navigare; (*a boat*) far navigare ‖ *intr* veleggiare, navigare; far vela; volare; (*said of a vessel*) partire; **to sail into** (coll) attaccare

sail'boat' *s* nave *f* a vela, veliero

sail'cloth' *s* tela di olona

sailing ['selɪŋ] *adj* in partenza ‖ *s* partenza; navigazione; navigazione a vela

sail'ing ship' *s* veliero

sail'mak'er *s* velaio

sailor ['selər] *s* marinaio

saint [sent] *adj* & *s* santo ‖ *tr* santificare, canonizzare

saint'hood *s* santità *f*

saintliness ['sentlɪnɪs] *s* santità *f*

Saint' Vi'tus's dance' ['vaɪtəsəz] *s* (pathol) ballo di San Vito

sake [sek] *s* causa, interesse *m;* **for the sake of** per il bene di, per l'amor di

salaam [sə'lɑm] *s* salamelecco ‖ *tr* fare salamelecchi a

salable ['seləbəl] *adj* vendibile

salacious [sə'leʃəs] *adj* salace

salad ['sæləd] *s* insalata

sal'ad bowl' *s* insalatiera

sal'ad oil' *s* olio da tavola

sala•ry ['sæləri] *s* (**-ries**) stipendio

sale [sel] *s* vendita; (*at reduced prices*) svendita, saldo; **for sale** in vendita; **si vende, si vendono**

sales'clerk' *s* commesso, impiegato

sales'la'dy s (-dies) commessa, impiegata

sales'man s (-men) venditore m; commesso; (traveling) piazzista m

sales'man·ship' s arte f di vendere

sales' promo'tion s promozione delle vendite, promotion f

sales'room' s sala di esposizione; sala vendite

sales' talk' s discorso da venditore; (e.g., of a barker) imbonimento

sales' tax' s imposta sulle vendite

saliva [səˈlaɪvə] s saliva

sallow [ˈsælo] adj giallastro, olivastro

sal·ly [ˈsælɪ] s (-lies) escursione, gita; (outburst) esplosione; (witty remark) uscita; (mil) sortita ‖ v pret & pp -lied) intr fare una sortita; **to sally forth** balzar fuori

salmon [ˈsæmən] s salmone m

salon [səˈlɑn] s salone m

saloon [səˈlun] s taverna; (on a passenger vessel) salone m

saloon' keep'er s taverniere m

salt [sɔlt] s sale m; **to be worth one's salt** valere il pane che si mangia ‖ tr salare; (cattle) dare sale a; **to salt away** (coll) metter via, conservare

salt' bed' s salina

salt'cel'lar s saliera

saltine [sɔlˈtin] s galletta salata

saltish [ˈsɔltɪʃ] adj salmastro

salt'pe'ter s (potassium nitrate) salnitro; (sodium nitrate) nitro del Cile

salt' shak'er s saliera

salt·y [ˈsɔltɪ] adj (-ier; -iest) salato

salubrious [səˈlubrɪ·əs] adj salubre

salutation [ˌsæljəˈteʃən] s saluto

salute [səˈlut] s saluto ‖ tr salutare

salvage [ˈsælvɪdʒ] s ricupero ‖ tr ricuperare

salvation [sælˈveʃən] s salvezza

Salva'tion Ar'my s Esercito della Salvezza

salve [sæv] or [sɑv] s unguento ‖ tr lenire, alleviare

sal·vo [ˈsælvo] s (-vos or -voes) salva

Samaritan [səˈmærɪtən] adj & s samaritano

same [sem] adj & pron indef medesimo, stesso; **it's all the same to me** a me fa lo stesso; **just the same** lo stesso, ugualmente; ciò nonostante; **same . . . as** lo stesso . . . che

sameness [ˈsemnɪs] s uniformità f; monotonia

sample [ˈsæmpəl] s campione m, saggio ‖ tr (to take a sample of) campionare; (to taste) assaggiare; provare

sam'ple cop'y s esemplare m di campione

sancti·fy [ˈsæŋktɪˌfaɪ] v (pret & pp -fied) tr santificare

sanctimonious [ˌsæŋktɪˈmonɪ·əs] adj che affetta devozione ipocrita

sanction [ˈsæŋkʃən] s sanzione ‖ tr sanzionare

sanctuar·y [ˈsæŋktʃʊˌɛrɪ] s (-ies) santuario; **to take sanctuary** prendere asilo, rifugiarsi

sand [sænd] s sabbia ‖ tr insabbiare;

(to polish) smerigliare; cospergere di sabbia

sandal [ˈsændəl] s sandalo

san'dal·wood' s sandalo

sand'bag' s sacchetto a terra

sand'bank' s banco di sabbia

sand' bar' s cordone m litorale, banco di sabbia

sand'blast' s sabbiatura ‖ tr pulire con sabbiatura, sabbiare

sand'box' s cassone m pieno di sabbia; (rr) sabbiera

sand'glass' s orologio a polvere or a sabbia

sand'pa'per s carta vetrata ‖ tr pulire con carta vetrata

sand'stone' s arenaria

sandwich [ˈsændwɪtʃ] s panino imbottito, tramezzino ‖ tr inserire

sand'wich man' s tramezzino, uomo sandwich

sand·y [ˈsændɪ] adj (-ier; -iest) sabbioso; (hair) biondo rossiccio

sane [sen] adj sensato

sanguinary [ˈsæŋgwɪnˌɛri] adj sanguinario

sanguine [ˈsæŋgwɪn] adj fiducioso; (complexion) sanguigno

sanitary [ˈsænɪˌtɛri] adj sanitario

san'itary nap'kin s pannolino igienico

sanitation [ˌsænɪˈteʃən] s sanità f

sanity [ˈsænɪti] s sanità f di mente

Santa Claus [ˈsæntəˌklɔz] s Babbo Natale

sap [sæp] s linfa, succhio; (mil) trincea; (coll) scemo ‖ v (pret & pp sapped; ger sapping) tr scavare; insidiare, minare; (to weaken) indebolire

sapling [ˈsæplɪŋ] s alberello; (youth) giovanetto

sapphire [ˈsæfaɪr] s zaffiro

Saracen [ˈsærəsən] adj & s saraceno

sarcasm [ˈsɑrkæzəm] s sarcasmo

sarcastic [sɑrˈkæstɪk] adj sarcastico

sardine [sɑrˈdin] s sardina; **packed in like sardines** pigiati come le acciughe

Sardinia [sɑrˈdɪnɪ·ə] s la Sardegna

Sardinian [sɑrˈdɪnɪ·ən] adj & s sardo

sarsaparilla [ˌsɑrsəpəˈrɪlə] s salsapariglia

sash [sæʃ] s sciarpa; (around one's waist) fusciacca; (of window) telaio

sash' win'dow s finestra a ghigliottina

sas·sy [ˈsæsi] adj (-ier; -iest) (coll) impertinente; (pert) (coll) vivace

satchel [ˈsætʃəl] s sacca; (of schoolboy) cartella

sateen [sæˈtin] s satin m

satellite [ˈsætəˌlaɪt] s satellite m

satiate [ˈseʃɪˌet] tr saziare

satin [ˈsætən] s raso

satire [ˈsætaɪr] s satira

satiric(al) [səˈtɪrɪk(əl)] adj satirico

satirist [ˈsætɪrɪst] s satirico

satirize [ˈsætɪˌraɪz] tr satireggiare

satisfaction [ˌsætɪsˈfækʃən] s soddisfazione

satisfactory [ˌsætɪsˈfæktəri] adj soddisfacente

satis·fy [ˈsætɪsˌfaɪ] v (pret & pp -fied) tr & intr soddisfare

saturate [ˈsætʃəˌret] tr saturare

Saturday ['sætərdi] s sabato

Saturn ['sætərn] s (astr) Saturno

sauce [sɔs] s salsa; (of fruit) conserva; (of chocolate) crema; (coll) insolenza, impertinenza || tr condire; rendere piccante || [sɔs] or [sæs] tr (coll) rispondere con impertinenza a

sauce'pan' s casseruola

saucer ['sɔsər] s piattino

sau·cy ['sɔsi] adj (-cier; -ciest) impertinente; (pert) vivace

sauerkraut ['saur‚kraut] s sarcrauti mpl, crauti mpl

saunter ['sɔntər] s giro, bighellonata || intr girandolare, bighellonare

sausage ['sɔsɪdʒ] s salsiccia

savage ['sævɪdʒ] adj & s selvaggio

savant ['sævənt] s erudito

save [sev] prep tranne, salvo || tr salvare; (money) risparmiare; (to set apart) serbare; **to save face** salvare le apparenze || intr fare economia

saving ['sevɪŋ] adj economico; che redime || **savings** spl risparmi mpl, economie fpl || **saving** prep eccetto, salvo

sav'ings account' s conto di risparmio

sav'ings and loan' associa'tion s cassa di risparmio che concede mutui

sav'ings bank' s cassa di risparmio

savior ['sevjər] s salvatore m

Saviour ['sevjər] s Salvatore m

savor ['sevər] s sapore m || tr assaporare; (to flavor) saporire || intr odorare; **to savor of** sapere di; odorare di

savor·y ['sevəri] adj (-ier; -iest) saporoso; piccante; delizioso || s (-ies) (bot) santoreggia

saw [sɔ] s (tool) sega; detto, proverbio || tr segare

saw'buck' s cavalletto

saw'dust' s segatura

saw'horse' s cavalletto

saw'mill' s segheria

Saxon ['sæksən] adj & s sassone m

saxophone ['sæksə‚fon] s sassofono

say [se] s dire m; **to have no say** non aver voce in capitolo; **to have one's say** esprimere la propria opinione; **to have the say** avere l'ultima parola || v (pret & pp said [sed]) tr dire; **I should say so!** certamente!; **it is said** si dice; **no sooner said than done** detto fatto; **that is to say** vale a dire; **to go without saying** essere ovvio

saying ['se·ɪŋ] s detto, proverbio

scab [skæb] s crosta; (strikebreaker) crumiro

scabbard ['skæbərd] s guaina, fodero

scab·by ['skæbi] adj (-bier; -biest) crostoso; (animal) rognoso; (slang) vile

scabrous ['skæbrəs] adj scabroso

scads [skædz] spl (slang) un mucchio

scaffold ['skæfəld] s impalcatura; (to execute a criminal) patibolo

scaffolding ['skæfəldɪŋ] s incastellatura, ponteggio

scald [skɔld] tr scottare; (e.g., milk) cuocere al disotto del punto d'ebollizione

scale [skel] s (e.g., of map) scala;

piatto della bilancia; (of fish) squama; **on a large scale** in grande scala; **scales** bilancia; **to tip the scales** far inclinare la bilancia || tr squamare; (to incrust) incrostare; (to weigh) pesare; scalare; graduare; ridurre a scala || intr squamarsi; scrostarsi

scallion ['skæljən] s scalogno

scallop ['skaləp] or ['skæləp] s (for cooking) conchiglia; (mollusk) pettine m; (slice of meat) scaloppina; (on edge of cloth) dentello, smerlo || tr (fish) cuocere in conchiglia; dentellare, smerlare

scalp [skælp] s cuoio capelluto || tr scotennare; (tickets) fare il bagarinaggio di

scalpel ['skælpəl] s scalpello

scalper ['skælpər] s bagarino

scal·y ['skeli] adj (-ier; -iest) squamoso; scrostato

scamp [skæmp] s cattivo soggetto, briccone m

scamper ['skæmpər] intr sgambettare; **to scamper away** darsela a gambe

scan [skæn] v (pret & pp scanned) ger scanning) tr scrutare; dare un'occhiata a; (verse) scandire; (telv) analizzare, scandire, esplorare

scandal ['skændəl] s scandalo

scandalize ['skændə‚laɪz] tr scandalizzare

scandalous ['skændələs] adj scandaloso

Scandinavian [‚skændɪ'nevɪ·ən] adj & s scandinavo

scanning ['skænɪŋ] s (telv) esplorazione

scan'ning line' s (telv) riga di analisi

scant [skænt] adj scarso; corto || tr diminuire; lesinare

scant·y ['skænti] adj (-ier; -iest) appena sufficiente; povero, magro; (clothing) succinto

scapegoat ['skep‚got] s capro espiatorio

scar [skar] s cicatrice f; (fig) sfregio || v (pret & pp scarred; ger scarring) tr segnare, marcare; sfregiare || intr cicatrizzarsi

scarce [skers] adj scarso, raro; **to make oneself scarce** (coll) non farsi vedere

scarcely ['skersli] adv appena; a mala pena; non . . . affatto; **scarcely ever** raramente; non . . . affatto

scarci·ty ['skersɪti] s (-ties) scarsità f, scarsezza; carestia

scare [sker] s spavento || tr spaventare, impaurire; **to scare away** fare scappare per lo spavento; **to scare up** (money) (coll) metter insieme

scare'crow' s spaventapasseri m

scarf [skarf] s (scarfs or scarves [skarvz]) sciarpa; cravattone m; (cover for table) centro, striscia

scarf'pin' s spilla da cravatta

scarlet ['skarlɪt] adj scarlatto

scar'let fe'ver s scarlattina

scar·y ['skeri] adj (-ier; -iest) (timid) (coll) fifone; (causing fright) (coll) spaventevole scathing ['skeðɪŋ] *adj* severo, bruciante

scatter ['skætər] *tr* disperdere, sparpagliare || *intr* disperdersi, sparpagliarsi

scatterbrained ['skætər,brend] *adj* scervellato, stordito

scenari·o [sɪ'nɛrɪ,o] *or* [sɪ'nɑrɪ,o] *s* (-os) scenario

scenarist [sɪ'nɛrɪst] *or* [sɪ'nɑrɪst] *s* scenarista *mf*, sceneggiatore *m*

scene [sin] *s* (*view*) paesaggio; (*place*) scena; (theat) scena, quadro; **behind the scenes** dietro le quinte; **to make a scene** fare una scenata

scener·y ['sinəri] *s* (-ies) paesaggio; (theat) scenario

scenic ['sinɪk] *or* ['sɛnɪk] *adj* pittoresco; (*pertaining to the stage*) scenico

scent [sɛnt] *s* odore *m*; profumo; (*sense of smell*) fiuto, odorato; (*trail*) traccia, pista || *tr* profumare; (*to detect*) fiutare, annusare

scepter ['sɛptər] *s* scettro

septic ['skɛptɪk] *adj & s* scettico

sceptical ['skɛptɪkəl] *adj* scettico

scepticism ['skɛptɪ,sɪzəm] *s* scetticismo

schedule ['skɛdjʊl] *s* lista; programma *m*; (*of trains, planes, etc.*) orario || *tr* programmare; mettere in orario

scheme [skim] *s* schema *m*; piano, progetto; (*plot*) trama || *tr* progettare; tramare

schemer ['skimər] *s* progettista *mf*; (*underhanded*) manipolatore *m*, concertatore *m*

scheming ['skimɪŋ] *adj* intrigante, scaltro

schism ['sɪzəm] *s* scisma *m*

schist [ʃɪst] *s* scisto

scholar ['skɑlər] *s* (*pupil*) alunno; detentore *m* di una borsa di studio; (*learned person*) dotto, studioso

scholarly ['skɑlərli] *adj* erudito, studioso

scholarship ['skɑlər,ʃɪp] *s* erudizione; (*money*) borsa di studio

scholasticism [skə'læstɪ,sɪzəm] *s* scolastica

school [skul] *s* scuola; (*of a university*) facoltà *f*; (*of fish*) banco || *tr* istruire, insegnare

school' age' *s* età scolastica

school'bag' *s* cartella

school' board' *s* comitato scolastico

school'boy' *s* alunno, scolaro

school' bus' *s* scuolabus *m*

school' day' *s* giorno di scuola; durata della giornata scolastica

school'girl' *s* alunna, scolara

school'house' *s* scuola, edificio scolastico

schooling ['skulɪŋ] *s* istruzione

school'mas'ter *s* maestro di scuola; direttore scolastico

school'mate' *s* compagno di scuola, condiscepolo

school'room' *s* aula scolastica

school'teach'er *s* maestro

school' year' *s* anno scolastico

schooner ['skunər] *s* goletta

sciatica [saɪ'ætɪkə] *s* (pathol) sciatica

science ['saɪəns] *s* scienza

sci'ence fic'tion *s* fantascienza

sci'ence-fic'tion *adj* fantascientifico

scientific [,saɪən'tɪfɪk] *adj* scientifico

scientist ['saɪəntɪst] *s* scienziato

scimitar ['sɪmɪtər] *s* scimitarra

scintillate ['sɪntɪ,let] *intr* scintillare

scion ['saɪən] *s* rampollo, discendente *m*

scissors ['sɪzərz] *ssg or spl* forbici *fpl*

scoff [skɔf] *or* [skɑf] *s* dileggio, beffa || *intr* burlarsi; **to scoff at** burlarsi di, dileggiare

scold [skold] *s* megera || *tr & intr* sgridare, rimproverare

scoop [skup] *s* (*ladlelike utensil*) paletta; (*kitchen utensil*) cucchiaio, cucchiaione *m*; cucchiaiata; palettata; (*of dredge*) benna; (*hollow*) buco; (naut) gottazza; (journ) primizia, esclusiva; (coll) colpo || *tr* vuotare a cucchiaiate; (journ) battere; (naut) gottare; **to scoop out** (*e.g., sand*) scavare; (*soup*) scodellare

scoot [skut] *s* (coll) corsa || *intr* (coll) correre precipitosamente

scooter ['skutər] *s* monopattino

scope [skop] *s* ampiezza; lunghezza; **to give full scope to** dare piena libertà d'azione a

scorch [skɔrtʃ] *s* scottatura || *tr* bruciacchiare; bruciare, inaridire; (fig) ferire || *intr* bruciarsi

scorching ['skɔrtʃɪŋ] *adj* bruciante

score [skor] *s* (*in a game*) punteggio; (*in an examination*) nota; linea, segno, marca; (*twenty*) ventina; (mus) partitura; **scores** un mucchio; **to keep score** segnare il punteggio; **to settle a score** (fig) saldare un conto || *tr* raggiungere il punteggio di, fare; marcare; guadagnare; (*to censure*) sgridare, rimproverare; (mus) orchestrare

score'board' *s* quadro del punteggio

score'keep'er *s* segnapunti *m*

scorn [skɔrn] *s* disdegno, disprezzo || *tr & intr* disdegnare, disprezzare

scornful ['skɔrnfəl] *adj* disdegnoso

Scorpio ['skɔrpi,o] *s* Scorpione *m*

scorpion ['skɔrpi·ən] *s* scorpione *m*

Scot [skɑt] *s* scozzese *mf*

Scotch [skɑtʃ] *adj* scozzese || *s* scozzese *m*; whisky *m* scozzese; **the Scotch** gli scozzesi

Scotch'man *s* (-men) scozzese *m*

Scotch' pine' *s* pino silvestre

Scotch' tape' *s* (trademark) nastro autoadesivo Scotch

scot'-free' *adj* impune; **to get off scot-free** farla franca

Scotland ['skɑtlənd] *s* la Scozia

Scottish ['skɑtɪʃ] *adj* scozzese || *s* scozzese *mf*; **the Scottish** gli scozzesi

scoundrel ['skaundrəl] *s* birbante *m*, farabutto, manigoldo

scour [skaur] *tr* sgrassare fregando, pulire fregando; (*the countryside*) battere

scourge [skʌrdʒ] *s* sferza; (fig) flagello || *tr* sferzare

scout [skaʊt] *s* esplorazione; giovane esploratore *m;* giovane esploratrice *f;* (mil) ricognitore *m;* (nav) esploratore *m;* (slang) tipo ‖ *tr* esplorare, riconoscere; cercar di trovare; disdegnare

scouting ['skaʊtɪŋ] *s* scoutismo

scowl [skaʊl] *s* cipiglio ‖ *intr* aggrottare le ciglia; guardare torvamente

scram [skræm] *v* (*pret & pp* **scrammed;** *ger* **scramming**) *intr* (coll) tagliare la corda; **scram!** (coll) vattene!, (coll) escimi di tra i piedi!

scramble ['skræmbəl] *s* ruffa, gara ‖ *tr* (*to grab up*) arraffare; confondere, mescolare; (*eggs*) strapazzare ‖ *intr* arrampicarsi; (*to struggle*) azzuffarsi

scram'bled eggs' *spl* uova strapazzate

scrap [skræp] *s* pezzetto, frammento; ritaglio, rottame *m;* (coll) baruffa; **scraps** avanzi *mpl;* ‖ *v* (*pret & pp* **scrapped;** *ger* **scrapping**) *tr* scartare ‖ *intr* (coll) fare baruffa

scrap'book' *s* album *m* di ritagli (di giornale o fotografie)

scrape [skrep] *s* impiccio, imbroglio; baruffa ‖ *tr* raschiare, graffiare; **to scrape together** racimolare ‖ *intr* raschiare; **to scrape along** vivacchiare; **to scrape through** passare per il rotto della cuffia

scraper ['skrepər] *s* raschietto

scrap' i'ron *s* rottami *mpl* di ferro

scrap' pa'per *s* carta straccia; carta da appunti

scratch [skrætʃ] *s* graffio, scalfittura; scarabocchio; (billiards) punto perduto; (sports) linea di partenza; **from scratch** da bel principio; dal niente; **up to scratch** soddisfacente ‖ *tr* graffiare, grattare; (*e.g., a horse*) cancellare ‖ *intr* graffiare; (*said of a chicken*) raspare; (*said of a pen*) grattare

scratch' pad' *s* quaderno per appunti

scratch' pa'per *s* carta da appunti

scrawl [skrɔl] *s* scarabocchio ‖ *tr & intr* scarabocchiare

scraw-ny ['skrɔni] *adj* (**-nier; -niest**) ossuto, scarno

scream [skrim] *s* grido, strillo; cosa divertentissima; persona divertentissima ‖ *intr* gridare, strillare

screech [skritʃ] *s* stridio ‖ *intr* stridere

screech' owl' *s* gufo; (*barn owl*) barbagianni *m*

screen [skrin] *s* (*movable partition*) paravento; (*in front of fire*) parafuoco; rete metallica; (*sieve*) vaglio; (mov; phys) schermo; (telv) teleschermo ‖ *tr* schermare; riparare, proteggere; (*to sieve*) vagliare; (*a film*) proiettare; (*to adapt*) (mov) sceneggiare

screen' grid' *s* (rad, telv) griglia schermo

screen' test' *s* provino

screw [skru] *s* vite *f;* giro di vite; (*of a boat*) elica; **to have a screw loose** (slang) avere una rotella fuori di posto; **to put the screws on** far pressione su ‖ *tr* avvitare; (*to twist*)

torcere; **to screw up** (slang) rovinare; **to screw up one's courage** prendere il coraggio a quattro mani ‖ *intr* avvitarsi

screw'ball' *s* (slang) pazzoide *m,* svitato

screw'driv'er *s* cacciavite *m*

screw' eye' *s* occhiello a vite

screw' jack' *s* martinetto a vite

screw' propel'ler *s* elica

screw-y ['skru·i] *adj* (**-ier; -iest**) (slang) pazzo; (slang) fuori di posto, strano

scribble ['skrɪbəl] *s* scarabocchio ‖ *tr & intr* scarabocchiare

scribe [skraɪb] *s* (*Jewish scholar*) scriba *m;* copista *mf* ‖ *tr* tracciare, incidere

scrimmage ['skrɪmɪdʒ] *s* ruffa; (*football*) azione

scrimp [skrɪmp] *tr & intr* lesinare

script [skrɪpt] *s* scrittura, scrittura a mano; manoscritto; testo; (*e.g., of a play*) copione *m;* (typ) carattere *m* inglese

scriptural ['skrɪptʃərəl] *adj* scritturale, biblico

scripture ['skrɪptʃər] *s* scrittura ‖ **Scripture** *s* Scrittura

script'writ'er *s* soggettista *mf*

scrofula ['skrɑfjələ] *s* scrofola

scroll [skrol] *s* rotolo di carta, rotolo di pergamena; (*of violin*) riccio; (archit) voluta, cartoccio

scroll'work' *s* ornamentazione a voluta

scro·tum ['skrotəm] *s* (**-ta** [tə] or **-tums**) scroto

scrub [skrʌb] *s* boscaglia; alberelli *mpl;* animale bastardo; persona di poco conto; (*act of scrubbing*) fregata; (sports) giocatore *m* di riserva ‖ *v* (*pret & pp* **scrubbed;** *ger* **scrubbing**) *tr* pulire, fregare

scrub' oak' *s* rovere basso

scrub'wom'an *s* (**-wom'en**) lavatrice *f,* donna a giornata

scruff [skrʌf] *s* nuca, collottola

scruple ['skrupəl] *s* scrupolo

scrupulous ['skrupjələs] *adj* scrupoloso

scrutinize ['skruti,naɪz] *tr* scrutare, disaminare

scruti·ny ['skrutɪni] *s* (**-nies**) attento esame, disamina

scuff [skʌf] *s* graffio, logorio ‖ *tr* logorare, graffiare

scuffle ['skʌfəl] *s* zuffa, rissa ‖ *intr* azzuffarsi, colluttare

scull [skʌl] *s* (*oar*) remo a bratto; (*boat*) canotto ‖ *tr* spingere a bratto ‖ *intr* vogare a bratto

sculler·y ['skʌləri] *s* (**-ies**) retrocucina

scul'lery maid' *s* sguattera

scullion ['skʌljən] *s* sguattero

sculptor ['skʌlptər] *s* scultore *m*

sculptress ['skʌlptrɪs] *s* scultrice *f*

sculpture ['skʌlptʃər] *s* scultura ‖ *tr & intr* scolpire

scum [skʌm] *s* schiuma; (slag) scoria; (*rabble*) feccia, gentaglia ‖ *v* (*pret & pp* **scummed;** *ger* **scumming**) *tr & intr* schiumare

scum·my ['skʌmi] *adj* (**-mier; -miest**) spumoso; (coll) vile, schifoso

scurf [skʌrf] *s* (*shed by the skin*) squama; incrostazione

scurrilous ['skʌrɪləs] *adj* scurrile

scur·ry ['skʌri] *v* (*pret & pp* **-ried**) *intr* affrettarsi; **to scurry around** dimenarsi

scur·vy ['skʌrvi] *adj* (**-vier; -viest**) spregevole, meschino ‖ *s* scorbuto

scuttle ['skʌtəl] *s* (*for coal*) secchio; (*trap door*) botola; corsa, fuga; (naut) boccaporto ‖ *tr* aprire una falla in, affondare ‖ *intr* affrettarsi, darsi alla corsa

scut'tle·butt' *s* (naut) barilozzo dell'acqua; (coll) rumore *m*, diceria

scuttling ['skʌtlɪŋ] *s* autoaffondamento

Scylla ['sɪlə] *s* Scilla; **between Scylla and Charybdis** fra Scilla e Cariddi

scythe [saɪð] *s* falce *f*

sea [si] *s* mare *m*; (*wave*) maroso; **at sea** in alto mare; **by the sea** a mare, sulla costa; **to follow the sea** farsi marinaio; **to put to sea** prendere il largo

sea'board' *adj* costiero ‖ *s* litorale *m*

sea' breeze' *s* brezza marina

sea'coast' *s* costa, litorale *m*

sea' dog' *s* (*seal*) foca; (*sailor*) lupo di mare

seafarer ['si‚ferər] *s* marinaio; viaggiatore marittimo

sea'food' *s* pesce *m*; (*shellfish*) frutti *mpl* di mare

seagoing ['si‚go·ɪŋ] *adj* di alto mare

sea' gull' *s* gabbiano

seal [sil] *s* sigillo; (*sea animal*) foca; (fig) suggello ‖ *tr* sigillare, apporre i sigilli a; (fig) suggellare

sea' legs' *spl*—**to have good sea legs** avere piede marino

sea' lev'el *s* livello del mare

seal'ing wax' *s* ceralacca

seal'skin' *s* pelle *f* di foca

seam [sim] *s* (*abutting of edges*) giuntura; (*stitches*) costura, cucitura; (*scar*) cicatrice *f*; (*wrinkle*) ruga; (in *metal*) commettitura; (min) filone *m*, vena

sea'man *s* (**-men**) marinaio

sea' mile' *s* miglio marino

seamless ['simlɪs] *adj* senza giuntura; (*stockings*) senza cucitura

seamstress ['simstrɪs] *s* cucitrice *f*

seam·y ['simi] *adj* (**-ier; -iest**) pieno di cuciture; basso, sordido; (*unpleasant*) spiacevole

séance ['se·ɑns] *s* seduta spiritica

sea'plane' *s* idrovolante *m*

sea'port' *s* porto di mare

sea' pow'er *s* potenza navale

sear [sɪr] *adj* secco ‖ *s* scottatura ‖ *tr* scottare, bruciare; (*to brand*) marcare a fuoco; inaridire; (fig) indurire

search [sʌrtʃ] *s* ricerca, investigazione; (*frisking a person*) perquisizione; **in search of** in cerca di ‖ *tr* cercare, investigare; perquisire, frugare ‖ *intr* investigare; **to search for** cercare; **to search into** investigare

searching ['sʌrtʃɪŋ] *adj* (e.g., *inspec-*

tion) profondo; (e.g., *glance*) indagatore, penetrante

search'light' *s* proiettore *m*, riflettore *m*; (mil) fotoelettrica

search' war'rant *s* mandato di perquisizione

sea'scape' *s* vista del mare; (*painting*) marina

sea' shell' *s* conchiglia

sea'shore' *s* costa, marina, mare *m*

sea'sick' *adj*—**to be seasick** aver mal di mare

sea'sick'ness *s* mal *m* di mare

sea'side' *s* costa, riviera, marina

season ['sizən] *s* stagione; **in season di** stagione; **in season and out of season** sempre, continuamente; **out of season** fuori stagione ‖ *tr* (*food*) condire; (*to mature*) stagionare; (e.g., *wood*) stagionare

seasonal ['sizənəl] *adj* stagionale

seasoning ['sizənɪŋ] *s* condimento; (of *wood*) stagionamento

sea'son's greet'ings *spl* migliori auguri *mpl* per le feste natalizie

sea'son tick'et *s* biglietto d'abbonamento

seat [sit] *s* sedia; (*part of chair*) sedile *m*; (*of human body*) sedere *m*; (*of pants*) fondo; sito, posto; (e.g., *of government*) sede *f*; (*in parliament*) seggio; (e.g., *of learning*) centro; (rr, theat) posto ‖ *tr* far sedere; aver posti per; (*a chair*) mettere il sedile a; (*pants*) mettere il fondo a; (*an official*) insediare; (mach) installare; **to be seated** essere seduto; **to seat oneself** sedersi

seat' belt' *s* cintura di sicurezza

seat' cov'er *s* guaina, foderina

seat'ing room' *s* posti *mpl* a sedere

sea' wall' *s* diga

sea'way' *s* via marittima; alto mare; mare grosso; rotta percorsa; via di fiume accessibile a navi da trasporto

sea'weed' *s* alga marina; pianta marina

sea'wor'thy *adj* atto a tenere il mare

secede [sɪ'sid] *intr* separarsi, distaccarsi

secession [sɪ'sɛʃən] *s* secessione

seclude [sɪ'klud] *tr* appartare; isolare

seclusion [sɪ'kluʒən] *s* reclusione; solitudine *f*, intimità *f*

second ['sɛkənd] *adj & pron* secondo; **to be second to none** non cederla a nessuno ‖ *s* secondo; (*in a duel*) padrino; (*in dates*) due *m*; (aut, mus) secondo; **seconds** (com) articoli *mpl* di seconda qualità; **to have seconds on** servirsi una seconda volta di ‖ *tr* assecondare; (*a motion*) appoggiare ‖ *adv* in secondo luogo

second·y ['sɛkən‚deri] *adj* secondario ‖ *s* (**-ies**) (elec) secondario

sec'ond-best' *adj* (il) migliore dopo il primo; **to come off second-best** arrivare secondo

sec'-ond-class' *adj* di seconda qualità; (aer, naut, rr) di seconda classe

sec'ond hand' *s* lancetta dei secondi

sec'ond-hand' *adj* di seconda mano, d'occasione

sec'ond lieuten'ant s sottotenente m

sec'ond-rate' adj di seconda categoria; (inferior) da strapazzo

sec'ond sight' s chiaroveggenza

sec'ond wind' [wind] s—to get one's second wind riprendere fiato

secre•cy ['sikrəsi] s (-cies) segretezza; in secrecy in segreto

secret ['sikrɪt] adj & s segreto; in secret in segreto

secretar•y ['sekrɪ,teri] s (-ies) segretario; (desk) scrittoio

se'cret bal'lot s scrutinio segreto

secrete [sɪ'krit] tr nascondere; (physiol) secernere

secretive ['sikrɪtɪv] or [sɪ'krɪtɪv] adj riservato, poco comunicativo

sect [sekt] s setta

sectarian ['sek'teri-ən] adj & s settario

section ['sekʃən] s sezione; (of city) rione m; (of fruit) spicchio; (of highway) tronco; (rr) tratta || tr sezionare

sectional ['sekʃənəl] adj (e.g., book-case) componibile; sezionale; locale, regionale

secular ['sekjələr] adj & s secolare m

secularism ['sekjələ,rɪzəm] s laicismo

secure [sɪ'kjʊr] adj salvo, sicuro || tr ottenere; assicurare; fissare; (law) garantire

securi•ty [sɪ'kjʊrɪti] s (-ties) sicurezza; protezione; garanzia; (person) garante m; securities valori mpl, titoli mpl

sedan [sɪ'dæn] s (aut) berlina

sedan' chair' s bussola, portantina

sedate [sɪ'det] adj calmo, posato

sedation [sɪ'deʃən] s ritorno alla calma; stato di calma mentale

sedative ['sedətɪv] adj & s sedativo

sedentary ['sedən,teri] adj sedentario

sedge [sedʒ] s carice m

sediment ['sedɪmənt] s sedimento

sedition [sɪ'dɪʃən] s sedizione

seditious [sɪ'dɪʃəs] adj sedizioso

seduce [sɪ'djus] or [sɪ'dus] tr sedurre

seducer [sɪ'djusər] or [sɪ'dusər] s seduttore m, corruttore m

seduction [sɪ'dʌkʃən] s seduzione

seductive [sɪ'dʌktɪv] adj seduttore

sedulous ['sedjələs] adj diligente

see [si] s (eccl) sede f || v (pret saw [sɔ]; pp seen [sin]) tr vedere; to see off andare ad accompagnare; to see through portare a termine || intr vedere; see here! faccia attenzione!; to see after prender cura di; to see through conoscere il gioco di

seed [sid] s seme m, semenza; to go to seed andare in semenza; deteriorarsi || tr seminare; (fruit) togliere i semi da || intr seminare; produrre semi

seed'bed' s semenzaio; (fig) vivaio

seeder ['sidər] s (person) seminatore m; (machine) seminatrice f

seedling ['sidlɪŋ] s piantina da trapianto

seed•y ['sidi] adj (-ier; -iest) pieno di semi; (unkempt) malmesso, malvestito

seeing ['si-ɪŋ] conj visto che, dato che

See'ing Eye' dog' s cane m guida per ciechi

seek [sik] v (pret & pp sought [sɔt]) tr cercare, ricercare; to be sought after essere ricercato; to seek to cercare di

seem [sim] intr parere, sembrare

seemingly ['simɪŋli] adv apparentemente

seem•ly ['simli] adj (-lier; -liest) decoroso; appropriato

seep [sip] intr colare, filtrare

seer [sɪr] s profeta m, veggente m

see'saw' s altalena; (motion) viavai m || intr altalenare

seethe [sið] intr bollire

segment ['segmənt] s segmento

segregate ['segrɪ,get] tr segregare

segregation [,segrɪ'geʃən] s segregazione

segregationist [,segrɪ'geʃənɪst] s segregazionista mf

Seine [sen] s Senna

seismograph ['saɪzmə,græf] or ['saɪzmə,graf] s sismografo

seismology [saɪz'mɑlədʒi] s sismologia

seize [siz] tr afferrare; impossessarsi di; (with one's clenched fist) impugnare; comprendere; (law) sequestrare, confiscare

seizure ['siʒər] s conquista, cattura; (of an illness) attacco; (law) sequestro, pignoramento

seldom ['seldəm] adj di raro, raramente

select [sɪ'lekt] adj scelto, selezionato || tr prescegliere, selezionare

selectee [sɪ,lek'ti] s (mil) recluta

selection [sɪ'lekʃən] s selezione, scelta

selective [sɪ'lektɪv] adj selettivo

self [self] adj stesso || s (selves [selvz]) sé stesso; io, personalità f; all by one's self senza aiuto altrui || pron sé stesso

self'-abuse' s abuso delle proprie forze; masturbazione

self'-addressed' adj col nome e l'indirizzo del mittente

self'-cen'tered adj egocentrico

self'-con'scious adj imbarazzato, vergognoso, timido

self'-control' s padronanza di sé stesso, autocontrollo

self'-defense' s autodifesa; in self-defense in legittima difesa

self'-deni'al s abnegazione

self'-deter'mina'tion s autodeterminazione

self'-dis'cipline s autodisciplina

self'-ed'ucat'ed adj autodidatta

self'-employed' adj che lavora in proprio

self'-ev'i•dent adj evidente, lampante

self'-ex•plan'a•tor'y adj ovvio, che si spiega da sé

self'-gov'ernment s autogoverno; controllo sopra sé stesso

self'-im•por'tant adj presuntuoso

self'-in•dul'gence s intemperanza

self'-in'terest s egoismo, interesse m

selfish ['selfɪʃ] adj egoista

selfishness ['selfɪʃnɪs] s egoismo

selfless ['sɛlflɪs] *adj* disinteressato; altruista

self'-liq'ui·dat'ing *adj* autoammortizzabile

self'-love' *s* amor proprio

self'-made' *adj* che si è fatto da sé

self'-por'trait *s* autoritratto

self'-pos·sessed' *adj* calmo, padrone di sé

self'-pres'er·va'tion *s* conservazione

self'-pro·pelled' *adj* semovente

self'-re·li'ant *adj* pieno di fiducia in sé stesso

self'-re·spect' *s* rispetto di sé stesso

self'-right'eous *adj* che si considera più morale degli altri, ipocrita

self'-sac'ri·fice' *s* sacrificio di sé, spirito di sacrificio

self'-same' *adj* stesso e medesimo

self'-sat'is·fied' *adj* contento di sé

self'-seek'ing *adj* egoista || *s* egoismo

self'-serv'ice *s* autoservizio

self'-start'er *s* motorino d'avviamento

self'-styled' *adj* sedicente

self'-support' *s* indipendenza economica

self'-tap'ping screw' *s* vite *f* autofilettante

self'-taught' *adj* autodidatta

self-threading ['sɛlf'θrɛdɪŋ] *adj* autofilettante

self'-willed' *adj* ostinato, caparbio

self'-wind'ing *adj* a carica automatica

sell [sɛl] *v* (*pret & pp* **sold** [sold]) *tr* vendere; (*an idea*) fare accettare; **to sell off** svendere, liquidare; **to sell out** smerciare; vendere a stralcio; (coll) tradire || *intr* vendere, vendersi; fare il venditore; **to sell off** (*said of the stock market*) essere in ribasso; **to sell out** vendere a stralcio; vendersi

seller ['sɛlər] *s* venditore *m*

Selt'zer wa'ter ['sɛltsər] *s* selz *m*

selvage ['sɛlvɪdʒ] *s* cimosa, vivagno

semantic [sɪ'mæntɪk] *adj* semantico || **semantics** *s* semantica

semaphore ['sɛmə,for] *s* semaforo

semblance ['sɛmbləns] *s* apparenza, specie *f*; apparizione

semen ['simɛn] *s* sperma *m*

semester [sɪ'mɛstər] *adj* semestrale || *s* semestre *m*

semicircle ['sɛmɪ,sʌrkəl] *s* semicircolo

semicolon ['sɛmɪ,kolən] *s* punto e virgola

semiconductor [,sɛmɪkən'dʌktər] *s* semiconduttore *m*

semiconscious [,sɛmi'kɑnʃəs] *adj* mezzo cosciente

semifinal [,sɛmi'faɪnəl] *s* semifinale *f*

semilearned [,sɛmi'lʌrnɪd] *adj* semidotto

semimonth·ly [,sɛmi'mʌnθli] or [,sɛmaɪ'mʌnθli] *adj* quindicinale || *s* (-lies) rivista quindicinale

seminar ['sɛmɪ,nɑr] or [,sɛmɪ'nɑr] *s* seminario

seminar·y ['sɛmɪ,nɛri] *s* (-ies) seminario

Semite ['sɛmaɪt] or ['simaɪt] *s* semita *mf*

Semitic [sɪ'mɪtɪk] *adj* semitico || *s* lingua semitica; (*family of languages*) semitico

semitrailer ['sɛmɪ,trelər] *s* semirimorchio

semiweek·ly [,sɛmi'wikli] or [,sɛmaɪ'wikli] *adj* bisettimanale || *s* (-lies) periodico bisettimanale

semiyearly [,sɛmi'jɪrli] or [,sɛmaɪ'jɪrli] *adj* semestrale || *adv* due volte all'anno

senate ['sɛnɪt] *s* senato

senator ['sɛnətər] *s* senatore *m*

send [sɛnd] *v* (*pret & pp* **sent** [sɛnt]) *tr* inviare, mandare; spedire; (*e.g., a punch*) lanciare; **to send back** rimandare; **to send forth** emettere; **to send packing** licenziare su due piedi || *intr* (rad) trasmettere; **to send for** mandare a chiamare, far venire

sender ['sɛndər] *s* speditore *m*, mittente *m*; (telg) trasmettitore *m*

send'-off' *s* (coll) addio affettuoso; (coll) lancio

senility [sɪ'nɪlɪti] *s* (pathol) senilismo

senior ['sinjər] *adj* maggiore, più anziano; seniore, di grado più elevato; dell'ultimo anno, laureando; senior, il vecchio || *s* maggiore *m*; seniore *m*, persona di grado più elevato; studente *m* dell'ultimo anno, laureando

sen'ior cit'izen *s* vecchio, pensionato

seniority [sin'jɑrɪti] or [sin'jɔrɪti] *s* anzianità *f*

sensation [sɛn'seʃən] *s* sensazione

sensational [sɛn'seʃənəl] *adj* sensazionale

sense [sɛns] *s* senso; **in a sense** in un certo senso; **to come to one's senses** riprendere il giudizio; **to make sense out of** arrivare a capire; **to take leave of one's senses** perdere il ben dell'intelletto || *tr* intuire; comprendere

senseless ['sɛnslɪs] *adj* (*unconscious*) privo di sensi; (*meaningless*) insensato, privo di senso

sense' or'gan *s* organo di senso

sensibili·ty [,sɛnsɪ'bɪlɪti] *s* (-ties) sensibilità *f*; **sensibilities** suscettibilità *f*

sensible ['sɛnsɪbəl] *adj* sensato; (*keenly aware*) sensibile; cosciente

sensitive ['sɛnsɪtɪv] *adj* sensitivo, sensibile; delicato

sensitize ['sɛnsɪ,taɪz] *tr* sensibilizzare

sensory ['sɛnsəri] *adj* sensorio

sensual ['sɛn/ʊ·əl] *adj* sensuale

sensuous ['sɛn/ʊ·əs] *adj* sensuale

sentence ['sɛntəns] *s* (gram) frase; (law) sentenza, condanna || *tr* sentenziare, condannare

sentiment ['sɛntɪmənt] *s* sentimento

sentimental [,sɛntɪ'mɛntəl] *adj* sentimentale

sentimentalism [,sɛntɪ'mɛntəl,ɪzəm] *s* sentimentalismo

sentinel ['sɛntɪnəl] *s* sentinella; **to stand sentinel** montare di sentinella

sen·try ['sɛntri] *s* (-tries) sentinella

sen'try box' *s* garitta, casotto

separate ['sɛpərɪt] *adj* separato ||

['sepə,ret] *tr* separare ‖ *intr* separarsi

separation [,sepə're∫ən] *s* separazione

Sephardic [sɪ'fɑrdɪk] *adj* sefardita

September [sep'tembər] *s* settembre *m*

septic ['septɪk] *adj* settico

sep'tic tank' *s* fossa settica

sepulcher ['sepəlkər] *s* sepolcro

sequel ['sikwəl] *s* seguito

sequence ['sikwəns] *s* serie *f*, sequenza, successione; conseguenza; (cards, eccl, mov) sequenza; (gram) correlazione

sequester [sɪ'kwestər] *tr* isolare, appartare; (law) sequestrare

sequin ['sikwɪn] *s* lustrino

ser·aph ['serəf] *s* (**-aphs** or **-aphim** [əfɪm]) serafino

Serbian ['sʌrbɪ-ən] *adj & s* serbo

Serbo-Croatian [,sʌrbokro'e∫ən] *adj & s* serbocroato

sere [sɪr] *adj* secco, appassito

serenade [,serə'ned] *s* serenata ‖ *tr* fare la serenata a ‖ *intr* fare la serenata

serene [sɪ'rin] *adj* sereno

serenity [sɪ'renɪti] *s* serenità *f*

serf [sʌrf] *s* servo della gleba

serfdom ['sʌrfdəm] *s* servitù *f* della gleba

serge [sʌrdʒ] *s* saia

sergeant ['sɑrdʒənt] *s* sergente *m*

ser'geant at arms' *s* (**ser'geants at arms'**) ufficiale *m* delegato a mantenere l'ordine

ser'geant ma'jor *s* (**sergeants major** or **sergeant majors**) (*in U.S. Army*) sergente *m* maggiore; (*in Italian Army*) maresciallo

serial ['sɪrɪ-əl] *adj* a puntate, a dispense ‖ *s* periodico; romanzo a puntate; programma *m* a serie

se'rial num'ber *s* matricola; (*of a book*) segnatura; (aut) matricola di telaio

se·ries ['sɪrɪz] *s* (**-ries**) serie *f*; (*works dealing with the same topic*) collana; **in series** (elec) in serie

serious ['sɪrɪ·əs] *adj* serio

seriousness ['sɪrɪ-əsnɪs] *s* serietà *f*; **in all seriousness** molto sul serio

sermon ['sʌrmən] *s* sermone *m*

sermonize ['sʌrmə,naɪz] *tr & intr* sermonare

serpent ['sʌrpənt] *s* serpente *m*

se·rum ['sɪrəm] *s* (**-rums** or **-ra** [rə]) siero

servant ['sʌrvənt] *s* servo, domestico; (*civil servant*) funzionario; (fig) servitore *m*

serv'ant girl' *s* serva, domestica

serv'ant prob'lem *s* crisi *f* ancillare

serve [sʌrv] *s* (*in tennis*) servizio ‖ *tr* servire; (*a sentence*) espiare; (*to suffice*) bastare (with *dat*); (*a writ*) notificare; **to serve s.o. right** stare bene (with *dat*), e.g., **it serves him right** gli sta bene ‖ *intr* servire; **to serve as** fare da

service ['sʌrvɪs] *s* servizio; (*of a writ*) notifica; (*branch of the armed forces*) arma; **at your service** per servirLa ‖ *tr* rifornire, riparare

serviceable ['sʌrvɪsəbəl] *adj* utile; durevole; pratico; riparabile

serv'ice club' *s* casa del soldato

serv'ice·man' *s* (**-men'**) militare *m;* riparatore *m*, aggiustatore *m*

serv'ice mod'ule *s* modulo di servizio

serv'ice rec'ord *s* stato di servizio

serv'ice sta'tion *s* stazione di servizio or di rifornimento

serv'ice-sta'tion attend'ant *s* benzinaio

serv'ice stripe' *s* gallone *m*

servile ['sʌrvɪl] *adj* servile

servitude ['sʌrvɪ,tjud] or ['sʌrvɪ,tud] *s* servitù *f;* lavori forzati

sesame ['sesəmi] *s* sesamo; **open sesame** apriti sesamo

session ['se∫ən] *s* sessione *f*, seduta

set [set] *adj* determinato, preordinato; abituale; fisso, rigido; (*ready*) pronto; meditato, studiato ‖ *s* (*e.g., of books*) collezione, serie *f*; (*e.g., of chess*) gioco; set *m*, insieme *m*, completo; (*of tires*) treno; (*of horses*) pariglia; (*of tennis*) partita; (*of dishes*) servizio; (*of kitchen utensils*) batteria; posizione, atteggiamento; (*of a garment*) linea; (*e.g., of cement*) presa; (*of people*) gruppo; (*of thieves*) genìa; (*of sails*) muta; (*of lines*) (geom) fascio; (rad, telv) apparato; (theat, mov) set *m* ‖ *v* (*pret & pp* **set**; *ger* **setting**) *tr* porre, deporre; mettere; (*fire*) dare; (*the table*) imbandire; (*a watch*) regolare; (*s.o. a certain number of tricks*) far cadere di; (*a price*) fissare; (*a gem*) incastonare; (*a fracture*) mettere a posto; (*a saw*) allicciare; (*a trap*) tendere; (*hair*) acconciare; stabilire; insediare; (*to plant*) piantare; (*a sail*) tendere; (*e.g., milk*) rapprendere; calibrare, tarare; (*cement*) solidificare; (typ) comporre; **to set back** ritardare; (*a clock*) mettere indietro; **to set forth** descrivere; **to set one's heart on** desiderare ardentemente; **to set store by** tenere in gran conto; **to set up** metter su; impiantare; (*drinks*) (slang) pagare ‖ *intr* (*said, e.g., of the sun*) tramontare; (*said of a liquid*) solidificarsi; (*said of cement*) fare presa; (*said of milk*) rapprendersi; (*said of a hen*) covare; (*said of a garment*) cascare; (*said of hair*) prendere la piega; **to set about** mettersi a; **to set out** porsi in cammino; **to set out to** mettersi a; **to set to work** mettersi a lavorare; **to set upon** attaccare

set'back' *s* rovescio, contrarietà *f*

set'screw' *s* vite *f* di pressione

setting ['setɪŋ] *s* (*environment*) ambiente *m;* (*of a gem*) montatura; (*of cement*) presa; (*e.g., of the sun*) tramonto; (theat) scenario; (mus) arrangiamento

set'ting-up' ex'ercises *spl* ginnastica da camera

settle ['setəl] *tr* determinare, risolvere; sistemare, regolare; (*a bill*) liquidare; installarsi in, colonizzare; calmare; (*a liquid*) far depositare; (law) conciliare || *intr* mettersi d'accordo; saldare un conto; stanziarsi, domiciliarsi; fermarsi, posare; (*said of a liquid*) depositare, calmarsi; solidificarsi; **to settle down to work** mettersi a lavorare di buzzo buono; **to settle on** scegliere, fissare

settlement ['sɛtlmənt] *s* stabilimento; sistemazione, regolamento; colonia, comunità *f*; (*of a building*) infossamento; agenzia di beneficenza

settler ['sɛtlər] *s* fondatore *m*; colono; conciliatore *m*

set'up' *s* portamento; (*e.g., of tools*) disposizione; quanto è necessario per mescolare una bibita alcolica; (coll) incontro truccato

seven ['sɛvən] *adj & pron* sette || *s* sette *m*; **seven o'clock** le sette

sev'en hun'dred *adj, s & pron* settecento

seventeen ['sɛvən'tin] *adj, s & pron* diciassette *m*

seventeenth ['sɛvən'tinθ] *adj, s & pron* diciassettesimo || *s* (*in dates*) diciassette *m*

seventh ['sɛvənθ] *adj, s & pron* settimo || *s* (*in dates*) sette *m*

seventieth ['sɛvənti·iθ] *adj, s & pron* settantesimo

seven·ty ['sɛvənti] *adj & pron* settanta || *s* (**-ties**) settanta *m*; **the seventies** gli anni settanta

sever ['sɛvər] *tr* tagliare, mozzare; (*relations*) troncare || *intr* separarsi

several ['sɛvərəl] *adj* parecchi, vari; rispettivi || *spl* parecchi *mpl*

sev'erance pay' ['sɛvərəns] *s* buonuscita, indennità *f* di licenziamento

severe [sɪ'vɪr] *adj* severo; (*weather*) rigido; (*pain*) acuto; (*illness*) grave

sew [so] *v* (*pret* **sewed**; *pp* **sewed** or **sewn**) *tr & intr* cucire

sewage ['su·ɪdʒ] or ['sju·ɪdʒ] *s* acque *fpl* di scolo or di rifiuto

sewer ['su·ər] or ['sju·ər] *s* fogna, chiavica

sewerage ['su·ərɪdʒ] or ['sju·ərɪdʒ] *s* fognatura; drenaggio, rimozione delle acque di rifiuto

sew'ing machine' ['so·ɪŋ] *s* macchina da cucire

sex [sɛks] *s* sesso

sex' appeal' *s* attrattiva fisica, sex appeal *m*

sextant ['sɛkstənt] *s* sestante *m*

sextet [sɛks'tɛt] *s* sestetto

sexton ['sɛkstən] *s* sagrestano

sexual ['sɛk/u·əl] *adj* sessuale

sex·y ['sɛksi] *adj* (**-ier; -iest**) (coll) erotico; (coll) procace

shab·by ['/æbi] *adj* (**-bier; -biest**) (*clothes*) frusto; (*house*) malandato; (*person*) malvestito; (*deal*) cattivo

shack [/æk] *s* baracca

shackle ['/ækəl] *s* ceppo; (*to tie an animal*) pastoia; (fig) ostacolo; **shackles** ceppi *mpl*, manette *fpl* || *tr* mettere in ceppi; (fig) inceppare

shad [/æd] *s* alosa

shade [/ed] *s* ombra; (*of lamp*) paralume *m*; (*of window*) tendina; (*for*

the eyes) visiera; (*hue*) tinta, sfumatura; **a shade of** un po' di; **shades** tenebre *fpl*; ombre *fpl* || *tr* ombreggiare; sfumare, digradare; (*a price*) ribassare leggermente

shadow ['/ædo] *s* ombra || *tr* ombreggiare; (*to follow*) pedinare; **to shadow forth** adombrare, preannunciare

shadowy ['/ædo·i] *adj* ombroso, ombreggiato; illusorio, chimerico

shad·y ['/edi] *adj* (**-ier; -iest**) ombroso; spettrale; (coll) losco; **to keep shady** (slang) starsene lontano

shaft [/æft] or [/ɑft] *s* (*of arrow*) asta; (*of feather*) rachide *f*; (*of light*) raggio; (*handle*) manico; (*of wagon*) stanga, timone *m*; (*of motor*) albero; (*of column*) fusto; (*of elevator*) pozzo; (*in a mountain*) camino; (min) fornello; (fig) frecciata

shag·gy ['/ægi] *adj* (**-gier; -giest**) peloso, irsuto; (*unkempt*) trasandato; (*cloth*) ruvido

shag'gy dog' sto'ry *s* storiella senza capo né coda

shake [/ek] *s* scossa; stretta di mano; momento, istante *m*; **the shakes** la tremarella || *v* (*pret* **shook** [/ʊk]; *pp* **shaken**) *tr* scuotere; scrollare; (*s.o.'s hands*) serrare; (*e.g., with a mixer*) sbattere; agitare, perturbare; eludere, disfarsi di || *intr* tremare; (*to totter*) traballare, tentennare; scuotere; darsi la mano

shake'down' *s* estorsione, concussione; (*bed*) lettuccio di fortuna

shake'down' cruise' *s* (naut) viaggio di prova

shaker ['/ekər] *s* (*e.g., for sugar*) spolverino; (*for cocktails*) sbattighiaccio, shaker *m*

shake'-up' *s* cambiamento completo, riorganizzazione, rimaneggiamento

shak·y ['/eki] *adj* (**-ier; -iest**) tremebondo; traballante, zoppicante

shall [/æl] *v* (*cond* **should** [/ʊd]) *v aux* si usa per formare (1) il futuro dell'indicativo, per es., **I shall do it** lo farò; (2) il futuro perfetto dell'indicativo, per es., **I shall have done it** l'avrò fatto; (3) espressioni di obbligo o necessità, per es., **what shall I do?** che devo fare?, che vuole che faccia?

shallow ['/ælo] *adj* basso, poco profondo; leggero, superficiale

sham [/æm] *adj* falso, finto || *s* frode *f*, contraffazione || *v* (*pret & pp* **shammed**; *ger* **shamming**) *tr & intr* fingere

sham' bat'tle *s* finta battaglia

shambles ['/æmbəlz] *s* macello; confusione, disordine

shame [/em] *s* vergogna; **shame on you!** vergogna!; **what a shame!** che peccato! || *tr* svergognare, disonorare

shame'faced' *adj* timido, vergognoso

shameful ['/emfəl] *adj* vergognoso

shameless ['/emlɪs] *adj* sfrontato, impudente, svergognato

shampoo [ʃæm'pu] *s* shampoo *m* ‖ *tr* fare lo shampoo a

shamrock ['ʃæmrɑk] *s* trifoglio irlandese

shanghai ['ʃæŋhaɪ] *or* [ʃæŋ'haɪ] *tr* imbarcare a viva forza ‖ **Shanghai** *s* Sciangai *f*

shank [ʃæŋk] *s* fusto; (*of tool*) codolo; (*stem*) gambo; (*of bird*) zampa; (*of anchor*) fuso; (coll) principio; (coll) fine *f*; **to ride shank's mare** andare col cavallo di San Francesco

shan·ty ['ʃænti] *s* (**-ties**) bicocca

shan'ty·town' *s* bidonville *f*

shape [ʃep] *s* forma; **in bad shape** in cattive condizioni; **out of shape** sformato ‖ *tr* formare, foggiare; plasmare, conformare ‖ *intr* formarsi; **to take shape** prender forma

shapeless ['ʃeplɪs] *adj* informe

shape·ly ['ʃepli] *adj* (**-lier; -liest**) ben fatto, formoso

share [ʃɛr] *s* parte *f*; interesse *m*; (*of stock*) azione *f*; (*of plow*) suola; **to go shares** dividere in parti eguali ‖ *tr* (*to enjoy jointly*) condividere; (*to apportion*) ripartire ‖ *intr* partecipare, prender parte

sharecropper ['ʃɛr,krɑpər] *s* mezzadro

share'hold'er *s* azionista *mf*

shark [ʃɑrk] *s* pescecane *m*; (*schemer*) piovra; (slang) esperto

sharp [ʃɑrp] *adj* affilato, acuto; angoloso; (*e.g., curve*) forte; distinto, ben delineato; (*taste*) pungente, salato; (*pain*) vivo; (*words*) mordace; (slang) elegante ‖ *s* (mus) diesis *m* ‖ *adv* acutamente; in punto, e.g., **at seven o'clock sharp** alle sette in punto

sharpen ['ʃɑrpən] *tr* affilare; (*a pencil*) fare la punta a ‖ *intr* affilarsi

sharpener ['ʃɑrpənər] *s* (*person*) affilatore *m*; (*machine*) affilatrice *f*

sharper ['ʃɑrpər] *s* gabbamondo

sharp'shoot'er *s* tiratore scelto

shatter ['ʃætər] *tr* frantumare; sfracellare; (*health*) rovinare; (*nerves*) sconvolgere; distruggere ‖ *intr* frantumarsi, andare in pezzi

shat'ter·proof' *adj* infrangibile

shave [ʃev] *s* rasatura; **to have a close shave** scapparla *or* scamparla bella ‖ *tr* (*the face*) radere, sbarbare; (*wood*) piallare; (*to scrape*) sfiorare; (*prices*) ridurre; (*a lawn*) tosare ‖ *intr* rasarsi

shaving ['ʃevɪŋ] *adj* da barba, per barba, e.g., **shaving cream** crema da *or* per barba ‖ *s* rasatura; **shavings** trucioli *mpl*

shav'ing brush' *s* pennello da barba

shav'ing soap' *s* sapone *m* per la barba

shawl [ʃɔl] *s* scialle *m*

she [ʃi] *s* (**shes**) femmina ‖ *pron pers* (**they**) essa, lei

sheaf [ʃif] *s* (**sheaves** [ʃivz]) covone *m*; (*of paper*) fascio

shear [ʃɪr] *s* lama di cesoia; tagliatura; **shears** cesoie *fpl* ‖ *v* (*pret* **sheared**; *pp* **sheared** *or* **shorn** [ʃorn]) *tr* (*sheep*) tosare; (*cloth*) tagliare; **to shear s.o. of** privare qlcu di

sheath [ʃiθ] *s* (**sheaths** [ʃiðz]) guaina, coperta; (*of a sword*) fodero

sheathe [ʃið] *tr* rinfoderare, inguainare

shed [ʃed] *s* portico, tettoia; (geog) spartiacque *m*, versante *m* ‖ *v* (*pret & pp* **shed**; *ger* **shedding**) *tr* (*e.g., blood*) spargere, versare; (*light*) dare, fare; (*feathers*) spogliarsi di, lasciar cadere

sheen [ʃin] *s* lucentezza

sheep [ʃip] *s* (**sheep**) pecora; **sheep's eyes** occhio di triglia; **to separate the sheep from the goats** separare i buoni dai cattivi

sheep'dog' *s* cane *m* da pastore

sheepish ['ʃipɪʃ] *adj* timido, goffo; pecoresco, pedissequo

sheep'skin' *s* pelle *f* di pecora; (*parchment*) cartapecora; (bb) bazzana; (coll) diploma *m*

sheer [ʃɪr] *adj* trasparente, fino, velato; puro; (*cliff*) stagliato ‖ *adv* completamente ‖ *intr* deviare

sheet [ʃit] *s* (*for bed*) lenzuolo; (*of paper*) foglio; (*of metal*) lamina; (*of water*) specchio; (naut) scotta

sheet' light'ning *s* lampeggio all'orizzonte

sheet' met'al *s* lamiera

sheet' mu'sic *s* spartito non rilegato

sheik [ʃik] *s* sceicco; (*great lover*) (slang) rubacuori *m*

shelf [ʃelf] *s* (**shelves** [ʃelvz]) scaffale *m*, scansia; (*ledge*) terrazzo, ripiano; banco di sabbia; **on the shelf** in disparte, dimenticato

shell [ʃel] *s* (*of egg or crustacean*) guscio; (*of mollusk*) conchiglia; (*of vegetable*) baccello; proietto, proiettile *m*; (*cartridge*) cartuccia; (*of a cartridge*) bossolo; (*framework*) armatura; (*of boiler*) involucro; imbarcazione da regata, schifo, iole *f* ‖ *tr* (*vegetables*) sgranare; bombardare, cannoneggiare; **to shell out** (slang) tirar fuori

shel·lac [ʃə'læk] *s* gomma lacca ‖ *v* (*pret & pp* **-lacked**; *ger* **-lacking**) *tr* verniciare con gomma lacca; (slang) dare una batosta a

shell'fish' *ssg* (**-fish**) frutto di mare; crostaceo; *spl* frutti *mpl* di mare; crostacei *mpl*

shell' hole' *s* cratere *m*

shell' shock' *s* psicosi traumatica bellica

shelter ['ʃeltər] *s* rifugio, ricovero; **to take shelter** rifugiarsi ‖ *tr* raccogliere, ospitare, dare rifugio a

shelve [ʃelv] *tr* mettere sullo scaffale; (*a bill*) insabbiare; mettere a riposo

shepherd ['ʃepərd] *s* pastore *m* ‖ *tr* guardare, curarsi di

shep'herd dog' *s* cane *m* da pastore

shepherdess ['ʃepərdɪs] *s* pastora

sherbet ['ʃɑrbət] *s* sorbetto

sheriff ['ʃerɪf] *s* sceriffo

sher·ry ['ʃeri] *s* (**-ries**) xeres *m*

shield [ʃild] *s* scudo; (*for armpit*) sottoascella *m*; (*badge*) scudetto; (elec) schermo ‖ *tr* proteggere; (elec) schermare

shift [ʃɪft] *s* cambio, cambiamento;

(period of work) turno; **(group of workmen)** operai *mpl* di turno, squadra di lavoro; espediente *m*, sotterfugio ‖ *tr* cambiare; spostare; **(blame)** riversare; ‖ *intr* cambiare; spostarsi; fare da sé; vivere di espedienti; **(rr)** manovrare; **(aut)** cambiare marcia

shift' key' *s* tasto maiuscole

shiftless [ˈʃɪftlɪs] *adj* pigro, ozioso

shift·y [ˈʃɪfti] *adj* (-ier; -iest) astuto; evasivo; pieno d'espedienti; **(glance)** sfuggente

shilling [ˈʃɪlɪŋ] *s* scellino

shimmer [ˈʃɪmər] *s* luccichìo ‖ *intr* luccicare, mandare bagliori

shim·my [ˈʃɪmi] *s* (-mies) **(dance)** shimmy *m*; **(aut)** farfallamento delle ruote, shimmy *m* ‖ *intr* ballare lo shimmy; vibrare

shin [ʃɪn] *s* stinco; **(of cattle)** cannone *m* ‖ *v* (pret & pp shinned; ger shinning) *tr* arrampicarsi su ‖ *intr* arrampicarsi

shin'bone' *s* stinco, tibia

shine [ʃaɪn] *s* splendore *m*; luce *f*; bel tempo; lucidatura, lucido; **to take a shine to** (coll) prender simpatia per ‖ *v* (pret & pp shined) *tr* pulire, lucidare ‖ *v* (pret & pp shone [ʃon]) *tr* **(e.g., a flashlight)** dirigere i raggi di ‖ *intr* brillare, luccicare, risplendere; **(to excel)** essere brillante, eccellere

shiner [ˈʃaɪnər] *s* (slang) occhio pesto

shingle [ˈʃɪŋɡəl] *s* assicella di copertura; **(to cover a wall)** mattoncino di rivestimento; **(Brit)** greto ciottoloso; **(coll)** capelli *mpl* alla bebé; **shingles** (pathol) erpete *m*, zona; **to hang out one's shingle** (coll) aprire un ufficio professionale ‖ *tr* coprire di assicelle or mattoncini; **(hair)** tagliare alla bebé

shining [ˈʃaɪnɪŋ] *adj* brillante, lucente

shin·y [ˈʃaɪni] *adj* (-ier; -iest) lucente, lucido; **(paper)** patinato

ship [ʃɪp] *s* nave *f*, bastimento; aeronave *f*; aeroplano; **(crew)** equipaggio ‖ *v* (pret & pp shipped; ger shipping) *tr* imbarcare; mandare, spedire; **(oars)** disarmare; **(water)** imbarcare ‖ *intr* imbarcarsi

ship'board' *s*—**on shipboard** a bordo

ship'build'er *s* costruttore *m* navale

ship'build'ing *s* architettura navale

ship'mate' *s* compagno di bordo

shipment [ˈʃɪpmənt] *s* invio, spedizione

ship'own'er *s* armatore *m*

shipper [ˈʃɪpər] *s* speditore *m*, spedizioniere *m*, mittente *m*

shipping [ˈʃɪpɪŋ] *s* imbarco; spedizione; **(naut)** trasporto marittimo

ship'ping clerk' *s* speditore *m*

ship'ping room' *s* ufficio impaccatura

ship'shape' *adj* & *adv* in perfette condizioni

ship'side' *s* molo

ship's' pa'pers *spl* documenti *mpl* di bordo

ship'wreck' *s* naufragio; **(remains)** relitto ‖ *tr* far naufragare ‖ *intr* naufragare

ship'yard' *s* cantiere *m* navale

shirk [ʃʌrk] *tr* **(work)** evitare; **(responsibility)** sottrarsi a ‖ *intr* imboscarsi

shirt [ʃʌrt] *s* camicia; **to keep one's shirt on** (slang) non perdere la calma; **to lose one's shirt** (slang) perdere la camicia

shirt' front' *s* sparato

shirt' sleeve' *s* manica di camicia

shirt'tail' *s* falda della camicia

shirt'waist' *s* blusa da donna

shiver [ˈʃɪvər] *s* brivido ‖ *intr* rabbrividire, battere i denti

shoal [ʃol] *s* secca, banco di sabbia

shock [ʃɑk] *s* urto, collisione; scossa; scossa elettrica; **(pathol)** shock *m* ‖ *tr* scuotere; **(to strike against)** urtare; scandalizzare, indignare; dare la scossa elettrica a; **(fig)** scioccare

shock' absorb'er [æbˈsɔrbər] *s* ammortizzatore *m* di colpi

shocking [ˈʃɑkɪŋ] *adj* disgustoso, scandalizzante

shock' ther'apy *s* terapia d'urto

shock' troops' *spl* truppe *fpl* d'assalto

shod·dy [ˈʃɑdi] *adj* (-dier; -diest) scadente, falso

shoe [ʃu] *s* scarpa; **(horseshoe)** ferro da cavallo; **(of a tire)** copertone *m*; **(of brake)** ganascia, ceppo ‖ *v* (pret & pp shod [ʃɑd]) *tr* calzare; **(a horse)** ferrare

shoe'black' *s* lustrascarpe *m*

shoe'horn' *s* corno da scarpe, calzatoio

shoe'lace' *s* laccio delle scarpe

shoe'mak'er *s* calzolaio

shoe' pol'ish *s* crema or cera da scarpe

shoe'shine' *s* lucidatura, lustramento di scarpe

shoe' store' *s* calzoleria

shoe'string' *s* laccio delle scarpe; **on a shoestring** con quattro soldi

shoe'tree' *s* tendiscarpe *m*

shoo [ʃu] *tr* fare sciò a ‖ *intr* fare sciò

shoot [ʃut] *s* **(e.g., with a firearm)** tiro; gara di tiro; **(chute)** scivolo; **(rok)** lancio; **(bot)** getto, virgulto ‖ *v* (pret & pp shot [ʃɑt]) *tr* **(any missile)** tirare; **(a bullet)** sparare; **(to execute with a bullet)** fucilare; **(to fling)** lanciare; **(the sun)** prendere l'altezza di; **(dice)** gettare; **(mov, telv)** girare, riprendere; **to shoot down** **(a plane)** abbattere; **to shoot up** (coll) terrorizzare sparando a casaccio ‖ *intr* tirare, sparare; passare rapidamente; nascere; **(said of pain)** dare fitte; **(mov)** cinematografare; **to shoot at** tirare a; (coll) cercare di ottenere

shoot'ing gal'lery *s* tiro a segno

shoot'ing match' *s* gara di tiro a segno; (slang) tutto, ogni cosa

shoot'ing star' *s* stella cadente

shop [ʃɑp] *s* **(store)** negozio, rivendita; **(workshop)** officina; **to talk shop** parlare del proprio lavoro ‖ *v* (pret & pp shopped; ger shopping) *intr* fare la spesa; **to go shopping** andare a fare la spesa; **to shop around** cercare un'occasione di negozio in negozio

shop'girl' *s* venditrice *f*

shop'keep'er s negoziante mf
shoplifter ['ʃɑp,lɪftər] s taccheggiatore m
shopper ['ʃɑpər] s compratore m
shopping ['ʃɑpɪŋ] s compra; (purchases) compre fpl, shopping m
shop'ping bag' s sporta, shopping m
shop'ping cen'ter s centro d'acquisto, ipermercato
shop'ping dis'trict s zona commerciale
shop'win'dow s vetrina
shop'worn' adj sciupato, usato
shore [ʃor] s costa, riva; spiaggia, lido; (fig) regione; (support) sostegno, puntello || tr puntellare
shore' din'ner s pranzo di pesce
shore' leave' s (naut) franchigia
shore'line' s frangia costiera
shore' patrol' s polizia della marina
short [ʃɔrt] adj (in stature) piccolo, basso; (in space, time) breve; (scanty) scarso; succinto; (in quantity) poco, piccolo; (rude) brusco; **in a short time** in breve; **in short** per farla breve; **on short notice** senza preavviso; **short of breath** corto di fiato; **to be short of** scarseggiare di || s (elec) cortocircuito; (mov) cortometraggio; **shorts** (underwear) mutande fpl; (sports attire) calzoncini mpl, shorts mpl || adv brevemente; bruscamente; (com) allo scoperto, e.g., **to sell short** vendere allo scoperto; **to run short of** essere a corto di; **to stop short** fermarsi di colpo || tr (elec) causare un cortocircuito in || intr (elec) andare in cortocircuito
shortage ['ʃɔrtɪdʒ] s mancanza; (of food) carestia; (from pilfering) ammanco
short'cake' s torta di pasta frolla; torta ricoperta di frutta fresca
short'-change' tr non dare il cambio giusto a; (coll) imbrogliare
short'cir'cuit s (elec) cortocircuito
short'-cir'cuit tr mandare in cortocircuito; (coll) rovinare || intr andare in cortocircuito
short'com'ing s difetto, manchevolezza
short'cut' s scorciatoia
shorten ['ʃɔrtən] tr raccorciare, abbreviare || intr raccorciarsi, abbreviarsi
shortening ['ʃɔrtnɪŋ] s raccorciamento; (culin) grasso, strutto
short'hand' adj stenografico || s stenografia; **to take shorthand** stenografare
short'hand' typ'ist s stenodattilografo
short-lived ['ʃɔrt'laɪvd] or ['ʃɔrt'lɪvd] adj effimero, di breve vita
shortly ['ʃɔrtli] adv in breve, brevemente; fra poco; bruscamente; **shortly after** poco dopo
short'-range' adj di corta portata
short' sale' s vendita allo scoperto
short-sighted ['ʃɔrt'saɪtɪd] adj miope; (fig) miope
short'stop' s (baseball) interbase m
short' sto'ry s novella
short-tempered ['ʃɔrt'tempərd] adj irascibile
short'-term' adj a breve scadenza

short'wave' adj alle onde corte || s onda corta
short' weight' s—**to give short weight** rubare sul peso
shot [ʃɑt] s tiro, sparo; (cartridge) cartuccia; (for cannon) palla; (pellets of lead) pallini mpl; (person) tiratore m; (hypodermic injection) iniezione; (of liquor) bicchierino; (phot) istantanea; (sports) peso; (mov) inquadratura; **not by a long shot** nemmeno a pensarci; **to start like a shot** partire come una palla da cannone; **to take a shot at** tirare un colpo a; (to attempt to) provarsi a
shot'gun' s schioppo, fucile m da caccia
shot' put' s lancio del peso
should [ʃud] v aux si usa nelle seguenti situazioni: 1) per formare il condizionale presente, per es., **if I should wait for him, I should miss the train** se lo aspettassi, perderei il treno; 2) per formare il perfetto del condizionale, per es., **if I had waited for him, I should have missed the train** se lo avessi aspettato, avrei perso il treno; 3) per indicare la necessità di un'azione, per es., **he should go at once** dovrebbe andare immediatamente; **he should have gone immediately** sarebbe dovuto andare immediatamente
shoulder ['ʃoldər] s spalla; (of highway) banchina; **across the shoulder** a bandoliera; **to put one's shoulders to the wheel** mettersi a lavorare di buzzo buono; **to turn a cold shoulder to** volgere le spalle a || tr portare sulle spalle; (a responsibility) addossarsi; spingere con le spalle
shoul'der blade' s scapola
shoul'der strap' s spallina; (mil) tracolla
shout [ʃaut] s urlo, grido || tr urlare, gridare; **to shout down far** tacere a forza di strilli || intr gridare
shove [ʃʌv] s spintone m || tr spingere || intr spingere, dare spintoni; **to shove off** allontanarsi dalla riva; (slang) andarsene
shov·el ['ʃʌvəl] s pala || v (pret & pp -eled or -elled; ger -eling or -elling) tr spalare || intr lavorare di pala
show [ʃo] s mostra; apparenza; traccia; ostentazione; (mov, telv, theat) spettacolo; **to make a show of** dar spettacolo di; **to steal the show from** ricevere tutti gli applausi invece di || tr mostrare, esporre; (a movie) presentare; dimostrare, insegnare; provare; (to register) segnare; (one's feelings) manifestare; (to the door) accompagnare; **to show in** fare entrare; **to show off** mettere in mostra || intr mostrarsi; presentarsi, apparire; (said of a horse) (sports) arrivare terzo, piazzarsi; **to show off** mettersi in mostra; **to show up** (coll) mostrarsi; (coll) farsi vedere
show' bill' s cartellone m
show'boat' s battello per spettacoli teatrali

show' busi'ness s industria dello spettacolo

show'case' s bacheca, vetrina

show'down' s carte scoperte; chiarificazione

shower ['∫au·ər] s (of rain) acquazzone m; (shower bath) doccia; (e.g., for a bride) ricevimento cui i partecipanti devono portare un regalo; (fig) pioggia || tr inaffiare; **to shower with** colmare di || intr diluviare; fare la doccia

show'er bath' s doccia

show' girl' s ballerina, girl f

show'man s (-men) impresario teatrale; persona che ha molta scena

show'-off' s reclamista m, strombazzatore m

show'piece' s capolavoro, oggetto d'arte

show'place' s luogo celebre; **to be a showplace** (said, e.g., of a house) essere arredato perfettamente

show'room' s sala di mostra

show' win'dow s vetrina

show·y ['∫o·i] adj (-ier; -iest) vistoso, sgargiante

shrapnel ['∫ræpnəl] s shrapnel m

shred [∫red] s brano, brandello; ritaglio; (fig) granello; **to cut to shreds** fare a brandelli || v (pret & pp shredded or shred; ger shredding) tr fare a brandelli; (paper) tagliuzzare

shrew [∫ru] s (woman) bisbetica; (animal) toporagno

shrewd [∫rud] adj astuto, scaltro

shriek [∫rik] s strido; strillo; risata stridula || intr stridere; strillare

shrill [∫rɪl] adj stridulo, squillante

shrimp [∫rɪmp] s gamberetto; (person) omiciattolo, nanerottolo

shrine [∫raɪn] s santuario, sacrario

shrink [∫rɪŋk] v (pret shrank [∫ræŋk] or shrunk [∫rʌŋk]; pp shrunk or shrunken [∫rʌŋkən]) tr contrarre, restringere || intr contrarsi, restringersi; ritirarsi

shrinkage ['∫rɪŋkɪdʒ] s restringimento; (in weight) calo

shriv·el ['∫rɪvəl] v (pret & pp -eled or -elled; ger -eling or -elling) tr raggrinzire; (from heat) raccartocciare; (to wither) avvizzire || intr raggrinzirsi; accartocciarsi; avvizzire; **to shrivel up** incartapecorire

shroud [∫raud] s sudario, lenzuolo funebre; (fig) cappa || tr avvolgere

Shrove' Tues'day [∫rov] s martedì grasso

shrub [∫rʌb] s arbusto

shrubber·y ['∫rʌbəri] s (-ies) arbusti mpl, cespugli mpl

shrug [∫rʌg] s scrollata di spalle || v (pret & pp shrugged; ger shrugging) tr scrollare; **to shrug one's shoulders** scrollare le spalle || intr fare spallucce

shudder ['∫ʌdər] s brivido, fremito || intr rabbrividire, fremere

shuffle ['∫ʌfəl] s (of cards) mescolata; turno di fare il mazzo; (of feet) strascichio; evasione || tr mescolare; strisciare, strascicare || intr fare il

mazzo; scalpicciare; ballare di striscio; **to shuffle off** strascicarsi, scalpicciare; **to shuffle out of** evadere da

shun [∫ʌn] v (pret & pp shunned; ger shunning) tr evitare, schivare

shunt [∫ʌnt] tr sviare; (elec) shuntare; (rr) deviare

shut [∫ʌt] adj chiuso || v (pret & pp shut; ger shutting) tr chiudere, serrare; **to shut in** rinchiudere; **to shut off** (e.g., gas) tagliare; **to shut up** tappare; imprigionare; (coll) fare star zitto || intr chiudersi; **to shut up** (coll) stare zitto, tacere

shut'down' s chiusura

shutter [∫ʌtər] s (outside a window) persiana, gelosia; (outside a store window) serranda, saracinesca; (phot) otturatore m

shuttle ['∫ʌtəl] s spola, navetta || intr fare la spola

shut'tle·cock' s volano, volante m

shut'tle train' s treno che fa la spola fra due stazioni

shy [∫aɪ] adj (shyer or shier; shyest or shiest) timido; (fearful) schivo, ritroso; corto, a corto, e.g., **he is shy of funds** è a corto di denaro || v (pret & pp shied) intr ritirarsi; schivarsi; (said of a horse) adombrarsi; **to shy away** tenersi discosto

shyster ['∫aɪstər] s (coll) azzeccagarbugli m

Sia·mese [,saɪ·ə'miz] adj siamese || s (-mese) siamese mf

Si'amese twins' spl fratelli mpl siamesi

Siberian [saɪ'bɪrɪ·ən] adj & s siberiano

sibilant ['sɪbɪlənt] adj & s sibilante f

sibyl ['sɪbɪl] s sibilla

sic [sɪk] adv sic || v (pret & pp sicked; ger sicking) tr aizzare; **sick 'em!** va!; **to sick on** aizzare contro

Sicilian [sɪ'sɪljən] adj & s siciliano

Sicily ['sɪsɪli] s la Sicilia

sick [sɪk] adj ammalato; nauseato; (bored) stucco; **sick at heart** con una spina nel cuore; **to be sick and tired** averne sin sopra i capelli; **to be sick of** at one's stomach avere la nausea; **to take sick** cader malato || tr (a dog) aizzare

sick'bed' s letto d'ammalato

sicken ['sɪkən] tr ammalare; disgustare || intr ammalarsi

sickening ['sɪkənɪŋ] adj stomachevole

sick' head'ache s emicrania accompagnata da nausea

sickle ['sɪkəl] s falce messoria, falcetto

sick' leave' s congedo per motivi di salute

sick·ly ['sɪkli] adj (-lier; -liest) cagionevole, malaticcio

sickness ['sɪknɪs] s malattia; nausea

side [saɪd] adj laterale || s parte f, lato; (e.g., of a coin) faccia; (slope) versante m; (of human body, of a ship) fianco; **to take sides** parteggiare || intr parteggiare; **to side with** schierarsi dalla parte di

side'board' s credenza

side'burns' spl basette fpl, favoriti mpl

side'car' s motocarrozzetta; carrozzino laterale (di motocarrozzetta)

side' dish' s portata extra

side' door' s porta laterale

side' effect' s effetto secondario

side'-glance' s occhiata di sbieco

side' is'sue s questione secondaria

side'line' s linea laterale; impiego secondario; attività secondaria

sidereal [saɪ'dɪrɪ‧əl] adj siderale

side'sad'dle adv all'amazzone

side' show' s spettacolo secondario di baraccone; affare secondario

side'slip' intr (aer) scivolare d'ala

side'split'ting adj che fa sbellicare dalle risa

side' step' s passo laterale; scartata

side'-step' v (pret & pp -stepped; ger -stepping) tr evitare || intr farsi da parte; fare una scartata

side'track' s binario morto di smistamento || tr sviare; (rr) smistare

side' view' s vista di profilo

side'walk' s marciapiede m

side'walk café' s caffè m con tavolini all'aperto

sideward ['saɪdwərd] adj obliquo, a sghembo || adv verso un lato; di sghembo

side'ways' adj sghembo || adv di sghembo; di fianco

side' whisk'ers spl favoriti mpl

siding ['saɪdɪŋ] s (rr) diramazione, binario morto, raccordo ferroviario

sidle ['saɪdəl] intr andare al lato; muoversi furtivamente

siege [sidʒ] s assedio; (of illness) ricorrenza d'attacchi; **to lay siege to** cingere d'assedio, assediare

siesta [si'estə] s siesta; **to take a siesta** fare la siesta

sieve [sɪv] s vaglio, setaccio || tr vagliare, setacciare

sift [sɪft] tr (flour) abburattare; setacciare; (to scatter with a sieve) spolverare; (fig) vagliare

sigh [saɪ] s sospiro || tr mormorare sospirando || intr sospirare; **to sigh for** sospirare

sight [saɪt] s vista, visione; spettacolo, veduta; (opt) mira, traguardo; (mil) mirino, tacca di mira; (coll) mucchio; **a sight of** (coll) molto; **at first sight** a prima vista; **at sight** ad apertura di libro; (com) a vista; **out of sight** fuori di vista; lontano dagli occhi; (prices) astronomico; **sights** luoghi mpl interessanti; **sight unseen** senza averlo visto prima, a occhi chiusi; **to be a sight** (coll) essere un orrore; **to catch sight of** arrivare a intravedere; **to know by sight** conoscere di vista; **to not be able to stand the sight of s.o.** not poter vedere qlcu nemmeno dipinto || tr avvistare; (a weapon) mirare || intr mirare, prendere di mira; osservare attentamente

sight' draft' s (com) tratta a vista

sight'-read' v (pret & pp -read [‚rɛd]) tr & intr leggere a libro aperto

sight'see'ing adj turistico || s turismo, visite fpl turistiche

sightseer ['saɪt‚si‧ər] s turista mf

sign [saɪn] s segno; segnale m; (e.g., on a store) insegna, cartello; **signs** tracce fpl || tr firmare; ingaggiare; indicare, segnalare || intr firmare; fare segno; **to sign off** (rad, telv) terminare la trasmissione; **to sign up** iscriversi

sig‧nal ['sɪgnəl] adj insigne, segnalato || s segnale m || v (pret & pp -naled or -nalled; ger -naling or -nalling) tr segnalare || intr fare segnalazioni

sig'nal corps' s (mil) armi fpl di trasmissione

sig'nal tow'er s (rr) posto di blocco

signato‧ry ['sɪgnɪ‚torɪ] s (-ries) firmatario

signature ['sɪgnət/ər] s firma; segno musicale; (typ) segnatura

sign'board' s cartellone m

signer ['saɪnər] s firmatario

sig'net ring' ['sɪgnɪt] s anello col sigillo

significance [sɪg'nɪfɪkəns] s importanza; (meaning) significato

significant [sɪg'nɪfɪkənt] adj importante

signi‧fy ['sɪgnɪ‚faɪ] v (pret & pp -fied) tr significare

sign'post' s palo indicatore

silence ['saɪləns] s silenzio || tr far tacere; (mil) ridurre al silenzio

silent ['saɪlənt] adj silenzioso, tacito

si'lent mov'ie s cinema muto

silhouette [‚sɪlu'et] s silhouette f, siluetta

silicon ['sɪlɪkən] s silicio

silicone ['sɪlɪ‚kon] s silicone m

silk [sɪlk] adj di seta || s seta; **to hit the silk** (slang) gettarsi col paracadute

silken ['sɪlkən] adj serico, di seta

silk' hat' s cappello a cilindro

silk'screen proc'ess s serigrafia

silk'-stock'ing adj & s aristocratico

silk'worm' s baco da seta, filugello

silk‧y ['sɪlkɪ] adj (-ier; -iest) di seta; come la seta

sill [sɪl] s basamento; (of a door) soglia; (of a window) davanzale m

sil‧ly ['sɪlɪ] adj (-lier; -liest) sciocco, scemo

si‧lo ['saɪlo] s (-los) silo || tr insilare

silt [sɪlt] s sedimento

silver ['sɪlvər] adj d'argento; (voice) argentino; (plated with silver) argentato || s argento || tr inargentare

sil'ver‧fish' s (ent) lepisma

sil'ver foil' s foglia d'argento

sil'ver fox' s volpe argentata

sil'ver lin'ing s spiraglio di speranza

sil'ver plate' s vasellame m d'argento; argentatura

sil'ver screen' s (mov) schermo

sil'ver‧smith' s argentiere m

sil'ver spoon' s ricchezza ereditata; **to be born with a silver spoon in one's mouth** esser nato con la camicia

sil'ver‧ware' s argenteria

sil'ver‧ware' chest' s portaposate m

similar ['sɪmɪlər] adj simile

similari‧ty [‚sɪmɪ'lærɪtɪ] s (-ties) similarità f, somiglianza

simile ['sɪmɪlɪ] s similitudine f

simmer ['sɪmər] *tr* cuocere a fuoco lento || *intr* cuocere a fuoco lento; (fig) ribollire; **to simmer down** (slang) calmarsi

simper ['sɪmpər] *s* sorriso scemo || *intr* fare un sorriso scemo

simple ['sɪmpəl] *adj* semplice

simple-minded ['sɪmpəl'maɪndɪd] *adj* sempliciuno, scemo

simpleton ['sɪmpəltən] *s* semplicione *m*

simulate ['sɪmjə,let] *tr* simulare

simultaneous [,saɪməl'teni·əs] or [,sɪməl'teni·əs] *adj* simultaneo

sin [sɪn] *s* peccato || *v* (*pret & pp* **sinned;** *ger* **sinning**) *intr* peccare

since [sɪns] *adv* da allora, da allora in poi; da tempo fa || *prep* da || *conj* dacché; poiché, dato che

sincere [sɪn'sɪr] *adj* sincero

sincerity [sɪn'serɪti] *s* sincerità *f*

sine [saɪn] *s* (math) seno

sinecure ['saɪnɪ,kjur] or ['sɪnɪ,kjur] *s* sinecura

sinew ['sɪnju] *s* tendine *m;* (fig) nerbo

sinful ['sɪnfəl] *adj* (*person*) peccatore; (*act, intention, etc.*) peccaminoso

sing [sɪŋ] *v* (*pret* **sang** [sæŋ] or **sung** [sʌŋ]; *pp* **sung**) *tr* cantare; **to sing to sleep** ninnare || *intr* cantare; (*said, e.g., of the ears*) fischiare

singe [sɪndʒ] *v* (*ger* **singeing**) *tr* strinare, bruciacchiare

singer ['sɪŋər] *s* cantante *mf;* (*in night club*) canzonettista *mf*

single ['sɪŋgəl] *adj* unico, solo; (*room*) a un letto; (*bed*) a una piazza; (*man*) celibe; (*woman*) nubile; (*combat*) corpo a corpo; semplice, sincero || **singles** *ssg* singolare *m* || *tr* scegliere; **to single out** individuare

single-breasted ['sɪŋgəl'brestɪd] *adj* a un petto, monopetto

sin'gle entry' *s* partita semplice

sin'gle file' *s* fila indiana

single-handed ['sɪŋgəl'hændɪd] *adj* da solo, senza aiuto altrui

sin'gle-phase' *adj* (elec) monofase

sin'gle room' *s* camera a un letto

sin'gle-track' *adj* (rr) a binario semplice; (fig) di corte vedute

sing'song' *adj* monotono || *s* cantilena

singular ['sɪŋgjələr] *adj & s* singolare *m*

sinister ['sɪnɪstər] *adj* sinistro

sink [sɪŋk] *s* acquaio; (*sewer*) scolo, fogna; (fig) sentina || *v* (*pret* **sank** [sæŋk] or **sunk** [sʌŋk]; *pp* **sunk**) *tr* sprofondare; infiggere; (*a well*) scavare; (*in tone*) abbassare; (*a boat*) mandare a picco, rovinare; investire; perdere || *intr* sprofondarsi; abbassarsi; (*said, of the sun, prices, etc.*) calare; andare a picco; lasciarsi cadere; (*in vice*) impantanarsi; (*said of one's cheeks*) infossarsi; (*in thought*) perdersi; **to sink down** sedersi; **to sink in** penetrare

sink'ing fund' *s* fondo d'ammortamento

sinner ['sɪnər] *s* peccatore *m*

Sinology [sɪ'nɑlədʒi] *s* sinologia

sinuous ['sɪnju·əs] *adj* sinuoso

sinus ['saɪnəs] *s* seno

sip [sɪp] *s* sorso || *v* (*pret & pp* **sipped;** *ger* **sipping**) *tr* sorbire, sorseggiare

siphon ['saɪfən] *s* sifone *m* || *tr* travasare con un sifone

si'phon bot'tle *s* sifone *m*

sir [sʌr] *s* signore *m;* (Brit) sir *m;* **Dear Sir** Illustrissimo signore; (com) Egregio signore

sire [saɪr] *s* (*king*) sire *m;* padre *m,* stallone *m* || *tr* generare

siren ['saɪrən] *s* sirena

sirloin ['sʌrlɔɪn] *s* lombata, lombo

sirup ['sɪrəp] or ['sʌrəp] *tr* sciroppo

sis·sy ['sɪsi] *s* (-sies) effeminato

sister ['sɪstər] *adj* (*ship*) gemello; (*language*) sorella; (*corporation*) consorella || *s* sorella; (*nun*) suora, monaca

sis'ter-in-law' *s* (**sis'ters-in-law'**) cognata

Sis'tine Chap'el *s* Cappella Sistina

sit [sɪt] *v* (*pret & pp* **sat** [sæt]; *ger* **sitting**) *intr* sedere; posare; (*said of a hen*) covare; (*said of a jacket*) stare; essere in sessione; **to sit down** sedersi; **to sit in on** partecipare a; assistere a; **to sit still** stare tranquillo; **to sit up** alzarsi; (coll) essere sorpreso

sit'-down strike' *s* sciopero bianco

site [saɪt] *s* sito, luogo, posizione

sitting ['sɪtɪŋ] *s* seduta; (*of a court*) sessione; (*of a hen*) covata; (*serving of a meal*) turno

sit'ting duck' *s* (slang) facile bersaglio

sit'ting room' *s* soggiorno

situate ['sɪtʃu,et] *tr* situare

situation [,sɪtʃu'eʃən] *s* situazione, posizione; posto

sitz' bath' [sɪts] *s* semicupio

six [sɪks] *adj & pron* sei || *s* sei *m;* **at sixes and sevens** in disordine; **six o'clock** le sei

six' hun'dred *adj, s & pron* seicento

sixteen ['sɪks'tin] *adj, s & pron* sedici *m*

sixteenth ['sɪks'tinθ] *adj, s & pron* sedicesimo || *s* (*in dates*) sedici *m*

sixth [sɪksθ] *adj, s & pron* sesto || *s* (*in dates*) sei *m*

sixtieth ['sɪkstɪ·ɪθ] *adj, s & pron* sessantesimo

six·ty ['sɪksti] *adj & pron* sessanta || *s* (-ies) sessanta *m;* **the sixties** gli anni sessanta

sizable ['saɪzəbəl] *adj* considerevole

size [saɪz] *s* grandezza; quantità *f;* (*of person or garment*) taglia; (*of shoes*) numero; (*of hat*) giro; (*of a pipe*) diametro; (*of gilding*) colla; (fig) situazione || *tr* misurare, classificare secondo grandezza; incollare; **to size up** (coll) stimare, giudicare

sizzle ['sɪzəl] *s* sfrigolio || *intr* sfriggere

skate [sket] *s* pattino; (slang) tipo || *intr* pattinare; **to skate on thin ice** andare in cerca di disgrazie

skat'ing rink' *s* pattinatoio

skein [sken] *s* gomitolo, matassa

skeleton ['skelɪtən] *adj* scheletrico || *s* scheletro

skel'eton key' *s* chiave maestra

skeptic ['skɛptɪk] *adj & s* scettico

skeptical ['skɛptɪkəl] *adj* scettico

sketch [skɛtʃ] *s* schizzo, disegno; abbozzo, bozzetto; (theat) scenetta || *tr* schizzare, disegnare; abbozzare

sketch'book' *s* album *m* di schizzi; quaderno per abbozzi

skew [skju] *adj* obliquo || *s* movimento obliquo; (chisel) scalpello a taglio obliquo || *tr* tagliare di sghembo || *intr* (to swerve) deviare; (to look obliquely) guardare di sghembo

skew' chis'el *s* scalpello a taglio obliquo

skewer ['skju·ər] *s* spiedino || *tr* mettere allo spiedo

ski [ski] *s* (skis or ski) sci *m* || *infr* sciare

ski' boot' *s* scarpa da sci

skid [skɪd] *s* (device to check a wheel) scarpa; (skidding forward) slittamento; (skidding sideway) sbandamento; (aer, mach) pattino || *v* (pret & pp skidded; ger skidding) *tr* frenare || *intr* (forward) slittare; (sideways) sbandare

skid' row' [ro] *s* quartiere malfamato

skier ['ski·ər] *s* sciatore *m*

skiff [skɪf] *s* skiff *m*, singolo

skiing ['ski·ɪŋ] *s* sci *m*

ski' jump' *s* salto con gli sci; trampolino di salto

ski' lift' *s* sciovia

skill [skɪl] *s* destrezza, perizia

skilled [skɪld] *adj* abile, esperto

skilled' la'bor *s* manodopera qualificata

skillet ['skɪlɪt] *s* padella

skillful ['skɪlfəl] *adj* destro, abile

skim [skɪm] *v* (pret & pp skimmed; ger skimming) *tr* (milk) scremare; (e.g., broth) sgrassare; (to graze) sfiorare; (the ground) radere; (a page) trascorrere || *intr* sfiorare; **to skim over** scorrere

ski' mask' *s* passamontagna *m*

skimmer ['skɪmər] *s* schiumaiola; (hat) canottiera

skim' milk' *s* latte scremato or magro

skimp [skɪmp] *tr* lesinare || *intr* economizzare, risparmiare

skimp·y ['skɪmpi] *adj* (-ier; -iest) corto, scarso; tarpato

skin [skɪn] *s* pelle *f*; (rind) scorza; (of onion) spoglia; **by the skin of one's teeth** (coll) per il rotto della cuffia; **soaked to the skin** bagnato fino all' ossa; **to have a thin skin** offendersi facilmente || *v* (pret & pp skinned; ger skinning) *tr* pelare, spellare; (e.g., one's knee) spellarsi; (slang) tosare; **to skin alive** (slang) scotennare; (slang) battere in pieno

skin'-deep' *adj* a fior di pelle

skin'-div'er *s* nuotatore subacqueo, sub *m*; (mil) sommozzatore *m*

skin'flint' *s* avaro

skin' game' *s* truffa

skin·ny ['skɪni] *adj* (-nier; -niest) magro, scarno

skin' test' *s* cutireazione

skip [skɪp] *s* salto || *v* (pret & pp

skipped; ger skipping) *tr* (a fence; a meal) saltare; (a subject) sorvolare; (school) (coll) marinare || *intr* saltare, salterellare; (said of typewriter) saltare uno spazio; (coll) svignarsela

ski' pole' *s* racchetta da sci

skipper ['skɪpər] *s* capitano, comandante *m*

skirmish ['skʌrmɪʃ] *s* scaramuccia || *intr* battersi in una scaramuccia

skirt [skʌrt] *s* sottana, gonna; (edge) orlo; (woman) (slang) gonnella || *tr* orlare; costeggiare; (a subject) evitare

ski' run' *s* pista da sci

skit [skɪt] *s* (theat) quadretto comico

skittish ['skɪtɪʃ] *adj* bizzarro, balzano; timido; (horse) ombroso

skulduggery [skʌl'dʌgəri] *s* trucco disonesto

skull [skʌl] *s* cranio, teschio

skull' and cross'bones *s* due tibie incrociate ed un teschio

skull'cap' *s* papalina

skunk [skʌŋk] *s* puzzola, moffetta; (coll) puzzone *m*

sky [skaɪ] *s* (skies) cielo; firmamento; **to praise to the skies** portare al cielo

sky'div'er *s* paracadutista *mf*

sky'jack'er *s* pirata *m* dell'aria

sky'lark' *s* allodola || *intr* (coll) darsi alla pazza gioia

sky'light' *s* lucernario

sky'line' *s* linea dell'orizzonte; (of city) profilo

sky'rock'et *s* razzo || *intr* salire come un razzo

sky'scrap'er *s* grattacielo

sky'writ'ing *s* scrittura pubblicitaria aerea

slab [slæb] *s* (of stone) lastra, lastrone *m*; (of wood) tavola; (slice) fetta

slack [slæk] *adj* lento, allentato; negligente, indolente; (fig) fiacco, morto || *s* lentezza; negligenza; stagione morta, inattività *f*; **slacks** pantaloni *mpl* da donna; pantaloni sciolti || *tr* allentare; trascurare; (lime) spegnere || *intr* rilasciarsi; essere negligente; **to slack up** rallentare

slacker ['slækər] *s* fannullone *m*; (mil) imboscato

slag [slæg] *s* scoria

slake [slek] *tr* spegnere

slalom ['slɑlom] *s* slalom *m*

slam [slæm] *s* colpo; (of door) sbatacchiamento; (in cards) cappotto; (coll) strapazzata || *v* (pret & pp slammed; ger slamming) *tr* sbattere, sbatacchiare; (coll) strapazzare || *intr* sbattere, sbatacchiare

slam'bang' *adv* (coll) con gran rumore, precipitosamente

slander ['slændər] *s* calunnia, maldicenza || *tr* calunniare, diffamare

slanderous ['slændərəs] *adj* calunnioso, diffamatorio

slang [slæŋ] *s* gergo

slant [slænt] *s* inclinazione; punto di vista || *tr* inclinare; (news) snaturare || *intr* inclinarsi; deviare

slap [slæp] *s* manata; (*in the face*) schiaffo, ceffone *m*; (*noise*) rumore *m*; insulto || *v* (*pret & pp* **slapped;** *ger* **slapping**) *tr* dare una manata a; schiaffeggiare

slap'dash' *adj* raffazzonato, fatto a casaccio || *adv* a casaccio

slap'hap'py *adj* (*punch-drunk*) stordito; (*giddy*) allegro, brillo

slap'stick' *adj* buffonesco || *s* bastone *m* d'Arlecchino; buffonata

slash [slæʃ] *s* sfregio; (*of prices*) riduzione || *tr* sfregiare; (*cloth*) tagliare; (*prices*) ridurre

slat [slæt] *s* travicello, regolo; (*for bed*) traversa; (*of shutter*) stecca

slate [slet] *s* ardesia, lavagna; lista elettorale; **clean slate** buon certificato || *tr* coprire con tegole d'ardesia; proporre la nomina di; (*to schedule*) mettere in cantiere

slate' roof' *s* tetto d'ardesia

slattern ['slætərn] *s* (*slovenly woman*) sciamannona; (*harlot*) puttana

slaughter ['slɔtər] *s* eccidio, carneficina || *tr* sgozzare, scannare

slaugh'ter-house' *s* macello, scannatoio

Slav [slav] or [slæv] *adj & s* slavo

slave [slev] *adj & s* schiavo || *intr* lavorare come uno schiavo

slave' driv'er *s* negriere *m*

slavery ['slevəri] *s* schiavitù *f*

slave' trade' *s* tratta degli schiavi

Slavic ['slavɪk] or ['slævɪk] *adj & s* slavo

slay [sle] *v* (*pret* **slew** [slu]; *pp* **slain** [slen]) *tr* scannare, uccidere

slayer ['sle·ər] *s* uccisore *m*

sled [slɛd] *s* slittino, slitta || *v* (*pret & pp* **sledded;** *ger* **sledding**) *intr* slittare

sledge' ham'mer *s* [slɛdʒ] *s* mazza

sleek [slik] *adj* liscio, lustro; elegante || *tr* lisciare, ammorbidire

sleep [slip] *s* sonno; **to go to sleep** addormentarsi; **to put to sleep** addormentare; uccidere con un anestetico || *v* (*pret & pp* **slept** [slɛpt]) *tr* dormire; aver posto a dormire per; **to sleep it over** dormirci sopra; **to sleep off a hangover** smaltire una sbornia dormendo || *intr* dormire; **to sleep in** dormire fino a tardi; passare la notte a casa; **to sleep out** passare la notte fuori di casa

sleeper ['slipər] *s* (*person*) dormiente *mf*; (*beam, timber*) trave *f*

sleep'ing bag' *s* sacco a pelo

sleep'ing car' *s* vettura letto

sleep'ing pill' *s* sonnifero

sleepless ['sliplɪs] *adj* insonne; (*night*) bianco

sleep'walk'er *s* sonnambulo

sleep·y ['slipi] *adj* (**-ier; -iest**) insonnolito, sonnolento; **to be sleepy** aver sonno

sleep'y-head' *s* dormiglione *m*

sleet [slit] *s* nevischio || *impers* **it is sleeting** cade il nevischio

sleeve [sliv] *s* manica; (*of phonograph record*) busta; (*mach*) manicotto; **to laugh in** or **up one's sleeve** ridere sotto i baffi

sleigh [sle] *s* slitta || *intr* andare in slitta

sleigh' bells' *spl* bubboli *mpl* da slitta, sonagliera da slitta

sleigh' ride' *s* passeggiata in slitta

sleight' of hand' [slaɪt] *s* gioco di prestigio

slender ['slɛndər] *adj* smilzo, snello; esiguo, esile

sleuth [sluθ] *s* segugio

slew [slu] *s* (coll) mucchio

slice [slaɪs] *s* fetta; (*of an orange*) spicchio || *tr* tagliare a fette; (fig) fendere

slick [slɪk] *adj* liscio, lustro; scivoloso; astuto; (slang) ottimo || *s* posto scivoloso; (coll) rivista stampata su carta patinata || *tr* lisciare, lustrare; **to slick up** (coll) acconciare

slicker ['slɪkər] *s* impermeabile *m* di tela cerata; (coll) furbo di tre cotte

slide [slaɪd] *s* scivolata, scivolone *m*; (*chute*) scivolo; (*landslide*) frana; (*for projection*) diapositiva; (*of a microscope*) vetrino; (mach) guida; (*of a slide rule*) (mach) cursore *m* || *v* (*pret & pp* **slid** [slɪd]) *tr* far scivolare || *intr* sdrucciolare, scivolare; (*said of a car*) pattinare, slittare; **to let slide** lasciar correre

slide' fas'tener *s* chiusura lampo

slide' projec'tor *s* diascopio

slide' rule' *s* regolo calcolatore

slide' valve' *s* (mach) cassetto di distribuzione

slid'ing door' *s* porta scorrevole

slid'ing scale' *s* scala mobile

slight [slaɪt] *adj* leggero, lieve; delicato || *s* noncuranza, disattenzione; affronto || *tr* fare con negligenza; (*to snub*) trattare con noncuranza, snobbare

slim [slɪm] *adj* (**slimmer; slimmest**) sottile; magro

slime [slaɪm] *s* melma; (*e.g., of a snail*) bava

slim·y ['slaɪmi] *adj* (**-ier; -iest**) melmoso; bavoso; sudicio

sling [slɪŋ] *s* (*to shoot stones*) fionda; (naut) braca; **in a sling** (*arm*) al collo || *v* (*pret & pp* **slung** [slʌŋ]) *tr* gettare; lanciare; (*freight*) imbracare; sospendere; mettere a bandoliera

sling'shot' *s* fionda

slink [slɪŋk] *v* (*pret & pp* **slunk** [slʌŋk]) *intr* andare furtivamente; **to slink away** eclissarsi

slip [slɪp] *s* scivolone *m*; svista, errore *m*; (*in prices*) discesa; (*underdress*) sottoveste *f*; (*pillowcase*) federa; (*of paper*) pezzo; (*space between two wharves*) darsena, imbarcatoio; (*form*) modulo; personcina; (*inclined plane*) (naut) scalo d'alaggio; (bot) innesto; **to give the slip to** eludere || *v* (*pret & pp* **slipped;** *ger* **slipping**) *tr* infilare; liberare; liberarsi da; omettere; **to slip off** togliersi; **to slip on** mettersi; **to slip one's mind** dimenticarsi di, e.g., **it slipped my mind** me ne sono dimenticato || *intr* scivolare, scorrere; sdrucciolare; sbagliare; peggiorare; **to let slip** lasciarsi sfuggire; **to slip away** svignarsela; **to slip by** (*said of time*) passare, fuggire; **to slip out of s.o.'s hands** sgusciare dalle mani di qlcu; **to slip up** sbagliarsi

slip′cov′er *s* fodera

slip′knot′ *s* nodo scorsoio

slip′ of the tongue′ *s* errore *m* nel parlare

slipper [ˈslɪpər] *s* pantofola

slippery [ˈslɪpəri] *adj* sdrucciolevole, scivoloso; evasivo; incerto

slip′shod′ *adj* trasandato, mal fatto

slip′-up′ *s* (coll) sbaglio

slit [slɪt] *s* taglio, fenditura ‖ *v* (*pret & pp* **slit**; *ger* **slitting**) *tr* tagliare, fendere; **to slit the throat of** sgozzare

slob [slɑb] *s* (slang) rozzo, villanzone *m*

slobber [ˈslɑbər] *s* bava; sdolcinatura ‖ *intr* sbavare; parlare sdolcinatamente

sloe [slo] *s* (*shrub*) prugnolo; (*fruit*) prugnola

slogan [ˈslogən] *s* slogan *m*

sloop [slup] *s* cutter *m*

slop [slɑp] *s* pastone *m*; (slang) sbobba ‖ *v* (*pret & pp* **slopped**; *ger* **slopping**) *tr* versare, imbrodare ‖ *intr* rovesciarsi, scorrere; (slang) perdersi in smancerie

slope [slop] *s* costa, pendice *f*; (*of mountain or roof*) spiovente *m* ‖ *tr* inclinare ‖ *intr* digradare, scendere

slop-py [ˈslɑpi] *adj* (**-pier; -piest**) fangoso; bagnato; (*slovenly*) sciatto; (*done badly*) abborracciato

slot [slɑt] *s* scanalatura; (*for letters*) buca; (*e.g., on a broadcasting schedule*) posizione

sloth [sloθ] *or* [slɔθ] *s* pigrizia; (zool) bradipo, poltrone *m*

slot′ machine′ *s* macchina a gettone

slouch [slaʊtʃ] *s* postura goffa; persona goffa; (coll) poltrone *m* ‖ *intr* muoversi goffamente; **to slouch in a chair** sdraiarsi

slouch′ hat′ *s* cappello floscio

slough [slaʊ] *s* pantano; (fig) abisso ‖ [slʌf] *s* (*of snake*) spoglia; (pathol) crosta ‖ *tr* — **to slough off** spogliarsi di ‖ *intr* sbucciarsi, cadere

Slovak [ˈslovæk] *or* [sloˈvæk] *adj & s* slovacco

sloven-ly [ˈslʌvənli] *adj* (**-lier; -liest**) sciatto, trasandato

slow [slo] *adj* lento; (*sluggish*) tardo; (*clock*) indietro, in ritardo; (*in understanding*) tardivo ‖ *adv* piano ‖ *tr* rallentare ‖ *intr* rallentarsi; (*said of a watch*) ritardare

slow′down′ *s* sciopero pignolo

slow′ mo′tion *s*—**in slow motion** al rallentatore

slow′-motion projec′tor *s* rallentatore *m*

slow′poke′ *s* (coll) poltrone *m*

slug [slʌg] *s* (*heavy piece of metal*) lingotto; (*metal disk*) gettone *m*; (fig) poltrone *m*; (zool) lumaca; (coll) colpo, mazzata ‖ *v* (*pret & pp*

slugged; *ger* **slugging**) *tr* picchiare sodo

sluggard [ˈslʌgərd] *s* poltrone *m*

sluggish [ˈslʌgɪʃ] *adj* pigro, indolente; lento, fiacco

sluice [slus] *s* canale *m*; stramazzo

sluice′ gate′ *s* paratoia

slum [slʌm] *s* bassifondi *mpl* ‖ *v* (*pret & pp* **slummed**; *ger* **slumming**) *intr* visitare i bassifondi

slumber [ˈslʌmbər] *s* dormiveglia *m*, sonnellino ‖ *intr* dormire, dormicchiare

slump [slʌmp] *s* depressione, crisi *f*; (*in prices*) ribasso, calo ‖ *intr* impantanarsi; peggiorare; (*said of prices*) ribassare, calare

slur [slʌr] *s* insulto, macchia; critica; (mus) legatura ‖ *v* (*pret & pp* **slurred**; *ger* **slurring**) *tr* pronunziare indistintamente; (*a subject*) sorvolare; insultare, calunniare; (mus) legare

slush [slʌʃ] *s* poltiglia di neve; fanghiglia; (fig) sdolcinatezza

slut [slʌt] *s* cagna; (*slovenly woman*) sciamannona; troia, puttana

sly [slaɪ] *adj* (**slyer** *or* **slier; slyest** *or* **sliest**) furbo; insidioso; (*hiding one's true feelings*) sornione; **on the sly** furtivamente

smack [smæk] *s* schiaffo; (*of whip or lips*) schiocco; (*taste*) traccia, sapore *m*; (coll) bacio collo schiocco ‖ *adv* di colpo, direttamente ‖ *tr* dare uno schiaffo a; colpire; (*the whip or one's lips*) schioccare; schioccare un bacio a ‖ *intr*—**to smack of** sapere di

small [smɔl] *adj* piccolo; povero; basso, umile; (*change*) spicciolo; (typ) minuscolo

small′ arms′ *spl* armi *fpl* portatili

small′ busi′ness *s* piccolo commercio

small′ cap′ital *s* (typ) maiuscoletto

small′ change′ *s* spiccioli *mpl*

small′ fry′ *s* minutaglia; bambini *mpl*; gente *f* di poca importanza

small′ hours′ *spl* ore *fpl* piccole

small′ intes′tine *s* intestino tenue

small-minded [ˈsmɔlˈmaɪndɪd] *adj* di corte vedute, gretto

small′ of the back′ *s* fine *f* della schiena, reni *fpl*

smallpox [ˈsmɔlˌpɑks] *s* vaiolo

small′ talk′ *s* conversazione futile

small′-time′ *adj* di poca importanza

small′-town′ *adj* di provincia

smart [smɑrt] *adj* intelligente; scaltro, furbo; (*pain*) acuto; (*in appearance*) elegante; (*pert*) impertinente; (coll) grande, abbondante ‖ *s* dolore acuto, sofferenza ‖ *intr* bruciare; dolere; soffrire

smart′ al′eck [ˈælɪk] *s* saputello

smart′ set′ *s* bel mondo

smash [smæʃ] *s* sconquasso; colpo; collisione; rovina, fallimento; (tennis) smash *m*, schiacciata ‖ *tr* sconquassare; sfracellare; rovinare; (tennis) schiacciare ‖ *intr* sconquassarsi; sfracellarsi; andare in rovina; **to smash into** scontrarsi con

smash′ hit′ *s* successone *m*

smash'-up' *s* sconquasso

smattering ['smætərɪŋ] *s* infarinatura, spolvero

smear [smɪr] *s* macchia, imbrattatura; calunnia; (bact) striscio ‖ *tr* imbrattare; spalmare; calunniare

smear' campaign' *s* campagna di vilipendio

smell [smɛl] *s* odore *m;* (*sense*) olfatto, odorato; profumo ‖ *v* (*pret & pp* **smelled** or **smelt**) *tr* fiutare, odorare ‖ *intr* odorare; (*to stink*) puzzare; profumare; **to smell of** odorare di; puzzare di

smell'ing salts' *spl* sali aromatici

smell•y ['smɛli] *adj* (*-ier; -iest*) puzzolente

smelt [smɛlt] *s* (ichth) eperlano ‖ *tr & intr* fondere

smile [smaɪl] *s* sorriso ‖ *intr* sorridere

smiling ['smaɪlɪŋ] *adj* sorridente

smirk [smʌrk] *s* ghigno ‖ *intr* ghignare

smite [smaɪt] *v* (*pret* **smote** [smot]; *pp* **smitten** ['smɪtən] or **smit** [smɪt]) *tr* colpire; percuotere; affliggere, castigare

smith [smɪθ] *s* fabbro

smith•y ['smɪθi] *s* (*-ies*) fucina

smit'ten *adj* afflitto; innamorato

smock [smɑk] *s* camice *m;* (*of mechanic*) camiciotto

smock' frock' *s* blusa da lavoro

smog [smɑg] *s* foschia, smog *m*

smoke [smok] *s* fumo; **to go up in smoke** andare in cenere ‖ *tr* affumicare; (*tobacco*) fumare; **to smoke out** cacciare col fumo; scoprire ‖ *intr* fumare; (*said, e.g., of the earth*) fumigare

smoke'-filled room' *s* stanza da riunioni piena di fumo

smoke'less pow'der ['smoklɪs] *s* polvere *f* senza fumo

smoker ['smokər] *s* fumatore *m;* salone *m* fumatori; (rr) vagone *m* fumatori

smoke' rings' *spl* anelli *mpl* di fumo

smoke' screen' *s* cortina di fumo

smoke'stack' *s* fumaiolo

smoking ['smokɪŋ] *s* (il) fumare; **no smoking** vietato fumare

smok'ing car' *s* vagone *m* fumatori

smok'ing jack'et *s* giacca da casa

smok'ing room' *s* stanza per fumatori

smok•y ['smoki] *adj* (*-ier; -iest*) fumoso

smolder ['smoldər] *s* fumo derivante da fuoco che cova ‖ *intr* covare; (*said of fire or passion*) covare; (*said of s.o.'s eyes*) ardere

smooch [smutʃ] *intr* (coll) baciarsi, baciucchiarsi

smooth [smuð] *adj* liscio, levigato; (*face*) glabro; di consistenza uniforme; (*flat*) piano; senza interruzioni; tranquillo; elegante; (*sound*) armonioso; (*taste*) gradevole; (*wine*) abboccato; (*sea*) calmo; (*style*) fluido ‖ *tr* lisciare, levigare; appianare, facilitare; calmare; **to smooth away** appianare

smooth-faced ['smuð ,fest] *adj* (*beardless*) glabro; liscio

smooth-spoken ['smuð,spokən] *adj* mellifluo

smooth•y ['smuði] *s* (*-ies*) galante *m*

smother ['smʌðər] *tr* affogare, soffocare

smudge [smʌdʒ] *s* macchia, imbrattatura ‖ *tr* macchiare, imbrattare; (*a garden*) affumicare

smudge' pot' *s* apparecchiatura per affumicare

smug [smʌg] *adj* (**smugger; smuggest**) pieno di sé stesso; liscio, lisciato

smuggle ['smʌgəl] *tr* contrabbandare ‖ *intr* praticare il contrabbando

smuggler ['smʌglər] *s* contrabbandiere *m*

smuggling ['smʌglɪŋ] *s* contrabbando

smut [smʌt] *s* sudiciume *m;* oscenità *f;* (agr) volpe *f,* golpe *f*

smut•y ['smʌti] *adj* (*-tier; -tiest*) sudicio; osceno; (agr) malato di volpe

snack [snæk] *s* spuntino, merenda; porzione

snack' bar' *s* tavola calda

snag [snæg] *s* tronco sommerso; protuberanza, sporgenza; (*tooth*) dente rotto; (fig) intoppo, ostacolo; **to hit a snag** incontrare un ostacolo ‖ *v* (*pret & pp* **snagged**) *ger* **snagging**) *tr* fare uno straccio a; (fig) ostacolare

snail [snel] *s* chiocciola, lumaca; **at a snail's pace** come una lumaca

snake [snek] *s* serpente *m;* (*nonvenomous*) biscia

snake' in the grass' *s* pericolo nascosto; (*person*) serpe *f* in seno

snap [snæp] *s* (*sharp sound*) schiocco; (*bite*) morso; (*fastener*) bottone automatico; (*of cold weather*) breve periodo; (*manner of speaking*) tono tagliente; (phot) istantanea; (coll) vigore *m;* (coll) cosa da nulla ‖ *v* (*pret & pp* **snapped**) *ger* **snapping**) *tr* schioccare; chiudere di colpo; spezzare di colpo; (*a picture*) scattare; **to snap one's fingers at** infischiarsi di; **to snap up** afferrare; (*a person*) tagliare la parola a ‖ *intr* schioccare; (*to crack*) rompersi di colpo; **to snap at** cercare di mordere; (*a bargain*) cercare di afferrare; **to snap out of it** (coll) riprendersi; **to snap shut** chiudersi di colpo

snap'drag'on *s* (bot) bocca di leone

snap' fas'tener *s* bottone automatico

snap' judg'ment *s* decisione presa senza riflessione

snap•py ['snæpi] *adj* (*-pier; -piest*) mordente, mordace; (coll) vivo, vivace; (coll) elegante; **to make it snappy** (slang) sbrigarsi

snap'shot' *s* istantanea

snare [snɛr] *s* laccio, lacciolo; (*of a drum*) corda

snare' drum' *s* cassa rullante

snarl [snɑrl] *s* (*of a dog*) ringhio; groviglio; (*of traffic*) ingorgo; (fig) confusione ‖ *tr* urlare con un ringhio; (*to tangle*) aggrovigliare; complicare ‖ *intr* ringhiare; aggrovigliarsi; complicarsi

snatch [snætʃ] *s* strappo, strappone *m;* presa; pezzetto; momentino ‖ *tr &*

intr strappare; **to snatch at** cercare di afferrare; **to snatch from** strappare a

sneak [snik] _s_ furfante _m_ || _tr_ mettere di nascosto; pigliare di nascosto || _intr_—**to sneak in** entrare di nascosto; **to sneak out** svignarsela

sneaker ['snikər] _s_ furfante _m;_ scarpetta da ginnastica

sneak' thief' _s_ ladro, topo

sneak·y ['sniki] _adj_ (-ier; -iest) furtivo

sneer [snɪr] _s_ ghigno || _intr_ sogghignare; **to sneer at** beffarsi si

sneeze [sniz] _s_ starnuto || _intr_ starnutare; **not to be sneezed at** (coll) non essere disprezzabile

snicker ['snɪkər] _s_ risatina || _intr_ fare una risatina

snide [snaɪd] _adj_ malizioso

sniff [snɪf] _s_ fiuto, fiutata; (_scent_) odore _m_ || _tr_ fiutare || _intr_ aspirare rumorosamente; (_with emotion_) moccicare; **to sniff at** annusare; mostrare disprezzo per

sniffle ['snɪfəl] _s_ moccio; **to have the sniffles** moccicare || _intr_ moccicare

snip [snɪp] _s_ taglio; pezzetto; (_person_) (coll) mezza cartuccia || _v_ (_pret & pp_ **snipped**) _ger_ **snipping**) _tr_ tagliuzzare

snipe [snaɪp] _s_ tiro di nascosto; (orn) beccaccino || _intr_ sparare in appostamento; attaccare da lontano

sniper ['snaɪpər] _s_ franco tiratore, cecchino

snippet ['snɪpɪt] _s_ ritaglio, frammento; (fig) mezza cartuccia

snip·py ['snɪpi] _adj_ (-pier; -piest) frammentario; (coll) corto, brusco; (coll) arrogante

snitch [snɪtʃ] _tr & intr_ (coll) graffignare, sgraffignare

sniv·el ['snɪvəl] _s_ moccio; singhiozzo; piagnisteo; falsa commozione || _v_ (_pret & pp_ **-eled** or **-elled;** _ger_ **-eling** or **-elling**) _intr_ singhiozzare, piagnucolare; (_to have a runny nose_) moccicare, avere il moccio

snob [snɑb] _s_ snob _mf_

snobbery ['snɑbəri] _s_ snobismo

snobbish ['snɑbɪʃ] _adj_ snobistico

snoop [snup] _s_ (coll) ficcanaso || _intr_ (coll) ficcare il naso

snoop·y ['snupi] _adj_ (-ier; -iest) (coll) curioso, invadente

snoot [snut] _s_ (slang) naso

snoot·y ['snuti] _adj_ (-ier; -iest) (coll) snobistico

snooze [snuz] _s_ (coll) sonnellino || _intr_ (coll) fare un sonnellino

snore [snor] _s_ russamento || _intr_ russare

snort [snɔrt] _s_ sbuffo || _intr_ sbuffare

snot [snɑt] _s_ (slang) moccio

snot·ty ['snɑti] _adj_ (-tier; -tiest) (coll) snobistico; (coll) arrogante; (slang) moccioso

snout [snaʊt] _s_ muso; (_of pig_) grugno; (_of person_) muso, grugno

snow [sno] _s_ neve _f_ || _intr_ nevicare

snow'ball' _s_ palla di neve || _tr_ gettare palle di neve a || _intr_ aumentare come una palla di neve

snow'blind' _adj_ accecato dalla neve

snow'bound' _adj_ prigioniero della neve

snow-capped ['sno ,kæpt] _adj_ coperto di neve

snow'drift' _s_ banco di neve

snow'fall' _s_ nevicata

snow' fence' _s_ barriera contro la neve

snow'flake' _s_ fiocco di neve

snow' flur'ry _s_ neve portata da raffiche

snow' line' _s_ limite _m_ delle nevi perenni

snow'man' _s_ (-men') uomo di neve

snow'plow' _s_ spazzaneve _m_

snow'shoe' _s_ racchetta da neve

snow'slide' _s_ valanga

snow'storm' _s_ bufera di neve

snow' tire' _s_ gomma da neve, pneumatico da neve

snow'-white' _adj_ bianco come la neve

snow·y ['sno-i] _adj_ (-ier; -iest) nevoso

snub [snʌb] _s_ affronto || _v_ (_pret & pp_ **snubbed;** _ger_ **snubbing**) _tr_ snobbare

snub·by ['snʌbi] _adj_ (-bier; -biest) camuso, rincagnato

snuff [snʌf] _s_ fiutata; tabacco da fiuto; (_of a candlewick_) moccolo; **up to snuff** (coll) soddisfacente; (coll) bene || _tr_ fiutare; tabaccare; (_a candle_) smoccolare; **to snuff out** spegnere; (fig) soffocare

snuff'box' _s_ tabacchiera

snuffers ['snʌfərz] _spl_ smoccolatoio

snug [snʌg] _adj_ (snugger; snuggest) comodo; (_dress_) attillato; compatto; (_well-off_) agiato; (_sum_) discreto; (_sheltered_) ben protetto; (_well-hidden_) nascosto

snuggle ['snʌgəl] _intr_ rannicchiarsi; **to snuggle up to** stringersi a

so [so] _adv_ così; così or tanto + _adj_ or _adv;_ per quanto; **and so** certamente; pure; **and so on** e così via; **or so** più o meno; **to think so** credere di sì; **so as to** + _inf_ per + _inf;_ **so far** sinora, finora; **so long!** arrivederci!; **so many** tanti; **so much** tanto; **so** così così; **so that** in maniera che, in modo che; **so to speak** per così dire || _conj_ cosicché || _interj_ bene!; basta!; così!

soak [sok] _s_ bagnata; (_toper_) (slang) ubriacone _m_ || _tr_ bagnare, inzuppare; imbevere; (coll) ubriacare; (slang) far pagare un prezzo esorbitante a; **to soak up** assorbire; **soaked to the skin** bagnato fino alle ossa || _intr_ stare a molle, macerare; inzupparsi

so'-and-so' _s_ (-sos) tal _m_ dei tali; tal cosa

soap [sop] _s_ sapone _m_ || _tr_ insaponare

soap'box' _s_ cassa di sapone; tribuna improvvisata

soap'box or'ator _s_ oratore _m_ che parla da una tribuna improvvisata

soap' bub'ble _s_ bolla di sapone

soap' dish' _s_ portasapone _m_

soap' flakes' _spl_ sapone _m_ a scaglie

soap' op'era _s_ (coll) trasmissione radiofonica o televisiva lacrimogena

soap' pow'der _s_ sapone _m_ in polvere

soap'stone' _s_ pietra di sarto

soap'suds' _spl_ saponata

soap·y ['sopi] _adj_ (-ier; -iest) saponoso

soar [sor] *intr* spaziare, slanciarsi; (aer) librarsi

sob [sab] *s* singhiozzo || *v* (*pret & pp* **sobbed;** *ger* **sobbing**) *tr* dire a singhiozzi || *intr* singhiozzare

sober ['sobər] *adj* sobrio; non ubriaco || *intr* smaltire la sbornia; **to sober down** calmarsi; **to sober up** smaltire la sbornia

sobriety [so'braɪ·əti] *s* sobrietà *f*

sobriquet ['sobrɪ‚ke] *s* nomignolo

sob' sis'ter *s* giornalista lacrimogeno

sob' sto'ry *s* storia lacrimogena

so'-called' *adj* cosiddetto

soccer ['sakər] *s* calcio, football *m*

sociable ['soʃəbəl] *adj* sociale, socievole

social ['soʃəl] *adj* sociale || *s* riunione sociale

so'cial climb'er ['klaɪmər] *s* arrampicatore *m* sociale

so'cial con'tract *s* patto sociale

socialism ['soʃə‚lɪzəm] *s* socialismo

socialist ['soʃəlɪst] *s* socialista *mf*

socialite ['soʃə‚laɪt] *s* persona che appartiene all'alta società

So'cial Reg'ister *s* (trademark) annuario dell'alta società

so'cial secu'rity *s* sicurezza sociale

so'cial work'er *s* visitatrice *f*, assistente *mf* sociale

socie·ty [sə'saɪ·əti] *s* (**-ties**) società *f*; (*companionship or company*) compagnia

soci'ety ed'itor *s* cronista mondano

sociology [‚sosɪ'alədʒi] or [‚soʃɪ'alədʒi] *s* sociologia

sock [sak] *s* calzino; (slang) colpo forte; (slang) attore *m* di prim'ordine; (slang) spettacolo eccezionale || *tr* (slang) dare un forte colpo a

socket ['sakɪt] *s* (*of eye*) occhiaia; (*of tooth*) alveolo; (*of candlestick*) bocciolo; (*wall socket*) (elec) presa di corrente; (elec) portalampada *m*

sock'et wrench' *s* chiave *f* a tubo

sod [sad] *s* zolla; terreno erboso || *v* (*pret & pp* **sodded;** *ger* **sodding**) *tr* piotare

soda ['sodə] *s* soda

so'da crack'er *s* galletta fatta al bicarbonato

so'da wa'ter *s* soda, gazosa

sodium ['sodɪ·əm] *adj* sodico || *s* sodio

sofa ['sofə] *s* sofà *m*, divano

so'fa bed' *s* sofà *m* letto

soft [sɔft] or [saft] *adj* molle; (*smooth*) morbido; (*iron*) dolce; (*hat*) floscio; (*person*) rammollito; (coll) facile

soft'-boiled' egg' ['sɔft'bɔɪld] or ['saft'bɔɪld] *s* uovo alla coque

soft' coal' *s* carbone bituminoso

soft' drink' *s* bibita

soften ['sɔfən] or ['safən] *tr* mollificare, rammollire; (fig) intenerire || *intr* intenerirsi

softener ['sɔfənər] or ['safənər] *s* ammorbidente *m*

soft' land'ing *s* allunaggio morbido

soft'-ped'al *v* (*pret & pp* **-aled** or **-alled;** *ger* **-aling** or **-alling**) *tr* mettere in sordina; (coll) moderare

soft'-shell crab' *s* mollecca

soft' soap' *s* sapone *m* molle; (coll) adulazione

soft'-soap' *tr* (coll) insaponare

sog·gy ['sagi] *adj* (**-gier; -giest**) rammollito, inzuppato

soil [sɔɪl] *s* suolo, terreno; territorio; (*spot*) macchia; (*filth*) porcheria, lordura || *tr* sporcare, macchiare || *intr* sporcarsi, macchiarsi

soil' pipe' *s* tubo di scarico

soiree or soirée [swɑ're] *s* serata

sojourn ['sodʒʌrn] *s* soggiorno || ['sodʒʌrn] or [so'dʒʌrn] *intr* soggiornare

solace ['salɪs] *s* conforto || *tr* confortare, consolare

solar ['solər] *adj* solare

so'lar bat'tery *s* batteria solare

solder ['sadər] *s* saldatura; lega per saldatura || *tr* saldare

sol'dering i'ron *s* saldatoio

soldier ['soldʒər] *s* (*man of rank and file*) soldato; (*man in military service*) militare *m* || *intr* fare il soldato

sol'dier of for'tune *s* soldato di ventura

soldier·y ['soldʒəri] *s* (**-ies**) soldatesca

sold-out ['sold‚aut] *adj* esaurito; (*e.g., theater*) completo

sole [sol] *adj* solo, unico; esclusivo || *s* (*of foot*) pianta; (*of stocking*) soletta; (*of shoe*) suola; (*fish*) sfoglia || *tr* solare

solely ['solli] *adv* solamente

solemn ['saləm] *adj* solenne

solicit [sə'lɪsɪt] *tr* sollecitare; adescare, accostare

solicitor [sə'lɪsɪtər] *s* sollecitatore *m;* agente *m;* (law) procuratore *m*

solicitous [sə'lɪsɪtəs] *adj* sollecito

solicitude [sə'lɪsɪ‚tjud] or [sə'lɪsɪ‚tud] *s* sollecitudine *f*

solid ['salɪd] *adj* solido; (*not hollow*) sodo; (*e.g., clouds*) denso; (*wall*) pieno, massiccio; (*word*) con grafia unita; intero; unanime, solidale; (*good*) buono; (*e.g., gold*) puro, massiccio

solidity [sə'lɪdɪti] *s* solidità *f*

sol'id-state' *adj* transistorizzato, senza valvole

solilo·quy [sə'lɪləkwi] *s* (**-quies**) soliloquio

solitaire ['salɪ‚ter] *s* solitario

solitar·y ['salɪ‚teri] *adj* solitario; unico || *s* (**-ies**) persona solitaria

sol'itary confine'ment *s* segregazione cellulare

solitude ['salɪ‚tjud] or ['salɪ‚tud] *s* solitudine *f*

so·lo ['solo] *adj* solo, solitario; (**mus**) solista || *s* (**-los**) (mus) solo

soloist ['solo·ɪst] *s* solista *mf*

so' long' *interj* (coll) ciao!; (coll) addio!; (coll) arrivederci!

solstice ['salstɪs] *s* solstizio

soluble ['saljəbəl] *adj* solubile

solution [sə'luʃən] *s* soluzione *f*

solvable ['salvəbəl] *adj* risolvibile

solve [salv] *tr* risolvere, sciogliere

solvency ['sɑlvənsi] s solvenza
solvent ['sɑlvənt] adj & s solvente m
somber ['sɑmbər] adj tetro
some [sʌm] adj indef qualche; di + art, e.g., **some apples** delle mele; (coll) forte, grande || pron indef alcuni, taluni; ne, e.g., **I have some** ne ho
some'bod'y pron indef taluno, qualcuno; **somebody else** qualcun altro || s (-ies) (coll) qualcuno
some'day' adv qualche giorno
some'how' adv in qualche modo; **somehow or other** in un modo o nell'altro
some'one' pron indef qualcuno, taluno; **someone else** qualcun altro
somersault ['sʌmər‚sɔlt] s salto mortale || intr fare un salto mortale
something ['sʌmθɪŋ] pron indef qualcosa; **something else** qualcos'altro || adv un po'; (coll) molto, moltissimo
some'time' adj antico, di un tempo || adv un giorno o l'altro, uno di questi giorni
some'times' adv talora, talvolta
some'way' adv in qualche modo
some'what' s qualcosa || adv piuttosto, un po'
some'where' adv in qualche luogo, da qualche parte; a qualche momento; **somewhere else** altrove
somnambulist [sɑm'næmbjəlɪst] s sonnambulo
somnolent ['sɑmnələnt] adj sonnolento
son [sʌn] s figlio
sonar ['sonɑr] s ecogoniometro, sonar m
song [sɔŋ] or [sɑŋ] s canto, canzone f; **for a song** per un soldo
song'bird' s uccello canoro
Song' of Songs' s Cantico dei Cantici
songster ['sɔŋstər] s cantante m, canzonettista m
songstress ['sɔŋstrɪs] s cantante f, canzonettista f
song'writ'er s canzoniere m
son'ic boom' ['sɑnɪk] s boato sonico
son'-in-law' s (sons'-in-law') genero
sonnet ['sɑnɪt] s sonetto
son·ny ['sʌni] s (-nies) figliolo
sonori·ty [sə'nɑrɪti] or [sə'nɔrɪti] s (-ties) sonorità f
soon [sun] adv in breve, ben presto; subito, presto; **as soon as** non appena, quanto prima; **as soon as possible** quanto prima; **I had sooner** preferirei; **how soon?** quando?; **soon after** poco dopo; **sooner or later** prima o poi, tosto o tardi
soot [sʊt] or [sut] s fuliggine f
soothe [suð] tr calmare, lenire
soothsayer ['suð‚se‚ər] s indovino
soot·y ['suti] or ['suti] adj (-ier; -iest) fuligginoso
sop [sɑp] s (soaked food) zuppa; (bribe) dono, offa || v (pret & pp sopped; ger sopping) tr intingere, inzuppare; **to sop up** assorbire
sophisticated [sə'fɪstɪ‚ketɪd] adj sofisticato, smalizioso
sophistication [sə‚fɪstɪ'ke/ən] s eccessiva ricercatezza; gusti mpl raffinati

sophomore ['sɑfə‚mor] s studente m del secondo anno, fagiolo
sophomoric [‚sɑfə'mɔrɪk] adj saputello, presuntuoso; ingenuo, imberbe
sopping ['sɑpɪŋ] adv—**sopping wet** inzuppato
sopran·o [sə'præno] or [sə'prɑno] adj per soprano, da soprano || s (-os) soprano mf
sorcerer ['sɔrsərər] s mago, stregone m
sorceress ['sɔrsərɪs] s maga, strega
sorcer·y ['sɔrsəri] s (-ies) stregoneria
sordid ['sɔrdɪd] adj sordido
sore [sor] adj irritato; indolenzito; estremo, grave; **to be sore at** (coll) aversela con || s piaga, ulcera; dolore m, afflizione; **to open an old sore** riaprire una ferita
sorely ['sorli] adv penosamente; gravemente, urgentemente
soreness ['sornɪs] s dolore m, afflizione
sore' spot' s (fig) piaga
sore' throat' s mal m di gola
sorori·ty [sə'rɑrɪti] or [sə'rɔrɪti] s (-ties) associazione femminile universitaria
sorrel ['sɔrəl] or ['sɑrəl] adj sauro
sorrow ['sɑro] or ['sɔro] s dolore m, cordoglio || intr affliggersi, provar cordoglio; **to sorrow for** rimpiangere
sorrowful ['sɑrəfəl] or ['sɔrəfəl] adj doloroso
sor·ry ['sɑri] or ['sɔri] adj (-rier; -riest) spiacente, desolato, dolente; povero, cattivo; **to be sorry** dolersi; dispiacere a, e.g., **he is sorry** gli dispiace || interj mi dispiace!, scusi!
sort [sɔrt] s tipo, specie f; maniera; **a sort of** una specie di; **out of sorts** depresso; ammalato; di mal umore; **sort of** (coll) piuttosto; (coll) un certo, e.g., **sort of a headache** un certo mal di testa || tr assortire; (mail) smistare
so'-so' adj passabile || adv così così
sot [sɑt] s ubriacone m
soubrette [su'brɛt] s (theat) soubrette f
soul [sol] s anima; **upon my soul!** sulla mia parola!
sound [saʊnd] adj sano; solido, forte; valido, buono; (sleep) profondo; valido, legale; onesto || s suono; rumore m; (of an animal) verso; (passage of water) stretto; (surg) sonda; (ichth) vescica natatoria; **within sound of** alla portata di || adv profondamente || tr (an instrument) sonare; pronunciare; (e.g., s.o.'s chest) auscultare; (praises) cantare; (to measure) sondare || intr sonare; parere, sembrare; fare uno scandaglio; **to sound like** avere il suono di; dare l'impressione di, parere
sound' bar'rier s muro del suono
sound' film' s pellicola sonora
soundly ['saʊndli] adv solidamente; profondamente; completamente
sound'proof' adj a prova di suono || tr insonorizzare

sound' track' *s* (mov) sonoro, colonna sonora

sound' truck' *s* autoveicolo con impianto sonoro

sound' wave' *s* onda sonora

soup [sup] *s* zuppa, minestra

soup' dish' *s* piatto fondo

soup' kitch'en *s* asilo dei poveri che serve zuppa gratuitamente

soup'spoon' *s* cucchiaio (da minestra)

sour [saur] *adj* acido; (*fruit*) acerbo || *tr* inacidire || *intr* inacidirsi

source [sors] *s* fonte *f*, sorgente *f*

source' lan'guage *s* lingua di partenza

source' mate'rial *s* fonti *fpl* originali

sour' cher'ry *s* (*fruit*) amarena; (*tree*) amareno

sour' grapes' *interj* l'uva è verde!

south [sauθ] *adj* meridionale, del sud || *s* sud *m*, meridione *m* || *adv* verso il sud

South' Amer'ica *s* l'America *f* del Sud

South' Amer'ican *adj & s* sudamericano

southeast [ˌsauθ'ist] *adj* di sud-est || *s* sud-est || *adv* al sud-est

southern ['sʌðərn] *adj* meridionale

South'ern Cross' *s* Croce *f* del Sud

southerner ['sʌðərnər] *s* meridionale *mf*

South' Kore'a *s* la Corea del Sud

south'paw' *adj & s* (coll) mancino

South' Pole' *s* Polo sud

South' Vietnam·ese' [vɪˌetnɑ'miz] *adj* vietnamita del sud || *s* (*-ese*) vietnamita *mf* del sud

southward ['sauθwərd] *adv* verso il sud

south'west' *adj* di sud-ovest || *s* sud-ovest *m* || *adv* al sud-ovest

souvenir [ˌsuvə'nɪr] or ['suvəˌnɪr] *s* ricordo, memoria

sovereign ['sɑvrɪn] or ['sʌvrɪn] *adj* sovrano || *s* (*king*) sovrano; (*queen; coin*) sovrana

sovereign·ty ['sɑvrɪnti] or ['sʌvrɪnti] *s* (*-ties*) sovranità *f*

soviet ['sovɪˌet] or [ˌsovi'et] *adj* sovietico || *s* soviet *m*

So'viet Rus'sia *s* la Russia Sovietica

sow [sau] *s* porca, troia || [so] *v* (*pret* sowed; *pp* sown or sowed) *tr* seminare

soybean ['sɔɪˌbin] *s* soia; seme *m* di soia

spa [spɑ] *s* terme *fpl*

space [spes] *adj* spaziale || *s* spazio; periodo; after a space dopo un po' || *tr* spaziare; to space out diradare

space' bar' *s* barra spaziatrice, spaziatrice *f*

space' cen'ter *s* cosmodromo

space'craft' *s* astronave *f*

space' flight' *s* volo spaziale

space'man' *s* (*-men'*) navigatore *m* spaziale

spacer ['spesər] *s* spaziatrice *f*, barra spaziatrice

space'ship' *s* astronave *f*

space'suit' *s* scafandro astronautico, tuta spaziale

spacious ['speʃəs] *adj* spazioso

spade [sped] *s* vanga; (cards) picca; to call a spade a spade dire pane al pane, vino al vino || *tr* vangare

spade'work' *s* lavoro preliminare

spaghetti [spə'geti] *s* spaghetti *mpl*

Spain [spen] *s* la Spagna

span [spæn] *s* (*of the hand*) spanna; (*of time*) tratto; (*of a bridge*) campata, luce *f;* (*of horses*) paio; (aer) apertura || *v* (*pret & pp* spanned) *ger* spanning) *tr* misurare a spanne; attraversare, oltrepassare; (*said of time*) abbracciare

spangle ['spæŋgəl] *s* lustrino || *tr* tempestare di lustrini; (*with bright objects*) stellare || *intr* brillare

Spaniard ['spænjərd] *s* spagnolo

Spanish ['spænɪʃ] *adj & s* spagnolo; the Spanish gli spagnoli

Span'ish-Amer'ican *adj & s* ispano-americano

Span'ish broom' *s* ginestra

Span'ish fly' *s* mosca cantaride

Span'ish om'elet *s* frittata di pomodori, cipolle e peperoni

Span'ish-speak'ing *adj* di lingua spagnola

spank [spæŋk] *tr* sculacciare

spanking ['spæŋkɪŋ] *adj* rapido; forte; (coll) eccellente, straordinario || *s* sculacciata

spar [spɑr] *s* (mineral) spato; (naut) asta, pennone *m;* (aer) longherone *m* || *v* (*pret & pp* sparred; *ger* sparring) *intr* fare la box

spare [sper] *adj* di riserva; libero, in eccesso; (*e.g., diet*) frugale; (*lean*) magro || *tr* salvare, risparmiare; perdonare; (*to do without*) fare a meno di, privarsi di; to have . . . to spare aver . . . d'avanzo; to spare oneself risparmiarsi

spare' parts' *s* pezzi *mpl* di ricambio

spare' room' *s* camera per gli ospiti

spare' tire' *s* ruota di scorta, pneumatico di scorta

spare' wheel' *s* ruota di scorta

sparing ['sperɪŋ] *adj* economico; (*scanty*) scarso

spark [spɑrk] *s* scintilla; traccia || *tr* (coll) rianimare; (coll) corteggiare || *intr* scintillare

spark' coil' *s* bobina d'accensione

spark' gap' *s* (elec) traferro, intraferro

sparkle ['spɑrkəl] *s* scintillio; (*luster*) scintillio; allegria, vivacità *f* || *intr* scintillare; (*said, e.g., of eyes*) brillare, luccicare; (*said of wine*) frizzare, spumeggiare

sparkling ['spɑrklɪŋ] *adj* scintillante; (*wine*) frizzante, spumeggiante; (*water*) gassoso

spark' plug' *s* candela

sparrow ['spæro] *s* passero

sparse [spɑrs] *adj* rado

Spartan ['spɑrtən] *adj & s* spartano

spasm ['spæzəm] *s* spasmo; sprazzo d'energia

spasmodic [spæz'mɑdɪk] *adj* spasmodico; intermittente, a sprazzi

spastic ['spæstɪk] *adj & s* spastico

spat [spæt] *s* litigio, battibecco; spats

ghette *fpl* || *v* (*pret & pp* **spatted; ger spatting**) *intr* avere un battibecco

spatial ['speʃəl] *adj* spaziale

spatter ['spætər] *tr* schizzare, spruzzare || *intr* gocciolare

spatula ['spætʃələ] *s* spatola

spawn [spɔn] *s* prole *f*, progenie *f;* risultato || *tr* produrre, generare || *intr* (ichth) deporre le uova

spay [spe] *tr* asportare le ovaie a

speak [spik] *v* (*pret* **spoke** [spok]; *pp* **spoken**) *tr* (*a language*) parlare; (*the truth*) dire || *intr* parlare; **so to speak** per così dire; **speaking!** al telefono!; **to speak of** importante, che valga parlarne; **to speak out** dire la propria opinione

speak'-eas'y *s* (**-ies**) bar clandestino

speaker ['spikər] *s* conferenziere *m*, oratore *m;* (*of a language*) parlante *mf;* (pol) presidente *m;* (rad) altoparlante *m*

speaking ['spikɪŋ] *adj* parlante; **to be on speaking terms** parlarsi || *s* parlare *m*, discorso

speak'ing tube' *s* tubo acustico

spear [spɪr] *s* lancia; (*for fishing*) arpione *m;* (*of grass*) stelo || *tr* trafiggere con la lancia

spear' gun' *s* fucile subacqueo

spear'head' *s* punta di lancia || *tr* condurre, dirigere

spear'mint' *s* menta romana spicata

special ['speʃəl] *adj* speciale || *s* prezzo speciale; treno speciale

spe'cial deliv'ery *s* espresso

spe'cial draw'ing rights' *spl* (econ) diritti *mpl* speciali di prelievo

specialist ['speʃəlɪst] *s* specialista *mf*

specialize ['speʃə,laɪz] *tr* specializzare || *intr* specializzarsi

spe'cial part'ner *s* accomandante *mf*

special·ty ['speʃəlti] *s* (**-ties**) specialità *f*

spe·cies ['spisiz] *s* (**-cies**) specie *f*

specific [spɪ'sɪfɪk] *adj* & *s* specifico

specification [,spesɪfɪ'keʃən] *s* specifica; (com) capitolato

specif'ic grav'ity *s* peso specifico

speci·fy ['spesɪ,faɪ] *v* (*pret & pp* **-fied**) *tr* specificare

specimen ['spesɪmən] *s* esemplare *m;* (coll) tipo

specious ['spiʃəs] *adj* specioso

speck [spek] *s* macchiolina *m;* (*of dust*) granello; (*of hope*) filo || *tr* macchiettare

speckle ['spekəl] *s* macchiolina || *tr* macchiettare, picchiettare

spectacle ['spektəkəl] *s* spettacolo; **spectacles** occhiali *mpl*

spectator ['spektetər] *or* [spek'tetər] *s* spettatore *m*

specter ['spektər] *s* spettro

spec·trum ['spektrəm] *s* (**-tra** [trə] *or* **-trums**) spettro; (fig) gamma

speculate ['spekjə,let] *intr* speculare

speech [spitʃ] *s* parola, parlata; (*before an audience*) discorso; (*of an actor*) elocuzione; **in speech** oralmente

speech' clin'ic *s* clinica per la correzione dei difetti del linguaggio

speechless ['spitʃlɪs] *adj* senza parole, muto

speed [spid] *s* velocità *f;* (aut) marcia || *tr* accelerare, affrettare || *intr* accelerare, affrettarsi; guidare oltre la velocità massima

speed'boat' *s* motoscafo da corsa

speeding ['spidɪŋ] *s* eccesso di velocità

speed' king' *s* asso del volante

speed' lim'it *s* limite *m* di velocità

speedometer [spi'dɑmɪtər] *s* tachimetro; (*to record the distance covered*) contachilometri *m*

speed'-up' *s* accelerazione

speed'way' *s* (*highway*) autostrada; (*for races*) pista

speed·y ['spidi] *adj* (**-ier; -iest**) veloce, rapido

spell [spel] *s* malia, incantesimo; fascino; turno; attacco; periodo di tempo; **to cast a spell on** incantare || *v* (*pret & pp* **spelled** *or* **spelt** [spelt]) *tr* compitare; scrivere in tutte lettere; voler dire; **to spell out** (coll) spiegare dettagliatamente || *intr* scrivere, sillabare || *v* (*pret & pp* **spelled**) *tr* rimpiazzare

spell'bind' *v* (*pret & pp* **-bound**) *tr* affascinare

spell'bind'er *s* oratore *m* abbagliante

spelling ['spelɪŋ] *adj* ortografico || *s* (*act*) compitazione; (*way a word is spelled*) grafia; (*subject of study*) ortografia

spell'ing bee' *s* gara di ortografia

spelunker [spɪ'lʌŋkər] *s* esploratore *m* di caverne

spend [spend] *v* (*pret & pp* **spent** [spent]) *tr* spendere; (*time*) passare

spender ['spendər] *s* spenditore *m*

spend'ing mon'ey *s* denaro per le piccole spese personali

spend'thrift' *s* sprecone *m*, spendaccione *m*

sperm [spʌrm] *s* sperma *m*

sperm' whale' *s* capodoglio

spew [spju] *tr* & *intr* vomitare

sphere [sfɪr] *s* sfera

spherical ['sferɪkəl] *adj* sferico

sphinx [sfɪŋks] *s* (**sphinxes** *or* **sphinges** ['sfɪndʒiz]) sfinge *f*

spice [spaɪs] *s* droga; spezie *fpl;* (fig) gusto, sapore *m* || *tr* drogare; dare gusto a, rendere piccante

spick-and-span ['spɪkənd'spæn] *adj* ordinato e pulito

spic·y ['spaɪsi] *adj* (**-ier; -iest**) drogato; piccante

spider ['spaɪdər] *s* ragno

spi'der·web' *s* ragnatela

spiff·y ['spɪfi] *adj* (**-ier; -iest**) (slang) elegante, bello

spigot ['spɪɡət] *s* (peg) zipolo; (faucet) rubinetto

spike [spaɪk] *s* chiodo, chiodone *m;* (*sharp-pointed piece*) spuntone *m;* (rr) arpione *m;* (bot) spiga || *tr* inchiodare; mettere chiodi a; (*a rumor*) porre fine a; (coll) alcolizzare

spill [spɪl] *s* rovesciamento; liquido rovesciato; (coll) caduta || *v* (*pret & pp* **spilled** *or* **spilt** [spɪlt]) *tr* rovesciare, spandere; versare; (naut) sventare; (coll) far cadere; (slang) snocciolare || *intr* rovesciarsi; versarsi

spill'way' *s* sfioratore *m*, stramazzo

spin [spɪn] *s* giro; (twirl) mulinello; corsa; **to go into a spin** (aer) cadere a vite || *v* (pret & pp **spun** [spʌn]) (ger **spinning**) *tr* far girare; (e.g., thread) filare; **to spin out** prolungare; **to spin a yarn** raccontare una storia || *intr* girare; (said of a top) prillare; filare

spinach ['spɪnɪtʃ] or ['spɪnɪdʒ] *s* spinacio; (leaves used as food) spinaci *mpl*

spi'nal col'umn ['spaɪnəl] *s* spina dorsale, colonna vertebrale

spi'nal cord' *s* midollo spinale

spindle ['spɪndəl] *s* (rounded rod) fuso; (shaft, axle) asse *m*; balaustro

spine [spaɪn] *s* spina; spina dorsale; (bb) costola; (fig) forza, carattere *m*

spineless ['spaɪnlɪs] *adj* senza spine; senza carattere

spinet ['spɪnɪt] *s* spinetta

spinner ['spɪnər] *s* filatore *m*; (machine) filatrice *f*

spinning ['spɪnɪŋ] *adj* filante || *s* filatura; rotazione

spin'ning mill' *s* filanda

spin'ning wheel' *s* filatoio

spinster ['spɪnstər] *s* zitella

spi·ral ['spaɪrəl] *adj & s* spirale *f* || *v* (pret & pp -raled or -ralled; ger -raling or -ralling) *intr* muoversi lungo una spirale

spi'ral stair'case *s* scala a chiocciola

spire [spaɪr] *s* (of a steeple) guglia, freccia; (of grass) foglia; (spiral) spirale *f*

spirit ['spɪrɪt] *s* spirito; valore *m*, vigore *m*; bevanda spiritosa); **out of spirits** giù di morale || *tr*—**to spirit away** portar via misteriosamente

spirited ['spɪrɪtɪd] *adj* brioso; (horse) superbo, vivace

spir'it lamp' *s* lampada a spirito

spiritless ['spɪrɪtlɪs] *adj* senza anima, senza vita

spir'it lev'el *s* livella a bolla d'aria

spiritual ['spɪrɪtʃu·əl] *adj* spirituale; (séance) spiritico

spiritualism ['spɪrɪtʃu·ə͵lɪzəm] *s* spiritismo; (philos) spiritualismo

spiritualist ['spɪrɪtʃu·əlɪst] *s* spiritista *mf*; (philos) spiritualista *mf*

spirituous ['spɪrɪtʃu·əs] *adj* alcolico

spit [spɪt] *s* sputo; (for roasting) spiedo, schidione *m*; punta; **the spit and image of** (coll) il ritratto parlante di || *v* (pret & pp **spat** [spæt] or **spit**; ger **spitting**) *tr & intr* sputare

spite [spaɪt] *s* dispetto, ripicco; **in spite of** a dispetto di, a onta di; **out of spite** per picca || *tr* far dispetto a; offendere; contrariare

spiteful ['spaɪtfəl] *adj* dispettoso

spit'fire' *s* persona collerica; (woman) bisbetica

spit'ting im'age *s* (coll) ritratto parlante

spittoon [spɪ'tun] *s* sputacchiera

splash [splæʃ] *s* schizzo, spruzzo; (of mud) zacchera; (sound) tonfo; **to make a splash** fare molto sci-sci || *tr & intr* sguazzare

splash'down' *s* (rok) ammaraggio, urto con l'acqua

spleen [splin] *s* cattivo umore, bile *f*; (anat) milza, splene *m*

splendid ['splendɪd] *adj* splendido; ottimo, magnifico

splendor ['splendər] *s* splendore *m*

splice [splaɪs] *s* giuntura || *tr* giuntare

splint [splɪnt] *s* stecca || *tr* steccare

splinter ['splɪntər] *s* scheggia || *tr* scheggiare || *intr* scheggiarsi

splin'ter group' *s* gruppo dissidente

split [splɪt] *adj* spaccato; diviso || *s* spaccatura; fessura; rottura, divisione; **splits** (sports) spaccato || *v* (pret & pp **split**; ger **splitting**) *tr* spaccare; dividere; **to split one's sides with laughter** scoppiare dalle risa || *intr* scindersi, dividersi; **to split up** separarsi

split' personal'ity *s* sdoppiamento della personalità

splitting ['splɪtɪŋ] *adj* che fende; che si fende; violento, fortissimo || *s*— **splittings** frammenti *mpl*

splotch [splɑtʃ] *s* macchia, chiazza || *tr* macchiare, chiazzare

splurge [splʌrdʒ] *s* ostentazione || *intr* fare ostentazione; fare una spesa matta

splutter ['splʌtər] *s* crepitio; (utterance) barbugliamento || *tr* barbugliare || *intr* crepitare; barbugliare

spoil [spɔɪl] *s* spoglia, bottino; **spoils** (mil) spoglie *fpl*; (pol) profitto, vantaggio || *v* (pret & pp **spoiled** or **spoilt** [spɔɪlt]) *tr* rovinare, sciupare; (a child) viziare; (food) deteriorare || *intr* guastarsi, andare a male

spoilage ['spɔɪlɪdʒ] *s* deterioramento

spoiled [spɔɪld] *adj* (child) viziato; (food) andato a male, passato

spoils' sys'tem *s* sistema politico secondo il quale le ·cariche vanno al partito vincitore

spoke [spok] *s* (of a wheel) raggio; (of a ladder) piolo

spokes'man *s* (-men) portavoce *m*

sponge [spʌndʒ] *s* spugna; **to throw in the sponge** (slang) gettare la spugna || *tr* pulire con spugna; assorbire; (coll) scroccare || *intr* assorbire; **to sponge off** (coll) vivere alle spalle di

sponge' bath' *s* spugnatura

sponge' cake' *s* pan *m* di Spagna

sponger ['spʌndʒər] *s* scroccatore *m*

sponge' rub'ber *s* gommapiuma

spon·gy ['spʌndʒi] *adj* (-gier; -giest) spugnoso

sponsor ['spɑnsər] *s* patrocinatore *m*; (of a charitable institution) patrono; (godfather) padrino; (godmother) madrina || *tr* patrocinare; (rad, telv) offrire

sponsorship ['spɑnsər͵ʃɪp] *s* patrocinio

spontaneous [spɑn'teni·əs] *adj* spontaneo

spoof [spuf] *s* mistificazione; parodia ‖ *tr* mistificare; parodiare ‖ *intr* mistificare; fare una parodia

spook [spuk] *s* (coll) spettro

spook·y ['spuki] *adj* (**-ier; -iest**) (coll) spettrale; (*horse*) (coll) nervoso

spool [spul] *s* spola, rocchetto

spoon [spun] *s* cucchiaio; (*lure*) cucchiaino; **born with a silver spoon in one's mouth** nato con la camicia ‖ *tr* servire col cucchiaio ‖ *intr* (coll) limonare

spoonerism ['spunə‚rızəm] *s* papera

spoon'-feed' *v* (*pret & pp* **-fed**) *tr* nutrire col cucchiaino; (fig) coccolare

spoonful ['spun‚ful] *s* cucchiaiata

spoon·y ['spuni] *adj* (**-ier; -iest**) (coll) svenevole

sporadic(al) [spə'rædɪk(əl)] *adj* sporadico

spore [spor] *s* spora

sport [sport] *adj* sportivo ‖ *s* sport *m*; gioco; (*laughingstock*) zimbello; (*gambler*) (coll) giocatore *m*; (*person who behaves in a sportsmanlike manner*) (coll) spirito sportivo; (*flashy fellow*) (coll) tipo fino; (biol) mutazione; **to make sport of** farsi gioco di ‖ *tr* (coll) sfoggiare; **to sport away** dissipare ‖ *intr* divertirsi; giocare; farsi beffe

sport' clothes' *spl* vestiti *mpl* sport

sport'ing chance' *s* pari opportunità *f* di vincere

sport'ing goods' *spl* articoli *mpl* sportivi

sport'ing house' *s* (coll) bordello

sports'cast'er *s* annunziatore sportivo

sports' fan' *s* appassionato agli spettacoli sportivi, tifoso

sports'man *s* (**-men**) sportivo

sports'man·ship' *s* sportività *f*, spirito sportivo

sports' news' *s* notiziario sportivo

sports'wear' *s* articoli *mpl* d'abbigliamento sportivo

sports'writ'er *s* cronista sportivo

sport·y ['sporti] *adj* (**-ier; -iest**) (coll) elegante; (coll) sportivo; (coll) appariscente

spot [spat] *s* macchia; luogo, punto, posto; (*e.g., of tea*) goccia; **spots** locali *mpl*; **on the spot** sul posto; (*right now*) seduta stante; (slang) in difficoltà; **to hit the spot** (slang) soddisfare completamente ‖ *v* (*pret & pp* **spotted;** *ger* **spotting**) *tr* macchiare; spargere; (coll) riconoscere ‖ *intr* macchiare; macchiarsi

spot' cash' *s* pronta cassa

spot'-check' *tr* fare un breve sondaggio di; controllare rapidamente

spot' check' *s* breve sondaggio; rapido controllo

spotless ['spatlıs] *adj* immacolato, senza macchia

spot'light' *s* riflettore *m*; (aut) proiettore *m*; **to be in the spotlight** (fig) essere il centro d'attenzione

spot' remov'er [rı'muvər] *s* smacchiatore *m*

spot' weld'ing *s* saldatura per punti

spouse [spauz] *or* [spaus] *s* consorte *mf*

spout [spaut] *s* (*to carry water from roof*) doccia; (*of jar, pitcher, etc.*) becco, beccuccio; (jet) zampillo, getto ‖ *tr & intr* sprizzare, zampillare; (coll) declamare

sprain [spren] *s* distorsione ‖ *tr* distorcere, distorcersi

sprawl [sprɔl] *intr* sdraiarsi

spray [spre] *s* spruzzo; (*of the sea*) schiuma; (*device*) spruzzatore *m*; (*twig*) ramoscello ‖ *tr & intr* spruzzare

sprayer ['spre·ər] *s* spruzzatore *m*, schizzetto, vaporizzatore *m*; (hort) irroratrice *f*

spray' gun' *s* pistola a spruzzo; (hort) irroratrice *f*

spray' paint' *s* vernice *f* a spruzzo

spread [spred] *s* espansione; diffusione; differenza; tappeto, coperta; elasticità *f*; (*of the wings of bird or airplane*) apertura; cibo da spalmare; (coll) festino; (journ) articolo di fondo or pubblicitario su varie colonne ‖ *v* (*pret & pp* **spread**) *tr* tendere, estendere; (*one's legs*) divaricare; (*wings*) spiegare; spargere, cospargere; (*the table*) preparare; (*butter*) spalmare; diffondere ‖ *intr* estendersi; spiegarsi; spargersi; spalmarsi; diffondersi

spree [spri] *s* baldoria, bisboccia; **to go on a spree** darsi alla pazza gioia

sprig [sprɪg] *s* ramoscello

spright·ly ['spraɪtli] *adj* (**-lier; -liest**) brioso, vivace

spring [sprɪŋ] *adj* primaverile; sorgivo; a molla ‖ *s* (*season*) primavera; (*issue of water from earth*) fonte *f*, polla; (*elastic device*) molla; elasticità *f*; (*leap*) salto; (*crack*) fenditura; (aut) balestra ‖ *v* (*pret* **sprang** [spræŋ] *or* **sprung** [sprʌŋ]; *pp* **sprung**) *tr* (*e.g., a lock*) far scattare; (*a leak*) aprire; (*a mine*) far brillare ‖ *intr* saltare; (*said of a metal spring*) scattare; scaturire, zampillare; nascere, derivare; esplodere; **to spring forth** or **up** sorgere

spring'board' *s* pedana, trampolino

spring' chick'en *s* pollo giovanissimo; (slang) ragazzina

spring' fe'ver *s* indolenza primaverile

spring' mat'tress *s* materasso a molle

spring' tide' *s* marea di sizigia

spring'time' *s* primavera

sprinkle ['sprɪŋkəl] *s* spruzzo, spruzzatina; (*small amount*) pizzico ‖ *tr* spruzzare; (*e.g., sugar*) spolverizzare ‖ *intr* sprizzare; piovigginare

sprinkler ['sprɪŋklər] *s* annaffiatoio; (*person*) annaffiattore *m*

sprinkling ['sprɪŋklɪŋ] *s* spruzzo, spruzzo; (*with holy water*) aspersione; (*with powder*) spolverizzamento; (*e.g., of knowledge*) spolvero, spolveratura; (*of people*) piccolo numero

sprin'kling can' *s* annaffiatoio

sprint [sprɪnt] *s* (sports) scatto, volata || *intr* (sports) scattare

sprite [spraɪt] *s* spirito folletto

sprocket ['sprɑkɪt] *s* moltiplica; (phot) trasportatore *m*

sprout [spraut] *s* germoglio || *intr* germogliare; crescere rapidamente

spruce [sprus] *adj* elegante, attillato || *s* abete rosso || *tr* attillare, azzimare || *intr* attillarsi, azzimarsi

spry [spraɪ] *adj* (**spryer or sprier; spryest or spriest**) vegeto

spud [spʌd] *s* vanghetto, tagliaradici *m;* (coll) patata

spun' glass' *s* lana di vetro

spunk [spʌŋk] *s* (coll) coraggio, fegato

spur [spʌr] *s* sperone *m;* (rr) raccordo ferroviario; (fig) pungolo; **on the spur of the moment** lì per lì || *v* (*pret & pp* **spurred**; *ger* **spurring**) *tr* spronare; **to spur on** spronare, incitare

spurious ['spjurɪ·əs] *adj* spurio

spurn [spʌrn] *s* disprezzo, sdegno; rifiuto || *tr* disprezzare, sdegnare; rifiutare

spurt [spʌrt] *s* spruzzo, zampillo; (*sudden burst*) scatto repentino || *intr* sprizzare, zampillare; scattare

sputter ['spʌtər] *s* barbugliamento; (*sizzling*) crepitio || *tr* barbugliare || *intr* barbugliare; crepitare

spu·tum ['spjutəm] *s* (*-ta* [tə]) sputo

spy [spaɪ] *s* (**spies**) spia || *v* (*pret & pp* **spied**) *tr* spiare; osservare || *intr* fare la spia; **to spy on** spiare

spy'glass' *s* cannocchiale *m*

spying ['spaɪ·ɪŋ] *s* spionaggio

squabble ['skwɑbəl] *s* battibecco || *intr* litigare

squad [skwɑd] *s* squadra

squadron ['skwɑdrən] *s* (*of cavalry*) squadrone *m;* (aer, nav) squadriglia; (mil) squadra

squalid ['skwɑlɪd] *adj* sordido; squallido, misero

squall [skwɔl] *s* groppo, turbine *m;* urlo || *intr* gridare, urlare

squalor ['skwɑlər] *s* sordidezza; squallore *m*, miseria

squander ['skwɑndər] *tr* scialacquare, dilapidare, sperperare

square [skwɛr] *adj* quadrato, e.g., **two square miles** due miglia quadrate; di . . . di lato, e.g., **two miles square** di due miglia di lato; ad angolo retto; solido; saldato; (coll) onesto; (coll) diretto; (coll) sostanzioso; (slang) all'antica; **to get square with** (coll) fargliela pagare a || *s* quadrato; (*small square, e.g., of checkerboard*) quadretto; (*city block*) isolato; (*open area in city*) piazza, piazzale *m;* (*of carpenter*) squadra; **on the square** ad angolo retto; (coll) onesto || *adv* ad angolo retto; (coll) onestamente || *tr* squadrare; dividere in quadretti; elevare al quadrato; quadrare; (*a debt*) saldare; **to square with** adattare a || *intr* quadrare; **to square off** prepararsi, mettersi in posizione difensiva

square' dance' *s* danza figurata americana

square' meal' *s* (coll) pasto abbondante

square' root' *s* radice quadrata

square' shoot'er ['ʃutər] *s* (coll) persona onesta

squash [skwɑʃ] *s* spappolamento; (bot) zucca; (sports) squash *m* || *tr* spappolare; spiaccicare; (*e.g., a rumor*) sopprimere; (*a person*) (coll) ridurre al silenzio || *intr* spiaccicarsi

squash·y ['skwɑʃi] *adj* (*-ier; -iest*) tenero; (*ground*) fangoso, pantanoso; (*fruit*) maturo

squat [skwɑt] *adj* tozzo || *v* (*pret & pp* **squatted**; *ger* **squatting**) *intr* accocolarsi; stabilirsi illegalmente su territorio altrui; stabilirsi su terreno pubblico per ottenere un titolo

squatter ['skwɑtər] *s* intruso

squaw [skwɔ] *s* squaw *f;* (coll) donna

squawk [skwɔk] *s* schiamazzo; (slang) lamento stridulo || *intr* schiamazzare; (slang) lamentarsi strillando

squaw' man' *s* bianco sposato con una pellirossa

squeak [skwik] *s* strido; cigolio || *intr* stridere; cigolare; (*said of a mouse*) squittire; **to squeak through** farcela per il rotto della cuffia

squeal [skwil] *s* strido || *intr* stridere; (slang) cantare, fare il delatore

squealer ['skwilər] *s* (slang) delatore *m*

squeamish ['skwimɪʃ] *adj* pudibondo; scrupoloso; (*easily nauseated*) schifiltoso, schizzinoso

squeeze [skwiz] *s* spremuta; stretta, abbraccio; **to put the squeeze on** (coll) far pressione su || *tr* premere; spremere, pigiare; stringere || *intr* stringere; **to squeeze through** aprirsi il passo attraverso; (fig) farcela a pena

squeezer ['skwizər] *s* spremifrutta *m*

squelch [skwɛltʃ] *s* osservazione schiacciante || *tr* schiacciare

squid [skwɪd] *s* calamaro, totano

squint [skwɪnt] *s* tendenza losca; (coll) occhiata; (pathol) strabismo || *tr* (*one's eyes*) socchiudere || *intr* socchiudere gli occhi; guardare furtivamente

squint-eyed ['skwɪnt‚aɪd] *adj* guercio, losco; malevolo

squire [skwaɪr] *s* (*of a lady*) cavalier *m* servente; (Brit) proprietario terriero; (U.S.A.) giudice *m* conciliatore || *tr* (*a woman*) accompagnare

squirm [skwʌrm] *s* contorsione || *intr* contorcersi; mostrare imbarazzo; **to squirm out of** cavarsela da

squirrel ['skwʌrəl] *s* scoiattolo

squirt [skwʌrt] *s* schizzo; (*instrument*) schizzetto; (coll) saputello || *tr & intr* schizzare

stab [stæb] *s* pugnalata; (*of pain*) fitta; **to make a stab at** (coll) provare || *v* (*pret & pp* **stabbed**; *ger* **stabbing**) *tr* pugnalare, trafiggere || *intr* pugnalare

stabilize ['stebəl‚aɪz] *tr* stabilizzare

stab' in the back' *s* pugnalata nella schiena or alle spalle

stable ['stebəl] *adj* stabile || *s* stalla; (*of race horses*) scuderia

sta'ble-boy' *s* stalliere *m*

stack [stæk] *s* pila; (*of hay or straw*) pagliaio; (*of firewood*) catasta; (*of books*) scaffale *m*; camino; (*coll*) mucchio, sacco || *tr* ammonticchiare, accatastare

stadi-um ['stedɪ-əm] *s* (-**ums** or -**a** [ə]) stadio

staff [stæf] or [staf] *s* bastone *m*; asta, albero; personale *m*, corpo; (*mil*) stato maggiore; (*mus*) rigo, pentagramma *m* || *tr* dotare di personale

staff' of'ficer *s* ufficiale *m* di stato maggiore

stag [stæg] *adj* per signori soli || *s* (*deer*) cervo; maschio; (*coll*) signore *m* || *adv* senza compagna

stage [stedʒ] *s* fase *f*, stadio; tappa, giornata; (*coach*) diligenza; teatro; piattaforma; (*of microscope*) piatto portaoggetti; (*theat*) scena, palcoscenico; **by easy stages** poco a poco; **to go on the stage** diventare attore || *tr* mettere in scena; organizzare

stage'coach' *s* diligenza

stage'craft' *s* scenotecnica

stage' door' *s* (*theat*) ingresso degli artisti

stage' fright' *s* tremarella

stage'hand' *s* macchinista *m*

stage' left' *s* (*theat*) la sinistra della scena guardando il pubblico

stage' man'ager *s* direttore *m* di scena

stage' right' *s* (*theat*) la destra della scena guardando il pubblico

stage'-struck' *adj* innamorato del teatro

stage' whis'per *s* a parte *m*

stagger ['stægər] *tr* far traballare; impressionare; (*troops; hours*) scaglionare || *intr* traballare

stag'gering *adj* traballante; impressionante, stupefacente

staging ['stedʒɪŋ] *s* impalcatura; (*theat*) messa in scena

stagnant ['stægnənt] *adj* stagnante

staid [sted] *adj* serio, grave

stain [sten] *s* macchia; tinta; colorante *m* || *tr* macchiare; tingere; colorare || *intr* macchiarsi

stained' glass' *s* vetro colorato

stained'-glass win'dow *s* vetrata a colori

stainless ['stenlɪs] *adj* immacolato; (*steel*) inossidabile

stair [stɛr] *s* scala

stair'case' *s* scala

stair'way' *s* scala

stair'well' *s* tromba delle scale

stake [stek] *s* picchetto; (*e.g., of cart*) staggio; (*to support a plant*) puntello; (*in gambling*) puglia, giocata; **at stake** in gioco; **to die at the stake** morire sul rogo; **to pull up stakes** (*coll*) andarsene, traslocare || *tr* picchettare; puntellare; attaccare a un palo; arrischiare; (*coll*) aiutare; **to stake out** picchettare; (*slang*) tenere sotto sorveglianza; **to stake out a claim** avanzare una pretesa

stale [stel] *adj* stantio; (*air*) viziato; (*fig*) ritrito

stale'mate' *s* (*chess*) stallo; **to reach a stalemate** essere in una posizione di stallo || *tr* mettere in una posizione di stallo

stalk [stɔk] *s* stelo; (*of corn*) stocco; (*of salad*) piede *m* || *tr* braccare || *intr* avanzare furtivamente; camminare con andatura maestosa

stall [stɔl] *s* (*in a stable*) posta; (*booth in a market*) bancarella; (*seat*) stallo; (*space in a parking lot*) spazio per il parcheggio || *tr* (*an animal*) stallare; (*a car*) parcheggiare; (*a motor*) far fermare; **to stall off** eludere, tenere a bada || *intr* impantanarsi; stare nella posta; (*said of a motor*) fermarsi; (*to temporize*) menare il can per l'aia

stallion ['stæljən] *s* stallone *m*

stalwart ['stɔlwərt] *adj* forte, gagliardo || *s* sostenitore *m*

stamen ['stemən] *s* stame *m*

stamina ['stæmɪnə] *s* forza, vigore *m*

stammer ['stæmər] *s* balbuzie *f* || *tr* & *intr* balbettare

stammerer ['stæmərər] *s* balbuziente *mf*

stamp [stæmp] *s* (*postage stamp*) francobollo; (*device to show that a fee has been paid*) timbro, bollo; impressione; carattere *m*; sigillo; (*tool for stamping coins*) conio; (*tool for crushing ore*) maglio || *tr* timbrare, stampigliare, bollare; sigillare; coniare; (*one's foot*) battere, pestare; imprimere; caratterizzare; (*mach*) stampare; **to stamp out** spegnere; sopprimere || *intr* battere il piede; (*said of a horse*) zampare

stampede [stæm'pid] *s* fuga precipitosa || *tr* precipitarsi verso; far fuggire precipitosamente || *intr* precipitarsi

stamp'ing ground' *s* (*coll*) luogo di ritrovo abituale

stamp' pad' *s* tampone *m*

stamp'-vend'ing machine' *s* distributore automatico di francobolli

stance [stæns] *s* posizione

stanch [stant∫] *adj* leale; forte; a tenuta d'acqua || *s* chiusa || *tr* arrestare il flusso da; (*blood*) stagnare

stand [stænd] *s* posizione; resistenza, difesa; tribuna, palco; sostegno, supporto; (*booth in market*) posteggio; posto di sosta || *v* (*pret & pp* **stood** [stud]) *tr* mettere in piedi; reggere, sostenere; sopportare, tollerare; (*one's ground*) mantenere; (*a chance*) avere; (*watch*) fare; (*coll*) pagare; **to stand off** tenere a distanza || *intr* stare; essere alto; fermarsi; stare in piedi; trovarsi; aver forza; essere; (*e.g., apart*) tenersi; **to stand back of** spalleggiare; **to stand by** appoggiare; **to stand for** rappresentare, voler dire; appoggiare, favorire; tenere a battesimo; (*coll*) tollerare; **to stand in line** fare la fila or la coda; **to stand in with** (*coll*) essere nelle buone grazie di; **to stand out** stagliarsi, distaccarsi, risaltare; **to stand up** tenersi in piedi; resistere, durare; **to stand up to** affrontare

standard ['stændərd] *adj* (*usual*) normale; uniforme, standard; *(language)* corretto, preferito ‖ *s* standard *m*; *(model)* modello, campione *m*; *(flag)* stendardo

stand'ard-bear'er *s* portabandiera *m*

standardize ['stændər ‚daɪz] *tr* standardizzare

stand'ard of liv'ing *s* tenore *m* di vita

stand'ard time' *s* ora ufficiale, ora legale

standee [stæn'di] *s* passeggero in piedi; spettatore *m* in piedi

stand'-in' *s* (mov) controfigura; **to have a stand-in with** (coll) essere nelle buone grazie di

standing ['stændɪŋ] *adj (jump)* da fermo; in piedi; fermo; *(water)* stagnante; vigente, permanente; *(idle)* fuori uso ‖ *s* posizione, rango, situazione; classifica; **in good standing** riconosciuto da tutti; **of long standing** vecchio, da lungo tempo

stand'ing ar'my *s* esercito permanente

stand'ing room' *s* posto in piedi

standpatter ['stænd‚pætər] *s* (coll) seguace *mf* dell'immobilismo

stand'point' *s* punto di vista

stand'still' *s* fermata; riposo; **to come to a standstill** fermarsi

stanza ['stænzə] *s* stanza

staple ['stepəl] *adj* principale ‖ *s* articolo di prima necessità; elemento indispensabile; *(e.g., to hold wire)* cavallottino, cambretta; *(to fasten papers)* grappetta; fibra tessile ‖ *tr* aggraffare

stapler ['steplər] *s* cucitrice *f* a grappe

star [star] *s (any heavenly body, except the moon, appearing in the sky)* astro; *(heavenly body radiating self-produced energy)* stella; *(actor)* divo; *(actress)* diva, stella *(athlete)* asso; (fig, mov) stella; (typ) stelletta; **to thank one's lucky stars** ringraziare la propria stella ‖ *v (pret & pp* **starred)** *ger* **starring)** *tr* costellare, stellare; presentare come stella; (typ) marcare con stelletta ‖ *intr* primeggiare

starboard ['starbərd] or ['star‚bord] *adj* di dritta, di tribordo ‖ *s* dritta, tribordo ‖ *adv* a dritta, a tribordo

starch [startʃ] *s* amido, fecola; *(in laundering)* salda; (coll) forza ‖ *tr* inamidare

starch-y ['startʃi] *adj* **(-ier; -iest)** amidaceo; *(e.g., collar)* inamidato; *(manner)* sostenuto, contegnoso

star' dust' *s* polveri *fpl* meteoriche; (fig) polvere *f* di stelle

stare [ster] *s* sguardo fisso ‖ *intr* rimirare; **to stare at** fissare gli occhi addosso a

star'fish' *s* stella di mare

star'gaze' *intr* guardare le stelle; sognare ad occhi aperti

stark [stark] *adj* completo; desolato; severo, serio; duro, rigido ‖ *adv* completamente

stark'-na'ked *adj* nudo e crudo

starlet ['starlɪt] *s* stellina, divetta

star'light' *s* lume *f* delle stelle

starling ['starlɪŋ] *s* storno, stornello

Stars' and Stripes' *s* bandiera stellata

Star'-Spangled Ban'ner *s* bandiera stellata

star' sys'tem *s* (mov) divismo

start [start] *s* inizio, principio; partenza; linea di partenza; *(sudden jerk)* sussulto, soprassalto; *(advantage)* vantaggio; *(spurt)* scatto ‖ *tr* iniziare, principiare; mettere in moto; dare il via a; *(a conversation)* intavolare; *(game)* stanare ‖ *intr* iniziare, principiare; mettersi in moto; incamminarsi; *(to be startled)* trasalire, sussultare; **to start** + *ger* mettersi a + *inf*; **to start** + *ger* + **again** rimettersi a + *inf*; **to start after** andare in cerca di

starter ['startər] *s (of a venture)* iniziatore *m*; partente *m*; (aut) motorino d'avviamento; (sports) mossiere *m*

starting ['startɪŋ] *adj* di partenza ‖ *s* messa in marcia

start'ing crank' *s* manovella d'avviamento

start'ing point' *s* punto di partenza

startle ['startəl] *tr* far trasalire ‖ *intr* trasalire, sussultare

startling ['startlɪŋ] *adj* allarmante, sorprendente

starvation [star'veʃən] *s* fame *f*, inedia, inanizione

starva'tion wag'es *spl* paga da fame

starve [starv] *tr* affamare; far morire di fame; **to starve out** prendere per fame ‖ *intr* essere affamato; morire di fame

starving ['starvɪŋ] *adj* famelico

state [stet] *adj* statale; ufficiale; di gala, di lusso ‖ *s* condizione; stato; gala, pompa; **to lie in state** essere esposto in camera ardente; **to live in state** vivere sfarzosamente ‖ *tr* dichiarare, affermare; *(a problem)* impostare

stateless ['stetlɪs] *adj* apolide

state-ly ['stetli] *adj* **(-lier; -liest)** maestoso, imponente

statement ['stetmənt] *s* dichiarazione, affermazione; comunicazione; (com) estratto conto

state' of mind' *s* stato d'animo

state'room' *s* cabina; (rr) compartimento privato

states'man *s* **(-men)** statista *m*, uomo di stato

static ['stætɪk] *adj* statico; (rad) atmosferico ‖ *s* disturbi *mpl* atmosferici

station ['steʃən] *s* stazione; rango, condizione ‖ *tr* stazionare

sta'tion a'gent *s* capostazione *m*

stationary ['steʃən ‚eri] *adj* stazionario

sta'tion break' *s* (rad, telv) intervallo

stationer ['steʃənər] *s* cartolaio

stationery ['steʃən ‚eri] *s (writing paper)* carta da lettere; *(writing materials)* cancelleria

sta'tionery store' *s* cartoleria

sta'tion house' *s* posto di polizia

sta'tion-mas'ter *s* capostazione *m*

sta'tion wag'on *s* giardinetta

statistical [stə'tɪstɪkəl] *adj* statistico

statistician [‚stætɪs'tɪʃən] *s* statistico

statistics [stə'tɪstɪks] *ssg (science)* statistica; *spl (data)* statistiche *fpl*
statue ['stæt∫u] *s* statua
statuesque [ˌstæt∫u'esk] *adj* statuario
stature ['stæt∫ər] *s* statura
status ['stetəs] *s* stato, condizione; condizione sociale
sta'tus sym'bol *s* simbolo della posizione sociale
statute ['stæt∫ut] *s* legge *f;* regolamento
stat'ute of limita'tions *s* legge *f* che governa la prescrizione
statutory ['stæt∫uˌtori] *adj* legale
staunch [stɔnt∫] or [stɑnt∫] *adj, s & tr* var of **stanch**
stave [stev] *s (of barrel)* doga; *(of ladder)* piolo; *(mus)* rigo, pentagramma *m* ‖ *v (pret & pp* **staved** or **stove** [stov]) *tr* bucare; *(to smash)* sfondare; **to stave off** tenere a bada
stay [ste] *s* permanenza, soggiorno; *(brace)* staggio; *(of corset)* stecca di balena; sostegno; (law) sospensione; (naut) strallo ‖ *tr* fermare; sospendere; poner freno a ‖ *intr* stare; mantenersi; restare, rimanere; *(at a hotel)* sostare; **to stay up** stare alzato
stay'-at-home' *adj* casalingo ‖ *s* persona casalinga
stead [stɛd] *s* posto; **in his stead** in suo luogo; **to stand in good stead** esser utile
stead'fast' *adj* fermo, risoluto
stead·y ['stedi] *adj (-ier; -iest)* stabile, fermo; regolare, costante; abituale; calmo, sicuro ‖ *v (pret & pp* **-ied**) *tr* rinforzare; calmare ‖ *intr* rinforzarsi; calmarsi
steak [stek] *s* bistecca
steal [stil] *s* (coll) furto ‖ *v (pret* **stole** [stol]; *pp* **stolen**) *tr* rubare; involare; *(the attention)* cattivare ‖ *intr* rubare; **to steal away** svignarsela; **to steal out** uscire di soppiatto; **to steal upon** approssimarsi silenziosamente a
stealth [stɛlθ] *s* clandestinità *f;* by **stealth** di straforo, di soppiatto
steam [stim] *adj* a vapore ‖ *s* vapore *m;* fumo; **to get up steam** aumentare la pressione; **to let off steam** scaricare la pressione; (slang) sfogarsi ‖ *tr (a steamship)* guidare; esalare; esporre al vapore; *(e.g., glasses)* appannare ‖ *intr* dar vapore, fumigare; bollire; *(to become clouded)* appannarsi; andare a vapore; **to steam ahead** avanzare a tutto vapore
steam'boat' *s* vapore *m*
steam' en'gine *s* macchina a vapore
steamer ['stimər] *s* vapore *m*
steam'er rug' *s* coperta da viaggio
steam'er trunk' *s* bauletto da cabina
steam' heat' *s* riscaldamento a vapore
steam' roll'er *s* rullo compressore; (fig) rullo compressore
steam'ship' *s* piroscafo, vapore *m*
steam' shov'el *s* escavatore *m* a vapore
steam' ta'ble *s* tavola riscaldata a vapore per mantenere calde le vivande
steed [stid] *s* destriere *m*

steel [stil] *adj* d'acciaio; *(industry)* siderurgico ‖ *s* acciaio; *(bar)* stecca d'acciaio; *(for sharpening knives)* affilacoltelli *m;* (fig) spada, brando ‖ *tr* acciaiare; **to steel oneself** corazzarsi, indurirsi; armarsi di coraggio
steel' wool' *s* paglia di ferro
steel'works' *spl* acciaieria
steelyard ['stil ˌjɑrd] or ['stiljərd] *s* stadera
steep [stip] *adj* erto, scosceso, ripido; *(price)* alto ‖ *tr* immergere, saturare, imbevere
steeple ['stipəl] *s* campanile *m;* *(spire)* cuspide *f*, guglia
stee'ple-chase' *s* corsa ad ostacoli
stee'ple-jack' *s* aggiustatore *m* di campanili
steer [stɪr] *s* bue *m*, manzo ‖ *tr* governare, guidare; (aer) pilotare ‖ *intr* governare; **to steer clear of** evitare
steerage ['stɪrɪdʒ] *s* (naut) alloggio passeggeri di terza classe
steer'ing wheel' *s* (aut) volante *m*, sterzo; (naut) ruota del timone
stellar ['stelər] *adj* stellare; *(role)* da stella
stem [stɛm] *s (of pipe, of key)* cannello; *(of goblet)* gambo; *(of column)* fusto; *(of spoon)* manico; *(of watch)* corona; *(of a word)* tema *m;* *(of note)* (mus) gamba; (bot) peduncolo, stelo; (bot) gambo; **from stem to stern** da poppa a prua ‖ *v (pret & pp* **stemmed**) *ger* **stemming**) *tr* togliere il gambo a; *(to check)* arrestare; *(to dam up)* arginare; *(to plug)* otturare; *(the tide)* risalire, andare contro ‖ *intr* originare, derivare
stem'-win'der *s* orologio a corona
stench [stent∫] *s* tanfo, fetore *m*
sten·cil ['stensəl] *s* stampo, stampino; parole *fpl* a stampo ‖ *v (pret & pp* **-ciled** or **-cilled**; *ger* **-ciling** or **-cilling**) *tr* stampinare
stenographer [stə'nɑgrəfər] *s* stenografo
stenography [stə'nɑgrəfi] *s* stenografia
step [stɛp] *s* passo; *(footprint)* orma, impronta; *(of ladder)* piolo; *(of staircase)* gradino; *(of carriage)* montatoio; **step by step** passo passo; **to watch one's step** fare molta attenzione ‖ *v (pret & pp* **stepped**; *ger* **stepping**) *tr* scaglionare; **to step off** misurare a passi ‖ *intr* camminare, andare a passi; mettere il piede; **to step aside** scostarsi; **to step back** indietreggiare; **to step on it** (slang) fare presto; **to step on the gas** (coll) accelerare; **to step on the starter** avviare il motore
step'broth'er *s* fratellastro, fratello consanguineo
step'child' *s (-children* [ˌt∫ɪldrən]) figliastro
step'daugh'ter *s* figliastra
step'fa'ther *s* patrigno
step'lad'der *s* scala a gradini or a libretto
step'moth'er *s* matrigna
steppe [step] *s* steppa

step'ping stone' s passatoio, pietra per guadare; (fig) gradino

step'sis'ter s sorellastra

step'son' s figliastro

stere·o ['steri ,o] or ['stiri ,o] adj stereofonico; stereoscopico || s (-os) musica stereofonica; sistema stereofonico; fotografia stereoscopica

stereotyped ['steri-ə,taɪpt] or ['stiri-ə-,taɪpt] adj stereotipato

sterile ['steril] adj sterile

sterilize ['steri ,laɪz] tr sterilizzare

sterling ['stʌrlɪŋ] adj di lira sterlina; d'argento; puro; eccellente || s argento .925; s vasellame m d'argento puro

stern [stʌrn] adj severo || s poppa

stet [stet] v (pret & pp stetted; ger stetting) tr marcare con la parola "vive"

stethoscope ['steθə ,skop] s stetoscopio

stevedore ['stivə ,dor] s stivatore m

stew [stju] or [stu] s stufato, guazzetto || tr stufare || intr cuocere a fuoco lento; (coll) preoccuparsi

steward ['stju·ərd] or ['stu·ərd] s amministratore m, agente m; maggiordomo; (aer, naut) cambusiere m, cameriere m

stewardess ['stju·ərdɪs] or ['stu·ərdɪs] s (naut) cameriera; (aer) hostess f, assistente f di volo

stewed' fruit' s composta di frutta

stewed' toma'toes spl pomodori mpl in umido

stick [stɪk] s stecco; legno; bacchetta; bastone m; (e.g., of candy) cannello; (naut) albero; (typ) compositoio; **in the sticks** (coll) in casa del diavolo || v (pret & pp stuck [stʌk]) tr pungere; ficcare, infiggere; attaccare; confondere; **to be stuck** essere insabbiato; essere attaccato; (fig) essere confuso; **to stick out** (the head) sporgere; (the tongue) cacciare; **to stick up** (slang) assaltare a mano armata, rapinare || intr rimanere attaccato; persistere; (said of glue) appiccicarsi; (to one opinion) tenersi; stare; **to stick out** sporgere; **to stick together** rimanere uniti; **to stick up** risaltare; (said, e.g., of quills) rizzarsi; **to stick up for** (coll) stare dalla parte di

sticker ['stɪkər] s etichetta gommata; spina; persona zelante; (coll) busillis m

stick'ing plas'ter s cerotto

stick'pin' s spilla da cravatta

stick'up' s (slang) grassazione

stick·y ['stɪki] adj (-ier; -iest) attaccaticcio; vischioso; (weather) afoso, soffocante; (fig) difficile

stiff [stɪf] adj rigido, duro; forte; (price) alto; denso || s (slang) cadavere m; **poor stiff** (slang) povero diavolo

stiff' col'lar s colletto duro

stiffen ['stɪfən] tr irrigidire || intr irrigidirsi

stiff' neck' s torcicollo; ostinazione

stiff'-necked' adj testardo

stiff' shirt' s camicia inamidata

stifle ['staɪfəl] tr soffocare

stigma ['stɪgmə] s (-mas or -mata [mətə]) stigma m

stigmatize ['stɪgmə ,taɪz] tr stigmatizzare

still [stɪl] adj fermo, tranquillo; silenzioso; (wine) non spumante || s calma; distillatore m; distilleria; (phot) fotografia singola || adv ancora; tuttora || conj tuttavia || tr calmare || intr calmarsi

still'birth' s parto di infante nato morto

still'born' adj nato morto

still' life' s (lifes') natura morta

stilt [stɪlt] s trampolo; (in water) palafitta; (orn) trampoliere m

stilted ['stɪltɪd] adj elevato; pomposo

stimulant ['stɪmjələnt] adj & s stimulante m, eccitante m

stimulate ['stɪmjə ,let] tr stimulare

stimu·lus ['stɪmjələs] s (-li [,laɪ]) stimolo

sting [stɪŋ] s puntura; (of insect) pungiglione; (fig) scottatura || v (pret & pp stung [stʌŋ]) tr & intr pungere

stin·gy ['stɪndʒi] adj (-gier; -giest) tirchio, taccagno

stink [stɪŋk] s puzza || v (pret stank [stæŋk] or stunk [stʌŋk]; pp stunk) tr far puzzare || intr puzzare; **to stink of money** (slang) aver soldi a palate

stinker ['stɪŋkər] s (slang) puzzone m

stint [stɪnt] s limite m; lavoro assegnato, compito || intr lesinarsi

stipend ['staɪpənd] s stipendio; assegno di studio, presalario

stipulate ['stɪpjə ,let] tr stipulare

stir [stʌr] s agitazione, movimento; (poke) spinta; **to create a stir** creare una sensazione || v (pret & pp stirred; ger stirring) tr mescolare; muovere; (fire) ravvivare; (pity) fare; **to stir up** eccitare, svegliare; (to rebellion) sommuovere || intr muoversi, agitarsi

stirring ['stʌrɪŋ] adj commovente

stirrup ['stʌrəp] or ['stɪrəp] s staffa

stitch [stɪtʃ] s punto; maglia; (pain) fitta; (bit) poco, po' m; **to be in stitches** (coll) sbellicarsi dalle risa || tr cucire; aggraffare || intr cucire

stock [stak] adj regolare, comune; banale, ordinario; di bestiame; borsistico; azionario; (aut) di serie; (theat) stabile || s provvista, scorta; capitale m sociale; azione f; azioni fpl, titoli mpl; (of tree) tronco; (of family; of anchor; of anvil) ceppo; razza, famiglia; materia prima; (of rifle) cassa; (broth) brodo; (handle) manico; (livestock) bestiame m; (theat) compagnia stabile; **in stock** in magazzino, disponibile; **out of stock** esaurito; **stocks** gogna, berlina; **to take stock** fare l'inventario; **to take stock in** (coll) aver fede in || tr fornire; fornire di bestiame; fornire di pesci || intr—**to stock up** fare rifornimenti

stockade [sta'ked] s staccionata

stock'breed'er s allevatore m di bestiame

stock'bro'ker s agente m di cambio
stock' car' s automobile f di serie; (rr) carro bestiame
stock' com'pany s (theat) compagnia stabile; (com) società anonima
stock' div'idend s dividendo pagato in azioni
stock' exchange' s borsa valori
stock'fish' s stoccafisso
stock'hold'er s azionista mf
stock'holder of rec'ord s azionista mf registrato nei libri della compagnia
Stockholm ['stakhom] s Stoccolma
stocking ['stakɪŋ] s calza
stock' in trade' s stock m; ferri mpl del mestiere
stock' mar'ket s borsa valori
stock'pile' s riserva, scorta || tr mettere in riserva || intr mettere in riserva materie prime
stock' rais'ing s allevamento bestiame
stock'room' s magazzino, deposito
stock•y ['staki] adj (-ier; -iest) tozzo, tarchiato
stock'yard' s chiuso per il bestiame
stoic ['sto·ɪk] adj & s stoico
stoicism ['sto·ɪ‚sɪzəm] s stoicismo
stoke [stok] tr (fire) attizzare; (a furnace) caricare
stoker ['stokər] s fochista m
stolid ['stalɪd] adj impassibile
stomach ['stʌmək] s stomaco || tr (fig) digerire
stone [ston] s sasso, pietra; (of fruit) osso; (pathol) calcolo || tr lapidare; affilare con la pietra; (fruit) snocciolare
stone'-broke' adj (coll) senza un soldo, senza il becco di un quattrino
stone'-deaf' adj sordo come una campana
stone'ma'son s tagliapietra m
stone' quar'ry s cava di pietra
stone's' throw' s tiro di sasso; within a stone's throw a un tiro di schioppo
ston•y ['stoni] adj (-ier; -iest) di sasso, sassoso, pietroso
stooge [studʒ] s (theat) spalla; (slang) complice mf
stool [stul] s sgabello, seggiolino; gabinetto; (mass evacuated) feci fpl
stool' pi'geon s piccione m di richiamo; (slang) spia
stoop [stup] s curvatura, inclinazione; scalini mpl d'ingresso || intr inclinarsi, piegarsi; degnarsi, umiliarsi
stoop-shouldered ['stup'‚ʃoldərd] adj con le spalle cadenti
stop [stap] s fermata, sosta; arresto; otturazione, blocco; cessazione; ostacolo; (of a check) fermo; (restraint) freno; (of organ) registro; to come to a stop fermarsi; cessare; to put a stop to metter fine a || v (pret & pp stopped; ger stopping) tr fermare, cessare; arrestare, sospendere; tappare, otturare; (a check) mettere il fermo a; to stop up tappare, otturare || intr fermarsi; arrestarsi; (said of a ship) fare scalo; (at an hotel) scendere; to stop + ger smettere di or cessare di + inf

stop'cock' s rubinetto di arresto
stop'gap' adj provvisorio || s soluzione provvisoria; (person) tappabuchi m
stop'light' s (traffic light) semaforo; (aut) luce f di stop
stop'o'ver s fermata intermedia
stoppage ['stapɪdʒ] s fermata, arresto; (of work, wages, etc.) sospensione
stopper ['stapər] s tappo, turacciolo
stop' sign' s segnale m di fermata
stop'watch' s cronometro a scatto
storage ['storɪdʒ] s magazzinaggio; (place for storing) magazzino; (of a computer) memoria
stor'age bat'tery s (elec) accumulatore m
store [stor] s negozio; magazzino; (supply) scorta; in store in serbo; to set store by dare molta importanza a || tr immagazzinare; to store away accumulare
store'house' s magazzino, deposito; (of knowledge) miniera
store'keep'er s negoziante m
store'room' s magazzino; (naut) dispensa
stork [stɔrk] s cicogna
storm [stɔrm] s tempesta, temporale m; (on the Beaufort scale) burrasca; (mil) assalto; (fig) scoppio || tr assaltare || intr tempestare; imperversare; (mil) andare all'attacco
storm' cloud' s nuvolone m
storm' door' s controporta
storm' sash' s controfinestra
storm' troops' spl truppe fpl d'assalto
storm' win'dow s controfinestra
storm•y ['stɔrmi] adj (-ier; -iest) tempestoso, burrascoso; (fig) inquieto, violento
sto•ry ['stori] s (-ries) storia, racconto; romanzo; (plot) trama; (level) piano; (coll) storia, menzogna || v (pret & pp -ried) tr istoriare
sto'ry-tell'er s narratore m, novelliere m; (coll) mentitore m
stoup [stup] s (eccl) acquasantiera
stout [staut] adj grasso, obeso; forte, robusto; leale, coraggioso || s birra nera forte
stout-hearted ['staut‚hartɪd] adj coraggioso
stove [stov] s (for warmth) stufa; (for cooking) fornello, cucina economica
stove'pipe' s tubo della stufa, cannone m; (hat) (coll) tuba
stow [sto] tr mettere in riserva; riempire; (naut) stivare || intr—to stow away imbarcarsi clandestinamente
stowage ['sto·ɪdʒ] s stivaggio; (place) stiva
stow'a·way' s passeggero clandestino
straddle ['strædəl] s divaricamento || tr (a horse) cavalcare; (the legs) divaricare; favorire entrambe le parti in || intr cavalcare; stare a gambe divaricate; (coll) tenere il piede tra due staffe
strafe [straf] or [stref] s attacco violento || tr attaccare violentemente con fuoco aereo; bombardare violentemente; (slang) punire

straggle ['strægəl] *intr* sbandarsi, sviarsi; sparpagliarsi, essere sparpagliato

straggler ['stræglər] *s* ritardatario

straight [stret] *adj* diritto, ritto; (*e.g., shoulders*) quadro; candido, franco; (*honest, upright*) retto; inalterato; (*hair; whiskey*) liscio; **to set s.o. straight** mettere qlcu sulla retta via; mostrare la verità a qlcu || *s* rettilinea; (*cards*) scala || *adv* dritto; sinceramente; rettamente; **straight ahead** sempre diritto; **straight away** immediatamente; **to go straight** vivere onestamente

straighten ['stretən] *tr* ordinare; raddrizzare || *intr* raddrizzarsi

straight' face' *s* faccia seria

straight' flush' *s* (cards) scala reale

straight'for'ward *adj* diretto; onesto

straight' man' *s* (theat) spalla

straight' ra'zor *s* rasoio a mano libera

straight'way' *adv* immediatamente

strain [stren] *s* sforzo; fatica eccessiva; tensione, pressione; strappo muscolare; tono, stile *m;* (*family*) famiglia; tendenza, vena; (coll) lavoro severo; (mus) aria, melodia || *tr* passare, colare; (*e.g., a rope*) tirare al massimo; (*one's ear*) tendere; (*a muscle*) strappare; (*the ankle*) slogare; (*e.g., words*) storcere, forzare || *intr* colare, filtrare; tendersi, tirare; sforzarsi; fare resistenza; **to strain at** tirare; resistere a

strained [strend] *adj* (*smile*) stentato; (*relations*) teso

strainer ['strenər] *s* scolatoio

strait [stret] *s* stretto; **straits** stretto; (fig) strettezze *fpl;* **to be in dire straits** essere nei frangenti

strait' jack'et *s* camicia di forza

strait'-laced' *adj* puritano, pudibondo

strand [strænd] *s* sponda, lido; (*of metal cable*) trefolo; (*of rope*) legnolo; (*of pearls*) filo || *tr* sfilare; (*e.g., a rope*) ritorcere, intrecciare; (*e.g., a boat*) lasciare incagliato; **to be stranded** trovarsi incagliato

stranded ['strændɪd] *adj* (ship) incagliato, arenato; (*e.g., rope*) ritorto, intrecciato

strange [strendʒ] *adj* strano; straniero; non abituato; inusitato

stranger ['strendʒər] *s* forestiero; nuovo venuto, intruso

strangle || ['stræŋgəl] *tr* strangolare; soffocare || *intr* strangolarsi; soffocarsi

strap [stræp] *s* (*of leather*) correggia; (*for holding things together*) tirante *m;* (*shoulder strap*) bretella; (*for passengers to hold on to*) manopola; (*to hold a sandal*) guiggia; (*to hold a baby*) falda; (*strop*) coramella || *v* (*pret & pp* **strapped;** *ger* **strapping**) *tr* legare con correggia or tirante; (*a razor*) affilare

strap'hang'er *s* (coll) passeggero senza posto a sedere

strapping ['stræpɪŋ] *adj* robusto; (coll) grande, enorme

stratagem ['strætedʒəm] *s* stratagemma *m*

strategic(al) [strə'tidʒɪk(əl)] *adj* strategico

strategist ['strætɪdʒɪst] *s* stratego

strate·gy ['strætɪdʒi] *s* (**-gies**) strategia

strati·fy ['strætɪ,faɪ] *v* (*pret & pp* **-fied**) *tr* stratificare || *intr* stratificarsi

stratosphere ['strætə,sfɪr] or ['stretə,sfɪr] *s* stratosfera

stra·tum ['stretəm] or ['strætəm] *s* (**-ta** [tə] or **-tums**) strato

straw [strɔ] *adj* di paglia; di nessun valore; falso, fittizio || *s* paglia; (*for drinking*) cannuccia; **I don't care a straw** non mi importa un fico; **to be the last straw** essere il colmo

straw·ber·ry *s* (**-ries**) fragola

straw'hat' *s* cappello di paglia; (*with hard crown*) paglietta

straw' man' *s* (*figurehead*) uomo di paglia; (*scarecrow*) spaventapasseri *m*

straw' mat'tress *s* pagliericcio

straw' vote' *s* votazione esplorativa

stray [stre] *adj* sbandato, randagio; casuale, fortuito || *s* animale randagio || *intr* sviarsi; (fig) sbandarsi

streak [strik] *s* stria; (*of light*) raggio; (*of madness*) ramo, vena; (*of luck*) (coll) periodo; **like a streak** (coll) come un lampo || *tr* striare, venare || *intr* striarsi, venarsi; andare come un lampo

stream [strim] *s* corrente *f;* (*of light*) raggio; (*of people*) fiumana, torrente *m;* (*of cars*) fila || *intr* colare; filtrare, penetrare; (*said of a flag*) fluttuare

streamer ['strimər] *s* pennone *m;* nastro; raggio di luce

streamlined ['strim,laɪnd] *adj* aerodinamico; (aer) carenato

stream'lin'er *s* treno dal profilo aerodinamico

street [strit] *adj* stradale || *s* via, strada

street'car' *s* tram *m*

street' clean'er *s* spazzino; (mach) spazzatrice *f*

street' clothes' *spl* vestiti *mpl* da passeggio; vestito da passeggio

street' floor' *s* pianterreno

street'light' *s* lampione *m*

street' map' *s* pianta della città; stradario

street' sign' *s* segnale *m* stradale

street' sprin'kler *s* carro annaffiatoio

street' walk'er *s* passeggiatrice *f*

strength [strenθ] *s* forza; resistenza; (*of spirituous liquors*) gradazione; (com) tendenza al rialzo; (mil) numero; **on the strength of** basandosi su

strengthen ['streŋθən] *tr* rinforzare; (fig) convalidare, rinsaldare || *intr* rinforzarsi, ingagliardirsi

strenuous ['strenju·əs] *adj* vigoroso; strenuo

stress [stres] *s* enfasi *f,* importanza; spinta; tensione, preoccupazione; accento; (mech) sollecitazione; **to lay**

stress on mettere in rilievo || *tr* (*a word*) accentare, accentuare; (*to emphasize*) accentuare; (*mech*) sollecitare

stress′ ac′cent *s* accento di intensità

stretch [stretʃ] *s* tiro, tirata; (*in time or space*) periodo; (*of road*) tratto, percorrenza; (*of imagination*) sforzo; (rr) tratta; (slang) periodo di detenzione; **at a stretch** di un tiro || *tr* tirare; tendere, distendere; (*the imagination*) forzare; (*facts*) esagerare; (*money*) stiracchiare; (*one's legs*) sgranchirsi; (*the truth*) esagerare; **to stretch oneself** sdraiarsi || *intr* estendersi; stiracchiarsi; distendersi; **to stretch out** sdraiarsi

stretcher [′stretʃər] *s* (*for a painting*) telaio; (*tool*) tenditore *m*, tenditoio; (*to carry wounded*) barella, lettiga

stretch′er-bear′er *s* portantino

strew [stru] *v* (*pret* **strewed**; *pp* **strewed** or **strewn**) *tr* spargere, cospargere; disseminare

stricken [′strɪkən] *adj* afflitto; ferito; danneggiato

strict [strɪkt] *adj* stretto, severo

stricture [′strɪktʃər] *s* aspra critica; (*pathol*) stenosi *f*

stride [straɪd] *s* passo; andatura; **rapid strides** grandi passi *mpl*; **to hit one's stride** avanzare a andatura regolare; **to take s.th in one's stride** fare qlco senza sforzi || *v* (*pret* **strode** [strod]; *pp* **stridden** [′strɪdən]) *tr* attraversare a grandi passi; attraversare di un salto || *intr* camminare a grandi passi; (*majestically*) incedere

strident [′straɪdənt] *adj* stridente

strife [straɪf] *s* discordia; concorrenza

strike [straɪk] *s* (*blow*) colpo; (*stopping of work*) sciopero; (*discovery of oil, ore, etc.*) scoperta; (*of fish*) abboccatura; colpo di fortuna || *v* (*pret* & *pp* **struck** [strʌk]) *tr* colpire, percuotere; infiggere; (*a match*) strofinare; (*fire*) accendere; fare impressione su; incontrare improvvisamente; (*e.g., ore*) scoprire; (*roots*) mettere; (*a coin*) coniare; andare in sciopero contro; arrivare a; (*a posture*) prendere; (*the hour*) scoccare; cancellare, eliminare; (*sails*) calare; (*attention*) richiamare; **to strike it rich** scoprire una miniera; avere un colpo di fortuna || *intr* dare un colpo; cadere; (*said of a bell*) suonare; accendersi; scioperare; (mil) attaccare; **to strike out** mettersi in marcia; (*to fail*) fallire, venir meno

strike′break′er *s* crumiro

striker [′straɪkər] *s* battitore *m*; (*clapper in clock*) martelletto; (*worker*) scioperante *m*

striking [′straɪkɪŋ] *adj* impressionante, sorprendente; notevole; scioperante

strik′ing pow′er *s* potere *m* d'assalto

string [strɪŋ] *s* spago, cordicella; (*e.g., of apron*) laccio; (*of pearls*) filo; (*of onions, of lies*) filza; (*row*) fila, infilata; (mus) corda; **no strings attached** (coll) senza condizioni;

strings strumenti *mpl* a corda; (coll) condizioni *fpl*; **to pull strings** usare influenza || *v* (*pret* & *pp* **strung** [strʌŋ]) *tr* legare; allacciare; infilare; infilzare; (*a racket*) munire di corde; (*to stretch*) tendere; (*a musical instrument*) mettere le corde a; (slang) ingannare; **to string along** (slang) menare per il naso; **to string up** impiccare || *intr*—**to string along with** (slang) andare d'accordo con

string′ bean′ *s* fagiolino

stringed′ in′strument *s* strumento a corda

stringent [′strɪndʒənt] *adj* stringente; urgente; severo

string′ quartet′ *s* quartetto d'archi

strip [strɪp] *s* striscia; (*of metal*) lamina; (*of land*) lingua || *v* (*pret* & *pp* **stripped**; *ger* **stripping**) *tr* spogliare; denudare; (*a fruit*) pelare; (*a ship*) sguarnire; (*tobacco*) togliere le nervature da; scortecciare; (*thread*) spanare; **to strip of** spogliare di || *intr* spogliarsi; denudarsi; fare lo spogliarello

stripe [straɪp] *s* stria, striscia, riga, lista; tipo, qualità *f*; (mil) gallone *m* || *tr* striare, filettare, rigare

strip′ min′ing *s* sfruttamento minerario a cielo aperto

strip′tease′ *s* spogliarello

stripteaser [′strɪp ˌtizər] *s* spogliarellista

strive [straɪv] *v* (*pret* **strove** [strov]; *pp* **striven** [′strɪvən]) *intr* sforzarsi; lottare; **to strive to** sforzarsi di

stroke [strok] *s* colpo; (*of bell or clock*) rintocco; (*of pen*) tratto, frego; (*of brush*) pennellata; (*of arms in swimming*) bracciata; colpo apoplettico; (*caress*) carezza; (*with oar*) vogata; (*of oar or paddle*) palata; (*of a master*) tocco; (*of a piston*) corsa; (*keystroke*) battuta; (*of genius*) lampo; (*of the hour*) scocco; **to not do a stroke of work** non muovere un dito || *tr* accarezzare

stroll [strol] *s* passeggiata; **to take a stroll** fare una passeggiata || *intr* fare una passeggiata, andare a zonzo; errare

stroller [′strolər] *s* girovago; carrozzella; (*itinerant performer*) (theat) guitto

strong [strɔŋ] or [straŋ] *adj* forte, vigoroso; valido; acceso, zelante; (*butter*) rancido; (*cheese*) piccante; (com) sostenuto

strong′box′ *s* cassaforte *f*

strong′ drink′ *s* bevanda alcolica

strong′hold′ *s* piazzaforte *f*

strong′ man′ *s* (*in a circus*) maciste *m*; (*leader*) anima; dittatore *m*

strong-minded [′strɔŋ ˌmaɪndɪd] or [′straŋ ˌmaɪndɪd] *adj* volitivo

strong′point′ *s* luogo fortificato

strontium [′strɑn/ɪ·əm] *s* stronzio

strop [strɔp] *s* coramella, affilarasoio || *v* (*pret* & *pp* **stropped**; *ger* **stropping**) *tr* affilare

strophe [′strofi] *s* strofa, strofe *f*

struc′tural steel′ [ˈstrʌktʃərəl] s profilato di acciaio

structure [ˈstrʌktʃər] s struttura; edificio ‖ tr strutturare

struggle [ˈstrʌgəl] s lotta; sforzo ‖ intr lottare; sforzare, dibattersi

strum [strʌm] v (pret & pp **strummed;** ger **strumming**) tr & intr strimpellare

strumpet [ˈstrʌmpɪt] s sgualdrina, puttana

strut [strʌt] s controvento, puntello, saettone m; incedere impettito; (aer) montante ‖ v (pret & pp **strutted;** ger **strutting**) intr pavoneggiarsi, fare la ruota

strychnine [ˈstrɪknaɪn] or [ˈstrɪknɪn] s stricnina

stub [stʌb] s (of tree) coppo; (e.g., of cigar) mozzicone m; (of a check) matrice f, madre f ‖ v (pret & pp **stubbed;** ger **stubbing**) tr sradicare; **to stub one's toe** inciampare

stubble [ˈstʌbəl] s (of beard) pelo ispido; **stubbles** stoppie fpl

stubborn [ˈstʌbərn] adj (headstrong) testardo; (resolute) accanito; (e.g., resistance) ostinato; (e.g., illness) ribelle; (soil) ingrato

stuc·co [ˈstʌko] s (-coes or -cos) stucco ‖ tr stuccare

stuck [stʌk] adj infisso; attaccato; (glued) incollato; (unable to continue) in panna; **stuck on** (slang) invaghito di

stuck′-up′ adj (coll) presuntuoso, arrogante

stud [stʌd] s (in upholstery) borchia; bottone m da sparato; (of walls) montante m; (stallion) stallone m; (for mares) monta; (archit) bugna, bugnato ‖ v (pret & pp **studded;** ger **studding**) tr cospergere; (with stars) costellare; (with jewels) incastonare, ingioiellare

stud′ bolt′ s prigioniero

stud′book′ s registro della genealogia

student [ˈstjudənt] or [ˈstudənt] adj studentesco ‖ s studente m; scolaro; (investigator) studioso

stu′dent bod′y s scolaresca

stud′horse′ s stallone m

studied [ˈstʌdid] adj premeditato; (affected) studiato

studi·o [ˈstudɪˌo] or [ˈstjudɪˌo] s (-os) studio

studious [ˈstjudɪ·əs] or [ˈstudɪ·əs] adj studioso; assiduo, zelante

stud·y [ˈstʌdi] s (-ies) studio ‖ v (pret & pp -ied) tr & intr studiare

stuff [stʌf] s roba, cosa; stoffa; materiale m; (nonsense) scemenze fpl; medicina; (coll) mestiere m ‖ tr riempire, inzeppare; (one's stomach) rimpinzare; (e.g., poultry) farcire; (e.g., salami) insaccare; (a dead animal) impagliare; **to stuff up** intasare ‖ intr rimpinzarsi

stuffed′ shirt′ s persona altezzosa

stuffing [ˈstʌfɪŋ] s ripieno

stuff·y [ˈstʌfi] adj (-ier; -iest) soffocante, opprimente; (nose) chiuso; pedante

stumble [ˈstʌmbəl] intr incespicare, inciampare; sbagliare, impaperarsi; **to stumble on** or **upon** intopparsi in

stum′bling block′ s inciampo, scoglio

stump [stʌmp] s (of tree) toppo, ceppo; (e.g., of arm) moncherino, moncone m; (of cigar, candle) mozzicone m; dente rotto; tribuna popolare; (for drawing) sfumino; **up a stump** (coll) completamente perplesso ‖ tr mozzare; lasciare perplesso; (coll) fare discorsi politici in

stump′ speech′ s discorso politico

stun [stʌn] v (pret & pp **stunned;** ger **stunning**) tr tramortire; (fig) sbalordire

stunning [ˈstʌnɪŋ] adj (blow) che stordisce; sbalorditivo, magnifico

stunt [stʌnt] s atrofia; creatura strimnzita; bravata, prodezza; (for publicity) montatura ‖ tr strimnzire; arrestare la crescita di ‖ intr fare delle acrobazie

stunt′ed adj strimnzito

stunt′ fly′ing s acrobazia aerea

stunt′ man′ s (mov) controfigura

stupe·fy [ˈstjupɪˌfaɪ] or [ˈstupɪˌfaɪ] v (pret & pp -fied) tr istupidire, intontire

stupendous [stjuˈpɛndəs] or [stuˈpɛndəs] adj stupendo

stupid [ˈstjupɪd] or [ˈstupɪd] adj stupido, ebete, scemo

stupor [ˈstjupər] or [ˈstupər] s torpore m, stupore m

stur·dy [ˈstʌrdi] adj (-dier; -diest) forte; (robust) tarchiato; risoluto

sturgeon [ˈstʌrdʒən] s storione m

stutter [ˈstʌtər] s tartagliamento ‖ tr & intr tartagliare

sty [staɪ] s (sties) porcile m; (pathol) orzaiolo

style [staɪl] s stile m; tono; (mode of living) treno ‖ tr chiamare col nome di

stylish [ˈstaɪlɪʃ] adj alla moda, di tono

sty·mie [ˈstaɪmi] v (pret & pp -mied; ger -mieing) tr ostacolare, contrastare

styp′tic pen′cil [ˈstɪptɪk] s matita emostatica

Styx [stɪks] s Stige m

suave [swɑv] or [swev] adj soave

subaltern [səbˈɔltərn] adj & s subalterno

subcommittee [ˈsʌbkəˌmɪti] s sottocommissione

subconscious [səbˈkɑnʃəs] adj & s subcosciente m

subconsciousness [səbˈkɑnʃəsnɪs] s subcosciente m, subcoscienza

sub′deb′ s (coll) signorina più giovane di una debuttante

subdivide [ˈsʌbdɪˌvaɪd] or [ˌsʌbdɪˈvaɪd] tr suddividere ‖ intr suddividersi

subdue [səbˈdju] or [səbˈdu] tr soggiogare, sottomettere; (color, voice) attenuare

subdued [səbˈdjud] or [səbˈdud] adj (voice) sommesso; (light) tenue

subheading ['sʌb‚hedɪŋ] s sottotitolo; (journ) sommario

subject ['sʌbdʒɪkt] adj soggetto; **subject to** (e.g., a cold) soggetto a; (e.g., a fine) passibile di ‖ s soggetto, materia, proposito; (of a ruler) suddito; (gram, med, philos) soggetto ‖ [səb'dʒɛkt] tr sottomettere

sub'ject cat'alogue s catalogo per materie

sub'ject in'dex s indice m per materie

subjection [səb'dʒɛkʃən] s soggezione

subjective [səb'dʒɛktɪv] adj soggettivo

sub'ject mat'ter s soggetto

subjugate ['sʌbdʒə‚get] tr soggiogare

subjunctive [səb'dʒʌŋktɪv] adj & s congiuntivo

sublease ['sʌb‚lis] s subaffitto ‖ [‚sʌb-'lis] tr subaffittare

sub·let [sʌb'let] or ['sʌb‚let] v (pret & pp -let; ger -letting) tr subaffittare

sub·machine' gun' [‚sʌbmə'ʃin] s mitra m

submarine ['sʌbmə‚rin] adj & s sottomarino

sub'marine chas'er ['tʃesər] s caccia-sommergibili m

submerge [səb'mʌrdʒ] tr sommergere ‖ intr sommergersi

submersion [səb'mʌrʒən] or [səb-'mʌrʃən] s sommersione

submission [səb'mɪʃən] s sottomissione

submissive [səb'mɪsɪv] adj sottomesso

sub·mit [səb'mɪt] v (pret & pp -mitted; ger -mitting) tr sottomettere; presentare, deferire; osservare rispettosamente ‖ intr sottomettersi

subordinate [səb'ɔrdɪnɪt] adj & s subordinato ‖ [səb'ɔrdɪ‚net] tr subordinare

suborna'tion of per'jury [‚sʌbər'neʃən] s subornazione

subplot ['sʌb‚plɑt] s intreccio secondario

subpoena or subpena [sʌb'pinə] or [sə-'pinə] s mandato di comparizione ‖ tr citare

sub rosa [sʌb'rozə] adv in segreto

subscribe [səb'skraɪb] tr sottoscrivere ‖ intr sottoscrivere; **to subscribe to** sottoscrivere a; (a magazine) abbonarsi a; (an opinion) approvare

subscriber [səb'skraɪbər] s sottoscrittore m; abbonato

subscription [səb'skrɪpʃən] s sottoscrizione; (e.g., to a newspaper) abbonamento; (e.g., to club) quota

subsequent ['sʌbsɪkwənt] adj susseguente, posteriore

subservient [səb'sʌrvɪ‚ənt] adj subordinato; ossequioso, servile

subside [səb'saɪd] intr calmarsi; (said of water) decrescere

subsidiar·y [səb'sɪdɪ‚eri] adj sussidiario ‖ s (-ies) sussidiario

subsidize ['sʌbsɪ‚daɪz] tr sussidiare, sovvenzionare; (by bribery) subornare

subsi·dy ['sʌbsɪdi] s (-dies) sussidio, sovvenzione

subsist [səb'sɪst] intr sussistere

subsistence [səb'sɪstəns] s sussistenza

subsoil ['sʌb‚sɔɪl] s sottosuolo

substance ['sʌbstəns] s sostanza

substandard [sʌb'stændərd] adj inferiore al livello normale

substantial [sʌb'stænʃəl] adj considerevole; ricco, influente; (food) sostanzioso; (e.g., reason) sostanziale

substantiate [səb'stænʃɪ‚et] tr provare, verificare; dare prova di, sostanziare

substantive ['sʌbstəntɪv] adj & s sostantivo

substation ['sʌb‚steʃən] s ufficio postale secondario; (elec) sottostazione

substitute ['sʌbstɪ‚tjut] or ['sʌbstɪ‚tut] adj provvisorio, interino ‖ s (thing) sostituto, surrogato; (person) sostituto, supplente mf; **beware of substitutes** guardarsi dalle contraffazioni ‖ tr—**to substitute for** sostituire (qlco or qlcu) a ‖ intr—**to substitute for** sostituire, rimpiazzare, e.g., **he substituted for the teacher** sostituì il maestro

substitution [‚sʌbstɪ'tjuʃən] or [‚sʌbstɪ'tuʃən] s sostituzione; (by fraud) contraffazione

substra·tum [sʌb'strætəm] s (-ta [tə]) sostrato, substrato

subterfuge ['sʌbtər‚fjudʒ] s sotterfugio

subterranean [‚sʌbtə'renɪ‚ən] adj sotterraneo

subtitle ['sʌb‚taɪtəl] s sottotitolo; (journ) titolo corrente; (mov) didascalia ‖ tr dare una didascalia a

subtle ['sʌtəl] adj sottile

subtle·ty ['sʌtəlti] s (-ties) sottigliezza

subtract [səb'trækt] tr sottrarre

subtraction [sʌb'trækʃən] s sottrazione

suburb ['sʌbʌrb] s suburbio, sobborgo; **the suburbs** la periferia

suburban [sə'bʌrbən] adj suburbano

suburbanite [sə'bʌrbə‚naɪt] s abitante mf dei suburbi

subvention [səb'venʃən] s sovvenzione ‖ tr sovvenzionare

subversive [səb'vʌrsɪv] adj & s sovversivo

subvert [səb'vʌrt] tr sovvertire

subway ['sʌb‚we] s sotterranea, metropolitana, metrovia; sottopassaggio

sub'way sta'tion s stazione della metropolitana

succeed [sək'sid] tr succedere (with dat), subentrare (with dat) ‖ intr riuscire; **to succeed to** (the throne) succedere a

success [sək'ses] s successo, riuscita

successful [sək'sesfəl] adj felice, fortunato; che ha avuto successo

succession [sək'seʃən] s successione; **in succession** in seguito, uno dopo l'altro

successive [sək'sesɪv] adj successivo

succor ['sʌkər] s soccorso ‖ tr soccorrere

succotash ['sʌkə‚tæʃ] s verdura di fagioli e granturco

succumb [sə'kʌm] intr soccombere

such [sʌtʃ] adj & pron indef tale, simile; **such a** un simile, un tale; **such**

a + *adj* tanto + *adj*, e.g., **such a beautiful story** una storia tanto bella; **such as** tale quale, come

suck [sʌk] *s* succhio || *tr* succhiare; *(air)* aspirare; **to suck in** (slang) ingannare

sucker ['sʌkər] *s* lattante *mf;* (bot) succhione *m;* (mach) pistone *m;* (coll) fesso, pollo, minchione *m*

suckle ['sʌkəl] *tr* allattare; nutrire || *intr* poppare

suck'ling pig' ['sʌklɪŋ] *s* maiale *m* di latte

suction ['sʌkʃən] *s* aspirazione

suc'tion cup' *s* ventosa

suc'tion pump' *s* pompa aspirante

sudden ['sʌdən] *adj* subito, improvviso; **all of a sudden** all'improvviso

suddenly ['sʌdənli] *adv* all'improvviso

suds [sʌdz] *spl* saponata; schiuma; (coll) birra

sue [su] or [sju] *tr* querelare || *intr* querelarsi; **to sue for damages** chiedere i danni; **to sue for peace** chiedere la pace

suede [swed] *s* pelle scamosciata

suet ['su·ɪt] or ['sju·ɪt] *s* grasso, sego

suffer ['sʌfər] *tr* soffrire; *(e.g., heavy losses)* subire || *intr* soffrire, patire

sufferance ['sʌfərəns] *s* tolleranza

suffering ['sʌfərɪŋ] *adj* sofferente || *s* sofferenza, strazio, patimento

suffice [sə'faɪs] *intr* bastare

sufficient [sə'fɪʃənt] *adj* sufficiente

suffix ['sʌfɪks] *s* suffisso

suffocate ['sʌfə͵ket] *tr & intr* soffocare

suffrage ['sʌfrɪdʒ] *s* suffragio

suffragette [͵sʌfrə'dʒɛt] *s* suffragetta

suffuse [sə'fjuz] *tr* soffondere

sugar ['ʃʊgər] *adj* (water) zuccherato; *(industry)* zuccheriero || *s* zucchero || *tr* zuccherare

sug'ar beet' *s* barbabietola da zucchero

sug'ar bowl' *s* zuccheriera

sug'ar cane' *s* canna da zucchero

sug'ar-coat' *tr* inzuccherare; *(e.g., the pill)* addolcire

sug'ar ma'ple *s* acero

sug'ar-plum' *s* zuccherino

sug'ar spoon' *s* cucchiaino per lo zucchero

sug'ar tongs' *spl* mollette *fpl* per lo zucchero

sugary ['ʃʊgəri] *adj* zuccherino, zuccheroso

suggest [səg'dʒɛst] *tr* suggerire

suggestion [səg'dʒɛst/ən] *s* suggerimento; (psychol) suggestione; ombra, traccia

suggestive [səg'dʒɛstɪv] *adj* suggestivo; *(risqué)* scabroso

suicidal [͵su·ɪ'saɪdəl] or [͵sju·ɪ-'saɪdəl] *adj* suicida

suicide ['su·ɪ͵saɪd] or ['sju·ɪ͵saɪd] *s* *(person)* suicida *mf;* *(act)* suicidio *m;* **to commit suicide** suicidarsi

suit [sut] or [sjut] *s* vestito da uomo; *(of a lady)* tailleur *m;* *(of cards)* seme *m,* colore *m;* *(for bathing)* costume *m;* corte *f,* corteggiamento; domanda, supplica; (law) causa; **to follow suit** seguire l'esempio; (cards)

rispondere a colore || *tr* adattarsi (with *dat*); convenire (with *dat*); **suit yourself** faccia come vuole || *intr* convenire, andare a proposito

suitable ['sutəbəl] or ['sjutəbəl] *adj* indicato, conveniente

suit'case' *s* valigia

suite [swit] *s* gruppo, serie *f;* serie *f* di stanze; *(of furniture)* mobilia; *(retinue)* seguito; (mus) suite *f*

suiting ['sutɪŋ] or ['sjutɪŋ] *s* taglio d'abito

suit' of clothes' *s* completo maschile

suitor ['sutər] or ['sjutər] *s* pretendente *m;* (law) querelante *mf*

sul'fa drugs' ['sʌlfə] *spl* sulfamidici *mpl*

sulfate ['sʌlfet] *s* solfato

sulfide ['sʌlfaɪd] *s* solfuro

sulfite ['sʌlfaɪt] *s* solfito

sulfur ['sʌlfər] *adj* solfiero || *s* zolfo; color *m* zolfo

sulfuric [sʌl'fjurɪk] *adj* solforico

sul'fur mine' *s* solfara

sulfurous ['sʌlfərəs] *adj* solforoso

sulk [sʌlk] *s* broncio || *intr* imbronciarsi

sulk·y ['sʌlki] *adj* (-ier; -iest) imbronciato || *s* (-ies) *(in horse racing)* sediolo, sulky *m*

sullen ['sʌlən] *adj* bieco, triste, tetro

sul·ly ['sʌli] *v* (pret & pp -lied) *tr* insudiciare, insozzare

sulphur ['sʌlfər] *adj & s* var of **sulfur**

sultan ['sʌltən] *s* sultano

sul·try ['sʌltri] *adj* (-trier; -triest) soffocante; infocato, appassionato

sum [sʌm] *s* somma; sommario; problema *m* di aritmetica || *v* (pret & pp summed; ger summing) *tr* sommare; **to sum up** riepilogare

sumac or **sumach** ['ʃumæk] or ['sumæk] *s* (bot) sommacco

summarize ['sʌmə͵raɪz] *tr* riassumere

summa·ry ['sʌməri] *adj* sommario || *s* (-ries) sommario, sunto

summer ['sʌmər] *adj* estivo || *s* estate *f* || *intr* passare l'estate

sum'mer resort' *s* stazione estiva

summersault ['sʌmər͵sɔlt] *s & intr* var of **somersault**

sum'mer school' *s* scuola estiva

summery ['sʌməri] *adj* estivo

summit ['sʌmɪt] *s* sommità *f*

sum'mit con'ference *s* riunione al vertice

summon ['sʌmən] *tr* convocare, invitare; evocare; (law) compulsare

summons ['sʌmənz] *s* ordine *m,* comando; (law) citazione || *tr* (law) citare

sumptuous ['sʌmptʃu·əs] *adj* sontuoso

sun [sʌn] *s* sole *m;* **place in the sun** posto al sole || *v* (pret & pp sunned; ger sunning) *tr* esporre al sole || *intr* prendere il sole

sun' bath' *s* bagno di sole

sun'beam' *s* raggio di sole

sun'burn' *s* abbronzatura || *v* (pret & pp -burned or -burnt) *tr* abbronzare || *intr* abbronzarsi

sundae ['sʌndi] s gelato con sciroppo, frutta o noci

Sunday ['sʌndi] adj domenicale ‖ s domenica

Sun'day best' s (coll) vestito da festa

Sun'day's child' s bambino nato con la camicia

Sun'day school' s scuola domenicale della dottrina

sunder ['sʌndər] tr separare

sun'di'al s meridiana

sun'down' s tramonto

sundries ['sʌndriz] spl generi mpl diversi

sundry ['sʌndri] adj vari, diversi

sun'fish' s pesce m mola, pesce m luna

sun'flow'er s girasole m

sun'glass'es spl occhiali mpl da sole

sunken ['sʌŋkən] adj affondato, sommerso; (hollow) incavato

sun' lamp' s sole m artificiale

sun'light' s luce f del sole

sun'lit' adj illuminato dal sole

sun·ny ['sʌni] adj (-nier; -niest) solatio, soleggiato; allegro, ridente; **it is sunny** fa sole

sun'ny side' s parte soleggiata; lato buono; **on the sunny side of** (e.g., thirty) al disotto dei . . . anni

sun' porch' s veranda a solatio

sun'rise' s sorgere m del sole; **from sunrise to sunset** dall'alba al tramonto

sun'set' s tramonto

sun'shade' s tenda; parasole m

sun'shine' s sole m, luce f del sole; **in the sunshine** al sole

sun'spot' s macchia solare

sun'stroke' s insolazione

sun' tan' s tintarella

sun'tan lo'tion s pomata antisole, abbronzante m

sun'up' s sorgere m, levare m del sole

sun' vi'sor s (aut) aletta parasole, parasole m

sup [sʌp] v (pret & pp supped; ger supping) intr cenare

super ['supər] adj (coll) superficiale; (coll) di prim'ordine, super ‖ s (coll) sovrintendente m; (coll) articolo di prim'ordine, super m

superabundant [,supərə'bʌndənt] adj sovrabbondante

superannuated [,super'ænju,etid] adj giubilato, pensionato; messo a riposo per limiti di età; antiquato

superb [su'pʌrb] or [sə'pʌrb] adj superbo

supercar·go ['supər,kargo] s (-goes) (naut) sopraccarico

supercharge [,supər't ʃardʒ] tr sovralimentare

supercilious [,supər'sɪlɪ·əs] adj altero, arrogante

superficial [,supər'fɪʃəl] adj superficiale

superfluous [su'pʌrflu·əs] adj superfluo

su'per-high'way s autostrada

superhuman [,supər'hjumən] adj sovrumano

superimpose [,supərɪm'poz] tr sovrapporre

superintendent [,supərɪn'tendənt] s soprintendente m; (of schools) provveditore m

superior [sə'pɪrɪ·ər] or [su'pɪrɪ·ər] adj superiore; di superiorità; (typ) esponente ‖ s superiore m

superiority [sə'pɪrɪ'ɔrɪti] or [su,pɪrɪ·'ɔrɪti] s superiorità f

superlative [sə'pʌrlətɪv] or [su'pʌrlətɪv] adj & s superlativo

su'per·man' s (-men') superuomo

supermarket ['supər,markɪt] s supermercato

supernatural [,supər'næt/ərəl] adj soprannaturale

superpose [,supər'poz] tr sovrapporre

supersede [,supər'sid] tr rimpiazzare, sostituire

supersensitive [,supər'sensɪtɪv] adj ipersensibile

supersonic [,supər'sɑnɪk] adj supersonico

superstition [,supər'stɪʃən] s superstizione

superstitious [,supər'stɪ/əs] adj superstizioso

supervene [,supər'vin] intr sopravvenire

supervise ['supər,vaɪz] tr sorvegliare, dirigere

supervision [,supər'vɪʃən] s supervisione, sorveglianza, direzione

supervisor ['supər,vaɪzər] s supervisore m, sorvegliante mf; ispettore m

supper ['sʌpər] s cena

sup'per-time' s ora di cena

supplant [sə'plænt] tr rimpiazzare

supple ['sʌpəl] adj flessibile; docile

supplement ['sʌplɪmənt] s supplemento ‖ ['sʌplɪ,ment] tr completare, supplire (with dat)

suppliant ['sʌplɪ·ənt] adj & s supplicante mf

supplicant ['sʌplɪkənt] s supplicante mf

supplication [,sʌplɪ'keʃən] s supplica

supplier [sʌ'plaɪ·ər] s fornitore m

sup·ply [sə'plaɪ] s (-plies) rifornimento, fornitura; provvista, scorta; (com) offerta; **supplies** rifornimenti mpl, vettovaglie fpl ‖ v (pret & pp -plied) tr fornire, provvedere; (food) vettovagliare

supply' and demand' s domanda ed offerta

support [sə'port] s sostegno, appoggio; puntello, rincalzo; mantenimento ‖ tr sostenere, appoggiare; puntellare; (a cause) caldeggiare; mantenere

supporter [sə'portər] s fautore m, sostenitore m; (jockstrap) sospensorio; giarrettiera; fascia elastica

suppose [sə'poz] tr supporre; ammettere; **suppose we take a walk?** che ne dice se facessimo una passeggiata?; **to be supposed to** be aver fama di essere; **to suppose so** credere di sì

supposed [sə'pozd] adj presunto

supposition [,sʌpə'zɪʃən] s supposizione

supposito·ry [sə'pazɪ,tori] s (-ries) suppositorio, supposta

suppress [sə'pres] tr sopprimere

suppression [sə'prɛʃən] *s* soppressione
suppurate ['sʌpjə ,ret] *intr* suppurare
supreme [sə'prim] *or* [su'prim] *adj* supremo, sommo
Supreme' Court' *s* (*in Italy*) Corte *f* di Cassazione; (*in U.S.A.*) tribunale *m* di ultima istanza
surcharge ['sʌr ,tʃɑrdʒ] *s* soprapprezzo; soprattassa; sovraccarico; (philately) sovrastampa || [,sʌr't/ɑrdʒ] *or* ['sʌr ,tʃɑrdʒ] *tr* sovraccaricare
sure [ʃur] *adj* sicuro; **to be sure!** certamentel, senza dubbiol || *interj* (coll) certamentel; **sure enough!** (coll) difatti
sure-footed ['ʃjur'futɪd] *adj* dal piede sicuro
sure' thing' *s* (coll) successo garantito || *adv* (coll) certamente || *interj* (coll) di sicuro!
sure•ty ['ʃurti] *or* ['ʃurɪti] *s* (**-ties**) malleveria
surf [sʌrf] *s* frangente *m*
surface ['sʌrfɪs] *adj* superficiale || *s* superficie *f* || *tr* rifinire; spianare; ricoprire || *intr* emergere
sur'face mail' *s* posta ordinaria
surf'board' *s* tavola per il surfing
surfeit ['sʌrfɪt] *s* eccesso; sazietà *f* || *tr* saziare, rimpinzare || *intr* saziarsi, rimpinzarsi
surf'ing *s* surfing *m*
surge [sʌrdʒ] *s* ondata; fiotto; (elec) sovratensione || *intr* ondeggiare, fluttuare; (*said, e.g., of a crowd*) affluire
surgeon ['sʌrdʒən] *s* (medico) chirurgo
surger•y ['sʌrdʒəri] *s* (**-ies**) chirurgia; sala operatoria
surgical ['sʌrdʒɪkəl] *adj* chirurgico
sur•ly ['sʌrli] *adj* (**-lier; -liest**) arcigno, imbronciato
surmise [sər'maɪz] *or* ['sʌrmaɪz] *s* congettura, supposizione || [sər'maɪz] *tr* & *intr* congetturare, supporre
surmount [sər'maunt] *tr* sormontare; coronare
surname ['sʌr ,nem] *s* cognome *m*; (*added name*) soprannome *m* || *tr* dare il cognome a; soprannominare
surpass [sər'pæs] *or* [sər'pɑs] *tr* sorpassare, superare
surplice ['sʌrplɪs] *s* cotta
surplus ['sʌrplʌs] *adj* eccedente || *s* sopravanzo, eccedenza
surprise [sər'praɪz] *s* sorpresa || *tr* sorprendere
surprise' par'ty *s* improvvisata
surprising [sər'praɪzɪŋ] *adj* sorprendente
surrender [sə'rɛndər] *s* resa || *tr* arrendere || *intr* arrendersi
surren'der val'ue *s* (ins) valore *m* di riscatto
surreptitious [,sʌrep'tɪʃəs] *adj* clandestino, nascosto, furtivo
surround [sə'raund] *tr* circondare, contornare; (mil) aggirare
surrounding [sə'raundɪŋ] *adj* circostante, circonvicino || **surroundings** *spl* dintorni *mpl*; ambiente *m*

surtax ['sʌr ,tæks] *s* sovrimposta, soprattassa; imposta complementare
surveillance [sər'velɑns] *or* [sər'veljəns] *s* sorveglianza, vigilanza
survey ['sʌrve] *s* quadro generale, schizzo; indagine *f*; (*of opinion*) sondaggio; rapporto; rilievo topografico; perizia || [sʌr've] *or* ['sʌrve] *tr* fare un'indagine di; sondare; rilevare; misurare || *intr* fare un rilievo
sur'vey course' *s* corso di rassegna generale
surveyor [sər've‐ər] *s* livellatore *m*, geometra *m*
survival [sər'vaɪvəl] *s* sopravvivenza
survive [sər'vaɪv] *tr* sopravvivere (with *dat*) || *intr* sopravvivere
surviving [sər'vaɪvɪŋ] *adj* superstite
survivor [sər'vaɪvər] *s* sopravvissuto, superstite *mf*
survivorship [sər'vaɪvər ,ʃɪp] *s* (law) sopravvivenza
susceptible [sə'sɛptɪbəl] *adj* suscettibile, ricettivo; impressionabile; **susceptible to** (*e.g., colds*) soggetto a
suspect ['sʌspɛkt] *or* [səs'pɛkt] *adj* sospetto || ['sʌspɛkt] *s* sospetto || [səs'pɛkt] *tr* sospettare
suspend [səs'pɛnd] *tr* sospendere || *intr* essere sospeso; fermarsi; fermare i pagamenti
suspenders [səs'pɛndərz] *spl* bretelle *fpl*
suspense [səs'pɛns] *s* sospensione; sospeso; **in suspense** in sospeso
suspen'sion bridge' [səs'pɛn/ən] *s* ponte sospeso
suspicion [səs'pɪʃən] *s* sospetto
suspicious [səs'pɪʃəs] *adj* (*subject to suspicion*) sospetto; (*inclined to suspect*) sospettoso
sustain [səs'ten] *tr* sostenere, sorreggere; (*with food*) sostentare; (*a conversation*) mantenere; (*a loss*) soffrire; (law) confermare
sustenance ['sʌstɪnəns] *s* sostentamento
sutler ['sʌtlər] *s* (mil) vivandiere *m*
swab [swab] *s* (mil) scovolo; (naut) redazza; (surg) batuffolo di cotone || *v* (*pret* & *pp* **swabbed**; *ger* **swabbing**) *tr* pulire con la redazza; spugnare; assorbire col cotone
swaddle ['swadəl] *tr* fasciare
swad'dling clothes' *spl* fasce *fpl* del neonato
swagger ['swægər] *s* spavalderia || *intr* fare lo spavaldo
swain [swen] *s* innamorato; (*lad*) contadinotto
swallow ['swalo] *s* (*of liquid*) sorso; (*of food*) boccone *m*; (orn) rondine *f* || *tr* & *intr* tranguggiare, inghiottire
swal'low-tailed coat' ['swalo ,teld] *s* frac *m*, marsina, abito a coda di rondine
swal'low-wort' *s* vincetossico
swamp [swamp] *s* pantano, palude *f* || *tr* inondare, sommergere
swamp•y ['swampi] *adj* (**-ier; -iest**) paludoso, pantanoso
swan [swan] *s* cigno
swan' dive' *s* volo dell'angelo

swank [swæŋk] *adj* (coll) **elegante, vistoso** ‖ *s* (coll) eleganza vistosa

swan's-down ['swɑnz‚daʊn] *s* piuma di cigno, piumino; mollettone *m*

swan' song' *s* canto del cigno

swap [swɑp] *s* scambio, baratto ‖ *v* (*pret* & *pp* **swapped**; *ger* **swapping**) *tr* & *intr* scambiare, barattare

swarm [sworm] *s* sciame *m* ‖ *intr* sciamare; (fig) formicolare

swarth·y ['sworði] or ['sworθi] *adj* (-ier; -iest) olivastro, abbronzato

swashbuckler ['swɑʃ‚bʌklər] *s* spadaccino, rodomonte *m*

swat [swɑt] *s* colpo ‖ *v* (*pret* & *pp* **swatted**; *ger* **swatting**) *tr* colpire; (*a fly*) schiacciare

sway [swe] *s* dondolio, ondeggiamento; dominio ‖ *tr* dondolare, fare oscillare; influenzare; dominare ‖ *intr* dondolarsi, ondulare; oscillare

swear [swer] *v* (*pret* **swore** [swor]; *pp* **sworn** [sworn]) *tr* giurare; (*to secrecy*) fare giurare; **to swear in** fare prestar giuramento a; **to swear off** giurare di rinunziare a; **to swear out a warrant** ottenere un atto di accusa sotto giuramento ‖ *intr* giurare; (*to blaspheme*) bestemmiare; **to swear at** maledire; **to swear by** giurare su, avere certezza di; **to swear to** dichiarare sotto giuramento; giurare di + *inf*

swear'word' *s* bestemmia, parolaccia

sweat [swet] *s* sudata; sudore *m* ‖ *v* (*pret* & *pp* **sweat** or **sweated**) *tr* sudare; far sudare; **to sweat it out** (slang) farcela fino alla fine; **to sweat off** (*weight*) perdere sudando ‖ *intr* sudare

sweater ['swetər] *s* maglione *m*, golf *m*, sweater *m*

sweat' shirt' *s* maglione *m* da ginnastica

sweat·y ['sweti] *adj* (-ier; -iest) sudato; che fa sudare

Swede [swid] *s* svedese *mf*

Sweden ['swidən] *s* la Svezia

Swedish ['swidɪʃ] *adj* & *s* svedese *m*

sweep [swip] *s* scopata; movimento circolare; estensione; curva; (*of wind*) soffio; (*of well*) mazzacavallo; **to make a clean sweep of** far piazza pulita di ‖ *v* (*pret* & *pp* **swept** [swept]) *tr* spazzare, scopare; percorrere con lo sguardo; (*eyes*) dirigere; travolgere ‖ *intr* scopare; passare; estendersi; dragare

sweeper ['swipər] *s* spazzino; (*machine*) spazzatrice *f*; (nav) dragamine *m*

sweeping ['swipɪŋ] *adj* esteso; travolgente, decisivo ‖ **sweepings** *spl* spazzatura

sweep'-sec'ond *s* lancetta dei secondi a perno centrale

sweep'stakes' *ssg* or *spl* lotteria abbinata alle corse dei cavalli

sweet [swit] *adj* dolce; (*butter*) senza sale; (*cider*) analcolico; **to be sweet on** (coll) essere innamorato di ‖

sweets *spl* dolci *mpl*; (coll) patate *fpl* dolci ‖ *adv* dolcemente; **to smell sweet** saper di buono

sweet'bread' *s* animella

sweet'bri'er *s* eglantina

sweeten ['switən] *tr* inzuccherare; raddolcire; purificare ‖ *intr* raddolcirsi; purificarsi

sweet'heart' *s* innamorato; innamorata; caro, amore *m*

sweet' mar'joram *s* maggiorana

sweet'meats' *spl* dolci *mpl*, confetti *mpl*

sweet' pea' *s* pisello odoroso

sweet' pota'to *s* batata, patata americana; (mus) ocarina

sweet-scented ['swit‚sentɪd] *adj* odoroso, profumato

sweet' tooth' *s* debole *m* per i dolci

sweet-toothed ['swit‚tuθt] *adj* goloso

sweet' wil'liam *s* garofano barbuto

swell [swel] *adj* (slang) elegante; (slang) eccellente, di prim'ordine ‖ *s* gonfiore *m*; onda, ondata; aumento; (mus) crescendo; (slang) elegantone *m* ‖ *v* (*pret* **swelled**; *pp* **swelled** or **swollen** ['swolən]) *tr* gonfiare, ingrossare; aumentare ‖ *intr* gonfiare, ingrossarsi; aumentare; (*said of the sea*) alzarsi; (*with pride*) montarsi

swelled' head' *s* borioso; **to have a swelled head** montarsi, essere pieno di sé

swelter ['sweltər] *intr* soffocare dal caldo

swept'back wing' *s* ala a freccia

swerve [swʌrv] *s* scarto, sbandamento ‖ *tr* sviare ‖ *intr* scartare, sbandare

swift [swift] *adj* rapido ‖ *s* rondone *m* ‖ *adv* rapidamente

swig [swig] *s* (coll) sorso ‖ *v* (*pret* & *pp* **swigged**; *ger* **swigging**) *tr* & *intr* (coll) bere a grandi sorsi

swill [swil] *s* imbratto; risciacquatura ‖ *tr* tracannare, trincare ‖ *intr* bere a lunghi sorsi

swim [swim] *s* nuoto; **the swim** (*in social activities*) la corrente ‖ *v* (*pret* **swam** [swæm]; *pp* **swum** [swʌm]; *ger* **swimming**) *tr* traversare a nuoto ‖ *intr* nuotare; essere inondato; (*said of one's head*) girare, e.g., **her head is swimming** le gira la testa

swimmer ['swimər] *s* nuotatore *m*

swimming ['swimɪŋ] *s* nuoto

swim'ming pool' *s* piscina

swim'ming trunks' *spl* mutandine *fpl* da bagno

swim'suit' *s* costume *m* da bagno

swindle ['swindəl] *s* truffa, imbroglio ‖ *tr* truffare, imbrogliare

swine [swain] *s* suino, maiale *m*, porco; **swine** *spl* suini *mpl*

swing [swiŋ] *s* oscillazione; dondolio; curva; (*suspended seat*) altalena; alternarsi *m*; piena attività; (boxing) sventola; (mus) swing *m*; **free swing** libertà *f* d'azione; **in full swing** (coll) in piena attività ‖ *v* (*pret* & *pp* **swung** [swʌŋ]) *tr* (*e.g., one's arms*) dondolare, oscillare; (*a weapon*) brandire; (*e.g., a club*) rotare; far girare; appendere; (*a deal*) (coll) riuscire ad ottenere || *intr* dondolare, dondolarsi, oscillare; girare; essere sospeso; cambiare; (boxing) dare una sventola; **to swing open** aprirsi di colpo

swing'ing door' ['swɪŋɪŋ] *s* porta oscillante

swinish ['swaɪnɪʃ] *adj* porcino

swipe [swaɪp] *s* (coll) colpo forte || *tr* (coll) dare un forte colpo a; (slang) portare via, rubare

swirl [swʌrl] *s* turbine *m*, vortice *m* || *tr* far girare || *intr* turbinare

swirling ['swʌrlɪŋ] *adj* vorticoso

swish [swɪʃ] *s* (*of whip*) schiocco; (*of silk*) fruscio || *tr* (*a whip*) schioccare; || *intr* schioccare; frusciare

Swiss [swɪs] *adj* svizzero || *s* svizzero; **the Swiss** gli svizzeri

Swiss' chard' [tʃɑrd] *s* bietola

Swiss' cheese' *s* groviera

Swiss' Guards' *spl* guardie *fpl* svizzere

switch [swɪtʃ] *s* verga; vergata; (*false hair*) posticcio; cambio, trapasso; (elec) interruttore *m*; (rr) scambio || *tr* battere, frustare; (elec) commutare; (rr) deviare; (fig) girare; **to switch off** (*light, radio, etc.*) spegnere; **to switch on** (*light, radio, etc.*) accendere || *intr* fustigare; cambiare; (rr) deviare

switch'back' *s* strada a zigzag; (rr) tracciato a zigzag

switch'blade knife' *s* coltello a serramanico

switch'board' *s* quadro

switch'board op'erator *s* centralinista *mf*

switch'ing en'gine *s* locomotiva da manovra

switch'man *s* (**-men**) deviatore *m*

switch'yard' *s* stazione smistamento

Switzerland ['swɪtsərlənd] *s* la Svizzera

swiv·el ['swɪvəl] *s* perno, gancio girevole || *v* (*pret & pp* **-eled** *or* **-elled**; *ger* **-eling** *or* **-elling**) *intr* girare

swiv'el chair' *s* sedia girevole

swoon [swun] *s* deliquio, svenimento || *intr* svenire

swoop [swup] *s* calata a piombo || *intr* calare a piombo, piombare

sword [sord] *s* spada; **at swords' points** pronti ad incrociare le spade; **to put to the sword** passare a fil di spada

sword' belt' *s* cinturone *m*

sword' cane' *s* bastone animato

sword'fish' *s* pesce *m* spada

swords'man *s* (**-men**) spadaccino

sword' swal'lower ['swɑloˌər] *s* giocoliere *m* che ingoia spade

sword' thrust' *s* stoccata

sworn [sworn] *adj* giurato

sycophant ['sɪkəfənt] *s* adulatore *m*; parassita *mf*

syllable ['sɪləbəl] *s* sillaba

sylla·bus ['sɪləbəs] *s* (**-bi** [ˌbaɪ]) sillabo, sommario scolastico

syllogism ['sɪləˌdʒɪzəm] *s* sillogismo

sylph [sɪlf] *s* silfo; silfide *f*; (fig) silfide *f*

sylvan ['sɪlvən] *adj* silvano

symbol ['sɪmbəl] *s* simbolo

symbolic(al) [sɪmˈbɑlɪk(əl)] *adj* simbolico

symbolism ['sɪmbəˌlɪzəm] *s* simbolismo

symbolize ['sɪmbəˌlaɪz] *tr* simboleggiare

symmetric(al) [sɪˈmetrɪk(əl)] *adj* simmetrico

symme·try ['sɪmɪtri] *s* (**-tries**) simmetria

sympathetic [ˌsɪmpəˈθetɪk] *adj* simpatetico; ben disposto

sympathize ['sɪmpəˌθaɪz] *intr*—**to sympathize with** aver compassione di; mostrar comprensione per; (*to be in accord with*) simpatizzare con

sympa·thy ['sɪmpəθi] *s* (**-thies**) compassione, commiserazione; **to be in sympathy with** essere d'accordo con; **to extend one's sympathy to** fare le condoglianze a

sym'pathy strike' *s* sciopero di solidarietà

symphonic [sɪmˈfɑnɪk] *adj* sinfonico

sympho·ny ['sɪmfəni] *s* (**-nies**) sinfonia

symposi·um [sɪmˈpozɪəm] *s* (**-a** [ə]) simposio, colloquio

symptom ['sɪmptəm] *s* sintomo

synagogue ['sɪnəˌgɔg] *or* ['sɪnəˌgɑg] *s* sinagoga

synchronize ['sɪŋkrəˌnaɪz] *tr & intr* sincronizzare

synchronous ['sɪŋkrənəs] *adj* sincrono

sincopation [ˌsɪŋkəˈpeʃən] *s* sincope *f*

syncope ['sɪŋkəˌpi] *s* (phonet) sincope *f*

syndicate ['sɪndɪkɪt] *s* sindacato || ['sɪndɪˌket] *tr* organizzare in un sindacato

synonym ['sɪnənɪm] *s* sinonimo

synonymous [sɪˈnɑnɪməs] *adj* sinonimo

synop·sis [sɪˈnɑpsɪs] *s* (**-ses** [siz]) sinossi *f*; (mov) sinopsi *f*

synoptic(al) [sɪˈnɑptɪk(əl)] *adj* sinottico

syntax ['sɪntæks] *s* sintassi *f*

synthe·sis ['sɪnθɪsɪs] *s* (**-ses** [ˌsiz]) sintesi *f*

synthesize ['sɪnθɪˌsaɪz] *tr* sintetizzare

synthetic(al) [sɪnˈθetɪk(əl)] *adj* sintetico

syphilis ['sɪfɪlɪs] *s* sifilide *f*

Syria ['sɪrɪə] *s* la Siria

Syrian ['sɪrɪən] *adj & s* siriano

syringe [sɪˈrɪndʒ] *or* ['sɪrɪndʒ] *s* (*fountain syringe*) schizzetto; (*for hypodermic injections*) siringa || *tr* schizzettare; iniettare

syrup ['sɪrəp] *or* ['sʌrəp] *s* sciroppo

system ['sɪstəm] *s* sistema *m*

systematic(al) [ˌsɪstəˈmætɪk(əl)] *adj* sistematico

systematize ['sɪstəməˌtaɪz] *tr* ridurre a sistema

systole ['sɪstəli] *s* sistole *f*

T

T, t [ti] *s* ventesima lettera dell'alfabeto inglese; **to fit to a T** calzare come un guanto

tab [tæb] *s* (*strap*) linguetta; (*of a pocket*) patta; targa; (*label*) etichetta; **to keep tabs on** (coll) sorvegliare; **to pick up the tab** (coll) pagare il conto

tab·by ['tæbi] *s* (**-bies**) gatto tigrato; gatta; (*spinster*) zitella; vecchia pettegola

tabernacle ['tæbər‚nækəl] *s* tabernacolo

table ['tebəl] *s* tavola; (*food*) mensa; (*people at a table*) tavolata; (*synopsis*) quadro, prospetto; (*list or catalogue*) indice *m*; **to turn the tables** rovesciare la posizione; **under the table** ubriaco fradicio ǁ *tr* aggiornare, rinviare

tab·leau ['tæblo] *s* (**-leaus** or **-leaux** [loz]) quadro vivente

ta'ble-cloth' *s* tovaglia

table d'hôte ['tabəl'dot] *s* pasto a prezzo fisso

tableful ['tebəl‚ful] *s* (*persons*) tavolata; (*food*) tavola apparecchiata

ta'ble-land' *s* tavoliere *m*

ta'ble lin'en *s* biancheria da tavola

ta'ble man'ners *spl* maniere *fpl* a tavola

ta'ble of con'tents *s* indice *m* delle materie

ta'ble-spoon' *s* cucchiaio

tablespoonful ['tebəl‚spun‚ful] *s* cucchiaiata

tablet ['tæblɪt] *s* (*writing pad*) blocco; (*slab*) lapide *f*; (*flat rigid sheet*) tabella, tavoletta; (pharm) disco, pastiglia

ta'ble talk' *s* conversazione familiare a tavola

ta'ble ten'nis *s* ping-pong *m*, tennis *m* da tavolo

ta'ble-ware' *s* servizio da tavola

ta'ble wine' *s* vino da pasto

tabloid ['tæblɔɪd] *s* giornale *m* a carattere sensazionale

taboo [tæ'bu] *adj & s* tabù *m* ǁ *tr* proibire assolutamente

tabulate ['tæbjə‚let] *tr* tabulare

tabulator ['tæbjə‚letər] *s* tabulatore *m*, incolonnatore *m*

tachometer [tə'kɑmɪtər] *s* tachimetro

tacit ['tæsɪt] *adj* tacito

taciturn ['tæsɪ‚tʌrn] *adj* taciturno

tack [tæk] *s* bulletta; cambio di direzione; (naut) virata; (sew) imbastitura ǁ *tr* imbullettare; attaccare; (naut) bordeggiare; (sew) imbastire ǁ *intr* virare; mutare di direzione

tackle ['tækəl] *s* attrezzatura; (mach) taglia, paranco; (gear) (naut) padiglione *m* ǁ *tr* attaccare, affrontare; (sports) placcare, bloccare

tack·y ['tæki] *adj* (**-ier**; **-iest**) appiccicaticcio; (coll) trasandato

tact [tækt] *s* tatto

tactful ['tæktfəl] *adj* pieno di tatto

tactical ['tæktɪkəl] *adj* tattico

tactician [tæk'tɪ/ən] *s* tattico

tactics ['tæktɪks] *ssg* (mil) tattica ǁ *spl* tatti a

tactless ['tæktlɪs] *adj* che non ha tatto, indiscreto

tadpole ['tæd‚pol] *s* girino

taffeta ['tæfɪtə] *s* taffettà *m*

taffy ['tæfi] *s* caramella, zucchero d'orzo; (coll) lisciata

tag [tæg] *s* etichetta; (*on a shoelace*) punta dell'aghetto; conclusione; (*last words of speech*) pistolotto finale; epiteto; frase fatta; (*of hair*) ciocca; (*in writing*) ghirigoro; (game) toccaferro ǁ *v* (*pret & pp* **tagged**) *ger* **tagging**) *tr* etichettare; (*to fine*) multare; aggiungere; soprannominare; accusare; stabilire il prezzo di; (coll) pedinare ǁ *intr* seguire da presso

tag' end' *s* (e.g., *of day*) fine *f*; estremità logorata; avanzo

tail [tel] *adj* di coda ǁ *s* coda; fine *f*; (*of coin*) croce *f*; **tails** falde *fpl*, frac *m*; **to turn tails** darsela a gambe ǁ *tr* attaccare; finire; (coll) pedinare

tail' assem'bly *s* (aer) impennaggio

tail' end' *s* coda, fine *f*

tail'light' *s* fanale *m* di coda

tailor ['telər] *s* sarto ǁ *tr* (*a suit*) tagliare, confezionare; (*one's conduct*) adattare ǁ *intr* fare il sarto

tailoring ['telərɪŋ] *s* sartoria

tai'lor-made' *adj* fatto su misura

tai'lor shop' *s* sartoria

tail'piece' *s* coda, estremità *f*; (mus) cordiera; (typ) fusello finale

tail'race' *s* canale *m* di scarico

tail'spin' *s* avvitamento

tail'wind' *s* (aer) vento di coda; (naut) vento in poppa

taint [tent] *s* macchia; infezione ǁ *tr* macchiare, infettare, corrompere

take [tek] *s* presa; (*of fish*) retata; (mov) presa; ripresa; (slang) incasso ǁ *v* (*pret* **took** [tuk]; *pp* **taken**) *tr* prendere, pigliare; ricevere, accettare; portare; (*to get by force*) portar via; (*a nap*) schiacciare; (*a bath*) fare; (*a joke*) stare a; (*an examination*) sostenere; (*one's own life*) togliersi; (*to deduct*) cavare; (*a purchase*) comprare; (*to convey*) portare; (time) impiegare; (*a step, a walk*) fare; (*a subject*) studiare; (*a responsibility, role, etc.*) assumere; (*an oath*) prestare; (*root*) mettere; (*exception*) sollevare; credere; (e.g., *a photograph*) fare, scattare; (slang) fregare; **it takes** ci vuole, ci vogliono; **to take amiss** prendere a male; **to take apart** scomporre; smontare; **to take back** riprendere; **to take down** abbassare; smontare; prender nota di; **to take for** prendere per; **to take from** portar via a; **to take in** (*to admit*) ammettere, ricevere; (*to encompass*) includere; (*a dress*) restringere; (*to cheat*) ingannare; (water) fare; (*a point of inter-*

est) visitare; **to take it** accettare, ammettere; (slang) resistere; **to take off** (*e.g., one's coat*) togliersi; portar via; scontare, defalcare; (slang) imitare; **to take on** ingaggiare; assumere; intraprendere; accettare la sfida di; **to take out** cavare, togliere; (*e.g., a girl*) portar fuori; (*e.g., a patent*) ottenere; **to take over** rilevare; (slang) imbrogliare; **to take p'ace** aver luogo; **to take s.o.'s eye** attrarre l'attenzione di qlcu; **to take the place of** sottentrare a; **to take up** cominciare a studiare; sollevare, tirar su; (*a duty*) assumere; (*time, space*) occupare || *intr* prendere; s'attare; darsi; diventare; **to take after** rassomigliare a; **to take off** (oll) partire, andarsene; (aer) decollare, involare; **to take up with** (coll) fare amicizia con; (coll) vivere con; **to take well** riuscire bene in fotografia

take'off' *s* parodia; (aer) decollaggio; (mach) presa di forza

tal'cum pow'der ['tælkəm] *s* talco

tale [tel] *s* storia, racconto; favola, fiaba; (*lie*) bugia, frottola; (*piece of gossip*) maldicenza

tale'bear'er *s* pettegolo

talent ['tælənt] *s* talento; persona di talento; gente *f* di talento

talented ['tæləntɪd] *adj* dotato di talento, dotato d'ingegno

tal'ent scout' *s* scopritore *m* di talenti

talk [tɔk] *s* chiacchierata; discorso, conferenza; (*language*) parlata; (*gossip*) pettegolezzo; **to cause talk** originare pettegolezzi || *tr* parlare; convincere parlando; **to talk up** elogiare || *intr* parlare; discutere; **to talk on** discutere; continuare a parlare; **to talk up** parlare apertamente

talkative ['tɔkətɪv] *adj* loquace

talker ['tɔkər] *s* parlatore *m*

talkie ['tɔki] *s* (coll) parlato

talk'ing machine' *s* grammofono

talk'ing pic'ture *s* film parlato

tall [tɔl] *adj* alto; (coll) stravagante, esagerato

tallow ['tælo] *s* sego

tal•ly ['tæli] *s* (**-lies**) tacca, taglia || *v* (*pret & pp* **-lied**) *tr* contare, registrare || *intr* riscontrare

tal'ly sheet' *s* foglio di spunta

talon ['tælən] *s* artiglio

tambourine [,tæmbə'rin] *s* tamburello

tame [tem] *adj* addomesticato; docile, mansueto; mite || *tr* addomesticare; domare; (*water power*) captare

tamp [tæmp] *tr* pigiare, comprimere; (*e.g., ground*) costipare

tamper ['tæmpər] *s* (*person*) pigiatore *m*; (*tool*) mazzeranga || *intr* intrigare; **to tamper with** (*a lock*) forzare; (*a document*) manomettere; (*a witness*) corrompere

tampon ['tæmpɑn] *s* (surg) tampone *m* || *tr* (surg) tamponare

tan [tæn] *adj* marrone; (*by sun*) abbronzato || *v* (*pret & pp* **tanned; ger tanning**) *tr* (*leather*) conciare; abbronzare; (coll) picchiare, sculacciare

tandem ['tændəm] *adj & adv* in tandem || *s* tandem *m*

tang [tæŋ] *s* sapore *m* piccante; odore *m* forte; traccia; (*of knife*) tallone *m*; (*sound*) tintinnio

tangent ['tændʒənt] *adj* tangente || *s* tangente *f*; **to fly off at a tangent** cambiare improvvisamente d'idea

tangerine [,tændʒə'rin] *s* mandarino

tangible ['tændʒɪbəl] *adj* tangibile

Tangier [tæn'dʒɪr] *s* Tangeri *f*

tangle ['tæŋɡəl] *s* intrico; (coll) litigio || *tr* intricare || *intr* intricarsi; (coll) litigare

tank [tæŋk] *s* conserva, serbatoio; (mil) carro armato

tankard ['tæŋkərd] *s* boccale *m*

tank' car' *s* (rr) carro botte

tanker ['tæŋkər] *s* petroliera; (aer) aerocisterna

tank' farm'ing *s* idroponica

tank' truck' *s* autocisterna

tanner ['tænər] *s* conciapelli *m*

tanner•y ['tænəri] *s* (**-ies**) conceria

tantalize ['tæntə,laɪz] *tr* stuzzicare con vane promesse

tantamount ['tæntə,maunt] *adj* equivalente

tantrum ['tæntrəm] *s* bizze *fpl*

tap [tæp] *s* colpetto, buffetto; (*in a keg*) spina, cannella; (*faucet*) rubinetto; (elec) presa; (mach) maschio; **on tap** alla spina; (coll) disponibile; **taps** (mil) silenzio || *v* (*pret & pp* **tapped; ger tapping**) *tr* battere; picchiare, picchiettare; (*from a barrel*) spillare; mettere il cannello a; (*resources*) usare; (*a telephone*) intercettare; (*water, electricity*) derivare; (mach) maschiare || *intr* picchiare

tap' dance' *s* tip tap *m*

tap'-dance' *intr* ballare il tip tap

tape [tep] *s* nastro; (sports) striscione *m* del traguardo || *tr* legare con nastro; misurare col metro a nastro; registrare su nastro magnetico

tape' meas'ure *s* metro a nastro; nastro per misurare

tape' play'er *s* riproduttore *m* a nastro magnetico

taper ['tepər] *s* cerino || *tr* affusolare || *intr* affusolarsi; **to taper off** rastremarsi; diminuire in intensità; diminuire a poco a poco

tape'-re•cord' *tr* registrare su nastro magnetico

tape' record'er *s* magnetofono, registratore *m* a nastro

tapes•try ['tæpɪstri] *s* (**-tries**) tappezzeria || *v* (*pret & pp* **-tried**) *tr* tappezzare

tape'worm' *s* verme solitario, tenia

tappet ['tæpɪt] *s* (aut) punteria

tap'room' *s* taverna, osteria

tap'root' *s* radice *f* a fittone

tap' wa'ter *s* acqua corrente

tap' wrench' *s* giramaschio

tar [tar] *s* catrame *m* || *v* (*pret & pp* **tarred; ger tarring**) *tr* incatramare tar·dy ['tɑrdɪ] *adj* (-dier; -diest) in ritardo; lento

tare [ter] *s* tara || *tr* tarare

target ['tɑrgɪt] *s* segno, bersaglio

tar'get date' *s* data progettata

tar'get lan'guage *s* lingua obbiettivo, lingua di arrivo

tar'get prac'tice *s* esercizio di tiro a segno

tariff ['tærɪf] *s* (*duties*) tariffa doganale; (*charge or fare*) tariffa

tarnish ['tɑrnɪʃ] *s* ossidazione; (fig) macchia || *tr* appannare || *intr* appannarsi, perdere il lustro

tar' pa'per *s* carta catramata

tarpaulin [tɑr'pɔlɪn] *s* telone *m* impermeabile catramato

tarragon ['tærəgən] *s* dragoncello

tar·ry ['tɑrɪ] *adj* incatramato || ['tærɪ] *v* (*pret & pp* -ried) *intr* rimanere; ritardare

tart [tɑrt] *adj* acido, pungente || *s* torta; (slang) puttana

tartar ['tɑrtər] *s* tartaro; cremore *m* di tartaro; (*shrew*) megera; **to catch a tartar** imbattersi in un muso duro

Tartarus ['tɑrtərəs] *s* Tartaro

task [tæsk] *or* [tɑsk] *s* compito, incarico; **to take to task** rimproverare

task' force' *s* gruppo formato per una missione speciale

task'mas'ter *s* sorvegliante *m*; sorvegliante severo

tassel ['tæsəl] *s* nappa; (bot) ciuffo

taste [test] *s* gusto, sapore *m*; buon gusto; (*sampling, e.g., of wine*) assaggio; esperienza; **to one's taste** a genio di qlcu || *tr* gustare, assaggiare || *intr* sentire, sapere; **to taste of** degustare; sapere di

tasteless ['testlɪs] *adj* insipido; di cattivo gusto

tast·y ['testɪ] *adj* (-ier; -iest) saporito; (coll) di buon gusto

tatter ['tætər] *s* brandello, sbrendolo || *tr* sbrindellare

tattered ['tætərd] *adj* sbrindellato

tattle ['tætəl] *s* chiacchiera; (*gossip*) pettegolezzo || *intr* chiacchierare; spettegolare

tat'tle·tale' *adj* rivelatore || *s* gazzetta, chiacchierone *m*

tattoo [tæ'tu] *s* tatuaggio; (mil) ritirata || *tr* tatuare

taunt [tɔnt] *or* [tɑnt] *s* rimprovero sarcastico, insulto || *tr* rimproverare sarcasticamente, insultare

Taurus ['tɔrəs] *s* (astr) Toro

taut [tɔt] *adj* teso, tirato

tavern ['tævərn] *s* osteria

taw·dry ['tɔdrɪ] *adj* (-drier; -driest) vistoso, sgargiante, pacchiano

taw·ny ['tɔnɪ] *adj* (-nier; -niest) falbo, fulvo

tax [tæks] *s* tassa, imposta || *tr* tassare; (*s.o.'s patience*) mettere a dura prova

taxable ['tæksəbəl] *adj* tassabile

tax'able in'come *s* imponibile *m*

taxation [tæk'seʃən] *s* imposizione, tassazione, contribuzione

tax' collec'tor *s* esattore *m* delle imposte

tax' deduc'tion *s* detrazione

tax'-ex·empt' *adj* esente da tasse

tax' evad'er [ɪ'vedər] *s* evasore *m*

tax·i ['tæksi] *s* (-is) tassì *m* || *v* (*pret & pp* -ied; *ger* -iing *or* -ying) *tr* far rullare || *intr* andare in tassì; (aer) rullare

tax'i·cab' *s* tassì *m*

tax'i driv'er *s* tassista *m*

tax'i·plane' *s* aeroplano da noleggio, aerotassì *m*

taxi' stand' *s* posteggio di tassì

tax'pay'er *s* contribuente *mf*

tax' rate' *s* imponibilità *f*

tea [ti] *s* tè *m*; (*medicinal infusion*) tisana; (*beef broth*) brodo di carne

tea' bag' *s* sacchetto di tè

tea' ball' *s* uovo da tè

tea'cart' *s* servitore *m*

teach [titʃ] *v* (*pret & pp* taught [tɔt]) *tr & intr* insegnare

teacher ['titʃər] *s* maestro, insegnante *mf*

teach'ers col'lege *s* scuola magistrale

teach'er's pet' *s* beniamino del maestro

teaching ['titʃɪŋ] *adj* insegnante || *s* insegnamento, dottrina

teach'ing aids' *spl* sussidi *mpl* didattici

teach'ing staff' *s* corpo insegnante

tea'cup' *s* tazza da tè

tea' dance' *s* tè *m* danzante

teak [tik] *s* tek *m*

tea'ket'tle *s* bricco del tè

team [tim] *s* (*e.g., of horses*) pariglia; (sports) squadra, equipaggio || *tr* apparigliare; tirare *or* trasportare con pariglia || *intr*—**to team up** unirsi, associarsi

team'mate' *s* compagno di squadra

teamster ['timstər] *s* (*of horses*) carrettiere *m*; (*of truck*) camionista *m*, autotrenista *m*

team'work' *s* affiatamento, collaborazione

tea'pot' *s* teiera

tear [tɪr] *s* lacrima; **to hold back one's tears** ingoiare le lacrime; **to laugh away one's tears** cambiare dal pianto al riso || [ter] *s* strappo || [ter] *v* (*pret* tore [tor]; *pp* torn [tɔrn]) *tr* strappare; stracciare; (*one's heart*) squarciare; (*to wound*) sbranare; (*one's hair*) strapparsi; **to tear apart** rompere in due; separare; **to tear down** demolire; (*a piece of equipment*) smontare; **to tear off** staccare; **to tear to pieces** dilaniare; fare a pezzi; **to tear up** (*a piece of paper*) stracciare; (*a street*) scavare || *intr* strapparsi, stracciarsi; **to tear along** precipitarsi; correre all'impazzata

tear' bomb' [tɪr] *s* bomba lacrimogena

tearful ['tɪrfəl] *adj* lacrimoso

tear' gas' [tɪr] *s* gas lacrimogeno

tear-jerker ['tɪr,dʒʌrkər] *s* (coll) storia lacrimogena

tear-off ['ter,ɔf] *adj* da staccarsi, perforato

tea'room' *s* sala da tè

tear' sheet' [ter] *s* copia di annuncio pubblicitario

tease [tiz] *tr* stuzzicare, molestare;

(hair) accotonare; *(e.g., wool)* cardare

tea'spoon' *s* cucchiaino

teaspoonful ['ti ,spun ,ful] *s* cucchiaino

teat [tit] *s* capezzolo

tea'time' *s* l'ora del tè

tea' wag'on *s* servitore *m*

technical ['tɛknɪkəl] *adj* tecnico

technicali•ty [,tɛknɪ'kælɪti] *s* **(-ties)** tecnicismo; dettaglio tecnico

technician [tɛk'nɪ/ən] *s* tecnico

technics ['tɛknɪks] *ssg* or *spl* tecnica

technique [tɛk'nik] *s* tecnica

ted'dy bear' ['tɛdi] *s* orsacchiotto

tedious ['tidɪ•əs] or ['tidʒəs] *adj* tedioso, noioso

tee [ti] *adj* fatto a T || *s* giunto a tre vie; *(golf)* piazzola di partenza || *tr*— **to tee off** *(slang)* cominciare || *intr*— **to be teed off** *(slang)* essere arrabbiato; **to tee off** *(golf)* colpire la palla dalla piazzola di partenza; **to tee off on** *(slang)* rimproverare severamente

teem [tim] *intr* brulicare; piovere a dirotto; **to teem with** abbondare di

teeming ['timɪŋ] *adj* brulicante; *(rain)* torrenziale

teen-ager ['tin ,edʒər] *s* giovane *mf* dai 13 ai 19 anni

teens [tinz] *spl* numeri inglesi che finiscono in -teen (dal 13 al 19); **to be in one's teens** avere dai 13 ai 19 anni

tee•ny ['tini] *adj* **(-nier; -niest)** *(coll)* piccolo, piccolissimo

teeter ['titər] *s* altalena, dondolio || *intr* dondolarsi, oscillare

teethe [tið] *intr* mettere i denti

teething ['tiðɪŋ] *s* dentizione

teeth'ing ring' *s* dentaruolo

teetotaler [ti'totələr] *s* astemio

tele•cast ['tɛlɪ ,kæst] or ['tɛlɪ ,kɑst] *s* teletrasmissione || *v* *(pret & pp* -cast *or* -casted) *tr & intr* teletrasmettere

telegram ['tɛlɪ ,græm] *s* telegramma *m*

telegraph ['tɛlɪ ,græf] or ['tɛlɪ ,grɑf] *s* telegrafo || *tr & intr* telegrafare

tel'egraph pole' *s* palo del telegrafo

Telemachus [tɪ'lɛməkəs] *s* Telemaco

telemeter [tɪ'lɛmɪtər] *s* telemetro || *tr* misurare col telemetro

telepathy [tɪ'lɛpəθi] *s* telepatia

telephone ['tɛlɪ ,fon] *s* telefono || *tr & intr* telefonare

tel'ephone book' *s* elenco or guida dei telefoni

tel'ephone booth' *s* cabina telefonica

tel'ephone call' *s* chiamata telefonica, colpo di telefono

tel'ephone direc'tory *s* elenco or guida dei telefoni

tel'ephone exchange' *s* centrale telefonica

tel'ephone op'erator *s* centralinista *mf*, telefonista *mf*

tel'ephone receiv'er *s* ricevitore *m*

tel'ephoto lens' ['tɛlɪ ,foto] *s* teleobbiettivo

teleplay ['tɛlɪ ,ple] *s* teledramma *m*

teleprinter ['tɛlɪ ,prɪntər] *s* telescrivente *f*

telescope ['tɛlɪ ,skop] *s* telescopio || *tr*

snodare; condensare || *intr* essere snodabile; *(in a collision)* incastrarsi

teletype ['tɛlɪ ,taɪp] *s* telescrivente *f* || *tr & intr* trasmettere per telescrivente

teleview ['tɛlɪ ,vju] *tr* telericevere

televiewer ['tɛlɪ ,vju•ər] *s* telespettatore *m*

televise ['tɛlɪ ,vaɪz] *tr* teletrasmettere

television ['tɛlɪ ,vɪ/ən] *adj* televisivo || *s* televisione

tel'evision screen' *s* teleschermo

tel'evision set' *s* televisore *m*

tell [tɛl] *v* *(pret & pp* told [told]) *tr* dire; *(to narrate)* raccontare; *(to count)* contare; distinguere; **I told you so!** te l'avevo detto!; **to tell off** *(coll)* dire il fatto suo a || *intr* dire; prevedere; avere effetto; **to tell on** *(s.o.'s health)* pesare a, e.g., **age was telling on his health** l'età pesava alla sua salute; *(coll)* denunciare

teller ['tɛlər] *s* narratore *m*; *(of bank)* cassiere *m*; *(of votes)* scrutatore *m*

temper ['tɛmpər] *s* indole *f*, temperamento; umore *m*; calma; *(metallurgy)* tempra; **to keep one's temper** mantenersi calmo; **to lose one's temper** perdere la pazienza || *tr* temprare || *intr* temprarsi

temperament ['tɛmpərəmənt] *s* indole *f*, temperamento, carattere *m*

temperamental [,tɛmpərə'mɛntəl] *adj* emotivo, capriccioso

temperance ['tɛmpərəns] *s* *(self-restraint in action)* temperanza; *(abstinence from alcoholic beverages)* sobrietà *f*

temperate ['tɛmpərɪt] *adj* temperato

temperature ['tɛmpərət/ər] *s* temperatura

tempest ['tɛmpɪst] *s* tempesta; **tempest in a teapot** tempesta in un bicchier d'acqua

tempestuous [tɛm'pɛst/ʊ•əs] *adj* tempestoso

temple ['tɛmpəl] *s* *(place of worship)* tempio; *(of spectacles)* susta, stanghetta; *(anat)* tempia

tem•po ['tɛmpo] *s* *(-pos or* -pi [pi]) *(mus)* tempo; *(fig)* ritmo

temporal ['tɛmpərəl] *adj* temporale

temporary ['tɛmpə ,rɛri] *adj* temporaneo, provvisorio, transitorio, interino

temporize ['tɛmpə ,raɪz] *intr* temporeggiare

tempt [tɛmpt] *tr* tentare

temptation [tɛmp'te/ən] *s* tentazione

tempter ['tɛmptər] *s* tentatore *m*

tempting ['tɛmptɪŋ] *adj* tentatore

ten [tɛn] *adj & pron* dieci || *s* dieci *m*; **ten o'clock** le dieci

tenable ['tɛnəbəl] *adj* difendibile

tenacious [tɪ'ne/əs] *adj* tenace

tenant ['tɛnənt] *s* inquilino, pigionante *mf*; *(of land)* fittavolo

tend [tɛnd] *tr* riguardare, governare; accudire (with *dat*), e.g., **he tends the fire** accudisce al fuoco || *intr* tendere; **to tend to** propendere verso; *(e.g., one's own business)* attendere a; **to tend to** + *inf* tendere a + *inf*

tenden•cy ['tɛndənsi] *s* **(-cies)** tendenza, propensione

tender ['tɛndər] *adj* tenero; sensibile, dolorante || *s* offerta; (naut) nave *f* rifornimento; (naut) lancia; (rr) carboniera || *tr* offrire
tender-hearted ['tɛndər ,hɑrtɪd] *adj* dal cuore tenero
ten'der·loin' *s* filetto || **Tenderloin** *s* rione *m* della mala vita
tenderness ['tɛndərnɪs] *s* tenerezza
tendon ['tɛndən] *s* tendine *m*
tendril ['tɛndrɪl] *s* viticcio
tenement ['tɛnɪmənt] *s* appartamento; casa; casamento
ten'ement house' *s* casamento
tenet ['tɛnɪt] *s* dogma *m*, dottrina
tennis ['tɛnɪs] *s* tennis *m*
ten'nis court' *s* campo da tennis
ten'nis play'er *s* tennista *mf*
tenor ['tɛnər] *s* tenore *m*
tense [tɛns] *adj* teso || *s* (gram) tempo
tension ['tɛn/ən] *s* tensione *f*
tent [tɛnt] *s* tenda; (*of circus*) tendone *m*
tentacle ['tɛntəkəl] *s* tentacolo
tentative ['tɛntətɪv] *adj* a titolo di prova; (*smile*) esile
tenth [tɛnθ] *adj, s & pron* decimo || *s* (*in dates*) dieci *m*
tenuous ['tɛnju·əs] *adj* tenue
tenure ['tɛnjər] *s* (*in office*) rafferma; (*permanency of employment*) inamovibilità *f*; (law) possesso
tepid ['tɛpɪd] *adj* tiepido
tercet ['tʌrsɪt] *s* terzina
term [tʌrm] *s* vocabolo, voce *f*; periodo, durata; termine *m*; (com) scadenza; **terms** condizioni *fpl*; **to be on good terms** essere in buone relazioni; **to come to terms** venire a patti || *tr* chiamare, definire
termagant ['tʌrməgənt] *s* megera
terminal ['tʌrmɪnəl] *adj* terminale || *s* (*end or extremity*) terminale *m*; (elec) morsetto; (rr) capolinea *m*
terminate ['tʌrmɪ ,net] *tr & intr* terminare
terminus ['tʌrmɪnəs] *s* termine *m*, fine *m*; (rr) capolinea *m*
termite ['tʌrmaɪt] *s* termite *f*
terrace ['tɛrəs] *s* terrazza, terrazzo; (agr) gradino, scaglione *m*
terra firma [tə'rɛrə 'fʌrmə] *s* terra ferma
terrain [tɛ'ren] *s* terreno
terrestrial [tə'tɛstrɪ·əl] *adj* terrestre
terrific [tə'rɪfɪk] *adj* terrificante; (coll) tremendo
terri·fy ['tɛrɪ ,faɪ] *v* (*pret & pp* **-fied**) *tr* terrificare, inorridire
territo·ry ['tɛrɪ ,tori] *s* (**-ries**) territorio
terror ['tɛrər] *s* terrore *m*
terrorize ['tɛrə ,raɪz] *tr* terrorizzare; dominare col terrore
ter'ry cloth' ['tɛri] *s* tessuto a spugna
terse [tʌrs] *adj* conciso, terso
tertiary ['tʌr/ɪ ,ɛri] *or* ['tʌr/əri] *adj* terziario
test [tɛst] *s* prova, saggio; esame *m* || *tr* provare, saggiare; esaminare; (*e.g., a machine*) collaudare
testament ['tɛstəmənt] *s* testamento || **Testament** *s* Testamento Nuovo
test' ban' *s* interdizione degli esperimenti nucleari

test' flight' *s* volo di prova
testicle ['tɛstɪkəl] *s* testicolo
testi·fy ['tɛstɪ ,faɪ] *v* (*pret & pp* **-fied**) *tr & intr* testimoniare
testimonial [,tɛstɪ'moni·əl] *s* (*certificate*) benservito, referenza; (*expression of esteem*) segno di gratitudine
testimo·ny ['tɛstɪ ,moni] *s* (**-nies**) testimonianza
test' pat'tern *s* (telv) monoscopio
test' pi'lot *s* pilota *m* collaudatore
test' tube' *s* provetta
tetanus ['tɛtənəs] *s* tetano
tether ['tɛðər] *s* cavezza, pastoia; **at the end of one's tether** al limite delle proprie risorse || *tr* legare; incavezzare, impastoiare
tetter ['tɛtər] *s* eczema *m*, impetigine *f*
text [tɛkst] *s* testo; tema *m*
text'book' *s* libro di testo
textile ['tɛkstɪl] *or* ['tɛkstaɪl] *adj & s* tessile *m*
textual ['tɛkst/ʊ·əl] *adj* testuale
texture ['tɛkst/ər] *s* (*of cloth*) trama; caratteristica, proprietà *f*
Thai ['tɑ·i] *or* ['taɪ] *adj & s* tailandese *mf*
Thailand ['taɪlənd] *s* la Tailandia
Thames [tɛmz] *s* Tamigi *m*
than [ðæn] *conj* di, e.g., **he is faster than you** è più veloce di te; (*before a verb*) di quanto, e.g., **he is smarter than I thought** è più intelligente di quanto pensavo; che, e.g., **he had barely begun to eat than it was time to leave** non aveva appena cominciato a mangiare che era ora di andarsene
thank [θæŋk] *s*—**thanks** ringraziamenti *mpl*; **thanks to** grazie a, in grazie di || *tr* ringraziare; **thanks** *interj* grazie!
thankful ['θæŋkfəl] *adj* grato
thankless ['θæŋklɪs] *adj* ingrato
Thanksgiv'ing Day' [,θæŋks'ɡɪvɪŋ] *s* giorno del Ringraziamento
that [ðæt] *adj dem* (**those**) quel; codesto; **that one** quello, quello là || *pron dem* (**those**) quello; codesto || *pron rel* che, quello che, il quale; **that is** cioè; **that's that** (coll) ecco fatto, ecco tutto || *adv* (coll) tanto, così; **that far** così lontano; **that many** tanti; **that much** tanto || *conj* che
thatch [θæt/] *s* paglia, copertura di paglia; (*hair*) capigliatura || *tr* coprire di paglia
thaw [θɔ] *s* sgelo || *tr* sgelare || *intr* sgelarsi
the [ðə], [ðɪ], *or* [ðɪ] *art def* il; al, e.g., **one dollar the dozen** un dollaro alla dozzina || *adv*—**so much the worse for him** tanto peggio per lui; **the more . . . the more** quanto più . . . tanto più
theater ['θi·ətər] *s* teatro
the'ater·go'er *s* frequentatore *m* abituale del teatro
the'ater news' *s* cronaca teatrale
theatrical [θɪ'ætrɪkəl] *adj* teatrale
Thebes [θibz] *s* Tebe *f*
thee [ðɪ] *pron pers* (Bib; poet) ti; te
theft [θɛft] *s* furto, ruberia

their [ðer] *adj poss* il loro, loro

theirs [ðerz] *pron poss* il loro

them [ðem] *pron pers* li; loro; **to them** loro

theme [θim] *s* tema *m*, soggetto; saggio; (mus) tema *m*

theme' song' *s* (mus) tema *m* centrale; (rad) sigla musicale

them·selves' *pron pers* essi stessi, loro stessi; si, e.g., **they enjoyed themselves** si divertirono

then [ðen] *adj* allora, di allora || *s* quel tempo; **by then** a quell'epoca; **from then on** da quel giorno in poi || *adv* allora; indi, poi; **then and there** a quel momento

thence [ðens] *adv* indi, quindi; da lì; da allora in poi

thence'forth' *adv* da allora in poi

theolo·gy [θi'ɑlədʒi] *s* (-gies) telogia

theorem ['θi·ərəm] *s* teorema *m*

theoretical [ˌθi·ə'retikəl] *adj* teoretico

theo·ry ['θi·əri] *s* (-ries) teoria

therapeutic [ˌθerə'pjutik] *adj* terapeutico || **therapeutics** *ssg* terapeutica

thera·py ['θerəpi] *s* (-ies) terapia

there [ðer] *adv* lì, là; **there are** ci sono; **there is** c'è; ecco, e.g., **there it is** eccolo

there'abouts' *adv* circa, approssimativamente, giù di lì

there'af'ter *adv* in seguito, dipoi

there'by' *adv* quindi, perciò, così

therefore ['ðerfor] *adv* per questo, quindi, dunque

there'in' *adv* lì; in quel rispetto

there'of' *adv* di ciò, da ciò

Theresa [tə'risə] or [tə'resə] *s* Teresa

there'upon' *adv* su questo; a quel momento; come conseguenza

thermal ['θʌrməl] *adj* (water) termale; (capacity) termico

thermistor [θər'mistər] *s* (elec) termistore *m*

thermocouple ['θʌrmoˌkʌpəl] *s* termocoppia

thermodynamic [ˌθʌrmodai'næmik] *adj* termodinamico || **thermodynamics** *ssg* termodinamica

thermometer [θər'mɑmitər] *s* termometro

thermonuclear [ˌθʌrmo'njuklɪ·ər] or [ˌθʌrmo'nuklɪ·ər] *adj* termonucleare

ther'mos bot'tle ['θʌrməs] *s* termos *m*

thermostat ['θʌrməˌstæt] *s* termostato

thesau·rus [θɪ'sɔrəs] *s* (-ri [rai] or -ruses) tesoro, lessico, compendio

these [ðiz] *pl* of **this**

the·sis ['θisis] *s* (-ses [siz]) tesi *f*

Thespis ['θespis] *s* Tespi *m*

they [ðe] *pron pers* essi, loro

thick [θik] *adj* spesso, grosso; folto, denso; pieno, coperto; viscoso; stupido; (coll) intimo || *s* spessore *m*; **in the thick of** nel folto di; **through thick and thin** nei tempi buoni e cattivi

thicken ['θikən] *tr* ispessire; ingrossare; infoltire || *intr* ispessirsi; ingrossarsi; (said of a plot) complicarsi

thicket ['θikit] *s* boscaglia, macchia

thick-headed ['θikˌhedid] *adj* indietro, stupido

thick'set' *adj* tarchiato; (hedge) fitto, denso

thief [θif] *s* (thieves [θivz]) ladro

thieve [θiv] *intr* rubare

thiever·y ['θivəri] *s* (-ies) furto

thigh [θai] *s* coscia

thigh'bone' *s* femore *m*

thimble ['θimbəl] *s* ditale *m*

thin [θin] *adj* (thinner; thinnest) (paper, ice) sottile; (lean) magro, smilzo; (e.g., hair) rado; (air) fine; (excuse) tenue; (voice) esile; (wine) leggero, annacquato || *v* (pret & pp thinned; ger thinning) *tr* assottigliare; (paint) diluire || *intr* assottigliarsi; **to thin out** (said of a crowd; one's hair) diradarsi

thine [ðain] *adj & pron poss* (Bib & poet) tuo, il tuo

thing [θiŋ] *s* cosa; **not to get a thing out of** non riuscire a capire; non cavare un briciolo d'informazione da; **of all things!** che cosa!; che sorpresa!; **the thing** l'ultima moda; **things** roba; **to see things** avere allucinazioni

think [θiŋk] *v* (pret & pp thought [θɔt]) *tr* pensare; credere; **to think it over** ripensarci; **to think nothing of it** non darci la minima importanza; **to think of** (to have as an opinion of) pensare di, e.g., **what do you think of that doctor?** cosa ne pensa di quel medico?; **to think out** decifrare; **to think up** immaginare || *intr* pensare; **to think of** (to imagine) immaginare; **to think not** credere di no; **to think of** (to turn one's thoughts to) pensare a, e.g., **he is thinking of the future** pensa al futuro; (to imagine) immaginare; **to think so** credere di sì; **to think well of** avere una buona opinione di

thinkable ['θiŋkəbəl] *adj* pensabile

thinker ['θiŋkər] *s* pensatore *m*

third [θʌrd] *adj, s & pron* terzo || *s* terzo; (in dates) tre *m*; (aut) terza

third' degree' *s* interrogatorio di terzo grado

third' rail' *s* (rr) rotaia elettrificata di contatto

third'-rate' *adj* di terz'ordine

Third' World' *s* Terzo Mondo

thirst [θʌrst] *s* sete *f* || *intr* aver sete; **to thirst for** aver sete di

thirst·y ['θʌrsti] *adj* (-ier; -iest) assetato, sitibondo; **to be thirsty** avere sete

thirteen ['θʌr'tin] *adj, s & pron* tredici *m*

thirteenth ['θʌr'tinθ] *adj, s & pron* tredicesimo || *s* (in dates) tredici *m*

thirtieth ['θʌrti·iθ] *adj, s & pron* trentesimo || *s* (in dates) trenta *m*

thir·ty ['θʌrti] *adj & pron* trenta || *s* (-ties) trenta *m*; **the thirties** gli anni trenta

this [ðis] *adj dem* (these) questo; **this one** questo, questo qui || *pron dem* (these) questo, questo qui || *adv* (coll) tanto, così

thistle ['θisəl] *s* cardo

thither ['θiðər] or ['ðiðər] *adv* là, da quella parte

Thomas ['tɑməs] *s* Tommaso
thong [θɔŋ] or [θɑŋ] *s* coreggia
thorax ['θoræks] *s* (**-raxes** or **-races** [rə ,siz]) torace *m*
thorn [θɔrn] *s* spina
thorn·y ['θɔrni] *adj* (**-ier; -iest**) spinoso
thorough ['θʌro] *adj* completo, esauriente
thor'ough·bred' *adj* di razza; (*horse*) purosangue || *s* individuo di razza; (*horse*) purosangue *mf*
thor'ough·fare' *s* passaggio; **no thoroughfare** divieto di passaggio
thor'ough·go'ing *adj* completo, esauriente
thoroughly ['θʌroli] *adv* a fondo
those [ðoz] *pl* of **that**
thou [ðau] *pron pers* (Bib; poet) tu || *tr* dare del tu a
though [ðo] *adv* tuttavia || *conj* malgrado, sebbene; **as though** come se
thought [θɔt] *s* pensiero; **perish the thought!** (coll) nemmeno a pensarci!
thoughtful ['θɔtfəl] *adj* pensieroso, riflessivo; (*considerate*) sollecito
thoughtless ['θɔtlɪs] *adj* irriflessivo, sconsiderato; (*reckless*) incurante
thought' transfer'ence *s* trasmissione del pensiero
thousand ['θauzənd] *adj, s & pron* mille *m*; **a thousand** or **one thousand** mille *m*
thousandth ['θauzəndθ] *adj, s & pron* millesimo
thralldom ['θrɔldəm] *s* schiavitù *f*
thrash [θræʃ] *tr* battere; (agr) trebbiare; **to thrash out** discutere a fondo || *intr* agitarsi, dibattersi
thread [θrɛd] *s* filo; (mach) filetto, verme *m*; **to lose the thread of** perdere il filo di || *tr* infilare; (fig) pervadere; (mach) filettare, impanare; **to thread one's way through** aprirsi il passaggio attraverso
thread'bare' *adj* frusto, logoro
threat [θrɛt] *s* minaccia
threaten ['θrɛtən] *tr & intr* minacciare
threatening ['θrɛtənɪŋ] *adj* minaccioso; (*e.g., letter*) minatorio
three [θri] *adj & pron* tre || *s* tre *m*; **three o'clock** le tre
three'-cor'nered *adj* triangolare; (*hat*) a tre punte
three' hun'dred *adj, s & pron* trecento
threepenny ['θrɛpənɪ] or ['θrɪpənɪ] *adj* del valore di tre penny; di nessun valore
three'-phase' *adj* trifase
three'-ply' *adj* a tre spessori
three' R's' [ɑrz] *spl* lettura, scrittura e aritmetica
three'score' *adj* sessanta
three' thou'sand *adj, s & pron* tre mila *mpl*
threno·dy ['θrɛnədi] *s* (**-dies**) trenodia
thresh [θrɛʃ] *tr* (agr) trebbiare; **to thresh out** discutere a fondo || *intr* trebbiare; battere
thresh'ing machine' *s* trebbiatrice *f*
threshold ['θrɛʃold] *s* soglia
thrice [θraɪs] *adv* tre volte; molto
thrift [θrɪft] *s* economia
thrift·y ['θrɪfti] *adj* (**-ier; -iest**) eco-

nomo, economico; vigoroso; prospero
thrill [θrɪl] *s* fremito d'emozione; esperienza emozionante || *tr* emozionare || *intr* emozionarsi; vibrare
thriller ['θrɪlər] *s* (coll) thrilling *m*
thrilling ['θrɪlɪŋ] *adj* emozionante, thrilling
thrive [θraɪv] *v* (*pret* **thrived** or **throve** [θrov]; *pp* **thrived** or **thriven** ['θrɪvən]) *intr* prosperare, fiorire
throat [θrot] *s* gola; **to clear one's throat** schiarirsi la voce
throb [θrɑb] *s* battito, palpito, tuffo || *v* (*pret & pp* **throbbed;** *ger* **throbbing**) *intr* palpitare, pulsare
throe [θro] *s* agonia, travaglio, spasimo; **in the throes of** nel travaglio di; (*e.g., battle*) nel momento più penoso di
throne [θron] *s* trono
throng [θrɔŋ] or [θrɑŋ] *s* folla, stuolo || *intr* affollarsi
throttle ['θrɑtəl] *s* (*of locomotive*) leva di comando; (*of motorcycle*) manetta; (*of car*) acceleratore *m*; (mach) valvola di controllo || *tr* soffocare; (mach) regolare
through [θru] *adj* diretto, senza fermate; **to be through** aver finito; **to be through with** farla finita con || *adv* attraverso; da una parte all'altra; completamente; || *prep* attraverso, per; durante; fino alla fine di; per mezzo di
through-out' *adv* completamente, da un capo all'altro; dappertutto || *prep* durante tutto, e.g., **throughout the afternoon** durante tutto il pomeriggio; per tutto, e.g., **throughout the house** per tutta la casa
throw [θro] *s* getto, tiro, lancio; gettata; coperta leggera || *v* (*pret* **threw** [θru]; *pp* **thrown**) *tr* gettare, tirare, lanciare; (*a shadow*) proiettare; (*the current*) connettere; (*said of a horse*) disarcionare; (*wrestling*) gettare a terra; (*a game*) (coll) perdere intenzionalmente; (coll) stupire; **to throw away** gettar via; perdere; **to throw back** rigettare; ritardare; **to throw in** (*the clutch*) innestare; (coll) aggiungere; **to throw oneself into** darsi a; **to throw out** sbatter fuori; (*the clutch*) disinnestare; **to throw over** abbandonare || *intr* gettare, tirare, lanciare; **to throw up** vomitare
thrum [θrʌm] *v* (*pret & pp* **thrummed;** *ger* **thrumming**) *intr* tamburreggiare; (mus) far scorrere la mano sulle corde di uno strumento
thrush [θrʌʃ] *s* tordo
thrust [θrʌst] *s* (*push*) spinta; botta; (*with dagger*) pugnalata; (*with sword*) stoccata || *v* (*pret & pp* **thrust**) *tr* spingere; conficcare, configgere; **to thrust oneself** (*e.g., into a conversation*) ficcarsi
thru'way' *s* autostrada
thud [θʌd] *s* tonfo || *v* (*pret & pp* **thudded;** *ger* **thudding**) *intr* fare un rumore sordo
thug [θʌg] *s* fascinoroso

thumb [θʌm] s pollice m; **all thumbs**
maldestro, goffo; **thumbs down** pollice verso; **to twiddle one's thumbs**
girare i pollici, essere ozioso; **under
the thumb of** sotto l'influenza di ‖
tr sporcare con le dita; (*a book*) sfogliare; **to thumb a ride** chiedere
l'autostop; **to thumb one's nose** (**at**)
fare marameo (a)

thumb′ in′dex s margine m a scaletta

thumb′nail′ *adj* breve, conciso ‖ s
unghia del pollice

thumb′screw′ s vite f ad aletta

thumb′tack′ s puntina

thump [θʌmp] s tonfo ‖ *tr* battere,
percuotere ‖ *intr* battere; cadere
con un tonfo; camminare a passi
pesanti; (*said of the heart*) palpitare
violentemente

thumping [′θʌmpɪŋ] *adj* (coll) straordinario, eccezionale; (coll) grande

thunder [′θʌndər] s tuono; (*of applause*) scroscio; (*of a cannon*)
rombo ‖ *tr* lanciare ‖ *intr* tonare,
rombare; (fig) scrosciare

thun′der-bolt′ s folgore f, fulmine m

thun′der-clap′ s scroscio di tuono

thunderous [′θʌndərəs] *adj* fragoroso

thun′der-show′er s acquazzone m accompagnato da tuoni

thun′der-storm′ s temporale m

thun′der-struck′ *adj* attonito

Thursday [′θʌrsdi] s giovedì m

thus [ðʌs] *adv* così; **thus far** sino qui

thwack [θwæk] s colpo ‖ *tr* colpire

thwart [θwɔrt] *adj* obliquo ‖ *adv* di
traverso ‖ *tr* contrariare, sventare

thy [ðaɪ] *adj poss* (Bib; poet) tuo, il
tuo

thyme [taɪm] s timo

thy′roid gland′ [′θaɪrɔɪd] s tiroide f

thyself [ðaɪ′sɛlf] *pron* (Bib; poet) te
stesso; te, ti

tiara [taɪ′ɑrə] or [taɪ′ærə] s (*female
adornment*) diadema m; (eccl) tiara

tick [tɪk] s (*of pillow*) fodera; (*of mattress*) guscio; (*of clock*) ticchettio;
(*dot*) punto; (ent) zecca; **on tick**
(coll) a credito ‖ *intr* fare ticchettio;
to make s.o. tick mandare avanti
qlcu

ticker [′tɪkər] s telescrivente f; (slang)
orologio; (slang) cuore m

tick′er tape′ s nastro della telescrivente

ticket [′tɪkɪt] s biglietto; (*e.g., of
pawnbroker*) polizza; (*slip of paper
or identifying tag*) bolletta, bollettino; (*summons*) verbale m; (*e.g., to
indicate price*) etichetta; lista dei
candidati; **that's the ticket** (coll)
questo è quello che fa

tick′et a′gent s biglietteria

tick′et of′fice s biglietteria

tick′et scalp′er [′skælpər] s bagarino

tick′et win′dow s sportello

ticking [′tɪkɪŋ] s traliccio

tickle [′tɪkəl] s solletico ‖ *tr* solleticare; divertire ‖ *intr* avere il solletico

ticklish [′tɪklɪʃ] *adj* sensibile al solletico; delicato; permaloso; **to be ticklish** soffrire il solletico

tick-tock [′tɪk ,tɑk] s tic tac m

tid′al wave′ [′taɪdəl] s onda di marea;
(fig) ondata

tidbit [′tɪd ,bɪt] s bocconcino

tiddlywinks [′tɪdli ,wɪŋks] s gioco
della pulce

tide [taɪd] s marea; **to go against the
tide** andare contro la corrente; **to
stem the tide** fermare la corrente ‖
tr portare sulla cresta delle onde; **to
tide over** aiutare; (*a difficulty*) sormontare

tide′wa′ter s marea; costa marina

tidings [′taɪdɪŋz] *spl* notizie fpl

ti-dy [′taɪdi] *adj* (**-dier; -diest**) pulito,
ordinato ‖ s (**-dies**) cofanetto, astuccio; appoggiacapo ‖ *v* (*pret & pp*
-died) *tr* rassettare, mettere in ordine
‖ *intr* rassettarsi

tie [taɪ] s laccio, nodo, vincolo; (*in
games*) patta; (*necktie*) cravatta;
(archit) traversa; (rr) traversina;
(mus) legatura ‖ *v* (*pret & pp* **tied**;
ger **tying**) *tr* allacciare, annodare;
legare; confinare; (*a game*) impattare; (*a person*) impattarla con; **to
be tied up** essere occupato; **to tie
down** confinare, limitare; **to tie up**
legare; impedire; (*e.g., traffic*) intasare ‖ *intr* allacciare; (*in games*)
impattare

tie′ beam′ s catena

tie′pin′ s spilla da cravatta

tier [tɪr] s gradinata; ordine m, livello

tiff [tɪf] s screzio, litigio

tiger [′taɪgər] s tigre f

ti′ger lil′y s giglio cinese

tight [taɪt] *adj* teso; stretto; compatto;
impermeabile, ermetico; pieno;
(*game*) (coll) serrato; (coll) tirato;
(slang) ubriaco ‖ **tights** *spl* calzamaglia ‖ *adv* strettamente; **to hold tight**
tenere stretto

tighten [′taɪtən] *tr* (*e.g., one's belt*)
tirare; (*e.g., a screw*) stringere ‖ *intr*
tirarsi; stringersi

tight-fisted [′taɪt′fɪstɪd] *adj* taccagno

tight′-fit′ting *adj* attillato

tight′rope′ s corda tesa

tight′ squeeze′ s—**to be in a tight
squeeze** (coll) essere alle strette

tight′wad′ s (coll) spilorcio

tigress [′taɪgrɪs] s tigre femmina

tile [taɪl] s mattonella; (*for floor*) piastrella; (*for roof*) tegola, coppo ‖ *tr*
coprire di mattonelle; coprire di piastrelle; coprire di coppi

tile′ roof′ s tetto di tegole

till [tɪl] s cassetto dei soldi ‖ *prep* fino
a ‖ *conj* fino a che . . . non, fino a
che, sinché . . . non, sinché ‖ *tr* lavorare, coltivare

tilt [tɪlt] s inclinazione; giostra, torneo;
full tilt di gran carriera; a tutta forza
‖ *tr* inclinare; (*a lance*) mettere in
resta; attaccare ‖ *intr* inclinarsi; giostrare; **to tilt at** combattere con

timber [′tɪmbər] s legno, legname m
da costruzione; alberi *mpl;* (fig)
tempra

tim′ber-land′ s bosco destinato a produrre legname

tim′ber line′ s linea della vegetazione

timbre ['tɪmbər] *s* (phonet & phys) timbro

time [taɪm] *s* tempo; ora, e.g., **what time is it?** che ora è?; volta, e.g., **three times** tre volte; giorni *mpl*, e.g., **in our time** ai giorni nostri; momento; ultima ora; ore *fpl* lavorative; periodo, e.g., **Xmas time** periodo natalizio; **for a long time** da lungo; **for the time being** per ora, per il momento; **in time** presto; col tempo; **on time** a tempo; a rate; *(said, e.g., of a bus)* in orario; **times** volte, e.g., **seven times** sette volte; **seven times sette** volte sette; **to bide one's time** aspettare l'ora propizia; **to do time** (coll) essere in prigione; **to have a good time** divertirsi; **to have no time for** non poter sopportare; **to lose time** *(said of a watch)* ritardare; **to make time** avanzare rapidamente; guadagnare terreno; **to pass the time of day** fare una chiacchierata; salutarsi; **to take one's time** fare le cose senza fretta; **to tell time** leggere l'orologio; *tr* fissare il momento di; calcolare il tempo di; (sports) cronometrare

time' bomb' *s* bomba a orologeria

time' card' *s* cartellino di presenza

time' clock' *s* orologio di controllo (delle presenze)

time' expo'sure *s* (phot) posa

time' fuse' *s* spoletta a tempo

time' keep'er *s* marcatempo; orologio; (sports) cronometrista *mf*

timeless ['taɪmlɪs] *adj* senza fine, eterno

time-ly ['taɪmli] *adj* (**-lier; -liest**) opportuno, tempestivo

time'piece' *s* orologio; cronometro

time' sig'nal *s* segnale orario

time'ta'ble *s* orario; tabella di marcia

time'work' *s* lavoro a ore

time'worn' *adj* logorato dal tempo

time' zone' *s* fuso orario

timid ['tɪmɪd] *adj* timido, pavido

tim'ing gears' ['taɪmɪŋ] *spl* ingranaggi *mpl* di distribuzione

timorous ['tɪmərəs] *adj* timoroso

tin [tɪn] *s* *(element)* stagno; *(tin plate; can)* latta ‖ *v* *(pret & pp* **tinned;** *ger* **tinning**) *tr* stagnare

tin' can' *s* latta

tincture ['tɪŋktʃər] *s* tintura

tin' cup' *s* tazzina metallica

tinder ['tɪndər] *s* esca

tin'der-box' *s* cassetta con l'esca e l'acciarino; persona eccitabile; (fig) polveriera

tin' foil' *s* stagnola

ting-a-ling ['tɪŋə,lɪŋ] *s* dindìn *m*

tinge [tɪndʒ] *s* sfumatura; pizzico, punta ‖ *v* *(ger* **tingeing** *or* **tinging**) *tr* sfumare; dare una traccia di sapore a

tingle ['tɪŋgəl] *s* formicolìo, pizzicore *m* ‖ *intr* informicolirsi, pizzicare; *(said of the ears)* ronzare; *(with enthusiasm)* fremere

tin' hat' *s* (slang) elmetto

tinker ['tɪŋkər] *s* calderaio, ramaio ‖ *intr* armeggiare

tinkle ['tɪŋkəl] *s* tintinnìo ‖ *tr* far tintinnare ‖ *intr* tintinnare

tin' plate' *s* latta

tin' roof' *s* tetto di lamiera di latta

tinsel ['tɪnsəl] *s* orpello, lustrino

tin'smith' *s* lattoniere *m*, stagnino

tin' sol'dier *s* soldatino di piombo

tint [tɪnt] *s* tinta, sfumatura ‖ *tr* tinteggiare

tin'ware' *s* articoli *mpl* di latta

ti-ny ['taɪni] *adj* (**-nier; -niest**) piccino

tip [tɪp] *s* punta; *(of mountain)* vetta; *(of umbrella)* gorbia; *(of shoe)* mascherina; *(of cigarette)* bocchino; *(of shoestring)* aghetto; colpetto; *(fee)* mancia; informazione confidenziale; inclinazione ‖ *v* *(pret & pp* **tipped;** *ger* **tipping**) *tr* mettere la punta a; inclinare, rovesciare; *(one's hat)* levarsi; dare la mancia a; toccare, battere; *(the scales)* far traboccare; **to tip in** (bb) inserire fuori testo; **to tip off** (coll) dare informazioni confidenziali a ‖ *intr* inclinarsi; dare la mancia

tip'cart' *s* carro ribaltabile

tip'-off' *s* (coll) avvertimento confidenziale

tipped'-in' *adj* (bb) fuori testo

tipple ['tɪpəl] *intr* sbevucchiare

tip'staff' *s* usciere *m*

tip-sy ['tɪpsi] *adj* (**-sier; -siest**) brillo

tip'toe' *s* punta di piedi ‖ *v* *(pret & pp* **-toed;** *ger* **-toeing**) *intr* camminare in punta di piedi

tirade ['taɪred] *s* tirata

tire [taɪr] *s* gomma, pneumatico; *(of metal)* cerchione *m* ‖ *tr* stancare ‖ *intr* stancarsi; infastidirsi

tire' chain' *s* catena antineve

tired [taɪrd] *adj* stanco, stracco

tire' gauge' *s* manometro della pressione delle gomme

tireless ['taɪrlɪs] *adj* infaticabile

tire' pres'sure *s* pressione (delle gomme)

tire' pump' *s* pompa (per i pneumatici)

tiresome ['taɪrsəm] *adj* faticoso; *(boring)* noioso

tissue ['tɪʃju] *s* tessuto; tessuto finissimo, velina

tis'sue pa'per *s* carta velina

titanium [taɪ'teni.əm] *or* [tɪ'teni.əm] *s* titanio

tithe [taɪð] *s* decima ‖ *tr* imporre la decima su; pagare la decima di

Titian ['tɪʃən] *adj* tizianesco ‖ *s* Tiziano

title ['taɪtəl] *s* titolo; (sports) campionato ‖ *tr* intitolare

ti'tle deed' *s* titolo di proprietà

ti'tle-hold'er *s* campione *m*, primatista *mf*

ti'tle page' *s* frontespizio

ti'tle role' *s* (theat) ruolo principale

tit'mouse' *s* (**-mice**) (orn) cincia

titter ['tɪtər] *s* risatina ‖ *intr* ridacchiare

titular ['tɪtʃələr] *adj* titolare

TNT ['ti,ɛn'ti] *s* (letterword) tritolo

to [tu], [tʊ] *or* [tə] *adv*—**to and fro** da una parte all'altra, avanti e indietro; **to come** to tornare in sè ‖ *prep* a, e.g., **he is going to Rome** va a Roma; **he gave a kiss to his mother**

diede un bacio a sua madre; **she is learning to sew** impara a cucire; per, e.g., **he has been a true friend to me** è stato un vero amico per me; da, e.g., **there is still a lot of work to do** c'è ancora molto lavoro da fare; con, e.g., **she was very kind to me** è stata molto gentile con me; in, e.g., **we went to church** siamo andati in chiesa; fino a, e.g., **to see s.o. to the station** accompagnare qlcu fino alla stazione; in confronto di, e.g., **the accounts are nothing to what really happened** le storie non sono nulla, in confronto di quanto è realmente successo; meno, e.g., **ten minutes to seven** le sette meno dieci

toad [tod] *s* rospo

toad'stool' *s* agarico, fungo velenoso

to-and-fro [tu-ənd'fro] *adj* avanti e indietro

toast [tost] *s* pane tostato; (*drink to s.o.'s health*) brindisi *m*; **a piece of toast** una fetta di pane tostato || *tr* tostare; brindare alla salute di || *intr* tostarsi; brindare

toaster ['tostər] *s* (*of bread*) tostapane *m*; persona che fa un brindisi

toast'mas'ter *s* persona che annuncia i brindisi, maestro di cerimonie

tobac·co [tə'bæko] *s* (**-cos**) tabacco

tobacconist [tə'bækənɪst] *s* tabaccaio

tobac'co pouch' *s* borsa da tabacco

toboggan [tə'bɑgən] *s* toboga *m*

tocsin ['tɑksɪn] *s* campana a martello; scampanata d'allarme

today [tu'de] *s & adv* oggi *m*

toddle ['tɑdəl] *s* passo vacillante || *intr* traballare, trotterellare

tod·dy ['tɑdi] *s* (**-dies**) ponce *m*

to-do [tə'du] *s* (**-dos**) (coll) daffare *m*, rumore *m*

toe [to] *s* dito del piede; (*of shoe*) punta — *v* (*pret & pp* **toed**; *ger* **toeing**) *tr*—**to toe the line** filare diritto

toe'nail' *s* unghia del piede

together [tu'gɛðər] *adv* insieme; **to bring together** riunire; riconciliare; **to call together** chiamare a raccolta; **to stick together** (coll) rimanere uniti, stare insieme

togs [tɑgz] *spl* vestiti *mpl*

toil [tɔɪl] *s* travaglio, sfacchinata; **toils** reti *fpl*, lacci *mpl* || *intr* travagliare, sfacchinare

toilet ['tɔɪlɪt] *s* toletta; gabinetto, ritirata; **to make one's toilet** farsi la toletta

toi'let pa'per *s* carta igienica

toi'let pow'der *s* polvere *f* di talco

toi'let soap' *s* sapone *m* da toletta

toi'let wa'ter *s* acqua da toletta

token ['tokən] *s* segno, marca; ricordo; (*used as money*) gettone *m*; **by the same token** per di più; **in token of** in segno di, come prova di

tolerance ['tɑlərəns] *s* tolleranza

tolerate ['tɑlə,ret] *tr* tollerare

toll [tol] *s* (*of bell*) rintocco; (*e.g., for passage over bridge*) pedaggio; (*tax*) dazio; (*compensation for grinding grains*) molenda; (*number of victims*) perdite *fpl*; (telp) tariffa inter-

urbana || *tr* (*a bell*) sonare a morto; (*the faithful*) chiamare a raccolta || *intr* sonare a morto

toll' bridge' *s* ponte *m* a pedaggio

toll' call' *s* (telp) chiamata interurbana

toll'gate' *s* barriera di pedaggio; (*in a turnpike*) casello

toma·to [tə'meto] *or* [tə'mɑto] *s* (**-toes**) pomodoro

toma'to juice' *s* sugo di pomodoro

tomb [tum] *s* tomba

tomboy ['tɑm,bɔɪ] *s* maschietta

tomb'stone' *s* pietra tombale, lapide *f*

tomcat ['tɑm,kæt] *s* gatto maschio

tome [tom] *s* tomo

tomorrow [tu'mɑro] *or* [tu'mɔro] *s* domani *m;* **the day after tomorrow** dopodomani *m* || *adv* domani

tom-tom ['tɑm,tɑm] *s* tam-tam *m*

ton [tʌn] *s* tonnellata; **tons** (coll) montagne *fpl*

tone [ton] *s* tono; (fig) tenore *m* || *tr* intonare; **to tone down** (*colors*) smorzare; (*sounds*) sfumare || *intr* intonarsi; **to tone down** moderarsi; **to tone up** rinforzarsi

tone' po'em *s* poema sinfonico

tongs [tɔŋz] *or* [tɑŋz] *spl* tenaglie *fpl;* (*e.g., for sugar*) molle *fpl*

tongue [tʌŋ] *s* (*language*) lingua; (*of bell*) battaglio; (*of shoe*) linguetta; (*of wagon*) timone *m;* (anat) lingua; (carp) maschio; **tongue in cheek** poco sinceramente; **to hold one's tongue** mordersi la lingua; **to speak with forked tongue** essere di due lingue

tongue' depres'sor *s* abbassalingua *m*

tongue'-lash'ing *s* sgridata

tongue' twist'er *s* scioglilingua *m*

tonic ['tɑnɪk] *adj & s* tonico

tonight [tu'naɪt] *s* questa sera, questa notte || *adv* stasera; stanotte

tonnage ['tʌnɪdʒ] *s* tonnellaggio, stazza

tonsil ['tɑnsəl] *s* tonsilla

ton·y ['toni] *adj* (**-ier; -iest**) (slang) elegante, di lusso

too [tu] *adv* (*also*) anche, pure; (*more than enough*) troppo; **too bad!** peccato!; **too many** troppi; **too much** troppo

tool [tul] *s* utensile *m*, attrezzo; (*person*) strumento; (*of lathe*) punta || *tr* lavorare; (bb) decorare

tool' bag' *s* borsa degli attrezzi

tool'box' *s* cassetta attrezzi

tool'mak'er *s* attrezzista *m*

tool'shed' *s* barchessa

toot [tut] *s* (*of horn*) suono; (*of locomotive*) fischio; (*of car's horn*) colpo; (coll) gazzarra || *tr* strombettare; **to toot one's own horn** strombazzare i propri meriti || *intr* strombettare

tooth [tuθ] *s* (**teeth** [tiθ]) dente *m*

tooth'ache' *s* mal *m* di denti

tooth'brush' *s* spazzolino da denti

toothless ['tuθlɪs] *adj* sdentato

tooth'paste' *s* pasta dentifricia

tooth'pick' *s* stuzzicadenti *m*

tooth' pow'der *s* polvere dentifricia

top [tɑp] *s* cima, sommo, vertice *m;* (*upper part of anything*) disopra *m;*

(of mountain, tree) vetta; (of box) coperchio; (beginning) principio; (of bottle) imboccatura; (of a bridge) testata; (of wagon) mantice m; (of car) tetto; (of wall) coronamento; (toy) trottola; (naut) gabbia; **at the top of one's voice** a perdifiato; **from top to bottom** daccapo a piedi, dal principio alla fine; **on top of** in cima di; subito dopo; **the tops** (coll) il migliore, il fiore; **to blow one's top** (slang) dare in escandescenze; **to sleep like a top** dormire come un ghiro ‖ v (pret & pp **topped**; ger **topping**) tr (a tree) svettare; coronare; superare

topaz ['topæz] s topazio

top' bil'ling s—**to get top billing** essere artista di cartello; (journ) ricevere il posto più importante

top' boot' s stivale m a tromba

top'coat' s soprabito di mezza stagione

toper ['topər] s ubriacone m

topgal'lant sail' [ˌtap'gælənt] s (naut) pappafico, veletta

top' hat' s cappello a staio o a cilindro

top'-heav'y adj troppo pesante in cima, sovraccarico in cima

topic ['tapik] s topica, tema m

top'knot' s crocchia

topless ['taplis] adj (mountain) di cui non si vede la vetta, eccelso; (bathing suit) topless

top'mast' s (naut) alberetto

top'most' adj il più alto

topogra·phy [tə'pagrəfi] s (-phies) topografia

topple ['tapəl] tr abbattere, rovesciare ‖ intr rovesciarsi, cadere

top' prior'ity s priorità massima

topsail ['tapsel] or ['tap ˌsel] s (naut) gabbia

top'-se'cret adj segretissimo

top'soil' s strato superiore del terreno

topsy-turvy ['tapsi'tʌrvi] adj rovesciato; confuso ‖ s soqquadro ‖ adv a soqquadro

torch [tortʃ] s fiaccola, torcia; **to carry the torch for** (slang) amare disperatamente

torch'bear'er s portatore m di fiaccola; (fig) capo, guida m

torch'light' s luce f di fiaccola

torch' song' s canzone f triste d'amore non corrisposto

torment ['torment] s tormento ‖ [tər'ment] tr tormentare

torna·do [tər'nedo] s (-dos or -does) tornado, tromba d'aria

torpe·do [tər'pido] s (-does) siluro ‖ tr silurare

torpe'do boat' s motosilurante f

torpe'do-boat destroy'er s torpediniera

torrent ['tarənt] or ['torənt] s torrente m

torrid ['tarid] or ['torid] adj torrido

torsion ['torʃən] s torsione

tor'sion bar' s barra di torsione

tor·so ['torso] s (-sos) torso

tortoise ['tortəs] s tartaruga

tor'toise shell' s tartaruga

torture ['tortʃər] s tortura ‖ tr torturare

toss [tɔs] or [tas] s lancio, getto ‖ tr lanciare, gettare; (to fling about) sballottare; (one's head) alzare sdegnosamente; agitare; rivoltare; (an opinion) avventare; **to toss off** fare rapidamente; (e.g., a drink) buttar giù; **to toss up** (a coin) gettar in aria, gettare a testa o croce; (coll) rigettare ‖ intr agitarsi, dimenarsi; **to toss and turn** (in bed) girarsi; **to toss up** giocare a testa o croce

toss'up' s testa e croce; (coll) eguale probabilità f

tot [tat] s bambino, piccolo

to·tal ['total] adj totale; (e.g., loss) completo ‖ s totale m ‖ v (pret & pp -taled or -talled; ger -taling or -talling) tr ammontare a; (to make a total of) sommare

totalitarian [to ˌtælɪ'teri·ən] adj totalitario ‖ s aderente mf al totalitarismo

totalitarismo

totter ['tatər] s vacillamento ‖ intr vacillare

touch [tʌtʃ] s (act) tocco; (sense) tatto; (of an illness) leggero attacco; (slight amount) punta; (for money) (slang) stoccata; **to get in touch with** mettersi in contatto con; **to lose one's touch** perdere il tocco personale ‖ tr toccare; raggiungere; riguardare; (for a loan) (slang) dare una stoccata a; **to touch on** menzionare; **to touch up** ritoccare ‖ intr toccare; **to touch down** (aer) atterrare

touching ['tʌtʃɪŋ] adj toccante, commovente ‖ prep riguardo a

touch'stone' s pietra di paragone

touch' type'writing s dattilografia a tatto

touch·y ['tʌtʃi] adj (-ier; -iest) suscettibile, permaloso; delicato, precario, rischioso

tough [tʌf] adj duro; forte; (luck) cattivo; violento ‖ s malvivente m

toughen ['tʌfən] tr indurire ‖ intr indurirsi

tough' luck' s disdetta, sfortuna

tour [tur] s gita, viaggio; (sports) giro; (mil) turno; (theat) tournée f ‖ tr girare; (theat) portare in tournée ‖ intr girare; (theat) andare in tournée

tour'ing car' ['turɪŋ] s automobile f da turismo

tourist ['turɪst] adj turistico ‖ s turista mf

tournament ['turnəmənt] or ['tʌrnəmənt] s torneo

tourney ['turni] or ['tʌrni] s torneo ‖ intr giostrare

tourniquet ['turnɪ ˌket] or ['tʌrnɪ ˌke] s laccio emostatico

tousle ['tauzəl] tr spettinare

tow [to] s rimorchio; (e.g., of hemp) stoppa; **to take in tow** prendere a rimorchio ‖ tr rimorchiare

toward(s) [tord(z)] or [tə'word(z)] prep (in the direction of) verso; (in respect to) per; (near) vicino a; (a certain hour) su, verso

tow'boat' s rimorchiatore m

tow' car' s rimorchiatore m

tow·el ['tau·əl] s asciugamano; (of paper) salvietta; **to throw in the**

towel (slang) gettare la spugna || *v* (*pret & pp* **-eled** or **-elled**; *ger* **-eling** or **-elling**) *tr* asciugare

tow'el rack' *s* portaasciugamani *m*

tower ['tauər] *s* torre *f* || *intr* torreggiare

towering ['tauərɪŋ] *adj* torreggiante; gigantesco; eccessivo

towline ['toʊˌlaɪn] *s* cavo· di rimorchio

town [taun] *s* città *f*; (*townspeople*) cittadinanza; **in town** in città

town' clerk' *s* segretario municipale

town' coun'cil *s* consiglio comunale

town' cri'er *s* banditore *m* municipale

town' hall' *s* municipio

township ['taunʃɪp] *s* suddivisione di contea

towns'man *s* (**-men**) cittadino; concittadino

towns'peo'ple *spl* cittadini *mpl*; gente *f* di città

town' talk' *s* dicerie *fpl*, pettegolezzi *mpl*

tow'path' *s* strada d'alaggio

tow'rope' *s* corda da rimorchio

tow' truck' *s* autogru *f*

toxic ['tɑksɪk] *adj & s* tossico

toy [tɔɪ] *adj* giocattolo; di giocattoli || *s* giocattolo; (*trifle*) nonnulla *m*; (*trinket*) gingillo || *intr* giocare; **to toy with** (*to play with*) giocare con; (*to trifle, e.g., with food*) baloccarsi con; (*an idea*) accarezzare; (*to flirt with*) flirtare con

toy' bank' *s* salvadanaio

toy' sol'dier *s* soldatino di piombo

trace [tres] *s* traccia, vestigio; (*tracing*) tracciato; (*of harness*) tirella; (fig) ombra || *tr* tracciare; (*e.g., s.o.'s ancestry*) rintracciare; (*a pattern*) lucidare

trac'er bul'let ['tresər] *s* pallottola tracciante

trache•a ['trekɪ•ə] *s* (**-ae** [ˌi]) trachea

tracing ['tresɪŋ] *s* tracciato

track [træk] *s* (*of foot*) traccia, pesta; (*rut*) solco, rotaia; (*of boat*) scia; corso; (*course followed by boat*) rotta; (*of tape recorder*) pista; (*of tractor*) cingolo; (*of ideas*) successione; (*width of a vehicle measured from wheel to wheel*) (aut) carreggiata; (rr) binario; (*track and field*) (sports) atletica leggera; (*for horses*) (sports) galoppatoio; (*for running*) (sports) pista, corsia; **to keep track of** non perder di vista; **to lose track of** perder di vista; **to make tracks** (coll) affrettarsi; **to stop in one's tracks** (coll) fermarsi di colpo || *tr* rintracciare, seguire le tracce di; lasciare tracce su; **to track down** rintracciare

track'ing sta'tion ['trækɪŋ] *s* (rok) stazione di avvistamento

track'less trol'ley ['træklɪs] *s* filobus *m*

track' meet' *s* incontro di atletica leggera

track'walk'er *s* (rr) guardialinee *m*

tract [trækt] *s* tratto, opuscolo, trattatello; (anat) tubo, canale *m*

traction ['trækʃən] *s* trazione

trac'tion com'pany *s* società *f* di trasporti urbani

tractor ['træktər] *s* trattore *m*; (*of a tractor-trailer*) motrice *f*

trac'tor-trail'er *s* treno stradale

trade [tred] *s* commercio; affare *m*; occupazione, mestiere *m*; (*people*) commercianti *mpl*, professionisti *mpl*; mercato; (*customers*) clientela; (*in slaves*) tratta || *tr* mercanteggiare; cambiare; **to trade in** dare come pagamento parziale || *intr* trafficare, commerciare; comprare; **to trade in** lavorare in; **to trade on** approfittarsi di

trade'mark' *s* marca or marchio di fabbrica

trade' name' *s* ragione sociale

trader ['tredər] *s* trafficante *m*

trade' school' *s* scuola d'avviamento professionale, scuola d'arti e mestieri

trades'man *s* (**-men**) commerciante *m*; artigiano

trade' un'ion *s* sindacato di lavoratori

trade' un'ionist *s* sindacalista *mf*

trade' winds' *spl* alisei *mpl*

trad'ing post' *s* centro di scambi commerciali; (*in stock exchange*) posto delle compravendite

trad'ing stamp' *s* buono premio

tradition [trə'dɪʃən] *s* tradizione

traditional [trə'dɪʃənəl] *adj* tradizionale

traduce [trə'djus] or [trə'dus] *tr* calunniare

traf•fic ['træfɪk] *s* traffico, circolazione; commercio; comunicazione || *v* (*pret & pp* **-ficked**; *ger* **-ficking**) *intr* trafficare

traf'fic cir'cle *s* raccordo a circolazione rotatoria

traf'fic court' *s* tribunale *m* della polizia stradale

traf'fic is'land *s* isola spartitraffico

traf'fic jam' *s* intralcio del traffico, ingorgo stradale

traf'fic light' *s* semaforo

traf'fic man'ager *s* dirigente *m* del traffico; (rr) gestore *m* di stazione

traf'fic sign' *s* segnale *m* di circolazione stradale, cartello indicatore

traf'fic tick'et *s* contravvenzione per violazione del traffico

tragedian [trə'dʒidɪ•ən] *s* tragico

trage•dy ['trædʒɪdi] *s* (**-dies**) tragedia

tragic ['trædʒɪk] *adj* tragico

trail [trel] *s* sentiero; (*track*) traccia, pista; (*of rope*) strascico, coda; (*of smoke*) pennacchio; (*left by an airplane*) striscia; (*of people*) codazzo || *tr* strascicare; essere sulla fatta di; (*e.g., dust on the road*) sollevare; (*mud*) lasciar cadere || *intr* strascicare; (*said, e.g., of a snake*) strisciare; (*said of a plant*) arrampicarsi; **to trail off** mutare; (*to weaken*) affievolirsi

trailer ['trelər] *s* traino; (*to haul freight*) semirimorchio; (*for living*) carovana, roulotte *f*; (bot) rampicante *m*

train [tren] *s* (*of vehicles*) convoglio; (*of robe*) strascico; (*of thought*) or-

dine *m;* (*of people*) coda; (rr) treno
|| *tr* addestrare, impratichire; (*a
weapon*) puntare, rivolgere; (*a
horse*) scozzonare; (*e.g., a dog*) ammaestrare; (*a plant*) far crescere;
(sports) allenare || *intr* addestrarsi;
ammaestrarsi; (sports) allenarsi

trained' nurse' *s* infermiera diplomata
trainer ['trenər] *s* allenatore *m*
training ['treniŋ] *s* esercizio, esercitazione; (sports) allenamento

train'ing camp' *s* campo addestramento
train'ing school' *s* scuola di addestramento professionale; riformatorio
train'ing ship' *s* nave *f* scuola
trait [tret] *s* tratto, caratteristica
traitor ['tretər] *s* traditore *m*
traitress ['tretris] *s* traditrice *f*
trajecto·ry [trə'dʒɛktəri] *s* (-ries)
traiettoria

tramp [træmp] *s* lunga camminata;
vagabondo; (*hussy*) sgualdrina || *tr*
attraversare; calpestare || *intr* cam-
minare a passi fermi; fare il vagabondo

trample ['træmpəl] *tr* calpestare; (fig)
conculcare || *intr*—**to trample on** or
upon calpestare

trampoline ['træmpə,lin] *s* trampolino
di olona per salti mortali

tramp' steam'er *s* carretta
trance [træns] or [trɑns] *s* **trance** *f;*
(*dazed condition*) estasi *f*
tranquil ['træŋkwɪl] *adj* tranquillo
tranquilize ['træŋkwɪ,laɪz] *tr* tranquil-
lizzare || *intr* tranquillizzarsi
tranquilizer ['træŋkwɪ,laɪzər] *s* tranquillante *m*
tranquillity [træŋ'kwɪlɪti] *s* tranquillità
f
transact [træn'zækt] or [træns'ækt] *tr*
sbrigare, trattare
transaction [træn'zækʃən] or [træns-
'ækʃən] *s* disbrigo, operazione
transatlantic [,trænsət'læntɪk] *adj* & *s*
transatlantico
transcend [træn'sɛnd] *tr* trascendere,
sorpassare || *intr* eccellere
transcribe [træn'skraɪb] *tr* trascrivere
transcript ['trænskrɪpt] *s* copia; traduzione; (educ) copia ufficiale del certificato di studi
transcription [træn'skrɪpʃən] *s* trascrizione
transept ['trænsɛpt] *s* transetto
trans·fer ['trænsfər] *s* trasferimento;
passaggio; (*pattern*) rapporto; (*of
funds*) giro; (*of real estate*) compra-
vendita; (law) voltura || [træns'fʌr]
or ['trænsfər] *v* (*pret* & *pp* **-ferred;**
ger **-ferring**) *tr* trasferire, trasportare; (*funds*) stornare; (*a design*)
rapportare; (*real estate*) comprarsi-
dere || *intr* trasferirsi; cambiare di
treno
trans'fer tax' *s* tassa di successione;
tassa sulla compravendita
transfix [træns'fɪks] *tr* trafiggere; paralizzare, inchiodare
transform [træns'fɔrm] *tr* trasformare;
(elec) trasformare || *intr* trasformarsi
transforma'tional gram'mar [,trænsfər-

'meʃənəl] *s* grammatica trasforma-
tiva
transformer [træns'fɔrmər] *s* trasfor-
matore *m*
transfusion [træns'fjuʒən] *s* trasfusione
transgress [træns'grɛs] *tr* trasgredire;
(*a limit or boundry*) oltrepassare ||
intr peccare
transgression [træns'grɛʃən] *s* trasgressione; peccato
transient ['trænʃənt] *adj* passeggero,
temporaneo; di passaggio || *s* ospite
mf di passaggio
transistor [træn'zɪstər] *s* transistore *m*
transit ['trænsɪt] or ['trænzɪt] *s* transito
transition [træn'zɪʃən] *s* transizione
transitional [træn'zɪʃənəl] *adj* di transizione
transitive ['trænsɪtɪv] *adj* transitivo ||
s verbo transitivo
transitory ['trænsɪ,tori] *adj* transitorio
translate [træns'let] or ['trænslet] *tr*
tradurre; convertire; (*to transfer*) tra-
sportare || *intr* tradursi
translation [træns'leʃən] *s* traduzione;
trasformazione; (telg) ritrasmissione
translator [træns'letər] *s* traduttore *m*
transliterate [træns'lɪtə,ret] *tr* traslitterare
translucent [træns'lusənt] *adj* traslu-
cido; (fig) chiaro
transmission [træns'mɪʃən] *s* trasmissione; (aut) trasmissione
trans·mit [træns'mɪt] *v* (*pret* & *pp*
-mitted; *ger* **-mitting**) *tr* & *intr* trasmettere
transmitter [træns'mɪtər] *s* trasmettitore *m*
transmit'ting set' *s* emittente *f*
transmit'ting sta'tion *s* stazione tra-
smettitrice
transmute [træns'mjut] *tr* & *intr* trasmutare
transom ['trænsəm] *s* (*crosspiece*) traversa; (*window over door*) vasistas
m; (naut) specchio di poppa
transparen·cy ['træns'pɛrənsi] *s* (-cies)
trasparenza; (*design on a translucent
substance*) trasparente *m;* (phot) diapositiva
transparent [træns'pɛrənt] *adj* trasparente
transpire [træns'paɪr] *intr* (*to happen*)
avvenire; (*to perspire*) traspirare; (*to
become known*) trapelare
transplant [træns'plænt] or [træns-
'plɑnt] *tr* trapiantare || *intr* trapian-
tarsi
transport ['trænspɔrt] *s* trasporto;
mezzo di trasporto || [træns'pɔrt] *tr*
trasportare
transportation [,trænspɔr'teʃən] *s* trasporto; trasporti *mpl,* locomozione;
biglietto di trasporto
trans'port work'er *s* ferrotranviere *m*
transpose [træns'poz] *tr* trasporre;
(mus) trasportare
trans·ship [træns'ʃɪp] *v* (*pret* & *pp*
-shipped; *ger* **-shipping**) *tr* trasbordare
trap [træp] *s* trappola, tranello;

(*double-curved pipe*) sifone *m*; (slang) bocca; (sports) congegno lanciapiattelli ‖ *v* (*pret & pp* **trapped; ger trapping**) *tr* intrappolare, accalappiare

trap′ door′ *s* trabocchetto, botola; (theat) ribalta

trapeze [trə'piz] *s* (sports) trapezio

trapezoid ['træpɪ‚zɔɪd] *s* (geom) trapezio, trapezoide *m*

trapper ['træpər] *s* cacciatore *m* di animali da pelliccia con trappole

trappings ['træpɪŋz] *spl* ornamenti *mpl*; (*for a horse*) gualdrappa

trap′shoot′ing *s* tiro al piattello

trash [træʃ] *s* immondizia, spazzatura; (*nonsense*) sciocchezze *fpl*; (*junk*) ciarpame *m*; (*worthless people*) gentaglia

trash′ can′ *s* portaimmondizie *m*

travail ['trævɪl] *or* [trə'vel] *s* travaglio; travaglio di parto

trav•el ['trævəl] *s* viaggio; traffico; (mach) corsa ‖ *v* (*pret & pp* **-eled** *or* **-elled**; *ger* **-eling** *or* **-elling**) *tr* viaggiare per, percorrere ‖ *intr* viaggiare; muoversi; (coll) andare

trav′el a′gency *s* ufficio turistico

traveler ['trævələr] *s* viaggiatore *m*

trav′eler's check′ *s* assegno viaggiatori

trav′eling bag′ *s* sacca da viaggio

trav′eling expens′es *spl* spese *fpl* di viaggio; (*per diem*) trasferta

trav′eling sales′man *s* (**-men**) commesso viaggiatore

traverse ['trævərs] *or* [trə'vʌrs] *tr* attraversare

traves•ty ['trævɪstɪ] *s* (**-ties**) parodia ‖ *v* (*pret & pp* **-tied**) *tr* parodiare

trawl [trɔl] *s* (*fishing net*) rete *f* a strascico; (*fishing line*) lenza al traino ‖ *tr & intr* pescare con la rete a strascico; pescare con la lenza al traino

trawling ['trɔlɪŋ] *s* pesca con la rete a strascico; pesca con la lenza al traino

tray [tre] *s* guantiera, vassoio; (chem, phot) bacinella

treacherous ['tretʃərəs] *adj* traditore, subdolo; incerto, pericoloso

treacher•y ['tretʃərɪ] *s* (**-ies**) tradimento

tread [tred] *s* (*step*) passo; (*of shoe*) suola; (*of tire*) battistrada *m*; (*of stairs*) pedata ‖ *v* (*pret* **trod** [trɑd]; *pp* **trodden** ['trɑdən] *or* **trod**) *tr* calpestare; (*the boards*) calcare; accoppiarsi con ‖ *intr* camminare; **to tread on** calpestare

treadle ['tredəl] *s* pedale *m*

tread′mill′ *s* ruota azionata col camminare; (fig) lavoro ingrato

treason ['trizən] *s* tradimento

treasonable ['trizənəbəl] *adj* traditore

treasure ['treʒər] *s* tesoro ‖ *tr* far tesoro di

treasurer ['treʒərər] *s* tesoriere *m*

treas′ure hunt′ *s* caccia al tesoro

treasur•y ['treʒərɪ] *s* (**-ies**) tesoreria; tesoro, erario

treat [trit] *s* trattenimento; (*something affording pleasure*) piacere *m*, diletto ‖ *tr* trattare; (*to cure*) curare, medi-

care; offrire un trattenimento a ‖ *intr* trattare; pagare per il trattenimento

treatise ['tritɪs] *s* trattato

treatment ['tritmənt] *s* trattamento; (*of a theme*) trattazione

trea•ty ['tritɪ] *s* (**-ties**) trattato

treble ['trebəl] *adj* (*threefold*) triplo; (mus) soprano ‖ *s* (*person*) soprano *mf*; (*voice*) soprano ‖ *tr* triplicare ‖ *intr* triplicarsi

tree [tri] *s* albero

tree′ farm′ *s* bosco ceduo

tree′ frog′ *s* raganella

treeless ['trilɪs] *adj* spoglio, senza alberi

tree′top′ *s* cima dell'albero

trellis ['trelɪs] *s* traliccio, graticcio

tremble ['trembəl] *s* tremito ‖ *intr* tremare

tremendous [trɪ'mendəs] *adj* tremendo

tremor ['tremər] *or* ['trimər] *s* tremito; (*of earth*) scossa

trench [trentʃ] *s* fosso, canale *m*; (mil) trincea

trenchant ['trentʃənt] *adj* mordace, caustico; vigoroso; incisivo

trench′ coat′ *s* trench *m*

trench′ mor′tar *s* lanciabombe *m*

trend [trend] *s* tendenza, orientamento ‖ *intr* tendere, dirigersi

Trent [trent] *s* Trento *f*

trespass ['trespæs] *s* (law) intrusione, violazione di proprietà ‖ *intr* entrare senza diritto, intrudersi; peccare; **no trespassing** divieto di passaggio; **to trespass against** peccare contro; **to trespass on** entrare abusivamente in; (*e.g., s.o.'s time*) abusare di; violare

tress [tres] *s* treccia

trestle ['tresəl] *s* cavalletto; viadotto a cavalletti; ponte *m* a cavalletti

trial ['traɪ-əl] *s* tentativo, prova; tribolazione, croce *f*; (law) giudizio, processo; **on trial** in prova; (law) sotto processo; **to bring to trial** sottoporre a processo

tri′al and er′ror *s* metodo per tentativo; **by trial and error** a tastoni

tri′al balloon′ *s* pallone *m* sonda

tri′al by ju′ry *s* processo con giuria

tri′al ju′ry *s* giuria civile o processuale

tri′al or′der *s* (com) ordine *m* di prova

tri′al run′ *s* viaggio di prova

triangle ['traɪ‚æŋgəl] *s* triangolo; (*in drafting*) quartabuono

tribe [traɪb] *s* tribù *f*

tribunal [trɪ'bjunəl] *or* [traɪ'bjunəl] *s* tribunale *m*

tribune ['trɪbjun] *s* tribuna

tributar•y ['trɪbjə‚terɪ] *adj* tributario ‖ *s* (**-ies**) tributario

tribute ['trɪbjut] *s* tributo; **to pay tribute to** (*e.g., beauty*) rendere omaggio a

trice [traɪs] *s* momento, istante *m*; **in a trice** in un batter d'occhio

trick [trɪk] *s* gherminella, inganno; trucco, tiro, scherzo; (*knack*) abilità *f*; (*feat*) atto; (*set of cards won*) presa; turno; (coll) piccola; **to be up to one's old tricks** farne una delle

sue; **to play a dirty trick on** fare un brutto tiro a|| *tr* giocare, ingannare
tricker·y ['trɪkəri] *s* (**-ies**) gherminella, inganno
trickle ['trɪkəl] *s* gocciolio, filo || *intr* gocciolare; (*said of people*) andare or venire alla spicciolata; (*said of news*) trapelare
trickster ['trɪkstər] *s* imbroglione *m*
trick·y ['trɪki] *adj* (**-ier; -iest**) ingannatore; (*machine*) complicato; (*ticklish to deal with*) delicato
tried [traɪd] *adj* fedele, provato
trifle ['traɪfəl] *s* bazzecola, bagattella; (*small amount of money*) piccolezza, miseria; **a trifle** un po' || *tr*—**to trifle away** sprecare || *intr* gingillarsi; **to trifle with** giocherellare con; scherzare con; divertirsi con
trifling ['traɪflɪŋ] *adj* futile; insignificante, trascurabile
trifocal [traɪ'fokəl] *adj* trifocale || **trifocals** *spl* occhiali *mpl* trifocali
trigger ['trɪgər] *s* (*of a firearm*) grilletto; (*of any device*) leva di sgancio || *tr* (*a gun*) far sparare; (*fig*) scatenare
trigonometry [‚trɪgə'nɑmɪtri] *s* trigonometria
trill [trɪl] *s* trillo, gorgheggio; vibrazione; (*speech sound*) (phonet) vibrante *f* || *tr* gorgheggiare; pronunziare con vibrazione || *intr* trillare, gorgheggiare
trillion ['trɪljən] *s* trilione *m*
trilo·gy ['trɪlədʒi] *s* (**-gies**) trilogia
trim [trɪm] *adj* (**trimmer; trimmest**) lindo, azzimato || *s* condizione; buona condizione; (*dress*) vestito; (*of hair*) taglio, sfumatura; decorazione, ornamento; (*of sails*) orientamento; (aut) attrezzatura della carrozzeria || *v* (*pret & pp* **trimmed**; *ger* **trimming**) *tr* tagliare; (*an edge*) rifilare; adattare; arrangiare; (*Christmas tree*) decorare; (*hair*) sfumare; (*a tree*) potare; ordinare, assettare; (*a sail*) orientare; (aer) equilibrare; (mach) sbavare; (coll) rimproverare; (coll) bastonare; (*to defeat* coll) battere, vincere
trimming ['trɪmɪŋ] *s* ornamento, guarnizione; (coll) battitura, batosta; **trimmings** guarnizioni *mpl*; (mach) sbavatura; (mach) rifilatura
trini·ty ['trɪnɪti] *s* (**-ties**) (*group of three*) triade *f* || **Trinity** *s* Trinità *f*
trinket ['trɪŋkɪt] *s* (*small ornament*) ninnolo, gingillo; **trinkets** (*trivial objects*) paccottiglia
tri·o ['tri·o] *s* (**-os**) terzetto
trip [trɪp] *s* viaggio; corsa; (*stumble*) inciampata; (*act of causing s.o. to stumble*) sgambetto; (*error*) passo falso; passo agile || *v* (*pret & pp* **tripped**; *ger* **tripping**) *tr* far inciampare, far cadere; fare lo sgambetto a; cogliere in fallo; (mach) far scattare || *intr* inciampare; fare un passo falso; avanzare saltellando, saltellare; **to trip over** inciampare in
tripartite [traɪ'pɑrtaɪt] *adj* tripartito

tripe [traɪp] *s* trippa; (slang) sciocchezze *fpl*
trip'ham'mer *s* maglio meccanico
triphthong ['trɪfθɔŋ] or ['trɪfθɑŋ] *s* trittongo
triple ['trɪpəl] *adj & s* triplo || *tr* triplicare || *intr* triplicarsi
triplet ['trɪplɪt] *s* (*offspring*) nato da un parto trigemino; (mus, poet) terzina
triplicate ['trɪplɪkɪt] *adj* triplicato || *s* triplice copia || ['trɪplɪ‚ket] *tr* triplicare
tripod ['traɪpɑd] *s* (*e.g., for a camera*) treppiede *m*; (*stool with three legs*) tripode *m*
triptych ['trɪptɪk] *s* trittico
trite [traɪt] *adj* trito, ritrito
triumph ['traɪ·əmf] *s* trionfo || *intr* trionfare
trium'phal arch' [traɪ'ʌmfəl] *s* arco trionfale
trivia ['trɪvɪ·ə] *spl* banalità *f*, futilità *f*
trivial ['trɪvɪ·əl] *adj* insignificante, futile, banale
Trojan ['trodʒən] *adj & s* troiano
Tro'jan Horse' *s* cavallo di Troia
Tro'jan War' *s* guerra troiana
troll [trol] *tr & intr* pescare con la lenza al traino, pescare con il cucchiaino
trolley ['trɑli] *s* asta di presa, trolley *m*; carrozza tranviaria, tram *m*
trol'ley bus' *s* filobus *m*
trol'ley car' *s* vettura tranviaria, tram *m*
trol'ley pole' *s* trolley *m*
trollop ['trɑləp] *s* (*slovenly woman*) sciattona; (*hussy*) sgualdrina
trombone ['trɑmbon] *s* trombone *m*
troop [trup] *s* truppa, gruppo; (*of animals*) branco; (*of cavalry*) squadrone *m*; **troops** soldati *mpl* || *intr* raggrupparsi; marciare insieme
trooper ['trupər] *s* soldato di cavalleria; poliziotto a cavallo; **to swear like a trooper** bestemmiare come un turco
tro·phy ['trofi] *s* (**-phies**) trofeo; (*any memento*) ricordo
tropic ['trɑpɪk] *adj* tropicale || *s* tropico; **tropics** zona tropicale
tropical ['trɑpɪkəl] *adj* tropicale
troposphere ['trɑpə‚sfɪr] *s* troposfera
trot [trɑt] *s* trotto || *v* (*pret & pp* **trotted**; *ger* **trotting**) *tr* far trottare; **to trot out** (coll) squadernare, esibire || *intr* trottare
troth [troθ] or [troθ] *s* promessa di matrimonio; **by my troth** affé di Dio; **in troth** in verità; **to plight one's troth** impegnarsi; dare la parola
troubadour ['trubə‚dor] or ['trubə‚dur] *s* trovatore *m*
trouble ['trʌbəl] *s* disturbo, fastidio; inconveniente *m*, grattacapo; disordine *m*, conflitto; (*of a mechanical nature*) panna, guasto; **not to be worth the trouble** non valere la pena; **that's the trouble** questo è il male; **the trouble is that** il guaio è che; **to be in trouble** essere nei guai; **to be**

looking for trouble andare a cercarsi le grane; **to get into trouble** mettersi nei pasticci; **to have trouble in** + *ger* durar fatica a + *inf*; **to take the trouble** incomodarsi ‖ *tr* molestare, disturbare; (*e.g., water*) intorbidare; dar del filo da torcere a; **to be troubled with** soffrire di; **to trouble one-self** scomodarsi

trouble' light' *s* lampada di soccorso

trou'ble-mak'er *s* mettimale *mf*

troubleshooter [ˈtrʌbəl ˌʃutər] *s* localizzatore *m* di guasti; (*in disputes*) paciere *m*, conciliatore *m*

troubleshooting [ˈtrʌbəl ˌʃutɪŋ] *s* localizzazione dei guasti; (*of disputes*) composizione

troublesome [ˈtrʌbəlsəm] *adj* molesto; difficile

trouble' spot' *s* luogo di disordini, polveriera

trough [trɔf] *or* [trɑf] *s* (*to knead bread*) madia; (*for feeding pigs*) trogolo; (*for feeding animals*) mangiatoia; (*for watering animals*) abbeveratoio; (*gutter*) doccia; (*between two waves*) cavo

troupe [trup] *s* troupe *f*

trouper [ˈtrupər] *s* membro della troupe; vecchio attore; tipo di cui ci si può fidare

trousers [ˈtrauzərz] *spl* pantaloni *mpl*

trousseau [truˈso] *or* [ˈtruso] *s* (**-seaux** *or* **-seaus**) corredo da sposa

trout [traut] *s* trota

trouvère [truˈver] *s* troviero

trowel [ˈtrau·əl] *s* cazzuola, mestola

Troy [trɔɪ] *s* Troia

truant [ˈtru·ənt] *s* fannullone *m*; **to play truant** marinare la scuola

truce [trus] *s* tregua

truck [trʌk] *s* autocarro, camion *m*; (*tractor-trailer*) autotreno; (*van*) furgone *m*; (*to be moved by hand*) carretto; verdura per il mercato; (*mach*, rr) carrello; (*coll*) robaccia; (*coll*) relazioni *fpl* ‖ *tr* trasportare per autocarro, autotrasportare

truck'driv'er *s* camionista *m*

truck' farm' *s* fattoria agricola per la produzione degli ortaggi

truculent [ˈtrʌkjələnt] *or* [ˈtrukjələnt] *adj* truculento

trudge [trʌdʒ] *intr* camminare; **to trudge along** camminare laboriosamente, scarpinare

true [tru] *adj* vero; esatto, conforme; legittimo; infallibile; a livello; **to come true** verificarsi; **true to life** conforme alla realtà

true' cop'y *s* copia conforme

true-hearted [ˈtru ˌhɑrtɪd] *adj* fedele

true'love knot' *s* nodo d'amore

truffle [ˈtrʌfəl] *or* [ˈtrufəl] *s* tartufo

truism [ˈtru·ɪzəm] *s* truismo

truly [ˈtruli] *adv* veramente, correttamente; **yours truly** distinti saluti

trump [trʌmp] *s* (cards) atout *m*; (Italian cards) briscola; **no trump** senza atout ‖ *tr* superare; (cards) pigliare con un atout o con una briscola; **to**

trump up inventare, fabbricare ‖ *intr* giocare un atout or una briscola

trumpet [ˈtrʌmpɪt] *s* tromba; (*toy*) trombetta; **to blow one's own trumpet** cantare le proprie lodi ‖ *tr* strombazzare ‖ *intr* sonar la tromba; strombazzare; (*said of an elephant*) barrire

truncheon [ˈtrʌntʃən] *s* bastone *m* del comando; (Brit) manganello

trunk [trʌŋk] *s* (*of living body, tree, family, railroad*) tronco; (*for clothes*) baule *m*; (*of elephant*) tromba; (aut) bagagliaio; (archit) fusto; (telp) linea principale; **trunks** pantaloncini *mpl*

trunk' hose' *s* (hist) brache *fpl*

truss [trʌs] *s* (*to support a roof*) capriata, incavallatura; (*based on cantilever system*) intralicciatura; (*for reducing a hernia*) cinto, brachiere *m*; (bot) infiorescenza ‖ *tr* legare, assicurare

trust [trʌst] *s* fede *f*; speranza; fiducia, custodia; (com) trust *m*, cartello; (law) fedecommesso; **in trust** in deposito; come fedecommesso; **on trust** a credito ‖ *tr* fidarsi di; credere (with *dat*); (*to entrust*) dare in deposito a; dare a credito a ‖ *intr* credere; fidarsi, prestar fede; **to trust in** (*e.g., a friend*) fidarsi di; (*God*) aver fede in

trust' com'pany *s* compagnia fedecommissaria; banca di deposito

trustee [trʌsˈti] *s* amministratore *m*; fiduciario; (*of a university*) curatore *m*; (*of an estate*) fedecommissario

trusteeship [trʌsˈti/ɪp] *s* amministrazione; (law) fedecommesso; (pol) amministrazione fiduciaria

trustful [ˈtrʌstfəl] *adj* fiducioso

trust'wor'thy *adj* fidato, di fiducia

trust·y [ˈtrʌsti] *adj* (**-ier**; **-iest**) fidato ‖ *s* (**-ies**) carcerato degno di fiducia

truth [truθ] *s* verità *f*; **in truth** in verità

truthful [ˈtruθfəl] *adj* verace, veritiero

try [traɪ] *s* (**tries**) tentativo, prova ‖ *v* (*pret & pp* **tried**) *tr* provare; (*s.o.'s patience*) mettere a dura prova; (*a person*) (law) processare; (*a case*) (law) giudicare; **to try on** (*clothes*) provare; **to try out** provare; esperimentare ‖ *intr* cercare, tentare; **to try out for** cercare di ottenere il posto di; (sports) cercare di farsi accettare in; **to try to** cercare di

trying [ˈtraɪ·ɪŋ] *adj* duro, penoso, difficile

tryst [trɪst] *or* [traɪst] *s* appuntamento

T'-shirt' *s* maglietta

tub [tʌb] *s* tino, bigoncia; vasca da bagno; (*clumsy boat*) (slang) carretta; (*fat person*) (slang) bombolo

tube [tjub] *or* [tub] *s* tubo; (*e.g., for toothpaste*) tubetto; (*of tire*) camera d'aria; (anat) tuba, tromba; (coll) ferrovia sotterranea

tuber [ˈtjubər] *or* [ˈtubər] *s* tubero

tubercle [ˈtjubərkəl] *or* [ˈtubərkəl] *s* tubercolo

tuberculosis [tju‚bɑrkjə'losɪs] or [tu‚bɑrkjə'losɪs] s tubercolosi f
tuck [tʌk] s basta ‖ tr ripiegare; **to tuck away** nascondere; (slang) fare una scorpacciata di; **to tuck in** rincalzare; **to tuck up** rimboccare
tucker ['tʌkər] s collarino di merletto ‖ tr—**to tucker out** (coll) stancare
Tuesday ['tjuzdɪ] or ['tuzdɪ] s martedì m
tuft [tʌft] s (of feathers) pennacchio; (of hair) cernecchio; (of flowers) cespo; (fluffy threads) fiocco, nappa ‖ tr impuntire; adornare di fiocchi ‖ intr crescere a cernecchio
tug [tʌg] s strattone m, strappata; (struggle) lotta; (boat) rimorchiatore m ‖ v (pret & pp **tugged**; ger **tugging**) tr tirare; (a boat) rimorchiare ‖ intr tirare con forza; lottare
tug'boat' s rimorchiatore m
tug' of war' s tiro alla fune
tuition [tju'ɪ/ən] or [tu'ɪ/ən] s (instruction) insegnamento; tassa scolastica
tulip ['tjulɪp] or ['tulɪp] s tulipano
tumble ['tʌmbəl] s rotolone m, ruzzolone m; (somersault) salto mortale; caduta; disordine m, confusione; (confused heap) mucchio ‖ intr rotolare, ruzzolare; cadere, capitombolare; gettarsi; rigirarsi; **to tumble down** cadere in rovina; **to tumble to** (coll) rendersi conto di
tum'ble-down' adj dilapidato
tumbler ['tʌmblər] s (acrobat) saltimbanco; (glass) bicchiere m; (in a lock) levetta; (toy) misirizzi m
tumor ['tjumər] or ['tumər] s tumore m
tumult ['tjumʌlt] or ['tumʌlt] s tumulto
tun [tʌn] s botte f, barile m
tuna ['tunə] s tonno
tune [tjun] or [tun] s (air) aria; (manner of speaking) tono; **in tune** intonato; **out of tune** stonato; **to change one's tune** cambiare di tono ‖ tr intonare; **to tune in** (rad) sintonizzare; **to tune out** (rad) interrompere la sintonizzazione di; **to tune up** (a motor) mettere a punto; (mus) intonare
tuner ['tunər] or ['tjunər] s (rad) sintonizzatore m; (mus) accordatore m
tungsten ['tʌŋstən] s tungsteno
tunic ['tjunɪk] or ['tunɪk] s tunica
tun'ing coil' ['tjunɪŋ] or ['tunɪŋ] s bobina di sintonia
tun'ing fork' s diapason m, corista m
Tunis ['tjunɪs] or ['tunɪs] s Tunisi f
Tunisia [tju'nɪʒə] or [tu'nɪʒə] s la Tunisia
Tunisian [tju'nɪʒən] or [tu'nɪʒən] adj & s tunisino
tun·nel ['tʌnəl] s tunnel m, traforo, galleria; (min) galleria ‖ v (pret & pp -neled or -nelled; ger -neling or -nelling) tr costruire un passaggio attraverso o sotto a
turban ['tʌrbən] s turbante m
turbid ['tʌrbɪd] adj turbido

turbine ['tʌrbɪn] or ['tʌrbaɪn] s turbina
turbojet ['tʌrbo‚dʒɛt] s turboreattore m
turboprop ['tʌrbo‚prɑp] s turboelica m
turbulent ['tʌrbjələnt] adj turbolento
tureen [tu'rin] or [tju'rin] s terrina
turf [tʌrf] s zolla erbosa; (peat) torba; **the turf** il campo delle corse; le corse, il turf
turf'man s (-men) amatore m delle corse ippiche
Turk [tʌrk] s turco
turkey ['tʌrki] s tacchino ‖ **Turkey** s la Turchia
turk'ey vul'ture s (Cathartes aura) avvoltoio americano
Turkish ['tʌrkɪʃ] adj & s turco
Turk'ish tow'el s asciugamano spugna
turmoil ['tʌrmɔɪl] s subbuglio
turn [tʌrn] s giro; (time for action) turno, volta; (change of direction) voltata; (bend) svolta, curva; (of events) piega; servizio; inclinazione, attitudine f; (of key) mandata; (of coil) spira; (coll) colpo, sussulto; (aer, naut) virata; **at every turn** a ogni pie sospinto; **in turn** a tua (Sua, vostra, etc.) volta; **to be one's turn** toccare a qlcu, e.g., **it's your turn** tocca a Lei; **to take turns** fare a turno ‖ tr girare, voltare; (soil) rovesciare; cambiare; (to make sour) coagulare; (to translate) tradurre; (e.g., ten years) raggiungere; (e.g., one's eyes) volgere; (on a lathe) tornire; (e.g., a coat) rivoltare; (to twist) torcere; (the wheel) (aut) sterzare; **to turn against** mettere su contro; **to turn around** rigirare; (s.o.'s words) ritorcere; **to turn aside** sviare; **to turn away** cacciare via; **to turn back** ricacciare; restituire; (the clock) ritardare; **to turn down** ripiegare; (the light) abbassare; (an offer) rifiutare; **to turn in** ripiegare; denunziare; rassegnare; **to turn off** (e.g., light) spegnere, smorzare; (gas, water, etc.) tagliare; (e.g., a faucet) chiudere; **to turn on** (e.g., light, radio, etc.) accendere; (e.g., a faucet) aprire; **to turn out** mettere alla porta; (animals) fare uscire dalla stalla; rivoltare; (light) spegnere; produrre, fabbricare; **to turn up** ripiegare in su, rimboccare; (on a lathe) tornire; tirar su; (a card) scoprire; trovare; (e.g., the radio) alzare ‖ intr girare; svoltare, voltare; **turn left at the corner** svolti a sinistra all'angolo; girarsi; cambiare; fermentare; cambiare di colore; diventare; (naut) virare; **to turn against** voltarsi contro; inimicarsi con; **to turn around** fare una giravolta; **to turn aside** or **away** sviarsi; **to turn back** ritornare; retrocedere; **to turn down** piegarsi in giù; rovesciarsi; **to turn in** piegarsi, ripiegarsi; tornare a casa; (coll) andare a dormire; **to turn into** sfogare in; trasformarsi in; **to turn on** voltarsi contro; girarsi su; dipendere da; occuparsi di; **to turn**

out riuscire; **to turn out to be** manifestarsi; riuscire ad essere; **to turn over** rotolarsi; rovesciarsi; **to turn up** voltarsi all'insù; alzarsi; apparire, farsi vedere

turn'buck'le s tenditore m

turn'coat' s voltagabbana mf; **to become a turncoat** voltar gabbano

turn'down' adj (collar) rovesciato ‖ s rifiuto

turn'ing point' s punto decisivo

turnip ['tʌrnɪp] s rapa

turn'key' s secondino, carceriere m

turn' of life' s menopausa

turn' of mind' s disposizione naturale

turn'out' s (gathering of people) concorso; (crowd) folla; produzione; (outfit) vestito; stile m, moda; (in a road) slargo, piazzola; (horse and carriage) equipaggio; (rr) binario laterale

turn'over' s (upset) rovesciamento, ribaltamento; (of customers) movimento di clienti; (of business) giro d'affari; rotazione di lavoratori; (com) ciclo operativo

turn'pike' s autostrada a pedaggio

turn' sig'nal s (aut) indicatore m di direzione, lampeggiatore m

turnstile ['tʌrn‚staɪl] s tornello

turn'ta'ble s (of phonograph) piatto rotante; (rr) piattaforma girevole

turpentine ['tʌrpən‚taɪn] s trementina

turpitude ['tʌrpɪ‚tjud] or ['tʌrpɪ‚tud] s turpitudine f

turquoise ['tʌrkɔɪz] or ['tʌrkwɔɪz] s turchese m

turret ['tʌrɪt] s torretta

turtle ['tʌrtəl] s tartaruga; **to turn turtle** rovesciarsi, capovolgersi

tur'tle-dove' s tortora

Tuscan ['tʌskən] adj & s toscano

Tuscany ['tʌskəni] s la Toscana

tusk [tʌsk] s zanna

tussle ['tʌsəl] s lotta, zuffa ‖ intr lottare, azzuffarsi

tutor ['tjutər] or ['tutər] s istitutore privato, ripetitore m; (guardian) tutore m ‖ tr dare ripetizione a ‖ intr dare ripetizioni; studiare con un ripetitore

tuxe·do [tʌk'sido] s (-dos) smoking m

twaddle ['twadəl] s sciocchezze fpl ‖ intr dire sciocchezze

twang [twæŋ] s (of musical instrument) suono vibrato; (of voice) timbro nasale ‖ tr pizzicare; dire con un timbro nasale ‖ intr parlare con voce nasale

twang·y ['twæŋi] adj (-ier; -iest) (tone) metallico; (voice) nasale

tweed [twid] s tweed m; **tweeds** abito di tweed

tweet [twit] s pigolio ‖ intr pigolare

tweeter ['twitər] s altoparlante m per alte audiofrequenze, tweeter m

tweezers ['twizərz] spl pinzette fpl

twelfth [twelfθ] adj, s & pron dodicesimo ‖ s (in dates) dodici m

Twelfth'-night' s vigilia dell'Epifania; sera dell'Epifania

twelve [twelv] adj & pron dodici ‖ s dodici m; **twelve o'clock** le dodici

twentieth ['twɛntɪ·ɪθ] adj, s & pron ventesimo ‖ s (in dates) venti m

twen·ty ['twɛnti] adj & pron venti ‖ s (-ties) venti m; **the twenties** gli anni venti

twice [twaɪs] adv due volte

twice'-told' adj detto più di una volta; detto e ridetto

twiddle ['twɪdəl] tr—**to twiddle one's thumbs** rigirare i pollici, oziare

twig [twɪg] s ramoscello; **twigs** sterpi mpl

twilight ['twaɪ‚laɪt] adj crepuscolare ‖ s crepuscolo

twill [twɪl] s diagonale m ‖ tr tessere in diagonale

twin [twɪn] adj & s gemello

twine [twaɪn] s spago ‖ tr intrecciare ‖ intr intrecciarsi

twinge [twɪndʒ] s punta, dolore acuto

twinkle ['twɪŋkəl] s scintillio; batter m d'occhio ‖ intr scintillare

twin'-screw' adj a due eliche

twirl [twʌrl] s giro, mulinello ‖ tr girare; (slang) lanciare ‖ intr girare rapidamente, frullare

twist [twɪst] s curva; giro; viluppo, intreccio; tendenza, inclinazione; (yarn) ritorno; (e.g., of lemon) fettina; (dance) twist m ‖ tr intrecciare; torcere; (e.g., the face) contorcere; (the meaning) stravolgere, stiracchiare; girare ‖ intr intrecciarsi; torcersi, divincolarsi; girare; serpeggiare; **to twist and turn** (in bed) girarsi e rigirarsi

twister ['twɪstər] s (coll) tromba d'aria

twit [twɪt] v (pret & pp **twitted**; ger **twitting**) tr ridicolizzare

twitch [twɪtʃ] s tic m; (jerk) strattone m; (to restrain a horse) torcinaso ‖ intr contrarsi; tremare; **to twitch at** tirare

twitter ['twɪtər] s garrito, cinguettio; (chatter) chiacchierio; ansia, agitazione ‖ intr garrire, cinguettare; chiacchierare; tremare d'ansia

two [tu] adj & pron due ‖ s due m; **to put two and two together** arrivare alle logiche conclusioni; **two o'clock** le due

two'-cy'cle adj a due tempi

two'-cyl'inder adj a due cilindri

two-edged ['tu‚ɛdʒd] adj a doppio filo

two'fold' adj duplice, doppio

two' hun'dred adj, s & pron duecento

twosome ['tusəm] s coppia

two'-time' tr (slang) fare le corna a

two'-way ra'dio s ricetrasmettitore m

tycoon [taɪ'kun] s magnate m

type [taɪp] s tipo; (typ) carattere m; (pieces collectively) (typ) caratteri mpl ‖ tr scrivere a macchina; simbolizzare ‖ intr scrivere a macchina

type'face' s stile m di carattere

type'script' s dattiloscritto

typesetter ['taɪp‚sɛtər] s (person) compositore m; (machine) compositrice f

type'write' *v* (*pret* **-wrote;** *pp* **-written**) *tr & intr* dattilografare, scrivere a macchina

type'writ'er *s* (*machine*) macchina da scrivere; (*typist*) dattilografo

type'writ'ing *s* dattilografia, scrittura a macchina; lavoro battuto a macchina

ty'phoid fe'ver ['taɪfɔɪd] *s* febbre *f* tifoide

typhoon [taɪ'fun] *s* tifone *m*

typical ['tɪpɪkəl] *adj* tipico

typi·fy ['tɪpɪ,faɪ] *v* (*pret & pp* **-fied**) *tr* simbolizzare

typist ['taɪpɪst] *s* dattilografo

typographic(al) [,taɪpə'græfɪk(əl)] *adj* tipografico

typograph'ical er'ror *s* errore *m* di stampa

typography [taɪ'pɑgrəfi] *s* tipografia

tyrannic(al) [tɪ'rænɪk(əl)] or [taɪ'rænɪk(əl)] *adj* tirannico

tyrannous ['tɪrənəs] *adj* tiranno

tyrant ['taɪrənt] *s* tiranno

ty·ro ['taɪro] *s* (**-ros**) principiante *m*

Tyrrhe'nian Sea' [tɪ'rini·ən] *s* Mare Tirreno

U

U, u [ju] *s* ventunesima lettera dell'alfabeto inglese

ubiquitous [ju'bɪkwɪtəs] *adj* ubiquo

udder ['ʌdər] *s* mammella

ugliness ['ʌglɪnɪs] *s* bruttezza

ug·ly ['ʌgli] *adj* (**-lier; -liest**) brutto

Ukraine, the ['jukren] or [ju'kren] *s* l'Ucraina *f*

Ukrainian [ju'kreni·ən] *adj & s* ucraino

ulcer ['ʌlsər] *s* piaga, ulcera; (*corrupting element*) (fig) piaga

ulcerate ['ʌlsə,ret] *tr* ulcerare ‖ *intr* ulcerarsi

ulterior [ʌl'tɪri·ər] *adj* ulteriore; (*motive*) nascosto, secondo

ultimate ['ʌltɪmɪt] *adj* ultimo

ultima·tum [,ʌltɪ'metəm] *s* (**-tums** or **-ta** [tə]) ultimato

ultimo ['ʌltɪ,mo] *adv* del mese scorso

ul'tra-high fre'quency ['ʌltrə'haɪ] *s* frequenza ultraelevata

ultrashort [,ʌltrə'ʃɔrt] *adj* ultracorto

ultraviolet [,ʌltrə'vaɪ·əlɪt] *adj & s* ultravioletto

umbil'ical cord' [ʌm'bɪlɪkəl] *s* cordone *m* ombelicale

umbrage ['ʌmbrɪdʒ] *s*—**to take umbrage at** adombrarsi per

umbrella [ʌm'brelə] *s* ombrello, paracqua *m*; (mil) ombrello

umbrel'la stand' *s* portaombrelli *m*

Umbrian ['ʌmbrɪ·ən] *adj & s* umbro

umlaut ['ʊmlaut] *s* metafonesi *f*; (*mark*) dieresi *f* ‖ *tr* cambiare il timbro di; scrivere con dieresi

umpire ['ʌmpaɪr] *s* arbitro ‖ *tr* arbitrare ‖ *intr* fare l'arbitro

UN ['ju'en] *s* (letterword) (**United Nations**) ONU *f*

unable [ʌn'ebəl] *adj* incapace; **to be unable to** essere impossibilitato a, non potere

unabridged [,ʌnə'brɪdʒd] *adj* integrale, non abbreviato

unaccented [ʌn'æksentɪd] or [,ʌnæk'sentɪd] *adj* non accentato, atono

unacceptable [,ʌnək'septəbəl] *adj* inaccettabile

unaccountable [,ʌnə'kauntəbəl] *adj* irresponsabile; inesplicabile

unaccounted-for [,ʌnə'kauntɪd,fɔr]

adj (*e.g., failure*) inesplicato; (*e.g., soldier*) irreperibile, mancante

unaccustomed [,ʌnə'kʌstəmd] *adj* (*unusual*) insolito; non abituato

unafraid [,ʌnə'fred] *adj* impavido

unaligned [ʌnə'laɪnd] *adj* non impegnato

unanimity [,junə'nɪmɪti] *s* unanimità *f*

unanimous [ju'nænɪməs] *adj* unanime

unanswerable [ʌn'ænsərəbəl] *adj* per cui non vi è risposta; (*argument*) irrefutabile, incontestabile

unappreciative [,ʌnə'priʃɪ,etɪv] *adj* sconoscente, ingrato

unapproachable [,ʌnə'protʃəbəl] *adj* inabbordabile; incomparabile

unarmed [ʌn'ɑrmd] *adj* disarmato, inerme

unascertainable [ʌn,æsər'tenəbəl] *adj* non verificabile

unassailable [,ʌnə'seləbəl] *adj* inattaccabile

unassembled [,ʌnə'sembəld] *adj* smontato

unassuming [,ʌnə'sumɪŋ] or [,ʌnə'sjumɪŋ] *adj* modesto, semplice

unattached [,ʌnə'tætʃt] *adj* indipendente; (*loose*) sciolto; non sposato; non fidanzato

unattainable [,ʌnə'tenəbəl] *adj* inarrivabile, irraggiungibile

unattractive [,ʌnə'træktɪv] *adj* poco attraente

unavailable [,ʌnə'veləbəl] *adj* non disponibile

unavailing [,ʌnə'velɪŋ] *adj* futile

unavoidable [,ʌnə'vɔɪdəbəl] *adj* inevitabile, ineluttabile

unaware [,ʌnə'wer] *adj* inconsapevole, ignaro ‖ (*un-knowingly*) inavvertitamente

unawares [,ʌnə'werz] *adv* inaspettatamente; (*unknowingly*) inavvertitamente

unbalanced [ʌn'bælənst] *adj* sbilanciato, squilibrato

unbandage [ʌn'bændɪdʒ] *tr* sbendare

un·bar [ʌn'bar] *v* (*pret & pp* **-barred;** *ger* **-barring**) *tr* disserrare il chiavistello di

unbearable [ʌn'berəbəl] *adj* insopportabile, insostenibile

unbeatable [ʌn'bitəbəl] *adj* imbattibile
unbecoming [ˌʌnbɪ'kʌmɪŋ] *adj* sconveniente, indegno; (*e.g., hat*) disadatto, che non sta bene
unbelievable [ˌʌnbɪ'livəbəl] *adj* incredibile
unbeliever [ˌʌnbɪ'livər] *s* miscredente *mf*
unbending [ʌn'bendɪŋ] *adj* inflessibile
unbiased [ʌn'baɪ·əst] *adj* imparziale, spassionato
un·bind [ʌn'baɪnd] *v* (*pret & pp* **-bound** ['baʊnd]) *tr* slegare
unbleached [ʌn'blit/t] *adj* non candeggiato, al colore naturale
unbolt [ʌn'bolt] *tr* (*a door*) togliere il chiavistello a; sbullonare
unborn [ʌn'bɔrn] *adj* nascituro
unbosom [ʌn'buzəm] *tr* (*a secret*) rivelare; **to unbosom oneself** aprire il proprio animo, sfogarsi
unbound [ʌn'baʊnd] *adj* sciolto, libero; (*book*) non rilegato
unbreakable [ʌn'brekəbəl] *adj* infrangibile
unbridle [ʌn'braɪdəl] *tr* sbrigliare
unbuckle [ʌn'bʌkəl] *tr* sfibbiare
unburden [ʌn'bʌrdən] *tr* scaricare; **to unburden oneself** (**of**) vuotare il sacco (di)
unburied [ʌn'berid] *adj* insepolto
unbutton [ʌn'bʌtən] *tr* sbottonare
uncalled-for [ʌn'kɔld ˌfɔr] *adj* superfluo, gratuito; fuori di posto, sconveniente
uncanny [ʌn'kæni] *adj* misterioso, straordinario
uncared-for [ʌn'kerd ˌfɔr] *adj* negletto, trascurato
unceasing [ʌn'sisɪŋ] *adj* incessante
unceremonious [ˌʌnserɪ'moni·əs] *adj* senza cerimonie
uncertain [ʌn'sʌrtən] *adj* incerto
uncertain·ty [ʌn'sʌrtənti] *s* (**-ties**) *s* certezza
unchain [ʌn't/en] *tr* scatenare, sferrare
unchangeable [ʌn't/endʒəbəl] *adj* immutabile
uncharted [ʌn't/artid] *adj* inesplorato
unchecked [ʌn't/ekt] *adj* incontrollato
uncivilized [ʌn'sɪvɪ ˌlaɪzd] *adj* incivile
unclad [ʌn'klæd] *adj* svestito
unclaimed [ʌn'klemd] *adj* non reclamato; (*letter*) giacente
unclasp [ʌn'klæsp] *or* [ʌn'klɑsp] *tr* sfibbiare
unclassified [ʌn'klæsɪ ˌfaɪd] *adj* non classificato; non secreto
uncle ['ʌŋkəl] *s* zio
unclean [ʌn'klin] *adj* immondo
un·clog [ʌn'klɑg] *v* (*pret & pp* **-clogged**) (*ger* **-clogging**) *tr* disintasare
unclouded [ʌn'klaʊdɪd] *adj* sereno, senza nubi
uncollectible [ˌʌnkə'lektɪbəl] *adj* inesigibile
uncomfortable [ʌn'kʌmfərtəbəl] *adj* scomodo, disagevole
uncommitted [ˌʌnkə'mɪtɪd] *adj* non impegnato
uncommon [ʌn'kɑmən] *adj* raro, straordinario

uncompromising [ʌn'kɑmprə ˌmaɪzɪŋ] *adj* intransigente
unconcerned [ˌʌnkən'sʌrnd] *adj* indifferente, noncurante
unconditional [ˌʌnkən'dɪ/ənəl] *adj* incondizionato
uncongenial [ˌʌnkən'dʒini·əl] *adj* antipatico, sgradito
unconquerable [ʌn'kɑŋkərəbəl] *adj* inconquistabile, inespugnabile
unconscionable [ʌn'kɑn/ənəbəl] *adj* senza scrupoli; eccessivo
unconscious [ʌn'kɑn/əs] *adj* (*without awareness*) inconscio, inconsapevole; (*temporarily devoid of consciousness*) incosciente; (*unintentional*) involontario
unconsciousness [ʌn'kɑn/əsnɪs] *s* incoscienza
unconstitutional [ˌʌnkɑnstɪ'tju/ənəl] *or* [ˌʌnkɑnstɪ'tu/ənəl] *adj* incostituzionale
uncontrollable [ˌʌnkən'troləbəl] *adj* incontrollabile, ingovernabile
unconventional [ˌʌnkən'ven/ənəl] *adj* non convenzionale, anticonformista
uncork [ʌn'kɔrk] *tr* stappare
uncouple [ʌn'kʌpəl] *tr* sganciare, disconnettere
uncouth [ʌn'kuθ] *adj* zotico, incivile, pacchiano
uncover [ʌn'kʌvər] *tr* scoprire
unction ['ʌŋk/ən] *s* unzione; (*fig*) untuosità *f*
unctuous ['ʌŋkt/ʊ·əs] *adj* untuoso
uncultivated [ʌn'kʌltɪ ˌvetɪd] *adj* incolto
uncultured [ʌn'kʌlt/ərd] *adj* incolto, rozzo
uncut [ʌn'kʌt] *adj* non tagliato; (*book*) intonso
undamaged [ʌn'dæmɪdʒd] *adj* indenne, illeso
undaunted [ʌn'dɔntɪd] *adj* imperterrito, impavido
undeceive [ˌʌndɪ'siv] *tr* disingannare
undecided [ˌʌndɪ'saɪdɪd] *adj* indeciso
undefeated [ˌʌndɪ'fitɪd] *adj* invitto
undefended [ˌʌndɪ'fendɪd] *adj* indifeso
undefensible [ˌʌndɪ'fensɪbəl] *adj* insostenibile
undefiled [ˌʌndɪ'faɪld] *adj* puro, immacolato
undeniable [ˌʌndɪ'naɪ·əbəl] *adj* innegabile, indubitato
under ['ʌndər] *adj* di sotto; (*lower*) inferiore; (*clothing*) intimo, personale || *adv* sotto; più sotto; **to go under** affondare; cedere; (coll) fallire || *prep* sotto; sotto a; (*e.g., 20 years old*) meno di; **under full sail** a vele spiegate; **under lock and key** sotto chiave; **under oath** sotto giuramento; **under penalty of death** sotto pena di morte; **under sail** a vela; **under separate cover** in plico separato; **under steam** sotto pressione; **under the hand and seal of** firmato di pugno di; **under the weather** (coll) un po' indisposto; **under way** già iniziato
un'der·age' *adj* minorenne
un'der·arm' pad' *s* sottoascella *m*

un'der·bid' v (pret & pp -bid; ger -bidding) tr fare un'offerta inferiore a quella di

un'der·brush' s sottobosco

un'der·car'riage s (aut) telaio; (aer) carrello d'atterraggio

un'der·clothes' spl biancheria intima

un'der·consump'tion s sottoconsumo

un'der·cov'er adj segreto

un'der·cur'rent s (of water) corrente subacquea; (of air) corrente f inferiore; (fig) controcorrente f

underdeveloped [ˌʌndərdɪˈvɛləpt] adj sottosviluppato

un'der·dog' s chi è destinato ad avere la peggio; vittima; the underdogs i diseredati

un'der·done' adj non cotto abbastanza

un'der·es'timate' tr sottovalutare

un'der·gar'ment s indumento intimo

un'der·go' v (pret -went; pp -gone) tr (a test) passare, sottostare (with dat); (surgery) subire, sottoporsi a; soffrire

un'der·grad'uate adj (student) non ancora laureato; (course) per studenti non ancora laureati || s studente universitario che non ha ancora ricevuto il primo diploma

un'der·ground' adj sotterraneo; segreto || s regione sotterranea; macchia, resistenza || adv sottoterra; alla macchia, segretamente

un'der·growth' s sterpaglia

underhanded [ˈʌndərˈhændəd] adj subdolo, di sottomano

un'der·line' or un'der·line' tr sottolineare

underling [ˈʌndərlɪŋ] s tirapiedi m

un'der·mine' tr scalzare, minare

underneath [ˌʌndərˈniθ] adj inferiore || s disotto || adv sotto, di sotto || prep sotto a, sotto

undernourished [ˌʌndərˈnʌrɪʃt] adj denutrito, malnutrito

un'der·pass' s sottopassaggio

un'der·pay' s (pret & pp -paid) tr & intr pagare insufficientemente

un'der·pin' v (pret & pp -pinned; ger -pinning) tr rincalzare

underprivileged [ˌʌndərˈprɪvɪlɪdʒd] adj derelitto, diseredato

un'der·rate' tr sottovalutare

un'der·score' tr sottolineare

un'der·sea' adj sottomarino || adv sotto il mare

un'der·seas' adv sotto il mare

un'der·sec'retar'y s (-ies) sottosegretario

un'der·sell' v (pret & pp -sold) tr vendere a prezzo minore di; (to sell for less than actual value) svendere

un'der·shirt' s camiciola, canottiera

undersigned [ˈʌndərˌsaɪnd] adj sottoscritto

un'der·skirt' s sottogonna

un'der·stand' v (pret & pp -stood) tr capire, comprendere; sottintendere; (to accept as true) constare, e.g., he understands that you are wrong gli consta che Lei ha torto || intr capire, comprendere

understandable [ˌʌndərˈstændəbəl] adj comprensibile

understanding [ˌʌndərˈstændɪŋ] adj comprensivo, tollerante || s (mind) intelletto; (knowledge) conoscenza; comprensione, intendimento; (agreement) intesa, accordo

understatement [ˌʌndərˈstetmənt] s sottovalutazione

un'der·stud'y s (-ies) (theat) doppio, sostituto || v (-ied) tr (an actor) fare il doppio di

un'der·take' v (pret -took; ger -taken) tr intraprendere; (to promise) promettere

undertaker [ˈʌndərˈtekər] or [ˈʌndərˌtekər] s impresario || [ˈʌndərˌtekər] s impresario di pompe funebri

undertaking [ˌʌndərˈtekɪŋ] s (task) impresa; (promise) promessa || [ˈʌndərˌtekɪŋ] s impresa di pompe funebri

un'der·tone' s bassa voce; (background sound) ronzio di fondo; tono; colore smorzato

un'der·tow' s (on the beach) risacca; (countercurrent below surface) controcorrente f

un'der·wa'ter adj subacqueo || adv sottacqua

un'der·wear' s biancheria intima

un'der·world' s (criminal world) malavita, teppa; (abode of spirits) ade m, averno; mondo sotterraneo; mondo sottomarino; antipodi mpl

un'der·write' v (pret -wrote; pp -written) tr sottoscrivere; (to insure) assicurare

un'der·writ'er s sottoscrittore m; (ins) assicuratore m

undeserved [ˌʌndɪˈzɑrvd] adj immeritato

undesirable [ˌʌndɪˈzaɪrəbəl] adj & s indesiderabile mf

undetachable [ˌʌndɪˈtætʃəbəl] adj non movibile

undeveloped [ˌʌndɪˈvɛləpt] adj (land) non sfruttato; (country) sottosviluppato

undigested [ˌʌndɪˈdʒɛstɪd] adj non digerito

undignified [ʌnˈdɪgnɪˌfaɪd] adj poco decoroso

undiscernible [ˌʌndɪˈzɑrnɪbəl] or [ˌʌndɪˈsɑrnɪbəl] adj impercettibile

undisputed [ˌʌndɪˈspjutəd] adj indiscusso, incontrastato

un·do [ʌnˈdu] v (pret -did; pp -done) tr sfare, disfare; rovinare; (a package) aprire; (a knot) sciogliere

undoing [ʌnˈduɪŋ] s rovina

undone [ʌnˈdʌn] adj non finito; to come undone disfarsi; to leave nothing undone non tralasciare di fare nulla

undoubtedly [ʌnˈdaʊtɪdli] adv indubbiamente, senza dubbio

undress [ˈʌnˌdrɛs] or [ʌnˈdrɛs] s vestaglia; vestito da ogni giorno || [ʌnˈdrɛs] tr spogliare, svestire; (a *wound*) sbendare || *intr* spogliarsi, svestirsi

undrinkable [ʌn'drɪŋkəbəl] *adj* imbevibile, non potabile

undue [ʌn'dju] or [ʌn'du] *adj* indebito; immeritato; eccessivo

undulate ['ʌndjə‚let] *intr* ondulare

unduly [ʌn'djuli] or [ʌn'duli] *adv* indebitamente, eccessivamente

unearned [ʌn'ʌrnd] *adj* non guadagnato col lavoro; immeritato; non ancora guadagnato

un'earned in'crement *s* plusvalenza

unearth [ʌn'ʌrθ] *tr* dissotterrare

unearthly [ʌn'ʌrθli] *adj* ultraterreno; spettrale; impossibile, straordinario

uneasy [ʌn'izi] *adj* (*worried*) preoccupato; (*constrained*) scomodo; (*not conducive to ease*) inquietante, a disagio

uneatable [ʌn'itəbəl] *adj* immangiabile

uneconomic(al) [‚ʌnikə'nɑmɪk(əl)] or [‚ʌnekə'nɑmɪk(əl)] *adj* antieconomico

uneducated [ʌn'edjə‚ketɪd] *adj* ineducato

unemployed [‚ʌnem'plɔɪd] *adj* disoccupato, incollocato; improduttivo || **the unemployed** i disoccupati

unemployment [‚ʌnem'plɔɪmənt] *s* disimpiego, disoccupazione

unemploy'ment compensa'tion *s* sussidio di disoccupazione

unending [ʌn'endɪŋ] *adj* interminabile

unequal [ʌn'ikwəl] *adj* disuguale, impari; **to be unequal to** (*a task*) non essere all'altezza di

unequaled or **unequalled** [ʌn'ikwəld] *adj* ineguagliato

unerring [ʌn'ʌrɪŋ] or [ʌn'erɪŋ] *adj* infallibile; corretto, preciso

unessential [‚ʌne'senʃəl] *adj* non essenziale

uneven [ʌn'ivən] *adj* disuguale, ineguale; (*number*) dispari

uneventful [‚ʌnɪ'ventfəl] *adj* senza avvenimenti importanti; (*life*) tranquillo

unexceptionable [‚ʌnek'sepʃənəbəl] *adj* ineccepibile, irreprensibile

unexpected [‚ʌnek'spektɪd] *adj* insospettato, imprevisto

unexplained [‚ʌnek'splend] *adj* inesplicato

unexplored [‚ʌnek'splɔrd] *adj* inesplorato

unexposed [‚ʌnek'spozd] *adj* (phot) non esposto alla luce

unfading [ʌn'fedɪŋ] *adj* immarcescibile; imperituro

unfailing [ʌn'felɪŋ] *adj* immancabile, infallibile; (*inexhaustible*) inesauribile; (*dependable*) sicuro

unfair [ʌn'fer] *adj* ingiusto; disonesto, sleale

unfaithful [ʌn'feθfəl] *adj* infedele

unfamiliar [‚ʌnfə'mɪljər] *adj* poco pratico; poco abituale, strano; non conosciuto

unfasten [ʌn'fæsən] or [ʌn'fɑsən] *tr* sfibbiare, sciogliere

unfathomable [ʌn'fæðəməbəl] *adj* insondabile

unfavorable [ʌn'fevərəbəl] *adj* sfavorevole

unfeeling [ʌn'filɪŋ] *adj* insensibile

unfetter [ʌn'fetər] *tr* sciogliere dalle catene

unfinished [ʌn'fɪnɪʃt] *adj* incompiuto; grezzo, non rifinito; (*business*) inevaso

unfit [ʌn'fɪt] *adj* disadatto; inabile

unfledged [ʌn'fledʒd] *adj* implume

unfold [ʌn'fold] *tr* schiudere; (*e.g., a newspaper*) spiegare || *intr* schiudersi; svolgersi

unforeseeable [‚ʌnfor'si‚əbəl] *adj* imprevedibile

unforeseen [‚ʌnfor'sin] *adj* imprevisto

unforgettable [‚ʌnfər'getəbəl] *adj* indimenticabile

unforgivable [‚ʌnfər'gɪvəbəl] *adj* imperdonabile

unfortunate [ʌn'fɔrtjənɪt] *adj & s* disgraziato, sfortunato

unfounded [ʌn'faundɪd] *adj* infondato

un-freeze [ʌn'friz] *v* (*pret* -**froze**; *pp* -**frozen**) *tr* disgelare; (*credit*) sbloccare

unfriend-ly [ʌn'frendli] *adj* (-**lier**; -**liest**) *adj* mal disposto, ostile; sfavorevole

unfruitful [ʌn'frutfəl] *adj* infruttuoso

unfulfilled [‚ʌnfəl'fɪld] *adj* incompiuto

unfurl [ʌn'fʌrl] *tr* spiegare, dispiegare

unfurnished [ʌn'fʌrnɪʃt] *adj* smobiliato

ungainly [ʌn'genli] *adj* sgraziato, maldestro

ungentlemanly [ʌn'dʒentəlmənli] *adj* indegno di un gentleman

ungird [ʌn'gʌrd] *tr* discingere

ungodly [ʌn'gɑdli] *adj* irreligioso, empio; (*dreadful*) (coll) atroce

ungracious [ʌn'greʃəs] *adj* rude, scortese; (*task*) sgradevole

ungrammatical [‚ʌngrə'mætɪkəl] *adj* sgrammaticato

ungrateful [ʌn'gretfəl] *adj* ingrato

ungrudgingly [ʌn'grʌdʒɪŋli] *adv* di buon grado, volentieri

unguarded [ʌn'gɑrdɪd] *adj* incustodito, indifeso; incauto, imprudente

unguent ['ʌŋgwənt] *s* unguento

unhappiness [ʌn'hæpɪnɪs] *s* infelicità *f*

unhap-py [ʌn'hæpi] *adj* (-**pier**; -**piest**) infelice, sfortunato

unharmed [ʌn'hɑrmd] *adj* illeso

unharness [ʌn'hɑrnɪs] *tr* togliere i finimenti a

unhealth-y [ʌn'helθi] *adj* (-**ier**; -**iest**) malsano

unheard-of [ʌn'hʌrd‚ɑv] *adj* (*unknown*) sconosciuto; inaudito

unhinge [ʌn'hɪndʒ] *tr* sgangherare; (fig) sconvolgere

unhitch [ʌn'hɪtʃ] *tr* sganciare; (*a horse*) staccare

unho-ly [ʌn'holi] *adj* (-**lier**; -**liest**) empio; terribile, atroce

unhook [ʌn'huk] *tr* sganciare

unhoped-for [ʌn'hopt‚fɔr] *adj* insperato

unhorse [ʌn'hɔrs] *tr* disarcionare

unhurt [ʌn'hʌrt] *adj* incolume, illeso

unicorn ['junɪ,kɔrn] *s* unicorno

unification [,junɪfɪ'keʃən] *s* unificazione

uniform ['junɪ,fɔrm] *adj & s* uniforme *f* || *tr* uniformare

uni·fy ['junɪ,faɪ] *v* (*pret & pp* **-fied**) *tr* unificare

unilateral [,junɪ'lætərəl] *adj* unilaterale

unimpeachable [,ʌnɪm'pitʃəbəl] *adj* irrefutabile; irreprensibile

unimportant [,ʌnɪm'pɔrtənt] *adj* poco importante

uninhabited [,ʌnɪn'hæbɪtɪd] *adj* inabitato, disabitato

uninspired [,ʌnɪn'spaɪrd] *adj* senza ispirazione, prosaico

unintelligent [,ʌnɪn'telɪdʒənt] *adj* non intelligente; stupido

unintelligible [,ʌnɪn'telɪdʒɪbəl] *adj* inintelligibile

uninterested [ʌn'ɪntrɪstɪd] *or* [ʌn-'ɪntə,restɪd] *adj* non interessato

uninteresting [ʌn'ɪntrɪstɪŋ] *or* [ʌn-'ɪntə,restɪŋ] *adj* poco interessante

uninterrupted [,ʌnɪntə'rʌptɪd] *adj* ininterrotto

union ['junjən] *s* unione; unione matrimoniale; (*of workers*) sindacato

unionize ['junjə,naɪz] *tr* organizzare in un sindacato || *intr* organizzarsi in un sindacato

un'ion shop' *s* fabbrica che assume solo sindacalisti

un'ion suit' *s* combinazione

unique [ju'nik] *adj* unico

unison ['junɪsən] *or* ['junɪzən] *s* unisono; **in unison** all'unisono

unit ['junɪt] *adj* unitario || *s* unità *f*; (mach, elec) gruppo

unite [ju'naɪt] *tr* unire || *intr* unirsi

united [ju'naɪtɪd] *adj* unito

Unit'ed King'dom *s* Regno Unito

Unit'ed Na'tions *spl* Organizzazione delle Nazioni Unite

Unit'ed States' *adj* statunitense || **the United States** *ssg* gli Stati Uniti

uni·ty ['junɪti] *s* (**-ties**) unità *f*

universal [,junɪ'vʌrsəl] *adj* universale

u'niver'sal joint' *s* giunto cardanico

universe ['junɪ,vʌrs] *s* universo

universi·ty [,junɪ'vʌrsɪti] *adj* universitario || *s* (**-ties**) università *f*

unjust [ʌn'dʒʌst] *adj* ingiusto

unjustified [ʌn'dʒʌstɪ,faɪd] *adj* ingiustificato

unkempt [ʌn'kempt] *adj* spettinato; trascurato

unkind [ʌn'kaɪnd] *adj* scortese; duro, crudele

unknowable [ʌn'no-əbəl] *adj* inconoscibile

unknowingly [ʌn'no-ɪŋli] *adv* inconsapevolmente

unknown [ʌn'non] *adj* sconosciuto || *s* incognito; (math) incognita

Un'known Sol'dier *s* Milite Ignoto

unlace [ʌn'les] *tr* slacciare

unlatch [ʌn'lætʃ] *tr* tirare il saliscendi a

unlawful [ʌn'lɔfəl] *adj* illegale

unleash [ʌn'liʃ] *tr* sguinzagliare; (fig) scatenare

unleavened [ʌn'levənd] *adj* azzimo

unless [ʌn'les] *conj* se non che, salvo che

unlettered [ʌn'letərd] *adj* ignorante; (*illiterate*) analfabeta

unlike [ʌn'laɪk] *adj* dissimile, differente; dissimile da, e.g., **a copy unlike the original** una copia dissimile dall'originale; (elec) di segno contrario || *prep* diversamente da, a differenza di; **it was unlike him to arrive late** non era cosa normale per lui arrivare in ritardo

unlikely [ʌn'laɪkli] *adj* improbabile

unlimber [ʌn'lɪmbər] *tr* mettere in batteria || *intr* prepararsi a fare fuoco; (fig) prepararsi

unlimited [ʌn'lɪmɪtɪd] *adj* illimitato

unlined [ʌn'laɪnd] *adj* (*e.g., coat*) non foderato; (*paper*) non rigato

unload [ʌn'lod] *tr* scaricare; (*passengers*) sbarcare; (*to get rid of*) liberarsi di || *intr* scaricare; sbarcare

unloading [ʌn'lodɪŋ] *s* discarica; sbarco

unlock [ʌn'lɑk] *tr* aprire

unloose [ʌn'lus] *tr* rilasciare; sciogliere

unloved [ʌn'lʌvd] *adj* poco amato

unlovely [ʌn'lʌvli] *adj* poco attraente

unluck·y [ʌn'lʌki] *adj* (**-ier; -iest**) sfortunato, disgraziato

un·make [ʌn'mek] *v* (*pret & pp* **-made** ['med]) *tr* disfare; deporre

unmanageable [ʌn'mænɪdʒəbəl] *adj* incontrollabile

unmanly [ʌn'mænli] *adj* non virile, effemminato; codardo

unmannerly [ʌn'mænərli] *adj* scortese

unmarketable [ʌn'mɑrkɪtəbəl] *adj* invendibile

unmarriageable [ʌn'mærɪdʒəbəl] *adj* che non si può sposare; non adatto al matrimonio

unmarried [ʌn'mærɪd] *adj* scapolo; (*female*) nubile

unmask [ʌn'mæsk] *or* [ʌn'mɑsk] *tr* smascherare || *intr* smascherarsi

unmatchable [ʌn'mætʃəbəl] *adj* impareggiabile

unmatched [ʌn'mætʃd] *adj* impareggiabile; (*unpaired*) sparigliato

unmentionable [ʌn'menʃənəbəl] *adj* innominabile

unmerciful [ʌn'mʌrsɪfəl] *adj* spietato

unmesh [ʌn'meʃ] *tr* disingranare || *intr* disingranarsi

unmindful [ʌn'maɪndfəl] *adj* immemore; incurante

unmistakable [,ʌnmɪs'tekəbəl] *adj* inconfondibile

unmitigated [ʌn'mɪtɪ,getɪd] *adj* completo; assoluto, perfetto

unmixed [ʌn'mɪkst] *adj* puro

unmoor [ʌn'mur] *tr* disormeggiare

unmoved [ʌn'muvd] *adj* immoto; fisso, immobile; (fig) impassibile

unmuzzle [ʌn'mʌzəl] *tr* togliere la museruola a

unnamed [ʌn'nemd] *adj* innominato

unnatural [ʌn'nætʃərəl] *adj* contro natura, snaturato; innaturale; affettato

unnecessary [ʌn'nesə,seri] *adj* inutile

unnerve [ʌn'nɜrv] *tr* snervare

unnoticeable [ʌn'notisəbəl] *adj* impercettibile

unnoticed [ʌn'notist] *adj* inosservato

unobserved [,ʌnəb'zɜrvd] *adj* inosservato

unobtainable [,ʌnəb'tenəbəl] *adj* non ottenibile, irraggiungibile

unobtrusive [,ʌnəb'trusɪv] *adj* discreto, riservato

unoccupied [ʌn'akjə,paɪd] *adj* libero, disponibile; *(not busy)* disoccupato

unofficial [,ʌnə'fɪʃəl] *adj* non ufficiale, ufficioso

unopened [ʌn'opənd] *adj* non aperto, chiuso; *(letter)* non dissuggellato; *(book)* intonso

unorthodox [ʌn'ɔrθə,daks] *adj* non ortodosso

unpack [ʌn'pæk] *tr* spaccare, sballare

unpalatable [ʌn'pælətəbəl] *adj* di gusto spiacevole

unparalleled [ʌn'pærə,leld] *adj* incomparabile, senza pari

unpardonable [ʌn'pardənəbəl] *adj* imperdonabile

unpatriotic [,ʌnpetri'atɪk] *or* [,ʌnpætri'atɪk] *adj* antipatriottico

unperceived [,ʌnpər'sivd] *adj* inosservato

unperturbable [,ʌnpər'tɜrbəbəl] *adj* imperterrito, imperturbato

unpleasant [ʌn'plezənt] *adj* spiacevole; *(person)* antipatico

unpopular [ʌn'papjələr] *adj* impopolare

unpopularity [ʌn,papjə'lærɪti] *s* impopolarità *f*

unprecedented [ʌn'presi,dentid] *adj* senza precedenti, inaudito

unprejudiced [ʌn'predʒədɪst] *adj* senza pregiudizio, imparziale

unpremeditated [,ʌnprɪ'medi,tetid] *adj* impremeditato

unprepared [,ʌnprɪ'perd] *adj* impreparato

unprepossessing [,ʌnprɪprə'zesɪŋ] *adj* poco attraente, antipatico

unpresentable [,ʌnprɪ'zentəbəl] *adj* impresentabile

unpretentious [,ʌnprɪ'tenʃəs] *adj* modesto, senza pretese

unprincipled [ʌn'prɪnsɪpəld] *adj* senza principi

unproductive [,ʌnprə'dʌktɪv] *adj* improduttivo

unprofitable [ʌn'prafɪtəbəl] *adj* infruttuoso

unpronounceable [,ʌnprə'naunsəbəl] *adj* impronunziabile

unpropitious [,ʌnprə'pɪʃəs] *adj* inauspicato

unpublished [ʌn'pʌblɪʃt] *adj* inedito

unpunished [ʌn'pʌnɪʃt] *adj* impunito

unqualified [ʌn'kwalɪ,faɪd] *adj* inabile, inidoneo; assoluto, completo

unquenchable [ʌn'kwentʃəbəl] *adj* inappagabile, inestinguibile

unquestionable [ʌn'kwestʃənəbəl] *adj* indiscutibile

unrav•el [ʌn'rævəl] *v (pret & pp -eled* or *-elled; ger -eling* or *-elling) tr* dipanare || *intr* districarsi; chiarirsi

unreachable [ʌn'ritʃəbəl] *adj* irraggiungibile

unreal [ʌn'ri-əl] *adj* irreale

unreali•ty [,ʌnri'ælɪti] *s (-ties)* irrealità *f*

unreasonable [ʌn'rizənəbəl] *adj* irragionevole

unrecognizable [ʌn'rekəg,naɪzəbəl] *adj* irriconoscibile

unreel [ʌn'ril] *tr* svolgere, srotolare || *intr* srotolarsi

unrefined [,ʌnrɪ'faɪnd] *adj* non raffinato, greggio; volgare, ordinario

unrelenting [,ʌnrɪ'lentɪŋ] *adj* inesorabile, inflessibile; indefesso

unreliable [,ʌnrɪ'laɪ-əbəl] *adj* malfido; *(news)* inattendibile

unremitting [,ʌnrɪ'mɪtɪŋ] *adj* incessante, costante

unrented [ʌn'rentɪd] *adj* da affittare

unrepeatable [,ʌnrɪpitəbəl] *adj* irripetibile

unrepentant [,ʌnrɪ'pentənt] *adj* impenitente

un'requit'ed love' [,ʌnrɪ'kwaɪtɪd] *s* amore non corrisposto

unresponsive [,ʌnrɪ'spansɪv] *adj* apatico, insensibile

unrest [ʌn'rest] *s* agitazione

un•rig [ʌn'rɪg] *v (pret & pp -rigged; ger -rigging) tr* (naut) disarmare

unrighteous [ʌn'raɪtʃəs] *adj* ingiusto

unripe [ʌn'raɪp] *adj* immaturo

unrivaled *or* **unrivalled** [ʌn'raɪvəld] *adj* senza pari

unroll [ʌn'rol] *tr* srotolare

unromantic [,ʌnro'mæntɪk] *adj* poco romantico

unruffled [ʌn'rʌfəld] *adj* calmo, imperturbabile

unruly [ʌn'ruli] *adj* turbolento; indisciplinato, insubordinato

unsaddle [ʌn'sædəl] *tr (a horse)* dissellare; *(a rider)* scavalcare

unsafe [ʌn'sef] *adj* malsicuro, pericolante

unsaid [ʌn'sed] *adj* non detto, taciuto; **to leave unsaid** passare sotto silenzio

unsalable [ʌn'seləbəl] *adj* invendibile

unsanitary [ʌn'sænɪ,teri] *adj* antigenico

unsatisfactory [ʌn,sætɪs'fæktəri] *adj* poco soddisfacente

unsatisfied [ʌn'sætɪs,faɪd] *adj* insoddisfatto, inappagato

unsavory [ʌn'severi] *adj* insipido; (fig) disgustoso, nauseabondo

un•say [ʌn'se] *v (pret & pp -said* [sed']*) tr* disdire

unscathed [ʌn'skeðd] *adj* incolume

unscheduled [ʌn'skedʒuld] *adj* non in elenco; *(event)* fuori programma; *(e.g., flight)* fuori orario; *(phase of production)* non programmato

unscientific [,ʌnsaɪ-ən'tɪfɪk] *adj* poco scientifico

unscrew [ʌn'skru] *tr* svitare || *intr* svitarsi

unscrupulous [ʌn'skrupjələs] *adj* senza scrupoli

unseal [ʌn'sil] *tr* dissigillare

unseasonable [ʌnˈsiznəbəl] *adj* fuori stagione; inopportuno

unseasoned [ʌnˈsiznd] *adj* scondito; (*crop*) immaturo; (*crew*) inesperto

unseat [ʌnˈsit] *tr* (*a rider*) scavalcare, disarcionare; (*e.g.*, *a congressman*) far perdere il seggio a, defenestrare

unseemly [ʌnˈsimli] *adj* disdicevole, sconveniente

unseen [ʌnˈsin] *adj* non visto, inosservato; nascosto, occulto; invisibile

unselfish [ʌnˈselfiʃ] *adj* disinteressato

unsettled [ʌnˈsetəld] *adj* disabitato; disorganizzato; disordinato, erratico; indeciso; (*bill*) da pagare

unshackle [ʌnˈʃækəl] *tr* liberare

unshaken [ʌnˈʃekən] *adj* inconcusso

unshapely [ʌnˈʃepli] *adj* senza forma, deforme

unshaven [ʌnˈʃevən] *adj* non rasato

unshatterable [ʌnˈʃætərəbəl] *adj* infrangibile

unsheathe [ʌnˈʃið] *tr* sguainare

unshod [ʌnˈʃad] *adj* scalzo; (*horse*) sferrato

unshrinkable [ʌnˈʃriŋkəbəl] *adj* irrestringibile

unsightly [ʌnˈsaitli] *adj* ripugnante, brutto

unsinkable [ʌnˈsiŋkəbəl] *adj* insommergibile

unskilled [ʌnˈskild] *adj* inesperto

un'skilled la'bor *s* lavoro manuale; mano d'opera non specializzata

unskillful [ʌnˈskilfəl] *adj* maldestro

unsnarl [ʌnˈsnɑrl] *tr* sbrogliare

unsociable [ʌnˈsoʃəbəl] *adj* insocievole

unsold [ʌnˈsold] *adj* invenduto

unsolder [ʌnˈsɑdər] *tr* dissaldare

unsophisticated [ˌʌnsəˈfisti‿ˌketid] *adj* semplice, puro

unsound [ʌnˈsaund] *adj* malsano, malato; (*decayed*) guasto, imputridito; falso, fallace; (*sleep*) leggero

unsown [ʌnˈson] *adj* incolto, non seminato

unspeakable [ʌnˈspikəbəl] *adj* indicibile; (*atrocious*) innominabile, inqualificabile

unsportsmanlike [ʌnˈsportsmənˌlaik] *adj* antisportivo

unstable [ʌnˈstebəl] *adj* instabile

unsteady [ʌnˈstedi] *adj* malfermo; incostante; irregolare

unstinted [ʌnˈstintid] *adj* generoso, senza limiti

unstitch [ʌnˈstitʃ] *tr* scucire

un·stop [ʌnˈstap] *v* (*pret & pp -stopped; ger -stopping*) *tr* stasare

unstressed [ʌnˈstrest] *adj* non accentuato; (*e.g.*, *syllable*) non accentato

unstrung [ʌnˈstrʌŋ] *adj* (*beads*) sfilato; (*instrument*) allentato; (*person*) snervato

unsuccessful [ˌʌnsəkˈsesfəl] *adj* (*person*) sfortunato; (*deal*) mancato; **to be unsuccessful** fallire

unsuitable [ʌnˈsutəbəl] or [ʌnˈsjutəbəl] *adj* inappropriato

unsurpassable [ʌnsərˈpæsəbəl] or [ˌʌnsərˈpɑsəbəl] *adj* insuperabile

unsuspected [ˌʌnsəsˈpektid] *adj* insospettato

unswerving [ʌnˈswɑrviŋ] *adj* diritto, fermo, costante

unsympathetic [ˌʌnsimpəˈθetik] *adj* indifferente, che non mostra comprensione

unsystematic(al) [ˌʌnsistəˈmætik(əl)] *adj* senza sistema

untactful [ʌnˈtæktfəl] *adj* senza tatto

untamed [ʌnˈtemd] *adj* indomito

untangle [ʌnˈtæŋgəl] *tr* sgrovigliare

unteachable [ʌnˈtitʃəbəl] *adj* indocile; refrattario agli studi

untenable [ʌnˈtenəbəl] *adj* insostenibile

unthankful [ʌnˈθæŋkfəl] *adj* ingrato

unthinkable [ʌnˈθiŋkəbəl] *adj* impensabile

unthinking [ʌnˈθiŋkiŋ] *adj* irriflessivo

untidy [ʌnˈtaidi] *adj* disordinato

un·tie [ʌnˈtai] *v* (*pret & pp -tied; ger -tying*) *tr* sciogliere; (*a knot*) slacciare, snodare ‖ *intr* sciogliersi

until [ʌnˈtil] *prep* fino, fino a ‖ *conj* fino a che, finché

untillable [ʌnˈtiləbəl] *adj* incoltivabile

untimely [ʌnˈtaimli] *adj* intempestivo; (*death*) prematuro

untiring [ʌnˈtairiŋ] *adj* instancabile

untold [ʌnˈtold] *adj* non detto, non raccontato; incalcolabile; (*inexpressable*) indicibile

untouchable [ʌnˈtʌtʃəbəl] *adj & s* intoccabile *mf*

untouched [ʌnˈtʌtʃt] *adj* intatto; insensibile; non menzionato

untoward [ʌnˈtord] *adj* sfavorevole; sconveniente, disdicevole

untrammeled or **untrammelled** [ʌnˈtræməld] *adj* non inceppato

untried [ʌnˈtraid] *adj* non provato

untroubled [ʌnˈtrʌbləd] *adj* tranquillo

untrue [ʌnˈtru] *adj* falso

untrustworthy [ʌnˈtrʌstˌwɑrði] *adj* infido, malfido

untruth [ʌnˈtruθ] *s* falsità *f*, menzogna

untruthful [ʌnˈtruθfəl] *adj* falso, menzognero

untwist [ʌnˈtwist] *tr* districare ‖ *intr* districarsi

unusable [ʌnˈjuzəbəl] *adj* inservibile

unused [ʌnˈjuzd] *adj* inutilizzato; **unused to** [ʌnˈjustu] disavvezzo a

unusual [ʌnˈjuʒʊ‿əl] *adj* insolito

unutterable [ʌnˈʌtərəbəl] *adj* impronunciabile; indicibile

unvanquished [ʌnˈvæŋkwiʃt] *adj* invitto

unvarnished [ʌnˈvɑrniʃt] *adj* non verniciato; puro, semplice

unveil [ʌnˈvel] *tr* svelare; (*a statue*) scoprire, inaugurare ‖ *intr* scoprirsi

unveiling [ˌʌnˈveliŋ] *s* scoprimento

unvoiced [ʌnˈvɔist] *adj* non espresso; (*phonet*) sordo

unwanted [ʌnˈwantid] *adj* non desiderato

unwarranted [ʌnˈwɑrəntid] *adj* ingiustificato

unwary [ʌnˈweri] *adj* incauto

unwavering [ʌnˈwevəriŋ] *adj* fermo, incrollabile

unwelcome [ʌnˈwelkəm] *adj* malaccetto, sgradito

unwell [ʌnˈwel] *adj* poco bene; **to be**

unwell (*said of a woman*) (**coll**) avere le mestruazioni

unwholesome [ʌnˈholsəm] *adj* malsano

unwieldy [ʌnˈwildi] *adj* ingombrante

unwilling [ʌnˈwɪlɪŋ] *adj* riluttante

unwillingly [ʌnˈwɪlɪŋli] *adv* a malincuore, a controvoglia

un·wind [ʌnˈwaɪnd] *v* (*pret & pp* **-wound** [ˈwaʊnd]) *tr* svolgere ‖ *intr* svolgersi; (*said of a watch*) scaricarsi; (*said of a person*) rilassiarsi

unwise [ʌnˈwaɪz] *adj* malaccorto

unwished-for [ʌnˈwɪʃt͵fər] *adj* indesiderato, non augurato

unwitting [ʌnˈwɪtɪŋ] *adj* involontario

unwonted [ʌnˈwʌntɪd] *adj* insolito

unworldly [ʌnˈwʌrdli] *adj* (*not of this world*) non terrestre; (*not interested in things of this world*) non mondano; (*naive*) semplice

unworthy [ʌnˈwʌrði] *adj* indegno

un·wrap [ʌnˈræp] *v* (*pret & pp* **-wrapped**; *ger* **-wrapping**) *tr* scartare, svolgere, scartocciare

unwrinkled [ʌnˈrɪŋkəld] *adj* senza una grinza

unwritten [ʌnˈrɪtən] *adj* orale; non scritto; (*blank*) in bianco

unyielding [ʌnˈjildɪŋ] *adj* inflessibile

unyoke [ʌnˈjok] *tr* liberare dal giogo

up [ʌp] *adj* che va verso la città; diretto al nord; al corrente; finito, terminato; alto; su; (*sports*) pari; **to be up and about essere in piedi** ‖ *s* salita; vantaggio; aumento; **ups and downs alti e bassi** *mpl* ‖ *adv* su; in alto; alla pari; **to be up essere alzato;** (*in sports or games*) essere avanti; **to be up in arms essere in armi;** essere indignato; **to be up to a person toccare a una persona; to get up alzarsi; to go up salire; to keep up mantenere; continuare; to keep up with mantenersi alla pari con; up above lassù; up against** (**coll**) contro; **up against it** (**coll**) in una strettoia; **up to fino a;** (*capable of*) (**coll**) all'altezza di; (*scheming*) (**coll**) tramando; **what's up?** che succede? ‖ *prep* su; sopra; fino a; **to go up a river risalire un fiume**

up-and-coming [ˈʌpənˈkʌmɪŋ] *adj* promettente

up-and-doing [ˈʌpənˈduɪŋ] *adj* (**coll**) intraprendente; (**coll**) attivo

up-and-up [ˈʌpənˈʌp] *s*—**on the up-and-up** (**coll**) aperto; (**coll**) apertamente; (**coll**) in ascesa

up·braid *tr* rimproverare, strapazzare

upbringing [ˈʌp͵brɪŋɪŋ] *s* educazione

up'coun'try *adj* all'interno ‖ *s* interno ‖ *adv* verso l'interno

up·date' *tr* aggiornare

upheaval [ʌpˈhivəl] *s* sommovimento; (*geol*) sconvolgimento tellurico

up'hill' *adj* erto, scosceso; arduo, faticoso ‖ *adv* in salita, all'insù

up·hold' *v* (*pret & pp* **-held**) *tr* alzare; sostenere; difendere

upholster [ʌpˈholstər] *tr* tappezzare

upholsterer [ʌpˈholstərər] *s* tappezziere *m*

upholster·y [ʌpˈholstəri] *s* (**-ies**) tap-

pezzeria; (*e.g., of cushions*) imbottitura; (*aut*) selleria

up'keep' *s* manutenzione; spese *fpl* di manutenzione

upland [ˈʌplənd] *or* [ˈʌplænd] *adj* alto, elevato ‖ *s* terreno elevato

up'lift' *s* elevazione; miglioramento sociale; edificazione ‖ **up'lift'** *tr* elevare

upon [ʌˈpɑn] *prep* su, sopra, in; **upon** + *ger* non appena + *pp*, e.g., **upon arising** non appena alzato; **upon my word!** sulla mia parola!

upper [ˈʌpər] *adj* superiore, disopra; (*town*) soprano; (*river*) alto ‖ *s* disopra *m*; (*of shoe*) tomaia; (rr) (**coll**) cuccetta; **on one's uppers ridotto al verde**

up'per berth' *s* cuccetta superiore

up'per case' *s* (typ) cassa delle maiuscole, cassa superiore

up'per-case' *adj* (typ) maiuscolo

up'per classes' *spl* classi *fpl* elevate

up'per hand' *s* vantaggio; **to have the upper hand prendere il disopra**

up'per·most' *adj* (il) più alto; principale ‖ *adv* principalmente, in primo luogo

uppish [ˈʌpɪʃ] *adj* (**coll**) arrogante, snob

up·raise' *tr* alzare, tirare su

up'right' *adj* ritto, verticale; dabbene, onesto ‖ *s* staggio, montante *m* ‖ *adv* verticalmente

uprising [ʌpˈraɪzɪŋ] *or* [ˈʌp͵raɪzɪŋ] *s* sollevazione, insurrezione

up'roar' *s* gazzarra, cagnara, fracasso

uproarious [ʌpˈrorɪ·əs] *adj* tumultuoso; (*noisy*) rumoroso; (*funny*) comico

up·root' *tr* sradicare

up·set' *adj* rovesciato; scompigliato; (*emotionally*) scombussolato; (*stomach*) imbarazzato ‖ **up'set'** *s* (*overturn*) rovesciamento; (*defeat*) rovescio; (*disorder*) scompiglio; (*illness*) imbarazzo, disturbo ‖ **up·set'** *v* (*pret & pp* **-set**; *ger* **-setting**) *tr* rovesciare; scompigliare; indisporre ‖ *intr* rovesciarsi, ribaltarsi

up'set' price' *s* prezzo minimo di vendita di un oggetto all'asta

upsetting [ʌpˈsetɪŋ] *adj* sconcertante

up'shot' *s* conclusione; essenziale *m*

up'side' *s* disopra *m*

up'side down' *adv* alla rovescia; **a gambe all'aria; a soqquadro**

up'stage' *adj* al fondo della scena; altiero, arrogante ‖ *adv* al fondo della scena ‖ *tr* trattare altezzosamente; (*theat*) rubare la scena a

up'stairs' *adj* del piano di sopra ‖ *s* piano di sopra ‖ *adv* su, al piano di sopra

upstanding [ʌpˈstændɪŋ] *adj* diritto; forte; onorevole

up'start' *s* arrivato, nuovo ricco

up'stream' *adv* a monte, controcorrente

up'stroke' *s* (*in handwriting*) tratto ascendente; (*mach*) corsa ascendente

up'swing' *s* (*in prices*) ascesa; miglioramento; **to be on the upswing migliorare**

up'-to-date' *adj* recentissimo; moderno; dell'ultima ora

up'town' *adj* della parte più alta della città || *adv* nella parte più alta della città

up'trend' *s* tendenza al rialzo

up'turn' *s* rivolta; (com) rialzo

upturned [ˌʌpˈtʌrnd] *adj* rivolto all'insù; (*upside down*) capovolto

upward [ˈʌpwərd] *adj* ascendente || *adv* all'insù; **upward of** più di

U'ral Moun'tains [ˈjʊrəl] *spl* Urali *mpl*

uranium [jʊˈrenɪˈəm] *s* uranio

urban [ˈʌrbən] *adj* urbano

urbane [ʌrˈben] *adj* urbano

urbanite [ˈʌrbəˌnaɪt] *s* abitante *mf* di una città

urbanity [ʌrˈbænɪti] *s* urbanità *f*

urbanize [ˈʌrbəˌnaɪz] *tr* urbanizzare

ur'ban renew'al *s* ricostruzione urbanistica

urchin [ˈʌrtʃɪn] *s* monello, birichino

ure·thra [jʊˈriθrə] *s* (**-thras** or **-thrae** [θri]) uretra

urge [ʌrdʒ] *s* stimolo || *tr* urgere, sollecitare, spronare; (*to endeavor to persuade*) esortare; (*an enterprise*) accelerare || *intr*—**to urge against** opporsi a

urgen·cy [ˈʌrdʒənsi] *s* (**-cies**) urgenza

urgent [ˈʌrdʒənt] *adj* urgente; (*desire*) prepotente

urinal [ˈjʊrɪnəl] *s* (*receptacle*) orinale *m*; (*for a bedridden person*) pappagallo; (*place*) orinatoio, vespasiano

urinary [ˈjʊrɪˌnɛri] *adj* urinario

urinate [ˈjʊrɪˌnet] *tr & intr* orinare

urine [ˈjʊrɪn] *s* urina

urn [ʌrn] *s* urna; (*for making coffee*) caffettiera; (*for making tea*) samovar *m*

urology [jʊˈrɑlədʒi] *s* urologia

Uruguay [ˈjʊrəˌgwe] or [ˈjʊrəˌgwaɪ] *s* l'Uruguai *m*

Uruguayan [ˌjʊrəˈgweˈən] or [ˌjʊrəˈgwaɪˈən] *adj & s* uruguaiano

us [ʌs] *pron pers* ci; noi; **to us** ci, a noi, per noi

U.S.A. [ˈjuˈɛsˈe] *s* (letterword) **(United States of America)** S.U.A. *mpl*

usable [ˈjuzəbəl] *adj* servibile, adoperabile

usage [ˈjusɪdʒ] or [ˈjuzɪdʒ] *s* uso, usanza; (*of a language*) uso

use [jus] *s* uso, impiego, usanza; **in use** in uso, in servizio; **it's no use** non giova; **out of use** disusato; **to be of no use** non servire a nulla; **to have**

no use for non aver bisogno di; non poter soffrire; **to make use of** servirsi di; **what's the use?** a che pro? || [juz] *tr* usare, impiegare, servirsi di; **to use badly** maltrattare; **to use up** consumare, esaurire || *intr*—**used to** translated in Italian in three ways: (1) by the imperfect indicative, e.g., **he used to go to church at seven o'clock** andava in chiesa alle sette; (2) by the imperfect indicative of **solere**, e.g., **he used to smoke all day** soleva fumare tutto il giorno; (3) by the imperfect indicative of **avere l'abitudine di**, e.g., **he used to go to the shore** aveva l'abitudine di andare alla spiaggia

used [juzd] *adj* uso, usato; **to get used to** [ˈjuzdtu] or [ˈjustu] fare la mano a, abituarsi a

useful [ˈjusfəl] *adj* utile

usefulness [ˈjusfəlnɪs] *s* utilità *f*

useless [ˈjuslɪs] *adj* inutile, inservibile

user [ˈjuzər] *s* utente *mf*

usher [ˈʌʃər] *s* (*doorkeeper*) portiere *m*; (hist) cerimoniere *m*; (theat) maschera; (mov) lucciola || *tr* introdurre; **to usher in** annunciare, introdurre

U.S.S.R. [ˈjuˈɛsˈɛsˈɑr] *s* (letterword) **(Union of Soviet Socialist Republics)** U.R.S.S. *f*

usual [ˈjuʒuˈəl] *adj* usuale, abituale; **as usual** come il solito

usually [ˈjuʒuˈəli] *adj* usualmente

usurp [juˈzʌrp] *tr* usurpare

usu·ry [ˈjuʒəri] *s* (**-ries**) usura

utensil [juˈtɛnsɪl] *s* utensile *m*

uter·us [ˈjutərəs] *s* (**-i** [ˌaɪ]) utero

utilitarian [ˌjutɪlɪˈtɛriˈən] *adj* utilitario

utili·ty [juˈtɪlɪti] *s* (**-ties**) utilità *f*; compagnia di servizi pubblici

utilize [ˈjutɪˌlaɪz] *tr* utilizzare

utmost [ˈʌtˌmost] *adj* sommo; estremo; massimo || *s*—**the utmost** il massimo; **to do one's utmost** fare tutto il possibile; **to the utmost** al massimo limite

utopia [juˈtopɪˈə] *s* utopia

utopian [juˈtopɪˈən] *adj* utopistico || *s* utopista *mf*

utter [ˈʌtər] *adj* completo, totale || *tr* proferire, pronunziare; (*a sigh*) dare, fare

utterly [ˈʌtərli] *adj* completamente

uxoricide [ʌkˈsɔriˌsaɪd] *s* (*husband*) uxoricida *m*; (*act*) uxoricidio

uxorious [ʌkˈsɔriˈəs] *adj* eccessivamente innamorato della propria moglie; dominato dalla moglie

V

V, v [vi] *s* ventiduesima lettera dell'alfabeto inglese

vacan·cy [ˈvekənsi] *s* (**-cies**) (*emptiness*) vuoto; (*unfilled position*) vacanza; (*unfilled job*) posto vacante; (*in a building*) appartamento libero;

(*in a hotel*) camera libera; **no vacancy** completo

vacant [ˈvekənt] *adj* (*empty*) vuoto; (*position*) vacante; (*expression of the face*) vago

vacate [ˈveket] *tr* sgombrare; (*a posi-*

tion) ritirarsi da; (law) annullare; **to vacate one's mind of worries** liberarsi dalle preoccupazioni || *intr* sloggiare; (coll) andarsene

vacation [ve'keʃən] *s* vacanza, villeggiatura; vacanze *fpl* || *intr* estivare, villeggiare

vacationer [ve'keʃənər] *s* villeggiante *mf*, vacanziere *m*

vacationist [ve'keʃənɪst] *s* villeggiante *mf*, vacanziere *m*

vaca'tion with pay' *s* vacanze *fpl* pagate

vaccinate ['væksɪ,net] *tr* vaccinare

vaccination [,væksɪ'neʃən] *s* vaccinazione

vaccine [væk'sin] *s* vaccino

vacillate ['væsɪ,let] *intr* vacillare

vacillating ['væsɪ,letɪŋ] *adj* vacillante

vacui·ty [væ'kju·rti] *s* (-**ties**) vacuità *f*

vacu·um ['vækju·əm] *s* (-**ums** or -**a** [ə]) vuoto; **in a vacuum** sotto vuoto || *tr* pulire con l'aspirapolvere

vac'uum clean'er *s* aspirapolvere *m*

vac'uum-pack'ed *adj* confezionato sotto vuoto

vac'uum tube' *s* tubo elettronico

vagabond ['vægə,bɑnd] *adj* & *s* vagabondo

vagar·y [və'gɛri] *s* (-**ies**) capriccio

vagran·cy ['vegrənsi] *s* (-**cies**) vagabondaggio

vagrant ['vegrənt] *adj* & *s* vagabondo

vague [veg] *adj* vago

va'gus nerve' ['vegəs] *s* (anat) vago

vain [ven] *adj* vano; (*conceited*) vanitoso; **in vain** in vano

vainglorious [ven'glorɪ·əs] *adj* vanaglorioso

valance ['væləns] *s* balza, mantovana

vale [vel] *s* valle *f*

valedictorian [,vælɪdɪk'torɪ·ən] *s* studente *m* che pronuncia il discorso di commiato

valence ['veləns] *s* (chem) valenza

valentine ['vælən,taɪn] *s* (*sweetheart*) valentino; (*card*) cartolina di San Valentino

valet ['vælɪt] or ['vælɪ] *s* valletto

valiant ['væljənt] *adj* valoroso

valid ['vælɪd] *adj* valido

validate ['vælɪ,det] *tr* convalidare, vidimare; (sports) omologare

validation [,vælɪ'deʃən] *s* convalida, vidimazione; (sports) omologazione

validi·ty [və'lɪdɪti] *s* (-**ties**) validità *f*

valise [və'lis] *s* valigetta

valley ['væli] *s* valle *f*, vallata; (*of roof*) linea di compluvio

valor ['vælər] *s* valore *m*, coraggio

valorous ['vælərəs] *adj* valoroso

valuable ['vælju·əbəl] or ['væljəbəl] *adj* (*having monetary worth*) prezioso; pregevole, pregiato || **valuables** *spl* valori *mpl*

value ['vælju] *s* valore *m*; importanza; (com) valuta, valore *m*; **an excellent value** un acquisto eccellente || *tr* stimare, valutare

value'-added tax' *s* imposta sul valore aggiunto

valueless ['væljulɪs] *adj* senza valore

valve [vælv] *s* (anat, mach, rad, telv)

valvola; (bot, zool) valva; (mus) pistone *m*

valve' gears' *spl* meccanismo di distribuzione

valve'-in-head' en'gine *s* motore *m* a valvole in testa

valve' lift'er ['lɪftər] *s* alzavalvole *m*

valve' seat' *s* sede *f* della valvola

valve' spring' *s* molla di valvola

valve' stem' *s* stelo di comando della valvola

vamp [væmp] *s* parte *f* anteriore della tomaia; (*patchwork*) rabberciatura; (*female*) vamp *f* || *tr* (*a shoe*) rimontare; rabberciare; (*to concoct*) inventare, raffazzonare; (*an accompaniment*) improvvisare; (*said of a female*) sedurre

vampire ['væmpaɪr] *s* vampiro; (*female*) vamp *f*

van [væn] *s* camionetta, autofurgone *m*; (mil & fig) avanguardia

vanadium [və'nedɪ·əm] *s* vanadio

vandal ['vændəl] *adj* & *s* vandalo || **Vandal** *adj* & *s* Vandalo

vandalism ['vændə,lɪzəm] *s* vandalismo

vane [ven] *s* (*weathervane*) banderuola; (*of windmill, of turbine*) pala; (*of feather*) barba

vanguard ['væn,gɑrd] *s* avanguardia; **in the vanguard** all'avanguardia

vanilla [və'nɪlə] *s* vaniglia

vanish ['vænɪʃ] *intr* svanire

van'ishing cream' ['vænɪʃɪŋ] *s* crema evanescente

vani·ty ['vænɪti] *s* (-**ties**) vanità *f*; (*table*) toletta; (*case*) astuccio di toletta

vanquish ['væŋkwɪʃ] *tr* superare, vincere

van'tage ground' ['væntɪdʒ] *s* posizione favorevole

vapid ['væpɪd] *adj* insipido

vapor ['vepər] *s* vapore *m*; (*visible vapor*) vapori *mpl*

vaporize ['vepə,raɪz] *tr* vaporizzare || *intr* vaporizzarsi

va'por lock' *s* tampone *m* di vapore

vaporous ['vepərəs] *adj* vaporoso

va'por trail' *s* scia di condensazione

variable ['vɛrɪ·əbəl] *adj* & *s* variabile *f*

variance ['vɛrɪ·əns] *s* divario, differenza; **at variance with** (*a thing*) differente da; differentemente da; (*a person*) in disaccordo con

variant ['vɛrɪ·ənt] *adj* & *s* variante *f*

variation [,vɛrɪ'eʃən] *s* variazione

varicose ['vɛrɪ,kos] *adj* varicoso

varied ['vɛrid] *adj* vario, svariato

variegated ['vɛrɪ·ə,getɪd] or ['vɛrɪ,getɪd] *adj* variegato, screziato

varie·ty [və'raɪ·ɪti] *s* (-**ties**) varietà *f*

vari'ety show' *s* spettacolo di varietà

varnish ['vɑrnɪʃ] *s* vernice *f* || *tr* verniciare; (fig) dare la vernice a

variola [və'raɪ·ələ] *s* (pathol) vaiolo

various ['vɛrɪ·əs] *adj* vari; (*varicolored*) vario, variegato

varsi·ty ['vɑrsɪti] *adj* (sports) universitario || *s* (-**ties**) (sports) squadra numero uno

var·y ['veri] v (pret & pp **-ied**) tr & intr variare

vase [ves] or [vez] s vaso

vaseline ['væsə ˌlin] s (trademark) vaselina

vassal ['væsəl] adj & s vassallo

vast [væst] or [vɑst] adj vasto

vastly ['væstli] or ['vɑstli] adv enormemente

vastness ['væstnɪs] or ['vɑstnɪs] s vastità f

vat [væt] s tino, bigoncia

Vatican ['vætɪkən] adj vaticano ‖ s Vaticano

Vat'ican Cit'y s Città f del Vaticano

vaudeville ['vodvɪl] or ['vɔdəvɪl] s spettacolo di varietà; (theatrical piece) vaudeville m, commedia musicale

vault [vɔlt] s volta; (underground chamber) cantina; (of a bank) camera di sicurezza; (burial chamber) cripta; (of heaven) cappa; (leap) salto ‖ tr formare a mo' di volta; saltare ‖ intr saltare

vaunt [vɔnt] or [vɑnt] s vanto, vanteria ‖ tr vantarsi di ‖ intr vantarsi

veal [vil] s vitello

veal' chop' s scaloppa, cotoletta di vitello

veal' cut'let s scaloppina

vedette [vɪ'dɛt] s (nav) vedetta; (mil) sentinella avanzata

veer [vɪr] s virata ‖ tr far cambiare di direzione a ‖ intr virare; (said of the wind) cambiare di direzione

vegetable ['vɛdʒɪtəbəl] adj vegetale ‖ s (plant) vegetale m; (edible plant) ortaggio; **vegetables** verdura, erbe fpl, erbaggi mpl, ortaggi mpl

veg'etable gar'den s orto

veg'etable soup' s minestra di verdura

vegetarian [ˌvɛdʒɪ'tɛrɪ-ən] adj & s vegetariano

vegetate ['vɛdʒɪ ˌtet] intr vegetare

vehemence ['vi-ɪməns] s veemenza

vehement ['vi-ɪmənt] adj veemente

vehicle ['vi-ɪkəl] s veicolo

vehic'ular traf'fic [vɪ'hɪkjələr] s circolazione stradale

veil [vel] s velo; **to take the veil** prendere il velo ‖ tr velare

vein [ven] s vena; (streak) ventatura; (of ore) filone m ‖ tr venare

velar ['vilər] adj & s velare f

vellum ['vɛləm] s pergamena

veloci·ty [vɪ'lɑsɪti] s (-ties) velocità f

velvet ['vɛlvɪt] adj di velluto ‖ s velluto; (slang) guadagno al gioco; (coll) situazione all'acqua di rose

velveteen [ˌvɛlvɪ'tin] s vellutino di cotone

velvety ['vɛlvɪti] adj vellutato

vend [vɛnd] tr vendere; (to peddle) fare il venditore ambulante di

vend'ing machine' s distributore automatico

vendor ['vɛndər] s venditore m

veneer [və'nɪr] s impiallacciatura, piallaccio; (fig) vernice f ‖ tr impiallacciare

venerable ['vɛnərəbəl] adj venerabile

venerate ['vɛnə ˌret] tr venerare

venereal [vɪ'nɪrɪ·əl] adj venereo

Venetia [vɪ'niʃɪ·ə] or [vɪ'niʃə] s (province) Venezia

Venetian [vɪ'niʃən] adj & s veneziano

Vene'tian blind' s veneziana, persiana avvolgibile

Venezuelan [ˌvɛnɪ'zwilən] adj & s venezolano

vengeance ['vɛndʒəns] s vendetta; **with a vengeance** violentemente; eccessivamente

vengeful ['vɛndʒfəl] adj vendicativo

Venice ['vɛnɪs] s Venezia

venire·man [vɪ'nairɪmən] s (-men) membro di un collegio di giurati

venison ['vɛnɪsən] or ['vɛnɪzən] s carne f di cervo

venom ['vɛnəm] s veleno

venomous ['vɛnəməs] adj velenoso

vent [vɛnt] s sfiatatoio; (of jacket) spacco; **to give vent to** dare sfogo a ‖ tr sfogare, sfuriare; mettere uno sfiatatoio a; **to vent one's spleen** sfogare la bile

vent' hole' s apertura di sfogo

ventilate ['vɛntɪ ˌlet] tr ventilare

ventilator ['vɛntɪ ˌletər] s ventilatore m

ventricle ['vɛntrɪkəl] s ventricolo

ventriloquist [vɛn'trɪləkwɪst] s ventriloquo

venture ['vɛntʃər] s azzardo, avventura rischiosa; **at a venture** alla ventura ‖ tr avventurare ‖ intr avventurarsi, arrischiarsi

venturesome ['vɛntʃərsəm] adj (risky) rischioso; (daring) avventuroso

venturous ['vɛntʃərəs] adj avventuroso

vent' win'dow s (aut) deflettore m

venue ['vɛnju] s (law) posto dove ha avuto luogo il reato; (law) luogo dove si riunisce la corte; **change of venue** cambio di giurisdizione

Venus ['vinəs] s (very beautiful woman) venere f; (astr) Venere m; (myth) Venere f

veracious [vɪ're ʃəs] adj verace

veraci·ty [vɪ'ræsɪti] s (-ties) veridicità f

veranda or **verandah** [və'rændə] s veranda

verb [vʌrb] adj verbale ‖ s verbo

verbalize ['vʌrbə ˌlaɪz] tr esprimere con parole; (gram) convertire in forma verbale ‖ intr essere verboso

verbatim [vər'betɪm] adj letterale ‖ adv parola per parola, testualmente

verbena [vər'binə] s (bot) verbena

verbiage ['vʌrbɪ·ɪdʒ] s verbosità f; (style of wording) espressione

verbose [vər'bos] adj verboso

verdant ['vʌrdənt] adj verde, verdeggiante

verdict ['vʌrdɪkt] s verdetto

verdigris ['vʌrdɪ ˌgris] s verderame m

verdure ['vʌrdʒər] s verde m

verge [vʌrdʒ] s orlo, limite m; bordo; (of a column) fusto; **on the verge of** al punto di; all'orlo di ‖ intr—**to verge on** costeggiare, rasentare

verification [ˌvɛrɪfɪ'keʃən] s verifica

veri·fy ['vɛrɪ ˌfaɪ] v (pret & pp **-fied**) tr verificare, confermare

verily ['vɛrɪlɪ] adv in verità

veritable ['vɛrɪtəbəl] adj vero

vermilion [vər'mɪljən] adj & s vermiglio

vermin ['vʌrmɪn] ssg (person) persona abominevole || spl (animals or persons) insetti mpl

vermouth [vər'muθ] or ['vʌrmuθ] s vermut m

vernacular [vər'nækjələr] adj volgare || s volgare m, vernacolo; (language peculiar to a class or profession) gergo

versatile ['vʌrsətɪl] adj (person) versatile; (tool or device) a vari usi

verse [vʌrs] s verso; (Bib) versetto

versed [vʌrst] adj versato

versification [ˌvʌrsɪfɪ'keʃən] s versificazione

versi·fy ['vʌrsɪ ˌfaɪ] v (pret & pp **-fied**) tr & intr versificare

version ['vʌrʒən] s versione

ver·so ['vʌrso] s (**-sos**) (of coin) rovescio; (of page) verso

versus ['vʌrsəs] prep contro; in confronto a

verte·bra ['vʌrtɪbrə] s (**-brae** [ˌbri] or **-bras**) vertebra

vertebrate ['vʌrtə ˌbret] adj & s vertebrato

ver·tex ['vʌrteks] s (**-texes** or **-tices** [tɪ ˌsiz]) vertice m

vertical ['vʌrtɪkəl] adj & s verticale f

ver'tical hold' s (telv) regolatore m del sincronismo verticale

ver'tical sta'bilizer s (aer) deriva

verti·go ['vʌrtɪ ˌgo] s (**-goes** or **-gos**) vertigine f

verve [vʌrv] s verve f, brio

very ['vɛrɪ] adj (utter) grande, completo; (precise) vero e proprio; (mere) stesso, e.g., **his very brother** suo fratello stesso || adv molto, e.g., **to be very rich** essere molto ricco

vesicle ['vɛsɪkəl] s vescichetta

vesper ['vɛspər] s vespro; **vespers** vespri mpl || **Vesper** s Vespero

ves'per bell' s campana a vespro

vessel ['vɛsəl] s (ship) nave f, vascello; (container) vaso; (anat) vaso; (fig) vasello

vest [vɛst] s (of man's suit) panciotto, gilè m; (of woman's garment) corpino || tr vestire; **to vest** (authority) in concedere a; **to vest with** investire di || intr vestirisi; **to vest in** passare a

vest'ed in'terest s interesse acquisito

vestibule ['vɛstɪ ˌbjul] s vestibolo

vestige ['vɛstɪdʒ] s vestigio

vestment ['vɛstmənt] s (eccl) paramento

vest'-pock'et adj da tasca, tascabile

ves·try ['vɛstrɪ] s (**-tries**) sagrestia; (chapel) cappella; giunta esecutiva della chiesa episcopaliana

ves'try·man s (**-men**) membro della giunta esecutiva della chiesa episcopaliana

Vesuvius [vɪ'suvɪ·əs] or [vɪ'sjuvɪ·əs] s il Vesuvio

vetch [vɛtʃ] s veccia; (grass pea) cicerchia

veteran ['vɛtərən] adj & s veterano

veterinarian [ˌvɛtərɪ'nɛrɪ·ən] s veterinario

veterinar·y ['vɛtərɪ ˌnɛrɪ] adj veterinario || s (**-ies**) veterinario

ve·to ['vito] s (**-toes**) veto || tr porre il veto a

vex [vɛks] tr irritare, tormentare

vexation [vɛk'seʃən] s fastidio, contrarietà f

vexatious [vɛk'seʃəs] adj irritante, fastidioso; (law) vessatorio

vexing ['vɛksɪŋ] adj noioso, fastidioso, irritante

via ['vaɪ·ə] prep via, per via di

viaduct ['vaɪ·ə ˌdʌkt] s viadotto

vial ['vaɪ·əl] s fiala, boccetta

viand ['vaɪ·ənd] s vivanda, manicaretto

viati·cum [vaɪ'ætɪkəm] s (**-cums** or **-ca** [kə]) (eccl) viatico

vibrate ['vaɪbret] tr & intr vibrare

vibration [vaɪ'breʃən] s vibrazione

vicar ['vɪkər] s vicario

vicarage ['vɪkərɪdʒ] s residenza del vicario; (office; duties) vicariato

vicarious [vaɪ'kɛrɪ·əs] or [vɪ'kɛrɪ·əs] adj sostituto; (punishment) ricevuto in vece di altra persona; (power) delegato; (enjoyment) di riflesso

vice [vaɪs] s vizio

vice'-ad'miral s viceammiraglio, ammiraglio di squadra

vice'-pres'ident s vicepresidente m

viceroy ['vaɪsrɔɪ] s viceré m

vice versa ['vaɪsɪ 'vʌrsə] or ['vaɪsə 'vʌrsə] adv viceversa

vicini·ty [vɪ'sɪnɪtɪ] s (**-ties**) vicinanze fpl, paraggi mpl

vicious ['vɪʃəs] adj vizioso; maligno; malvagio; (dog) cattivo, che morde; (horse) selvaggio; (headache) tremendo; (reasoning; circle) vizioso

victim ['vɪktɪm] s vittima

victimize ['vɪktɪ ˌmaɪz] tr fare una vittima di; ingannare; (hist) sacrificare

victor ['vɪktər] s vincitore m

victorious [vɪk'torɪ·əs] adj vittorioso

victo·ry ['vɪktərɪ] s (**-ries**) vittoria

victuals ['vɪtəlz] spl vettovaglie fpl

vid'eo cassette' ['vɪdɪ ˌo] s videocassetta

vid'eo sig'nal s segnale m video

vid'eo tape' s nastro televisivo

vie [vaɪ] v (pret & pp **vied**; ger **vying**) intr gareggiare; **to vie for** disputarsi

Vien·nese [ˌvi·ə'niz] adj viennese || s (**-nese**) viennese mf

Vietnam [ˌviɛt'nam] s il Vietnam

Vietnam·ese [vɪ ˌɛtnə'miz] adj vietnamita || s (**-ese**) vietnamita mf; (language) vietnamita m

view [vju] s vista; (picture) veduta; prospetto; esame m; punto di vista; **to be on view** (said of a corpse) essere esposto; **to keep in view** non perdere di vista; **to take a dim view of** avere un'opinione scettica di; **with a view to** con lo scopo di || tr guardare, osservare; considerare

viewer ['vju-ər] s spettatore m; (telv) telespettatore m; (phot) visore m; (phot) proiettore m di diapositive

view'find'er s (phot) traguardo, visore m

view'point' s punto di vista

vigil ['vɪdʒɪl] s vigilia; **to keep vigil** vegliare

vigilance ['vɪdʒɪləns] s vigilanza

vigilant ['vɪdʒɪlənt] adj vigilante

vignette [vɪn'jet] s vignetta

vigor ['vɪgər] s vigore m, gagliardia

vigorous ['vɪgərəs] adj vigoroso

Viking ['vaɪkɪŋ] s vichingo

vile [vaɪl] adj vile, malvagio; (wretchedly bad) orribile; disgustoso, ripugnante; (filthy) sporco; (poor) povero, basso

vili-fy ['vɪlɪ‚faɪ] v (pret & pp -fied) tr vilificare

villa ['vɪlə] s villa

village ['vɪlɪdʒ] s villaggio, paese m

villager ['vɪlɪdʒər] s paesano

villain ['vɪlən] s scellerato; (of a play) cattivo, anima nera

villainous ['vɪlənəs] adj vile, infame

villain-y ['vɪləni] s (-ies) scelleratezza, malvagità f

vim [vɪm] s vigore m, brio

vinaigrette [‚vɪnə'gret] s boccetta dell'aceto aromatico

vinaigrette' sauce' s salsa verde

vindicate ['vɪndɪ‚ket] tr scolpare; difendere, sostenere; (e.g., a claim) rivendicare

vindictive [vɪn'dɪktɪv] adj vendicativo

vine [vaɪn] s (climber) rampicante f; (grape plant) vite f

vine'dress'er s vignaiolo

vinegar ['vɪnɪgər] s aceto

vinegarish ['vɪnɪgərɪ] adj acetoso; (fig) acre, mordace

vinegary ['vɪnɪgəri] adj acetoso; (fig) irritabile, irascibile

vineyard ['vɪnjərd] s vigna, vigneto

vintage ['vɪntɪdʒ] s vendemmia; vino di annata eccezionale; (fig) edizione antiquata

vintager ['vɪntɪdʒər] s vendemmiatore m

vin'tage wine' s vino di marca

vin'tage year' s buona annata

vintner ['vɪntnər] s produttore m di vino; vinaio

vinyl ['vaɪnɪl] or ['vɪnɪl] s vinile m

violate ['vaɪ-ə‚let] tr violare

violation [‚vaɪ-ə'leʃən] s violazione

violence ['vaɪ-ələns] s violenza

violent ['vaɪ-ələnt] adj violento

violet ['vaɪ-əlɪt] adj violetto || s (color) violetto, viola; (bot) violetta; (Viola odorata) viola mammola

violin [‚vaɪ-ə'lɪn] s violino

violinist [‚vaɪ-ə'lɪnɪst] s violinista m

violoncellist [‚vaɪ-ələn't[elɪst] or [‚vi-ələn't[elɪst] s violoncellista mf

violoncel-lo [‚vaɪ-ələn't[elo] or [‚vi-ələn't[elo] s (-los) violoncello

VIP ['vi'aɪ'pi] s (letterword) (Very Important Person) persona di maggiore riguardo

viper ['vaɪpər] s vipera; (any snake) serpe f; (spiteful person) vipera

vira·go [vɪ'rego] s (-goes or -gos) megera, donna dal caratteraccio impossibile

virgin ['vʌrdʒɪn] adj & s vergine f || **Virgin** s Vergine f

vir'gin birth' s parto verginale della Madonna; (zool) partenogenesi f

Virgin'ia creep'er [vər'dʒɪnɪ-ə] s vite f del Canada

virginity [vər'dʒɪnɪti] s verginità f

Virgo ['vʌrgo] s (astr) Vergine f

virility [vɪ'rɪlɪti] s virilità f

virology [vaɪ'rɑledʒi] s virologia

virtual ['vʌrt[u-əl] adj virtuale

virtue ['vʌrt[u] s virtù f

virtuosi·ty [‚vʌrt[u'ɑsɪti] s (-ties) virtuosità f, virtuosismo

virtuo·so [‚vʌrt[u'oso] s (-sos or -si [si]) virtuoso

virtuous ['vʌrt[u-əs] adj virtuoso

virulence ['vɪrjələns] s virulenza

virulent ['vɪrjələnt] adj virulento

virus ['vaɪrəs] s virus m

visa ['vizə] s visto || tr vistare

visage ['vɪzɪdʒ] s faccia; apparenza

vis-à-vis [‚vizə'vi] adj l'uno di fronte all'altro || adv vis-à-vis || prep di fronte a

viscera ['vɪsərə] spl visceri mpl, viscere fpl

viscount ['vaɪkaunt] s visconte m

viscountess ['vaɪkauntɪs] s viscontessa

viscous ['vɪskəs] adj viscoso

vise [vaɪs] s morsa

visé ['vize] or [vi'ze] s & tr var of visa

visible ['vɪzɪbəl] adj visibile

Visigoth ['vɪzɪ‚gɑθ] s visigoto

vision ['vɪʒən] s visione; (sense) vista

visionar-y ['vɪʒə‚neri] adj visionario || s (-ies) visionario

visit ['vɪzɪt] s visitare; affliggere, colpire; (a punishment) far ricadere || intr visitare; (to chat) fare un chiacchierata

visitation [‚vɪzɪ'teʃən] s visitazione; punizione divina, visita del Signore

vis'iting card' s biglietto da visita

vis'iting hours' spl orario delle visite

vis'iting nurse' s infermiera che visita i pazienti a domicilio

visitor ['vɪzɪtər] s visitatore m

visor ['vaɪzər] s visiera; (fig) maschera

vista ['vɪstə] s vista, prospettiva

visual ['vɪʒu-əl] adj visivo; visuale

vis'ual acu'ity s acutezza visiva

visualize ['vɪʒu-ə‚laɪz] tr formare l'immagine mentale di; (to make visible) visualizzare

vital ['vaɪtəl] adj vitale; (deadly) mortale || **vitals** spl organi vitali

vitality [vaɪ'tælɪti] s vitalità f

vitalize ['vaɪtə‚laɪz] tr animare, infondere vita a

vi'tal statis'tics spl statistiche fpl anagrafiche

vitamin ['vaɪtəmɪn] s vitamina

vitiate ['vɪʃɪ‚et] tr viziare

vitreous ['vɪtrɪ-əs] adj vitreo, vetroso

vitriolic [‚vɪtrɪ'ɑlɪk] adj di vetriolo; (fig) caustico

vituperate [vaɪ'tupə‚ret] or [vaɪ'tjupə‚ret] tr vituperare

viva ['vivə] s evviva || *interj* viva!
vivacious [vɪ'veʃəs] or [vaɪ'veʃəs] *adj* vivace
vivaci·ty [vɪ'væsɪti] or [vaɪ'væsɪti] s (-ties) vivacità *f*, gaiezza
viva voce ['vaɪvə 'vosi] *adv* a viva voce
vivid ['vɪvɪd] *adj* vivido
vivi·fy ['vɪvɪ,faɪ] *v* (*pret & pp* -fied) *tr* vivificare
vivisection [,vɪvɪ'sekʃən] s vivisezione
vixen ['vɪksən] s volpe femmina; (*ill-tempered woman*) megera
vizier [vɪ'zɪr] or ['vɪzjər] s visir *m*
vocabular·y [vo'kæbjə,leri] s (-ies) vocabolario
vocal ['vokəl] *adj* vocale; (*inclined to express oneself freely*) che si fa sentire, loquace; (*e.g., outburst*) verbale
vocalist ['vokəlɪst] s cantante *mf*; (*of jazz*) vocalist *mf*
vocalize ['vokə,laɪz] *tr* vocalizzare || *intr* vocalizzarsi
vocation [vo'keʃən] s vocazione; professione, impiego
voca'tional educa'tion s istruzione professionale
vocative ['vakətɪv] *adj* vocativo
vociferate [vo'sɪfə,ret] *intr* vociferare
vociferous [vo'sɪfərəs] *adj* rumoroso, vociferante
vogue [vog] s voga, moda; **in vogue** in voga, di moda
voice [vɔɪs] s voce *f*; (*of animals*) verso; **in a loud voice** a voce alta; **in a low voice** a voce bassa; **to give voice to** esprimere; **with one voice** con una sola voce || *tr* esprimere; (phonet) sonorizzare || *intr* sonorizzarsi
voiced [vɔɪst] *adj* (phonet) sonoro
voiceless ['vɔɪslɪs] *adj* senza voce; muto; (phonet) sordo, duro
void [vɔɪd] *adj* (*useless*) inutile; (*empty*) vuoto; (law) invalido, nullo; **void of** sprovvisto di || s vuoto; (*gap*) buco || *tr* vuotare; (*the bowels*) evacuare; annullare || *intr* andare di corpo
volatile ['valətɪl] *adj* volatile; instabile; (*disposition*) volubile, incostante
volatilize ['valətɪ,laɪz] *tr* volatilizzare || *intr* volatilizzarsi
volcanic [val'kænɪk] *adj* vulcanico
volca·no [val'keno] s (-noes or -nos) vulcano
volition [və'lɪʃən] s volontà *f*; **of one's own volition** di propria volontà
volley ['vali] s (*e.g., of bullets*) scarica, sventagliata; (tennis) volata || *tr* colpire a volo || *intr* colpire la palla a volo
vol'ley·ball' s pallavolo *f*
volplane ['val,plen] s planata || *intr* planare
volt [volt] s volt *m*
voltage ['voltɪdʒ] s voltaggio
volt'age divid'er [dɪ'vaɪdər] s divisore *m* del voltaggio
voltaic [val'te·ɪk] *adj* voltaico
volte-face [volt'fas] s voltafaccia *m*

volt'me'ter s voltmetro
voluble ['valjəbəl] *adj* locuace
volume ['valjəm] s volume *m*; **to speak volumes** avere molta importanza; essere molto espressivo
voluminous [və'lumɪnəs] *adj* voluminoso
voluntar·y ['valən,teri] *adj* volontario || s (-ies) assolo di organo
volunteer [,valən'tɪr] *adj & s* volontario || *tr* dare o dire volontariamente || *intr* offrirsi; arruolarsi come volontario; **to volunteer to** + *inf* offrirsi di + *inf*
voluptuar·y [və'lʌptʃʊ,eri] *adj* voluttuoso || s (-ies) sibarita *m*, epicureo
voluptuous [və'lʌptʃu·əs] *adj* voluttuoso
volute [və'lut] s voluta
vomit ['vamɪt] s vomito || *tr & intr* vomitare, rigettare
voodoo ['vudu] *adj* di vudù || s (*practice*) vudù *m*; (*person*) vuduista *mf*
voracious [və're/əs] *adj* vorace
voracity [və'ræsɪti] s voracità *f*
vor·tex ['vortəks] s (-texes or -tices [tɪ,siz]) vortice *m*
vota·ry ['votəri] s (-ries) persona legata da un voto; amante *mf*, appassionato
vote [vot] s voto; **to put to the vote** mettere ai voti; **to tally the votes** procedere allo scrutinio dei voti || *tr* votare; dichiarare; **to vote down** respingere; **to vote in** eleggere; **to vote out** scacciare || *intr* votare
vote' get'ter ['getər] s accaparratore *m* di voti; slogan *m* che conquista voti
voter ['votər] s elettore *m*
vot'ing machine' ['votɪŋ] s macchina per registrare lo scrutinio dei voti
votive ['votɪv] *adj* votivo
vo'tive of'fering s voto, ex voto, offerta votiva
vouch [vautʃ] *tr* garantire || *intr*—**to vouch for** (*s.th*) garantire; (*s.o.*) rendersi garante per, garantire per
voucher ['vautʃər] s garante *mf*; (*certificate*) ricevuta, pezza d'appoggio
vouch·safe' *tr* concedere, accordare || *intr*—**to vouchsafe to** + *inf* degnarsi di + *inf*
voussoir [vu'swar] s cuneo
vow [vau] s voto; **to take vows** pronunciare i voti || *tr* promettere; (*vengeance*) giurare || *intr* fare un voto
vowel ['vau·əl] s vocale *f*
voyage ['vɔɪ·ɪdʒ] s viaggio; (*by sea*) traversata || *tr* attraversare || *intr* viaggiare
voyager ['vɔɪ·ɪdʒər] s viaggiatore *m*, passeggero
vulcanize ['vʌlkə,naɪz] *tr* vulcanizzare
vulgar ['vʌlgər] *adj* volgare; comune, popolare
vulgari·ty [vʌl'gærɪti] s (-ties) volgarità *f*
Vul'gar Lat'in s latino volgare
Vulgate ['vʌlget] s Vulgata
vulnerable ['vʌlnərəbəl] *adj* vulnerabile
vulture ['vʌltʃər] s avvoltoio

W, w ['dʌbəl ,ju] s ventitreesima lettera dell'alfabeto inglese

wad [wɑd] s (of cotton) batuffolo, bioccolo; (of money) mazzetta, rotolo; (of tobacco) pallottola; (in a gun) stoppaccio || v (pret & pp **wadded; ger wadding**) tr arrotolare; (shot) comprimere; (fig) imbottire

waddle ['wɑdəl] s andatura a mo' di anitra || intr scuellettare

wade [wed] tr guadare || intr guadare; avanzare faticosamente; sguazzare; **to wade into** (coll) attaccare violentemente; **to wade through** procedere a stento per; leggere con difficoltà

wad'ing bird' ['wedɪŋ] s trampoliere m

wafer ['wefər] s disco adesivo di carta per chiudere lettere; (cake) wafer m, cialda; (eccl, med) ostia

waffle ['wɑfəl] s cialda

waf'fle i'ron s schiacce fpl

waft [wæft] or [wɑft] tr portare leggermente or a volo || intr librarsi, spandersi

wag [wæg] s (of head) cenno; (of tail) scodinzolio; (person) burlone m || v (pret & pp **wagged; ger wagging**) tr (the head) scuotere; (the tail) dimenare || intr scodinzolare

wage [wedʒ] s salario, paga; **wages** salario, paga; ricompensa; prezzo, e.g., **the wages of sin is death** la morte è il prezzo del peccato || tr (war) fare

wage' earn'er ['ʌrnər] s salariato

wager ['wedʒər] s scommessa; **to lay a wager** fare una scommessa || tr & intr scommettere

wage'work'er s lavoratore salariato

waggish ['wægɪʃ] adj scherzoso, comico, burlone

Wagnerian [vɑg'nɪrɪ-ən] adj & s wagneriano

wagon ['wægən] s carro, carretto; (e.g., Conestoga wagon) carriaggio; furgone m; carrozzone m; **to be on the wagon** (slang) astenersi dal bere; **to hitch one's wagon to a star** avere altissime ambizioni

wag'tail' s (orn) ballerina, cutrettola

waif [wef] s (foundling) trovatello; abbandonato; animale smarrito

wail [wel] s gemito, lamento || intr gemere, lamentarsi

wain·scot ['wenskət] or ['wenskɑt] s pannello per rivestimenti || v (pret & pp **-scoted** or **-scotted; ger -scoting** or **-scotting**) tr rivestire di pannelli di legno

waist [west] s vita, cintura; blusa, camicetta, corpetto

waist'band' s cintola

waist'cloth' s perizoma m

waistcoat ['west ,kot] or ['westkət] s corpetto, gilè m

waist'line' s vita, cintura; **to keep or watch one's waistline** conservare la linea

wait [wet] s attesa; **to lie in wait** atten-

dere al varco || tr (one's turn) attendere || intr attendere, aspettare; **to wait for** attendere, aspettare; **to wait on** servire; **to wait up for** (coll) aspettare alzato

wait'-and-see' pol'icy s attendismo

waiter ['wetər] s cameriere m; (tray) vassoio

wait'ing list' s lista d'aspettativa

wait'ing room' s sala d'aspetto

waitress ['wetrɪs] s cameriera

waive [wev] tr (one's rights) rinunciare (with dat); differire; mettere da parte

waiver ['wevər] s rinuncia

wake [wek] s (any watch) veglia; (watch by a dead body) veglia funebre; (of a boat) solco, scia; **in the wake of** come risultato di; nelle orme di || v (pret **waked** or **woke** [wok]; pp **waked**) tr svegliare || intr svegliarsi; **to wake to** darsi conto di; **to wake up** svegliarsi

wakeful ['wekfəl] adj sveglio; insonne

waken ['wekən] tr svegliare || intr svegliarsi

wale [wel] s segno lasciato da una frustata, vescica; (in fabric) riga, costa

Wales [welz] s la Galles

walk [wɔk] s (act) camminata; (distance) cammino; (for pleasure) passeggiata; (gait) andatura; (line of work) attività f, mestiere m; (sidewalk) marciapiede m; (in a garden) sentiero; (yard for domestic animals to exercise in) recinto; (sports) marcia; **to go for a walk** andare a fare una passeggiata || tr (a street) percorrere; (a horse) passeggiare; (a patient) far camminare; (a heavy piece of furniture) abbambinare; **to walk off** (a headache) far passare camminando || intr camminare; passeggiare; (said of a horse) andare al passo; (sports) marciare; **to walk away from** andarsene a piedi da; **to walk off with** rubare; vincere con facilità; **to walk out** uscire in segno di protesta; (coll) mettersi in sciopero; **to walk out on** (coll) piantare in asso

walkaway ['wɔkə ,we] s facile vittoria

walker ['wɔkər] s camminatore m; (to teach a baby to walk) girello

walkie-talkie ['wɔki'tɔki] s trasmettitore-ricevitore m portatile

walk'ing pa'pers spl—**to give s.o. his walking papers** (coll) dare gli otto giorni a qlcu

walk'-in refrig'erator s cella frigorifera

walk'ing stick' s bastone m da passeggio

walk'-on' s (actor) figurante m, comparsa; (role) particina

walk'out' s sciopero

walk'o'ver s facile vittoria, passeggiata

wall [wɔl] s muro; (between rooms; of a vein) parete f; (rampart) muraglia; **to drive to the wall** ridurre alla disperazione; **to go to the wall** perdere; fare fallimento || *tr* murare; **to wall up** circondare con muro

wall'board' *s* pannello da costruzione

wallet | 'walɪt| *s* portafoglio

wall'flow'er *s* violacciocca gialla; **to be a wallflower** fare tappe..eria

Walloon |wa'lun| *adj & s* vallone *mf*

wallop ['waləp] *s* (coll) colpo violento; (coll) effetto || *tr* (coll) dare un colpo violento a; (coll) battere completamente

wallow ['walo] *s* diguazzamento; (*place*) brago, pantano || *intr* diguazzare; (*in wealth*) nuotare

wall'pa'per *s* tappezzeria || *tr* tappezzare

walnut ['wɔlnət] *s* (*tree; wood*) noce *m;* (*fruit*) noce *f*

walrus ['wɔlrəs] or ['wɑlrəs] *s* tricheco

Walter ['wɔltər] *s* Gualtiero

waltz [wɔlts] *s* valzer *m* || *tr* ballare il valzer con; (coll) condurre con disinvoltura || *intr* ballare il valzer

wan [wan] *adj* (**wanner; wannest**) (*face*) smunto, sparuto, smorto; (*light*) debole

wand [wand] *s* bacchetta

wander ['wandər] *tr* vagare per || *intr* vagare, vagabondare; errare

wanderer ['wandərər] *s* vagabondo; pellegrino

Wan'dering Jew' *s* ebreo errante

wan'der-lust' *s* passione del vagabondaggio

wane [wen] *s* decadenza, declino; calare *m* della luna; **on the wane** in declino; (*moon*) calante || *intr* decadere, declinare; (*said of the moon*) calare

wangle ['wæŋgəl] *tr* (coll) ottenere con l'astuzia, rimediare; (coll) falsificare; **to wangle one's way out of** (coll) tirarsi fuori da . . . con l'astuzia || *intr* (coll) arrangiarsi

want [want] or [wɔnt] *s* bisogno, necessità *f;* domanda; miseria; **for want of** a causa della mancanza di; **to be in want** essere in miseria; **to be in want of** aver bisogno di || *tr* volere, desiderare; mancare; aver bisogno di || *intr* desiderare; **to be wanting** mancare, e.g., **three cards are wanting** mancano tre carte; **to want for** aver bisogno di

want' ad' *s* annunzio economico

wanton ['wantən] *adj* di proposito, deliberato; arbitrario; licenzioso, sfrenato; (*archaic*) lussureggiante

war [wɔr] *s* guerra; **to go to war** entrare in guerra; (*said of a soldier*) andare in guerra; **to wage war** fare la guerra || *v* (*pret & pp* **warred**); *ger* **warring**) *intr* guerreggiare; **to war on** fare la guerra a

warble ['wɔrbəl] *s* gorgheggio || *intr* gorgheggiare

warbler ['wɔrblər] *s* canterino; uccello canoro; (orn) beccafico

war' cloud' *s* minaccia di guerra

ward [word] *s* (*of city*) distretto; (*division of hospital*) corsia; (*separate building in hospital*) padiglione *m;*

(*guardianship*) tutela; (*minor*) pupillo; (*of lock*) scontro || *tr*—**to ward off** stornare, schermirsi da

warden ['wordən] *s* guardiano; (*of jail*) direttore *m;* (*in wartime*) capofabbri..ato

ward' heel'er *s* politicantuccio

ward'robe *s* guardaroba *m*

ward' robe trunk' *s* baule *m* armadio

ward'room *s* (nav) quadrato

ware [wer] *s* vasellame *m; wares* merce *f*

war' ef'fort *s* sforzo bellico

ware'house' *s* deposito, magazzino

ware'house'man *s* (-**men**) magazziniere *m*

war'fare' *s* guerra

war'head' *s* (mil) testa

war'horse' *s* cavallo di battaglia; (coll) veterano

warily ['werɪli] *adv* con cautela

wariness ['werɪnɪs] *s* cautela

war'like' *adj* guerresco, guerriero

war' loan' *s* prestito di guerra

war' lord' *s* generalissimo

warm [wɔrm] *adj* caldo; (*lukewarm*) tiepido; (*clothes*) che tiene caldo; (*with anger*) acceso; **to be warm** (*said of a person*) avere caldo; (*said of the weather*) fare caldo || *tr* scaldare, riscaldare; (*s.o.'s heart*) slargare; **to warm up** riscaldare || *intr* scaldarsi, riscaldarsi; **to warm up** (*said, e.g., of a room*) riscaldarsi; (*with emotion*) eccitarsi, accalorarsi; **to warm up to** prender simpatia per

warm-blooded ['wɔrm'blʌdɪd] *adj* (*animal*) a sangue caldo; impetuoso, ardente

war' memo'rial *s* monumento ai caduti

warmer ['wɔrmər] *s* scaldino

warm-hearted ['wɔrm'hɑrtɪd] *adj* caloroso, cordiale

warm'ing pan' *s* scaldaletto

warmonger ['wɔr,mʌŋgər] *s* guerrafondaio

war' moth'er *s* madrina di guerra

warmth [wɔrmθ] *s* calore *m*, tepore *m;* foga, entusiasmo

warm'up' *s* preparazione; (*of radio, engine, etc.*) riscaldamento

warn [wɔrn] *tr* avvertire, mettere in guardia; (*to admonish*) ammonire; informare; **to warn off** intimare di allontanarsi (da)

warn'ing *adj* di avvertimento || *s* avvertimento, ammonimento; (law) diffida

war' nose' *s* acciarino, testa

war' of nerves' *s* guerra dei nervi

War' of the Roses' *s* Guerra delle due Rose

warp [wɔrp] *s* (*of a fabric*) ordito; (*of a board*) svergolamento, curvatura; aberrazione mentale; (naut) gherlino || *tr* curvare, svergolare; (*a fabric*) ordire; falsare, alterare; (naut) tirare col gherlino || *intr* curvarsi; falsarsi, alterarsi; (naut) alare

war'path' *s*—**to be on the warpath** essere sul sentiero della guerra, prepararsi alla guerra; (*to be angry*) essere arrabiato, essere di cattivo umore

war'plane' *s* aeroplano da guerra

war' prof'iteer *s* pescecane *m*

warrant ['wɑrənt] or ['wɔrənt] *s* garanzia; certificato; ricevuta; (com) nota di pegno; (law) ordine *m*, mandato ‖ *tr* garantire; autorizzare

warrantable ['wɑrəntəbəl] or ['wɔrəntəbəl] *adj* giustificabile, legittimo

war'rant of'ficer *s* sottufficiale *m*

warran·ty ['wɑrənti] or ['wɔrənti] *s* (**-ties**) garanzia; autorizzazione

warren ['wɑrən] or ['wɔrən] *s* conigliera; (fig) formicaio

warrior ['wɔrjər] or ['wɑrjər] *s* guerriero

Warsaw ['wɔrsɔ] *s* Varsavia

war'ship' *s* nave *f* da guerra

wart [wɔrt] *s* verruca

war'time' *s* tempo di guerra

war'-torn' *adj* devastato dalla guerra

war' to the death' *s* guerra a morte

war-y ['wɛri] *adj* (**-ier; -iest**) guardingo

wash [wɑʃ] or [wɔʃ] *s* lavata; (*clothes washed or to be washed*) bucato; (*rushing movement of water*) sciacquio; (*dirty water*) lavatura; (*painting*) mano *f* di colore; (aer, naut) scia ‖ *tr* lavare; (*dishes*) rigovernare; (*said of sea or river*) bagnare; **to be washed up** essere finito; **to wash away** (*soil of river bank*) dilavare; portar via ‖ *intr* lavarsi; fare il bucato; essere lavabile; (*said of waves*) battere

washable ['wɑʃəbəl] or ['wɔʃəbəl] *adj* lavabile

wash'-and-wear' *adj* non-stiro

wash'ba'sin *s* conca, catinella

wash'bas'ket *s* cesto del bucato

wash'board' *s* asse *m* da lavanda; (*baseboard*) battiscopa *m*

wash'bowl' *s* conca, catinella

wash'cloth' *s* pezzuola per lavarsi

wash'day' *s* giorno del bucato

washed-out ['wɑʃt ‚aut] or ['wɔʃt ‚aut] *adj* slavato; (coll) stanco; (coll) abbattuto, accasciato

washed-up ['wɑʃt‚ʌp] or ['wɔʃt‚ʌp] *adj* (coll) finito

washer ['wɑʃər] or ['wɔʃər] *s* (*person*) lavatore *m*; (*machine*) lavatrice *f*; (*under head of bolt*) rondella, rosetta; (*ring to prevent leakage*) guarnizione

wash'er·man *s* (**-men**) lavatore *m*

wash'er·wom'an *s* (**-wom'en**) lavatrice *f*, lavandaia

wash' goods' *spl* tessuti *mpl* lavabili

washing ['wɑʃɪŋ] or ['wɔʃɪŋ] *s* lavata, lavaggio, lavanda; (*of clothes*) bucato; **washings** lavaggio

wash'ing machine' *s* lavabiancheria, lavatrice *f*

wash'ing so'da *s* soda da lavare

wash'out' *s* erosione; (aer) svergolamento negativo; (coll) rovina completa

wash'rag' *s* pezzuola per lavarsi; straccio di cucina

wash'room' *s* gabinetto, toletta

wash'stand' *s* lavabo, lavamano

wash'tub' *s* mastello, lavatoio

wash' wa'ter *s* lavatura

wasp [wɑsp] *s* vespa

waste [west] *s* spreco; (*refuse*) scarico, rifiuto; (*desolate country*) landa; (*excess material*) scarto; (*for wiping machinery*) cascame *m* di cotone; **to go to waste** essere sciupato; **to lay waste** devastare ‖ *tr* perdere, sciupare, sprecare ‖ *intr*—**to waste away** intristire, consumarsi

waste'bas'ket *s* cestino della carta straccia

wasteful ['westfəl] *adj* dispendioso; distruttivo

waste'pa'per *s* cartastraccia

waste' pipe' *s* tubo di scarico

waste' prod'uct *s* scarto; (*body excretion*) escremento

wastrel ['westrəl] *s* sciupone *m*; spendaccione *m*, prodigo

watch [wɑtʃ] *s* orologio; (*lookout*) guardia; (mil) guardia; (naut) turno; **to be on the watch for** essere all'erta per; **to keep watch over** vegliare su ‖ *tr* (*to look at*) osservare; (*to oversee*) vigilare; guardare; fare attenzione a ‖ *intr* guardare; (*to keep awake*) vegliare; **to watch for** fare attenzione a; **to watch out** fare attenzione; **to watch out for** fare attenzione a; essere all'erta per; **to watch over** sorvegliare; **watch out!** attenzione!

watch'band' *s* cinturino dell'orologio

watch'case' *s* cassa dell'orologio

watch' charm' *s* ciondolo dell'orologio

watch' crys'tal *s* cristallo dell'orologio

watch'dog' *s* cane *m* da guardia; (fig) guardiano

watch'dog' commit'tee *s* comitato di sorveglianza

watchful ['wɑtʃfəl] *adj* vigile

watchfulness ['wɑtʃfəlnɪs] *s* vigilanza

watch'mak'er *s* orologiaio

watch'man *s* (**-men**) guardiano, sorvegliante *m*; (*at night*) guardia notturna, metronotte *m*

watch' night' *s* notte *f* di San Silvestro; ufficio religioso della vigilia di Capodanno

watch' pock'et *s* taschino dell'orologio

watch'tow'er *s* torre *f* d'osservazione

watch'word' *s* parola d'ordine, consegna; slogan *m*

water ['wɔtər] or ['wɑtər] *s* acqua; **of the first water** di prim'ordine; (*e.g., a thief*) della più bell'acqua; **to back water** retrocedere; **to be in deep water** essere in cattive acque; **to fish in troubled waters** pescare nel torbido; **to hold water** aver fondamento; **to keep above water** (fig) tenersi a galla; **to make water** (*to urinate*) urinare; (naut) fare acqua; **to throw cold water on** scoraggiare ‖ *tr* bagnare; dare acqua a; (*cattle*) abbeverare; (*wine*) annacquare ‖ *intr* abbeverarsi; (*said of the mouth*) aver l'acquolina; (*said, e.g., of a ship*) fare acqua; (*said of the eyes*) lacrimare

wa'ter bug' s bacherozzolo
wa'ter car'rier s acquaiolo
wa'ter·col'or s acquerello
wa'ter-cooled' adj a raffreddamento ad acqua
wa'ter·course' s corso d'acqua
wa'ter·cress' s crescione m
wa'ter cure' s cura delle acque
wa'ter·fall' s cascata
wa'ter-front' s riva, banchina
wa'ter gap' s gola, passo
wa'ter ham'mer s colpo d'ariete
wa'ter heat'er s scaldabagno, scalda-acqua m
wa'ter ice' s granita
wa'tering can' s annaffiatoio
wa'tering place' s stabilimento balneare; stazione termale; (drinking place) abbeveratoio
wa'tering pot' s annaffiatoio
wa'tering trough' s abbeveratoio
wa'ter jack'et s camicia d'acqua
wa'ter lil'y s nenufaro
wa'ter line' s linea di galleggiamento or d'acqua; linea di livello
wa'ter main' s tubo di flusso principale
wa'ter-mark' s linea di livello massimo; (in paper) filigrana
wa'ter·mel'on s cocomero, anguria
wa'ter me'ter s contatore m dell'acqua
wa'ter mill' s mulino ad acqua
wa'ter pipe' s tubo dell'acqua
wa'ter po'lo s pallanuoto f
wa'ter pow'er s forza idrica
wa'ter·proof' adj & s impermeabile m
wa'ter·repel'lent adj idroripellente
wa'ter·shed' s spartiacque m, displuvio
wa'ter ski' s idrosci m
wa'ter sof'tener s decalcificatore m
wa'ter·spout' s (to carry water from roof) pluviale m; (meteor) tromba marina
wa'ter sys'tem s (of a river) sistema m fluviale; (of city) conduttura dell'acqua, impianto idrico
wa'ter-tight' adj stagno, ermetico; (fig) perfetto, inconfutabile
wa'ter tow'er s torre f serbatoio
wa'ter wag'on s (mil) carro dell'acqua; to be on the water wagon (slang) astenersi dal bere
wa'ter·way' s via d'acqua, idrovia
wa'ter wheel' s ruota or turbina idraulica; (of steamboat) ruota a pale
wa'ter wings' spl galleggiante m per nuotare
wa'ter·works' s impianto idrico; (pumping station) impianto di pompaggio
watery ['wɔtəri] or ['wɑtəri] adj acquoso; lacrimoso; povero, insipido; umido, acquitrinoso
watt [wɑt] s watt m
watt'-hour' s (-hours) wattora m
wattle ['wɑtəl] s (of bird) bargiglio
watt'me'ter s wattmetro
wave [wev] s onda; (of cold; of feeling) ondata; (of the hand) cenno; (of hair) onda, ondulazione || tr (a flag) sventolare; (the hair) ondulare; (the hand) fare cenno con; to wave aside fare cenno di allontanarsi a; (e.g., a

proposal) rifiutare || intr ondeggiare, fare cenni con la mano
wave'length' s lunghezza d'onda
wave' mo'tion s movimento ondulatorio
waver ['wevər] intr ondeggiare, oscillare; (to hesitate) titubare, tentennare; (to totter) pencolare
wav·y ['wevi] adj (-ier; -iest) (sea) ondoso; (hair) ondulato
wax [wæks] s cera; (fig) fantoccio || tr incerare; (a recording) (coll) registrare || intr aumentare; diventare; (said of the moon) crescere; to wax indignant indignarsi
wax' pa'per s carta cerata, carta oleata
wax'works' s museo di statue di cera
way [we] s maniera, modo; via; condizione; across the way di fronte; a good way un buon tratto; all the way fino alla fine della strada; completamente; all the way to fino a; any way ad ogni modo; by the way a proposito; in a way in un certo modo; fino a un certo punto; in every way per ogni verso; in this way in questa maniera; one way senso unico; on the way to andando a; on the way out uscendo; diminuendo, sparendo; out of the way eliminato; fuori mano; strano; irregolare; that way in quella direzione; per di lì; in quella maniera; this way in questa direzione; per di qui; in questa maniera; to be in the way essere d'impaccio; to feel one's way avanzare a tentoni; to force one's way aprirsi il passo a viva forza; to get out of the way togliersi di mezzo; to give way ritirarsi, cedere; (said of a rope) rompersi; to give way to cedere a, darsi a; to go out of one's way darsi da fare, disturbarsi; to have one's way vincerla; to keep out of the way stare fuori dai piedi; to know one's way around conoscere bene la via; (fig) sapere il fatto proprio; to know one's way to sapere andare a; to lead the way guidare, fare da guida; prendere l'iniziativa; to lose one's way perdersi; to make one's way avanzare; fare carriera; to make way for far largo a; to mend one's ways mettere la testa a partito; to not know which way to turn non sapere a che santo votarsi; to put out of the way togliere di mezzo; to see one's way to vedere la possibilità di; to take one's way andarsene; to wind one's way through andare a zig zag per; to wing one's way andare a volo; under way in moto; in cammino, avviato; way in entrata; way out uscita; ways modi mpl, maniere fpl; (naut) scalo; which way? da che parte?; in che modo?, per dove?
way'bill' s lettera di vettura
wayfarer ['we,ferər] s viandante m
way'lay' v (pret & pp -laid) tr tendere un agguato a; fermare improvvisamente
way' of life' s tenore m di vita

way'side' *s* bordo della strada; **to fall by the wayside** cadere per istrada; (fig) fare fiasco

way' sta'tion *s* stazione con fermata facoltativa

way' train' *s* treno omnibus

wayward ['wewərd] *adj* indocile, caparbio; irregolare; capriccioso

we [wi] *pron pers* noi; noialtri, e.g., **we Italians** noialtri italiani

weak [wik] *adj* debole

weaken ['wikən] *tr* indebolire, infiacchire || *intr* indebolirsi, infiacchirsi

weakling ['wiklɪŋ] *s* debolino, rammollito

weak-minded ['wik'maɪndɪd] *adj* irresoluto; scemo

weakness ['wiknɪs] *s* debolezza, fiacchezza; (*liking*) debole *m*

wealth [welθ] *s* ricchezza

wealth·y ['welθi] *adj* (*-ier; -iest*) ricco

wean [win] *tr* svezzare, slattare; **to wean away from** disavvezzare da

weanling ['winlɪŋ] *adj* appena svezzato || *s* bambino or animale appena svezzato

weapon ['wepən] *s* arma

weaponry ['wepənri] *s* armi *fpl*, armamento

wear [wer] *s* uso, servizio; (*clothing*) vestiti *mpl*, indumenti *mpl*; (*wasting away from use*) consumo, logorio; (*lasting quality*) durata, durabilità *f*; **for everyday wear** per ogni giorno || *v* (*pret* **wore** [wor]; *pp* **worn** [worn]) *tr* portare, avere indosso; (*to cause to deteriorate*) logorare, consumare; (*to tire*) stancare; **to wear out** logorare, strusciare; (*a horse*) sfiancare; (*one's patience*) esaurire; (*s.o.'s hospitality*) abusare di || *intr* logorarsi, consumarsi; **to wear off** diminuire, sparire; **to wear out** logorarsi; stancarsi; esaurirsi; **to wear well** essere di ottima durata

wear' and tear' [ter] *s* logorio

weariness ['wɪrɪnɪs] *s* fatica, stanchezza

wear'ing appar'el ['werɪŋ] *s* abbigliamento, articoli *mpl* d'abbigliamento

wearisome ['wɪrɪsəm] *adj* affaticante; (*tedious*) noioso

wea·ry ['wɪri] *adj* (*-rier; -riest*) stanco || *v* (*pret & pp* **-ried**) *tr* stancare || *intr* stancarsi

weasel ['wizəl] *s* donnola

wea'sel words' *spl* parole *fpl* ambigue

weather ['weðər] *s* tempo; maltempo; **to be under the weather** (coll) non sentirsi bene; (*to be slightly drunk*) (coll) essere alticcio || *tr* (*lumber*) stagionare; (*adversities*) superare, resistere (with *dat*)

weather-beaten ['weðər,bitən] *adj* segnato dalle intemperie

weath'er bu'reau *s* servizio metereologico

weath'er·cock' *s* banderuola

weath'er fore'cast *s* previsioni *fpl* del tempo, bollettino metereologico

weath'er-man' *s* (*-men'*) metereologo

weath'er report' *s* bollettino metereologico

weath'er strip'ping ['strɪpɪŋ] *s* guarnizione a nastro per inzeppare

weath'er vane' *s* banderuola, ventarola

weave [wiv] *s* tessitura || *v* (*pret* **wove** [wov] or **weaved**; *pp* **wove** or **woven** ['wovən]) *tr* tessere; (fig) inserire; **to weave one's way** aprirsi un varco serpeggiando || *intr* tessere; serpeggiare

weaver ['wivər] *s* tessitore *m*

web [web] *s* tessuto; (*of spider*) tela; (*of rail*) anima, gambo; (zool) membrana; (fig) rete *f*, maglia

web-footed ['web,fʊtɪd] *adj* palmipede

wed [wed] *v* (*pret & pp* **wed** or **wedded**; *ger* **wedding**) *tr* sposare; (*said of the groom*) impalmare; (*said of the bride*) andare in sposa a || *intr* sposarsi

wedding ['wedɪŋ] *adj* nuziale || *s* sposalizio, nozze *fpl*, matrimonio

wed'ding cake' *s* torta nuziale

wed'ding day' *s* giorno di nozze

wed'ding invita'tion *s* invito a nozze

wed'ding march' *s* marcia nuziale

wed'ding ring' *s* fede *f*, vera

wedge [wedʒ] *s* cuneo; (*of pie*) spicchio; (*to split wood*) bietta; (*to hold a wheel*) scarpa || *tr* incuneare

wed'lock *s* matrimonio

Wednesday ['wenzdi] *s* mercoledì *m*

wee [wi] *adj* piccolo piccolo

weed [wid] *s* malerba, erbaccia; (coll) sigaretta; (slang) marijuana; **weeds** vestito da lutto, gramaglie *fpl* || *tr* sarchiare, mondare

weeder ['widər] *s* (agr) estirpatore *m*

weed'ing hoe' *s* sarchio, zappa

weed'-kill'er *s* diserbante *m*

week [wik] *s* settimana; **week in, week out** una settimana dopo l'altra

week'day' *s* giorno feriale

week'end' *s* fine-settimana *m*, fine *f* di settimana, week-end *m* || *intr* passare il fine-settimana

week·ly ['wikli] *adj* settimanale || *s* (*-lies*) settimanale *m* || *adv* settimanalmente

weep [wip] *v* (*pret & pp* **wept** [wept]) *tr* piangere; **to weep oneself to sleep** addormentarsi piangendo; **to weep one's eyes out** piangere a calde lacrime || *intr* piangere; **to weep for joy** piangere di gioia

weeper ['wipər] *s* piagnone *m*; (*hired mourner*) prefica

weep'ing wil'low *s* salice *m* piangente

weep·y ['wipi] *adj* (*-ier; -iest*) piangente, lacrimoso

weevil ['wivəl] *s* curculione *m*

weft [weft] *s* (*yarns running across warp*) trama; (*fabric*) tela, tessuto

weigh [we] *tr* pesare; (*anchor*) levare; (*to make heavy*) appesantire; (fig) soppesare, ponderare; **to weigh down** piegare || *intr* pesare; gravitare; **to weigh in** (sports) pesarsi; **to weigh upon** gravare a

weigh'bridge' *s* stadera

weight [wet] *s* peso; (fig) peso; **to carry weight** aver del peso; **to lose weight** diminuire di peso; **to put on weight** crescere di peso; **to throw**

one's **weight around** far sentire la propria importanza || tr appesantire; (statistically) ponderare, dare un certo peso a

weightless ['wetlɪs] adj senza peso, imponderabile

weightlessness ['wetlɪsnɪs] s imponderabilità f

weight·y ['weti] adj (-ier; -lest) pesante; importante

weir [wɪr] s sbarramento; (for catching fish) pescaia

weird [wɪrd] adj soprannaturale, misterioso; strano, bizzarro

welcome ['welkəm] adj benvenuto; gradito; **you are welcome** (i.e., gladly received) sia il benvenuto; (in answer to thanks) prego; **you are welcome to it** è a Sua disposizione; **you are welcome to your opinion** pensi come la vuole || s benvenuto || tr dare il benvenuto a; accettare; gradire || interj benvenuto!

weld [weld] s saldatura autogena; (bot) guaderella || tr saldare || intr saldarsi

welder ['weldər] s saldatore m; (machine) saldatrice f

welding ['weldɪŋ] s saldatura autogena

wel'fare' s benessere m; (effort to improve living conditions) beneficenza, assistenza; **to be on welfare** ricevere assistenza pubblica

wel'fare state' s stato sociale or assistenziale

well [wel] adj bene; in buona salute || s pozzo; (for ink) pozzetto, serbatoio; (spring) sorgente f; (shaft for stairs) tromba || adv bene; **as well** pure; **as well . . . as** tanto . . . come; **as well as** tanto come, non meno che || intr —**to well up** sgorgare || interj behl; benel; alloral, dunquel

well-appointed ['welə'pɔɪntɪd] adj ben ammobiliato

well-attended ['welə'tendɪd] adj molto frequentato

well-behaved ['welbɪ'hevd] adj beneducato; **to be well-behaved** comportarsi bene

well'-be'ing s benessere m

well'born' adj bennato

well-bred ['wel'bred] adj educato, costumato

well-disposed ['weldɪs'pozd] adj bendisposto

well-done ['wel'dʌn] adj benfatto; (meat) ben cotto

well-fixed ['wel'fɪkst] adj (coll) agiato, abbiente

well-formed ['wel'fɔrmd] adj benfatto

well-founded ['wel'faʊndɪd] adj fondato

well-groomed ['wel'grumd] adj (person) curato; (horse) ben governato

well-heeled ['wel'hild] adj (coll) agiato, benestante

well-informed ['welɪn'fɔrmd] adj bene informato

well-intentioned ['welɪn'tenʃənd] adj benintenzionato

well'-kept' adj ben conservato; (person) benportante; (secret) ben mantenuto

well-known ['wel'non] adj notorio, ben noto

well-meaning ['wel'minɪŋ] adj benevolo, benintenzionato

well-nigh ['wel'naɪ] adv quasi

well'-off' adj agiato, benestante

well-preserved ['welprɪ'zɑrvd] adj ben conservato; (person) benportante

well-read ['wel'red] adj colto, che ha letto molto

well-spoken ['wel'spokən] adj (person) raffinato nel parlare; (word) a proposito

well'spring' s sorgente f

well' sweep' s mazzacavallo del pozzo

well-tempered ['wel'tempərd] adj ben temperato

well-thought-of ['wel'θɔt,ɑv] adj tenuto in alta considerazione

well-timed ['wel'taɪmd] adj opportuno

well-to-do ['weltə'du] adj benestante

well-wisher ['wel'wɪʃər] s amico, sostenitore m

well-worn ['wel'worn] adj (clothing) liso, consunto, trito; (argument) logoro, banale; portato con eleganza

welsh [welʃ] intr—**to welsh on** (a promise) (slang) mancare a; (a person) (slang) fregare || **Welsh** adj & s gallese m f; **the Welsh** i gallesi

Welsh'man s (-men) gallese m

Welsh' rab'bit or **rare'bit** ['rerbɪt] s fonduta fatta con la birra servita su pane abbrustolito

welt [welt] s (finish along a seam) costa; (of shoe) guardolo; (wale from a blow) riga, sferzata

welter ['weltər] s guazzabuglio; confusione; (a tumbling about) rotolio || intr rotolarsi, guazzare

wel'ter·weight' s (boxing) peso welter, peso medio-leggero

wench [wentʃ] s ragazza, giovane f

wend [wend] tr—**to wend one's way** dirigere i propri passi

werewolf ['wɪr,wʊlf] s lupo mannaro

west [west] adj occidentale || s ovest m, occidente m || adv verso l'ovest

western ['westərn] adj occidentale || s western m

West' In'dies ['ɪndɪz] spl Indie fpl Occidentali

westward ['westwərd] adv verso l'ovest

wet [wet] adj (wetter; wettest) bagnato; (paint) fresco; (damp) umido; (rainy) piovoso; che permette la vendita delle bevande alcoliche || s umidità f; antiproibizionista mf || v (pret & pp wet or wetted; ger wetting) tr bagnare || intr bagnarsi

wet' blan'ket s guastafeste mf

wether ['weðər] s castrone m

wet' nurse' s nutrice f, balia

whack [hwæk] s (slang) colpo, percossa; (slang) prova, tentativo || tr (slang) percuotere

whale [hwel] s balena; **a whale of** (slang) gigantesco, e.g., **a whale of a lie** una bugia gigantesca; enorme, e.g., **a whale of a difference** una differenza enorme || tr (coll) battere || intr pescare balene

whale'bone' s osso di balena, fanone m

wharf [hwɔrf] s (wharves [hwɔrvz] or wharfs) molo

what [hwɑt] adj interr che; quale ‖ adj rel quello . . . che; il . . . che, e.g., wear what tie you prefer mettiti la cravatta che preferisci ‖ pron interr che; quale; what else? che altro?; what if . . . ? e se . . . ?; what of it? e che me ne importa? ‖ pron rel quello che; what's what (coll) tutta la situazione ‖ interj what a . . . ! che . . . !, e.g., what a beautiful day! che splendida giornata!

what·ev'er adj qualsiasi; qualunque ‖ pron quanto; che; quello che

what'not' s scaffaletto

wheal [hwil] s vescichetta

wheat [hwit] s grano, frumento

wheedle ['hwidəl] tr adulare; persuadere con lusinghe; (money) spillare

wheel [hwil] s ruota; (of cheese) forma; (coll) bicicletta; at the wheel al volante; in controllo ‖ tr roteare; portare in carrozzella ‖ intr girare

wheelbarrow ['hwil ˌbæro] s carriola

wheel'base' s passo

wheel'chair' s carrozzella

wheel' col'umn s (aut) piantone m di guida

wheeler-dealer ['hwilər'dilər] s (slang) grande affarista m

wheel' horse' s cavallo di timone; lavoratore m di fiducia

wheelwright ['hwil ˌrait] s carradore m

wheeze [hwiz] s affanno; (pathol) rantolo ‖ intr respirare affannosamente; (pathol) rantolare

whelp [hwelp] s cucciolo ‖ tr & intr figliare, partorire

when [hwen] adv & conj quando

whence [hwens] adv donde, di dove ‖ conj donde; per che ragione

when·ev'er conj ogniqualvolta, qualora

where [hwer] adv & conj dove

whereabouts ['hwera ˌbauts] s luogo dove uno si trova ‖ adv & conj dove

whereas [hwer'æz] conj mentre; visto che, considerato che

where·by' adv per cui, col quale

wherever [hwer'evər] adv dove mai ‖ conj dovunque

wherefore ['hwerfor] s perché m ‖ adv perché ‖ conj per cui, percome

where·from' adv donde

where·in' adv dove; in che modo ‖ conj dove; nel quale

where·of' adv di che ‖ conj di che; del quale

where·upon' adv sul che; laonde, dopodiché

wherewithal ['hwerwɪð ˌɔl] s mezzi mpl

whet [hwet] v (pret & pp whetted; ger whetting) tr affilare; (the appetite) aguzzare

whether ['weðər] conj se; whether or no ad ogni modo, in ogni caso; whether or not che . . . o che non

whet'stone' s pietra da affilare

whey [hwe] s scotta

which [hwitʃ] adj interr quale ‖ adj rel il (la, etc.) quale ‖ pron interr che; quale; which is which qual'è

l'uno e qual'è l'altro ‖ pron rel che; il quale; quello che

which·ev'er adj & pron rel qualunque

whiff [hwif] s (of air) soffio; fiutata; (trace of odor) zaffata; to get a whiff of sentire l'odore di ‖ intr soffiare; (said of a smoker) dare boccate

while [hwail] s tempo; a long while un bel pezzo; a while ago un tratto fa; to be worth one's while valere la pena ‖ conj mentre ‖ tr—to while away passare piacevolmente

whim [hwim] s capriccio, estro

whimper ['hwimpər] s piagnucolio ‖ tr & intr piagnucolare

whimsical ['hwimzikəl] adj capriccioso, estroso, stravagante

whine [hwain] s (of dog) guaito; (of person) piagnucolio ‖ intr (said of a dog) guaire, uggiolare; (said of a person) piagnucolare

whin·ny ['hwini] s (-nies) nitrito ‖ v (pret & pp -nied) intr nitrire

whip [hwip] s frusta; uova fpl sbattute con frutta ‖ v (pret & pp whipped or whipt; ger whipping) tr frustare, battere; (eggs) frullare; (coll) vincere, sconfiggere; to whip off (coll) buttar giù; to whip out tirar fuori rapidamente; to whip up (coll) preparare in quattro e quattr'otto; (coll) eccitare, incitare

whip'cord' s cordino della frusta; (fabric) saia a diagonale

whip' hand' s mano che tiene la frusta; vantaggio, posizione vantaggiosa

whip'lash' s scudisciata

whipped' cream' s panna montata

whipper-snapper ['hwipər ˌsnæpər] s pivello

whippet ['hwipit] s piccolo levriere

whip'ping boy' ['hwipiŋ] s testa di turco

whip'ping post' s palo per la fustigazione

whippoorwill [ˌhwipər'wil] s caprimulgo, succiacapre m

whir [hwʌr] s ronzio ‖ v (pret & pp whirred; ger whirring) intr ronzare; volare ronzando

whirl [hwʌrl] s giro improvviso; corsa; mulinello; (fig) successione ‖ tr & intr mulinare; my head whirls mi gira la testa

whirligig ['hwʌrli ˌgig] s turbine m; (carrousel) giostra; (toy) girandola; (ent) ragno d'acqua

whirl'pool' s risucchio, mulinello

whirl'wind' s turbine m, tromba d'aria

whirlybird ['hwʌrli ˌbʌrd] s (coll) elicottero

whish [hwiʃ] s fruscio ‖ intr frusciare

whisk [hwisk] s scopatina ‖ tr scopare, spolverare; (eggs) sbattere; to whisk out of sight far sparire ‖ intr guizzare

whisk' broom' s scopetta per i vestiti, spolverino

whiskers ['hwiskərz] spl barba; (on side of man's face) basette fpl; (of cat) baffi mpl

whiskey ['hwiski] s whisky m

whisper ['hwɪspər] s sussurro, bisbiglio, mormorio; **in a whisper** in un sussurro || tr & intr sussurrare, bisbigliare, mormorare

whisperer ['hwɪspərər] s sussurrone m

whispering ['hwɪspərɪŋ] adj di maldicenze || s sussurrio; maldicenza

whistle ['hwɪsəl] s fischio; **to wet one's whistle** (coll) bagnarsi l'ugola || tr fischiare || intr fischiare, zufolare; **to whistle for** chiamare con un fischio; (money) aspettare in vano

whis'tle stop' s stazioncina, paesetto

whit [hwɪt] s—**not a whit** niente affatto

white [hwaɪt] adj bianco || s bianco; **whites** (pathol) leucorrea

white'cap' s frangente m, cavallone m, onda crespa

white' coal' s carbone bianco

white'-col'lar adj impiegatizio

white' feath'er s—**to show the white feather** mostrarsi vile

white' goods' spl biancheria da casa; articoli mpl di cotone; apparecchi mpl elettrodomestici

white-haired ['hwaɪt,herd] adj dai capelli bianchi; (coll) favorito

white' heat' s calor bianco

white' lead' [led] s biacca

white' lie' s bugia innocente

white' meat' s bianco, carne f del petto

whiten ['hwaɪtən] tr imbiancare, sbiancare || intr imbiancarsi, sbiancarsi; impallidire

whiteness ['hwaɪtnɪs] s bianchezza

white' plague' s tubercolosi f

white' slav'ery s tratta delle bianche

white' tie' s cravatta da frac; marsina, abito da cerimonia

white'wash' s imbiancatura; (fig) copertura || tr imbiancare, intonacare; (fig) coprire

white' wa'ter lil'y s ninfea

whither ['hwɪθər] adv dove, a che luogo || conj dove

whiting ['hwaɪtɪŋ] s (ichth) nasello; (ichth) merlango

whitish ['hwaɪtɪʃ] adj biancastro

whitlow ['hwɪtlo] s patereccio

Whitsuntide ['hwɪtsən,taɪd] s settimana di Pentecoste

whittle ['hwɪtəl] tr digrossare; **to whittle away or down** ridurre gradualmente

whiz or whizz [hwɪz] s sibilo; (coll) asso || v (pret & pp whizzed; ger whizzing) intr—**to whiz by** passare sibilando; passare come una freccia

who [hu] pron interr chi; **who else?** chi altri?; **who goes there?** (mil) chi va là?; **who's who** chi è l'uno e chi è l'altro; **chi è la gente importante** || pron rel chi; il quale

whoa [hwo] or [wo] interj fermo!

who·ev'er pron rel chiunque

whole [hol] adj tutto, intero; sano, intatto; **made out of the whole cloth** completamente immaginario || s tutto; **as a whole** nell'insieme; **on the whole** in generale

wholehearted ['hol,hɑrtɪd] adj molto sincero, generoso

whole' note' s (mus) semibreve f

whole'sale' adj & adv all'ingrosso || s ingrosso || tr vendere all'ingrosso || intr vendersi all'ingrosso

wholesaler ['hol,selər] s grossista mf

wholesome ['holsəm] adj (beneficial) salutare; (in good health) sano

wholly ['holɪ] adv interamente

whom [hum] pron interr chi || pron rel che; il quale

whom·ev'er pron rel chiunque

whoop [hup] or [hwup] s urlo; (pathol) urlo della pertosse; **to not be worth a whoop** (coll) non valere un fico secco || tr—**to whoop it up** (slang) fare il diavolo a quattro || intr urlare

whoop'ing cough' ['hupɪŋ] or ['hwupɪŋ] s pertosse f

whopper ['hwɑpər] s (coll) enormità f; (coll) fandonia, bugia enorme

whopping ['hwɑpɪŋ] adj (coll) enorme

whore [hor] s puttana || intr—**to whore around** puttaneggiare; andare a puttane

whortleber·ry ['hwʌrtəl,beri] s (-ries) mirtillo

whose [huz] pron interr di chi || pron rel di chi; del quale; di cui

why [hwaɪ] s (whys) perché m; **the whys and the wherefores** il perché e il percome || adv perché || interj diamine!; **why, certainly!** certamente!; **why, yes!** evidentemente!

wick [wɪk] s stoppino, lucignolo

wicked ['wɪkɪd] adj malvagio; (mischievous) cattivo; (dreadful) terribile, bestiale

wicker ['wɪkər] adj di vimini || s vimine m

wicket ['wɪkɪt] s (small door) portello; (ticket window) sportello; (of a canal) chiusa; (cricket) porta; (croquet) archetto

wide [waɪd] adj largo; esteso; (eyes) aperto; (sense of a word) lato || adv largamente; completamente; lontano; **wide of the mark** lontano dal bersaglio

wide'-an'gle adj grandangolare

wide'-awake' adj sveglio

widen ['waɪdən] tr slargare, estendere || intr slargarsi, estendersi

wide'-o'pen adj spalancato; (to a gambler) accessibile

wide'-spread' adj (e.g., arms) aperto; diffuso

widow ['wɪdo] s vedova; (cards) morto || tr lasciar vedova

widower ['wɪdo·ər] s vedovo

widowhood ['wɪdo,hud] s vedovanza

wid'ow's mite' s obolo della vedova

wid'ow's weeds' spl gramaglie fpl vedovili

width [wɪdθ] s larghezza

wield [wild] tr (e.g., a sword) brandire; (e.g., a hammer) maneggiare; (power) esercitare

wife [waɪf] s (wives [waɪvz]) moglie f

wig [wɪg] s parrucca

wiggle ['wɪgəl] s dimenio; (of fish)

guizzo || *tr* dimenare || *intr* dimenarsi; guizzare

wig′wag′ *s* segnalazione con bandierine || *v* (*pret* & *pp* -**wagged**; *ger* -**wagging**) *tr* & *intr* segnalare con bandierine

wigwam [′wɪgwɑm] *s* tenda a cupola dei pellirosse, wigwam *m*

wild [waɪld] *adj* (*animal*) feroce; (*e.g.*, *berry*) selvatico; (*barbarous*) selvaggio; (*violent*) furioso; (*mad*) pazzo; (*unruly*) discolo, indisciplinato; (*extravagant*) pazzesco; (*shot or throw*) lanciato all'impazzata; **wild about** pazzo per || *s* regione deserta; **the wild** la foresta; **wilds** regioni selvagge || *adv* pazzamente; **to go wild** andare in delirio; **to run wild** crescere all'impazzata; correre senza freno

wild′ boar′ *s* cinghiale *m*

wild′ card′ *s* matta

wild′cat′ *s* gatto selvatico; lince *f*; impresa arrischiata || *v* (*pret* & *pp* -**catted**) *ger* -**catting**) *tr* & *intr* esplorare per conto proprio

wild′cat strike′ *s* sciopero non autorizzato dal sindacato

wilderness [′wɪldərnɪs] *s* deserto

wild-eyed [′waɪld ,aɪd] *adj* stralunato; (*scheme*) pazzesco

wild′fire′ *s* fuoco greco; fuoco fatuo; **to spread like wildfire** crescere come la gramigna; (*said of news*) spargersi come il baleno

wild′ flow′er *s* fiore *m* di campo

wild′ goose′ *s* oca selvatica

wild′-goose′ chase′ *s* ricerca della luna nel pozzo

wild′life′ *s* animali *spl* selvatici

wild′ oat′ *s* avena selvatica; **to sow one's wild oats** correre la cavallina

wild′ ol′ive *s* olivastro, oleastro

wile [waɪl] *s* stratagemma *m*, inganno; (*cunning*) astuzia || *tr* allettare; **to wile away** passare piacevolmente

will [wɪl] *s* volontà *f*, volere *m*; (*law*) testamento; **at will** a volontà || *tr* volere; (*law*) legare || *intr* volere; **do as you will** faccia come vuole || *v* (*pret* & *cond* **would**) *aux* **she will leave tomorrow** partirà domani; **a cactus plant will live two months without water** una pianta grassa può vivere due mesi senz'acqua

willful [′wɪlfəl] *adj* volontario; ostinato

willfulness [′wɪlfəlnɪs] *s* volontarietà *f*; ostinatezza

William [′wɪljəm] *s* Guglielmo

willing [′wɪlɪŋ] *adj* volonteroso; **to be willing** essere disposto

willingly [′wɪlɪŋli] *adv* di buon grado, volentieri

willingness [′wɪlɪŋnɪs] *s* buona voglia, propensione

will-o′-the-wisp [′wɪləðə′wɪsp] *s* fuoco fatuo; (fig) illusione, chimera

willow [′wɪlo] *s* salice *m*

willowy [′wɪlo·i] *adj* pieghevole; (*slender*) snello; pieno di giunchi

will′ pow′er *s* forza di volontà

willy-nilly [′wɪli′nɪli] *adv* volente o nolente

wilt [wɪlt] *tr* far appassire || *intr* appassire, avvizzire

wil·y [′waɪli] *adj* (-**ier**; -**iest**) astuto, scaltro

wimple [′wɪmpəl] *s* soggolo

win [wɪn] *s* vittoria, vincita || *v* (*pret* & *pp* **won** [wʌn]; *ger* **winning**) *tr* & *intr* guadagnare; **to win out** vincere, aver successo

wince [wɪns] *s* sussulto || *intr* sussultare

winch [wɪntʃ] *s* verricello; (*handle*) manovella; (naut) molinello

wind [wɪnd] *s* vento; (*gas in intestines*) vento; (*breath*) fiato, tenuta; **to break wind** scoreggiare; **to get wind of** subodorare; **to sail close to the wind** (naut) andare all'orza; **to take the wind out of the sails of** sconcertare; **winds** (mus) fiati *mpl* || *tr* far perdere il fiato a || [waɪnd] *v* (*pret* & *pp* **wound** [waʊnd]) *tr* (*to wrap up*) arrotolare; (*thread*, *wool*) dipanare, aggomitolare; (*a clock*) caricare; (*a handle*) far girare; **to wind one's way through** serpeggiare per; **to wind up** arrotolare; eccitare; finire, portare a termine || *intr* serpeggiare, snodarsi

windbag [′wɪnd ,bæg] *s* (*of a bagpipe*) otre *m*; (fig) parolaio, otre *m* di vento

windbreak [′wɪnd ,brek] *s* frangivento

wind′ cone′ [wɪnd] *s* manica a vento

winded [′wɪndɪd] *adj* senza fiato

windfall [′wɪnd ,fɔl] *s* frutta abbattuta dal vento; provvidenza, manna del cielo

wind′ing sheet′ [′waɪndɪŋ] *s* lenzuolo funebre

wind′ing stairs′ [′waɪndɪŋ] *spl* scala a chiocciola

wind′ in′strument [wɪnd] *s* (mus) strumento a fiato

windlass [′wɪndləs] *s* verricello

windmill [′wɪnd ,mɪl] *s* mulino a vento; (*air turbine*) aeromotore *m*; **to tilt at windmills** combattere i mulini a vento

window [′wɪndo] *s* finestra; (*of ticket office*) sportello; (*of car or coach*) finestrino

win′dow dress′er *s* vetrinista *mf*

win′dow dress′ing *s* vetrinistica; (fig) facciata, apparenza

win′dow en′velope *s* busta a finestrella

win′dow frame′ *s* intelaiatura della finestra

win′dow-pane′ *s* vetro, invetriata

win′dow sash′ *s* intelaiatura della finestra

win′dow screen′ *s* zanzariera

win′dow shade′ *s* tendina avvolgibile

win′dow-shop′ *v* (*pret* & *pp* -**shopped**; *ger* -**shopping**) *intr* guardare nelle vetrine senza comprare

win′dow sill′ *s* davanzale *m* della finestra

windpipe [′wɪnd ,paɪp] *s* trachea

windproof [′wɪnd ,pruf] *adj* resistente al vento

windshield [′wɪnd ,ʃild] *s* parabrezza *m*

wind′shield wash′er *s* lavacristallo

wind'shield wip'er s tergicristallo

windsock ['wɪnd ,sɑk] s (aer) manica a vento

windstorm ['wɪnd ,stɔrm] s bufera di vento

wind' tun'nel [wɪnd] s (aer) galleria aerodinamica

wind-up ['waɪnd ,ʌp] s conclusione

windward ['wɪndwərd] s orza, soprav-vento; to turn to windward mettersi al sopravvento

Wind'ward Is'lands spl Isole fpl So-pravvento

wind·y ['wɪndi] adj (-ier; -iest) ven-toso; verboso, ampolloso; it is windy fa vento

wine [waɪn] s vino || tr offrire vino a || intr bere del vino

wine' cel'lar s cantina

wine'glass' s bicchiere da vino

winegrower ['waɪn ,groʊ·ər] s vinifica-tore m, viticoltore m

wine' press' s torchio per l'uva

winer·y ['waɪnəri] s (-ies) stabilimento vinicolo

wine'shop' s fiaschetteria

wine'skin' s otre m

wine' stew'ard s sommelier m

winetaster ['waɪn ,testər] s degustatore m di vini

wing [wɪŋ] s ala; (unit of air force) aerobrigata; (theat) quinta; to take wing levarsi a volo; under one's wing sotto la protezione di qlcu. || tr ferire nell'ala; to wing one's way volare, portarsi a volo

wing' chair' s poltrona a orecchioni

wing' col'lar s colletto per marsina

wing' nut' s (mach) galletto

wing'span' s (of airplane) apertura alare

wing'spread' s (of bird) apertura alare

wink [wɪŋk] s ammicco; in a wink in un batter d'occhio; to not sleep a wink non chiudere occhio; to take forty winks (coll) schiacciare un pi-solino || tr (the eye) strizzare || intr ammiccare, strizzare l'occhio; (to blink) battere le ciglia; to wink at ammiccare a; far finta di non vedere

winner ['wɪnər] s vincitore m

winning ['wɪnɪŋ] adj vincente, vinci-tore; attraente, simpatico || winnings spl vincita

winnow ['wɪno] tr ventilare, brezzare; (fig) vagliare || intr svolazzare

winsome ['wɪnsəm] adj attraente

winter ['wɪntər] adj invernale || s in-verno || intr svernare

win'ter-green' s tè m del Canadà; olio di gaulteria

win·try ['wɪntri] adj (-trier; -triest) invernale; freddo

wipe [waɪp] tr forbire, detergere; (to dry) asciugare; to wipe away (tears) asciugare; to wipe off pulire, forbire; to wipe out distruggere completa-mente; (coll) eliminare

wiper ['waɪpər] s strofinaccio; (mach) camma; (elec) contatto scorrevole

wire [waɪr] s filo metallico; tele-gramma m; (coll) telegrafo; to pull wires manovrare di dietro le quinte

|| tr legare con filo metallico; attrez-zare l'elettricità in; (coll) mandare per telegrafo; (coll) telegrafare || intr (coll) telegrafare

wire' cut'ter s pinza tagliafili

wire' entan'glement s reticolato di filo spinato

wire' gauge' s calibro da fili

wire-haired ['waɪr ,herd] adj a pelo ruvido

wireless ['waɪrlɪs] adj senza fili || s telegrafo senza fili; telegrafia senza fili

wire' nail' s chiodo da falegname

wirepulling ['waɪr ,pʊlɪŋ] s manovra dietro alle quinte

wire' record'er s magnetofono a filo

wire' screen' s rete metallica

wire'tap' v (pret & pp -tapped; ger -tapping) tr (a conversation) inter-cettare

wiring ['waɪrɪŋ] s sistema m di fili elettrici

wir·y ['waɪri] adj (-ier; -iest) fatto di filo; (hair) ispido; (tone) metallico, vibrante; (sinewy) segaligno

wisdom ['wɪzdəm] s senno, sapienza, saggezza

wis'dom tooth' s dente m del giudizio

wise [waɪz] adj saggio, sapiente; (deci-sion) giudizioso; to be wise to (slang) accorgersi del gioco di; to get wise (slang) mangiare la foglia; (slang) diventare impertinente || s modo, maniera; in no wise in nessun modo || tr—to wise up (slang) avvertire || intr—to wise up (slang) accorgersi

wiseacre ['waɪz ,ekər] s sapientone m

wise'crack' s (coll) spiritosaggine f || intr (coll) dire spiritosaggini

wise' guy' s (slang) sputasentenze m

wish [wɪʃ] s desiderio; augurio; to make a wish formulare un desiderio || tr desiderare; augurare; to wish s.o. a good day dare il buon giorno a qlcu || intr desiderare; to wish for desiderare

wish'bone' s forcella

wishful ['wɪʃfəl] adj desideroso

wish'ful think'ing s pio desiderio

wistful ['wɪstfəl] adj melanconico, pensoso, meditabondo

wit [wɪt] s spirito; (person) bellospi-rito; (understanding) senso; to be at one's wits' end non sapere a che santo votarsi; to have one's wits about one avere presenza di spirito; to live by one's wits vivere di espe-dienti

witch [wɪtʃ] s strega

witch'craft' s stregoneria

witch' doc'tor s stregone m

witch'es' Sab'bath s sabba m

witch' ha'zel s (shrub) amamelide f; (liquid) estratto di amamelide

witch' hunt' s caccia alle streghe

with [wɪð] or [wɪθ] prep con; a, e.g., with open arms a braccia aperte; di, e.g., covered with silk coperto di seta; to be satisfied with the per-formance essere contento della rap-presentazione; da, e.g., with the In-

dians dagli indiani; **to part with** separarsi da

with·draw' v (pret **-drew;** pp **-drawn**) tr ritirare || intr ritirarsi

withdrawal [wɪðˈdrɔ·əl] or [wɪθˈdrɔ·əl] s ritiro, ritirata; (of funds) prelevamento

wither [ˈwɪðər] tr intisichire; (with a glance) incenerire || intr avvizzire, intisichire

with·hold' v (pret & pp **-held**) tr trattenere; (information) sottacere; (payment) defalcare; (permission) negare

withhold'ing tax' s imposta trattenuta

with·in' adv dentro, didentro || prep entro, entro di, dentro a, dentro di; fra; in; (a time period) nel giro di

with·out' adv fuori || prep senza; fuori, fuori di; to do without fare a meno di; without + ger senza + inf, e.g., without saying a word senza dire una parola; senza che + subj, e.g., she fell without anyone helping her cadde senza che nessuno l'aiutasse

with·stand' v (pret & pp **-stood**) tr resistere (with dat), reggere (with dat)

witness [ˈwɪtnɪs] s testimone mf; in witness whereof in fé di che; to bear witness far fede || tr (to be present at) presenziare; (to attest) testimoniare, firmare come testimone

wit'ness stand' s banco dei testimoni

witticism [ˈwɪtɪˌsɪzəm] s motto, battuta spiritosa, spiritosaggine f

wittingly [ˈwɪtɪŋlɪ] adv consapevolmente

wit·ty [ˈwɪtɪ] adj (**-tier; -tiest**) spiritoso, divertente

wizard [ˈwɪzərd] s mago

wizardry [ˈwɪzərdrɪ] s magia

wizened [ˈwɪzənd] adj raggrinzito

woad [wod] s (bot) guado

wobble [ˈwɑbəl] s oscillazione, dondolio || intr oscillare, dondolare; (said of a chair) zoppicare; (fig) titubare

wob·bly [ˈwɑblɪ] adj (**-blier; -bliest**) oscillante, zoppo, malfermo

woe [wo] s disgrazia, afflizione, sventura; || interj—**woe is me!** ahimè!

woebegone [ˈwobɪˌgɔn] or [ˈwobɪˌgɑn] adj triste, abbattuto

woeful [ˈwofəl] adj sfortunato, disgraziato; (of poor quality) orribile

wolf [wulf] s (wolves [wulvz]) lupo; (coll) dongiovanni m; **to cry wolf** gridare al lupo; **to keep the wolf from the door** tener lontana la miseria || tr & intr mangiare come un lupo

wolf'hound' s cane m da pastore alsaziano

wolfram [ˈwulfrəm] s wolframio

wolf's-bane or **wolfsbane** [ˈwulfsˌben] s (bot) aconito

wolverine [ˌwulvəˈrin] s (zool) ghiottone m

woman [ˈwumən] s (women [ˈwɪmɪn]) donna

womanhood [ˈwumənˌhud] s (quality) femminilità f; (women collectively) donne fpl, sesso femminile

womanish [ˈwumənɪʃ] adj femminile; (effeminate) effeminato

wom'an·kind' s sesso femminile

woman·ly [ˈwumənlɪ] adj (**-lier; -liest**) femminile, muliebre

wom'an suf'frage s suffragio alle donne

woman-suffragist [ˈwumənˈsʌfrədʒɪst] s suffragista mf

womb [wum] s utero; (fig) seno

womenfolk [ˈwɪmɪnˌfok] spl le donne

wonder [ˈwʌndər] s (something strange and surprising) meraviglia; (feeling) ammirazione; (miracle) prodigio, miracolo; **for a wonder** cosa strana; **no wonder that** non fa meraviglia che; **to work wonders** fare miracoli || tr—to wonder that meravigliarsi che; **to wonder how, if, when, where, who, why** domandarsi o chiedersi come, se, quando, dove, chi, perché || intr meravigliarsi; chiedersi; **to wonder at** ammirare

won'der drug' s medicina miracolosa

wonderful [ˈwʌndərfəl] adj meraviglioso

won'der·land' s paese m delle meraviglie

wonderment [ˈwʌndərmənt] s sorpresa, meraviglia, stupore m

won'der-work'er s taumaturgo

wont [wʌnt] or [wɔnt] adj abituato, solito || s abitudine f, costume m

wonted [ˈwʌntɪd] or [ˈwɔntɪd] adj solito, abituale

woo [wu] tr (a woman) corteggiare; (to seek to win) allettare; (good or bad consequences) andare in cerca di

wood [wud] s legno; (firewood) legna; (keg) barile m; **out of the woods** fuori pericolo; al sicuro; **woods** bosco, selva

woodbine [ˈwudˌbaɪn] s (honeysuckle) abbracciabosco; (Virginia creeper) vite f del Canadà

wood' carv'ing s intaglio in legno, statua in legno

wood'chuck' s marmotta americana

wood'cock' s beccaccia

wood'cut' s silografia

wood'cut'ter s boscaiolo

wooded [ˈwudɪd] adj legnoso, boschivo

wooden [ˈwudən] adj di legno; duro, rigido; inespressivo

wood' engrav'ing s silografia

wooden-headed [ˈwudənˌhɛdɪd] adj (coll) dalla testa dura

wood'en leg' s gamba di legno

wood'en shoe' s zoccolo

wood' grouse' s gallo cedrone

woodland [ˈwudlənd] adj boschivo || s foresta, bosco

wood'man s (**-men**) boscaiolo

woodpecker [ˈwudˌpɛkər] s picchio

wood'pile' s legnaia

wood' screw' s vite f per legno

wood'shed' s legnaia

woods'man s (**-men**) abitatore m dei boschi; boscaiolo

wood'wind' s strumento a fiato di legno

wood'work' s lavoro in legno; parti fpl di legno

wood'work'er s ebanista m, falegname m

wood'worm' s tarlo

wood·y ['wʊdi] *adj* (**-ier; -iest**) boscoso, alberato; (*like wood*) legnoso
wooer ['wu-ər] *s* corteggiatore *m*
woof [wʊf] *s* (*yarns running across warp*) trama; (*fabric*) tessuto
woofer ['wʊfər] *s* altoparlante *m* per basse audiofrequenze, woofer *m*
wool [wʊl] *s* lana
woolen ['wʊlən] *adj* di lana || *s* tessuto di lana; **woolens** laneria
woolgrower ['wʊl‚groʊ-ər] *s* allevatore *m* di pecore
wool·ly ['wʊli] *adj* (**-ier; -iest**) (di lana; lanoso; (coll) confuso
word [wʌrd] *s* parola; **by word of mouth** oralmente; **to be as good as one's word** essere di parola; **to have a word with** dire quattro parole a; **to have word from** aver notizie da; **to keep one's word** essere di parola; **to leave word** lasciar detto; **to send word** that mandare a dire che; **words** (*quarrel*) baruffa || *tr* esprimere, formulare || **Word** *s* (theol) Verbo
word' count' *s* conto lessicale
word' forma'tion *s* formazione delle parole
wording ['wʌrdɪŋ] *s* fraseologia, dicitura
word' or'der *s* disposizione delle parole in una frase
word' stock' *s* lessico
word·y ['wʌrdi] *adj* (**-ier; -iest**) verboso, paroláio
work [wʌrk] *s* lavoro; (*of art, fortification, etc.*) opera; **at work** al lavoro, in ufficio; (*in operation*) in servizio; **out of work** senza lavoro, disoccupato; **to give s.o. the works** (slang) trattare male; (slang) ammazzare; **to shoot the works** (slang) scialare; **works** opificio; meccanismo; (*of clock*) castello || *tr* far funzionare; lavorare, maneggiare; (*e.g., a miracle*) operare; (*e.g., iron*) trattare; **to work up** preparare; stimulare, eccitare || *intr* lavorare; (*said of a machine*) funzionare; (*said of a remedy*) avere effetto; **to work loose** sciogliersi; **to work out** andare a finire; (*said of a problem*) sciogliersi; (*said of a total*) ammontare; (sports) allenarsi
workable ['wʌrkəbəl] *adj* (*feasible*) praticabile; (*e.g., iron*) lavorabile
work'bench' *s* banco
work'book' *s* manuale *m* d'istruzioni; (*for students*) quaderno d'esercizi
work'box' *s* cassetta dei ferri del mestiere; (*for needlework*) cestino da lavoro
work'day' *adj* lavorativo; ordinario, di tutti i giorni || *s* (*working day*) giorno feriale, giornata lavorativa
worked-up ['wʌrkt‚ʌp] *adj* sovreccitato
worker ['wʌrkər] *s* lavorante *m*, lavoratore *m*, operaio
work' force' *s* mano *f* d'opera
work'horse' *s* cavallo da tiro; (*tireless worker*) lavoratore indefesso
work'house' *s* carcere *m* con lavoro obbligatorio; (Brit) istituto dei poveri
work'ing class' *s* classe operaia

work'ing condi'tions *spl* trattamento, condizioni *fpl* di lavoro
work'ing girl' *s* ragazza lavoratrice
work'ing hours' *spl* orario di lavoro
working'man *s* (**-men**) lavoratore *m*
work'ing or'der *s* buone condizioni, efficienza
work'ing·wom'an *s* (**-wom'en**) operaia, lavoratrice *f*
work'man *s* (**-men**) lavoratore *m;* (*skilled worker*) operaio specializzato
workmanship ['wʌrkmən‚ʃɪp] *s* fattura; (*work executed*) opera
work' of art' *s* opera d'arte
work'out' *s* (sports) esercizio, allenamento
work'room' *s* (*for manual work*) officina; (*study*) gabinetto, laboratorio
work'shop' *s* officina
work' stop'page *s* sospensione del lavoro
world [wʌrld] *adj* mondiale || *s* mondo; **a world of** un monte di; **for all the world** per tutto l'oro del mondo; **in the world** al mondo; **since the world began** da che mondo è mondo; **the other world** l'altro mondo; **to bring into the world** mettere al mondo; **to see the world** conoscere il mondo; **to think the world of** tenere in altissima considerazione
world' affairs' *spl* relazioni *fpl* internazionali
world·ly ['wʌrldli] *adj* (**-ier; -iest**) mondano, secolare
world'ly-wise' *adj* vissuto
world's' fair' *s* esposizione *f* mondiale
world' war' *s* guerra mondiale
world'-wide' *adj* mondiale
worm [wʌrm] *s* verme *m* || *tr* liberare dai vermi; **to worm a secret out of s.o.** carpire un segreto a qlcu; **to worm one's way into** insinuarsi in
worm-eaten ['wʌrm‚itən] *adj* tarlato, bacato
worm' gear' *s* meccanismo a vite perpetua, ingranaggio elicoidale
worm'wood' *s* assenzio; (fig) amarezza
worm·y ['wʌrmi] *adj* (**-ier; -iest**) verminoso; (*worm-eaten*) bacato; (*groveling*) vile, strasciacante
worn [wʌrn] *adj* usato; (*look*) stanco, esausto
worn'-out' *adj* logoro, scalcinato; (*by illness*) consunto; (fig) trito
worrisome ['wʌrisəm] *adj* preoccupante; (*inclined to worry*) preoccupato
wor·ry ['wʌri] *s* (**-ries**) preoccupazione, inquietudine *f;* (*trouble*) fastidio || *v* (*pret & pp* **-ried**) *tr* preoccupare, inquietare; **to be worried** essere impensierito || *intr* preoccuparsi, inquietarsi; **don't worry!** non si preoccupi!
worse [wʌrs] *adj & s* peggiore *m*, peggio || *adv* peggio; **worse and worse** di male in peggio
worsen ['wʌrsən] *tr & intr* peggiorare
wor·ship ['wʌrʃɪp] *s* venerazione, adorazione; servizio religioso; **your Worship** La Signoria Vostra || *v* (*pret &*

pp **-shiped** or **-shipped; ger -shiping** or **-shipping** *tr* venerare, adorare

worshiper or **worshipper** ['wʌrʃɪpər] *s* adoratore *m; (in church)* devoto, fedele *m*

worst [wʌrst] *adj* (il) peggiore; pessimo ‖ *s* peggio, peggiore *m; at* worst alla peggio; if worst comes to worst alla peggio; to get the worst averne la peggio ‖ *adv* peggio

worsted ['wustɪd] *adj* di lana pettinata ‖ *s* tessuto di lana pettinata

wort [wʌrt] *s* mosto di malto; pianta, erba

worth [wʌrθ] *adj* che vale, da, e.g., worth ten dollars da dieci dollari; to be worth valere; essere di pregio; to be worth + ger valere la pena (di) + inf, e.g., it is worth reading vale la pena (di) leggerlo ‖ *s* pregio, valore *m; a dollar's worth* un dollaro di

worthless ['wʌrθlɪs] *adj* senza valore; inutile; inservibile; *(person)* indegno

worth'while' *adj* meritevole, meritevole d'attenzione

wor·thy ['wʌrði] *adj* (-thier; -thiest) degno, meritevole ‖ *s* (-thies) maggiorente *mf*

would [wud] *v aux* they said they would come dissero che sarebbero venuti; he would buy it if he had the money lo comprerebbe se avesse i soldi; would you be so kind to avrebbe la cortesia di; he would spend every winter in Florida passava tutti gli inverni in Florida; would that . . . ! oh se . . . !, volesse il cielo che . . . !, magari . . . !

would'-be' *adj* preteso, sedicente; *(intended to be)* inteso

wound [wund] *s* ferita ‖ *tr* ferire

wounded ['wundɪd] *adj* ferito ‖ the wounded i feriti

wow [wau] *s* distorsione acustica di suono riprodotto; *(slang)* successone *m* ‖ *tr* (slang) entusiasmare ‖ *interj* (coll) accidenti

wrack [ræk] *s* naufragio; vestigio; *(seaweed)* alghe marine gettate sulla spiaggia; to go to wrack and ruin andare completamente in rovina

wraith [reθ] *s* spettro, fantasma *m*

wrangle ['ræŋɡəl] *s* baruffa, alterco ‖ *intr* altercare, rissare

wrap [ræp] *s* sciarpa; mantello ‖ *v* (pret & pp wrapped; ger wrapping) *tr* involgere; impaccare; to be wrapped up in essere assorto in; to wrap up avvolgere; *(in paper)* incartare; *(in clothing)* imbacuccare; (coll) concludere ‖ *intr*—to wrap up imbacuccarsi, avvolgersi

wrapper ['ræpər] *s* veste *f* da camera, peignoir *m; (of newspaper)* fascia, fascetta; *(of cigars)* involto

wrap'ping pa'per ['ræpɪŋ] *s* carta d'impacco d'imballaggio

wrath [ræθ] or [rɑθ] *s* ira; vendetta

wrathful ['ræθfəl] or ['rɑθfəl] *adj* collerico, iracondo

wreak [rik] *tr* (vengeance) infliggere; (anger) scaricare

wreath [riθ] *s* (wreaths [riðz]) ghirlanda; *(of laurel)* laurea; *(of smoke)* spirale *f*

wreathe [rið] *tr* inghirlandare; avviluppare; *(a garland)* intessere ‖ *intr* (said of smoke) innalzarsi in spire

wreck [rek] *s* rottame *m*, relitto; naufragio; rovina; catastrofe *f*, disastro; (fig) rottame *m*, relitto ‖ *tr* far naufragare; distruggere, rovinare; *(a train)* fare scontrare, fare deragliare; *(a building)* demolire

wreckage ['rekɪdʒ] *s* rottami *mpl*, relitti *mpl*; rovine *fpl*

wrecker ['rekər] *s* (tow truck) autogrù *f; (housewrecker)* demolitore *m*

wreck'ing ball' *s* martello demolitore

wreck'ing car' *s* autogrù *f*

wrecking' crane' *s* (rr) carro gru

wren [ren] *s* scricciolo

wrench [rentʃ] *s* chiave *f; (pull)* tiro; *(of a joint)* distorsione ‖ *tr* torcere, distorcere; *(one's limb)* torcersi, distorcersi

wrest [rest] *tr* strappare, togliere a viva forza; *(to twist)* torcere

wrestle ['resəl] *s* lotta, combattimento ‖ *intr* fare la lotta, lottare

wrestler ['restlər] *s* lottatore *m*

wrestling ['reslɪŋ] *s* lotta

wretch [retʃ] *s* disgraziato, tapino

wretched ['retʃɪd] *adj* (pitiable) misero, disgraziato, tapino; *(poor, worthless)* miserabile

wriggle ['rɪɡəl] *s* (e.g., of a snake) guizzo; dondolio ‖ *tr* dondolare, dimenare ‖ *intr* guizzare; dimenarsi; to wriggle out of sgattaiolare da, divincolarsi da

wrig·gly ['rɪɡli] *adj* (-glier; -gliest) che si contorce; (fig) evasivo

wring [rɪŋ] *v* (pret & pp wrung [rʌŋ]) *tr* torcere; *(wet clothing)* strizzare; *(one's heart)* stringersi; *(e.g., one's hands)* torcersi; to wring the truth out of strappare la verità a

wringer ['rɪŋər] *s* strizzatoio

wrinkle ['rɪŋkəl] *s* (on skin) ruga; *(on fabric)* crespa, grinza; (coll) trovata, espediente *m* ‖ *tr* corrugare, raggrinzire; *(fabric)* increspare

wrin'kle-proof' *adj* antipiega, ingualcibile

wrin·kly ['rɪŋkli] *adj* (-klier; -kliest) rugoso, grinzoso

wrist [rɪst] *s* polso

wrist'band' *s* polso

wrist' pin' *s* spinotto

wrist' watch' *s* orologio da polso

writ [rɪt] *s* scritto; (law) ordine *m*

write [raɪt] *v* (pret wrote [rot]; pp written ['rɪtən]) *tr* scrivere; to write down mettere in iscritto; *(to disparage)* menomare; to write off *(a debt)* cancellare; (com) stornare; to write up redigere, scrivere in pieno; *(to ballyhoo)* scrivere le lodi di ‖ *intr* scrivere; to write back rispondere per lettera

write'-in-vote' *s* voto per candidato il cui nome non è nella lista

writer ['raɪtər] *s* scrittore *m*

write'-up' *s* descrizione scritta, conto; stamburata, elogio; (com) valutazione eccesiva

writhe [raɪð] *intr* contorcersi, spasimare, dibattersi

writing ['raɪtɪŋ] *s* lo scrivere; (*something written*) scritto; (*characters written*) scrittura; professione di scrittore; **at this writing** scrivendo questa mia; **in one's own writing** di proprio pugno; **to put in writing** mettere in iscritto

writ'ing desk' *s* scrittoio

writ'ing mate'rials *spl* l'occorrente *m* per scrivere, oggetti *mpl* di cancelleria

writ'ing pa'per *s* carta da lettere

writ'ten ac'cent ['rɪtən] *s* accento grafico

wrong [rɔŋ] or [rɑŋ] *adj* sbagliato, erroneo; (*awry*) guasto; (*step*) falso; cattivo, ingiusto; **there is nothing wrong with him** non ha niente; **to be wrong** (*mistaken*) aver torto; (*guilty*) aver la colpa || *s* torto; **to**

be in the wrong essere in errore; **to do wrong** fare del male; commettere un'ingiustizia || *adv* male; (*backward*) alla rovescia; **to go wrong** andare alla rovescia; andare per la cattiva strada || *tr* far torto a, offendere, maltrattare

wrongdoer ['rɔŋ,duˑər] or ['rɑŋ,duˑər] *s* peccatore *m*, trasgressore *m*

wrongdoing ['rɔŋ,duˑɪŋ] or ['rɑŋ,duˑɪŋ] *s* peccato, offesa, trasgressione

wrong' num'ber *s* (telp) numero sbagliato; **you have the wrong number** Lei si è sbagliato di numero

wrong' side' *s* rovescio; (*of street*) altra parte; **to get out of bed on the wrong side** alzarsi di malumore; **wrong side out** alla rovescia

wrought' i'ron [rət] *s* ferro battuto

wrought'-up' *adj* sovreccitato

wry [raɪ] *adj* (wrier; wriest) sbieco, storto; pervertito, alterato; ironico

wry'neck' *s* (orn & pathol) torcicollo

X

X, x [eks] *s* ventiquattresima lettera dell'alfabeto inglese

Xanthippe [zæn'tɪpɪ] *s* Santippe *f*

Xavier ['zævɪˑər] or ['zevɪˑər] *s* Saverio

xebec ['zibek] *s* (naut) sciabecco

xenon ['zinɑn] or ['zenɑn] *s* xeno

xenophobe ['zenəˌfob] *s* xenofobo

Xenophon ['zenəfɑn] *s* Senofonte *m*

xerography [zɪ'rɑgrəfɪ] *s* xerografia

xerophyte [zɪrə,faɪt] *s* xerofito

Xerxes ['zɑrksɪs] *s* Serse *m*

Xmas ['krɪsməs] *s* Natale *m*

x-ray ['eks,re] *adj* radiografico || *s* raggio X; (*photograph*) radiogramma *m*, radiografia || *tr* radiografare

xylograph ['zaɪlə,græf] or ['zaɪlə,graf] *s* silografia

xylophone ['zaɪlə,fon] *s* silofono

Y

Y, y [waɪ] *s* venticinquesima lettera dell'alfabeto inglese

yacht [jɑt] *s* yacht *m*, panfilo

yacht' club' *s* club *m* nautico, associazione velica

yak [jæk] *s* yak *m* || *v* (pret & pp yakked; ger yakking) *intr* (slang) ciarlare, chiacchierare

yam [jæm] *s* igname *m;* (sweet potato) patata dolce, batata

yank [jæŋk] *s* tiro, strattone *m* || *tr* dare uno strattone a, tirare || *intr* dare uno strattone, tirare

Yankee ['jæŋki] *adj & s* yankee *mf*

yap [jæp] *s* guaito; (slang) chiacchierio, ciancia || *v* (pret & pp yapped; ger yapping) *intr* latrare, guaire; (slang) chiacchierare, ciarlare

yard [jɑrd] *s* cortile *m;* recinto; yard *m*, iarda; (naut) pennone *m;* (rr) scalo smistamento

yard'arm' *s* estremità *f* del pennone

yard' goods' *spl* tessuti *mpl* in pezza

yard'mas'ter *s* (rr) capo dello scalo smistamento

yard'stick' *s* stecca di una iarda di lunghezza; (fig) metro

yarn [jɑrn] *s* filo, filato; (coll) storia

yarrow ['jæro] *s* millefoglie *m*

yaw [jɔ] *s* (naut) straorzata; (aer) imbardata || *intr* (naut) straorzare, guizzare; (aer) imbardare

yawl [jɔl] *s* barca a remi; (naut) iolla

yawn [jɔn] *s* sbadiglio || *intr* sbadigliare; (said, e.g., of a hole) vaneggiare, aprirsi

yea [je] *s & adv* sì *m*

yean [jin] *intr* (said of sheep or goat) partorire

year [jɪr] *s* anno; **to be . . . years old** avere . . . anni; **year in, year out** un anno dopo l'altro

year'book' *s* annuario

yearling ['jɪrlɪŋ] *adj* di un anno di età || *s* animale *m* di un anno di età

yearly ['jɪrlɪ] *adj* annuale || *adv* annualmente

yearn [jʌrn] *intr* smaniare, sospirare; **to yearn for** anelare per

yearning ['jʌrnɪŋ] *s* anelo, sospiro ardente

yeast [jist] *s* lievito

yeast' cake' *s* compressa di lievito

yell [jel] *s* urlo || *tr* gridare || *intr* urlare

yellow ['jelo] *adj* giallo; (*newspaper*) sensazionale; (*cowardly*) (coll) vile || *s* giallo; giallo d'uovo || *intr* ingiallire

yellowish ['jelo‧ɪʃ] *adj* giallastro

yel'low‧jack'et *s* vespa, calabrone *m*

yel'low streak' *s* (coll) vena di codardia

yelp [jelp] *s* guaito || *intr* guaire

yeo'man *s* (-**men**) (naut) sottufficiale *m;* (Brit) piccolo proprietario terriero

yeo'man of the guard' *s* guardia del servizio reale

yeo'man's serv'ice *s* lavoro onesto

yes [jes] *s* sì *m;* **to say yes** dire di sì || *adv* sì || *v* (*pret* & *pp* **yessed;** *ger* **yessing**) *tr* dire di sì a || *intr* dire di sì

yes' man' *s* (coll) persona che approva sempre; (coll) leccapiedi *m*

yesterday ['jestərdɪ] *or* ['jestər‧de] *s* & *adv* ieri *m*

yet [jet] *adv* ancora; tuttavia; **as yet** sinora; **nor yet** nemmeno; **not yet** non ancora || *conj* ma, però, pure

yew' tree' [ju] *s* tasso

Yiddish ['jɪdɪʃ] *adj* & *s* yiddish *m*

yield [jild] *s* rendimento, resa; (*crop*) raccolto; (com) reddito, gettito || *tr* rendere, fruttare || *intr* rendere, fruttare, produrre; (*to surrender*) cedere, arrendersi; sottomettersi; cedere il posto

yodeling *or* **yodelling** ['jodəlɪŋ] *s* tirolesa

yoke [jok] *s* (*contrivance*) giogo; (*pair, e.g., of oxen*) paio; (*of shirt*) sprone *m;* (naut) barra del timone; **to throw**

off the yoke scuotere il giogo || *tr* aggiogare

yokel ['jokəl] *s* zoticone *m*

yolk [jok] *s* tuorlo

yonder ['jɑndər] *adj* situato lassù; situato laggiù || *adv* lassù; laggiù

yore [jor] *s*—**of yore** del tempo antico, del tempo in cui Berta filava

you [ju] *pron pers* Lei; tu; Le, La; te, ti; voi; vi; Loro || *pron indef* si, e.g., **you eat at noon** si mangia a mezzogiorno

young [jʌŋ] *adj* (**younger** ['jʌŋgər]; **youngest** ['jʌŋgɪst]) giovane || **the young** i giovani

young' hope'ful *s* giovane *m* di belle speranze

young' la'dy *s* giovane *f;* (*married*) giovane signora

young' man' *s* giovane *m*, giovanotto

young' peo'ple *s* i giovani

youngster ['jʌŋstər] *s* giovanetto; (*child*) bambino

your [jur] *adj* Suo, il Suo; tuo, il tuo; vostro, il vostro

yours [jurz] *pron poss* Suo, il Suo; tuo, il tuo; vostro, il vostro; **of yours** Suo; **very truly yours** distinti saluti

your‧self [jur'self] *pron pers* (-**selves** ['selvz]) Lei stesso; sé stesso; si, e.g., **are your enjoying yourself?** si diverte?

youth [juθ] *s* (**youths** [juθs] *or* [juðz]) gioventù *f*, giovinezza; (*person*) giovane *mf;* i giovani

youthful ['juθfəl] *adj* giovane, giovanile

yowl [jaul] *s* urlo || *intr* urlare

Yugoslav ['jugo'slɑv] *adj* & *s* iugoslavo

Yugoslavia ['jugo'slɑvɪ‧ə] *s* la Iugoslavia

Yule [jul] *s* il Natale; le feste natalizie

Yule' log' *s* ceppo

Yuletide ['jul‧taɪd] *s* le feste natalizie

Z

Z, z [zi] *s* ventiseiesima lettera dell'alfabeto inglese

za‧ny ['zenɪ] *adj* (-**nier; -niest**) comico, buffonesco || *s* (-**nies**) buffone *m*, pagliaccio

zeal [zil] *s* zelo, entusiasmo

zealot ['zelət] *s* zelante *mf*, fanatico

zealotry ['zelətrɪ] *s* fanatismo

zealous ['zeləs] *adj* zelante, volenteroso

zebra ['zibrə] *s* zebra

ze'bra cross'ing *s* zebre *fpl*

zebu ['zibju] *s* zebù *m*

zenith ['zɪnɪθ] *s* zenit *m*

zephyr ['zɛfər] *s* zefiro

ze‧ro ['zɪro] *s* (-**roes**) zero || *tr*—**to zero in** (mil) aggiustare il mirino di || *intr*—**to zero in on** (mil) concentrare il fuoco su

ze'ro grav'ity *s* gravità *f* zero

ze'ro hour' *s* ora zero

zest [zest] *s* entusiasmo; (*flavor*) aroma *m*, sapore *m*

Zeus [zus] *s* Zeus *m*

zig-zag ['zɪg‧zæg] *adj* & *adv* a zigzag || *s* zigzag *m;* serpentina || *v* (*pret* & *pp* -**zagged;** *ger* -**zagging**) *intr* zigzagare; serpeggiare

zinc [zɪŋk] *s* zinco

zinnia ['zɪnɪ‧ə] *s* zinnia

Zionism ['zaɪ‧ə‧nɪzəm] *s* sionismo

zip [zɪp] *s* (coll) sibilo; (coll) energia, vigore *m* || *v* (*pret* & *pp* **zipped;** *ger* **zipping**) *tr* chiudere con cerniera lampo; aprire con cerniera lampo; (coll) portare rapidamente; **to zip up** (*to add zest to*) dare gusto a || *intr* aprirsi con cerniera lampo; sibilare; (coll) filare, correre; **to zip by** (coll) passare come un lampo

zip' code' *s* codice *m* di avviamento postale
zipper ['zɪpər] *s* cerniera *or* serratura lampo
zircon ['zʌrkɑn] *s* zircone *m*
zirconium [zər'konɪ·əm] *s* zirconio
zither ['zɪθər] *s* cetra tirolese
zodiac ['zodɪˌæk] *s* zodiaco
zone [zon] *s* zona; distretto postale ‖ *tr* dividere in zone
zoo [zu] *s* giardino zoologico
zoologic(al) [ˌzo·əˈlɑdʒɪk(əl)] *adj* zoologico

zoologist [zoˈɑlədʒɪst] *s* zoologo
zoology [zoˈɑlədʒi] *s* zoologia
zoom [zum] *s* ronzio; (aer) cabrata, impennata; (mov, telv) zumata ‖ *tr* (aer) far cabrare, fare impennare; (mov, telv) zumare ‖ *intr* ronzare; (aer) cabrare, impennarsi; (mov, telv) zumare
zoom' lens' *s* (phot) transfocatore *m*
zoophite ['zo·əˌfaɪt] *s* zoofito
Zu·lu ['zulu] *adj* zulù ‖ *s* (**-lus**) zulù *mf*
Zurich ['zurɪk] *s* Zurigo *f*